The

CHELSEA HOUSE LIBRARY *of* LITERARY CRITICISM

The

CHELSEA HOUSE LIBRARY *of* LITERARY CRITICISM

TWENTIETH-CENTURY AMERICAN LITERATURE

Volume 3

General Editor

HAROLD BLOOM

1986
Chelsea House Publishers
New York
New Haven Philadelphia

Printed and bound in the United States of America.

Library of Congress Cataloging in Publication Data

Twentieth-century American literature.
(The Chelsea House library of literary criticism)
Includes bibliographies and index.
1. American literature—20th century—History and criticism—Collected works. 2. Authors, American—20th century—Biography—Dictionaries. I. Bloom, Harold.
PS221.T834 1986 810'.9'005
84-27430
ISBN 0-87754-803-X

Chelsea House Publishers
Harold Steinberg, Chairman & Publisher
Susan Lusk, Vice President
A Division of Chelsea House Educational Communications, Inc.

133 Christopher Street, New York, NY 10014

345 Whitney Avenue, New Haven, CT 06510

5014 West Chester Pike, Edgemont, PA 19028

Acknowledgments for selections used in this volume commence on page 1897.

CONTENTS

The Index to this series, *Twentieth-Century American Literature*, appears in Volume 7.

ILLUSTRATIONS

ABBREVIATIONS

Am	America
AM	American Mercury
AmSt	American Studies
APR	American Poetry Review
AS	American Scholar
ASp	American Spectator
At	Atlantic
B&B	Books and Bookmen
BF	Book Forum
Bkm	Bookman (New York)
CE	College English
CF	Canadian Forum
CLAJ	CLA Journal
Cmty	Commentary
CoL	Contemporary Literature (formerly Wisconsin Studies in Contemporary Literature)
Com	Commonweal
Crt	Critique
DQ	Denver Quarterly
Enc	Encounter
ETJ	Educational Theatre Journal
Fndtn	Foundation
GR	Georgia Review
HA	Harvard Advocate
HB	Harper's Bazaar
HdR	Hudson Review
Ind	Independent
KR	Kenyon Review
Lit	Literature
LitM	The Little Magazine
LM	London Mercury
Lon	London Magazine
LT	Listener
MFS	Modern Fiction Studies
MLN	Modern Language Notes
MPS	Modern Poetry Studies
MR	Massachusetts Review
NaR	National Review
ND	Negro Digest
NEQ	New England Quarterly
NMQ	New Mexico Quarterly
NR	New Republic
NS	New Statesman
Nwk	Newsweek
NY	New Yorker
NYHT	New York Herald Tribune
NYRB	New York Review of Books
NYT	New York Times
NYTBR	New York Times Book Review
NYTr	New York Tribune
Obs	Observer
Opy	Opportunity
PR	Partisan Review
PRev	Paris Review
Prog	Progressive
RCF	Review of Contemporary Fiction
Ren	Renascence
Rep	Reporter
Salm	Salmagundi
SAQ	South Atlantic Quarterly
SHR	Southern Humanities Review
SLJ	Southern Literary Journal
SoR	Southern Review
Spec	Spectator
SR	Saturday Review
SRL	Saturday Review (London)
SS	Smart Set
SSF	Studies in Short Fiction
SvR	Soviet Review
SwR	Sewanee Review
SWR	Southwest Review
TLS	Times Literary Supplement
WAL	Western American Literature
WPBW	Washington Post Book World
YR	Yale Review

Stanley Elkin

1930–

Stanley Lawrence Elkin was born in New York City on May 11, 1930. He was educated at the University of Illinois, from which he received a B.A. in 1952, an M.A. in 1953, and a Ph.D. in 1961. Elkin married Joan Jacobson in 1953; they have three children. He served in the Army from 1957 to 1959, and has taught at Washington University in St. Louis since 1960. He has been a visiting professor at Smith, Yale, Boston University, the University of California, the University of Wisconsin, and the University of Iowa.

Elkin's writing career began with short stories, collected in *Criers and Kibitzers, Kibitzers and Criers* (1966) and *Stanley Elkin's Greatest Hits* (1980), which won a *Sewanee Review* Prize. *Boswell: A Modern Comedy* (1964) was the first of many critically successful novels, distinguished by Elkin's antic use of language and his fascination with "the strange displacements of the ordinary." They include *A Bad Man* (1967), *The Dick Gibson Show* (1971), *The Franchiser* (1976), *The Living End* (1979), *George Mills* (1982), and *The Magic Kingdom* (1985). Like Ben Flesh, the titular protagonist of *The Franchiser,* Elkin has multiple sclerosis. Both *The Dick Gibson Show* and the collection of novellas *Searches and Seizures* (1973) were nominated for National Book Awards; *The Living End,* Elkin's sardonic vision of heaven and hell, won a Rosenthal Foundation Award; *George Mills* won a National Book Critics Circle Award. His other awards include a Longview Foundation Award in 1962, a *Paris Review* Prize in 1965, a Guggenheim Fellowship in 1966, a Rockefeller Foundation grant in 1968, a National Endowment for the Arts grant in 1971, and a grant from the American Academy of Arts and Letters in 1974. He was elected to the Academy in 1982. Elkin lives in University City, Missouri.

General

"There are only two kinds of intelligences, the obsessive and the perspectual," says James Boswell, hero of Stanley Elkin's first novel, *Boswell.* In statement and act Boswell affirms the obsessive and thereby points to what I believe is the single most important theme—and description of technique—in Elkin's work. In Elkin's fictional world, the perspectual intelligence—rational, balanced, Apollonian—gives way to the obsessive imagination, the willful, kinetic force that destroys accepted perspective with its compulsively straight and irrationally jagged lines. For Elkin, perspective means objectivity, ordinariness, and compromise. Obsession is subjective, strange, and extreme; it is characterized by a narrow focus on fixed ends, by intense desire and extravagant means, and by the lack of relations and options. Elkin does create perspectives on his characters' actions through comedy and invites the reader to analyze the nature and effects of obsession. But within the work itself, "Drive drives the world," obsession dominates. It rules character, dictates structure, and permeates the voices Elkin loves to throw.

Elkin's protagonists are ordinary men with extraordinary purposes and singular dreams, men who become obsessed with the improbable possibilities of the self's expansion. Isolated by their obsessions, these manic heros mount single-minded assaults upon the world and force themselves toward ultimate fulfillments. Although development is their end, plot becomes the compulsive repetition of action and complex situation is reduced to simplicity by their obsessions. Even setting is defined by the radical subjectivity of the obsessive inhabiting it. Sellers of singleness, pitchmen of transcendence, Elkin's narrators and heroes have a high-energy, repetitive rhetoric, an exclamatory prose that intensifies the ordinary, presses the impossible, and registers the urgency of their fixations. The result is a unity of effect, a Siamese connection of substance and style.

It is probably a truism that characters in contemporary American fiction are obsessional, but Elkin's heroes, unlike those, say, of Mailer, Hawkes, or O'Connor, develop their obsessions from natural authorities, common needs, or the promises of a popular culture rather than from some social, psychological, or religious ideology. Elkin's are not the exotic products of a subculture nor the constructs of an experimental theory but the distortions of the American almost-ordinary. Because their obsessions arise from areas of mass fascination and because they expend their energies within recognizable—if sometimes dislocated—systems of value, their private thoughts and public careers reveal truths particularly relevant and available to the American present. Theirs is the singleness that illuminates multiplicity, the focus that creates perspective, and Elkin uses them to examine both the normalities and aberrancies of our time.—Thomas LeClair, "The Obsessional Fiction of Stanley Elkin," *CoL,* Winter 1975, pp. 146–47

Works

Obviously, the novelist of today is operating under the terms of a new chemistry. The old visions will no longer serve him and so he looks for new ones, and one avenue that the search takes is exemplified by Stanley Elkin. Leo Feldman, the hero of *A Bad Man,* is not so much bigger than life as realer than real, the only familiar anchor in a world of fantasy. Feldman is the quintessential merchant to whom trade is not a means to profit or even a way of life, but an obsession, a religion, the way to whatever salvation there might be. His sense of competition is so monstrously developed that he must destroy other people compulsively for the joy that is in it. In the games he plays with his own son, he cheats. And yet, it is not his viciousness that leads to his downfall, but his desire to sell more and more, to be of greater service to his customers.

He starts with obscene books and dirty records, contraceptive dispensers near the elevators, and goes on to offer loose women, abortions, drugs. Now, we know that such a thing as this never happened, will never happen in the foreseeable future, and Feldman's career in prison—which is the stuff of the greater part of the novel—is just as far-fetched. Feldman is persecuted under a dispensation that allows the warden to change the rules continually so that a prisoner never knows when yesterday's good behavior will become today's offense. Or, rather, Feldman never knows, for it seems that he alone is made to suffer the vagaries of the system. Yet he continues in his old habits. Set to work in the commissary, he soon perverts its operation by offering only the shabbiest, most worthless goods at outrageous prices. Even while he is being punished for one misdeed, he is plotting the next, figuring the angles.

Feldman has near his heart an homunculus, an undeveloped physical being which I take to be symbolic of that decent part of his character which died unborn. He himself faces death at the end of the book totally unrepentant: he loves his life for what it has been, for the disasters it has caused, the suffering it has engendered for others. "I accept wars, history, the deaths of the past, other people's poverties and losses. Their casualties and bad dreams, I write off." His own life, Feldman thinks, is "the single holiness".

I have considerable admiration for Elkin's talent and accomplishments. He has a superb parodic gift, a sharp wit, a genuine comic sense which he allows to range widely, but which he keeps under the control of the novel's general concept. Many black humorists fall victim to their own excesses: they will include anything that comes to mind. Elkin avoids this and the accompanying effects of blunting and diffusion. But when all the virtues of *A Bad Man* have been counted, the final evaluation remains to be made. The satire seems to me to be finally shallow because the concept of Feldman as man is grossly oversimplified. And though moments of vitality occur here and there, no sense of life is maintained. The approach Elkin takes will not sustain it. —WALTER SULLIVAN, "The Novel in the Gnostic Twilight," *SwR*, Oct. 1970, pp. 659–60

Stanley Elkin's characters suffer from an interesting variety of the same basic disease. The "Eligible Men" are word kings. They build up glittering verbal palaces around themselves in cascading rhetorical monologues, in dreams, in deep wordy caverns of introspection. Their worlds are perfected right down to the final bauble on the last minaret. Then the crunch comes. They discover that no one else is living there but them. The brilliant talker is the proprietor and sole inhabitant of his universe; and he might as well be adrift in outer space. His fatal proficiency in language has taken him clean out of the world of other people.

This is the central theme of the three short novels that make up the book; one about a talking bailbondsman, one about a dreaming Kennedy-Plimpton playboy, and one about an introspective lecturer on the lunch-party circuit. Elkin has perfected a form of garrulous baroque, a sort of solipsist's Scrabble. Like grotesque illustrations to a theory of Chomskian linguistics, his characters seem to have been born with outsize generative grammars installed inside their craniums.

Alexander Main, the bailbondsman, known in Cincinnati as "Phoenician," is, he boasts, renowned in the city for his smart dialogue, but he hasn't had a conversation since his wife died. Down telephones, through taxi grilles, across office desks and over lunch-parlour counters, he rants on about the universe, and ends up by terrorising his clerk (for whom he has bought a high stool and a quill pen so that he can look like a "real clerk" out of Charles Dickens) in a hotel room.

> "And for every black hole there's a *white* hole. That's what Hjellming thinks, how he accounts for the quasars. Are you reading me, Crainpool? The universes are leaking into each other. There's this transfusion of law in the sky. I'm honest, I'm an honest man. Upright and respectable here in this universe I inhabit. I'm honest, but the fucking laws are leaking, the physical constants bleeding into each other like madras. God Himself nothing but a slow leak, some holy puncture, Nature's and reality's sacred flat. Matter and anti-matter. Inside our universe is another. Dig? Chinese boxes of universes. When I kill you in your room here tonight, maybe that's virtue next-door. You think?"
>
> "Why? Please, Mr Main, *why?*"
>
> "Shut up about why. I don't *know* why!"
>
> Crainpool changes his tactics. He stops whining and becomes almost angry. "You always have to have the last word," he says. "You always have to do things big, don't you? Big shot. You'd kill me for nothing, for the sake of your style."
>
> "My style? Nah."

But he would. Given a style like that, bullets are superfluous; and Elkin's inspired gasbags write and talk themselves out to the realm of human relations. Ashenden, the scrupulous New England aristocrat, has a sensibility so fine he cannot bring himself to violate his friends' wives; he wanders out of an English country house into a painting by Edward Hicks and into the embrace of an enormous she-bear whom he has to satisfy in coitus. The ordinary laws of physics and human conduct just don't apply to these cursed language-using animals, and that is their tragedy.

For the power of Elkin's writing lies in his capacity to move smoothly from the real into the fantastic and back again. His characters, no matter how wild their imaginative and linguistic flights, are always rooted in the ordinary. He can create a city street, or a hideous housing complex for the retired middle class (in "The Condominium," the best novella of all), as ably as any devoted realist. And around the terrifying limitlessness of characters who have not learned that language has its limits, he has moulded a sad, sour, entirely satisfying fiction.—JONATHAN RABAN, "Taking Possession," *Enc*, Feb. 1975, pp. 83–84

For all ⟨Elkin's⟩ novels' similarities of tone, structure, and comic method, *The Franchiser* is a clear advance in Elkin's art. In *The Dick Gibson Show* Elkin achieved a wide range of effects through mimicry and parody of the great variety of radio voices sent out over the airwaves from the thirties through the late sixties. Finally, the book's achievement has a certain narrowness in that the variety of treatment and technique lies within the narrow compass of one medium only, that of radio. Elkin's art registers a significant advance in *The Franchiser* in that he is able to make use of many of the techniques and talents displayed in the earlier novel and place them in the service of a decidedly larger, more ambitious social portraiture—one which entails nothing less than the re-creation of the look and feel, the tones and textures of American popular culture. The more recent book examines not just a single medium but an entire civilization—commercial America, the evermore increasingly commercialized America of the past two decades.

One would make a mistake, however, to read *The Franchiser* as a predominantly satiric novel; for while it has satiric moments, the whole weight of the book is on the side of comedy, a comedy not infrequently celebratory—Whitman with a smile. Elkin's regard for the sights and sounds, the tones and textures, of our commercial civilization is one of absolute and absorbed fascination (he has elsewhere referred to himself as a "passionate voyeur" of the life he re-creates). Here, for example is his "celebration" of one of our culture's basic foodstuffs; fresh from a visit to one of his Baskin-Robbins franchise openings, the hero exclaims to a friend: "The colors of those ice creams! Chocolate like new shoes, cherry like bright fingernail polish. We do a Maple Ripple it looks like fine-grained wood, a peach like light coming through a lampshade. The ice-cream paints bright as posters, fifty Day-Glo colors. You scoop the stuff up you feel like Jackson Pollock. . . . I take one look at the ice-cream acrylics and I'm happy as Looney Tunes."

This dithyrambic spectator is clearly designed as an exemplary figure: "The culture? *I'm* the culture." His interests, for example, are very often those of a quintessential American male; he, like his creator, is fascinated by the accessories of car washes and ultramodern gadget-and-gimmick stuffed motels. The very name Elkin gives his protagonist—Flesh—testifies to his representative function: he is clearly designed as a modern American Everyman. By making him an orphan, Elkin strips away virtually all formative influences save those of the culture at large: Ben Flesh is a creation not of any one set of parents but of the whole American popular culture (even his fortune, his inheritance from his godfather, has its origin in immensely successful musical comedy productions of the 1930's and 40's; American show tunes, the names of Gershwin, of Rodgers and Hart, of Jolson and Cantor—these are frequently on the hero's lips). If he is "Flesh," our common American flesh with all its attendant needs for the simple, the basic, the mundane (those needs supplied in such profusion by "Flesh's" franchises—the basic foods from McDonald's and The Colonel's, the staple of tears-and-laughter from Cinema I and Cinema II, the staples of personal hygiene from One-Hour Martinizing); if the hero is Flesh, he is also *Ben—Benjamin*. With this name Elkin signals the peculiarly *American* nature of the hero's entrepreneurship. The name surely points to the great-granddaddy of American business shrewdness, the virtual founder of American entrepreneurdom, Benjamin Franklin, that other, earlier, inspired figure whose passion and inspiration were all placed in the service of the utterly practical. Flesh, like his prototype, is the common man writ large.—ROBERT EDWARD COLBERT, "The American Salesman as Pitchman and Poet in the Fiction of Stanley Elkin," *Crt*, Vol. 21, No. 2 (1979), pp. 54–56

"It was always Art," God explains. "I work by the contrast and metrics, by beats and the silences. It was all Art. *Because it makes a better story is why.*" At this announcement, Christ holds up "his damaged hands." He is furious. "Because it makes a better *story?*" Christ screams. "Is this true? *Is* it?"

Sadly, and wonderfully, it's all true. In fact, so much recognizable truth permeates ⟨*The Living End*⟩ that one must remind oneself, during the most realistic and visceral detail, that we are—most of the time—in that fantasy land which is commonly called life after death. It is no fantasy as Elkin describes it. When God summons Doomsday, and the dead join the living to receive the Last Judgment, we feel more familiar with the dead than we feel akin to the living—in *The Living End* we spend more time with the dead than with the living, and we spend the time vividly. "Their bodies shone with gore like wet paint. They sooted the world as if it were carpet. The living and dead were thrown together, and the dead looked away first.". . .

The doomed and dying are Elkin's loved ones; it's only logical that he should have expanded his universe to include the afterlife—and God's terrible explanation. But the reader of Elkin's earlier work will be surprised by *The Living End* for another reason. The book is a narrative marvel; the novel has a plot—and such a fast pace that a veteran Elkin reader may wonder about the places where he lost interest, or lost his way, in reading Elkin before. A common criticism of Elkin is that he can't sustain the narrative momentum necessary in a novel. . . .

The best of Elkin's work (before *The Living End*) is the collection of three novellas, *Searches and Seizures*. It is as if the short-novel form forced Elkin to contain himself and move ahead with his storytelling while he nonetheless dazzled us with his language. But in *The Living End* all that Elkin has done well before he does again, and does better; and what's different in this new work is also better. *The Living End* has a linear narrative that is as seductive and hooking, in that old-fashioned what's-going-to-happen-next way, as any thriller. From the moment the gentle liquor store owner, Ellerbee, is shot and killed and sent to heaven—and then sent to hell—we (like poor Ellerbee) want to meet God and find out why. "You're quite a guy," a woman tells Ellerbee, when he's still alive. Indeed, that's the point: Ellerbee is a good guy; he's supporting the widow of a slain employee (and another who's crippled for life); he does not accept sex in payment for his charity; he loves and is faithful to his nagging, bitchy wife. When we see how Ellerbee is treated in the afterlife, we can't wait to hear God's reasons.

"I was definitely slain," complains another of the damned in hell. "Smited. Blasted. Here today gone today. Slain absolutely. And none of the amenities, let me tell you, no last words or final cigarette, the blindfold unoffered. It was as if I'd gotten in to start my car and—boom! Like someone ambushed, snuffed by onions, eating in restaurants and rushed by hit men."

"Do you know who did it?" asks another of the damned.

"I've got my suspicions, I'm working on it, I've got my leads."

The leads point to God, of course, and in the third part of this triptych we know we're going to hear the Why and What for of the Holy Family. They are grisly answers, deadly funny, completely serious. Among other things we discover: God makes mistakes. That He is human is not necessarily appealing. . . .

What Ellerbee discovers is that everything is true. Says a resident of hell, "We hit the Wall with every step. It's all Wall down here. It's wall-to-wall Wall."

It's like life itself, of course, but so keenly exaggerated that Elkin manages to make the pain more painful, and the comedy more comic. His descriptions of hell lose nothing by comparison to Bosch and Bruegel—its deception, its rarefied air of phony goodness. The unveiling of the Virgin Birth is too inspired a tale to spoil for the readers of this novel; nor should I tell too much about the quarreling between Jesus and God—or about the compromised, complaining carpenter that Joseph is. It would be a kind of heresy for me to tell you what God's final act is—when He has assembled all the living and dead to hear His verdict on Judgment Day. "There was not a bad seat in the house," Elkin writes of Doomsday, "strangely, all could see Him."

Bitching to the multitude, God says, "I give you pain. Do you appreciate the miracle? To make it up out of thin air, deep, free-fall space, the gifted, driven atoms of remonstrance? Trickier than orange juice or the taste of Brie."

On Judgment Day "a woman who had given her eyes away stirred her fingers in her weeping holes. 'So grotesque,' she moaned, 'death grotesque as life. All, all grotesque.'" But in *The Living End* Elkin provides us with more than the grotesque perspective; as in most profoundly moving and enduring novels the evidence of how humanity behaves is overwhelmingly sad, yet there is a spirit of resistance and an energy that cries out how tenaciously worthwhile living is.

It is an ambitious undertaking to reveal the similarities life after death bears with life before death; it is all the more remarkable that Elkin has rendered such a grand scheme so comically and so succinctly. A mere 148 pages—some will doubtlessly describe this book as a little novel, but most writers will be envious of Elkin's economy. His talent and his compassionate laughter have always been huge. Now here is a novel—a narrative and a vision—that can contain the tendency of his robust imagination and his ribald language to run amok. *The Living End* is a big book for Stanley Elkin, and a fine and daring novel for our literature.—JOHN IRVING, "An Exposé of Heaven and Hell," *NYTBR*, June 10, 1979, pp. 7, 30

In *The Magic Kingdom*, the wild language that has always been Mr. Elkin's meets the least likely subject of rich playful prose, a group of dying children. Suffering and death usually wear the mourning clothes of language, but not in this novel. "Noah Cloth, confined to hospitals at a time in his life when other boys his age were in school, could not read well or do his maths. His history was weak, his geography, most of his subjects. Only in art had he done well, and now he'd lost his ability to draw. Nine times he'd been operated on for bone tumors: in his right wrist, along his left and right femurs, on both elbows, once at the base of his skull, and once for little garnetlike tumors around a necklace of collarbone."

The narrative concerns the trip Noah and his companions are taking from England to Disney World for their dream holiday. When we read of such journeys in the newspapers, we see the sweetness in the gesture of such arranged happiness. We see the sentimental kindness of granting a last wish. We see everything except the dying children as they are. Mr. Elkin strips away the sentimentality and replaces it with an honest look at the grotesque possibilities we all carry around and prefer not to see, not even in fiction.

The seven children in *The Magic Kingdom* are traveling, but they have lost the one passport that matters—they cannot be admitted to the province of health and longevity, but everything else is theirs, including this well-intentioned journey to Disney World.

Even fiction, that familiar opener of eyes, rarely opens our eyes to the interior terrors. We are accustomed to metaphores of disease and decay. Mr. Elkin presents the real thing; not metaphors, kids. Novelists may X-ray the soul and the psyche, but we leave the body to technicians.

Not Stanley Elkin. His magic kingdom is the domain of "fallen pediatric angels," the province of children defined by their diseases, children who have slipped through not only the safety net, so cozy to politicians, but children who have defied the trickiness of evolution. They are the owners of blasted genes, they are hopeless, doomed beings, and on their way to Disney World in a hysterical farce that sounds like Shakespeare reading aloud from *The National Enquirer.*

These children on a Disney World holiday are nothing like the adult sufferers to whom we are accustomed. This is the magic kingdom, not the magic mountain, nothing as pastoral as tuberculosis for this crew, no philosophical discussions, just a pretty good shot at living out the week. And the work is aptly titled. It is not Disney's magic kingom but Stanley Elkin's. Disney's mechanical and electrical shenanigans, his puppets and animals, are no match for the fireworks of Mr. Elkin's imagination.

In this novel, as in no other, the lyrical merges with the clinical, the romantic motif of the journey couples with the vocabulary of the hospital ward. People are the incarnations of their diseases and the names of their drugs and chemical medicines ring out as harmoniously as the names of Homeric gods in the *Odyssey*. Mr. Elkin is weaving the tapestry of disease, the language and the technique of having your last good time. In this tapestry, pharmacology replaces mythology. The doctors attending the blood cell of a leukemia patient are "careful as art restorers . . . chipping away at the white smear that poisoned it, bringing back the brisk, original color from their tubes of vincristine and prednisone and asparaginase and dexamethasone and mercaptopurine and allopurinol and methotrexate and cyclophosphamide and doxorubicin and other assorted hues.". . .

We are accustomed to using the language of health even when we speak of those in the kingdom of disease. We use active images, we "battle" illness, we "conquer" adversity. Mr. Elkin strips away this false language of valor and health. He creates a crazy quilt, words connect wildly, as desperate as the characters who wish to connect to the healthy world.

But there is also a quiet language in this work. A language that draws on James Joyce. And in a way Eddy Bale, leading the dying children, is Mr. Elkin's version of Leopold Bloom, yet another mock Ulysses, this one even more hopeless than Joyce's.

These doomed children, the barely living, first glimpse Disney World in a rich prose that echoes the end of Joyce's story "The Dead."

> Snow was falling on Cinderella Castle, snow was falling on Main Street and Liberty Square. It was falling on Adventureland and on Fantasyland. It sheathed the spires on the Haunted Mansion and clung to the umbrellalike strutted sides of Space Mountain and looked grim and oddly bruised against the spiky red slopes of Big Thunder Mountain. It coated the crazed, bulging eyes of Captain Nemo's surfaced craft and collected as slush in the saucers of the Mad Tea Party and left powdery traces along the big ledges and sills of the Liberty Tree Tavern's wide leaded windows. Discrete drifts of the stuff were swept against the heavily weathered stockade fences of Frontierland and intensified the gleam of Tomorrowland's crisp concretes and metals and alloys. A fine powder dusted the notched and scalloped foliage along the banks of the steaming river that bent and flexed, hooked and curled past tropical rain forest and choked veldt, past the Asian jungle and the rich green growth of the Nile Valley. It filled the pocked surfaces of Spaceship Earth and lent the entire park the look of some new, raw terrible Ice Age.

The resonance of "The Dead" is not only a literary suggestion, it is the melancholy truth that we prefer not to hear. Mr. Moorhead, the pediatrician, understands it. "He had to revise all his old theories. Disease, not health, was at the core of things."

For Charles Mudd-Gaddis, a 9-year-old geriatric, middle age lasts a few days. For Liam, an outing means peeking out the hospital window at the passing traffic. For Nurse Bible, immortality is a group pose in Madame Tussaud's wax museum.

"'Madame Tussaud's!' Liam says. 'Me in Madame Tussaud's! That's a stunner. I mean, no boy *wants* to die, but that's a stunner. I can almost see the expression on my mate's faces when they see me.'"

If not for the hyperbolic comic voice, we could hardly bear the pathos of these young sufferers. When the comic lets down its guard even for a half sentence, the effect is devastating.

"Tony is now two years beyond his last remission but

freckles have begun to reappear around his jawline and his renal functions are in an early stage of failure."

That mixture, the emerging freckles combined with the emerging renal failure is the sad sweet music of this prose, as pervasive as the snow upon the living and the dead.

For Eddy Bale, Mr. Elkin's Ulysses, the passage to Disney World includes no exotic temptations, no one-eyed giants, no offers of beauty or eternal life. Eddy is a fool, he has lost his son to nature, his wife to the corner tobacconist. The Queen asks for her money back, even the children disappoint him by acting like normal children. Yet the farcical plot of *The Magic Kingdom* moves Eddy to the bed as surely as the adventures of the *Odyssey* moved Ulysses to Penelope. Eddy Bale encounters his Penelope but there are none of the glories of stony Ithaca, not even the brown solemnity of Bloom's Dublin.

Eddy Bale's Penelope has been weaving the poison web of herself. Instead of Molly Bloom's "Yes," she becomes a chorus of "Now." Her other suitors are her own hands, her offsprings are stillbirths. She and Eddy are as hopeless as the group they shepherd, yet the fun goes on.

The comic vision of this work is both hysterical and profound. Part sick joke, part lyrical meditation on the nature of disease, the journey to this magic kingdom earns its place among the dark voyages that fiction must chronicle.—MAX APPLE, "Having Their Last Good Time," *NYTBR*, March 24, 1985, pp. 34–35

SCOTT SANDERS
Interview with Stanley Elkin (1973)

Contemporary Literature, Winter 1975, pp. 131–45

A: I'm attracted to the extreme. The air-conditioner on super-cool and the steak bloody. I'm attracted to extremes of personality, too. When I was a graduate student, I was a reader and admirer of William Faulkner. Ultimately I wrote my thesis on him. It wasn't a good thesis and it had to do with religious symbolism in Faulkner's work. What I then took for religious symbolism, I now see as a kind of religious *awe*. I'm not comparing my talent to Faulkner's of course, but it seems to me that as human beings, we may both be hyper-impressionable. I stand in awe of the *outré*. Those characters who are exaggerated seem, to me at least, more vital than the ordinary character, certainly more energetic. It's this energy which engines my work.

Q: It seems to me this awe that you're describing, this fascination with extreme figures, although present in all of your works, is most evident in *The Dick Gibson Show*, the latter part of which presents a collection of exaggerated figures. The book becomes a record of extreme voices, of eccentrics who call into Gibson's talkshow from all over America.

A: Yes, but those are figures who are out of control. They're amok men. Gibson himself, like myself and Faulkner, is interested in the outrageous. But when the outrageous becomes the *italicized* outrageous, it becomes dangerous. When Gibson makes a speech to his callers and says, "What's the matter with everybody? I'm sick of obsession. I've eaten my ton and can't swallow another bite. Where are the ones who used to call with their good news and their recipes for Brunswick stew and their tips about speed traps between here and Chicago? What is with the crabgrass? What'll it be this summer, the sea or the mountains?" he's getting scared, denying the very types to whom he'd originally been attracted.

Q: Your fiction is full of hustlers, con men, and salesmen. Feldman's father, for example, in *A Bad Man* or Lome in *Boswell* sell their wares by overwhelming their listeners with language. Is your prose also in places a kind of pitchman's rhetoric, a way of persuading an audience of the outlandish or the unlikely? I'm thinking, for example, of the wrestling scene with The Grim Reaper in *Boswell*, or the kangaroo court in *A Bad Man*, or the bear rape scene in *The Making of Ashenden*.

A: It's not so much a question of persuading an audience of the outlandish or unlikely, as of persuading them of the possibilities inherent in rhetoric. Rhetoric doesn't occur in life. It occurs in fiction. Fiction gives an opportunity for rhetoric to happen. It provides a stage where language can stand. It's what I admire in the fiction of other people and what I aspire to in my own fiction. I'd rather have a metaphor than a good cigar. Certainly there's a pitchman aspect to my prose, but *I'm* not trying to sell anybody anything. I *am* trying to upset the applecarts of expectation and ordinary grammar, and you can only do that with fierce language. You can only do that with aggression: the aggression of syntax and metaphor, the aggression, really, of actual, by God metered prose, which I try for from time to time in my novels. But there's an element, too, of the other thing—persuading people of the unlikely. To take what today everybody is so fond of calling the conventional wisdom and to show that there is no conventional wisdom. That truth comes in fifty-seven day-glo flavors. . . .

Q: So far you've talked about the role of personality and language in your fiction, but you haven't mentioned the abstractions that other writers commonly mention—social issues, politics, ideology. What is your feeling regarding those other concerns of fiction?

A: That they're off-limits, out of bounds. The writer doesn't have the moral authority to prescribe for others. A novel's function is not sociological. A book doesn't have to sell people anything but language. Style, yes; lifestyle, no. As for ideas, it seems to me that no writer I can think of—there are exceptions—*thinks*. He comes to ideas late. The writer uses the techniques of other arts. For example, "Nude Descending a Staircase" precedes Joyce's stream-of-consciousness technique in *Ulysses*. Freud precedes Joyce. Writers pick up on ideas, perhaps, and use them in their work, but they do not invent them. Writers come to the idea of community only after the notion has occurred to some social scientist.

Q: Is this tardiness, do you feel, due to the fact that the writer's medium puts up a greater resistance than, say, the musician's or painter's?

A: No, it's because, if the writer is doing his job, he is thinking only in terms of sentences and metaphor and syntax. These are the only things that are really real to him. That's all I care to be admired for.

Q: What writers, living or otherwise, offer you models for this passionate interest in language?

A: Well, I've mentioned Faulkner, who is "otherwise." Living writers? Certainly William Gass—above all others, probably. Then John Barth—though when I say John Barth I mean early Barth, the Barth of *The Sotweed Factor.* Gass has said that his art is the sentence, that he knows more about the sentence than any other living being. It's not a boast; it's simply a statement of fact. When I was a graduate student, and working on *Accent* magazine, I shared an office with Bill Gass at the University of Illinois, and I used to watch him scribble scribble scribble, and what he was doing was practicing his sentences, doing these endless, silent scales. He had a kaleidoscope on his desk, and he would turn it to the window to catch the light, and then try to write down what the kaleidoscope saw. You know, taking from the one medium and translating into the other. That's a marvellous thing. It's much more important than the writer doing the social scientist's job.

Q: This focus upon syntax, this close craft of the sentence, seems uncharacteristic of American fiction.

A: Certainly. As a matter of fact, when a popular critic becomes aware that a writer *is* handling language, he tends to write off that novelist. For example, John Updike for years has been criticized as a man of no substance, as a man who "*writes well.*" The criticism of Updike's novels it that they are *written* well. That's absurd.

Q: Because language is the one domain that no one else but the writer masters? Other people tell stories—film-makers, for example—but no one else performs in the realm of language except the writer?

A: Right. I've yet to read a review of my own work—maybe it's not *true* of my own work, but I hope it is; it's certainly the thing I most strive for—where the reviewer simply says, "This man writes well.". . .

Q: You seem to have a fascination for the *stuff* of modern America, of consumer America—the ticky-tacky highway culture, merchandise . . .

A: That's only because I *live* in modern America. If I had lived in seventeenth-century Germany, I would be fascinated with stuff in palaces, the swords and steins and dueling scars.

Q: The reason I ask is because many contemporary American writers feel hostile toward precisely those features of our society which fascinate you and fill your fiction.

A: Not only fascinate me. I *approve* of plenty. I dig cornucopia. I eat excess up. In the same way that I'm attracted to the bizarre personality, I'm attracted to overstatement of all kinds—whether it's material overstatement, the overstatement of the neon signs on our Broadways, or spiritual overstatements, which others see as spiritual understatement. It seems to me that all these *things*, all this *crap*, is the true American graffiti, the perfect queer calligraphy of the American signature—what gives us meaning and makes us fun.

Q: Roth and Bellow, among others, have complained that contemporary American reality beggars the writer's imagination, because the reality itself is more fabulous than any fictions they can generate. You as a writer seem to thrive on the fabulous, on the extreme, in American culture.

A: I hope so.

Q: Whom do you think of as your audience, as your readers?

A: Primarily I try to please myself. Next, Bill Gass. After that, no one.

Q: Do you mean that when you're writing, you're not conscious of, you're not trying to affect, some larger audience?

A: That may sound arrogant, as if I'm not concerned with my audience. But if I were to tell you about my concern for my audience, it would sound even more arrogant. Obviously I want people to like what I do, but primarily I would like them to understand that what I'm doing is *writing*, and to appreciate the work for the quality of the writing. Now most readers are not accustomed to reading that way, they really aren't. I teach literature in a university. And obviously, because it's the easiest thing to do, because it provides a kind of handle to the book, one talks about themes, one talks about symbols, one talks about ideas, one talks—in a vague way—about characterization and personality. But that isn't really what we ought to be talking about. What we really ought to be talking about is the individual sentence. . . .

Q: Although the language is dense throughout your fiction—and by dense I mean it offers resistance to the eye and the mind—it seems to have become even more intricate recently, more dense, especially in the three novellas which you've just finished. Do you feel this is true?

A: I hope it's true. And I hope it gets truer. My next novel—if I live and nothing happens—is going to be a book which I'm tentatively calling *The Franchiser* (though I think that this title is a particularly ugly one), about a man who goes out and buys franchises across the country. He's the man who's responsible for making America look like America, and to the degree that that's so, according to my lights, that makes him a hero. Because he makes plenty look like plenty. Or because he makes plenty look like plentiest. And this will give me an opportunity to check into a Ramada Inn, which is a franchise organization, and make my notes, as I did in the Natural History Museum, and do for the Ramada Inn what I hope I did for teeth. It will give me a splendid opportunity to discuss thirty-two of Mr. Howard Johnson's flavors, and to try to get the colors of his ice creams down. It will give me an opportunity to get down the late forties quality of the Fred Astaire Dance Studios, which still exist as franchises. So, hopefully, I have a form which will serve intentions I've had all my life. Not just a form—a concept particularly serviceable to me, the beauty that sleeps in the vulgar.

Q: Do you anticipate that *things* will displace personality in your fiction?

A: No. I'm no admirer of the French *nouveau roman*. No people live there. Things are a necessary backdrop to personalities and character, but personality must be the organizing principle of the novel. You can't have a novel about a television set. You can't have a novel about the texture of towels. It would be unbearable. So you've got to invent people to use those towels, you've got to invent a guy to watch that television set. You see, to the extent that there is a persistent theme in my work it's the theme of the human being as consumed consumer. . . .

Q: This mix of what linguists call register, added to the aggressive metaphor we've already talked about—the yoking of incongruous images—gives your prose a free-for-all quality. Any kind of language seems to be available to every character. Any given sentence might combine language drawn from radically separated realms of experience.

A: Yes. And I suppose what you're also saying is that there are people in my work who may suddenly speak like Ph.D.'s or Ph.D.'s like slumlords, but this is simply a convention of fiction and drama. Did the people in Elizabeth's court speak blank verse? Did the children in the nineteenth century speak the way that children in Henry James speak? I allow every character my diction. And may it serve him better than it serves me.

Q: That diction includes a variety which would not be available to anyone but the writer?

A: Probably, though writers do not own the language. We may copyright only what we use.

Q: Morty Perlmutter, who appears in a couple of your works, an anthropologist and Nobel Laureate, defines morality as "the awareness of others." Is Stanley Elkin, like Perlmutter, a kind of fictional anthropologist, a man who takes all humanity for his subject, and on equal terms?

A: Well, it's a question which is self-serving in the answer. The answer being yes. On the other hand, maybe it's not so self-serving if stated in another way: which is, human beings amuse me. But they *do* amuse me, and I do *like* them. One of the things that gets my back up—I'm still thinking about your question concerning critics—is that when critics aren't calling me a satirist, and when they aren't calling me a black humorist—a term I reject—they're saying that my characters are losers. I don't regard them as losers. The fact that they may be unhappy doesn't mean that they're losers. The fact that they may be outrageous or immoral doesn't mean that they're losers. The fact that they're obsessed, that they have obsessions which would get real people arrested, doesn't mean that they're losers. It means that they are simply demonstrating the kind of extravagance—the kind of *heroic* extravagance, if you will—that makes them, in my view, winners—winners, inasmuch as they *impress* me. Alas, they put others off.

Q: By saying you're not a black humorist, I take it you mean that you do not set out deliberately to ward off tragedy through humor. Yet your works are very funny in places, all of them. Is that humor a by-product of your amusement—to use your word—over your extravagant types?

A: I never deliberately set out to be funny. As a matter of fact, I didn't even *know* I was funny until a friend of mine told me that I wrote funny stuff. This was years ago, before I wrote my first novel, and before I had very much published, and I became very self-conscious about being "funny," and began, I think, to cultivate those aspects of my work which were amenable to humor. But I don't distinguish between race, creed, and color regarding comedy. I mean I do not know what the hell "black humor" even *means*. That's why I resent the title. Humor is humor. A joke is a joke, whether it's performed on a vaudeville stage, or in a church, or on a gallows. As a comic writer I think I'm something of an opportunist. That is, I write X, then discover two or three pages later that X is susceptible of being turned into a joke. Even if it is destructive of structure, even if it is distracting, I make the joke. I take the money and run, as it were. I make the joke because it amuses me to make the joke.

Q: You mentioned that even at the expense of structure you would make the joke. One criticism that might be raised against your novels is that they tend to be episodic; you seem to be less interested in structure, in the sense of plot or sequence of events, than you are in personality, or in rhetoric. Do you think this is true?

A: I think it is true. But I see nothing *necessarily* negative in that. I'm incapable of writing a detective story, which requires, it would seem to me, a knowledge of the end before one begins the first sentence. I'm incapable of long-distance plotting. I plot as I go along. This is true of my novels, not of my short stories. Something happens when I write a short story. That is, I have the entire story in view before I begin to write it. But it is not true when I am writing a novel. When I'm writing a novel I begin with a character, and with a character who has a particular occupation, an unusual occupation, and then I find out about the character, through the disparate episodes in which the character is involved. One discovers what one wants to say by saying it, as other people have pointed out.

Q: Is this another way of saying what you have said before, namely, that, because your prime interest is in the energy and impulse of the language, you have to follow the momentum of the language wherever it leads, regardless of structure?

A: Yes. The language blinds me to goals. It blinds me to ends, and that may very well be a flaw in my work. Certainly I admire what I cannot do. I also admire, as I've indicated before, what I *can* do. But I admire, let's say, a writer like Iris Murdoch, whose novels are superbly plotted. I admire a writer like William Trevor, whose novels are masterpieces of plot. An attention to writing ought not to exclude an attention to plot. In my case it does. . . .

Q: There's another form of momentum in your language, where one metaphor seems to generate a whole series of metaphors.

A: Yes. Well, this is the old business of cataloguing. I'm fascinated by catalogues. I love making them up. What Gass is to the sentence, I would like to be to the catalogue.

Q: You've mentioned some of your experiences and practices as a teacher. I wonder if you feel your experiences in the university have affected—or enabled—your work in any way?

A: Well, it has permitted my work in one way by cutting the work off at the pass. What I mean is, I am not one of those people with unlimited sources of energy. I cannot conceive of having to write all the time. I hold to the Hemingway notion of recharging the batteries. The ideal life, it seems to me, would be to write for nine or ten months, then teach for even more than that. Then write for another nine or ten months, teach for another year. I couldn't teach all the time. So the one thing reinforces the other.

Q: While you are in the process of writing a work, you've mentioned elsewhere, serendipity plays an important role in providing you with new materials. Could you talk about that?

A: . . . The idea for *Boswell* came to me while I was talking with a friend of mine named Phil London, who was regaling me with stories of how Boswell got to meet Voltaire, and I got the idea for *A Bad Man* talking with my friend Al Lebowitz who was telling me a sad story about a lawyer pal of his who was about to be put away for a year, thrown into jail for malpractice or something. And I thought, gee, what would it be like for a middle-class man to spend a year in a penitentiary? So I guess I would never have written *A Bad Man* had I not been told this story. That's an accident. They've all been accidents. You can tell my critics—"Leave him alone, he didn't mean it, it was an accident." Anyway, yes. I believe in the muse. And Her name is Serendipity.

LARRY McCAFFERY

"Stanley Elkin's Recovery of the Ordinary"

Critique, Volume 21, Number 2 (1979), pp. 39–51

The Franchiser (1976), Stanley Elkin's most successful novel to date, begins with the following paragraph:

> Past the orange roof and turquoise tower, past the immense sunburst of the green and yellow sign, past the golden arches, beyond the low buff building, beside the discrete hut, the dark top hat on the studio window shade, beneath the red and white longitudes of the enormous bucket, coming up to the thick shaft of the yellow arrow piercing the royal-blue field, he feels he is home. Is it Nashville? Elmira, New York? St. Louis County? A Florida key? The Illinois Arrowhead? Indiana like a holster, Ohio like a badge? Is he North? St. Paul, Minn.? Northeast? Boston, Mass.? The other side of America? Salt Lake? Los Angeles? At the bottom of the country? The Texas udder? Where? In Colorado's frame? Wyoming like a postage stamp? Michigan like a mitten? The chipped, eroding bays of the Northwest? Seattle? Bellingham, Washington?[1]

Like virtually all of Elkin's paragraphs, this one demonstrates his remarkable ability to transform the ordinary into the exceptional through fierce, energetic language. The elaborate, lengthy opening sentence, with its repetitious and alliterative prepositions ("past . . . past . . . past . . . beyond . . . beside . . . beneath"), leads to the simple declaration that some as-yet-unnamed "he" "feels he is home." We are surely surprised by the catalogue of towns and states that follow, many trailing similes behind them like lettering from a skywriting plane—how, we wonder, can this "he" feel at home if he doesn't know where he is? No matter; the similes rescue the list from boredom: Illinois is an "arrowhead" (yes, we nod, we can see that); Ohio is a badge, Indiana a holster, Michigan a mitten (of course, we never noticed that before); the lower part of Texas is an udder. Suddenly, these states have been changed for us, charged with a significance that they have never had before. We have now begun Elkin's most extreme, complex, and difficult work, a book which brings together all of his major themes with an energy and power—words difficult to resist in trying to label his fiction—that surpass anything he has written before. The book can serve, then, as a convenient vehicle to discuss all of Elkin's characteristic concerns. It also pushes his stylistic and structural oddities to their natural and perhaps even ultimate limits, but in such a way as to embody perfectly what has always been his major intention as a writer: the creation of wonderfully rich and excessive language which operates to unmask the beauty and wonder that is normally locked within the vulgar and ordinary.

All of Elkin's novels have dealt with the by-now familiar modern issues of isolation, alienation, and the existential construction of value systems to help fill the void, pass the time in the face of mortality and an absurd but potentially destructive exterior environment. Like many modern characters, Elkin's heroes all have the same primitive need to say, like Bellow's Henderson, *I want, I want,* but unlike Henderson or Huck or Hemingway's characters, and unlike Nabokov's Kinbote and Humbert, Coover's J. Henry Waugh, or Kesey's McMurtry, Elkin's characters find their transcendence and freedom not in lighting out for some literal or imagined territory, but in seeking out the familiar, in filling themselves with the drek and ticky-tack of modern America. These people hope to conquer transience with their childishly egocentric effort to incorporate as much into themselves as possible, to stuff themselves to the exploding point with Big Macs and Kentucky Fried Chicken, with Howard Johnson's Ice Cream for dessert; meanwhile, they are surreptitiously slipping napkins and plastic forks into their pockets, picking up stationery and envelopes from motel drawers, admiring their handfuls of matchbook covers which testify to their wanderings as surely as their Fotomat slides. Leo Feldman, the "Bad Man" of Elkin's second novel (1967), arrested and put in prison for "doing favors" for others, testifies for several pages at his trial about all the things of his past that have moved him. One of these magical catalogues reads as follows—like many of Elkin's catalogues, this one begins with a clear topic sentence (but a fragment) and then "moves" nowhere at all except by mere accretion of detail. The details show Elkin's wonderful eye for them and also generate a force of their own by their sheer rhythm and momentum:

> Glamour, magic and plentitude, I tell you. Plenty of plentitude. High waste in restaurants. Steaks no man can finish by himself, bottomless cups of coffee and lots of butter. Balloons for the kiddies, and the waiter passing mints. Ditto the individual machinery of motel rooms: Vibrabeds and the chamois for shoes, packets of instant coffee and powdered cream—the gizmo to boil the water. The paper ribbon in deference to my ass across the toilet seat breaks my heart. The magician's shy stooges and the tears of Miss America and her runners-up. Listen. 'Happy Birthday' in the night clubs and the 'Anniversary Waltz.' God bless people who take their celebrations to night clubs, I say. *Listen.* Miracle drugs, the eye bank, and the first crude words of mutes. The moment they unwrap the bandages four weeks after the operation. *Listen. Listen to me.* The oaths of foreigners for their final papers. Night-school graduation. A cake for the new nigger in the neighborhood. Towns chipping in for anything. People cured of cancer, and the singing in the London Underground during the Blitz. *Listen, listen to me now. Listen to me!* Sheriffs shaming lynch mobs. Boys who ask ugly girls to dance, and vice versa. Last stands of individual men, and generosity from unexpected quarters.[2]

Elkin's heroes are moved by these kinds of excesses because they are obsessively aware of death and because they are isolated in the midst of a world of plenty. Filled with the energy of wonder, they seek out mystery, constantly asking themselves, like Alexander Main in "The Bailbondsman," "What do I do with my wonder, I wonder?"[3] For Elkin's characters, the sources of mystery are everywhere, in both "The Great" or extraordinary (for Boswell), and (more typically) in the loneliness and suffering of the ordinary (for Dick Gibson, Alexander Main, and Feldman). These men desire to restore their "open-ended sense of mystery"[4] and to achieve it they constantly seek ways to intensify their ordinary experience, to arm and protect themselves against the primal emptiness by overwhelming themselves with profusion and excess.

Elkin's heroes are also outcasts and outsiders, men who typically operate on the fringes of society even as they control it, and who even prefer it that way for fear that they will have to share their bounty with others. Such basic selfishness may help explain why no truly significant women or satisfying love affairs occur in Elkin's fiction, except possibly for Ashenden's encounter with the Bear. As Boswell explains, "You had to go it alone for it to mean anything. To share experience with so much as one other person was immediately to halve it. . . . In the long run it was the deepest wisdom to be a pirate, to plot among the survivors on the beach to kill off the other survivors, and then to scheme how to somehow dispose of whoever remained."[5] The major resource of these characters, then, is simply their incredible energy and drive, their willingness to pursue their goals with what Elkin himself has termed their "heroic extravagance,"[6] which leads to their "obsessive" qualities, well described in the only significant critical overview of Elkin's work.[7] Ben Flesh in *The Franchiser* brings all of Elkin's previous concerns into sharper focus than ever before, and the reason he does is that Elkin finally has discovered an occupation for one of his major characters that serves his intentions perfectly.

Elkin has acknowledged in two interviews that his stories are usually generated by the occupations of his characters;[8] once he has the occupation, he pursues its implication as far as his language allows him. The occupations—Feldman is a department store owner, Dick Gibson is a radio announcer, Alexander Main is a bailbondsman—allow his characters to pursue their drive for extreme demands while at the same time constantly coming into contact with the ordinary. In Ben Flesh, however, Elkin has created a man who not only comes into contact with ordinary America but who is actually "the man who made America look like America, who made America famous" (262). Ben buys franchises and, as Elkin summarizes, is "a man of franchise, a true democrat who would make Bar Harbor, Maine look like Chicago, who would quell distinction, obliterate difference, who would common denominate until Americans recognize that it was America everywhere" (164). In one of his wonderful lists of things, Ben explains to one of his god-cousins exactly who he is:

> I'm Mr. Softee, I'm the chicken from the Colonel. Cock-a-doodle-do and the sky is falling. I'm the Fred Astaire man. I'm the Exxon dealer, we thought you'd like to know. . . . I'm a cultured man. I'm One Hour Martinizing and the Cinema I, Cinema II in the shopping center. I'm America's Innkeeper, I'm

> Robo-Wash. I'm Benny Flesh, K-O-A, and Econo-Car International. I'm H & R Block, but it's seasonal. The culture? *I'm* the culture! Ben Flesh, the Avon lady, Ben, the Burger King. Or maybe you meant something more academic? Sure. Okay. How-doyoudo? I'm EvelynWoodofEvelynWoodReading-Dynamics. Pleasedtomeetcha. WannareadW*arand-Peace*onyourlunchbreak? The culture. Sweetie, I've got ice-vending machines in every Big Ten campus town in the Midwest. Want, want to know something? My hand don't work but I'm—hah hah, this'll kill you—Mister Magic Fingers. Yes! (192–93)

Thus Ben is not just an observer of the vulgar, of the ordinary crap that Elkin has called "the true American graffiti, the perfect queer calligraphy of the American signature—which gives us meaning and makes us fun."[9] No, Ben is the shaper of appearance, the man who brings all these things into being. Unlike so many other recent American characters who despair of such things, Ben is no snob about the job a One Hour Martinizer can do with your suit, and he appreciates the fact that Ronald MacDonald is, after Santa Claus, the most recognized person in the world to children. Indeed, Ben's tendency to appreciate and embrace these aspects of American culture may be an ultimately healthier response than the ones we've seen in most contemporary books—especially if we accept the plastic buffalo-hump dealer in Barthelme's *Snow White*, who suggests that since "trash" may soon be all we have left around us, we had better stop trying to figure out how to "dispose" of it and learn, instead, how to "dig" it.[10] Commanded by his dying godfather, who made his fortune as a costume designer for musical comedies in the 1930's, to "recover the ordinary" (40), Ben sets out to costume America with his own bright colors and gaudy set decorations; his rapid rise to power and money closely parallels America's own growth during the 1950's and 60's.

Ben is also pursued, though, by the spectre of what haunts all of Elkin's characters since *Boswell* (1964): death, bodily decay, and the prospect of his own loss of literal and figurative potency. Like Boswell's allegoric confrontation with John Sallow ("The Grim Reaper") in the wrestling ring, Ben's battle with multiple sclerosis is a fight which he quickly realizes he cannot win but only delay. His initial reaction to the diagnosis of his disease is simply to flee, to hop in his huge Cadillac and drive through a hellishly hot Midwestern landscape, made all the more uncomfortable by the sudden failure of America's energy sources (thus making Ben's identification with America all the more evident). Later, when he obtains a remission from his disease, he understands that "we live mostly in remission. Death and pain being the conditions of our pardon" (214). Ben had been told by his godfather that he should savor the fact that he is alive at all: "How crowded is the universe," his godfather said. "How stuffed to bursting with its cargo of crap. . . . I am talking the long shot of existence, the odds no gambler in the world would take, that you would ever come to life as a person, a boy called Ben Flesh. . . . It's incredible really. Amazing. . . . My God, lad, you're a fucking celebration" (22). Until his numbing bout with m.s., Ben pursued the ordinary, although dedicatedly, at least partially as a matter of obligation. Now, however, when he walks into one of his movie franchises during a period of remission, he find himself filled with wonder and excitement; when he lists its features, he fleshes them out with familiar details which somehow suggest his sense of mystery:

> The movie's glass candy cases as big around as a boy's bedroom. With their gorgeous tiers of cellophane-wrapped, cardboard candy boxes with their miniatures—their individually sheathed Heaths and Peter Paul's Mounds and Almond Joys and Milky Ways and Mars. Milk Duds and jujubes like boxes of marble. No *bars* any more. Oh, the immense dark Hershey's of course, yellow Butterfingers long as a ruler (seventy-five cents some of them, practically nothing under forty-five cents). . . . The movie's thick carpets, a bright, gentle meld and die-dye of color giving ground to color like the progress of landscape, laws of geography. My movie's toilets, its Women's room and Men's, with its urinals white as pillowcase, its stalls of decorator colors not found in nature, and its tiny discrete colored tiles like squares on a board game. (230)

Ben's losing battle with m.s. is not his only reminder of the potential for decline and loss. His eighteen godcousins, whose sameness mirrors the effect that Ben spreads wherever he goes, are a sort of conglomerate alter ego for Ben. Their various grotesque diseases, which rapidly begin to kill them off late in the novel, are a constant, cumulative reminder to Ben of his own precarious existence. Then, too, the momentum of his franchise success begins to slacken and then to fail alarmingly; Ben is forced to close many of them, consolidates his finances, and then eventually puts all his money and hope into one final gamble: a Travel Inn which he builds just south of Chattanooga in the hopes of attracting tourists traveling south to Disney World. The forces of decline are all around; his carefully made plans are foiled by the Arab oil embargo which lowers the speed limit to 55 m.p.h. and thus makes Chattanooga too far away for one day's drive from the big Midwestern cities. On the night of his grand opening, Ben realizes that he is ruined; but on this, the night of his greatest failure—with his own physical decay an imminent reality—Ben receives one of his miraculous insights: listening in on all the love-making that is occurring in the few rooms of his motel that are occupied, he is suddenly moved (as Feldman is just before being found guilty at the end of *A Bad Man*); when his clerk asks why he seems so upset, Flesh answers, "Why? Because love happens . . . It really happens. It actually takes place. It occurs. Why am I upset? Because love is sweeping the country and lyrics are the ground of being, singing the literature of the ordinary, and romance is real as heartburn. Because guys score and stare at the women next to them and trace their fingers gently over their sweetheart's eyebrow breaking like a wave" (330).

Ben's reaction is not a deliberate, sentimental decision to ignore the forces of ugliness and destruction around him. Indeed, Elkin's characters rarely seem to ignore *anything*, even the repellent. Earlier in the novel, during one of Ben's marvelous set pieces at an Arthur Murry Dance Studio, he had announced after looking into one woman's shopping bag, "There are Hefties there, liners for garbage cans. How civilized! Maybe all that distinguishes man from the beasts is that man had the consideration to invent garbage can liners. What a convenience! We die, yes, but are compensated by a million conveniences" (63). With characteristic manic energy, Ben begins to list for his motel clients all the major killers of people in the United States, including the horrible diseases that killed his godcousins. As with nearly all of Elkin's characters, facing the gruesome and the deadly is not nearly enough to cover up Ben's sense of amazement and mystery at what Nick Carraway called, under rather similarly disturbing circumstances, "the inexhaustible variety of life."[11] "And *still* they still smooch," Ben says wonderingly when he has finished his mortality list: "They come calling, call coming, go courting, hold hands, sip soda through a straw, French kiss with their throats sore and their noses running" (331). For Ben this

"Night of Love" acts as a confirmation of his own desire to shout affirmation even as he hurtles toward the abyss.[12] Soon he is renewing his egocentric desire to be at the center of things, the axis around which all else revolves. Looking at the Ptolemaic map on the big display board opposite the registration desk, with his own Travel Lodge located at the center of the universe, Ben "suddenly sees it not as a wheel of distances but of options. . . . He is surrounded by place, by tiers of geography like bands of amphitheater. He is at the center. . . . Anywhere he went would be the center. He would pull the center with him, the world rearranging itself around him like a woman smoothing her skirt, touching her hair" (331–32).

The Franchiser concludes by taking us back to its opening scene, with Ben sitting in a gasoline station, thinking to himself that "People were good . . . Life was exciting" (341). The book's final paragraph is a powerful and moving testimony to the total commitment that Elkin's characters are able to make to the "fucking celebration" that is life and to the transformational ability of their energetic imaginations:

> He was broken, they would kill him. The Finsbergs were an endangered species and his Travel Inn a disaster. They would kill him. Within weeks he would be strapped to a wheelchair. And ah, he thought, euphorically, ecstatically, this privileged man who could have been a vegetable or mineral instead of an animal, and a lower animal instead of a higher, who could have been a pencil or a dot on a die, who could have been a stitch in a glove or change in someone's pocket, or a lost dollar nobody found, who could have been stillborn or less sentient than sand, or the chemical flash of somebody else's fear, ahh. *Ahh!* (343)[13]

The second and more important part of this discussion—an analysis of Elkin's style and structural approach in *The Franchiser*—is needed to correct a misunderstanding of Elkin's style that has prevented him from taking his rightful place as one of America's most gifted and original voices. Anyone familiar with the critical reception of Elkin's books knows the consistency with which critics comment that although they are immensely entertained by his novels, they find that the whole is less than the parts. When the point was brought up in an interview, Elkin commented, appropriately, that "Although I am immensely entertained by their reviews, I end up saying that the whole is less than the parts."[14] Still, the major charge made against Elkin is that his books are unstructured and episodic in nature—an obvious flaw in a critical climate that champions the intricate and finely wrought constructions of Barth, Nabokov, and Gass. In the same interview, Elkin, with his dander obviously up, replied to this charge that, "As a matter of fact, I *am* concerned with structure and form and my novels *are* structured and formed. There isn't a novel I have written which does not have a very well-defined structure. . . . Now, if people don't recognize the structure, that isn't my fault."[15]

Actually, Elkin's claims that his novels have a "well-defined structure" are rather misleading and were probably induced by his simply getting tired of critics blaming him for something that does not have anything to do with the success of what he is aiming for in his novels. When we examine the way his books work, they really *do not* have a tightly woven structure, at least not in any usual notion of plot. Oh, they have a development of a sort, although Elkin's books develop more by a principle of repetition than by subtle shifts in personal motivation or by the gradual introduction of narrative complexities; and they usually have a sense of progression—as in *The Franchiser* with the decline of Ben's fortunes—although even it is created more by accretion than anything else. If we really take Elkin's books apart paragraph by paragraph, we hardly find the carefully balanced blend of elements and subtle interrelationships among significant details that we would find, say, in Nabokov's novels. Quite the contrary, we find constant digression, tall tales, jokes, and descriptions, none of which seems to lead anywhere. Above all, we discover that Elkin loves to stop the action of his novels to present what is his most singular and successful stylistic feature: his catalogues and lists. These catalogues do not contribute to the action nor even directly assist in illuminating anything related to the plot except insofar as they demonstrate the incredible vitality of the characters' rhetoric and imaginations. If we complain that Elkin has stopped the action "merely" to create a catalogue, tell a joke, or make a sales pitch, we are missing the point. As he explained in an earlier interview, he is interested in using his prose as a means of persuading his readers of "the possibilities inherent in rhetoric. . . . Fiction gives an opportunity for rhetoric to happen. It provides a stage where language can stand."[16] Not aspects of the plot, Elkin's jokes, catalogues, and digressions are the stages where rhetoric surely does happen.

Elkin goes on to define what he calls his "opportunist" approach to fiction: "As a comic writer I think I'm something of an opportunist. That is, I write X, then discover two or three pages later that X is susceptible of being turned into a joke. Even if it is destructive of structure, even if it is distracting, I make the joke. I take the money and run, as it were."[17] Such self-evaluation—which seems more accurate than the earlier claims about "tight-structure"—is further clarified when he explains that his goal in writing is the creation of a fierce language capable of introducing new perspectives and significance where none had previously existed. "The language blinds me to goals," he admits—and then adds, "It blinds me to ends."[18] After having read a lengthy digressive passage from "The Condominium," Elkin remarks that, "Well, that passage hasn't got a damn thing to do with the flow of the story. Indeed, it interrupts it. . . . Yet it seemed to me at the time, and seems to me now on rereading it, to be more important than anything that happens in the scene."[19] Of course, from Elkin's standpoint the passage *is* the most important element in the scene simply because it has the best language. Critics regularly seem to condemn Elkin for what they applaud in, say, Barthelme: "Give me the odd linguistic trip, stutter, and fall, and I will be content," we read in *Snow White*,[20] and we forgive Barthelme for his plotless narrative, his unusual digressions and lists, knowing full well that what he is doing is creating a linguistic object, a rhetorical free-for-all. The difference, it seems to me, is that we forgive—even applaud—Barthelme for his high-wire performances because he does not bother to pretend, even remotely, that he is doing anything other than writing beautifully constructed sentences. Because Elkin's eye sees realistic rather than surrealistic details, we take him to task for not adhering to the structural norms of realistic fiction. Probably the best way we can see how his novels work is to consider his use of the catalogue, the key to both the structure of his books and the peculiar, obsessive quality of his major characters.

"I'm fascinated by catalogues," Elkin has commented; "I love making them up. What Gass is to the sentence, I would like to be to the catalogue."[21] The structure of *The Franchiser* relies on catalogues the way that off-shore derricks rely on their piles for support. The book contains literally hundreds of these catalogues, and the plot often seems little more than an excuse to carry Ben Flesh from one scene to another which he can then describe in vibrant detail. There are lists of stereo accessories and love affairs, descriptions of movie theaters and the people who attend them, of the smells to be found in One Hour Martinizers, of the sight and textures of conventioneers' suits, of different kinds of cereal boxes and the variety of tactile experiences you get while standing under a shower; in his longest list, which goes on for over three pages, we have a complete inventory of every standard item to be found in a Travel Inn. These catalogues frequently seem to begin as simply a mode of description, but verisimilitude quickly gives way to deliberate excess and overstatement, a profusion of metaphor and simile which seems almost self-generating. Consider the following description of a guard early in the book:

> He spotted Mopiani from the Caddy as he drove up, the man pneumatic in the cop's criss-crossed leather that bound Mopiani's tunic, the thick straps and ammunition loops potted with bullets, the long holster like a weapon, its pistol some bent brute at a waterhole, the trigger like a visible genital, the uniform itself a weapon, the metal blades of Mopiani's badge, the big key ring with its brass claws, a tunnel of handcuffs doubled on his backside, the weighted, tapered cosh, the sergelike grainy blue hide, the stout black brogans, and the patent-leather bill of his cap like wet ink. He leaned against the blond boards that covered the entrance to the building and smoked a cigarette. In his other hand he held a walkie-talkie. (7)

Such rhetorical excesses, of course, destroy the linear movement of the book's plot and actually become the center of focus rather than serving as subsidiary aspects of realism. They are entirely appropriate since Elkin, like Gass, is primarily interested in keeping the reader imprisoned on the page, entrapped and entranced not by themes or mimetic illusions but by sentences. Elkin remarks that "A book doesn't have to sell people anything but language . . . If the writer is doing his job, he is thinking only in terms of sentences and metaphor and syntax. These are the only things that are really real to him. That's all I care to be admired for."[22]

In addition to serving as rhetorical sounding boards for Elkin's remarkable prose, the catalogues serve to reinforce the central aspect of his characters. The over-richness of the language in Elkin's novels is entirely in keeping with the compulsive and obsessive nature of his heroes; indeed, as the details spew forth like quarters from some lucky slot machine, we find a linguistic reflection of his heroes' desire to contain the world, to enrich their beings as fully as possible: "Elkin's narrators repeat and exaggerate, even refurbish old cliches to express the reality of their obsessed lives. Their prose expands, runs on, grabs at any possibility, even when describing an ordinary occasion. For Elkin's hyperconscious heroes, though, few occasions are ordinary: everything is turned strange and significant by their obsessions."[23] One justification for the richness of details in *The Franchiser* is provided by Ben Flesh's godfather's desire that Ben "recover the ordinary"—a recovery which is made possible for the reader in large measure by the catalogues throughout the novel. The *real* justification for Elkin's catalogue method, however, is that the catalogues typically do rescue the ordinary by transforming the mundane details of American life into expansive, energetic prose.

"All I want from a reviewer," Elkin has said almost wistfully, "is for the man to say, 'This fellow writes well.'"[24] Ladies and gentlemen, it is about time the word started getting out: this fellow Stanley Elkin writes *well*.

Notes

1. Stanley Elkin, *The Franchiser* (New York: Farrar, Straus & Giroux, 1976), p. 3. Subsequent references are to this edition. For a listing of Elkin's works, together with critical articles and reviews of those works, see my "Stanley Elkin: a Bibliography, 1957–1977," *Bulletin of Bibliography*, 34, 2 (1977), 73–76.
2. Stanley Elkin, *A Bad Man* (New York: Random House, 1967), p. 321.
3. Stanley Elkin, "The Bailbondsman," in *Searches and Seizures* (New York: Random House, 1973), p. 124.
4. Raymond Olderman, "The Six Crises of Dick Gibson," *Iowa Review*, 8 (Winter 1976), 130.
5. Stanley Elkin, *Boswell* (1964; rpt. New York: Berkley Medallion, 1967), p. 272. The desire to hold on to things is evident in Boswell's earlier remark: "That was the important thing: was it possible to keep anything? Was it possible to keep one solitary thing? Never mind the money in the minds, the good looks, the health—*could you keep your fingernails?*" (p. 242).
6. Scott Sanders, "An Interview with Stanley Elkin," *Contemporary Literature*, 16, 2 (Spring 1975), 141.
7. Thomas LeClair, "The Obsessional Fiction of Stanley Elkin," *Contemporary Literature*, 16, 2 (Spring 1975), 146–62.
8. See the interview by Sanders and also Thomas LeClair, "The Art of Fiction LXI" (interview with Stanley Elkin), *Paris Review*, No. 66 (Summer 1976), 54–86.
9. Sanders, p. 137; Elkin also repeats this phrase verbatim in *The Franchiser* (p. 270).
10. Donald Barthelme, *Snow White* (1967; rpt. New York: Bantam, 1968) p. 97.
11. F. Scott Fitzgerald, *The Great Gatsby* (1925; rpt. New York: Scribners, 1955), p. 24.
12. Perhaps the most extreme example of this kind of defiance appears in the last scene of "The Condominium" as Preminger hurtles to the suicidal death thinking, "*And the hole, the hole I'm going to make when I hit that ground!*"; in *Searches and Seizures*, p. 304.
13. Nearly all of Elkin's works conclude in this open-ended, affirmative manner; even though most of the novels have moved their major characters to a dissipation of their energy, there remain new prospects, new possibilities when the book concludes (cf. *Boswell*, *A Bad Man*, *The Dick Gibson Show*, "The Bailbondsman," "The Making of Ashenden," and many of the short stories). *A Bad Man*, for example, concludes as follows: "And possibly they would only beat him very badly, inexpertly. The homunculus would not rip his heart. He would recover. Or perhaps such an 'accident' was God's sign that the Diaspora was still unfinished, and that until it was, until everything had happened, until Feldman had filled the world, all its desert places and each of its precipices, all of its surfaces and everywhere under the seas, and along its beaches, he could not be punished or suffer the eternal lean years of death. Why, I *am* innocent, he thought, even as they beat him. And indeed, he felt so" (p. 336).
14. LeClair (Interview with Stanley Elkin), p. 67.
15. Ibid.
16. Sanders, p. 132.
17. Sanders, p. 142.
18. Sanders, p. 143.
19. Sanders, p. 144.
20. Barthelme, p. 139.
21. Sanders, p. 144.
22. Sanders, p. 135.
23. LeClair, "The Obsessional Fiction of Stanley Elkin," p. 150.
24. Jeffrey Duncan, "A Conversation with Stanley Elkin and William Gass," *Iowa Review*, 7 (Winter 1976), 54.

Ralph Ellison

1914–

On March 1, 1914, American novelist and essayist Ralph Waldo Ellison was born in Oklahoma City, Oklahoma. His father, Lewis Ellison, was a construction worker and tradesman who died when Ellison was three. His mother, the former Ida Millsap, worked as a domestic servant while Ellison grew up thriving on the discarded magazines and phono records she brought home from the white households where she worked.

In 1933 Ellison began studying music at the Tuskegee Institute in Alabama, where he remained three years before coming to New York in 1936 to study sculpture and work at the Federal Writers' Project. In New York he met Langston Hughes and Richard Wright, who gave him great encouragement in his writing. Ellison's short stories, essays, and reviews began appearing in the *Antioch Review*, the *New Masses*, and many other magazines and journals in the late thirties. In 1942 Ellison edited the *Negro Quarterly*. After World War II he received a Rosenwald Fellowship which enabled him to write the widely acclaimed *Invisible Man*, published in 1952. This long novel is both an historical biography of the black man in America and an allegory of man's quest for identity. *Invisible Man* received the National Book Award for fiction in 1953 and, according to a *Book Week* poll in 1965, had been the most distinguished novel published during the preceding twenty years. *Shadow and Act*, Ellison's second book, is a collection of personal essays about literature, folklore, jazz, and the author's life.

Ralph Ellison has been both lecturer and professor at Yale, Chicago, New York, and numerous other American universities; he also lectured extensively in Germany in 1954. Ellison held the Rome Fellowship of the American Academy of Arts and Letters from 1955 to 1957, and received the United States Medal of Freedom in 1969. He is on the editorial board of the *American Scholar*, has served as trustee of the John F. Kennedy Center for the Performing Arts, and as honorary consultant in American Letters at the Library of Congress. In 1946 Ellison married Fanny McConnell, and they now live in New York City.

A few years ago, in an otherwise dreary and better forgotten number of *Horizon* devoted to a louse-up of life in the United States, I read with great excitement an episode from *Invisible Man*. It described a free-for-all of blindfolded Negro boys at a stag party of the leading citizens of a small Southern town. Before being blindfolded the boys are made to stare at a naked white woman; then they are herded into the ring, and, after the battle royal, one of the fighters, his mouth full of blood, is called upon to give his high school valedictorian's address. As he stands under the lights of the noisy room, the citizens rib him and make him repeat himself; an accidental reference to equality nearly ruins him, but everything ends well and he receives a handsome briefcase containing a scholarship to a Negro college.

This episode, I thought, might well be the high point of an excellent novel. It has turned out to be not *the* high point but rather one of the many peaks of a book of the very first order, a superb book. The valedictorian is himself Invisible Man. He adores the college but is thrown out before long by its president, Dr. Bledsoe, a great educator and leader of his race, for permitting a white visitor to visit the wrong places in the vicinity. Bearing what he believes to be a letter of recommendation from Dr. Bledsoe he comes to New York. The letter actually warns prospective employers against him. He is recruited by white radicals and becomes a Negro leader, and in the radical movement he learns eventually that throughout his entire life his relations with other men have been schematic; neither with Negros nor with whites has he ever been visible, real. I think that in reading the *Horizon* excerpt I may have underestimated Mr. Ellison's ambition and power for the following very good reason, that one is accustomed to expect excellent novels about boys, but a modern novel about men is exceedingly rare. For this enormously complex and difficult American experience of ours very few people are willing to make themselves morally and intellectually responsible. Consequently, maturity is hard to find.

It is commonly felt that there is no strength to match the strength of those powers which attack and cripple modern mankind. And this feeling is, for the reader of modern fiction, all too often confirmed when he approaches a new book. He is prepared, skeptically, to find what he has found before, namely, that family and class, university, fashion, the giants of publicity and manufacture, have had a larger share in the creation of someone called a writer than truth or imagination—that Bendix and Studebaker and the nylon division of Du Pont, and the University of Chicago, or Columbia or Harvard or Kenyon College, have once more proved mightier than the single soul of an individual; to find that one more lightly manned position has been taken. But what a great thing it is when a brilliant individual victory occurs, like Mr. Ellison's, proving that a truly heroic quality can exist among our contemporaries. People too thoroughly determined—and our institutions by their size and force too thoroughly determine—can't approach this quality. That can only be done by those who resist the heavy influences and make their own synthesis out of the vast mass of phenomena, the seething, swarming body of appearances, facts, and details. From this harassment and threatened dissolution by details, a writer tries to rescue what is important. Even when he is most bitter, he makes by his tone a declaration of values and he says, in effect: "There is something nevertheless that a man may hope to be." This tone, in the best pages of *Invisible Man*, those pages, for instance, in which an incestuous Negro farmer tells his tale to a white New England philanthropist, comes through very powerfully; it is tragicomic, poetic, the tone of the very strongest sort of creative intelligence.

In a time of specialized intelligences, modern imaginative writers make the effort to maintain themselves as *un*specialists, and their quest is for a true middle-of-consciousness for everyone. What language is it that we can all speak, and what is it that we can all recognize, burn at, weep over; what is the stature we can without exaggeration claim for ourselves; what is the main address of consciousness?

I was keenly aware, as I read this book, of a very significant kind of independence in the writing. For there is a "way" for Negro novelists to go at their problems, just as there are Jewish or Italian "ways." Mr. Ellison has not adopted a minority tone. If he had done so, he would have failed to establish a true middle-of-consciousness for everyone.

Negro Harlem is at once primitive and sophisticated; it exhibits the extremes of instinct and civilization as few other American communities do. If a writer dwells on the peculiarity of this, he ends with an exotic effect. And Mr. Ellison is not exotic. For him this balance of instinct and culture or civilization is not a Harlem matter; it is *the* matter, German, French, Russian, American, universal, a matter very little understood. It is thought that Negroes and other minority people, kept under in the great status battle, are in the instinct cellar of dark enjoyment. This imagined enjoyment provokes envious rage and murder; and then it is a large portion of human nature itself which becomes the fugitive murderously pursued. In our society Man—Himself—is idolized and publicly worshipped, but the single individual must hide himself underground and try to save his desires, his thoughts, his soul, in invisibility. He must return to himself, learning self-acceptance and rejecting all that threatens to deprive him of his manhood.

This is what I make of *Invisible Man*. It is not by any means faultless; I don't think the hero's experiences in the Communist party are as original in conception as other parts of the book, and his love affair with a white woman is all too brief, but it is an immensely moving novel and it has greatness.

So many hands have been busy at the interment of the novel—the hands of Paul Valéry, the hands of the editors of literary magazines, of scholars who decide when genres come and go, the hands of innumerable pipsqueaks as well—that I can't help feeling elated when a resurrection occurs. People read history and then seem to feel that everything has to conclude in their own time. "We have read history, and therefore history is over," they appear to say. Really, all that such critics have the right to say is that fine novels are few and far between. That's perfectly true. But then fine anythings are few and far between. If these critics wanted to be extremely truthful, they'd say they were bored. Boredom, of course, like any mighty force, you must respect. There is something terribly impressive about the boredom of a man like Valéry who could no longer bear to read that the carriage had come for the duchess at four in the afternoon. And certainly there are some notably boring things to which we owe admiration of a sort.

Not all the gravediggers of the novel have such distinction as Valéry's, however. Hardly. And it's difficult to think of them as rising dazzled from a volume of Stendhal, exclaiming "God!" and then with angry determination seizing their shovels to go and heap more clods on the coffin. No, theirs unfortunately isn't often the disappointment of spirits formed under the influence of the masters. They make you wonder how, indeed, they *would* be satisfied. A recent contributor to *Partisan Review*, for instance, complains that modern fiction does not keep pace with his swift-wheeling modern consciousness which apparently leaves the photon far behind in its speed. He names a few *really* modern writers of fiction, their work unfortunately still unpublished, and makes a patronizing reference to *Invisible Man:* almost, but not quite, the real thing, it is "raw" and "overambitious." And the editors of *Partisan Review* who have published so much of this modern fiction that their contributor attacks, what do they think of this? They do not say what they think; neither of this piece nor of another lulu on the same subject and in the same issue by John Aldridge. Mr. Aldridge writes: "There are only two cultural pockets left in America, and they are the Deep South and that area of northeastern United States whose moral capital is Boston, Massachusetts. This is to say that these are the only places where there are any manners. In all other parts of the country people live in a kind of vastly standardized cultural prairie, a sort of infinite Middle West, and that means that they don't really live and they don't really do anything."

Most Americans thus are Invisible. Can we wonder at the cruelty of dictators when even a literary critic, without turning a hair, announces the death of a hundred million people?

Let us suppose that the novel is, as they say, played out. Let us only suppose it, for I don't believe it. But what if it is so? Will such tasks as Mr. Ellison has set himself no more be performed? Nonsense. New means, when new means are necessary, will be found. To find them is easier than to suit the disappointed consciousness and to penetrate the thick walls of boredom within which life lies dying.—SAUL BELLOW, "Man Underground," *Cmty*, June 1952, pp. 608–10

Interviewer: When did you begin *Invisible Man?*

Ellison: In the summer of 1945. I had returned from the sea, ill, with advice to get some rest. Part of my illness was due, no doubt, to the fact that I had not been able to write a novel for which I'd received a Rosenwald Fellowship the previous winter. So on a farm in Vermont where I was reading *The Hero* by Lord Raglan and speculating on the nature of Negro leadership in the United States, I wrote the first paragraph of *Invisible Man*, and was soon involved in the struggle of creating the novel.

Interviewers: How long did it take you to write it?

Ellison: Five years, with one year out for a short novel which was unsatisfactory, ill-conceived and never submitted for publication.

Interviewers: Did you have everything thought out before you began to write *Invisible Man?*

Ellison: The symbols and their connections were known to me. I began it with a chart of the three-part division. It was a conceptual frame with most of the ideas and some incidents indicated. The three parts represent the narrator's movement from, using Kenneth Burke's terms, purpose to passion to perception. These three major sections are built up of smaller units of three which mark the course of the action and which depend for their development upon what I hoped was a consistent and developing motivation. However, you'll note that the maximum insight on the hero's part isn't reached until the final section. After all, it's a novel about innocence and human error, a struggle through illusion to reality. Each section begins with a sheet of paper; each piece of paper is exchanged for another and contains a definition of his identity, or the social role he is to play as defined for him by others. But all say essentially the same thing, "Keep this nigger boy running." Before he could have some voice in his own destiny he had to discard these old identities and illusions; his enlightenment couldn't come until then. Once he recognizes the hole of darkness into which these papers put him, he has to burn them. That's the plan and the intention; whether I achieved this is something else. . . .

Interviewers: Do you have any difficulty controlling your characters? E. M. Forster says that he sometimes finds a character running away with him.

Ellison No, because I find that a sense of the ritual understructure of the fiction helps to guide the creation of characters. Action is the thing. We are what we do and do not do. The problem for me is to get from A to B to C. My anxiety about transitions greatly prolonged the writing of my book. The naturalists stick to case histories and sociology and are willing to compete with the camera and the tape recorder. I despise concreteness in writing, but when reality is deranged in fiction, one must worry about the seams. . . .

You know, I'm still thinking of your question about the use of Negro experience as material for fiction. One function of serious literature is to deal with the moral core of a given society. Well, in the United States the Negro and his status have always stood for that moral concern. He symbolizes among other things the human and social possibility of equality. This is the moral question raised in our two great nineteenth-century novels, *Moby-Dick* and *Huckleberry Finn*. The very center of Twain's book revolves finally around the boy's relations with Nigger Jim and the question of what Huck should do about getting Jim free after the two scoundrels had sold him. There is a magic here worth conjuring, and that reaches to the very nerve of the American consciousness—so why should I abandon it? Our so-called race problem has now lined up with the world problems of colonialism and the struggle of the West to gain the allegiance of the remaining non-white people who have thus far remained outside the Communist sphere; thus its possibilities for art have increased rather than lessened. Looking at the novelist as manipulator and depictor of moral problems, I ask myself how much of the achievement of democratic ideals in the United States has been affected by the steady pressure of Negroes and those whites who were sensitive to the implications of our condition; and I know that without that pressure the position of our country before the world would be much more serious than it is even now. Here is part of the social dynamics of a great society. Perhaps the discomfort about protest in books by Negro authors comes because since the nineteenth century American literature has avoided profound moral searching. It was too painful, and besides, there were specific problems of language and form to which the writers could address themselves. They did wonderful things, but perhaps they left the real problems untouched. There are exceptions, of course, like Faulkner, who has been working the great moral theme all along, taking it up where Mark Twain put it down.

I feel that with my decision to devote myself to the novel I took on one of the responsibilities inherited by those who practice the craft in the United States: that of describing for all that fragment of the huge diverse American experience which I know best, and which offers me the possibility of contributing not only to the growth of the literature but to the shaping of the culture as I should like it to be. The American novel is in this sense a conquest of the frontier; as it describes our experience, it creates it.—Ralph Ellison, Interview by Alfred Chester, Vilma Howard, *PRev*, Spring 1955, pp. 180–83

The basic unity of human experience—that is what Ellison asserts; and he sets the richness of his own experience and that of many Negroes he has known, and his own early capacity to absorb the general values of Western culture, over against what Wright called "the essential bleakness of black life in America." What he is saying here is not that "bleakness" does not exist, and exist for many, but that it has not been the key fact of his own experience, and that his own experience is part of the story. It must be reckoned with, too:

> For even as his life toughens the Negro, even as it brutalizes him, sensitizes him, dulls him, goads him to anger, moves him to irony, sometimes fracturing and sometimes affirming his hopes . . . it *conditions* him to deal with his life and with himself. Because it is *his* life, and no mere abstraction in somebody's head.

Not only the basic unity, but the rich variety, of life is what concerns him; and this fact is connected with his personal vision of the opportunity in being an American: "The diversity of American life is often painful, frequently burdensome and always a source of conflict, but in it lies our fate and our hope." In many places, Ellison insists on his love of diversity and a pluralistic society. For instance, in "That Same Pain, That Same Pleasure": "I believe in diversity, and I think that the real death of the United States will come when everyone is just alike." The appreciation of this variety is, in itself, a school for the imagination and moral sympathy. And, for Ellison, being a "Negro American" has to do with this appreciation, not only of the Negro past in America, but with the complex fluidity of the present:

> It has to do with a special perspective on the national ideals and the national conduct, and with a tragicomic attitude toward the universe. It has to do with special emotions evoked by the details of cities and countrysides, with forms of labor and with forms of pleasure; with sex and with love, with food and with drink, with machines and with animals; with climates and with dwellings, with places of worship and places of entertainment; with garments and dreams and idioms of speech; with manners and customs, with religion and art, with life styles and hoping, and with that special sense of predicament and fate which gives directions and resonance to the Freedom Movement. It involves a rugged initiation into the mysteries and rites of color which makes it possible for Negro Americans to suffer the injustice which race and color are used to excuse without losing sight of either the humanity of those who inflict that injustice or the motives, rational or irrational, out of which they act. It imposes the uneasy burden and occasional joy of a complex double vision, a fluid, ambivalent response to men and events which represents, at its finest, a profoundly civilized adjustment to the cost of being human in this modern world.

Out of this view of the life of the "Negro American"—which is a view of *life*—it is no wonder that Ellison does not accept a distinction between the novel as "protest" and the novel as "art"—or rather, sees this distinction as a merely superficial one, not to be trusted. His own approach is twofold. On the one hand, he says "protest is an element of all art," but he would not limit protest to the social or political objection. In one sense, it might be a "technical assault" on earlier styles—but we know that Ellison regards "techniques" as moral vision, and a way of creating the self. In another sense, the protest may be, as in *Oedipus Rex* or *The Trial*, "against the limitation of human life itself." In yet another sense, it may be—and I take it that Ellison assumes that it always is—a protest against some aspect of a personal fate:

> . . . that intensity of personal anguish which compels the artist to seek relief by projecting it into the world in conjunction with other things; that anguish might take the form of an acute sense of inferiority for one [person], homosexuality for another, an overwhelming sense of the absurdity of human life for still another . . . the experience that might be caused by humiliation, by a harelip, by a stutter, by epilepsy—indeed, by any and everything in life which plunges the talented individual into solitude while leaving him the will to transcend his condition through art.

And the last words of this preceding quotation bring us to the second idea in his twofold approach to the distinction between the novel as protest and the novel as art: the ideal of the novel is a transmutation of protest into art. In speaking of Howe's evaluation of his own novel, Ellison says:

> If *Invisible Man* is even "apparently" free from "the ideological and emotional penalties suffered by Negroes in this country," it is because I tried to the best of my ability to transform these elements into art. My goal was not to escape, or hold back, but to work through; to transcend, as the blues transcend the painful conditions with which they deal.

And he relates this impulse toward transcendence into art to a stoical American Negro tradition which teaches one to master and contain pain; "which abhors as obscene any trading on one's own anguish for gain or sympathy"; which deals with the harshness of existence" "as men at their best have always done." And he summarizes the relevance of this tradition: "It takes fortitude to be a man and no less to be an artist."

In other words, to be an artist partakes, in its special way, of the moral force of being a man. And with this we come again, in a new perspective, to Ellison's view of the "basic unity of experience." If there is anguish, there is also the possibility of the transmutation of anguish, "the occasional joy of a complex double vision."

For in this "double vision" the "basic unity" can be received, and life can be celebrated. "I believe," he says to Howe, "that true novels, even when most pessimistic and bitter, arise out of an impulse to celebrate human life, and therefore are ritualistic and ceremonial at their core." The celebration of life—that is what Ellison sees as the final nature of his fiction, or of any art. And in this "double vision" and the celebration which it permits—no, entails—we find, even, the reconciliation possible in recognizing "the humanity of those who inflict injustice." And with this Ellison has arrived, I take it, at his own secular version of Martin Luther King's conception of *agapé*.

If, in pursuing this line of thought about Ralph Ellison, I have made him seem unaware of the plight of the Negro American in the past or the present, I have done him a grave wrong. He is fully aware of the blankness of the fate of many Negroes, and the last thing to be found in him is any trace of that cruel complacency of some who have, they think, mastered fate. If he emphasizes the values of challenge in the plight of the Negro, he would not use this to justify that plight; and if he applauds the disciplines induced by that plight, he does so in no spirit of self-congratulation, but in a spirit of pride in being numbered with those people.

No one has made more unrelenting statements of the dehumanizing pressures that have been put upon the Negro. And *Invisible Man* is, I should say, the most powerful artistic representation we have of the Negro under these dehumanizing conditions; and, at the same time, a statement of the human triumph over those conditions.—ROBERT PENN WARREN, "The Unity of Experience," *Cmty*, May 1965, pp. 91–96

The stark years of the thirties forced the Negro author to take a more realistic assessment of his situation. Frequently he labored under a structured ideology not altogether suited to his problems, but in any event he was required by this kind of discipline to relate what was unique in his culture to a broader over-all concept of history. During the first half of the decade the Communists appeared to champion an independent state located somewhere in the South, but after 1934 more and more stress was laid on full-fledged assimilation and integration into American life. This forced Negro intellectuals to examine even more closely their own ambivalent assimilationist and separatist views.

One of these was a young college student, Ralph Ellison, who came to New York in 1937 and began writing under the guidance and encouragement of a confirmed Party member, Richard Wright. Wright himself had written about the problem of Negro cultural identity and its place in a pluralistic society. Ellison almost immediately took up the dilemma, and in a sense devoted all his energies to its pursuit. After a long period of fits and starts in short stories, essays, and reviews, he achieved a major American novel, *Invisible Man* (1952).

No one could have been better suited, by virtue of his training and upbringing and experience, to undertake the challenge. Born in Oklahoma City in 1914, when caste lines were not yet so rigidly drawn as in other parts of the South, Ellison enjoyed a freedom to partake of the various crosscurrents of American life that were still sweeping across that near-frontier area. Not only did he encounter in his day-to-day experiences persons of different backgrounds, but he learned their songs, dances, and literature in the public schools. Moreover, he attended films and theater and read books avidly, and none of these suggested to him the "limitations" of Negro life. He dreamed the dreams of other American boys where the frontier spirit still obtained, and although he was aware of racism in the community, it never once occurred to him he was inferior because he was a Negro. "It was no more incongruous for young Negro Oklahomans to project themselves as Renaissance Men than for white Mississippians to see themselves as ancient Greeks or noblemen out of Sir Walter Scott."

He knew best, of course, his Negro culture, and he projected on his vision of the outside world the specificities of a Negro outlook. In his boyhood fantasies there existed Negro gamblers, scholars, cowboys, soldiers, movie stars, athletes, physicians, and figures from popular and classical literature. But jazz and especially blues provided him with the greatest sources of satisfaction. In his growing years, Kansas City jazz attained its ultimate refinement in the environs of Oklahoma City, and figures like Jimmie Rushing, Hot Lips Paige, Charlie Christian, and others became heroes to hosts of Negro boys. And if jazz was not regarded as being quite respectable in the schools he attended, he was given a rather impressive training in classical music so that he could make comparisons and perceive relationships. Thus for Ellison it was not simply a case of Negro culture standing apart, but a convergence in which Negro culture maintained its separate identity in a wider spectrum.

Not surprisingly, Ellison's understanding of his early life corresponds to his definition of Negro jazz. And ultimately it is jazz, and blues especially, that becomes the aesthetic mainspring of his writing. If literature serves as a ritualistic means of ordering experience, so does music, as Ellison well understands. And it is more to the rites of the jazz band than to the teachings of Kenneth Burke or the influences of Hemingway, Stein, Eliot, Malraux, or Conrad (persons whom Ellison mentions as literary ancestors and preceptors) that Ellison owes the structure and informing ideas of his novel. Particularly relevant is the attention Ellison casts on the jazz soloist. Within and against a frame of chordal progressions and rhythmic patterns, the soloist is free to explore a variety of ideas and emotions. But this freedom is not absolute. The chordal background of the other musicians demands a discipline that the soloist dare not breach. He is as much a part of the whole as he is an individual, and he may well lose himself in the whole before he recovers his individual identity. Finally, music, however tragic its message, is an affirmation of life, a celebration of the indomitable human spirit, in that it imposes order and form on the chaos of experience.

> The delicate balance struck between strong individual personality and the group . . . was a marvel of social organization. I had learned too that the end of all this discipline and technical mastery was the desire to express an affirmative way of life through its musical tradition and that this tradition insisted that each artist achieve his creativity within its frame. He must learn the best of the past, and add to it his personal vision. Life could be harsh, loud and wrong if it wished, but they lived it fully, and when they expressed their attitude toward the world it was with a fluid style that reduced the chaos of living to form.
>
> For true jazz is an art of individual assertion within and against the group. Each true jazz moment . . . springs from a contest in which each artist challenges all the rest; each solo flight, or improvisation, represents (like the successive canvases of a painter) a definition of his identity: as individual, as member of the collectivity and as a link in the chain of tradition. Thus, because jazz finds its very life in an endless improvisation upon traditional materials, the jazzman must lose his identity even as he finds it.
>
> —EDWARD MARGOLIES, "History as Blues: Ralph Ellison's *Invisible Man*," *Native Sons*, 1968, pp. 128–31

EARL H. ROVIT

"Ralph Ellison and the American Comic Tradition"

Wisconsin Studies in Contemporary Literature
Fall 1960, pp. 34–42

The most obvious comment one can make about Ralph Ellison's *Invisible Man* is that it is a profoundly comic work. But the obvious is not necessarily either simple or self-explanatory, and it seems to me that the comic implications of Ellison's novel are elusive and provocative enough to warrant careful examination both in relation to the total effect of the novel itself and the American cultural pattern from which it derives. It is generally recognized that Ellison's novel is a highly conscious attempt to embody a particular kind of experience—the experience of the "outsider" (in this case, a Negro) who manages to come to some sort of temporary acceptance, and thus, definition, of his status in the universe; it is not so generally recognized that *Invisible Man* is an integral link in a cumulative chain of great American creations, bearing an unmistakable brand of kinship to such seemingly incongruous works as *The Divinity School Address*, *Song of Myself*, *Moby-Dick*, and *The Education of Henry Adams*. But the later proposition is, I think, at least as valid as the former, and unless it is given proper recognition, a good deal of the value of the novel will be ignored.

First it should be noted that Ellison's commitment to what Henry James has termed "the American joke" has been thoroughly deliberate and undisguised. Ellison once described penetratingly the ambiguous *locus* of conflicting forces within which the American artist has had always to work: "For the ex-colonials, the declaration of an American identity meant the assumption of a mask, and it imposed not only the discipline of national self-consciousness, it gave Americans an ironic awareness of the joke that always lies between appearance and reality, between the discontinuity of social tradition and that sense of the past which clings to the mind. And perhaps even an awareness of the joke that society is man's creation, not God's." This kind of ironic awareness may contain bitterness and may even become susceptible to the heavy shadow of despair, but the art which it produces has been ultimately comic. It will inevitably probe the masks of identity and value searching relentlessly for some deeper buried reality, but it will do this while accepting the fundamental necessity for masks and the impossibility of ever discovering an essential face beneath a mask. That is to say, this comic stance will accept with the same triumphant gesture both the basic absurdity of all attempts to impose meaning on the chaos of life, and the necessary converse of this, the ultimate significance of absurdity itself.

Ellison's *Invisible Man* is comic in this sense almost in spite of its overtly satirical interests and its excursions into the broadly farcical. Humorous as many of its episodes are in themselves—the surreal hysteria of the scene at the Golden Day, the hero's employment at the Liberty Paint Company, or the expert dissection of political entanglements in Harlem—these are the materials which clothe Ellison's joke and which, in turn, suggest the shape by which the joke can be comprehended. The pith of Ellison's comedy reverberates on a level much deeper than these incidents, and as in all true humor, the joke affirms and denies simultaneously—accepts and rejects with the same uncompromising passion, leaving not a self-cancelling neutralization of momentum, but a sphere of moral conquest, a humanized cone of light at the very heart of the heart of darkness. *Invisible Man*, as Ellison has needlessly insisted in rebuttal to those critics who would treat the novel as fictionalized sociology or as a dramatization of archetypal images, is an artist's attempt to create a *form*. And fortunately Ellison has been quite explicit in describing what he means by *form*; in specific reference to the improvisation of the jazz-musician he suggests that form represents "a definition of his identity: as an individual, as a member of the collectivity, and as a link in the chain of tradition." But note that each of these definitions of identity must be individually exclusive and mutually contradictory on any logical terms. Because of its very pursuit after the uniqueness of individuality, the successful definition of an individual must define out the possibilities of generalization into "collectivity" or "tradition." But herein for Ellison in his embrace of a notion of fluid amorphous identity lies the real morality and humor in mankind's art and men's lives—neither of which have much respect for the laws of formal logic.

At one time during the novel when Ellison's protagonist is enthusiastically convinced that his membership in the Brotherhood is the only effective means to individual and social salvation, he recalls these words from a college lecture on Stephen Dedalus: "Stephen's problem, like ours, was not actually one of creating the uncreated conscience of his race, but of creating the *uncreated features of his face*. Our task is that of making ourselves individuals. The conscience of a race is the gift of its individuals who see, evaluate, record. . . . We create the race by creating ourselves and then to our great astonishment we will have created something far more important: We will have created a culture. Why waste time creating a conscience for something that doesn't exist? For, you see, blood and skin do not think!" This is one of the most significant passages in the novel, and one which must be appreciated within the context of the total form if the subtle pressure of that form is to be adequately weighed. And this can be done only if the Prologue and the Epilogue are viewed as functional elements in the novel which set the tempo for its moral action and modulate ironically upon its emergent meanings.

The Prologue introduces the narrator in his underground

hibernation musing upon the events of his life, eating vanilla ice cream and sloe gin, listening to Louis Armstrong's recording, "What Did I Do to Be So Black and Blue?" and trying to wrest out of the confusions of his experiences some pattern of meaning and/or resilient core of identity. The next twenty-five chapters are a first-person narrative flashback which covers some twenty years of the protagonist's life ending with the beginning, the hero's descent into the underground hole. The concluding Epilogue picks up the tonal patterns of the Prologue, implies that both meaning and identity have been discovered, and dramatically forces a direct identification between the narrator and the reader. Ostensibly this is another novel of the initiation of a boy into manhood—a *Bildungsroman* in the episodic picaresque tradition. The advice of the literature teacher has been realized; the hero has created the features of his face from the malleable stuff of his experience. He who accepts himself as "invisible" has ironically achieved a concrete tangibility, while those characters in the novel who seemed to be "visible" and substantial men (Norton, Brother Jack, and even Tod Clifton) are discovered to be really "invisible" since they are self-imprisoned captives of their own capacities to see and be seen in stereotyped images. However, to read the novel in this way and to go no further is to miss the cream of the jest and the total significance of the whole form which pivots on the ironic fulcrum of the blues theme introduced in the Prologue and given resolution in the Epilogue. As in all seriously comic works the reader is left not with an answer, but with a challenging question—a question which soars beyond the novel on the unanswered notes of Armstrong's trumpet: "What did I do to be so black and blue?"

For the protagonist *is* finally and most comically *invisible* at the end of the novel; he has learned that to create the uncreated features of his face is at best a half-value, and at worst, potentially more self-destructive than not to strive after identity at all. For Ellison ours is a time when "you prepare a face to meet the faces that you meet"—a time when we have learned to shuffle and deal our personalities with a protean dexterity that, as is characterized through Rinehart, is a wholesale exploitation of and surrender to chaos. After the narrator's fall into the coalpit he discovers that his arrogantly naïve construction of personality is nothing more than the accumulated fragments in his briefcase: the high-school diploma, Bledsoe's letter, Clifton's dancing doll, Mary's bank, Brother Tarp's iron. And most ironically, even these meager artifacts—the fragments he has shored against his ruin—represent not him, but the world's variegated projections of him. The narrator learns then that his educational romance is a farcical melodrama of the most garish variety; the successive births and rebirths of his life (his Caesarean delivery from college, his birth by electronics at the factory hospital, the christening by the Brotherhood) were not the organic gestations of personality that he idealized so much as they were the cold manipulations of artificial insemination. His final acceptance of his invisibility reminds us of the demand of the Zen Master: "Show me the face you had before you were born."

However, we must note also that this acceptance of invisibility, of amorphous nonidentity, is far from a resignation to chaos. The protagonist has successfully rebelled against the imposition of social masks whether externally (like Clifton's) or internally (like Brother Tarp's) bestowed; his is not a surrender of personality so much as a descent to a deeper level of personality where the accent is heavier on possibilities than on limitations. The 1,369 glowing light bulbs in his cellar retreat attest to the increased power and enlightenment which are positive gains from his experience, as well as to the strategic advantages of his recourse to invisibility. The literature teacher unwittingly pointed out the flaw in his exhortation even as he declaimed it: "Blood and skin do not think!" For to think is to be as much concerned with analysis as it is with synthesis; the ironic mind tears radiant unities apart even as it forges them. Accordingly Ellison's narrator assumes the ultimate mask of facelessness and emphasizes the fluid chaos which is the secret substance of form, the dynamic interplay of possibilities which creates limitations. The narrator is backed into the blank corner where he must realize that "the mind that has conceived a plan of living must never lose sight of the chaos against which that pattern was conceived." In accepting himself as the Invisible Man he assumes the historic role which Emerson unerringly assigned to the American poet; he becomes "the world's eye"—something through which one sees, even though it cannot itself be seen.

And here it may be fruitful to investigate briefly the peculiar relationship of Emerson's work to Ellison (whose middle name is propitiously Waldo). In the recently published excerpt from a novel in progress, "And Hickman Arrives," Ellison has his main character, Alonzo Zuber, Daddy Hickman, make some complimentary remarks about Emerson, "a preacher . . . who knew that every tub has to sit on its own bottom." Daddy Hickman, a Negro preacher ("Better known as GOD'S TROMBONE"), is vividly characterized as a wise and shrewd virtuoso of the evangelical circuit who might not unfairly be taken as a modern-day Emerson, preaching eloquently the gospel of humanity. These facts may be significant when we remember that Emerson's work is given short shrift as rhetorical nonsense in *Invisible Man* and his name is bestowed upon a character whose minor function in the novel is to be a self-righteous hypocrite. This shift in attitude may indicate that Ellison has come to realize that there are some major affinities binding him to his famous namesake, and, more important, it may enable us to understand more clearly the remarkable consistency of the American struggle to create art and the relatively harmonious visions which these unique struggles have attained.

Superficially there would seem to be little to link the two men beyond the somewhat labored pun of their names and Ellison's awareness of the pun. The one, an ex-Unitarian minister of respectable, if modest, Yankee background, whose orotund explorations in autobiography gave fullest form to the American dream—whose public pose attained an Olympian serenity and optimistic faith which have caused him to be associated with a wide range of sentimentalities from Mary Baker Eddy to Norman Vincent Peale; the other, an Oklahoma City Negro, born in 1914, ex-Leftist propagandist and editor, who would seem to have belied the Emersonian prophecy of individualism and self-reliance by the very title of his novel, *Invisible Man*. The one, nurtured by the most classical education that America had to offer; the other, a rapt disciple of jazzmen like Charlie Christian and Jimmy Rushing who has attributed to their lyric improvisations his deepest understanding of aesthetic form. The one, white and given to the Delphic utterance; the other, black and adept in the cautery of bitter humor. But in their respective searches for identity, in their mutual concern with defining the possibilities and limitations which give form and shape to that which is human, the poet who called man "a golden impossibility" and the novelist who teaches his protagonist that life is a latent hive of infinite possibilities draw close together in their attempts to find an artistic resolution of the contrarieties of existence.

"Only he can give, who has," wrote Emerson; "he only can create, who is." Experience is the fluxional material from which these all-important values and identities are created, and

Emerson's great essays are processive incantations whose ultimate function is to bring identity into being, even as they chant the fundamental fluidity of all forms spontaneously and eternally merging into other forms. When we remember that Emerson once wrote: "A believer in Unity, a seer of Unity, I yet behold two," it may be worth a speculation that the Emerson behind the triumphant artifices of the *Essays* was not a terribly different person from the Invisible Man in the coalpit whose submersion into the lower frequencies had given him an entree to the consciousnesses of all men. This awareness of the absurdity of meaning (and the potential meaningfulness of chaos) is at the heart of Emerson's delight in paradox, his seeming inconsistencies, his "dialogistic" techniques, his highly functional approach to language. "All symbols are fluxional," he declaimed; "all language is vehicular and transitive and is good for conveyance not for homestead." Thus Melville's attempted criticism of Emerson in *The Confidence Man* misses widely the mark; Emerson isn't there when the satire strikes home. Melville, who above all of Emerson's contemporaries should have known better, mistook the Olympian pasteboard mask for a reality and misread the eloquent quest for identity as a pretentious melodrama. For, as Constance Rourke recognized, Emerson is one of our most deft practitioners of the American joke, and the magnitude of his success may be measured by the continued effectiveness of his disguises after more than a hundred years.

But again we must return to the *form* of *Invisible Man* to appreciate how deeply involved Ellison's work is with the most basic American vision of reality. Although it is probably true as some critics have pointed out that the dominating metaphor of the novel—the "underground man" theme—was suggested by Dostoevski and Richard Wright, it is for our purposes more interesting to note a similar metaphor in Hart Crane's poem, "Black Tambourine":

The interests of a black man in a cellar
Mark tardy judgment on the world's closed door.
Gnats toss in the shadow of a bottle,
And a roach spans a crevice in the floor.

. . .

The black man, forlorn in the cellar,
Wanders in some mid-kingdom, dark, that lies,
Between his tambourine, stuck on the wall,
And, in Africa, a carcass quick with flies.

Invisible Man achieves an expert evocation of that "mid-kingdom," that demimonde of constant metamorphosis where good and evil, appearance and reality, pattern and chaos are continually shifting their shapes even as the eye strains to focus and the imagination to comprehend. The Kafkaesque surrealism of the novel's action, the thematic entwinement of black-white and dark-light, and the psychic distance from the plot-development which the use of the Prologue and the Epilogue achieves posit the moral center of the novel in that fluid area where experience is in the very process of being transformed into value. The narrator, the author, and the reader as well are caught in the "mid-kingdom" which seems to me to be the characteristic and unavoidable focus of American literature. For this mid-kingdom, this unutterable silence which is "zero at the bone," seems to me to be the one really inalienable birthright of being an American. Some Americans following Swedenborg named it "vastation"; others gave it no name and lamented the dearth of an American tradition within which the artist could work; at least one commissioned the sculptor, St. Gaudens, to incarnate it in a statue. One way of attempting to describe the sense of being within this mid-kingdom can be most dramatically seen in "The Castaway" chapter of *Moby-Dick* where Pip is left floundering in the boundless Pacific. And although the techniques of approaching the experience have been richly various, the experience itself, an incontrovertible sense of absolute metaphysical isolation, can be found at the core of the most vital American creations.

"American history," writes James Baldwin in *Notes of a Native Son*, is "the history of the total, and willing, alienation of entire peoples from their forbears. What is overwhelmingly clear . . . is that this history has created an entirely unprecedented people, with a unique and individual past." The alienation, of course, is more than sociological and ideological; it seeps down into the very depths whence the sureties of identity and value are wrought; and it imprisons the American in this mid-kingdom where the boundaries—the distance from the tambourine on the wall to the carcass quick with flies—cannot be measured in either years or miles. The American seeking himself—as an individual, a member of the collectivity, a link in the chain of tradition—can never discover or create that identity in fixed restrictive terms. The past is dead and yet it lives: note Ellison's use of the narrator's grandfather, the yams, the techniques of the evangelical sermon. Individuals are frozen in mute isolation, and yet communication is possible between them: the Harlem riot, the way the narrator listens to music. Ellison's novel is the unique metaphor of his own thoroughly personal experience, and yet it makes a fitting link in the chain of the American tradition.

That Ellison and his narrator are Negroes both is and is not important. From the severe standpoint of art the racial fact is negligible, although there are doubtless areas of meaning and influence in *Invisible Man* which sociological examination might fruitfully develop. From the viewpoint of cultural history, however, the racial fact is enormously provocative. It is strikingly clear that contemporary American writing, particularly the writing of fiction, is dominated by two categories of writers: members of religious and racial minorities, and writers who possess powerful regional heritages. Both groups have an instinctive leasehold within the boundaries of the "mid-kingdom"; the Negro, the Catholic, the Jew, and the Southerner share the immediate experience of living on the razor's edge of time, at the very point where traditions come into desperate conflict with the human need to adapt to change. And, of equal importance, both groups—in varying degrees—are marked out on the contemporary scene as being "different"; both groups cannot avoid the terrible problem of identity, because it is ever thrust upon them whether they like it or not. These are the conditions which in the American past have nourished our spasmodic exfoliations of significant literary activity: the great "Renaissance" of the 1840's and '50's, the Twain-James-Adams "alliance" of the late nineteenth century, the post–World War One literary fluorescence from which we have just begun to break away. But the Lost Generation was the last generation which could practice the necessary expatriation or "fugitivism" in which these factors—the disseverance from the past and the search for identity—could operate on nonminority or nonregional American writers. Thus Ralph Ellison—and contemporaries like Saul Bellow, Flannery O'Connor, and William Styron—are *inside* the heart of the American experience by the very virtue of their being in some way "outsiders." Like Emerson, himself a royal inhabitant of the mid-kingdom over a century ago, they are challenged to create form, or else succumb to the enveloping chaos within and without.

And the answers which they arrive at—again as with Emerson—are answers which cannot be taken out of the context of their individually achieved forms without being reduced to platitude or nonsense. Form, the creation of a radical, self-defining metaphor, is the one rational technique which human beings have developed to deal adequately with the basic irrationality of existence. The answer which *Invisible Man* gives to the unanswerable demands which life imposes on the human being has something to do with human limitation and a good deal to do with freedom; it has something to do with hatred, and a good deal more to do with love. It defines the human distance between the tambourine and the carcass and it accepts with wonder and dignity the immeasurable gift of life. The black man in the cellar transforms his isolation into elevation without denying the brute facts of existence and without losing his ironic grip on the transiency of the moment. The amorphous ambiguity of the mid-kingdom is for a timeless instant conquered and made fit for habitation. Perhaps tragedy teaches man to become divine, but before man can aspire to divinity, he must first accept completely the responsibilities and limitations of being human. The American experience, cutting away the bonds of tradition which assure man of his humanity, has not allowed a tragic art to develop. But there has developed a rich and vigorous comic tradition to which *Invisible Man* is a welcome embellishment, and it is this art which promises most as a healthy direction into the future.

JONATHAN BAUMBACH
"Nightmare of a Native Son"
The Landscape of Nightmare
1965, pp. 68–86

> "Who knows but that, on the lower frequencies, I speak for you?"
> *(Invisible Man)*

I hesitate to call Ralph Ellison's *Invisible Man* (1953) a Negro novel, though of course it is written by a Negro and is centrally concerned with the experiences of a Negro. The appellation is not so much inaccurate as it is misleading. A novelist treating the invisibility and phantasmagoria of the Negro's life in this "democracy" is, if he tells the truth, necessarily writing a very special kind of book. Yet if his novel is interesting only because of its specialness, he has not violated the surface of his subject; he has not, after all, been serious. Despite the differences in their external concerns, Ellison has more in common as a novelist with Joyce, Melville, Camus, Kafka, West, and Faulkner than he does with other serious Negro writers like James Baldwin and Richard Wright. To concentrate on the idiom of a serious novel, no matter how distinctive its peculiarities, is to depreciate it, to minimize the universality of its implications. Though the protagonist of *Invisible Man* is a southern Negro, he is, in Ellison's rendering, profoundly all of us.

Despite its obvious social implications, Ellison's novel is a modern gothic, a Candide-like picaresque set in a dimly familiar nightmare landscape called the United States. Like *The Catcher in the Rye*, *A Member of the Wedding*, and *The Adventures of Augie March*, Ellison's novel chronicles a series of initiatory experiences through which its naïve hero learns, to his disillusion and horror, the way of the world. However, unlike these other novels of passage, *Invisible Man* takes place, for the most part, in the uncharted spaces between the conscious and the unconscious, in the semilit darkness where nightmare verges on reality and the external world has all the aspects of a disturbing dream. Refracted by satire, at times, cartooned, Ellison's world is at once surreal and real, comic and tragic, grotesque and normal—our world viewed in its essentials rather than its externals.

The Negro's life in our white land and time is, as Ellison knows it, a relentless unreality, unreal in that the Negro as a group is loved, hated, persecuted, feared, and envied, while as an individual he is unfelt, unheard, unseen—to all intents and purposes invisible. The narrator, who is also the novel's central participant, never identifies himself by name. Though he experiences several changes of identity in the course of the novel, Ellison's hero exists to the reader as a man without an identity, an invisible "I." In taking on a succession of identities, the invisible hero undergoes an increasingly intense succession of disillusioning experiences, each one paralleling and anticipating the one following it. The hero's final loss of illusion forces him underground into the coffin (and womb) of the earth to be either finally buried or finally reborn.

The narrator's grandfather, whom he resembles (identity is one of the major concerns of the novel), is the first to define the terms of existence for him. An apparently meek man all his life, on his deathbed the grandfather reveals:

> "Son, after I'm gone I want you to keep up the good fight. I never told you, but our life is a war and I have been a traitor all my born days, a spy in the enemy's country ever since I give up my gun back in the Reconstruction. Live with your head in the lion's mouth. I want you to overcome 'em with yesses, undermine 'em with grins, agree 'em to death and destruction, let 'em swoller you till they vomit or bust wide open."[1]

Though at the time he understands his grandfather's ambiguous creed only imperfectly, the hero recognizes that it is somehow his heritage. In a sense, the old man's code of acquiescent resistance is an involved justification of his nonresistance; it is a parody on itself, yet the possibility always remains that it is, in some profound, mysterious way, a meaningful ethic. On a succession of occasions, the hero applies his grandfather's advice, "agreeing 'em to death," in order to understand its import through discovering its efficacy. On each occasion, however, it is he, not "'em," who is victimized. Consequently, the hero suffers a sense of guilt—not for having compromised himself but for failing somehow to effect his grandfather's ends. Ironically, he also feels guilty for deceiving the white "enemy," though he has "agreed them" not to death or destruction, only to renewed complacency. For example:

> When I was praised for my conduct I felt a guilt that in some way I was doing something that was really against the wishes of the white folks, that if they had understood they would have desired me to act just the opposite, that I should have been sulky and mean, and that really would have been what they wanted, even though they were fooled and thought they wanted me to act as I did. [p. 20]

The hero's cynical obsequiousness has self-destructive consequences. Having delivered a high school graduation speech advocating humility as the essence of progress, he is invited to deliver his agreeable oration to a meeting of the town's leading white citizens. Before he is allowed to speak, however, he is subjected to a series of brutal degradations, which teach him, in effect, the horror of the humility he advocates. In this episode, the first of his initiatory experiences, the invisible man's role is symbolically prophesied. The hero, along with nine other Negro boys, is put into a prize ring, then is blindfolded and coerced into battling his compatriots. Duped by the whites, the Negro unwittingly fights himself; his potency, which the white man envies and fears, is mocked and turned against him to satisfy the brutal whims of his persecutor. That the bout is preceded by a nude, blond belly dancer whom the boys are forced to watch suggests the prurience underlying the victimizer's treatment of his victim. The degrading prizefight, a demonstration of potency to titillate the impotent, in which the Negro boys blindly flail one another to entertain the sexually aroused stag audience, parallels the riot in Harlem at the end of the novel, which is induced by another institution of white civilization, the Brotherhood (a fictional guise for the Communist party). Once again Negro fights against Negro (Ras the Destroyer against the hero), although this time it is for the sake of "Brotherhood," a euphemism for the same inhumanity. In both cases, the Negro unwittingly performs the obscene demands of his enemy. In magnification, Harlem is the prize ring where the Negroes, blindfolded this time by demagoguery, flail at each other with misdirected violence. The context has changed from South to North, from white citizens to the Brotherhood, from a hired ballroom to all of Harlem, but the implication remains the same: the Negro is victimized by having his potency turned against himself by his impotent persecutor.

After the boxing match, what appears to be gold is placed on a rug in the center of the room and the boys are told to scramble for their rewards. The hero reacts: "I trembled with excitement, forgetting my pain. I would get the gold and the bills, I thought. I would use both hands. I would throw my body against the boys nearest me to block them from the gold" (p. 29).

He is, on the rug as in the boxing ring, degraded by self-interest. Though his reaction is unpleasant, it is, given the provocation, the normal, calculable one. He has been tempted and, unaware of any practicable ethical alternative, has succumbed in innocence. When the temptation recurs in more complex guises later in the novel and Ellison's nameless hero as adult falls victim to his self-interest, he is, despite his larger moral purposes, culpable and must assume responsibility for the terrible consequences of his deeds. In each of the various analogous episodes, the hero is torn between his implicit commitment to his grandfather's position—subversive acquiescence—and his will to identity—the primal instinct of self-assertion. Both commitments dictate pragmatic, as opposed to purely ethical, action, with, inevitably, immoral and impractical consequences. The rug becomes electrified, the gold coins turn out to be brass—a means, like the bout, of mocking the Negro's envied potency. That the fight and electrification follow in sequence the naked belly dancer in the course of an evening of stag entertainment for tired white businessmen indicates the obscene prurience behind the white citizen's hatred of the Negro. By debasing and manipulating the Negro's potency, the white mutes its threat and at the same time experiences it vicariously. It is in all a mordant evocation, satiric in its rendering and frightening in its implications. The white man's fascination with the Negro as a source of power (potency) is another of the thematic threads that holds together what might otherwise be a picaresque succession of disparate episodes. The ballroom humiliation serves as a gloss on the following scene, in which the hero is expelled from the Negro state college for, ironically, the consequence of his obedience to a white trustee.

The president of the Negro college, Dr. Bledsoe (all of Ellison's names characterize their bearers), entrusts the hero, up to then a model student, with the responsibility of chauffeuring a philanthropic white trustee, Mr. Norton, on a tour of the manicured country surrounding the campus. Driving aimlessly—or perhaps with more aim than he knows—the hero suddenly discovers that he has taken the trustee to the backwoods homestead of Jim Trueblood, the area's black sheep, an "unenlightened" Negro whose sharecropper existence (and incestuous, child producing, accident with his daughter) is a source of continued embarrassment to the "progressive" community of the college. The hero would like to leave, but Norton, curiously fascinated by the fact that Trueblood has committed incest (and survived), insists on talking with the sharecropper. At Norton's prodding, Trueblood tells his story, an extended and graphically detailed account of how he was induced by a dream into having physical relations with his daughter. The story itself is a masterpiece of narrative invention and perhaps the single most brilliant scene in the novel.

As Trueblood finishes his story, we discover in a moment of ironic revelation that the bloodless Norton is a kind of euphemistic alter ego—a secret sharer—of the atavistic Trueblood. Earlier, while being driven deeper into the backwoods country—the reality behind the ivy league façade of the college—Norton had rhapsodized to the narrator about the unearthly charms of his own daughter, for whose death he feels unaccountably guilty:

> "Her beauty was a well-spring of purest water-of-life, and to look upon her was to drink and drink and drink again. . . . She was rare, a perfect creation, a work of purest art. . . . I found it difficult to believe her my own. . . ."
>
> "I have never forgiven myself. Everything I've done since her passing has been a monument to her memory." [pp. 43–44]

Trueblood, then, has committed the very sin that Norton has, in the dark places of his spirit, impotently coveted. Upon hearing Trueblood's story, Norton participates vicariously in his experience, has his own quiescent desires fulfilled while exempted, since Trueblood has acted for him, from the stigma of the act. Underlying Norton's recurrent platitude that "the Negro is my fate" (he means that they are his potency) is the same prurience that motivates the sadism of the white citizens in the preceding scene. However, in an ironic way, Trueblood *is* Norton's fate. When Trueblood finishes his story, Norton feels compelled to pay him, as the white citizens reward the Negro boxers, in exchange for, in a double sense, having performed for him. When Norton (who exists here really as idea rather than character) leaves Trueblood's farm, he is exhausted and colorless, as if he had in fact just committed incest with his own daughter.

Having exposed Norton to the horror of his own philanthropic motives, after a further misadventure among inmates of a Negro insane asylum, the hero is expelled from school by Bledsoe because "any act that endangered the continuity of the dream is an act of treason." The boy, sensing his innocence, feels haunted by his grandfather's curse. Through Ellison's surrealistic rendering, we sense the nightmare reality of the hero's experience (as we do not with Norton's comparable nightmare):

> How had I come to this? I had kept unswervingly to the path before me, had tried to be exactly what I was expected to be, had done exactly what I was expected to do—yet, instead of winning the expected reward, here I was stumbling along, holding on desperately to one of my eyes in order to keep from bursting out my brain against some familiar object swerved into my path by my distorted vision. And now to drive me wild I felt suddenly that my grandfather was hovering over me, grinning triumphantly out of the dark. [p. 131]

Accepting responsibility for the sins of his innocence, the hero goes to New York, armed with several letters of "identification" which Bledsoe had addressed to various trustees for the ostensible purpose of finding him a job. When the hero discovers that the letters have been written "to hope him to death, and keep him running," that the renowned Negro educator Bledsoe has betrayed him treacherously, has in effect ordered him killed as an almost gratuitous display of power, he experiences a moment of terrible disillusion. At the same time he senses that this betrayal is in some way a re-enactment of the past: "Twenty-five years seemed to have lapsed between his handing me the letter and my grasping its message. I could not believe it, yet I had a feeling that it all had happened before. I rubbed my eyes, and they felt sandy as though all the fluids had suddenly dried" (p. 168).

In a way, it *has* happened before; for Bledsoe's act of victimization (the beating of Negro by Negro) is analogous to the punishment the hero received in the prize ring at the hands of the largest of the other Negro boys. Bledsoe's deceit, like its analog, is motivated by the desire to ingratiate himself with the white society which dispenses rewards—which provides, or so he believes, the source of his power.

As one episode parallels another, each vignette in itself has allegorical extensions. Employed by Liberty Paints, a factory "the size of a small city," the narrator is ordered to put ten drops of "black dope" into buckets of optic white paint in order, he is told, to make it whiter. The mixing of the black into the white is, of course, symbolic: the ten drops are analogous to the ten boys in the prize ring, and in each case the white becomes whiter by absorbing the Negro's virility, by using the black to increase the strength of the white. Yet the name "optic white" suggests it is all some kind of visual illusion. When the black dope runs out, the hero as apprentice paint mixer is ordered by his boss, "the terrible Mr. Kimbro," to replace it, without being told which of seven possible vats has the right substance. Left to his own discretion, the hero chooses the wrong black liquid, concentrated paint remover, which makes the white paint transparent and grayish; this act symbolizes the implicit threat of Negro potency left to its own devices. The paint-mixing scene is paralleled by the violence of the insane Negro veterans at the bar (the Golden Day) in which they beat their white attendant Supercargo into grayness and terrorize the already depleted Norton. It anticipates the antiwhite violence of Ras the exhorter-turned-destroyer, the only alternative to invisibility the white man has left the Negro.

Yet there is the illusion of another alternative: when the narrator adds the black drops to the paint which already contains the black remover, though the mixture appears gray to him, it passes for white in Kimbro's eyes. This is, in symbol, the role of subterfuge and infiltration—his grandfather's legacy and curse.

> I looked at the painted slab. It appeared the same: a gray tinge glowed through the whiteness, and Kimbro had failed to detect it. I stared for a minute, wondering if I were seeing things, inspected another and another. All were the same, a brilliant white diffused with gray. I closed my eyes for a moment and looked again and still no change. Well, I thought as long as he's satisfied. . . . [p. 180]

Kimbro permits the gray-tinged paint to be shipped out and the hero wonders whether, after all, he has been the deceiver or the deceived. He suspects, when Kimbro dismisses him, that he somehow has been the dupe. That the paint passes for white in Kimbro's eyes suggests that the black with which it was mixed was, like the hero's existence, to all intents and purposes, invisible.

Essentially invisible, the narrator undergoes a succession of superficial changes of identity—in a sense, changes of mask—each entailing a symbolic, though illusory, death and rebirth. Knocked unconscious by the explosion of a machine which makes the base of a white paint, a machine that he was unable to control, the hero is placed in another machine, a coffin-like electrified box, in order to be "started again." The shock treatments surrealistically rendered recall the electrification from the rug, however magnified in intensity. Like most of the episodes in the novel, it is on the surface a comic scene, though in its implications (lobotomy and castration) it is a singularly unpleasant nightmare. The hero's first awareness upon awakening is that he is enclosed in a glass box with an electric cap attached to his head, a combination coffin-womb and electrocutor. When he is blasted with a charge of electricity, he instinctively screams in agonized protest, only to be told in response as if he were indeed a piece of equipment, "'Hush goddamit . . . We're trying to get you started again. Now shut up!'" (p. 203). After a while he is unable to remember who he is or whether he has in fact existed before his present moment of consciousness: "My mind was blank, as though I'd just begun to live." Like the charged rug, though considerably more cruel, the shock treatments are intended to neutralize him, in effect to castrate him. In his moments of confused consciousness he hears two voices arguing over the proper method to treat his case. One is in favor of surgery, the other in favor of the machine.

> "The machine will produce the results of a prefrontal lobotomy without the negative effect of the knife," the voice said. "You see, instead of severing the prefrontal lobe, a single lobe, that is, we apply pressure in the proper degrees to the major centers of nerve control—our concept is Gestalt—and the result is as complete a change of personality as you'll find in your famous fairy-tale cases of criminals transformed into amiable fellows after all that bloody business of a brain operation. And what's more," the voice went on triumphantly, "the patient is both physically and neurally whole."
>
> "But what of his psychology?"
>
> "Absolutely of no importance!" the voice said. "The patient will live as he has to live, with absolute integrity. Who could ask more? He'll experience no major conflict of motives, and what is even better, society will suffer no traumata on his account."
>
> There was a pause. A pen scratched upon paper. Then, "Why not castration, doctor?" a voice asked waggishly, causing me to start, a pain tearing through me.
>
> "There goes your love of blood again," the first voice laughed. "What's that definition of a surgeon, 'A butcher with a bad conscience'?"
>
> They laughed. [pp. 206–207]

I quote this passage at length to suggest the high-voltage charge of Ellison's satire, capable at once of being mordantly comic and profoundly terrifying. The clinical attitude of the psychologist ("society will suffer no traumata on his account") suggests the northern white position toward the Negro, as opposed to the butcher-surgeon who represents the more overtly violent southern position. The ends of both, however, are approximately the same—emasculation; the difference is essentially one of means.

The narrator is, in this scene, almost visibly invisible, discussed impersonally in his presence as if he were not there. When he is unable to recall his name, his mother's name, any form of his identity, any form of his past, the doctors seem pleased and deliver him from the machine, the only mother he knows.

> I felt a tug at my belly and looked down to see one of the physicians pull the cord which was attached to the stomach node, jerking me forward. . . .
>
> "Get the shears," he said. "Let's not waste time."
>
> "Sure," the other said. "Let's not waste time."
>
> I recoiled inwardly as though the cord were part of me. Then they had it free and the nurse clipped through the belly band and removed the heavy node. [p. 213]

In describing the birth from the machine, Ellison suggests through evocation that it is also a kind of castration. Insofar as it leaves the hero without the potency of self, it is, in implication, just that.

Aside from the Prologue and parts of the Epilogue, which have an enlightened madness all their own, the experience of the machine birth is the least realistic, the most surrealistic, in the novel. And this brings us to what I think is the novel's crucial flaw, its inconsistency of method, its often violent transformations from a kind of detailed surface realism in which probability is limited to the context of ordinary, everyday experiences to an allegorical world of almost endless imaginative possibilities. Often the shift is dramatically effective, as when the hero and Norton enter the insane world of the Golden Day (here the truth is illuminated by a nominal madman who has the insane virtue of pure sight) and Norton is forced into a frightening moment of self-recognition. On other occasions, the visional shifts jar us away from the novel's amazing world into an awareness of the ingenuity of its creator. Since Ellison is at once prodigiously talented and prodigiously reckless, *Invisible Man* is astonishingly good at its best. By the same token the book is uneven; on occasion it is very bad as only very good novels can be. Given the nature of his vision, Ellison's world seems real—or alive—when it is surrealistically distorted, and for the most part made-up—or abstract—when it imitates the real world. Largely recounted in the manner of traditional realism, the hero's adventures in the Brotherhood up until the Harlem riot constitute the least interesting section of the novel.

In joining the Brotherhood, the narrator gives up his past to assume a new identity or rather new nonidentity, Brother ———. Because of his remarkable speech-making abilities, as well as his conscious ambition to be some kind of savior, he becomes one of the leading figures of the Harlem Brotherhood. Finally, his controversial activities make it necessary for him to disguise himself in order to get through Harlem safely. Brother ———'s disguise—dark glasses and a wide-brimmed hat—which he has hoped would make him inconspicuous in Harlem, creates for him still another identity, which is, in effect, just a new aspect of nonidentity. Wearing the hat and glasses, Brother ——— is unrecognized as his Brotherhood self, but is mistaken for a man named Rinehart, a charlatan of incredible diversification. Rinehart, whose identities include numbers runner, police briber, lover, pimp, and Reverend, is, the hero discovers, a kind of alter ego to his invisibility. If you are no one, you are at the same time potentially everyone. The hero has disguised himself in order to avoid the consequences of his acts and instead finds himself held responsible for Rinehart's inordinate sins—for all sins—which are, in the Dostoyevskian sense, his own. When the Brotherhood's theoretician Hambro informs the hero that, with the alteration of the larger plan, his role has changed from exhorter to pacifier, he senses his likeness to his dazzling alter ego:

> ". . . Besides I'd feel like Rinehart. . . ." It slipped out and he looked at me.
>
> "Like who?"
>
> "Like a charlatan," I said.
>
> Hambro laughed. "I thought you learned about that, Brother."
>
> I looked at him quickly. "Learned what?"
>
> "That it's impossible *not* to take advantage of the people."
>
> "That's Rinehartism—cynicism. . . ." [p. 436]

In following the dictates of the Brotherhood, the hero has hurt, he discovers to his pain, the very people he has intended to help. Without benefit of glasses and hat, he has been a Rinehart in disguise all the time. He has been, paradoxically, an unwitting cynic. Duped by his self-conscious, romantic ambitions to be another Booker T. Washington, the hero has let the Brotherhood use him for their cynical "historic" purposes. As a Brotherhood agent, he demagogically incites the Harlem Negroes to potential action only to leave them prey to the misdirected violence of Ras, their violence ultimately turned, like that of the boys in the prize ring, against themselves. With awareness comes responsibility, and the hero recognizes that he alone must bear the guilt for the Brotherhood's betrayal of the Negro. The ramifications of his awful responsibility are manifested generally in the hellish Harlem riot at the end of the novel and particularly in the disillusion and death of the most admirable of the Brotherhood, Tod Clifton (the name suggests a kind of Promethean entrapment), whose career prophesies and parallels that of the hero.

Earlier in the novel, Ras, after sparing Tod's life, has exhorted his adversary to leave the Brotherhood and join his racist movement (a fictionalized version of the Black Muslims). Their confrontation, an objectification of the hero's interior struggle, anticipates Tod's defection from the Brotherhood.

> "Come with us, mahn. We build a glorious movement of black people. *Black people!* What do they do, give you money? Who wahnt the damn stuff? Their money bleed black blood, mahn. It's unclean! Taking their money is shit, mahn. Money without dignity—that's *bahd* shit!"
>
> Clifton lunged toward him. I held him, shaking my head. "Come on, the man's crazy," I said, pulling on his arm.
>
> Ras struck his thighs with his fists. "Me crazy, mahn? You call me crazy? Look at you two and look at me—is this sanity? Standing here in three shades of blackness! Three black men fighting in the street because of the white enslaver? Is that sanity? Is that consciousness, scientific understanding? Is that the modern black mahn of the twentieth century? Hell, mahn! Is it self-respect—black against black? What they give you to betray—their women? You fall for that?"
>
> "Let's go," I repeated. He stood there, looking.
>
> "Sure, you go," Ras said, "but not him. You contahminated but he the real black mahn. In Africa this mahn be a chief, a black king!" [pp. 322–23]

In this eloquent scene, Clifton finally rejects Ras, but he is undeniably moved by his enemy's crude exhortation. Ras—the name suggests an amalgam of race and rash—is a fanatic, but given his basic premise, that the white man is the Negro's natural enemy, his arguments are not easily refutable. Unable to answer Ras, Clifton, out of a sense of shame or guilt, knocks the Exhorter down, committing an act of Rasian violence. The punch is an acknowledgment, a communion, an act of love. As they leave, the hero discovers that Clifton has tears in his eyes. Clifton says, referring to Ras, "'That poor misguided son of a bitch.' 'He thinks a lot of you, too,' I said" (p. 326).

Clifton is sympathetic to Ras's motives, but he is nevertheless too civilized to accept his methods. The Brotherhood, then, with its cant of "historic necessity," represents to Clifton the enlightened alternative to racist violence through which the Negro can effect his protest. Entrapped by the Brotherhood through the commitment imposed by his integrity, Clifton becomes, even more than the narrator, a victim of the Brotherhood's betrayal. Like the implicit suicide of Conrad's Lord Jim, Clifton's death (he provokes a policeman into shooting him) is a sacrifice to a culpability too egregious to be redeemed in any other way, and, at the same time, a final if gratuitous act of heroism. In giving himself up to be murdered, Clifton takes on the whole responsibility for the Brotherhood's betrayal of the Negro. If by his sacrifice he does not redeem the hero from his own culpability, he at least through his example sets up the possibility of Brother ———'s redemption. If the various characters with whom the "invisible" hero is confronted represent possible states of being, Clifton symbolizes the nearest thing to an idea.

Clifton's death, because it permits the hero to organize the Negroes around a common cause (the narrator's funeral oration is a magnificent parody of Antony's), is potentially an agency of good, for Clifton can be considered in a meaningful sense a sacrifice. However, even that is denied him. At the last minute the Brotherhood withdraws its support from the hero, and, left to their own devices and the exhortation of Ras, the aroused Negroes perform arbitrary acts of plunder and violence. That Clifton's death initiates the Harlem riots, which serve the Brotherhood's new purpose of pacifying the Negro by exhausting his hate-charged energies in meaningless self-conflict, is a last terrible mockery of his decent intentions.

In hawking the chauvinistic "Sambo dolls" which dance at the tug of an invisible string, Clifton was not so much mocking the Brotherhood's attitude toward the Negro as he was parodying himself. His own comment about Ras suggests in a way the impulse of his nihilistic act:

> "I don't know," he said. "I suppose sometimes a man *has* to plunge outside history. . . ."
> "What?"
> "Plunge outside, turn his back. . . . Otherwise, he might kill somebody, go nuts." [p. 328]

Deceived by the bogus historians of the Brotherhood, Clifton has "plunged outside history," though in punching the white policeman he demonstrated that he had not quite "turned his back." As an alternative to violent reprisal—Clifton was an essentially gentle man racked by rage—he became a heckler of the Brotherhood, of the Negro, of the white man's treatment of the Negro, of himself, of the universe. Though he is one of the few noble characters in Ellison's world, his destruction is less than tragic. A man of tragic stature, Clifton is a captive participant in an absurd world which derogates him and mocks the significance of his death as it did his life. Clifton's sacrificial act, its intention perverted, is mostly invisible. The others of the Brotherhood—Wrestrum (rest room), Tobitt (two bit), Jack (money, masturbation)—who in their commitment to "science" have become as dehumanized and corrupt as those they oppose, survive the shift in tactical policy.

When the hero discovers that it is through him that the Brotherhood has betrayed Clifton, he feels responsible for his friend's death. Earlier, in outrage he spat at one of Clifton's dancing puppets, knocking it "lifeless," performing symbolically what the policeman does actually—the murder of Clifton. When the hero knocks over the doll, an onlooker laughs at what he thinks is the likeness between the spitter and the spat-on doll. Just as Clifton in selling the obscene doll has been mocking himself, the hero in spitting at the doll has been attacking himself as well as Clifton, though without benefit of awareness. Only after his showdown with the Brotherhood, and even then incompletely, does the hero become aware that he has been performing all along as if he were, in life size, the dancing puppet doll.

At his moment of greatest self-awareness, the hero suffers his most intense sense of guilt. Watching two nuns in the subway (one black, one white), he remembers a ritual verse he had once heard.

> Bread and wine,
> Bread and wine,
>   Your cross ain't nearly so
>   Heavy as mine. . . . [p. 382]

The rhyme comes to him as an automatic response, its singsong at first over-riding its sense. Momentarily, almost without awareness, as the pain of wound travels from flesh to brain, he comes to assume its implications. As he watches some Negroes maltreat a white shopkeeper, he experiences a terrible revelation:

> A pressure of guilt came over me. I stood on the edge of the walk watching the crowd threatening to attack the man until a policeman appeared and dispersed them. And although I knew no one could do much about it, I felt responsible. All our work had been very little, no great change had been made. And it was all my fault. I'd been so fascinated by the motion that I'd forgotten to measure what it was bringing forth. I'd been asleep, dreaming. [p. 384]

A sleepwalker in a world never real enough for him to believe in, the hero experiences a succession of awakenings, only to find himself participating in still another level of nightmare. In accepting Clifton's role as martyr-saint, in taking on the responsibility for all of Harlem, all of Brotherhood, in extension, *all*, he succeeds only in setting himself up for a final, self-destroying victimization. Aware of the futility of all his past acts and, in implication, all acts in the absurd context of his world, the hero commits an act of meaningless violence. Entrapped by a situation for which he is at least partly responsible, with his neck quite literally at stake (Ras wants to hang him), he impales the demonic innocent, Ras, through the jaw with his own spear.

That Jack, the leader of the Brotherhood, has one eye (as earlier the euphemistic preacher Barbee is revealed as blind) is symbolic of the distorted perspective of the Brotherhood's "scientifically objective view" of society, in which the human being is a casual puppet in the service of the "historic" strings that manipulate him. Clifton makes only *paper* Negroes dance; it is Jack and Tobitt who treat flesh-and-blood Negroes as if they were puppet Sambo dolls. (By having Clifton charge a "brotherly two bits" for the puppet dolls, Ellison, through suggestion, transfers the onus of traitor to Tobitt and in extension to the Brotherhood itself.) When the hero discovers that the Brotherhood has betrayed him, he consciously resolves to impersonate the puppet doll he has so long mimicked unwittingly—to, as his grandfather advised, "overcome 'em with yeses . . . agree 'em to death and destruction." For all his Rinehartian machinations, he manages, however, only to abet the scheme of the Brotherhood.

Seeking redemption from his compounded guilt, he is sucked into the maelstrom of the Harlem riot for which he suffers a sense of limitless, unreclaimable responsibility. He realizes that "By pretending to agree I had indeed agreed, had made myself responsible for that huddled form lighted by flame and gunfire in the street, and all others whom now the night was making ripe for death" (p. 478). The flaming buildings and streets, the burnt tar stench, the black figures moving shadow-like through the eerily illumined night become an evocation of Hell, a mirror for the hero's raging interior guilt. At the center of the riot—at the very seat of Hell—he experiences the deaths of his various corrupted identities, shedding the false skins to get at the pure invisibility underneath. As Ras approaches, the hero searches for his "Rineharts," his dark glasses, only to see the crushed lenses fall to the street. "'Rinehart, I thought, Rinehart!'" as if he had just witnessed Rinehart himself—his Rinehart self—collapse in death before him. To propitiate Ras and stop the riots, the hero disavows allegiance to the Brotherhood, killing in effect his Brotherhood self. But as he is invisible, he is unheard, his words as always not communicating his meanings. Struck by the absurdity of the demonic Ras on horseback, of the senseless pillage and murder around him, and, after all, of existence itself, the hero is for the moment willing to relinquish his life if it will make the white man see him and consequently see himself. But the example of Clifton's meaningless sacrifice dissuades him. The hero, faced with death, decides that it is "better to live out one's own absurdity than to die for that of others, whether for Ras's or Jack's." When in self-protection he impales Ras, who is in a sense the deepest of his identities, he experiences the illusion of death and rebirth: "It was as though for a moment I had surrendered my life and begun to live again" (p. 484).

Newly baptized by an exploded water main, like the birth from the machine, a somewhat illusory (and comic) resurrection, the hero seeks to return to Mary, his exlandlady, who has become a symbolic mother to him. But as he is unable to imitate Christ, he is unable to reach Mary. Instead, chased by two white looters, he falls through an open manhole. Unable to find the exit to his coffinlike cell, he burns various papers of his past (high school diploma, Sambo doll, Brotherhood card) for torches to light his way out, only to discover in a moment of terrible realization that the Jacks and Nortons have left him no exit, that without his paper symbols he has no past and consequently no home, no identity. With this knowledge he relaxes in the carrion comfort of his dank hole, having returned at last to the womb of the earth. It is, as he puts it, a "death alive," from which emergence will be rebirth, his victimization transcended, his guilt perhaps purged, his soul if possible redeemed. A nonparticipant in existence, an invisible man by choice, the hero continues to live in his private cellar, which he has illumined by 1,369 lights (a symbolic attempt at transcending his invisibility—at seeing himself), the electricity supplied gratuitously in spite of themselves by Monopolated Light and Power. As the whites had mocked his potency and used it for their own ends, he is now paying them back in kind. Though he is protected from the pain of disillusion while isolated from the brutal, absurd world he hates and, in spite of himself, loves, the hero plans some day to emerge into the outside world because, a son of God and man, one of us, he is willing to believe that "even the invisible victim is responsible for the fate of all" (p. 487).

Much of the experience in Ellison's novel is externally imposed; that is, each scene, through allusive reference, is made to carry a burden of implication beyond that generated by its particular experience. Consequently the weight of the novel, its profound moral seriousness, resides primarily in conception rather than rendering. Given the problem of transforming large abstractions into evocative experiences, Ellison is nevertheless able more often than not to create occasions resonant enough to accommodate his allegorical purposes. Finally, one senses that the novel, for all its picaresque variety of incident, has a curiously static quality. This is not because the episodes are the same or even similar—on the contrary, one is compelled to admire the range and resourcefulness of Ellison's imaginative constructions—but because they are all extensions of the same externally imposed idea; they all *mean* approximately the same thing.

Like so many of our serious writers, Ellison is not prolific. It took him, by his own testimony, some seven years to write *Invisible Man*, and now eleven years after its publication his second novel is still not completed. If Ellison's reputation had to rest, as it does at the time of this writing, on his one impressive if uneven novel, *Invisible Man* is, I suspect, vital and profound enough to survive its faults—to endure the erosions of time. As a satirist and surrealist, Ellison excels among his contemporaries and can bear comparison with his mentors—Kafka, Joyce, and Faulkner. As a realist, he is less adept: talky, didactic, even at times, if the term is possible for so otherwise exciting a writer, tedious. For all that, Ellison has written a major novel, perhaps one of the three or four most considerable American novels of the past two decades.

An excerpt from his forthcoming novel, "And Hickman Arrives," published in the first issue of *The Noble Savage*, exhibits some of the same evangelical rhetoric that gives *Invisible Man* its terrible impact. Still, it is idle from a fifty-page fragment to prophesy what kind of novel it will make. Moreover, "And Hickman Arrives" has many of the damaging excesses of the first novel. Ellison has a penchant for letting good things go on past their maximum effectiveness. Yet his excesses are also his strength; like Faulkner before him, Ellison is a writer of amazing verbal energy and at his best he creates experiences that touch our deepest selves, that haunt us with the suffocating wisdom of nightmare. American novelists have often had a predilection for large, protracted books, as if great length were a virtue in itself. Ellison is no exception. However, he is one of the few novelists on the scene today who seems capable of producing a large, serious novel, justified by the size of its experience and the depth of its informing intelligence. On the lowest (and highest) frequencies, he speaks for us.

Notes

1. Ralph Ellison, *Invisible Man* (New York; New American Library, 1953), p. 19. All quotations are from this edition.

BARBARA CHRISTIAN
"Ralph Ellison: A Critical Study"
Black Expression, ed. Addison Gayle, Jr.
1969, pp. 353–65

In 1952, reviewers across the country in both black and white periodicals hailed the then newly published book, *Invisible Man*, as a most impressive work of fiction. In that same year, Ralph Ellison's first novel was given collective critical acclaim for it was called the best novel of the last twenty years. There is no doubt that Ellison, although not very prolific (*Invisible Man* is his only completed creative work), is a skilled, impressive and lyrical writer. But he is not only a novelist; Ellison is also a critic with a particular point of view. His point of view can be seen in almost any paragraph in his collected essays, *Shadow and Act* (1966). Ellison's speech when he received the National Book Award reveals his particular slant:

> Thus to see America with an awareness of its rich diversity and its almost magical fluidity and freedom, I was forced to conceive of a novel unburdened by the narrow naturalism which has led, after so many

> triumphs, to the final and unrelieved despair which marks so much of our current fiction. I was to dream of a prose which was flexible and swift as American change is swift, confronting the inequalities, but yet thrusting forth its images of hope, human fraternity and individual self-realization. It would use the richness of our speech, the idiomatic expression and the rhetorical flourishes from past periods which are still alive among us. And despite my personal failures, there must be possible a fiction, which, leaving sociology to the scientists, can arrive at the truth about the human condition, here and now, with all the bright magic of a fairy tale.

The emphasis in this acceptance speech is without a doubt on the aesthetic problems of the artist. Unlike Wright and other notable black writers, Ellison is the spokesman for the "infinite possibilities" that he feels are inherent in the condition of being an artist rather than a Negro artist. He repeatedly states in his essays that his primary concern is not the social but rather the aesthetic responsibilities of the writer.

As we shall see, Ellison's positions in many of his essays do not always coincide with the ideas expressed in *Invisible Man*. Nonetheless, the essays, such as "Richard Wright's Blues," his interview with *Partisan Review*, and many of his essays on music are worth our attention for they reveal his interests and philosophy as they have developed and in this sense are a means of clarifying certain sections of *Invisible Man*.

There is one word that crops up repeatedly in both the essays and *Invisible Man* and which is at the base of Ellison's aesthetic beliefs. That word is *myth*, the magical transformer of life. Influenced by T. S. Eliot whom he calls his literary ancestor, Ellison combines the literary past and the memory and culture of the individual with the present, thus placing the contemporary writer alongside the other men who have written in the English language. Baldwin stresses the fact that the writer creates out of his own experience. Ellison would add that one writes out of one's experience as understood through one's knowledge of self, culture, and literature. Self, in Ellison's case, refers to his own past and background, culture to the American culture and more specifically to Negro American culture, and literature to the entire range of works in European literature that help to make up Western sensibility.

Even Ellison's name itself is steeped in myth as he points out in the essay, "Hidden Names and Complex Fate." His father had named him after Ralph Waldo Emerson and Ellison recalls that "much later after I began to write and work with words, I came to suspect that my father had been aware of the suggestive powers of names and the magic involved in naming." The name *Ralph Waldo* indeed had magic for it enabled Ellison to see the power of the myth and to envision the role that myth could play in achieving his aim which was, as he put it, "to add to literature the wonderful American speech and idiom and to bring into range as fully as possible the complex reality of American experience as it shaped and was shaped by the lives of my own people." Myths in order to be preserved and appreciated must be written down and Ellison, in his comments on Hemingway and Faulkner, is constantly aware that one element of the American past is sorely missing from most American literature. As Ralph Waldo Emerson could merge the myths and attitudes of New England into his philosophy of Transcendentalism, Ralph Waldo Ellison would merge that essential element, the nature of black folklore and life style, into American literature—and myth could be the carrier.

The past, especially the American past, is also a magical word for Ellison. Perhaps the impact of this concept on Ellison can be seen only when one looks at this writer's individual history. He was born and grew up in Oklahoma City in the 20's; he was raised in a virtual frontier town which had been a state only seven years when he was born. The newness of the state, the lack of a tradition of slavery allowed the boy to believe that nothing was hopelessly beyond the reach of the black world really, "because if you worked and you fought for your rights, and so on, you could finally achieve it." By early adolescence, Ellison remembers that "the idea of the Renaissance Man had drifted down to him and his friends and that they discussed mastering themselves and everything in sight as though no such thing as racial discrimination existed." No doubt, Ellison's background, with its illusion of personal freedom, is a strong determinant in his philosophy of "infinite possibilities."

In addition to the belief that he could be a Renaissance man, Ellison wanted to be a great musician. His youth and dreams were obsessed by his love of music both in the classical field which he studied at school and in the blues and jazz that he heard in the black community around him. The sense of timing, the flow of lyricism developed through this first love comes to fruition in *Invisible Man* and is one of the most beautiful aspects of the book. Music, too, gave Ellison an insight into the life around him. He tells us:

> The blues speak to us simultaneously of the tragic and comic aspects of the human condition and they express a profound sense of life shared by many Negro Americans precisely because their lives have combined these modes. This has been the heritage of a people who for hundreds of years could not celebrate birth or dignify death and whose need to live despite the dehumanizing pressures of slavery developed an endless capacity for laughter at their painful experience.

This analysis of the blues as a tragic-comic form was to contribute a great deal to *Invisible Man*, for this is precisely the stance that the hero takes when he explains his invisibility to us. But more important for Ellison, the craftsman, music taught him that "technique was that which transforms the individual before he is able to transform it. The artist discovers that he has taken on certain obligations; that he must not embarrass his chosen form, and that in order to avoid this he must develop taste." The meditation on form led Ellison to one of his basic tenets:

> He (the artist) learns—and this is most discouraging—that he is involved with values which turn in their own way, and not in the way of politics, upon the central issues affecting his nation and his time.

The aesthetic, rather than the political, was to be Ellison's concern; his grand social gesture was to be his creative work.

After graduating from high school, Ellison's love of music took him to Tuskegee where he planned to study under a famous musician. But like the hero in *Invisible Man*, he left the shelter of the dream-like college to work in New York for the summer, and never came back. Unable to find work, and disappointed with the sculpture he had come to study, the young man began to write. In his travels through Harlem he met Richard Wright who was then writing *Native Son* and who got Ellison's first piece, a book review, published. Wright encouraged the young musician in the art of writing, stressing not so much a mystical process but emphasizing craft, hard work, and thought. He guided Ellison to such writers as Henry James, and discussed the literary effects of Conrad, Joyce, and Dostoevsky with his new student. Although Ellison was overwhelmed by the towering personality of Richard Wright and though he learned a great deal about writing from him, he, even at that time, found Wright's novels disturbing. His comment on *Native Son* was that "Bigger Thomas had none of the fine qualities of Richard Wright, none of the imagination, none of the sense of poetry, the sense of gaiety," and Ellison summarily preferred Wright to Bigger Thomas. The younger writer always thought of himself as an artist taken up with the magical quality of writing and the poetry of it, while Richard Wright, he felt, was overcommitted to ideology.

By 1945, Ellison had devised a plan for a book which would incorporate the myth and literature of the Western world into the experience of the American black man. This book would reveal the travelings of the mind as it escaped from the darkness of illusion into the light of reality. Just as Dante had summarized the whole of medieval myth in his passing from dark circles of Hell to the light of the Paradiso, Ellison would use the literature and legends of American society, both black and white, as a means of clarifying and transforming the meaning of twentieth century existence. This was a grand aim and it took Ellison seven years, from 1945 to 1952, to create and revise the book.

Like Joyce's *Portrait of the Artist as a Young Man*, a book which has greatly influenced Ellison's work, *Invisible Man* has been called the story of a young man's search for his identity. Both heroes must escape from the illusions and limitations of their environments in order to find themselves. Joyce's Stephen has to confront his Irish, Catholic, and family traditions. Ellison's hero has to penetrate the illusions built around the fact that he is black, not only in others, but more importantly in himself. As he moves from darkness to light, a basic motif in the book, the hero must encounter variations of deception which attempt to blind him to his image, that as a black man in America, he does not in relation to the rest of his world really exist.

This is the substance of the book but actually the hero has found his identity before the book opens. His first statement is to assure us that he knows who he is. "I am an invisible man," he proclaims with mingled pride and fear. Rather than searching for his identity, he is more interested in clarifying for himself his reasons for descending into his hell-like hole, and possibly for rising out of it, if and when he decides to do so. His goal in telling us his story is to separate the pride from the fear to make sense out of his experience. He is forced to explain himself not because it is necessary in that hole of his, but because he needs to face the world outside: "What did I do to be so black and blue?" Just as hibernation could not work for Dostoevsky's hero in his underground, so it cannot work for Ellison's hero. It is impossible for both of these intellectuals to protest their situation silently (hibernation is nothing less than passive protest) because of the nature of their minds.

> So I took to the cellar; I hibernated, I got away from it all. But that wasn't enough. I couldn't be still in hibernation. Because, damn it, there's the mind, the mind. It wouldn't let me rest.

It is the mind that puts these heroes in hell and it is the pain of consciousness that forces them to murder an old self and create a new one.

Actually the invisible man's mind hadn't been at rest since his grandfather had uttered that loathsome curse on his deathbed. The old man, usually meek and gentle, turned violent on his deathbed and hissed out his last words of advice:

> Live with your head in the lion's mouth. I want you to overcome 'em with yeses, undermine 'em with grins, agree 'em to death and destruction, let them swoller you till they vomit or bust wide open.

The snake had crawled into the garden of Paradise. These words were to haunt the life and dreams of the hero throughout the book not so much because he does not understand them but because he senses the irony that lies beneath them.

It is with this mental assault, rather than with a physical attack, that Ellison begins the book (contrast this with the beginning of *Native Son*); it is with his first disturbance of a child's mind. The narrator's grandfather had simply accepted the fact that Negroes survived by lying to white people and he suggests that the lie is not only the tool for survival but a means of victory as well. But the narrator does not want to believe this and it is precisely by telling the truth, accidentally sometimes, as in the speech he makes at the Battle Royale, that he continues to get into trouble. His grandfather's warnings, though, held another meaning—that a person, a race, a people must not fool itself into believing its own lies. Our narrator does believe in his own deceptive speech at the Battle Royale, in his own behavior at the college; he believes the actions that are meant to fool white people. But in spite of his resistance to the truth, his grandfather's swan song is harsh enough to unsettle him for the rest of his life.

The power of the lie, the fact that it is at the base of the relations between whites and blacks in this country, is forced home traumatically to the hero in the junior year at his dream-world college which had been built on and had survived exactly by those very lies. And Ellison, anxious to show the complexity and attractiveness of the illusion, literally flushes this section with pseudo myth and ritual. The college is the hero's religion, its ceremonies, his act of worship. Presiding over this universe, untouchable and benevolent, are the great white fathers, like Mr. Norton who had created this world through the mediation of the Christ-like Negro teacher and leader of his people. Barbee, the blind minister, gives us the full impact of the Founder who could effectively mediate between the gods and the people, since he was brother racially to the people and understood mentally the wishes of the gods. The religious overtones in this section are heightened even more by the hero's encounter with one of these white gods. Mr. Norton. Such words as *destiny, fate, salvation* regularly flow out of Norton's lips just as sums of money for the benefit of the college flow out of his pocketbook. In exchange for creating this dream-world, Mr. Norton expects, kindly it is true, adoration and power.

In this setting, Ellison then introduces Jim Trueblood and the vet, two demoniac characters, companions no doubt of the hissing grandfather. Both are blasphemers, for Jim Trueblood (the pun is marvellous) commits the unforgivable sin and lives, despite the pronouncement of the gods, while the vet deliberately attacks the supremacy and benevolence of the gods who had supposedly given him so much. During Norton's talk with Trueblood and the vet, the narrator shows signs of increasing disturbance and fear, for these men were talking to white men as if they were simply other men, not gods. These men were speaking the truth. The vet, protected by his status as an insane man, says ironically:

> You don't have to be a complete fool to succeed. Play the game but don't believe in it.

Bledsoe, president of the college, tells the narrator the whole truth, puts his finger exactly on what was wrong with the Golden-Day episode, why it was actual treason, and why the hero must be expelled from the college:

> You're dangerous, boy, why the dumbest black bastard in the cotton patch knows that the only way to please a white man is to tell him a lie. What kind of education are you getting around here?

So much for the American Dream. The dream-world college is built on a lie, Bledsoe knows it, he assumes every Negro does; but our narrator naively believes that he is telling the truth when in fact he has not even found it. Bledsoe lives the doctrine of the grandfather. He is the first of the long line of yes-ers in the book, of people who are used by and use white people and who know exactly where it's at. He represents for the invisible man his first concrete glimpse into the real world and the narrator never forgives him for it.

The trip North, archetypal for the black man in this country, precipitates the hero's search for work and then for his own identity. Cast out from the dream-world college, both physically and spiritually, he descends into *Mister* Brockway's underground hole where Optic White paint is made. The irony of this scene is hilarious as Ellison juxtaposes the supreme lie of the Negro "white is right" with the slogan of the company, "If it's Optic White, it's the right white." Why not whitewash everything? Just as Negroes had conveniently told whites that they were right when in fact they knew they weren't, Lucius Brockway improves on the saying by turning it into a slogan which gives him prestige in the eyes of the man upstairs. The whole nightmarish experience, underlined by the hero's first attempt at violence and by the serious injury he receives, his first literal blow on the head, is a preparation for one of Ellison's most impressive pieces, the surrealistic hospital dream of castration and loss of identity that the narrator suffers. Dreams had been used before in the book. "Keep that nigger running," the dream caused by his grandfather's words, is a father to the horrifying dream sequence that the hero now experiences. Music, too, plays an essential part in dramatizing the trauma of the nightmare. Beethoven's Fifth becomes unbearable and is pitted against the hero's childhood songs now magnified in horrifying proportions in his dream. Although the Invisible Man knows who Brer Rabbit is, he hasn't learned what this cunning fellow, essential to Negro folklore, really represents. Brer Rabbit, the symbol of the yes-er who destroys through yessing, knows when he is conning and when he is not. The hero is still trapped by his wish to believe that in fact he can survive by deceiving himself.

The nightmare with all its grotesque images of the hero's past indicates that he does know unconsciously the truth but that the mind with its affinity for rationality cannot stand for the absurdity that is implied in the truth. How can his mind grasp the fact that he does not really exist? The dream does rid the narrator of one fear though. When he is released from the factory hospital he reflects:

> Leaving him and going out into the paint-fuming air I had the feeling that I had been talking beyond myself, had used words and expressed attitudes not my own, that I was in the grip of some alien personality lodged deep within me. It was as though I were acting out a scene from some crazy movie. Or perhaps I was catching up with myself and had put into words feelings which I had hitherto suppressed. Or was it I thought that I was no longer afraid? I was no longer afraid. Not of important men, not of trustees and such; for knowing now that there was nothing which I could expect from them, there was no reason to be afraid.

At this point in the story, the intensity of the action subsides; the narrator becomes "cool" as he withdraws from society for the first time. This time it is not into the hole but into the warm generous arms of Mary, Mary Rambo, whom he does not think of as a friend but as a force, familiar and stabilizing. And during this hibernation with Mary, we see the hero wrestle with his benefactor. Mary belongs to his past for she insists that he do something, that he be one of those men who will save his people. But he becomes more and more convinced that anything he could do would only be futile.

This time the feeling of futility lasts only for a little while. The voice of the past wins out. The hero returns to sociey as he is reminded by those hot juicy yams as to who he is and that he had tried to suppress his past in his dream-world college. It is no accident, I think, that Ellison follows up the eating of yams with the eviction scene in which the hero speaks his mind. But this time he speaks an accepted lie, "We are a law-abiding people," in order to provoke and arouse the crowd to action. For the first time in the book he feels potent and alive. Just as Bigger Thomas becomes aware of his own life through the murder he had unintentionally committed, so too Ellison's hero comes to life as he destroys the false myth that Negroes can and will suffer anything.

But another obstacle is placed in the hero's path before he can see it like it is. Intrigued by the power and stability which the brotherhood represents, he becomes a part of their group. Again, he feels, as he had at college, that he is engaged in discovering and promoting the truth, that he has gained recognition, that he is living a significant life. However, just as Barbee, the blind minister, had perpetuated the myth of the great Christ-like Founder, so Jack, the one-eyed leader of the Brotherhood, worships the myth of history. As patronizing as Norton, Jack leads the hero into another deception, that in history, there is salvation and that salvation can be attained through subordinating the individual to a cause bigger than himself. Thus, in dealing with Christianity and Communism, and in relating them to each other, Ellison presents two important paths by which black people have tried to find themselves.

That Ellison calls his organization the Brotherhood rather than the Communist Party, which it obviously is, is significant, I believe. For what he might be suggesting is that the essence of any such *ism* is an abstraction such as "history saves." And that when push comes to shove, this abstraction rules and controls the living entities within it. Harlem is only a political entity to Jack. He doesn't know nor want to know

> the gin mills, and the barber shops and the juke joints and the churches and the beauty parlors on Saturday when they're frying hair, the whole of unrecorded history called reality.

History, as Jack sees it, is a means of imposing order on chaos. It is not the reality itself; it is an ideal which is imposed on the real. Thus, the problem of scientific objectivity, the ritual of this organization, is the first obstacle that the hero now turned orator faces when he joins the Brotherhood. Many brothers protest that although his speeches are effective, they are not scientific. And when the narrator, angered by the fact that the organization will not avenge the death of Tod Clifton, accuses Brother Hambro of being mechanical, communication between him and the organization falls apart. The organization called for the sacrifice of Harlem, but the narrator sees that "for them it is simple, but hell, I was both sacrificer and victim. *That was reality.* They did not have to put the knives to their own throats."

Enraged by the brotherhood's betrayal, the hero looks for another alternative. Ras and Rinehart, the two powerful figures who dominate the rest of the book, represent other means of existence. The narrator's introduction to Ras is worth looking at closely since Ras represents a complete departure from the other characters in the book. He is definitely visible (perhaps the only completely visible person in the book) in the most dangerous fashion imaginable. Tod Clifton acknowledges after his street brawl with Ras: "But it's on the inside that Ras is strong. On the inside he's dangerous." The narrator misreads Clifton's comment as he believes the inside that Tod is talking about to be the inside of the Brotherhood. Tod's tragic end itself, though, is a testimony to the truth of Ras's philosophy. The narrator, helpless, looks on as Tod, months later, goes nuts, peddling Sambo dolls on Times Square, and is finally gunned down by the police. "I don't know," Tod had said, "I suppose sometimes a man has to plunge outside history . . . otherwise he might kill somebody, go nuts." And Ras is nuts to those who do not understand his logic, his existence, his visibility. The narrator obviously does not understand that the militant Ras is an alternative to his present existence, as can be seen in their encounter during the riots.

Rinehart, however, is an alternative to our nameless hero—Rinehart, numbers runner, preacher, lover, conman, whose invisibility gives him the potential to live more than one life at the same time—who indulges in the infinite possibilities of life. Rinehart is an urban Brer Rabbit; he yesses everybody. This multiple personality knows that the people around him recognize him only by his outer trappings, that the people are blind and that he can take advantage of their blindness. Rinehart is a boldface liar, but he has flair and is effective precisely because he knows that he does not really exist. The hero's one night transformation into Rinehart brings him to the realization that "the people who define him are blind, bat blind, hearing only the echoes of their own voices. And because they were blind, they would destroy themselves and he would help them." In a Rinehart fashion, the hero sees that "it was a joke, an absurd joke." Once the narrator's mind accepts the absurdity of his world, he is able to see himself as he really is:

> And now I looked around a corner in my mind and saw Jack and Norton and Emerson merge into one single white figure. They were very much the same, each attempting to force his picture of reality upon me and neither giving a hoot in hell for how things looked to me. I was simply a material, a natural resource to be used. I had switched from the arrogant absurdity of Norton and Emerson to that of Jack and the Brotherhood, and it all came out the same—except that now I recognize my invisibility.

Now that he knows he is invisible, what should he do? Well, he could be a Rinehart, "he could overcome them with yesses, undermine them with grins, he could agree them to death and destruction."

But it is too late to become Brer Rabbit. The truth will out and it bursts out violently in the riots, a scene which is packed full of the swift American idiom that Ellison delights in. Rinehartism eventually is bound to fail for the acrobatics that one has to perform to keep it up tries the nerves. As the hero says at the beginning of the book:

> You often doubt if you really exist. You wonder whether you aren't simply a phantom in other people's minds. Shy, a figure in a nightmare which the sleeper tries with all his strength to destroy. It's when you feel like this that out of resentment, you begin to bump people back. And let me confess, you feel that way most of the time. You ache with the need to convince yourself that you do exist in the real world, that you're a part of all the sound and anguish, and you strike out with your fists, you curse and you swear to make them recognize you. And alas, it's seldom successful.

Alas it is seldom successful. The hero, buried alive in his hole at the end of the riots, is most painfully aware of that fact. The horror of that realization calls up the maddening, powerful, and tortuous dream that keeps him in his hole. Accosted by the grotesque figures of Jack, Norton, Bledsoe, and the rest, tortured by their question: "How does it feel to be free of illusions?", the crushed invisible man can only scream with intense ferocity, "Painful and empty, painful and empty." What is an invisible man but a man who doesn't exist?

If Ellison's novel had ended with that dream, it would fall into the well-known category of the absurd along with the French existentialists of the '40's and the American playwrights of today. But that mind won't leave the hero be. He has progressed from being blind to being invisible. He has traveled a long way. Nonetheless he must deal with invisibility as a concept which is still an unknown quality to him, a concept that eludes even his imagination, far less his rational mind.

The epilogue reasserts his need to make his past rational. By reliving his experience he sees that many false ideas have been cleared away. Still, he is left with his will to transcend invisibility. Pushed by his instinct for survival, the narrator stumbles into the efficacy of diversity, the inevitability of necessity. "Life," he says, "is to be lived not controlled and humanity is won by continuing to play in the face of certain defeat." A worthy and noble ideal but not very convincing. As the invisible man prepares (perhaps) to leave his hole, he gives us a more credible reason for doing so. Could it be that we're all invisible men? That white men could blind themselves to their own invisibility, but black men could not? And he settles on this point with a howl, a sense of triumph as well as a sense of terror,

> Who knows that on the lower frequencies
> I speak for you.

TONY TANNER

"The Music of Invisibility"

City of Words: American Fiction, 1950–1970

1971, pp. 50–64

> Could this compulsion to put invisibility down in black and white be thus an urge to make music of invisibility? *(Invisible Man)*

In the Introduction to his essays *(Shadow and Act)*, Ralph Ellison, recalling the circumstances of his youth, stresses the significance of the fact that while Oklahoman jazz musicians were developing "a freer, more complex and driving form of jazz, my friends and I were exploring an idea of human versatility and possibility which went against the barbs or over the palings of almost every fence which those who controlled social and political power had erected to restrict our roles in the life of the country." The fact that these musicians working with "tradition, imagination and the sounds and emotions around them," could create something new which was both free yet recognizably formed (this is the essence of improvisation) was clearly of the first importance for Ralph Ellison; the ideas of versatility and possibility which he and his friends were exploring provide the ultimate subject-matter, and nourish the style, of his one novel to date, *Invisible Man* (1952), a novel which in many ways is seminal for subsequent American fiction. His title may owe something to H. G. Wells's novel *The Invisible Man*, for the alienated Griffin in Wells's novel also comes to realize "what a helpless absurdity an Invisible Man was—in a cold and dirty climate and a crowded, civilized city" and there is a very suggestive scene in which he tries to assemble an identity, which is at the same time a disguise, from the wigs, masks, artificial noses, and clothes of Omniums, the large London store. It would not be surprising if Wells's potentially very probing little novel about the ambiguity involved in achieving social "identity" had stayed in Ellison's extremely literate memory. But if it did so it would be because Ellison's experience as a Negro had taught him a profounder sort of invisibility than any chemically induced vanishing trick. As the narrator says in the opening paragraph, it is as though he lives surrounded by mirrors of distorting glass, so that other people do not see him but only his surroundings, or reflections of themselves, or their fantasies. It is an aspect of recent American fiction that work coming from members of so-called minority groups has proved to be relevant and applicable to the situation of people not sharing their immediate racial experience or, as it may be, sexual inclination; and *Invisible Man*, so far from being limited to an expression of an anguish and injustice experienced peculiarly by Negroes, is quite simply the most profound novel about American identity written since the war.

The book begins and ends in a small underground room, situated significantly in a "border area." It is there that the unnamed narrator—unnamed because invisible on the social surface—is arranging his memories, structuring his experiences, creating his life. It is important to bear this in mind since the book is not only an account of events but quite as importantly about what the consciousness of the narrator has managed to make of those events, how it has managed to change because of them. His little room is flooded with the light from 1,369 light bulbs, run by free current drained off from the Monopolated Light and Power Company. It is an echo of Hemingway's "clean, well-lighted place" but with many significant differences. The narrator has had experience of electricity before. As a child he had been engaged in one of those grotesque entertainments in which white Southerners make negro youths fight among themselves for coins which they are then invited to pick up from an electrified rug. The narrator discovers that if he is careful he can contain the electricity, but then he is thrown bodily on to the rug by the white men who persist in shouting misleading cues and directions. The agony is intense and it seems that a century will pass before he can roll free.

The whole experience is an early paradigm of the treatment he is to receive all through his adult life. Later in life he is given electric shock "treatment" which is intended to have the effect of a pre-frontal lobotomy without actually cutting into the brain. The white doctor explains his technique, describing how they apply pressure to the centres of nerve control—"our concept is Gestalt." This implies that simply by applying the appropriate pressures they can alter the way a man reads reality, another device for that monitoring of consciousness which is so abhorrent to the American hero. And the electricity is important here. It can be seen as the indispensable force by which society warms and lights its way. That power can be also used to make cruel sport of the individual, to condition him, make him jump to the whim of the man at the controls. The question is, can the narrator find a way to "contain" this power, to use it without being its helpless victim or its ruthless exerciser?

The first time he finds himself in opposition to the existing authorities, Dr Bledsoe, who runs the Uncle Tom–like State College for negroes in the South, tells him, "This is a power set-up, son, and I'm at the controls." The moral would seem to be—control or be controlled; as when, later in his life, he sees two pictures of bull-fighting in a bar in one of which the matador gracefully dominates the bull while in the second he is being tossed on the black bull's horns. There is a black powerhouse close to the white buildings of the college, and while the notion of black power which has since emerged in America is not entirely irrelevant here, Ellison is making the much more profound point that power is what keeps society going at all levels; the lights in the library and the chapel, the machines in the factory and the hospitals all derive from the morally neutral force of electricity. Morality starts when man diverts this power to specific ends. The experience of the narrator is that it is usually used for the more or less cynical manipulation of individuals. Yet electricity is also a source of light, and the achievement of the narrator must be to find a way out of the power set-up altogether (for to be a controller is more pernicious than to be one who is controlled) and tap some of that power for his own private purpose—to "illuminate the blackness of my invisibility," to become aware of his own form.

The odyssey which the narrator, with the aid of 1,369 lights bulbs, looks back on takes place on many levels. His travelling is geographic, social, historical and philosophical. In an early dream he finds inside his brief-case an envelope which contains an endless recession of smaller envelopes, the last of which contains the simple message "Keep this Nigger-Boy Running." It is only at the end when he finally burns all the contents of his real brief-case that he can start to control his own momentum. Up to that point his movements are really controlled from without, just like the people in the New York streets who to him seem to walk as though they were directed by "some unseen control." The pattern of his life is one of constraint and eviction; he is alternately cramped and dispossessed. This is true of his experience in the college, the factory, the hospital, the Party. What he discovers is that every institution is bent on processing and programming the individual in a certain way; yet if a man does not have a place in any of the social structures the danger is that he might fall into chaos.

At his college, in the chapel everybody seems to have eyes of robots and faces like frozen masks (i.e. "fixed" in rigid roles), and the blind preacher telling them "the way" inaugurates a theme of the blindness or warped vision of all the creatures of the given structures of society, whether leaders or led—a point underlined when Brother Jack's glass eye falls out. References to dolls, actors, masks, dummies, and so on, proliferate throughout, and before the narrator is startled or pushed out of his first given role—at the state college—he too is described, by a man of accredited perceptions, as a "mechanical man." The speaker is addressing Mr Norton, a trustee of the college, whom he aptly calls "a trustee of consciousness." He is making the point that such institutions turn out automata, who accept the rigid and restraining role imposed on them as true identity, and defer to the white man's version of reality.

The point about all the representatives of social power that the narrator encounters—teacher, preacher, doctor, factory-owner, Party member, whatever—is that they all seek to control reality and they believe that they can run it according to their plan. To this extent one can say that they have a mechanizing attitude towards reality, and it is no accident that the narrator is constantly getting involved with literal machines (in the factory, the hospital, etc.) as well as with what one might call the mechanizers of consciousness, the servants of church, college or Party. On the other hand there is the point that these institutions, these people at the social controls, do seem to give the individual a role, a place in the scheme of things. At one stage the narrator is enthusiastic about the Party, because it gives the world a meaningful shape and himself an important role in it: "everything could be controlled by our science. Life was all pattern and discipline."

The alternative to the servile docility and rigid regulations of the state college would seem to be the utter chaos of The Golden Day Saloon, which with its fighting and drinking and debauchery seems to be in continuous rehearsal for "the end of the world," as one mad participant proclaims it (see R. W. B. Lewis's fine essay "Days of Wrath and Laughter"[1] for a discussion of the apocalyptic hints in the novel). It may be more real, more authentic than the fabricated performances in the chapel at the college, but in its utterly shapeless confusion it offers no opportunities for self-development or self-discovery. Society does indeed impose false surfaces on things; a point well made at the paint factory where the narrator has to mix in a black constituent which nevertheless produces a dazzling Optic White paint used for government buildings. It reminds the narrator of the white painted buildings of the campus; it also reminds him that The Golden Day had once been painted white but that now it was all flaking away. The fact that the paint is called Liberty Paint in conjunction with the suggestion that it is at least in part an optical illusion (the narrator can see a grey in the white which his overseer ignores or cannot detect) is a fairly clear irony; we are in fact "caught" in the official version of reality—the painted surfaces—maintained by the constituted authorities. On the other hand, if you strip all the false paint away you are likely to be confronted with the merely chaotic "truth" of The Golden Day. In the same way, the mechanizers and controllers of reality turn people into automata and manipulable dummies; but can a man achieve any visible shape or role if he refuses to join any of the existing patterns?

This is indeed the narrator's problem. When he is about to be sent away from the college he feels that he is losing the only identity that he has ever known. At this stage he equates a stable niche in the social structure with an identity, and for a long time his quest is for some defining and recognized employment. The matter of the letters from Bledsoe is instructive; they are supposed to be helping him find a job which might enable him to return to his higher education, whereas in fact they are treacherously advancing Bledsoe's scheme of keeping him as far away from college as possible. He feels all along that he is playing a part in some incomprehensible "scheme," but it is only when the younger Emerson shows him one of the letters that he begins to understand. "Everyone seemed to have some plan for me, and beneath that some more secret plan." It is an essential part of his education that he should come to realize that "everybody wanted to use you for some purpose" and that the way they recognize you, on and in their own terms, is not to be confused with your identity.

After his accident in the factory he undergoes what is in effect a process of rebirth—not organically but electrically. From his fall into the lake of heavy water and on to his coming to consciousness with a completely blank mind in a small glass-and-nickel box, and his subsequent struggle to get out, it reads like a mechanized parody of the birth process. The electrical treatment has temporarily erased his earlier consciousness and he cannot say who he is or what his name is. His only concern is to get out of the machine without electrocuting himself. "I wanted freedom, not destruction . . . I could no more escape than I could think of my identity. Perhaps, I thought, the two things are involved with each other. When I discover who I am, I'll be free." This, coming nearly halfway through the book, is a crucial turning-point. The machine is every system by which other people want to manipulate him and regulate his actions. In much the same way the Party gives him a new identity and tries to reprogramme him for its ends. The narrator is not a nihilist—he does not wish to smash the machine, knowing that he will probably be destroyed with it—but he wants to find some sort of freedom from the interlocking systems which make up society, and he realizes that it will have to be mainly an inner freedom. At the end he can look back and see that the individuals from various professions or parties who had sought to direct and use him "were very much the same, each attempting to force his picture of reality upon me and neither giving a hoot in hell for how things looked to me." This is why he wants to be free of all parties, all partial pictures, all the imposed and imprisoning constructs of society. This urge will bring him to a second rebirth near the end—this time a private, self-managed one. But before coming to that we should consider some of the advice and examples he has received from figures who are not on the side of the system-makers, not enlisted among the controllers.

His grandfather on his deathbed has given the advice to "overcome 'em with yeses," and only by the end can the narrator see a possible hidden meaning in this exhortation. Before he leaves for New York, the vet in The Golden Day advises him that, once there, he should play the game without believing it: he explains that he will be "hidden right out in the open" because "they" will not expect him to know anything and therefore will not be able to see him. When asked by the narrator who "they" refers to, he answers, "Why the same *they* we always mean, the white folks, authority, the gods, fate, circumstances—the force that pulls your strings until you refuse to be pulled any more." Three further things he says to the narrator are of particular importance. He tells him that much of his freedom will have to be "symbolic"—a deeper truth perhaps than he knows for the boy who will ultimately find his freedom in the symbols called words. He says, "Be your own father, young man," an Oedipal echo (picking up the description we have already had of the narrator standing where three roads converge) and a warning to the boy that he will have to create an identity, not rely on assuming one already waiting for him. Thirdly, he bids him remember that the world is "possibility." And this anticipates the narrator's encounter with Rinehart which is perhaps the most important "epiphany" in the book.

Before this encounter there is the decisive incident connected with Tod Clifton, the narrator's friend who suddenly drops all Party work and makes himself into a sort of parody Negro. Tod becomes a street-hawker in Harlem, mongering self-mocking black dolls. He is duly killed, as his name forewarns us, by a policeman—the cause of his death being described as "resisting reality." It is Tod who, after a bitter encounter with the black fantatic Ras, speculates that, "I suppose sometimes a man *has* to plunge outside history." History is the temporal dimension of the social structure, its emerging shape, as well as being the accumulation of memories which weigh on us. It is everything that has conditioned society and the individual within it. History we could say is the visible part of society's progress or change, the fraction that shows above the surface. It is worth stressing this because we often see the narrator entering, or falling into, or retreating to, dark subterranean places. It is in a subway, looking at some sharply dressed black boys, that the narrator has his vision of the significance of all those anonymous people who play no part in history, the transitory ones who will never be classified, too silent to be recorded, too ambiguous to be caught in "the most ambiguous words." "What if history was a gambler . . . What if history was not a reasonable citizen, but a madman full of paranoid guile and these boys his agents, his big surprise? For they were outside . . . running and dodging the forces of history instead of making a dominating stand." If history is a gambler—and truth tends to come in underground places in this book—then all those people up on the surface who regard it as a manipulable machine are wrong. Up there they "distort" people in the interests of some abstract "design"; they force people into tight little boxes, just as Tod is literally trapped in the ulimate confinement of the coffin. Having seen this much the narrator is effectively through with all parties of the surface. It remains for him to see whether there is any alternative mode of life.

This is when he encounters Rinehart, or rather the phenomenon of Rinehart, since Rinehart is not a man to be met so much as a strategy to be made aware of. The narrator comes to "know" Rinehart by being mistaken for him when he adopts a safety disguise. After being taken for a number of contradictory Rineharts—from gambler to Reverend—the narrator suddenly understands and appreciates the significance of this figure. "His world was possibility and he knew it. He was years ahead of me and I was a fool . . . The world in which we lived was without boundaries. A vast seething, hot world of fluidity, and Rine the rascal was at home. Perhaps *only* Rine the rascal was at home in it." The realization makes him feel as though he has just been released from a plaster cast; it suggests what life on the surface never suggested: "new freedom of movement." "You could actually make yourself anew. The notion was frightening, for now the world seemed to flow before my eyes. All boundaries down, freedom was not only the recognition of necessity, it was the recognition of possibility." This is as succinct an expression of the discovery earned in this book as one could wish for. But what follows is also important. "And sitting there trembling I caught a brief glimpse of the possibilities posed by Rinehart's multiple personalities and turned away." I stress this because although the narrator learns his most important lesson from the spectacle of Rinehart he does not wish to emulate him.

If we can simplify the structuring of reality implicit in the book for a moment, we could say that just as figures like Norton, Emerson, Bledsoe and Brother Jack are at home on the surface, which is the realm of social rigidification and the mechanistic manipulations of history; just so Rinehart is the figure most at home in the subterranean world, a fluid darkness flowing on underneath history and society, beneath their shaping powers. This lower realm clearly has its potencies and its truths. But a world of no boundaries, a world given over to "the merging fluidity of forms," which the narrator sees when he puts on his dark glasses, such a world can finally only be a chaos. And Ellison himself has made this point very clear in an interview.[2] Rinehart's middle name is "Proteus" and Ellison intended something quite specific by his character.

> Rinehart is my name for the personification of chaos. He is also intended to represent America and change. He has lived so long with chaos that he knows how to manipulate it. It is the old theme of *The Confidence Man*. He is a figure in a country with no solid past or stable class lines; therefore he is able to move about easily from one to the other.

To emulate Rinehart would be to submit to chaos. Rinehart, whose heart is in fact all rind, really represents the ultimate diffusion and loss of self; a freedom, indeed, which might easily turn into that nightmare of jelly. The narrator, attempting to discover or create his own identity, does not want to dissolve in fluidity. Yet if he rejects both the life-denying mechanical fixities of the surface operators, and the fluid adaptations and adaptive improvisations of a Rinehart, the question emerges—where can he go, what can he do?

Perhaps we can get nearer the answer if we ask, not where will he go, but how will he move? One thing he learns after all his experiences on different levels is that the prevailing notion that success involved rising *upward* is a lie used by society to dominate its members. "Not only could you travel upward toward success but you could travel downward as well; up *and* down, in retreat as well as in advance, crabways and crossways and around in a circle, meeting your old selves coming and going and perhaps all at the same time." This notion of movement is related to that "running and dodging" of the forces of history he had earlier discerned as a possibility, and is of special importance as it provides the plot lines of many of the novels we will be considering. At the height of the Harlem riots the narrator finds himself running from all parties, but with the new realization that he no longer has to run either for or from the Jacks and Emersons and the Bledsoes and Nortons, "but only from their confusion, impatience, and refusal to recognize the beautiful absurdity of their American identity and mine." And just when it seems that he will be killed in the converging forces of that apocalyptic night (which, like the battle royal he was involved in as a child, is in fact engineered by unscrupulous white people so that the rebels and rioters who think they are generating a scheme of their own are in fact fulfilling someone else's) the narrator falls down a hole into the dark chamber of his second rebirth.

First of all he has to burn all the papers in his brief-case to find his way out of the hole: those papers represent all the schemes and treacheries that his various controllers have planned for him. He is in fact burning up his past and all the false roles it has sought to trap him in. With the aid of the light from the flames (i.e. he has learned something from his past experience) he enters another dimensionless room where he loses all sense of time. He has to go down a long dark passage and then he lies down in a state between waking and dreaming. Subsequently he has a dream of being castrated by a group consisting of all those who had sought to direct and control his previous life. But when he wakes, he is beyond them. "They were all up there, somewhere, making a mess of the world. Well, let them. I was through and, in spite of the dream, I was whole." At this point he decides to take up residence underground and with this gesture of repudiation—a plague on both your houses—so characteristic of American literature, the book might well have ended. But there is an Epilogue, and in some ways this is the most important part of the book.

As was noted, while writing the book the narrator has been living underground and in a "border area." The point is worth remembering because throughout his life he has been striving to avoid being forced into either of the two extremes of life-style exemplified by Emerson's and Jack's surface New York and Rinehart's Harlem. "I don't belong to anything," he cries at one point. To be able to exist in a border area is to resist being wholly drawn into one or the other, to secure a bit of private freedom on the edge. And what he has been doing in his refuge of secret illumination is best suggested by a sentence he remembers from his school-teacher, talking about *A Portrait of the Artist as a Young Man*. "Stephen's problem, like ours, was not actually one of creating the uncreated conscience of his race, but of creating the *uncreated features of his face*." The narrator has discovered what many American heroes have discovered, that he is not free to reorganize and order the world, but he can at least exercise the freedom to arrange and name his perceptions of the world. He cannot perhaps assert and define himself in action, but sometimes at least he can assert and create himself in some private space not in the grip of historical forces. While running and dodging in the outside world, the hero may be evolving and discovering and defining his true features in his inner world, like this narrator. His most important affirmation may be, not of any pattern in the outside world, but of the patterning power of his own mind.

This is not the artist as hero so much as the hero out of dire necessity having to become an artist. For it is only in the "symbolic" freedom of lexical space that he can both find and be himself. In writing his book the narrator has created his face. He is aware of the paradox involved in the compulsion "to put invisibility down in black and white"—the phrase pointing nicely both to the black and white which make up the legibility of print, and the patterning of symbolic black and white which in the book itself is one of his main strategies for rendering his experience visible. But in the pursuit of this paradox lies his only freedom. He tells the story of a yokel who beat a prizefighter against all the odds because he simply stepped "inside of his opponent's sense of time." Just so the narrator can step out of other people's times and schemes, but only by creating his own in his writing. He has a memory or dream of asking his mother to define freedom and she answers, "I guess now it ain't nothing but knowing how to say what I got up in my head." This is the freedom which the narrator achieves in the act of seeking it in his writing.

But the problem remains of "the next step." He had every reason for going underground: "my problem was that I always tried to go in everyone's way but my own," which meant that he had never been master of his own direction, and "to lose your direction is to lose your face." He has gone into hibernation in his cellar to find direction and face. But he makes another discovery there. "I couldn't be still even in hibernation. Because, damn it, there's the mind, the *mind*. It wouldn't let me rest." Here indeed we find a conflict of urges shared by many American heroes—the desire to hibernate (celebrated definitively in Washington Irving's tale of Rip Van Winkle—one of the first American "outsiders"!), and the inability to remain still in hibernation. Ellison's narrator speaks both of his "craving for tranquillity, for peace and quiet," and of the "ache" to "convince yourself that you do exist in the real world." The difficulty here is that if you remain in hibernation you are likely to stagnate in unseen inertia; but if you rejoin the shared reality of the surface you are going to be forced into role-playing.

Ellison's narrator defends the value of hibernation as a covert preparation for some subsequent action, but after writing his book he is still wrestling with the problem of defining the nature of that ensuing action. "Yes, but what *is* the next phase?" In hibernation you can become visible to yourself, but to remain in hibernation indefinitely is simply to die. So at the end the narrator says, "the old fascination with playing a role returns, and I'm drawn upward again," and ends his book with the confession that perhaps "I've over-stayed my hibernation, since there's a possibility that even an invisible man has a socially responsible role to play." At the same time there is the recognition that "up above there's an increasing passion to make men conform to a pattern." What the narrator seeks is a way of rejoining the reality of the surface without being forced into another man's pattern or made to play a role to fit an alien scheme. In this he is only one of many recent American heroes who seek some other alternative to the twin "deaths" of total inertia and diffusion into role-playing. It is as though they are bound to oscillate between the reality-starvation involved in complete ego-autonomy, as defined by David Rapaport, and the loss of ego-autonomy involved in the other-directed behaviour of Erving Goffman's hollow role-players. . . . Confronting this problem—sometimes an impasse—is one of the main subjects of recent American fiction. No wonder the Invisible Man says he has "become acquainted with ambivalence."

We could say then that the Invisible Man, like many after him, is seeking a new way of being in reality. We do not see him rejoin the surface; again like many after him, he leaves us with a verbal definition of the nature of his resolve. He has learned a whole new way of looking at reality and his relation to it. As he now sees it "my world has become one of infinite possibilities" and "life is to be lived, not controlled." What he also recognizes, and this is crucial, is that he too is imposing a pattern on reality by writing the book. Of course, his motive is different and it is the sort of pattern which clarifies and extends his own consciousness rather than one which cramps and limits someone else. But it is important to keep the fact in mind: "the mind that has conceived a plan of living must never lose sight of the chaos against which that pattern was conceived. That goes for societies as well as for individuals."

He is including here a recognition of the fact that even to perceive reality is to organize it in a certain way in one's consciousness—that too is a Gestalt principle. This is another reason why the novel is so preoccupied with eyesight and the problems involved in the fact that we live at the intersections of endlessly different paths of vision. Without some patterning we cannot even experience reality, let alone participate in it. What he has learned is that it is always dangerous to start to confuse your own particular patterning with reality itself. From that point of view reality *is* chaos, and we live only in the patterns we derive from it or impose on it. But if you live too long in any one pattern you are likely to become completely sealed off from all contact with reality—like those people D. H. Lawrence describes as living under an unbrella.[3]

> Man must wrap himself in a vision, make a house of apparent form and stability, fixity. In his terror of chaos he begins by putting up an umbrella between himself and the everlasting whirl. Then he paints the underside of his umbrella like a firmament . . . Man fixes some wonderful erection of his own between himself and the wild chaos, and gradually goes bleached and stifled under his parasol. Then comes a poet, enemy of convention, and makes a slit in the umbrella; and lo! the glimpse of chaos is a vision, a window to the sun.

Ellison's narrator has made this discovery in his own way for himself. What he also recognizes is that his book, too, like any work of art, is a "fixity" of "apparent form." A glimpse of chaos is also a glimpse of The Golden Day: to achieve any sense of ongoing identity man needs those houses and umbrellas. Consciousness depends on architecture. What is important is not to forget the fluidity in which it stands.

When he has only been in New York for a short time, the Invisible Man meets a man pushing a cart loaded down with thousands of abandoned blueprints and scrapped plans for houses and buildings. As the man says, "Folks is always making plans and changing 'em." The narrator in his naivety says, "but that's a mistake. You have to stick to the plan," and the man answers, "you kinda young, daddy-o." It is a little parable in passing. Human beings are inveterate planners, but plans are just so many clues for arranging which ultimately go to the scrap heap. What the narrator has to learn is that there are bound to be plans, but that any one plan you get involved in may well involve some falsification or constriction of your essential self. He drops out of all plans for a while to draw up his own. But once drawn up that too has to be left behind, as it were. The highest aspiration would seem to be not to get trapped in any one plan, while recognizing that to achieve any identity is to be involved in plans. One could envisage for the narrator a continuing life of moving in and out of plans; like the rest of us oscillating between chaos and pattern but much more aware of it than most. In that awareness lies a measure of his freedom.

In this connection his final comment that he is sloughing off his old skin is an important metaphor. For "skin," read "plan of any kind." And just as the narrator sheds skins, so Ellison himself "sheds" styles, an example of what I meant when I said that the activity of the American hero was often an analogue of the activity of his author. Ellison is quite explicit about this. In the interview referred to he describes how he deliberately changed the style of the book as the narrator moved from the South to the North and from thence into a more private territory; at first it is more naturalistic, then expressionistic, and finally surrealistic, each modulation intended to express both the state of mind of the narrator and the society he is involved in. As the hero manages to extract himself from a series of fixed environments, so the author manifests a comparable suppleness by avoiding getting trapped in one style.

Another statement from Ellison makes this very clear and helps to explain the extraordinary proliferation—and sometimes convulsion of styles which is so especially characteristic of recent American fiction (it is seldom indeed one finds a serious writer committing himself to the sort of naturalism which earlier American writers had helped to develop). Naturalism, Ellison maintains, tends to lead writers to despair, and it fails to confront the diversity of America. Instead, he says,

> I was to dream of a prose which was flexible, and swift, confronting the inequalities and brutalities of our society forthrightly, but yet thrusting forth its images of hope, human fraternity and individual self-realization. It would use the riches of our speech, the idiomatic expression and the rhetorical flourishes from past periods which are still alive among us.

He feels that it must be possible to write a kind of fiction which can arrive at relevant truths "with all the bright magic of a fairy tale." Ellison's prose in the novel is heavily foregrounded, demonstrating quite deliberately an ability to draw on sources as disparate as Revelations, the blues, classical literature, Dante, Southern white rhetoric, Harlem slang, and so on. This should not be seen as a wildly eclectic attempt to import significance but rather as a delighted display of the resources of consciousness and imagination which he can bring to bear against the pressures of a changing environment. In such a way the American writer procures some verbal freedom from the conditioning forces which surround him.

Ellison has not at this time published another novel, although one called *And Hickman Comes* has long been promised. Considering the wealth of *Invisible Man* one might wonder whether he had not put all his material into that one book. He has published a book of essays called *Shadow and Act*, however, and in these he is visibly concerned with the same basic themes and problems; whether reviewing books on the Negro question or peering back into his own past, he is always exploring the nature of his American identity and its relations with the reality around him. And like his fictional narrator he particularly resents those who would pre-empt his reality by defining it in their terms.

Both as a novelist and as an essayist, one of his primary aims in writing is to challenge any "patterning" of life—whether fictional, ideological or sociological—which is a falsification of existence as he has experienced it. Perhaps the best image Ellison has for the American writer is the one he takes from the story of Menelaus and Proteus. Eidothea's advice to Menelaus is to keep a firm hold on Proteus until, after all his changes of shape, he appears as himself, at which point he will reveal the name of the offended god and how they can make their way home without further interruption.

> For the novelist, Proteus stands for both America and the inheritance of illusion through which all men fight to achieve reality. Our task then is always to challenge the apparent forms of reality . . . and to struggle with it until it reveals its mad, vari-implicated chaos, its false faces, and on until it surrenders its insight, its truth.

What we should notice is that the Invisible Man does not emulate Proteus Rinehart any more than Ellison envisages the American writer capitulating to the Protean reality around him. In many recent American novels we will find the hero in quest of identity confronting a Protean figure whose quick metamorphoses seem to make him enviably well adapted to reality; but the hero seldom takes him for a model, no matter how much he may learn from him, for that way lies chaos, the nightmare jelly, the ultimate dissolution of self. No fixed patterns, then, but not a reversion to Protean fluidity either; instead a struggle with, a resistance to, both, conducted in some "border area" where author and hero alike attempt to create themselves and come into the meaning of their experience. In projecting his situation in these terms, or in this "Gestalt," Ellison was, to take up the last line of his novel, speaking albeit "on the lower frequencies" for more American writers than he can have realized.

Notes

1. In *Trials of the Word* (New Haven: Yale University Press, 1965).
2. In *Paris Review*, Spring, 1965; reprinted in *Shadow and Act* (London: Secker and Warburg, 1967).
3. "Chaos in Poetry," reprinted in *Selected Literary Criticism*, edited by Anthony Beal (London: William Heinemann, 1955).

BERNDT OSTENDORF

From "Oral Tradition and the Quest for Literacy"

Black Literature in White America

1982, pp. 127–47

Though indebted to the modernist tradition of European literature, particularly to Hemingway, Conrad, Joyce, Eliot, and Malraux, whose distrust in socialist or other realism he shared, ⟨Ellison's⟩ chief allegiance is to his own untapped and rich cultural tradition: black folklore. Like Joyce he endeavors to recreate the consciousness of his race in its very forms and structures. He will not provide the security of a political vision or a rational orientation outside or above the forms of communication which its own black culture has produced in reaction to a long history of contradictions. Like his modernist masters Ellison has tried to recreate the 'webs of significance', the symbolic structures, and patterns of behavior of his specific culture. In other words, he has refused to arrange the data of black culture to fit a current world view, a political platform, or a sociological paradigm. Instead he seeks out the ambiguities and conflicts which have gone into the making of the modern and particularly the modern Afro-American identity and its social system of communication. The charge may be made, and has been made, that Ellison counsels reconciliation with the problem-solving strategies of black folklore and thus with the circumscribed social space of a folk horizon and that he existentializes the politics of slavery by equating the black condition with the 'human condition'. Ellison is, like Faulkner, ambiguous in his attitude toward Southern culture and black folklore. One suspects that Ellison, who grew up in an urban middle class home and received a larger than ordinary sense of entitlement from his mother, was socially and psychologically secure enough to accept the self-contradictory tradition of black folklore. This is a pattern that one may observe in the literature of many other ethnic groups as well: that only the most assimilated members of American minorities have been able to fully articulate what it means to be a 'minority' and to create an art out of the experience and 'privilege' of being a marginal man. In other words, the actual battle of 'integration' had to be won for those who wanted to write about their past in other than wound-worshipping terms. Those trapped in the actual political systems of oppression (e.g. the oral culture of the South) knew instinctively that their old culture was a barrier on the road toward American self-hood, and therefore used it only as a source of political energy.

They had to deny its redeeming function and had to let the next generation rescue it. Cultural identity, in other words, is the privilege of the socially secure. Thus the apparent paradox: the rural folk culture of blacks could only be rescued artistically from the *urban* perspective and by those who were not themselves trapped by it. Ellison brought that type of self-confidence into his work. Perhaps it had to do with a singular fact that he began as a musician. Of all black artists musicians have the strongest sense of self, and justifiably so. For musicians know first hand what America owes to blacks. With such a strong sense of self the quest for a past and the previous condition may invite celebration rather than self-hatred. Ellison describes his first contact with folk culture in *Shadow and Act:*

> I was of the city, you see. But during the fall cotton-picking season certain kids left school and went with their parents to work in the cotton fields . . . those trips to the cotton patch seemed to me an enviable experience because the kids came back with such wonderful stories. And it wasn't the hard work which they stressed, but the communion, the playing, the eating, the dancing and the singing. And they brought back jokes, our Negro jokes—not those told about Negroes by whites—and they always returned with Negro folk stories which I'd never heard before and which couldn't be found in any books I know about. This was something to affirm and I felt there was a richness in it.[1]

It is perhaps easier to celebrate that which does not enslave you, and indeed there are hints of pastoralism in his urban appreciation of rural folklore. But Ellison's political act lies elsewhere: first, in combatting the notion of pathology in black life (a sociological diagnosis with built-in therapeutic strategies that tend to perpetuate the disease of 'victimism'). Secondly, in making a conscious effort to rescue black folklore and folk consciousness, to open the shackles of folklore and to utilize the productive energy in it. Invisibility is the key metaphor of his novel, but it explains his aesthetic and his social criticism as well. The thrust of his art is toward literacy and consciousness. By recreating the deep structures of black oral cultural as literature, he makes them both visible and available outside the social organization which created them. It may have been an advantage that Ellison was not trapped in the folk culture that he so lovingly (and optimistically) restores. And his ability may explain Richard Wright's inability or hesitation to deal affirmatively with folk materials; for Wright carried the scars of his Southern folk tradition into exile. Perhaps Wright knew the sedentary and conservative power of folklore only too well and therefore created a Bigger Thomas who lacked the compensatory resources and the escape mechanisms of a folk culture—imagine Bigger singing the Blues! Wright radicalized the psychological aspect of blackness and racism. Ellison, on the other hand, realized that preaching pathology perpetuates it and worshipping wounds ultimately leads to 'victimism'. Instead he has tried to bolster black pride and self-respect by stressing the celebration, the self-help and survival wisdom in black life. Ellison and Wright are—as relatives—two chips off the same block of black history and experience.

The modernist authors, whom Ellison often cites as his teachers, used universal or mythological 'codes' and therefore encouraged readings which stressed the universal or apolitical appeal of their work. Inspired by T. S. Eliot's directives on reading Joyce, an entire generation of critics joined the exodus from the nightmare of history into mythic universality and spatial form.[2] Ellison, though not denying the universal substratum of his folkloristic code, would insist on its historical singularity. Black folklore, which is an ironic commentary on some of the most cherished background assumptions or myths of American history, refuses to be reduced to purely archetypal or universal paradigms. To wit, Oedipus and Brer Rabbit represent paradigmatic patterns of behavior and ritual which are part of a larger cultural 'web of significance', but the former is now truly universal whereas the latter is still rooted in Afro-American history. In other words, Brer Rabbit may well have oedipal features, but Oedipus lacks the specific *historical* wisdom of Brer Rabbit.

Black folklore represents a sedimentation of behavior and ritual developed in labor and perfected in play. In a world of necessity it carved out areas of freedom. Ellison, in keeping with his childhood encounter with folklore, stresses the celebration. He writes 'It (folklore) announced the Negro's willingness to trust his own experience, his own sensibilities as to the definition of reality, rather than allow his masters to define these crucial matters for him.' Yet, neither his experience nor his sensibility were shaped outside the range of his master's voice or influence. The color line demarcated also the area of safety for fantasy and consciousness. Fantasy had to be put on a leash as animal story, consciousness was camouflaged as 'lie', and rebellion masqueraded as self-irony. These strategies of *Verfremdung* guaranteed survival in an oppressive symbolic universe, but the strategy itself was also a mark of oppression. They sharpened the appreciation of style and ingenuity, but they also counseled evasion and deception. Its 'grammar' is double-edged. Today these strategies and their cultural results do not always appeal to militant readers who tend to underestimate the radical edge in them. But as Ellison says, Sambo, Jack and Uncle Tom were in their own way heroic, given the circumstances in which they had to operate. They were determined to maintain a sense of self beyond the definition which the white man forced on them. Black folklore could not ignore the white man's definition of reality, but it could lampoon and transcend it. Though not unburdened by the white presence, it was never unhinged by it. Ellison writes:

> It preserves mainly those situations which have repeated themselves again and again in the history of any given group. It describes those rites, manners, customs, and so forth, which insure the good life, or destroy it; and it describes those boundaries of feeling, thought and action which that particular group had found to be the limitation of the human condition. It projects this wisdom in symbols which express the group's will to survive; it embodies those values by which the group lives and dies.[3]

But for the black folk in the South 'the limitations of the human condition' were largely man-made, they were political, and not existential nor anthropological. The group's will to survive is evident in folklore, but those rituals in preservation of the caste line and in protection from violence 'were thoughtlessly accepted by blacks and whites.' The adverb is significant. It indicates the rigorous social determination of these forms and the taboo or ban on a conscious exploration of the 'human condition'. The revolutionary message of black folklore had to stay in allegorical hiding, had to be displaced as comedy, must hibernate in invisibility, until a poet of consciousness would come and rescue it.

Ever since the Greeks freed art from its mythical shackles its grammar of forms has moved toward consciousness. Though the evolution of poetic and social forms of communication has always been interdependent, poetry has constantly transcended the purely social. The emancipatory promise of art is its ability to explore the not-yet-conscious and not-yet-possible on the one hand, and its drive towards ever greater self-consciousness on the other. Literary fantasy and the dreams of poets are infinite, bounded by their adventurous spirit, but folklore and myth are by comparison finite provinces of communally sanctioned behavior and meaning. Unlike forms of private fantasy they are moored to the context and dynamics of lived reality. Though the highest praise has often been given to those Western artists who have become the antennae or conscience of their race, they did not merely 'reproduce' the folklore of their people, but brought it into self-critical light. Moreover, these modernist authors took the freedom to ransack the arsenal of formal and thematic archetypes of literate and oral traditions anywhere and transform them into private systems of aesthetic communication. In contrast, neither the form nor content of myth or folklore may be changed at the whim of a creative individual. Aristotle warned his contemporary artists not to tamper with ancient myths since these had achieved a paradigmatic perfection. Folklore, far less venerable, but equally public, is subject to what Jakobson called 'die Präventivzensur der Gemeinschaft'. It is an intersubjectively controlled sedimentation of experience and therefore answerable to a shared horizon. Consequently it exerts strong social control, a power which it loses as it becomes 'poeticized' and turns into fiction. (One is reminded of Heraclitus' complaint that Homer destroyed the power of the Olympians by turning them into a fiction.) A member of a folk group may not treat the oral forms or traditions of his community disrespectfully. In art the poet is in control of his fantasy—like a God paring his fingernails—as much as the reader is in control of his response.

Within its social organization folklore promotes solidarity and in-group cohesion by providing a set of solutions to common, not individual, problems. It creates and maintains survival strategies and provides protection for the individual as long as he remains loyal to the group and its horizon. As was noted above, this protection may also turn into a trap. Unless made conscious, 'the patterns of behavior maintained by folklore tend to reproduce the pathology of sociopsychological bondage even after the material causes of this pathology have been changed and removed.'[4] This is the conservative and sedentary force of folklore. At the same time folklore may be liberating in another respect. While restrictive in conceptual freedom, it emancipates the senses and liberates through rituals of catharsis. There is a potentially emancipatory force in folklore, which is often lacking in our Victorian notion of high cultural response. This is its unabashed delight in innocent carnality and its ability to squeeze a large measure of freedom from the enjoyment and acceptance of the here and now. Though freedom of choice and poetic license, so typical of Western art, are lacking in folklore, it enjoys a wealth of collective rituals of catharsis, rituals which may seem compulsive to the uninitiated but which provide quite another area of freedom, an area where the folk artist can enjoy his licence: this is in terms of performance and style. Individual talent in folk art surfaces as style. It is in this area that folk-trained artists have most to offer. This talent has carried over into literature: public poetry readings by black poets are probably the most successful branch of black literary activity.

Ellison's function as a writer, his social act, is to counteract the repressive forces of ritualized behavior by lifting it from thoughtlessness into consciousness, from social habit into poetic form. At the same time Ellison has tried to salvage the affirmative and cathartic power of folklore, its delight in histrionics, and its supple, jazz-like style. The importance of performance and style is evident in all forms of black folklore, and Ellison freely draws on these resources of his culture. In short, the function of folklore in Ellison's fiction is neither ornamental, nor purely comical, nor universal. Folklore is his semiotic cultural code, a system of shared meanings and a pragmatic charter of behavior. Its forms are sedimentations of historical consciousness and deeply rooted cultural mores. Characteristic of these forms is a persistent ambivalence toward white America. They teach a strategy of suspending affirmation or rejection and withholding judgement until the situation in which they are used either forces, permits, or invites it. Some folk stories cherished most by the folk for their deep truths are told as lies. The label 'lie' is the visa which permits their being told at large. This licencing mechanism is similar in folklore or fiction; for fiction, as the French say, is a form of *mentir vrai*, of lying truthfully. The subterfuge is particularly called for at those times or in those places which render telling the truth dangerous.

The short story 'Flying Home' (1944) which is based on one such folk lie is an excellent vehicle to illustrate Ellison's use of black folklore.[5] A close examination of this story will show why so much praise and criticism of his work, particularly of *Invisible Man* (1953) which is remarkably similar, is based on an inadequate and incomplete understanding of black folk forms.[6]

The title 'Flying Home' is full of irony; it alludes to black history, myth, and current politics. 'Flying' is an old metaphor of freedom, popularized by spirituals and politicized by the underground railway. Richard Wright picked this symbol as a metaphor of Bigger's crude aspirations, and Jesse B. Semple playfully links NASA and freedom.[7] Flying also recalls the hope which blacks had placed in the air force as an agency of integration, and what became of that hope. The title is identical with that of a popular tune which Lionel Hampton wrote as a tribute to a largely white air force. Archetypal burrowers have come up with a number of mythological allusions, all of which are irreverently and ironically deflated by the folk tale (the lie) within the story:[8] Todd-Icarus, the black pilot, tries to reach the light, that is, whiteness. The *hubris* of his aspirations causes his downfall and he returns 'home' as the prodigal son. But, as the folk tale underlines, his homecoming is ambivalent. He returns to the repressed history of the 'previous' (folk) tradition and to that class from which he had fled for the sake of a white bourgeois mirage. The very title unites various contexts of meaning under one multilayered symbol. 'Flying Home' is meaningful in the context of mythology, black folklore, black history, current politics, psychology, and jazz. Of all these contexts folklore has the last word, for it comments and reflects upon every other possible analogy in an ironical manner. The high seriousness of the mythological tale, the depressing facts of black history, the sociology of race relations, the aspirations of the middle class—all these are lampooned and deflated by the wisdom of the folk tale. Ellison uses the affirmation and rejection of the folk tale for ironic purposes; a sort of double fiction built into his fiction. Folklore is—so to speak—his metafiction. The folk story Ellison makes use of acquired shape and meaning through generations of shared experience. It was shaped by the 'Präventivzensur der Gemeinschaft'. Thus its structure is the product of spontaneous social interaction; in Ellison's word a 'thoughtless' process. Ellison's method of artistic composition is that of the modernist poets, that is, it is highly conscious. Though his story is manifestly simple, it has a deliberate structure, a substratum of symbolic correspondences and parallelisms. But this deliberate structure stays close to the folk experience. Ellison merely parallels and thus concentrates folk forms by finding the appropriate connection in action, incident, and character. His story is folklore in poetically condensed form. His remarkable talent lies in making the right choice from black folk forms and themes and combining them into a new coherent symbolic system.

The episode and its prehistory are short. A black pilot named Todd is stationed in a training camp in Alabama impatiently waiting for his call to active duty. Caught between the 'ignorant black men' of his past and the condescending white officers of his present situation, he expects to achieve his manhood and identity by meeting the enemy. (Todd seems to have internalized the practice of transferring inner-societal conflicts to an outside enemy.) On a practice run with an airplane which is appropriately called 'advanced trainer,' he pulls the plane into a steep climb and loses control. Before he can correct his error by going into a dive, a buzzard hits the propeller, blurs his vision, and he panics into an emergency landing. All this is prehistory. The story begins as Todd regains consciousness. A black sharecropper with the historically significant name of Jefferson and his son find him and try to help him up, but his foot is broken. While the son runs for help, the old man helps Todd pass the time. A conversation ensues between this old, resigned, but eminently wise sharecropper and the achievement-oriented Todd, a conversation which gradually unveils the repressed identity conflicts in Todd and his mindless overassimilation to a white world which rejects him. Todd feels the danger instinctively: 'It came to him suddenly that there was something sinister about the conversation, that he was flying unwilling into unsafe and uncharted regions,' namely into his repressed knowledge of racial reality which had anticipated the inevitable wreck of his ambitions. Todd believes that he is one hundred years ahead of Jefferson in terms of consciousness and civil liberties ('that buzzard knocked me back a hundred years') and he rationalizes this difference as a negative definition of his identity. "Sure he's all right. Nice and kind and helpful. But he's not you.'

This social advancement, which has alienated him from the spontaneous racial solidarity of his group and which feeds his subconscious anxiety and panic, forbids him to accept Jefferson's rather relentless folk wisdom.[9] Jefferson, to be sure, is proud of Todd's achievement, but he knows its limitations better than Todd. His rather naive attempt to kill time and entertain Todd turns into a Freudian blunder, which triggers the conflict; for the tale of the 'Flying Fool' is an allegory of the hopes generated by the Emancipation and the sobering experiences of Reconstruction which uses the concrete metaphors of flight to drive its point home. Todd is doubly affected by this tale: allegorically he is a member of that group whose aspiration the tale calls 'foolish', concretely he is trying to fly into a higher class. Todd does not want to be reminded of the tale's moral which Jefferson specifies as 'you have to come by the white folks, too.' It is the 'too' implied in the story which angers him, since he would like to be taken as an individual person with unalienable rights rather than as a member of a group, a class, or a race.

Todd's rage surprises Jefferson who had not intended any harm. The unresolved tension between Jefferson and Todd is then interrupted by the white landowner, Graves, accompanied by two attendants from a lunatic asylum who threaten to put him into a strait jacket. Now the presumptive threat to his identity by a member of his race turns into a real threat to his life by a racist; Todd's resistance to the moral of Jefferson's story explodes into hysteria, an indication that Todd has totally lost control of himself and his ambivalent situation.[10] At the same time the confirmation of Jeff's wisdom by Graves' act forces Todd's repressed knowledge back into his consciousness: 'And then a part of him stood behind it all, watching the surprise in Graves' red face and his own hysteria.' The threat to identity and life is then resolved by Jefferson who becomes his 'sole salvation in an insane world of outrage and humiliation.' Jefferson's subtle act of Tomism deflects Graves' aggression by humoring his prejudice. The story ends with a scene, not totally convincing in its latent optimism, which takes the return of the prodigal son more or less seriously. Against the backdrop of harmonious nature, which has always been a hackneyed cipher of human peace and solidarity, Todd is carried away by Jefferson and his son. The structural necessity of having to put a story to bed seems to have gotten the better of reality. . . .

For many years Ralph Ellison has been fighting single-handedly to rescue the black usable past which is stored in folklore. In interviews, essays, addresses and seminars all over the United States he has been arguing for a respect and appreciation of black folklore which according to him it has not received at the hands of white or black poets or critics. He does not want to minimize slavery by romantically praising its cultural results, but he argues that this culture is not only a 'mark of oppression' but primarily a celebration of survival. Although Jefferson is caught in a pattern of behavior which is, to a certain degree, thoughtless and although the wisdom of his folk tale is so much part of his 'thoughtless' behavior that its actuality escapes him, his accommodation to the situation has not unhinged his identity. Todd, on the other hand, is alienated from his group heritage and clings to a pseudo-identity which he can only maintain at the cost of blindness, self-hatred and self-deception. Not being himself, he cannot laugh about himself, as can Jefferson who draws pleasure from narrating painful truths. Jefferson's is the power of the blues; he can create catharsis out of conflict and oppression. This human power is a dialectical result of his political weakness. Todd, who is painfully made aware of his own weakness, lost this power when he moved up and away from his group. His 'fortunate fall' results in a new solidarity between Jefferson and himself and a deeper understanding of what his real buried self may be. Thus oral culture, particularly when it meets with false consciousness, may become an agent of de-alienation.

Ellison has explored the richness of the black oral tradition. Ironically this makes him a forerunner of the very cultural nationalism whose militant fringe has been rejecting him for years as an Uncle Tom. It should satisfy his sense of irony that this state of affairs forms the main theme of his work.

Notes

1. *Shadow and Act* (London, 1967), p. 7. George Kent, 'Ralph Ellison and Afro-American Folk and Cultural Tradition,' *Blackness and the Adventure of Western Culture* (Chicago, 1972), looks at Ellison's use of folklore with 'a certain unease' and Larry Neal, 'Ellison's Zoot Suit,' in *Ralph Ellison: A Collection of Critical*

Essays, ed. John Hersey (Englewood Cliffs, 1974), praises Ellison's return to folk roots, but finds it hard to swallow his appeals to universality. Susan Blake, 'Ritual and Rationalization: Black Folklore in the Works of Ralph Ellison,' *PMLA* 94 (1979): 121–35, blames Ellison for ignoring, minimizing, distorting and denying the true folk expression. Though her analysis is the most probing to date she seems to miss the irony and conscious jive in Ellison's use of folklore. Ultimately she will not and cannot stand ambivalence and contradiction. Black folklore is not universalized into myth; myth is teased by folklore, and reality is teased by both.

2. The conservative bias of the modernist tradition is discussed in Ostendorf, *Der Mythos in der Neuen Welt: Eine Untersuchung zum amerikanischen Myth Criticism* (Frankfurt, 1971) and in Robert Weimann, *Literaturgeschichte und Mythologie* (Berlin und Weimar, 1971).
3. *Shadow and Act*, p. 175.
4. P. Bogatyrev and R. Jakobson, 'Die Folklore als eine besondere Form des Schaffens,' *Donum Natalicium Schrijnen* (Utrecht, 1929). See also Roger D. Abrahams on the social control function of folklore in 'Personal Power and Social Restraint in the Definition of Folklore,' *Journal of American Folklore* 84 (1971): 16–30; and Richard Bauman, 'Differential Identity and the Social Base of Folklore,' *Journal of American Folklore* 84 (1971): 31–41. Useful suggestions are made by Peter L. Berger and Thomas Luckmann, *The Social Construction of Reality: A Treatise in the Sociology of Knowledge* (New York, 1966), particularly on 'Sedimentation and Tradition' and on the 'Origins of Symbolic Universes.'
5. The story may be found in the following anthologies: E. Seaver, ed., *Cross Section* (New York, 1944); C. A. Fenton, ed., *Best Short Stories of World War II* (New York, 1957); Langston Hughes, ed., *The Best Short Stories by Negro Writers* (Boston, 1967); James Emanuel and Theodore Gross, eds., *Dark Symphony: Negro Literature in America* (New York, 1968); Darwin Turner, ed., *Black American Literature: Fiction* (New York, 1969); Eva Kissin, ed., *Stories in Black and White* (Philadelphia, 1970); Francis Dearns, ed., *Black Identity* (New York, 1970); William Adams et al., eds., *Afro-American Literature: Fiction* (Boston, 1970).
6. The deceptive quality of black folklore has sent liberals, militants, and well meaning translators in all directions of arbitrary interpretation. Liberals tend to universalize its meaning thus pulling its teeth, militants call it 'irrelevant for the cause of black liberation', and translators simply ignore it. Ellison, who seemed content that in Germany his novel was read and treated as a novel, not as protest fiction, would be appalled by the translation of his work: folklore gets knocked straight out of the picture. 'Blues' is translated as 'sad song', and Brer Rabbit or Brer Bear don't make it at all into German. This is unfortunate, for German has by now acculturated the Blues and there is a perfectly fine tradition of animal tales that could have been utilized for the folkloric resonances of his novel. It simply did not seem important enough to the translator. The story 'Flying Home' was literally massacred at the hands of the translator. None of the folkloric allusions survive the translation into German. Heinz Politzer (ed.) *Amerika erzählt* (Frankfurt, 1971).
7. Langston Hughes is quoted in Dundes, ed., *Mother Wit from the Laughing Barrel* (Englewood Cliffs, 1973), p. 52: 'The sky would be my roadway and the stars my stopping place. Man if I had a rocket plane, I would rock off into space and be solid gone. Gone. Real gone! I mean *gone*,' The hyperbolic finale is reminiscent of the folk tale within the story.
8. Joseph Trimmer, 'Ralph Ellison's "Flying Home",' *Studies in Short Fiction* 9 (1972): 175–82.
9. On anxiety and panic due to isolation from the group see Ellison, *Shadow and Act*, p. 99ff.; also William Greer and Price Cobbs, *Black Rage* (New York, 1968), and Francois Raveau, 'An Outline of the Role of Color in Adaptation Phenomena,' in *Color and Race*, ed. John Hope Franklin (Boston, 1968). See also Erik H. Erikson, 'The Concept of Identity in Race Relations,' in *The Negro American*, eds. Talcott Parsons and Kenneth Clarke (Boston, 1965). On the strategies of repression required for a 'change' or 'alternation' of consciousness see Berger and Luckmann, *The Social Construction of Reality*, pp. 180–81.
10. Ellison, *Shadow and Act*, p. 99ff.

WILLIAM EVERSON

1912–

William Oliver Everson was born in Sacramento on September 10, 1912. He attended Fresno State College in the early 1930s, then worked in the Civilian Conservation Corps. After reading Robinson Jeffers, Everson not only began to write poetry but found God as well. He published his first book, *These Are the Ravens*, in 1935, and in 1938 married his high school sweetheart Edwa Poulson. A second volume, *San Joaquin*, followed in 1939. As a conscientious objector, Everson spent World War II in the Civilian Public Service. At this time he founded the Untide Press, and wrote the poems collected in *The Masculine Dead* (1942) and *The Residual Years*, which was twice expanded to include all Everson's work between 1934 and 1948.

After the war Everson met Kenneth Rexroth, who introduced him to the anarcho-pacifist community in San Francisco that gave birth to the Beat movement. There Everson met Mary Fabilli, who was instrumental in converting him to Catholicism. Their marriage in 1948 was annulled in 1951 when Everson entered the Dominican Order as "Brother Antoninus." From 1954 to 1957 he wrote no poetry; in 1957 he ended a period of seclusion, giving readings and publishing books like the Pulitzer-nominated *The Crooked Lines of God* (1959) and *The Hazards of Holiness* (1962), which were both eventually subsumed under *The Veritable Years 1949–1966* (1978).

Everson met Susanna Rickson in 1965, and wrote of his unconsummated passion for her in *The Rose of Solitude* (1967). In 1969 he left the order and married her; they had one son. Since 1971 Everson has been poet-in-residence at the University of California at Santa Cruz. He has written books such as *Man-Fate: The Swan Song of Brother Antoninus* (1974) and *The Masks of Drought* (1979), and has also been active as a printer. Everson's awards include a Guggenheim Fellowship in 1949, a Commonwealth Club of California Silver Medal in 1967, a Shelley Memorial Award in 1978, and a National Endowment for the Arts grant in 1981. He lives in Santa Cruz, California.

It's long ago now, another epoch in the life of mankind, before the Second War, that I got a pamphlet of poems from a press in a small California town—*These Are the Ravens*—and then a handsome book from the Ward Ritchie Press in Los Angeles—*San Joaquin*. They weren't much like the poems being written in those days, either in *New Masses*, *Partisan Review* or *The Southern Review*. They were native poems, autochthonous in a way the fashionable poems of the day could not manage. Being an autochthon of course is something you don't manage, you are. It was not just the subjects, the daily experience of a young man raising grapes in the Great Valley of California, or the rhythms, which were of the same organic pulse you find in Isaiah, or Blake's prophecies, or Whitman, or Lawrence, or Sandburg at his best, or Wallace Gould, or Robinson Jeffers. This, it seemed to me, was a young fellow out to make himself unknown and forgotten in literary circles. The age has turned round, and the momentary reputations of that day are gone, and William Everson, now Brother Antoninus, is very far from being unknown and forgotten.

I say this, not in a spirit of literary controversy, but to try to bring home to a time that accepts his idiom and his sensibility, how unusual these poems were thirty years ago. Everson has won through, and in a very real sense this whole book—a new edition of his early poems—is a record of that struggle. It is a journal of a singlehanded war for a different definition of poetic integrity. There is nothing abstract or impersonal about these poems. They are not clockwork aesthetic objects, wound up to go off and upset the reader. T. S. Eliot and Paul Valéry told the young of the last generation that that's what poems were, and the young dutifully tried their best to make such infernal machines, never noticing that their masters never wrote that way at all. Everson paid no attention. He cultivated and irrigated and tied up the vines and went home in the sunset and ate dinner and made love and wrote about how he felt doing it and about the turning of the year, the intimate rites of passage, and the rites of the season of a man and a woman. He used the first person singular pronoun often, because that, as far as he could see, was the central figure in the cast of the only existential drama he knew. And what is wrong with that? Nothing at all, the critics of the last generation to the contrary notwithstanding. It wasn't an alarm clock that meditated in the marine cemetery or suffered in the wasteland of London.

Everson has been accused of self-dramatization. Justly. All of his poetry, that under the name of Brother Antoninus, too, is concerned with the drama of his own self, rising and falling along the sine curve of life, from comedy to tragedy and back again, never quite going under, never quite escaping for good into transcendence. This is a man who sees his shadow projected on the sky, like Whymper after the melodramatic achievement and the tragedy on the Matterhorn. Everything is larger than life with a terrible beauty and pain. Life isn't like that to some people and to them these poems will seem too strong a wine. But of course life is like that. Night alone, storm over the cabin, the sleepless watcher whipsawed by past and future—life is like that, of course, just as a walk on the beach is like "Out of the Cradle Endlessly Rocking," or playing on the floor while mother played the piano is like Lawrence's "Piano." Hadn't you ever noticed?

Something terribly important and infinitely mysterious is happening. It is necessary to hold steady like Odysseus steering past the sirens, to that rudder called the integrity of the self or the ship will smash up in the trivial and the commonplace. This is what Everson's poetry is about—but then, sometimes less obviously, so is most other poetry worth its salt.

I don't think there is any question but that William Everson is one of the three or four most important poets of the now-notorious San Francisco school. Most of the people wished on the community by the press are in fact from New York and elsewhere. The thing that distinguishes Robert Duncan, Philip Lamantia, William Everson and their associates is that they are all religious poets. Their subjects are the varied guises of the trials of the soul and the achievement of illumination. Everson's poems are mystical poems, records of the struggle towards peace and illumination on the stairs of natural mysticism. Peace comes only in communion with nature or momentarily with a woman, and far off, the light is at the end of a tunnel. So this is an incomplete autobiography—as whose isn't?"

How deeply personal these poems are, and how convincingly you touch the living man through them. I have read them for years. Brother Antoninus is one of my oldest and best friends and the godfather of my daughters. As I turn over the pages, some of them thirty years old, I feel again, as always, a comradeship strong as blood. Evil men may have degraded those words, but they are still true and apposite for the real thing. Blood brotherhood.—KENNETH REXROTH, "Introduction" to *The Residual Years*, 1935, pp. xv–xvii

About ten years ago I sat in a Yale auditorium and listened to William Everson, then Brother Antoninus, O.P., read his poems. It was an astonishing performance. The poems seethed with a sometimes violent erotic mysticism and the Dominican lay brother seemed to drag each phrase out of anguished personal depths. But the audience, comprised mostly of Yale students, sat mesmerized. I remember hearing, during one long pause in the poet's reading, the distinct tapping of snowflakes on the auditorium windows. The control that Everson exerted was not all dramatic performance. His poetry was powerful and moving as it stood alone on the printed page. Brother Antoninus had achieved at this point in his career considerable stature as a poet of the "San Francisco Renaissance."

Now, after a long silence, William Everson offers his readers a collection of poems: *Man-Fate: The Swan Song of Brother Antoninus*. These poems are, as he tells us, "a love poem sequence." They explore the implications of his break with monastic life and his new union with Susanna and her infant son. This volume is comprised, he says, "of troubled verse." Indeed. But the trouble does not lie with the subject matter, as Everson fears. Most contemporary readers are sophisticated enough to accept with equanimity the transition of a monk to the lay marital status. My quarrel with Everson arises from his squandering of an enormous talent in gusts of undisciplined verse. The long introductory poem, "Tendril in the Mesh," with its heavy thump of alliteration, affected diction, and baroque metaphors reads like a bad translation of some fourteenth century Northumbrian verse. Who could endure much of this?

> Your face is flensed with an awesome devouring passion.
> In the flukes of contortion I fear what I see as I need it.
> My body is written with poems your fingers enscrolled on my flesh.

But I am a stubborn reader and endure I did for some 280 lines. After such a buffeting of bathos I probably over-reacted in joy to the quietly lovely "Ebb at Evening." However, this poem and "Man-Fate" seem to me to be eminently successful works of art. Here Everson is master of his craft. The agony that pulses just beneath the surface of his work establishes a rhythm that is dangerous, threatening, but controlled. Poems such as these and "The Black Hills" demonstrate that Everson remains an artist with reserves of power he has yet to tap.—CLAIRE HAHN, *Com*, May 9, 1975, pp. 124–25

A poet whose religion was of as much interest as his writing, William Everson (then Brother Antoninus) has republished the work of his eighteen years as a Dominican lay brother. The volume ⟨*The Veritable Years: 1949–1966*⟩ is the second in a trilogy called *The Crooked Ways of God*. Reading these poems again several decades later, one wonders what the fuss was all about. Where Hart discovers original imagery, Everson falls back on imitations of Jeremiah and Jeffers. Did Everson's reputation depend on the verbally sensational, the mock-biblical, and the autobiographical shock rather than on content and style? It appears so. Tip over the first exclamation point and line after line of poetry collapses like dominoes. Here pseudo-Donne ("Make me! Slake me! Back me!"), pseudo-Song of Songs (the poet's affair with "Rose"), and pseudo-Aquinas (Being exists, etc.) exploit the Christian tradition, not explore it. Everson explains too much, whether about his sexuality or his spirituality. Take the lines from "The Word": "Not willed but perceived, / Not declared but acknowledged, / Yielded into the dimensional, / A salutation from the without." Nothing has been anchored in the humble hints of incarnation. In the end, however, one prefers such abstractions to the masochism of many other poems.—JAMES FINN COTTER, "Familiar Poetry," *HdR*, Spring 1979, p. 117

SAMUEL CHARTERS
"Brother Antoninus"
Some Poems/Poets
1971, pp. 97–106

How can a poet like Antoninus be made to fit any group of American poets or poetry? It's hard to believe that at this point there could even be an Antoninus, that somehow out of the doubt and the questioning of much American poetry of the last twenty or thirty years there could still be a poet as fervent and as stripped bare as Antoninus. He has fully invested himself in each of the dimensions of his work—from the first nature elegies that were his early response to the poetry of Robinson Jeffers to the complex, passionate poems that marked his conversion to Catholicism and his acceptance of Dominican vows. It is almost as difficult to place Jeffers' work into any kind of perspective; so it isn't surprising that the work of a disciple—as Antoninus has always described himself—has some of the same problem. The surprise is that there could *be* poetry like this being written.

It isn't only the insistence on the urgency of the poet's self that sets Antoninus's work apart from other poetry of the last twenty years. There have been other poets who have tried to scrape away as many layers of the skin. Antoninus, in a period when the poetic idiom has become dry and understated, has an almost seventeenth century richness of language and expression. He has a closer affinity to Vaughn, Crashaw, Alabaster—the Christopher Smart of *A Song to David*—than he does to the insistent objectivity of Robert Creeley or Denise Levertov, or to the complex allusiveness of Charles Olson or Robert Duncan. I don't think he was influenced by the metaphysical poets—he was from the beginning a Jeffers' disciple—but the feeling in the poetry is of a man, like the earlier poets, who has been driven by the torment of his life to the most intense poetry he can find language to express.

Antoninus's language is so intense, so vivid, that the poems can almost be read in clusters of words and phrases—"Far trumpets of succinctness," "a treading of feet on the stairs of redness," "I think moons of kept measure," "I felt the new wind, south/Grope her tonguing mouth on the wall," "The wind breaking its knees on this hurdle, the house," "Birds beak for her!" "In the high peal of rivering lips," "The low freighters at sea/Take in their sides the nuzzling dolphins that are their death." He has a brilliant sense of alliteration. From *In the Fictive Wish*,

Wader
Watcher by water,
Walker alone by the wave-worn shore
In water woven.

And he doesn't hesitate to extend the flash of phrase into a poem's inner tensions. He uses a long, wavering line at points that near the stillness of a moment of contemplation. From *The Rose of Solitude*,

For what blooms behind your lips moves ever within
my sight
the kept diffusion of the smile;
And what dawns behind your brow subsists within
my thought
the somnolent mystery of mind;
And what trembles in your words lives on forever in
my heart
the immutable innerness of speech

But at moments of deepening intensity the line tightens to an abrupt, insistent rhythmic unit. From earlier in *The Rose*,

I crept
I brought Him gifts
Hushed in my heart
I brought what I had
I crept.

None of this has the flat speech rhythm that sets the dominant tone of most contemporary poetry. Duncan has his own kind of rhetorical verbosity, and Ginsberg has some of the rhythm of the synagogue chant, but the modern poet has usually been less emotional—his own responses kept at an objective distance from the poem. Antoninus has none of this restraint—the phrase, the phrase rhythm, function as a direct expression of his emotions. Part of the felt affinity with the earlier group of metaphysical poets is this emotional extravagance, this sense of poetic hyperbole. From *The Rose*,

Heart to be hushed.
Let it howk and then hush.
Let the black wave break.
Let the terrible tongue
Engorge my deeps
Let the loins of ferocity
Lave my shut flesh.

From "The Song the Body Dreamed in the Spirit's Mad Behest,"

Born and reborn we will be groped, be clenched
On ecstasies that shudder toward crude birth,
When His great Godhead peels its stripping strength
In my red earth

The image and the language could almost have come from Donne's sonnet,

Divorce mee, 'untie, or breake that knot againe,
Take mee to you, imprison mee, for I
Except you 'enthrall mee, never shall be free,
Nor ever chast, except you ravish mee.

It's true that of all the contemporary poets Antoninus is the only one with some kind of persona—his identification with his holy order—that he can put between himself and his work, and it could be that this has given him the situation he needed to open his emotional stance. When he took his vows in 1951, after more than a dozen years of publication as William Everson, he had, as Brother Antoninus, a reach of expression opened to him that had been inhibited while he was still writing as William Everson. Nothing in his secular poetry has the grinding fervor of his religious writing. But is the poet William Everson? Is the poet Brother Antoninus? The two persons of Antoninus have never fully merged—even now that he has left the order and married, and the complex currents of his poetry express this continuing duality. Not confusion—I don't think there is any confusion of his separate identities in Antoninus, only a deep consciousness of their differences. But the emphasis of the poetry has moved—since 1951, when he was thirty-nine—from the preoccupations with the self to the more specific emotions of his religious self. Everson is still present in Antoninus, as the man who is Antoninus was a presence in the poems of Everson.

It is the poems from his deepest point of spiritual crisis that in some ways most intensely involve anyone reading his poetry. The poems from this point of decision, from about 1945 and 6 to 1948, have a desperate, immediate poignancy. It is possible to be unmoved by the religiosity of the later work, and to pass over the Jeffers-like cadences of the first poems, but this period of his life was one of deep personal unhappiness, and the humanness of his loss is directly, and strongly, moving. So much seems to be slipping through his hands, and one moment of loss slides uncertain and confused into only another moment of loss. Artistically they become some of his most fully formed poems. The images of his earlier work—earth, the sea, the smells of weeds, the distances of hills and fields—have spread and extended through the lengthened lyric impulse of his dominating unhappiness. Since the poems come near his moment of crisis their resolutions are temporary—their sense of imminent despair tangled and heavy through their loping lines. *In the Fictive Wish*, from Oregon, 1946, has perhaps the most fully realized flowering of beauty, since it centers on one of his points of almost complete resolution. *The Blowing of the Seed*, from Sebastopol, California, in 1946, is agonizing in its pained cutting of his body in its sudden despair. "There Will Be Harvest," from Berkeley the next year, in the collection *The Springing of the Blade*, is dominated with the weight of his life's details, and its involvement with the crisis of his physical love.

In the Fictive Wish is a sustained lyric outburst, its syntax and form left ambiguous, but its emotional clarities brilliantly sustained. From its opening lines the difficulties of understanding are obvious, but the poem's great beauty also begins to unfold with its first hesitant breath.

> So him in dream
> Does celibate wander
> Where woman waits,
> Of whom he may come to,
> Does woman wait
> Who now is
> Of his.

Instead of "So he in dream . . ." the other pronoun form "him" for its alliteration with the final *m* of dream; the first sound of the *s* of So returning in the soft *c* of celibate, the two opening lines making a loosely conjoined phrase of four accents ending on the feminine cadence of wander. The language has an almost medieval sense of word usage in its inversions of sentence structure, "Of whom he may come to," "Does now the Lord retain," "Of that they then came to," and there is a suggestion of the medieval poem of physical rapture in his description of the woman's body,

> Of such body and of such croft,
> Where ache of sex could so conjoin,
> Could so sink,
> As dreams sunken;
> Of such cunted closure
> Built broad in the love grip;
> As of bed,
> Broad,
> As of width for woman;
> And of belly
> Broad for the grapple.

The language could be from Skelton, or an anonymous 15th Century carol. The poem's ending is one of his most beautifully moulded series of enfolding alliterations—the opening lines of the last section,

> Wader
> Watcher by water,
> Walker alone by the wave-worn shore,
> In water woven.

with their soft sounds of *w*, *wa*, *wo*—in the next line mingling the *w* with a beginning *m* sound

> She moves now where the wave glistens,

and in the next line it is the *m*,

> Her mouth mocking with laughter

then the *s* of glistening returns again with,

> In the slosh unheard

the sound opens to

> When the sea slurs after;
> In the sleepy suckle

and the verse ends with a long rhythmic unit developing the *l* of sleepy and suckle—and leaves the sound poised for the opening line of the next verse.

> That laps at her heel where the ripple hastens,
> And the laughing look laid over her arm

The final lines are one of his most intensely moving images of loss and unhappiness.

> Lurker,
> She leaves with laughter,
> She fades where the combers falter,
> Is gone where the dream is gone
> Or the sleeper's murmur;
> Is gone as the wave withdrawing
> Sobs on the shore, and the stones are shaken
> As the ruined wave
> Sucks and sobs in the rustling stones,
> When the tide is taken.

The physical insistence of the poetry has continued since this period of his life. The pain was only briefly resolved in the certitudes of the Church. On some levels of his expression there has even been an intensification. The poetry that emerged from his years in the Dominican Order increasingly shared the violent physicality of the metaphysical poets—the acerbation of celibacy on a body that is unable to deny its desire for fulfillment. In his book *The Rose of Solitude* the violence of desire and its turmoil becomes the central problem of the poem—and the desire expressed in the poem is open and explicit, forced in on him by the real embrace of a woman, the rose, on the floor of a San Francisco apartment,

> Now up from down under
> The long stitch of manflesh
> Goes suckering in.
> All that fretfulness
> Shucked now,
> Purled shuddering under.
> It is the make of the male.

He even questions the meanings of his continence.

O God and Riddler,
Why?
Is this sin?
I seek no sin.
I would never offend Thee.

In an earlier verse,

Is truly a sin
That her name is written,
Stroked in primal fire,
On my stultified heart?

In "The Song the Body Dreamed in the Spirit's Mad Behest" it is a sublimated desire suffusing his response to God.

Call Him the Lover and call me the Bride,
Lapsing on the couch of His repose
I heard the elemental waters rise,
Divide and close . . .
He is the Spirit but I am the Flesh
Out of my body must he be reborn,
Soul from the sundered soul, Creation's gout
In the world's bourn . . .
Mounted between the thermals of my thighs
Hawklike He hovers surging at the sun,
And feathers me a frenzy ring around
That deep drunk tongue.

The poem has an indelible, raw energy. But in all of his mature work there has been this same sense of urgent need, and it has been as strong a force in the poems not immediately physical in their confrontations. It could be that the difference between Antoninus and most of the other poets of the last twenty years is that his blood runs closer to his skin, and that his involvement with the emotional realities of his life is more intensely felt than theirs. The guarded tone of most modern poetry does give the impression of a cautious withdrawal from a social environment so hostile that anything except a kind of guarded mistrust seems too naive as an emotional response. Whatever anyone has believed in as a kind of center for himself or the society has turned out to be mostly useless. This doesn't mean that other poets haven't been involved with the implications of sexuality, haven't brooded over the failure of what Antoninus would call Man and Woman to resolve their differences—it only means that they've decided to let less of themselves be measured against the force of this confrontation. Antoninus refuses to step out of the way, just as he has refused to deny any of the physical implications of his mature work.

At points in the poetry Antoninus seems to be overwhelmed by some of the forces he's thrust himself against. The texture of the line becomes strained, the force of the language becomes excessive. The experience of the sexual embrace is almost beyond any verbal expression, but he keeps trying to find an explicit imagery that would break through to the physical reality.

In my emptiness
These arms gall for her, bride's mouth,
Spent-breathed in laughter, or that night's
First unblushing revealment, the flexed
Probity of the flesh, the hymen-tilted troth,
We closed, we clung on it, the stroked
And clangorous rapture!

The imagery is so forced that it loses its effect of moving through to the experience itself. Sometimes his despair cries out too strongly—almost with a kind of self-indulgence.

The face I know
Becomes the night-black rose
And I cry out of a shambling of pain,
A clothing of anguish . . .
Great tongs
Tear rents of speechlessness
Cut from my lips . . .
I drunkenly stagger. I flay
Segments of numbness,
A stuff of wretchedness
Tatters my shanks . . .

But the outburst is no more naked than Shelley's,

As thus with thee in prayer in my sore need.
Oh, lift me as a wave, a leaf, a cloud!
I fall upon the thorns of life! I bleed!

Even when the imagery is most strained, the language most driven, these moments in the later work only more deeply etch the complex portrait of himself that the poetry gives us. It is poetry that meets us so strongly—even when it looms at us from directions where we hadn't expected poetry to come. And the only thing that matters now is that the poetry has come, that he has written the poems, that there is, almost unbelievably, an Antoninus.

LEE BARTLETT
From "God's Crooked Lines: William Everson and C. G. Jung"
William Everson

1983, pp. 7–20

In 1932 Jung had written that "among my patients in the second half of life—that is to say, over thirty-five—there has not been one whose problem in the last resort was not that of finding a religious outlook on life."[1] In 1948 Everson was a year beyond Jung's climacteric. He had undergone a series of traumas, including the deaths of both his mother (to whom he was very close) and his father (from whom he was more or less estranged), internment during the war in a camp for conscientious objectors, divorce from his first wife Edwa Poulson, and finally a second marriage, to the poet Mary Fabilli, which was on unstable ground to say the least. In the fall, Fabilli (who at this time was re-discovering her lost Catholic faith) gave Everson a copy of St. Augustine's *Confessions*, wherein he discovered something he "most desperately needed—a man's religion" to replace his rather vaguely defined and failing pantheism. On Christmas Eve, Fabilli took Everson to Midnight Mass in a San Francisco cathedral where "the nuns had prepared the Crib to one side of the sanctuary, with fir trees banked about a miniature stable." There, suddenly, as he

> crouched out there on the sheepflats of man's terrestrial ambiguity, with nothing but the rags of pitiful pride between me and that death, something was spoken into my soul, and hearing I followed. When the fir-smell reached me across the closed interior air of the Cathedral, binding as it did the best of my past and the best of my future, shaping for the first time that synthesis of spirit and sense I had needed and never found, I was drawn across, and in the smell of the fir saw it for the first time, not merely as an existent thing, but as a *created* thing, witness of the Word, the divine Logos, who made all earth, and me, a soul in His own image, out of very love. And I saw in the fact of Creation the end of Creation; and in the end of Creation saw indeed the unspeakable Lover who draws the loved one out of the web of affliction, remakes him as His own. It was then that I could rise from the pew, and, following like a hound the trace on the

> air, go where the little images lay, in the Crib there, so tiny, among the simple beasts, watched over by the cleanly woman and the decent man, and these humble ones, my good friends the sheepherders, who in that instant outleaped the philosophers. That was the night I entered into the family and fellowship of Christ—made my assent, such as it was—one more poor wretch, who had nothing to bring but his iniquities.[2]

Following this experience, Everson took instruction in the Catholic faith, converted, worked for a time with the Catholic Workers Movement in Oakland, California, then eventually entered the Dominican Order as Brother Antoninus. Until this time, he had a rising reputation as a poet of the California Central Valley; after a few years of monastic silence, Everson emerged again on the literary scene replacing in books like *The Crooked Lines of God*, *The Hazards of Holiness*, and *The Rose of Solitude* his early concerns with man's relationship to the land with man's relationship to God. As Antoninus, Everson became the leading exponent of erotic mysticism in the Church, and with Thomas Merton he enjoyed a reputation as one of the two finest Catholic poets since Gerard Manley Hopkins. This reputation went into slight eclipse when Everson left the Order to marry in 1969, but the 1978 publication of his collected Catholic poetry, *The Veritable Years*, reawakened critical interest in his achievement. And it is this work from Everson's Catholic period (from which the bulk of these forewords and afterwords are drawn) which is most thoroughly grounded in analytical psychology.

Everson came to Jung through Father Victor White. White, like the poet a Dominican, was Reader in Theology at Blackfriars College at Oxford. Additionally, he was a foundation member and lecturer at the Jung Institute of Analytical Psychology, and he knew Jung as both a teacher and a friend. White visited Jung at Bollingen numerous times, and carried on a substantial correspondence with him which led, unfortunately, to an alienation between the two men late in Jung's life. For many years White had planned to write an extended historical, psychoanalytical, and theological treatise on the relationship between God and the unconscious, but his work was, he felt, pre-empted by Albert Beguin's *L'Art romantique et la rêve*, A. Wilwol's *Rätsel der Seele*, and Josef Goldbrunner's *Heligkeit und Gesundheit*, among other books. However, the first two chapters of this unfinished project, along with ten other related papers, were collected in 1952 in White's *God and the Unconscious*.

Everson did not read that book until a few years after its publication, and even then, as he explains in his introduction to the volume's recent reissue, he was "suspicious of depth psychology's pertinence to the spiritual life, preferring to suffer it out with St. John of the Cross." Everson met White in the fall of 1955, when the priest was a visiting lecturer at St. Albert's College in Oakland, where Everson lived as a lay brother. There the two men had discussions centering on "the doctrine of the non-essentiality of evil as seen in the abiding tradition of the Church since Augustine, which Jung opposed." Eventually, however, as Everson outlined to me in a letter, White's work on Jung took hold of the poet. White

> went back to England after the Spring Semester in 1956. He had been sent Marcuse's *Eros and Civilization* to review, but had no room for it in his bag and left it with me. I began to browse in it, then settled down with the analysis of Freudian psychology which is featured there. I had been introduced to Freud back in 1946 at Cascade Locks, Oregon, awaiting demobilization, via *The Function of the Orgasm* by Wilhelm Reich, but put it out of my mind since my conversion. I had just gone through a series of depressions, and one of the brethren suggested I seek psychiatric help. Then I got a letter from a professor writing a book; he asked me to reprint "The Raid" and, moreover, comment on my intentions. I made to reply that it was simply "they who live by the sword will die by the sword," but suddenly I caught myself saying "wait a minute." The Freudian analysis was clicking in my mind. I saw the Oedipus complex in the poem for the first time. It was shockingly revelatory. That night a crucial dream came and next day I began to write an erotic fantasy of the union with the mother. In Jungian terms the anima invaded. But still I did not read Jung, only Freudian books. . . . Then arrived Neumann's *The Origins and History of Consciousness*, which won me over and took me back to *God and the Unconscious*. I put aside Freud and plunged into Jung. It was now 1957.

For Everson, this return to White's study, which was to have a central influence on the development of his thought, coincided with an interest in the religious aspect of the emergence of the Beat Generation writers, a surfacing which the poet came to argue was in fact the re-emergence in the 20th century of the Dionysian spirit.[3]

Because Freud's "system" is at its center atheist, it is not finally really available to Catholics; there have been, of course, attempts to bring the two programs into registration but, as Everson points out, these have ended in "the uneasy *modus vivendi* between Catholic psychiatry and Freudian psychoanalysis, based on a moot distinction between *soul* and *psyche*, wherein the mentally distressed religionist placed his immortal soul in the hands of his shrink."[4] In a paper which must have been extremely important to Everson once he began to see his new-found religious faith balanced with the perspectives of analytical psychology, "Freud, Jung and God," White argues that while Jung's split with Freud had various causes, one of the most significant was the disagreement over the nature of God and religion. "Freud's presentation of psycho-analysis," White maintains, "assumes atheism, it does not even claim to prove it." From the relatively early *Totem and Taboo* to the late *The Future of an Illusion*, Freud developed one of his central concepts—that God is simply a "phantasy substitute for the actual, and never wholly satisfactory, parent: a projection to compensate for an infantile sense of helplessness." In his later work, however, Jung argued that the inverse was true, that once we come to see Freud's notion of the sexual libido as simply a particular instance of a much more pervasive universal Spirit, the way becomes open "to us," for instance, no longer to conceive of God as a substitute for the physical father, but rather the physical father as the infant's first substitute for god, the genetically prior bearer of the image of the All-Father. God less a Big Father than the physical father a little God."[5] In short, where for Freud religion was merely a symptom of psychosis, for Jung the *absence* of religion became the psychological dis-ease.

A second of White's papers which certainly must have appealed to Everson was "Revelation and the Unconscious." Here White outlines the idea of prophecy and the prophet in the work of St. Thomas from an implicitly Jungian perspective. St. Thomas believied, White reminds us, in the necessity of divine revelation "because the purpose and meaning of human existence is ultimately to be found only in the invisible and incomprehensible Divinity"; the nature of this purpose must, however, somehow be made manifest to us, and this is the function of prophecy. Further, White argues, St. Thomas (following St. Paul) regarded revelation as the most important of all *charismata*, one which "is no permanent disposition (habitus) to be used at will, but something momentarily undergone (passio); something, not that the recipient does, but that is done to him, which seizes him and overpowers him."[6]

The idea of revelation predates Christianity, of course, and Everson's sense of prophetic voice as it relates to the function of the shaman has been abiding, informing his best essays and interviews as well as his own poetic practice since at least his conversion. "The poet knows that he speaks adequately then only when he speaks somewhat wildly," says Emerson in "The Poet," and it is the ecstasy produced through controlled possession which Everson feels the shaman, like the poet, channels into artistic activity. Taking the pictographs on the cave walls of Lascaux and Altamira as evidence, Andreas Lommel (whom the poet has often used as a source) judges paleolithic shamans to be the first artistically creative figures known to us.[7] Indeed, while they often functioned as physicians or high priests or priestesses, they were not simply witch doctors. Tribal witch doctors gained their status through a will to power, and were successful according to their abilities for the power of suggestion and hypnosis. Shamans, on the other hand, acted not out of a will to power but to escape from possession (or, in clinical terms, psychosis) by entering into shamanistic activity—drawing, dance, song. Thus, while in some primitive cultures shamans and witch doctors filled many of the same roles, shamans were primarily distinguished by their call to be artistically creative. . . .

Of all Jung's concepts, though, it is the idea of the anima/animus which has taken a central place in Everson's program: that each man carries "a spontaneous product of the unconscious" which is the feminine within him, while each woman's "unconscious has, so to speak, a masculine imprint."[8] These contra-sexual aspects, Jung argues, must be recognized and reconciled within each individual and finally, by extension, within the collective to form an androgynous whole if psychic stability is to be realized. For the eighteen and a half years Everson lived as a Dominican monk, as Antoninus, almost all his work derived its substance and power from the very real tension produced by an ongoing struggle between the spirit and the flesh. *The Rose of Solitude* (1967) is probably Everson's finest achievement as Antoninus, and in the prose foreword to that book the poet recognizes this theme: "The spiritual life is both speculative and practical, but a painful tension obtains between the world of the ideal and the world of immediate experience." The subject of *Rose* is a monk's interior struggle with sexuality in his relationship with a divorced Mexican dancer. Yet even deeper, the poem sequence traces the transformation of a sexual struggle through a Jungian mergence of the masculine and feminine aspects of the Self as a path to *gnosis*. . . .

Everson's concern with "the woman within" appears as early as the pre-Dominican, pre-Jungian *In the Fictive Wish*, though it becomes progressively more central to his poetic project through the Catholic poetry leading up to *The Rose of Solitude*. As Albert Gelpi points out, "in 'The Encounter' and several other remarkable poems towards the end of *Crooked Lines* Antoninus becomes the woman before God, his/her whole being called into activity by His totally mastering love."[9] Further, in "Annul in Me My Manhood" the poet reverses Lady Macbeth's aspostrophe "unsex me here," asking that God might make him "woman-sexed and weak, / If by that total transformation / I might know Thee more," while the later "God Germed in Raw Granite" asks "Is this she? Woman within! / . . . when we / Well-wedded merge, by Him / Twained into one and solved there." But it is not until *Rose* that Everson moves beyond a sense of the recognition of the anima as a facet of his quest to, like Whitman, a realization that in fact the woman within is its object.

The "Prologue" to *Rose* announces that volume's theme, one that parallels Whitman's while significantly altering its situation in that here the struggle is overtly male-female:

> The dark roots of the rose cry in my heart.
> They pierce through rock-ribs of my stony flesh,
> Invest the element, the loam of life.
> They twist and mesh.
>
> The red blood of the rose beats on, beats on,
> Of passion poured, of fiery love composed,
> Virtue redeemed, the singular crest of life,
> And pride deposed.
>
> Love cries regenerate and lust moans consumed,
> Shaken in terror on that rage of breath.
> Untrammeled still the red rose burns on
> And knows no death.
>
> Petal by crimson petal, leaf by leaf,
> Unfolds the luminous core, the bright abyss,
> Proffers at last the exquisite delight
> Of the long kiss.
>
> Until shall pass away the wasted means
> Leaving in essence what time held congealed:
> The Sign of God evoked from the splendid flesh
> Of the Rose revealed.

The opening lines of the poem present a traditional symbol, though the situation is ambiguous: we have a rose (and we think here of Dante or, perhaps because the "roots" are "dark," of Blake or Roethke), yet at the same instant the rose seems to be a thing both external to the poet (i.e., a woman) and part of him as well. The question becomes one of direction—is the rose something that has invaded him (his infatuation with an Other) or is it something already resident in the poet, buried deep in his soul, crying to emerge? Because Antoninus' affair with Rose Tunneland, the divorced Mexican dancer, occasions the poem, the first possibility seems the obvious. However, the first line is telling: the rose is crying *in* his heart; that is, we do not necessarily have a movement inward "through rock-ribs" of "stony flesh," but possibly a movement outward to the "loam of life" which is psychic wholeness. In this sense, the rose becomes symbolic of the poet's feminine aspect, and the movement of the poem, the unfolding "petal by crimson petal, leaf by leaf" of the rose, becomes as much a figurative enactment of the poet's emerging recognition of his own androgynous nature as a specifically sexual circumstance. On the one hand, the monk finds in the body of his woman "The Sign of God"; on the other, it is the "splendid flesh of the Rose" of his anima which reveals to him the core of his religion and affords him regeneration.

Throughout the sequence's five sections, Whitman's Adam is transformed into the Christ-figure, the poet crucified, having nailed himself "to the Mexican cross, / The flint knife of her beauty." Of course such symbolism is perhaps rather unextraordinary given Everson's situation—a monk whose vow of celibacy is undergoing a rigorous test—but it works on a level deeper than the immediate. According to Jung's studies, the cross (which is a primary symbol in *Rose*) "is a many-faceted symbol, and its chief meaning is that of the 'tree of life' and the 'mother,'" certainly an instrument of pain, but one leading to regeneration.[10] Further, Christ's crucifixion (which the poet here re-enacts in the passion of his own life) is often identified with a passing into androgyny. In his *Sermo Suppositus* Augustine writes,

> Like a bridegroom Christ went forth from his chamber, he went out with a presage of his nuptials into the field of the world. . . . He came to the marriage-bed of the cross, and there, in mounting it, he consummated his marriage. And when he perceived the sighs of the creature, he lovingly gave himself up to the torment in place of his bride, and he joined himself to the woman forever.[11]

Jung points out that the sense of the Christ-figure himself as androgynous has played a crucial role in the Christian tradition, relating specifically to the Adamic myth:

> The Church symbolism of *sponsus* and *sponsa* leads to the mystic union of the two, i.e., to the *anima Christi* which lives in the *corpus mysticum* of the Church. This unity underlies the idea of Christ's androgyny . . . which is no doubt connected with the Platonic conception of the bisexual First Man, for Christ is ultimately the Anthropos.[12]

In *Aion*, Jung goes on to remind us that iconography often pictures Christ with breasts (in the manner of "The New Birth" from the *Rosarium philosophorum secunda pars alchimiae de lapide philosophico*, Frankfurt, 1550, page 19), "in accordance with the Song of Solomon 1:1: 'For thy breasts are better than wine.' "[13] Finally, the "symbol of the hermaphrodite, it must be remembered, is one of the many synonyms for the goal of the art"[14] of alchemy, which like poetry seeks to reunite the contradictions of the fallen phenomenal world into their primal unity.

The scandal surrounding the publication of *The Rose of Solitude* in the more conservative quarters of the Church can thus be seen as a reaction not so much to the situation of the sequence (in 1967 a narrative of a monk's fall, especially a *felix culpa*, would raise few eyebrows) but rather in the Lawrentian implications of Everson's erotic vision:

> My act lives.
>
> From its life delivered
> I stand free.
>
> Of the Rose renewed
> I rise, I rise.
> I stand free.
>
> In the wisdom of the flesh,
> In the truth of the touch,
> In the silence of the smile
> Redeemed.
>
> ("Immortal Strangeness")

And further,

> I have said before:
> All the destinies of the divine
> In her converge.
>
> . . .
>
> To love her more
> Is to love self less.
> And to love self less
> Is to love God more.
>
> To love selflessly
> Is to love:
>
> Him in her.
>
> Amen.
>
> ("On the Thorn")

As the Christ figure, Everson, like Whitman's Anthropos, finds regeneration not in mortification and denial. Rather, as these powerful poems trace the poet's sexual dark night in his conflict with the flesh, it is finally his submission to his passion for the Rose—the woman within—which affords him wholeness: " 'When the devil / Can't find a way / He sends a woman.' / So does God."

Notes

1. See especially Jung's 1934 "interview," "Does the World Stand on the Verge of Spiritual Rebirth?" in *C. G. Jung Speaking*, edited by William McGuire and R. F. C. Hull (Princeton: Princeton University Press, 1977), pp. 67–75.
2. Everson, "From the Depths of a Void" in *Earth Poetry: Selected Essays and Interviews of William Everson*, edited by Lee Bartlett (Berkeley: Oyez, 1980), p. 75.
3. "Dionysus and the Beat Generation," *Earth Poetry*, pp. 21–8.
4. From the manuscript of Everson's introduction to the reissue of White's *God and the Unconscious*, forthcoming from Spring Publications.
5. White, *God and the Unconscious* (Cleveland: World Publishing Company, 1952), pp. 67, 78.
6. White, p. 126.
7. Information on shamanism in the following paragraphs is drawn from Everson's source, Andreas Lommel, *Shamanism: The Beginnings of Art* (New York: McGraw-Hill, 1966).
8. C. G. Jung, *Aion* (Princeton: Princeton University Press, 1968), pp. 11–22.
9. Albert Gelpi, "Everson/Antoninus: Contending with the Shadow," an afterword to Everson's *The Veritable Years* (Santa Barbara: Black Sparrow Press, 1978), p. 361.
10. C. G. Jung, *Symbols of Transformation* (Princeton: Princeton University Press, 1956), p. 269.
11. Ibid.
12. C. G. Jung, *The Psychology of the Transference* (Princeton: Princeton University Press, 1969), p. 146.
13. *Aion*, p. 205.
14. See June Singer, *Androgyny* (New York: Anchor Press, 1976), pp. 125–50.

JAMES T. FARRELL

1904–1979

James Thomas Farrell, a second-generation Irish-American, was born to working-class parents on February 27, 1904, on the south side of Chicago. The city, where he lived until 1931, provides the background for many of his realistic novels of urban life. After graduating from high school he worked at various jobs, and between 1925 and 1929 managed to take a number of courses at the University of Chicago, notably in composition. Supporting himself by journalism and by publishing stories and essays, he married in 1931 and spent a year in Paris, where he was encouraged in his writing by Ezra Pound, before taking up residence in New York City in 1932.

Farrell's first novel, *Young Lonigan*, was published in 1932, followed in 1934 by *The Young Manhood of Studs Lonigan*, and in 1935 by *Judgment Day*. These three novels make up the trilogy *Studs Lonigan*, which brought him to prominence, winning him a Guggenheim Fellowship in 1936 and a Book-of-the-Month Club award in 1937. Farrell's broad depiction of American society continued with the O'Neill-O'Flaherty pentalogy, which occupied him from 1936 to 1953. At the same time he produced other novels, short stories, essays on literature, philosophy and history, and journalism, and was actively engaged as a pragmatist and liberal internationalist in New York intellectual and political life. In 1941 he helped to organize the Civil Rights Defense Committee, and in 1947 became a member of the Workers' Defense Committee. From 1954 to 1956 he was chairman of the American Committee for Cultural Freedom, and spoke at conferences in America and Europe. A 1956 lecture tour to Israel provided the experiences recorded in *It Has Come to Pass*, 1958.

Among Farrell's collections of essays are *A Note on Literary Criticism* (1936); *Literature and Morality* (1947); and *Reflections at Fifty* (1954). *The Short Stories of James T. Farrell* appeared in 1937, and *An Omnibus of Short Stories* in 1957. *The Collected Poems of James T. Farrell* was issued in 1965. An ambitious multicycled series of novels, *A Universe of Time*, which began appearing in 1963 with *The Silence of Time*, was still incomplete at his death in Manhattan on August 22, 1979.

JAMES T. FARRELL

From "How *Studs Lonigan* Was Written" (1938)

The League of Frightened Philistines

1945, pp. 82–89

I

I began writing what has developed into this trilogy in June, 1929. *Judgment Day* was finally completed at the end of January, 1935. In June, 1929, I was a young man who had burned other bridges behind him with the determination to write, whether my efforts brought me success or failure. I was then finishing what happened to be my last quarter as a student at the University of Chicago. Three times before I had dropped out of classes because I was restless and dissatisfied, resolved to devote my time to writing and to educating myself in my own haphazard manner. For a fourth and last time I had matriculated and I managed to finish the quarter. Although I read continuously and rather broadly, after my sophomore year I could not maintain a steady interest in any of my courses except in composition, where I could write as much as I pleased. I would cut other classes, day after day, finally dropping out, heedless of the loss of credit and the waste of money I had spent for tuition.

My mood and state of mind in those days were, I believe, of the kind which most young writers will recognize. To be a young man with literary aspirations is not to be particularly happy. At first, the desire to write is more strong than is a clear perception of what one wants to write and how one will write it. There are surprising oscillations of mood. One moment the young writer is energetic and hopeful. The next he is catapulted into a fit of despair, his faith in himself infirm, his self-confidence shattered and broken, his view of the future one in which he sees self-sacrifice ending only in dismal failure. There are times when he cannot look his friends in the eye. There are moments when he feels himself to be set against the opposition of the entire world. There are occasions when he turns a caustic wit, a brutal sarcasm, and a savage arrogance on others only because he is defending himself from himself. Suddenly he will be devastated by an image of himself in which he sees a nobody who has had the temerity and egotism to want to call himself a writer. He measures himself, with his few unpublished manuscripts, against the accomplishments of great writers, and his ambition suddenly seems like insanity. Even though he is not particularly conscious of clothes, there are periods when he gazes upon his own shabbiness—his unshined shoes, his worn and unpressed shiny suit, his frayed overcoat, his uncut hair—and he sees these as a badge of his own miserable mediocrity. A sense of failure dogs his steps. Living with himself becomes almost unendurable.

Writing is one of the cruelest of professions. The sense of possible failure in a literary career can torment one pitilessly. And failure in a literary career cannot be measured in dollars and cents. Poverty and the struggle for bread are not the only features of a literary career that can make it so cruel. There is the self-imposed loneliness. There is the endless struggle to perceive freshly and clearly, to realize and re-create on paper a sense of life. There is more than economic competition involved. The writer feels frequently that he is competing with time and with life itself. His hopes will sometimes ride high. His ambitions will soar until they have become so grandiose that they cannot be realized within the space of a single lifetime. The world opens up before the young writer as a grand and glorious adventure in feeling and in understanding. Nothing human is unimportant to him. Everything he sees is germane to his purpose. Every word that he hears uttered is of potential use to him. Every mood, every passing fancy, every trivial thought can have its meaning and its place in the store of experience he is accumulating. The opportunities for assimilation are enormous, endless. And there is only one single short life of struggle in which to assimilate. A melancholy sense of time becomes a torment. One's whole spirit rebels against a truism that all men must realize, because it applies to all men. One seethes in rebellion against the realization that the human being must accept limitations, that he can develop in one line of effort only at the cost of making many sacrifices in other lines. Time becomes for the writer the most precious good in all the world. And how often will he not feel that he is squandering this precious good? His life then seems like a sieve through which his days are filtering, leaving behind only a few, a very few, miserable grains of experience. If he is wasting time today, what assurance can he give himself that he will not be doing likewise tomorrow? He is struggling with himself to attain self-discipline. He weighs every failure in his struggle. He begins to find a sense of death—death before he has fulfilled any of his potentialities—like a dark shadow cast constantly close to his awareness.

Such were some of the components of my own state of mind when *Studs Lonigan* was begun.

II

In the spring of 1929 I took a course in advanced composition conducted by Professor James Weber Linn. Professor Linn—with whom I was constantly at loggerheads concerning literary questions—was encouraging. His encouragement, as well as my arguments with him and with the majority of the class, assisted me in maintaining my own self-confidence. I wrote thousands of words for his course. I wrote stories, sketches, book reviews, essays, impressions, anecdotes. Most of these manuscripts related to death, disintegration, human indignity, poverty, drunkenness, ignorance, human cruelty. They attempted to describe dusty and deserted streets, street corners, miserable homes, pool rooms, brothels, dance halls, taxi dances, bohemian sections, express offices, gasoline filling stations, scenes laid in slum districts. The characters were boys, boys' gangs, drunkards, Negroes, expressmen, homosexuals, immigrants and immigrant landlords, filling-station attendants, straw bosses, hitch hikers, bums, bewildered parents. Most of the manuscripts were written with the ideal of objectivity in mind. I realized then that the writer should submit himself to an objective discipline. These early manuscripts of mine were written, in the main, out of such an intention.

One of the stories I wrote for Professor Linn's course was titled *Studs*. It was originally published in *This Quarter*. *Studs* is the story of a wake, written in the first person. The corpse is a lad from the Fifty-eighth Street neighborhood who had died suddenly at the age of twenty-six. The story describes his background and friends. They have come to the wake and they sit in the rear of the apartment, discussing the mysteries of death in banalities, nostalgically remembering the good old days, contentedly describing the dull details of their current life. The author of the story sits there, half-heartedly trying to join in the conversation, recollecting the past vividly, remembering how these fellows, who are now corpulent and sunk in the trivialities of day-to-day living, were once adventurous boys.

Professor Linn read this story in class and praised it most enthusiastically. I had no genuine opinion concerning it. I had tried to write it as honestly, as clearly, and as well as I could. I did not know what I thought of it. The praise this story received in class greatly encouraged me. I asked Professor Robert Morss Lovett to read it. He kindly consented, and after doing so, he called me to his office and suggested that this story should be developed at greater length, and the milieu described in it should be put down in greater detail. I had already begun to think of doing this, and Professor Linn and Professor Lovett are the spiritual godfathers of *Studs Lonigan*.

III

. . . The story of Studs Lonigan opens on the day that Woodrow Wilson is renominated to run for a second term as President of the United States. It closes in the depths of the Hoover era.

It was during the period of the Wilson Administration that this nation reached upward toward the zenith of its power and became, perhaps, the richest and the most powerful nation in all history. The story of Studs Lonigan was conceived as the story of the education of a normal American boy in this period. The important institutions in the education of Studs Lonigan were the home and the family, the church, the school, and the playground. These institutions broke down and did not serve their desired function. The streets become a potent educative factor in the boy's life. In time, the pool room becomes an important institution in his life. When Studs reaches his young manhood, this nation is moving headlong into one of the most insane eras of our history—the Prohibition era. A word here is necessary concerning the drinking of Studs and his companions. This drinking has a definite social character. When Studs and his companions drink, they do so as a gesture of defiance which is in the spirit of the times. Drinking in those days became a social ritual. Furthermore, when Studs and his companions began drinking, the worst liquor of the Prohibition era was being sold. Those were the days when the newspapers published daily death lists of the number of persons who had died from bootleg liquor and wood alcohol. That was the time when men and boys would take one or two drinks, pass out into unconsciousness and come to their senses only to learn that they would never again have their eyesight. All generations drink more or less in the period of young manhood. But all generations do not drink the kind of bootleg liquor that Studs Lonigan and his companions drank. The health of Studs and many of his friends is impaired and permanently ruined in this story. That very loss of health has, it can be seen now, a social character.

Studs Lonigan is neither a tough nor a gangster. He is not really a hard guy. He is a normal young American of his time and his class. His values become the values of his world. He has as many good impulses as normal human beings have. In time, because of defeat, of frustration, of a total situation characterized by spiritual poverty, these good impulses are expressed more and more in the stream of his reverie. Here we find the source of Studs's constant dream of himself. Studs's dream of himself changes in character as the story progresses. In the beginning, it is a vision of what he is going to be. He is a boy waiting at the threshold of life. His dream of himself is a romantic projection of his future, conceived in the terms and the values of his world. In time, this dream of himself turns backward. It is no longer a romantic projection of things to come. More and more it becomes a nostalgic image turned toward the past. Does this not happen in greater or lesser degree to all of us?

Shortly after I began working on *Studs Lonigan*, I happened to be reading John Dewey's *Human Nature and Conduct*, and I came upon the following sentence which I used as a quotation in *Young Lonigan*: "The poignancy of situations which evoke reflection lies in the fact that we do not know the meaning of the tendencies that are pressing for action." This observation crystallized for me what I was seeking to do. This work grew out of a situation which evoked reflection. The situation revealed to me the final meaning of tendencies which had been pressing for action. And that final situation became death, turning poignancy into tragedy. *Studs Lonigan* was conceived as the story of an American destiny in our time. It deals with the making and the education of an ordinary American boy. My attitude toward it and toward my character here is essentially a simple one. "There but for the grace of God go I." . . . There but for the grace of God go—many others.

ALFRED KAZIN

From "The Revival of Naturalism"
On Native Grounds
1942, pp. 381–85

Farrell was perhaps the most powerful naturalist who ever worked in the American tradition, but the raw intensity of that power suggested that naturalism was really exhausted and could now thrive only on a mechanical energy bent on forcing itself to the uttermost. There is a total and moving design unfolded in his conflicting histories of Studs Lonigan and Danny O'Neill—the history of the South Chicago world out of which both sprang; the history of these two careers, one descending and the other ascending, with the ascendant Danny

O'Neill giving back the life that had almost crushed him as a youth—*giving it all back*. But scene by scene, character by character, Farrell's books are built by force rather than imagination, and it is the laboriously contrived solidity, the perfect literalness of each representation, that give his work its density and harsh power. As an example for novelists Farrell was as much a blind alley as Dreiser, but where Dreiser remained a kind of tribal poet, a barbaric Homer who exercised a peculiar influence because of his early isolation and his place in the formation of naturalism, Farrell, so much less sentient a mind, grew out of the materialism of the early thirties. For while Dreiser was the epic recorder of the American tragedy in the first great period of naturalism, his awkwardness seemed merely a personal trait, and one that did not conceal the great depths in his work. Farrell was the archetypal novelist of the crisis and its inflictions, and the atmosphere of crisis supported his work as appropriately as his own conception of life satisfied the contemporary need to shock and to humiliate. It is not only that all the rawness and distemper of the thirties seem to live in Farrell's novels; though written as the story of his own education, they are at the same time the most striking example of that literalness of mind which showed all through the depression literature in the surrender of imagination and in the attraction to pure force and power.

It is this literalness, this instinctive trust in the necessity of violence, which makes Farrell's practice in fiction so livid a symbol of the mind of depression America. In his hands the cult of violence was something different from Faulkner's overstylized Gothic, which had to be seen through a maze of confused lyricism and technical legerdemain, or Caldwell's pellagra Frankenstein, which was wryly comic. It was naturalism proving its bravado to itself, and expanding by the sheer accumulation of sensations. The technique was a kind of arithmetical progression, notably in such furious scenes as the famous New Year's Eve bacchanal in *The Young Manhood of Studs Lonigan*, the nightmare initiation scene in *Judgment Day*, and that apocalyptic passage in *No Star Is Lost* which portrayed Aunt Margaret O'Flaherty, drunk to the hilt, thrown out by her latest lover, sitting on the steps and counting her fingers in a devouring rush of the D.T.'s. Farrell's style was like a pneumatic drill pounding at the mind, stripping off the last covers of the nervous system. Primitive in their design, his scenes aroused a maximum intensity of repulsion by the sheer pressure of their accumulative weight. If one submitted to that pressure, every other consideration seemed irrelevant or falsely "literary," like Farrell's tone-deafness, or the fact that he improvised his scenes within so narrow a range that the final impression was black unrelieved dullness. This was Life, or at the very least the nerve-jangled and catastrophic life the thirties knew.

What gave Farrell his edge over other left-wing naturalists, many of whom perished singly even before their movement did, was his complete confidence in his material and gifts, in the very significance of his literary existence. Cantwell gave up after two novels; Dahlberg was exhausted by his own sensibility; Caldwell, as Kenneth Burke once said, became so repetitious that he seemed to be playing with his toes; Gold wrote nothing after *Jews without Money*, which expressed all he had to say, except his *Daily Worker* twaddle; Schneider, Seaver, Rollins, Conroy, Burke, Lumpkin, were all unable to follow up their early novels. Of the host of younger writers who seemed to promise so much to Marxist critics in the early thirties—the Tillie Lerners, the Arnold Armstrongs, the Ben Fields—only Richard Wright and Albert Maltz went on writing at all. But Farrell's will to endure gave him the energetic faith to write a trilogy and to launch one of the most expansive autobiographical epics in literary history. If his grimness often became the very tone of his work, it also served as a rationale, a formal conception as grandiose as Jules Romains's. Farrell's very need to write along a line of single concentration was, like his complete dependence upon his own resources, a kind of spiritual autarchy—there was only one subject in his work, and the spirit with which he pursued it soon became one with it. For Farrell was not "making" subjects out of proletarian life, like those occupational novelists whose books reflected their special knowledge of automobile workers, textile hands, relief supervisors; or those nationality novelists who were as crude as the Communist party's program for a "black belt" in the South to be composed exclusively for Negroes. He never wrote about his fellow Irish in that fake sociological spirit; Studs Lonigan's gang, the O'Flaherty and O'Neill families, the priests and nuns, were all dramatis personae in the story of Danny James Farrell O'Neill, whose story *was* his will to endure, to be free of the influences that had threatened to stifle his spirit.

Farrell's distinction was thus a very real one: in a period of moral collapse, he believed in himself with an almost monumental seriousness. Far more than Dreiser, whose career was spotted with failure, who wrote his books by intermittent and devastating exertions, Farrell represented the supremacy of the naturalist's imagination in, rather than over, a period of tormented materialism. He did not rise above the hazards of writing, he was fiercely unconscious of them; his personal victory over the first enemies of his freedom—the Church and Studs Lonigan and the slums of Chicago—became a literary victory by the sheer force of his remorseless attack upon them. If all writers remember longest what they learned in their youth, Farrell's work suggests that he remembered nothing and learned from nothing but his youth. Unlike all the little people in left-wing letters who loved the working class to death but could never touch them, Farrell was joined by every instinct to men and women who have never known the barest security, who have clawed the earth to live from one day to the next. What more was needed in *Studs Lonigan* than the literal transcription of the Irish Babbittry's inhuman yammering, with abysmal cruelty banging against animal insolence, where only Celtic blood could get back at Celts with so much grisly humor? What more was needed in *A World I Never Made* and after than the toneless saga of drink, of a new child every year, of meat once a week, of endless, life-shattering recrimination, of a little boy named Danny O'Neill who wanted baseball and a quiet table, but who could never forget, though his grandmother took him away, that at home his parents and brothers and sisters were slowly dying together?

Unlike some sentimentalists, Farrell certainly never defended his work by calling it "sociology." Although he quickly became a convenient symbol to cultural historians who saw in him a student of the American city, to sociologists and social-settlement liberals and literary anthropologists of the lives and morals of the poor, Farrell insisted, with the traditional justice and something more than the traditional vehemence of the naturalist, that his work had the self-sufficient form and self-justifying power of a solidly written and precise literary record. And it was not the Marxist critics alone—who, indeed, were often cold to Farrell's work because it was not formally "revolutionary"—who supported this view; it was a kind of collective esthetic simplicity, or paralysis, of men of goodwill in the thirties who, having rejected genteel objections that *Studs Lonigan* was sociology, decided that it must be art—and obviously very powerful art. These genteel objections, which occurred only to those who feared the widest possible democracy of subject in the nobel, were, as John Chamberlain wrote in his introduction to the Lonigan trilogy, "an incantation designed to exorcise the uncomfortable memory of Studs and his frightening palsy-walsies, with their broads, their movies, their pool, their alky, their poker and their craps. . . . Like all incantations, it masks a real respect. People don't usually bother to spin fine distinctions between documentary and artistic excellence when they are not disturbed by a book." Whereupon one asked, as Mr. Chamberlain did, impatiently, "What in hell is art, anyway?"

What was it indeed? To a democracy slowly arming against Fascism and conscious of its latent forms in the United States, *Studs Lonigan* did, at the very least, rank as a brilliant exposure of brutality and ignorance and corruption. If a healthy literature, as the Marxists insisted, meant an aroused concern with social analysis and the pressure of class forces in capitalist society, *Studs Lonigan* was a dynamic naturalism whose depth of insight and furious vitality gave it the stamp of creative power. To an America obsessed by the atmosphere of dissolution, proud of its "realism" and urgently in need of stimulation, Farrell's violence was salutary—a vigorous demonstration that art had to respond, at some stage of human development, with as much vigor as the strident life that gave it birth. "When a book has depth and pace," John Chamberlain wrote of *Studs Lonigan*, "when it continually flashes with meanings, when it coördinates one's own scattered and spasmodic experiences and reflections, when it mounts to climaxes that suddenly reveal by artistic mutation what has been imperceptible and latent in a character, then aren't we justified in calling it art, no matter how 'photographic' the realism?"

Yes; but in these terms art became only another abstraction, a hypothetical end-product as unreal as the famous "withering away of the state" in Leninist theory. For what if the realism was as brutal in its way as the brutality it exposed? It was not that Farrell's work was "amoral"; on the contrary, the moral judgment Danny O'Neill was forever making on his world—though familiarly mechanical as in most books of the kind, forever declaiming *J'accuse!*—was the most pervasive element in his work. It was art, powerful and vital art; but it was also a perfect example of that unconscious and benevolent philistinism which believes that one escapes from materialism by surrendering to it; that the principle of action, for writers as well as for revolutionaries, is to gain freedom for oneself by denying it to others. In the Marxist-Leninist theory of the state, one began as a terrorist and ended theoretically as a free man living in a more "human" world that had never practiced a conscious humanity. In the left-wing theory of literature, which was so riddled with determinism that it employed only half one's mind and soul, spiritual insight was to be won only by proving how little there was of it in life.

EDGAR M. BRANCH
From "Conclusion"
James T. Farrell
1971, pp. 161–65

Viewed in a larger context, Farrell's fiction clearly falls within the classical line of the novel's development: the tradition of critical Realism. He has sought his meanings in actual experience by representing characters in a definite time and place and in complex relationship to other individuals. He has shown their destinies being shaped by the milieu and the period, by their particular roles in society, and by their qualities of character. In being faithful to the cultural and material environments that shape his characters' spirits, Farrell has avoided reliance upon the transcendent or upon the legendary and mythological—the resources of the symbolic novelist. The symbols immanent in Farrell's writing intensify and focus the meaning of the concrete reality portrayed, but they remain organic with it. Nor do they emerge as semi-independent allegories.

Similarly, Farrell's narrative techniques and his non-poetic language are appropriate to his concentration upon reality as it actually is felt by specific individuals in a particular time and place, usually, but by no means invariably, Chicago and New York neighborhoods of the 1920's and 1930's. Technique and language are used to communicate and to objectify the empirically experienced reality, whether manifested as "environment" or as subjective impression, reverie and dream. In short, Farrell has employed the classic means of the Realist in combination with modern themes to highlight important human problems and to provide, through the carefully developed destinies of his characters, a vision of humanity and of some alternatives open to men in this world.

The literary means Farrell employed are deeply appropriate to his ontology, which is naturalistic, empirical, secular. "By naturalism," Farrell has written, "I mean that whatever happens in this world must ultimately be explainable in terms of events in this world. I assume or believe that all events are explainable in terms of natural origins rather than of extranatural or supernatural origins." Philosophically, Farrell's world is not one of essence but one of relationship, process, tendency, change, emergence, and time leading onward to death. Most of his fiction, sometimes thought of as a formless overflow of memory, may reasonably be regarded as a selection of experience that imaginatively embodies the world as process, adhering to the logic of life as he conceives it. For his fiction is faithful to the concreteness and the flow of events, to psychological relativism, and to natural causation. Farrell's ambiguous and shifting status early in life, so deeply felt, was an ideal ground for the development of this philosophy, just as this philosophy formulates the assumptions underlying what and how he has written.

One of Farrell's distinctions is the literary form he evolved—most successfully in the Studs Lonigan and the Danny O'Neill series. In those works, the particular blend of a bold architectural structure, an objective narrative method, and a style attuned to the idiom of his characters and to the quality of their experience was his own creation, one designed to express the life he knew intimately in Chicago. Nevertheless, his avid consumption of books that began in 1925 inevitably shaped his thinking and writing.

Among the writers of fiction who influenced him in the 1920's, a few deserve particular mention. To Farrell, Theodore Dreiser was a symbol of integrity, an uncompromising fighter against great odds who broke fresh ground for later writers. Farrell's style and method, and indeed the effects he creates, have little resemblance to Dreiser's, nor could Farrell accept Dreiser's gloomy philosophy; but he valued the older man's depth of feeling and his broad sympathy and respect for humanity. Moreover, Dreiser's picture of Chicago and of boyhood was meaningful to Farrell, who imaginatively identified Dreiser's Clyde Griffiths with boys he had known, and Carrie and Jennie with his aunts. Sherwood Anderson's fiction, even more than Dreiser's, gave Farrell confidence in his boyhood as material for literature, in part because Farrell intimately identified with Anderson's deviate characters who affected him deeply. Their inner life, Farrell recognized, was presented as meaningful and important. Anderson's ordinary, inarticulate persons, like Farrell's Studs and Danny, craved understanding; they were beset by frustrations that spawned lonely, cramped selves, and even aggression.

From Hemingway's fiction Farrell gained some suggestions for stories and, more important, an electric impression of immediacy, of the intensely vernacular, as though the action were taking place next door in America even when it was occurring in Europe. Hemingway's use of dialogue for narration was a revelation to Farrell, and his style helped Farrell discard an adolescent subjectivity and a constant striving for metaphors apparent in his 1927 college writing. James Joyce's fiction, which also helped Farrell acquire objectivity in his prose, presented dramatic action through the interior monologue, the dream, and the staccato-like progression of snapshot episodes like that in the party scene ending *The Young Manhood of Studs Lonigan*. Joyce as Irish rebel and spoiled priest was significant to Farrell, for Joyce's exploration of the themes of self-discovery and of the artist's developing of consciousness struck home.

Numerous philosophers, social scientists, and others redirected Farrell's thinking during the 1920's and thereby opened up perspectives within his writing. In 1927 Farrell, somewhat like Bernard Clare, briefly acted the part of a Nietzschean rebel—self-assertive and superior, a Dionysian truth-seeker and destroyer, the archenemy of Christianity and all shackling delusions—even though Dreiser's attitudes of sympathy and acceptance served as a counterpoise in his total consciousness at the time. Today it is possible to say that Nietzsche's influence pervades Farrell's writing. It merges importantly into the total ethical and social thrust of his fiction, for it helped give form to the individualistic, revolutionary strain native to Farrell.

Even more significant in Farrell's development were the American pragmatists William James, John Dewey, and George H. Mead. (Farrell's intimate knowledge of the writing of these men, especially Dewey's and Mead's, and his close alliance with their intellectual tradition, are evident in *Dialogue on John Dewey* [1959].) Separate studies have examined this relationship, and here it is enough to indicate the profundity of Farrell's indebtedness. Pragmatist thought shaped his social values and his concept of man in freedom and in bondage. It enlarged his understanding of social and individual growth. Especially Dewey and Mead have had much to do with Farrell's stand in ethics, esthetics, and metaphysics. And because Farrell absorbed their concepts of time, emergence, reverie, habit, and the interaction of the self with other selves and the environment, their influence may be seen as a kind of stance toward experience that he developed, or even as an organizing principle affecting the style and structure of his fiction.

Thorstein Veblen's ideas excited Farrell in the 1920's. Veblen's theory of business enterprise clarified Farrell's understanding of the economic system and of his experience within it as a lowly service-station attendant. Veblen helped Farrell see that an acquisitive society and a standardized industrial order often thwart man's best instincts and stunt personal creativity. Similarly Charles Beard's *An Economic Interpretation of the Constitution of the United States* shaped Farrell's view of historical cause and effect, and John Maynard Keynes' *The Economic Consequences of the Peace* revealed to Farrell a new, unhappy vista of a violent future. Just as unhappy was the longer vista ending in universal death presented in Bertrand Russell's "A Free Man's Worship," but Russell taught Farrell the value of stoicism and the dignity of human striving for a better life on earth. Walter Pater also spoke to Farrell about the proper use of time and consciousness. As Farrell moved from the 1920's into the 1930's, the influences of Sigmund Freud and of Karl Marx, Leon Trotsky, and other revolutionists became more pronounced, although not so basic as that of the pragmatists.

ALAN M. WALD
From "The Literary Record"
James T. Farrell: The Revolutionary Socialist Years
1978, pp. 134–43

If one surveys the large quantity of Farrell's fiction which concerns radical intellectuals and particularly the Stalinist movement, there is one overriding characteristic: the conception of Stalinism, with its cultural arm, as a deforming and perfidious social movement. V. F. Calverton noted the absence of this approach in *A Note on Literary Criticism;* Farrell's polemic, Calverton had argued, seemed to be mainly against the ignorance of various Communist party critics. However, if the Trotskyist notion of Stalinism remained undiscussed in *A Note on Literary Criticism* for tactical reasons, the situation was soon reversed. In the following months and years Farrell demonstrated no lack of aggressiveness in promoting a Trotskyist understanding of political and cultural Stalinism in its Third Period, Popular Front, wartime, and post-Browder phases. (It was precisely this kind of incisive political critique which made Farrell anathema to the Stalinists and to those liberals who chose to ally with them.) And to some degree, Trotskyist critiques of the phases of Stalinism are concepts underlying parts of two novels *(The Road Between* and *Yet Other Waters)*, scores of short stories, and one important play, *The Mowbray Family.*

Farrell's fictional world of the Stalinist political-cultural movement is not peopled with simple scoundrels, conspirators, or especially naive or warped individuals (although some of these types are present). As a social force, Stalinism is portrayed as a magnet of attraction, offering (in its different periods) combinations of material and spiritual rewards. In the beginning of *Yet Other Waters* (depicting Stalinism in transition from the Third Period to the Popular Front), novelist Bernard Carr and Mel Morris (the editor of *Social Theatre)* have a revealing discussion. Mel, to whom the party has given a magazine and an audience, sings praises to what the Stalinists have done for him in a very material sense:

> "Look how we've both got ahead already," Mel went on. "We're going places. And the Movement's going places. After the Writers Congress next month, Bernie, there's going to be nothing to stop us in American culture. You remember how we both came to New York a few years ago, poor and unknown, without a pot to piss in?"[1]

The pull and appeal of the Communist movement is described in other Farrell stories, such as "John Hitchcock," which treats a starving book reviewer attracted as well as repelled by the movement:

> Many writers . . . had gone left. In the circles in which he moved, Marxism, Revolution, the Communist Party, were constant subjects of loud discussion. . . . Few of those who participated in these discussions were well read in Marxism; few knew the history of the Russian Revolution; and the level of the discussions was generally rigid, sloganistic. The Communists and fellow travelers who defended the

> Party line consistently spoke with great confidence and self-assurance, with, literally, the conceit of history in their voices. . . . Most of them were in circumstances essentially similar to those in which John found himself. They were declassed intellectuals. They wanted to be writers, critics, employees in publishing houses, figures in the literary life of New York. Times were bad, very bad in the publishing business. America was in the depths of the Hoover era. There was widespread unemployment. There were riots, starvation, hunger marches. American economy was shaken. The future looked miserable. The declassed intellectuals were insecure, shaky, worried. They did not know where to turn. The effort to survive harried them, warped their character. Communists and fellow travelers spoke to them with assurance and self-confidence, convinced that they were absolutely right.[2]

Fear and insecurity made them more susceptible to the pull; there was also idealism—the kind of idealism which moved Bernard Carr during the 1927 Sacco-Vanzetti demonstration (and which he tended to associate with the Communists). As Farrell later wrote: "Stalinism was . . . a house of cultural assignation, where one guy could get two girls for the night, the glamour girl of success, and poor little Nell, the beautiful but ragged proletarian girl of integrity."[3] Yet, as Farrell's stories reveal—and as the record authenticates—for most of the plebeian writers the success was short-lived. Many pro-Stalinists (such as Henry Roth, Robert Cantwell, Jack Conroy, Clara Weatherwax, Leane Zugsmith, Edwin Seaver, Isadore Schneider, Mike Gold, Edwin Rolfe, and Edward Newhouse) ended up writing little fiction, and much of that was soon forgotten. And, like many other characters in Farrell's stories, his literary representations of these pro-Stalinist writers end up as middle-aged men with lost dreams.[4] . . .

The Bernard Carr trilogy, although it relies heavily on Farrell's personal experiences, was intended to portray the process of the political and moral corruption of writers in the 1930's. Carr was to become the half-willing prey of Stalinism at first, and then probably fall victim to commercial corruption. Obviously the original plan never materialized. And if one studies the Carr trilogy seeking an autobiographical representation of Farrell's experiences in the thirties, the books are especially disconcerting because they compress nearly fifteen subsequent years into the story. Thus Carr's break with the Stalinists in *Yet Other Waters* becomes a separation from the revolutionary movement per se. As one commentator noted, *Yet Other Waters* is not at all the kind of book Farrell would have written in the thirties or early forties. It has the distinct flavor of Farrell's views of the very late forties and after.[5]

For example, in *Yet Other Waters* the Trotskyists are presented essentially as a wing of the Stalinist movement—an opinion Farrell came to hold during those later years in direct contradiction to his earlier views. This portrayal is accomplished through the character of Lester Owens (suggestive of James Rorty), the anarchist poet who once served on the editorial board of *Mass Action*. In *Yet Other Waters*, Owens organizes an Open Letter of Protest against the Stalinists' disruption of a Socialist party meeting. Owens explains to Carr that although Leon Trotsky was a great man, his followers are about as bad as the Stalinists. He describes how the Trotskyists broke up a Non-Partisan Labor Committee because they (the Trotskyists) were planning to amalgamate with another group. The period of brief collaboration with the Trotskyists, for Owens, was simply a "second merry-go-round." Consequently, when Carr draws back from the Stalinists, he is left only with some vague literary projects and his shaky relationship with his wife as alternatives to politics. Although it concerns the 1930's, *Yet Other Waters* is in viewpoint a novel of the late forties and early fifties, and can be fully assessed only in the context of Farrell's political and personal life in those years. Nevertheless, this *roman à clef* about the tribulations of literary intellectuals is in the genre which seems most typical of novelists in the radical anti-Stalinist current. . . .

It was frequently because of their approach to character development that Farrell judged novels of the pro-Stalinist writers to be shallow; no doubt Farrell felt drawn to and was influenced by Trotsky on a literary plane because of the marvelous character portraits contained in *The History of the Russian Revolution*. Of these, Farrell once wrote:

> He [Trotsky] saw in everyone the representative of a class or of a social group, and in everyone's ideas he perceived their political consequences. His estimates of character, despite the charges of his critics, were generally not personal: they were political and intellectual. His brilliant character vignettes in *The History of the Russian Revolution* are actually social studies in miniature.[6]

Although the class differences of characters—for example, in the O'Neill-O'Flaherty books, Jim O'Neill, the worker, and Al O'Flaherty, the salesman—were in the material itself, Trotsky's approach may have helped Farrell make full use of all possibilities. The crowning achievement was probably Farrell's magnificent portrait of his father, represented by Jim O'Neill, as the embodiment of the American working man in *Father and Son*.[7] . . .

Especially when Farrell is compared to other American realists like Dreiser, his work shows indications of an international and historical consciousness which Trotsky's Marxism may have partially inspired and partially broadened. In a taped interview with David Madden, Farrell emphasized the importance of the first World War at the beginning of the second volume of the Studs Lonigan books, an event which resulted in an "unsure moral consciousness" after its occurrence.[8] Apparently an important conception underlying Farrell's forthcoming book *How Our Day Began* (of which some excerpts have been published), is the world-shaking opening of what Lenin deemed "the imperialist epoch" of war and revolution, in 1914:

> We were born the same year and, thus, we can say that we are of the same generation and have felt some of the same general pressures of history on our own lives. Our characters, our minds, our feelings, have grown, developed, evolved within the field where these pressures are at work. You are Dutch and Jewish and were born in Amsterdam, and I am American and Irish, and was born in Chicago. We are children of the twentieth century, but we were born before the twentieth century became fully what it is. In 1914, this century exploded in its own face, and ever since it has been face-lifting and doctoring itself, and seeking to develop a better mirror in order that it may see its own reflected image more clearly.[9]

Nevertheless, it is not the ⟨case⟩ that Farrell's outlook derives from a single source of influence—be it a man like Trotsky, a historic movement like socialism, or a liberal philosophy like pragmatism. Rather, what has been demonstrated is how Farrell's social, moral, and political concerns not only underlie much of his fiction but also how they are expressed in his fiction—sometimes more directly than at other times. A comprehensive and judicious assessment of Farrell's contributions to American letters is thus impossible without taking into account his long and intense involvement with Marxism and Trotskyism. If Farrell's work had been exclusively provincial rather than intertwined with political events of the day (even, in some instances, virtually rotating around international events), then one might be justified in ignoring the relationship between Farrell's literary output and his involvement with Trotsky and revolutionary Marxism. But Farrell's work is not provincial—nor divorced from his Marxist experience.

Notes

1. *Yet Other Waters* (New York: Vanguard, 1952), p. 10.
2. *When Boyhood Dreams Come True* (New York: Signet, 1953), p. 149.
3. Unpublished manuscript, Farrell Collection.
4. This is especially true of "The Martyr."
5. David Sanders, "Pattern of Rejection: Three American Novelists and the Communist Party Line, 1919–1949," Diss. U.C.L.A., 1956, p. 266.
6. *Partisan Review*, 7 (September–October 1940), 390.
7. The significance of the character Jim O'Neill was captured in Stephen Vincent Benét's review of *Father and Son* in the *Saturday Review of Literature*, 23 (October 12, 1940), 40.
8. David Madden, ed., *Talks with Authors* (Carbondale: Southern Illinois University Press, 1968), p. 94.
9. "How Our Day Began," *The Smith*, 3 (February 15, 1968), 9.

WILLIAM FAULKNER

1897–1962

William Harrison Faulkner was born in New Albany, Mississippi, on September 25, 1897, into the Falkner family, which had lived in northern Mississippi since before the Civil War. In 1902 the family moved to Oxford, Mississippi, where Faulkner spent most of his life, and which forms the basis for the town of Jefferson in his Yoknapatawpha cycle. A poor student, he left high school after tenth grade, but taught himself French in order to read the Symbolist poets and read widely in modern English literature. After the First World War, in which he was enrolled in the Royal Flying Corps in Toronto but did not see action, he studied for one year at the University of Mississippi, and was variously employed. His first publication was a volume of poems, *The Marble Faun* (1924); apparently as a result of a printer's error, a "u" was added to his family name, and was kept by the author in subsequent works.

After six months in New Orleans, Faulkner visited Europe, returning on the publication of his first novel, *Soldiers' Pay*, in 1926. The Yoknapatawpha cycle began to appear in 1929, with *Sartoris* and *The Sound and the Fury*, followed in 1930 by *As I Lay Dying*. Early critical attention turned to notoriety with the publication of *Sanctuary* (1931) on account of the novel's sensational subject matter. *Light in August* (1932) and *Absalom, Absalom!* (1936) appeared to have established Faulkner, but by the early 1940s he was neglected in America and had to earn a living as a script writer in Hollywood.

Faulkner's second and enduring rise to fame began in 1946 with the publication of *The Portable Faulkner*, edited by Malcolm Cowley. He published *Intruder in the Dust* in 1948. His *Collected Stories* (1950) won him a National Book Award, and the same year he was awarded the Nobel Prize for Literature for 1949 and traveled to Stockholm to make a speech of acceptance which has become famous. Thus established as a public figure, he traveled abroad for the State Department, visiting South America in 1954 and 1961, the Far East in 1955, and Europe in 1955 and 1957. From 1957 to 1958 he was writer in residence at the University of Virginia. He was awarded the Pulitzer Prize twice, for *The Town* (1957) and *The Reivers* (1962). Among his other books are *The Unvanquished* (1938); *Go Down, Moses* (1942); *Requiem for a Nun* (1951); and *A Fable* (1954).

William Faulkner married in 1929 and had one daughter. He died of a heart attack in Oxford, Mississippi, on July 6, 1962.

Personal

⟨To Malcolm Cowley, October 17 and November 14, 1945.⟩ I had no idea Faulkner was in bad shape and very happy you are putting together the Portable of him. He has the most talent of anybody and he just needs a sort of conscience that isn't there. Certainly if no nation can exist half free and half slave no man can write half whore and half straight. But he will write absolutely perfectly straight and then go on and on and not be able to end it. I wish the christ I owned him like you'd own a horse and train him like a horse and race him like a horse—only in writing. How beautifully he can write and as simple and as complicated as autumn or as spring.

I'll try and write him and cheer him up.

⟨To William Faulkner, July 23, 1947.⟩ You are a better writer than Fielding or any of those guys and you should just know it and keep on writing. You have things writen that come back to me better than any of them and I am not dopy, really. You shouldn't read the shit about liveing writers. You should always write your best against dead writers that we know what stature (not stature: evocative power) that they have and beat them one by one. Why do you want to fight Dostoevsky in your first fight? Beat Turgenieff—which we both did soundly and for time which I hear tick too with a pressure of 205 over 115 (not bad for the way things have run at all). Then nail yourself

DeMaupassant (tough boy until he got the old rale. Still dangerous for three rounds). Then try and take Stendhal. (Take him and we're all happy.) But don't fight with the poor pathological characters of our time (we won't name). You and I can both beat Flaubert who is our most respected, honored master. But to do that you have to be able to accept the command of a battalion when it is given (when you are a great company commander), to relinquish it to be second in command of a regiment (walk with shits nor lose the common touch) and then be able to take a regiment when you loathe the takeing of it and were happy where you were (or were unhappy but didn't want to go over Niagara Falls in a barrel) (I can't go up higher in this hierarchy because have no higher experience and anyway probably bore the shit out of you). Anyway I am your Bro. if you want one that writes and I'd like us to keep in touch.

⟨To Lillian Ross, February 20, 1953.⟩ Thanks very much for your letter and the news about Mr. Faulkner the writer. What's he doing in N.Y. again? Thought he never left that little old Homestead in Mississippi.

I cannot help out very much with the true dope on God as I have never played footy-footy with him; nor been a cane brake God hopper; nor won the Nobel prize. It would be best to get the true word on God from Mr. Faulkner.

I know the same amount about God as you do. Have not been vouchsafed any revelations. It is quite possible that Mr. Faulkner sits at table with him each night and that the deity comforts him if he has a bad dream or wipes his mouth and helps him eat his corn pone or hominy grits or wheaties in the morning.

I hope Mr. Faulkner never forgets himself and gives it to the deity with his corn cob. It is nice to know he has good taste and judgement but, as one of my oldest friends, remember never to trust a man with a southern accent and never trust a God-hopper either North or South of the Macy-Dixie line.

You ask if I know what he means. What he means is that he is spooked to die and he is moving in on the side of the strongest battalions. We will fight it out here and if there are no reserves it is too Faulking bad and they will find what is left of Dog company on that hill.

Please do not quote me on any of the above as it is controversial.

Lillian I cannot help but think that people who talk about God as though they knew him intimately and had received The Word etc. are frauds. Faulkner has always been fairly fraudulent but it is only recently that he has introduced God when he is conning people. . . .

I have no message to give to Mr. Faulkner except to tell him I wish him the grace of a happy death and I hope he will not continue to write after he has lost his talent. Don't give him that message either. But that is what I would really tell him. —ERNEST HEMINGWAY, *Ernest Hemingway: Selected Letters, 1917–1961*, ed. Carlos Baker, 1981, pp. 603–4, 624–25, 769–72

Working at the big book ⟨probably *A Fable*⟩. . . . I know now—believe now—that this may be the last major, ambitious work; there will be short things, of course. I know now that I am getting toward the end, the bottom of the barrel. The stuff is still good, but I know now there is not very much more of it, a little trash comes up constantly now, which must be sifted out. And now, at last, I have some perspective on all I have done. I mean, the work apart from me, the work which I did, apart from what I am. . . . And now I realise for the first time what an amazing gift I had: uneducated in every formal sense, without even very literate, let alone literary, companions, yet to have made the things I made. I dont know where it came from. I dont know why God or gods or whoever it was, selected me to be the vessel. Believe me, this is not humility, false modesty: it is simply amazement. I wonder if you have ever had that thought about the work and the country man whom you know as Bill Faulkner—what little connection there seems to be between them.—WILLIAM FAULKNER, Letter to Joan Williams (April 29, 1953), *Selected Letters of William Faulkner*, ed. Joseph Blotner, 1977, p. 348

William Faulkner had a firm belief that the author writes the book and the publisher publishes it. He would bring in a manuscript, and I'd say, "Bill, do you have any ideas about the book jacket and the advertising?" Bill would say, "Bennett, that's your job. If I didn't think you did it well, I'd go somewhere else." The result was that William Faulkner got more attention in our office than most others, perhaps to prove to him that he was right in trusting us. . . .

One time he was going to be here for ten days, and we arranged all kinds of interviews for him—*The New York Times*, the *Herald Tribune*, *Time* magazine, and so forth. Everything was beautifully scheduled ahead of time. Faulkner arrived and he and I had dinner together. Hal Smith came along and also a gentleman named Dashiell Hammett, author of *The Maltese Falcon* and some of the best detective stories ever written.

Dash was quite a boy at putting away the liquor, and Hal was no slouch either. And as for Faulkner—well, I couldn't stand the pace. I went home, first saying to Bill, "Remember, there'll be a fellow from the *Times* at the office at ten o'clock in the morning." That was the last we saw of him until I got a call from the Algonquin Hotel several days later; Bill had gone into the bathroom, slipped down against the steam radiator and was badly burned. We rushed him to the hospital, where he spent a good part of his vacation. The day before he went home, I said, "Bill, aren't you ashamed of yourself? You come up here for your first vacation in five years and you spend the whole time in the hospital." Very quietly—he was always very quiet—Bill said, "Bennett, it was *my* vacation."

The maddening thing about Bill Faulkner was that he'd go off on one of those benders, which were sometimes deliberate, and when he came out of it, he'd come walking into the office clear-eyed, ready for action, as though he hadn't had a drink in six months. But during those bouts he didn't know what he was doing. He was helpless. His capacity wasn't very great; it didn't take too much to send him off. Occasionally, at a good dinner, with the fine wines and brandy he loved, he would miscalculate. Other times I think he pretended to be drunk to avoid doing something he didn't want to do.

Bill was one of the most impressive men I ever met. Though he was not tall, his bearing and his fine features made him distinguished-looking. Sometimes he wore what seemed to be rather weather-beaten clothes, but actually were outfits that he had had made to order in England. And he always took time to answer even the most trivial question. You'd say, "Nice day, Bill, isn't it?" and he'd stop and consider it as though you'd asked him something very important.

On November 10, 1950, when it was announced that William Faulkner had been awarded the Nobel Prize for Literature, he said he would not go to Stockholm to get the award. His daughter Jill, whom he adored, was by this time a young lady of seventeen, and when it was pointed out to him that the trip would be a wonderful experience for her, he finally consented. He called from Mississippi, gave us his measurements and asked us to rent a full-dress suit for him and have it ready by the time he arrived in New York.

Bill went to Stockholm and made a superb speech—but

he came back a little annoyed because the suit I'd rented for him had only one stripe on the pants, and he discovered that European dress suits had two stripes. But he concluded, "You know, Bennett, I think I'll keep that suit."

I said, "What do you mean? I rented it. It's got to go back."

He said, "You just treat me to that suit. I'm going to keep it!"

I don't know whether he ever wore it again, but he took it back home with him.

Well, now he was famous and recognized as one of the great American novelists. His previous books began to be in demand, although a lot of them had gone out of print for a while. Today they are all in print and all sell. They're classics. *A Fable* put him suddenly into the best-seller class. He was on a rising tide, and more colleges were beginning to make him "Required Reading."

I got a call one day from the governor of Mississippi. At first I thought somebody was kidding me. (Norman Cousins of *The Saturday Review* was always identifying himself as the President, or something like that.) But it *was* the governor of Mississippi, and he said, "You've got to do me a favor, Mr. Cerf. This great sovereign state of Mississippi wants to give a dinner in honor of our Nobel Prize winner, William Faulkner, but he won't even talk to me."

I said, "What do you mean?"

He said, "I've called him about five times. He won't come to the phone. And all we want is to fix up a dinner in his honor. I want you to tell him this."

I said, "Well, he's in the middle of a novel. When he's working on a book, he doesn't like to be interrupted. But I'll see what I can do."

I immediately called Bill, who was in Oxford, and said, "Bill, I hear you won't talk to the governor of Mississippi."

He said, "That's right."

I said, "Well, all he wants is for the state to give a dinner in your honor."

And Bill said, "When I needed Mississippi, they had no respect for me. And now that I've got the Nobel Prize, you tell the governor of Mississippi he can go . . ."

When I called back the governor I couldn't quote Bill exactly, so I said, "It's as I suspected, Governor. He's in the middle of a novel. I'm terribly sorry, but he can't be disturbed."

How we laughed over this!

As a man he was so utterly without guile. He would come into the office—he made our office his headquarters when he came to New York—and peel off his coat. I had given him a pair of the red suspenders the Stork Club handed out to favored patrons, and Bill loved them. He would sit there in those red suspenders, smoking a pipe and reading mystery paperbacks. He liked mystery stories. When young writers would come in I'd say, "How would you like to meet William Faulkner?" This always gave them quite a thrill. I'd walk them in, and they'd see this man reading, with his feet up and the red suspenders and the pipe. And I'd say, "This is William Faulkner." And Bill would take the pipe out of his mouth and affably say "Howdy" and return to his book. . . .

The very last time we were with him was at "21" in 1962. It was then that he talked to me about Albert Erskine, who became his editor after Saxe Commins died. Faulkner said, "You know, I think Albert is the best book editor I know." I said, "Golly, Bill, coming from William Faulkner, that's quite an encomium. Have you told Albert?" He paused for a minute, then said, "No, I haven't. Bennett, when I've got a horse that's running good, I don't stop him to give him some sugar."

It had always been Faulkner's plan that when he finished the third volume of the Snopes trilogy, it should be done as a set: *The Hamlet, The Town, The Mansion*—the three separate books about the Snopes family which he wrote over a period of many years. When the manuscript of *The Mansion* was delivered, Albert pointed out that there were certain discrepancies among the three volumes. Bill explained calmly, "That doesn't prove a thing, Albert. As I wrote those books, I got to know the people better. By the time I did the third volume, I knew a lot more about them than I did in the first volume"—as though they were actually real people.—BENNETT CERF, *At Random*, 1977, pp. 129–33

Before he began to write and long before he became famous, Faulkner learned to protect his privacy. He often sought adventures, and he persistently forced himself to take great chances: he wanted to be "man in his sorry clay braving chance and circumstance." But he remained divided and elusive. In some moods he simply enjoyed being outrageous; in others he tended to be evasive and deceptive; in still others he became deliberately misleading. Almost as deep as the shyness he felt toward strangers lay an aristocratic distaste for public exposure except on his own terms. Although he had committed no major crimes, nor even many acts he thought shameful, he still did not like people prying into his life. But he was cautious not only with rivals and strangers but also with members of his own family and with people he thought of as friends—which suggests that the sources of his wariness go back to the beginning. Our earliest accounts of him vary remarkably, and what they imply, later recollections confirm: that he developed early both a need and a capacity for establishing a wide variety of carefully delimited relationships with the people around him.

Since the implications of Faulkner's kind of cautious variety are subtle and diverse, we must come to them slowly, but both his need and his capacity for such variety can be located. During his earliest years he experienced an unusually strong sense of holistic unity with his family, and especially with his mother. From these years, he gathered a sense of his world as blessed and of himself as virtually omnipotent. Although he suffered no great trauma, he lost this double sense of well-being at an early age, and he found the experience painful. Troubled in part by the loss itself and in part by the feeling that those who had bequeathed blessedness had also destroyed it, he emerged from childhood determined to control his relations to his world. In the small, seemingly limited towns in which he grew up, he met a variety of people both within and beyond his prominent, extended family, and he had easy access to all of them. Moving among them as a sensitive, curious boy, he tended to approach them on their own terms, and as he did, different sides of his character began to emerge. But since he was wary and determined as well as curious, he kept himself to himself, not so much by pulling back as by cultivating highly stylized relationships with acquaintances, friends, and relatives alike—a habit that lasted a lifetime.

In the stories he was reading as well as in the manners he was acquiring, he discovered a variety of guises, roles, and masks that enabled him to keep people at a distance. Eventually a sense of urgency reinforced his sense of caution. From the twenties into the forties, he was driven by the feeling that he had great work to do; and even after his powers had begun to fade, he was dogged by the feeling that he had to remain a "man working." Yet the work he did, he did alone. When he was with other people, he tended to play—sometimes for the purpose of resting and sometimes for the purpose of putting "things over on people," but always for the purpose of protecting himself. Spurred by wariness and urgency, then by wariness and weariness, he insisted upon delimiting and stylizing his associations with people. As a result, many who saw him regularly, or at least repeatedly, saw him partially and yet took the discernible part for the evasive whole. The reports we have, then, are confused as well as confusing, not only because some people have inevitably claimed to know him better than they did, nor merely because some friends and relatives have tried to settle old grievances, but also because he was a shy and troubled boy who became a shy and troubled man. Throughout his life—from the years of apprenticeship through the years of great innovation and achievement to the years of painful decline—his manners tended to be formal, his statements formulaic, and his life ceremonial.

Like his life, Faulkner's art serves the double purpose of deception and expression. Unlike his life, which shows much change and little development, his art shows great development as well as great change. The same man who insisted on establishing fixed, stylized relations with other people insisted on cultivating fluid and intimate relations with his fictions and his characters. During his career as a poet, when his voice remained rather directly his own, his art tended to reiterate his manners: it was primarily a way of controlling and delimiting his interaction with his world. As he began writing prose, however, he began mastering techniques and strategies that permitted greater displacement and disguise. His art not only became more supple and subtle as it became more indirect; it also became more personal. Though it remained his way of insisting on unity and harmony, it became his way of confronting the radical variety, fluidity, and power both of his world and of his own consciousness. The separations and losses that enter his poetry primarily as borrowed emotions and borrowed phrases soon began to shape his fiction. In the years of his greatness, he permitted even the most familiar and essential demarcations—clear beginnings and endings—to become ghostly. Although he continued to seek a formal, ceremonial life, he experimented in art with the dissolution of everything: one part of the radically venturesome quality of his writing derives from his willingness to brave the loss of all familiar procedures and the disintegration of all familiar forms. His fictions are replete with false starts, hesitations, and regressions; and they insist upon giving us, not beginnings, harmonies, and endings, but the sense of beginnings, the sense of harmonies, the sense of endings. In his novels and stories, forms flow, alter, disintegrate, displacing and replacing one another without end. Yet, if one part of the richness of his art comes from all the things it resists, withholds, and disguises, another part comes from all the things it explores, discloses, and bequeathes.—DAVID MINTER, "Preface" to *William Faulkner: His Life and Work*, 1980, pp. xi–xii

General

Isn't there something familiar about ⟨the nature of Faulkner's time⟩? This unspeakable present, leaking at every seam, these sudden invasions of the past, this emotional order, the opposite of the voluntary and intellectual order that is chronological but lacking in reality, these memories, these monstrous and discontinous obsessions, these intermittences of the heart—are not these reminiscent of the lost and recaptured time of Marcel Proust? I am not unaware of the differences between the two; I know, for instance, that for Proust salvation lies in time itself, in the full reappearance of the past. For Faulkner, on the contrary, the past is never lost, unfortunately; it is always there, it is an obsession. One escapes from the temporal world only through mystic ecstasies. A mystic is always a man who wishes to forget something, his self or, more often, language or objective representations. For Faulkner, time must be forgotten.

> 'Quentin, I give you the mausoleum of all hope and desire; it's rather excruciatingly apt that you will use it to gain the reductio ad absurdum of all human experience which can fit your individual needs no better than it fitted his or his father's. I give it to you not that you may remember time, *but that you might forget it now and then for a moment* and not spend all your breath trying to conquer it. Because no battle is ever won he said. They are not even fought. The field only reveals to man his own folly and despair, and victory is an illusion of philosophers and fools.'

It is because he has forgotten time that the hunted negro in *Light in August* suddenly achieves his strange and horrible happiness.

> It's not when you realize that nothing can help you—religion, pride, anything—it's when you realize that you don't need any aid.

But for Faulkner, as for Proust, time is, above all, *that which separates*. One recalls the astonishment of the Proustian heroes who can no longer enter into their past loves, of those lovers depicted in *Les Plaisirs et les jours*, clutching their passions, afraid they will pass and knowing they will. We find the same anguish in Faulkner.

> . . . people cannot do anything very dreadful at all, they cannot even remember tomorrow what seemed dreadful today.

and

> . . . a love or a sorrow is a bond purchased without design and which matures willynilly and is recalled without warning to be replaced by whatever issue the gods happen to be floating at the time.

To tell the truth, Proust's fictional technique *should have been* Faulkner's. It was the logical conclusion of his metaphysics. But Faulkner is a lost man, and it is because he feels lost that he takes risks and pursues his thought to its uttermost consequences. Proust is a Frenchman and a classicist. The French lose themselves only a little at a time and always manage to find themselves again. Eloquence, intellectuality and a liking for clear ideas were responsible for Proust's retaining at least the semblance of chronology.

The basic reason for this relationship is to be found in a very general literary phenomenon. Most of the great contemporary authors, Proust, Joyce, Dos Passos, Faulkner, Gide and Virginia Woolf, have tried, each in his own way, to distort time. Some of them have deprived it of its past and future in order to reduce it to the pure intuition of the instant; others, like Dos Passos, have made of it a dead and closed memory. Proust and Faulkner have simply decapitated it. They have deprived it of its future, that is, its dimension of deeds and freedom. Proust's heroes never undertake anything. They do, of course, make plans, but their plans remain stuck to them and cannot be projected like a bridge beyond the present. They are day-dreams that are put to flight by reality. The Albertine who appears is not the one we were expecting, and the expectation was merely a slight, inconsequential hesitation, limited to the moment only. As to Faulkner's heroes, they never look ahead. They face backwards as the car carries them along. The coming suicide which casts its shadow over Quentin's last day is not a human possibility; not for a second does Quentin envisage the possibility of *not* killing himself. This suicide is an immobile wall, a *thing* which he approaches backwards, and which he neither wants to nor can conceive.

. . . you seem to regard it merely as an experience that will whiten your hair overnight so to speak without altering your appearance at all.

It is not an *undertaking*, but a fatality. In losing its element of possibility it ceases to exist in the future. It is already present, and Faulkner's entire art aims at suggesting to us that Quentin's monologues and his last walk *are already* his suicide. This, I think, explains the following curious paradox: Quentin thinks of his last day in the past, like someone who is remembering. But in that case, since the hero's last thoughts coincide approximately with the bursting of his memory and its annihilation, who is remembering? The inevitable reply is that the novelist's skill consists in the choice of the present moment from which he narrates the past. And Faulkner, like Salacrou in *L'Inconnu d'Arras*, has chosen the infinitesimal instant of death. Thus, when Quentin's memory begins to unravel its recollections ("Through the wall I heard Shreve's bed-springs and then his slippers on the floor hishing. I got up . . .") *he is already dead*. All this artistry and, to speak frankly, all this illusion are meant, then, merely as substitutions for the intuition of the future lacking in the author himself. This explains everything, particularly the irrationality of time; since the present is the unexpected, the formless can be determined only by an excess of memories. We now also understand why duration is "man's characteristic misfortune". If the future has reality, time withdraws us from the past and brings us nearer to the future; but if you do away with the future, time is no longer that which separates, that which cuts the present off from itself. "You cannot bear to think that someday it will no longer hurt you like this." Man spends his life struggling against time, and time, like an acid, eats away at man, eats him away from himself and prevents him from fulfilling his human character. Everything is absurd. "Life is a tale told by an idiot, full of sound and fury, signifying nothing."

But is man's time without a future? I can understand that the nail's time, or the clod's or the atom's is a perpetual present. But is man a thinking nail? If you begin by plunging him into universal time, the time of planets and nebulae, of tertiary flexures and animal species, as into a bath of sulphuric acid, then the question is settled. However, a consciousness buffeted so from one instant to another ought, *first of all*, to be a consciousness and then, *afterwards*, to be temporal; does anyone believe that time can come to it from the outside? Consciousness can "exist within time" only on condition that it become time as a result of the very movement by which it becomes consciousness. It must become "temporalized", as Heidegger says. We can no longer arrest man at each present and define him as "the sum of what he has". The nature of consciousness implies, on the contrary, that it project itself into the future. We can understand what it is only through what it will be. It is determined in its present being by its own possibilities. This is what Heidegger calls "the silent force of the possible". You will not recognize within yourself Faulkner's man, a creature bereft of possibilities and explicable only in terms of what he has been. Try to pin down your consciousness and probe it. You will see that it is hollow. In it you will find only the future.

I do not even speak of your plans and expectations. But the very gesture that you catch in passing has meaning for you only if you project its fulfilment out of it, out of yourself, into the not-yet. This very cup, with its bottom that you do not see—that you might see, that is, at the end of a movement you have not yet made—this white sheet of paper, whose underside is hidden (but you could turn over the sheet) and all the stable and bulky objects that surround us display their most immediate and densest qualities in the future. Man is not the sum of what he has, but the totality of what he does not yet have, of what he might have. And if we steep ourselves thus in the future, is not the formless brutality of the present thereby attenuated? The single event does not spring on us like a thief, since it is, by nature, a Having-been-future. And if a historian wishes to explain the past, must he not first seek out its future? I am afraid that the absurdity that Faulkner finds in a human life is one that he himself has put there. Not that life is not absurd, but there is another kind of absurdity.

Why have Faulkner and so many other writers chosen this particular absurdity which is so un-novelistic and so untrue? I think we should have to look for the reason in the social conditions of our present life. Faulkner's despair seems to me to precede his metaphysics. For him, as for all of us, the future is closed. Everything we see and experience impels us to say, "This can't last." And yet change is not even conceivable, except in the form of a cataclysm. We are living in a time of impossible revolutions, and Faulkner uses his extraordinary art to describe our suffocation and a world dying of old age. I like his art, but I do not believe in his metaphysics. A closed future is still a future. "Even if human reality has nothing more 'before' it, even if 'its account is closed', its being is still determined by this 'self-anticipation'. The loss of all hope, for example, does not deprive human reality of its possibilities; it is simply a way of *being* toward these same possibilities." ⟨Heidegger, *Sein und Zeit*⟩—JEAN-PAUL SARTRE, "On *The Sound and the Fury:* Time in the Work of Faulkner" (1939), *Literary Essays*, tr. Annette Michelson, 1957, pp. 83–87

William Faulkner is really a traditional moralist, in the best sense. One principle holds together his thirteen books of prose—including his new novel, *The Wild Palms*—giving his work unity and giving it, at times, the significance that belongs to great myth. That principle is the Southern social-economic-ethical tradition which Mr. Faulkner possesses naturally, as a part of his sensibility.

However, Mr. Faulkner is a traditional man in a modern South. All around him the anti-traditional forces are at work; and he lives among evidences of their past activity. He could not fail to be aware of them. It is not strange, then, that his novels are, primarily, a series of related myths (or aspects of a single myth) built around the conflict between traditionalism and the anti-traditional modern world in which it is immersed.

In a re-arrangement of the novels, say for a collected edition, *The Unvanquished* might well stand first; for the action occurs earlier, historically, than in any other of the books, and it objectifies, in the essential terms of Mr. Faulkner's mythology, the central dramatic tension of his work. On one side of the conflict there are the Sartorises, recognizable human beings who act traditionally. Against them the invading Northern armies, and their diversified allies in the reconstruction era, wage open war, aiming to make the traditional actions of the Sartorises impossible.

The invaders are unable to cope with the Sartorises; but their invasion provides another antagonist with an occasion within which his special anti-Sartoris talent makes him singularly powerful. This antagonist is the landless poor-white horse-trader, Ab Snopes; his special talent is his low cunning as an *entrepreneur*. He acts without regard for the legitimacy of his means; he has no ethical code. In the crisis brought about by the war, he is enabled to use a member of the Sartoris family for his own advantage because, for the first time, he can be useful to the Sartorises. Moreover, he is enabled to make this Sartoris (Mrs. Rosa Millard) betray herself into an act of self-interest such as his, and to cause her death while using her as his tool.

The characters and the conflict are particular and credible. But they are also mythological. In Mr. Faulkner's mythology there are two kinds of characters; they are Sartorises or Snopeses, whatever the family names may be. And in the spiritual geography of Mr. Faulkner's work there are two worlds: the Sartoris world and the Snopes world. In all of his successful books, he is exploring the two worlds in detail, dramatizing the inevitable conflict between them.

It is a universal conflict. The Sartorises act traditionally; that is to say, they act always with an ethically responsible will. They represent vital morality, humanism. Being anti-traditional, the Snopeses are immoral from the Sartoris point-of-view. But the Snopeses do not recognize this point-of-view; acting only for self-interest, they acknowledge no ethical duty. Really, then, they are a-moral; they represent naturalism or animalism. And the Sartoris-Snopes conflict is fundamentally a struggle between humanism and naturalism.

As a universal conflict, it is important only philosophically. But it is important artistically, in this instance, because Mr. Faulkner has dramatized it convincingly in the terms of particular history and of actual life in his own part of the South—in the terms of his own tradition.

In *Sartoris*, which was published before *The Unvanquished* but which follows it in historical sequence, the conflict is between young Bayard Sartoris (the grandson of the Bayard Sartoris who was a youth in *The Unvanquished*) and the Snopes world of the 1920's. "General Johnston or General Forrest wouldn't have took a Snopes into his army at all," one of the characters say; but, significantly enough, one Flem Snopes has come, by way of local political usefulness, to be vice-president of old Bayard Sartoris' bank. Young Bayard's brother, John, has been killed in a war; but it is clear that it was a Snopes war and not a Sartoris war. Bayard himself is extremely conscious of his family's doom; he feels cheated because he did not die violently, in the tradition, like his brother; finally, he kills himself, taking up an aeroplane that he knows will crash.

The Snopes world has done more than oppose the Sartorises. It has weakened them internally (as it weakened Rosa Millard) in using them for its advantage; it has made them self-conscious, queer, psychologically tortured. Bayard Sartoris has something of the traditional instinct for noble and disinterested action, under a vital ethical code. But the strength is so warped internally by the psychological effects of the Snopes world upon it, and it is so alien to the habitual actions of that world, that it can only manifest itself in meaningless violence, ending in self-destruction.

The same pattern recurs, varied somewhat and handled in miniature, in the short story about the Sartorises—"There Was a Queen." Here the real conflict centers in Narcissa Benbow, the widow of young Bayard Sartoris, who has given herself to a detective in order to recover from his possession a collection of obscene letters that one of the Snopeses had written to her anonymously and afterwards stolen. The consciousness of Narcissa's deed kills the embodiment of the virile tradition, old Miss Jennie Sartoris (Mrs. DuPré). Narcissa's yielding to the detective is the result of the *formalization* of one aspect of her traditional morality—her pride—through the constant opposition of the Snopes world to it; this formalization allows the Snopes world to betray her into anti-traditionalism by creating a situation in which she must make a formalized response. It is a highly significant tactic. For the moment a tradition begins to be formalized into a code, it commences to lose vitality; when it is entirely formalized, it is dead—it becomes pseudo-tradition.

As early as *Soldiers' Pay* (1926) the same theme is the basis for Mr. Faulkner's organization of experience; and it is the best possible indication of the urgency of the theme with him that it should be central in his first novel. Mahon, the old Episcopal clergyman, conscious of sin, tolerant of human weakness, is still unaware of the vital opponent to his formalized, and so impotent, tradition—the a-morality with which history has surrounded him. Donald Mahon, his son, is brought home from the World War, dying; in him, the minister's code has faced anti-traditional history. Because Donald is not dead, the conflict must continue; locally, it is between the preacher and Cecily Saunders (Donald's fiancée before he went to war) with her family and associates who are typical of the new Jazz Era. Obviously, Cecily's world of jazz and flappers and sleek-haired jelly-beans represents the same anti-traditional historical movement that brought Flem Snopes into Bayard Sartoris' bank. The names and the settings are different; that is all.

In *The Sound and the Fury*, Quentin Compson represents all that is left of the Sartoris tradition. The rest of his family have either succumbed entirely to the Snopes world, like Jason Compson, or else have drugs to isolate them from it—Mr. Compson his fragments of philosophy, Uncle Maury his liquor, Mrs. Compson her religion and her invalidism, Benjy his idiocy. But Quentin's very body is "an empty hall echoing with sonorous defeated names." His world is peopled with "baffled, outraged ghosts"; and although Quentin himself is "still too young to deserve yet to be a ghost," he is one of them. However, it is evident that Quentin's traditionalism is far gone in the direction of formalization, with its concomitant lack of vitality; he is psychologically kin to Bayard Sartoris and to Narcissa Benbow. When he discovers that his sister Candace has been giving herself to the town boys of Jefferson, Mississippi, and is pregnant, he attempts to change her situation by telling their father that he has committed incest with her. It is a key incident. Quentin is attempting to transform Candace's yielding to the a-morality of the Snopes world into a sin, within the Sartoris morality; but the means he employs are more nearly pseudo-traditional and romantic than traditional; and he fails.

Quentin tells his father: "It was to isolate her out of the loud world so that it would have to flee us of necessity." Precisely. The loud world is the Snopes world, with which the Compson house has become thoroughly infected and to which it is subject. Quentin is really *striving toward the condition of tragedy* for his family; he is trying to transform meaningless degeneracy into significant doom. But because his moral code is no longer vital, he fails and ends in a kind of escapism, breaking his watch to put himself beyond time, finally killing himself to escape consciousness. Only he is aware of the real meaning of his struggle, which sets up the dramatic tension in *The Sound and the Fury*.

In a way, Quentin's struggle is Mr. Faulkner's own struggle as an artist. In *Sartoris*, Mr. Faulkner wrote of the name: "There is death in the sound of it, and a glamorous fatality." Sartoris—all that the name implies—is the tragic hero of his work; it is doomed, like any tragic hero. But the doom toward which the Sartoris world moves should be a noble one. In *Absalom, Absalom!* although apparently with great difficulty, as if he were wrestling with the Snopes world all the while, Mr. Faulkner finally achieves the presentation of a kind of "glamorous fatality" for the Sartoris world—embodied in Thomas Sutpen and his house.

The book is really a summary of the whole career of the

tradition—its rise, its fatal defects, its opponents, its decline, and its destruction. The action is of heroic proportions. The figures are larger than life; but, as Mr. T. S. Eliot has suggested of Tourneur's characters, they are all distorted to scale, so that the whole action has a self-subsistent reality. And the book ends with a ritualistic purgation of the doomed house, by fire, which is as nearly a genuine tragic scene as anything in modern fiction.

For the first time, Mr. Faulkner makes explicit here the contrast between traditional (Sartoris) man and modern (Snopes) man, dissociated into a sequence of animal functions, lacking in unity under essential morality. One of the characters says of traditional men:

> People too as we are, victims of a different circumstance, simpler and therefore, integer for integer, larger, more heroic and the figures therefore more heroic too, not dwarfed and involved but distinct, uncomplex who had the gift of loving once or dying once instead of being diffused and scattered creatures drawn blindly from a grab bag and assembled.

It was the world of these "diffused and scattered creatures" in which Quentin Compson lived; and it was the effort not to be "diffused and scattered"—to transform his own family's doom into the proportions of the world of Sutpen and Sartoris—that led to his death. But it is significant that it should be Quentin through whose gradual understanding the story of Sutpen is told, and that it should be Quentin who watches the final destruction of Sutpen's house. For Sutpen's tradition was defective, but it was not formalized as Quentin's was; and his story approaches tragedy.

As I Lay Dying stands a little apart from the rest of Mr. Faulkner's novels, but it is based upon the philosophical essence of his Sartoris-Snopes theme—the struggle between humanism and naturalism. The naif hill folk who appear in the book are poor and ungraceful, certainly; they are of low mentality; sexually, they are almost animalistic. But when Anse Bundren promises his dying wife that he will bury her in Jefferson, he sets up for himself an ethical duty which he recognizes as such—though not in these terms. It is the fulfillment of this obligation, in spite of constant temptation to abandon it, and in spite of multiplied difficulties put in his way by nature itself, that makes up the action of the novel.

Fundamentally, *As I Lay Dying* is a legend; and the procession of ragged, depraved hillmen, carrying Addie Bundren's body through water and through fire to the cemetery in Jefferson, while people flee from the smell and buzzards circle overhead—this progress is not unlike that of the medieval soul toward redemption. The allegories of Alanus de Insulis and the visions of Sister Hildegard of Bingen would yield a good many parallels. On a less esoteric plane, however, the legend is more instructive for us. Because they are simpler in mind and live more remotely from the Snopes world than the younger Sartorises and Compsons, the Bundrens are able to carry a genuine act of traditional morality through to its end. They are infected with a-morality; but it is the a-morality of physical nature, not the artificial, self-interested a-morality of the Snopeses. More heroism is possible among them than among the inhabitants of Jefferson. . . .

William Faulkner's myth finds expression in work that is definitely romantic; when he comes near to tragedy, it is the tragedy of Webster. His art, like Webster's, is tortured. In form, each of his novels resembles a late-Elizabethan blank verse line, where the meter is strained, threatens to break, sometimes breaks, but is always exciting. He is an original craftsman, making his own solutions to his problems of form, often blundering, but occasionally striking upon an effect that no amount of studious craftsmanship could achieve. Consequently, like Dostoievski, or like Miss Djuna Barnes in our own time, he is very special; and his work cannot be imitated except futilely, for he works within no general tradition of craft and hands on no tradition to his successors.

But Mr. Faulkner's difficulties of form derive, in part, from the struggle that he has to make to inform his material. The struggle is manifest, even in the prose itself. Discounting the results of plain carelessness in all of the books, the correlation between the fictions and the quality of the prose in Mr. Faulkner's books is instructive. It appears significant that *The Unvanquished* contains his least tortured, *Pylon* his most tortured prose.

He has worked to project in fiction the conflict between his inherent traditional values and the modern world; and the conflict has affected his fictional projection, so that all of his work is really a *striving toward* the condition of tragedy. He is the Quentin Compson or the Bayard Sartoris of modern fiction. He does not always fail; but when he does, his failure is like theirs—he ends in confused or meaningless violence. And for the same reasons: His heritage is theirs, and it is subject to the same opposition to which they are subject as characters. When he is partially successful, the result is tortured but major romantic art.

Now, in 1939, Mr. Faulkner's work may seem melodramatic. Melodrama differs from tragedy only in the amount of meaning that is subsistent in the pattern of events; and in our time the values of Mr. Faulkner's tradition are available to most men only historically, in the same way that, let us say, medieval values are available. The significance of the work as myth depends, then, upon the willingness of the reader to recover the meaning of the tradition—even historically. —GEORGE MARION O'DONNELL, "Faulkner's Mythology," *KR*, Summer 1939, pp. 285–99

. . . Mr. Faulkner's style, though often brilliant and always interesting, is all too frequently downright bad; and it has inevitably offered an all-too-easy mark for the sharpshooting of such alert critics as Mr. Wyndham Lewis. But if it is easy enough to make fun of Mr. Faulkner's obsessions for particular words, or his indifference and violence to them, or the parrotlike mechanical mysticism (for it is really like a stammer) with which he will go on endlessly repeating such favorites as 'myriad, sourceless, impalpable, outrageous, risible, profound,' there is nevertheless something more to be said for his passion for overelaborate sentence structure.

Overelaborate they certainly are, baroque and involuted in the extreme, these sentences: trailing clauses, one after another, shadowily in apposition, or perhaps not even with so much connection as that; parenthesis after parenthesis, the parenthesis itself often containing one or more parentheses—they remind one of those brightly colored Chinese eggs of one's childhood, which when opened disclosed egg after egg, each smaller and subtler than the last. It is as if Mr. Faulkner, in a sort of hurried despair, had decided to try to tell us everything, absolutely everything, every last origin or source or quality or qualification, and every possible future or permutation as well, in one terrifically concentrated effort: each sentence to be, as it were, a microcosm. And it must be admitted that the practice is annoying and distracting.

It is annoying, at the end of a sentence, to find that one does not know in the least what was the subject of the verb that dangles *in vacuo*—it is distracting to have to go back and sort out the meaning, track down the structure from clause to clause, then only to find that after all it doesn't much matter, and that the obscurity was perhaps neither subtle nor important. And to the extent that one *is* annoyed and distracted, and *does* thus go back and work it out, it may be at once added that Mr. Faulkner has defeated his own ends. One has had, of course, to emerge from the stream, and to step away from it, in order properly to see it; and as Mr. Faulkner works precisely by a process of *immersion*, of hypnotizing his reader into *remaining immersed* in his stream, this occasional blunder produces irritation and failure.

Nevertheless, despite the blunders, and despite the bad habits and the willful bad writing (and willful it obviously is), the style as a whole is extraordinarily effective; the reader *does* remain immersed, *wants* to remain immersed, and it is interesting to look into the reasons for this. And at once, if one considers these queer sentences not simply by themselves, as monsters of grammar or awkwardness, but in their relation to the book as a whole, one sees a functional reason and necessity for their being as they are. They parallel in a curious and perhaps inevitable way, and not without æsthetic justification, the whole elaborate method of *deliberately withheld meaning*, of progressive and partial and delayed disclosure, which so often gives the characteristic shape to the novels themselves. It is a persistent offering of obstacles, a calculated system of screens and obtrusions, of confusions and ambiguous interpolations and delays, with one express purpose; and that purpose is simply to keep the form—and the idea—fluid and unfinished, still in motion, as it were, and unknown, until the dropping into place of the very last syllable.

What Mr. Faulkner is after, in a sense, is a *continuum*. He wants a medium without stops or pauses, a medium which is always *of the moment*, and of which the passage from moment to moment is as fluid and undetectable as in the life itself which he is purporting to give. It is all inside and underneath, or as seen from within and below; the reader must therefore be steadily *drawn in*; he must be powerfully and unremittingly hypnotized inward and downward to that image-stream; and this suggests, perhaps, a reason not only for the length and elaborateness of the sentence structure, but for the repetitiveness as well. The repetitiveness, and the steady iterative emphasis—like a kind of chanting or invocation—on certain relatively abstract words ('sonorous, latin, *vaguely* eloquent'), has the effect at last of producing, for Mr. Faulkner, a special language, a conglomerate of his own, which he uses with an astonishing virtuosity, and which, although in detailed analysis it may look shoddy, is actually for his purpose a life stream of almost miraculous adaptability. At the one extreme it is abstract, cerebral, time-and-space-obsessed, tortured and twisted, but nevertheless always with a living *pulse* in it; and at the other it can be as overwhelming in its simple vividness, its richness in the actual, as the flood scenes in *The Wild Palms*.

Obviously, such a style, especially when allied with such a method, and such a *concern* for method, must make difficulties for the reader; and it must be admitted that Mr. Faulkner does little or nothing as a rule to make his highly complex 'situation' easily available or perceptible. The reader must simply make up his mind to go to work, and in a sense to coöperate; his reward being that there *is* a situation to be given shape, a meaning to be extracted, and that half the fun is precisely in watching the queer, difficult, and often so laborious, evolution of Mr. Faulkner's idea. And not so much idea, either, as form. For, like the great predecessor whom at least in this regard he so oddly resembles, Mr. Faulkner could say with Henry James that it is practically impossible to make any real distinction between theme and form. What immoderately delights him, alike in *Sanctuary, The Sound and the Fury, As I Lay Dying, Light in August, Pylon, Absalom, Absalom!* and now again in *The Wild Palms*, and what sets him above—shall we say it firmly—all his American contemporaries, is his continuous preoccupation with the novel *as form*, his passionate concern with it, and a degree of success with it which would clearly have commanded the interest and respect of Henry James himself. The novel as revelation, the novel as slice-of-life, the novel as mere story, do not interest him: these he would say, like James again, 'are the circumstances of the interest,' but not the interest itself. The interest itself will be the *use* to which these circumstances are put, the degree to which they can be organized.—CONRAD AIKEN, "William Faulkner: The Novel as Form," *At*, Nov. 1939, pp. 651–52

It is sometimes said that Faulkner's theme is the disintegration of the Southern traditional life. For instance, Malcolm Cowley, in his fine introduction to the *Portable Faulkner*, says that the violence of Faulkner's work is "an example of the Freudian method turned backward, being full of sexual nightmares that are in reality social symbols. It is somehow connected in the author's mind with what he regards as the rape and corruption of the South." And Maxwell Geismar, whose lack of comprehension of Faulkner strikes me as monumental, interprets Faulkner's work as merely Southern apologetics, as "the extreme hallucinations" of a "cultural psychosis."

It is true that Faulkner deals almost exclusively with the Southern scene, it is true that the conflict between past and present is a constant concern for him, it is true that the Civil War is always behind his work as a kind of backdrop, and it is true, or at least I think it is true, that in Faulkner's work there is the implication that Northern arms were the cutting edge of modernism. But granting all this, I should put the emphasis not in terms of South and North, but in terms of issues common to our modern world.

The Faulkner legend is not merely a legend of the South but of a general plight and problem. The modern world is in moral confusion. It does suffer from a lack of discipline, of sanction, of community of values, of a sense of mission. We don't have to go to Faulkner to find that out—or to find that it is a world in which self-interest, workableness, success provide the standards of conduct. It was a Yankee who first referred to the bitch goddess Success. It is a world in which the individual has lost his relation to society, the world of the power state in which man is a cipher. It is a world in which man is the victim of abstraction and mechanism, or at least, at moments, feels himself to be. It can look back nostalgically upon various worlds of the past, Dante's world of the Catholic synthesis, Shakespeare's world of Renaissance energy, or the world of our grandfathers who lived before Shiloh and Gettysburg, and feel loss of traditional values and despair in its own aimlessness and fragmentation. Any of those older worlds, so it seems now, was a world in which, as one of Faulkner's characters puts it, men "had the gift of living once or dying once instead of being diffused and scattered creatures drawn blindly from a grab bag and assembled"—a world in which men were, "integer for integer," more simple and complete.

At this point we must pause to consider an objection. Someone will say, and quite properly, that there never was a golden age in which man was simple and complete. Let us grant that. But we must grant that even with that realistic reservation man's conception of his own role and position has changed from time to time. It is unhistorical to reduce history to some dead level, and the mere fact that man in the modern world is worried about his role and position is in itself significant.

Again, it may be objected, and quite properly, that any old order that had satisfied human needs would have survived; that it is sentimental to hold that an old order is killed from the outside by certain wicked people or forces. But when this objection is applied to Faulkner it is based on a misreading of his work. The old order, he clearly indicates, did *not* satisfy human needs, did *not* afford justice, and therefore was "accurst" and held the seeds of its own ruin. But the point is this: the old order, even with its bad conscience and confusion of mind, even as it failed to live up to its ideal, cherished the concept of justice. Even in terms of the curse, the old order as opposed to the new order (in so far as the new order is equated with Snopesism) allowed the traditional man to define himself as human by setting up codes, ideas of virtue, however mistaken; by affirming obligations, however arbitrary; by accepting the risks of humanity. But Snopesism has abolished the concept, the very possibility of entertaining the idea of virtue. It is not a question of one idea and interpretation. It is simply that no idea of virtue is conceivable in the world in which practical success is the criterion.

Within the traditional world there had been a notion of truth, even if man in the flow of things could not readily define or realize his truth. Take, for instance, a passage from "The Bear."

> 'All right,' he said. 'Listen,' and read again, but only one stanza this time and closed the book and laid it on the table. 'She cannot fade, though thou has not thy bliss,' McCaslin said: 'Forever wilt thou love, and she be fair.'
>
> 'He's talking about a girl,' he said.
>
> 'He had to talk about something,' McCaslin said. Then he said, 'He was talking about truth. Truth is one. It doesn't change. It covers all things which touch the heart—honor and pride and pity and justice and courage and love. Do you see now?'

The important thing, then, is the presence of the concept of truth—that covers all things which touch the heart and define the effort of man to rise above the mechanical process of life.

When it is said, as it is sometimes said, that Faulkner is "backward-looking," the answer lies, I think, in the notion expressed above. The "truth" is neither of the past nor of the future. Or rather, it is of both. The constant ethical center of Faulkner's work is to be found in the glorification of human effort and human endurance, which are not confined to any one time. It is true that Faulkner's work contains a savage attack on modernity, but the values he admires *are* found in our time. The point is that they are found most often in people who are outside the stream of the dominant world, the "loud world," as it is called in *The Sound and the Fury*. Faulkner's world is full of "good" people—Byron Bunch, Lucas Beauchamp, Dilsey, Ike McCaslin, Uncle Gavin, Benbow, the justice of the peace in *The Hamlet*, Ratliff of the same book, Hightower of *Light in August*—we could make an impressive list, probably a longer list from Faulkner than from any other modern writer. "There are good men everywhere, at all times," Ike McCaslin says in "Delta Autumn."

It is not ultimately important whether the traditional order (Southern or other) as depicted by Faulkner fits exactly the picture which critical historical method provides. Let it be granted that Faulkner does simplify the matter. What remains important is that his picture of the traditional order has a symbolic function in contrast to the modern world which he gives us. It is a way of embodying his values—his "truth."
—ROBERT PENN WARREN, "William Faulkner" (1946–50), *Selected Essays*, 1958, pp. 65–68

I feel that this award was not made to me as a man, but to my work—a life's work in the agony and sweat of the human spirit, not for glory and least of all for profit, but to create out of the materials of the human spirit something which did not exist before. So this award is only mine in trust. It will not be difficult to find a dedication for the money part of it commensurate with the purpose and significance of its origin. But I would like to do the same with the acclaim too, by using this moment as a pinnacle from which I might be listened to by the young men and women already dedicated to the same anguish and travail, among whom is already that one who will some day stand here where I am standing.

Our tragedy today is a general and universal physical fear so long sustained by now that we can even bear it. There are no longer problems of the spirit. There is only the question: When will I be blown up? Because of this, the young man or woman writing today has forgotten the problems of the human heart in conflict with itself which alone can make good writing because only that is worth writing about, worth the agony and the sweat.

He must learn them again. He must teach himself that the basest of all things is to be afraid; and, teaching himself that, forget it forever, leaving no room in his workshop for anything but the old verities and truths of the heart, the old universal truths lacking which any story is ephemeral and doomed—love and honor and pity and pride and compassion and sacrifice. Until he does so, he labors under a curse. He writes not of love but of lust, of defeats in which nobody loses anything of value, of victories without hope and, worst of all, without pity or compassion. His griefs grieve on no universal bones, leaving no scars. He writes not of the heart but of the glands.

Until he relearns these things, he will write as though he stood among and watched the end of man. I decline to accept the end of man. It is easy enough to say that man is immortal simply because he will endure: that when the last ding-dong of doom has clanged and faded from the last worthless rock hanging tideless in the last red and dying evening, that even then there will still be one more sound: that of his puny inexhaustible voice, still talking. I refuse to accept this. I believe that man will not merely endure: he will prevail. He is immortal, not because he alone among creatures has an inexhaustible voice, but because he has a soul, a spirit capable of compassion and sacrifice and endurance. The poet's, the writer's, duty is to write about these things. It is his privilege to help man endure by lifting his heart, by reminding him of the courage and honor and hope and pride and compassion and pity and sacrifice which have been the glory of his past. The poet's voice need not merely be the record of man, it can be one of the props, the pillars to help him endure and prevail.
—WILLIAM FAULKNER, Address upon receiving the Nobel prize for Literature (1950), *Essays, Speeches and Public Letters*, ed. James B. Merriwether, 1965, pp. 119–20

He is a good writer when he is good and could be better than anyone if he knew how to finish a book and didn't get that old heat prostration like Honest Sugar Ray at the end. I enjoy reading him when he is good but always feel like hell that he is not better. I wish him luck and he needs it because he has the one great and un-curable defect; you can't re-read him. When you re-read him you are conscious all the time of how he fooled you the first time. In truly good writing no matter how many times you read it you do not know how it is done. That is because there is a mystery in all great writing and that mystery does not dis-sect out. It continues and it is always valid. Each time you re-read you see or learn something new. You do not just see the mechanics of how you were tricked in the first place. Bill had some of this at one time. But it is long gone. A real writer should be able to make this thing which we do not define with a simple declarative sentence.

Criticism class is out.—ERNEST HEMINGWAY, Letter to Harvey Breit (June 27, 1952), *Ernest Hemingway: Selected Letters: 1917–1961*, ed. Carlos Baker, 1981, p. 770

Professor Randall Stewart, in his very stimulating little book *American Literature and Christian Doctrine*, asserts that "Faulkner embodies and dramatizes the basic Christian concepts so effectively that he can with justice be regarded as one of the most profoundly Christian writers in our time. There is everywhere in his writings the basic premise of Original Sin: everywhere the conflict between the flesh and the spirit. One finds also the necessity of discipline, of trial by fire in the furnace of affliction, of sacrifice and the sacrificial death, of redemption through sacrifice. Man in Faulkner is a heroic, tragic figure." This is a view with which I am in basic sympathy. I agree heartily with Professor Stewart on the matter of Faulkner's concern with what he calls "original sin," and with Faulkner's emphasis upon discipline, sacrifice, and redemption. But to call Faulkner "one of the most profoundly Christian writers in our time" seems somewhat incautious. Perhaps it would be safer to say that Faulkner is a profoundly religious writer; that his characters come out of a Christian environment, and represent, whatever their shortcomings and whatever their theological heresies, Christian concerns; and that they are finally to be understood only by reference to Christian premises.

. . . A very important theme in his earlier work is the discovery of evil, which is part of man's initiation into the nature of reality. That brilliant and horrifying early novel *Sanctuary* is, it seems to me, to be understood primarily in terms of such an initiation. Horace Benbow is the sentimental idealist, the man of academic temper, who finds out that the world is not a place of moral tidiness or even of justice. He discovers with increasing horror that evil is rooted in the very nature of things. As an intellectual, he likes to ponder meanings and events, he has a great capacity for belief in ideas, and a great confidence in the efficacy of reason. What he comes to discover is the horrifying presence of evil, its insidiousness, and its penetration of every kind of rational or civilized order. There is in this story, to be sure, the unnatural rape of a seventeen-year-old girl by the gangster Popeye, and the story of Popeye's wanton murder of Tommy, but Horace Benbow might conceivably accept both of these things as the kinds of cruel accidents to which human life is subject. What crumples him up is the moral corruption of the girl, which follows on her rape; she actually accepts her life in the brothel and testifies at the trial in favor of the man who had abducted her. What Horace also discovers is that the forces of law and order are also corruptible. His opponent in the trial, the district attorney, plays fast and loose with the evidence and actually ensures that the innocent man will not only be convicted but burned to death by a mob. And what perhaps Horace himself does not discover (but it is made plainly evident to the reader) is that Horace's betrayal at the trial is finally a bosom betrayal: Horace's own sister gives the district attorney the tip-off that will allow him to defeat her brother and make a mockery of justice. Indeed, Horace's sister, the calm and serene Narcissa, is, next to Popeye, the most terrifying person in the novel. She simply does not want her brother associated with people like the accused man, Lee Goodwin, the bootlegger, and his common-law wife. She exclaims to her brother, "I don't see that it makes any difference who [committed the murder]. The question is, are you going to stay mixed up with it?" And she sees to it with quiet and efficient ruthlessness that the trial ends at the first possible date, even though this costs an innocent man's life.

Sanctuary is clearly Faulkner's bitterest novel. It is a novel in which the initiation which every male must undergo is experienced in its most shattering and disillusioning form. Horace not only discovers the existence of evil: he experiences it, not as an abstract idea but as an integral portion of reality. After he has had his interview with Temple Drake in the brothel, he thinks: "Perhaps it is upon the instant that we realize, admit, that there is a logical pattern to evil, that we die," and he thinks of the expression he had once seen in the eyes of a dead child and in the eyes of the other dead: "the cooling indignation, the shocked despair fading, leaving two empty globes in which the motionless world lurked profoundly in miniature.

One of the most important connections has already been touched upon in what I have said earlier. Horace Benbow's initiation into the nature of reality and the nature of evil is intimately associated with his discovery of the true nature of woman. His discovery is quite typical of Faulkner's male characters. In the Faulknerian notion of things, men have to lose their innocence, confront the hard choice, and through a process of initiation discover reality. The women are already in possession of this knowledge, naturally and instinctively. That is why in moments of bitterness Faulkner's male characters—Mr. Compson in *The Sound and the Fury*, for example—assert that women are not innocent. Mr. Compson tells his son Quentin: "Women are like that[;] they don't acquire knowledge of people[. Men] are for that[. Women] are just born with a practical fertility of suspicion. . . . they have an affinity for evil[—]for supplying whatever the evil lacks in itself [—]drawing it about them instinctively as you do bed clothing in slumber. . . ." Again, "Women only use other people's code of honour."

I suppose that we need not take these Schopenhauerian profundities of the bourbon-soaked Mr. Compson too seriously. It might on the whole be more accurate to say that Faulkner's women lack the callow idealism of the men, have fewer illusions about human nature, and are less trammeled by legalistic distinctions and niceties of any code of conduct.

Faulkner's view of women, then, is radically old-fashioned—even medieval. Woman is the source and sustainer of virtue and also a prime source of evil. She can be either, because she is, as man is not, always a little beyond good and evil. With her powerful natural drives and her instinct for the concrete and personal, she does not need to agonize over her decisions. There is no code for her to master—no initiation for her to undergo. For this reason she has access to a wisdom which is veiled from man; and man's codes, good or bad, are always, in their formal abstraction, a little absurd in her eyes. Women are close to nature; the feminine principle is closely related to the instinctive and natural: woman typically manifests pathos rather than ethos. . . .

Evil for Faulkner . . . involves a violation of nature and runs counter to the natural appetites and affections. And yet . . . the converse is not true; Faulkner does not consider the natural and instinctive and impulsive as automatically and necessarily good. Here I think rests the best warrant for maintaining that Faulkner holds an orthodox view of man and reality. For his men, at least, cannot be content merely with being natural. They cannot live merely by their instincts and natural appetites. They must confront the fact of evil. They are constrained to moral choices. They have to undergo a test of their courage, in making and abiding by the choice. They achieve goodness by discipline and effort. This proposition is perhaps most fully and brilliantly illustrated in Faulkner's story "The Bear." Issac McCaslin, when he comes of age, decides to repudiate his inheritance. He refuses to accept his father's plantation and chooses to earn his living as a carpenter and to live in a rented room. There are two powerful motives that shape this decision: the sacramental view of nature which he has been taught by the old hunter, Sam Fathers, and the discovery of his grandfather's guilt in his treatment of one of his slaves: the grandfather had incestuously begotten a child upon his own half-Negro daughter.

"The Bear" is thus a story of penance and expiation, as also of a difficult moral decision made and maintained.

. . . I am very anxious to sketch in, even at the risk of overbold strokes, the general nature of Faulkner's conception of good and evil, and so I mean to stand by this summary: Faulkner sees the role of man as active; man makes choices and lives up to the choices. Faulkner sees the role of woman as characteristically fostering and sustaining. She undergirds society, upholding the family and community mores, sending her men out into battle, including the ethical battle. This generalization I believe, is, if oversimplified, basically true. And I should like to relate it to Faulkner's "Calvinistic" Protestantism. In so far as his Calvinism represents a violent repression and constriction of natural impulse, a denial of nature itself, Faulkner tends to regard it as a terrible and evil thing. And the natural foil to characters who have so hardened their hearts in accordance with their notion of a harsh and vindictive God is the feminine principle as exemplified by a person like Lena Grove, the heroine of *Light in August*. Lena has a childlike confidence in herself and in mankind. She is a creature of warm natural sympathies and a deep instinctive commitment to her natural function.

But Faulkner has still another relation to Calvinistic Protestantism. Insofar as the tradition insists that man must be brought up to the urgency of decision, must be set tests of courage and endurance, must have his sinews strung tight for some moral leap or his back braced so as to stand firm against the push of circumstance, Faulkner evidently derives from this tradition. From it may be derived the very necessity that compels his male characters to undergo an initiation. The required initiation may be analogous to the crisis of conversion and the character's successful entrance into knowledge of himself, analogous to the sinner's experiencing salvation.

On the conscious level, Faulkner is obviously a Protestant anticleric, fascinated, but also infuriated, by some of the more violently repressive features of the religion that dominates his country. This matter is easily illustrated. One of his masterpieces, *Light in August*, provides a stinging criticism of the harsher aspects of Protestantism. Indeed a basic theme in *Light in August* is man's strained attempt to hold himself up in a rigid aloofness above the relaxed female world. The struggle to do so is, as Faulkner portrays it in this novel, at once monstrous, comic, and heroic, as the various characters take up their special postures. . . .

To try for a summary of a very difficult and complicated topic: Evil for Faulkner involves the violation of the natural and the denial of the human. As Isaac's older kinsman says in "The Bear," "Courage and honor and pride, and pity and love of justice and of liberty. They all touch the heart, and what the heart holds to becomes truth, as far as we know truth." A meanness of spirit and coldness of calculation which would deny the virtues that touch the heart is by that very fact proven false. Yet Faulkner is no disciple of Jean-Jacques Rousseau. He has no illusions that man is naturally good or that he can safely trust to his instincts and emotions. Man is capable of evil, and this means that goodness has to be achieved by struggle and discipline and effort. Like T. S. Eliot, Faulkner has small faith in social arrangements so perfectly organized that nobody has to take the trouble to be good. Finally Faulkner's noblest characters are willing to face the fact that most men can learn the deepest truths about themselves and about reality only through suffering. Hurt and pain and loss are not mere accidents to which the human being is subject; nor are they mere punishments incurred by human error; they can be the means to the deeper knowledge and to the more abundant life.—CLEANTH BROOKS, "William Faulkner: The Vision of Good and Evil," *The Hidden God*, 1963, pp. 22–43

Works

THE SOUND AND THE FURY

The technique in this section ⟨"June 2, 1910" in *The Sound and the Fury*⟩ is not quite the same as that employed in the first section. The difference is due to the fact that Quentin's mind is much more complex than Benjy's. Since Benjy is incapable of the simplest abstraction, there is in his section nothing that can truly be called soliloquy. Quentin, however, is capable of thought, and we find throughout his section numerous soliloquies. Since Quentin's intellect is more highly developed than Benjy's, it is more nimble in shifting from one experience or idea to another. Although such capriciousness often makes Quentin's mental processes difficult to follow, this is no mere personal whim on the part of the author to make the section unduly perplexing. Even in the most complex and realistic passages, Faulkner has greatly simplified Quentin's mental processes in order that the reader may be able to understand them. The following representative excerpt will illustrate this point. Quentin is on a street car in Cambridge, but his mind is preoccupied with recalling a drive with his mother, his sister Candace, and her husband Herbert, shortly after their marriage on April 25, 1910. The mother is doing most of the talking:

> Herbert has spoiled us all to death Quentin did I write you that he is going to take Jason into his bank when Jason finishes high school Jason will make a splendid banker he is the only one of my children with any practical sense you can thank me for that he takes after my people the others are all Compson *Jason furnished the flour. They made kites on the back porch and sold them for a nickel a piece, he and the Patterson boy. Jason was treasurer.*
>
> There was no nigger on this street car, and the hats unbleached as yet flowing past under the window. Going to Harvard. We have sold Benjy's *He lay on the ground under the window, bellowing We have sold Benjy's pasture so that Quentin may go to Harvard* a brother to you. Your little brother.
>
> You should have a car it's done you no end of good dont you think so Quentin I call him Quentin at once you see I have heard so much about him from Candace.
>
> Why shouldn't you I want my boys to be more than friends yes Candace and Quentin more than friends *Father I have committed* what a pity you had no brother or sister *No sister no sister had no sister* Dont ask Quentin he and Mr. Compson both feel a little insulted when I am strong enough to come down to the table I am going on nerve now I'll pay for it after it's over and you have taken my little daughter away from me *My little sister had no. If I could say Mother. Mother.*

. . . Since this short passage contains fragments dealing with six different time-scenes, the reader may conclude that the author has unnecessarily exaggerated the complexity of Quentin's mind. However, if he will try to imagine what a representative excerpt from his own mind would look like if transcribed onto the printed page, the reader will realize that Faulkner has actually simplified Quentin's mental activity in this passage (and throughout his section). He has eliminated all extraneous details which would not contribute to the main theme, and he has presented Quentin's mind as operating much more logically than it would in reality.

In one instance, Faulkner carries this simplification to the extreme of having Quentin's mind continue in chronological order in the same recalled experience for eighteen pages. He wants to present in an uninterrupted, dramatic unit the central memory which is the basis of Quentin's internal struggle. Since it would be unusual and out of character for Quentin's mind to recall this much of one past experience at one time without interruption, the author makes this particular instance plausible by having the recalled unit pass through Quentin's mind while he is temporarily unconscious. The unit is not difficult to understand, but it does raise certain interesting questions. A short excerpt from near the first of the unit will illustrate the technique. Caddy has just come home after being out with Dalton Ames, and Benjy has sensed her shame and started screaming. She runs out to a nearby stream and plunges in. Quentin follows her:

> the water sucked and gurgled across the sand spit and on in the dark among the willows across the shallow the water rippled like a piece of cloth holding still a little light as water does
>
> he's crossed all the oceans all around the world
>
> then she talked about him clasping her wet knees her face tilted back in the grey light the smell of honeysuckle there was a light in mothers room and in Benjys where T. P. was putting him to bed
>
> do you love him
>
> her hand came out I didnt move it fumbled down my arm and she held my hand flat against her chest her heart thudding
>
> no no
>
> did he make you then he made you do it let him be was stronger than you and he tomorrow Ill kill him I swear I will father neednt know until afterward

In this passage and throughout the unit, the author steers a middle course between making the material comprehensible and at the same time keeping it convincing as a stream of consciousness rendering of a past experience. The speeches and the descriptive fragments are paragraphed separately to avoid confusion. The general absence of orthodox punctuation and capitalization causes no real difficulty but does succeed in distinguishing the unit from ordinary narration and giving it the desired appearance.

One may ask: why did the author not render all of Quentin's recalled experiences in some such simplified, chronological manner as this? It would certainly have made it far less difficult for the reader to follow the main threads of the plot. This is just the question raised by Mr. Hicks's remark that Faulkner seems first to have invented his stories in the regular chronological order and then recast them in a distorted form. The answer is that in the first three sections of *The Sound and the Fury* the author is not primarily concerned with presenting the facts of a story, but with presenting the *reactions* of certain characters to these facts and thereby revealing individual states of mind. Every simplification of the technique necessitates a corresponding simplification of the character's mental reaction and alters his state of mind to a slightly different state of mind. In the particular unit under discussion, for example, Quentin's state of mind is much less complex than it is in other parts of his section. The author had to sacrifice complexity in order to gain something else which he considered worth the temporary sacrifice. However, if the whole of Quentin's recalled experiences were rendered in this manner, the distinguishing characteristics of Quentin's state of mind would certainly be lost. That this would be the case can be seen by comparing the first three sections of the book. In each section a different variation of the stream of consciousness technique is used, and in each case the resulting state of mind of the character is different and the effect upon the reader is different.

While dealing with the interrelations of technique, content, and the desired effect upon the reader, one may ask another question: if the absence of standard punctuation and capitalization in the above passage is effective in setting it apart and giving it the illusion of a recalled experience, why did the author not use some such method as this in the first section for presenting Benjy's recalled experiences? The answer is that, by using the same punctuation and capitalization for the past experiences as for the present, the author is trying to suggest that to Benjy's undiscriminating mind the past is no less real and immediate than the present. To have made even a formal distinction between the two would have implied that Benjy was himself aware of a difference.

The third section of *The Sound and the Fury* is almost wholly orthodox both in content and in technique and requires no detailed analysis. Although one can detect on examination that Jason's section, "April 6, 1928," is presented through a simplified version of the stream of consciousness technique, it is not necessary that the reader give any particular attention to this fact in order to understand the section. Except for a few recalled fragments, Jason's section is a straightforward first-person narrative of events taking place on April 6.

The last section, "April 8, 1928," is the most orthodox of all the sections, for it is a regular omniscient rendering of this day's events. The only characteristic which it has in common with the other three sections is the strictly objective attitude which the author maintains toward his material. Although there are a few interpretative statements in this section, these are kept at a minimum and incorporated into the main body of the material in such a way as not to attract attention to themselves or alter the prevailing tone of the section.

Most readers and critics have been baffled by the unusual arrangement of the four sections in the following unchronological order: "April 7, 1928," "June 2, 1910," "April 6, 1928," "April 8, 1928." Commenting upon this aspect of the novel, Granville Hicks says, "It is not certain that Benjy was the inevitable narrator of the history of the Compson family, or that the story could only have been told in four episodes, or that in the arrangement of these episodes chronological order had to be violated." This statement, as well as the other one quoted earlier, assumes that *The Sound and the Fury* is fundamentally a conventional type of "story" which the author is unnecessarily distorting into a difficult form. But this is hardly the case. According to this method of reckoning, Benjy's section is almost eighteen years out of its chronological order. This conclusion would be correct if each section were devoted entirely to events of the designated date. But this is true for only one section of the book, "April 8, 1928." Each of the other sections deals with two sets of events: those which take place on the designated date and those which are recalled from the past; and these recalled events are no less important than the present. In the first two sections, recalled experiences are far more important than the present enveloping action. If one is to determine the fundamental chronology of the four sections, he must consider the dates of the recalled experiences.

In his introduction to *The Portable Faulkner*, Malcolm Cowley raises another stimulating question for discussion. "In *The Sound and the Fury*, which is superb as a whole," he says, "we can't be sure that the four sections of the novel are presented in the most effective order." What disturbs Mr. Cowley is not the violation of surface chronology but the fact that "we can't fully understand and perhaps can't even read the first section until we have read the other three." By "most effective order" he seems to mean the order in which a section would be most easily understood and most effective individually. One may very well agree with Mr. Cowley that some other order of arrangement might have made Benjy's section more comprehensible on the first reading; however, the shifting of this section would merely mean that some other section would then come into first position, and the same trouble would start all over again, for each of the four sections is interdependent upon the other three. This is true even of the fourth and simplest section—as Cowley discovered when he considered printing this unit in *The Portable Faulkner*. "I thought that the last part of the book would be most effective as a separate episode, but still it depended too much on what had gone before."

Let us consider some of the ways in which the present position of Benjy's section does contribute to the desired effect of the novel as a whole. If the childhood experiences are to be included at all, it does seem definitely preferable that they be presented early, before the reader advances too far into the problems of adult life dealt with in the following three sections. But Benjy's section is far more than a mere background summary of ordinary childhood experiences. From one point of view, it is the whole novel in miniature. It presents all the main characters in situations which foreshadow the main action. This is particularly true of the recalled water-splashing episode which took place when Caddy was seven, Quentin nine, Jason about five, and Benjy about three. These children and a little colored boy, Versh, are playing in the branch one evening. Caddy gets her dress wet and, in order to avoid punishment, pulls off the dress to let it dry. Quentin is perturbed because she gets her dress wet and also because she pulls it off before Versh and the other children. He slaps her and she falls down in the water, getting her bodice and drawers wet. He then feels partly responsible for Caddy's guilt and says that they will both get whipped. She says it was all his fault. However he and she and Versh agree not to tell; but Jason decides to tell if Caddy and Quentin do not give him a bribe. When the children go to bed, Dilsey the Negro cook discovers the stain on Caddy's buttocks, but she is unable to remove the spot.

The parallels between this and the main plot are obvious. When Caddy becomes a young woman, she soils her honor with a serious stain which will not come off; Quentin assumes responsibility for her shame and finally commits suicide in an attempt to expiate her sin; Jason, true to form, makes the most of Caddy's shame by blackmailing her for all he can get. In the childhood experience, Jason walks with his hands in his pockets (as if "holding his money") and once falls down because he does not have his arms free to balance himself; in the main action later, his "holding his money" (by keeping it at home in a box instead of banking it) results in his being robbed by his niece. Since this childhood experience is obviously intended to foreshadow the adult action, it can accomplish this purpose only if it comes before the other three sections.

The Sound and the Fury is a novel about disorder, disintegration, and the absence of perspective. As an introduction to this theme, what could be more appropriate than the flat, perspectiveless language of Benjy's section? The novel is essentially about the internal chaos of the characters—their intellectual, moral, and spiritual confusion. It is therefore appropriate that the first section be presented from the point of view of an idiot who symbolizes this general disorder and exemplifies the simplest variation of it—intellectual confusion. Benjy is incapable of intellectual discrimination, constantly mistaking the past for the present.

Two of the four sections are restricted in two respects and two are restricted in only one respect. Quentin's and Jason's sections are restricted to the internal point of view and to a limited phase of Caddy's transgression. Quentin is preoccupied almost exclusively with Caddy's loss of honor; Jason's attention is concentrated upon Caddy's illegitimate daughter. Benjy's section, although it is restricted in point of view to the mind of Benjy, is not restricted to Caddy or to any one phase of her problem to the exclusion of other matters and other characters. The last section of the novel is similar to Benjy's section in that it too deals with the Compson situation in a general manner, but it accomplishes the effect of comprehensiveness by another means. Whereas Benjy's section is restricted in point of view and not narrowly restricted in time-span, the last section is restricted in time-span to the events of one day but still acquires breadth of outlook by being written from the omniscient-omnipresent point of view, which gives the reader the impression of being outside the characters and at a sufficient remove to view the whole general panorama. The comprehensive quality of the first and the last sections, as contrasted with the two middle sections, gives a good architectural balance to the structure of the novel as a whole. It also allows the reader to begin with the general situation, move into two particular phases of this situation, and emerge again on the other side with a broad, general view. By beginning and ending the novel in this way, the author gives extension to the theme by making clear that the novel is not merely about Caddy's transgression and the reaction of her family, but about a much more comprehensive theme. The disorder, disintegration, and absence of perspective in the lives of the Compsons is intended to be symbolic and representative of a whole social order, or perhaps it would be better to say a whole social disorder.
—LAWRENCE BOWLING, "Faulkner: Technique of *The Sound and the Fury*," *KR*, Autumn 1948, pp. 558–66

AS I LAY DYING

The difficulty of arriving at any satisfactory and consistent interpretation of *As I Lay Dying* disturbs critics of Faulkner. As one of the most recent, Walter J. Slatoff, says:

> One is uncertain about the qualities of some of the important characters and about how to feel toward them; one is puzzled by the meanings of many of the events; one is far from sure what the book is chiefly about, and above all one is uncertain to what extent one has been watching an epic or tragedy or farce.

Although no approach to the novel can wholly resolve its difficulties and remove its complexities, interpretation of *As I Lay Dying* as an ironic inversion of the quest romance, rather than as "epic or tragedy or farce," serves to reconcile diverse elements, to clarify patterns of action and functions of characters, and to invest the whole with meaning which corrects sentimental misconceptions and softens the savage irony apparent to those who shun sentimentality. Northrop Frye's analysis of the "Mythos of Summer: Romance," which is part of his "rational account of some of the structural principles of Western literature in the context of its Classical and Christian heritage," presents so many points which have parallels in *As I Lay Dying* that a systematic comparison of the novel with the traditional structure would seem logical. This comparison proves richly rewarding.

The validity of an interpretation based on a conceptual antithesis between one of the most cherished narrative patterns in Western literature and the unheroic adventures of a family of Southern poor whites is strengthened by Slatoff's well-supported observation that "Faulkner's thought and writing are dominated by thematic and conceptual antitheses of all sorts." But Slatoff fails to note the implicit antithesis exemplified here.

The obscure and difficult technique, with the many short sections in the first person, somewhat conceals the essential simplicity of the central action, the journey of the Bundren family from Frenchman's Bend to Jefferson, beset by perils of flood and difficulties of transportation and supplies, to bury the dead wife and mother, Addie Bundren. The feckless father, Anse, the sons—Cash, Darl, Jewel, and little Vardaman—and the daughter, Dewey Dell, are the central characters. Neighbors, country people along the way, and townspeople in Mottson and Jefferson are the minor characters. The Bundrens have a hill farm from which, with the aid of their kindly but exasperated neighbors, they derive a bare subsistence. Therefore the journey to Jefferson is a major event in their lives, justified only by the extraordinary circumstance that Anse gave Addie a solemn promise to bury her with her family in Jefferson. So welcome is the prospect of the journey to the whole family that one might well suspect the genuineness of the promise were it not confirmed in the one section dealing with Addie's stream of consciousness. The title may be interpreted as a reflection of the irony of the initial situation: as Addie lay dying, the plans for her burial were given impetus by other motives and objectives. Jewel thinks that everyone is "burning hell" to get Addie dead and buried. Anse's comment, in Darl's clairvoyant account of Addie's death during his absence, epitomizes the irony: "God's will be done. . . . Now I can get them teeth." As Olga Vickery points out, Anse's "desire for new teeth and Jewel's savage determination to perform the promised act" are all that keep Anse from letting the word serve for the deed.

The diverse dreams for which the characters seek fulfillment and the time of action, July, furnish a parallel to the "Mythos of Summer: Romance," which Frye describes as "nearest of all literary forms to the wish-fulfilment dream." Each of the main characters has a dream, "the search of the libido or desiring self for a fulfilment that will deliver it from the anxieties of reality but will still contain that reality." Barbara Giles neatly sums up the desired fulfillment: "the simple but powerful wish of poor rural folk to go to town." The fact that the dreams are trivial or ludicrous to begin with is the basis of the other ironic inversions. The attempt to read into *As I Lay Dying* the heroic quality that the quest makes one expect is due to a failure to detect this primary inversion. Anse longs for new teeth and, secretly, a new wife. Cash, the carpenter, has saved money for a graphophone. Dewey Dell wants bananas and an abortion. Vardaman wants to look at a toy train in a store window but will take bananas as second best delight. Darl and Jewel, the rejected and the favorite son, are the only ones concerned chiefly with the ostensible object of the quest.

These are the dreams. The "sequential and processional form" (Frye), familiar as it is romantically idealized by a conventional narrator or author, so loses its outlines in the complexities and ambiguities of the multiple views of the characters that events are sometimes not clear. Disagreement among critics on such essential points as whether Darl is really insane, whether Vardaman is merely a small boy or an idiot, and whether the journey is heroic evidence of devotion or a comedy of errors has some justification. If my reading is correct, Darl and Jewel are the central characters, but they are also the most ambiguous ones. Olga Vickery gives the reason for only one section being devoted to Jewel's stream of consciousness: his world "consists of a welter of emotions, centering on Addie, which cannot be communicated." These emotions "are translated immediately into actions." The self revelation of Darl and the contrasting interpretations of him by other characters cause confusion which the reader is left to elucidate as best he may.

And the setting likewise shows ironic inversion. The Mississippi countryside in July should have some idyllic qualities, despite the heat. It is a peaceful region of pine hills and rivers, very sparsely settled. But a flood broke the idyllic summer calm with a destroying fury that seems almost maleficent, and then the heat caused the procession to be enveloped in the stench of corruption. From death to burial, Addie with her attendants became a nine day's wonder. Olga Vickery denies that the journey is "an inspiring gesture of humanity or a heroic act of traditional morality." The journey is rather "a travesty of the ritual of interment" because the individuals do not give meaning to the ritual. Anse and Dewey Dell lack the proper spirit and Cash and Darl are in conflict with it.

The inversion or the perversion of the idealized quest of the old romances is apparent in the object of the quest, the characters who take part in it, the incidents, the precious objects and symbols associated with the ritual, and the results finally achieved.

Instead of a treasure to be found or a prize to be won, there is a body to be buried. The characters, though not so sharply polarized nor so simply drawn as in quest-romance, are largely ironic counterparts of familiar types. Instead of saving a sleeping beauty, the hero, Jewel, buried Addie, from three to nine days dead, "in summer, and we're running out of ice." Addie, emotionally and structurally the heroine, is also the mother figure. But Addie when alive was not the wise mother of romance, "often the lady for whose sake or at whose bidding the quest is performed," but was an unmaternal mother who rejected her second son and gave Vardaman and Dewey Dell to Anse to make up for the child she had robbed him of and to negative Jewel, a mother who knew that "only through the blows of the switch could my blood and their blood flow as one stream" *(As I Lay Dying)*. She was a true mother only to Jewel. "She rejected not only the children she taught and all but one of the children she bore, she rejected life itself . . . ." As Waggoner observes, Addie alive was not a redemptive figure. Dead, she was a peril and an offense. No quest-romance is complete without a distressed damsel, but nowhere in romance is there a distressed damsel like Dewey Dell, who fatalistically lingered with Lafe at the end of the cotton row when the cotton sack was full and who felt "like a wet seed wild in the hot blind earth" *(As I Lay Dying)*—and hoped for a crop failure. If Addie is the "lady of duty" to Anse and her family, a most apt term, Anse's second wife is the "lady of pleasure" (Frye), less seductive than her prototypes. A possible implication of Cash's mysterious first reference to her house as "Mrs. Bundren's house," in a passage otherwise limited to the events and, one would suppose, to the consciousness of Cash *before* Anse presented her to the family in the last sentence in the book, is that she was Mrs. Bundren before she married Anse. The lady of pleasure would then suggest a Gertrude-Claudius situation with a hint of the incest feared in connection with the black queen (Frye). Maybe the inversion is inverted!

Anse, as the husband of Addie, the ironic counterpart of the wise mother figure, should be an unwise old man, the white king to Addie's white queen (Frye). And so he is. Though he is inept and helpless, avoiding exertion for fear that to sweat will kill him, Anse is described on one occasion in terms that definitely recall mysterious sages like Merlin:

> Pa leans above the bed in the twilight, his humped silhouette partaking of that owl-like quality of awry-feathered, disgruntled outrage within which lurks a wisdom too profound or too inert for even thought.

His ability to secure aid from everyone else while asserting his determination not to be beholden to anyone suggests a magic power: Armstid said, "I be durn if Anse don't conjure a man . . . ." Even the other characters regard him as the special concern of the Lord, so contagious is Anse's view of himself: "I am the chosen of the Lord, for who He loveth, so doeth He chastiseth. But I be durn if He don't take some curious ways to show it, seems like." The secret of his power is, as Vickery notes, that "His words create an image of himself as the meek and magnanimous victim forgiving a cruel and heartless world": no one dares justify his implications by refusing him help. What dignity Anse possesses and what grief he might feel would detract from the irony. But after selling Jewel's horses and taking the helpless Cash's graphophone money to buy the mules and using Dewey Dell's abortion money for his teeth, he finally loses all sympathy when, shaved, combed, and "perfumed like a milliner," he leads forth his bride, "kind of hangdog and proud too, with his teeth and all." Through the sacrifice of others he buried one wife, but he got the second by his unaided efforts and used the "hearse" to take her home in.

The traditional conflict between father and son occurs between Anse and Jewel, from the time when, by taking work from his flesh and blood, as Anse saw it, Jewel earned money to buy the horse. The true reason for the hostility is that Jewel is not Anse's son; though there is no indication that Anse was aware of the fact, he would be aware that Jewel was Addie's favorite and his rival.

Cash, the eldest son, is the artificer; he forges no sword, but the care with which he made the coffin on the bevel to withstand the slanting stress of the animal magnetism of a dead body recalls the craftsmanship of his legendary predecessors. His concern for his tools, lost in the flood, is like a hero's concern for an Excalibur.

Darl, the second son, can be viewed in two ways, dependent on whether one considers him insane or sane: he is either the enchanted knight who is not released from the evil spell or he is the unenchanted victim of the forces of evil and sterility which deliver him over to be imprisoned in a dungeon. He is the son rejected by his mother, as Jewel is the one most dear to her. . . .

Vernon Tull provides another ironic inversion as the faithful, practical helper to the "wise" old man, like Sancho Panza to Don Quixote (Frye). Tull is actually superior to Anse, whom he helps against his own better judgment. His most striking capitulation, however, is not to Anse's fecklessness but to Vardaman's childlike confidence: "Because a fellow can see ever now and then that children have more sense than him." Here the irony vanishes: Faulkner consistently pays tribute to the innate wisdom of children and to their gift for direct action and for making adults act against their own convictions. Perhaps Vardaman has no parallel in romance because he is not ironically conceived.

The parallels between both major and minor characters in quest-romance and in Faulkner's journey explain what seems to Slatoff to be a deviation in *As I Lay Dying* from Faulkner's use of antithesis in characterization: the antithesis exists, but between the characters in the novel and those in romances. Although there is also antithesis between characters within the novel, especially the antithesis between those who respond by words and those who respond by action, providing the structural pattern traced by Olga Vickery, the sharp black and white contrasts of romance are lacking.

In the incidents of the quest, the traditional perils of fire and water are the ones Addie, talking to Cora Tull, had imagined Jewel facing for her sake: "He is my cross and he will be my salvation. He will save me from the water and from the fire. Even though I have laid down my life, he will save me." On the basis of Addie's words and of Jewel's actions, Jewel emerges as the hero, despite the fact that only one passage presents Jewel directly. Slatoff raises the question of what salvation she can mean, "especially if she is going to Jefferson because her father is right or to revenge herself on Anse." Jewel does fulfill the promise Anse made that Addie should be buried in Jefferson. He rescues her from the flood by keeping the wagon from being swept downstream. He sacrifices his horse for a team of mules to pull the wagon. He rescues her from the fire by bringing her coffin out of the burning barn, end over end, himself "enclosed in a thin nimbus of fire." He is the hero of the myth who braves flood and fire to reach or rescue his beloved. The symbolic significance of both the flood and the fire goes back farther than romances, to myth. Interpretation of the flood in *As I Lay Dying* as a rebirth, freeing the sons for their destinies, or as a fable of the testing of the three sons in which the river is the symbol of another world and the journey a journey to salvation relates the story of the Bundrens ultimately to "the archetypal myth of the history of the world," in which the "deluge hero is a symbol of the germinal vitality of man surviving even the worst tides of catastrophe and sin." No dove, no raven marks the end of this flood, but, instead, buzzards. Moreover, the hero sacrifices life to death: Jewel makes good Anse's bargain with Snopes and gives up his horse, the horse which in romance "gets the hero to his quest" and consequently keeps a central place (Frye). The lineage of Jewel's horse, descendant of one of the famous spotted horses Flem Snopes brought from Texas, suggests legendary steeds with noble ancestry. Upon the humble mules, unlike their parallels in romance, the success of the quest depends. . . .

What has the quest achieved? Cash, the artificer son, has suffered the mutilation which for Hephaistos or Weyland the smith was a kind of ritual death (Frye). Cash's analysis of Darl may be the ironic equivalent of the "unusual wisdom or power" gained by mutilation, but it cannot aid Darl. Cash also dwells upon the idea that "nothing justifies the deliberate destruction of what a man has built with his own sweat," referring to the coffin which Darl had tried to burn and reflecting his craftsman's pride. Olga Vickery credits his suffering with "the extension of his range of awareness and . . . his increased sensitivity both to events and to people." This is Cash's wisdom; his only power gained is that of unselfish and silent endurance, at the cost perhaps of the skill he prizes. His only consolation is the music of the "duck-shaped" woman's graphophone. Darl, the most sensitive son, saved nothing in the flood in which Cash saved the horse and had his leg broken and Jewel saved the wagon and coffin and Cash's tools. He is sent to an insane asylum. Dewey Dell wants to destroy the new life within her and will no doubt succeed.

True, a bride has been won, Anse's second wife, the "duck-shaped woman" with the "hard-looking pop eyes," like one of the loathly ladies but incapable of magic transformation. Furthermore, she is won by infidelity to the memory of the dead Addie, the heroine for whom the quest was undertaken. Anse's economy in making the borrowing of spades to dig his first wife's grave serve as prelude to his second marriage outdoes the thrift in Elsinore. The lack of hesitation on Anse's part—"it was like he knowed"— would seem to have only one plausible explanation: the bride was an object of the quest, not just a happy coincidence. Jewel, the hero, has lost both his mother and his horse, the substitute for a woman's love as well as a symbol of virility. Whereas the "quest-romance is the victory of fertility over the wasteland" (Frye), *As I Lay Dying* represents the victory of death and sterility and infidelity.—ELIZABETH M. KERR, "*As I Lay Dying* as Ironic Quest," *CoL*, Winter 1962, pp. 5–13

LIGHT IN AUGUST

Of all the readers who have sought the thread which would afford safe entrance into *Light in August*, a labyrinth of tangled lives, creeds, fates, and destinies, Cleanth Brooks seems to me to have come closest to comprehending the novel in its totality. He says, "The community is everywhere in this novel." And he says, "Unless the controlling purposes of the individual are related in some fashion to those which other men assume, the individual is indeed isolated, and is forced to fall back on his own personal values with all the liability to fanaticism and distortion." I subscribe fully to these statements, but it seems to me that Mr. Brooks may be oversimplifying and limiting *Light in August* when he says: "The various characters who act and suffer in this novel are all people outside the community, and whatever their special psychological isolation, it is given objective reference and dramatic meaning by their alienation from the community in which they live or into which they have come."

Solidarity within the community is certainly the central subject, but the characters are not all outside the community. Furthermore, those who are outside are outside in different degrees, and the book achieves its particular form because the different degrees are so intermeshed as to constitute a narrative and dramatic presentation of an essentially thematic structure. If we are to attain a Coleridgean ideal and account for the work as a structural whole, we must account for the presence in the novel of these "special psychological isolations" and the battles which the characters fight, or refuse to fight, or are unable because of important limitations to fight; and we must so phrase a statement of theme as to account for the presence and the relationships of these particular lives.

Light in August rises out of Faulkner's tragic vision of man as inescapably dual in nature. In the psychological dialectic sustaining it the thesis is: the world in which we live is a chaos of mixed evil and good, a chaos which stems from (1) limited or lip service to moral (community) orders which are selfishly conceived and so corrupted, (2) human incapacity to adopt any code without its ultimately becoming rigid—humane conviction inevitably hardens into inhumane convention. The antithesis: despite the moral anarchy arising necessarily from this thesis, the individual realizes himself only in terms of community values, and he must submit himself to the larger good or perish.

The dramatically demonstrated impossibility of molding a compassionate community of isolative and selfish motives and ideals makes *Light in August* Faulkner's most pessimistic novel. As the theme is worked out, we are made increasingly aware of the ultimately insoluble ethic problem which is the core of the tragedy: Man is not simply a moral being with dual leanings towards self-realization and communal obligations; the two become in actual life (in the microcosm of Jefferson in *Light in August*) so interwoven that one may convince himself that his own private demands are, or should be, those of the community; or he may seize upon certain commonly esteemed values with such fervor that he cannot allow his views to be questioned. We are reminded of Sherwood Anderson's story of the old writer with his theory of how truths become grotesque. "It was his notion," says Anderson, "that the moment one of the people took one of the truths to himself, called it his truth, and tried to live his life by it, he became a grotesque and the truth he embraced became a falsehood."

In *Light in August* Faulkner is dealing with a group of such grotesques; but Faulkner cuts deeper than Anderson's old writer, because Faulkner's grotesques, despite their strangeness and despite the illusions which render them grotesque, are all too human to allow us to conclude that Faulkner is simply asserting the overriding importance of community obligation. He is insisting that there are within man and within the community itself forces that are inherently divisive. He accomplishes his intent by exploring the rationale of various types of alienation and illusion and by postulating a graded scale of illusions and their effects upon their possessors as communal beings. This graded scale constitutes the complex of ethic judgment upon which the comprehension of the novel as a whole depends.

What we have to deal with in *Light in August* is the peculiar collocation in Jefferson, Mississippi, of various lives whose stories cannot be accounted for on the basis of narrative alone. If, however, we see that the thematic conflict is between rigid patterns of self-involvement on the one hand and commitment to a solidarity that transcends self on the other, we must see that the chief character, the moral protagonist, because he alone can serve as an ethic slide rule by means of which we can compute the relative failures and successes of the other characters, is Gail Hightower, the old unchurched minister who is, as we open the story, ironically, "Done Damned in Jefferson." It may be that at the end he is still damned as far as Jefferson is concerned, but through him the reader who inhabits a larger, though not dissimilar, community is enabled to estimate the relative moral worth of the other characters and the fixations which inhibit or limit their participation in society. . . .

In summoning before himself for review and rejection his past life, Hightower reveals the source of moral achievement: he manifests the power of choice, of free will. Just as it was within his power as moral agent to reject the community for immunity, so also it is within his power to reject immunity—to earn his redemption, as Robert Penn Warren might say, by being judge at his own trial before the bar of communal justice. In exercising the power of choice and in becoming the compassionate observer, Hightower seems to speak for Faulkner and to be raised out of himself into a sort of mediate figure between the community, including the readers, and the more alienated figures of the novel. I think Warren Beck has something like this in mind when, in speaking of the "Compassionate troubled observers" of several of Faulkner's works, he says, "It is no doubt significant of Faulkner's own attitude that these compassionate observers so largely provide the reflective point of view from which the story is told and thereby determine its moral atmosphere." . . .

Faulkner is sometimes willing to voice his own moral convictions; this is true in the case of a bit of literary criticism which appears in the midst of *Light in August*. When Byron first tells Hightower that he has taken Lena to the cabin on the Burden place and asks for Hightower's aid, the old minister's desire for immunity still rules; when Byron leaves, he tries to escape into Tennyson. Then Faulkner says:

> It does not take long. Soon the fine galloping language, the gutless swooning full of sapless trees and dehydrated lusts begins to swim smooth and swift and peaceful. It is better than praying without having to think aloud. It is like listening in a cathedral to a eunuch chanting in a language which he does not even need to not understand.

I do not believe that this is wilfully capricious denigration. It is in keeping with Faulkner's conviction that a relevant moral order must be applicable in a world of hardened convention, of men and women of selfish desires, self-deception, and chicanery. Instead of a reaffirmation of new or old community ideals, the best Faulkner can offer is a Hightower compassion, grounded on an understanding of the need to recognize human weakness. As another of Faulkner's characters has phrased it elsewhere, all that God Himself asks of man is that he "hold the earth mutual and intact in communal anonymity of brotherhood, and all the fee he asked was pity and humility and sufferance and endurance and the sweat of his face for bread." So the moral power of Tennyson's never-never land is meaningless, does not answer to man's nature and needs as they are; it is significant that after delivering Lena's baby, Hightower reads *Henry IV*, which Faulkner calls "food for a man." By then Hightower's compassion is in the ascendant, and it is capable of causing him to struggle to transcend himself. In the final analysis it is the struggle that is important, and perhaps its importance is emphasized by the fact that it takes place within the unlikely breast of Hightower. At any rate, through Hightower we see that even moral splendor is relative and can be achieved by a man who rises from the stench of selfish isolation to assert the absolute value of pity. Of course, the proper understanding comes too late for much social efficacy; and as Hightower sits before his window awaiting death, the habitual thundering horses and flashing sabers tumble again into his revery. But before that there has come his realization of his sins and of his duty as communal man; and this realization for a moment triumphs, though the one man dies.—CARL BENSON, "Thematic Design in *Light in August*," *SAQ*, Oct. 1954, pp. 540–55

Faulkner's world is grim—a world in which the past exerts an irresistible force, but against which there is no supernatural sanction, no redeeming belief. He believes in original sin, but not in divine love, and he is endlessly bemused by the human effort to read fate or to avoid it. The highest reach of his belief is the effort to become "a saint without God" (Albert Camus), but this is a point not yet tried for in *Light in August*. Correspondingly, there is great power in his work, but little color, and *Light in August*, for all its brilliance, somehow wears the lack-lustre look of the year in which it was published, 1932. It is a grim book, and the countryside described in it already has the pinched, rotted look that one sees in so many depression novels about the South. The greatest fault of the book is its over-schematic, intellectualized past. Although Faulkner himself has lived more like Joe Christmas than like the Sartorises, he is socially far from the world of Joe Christmas and Lena Grove, and there are tell-tale signs in the novel that it is written *down*—for Faulkner, too much from his head down, and about people whom he tends to generalize and to overpraise, as if he saw them only as symbols rather than as entirely complex beings. And it is a simple fact that the opening of *Light in August* is so beautiful that nothing after quite comes up to it.

On the other hand, it is one of Faulkner's greatest books, and although it does not have the blazing directness of *The Sound and the Fury* (a book written more directly out of Faulkner's own experience), it has much of the creative audacity which is Faulkner's highest ideal in art. With this book, published in 1932, Faulkner completed a period of extraordinary fertility. He was only thirty-five; since 1929, he had published, in rapid order, *Sartoris, The Sound and the Fury, As I Lay Dying, Sanctuary,* and *Light in August*. It was a period of tremendous creative power. When he was recently in Japan, Faulkner said of this period:

> I think there's a period in a writer's life when he, well, simply for lack of any other word, is fertile and he just produces. Later on, his blood slows, his bones get a little more brittle, his muscles get a little stiff, he gets perhaps other interests, but I think there's one time in his life when he writes at the top of his talent plus his speed, too. Later the speed slows; the talent doesn't necessarily have to fade at the same time. But there's a time in his life, one matchless time, when they are matched completely. The speed, and the power and the talent, they're all there and then he is . . . 'hot.'

Light in August comes out of that "one matchless time." The only possible objection one can have to the book is the number of implications which Faulkner tries to bring out of his material—for just as the characters' own lives are "set" for them to mull over, so Faulkner constantly mulls over them, wringing a poetry that has grandeur but also an intensity of contemplation that is sometimes more furious in expression than meaningful in content. If we see Faulkner's narrative method as essentially recollective, in the form of individual meditation over past events, we can recognize the advantage he has over most "naturalistic" writers and we understand why Faulkner refers to himself as a "poet." For what makes the portrait of Joe Christmas so astonishing is the energy of imagination lavished upon it, the consistency of texture that derives from the poet's sense that he has not only to *show*, in the modern realistic sense, but to *say*—that is, to tell a story which follows from his contemplation of the world, and which preserves, in the nobility of its style and in the serene independence of its technique, the human victory over circumstances.

It is this that makes us hear Faulkner's own voice throughout the book, that allows him to pull off the tremendous feat of making us believe in a character who in many ways is not a human being at all—but struggling to become one. And this, after all, is the great problem of the novelist today. Joe Christmas is an incarnation not only of the "race problem" in America, but of the condition of man. More and more, not merely the American novel, but all serious contemporary novels, are concerned with men who are not real enough to themselves to be seriously in conflict with other men. Their conflicts, as we say, are "internal"; for they are seeking to become *someone*. Joe Christmas lives a life that is not only solitary but detached. He lives in society physically, but actually he is concerned only with the process of self-discovery, or of self-naming, even of self-legalization. This is a fate which, as we know, can be as arduous and deadly as that of the classic heroes. But in Joe Christmas's case, there is no conflict from positions of strength, no engagement between man and man—only the search of the "stranger," *l'étranger*, to become man.—ALFRED KAZIN, "The Stillness of *Light in August*," *Twelve Original Essays on Great American Novels*, ed. Charles Shapiro, 1958, pp. 281–83

The community demands special consideration . . . , for the community is the powerful though invisible force that quietly exerts itself in so much of Faulkner's work. It is the circumambient atmosphere, the essential ether of Faulkner's fiction. But for many a reader, the community is indeed invisible and quite imperceptible: it exerts no pressure on him at all—and lacking any awareness of this force, he may miss the meaning of the work. Such readers find *Light in August* quite baffling simply because they are unaware of the force of community that pervades it and thus miss the clue to its central structure.

Yet a little reflection will show that nearly all the characters in *Light in August* bear a special relation to the community. They are outcasts—they are pariahs, defiant exiles, withdrawn quietists, or simply strangers. Miss Burden, the daughter of carpetbagger intruders, has lived for years within what can be described only as a kind of cultural cyst. The community has tried its best to expel the Reverend Mr. Hightower, though having failed in the attempt it has finally accorded him a sort of grudging acceptance. Joe Christmas is, of course, Ishmael himself, actively defying the community. Even Byron Bunch fits into this pattern of alienation. Byron, with his methodical earnestness and his countrified asceticism, is regarded as a kind of eccentric—a "character." For "seven years [he] had been a minor mystery to the town."

But the community itself, the great counterforce to which these characters are attracted or against which they are reacting, has no special representatives in the novel and need have none. For the community, everywhere in the novel, is visible to the reader who is prepared to see it. It expresses itself through Mrs. Armstid emptying her china bank and knotting the coins into a sack for Lena; through the sheriff kicking the ineffectual bloodhounds or ordering the thrill-seekers away from his examination of the Negro witness; through the second-hand furniture dealer who relates the closing episode of the novel; and through a dozen other minor or anonymous characters.

Sometimes the author makes an explicit comment upon the community, as he does in the long and brilliantly handled account of Gail Hightower in chapter 3. After Mrs. Hightower's shameful death, the community is sure that Hightower will resign his church. When he does so at last, after persistent moral pressure, the town is glad. "Then the town was sorry with being glad, as people sometimes are sorry for those whom they have at last forced to do as they wanted them to." But Hightower still would not leave the town, and the community was furious with him for his stubbornness. Finally, some men took him out and beat him, and the townspeople, now horrified, offered "to prosecute the men who had done it." But Hightower refused to tell who his assailants were. "Then all of a sudden the whole thing seemed to blow away, like an evil wind. It was as though the town realized at last that he would be a part of its life until he died, and that they might as well become reconciled." Neighbors once more began to leave baskets of food upon his porch—"though they were the sort of dishes which they would have sent to a poor mill family. But it was food, and wellmeant."

One way in which to gauge the importance of the community in this novel is by imagining the action to have taken place in Chicago or Manhattan Island, where the community—at least in Faulkner's sense—does not exist. As far as the general plot is concerned, everything in the novel could be easily accounted for: The frustration and rage of Joe Christmas, the murder of the lonely old maid, Miss Burden, and the moral impotence and isolation of Hightower are situations and events that occur frequently enough in the setting of our great modern world cities. The plight of the isolated individual cut off from any community of values is of course a dominant theme of contemporary literature. But by developing this theme in a rural setting in which a powerful sense of community still exists, Faulkner has given us a kind of pastoral—that is, he has let us see our modern and complex problems mirrored in a simpler and more primitive world. *Light in August* is, in some respects, a bloody and violent pastoral. The plight of the lost sheep and of the black sheep can be given special point and meaning because there is still visible in the background a recognizable flock with its shepherds, its watchdogs, sometimes fierce and cruel, and its bellwethers.

Yet the reader of *Light in August* may still question the relation of the fact of community to the meaning of the novel. Granted that the community is a living force, what does that have to do with the meaning of the novel? And he can scarcely be blamed if he goes on to ask whether *Light in August* is a novel at all. What possible relation is there between the two main characters, Lena and Joe Christmas, who never meet and who go their separate ways, the one placidly, the other violently? There is obviously the bare fact of contrast; but is there anything more? Do not these characters between them rend the book in two?

Both questions are in order. A proper answer to the first (the relation of the community to the meaning of this novel) will suggest an answer to the second (the unity of the novel). But the answer to the first cannot be succinct, and in any case we must begin by considering more fully the relations of the various characters—to each other and to the world around them.

Lena and Joe Christmas, as everyone has seen, stand in obvious contrast to each other. Their very likenesses stress their basic differences. Both are orphans; both escape from home by crawling out a window; both are betrayed by their first loves; both in the course of their wanderings come to Jefferson. But how different they are in relation to society! Every man's hand is sooner or later lifted against Joe Christmas; he demands that it be so. But Lena, heavy with child, on an obviously ridiculous quest to find the father of her child, leads a charmed life. Even the women who look upon her swollen belly with evident disapproval press their small store of coins upon her, and the community in general rallies to help her. As Mrs. Beard remarks to Byron Bunch: "Aint you and that preacher and ever other man that knows about her already done everything for her that she could think to want?" In the person of Bunch, her quixotic errand actually raises up for her an authentic though clumsy knight-errant, who becomes her protector and fights her battles.

Joe repels, Lena attracts the force of the community into which they both come as strangers. But the point is not that Lena is "good" and Joe "bad." Joe's alienation from the community is not simply "willed"—there are deep-seated reasons for it, and, moreover, his is only the most extreme of a whole series of such alienations. . . .

If in Faulkner's work the community can still serve as a positive norm, does that mean that in his fiction there is no room for the roles of the prophet and the saint? Can one ever find implicit approval of the individual's effort to amend or transcend the values held by the community? The answer is yes, and often. Faulkner was always fascinated by rebels and has usually accorded them a full measure of dramatic sympathy. But his fiction also reveals keen awareness of the perils risked by the individual who attempts to run counter to the community. The divergent individual may invite martyrdom; he certainly risks fanaticism and madness. In *Light in August*

Faulkner's emphasis is primarily on the distortion and perversion and sterility which isolation from the community entails, though even here there is a clear recognition of a heroic element in Hightower, Joanna Burden, and Joe Christmas. —CLEANTH BROOKS, "The Community and the Pariah," *William Faulkner: The Yoknapatawpha Country*, 1963, pp. 52–55, 69–70

ABSALOM, ABSALOM!

The Sutpen tragedy is the means of conveying the larger social tragedy. In its broader outlines, the Sutpen tragedy is in many ways analogous to the social. Sutpen had two sons: one white, the other Negro. He denied the Negro; fratricide resulted. The Civil War, too, was a fratricidal conflict caused by denial of the Negro. In the passage which designates the Mississippi River as the "geological umbilicus" of the continent, uniting Quentin and Shreve in a "sort of geographical substantiation," the brotherhood of North and South is established explicitly.

Sutpen's sin, his failure of humanity, is the equivalent in personal terms of the sin of plantation culture, its failure to accept the brotherhood of all mankind. Both failures are provided with the suggestion of an ancestry. Sutpen's progenitors go back to the criminal element in England; slavery, when first introduced into the West Indies, was begun by men "whom the civilized land and people had expelled": "whose thinking and desires had become too crass to be faced and borne longer," and who had been set, "homeless and desperate upon the lonely ocean." In the description of Haiti as "the halfway point between what we call the jungle and what we call civilization," we are not far from Mr. Compson's description of the half-civilized Methodist South: "(. . . Sutpen and Henry and the Coldfields too) who have not quite yet emerged from barbarism, who two thousand years hence will still be throwing off the yoke of Latin culture and intelligence from which they never were in any great permanent danger to begin with."

The social tragedy is conveyed through the Sutpen tragedy concretely as well as abstractly. As the biggest single plantation owner in the county, Sutpen is the very incarnation of the Old South. In describing the conception, attainment, and destruction of Sutpen's design, Faulkner shows the tragedy of that society in terms of the presiding theme.

The social panorama which first unfolds itself to young Sutpen's eye when he descends the mountain is of "a country all divided and fixed and neat with people living on it all divided and fixed and neat because of what color their skins happened to be and what they happened to own." The division upon which the plantation system rests is seen as already established. He sees "niggers working in the fields . . . while fine men sat fine horses and watched them." Poor whites find miscellaneous work in connection with the plantations, getting their overalls and calico dresses from the "plantation commissary," or on store credit, and taking shelter in cabins "not quite as well kept up and preserved as the ones the nigger slaves lived in." The poor whites are physically less well provided for than the Negroes, but their dwellings are "nimbused with freedom's bright aura." In the theoretical concession to worth which freedom implies lies their torment. Only the exceptionally strong and ruthless of purpose, like Sutpen, could accept the challenge to equality with the men who sat the fine horses. Their more typical responses of indignation, blocking the road to an oncoming carriage or throwing dust after its proud wheels, were purely symbolic.

During the years in which Sutpen completes his house, obtains the appropriate wife, and raises to near adulthood the two perfectly suitable heirs of his caste ambitions, plantation society is depicted as reaching the pinnacle of civilized refinement in manners, arts, dress, ceremony and entertainment. The exquisiteness of these attainments is in part symbolized in the beauty of the house itself, its grace deriving from the enforced labors of the French architect and from the objects which go to furnish it: the crystal chandeliers, the candelabra, the tapestries, silver, linen, Damask, crystal, Wedgwood, carpets, and—above all—the great formal white door with its fanlight "imported pane by pane from Europe." (Shreve's garbled review of "crystal tapestries and Wedgwood chairs" is final evidence of the hopelessness of his ever comprehending this aspect of Quentin's cultural past.) Sutpen's marble monument, imported from Italy and brought past the Civil War blockade to be toted in the regimental forage wagon all the way from Charleston, symbolizes a sense of social grandeur and dignity which had become so completely assimilated by the upper classes as to be projected for immortality.

Sutpen's wife, Ellen, the vacuous "butterfly" who chaperones for Judith and Bon a courtship of patterned walks in a formal garden, is the female who presides over the rituals of refined existence. The shopping expeditions with her marriageable daughter, during which she would "finger and handle and disarrange and then reject . . . the meagre fripperies and baubles" of local shops, conveys the luxury of taste made possible by plantation prosperity. Henry's social experience, a round of hunting and cockfighting, amateur horse racing, and dancing at "other plantations almost interchangeable with his own," is the model of socially prescribed leisure. Judith's pattern, likewise, is conveyed by "riding habits" and "ball gowns." The library of the magnificent house, decked in the consummate festiveness of Southern Yuletide, is the scene where the gentlemanly young Henry renounces his birthright in favor of the even more gentlemanly, New Orleans–bred Bon, whose poised indolence and silken dressing gown had first won him his country brother's idolatry.

The image of that society is captured in briefly-sketched word pictures which are as conventional and set as old-time calendar prints. The slave belongs in this picture, and he is never omitted. There are the ladies going to church "with house negroes to carry the parasols and flyswishes . . . moving in hoops among the miniature broadcloth of the . . . little boys and pantelettes of the little girls." There is the evocation of Southern Christmas in a view of the plantation houses "with . . . holly thrust beneath the knockers . . . eggnog and toddy . . . and blue unwinded wood smoke standing above the plastered chimneys of the slave quarters." There is "music at night—fiddle and triangle among the blazing candles." On such occasions the best champagne is "dispensed out of the burlesqued pantomime elegance of negro butlers." When the young Confederates make their farewells for battle, after an evening of waltzing with their crinolined ladies, the view of their departure includes their grooms and "body servants." The glory and romance are conveyed unforgettably, but the shadow of the slave haunts the scene. As Ellen and Judith return in their carriage from a triumphant shopping expedition, they ride with "an extra nigger on the box with the coachman to stop every few miles and build a fire and re-heat the bricks on which Ellen and Judith's feet rested."

The extent to which the entire social superstructure is set upon treacherous foundations is hinted at repeatedly. Graciousness prevails, but at too great a remove from the elementary facts of life. Private and colonel, on the eve of enlistment, are united in honor and pride. They "call each by their given names . . . one man to another above the suave powdered shoulders of the women." But they do so as gentleman to gentleman, "not . . . as one farmer to another across a halted plow in a field."

The delicacy of consideration accorded the young gentlewomen is not truly earned. Mr. Compson distinguishes three types of females in the society: "the virgins whom gentlemen someday married, the courtesans to whom they went while on sabbaticals to the cities, [and] the slave-girls and women upon whom that first caste rested and to whom in certain cases it doubtless owed the very fact of its virginity." He describes the simple commandeering of the slave girls from the fields; no more respect was accorded the well kept octoroon mistresses, like Bon's, who for all their loyalty and careful nurturing were valuable only as "commodities." Except for the selective interest of the white man in these few, Mr. Compson has Bon explain to Henry, they "would have been sold to any brute for the price . . . body and soul for life . . . [to be used] with no more impunity than he would dare to use an animal." In their incredible beauty and helplessness, these women are "the supreme apotheosis of chattelry."

Upon the maintained difference between slave-girl and gentlewoman, slave laborer and gentleman, plantation society rested. Yet how different were Henry and the young men of his class from their darker-skinned contemporaries? It is Mr. Compson who asks this question and gives the answer: ". . . only in the surface matter of food and clothing and daily occupation any different from the negro slaves who supported them—the same sweat, the only difference being that on the one hand it went for labor in the fields where on the other it went for the spartan pleasures which were available to them because they did not have to sweat in the field."

From the utmost heights comes the fall to utter devastation, economically, socially and spiritually. The war is lost, and not merely because of the superior strategy and numbers of the enemy, but through the transposition into military terms of the very flaw by which the society was marred, through "generals . . . who should not have been generals . . . who were generals not through training or aptitude . . . but, by divine right to say 'Go there' conferred upon them by an absolute caste system."

Girls of Judith's kind, created by "a hundred years of careful nurturing . . . by the tradition in which Thomas Sutpen's ruthless will had carved a niche," must now dress the "self-fouled bodies of the strange injured and dead," must learn to tend household without money or servants, to harness the mule, and go clad in faded gingham. The house, too, must surrender its objects of beauty and pride, "giving of itself in slow driblets of furniture and carpet, linen and silver."

Sutpen comes home to find "his plantation ruined, fields fallow . . . taxes and levies and penalties sowed by United States marshals . . . and all his niggers gone." Defeat has brought about a leveling of whites; Wash Jones, who never before would have dared, now freely crosses the threshold. Sutpen is reduced to running a country store with Wash. His persistence in his design becomes fantastic.

Most devastating is the spiritual alteration in the people. The gallantry of those who were the first to go is contrasted strikingly with the sullenness of those who were the first to come home: " . . . not all of them tramps, ruffians, but men who had risked and lost everything, suffered beyond endurance and had returned now to the ruined land, not the same men who had marched away but transformed . . . into the likeness of that man who abuses from very despair and pity the beloved wife or mistress who in his absence has been raped." Frustrated and embittered, these men strike fear into their compatriots who remained. During the era of carpetbaggers, they organize into night raiders, draining off in these excesses the "suppurations" of defeat. The more reflective exist, like Bon, "mindless and irrational companion and inmate of a body which . . . is still immersed . . . in recollections of old peace" but in whom consciousness enforces the knowledge that "what Was is one thing and now it is not because it is dead, it died in 1861."

Forty years later the Sutpen mansion, symbol of a social design, still stands. Its "rotting portico and scaling walls" bespeak "some desolation more profound than ruin." Three generations of Sutpens had met doom within it; three generations of Southerners, brooding upon the mystery of its decay, had lived within the shadow of its prefigured annihilation. The desolation of the mansion is the key to Quentin's own, and in the story of a design that failed we may read the meaning of the decline of the South. And more: this novel, which holds an instant in history timeless and infinite in sombre implication, is a new revelation of "the dark and simple heart of things," pulsing forever in the world. All human history in its recurrence of error and anguish is represented in the myth of Quentin, Sutpen, and the South. In this fall of a man, a house, a class, and a culture, we know again, with terrifying nearness, the inexorability of "fate." Hybris and its punishment, sin and atonement, psychological compulsions and their proliferating destructiveness—these concepts, ancient and modern, endow *Absalom, Absalom!* with the poetic reality of classic moral tragedy.—ILSE DUSOIR LIND, "The Design and Meaning of *Absalom, Absalom!*," *PMLA*, Dec. 1955, pp. 908–12

GO DOWN, MOSES

William Faulkner's latest volume ⟨*Go Down, Moses*⟩ is brought out as a collection of stories, but six of the seven stories deal with a single theme, the relation of the Mississippi McCaslins to the Negroes about them, and they have a coherence strong enough to constitute, if not exactly a novel, then at least a narrative which begins, develops, and concludes. The seventh and alien story, "Pantaloon in Black," is inferior both in conception and in execution; why it was placed in the midst of the others is hard to understand, for it diminishes their coherence. But conceivably Mr. Faulkner intended it to do just that, wishing to exempt the collection from being taken for a novel and judged as such. Yet it is only as an integrated work that the group of McCaslin stories can be read.

Mr. Faulkner's literary mannerisms are somewhat less obtrusive than they have been, but they are still dominant in his writing, and to me they are faults. For one thing, I find tiresome Mr. Faulkner's reliance on the method of memory to tell his stories. No doubt we can accept what so many Southern novelists imply, that in the South a continuous acute awareness of regional, local, and family history is one of the conditions of thought. But the prose in which Mr. Faulkner renders this element of his stories is, to me, most irritating; it drones so lyrically on its way, so intentionally losing its syntax in its long sentences, so full of self-pity expressed through somniloquism or ventriloquism. Then, too, while I am sure that prose fiction may make great demands on our attention, it ought not to make these demands arbitrarily, and there is no reason why Mr. Faulkner cannot settle to whom the pronoun "he" refers. Mr. Faulkner's new book is worth effort but not, I think, the kind of effort which I found necessary: I had to read it twice to get clear not only the finer shades of meaning but the simple primary intentions, and I had to construct an elaborate genealogical table to understand the family connections.

These considerations aside, Mr. Faulkner's book is in

many ways admirable. The six McCaslin stories are temperate and passionate, and they suggest more convincingly than anything I have read the complex tragedy of the South's racial dilemma. The first of the stories is set in 1856; it is the humorous tale of the chase after the runaway Tomey's Turl—it takes a certain effort to make sure that this is a slave, not a dog—of how old Buck McCaslin is trapped into marriage by Miss Sophonisba Beauchamp and her brother Hubert (rightfully the Earl of Warwick), and of the poker game that is played for Tomey's Turl; the humor is abated when we learn that Turl is half-brother to one of the poker players. The last story is set in 1940; its central figure is the Negro murderer Samuel Worsham Beauchamp, descendant of Tomey's Turl, and related to the McCaslins through more lines than one.

The best of the book does not deal directly with the Negro fate but with the spiritual condition of the white men who have that fate at their disposal. The Edmonds branch of the McCaslin family—there are three generations of Edmonds, but Mr. Faulkner likes to telescope the generations and all the Edmondses are really the same person: this does not exactly make for clarity—represents the traditional South; Isaac McCaslin, who is by way of being the hero of the narrative, represents the way of regeneration. The Edmondses are shown as being far from bad; in their relation to their Negroes they are often generous, never brutal, scarcely even irresponsible; but they accept their tradition and act upon their superiority and their rights, and the result is tragedy and degeneration both for the Negroes and for themselves. The effects are not always immediate and obvious; one of the best passages in the book, and one of the most crucial, is that in which, as a boy, Carothers Edmonds asserts his superiority over his Negro foster-brother and then, seeking later to repent, finds the tie irrevocably broken and his foster-family, though wonderfully cordial, stonily implacable; and this failure of love which Edmonds's tradition imposed upon him seems to affect his whole life.

As against the tradition which arrests the dignity of possession and the family, Issac McCaslin sets the dignity of freedom and the unpossessable wilderness. The experience by which his moral sensibility is developed is a kind of compendium of the best American romantic and transcendental feeling. Cooper, Thoreau, and Melville are all comprised in what he learns from Sam Fathers, the Chickasaw Indian (but he was enough of a Negro to be glad to die), from the humility and discipline of hunting, from the quest after a great bear, a kind of forest cousin to Moby Dick, from the mysterious wilderness itself. So taught, he can no longer continue in the tradition to which he is born; at great and lasting cost to himself he surrenders his ancestral farm to the Edmonds branch.

It will of course be obvious that so personal and romantic a resolution as Ike McCaslin's is not being offered by Mr. Faulkner as a "solution" to the racial problem of the South; nor, in representing that problem through the sexual and blood relations of Negro and white, is he offering a comprehensive description of the problem in all its literalness. (Though here I should like to suggest that Mr. Faulkner may be hinting that the Southern problem, in so far as it is cultural, is to be found crystallized in its sexual attitudes: it is certainly worth remarking of this book that white women are singularly absent from it and are scarcely mentioned, that all the significant relations are between men, and that Isaac McCaslin is the only man who loves a woman.) But the romantic and transcendental resolution and the blood and sexual ties are useful fictional symbols to represent the urgency and the iniquity of the literal fact. They suggest that its depth and its complication go beyond what committees and commissions can conceive, beyond even the most liberal "understanding" and the most humanitarian "sympathy." Mr. Faulkner not only states this in the course of his book; he himself provides the proof: the story "Pantaloon in Black" is conceived in "understanding" and "sympathy," like every other lynching story we have ever read, and when it is set beside the McCaslin stories with their complicated insights it appears not only inadequate but merely formal, almost insincere.—Lionel Trilling, "The McCaslins of Mississippi," *Nation*, May 30, 1942, pp. 632–33

We have grown used to reading collections of short stories that masqueraded as novels so as to have a wider sale. Here is another sort of hybrid: a loosely jointed but ambitious novel masquerading as a collection of stories, possibly because William Faulkner was too proud or indifferent to call them chapters in a book.

Six of the seven episodes in *Go Down, Moses* deal with the McCaslin family, on its big plantation in northwestern Mississippi. These six have the same underlying theme, which is the price paid by many generations for the first McCaslin's relations with a slave girl who was also—trust Faulkner for this added detail—his illegitimate daughter. Four of the stories are concerned with his white grandson, Isaac McCaslin; they deal respectively with his parentage, his training as a hunter, his abnegation—if that is the word for what he did when he surrendered his plantation for the humbler inheritance he received from a half-Indian guide—and his last hunting trip into the wilderness. Two other stories deal with the first McCaslin's colored descendants, who also appear more briefly in the tales about old Isaac. One of them bears a child by her white cousin; another is electrocuted for shooting a Chicago policeman, and the white merchants of Jefferson pay for bringing his body home. Only one story, "Black Pantaloon," ⟨"Pantaloon in Black"⟩ has nothing to do with the McCaslin clan; it describes a murder and a lynching as a sequence of tragic events beyond good and evil.

The first story, "Was," comes close to being Faulkner's funniest, and the first half of "The Bear" is almost the best hunting yarn I have ever read. The trouble is that the book as a whole is a little too formless and repetitive to make a satisfactory novel, just as the seven episodes are a little too interdependent to stand completely alone. And there is another sense, too, in which *Go Down, Moses* is a hybrid. Most of the stories were first published in various magazines and met the strict rules they set for contributors; then afterwards they were revised and fitted together to meet the equally strict but quite different rules that Faulkner sets for himself. The magazine sections can still be recognized; they are straightforward prose, concerned only with telling a story. The later additions are in the curious idiom which Faulkner invented and sometimes writes magnificently, but which he writes at other times with no consideration for the reader.

Perhaps the best way to judge the book is neither as a novel nor as a series of novellas; neither as magazine nor as personal writing; but simply as another instalment of the Mississippi legend on which Faulkner has now been working for more than fifteen years. It is, as everyone knows by this time, the story of an imaginary county called Yoknapatawpha—area, 2,400 square miles; population, 15,611 by Faulkner's last census, which was printed at the end of *Absalom, Absalom!* At least a fifth of its people, Negro and white, have by now appeared in one or more of his stories. And these stories, although they differ in quality, and although the seven in *Go Down, Moses* are only his second-best, have each the effect of making the legend as a whole seem more impressive. There is no other American writer, and not many novelists anywhere, who have succeeded in presenting the life of a whole neighborhood, with all its social strata, all its personal conflicts, all its humor and much more than its share of violent crimes.

And there is no other American writer who has been so consistently misrepresented by his critics, including myself. William Faulkner is not a pure Romantic in the Poe tradition, as I asserted some years ago; on the contrary, some of his recent work seems closer to Mark Twain, with overtones of Turgenev. He does not hate the South, as several of the Nashville critics used to say; on the contrary, his work from beginning to end is inspired by deep love for this land, with its "woods for game and streams for fish and deep rich soil for seed and lush springs to sprout it and long summers to mature it and serene falls to harvest it and short mild winters for men and animals." He does not blame women or the Negro, or both together, for the decline of Southern culture, as Maxwell Geismar asserts in a recent essay; on the contrary, he feels that the planters themselves were guilty. He is not unable, as Mr. Geismar also says, to create a sympathetic character who is not a child or an idiot; on the contrary, his last two books have been full of sympathetic characters, and old Isaac McCaslin comes close to being a Christian saint. Finally he is not a negligible writer, a mere "Sax Rohmer for the sophisticated," as Granville Hicks once wrote; on the contrary he is, after Hemingway and perhaps Dos Passos, the most considerable novelist of this generation.—MALCOLM COWLEY, "Go Down to Faulkner's Land," *NR*, June 29, 1942, pp. 900–901

INTRUDER IN THE DUST

. . . ⟨It⟩ ought to be said that, from the point of view of the writing, ⟨*Intruder in the Dust*⟩ is one of the more snarled-up of Faulkner's books. It is not so bad as "The Bear," which has pages that are almost opaque. But in his attempt to record the perceptions—the instinctive sensations and the half-formed thoughts—of his adolescent boy, in aiming at prisms of prose which will concentrate the infrared as well as the ultraviolet, he leaves these rays sometimes still invisible, and only tosses into our hands some rather clumsy and badly cut polygons. It would require a good deal of very diligent work and very nice calculation always to turn out the combinations of words that would do what Faulkner wants. His energy, his image-making genius get him where he wants to go about seventy per cent of the time, but when he misses it, he lands in a mess. . . .

. . . ⟨Is⟩ pressure from outside worth nothing? Has it had no moral effect on the South? It seems to me that this book itself, which rejects outside interference, is a conspicuous sign that it has. The champions of Lucas Beauchamp are shown as rather reluctant, as even, at moments, resentful, in recognizing his rectitude and dignity, but they do rally energetically to clear him—all of them of the best old stock—in a way that I do not remember the inhabitants of Jefferson behaving in any other of Faulkner's books. Young Charles and his young Negro pal become regular Boy Scouts. Miss Habersham proves herself a dear, gallant old thoroughbred. The uncle is as ironic and delightful as the uncle of the boy next door in E. Nesbit's books about the Bastable children. And when this wonderful posse is on the march, they have hairbreadth escapes but get all the breaks. And, in the end, the vulgar people who wanted to see Lucas lynched get into their vulgar cars and turn tail and run away. There has been nothing so exhilarating in its way since the triumphs of the Communist-led workers in the early Soviet films; we are thrilled with the same kind of emotion that one got from some of the better dramatizations of the career of Abraham Lincoln.

This is a new note to come from the South; and it may really represent something more than Faulkner's own courageous and generous spirit, some new stirring of public conscience. In the meantime, in harping on this message, I do not want to divert attention from the excellence and interest of the book, which sustains the polymorphous vitality, the poetic truth to experience, of Faulkner's Balzacian chronicle of Yoknapatawpha County. Old Lucas and certain of the other characters have already appeared in *Go Down, Moses*, to which *Intruder in the Dust* is, indeed, more or less of a sequel, and the later adventures of Lucas are more interesting if you know his past history as recounted in the earlier volume, and understand his role in the tangle of black-and-white relationships which Faulkner has presented there. This subject of the complicated consequences of the mixture of white with Negro blood has been explored by Faulkner with remarkable intelligence and subtlety and variety of dramatic imagination; and Lucas himself, the black man who embarrasses a set of white relatives by having inherited the strongest traits of a common white ancestor, is one of the author's most impressive creations. Even when the prose goes to pieces, the man and his milieu live.—EDMUND WILSON, "William Faulkner's Reply to the Civil Rights Program," *NY*, Oct. 23, 1948, pp. 120, 127–28

There are probably very few novelists in America who have not in some depressed, sterile hour wished for Faulkner's madness. He is authentically, romantically possessed by his genius; he can lose himself not only in the act of writing but in the world his imagination has created and populated. He believes all of it, concretely, amazingly: the map of Yoknapatawpha County is not a joke. Here is a man who can take a walk in the morning and point to the spot where Wash Jones killed Sutpen or visit Compson's Mile for which Jason I swapped Ikkemotubbe a race horse. And he is so beautifully our young writer's image of the artist: he has done it by himself, in solitude, far from New York, in spite of critics, little magazines, fads, and professors—our natural genius, isolated, sure of himself, magnificently hallucinated as we feel the artist ought to be. And what a happy man he must have been, for what is there except the furious ecstasy of art's triumph over the artist's life in his extraordinary recent comments on the characters in *The Sound and the Fury*? He tells us that Candace, the heroine of a novel published in 1929, has vanished in Paris with the German occupation in 1940, that she is still beautiful and does not show her age. He's mad, of course; we remind ourselves that there is no Candace, nor a Jason, after the pages of the book are closed, to live on into a sour middle age and to sneak up the steps with his "big, plain, brazenhaired" mistress from Memphis. Still we cannot help but envy a writer so splendidly deluded; we feel an irrevocable calling to art ought to give us indifference to reality, that creative work should heal the misery of an unhappy love affair, pull us through nervous breakdowns, discount personal deficiencies, and in that sense most artists strive desperately for the same fantastic identification with their work and characters, the wondrous involvement with the imagination which Faulkner's little map symbolizes with an accuracy and simplicity almost beyond credulity. For it is either this or the slow, painful workings of the mind; either Faulkner's madness, large and self-sufficient, his stunning belief in his imaginary world, or something we secretly believe to be smaller: autobiographies, social observation, the neat situation, "the interesting but not creative."

His limitations, his overwriting and obfuscation are apparent; it is easy enough, if reckless, for Clifton Fadiman to satirize one of his most dazzling works ("One may sum up both substance and style by saying that every person in *Absalom, Absalom!* comes to no good end, and they all take a hell of a time coming even that far."), or to be really dreary about him, as Maxwell Geismar is, and hint at Fascism, the great "hatred," and the threat to the body politic in Faulkner's love of the past. But his six or seven superb novels insinuate themselves, no matter, and someone is always discovering that Faulkner is our greatest living novelist and saying it with a chip on his shoulder, belligerently, as though he expected to be booted out of the room. Indeed, Faulkner's reputation is curiously incomplete, somehow not authorized and catalogued. Like a patch of thrilling and famous scenery, almost everyone admires him but no one has anything very thrilling or famous to say about him.

One does not know whether to be glad or sorry that even Faulkner, the possessed, legendary writer, could not escape forever from the real Mississippi. His new novel, *Intruder in the Dust*, is astonishing: it is a tract, a polemic, even in its odd way a "novel of ideas." It is not what we expected and in it Faulkner appears as a hermit, perfect and necessary to our urban sentiments, who by chance picked up yesterday's newspaper, became annoyed with the state of the world and ran down from the hills to make a speech in the public square. It is less than his previous work, but fascinating because of that work and because it reveals the desperation of his present condition, the possibility that his inspired madness has disintegrated, leaving him, like everyone else, hollow and uncertain with the sickness and perplexity not of the past but of the present. The sickness of *Intruder in the Dust*, the fear and despair, are intimately connected with the future of Faulkner's career, a career which demands that there be a South, not just a geographical section and an accent, but a reasonably autonomous unit, a kind of family ready, and even with a measure of geniality, to admit the existence of the people next door and to cooperate in the necessary civic responsibilities, such as the removal of garbage and the maintenance of highways, but beyond that unique and separate, not to be reproached, advised, or mourned for the goings on behind the door. . . .

The brilliance of ⟨the novel's⟩ situation is that it is not so much about the Negro as about the South's appalled recognition of its sins, its confusion before the unforgiving, alienated faces of the Negroes whose suffering has given them immense pride and dignity, the moral superiority of the victim. The Negro must be saved, Faulkner seems to be saying, so that the white man can become his moral equal, be relieved of the bondage to his terrible mistake. . . .

Faulkner acknowledges the Negro's moral victory over the South, yields and desires his total civic equality ("Someday Lucas Beauchamp . . . will vote anywhen and anywhere a white man can and send his children to the same schools anywhere the white man's children go and travel anywhere the white man does as the white man does it"), scorns as he always has the depraved Southern murderer, the Percy Grimm who killed and emasculated Joe Christmas, and whose portrait Faulkner has drawn with a passionate condemnation not achieved to my knowledge, by any other writer.

This perception of the final emancipation of the Negro is real and historical, a fact and a victory only Stalinists and certain liberals feel compelled to underestimate. The sadistic passion these people take in disowning every triumph of the Negro in America, in predicting greater and greater injustice to him, is one of the most detestable aberrations of their minds. One can only believe they want violence in order to prove themselves right, as the deluded maniac, faced with the infuriating reason of the doctor, wishes to have a great bloody wound the next day to testify to the actual existence of his imaginary attackers. And when the Negroes are won over to the Communist Party have they not fallen in love with their own misfortune, since at no time is there so much discussion of lynchings, humiliating segregation, such delicious examination of white deceitfulness as between Stalinists and Negroes? The one never tires of "exposing" to the other an endless chronicle of dangers past and to come, as if the Negro did not know them well enough but had to taste, touch, and fondle them over and over until both are in a frenzy of indescribable perversity.

Faulkner's best intuitions have something to do with this phenomenon and there is at least a measure of psychological truth in his understanding that a cruel, lost South is necessary to the idea of America held by certain radicals. This intuition partly informs his plea that the South be allowed to redeem itself. Unfortunately he was not content with psychological perceptions, but had to compose a states' rights, leave us alone, don't be coming down here and telling us what to do, pamphlet which falsifies and degrades his fine comprehension of the moral dilemma of the decent guilt-ridden Southerner.

I think he was compelled to this not alone by a compulsive love of the South but also by the fact that he has lost his belief in the South as a unique region; he can reaffirm that belief only by imagining a mystic separation from the North, since his will to justice does not want a South unique because of its brutality to Negroes. He must believe that the contemporary Southerner is still close to his history, still romantically doomed, unable to forget the old disgrace, a proud, driven, image of the past. "For every Southern boy fourteen years old, not once but whenever he wants it, there is the instant when it's still not yet two o'clock on that July afternoon in 1863, the brigades are in position behind the rail fence, the guns are laid and ready in the woods and the furled flags are already loosened to break out and Pickett himself with his long oiled ringlets and his hat in one hand probably and his sword in the other looking up the hill waiting for Longstreet to give the word. . . ."

But this is unimaginable; it is literary, flamboyant, historically ridiculous in terms of America today. And it is also inconceivable, that the citizens of a few states are actually prepared, as Faulkner suggests, to risk their lives, their children, their futures, their wealth, or even their time in any sustained, hopeless revolt against the will of the country to which they are tied and which they need as much as anyone else. This is romantic, cowboy play acting, the election of Talmadge, the hootings and posturings of the Dixiecrats notwithstanding. The rebel yell on the radio—an unmistakable scream of buffoonery and self-mockery. It is the end, not the beginning, the end of Faulkner's imaginary kingdom and he is terrified by it.

The Negroes have migrated in vast numbers to the North and those who are left no longer feel tragically or gloriously fused with the destiny of the South. There are no Dilseys today, neither in the South nor in the North, neither black nor white, and Faulkner's immense, loving memorial to the Negro servant is not only a remarkable creative achievement but a contribution to social history, a painstaking study of a lost relationship which will appear, a few generations from now, as queer and archaic to the American as the role of a duenna. The white Southerner himself is ruled by the ambitions of the rest of the country which are all he can call upon if he is to survive and manage the American present.

Faulkner has caught up with the confusion of the country

today, and with bitterness he finds that it cannot be controlled and ordered or even thought about in the intimate, vitalizing way in which he knew and used the past. The language of *Intruder in the Dust* is fatefully indicative of what has happened to him and his vision. Upon a realistic, contemporary situation he has tried hopelessly, impossibly, to impose the grandiloquent cadences of *Absalom, Absalom!* and nothing could be more out of key, more jarring and defeating. The rhetoric of that gloomy marvel cannot give epic grandeur, vast passionate design to his parable of the present. Here everything is real, small, and practical. What we hear, in spite of every effort to disguise it, is not the old Faulknerian music, but the sour stutters and complaints of a writer fretting over his new, urgent, difficult material.—ELIZABETH HARDWICK, "Faulkner and the South Today," *PR*, Oct. 1948, pp. 1130–35

Intruder ⟨*in the Dust*⟩ is marvelously funny. Faulkner's veracity and accuracy about the world around keeps the comic thread from ever being lost or fouled, but that's a simple part of the matter. The complicated and intricate thing is that his stories aren't decked out in humor, but the humor is born in them, as much their blood and bones as the passion and poetry. Put one of his stories into a single factual statement and it's pure outrage—so would life be—too terrifying, too probable and too symbolic too, too funny to bear. There has to be the story, to bear it—wherein the statement, conjured up and implied and demonstrated, not said or the sky would fall on our heads, is yet the living source of his comedy—and a good part of that comedy's adjoining terror, of course.

It doesn't follow that *Intruder*, short, funny, of simple outline, with its detective-story casing, is one of the less difficult of Faulkner's novels. Offering side-by-side variations of numerous words, daringly long, building ever-working sentences (longer than *The Bear*'s, maybe, if anybody is counting), moods and moments arrested, pulled up to peaks, wilfully crowned with beauty and terror and surprise and comedy, Faulkner has at once re-explored his world with his marvelous style that can always search in new ways, and also appeared to use from beginning to end the prerogatives of an impromptu piece of work. It could be that to seem impromptu is an illusion great art can always give as long as profundities of theme, organization, and passionate content can come at a calling, but the art of what other has these cadenzas? Even the witty turns and the perfect neatness of plot look like the marks of a flash inspiration. If *Intruder* did come intruding in a literal way, shaped from the dust into life before the eyes, then we have a special wonder here; but it's none of our business, and the important thing is the wonder, special or not.

Time shifts its particles over a scene now and then, past and future like seasoning from a shaker, and Yoknapatawpha County we know now too, while the new story in its year, month, and ticking hour of day and night, emerges in that illumination and shading which Faulkner supplies to the last inch and the ultimate moment. The political views in *Intruder*, delivered outright as a speech, are made, rightly enough, another such shading to the story.

As in all Faulkner's work, the separate scenes leap up on their own, we progress as if by bonfires lighted on the way, and the essence of each scene takes form before the eyes, a shape in the fire. We see in matchless, "substituteless" (Faulkner's word for swearing) actuality and also by its contained vision: "Miss Habersham's round hat on the exact top of her head such as few people had seen in fifty years and probably no one at any time looking up out of a halfway rifled grave." Every aspect of vision is unique, springs absolute out of the material and the moment, only nominally out of "character" or "point of view," and so we see hats and happenings and every other thing, if not upwards from a half rifled grave, then down the road of the dark shuttered cabins, or up a jail stair, from the lonely ridge where Gowries come; or see in accompaniment with the smell of quicksand (a horse is there to get the smell and rear up), by the light even of impending conflagrations. Old Man Gowrie turning over a body that's the wrong body, not his son's, becomes "only an old man for whom grief was not even a component of his own but merely a temporary phenomenon of his slain son, jerking a strange corpse over onto its back not in appeasement to its one mute indicting cry not for pity not for vengeance not for justice but just to be sure he had the wrong one, crying cheery abashless and loud, 'Yep it's that damned Montgomery damned if it ain't!' " The boy's feverish dream of Miss Habersham trying to drive around the mob to get back to her own house, a vision of How the Old Woman Got Home, is this writer's imagination soaring like the lark.

Of course it's a feat, this novel—a double and delightful feat, because the mystery of the detective-story plot is being ravelled out while the mystery of Faulkner's prose is being spun and woven before our eyes. And with his first novel in eight years, the foremost critics are all giving cries as if (to change the image) to tree it. It's likely that Faulkner's prose can't be satisfactorily analyzed and accounted for, until it can be predicted, God save the day. Faulkner's prose, let's suspect, is intolerantly and intolerably unanalyzable and quite pure, something more than a possum in a tree—with its motes bright-pure and dark-pure falling on us, critics and non-critics alike.—EUDORA WELTY, "In Yoknapatawpha," *HdR*, Winter 1949, pp. 597–98

A FABLE

What Faulkner is trying to say in ⟨*A Fable*⟩ is matter for perplexity on a first reading, and far from pellucid thereafter; it will almost certainly be distorted wilfully by reviewers with axes of their own to grind. Yet his explicit message—for so it must be roundly named—is put in the novel itself in almost the same summary words in which he stated it in his Nobel Prize speech and in his Foreword to *The Faulkner Reader*. It is clear at least that Faulkner is totally engaged by this message, that for him it represents the consummation of "a life's work in the agony and sweat of the human spirit." That he has failed to find adequate incidents, agonists and symbols to realize it dramatically and poetically is a conviction that grows steadily and painfully upon the reader; that he has failed to dominate the intellectual problems with which he has been struggling—for the book cannot be taken as other than an effort at something like a social, a theological, a philosophical novel—is quite as evident. On the terms it sets for itself, the book demands to be judged not merely against the background of the author's own work, nor that of the current American novel, but by comparison with such awesomely mentionable names as Melville, Tolstoy, Dostoevsky and Mann. . . .

However labored the retelling of the Christ story, the book leaves no doubt that Faulkner's possession by it is profound and shaking. The precise nature of his religious commitment is less easy to determine. His Christianity is not of a conventional sort, though without doubt it will be both welcomed as such and repudiated as a "failure of nerve"; nor is it an orthodox one, though it has much in common with certain types of neo-orthodox and existential theology. Neither can it bulwark the Church Visible, which Faulkner with some allowance for exceptions assigns to the ranks of Caesarism and Rapacity. Faulkner's is most likely a humanistic—or, more accurately, a non-supernaturalistic—rendering of the Christian symbolism, and it offers no theodicy and no other-worldly beatitude. In his Nobel Prize speech and in his Foreword to *The Faulkner Reader*, he has defined his crystallizing purpose as a writer: "to uplift man's heart," "to say No to death," to show that "at least we are not vegetables," to help man to "teach himself that the basest of all things is to be afraid"; and he has summed up his credo quite simply—for our understanding of the novel, much too simply—in words that have already reverberated widely:

> I decline to accept the end of man. It is easy enough to say that man is immortal simply because he will endure: that when the last ding-dong of doom has clanged and faded from the last worthless rock hanging tideless in the last red and dying evening, that even then there will still be one more sound: that of his puny inexhaustible voice, still talking. I refuse to accept this. I believe that man will not merely endure: he will prevail. He is immortal, not alone because he alone among creatures has an inexhaustible voice, but because he has a soul, a spirit capable of compassion and sacrifice and endurance.

Both the corporal and the Negro preacher echo part of this credo, but a part only. Asked if he is an ordained minister, the Negro replies:

> I dont know. I bears witness."
>
> "To what? God?"
>
> "To man. God dont need me. I bears witness to Him of course, but my main witness is to man."
>
> "The most damning thing man could suffer would be a valid witness before God."
>
> "You're wrong there," the Negro said. "Man is full of sin and nature, and all he does dont bear looking at, and a heap of what he says is a shame and a mawkery. But cant no witness hurt him. Some day something might beat him, but it wont be Satan."

For all the primitive Christian attitudes which Faulkner expresses sympathetically—humility, a mystique of suffering, *agape*, victory through passive resistance—it is neither his Messianic figure nor the apostles who utter the crowning article in his credo, that man will not merely endure but prevail, but, by a breath-taking reversal, the generalissimo, who functions as both Pontius Pilate and Tempter, and is functionally the supreme representative of Caesarism. The generalissimo is, indeed, an ambiguous figure from the beginning. Scion of a noble family and the *Comité de Ferrovie*, the most brilliant graduate of St. Cyr, he refuses as a young officer to take the direct road to a marshal's baton but chooses for a hermitage a desert post in North Africa where he flouts his superiors by preventing a desired colonial war. We hear of him afterwards in a Tibetan lamasery and on his mysterious Balkan excursion; he reappears without explanation decades later as supreme commander in the war. He is compared to St. Anthony, but he is an anchorite of military austerity and patriotic devotion. And he engineers the quelling of the mutiny and the continuance of the war.

It is, then, with the surprise of shock that in the last conversation between father and son we hear the generalissimo expressing the more difficult faith in man, one which survives even the acceptance of the inevitability of wars and the multiplication of the Frankenstein machines which make man's plight ever less controllable and his wars more devastating. He says to the corporal at the end of the Temptation scene:

> "Afraid? No no, it's not I but you who are afraid of man; not I but you who believe that nothing but a death can save him. I know better. I know that he has that in him which will enable him to outlast even his wars; that in him more durable than all his vices, even that last and most fearsome one; to outlast even this next avatar of his servitude which he now faces: his enslavement to the demonic progeny of his own mechanical curiosity, from which he will emancipate himself by that ancient tried-and-true method by which slaves have always freed themselves: by inculcating their masters with the slaves' own vices—in this case the vice of war and that other one which is no vice at all but instead is the quality-mark and warrant of man's immortality: his deathless folly. . . ."

And it is the old marshal rather than the Messiah who ventures an apocalypse—not of a New Jerusalem where lion and lamb will lie down together but of an endless blood-letting and even the final devastation of the planet. Man, he foresees, will endure through all this, though the prophecy has to invoke science fiction to support the faith:

> ". . . already the next star in the blue immensity of space will be already clamorous with the uproar of his debarkation, his puny and inexhaustible voice still talking, still planning; and there too after the last ding dong of doom has rung and died there will still be one sound more: his voice, planning to build something higher and faster and louder; more efficient and louder and faster than ever before, yet it too inherent with the same old primordial fault since it too in the end will fail to eradicate him from the earth. I dont fear man. I do better: I respect and admire him. And pride: I am ten times prouder of that immortality which he does possess than ever he of that heavenly one of his delusion. Because man and his folly—"
>
> "Will endure," the corporal said.
>
> "They will do more," the old general said proudly. "They will prevail.—Shall we return?"

Although this is the last explicit word on the subject, we should not in consequence accept the marshal as the author's final spokesman. It is possible to take the corporal's subsequent apotheosis as the Unknown Soldier to be a forecast of the victory of Christ over Caesar; the incident has too much irony, however, for us to be happy about such a construction: the undying flame beneath the Arc de Triomphe after all commemorates devotion to country and therefore, in terms of Faulknerian Christianity, to Caesar. Nor, I believe, can we simply take the generalissimo to be the devil or the devil's advocate and treat the scene as the equivalent of the Grand Inquisitor section of *The Brothers Karamazov*, though the partial correspondence is obvious. Against this interpretation obtrudes not only the fact that it is the marshal who voices, even though for radically different reasons, the author's belief that man will not merely endure but prevail, but also the fact that he is the Messiah's father, and consequently stands to him in the relation of the first person of the Trinity, however much we must depart from the orthodox conceptions of this. The puzzle is heightened by the difference between the passage in the novel and the affirmation in the Nobel Prize speech. The former says that man will prevail because of his magnificent pride and folly; the latter says he will prevail because of his compassion and sacrifice (endurance is comprised in both versions).

To try to resolve this puzzle would get us into theological and moral questions which Faulkner himself steers clear of and probably has never confronted in abstract terms. One way out would be to construe the ending as a monstrous irony and nothing more: a forecast of the defeat of Christian virtues and even a repudiation of them. Another way, which would also account for the fusion of God and Satan in the ambivalent person of the generalissimo, would take the heretical tack—in Faulkner's case we cannot rule out the likelihood of some kind of heresy—that the New Covenant has not fulfilled and superseded the Old but inverted it; in which case Faulkner would be leaving open the Nietzschean possibility that a second transvaluation of values is called for. Still a third alternative would be that of Barthian neo-orthodoxy: the victory of Christ over Caesar is purely other-worldly and not even a partial redemption of man in time and history. None of these solutions fits the novel.

From a European writer of Faulkner's stature we would expect in the treatment of such a theme, even if no answer, at least a sharper and richer debate in contemporary theological and philosophical terms than Faulkner gives us: there is a considerable amount of debate in the book, but it tapers off into nebulous language. Lionel Trilling has commented at length and penetratingly on both the limitations and the partial advantages that Faulkner and Hemingway as representative American writers exhibit because of their chosen and even vaunted "indifference to the conscious intellectual tradition of the time." Faulkner's explicit handling of ideas, outside as well as within the domain of theology, is usually amateurish. When, for example, as happens repeatedly in the novel, a cause is assigned to the war, it is the familiar simplification current in the 1920's: that it was an international conspiracy of the munitions makers and the generals. The generalissimo could, speaking in character, have introduced some needed complications, but he does not do so.

In trying to get some kind of foothold on the implicit ideational purport of the book, we can at least note some remote parallels to doctrines of such theologians as Tillich and Niebuhr. For the former, man's precarious triumph consists in his Courage to Be, which includes the courage to face anxiety and the eventual non-being in time which is his individual destiny: the Christ figure as the "concrete absolute" is the paradigm for this courage. For both theologians, man's redemption is not an ultimate victory of the Christian message in time, but both a timeless realization and a never-ending battle to wring some approximation to it from the relativities of history.

We can't be confident as to what intellectualized beliefs if any undergird the novel, and it is useless to conjecture what Faulkner would say if he articulated them fully. What we are compelled to do is to ask what sort of vision has been earned by the raw experience that the author has put into his work beyond the half-explicit formulations. The new book is not a simple about-face from Faulkner's previous writing, but has a positive continuity with it. Aside from his "primitives"—such as the frontiersmen and Indians who represent a golden age that is gone beyond recovery—in his fiction of the South two kinds of characters chiefly have dignity: Negroes and unreconstructed aristocrats. Faulkner's allegiance is divided between the two sets of virtues which they exhibit. His sympathies are enlisted both by the virtues of slave-morality and those of master-morality (each in a Mississippian rather than a Nietzschean version), without his being able to commit himself wholeheartedly to either. His Negroes, the insulted and injured yet faithful, alone are "Christians," and they have found a way to endure while accepting their status as victims. The unvanquished among the Sartorises and Compsons do not endure literally; in fact they come to an early end. But they achieve a kind of immortality by style and gesture, through a code of honor. Their self-destructive pride and bravado make them live in the imaginations of men. Both sets of characters in their different ways endure and prevail. That such classic qualities as reason, moderation, disciplined imagination and political acumen can also help man to survive and intermittently triumph is nowhere acknowledged by Faulkner, though they are sometimes approximated in his sturdier but less glamorous characters, usually poor whites by origin. Anything Greek in Faulkner's world is of the Saturnian reign and the Dionysian rebellion: Apollo and Athene are absent from his pantheon.

When Faulkner leaves the microcosm of Yoknapatawpha for the great world of contemporary society, he maintains the same attitudes at whatever cost of oversimplification. The suffering servant is now the common soldier or the European peasant; the man of deathless folly is the army flyer, the stunt pilot or the professional military leader. In *A Fable*, despite the violent and forced invocation of Christian allegory, it is possible to see why the triumph of man is proclaimed by the generalissimo, regardless of consistency with the Nobel Prize speech. For the aesthetic vision, of a high romantic mold, struggles to some kind of victory over the moral: the meek may inherit the earth, but the "aristocratic" virtues, however tarnished, hold the allegiance of the novelist.

Even though *A Fable* is an eccentric and dreamlike commentary on modern society, and artistically unachieved, it at times commands partial respect by the heat of the vision and the depth of the concern. It is brave in these days to have persisted in seeking some kind of faith in man. But for evidence of Faulkner's mastery we must return to those books in which his troubled spiritual questings had not burst the bounds of his resources. In this book only those sections are convincing that, like the episode of the race horse and the doings of the airmen, are deeply imbued by the author's experience and encompassed by his intellect.—PHILIP BLAIR RICE, "Faulkner's Crucifixion," *KR*, Autumn 1954, pp. 662–70

WALTER J. SLATOFF
"Conclusions"
Quest for Failure: A Study of William Faulkner
1960, pp. 239–65

Faulkner's ambiguity and irresolution, at bottom, are more a matter of temperament than of deliberate artistic intent, as will be shown later. Up to a point, however, we may understand them as serving or reflecting two general intentions.

The first of these is to achieve powerful emotive and perhaps even hypnotic effects. This intention becomes clear when we understand something of Faulkner's generally irrationalistic attitudes. Conrad Aiken has suggested that what Faulkner is after, in part, is a "medium without stops or pauses," an "image stream" toward which the reader "must be powerfully and unremittingly hypnotized," and Aiken suggests that this intent to hypnotize accounts, perhaps, not only for the length and elaborateness of Faulkner's sentence structure but for his repetitiveness as well.[1] It is likely that the frequent resistance of Faulkner's work to rational analysis also contributes to this hypnotic effect. Some passages from Edward Snyder's *Hypnotic Poetry* strongly suggest that this may be true. Professor Snyder notes that in actual hypnosis the stimuli used "are such as to fix the attention while retarding mental activity," and he concludes that the same retardation of mental activity is helpful in producing the less complete hypnoidal state which he calls "emotional trance," a state in which the subject's emotional susceptibility is highly intensified.[2] In his Foreword to Snyder's book, the psychologist James Leuba writes that Snyder has "demonstrated the existence of a type of poetry which owes its attraction to a method of composition, the effect of which is to limit the intellectual activity, i.e., to induce a state of partial trance, and thereby to free in some measure the emotional life from the trammel of critical thinking."[3]

Whether Faulkner actually induces a state of partial trance is not especially important here. And I do not wish to suggest that the spell he puts upon us is deadening or paralyzing. Quite the contrary. It does seem likely, however, that the purpose and effect of much of his presentation is to free the emotional life from the "trammel" of critical thinking, so that like the preacher in *The Sound and the Fury*, who is also in a sense a hypnotist, he might speak directly to the "heart." To some extent, we can say of Faulkner, as McCaslin says was true for God, that he "didn't have His Book written to be read by what must elect and choose, but by the heart" (*GDM*, 260). I do not mean to connect the word "heart" entirely with the words "emotive" or "hypnotic," and Faulkner's own use of the word "heart" is inconsistent, but there is no doubt that he sees the heart essentially as an organ of feeling and as antithetic to the head and that he regards it, not the head, as providing the way to truth. "Ideas and facts," he has said in an interview, "have very little connection with truth."[4] We give ourselves "mind's reason[s]," says Ike McCaslin, "because the heart dont always have time to bother with thinking up words that fit together" (*GDM*, 348).

An even greater distrust of the head is suggested when he speaks of "fact and probability" as "rubble-dross" (*RN*, 261) and when he equates "that best of ratiocination," to which Quentin and Shreve are dedicated, with Sutpen's dead morality and Miss Coldfield's "demonizing" (*AA*, 280). Jason Compson, whom Faulkner has said he considers the most vicious and detestable of his creations, is in a sense the most logical of his characters. Faulkner describes him as "the first sane Compson since before Culloden. . . . Logical, rational" (*SF*, 16). Faulkner's most sympathetically presented characters, on the other hand, tend to be virtually inchoate or else, like Gavin Stevens, they speak with little regard for rational sequence or organization. And, of course, Faulkner's own style—with its syntactical violations, pseudo syntax, shifting metaphors, and oxymorons—suggests, at the least, a desire to transcend the usual rational processes of comprehension. So does his deprecation of Hemingway for staying within limits and his affirmation of his own and Thomas Wolfe's desire to go beyond this, to attempt the impossible.

Allied with his desire to transcend the usual rational processes is an obvious discontent with the ability of language to convey truth. This is evident not only in his stylistic straining at the limits of language but in his various comments about the chasm between life and print or, as Addie Bundren puts it, between "words" and "doing." Like Addie, he also seems to fear not only that "words don't ever fit even what they are trying to say at" (*AILD*, 463) but that they are empty substitutes for feeling and experience: "sounds that people who never sinned nor loved nor feared have for what they never had and cannot have until they forget the words" (*AILD*, 465).

Much of Faulkner's presentation, I think, is designed to prevent his readers from substituting language and "mind's reasons" for the actual experiences he is trying to suggest. The equation of a single word with a feeling, the suggestion that they can possibly be synonymous, is especially to be avoided. This helps to explain why Faulkner so often begins his descriptions negatively, by saying it was not one thing but another, or describes feelings or conditions as a tension between poles or an approximation of a pole or even something beyond a pole, gives us a term like fear (or love or rage) and then says it was not that but almost that or something beyond that. Perhaps it helps to explain, also, why he uses so many words. Similarly, his oxymorons, synesthetic images, mixed metaphors, pseudo syntax, noncoherent "explanations," and alternate and multiple suggestions, all prevent us from comfortably substituting language and logic for feelings; they all counteract our tendency to construct pigeon holes in order to forget the things we put in them. This same intention, I think, has much to do with the larger and more general ambiguities and irresolution that prevent us from integrating our responses to the novels as wholes. For so long as our reactions are in a suspension rather than in crystallized form, they remain feelings and experiences rather than rational or verbal constructions.

The foregoing would seem to be reasonably safe, though partial, conclusions. But I would like to suggest a further, somewhat more tenuous aspect of Faulkner's irrationalism: his tendency to take and present a somewhat Bergsonian view of both experience and comprehension.

Like Bergson, he often tends to view experience as a state of the whole being or of the self and to conceive of the self as an indivisible internal process which can only be intuited and cannot really be defined either by analysis or images. It is this notion of experience and self which Rosa suggests when she refers to herself as, "not my body . . . but I, myself, that deep existence which we lead" (*AA*, 137). It is this which Faulkner suggests in his frequent descriptions of an experience or act as something participated in by the "whole" or "entire" being. For example, when Joe Christmas tries to feel what it is like to be a Negro he can feel "his whole being writhe and strain with physical outrage and spiritual denial" (*LIA*, 197). Faulkner's presentation often seems in accord also with Bergson's view that "every feeling . . . contains within it the whole past and present of the being experiencing it."[5] We find Faulkner again and again using the flashback to add to a feeling or event the whole past of the being experiencing it. Again and again he interrupts an important experience not merely to describe one past event or a few associations called up by the present experience but to recapitulate much and sometimes all of a character's essential past up to that point. His description of experience as both cumulative and retroactive (*U*, 145) is in accord with this view.

More significant, however, is Faulkner's attempt to present this experiencing self through images of motion and tension. Although Bergson insists that no image can fully express the nature of the self, he does view the self essentially as motion and tension. After comparing the inner life to "the unrolling of a coil" or "a continual rolling up, like that of a thread on a ball,"[6] he writes: "Finally let us free ourselves from the space which underlies the movement in order to continue only the movement itself, the act of tension or extension; in short pure mobility. We shall have this time a more faithful image of the development of our self in duration."[7] Later he says that "intuition" is as distinct from a summary or synthesis of knowledge "as the motor impulse is distinct from the path traversed by the moving body, as the tension of the spring is distinct from the visible movements of the pendulum."[8]

Again and again . . . Faulkner presents important psychological experiences of his characters as sensations of movement or tension of an undefined internal self or as tensions between the velocities of different parts of the self, as though the self were a series of motions. His even more frequent presentations of psychological conditions as generalized states of quiescence and turbulence and as gatherings and releases, although not in strict keeping, perhaps, with a Bergsonian view of self, all suggest that he frequently conceives of the self as an indivisible organic and dynamic process and that he views experiences as conditions of that dynamic process rather than as specific and analyzable reactions. What we know about Faulkner's characters, as pointed out earlier, is not their thoughts or specific emotions or even their likes and dislikes so much as their general state of quiescence or turbulence, usually a state of tension. What we witness then in Faulkner's works is in large measure a vision of the dynamics of the human psyche or the process which some psychologists have labeled "primitive sensation," a vision of the quiescences, turbulences, tensions and releases, writhings and strainings of man viewed not from without, as mosaic, but from within, as whole being.

Faulkner often thinks of comprehension in a similar way, seeing true understanding not as intellectual act but as experience—experience again defined as feeling, sensation, and dynamic process of the whole being, something very different from the words and sentences usually used to convey it. This comprehension comes not from disinterested detachment but from involvement, empathy, identity. It is the kind of comprehension Quentin has of part of the Sutpen story, having "absorbed it . . . without the medium of speech somehow from having been born and living beside it, with it, as children will and do" (AA, 212–213). It is the kind Judith and Sutpen have of each other "who seem to know one another so well or are so much alike that" they comprehend "without need of the medium of ear or intellect" (AA, 122). Will Varner wants "to find out what it must have felt like to be the fool that would need all this [a large mansion] just to eat and sleep in" (*H*, 7). That is, he wants to imaginatively re-experience it. What Rosa, Hightower, and other of Faulkner's narrators explicitly demand of their listeners is not that they understand or even sympathize in the usual sense so much as feel what happened, share in the experience: hear it, smell it, above all "feel" it. Addie beats her pupils so that her blood in them will run and make them "aware" of her, make her something in their "secret and selfish" lives.

The fullest comprehension of something, Faulkner sometimes suggests, would come not merely from being close to it, feeling it, or even from imaginatively projecting oneself into it, but from a kind of mystical union with it. Thus Quentin and Shreve are finally described not only as riding along with Charles and Henry but as somehow merging with them into a new twosome "smelling the very smoke which had blown and faded away forty-six years ago" (AA, 351). Thus Gavin Stevens muses that "by the act of eating and maybe only by that" can man

> actually enter the world, get himself into the world: not through it but into it, burrowing into the world's teeming solidarity like a moth into wool by the physical act of chewing and swallowing the substance of its warp and woof and so making, translating into a part of himself and his memory, the whole history of man. [*ID*, 207]

Here again Faulkner's view is close to Bergson's belief that real understanding comes only through "intuition," which he defines as an entering into an object, a coincidence with it, rather than a viewing from without.

> The author may multiply the traits of his hero's character, may make him speak and act as much as he pleases, but all this can never be equal to the simple and indivisible feeling which I should experience if I were able for an instant to identify myself with the person of the hero himself. . . . [T]hat which is properly himself, that which constitutes his essence cannot be perceived from without, being internal by definition. . . . Coincidence with the person himself would alone give me the absolute.[9]

It is this kind of comprehension Joe Christmas so desperately seeks as he tries "to breathe into himself the dark odor, the dark and inscrutable thinking and being of Negroes" (*LIA*, 197).

If the essence or inmost self of another person is a dynamic process, the ultimate act of empathy or identity would be to experience that dynamic process. To empathize would not mean merely to think the thoughts the other person thinks or to feel the specific sensory responses he feels; it would mean to share the movements, quiescences, turbulences, tensions, releases, writhings, and strainings of his inmost self. This, I believe, is the kind of response Faulkner often wants to produce in the reader. The reader's act of comprehension is not to be from without, not a detached contemplative or evaluative act, but rather an empathic experience, a comprehension from within. He is not so much to observe and judge characters, as to feel what they feel, as nearly as possible, to be them. He is to comprehend as much as possible as Quentin comprehends the South, through somehow absorbed heritage, and as Quentin and Shreve come to comprehend Henry and Charles, through identity. Like Will Varner he is to experience what things and people "felt like." And since the ultimate act of comprehending something would be to empathize or identify with its essence, essence seen as dynamic process, much of the reader's experience is to be the experience of tensions and dynamic process within his own being.

It is the degree to which Faulkner provides this last kind of experience that most marks him off from other modern novelists who try, as he does, to give their readers an essentially empathetic experience through interior monologues, spiral movement, sensory emphasis, hypnotic repetition, evocative images, and symbols. And it is this which accounts for much of the peculiar force of his work. We can say that he produces these deep inner movements and tensions largely by his persistent and many-pronged stimulation of the kinesthetic and visceral senses, but we must understand that the phrase "kinesthetic and visceral senses" is inadequate here and that there is undoubtedly a profound kinship between the responses we call "kinesthetic" and "visceral" and our fundamental sense of life and of our own being; certainly there is a deep kinship between those responses and the experiences of the kind of inmost self Faulkner assumes. We must understand, also, that empathy is largely dependent upon such motor and visceral responses.[10]

These responses to Faulkner's work are brought about in part by his continual emphasis on motion, quiescence and turbulence, and tension and release, that is, by the consistency with which the external and internal worlds are presented as dynamic process. They are even more powerfully stimulated by Faulkner's persistent use of certain kinds of antithesis, those antitheses which juxtapose irreconcilable elements and leave the reader with the tension of an impasse and those antitheses which simultaneously suggest movement, activity, or impulse and restraint of movement, activity, or impulse. I am thinking now not only of images like "rapt dynamic immobility," "hanging immobilised by the heels in attitudes of frantic running," or "calm and contained and rigidly boiling," but of the many larger struggles within and between characters and between characters and natural forces, which have the same qualities and effects as such images.

In a more general way the same sorts of deep inner tension are induced by Faulkner's techniques of "deliberately withheld meaning" and "of progressive and partial and delayed disclosure," as Conrad Aiken puts it, and by his long involuted and interrupted sentences and paragraphs, for they continually block or retard the urge of eye and intellect to move forward. It is no accident that Joseph Warren Beach chooses powerful visceral images to describe the effect of these techniques. "Half the time we are swimming under water, holding our breath and straining our eyes to read off the meaning of submarine phenomena. . . . From time to time we come to the surface, gasping, to breathe the air of concrete fact and recorded truth, only to go floundering again the next moment through crashing waves of doubt and speculation."[11]

Finally, I think, our total response to the novels is to a large extent one of deep and profound tension. For unless we possess an unusually high degree of negative capability, we are not content with complex unresolved suspensions and are deeply frustrated and strained by our inability to integrate our thoughts and feelings. To the extent that the experience of Faulkner's characters has been a matter of powerful inner movements and tensions we are by our own similar responses sharing their experience and thereby, in a Bergsonian sense, most deeply "intuiting" and comprehending it.

To what extent Faulkner is consciously seeking the kinds of effects just described I am not sure. At one time I felt that one could trace in Faulkner's works and public statements a fairly consistent mystical vision very much in accord with Bergson's philosophy, a vision of time being defeated by a process in which the past experience of men, experience understood primarily as tension, is involved with the past and future in the form of tension, a vision, in the largest sense, of the *élan vital*, the life force itself, enduring in time. And I felt that Faulkner's reiterated assertion that "man will endure" was to be understood essentially in those terms, as was his assertion that both the writer and reader were enabled to "say No to death" by means of the capacity of the writer's words to engender "the old deathless excitement in hearts and glands."[12] I have come to feel, however, that, although one can make a case for the existence of such a vision in the works, it is too intermittent and partial, and too often contradicted, to be seen as anything other than one more of the many ideas and themes that lie in loose suspension with one another.

I have dwelt upon the Bergsonian approach to experience and comprehension because, regardless of Faulkner's intention, it seems a valid and illuminating way to look at his works. It explains much of his power and makes the tension he produces in the reader more purposeful and meaningful than it might seem if we see it merely as the consequence of a less specific irrationalism which desires only to prevent us from translating feeling into language or abstract formulations.

Yet even to see a general sort of irrationalism as the governing principle behind Faulkner's works is not entirely satisfactory, for there is too much that it does not explain. Faulkner's ambiguity and irresolution must also be understood as asserting and reflecting a somewhat more intellectual intention and view of life. It is difficult to define this view and almost impossible to draw a dividing line between the view and Faulkner's temperament. Warren Beck has helped to illuminate this view of life:

> If Faulkner's sentences sometimes soar and circle involved and prolonged, if his scenes become halls of mirrors repeating tableaux in a progressive magnification, if echoes multiply into the dissonance of infinite overtones, it is because the meanings his stories unfold are complex, mysterious, obscure, and incomplete. There is no absolute, no eternal pure white radiance in such presentations, but rather the stain of many colors, refracted and shifting in kaleidoscopic suspension, about the center of man's enigmatic behavior and fate, within the drastic orbit of mortality. Such being Faulkner's view of life, such is his style.[13]

Karl Zink asserts that "at its best, form in Faulkner's art constitutes a living effort to penetrate and to realize in art an ineffable complexity."[14]

Certainly these critics are right that Faulkner's work often embodies and suggests a view that life is enigmatic and ineffably complex. To a large extent his shifts in tone and point of view, his avoidance of resolution, and his various obstacles to rational understanding may be seen as an effort so to present life and experience as to make facile interpretation impossible. The meaning of the stories of Sutpen and Joe Christmas and others, Faulkner is saying, is largely ambiguous: Whether they are free agents or pawns, heroes or villains, is ambiguous, just as it is uncertain whether the tall convict is a hero or a fool, whether Darl Bundren is a seer or a madman, and whether the desperate struggles of the convict, the Bundrens, and others are tragic or comic, significant or futile. Whether or not there is a God is also problematical and, if there is, whether he is to be thought of as Jehovah, Christ, Satan, Joker, Umpire, Chess Player, or life force. Even about the one certainty—that "man will endure"—we are to wonder whether he will endure by virtue of his soul or his folly and whether enduring means primarily to suffer or to transcend time. These "alternative" views, we must remember, are usually presented in such a way that we can neither choose between them nor combine them. Faulkner does not permit us to think of a character as part hero and part fool or of events as partly significant and partly futile. Like the terms of most of Faulkner's oxymorons the "alternatives" remain at once together and apart.

To say that Faulkner sees and presents life as enigmatic and ineffably complex is not enough, however; such a description leaves out important qualities of his feeling about life, qualities that are inseparable from his view of life.

> You get born and you try this and you dont know why only you keep on trying it and you are born at the same time with a lot of other people, all mixed up with them, like trying to, having to, move your arms and legs with strings only the same strings are hitched to all the other arms and legs and the others all trying and they dont know why either except that the strings are all in one another's way like five or six people all trying to make a rug on the same loom only each one wants to weave his own pattern into the rug; and it cant matter, you know that, or the Ones that set up the loom would have arranged things a little better, and yet it must matter because you keep on trying. [AA, 127]

The words are Judith Sutpen's, but the passage communicates more clearly than any other, I believe, the essence of Faulkner's view of life and his feeling toward it. The passage suggests not only the complex and enigmatic qualities of life, but the sense of life as conflict, tension, and frustration, which persistently informs Faulkner's presentation. Above all, it suggests the intense contradictory feelings which, as much as anything else, I think, explain Faulkner's attitude toward life and toward his own art: "It cant matter, you know that, . . . and yet it must matter." It cannot have meaning and yet it must. The statement does not simply describe a dual perspective (sometimes seems to matter, sometimes not) or an uncertainty (may or may not matter) or even a paradox (does and does not matter). The simultaneous "cant" and "must" suggests a desperately divided and tormented perspective, a condition of mind which tries to move simultaneously and intensely toward both order and chaos and which understandably seizes upon the figure which most nearly moves in both directions, the oxymoron.

This division in view and feeling about the meaningfulness of life and effort accounts, undoubtedly, for Faulkner's frequent explicit and implicit coupling of terms like "empty" and "profound," "futile" and "tragic," and for phrases such as "the substance itself [life] not only not dead, not complete, but in its very insoluble enigma of human folly and blundering possessing a futile and tragic immortality" (*P*, 85), and "profound and irrevocable if only in the sense of being profoundly and irrevocably unimportant" (*P*, 111). This division helps us also to understand Faulkner's seemingly obsessive assertion and denial of immortality and to account for his often perceptive idiots and incoherent intellectuals. It accounts, in part, for his failure to pursue thoroughly many of the ideas and meanings which he has suggested, even more, for his ability to urge certain meanings intensely and then to ignore them or to contradict them with equal intensity, and also for his use of form both to illuminate and to obscure. It is a view and feeling which, in general, makes it necessary for him to try continuously to affirm and deny, to illuminate and obscure, the meaning of his own artistic creations and the significance of the lives and experiences he presents. It accounts, perhaps, for his inability finally to commit himself and for his ability to treat art both as a plaything and a dedication. Undoubtedly it helps to explain the utterly divergent critical estimates and interpretations of his work. Finally, I believe, it accounts in large measure for the peculiarly compelling and disturbing power of his works, for it reminds us of the similar schizophrenia within ourselves which we have worked hard to bury.

Generally skeptical views of life, or dual perspectives in which life appears in some ways meaningful and in some ways meaningless, are not uncommon, are certainly comprehensible, and have informed much great art, including that of Shakespeare. Metaphysical poetry and Jacobean drama, at times, seem to suggest a division of feeling, as well as of view, about life's meaningfulness, which is as intense as Faulkner's. There is still, however, an important difference. Whatever the tensions and opposing suggestions, explicit or implicit, in a poem by Donne or a play by Webster, one feels behind them, I think, a governing mind which never really doubts the validity of its own ideas and perceptions or the possibility, if not the existence, of a moral universe in which such ideas and perceptions are relevant, which never abandons the effort to order its thoughts and emotions. Like many modern artists Faulkner has no such certainty.

Unlike any other modern of comparable stature, however, Faulkner's uncertainty also embraces his art. Virginia Woolf, Joyce, and even Kafka never seem to have really doubted the validity of art, and they have used it always to resist and to recreate as well as to reflect the dissolving worlds they saw and felt about them. They remain committed to order and reason. There have been some writers and painters, the surrealists and Dadaists, who have not resisted, whose uncertainty or despair has led them to deny reason, whose desperation has led them to protest against disorder with disorder. A part of Faulkner remains intensely committed to art and order and seeks desperately, and of course paradoxically, to find a way by which art can order equally intense convictions that life and art do and do not matter. A part of him is content with disorder.

Finally, however, I do not think we can adequately explain the kinds of tensions and suspensions we find in Faulkner's work except in terms of temperament. At bottom, his works seem governed not so much by a view of life, or by a particular gap in his thought and feeling, or by particular principles of organization as by his temperament, that is, by the particular compound of intellectual and emotional inclinations, tendencies, and responses that characterize his mental life and shape his reactions to experience. It is his temperamental responses, rather than any theories or ideas or particular torments, which he undoubtedly trusts to produce and to order his art. Any work of art, of course, reflects the temperament of its author and in some ultimate sense is governed by his temperament. But in Faulkner's case, the relationship between art and temperament seems far more immediate, direct, and pervasive than is true for most novelists. With most writers we can think of temperament as providing coloring or flavoring or at most as affecting their choice and treatment of material; with Faulkner it becomes an inextricable part of the very structure and meaning of his work. I mean this quite literally—that both the form and meanings of his works are governed much less by any controlling ideas, or themes, or dramatic or aesthetic considerations than by a succession of temperamental impulses and responses. The finished work becomes, in a sense, the record of a process, the record of the artist's struggle with his materials, rather than the record of his victory over his materials. Yet even this way of putting it is misleading, for it suggests a priority to the materials that I do not think they possess in Faulkner's case. To a large extent the materials, themselves, are proliferations which come into being as a direct result of temperamental impulse. In many cases the proliferations become the chief substance of the books.

When asked about the composition of *The Sound and the Fury*, Faulkner answered as follows:

> That began as a short story, it was a story without plot, of some children being sent away from the house during the grandmother's funeral. They were too young to be told what was going on and they saw things only incidentally to the childish games they were playing, which was the lugubrious matter of removing the corpse from the house, etc., and then the idea struck me to see how much more I could have got out of the idea of the blind, self-centeredness of innocence, typified by children, if one of those children had been truly innocent, that is, an idiot. So the idiot was born and then I became interested in the relationship of the idiot to the world that he was in but would never be able to cope with and just where could he get the tenderness, the help, to shield him in his innocence. I mean "innocence" in the sense that God had stricken him blind at birth, that is, mindless at birth, there was nothing he could ever do about it. And so the character of his sister began to emerge, then the brother, who, that Jason (who to me represented complete evil. He's the most vicious character in my opinion I ever thought of), then he appeared. Then it needs the protagonist, someone to tell the story, so Quentin appeared. By that time I found out I couldn't possibly tell that in a short story. And so I told the idiot's experience of that day, and that was incomprehensible, even I could not have told what was going on then, so I had to write another chapter. Then I decided to let Quentin tell his version of that same day, or that same occasion, so he told it. Then there had to be the counterpoint, which was the older brother, Jason. By that time it was completely confusing. I knew that it was not anywhere near finished and then I had to write another section from the outside with an outsider, which was the writer, to tell what had

> happened on that particular day. And that's how that book grew. That is, I wrote that same story four times. None of them were right, but I had anguished so much that I could not throw any of it away and start over, so I printed it in the four sections. That was not a deliberate *tour de force* at all, the book just grew that way. That I was still trying to tell one story which moved me very much and each time I failed, but I had put so much anguish into it that I couldn't throw it away, like the mother that had four bad children, that she would have been better off if they all had been eliminated, but she couldn't relinquish any of them. And that's the reason I have the most tenderness for that book, because it failed four times.[15]

Although we probably cannot accept this as an entirely literal or accurate account in view of other statements Faulkner has made about the book,[16] I believe it nevertheless reveals much about the way his works come into being and about the kind of entities they are. It does so especially when we remember that the various narrators do not, as Faulkner says they do, focus upon the same day or the same occasion and that each section develops and emphasizes a new set of events, builds a new story. Faulkner's insistence that he was trying to tell "one story" may not at first seem in entire accord with the notion that Faulkner's proliferations become the substance of his books, but it does fit if we recognize that the "story" was not something Faulkner had clearly in mind but something he vaguely sensed and was reaching for. The book, then, as we have it, is in a sense the record of the process of reaching. We can say the reason he failed is that, each time he reached, his proliferations and temperamental impulses put the "story" farther out of reach. Interesting also is Faulkner's statement that "there had to be the counterpoint," a notion I shall comment on later.

Perhaps even more suggestive of how much the proliferations can overwhelm a germinal idea is Faulkner's insistence that in *A Fable* he was "primarily" telling the tragic story of "the father who had to choose between the sacrifice or the saving of his son."[17] It is not too much to say, I think, that in the completed work this story is virtually lost amid the other stories and other emphases. One even feels that Faulkner has neglected this aspect of the story. As finally presented, in fact, the choice seems entirely the son's.

Probably the most graphic illustration of the process by which Faulkner constructs his stories is the section of *Absalom, Absalom!* in which Shreve and Quentin, giving full vent to their temperaments and emotions of the moment, elaborate upon the Sutpen story: at times they are carried away by a minor detail; at times one or the other becomes too excited to be coherent or to finish a thought or to heed the other's cry of "Wait. Wait"; at times they retrace something they have said and are dissatisfied with; at times they are horrified, shocked, or amazed at what they have said, or they become lost and confused about where they are going; at times their conflicting attitudes lead them to quarrel and to take conflicting views of the same event or conflicting tones toward it, which they cannot take time to argue out or resolve; at times they simply luxuriate in the spectacle of their own creative process; and they continually keep thinking of one more thing that must or may or might have happened and one more way of interpreting what happened until they have built a structure so complex and involved and so impossible to embrace that they can respond to it only in violent emotional terms. Faulkner, I believe, writes his books in much the same way.

Perhaps all this seems obvious and unnecessary to belabor. Yet it cannot have been obvious if one is to judge from the enormous number of attempts to explain the novels in terms of one or another specific theme or specific aesthetic or strategic intention, or to judge from the apparently overwhelming inclination of critics to treat the novels as though they entirely resembled *Madame Bovary* and were nothing at all like *Tristram Shandy.*

What is most significant, of course, about Faulkner's novels is not the mere fact that they are largely governed by temperamental responses, but the kinds of responses these are. For it is the kind of temperament he has that gives his works their characteristic shape (or shapelessness, depending on how narrowly one conceives the term shape), and that makes the search for the meaning or design of his novels so enticing and yet so futile an occupation.

Obviously it is premature to attempt any full or final analysis of Faulkner's temperament, but I believe this study has shown certain fundamental aspects of that temperament which more than any others determine the form of his novels. One of these aspects is the group of tendencies I have labeled the polar imagination: the tendency to view and interpret experience in extreme terms, to see life and feel it on all levels as composed essentially of pairs of warring entities, and to be fascinated by those especially tense sorts of antitheses in which the opposed entities are in a state of conflict which can neither be ended nor resolved. Clearly, the creative process for Faulkner is in large measure a series of responses by this sort of imagination, a series of movements or leaps from a thing to its opposite, and this process seems to take place regardless of what that thing is—a word, character, idea, or tone. It may even occur with respect to a whole story. When asked about the composition of *The Wild Palms,* he answered that his object was

> To tell the story I wanted to tell, which was the one of the intern and the woman who gave up her family and husband to run off with him. To tell it like that, somehow or another I had to discover counterpoint for it, so I invented the other story, its complete antithesis, to use as counterpoint. And I did not write those two stories and then cut one into the other. I wrote them, as you read it, as the chapters. The chapter of the *Wild Palms,* chapter of the *River Story,* another chapter of the *Wild Palms,* and then I used the counterpoint of another chapter of the *River Story.* I imagine as a musician would do to compose a piece of music in which he needed a balance, a counterpoint.[18]

What is revealing here is not only his desire for a counterpoint but his desire to make it a "complete antithesis" and his need to move back and forth between the two as he goes along. Even if, as is possible, he did not actually write the book that way, his desire to explain it in those terms and to publish the stories in that form is significant. It is also illuminating that, despite his assertion that the primary story is the one about the woman and the intern, he ends the book with the story of the convict. Moreover, the antithesis, or proliferation, comes to seem the dominant and more powerful story. Unlike the musician, who at the end of his composition resolves the counterpoint, Faulkner leaves us simply with the counterpoint itself.

Again and again throughout his work Faulkner obviously feels a need to counterbalance what he thinks or feels with some kind of antithesis. I suspect that he experiences much the same sense of completion and satisfaction from the tension of an unresolved antithesis that most other writers do from harmony and resolution, that like a juggler he feels fulfilled only when his materials are in motion.

It may seem odd at first glance that a polar imagination,

which is after all a rather simple and orderly form of imagination, should result in novels as complex and ambiguous as Faulkner's. Yet it is not strange at all when one realizes that the kinds of tense relationships Faulkner keeps establishing must by their very nature remain unexplored and that the effect of an accumulation of antitheses differs greatly from that of a single one. A single antithesis has the sharpness and clarity of a single combat; an accumulation of antitheses much more resembles a war of each against each and all against all, which is chaos. One can see this quite clearly on a small scale when one examines some of the almost unintelligible thoughts and statements of characters like Rosa Coldfield and Darl Bundren and finds that they are essentially accumulations of antitheses.[19] One can see it on a larger scale when one closely examines a complex whole like *Light in August* and discovers that its scenes consist largely of fairly simple "pairings" in which characters are in antithesis with each other or with a group.[20]

But the polar imagination alone would not account for the immensely varied kinds of ambiguity and irresolution we find in the novels. These can be explained, I think, only by two other aspects of Faulkner's temperament. One is his remarkable fecundity. It is this, of course, which has enabled him to create so rich and varied a fictional world and to provide for his reader such a profusion of effects and suggestions. In a sense he is so busy giving birth that he has no time to train or discipline his children. Too much of the irresolution is deliberate, however, for it to be the result merely of undisciplined fecundity or for it to be explained by his own statement: "I didn't like school and I quit about sixth grade. So I don't know anything about rational and logical processes of thought at all. I didn't have enough mathematics to have a disciplined mind."[21] If nothing else, Faulkner's quite careful consistency about the physical details of his stories and the clearly deliberate irrationality of much that he does make such explanations insufficient.

The other of these two aspects of his temperament is what must be an almost compulsive desire to leave things unresolved and indeterminate. This desire seems quite different from the kind of tolerance for inconclusiveness that has sometimes been called "negative capability." One senses, rather, in both Faulkner's novels and public statements an active willingness to close in on things, to narrow or define, to clarify or explore relationships, to commit himself, whether it be to a particular view of a character, particular explanation of an action, or particular meaning of a word. I cannot help feeling that many of his leaps and shifts of ground are as much a way of escaping having to resolve his thoughts or feelings as they are a way of reaching for something farther. It is as though he is determined to avoid clarifying or finishing his ideas, almost as though he feared to take hold of them, to give them full shape or realization, as though in some obscure way he wished to fail so that he would be able to go on trying.[22]

Insofar as there is any single key to understand both Faulkner's mind and work, it is, I believe, his notion and feeling that what is important about life is the act of trying and that completion or success or resolution would mean both an end to trying and a sign that not enough had been tried.

Earlier I suggested that Faulkner's comments to Harvey Breit about contemporary authors indicated that in a very real sense Faulkner was seeking failure, that he saw failure as a kind of measure or objective. In a later interview he makes that attitude quite explicit. He says of Hemingway:

> I thought that he found out early what he could do and he stayed inside of that. He never did try to get outside the boundary of what he really could do and risk failure. He did what he really could do marvelously well, first rate, but to me that is not success but failure . . . failure to me is the best. To try something you can't do, because it's too much (to hope for), but still to try it and fail, then try it again. That to me is success.[23]

A moment later, in answer to the question "Do you consider human life basically a tragedy?" he says: "Actually, yes. But man's immortality is that he is faced with a tragedy which he can't beat and he still tries to do something with it."[24] If the absolutely crucial thing is to go on trying—if it is the act of trying which gives man his immortality and which even, as Judith Sutpen suggests, makes life matter and gives it meaning—then one cannot really risk success, and failure becomes a kind of success.

I think it is not mere verbal paradox to call Faulkner's effort a "quest for failure." It is a quixotic ideal, certainly. But Faulkner is a Southerner and he has said that he usually reads *Don Quixote* once every year.[25] Earlier I commented on the number of Faulkner's characters who behave in precisely the ways which will prolong their torment and ensure their failure or doom. They, too, seem driven by a quest for failure. This kind of quest is a compelling and moving thing to witness. But it is a tormenting and discouraging thing to have to take part in. That is what, consciously or no, Faulkner makes the reader do. The reader, too, must try and try to grasp the novels and is doomed to fail. The "jigsaw puzzle picture integers" remain always "inextricable, jumbled, and unrecognizable," "just beyond his reach."

Many readers, I am sure, will be dissatisfied and disappointed by these conclusions, and they will go on trying to weave their own patterns on the loom that Faulkner has provided, feeling as Judith Sutpen did, and as part of Faulkner does, that it must be possible to do so "because you keep on trying." That they will keep trying, will face something they "can't beat and still tr[y] to do something with it," would surely win Faulkner's approval, for it is this quality in man which, as he puts it, "gives him his immortality."

What I have tried to assert and make clear is the other side of this terrible paradox: that we as readers are faced with something we "can't beat," that the pattern in Faulkner's world cannot be found, or woven, else the one "that set up the loom would have arranged things a little better."

If Faulkner is right about man's quixotic propensities, and I believe he is, some of my conclusions can never fully be accepted. The most I can hope is that they are not misunderstood.

First, I am not asserting that there is no ordering or unifying principle in Faulkner's art, but rather that the dominant principle is the persistent placement of entities of all sorts into highly tense relationships with one another, relationships which to varying degrees resemble the relationship between the terms of an oxymoron. This is, of course, a curiously complex and puzzling kind of ordering principle, since it contains within itself a kind of disorder and disintegration and works against the attainment of any final, over-all order and unity.

Second, I am not saying that there is no unifying perspective in Faulkner's vision, but rather that his perspective is an intensely ambivalent one and that the ambivalence exists with respect to almost every important aspect of human experience, including reason and the question of whether life and art have any point or meaning. This, too, is a curiously complex and puzzling sort of perspective, for it, too, contains within itself a form of self-destruction, since it allows the artist almost any kind of freedom in his presentation, including the freedom to neglect or negate his own conceptions. Beyond this, Faulkner's art and vision both are ordered chiefly by his temperament and by the persistent patterns of rhetoric and perception described earlier in this book—by his powerful tendency to polarize experience of all varieties and to render it in terms of motion and immobility, sound and silence, quiescence and turbulence, and tension.

This is not to say that his works are devoid of major ordering themes, ideas, values, or attitudes, but rather that they embody a great many of these, that different and often conflicting ones are urged or embodied at various times or at the same time, and that none dominates his work sufficiently or consistently enough to serve as a unifying center. When one looks at his works as a whole, I do not think one can say that they consistently support even the rather loose group of values usually associated with the Christian and chivalric traditions, for in opposition we find a celebration of any and all kinds of dynamic and intense activity. To put it a little differently, Faulkner seems to be saying sometimes that the way in which man endures is terribly important and sometimes that the way does not matter just so long as the process of enduring goes on. Sometimes he makes Christ and Caesar mortal enemies, sometimes quite literally celebrates them in the same breath.

On the metaphysical level, too, there is a fundamental division in his thought, for we can find embodied in his works, as I have suggested, an essentially monistic philosophy which fuses body and mind into "whole being," which sees reality and truth as dynamic, a matter of action, involvement, and emotion, and which makes immortality a continuing process within the world of time and change. At the same time we can find a sharply dualistic view which might roughly be labeled Platonic, a view which dichotomizes body and mind, which sees reality and truth and immortality as static and immutable, and which leads Faulkner to create in his works an extensive realm outside time.

The only major idea, I believe, that he never abandons or seriously undercuts is that man should and must keep on trying whatever it is he must try and that his greatness consists in this.

All this does not mean that there is no point or profit in tracing the various patterns, themes, ideas, and attitudes that recur in Faulkner's novels. But we must come to recognize the extent to which any of these are partial and fragmentary and part of a suspension which will not be resolved.

The reader may well wonder why, despite my admiration for much that Faulkner does and despite my belief that ambivalence is a valid point of view, my tone is often irritable and annoyed. It may seem even stranger when I say that I share much of Faulkner's uncertainty about whether life has pattern or meaning. My irritation comes, I believe, from my feeling that Faulkner's fictional world is in many respects even more ambiguous and complex than the real one and that this is, in part, the result of a deliberate quest for failure. I understand that this will be the least palatable of my conclusions, but I must insist that I mean it quite literally and soberly. I do not mean by it that Faulkner has failed merely because he has been in quest of perfection or of "the impossible" and therefore had to fall short, as one feels was often true of Conrad, for example. I mean that in a very real sense he has seen complexity and inconclusiveness and baffling relationships as both means and end and has welcomed them too easily. He has not always so much fought his way through experience and, after his best efforts to understand and clarify it, arrived at certain ambiguities and paradoxes that represent the farthest he can go. He often seems rather to start with paradoxes and to delight in finding them and in remaining with them. When an enormous number of relatively simple things like faces, movements, and sounds have been described in oxymoronic or paradoxical terms and when numerous insignificant experiences have been presented ambiguously, one is less respectful of the major paradoxes and ambiguities, less certain that they are the result of reaching too far. When virtually every technique of an author is a movement away from coherence and resolution, one cannot easily feel that the final disorder is merely the result of too high an aim. When a writer consistently uses the ends of his novels to put his meanings farther out of reach, there is a sense in which he is not only reaching but is pushing as well. Let me make perfectly clear that I am not quarreling with the use of these techniques or with deliberate disorder as such. What troubles me is the amount of such disorder in Faulkner's work and his degree of reliance upon it, so that, finally, we cannot distinguish between the real mysteries and the manufactured ones. It is difficult, as I have said, to believe that a man can seek failure, though perhaps all men in some sense do so, but if one believes, as Faulkner does, in the crucial importance of endless trying, then failure can become not only a proof that enough has been tried but a need and a quest.

Notes

The abbreviations and editions of Faulkner's works used in this study are as follows. All the editions are published at New York by Random House unless otherwise noted. *AA: Absalom, Absalom!* (Modern Library, 1951); *AILD: As I Lay Dying* (Modern Library, 1946); *GDM: Go Down, Moses* (1942); *H: The Hamlet* (1940); *ID: Intruder in the Dust* (1948); *LIA: Light in August* (Modern Library, 1950); *P: Pylon* (New York: Harrison Smith and Robert Haas, 1935); *RN: Requiem for a Nun* (1950); *SF: The Sound and the Fury* (Modern Library, 1946); *U: The Unvanquished* (1938).

1. Conrad Aiken, "William Faulkner: The Novel as Form," *Atlantic Monthly*, 164 (1939), pp. 650–654. Reprinted in *William Faulkner: Two Decades of Criticism*, edited by Hoffman and Vickery (East Lansing: Michigan State College, 1951), pp. 139–147.
2. *Hypnotic Poetry: A Study of Trance-Inducing Techniques in Certain Poems and Its Literary Significance* (Philadelphia: University of Pennsylvania Press, 1930), pp. 25, 32–33.
3. Ibid., p. x.
4. Jean Stein, "The Art of Fiction XII: William Faulkner" (an interview with Faulkner), *Paris Review*, no. 12 (Spring, 1956), pp. 28–52.
5. Henri Bergson, *An Introduction to Metaphysics*, tr. T. E. Hulme (New York and London: Putnam, 1912), p. 25.
6. Ibid., pp. 11–12.
7. Ibid., p. 12.
8. Ibid., p. 92.
9. Ibid., pp. 3–5.
10. See Walter J. Slatoff, *Quest for Failure: A Study of William Faulkner* (Westport, Conn.: Greenwood Press, 1960), note 10, p. 25.
11. Joseph Warren Beach, quoted in *Two Decades*, p. 29.
12. William Faulkner, *Faulkner Reader* (New York: Random House, 1954), pp. x–xi.
13. "William Faulkner's Style," in *Two Decades*, p. 162.
14. Karl W. Zink, "William Faulkner: Form as Experience," *South Atlantic Quarterly*, LIII (1954), p. 384.
15. *Faulkner at Nagano*, ed. Robert A. Jelliffe (Tokyo: Kenkyusha, Ltd., 1956), pp. 103–105.
16. These statements, however, are similar enough to the one quoted to indicate that it is at least roughly true. See, for example, Stein, "Art of Fiction," pp. 39–40, and Cynthia Grenier, "The Art of Fiction," *Accent*, XVI (1956), pp. 172–173.
17. *Faulkner at Nagano*, pp. 159–160.
18. Ibid., pp. 79–80. See also Stein, "Art of Fiction," p. 43.
19. See Slatoff, *Quest for Failure*, pp. 100–101, 105.
20. Lena–Mrs. Armstid (pp. 15–18); sawmill workers–Christmas (pp. 27–31); sawmill workers–Brown (pp. 31–34); Brown–Christmas (pp. 34–35, 89–91, 239–240); Bunch–Lena (pp. 45–48, 434–444);

Hightower–townspeople (pp. 52–62); Bunch–Hightower (pp. 67–88, 261–269, 272–278, 318–320); Christmas–dietitian (pp. 107–109); dietitian–Doc Hines (pp. 110–116); dietitian–matron (pp. 116–118); Christmas–McEachern (pp. 128–134, 139–144, 177–178); Christmas–Mrs. McEachern (pp. 146–147, 181–182); Christmas–Bobbie (pp. 156–157, 160, 162–164, 170–173); Bobbie–Max (pp. 167–168); Christmas–Bobbie, Max, blonde lady, and so on (pp. 185–191); Christmas–Joanna (pp. 210–211, 224–247); sheriff–Negro (pp. 255–256); Christmas–Negro congregation (pp. 281–285); Hightower–Byron, Hineses (pp. 323–328, 334, 338–343); Hightower–Lena (pp. 357–361); Brown–Lena (pp. 376–379); Bunch–Brown (pp. 384–385); Christmas–Grimm (pp. 404–407).

21. *Faulkner at Nagano*, p. 38
22. For another discussion which emphasizes the importance of Faulkner's temperament and divided sensibility see Alfred Kazin, *On Native Grounds* (New York: Reynal and Hitchcock, 1942), pp. 453–470.
23. *Faulkner at Nagano*, pp. 3–4. The three periods after "failure" appear in the original.
24. Ibid., p. 4. See also Stein, "Art of Fiction," pp. 29–30, where Faulkner writes that if the artist were really successful in matching his work to his dream of perfection, "nothing would remain but to cut his throat."
25. *Faulkner at Nagano*, p. 42.

JOSEPH GOLD

"Introduction: 'What I Was Talking About'"
William Faulkner: A Study in Humanism, from Metaphor to Discourse
1966, pp. 3–20

When William Faulkner was in Japan in 1955, he made one statement which seems to me to stand out among his many public utterances as singularly revealing: "[To] me the Old Testament is some of the finest, most robust and most amusing folklore I know. The New Testament is philosophy and ideas, and something of the quality of poetry."[1]

What gives this comment special significance, coming as it does from this particular author, is that it unwittingly describes a transition that has taken place in Faulkner's own work, dividing it roughly into those novels and stories written before he received the Nobel Prize and those written after.

There is no doubt that Faulkner's description of the Old Testament is a convincing one. There is a power and a color, a vivid intensity in the characterization, a vitality in narration, a beauty in the language, a general dynamism that is incomparable. Dogma and theology are conveniently confined to the first five books, leaving the rest free for metaphor and narration with the grandeur of myth. Everything is concrete and alive and human, and only the vigorous drawings of a Blake could give the work an even remotely adequate pictorial rendering. The God of the Old Testament speaks, acts, and feels, and rapidly emerges with a strong personality comprehended as a force acting in and through the doings of men. On the other hand, the New Testament, as Faulkner pointed out, is an intellectual extension and elaboration of the Old, an attempt to explain, to make rationally apprehensible the nature of God, man, and Heaven and to prescribe a pattern of conduct and attitude by which man can attain eternal life. The New Testament is a book of ideas; God, though He is a prominent part of the subject matter, stays essentially in the background. We may believe that He is there, but we never see Him, hear Him, or feel Him.

Now all this seems fairly obvious, and these observations would hardly be worth making, were it not for the fact that they are equally applicable to Faulkner's writing, falling as it does into two phases, two bodies of work, roughly divided by World War II. Indeed, perhaps it was that war, or perhaps it was international public recognition, finally symbolized and made real for Faulkner by the Nobel Prize, that caused this shift in his writing. Whatever the reason, there is a major stylistic shift, and it seems to be characterized by the same distinctions that separate the literary features of the Old and New Testaments. One detects in Faulkner's later fiction an urgency, almost a desperation, to convince and explain. There is an overabundance of rhetoric and speech-making, dragged into the novels with little justification; there is an emphasis on ideas rather than on people—altogether a concentration on saying rather than on doing. When the critic takes into account the religious tone of what Faulkner is saying (for instance in a work like *Requiem for a Nun*), there is a natural temptation to relate this later emphasis to the author's sudden realization that he was a figure of international prominence, called upon by his eminence to serve as a spokesman for mankind.

In his early work Faulkner approaches the creation of myth. That is to say, his characters are so convincing and universal and so recognizable that they attain the stature of archetypes while retaining the complexities of human beings. Their actions evolve into metaphors about the nature of human experience. In contrast, after 1948, Faulkner created Christ-figures instead of Christ-like figures. Faulkner's language must reasonably be called unjustifiable rhetoric when it bears little relationship to its subject. The complexity of the language that is applied to Joe Christmas is appropriate because of the equally complex agony of the character's psyche and situation, but this kind of writing becomes mere verbal gymnastics when applied to a character as decided and single-minded and untroubled as the corporal in *A Fable*.

This major shift in emphasis can be illustrated by what happened in the composition of the last two works of the Snopes trilogy. *The Town* and *The Mansion* seem to have come from an artist who was torn between a compulsion to sermonize and a wish to recapture the vigor of the imaginative early work. The frequent use of early-story material in these novels would seem to illustrate this latter desire, while the persistent use of Gavin Stevens and his rhetorical tendencies indicates that Faulkner could not overcome his need to make forthright and unveiled statements.

The first real indication of this pulpit tendency is observable in the 1942 version of "The Bear," which heralds the coming of what might be called the public years. To that story, which had its origins years before, Faulkner added a long, sententious debate between Isaac and his cousin McCaslin which amounts to an analysis of the significance and meaning of what has passed before in the more convincing narrative part of the story. Faulkner is virtually being his own commentator, as though he feared that the ideas embodied in the action were not clear enough. If it be objected that the same technique was employed much earlier in *Absalom, Absalom!* we might observe that the Quentin-Shreve discussion differs substantially from the Ike-McCaslin debate by virtue of the difference in context. Quentin's opinion is merely one of a number of points of view on which the novel is constructed. His discussion with Shreve is not about the events of the novel—it is a method by which the events are actually revealed. The novel's fabric is tightly woven together, and from the beginning Quentin is shown to be striving desperately to understand the implications of the events that emerge in the telling. In other words, Quentin's reactions to events are not separated in time or space from the events themselves. Quentin is a convincing part of the problematical world of the South which he carries around with him. His exchanges with Shreve are woven into the complex relationships and intricate psychological explorations that characterize the fictional technique. None of these observations can be convincingly applied to Isaac of "The Bear," who is a different person in his debate with his cousin from the younger Ike of the earlier hunting episodes. He has shifted in time and place and thus "stepped out," as it were, to comment on his own actions.

What then is this "message" that Faulkner has felt driven to express, so overtly that it has altered the whole tone and shape of his work? Before we choose any one label for his position, let us look at some of the significant statements, public and fictional, that together constitute a consistent attitude towards man. The most obvious choice is the Stockholm Address.

> [The writer] must teach himself that the basest of all things is to be afraid; and, teaching himself that, forget it forever, leaving no room in his workshop for anything but the old verities and truths of the heart, the old universal truths lacking which any story is ephemeral and doomed—love and honor and pity and pride and compassion and sacrifice. . . . I believe that man will not merely endure: he will prevail. He is immortal, not because he alone among creatures has an inexhaustible voice, but because he has a soul, a spirit capable of compassion and sacrifice and endurance.[2]

In Japan, Faulkner made similar statements about the goals of writers like the following:

> *Q:* I think that what you said just now is a very good and proper message for us, but if there is any other thing that you can say to encourage us . . . .
>
> *F:* Yes—to work, to believe always in man, that man will prevail, that there's no suffering, no anguish, that man is not suitable to changing, if he wants to, then to work hard.[3]
>
> *F:* People can always be saved from injustice by some man. . . . Anyone can save anyone from injustice if he just will, if he just tries, just raises his voice. . . .[4]
>
> We must cure them [errors]; we mustn't go back to a condition, an idyllic condition, in which the dream [made us think] we were happy, we were free of trouble and sin. We must take the trouble and sin along with us, and we must cure that trouble and sin as we go.[5]
>
> He's [the writer] not really writing about his environment, he's simply telling a story about human beings in the terms of environment . . . . The novelist is talking about people, about man in conflict with himself, his fellows, or his environment. . . .[6]
>
> I still believe in man. That he still wishes, desires, wants to do better than he knows he can and occasionally he does do a little better than anybody expects of him. This man [is immortal]. . . .[7]
>
> Well, I believe in God. Sometimes Christianity gets pretty debased, but I do believe in God, yes. I believe that man has a soul that aspires towards what we call God, what we mean by God. . . .[8]
>
> I would say, and I hope, the only school I belong to, that I want to belong to, is the humanist school.[9]

I have quoted at length because the overwhelming impact of so many separate pronouncements cannot be ignored or treated lightly.

Consider again that at the University of Virginia, Faulkner said:

> *Q:* Sir, it means that your basic conception of life is optimistic?
>
> *F:* Yes.
>
> *Q:* But not of the individual.
>
> *F:* Well, the individual is not too much, he's only a pinch of dust, he won't be here very long anyway, but his species, his dreams, they go on. There's always somebody that will keep on creating the Bach and the Shakespeare as long as man keeps on producing. . . .[10]
>
> What we need are people who will say, This is bad and I'm going to do something about it, I'm going to change it.[11]
>
> . . . there is no place anymore where individual man can speak quietly to individual man of such simple things as honesty with oneself and responsibility towards others and protection for the weak and compassion and pity for all.[12]

The generally humanistic attitude that emerges so strongly seems, to judge from the fiction, to be grounded in a religious faith, a belief in God as a prevailing force of good when working through natural, instinctive, "innocent" man. *A Fable* is an allegory that retells the Christ myth in humanistic terms. It seems that for Faulkner, as for many Western writers and thinkers, Christ was a living substance of a man under the domination of the divine element in him. Like Emerson, Faulkner seems to believe in an immanent Christ. If Faulkner believes in God, it is in a God that resides in some way in the heart of man. Emerson says without the guise of fiction what Faulkner says in *A Fable*.

> Jesus Christ belonged to the true race of prophets. He saw with open eye the mystery of the soul. Drawn by its severe harmony, ravished with its beauty, he lived in it, and had his being there. Alone in all history he estimated the greatness of man. One man was true to what is in you and me. He saw that God incarnates himself in man, and evermore goes forth anew to take possession of his World. He said, in this jubilee of sublime emotion, "I am divine. Through me, God acts; through me, speaks. Would you see God, see me; or see thee, when thou also thinkest as I now think."[13]

God becomes man when man becomes God. Faulkner demonstrates this by having his old general, of *A Fable*, give man completely free choice in the matter of his own salvation.[14] God, in this later work, is not a controlling force but a kind of servant of human wishes. Man collectively controls his own destiny. Nancy, in *Requiem for a Nun*, is a drug addict, a whore, and finally a murderer, but she is "innocent," which is to say that she can never be condemned for wickedness of motivation because her intentions and the results of her acts, Faulkner would have us believe, are good. Faulkner is convinced, apparently, that no act can be good or evil in itself. He has plentifully peopled his novels to show that evil resides in attitude. Grimm, Hines, Flem Snopes, Jason, Sutpen, Januarius Jones, and many others are people who commit acts which might also conceivably have been attributed to the "heroic" figures in the novels. What distinguishes them is their consciousness of their own separateness, their nonhuman estimates of others, and their insistence on the gratification of self-hood. They are cold and lack the compassion which is man's highest attribute.

The best illustration of this attitude is in Faulkner's treatment of man's relationship to nature. Old Ben, the bear, is the incarnation of innocence; he is incapable of evil, killing as he does out of pure need or pure anger, but incapable of violating his natural integrity. "It [the bear] did things that were evil, by a more intelligent code, but by its own code they were not evil and it was strong and brave to live up to its own code of morality."[15] Thus he ought to be killed by an equally pure and appropriate force—killed, but killed with regret since compassion is the "code of morality" to which man must "live up." Isaac, for instance, shows equal respect for bear, deer, and snakes; the hunters in this story and the convict in the *Old Man* are able to live in perfect harmony with nature.[16] This concept is like nothing so much as William Blake's concept of innocence. It is a belief which involves the necessity and possibility of throwing over the past, of being better than one is, of creating paradise here and now in a world that is Eden if only we will see it and love it and in which man is either the creative or the destructive force depending on the choice he makes.

> . . . He had created them, upon this land this South for which He had done so much with woods for game and streams for fish and deep rich soil for seed and lush springs to sprout it and long summers to mature it and serene falls to harvest it and short mild winters for men and animals and saw no hope anywhere and looked beyond it where hope should have been.[17]

But Faulkner, unlike Blake, does not have his own carefully wrought mythology or a system of dialectic in which some part of man, like the imagination which Blake employs, can be considered the shaping and creative best impulse. Like "Humanism" itself, or any other strongly held religious conviction, Faulkner's belief is based on faith. Faulkner is therefore obliged to fall back on tradition and finds himself in the difficult position of selecting and reworking elements in a past to which he does not subscribe. He is unable to provide a "how" and can only show us an "is." This he does dynamically in his early work in the figures of people like Dilsey, Lena Grove, the tall convict, Nancy Mannigoe, Chick Mallison, Byron Bunch, and in the later work he does it by the more wooden presentation of characters like the corporal of *A Fable* and the Ratliff of his last two novels.

The nearest formal arrangement of these views that one can detect as an influence on Faulkner is the Baptist, revivalist, evangelistic tradition in the South, with which he must surely have come into contact and which he brilliantly depicts in the Negro church meeting in *The Sound and the Fury*:

> Remember, the writer must write out of his background. He must write out of what he knows and the Christian legend is part of any Christian's background, especially the background of a country boy, a Southern country boy. My life was passed, my childhood, in a very small Mississippi town, and that was a part of my background. I grew up with that. I assimilated that, took that in without even knowing it. It's just there.[18]

The kind of religionism that Faulkner most likely encountered, permeating the South, is sought for through exhortation. It is a demand to vision through decision. "Believe," says Nancy Mannigoe, and the religious life is thus made to seem deceptively easy. Faulkner's heroes are most frequently simple-minded, sometimes country people, sometimes children, even idiots. They are chosen because in such people the wished-for state of mind is more readily observable. It is not their usual poverty or their often unfortunate physical situation that is offered to us for imitation, but the state of mind which they demonstrate by their living. When, as in his later fiction, Faulkner tries to intellectualize these beliefs, he fails on all fronts. He finds himself unable to systematize the faith which he advocates, and the effort required by the attempt undermines the imaginative conception which so powerfully infuses the fully realized and vividly delineated characters of the early novels. Had Faulkner tried carefully to explain why Dilsey is as she is, he would have been unable to visualize fully the completed person, and we would have received an early version of the pseudo-Christ of *A Fable*. Dilsey's very dynamism comes from a total, unexplained commitment. Like all of Faulkner's heroes, she is fully alive in the spirit and has no concern with doctrines and dogma and the intellectual minutiae of the religious word. Her faith represents the solid foundation of religion and signifies a distillation of the Christian idea. She is full of love and tolerance and, much of the time, even joy. This last characteristic is best illustrated, however, in Lena Grove, who moves through a hostile world transforming it by her trusting serenity into a place of mystery and wonder. She does not doubt that people are essentially good and kind, and in a magical way this assurance calls forth goodness and kindness.

Faulkner is unable to systematize in any way the absolutes towards which he seems to be imaginatively driven. However, we can glean a fairly consistent view which, though it is without the sanction of theology and though it lacks an explicable dialectic, does provide a forceful vision of the wished-for state of mind. Lena Grove and Dilsey most obviously represent the kind of attitude which not only makes their own lives possible and meaningful but also affects the world around them. In Christian evangelism there is a phrase about making "the decision for God." These noble women seem to have made this decision. They illustrate what happens when by an act of will one decides to believe in fundamental human goodness, in the possibility of human improvement, and in the essential oneness of man.

In at least three obvious cases Faulkner's heroic protagonists are women, which seems to indicate his perhaps romantic mistrust of reason and intellect as a means of attaining truth. Chick Mallison in *The Town* observes:

> Since women learn at about two or three years old and then forget it, the knowledge about their-selves that a man stumbles on by accident forty odd years later with the same kind of startled amazement of finding a twenty-five-cent piece in an old pair of britches you had started to throw away.[19]

And in *Go Down, Moses* Isaac thinks: "*They are born already bored with what a boy approaches only at fourteen and fifteen with blundering and aghast trembling.*"[20] As women understand their own sexual natures, so they seem to understand their own relationship to the world, and so presumably, through feeling and emotion, one can arrive at a sense of mystery and wonder and unity in the universal situation in the way that Lena does. Such an ideal state has all the aspects of humanism, and leads to all the acts that Dilsey performs and that are embodied in other humanistic or existential twentieth-century works, for instance via the doctor of Camus' *La Peste*. But Faulkner's humanism rests on a rock foundation of faith, almost of mysticism. There is a God, and He is visible in the universe through man, and in nature. He is available to all men at all times if they will throw over systems and act out of acceptance and love. Faulkner can no more than any other "believer" transmit the means of spiritual commitment; he can only illustrate the appearance and the effect of such commitment.

Faulkner says that it is the writer's task to illustrate and elaborate the human qualities of "love and honor and pity and pride and compassion and sacrifice." By reoffering these "old verities," the artist reminds man of the best in himself and helps him to see the beauty, the nobility that is possible in life. And these qualities are not arrived at rationally; they are the "truths of the heart." One thinks of Wordsworth or the transcendentalists more than anyone else. By 1950, then, Faulkner clearly saw his role as that of a kind of preacher, an inspired illustrator and celebrant of man's basic qualities. But, as I have said above, this was not a new self-awareness that he came to. A glance at some of the early works, those written in the late 1920's and early 1930's, will, I hope, further reveal that Faulkner was always writing from a single point of view.

The "shift" then in Faulkner's writing is a shift of emphasis or technique, rather than a change of ideas, and it is perhaps illuminated by regarding it as a move from the making of myth to the construction of allegory. Perhaps it is necessary at this point to say something about literary symbolism. Language and therefore literature is structured on the use of symbols. The degree to which a reader's responses to symbols vary is the degree to which the symbols vary. For instance, a letter of the alphabet is not a symbol (except as it may be read aloud when it symbolizes a sound), but as a mark on paper it is a thing in itself. As part of a word it becomes an integral part of a symbol, as in "whale," where the word is designed to evoke a picture of a sea creature, already previsioned in the reader's mind. This is the simplest kind of symbol usage. The phrase "ferocious whale" enriches the mental picture by increasing the vitality of our necessary imaginative response. We move in our minds from a dictionary illustration, from a "still," to a "film strip." The phrase "white whale" enriches our response infinitely more (if we have read *Moby-Dick*, though to some extent even if we have not), conjuring up the entire complex of ideas and images that constitute Melville's novel and all the emotional responses that he explains in the chapter on the "whiteness of the whale." We thus see that a literary symbolic structure is possible on three levels. A word produces an object; a phrase produces a qualified object; a series of phrases, an elaborate pattern, produces an object so qualified and of such complex associations that it in turn evokes something further, perhaps a whole range of associations. It may thus be said that symbols have a range of reference, some extending further in their association than others, as the ripples of water extend in proportion to the size of the disturbance.

I would say then that one way of distinguishing symbols is according to the degree of complexity of the emotional and intellectual response that they evoke in the reader. Now the nature of a symbol which represents an abstraction, as the white whale represents, say evil, is that it evokes a relatively great complexity of responses, or one might say, disturbances in the reader. This is so because no single image can be supplied to match the symbol, and the mind searches for equivalents and involuntarily produces associations in order to try to comprehend the abstract idea. In other words, such a symbol forces upon the intelligent reader the problem of encountering the concept for which it stands, and this is a stimulating exercise. I call this literary process, for want of a better term, associative symbolism, and, in specific instances, echoing symbols.

There is another kind of symbolism, which might be called directive, which works against richness and complexity in the literature where it is employed. This is because it uses symbolic equivalents or signs to call forth concrete secondaries. Such symbolism produces what Northrop Frye calls "naïve allegory" of the kind employed in local pageants and in some literature.[21] Echoing symbols, on the other hand, tend to produce myth and archetype.

In naïve allegory the object of the game is to find the shoe which fits the foot, and this is usually easy to do—must be easy to do since the writer is really only interested in secondaries, not in symbols, and therefore the literary construction is based on the assumption that the reader is a reasonably good judge of shoes and the author is an expert salesman. Once the reader has found the exact shoe, he has found it, and he is left with it. The scheme is simple because in such cases the author's motive is usually discursive rather than exploratory and his impulse is didactic rather than visionary. It may thus be seen that a collection of echoing symbols will increase the complexity and profundity of a work of art by a complex kind of progressive presentation, as three dimensions in chess would make the game more than 50 per cent more difficult. A collection of directive symbols, on the other hand, will produce no more than what amounts to a repetition and duplication of a single symbol, as though one were to play the same game of chess again and again with different-colored pieces.

So far we have been cursorily discussing the over-all impact of kinds of symbolic fiction, what we might call the general dynamics of fiction. We must ask further how and why an echoing symbol differs in itself from a directive symbol. An echoing symbol is usually complex in itself and realistic. Thus, *Moby-Dick* is interesting in his own right; he has a personality, a vitality, and a thorough characterization of his own. So, indeed, does Dilsey of *The Sound and the Fury*, Christian Pilgrim of *Pilgrim's Progress*, and Gulliver, along with countless other symbolic figures in the greatest literature. The corporal of *A Fable* does not have such characteristics—he is not real, not imaginable in human terms, and not an emotionally evocative figure, whereas his counterpart in *Light in August*, Joe Christmas, does have all the literary qualities that the former lacks. This situation is also true of the cardboard Nancy Mannigoe as opposed to the flesh-and-blood Dilsey, and, to a lesser extent, of Gavin Stevens, as he reappears from *Light in August* to *The Mansion*. In other words, Faulkner has moved from the presentation of archetypal images to the presentation of "disguised ideas." But why is a directive symbol, like the corporal, so different from Joe Christmas? Because the corporal is transposable for Christ and, in fact, Faulkner is primarily interested in Christ; the corporal is only an intellectual contrivance, not a product of the imagination. Joe Christmas, on the other hand, is not transposable for anything, and while he symbolizes many ideas and situations, he is still himself, the focus of a web of associations. In other words a symbolic figure of this kind is a total substitution for the ideas which we can thereafter abstract; being a synthesis, an integration, he is a new reality and not any one of the parts that compose him. An allegorical symbol like the corporal is not a substitution, but a preparation for his equivalent. Concretions are not abstractions, the "Mona Lisa" is not enigma itself, so a concretion like Joe Christmas must absorb and embody the abstractions he represents and thus become all important in himself. Any critical analysis of such a figure must violate the completeness of the original literary construct, unless the critic ultimately returns to the whole man as he acts out his drama. The corporal, however, is not the corporal but somebody else and will, therefore, never be himself.

Now it seems that the degree of integrity produced by symbols results not from what the symbols represent, but from the motivation of the writer, as Mr. Frye points out.[22] In discursive writing, the power of the images is diminished while in truly literary constructs the precision or rigidity of the ideas is diminished.

When Faulkner answered a question at Virginia in the following way, he perhaps revealed more of himself than he knew:

> *Q*: Mr. Faulkner, in your speech at Stockholm you expressed great faith in mankind . . . not only to endure but to prevail. . . . Do you think that's the impression the average reader would get after reading *The Sound and the Fury?*
>
> *F*: . . . yes, that is what I was talking about in all the books, and I failed to say it.[23]

The increasing desire to speak about his faith in mankind led Faulkner to take a more conscious and a more desperate hand in planting that "talking" in his later work. Faulkner also said, "I wrote for years before it occurred to me that strangers might read the stuff, and I've never broken that habit."[24] But the latter part of the comment cannot be true—was not true because the Nobel Prize must have made Faulkner intensely aware all of the time that strangers were reading his "stuff." This awareness, coupled with his convictions, produced the state of affairs that is the subject of this approach. Faulkner described his own magnificent early work in fitting terms:

> You write a story to tell about people, man in his constant struggle with his own heart, with the hearts of others, or with his environment. It's man in the ageless, eternal struggles which we inherit and we go through as though they'd never happened before, shown for a moment in a dramatic instant of the furious motion of being alive, that's all my story is. You catch this fluidity which is human life and you focus a light on it and you stop it long enough for people to be able to see it.[25]

In his later writing, however, the people are not alive. Of "The Bear," Faulkner could say, "That is symbolism," but of the symbolism that critics have found in *The Sound and the Fury,* he said instead:

> Well, I would say that the author didn't deliberately intend but I think that in the same culture the background of the critic and of the writer are so similar that a part of each one's history is the seed which can be translated into the symbols which are standardized within that culture. That is, the writer don't have to know Freud to have written things which anyone who does know Freud can divine and reduce into symbols.[26]

Faulkner's personal history in the use of symbolism was clearly summarized in one other speech in Japan:

> And when I found that people read the books and got pleasure from them and found in them something of what I tried to put [in], I was very pleased, I was very flattered. Though they found things in those books that I was too busy to realize I was putting in the books. They found symbolism that I had no background in symbolism to put in the books. But what symbolism is in the books is evidently instinct in man, not in man's knowledge but in his inheritance of his old dreams, in his blood, perhaps his bones, rather than in the storehouse of his memory, his intellect.[27]

Having been "pleased" and "flattered," Faulkner became self-conscious. He began to write of the old verities as his intellect now conceived them, and perhaps he started "putting in" a little symbolism, just to make sure that some was there.

Notes

1. Robert A. Jelliffe (ed.), *Faulkner at Nagano* (Tokyo, 1956), 45; hereafter cited as *Nagano.*
2. "The Stockholm Address," *American Literary Essays* (ed. by Lewis Leary) (New York, 1960), 313.
3. *Nagano,* 18.
4. Ibid., 76.
5. Ibid., 77–78.
6. Ibid., 157.
7. Ibid., 5.
8. Ibid., 23–24.
9. Ibid., 95.
10. Frederick L. Gwynn and Joseph L. Blotner (eds.), *Faulkner in the University* (Charlottesville, Virginia, 1959), 286.
11. Ibid., 246.
12. Ibid., 242.
13. "The Divinity School Address," *Selections from Ralph Waldo Emerson* (New York, 1957), 105.
14. A thorough discussion of the allegorical God of A *Fable* is contained in Joseph Gold, *William Faulkner: A Study in Humanism, from Metaphor to Discourse* (Norman, Oklahoma, 1966), chapter six. See also *Modern Fiction Studies,* Vol. VII (Summer, 1961), 145–56.
15. *Nagano,* 93.
16. It is significant, however, that it is not Isaac who kills the bear. This situation is dealt with at length in Gold, *William Faulkner,* chapter three.
17. William Faulkner, *Go Down, Moses* (New York, 1942), 283.
18. Gwynn and Blotner (eds.), *Faulkner in the University,* 86.
19. William Faulkner, *The Town* (New York, 1957), 101.
20. *Go Down, Moses,* 314.
21. *Anatomy of Criticism* (Princeton, N.J., 1957).
22. Ibid., 75.
23. Gwynn and Blotner (eds.), *Faulkner in the University,* 4.
24. Ibid., 14.
25. Ibid., 25.
26. Ibid., 147.
27. *Nagano,* 68.

FLOYD C. WATKINS

From *The Flesh and the Word: Eliot, Hemingway, Faulkner*

1971, pp. 254–76

The Truth Shall Make You Fail

A major influence which made the older Faulkner conscious of his messages was his relationship with Malcolm Cowley, which began in May 1944 when Faulkner found a letter that had been lying in his desk drawer since February.[1] One result of a lengthy correspondence and of Cowley's arranging some of Faulkner's works into a historical sequence in *The Portable Faulkner* was a growing awareness by the artist of chronology, the stream of history, the pattern of his works. It is inconceivable that Faulkner was unaware of the complex interrelationships between the works in his Yoknapatawpha cycle, but perhaps Cowley's letters changed the kind of awareness. Faulkner had known the history and the people intuitively, as an artist; he learned from Cowley the critical statements about the uniqueness of the County in literary history and American literature. He had known the people, his characters. He learned to think of his accomplishments. He had created the actions, the plots, and the lives of his characters; it was, he said many times, that strange creative process in which he started the fiction about his characters and then let them work out their own destinies. He had written about what the characters did as the novels unfolded; he began to write critically and historically about what his characters had already done in fiction written earlier. He had recorded merely his characters' thoughts and their actions; he began to interpret the meanings of what he had previously written. Before Cowley, Faulkner had written almost no nonfiction; after Cowley, he composed the Nobel Prize speech, made addresses to historical associations, gave graduation addresses, allowed his interviews to be published in numerous periodicals and books. Before Cowley, he created the concrete actions and specific thoughts of the characters in *The Sound and the Fury*; at the specific instigation of Cowley, he wrote an appendix to that novel in which he said that the Negroes "endured"—the late vocabulary of abstraction—rather than showing how they did without stating it. He began to speak a nearly new vocabulary of the old virtues and verities which formerly he had seen merely in the characters rather than heard from their tongues and his own; he began to talk about "loved . . . honor . . . doomed . . . doom . . . loved . . . decency . . . pride . . . integrity . . . vanity . . . defeat. . . ." As a critic, a commentator, he thought of the county seat of Jefferson, "where life lived too with all its incomprehensible passion and turmoil and grief and fury and despair."[2]

The tendencies, of course, were already present before Cowley; they were noticeable in "The Bear." But the very arrangement of *The Portable Faulkner* made Faulkner critically aware of what he had done with the intuition of an artist. And in the preface, Cowley argued that Faulkner "had created a mythical county in Northern Mississippi and had told its story to what he regarded as the morally disastrous present. . . . Apparently no one knew that Faulkner had attempted it." Faulkner wrote Cowley that he had "thought of spending my old age doing something of that nature: an alphabetical, rambling genealogy of the people, father to son to son."[3] But this was a statement made after Cowley had given him his new critical consciousness of his accomplishment. He suggested that Faulkner "collect his short stories in a volume arranged by cycles"—a task which would make him intensely aware of the historical scheme. The change is apparent in every late work, but the responsibility of Cowley for the change is most evident in a statement Faulkner wrote to him: "By God, I didn't know myself what I had tried to do, and how much I had succeeded."[4] Surely he had known, but in the way of an artist. Now for the first time he knew as a critic and historian of his own works. For the rest of his career, he would compile genealogies, write histories, preach and moralize about his own past themes. Old age, the times, and Malcolm Cowley changed and diminished Faulkner's art.[5]

Faulkner had to interpret his own works before many of his readers and critics could understand his larger faith in the possibility of man if not the power of God. Beginning with *Intruder in the Dust*, he made longer and longer statements of his faith. The sermons on human and race relations in that novel are bearable for one critic only because of "Faulkner's mastery of language."[6] R. W. B. Lewis admires the book because of its "larger conviction of human freedom";[7] and Cleanth Brooks maintains that "Charles Mallison's conflict of loyalties and his relation to his own community" provide some justification for the sermons of Gavin Stevens.[8]

The sermons by Faulkner and his characters are too many and too long, and the justifications are insufficient. Message dominates art so much that *Intruder in the Dust* has many failings. It takes man in mass and in mob to the level of false abstraction and sweeping generalization. The killer of Joe Christmas was the individual Percy Grimm, and even the antagonists of Rider in "Pantaloon in Black" were particular persons. But the mob which plans to lynch Lucas Beauchamp and which is made foolish when Lucas's innocence is established exists only as an abstract mass. Gavin Stevens and Faulkner reduce men to mere idea when they describe the mob as "not faces but a face, not a mass nor even a mosaic of them but a Face: not even ravening nor uninsatiate but just in motion, insensate, vacant of thought or even passion: an Expression significantless and without past. . . ."[9] The lack of humanity in person and in group is Faulkner's failure. To this point he had made the bad and the weak characters concrete and comprehensible as persons. Now, people are mere illustrations of doctrines.

A novel may be too homiletic and didactic even when the characters do all the preaching. If the author's views are indistinguishable from those of his characters, the failure of art is likely to be more pronounced. But even when the reader may distinguish between the argument of character and author, the novel may still fail if there is more social, political, or philosophical discussion than action. *Intruder in the Dust* has a small core of concrete art: the personal relationships between Chick Mallison and the silent Lucas Beauchamp; the love and wisdom in the depths of old man Gowrie, who superficially seems to be only a caricature of a violent hillbilly; the images and events during the disinterments of various corpses.

But essays prevail, and not all of them come from the mouth of the garrulous Gavin Stevens. Charles Mallison's meditations have a political, regional, and geographical context too broad for a sixteen-year-old boy. He helps a Negro boy and an old lady dig up a corpse at night to prove the innocence of "a damned highnose impudent Negro," but he thinks more abstrusely than the contemplative Quentin Compson and more broadly than the prophetic Isaac McCaslin. Chick's mind moves from event to generalization, from Lucas to "the whole dark people on which the very economy of the land itself was founded" (*ID*, p. 97). From Chick come sermonettes on the smell of Negroes, "a rich part of his heritage as a Southerner" (*ID*, p. 12), on women (*ID*, pp. 105–106), innocence and murder (*ID*, pp. 116–117), permission, motherhood (*ID*, pp. 123–124), fatherhood (*ID*, p. 133), truth and the way it is expressed in vocabulary (*ID*, pp. 80, 89). Chick's poetry nearly becomes absurdity when Faulkner's sonorousness exalts the trivial. The courthouse bells are "skydwellers, groundless denizens of the topless air too high too far insentient to the crawling earth then ceasing stroke by hasteless stroke from the subterrene shudder of organs and the cool frantic monotone of the settled pigeons" (*ID*, p. 42). Going with the sheriff and his uncle to the cemetery to dig up a corpse for a second time, he thinks of

> the blue and gauzed horizon beyond which lay at last like a cloud the long wall of the levee and the great River itself flowing not merely from the north but out of the North circumscribing an outland—the umbilicus of America joining the soil which was his home to the parent which three generations ago it had failed in blood to repudiate. . . . (*ID*, p. 151)

He sentimentally sees even hogs as "alerted as though sensing already their rich and immanent destiny" (*ID*, p. 4). Faulkner does not seem to recognize the absurdity of Gavin Stevens's figure of the manner of birth: he "had said that man didn't necessarily eat his way through the world but by the act of eating and maybe only by that did he actually enter the world, get himself into the world . . ." (*ID*, p. 207). The best of intentions cannot prevent the image of a well-toothed fetus cannibalistically gnawing its way out of the womb. Faulkner himself interrupts a scene of terror and suspense to write an essay on the right of man to dignity and decorum in death (*ID*, p. 135).

Chick Mallison's pattern of thinking violates the most fundamental law of the good people in Faulkner's best fiction. A good deed by Caddy or Addie or Cash or the convict was done not for the sake of duty or principle but for the person who could benefit. The convict, for example, tries to do the right thing, "not for himself, but for her" (*WP*, p. 161). In contrast, Chick Mallison acts not for Lucas but for principle, and seemingly Faulkner approves. Chick "had wanted of course to leave his mark too on his time in man but only that, no more than that, some mark on his part in earth but humbly, waiting wanting humbly even, not really hoping even, nothing (which of course was everything) except his own one anonymous chance too to perform something passionate and brave and austere not just in but into man's enduring chronicle worthy of a place in it . . ." (*ID*, p. 193). Reputation and fame have replaced the selfless act. A hero of a later work acts for self because he thinks too much, and Faulkner does not condemn the thinking.

The ratiocinative detective stories of *Knight's Gambit*, published one year after *Intruder in the Dust*, mark a further decline in Faulkner's powers. Gavin Stevens's love of talk is a severe limitation. Faulkner was apparently moved to write these stories by his concept of justice, his belief that justice may be achieved only by a wise man and not by legal systems. Gavin defines justice as "composed of injustice and luck and platitude in unequal parts,"[10] and the plots of the stories are contrived to show how he thinks and talks to make luck and platitude, especially platitude, prevail over injustice. There are a number of well-created characters in *Knight's Gambit*, but always they are filtered through too much talk and a method of narration that tends far too much to abstraction, far too little to the dramatic. Gavin's voice talks constantly, Faulkner admits, "not because its owner loved talking but because he knew that while it was talking, nobody else could tell what he was not saying" (*KG*, p. 148). But this confusion persists in the reader as well as in Gavin's fellow-characters. Together, Faulkner and Gavin now see a character impersonally as belonging to "a still older and firmer American tradition" (*KG*, p. 151), and they discuss the fiction and their own self-conscious myth-building in literary terms: "the parent's lines and character" (*KG*, p. 148), "an appendix or anyway appendage; a legend to or within or behind the actual or original or initial legend; apocryphal's apocrypha" (*KG*, p. 144). "The whole plot was hind-part-before . . ." (*KG*, p. 148). The title story places country above person and character. A bickering and violent family come together in love because of their devotion to country. The book ends with an essay on America, patriotism, and war:

> he thought how perhaps that country, that nation, that way of living really was invincible which could not only accept war but even assimilate it in stride by compromising with it; with the left hand so to speak, without really impeding or even deflecting, aberrating, even compelling the attention of the right hand still engaged in the way's old prime durable business. (*KG*, p. 245)

Compared with Faulkner's best fiction, many passages in *Knight's Gambit* are almost embarrassing.

In 1951 Faulkner became the historian of his own fictional domain and published *Requiem for a Nun*, which alternates chapters of pageant-history with a drama about the later life of Temple Drake, the anti-heroine of *Sanctuary*. The chapters provide historical accounts of the naming of Jefferson, the building of a courthouse, and the establishment of the state capital in Jackson. Faulkner is expanding the background of Yoknapatawpha County as he had that of the Compson family in the appendix to *The Sound and the Fury*. It is as if he had written a history of the county as a background for the life and loves of Caddy without any more connection between the parts of the book than the description of what had happened historically on the sites of the events of Caddy's life. The very separation of the historical chapters from the drama of the lives of Temple, her husband (Gowan Stevens), and Nancy Mannigoe is a didactic method. In a review of *Requiem for a Nun* Malcolm Cowley praises Faulkner's new moral vision. He is regenerated. "Now there is a reformed Faulkner, conscious of his public duties, who has become the spokesman for the human spirit. . . ."[11] For Cowley as for most critics and readers, Faulkner had to state his beliefs before they were apparent. He had not been reborn; his later and inferior works should have taught the critic that his technique had changed—not his beliefs. Cowley praised the "historical account" before each scene of the drama, and he placed *Requiem for a Nun* "among the most successful of Faulkner's many experiments in narrative form." Even the reservations in the review praise the new moral Faulkner and damn the older and greater writer on moral grounds. Admitting that *Requiem for a Nun* probably has "less beneath the surface" than the story of Temple in *Sanctuary*, Cowley separates art and morality in the early books: "I'm not sure the old unregenerate and scampish Faulkner wasn't the greater novelist."

Cowley made contributions to the reading of Faulkner, but a better understanding of his art and the weakness of such later books as *Requiem* comes in later criticism. Lawrance Thompson, for example, sees "the themes" of "the final phase of the drama . . . being discussed in general terms which are so blatant and propagandistic that Faulkner's art has become completely eclipsed."[12] And Cleanth Brooks writes, "The use of this material in just this fashion constitutes the most daring but perhaps the least successful solution of the structural problems attempted by Faulkner in any of his novels."[13]

If the historical fables which introduce the supposedly dramatic scenes in the play are didactic, so is the drama itself. Gavin Stevens, the first main talker, speaks moralistically and abstractly in the very words which writers in the early twentieth century thought were denied them. A full page[14] lifted out of the text may exist as an abstract essay on truth without any stated application to the little drama of Nancy's killing Temple's child so that she will not leave her family to become the mistress of the brother of Red, her lover in *Sanctuary*. Soon the nun, Nancy, "dopefiend," murderer, and "nigger whore," develops her own moral vocabulary; and when Temple starts talking in similar fashion, even the drama of *Requiem for a Nun* has become pure morality play.

The historical commentaries are much more than a compilation of the old facts of the history of Yoknapatawpha County: Faulkner presents an image such as the name of the girl scratched on the window of the jail and then interprets in long moralizing passages; he tells a serio-comic story of a fifteen-pound lock on the "bi-monthly mail pouch" and then interprets his own image as "the power and the will to liberty"; using such terms as *symbolism* and *mythical*, he expounds his views on modern life; he comments on "one nation, one world," on changes in education, on the niseis in World War II, on materialistic progress, on architecture, government and alphabetized agencies, the automobile, criminal gangs, the frontier and its virtues and the demise thereof, the rise of bureaucracy, credit, the land, states' rights, the boosterism of Rotary and Lions clubs. And never does he establish an adequate connection between his historical views and the moral histories of Temple and Nancy.

From writing about persons and families in *As I Lay Dying*, *The Sound and the Fury*, and *Absalom, Absalom!*, Faulkner moved to the general history of his county in *Requiem for a Nun* and on to the subject of the condition of man in *A Fable*. After *Go Down, Moses*, his major accomplishments are to be found in *The Town* and *The Mansion*, the last two books of the trilogy, *Snopes*, especially in the creation of the poor-white Mink. Flem Snopes, the main exploiter of his community, is silent like Faulkner's good people, but not because of the inability of virtue to find words for goodness. His silence is the inarticulateness of pure materialism and negation. The community which must triumph over the silent evil is itself usually impotent; it spells out its horrors and its ineffectiveness, especially in the last two works of the trilogy, as it talks too much and does too little about the central evil. Mink Snopes in *The Mansion*, the real moral avenger of the wrongs done to the community, is one of the most successful characterizations in Faulkner's later works partly because he can do good and evil, perhaps in the same deed, even when he cannot articulate his moral positions except in very short and mysterious simple sentences. But while Faulkner returned to the creation of a character very much like the old and silent ones, he also moved again toward the more universal. Yoknapatawpha steadily becomes more cosmopolitan. Ratliff's nationality is changed from Anglo-Saxon to Russian, and Chinese begin to appear in Jefferson.

Obviously these views of Faulkner's late works exaggerate the flaws and ignore some of the accomplishments in order to demonstrate the increasing failures of his art because of his wish to say what really never needed saying if his readers and critics had been perceptive. Even *A Fable* is not always so abstract and moralistic as its title might indicate.

A martyred saint stands at the center of many novels by Faulkner. Caddy's love for her family and her seducers is sacrificial; Joe Christmas is a sort of black martyr who suffers for his own error as well as the sins of the community; the convict endures ordeals merely carrying out his man-given duty only to find that bureaucracy adds ten years to his sentence to protect itself; Ike McCaslin suffers for his people and for the curse which servitude has imposed on the white and black races; Lucas Beauchamp is potentially such a victim in *Intruder in the Dust*. As Faulkner's styles and techniques become more moralistic in the later works, the martyrdom of the protagonists becomes more extreme, the martyrdom is decreed by a legal system established by the forces of civilization, the protagonist is less guilty and criminal, his virtues are greater, and he has fewer flaws. To put it simply, the moral systems of the later novels are great over-simplifications; principle or meaning is placed far above the concreteness, credibility, and particularity of character. Nancy in *Requiem for a Nun* and the corporal in *A Fable* are Faulkner's most saintly martyrs and his least successful protagonists. Their humanity and their saintliness are exaggerated beyond the prerogatives of fiction. Message becomes more important than person; the characters preach much; and the author preaches about them.

In the older works the character worked out his life in the events in the novel, and the reader was left to deduce the principle if he could. By smothering Temple's child, Nancy saved Temple's family and ultimately her soul. But Nancy and the governor who refuses to commute her sentence and Faulkner make her too saintly to be a good character. Refusing clemency, the governor says, "'Who am I, to have the brazen temerity and hardihood to set the puny appanage of my office in the balance against that simple undeviable aim? Who am I, to render null and abrogate the purchase she made with that poor crazed lost and worthless life?'" (*RN*, p. 210). If Nancy sacrifices herself for a family and if the state participates in the sacrifice, the corporal in *A Fable* tries to achieve peace for mankind and sacrifices himself for a concept of humanity. And the allegorical old general, who at once represents worldly authority, Satan, and God the Father, must permit the sacrifice, must have the corporal executed, for the same reason that the governor could not allow Nancy to be saved. The themes of the two books are generally the same; the most significant change is that Faulkner has didactically extended and broadened his moral principles. The general specifically echoes the governor: "'If I gave him his life tonight, I myself could render null and void what you call the hope and the dream of his sacrifice. By destroying his life tomorrow morning, I will establish forever that he didn't even live in vain, let alone die so. . . .'"[15] The general's "render null and void" echoes the governor's "render null and abrogate," and he adds *sacrifice* and *live in vain*. Faulkner has accepted the vocabulary denied by Frederic Henry and Addie Bundren.

The corporal, Andrew Lytle has said, is never

> seen . . . as a person. . . . He is begot of the sound of the author's voice upon an idea. This makes the great scene above the city between father and son miscarry, for there is no son but an abstraction to be tempted. In spite of the variety of the general's plea it never quite has the human warmth of a parent trying to save his child.[16]

Christ was "incarnate." The corporal is not. Surely, Lytle continues, Faulkner "should have given him flesh and the body's needs. Action should never be resolved in symbolic terms only. Reality and symbol should fit as the glove the hand."[17] When the poetry and fiction of Eliot, Hemingway, and Faulkner move from the flesh of their works of the early twentieth century to the morality of the late twentieth century, they have violated their own early critical dicta and pleased some of the moral aims of the time at the expense of their art. Again Lytle explains it best:

> And so it seems that a morality, or an allegory, whose materials are mortal sins and moral principles, and not the uniqueness of individual men, could make a better effect in an age of belief, because this belief suffused all degrees of rank and particularity. . . . But today where we have conventions empty of belief and institutions being reduced to organizations and forms which have lost the natural object, a morality lacks authority [I would say art]. It is why fiction as a literary form appears now and not in the fourteenth century. Everyman now must first become unique man.[18]

He had been unique as late as the 1920s, though partly in denial and disbelief. The difference between *A Fable* and the best literature of the twenties is striking when the strange similarities between this work and *A Farewell to Arms* are considered. Frederic Henry says farewell even in principle as a person; the corporal's opposition to war is mainly a statement of the author's belief.

Art never vanishes from Faulkner's fiction; it merely diminishes. The old touch of the master appears at times—in the creation of the drunkenness of the soldiers searching for a corpse to be buried as the unknown soldier (they ultimately use the body of the corporal); in the account of the general's tour of duty in Asia; in the presentation of the execution of the corporal between two thieves; in the story of the three-legged race horse except when it turns into a sermon on history and similar topics by a lawyer and the omniscient Faulkner.

But even the patterns of concrete images in Faulkner are

in part determined by his wish to create a moral pageant. Sound, I believe, is more preponderant in the imagery in Faulkner's fiction than it had ever been before. As Eliot had used sound to suggest the supernatural in the *Four Quartets*, Faulkner in *A Fable* used the same sense to suggest the mysterious awesomeness of man. Despite the Christ-like corporal, Faulkner's beliefs were more human-oriented than religious. But he uses sounds often associated with religious beliefs and events to add to the significance of man in his morality-novel. *A Fable* begins with sounds representing the authoritarian military establishment; the people fearing for the life of the corporal gather "Long before the first bugles sounded from the barracks" (*F*, p. 3). The compulsions of the symbolic bugle are opposed by the mysterious, almost supernatural, almost sourceless sounds of all the good people of the earth. They express their beliefs, their love of the corporal and his cause, in a sound which "was not voices yet so much as a sigh, an exhalation, travelling from breast to breast up the boulevard. It was as if the night's anxiety . . . was gathering itself to flow over them like the new day itself in one great blinding wave . . ." (*F*, pp. 12–13).

Often Faulkner's images pose an antithesis between crass sounds of authority or orthodoxy and mysterious sounds and silences among the little people.[19] A car containing three generals seems "to progress on one prolonged crash of iron as on invisible wings with steel feathers" (*F*, p. 13), and it moves through people standing in "that silence which was still aghast and not quite believing" (*F*, p. 13). Finally there is a sound among the crowd, "a concerted sound: a faint yelling" (*F*, p. 14); and Faulkner labors to make it more mysterious, sourceless, and supermortal than the cries of the hounds pursuing the mythical bear in *Go Down, Moses*: "It was high, thin with distance, prolonged, not vindictive but defiant, with at the same time a curiously impersonal quality, as if the men it came from were not making, producing it . . ." (*F*, p. 14).

Just as silence and sourceless sounds among the people oppose the crass sounds of the establishment, the armistice achieved by the corporal produces silence broken only by sounds of beauty: Faulkner points out "the ringing silence" which a division commander "hadn't even heard yet because he had never heard anything here before but guns" (*F*, p. 37). The peace during this armistice makes even the commander remember the sounds of childhood innocence: the

> cicada chirring and buzzing . . . the lark too, high and invisible, almost liquid but not quite, like four small gold coins dropped without haste into a cup of soft silver, . . . the lark again, incredible and serene, and then again the unbearable golden silence, so that he wanted to clap his hands to his ears, bury his head, until at last the lark once more relieved it. (*F*, p. 37)

A story of the hanged man and the bird, which Faulkner says he found in a novel by James Street, is told by the old general when he tempts the corporal to live. Here the sound of the bird again may suggest beauty, peace, and something of immortality. But the general mistakenly uses its song as a symbol of earthly life. " 'Then take that bird. Recant, confess, say you were wrong . . .' " (*F*, p. 351). Beautiful sounds accompany the cart carrying the corpse of the corporal. Twice Faulkner writes that it moves through a "faint visible soundless rustling" and among "silent arrested faces" (*F*, p. 391).

At the crucial time when soldiers walk unarmed toward the enemy hoping to attain peace (*F*, p. 322), the harsh sound of a bugle blowing reveille is followed by the song of a lark (*F*, p. 324). And the "eternal and perennial larks" sing during the journey of the van that carries the corpse of the executed corporal—perhaps in echo of the swallows that flew over the cross crying "Console, console."[20] Always the silence or the sound of the people is mysterious, "murmurous not with the voices but as though with the simple breathing, the inspiration and suspiration of the people" (*F*, pp. 137, 149, 222), "choral almost . . . thin hysteric nearer screams and cries . . . still filling the horizon even after the voices themselves had ceased with a resonant humming" (*F*, p. 243). The voices of women become "the mass voice of the ancient limitless mammalian capacity not for suffering but for grieving, wailing, to endure incredible anguish because it could become vocal without shame or self-consciousness, passing from gland to tongue without transition through thought . . ." (*F*, p. 222). The Christ-like corporal who strives for peace and for the hopes of the people is silent, and even the lorry which carries him and his disciples to prison for mutiny moves in silence (*F*, p. 13). It is almost as if he were in the silence of Eliot's "still point of the turning world" in the *Four Quartets*. At the time of the scene representing the Last Supper, the corporal is silent, a door of the prison is "clashed shut again" by a sergeant, and the corporal's disciples yell in a supernatural "sound hoarse, loud, without language, not of threat or indictment either: just a hoarse concerted affirmation of repudiation . . ." (*F*, p. 334).

Although these sounds and silences are effectively described and dramatically created, they exist almost as much on the level of idea as on the level of image. Obviously, the division commander, a representative of the forces of war, cannot tolerate the serenity of the silence of peace. Similarly, an adjutant has "never heard silence before" (*F*, p. 95). The generals who cannot tolerate the silence of peace create in the city the sounds of war: "an orderly discordant diapason of bugles" represents the warmongers of three nations (French, English, American); they are "the bronze throat of orderly and regulated War" (*F*, p. 138). And the soldiers still in the service of authority bark their symbolic commands in three languages "in the same discordant unison as the bugles" (*F*, p. 138). Officialdom is always noisy with frantic bugles, shrill whistles, and boots tramping and clashing. The executioners of the corporal talk in a "steady unemphatic gabble," and their noncommissioned officers shout in "harsh abrupt ejaculations" (*F*, p. 383).

The harsh sounds of the establishment and the silences and the symbolic sounds of the little people and the natural world are schematized in true symbolic and psychological terms, but they are as moralistic and allegorical as they are sensuous. The sounds of Yoknapatawpha County strike even urban ears with more reality and less morality. Faulkner can still write concretely, but the sound of allegory rings through the sounds of the physical world. It is symptomatic that Faulkner and Eliot stressed images of sounds of a supramundane world in their most abstract, affirmative, moralistic, and discursive works.

The sounds of *A Fable* first stress Faulkner's concepts, his beliefs in humanity in general. No matter how good the parts of the novel, every aspect emphasizes belief. More than ever before, Faulkner's fiction exists first for idea. Myths found by critics of the early works may be true or imposed—Addie, for example, represents "Demeter-Persephone-Kore."[21] In *A Fable* Faulkner labors not to let any myth escape the reader. He embodies the idea of the main myth of the corporal in a subplot, a story-within-a-story of a three-legged race horse pursued by an owner who wishes to use the horse only as a stud. The horse is aided in flight by an English groom, an old Negro, and a twelve-year-old boy. Lest the clear mythological connection between the subplot and the main story be lost, Faulkner states the backgrounds for his own work. The story of the horse is a story of love, of the fall of man, the Garden of Eden, Pyramus and Thisbe, Adam and Lilith (*F*, p. 153). It is "the immortal pageant-piece of the tender legend which was the crowning glory of man's own legend beginning when his first paired children lost well the world and from which paired prototypes they still challenged paradise . . ." (*F*, p. 153). Thomas Sutpen as person is more important in *Absalom, Absalom!* than any historical, Biblical, or archetypal mythology which he plays out in the novel. The person now hardly matters as person in comparison with the significance of the mythology which he enacts: "the story, the legend, was not to be owned by any one of the pairs who added to its shining and tragic increment, but only to be used, passed through, by each in their doomed and homeless turn" (*F*, p. 154).

Often Faulkner lets his eyes stray from his story while characters preach sermons on such subjects as "the rise of man." Without any narrative specificity, he lists mythical and historical parallels:

> the giants who coerced compelled directed and, on occasion, actually led his [man's] myriad moil: Caesar and Christ, Bonaparte and Peter and Mazarin and Alexander, Genghis and Talleyrand and Warwick, Marlborough and Bryan, Bill Sunday, General Booth and Prester John, prince and bishop, Norman, dervish, plotter and khan. . . . (*F*, p. 181)

At times *A Fable* becomes a miscellany of names, like an unalphabetized index to mythology. A sergeant looks at the corporal and the mob witnessing his entrance into Paris and sees "the whole human race" (*F*, p. 9). The humane and wise sheriff who refuses to help Jason Compson recover his money because it has been gained immorally now has become a mythical figure—a federal deputy who refuses to search for the race horse. Faulkner creates a scene between the owner of the horse and the deputy in three fourths of a page of dialogue but writes seven eighths of a page of abstraction about this "poet, not the writing kind, or anyway not yet, but rather still one of Homer's mere mute orphan godchildren" (*F*, pp. 158–159).

A Fable is a re-enactment of the life of Christ in the twentieth century with Christ again crucified as Faulkner said he would be in *Faulkner in the University*. But the meaning of the religious myth is much more important to Faulkner than the vehicle of the narrative of modern times. Idea came before images and characters. "The notion occurred to me. . . . I had to—then it became *tour de force*, because I had to invent enough stuff to carry this notion."[22] Again and again the dialogue and the event are mythical but implausible, as in dialogue like the following:

> 'With Christ in God,' he said. 'Go now.'
> 'So I'm to save France,' the other said.
> 'France,' he said, not even brusquely, not even contemptuously. 'You will save man. Farewell.' (*F*, p. 264)

The weight of the myth in some scenes which re-enact the Christ story is so heavy that events—the "stuff," Faulkner called it—become ludicrous and abstract. It is difficult if not impossible to re-create the crucifixion in our time with the physical paraphernalia of Biblical times, but for the sake of meaning Faulkner at least attempted it. The corporal is tied to a post (the cross) and shot. The post is rotten, and "the corporal's body, post bonds and all, went over backward as one intact unit . . ." (*F*, p. 385). The sergeant-major administering the coup de grâce finds "that the plunge of the post had jammed it and its burden too into a tangled mass of old barbed wire, a strand of which had looped up and around the top of the post and the man's head as though to assoil them both in one unbroken continuation of the fall, into the anonymity of the earth. The wire was rusted and pitted and would not have deflected the bullet anyway, nevertheless the sergeant-major flicked it carefully away with his toe before setting the pistol's muzzle against the ear" (*F*, pp. 385–386). How much fable dominates even the plot here is apparent if a similar death in the older fiction is recalled—the drama of event when Henry Sutpen kills Charles Bon at the gate to the Sutpen mansion. The gate is symbolic in *Absalom, Absalom!*, but first it is an actual gate, a concrete place of a tragic meeting. The wire in *A Fable* recalls the crown of thorns more than the old barbed wire of the trenches in World War I.

Many of the re-enactments of events in the life of Christ seem almost as much parody as true narration of true events. There is far too much fable in this novel. Faulkner attempts to state the most he can believe, writes his longest sermons. Like the abstract dedication of Anse Bundren to talk and word, Faulkner's *A Fable* is almost words that "go straight up in a thin line." And the plot and deeds no longer move "terribly . . . along the earth, clinging to it." The beauty of concrete event is almost gone, and the abstractions are now too much like those "sounds that people who never sinned nor loved nor feared have for what they never had and cannot have until they forget the words."[23] The religious parallels are imposed on plot, event, and character.

In *A Fable*, Faulkner treated the largest possible mythical, moral, and spiritual subject he could imagine in a scene as geographically universal as he could make it. In his last book, *The Reivers*, he turns to a story about the private conscience of a small boy as remembered in the old age of a moralizing and talkative old man. Faulkner and his narrator, Lucius Priest, retell much of the history of Yoknapatawpha County somewhat in the fashion of the historical parts of *Requiem for a Nun*. And in every instance the history moves toward greater universality and significance and away from particularity. The county is older—founded in the 1790s rather than in the 1820s and 1830s.[24] There are histories of the hunting camp, old hotels, the first car in the county, dress and customs with the car, frontier travel.[25] There are long and tedious historical remembrances and visions and moral essays on "Virtue" (55, 133, 143), lies (64), automobiles and mudholes (87), the smell of a whorehouse (99), the life of a pimp (113–114), the wonderfulness of the wisdom of women (111), the moral hierarchy of animals (the rat first, the mule second, the cat third, the dog fourth—121–123), the loss of innocence (155), racism (174–175), policemen (176), population (193), integration and the limits of the law (243), air conditioning (193), sex (194–195), childhood (46), death (47), badges (206), the democracy of horse racing (215, 234).

As in "Pantaloon in Black," the Negro is idealized in a perfect character who says grace perfectly and who eats with good manners just like a white man, "exactly as Grandfather did" (*R*, p. 247). Everbe is a sentimentalized Caddy Compson in *The Reivers* with much of the silence and all of the tragedy distilled from her character. "She worked in a bawdy-house but her heart was clean. Outside of that, what can one say against her?"[26] She reforms because of true love for Boon Hogganbeck, but when the racehorse is taken from Ned and Boon and Lucius, Everbe's love provides the only opportunity to get him back. Melodrama and sentimentality prevail in Boon's violent whipping of Everbe and Lucius's exclamations of his disappointment at her presumed fall from renewed virtue. Miss Reba attempts to treat the serious matter with superficial humor: "'What the hell does [sleeping with] one more [man] matter? aint she been proving ever since Sunday she's quit? If you'd been sawing logs as long as she has, what the hell does one more log matter when you've already cancelled the lease and even took down the sign?'" (*R*, p. 280). And Lucius forgives:

> "It's all right," I said.
> "I thought I had to," she said. "I didn't know no other way."
> . . .
> "You did have to," I said. (*R*, p. 280)

Rejected by Boon, Everbe reforms "from the temptation business" and virtuously takes a job nursing the invalid wife of a wonderfully devoted and virtuous constable, "washing and cooking and lifting his wife in and out of bed and washing her off, for that constable" (*R*, p. 281). Shades of the saintliness of Bret Harte's Mother Shipton! The confusion of Quentin Compson is replaced by the wonderful understanding of Lucius and a sentimental novelist. When Boon marries Everbe despite her past and her fall, sentimentality and comedy have saved a Caddy-like woman from whoredom; and the novel ends with the birth of Boon and Everbe's baby, Lucius Priest Hogganbeck.

Faulkner has reformed his loose woman, made the boisterous and retarded Boon Hogganbeck tender and loving, given understanding and wisdom to the once-confused young narrator, given up a tragic view of the world for farce and happiness. Almost all is right with the world in the last book about Yoknapatawpha County, which becomes at the end almost the best of all possible worlds. Virtue has mostly triumphed, and much of the art has disappeared.

The Summing Up

Some of the greatest literature of the twentieth century was written by T. S. Eliot, William Faulkner, and Ernest Hemingway in their early careers. The best works of all three were written according to similar standards: they denied the abstract word, depended on image and act rather than statement, left much unsaid, created admirable doers and contemptible talkers, kept the poet out of his poem and the novelist out of his fiction, preferred the dramatic to the lyric. The standards they followed were so rigid that, extended too far, they would exclude much of the greatest literature of the world and many of the beliefs about person, nation, and God. But the standards are meaningful and useful in interpreting and evaluating most of the writing of the twentieth century.

All three writers followed the same trend. The eldest one, Eliot, changed first. All became users of abstract words, stated instead of relying on image and act, preached, tried to create admirable talkers, invaded their own poems and fiction, preferred the discursive instead of the lyric. And by the standards they had themselves followed, their later works fall short of the early ones.

Why the change?

The times caused it in part. The depression and World War II began to incline the writer more and more toward new techniques and new faiths in the person, the nation, and a supreme being.

Time and old age softened the hard young men. Age does not convert all to a rosier optimism. Hardy, Housman, Arnold, Melville, Mark Twain, Tennyson, Camus, James—many stick with moral, religious, and social skepticism of some kind until the bitter end. Eliot, Hemingway, and Faulkner did not.

Whatever the reasons, literature and the language reacted against obvious sentimentalities and then reacted against its own hard-boiled objectivity. F. W. Bateson has argued that "The real history of poetry is . . . the history of the changes in the kind of language in which successive poems have been written. *And it is these changes of language only that are due to the pressure of social and intellectual tendencies.*"[27] The artistic development of Eliot, Hemingway, and Faulkner may be traced, but the causes lie buried in the numerous forces of one of the most complex ages of man. Each of these writers, and other distinguished men of letters, felt in his old age a new responsibility to the world; the high rate of literacy, the acceleration of population growth, and the devices of mass communication made each more responsible to more peoples than authors had ever before dreamed of. The personal and even private human fears before the abstractions of the twentieth century—the bomb and international political power—made elderly writers who had endured earlier sufferings wish to preach on universal meanings and potentialities. To some extent, Eliot, Hemingway, and Faulkner all became victimized by old age in the manner that Eliot had described it.

> Now, in theory, there is no reason why a poet's inspiration or material should fail, in middle age or at any time before senility. For a man who is capable of experience finds himself in a different world in every decade of his life; as he sees it with different eyes, the material of his art is continually renewed.[28]

Elderly writers, Eliot continued, "cling to the experiences of youth" or "leave their passion behind" or become "dignified . . . public figures with only a public existence." They do, say, think, and feel "only what they believe the public expects of them." Thus the public composes the poet. None of these three writers became this bad, but all of them yielded to the pressures and changed their techniques, their language, their styles—and for the worse.

But of course Eliot, Hemingway, and Faulkner should not be remembered for their declines. With some exceptions, the best literary works by Americans have been written when the author still had some of the sap of young manhood. And I believe that the best poetry and fiction of the first half of the twentieth century in America came from the earlier years and the severe standards of Eliot, Hemingway, and Faulkner. This study has not shown why they changed; it has attempted to describe what they did.

Notes

1. Malcolm Cowley, *The Faulkner-Cowley File: Letters and Memories, 1944–1962*, A Viking Compass Book (New York: The Viking Press, 1968), p. 6.
2. Faulkner, "Appendix," *The Sound and the Fury*, The Modern Library (New York: Random House, 1946), pp. 9, 10, 13, 16.
3. Cowley, p. 25.
4. Cowley, p. 91.
5. Warren Beck may have had a similar influence on Faulkner. See "Faulkner: A Preface and a Letter," *The Yale Review*, 52 (October 1962), 159.
6. Tommy Hudson, "William Faulkner: Mystic and Traditionalist," *Perspective*, 3 (Autumn 1950), 227.
7. R. W. B. Lewis, "The Hero in the New World: William Faulkner's *The Bear*," *The Kenyon Review*, 13 (Autumn 1951), 642.
8. Cleanth Brooks, *William Faulkner: The Yoknapatawpha Country* (New Haven: Yale University Press, 1963, 1964), p. 228.
9. Faulkner, *Intruder in the Dust* (New York: Random House, 1949), p. 182. Hereafter cited in text with abbreviation *ID*.
10. Faulkner, *Knight's Gambit* (New York: Random House, 1949), p. 24. Hereafter cited in text with abbreviation *KG*.
11. Malcolm Cowley, "In Which Mr. Faulkner Translates Past into Present," *New York Herald Tribune Book Review*, September 30, 1951, p. 1.
12. Lawrance Thompson, *William Faulkner: An Introduction and Interpretation*, American Authors and Critics Series, Second

Edition (New York: Holt, Rinehart and Winston, Inc., 1967), p. 130.
13. Brooks, p. 140.
14. Faulkner, *Requiem for a Nun* (New York: Random House, 1951), pp. 165–166. Hereafter cited in text with abbreviation *RN*. See also Joseph Gold, *William Faulkner: A Study in Humanism, from Metaphor to Discourse* (Norman: University of Oklahoma Press, 1966), p. 107.
15. Faulkner, *A Fable* (New York: Random House, 1950, 1954), p. 332. Hereafter cited in text with abbreviation *F*.
16. Andrew Nelson Lytle, "The Son of Man: He Will Prevail," *The Sewanee Review*, 63 (1955), 126.
17. Lytle, p. 126.
18. Lytle, p. 125.
19. See Frank Turaj's excellent article, "The Dialectic in Faulkner's *A Fable*," *Texas Studies in Literature and Language*, 8 (Spring 1966), 94, 101.
20. Kimon Friar and John Malcolm Brinnin, *Modern Poetry: American and British* (New York: Appleton-Century-Crofts, Inc., 1951), p. 496.
21. Carvel Collins, "The Pairing of *The Sound and the Fury* and *As I Lay Dying*," *The Princeton University Library Chronicle*, 18 (Spring 1957), 120–121.
22. Faulkner, *Faulkner in the University: Class Conferences at the University of Virginia 1957–1958*, ed. Gwynn and Blotner (Charlottesville: The University of Virginia Press, 1959), p. 27.
23. Faulkner, *As I Lay Dying*, The Modern Library (New York: Random House, 1930, 1964), pp. 165–166.
24. Faulkner, *The Reivers: A Reminiscence* (New York: Random House, 1962), p. 8. Hereafter cited in text with abbreviation *R*.
25. See pp. 20, 24, 23–27, 28–29, 73–74.
26. Thomas Wolfe, *Look Homeward, Angel* (New York: Charles Scribner's Sons, 1929), p. 274.
27. F. W. Bateson, *English Poetry and the English Language: An Experiment in Literary History* (Oxford: At the Clarendon Press, 1934), p. vi.
28. Eliot, "Yeats," *On Poetry and Poets* (New York: The Noonday Press, 1957), p. 301.

GLENN O. CAREY

"Faulkner and His Carpenter's Hammer" (1976)

Faulkner: The Unappeased Imagination
ed. Glenn O. Carey
1980, pp. 259–69

> After all, there must be some things for which God cannot be accused by man and held responsible. There must be.
>
> (*Light in August*)
>
> If Jesus returned today we would have to crucify him quick in our own defense, to justify and preserve the civilization we have worked and suffered and died shrieking and cursing in rage and impotence and terror for two thousand years to create and perfect in man's own image; if Venus returned she would be a soiled man in a subway lavatory with a palm full of French post-cards—
>
> (*The Wild Palms*)

In *Knight's Gambit*, a Faulkner character says, "In fact, I sometimes think that the whole twentieth century is a sorry thing, smelling to high heaven in somebody's nose."[1] The reader of Faulkner's fiction often realizes that it is Faulkner himself who was offended by the noisome smell of civilization. Throughout Faulkner's work one notices his deep emotional reaction whenever he presented an aspect of civilization that he despised and that he believed should and could be changed and improved. In dramatizing this condemnation, Faulkner consistently underscored the evil in the man-made world. As the old Negro preacher says in *A Fable*, "Evil is a part of man, evil and sin and cowardice, the same as repentance and being brave. You got to believe in all of them, or believe in none of them. Believe that man is capable of all of them, or he aint capable of none."[2] Faulkner's strong emphasis on evil caused some early critics who superficially read his fiction to pronounce derogatory judgments, saying that Faulkner was concerned with evil and violence too often, too much, and too shockingly. One of the answers to these critics could begin with a reminder that the writers of the greatest literature in English—Chaucer, Milton, Shakespeare, Fielding, Melville, to name only a familiar few—were also concerned in their writings with evil, not because of evil alone, but because they were aware that through the dramatic presentation of evil the author often can create a meaningful artistic achievement that will include the writer's acknowledgement and acceptance of man's responsibility to his fellow man. Thus it is with Faulkner.

At Nagano Faulkner was asked, "Can you please explain a little about your works, in which things of evil or violence come in and you have used them as material in expressing your ideas?" Faulkner's reply explains why he used evil and violence to dramatize his social criticism.

> Yes—never to use the evil for the sake of the evil—you must use the evil to try to tell some truth which you think is important; there are times when man needs to be reminded of evil, to correct it, to change it; he should not be reminded always only of the good and the beautiful. I think the writer or the poet or the novelist should not just be a "recorder" of man—he should give man some reason to believe that man can be better than he is. If the writer is to accomplish anything, it is to make the world a little better than he found it, to do what he can, in whatever way he can, to get rid of the evils like war, injustice—that's his job. And not to do this by describing merely the pleasant things—he must show man the base, the evil things that man can do and still hate himself for doing it, to still prevail and endure and last, to believe always that he can be better than he probably will.[3]

In conjunction with this concern of Faulkner with evil, and in answer to those who may still believe that Faulkner was writing about evil and corruption only as it is found in the South, one should remember that evil is universal and that the microcosm of Jefferson, Yoknapatawpha County, Mississippi, can have acceptance as a universal symbol just as the Mississippi River has in *Huckleberry Finn*, the lifeboat has in "The Open Boat," and the *Pequod* has in *Moby-Dick*. Many of Faulkner's novels clearly have universal implications. As an example, *The Sound and the Fury* has received much interpretation of this kind. Irving Howe in a classic 1952 study wrote that it is not only about "modern humanity in Mississippi" but modern humanity in New York, Paris, and thus everywhere: "*The Sound and the Fury* seems a terrible criticism not of the South alone but of the entire modern world. The more severe Faulkner's view of the South, the more readily does one forget he is writing about the South."[4] Jean-Paul Sartre also readily perceived this universality in *The Sound and the Fury*: "We are living in a time of impossible revolutions, and Faulkner uses his extraordinary art to describe our suffocation and a world dying of old age."[5] A year earlier William Van O'Connor saw that Faulkner applied in this novel ". . . his most characteristic subject matter, his heritage as a southerner, and modern man in search of belief."[6] Relevant to Faulkner is what Herbert Read said elsewhere: "regionalism, in spite of its local origins, is always universal—that is to say, it appeals, not to the limited audience of the region in which it is written, but to mankind everywhere and at all time."[7] When Read's viewpoint is directed towards Faulkner's fiction, his regionalism achieves a universality that gives major importance to his criticism of civilization's effects and consequences. It seems further pertinent to refer those few remaining diehard doubters of Faulkner's use of evil to John Milton's *Areopagitica*, in which he wrote that "the knowledge and survey of vice is in this world so necessary to the constituting of human virtue, and the scanning of error to the confirmation of truth. . . ." Finally, again to use some of Milton's own words, Faulkner can be called a truly universal "champion of truth."

Faulkner demonstrated in his writings and in his personal statements that he was profoundly disturbed by some of the actions of modern man and by what is called civilized progress. In his concern Faulkner said that some people,

> . . . the humanitarian in science and the scientist in the humanity of man, who might yet save that civilization which the professionals at saving it—the publishers who condone their own battening on man's lust and folly, the politicians who condone their own trafficking in his stupidity and greed, and the churchmen who condone their own trading on his fear and superstition—seem to be proving that they can't.[8]

Faulkner made true religion—sometimes, for convenience, he called it Christianity—or the acceptance of responsibility for one's fellow man an important element in his fiction. Once he was asked, "Does that mean an artist can use Christianity simply as just another tool, as a carpenter would borrow a hammer?" Faulkner's reply shows his panoramic social vision:

> The carpenter we were speaking of never lacks that hammer. No one is without Christianity, if we agree on what we mean by the word. It is every individual's individual code of behavior by means of which he makes himself a better human being than his nature wants to be, if he followed his nature only. Whatever its symbol—cross or crescent or whatever—that symbol is man's reminder of his duty inside the human race.[9]

Faulkner consistently reminded himself of his duty, his responsibility to his fellow man. Interspersed in his fiction are observations and criticisms of civilized man, who is the "author and victim too of a thousand homicides and a thousand copulations and divorcements."[10] To Faulkner, modern man is drowning himself in "*this seething turmoil we call progress.*"[11] He called sharp attention to man's spiritual dryness and self-designed destruction in his Nobel Prize Speech. "Our tragedy today is a general and universal physical fear so long sustained by now that we can even bear it. There are no longer problems of the spirit. There is only the question: When will I be blown up?"

As Faulkner watched what he called "*the miragy antics of men and women,*"[12] one remembers that he described humanity in *Mosquitoes* as "a kind of sterile race: women too masculine to conceive, men to feminine to beget. . . ."[13] Twenty years later he wrote that modern life is "that agony of naked inanesthetisable nerve-ends which for lack of a better word men call being alive."[14] He wrote in *The Wild Palms*, "*you are born submerged in anonymous lockstep with the teeming anonymous myriads of your time and generation; you get out of step once, falter once, and you are trampled to death.*"[15] Again, in *Mosquitoes*, of relevance are Fairchild's final words to Talliaferro, a vain, frustrated, unhappy man. First Fairchild looked at Talliaferro, then he looked up, "O Thou above the thunder and above the excursions and alarms, regard Your masterpiece!" When Fairchild looked down again at Talliaferro, "'Get to hell out of here,' he roared. 'You have made me sick!'"[16] In *Absalom, Absalom!*, Faulkner wrote that two of the principal characters are symbolically "doomed to live," and that only a few of us in this world are able "to make that scratch, that undying mark on the blank face of the oblivion to which we are all doomed. . . ."[17] It is just as Judith Sutpen also says,

> . . . you make so little impression, you see. You get born and you try this and you don't know why only you keep on trying it and you are born at the same time with a lot of other people, all mixed up with them, like trying to, having to, move your arms and legs with strings only the same strings are hitched to all the other arms and legs and the others all trying and they dont know why either except that the strings are all in one another's way like five or six people all trying to make a rug on the same loom only each one wants to weave his own pattern into the rug; and it cant matter, you know that, or the Ones that set up the loom would have arranged things a little better, and yet it must matter because you keep on trying or having to keep on trying and then all of a sudden it's all over and all you have left is a block of stone with scratches on it provided there was someone to remember to have the marble scratched and set up or had time to, and it rains on it and the sun shines on it and after a while they dont even remember the name and what the scratches were trying to tell, and it doesn't matter.[18]

On the other hand, especially in "Faith or Fear," Faulkner stressed the hopeful side of life as he described a list of those God-like men who are remembered century after century.

> They are the long annal of the men and women who have anguished over man's condition and who have held up to us not only the mirror of our follies and greeds and lusts and fears, but have reminded us constantly of the tremendous shape of our godhead too—the godhead and immortality which we cannot repudiate even if we dared, since we cannot rid ourselves of it but only it can rid itself of us—the philosophers and artists, the articulate and grieving who have reminded us always of our capacity for honor and courage and compassion and pity and sacrifice.[19]

One could further note what that sensitive Faulkner character the Reverend Gail Hightower says about modern man in *Light in August*: "Poor man. Poor mankind,"[20] as well as what the gruff, perceptive Revered Joe Goodyhay says in *The Mansion*, "Save us, Christ. The poor sons of bitches."[21]

We can see that Faulkner often condemned and yet pitied mankind. He also repeatedly said that man creates his own disasters and that he should try to rise above these self-created calamities:

> Well, there are some people in any time and age that cannot face and cope with the problems. There seem to be three stages: The first says, This is rotten, I'll have no part of it, I will take death first. The second says, This is rotten, I don't like it, I can't do anything about it, but at least I will not participate in it myself, I will go off into a cave or climb a pillar to sit on. The third says, This stinks and I'm going to do something about it.[22]

Faulkner then added, "What we need are people who will say, This is bad and I'm going to do something about it, I'm going to change it."[23] In trying to change it, Faulkner included in his fiction much about evil in society, and this is particularly evident in *Sanctuary*, which is full of the "current trends" (Faulkner's term) of man's mass compulsions to be famous, rich and successful, as well as calling attention to our mechanized and specialized way of life where sex, love, and personal involvement in life have become less a matter for individual judgment and decision than a reflection of mass society's current desires and pressures. In *Sanctuary* Faulkner, through the main characters, etched the deformed body and spirit of modern man. He not only depicted the moral confusion and the social decay of the South, but he indicted contemporary man everywhere in modern life where people in their hurried and harried life consistently minimize the worth of the individual and where many of us continue to remain unconcerned about the excessive loss and degradation of human life through drugs and suicide, the excessive highway accidents, and the steadily rising crime and terrorism throughout the United States and the world. Many of us today have learned to accept the ever-present specter of mass murder as wars come and go so quickly that an American born around 1910 can see in the retrospect of adulthood that his lifespan includes at least two world wars, one so-called police action, the Vietnam conflict, and, by today, the omnipresent threat of a worldwide holocaust that has the potential to destroy man completely. The "current trends" of *Sanctuary* emphasize man's debasement of his moral, ethical, and religious beliefs, as well as his reliance on hypocrisy as a routine way of life.

The motivating character in *Sanctuary* is Popeye, a big-time Memphis gangster of the 1920's, a bootlegger who strongly affects the lives of Temple Drake and Horace Benbow. Although some of these changes are caused by the character traits of Temple and Benbow, Popeye ignites the fuse that sets off the upheavals in their already disturbed lives. Popeye is one of those Faulkner characters who represent the mechanical civilization that has invaded and partially conquered the South,[24] and Faulkner frequently describes Popeye in "mechanical" terms. This kind of description comes in swift order, for early in the novel Popeye enters wearing his stiff straw sailor "like a modernistic lampshade," his eyes looked like "two knobs of soft black rubber," and his face had a "bloodless color, as though seen by electric light." He wore a tight black suit, had "doll-like hands," and "his skin had a dead, dark pallor. His nose was faintly aquiline, and he had no chin at all. His face just went away, like the face of a wax doll set too near a hot fire and forgotten." Popeye's whole appearance has "that vicious depthless quality of stamped tin."[25]

Popeye is a lost human being, Faulkner said, who became a symbol of evil in modern society only by coincidence.[26] Coincidence or not, Popeye represents evil in *Sanctuary*, and evil unadulterated with good. The only "good" action is Popeye's yearly trip to Pensacola to see his mother, but these journeys are more habit than filial concern.

This epitome of modern evil is depicted as the all-powerful gang leader who fears no one and who is feared by everyone he meets; but Popeye, if he has reached the zenith of underworld power, has also reached the nadir of physical and spiritual life. Popeye cannot enjoy his wealth because he has nothing he can do with it, and he cannot drink liquor because it poisons him (10, 370). He has "no friends and had never known a woman and knew he could never . . ." (370). Because he is impotent, he uses either a corncob as his sexual instrument (as he did once with Temple) or a substitute (his henchman Red) to obtain a vicarious sexual and emotional release. Popeye's heredity and inferior environment have given him an unusually sordid background. He was unable to talk and walk until he was four because of congenital syphilis from his father, who married Popeye's mother only because he was forced to after he had made her pregnant. His grandmother who lived with him and his mother was a pyromaniac, and his adult associates are gangsters, prostitutes, and morons, or as Ruby Lamar calls most of them, "crimps, and spungs and feebs" (8).

Remarkably, Popeye has one outstanding physical trait. He shoots with amazing accuracy, and he kills Tommy the feeb, and Red the handsome gangster who, following Popeye's orders, has had frequent intercourse with Temple while Popeye watched in ecstasy, making a "high whinnying sound like a horse" (191). The ironic justice of *Sanctuary* has Popeye arrested near Birmingham while on the way home from seeing his mother: "they arrested him for killing a man in one town and at an hour when he was in another town killing somebody else . . . and he said 'For Christ's sake . . .'" (370–71).

Loveless, hopeless, purposeless, and almost faceless—this is Popeye in *Sanctuary*—a monstrous embodiment of twentieth century man. Popeye could be called an end product of our spiritually sterile modern civilization, as one recalls that Faulkner said that Popeye is a symbol of evil in society, and that this incarnation of evil was born out of society's virulence. But, even so, Faulkner gives Popeye some redeeming qualities at the end—seemingly instinctive insights into the futility of his success and the emptiness of his life. In jail, after calmly hearing his death sentence, Popeye accepts the double irony of fate and justice by rejecting help from his high-priced Memphis lawyer.

Popeye then permits a minister to pray for him, saying, "Sure . . . go ahead. Dont mind me," and while the minister prays Popeye smokes. As an added note of rejection, Popeye says to the turnkey who wants to return the change from a $100 bill, "Keep it . . . Buy yourself a hoop" (378).

During his last living hours Popeye turns from many things modern-day society considers compellingly important: a powerful influence that can "fix" anything; an excessive abundance of money that seemingly can buy everything, including influence; and a calculated religious attitude, which in moments of need frequently becomes immediately important for the safety and comfort of one's present and future life. In these final scenes, Popeye's physical and mental rejection of what modern man too often considers overwhelmingly important—power, money, religion—symbolically separates him at the end of his life from the society that produced and shaped him.

In *Sanctuary* society left its stigma on Popeye in his twisted physical, mental, and spiritual growth, and Faulkner through exaggerated irony and satire presented Popeye as an extreme symbol of modern man. Yet, before he dies, Popeye significantly turns away from all that he had been conditioned by society to accept as success, as he impassively allows himself to be destroyed, seemingly because nothing he has achieved is worth living for.

Elsewhere in his fiction Faulkner chose other aspects of current trends and self-created destructiveness to underscore man's moral and ethical violations. In *Pylon*, *Requiem for a Nun*, *The Town*, and particularly in *Intruder in the Dust* and *Sartoris*, Faulkner scathingly censures modern man's manic prostitution to the automobile, a mechanism daily destroying human, animal, and plant health and life.[27] The world's incessant obsession with war—"man's fatal vice" as Faulkner called it—is reprobated in *The Mansion, Light in August,* and impressively excoriated in *Soldiers' Pay* and *A Fable.*[28]

Faulkner in his writings used what he called his carpenter's hammer to design a superstructure of criticism and condemnation for certain aspects of civilization that he scorned and that he believed should and could be changed and improved. In his entire creative life Faulkner manifested his profound belief that "the whole twentieth century is a sorry thing."

Notes

1. William Faulkner, *Knight's Gambit* (New York: Random House, 1949), p. 54.
2. William Faulkner, *A Fable* (New York: Random House, 1954), p. 203.
3. *Faulkner at Nagano*, ed. Robert A Jeliffe (Tokyo: Kenkyusha Ltd., 1959), pp. 13–14.
4. Irving Howe, *William Faulkner: A Critical Study* (New York: Random House, 1952), p. 6. (Available in a third and expanded edition, University of Chicago Press.)
5. Jean-Paul Sartre, *Literary and Philosophical Essays* (New York: Criterion Books, Inc., 1955), p. 87.
6. William Van O'Connor, *The Tangled Fire of William Faulkner* (Minneapolis: University of Minnesota Press, 1954), p. 41.
7. Herbert Read, *The Tenth Muse* (New York: Grove Press, Inc., 1957), p. 69. Of interest in a consideration of Faulkner's attacks on civilization is his attitude towards primitivism. Important in any discussion of primitivism in Faulkner's work would be the early criticisms of Ursula Brumm and R. W. B. Lewis. See Brumm, "Wilderness and Civilization: A Note on William Faulkner," *Partisan Review,* 22 (Summer 1955), 340–350; and Lewis, "The Hero in the New World: William Faulkner's 'The Bear,'" *Kenyon Review,* 13 (Autumn 1951), 641–660.
8. William Faulkner, "On Privacy: The American Dream: What Happened to It," *Harper's Magazine,* 211 (July 1955), 38.
9. Jean Stein, "The Art of Fiction XII: William Faulkner," *Paris Review,* 4 (Spring 1956), 42.
10. William Faulkner, *Absalom, Absalom!* (New York: Random House, 1936), p. 89.
11. Ibid., p. 147.
12. Ibid., p. 162.
13. William Faulkner, *Mosquitoes* (New York: Liveright Publishing Corp., 1927), p. 252.
14. William Faulkner, *Intruder in the Dust* (New York: Random House, 1948), p. 26.
15. William Faulkner, *The Wild Palms* (New York: Random House, 1939), p. 54.
16. *Mosquitoes*, p. 345.
17. *Absalom, Absalom!*, pp. 132, 129.
18. Ibid., p. 127.
19. William Faulkner, "Faith or Fear," *Atlantic Monthly,* 192 (August 1953), 54.
20. William Faulkner, *Light in August* (New York: Random House, 1932), p. 87.
21. William Faulkner, *The Mansion* (New York: Random House, 1959), p. 282.
22. *Faulkner in the University*, ed. Frederick L. Gwynn and Joseph L. Blotner (Charlottesville: University of Virginia Press, 1959), pp. 245–246.
23. Ibid., p. 246.
24. See Malcolm Cowley, "Introduction," *The Portable Faulkner* (New York: The Viking Press, 1967). Cowley was among the first to make this observation.
25. William Faulkner, *Sanctuary* (New York: Random House, 1932), pp. 2–5. Further reference will be included in the text.
26. *Faulkner in the University*, p. 74.
27. See Glenn O. Carey, "William Faulkner on the Automobile as Socio-Sexual Symbol," *The CEA Critic,* 36 (January 1974), 15–17.
28. See Glenn O. Carey, "William Faulkner: Man's Fatal Vice," *Arizona Quarterly,* 28 (Winter 1972), 293–300.

ARTHUR F. KINNEY
"Narrative Consciousness"
Faulkner's Narrative Poetics: Style as Vision
1978, pp. 86–101

"If experience consists of impressions," writes Henry James, "it may be said that impressions *are* experience"[1]: we are helped to the meanings of Faulkner's novels by the pressures of their *narrative consciousness* on events. It is a necessary limitation, for few of us are tolerant enough to observe fictional events in full neutrality; one task of fiction, Simon O. Lesser reminds us, is "the scaling of time to a dimension our minds can compass."[2] Our conscious act of reading is controlled in large measure by what R. S. Crane calls "determinate desires,"[3] initial formulations of the narrative consciousness, the primary function of which is to shape events for us. In Faulkner our visual thinking relies on the orientation, authority, bias, and involvement of the screening perspective, on the logic of the narrative subjectivity. Jason's frantic chase after the man from the circus in chapter 4 of *The Sound and the Fury* could, in any other context than that in which we have it, become low comedy. But we have shared a day with Jason in chapter 3; we know how he is mocked and scorned and ignored by others, and we are accustomed to the elaborate behavior and sentiment which he employs in order to move with a little freedom and self-respect in his sharply constricted world. In *The Wild Palms,* the young couple in the emergency warship would seem gratuitous if Harry Wilbourne had not implied, through his presiding intelligence, that he has not known any happily married couples. If Bayard did not tell us the events of *The Unvanquished* retrospectively, *after* he had faced Redmond, we should not be as aware as he may be of the alternatives, posed first in the novel by the Yankee colonel, on the day of his final duel. With Faulkner (as with Melville or Conrad) this open but dislocated narrative consciousness requires us to enter the fictional field, yet it is this same narrative consciousness that provides us with our point of entry. We know Faulkner's characters, says Mary Cooper Robb, "inside-out, not outside-in."[4]

But we must also be aware that the screening perspective will necessarily be somewhat distorted because it comes directly from the simulated human source. We have seen that Granny's vision is astigmatic in *The Unvanquished*, for instance, because the older Bayard recalls it that way; seen frontally between Bayard and Ringo and caught in the havoc of the War between the States, she would appear to us quite differently. McEachern sees Joe's tendency to sin because he *wants* to see it: sinning is for McEachern a natural condition of the human personality and a verification of God. The matter of race is more complicated yet. Faulkner's narrative consciousness, participant in the regional consciousness of Yoknapatawpha, is open enough in Quentin's and Chick's observations on blacks in *The Sound and the Fury* and in *Intruder in the Dust,* but it is less visible (yet more significant) in other instances: Caspey's return from the war provides Young Bayard with a secret self that determines many of his early actions in *Flags in the Dust;* Dilsey's natural affinity for motherhood shames Caroline Compson while her insinuating authority often undermines Jason; and Nancy Mannigoe's trust in her ability to teach Temple to "believe"[5] is modified . . . because she neglects to take race into account. Yet here as elsewhere, Faulkner removes himself from the narrative perspective; his "Craft and raw material are in such lucid balance," says Wright Morris in reference to *The Sound and the Fury,* "that it seems the craftsman himself is missing. We are *within* the picture; it seems no outside force had a hand in it."[6] Faulkner's ideal as a functioning artist is simply to provide and juxtapose the necessary episodes; ideas renewed in patchwork, while the role of the artist remains, as Stephen Dedalus notes, "within or behind or beyond or above his handiwork, invisible, refined out of existence, indifferent, paring his fingernails."[7]

Faulkner also shares with his predecessors in the fiction of consciousness an unfolding perspective: it is fundamental to his narrative poetics that the material which prompts visual thinking is relatively static while the narrative consciousness in its act of recording and integrating is in constant movement. "What I see and hear in the soar and thud of [Faulkner's] details," Alfred Kazin remarks, "is an effort to convey—not merely *to* the consciousness of a single mind but *along* the whole circuit of time and thought through which we move—that which *is* our life in all its presentness."[8] In *The Unvanquished*, visual thinking grows before us as Bayard matures, much as the language and perceptual awareness deepen in *A Portrait of the Artist as a Young Man*. Chick's early bewilderment at his rescue and subsequent treatment by the black man Lucas after falling into the creek in *Intruder in the Dust* is pointedly differentiated from his later, more mature determination to dig up the Gowrie grave to ascertain Lucas's innocence of a white man's murder. The single, puzzled response to Lucas on the earlier occasion is likewise changed into a capacity for those multiple meanings he is able to bring to this later act, for the dust into which he intrudes is not just the dust of the ground and the dead, but the dust of history, of superstition, of prejudice, and of myth—all the dust that blurs and obscures our insight. This progressive perspective in Faulkner is accretive—by impressions—rather than causal by observation or chronological in time, additive in a way that allows us, by recurrence and selective emphasis, to anticipate, to understand, and finally to interpret and judge.

Our response is shared by Faulkner's characters themselves; they like to tell stories. Grandfather Priest sees his childhood as a kind of fable; Shreve requests a story from Quentin as Quentin received an account from his father; and Ike, when confronted by the commissary ledgers, attempts to decode them as a narrative. Some of Faulkner's narrators, like Old Bayard, Aunt Jenny, and Temple Stevens, are compulsive storytellers, and some novels, like *Sanctuary*, retell the same story: we have alternative versions of Temple's provocation and rape from Ruby, Lee, Horace, Temple, and Eustace Graham, Temple's lawyer. At times it is difficult, as it is with Ratliff in *Snopes*, to know when the storyteller is reporting events and when he is fabricating them. *Light in August* is one of Faulkner's most popular works in direct proportion to the relatively easy availability of its narrative consciousness; *A Fable* and *Absalom, Absalom!* have been, historically, the least accessible because the narrative consciousnesses there are multiple and unusually guarded.

But the progressive perspective in Faulkner . . . in *A Fable* and *The Unvanquished* is probationary: it stops at provisional truths. Habitually searching, it refuses to accept conclusive opinions but seeks to integrate contingent images and structures in the consciousness. Isaac's vision of the magnificent buck in "The Old People" chapter of *Go Down, Moses* is evanescent, fleeting; his incantatory experiences with Old Ben are transcendent; his recollections of the former hunts in the chapter "Delta Autumn" are deliberately nostalgic and incomplete: he refuses at each stage in his life as a hunter to assess with any finality the experience of the hunt or the significance of his quarry. Before Ratliff is tricked by Flem at the Grenier place and especially after his fool's hunt for gold, he is unwilling to predict the next movement of any Snopes; the tribe of young Snopeses that arrives from Texas at the close of *The Town* is essentially a metaphor for the inherent boundlessness of truth. Despite the progressively detailed conjectures of Quentin and Shreve and the hypotheses of Rosa and Mr. Compson, the final assessment of Thomas Sutpen lies beyond the boundaries of *Absalom, Absalom!*

The hesitation to limit the range of perceptual experience is both encouraged and discouraged by ritual, legend, and myth. Harry Wilbourne and the tall convict use the ready-made formulas of pulp fiction to define their lives and to trace their own relative success, but they are unwilling, finally, to recognize their own practice. Neither Aunt Jenny nor Narcissa Benbow is willing to subscribe to the Sartoris legend absolutely, but it is a useful index for them in appraising the actions of their ancestors and in assimilating the death of young John. Hightower is able to accept his grandfather's raid on the hen house by transforming it into an act of great bravery during a wartime mission, but in moments of illumination he knows that he has been able to live with his past only by lying about it, by avoiding it. It is this unfolding narrative vision, along with a passion to explain contingencies, that gives narrative consciousness in Faulkner its dynamic quality. "Our eyes [are] hypnotically fixed on the skein of plot as it unravels itself," as Simon Lesser puts it elsewhere, "on the moving tip of the story line."[9] This progressive unfolding, which runs counter to Faulkner's arrangements of discrete episodes, provides his novels with their own inner energies and a dialectic of forces we, as readers, must resolve.

The narrative consciousness in Faulkner focuses first on images. "Things, it is true, are not complete without minds," Bosanquet reminds us, "but minds, again, are not complete without things."[10] The primacy Faulkner awards to visual thinking suggests the intensity of experience as well as its shape. Visual thinking is essential to his narrative poetics, as the revisions in his holographs and typescripts repeatedly indicate. In the holograph of *As I Lay Dying*, for example, Darl describes seeing Jewel's horse as "a gaudy instance among the pines"; in the book, this has become "a gaudy instant among the blue shadows."[11] In the holograph, Dewey Dell says, "I sit naked on the seat above the mules"; the book reads, "the unhurrying mules."[12] Such revisions attempt not only to capture the angle of vision but to employ the special language of the particular narrative consciousness. In the holograph, Faulkner has pasted in this additional passage for Darl:

> For an instant it resists, as though volitional, as though within it her pole-thin body clings furiously, even though dead, to a sort of modesty, as she would have tried to conceal a soiled garment that she could not prevent her body soiling. Then it breaks free, rising as though the emancipation of her body had added lightness buoyancy to the boards or as though, seeing that the garment is about to be torn from her, she rushes suddenly after it in a passionate reversal of concealment. The reason lost in the compulsion of the need. Jewel's face goes completely green and I can hear teeth in his breath.

Moreover, the visual possibilities of Addie's coffin are heightened in the revisions in numerous places. In the holograph, Faulkner adds to Tull's monologue this description of the flood:

> It was nigh up to the levee on both sides, the earth hid except for the tongue of it we was on going out to the bridge and then down into the water, and except for knowing how the road and the bridge used to look, a fellow couldn't tell where was the river and

where the land. It was just a tangle of yellow and the levee not less wider than a knife-back kind of, with us setting in the wagon and on the horse and the mule.

Elsewhere Whitfield's language is also intensified. What reads "I won" in the holograph is published as "I emerged victorious"[13]; "His holy love" becomes "His holy peace and love"[14]; "for by those dangers and difficulties" becomes "for by those dangers and difficulties which I should have to surmount"[15]; "I deceived" becomes "'I betrayed'"[16]; "let the tale come from my lips and not hers" becomes "'let not the tale of mine and her transgression come from her lips instead of mine.'"[17] Holograph 96 has Cash thinking, "So he stopped there like he knowed, before that little house" but the book changes the passage to "So he stopped there like he knowed, before that little new house, where the music was. We waited there, hearing it. I believe I could have dickered Suratt down to five dollars on that one of his. It's a comfortable thing, music is."[18] Dewey Dell's language is made less similar to Darl's throughout, and a number of Christian overtones are added to monologues by Darl and Vardaman. In each instance, the change is toward perceptual consciousness, within the confines of the narrative angle of vision.

"An 'image,'" Gombrich writes, "is not an imitation of an object's external form, but an imitation of certain privileged or relevant aspects."[19] For Faulkner, images are synedoches for the narrative consciousness which they help to define. There are the soap bubbles which characterize the beauty and vulnerability of antebellum life for Bayard as he looks backward on the first chapter of *The Unvanquished*, and—later, after his baptism in war—the mutilated hand of Grumby. The roadsign for New Hope which is registered in the consciousness of Dewey Dell not only comments on her own interest in the trip to Jefferson but reminds us of the real motivations for other members of the Bundren family who are making up the arduous journey. The tube of toothpaste which Joe Christmas squeezes when he innocently eavesdrops on the dietitian's sexual encounter has later ramifications in scenes with Bobbie Allen and Joanna Burden and (for us, if not Joe) is finally correlated with his castration by a butcher knife at the hands of Percy Grimm. The smell of Lucas Beauchamp's house for Chick, the black man's food, and Chick's inability to recognize Molly in a picture because she is not wearing her headrag all remind us, at the outset of *Intruder in the Dust*, of the depth of Chick's racial consciousness. In *The Mansion*, Linda's gift to Gavin of a cigarette lighter engraved with both their initials—*GLS*—suggests the warmth of her feeling for him and her desire to be remembered by him after she leaves Jefferson. "'It's by pictures, pictures . . . that one must get at you,'" says one of Dostoyevsky's characters.[20]

Often Faulkner uses perceptual imagery to suggest the associations within the unconscious rather than in the conscious recognitions. We define the Sartorises initially in part by their house; we measure Sutpen's fate by the damage done to Sutpen's Hundred during the war, and mourn its final destruction by Clytie; we are able to judge Fonsiba ironically (although Isaac cannot at first) by her mean dwelling: "just a log cabin built by hand and no clever hand either, a meagre pile of clumsily-cut firewood sufficient for about one day."[21] Temple's appearance in *Sanctuary*—first seen in a dancing dress, then in a Chinese smock, finally identified only by her cosmetics—helps us to trace her decline and her corruption. Byron Bunch aids us in identifying Hightower by personifying his canvas deck chair, "mended and faded and sagged so long to the shape of Hightower's body that even when empty it seems to hold still in ghostly embrace the owner's obese shapelessness; approaching, Byron thinks how the mute chair evocative of disuse and supineness and shabby remoteness from the world, is somehow the symbol and the being too of the man himself."[22] When such possessions become consciously important and jealously guarded, the narrative consciousness works from another direction. There are Flem's restaurant, water tower, bank, and mansion, and Granny Millard's expanding horse pen, Boss Priest's car and the MacCullum's dogs, the coins Lucas saves to pay for Gavin and Linda's foreign Jaguar. Most revealing of all are the images of other people rather than the realities themselves to which narrative consciousnesses cling: images of Caddy, Thomas Sutpen, and Lucius Quintus Carothers McCaslin—those characters in Faulkner whom we never seem to meet in the novels, except in the memories of others.

In such instances as these last, visual thinking in the Faulknerian narrative consciousness becomes metaphoric. The narcissus which Benjy carries not only suggests his essential self-centeredness, even when he thinks of Caddy, but, like the cornflower and jimson weed with which he is also associated, it is a superstitious sign of death. In *Sanctuary*, Popeye carries a pistol (a "sex-surrogate," Swiggart calls it[23]), Horace carries a book, while our introduction to Ruby—"A woman stood at the stove. She wore a faded calico dress. About her naked ankles a worn pair of man's brogans, unlaced, flapped when she moved"[24]—tells us of the drudgery of her labor, her poverty, and her dependence on others as well as her capacity to be satisfied with very little (Later she will finger the chocolates Horace brings her in Jefferson, but she will not eat them.) The elaborately "flowered china"[25] clock in Temple's room in Memphis is stopped at 10:30: the hour of college chapel and, at evening, of college dances. The oleanders which divide Harry's and Charlotte's beach cabin from the doctor's and which reappear at the hospital and the jail are poisonous evergreen bushes. The spotted horses from Texas—strange, uncontrollable, fantastic, yet always fascinating—become metaphors for the Snopeses themselves, just as Flem is mirrored at the last in a mansion which he reconstructs on the outside but which is rotting away within. Chains of such metaphors can become choric, as with the buzzards in *As I Lay Dying*, the bird call which is simultaneously a sign of life and a warning of death in *A Fable*, and Mink's various relationships to the land throughout *Snopes*. Such poetic images, Northrop Frye reminds us in his *Anatomy of Criticism*, "do not state or point to anything, but, by pointing to each other, they suggest or evoke the mood which informs."[26] Donald Mahon's blindness is an ironic commentary on all the characters in *Soldiers' Pay*, just as the mosquitoes of Faulkner's second novel are the basic metaphor for the vicious, pointless, and disgusting behavior of Mrs. Maurier's guests aboard her yacht on Lake Ponchartrain.

The developing narrative consciousness in Faulkner proceeds by correlations of whole chains of such images as these. Uncle Buck and Uncle Buddy open *Go Down, Moses* with their deliberate analogy between their ritualistic hunts for the fox and for Tomey's Turl, insinuating a moral equivalency that becomes a central belief of the McCaslins throughout the remainder of the novel. In *Knight's Gambit*, Gavin Stevens moves from a relatively simple problem of deduction in which he comes to realize that crime is a matter of understanding human nature and that solving crime is less important than preventing it; the final chapter, "Knight's Gambit," conflates both the psychological and the moral lessons in the chess metaphor which Gavin and Chick use to describe their protection of Captain Gualdres and Melisandre Harriss before forcing the Captain's departure in order to save her. Our awareness of such correlations, often implicit in the novels and stories, helps us to understand the action. When in *Flags in the Dust*, for instance, we hear Virginius MacCallum question the need to buy a Christmas turkey since there is already so much food on hand—using almost precisely the words Old Bayard uses about Thanksgiving dinner just before Young Bayard accidentally kills him—we can see the efficient cause for Young Bayard's abrupt departure. Emily Grierson refuses to admit Colonel Sartoris's death in "A Rose for Emily," not because she wishes to avoid paying taxes but because in her mind his death is correlative to that of her father and of Homer Barron: and the death of the old order and of herself as well.

Such analogous perceptions lead to habitual behavior. Apparently Quentin has a strong memory of brushing Caddy when she falls into the branch, for he brushes Natalie's back and pauses to brush his teeth just before drowning himself, as if preparing to meet Caddy again. Quentin views his entire last day in creative analogies, the one between Caddy and the little Italian girl only the most explicit of them. Mink discloses his years of single-minded concentration on Flem's death and his opinion of his cousin when he plans the murder by ambush with an archaic weapon: the act as performed is a counterpart to his killing of Jack Houston. The ability to analogize does not merely supply models of action, however. It can also lead to original and ingenious actions. Flem learns how to relate two things so that he may deal with them both at once: he arranges to rid himself of the Old Frenchman place as well as Henry Armstid and Ratliff with the same land-salting plan, and in exposing Montgomery Ward Snopes's parlor of pornography, he rids himself of a troublesome cousin, finds a way to keep Mink under observation at Parchman, and begins to form his public reputation as a leading citizen of Jefferson. In other instances, creative analogies are meant as implicit replies or reprimands, as when Mrs. Hines in showing warmth to Joe and to Lena's baby at their births tries to counteract and so compensate for the brutal treatment by her husband. The depth of human need for analogies in the formation of consciousness is made most forceful, though, when there is only incomplete correlation, as Joe Christmas and Temple Drake, Thomas Sutpen and Ike McCaslin learn to their own final ruin.

A particularly common method of creative analogy in Faulkner's narrative consciousness is doubling, in which characters reify themselves or portions of themselves in other characters, similar to the double in Dostoyevsky, or the secret sharer in Conrad. Otto Rank tells us that the double may project the character's narcissism or his wish fulfillment; or as a haunting presence from the past he may serve as an embodiment of guilt, shame, or envy, acting as a kind of conscience control. Ovid's Narcissus is an instance of doubling in its simplest forms: "Am I the lover / Or beloved?"[27] he asks. This is the conception behind the numerous mirror images in *The Marble Faun*, Faulkner's early book of poetry—but it is also Quentin's silent question when he confronts Caddy and when, thinking of her still, he sees his own mirrored self in Dalton Ames or Julio or Gerald Bland. The relationship between Horace and Popeye in *Sanctuary* is first established when Horace sees Popeye's straw hat instead of his own face reflected in the natural spring at the old Frenchman place. It is Temple who keeps looking in a mirror in this novel, however, illustrating Rank's theory that the mirror often images both the libidinous desire and a death wish (as it does elsewhere with Benjy and Quentin). "Maeterlinck says: *If Socrates leave his house today he will find the sage seated on his doorsteps. If Judas go forth tonight it is to Judas his steps will tend,*" Stephen Dedalus recalls in *Ulysses*. "Every life is many days, day after day. We walk through ourselves, meeting robbers, ghosts, giants, old men, young men, wives, widows, brothers-in-love. But always meeting ourselves."[28]

This sense of the other self often directs the narrative consciousness in Faulkner, as it does in Dostoyevsky, Melville, Conrad, and Proust. Jason and Caroline Compson facing each other across the dining table recognize their own deep similarities; so do Joe Christmas and Bobbie Allen across the counter of the restaurant, confessing their own guilt and their own sexual longings while believing, somehow, in their trapped innocence. Marthe sees in the corporal her own capacity to love and her own victimization by others who misunderstand her; Boon Hogganbeck finds a suitable companion for his journey into Non-Virtue in the eleven-year-old Lucius Priest. Temple Drake, "with her high delicate head and her bold painted mouth and soft chin, her eyes blankly right and left looking, cool, predatory, and discreet,"[29] sees an open resemblance in Popeye, to whom she is drawn as a kind of secret sharer. Emmy's conscious doubling of Donald Mahon as a boy and Januarius Jones as a man, permitting her to surrender to Jones at last, is one of the chief revelations of Emmy's character (as well as Mahon's) in *Soldiers' Pay*. Ike sees himself as the secret sharer of Sam Fathers, childlike and pure, but in repeating Sam's "'Grandfather!'"[30] to a snake rather than to the magnificent buck and omitting the word "Oleh!," Ike betrays his own inner sense of fatality and unintentionally mocks Sam's earlier transcendent vision.

This secret selving as a form of wish fulfillment explains Quentin's strong attraction to Caddy; it also explains Harry Wilbourne's uncommon fascination for the young couple on the World War I hulk. Thomas Sutpen functions as a wish fulfillment for a number of characters in *Absalom, Absalom!* Henry sees him as patriarch, Charles as the means to self-respect, Wash as a sign of his own chance for advancement, Mr. Coldfield as a wise if immoral business investment, and Rosa (like Ellen) as the means for a marriage which advances the cherished values of the antebellum Southern culture. But here as elsewhere in Faulkner, intense doubling can lead to anxiety. The double can become a "love-hate object," Robert Rogers informs us, "the object of conflicting emotions so powerful that the unstable perceiver cannot tolerate the resultant anxiety. The perceiver attempts to dispel this anxiety by the magical gesture of separating the seemingly untidy whole into tidy compartments. Actuality is denied, a good-bad father becoming in the sublogic of the primary process the good, loved father and the bad, hated father."[31] This psychological interpretation clarifies Rosa's demonic hatred alongside her intense admiration of Sutpen. Quentin's and Benjy's profoundly felt ambivalence toward Caddy shows how their own identities are essentially grounded in their view of her: she is both the faithful companion—the beloved—and the greatest possible loss—the chief threat. But they cannot rid themselves of thinking of her as their other self.

Furthermore, the sense of the secret self can become so powerful to the inner vision that the narrative consciousness is obsessed with annihilating it. Rank tells us that shadows and reflections in water and mirrors are ways in which the consciousness tries to destroy what it most cherishes and fears. Faulkner, who had heard some Freudian ideas by the mid-1920s, seems to have this in mind in charting Quentin's last day among shadows, the Charles River, and his projections of himself on the men and boys he meets and remembers. Even the secret sharer with whom the narrative conscious may profess friendship on the surface can represent a bitter antagonist beneath conscious statement, as Rat Rittenmeyer hates Harry Wilbourne and as Darl fears and hates Jewel. The same relationship may exist between Thomas Sutpen and Charles Bon, if the reconstruction of them by Quentin and Shreve has merit; it is surely true of Mink Snopes and Jack Houston. Mink is drawn to destroy Houston not simply because of the extra pound fee for a month's feeding and pasturage of his cow, but because Houston so resembles Mink's hated self in his pride, his irascibility, his toughness—and in his subjection to a woman who, however admirable she may have been, consumes him in marriage. This secret selving in Faulkner is often decisive in the behavior of the narrative consciousness and often reinforces its actions: in hanging on to each other inside their rotting house, the Compsons cling to the several symbolic presences (in love and hate) which provide companionship in the irrevocable erosion of whatever claims to merit and stature they and their family once possessed.

Hume believed that the mind perceives no more than a composite of sense impressions; its only creative act, he said, is to juxtapose them. "Creation of this kind we practise every day," Percy Lubbock adds in *The Craft of Fiction*. "We are continually piecing together our fragmentary evidence about the people around us and moulding their images in thought. It is the way in which we make our world; partially, imperfectly, very much at haphazard, but still perpetually, everybody deals with his experience like an artist."[32] Bayard Sartoris fashions his crucial responses because of his juxtaposition of Yankee courtesy and Confederate deceit. Anse Bundren's remarriage on the day of Addie's burial is prompted by his lifelong commitment to the forces of growth over the forces of decay. Much of the dramatic impact of the Jefferson scenes in *Sanctuary* is the juxtaposition, in Horace's mind, of the carelessness of Popeye and Temple on the one hand and Narcissa's lack of concern on the other; the dry rot of inhumanity which he comes to see as characteristic of his hometown ironically enervates him at the crucial moment in Lee Goodwin's trial. Rider is likewise enervated in *Go Down, Moses* when he discovers that whites and blacks treat him the same after Mannie's death as before: the world has not trembled nor graves yawned at the incomprehensible death of so central a force in his life. In comparing the commercial force of the plantation to that of the woods by juxtaposing the images of the ledger books and the railroad, Isaac McCaslin rejects two tainted landscapes only to learn, in later years, that he has left himself no suitable geography in which to continue living.

This juxtaposition of mental geographies is peculiarly strong in the narrative consciousness in Faulkner. The American backwoods freedom afforded the British groom in *A Fable* is sharply curtailed in wartime France, where he changes his position to that of a sentry; and his black companion, once the lay preacher and stablehand the Reverend Tobe Sutterfield, is likewise corrupted by the war, changing his name to "Monsieur Tooleyman" of the Association Les Amis Myriades et Anonymes à la France de Tout le Monde of Paris, his second, grander, but more institutionalized self. In *Intruder in the Dust*, Chick Mallison finds that his growth—his baptism, maturity, and awareness of last things—comes in the country; Jefferson images only stratification, and a kind of numbness and sterility, a stasis. Chick is drawn to the Gowrie grave not only to save Lucas Beauchamp, although that is his first conscious motive, but, finally, to save himself. "If William Faulkner is occasionally obscure, he is not willfully so," Coindreau remarks. "His complexities, whether of content or of form, are never gratuitous"[33]: the narrative consciousness in Faulkner, by its combinations and correlations of images, exposes in much of Faulkner's fiction the fundamental significations of his novels.

Faulkner's characters are first defined, then grow, by developing intricate conscious and unconscious relations between their inner and outer worlds. This takes most of their time, attention, and psychic energy, yet often the rewards are frustrating or sharply restrictive; often they reduce their spheres of choice and action, ending up confused, alone, and shut off from the main currents of life. They are unable or unwilling to reconcile their deepest needs in their restricted worlds. *Pylon*, while it lacks the inner density and resonance of many of Faulkner's novels and while it does not have the consistency of a singular presiding intelligence, is nevertheless illustrative of several of his methods of narrative consciousness.

The central perspective in *Pylon* is that of the reporter; he is the one who is able to draw the similarities between the opening celebration for Feinman Airport and the Mardi Gras of New Valois. The new airport, built on land reclaimed from Lake Rambaud, is named in honor of the chairman of the Sewage Board who is more interested in the profit motive than in human safety; its buildings and runways are modernistic and ugly, twisted by the needs of the planes and equipment and by the donor's desire to engrave his initial into the design wherever possible, both consequences of the dehumanization which characterizes the contemporary world in the reporter's consciousness. Yet the gold and purple pennons at the airport have their correlative in the gold and purple tinsel which transforms the noisy, mechanical, stinking city into a festival that mocks both pagan and Christian beliefs with its excessiveness and its excrement: the crepe streamers in New Valois read *inri* ("Jesus of Nazareth, King of the Jews"), an ironic allusion to Feinman himself. Fundamentally, it is the mechanical life that is common to both, Feinman Airport filled with its stunt planes which turn around metal pylons and New Valois directed by newspapers and clocks. The telephones and cars which connect both locations tie them together more securely. The reporter's dilemma is that from such a world corrupted by technology he is constantly urged by his editor Hagood to write stories of moving human interest.

Like most narrative consciousness in Faulkner, the reporter is mirrored in the objects he perceives. He is not alien to this city, much as he might wish to be. He depends on its gadgets, contributes to its newspaper, lives on a street labeled "The Drowned," and drinks absinthe, which is made from wormwood. But we know that he has some pretensions to art from his apartment in the Vieux Carré (although we can also see that his taste is limited).

> It was a gaunt cavern roofed like a barn, with scuffed and worn and even rotted floorboards and scrofulous walls and cut into two uneven halves, bedroom and studio, by an old theatre curtain and cluttered with slovenly mended and useless tables draped with imitation batik bearing precarious lamps made of liquorbottles, and other objects of oxidised metal made for what original purpose no man knew, and hung with more batik and machine-made Indian blankets and indecipherable basrelief plaques vaguely religio-Italian primitive.[34]

The reporter's insufficient appreciation of art is revealed more pointedly by Jiggs, his surrogate consciousness in the opening pages, whose unrealistic desire is for riding boots which are lavishly displayed rather than beautiful in themselves and which represent wealth rather than utility, for he has no horse; he buys them without even trying them on for size. Although the reporter and Jiggs are from different worlds, they have striking similarities. Both are derelicts of humanity whose labor causes machines to run, yet, while contributing to this mechanical society, they profess close relationships to humanity, living on borrowed money and dependent on others.

Because the reporter sees in the fliers the loneliness and tawdriness that he wishes to escape, he does not like or admire them at first; he sees them as robotlike; "'they aint human like us.'"[35] He makes the plane, rather than the attractive Laverne or the young boy Jackie, the center of their perverted, modern and mechanical life; he is quick to image them as objects rather than as human beings, as Hagood might have predicted he would. But the reporter is an example of the unfolding perspective in Faulkner. From the moment he begins to study the fliers, the reporter finds his observations challenged. He feels sexual attraction for the woman and to his surprise learns that she is genuinely concerned about the safety of Jack Holmes during his free fall; she is obviously in love with Roger Shumann; and she oversees her boy (even though she does not know which of her lovers is his father) by teaching him how to handle taunts from others. Moreover, the ability of the fliers to create a form of art within their machine-ridden environment, along with their insistence on a kind of independence, generosity, and freedom which sets them apart from modern society, attracts the reporter's admiration as well as his bewilderment, and he invites them to spend the night with him. Although his motives are mixed, for he hopes to make love with Laverne, the reporter shows us by his change of attitude, behavior, and language that the fliers are awakening their emotions in him. He sees them, though unconsciously at first, as secret selves.

The reporter has a reputation for gathering facts, but he is not skilled at understanding human psychology. He does not understand the dynamics of the group of fliers, and, ignorant of the fact that Holmes is threatened by Shumann's leadership, he is surprised when Jack turns him out of his own apartment. The next day, he avoids Jack and seeks out Roger as his secret self. The two men are instinctively friends, bonded by their seriousness, their professionalism, their concern for Laverne and the baby soon to be born, and their anxiety to win big money to provide for them. From the start it is a bad match; both the reporter and Roger are romantic and well intentioned, even courageous, but they lack sufficient mechanical knowledge and realistic self-appraisal. In their misguided attempt to show their concern for others, both become *un*professional; they arrange, at some illegality, for Roger to fly Ord's unsafe plane in the big race. As the reporter takes the fliers on a taxi ride nowhere, as he betrays them in getting their mechanic drunk, he is now a direct participant causing Roger's death. This scarecrow, this cadaverous corpse of a man has helped to create his own double in the corpse of the best flier of the group and the man he sees as his only friend. Ironically, neither makes the correlation to Roger's prototype, Lieut. Frank Burnham, described only the day before in the reporter's own newspaper as being burned alive, the air meet's first fatality.

But if Roger Shumann dies in an effort to provide for Laverne, Jack, Jackie, and the baby, he also inadvertently provides for the reporter. Awakened to a love of mankind which he finds impossible to bear, the reporter leaves three accounts of the death of his other self. The first is his initial attempt at poetry; the second, a turgid journalistic report; the third, his first openly confessional and autobiographical writing. The reporter has learned at last to give Hagood the humanity and warmth his employer has wanted, for it is Hagood, not Shumann, who we discover has—through cajolery, concern, and patience—been the reporter's real secret sharer all along. Because Hagood remains the living double who represents to the reporter his own guilt and shortcomings, for Hagood is a generous man who has succeeded professionally in the world of New Valois, there is some doubt that the reporter will be able to return to this father figure whom he both hates and loves. But there is no doubt that he has moved beyond the contrived and the mocking which his world, until now, has stood for. *Pylon* concludes with its own balance of forces; the reporter with his newly found love for others has returned to the world of absinthe, but he has left behind a letter in an attempt to save himself, as he was not, in the end, able to save Shumann and the rest. The birth and growth of the human consciousness of a reporter forced to anonymity by his gadget-ridden culture is the theme—and the triumph and the tragedy—of *Pylon*.

Notes

Regarding Faulkner's fiction, references are to the present standard modern Library and Vintage editions published by Random House, Inc.

1. Henry James, "The Art of Fiction," *Theory of Fiction: Henry James*, ed. James E. Miller, Jr. (Lincoln, Neb., 1972), p. 35.
2. Simon O. Lesser, *Fiction and the Unconscious* (New York, 1957), p. 171.
3. R. S. Crane, "The Concept of Plot and the Plot of *Tom Jones*," in *Critics and Criticism*, abr. ed. (Chicago, 1957), p. 67.
4. Mary Cooper Robb, *William Faulkner: An Estimate of His Contribution to the Modern American Novel* (Pittsburgh, 1957), p. 15.
5. *Requiem for a Nun*, p. 234.
6. Wright Morris, *The Territory Ahead* (New York, 1963), p. 177.
7. James Joyce, *Portrait of the Artist as a Young Man* (New York, 1956), p. 215.
8. Alfred Kazin, *The Inmost Leaf* (New York, 1959), p. 271.
9. Lesser, p. 166.
10. Bernard Bosanquet, *Three Lectures on Aesthetics* (London, 1915), p. 70.
11. *As I Lay Dying*, p. 11.
12. Ibid., p. 115.
13. Ibid., p. 169.
14. Ibid., p. 169.
15. Ibid., p. 169.
16. Ibid., p. 170.
17. Ibid., p. 170.
18. Ibid., p. 226.
19. E. H. Gombrich, "Meditations on a Hobby Horse of the Roots of Artistic Form," in *Aesthetics Today*, ed. Morris Philipson (Cleveland, 1961), p. 120.
20. q. v. Lesser, p. 149.
21. *Go Down, Moses*, p. 277.
22. *Light in August*, p. 342.
23. Peter Swiggart, *The Art of Faulkner's Novels* (Austin, Tex., 1962), p. 22.
24. *Sanctuary*, p. 8.
25. Ibid., p. 144.
26. Northrop Frye, *Anatomy of Criticism: Four Essays* (Princeton, 1957), p. 81.
27. Ovid, *Metamorphoses*, III 466–67.
28. James Joyce, *Ulysses* (New York, 1934), p. 210.
29. *Sanctuary*, p. 29.
30. *Go Down, Moses*, p. 330.
31. Robert Rogers, *A Psychoanalytic Study of the Double in Literature* (Detroit, 1970), pp. 109–10.
32. Percy Lubbock, *The Craft of Fiction* (New York, 1957), p. 7.
33. Maurice Edgar Coindreau, *The Time of William Faulkner: A French View of Modern American Fiction*, trans. George McMillan Reeves (Columbia, S. C., 1971), p. 62. He is speaking of *The Wild Palms* in particular.
34. *Pylon*, p. 90.
35. Ibid., p. 45.

HUGH KENNER
"Faulkner and the Avant-Garde"
Faulkner, Modernism, and Film
1979, pp. 182–96

Faulkner is clearly part of something modern: we have no difficulty thinking of whole pages and chapters of *The Sound and the Fury* or *Absalom, Absalom!* which it is inconceivable that anyone could have written before the complex revolution of verbal and narrative techniques we associate with the early twentieth century. Yet avant-garde is a metaphor of which we sense the wrongness as soon as we apply it. It is a military metaphor; the avant-garde is the forward edge of an army, or perhaps a scouting party, or a clutch of purposeful dynamiters—in any case a coherent group under discipline. Applied to the arts, this metaphor reflects a bourgeois fear of being plotted against, and a plot entails a group. Faulkner wasn't a group man. No other major twentieth-century writer was so isolated from his peers. The list of men he admired but never met would astonish by its length. In Paris, in 1925, he seems to have glimpsed Joyce once, at a cafe. They did not meet; nor did Faulkner meet Pound, nor Hemingway, nor Gertrude Stein, nor even Sylvia Beach.

Poets, it may be, congregate more than novelists, perhaps because, putting fewer words on fewer pages, they have more time to spare from driving the pen. Though Joyce seems to have met nearly everybody, it was because they sought him out, during the nearly twenty years he lived in Paris, and revolutionaries of the word had more reasons for coming to Paris than to Oxford, Mississippi. Still, allowing for the fact that professional gregariousness has not been a conspicuous trait of novelists, there is something idiosyncratic about Faulkner's isolation. He did not even talk much about his reading—his equivocation about his knowledge of *Ulysses* is famous—and when, in late years, confronting undergraduate audiences, he was asked about his peers he tended to answer in lists: "Wolfe, John Dos Passos, Hemingway, Willa Cather, John Steinbeck" ran one such list; and as for detailed comment, he would merely rank them according to what he called "the splendor of the failure": that ranking ran "Wolfe, Faulkner, Dos Passos, Hemingway and Steinbeck."[1]

Such evasiveness seems meant to create a presumption: that the heart of writing is ultimately moral, that each writer confronts his aspiration and his failure alone, and that what writers learn from one another is either private or trivial. But avant-garde by definition professes a community of aim. It is held together by what its members profess in common, by interchange, by an emphasis on the part of the craft that is learned, shared, exchanged, sharpened in the phrasing and the exchanging. Manifestoes are its staple, and cafe talk; and if Joyce for example signed no manifestoes, he is nonetheless legitimately claimed by a modernism that learned from his example, in part because he had so clearly thought out his methods that his example could teach them, and teach the attitudes behind them.

Faulkner clearly wanted no part of pedagogy, nor of literary politics. But in talking as he did about the intensities of solitary aspiration and failure, he seemed to disavow the other face of avant-gardism as well, its emphasis on what can be defined as a community of aim and means: the deliberate craft, the statable grounds of self-criticism. Faulkner it seems, did not mind anyone's believing that the hard work he did came from his gut: that there was nothing to talk about save the sense of dedicated effort.

This proposition may be conveniently illustrated from the history of one twentieth-century group, the imagists, who were united, insofar as anything united them save mutal acquaintance, by a program with three points: (1) "Direct treatment of the 'thing,' whether subjective or objective"; (2) no unnecessary word; (3) a metric obeying the phrase rather than the metronome. We may think of this program under either of two aspects, the public and the technical. One part of its intent—and the purpose of publishing it rather than confining it to talk and private circulation—was pedagogic: to alter public taste, to define criteria that will exclude much that gets readily admired, and focus attention on much that gets forgotten, or admired without perception. For it does not describe only future poems: it isolates certain past ones. Sappho meets these criteria; so does Catullus; so does Villon. Swinburne does not, running riot with unnecessary words; and if many Greek writers were, as Pound said, "rather Swinburnian," the effect of the imagist canon is to isolate Sappho and the epigrammatists of the Greek anthology from what is inertly celebrated as "Greek Literature." So a manifesto that seems phrased for the use of poets can alter the perceptions of a reader of poetry who has no ambition to write a line.

The other aspect of the program is technical; it gives a poet criteria for revision. Have I worked for direct presentation, or contented myself with abstraction? Have I admitted nonfuncting words, words maybe that swarm out of habit, or that fill out a rhythm and do nothing else? Have I permitted my rhythm to sway mechanically?

We may add that in redefining a tradition, and in isolating technical matters from it, the imagist canon allowed poets to admire Sappho or Catullus, and aspire to emulate their excellence, without imitating them directly, thus saving young writers much time they might otherwise lose executing pastiche. In this respect it defines prose canons too; Stendhal for instance is by extension an imagist, Stendhal who based his style, he said, on that of the *Code Napoleon*. So is Jane Austen, so is the Joyce of *Dubliners*, but not Dickens, nor Walter Scott.

Now clearly William Faulkner would not have subscribed to this particular set of criteria, beyond perhaps agreeing, through a cloud of pipe smoke, that in some ways what was proposed was a pretty good thing. The famous description of Popeye in the opening paragraphs of *Sanctuary* might pass for the writing of a writer of imagist prose: "His face had a queer, bloodless color, as though seen by electric light; against the sunny silence, in his slanted straw hat and his slightly akimbo arms, he had that vicious depthless quality of stamped tin." "Sunny silence" looks like a mannered synaesthesia, but "sunny" is needed to offset "electric light": under the sky, this face is unnatural in color. And the superb "stamped tin," with its clanked dull rhythm—how much contempt resonates in the sound of the words, a "musical phrase" indeed if we eschew the sentimental connotations of "musical," to reinforce the absolute finality of the image. Still, no manifesto would have made Faulkner forego his love of many words, superfluous if we examine them one by one but defensible as contributing to a copiousness, a garrulousness, a quality of psychic overflowing he discerned in the tradition of oral storytelling and prized above any satisfactions to be obtained from erasure, paring, spareness.

But the real point is not an incompatibility between Faulkner's practice and any particular set of modernist criteria. The real point is that he had no special use for either of the two aspects of any program. He had no special ambition to reform public taste, none of the pedagogical fervor of the born avant-gardist. And he had no desire, by any commitment now, to limit the scope of his operations in the future.

We have already glanced at one reason for this temperamental aversion. The base of Faulkner's storytelling was oral, and every twentieth-century avant-garde movement one can think of was dedicated to canons not oral but literary, canons which if they admit copiousness require even it to seem a little synthetic, like the lists in *Ulysses*, every item of which Joyce means us to feel can be justified on deliberated and specifiable grounds. The assumption that we are free to weigh and question every word is an assumption peculiar to written literature, where the words stay still for inspection as they do not when someone is talking; to written literature, moreover, which has accepted and come to terms with its status as writing, in fact as writing for a printing press, and envisions a reader silent before printed pages. In this sense the entire thrust of twentieth-century modernism—the Revolution of the Word which commenced in English about 1910, inheriting French developments that date from 1880 and before; the complex eponymous movement that gave us *Ulysses*, *The Waste Land*, the *Cantos*, the *Paterson* of Williams, and the poems of Marianne Moore—its thrust was toward a consolidation of all that printed paper implies: the well-wrought artifact, the tireless revision, the skilled reader, the habitual rereader, in an economy of typescripts, numbered pages, typographic cues for which a speaking voice has no equivalent, etymologies, dictionaries. (Shakespeare had no dictionary.) Questioned about his relationship to this context of creativity, questioned moreover by questioners in classrooms who had no idea that any other context was pertinent, Faulkner was understandably either brusque or evasively polite, feeling perhaps like a shaman who has wandered into a conference of brain surgeons, knowing that he commands skills of incantation incompatible with their discourse of subtle instruments.

A narrative passage from *The Hamlet* runs like this:

> And after that, not nothing to do until morning except to stay close enough where Henry can call her until it's light enough to chop the wood to cook breakfast and then help Mrs. Littlejohn wash the dishes and make the beds and sweep while watching the road. Because likely any time now Flem Snopes will get back from wherever he has been since the auction, which of course is to town naturally to see about his cousin that's got into a little legal trouble and so get that five dollars. 'Only maybe he won't give it back to me,' she says, and maybe that's what Mrs. Littlejohn thought too, because she never said nothing.

Though written, this is not *writing*, not by the criteria Stendhal taught us, or Flaubert, or Conrad, or Joyce. Not merely are its sentence rhythms those of oral narrative (rhythms Conrad eschewed despite his fondness for oral narrators; rhythms Joyce in synthesizing them beautifully in "Cyclops" nevertheless interrupted thirty-two times with interpolations from the domain of print): not only that, but it requires the reader to play the role of hearer, participating in the "now" of "any time now" and in the speculation about where Flem had been. Not the sentence rhythms but the role forced on the reader will serve to discriminate what is radically written from what is radically oral. The reader-as-listener must pretend as listeners do that he does not confront anonymously the anonymity of print, that he is acquainted with time and place and genealogy, that he knows people who are barely named, that characters and their pasts need not be cunningly "introduced" because knowledge of all that attaches to a name is part of the communal stock the reader shares with a community which includes the storyteller and of which the bounds are indefinite.

This is of course a radically unreal supposition, but we brave it out and pick up such knowledge the way a tactful stranger does, never impeding nor embarrassing the storyteller. We pick it up from clues, which means close reading: which means, since reading despite the oral convention is what we are after all doing, that we approach the Faulkner text very like New Critics, as if it had been written by James Joyce. Hence a curious strain at the heart of anyone's confrontation with a Faulkner novel. For ideal comprehension we must take notes, turn back to an earlier page, keep track of time schemes and family trees; we must simultaneously pretend that we need do none of this, need only listen to a voice we ourselves supply. The puzzle we are put to, making out what really did happen, is exactly the trouble we incur with a difficult written text in which the paring away of unnecessary words has been carried perhaps excessively far.

What Faulkner tended to pare away, or perhaps didn't think of supplying in the first place, isn't the verbiage which both imagism and the more general canons of international modernism have interdicted, but information, the sort of information a storyteller's hearers take for granted because they are part of this community. Take, for a brief and amusing illustration, the story "An Error in Chemistry," an unimportant potboiler nine editors rejected before *Ellery Queen's Mystery Magazine* paid $300 for it in 1945. The story turns on a mystery writer's gimmick: an impostor exposes himself by not knowing how a Mississippian would make a cold toddy. He spoons sugar into raw whiskey, which won't dissolve it, instead of into water to which the whiskey will then be added, and everybody in the room is aghast at this violation not only of chemistry but of an immutable folkway. As the narrator tells us, "I had not only watched Uncle Gavin, and the sheriff when he would come to play chess with Uncle Gavin, but Uncle Gavin's father too who was my grandfather, and my own father before he died, and all the other men who would come to Grandfather's house who drank cold toddies": that is how you acquire that sort of information; any member of the storyteller's community has acquired it likewise; the northern imposter hasn't. And in the first version of the story, the one his agent tried in vain to place for five years, Faulkner apparently forgot that most of his readers would be in the position of the northern impostor: failed at the very climax of his tale to specify what error the impostor made: forgot in short to tell us outlanders what any Mississippian would know.[2] The incident illuminates his principle of omission, which isn't that of a disciplined imagist at all.

So he makes the modernist demand that we read slowly and closely for reasons diametrically opposite to those that govern modernist orthodoxy. The modernist assumption, arising from the economy of print, is that to tell your story, secure your effect, there exists a discoverable combination of just the right words, a minimal set of words, not to be exceeded, and to be arranged in exactly the right order. The James Joyce of a famous anecdote spent all day on two sentences, not seeking the exact word—he had his words already—but seeking the perfect order of fiteen words in two sentences. "There is an order in every way appropriate. I think I have it."[3] But the storyteller confronting a living audience hasn't time for that order of research; if he began to fumble over two sentences he would rapidly lose his audience. He is apt to tell his story over and over again, never twice in quite the same way. His unit of attention is not the word but the event, and the practice that shapes the tale toward its definitive ordering is likely to experiment as Faulkner often did, rearranging whole blocks of narrative, placing this incident now before, now after that one, until the most satisfying version is certified by communal agreement and embedded in his repertoire. But even the "final" version will not be told twice in quite the same words.

Being engaged with his audience, the storyteller (or the bardic singer of tales) is little tempted to be engaged with himself. Walter Ong, our prime theorist of these matters, remarks that "You cannot find Homer's personality in the *Iliad*, although you might find the personality of an entire culture there."[4] Nor can you find Faulkner's personality in *Light in August*—not because, like Joyce, he took conscious steps to keep it out, playing "the God of creation, . . . within or behind or beyond or above his handiwork, invisible, refined out of existence, indifferent, paring his fingernails," but because his absorption with tale and audience make it unlikely that self-consciousness will creep in. It is the writer who is conscious of being alone with a sheet of paper, making word-by-word decisions and revisions, hesitating all day over two sentences, who is apt to find a self-absorption invading his work unless he makes deliberate resolves to keep it out.

Faulkner's oral storytelling mode, it is commonplace to observe, is that of a provincial culture with its small towns, its agriculture, its still living religion, its implicit norms of conduct. Drawing an analogy between Faulkner and Yeats, Cleanth Brooks has quoted the Irishman Seán O'Faoláin, who thought that life in Mississippi sounded very like life in County Cork:

> There is the same passionate provincialism; the same local patriotism; the same southern nationalism—those long explicit speeches of Gavin Stevens in *Intruder in the Dust* might, *mutatis mutandis*, be uttered by a southern Irishman—the same feeling that whatever happens in Ballydehob or in Jefferson has never happened anywhere else before, and is more important than anything that happened in any period of history in any part of the cosmos; there is the same vanity of an old race; the same gnawing sense of old defeat; the same capacity for intense hatred; a good deal of the same harsh folk-humor; the same acidity; the same oscillation between unbounded self-confidence and total despair; the same escape through sport and drink.[5]

We may next note that of the two great writers born in nineteenth-century Ireland, the elder, W. B. Yeats, was excited by collections of folk narratives and even helped Lady Gregory collect them, while the younger, James Joyce, affected a bored contempt for such materials though he put them to covert use in *Finnegans Wake*. Yeats (who like Faulkner went on to win the Nobel Prize, bestowed by a committee with a demonstrable predilection for regional writers) argued memorably that

> All that we did, all that we said or sang
> Must come from contact with the soil, from that
> Contact everything Antaeus-like grew strong.

Joyce (whom the Nobel committee overlooked, omitting as it did so to honor the greatest man of letters of the twentieth century) called Ireland "the afterthought of Europe" and spent his last decades in Europe's most cosmopolitan capital, Paris.

One cannot imagine modern letters without Joyce; one cannot imagine modern Ireland without Yeats. To say that is not to confine the interest of Yeats to the Irish; without Yeats we should all be deprived of a memorable, an irreplaceable body of work. (Many curricula moreover would be impoverished, so great is his pedagogical usefulness.) But it is difficult to specify the difference Yeats made to any other major writer, whatever moral difference his existence assuredly made to the next generation in Ireland; whereas Joyce was so great an innovator his mark is on all prose narrative since the publication of *Ulysses*.

In making this distinction we are preparing for a clarification of twentieth-century modernism which in turn will help clarify Faulkner's relationship to it. One way of describing what happened to English in the twentieth century is this: English ceased to be the language of a country and its former colonies; it became instead simply an available language, regarded differently by writers in England, in the United States, in Ireland. Three regional literatures arose: the English, the American, the Irish, writers in each country bringing different social assumptions to their common dictionary. Take the word "accurate." An Englishman, guided by the latin *cura*, "care," in an etymology he may not even know, feels *trouble* in accuracy; it is achieved by taking care. William Carlos Williams said of something he was writing, "As far as I have gone it is accurate": "it," not "I"; the emphasis is not on the trouble but on the close tolerances of the result. An American senses in accuracy a technological *precision*. James Joyce in *Ulysses* presents Mr. Philip Beaufoy "in accurate morning dress"; we may be tempted to say that an Englishman who invokes accuracy is being troubled, an American is being precise, and an Irishman is being funny. Such examples could be multiplied by the thousand. James Joyce wrote of an English priest, "How different are the words *home, Christ, ale, master*, on his lips and on mine! . . . His language, so familiar and so foreign, will always be for me an acquired speech." Yet Joyce had grown up speaking no language save what everyone called "English."

Three languages then, drawn from the same dictionary; three social experiences likewise; and by the mid-twentieth century, for the first time, three literatures. Earlier Irish writers had won their fame in England, earlier American ones had hoped to. We may speak now of the literatures of the three provinces, England too a province like the others. For the twentieth century also gave birth to a fourth English, that of international modernism.

It seems clear, for instance, that *Ulysses* is in no meaningful way a part of Irish literature; nor is *Waiting for Godot* (which is not part of French literature either, though the first version was written, by an Irishman, in French). Is *The Waste Land* part of English literature? Probably not; not the way *The Vanity of Human Wishes* is, or *Mrs. Dalloway*. It is easier to assign these works, and others, to a new international tradition, the language of which is to be found in an English dictionary; much as it is easier to assign the oeuvre of Picasso to something analogously international than to the history of Spanish art, or the history of French. Virginia Woolf's work on the other hand, despite certain avant-garde mannerisms, is simply English; Sean O'Casey's is Irish; Ernest Hemingway's is American; and so is Scott Fitzgerald's and most of Faulkner's.

Such a taxonomy is not a means of assigning value but a way of assessing relationships. The masters of international modernism were the century's great innovators, on whose innovations the writers of the three provinces habitually drew. They pay for their grandeur, though, with a certain abstractness—an attentuation of the richness and power that is available to a novelist or poet who is working within a culture, with the culture's norms and its minute signals. Little that is specifically Irish, except the precision of speech rhythm and a taste for the comedy of logic, has survived the process by which Samuel Beckett's novels and plays were extracted from the language he learned in Dublin. Joyce bent his intention not on being Irish but on being a pupil of the Jesuits who chanced to have grown up in Ireland. But remove his southernness from

Faulkner, or remove Sligo and the Anglo-Irish pride from Yeats, and nothing much is left.

We have in Faulkner, then, a distinguished and powerful instance of the sort of local literary tradition the modernism of the twentieth century has made possible: a way of being intensely local which profits from a range of expressive devices not local at all but developed by several great contemporary innovators whose intention was to see their native region from afar, with cosmopolitan eyes. Joyce could not have written in Dublin, nor Eliot in St. Louis, nor Pound in either Idaho (where he was born) or Pennsylvania (where he grew up). They went to the great capitals, never forgetting their roots, always looking back.

But Faulkner could not have written *The Sound and the Fury* in Paris, nor could William Carlos Williams have carried his Jersey materials there. And yet every page of theirs bespeaks their contemporaneity with Joyce and with Pound, but for whom neither could have written as he did.

We may want to ask, finally, what all this implies about Faulkner's reader. We have employed, for expository convenience, the model of the communal storyteller, who tells tall tales, tales his hearers already half know, and tells them over and over, he and those who hear knit in a web of comprehension a great deal of which need not even entail what is spoken. Such a man enjoys extraordinary intimacy with the hearers he knows, and may be half-incomprehensible fifty miles away, where certain names have no potency.

Moving such a model from folklorists' Platonism toward reality, we obtain for instance Faulkner's V. K. Ratliff, with his perfect assurance of how to enter a store "on the gallery of which apparently the same men who had been there when he saw it last a year ago were still sitting," and his sense of how to obtain an audience by dropping the impenetrable phrase "Goat-rancher." People who feign indifference to Ratliff's presence absorb every word he says, as a story perfectly shaped to pique curiosity winds from a teasing opener to a climax that restates the opening in new light. He is like the bard Demodokos in the *Odyssey*, a portrait within the work of the shaper of the work itself.

But this too is Platonized. Demodokos may give us Homer's sense of himself, but Faulkner, a man in a study with a pen, is no V. K. Ratliff, nor do his readers sit on the gallery of even an ideal store. Faulkner's fame did not start in Oxford and spread outward. It started in places like Paris and New York, and eventually reached Mississippi. "Mr. Faulkner a great writer?" ran an Oxford comment on the 1939 cover story in *Time*; "Well, they sure wouldn't hire him to write a Chamber of Commerce booklet for the town."[6]

Print is perilous stuff, like electricity. They read print as far away as New York, and stories should be kept in the family. And Dublin, by the way, contains dozens of raconteurs who will tell you that the city contained and still contains a host of storytellers more gifted than Joyce. As it may; he was more than a storyteller. And they say his great gift was for taking in Americans.

No, the ideal Faulkner reader is not the ideal listener the communal storyteller supposes. Nor is he that "ideal reader suffering from an ideal insomnia" whom Joyce presupposed and did so much to train: the patient correlator of clues and looker-up of stray facts. The ideal Faulkner reader must combine New-Critical skills of textual response with an imaginative flexibility that can bend salmon-supple in and out of the Yoknapatawpha community: for if you read him as if he were Joyce you are repeatedly snagged by what seem like hundreds of running feet of lazily coiled rusty rhetoric and thickets of unregarded narrative gestures, whereas if you read him as if he were a comfortable old-fashioned novelist the coinages, the neologisms, the inner monologues and resonant italics—all the contrivances of literary technology—betray you. And if you read him as if he were an awkward amalgam of both you get no satisfaction at all. It is a unique role that the reader must play, seeing folk material imitated, synthesized, by the devices of the twentieth-century avant-garde, being aware that that is what is going on and yet responding as if he were what he cannot be, a sympathetic member of a vanished community. Our role demands tact and resourcefulness, an ability to adjust repeatedly to altered focus, and we may be years learning it. The avant-garde created Faulkner's techniques but did not train his reader. We must acquire our training from his books.

Notes

1. Joseph Blotner, *Faulkner: A Biography* (New York: Random House, 1974), II, 1232.
2. Blotner, *Faulkner*, II, 1189*n*.
3. Frank Budgen, *James Joyce and the Making of* Ulysses (New York: H. Smith and R. Haas, 1934), 20.
4. Walter J. Ong, *Interfaces of the Word* (Ithaca, New York: Cornell University Press, 1977), 221.
5. Seán O'Faoláin, *The Vanishing Hero*, as quoted in Cleanth Brooks, *William Faulkner: The Yoknapatawpha Country* (New Haven: Yale University Press, 1963), 2.
6. Blotner, *Faulkner*, II, 1016.

LYALL H. POWERS

"The Yoknapatawpha Comedy"

Faulkner's Yoknapatawpha Comedy

1980, pp. 253–61

> But he must read it again. He could not remember the whole shape of the thing.
>
> (Virginia Woolf, *To the Lighthouse*, "The Window," XIX)

The Yoknapatawpha novels, taken together, express a fundamental faith in mankind—that faith which Faulkner uttered in his Nobel Prize acceptance speech: "I decline to accept the end of man. . . . I believe that man will not merely endure: he will prevail."[1] As we have seen, the richly realistic "record of man" as it appears in these novels also gives expression to the persistent themes responsible for the sense of affirmation and optimism arising from the fiction—the theme of the Self-Destructiveness of Evil and the theme of the Second Chance (or the Quo Vadis theme). We have seen that those characters who act in the service of evil are regularly frustrated and ultimately provoke their own defeat—both those who actively pursue evil ends and those who passively serve evil ends by failing to do what they know is good. These latter are often the intelligent and perhaps even well-intentioned characters, principally Horace Benbow, Quentin Compson, Isaac McCaslin, and Gavin Stevens—men whose failure of courage and, hence, of love prevents them from acting on their good ideals. They are Faulkner's quasi-tragic heroes; they are tragically self-destructive. And while we have seen that many of Faulkner's characters fail to grasp the Second Chance when it is presented to them, we have also seen that not all fail. The blessed few, the Saving Remnant,[2] emphatically exhibit "a soul, a spirit capable of compassion and sacrifice and endurance." Not only do they discount, finally, the inevitability of the tragic careers of Faulkner's "good, weak heroes," they also complement effectively those self-destructive characters who flourish briefly in the service of evil.

I would by no means suggest that Faulkner was always

quite clear about and consciously aware of his intentions. Like most artists he tended to discover his proper themes in the process of developing his stories, to recognize his intentions during the task of revision—and especially revision of short story material for inclusion in his novels. Yet the very persistence of these themes suggests that a singleness of purpose—whenever, and however consciously, recognized by the author—did indeed motivate the creation of the Yoknapatawpha novels. The consistency of expression in the development of these themes yields a unity of impression; and it is perhaps for that reason that the Yoknapatawpha fiction has come commonly to be called a Saga.

It is well over a quarter of a century since Malcolm Cowley quietly observed that Faulkner's Yoknapatawpha fiction comprises a single unified work. "It sometimes seems to me," he wrote, ". . . that all the people of the imaginary county, black and white, townsmen, farmers, and housewives, have played their parts in one connected story."[3] Other critics since then have at times briefly assented to that observation, but I think no one has seriously examined the implications of Mr. Cowley's perceptive remark and thus grasped its profundity.[4] It is frequently noted that the work of a major novelist does exhibit a peculiar unity; but the unity to be found (and which I believe Mr. Cowley observed) in Faulkner's Yoknapatawpha fiction is the kind of unity one might expect in a single novel—not only persistence of theme, setting, and characters but also the progress and development, the effect of cumulation from *Sartoris* to *The Mansion*, that convey the sense of organic unity and focussed significance that one gets from a single novel. The baker's dozen of Faulkner's Yoknapatawpha novels are indeed very much a single opus. In this respect the Yoknapatawpha Saga resembles Zola's fictional history of the Rougon-Macquart family, or Proust's extended chronicle, *A la recherche du temps perdu*, or, best of all, Balzac's *Comédie humaine*.

We have biographer Joseph Blotner's word for it that "As for prose fiction, there was no doubt in Faulkner's mind, or Phil Stone's, about who was the greatest artist in the field. It was Balzac."[5] And it is interesting to consider what in that writer's work particularly appealed to Faulkner. He told Cynthia Grenier (in September 1955), "I like the fact that in Balzac there is an intact world of his own. His people don't just move from page one to page 320 of one book. There is continuity between them all like a blood-stream which flows from page one on through page 20,000 of one book. The same blood, muscle and tissue binds the characters together."[6] He said essentially the same thing to Jean Stein vanden Heuvel, and later in the interview gave the familiar account of his discovery of Yoknapatawpha.

> *Q*: What happened to you between *Soldiers Pay* and *Sartoris*—that is what caused you to begin the Yoknapatawpha Saga?
>
> *Faulkner*: With *Soldiers Pay* I found out that writing was fun. But I found out after that not only each book had to have a design but the whole output or sum of an artist's work had to have a design. . . . Beginning with *Sartoris* I discovered that my own little postage stamp of native soil was worth writing about. . . .[7]

One feels that the informing design of the whole Saga had existed in Faulkner's imagination from the outset of his career—or from the middle twenties, at least—and was constantly available to him, and that for any given story he had merely to reach in and break off a convenient piece from the rich basic stock. Or, to borrow from Malcolm Cowley's apt metaphor, to cut another plank from the living tree:

> All his books in the Yoknapatawpha saga are part of the same living pattern. It is this pattern, and not the printed volumes in which part of it is recorded, that is Faulkner's real achievement. . . . All the separate works are . . . like wooden planks that were cut, not from a log, but from a still living tree.[8]

The available evidence proves the soundness of Mr. Cowley's observation and the aptness of his metaphor. Faulkner frequently explained, during the middle fifties, that he had conceived the whole story of the swarming Snopeses instantaneously—"like a bolt of lightning lights up a landscape and you see everything but it takes time to write it, and this story I had in my mind for about thirty years. . . ."[9] And the testimony of the "Father Abraham" story indicates clearly enough that he had at least the broad, general scheme of the Snopes plague in his mind in the middle twenties. (It was further fleshed out, tentatively, in Faulkner's letter to Robert Haas in 1930.)[10] Furthermore, at about the same time he wrote the extensive *Flags in the Dust* (out of which *Sartoris* was carved by Ben Wasson for publication). Before 1929, then, Faulkner had set down the two complementary stories that would be his principal literary concerns for the next thirty years—that of the decadent Southern pseudoaristocracy and its immediate descendants, and that of the rise and threatened success of the traditionless, vulgar, and grossly immoral rednecks.[11]

It is the case with Faulkner, as with Balzac, Zola, and perhaps Proust, that each individual novel is satisfactory as a discrete item; yet the whole of the Saga is impressively more than the sum of its parts. In that respect the Saga resembles certain works of Faulkner's contemporaries which are made up of satisfactorily separable pieces but which are far richer in their totality—Sherwood Anderson's *Winesburg, Ohio*, Joyce's *Dubliners*, Hemingway's *In Our Time*. And Faulkner's *The Unvanquished* and *Go Down, Moses* are themselves interesting examples of the same composite form.

The unity of the Saga is due, in part, to the consistent geographic setting of the novels, Faulkner's postage stamp of native soil—Yoknapatawpha Saga resembles *Dubliners* and *Winesburg, Ohio* in the consistent reliance on specific setting as unifying device. The unity of Faulkner's Saga is due also to the regular reappearance of various Yoknapatawpha inhabitants—generations of them, indeed: the old pseudoaristocratic families of Sartorises, Compsons, and De Spains; the solid white peasantry of MacCallums, Bookwrights, and Tulls; the black families of Dilsey and Roskus, Molly and Lucas, Ringo, and Aleck Sander; and the poor whites and rednecks like the Gowries, the Armstids, the Bundrens, and of course the Snopeses. It is not simply that the novels resume and further develop the careers of these families as the main concerns of their plots—as *The Unvanquished* completes *Sartoris* by flashback and *Absalom, Absalom!* similarly completes *The Sound and the Fury*, *Requiem for a Nun* completes *Sanctuary*, and *The Town* and *The Mansion* complete the trilogy begun with *The Hamlet*; it is, further, that we find passing references in a given novel to other characters and events than those with which that particular novel is concerned—characters, events, and careers which belong to other parts of the Saga, and not even always to parts already published. Sometimes, indeed, these passing references seem almost like little loose ends that simply don't "belong"—until one has read the whole of the Saga, finished the chronicle, and sees the ultimate connections.

The Saga, then, does not develop as a steady chronological progression. It has a significant informing structure. It divides readily into two parts, what I have called two "movements": the first (from *Sartoris* through *The Unvanquished*) is defined by the two accounts of Sartoris history which bracket it, and the second (from *The Hamlet* through *The Mansion*) by the initial and the final volumes of the Snopes trilogy which bracket it. Two additional unifying threads which help bind the two parts are: (1) the metamorphosis of Horace Benbow into Gavin Stevens, and (2) the return of the sewing-machine salesman, whom we first met as V. K. Suratt in *Sartoris*, as V. K. Ratliff in *The Hamlet*, where he begins his anti-Snopes campaign which burgeons through the trilogy. And the final volume, as I have indicated in the preceding chapter, successfully concludes both the Snopes trilogy and the Yoknapatawpha Saga as a whole. If Faulkner did not "break the pencil" after completing *The Mansion*, he abandoned it in favor of an instrument of softer lead to set down *The Reivers*.

The mode of nostalgia dominates the first movement of the Saga; its concern is with the past, its view "back-looking," and its progress generally retrogressive. The stories of the first two novels (*Sartoris* and *The Sound and the Fury*) find their completion respectively in the last novel of this movement (*The Unvanquished*), which is a flashback to a time two generations earlier, and in the second last (*Absalom, Absalom!*), which is a flashback to a much more recent past but contains within it material contemporary with that of *The Unvanquished*—the Civil War. This first movement seems concerned with answering such questions as Why did the South fall? Why did God let the South lose the Civil War? What legacy has been left from antebellum days? The action of this movement serves to discover the evil that was gnawing at the base of the glorious antebellum Southern structure and caused it to topple, to identify the consequent evil that poisons the modern postbellum world, and to recognize the virtue of the unspoiled, simple people who have remained in touch with and so been nourished by the source of Good. The mode of anticipation dominates the second movement of the Saga—and it is increasingly hopeful anticipation; its concern is with the present and the future, its view forward looking, and its progress advancement. If the first movement has seemed to emphasize human failure—of courage, of love, of responsibility—the second even more clearly emphasizes success. The second movement as a whole may, indeed, be seen as predominantly a successful grasping of the Second Chance, even as the first movement predominantly expresses the Self-Destructiveness of failure, that failure which results from the evil of man's inhumanity. The second movement seems to pose the single question: How can the fallen South be redeemed?—i.e., given the failure of the pseudoaristocratic way and the subsequent destructive dominance of the plague of Snopesism and redneckism, where can be found the heroic qualities needed to redeem fallen society? The coin of evil here shows its "democratic" face—the obverse of the "aristocratic," with which the first movement principally dealt.

These two movements of the Saga—the two acts of this drama—are further united by the persistent development of the career of the familiar Faulknerian "good, weak hero." In reading through the whole opus of the Yoknapatawpha Saga, one has the same sense of following the career of a definite protagonist as in reading Hemingway's *In Our Time* or, indeed, Eliot's *The Waste Land*. And the Yoknapatawpha protagonist is strikingly consistent. He is intelligent, full of rhetoric and exalted moral principles, but afraid of life's actuality; he is thus fundamentally an escapist and consequently a figure of impotence. He is romantically chivalrous yet loveless, despite his characteristic incestuousness or nympholepsy. His love (or lust) is merely cerebral; his virtue mainly theoretic. He is wise and sensitive enough to define most of the threatening evils of his world, but lacks the courage to oppose those evils effectively. He represents the antebellum, white, pseudoaristocratic establishment, and he usually defines the principal evil as the political, social, and moral threat posed by the rising rednecks—focussed in the Snopeses and chiefly in Flem. He presents himself as the principal opponent to that threat, but his opposition is verbal merely, like that of a member of a debating team. He is usually, of course, singularly ineffectual. His name is Horace Benbow or Quentin Compson or Isaac McCaslin or Gavin Stevens.

He yearns to slough off the legacy of responsibility he has inherited as a burden from his predecessors, and the legacy involves responsibility for the condition of the Negroes—the transmitted curse of slavery—and for the very rise of the rednecks. And while the redneck threat is not quite so clearly defined in the first movement of the Saga as it will be in the second, it is evident enough. The spreading stain of Snopesism is already detectable and even its ultimate achievement distinctly anticipated there. *Sartoris* retains, from both the "Father Abraham" manuscript and *Flags in the Dust*, the prophetic thumbnail sketch of Flem Snopes's success.

> Flem, the first Snopes, had appeared unheralded one day behind the counter of a small restaurant on a side street, patronized by country folk. With this foothold and like Abraham of old, he brought his blood and legal kin household by household, individual by individual, into town, and established them where they could gain money. Flem himself was presently manager of the city light and water plant, and for the following few years he was a sort of handy man to the municipal government; and three years ago, to old Bayard's profane astonishment and unconcealed annoyance, he became vice president of the Sartoris bank, where already a relation of his was a bookkeeper.[12]

The protagonist's unwillingness to accept real responsibility for the world he has created—or at least for the conditions his predecessors created and willed to him—is expressed in his fundamental exclusiveness. He can be friendly and protectively avuncular with the Negroes and his white inferiors, but he will involve himself seriously only with his own kind. His exclusiveness is given dramatic expression in the protagonist's typical incestuous tendencies. We find this in Horace Benbow's attitude toward Narcissa, in Quentin's toward Caddy, in Henry Sutpen's toward Judith (which Quentin sees as a startling reflection of his own situation), and even in the enforced relationship of Colonel John Sartoris and Drusilla Hawk. But this incestuous love remains theoretic, cerebral, for it never achieves physical consummation. The protagonist moves through a world which is (certainly for him, at least) largely loveless—for he has made it so; and he moves relentlessly to his own defeat, for his bent is fundamentally suicidal.

The significance of the weakness, of the impotence and futility of the protagonist is augmented in the first movement of the Saga by the added dimension of the specific evil of racial discrimination, of slavery and its legacy, which is a central concern of *Light in August* and *Absalom, Absalom!* The last phase of this movement, however, presents the strong implicit statement of *The Unvanquished*—that each generation, each cycle of the wheel, needs and may indeed effect the return of a truly heroic champion who embodies the redeeming and sustaining virtues, and who will act on them; that is Bayard Sartoris.

In the second movement of the Saga the career of the

protagonist (now consistently Gavin Stevens) shows a steady decline, in spite of his helpful discussions with Temple Drake in *Requiem for a Nun;* and that decline persists precipitously into the terminal phase, *The Mansion*. Yet as we proceed through the second movement we find that *Intruder in the Dust* has begun the development of what will become a most encouraging figure, properly part of the Saving Remnant, who will increase in wisdom as in stature through the balance of the second movement of the Saga to emerge finally (in *The Mansion*) as a proper hero—the man the protagonist is never able to become, in fact something very close to the modern equivalent of Bayard Sartoris as he is developed in *The Unvanquished*, a Second-Chance Bayard: Charles "Chick" Mallison, nephew of Gavin Stevens.

The important idea discussed at length by Gavin and Temple in *Requiem*—that good not only can but must come out of evil—is realized in the emergence and progress of Wallstreet Panic Snopes. In his review of the clan, Montgomery Ward Snopes has explained with pleasant irony that Eck and Wall are "our shame": for they are atypical Snopeses. I would reemphasize my opposition to the frequent suggestion (even apparently supported by some of Faulkner's subsequent comments) that Wall and his father are not really Snopeses at all. In a sense they are not, of course, for they do not behave like typical Snopeses. But Faulkner made them part of the clan as though to insist on the idea that from the heart of this most despicable and threatening group could arise a useful and admirable human character. Wall has the necessary virtues of courage and industry and compassion and responsibility, and he has the wit to rely, in time of financial difficulty, upon the aid of Ratliff while refusing the aid of Flem.[13] And in those two, Wall and Ratliff, we have two more members of the Saving Remnant who have emerged clearly and hopefully again at the end of the trilogy; with them, of course, is the figure of the young man Charles Mallison, who is the potential hero of the new era.

The central *agon* of the Saga has been resolved; yet it has in a sense ended in what seems to be a stalemate. The theme of the Self-Destructiveness of Evil has closely embraced both protagonist and antagonist: both are figures of impotence. Nevertheless, the basic conflict sustained throughout the Saga has involved two impotent forces; and it has been a conflict between two sorts of evil, either of which, if triumphant, would prevent true progress in the modern world—neither could effectively "redeem the time." By cancelling each other out in impotent stalemate they leave the field open to the enduring Saving Remnant and to the emergence of the potentially redemptive figure of the true hero. Chick Mallison has been well prepared by his early association with the powerful Lucas Beauchamp and also with Aleck Sander, and by the precepts of his uncle Gavin and the common sense of V. K. Ratliff. He has furthermore been tested in the recent war—and a war, it is worth noting in this context, that is not quite of his own making, in contrast to the crucial war which involved his Sartoris and Compson predecessors in the 1860s. If Chick in all this is reminiscent of Bayard Sartoris, he is yet something of a modern, democratic equivalent of Bayard. The young Sartoris did, after all, belong to the pseudoaristocracy of the antebellum world, and it is precisely the absence of such as he in the modern, postbellum world that has been the motive force through much of the Saga's searching concern.

With the establishing of the potential of Chick Mallison at the close of *The Mansion* the Saga has really completed its cycle, which began with the figure of the superannuated Bayard and his incapacitated heir—grandson of the same name—and ends with a capable and figurative heir, a "new Bayard" named Charles, who participates in the final and distinctly hopeful expression of the theme of the Second Chance. The Saga, then, comes to a successful resolution, a complete and satisfying denouement. The sense of completeness derives in part from the brief resumption of several narrative motifs from earlier pieces of the Saga in order to bring them to conclusion, in part from the impression of unity focussed by the composite protagonist engaged in a persistent *agon*, in part from the culmination of that *agon* with the cancelling out of impotent protagonist and antagonist and thus the fruitful resolution of the Saga's consistent dominant themes. The resolution is not only successful but inescapably hopeful as it leaves us with the distinct emergence of a new and legitimate hero, the young representative of the constant Saving Remnant.

> *Question*: Sir, it means that your basic conception of life is optimistic?
> *[Faulkner]*: Yes.[14]

The Yoknapatawpha Saga is our modern American divine comedy.

Notes

1. *Essays, Speeches and Public Letters by William Faulkner*, ed. James B. Merriwether (New York: Random House, 1965), p. 120. Cf. the comment Faulkner made to Loïc Bouvard in 1952: "I have tremendous faith in man, in spite of all his faults, his limitations." The interview, translated, is reprinted in James B. Merriwether and Michael Millgate, eds., *The Lion in the Garden: Interviews with William Faulkner, 1926–1962* (New York: Random House, 1968) (hereafter cited as *Lion in the Garden*); see p. 71 for the quotation.
2. While Faulkner seems to have explicitly rejected the term, he obviously accepted the concept in his answers to a questioner at the University of Virginia. Faulkner began by explaining his idea of the type of man who will prevail:

   > A: . . . there's always someone . . . that will never stop trying to get rid of Snopes.
   > Q: . . . . A remnant?
   > A: No, the impulse to eradicate Snopes is in my opinion so strong that it selects its champions when the crisis comes. When the battle comes it always produces a Roland. It doesn't mean that they will get rid of Snopes or the impulse which produces Snopes, but always there's something in man that don't like Snopes and objects to Snopes and if necessary will step in to keep Snopes from doing some irreparable harm.

   See Frederick C. Gwynn and Joseph L. Blotner, eds., *Faulkner in the University* (New York: Random House, Vintage Books, 1959), p. 34.
3. Introduction, Malcolm Cowley, ed., *The Portable Faulkner* (New York: Viking Press, 1946), p. 5. Cowley had written to Faulkner, August 9, 1945: "The chief thing is that your Mississippi work hangs together beautifully as a whole—as an entire creation there is nothing like it in American literature"; see Malcolm Cowley, ed., *The Faulkner-Cowley File: Letters and Memories 1944–1962* (New York: Viking Press, 1966), p. 24 (hereafter cited as *File*). Cowley there makes quite clear his intention in putting together the *Portable Faulkner*: "I still feel . . . that Faulkner's genius was not primarily novelistic, in the usual sense of the word, but rather epic or bardic. My purpose in 1945 was to reveal that epic quality by emphasizing what others had overlooked: the scope and force and interdependence of his work as a whole" (*File*, p. 31). Faulkner's remarkable response of April 23, 1946, to Cowley's achievement is revealing: "The job is splendid. Damn you to hell anyway. . . . By God, I didn't know myself what I had tried to do, and how much I had succeeded" (*File*, pp. 90–91).
4. A notable exception is my former student, Mrs. Joanne Vanish Creighton, whose *William Faulkner's Craft of Revision* (Detroit: Wayne State University Press, 1977), is an excellent study of Faulkner's revision of short pieces for incorporation into the novels. There, Mrs. Creighton offers this acute perception: "the

Yoknapatawpha County fiction becomes a kind of 'meta-novel' that exists above and beyond the individual stories and novels which inform it . . ." (p. 12).

5. Joseph Blotner, *Faulkner: A Biography*, 2 vols. (New York: Random House, 1974), p. 301. In the interview with Loïc Bouvard, Faulkner coupled Balzac significantly with two others: "I was influenced by Flaubert and by Balzac. . . . And I feel very close to Proust. After I had read *A la recherche du temps perdu* I said 'This is it!'—and I wished I had written it myself." See *Lion in the Garden*, p. 72.
6. Interview with Cynthia Grenier, *Lion in the Garden*, p. 217. It is encouraging also to recall that the late Edmund Wilson was moved to make the association with Balzac in his review of *Intruder in the Dust*: "the book . . . sustains, like its predecessors, the polymorphous, polychromatic vitality, the poetic truth to experience, of Faulkner's Balzacian chronicle of Yoknapatawpha County." From *Classics and Commercials* (1950), reprinted in Robert Penn Warren, ed., *Faulkner: A Collection of Critical Essays* (Englewood Cliffs, N. J.: Prentice-Hall, 1960), p. 225.
7. Interview with Jean Stein vanden Heuvel, *Lion in the Garden*, pp. 251, 255.
8. Introduction, *Portable Faulkner*, p. 8.
9. *Faulkner in the University*, p. 90 (April 25, 1957); see also p. 201 (June 5, 1957): "I thought of these people [the Snopeses] thirty years ago. . . ."
10. Quoted in Blotner, *Biography*, pp. 1006–8.
11. Consider the perceptive observation of George Marion O'Donnell, one of the earliest serious critics of Faulkner: "In Mr. Faulkner's mythology there are two kinds of characters; they are Sartorises or Snopeses, whatever the family names may be. And in the spiritual geography of Mr. Faulkner's work there are two worlds: the Sartoris world and the Snopes world. In all of his successful books, he is exploring the two worlds in detail, dramatizing the inevitable conflict between them." From *The Kenyon Review*, Summer 1939, reprinted in Linda Wagner, ed., *Four Decades of Faulkner Criticism* (East Lansing: Michigan State University Press, 1973), p. 84.
12. *Sartoris* (New York: New American Library, Signet Books, 1961), p. 147.
13. At the University of Virginia Faulkner promised that the completion of the Snopes trilogy would involve the emergence of "an accepted type of Snopes" (*Faulkner in the University*, p. 283); that is fulfilled in the development of Wall Snopes. He also promised that "Snopeses will destroy themselves" (*Faulkner in the University*, p. 282); that is graphically realized in Mink's slaying of Flem.
14. *Faulkner in the University*, p. 286.

VICTOR STRANDBERG
"Between Truth and Fact: Symbols of Identity"
A Faulkner Overview: Six Perspectives
1981, pp. 43–55

. . . the story behind every brow

When William Faulkner wrote to Malcolm Cowley that he did not care much for facts but only for truth, he was touching upon a discrepancy that is fundamental to his style, characterization, and sense of purpose in literature; for the conflict between the truth—that personal, subjective vision that every man privately lives by—and the facts, or objective realities of the outer world, is typically the essence of the predicament of Faulkner's characters. In simplest terms, the truth is how one appears to oneself; the facts are how one appears to others. In terms of style, Faulkner rendered this conflict most powerfully by combining the interior monologue form, which renders in full the truth of each speaker's life, with the technique of multiple narrators, thereby subjecting each of these "truths" to the uncomprehending—and often hostile—eye of outside observers. In *The Sound and the Fury* and *As I Lay Dying* (and *Absalom, Absalom!* too, in its own way), each character thus rolls from subject to object; from truth to fact; from being the center of almost infinite horizons of consciousness within his own monologue to becoming a mere spectacle in the eye of his neighboring speaker, who for the most part can see only the outer facts about his fellows. In the end, the psychological integrity of Faulkner's people depends upon their ability to construct a bridge, however fragile, that can mediate between the facts and the truth of their lives, thereby subserving each character's central mode of identity.

This bridge, mediating between truth and fact, or subject and object, constitutes Faulkner's version of what T. S. Eliot called the objective correlative—a term Mr. Eliot had to stop and define by way of justifying his opinion that *Hamlet*, "so far from being Shakespeare's masterpiece, . . . is most certainly an artistic failure":

> The only way of expressing emotion in the form of art is by finding an "objective correlative"; in other words, a set of objects, a situation, a chain of events which shall be the formula of that *particular* emotion; such that when the external facts . . . are given, the emotion is immediately evoked.

Hamlet's failure, Mr. Eliot wrote, consists in its lack of an understandable motivation for the main character's inflamed emotions: "This complete adequacy of the external to the emotion . . . is precisely what is deficient in *Hamlet*. Hamlet (the man) is dominated by an emotion which . . . is in *excess* of the facts as they appear. . . . His disgust is occasioned by his mother, but . . . his mother is not an adequate equivalent for it; his disgust envelops and exceeds her. It is thus a feeling which he cannot understand; he cannot objectify it, and it therefore remains to poison life and obstruct action" (p. 125).[1] The true emotional motivation for Hamlet, Eliot suspected, lay somewhere outside the play, most probably in the emotional catastrophe that evidently befell Shakespeare himself in the Sonnets: "*Hamlet*, like the sonnets, is full of some stuff that the writer could not drag to light, contemplate, or manipulate into art." (The "stuff" that Eliot cannot quite define is quite obviously the break-up of Shakespeare's great love affair with his Dark Lady and with his "golden boy," an emotional disaster that left its mark preeminently in the grand theme of betrayal over the next dozen years of Shakespeare's writing career.)

Mr. Eliot's formula, though stated as an aesthetic principle, describes with remarkable accuracy the personal psychology of Faulkner's people, whose objective correlatives, in providing "complete adequacy of the external to the emotion," bridge the gap between truth and fact. To illustrate, we might begin with a few symbols on the personal or idiosyncratic level, moving from there to the larger modes of identity such as sex, class, race, and culture. Faulkner's artist figures work mostly on this level of private symbolism, their handiwork comprising the visible object that manifests their inner truth to the outer world. Given sufficiently large obstacles to achievement, these artist figures may attain genuine comic-heroic status, as Cash Bundren does in beveling his mother's coffin out in a cloudburst rather than ripping a few boards off the barn to finish the job, as Vernon Tull advises. Later he makes painstaking wooden plugs rather than putty over the holes Vardaman bored so his mother could breathe—never minding that this same coffin, a few days hence, will disappear from the eyes of men forever. The coffin, then, represents not only his affirmation of existential freedom—he could do this much for his mother, though he could do nothing about her dying—it is also the objective correlative for his craft as a carpenter, the central truth of his identity. Another artist hero, the French architect in *Absalom, Absalom!*, invests his identity in two objects: his plumed hat, representing his status as a Frenchman, and Sutpen's mansion. Loss of the hat causes a memorable gesture of despair—"He . . . flung the hand up in a gesture that Grandfather said you simply could not describe, that seemed to gather all misfortune and defeat that the human race ever suffered into a little pinch in his fingers like dust and fling it backward over his head" (pp. 257–58)—but the artist recoups by dint of his other identity symbol, "a house which he doubtless not only expected but firmly intended never to see again" (like Cash's coffin). The art object in this case represents not only a manifestation of its maker's inner being but a stunning triumph—the only one in the book—over Thomas Sutpen's otherwise invincible will, the latter's "dream of grim and castlelike magnificence" (p. 38) giving way at last to the Frenchman's stubborn craft. A similar symbol of personal identity is Labove's diploma in *The Hamlet*, no mere instrument for upward social mobility to him but a totem that objectifies, from his innermost being, "his hill-man's purely emotional and foundationless faith in education, the white magic of Latin degrees, which was an actual counterpart of the old monk's faith in his wooden cross." For Popeye too, in *Sanctuary*, a private symbolism compensates for an otherwise inadequate sense of identity. The absence of a father figure—Popeye's basic problem—calls forth as a substitute role model the 1920s image of the Italian-American gangster (Popeye's name is Vitelli), whom he emulates in every particular of dress (a tight black suit, hair with brilliantine), mannerism (smoking without use of fingers, holding his head at a wary angle), and code (the tough witticisms, the silence unto death when in the hands of the law). And by developing masterly skill with gun and car in this role, Popeye symbolically compensates for his lack of male potency. To complete our brief catalogue of private symbols, the final entry would have to be Benjy's slipper, again a palpable object that, when rubbed like Aladdin's lamp, magically bridges the chasm between fact, the barrenness of time present, and truth, the paradisiacal time past when he was Maury, not Benjy, and was surrounded by people who loved him.

In turning from these private symbols to the larger modes of identity, we again find in every instance a gap between inner truth and external reality that must be bridged by "a set of objects, a situation, a chain of events" peculiar to the character in question. With respect to sexual identity, both the male and female principles offer a rich study in this psychology. Because they lack the male initiative, Faulkner's women face the worse plight concerning sexual identity, and their facts-versus-truth predicament is the more intractable. With their identity as females dependent upon acquiring a lover/husband and children, Faulkner's old maids must resort largely to fantasy in order to have a satisfactory identity. Yet, in every case, the Faulkner old maid reposes her fantasy, and her identity with it, upon some actual object in the outer world, charging it with her private emotional integrity. The facts in Judith Sutpen's life, for example, are that she is a virgin spinster; the truth of her heart, however, is that she is Charles Bon's wedded bride; and the tangible object that bridges between fact and truth is the wedding dress that she and her female helpers somehow sewed from scraps and stitches during the grinding privation of the Civil War. For Rosa Coldfield the schism between truth and facts is all the more striking. The facts declare that she too is a virginal old maid and, unlike Judith Sutpen, one who hates and fears all men because of her mother's death in childbirth and what she interprets to be her sister's murder at the hands of that devil figure, Thomas Sutpen. Her truth, however, is that she too has acquired a betrothed and prospective husband—and it does not matter that he is that same devil figure whom she hates and loathes above all men. What bridges the chasm between truth and fact in her case are the words that Sutpen has factually uttered, his casual and impersonal invitation to marry. When Sutpen later qualifies his offer, so that he will marry her only after she gives birth to living male issue, her towering bitterness rises not so much against Sutpen's offense to Southern gentility as against his crime in destroying her bridge between fact and truth—and leaving both fantasy and identity in permanent ruins. A yet more striking case is that of Emily Grierson in "A Rose for Emily." The facts in her instance are that she is a murderous necrophiliac; her truth is that she is a romantic heroine who, having yielded up her father to time and death and the townspeople (it took three days to persuade her to give up the body), would never make that mistake again, and so maintained her lover against time, death, townspeople, and the lover's imminent desertion, all together. Crazed though she is, it suits my thesis that even Emily cannot live by fantasy alone; she too requires an objective correlative, an actual, tangible object in the real world that might confirm her inner truth—the object being, in her case, the bridal chamber in the attic complete with rose and silver trimmings and skeletal bridegroom. Among Faulkner's unmarried women, as our final example, Joanna Burden requires an objective correlative of special complexity to serve her double identity as secret sexual tigress and public benefactress of the Negro. Her bridge between these truths and their opposing facts—that she has reached menopause and is subtly a racist—is her sexual and philanthropic relationship to Joe Christmas, whose identity as a "Negro" male nicely complements her need for both sexual and racial connection until his decision to leave her precipitates their final crisis.

Normally the Female Principle finds its objective correlative in lover, child, and marriage contract, but one of Faulkner's great achievements in literature is his apprehension of the women's liberation psychology a generation ahead of its time. A recent statement by Anaïs Nin, "We are all engaged in the task of peeling off the false selves, the programmed selves, the selves created by our families, our culture, our religions," nicely corroborates the truth-versus-fact dilemma that Faulkner portrayed decades earlier in rebellious females like Caddie Compson, Charlotte Rittenmeyer, and the girl parachutist in *Pylon*. Intense, tragic, doomed and damned from the start, these free spirits drew forth great gouts of their author's most impassioned rhetoric. The most tragic victim of them all, it seems fair to say—because the most terribly trapped and alone—is Addie Bundren of *As I Lay Dying*, whose truth/facts dichotomy is totally intractable. The facts in her case are the marriage and children that devolved from her decision, years ago, to accept as husband a slobbish nincompoop, infinitely her inferior, rather than live on as an old maid schoolteacher. Her rage at having to make such a terrible choice, literally the only choice open to a woman in her social position, has turned into hatred of her husband and children; but at least once she did have an opposing truth to live by: her search for transcendence in the illicit affair with the preacher Whitfield. Subsequently, the visible object that mediates between the facts and her truth is her son Jewel, so named because she loves him alone of her five children, not because he resembles her (it is obviously Darl who resembles her most in his keen intelligence), but solely because he was born of the illicit affair and so can objectify her secret rebellion against the awful entrapment of the marriage.

By contrast with the Female Principle, Faulkner's men

have a great advantage in that their expression of sexual identity is free from the terrible female dependency on other people. Indeed, the male's identity does not even require the existence of the opposite sex, much less its cooperation, since the Male Principle manifests itself through competition with male rivals, much in the mode of Alfred Adler's individual psychology: "A thorough-going study has taught us. . . , as our *most general pre-supposition*, that the psyche has as its objective the *goal of superiority*" (emphasis Adler's). The male's disadvantage is that he has got to be brave, braver and stronger than the rival who himself is seeking the goal of superiority. For this reason, although Faulkner's objectification of the Male Principle may sometimes take symbolic form (like Jewel's and Houston's untamable stallions in *As I Lay Dying* and *The Hamlet* or like Ikkemotubbe's steamboat), in most cases the object that mediates between the inner truth of a man's superiority and the outer world of fact-minded skepticism is the heroic deed or act that compels recognition from other males. Jewel's rescue of his mother's coffin from flood and fire is one such bridge between truth and fact; and another is Labove's invincible play in football and basketball, which leads to the valley conference championship in *The Hamlet*. Towering over them all is the awesome figure of Thomas Sutpen, the Male Principle in pristine form and the single-handed victor over a slave rebellion ("He put the musket down and went out and subdued them") and the Ku Klux Klan (to "This may mean war, Sutpen," he answered, "I am used to it" [*Absalom!*, pp. 254, 162]). In Sutpen's case, a handwritten letter from General Lee saying "This man is brave" objectifies the essential nature of the man but, in general, the Male Principle operates through what Eliot called "a situation, a chain of events," rather than through a "set of objects." In either case, however, the principle of the objective correlative remains functional.

In moving from sexual to social identity, the terms of the objective correlative become greatly more various and subtle. For this reason, it will be useful to pause for a moment and draw upon the psychology of William James and Jean-Paul Sartre in so far as they illuminate Faulkner's thinking. From James we learn that the matrix of identity—in all its modes—is the body: "The world experienced—otherwise called 'the field of consciousness'—comes at all times with our body as its center. . . . Everything circles around it, and is felt from its point of view. The word 'I,' then, is primarily a noun of position, like 'this' and 'here.'" From Sartre we learn that the psychic consequence attending this constraint of one's identity within its cylinder of flesh is nausea. Writing in the Victorian era, Professor James was too genteel to press this point, but Sartre, with characteristic unpleasantness, seems rather to relish his humiliating realization: "A dull and inescapable nausea perpetually reveals my body to my consciousness. . . . We must realize that it is on the foundation of this nausea that all concrete and empirical nauseas (nausea caused by spoiled meat, fresh blood, excrement, etc.) are produced and make us vomit." In terms of our truth/facts dichotomy, then, consciousness is the truth we live by; the body, with its blood, vomit, excrement (Faulkner's "old meat"), is its opposing fact; and nausea is the connecting bridge between them. Supporting Sartre's system, two literary cognates that come immediately to mind are T. S. Eliot's Prufrock and Lil (of "The Fire Sermon"), whose amorous intentions (truth) succumb hopelessly to the facts of bodily decrepitude—thin hair and physique, and rotten teeth, respectively. (Occasionally, as in Kafka, the reverse is true—perfect physical health being at odds with a fatal spiritual disease—but nausea is still the predominant feeling.)

Although more subtly than is true of race, sex, or age, social identity also operates around the matrix of the body. Here a further linkup between William James and Sartre will prove directly relevant to Faulkner's rendering of the subject. We begin with Professor James's classic formulation concerning the social self: "*A man has as many social selves as there are individuals who recognize him* and carry an image of him in their mind. To wound any of these images is to wound him" (emphasis James's). By way of pointing out just where this image of self may most readily be wounded, James added—perhaps with a nod to Carlyle and Dickens—a bit of clothes philosophy to his discussion: "The old saying that the human person is composed of three parts—soul, body, and clothes—is more than a joke. We . . . appropriate our clothes and identify ourselves with them. . . ." Sartre's refinement of this psychology consists of the Sartrean look or stare, which—again reminding us of Prufrock ("eyes that fix you in a formulated phrase") and Lil ("I swear, I can't bear to look at you")—confers an unacceptable identity upon its victim:

> What does *being seen* mean for me?
>
> Let us imagine that moved by jealousy, curiosity, or vice I have just glued my ear to the door and looked through a keyhole. . . . I am a pure consciousness *of* things. . . . But all of a sudden I hear footsteps in the hall. Someone is looking at me! . . . I shudder as a wave of shame sweeps over me. . . . Now shame . . . is shame of *self*; it is the recognition of the fact that I am indeed that object which the Other is looking at and judging. . . . Thus in the shock which seizes me when I apprehend the Other's look, this happens—that suddenly I experience a subtle alienation of all my possibilities.

In this sudden shift from seer to thing seen, from subjective consciousness to being an object of the Other's judgment, Sartre's peeper at the keyhole nicely paradigms the mirror analogues of Faulkner's fiction. With respect to Faulkner's rendering of social identity, Thomas Sutpen must stand as both the chief victim and chief perpetrator of the Jamesian/Sartrean dilemma. Invincible though he is as champion of the Male Principle, Sutpen learns in moving from hillbilly to tidewater country that "there was a difference between . . . men, not to be measured by lifting anvils or gouging eyes or how much whiskey you could drink and then get up and walk out of the room" (*Absalom!*, p. 226). The Sartrean stare that mortally wounds Sutpen's social self comes from the elegant Negro butler who, after a glance at Sutpen's clothes and grooming, orders him away from the mansion's front door and around to the kitchen:

> And now he stood there before that white door with the monkey nigger barring it and looking down at him in his patched made-over jeans clothes and no shoes, and I don't reckon he had even ever experimented with a comb. . . . He had never thought about his own hair or clothes or anybody else's hair or clothes until he saw that monkey nigger . . . looking at them and . . . the nigger told him, even before he had had time to say what he came for, never to come to that front door again but to go around to the back. [*Absalom!*, p. 232]

From this moment on, for Sutpen as for Sartre, hell is other people; and he must invest the whole of his works and days trying to bridge the facts of his social identity (white trash) with his inner truth (I'm as good as any man).

Tragically, the objective correlative that Sutpen chooses, his "design" of an aristocratic dynasty, fatally clashes with the identity-needs of his various psychic dependents; so that he can sustain his bridge between fact and truth only by destroying theirs. Among those dependents, Sutpen's victims make up a checklist of all the important modes of identity: racial (Eulalia Bon, "face filled with furious and almost unbearable unforgiving almost like fever" [*Absalom!*, p. 297]); filial (Charles Bon, "thinking *That's all I want. He need not even acknowledge me . . . just as he will let me know . . . I am his son*" [*Absalom!*, p. 319]); sexual ("Rosie Coldfield, lose him, weep him; caught a man but couldn't keep him" [*Absalom!*, p. 168]); and class (Wash Jones, "thinking quietly, like in a dream: *I kaint have heard what I know I heard*. . . . 'You said if she was a mare you could give her a decent stall in the stable' " [*Absalom!*, p. 288]).

It is appropriate that this last bid of bridge-busting is Sutpen's last, breaking the most spectacularly far-reaching connection of them all between truth (Wash's Bible-ordained supremacy to all Negroes and equality with all men of white skin) and fact—Wash's exceptionally degraded status at the bottom of the social heap, such that a Negro woman can even block his entrance to Sutpen's kitchen: "Stop right there, white man. Stop right where you is. You aint never crossed this door while Colonel was here and you aint going to cross it now" (*Absalom!*, p. 281). In Wash's case, the objective correlative that visibly bridges this awful chasm is his infant great-granddaughter who, in being fathered by Thomas Sutpen, represents a miraculous confluence of blood lines between Wash's white trash family and that of the godlike aristocrat. It is interesting that what calls forth Wash's instantaneous metamorphosis of character is a humiliation directed not at him personally but at his family—precisely the mode of identity that Sutpen has most grievously injured with respect to his own families. When Sutpen dismisses the infant he has sired, thereby causing Wash Jones to "see his whole life shredded from him . . . like a dried shuck thrown onto the fire," Wash avenges his ruined social and family honor through recourse to something out of the Male Principle: the heroic act that says, "This man is brave." In rising, scythe in hand, against the transgressor and later against the whole posse of Sutpen's peers—"and now Wash was running . . . straight into the lanterns and the gun barrels . . . while de Spain ran backward before him, saying, 'Jones! Stop! Stop, or I'll kill you. Jones! Jones! *Jones!*' "—Wash displays what William James called "life's supreme mystery," involving an ultimate transformation of identity:

> In heroism, we feel, life's supreme mystery is hidden. . . . No matter what a man's frailties otherwise may be, if he be willing to risk death, and still more if he suffer it heroically, in the service he has chosen, the fact consecrates him forever. Inferior to ourselves in this or that way, if yet we cling to life, and he is able "to fling it away like a flower" as caring nothing for it, we account him in the deepest way our born superior.

So Wash, in losing his most cherished symbol of identity, becomes twice-born, in William James's phraseology. Thomas Sutpen's witness to some such transformation is evident in the type of Sartrean stare he fixes—in his last seconds of life—upon his erstwhile lackey:

> His eyes widened and narrowed, almost like a man's fists flexing and shutting, as Wash began to advance toward him, stooping a little. Very astonishment kept Sutpen still for the moment, watching that man whom in twenty years he had no more known to make any motion save at command than he had the horse upon which he rode. Again his eyes narrowed and widened . . . "Stand back," he said suddenly and sharply. "Don't touch me."
>
> "I'm going to tech you, Kernel," Wash said. . . .

If class identity operates around the matrix of the body, with the Sartrean stare assigning one a place according to one's grooming, clothing, and dental health, the principle holds true all the more obviously with respect to race. Unable to escape their inferior status through either the heroic deed or upward social mobility, Faulkner's racial scapegoats provoked their author's moral imagination most largely when mixed blood excluded a Joe Christmas or an Etienne de St. Velery Bon from their respective black and white communities. For Etienne, after his subjection to the Sartrean stare in the courtroom ("Every face in the room turned toward the prisoner"—p. 203), the object that conveys his identity to the world is the Negress he marries, a wholly symbolic wife chosen to represent his rage and defiance towards the South's ethnic hierarchy. Joe Christmas's choice of a black rather than white identity is objectified in his razor, the instrument of gruesome murder and castration. In these instances the scapegoat's loss of identity turns his objective correlative into a mere negative symbol, a weapon of hostility and defiance. Faulkner's fully socialized Negroes, however, affirm their identity through positive rituals and objects, like Bayard's host enjoying his Christmas in *Sartoris* and Lucas Beauchamp reversing the white boy's largesse in *Intruder in the Dust*.

We come finally to the broadest of all modes of identity, that of culture, where the truth/facts schism has its most ruinous impact. Historically, every culture begins with a perfect coalescence between truth and fact, so that no bridge is necessary between them. From St. Paul through John Milton, we may say that the truths of Christian culture were regarded as facts, credible enough to sustain the innermost identity of the true believer. But with the rise of the Age of Reason, Christian truth parted from the facts of science, each going its own way in the eighteenth century and clashing head-on—via Darwin, Nietzsche, and company—in the nineteenth. By the early twentieth century Herman Hesse was saying, "Human life is reduced to real suffering, to hell, only when two ages, two cultures and religions overlap"; and Quentin Compson would shortly be watching Jesus walk down the long and lonely light-rays. Faulkner's most tragic and pathetic characters are thus his doomed intellectuals, like Quentin Compson and his father, Horace Benbow, Bayard Sartoris, and Gail Hightower, who, unable to bridge the gulf between their genteel heritage and the total anarchy that confronts them, seek their various escapes in withdrawal, suicide, and alcohol. In a contrary way, because they are a generation ahead of their time rather than attached to the past, Harry and Charlotte are also victims of the overlap of cultures in *The Wild Palms*. Here, too, there is no bridge to mediate between the lovers' truths—love, freedom, the search for transcendence—and the facts that oppose them: their need for money and society's definition of adultery, cohabitation, and abortion as crimes. So they, too, futilely seek escape rather than a bridge across the truth/facts schism. Henry Sutpen is also a victim of his culture, forced to choose between his truth, "*You* [Charles Bon] *are my brother*," and the facts of his Old South heritage: "*No I'm not. I'm the nigger that's going to sleep with your sister. Unless you stop me Henry*" (*Absalom!*, pp. 357–58). Various modes of identity converge in this scene—sexual, racial, familial—but it is the cultural taboo against miscegenation that finally forces Henry's hand against his brother, after the lesser taboos of bigamy and incest had failed of this effect.

It is a terrible thing to be torn, like Henry Sutpen,

between truth and fact, but more terrible still is the state of having facts with no truth to live by. Faulkner's most striking victim of this condition would have to be Darl Bundren in *As I Lay Dying*, a clairvoyant seer of fact—he knows all about his brother's bastardom, his sister's pregnancy, his mother's hatred of her children—whose total lack of any truth to live by is the basis of his alienation from the others. Darl's truth, like Charles Bon's, would have inhered in his sense of family had his parents not been so totally inadequate. For both Darl and Charles Bon, the missing symbol of identity is best defined (perhaps) in a sentence from Thomas Wolfe; "The deepest search in life, it seemed to me, the thing that in one way or another was central to all living was man's search to find a father, not merely the father of his flesh, not merely the lost father of his youth, but the image of a strength and wisdom external to his need and superior to his hunger." Thomas Sutpen, by a glance, could have filled this need: Anse Bundren is something else again.

Faulkner's social philosophy, and most notably his quarrel with the Law, turned very largely upon the truth/facts schism. The trouble with the Law is that it deals solely in facts, not in truth, and so it treats uncomprehendingly at best and unjustly at worst a long series of characters whom Faulkner hales into the courtroom: Quentin Compson in *The Sound and the Fury*, Goodwin in *Sanctuary*, Mink in the Snopes trilogy, Harry Wilbourne in *The Wild Palms*, the convict in *Old Man*, Charles Etienne de St. Velery in *Absalom, Absalom!*, Lucas Beauchamp in *Intruder in the Dust*, Nancy Mannigoe in *Requiem for a Nun*. As one who sided with truth over fact, Faulkner was especially harsh on minor villains like the lawyer in *Absalom!*, legalistically computing the dollar value of incest and bigamy at Sutpen's Hundred. His own search for the truth behind the facts of murder, theft, arson, or whatever is nicely rendered in a comment by Mr. Compson in *Absalom!*:

> Have you noticed how so often when we try to reconstruct the causes which lead up to the actions of men and women, how with a sort of astonishment we find ourselves now and then reduced to the belief, the only possible belief, that they stemmed from some of the old virtues? The thief who steals not for greed but for love, the murderer who kills not out of lust but pity? [*Absalom!*, p. 121]

Faulkner's treatment of history likewise prefers truth over fact, especially since the facts—"a few old mouth-to-mouth tales," "letters without salutation or signature"—are so thin as to leave it mostly to the imagination to conjure up "the people in whose living blood and seed we ourselves lay dormant and waiting" (*Absalom!*, pp. 100–101). The moral imagination in particular—which means the ability to lead other people's lives—provided Faulkner's own bridge between truth and fact. The facts, for Faulkner, meant mainly the sweep of time and change and loss such as we see in the "Domesday Book"—that authorial commentary on Yoknapatawpha history that runs from *The Bear* and the appendix to *The Sound and the Fury* through *Requiem for a Nun* and the later Snopes trilogy. The reduction of the old Compson place to "row after row of small crowded jerrybuilt individually owned demiurban bungalows," for example, and the destruction of the wilderness in "The Bear," were facts that Faulkner accepted with the observation that, "No matter how fine anything seems, it can't endure, because once it stops, abandons motion, it is dead." What sanctifies such facts is the "truth" of honor, courage, sacrifice, and compassion that prevails in any age, from Indian times to our own. To spotlight those truths is to "create much better people than God can," as Faulkner claimed any writer worth his salt tries to do. Creating better people than God can is in turn to risk unrealism in fiction, mere romantic escapism. Greatly offsetting that risk, so as to make the old truths of the heart credible and efficacious for us, are Faulkner's symbols of identity that enable us to cross over from the facts to the truth of those wonderful Faulkner people, truly getting the story behind every brow.

Notes

1. The following sources have used: Malcolm Cowley, *The Faulkner-Cowley File: Letters and Memories, 1944–1962* (Viking, 1966), p. 89; T. S. Eliot, "Hamlet and His Problems," in *Selected Essays of T. S. Eliot* (Harcourt, Brace, 1950), pp. 123–25; Anais Nin, "Eroticism in Women," *Playgirl*, April 1974, p. 30; Alfred Adler, preface to *The Practice and Theory of Individual Psychology* (Harcourt, Brace, 1927); Horce M. Kallen, ed., *The Philosophy of William James* (Modern Library, 1925), pp. 126, 128, 156; William James, *The Varieties of Religious Experience* (Longmans, Green, 1902), p. 364; Jean-Paul Sartre, *Being and Nothingness* (Washington Square Press, 1966), pp. 347–54, 445; Herman Hesse, *Steppenwolf* (Modern Library, 1963), p. 23; Maxwell Geismar, ed., *The Portable* [Thomas] *Wolfe* (Viking, 1946), p. 582; Frederick L. Gwynn and Joseph Blotner, eds., *Faulkner in the University* (Vintage, 1965), pp. 118, 131–32, 277; William Faulkner, *Absalom, Absalom!* (Modern Library, 1951); *The Faulkner Reader* (Modern Library, 1961), p. 610; Faulkner, *The Hamlet* (Modern Library, 1940), p. 118.

EDNA FERBER

1887–1968

Edna Ferber was born on August 15, 1887, in Kalamazoo, Michigan, and grew up in Appleton, Wisconsin. After working as a reporter, she published her first novel, *Dawn O'Hara*, in 1911, and gained popularity in the following years with collections of short stories, including *Emma McChesney & Co.* (1915) and *Cheerful—By Request* (1918). Her energetic female characters caused her to be seen as a spokeswoman for evolving woman, and she was a frequent lecturer at women's clubs.

Ferber's career as a best-selling novelist began in 1924 with *So Big*, which won her a Pulitzer Prize and sold well in America and Europe. *Show Boat* (1926) became the basis for the classic musical which opened in 1927, coinciding with the Broadway success of *The Royal Family*, the first of five plays Ferber wrote in collaboration with George S. Kaufman. By the time her novel *Cimarron* appeared in 1929, Ferber was enjoying extraordinary recognition, and had become a leading figure in New York social circles.

A militant pro-American, Ferber depicted life in varying parts of the country in her well-researched novels, which continued with *American Beauty* (1931), *Come and Get It* (1935), and *Saratoga Trunk* (1941). The most notable of her post-war works are *Giant* (1952), set in Texas, and *Ice Palace* (1958), which celebrates Alaska. The many films based on her fiction provided starring roles for, among others, Gary Cooper, Ingrid Bergman, Rock Hudson, James Dean, and Elizabeth Taylor. She enjoyed two further Broadway successes with Kaufman, *Dinner at Eight* (1932) and *Stage Door* (1936).

Ferber wrote two volumes of autobiography, *A Peculiar Treasure* (1939) and *A Kind Of Magic* (1963), which was her last publication. Although a best-selling author until her death on April 16, 1968, her standing with literary critics was less secure, and she is little read today.

A dedicated and disciplined writer, Edna Ferber never married.

General

Most writers lie about the way in which they came to write this or that story. I know I do. Perhaps, though, this act can't quite be classified as lying. It is not deliberate falsifying. Usually we roll a retrospective eye while weaving a fantastic confession that we actually believe to be true. It is much as when a girl says to her sweetheart, "When did you begin to love me?" and he replies, "Oh, it was the very first time I saw you, when—" etc. Which probably isn't true at all. But he thinks it is, and she wants to think it is. And that makes it almost true.

It is almost impossible to tell just how a story was born. The process is such an intricate, painful, and complicated one. Often the idea that makes up a story is only a nucleus. The finished story may represent an accumulation of years. It was so in the case of the short story entitled "The Gay Old Dog."

I like "The Gay Old Dog" better than any other short story I've written (though I've a weakness for "Old Man Minick") because it is a human story without being a sentimental one; because it presents a picture of everyday American family life; because its characters are of the type known as commonplace, and I find the commonplace infinitely more romantic and fascinating than the bizarre, the spectacular, the rich, or the poor; it is a story about a man's life, and I like to write about men; because it is a steadily progressive thing; because its ending is inevitable.

It seems to me that I first thought of this character as short-story material (and my short stories are almost invariably founded on character, rather than on plot or situation) when I read in a Chicago newspaper that the old Windsor Hotel, a landmark, was to be torn down. The newspaper carried what is known as a feature story about this. The article told of a rather sporty old Chicago bachelor who had lived at this hotel for years. Its red plush interior represented home for him. Now he was to be turned out of his hotel refuge. The papers called him The Waif of the Loop. That part of Chicago's downtown which is encircled by the elevated tracks is known as the Loop. I thought, idly, that here was short-story material; the story of this middle-aged, well-to-do rounder whose only home was a hotel. Why had he lived there all these years? Was he happy? Why hadn't he married? I put it down in my note-book (yes, we have them)—The Waif of the Loop. Later I discarded that title as being too cumbersome and too difficult to grasp. Non-Chicagoans wouldn't know what the Loop meant.

So there it was in my note-book. A year or two went by. In all I think that story must have lain in my mind for five years before I actually wrote it. That usually is the way with a short story that is rich, deep, and true. The maturing process is slow. It ripens in the mind. In such cases the actual mechanical matter of writing is a brief business. It plumps into the hand like a juicy peach that has hung, all golden and luscious, on the tree in the sun.

From time to time I found myself setting down odd fragments related vaguely to this character. I noticed these overfed, gay-dog men of middle age whom one sees in restaurants, at the theater, accompanied, usually, by a woman younger than they—a hard, artificial, expensively gowned woman who wears a diamond bracelet so glittering that you scarcely notice the absence of ornament on the third finger of the left hand. Bits of characterization went into the note-book . . . "The kind of man who knows head waiters by name . . . the kind of man who insists on mixing his own salad dressing . . . he was always present on first nights, third row, aisle, right." I watched them. They were lonely, ponderous, pathetic, generous, wistful, drifting.

Why hadn't he married? Why hadn't he married? It's always interesting to know why people have missed such an almost universal experience as marriage. Well, he had had duties, responsibilities. Um-m-m—a mother, perhaps, and sisters. Unmarried sisters to support. The thing to do then was to ferret out some business that began to decline in about 1896 and that kept going steadily downhill. A business of the sort to pinch Jo's household and make the upkeep of two families impossible for him. It must, too, be a business that would boom suddenly, because of the War, when Jo was a middle-aged man. I heard of a man made suddenly rich in 1914 when there came a world-wide demand for leather—leather for harnesses, straps, men's wrist watches. Slowly, bit by bit, the story began to set—to solidify—to take shape.

Finally, that happened which always reassures me and makes me happy and confident. The last paragraph of the story came to me, complete. I set down that last paragraph, in lead pencil, before the first line of the story was written. That ending literally wrote itself. I had no power over it. People have said to me: "Why didn't you make Emily a widow when they met after years of separation? Then they could have married."

The thing simply hadn't written itself that way. It was unchangeable. The end of the story and the beginning both were by now inevitable. I knew then that no matter what happened in the middle, that story would be—perhaps not a pleasant story, not a happy one, though it might contain humor—but a story honest, truthful, courageous and human.—EDNA FERBER, "Foreword" to "The Gay Old Dog," *My Story That I Like Best*, ed. Ray Long, 1925, pp. 11–14

Edna Ferber's first stories had to do with women who pushed their way into competition in business with men. She glorified the woman commercial traveler and the woman producer. They were case histories of actual go-getting women, and she related them by her astute journalistic sense to the subconscious opinion which all women were holding of themselves. The combination was excellent for her own bank account, and excellent stimulus for the progress of feminist enterprise, and excellent also for the increase of the primary documentary sources of the feminist movement. Unquestionably, future historians will turn to Edna Ferber for the gathering of vivid first-hand reporting of the time in fiction. She is, therefore, to an almost final extent, the supreme feminist.

Whether it was out of utter feminist conviction, or out of the accidental attraction of the keen journalist for good material, only Miss Ferber herself will know. But whatever the conscious, or subconscious, motivation might have been at the beginning, she stands now as the supreme fictional annalist of careerist women in the heyday of their careers. . . .

There is nothing in her stories borrowed from Europe. There is no shadow of sophisticated weariness. Sometimes there are touches of naïveté, but these touches come from the author's sense of the zest for living, which is the breath of any new civilization.

She writes as if none of the authors of Europe existed. From the classical standpoint she has no style whatever. But from the vital standpoint of how style is associated with the emotion of time and place, she has perfect style.

Apart entirely from her fidelity to the rhythm of primitive pioneer story-telling, and apart entirely from her absorption in the current of the American scene, Edna Ferber is of towering importance to the School of Femininity. She belongs to the great procession—Austen, the Brontës and Eliot—who presented the feminist picture.

Serena de Jong, the heroine of her greatest book, *So Big*, belongs with Elizabeth Bennett and Jane Eyre and Maggie Tulliver. Her other women are like the other women of Miss Austern, the Brontës and George Eliot. They are the Elizabeths and the Janes and the Maggies out in a new world on the make, selling lingerie, performing on show boats, running newspapers and raising prize asparagus, struggling with emotion and finding themselves relief in action. But there is one great difference, and it is the difference between the nineteenth-century lady and the twentieth-century woman—her women are not dependent upon men for the adequate conduct of their lives. Elizabeth Bennett, had she been disappointed in Mr. Darcy after marriage, would have been in an emotional whirlwind, and Miss Austen, had she tackled such a situation, would have been hard put to it to find a neat conclusion. Little Jane Eyre, if fate had not taken the wild and fascinating Mr. Rochester by the scruff of his unrighteous neck and handed him over to her, would have been a flattened out little mortal. Poor Maggie Tulliver had to be drowned after a purgatory of isolation because she had magnetism which she could not use to her own advantage. But Serena and all the women of Edna Ferber take erotic disappointment in their twentieth-century stride and do not expect anything from men. They say to themselves—men are like that—and find plenty to do besides looking around for another hero or getting drowned. And this in spite of the fact that they are women of deep emotions and strong passionate attachments. They observe their husbands; they mother their sons and their daughters, and expect no undue amount either of love or of great stature from any of them in return. Life to them is worth what it brings in experience. They live in the feminist era in the new world.

Serena de Jong, facing disappointment both in her husband and her son and raising the best asparagus in the State, is a symbol of the new woman. She is not a romantic figure in the old sense, yet she is a woman of new romance, courageous, real and vital.

In all Edna Ferber's work there is an undercurrent of dissatisfaction with men which is characteristic of all the general writing of the modern School of Femininity in its present phase. It may be a half-way phase. The woman of the next phase may come to the conclusion that her real work for the race is to maintain at all cost and with great creative effort the illusion of romance and greatness in men. But for the present she seems to be of the general opinion that men are weak, or that at least the men of this period are not strong enough for the women whose strength has been bred of the feminist pioneering era. Serena de Jong met no man who was as strong as herself, and this is true of all Edna Ferber's women. It is the plaint of all strong women, and women for the time are through with the nursing of an illusion. There is too much to do in the big impersonal world. It is the tragedy which Olive Schreiner foresaw when she wrote *The Story of an African Farm*. Men would inevitably be a step behind the new woman. But it is an even greater tragedy than Olive Schreiner foresaw. She believed in the race. She taught that strong women would breed strong sons. Edna Ferber shows her women disappointed in their sons; for the sons are never quite so rugged in fiber as their pioneering mothers; and the conclusion is that strength needs more than one parent. So has the feminist story reached one of its plateaux of experience, and what is to be done about it? For nature created women normally incapable of happiness in companionship with men weaker than themselves. Meanwhile there remains much of the world yet to be conquered for women, and this is the real love of the women she portrays in the height of their powers.—MARGARET LAWRENCE, "Go-Getters," *The School of Femininity*, 1936, pp. 188–93

Works

Dawn O'Hara, by Edna Ferber, is a book that does offer a problem and in a certain sense answers it in its own sub-title. The problem is this: supposing a girl, after a few months of mad happiness, finds that she is bound for life to a man who has suddenly broken down and whom the doctors pronounce incurably insane. The sub-title of the book is "The Girl Who Laughed;" and that is not a bad answer to a good many of life's most trying problems. At the opening of the story, however, Dawn is very far from being in a mood for laughter. Ten years of unrelieved strain on a New York daily paper, with the driving necessity of paying her husband's hospital bills ever at her heels, at last breaks her down; and her sister and her fairly well-to-do brother-in-law pick her up bodily and transfer her to the peace and quiet of their home somewhere not many miles from Milwaukee. At this point it is not surprising for the reviewer to discover that he has a story before him which he is simply going to spoil if he tries to retell it. Supposing, for instance, he should say bluntly: This is the story of a young woman who has no right to think of love and marriage, and to whom a perverse fate has sent the kindest, staunchest, most lovable young German doctor you can well imagine. He makes a well woman of her by the sheer magnetic force of his will to have her live. And then, when they both realise what they mean to each other and what the hopelessness of their case means to both, they try to bury themselves in hard work, he in his Milwaukee practice, she in newspaper reporting on a paper in the same city, where his influence has found an opening for her. And then, at an hour when it seems as though nothing worse could overtake them, fate does give one added twist of the screw and her husband is released from the asylum as cured and comes to Milwaukee to claim her. None of this begins to touch the real essence of the book because, although it deals in tragedy, it is a fabric woven from threads of sheer light heartedness, unquenchable courage, warm-hearted understanding of the things which go to make the essential joy of living. There are, for instance, certain chapters in the book picturing a delightful, unique, inimitable German boarding-house in Milwaukee that makes one sigh while reading them, partly from a vague nostalgia for happy bygone days in German pensions, partly also from sheer envy of the subtle touch that penned them. And then, too, there is one portrait of a broken-down sporting editor, a man whose days are numbered, a man vulgar in speech and with many sins upon his conscience, but who, nevertheless, is rich in some of the rarest gifts that human nature knows and whose final tragedy leaves a vacant spot in the heart akin to that of a personal bereavement. For these reasons it seems the part of wisdom to inscribe the name of Edna Ferber in some easily accessible part of our memory whereby there shall be no danger in the future of missing anything that may come from her pen. It would seem that she is a young woman who has gone some distance already on the road of achievement and is likely to go much further.—FREDERIC TABER COOPER, *Bkm*, June 1911, p. 534

We need not be sentimentalists to regard the past with a romantic eye. It is the normal way of regarding it. The past is, at first hand, romantic. Disenchantment comes only when we reconstruct it laboriously with the aid of history books and contemporary documents, or when we treat it in terms of the present. Flaubert pored for many years over source-material, and *Salammbô* is not romantic. John Erskine brought Helen up to date, and *The Private Life of Helen of Troy* is not romantic. But in general the realists have considered their own age and the romanticists an earlier one.

At a time when realism is all but monopolizing literature, one experiences a sensation of delighted relief in encountering *Show Boat*. It is gorgeously romantic—not in the flamboyant and artificial manner of the historical romance which twenty-five years ago, under the titles of *Janice Meredith* and *Richard Carvel*, came definitely labeled before the American public; not staggering beneath a weight of costume and local color. *Show Boat* comes as a spirited, full-breasted, tireless story, romantic because it is too alive to be what the realists call real; because it bears within itself a spirit of life which we seek rather than have; because it makes a period and mode of existence live again, not actually different from what they were, but more alluring than they could have been. *Show Boat* is romantic not because its people and events violate any principle of possibility, but because they express a principle of selection. Miss Ferber has chosen the brightest colors and let the dull ones go. She has avoided the contrasts by which the brightness would fade into the common light of day. *Show Boat* is dominated by one tone as Hergesheimer's *Balisand* is dominated by another.

After the days of Mark Twain, the Mississippi holds small place in American literature. Now it reclaims its place, happily as the scene of later days than Mark Twain's. River travel such as he described had fallen off with the coming of railroads, and Captain Andy Hawks of *Show Boat*, facing the fact in the late '70s but satisfied by no life save that of the river, compromised with buying a show boat—one of those floating theatres which moved from town to town for a one or two night stand, by day approaching the town with calliope screaming and flags flying, by night shining with hundreds of lights above the river. On board with him was his wife Parthy, a hard, gaunt New Englander who should have been a spinster; his daughter Magnolia, at first a child, later on the ingenue of his troupe; the troupe itself, all "picked" characters for the purposes of the novel; and, when the time was ripe, that most engrossing and romantic character of all—Gaylord Ravenal.

Magnolia Hawks was as much in sympathy with her spry half-Gallic little father as his wife was out of it. Parthy Hawks mistrusted the show-boat existence, though in the end her repressions conquered her and made her the show boat's worst slave. She also mistrusted Gaylord Ravenal, who came aboard it to act, only because he fell in love with Magnolia. She found out all about him, but she could not keep Magnolia from marrying him. They stole off and were married in a small river town, Ravenal paying the minister with his last $10. How enjoyable a figure he is from start to finish and how flawlessly he comes up to every requirement of his romantic part! Exiled from New Orleans for killing a man in self-defense; aristocratic and nonchalant, perfectly groomed, a cool, inveterate gambler, leading Magnolia, in after years when Andy Hawks had been drowned, to a seesaw existence in Chicago, fluctuating with his gains and losses at faro—a delightful figure from start to finish, and a delightful finish, when he leaves Magnolia $600 and goes away forever.

The third generation in Magnolia's family is her daughter Kim; and though she brings the story up to modern times, she leaves its tone of romance unimpaired. She becomes a great actress in the New York City of today, moving about in a social millieu in which appear such actual figures as Woollcott and Broun, Crowninshield and Swope, Katharine Cornell and Ethel Barrymore, all of them glimpsed fleetingly. But Miss Ferber carries her story further, makes it swing full-circle. When old Parthy dies, having made half a million with her show boat, Magnolia goes back for the funeral and feels the call of the past. She can't leave the *Cotton Blossom*, and down the Mississippi, presumably in this year 1926, she goes with it, stopping on June 2 at a town called Lulu. By bringing the story of the show boat up to date Miss Ferber almost makes the cord snap; but it holds somehow, perhaps because Magnolia herself makes the last romantic gesture.

All art is a luxury in the sense that it fills a place beyond the physical necessities of life, but some art there is which is entirely ornamental, which does not reveal life, or probe character, or feed the soul. *Show Boat* is such a piece of writing—a gorgeous thing to read for the reading's sake alone. Some, perhaps, will conscientiously refer to it as a document which reanimates a part of the American scene that once existed and does no more. But this writer cannot believe it is that; rather it is a glorification of that scene, a heightening, an expression of its full romantic possibilities. There was, no doubt, a gallant Andy Hawks in the old days, and a Magnolia, and more Gaylord Ravenals than one; there was such a scene as that recorded of Julie Dozier when she was discovered to have negro blood; there was a Parthy Hawks who ran a show boat down the river, an indomitable woman who formed an anomaly among show boat proprietors; but they were never the one group who lived on the *Cotton Blossom*. Plenty of prose intermingled with the poetry of the true scene, plenty of realism with the romance. And all these things, of course, Miss Ferber knew before and while and after she wrote *Show Boat*.

But Life, here, gives way unrestrainedly to Art. And Art functions in one tone—the romantic. Some will not submit to this, and will object to a piece of melodrama here, a wild coincidence there, an unconvincing character somewhere else. That will be an esthetic mistake. Let us accept the delightful lives these people lead. All in all, when you look back upon the story it is amazing how little that is exciting and complicated has happened; this is biography rather than "plot." Miss Ferber has told her story without stint, a long free-breathing story, safe from the careful selectiveness and lacunation of modern schools of writing. It never becomes sentimental; at times it is

Emendatione of Benedict Spinoza. Beyond sense perception, the first, and reasoning, the second, Spinoza placed a third kind of knowledge, *scientia intuitiva,* which he credited with an adequate grasp of the Real and even (or therefore) of God in certain attributes. About all Broad in his lectures had had to say on this subject was that no doubt Spinoza had had "mystical experiences," rather a thorn in the side of philosophy, one gathered, and at any rate outside philosophy's province. The snub shocked me a little, as did the catchall category. I thought I might make Broad see what Spinoza possibly meant if I told him with exactitude the nature of the third kind of knowledge in my own experience. I wrote:

"The mind or consciousness or identity most familiar to me has on certain occasions been in a superior state which it is difficult to describe. But then it is difficult really to describe anything.

"A. The state I refer to is not the same as a dream. In dreams the waking powers of introspection and memory and the sense of space-time relations are not only disturbed but enfeebled. The kind of experience I am speaking of involves a transformation, but not an enfeeblement, of these faculties. It is quite definitely an extreme state of being awake.

"B. It is a concentration of self-consciousness and a release from thoughts irrelevant to the present reality. It is like the feeling of loneliness and reality which a child has when it is seized by a terror of actual death, only in this case the imagined death of the body is not in the mind's focus. What is there is the perceptual situation perceived, together with a sudden loss of the ordinary habit of assuming that such a situation is a consequence of something and that what happens in it is reasonable. The mind is acutely and even masterfully conscious of itself and of others and of our actual life of movement and thought in a space-time transparency. It regards things and events in isolation, since they are no longer parts of a progression or included in any obvious scheme, and isolated they appear more beautifully distinct from each other, they take on an individuality for which names and other general symbols are entirely inadequate, and they lose the relative values formerly attributed to them. For example, it would be of no consequence to a man whose mind was so clarified whether the waiter brought him his dinner or stabbed him in the back: either action would be valued for itself.

"C. A pleasant experience, but wholly without emotion of one kind or another. . . . Each thing and each occurrence being as valuable as any other, the expectance of pleasure or pain is simply obliterated from the consciousness and motives and emotions no longer exist.

"D. This is not because a certain Necessity is realized in everything apprehended. The point is perhaps important. If there were a Necessity in any ordinary sense of the term an apprehension of the necessity would include a resignation to it. There is no resignation; there is neither passivity nor activity; there is simply existence and the things that exist.

"E. Not Intellectual Detachment. It is possible for the ironic mind to withdraw indefinitely behind the scenes to which it is a witness, and behind itself. In the state I am describing there is no withdrawal from the object, but a sort of expansion and inclusion of it, the total consciousness participating.

"F. Not Heightened Consciousness. I am not speaking of a mere sharpening of the senses or a more sensitive awareness of tones in a situation, such as most good artists and many other people possess and improve by training. A "heightened consciousness" of this kind may exist without undergoing the transformation necessary to the condition of emotional vacuum I have described.

"G. Example in Literature. Dostoevsky must have experienced this state of consciousness to have been able to use it in the novel *The Possessed.* Having had the experience, he created a character whose state of consciousness should be constantly so clarified, and followed his life from the ordinary point of view. The hero of the novel was so keenly alive and in such complete unemotional control that he could experiment with the perceptual situation in ways which might be and were judged insane. It is this which makes the incident in which he pulls Garganov's nose so much more interesting than, for example, the incident in *Point Counter Point* in which Spandrell kills Webley to find out what it's like. Huxley's character is merely affected to an extreme with a conventional "disillusionment" and his motive in killing Webley is a vulgar one, despite the author's pains to surround it with ideas. . . .

"I have now said what I mean exactly insofar as I am able to say it, and what I mean is now understood exactly to that extent. . . . My suggestion is that Spinoza had this experience, or one essentially like it, that he found it superior, and that he went so far as to believe that it was, in fact, a perception of Reality. He consequently tried to induce it more often and to think up a method of inducing it in others, and his philosophy grew out of the necessity of explaining coherently in current philosophical terms the Reality so perceived. . . ."

In conclusion, I took up several points that had been questioned by the lecturer, suggesting ways of interpreting them. Broad had, for example, objected to Spinoza's attribution of a kind of pleasure, *beatitudo,* to the third kind of knowledge on the ground that this was to make an emotional experience out of a purely intellectual one. "Nowhere in Spinoza's system," I zealously pointed out, "is *beatitudo* classed as an emotion. . . ."

It ensued from this effort that one afternoon I climbed a Trinity staircase to Dr. Broad's rooms. Nobody had told me, or ever did tell me—I have only lately discovered it—that they had once been Isaac Newton's. Had I known this, I would have realized dimly that Broad occupied them by merit. They were dusky, bookish, low-ceilinged. My host received me gravely and kindly. His polished skull and brow shone faintly, his speculative gray eyes shone not at all. His questions and remarks were deliberative. At one point he said, "I rarely go abroad because I can't speak other languages." It was a thinker's decision, neither insular nor affected, and very much in character. If we ever got around to talking about Spinoza, I cannot remember what we said, but I do remember asking myself if it had been somehow bad form on my part to pursue the matter. A year later, back at Harvard, I had a letter from him on academic points in the course of which he asked, "Have you had any more mystical experiences?" As he again used the term to the use of which I had taken exception, I felt this, then, to be a little insistent, or a little absentminded, or perhaps he even meant to pull my leg.

It is easy in retrospect to think this shyness and touchiness unreasonable. Certainly Broad was neither patronizing me nor making fun of me. The truth is that whatever value could be placed on my affliction or privilege—and I still wonder—it probably did not correspond to Spinoza's *scientia intuitiva,* which seems to have been a mathematician's rapture at grasping the logical order of the universe. I had, as it happened, addressed my submission to a man who was to become years later president of the Society for Physical Research and to deliver at Trinity in the Lent terms of 1959 and

1960 two magisterial courses of lectures on that subject. Is this an example of the irony that dogs our lives? At any rate, in the spring of 1932 I went no further with my study of the saintly metaphysician and lens grinder of The Hague. I had tried to put my amazement into words and had received perhaps the only possible comment on it.—ROBERT FITZGERALD, "The Third Kind of Knowledge," *At*, June 1980, pp. 81–82

Works

POETRY AND CRITICISM

Robert Fitzgerald's sometimes distinguished collection of poems ⟨*In the Rose of Time*⟩ will have, very likely, only a small audience, for it is Mr. Fitzgerald's achievement to be, in R. P. Blackmur's phrase, an "executive" poet, a poet who reminds other poets how it is done, who reassures them that it can be done with the old graciousness, the ancient control.

It is, however, just this perfect sureness of touch which raises doubts about the total success of the poems; the doubts, it should be said quickly, are never about the sincerity of the poet. Mr. Fitzgerald's poems come always deeply out of himself, but it is the scope and the manner of the feelings which, provoking hesitant assent instead of acquiescence, limit the poems.

The announced scope is large enough, and traditional enough: Death, Marriage, Despair, Youth. Most of the capitalized troubles which are a poet's materials are here, but there is a failure often to recreate them with the full sweep of the understanding. My impression is that this failure is the result of a certain kind of narrow vision abetted by a narrowing manner. His vision, that of a cultivated man in a troubled world, is by now a familiar one; and his manner, implying as it does an elegance of gesture and a muteness of tone, is, I'm afraid, equally familiar. It is not surprising at all that many of his poems focus on classical subjects or are direct imitations of the classic style; nor is it surprising that the quality of light he is oftenest fond of should be half-light, morning or evening time. In the sure necessities of his "Georgic" or in the comfortably triste "Aubade" one perceives a refined talent, holding itself still, shutting out the glare.

What I am trying to say is that Mr. Fitzgerald misses violence. It is not that he fails to recognize it but that, given his kind of sensibility, he tends to turn away from it. In a poem called "Sea Pieces," for instance, that tender evening moment which descends on people at a beach and which waits for a poem to shape it into meaning, continues, on Mr. Fitzgerald's page, to wait through two delicate, breathless sections. The reader turns the page expecting the crystallized moment, only to find himself staring at the stern Latin title of the next poem. And often, this is what happens: the poet stands before an event, describes it with sometimes stunning accuracy, and then, as if understanding or response were beneath his dignity, he turns away leaving his reader with a rich, if delicate sense of incompletion. I think, for instance. of "Augustan Suite," an autobiographical meditative poem which contents itself with half-indications, understatements, faint stirrings. "Manuscript with Illumination," "Georgic," "Patruus" are other instances of poems in which anger is displayed, arranged, even copied, but not fully believed because it is spoken of in the tone of "fortunate weariness the world envied."

When he is not so weary or classic or crepuscular Fitzgerald threatens us with a different kind of excellence. "Adulescentia," for instance, is a piece of poignancy, almost of fury, because he remembers shamelessly and well "that clear lake and dazzlement of youth . . . Shame's burning kingdom, vanity's new world." He does not deny himself the full dangers of re-creation; and the poem renews the terror of his childhood when, lying in bed, he imagined enemies at night and willed himself to be frightened when "Something held its breath in the tight dark" and he thought, "God, let there be some midnight walker/Heavy heeled and solid; let me turn over."

In "The Winter Night's Dream," Mr. Fitzgerald shows that he knows where the trouble lies. Directing the lightning stroke against himself, he describes his failure in a dream life in which, in his own words, he

> dwelt to windward of a mob;
> And would not sortie in the wind.
> But when the wind fell, then I cried
> In a low voice to my hunted kindred to run for it
> outside.

The other life, and the life to which he wakes are the same. I think that Mr. Fitzgerald knows here, and in "The Glass" and in "The Sympathy of Peoples," that to join the life of the world by one's own permission is to be contemptuous of it. The deliberately shaded eye complains against the light. In these later poems the trouble, the violence and the light are richly creeping in.—LEONARD WOLF, "The Shaded Eye," *Com*, April 26, 1957, pp. 99–101

Conventionally, the publication of a volume of collected poems provides an occasion for revaluation. Such a book is the "big" one by which a writer may be measured with a kind of finality that appears to be judicious and reasonable. More often than not, however, it provides the occasion to discover for the first time the real character of the poet. The judgments it permits may be as partial and inconclusive as those deduced from a first volume, although for different reasons. But the reader of a collected volume has the advantage, if he will take it, of being able to range at will through the poet's world; he may discover much that is new and come to see old landmarks in a new light. *In the Rose of Time* is a perfect case in point. Robert Fitzgerald first appeared in *Ten Introductions* (1934), where he was represented by a handful of well-wrought pieces. *Poems* (1935) enriched a favorable first impression. *A Wreath for the Sea* (1943), which accounts for about two-thirds of *In the Rose of Time*, established Fitzgerald as one of the ablest poets of his generation. The fifteen poems selected from the work written over the past twelve or so years will, I think, add to his reputation, although fifteen poems in so many years seems a small number. Much of his time Fitzgerald has spent on his translations, of course; and these must be reckoned as anything but time lost.

A collected volume also offers the poet an opportunity to make his own choice of the work he wishes to keep. Fitzgerald has included all but a few of the poems from his earlier books. Those that he has omitted are not likely to be missed; on the whole, they reflect the double image of Eliot and Pound, although without embarrassment to their author. Nor has Fitzgerald found occasion to revise his earlier work: a title has been changed, but that is all. So much, then, for externals.

In a comment on *Ten Introductions*, William Plomer characterized Fitzgerald's work as "graceful." Certainly the adjective is a precise one, for the continuing and notable quality of this poetry is its grace. It is not, however, a grace that has been achieved at the expense of the tensile strength and precision which are also characteristic of Fitzgerald's work. These qualities can be illustrated almost at random; but the first stanza of "Sympathy of Peoples" is especially notable as a revelation of these and other aspects of this poetry:

No but come closer. Come a little
Closer. Let the wall-eyed hornyhanded
Panhandler hit you for a dime
Sir and shiver. Snow like this
Drives its pelting shadows over Bremen,
Over sad Louvain and the eastern
Marshes, the black wold. It sighs
Into the cold sea of the north,
That vast contemptuous revery between
Antiquity and you. Turn up your collar,
Pull your hatbrim down. Commune
Briefly with your ignorant heart
For those bewildered raging children
Europe surrenders her old gentry to.

Deceptive in its juxtaposition of the colloquial and highly organized and self-conscious rhetoric that one associates with the classicism of Allen Tate, such writing gives up its secrets slowly. Its subtleties are not those, however, of a poet for whom poetry is simply a verbal or intellectual construct. The "wit," apparent in the play of high seriousness and the colloquial idiom, has not been laid on to disguise an essential lack of substance. Fitzgerald does not, in other words, ever seem to strain for his effects; yet everything he does carries artistic conviction.

His particular skill as a translator may well have had its influence upon the poems. In the translations included in the present volume—from Horace, Catullus, Villon, and most notably from Vergil—Fitzgerald conveys something more than either the mere sense or atmosphere of the original. In his translation of one of the *Georgics* he prunes and reshapes the original so unobtrusively that he achieves that rare thing, a real translation that is also an original. It is worth noting that the poem has been generally praised as if it were altogether an original work.

Almost as important for Fitzgerald, at least from the point of view of the reader who would judge on the evidence of the poems themselves, has been a continuing interest in the possibilities of what the neo-classic writers used to call "imitation." The more obvious experiments of this sort are to be found in the first section of the book: Song after Campion," "Night Song," "Elegy," "First Movement" (the ambitious prelude to the later longer poems such as "Counselors," "Augustan Suite," and "In the Glass"), "Petit Jour," and "Epithalamion." In *A Weath for the Sea*, Fitzgerald experiments with a form that is very much his own, of which "Sea Pieces," "Horae," and "Mementoes" are typical. In each case, the title binds two or three separate poems together to produce an impressive total effect that the parts, although self-contained, would not have achieved. Elsewhere the parts do achieve impressive wholeness; this is especially true of the first of three "Portraits," an elegy for John Wheelwright, which is as moving as any modern elegy I know, and which really requires quotation in full, although the concluding stanzas may partly suggest its quality:

Yet upward in LaFarge's flame
His savior twisted, and does still;
The true line comes as once it came
To masculine Homer's steady will;

Control and charity of the just,
And their wild laughter flung at night,
Commemorate his death, his dust,
His gaiety. John Wheelwright.

The poems written since *A Wreath for the Sea* continue to explore the mingling worlds of past and present that have furnished Fitzgerald much of his raw material. Slight as some of them look on first reading, they are all endowed with those qualities of grace and tensile strength. "The Winter Night's Dream" reveals one aspect—the more idiomatic one—of this section:

The mind in double gloom detained,
The slow dawn, filling up with snow,
Return me to the dream I feigned
Of some dark life-time long ago.

Whether by dream or feigning true,
In a vast city's drift and throb,
Keeping a bare house known to few
I dwelt to windward of a mob;

And would not sortie in the wind,
But when the wind fell, then I cried
In a low voice to my hunted kind-
red to run for it outside.

"History" reveals the more ruminative aspects of the poetry:

A man, this man,
Bred among lakes and railway cars and smoke,
The salt of childhood on his wintry lips,
His full heart ebbing toward the new tide
Arriving, arriving, in laughter and cries,
Down the chaotic dawn and eastern drift,
Would hail the unforeseen, and celebrate
On the great mountainside those sprites,
Tongues of delight, that may remember him—
The yet unborn, trembling in the same rooms,
Breakfasting before the same grey windows,
Lying, grieving again; yet all beyond him,
Who knew he lived in rough Jehovah's breath,
And burned, a quiet wick in a wild night,
Loving what he beheld and will behold.

It is a comment upon the curious nature of the literary fashions of our time that Robert Fitzgerald has not yet found its way into anthologies. There are one or two exceptions: "Cobb Would Have Caught It" and "Colorado" have been reprinted by one or two editors. But there has been no adequate representation of his work in any of the important anthologies. The publication of *In the Rose of Time* may bring to Fitzgerald the recognition he deserves; even so, he has written at least a dozen poems that could replace some of the less-deserving "landmarks" of contemporary poetry.—SAMUEL FRENCH MORSE, "The Time Made Good," *Poetry*, May 1957, pp. 110–13

Robert Fitzgerald, the noted poet and translator, has written an unexpectedly ingratiating account of an intrinsically arcane subject—the Princeton seminars in literary criticism held in 1949–1951, a forum in which he was participant and official scribe. A book recounting the discussions of a literary seminar might not be expected to hold much interest for the general reader—particularly when the seminar concerns such esoterica as the stylistics of Pascal. But it does—and that is a mysterious and noteworthy accomplishment.

Enlarging the Change is based on Mr. Fitzgerald's original transcriptions which lay forgotten in his files for 30 years. His opinions seem not to have changed too much. He still holds in high regard the scholarship of Francis Fergusson and Jacques Maritain, still differs sharply with Erich Auerbach, Mark Schorer and René Wellek. With remarkable skill he recreates the discussions of these and other midcentury literary luminaries, vividly bringing their words back to life, unearthing treasured bits that might otherwise have been lost.

Here, for example, is Schorer on the novel: "Plot, in a great novel, is not first of all a means to demonstrate a view of life, but rather of forcing characters into positions where they will experience life at its fullest, its most intense and crucial, under the particular social circumstances. . . . *Tested* morality requires sustained *pressure* and *crisis*."

Many of the participants were engaged at the time of the seminars in works of wide literary interest and importance—John Berryman's *Stephen Crane*, Irving Howe's *Sherwood Anderson* and Delmore Schwartz's *Vaudeville for a Princess* were all about to be published. Auerbach's *Mimesis* had not yet been published in English. Maritain's papers became his Andrew Mellon Lecture papers and, later, his acclaimed "Creative Intuition in Art and Poetry." Delmore Schwartz, daunted by the reception of his seminar presentation as "thin and even weak," never published his study of T. S. Eliot, one which in crucial ways inspired his own career.

Simply and modestly, "the writer" reports on the triumphs and deflations, the petty politics and intellectual flights of the personalities, great and not so great, who attended the seminars. Scholars interrupt scholars. "But where is literature?" one asks, impatiently cutting off a thought on Pascal's Christianity. Auerbach isn't interested in Baudelaire's soul. Mr. Wellek disparages the visualizing power of Henry James—"There was a kind of roughness" in that, notes the writer. Auerbach never comes back after his own readings, except once for one by his friend Ferguson.

Mr. Fitzgerald recounts many instances of annoying academic certitudes, high-toned vagaries and unembarrassed arrogance in outlining "correct" critical standards—the denigration of D. H. Lawrence, the stress on "conscious reason" and the intellect's "superior intuition." William Meredith was "unable to discuss a second-rate mind in a great poem, such as some by Tennyson and Hugo." But the smug assertions were not unchallenged. Mr. Fitzgerald calmly records the frequent and angry objections that played off as sub-theme to the confident—at times even fatuous—tone which dominated the gatherings.

Mr. Fitzgerald's book shows how much more confidence existed in 1950 than today about the possibility of literary absolutes. And we cannot help but feel envy. Scrupulously evoking the earlier era, the account makes our nostalgia not only palpable, but justified. He invites us to tally what has been lost and gained in the years since—modesty, perhaps, on the one hand, certitude on the other. But however stifling or narrow or arrogant that community was, the current anomie attendant on the loss of community is, by contrast, even more debilitating. This is perhaps the tacit message behind the reportage.—MARTIN DUBERMAN, "Literary Summitry," *NYTBR*, Jan. 13, 1985, p. 39

TRANSLATIONS

There can be little doubt that Fitzgerald's approach to a twentieth-century version of *The Odyssey* travels the same road so clearly marked before him by Ezra Pound, W. H. D. Rouse and particularly Dudley Fitts, who collaborated with Fitzgerald in translations of *The Alcestis of Euripides* and *The Antigone of Sophocles*. This in itself is an excellent beginning, for it insures the reader against all trials of boredom in a rediscovery of Homer's epic.

Any new version of Homer's *The Odyssey* is an ambitious task, and it carries with it the language of the translator's day as well as the translator's interpretation of the original text. One of the great merits of Fitzgerald's book is its rendering of Homer's heroic dignity, his moral force, his religious spirit—and this without loss of narrative clarity and action. Fitzgerald's Homer is a noble Homer who almost never nods.

In reading Fitzgerald's Homer one never forgets that Homer was a poet, a poet of serious purpose and austere imagery—and Fitzgerald has wisely chosen as his medium English blank verse. This aspect of Homer is shown in the following lines:

Now Zeus who views the wide world sent a sign to
him,
launching a pair of eagles from a mountain crest
in gliding flight down the soft blowing wind,
wing-tip to wing-tip quivering taut, companions,
till high above the assembly of many voices
they wheeled, their dense wings beating, and in
havoc
dropped on the heads of the crowd—a deathly
omen—
wielding their talons, tearing cheeks and throats;
then veered away on the right hand through the city.
Astonished, gaping after the birds, the men
felt their hearts flood, foreboding things to come.

This is proof, aside from its faithful austerities, that Fitzgerald has read Homer with reverence. Fitzgerald himself is a poet of fine distinction whose early work held promise of mature achievement—and a large measure of that achievement is shown in his version of *The Odyssey*.

Fitzgerald's version is not without its lyrical ingenuities, and the happiest of these is the song he makes the Seirenes sing:

Sweet coupled airs we sing.
No lonely seafarer
Holds clear of entering
Our green mirror.

. . .

Sea rovers here take joy
Voyaging onward,
As from our song of Troy
Greybeard and rower-boy
Goeth more learned.

All feats on that great field
In the long warfare,
Dark days the bright gods willed,
Wounds you bore there,
Argos' old soldiery
On Troy beach teeming,
Charmed out of time we see.
No life on earth can be
Hid from our dreaming.

In this manner Fitzgerald has recaptured the legendary magic of the Seirenes' song. If "a book is a mirror," then Fitzgerald has looked deeply into Homer's epic of Odysseus, and what we now see looking out of it are the features of a poet.

There is a moral to be drawn from the publication of Fitzgerald's fine version. It is this: only poets who have gifts for understanding the meaning of our classical heritage should be encouraged to translate the poetry of the ancient world. Only they can endow it with renewed life and meaning. Fitzgerald belongs to that rare company.—HORACE GREGORY, "A Noble Homer Who Almost Never Nods," *NYTBR*, Apr. 16, 1961, p. 7

Robert Fitzgerald . . . listens to the sounds the whole passage makes, and his various dealings with this famous word ⟨*polyphloisboio*⟩ are elucidative.

So harsh he was, the old man feared and obeyed
him,
in silence trailing away
by the shore of the tumbling dangerous whispering
sea . . .

Fourteen years ago, in his *Odyssey*, he dealt with its two occurrences in that poem in two wholly different ways, responding to different local effects. Once, quickening

Homer's narrative, he has only "foaming": the Phaeacian ship bore Odysseus back to Ithaca,

her bow wave
riding after, and her wake
on the purple night-sea foaming.

The other time, when Odysseus walks despairing by the sea as Chryses had walked by the sea near Troy, and Homer employs the identical phrase he had used in the *Iliad*, Fitzgerald writes

And then he wept,
despairing for his own land, trudging down
beside the endless wash of the wide, wide sea
weary and desolate as the sea.

The endless wash, the wideness, the desolation, these do not answer to separate Greek words, they are all extrapolated from that polysemous *polyphloisboio*.

Such multifariousness tends to bewilder scholars, who prefer the Lincoln-log verse of Richmond Lattimore, sturdy, opaque, its members trundled to the site and pegged together. But it is Fitzgerald, unafraid of being thought "rather free," who has accomplished our time's penetration into the enduring mysteries of Homeric rhetoric. He can manage the famous similes as deftly as the captains by Skamander managed their troops:

And as migrating birds, nation by nation,
wild geese and arrow-throated cranes and swans,
over Asia's meadowland and marshes
around the streams of Kaystrios, with giant
flight and glorying wings keep beating down
in tumult on that verdant land
that echoes to their pinions, even so,
nation by nation, from the shops and huts,
the host debouched upon Skamander plain.
With noise like thunder pent in earth
under their trampling, under the horses' hooves,
they filled the flowering land beside Skamander,
as countless as the leaves and blades of spring.

One needs a good deal of context to gauge the local excellences.

What Homer said of the cranes and swans was "long-necked," a bit of lore worth fixing with language in a time of no zoos nor picture-books, but pointless today. "Arrow-throated" is Fitzgerald's admirably martial invention, and a mark of his concern that nothing shall seem pointless. Then Homer built his first long sentence around eight syllables that resound like anvils, *klangedōn prokathizóntōn*, "uttering their cries the birds keep settling ever forwards." English has no equivalent for that verb, and no strident word with the authority of *klangedōn*. Fitzgerald's

with giant
flight and glorying wings keep beating down
in tumult

gets its effect not by word-for-word substitution but by disrupting with enjambment and splendor of diction ("glorying") the progress of his equable measure. And

With noise like thunder pent in earth

—two syllables short, that line tramps like a host.

Fitzgerald's secret—so far as we can disentangle it from his immense resourcefulness—is a straight-running unobtrusive idiom and a straightforward ten-syllable line in which the slightest deviations become expressive. (Shine polarized light through clear Lucite: every strain makes a rainbow pattern.) It yielded him in the Fifties a magnificent *Odyssey*, arguably *the* Homeric version of our century. If his *Iliad* is a little less successful, that tells us something both about our time's idiom and about the *Iliad*, which will capitulate less often to a technique of iridescences.—HUGH KENNER, "Mirror of Language," *NaR*, Apr. 25, 1975, pp. 462–63

Robert Fitzgerald: In a way you can feel that the poet himself is looking over your shoulder, and you say to yourself, now, how would this go for him? Would this do or not? And that, I think, is leading us pretty close to the heart of the matter. I have an example that I'm very fond of, in one of Richard Wilbur's translations of Villon. It is "The Ballade of the Dead Ladies." It begins,

Dites-moi ou, n'en quel pays,
Est Flora, la belle Romaine,
Archipiadès ni Thaïs,
Qui fut sa cousine germaine

Oh, "Tell me where, on lands or seas, Flora the Roman belle has strayed/Archipiades or Thais, who put each other in the shade." Now, the French says of the second of these dead lovelies—two courtesans, as he understood them—that she was the *cousine germaine* of the first. In what respect was she a first cousin? She was first cousin in respect to her beauty. Now Wilbur found in English idiom a lovely phrase for what one beauty does to another beauty. She puts her in the shade, if she can, and he translates that line, "who put each other in the shade"—literally utterly remote from the French. But, my point is: that had Villon been using our language, and had he found that idiom, that same phrase, he would have been delighted to use it in that place.

Edward Honig: Yes, indeed.

Robert Fitzgerald: His job being to make a ballade, a rhymed composition, with lines that would of course make sense, that was the nature of what he was doing, and Wilbur, to my mind perfectly, exemplifies one of the principles of good translation.

Edward Honig: That's a fine example; it tells me something about the nature of lyric poetry. You can extend it to any poetry that rhymes and is not necessarily lyric but dramatic: that the right conjunction of words must be sought and found, words in perhaps a more extended form, as in narrative poetry. This isn't the main point of such poetry, but then you're the authority on narrative poetry—Homer, in this regard.

Robert Fitzgerald: Well, I would then go on to say that Homer, as we now know, was working in what they call an oral tradition. Now the performer—because that's what he was—had at his disposal a great repertory of themes, narrative and dramatic situations, and he had at his disposal a great repertory of formulae, of lines, half lines, phrases, all metrical, let it be observed, that could be modified or used in many contexts during his performance, which was always to some extent extemporary. Now, as he went along with his tale, he could and did invent new ways of handling episodes and passages that made each performance, in some way, a new thing. Do you see how this fact liberates, to a certain extent, the translator?

Edward Honig: Yes.

Robert Fitzgerald: If his obligation as I have thought is always to the originator, to the original imagination, then he knows that for that imagination no text, no text sacred or otherwise, existed, that free improvisation was part of the essence of each performance. Therefore, what is known as freedom in translation would be nearer to what the original performer expected of a translator than it might be in the case of someone who had, like say Paul Valéry, labored over every line and for whom the final text in every detail had more importance than for the Homeric singer.

Edward Honig: Your emphasis makes me understand the term "poetic license" in an entirely different way. The slightly perjorative sense of the phrase suddenly seems to have another meaning.

Robert Fitzgerald: Yes, one sees by virtue of this slight liberation that in fact all works of imagination are improvisation at some stage, at the beginning certainly. And one sees how precious this sheer invention is in the making of a work of art. I remember at a certain point in working on the *Odyssey* that Rudyard Kipling's stories, which I was reading as it happened to my children in Italian versions, reminded me of the possibilities of sheer invention. In one of the stories there is a seal, who is the hero, and his life is spent in the oceans of the world. He has as part of his private language phrases and exclamations that refer to his life as a seal in the great cold South Atlantic waters, like swearing "by the foaming straits of Magellan." I can't recall now—I wish I could—some of the language that Kipling invented for his seal, but all of this is important, it seems to me in the imaginative field of someone working on something so tremendously inventive as the Homeric poems. If you think that someone was able to invent those actions and sustain them and elaborate them over such a span with such constant resources of surprise, dramatic scene-making, and dramatic language, then I think the interest that this kind of consideration has will not seem too remote.

Edward Honig: That may relate to something I was thinking in reading your translations, and perhaps it's what makes your Homeric poems unique as translations. It's the supposition that in being aware of the oral tradition behind the compositions, the kind of performance-invention you just described, you become the first translator of Homer who consciously used it in working out a variety of possibilities in voice and characterization.

Robert Fitzgerald: Well, to some extent maybe that's true, but one may imagine that in the future, as this understanding deepens and widens, more appropriate forms may be found for it. I'd say I made a beginning.

Edward Honig: A very important one. But you seem also to bring with it as a principle something that belies the idea that there are only two possibilities in writing poetry: writing in closed and writing in open forms—that is, free verse as against metered and rhymed verse—by indicating that with a consciousness of all traditions one's sense of the techniques of verse, meter and sound becomes indeed the tool by which one finds the freedom to write or to perform and invent through translation.

Robert Fitzgerald: Let's bring our talk back to earth a little and remember that what the translator—myself in particular—does is not comparable to what the Homeric performer was doing. His art was comparable to the art of the great musical virtuosos who can improvise, who can sit at the piano and by his mastery, both of the performing technique and of the musical background, can make music. The translator—and I now think of my own sweating days and nights—does one draft after another; he's a sedentary craftsman trying through repeated trials and failures to arrive at a readable English page. I did it by writing out the Greek of each book in a ledger-type notebook: each Greek line followed by two blank lines. While I did this, I would use the dictionary and what scholarship I could find to clear up puzzles in the text. When I went to work I had nothing but my own Greek in my own hand before me to try to match with English in the blank lines underneath the Greek. Then the typewritten drafts began, and every evening I would destroy half of what I had done every morning, and often a day's work would be only a few lines. I had from the beginning the sense that I didn't care how long it took and if I had to wait a week for a suitable version of one exclamation I would wait a week and, you know—no hurry. Patience. Patience.—ROBERT FITZGERALD, Interview by Edward Honig, *MLN*, 1976, pp. 1577–80

Virgil is the poet everyone used to read at school; a few still do, and, as Virgil said about farmers, they are fortunate if only they knew it. More than any other, he is the central poet of the West, honored and even read from the first days of the Roman Empire. No wonder that Robert Fitzgerald, the emeritus Professor of Rhetoric and Oratory at Harvard, should turn his attention to Virgil. What is remarkable is that the translator should qualify for the *Guinness Book of Records* by becoming, as his publisher says, the first poet to have translated the *Iliad*, the *Odyssey*, and the *Aeneid*. . . .

How far does Mr. Fitzgerald succeed? The proof of the pudding is in the eating and each reader must try for himself. The scholarship of the version is sufficiently guaranteed; Mr. Fitzgerald has had the support and advice of his Harvard colleagues. But what about the English which, rather than the Latin, is the point in which most verse translators fail? Has Mr. Fitzgerald, following his original, really given us a convincing narrative poem in the language and rhythms of the late 20th century? Hardly, but what examples are there of such a poem, original or translated? The blank verse is that of a practiced hand, better than that of the recent version of the *Aeneid* by Allen Mandelbaum but not nearly as good as that of Longfellow's Dante (however pedestrian that version may now be considered to be). More than Dante, Virgil tempts the translator to a grandeur which our contemporary language has not shown that it can bear. This is the *pons asinorum* of the Virgilian translator. Mr. Fitzgerald gets over it on the whole with skill, but it is with an academic dignity rather than a verbal resourcefulness in which one can recognize the hand of a poet.

The narrative force of the *Aeneid* is very great, and it is in telling the story well, in language that does not attract attention to itself but to the matter, that the translator must try to compensate for the many qualities of the original that cannot be rendered. Virgil is a deep sea in which we can fish, rather than a text for which we can hope to find an equivalent. Mr. Fitzgerald is tempted by a certain eloquence that is virtually impossible in contemporary English, and the result is a deliberateness of language that takes the shuddering life out of it. A certain, not altogether ineffective rhetoric remains and the translator makes few concessions to the sort of limp poeticism that still tempts so many versifiers translating classical texts, and none to that smart-aleckry of pretended up-to-dateness that tempts many more.

There is dignity in this version, but it is too much something put on the surface and too little the outcome of sympathy with the Virgilian sentiments trying to find expression in the natural language of our own time. The narrative does emerge as a genuine story one can follow with interest, but a reader who knows nothing of Virgil could never suppose that he was reading anything other than a translation; no one in our day, or indeed any other, could conceivably write a poem in this tone.—C. H. SISSON, "Accepting a Heroic Challenge," *NYTBR*, Oct. 16, 1983, p. 13

JOHN GOULD FLETCHER

1886–1950

John Gould Fletcher was born in Little Rock, Arkansas, on January 3, 1886. He was the only son of John Gould Fletcher, a wealthy, middle-aged Confederate soldier, and of Adolphine Krause Fletcher, a young woman of a German-Danish family. Fletcher was educated mostly by private tutors in his father's home, but spent a year at Phillips Andover; he entered Harvard at seventeen, where he began to write verse. A year before his graduation Fletcher's father died, leaving him a large inheritance. Months later Fletcher left Harvard, and drifted until 1908, when he made his decisive move and set sail for Italy to begin his writing career. He settled in Europe until 1914, but the outbreak of World War I drove him back to America. During this period Fletcher published five volumes of poetry at his own expense; his more serious work began on his return to the U.S., when he became associated with Amy Lowell and the Imagist movement. In 1916 he went back to Europe and married Daisy Arbuthnot, an Englishwoman whose acquaintance he had made while assisting her husband with an exhibition of paintings. He published several collections of verse, including *Goblins and Pagodas* (1916), *Japanese Prints* (1918), and *The Black Rock* (1928).

He stayed abroad for seventeen years, but returned permanently to America in 1933 at the dissolution of his marriage. Fletcher married Charlie May Simon in 1936, and traveled extensively with her in the United States. In the year of his marriage he published his ambitious *Epic of Arkansas*. He received a Pulitzer Prize in 1939 for his *Selected Poems*.

On May 20, 1950, Fletcher was found drowned in a swimming pool near his home in Little Rock, apparently a suicide. His wife explained the suicide as a reaction of a sensitive man to a mechanized and barbarous age.

The reader who makes his first acquaintance with Mr. Fletcher's work through these two volumes ⟨*Japanese Prints* and *The Tree of Life*⟩ will have a very unfair impression of the author's real worth; for these in no sense compare with his best work as it is revealed in *Irradiations: Sand and Spray* or in *Goblins and Pagodas*. The brevity of the small poems in *Japanese Prints*, and possibly their subject matter, are the only points of similarity with Japanese poetry; they are decorative in phrasing, but perhaps because of this very "decorative" element, they seem to escape that union of spiritual delicacy and profundity which is characteristic of even the slightest Japanese verse. We, as westerners, are too prone to overlook the underlying humanism of Japanese or Oriental art and to get only the outward appearance. Of course the outward mask is in itself wonderful, and "decorative" in truth, but this is not all; and when one in turn undertakes to create another mask, one must not forget that there should be a face underneath it. Otherwise the mask will be empty. Masks that only imitate other masks eventually become lifeless.

That is, I think, why these small poems by Mr. Fletcher do not move us, either as art or life. They appeal rather as a sort of literary bric-à-brack. This is perhaps too harsh for their intention, which is relatively slight. Nevertheless, unless interpretation really adds something, it is better discarded, and these poems which continually suggest not the author, but the double art from which they are derived, do not after all do justice to the original. For Japanese poetry, however brief, is not slight, and it does not pose or attitudinize as these poems often seem to do. If, forgetting Japanese prints and Japanese *tankas*, Mr. Fletcher had written a series of small poems independently of Japanese models, the spirit, one believes, would have been much closer to that of Japanese poetry.

The Tree of Life represents a completely different phase of art from that exemplified in *Japanese Prints*. In these love poems, emotion has completely run away with the author. It is impossible to retain any definite impression of the book or of single poems—only a confused, vague tangle of sifting moods and images, none with enough contour to stay fixed even for a moment. The book is a welter of emotion, but it remains chaotic and without form. All poets have lapses. Only a comparatively small proportion of the work of the biggest men is retained and treasured. So there is no reason to be too despairing because these two books do not come up to Mr. Fletcher's already achieved level. But any man who has the "Ghosts of an Old House," the "Blue Symphony" and some of the poems in *Irradiations* to his credit need not expect us to be satisfied with anything less.—ALICE CORBIN HENDERSON, "Two Books by Fletcher," *Poetry*, March 1919, pp. 340–41

It is a hard thing to write a man of talent, sincerity, and verve down to the level where his work leaves him. Yet the easier approach of accepting his work at its face value is more disheartening in the end; instead of a small thing to keep we have an inflated thing to let go. It is the old question, with Mr. Fletcher, of how much intention can outrun ability, how much mere feeling can replace the barrier of form, how much, finally, words used conventionally can substitute for the force of idiom—and still leave a sound body of poetry. If we take Mr. Fletcher at his declared value, and try to achieve it for ourselves, we shall find, I think, that he has failed by going too far on all three counts. Taken solemnly, his poems ⟨in *XXIV Elegies*⟩ are inflations of his private experience: you feel what he feels, not what the object felt like. Taken seriously, for what there is in them, what stays in the mind, we have again and again to recognize, strikingly deployed, the elements of poetry presided over by a genuinely poetic figure. There is hardly more in many than a greater reputation; and it makes an amount, with a value, large enough to keep if not great enough to incorporate; there is always the possibility, the suggestion, the fragment—if never the achieved composition.

The causes of his substantial failure lie partly in his mode of using language and partly in the personal relation between his language and his themes. Mr. Fletcher's language is rhetorical, loose, and unsyntactical. It would never stand up as prose; without rhythm and line structure it would seem only a vocabulary. At his worst he takes words by their colored covers and opens and shuts them loudly. At his best he does not put much meaning into his words, only colors them with his moods; hence it takes a great many words piling up, clattering, singing, to collect a semblance of the meaning that was in him. Never concerned with what words force into each other from their insides, his words change little and are a good deal alike in their different appearances. He takes—and this is his rhetoric—the nearest statement, image, or phrase to be the ultimate. Master his vocabulary and you have mastered his rhetoric. When it succeeds, his rhetoric is fresh because it is right with the usual poetic rightness; but it is not right because it is fresh, or organic, or inexhaustibly alive. The words clatter, they do not clash.

As with the words so with the larger units of expression. There is nothing to burrow in to find and feel the meaning out. There is more meaning immediately, at first glance, than can ever be found on subsequent intimacy; that is because the general intent, not the specific datum, is viable. You do not anywhere weigh these poems; you run through them. If you run through a lot of them you will get quite a lot of Mr. Fletcher himself, a generous, brilliant, prodigal lot; and you will come to know what obsessed him, drove him—in love and death, machinery and the sea, cities and landscapes—to write verse.

His poems are not objects but media. Within themselves the parts do not modify and compose, do not share and discover and brim with an inner light; they make a light-shot procession, almost a mob, that cannot be added up. You get the breathlessness but not the breath of experience. Take as good a line as any: "God is the thunderbolt that falls, when the heart otherwise would be broken." It is best in its breathless immediacy. Look for the breath, its ultimate quake and savor, and it will have been stopped; it was never there, in the poem.

As Mr. Fletcher is to his language so his language is to his themes. The relation is personal and immediate, and there is no barrier of form. Or his form is of that looseness that it exists only in the degree that it cannot help itself. Mr. Fletcher is a personal poet in that it is the prevalent sense of his personality that animates his poems and alone gives them form. As the poems are never made objects, so they never become their own subjects but remain in both respects fragments preserved of their author. The striking result—always to be observed of this mode of language—that his subjects fit into words as given; the subjects neither add to the life of the language nor stretch its scope, nor does the language absorb the subjects and become idiom. Thus the poems are versions, not discoveries.—R. P. BLACKMUR, "Versions of Fletcher," *Poetry*, March 1936, pp. 344–47

"Who recalls the address now of the Imagists?" asked MacLeish in his *Invocation to the Social Muse.* Those of us with long memories recall a hospitable place, where several people having no real business there temporarily checked their poetic luggage. Among these was John Gould Fletcher. From the first it was obvious that this author, while interested in technical experiments, cared little for the principles of the group with which he was associated. The present volume (*Selected Poems*) emphasizes his divergence from them. There is not a poem in the book handled with the directness, the terse precision, that mark the best work of the school, and while some of the early poems are written in "the sequence of the musical phrase", the later ones incline to follow "the sequence of the metronome". Nevertheless, Fletcher's *Selected Poems* offer, in however oblique a manner, a tribute to imagism. For they exhibit, on page after page, the faults against which the group so loudly, so vigorously, and not altogether vainly, inveighed.

Throughout the volume one finds the helpless elision, the ineffective inversion, the careless cliché. On the first page "'gainst" appears twice, nor does the poet hesitate later to write "'mid", "'neath", "'gain", or to speak of thickets "where once *did* climb the wild grape-cables". Such banalities as "You were I and I was you", "haunted by hopeless sin", are not exceptional. In the midst of a piece of rhymed prose, the flexible form of which should encourage lively writing, Fletcher shamelessly asserts, "Life is a dream". Some pieces are marred by rhetorical vagueness, exemplified in

Towards the impossible,
Towards the inaccessible,
Towards the ultimate,
Towards the silence,
Towards the eternal,
These blossoms go.

Others make flat prose statements without the saving touch of a concrete detail, as in the poem mysteriously entitled "Elegy on the Building of the Washington Bridge":

There is a bridge before us we have need
To build; a bridge whose links
Are consciousness, whose roadway faith; whose
anchoring towers
Are the flesh acting and the mind that thinks.

Was there a poet once who wrote about "the pierless bridge" of faith? Was there a poet who hymned *The Bridge?* Shades of Emily and Hart Crane! Do you laugh or weep?

The book holds a few pieces that continue to please, either by the splendor of their imagery or the richness of their internal rhymes. Thus, one returns with delight to the third section of the opening piece, "Irradiations," a passage which is indeed a complete poem in itself:

Over the roof-tops race the shadows of clouds;
Like horses the shadows of clouds charge down the
street.
Whirlpools of purple and gold,
Winds from the mountains of cinnabar,
Lacquered mandarin moments, palanquins swaying
and balancing
Amid the vermilion pavilions, against the jade
balustrades.
Glint of the glittering wings of dragon-flies in the
light:
Silver filaments, golden flakes settling downwards,
Rippling, quivering flutters, repulse and surrender,
The sun broidered upon the rain.
The rain rustling with the sun.

Over the roof-tops race the shadows of clouds;
Like horses the shadows of clouds charge down the
street.

"The Blue Symphony," another early poem, contains a passage that skilfully evokes the cold charm of a goblin stream:

One chuckles by the brook for me:
One rages under the stone.
One makes a spout of his mouth;
One whispers—one is gone.

One over there on the water
Spreads cold ripples
For me
Enticingly.

The vast dark trees
Flow like blue veils
Of tears
Into the water.

Sour sprites,
Moaning and chuckling.
What have you hidden from me?

But not content to conclude here, the poet adds another six lines which blur the picture. "Clipper Ships," a prose poem, opens stirringly: "Beautifully as a tiered cloud, skysails set and shrouds twanging, she emerges from the surges that keep running away before day on the low Pacific shore." But this vividness is not sustained. The two other pieces of symphonic prose, "The Old South" and "The Passing of the South," are nearer prose than poetry, and the casual rhymes are obtrusive.

The penultimate section of the book consists of thirteen elegies, on a variety of subjects which include a transatlantic voyage, the Jewish people, Thomas A. Edison, an empty skyscraper, the Russian revolution, Tintern Abbey, and The Last Judgment. Just why Fletcher chooses to call these effusions "elegies" is not clear, though some of them are mournful enough. It is in these ambitious pieces that one expects to find the poet's attitude toward the problems of his generation stated or implied, but it is not clear whether he hopes for "the great renewal of the coming spring" that will flower out of revolution, or whether he shares the bleak view of Thomas Hardy, to whom he dedicates "The Black Rock." It is evident that he admires such intransigeants as Columbus, Blake, Nietzsche, and Whitman, but the volume fails to reveal any integrated philosophy. It is interesting to note that one looks in vain for an expression of the viewpoint stated in *I Take My Stand*, the manifesto of the southern agrarians with whom Fletcher at one time allied himself.

The book is flawed, however, less by the poet's failure to declare himself than by the weakness of his execution. The good work fails to balance the shocking faults of the volume as a whole. Oddly enough, Fletcher saw fit to exclude some of his neatest work, as, for example, the delicate hokkus from his book of *Japanese Prints*. While rejecting the lessons that the imagists could have taught him, he has apparently failed to heed the instructions of the symbolists. His is neither the chiselled line nor the musical nuance. He lost an address that was worth remembering, and in all his further peregrinations found no better home.—BABETTE DEUTSCH, "A Lost Address," *Poetry*, Sept. 1938, pp. 347–51

Fletcher's major effort during the years to 1917 was a series of "Symphonies," which were to present important phases in the intellectual and emotional development of an artist. Each phase was to be symbolized by a color, each color evoking in the poet's mind certain pictures which were to impress the desired emotional and imaginative effect upon the reader.

> I have tried to state each phase in the terms of a certain color, or combination of colors which is emotionally akin to that phase. This color, and the imaginative phantasmagoria of landscape which it evokes, thereby creates, in a definite and tangible form, the dominant mood of each poem.

The "Blue Symphony" deals with the young artist's search for beauty; confused at first by his own immaturity and by the influence of other men, he finally attains self-assurance through recognition that the vision which he pursues will always elude him. The color *blue* was suggested to Fletcher by the emotions accompanying perception of mystery, depth, distance—emotions which he thought appropriate to the theme; at the same time, it evoked in his mind the specific images of mist, smoke, death-mountains, which would stimulate these emotions in the reader. To heighten the effect of unreality, Fletcher introduced his imagery in the logically unrelated pattern characteristic of certain poems by Rimbaud.

The "White Symphony" follows a pattern that resembles the Rimbaud technique even more closely. The title of the poem recalls Gautier's "Symphonie en blanc majeur"; its "symphonic" progression (by sections or movements, each developing a mood through its color symbolism) also derives, in some measure, from the possibilities suggested by the title of the French poem. However, its theme, the struggle for the inaccessible, the eternal, is neither Parnassian nor Imagist, and its use of *white* to symbolize this absolute repeats a Symbolist device. Its images, products of the hallucinatory imagination, directed by the subconscious, resemble the phantasmagoria of *Les Illuminations*. In the opening passage, for example, white petals of peonies thrust out to embrace the onlooker, thrust out until they lose their identity and are transformed first into flakes of snow, then the dazzling white of clouds; the transition from one image to the next is handled in such a way as to recreate the "impossible" behavior of images in dreams.

Fletcher, in fact, develops his imagery from the correspondences for *E* (white—mists, lancelike glaciers, etc.) and for *O* (blue—Omega, silences of the heavens) indicated by Rimbaud in his "Vowels" sonnet—"White Symphony" moving from the radiance of the ecstasy in section I to the blue of the eternal in section II and back to white in section III, now the pallor of death as the human dream fails. In the "Symphonies," Fletcher tries to state each mood, through his color imagery, in terms the reader can see or feel, and the poems have little meaning in the conventional sense: to this extent they are Imagistic (as are the Japanese poems which interested Fletcher and Amy Lowell, as well as Pound). Yet they make assumptions which Imagism, at least implicitly, denies; they deal with the imprecise—no matter how precisely—and go beyond the Imagist's tendency to make language more scientific and precise, its almost naturalistic tendency to confine expression within the limits of the solid, physical sensation or feeling.

Fletcher used this technique in poetry that was to be Imagistic. "Blue Symphony," again with its *long-O* words to establish the correspondences suggested by Rimbaud, was written as an Imagist poem; "London Excursion," which employs the same "unrelated" method of progression, was also published in the anthology of 1915. Its attempt to communicate a reaction to the modern city is not inconsistent with Imagism, because the poet sees no transcendental significance in his object. Its method, however, is not to bring the reader closer to the object that he may react to it or see it more clearly as it is, but to interpose the poet's quite subjective impressions of the scene. The images are wholly impressionistic, and their final effect derives from the strangeness and individuality of the poet's view; being one significant step removed from reality, they lose the hardness and objectivity of Imagism: domes of bowler hats vibrate in the heat, the city seems to throw its streets after those who flee from it.

Certain descriptive poems that Fletcher contributed to the anthologies demonstrate other characteristics not inconsistent with Imagism. For example, they reveal his ability to depict color vividly:

Shadows of blue hands passing
Over a curtain of flame.

Grey rain curtains wave afar off,
Wisps of vapor curl and vanish.
The sun throws soft shades of golden light
Over rose-buttressed palisades.

Now the clouds are a lazy procession,
Blue balloons bobbing solemnly
Over black-dappled walls.
("Clouds across the Canyon")

On occasion, he could create an image like that advocated by Hulme. He wrote of "The Unquiet Street":

> On rainy nights
> It dully gleams
> Like the cold tarnished scales of a snake;
> And over it hang arc-lamps,
> Blue-white death lilies on black stems.

Or

> And the grinding click of their skates as they
> impinge on the surface
> Is like the brushing together of their wing-tips
> of silver.
>
> ("The Skaters")

Such imagery, however, is so rare as to pass unnoticed in his predominantly Symbolist technique, and would not seem to justify his inclusion in Imagist volumes. Privately, to Amy Lowell, Fletcher admitted the anomaly of his association with the three anthologies.

> I do not believe that a poem should present an "image," I believe it should present an emotion. I do not believe in "clear, hard, and definite presentation." I believe in a complete, that is to say, shifting and fluid presentation. I do not believe in "absolute freedom in choice of subject."—I believe that the very word "choice" means lack of freedom. If one chooses, one has certain standards whereby one chooses. I do not believe that the "exact word" is possible. I do not believe in cadence, but in rhythm (a different thing altogether). I do not believe altogether in "externality." Therefore I do not accept Imagism. I am a Rhythmist or a Symbolist, but not an Imagist.
>
> —Stanley Coffman, Jr., "Amygism," *Imagism*, 1951, pp. 176–80

Not surprisingly, Fletcher ⟨in later life⟩ decided "that what was, after all, interesting about humanity was less the accidents of any individual life than the tendencies inherent in humanity as a whole." The prose and later poetry show a natural trend towards abstraction, towards jumping from, and at times over, the individual to the general.

This point brings up the most difficult of Fletcher's poems to discuss, the philosophical poems of the Twenties in which he set out to examine the "tendencies inherent in humanity as a whole," *Parables* and *Branches of Adam*. They are poems (or, for part of *Parables*, prose sketches) about the "eternal" problems of good and evil and man's search for God. *Branches of Adam* is Fletcher's most ambitious work, an epic on the Creation, the Fall of Man, and the Flood. As he himself says, it is a prime example of his untimeliness—no one in the Twenties was interested. The fact that he did not include it or any of the *Parables* in his *Selected Poems*, together with the brief and hesitant remarks he makes about them in *Life Is My Song*, may indicate that he felt more lacking here than timeliness.

In *Branches of Adam* Fletcher comes close to creating the grand style he needs. He builds on the Bible and on Blake, whose influence almost overwhelm him, but there are long passages, especially of description, which are not derivative in tone. His love of hugeness and violence, which threatens at times to split some of the symphonies as it does some of the later elegies, is here in place. The poem blazes and throbs. The figures are superhuman, and the might of their passions is conveyed in a series of elemental nature images rolled along on a long line which can both thunder and flash. For a poem which had to make its own technique unlike anything other poets at the time were interested in making, *Branches of Adam* is an amazing achievement, and it deserves to be known as one of the few impressive long poems of the century.

If Fletcher recognized a partial failure, it was probably due to his basic plan. He set out to make a myth. There is no evidence that myths have ever been "made" in this way—a myth which is recognized by its maker as a myth is merely a symbol. And the symbol in this demonic, reversed version of Genesis only partly covers the abstract message, so that the concrete and abstract do not fuse but merely exist side by side. In Cain, at least, Fletcher finds a symbol of one side of man's nature which is perhaps his most striking single creation.

He is not, of course, to blame for not having a more positive message than the misery of man in his search for God. The lack of God and the longing for Him Fletcher strongly felt, and, of course, they have made poetry before. Perhaps the contrast between the terrific framework of the poem and its inability to affirm anything seems somewhat incongruous.

In *The Black Rock* Fletcher found another way of dealing with the same problem, and such little-known lyrics as "The Last Frontier," "The Future," "Isle Iranim" and "Brahma" solve temporarily his difficulty of finding an individual poetic idiom for philosophic poetry. That there are so few of these lyrics may be a sign that Fletcher had said what he had to say. The title poem of the volume is only less striking because it suffers from one of Fletcher's commonest faults, not knowing when to stop. In *The Black Rock* Fletcher gets his second wind and writes the second group of poems that is indisputably his, poems he regarded as dealing with more important themes. Unfortunately he never reached a third period of such sureness of style.—Ben Kimpel, "John Gould Fletcher in Retrospect," *Poetry*, Aug. 1954, pp. 290–92

. . . ⟨A⟩ survey of Fletcher's poetry from 1913 to 1916 reveals that very little of his large and varied output was, strictly speaking, imagistic. Certainly the "Symphonies," "London Excursion," polyphonic prose pieces, "Mississippi" and "Arizona" poems, and most of *The Tree of Life*, in their length, frequent abstraction, and courting of the infinite, do not even remotely approach imagist ideals. As for the many short, objective, free-verse poems that Fletcher composed—*Irradiations*, "The Ghosts of an Old House," *Japanese Prints*, "The Skaters," and other 1916 and 1917 anthology pieces—these have often passed for being imagistic, but they do not consistently possess the qualities of precision and "hardness" so crucial to the imagist aesthetic; nor do they aim at the sudden, intense release of energy that Pound associated with his image. At no time did Fletcher wholeheartedly adopt or try to realize imagist goals, i.e., to write poetry of a plastic nature or to "present an Image." Indeed, that he could produce the glaringly non-imagistic love poems that comprise *The Tree of Life* throughout the period of his association with the movement indicates that he was indifferent to some of the central tenets of imagism.

Fletcher's own beliefs in regard to the function of poetry as compared to those of the early imagists may be summarized as follows. He did not favor a maximum of visual content but felt that poetic style should be an attempt to develop the musical quality of literature. As a result, his poems cultivate not a sharpness of outline, but a richness of sound. Furthermore, while the early imagists focused on concrete objects and small pieces of reality, Fletcher tried to bring out the underlying essence of a scene. His most common way of doing this was through his "symphonic" method, which led to the quiet prolongation of effect rather than to the forceful "hit" or impact

Pound tried to attain in his "image." It also resulted in the writing of many long poems, something the imagists were not known for. Lastly, Fletcher's manner of composition was different from that of the early imagists. They prided themselves on paring down their utterances to the fewest words possible and strove, through careful pruning, to give their compositions a finished, "made" quality. Fletcher customarily dashed off his poems in improvisational bursts and left them essentially unrevised. His work, characteristically, is not restrained and severe in tone, but has an exuberant and overflowing quality.

In spite of these differences, Fletcher was a bona fide participant in the movement, strongly involved in its intrigues, active in helping to write its prefaces, and a vocal defender of some of its tenets. How do we account for this paradox? The explanation is that Fletcher and his fellow imagists had a very broad concept of what constituted a literary school. Imagism, like the French "-isms" from which it took its cue, did not demand from its members rigid adherence to a specific doctrine, but only required that they agree to follow loose guidelines in writing poetry and share a common attitude toward life. It was this undefinable but real "attitude toward life" that Fletcher held in common with his imagist colleagues. Much more important than the flexible principles in the various manifestoes was their belief that they could rely on each other to write directly and "sincerely" about whatever moved them. Something was in the air, a new attitude toward experience which the principles of the manifestoes could only intimate, but which was, above all, their reason for banding together. Fletcher, by expressing his distaste for the mannerisms of recent poetry and by committing himself to metric freedom and definite treatment of a subject—indeed, by his whole artistic demeanor—showed that he shared this attitude toward experience and as a result could unhesitatingly be accepted as a peer.

John Gould Fletcher, imagist, fought many battles for Amy Lowell and the movement, but he was much more than one of her troopers: he was a gifted poet and intelligent man of letters whose work deserves a better fate than it has received.
—EDMUND S. DE CHASCA, "Fletcher's Poetry, 1913–1916," *John Gould Fletcher and Imagism*, 1978, pp. 220–22

CONRAD AIKEN
From "Possessor and Possessed: John Gould Fletcher"
Scepticisms
1919, pp. 105–14

The work of Mr. John Gould Fletcher has hardly attained the eminence in contemporary poetry that it deserves. One is doubtful, indeed, whether it will. For not only is it of that sort which inevitably attracts only a small audience, but it is also singularly uneven in quality, and many readers who would like Mr. Fletcher at his best cannot muster the patience to read beyond his worst. Mr. Fletcher is his own implacable enemy. He has not yet published a book in which his excellent qualities are single, candid, and undivided: a great many dead leaves are always to be turned. The reward for the search is conspicuous, but unfortunately it is one which few will take the trouble to find.

Mr. Fletcher's latest book, *The Tree of Life* is no exception to this rule: it is perhaps if we leave out of account his five early books of orthodox and nugatory self-exploration, the most remarkably uneven of them all. It has neither the level technical excellence, the economical terseness of his *Japanese Prints*, nor, on the other hand, the amazing flight of many pages in *Goblins and Pagodas*. Yet certainly one would rather have it than *Japanese Prints*; and even if it contains a greater proportion of dross than is to be found in the symphonies, it has compensating qualities, qualities which one feels are new in the work of Mr. Fletcher, and which make one hesitate to rate it too far below *Goblins and Pagodas*, or, at any rate, *Irradiations*.

. . . Mr. Fletcher has a very original sensibility, and it is also true that his initial stimulus sometimes comes from without, but whereas in the work of certain other poets these factors might be paramount, in the case of Mr. Fletcher the striking feature has always been his habit of surrendering himself, almost completely, to the power of these automatically, unravelling verbal reflexes. In fact the poetry of Mr. Fletcher is as remarkable an illustration of this principle as one could find.

The implications are rich. What occurs to one immediately is that, as the functioning of these verbal reflexes is most rapid when least consciously controlled, the poet will be at his best when the initial stimulus is of a nature to leave him greatest freedom. To such a poet, it will be seen, it would be a great handicap, to have to adhere too closely, throughout a longish poem, to a fixed and unalterable idea. The best theme for him will be the one which is least definite, one which will start him off at top speed but will be rather enhanced than impaired by the introduction and development of new elements, by rapid successive improvisations in unforeseen directions. Any sort of conceptual framework prepared in advance with regard either to subject or form would be perpetually retarding him, perpetually bringing him back to a more severely conscious plane of effort, a plane on which, the chances are, he would be far less effective. These suppositions gain force when we turn, in their light, to Mr. Fletcher's work. In *Irradiations* we find him taking his first ecstatic plunge into improvisation—formalism is thrown to the winds, and with it much which for this poet perplexes and retards; and an amazingly rich treasure house of verbal reflexes, the gift of a temperament almost hyperaesthetic in its sensitiveness to colour, line, and texture—a temperament in which some profound disharmony is most easily struck at and shaken through these senses—is for the first time rifled. It is in this stage of a lyric poet's career that his speech most glistens. Impressions come up shining from their long burial in the subconscious. The poet is perhaps a little breathless with his sudden wealth—he is at first content to bring up only small handfuls of the most glittering coin; he is even perhaps a little distrustful of it. But the habit of allowing himself to be possessed by this wealth grows rapidly. The mechanism becomes more familiar, if anything so vague as this kind of apperception can be said to be truly recognizable, and the poet learns the trick of shutting his eyes and not merely allowing, but precisely inviting, his subconscious to take possession of him. The trick consists largely in a knowledge, abruptly acquired, of his own character, and of such ideas as are, therefore, the "Open Sesame!" to this cave. It was in colourism that Mr. Fletcher found this password. And it was in *Goblins and Pagodas* that he first put it to full and gorgeous use.

For in the idea of a series of symphonies in which the sole unity was to be a harmony of colour, in which form and emotional tone could follow the lead of colouristic word-associations no matter how far afield, Mr. Fletcher discovered an "Open Sesame!" so ideal to his nature, and so powerful, as not merely to open the door, but at one stroke to lay bare his treasure entire. One should not overlook here also an important secondary element in Mr. Fletcher's nature, a strong but partial affinity for musical construction, a feeling for powerful submerged rhythms less ordered than those of metrical verse, but more ordered than those of prose; and this element, too, found its ideal opportunity in the colour symphonies. The result was, naturally, the most brilliant and powerful work which Mr. Fletcher has yet given us—a poetry unlike any other. It contains no thought: Mr. Fletcher is not a conceptual poet. It contains, in the strictly human sense, extraordinarily little of the sort of emotion which relates to the daily life of men and women; there are despairs and exaltations and sorrows and hopes, and the furious energy of ambition, and the weariness of resignation, but they are the emotions of someone incorporeal, and their sphere of action is among winds and clouds, the colours of sky and sea, the glittering of rain and jewels, and not among the perplexed hearts of humanity. In a sense it is like the symbolism of such poets as Mallarmé, but with the difference that here the symbols have no meaning. It is a sort of absolute poetry, a poetry of detached waver and brilliance, a beautiful flowering of language alone, a parthenogenesis, as if language were fertilized by itself rather than by thought or feeling. Remove the magic of phrase and sound, and there is nothing left: no thread of continuity, no relation between one page and the next, no thought, no story, no emotion. But the magic of phrase and sound is powerful, and it takes one into a fantastic world where one is etherealized, where one has deep emotions indeed, but emotions star-powdered, and blown to flame by speed and intensity rather than by thought or human warmth.

Unfortunately it is only for a little while that a poet can be so completely possessed by the subconscious: the more complete the possession the more rapid the exhaustion. One or two of Mr. Fletcher's colour symphonies showed already a flagging of energy, and in addition to the unevenness which is inevitable in a blind obedience to the lead of word-association alone (since it leads as often to verbosity as to magic) that unevenness also is noticed which comes of the poet's attempt to substitute the consciously for the unconsciously found—an attempt which for such a temperament as Mr. Fletcher's is frequently doomed to failure. There are limits, moreover, as we have seen, to the number of themes which will draw out the best of the possessed type of poet. Failing to discover new themes, he must repeat the old ones; and here it is not long before he feels his consciousness intruding, and saying to him, "You have said this before," a consciousness which at once inhibits the unravelling of word-association, and brings him back to that more deliberate sort of art for which he is not so well fitted. It is to this point that Mr. Fletcher has come, recently in *Japanese Prints*, and now in *The Tree of Life*. Here and there for a moment is a flash of magic and power—there are pages, even whole poems, which are only less delightful than the symphonies—but intermingled with how much that is lame, stiltedly metrical, verbose, or downright ugly. The use of regular metre or rhyme brings him down with a thud. . . . *The Tree of Life* is a volume of love poems, more personal than Mr. Fletcher has given us hitherto, and that has an interest of its own. But the colourism has begun to dim, it is often merely a wordy and tediously overcrowded imitation of the coloured swiftness of *Goblins and Pagodas*, the images indistinct and conflicting; and if one is to hope for further brilliance it is not in this but in a new note, audible here and there in the shorter lyrics, a note of ironlike resonance, bitterly personal, and written in a free verse akin to the stark eloquence of Biblical prose. . . . Are these lyrics an earnest of further development, and will Mr. Fletcher pass to that other plane of art, that of the possessor artist, the artist who foresees and forges, who calculates his effects? There is hardly enough evidence here to make one sure.

ALFRED KREYMBORG
From "A Free Verse Revolt"
A History of American Poetry
1934, pp. 361–67

His restless nature is rarely at home anywhere, and his gorgeous imagination, a lonely spirit afire with mystic yearning, now roves among insoluble vistas and horizons. He marches toward the unattainable with singular courage and reduces his discoveries to what Conrad Aiken once termed, absolute poetry. This term has a kinship with absolute music, as opposed to program music. "It is," wrote his fellow Southerner, "a beautiful flowering of language alone, a parthenogenesis, as if language were fertilized by itself rather than by thought or feeling. . . . But the magic of phrase and sound is powerful, and takes one into a fantastic world where one is etherealized, where one has deep emotions indeed, but emotions star-powdered, and blown to flame by speed and intensity rather than by thought or human warmth." This analysis refers to Fletcher the Imagist, author of *Irradiations* and *Goblins and Pagodas*, reissued later under the musical title, *Preludes and Symphonies*. Aiken's conclusions are often cramped by his devotion to fascinating theses, logically carried through. The early Fletcher poems have Southern soil as their source. His rich embroidery of images is to be found throughout Southern poetry, from Poe to Lanier, from Aiken to John Crowe Ransom. All Southerners, whether they write poetry or prose or take to religion or oratory, have a love of rhetoric, a love which qualified Fletcher for Symbolism and Imagism. But he did not completely divorce himself from life, nor from sex either—as parthenogenesis implies. His later books show a closer communion with life; they are more realistic and concern themselves with things definitely American, as well as superterrestrial. Aiken's approach to Fletcher was correct, but his deductions were too restricted, a little ungenerous.

Fletcher may have been the least popular of the Imagists—an unpopularity which pursues him even now, in the course of a broader development. But the fault is due, not to the poet, but to his readers. Fletcher has faults—more than many lesser poets. He is another of the reckless blunderers whose progress with the public is slow. A hermit by disposition, an impassioned monk, he has the virtues and vices of any egocentric artist. But he has a great deal to give, despite his failure to communicate himself fully and clearly. His symphonic instrument is erratic. At times he writes like an inspired god in chaos, and then falls away and fumbles about like a tyro. A tremendously prolific person, he lacks the power of self-criticism essential to major artistry. He has major intentions without the minor talents for revising his tumultuous output. If Fletcher had Amy Lowell's talent, or Miss Lowell had had his genius, a first-rate lyric poet would have emerged. They were great friends: *Preludes and Symphonies* was dedicated to her. For sheer lyric artistry—passion welded to cold hard form—both poets were surpassed by H. D. But H. D. perfected a single string: a simpler task than Fletcher's endeavor to master all instruments, natural and supernatural. His quest of the divine is another reason for his unpopularity. The public has never followed—certainly not of late years—the visions of mystics. People prefer something closer at hand, something more comfortable, something to read in rocking chairs.

The gorgeous *Irradiations* are not alone Imagistic: many of the rhetoric figures depend upon languorous Southern landscapes. The opening poem, with its swift movement, may have been written abroad, but the mood and language are native.

the passing of the wind
Upon the pale lower terraces of my dream
Is like the crinkling of the wet grey robes
Of the hours that come to turn over the urn
Of the day and spill its rainy dream.

Sails and rivers abound in other Irradiations. Though exotic images, many of them Oriental, color the lines, one can feel the Mississippi flow through them. Always the phrases are gorgeous, their progressions harmonious. Umbrellas are "recurved blossoms of the storm." Here is a love motif in two lines:

The fountain blows its breathless spray
From me to you and back to me.

The trees are like "great jade elephants" and "the clouds are their crimson howdah-canopies." In a city at night, "the wind of the darkness whispered, Hush! to my soul." The "seeded grass" is "an army of little men crawling up the long slope with quivering, quick blades of steel." "The dancing dunes" are "labyrinths of shifting sand." And the poet's happiness is like the sand: "I let it run out of my hand." Addressing a child, his vision embraces infinitude in four lines:

Strange, old, and silent being, there is something
Infinitely vast in your intense tininess:
I think you could point out, with a smile, some
curious star
Far off in the heavens, which no man has seen
before.

Walking the nocturnal town, the poet remembers only a "gaudy, shameless night-orchid," which he prefers to "the feeble forget-me-nots of the world." The orchid was alive, "when all the rest were but puppets of the night." These poems are anything but sexless. And Fletcher, intensely serious though he is, is never too serious for dancing:

I drink of the red bowl of the sunlight:
I swim through seas of rain:
I dig my toes into earth:
I taste the smack of the wind:
I am myself:
I live.

This Southern poet owes more to Whitman than he does to the French or the Oriental. He is not as democratic as Walt; he is a lover of jungles, of an almost inhuman god, of asperities and solitudes. His soul is "a gorge that was filled with the warring echoes of song." . . .

In the later volumes, *The Tree of Life*, *Breakers and Granite*, *Branches of Adam*, *The Black Rock*, the mystic visions of Fletcher become intensified through a fiercer, more intimate warfare on the forces of reality. During the last ten years, the poet has penetrated beyond the self-imposed restraints of Imagism. Through an ever-increasing interest in his native soil, he is now swayed by humanity, without, however, being able to rid himself of his loneliness. Something of the old savage clings to him still, but the savage has grown simpler, more concrete, more conscious of things outside the ego. He is just as impassioned as ever, but the passion has mellowed, without growing soft. He is just as prophetic, but the biblical tone no longer sounds so remote. Unable to master his idealism or compromise with a middle course, he does not yet accept life or humanity, here or anywhere else, just as they are. There is too much evil abroad, evil he cannot accept. He continues to thunder away like an old Calvinist. His jeremiads attack the earth of his ancestors, and of his own time. Nothing could be more sweeping than the denunciatory lines of "To a Survivor of the Flood." Rhyme makes an entrance with poignant drum-beat. The flood is not the flood of old, but a modern flood, with but one survivor, a "Titan standing on wrecked peaks upright, Olympus piled on Sinai." This Titan, grown Everyman, is harangued with fiery symbols of dissolution:

Will you speed forth on some chance lava flow
Torn from a ruined sun you do not know,
Towards a state no human tongue can tell
After wrecked heaven has fallen below dead hell?
Or will you sink down sluggishly within,
Dropping below the waters cheek and chin,
And last of all, now nevermore to rise,
The huge unspeaking orbits of your eyes?
Will you rest rotting darkly in that sea,
To an eternity of vacancy?

This is no longer the spirit of Whitman, but a recrudescence of the darker genius of the misanthropic Melville. And yet, like Whitman, Lowell, Markham, Robinson, Lindsay, Sandburg, this poet, in the midst of whatever hatred or despair he may feel concerning his race, was moved by Lincoln. One of the noblest tributes to the all-saving Rail-splitter is Fletcher's. He compares Lincoln to a pine:

Ungainly, labouring, huge,
The wind of the north has twisted and gnarled its
branches;
Yet in the heat of midsummer days, when thunder-
clouds ring the horizon,
A nation of men shall rest beneath its shade.

Like Robinson, Fletcher goes back to the days when Lincoln was held in doubt:

But he whom we mocked and obeyed not, he whom
we scorned and mistrusted,
He has descended, like a god, to his rest.

Fletcher calls for flowers to be strewn over the grave: Northern forget-me-nots, Eastern arbutus, Western orange blossoms and "from the heart of the land the passion-flower."

Rayed, violet, dim,
With the nails that pierced, the cross that he bore and
the circlet,
And beside it there lay also one lonely snow-white
magnolia,
Bitter for remembrance of the healing which has
passed.

The Southern magnolia closes the poem, and bitterness for remembrance has spread throughout the land. The wiser Robinson saw that we can have but one Titan at a time. It is true of all races and all ages.

Of the other poems on American themes, those about the Southwest and the group called *Down the Mississippi* belong to the Imagistic period. *Granite and Breakers* contains most of the rugged poems. Somehow, the poet is more at home among cosmic vistas and among his modern versions of biblical scenes. "The Creation and Fall" from *Branches of Adam* is a blending of fable and fact set to a powerful swiftness of movement and intensity of design. The poem is weakened by lapses from the opening fortissimo trumpets. There is too much fortissimo, too much orotundity. Nuances, where nuances would have aided the unfolding tale, are too rare. Fletcher is not a dramatist, but a rhapsodist. Yet the poem teems with moving emotions and images. And Adam, like Miss Branch's Nimrod, is the hero of the old days. "Lazarus" is an even finer poem, though equally awkward at times. It is divided into eleven movements: the awakening, his attempt to remember his former life, his quest of the Preacher who had saved him, his encounter with Jesus and the thieves on the way to the Crucifixion, a mob scene, Golgotha, the visit to Joseph's tomb, and little by little, the mistaken recognition of Lazarus as Christ risen from the tomb. Fletcher's own faith in the Savior is intoned in a simple song: "Advent." But the poet's mysticism is most appealing when addressed directly to Nature, as in "Autumnal Clouds." This is a superb chant, the song of a modern Solomon:

Autumnal clouds,
Look! far there in the sunlight,
The glory floods you now, I see you plainly:
You are no more clouds to me, you are a woman,
White and rosy and gold and blue and beautiful.
You move across the sky, the dusk is at your feet,
The night is in your arms, the moon is on your breast,
The stars are in your eyes, the dawn is on your hair.
Drench me, drown me, darken me, make me
drunken with deep red torrents of joy,
Till I forget all things in the world but this,
The glory of God everlasting, the fire of passion and
death.

CAROLYN FORCHÉ

1950–

Carolyn Louise Forché was born in Detroit, Michigan, on April 28, 1950. She first published poems in periodicals while an undergraduate at the Justin Morrill College of Michigan State University, where she majored in creative writing. In both 1970 and 1971 she won the first prize in the Michigan State University poetry competition, and has steadily extended her reputation as a poet and teacher of poetry since her graduation in 1972.

After receiving an Award in Poetry from the *Chicago Review* in 1975, Forché published her first book, *Gathering the Tribes*, in 1976, winning the Yale Series of Younger Poets Award. Further honors followed, with a National Endowment for the Arts grant in 1977 and a Guggenheim Fellowship in 1978. From 1978 to 1980 she was a journalist in El Salvador, reporting on human rights violations for Amnesty International. Her second collection of poems, *The Country between Us*, was the Lamont Poetry Selection of the Academy of American Poets in 1981.

Forché's interest in foreign languages and cultures extends to Serbo-Croatian, Russian, Spanish and Tewa, and her translations include versions of the Spanish poems of Claribel Alegría, published in a parallel text, *Flowers from the Volcano*, in 1981. As well as writing, she has given readings and taught at colleges and universities across the country, including San Diego State University, the University of Arkansas, and the University of Virginia.

Next to ⟨Marilyn⟩ Hacker, Carolyn Forché seems like a little girl playing with dolls, yet she also has won a prize, her first book, *Gathering the Tribes*, being the 71st in the Yale Series of Younger Poets. When one looks over the names of the previous 70, one is struck by how few have gone on to significant accomplishment and by how much those few altered their first work to achieve maturity. No doubt Forché will find alteration too. For the present she has a slick technical veneer—the standard low-keyed free metric taught to thousands each semester in our "creative writing schools." But beyond that there is certain depth of feeling, particularly in her poems about Hispano-Indian life near Truchas Peake, N.M. In short, her work is promising. I'm sorry to use a term made depreciative by custom, but in this case it is exactly, literally right, and so not depreciative after all.—HAYDEN CARRUTH, *NYTBR*, Aug. 8, 1976, p. 12

Carolyn Forché, like Neruda, Philip Levine, Denise Levertov and others who have, in recent years, wed the "political" and the "personal," addresses herself unflinchingly to the exterior, historical world. In ⟨*The Country between Us*⟩ her subject is primarily El Salvador, and her news is bleakly and succinctly stated: "What you have heard is true."

. . . The "public" world is Carolyn Forché's bitter and often lacerating subject. *The Country between Us* concerns itself variously with the voices of El Salvador (where Miss Forché lived for two years, working as a journalist), Belgrade, Prague, Detroit and other unnamed cities; its tone is restrained, uninflected, even melancholic, its subject is the ongoing tragedy of political—or is it simply human?—cruelty. "There is nothing one man will not do to another" is the jarring final line of a short poem set in El Salvador, but this judgement is applicable elsewhere and everywhere:

In the mass graves, a woman's hand
caged in the ribs of her child,
a single stone in Spain beneath olives,
in Germany the silent windy fields,
in the Soviet Union where the snow
is scarred with wire, in Salvador
where the blood will never soak
into the ground, everywhere and always
go after that which is lost.
There is a cyclone fence between
ourselves and the slaughter and behind it
we hover in a clam protected world like
netted fish, exactly like netted fish.
It is either the beginning or the end
of the world, and the choice is ourselves
or nothing.

("Ourselves or Nothing")

. . . Carolyn Forché is blunt, unremitting, candid. There may be readers who object to her somewhat abstract—

and apoetic—endorsement of a grief too great to have been experienced by any individual ("all the mass graves of the century's dead / will open into your early waking hours: / Belsen, Dachau, Saigon, Phnom Penh / and the one meaning Bridge of Ravens / Sao Paulo, Armagh, Calcutta, Salvador"), but her voice is never shrill or strident, and the horrific visions are nearly always contained within fully realized poems.

In Salvador, after a luxurious dinner, the dried ears of "rebels" are dropped playfully into a glass by a colonel who says, "Something for your poetry, no?" There are "reports / of mice introduced into women, of men / whose testicles are crushed like eggs"; visions of starving children "like a supper scrap / filling with worms." It is unavoidable in poems so intensely political that names (Carolina, Francisco, Jara, Torres, etc.) are evoked that cannot communicate any particular meaning to the reader, and that the self-effacing technique produces an impersonal and at times rhetorical poetry. Can the language of poetry compete with journalism, one wonders, in limning the graphic outrages of mass shootings, mutilations, tortures? This is the country of "the razor, the live wire / dry ice and concrete, gray rats," where a man's hands are chopped off by his captors and flung into a field; it is a nightmare country lucidly presented:

> When Virea was burned we knew it had come to an end,
> his coffin rocking into the ground like a boat or a cradle.
> I could take my heart, he said, and give it to a *campesino*
> and he would cut it up and give it back:
> you can't eat heart in those four dark
> chambers where a man can be kept for years.
> A boy soldier in the bone-hot sun works his knife
> to peel the face from a dead man
> and hang it from the branch of a tree
> flowering with such faces
> ("Because One Is Always Forgotten")

Caroyln Forché's first book, *Gathering the Tribes*, a winner of the Yale Younger Poets award, introduced a poet of uncommon vigor and assurance. *The Country between Us* is a distinct step forward. Though one tends to remember vivid fragments of poems rather than wholes, the cumulative power of the volume is considerable. "In what time do we live," the poet asks, "that it is too late to have children?"—a partial view, but no less compelling, no less authentic. One feels that the poet has earned her bleak and wintry vision:

> We do not rid ourselves of these things
> even when we are cured of personal silence
> when for no reason one morning
> we begin to hear the noise of the world again.
> ("City Walk-Up, Winter 1969")

—Joyce Carol Oates, *NYTBR*, April 4, 1982, pp. 13, 29

⟨*The Country between Us*⟩ seethes with anger at man's inhumanity and stupidity. And what instances she reports in her poems about El Salvador: corpses eviscerated, living men stacked like corpses, human ears collected in a sack. Hardly by chance, she previously lived with a man writing a book on the Holocaust who in turn could not free himself from the constricting nightmare. Clearly—even calmly—the poet raises her voice in opposition to this hysteria. She divides her book into three parts: "In Salvador, 1978–80," "Reunion," and "Ourselves or Nothing." The opposites in her poetry find expression in the last title, a long poem about our freedom still to choose. Here "nothing" means exactly that; it is not an existential concept but possible annihilation of all life after every value we have held has been wiped out. "Message" bleakly critiques "ideas or men that amounted to nothing." "For the Stranger" describes a meeting on a train when two opposites, an older worker from a communist country and the author, attract: "We have, each of us, nothing. / We will give it to each other." The scene offers a parable on the world situation when the Superpowers sit down to talk. "Nothing" resonates through the poems: "I have nothing," "I give nothing," "There is nothing." In "Joseph," a poem about a Vietnam veteran who calls her for comfort, Forché closes with the observation that even the phone "has nothing to say to you." In her fluently reportorial style the poet exercises perfect control over her material, which ranges also into her own past life in Eastern European cities—Belgrade and Prague—and her Mid-West childhood. Her style levels everything out and is highly readable; however, the alternatives for "ourselves" never glow with life. Bleakness is all. The moral force that lies behind the lines too often fails to break through. "Return" grieves that "you were born to an island of greed / and grace where you have this sense of yourself / as apart from others." That very alienation becomes the one difficulty of these honest, searching poems. Their opposition needs more inwardness.—James Finn Cotter, *HdR*, Autumn 1982, pp. 474–75

STANLEY KUNITZ
"Foreword"
Gathering the Tribes
1976, pp. xi–xv

Kinship is the theme that preoccupies Carolyn Forché. Although she belongs to a generation that is reputed to be rootless and disaffiliated, you would never guess it from reading her poems. Her imagination, animated by a generous life-force, is at once passionate and tribal. Narrative is her preferred mode, leavened by meditation. She remembers her childhood in rural Michigan, evokes her Slovak ancestors, immerses herself in the American Indian culture of the Southwest, explores the mysteries of flesh, tries to understand the bonds of family, race, and sex. In the course of her adventures she dares to confront, as a sentient being, the overwhelming questions by which reason itself is confounded: Who am I? Why am I here? Where am I going?

In "Burning the Tomato Worms," a central poem, the narrative focuses on Anna, "heavy sweatered winter woman" seen "in horse-breath weather." She was the poet's paternal grandmother, who spoke a Slovak of the Russian-Czech borderlands and who, with her Old World lore and old wives' tales, profoundly influenced the poet's childhood.

> Anna's hands were like wheat rolls
> Shelling snow peas, Anna's hands
> Are both dead, they were Uzbek,
> Uzbek hands known for weaving fine rugs
> Eat Bread and Salt and Speak the Truth

Here as elsewhere the local color is vivid and unforced. But the poem is not to be construed as an exercise in sentimentality or ethnic nostalgia: it is woven of two strands, one commemorating a beloved person and place, the other recounting a girl's sexual initiation. The burning of the tomato worms can be read as a ritual of purification. Everywhere in these pages ritual and litany are close at hand. Even the act of bread making, a recurrent image, assumes a ceremonial aspect.

Love of people, love of place. Carolyn Forché's poems give an illusion of artlessness because they spring from the simplest and deepest human feelings, from an earthling's awareness of the systemic pulse of creation. The poems tell us she is at home anyplace under the stars, wherever there are fields or mountains, lakes or rivers, persons who stir her atavistic bond-sense. In "Song Coming toward Us" she writes:

I am spirit entering
the stomach of the stones.

Bowls of clay and water sing,
set on the fires to dry.
The mountain moves
like the spirit of southeast morning.

You walk where drums are buried.
Feel their skins tapping all night.
Snow flutes swell ahead of your life.
Listen to yourself.

She listens. At Justin Morrill College, an experimental residential branch of Michigan State University, where five years ago the earliest parts of *Gathering the Tribes* were conceived, she began her avid consumption of languages. Now she studies Russian, Spanish, Serbo-Croatian, French and Tewa (Pueblo Indian), listening beyond grammar for the secret texts. She acknowledges a primal sense of the power of words. The power to "make words"—in the mouth, in the heart, on the page—is the same to her as to give substance. Aiming at wholeness, strength, and clarity, she works at language as if it were a lump of clay or dough in her hands. In her search for poetry, in her effort to understand it, she has bent over the potter's wheel, climbed mountain ranges, ventured into the Mojave Desert. And she has sought out teachers. Among her teachers she lists her grandmother Anna, who died in 1968 ("Grandma, come back, I forgot/How much lard for these rolls"); her father, Michael Sidlosky, a tool and die maker, and her mother, Louise, who bore seven children before going to college, from which she graduated the same year as Carolyn, her eldest daughter; Teles Goodmorning of the Taos pueblo ("His voice scoops a swarm of coals,/dust rising from it"); Rosita of the same pueblo ("Her laugh is a music/from the time of Christ"); and Lama Kalu Rimpoche (an unknown and humble, very old man encountered in the mountains of New Mexico).

The place dearest to her include the south Michigan heartland where she was raised, Truchas and the Pueblo village of Taos in New Mexico, the Washington coast, and the Okanogan region of southern British Columbia. Anna, Alfansa, Teles Goodmorning, the dulcimer maker, Rosita, Jacynthe, the child born in the Okanogan, the monks of the mountain abbey, and Joey, a first love, who went off to study for the priesthood, are all characters clearly drawn from life and attached to specific locations. One might say that they are embodiments of the reality of their settings.

If I am right in supposing that "Year at Mudstraw," "Taking Off My Clothes," and "Kalaloch" are among the last poems written for this book, it would appear that Forché is moving toward a tauter line, packed with incisive detail, and a firmer dramatic structure than is evident in her earlier narratives. "Taking Off My Clothes" begins

I take off my shirt, I show you.
I shaved the hair out under my arms.
I roll up my pants, I scraped off the hair
on my legs with a knife, getting white.

My hair is the color of chopped maples.
My eyes dark as beans cooked in the south.
(Coal fields in the moon on torn-up hills)

I have little doubt that the poem in *Gathering the Tribes* that will be most discussed, quoted, and anthologized is "Kalaloch" (pronounced ka-lā´-lok), an almost faultlessly controlled erotic narrative of 101 lines. In its boldness and innocence and tender, sensuous delight it may very well prove to be the outstanding Sapphic poem of an era. Here is its concluding section:

Flies crawled us,
Jacynthe crawled.
With her palms she
spread my calves, she
moved my heels from each other.
A woman's mouth is
not different, sand moved
wild beneath me, her long
hair wiped my legs, with women
there is sucking, the water
slops our bodies. We come
clean, our clits beat like
twins to the loons rising up.

We are awake.
Snails sprinkle our gulps.
Fish die in our grips, there is
sand in the anus of dancing.
Tatoosh Island.
hardens in the distance.
We see its empty stones
sticking out of the sea again.
Jacynthe holds tinder
under fire to cook the night's wood.

If we had men I would make
milk in me simply. She is
quiet. *I like that you*
cover your teeth.

KATHA POLLITT

"Poems on Public Subjects"

Nation, May 8, 1982, pp. 562–63

Why is so little good political poetry written in America today? The very phrase "political poetry" conjures up visions of smudgy sectarian newspapers where verses with titles like "Death to All Fascists" appear next to letters signed "A Brother in Detroit." And yet, it wasn't so long ago that poets wrote about the major issues of the day as a matter of course. Subjects like Italian (or Greek or Polish) independence, slavery and the plight of the industrial poor were as much a staple of nineteenth-century verse as were the deaths of beautiful girls. Our own century offers Pound, Auden and his circle, and Lowell. Among poets working now, however, only a few treat the sorts of events and issues one reads about in the newspapers or demonstrates about in the streets, and I think it's significant that those who do—Bly, Levertov, Rich, Ginsberg—are middle-aged. For most young poets, I suspect, the prospect that a poem might address the election of Ronald Reagan, the arms race or the organizing of office workers must seem both comical and insulting. Many would quarrel with the whole notion of thinking of poems in terms of what they are "about."

The problem is not that poets are apolitical. It's that they have inherited a literary form so diminished and so privatized that many things lie outside its purview. If the prototypical magazine poem of 1910 was a sonnet to Eleonora Duse adorned with allusions to nightingales, Greek gods and the poet's fainting heart, ours is a free-verse elegy on the isolation of the self, set on a campus in the Middle West and decorated with references to snow, light, angels and the poet's nostalgia for his childhood. Ours is a poetry, in other words, of wistful longings, of failed connections, of inevitable personal loss, expressed in a set of poetic strategies that suit such themes—a lax syntax and simplified vocabulary that disclaim intellectual pretension, and ethereal, numinous images that testify to the poet's sensibility. There is little place in this sort of poetry for politics, for whatever its repercussions in the realm of private feeling, politics is fundamentally a public affair.

Carolyn Forché's second book of poems ⟨*The Country between Us*⟩ is interesting both because Forché is a talented poet—her first book, *Gathering the Tribes*, was a Yale Younger Poets selection—and because it tackles the political subject matter I am arguing is so uncongenial to young poets. The first section, dedicated to the memory of Oscar Romero, the murdered archbishop of San Salvador, is set in El Salvador, where Forché lived for two years and worked as a journalist. Other poems are addressed to old friends from the working-class Detroit neighborhood of Forché's childhood: one has become a steelworker haunted by memories of Vietnam; another, with whom Forché had shared adolescent dreams of travel and romance, lives with her husband and kids in a trailer. Elsewhere in the poems we meet a jailed Czech dissident, the wife of a "disappeared" Argentine and Terrence Des Pres, author of *The Survivor*, a study of the death camps. This is strong stuff, and the excited response *The Country between Us* has already provoked shows, I think, how eager people are for poetry that acknowledges the grim political realities of our time.

At their best, Forché's poems have the immediacy of war correspondence, postcards from the volcano of twentieth-century barbarism:

> A boy soldier in the bone-hot sun works his knife
> to peel the face from a dead man
> and hang it from the branch of tree
> flowering with such faces.
> ("Because One Is Always Forgotten")

> a labor leader was cut to pieces and buried.
> Tell them how his friends found
> the soldiers and made them dig up
> and ask forgiveness of the corpse, once
> it was assembled on the ground
> like a man.
> ("Return")

Testicles are "crushed like eggs," rats are introduced into vaginas, José waves his bloody stumps in the air, Lil Milagro is raped and forced to defecate in public. "There is nothing one man will not do to another," Forché tells us. So shocking are the incidents reported here—so automatic is our horror at a mere list of places where atrocities have occurred ("Belsen, Dachau, Saigon, Phnom Penh")—that one feels almost guilty discussing these poems as poems, as though by doing so one were saying that style and tone and diction mattered more than bloody stumps, and murdered peasants and the Holocaust.

This unease, though, should not have arisen in the first place, and it points to an underlying problem: the incongruity between Forché's themes and her poetic strategies. Forché's topics could not be more urgent, more extreme or more public, and at least one of her stated intentions is to make us look at them squarely. And yet, she uses a language designed for quite other purposes, the misty "poetic" language of the isolated, private self. She gives us bloody stumps, but she also gives us snow, light and angels. You have to read "The Island" several times, for instance, to get past the exotic tropical scenery, the white dresses, the "seven different shawls of wind," the mist that is like bread and so forth, and realize that this is a poem of homage to Claribel Alegría, a heroic woman whom Forché would like to resemble, and that Claribel is telling Forché not to give up hope for El Salvador. At least, I think that's what it's about.

In other poems, a man manufactures bullets in "the spray of stars that is/a steel mill"; a political prisoner sees people as "those cold/globes of breath that shape/themselves into bodies"; the coffin of a Salvadoran martyr is seen "rocking into the ground like a boat or a cradle." The trouble is, if her images are to bear the burdens Forché places on them and move us in the way she wants, a steel mill can't be a lovely play of light, or bodies dreamlike apparitions, or death either a calm voyage or the sleep of a baby. They have to be real.

When Forché speaks plainly, she can be very good indeed. "The Expatriate" is a clever satire on a young American left-wing poet whose idea of solidarity with the Third World is to move to Turkey and sleep with women who speak no English. "It would be good if you could wind up/in prison and so write your prison poems," says Forché ironically, and we know she's got his number:

> You have been in Turkey a year now.
> What have you found? Your letters
> describe the boring ritual of tea,
> the pittance you are paid to teach
> English, the bribery required for so much
> as a postage stamp. Twenty-year-old poet,
> Hikmet did not ask to be Hikmet.

Equally memorable is "The Colonel," an account of dinner at the home of a right-wing Salvadoran officer, who, after the wine and the rack of lamb, dumps his collection of human ears on the table: "Something for your poetry, no?" The precise, observed details—the bored daughter filing her nails, the American cop show on TV, the parrot in the corner and the gold bell for the maid—work together to make a single impression, and the colonel himself, with his unpredictable swings between domestic boredom and jaunty brutality, is a vivid character, as Claribel Alegría is not. Interestingly, in view of what I've been saying about Forché's poetics, "The Colonel" is written in prose.

Perhaps what I miss in this collection is simply verbal energy. The poems, especially the longer ones, do tend to blur in the mind. Forché insists more than once on the transforming power of what she has seen, on the gulf it has created between herself and those who have seen less and dared less:

> And when I speak with American men
> there is some absence of recognition:
> their constant Scotch and fine white
> hands, many hours of business, penises
> hardened by motor inns and a faint
> resemblance to their wives. I cannot
> keep going.
> ("The Return")

But how can we grasp the power of this transforming vision when it is expressed in lackluster assertions. ("I cannot keep going") and facile caricatures of "American men" as adulterous Babbitts?

Whether or not one admires Forché for stressing the intensity of her responses to the sufferings of others—many readers, I should point out, do not share my discomfort with this emphasis—the intensity is vitiated by the inadequate means by which it is conveyed. It is embarrassing to read that Forché goes "mad, for example,/in the Safeway, at the many heads/of lettuce, papayas and sugar, pineapples/and coffee, especially the coffee." It trivializes torture to present it in terms of lunch:

> The *paella* comes, a bed of rice
> and *camarones*, fingers and shells,

the lips of those whose lips
have been removed, mussels
the soft blue of a leg socket.
("In Memory of Elena")

It is wildly histrionic—and slanderous, too—to accuse politically moderate human-rights activists of deriving masturbatory pleasure from torture reports:

they cup their own parts
with their bedsheets and move themselves
slowly, imagining bracelets affixing
their wrists to a wall
("The Return")

Does Forché think we read her poems as pornography?

It is not enough—this too may be a minority opinion—to dedicate one's poetry to the defeat of the torturers, to swear that

I will live
and living cry out until my voice is gone
to its hollow of earth where with our
hands and by the lives we have chosen
we will dig deep into our deaths.
("Message")

The boldness of the promise is undermined by the commonplace rhetoric ("hollow of earth" for "grave") and woolly syntax (the hands and lives dig into our deaths *after* the voice is dead?)

On the other hand, to make such a promise is not nothing, either. If poetry is to be more than a genteel and minor art form, it needs to encompass the material Forché presents. Much credit, then, belongs to Forché for her brave and impassioned attempt to make a place in her poems for starving children and bullet factories, for torturers and victims, for Margarita with her plastique bombs and José with his bloody stumps. What she needs now is language and imagery equal to her subjects and her convictions. The mists and angels of contemporary magazine verse are beneath her: she *has* seen too much, she has too much to say. Of how many poets today, I wonder, could that be said?

JUDITH GLEASON
From "The Lesson of Bread"

Parnassus: Poetry in Review, Spring-Summer 1982, pp. 15–20

An important variant of the Dionysian *pathos* which is beginning to surface among those of us concerned with healing arts is the Shamanic. Indeed, what the poet bears witness to "In Salvador, 1978–80" might be compared to a Shamanic voyage of dismemberment, a process with imaginative agony undergone in order to remake one's self whole for the benefit of others. As the traditional Shaman's dramatic passion is re-enacted in the enabling-space of his "theatre," a magic circle centered in his body-mind, those present not only benefit from his charismatic power (through suffering hard won) but also vicariously (as in tragic drama) go through his motions. Souls stolen by demons of various sorts are brought back into their proper bodies. Order and form are given to otherwise seemingly inchoate and disintegrative forces at large in the universe as in the uninitiated and undisciplined human soul. That El Salvador was not Carolyn Forché's first journey of this sort, a bleak poem called "City Walk-Up, Winter 1969" is sufficient testimony. We know that country too, a place characterized by absence of ordinary, living time:

A previous month is pinned to the wall where
days are numbered differently and described by
the photograph of a dead season. . . .

We do not rid ourselves of these things
even when we are cured of personal silence
when for no reason one morning
we begin to hear the noise of the world again.

Madness is small doses. A natural homeopath, the poet. Contained within the enabling format of her poems "In Salvador" are metonyms of violence which are the very substance of cure. In "Return" the severed hand clutches the soil. And so, as a last resort, must we. In "San Onofre," the last step before the frontier dividing us from a Latin America where hands are tied together and disappearance probable, Carolyn Forché sees "children patting the mud." A reassuring image rooted in most childhoods, in this poet's life-work it has a special resonance. For behind Carolyn Forché as a child stands the grandmother baking bread, stands Anna, heroine of her first volume ⟨*Gathering the Tribes*⟩ and of that "Endurance" with which the second section of the present collection ⟨*The Country between Us*⟩ begins. "There is nothing one man will not do to another," concludes the visitor to a Salvadorian prison. By implication, then, may our cure come from the observation of women? And the final couplet of one of those devastating ballads of dismemberment reads:

The heart is the toughest part of the body
Tenderness is in the hands.
("Because One Is Always Forgotten")

The bread-maker's hands are strong, rhythmic, and respectful of the "otherness' of an increasingly lively substance whose consistency is subtly programmed by an experienced human intelligence. No cookbook can tell you how. It's a process you have to develop a feel for. When an overly sticky dough invades the hands—helpless dismay, a taste of what it would be like to be passively trapped by a tar baby. At the other extreme, matter rears its stiff upper lip and retreats into that friable, clod-like obstinacy which we so often defensively project upon the world in other contexts. In the destructive element immerse? No! Rather up to the elbows in the glutinous, the albuminous! Look into what straits Conrad's advice has led us! The bread-maker discloses the recipe for a different type of heroism.

Grandma, come back, I forgot
How much lard for these rolls

Already in this first poem of her first volume Carolyn Forché establishes the eucharistic parameters of her moral world. It is an intentionality which offers itself willingly, and with a ready dexterity. To what? Ah, often to that which is on the way out, or walled up, to a vital ingredient in life that's missing.

I'll tell you I don't remember any kind of bread
Your wavy loaves of flesh
Stink through my sleep
The stars on your silk robes
("The Morning Baking")

Anna is the peasant ancestress, Queen of the poet's Revelations, whose hands—primary metonym of a working connectedness to the world—are imagined to be of that self-same material they manipulate.

Anna's hands were like wheat rolls
Shelling snow peas, Anna's hands
("Burning the Tomato Worms")

Years later, visiting Belgrade, the poet is haunted by visions of Anna:

hard yellow beans in her lap
her babushka of white summer cotton,
her eyes the hard pits of her past. . . .

Peeling her hands
with a paring knife, *saying in your country*
you have nothing

The hands of the ancestress have vegetatively rooted themselves in the old country from whose bourn the young traveller must return to make something come of nothing. Hamlet too was fat. And Anna always of great age and a prophetess:

Each word was the husk
of a vegetable tossed to the street
or a mountain rounded by trains
with cargoes of sheep dung and grief.
("Endurance")

What is Anna, through the poet as medium, trying to tell us, if we would only shut up and listen? Is it about love? Whatever it is we have to be patient, for, as the poet continually cautions, it takes a long time for voices to reach each other, to percolate through the loam of the country between us. Meanwhile, one readies the ingredients for lovemaking. . . .

I'd roll off my hands and let the wind come dust me, shape my pillow into Joey's chest and sleep. I work the dough between my fists, pull it back toward me, punch it then dust it with flour again. ("This Is Their Fault," *Gathering the Tribes)*

These are my breasts, your eyelids
on my throat, *are you hungry?*
("Taproot," *Gathering the Tribes)*

take our clothes
in our fingers and open
ourselves to their hands.
("Poem for Maya")

the tongues swishing
in my dress, some yours, some
left by other men.
("Reunion")

As if preparing a meal of herself, in poem after poem the poet is seen peeling her potatoes, unbuttoning her blouse, taking off her clothes. But what should be the prelude to a shaping, mutually self-constituting experience so often turns subjected to Salvadorian dismemberment. The hands of the jailors down there efface what they touch. The iron weapons but bestow the *coup de grâce*. And a lover's hands may lie because his heart is cold. For a while, the poet finds hope in a woman's mouth, which is "not different," and being akin is more than kind, but in the end it is "the stranger" with whom she would share that scrap of bread which is our transubstantiated "nothing."

Hers not the hand which seizes the part of fire, hers not the chameleon self which feeds on air, nor does she dive for safety into the depths of water. Carolyn Forché's erotic landscape is horizontal, its contours shaped by the intimacy (or the denial) of touch. It requires time and the vastness of the southwest to unfold itself:

The creator smoothed over the valley. The man and woman were quiet and their thoughts passed between them. These were of the substance of motionless wind., awake to the quiet, quiet within the hungry space of their presence. ("The Place That Is Feared I Inhabit," *Gathering the Tribes)*

But modern life reduces it to the size of a window box, to the space between rushing railway cars, to the confines of a hastily rented room (the same in every city).

how much tenderness we could
wedge between a stairwell
and a police lock
("Reunion")

What landlord is responsible for such a *lebensraum* of lock-up/bolt out?

In the long poem "Ourselves or Nothing," which concludes *The Country between Us*, Carolyn Forché gives us the portrait of a present-day Faust working night after night in a "ruined house" going after "that which is lost," a minute reconstruction of the ravages of the Holocaust, of the last hours of those who

turned to face the worst
straight-on, without sentiment or hope
simply to keep watch over life

But ironically, though this driven researcher's words, italicized, ring out strong and true, they come from beyond the pale, from beyond the bourn of that other country from which ghosts, moistening their dried lips with blood, speak to us. What the italicized voice on the page lacks is a body. The poet in memory walks through that house, impatiently smoking, her nightdress characteristically open, but the advocate of self-healing time, of didactic, politically committed poetry upon the slopes of *Parnassus*[1] doesn't even notice her. What is the meaning?

It is either the beginning or the end
of the world, and the choice is ourselves—
or nothing.

Notes

1. "Poetry in Dark Times," *Parnassus*, vol. 8, no. 2 (1980).

ROBERT FRANCIS

1901–

The son of a Baptist pastor of Irish descent, Robert Francis was born on August 12, 1901, in Upland, Pennsylvania. He was educated at Harvard University, receiving a B.A. in 1923, and taught for a year at the preparatory school of the American University of Beirut before returning to Harvard to take an Ed.M. in 1926. After only a year of teaching he decided to devote himself full time to his writing, though he had to supplement his meager income from poems and essays by giving violin lessons until 1942. Since 1926 he has lived in rural solitude in the Amherst area, from 1940 on in his own one-man house.

Francis' first book publication was *Stand with Me Here*, 1936, but he received little recognition even after his second volume, *Valhalla and Other Poems* (1938), made him co-recipient of the Shelley Memorial Award in 1939. A venture into fiction, *We Fly Away* (1948), was no more successful than his poetry, but his inclusion in the anthology *New Poems by American Poets* (1953) brought a change of fortune, and particularly since the appearance of a further volume of poems, *The Orb Weavers*, in 1960, he has been in demand as a lecturer and teacher at writers' workshops and colleges across the country, and has received numerous honors.

In 1957–58 Francis was the Prix de Rome Fellow of the American Academy of Arts and Letters, and the Amy Lowell Travelling Scholarship in 1967–68 gave him the opportunity to return to Italy, where he worked on his autobiography, *The Trouble with Francis* (1971). *Come Out into the Sun: Poems New and Selected* appeared in 1965, and *Collected Poems 1936–1976* in 1976. Francis' most recent poems were published in 1984 in *Butter Hill and Other Poems*, and he has also produced such essays as *The Satirical Rogue on Poetry* (1968) and *Pot Shots at Poetry* (1980).

"Man working"—the hand-lettered sign on the poet's door made me pause. I had barely begun to weigh the frustration of a wasted journey against the risk of becoming a latter-day person from Porlock when the door opened, and Robert Francis, tall, spare, white-haired, welcomed me in. . . .

Many of the poems and much of the prose that have filled Francis's books were written here, and at the age of 75, a year after the publication of his highly regarded *Collected Poems* by University of Massachusetts Press, it is here that he continues to work. Never before, in fact, has he been involved in so many projects: a second volume to his autobiography, a philosophical book, a piece on Emily Dickinson and an essay that will be the principal address at the Annual Meeting of the Thoreau Society in Concord. "And I do poems now and then," he was quick to add. "So you see, I'm not a retired person."

In the still seclusion of Fort Juniper—Francis's name for the cottage in Amherst, Massachusetts, where he has lived for nearly forty years—Thoreau seemed a natural subject. "I've never been a Thoreau scholar," the poet said, in a gentle, resonant voice. "I've never been a Thoreau follower. But it just happens that my life, my humble, obscure life, has somewhat paralleled his. So that people sometimes compare us—sometimes to my embarrassment. But Thoreau does figure. I've been aware of him, as sort of a stimulating and sustaining presence." He walked over to the bookcase, and indicated a little section of some half dozen books on Thoreau. "I don't do that for many writers," he said.

Surely, Thoreau would approve of the way Francis lives. For most of his life, he has made little money, and needed less. Living alone, he does his own cooking and cleaning, and takes care of his house and the land around it. In winter, all the heat for the cottage comes from the fireplace and the cast iron stove. When Francis had Fort Juniper built, it was very much in the country, in the corner of a cow pasture. "Indeed," he recalls, "for a year or two, cows continued to pasture around me, on one side or another." In the years since, the town has come closer: houses have taken the place of cows. But the trees that the poet has "encouraged" to grow up all around his dwelling screen Fort Juniper from the other houses and from Market Hill Road. As we talked, a flight of crows settled into the trees, and stridently punctuated the conversation.

Quietly, with a note of gratitude in his voice, Francis praised the life he has been able to live at Fort Juniper. "It is true that I have had to live simply and inexpensively to give myself to writing, rather than taking a paying job." (For over thirty years, even through lean times of obscurity, he has supported himself entirely by his work.) "If I wanted to be a writer, I just *had* to live simply. That's one reason I've lived this way, but the other is that I like it in itself. Poets have often praised this very thing—not destitution, but just enough to get along. Simplicity is not only a necessity, but it's an ideal, for the reasons that Thoreau taught and exemplified, an esthetic principle.

"I think this relates to my ideals in writing. I believe in clarity, in getting rid of superfluities. You know, if you can say a thing in a few words, it's really more effective than if you use a lot of words. I think in living, if you can make things simple, get along without a lot of junk, it's more satisfying esthetically as well as economically.

His way of life has given Francis the three things he needs for writing: "nature, leisure and solitude." By leisure, he is quick to explain, he means "not idleness, but the freedom to use my time for my own purposes." By solitude, "not isolation, but having periods when I am alone." As for nature, "it's important in living. You're surrounded by beauty, fresh air, quiet. If you live in such surroundings, it's only natural that you write about it, let nature stand. It's your vocabulary in writing. . . .

"I came to the conclusion that, for better or worse, being a poet was what I had to do, wanted to do, the most rewarding thing, and I had to keep on. I thought of myself as defended by three lines of defense. I couldn't command publication: this was something that other people determined. I could go on writing, doing my work, but I wasn't in full control of the success even of it. But I could live the life of a poet. I could live those values—introspection, observation, enjoyment of nature—out of which my poems grew. Nothing could prevent my doing that. I was completely in control. With that sense of an inner line of fortification that was impregnable, I managed to go on, and very soon after that I began to have some acceptances and some recognition.". . .

Apparently moved even at the recollection, Francis described a recent reading at Providence College. "When I had finished that reading they clapped and clapped till I thought they'd never stop. And yet," he paused reflectively, "the poetry they write is so different from mine. Why should they be enthusiastic about my poetry, which you'd think they would brush aside as old-fashioned? It's kind of a puzzle."

A puzzle? There is something in the unassuming simplicity of Francis's poems, their craftsmanship and poise, that transcends fashion. And surely there is much in Francis himself, a poet and a gentle man rejecting worldly satisfactions for the simple rewards of work, peace and beauty, to make him an attractive figure to young people who seek to find in their lives what he has made of his.

Not the least attractive aspect of Francis is the grace with which he bears his recent acclaim: he places himself behind his work. Recognition, he says, "has given me much more confidence that when I start to do a piece of writing that people are going to be interested. But I know that ultimately the power of my work is going to depend on the quality of my work, and that's out of my hands."

Among the trees that surround Fort Juniper is a thin red maple on which Wang Hui-Ming, a local poet and engraver carved three of Francis's poems. One of them, "Waxwings," illuminates the poet himself beyond all paraphrase:

> Four Tao philosophers as cedar waxwings
> chat on a February berrybush
> in sun, and I am one.
>
> Such merriment and such sobriety—
> the small wild fruit on the tall stalk—
> was this not always my true style?
>
> Above an elegance of snow, beneath
> a silk-blue sky a brotherhood of four
> birds. Can you mistake us?
>
> To sun, to feast, and to converse
> and all together—for this I have abandoned
> all my other lives.
>
> —CARL E. SHERMAN, "Man Working," *BF*, 1977, pp. 436–40

In an era of the Avant-Avant-Garde, Robert Francis, who can be passionate without being puffy, is a poet daringly Horatian. *Ars celare artem*. The art is to hide the art. Like Herbert or Herrick a technician, a metrical Swiss-watchmaker, fond of the chime and the golden cogs, he happily relishes versing. His poems wound us cleanly by their diminutive and lovely precisions.

Consider, because it has so much to say on the matter, his poem "Excellence." Little seems at first to astonish. The words are plain, the syntax easy. The meaning seems a truth so common we need hardly acknowledge it. The athletic metaphor earns its force by being obvious. But the poem sticks in the mind and its phrases come to hand. "From poor to good is great. From good to best is small." The simplicity of the elements makes the precision, when at last we attend, surprising.

Not many poets are worth scanning, and only a few, a very few, make it delightful. Here's how it might go for "Excellence":

> (x) Éx|cĕllĕ(ńce)|ĭs míl|lĭmé|tĕrs (á)nd|(nó)t míles.
>
> Frŏm póor|tŏ góod|ĭs gréat.|Frŏm góod|tŏ bést|ĭs smáll.
>
> Frŏm ál|mŏst bést|tŏ bést|(só)metímes|(nó)t méas|ŭ(rá)|blĕ.
>
> Thĕ mán|whŏ léaps|thĕ hígh|ĕst léaps|pĕrháps|ăn ínch
>
> Ăbóve|thĕ rún|nĕr-úp.|Hów glór|i(óu)s|thát ínch
>
> Ănd thát|splít-séc|ŏnd lóng|ĕr (í)n|thĕ áir|bĕfóre|thĕ fáll.

The first surprise is that the poet has chosen hexameters for a poem about legerity. The headless first line—(x) Éx|cĕll(é)nce—at first disguises the choice. Perhaps the line, with its alliteration, gave Francis the meter. Having said that to himself, or written it down, he had at least to consider writing the poem in hexameters. He might have changed to "Excellence is inches and not miles" for a lighter, pentameter line. (As he uses "inch" later in the poem, it wouldn't have been out of place.) But the poem, we realize, is less about the jumper's ease than about his difficulty, the long training, the extra effort that earns excellence, that buys "that split-second longer in the air." Possibly because hexameter feels as though it goes a little beyond the pentameter norm of English—seems to have to somehow push its way to its end—it was a perfect choice.

Having made that choice, the poet exploits it beautifully, especially in the last line where, after we have become accustomed to lines of six feet, he pushes yet a little farther and ends with a heptameter. We don't see that extra length because the words are shorter; but we hear it. The line lasts in the ear just a split-second longer than the others.

Once we begin noticing, the poem grows richer and richer in meaning. It isn't only the handy alliteration that makes "millimeters and not miles" so exact and contrasting, but the short "i" of "mil-" and the long "i" of "miles." In line 2, the unrelenting monosyllables and the caesura suggest the distance between "poor" and "best," a distance that can only be crossed by such a dogged pace as the line itself has. In line 3, the almost completely unaccented secondary accent of the word "measurable," followed by the unaccented feminine syllable, blurs the beat so much that we almost have to force the voice to record it. (We can't bring ourselves to say "MÉAS-ŭr-Áblĕ.") And so, coming after the nearly level accents of "bést| (só)metimes|(nó)t méas-," the line's end mimes the meaning of "not measurable." Even the slight temptation to hear an off-rhyme of "-ble" with "miles" and "small"—and so to displace the accent falsely onto that syllable—reenforces the effect. The run-on from line 4 to line 5, the poem's first, marks the effort, the spring. The more static second run-on, from line 5 to line 6, and the clustering of accents in the first half of the sentence fragment, followed by the light accent of "(í)n | thĕ áir," give the final line its appropriate rhythm.

Robert Francis' poems are filled with such minor, hidden exactness that bring the poems alive to the ear and so to the attentive mind. The wonderfully elusive syntax of "The Base Stealer" is such an effect, or that poem's gaily metered last line, which leans backward until the very end and forces us to scan it "Délĭcăte,|délĭcăte,|délĭcăte,|délĭcăte—|(x)nów!" Or the knuckle-ball off-rhyming of "Pitcher," which keeps us unsure the poem's couplets are being rhymed until the final

> Not to, yet still, still to communicate
> Making the batter understand too late.

Or the dazzlingly unlikely "rhyme" words of "Hallelujah: A Sestina": *Hallelujah*, *boy*, *hair*, *praise*, *father*, and *Ebenezer*, which Francis turns and returns with apparent ease.

A reader may well feel, perhaps due to the word "meters" buried in "millimeters," that "Excellence" is also, intentionally, about poetry. Several of Francis' poems about sports suggest a similar resonance. In "Catch," for instance: "Two boys uncoached are tossing a poem together, / Overhand, underhand, backhand, sleight of hand, every hand, /. . . to outwit the prosy." "Pitcher," "The Base Stealer," "High Diver," and "Sailboat, Your Secret" offer tempting symbols of the poet's craft and methods, as do "Skier" ("He swings down like the flourish of a pen") and of course "Apple Peeler" (the spiral of peel is "Like a trick sonnet in one long, versatile sentence"). They make a delicious cluster.

Small though Francis' poems mostly are, and unpretentious, they are magical. Not the least of the magic is the almost unnoticed "formality and formal ease" by means of which the poet so slyly and surely gets the rabbits *into* the hat.—ROBERT WALLACE, "The Excellence of 'Excellence,'" *Field*, Fall 1981, pp. 16–18

JOHN HOLMES
From "Constants Carried Forward: Naturalness in Robert Francis' Poems"

Massachusetts Review, August 1960, pp. 766–74

The Orb Weaver is a book that adds an almost-lost quality to modern American poetry. This quality is the finality and naturalness, so unassertive as to be simply there, not to have been devised, of a poem that is thought through, worked through, and then kept for contemplation of its wholeness, for a long time before it is displayed in print. I read the manuscript of this book years ago, and so have some of the poet's friends. There was nothing hasty about it, nor about any of the poems in it, nor any of the lines in any of the poems. Not many poets nowadays in their platform appearances can say their poems without book or typescript in hand. Robert Francis has all his poems in his head, where they were made. When he says his poems to an audience, it is as if he is listening, too; the testing and polishing goes on a long time. But I am sure his poems have been talked walking, talked eating, or falling asleep, talked to himself over and over until there are no seams of grammar showing, no stiffness of moving parts, no hollows in logic or expectation, long before any audience hears them. It is hard for me not to be metaphorical about it, as he often is, but if he were a woodcarver, he is the patient kind who puts the finished piece where it gets a good light. He looks at it for months, for years, sometimes taking the knife to it again. When it is sold, it has not only been finished, it has taken on its color in depth, and wholly claimed its shape. But he says this better in the poem "Glass":

> Words of a poem should be glass
> But glass so simple-subtle its shape
> Is nothing but the shape of what it holds.
>
> A glass spun for itself is empty,
> Brittle, at best Venetian trinket.
> Embossed glass hides the poem or its absence.
>
> Words should be looked through, should be windows.
> The best word were invisible.
> The poem is the thing the poet thinks.
>
> If the impossible were not
> And if the glass, only the glass,
> Could be removed, the poem would remain.

Much of today's poetry has the quality of intensity and surprise, delivered with skillful, flourishing thrust. One gets the point, and is left dazed by the attack. But as time has been used to make the poems in this book, time itself is one of the ingredients. They do not burst in the reader's mind, they grow. This poet has all the time in the world to look at and into a thing or a feeling, and he takes it. When he has looked enough, there is nothing more to be seen. We say in critical approval of poetic technique that the writer exhausts the image he has chosen, meaning that he has employed all its possibilities and aspects. Robert Francis does that, but what he does should not be described that way. He exhausts the object, the quality, or the movement. His best poems are not merely technically completed and polished, they contain everything there is about it, so that, as he says, if the words were taken away, the subject would be there.

This complete containment is perhaps most obvious in "Gold," which, because the poet must gather from many instances the goldenness he rejoices in, seems a catalogue. But we do not check off the examples, though we see each one. We feel gold, all the gold there is.

> Suddenly all the gold I ever wanted
> Let loose and fell on me. A storm of gold
> Starting with rain a quick sun catches falling
> And in the rain (fall within fall) a whirl
> Of yellow leaves, glitter of paper nuggets.
>
> And there were puddles the sun was winking at
> And fountains saucy with goldfish, fantails, sunfish,
> And trout slipping in streams it would be insult
> To call gold and, trailing their incandescent
> Fingers, meteors and a swimming moon.
>
> Flowers of course. Chrysanthemums and clouds
> Of twisted cool witch-hazel and marigolds,
> Late dandelions and all the goldenrods.
> And bees all pollen and honey, wasps gold-banded
> And hornets dangling their legs, cruising the sun.
>
> The luminous birds, goldfinches and orioles,
> Were gone or going, leaving some of their gold
> Behind in near-gold, off-gold, ultra-golden
> Beeches, birches, maples, apples. And under
> The appletrees the lost, the long-lost names.
>
> Pumpkins and squashes heaped in a cold-gold sunset—
> Oh, I was crushed like Croesus, Midas-smothered
> And I died in a maple-fall a boy was raking
> Nightward to burst all bonfire-gold together—
> And leave at last in a thin blue prayer of smoke.

A very Francis kind of wording comes in the third line of the next to last stanza of this poem, and runs into the fourth. It seems to me that in "near-gold, off-gold, ultra-golden," we catch him at work, seeing, remembering, completing all the gradations and kinds of gold there are. The way he carries the action onward from the golden-sounding, gold-colored birds, to their motion, to gold in the apples, and trees, and to names of old apples is part of still another skill. But in the third and fourth lines the vowels in *near, off*, and *ultra*, then the consonants in *beeches, birches, maples, apples*—with of course consonants helping vowels, and vowels helping consonants—is one of those times when Francis is walking his poem, trying it, saying it, turning it. No one else can know how long he was in finding all the words and sentence-movement. But the rain caught in sun, and leaves in the sun and rain, is not easy to write, nor could "saucy" have come quickly to mind, nor the self-control of "Flowers of course."

When the subject of the poem is movement, this poet's eye looks often at the action itself, and each time further into the intention, so that when he makes the poem "Pitcher," it is a naming of inner qualities, purposes, strategies. Somehow it is all the more a poem of constant action, and the reader does the pitching because he knows why he is doing it.

> His art is eccentricity, his aim
> How not to hit the mark he seems to aim at,
>
> His passion how to avoid the obvious,
> His technique how to vary the avoidance.
>
> The others throw to be comprehended. He
> Throws to be a moment misunderstood.
>
> Yet not too much. Not errant, wild,
> But every seeming aberration willed.
>
> Not to, yet still, still to communicate
> Making the batter understand too late.

The ingredient of time is in this poem, too. None of these definings came in a flash. Pitchers were watched through many innings of many games, and the exact word for the purpose behind several kinds of movements, in different situations in the game, were noted and considered. Robert Francis brings the long look back to poetry, in a most un-twentieth-century way. Often it gives us poems about sports, or physical action, several about baseball, as "Catch" and "The Base Stealer," and others like "Two Wrestlers," "Swimmer," "High Diver," and "The Rock Climbers," and in every one he gets us inside the player's skin.

As much as most poets do, Robert Francis uses anecdote, or narrative, as a framework for a poem. Yet he is never merely anecdotal, nor dependent only on narration, and it would need deep digging to uncover any moralizing. What is good, that is, not evil, is total realization of the object, almost any object. There is not much recorded evil in Robert Francis' world, yet one has a feeling that this infinitely wary, moccasin-footed, sharp-eyed poet is on guard against it all the time. By implication, it is a wrong not to notice the world, not to give the world a long look, not to see all its surface, and all the under-meaning. Not to see would be a kind of murder by carelessness, or by indifference. If perceiving and telling a sort of small story, a fragment of happening, will save life, of course he will tell it, and then it becomes an example of something worth saving. He is totally on the side of life. . . .

Robert Francis' poems have in a high degree the fulfillment of expectation raised. It is present because of the long, close observation, the life-giving look, the full report of the senses, and the patience—qualities already named. I have another extraordinarily vivid memory of hearing him read a poem, again from his 1944 book, called "Serpent as Vine." It is an incident, anecdote maybe. At any rate it begins with immediacy, "Once I observed—" and we are there, with him. I hear his voice again, making it more real than I can be sure it would be for me on the page, if I had not heard it.

> Once I observed a serpent climb a tree.
> Just once. It went up twisting like a vine,
> Around, around, then out across a branch,
> And though it went up faster than a vine,
> It did not seem to hurry as it went.
>
> And having reached a certain bough, it lay
> As quiet as a vine. I could not tell
> Its secret there among the summer leaves.
> But what I knew I knew exceedingly well:
> That something underfoot was overhead.

The "just once" is the startlement of coming on the sight, while walking in the woods. The natural likeness to make in that surprise is to a vine, but second thought, and the first expectation fulfilled, comes at once, with "And though it went up faster than a vine." In the pause between stanzas, I shivered, tense and waiting for what the snake would do next. "And having reached a certain bough, it lay as quiet as a vine." Most likely, of course, but unpredictable; and then nothing, the unknowable snake. Then the human reaction, not of the walker in the woods, but in the world gone wrong—"something underfoot was overhead." This is masterly brief, and a prime example of Robert Francis' power, the delayed thrust that goes deep, then deeper.

In the next to last line of the serpent poem is a touch of a characteristic of this poet, the repetition, with a turn in meaning, of the same or similar or suggested-expected rhyming word. This is a kind of trademark in Robert Francis' poems, as we say of a person's habitual mannerism. This particular thing comes, I think, out of his unhurried way of finding and using words. In this self-given leisure there is room enough for some play, playfulness, playing—some saying and trying nearby words. Suddenly he sees that they enlarge his meaning, add to the music of the poem, and then throw criss-cross beams of extra meaning because he has placed them where they reflect each other's glint. Beyond the delight this multiplicity gives the reader is the awareness yet again that in the world of Robert Francis there need be no haste. Doom does not hover, time is not running out, there is all the world to look at, and all the time in the world to look. We have nearly forgotten this. Robert Francis is no exhorter, and not overt as a teacher. He is an example, and even in this never looks over his shoulder to see if anyone is noticing him. . . .

All of Robert Francis' wit, skill, warmth, and life-sense come together in "Hallelujah: A Sestina," a poem which will surely rejoice every reader of this book, as it surely did those friends of the poet who had it last Christmas from him. His father recurs in his poems, in this and the other books, a figure of strength and excellence. His father was the tenth child of the family, named Ebenezer, but the son's love and joy in him was such that he wishes in this poem a different name for fitness, not one that means Stone of Help.

> A wind's word, the Hebrew Hallelujah.
> I wonder they never give it to a boy
> (Hal for short) boy with wind-wild hair.
> It means Praise God, as well it should since praise
> Is what God's for. Why didn't they call my father
> Hallelujah instead of Ebenezer?

Turning and turning through all the possibilities of names, choice and no choice of names, being a boy, becoming a father, praising God and father, the poem runs exuberantly through the six and a half stanzas required. Incidentally the old fixed form is shaken loose, shot full of new life, and set running in the wind, love and joy in the wind of the generations. A few times in a poet's life, maybe for some only once, along comes the poem he was born to write. This is one of the poems Robert Francis was born to write. All his particularities come together, at the height of his liveliest manner, on a subject long and deep in his life and personality. It ends:

> But what I'm coming to—Could I ever praise
> My father half enough for being a father
> Who let me be myself? Sing hallelujah.
> Preacher he was with a prophet's head of hair
> And what but a prophet's name was Ebenezer,
> However little I guessed it as a boy?
>
> Outlandish names of course are never a boy's
> Choice. And it takes time to learn to praise.
> Stones of Help is the meaning of Ebenezer,
> Stone of Help—what fitter name for my father?
> Always the Stone of Help however his hair
> Might graduate from black to Hallelujah.
>
> Such is the old drama of boy and father.
> Praise from a grayhead now with thinning hair.
> Sing Ebenezer, Robert, sing Hallelujah!

The qualities that have made Robert Francis known to poets are of course the same that will be enjoyed for a long time by his readers. First of all, the poems are readable, because they have life in them. They have been slowly and thoughtfully made, and kept until ready to go out on their own. They have, as one important ingredient, time. Time went into the making, and one feels a freedom and quiet and amplitude in reading them. The poems satisfy every expectation they create, as a work of art in any medium should. As the poet has delighted in discovering words that belong in the poem, the reader feels his own pleasure in finding them unexpectedly and rightfully there. Serious as he can sometimes be, Robert Francis can often be amused and amusing, joyfully saying so. He is that rare figure in present-day poetry, both a poet's poet and a reader's poet.

HOWARD NELSON
From "Moving Unnoticed: Notes on Robert Francis's Poetry"
Hollins Critic, October 1977, pp. 1–11

I

September, 1976, marked the publication of the *Collected Poems* of an American poet who at seventy-six has written quietly over the past half-century a body of poems which deserves to be celebrated. The poet is Robert Francis. His career was long characterized by a lack of recognition—Robert Frost called him America's "best neglected poet"—and even after the publication of *The Orb Weaver* by Wesleyan in 1960 and *Come Out into the Sun* by the University of Massachusetts in 1968 helped change this situation to some degree, his work has continued to be omitted from most of the anthologies which have tried to represent the best contemporary American poetry. It seems to me that any sampling of "the best" of our poetry that doesn't include Francis is incomplete.

Since 1940 Francis has lived in a small house on the outskirts of Amherst, Massachusetts, which he calls Fort Juniper, liking the tenacity and naturalness the name suggests. He has taken Thoreau more literally than most of the rest of us have dared, not only appreciating some of his attitudes, but taking up the practical challenge of achieving independence and integrity through simplicity as well. He has lived alone, foregone many of the luxuries we have learned to consider necessities, earned only enough money to meet the demands of his frugal budget, lived philosophically in Thoreau's sense of the word ("To be a philosopher is not merely to have subtle thoughts, nor even to found a school, but so to love wisdom as to live according to its dictates, a life of simplicity, independence, magnanimity, and trust."—"Economy"); and written poetry.

In poetry as in living, his path and style have been governed by a spirit of independence and radical common sense. When Thoreau set out to go his own way at Walden, he looked around him and into tradition and selected a few basic tools and resources he found sound and useful—an ax, some boards he could unwarp in the sun, a copy of Homer. Similarly, Francis has founded his poetry on a few simple, solid, timeless poetic values.

In the experimentation and vital restlessness of the American poetry of the past twenty years or so, certain basic poetic values—e.g., music, clarity of statement, the calm light of a reflective mind, a polished surface—have often been overshadowed or shunted aside. Not without a certain growing interest of his own in more open variations of form, Francis throughout his career has been calmly stubborn in his devotion to a kind of poem that exists in the currents of literary experiment and opinion like a smooth, deeply imbedded stone in a stream: the short, clear, meditative, lyrical poem. Francis has followed no poetic movements but those of his own imagination, and he has become a master of this kind of poem.

II

On the question of attitude toward language, modern American poetry has tended to polarize. On one side there is the movement, with William Carlos Williams as its master, into language that is plain, stripped of ornament and allusion, and colloquial. Increasingly the dominant mode in the last twenty years, this approach is perpetually vital in the right hands, but often leads to verbal flatness and boredom as well. Reading even accomplished poets, as with some of the Black Mountain poets twenty years later, we sometimes feel as if we are experiencing a long drought, and yearn for the "simple, colloquial" language to give way to a single memorable, beautiful phrase.

At the other pole are poets who favor a more imposing language, who feel that language itself is the prime concern in poetry, and sometimes say it is in fact the ultimate subject of poetry. This attitude sometimes produces poetry that lodges itself permanently in the imagination, lines whose vividness or originality or music seem to present us with "what will suffice." Everyone is too familiar, however, with this kind of craft when it is nothing more than craft—the poetry of a brilliant shallowness, self-conscious cleverness, conspicuous sounds that resonate only for a second. Either attitude toward language can produce a form of dullness.

Robert Francis transforms the dichotomy into a paradox. Like most true poets, he is good at living with paradoxes. He has written poems on both sides of the qestion.

GLASS

Words of a poem should be glass
But glass so simple-subtle its shape
Is nothing but the shape of what it holds.

A glass spun for itself is empty.
Brittle, at best Venetian trinket.
Embossed glass hides the poem or its absence.

Words should be looked through, should be windows.
The best word were invisible.
The poem is the thing the poet thinks.

If the impossible were not.
And if the glass, only the glass,
Could be removed, the poem would remain.

Reading through Francis's poetry, one of the most strongly pervasive qualities one notices is the clarity, the subtle lustre, of the language. The poems have certainly been polished, but toward a greater transparence and directness rather than glittering effects. The language is fresh, exact, attractive, but it rarely stops the reader in his tracks, not for overcleverness, nor obscurity, nor even a sudden stab of power. (Emily Dickinson often stops her reader dead every line or so.) Francis's diction is lucid. He almost never sacrifices the movement or clarity of a poem for complicated phrases or images. "Glass" itself is a good example of language that falls away, silent and transparent. The lines are clear, clean, declarative. The only place the diction begins to clink a little—"Venetian trinket"—is in the second stanza, where poetry made from such language is being described. The poem's rhetoric is quiet—parallelisms that we hear but which would move easily through ordinary conversation.

Then in a recent poem, "Poppycock," Francis precisely contradicts the statement of "Glass." The poem is a celebration of the delicious eccentricity of words, and concludes with these lines:

But to get back to poppycock
what a word!
God, what a word!
Just the word!

Keep your damn poems
only give me the words
they are made of.
Poppycock!

The poem is not a very good one—Francis has a playfulness that sometimes turns cute, and then soft spots appear—but those closing lines express an important element in his poetry: his relish for language, the weight of it on the tongue, the texture of it in the mind. While his love of words themselves at times leads him into preciousness and ornament, more often it helps him to become a *namer:* one of those poets—such as Whitman could be, enumerating the objects of the world, the "dumb, beautiful ministers"—whose noticing and mentioning of a thing captures the resonance a poem needs, whose naming is an act of creation and love. Here is a poem which exemplifies the way Francis notices language and the world he is describing both—almost as if they were one thing.

REMIND ME OF APPLES

When the cicada celebrates the heat,
Intoning that tomorrow and today
Are only yesterday with the same dust
To dust on plantain and on roadside yarrow—
Remind me, someone, of the apples coming,
Cold in the dew of deep October grass,
A prophecy of snow in their white flesh.

In the long haze of dog days, or by night
When thunder growls and prowls but will not go
Or come, I lose the memory of apples.
Name me the names, the goldens, russets, sweets,
Pippin and blue pearmain and seek-no-further
And the lost apples on forgotten farms
And the wild pasture apples of no name.

Here is another poem—in a form Francis calls "fragmented surface," abandoning grammar and discursiveness—a poem which takes him deep into pure naming.

SILENT POEM

backroad leafmold stonewall chipmunk
underbrush grapevine woodchuck shadblow

woodsmoke cowbarn honeysuckle woodpile
sawhorse bucksaw outhouse wellsweep

backdoor flagstone bulkhead buttermilk
candlestick ragrug firedog brownbread

hilltop outcrop cowbell buttercup
whetstone Thunderstorm pitchfork steeplebush

gristmill millstone cornmeal waterwheel
watercress buckwheat firefly jewelweed

gravestone groundpine windbreak bedrock
weathercock snowfall starlight cockcrow

Such a poem might serve to answer the complaint of those who think Francis is too traditional or backward-looking in his form. But "Silent Poem" is actually among the most backward-looking of poems: it takes poetry back to that condition of quiet and wonder when sounds were first formed and linked to objects of the world, when every word was fresh and a poem.

In less skilled and loving hands, such a poem would become a curiosity or an exercise. As rendered by Francis's subtle hands, it has become beautiful poetry. Few poets have made silence, both external and internal, so palpable.

If there is poetry that celebrates words, and poetry that tries to make words disappear, then Francis has written poems that could be assigned to one category or the other, but in most of his poetry he accomplishes the paradox of language which seems to move in both directions at once, to a degree not many modern poets have been able to sustain. Almost always there is in Francis's poetry the savor of the balance between memorable language and a relaxed lucidity.

III

There is a quality of crispness in Francis's work. Partly it derives from his clear eye, his closely observed imagery. His use of imagery is steady and sure, never bizarre or spectacular. An inward man by nature and lifestyle, when Francis writes of inward things, he carries the solidity and delicacy of the things of the world with him.

The crispness comes also from Francis's ear. Compared to most recent poetry, Francis's work is unfashionably musical. The general abandonment of rhyme and meter in the last decade has been a healthy thing for our poetry, helping many of our best poets to do their most authentic and moving work. But the reaction against measured, regular music has led eventually to a scarcity of strong verbal music of any kind. There has been some strong music returning in recent years in the work of black poets such as Etheridge Knight and Lucille Clifton, with its use of the fundamental repetitions of oral poetry, but many of our prominent poets now have developed ears so subtle and reactionary that almost any speech is musical enough for them.

Early and late, Francis has been a lyrical poet. Many of his poems have the small, sharp music of epigrams and couplets, but his poetry also has more flowing rhythms and the more beautiful and haunting music of older repetitions—alliteration, assonance, refrain—and often they are quietly chant-like.

LIKE GHOSTS OF EAGLES

The Indians have mostly gone
but not before they named the rivers
the rivers flow on
and the names of the rivers flow with them
  Susquehanna Shenandoah

The rivers are now polluted plundered
but not the names of the rivers
cool and inviolate as ever
pure as on the morning of creation
  Tennessee Tombigbee

If the rivers themselves should ever perish
I think the names will somehow somewhere hover
like ghosts of eagles
those mighty whisperers
  Missouri Mississippi

And there is the clarity of his intelligence. There is a wonderful crispness in Francis's thinking in his poems—the sense of a mind that has been given a long time to work, for the ideas to grow slowly, like crystals.

Many of Francis's poems are poems of direct, rational statement. This sort of poem seems especially prone to becoming stiff and unmysterious. Yvor Winters is the outstanding example of a poet whose dedication to reason gave his poems a grave, graven quality. But this kind of thinking in poems of course has a beauty of its own. Francis's grasp is firm and sure, but there is nothing stiff or didactic in its strength and precision. . . .

Francis is frequently a poet of wit, both in the modern and the Seventeenth Century sense of the word. It leads him sometimes to light verse—some of it, the recent poem "History" for example, very keen, some of it merely light. It also leads him to some of his finest poems. Here is a poem based on an elaborate metaphor, but the intelligence works with such smoothness that the connotations of the word "conceit" do not apply at all.

SWIMMER

I

Observe how he negotiates his way
With trust and the least violence, making
The stranger friend, the enemy ally.
The depth that could destroy gently supports him.
With water he defends himself from water.
Danger he leans on, rests in. The drowning sea
Is all he has between himself and drowning.

II

What lover ever lay more mutually
With his beloved, his always-reaching arms
Stroking in smooth and powerful caresses?
Some drown in love as in dark water, and some
By love are strongly held as the green sea
Now holds the swimmer. Indolently he turns
To float.—The swimmer floats, the lover sleeps.

Happily Francis's *Collected Poems* is already incomplete: he continues to produce excellent work. In 1976 he published a collection called *A Certain Distance*, which includes previously published poems but is primarily made up of prose poems—"portraits and sketches . . . done in words" Francis calls them—collected for the first time. The pieces in the book are contemplations and celebrations of young men. As Francis moves to the looser form of the prose poem, he retains the poise and perception of his poems written in verse. I want to include a brief prosepoem here, because it represents new work published so far only in a limited edition, and because when a poet writes about art he makes a statement relevant to his own art.

TENOR

As rare as an absolutely cloudless day
is the tenor who achieves his high notes without
any sense of strain. Who does not climb, strive,
and reach for them but simply floats up.
In opera, of course, a tenor like the bass
or baritone must at all times be dramatic,
assertive, asserting in addition to all else
his virility. He throbs, he sobs, he all but
splits a gut.
With the throbbing tenor I do not identify.
But in that happy instance when a tenor merely
lifts to a high note I too am lifted.

IV

I haven't talked directly about content.

Francis has no ideology or personal mythology, but his work has a great pervasive theme. This is one of the major themes of modern poetry especially, the theme of Williams and Stevens, of Richard Wilbur and Gary Snyder, in their different ways: the engagement of the imagination and the actual, poetry's effort to focus the material world in a new light and make us more awake to it. Francis's poems are mostly about *things*, observations, actions, seasons: bells, and earthworm, a sailboat, blueberries, a wasp: a baserunner about to steal, old men gathering apples, a man diving for coins, and another diving for "Some uncouth thing/That we could swear . . . / Was never born/Or could ever be/Anywhere. . . .": April thunder, summer dog-days, the year's cooling, blue winter. His poems only occasionally discuss this theme: continually, they embody it. He uses the things of the world for symbolic and moral purposes, but this is simply a part of the interplay of mind and subject, of the homage to awareness and the world. Since there is no heaven, we had better pay attention to the earth. . . .

In the poem "Statement," Francis avows his devotion to earthly rather than any ideal beauty, and says "I want a beauty I must dig for. . . ./I am in love with what resists my loving./ With what I have to labor to make live." This supports what I've said above, but it also brings to mind one of the limitations of Francis's poetry. The things that he writes about are commonplace and plain enough, but they are not things which require the greatest labor to love and make live. Imaginative renderings and meditations on juniper bushes and baseball players are welcome, but Francis stops about there in pursuing the lowly and the ordinary. One of the fine things about Williams is his insistence on including the ugly and forsaken in his poetic vision, which Francis does not do. He is a bit too decorous to do so.

Another theme which Francis has written on often is death, and he has done many beautiful poems on the subject. Reading such poems as "The Quiet Thing," "Past Tense," and "When I Come," one notices especially their calm, their clear-headedness and restraint. This is an admirable quality in elegiac poems, but it is part of another, related limitation, that of emotional intensity and range. Francis is not a poet of the depths and heights of emotion. His poems, whether acknowledgements of evil or expressions of joy, have an air of controlled grace. There is little if any terror or despair or exaltation in them. They lack the kind of power strong grief can give. This reserve is, of course, a matter of principle for Francis, as the poem about the tenor and others in praise of artists, workers, and athletes whose effectiveness lies in their control and self-possession suggest.

This is not at all to say that Francis's poetry is not moving. Within the reserve, a marvelous sensitivity, an eloquence of emotion, is present. . . .

V

Some of Francis's poems are aimed primarily at the ear, some at the eye: some are satiric, some are straightforward celebrations: some are discursive, some are "silent." Central to his work, however, is that it brings music and image, a steady light of the mind and things simple and mysterious, together into a union, a wholeness. Francis provides a valuable counterpoint to the solipsism of much of our poetry now. There is a nice irony in the *Collected Poems* of this lucid, uncelebrated poet having appeared in the year that John Ashbery won the prizes.

There is a magnificence in poets—like Hart Crane or Galway Kinnel—who strain a lyric genius toward something epic or transcendent. But there is another kind of beauty in poets who write short, lyrical, haunting, moving, clear, clarifying poems all their lives. In such poems there is a union of sense and sound, thought and feeling, that implies a union and condition of aliveness that might exist in human beings as well. This is the work this poet has done for us.

MARY E. WILKINS FREEMAN

1852–1930

Late in life Mary E. Wilkins Freeman claimed to have been born on October 31, 1862, but the true date was a decade earlier. She was the daughter of a Randolph, Massachusetts, architect, Warren E. Wilkins, and his wife Eleanor Lothrop Wilkins. Both parents were of a long line of New Englanders. Freeman was a fragile child, and received most of her education at home. Because of ill health she was only able to attend Mount Holyoke Seminary for a year. But Freeman was an enthusiastic reader, and she gave herself a broad, albeit spotty, education which may have made for the peculiar originality of her own works. She began publishing children's verses, but turned to adult stories in order to support herself and an elderly aunt. By the time she was thirty Freeman had lost all the rest of her family and was a professional writer by necessity. She served as secretary to Oliver Wendell Holmes, Sr., and entered the Massachusetts literary society. Her collection of stories, *A New England Nun*, was published in 1891, and it established her reputation. Her first novel, *Jane Field*, appeared in 1893. Volumes of short and long fiction tumbled from her pen every few months over the next ten years.

She married Dr. Charles Manning Freeman in 1902. Although she had been prolific, Freeman wrote less and less after her marriage. She lived with her husband in Metuchen, New Jersey, until her death on March 13, 1930.

I confess I find her tales delightful, and I often read them, but as you know I am not content to rest on my own pleasure in literary criticism. We are no longer talking of the great masterpieces, of the gigantic achievements of such men as Homer, Sophocles, Rabelais, Cervantes; we agreed that when we spoke of these great, enduring miracles of art, it was best to lay aside all question of liking or not liking, of reading often or reading seldom. But when one comes to modern days, to books which have yet to prove their merit by the test of their endurance, it is pardonable if one is sometimes a little confused, if one fails to discriminate at once between the merely interesting and the really artistic. I may be so delighted with a book for reasons that have nothing to do with art, that, by an unconscious trick of the mind, I persuade myself that I am reading literature while there is only reading-matter. And at one time I was inclined to think that I had "confused" Miss Wilkins in this manner. For, on the surface, you have in her books merely village tales of New Englanders, tales often sentimental, often trivial enough, and sometimes, it would seem, of scarcely more than local interest. Hardly can one conceive the possibility of any ecstasy in these pleasant stories; for they deal, ostentatiously, with the surface of things, with a breed of Englishmen whose chief pride it was to hide away and smother all those passions and emotions which are the peculiar mark of man as man.

Yet, I believe that I can justify my love of Miss Wilkins's work on a higher ground than that of mere liking. In the first place I agree with Mr. T. P. O'Connor, who pointed out very well that the passion does come through the reserve, and occasionally in the most volcanic manner. He selects a scene from *Pembroke*, in which the young people play at some dancing game called Copenhagen, and Mr. O'Connor shows that though the boys and girls of Pembroke knew nothing of it, they were really animated by the spirit of the Bacchanals, that the fire and glow of passion of the youthful ecstasy burst through all the hard crusts of Calvinism and New England reserve. And we have agreed that if a writer can make passion for us, if he can create the image of the eternal human ecstasy, we have agreed that in such a case the writer is an artist.

But I think that there are other things, more subtle, more delicately hinted things in Miss Wilkins's tales; or rather I should say that they are all pervaded and filled with an emotion which I can hardly think that the writer has realised. Well, I find it difficult to express exactly what I mean, but I think that the whole impression which one receives from these tales is one of loneliness, of isolation. Compare Miss Wilkins with Jane Austen, the New England stories with *Pride and Prejudice*. You might imagine, at first, that in one case as in the other there is a sense of retirement, of separation from the world, that Miss Austen's heroines are as remote from the great streams and whirlpools of life as any Jane Field or Charlotte of Massachusetts. But in reality this is not so. The people in the English novels are in no sense remote; they are merely dull; they cannot be remote, indeed, since they are not human beings at all but merely the representatives of certain superficial manners and tricks of manner which were common in the rural England of a hundred years ago. "Remoteness" is an affection of the soul, and wicker-figures, dressed up in the clothes of a period, cannot have any such affections predicated of them; and consequently though Emma or Elizabeth may appear very quaint to us from the contrast between the manners of this century and the last, they cannot be remote. But that does seem to me the quality of those books of Miss Wilkins's; the people appear to be very far off from the world, to live in an isolated sphere, and each one lives his own life, and dwells apart with his own soul, and in spite of all the trivial chatter and circumstance of the village one feels that each is a human being moved by eminently human affections.—ARTHUR MACHEN, *Hieroglyphics: A Note upon Ecstasy in Literature* (1902), 1923, pp. 151–54

From the religious intolerance of Cotton Mather to the imaginative isolation of Hawthorne and from that to the nervous impotence of Mrs. Freeman's men and women, is a regular progress. The great preacher sought to suppress all worldly emotions; the artist made of the solitude which follows this suppression one of the tragic symbols of human destiny; the living novelist portrays a people in whom some native spring of action has been dried up, and who suffer in a dumb, unreasoning inability to express any outreaching passion of the heart or to surrender to any common impulse of the body. It is true, of course, that Mrs. Freeman describes only a single phase of New England character, just as Hawthorne did before her; but the very genealogy of her genius shows that she has laid hold of an essential trait of that character, and, indeed, it needs but little acquaintance with the stagnant towns of coast and mountains to have met more than one of the people of her books actual in the flesh. Her stories are not tragic in the ordinary sense of the word; they have no universal meaning and contain no problem of the struggle between human desires and the human will, or between the will and the burden of circumstances. They are, as it were, the echo of a tragedy long ago enacted; they touch the heart with the faint pathos of flowers pressed and withered in a book, which, found by chance, awaken the vague recollection of outlived emotions. They are very beautiful in their own way, but they are thoroughly provincial, just as the treatises of Cotton Mather were provincial; they have passed from the imagination to the nerves.

Already in Hawthorne we find the beginnings of this strangely repressed life. Hepzibah Pyncheon, struggling in an agony of shame and impotence to submit to the rude contact of the world, is the true parent of all those stiffened, lonely women that haunt the scenes of Mrs. Freeman's little stage. Only there is this signal difference: poor, blighted Hepzibah is part of a great drama of the conscience which in its brooding over the curse of ancestral sin can only be compared with the Atë of the Æschylean theatre. All the characters that move within the shadow of that *House of the Seven Gables* are involved in one tragic idea assimilated by the author's imagination from the religious inheritance of the society about him—the idea that pride, whether worldly or unworldly, works out its penalty in the separation of the possessor from the common heart of humanity. But in Mrs. Freeman's tales this moral has utterly vanished; they have no significance beyond the pathos of the lonely desolation depicted. Her first book, *A Humble Romance*, is made up of these frustrate lives, which are withheld by some incomprehensible paralysis of the heart from accepting the ordinary joys of humanity, and her latest book, *The Givers*, appeals to our sympathy by the same shadow of a fore-gone tragedy.—PAUL ELMER MORE, "Hawthorne: Looking Before and After," *Shelburne Essays: Second Series*, 1905, pp. 180–82

In the year when Boston was celebrating three hundred glorious years Mary Wilkins Freeman died. Newspapers and literary journals outside Boston noticed her death but made little of it. All her important work was done thirty years ago; her body had outlived her power and her reputation, and she had passed into literary history as a writer of village tales once admired but no longer read. Her genius was original, not of a school. Her traceable forerunners in New England, mostly women, Rose Terry Cooke and Harriet Beecher Stowe of *Oldtown Folks*, were more sentimental, and let their tears leak into their stories. Mary Wilkins had no tears except the tears of things. And theories of style and construction would have puzzled her, except for such elementary matters as correct syntax and accuracy in the use of words, which she had learned and taught in a strict schoolroom. She must have been bewildered and perhaps was spoiled later by the praise of too literary critics who said that her story, "A Village Lear," was worthy of Maupassant. Probably she was not aware of the existence of Russian writers who were digging into hard soil and narrow lives and finding values at once local and universal. Her material was close at hand, plain and simple; she had the genius to see it and render it objectively. Her stories are as primitive as folk-tales and almost as anonymous. This does not mean that she was a blind genius stumbling on masterpieces by the grace of God. She knew her material thoroughly, believed in it intensely, and early discovered what she could do with it. She repeated a score of times the unmistakable Mary Wilkins story, did it more and more deliberately, until finally fame overtook her and she became too much aware of herself as a literary person. Then the young Mary Wilkins died and the older woman produced nothing memorable. Perhaps she had exhausted her real material.

Her material is the village, partly stricken with senility by weakening emigrations of youth to the West and to neighbouring cities, and not yet modernized by the city influences which have obliterated old-fashioned country characteristics. Mary Wilkins does not see and convey the idyllic charm of the village or its lighter comedy; she is no humorist. She feels the pathos, the tragedy, the hardness, the bitterness of village life, but she does not hold her people up to pity or scorn. There is no bitterness in her own attitude and not a touch of deliberate satire. So far as her personality shows at all, she is rather timid and tender. The gentle woman merely records a grimness for which she is not responsible, in limited and thwarted lives which she understands but does not wilfully create. It would be more difficult to read a life of her into her stories, or from them, than to conjecture the shadowy biography of Emily Dickinson from her poems. The lingo of our time would deal with Mary Wilkins and her characters in terms of "repressions", of libidos confined in narrow human barrels with the bungs driven in tight by a Puritan mallet. Some critics have noted a resemblance between the contours of her characters and her angular bony phrasing. This may mean simply that her style fits her substance. Her phrasing is economical and unadorned, but it is easy, flexible, muscular, both when it reproduces the talk of her people and when it is her own essential pure English. She has neither the grace of Miss Jewett nor the poetry of Miss Alice Brown, but at times the hard, unlovely substance is wrought into an exquisitely delicate fabric. Mary Wilkins never defends the dignity of New England country folk, as Miss Jewett does, or questions the value of the life about her. She merely accepts it and lets it speak for itself. Only an artist can do that.—JOHN MACY, "The Passing of the Yankee," *Bkm*, Aug. 1931, pp. 617–18

Mary E. Wilkins, if one read between her lines, revealed, if not its terribleness, at least its strength; and there was a certain truth in Louise Imogen Guiney's phrase,—she was "a sort of sordid Æschylus." There was something fierce and primitive in her view of life, and the Furies existed for her, and for her, in the laws of range sublime, there was a mighty god that grew not old. It was a pity that her later books obscured the stories of her prime. Tragic at first, they became pathetic and often sentimental,—because Miss Wilkins had a village mind. As long as she wrote in terms of the village, she possessed the village integrity and all the grand inheritance of the Puritan faith; and this gave her a profundity that made her point of view, at moments, all but universal. But when she attempted to write novels, for which she was not qualified, and when she dealt with other than village types, she lost her universality and, along with this, the integrity that sprang from her village birthright. She did not understand the types Miss Jewett understood so well, the more cultivated life of the "mansion-houses," where the women wore "blue-lavender silk" instead of the calico dresses she knew, or instead of the "one black silk that stood alone." Her attitude towards all this was that of the other village women, resentful yet romantically dazzled; and as, with success, she moved from her early position and outgrew her resentment of the rich, her romantic admiration of them took the upper hand and she lost her hold on the verities for which she had spoken. She became unreal and self-conscious in the presence of high life, regarding which she was driven to write too much, and she cut her people to fit the story instead of letting the story spring out of the people. But in some of her early tales, perhaps twenty or thirty, she was an eminent artist, as eminent as Miss Jewett, and even more so, because of the depth of feeling that informed her art. In one sense, Miss Wilkins warranted all the laments of Boston. She revealed the desolation of the Yankee ebb-tide. But, better than anyone else, she also pictured the powers of last resistance in the Yankee soul. Was the Yankee soul at bay? At least, its lights were burning,—this was the fact at the heart of Miss Wilkins's tales. It was quick to fight for its self-respect, and even for perfection, whatever the odds might be and whatever its fate.

. . . Underneath Miss Wilkins's village something lurked that was still sublime, although it was true that the village guarded its secret. It exacted from fate every last penny of tribute. Those who, like many Bostonians, were already disheartened found evidence in Miss Wilkins's dun-coloured stories to suppose that Yankeeland had come to an end. Perhaps it had, on the old basis; and there was always the chance that it could not react any longer to new conditions. It may have been pushed to the wall and beyond the wall. But is it not a law of life that, the more it is repressed, the more intense the will to live becomes,—provided it is able to survive at all,—and that if, at last, it finds an outlet, it expresses itself in proportion to its former repression? What fate was in store for New England? Were the Barrett Wendells right? Was its prospect really as dark as Miss Wilkins seemed to show it? In so far as writers counted, the prospect was reassuring; for writers emerging all over the region were to suggest before long that the Yankee stock was hale and as virile as ever. They were a proof that the real New England was not to be found in the Barrett Wendells or in what Miss Wilkins's stories appeared to show. They proved that the reality was what Miss Wilkins really showed, in her plain, stark, factual tales.—VAN WYCK BROOKS, "Country Pictures," *New England: Indian Summer 1865–1915*, 1940, pp. 464–73

AUSTIN WARREN

From "Mary E. Wilkins (1852–1930)"
The New England Conscience
1966, pp. 158–69

In a Wilkins village, the women—widows and spinsters—outnumber the men: a young woman has to think three times before she rejects an offer of marriage. And the men, such as they are, are weaker than the women: less determined of character, less sharply defined. The older women—many if not most of them—are what New England calls 'characters.' They are mostly genteelly poor. Think of the huge meals Dickens' people eat, and then of the supper in a Wilkins' lady's cottage: some thinly sliced white bread, a glass saucer of currants, a pot of tea. The Babcock sisters (in "A Gala Dress") lack even the saucer of currants, or its equivalent; and "No sauce for tea was regarded as very poor living by the village women." To have an egg is a luxury. Cruder folk (like men and Matilda Jennings—also in "A Gala Dress") may have salt pork, cold potatoes, baked beans, or mackerel. But these are concessions to the flesh.

The Wilkins people have all been "brought up on the rigid New England plan"—the one I not only remember but feel. It *seemed absolute morality*; it was actually, I can take in, though I but imperfectly feel it, only *a morality:* one which antedated even the approach to the Socialized State ('social security' and the like) which the United States had reached by 1965. According to the "rigid New England plan," a mortgage is an immorality; buying anything on 'the installment plan' is immoral: one shouldn't buy anything until he can pay the full price in 'ready money.' Increasing one's income by investment (however conservative) in stocks and bonds is immoral. Perhaps the most solemn injunction of this now archaic New England morality is that it is immoral "to be beholden" to anyone. Loans, gifts, and charity are not to be accepted. What one can't pay for in cash or reciprocity of services rendered (estimated in terms of time and money), one goes without: "I have my pride."

Pride: how ambivalent that quality is among the genteel poor. In that context it can hardly be called a great splendid 'deadly sin.' Without it Miss Wilkins' women would lose their desire to live, their psychic *structure*. It may be founded on faint distinctions and on the slight eminences, social, mental and artistic (the "Village Singer," the village "Poetess," the "Old Arithmetician," who, having a "faculty" and "gift" for ciphering, solves a sum the young male high-school teacher can't solve); the pride of the "Independent Thinker," who, too deaf to hear the sermon, doesn't go to church but works defiantly at her knitting, the proceeds from which go, anonymously, to help the very neighbor who censures her for not keeping the Sabbath; but fundamentally it seems a willingness to suffer for nonconformity to standards which one cannot accept.

This is an 'Orthodox' community in the New England sense: there is no Unitarian Church which has, legally, stolen the white meetinghouse on the green and the communion silver. The old ladies, whether they 'go to meeting' or not, read a chapter in the Bible before bedtime. The Ten Commandments are as real as the New England rocks and hills: especially, thou shalt not steal; thou shalt not covet thy neighbor's goods; thou shalt not bear false witness; honor thy father and thy mother, and more especially thy mother.

As the 'bed-rock' beneath any such specificities is the First and Greatest Commandment, Thou Ought. It's your Duty. How charmingly ingenuous and supernaturally innocent is that quatrain of Emerson's learned at 'school':

So nigh is grandeur to our dust
  So near is God to man
When Duty whispers low, 'Thou must',
  The youth replies, 'I can'.

Easy for Emerson; but how hard for the battered and worn, who hesitatingly say, "It's my Dooty and I must do it," or who, like Ann Millet (a cat her only "Object of Love"), says its ritual equivalent.

As Ann looks at her squashes (upon which she and her pussy cat, Willy, feed), she says to herself, " 'A splendid lot they *air* . . . I'd *orter to be thankful*' " "Ann always spoke of her *obligation to duty*"—her duty to duty—"and never seemed to think of herself as performing the duty itself. 'I'd *orter* be thankful', said she always."

I have written of nonconformist pride, the pride of what, in the title of one of her stories, Miss Wilkins calls the "Independent Thinker." In its own way, this is the Thoreauvian pride at "signing off" from a society, or the rules of a society, which one does not accept. It seems to say, "Every man *ought to be* an island to himself"—or perhaps we should add, a mountain, or at least a hill. Emerson says—so elegantly and urbanely that the bark *and bite* may be missed—"We *descend to meet*"—one of those half-truths salutary in certain contexts. But this fine utterance is perhaps less true than the opposite half-truth, that we ascend to meet: we put on our best Sunday clothes and try to behave and think and talk better than our solitary routine.

A friend used to say to me when we were both young, "Only the strong can love the strong"; and his axiom much impressed me. One can argue, of course, that strength is not all of the same kind; and in real friendship or real marriage one of the partners is strong in one way and the other in another: they pool their strengths.

But, on the whole, I have no wish to argue or to subtilize. We must be selves, possessed of a proper degree of self-love and self-respect, before we can, in any real way, love others. You must have a self before you can give it away. To a neurotic, Jesus' saying, "Thou shalt love thy neighbor as theyself," is high, lofty, and so on but baffling—because one can't love oneself with that normal degree of self-love and self-respect which the injunction seems to presuppose.

'Neurotic pride' (which keeps people going but which also isolates them) has, finally, to be broken down—if not through a "breakdown" through a public confession. Secret penance is inadequate. Penitence—a different thing—involves confession to the one we have wronged, either to the wronged one or, ideally, to the community, and involves restitution. A wrong we have done is not only a 'sin against God' and a wrong against our particular neighbor but a wrong against society, or community, that which constitutes an organic continuum between the individual and God. Touching examples drawn from Miss Wilkins' tales are "A Stolen Christmas," "Calla-Lilies and Hannah" (with confession before the church congregation), and "Sister Liddy" (who, dying in the almshouse, has to confess that, not having once 'had' and now 'lost' 'things'—having no past glories or connections about which to boast—she has invented the sister upon whose surpassing grandeur she has dilated to her fellow inmates).

Something approximating a majority of Miss Wilkins' stories seem to me to deal with 'cases of conscience'—that is, with situations in which the protagonist is confronted with principles or duties which present rival claims. As—in latter-day Protestantism at least—one can tell what one's duty is by its giving neither pleasure or joy, but, at the most, a kind of grim self-approbation—it is fair to say that Wilkins women do not always recognize that they are confronted with 'rival duties'—though a Jesuit or an Anglican like Bishop Jeremy Taylor or Bishop Kirk would certainly say that they were. Self-fulfillment is—if abstractly put—as much a duty as 'self-sacrifice.' It is as much a duty to receive—especially with grateful grace—as it is to give (something often done in New England with such absence of tenderness or delicacy that one would be grateful indeed not to have to be "beholden").

The habitual problems of conscience for fairly decent people less concern the "struggle between good and evil"—or virtue and sin—than they do that of finding, in a particular case, which good principle should be allowed precedence over which other good principle. And as for "sin"—the practical problem (as the 'permissive' psychiatrist, at least, knows—and doubtless the wise and generous priest as well) is that if one can't keep every jot and tittle of the Law (and who can?) it is better to commit the venial rather than the 'mortal' or 'deadly' sin. Your principles, to be sure, ought to be clear, but your application of them should be flexible.

But, as Anglican Bishop Kirk's *Conscience and Its Problems* should make clear—not, indeed, to the subtle and sinuous though entirely sincere John Henry Newman, who wouldn't need it, but to his manly and muscularly Christian opponent, Charles Kingsley—the province of casuistry, rightly understood, is coterminous with practical ethics (that is, the adjustment of collisions between *duties*; the sensible and sensitive judgment of how to apply more or less permanent 'principles' to 'situations' or 'cases' which constantly vary).

Most of Henry James's short stories and *novellas* deal with 'cases of conscience,' but with such cases as exist at relatively high social, intellectual, and moral altitudes. Miss Wilkins' stories, which deal with the 'genteel poor' and 'humble folk,' show that casuistry has no social or intellectual limitation to its scope.

Perhaps these 'cases' (what might, more simply, be called 'moral problems') are—like psychiatric treatment—easier to manage with people of a relatively high intelligence—and with a clergyman or an equivalent person of relatively high intelligence and intuition: it is notable that the Protestant clergymen in Miss Wilkins' tales are practically useless as analysts and counsellors. But over this 'perhaps' I hesitate, knowing all the ways that intelligence can avoid and evade the simplest moral obligations; how you can be too smart for your own good, and too brilliant to be wise,—knowing also that the counsellor need not be more brilliant than the counselled, but must be more steadfast, more balanced, more centered.

The fact remains that Wilkins people have little guidance from without. They are all Bible readers; but they certainly show the comparative uselessness of Bible-reading unaccompanied by interpretative theology,—Bible-reading, that is, of texts read uncontextually. It seems that—as with the ancestral New England Puritans who landed on "the stern and rock-bound coast"—it is the Old Testament rather than the New, the Law rather than the Gospel, which, chiefly, they have understood. And it follows, I think, that in the 'cases of conscience' Miss Wilkins gives us, it is often a struggle between the authority of the Old Testament (as her people understand it) and something they don't think of as 'religious' at all—the voice of common sense, the voice of private conscience, the voice of 'charity'—that is, of love.

Apposite is the story "Gentian," told almost entirely from the point of view of Lucy Tollet, the elderly wife of Alfred Tollet. "Alferd," the household autocrat, has all his life been very healthy; but now, all spring, he complains of "great depression and languor" and has not attempted to work in his garden. His wife can't induce him to see a doctor; as she tells her sister, "Alferd was allus jest so. He ain't never thought nothin' of doctors, nor doctors' stuff."

Lucy's unmarried sister, to whom she reports, has her own brand of impatience with "Alferd" and theories. If he won't see a doctor, he should certainly be made to "take somethin'"—"Somethin' bitter"—probably gentian. Says sister Hannah, "I'd make him, ef I put it in his tea unbeknownst to him"; and Hannah continues, "I don't *believe in deceivin' generally*, but I don't believe the Lord would hev let folk hed the *faculty* for deceivin' in 'em ef it wan't to be used fur good sometimes."

Lucy takes Hannah's advice—only, as "Alferd" complains of the tea tasting bitter, she takes to putting little sprinklings of it in the bread, pies, and everything she cooks. And Alfred immediately begins to be better, and by September is as hearty as ever. "But his wife seemed to lose as he gained. . . . She did *not go to church at all*, and she had been a devout church-goer."

Lucy is unable to take, with 'good conscience,' the sister's casuistical advice upon which, with results so beneficial to her old husband, she has acted. And finally she bursts out in confession to her sister: "I deceived him, an' it's been 'most killin' me to think on't ever since." And then Lucy feels compelled to confess to her husband—whereupon, first, he will eat nothing she cooks, and, shortly after, he allows her to go to live with her sister.

The ending of the story is perhaps here irrelevant—though it is psychologically sound to New England character. After a separation of autumn and winter, Lucy visits her own house and begs her husband, standing there with his hat, to let her return. He sends her back to her sister's, though with a new tone in his voice. In a few minutes her husband appears, obstinate in carrying out his ritual idea that it is he who should confess and beg forgiveness. "I've come to ask you to come home, Lucy. I'm a-feelin' kinder poorly this spring, an'—I want you ter stew me up a little gentian. What you give me afore did me a sight of good." Certainly, the love behind it, the love which prompted Lucy to do something so contrary to her conscience as to deceive—that love had done him "a world of good."

Pride can easily beget solitude: one isn't willing to bow to one's superiors, nor associate with one's inferiors; and—in a village, at least, with its small distinctions of eminence and lowness—it is difficult to think of others who are admitted to be one's equals. This is not to say that solitude begets pride; but that, too, is a 'genealogy of morals' which could be illustrated out of Helen Wadell's wonderful *Desert Fathers*, the early Christian hermits of Egypt.

There is an extraordinary short story of Miss Wilkins which I long overlooked—perhaps because of its deviation from type. It is about an isolated *man;* and its 'chorus' is not that of village women but of that 'club' of rural philosophers and yarn-spinners who make the 'general store' their headquarters; and it comes nearer to the explicitness of a 'moral' than any other I can remember—a 'moral' not merely of this story but of all the stories one could tell, whether about New England or India.

For six years, Nicholas Gunn, once married, had lived alone in an unheated cabin distant from the village. During a snowstorm, he sits at his open door, as "calmly passive . . . as a Buddhist monk." He leads a thoroughly ascetic life. Though he has a stove, he makes himself eat his hasty pudding cold. Though he has a cot bed, he sleeps "rolled in a blanket, on the bare floor." He reads his Bible by the light of a candle. Whatever the cause of his eccentricities—whether "mystical religious fervor" or "his own personal sorrows, [he] would have been revered and worshipped as a saintly ascetic among some nations." But in his native New England, he was ridiculed as either a "darned fool" or "cracked."

Reiterated circumstance forces his conscience to take in—to adopt—a feeble and consumptive old peddler whose half-sister is going to commit him to the poor farm.

The reluctant host tries to explain how he became an ascetic. Having had "lots of trouble," "mainly through folks I set by," he had figured out that if he didn't care anything for anybody he wouldn't have trouble from them, and if he didn't care anything about himself he wouldn't have any trouble from that quarter. "I kept cold when I wanted to be warm, an' warm when I wanted to be cold. I didn't eat anything I liked, an' I left things around that hurt me to see." He read the Bible because he no longer believed in it, and so reading it made him feel worse. "I did about everything I could to spite myself an' get all the feelin' out of me. . . ."

But now the ex-hermit sees that his solution was wrong, though he expresses his change of mind in a characteristically New England way, a negatively toned version of Margaret Fuller's exuberant, conceited, and un-New England declaration—her "I accept the universe." Nicholas Gunn says of the 'world,' of life, with its unpredictable anxieties and pains, "I've got to go through with the whole of it *like other folks*, an' I guess I've got grit enough. I've made up my mind that men's tracks cover the whole world, and there ain't standin'-room outside of 'em. I've got to go with the rest."

Miss Wilkins does not spoil the ending of the story, despite two closing paragraphs which give a mildly poetic and symbolic sign that a 'conversion experience' has taken place. She keeps her balance steady by a maxim of her own, less picturesque and more abstract than Gunn's speech. His guest, she says, "did not in the least understand him, *but that did not matter.* There is a *higher*"—delightful substitute for the expected *lower*—or even *deeper*—"There is a higher congeniality than that of mutual understanding; there is that of need and supply."

Miss Wilkins' stories are not autobiographical. She wrote the best of them while she was a spinster, yet not (like her *New England Nun*) vowed by her habits to celibacy, only waiting—waiting, in her case, till she married in her late forties the handsome Dr. Freeman of Metuchen, New Jersey. Her family were genteelly poor Congregationalists; and she wrote to support herself, not primarily to be 'creative,' as Sarah Orne Jewett professed to do, or to defend village people ('the natives,' as they were called in my youth) against the patronage of 'summer boarders.' Yet she had the conscience of a literary craftsman. Her stories have neither extraneous descriptive passages exhibiting her own sensibility nor passages (such as Mrs. Stowe, in her exuberance, poured out) explaining the New England character or expositing its theologies. There are few words, let alone sentences, which one would like to cross out as 'redundant.' She is spare and stripped, like Maupassant, whom she surely read, and the later Tolstoi, for whose "Three Lives" she expressed admiration. Best of all, in contrast to the Miss Jewett of *Country of the Pointed Firs*, Miss Wilkins does not tell her tales from the point of view of a city visitor, however sympathetic, nor swathe the dialogue of her characters in her own prose: her stories are almost entirely told in dialogue.

Her literary objectivity may have been helped by her own unromantic character. To one woman friend she deeply cared about, she wrote—in an undated but fairly early letter, "You are fond of people, and I never have been." In the sense she meant it, this was always true of her: she was *interested* by people and their motives—as devoid of hostility or satire as of "fondness." And this extended into something even rarer: she could view herself and own life and the ups and downs of her 'bachelor days' and her not particularly fortunate marriage as though they all belonged to somebody else.

As for her personal involvement in the ethical rigorism and scrupulosity she so often narratively described, the best testimony is a letter she wrote about her year at Mount Holyoke in 1870, twenty years after the death of Mary Lyon, its celebrated founder, under whom Emily Dickinson suffered and stood her own ground: "As I remember, I did not behave as well at Mount Holyoke; and I am inclined to attribute it to monotony of diet and *too strenuous goadings* of conscience."

Miss Wilkins' mind, like that of Henry James (who read her first two and best collections with admiration), was not "violated by ideas." She was neither a rebel against New England orthodoxy nor a belated and belligerent advocate of it. Nicholas Gunn's speech in "A Solitary," negative and cautious as it is, is singularly abstract for her, who was—strange to say of one who, at a certain level, knew New England so well—not at all a theoretician. If her common sense and moderation are not more quickly observed, it is because her nature was so much that of an artist that she can glow with the aberrations—understood but scarcely shared—of her characters.

Bruce Jay Friedman

1930–

Bruce Jay Friedman was born on April 26, 1930, in the Bronx, New York, where he also grew up. After taking a degree in journalism at the University of Missouri, he saw military service with the U.S. Air Force, being discharged as a first lieutenant in 1953. Having joined the Magazine Management Company as an editorial director in 1954, he had spells as executive editor in charge of *Men*, *Male*, and *Man's World* before devoting himself full time to his own writing in 1966.

Friedman's first novel, *Stern*, was published in 1962, setting the tone for his wildly humorous fiction and plays about Jewish characters. Further novels include *A Mother's Kisses* (1964), *The Dick* (1970), and *About Harry Towns* (1974). His short fiction first appeared in *Far from the City of Class and Other Stories* (1963) and in 1965 he edited the anthology *Black Humor*. More of his own stories were published in *Black Angels* (1966).

Friedman has had a number of plays produced off-Broadway, notably *Scuba Duba: A Tense Comedy*, which enjoyed a successful run from 1967 to 1969, *Steambath* (1970), *First Offenders* (1973), and *A Foot in the Door* (1979). He has also written screenplays, and a volume of anecdotes and satire, *The Lonely Guy's Book of Life* (1978).

Friedman has been married once, and has three children. He lives in New York.

Although *Time* magazine described Bruce Jay Friedman's *Stern* as a novel "in the tradition of the Jewish *schlemiel* story and the Charlie Chaplin movie," and its author as a Jewish protagonist, *Stern* was a satire too angry, a farce too anguished, ever to reach the American screen; Stern himself has precisely nothing to do with the legendary ghetto chump; and Friedman is not a Jewish protagonist.

In placing Friedman in the "The Whole World Looks Jewish When You're In Love" school of Norman Podhoretz and Gertrude Berg, *Time's* appraisers missed by a margin as wide as if they had identified LeRoi Jones with Uncle Remus. *Stern* is not about Jewishness; it is about un-Jewishness.

> When the Seder began, Uncle Sweets would take long difficult passages to himself, which gave him an opportunity to hit high notes galore, but soon Uncle Mackie would break in with great clamor, doing a series of heroic-sounding but clashing chants that seemed to have been developed outdoors in Arizona. Uncle Sweets would stop and say to him, "What the hell do you know? You shit in your hat in Phoenix." And Uncle Mackie would fly at him, saying, "I'll kick your two-bit ass through the window." . . . And thus the curtain would come down on another religious holiday.

The time when the East 10th Street kitchen was a sanctuary that returned, by evening, the dignity lost in the day's humiliations, is past: and all the greenery of suburbia cannot bring it back. Indeed, a task force of caterpillars ravage Stern's suburban greenery as if they had been sent, while his neighbors' gardens bloom unblighted. Who sends caterpillars?

In his own country, Stern lives in a far-off land. Of his ancestral heritage nothing remains but an ancient shame. Neither his wife nor his father nor a friend speak to him as though he were related to them. Masterless dogs arrest him.

> On the second night of the estate-crossing, it was not quite so dark as it was to be later on, and Stern was able to see two thin, huge dogs vault a fence and make for him with a whistling sound. They skimmed through the night and came to an abrupt halt at his feet, their gums drawn back, teeth white, both high above his waist. One took Stern's wrist between his teeth and the two animals, hugging close to his side, walked with him between them, as though they were guards taking a man to prison. He tried not to perspire, having heard you showed your fear that way. They walked him until the dog released his wrist, which was soaking wet; then both turned and went back, trotting swiftly through the night.

Friedman has nothing of the cleverness of Roth; he lacks Bellow's intellectualism altogether. Unlike Malamud, his people don't even have connections to a life of the past. Their severance is demonstrated by Stern's own hallucinatory progress. For he embodies not tradition but disorder, the disorder of the great city. And Stern's way marks the end of a time, for American multitudes, when each man belonged to the company of men. "Plunged in torment plunged in fire"—Friedman's sources, if he must be categorized, are nearer to those of Beckett than to his New York colleagues. His people were weak in the head when they came into the world. It is Stern who drags along at the end of Pozzo's rope. And when Stern enters the Grove Rest Home for the cure of an ulcer ("a hairy coarse-tufted little animal that squawked for nourishment") we are truly among those whose birth was astride a grave.

"A guy has to have freedom," a tall youth with flaring pimples assures Stern at Grove Rest, "the whole trouble with everything is there's always somebody stepping on your head when you're eating a bowl of kraut. You live, you live. You die, you die. Only thing I care about is old guys not pushing me around."

The difference between Friedman and Beckett is that while Beckett assigns a separate ash can to each of his characters, Friedman uses no props: his people simply live ash-can lives. Grove Rest itself is such a can, electrified and provided with cots, through which time alternates not between day and night but between Pill-and-Bandage Time and Milk-and-Cookie Time. . . .

The satire is sustained in Friedman's second volume, *Far from the City of Class*. In one of these stories, "A Foot in the Door," the author has adapted the Faustian legend to the burlesque stage, in a take-off of the values that propel The Young Man on the Way Up. Here the ambitious *petit-bourgeois*, Gordon, is seduced by his insurance man, Merz, into giving up his hair in return for Merz's word that Gordon's rival, in a race for office promotion, will be put out of the running. Gordon's hair falls out within a month, and the rival is shipped to Dubuque. As Gordon's gains in money and prestige increase, his emotional life is diminished until he has no love left in his life. Here, Friedman has put the Biblical wisdom, that he who gains his life must lose it, into fresh phrasing: "Beware of what you ask for—you may get it."

The same sense of loss, and of longing to belong, invests his current novel, *A Mother's Kisses*. "Wait till you have to say hello to life," the 17-year-old Joseph's mother warns him, "have you got surprises coming. Take a look over your shoulder and see what's really coming." . . .

What makes Friedman more interesting than most of Malamud, Roth and Bellow is the sense he affords of possibilities larger than the doings and undoings of the Jewish urban bourgeois, which, after all, comprises but an infinitesimal aspect of American life. What makes him more important is that he writes out of the viscera instead of the cerebrum. What makes him more dangerous is that while they distribute prose designed by careful planning for careful living, Friedman really doesn't know what he's doing. "I can remember being inside Mommy," Stern's infant son tells him, "I knew about the Three Stooges in there."

Bruce Jay Friedman is that rarity, a compulsive writer whose innocence makes his flaws of greater value, ultimately, than the perfections of skilled mechanics.—NELSON ALGREN, "The Radical Innocent," *Nation*, Sept. 21, 1964, pp. 142–43

Bruce Jay Friedman, who is two years older than Updike, has published two novels, and now we have his second collection of short stories, *Black Angels*. I liked his first novel, *Stern*, though I was not so extravagantly enthusiastic about it as Stanley Edgar Hyman, perhaps because, as Hyman suggested, the humor is likely to have a special appeal for Jewish readers. Parts of *A Mother's Kisses* seemed to me very funny indeed, but I felt that the joke was worn out some time before the novel ended. Yet, despite reservations, I was impressed by Friedman's orginality and talent, and I was eager to read the stories in *Black Angels*.

Friedman takes more risks than Updike and has a larger percentage of failures. Many of the stories are fantasies, some startlingly successful, some not quite successful enough. In the title story a man who is in domestic and financial difficulties is rescued by a quartet of Negro handymen, miraculously efficient and incredibly cheap. The reader has no doubt that the arrangement is too good to last, but Friedman's ending is a walloping surprise. In "The Investor" a man's temperature follows the fluctuations of a particular stock. It is a crazy idea but amusing, and again the question is whether Friedman can create an adequate climax; he does so, in the tradition of the tall story, by topping a wild idea with an even wilder one. One of the less successful fantasies is "Show Biz Connections," in which the wild idea is too far out to hold the reader's interest. In "The Mission" the idea is ingeniously developed, but the story turns out to be too much like a television gag.

In "The Interview" the fantasies exist only in the mind of the main character, who, as he interviews a candidate for a job, invents for her an excitingly lurid past. In "Brazzaville Teenager" a young man acts out his own fantasy. "Let Me See Faces" is a monologue, somewhat in the old Dorothy Parker manner, in which a woman of doubtful virtue and uninhibited speech tells us about her dreams and her actions. Perhaps the greatest surprise of all is "A Change in Plans," in which the expected twist never comes.

In Albee's *Who's Afraid of Virginia Woolf?* George informs his younger colleague that you can't tell the difference between illusion and reality and it doesn't matter anyhow. But in practical affairs at any rate the difference does matter, and one has to make the distinction as well as one can. Many contemporary writers have discovered that fantasy is one way of apprehending as much reality as we are capable of coping with, and Friedman is one of them. He is sometimes playful, as of course he has a right to be; but in the best of the stories he is grappling with human reality.

Friedman has much to learn about problems of his craft that Updike seems to have mastered soon after he got out of diapers, but he is a lively and interesting writer with an unusual kind of imagination. Updike's stories give great pleasure because of their technical perfection, but they don't offer many surprises. This is the last thing one could say about the stories in *Black Angels*.—GRANVILLE HICKS, "Domestic Felicity?," *SR*, Sept. 24, 1966, pp. 31–32

For some writers, particularly Americans, fiction seems to have taken on a special function in the last decade or so. Besides fulfilling its traditional relations with the reader, it has become a means for the author himself to cope with life. The very writing seems to be the author's means of making it possible for him to live, serving as exorcism of the era's dark spirits and as resolution of the nebulous.

This phenomenon has been especially manifested in the mode called black humor. One definition of black humor—a term now so commonplace and loosely used that we ought to keep redefining it—is the perception of what is funny in the terrible. Barth and Barthelme, Southern and Heller share at least this characteristic: much of their satire is not the traditional effort of sane men to purge the world of insanity, putting a fix on it, and attempting to mark out a *cordon sanitaire* of laughter. These men seem to be saying, "If you can look at the scary stuff from this angle, at least you can get a few laughs out of it, possibly not go crazy, and perhaps make your way through your life in a casually decent way."

No young writer is more frightened than Bruce Jay Friedman. From the first pages of his first novel, *Stern*, he has been using fiction as juju—to control or appease or amuse the pressing uglinesses of modern life. Superfluously, I note that his work is such good art that it also functions for us or else he would be a mere autistic diarist; but Friedman's public work seems to be Friedman's personal charm and rabbit's foot, making it (presumably) possible to feel fairly safe among the Boygs of our era. *Stern*, movingly and bitterly, fixes—one may say, immobilizes—the ridiculousness of anti-Semitism and the way it can make Jews ridiculous. In his first book of stories, *Far from the City of Class*, assorted fears and fallacies are tickled into momentary lulls. In his second novel, *A Mother's Kisses*, he depicts the possessiveness of motherhood as a hilarious horror, with the Bosch-like image of a young man tied by an unbilical cord to a gaping womb that he drags after him as he flees it.

Now Friedman publishes a book of stories, *Black Angels*, in which he pushes, or is pushed, past black humor into black fantasy. In the past, like other black humorists, he has had fantastic visions of reality; most of these new stories are realistic visions of fantasy. He fixes on particular dreads or threats, highly recognizable and depicted highly realistically; then without a lapse in naturalistic method, he pushes them into imaginative amplification that makes them more, not less, vivid: yet somehow kept at a safe distance. They have been magnified in effect on the panavision screen of imagination, but at least they are not—at the moment—flying all about our heads down in the audience.

For example, the title story of the book concerns a suburbanite, deserted by his wife and child, who hires some Negro gardeners to tend his lawn. They work well and taciturnly but charge him so very little that he is embarrassed and pays them more than they ask. He gives them other work—painting his house, and so on; again they say little, work well, charge almost nothing. Their silence and content at last bring his guilt and loneliness to a boil. He invites the chief of the bunch in for a beer and just starts talking to him. He feels better for the talking and asks the Negro "just for fun" what he would charge by the hour to listen. Instantly the Negro, whose gardening rates have been low, replies, "Fo' hunnid." When the white man remonstrates, the Negro starts to leave. The white man relents, agrees to pay, and asks whether this first hour counts. "'It do,' said the Negro, sinking into the couch and snapping out a pad and pencil."

Far off and happily out of the reach of clinical dissection is a mysterious nimbus, combining racial assumptions, economic injustice, the loneliness of a foolishly patterned life, the stolid inevitability of the conquest by the genial natural of the neurotic unnatural. All these elements are quickened in a story that is fantastic, yet whose every syllable, as far as stenographic ear is concerned, might come from John O'Hara.

In varying ways this paradox applies to many of the other stories. "The Investor" ties the movement of a sick man's fever to the movements of a stock on the Exchange, point by point, up or down. While it is being splittingly funny and of course fantastic, it is dealing in truths about money-grubbing and doctoring and sex, and such other matters as life and death.

The sharpness of Friedman's distilling imagination, his power to grasp large and ancient intangibles through corners of the ludicrous present, are nowhere better shown than in "Brazzaville Teen-ager." Here is the first paragraph:

> He had always felt that perhaps a deathbed scene would unite them; he and his father would clutch at each other in a sicklied fusion of sweetness and truth, the older man dropping his lifelong cool, finally spilling the beans, telling Gunther what it was all about, philosophy, stories of extramarital rascality, the straight dope on how much dough he had to the penny, was Mom any good in the hay! Did it hurt to be old? Was death a breeze?

The slang, the jazz rhythm, the desperation to rip into cores with shock that (as Friedman knows) fails quite to shock by the very act of being used—these are typical Friedman poignancies.

Much of modern vernacular writing settles for facile effects, plays to an easily titillated gallery of glib emotions. One sure sign is the movie metaphor: "He had that Marlon Brando fake-sweet smile just before the punch," etc. etc. But some contemporary Americans, like Friedman, like Irvin Faust, are crystallizing vernacular language and reference and emotion into something keener than easy recognition—in the tradition of Europe's dialect poets. "Did it hurt to be old? Was death a breeze?" The lines might have been translated from G. G. Belli, the profane poet of old Rome. . . .

Not all of the stories launch from earthly pads to outer space. And not all of them—particularly the last two—are successful. Sometimes one catches a glimpse of Ray Bradbury or James Thurber or John Collier hurrying by. But predominantly Friedman is fending—and fearing—for himself.

His protagonists, rich or poor, young or otherwise, tend to blend into one another in retrospect. He reserves individualizing touches for subsidiary characters, a flaw which, like the virtues mentioned earlier, he shares with some of his gifted contemporaries. But though the scale is limited, the matter is large. The successes among these 16 stories, which is to say most of them, are small bizarre offerings to forces that threaten all of us. One feels that the mere ritual of writing them has helped, momentarily at least, to mollify or perhaps entertain those spirits; and in so doing, the stories serve both the author and us.—STANLEY KAUFFMANN, "Frightened Writer," *NR*, Oct. 8, 1966, pp. 20, 37

Bruce Jay Friedman's *Scuba Duba* is a nearly perfect product of the new pseudo-sophistication, being a compendium of varieties of dishonesty, an icon of simulated seriousness and fake wit, a gross indulgence masquerading as a work. And it has been taken up overnight by an audience which constitutes the complement of the exploiters, their target and body politic, an audience wised up to Broadway and avid for what it considers—or has been told to consider—"real," au courant, hit-em-where-they-live drama, absurd, cocky and daring as hell. When I saw the play on its second night there was a long line at the box-office (which was selling tickets through next April), the first time I have ever seen one at an off-Broadway theatre in my seven years of reviewing.

This line had formed almost wholly in response to a rave review in that morning's *New York Times*. . . . It was the kind of review which, whether you saw the play before or after reading it, went to deepen your sense of living in a culture of absolute unreality.

The way Friedman's own contribution to unreality masks itself as actual is twofold. Thematically he seems to be dealing with some exceedingly pertinent contemporary social and psychological material, and dramaturgically he appears to be in the full recent tradition of what we might call the scatological-absurd. In the stage's new climate, where anything goes and everything is bound to come, it is nevertheless an impressive feat of exploitive playwriting to fuse two such disparate elements of audience appeal—hip sociology and advanced bawdry—into the simulacrum of a dramatic experience. Negroes and tits, together with a dash of Jewish mother-fixation, all of it served up with what has come to be known as "irreverence" or "if cultural rape is inevitable, lie back and enjoy it": such is *Scuba Duba*, whose very title conveys that distinctive lilt of the current imagination as it sets off to appropriate the games other people play.

In not much more than five minutes after the curtain goes up, we are aware that in his first play novelist Friedman is presenting us once again with Stern and the protagonist of *A Mother's Kisses*, those archetypes of brash Jewish male exteriors which cover victims' souls. He has been diluted and transplanted to the French Riviera in the guise of a vacationing copywriter for outdoor advertising who thinks his wife has run off with a Negro frogman. It is early evening and he must somehow get through the night. He manages this flaccid movement (which is what has been praised as the "plot") with the help of an assortment of characters of the kind that are popularly known now as "zany," until the morning brings showdown, a sort of interracial, Borscht belt *High Noon*.

The wife returns with the frogman, a caricature of hipsterism cum Black Power, and another Negro, a genteel, poetry-writing fellow who turns out to be the actual lover. Her husband, as we have been made intolerably aware all evening, is terrified of losing her and moves through a rapid series of last-ditch ploys designed to get her back, which range from frontal assaults on the Negroes to appeals to her pity, culminating in an abject announcement that he will be willing for the man to stay in the house as her lover if she will remain there as his wife. Throughout this final scene the play, which has hitherto been trying to be funny, is making a stab at seriousness, at what we have to call the new realism, and in keeping with this impulse *Scuba Duba* ends with the wife *really* going off with the Negro, a smashing triumph over the formulas and pallid sociology of the Broadway stage.

It is as entirely unconvincing as if she had stayed. The point in fact is that nothing is going to bring conviction, comic or otherwise, to a play that has been existing all along as a fraud, an exercise in self-indulgence, and one whose chief interest in social phenomena lies in literally getting back at their seriousness through japes, fashionable wit and the most vulgar kind of mockery. For Friedman's comic impulse, whenever it isn't simply drilling down into that exhausted mine of neurotic Jewishness (mothers, psychiatrists, hypochondria, self-pity) is capitalizing on the tensions and terrors of the interracial situation by letting us hear, in that liberating communal atmosphere the theatre is supposed to provide, the "things we haven't yet dared say" about it. "We" are the Jewish liberals and anybody who has been passing as one. And what we haven't said, at least publicly, is "coon," "spade," "coal-dusting nigger," "monkey," "chocolate shithead" and a good deal more in a progressive action of getting it off our chests through Friedman's heroism, a high point of which may lie in calling a Negro girl in an anecdote "Urethra."

This vocabulary of insult and invective runs through the play as its verbal leitmotif and functions as that kind of sterile catharsis which is obtained whenever something previously forbidden is allowed a temporary and revocable release. It is hermetic, cut off from true feeling and thought, not part of any dramatic action or purpose, sent up into the air in the interests of coarse therapy, of "acting-out." And yet in the play's most cowardly procedure it is all made safe, legitimized by the playwright's having seen to it that we are made aware of our inferiority, that the Negroes come off better, that they get the girl while we, poor schnooks who have been suffering with the hero all along, get the bird. That masochism has long been a mainstay of American commercial theatre, Broadway audiences having reveled in the exposure of their middle-class deficiencies and delusions, is a commonplace observation; the bright new fact is that masochism has spread to the outlying precincts where an audience purportedly hungry for truth and art has really been waiting for its chance at homeotherapy.

If I turn now from substance to craft, it isn't because I see them as separate but because reviews have their own order of business. The fact is that if Friedman had written a true play, if he had a dramatic imagination (as *Stern* clearly showed he has a novelistic one), his substance would have altered under its pressure, even while his "subject" remained the same. But lacking a dramatic imagination, not knowing how to set people or faculties in confrontation or how to force a histrionic reality out of raw experience, he is left with that experience at its level of deprivation of meaning and form. What he seems to have done to compensate for this is to have picked up information on how other writers have gotten by with their non-plays in this era of formlessness and the cash value of gratuitous outrage.

The chief asset, of course, is that battalion of zany characters whom you can shuttle on and off the stage as purveyors of fresh *schticks*, new routines to vary your central one. They include here a zany American tourist fresh from *Babbitt* and the Elks Wednesday meeting; a zany landlady who thinks everyone's a celebrity ("Oh, Sidney!" she mistakes the frogman for the movie star); a zany gendarme straight out of a perfume ad who says "everyzing" and "nozzing," a zany effete psychiatrist who simply can't *help* our hero any longer; a zany neighbor girl in a bikini who tells "absurd" anecdotes and helps him sexually through the ordeal; a zany anarchist who runs through the set shouting that all men are "teefs"; and a zany Englishwoman named Cheyenne who walks around in thigh-length boots, a merry widow and bare bulbous breasts, asks if there's "a crapper in the house," announces that she's trying to cut down to five climaxes a night and is hung up, culturally, on Bernie [sic] Malamud. . . .

Most of the time the actors are left to perform in a style of frenetic naturalism, what we might call domestic-absurd. Cut off from each other by Friedman's failure to achieve any kind of dramatic structure, they occupy their islands of speech and gesture to the best of their abilities, which in most cases are extraordinarily small. . . . A black comedy if you will, but one whose darkness seemed to me to lie in its revelations of what is likely to be esteemed for some time to come in certain quarters as wit, imagination, theatrical zest and social sophistication.—RICHARD GILMAN, "Anatomy of a Hit," *NR*, Oct. 28, 1967, pp. 31–33

MAX F. SCHULTZ

From "Towards a Definition of Black Humor"

Southern Review, Winter 1973, pp. 117–34

I

Conrad Knickerbocker is its theoretician; Bruce Jay Friedman, its field commander. Yet neither they nor their fellow partisans can agree on a common article of faith or theater of operations. Black Humor is a movement without unity, a group of guerrillas who huddle around the same campfire only because they know that they are in Indian territory. Even though they grudgingly concur about the enemy, they anarchistically refuse to coordinate their attack. Desperate men, they have abandoned not only the safety of received opinions but have also left to the news media the advance positions of satirical shock treatment, charging instead the exposed flanks of undiscovered lands "somewhere out beyond satire," which require "a new set of filters" to be seen.[1]

The irony is that Friedman inadvertently gave literary respectability and philosophical cohesion to the group when he patched together thirteen pieces (short stories and excerpts from novels, including one of his own, "Black Angels") for Bantam Books in 1965 and nonchalantly entitled them *Black Humor*. The other twelve writers on whom he had perpetrated this travesty were Terry Southern, John Rechy, J. P. Donleavy, Edward Albee, Charles Simmons, Louis-Ferdinand Céline, James Purdy, Joseph Heller, Thomas Pynchon, Vladimir Nabokov, Conrad Knickerbocker, and John Barth. The venture was an exercise in bookmaking. Friedman's novels had had good critical reception but modest sales; he had a living to earn, a family to support. Much to his surprise he found himself tarred with his own black label. Dumbfounded, like one of his fictional characters, to learn that someone was indeed listening, he now regrets his part in this bit of carpentry for the trade. The tag has been applied to his own fiction until he winces when he hears the words. "What I ended up with was 13 separate writers with completely private and unique visions," he admitted with ingratiating candor as early as his foreword to the collection, "who in so many ways have nothing at all to do with one another and would not know or perhaps even understand one another's work if they tripped over it" (pp. vii–viii).

Despite Friedman's protestations and a recent effort to describe his play *Scuba Duba* with the more critically usable phrase "tense comedy," the Black Humor tag seems to have stuck. If, however, the term is to have any critical usefulness, aside from an opaque impressionistic meaning, it must be more clearly defined than hitherto. For as a term Black Humor *is* vague. It fails to distinguish among the genres. It fails to differentiate the contemporary movement from the many instances in the past of similar literary reactions to human experience. It fails to focus the means (plot, character, thought, and diction) and the end (effect on reader: laughter, tears, etc.) of literary expression, as Friedman's alternative "tense comedy" attempts more successfully to do. Indeed, Black Humor needs a definition that will be not only inclusive but exclusive.

Although several attempts have been made to date and define Black Humor, the results have been elusive and chimerical. (1) Despairing of any substantive formula, Friedman opts for a mystery that has been around as long as the human mind has had an iconoclastic itch to peel back disguises and to probe "thoughts no one else cares to think." (2) In *The Fabulators*, Robert Scholes tries to channel Friedman's all-out purchase on history by shifting to formalist concerns and identifying Black Humor with the recurrent intellectual reaction of artists to the limitations of realism. As with the painterly aims of some modern artists, Black Humorists, he believes, are absorbed by the possibilities of playful and artful construction. They are master fabulators in the tradition of the Romance and its baroque configurations. Like Plato's "all-in-one," unfortunately, Scholes's "fabulation" becomes in practice a nondiscriminating standard, subsuming in its alembic all "artful contrivance," for is not the artist by nature a maker of patterns? Are not the stark fables of Isaac Bashevis Singer as contrived as the mannered convolutions of Vladimir Nabokov? Surely Scholes's already disparate group of fabulators, ranging from Lawrence Durrell to John Hawkes, could not deny membership to the master fabulator—and ironist—Henry James. *Hic reductio ad absurdum!* If, on the other hand, Scholes sees this fabulation as a game to be enjoyed in part for its own sake, a decadence appreciated by a specially developed taste for the sophisticated, the artful—as his emphasis on Nabokov and Barth as arch-fabulators would suggest—then, of course, the earnest moral position of a Henry James or the sincere social gesture of a Bruce Jay Friedman, a Louis-Ferdinand Céline, a Terry Southern, or a Kurt Vonnegut becomes an important distinction. This is not to deny that Nabokov and Barth have their serious themes, or that Friedman has his aestheticism, but to suggest that the ways Nabokov and Barth handle their subjects loom larger in their calculations than the stylisms of Friedman loom in his. The verbal conundrums of Nabokov and Barth in any final analysis would appear more the stance of the aesthete than would the verbal uniqueness of Friedman. And Scholes's definition would seem inevitably to polarize the practitioners of Black Humor into at least two groups distinguishable by the formalist means they employ. (3) Conrad Knickerbocker, in his groundbreaking essay,[2] diminishes the Black Humorist to *poète maudit*, a scorpion to the status quo, so full of the poison of self-loathing for the "specially tailored, ready-to-wear identities" given to us by television, movies, the press, universities, the government, the military, medicine, and business that he mortally stings himself, pricking the surrogate skin of society.

We unnecessarily compound the problem of determining what Black Humor is when we try, like Scholes, to see it as a universal attitude of mind, periodically emerging in the history of literature. Such a *via media* leads to an impasse not unlike that reached by those critics who make Romanticism and Classicism out to be constant modes of apprehending human experience. More limiting, certainly, but more useful in the long run is to recognize that Black Humor is a phenomenon of the 1960s, comprising a group of writers who share a viewpoint and an aesthetics for pacing off the boundaries of a nuclear-powered, war-saturated, chemically oriented world. Equally useful is to discriminate Black Humor from the oral techniques of sick humor and from the dramatic conventions of the theater of the absurd, even though it shares with these modes of expression some of the same assumptions about our century.

Like all comic visions of life, Black Humor concerns itself with social realities. In this respect, it is not anti-realistic romance (as Scholes argues) so much as realism forced to the extreme of a metaphysical truth—an intensified, at times *sur*realistic, concentration on those details of contemporary existence illustrative of a disoriented world.

II

In the metaphysical assumptions that underlie their views of the relationship of man to society, traditional comedy and Black Humor differ radically. New Comedy, according to Northrop Frye's "The Argument of Comedy,"[3] always worked toward a reconciliation between the individual and society. Either the normal individual was freed from the bonds of an arbitrary humor society, or a normal society was rescued from the whims imposed by humor individuals. As might be suspected, Frye finds lurking beneath this realignment of social forces the yearly triumph of spring over winter. He sees the victory of normality over abnormality as a formalized celebration of the archetypal pattern of death and resurrection. In the marriage of the young hero, in his triumph over the old pursuer (*senex*), in the freeing of the slave, New Comedy rehearsed the victory of life over death.

Black Humor stops short of any such victory. It enacts no individual release or social reconciliation; it often moves toward, but ordinarily fails to reach, that goal. Like Shakespeare's dark comedies, Black Humor condemns man to a dying world; it never envisions, as do Shakespeare's early and late comedies, the possibilities of human escape from an aberrant environment into a forest milieu, as a ritual of the triumph of the green world over the wasteland. Thus, at the conclusion of Bruce Jay Friedman's first novel, *Stern*, the protagonist is as alienated from "the kike man" and the suburban neighborhood he lives in as he was at the outset. Despite his efforts at *rapprochement*, he and society persist in the bonds of abnormality separating each other. Similarly, in *A Mother's Kisses*, Joseph tugs at the symbolic end of his mother's silver cord, reaching out for girls of his own age; but the gulf between him and normal sexual experience remains unbridged at the novel's conclusion. That the expanse has been shortened, that Joseph has moved away from his mother toward his contemporaries, explains in part the dim penetration of light in this novel as compared to the impenetrable blackness blanketing *Stern*. In *A Mother's Kisses* Friedman skillfully hints at an eventual release when Joseph puts Meg on the train for home in the final scene and when his last encounter with a girl (in a Saturday night foray at a nearby college) breaks off at the interruption of someone else and not at his own timid withdrawal. Still, full accommodation of Joseph with his milieu fails to "come off" within the novel. . . .

The divisiveness of society is certainly one consequence of the individualizing bent of Protestant humanism in the past 500 years. But other causes peculiar to our century are equally discernible. One need only contrast the Rome of Plautus and the London of Shakespeare to the New York City of Friedman and the Los Angeles of Pynchon to see the change in social cohesion that has taken place. Whereas the Plautean Romans and the Shakespearean Londoners were united by a common class and culture, Friedman's New Yorkers and Pynchon's Angelenos are connected to each other by subways and freeways. Although people live elbow to elbow, they are separated by vast distances from the places of personal relationships: work, church, parental homes, recreation. Friedman's Everyman, Stern, daily faces a harrowing multi-houred trip to the office among indifferent, or outright hostile, fellow commuters. Angelenos spend equal numbers of hours speeding down ribbons of concrete, each encased in his metal cocoon of an automobile, cut off from the intimate sounds and smells of human voices and bodies, permitted only the occasional blurred glimpse of a face through two panes of window glass as they whisk past one another. It is this divisive world that moves the Black Humorist, in part, to arrest the traditional comic reconciliation of individual and society.

Black Humor differs also from current existentialist views of man in refusing to treat his isolation as an ethical situation. Friedman slyly ribs Stern's effort to offset his fearful solitariness. For example, in the last scene, Stern's self-conscious embrace of wife and child in the nursery becomes a parodic tableau of the Holy Family, mistimed, and miscued:

> Now Stern walked around the room, touching the rugs to make sure they wouldn't fall on his son's face. Then he said, "I feel like doing some hugging," and knelt beside the sleeping boy, inhaling his pajamas and putting his arm over him. His wife was at the door and Stern said, "I want you in here, too." She came over, and it occurred to him that he would like to try something a little theatrical, just kneel there quietly with his arms protectively draped around his wife and child. He tried it and wound up holding them a fraction longer than he'd intended.

. . . Like Böll's Clown, the protagonist of Black Humor does not despair with the savage bitterness of a Miss Lonelyhearts. Nor does he remain aloof, dismissing society with cold imperviousness, like Dennis Barlow. Rather, he worries about his place in it. Only after repeated rebuffs in his search for a relationship with others does he accept his empty existence with an angry shrug like Ferdinand Bardamu. He may be a booby like Friedman's Stern, a *naïf* like his Joseph, an anti-hero like Céline's Bardamu, a silly like Vonnegut's Eliot Rosewater, a pervert like Nabokov's Humbert Humbert, a clown like Heller's Yossarian, a fool like Barth's Ebenezer Cooke—but he is never an untouched innocent like Waugh's Paul Pennyfeather, nor a dismembered scapegoat like West's Lemuel Pitkin, nor an unwitting gull like Swift's Gulliver. At the end of *Decline and Fall*, Paul Pennyfeather returns to college unchanged by his scarifying mishaps. At the end of *A Cool Million* Lemuel Pitkin is without thumb, leg, eye, teeth, scalp, indeed his very existence; yet he is ironically a heroic witness to the American dream of success. The Black Humor protagonist does not simply function, like these satiric foils, as an authorial lens for analyzing the real, corrupt object of the satire. For him detachment does not mean withdrawal from the world, as it does for Gulliver, Candide, or Dennis Barlow in Waugh's *The Loved One*. He is at once observer of, and participant in, the drama of dissidence, detached from and yet affected by what happens around him. Extremely conscious of his situation, he is radically different from the satiric puppets of Waugh and West, who bounce back like Krazy Kat from every cruel flattening as smooth and round as before, their minds unviolated by experience. His—and the author's—gaze is more often than not inward, concentrated on what Conrad Knickerbocker has called the terrors and possibilities of self-knowledge ("Humor with a Mortal Sting,"p. 61). His prison-house loneliness, forced upon him by existence, becomes an odyssey into being, a Célinesque journey to the end of the night.

The moral quality of society—the aim of satire—is not, according to Northrop Frye, the point of the comic resolution of an individual and a group. Nor is it the objective of Black Humor, which resists any final accommodation. As Scholes notes, the Black Humorist is not concerned with what to do about life but with how to take it. This is not to say that he has no moral position, but only to suggest that this position is *implicit*. He may challenge the trances and hysterias of society, as Conrad Knickerbocker suggests, but he does not ordinarily urge choice on us. He seeks rather a comic perspective on both tragic fact and moralistic certitude. In extreme instances (some of Kurt Vonnegut's writings, for example) this attitude of mind will lead to the novel's refusal to take its implied moral position seriously. *The Sot-Weed Factor* has been faulted for its abdication of responsibility to answer the questions it raises about intrinsic values, and *Catch-22* for its central evasiveness as regards war, for its not having a point of view, an awareness of what things should or should not be. Such is the ultimate ethical and aesthetic chaos that these novels risk in their rage for an inclusive purchase on reality.

III

To the satirist there are false versions of reality and true versions. Whispering Glades in Waugh's *The Loved One* is a false ordering of reality, the traditionalism identified with English country houses a true ordering. The illogicality of action rampant in the Algerian world of West's *A Cool Million* does not ultimately deny an underlying faith in the Puritan ethic of industry and perseverence. To the Black Humorist, contrariwise, all versions of reality are mental constructs. No one is aprioristically truer than another. Falsity obtains only when we mistakenly assume that one verbal construct morally or intellectually preempts all others. . . .

The Black Humorist is a social critic, as Bruce Jay Friedman claims, only in that he "lays bare" the perversions, "hang-ups," sacred cows, and taboos of society. They may be as universal as Céline's preoccupations with the absurdity of war and institutionalized inhumanities, or as personal as Friedman's catharses of sexual blocks. That which familiarity, semantic blur, and such intellectual opiates as patriotism, sanctity of family, religious allegiance, and racial ideals have numbed us into accepting without demur as commonplace and unquestionable, the Black Humorist uncovers anew as murderous and frightening. Focusing our attention on such things, he forces us to share with him the painful laughter of examining and analyzing our mutually hidden and camouflaged obsessions. He exorcises as comical and lighthearted that from which we customarily recoil in horror. But where satire would perform a lobotomy on these sudden terrors, Black Humor simply records them for future reference, though not without a wink so tight that it brings an empathic tear to both author's and reader's eyes. It is more a detached history of the black thoughts of the human mind and the unspoken fears of society than its scourge. *Lolita* documents without editorial indignation the drab and furtive bowers of Hymen that masquerade as the proud American institution, the Motel. *The Sot-Weed Factor* luxuriates in the venery and political venality of the colonial American. *A Mother's Kisses* counts the prurient glimpses of sex by a seventeen-year-old as the boyish collecting of baseball cards; it defines the sacrosanct fellowship of father and son as a tension of day-long silence broken only by such intimacies as "I buy a paper here," "I usually stand at this end [of the subway] and hold on to a strap," and "I only take a fast bite" for lunch. Thomas Pynchon in *V.* soberly tells us about employment in the sewers of New York City, where daily there are wild disoriented hunts for alligators, grown from pet reptiles flushed down the toilet by urban children.

Any irreverent gesture toward the sanctified and the sanctimonious risks ostracism. Such is the fate of all who would parody the status quo. Black Humor often works to control such potential disaffection, especially acute in a fiction where the protagonist is a reject of society, through the device of the first-person narrator. The space we inhabit is suddenly part of the space that the narrator also occupies. We are drawn into his environment and merged with his point of view. But the "inside" point of view (as Wayne Booth calls it) creates for the author as serious a narrative problem as it solves. Not only is the world depicted from the idiosyncratic stance of an outsider perverse, but it is necessarily limited and incomplete. For, unless the narrator's vision is identical to the author's, the narrator's world must be a restricted one. Such a limited sensibility militates against the inclusiveness, irony, and impurity that is central to Black Humor's posit of a disorderly, infinitely Protean universe. Hence writers of Black Humor have had to devise fictional forms that are enormously self-conscious, aware not only of their position but of the endless other possible orbits that stand in relation to them. . . .

At least six kinds of deployment are used to suggest the self-conscious awareness that the world of our sensibility impinges upon, and is invaded in turn by, the worlds of other sensibilities. (1) The careful Jamesian distinction between narrator and author is blurred, allowing for the introduction of authorial responses to the narrator's vision not verified by the experience of the narrative. Both Céline and Nabokov adopt this maneuver in the conclusions of *Journey to the End of the Night* and *Lolita*. A startling variation is the homogenizing, as Barth terms it, of first and third person in some of Donleavy's and Nabokov's work. (2) Corollary to the narratorial blur is the felt presence of the author throughout the novel. Nabokov employs this tactic in *Lolita* with the skill of a master chess player. He plants clues, introduces his own signature of the passionate pursuit of lepidoptery, arbitrarily alters Humbert's physical appearance—all as a reminder to the reader that the omniscient control of the author is never in doubt. (3) The human sense of time and the distinctions of history are blurred, until the present becomes a parodic reconstruction of the past, a compendium of all the human exercises in abstraction designed to impose connectiveness on the intervals of time. Barth and Pynchon are the most inventive practitioners of this ardent "betrayal" or experience. (4) Literary parody offers these writers another dimension of self-consciousness, for disclosing how our verbal constructs are subjective perceptions of reality. The parodies of Nabokov, Barth, and Terry Southern, for example, comically remind us that other worlds, other patterns of reality exist concurrently with the ones of our making. Their multidimensional presentations of human experience correct our tragic tendency (one thinks of Humbert Humbert's error) to mistake the mirror of one's mind as a true record of the *ding an sich*. Epistemologically they represent efforts, in the phrase of Alfred Appel, "to exhaust the 'fictional gestures'" which would reduce the ineffable qualities of human experience to a convention of language. (5) The revered Aristotelian dogma of plot, while not read out of the canon, is obscured by a broadening of the independent role of incidents and surface details. The usual functional connection between plot and theme is blurred, permitting apparently irrelevant incidents to develop bifocally in concurrence with the plot a related but more inconclusive vision of life. Friedman, along with Céline and Heller and Vonnegut whom he admires, generally employs this tactic in his novels. (6) Activities and thoughts appear in their negative aspects, expanding our sensibilities, like Alice through the Looking Glass, with a hint of "New thresholds, new anatomies." Thus is suggested to our consciousness the suspicion that the arrangement of experience into either/or equations falsifies by delimitation the alternative infinites of *and* and *and*. Heller and Vonnegut frequently conceive of actions and events in such terms.

As one of its anthologists has remarked, "There are no certainties in Black Humor,"[4], as there are none in the world it chronicles. . . . Borges' vision of human experience as a labyrinth is a near perfect metaphysical conceit for Black Humor's world picture. Another almost equally appropriate is undiagnosed illness. One thinks of Yossarian's puzzling liver condition, Eliot Rosewater's amnesia, Sebastian Dangerfield's debilitating *malaises*, Cabot Wright's blackouts, Jacob Horner's and Ebenezer Cooke's recurrent immobilities, Stern's ulcer, Joseph's father's mysterious back ailment, Meg's periodic sieges of sitting around in a bathrobe. Friedman's novels, particularly, abound in enigmatic balloonings of arm and head, in inexplicable lapses and convalescences. While recovering from an attack of swelling, Joseph expresses surprise that anything sick ever heals: "One day, he felt, it would be announced that the whole germ theory of disease was a hoax, that there was no such thing as a germ . . . that all medicines were silly, doctors could learn all they needed to know in two weeks of school and that when people got better it was a wild coincidence" (*A Mother's Kisses*). Implicit in Joseph's expectations is a denial of the meaningful relatedness of actions, on which the accepted empirical notions of the physical world are posited. If casual sequence (*non sequitur*) and temporal sequence (*post hoc; ergo, propter hoc*) are questioned, then technically all history may be a sham—as Barth and Pynchon have been pointing out delightedly at great length. Without a logic of events to narrow the possibilities of an action to one or several consequences, a Pandora's box of possibilities is uncapped. Thus, at a signal from the leader of an overcoated gang after he had distributed bars of halvah, a girl may undress "as though she always disrobed after halvah servings." If her nudity follows such illogical directives, why could it not just as easily be triggered by an afternoon on the ski slopes, or a snappy speech by the Vice-President, or an hour of television cartoons?

To an individual assailed by an infinite number of possibilities of action, the terror of daily life with its mandatory decisions will automatically wax out of all proportion to the situation. Hence an assemblage of the familiar, as in much Pop art, becomes a strategy for encroachment on the unknown. In this light the structural peculiarities of some other well-known Black Humor novels, which have attracted critical attention on that account, become explicable: the compulsive return again and again to the same action in Heller's *Catch-22;* the inexhaustible guises and disguises in Barth's *The Sot-Weed Factor*; the transformations of places and persons with the same initial letter in Pynchon's V.; and the endless refractions of mirror words and images, puns, parodies, and doubles in Nabokov's *Lolita*.

Even more to the point is the shift from refined selectivity to omnibus appetite for experience in so many of these novels. . . . What preoccupies these authors is not desire for experience itself so much as a need to find, in Ebenezer Cooke's words, an Ariadne's thread marking our "path through the labyrinth of Life" (ch. 3)—a need to cajole out of experience all its variations, as a way of getting at the causes of reality, of connecting us with our starting place. Like Menelaus on the shores of Pharos in Euripides' play, exhorting direction from the Proteus of life, they are less bent on judging the multiple appearances of reality than on simply knowing them, as the only desperate way left to wring from experience a modicum of sanity, perhaps of salvation.

In a limited sense, then, Robert Scholes is right in noting the interest of the Black Humorists with construction; but he minimizes their seriousness when he characterizes this concern as playful or artful. Like the Painterly and Post-Painterly movements, the Black Humorist's intensive search through form for the springs of twentieth-century existence is worthy of our attention. If he cannot be numbered among those moral activists who change the visible face of things, he is nevertheless, in his passionate concentration on the hallucinations of reality, as Knickerbocker insists, one of the "keepers of conscience." Among the writers of contemporary fiction, the Black Humorist is conspicuously risking the resources of the imagination to find new modes of order for the raw materials of experience. One of today's adventurers into the murky corners of the human mind and the social soul, his vision is as necessary to individual health as the discovery of the Salk vaccine, for he is working a revolution in our sensibilities, he is instructing us anew in ways of perceiving reality.

Notes

1. Bruce Jay Friedman, *Black Humor* (New York, 1965), pp. x-xi.
2. "Humor with a Mortal Sting," *New York Times Book Review*, LXIX, pt. 2, pp. 3+.
3. In *Theories of Comedy*, edited by Paul Lauter (New York, 1964), pp. 450–60.
4. Douglas M. Davis, *The World of Black Humor* (New York, 1967), p. 30.

ROBERT FROST

1874–1963

Robert Lee Frost was born in San Francisco on March 26, 1874. After the death of his father, a journalist and unsuccessful politician, the family moved to Massachussetts in 1885. In spite of a distinguished high school career, Frost left Dartmouth College after a single semester and found work first in a woolen mill, then as a teacher. In 1887 he entered Harvard University, but again abandoned his studies without a degree, and on the advice of his doctor moved with his wife to a farm in New Hampshire. Though he enjoyed country life, Frost was never much of a farmer, and had more success as a teacher at a local school.

Frost had published poems in *The Independent* as early as 1894, and in 1912 took his family to England in an attempt to further his writing career. In 1913 his first collection of poems, *A Boy's Will*, was published in London, followed a year later by *North of Boston*, which won him admirers in America, so that, on his return in 1915, he found himself in demand for poetry readings and lectures on poetry and teaching. In 1916 he was Phi Beta Kappa poet at Harvard, and in 1917 began a long association with Amherst College, which did not exclude him from teaching for several years at the University of Michigan.

Although a popular and innovative teacher, Frost viewed this role primarily as a means to finance his writing, and his production in the following years established him as a leading American poet. *New Hampshire* (1923) won him the first of four Pulitzer Prizes, the others being awarded for *Collected Poems* (1930), *A Further Range* (1936), and *A Witness Tree* (1942). His public success in these years was accompanied by family problems, with the death of his wife in 1938 and the suicide of his son in 1940.

Frost's philosophical and religious convictions found extended expression in the dramatic poems *A Masque of Reason* (1945) and *A Masque of Mercy* (1947). After the lyric poetry *Steeple Bush* (1947) and the issuing of a new edition of *Collected Poems* in 1949, Frost's poetic activity declined, but the 1950s brought him increased honors and renown. By the end of his life, he had received forty-four honorary degrees, and his status as a public figure was reflected in an invitation to read a poem at the inauguration of John F. Kennedy in 1960, and in a meeting with Khrushchev in the Soviet Union in 1962, when he attempted to promote his vision of magnanimous rivalry between the superpowers. Other visits abroad were made in 1954 to Brazil, on behalf of the State Department, in 1956 to England, to receive honorary degrees at Oxford and Cambridge, and in 1960 to Israel and Greece.

After the appearance of a final volume of poems, *In the Clearing*, in 1962, Robert Frost died as America's most popular poet on January 29, 1963.

Personal

A man is more than the sum of his qualities, and Frost is not different from other men in this respect. To isolate and describe his qualities will not give a rounded picture, but it will give us an impression of the kind of human being he is. . . . There have been subtle changes over the years, yet they indicate not a difference in but an intensification of personal traits. Friendliness and cordial warmth are compounded in his camaraderie, the vigorous, virile companionableness of a man for his own kind. In his presence one feels something salutary and restorative. He attracts the young like a bright light, and not only the young but others, too, for someone of prominence—an editor, or former student, or friend, or neighbor—is always beating a path to his door, seeking him out.

His camaraderie is an intrinsic part of his personal raciness. No matter where you meet him, whether in his Cambridge study, on a lecture platform, in the local grocery store, in a suburban street, in his mountain cabin, whether in the pasture grazing a horse on tether, or among the tall poles in a garden where the broad-leafed bean flowers, or in a thicket with axe and long-handled cutting hook, the special quality of his raciness is apparent. There is no pose, no pretentiousness, no mask. Such bonhomie seemed incredible to a Spanish friend reared in the formal tradition of Madrid and Salamanca. He was fairly bowled over when he met Frost in a jumper and overalls, and blue canvas-topped shoes, dressed simply but comfortably, and completely relaxed. It is almost too much for the European, who apparently expects the guard of a notable writer to be up and his mask to be well fitted. Frost is genuine enough to be very natural, and this is the essence of his charm. He is what he is. The European "genius" has a reputation at stake. The democratic American poet is only like the rest of us; his difference is his genius.

Physically, Frost has the solidity of the close-sodded native soil. He stands about five feet nine, and you are aware at once of his strong-armed, full-chested, rugged build. In his old clothes he looks bigger than he actually is. When approached in the garden, he appears to loom; but when dressed up, he shrinks to medium height. Close up you notice the full, thick, muscular, workmanlike hands, the backs of them rough, the thumb large, the fingers long, the tips blunt, the nails wide and thick—firm fingers to grasp an ax, strong shoulders to start the swing, muscular forearms to follow through. His practical truths are the tougher, you think, recalling Thoreau, for the calluses on the broad, well-lined palms. His blue eyes, which are rarely measuring, nevertheless take you in. He looks, listens, appraises. And he sizes up memorably, saying, "I see what I see." His nose is strong and aggressive. His lips are full but not sensual; the chin is firm. Altogether, the quality of raciness is in the big-framed, shaggy-headed appearance. It is in manner, carriage and speech. It is in his manner which is neighborly, but not unurban; in his carriage which is not to be distinguished from any city dweller's; in his speech which is not gauche or clumsy, and not identifiable with rustic voices.

He describes himself as lazy, but this is hardly the word that characterizes a relaxed calmness. He is relaxed, not lazy, because he has known how to economize energy. His so-called "laziness" and "evasiveness" have protected him, enabled him to get the important work done. He is always active about the real work, which is writing poetry, and, in a sense, his talking contributes to the writing, for it is while talking he tries out the ideas and expressions that go into making a poem. In his talk a process is always going on: it is the reflection upon ideas in experience and the conversion of experience into ideas. This is the nub of it. He turns interior meditation inside out and lengthens a thought in conversation.

What Henry James said of Ivan Turgenev is certainly true of Frost. "He was the richest, the most delightful, of talkers, and his face, his person, his temper, the thoroughness with which he had been equipped with human intercourse, make, in the memory of his friends, an image which is completed, but not thrown into the shade by his literary distinction." Frost is one of the readiest of the vanishing tribe of original talkers in the twentieth century, a tribe that includes William Butler Yeats, James Stephens, Paul Claudel, George Santayana and D. H. Lawrence. He belongs with them; not, perhaps, with Coleridge whose monologues were said to ascend, in De Quincey's description, "like Jacob's ladder, by just gradations, into the Heaven of Heavens and the thrones of the Trinity." Not yet with Swinburne, whose spellbinding talk, the exhilarated Henry Adams described as a "wild Walpurgis-night." Frost's talk is not pyrotechnic or febrile. On the contrary, it is social, genial and expansive. There are few unintended pauses in it. One thought starts another, and he rambles on while the deep-set blue eyes, the blunt nose, the expressive lips, the formidable chin and the shock of white hair all help to pin a point down.

Best in a small group, preferably man to man, it is true, as a friend says, in idiom, "He'll stay there talking until the last dog is dead." Yet what he says makes good listening. Where all of it comes from, different almost every time, is a wonder. He is hard to corner, and you soon learn to watch both holes for his appearance. His manoeuvrability is positively ingenious. He always seems at random like a bluebottle fly on a hot midsummer day. "I have an endless resourcefulness to change my ground," he says, and it is this endless resourcefulness which animates the conversation. Almost any topic trips the trigger of his loaded memory. He talks about twelfth-century jongleurs as readily as about witchcraft, about Ezra Pound and the Bollingen Award as sharply as about submarginal economy, about Bohr's atom as informatively as about T. S. Eliot's *Four Quartets*. At any given time he may make allusions to the Mormons and their art, the Mayas in Yucatan, Swedenborgianism, the Parmenidean idea of identity, the Nietzschean *Will to Power*, glass shirts, water witches or Morgan horses.

Although he mentions simple, natural things—a fresh flower found in an upper pasture, or the white throated sparrows at the field's edge, or a cornered fox—there is a wide sweep to his conversational interests, which include internationalism (like Thoreau, he's a "home-cosmographer"), politics (he's an independent Democrat), athletics (usually baseball), literature (chiefly poetry), America (notably Vermont), teaching (as "performance"), philosophy (out of the grass roots), and people (individuals, not types). Ranging the humanities, he explores rather than exploits his reading. Using it as a man does who makes it a part of himself, he is Bacon's ready man and brandishes like trophies quotations from the classics and his contemporaries. He talks nimbly at the surface, but he arrives there from a distance. It is the very fact that he has this surface which makes him a ready talker. Edwin Arlington Robinson lacked it and envied Frost the satisfying gift of being a conversable man.

Playing superbly, he touches nimbly the keys of many moods and ranges with agility from banter to seriousness. His voice is medium in pitch, rather low than high, but not guttural; and it registers sensitively shades of feeling—elation or scorn, exultance or sadness. Just as the charm of the man comes to focus in his talk, so the total force of the poet comes to focus in the resonant voice. It is the voice of a man who is readily able to reproduce the brogue of Irish speech tones, or nuances in colloquial idiom and the accent of a countryman, or blank-verse paragraphs of Miltonic eloquence. Those with whom we talk usually have a control of language only at the level of sense, and even at this level usage may lapse into slang or stiffen into formal phrasing as in a book. There is another level—the tonal—that comes from the arrangement of words in sequences of sound. In Frost's poetry the meaning is partly in the tone. Similarly, in his conversation one has to hear the voice intonate the thought to catch the total meaning. His habitual speech is idiomatic. Whether in letter or poem, reading, preface or introduction, the phrasing has an idiosyncratic intonation.

Sauntering along at an unhurried clip, his voice not only expresses an amiable and sensitive personality, it also expresses the phonetics of thought—the way a thought sounds. His thoughts have the creative touch of personal language. In the native tradition he uses a concrete illustration, a homely allusion or a folksy story to make a point. But the style is the man himself. Strongest and most enkindling is the explorative thrust of the mind. He is always reacting, and always unpredictably, for his mind is refractive as well as reactive. Anyone would have difficulty outguessing him. The natural variability of his weathered mind is its life. Fluently, he ranges from the speech of common sense to lyrical eloquence. Quite unexpectedly there will be a run of speech that has the lilt of poetry in it. So I have heard it often as the poet's aroused sensibility raised the listener as by verbal levitation on a sequence of metaphor, or released in him by flashes of phrase the rich joy of *The Odyssey* or *Walden*.—REGINALD L. COOK, *The Dimensions of Robert Frost*, 1958, pp. 10–14

ROBERT FROST 13 DECEMBER 1960
43 [35] BREWSTER ST WASHINGTON
CAMBRIDGE MASS
I WOULD BE DELIGHTED IF YOU WOULD PARTICIPATE IN THE INAUGURAL CEREMONIES JANUARY TWENTIETH. I KNOW THAT IT WOULD GIVE THE AMERICAN PUBLIC AS MUCH PLEASURE AS IT WOULD MY FAMILY AND ME. THE JOINT CONGRESSIONAL INAUGURAL COMMITTEE WILL SEND YOU A FORMAL INVITATION IN THE NEAR FUTURE. WITH BEST PERSONAL WISHES,
JOHN F. KENNEDY.

PRESIDENT ELECT JOHN F. KENNEDY 14 DECEMBER 1960
WASHINGTON DC CAMBRIDGE
IF YOU CAN BEAR AT YOUR AGE THE HONOR OF BEING MADE PRESIDENT OF THE UNITED STATES, I OUGHT TO BE ABLE AT MY AGE TO BEAR THE HONOR OF TAKING SOME PART IN YOUR INAUGURATION. I MAY NOT BE EQUAL TO IT BUT I CAN ACCEPT IT FOR MY CAUSE—THE ARTS, POETRY, NOW FOR THE FIRST TIME TAKEN INTO THE AFFAIRS OF STATESMEN. I AM GLAD THE INVITATION PLEASES YOUR FAMILY. IT WILL PLEASE MY FAMILY TO THE FOURTH GENERATION AND MY FAMILY OF FRIENDS AND WERE THEY LIVING IT WOULD HAVE PLEASED INORDINATELY THE KIND OF GROVER CLEVELAND DEMOCRATS I HAD FOR PARENTS.
ROBERT FROST

—*Selected Letters of Robert Frost*, ed. Lawrance Thomson, 1964, pp. 585–86

One evening in May 1962, Robert Frost and Anatoly Dobrynin, Soviet Ambassador to the United States, dined at the house of Stewart Udall, Secretary of the Interior. Out of that evening came a proposal for a cultural exchange between two poets, one American, one Russian. In July, President John F. Kennedy requested Frost to be the American participant. Frost accepted, and details of the exchange were soon arranged, for Udall himself was going to Russia in late August at the head of a delegation to visit hydroelectric installations.

Frost asked Frederick Adams, director of the Pierpont Morgan Library in New York and a friend of long standing, to go with him. I was asked to go along to help with arrangements and the language. . . .

We landed in Moscow at five. A delegation of Soviet writers met Frost. Alexander Tvardovsky was there, poet, editor of *Novy Mir* (New World), and a Lenin Prize winner, who was to have visited the United States soon after Frost's return but who never came. Alexei Surkov was there, poet, secretary of the Writers Union and one of the key figures in the administration of the Soviet intellectual world. Evgeny Evtushenko was there, slim and confident. Mikhail Zenkevich, a poet, and Ivan Kashkin, a professor, were also there, the men who published the first Russian translations of Frost in their 1939 anthology *American Poets of the Twentieth Century*. Although the Russians were obviously not yet sure of their guest and of what to make of him, they were polite and dutifully attentive. Frost was much wearied by the long plane ride. Arrangements seemed to be in the hands of two women, specialists in American literature, from the Foreign Section of the Writers Union.

Evtushenko had to duck out early to keep another appointment. There was a press conference in the airport waiting room. But despite the gray weather and Frost's fatigue, you could sense a special and optimistic tone in the Russian intellectual world. As the saying goes, they had put their best foot forward. Here was Tvardovsky, the man most responsible for engineering the success of the liberal *New World* in which, two months later, *One Day in the Life of Ivan Denisovich* was to appear. Here was Surkov, who in 1960–1962 temporarily assumed a new position sympathetic to the intelligentsia by having edited a little volume of Pasternak's poems and the first volume of the new *Concise Literary Encyclopedia*. Here was Evtushenko, world famous, whose "Babyi Yar" had caused a sensation the year before and whose politically electrifying "Stalin's Heirs" was to be published six weeks later. These men, along with Zenkevich and Kashkin, had come not only to greet Frost but also to express their allegiance to those independent, humanistic values expounded in Frost's poetry which they were trying to make operating principles in their own new literature.

Greeting Frost, they greeted the West of their own cultural tradition. For them Frost personified this tradition. Frost's most important accomplishment in Russia was not the political embassy he aspired to but the enactment of freewheeling literary activity which he, by his poetry readings and by his talk, encouraged among the Russians. Won by the Russians away from some of his preconceptions about them, Frost was an example and a reminder to them not of the politics of literature but of vitality of the literary tradition. Evtushenko, for example, who had not stayed for the whole conference at the airport, subsequently invited Frost to dinner and talked to him informally several times. Sharply criticized in late 1962 as a self-aggrandizing showoff, in January 1963 Evtushenko sent Frost a simple, sincere telegram: TODAY IVE READ AGAIN AND AGAIN YOUR POEMS I AM HAPPY THAT YOU LIVE ON THE EARTH.
—F. D. REEVE, *Robert Frost in Russia*, 1963, pp. 3, 19–21

It may seem a paradox that, from all accounts (I never asked her), my mother was an atheist or at least an agnostic. Yet the power she exercised on all about her was a spiritual force, a *depth* of godliness (or goodness) that did not need God for backing—only love, human love. She refused to accept the cruelty of life and death, but neither did she cry out against it, or ask for mercy, or blame herself—or anyone else. In contrast, my father tended to self-pity. He was given to self-torture, even taking a certain pride in the idea that God had possibly *chosen* to give him a hard time. There was Job, wasn't there?

The difference between my parents lay in this sphere. It is a common difference between a man and a woman—particularly when one or the other has the creative genius. Creative man is given to wildness, and thence to wilderness, of soul—"desert places." This was true of Robert Frost. He gloried in wildness, in saying, "Poets get their knowledge cavalierly . . . They stick to nothing deliberately, but let what will stick to them like burrs where they walk in the fields. . . . No tears in the writer, no tears in the reader." While this could mean, and did, that life in his vicinity was both intellectually and emotionally exciting and rewarding, it also had its dangers for himself and others. It was by miraculous good fortune, or by the figure a poem makes ("it begins in delight and ends in wisdom—the figure is the same as for love") that he was saved through discovering the protection of "The Silken Tent." Pascal said, "We know the truth not only by the reason but by the heart.The heart has its reasons that reason knows not of."—Leslie Frost, "Introduction" to *New Hampshire's Child*, 1969

If his poetry-writing mother had lived to share the excitement of ⟨his⟩ triumphs, she might have understood, even better than he, some of the complicated relationships between his earliest humiliations and his consequent craving for glory. She knew how deeply he had been hurt and confused throughout his childhood by family difficulties and the marital estrangements of his parents; difficulties which had made the home in San Francisco more nearly a battleground than a place where a child might acquire a sense of security. Although the boy's father had rebelled against the austere puritanism of his own New England upbringing, the man had clung to a belief in the biblical precept that he who spareth the rod hateth his son, and in his attempt to be a good father he had cast the fury of his impatience on Robbie through frequent whippings, some of which caused lasting scars.

The boy's mother, shocked by the brutality of these punishments, often fled in tears to her bedroom and prayed for mercy while the whippings were being administered. Trying to make amends, she taught her son and her younger child, Jeanie, the consolations of religious belief. The children were made to understand that while the ways of God are indeed mysterious and beyond finding out, they are ultimately just. She also explained that if her children bravely accepted God's way of testing them in this world, they would be rewarded with life everlasting in the perfect world to come. Mrs. Frost read Bible stories to her children and helped them fashion their ideals around the achievements of heroes and heroines who overcame all painful hardships through actions which reflected courage, skill, cunning, wit, nobility, compassion, and persistent striving for glory.

Perhaps, during his boyhood, Robert Frost became so nervously upset that he confused the ideas of heavenly and earthly punishment. If God could punish by striking back at those who offended him, then there seemed to be divine justification for any man or boy to punish his enemies by striking back. These earliest hurts merely took new forms after the boy's father died; after the widowed mother moved from San Francisco to New England with her two children. Mrs. Frost, trying to earn a living as a public school teacher in Salem, New Hampshire, failed so completely that some of the students and townspeople insulted her and her children until she was forced to resign. The night before the Frosts moved from Salem, the boy said through furious tears, "You wait. Some day I'll come back . . . and show them."

He was determined that some day, somehow, he would be able to strike back, in self-vindication, and beneath all of his later ambition to triumph as a poet was at least the subconscious desire to make amends by retaliating against those who had humiliated him—and his mother. She had indeed made him want to achieve honor and glory based on heroic accomplishment, and this ideal became inextricably bound up with his desire to retaliate. . . .

He brought back from England all the hopes and fears he had taken with him. At the beginning of his triumph in America, he became depressed by a lack of confidence in his ability to continue writing poetry. In one mood of depression he hinted that his immediate poetic concern was with nothing except darkness. Half seriously and half playfully he once claimed he had nearly completed two books of verse, one to be called "Melanism" and the other "The Sense of Wrong." At another time he said, insinuatively, that "Pitchblende" was the title of a manuscript he had completed. These typically cryptic remarks are enough to illuminate a stanza of his poem, "Afterflakes":

If I shed such a darkness,
If the reason was in me,
That shadow of mine should show in form
Against the shapeless shadow of storm,
How swarthy I must be.

Sometimes, in these moods of darkness, when the sense of wrongs done to him was intermingled with the sense of his inability to carry on as a successful poet, his lack of confidence expressed itself in jealous fears. At the time of his return from England, Frost knew that the most highly praised New England poet was Edwin Arlington Robinson, and his jealousy of Robinson was caused largely by his fear that he might never be able to match Robinson's literary achievement. He felt that another serious competitor, in 1915, was the Imagist poet Amy Lowell, and he initially cultivated her friendship. As soon as he acquired more literary stature than she, however, he began to confide that he would soon "throw off the light mask" he wore when speaking of her in public. Some day he would expose her "for a fool as well as a fraud." Just before Amy Lowell died in 1925, Frost felt that he had managed to triumph over her, in a way which satisfied him. Edgar Lee Masters was another competitor who aroused Frost's jealousy for a time, but he was relieved—and even delighted—when the reputation of Masters began to slip. Sandburg threatened to become the most dangerous rival for popularity, and as a result Frost gradually intensified the harshness of his jealous remarks about Sandburg. Later, an attractive competitor for honors was young Edna St. Vincent Millay, whose vividly successful appeal to college audiences infuriated Frost. When he was elected to membership in the American Academy, in 1930, he privately confessed that he took an "evil pleasure" in this triumph over her. Beneath all these fears and jealousies was his lack of confidence in himself, inseparably tied in with his uncontrollable ambition to triumph over all rivals, and he justified his attitude by drawing one analogy from prizefighting: "There can be only one heavyweight champion at a time." . . .

The alternations of fact, as used by Frost in his gossiping, were not unrelated to those he made in his improved versions of his own life story. Even as his platform manner dramatized his ideal image of how he wanted to be viewed, so his accounts of his early experiences fulfilled his ideal of what he wished the story of his life to become. Although he tried to make the story distinct from any other in its uniqueness and originality, he often made it sound similar to one of Horatio Alger's accounts of how Ragged Dick or Tattered Tom, battling poverty and humiliation, grew up to win honor and glory—and wealth. Repeatedly claiming that he seemed to be doomed from the start, Frost liked to tell of how he had sold newspapers for pennies on the streets of San Francisco, and of how his father's great promise had been wasted in gambling and drunkenness. He always described his mother as an aristocratic Scots lady, defeated by her marital misfortunes, and subsequently humiliated by cruel circumstances, while the wealthy relatives who might have helped her turned their backs. Later, Frost said, these wealthy relatives turned against him simply because he wanted to be a poet instead of a lawyer. Although the fact do not support these claims, he seemed to convince himself that he was telling the truth most of the time. And in rounding out his mythic autobiography he usually stressed the point that in spite of seemingly insurmountable hindrances he had managed to achieve his goal in a way which was a complete triumph over all his enemies.

There were times when Frost did acknowledge the discrepancies between autobiographical facts and fictions. On one occasion he said in public, "Don't trust me too far. I'm liable to tell you anything. Trust me on the poetry, but don't trust me on my life. Check up on me some." This warning to others may have indicated some of the warnings he also tried to give himself. Earlier, as a teacher of psychology, he had used a text in which William James divided "the self" into "the Me" and "the I" to represent a dangerous aspect of inner conflict. James may have heightened Frost's awareness of the perpetual clash between his idealizing and his realizing responses.

An even more vivid warning, in his own family, caused him to try to reconcile these opposing drives. Over the years, he became increasingly frightened by what he saw happening to his younger sister Jeanie. She found her own ways of coping with her hurts and humiliations: more and more she withdrew into fantasies until she had to be placed in a mental institution, where she spent the remainder of her life. Before and after Jeanie's collapse, her brother warned others about similar dangers confronting anyone who became too self-indulgent in making retreats from realities. Repeatedly he referred to occasions in the past when he had felt himself standing on the edge of an abyss into which he might have fallen if he had not taken firm action to save himself.

One saving action, for Frost, was the writing of poetry, and he repeatedly said his art gave him a way of dealing with confusions which intermittently threatened to overwhelm him. When in an ugly mood, he could not resist using poems as weapons for striking back at those who had perhaps unconciously and unintentionally injured him. Even in these cases, he was inclined to conceal his purpose by intermingling seriousness with playfulness, to such an extent that his ambiguous meanings left his readers in doubt. Usually, however, he made his poetry dramatize and try to resolve the conflicts between the opposing sides of his consciousness—conflicts between affirming and denying, between hope and fear, between loving and hating.

It might seem that only those who knew Robert Frost well could understand and admire the hard-earned and always precarious triumph he gained over the constant threat of inner chaos. If so, however, he would not have won such widespread and continuous public response with his poetry. Perhaps the major reason why he remains the best-known and best-loved American poet, at home and abroad, is that no themes are more universal and attractive than those which try to offer affirmative resolutions for the conflicts dramatized in his life and in his poetry. Readers old and young, waging their own struggles against the constant threat of chaos, seem to find comfort and encouragement in many of his aphoristic lines which are so cherished that they have become familiar quotations: "Earth's the right place for love: I don't know where it's likely to go better." "The utmost reward of daring should be still to dare." "Ah, when to the heart of man was it ever less than a treason, to go with the drift of things?" "Something there is that doesn't love a wall, that wants it down." "Good fences make good neighbors." "But oh, the agitated heart till someone really find us out."—LAWRANCE THOMPSON, "Introduction" to *Robert Frost: The Years of Triumph, 1915–1938*, 1970, pp. xiii–xix

Years ago I heard Robert Frost define a mugwump as a little bird balancing on a twig with his mug pointing one way and his wump the other. Wasn't Frost himself a perfect illustration?

He laughed at educators, and was one. He twitted scientists but kept up with what they were doing. He was proart and antiart: an artist to his fingertips when writing poems, but a plain man and no nonsense on the platform speaking those poems. Also a plain man and no nonsense speaking *in* those poems. As for religion, you can make out as good a case for Frost the skeptic as for Frost the believer.

He was in favor of walls and he was scornful of walls. In "Mending Wall" the speaker kids his neighbor for insisting on repairing an unnecessary wall; but the speaker keeps right on doing his share of repairing nevertheless. That was not the only fence that Frost was on both sides of.

Did his mugwumpism help him as a poet? I wouldn't venture to say. Some great poets have been middle-of-the-road, others have been extremists. But one thing certain is that his mugwumpism helped Frost as a wise man. In the popular mind a wise man can't be an extremist. If he is so broadly and centrally located that he speaks, or seems to speak, for everybody, then he is a wise man indeed.

Of course Frost's definition of mugwump is far from accurate, and Frost probably only picked it up somewhere. Strictly speaking, a mugwump is a member of one political party who now and then switches his vote to the other party. This is what many Republicans did in 1884 to help elect Grover Cleveland. A mugwump by rights is a little bird that flits back and forth between two twigs. Or that changes his direction on the same twig.

Frost had good reason to be interested in mugwumps, for in politics he was close to being one in the true meaning of the word. A passionate Democrat at nine years of age, he helped elect Cleveland. At eighty-six he not only helped elect another Democrat for President, he helped inaugurate him. But in between, during those New Deal years, that was another story.

My guess is that Frost would not object to being called a mugwump. The word was pure American even before the coming of the white man. In the Algonquin tongue it means "big chief." No, Frost would not object. I can almost hear him chuckle.—ROBERT FRANCIS, "Frost as Mugwump," *Pot Shots at Poetry*, 1980, pp. 30–31

It may be only retrospection that makes it seem as if, in the late fall of 1962, Frost knew the end was in sight. *In the Clearing* had, after many delays, been published in the previous March to a response which could at best be called polite. There had been a large eighty-eighth birthday party in Washington, at which he presented a copy of his new book to the president; then came the Russian adventure with its less than glorious conclusion. In late November and early December of the year, he made what were to be his last two public appearances, the first of them at the newly opened Hopkins Center at Dartmouth. There he delivered his usual blend of talking and reading from his poetry; it was posthumously published as "On Extravagance"—his main theme for the evening. Five days later, he made his annual Ford Forum appearance at Jordan Hall in Boston. The Dartmouth talk celebrated "extravagance," the extravagance of the universe, and of man as "the most wasteful, spending thing in it—in all his luxuriance." Poetry was an "extravagance about grief," springing from great impulses such as the one to say "It sometimes seems as if" or (and as he would repeat in the Ford Forum talk) "If I could only tell you." After reading various poems, including, "The Most of It" and "Never Again Would Birds' Song . . ." as examples of extravagance, he ended with a short one from *Steeple Bush* which he seldom read aloud (first of a group titled *Five Nocturnes*, it was titled "The Night Light"):

She always had to burn a light
Beside her attic bed at night.
It gave bad dreams and broken sleep,
But helped the Lord her soul to keep.
Good gloom on her was thrown away.
It is on me by night or day,

Who have, as I suppose, ahead
The darkest of it still to dread.

"Suppose I end on that dark note. Good night," he concluded his talk. It was an unusual place for him to end, and carried a hint that the foreseeing "I" in the poem had a human counterpart in the old and tired poet.—WILLIAM H. PRITCHARD, "Deeper into Life," *Frost*, 1984, pp. 256–57

General

You asked me to look at the poem, "My Butterfly," in this week's paper, by Mr. Frost.

I am a trifle dizzy over the election, feel as if a hogshead of salt had rolled over me; but I am not stupid enough yet to fail to see the extreme beauty of that little ode. It gives me a pang to know that its author is poor. To be a poet and be poor is a terrible lot. What hope is there? I have felt the gag in my teeth whenever I wanted to sing—and I'm not much of a poet—a gag that can speak and say to me: "No! go grind for bread! Let the rich men like Tennyson and Swinburne and Lowell and Browning and Holmes do the singing; what right has a poor man to waste his time and breath with song." But all the same were I a rich man that young Frost should not leave school "for financial reasons." Going back to the poem "My Butterfly," it has some secret of genius between the lines, an appeal to sympathy lying deep in one's sources of tenderness; and moreover its art is singular and biting, even where the faulty places are almost obtruded. My wife read it aloud to me the other evening when my eyes ached after too hard a day's work; and it made me ashamed that I could feel discouraged when I thought of the probable disappointment in store for young Frost all his life long. If I had a chance to say my say to him I should tell him to forget that he ever made a poem and to never pen another rhyme. I told my brother that years ago and now he is a great lawyer instead of a disappointed poet with a gag in his mouth! I was a better lawyer than he when I was lured away by the Muses. If Frost has good health tell him to learn a trade or profession and carry a sling-shot in his pocket for Hoede. —MAURICE THOMPSON, Letter to W. H. Ward (Nov. 10, 1894), *Recognition of Robert Frost*, ed. Richard Thornton, 1937, pp. 17–18

It is a sinister thing that so American, I might even say so parochial, a talent as that of Robert Frost should have to be exported before it can find due encouragement and recognition.

Even Emerson had sufficient elasticity of mind to find something in the 'yawp'. One doesn't need to like a book or a poem or a picture in order to recognize artistic vigor. But the typical American editor of the last twenty years has resolutely shut his mind against serious American writing. I do not exaggerate, I quote exactly, when I say that these gentlemen deliberately write to authors that such and such a matter is 'too unfamiliar to our readers'.

There was once an American editor who would even print me, so I showed him Frost's *Death of the Hired Man*. He wouldn't have it; he had printed a weak pseudo-Masefieldian poem about a hired man two months before, one written in a stilted pseudo-literary language, with all sorts of floridities and worn-out ornaments.

Mr Frost is an honest writer, writing from himself, from his own knowledge and emotion; not simply picking up the manner which magazines are accepting at the moment, and applying it to topics in vogue. He is quite consciously and definitely putting New England rural life into verse. He is not using themes that anybody could have cribbed out of Ovid.

There are only two passions in art; there are only love and hate—with endless modifications. Frost has been honestly fond of the New England people, I dare say with spells of irritation. He has given their life honestly and seriously. He has never turned aside to make fun of it. He has taken their tragedy as tragedy, their stubbornness as stubbornness. I know more of farm life than I did before I had read his poems. That means I know more of 'Life'.

Mr Frost has dared to write, and for the most part with success, in the natural speech of New England; in natural spoken speech, which is very different from the 'natural' speech of the newspapers, and of many professors. His poetry is a bit slow, but you aren't held up every five minutes by the feeling that you are listening to a fool; so perhaps you read it just as easily and quickly as you might read the verse of some of the sillier and more 'vivacious' writers.

A sane man knows that a prose story can't be much better than the short stories of De Maupassant or of 'Steve' Crane. Frost's work is interesting, incidentally, because there has been during the last few years an effort to proceed from the prose short story to the short story in verse. Francis Jammes has done a successful novel in verse, in a third of the space a prose novel would have taken—*Existences* in *La Triomphe de la vie*. Vildrac and D. H. Lawrence have employed verse successfully for short stories. Masefield is not part of this movement. He has avoided all the difficulties of the immeasurably difficult art of good prose by using a slap-dash, flabby verse which has been accepted in New Zealand. Jammes, Vildrac and Lawrence have lived up to the exigencies of prose and have gained by brevity. This counts with serious artists.

Very well, then, Mr Frost holds up a mirror to nature, not an oleograph. It is natural and proper that I should have to come abroad to get printed, or that 'H.D.'—with her clear-cut derivations and her revivifications of Greece—should have to come abroad; or that Fletcher—with his *tic* and his discords and his contrariety and extended knowledge of everything—should have to come abroad. One need not censure the country; it is easier for us to emigrate than for America to change her civilization fast enough to please us. But why, IF there are serious people in America, desiring literature of America, literature accepting present conditions, rendering American life with sober fidelity— why, in heaven's name, is this book of New England eclogues given us under a foreign imprint?

Professors to the contrary notwithstanding, no one expects Jane Austen to be as interesting as Stendhal. A book about a dull, stupid, hemmed-in sort of life, by a person who has lived it, will never be as interesting as the work of some author who has comprehended many men's manners and seen many grades and conditions of existence. But Mr Frost's people are distinctly real. Their speech is real; he has known them. I don't want much to meet them, but I know that they exist, and what is more, that they exist as he has portrayed them.

Mr Frost has humour, but he is not its victim. *The Code* has a pervasive humor, the humor of things as they are, not that of an author trying to be funny, or trying to 'bring out' the ludicrous phase of some incident or character because he dares not rely on sheer presentation. There is nothing more nauseating to the developed mind than that sort of local buffoonery which the advertisements call 'racy'—the village wit presenting some village joke which is worn out everywhere else. It is a great comfort to find someone who tries to give life, the life of the rural district, as a whole, evenly, and not merely as a hook to hang jokes on. The easiest thing to see about a man is an eccentric or worn-out garment, and one is godforsakenly tired of the post–Bret-Hartian, post–Mark-Twainian humorist.

Mr Frost's work is not 'accomplished', but it is the work of a man who will make neither concessions nor pretences. He will perform no monkey-tricks. His stuff sticks in your head—not his words, nor his phrases, nor his cadences, but his subject matter. You do not confuse one of his poems with another in your memory.—EZRA POUND, "Robert Frost" (1914), *Literary Essays*, 1954, pp. 384–86

I have said that Mr. Frost's work is almost photographic. The qualification was unnecessary, it is photographic. The pictures, the characters, are reproduced directly from life, they are burnt into his mind as though it were a sensitive plate. He gives out what has been put in, unchanged by any personal mental process. His imagination is bounded by what he has seen, he is confined within the limits of his experience (or at least what might have been his experience) and bent all one way like the wind-blown trees of New England hillsides.

In America we are always a little late in following artistic leads. *Les Soirées de Médan*, and all Zola's long influence, are passing away in Europe. In England, even such a would-be realist as Masefield lights his stories with bursts of a very rare imagination. No such bursts flame over Mr. Frost's work. He tells you what he has seen *exactly* as he has seen it. And in the word *exactly* lies the half of his talent. The other half is a great and beautiful simplicity or phrase, the inheritance of a race brought up on the English Bible. Mr. Frost's work is not in the least objective. He is not writing of people whom he has met in summer vacations, who strike him as interesting, and whose life he thinks worthy of perpetuation. Mr. Frost writes as a man under the spell of a fixed idea. He is as racial as his own puppets. One of the great interests of the book is the uncompromising New Englander it reveals. That he could have written half so valuable a book had such not been the case I very much doubt. Art is rooted in the soil, and only the very greatest men can be both cosmopolitan and great. Mr. Frost is as New England as Burns is Scotch, Synge Irish, or Mistral Provençal.

And Mr. Frost has chosen his medium with an unerring sense of fitness. As there is no rare and vivid imaginative force playing over his subjects, so there is no exotic music pulsing through his verse. He has not been seduced into subtleties of expression which would be painfully out of place. His words are simple, straightforward, direct, manly, and there is an elemental quality in all he does which would surely be lost if he chose to pursue niceties of phrase. He writes in classic metres in a way to set the teeth of all the poets of the older schools on edge; and he writes in classic metres, and uses inversions and *clichés* whenever he pleases, those devices so abhorred by the newest generation. He goes his own way, regardless of anyone else's rules, and the result is a⟨n⟩ . . . unusual power and sincerity.—AMY LOWELL, *NR*, Feb. 20, 1915, pp. 81–82

We find in Frost's work the same homely, tough, colloquial humour as in the fifteenth Idyll of Theocritus. Like Virgil, he has been a farmer; and this ensured that his nature-poetry should not degenerate into false romanticism, whimsicality, heartiness, or mere botanizing. It is also important that Frost is a highly civilized man. He feels nature deeply: but his emotion is always passed through a filter of ironic detachment before it emerges in his verse. This renders impossible for him both the savage intensity of vision and the naive magniloquence which we find in Clare. Frost, like Clare, is first and foremost a simple soul; but he is also a complex intelligence, and the simplicity of his verse is the simplicity—not of nature—but of a serious and profoundly critical spirit.

It is this fundamental seriousness which makes him most akin to Wordsworth. Detachment, for him as for Wordsworth, is a necessary condition of the creative power. It is worth noticing that his most consistently successful work, *North of Boston*, which is concerned throughout with the New England landscape and character, was written while he was living in Gloucestershire. This is as clear an example of "emotion recollected in tranquillity" as the lines on Tintern Abbey. Frost's most remarkable affinity with Wordsworth, however, lies in the temper (or tempo, or temperature) of his verse. Most poets, when the poetic impulse flags, attempt to conceal and compensate for this by a display of virtuosity, by passages of verbal decoration, by complicating the verse-texture. This, in a long poem, results in a break of tempo, a feverish heightening of temperature which can never be quite hidden by artistic dexterity. Wordsworth never does this. His idiom is already so level that it can carry off even the "flat" passages. The same, on a smaller scale, is true of Frost. By consciously and consistently maintaining a conversational tone, he keeps the texture of his verse remarkably even. His poems are sometimes dull: they are never false, pretentious, artificially stimulated. As he writes in his poem, "The Oven Bird":

> The bird would cease and be as other birds
> But he knows in singing not to sing.
> The question that he frames in all but words
> Is what to make of a diminished thing.

The subdued, ironic twist at the end of this poem is typical of Frost. He is a serious moralist as well as a serious artist. But his peculiar intimacy with nature prevents him from being openly didactic. He teaches, like nature, in parables: sometimes merely presenting a picture, a mood, a narrative, and leaving you to draw your own conclusions; never permitting himself more than the tender, humorous sort of comment we find at the end of "Birches":

> Earth's the right place for love:
> I don't know where it's likely to go better.
> I'd like to go by climbing a birch tree,
> And climb black branches up a snow-white trunk
> *Toward* heaven, till the tree could bear no more,
> But dipped its top and set me down again.
> That would be good both going and coming back.
> One could do worse than be a swinger of birches.

There is something more deeply American here, and in the whole tenor of Frost's work, than the mere idiom of humour. The morality we find implicit in such admirable poems as "Birches," "Mending Wall," "Good-Bye and Keep Cold," "The Sound of the Trees," and "Mowing," is best summed up in these two extracts:

> We love the things we love for what they are.
>
> Anything more than the truth would have seemed
> too weak
> To the earnest love that laid the swale in rows,
> Not without feeble-pointed spikes of flowers
> (Pale orchises), and scared a bright green snake.
> The fact is the sweetest dream that labor knows.

This "earnest love" for things as they are, the mainspring of Frost's poetry, is not an exclusively American virtue: but it proceeds from the same sober, passionate puritanism that, breathing the genius of its local habitation, reached highest expression in the work of another New England poet, Emily Dickinson: it gives their poems a personal quality, a moral "feel," which would have been different if their authors had inherited any other national tradition. This "earnest love" is also the final refutation of anyone who asserts that Frost's nature poetry is escape-poetry.

Escapist nature-poetry represents a running away, in the first place, from human emotions. If further proof were needed that Frost is not guilty of this, we should find it in his narrative poems. These show the same contemplative loving-kindness that we feel in the narrative poems of Wordsworth: human emotions are related to earth and the seasons by a "natural piety": women are not turned into nymphs, nor nature into god or satyr. Here again we see the peculiar blend of honesty and subtlety which characterizes Frost's imagination. He is downright, yet seldom crude. His is not the innocence of the primitive mind, but the honesty of the civilized—an honesty that can be attained by the modern poet only after severe discipline, whose balance any relaxation will instantly destroy. Integrity is an overworked term today: but it can be applied with accuracy to the work of Robert Frost. His poetry is by no means so widely known in England as it should be, though he has for long commanded the respect of his fellow-poets. It is to be hoped that this edition will extend his popularity. It is time we did him what honour we can.—C. DAY LEWIS, "Preface" to *Selected Poems of Robert Frost*, 1936

Perhaps the best way to acquire an idea of Robert Frost's poetic method is to take one of his poems and follow out its development. "The Axe-Helve" is as good an example as any, and it expresses, I think, an attitude which is both somewhat unusual in poetry and at the same time perfectly comprehensible.

It begins:

I've known ere now an interfering branch
Of alder catch my lifted axe behind me.

These lines define a feeling which is fairly constant in Mr. Frost's poetry: that all action presents not only straightforward difficulties but unexpected ones as well, so that one has to be on one's guard against unforeseen resistances. In the next few lines he qualifies the danger—his final statements are generally arrived at by a series of qualifications—and insists that the branch "was, as I say, an alder branch." Then he goes on:

This was a man, Baptiste, who stole one day
Behind me on the snow in my own yard
Where I was working at the chopping block,
And cutting nothing not cut down already.
He caught my axe expertly on the rise,
When all my strength put forth was in his favor,
Held it a moment where it was, to calm me,
Then took it from me—and I let him take it.
I didn't know him well enough to know
What it was all about. There might be something
He had in mind to say to a bad neighbor
He might prefer to say to him disarmed.

Here once more there is a real or potential danger to be allowed for; it is indicated merely as a humorous contingency, though the humour is considerably discounted by the complete helplessness expressed in the line:

When all my strength put forth was in his favor.

But after all Baptiste merely wished to speak about the axe.

It was the bad axe-helve someone had sold me—
"Made on machine," he said, ploughing the grain
With a thick thumbnail to show how it ran
Across the handle's long drawn serpentine,
Like the two strokes across a dollar sign.
"You give her one good crack, she's snap raght off.
Den where's your hax-ead flying t'rough de hair?"
Admitted; and yet, what was that to him?

And so the poem continues in an almost dialectically strict progression where one false possibility is rejected after another. Baptiste offers to put in another helve that will last better.

Something to sell? That wasn't how it sounded,

is the narrator's response. Baptiste continues:

"Den when you say you come? It's cost you nothing.
Tonaght?"
As well tonight as any other night.

When the narrator goes to Baptiste's house he takes care to observe:

My welcome differed from no other welcome.
Baptiste knew best why I was where I was.
So long as he would leave enough unsaid,
I shouldn't mind his being overjoyed
(If overjoyed he was) at having got me
Where I must judge if what he knew about an axe
That not everybody else knew was to count
For nothing in the measure of a neighbor.
Hard if, though cast away for life with Yankees,
A Frenchman couldn't get his human rating!

There is in all this an extraordinary caution and watchfulness. The narrator now suspects that Baptiste has got him to his house under false pretences, and that the axe-helve is a mere excuse. Mrs. Baptiste does not know much English. So

I was afraid, in brightening first on me,
Then on Baptiste, as if she understood
What passed between us, she was only feigning.

And then the definite suspicion crystallizes:

Baptiste was anxious for her; but no more
Than for himself, so placed he couldn't hope
To keep his bargain of the morning with me
In time to keep me from suspecting him
Of really never having meant to keep it.

The poem does not end there, however, for:

Needlessly soon he had his axe-helves out . . .
He showed me that the lines of a good helve
Were native to the grain before the knife
Expressed them, and its curves were no false curves
Put on it from without.

Here we come to another perception which is constant in Mr. Frost's poetry: that things, and feelings too, have a rightness which is finally dependent on the natural material out of which they are made, a rightness which can be achieved only by a kind of patience:

Baptiste knew how to make a short job long
For love of it, and yet not waste time either.

The poem ends:

Do you know, what we talked about was knowledge?
Baptiste on his defense about the children
He kept from school, or did his best to keep—
Whatever school and children and our doubts
Of laid-on education had to do
With the curves of his axe-helves and his having
Used these unscrupulously to bring me
To see for once the inside of his house.
Was I desired in friendship, partly as some one
To leave it to, whether the right to hold
Such doubts of education should depend
Upon the education of those who held them?
But now he brushed the shavings from his knee
And stood the axe there on its horse's hoof,
Erect, but not without its waves, as when
The snake stood up for evil in the Garden,—
Top-heavy with a heaviness his short,
Thick hand made light of, steel-blue chin drawn
down
And in a little—a French touch in that.
Baptiste drew back and squinted at it, pleased;
"See how she's cock her head!"

The development of this poem gives us a pleasure somewhat analogous to that we have from reading Plato's *Dialogues;* the only method used seems to be the rejection of false hypotheses; yet starting from a perfectly simple position we reach one we could never have foreseen. It is in this strict and watchful development of his theme, this steady movement towards a point related to his starting-point and yet not obviously implicit in it, that Mr. Frost is perhaps most remarkable as a poet. His revelation of his theme is gradual; it is not contained in an instantaneous flash, but in the whole movement. And it is achieved almost entirely by the use of what Mr. W. B. Yeats, speaking in another connection, calls "dull, numb words." By these Mr. Frost sets out to define the truth implicit in a situation as the lines of a good helve are implicit in the lines of the wood.

Mr. Frost uses these words with consummate skill; but as his constant aim is to define them, that is to select one meaning out of the many they possess and use that only, his poetry is of a very peculiar kind; for most of the poetry we know proceeds by the opposite method, giving words a many-sided significance. In a sense Mr. Frost's poetry may be called a sort of anti-poetry. It is not only unlike

> And peace proclaims olives of endless age,

but inimical to it. It is much nearer, in a curious way, to the stories of Franz Kafka, who also started from a simple position and by rejecting false hypotheses arrived at very strange conclusions, than to any other poetry one can think of. —EDWIN MUIR, "Preface" to *Selected Poems of Robert Frost*, 1936

Abstraction is an old story with the philosophers, but it has been like a new toy in the hands of the artists of our day. Why can't we have any one quality of poetry we choose by itself? We can have in thought. Then it will go hard if we can't in practice. Our lives for it.

Granted no one but a humanist much cares how sound a poem is if it is only *a* sound. The sound is the gold in the ore. Then we will have the sound out alone and dispense with the inessential. We do till we make the discovery that the object in writing poetry is to make all poems sound as different as possible from each other, and the resources for that of vowels, consonants, punctuation, syntax, words, sentences, meter are not enough. We need the help of context—meaning—subject matter. That is the greatest help towards variety. All that can be done with words is soon told. So also with meters—particularly in our language where there are virtually but two, strict iambic and loose iambic. The ancients with many were still poor if they depended on meters for all tune. It is painful to watch our sprung-rhythmists straining at the point of omitting one short from a foot for relief from monotony. The possibilities for tune from the dramatic tones of meaning struck across the rigidity of a limited meter are endless. And we are back in poetry as merely one more art of having something to say, sound or unsound. Probably better if sound, because deeper and from wider experience.

Then there is this wildness whereof it is spoken. Granted again that it has an equal claim with sound to being a poem's better half. If it is a wild tune, it is a poem. Our problem then is, as modern abstractionists, to have the wildness pure; to be wild with nothing to be wild about. We bring up as aberrationists, giving way to undirected associations and kicking ourselves from one chance suggestion to another in all directions as of a hot afternoon in the life of a grasshopper. Theme alone can steady us down. Just as the first mystery was how a poem could have a tune in such a straightness as meter, so the second mystery is how a poem can have wildness and at the same time a subject that shall be fulfilled.

It should be of the pleasure of a poem itself to tell how it can. The figure a poem makes. It begins in delight and ends in wisdom. The figure is the same as for love. No one can really hold that the ecstasy should be static and stand still in one place. It begins in delight, it inclines to the impulse, it assumes direction with the first line laid down, it runs a course of lucky events, and ends in a clarification of life—not necessarily a great clarification, such as sects and cults are founded on, but in a momentary stay against confusion. It has denouement. It has an outcome that though unforeseen was predestined from the first image of the original mood—and indeed from the very mood. It is but a trick poem and no poem at all if the best of it was thought of first and saved for the last. It finds its own name as it goes and discovers the best waiting for it in some final phrase at once wise and sad—the happy-sad blend of the drinking song.

No tears in the writer, no tears in the reader. No surprise for the writer, no surprise for the reader. For me the initial delight is in the surprise of remembering something I didn't know I knew. I am in a place, in a situation, as if I had materialized from cloud or risen out of the ground. There is a glad recognition of the long lost and the rest follows. Step by step the wonder of unexpected supply keeps growing. The impressions most useful to my purpose seems always those I was unaware of and so made no note of at the time when taken, and the conclusion is come to that like giants we are always hurling experience ahead of us to pave the future with against the day when we may want to strike a line of purpose across it for somewhere. The line will have the more charm for not being mechanically straight. We enjoy the straight crookedness of a good walking stick. Modern instruments of precision are being used to make things crooked as if by eye and hand in the old days.

I tell how there may be a better wildness of logic than of inconsequence. But the logic is backward, in retrospect, after the act. It must be more felt than seen ahead like prophecy. It must be a revelation, or a series of revelations, as much for the poet as for the reader. For it to be that there must have been the greatest freedom of the material to move about in it and to establish relations in it regardless of time and space, previous relation, and everything but affinity. We prate of freedom. We call our schools free because we are not free to stay away from them till we are sixteen years of age. I have given up my democratic prejudices and now willingly set the lower classes free to be completely taken care of by the upper classes. Political freedom is nothing to me. I bestow it right and left. All I would keep for myself is the freedom of my material—the condition of body and mind now and then to summons aptly from the vast chaos of all I have lived through.

Scholars and artists thrown together are often annoyed at the puzzle of where they differ. Both work from knowledge; but I suspect they differ most importantly in the way their knowledge is come by. Scholars get theirs with conscientious thoroughness along projected lines of logic; poets theirs cavalierly and as it happens in and out of books. They stick to nothing deliberately, but let what will stick to them like burrs where they walk in the fields. No acquirement is on assignment, or even self-assignment. Knowledge of the second kind is much more available in the wild free ways of wit and art. A schoolboy may be defined as one who can tell you what he knows in the order in which he learned it. The artist must value himself as he snatches a thing from some previous order in time and space into a new order with not so much as a ligature clinging to it of the old place where it was organic.

More than once I should have lost my soul to radicalism if it had been the originality it was mistaken for by its young converts. Originality and initiative are what I ask for my country. For myself the originality need be no more than the freshness of a poem run in the way I have described: from delight to wisdom. The figure is the same as for love. Like a piece of ice on a hot stove the poem must ride on its own melting. A poem may be worked over once it is in being, but may not be worried into being. Its most precious quality will remain its having run itself and carried away the poet with it. Read it a hundred times: it will forever keep its freshness as a metal keeps its fragrance. It can never lose its sense of a meaning that once unfolded by surprise as it went.—ROBERT FROST, "The Figure a Poem Makes," *Selected Poems of Robert Frost*, 1963, pp. 1–4

Robert Frost never offends against the decencies by boasting of what he has achieved as a poet. Though he must be well aware that nobody else could have written these poems, which are stamped all over with his own seal, and though plenty of people would give their right hands to have done so, he says simply: 'It's for the world to decide whether you're a poet or not.' The truth is that Frost was the first American who could be honestly reckoned a master-poet by world standards. Poe, Longfellow, Whittier, and many more of his American predecessors had written good provincial verse; and Whitman, a homespun eccentric, had fallen short of the master-post title only through failing to realize how much more was required of him. Frost has won the title fairly, not by turning his back on ancient European tradition, nor by imitating its successes, but by developing it in a way that at last matches the American climate and the American language.

'Master-poet' has been wrongly read by teachers and college professors who use Frost's work as a ruler to whack on their pupils' knuckles. It means that, like a master-goldsmith or a master-mason, he knows exactly what he is doing and why; not that he is in need of disciples to applaud him. Frost has remarked that being taught poems at school reduces them to the rank of mere information, and that he doubts whether 'poetic literature' deserves a place in the educational curriculum. In other words, poetry should be treated as a private matter. To teach it as class-room literature is like reducing love to public philanthropy, or religion to Church history and doctrine. Nevertheless, most people first become aware of poetry at their schools or colleges; and a few of these, at least, make it a free gift, not a subject for grades.

One good way of judging poets is to pretend that they are still living, even if they have been dead two thousand years or more, and to decide what personal immediacy they still have for you. Imagine yourself saying: 'Tonight there's to be a moonlight barbecue down by the creek. Just ourselves, and maybe two or three special others . . . Would it be fun if John Milton came along? Or Will Shakespeare? Or Johnny Keats? Or Mr. Percy Bysshe Shelley? Or Herr Professor Johann Wolfgang von Goethe? Or Old Homer, the harpist? Or Signor Dante Alighieri?' A quick leaf-through of their poems will give you a pretty shrewd notion which of them would be readily accepted by everyone at the barbecue, including the non-intellectuals, and make you all feel warmer towards each other than before, and perhaps keep an unforgettable conversation going until the small hours. Those special ones would be the master-poets; of whom there have been very few in history.

I agree with Frost that a poem planned beforehand never comes off. Real ones appear unexpectedly, and always at a time when the poet is in a so-called state of grace: which means a clear mind, tense heart, and no worries about fame, money, or other people, but only the excitement of a unique revelation about to be given.

Frost is a quick worker; many of his poems are written straight off. Some, he admits, have trouble in one or two spots that he may never put right, because it is so difficult to recover the trance-like mood in which a poem first entered the mind. A poem's most precious quality, he says, will always be that it ran in from nowhere and carried the poet away with it. Yet sometimes the trouble can be removed, by a sudden insight, twenty or thirty years later. . . .

Frost has always respected metre. When, during the *Vers Libre* period of the Nineteen Twenties and Thirties his poems were disdained as old-fashioned, he remarked disdainfully that writing free verse was like playing tennis without a net. The *Vers Librists*, it should be explained, had rebelled against a degenerate sort of poetry in which nothing mattered except getting the ball neatly over the net. Few games are so wearisome to watch as a methodical ping-pong, ping-pong tennis match in which each player allows his opponent an easy forehand return from the same court. The *Vers Librists*, therefore, abandoned the tennis-net of metre altogether, and concentrated on rhythm. But though metre is boring without rhythm, the reverse is equally true. A rhythmic manipulation of metre means—in this tennis metaphor—so placing your shots that you force the other fellow to dart all round his territory, using backhand, forehand, volley or half-volley as the play demands. Only the 'strain of rhythm upon metre' (Frost's own phrase), makes a poem worth reading, or a long rally in tennis worth watching. That you can't achieve much in poetry without, so to speak, a taut net and straight whitewashed lines, is shown by the difficulty of memorizing free verse; it does not fix itself firmly enough in the imagination.

Frost farmed for ten years among the well-wooded hills of Vermont. The four natural objects most proper to poems are, by common consent, the moon, water, hills and trees; with sun, birds, beasts and flowers as useful subsidiaries. It is remarkable that, among the ancient Irish, Highland Scots and Welsh, from whose tradition (though at second or third hand) English poetry derives most of its strange magic—the Muse was a Moon, Mountain and Water-goddess, and the word for poetic literature was always 'trees'. Bardic schools were built in forests, not in towns; and every letter of the alphabet had a tree name. Frost's most haunting poems, such as 'The Wood-Pile,' 'Birches,' 'An Encounter,' 'Stopping by Woods on a Snowy Evening,' are set in woods. The moon floats above, and water rushes down from every hill. The farmhouse in the clearing—unless it is staging one of those poignant country dramas which are his specialty—provides him with a convenient centre from which to saunter out and commune in thought with the birches, maples, hickories, pines, or wild apples. 'Into My Own,' the first poem of Frost's apprentice-work, 'A Boy's Will' (1913), begins:

> One of my wishes is that those dark trees,
> So old and firm they scarcely show the breeze,
> Were not, as 'twere, the merest mask of gloom,
> But stretched away unto the edge of doom

Among trees, you are usually alone, but seldom lonely: they are companionable presences for those in love and, although Frost seldom uses the word 'love', all his poems are instinct with it.

He reminds us that poems, like love, begin in surprise, delight and tears, and end in wisdom. Whereas scholars follow projected lines of logic, he collects his knowledge undeliberately, he says, like burrs that stick to your legs when you walk through a field. Surprise always clings to a real poem, however often it is read; but must come naturally, cannot be achieved by the cunning formula of a short story or detective thriller. If there have been no tears of surprise in the writer, then there will be no tears of surprise in the reader. The poetic impulse, though unforeseeable, can be discouraged all too easily. Most poets sell themselves to money, religion, literature, politics, philosophy or social position, before they have reached their middle 'twenties, and that is the end of them. Frost has never sold himself, though not shy of mixed company.

One good way of judging a particular poem (once you have saved time by first judging the poet) is to ask yourself whether the package contains anything irrelevant to its declared contents, and whether anything essential has been left out. I admit that even Frost lapses at times into literary references, philosophy, political argument and idle play with words; yet has any other man now alive written more poems that stand up to this packaging test? His chief preoccupation is freedom: freedom to be himself, to make discoveries, to work, to love, and not to be limited by any power except personal conscience or commonsense.

One of his best-known poems, 'Mending Wall,' begins:

> Something there is that doesn't love a wall,
> That sends the frozen-ground-swell under it,
> And spills the upper boulders in the sun;

He and his neighbour, between them, annually repaired the wall that separates their farms, each working from his own side and keeping pace with the other. Although neither of them raised sheep or cows that might stray into the crops—Frost had only apple-trees; his neighbour, pines—the repairs were made to justify the proverb 'Good fences make good neighbours!' And if anyone asks: 'But what *is* the something that doesn't love a wall?', the answer is, of course, 'frost'—also its open-hearted namesake, Robert Frost.

The old Vermont way of life ended long ago. Solitude among trees, solitude beside running water or under the moon, fostered these poems. Now the backwoodsman buys himself a television set and finds company enough in the commercials:

> Four-room shack aspiring high
> With an arm of scrawny mast
> For the visions in the sky
> That go blindly pouring past.
> In the ear and in the eye
> What you get is what to buy.
> Hope you're satisfied to last.

Though Frost owns to the growing materialism of the United States, which stultifies the Founding Fathers' prayer for courage and self-control among those destined to occupy the land, he refuses to lament bygone times. The land, the tools, and the language are all still available, and he has himself proved how nobly they can be used. Nevertheless, it would be rash to expect that another master-poet of the same quality will appear under the present economic system, despite a shorter working week, improvements in transport, and a greater ease in living. To resist the social pressure now put even on one's leisure time, requires a tougher upbringing and a more obstinate wilfulness about going one's own way, than ever before. A great part of the countryside has been scheduled for industrialization and, as everyone tells me, this is a critical, rather than a creative age. But give thanks, at least, that you still have Frost's poems; and when you feel the need of solitude, retreat to the companionship of moon, water, hills and trees. Retreat, he reminds us, should not be confused with escape. And take these poems along for good luck!—ROBERT GRAVES, "Introduction" to *Selected Poems of Robert Frost*, 1963, pp. ix–xiv

The best of all, he recognized, is "belief," belief that lies beyond the need of defenses, humorous or otherwise. This is what the great poets have. "Belief is better than anything else, and it is best when rapt, above paying its respects to anybody's doubt whatsoever. At bottom the world isn't a joke." What is important is not simply to have "belief" (Frost in fact had plenty), but, poetically, to make no apology for having it. Not, at any rate, the kind of apology that lies behind the ironic personas of so many of Frost's serious poems.

"Humor is the most engaging cowardice." Although Frost's manner is not always humorous, and although much of his ironic defensiveness represents, as we shall see later, a conscious pragmatism, an awareness of the moral and psychological value of a humorous perspective, this statement perhaps sums up best of all why Frost is not among the great poets, though he is among the very good ones. We reserve greatness for "believers"—in no matter what. Frost's concern "not to set down an idea that is of [his] own thinking," but rather "to give it as in character" certainly made for liveliness, immediacy, and variety in his work. He greatly extended the "sound" of poetry. But all too often the "voice" of a poem acts as a mask, "simply a kind of guardedness," shielding the poet from the full implications of his serious subjects and preventing any real intellectual grappling with them.

It would be a mistake, of course, to assume that in every Frost poem the voice is humorous or whimsical, or indeed that a persona is clearly characterized at all. In some poems there are no idiosyncrasies of voice to render personality, no intruding touches of characterization. In such poems as "Design," for instance, or "Neither Out Far Nor In Deep," Frost is more concerned with the subject than with the speaker's apprehension of it, and there is a direct commerce between poet and reader. Whether or not Frost is using his "own" voice here is debatable. Suffice it to say that in some of Frost's poems we are unaware of an individualized persona taking delight in "saying a thing," but that most of his poems do "shape on some speaking tone of voice," and that an awareness of "voice" is perhaps the most fruitful way of approaching his poetry.

Apart from the interpretation of individual poems, a proper attention to the tones of voice in his poetry enables us to appreciate more exactly the nature of Frost's distinctive contribution to American literature. The sheer variety of sound in Frost's poetry makes most other poets seem one-dimensional. Working with the cadences of New England speech, and declining "music" in favor of "the sound of the talking voice," Frost ranged in tone from the lyric to the narrative, from the dramatic to the meditative, from the "terrifying" to the humorous. All the fun's in how you say a thing.—ELAINE BARRY, "Introduction" to *Robert Frost*, 1973, pp. 15–17

Our concern is with Frost's poetry; the main question is, "Are we reading his poetry correctly?" To begin with, if we accede to the Frost myth, we oversimplify our reading. The myth implies, for one thing, that Frost's work is explicit, that everything in it is immediately available on the surface. Further, it suggests that his work is not so much "poetry" as "verse" (to make the snobbish distinction), hence less worth critical attention. It may be taken as simple stuff, casually tossed off—or at least not as painstakingly wrought as the poetry of Eliot or Yeats—and therefore not worth as much aesthetic attention.

Let us consider "Mending Wall" as a kind of test case, for there the speaker seems to be the very image of the Frost myth. Here we find the typical rural activity of mending a stone wall in the spring, one shared by the poet and a neighbor, both farmers:

Something there is that doesn't love a wall,
That sends the frozen-ground-swell under it
And spills the upper boulders in the sun,
And makes gaps even two can pass abreast.
The work of hunters is another thing:
I have come after them and made repair
Where they have left not one stone on a stone,
But they would have the rabbit out of hiding,
To please the yelping dogs . . .
I let my neighbor know beyond the hill;
And on a day we meet to walk the line
And set the wall between us once again. . . .
There where it is we do not need the wall:
He is all pine and I am apple orchard.
My apple trees will never get across
And eat the cones under his pines, I tell him.
He only says, "Good fences make good neighbors . . ."
I see him there,
Bringing a stone grasped firmly by the top
In each hand, like an old-stone savage armed.
He moves in darkness as it seems to me,
Not of woods only and the shade of trees.
He will not go behind his father's saying,
And he likes having thought of it so well
He says again, "Good fences make good neighbors."

On the simplest level, the poem pictures the activity clearly, in plain language, and makes gentle fun of the neighbor for insisting that "good fences make good neighbors" when it is clear that there is no practical reason for this one, and that in addition there is something unnatural about walls in general. This simplistic interpretation is hardly all there is to it, however, as experienced readers know. The Frost "myth" of the benevolent country thinker who "says" his poems straight out as if for people who don't like poetry has been sharply modified by our growing consciousness of Frost's complexity. Inevitably, as his poetry is read more closely and thoughtfully (and as we acquire information about Frost himself like that in Thompson's biography in support of our literary insights), further implications and problems in his work emerge more fully. In "Mending Wall," it becomes clear that the speaker really favors mending the wall—he initiates the process every year, and inveighs against the destructive hunters, even though there seems little overt reason for this particular wall. Thus the speaker accepts the activity as a ritual, restoring a symbol of manmade barriers that have the general function of restricting the chaos of ungoverned nature. The poem may be taken mainly as an attack on the neighbor's mindless "darkness"—yet he seems, as a "natural" man, essentially sound in his inherited respect for walls.

In the last analysis the wall is both good and bad. The barrier serves both to separate the men and to bring them together, and each of these functions is ambivalent. Individuation, maintained by barriers, is necessary to personal integrity, but understanding and cooperation are just as humanly important. The neighbor farmer simply sees that barriers are necessary without understanding why, while the speaker knows why they are and sees the defects of barriers, too. He accepts the paradox and works within it.

Yet a further dimension to the poem is offered by psychoanalytic analysis. Few now deny that poetry is always to some extent a projection of the author's psyche, unconscious as well as conscious, although there is much dispute about particular interpretations. The number of images in the poem concerning the mouth, eating, and speech suggest to Norman Holland an oral "nucleus of fantasy" that embodies the desire to destroy all barriers between the self and the outside world—an impulse at the root of much that is consciously expressed in the poem. Whether one accepts such interpretations or not, many critics acknowledge the validity of the approach as a means of providing further insight into poetry that has all too often been taken superficially as the work of a kindly old farmer-philosopher.—James L. Potter, *Robert Frost Handbook*, 1980, pp. 48–50

EDWARD GARNETT
"A New American Poet"

Atlantic, August 1915, pp. 214–21

A short time ago I found on a London bookstall an odd number of *The Poetry Review*, with examples of and comments on 'Modern American Poets,'—examples which whetted my curiosity. But the few quotations given appeared to me literary bric-à-brac, the fruit of light *liaisons* between American dilettantism and European models. Such poetry, æsthetic or sentimental,—reflections of vagrant influences, lyrical embroideries in the latest designs, with little imaginative insight into life or nature,—abounds in every generation. If sufficiently bizarre its pretensions are cried up in small Bohemian coteries; if sufficiently orthodox in tone and form, it may impress itself on that public which reads poetry as it looks idly at pictures, with sentimental appetite or from a vague respect for 'culture.' Next I turned to some American magazines at hand, and was brought to a pause by discovering some interesting verse by modern American poets, especially by women whose sincerity in the expression of the inner life of love compared well with the ambitious flights of some of their rivals. I learned indeed from a magazine article that the 'New Poetry' was in process of being hatched out by the younger school; and, no doubt, further researches would have yielded a harvest, had not a literary friend chanced to place in my hands a slim green volume, *North of Boston*, by Robert Frost. I read it, and reread it. It seemed to me that this poet was destined to take a permanent place in American literature. I asked myself why this book was issued by an English and not by an American publisher. And to this question I have found no answer. I may add here, in parenthesis, that I know nothing of Mr. Robert Frost save the three or four particulars I gleaned from the English friend who sent me *North of Boston*.

In an illuminating paper on recent American fiction which I hope by and by, with the editor's permission, to discuss along with Mr. Owen Wister's smashing onslaught in the *Atlantic Monthly*, Mr. W. D. Howells remarks, 'By test of the native touch we should not find genuine some of the American writers whom Mr. Garnett accounts so.' No doubt Mr. Howells's stricture is just, and certain American novelists—whom he does not however particularize—have been too affected in spirit by European models. Indeed Frank Norris's early work, *Vandover and the Brute*, is quite continental in tone; and it is arguable that his study of the French Naturalists may have shown beneficial results later, in the breadth of scheme and clarity of *The Pit*.

This point of 'the native touch' raises difficult questions, for the ferment of foreign influence has often marked the point of departure and rise of powerful native writers, such as

Pushkin in Russia and Fenimore Cooper in America. Again, if we consider the fiction of Poe and Herman Melville, would it not be difficult to assess their genuineness by any standard or measure of 'native touch'? But I take it that Mr. Howells would ban as 'not genuine' only those writers whose originality in vision, tone, and style has been patently marred or nullified by their surrender to exotic influences.

So complex may be the interlacing strains that blend in a writer's literary ancestry and determine his style, that the question first to ask seems to me whether a given author is a fresh creative force, an original voice in literature. Such an authentic original force to me speaks from *North of Boston*. Surely a genuine New England voice, whatever be its literary debt to old-world English ancestry. Originality, the point is there,—for we may note that originality of tone and vision is always the stumbling-block to the common taste when the latter is invited to readjust its accepted standards.

On opening *North of Boston* we see the first line to be stamped with the magic of *style*, of a style that obeys its own laws of grace and beauty and inner harmony.

Something there is that doesn't love a wall,
That sends the frozen-ground-swell under it,
And spills the upper boulders in the sun;
And makes gaps even two can pass abreast.
The work of hunters is another thing:
I have come after them and made repair
Where they have left not one stone on stone,
But they would have the rabbit out of hiding,
To please the yelping dogs.

Note the clarity of the images, the firm outline. How delicately the unobtrusive opening suggests the countryman's contemplative pleasure in his fields and woods. It seems so very quiet, the modern reader may complain, forgetting Wordsworth; and indeed, had Wordsworth written these lines, I think they must have stood in every English anthology. And when we turn the page, the second poem, 'The Death of the Hired Man,' proves that this American poet has arrived, not indeed to challenge the English poet's possession of his territory, but to show how untrodden, how limitless are the stretching adjacent lands. 'The Death of the Hired Man' is a dramatic dialogue between husband and wife, a dialogue characterized by an exquisite precision of psychological insight. I note that two college professors have lately been taking Mr. Ruckstuhl to task for a new definition of poetry. Let us fly all such debates, following Goethe, who, condemning the 'æsthete who labors to express the nature of poetry and of poets,' exclaimed, 'What do we want with so much definition? A lively feeling of situations and an aptitude to describe them makes the poet.' This definition, though it does not cover the whole ground, is apropos to our purpose.

Mr. Frost possesses a keen feeling for situation. And his fine, sure touch in clarifying our obscure instincts and clashing impulses, and in crystallizing them in sharp, precise images,—for that we cannot be too grateful. Observe the tense, simple dramatic action, foreshadowing conflict, in the opening lines of 'The Death of the Hired Man':

Mary sat musing on the lamp-flame at the table
Waiting for Warren. When she heard his step,
She ran on tip-toe down the darkened passage
To meet him in the doorway with the news
And put him on his guard. 'Silas is back.'
She pushed him outward with her through the door
And shut it after her. 'Be kind,' she said.

'It's we who must be good to him now,' she urges. I wish I had space to quote the debate so simple in its homely force, so comprehending in its spiritual veracity; but I must restrict myself to these arresting lines and to the hushed, tragic close:—

Part of a moon was falling down the west
Dragging the whole sky with it to the hills.
Its light poured softly in her lap. She saw
And spread her apron on it. She put out her hand
Among the harp-like morning-glory strings
Taut with the dew from garden bed to eaves,
As if she played unheard the tenderness
That wrought on him beside her in the night.
'Warren,' she said, 'he has come home to die:
You need n't be afraid he'll leave you this time.'
'Home,' he mocked gently.
'Yes, what else but home?
It all depends on what you mean by home.
Of course he's nothing to us, any more
Than was the hound that came a stranger to us
Out of the woods, worn out upon the trail.'
'Home is the place where, when you have to go there,
They have to take you in.'
'I should have called it
Something you somehow have n't to deserve.'
. . .
'You'll be surprised at him—how much he's broken,
His working days are done; I'm sure of it.'
'I'd not be in a hurry to say that.'
'I have n't been. Go, look, see for yourself.
But, Warren, please remember how it is:
He's come to help you ditch the meadow.
He has a plan. You must n't laugh at him.
He may not speak of it, and then he may.
I'll sit and see if that small sailing cloud
Will hit or miss the moon.'
It hit the moon.
Then there were three there making a dim row,
The moon, the little silver cloud, and she.
Warren returned—too soon, it seemed to her,
Slipped to her side, caught up her hand and waited.
'Warren,' she questioned.
'Dead,' was all he answered.

Yes, this is poetry, but of what order? the people may question, to whom for some reason poetry connotes the fervor of lyrical passion, the glow of romantic color, or the play of picturesque fancy. But it is precisely its quiet passion and spiritual tenderness that betray this to be poetry of a rare order, 'the poetry of a true real natural vision of life,' which, as Goethe declared, 'demands descriptive power of the highest degree, rendering a poet's pictures so lifelike that they become actualities to every reader.' One may indeed anticipate that the 'honorable minority' will appraise highly the spiritual beauty of the lines above quoted.

But what of his unconventional *genre* picture, such as 'A Hundred Collars'? Is it necessary to carry the war against the enemy's cardboard fortresses of convention by using Goethe's further declaration:—

'At bottom no subject is unpoetical, if only the poet knows how to treat it alright.' The dictum is explicit: 'A true, real, natural vision of life . . . high descriptive power . . . pictures of life-like actuality . . . a lively feeling of situation'—if a poet possess these qualifications he may treat any theme or situation he pleases. Indeed, the more prosaic appears the vesture of everyday life, the greater is the poet's triumph in seizing and representing the enduring human interest of its familiar features. In the characteristic fact, form, or feature the poet no less than the artist will discover essential lines and aspects of beauty. Nothing is barred to him, if he only have *vision*. Even the most eccentric divagations in human conduct can be exhibited in their true spiritual perspective by the psychologist of insight, as Browning repeatedly demonstrates. One sees no reason why Browning's 'Fra Lippo Lippi' with all its roughcast philosophic speculation should be 'poetry' and Mr. Frost's 'A Hundred Collars' should not; and indeed the purist must keep the gate closed on both or on neither. If I desired indeed to know whether a reader could really detect the genuine poet, when he appears amid the crowd of *dilettanti*, I should ask his judgment on a typical uncompromising passage in 'A Hundred Collars,' such as the following:—

'No room,' the night clerk said, 'Unless—'
Woodville's a place of shrieks and wandering lamps
And scars that shook and rattle—and *one* hotel.
'You say "unless."'
'Unless you would n't mind
Sharing a room with some one else.'
'Who is it?'
'A man.'
'So I should hope. What kind of man?'
'I know him: he's all right. A man's a man.
Separate beds of course you understand.'
The night clerk blinked his eyes and dared him on.
'Who's the man sleeping in the office chair?
Has he had the refusal of my chance?'
'He was afraid of being robbed or murdered.
What do you say?'
'I'll have to have a bed.'
The night clerk led him up three flights of stairs
And down a narrow passage full of doors,
At the last one of which he knocked and entered.
'Lafe, here's a fellow wants to share your room.'
'Show him this way. I'm not afraid of him.
I'm not so drunk I can't take care of myself.'
The night clerk clapped a bedstead on the foot.
'This will be yours. Good night,' he said, and went.
. . .
The Doctor looked at Lafe and looked away.
A man? A brute. Naked above the waist,
He sat there creased and shining in the light,
Fumbling the buttons in a well-starched shirt.
'I'm moving into a size-larger shirt.
I've felt mean lately; mean's no name for it.
I've found just what the matter was to-night:
I've been a-choking like a nursery tree
When it outgrows the wire band of its name-tag.
I blamed it on the hot spell we've been having.
'Twas nothing but my foolish hanging back,
Not liking to own up I'd grown a size.
Number eighteen this is. What size do you wear?'
The Doctor caught his throat convulsively.
'Oh-ah-fourteen-fourteen.'

The whole colloquy between this tipsy provincial reporter, Lafayette, and the scared doctor, will, at the first blush, seem to be out of court to the ordinary citizen trained from childhood to recognize as 'poetical,' say Bryant's *Thanatopsis*. The latter is a good example of 'the noble manner,' but the reader who enjoys it does not therefore turn away with a puzzled frown from Holmes's 'The Wonderful One-Hoss Shay.'

But is Mr. Frost then a humorist? the reader may inquire, seeing a gleam of light. Humor has its place in his work; that is to say, our author's moods take their rise from his contemplative scrutiny of *character* in men and nature, and he responds equally to a tragic episode or a humorous situation. But, like creators greater in achievement, his humorous perception is interwoven with many other strands of apprehension, and in his *genre* pictures, sympathy blends with ironical appreciation of grave issues, to endow them with unique temperamental flavor. If one styled 'Mending Wall' and 'A Hundred Collars' idyls of New England life, the reader might remark sarcastically that they do not seem very idyllic; but idyls they are none the less, not in the corrupted sense of pseudo-Arcadian pastorals, but in the original meaning of 'little pictures.' One may contend that 'The Housekeeper' is cast in much the same gossiping style as Theocritus's idyl, 'The Ladies of Syracuse,' with its prattle of provincial ladies over their household affairs and the crush in the Alexandrian streets at the Festival of Adonis. And one may wager that this famous poem shocked the academic taste of the day by its unconventionality, and would not indeed, please modern professors, were it not the work of a Greek poet who lived three hundred years before Christ.

It is not indeed a bad precept for readers who wish to savor the distinctive quality of new original talents to judge them first by the *human interest* of what they present. Were this simple plan followed, a Browning or a Whitman would not be kept waiting so long in the chilling shadows of contemporary disapproval. Regard simply the people in Mr. Frost's dramatic dialogues, their motives and feelings, their intercourse and the clash of their outlooks, and note how these little canvases, painted with quiet, deep understanding of life's incongruous everyday web, begin to glow with subtle color. Observe how the author in 'A Servant to Servants,' picturing the native or local surroundings, makes the *essentials* live and speak in a woman's homely confession of her fear of madness.

But it is best to give an example of Mr. Frost's emotional force, and in quoting a passage from 'Home Burial' I say unhesitatingly that for tragic poignancy this piece stands by itself in American poetry. How dramatic is the action, in this moment of revelation of the tragic rift sundering man and wife!

He saw her from the bottom of the stairs
Before she saw him. She was starting down,
Looking back over her shoulder at some fear.
She took a doubtful step and then undid it
To raise herself and look again. He spoke,
Advancing toward her: 'What is it you see
From up there always—for I want to know.'
She turned and sank upon her skirts at that,
And her face changed from terrified to dull,
He said to gain time: 'What is it you see,'
Mounting until she cowered under him.
'I will find out now—you must tell me, dear.'
She, in her place, refused him any help
With the least stiffening of her neck and silence.
She let him look, sure that he would n't see,
Blind creature; and a while he did n't see.
But at last he murmured, 'Oh,' and again, 'Oh.'
'What is it—what?' she said.
'Just that I see.'
'You don't,' she challenged. 'Tell me what it is.'
'The wonder is I did n't see at once,
I never noticed it from here before.
I must be wonted to it—that's the reason.
The little graveyard where my people are!
So small the window frames the whole of it.
Not so much larger than a bedroom, is it?
There are three stones of slate and one of marble,
Broad-shouldered little slabs there in the sunlight,

On the sidehill. We have n't to mind *those*.
But I understand: it is not the stones,
But the child's mound—'

'Don't, don't, don't, don't,' she cried.

He entreats his wife to let him into her grief, and not to carry it, this time, to some one else. He entreats her to tell him why the loss of her first child has bred in her such rankling bitterness toward him, and why every word of his about the dead child gives her such offense.

—'And it's come to this,
A man can't speak of his own child that's dead.'

'You can't because you don't know how.
If you had any feelings, you that dug
With your own hand—how could you?—his little grave;
I saw you from that very window there,
Making the gravel leap and leap in air,
Leap up like that, like that, and land so lightly
And roll back down the mound beside the hole.
I thought, Who is that man? I did n't know you.
And I crept down the stairs and up the stairs
To look again, and still your spade kept lifting.
Then you came in. I heard your rumbling voice
Out in the kitchen, and I don't know why,
But I went near to see with my own eyes.
You could sit there with the stains on your shoes
Of the fresh earth from your own baby's grave
And talk about your everyday concerns.
You had stood the spade up against the wall
Outside there in the entry, for I saw it.'

'I shall laugh the worst laugh I ever laughed.
I'm cursed, God, if I don't believe I'm cursed.'

'I can repeat the very words you were saying.
"Three foggy mornings and one rainy day
Will rot the best birch fence a man can build."
Think of it, talk like that at such a time?
What had how long it take a birch to rot,
To do with what was in the darkened parlor.
You *could n't* care! The nearest friends can go
With any one to death, comes so far short
They might as well not try to go at all.
No, from the time when one is sick to death,
One is alone, and he dies more alone.
Friends make pretence of following to the grave,
But before one is in it, their minds are turned
And making the best of their way back to life
And living people, and things they understand.
But the world's evil. I won't have grief so
If I can change it. Oh, I won't, I won't.'

Here is vision, bearing the flame of piercing feeling in the living word. How exquisitely the strain of the mother's anguish is felt in that naked image,—

'Making the gravel leap and leap in air,
Leap up like that, like that, and land so lightly.'

Perhaps some readers, deceived by the supreme simplicity of this passage, may not see what art has inspired its perfect naturalness. It is indeed the perfection of poetic realism, both in observation and in deep insight into the heart. How well most of us know, after we have followed the funeral and stood by the grave-side of some man near to us, that baffled, uneasy self-questioning, 'Why do I feel so little? Is it possible I have no more sorrow or regret to feel at this death?' But what other poet has said this with such moving, exquisite felicity?

I have quoted 'Home Burial' partly from the belief that its dramatic intensity will best level any popular barrier to the recognition of its author's creative originality. But one does not expect that even a sensitive taste will respond so readily to the rare flavor of 'The Mountain' as did the American people to Whittier's 'Snowbound,' fifty years back. The imagery of the Quaker poet's idyl, perfectly suited to its purpose of mirroring with faithful sincerity the wintry landscape and the pursuits and character of a New England farmer's family, is marked by no peculiar delicacy or originality of style. Mr. Frost, on the other hand, may disappoint readers who prefer grandeur and breadth of outline or magical depth of coloring to delicate atmospheric imagery.

But the attentive reader will soon discover that Mr. Frost's cunning impressionism produces a subtle cumulative effect, and that by his use of pauses, digressions, and the crafty envisagement of his subject at fresh angles, he secures a pervading feeling of the mass and movement and elusive force of nature. He is a master of his exacting medium, blank verse,—a new master. The reader must pause and pause again before he can judge him, so unobtrusive and quiet are these 'effects,' so subtle the appeal of the whole. One can, indeed, return to his poems again and again without exhausting their quiet imaginative spell. For instance, the reader will note how the feeling of the mountain's mighty bulk and hanging mass, its vast elbowing flanks, its watching domination of the near fields and scattered farmsteads, begins to grow upon him, till he too is possessed by the idea of exploring its high ravines, its fountain springs and granite terraces. One of the surest tests of fine art is whether our imagination harks back to it, fascinated in after contemplation, or whether our interest is suddenly exhausted both in it and the subject. And 'The Mountain' shows that the poet has known how to seize and present the mysterious force and essence of living nature.

In nearly all Mr. Frost's quiet dramatic dialogues, his record of the present passing scene suggests how much has gone before, how much these people have lived through, what a lengthy chain of feelings and motives and circumstances has shaped their actions and mental attitudes. Thus in 'The Housekeeper,' his picture of the stout old woman sitting there in her chair, talking over Estelle, her grown-up daughter, who, weary of her anomalous position in the household, has left John and gone off and married another man, carries with it a rich sensation of the women's sharp criticism of a procrastinating obstinate man. John is too dense in his masculine way to know how much he owes to them. This psychological sketch in its sharp actuality is worthy of Sarah Orne Jewett.

But why put it in poetry and not in prose? the reader may hazard. Well, it comes with greater intensity in rhythm and is more heightened and concentrated in effect thereby. If the reader will examine 'A Servant to Servants,' he will recognize that this narrative of a woman's haunting fear that she has inherited the streak of madness in her family, would lose in distinction and clarity were it told in prose. Yet so extraordinarily close to normal everyday speech is it that I anticipate some academic person may test its metre with a metronome, and declare that the verse is often awkward in its scansion. No doubt. But so also is the blank verse of many a master hard to scan, if the academic footrule be not applied with a nice comprehension of where to give and when to take. In 'A Servant to Servants' the tragic effect of this overdriven woman's unburdening herself of her load of painful memories and gloomy forebodings is to my mind a rare artistic achievement,—one that graves itself on the memory.

And now that we have praised *North of Boston* so freely, shall we not make certain stiff, critical reservations? Doubtless one would do so were one not conscious that Mr. Frost's fellow poets, his deserving rivals, will relieve one of the task. May I say to them here that because I believe Mr. Frost in *North of Boston* had found a way for himself, so I believe their roads lie also open before them. These roads are infinite, and will surely yield, now or to-morrow, vital discoveries. A slight defect of Mr. Frost's subtle realistic method, and one does not wish to slur it over, is that it is sometimes difficult to grasp all the implications and bearings of his situations. His language in 'The Self-Seeker' is highly figurative, too figurative perhaps for poetry. Again in 'The Generations of Men,' his method as art seems to be both a little casual and long-winded. In several of his poems, his fineness of psychological truth is perhaps in excess of his poetic beauty,—and inevitable defect of cool, fearless realism. And the corollary criticism no doubt will be heard, that from the intensity with which he makes us realize things we should gain a little more pleasure. But here one may add that there is pleasure and pleasure, and that it seems remarkable that this New England poet, so absorbed by the psychological drama of people's temperaments and conduct, should preserve such pure outlines and clear objectivity of style.

Is his talent a pure product of New England soil? I take it that just as Hawthorne owed a debt to English influence, so Mr. Frost owes one also. But his 'native touch' is declared by the subtle blend of outspokenness and reticence, of brooding conscience and grave humor. Speaking under correction, it appears to me that his creative vision, springing from New England soil, and calmly handing on the best and oldest American tradition, may be a little at variance with the cosmopolitan clamor of New York. It would be quaint indeed if Americans who, according to their magazines, are opening their hospitable bosoms to Mr. Rabindranath Tagore's spiritual poems and dramas of Bengal life, should rest oblivious of their own countryman. To certain citizens Mr. Frost's poems of the life of inconspicuous, humble New England folk may seem unattractively homely in comparison with the Eastern poet's lofty, mystical dramas; but by American critics this view will doubtless be characterized as a manifestation of American provincialism. The critics know that a poet who has no 'message' to deliver to the world, whose work is not only bare of prettiness and sentimentality but is isolated and unaffected by this or that 'movement,' is easily set aside. Nothing is easier, since his appeal is neither to the interests nor caprices of the market. Ours indeed is peculiarly the day when everything pure, shy, and independent in art seems at the mercy of those who beat the big drum and shout their wares through the megaphone. And knowing this, the critic of conscience will take for his watchword *quality*.

'Mr. Frost is a true poet, but not a *poetical* poet,' remarked a listener to whom I read 'A Servant to Servants,' leaving me wondering whether his verdict inclined the scales definitely to praise or blame. Of poetical poets we have so many! of literary poets so many! of drawing-room poets so many!—of academic and dilettanti poets so many! of imitative poets so many! but of original poets how few!

MARK VAN DOREN

From "The Permanence of Robert Frost"

American Scholar, Spring 1936, pp. 192–98

Mr. Frost was a "modern" poet in 1914 when *North of Boston* appeared in this country after twenty years during which nothing of his had been known. And it might have been expected that he would experience at least some of the difficulty which other "modern" poets have faced before they could be recognized. For the one thing which all new poets possess in common is strangeness. Such poets do not seem to their first readers to be writing poetry at all. And some of them, indeed, are not. But some of them are, and it usually takes several years for the world to find this out. Mr. Frost had his strangeness, too, and for all anyone knows there may still be many persons who would declare him no poet because of it. In general, however, he has met with remarkably little resistance. His strangeness consisted, and still consists, in the conversational tone he builds into his verse. His poems are said, not sung; his poems are people talking. If this cannot be poetry, then Mr. Frost is no poet. If it can be poetry, Mr. Frost has supplied the proof. And he has been the only one to do so, despite the fact that almost every American poet younger than he has tried to imitate him. Coming upon the scene with a gift which not everyone was capable of acknowledging as the gift of a poet for the reason that it had never been the gift of one before, he has ended by establishing it as one of the gifts most easy to recognize, however impossible it may be to achieve. This is still another sign not only of his originality but of his genuineness. For no two good poets are alike in any other respect than that they are good. No one of them ever explains another.

Mr. Frost has an amusing story to tell in this connection. Some time during the dark years he sent a number of his poems to a friend for criticism, saying that the magazines would not have them but that they might be worth some one's reading anyhow, and asked the friend to discuss them frankly. The friend's report was that they did not seem to him to be poetry. If he were asked what they did seem to be he would have to say: Conversation. Mr. Frost, far from being discouraged, knew that he had found out something. His poems had one quality at least. They sounded like something. There was something in them that could be named. So he said to himself: I will develop this quality until it becomes not my weakness but my strength; I will prove that conversation can *be* poetry. And that is precisely what he has done. His characteristic line is the spoken, not the singing one, and whenever he presents any difficulty to the reader the reason is right there. Not a few of his lines, in fact, are unintelligible until they are heard by the conversing ear of the reader. For instance this one:

> Before we met and you what I had passed.

It is necessary to approach this line in its context if one is to know that it means: "Before we met and you had passed what I had passed." As the concluding line of a sonnet called "Meeting and Passing" it compresses into itself the whole meaning of the thirteen lines that have gone before it and seems, indeed, in its very compression to partake of the quality which most distinguishes human speech at its best. For the man who talks under the name of Robert Frost knows how to say a great deal in a short space, just as the many men and women whom he has listened to in New England and elsewhere have known how to express in the few words they use more truth than volumes of rhetoric can express. Another line from another poem is unintelligible in still another sense:

> As that I can see no way out but through.

Here we have not only compression, which disappears when we read the line as one of four:

Len says one steady pull more ought to do it.
He says the best way out is always through.
And I agree to that, or in so far
As that I can see no way out but through.

We have also a lack of accent, a lack which disappears as soon as we hear all that the woman says—she is afraid, by the way, that she will go insane unless she extracts herself from a certain state of mind—and hear her place a strong but natural emphasis upon the word "but" in that otherwise perplexing line. Here our perplexity was, perhaps, that we could not see how Mr. Frost could have presumed to call the line in question a blank verse line. It did not sound like one, certainly, until we heard this woman saying it. But then it did, as every one of Mr. Frost's blank verse line does in the same circumstances, the tendency coming to a famous climax in the two definitions of home that are spoken in "The Death of the Hired Man":

"Home is the place where, when you have to go
there,
They have to take you in."
"I should have called it
Something you somehow haven't to deserve."

In the first of these lines it must be plain that the only cue to the reading of the words "where, when" is the cue of the voice; as in the last line only the voice, pausing in the midst of speech, can direct the reader how to say "somehow" three or four times as slowly as he says "something."

Now this "difficulty" in Mr. Frost is something for which the specialists in poetry admired him at the beginning of his career. It was also, however, something which made his more general audience love him. For once, then, a poet's particular quality was no barrier to his communication. That is one thing which was meant a while back by the assertion that he occupied a middle ground. Another thing that might have been meant is this. He, like perhaps any other poet today who has received critical acclaim, is something of a Symbolist. He deals, that is to say, in indirection. The thing he seems to be talking about is never quite the thing he means to be talking about. He selects an object, an animal, a person, a life, or whatever other thing he likes, and makes it a symbol of something else which is larger or deeper than itself, so that as we read him we seem to see behind or through his subject matter, and derive a pleasure from so doing. Yet here again Mr. Frost has not suffered the common penalty—which is that the poet, retreating ever and ever from us into a world of his own experience, a world whose light is all shadowy with reflected meanings, becomes in the end unintelligible and writes only for himself. Mr. Frost is as skilful a Symbolist as anyone, and his critics acknowledge that this is so; but the mystery in his poems is never of the sort which makes so many contemporary poems sound like puzzles. It is merely the mystery which there is in all existence and which he has his own personal way of feeling. Just as his untrained readers have enjoyed hearing the voice of his verse because it is a singularly human voice, so they have enjoyed the additional and deeper layers of meaning which underlie all his apparently simple pieces. It is not that nothing is clear. The surface is as clear as daybreak. It is that the things which are unclear are the things which elsewhere in the world are unclear—in all our life, no less. The poem called "The Runaway" is a perfect picture, merely on the level of photography, of a young colt escaped from its mother in a snowstorm. It is also, though there are no words in it which say this, a complete reminder of a universe full of young, lost things, of a universe in which every creature, indeed, lives touchingly and amusingly alone. And there is no human being alive who would miss this in the poem. At the same time it is one of the most ingenious exercises in Symbolism produced by any poet during half a century, whether in France, in England, or in America.

The Symbolists have been on the whole shy and special souls, somewhat withdrawn from the common path. Something about the modern world has brought it about that its poets are by and large its least wise and sensible persons. Mr. Frost has his shynesses; he tells us he has turned his back on most of the United States; he is constantly threatening the minor note; and yet he has never spoken with anything less complete than the human voice at its ripest and wisest. He is romantic, granted; but he knows the world and knows therefore whereof he speaks—why he doesn't like most of it, why he likes the portions of it he does like, and why in the most general sense he is what he is. An early poem in his earliest volume, *A Boy's Will*, put this feeling in a fairly callow form; yet even there the theme had its connection with the larger world, its roots in life.

One of my wishes is that those dark trees,
So old and firm they scarcely show the breeze,
Were not, as 'twere, the merest mask of gloom,
But stretched away unto the edge of doom.

I should not be withheld but that some day
Into their vastness I should steal away,
Fearless of ever finding open land,
Or highway where the slow wheel pours the sand.

I do not see why I should e'er turn back,
Or those should not set forth upon my track
To overtake me, who should miss me here
And long to know if still I held them dear.

They would not find me changed from him they
knew—
Only more sure of what I thought was true.

Escape here is not a sentiment; it is a fact, and the man who speaks of it is not in so doing a pretty fool of the sort we are used to. He has seen the world—the eighth line alone would prove that—and has accepted it. He is not leaving it, actually. He is only taking this way to describe it and comment upon it. So, years later, Mr. Frost in his *New Hampshire* was to talk at considerable length—it is much his longest poem—about the absurdities of modern society. But there again he was not to damn something which he somehow wasn't up to understanding. He had been through it and was now on the other side of it; his criticism was mature. Any quaintness in the poem, too, was more than quaintness; it was the peculiar twist of a seasoned and of course not quite symmetrical character. *New Hampshire*, in other words, carried conviction, as Mr. Frost's poems always do, no matter how personal and particular they sound. When, for another instance, he says that there is nothing new under the sun—nothing at least worth wondering about—he seems neither to be speaking a commonplace nor to be evading the human responsibility to "keep up."

New is a word for fools in town who think
Style upon style in dress and thought at last
Must get somewhere.

For, dear me, why abandon a belief
Merely because it ceases to be true.

Cling to it long enough, and not a doubt
It will turn true again, for so it goes.
Most of the change we think we see in life
Is due to truths being in and out of favor.

These for him are no light sayings. They are the truth, for him; they have that sound.

The last of his dualities is by no means the least important, though it must be stated briefly. He is a New England poet, perhaps the New England poet, and reaps all the advantage there is in being true to a particular piece of earth—true to its landscape, its climate, its history, its morality, its tongue. But he is in the same breath a poet of and for the world. One need not have lived in New England to understand him. He has induced, it happens, a nostalgia for New England in persons who never saw the place. But what is of greater consequence, his voice is immediately recognizable anywhere as a human voice, and recognizable for the much that it has to say. He has his roots, as literature must always have them; but he grows at the top into the wide air that flows around the world where men and women listen.

MALCOLM COWLEY

From "The Case against Mr. Frost"

New Republic, September 11, 1944, pp. 312–13; September 18, 1944, pp. 345–47

Robert Frost has been heaped with more official and academic honors than any other American poet, living or dead. Although he was never graduated from college, having left Dartmouth after two months and Harvard after two years (and more credit to his dogged independence), he holds by the last count seventeen honorary degrees. He was twice made a Master of Arts (by Amherst and Michigan), three times a Doctor of the Humanities (by Vermont, Wesleyan and St. Lawrence) and twelve times a Doctor of Letters (by Yale, Middlebury, Bowdoin, New Hampshire, Columbia, Williams, Dartmouth, Bates, Pennsylvania, Harvard, Colorado and Princeton). He has been chosen a Phi Beta Kappa poet by Tufts, William and Mary, Harvard (twice) and Columbia. He has been a professor at Amherst; a poet in residence and a fellow in letters at Michigan; a Charles Eliot Norton professor, a Ralph Waldo Emerson fellow and a fellow in American civilization at Harvard, all these being fairly lucrative appointments. He has been awarded four Pulitzer Prizes, one more than E. A. Robinson and two more than Stephen Vincent Benét, the only other poets to be named more than once. He has also received the Loines Prize for poetry, the Mark Twain medal, the gold medal of the National Institute of Arts and Letters and the silver medal of the Poetry Society of America. His work has been the subject of at least two full-length critical studies, many brochures, pamphlets, bibliographies and a memorial volume, *Recognition of Robert Frost*, not to mention hundreds of essays which, some discordant notes in the early years, have ended as a vast diapason of praise.

And Frost deserves all these honors, both for his poetry in itself and for a long career devoted to the art of verse. In a country where poets go to seed, he has kept his talent ready to produce perfect blossoms (together with some that are misshapen or overgrown). It is a pleasure to name over the poems of his youth and age that become more vivid in one's memory with each new reading: the dramatic dialogues like "The Death of the Hired Man" and "The Witch of Coös," besides half a dozen others almost equally good; the descriptions or narrations that turn imperceptibly into Aesop's fables, like "The Grindstone" and "Cow in Apple Time"; and, best of all, the short lyrics like "The Pasture," "Now Close the Windows," "The Sound of the Trees," "Fire and Ice," "Stopping by Woods on a Snowy Evening" (always a favorite with anthologists), "To Earthward," "Tree at My Window," "Acquainted with the Night," "Neither Out Far Nor In Deep," "Beech," "Willful Homing," "Come In" . . . and I could easily add to the list. One of his best lyrics was written in 1892, when Frost was a freshman at Dartmouth; three or four others were included in his latest book, *A Witness Tree*, published just fifty years later; and these recent poems show more skill and density of expression than almost anything he had written before. This same volume and the one that preceded it—*A Further Range*, published in 1936—also contain bad poems that have been almost equally admired: long monologues in pedestrian blank verse, spoken as if from a cracker barrel among the clouds, and doggerel anecdotes directed (or rather, indirected) against the New Deal; but a poet has the right to be judged by his best work, and Frost at his best has added to our little store of authentic poetry.

If in spite of this I still say that there is a case against him and room for a dissenting opinion, perhaps I chiefly mean that there is a case against the zealous admirers who are not content to take the poet for what he is, but insist on using him as a sort of banner for their own moral or political crusades.

We have lately been watching the growth in this country of a narrow nationalism that has spread from politics into literature (although its literary adherents are usually not political isolationists). They demand, however, that American literature should be affirmative, optimistic, uncritical and "truly of this nation." They have been looking round for a poet to exalt; and Frost, through no fault of his own (but chiefly through the weaker qualities of his work), has been adopted as their symbol. Some of the honors heaped on him are less poetic than political. He is being praised too often and with too great vehemence by people who don't like poetry. And the result is that his honors shed very little of their luster on other poets, who in turn feel none of the pride in his achievements that a battalion feels, for example, when one of its officers is cited for outstanding services. Instead Frost is depicted by his admirers as a sort of Sunday-school paragon, a saint among miserable sinners. His common sense and strict Americanism are used as an excuse for berating and belittling other poets, who have supposedly fallen into the sins of pessimism, obscurity, obscenity and yielding to foreign influences; we even hear of their treachery to the American dream. Frost, on the other hand, is depicted as loyal, autochthonous and almost aboriginal. We are told not only that he is "the purest classical poet of America today"—and there is some truth in Gorham B. Munson's early jugdment—but also that he is "the one great American poet of our time" and "the only living New Englander in the great tradition, fit to be placed beside Emerson, Hawthorne and Thoreau."

But when Frost is so placed and measured, his stature seems greatly diminished; it is almost as if a tough little Morgan horse, the best of its breed, had been judged by the standards that apply to Clydesdales and Percherons. Height, breadth and strength: he falls short in all these qualities of the great New Englanders. And the other quality for which he is often praised, his utter faithfulness to the New England spirit, is not one of the virtues they knowingly cultivated. They realized that the New England spirit, when it stands alone, is inclined to be narrow and arithmetical. It has reached its finest growth only when cross-fertilized with alien philosophies.

Hinduism, Sufism, Fourierism and German Romanticism: each of these doctrines contributed its own share to the New England renaissance of the 1850's. Even Thoreau, who died almost in sight of his birthplace, said that he had traveled much in Concord; he spoke of bathing his intellect "in the stupendous and cosmogonal philosophy of the Bhagvat-Geeta. . . . The pure Walden water," he said, "is mingled with the sacred water of the Ganges." And Hawthorne, who told us that "New England is quite as large a lump on earth as my heart can really take in," was eager for any new ideas that might help to explain the nature of New Englanders as individuals or as members of society. The books he borrowed from the Salem Athenaeum during the ten lonely years he spent at home included the complete works, in French, of Rousseau, Voltaire (several times), Pascal, Racine (several times) and the "Essais" of Montaigne, as well as a great number of volumes on science, philosophy, general history and the past of New England.[1] Some of his weaker contemporaries were quite unbalanced by the foreign learning with which they overloaded their minds; but the stronger ones assimilated everything and, in the end, reasserted their own New England natures, which had become immensely richer.

And even Frost, as purely Yankee as his character seems today, was partly formed by his three years abroad. The turning point in his life was when he sold his first New Hampshire farm (which his grandfather had bought for him on condition that he live there at least ten years) and when, in 1912, his wife said, "Let's go to England and live under thatch." In England he made the reputation that enabled him to continue his career as a poet (and also as a "poet in residence"). In England, too, he had the experience of meeting other poets who understood what he was trying to say: Lascelles Abercrombie, Rupert Brooke, Wilfred Wilson Gibson and Edward Thomas. They were willing to learn from him, and Frost, in a sense, learned even more from them: that is, he learned to abandon the conventional language of the Late Victorians and to use his own speech without embarrassment. It is interesting to compare *A Boy's Will*, published in London but written in New Hampshire before his English journey, with "Mountain Interval," published after his return to this country in 1915 but written chiefly in England. The poems in *A Boy's Will* gave his own picture of the world, but in the language of the genteel poets; they were full of "maidens pale," "sweet pangs" and "airy dalliance." The poems written in the English countryside used the language that is spoken north of Boston. Once it had been regarded as a mere dialect only to be used in ballads like "Skipper Ireson's Ride" and in satirical comments like "The Biglow Papers"; but Frost in England had done what Hemingway would later do in Paris: he had raised his own idiom to the dignity of a literary language.

It was after his return that he carried the process further. Having learned to write New Hampshire, he also began to think New Hampshire, in the sense of accepting its older customs as immutable laws. . . .

II

In spite of his achievements as a narrative and lyric poet . . . there is a case against Robert Frost as a social philosopher in verse and as a representative of the New England tradition. He is too much walled in by the past. Unlike the great Yankees of an earlier age, he is opposed to innovations in art, ethics, science, industry or politics. Thus, in one of his longer blank-verse monologues, he bridles when he hears a "New York alec" discussing Freudian psychology, which Frost dismisses as "the new school of the pseudo-phallic." Elsewhere he objects to researches in animal behavior (which he calls "instituting downward comparisons"), to new inventions (saying that ingenuity should be held in check) and even to the theory of evolution—or at least he ridicules one farmer who speaks of it admiringly, whereas he sympathizes with another who stops him on the road to say:

The trouble with the Mid-Victorians
Seems to have been a man named John L. Darwin.

New ideas seem worse to him if they come from abroad, and worst of all if they come from Russia. He is continually declaiming against the Russians of all categories: the pessimistic Russians, the revolutionary Russians, the collectivistic Russians, the five-year-planning Russians: he seems to embrace them all in a global and historical dislike that extends from Dostoevsky to Dnieperstroy. He is horrified by the thought that New England might be exposed to the possibility of adopting any good or bad feature of the Russian program. Thus, after reading about a project for rural rehabilitation, he hastened to write:

It is in the news that all these pitiful kin
Are to be bought out and mercifully gathered in
To live in villages next to the theatre and store
Where they won't have to think for themselves any
more;
While greedy good-doers, beneficent beasts of prey,
Swarm over their lives, enforcing benefits
That are calculated to soothe them out of their wits,
And by teaching them how to sleep the sleep all day,
Destroy their sleeping at night the ancient way.

Sometimes Frost decides that it would be a relief "To put these people at one stroke out of their pain"—these people being the marginal farmers; then next day he wonders how it would be if someone offered to put an end to his own troubles. The upshot is that he proposes to do nothing whatever, being satisfied with the New England countryside as it is—or rather, as it was in his early manhood—and outraged by anyone who tries to improve it.

Yet there are other poems in which he suggests that his faithfulness to "the ancient way" is more a matter of habit than conviction. In "The Black Cottage," he remembers an old woman who had lost her husband in the Civil War and who used to say (in her "quaint phrase," as Frost calls it) that all men were created free and equal. The old woman was also an orthodox Christian, and her presence in church kept the minister from changing any phrases in the Creed. The minister says, recalling "her old tremulous bonnet in the pew":

I'm just as glad she made me keep hands off,
For, dear me, why abandon a belief
Merely because it ceases to be true.
Cling to it long enough, and not a doubt
It will turn true again.

Although the minister is speaking, he seems to express Frost's attitude toward the old New England standards. The poet is more conventional than convinced, more concerned with prudence than with virtue, and very little concerned with sin or suffering; you might say that he is more Puritan, or even prudish, than he is Christian. All the figures in his poems are decently draped; all the love affairs (except in a very late narrative, "The Subverted Flower") are etherealized or intellectualized; and although he sometimes refers to very old adulteries, it is only after they have been wrapped in brown paper and locked away in cupboards. On the other hand, there is little in his work to suggest Christian charity or universal brotherhood under God. He wants us to understand once and for all that he is not his brother's keeper:

I have none of the tenderer-than-thou
Collectivistic regimenting love
With which the modern world is being swept

—and the ancient world was also swept, in the first centuries after Christ. There is one of his narratives, "Two Tramps in Mud Time," that has often been praised for the admirable lesson with which it ends; and yet a professor told me not long ago that his classes always seemed vaguely uncomfortable when they heard it read aloud. It was first published in 1934, and it deals with what seems to have been an incident of the depression years. The poet tells us that he was working in his door-yard on an April day between winter and spring; he was splitting great blocks of straight-grained beech with a lively sense of satisfaction. Two tramps came walking down the muddy road. One of them said, "Hit them hard," and then lingered by the roadside, suggesting wordlessly that he might take the poet's job for pay. The poet assumed that they had spent the winter in a lumber camp, that they were now unemployed and that they had slept "God knows where last night." In life the meeting may have had a different sequel. Perhaps the poet explained to the homeless men that he liked to split his own wood, but that he had other work for them to do; or perhaps he invited them into the kitchen for a slab of home-baked bread spread thick with apple butter. In the poem, however, he lets them walk away without a promise or a penny; and perhaps that explains why a college class—west of the Alleghanies, at least—cannot hear it read without feeling uneasy. Instead of helping these men who wanted to work, Frost turns to the reader with a sound but rather sententious sermon on the ethical value of the chopping block:

> But yield who will to their separation,
> My object in living is to unite
> My avocation and my vocation
> As my two eyes make one in sight.
> Only where love and need are one,
> And the work is play for mortal stakes,
> Is the deed ever really done
> For heaven and the future's sakes.

The meter and tone of the passage remind us of another narrative poem written in New England almost a hundred years before; but "The Vision of Sir Launfal" had a different moral to point:

> Not what we give but what we share,
> For the gift without the giver is bare;
> Who gives himself with his alms feeds three,
> Himself, his hungering neighbor and me.

What Frost sets before us is an ideal, not of charity or brotherhood, but of separateness. "Keep off each other and keep each other off," he tells us in "Build Soil." "We're too unseparate out among each other. . . . Steal away and stay away." In some of his poems he faintly suggests Emerson, and yet he is preaching only half the doctrine of self-reliance, which embraced the community as well as the individual. Emerson said, for example, "He only who is able to stand alone is qualified for society," thus implying that the self-reliant individual was to use his energies for social ends. Frost, on the other hand, makes no distinction between separateness and self-centeredness. In his poems, fine as the best of them are, the social passions of the great New Englanders are diverted into narrower channels. One cannot imagine him thundering against the Fugitive Slave Law, like Emerson; or rising like Thoreau to defend John Brown after the Harpers Ferry raid; or even conducting a quietly persistent campaign against brutality on American ships, as Hawthorne did when he was consul at Liverpool. He is concerned chiefly with himself and his near neighbors, or rather with the Yankees among his neighbors (for although his section of New England is largely inhabited by Poles and French Canadians, there are only two poems in which these foreigners are mentioned). He says when splitting his straight-grained beech blocks:

> The blows that a life of self-control
> Spares to strike for the common good
> That day, giving a loose to my soul,
> I spent on the unimportant wood;

—and one feels that these blows might symbolize the inward or backward turning of energies in a region that once had wider horizons.

And Frost does not strive toward greater depth to compensate for what he lacks in breadth; he does not strike far inward into the wilderness of human nature. It is true that he often talks about the need for inwardness. He says, for example, in "Build Soil," which for all its limitations of doctrine is the best of his long philosophical poems and perhaps the only one worth preserving:

> We're always too much out or too much in.
> At present from a cosmical dilation
> We're so much out that the odds are against
> Our ever getting inside in again:

—yet still he sets limits on the exploration of himself, as he sets them on almost every other human activity; here again he displays the sense of measure and decorum that puts him in the classical, or rather the neo-classical, tradition. He is always building defenses against the infinite, walls that stand "Between too much and me." In the woods, there is a pile of rocks and an iron stake to mark the limit of his land; and here too:

> One tree, by being deeply wounded,
> Has been impressed as Witness Tree
> And made commit to memory
> My proof of being not unbounded.

The woods play a curious part in Frost's poems; they seem to be his symbol for the uncharted country within ourselves, full of possible beauty, but also full of horror. From the woods at dusk, you might hear the hidden music of the brook, "a slender, tinkling fall"; or you might see wood creatures, a buck and a doe, looking at you over the stone fence that marks the limit of the pasture lot. But you don't cross the fence, except in dreams; and then, instead of brook or deer, you are likely to meet a strange Demon rising "from his wallow to laugh." And so, for fear of the Demon, and also because of your moral obligations, you merely stand at the edge of the woods to listen:

> Far in the pillared dark
> Thrush music went—
> Almost like a call to come in
> To the dark and lament.
>
> But no, I was out for stars:
> I would not come in.
> I meant, not even if asked,
> And I hadn't been.

But Hawthorne before him, timid and thin and conventional as he was in many of his tales, still plucked up his courage and ventured into the inner wilderness; and Conrad Aiken's poems (to mention one example of New England work today) are written almost wholly from within that haunted mid-region. To explore the real horrors of the mind is a long tradition in American letters, one that goes back to our first professional novelist, Charles Brockden Brown. He said in one of his letters, quoted in a footnote by Van Wyck Brooks, "You, you tell me, are one of those who would rather travel into the mind of a plowman than into the interior of Africa. I confess myself of your way of thinking." The same tendency was continued by Poe and Melville and Henry James, and it extends in an almost unbroken line into the late work of Hemingway and Faulkner. But Frost, even in his finest lyrics, is content to stop outside the woods, either in the thrush-haunted dusk or on a snowy evening:

> The woods are lovely, dark and deep.
> But I have promises to keep,
> And miles to go before I sleep,
> And miles to go before I sleep.

If he does not strike far inward, neither does he follow the other great American tradition (extending from Whitman through Dos Passos) of standing on a height to observe the panorama of nature and society. Let us say that he is a poet neither of the mountains nor of the woods, although he lives among both, but rather of the hill pastures, the intervales, the dooryard in autumn with the leaves swirling, the closed house shaking in the winter storms (and who else has described these scenes more accurately, in more lasting colors?). In the same way, he is not the poet of New England in its great days, or in its late–nineteenth-century decline (except in some of his earlier poems): he is rather a poet who celebrates the diminished but prosperous and self-respecting New England of the tourist home and the antique shop in the abandoned gristmill. And the praise heaped on Frost in recent years is somehow connected in one's mind with the search for ancestors and authentic old furniture. You imagine a saltbox cottage restored to its original lines; outside it a wellsweep preserved for its picturesque quality, even though there is also an electric pump; at the doorway a coach lamp wired and polished; inside the house a set of Hitchcock chairs, a Salem rocker, willow-ware plates and Sandwich glass; and, on the tip-top table, carefully dusted, a first edition of Robert Frost.

Notes

1. These facts about Hawthorne are taken from F. O. Matthiessen's *American Renaissance* (New York: Oxford University Press, 1941), a book that has never been sufficiently praised.

YVOR WINTERS

From "Robert Frost: or, the Spiritual Drifter as Poet"

Sewanee Review, August 1948, pp. 564–96

Robert Frost is one of the most talented poets of our time, but I believe that his work is both overestimated and misunderstood; and it seems to me of the utmost importance that we should understand him with some accuracy. If we can arrive at a reasonably sound understanding of him, we can profit by his virtues without risk of acquiring his defects; and we may incidentally arrive at a better understanding of our present culture.

A popular poet is always a spectacle of some interest, for poetry in general is not popular; and when the popular poet is also within limits a distinguished poet, the spectacle is even more curious, for commonly it is bad poetry which is popular. When we encounter such a spectacle, we may be reasonably sure of finding certain social and historical reasons for the popularity. Frost is similar in his ways and attitudes and perceptions to a very large number of the more intelligent, if not the most intelligent, of his contemporaries: to the school teachers, the English professors, the more or less literate undergraduates, the journalists, and the casual readers of every class. These people are numerous and are in a position to perpetuate their ways and attitudes; this similarity, therefore, is worth examining.

Frost has been praised as a classical poet, but he is not classical in any sense which I can understand. Like many of his contemporaries, he is an Emersonian Romantic, although with certain mutings and modifications which I shall mention presently, and he has labeled himself as such with a good deal of care. He is a poet of the minor theme, the casual approach, and the discreetly eccentric attitude. When a reader calls Frost a classical poet, he probably means that Frost strikes him as a "natural" poet, a poet who somehow resembles himself and his neighbors; but this is merely another way of saying that the reader feels a kinship to him and likes him easily. Classical literature is said to judge human experience with respect to the norm; but it does so with respect to the norm of what humanity ought to be, not with respect to the norm of what it happens to be in a particular place and time. The human average has never been admirable, and in certain cultures it has departed very far from the admirable; that is why in the great classical periods of literature we are likely to observe great works in tragedy and satire, the works of a Racine and a Molière, of a Shakespeare and a Jonson, works which deal in their respective ways with sharp deviations from the ideal norm; and that is why literature which glorifies the average is sentimental rather than classical.

Frost writes of rural subjects, and the American reader of our time has an affection for rural subjects which is partly the product of the Romantic sentimentalization of "nature," but which is partly also a nostalgic looking back to the rural life which predominated in this nation a generation or two ago; the rural life is somehow regarded as the truly American life. I have no objection to the poet's employing rural settings; but we should remember that it is the poet's business to evaluate human experience, and the rural setting is no more valuable for this purpose than any other or than no particular setting, and one could argue with some plausibility that an exclusive concentration on it may be limiting.

Frost early began his endeavor to make his style approximate as closely as possible the style of conversation, and this endeavor has added to his reputation: it has helped to make him seem "natural." But poetry is not conversation, and I see no reason why poetry should be called upon to imitate conversation. Conversation is the most careless and formless of human utterance; it is spontaneous and unrevised, and its vocabulary is commonly limited. Poetry is the most difficult form of human utterance; we revise poems carefully in order to make them more nearly perfect. The two forms of expression are extremes, they are not close to each other. We do not praise a violinist for playing as if he were improvising; we praise him for playing well. And when a man plays well or writes well, his audience must have intelligence, training, and patience in order to appreciate him. We do not understand difficult matters "naturally."

The business of the poet can be stated simply. The poet deals with human experience in words. Words are symbols of concepts, which have acquired connotation of feeling in addition to their denotation of concept. The poet, then, as a result of the very nature of his medium, must make a rational statement about an experience, and as rationality is a part of the medium, the ultimate value of the poem will depend in a fair measure on the soundness of the rationality: it is possible, of course, to reason badly, just as it is possible to reason well. But the poet is deliberately employing the connotative content of language as well as the denotative: so that what he must do is make a rational statement about an experience, at the same time employing his language in such a manner as to communicate the emotion which ought to be communicated by that rational understanding of the particular subject. In so far as he is able to do this, the poem will be good; in so far as the subject itself is important, the poem will be great. That is, a poem which merely describes a stone may be excellent but will certainly be minor; whereas a poem which deals with man's contemplation of death and eternity, or with a formative decision of some kind, may be great. It is possible, of course, that the stone may be treated in such a way that it symbolizes something greater than itself; but if this occurs, the poem is about something greater than the stone. The poet is valuable, therefore, in proportion to his ability to apprehend certain kinds of objective truth; in proportion as he is great, he will not resemble ourselves but will resemble what we ought to be. It becomes our business, then, to endeavor to resemble him, and this endeavor is not easy and for this reason few persons make it. Country conversation and colloquial charm are irrelevant to the real issue. The great poets, men like Ben Jonson, Fulke Greville, and Richard Crashaw, have few readers; though some of them, like Milton, are widely admired from a distance. But they offer us, in their best efforts, the finest understanding of human experience to which we have access; some people are able and willing to understand them; and the human intelligence, however precariously, is thus kept alive. If we set up false ideals of human nature, and our best poets judge experience in terms of them and so beguile us into doing likewise, the human intelligence is to that extent diminished.

Frost has said that Emerson is his favorite American poet, and he himself appears to be something of an Emersonian. Emerson was a Romantic pantheist: he identified God with the universe; he taught that impulse comes directly from God and should be obeyed, that through surrender to impulse we become one with God; he taught that reason is man-made and bungling and should be suppressed. In moral and aesthetic doctrine, Emerson was a relativist; his most thorough-going disciples in American literature were Walt Whitman and Hart Crane. In Frost, on the other hand, we find a disciple without Emerson's religious conviction: Frost believes in the rightness of impulse, but does not discuss the pantheistic doctrine which would give authority to impulse; as a result of his belief in impulse, he is of necessity a relativist, but his relativism, apparently since it dervies from no intense religious conviction, has resulted mainly in ill-natured eccentricity and in increasing melancholy. He is an Emersonian who has become sceptical and uncertain without having reformed; and the scepticism and uncertainty do not appear to have been so much the result of thought as the result of the impact upon his sensibility of conflicting notions of his own era—they appear to be the result of his having taken the easy way and having drifted with the various currents of his time.

II

I should like first of all to describe a few poems which deal with what in the hands of a more serious writer one could describe as the theme of moral choice. These poems throw more light on Frost as a whole, perhaps, than do any others, and they may serve as an introduction to his work. I have in mind especially three poems from *Mountain Interval:* the introductory piece entitled "The Road Not Taken," the post-scriptive piece entitled "The Sound of the Trees," and the lyrical narrative called "The Hill Wife"; and one poem from *A Further Range:* the poem entitled "The Bearer of Evil Tidings." These poems all have a single theme: the whimsical, accidental, and incomprehensible nature of the formative decision; and I should like to point out that if one takes this view of the formative decision, one has cut oneself off from understanding most of human experience, for in these terms there is nothing to be understood—one can write of human experience with sentimental approval or with sentimental melancholy, but with little else.

"The Road Not Taken," for example, is the poem of a man whom one might fairly call a spiritual drifter; and a spiritual drifter is unlikely to have either the intelligence or the energy to become a major poet. Yet the poem has definite virtues, and these should not be overlooked. In the first place, spiritual drifters exist, they are real; and although their decisions may not be comprehensible, their predicament is comprehensible. The poem renders the experience of such a person, and renders the uncertain melancholy of his plight. Had Frost been a more intelligent man, he might have seen that the plight of the spiritual drifter was not inevitable, he might have judged it in the light of a more comprehensive wisdom. Had he done this, he might have written a greater poem. But his poem is good as far as it goes; the trouble is that it does not go far enough, it is incomplete, and it puts on the reader a burden of critical intelligence which ought to be borne by the poet. We are confronted with a similar critical problem when the Earl of Rochester writes remarkably beautiful poems to invite us to share in the pleasures of drunkenness. The pleasure of drunkenness are real—let no one delude himself on that score—and the Earl of Rochester is one of the most brilliant masters of English verse. But if the pleasures of drunkenness are regarded in what the sentimental critics are wont to term a true perspective, they are seen to be obstacles to other experiences of far greater value, and then they take on the appearance of temptations to sin. Dante would have dealt with these pleasures truly, placing them where they belonged in the hierarchy of values; Rochester was not equal to the task, but Rochester gave us a good evaluation of the experience of a man in his predicament as he himself sees it. He is like the demon defined by Aquinas: good in so far as he may be said to exist, but a demon in so far as his existence is incomplete. And like the demon he is also enticing, for he has more than usual powers of persuasion. We are protected against his incompleteness and against his enticements if we understand his limitations, and we can then profit by what he possesses; but without understanding, we may be drawn to emulate him, to form outselves upon him—we may, in a sense, become possessed by an evil power which is great enough to control us and diminish our own being.

The comparison of Rochester to Frost is unjust in one respect, for Rochester was a consciously vicious man; whereas Robert Frost would not willingly injure anyone. Yet the comparison in other ways is just, for Frost, as I shall show, has willfully refrained from careful thinking and so is largely responsible for his own condition; and his condition is less dramatic and more easily shared by large numbers of his contemporaries than was the condition of Rochester, so that he is probably a greater menace to the general intelligence. Rochester knew himself to be a sinner, and he knew that he would be regarded as one. Frost by a process of devious evasions has convinced himself that he is a wise and virtuous man, and he is regarded as a kind of embodiment of human wisdom by hundreds of thousands of Americans from high school age to the brink of senility. He embodies a common delusion regarding human nature, and he is strongly reinforcing that delusion in the minds of his contemporaries.

"The Sound of the Trees" deals with a longing to depart which has never quite been realized. The trees

> are that which talks of going
> But never gets away.

The poem ends as follows:

> I shall make the reckless choice
> Some day when they are in voice
> And tossing so as to scare
> The white clouds over them on.
> I shall have less to say,
> But I shall be gone.

The poem has the same quality of uncertainty and incomprehension as "The Road Not Taken"; it is written with about the same degree of success, with about the same charm, and with about the same quality of vague melancholy. In considering either of these poems, especially if one compares them even to minor works by sixteenth- and seventeenth-century masters, one will observe not only the limitations of intelligence which I have mentioned, but a quality, slight though it may be, of imprecision in the rendering of the detail and of the total attitude, which is the result of the limitations. Such a poem as Robert Herrick's "Night-Piece to Julia" is as sharp as a knife in comparison. Herrick knew exactly what he was saying and exactly what it was worth. Frost, on the other hand, is mistaking whimsical impulse for moral choice, and the blunder obscures his understanding and even leaves his mood uncertain with regard to the value of the whole business. He is vaguely afraid that he may be neither wrong nor right.

"The Hill Wife" is a less happy specimen than the poems just mentioned. It deals, not with a personal experience of the author, but with a dramatic situation seen from without; and the dramatic crisis is offered as something incomprehensible. The wife leaves her husband because she is lonely on their back-country farm, but there is no clear understanding of her motive; we are told that she is disturbed when the birds leave in the fall, and frightened by a casual tramp, and that a pine near the window obsesses her thoughts. The last section, characteristically entitled "The Impulse," describes her final act as a sudden and unpremeditated one. The poem has an eerie quality, like that of dream or of neurosis, but it has little else. As a study in human relationships, it amounts to nothing, and one has only to compare it to "Eros Turannos" by Robinson to discern its triviality. "The Bearer of Evil Tidings" deals with a similarly casual and sudden decision, although it is a more interesting poem. And one might mention also the poem from *A Witness Tree* entitled "A Serious Step Lightly Taken": the serious step in question is merely the buying of a farm; but the title is characteristic, and the title implies approval and not disapproval—it implies that serious steps ought to be lightly taken. But if serious steps are to be lightly taken, then poetry, at least, is impoverished, and the poet can have very little to say. Most of the world's great poetry has had to do with serious steps seriously taken, and when the seriousness goes from life, it goes from the poetry.

III

I shall consider next some of the more clearly didactic poems, which will reinforce what I have been saying. I should perhaps mention briefly as one of these, a short lyric in *West-Running Brook*, a lyric called "Sand Dunes," of which the clearly stated theme is the Emersonian notion that man can think better if he frees himself wholly from the past. The last poem in the same volume, at least as the volume originally appeared, is called "The Bear." The poem compares the wild bear to the bear in a cage; the uncaged bear is a creature of free impulse and is compared by implication to man as he would be were he guided by impulse; and the caged bear is compared to rational man as he is. The poem is amusing on first reading, but it wears thin with time. The difficulty is this, that satirical poetry is a branch of didactic poetry, for whereas purely didactic poetry endeavors to convince directly, satirical poetry endeavors to convince indirectly by ridiculing what the poet takes to be a deviation from wisdom; and both forms depend rather obviously upon the soundness of the ideas which they expound or assume. Frost tells us in this poem that reasoning man is ridiculous because he appears to labor and to change his mind; and he implies that impulsive man would be a wiser and a nobler creature. The fact of the matter is, however, that impulsive man, if he is restrained, like Frost, by conventions and habits the nature and origins of which he does not understand, is likely to be merely confused, uncertain, and melancholy; and if he is not so restrained may degenerate to madness or to criminality. Within relatively recent years, we have had two tragic examples, in Hart Crane and in Ezra Pound, of what a man of genius can do to himself and to his work by energetically living the life of impulse. It is not foolish to change one's mind; one learns by changing one's mind. Life is a process of revision in the interests of greater understanding, and it is by means of this process that men came down from the trees and out of the caves; and although civilization is very far from what it should be, nevertheless mankind have shown a marked improvement over the past ten thousand years. This improvement is the result of the fact that man is a rational animal, as I believe that a certain Greek once remarked. The uncaged bear, or the unreflective cave-man, is inferior to Thomas Aquinas and to Richard Hooker, to Dante and to Ben Jonson, and to assert the contrary is merely irresponsible foolishness. Frost then is satirizing the intelligent man from the point of view of the unintelligent; and the more often one reads the poem, the more obvious this fact becomes, and the more trivial the poem appears.

Frost expounds the same ideas more directly still in his poem "To a Thinker," in *A Further Range*. The idea in this poem is the same as that in "The Bear," but is even more plainly stated; we have the commonplace Romantic distrust of reason and trust in instinct. The poem ends as follows:

> So if you find you must repent
> From side to side in argument,
> At least don't use your mind too hard,
> But trust my instinct—I'm a bard.

The poem is badly written, but one couplet is momentarily amusing:

> I own I never really warmed
> To the reformer or reformed.

Yet when we examine it more carefully, there is something almost contemptible about it. There are, of course, reformers and reformers, and many of them have been ludicrous or worse. Frost is invoking the image of the soap-box politician or the street-corner preacher in order to discredit reason. But the word *reform* can be best evaluated if one separates the syllables for a moment. To reform means to re-form. And the progress of civilization has been a process of re-forming human nature. Socrates re-formed the human mind; Jesus re-formed man's moral and religious nature; Aquinas re-formed philosophical method and content; and William the Silent re-formed the idea of the state. Frost endeavors to gain his point by sleight-of-hand; he endeavors to obscure the difference between St. Thomas Aquinas and Pussyfoot Johnson.

Even Frost, with his instinct to guide him, is not proof against wavering, however. In the same volume with the poem just described is a poem called "The White-Tailed Hornet," in which Frost describes the activities of a hornet and the errors it commits under the guidance of instinct, and he reprehends mankind for having engaged in "downward comparisons":

> As long on earth
> As our comparisons were stoutly upward
> With gods and angels, we were men at least,
> But little lower than the gods and angels.
> But once comparisons were yielded downward,
> Once we began to see our images
> Reflected in the mud and even dust,
> 'Twas disillusion upon disillusion.
> We were lost piecemeal to the animals
> Like people thrown out to delay the wolves.

Yet we have seen Frost himself engaging in downward comparisons, and we shall see him doing it again. This is the only poem in Frost's works which seems to represent a conscious rejection of his usual ideas, and this poem, as I have said, even occurs in the same volume with the poem which I quoted previously, "To a Thinker." It is possible that Frost shares the contempt felt by Emerson and by Whitman for consistency, or he may be so inexperienced a thinker as to be unaware of his inconsistency; the point is of little importance, for he nowhere else takes up this argument.

Frost has something to say of the relationship of the individual to society. His most extensive poem on this subject is called "Build Soil—A Political Pastoral," and was delivered at Columbia University, May 31, 1932, before the national party conventions of that year. It will be remembered that these were the conventions which led to the first election of Franklin D. Roosevelt, and that the time was one of the darkest periods in the history of the nation. The poem is Frost's most ambitious effort to deal with his social, political, and economic views. As to his economic views, he says that if he were dictator of the country:

> I'd let things take their course
> And then I'd claim the credit for the outcome.

This statement, if it means anything at all, is a statement of belief in an unrestrained laissez-faire system, of the sort that Emerson would have approved; a belief that if things are left alone they must come right. It represents a doctrine of political drifting which corresponds to the doctrine of personal drifting which we have already seen; in practice, it could lead only to the withdrawal from public affairs of the citizen not concerned primarily with personal aggrandizement, and to the surrender of the nation to the unscrupulous go-getter, who, though he may not be a drifter, is not governed by admirable aims. It is similarly an obscurantist doctrine: it implies that this realm of human activity, like others, cannot be dealt with rationally and is better if not understood. As to the behavior of the private citizen, Frost says:

> I bid you to a one-man revolution—
> The only revolution that is coming.
> We're too unseparate out among each other—
> With goods to sell and notions to impart . . .
> We congregate embracing from distrust
> As much as love, and too close in to strike
> And so be very striking. Steal away
> The song says. Steal away and stay away.
> Don't join too many gangs. Join few if any.
> Join the United States and join the family—
> But not much in between unless a college.

The individual is thus advised against any kind of political activity in a time of national collapse. The difficulties of effective political action are obvious; the English-speaking peoples have been struggling with the problems of constitutional government for centuries. But if the reality of the difficulties results in our stealing away from them, society will be taken over, as I have said, by the efficient scoundrels who are always ready to take over when everyone else abdicates. In a dictatorship by scoundrels, the Frosts and the Thoreaus, the amateur anarchists and village eccentrics, would find life somewhat more difficult than they have found it to date. Frost objects in the last passage to the commerce of minds, and he objects to it earlier in the poem:

> Suppose someone comes near me who in rate
> Of speech and thinking is so much my better
> I am imposed on, silenced and discouraged.
> Do I submit to being supplied by him
> As the more economical producer?
> No, I unostentatiously move off
> Far enough for my thought-flow to resume.

It does not occur to Frost that he might learn from his betters and improve himself; he can see only two possibilities in his relationship with them—he can be silenced by them or he can ignore them and proceed as before. There is the implication in this passage that his personal "thought-flow" is valuable merely because it is his own, that it should remain uncontaminated. He believes that the man and the nation equally will reach their fullest development through a kind of retreat to passivity, through letting things happen as they may with a minimum of influence from without.

The same sentimental dislike for society, for community of interest, can be found in the poem called "The Egg and the Machine," a poem appended in the *Collected Poems* to the group called *West-Running Brook*. The poem tells of a Thoreau-like adventurer who is exasperated to encounter a railroad running through his favorite marsh. After a locomotive passes him, he proceeds to find a nestful of turtle eggs, and Frost writes:

> If there was one egg in it there were nine,
> Torpedo-like, with shell of gritty leather
> All packed in sand to wait the trump together.
> 'You'd better not disturb me any more,'
> He told the distance, 'I am armed for war.
> The next machine that has the power to pass
> Will get this plasm in its goggle-glass.'

Here are several familiar Romantic attitudes: resentment at being unable to achieve the absolute privacy which Frost names as a primary desideratum in "Build Soil," the sentimental regard for the untouched wilderness (the untouched wilderness would provide absolute privacy for the unique Romantic), and the sentimental hatred for the machine. I am willing to admit, in connection with the last matter, that machinery is sometimes far from beautiful, both in itself and in some of its effects; but its benefits have been overwhelmingly great, and the literary farmer in Vermont could scarcely hope to subsist either as farmer or as writer without its help, any more than he could hope to subsist unless a good many people faced moral and political realities; and it is curiously unjust that the locomotive, that patient and innocuous draft horse of civilization, should be selected to symbolize the viciousness of machinery. Frost's real objection to the machine, I suspect, is its social nature; it requires and facilitates cooperation, and Frost is unwilling to recognize its respectability mainly for this reason. . . .

Frost, as far as we have examined him, then, is a poet who holds the following views: he believes that impulse is trustworthy and reason contemptible, that formative decisions should be made casually and passively, that the individual should retreat from cooperative action with his kind, should retreat not to engage in intellectual activity but in order to protect himself from the contamination of outside influence, that affairs manage themselves for the best if left alone, that ideas of good and evil need not be taken very seriously. These views are sure to be a hindrance to self-development, and they effectually cut Frost off from any really profound understanding of human experience, whether political, moral, metaphysical, or religious. The result in the didactic poems is the perversity and incoherence of thought; the result in the narrative poems is either slightness of subject or a flat and uninteresting apprehension of the subject; the result in the symbolic lyrics is a disturbing dislocation between the descriptive surface, which is frequently lovely, and the ultimate meaning, which is usually sentimental and unacceptable. The result in nearly all the poems is a measure of carelessness in the style, sometimes small and sometimes great, but usually evident: the conversational manner will naturally suit a poet who takes all experience so casually, and it is only natural that the conversational manner should often become very conversational indeed.

It is worth while to mention one other poem in connection with Frost's retreat from the serious subject. The poem I have in mind is called "The Times Table." The poem deals with a farmer who is given to commenting on death and who is reproved by Frost: Frost remarks that such comments should not be made

> Unless our purpose is doing harm,
> And then I know of no better way
> To close a road, abandon a farm,
> Reduce the births of the human race,
> And bring back nature in people's place.

We should remember that Frost is a poet and normally speaks with full consciousness of his role as poet; it is reasonable to assume that this poem applies to the poet as well as to other persons. The poet, then, should not deal with death or with comparably disturbing topics, because these topics distress and discourage people. Yet I wish to point out that all people die, that human life is filled with tragedy, and that commonly the tragedies accumulate all but overwhelmingly toward the end. To ignore the tragic subject is to leave oneself unprepared for the tragic experience; it is likely to lead to disaster and collapse. It is the business of the poet, let me repeat, to understand his subjects, and as far as may be the most difficult and important subjects, in rational terms, and at the same time to communicate the feeling which ought to be communicated by that rational understanding. The great poet judges the tragic subject completely, that is, rationally and emotionally; the nature of the human mind is such that we can enter the poet's mind by way of his poem, if we are willing to make the effort, and share his judgment. In this way we may gain both understanding and strength, for the human mind is so made that it is capable of growth and of growth in part through its own self-directed effort. This is the virtue of poetry; in so far as it is good, and we understand both its goodness and its limitations, it enables us to achieve a more nearly perfect and comprehensive being, to reduce that margin of spiritual privation which is evil. But Frost advises us to turn away from serious topics, and for the greater part he confines himself to minor topics. The major topics impinge upon his personal experience, however, for after all they are unavoidable; but his treatment of them is usually whimsical, sentimental, and evasive; and in his later years his poetry is more and more pervaded by an obscure melancholy which he can neither control nor understand.

RANDALL JARRELL
From "To the Laodiceans"
Poetry and the Age (1953)
1955, pp. 34–62

Back in the days when "serious readers of modern poetry" were most patronizing to Frost's poems, one was often moved to argument, or to article-writing, or to saying under one's breath: *What is man that Thou art mindful of him?* In these days it's better—a little, not much: the lips are pursed that ought to be parted, and they still pay lip-service, or little more. But Frost's best poetry—and there is a great deal of it, at once wonderfully different and wonderfully alike—deserves the attention, submission, and astonished awe that real art always requires of us; to give it a couple of readings and a ribbon lettered First in the Old-Fashioned (or Before 1900) Class of Modern Poetry is worse, almost, than not to read it at all. Surely *we* [I don't know exactly whom this *we* includes, but perhaps I could say that it means "the friends of things in the spirit," even when the things are difficult, even when the things are in the flesh] are not going to be like the *Saturday Review* readers and writers who tell one how completely good Frost is, and in the next breath tell how narrowly good, limitedly good, badly good Eliot is. Surely it is the excellence most unlike our own that we will be most eager to acknowledge, since it not only extends but completes us—and since only we, not the excellence, are harmed by our rejection of it.

Frost has limitations of a kind very noticeable to us, but they are no more important than those of other contemporary poets; and most of the limitations, less noticeable to us, that these poets share, Frost is free of. If it makes good sense (but a narrow and ungenerous, though essential, sense) to say about Frost, "As a poet he isn't in Rilke's class at all," it does *not* make such sense if you substitute for Rilke's name that of Eliot or Moore or Stevens or Auden, that of any living poet. We can already see, most vividly, how ridiculous posterity is going to find the people who thought Marianne Moore's poems "not poetry at all," *The Waste Land* a hoax, and so on; but is posterity going to find any less ridiculous the intellectuals who admitted Frost only as a second-class citizen of the Republic of Letters, a "bard" whom it would be absurd to compare with real modern poets like—oh, E. E. Cummings? Frost's daemonic gift of always getting on the buttered side of both God and Mammon; of doing and saying anything and everything that he pleases, and still getting the World to approve or tactfully ignore every bit of it; of not only allowing, but taking a hard pleasure in encouraging, fools and pedants to adore him as their own image magnified—all this has helped to keep us from seeing Frost for what he really is. And here one has no right to be humble and agreeable, and to concede beforehand that *what he really is* is only one's own "view" or "interpretation" of him: the regular ways of looking at Frost's poetry are grotesque simplifications, distortions, falsifications—coming to know his poetry well ought to be enough, in itself, to dispel any of them, and to make plain the necessity of finding some other way of talking about his work.

Any of us but Frost himself (and all the little Frostlings who sit round him wondering with a foolish face of praise, dealing out ten monosyllables to the homey line) can by now afford just to wonder at his qualities, not to sadden at his defects, and can gladly risk looking a little foolish in the process. The real complication, sophistication, and ambiguity of Frost's thought [what poet since Arnold has written so much about isolation, and said so much more about it than even Arnold? what other poet, long before we had begun to perfect the means of altogether doing away with humanity, had taken as an obsessive subject the wiping-out of man, his replacement by the nature out of which he arose?], the range and depth and height of his poems, have had justice done to them by neither his admirers nor his detractors—and, alas, aren't going to have justice done to them by me now. If one is talking about Frost's poetry to friends, or giving a course in it to students, one can go over thirty or forty of his best poems and feel sure about everything: one doesn't need, then, to praise or blame or generalize—the poems speak for themselves almost as well as poems can. But when one writes a little article about Frost, one feels lamentably sure of how lamentably short of his world the article is going to fall; one can never write about him without wishing that it were a whole book, a book in which one could talk about hundreds of poems and hundreds of other things, and fall short by one's essential and not accidental limitations.

I have sometimes written, and often talked, about Frost's willful, helpless, all too human mixture of virtues and vices, so I hope that this time I will be allowed simply—in the nice, old-fashioned, looked-down-on phrase—to appreciate. And I want to appreciate more than his best poems, I want to exclaim over some of the unimportantly delightful and marvellously characteristic ones, and over some of the places where all of Frost and all of what is being described are married and indistinguishable in one line. But first let me get rid, in a few sentences, of that Skeleton on the Doorstep that is the joy of his enemies and the despair of his friends. Just as a star will have, sometimes, a dark companion, so Frost has a pigheaded one, a shadowy self that grows longer and darker as the sun gets lower. I am speaking of that other self that might be called the Grey Eminence of Robert Taft, or the Peter Pan of the National Association of Manufacturers, or any such thing—this public self incarnates all the institutionalized complacency that Frost once mocked at and fled from, and later pretended to become a part of and became a part of. This Yankee Editorialist side of Frost gets in the way of *everything*—of us, of the real Frost, of the real poems and their real subject-matter. And a poet so magically good at making the subtlest of points surely shouldn't evolve into one who regularly comes out and tells you the point after it's been made—and comes out and tells you, in such trudging doctrinaire lines, a point like the end of a baseball bat. Frost says in a piece of homely doggerel that he has hoped wisdom could be not only Attic but Laconic, Boeotian even—"at least not systematic"; but how systematically Frostian the worst of his later poems are! His good poems are the best refutation of, the most damning comment on, his bad: his *Complete Poems* have the air of being able to educate any faithful reader into tearing out a third of the pages, reading a third, and practically wearing out the rest.

We begin to read Frost, always, with the taste of "Birches" in our mouth—a taste a little brassy, a little sugary; and to take it out I will not use such good and familiar poems as "Mending Wall" and "After Apple-Picking," or such a wonderful and familiar (and misunderstood) poem as "An Old Man's Winter Night," but four or five of Frost's best and least familiar poems. Let me begin with a poem that, at first glance, hardly seems a Frost poem at all, but reminds us more of another kind of unfamiliar poem that Housman wrote; this poem is called "Neither Out Far Nor In Deep":

The people along the sand
All turn and look one way.
They turn their back on the land.
They look at the sea all day.

As long as it takes to pass
A ship keeps raising its hull;
The wetter ground like glass
Reflects a standing gull.

The land may vary more;
But wherever the truth may be—
The water comes ashore,
And the people look at the sea.

They cannot look out far.
They cannot look in deep.
But when was that ever a bar
To any watch they keep?

First of all, of course, the poem is simply there, in indifferent unchanging actuality; but our thought about it, what we are made to make of it, is there too, made to be there. When we choose between land and sea, the human and the inhuman, the finite and the infinite, the sea *has* to be the infinite that floods in over us endlessly, the hypnotic monotony of the universe that is incommensurable with us—everything into which we look neither very far nor very deep, but look, look just the same. And yet Frost doesn't say so—it is the geometry of this very geometrical poem, its inescapable structure, that says so. There is the deepest tact and restraint in the symbolism; it is like Housman's

Stars, I have seen them fall,
But when they drop and die
No star is lost at all
From all the star-sown sky.

The toil of all that be
Helps not the primal fault:
It rains into the sea
And still the sea is salt.

But Frost's poem is flatter, greyer, and at once tenderer and more terrible, without even the consolations of rhetoric and exaggeration—there is no "primal fault" in Frost's poem, but only the faint Biblical memories of "any watch they keep." What we do know we don't care about; what we do care about we don't know: we can't look out very far, or in very deep; and when did that ever bother *us?* It would be hard to find anything more unpleasant to say about people than that last stanza; but Frost doesn't say it unpleasantly—he says it with flat ease, takes everything with something harder than contempt, more passive than acceptance. And isn't there something heroic about the whole business, too—something touching about our absurdity? if the fool persisted in his folly he would become a wise man, Blake said, and we have persisted. The tone of the last lines—or, rather, their careful suspension between several tones, as a piece of iron can be held in the air between powerful enough magnets—allows for this too. This recognition of the essential limitations of man, without denial or protest or rhetoric or palliation, is very rare and very valuable, and rather usual in Frost's best poetry. One is reminded of Empson's thoughtful and truthful comment on Gray's *Elegy*: "Many people, without being communists, have been irritated by the complacence in the massive calm of the poem . . . And yet what is said is one of the permanent truths; it is only in degree that any improvement of society would prevent wastage of human powers; the waste even in a fortunate life, the isolation even of a life rich in intimacy, cannot but be felt deeply, and is the central feeling of tragedy."

Another of Frost's less familiar poems is called "Provide Provide":

The witch that came (the withered hag)
To wash the steps with pail and rag
Was once the beauty Abishag,

The picture pride of Hollywood.
Too many fall from great and good
For you to doubt the likelihood.

Die early and avoid the fate.
Or if predestined to die late,
Make up your mind to die in state.

Make the whole stock exchange your own!
If need be occupy a throne,
Where nobody can call *you* crone.

Some have relied on what they knew;
Others on being simply true.
What worked for them might work for you.

No memory of having starred
Atones for later disregard
Or keeps the end from being hard.

Better to go down dignified
With boughten friendship at your side
Than none at all. Provide, provide!

For many readers this poem will need no comment at all, and for others it will need rather more than I could ever give. The poem is—to put it as crudely as possible—an immortal masterpiece; and if we murmur something about its crudities and provincialisms, History will smile tenderly at us and lay us in the corner beside those cultivated people from Oxford and Cambridge who thought Shakespeare a Hollywood scenario-writer. Since I can't write five or six pages about the poem, it might be better to say only that it is full of the deepest, and most touching, moral wisdom—and it is full, too, of the life we have to try to be wise about and moral in (the sixth stanza is almost unbearably actual). The Wisdom of this World and the wisdom that comes we know not whence exist together in the poem, not side by side but one inside the other; yet the whole poem exists for, lives around, the fifth stanza and its *others on being simply true*—was restraint ever more moving? One can quote about that line Rilke's *In the end the only defence is defencelessness*, and need to say no more. But the rest of the poem is the more that we need to say, if we decide to say any more: it says, in the worldliest and homeliest of terms, that expediency won't work—the poem is, even in its form, a marvellous *reductio ad absurdum* of expediency—but since you *will* try it, since you *will* provide for the morrow, then provide hard for it, be really expedient, settle yourself for life in the second-best bed around which the heirs gather, the very best second-best bed. The poem is so particularly effective because it is the Wisdom of this World which demonstrates to us that the Wisdom of this World isn't enough. The poem puts, so to speak, the minimal case for morality, and then makes the minimal recommendation of it (*what worked for them might work for you*); but this has a beauty and conclusiveness that aren't minimal.

The most awful of Frost's smaller poems is one called "Design":

I found a dimpled spider, fat and white,
On a white heal-all, holding up a moth
Like a white piece of rigid satin cloth—
Assorted characters of death and blight
Mixed ready to begin the morning right,
Like the ingredients of a witches' broth—
A snow-drop spider, a flower like froth,
And dead wings carried like a paper kite.

What had that flower to do with being white,
The wayside blue and innocent heal-all?
What brought the kindred spider to that height,
Then steered the white moth thither in the night?
What but design of darkness to appall?—
If design govern in a thing so small.

This is the Argument from Design with a vengeance; is the terrible negative from which the eighteenth century's Kodak picture (with its *Having wonderful time. Wish you were here* on the margin) had to be printed. If a watch, then a watch-maker; if a diabolical machine, then a diabolical mechanic—Frost uses exactly the logic that has always been used. And this little albino catastrophe is too whitely catastrophic to be accidental, too impossibly unlikely ever to be a coincidence: accident, chance, statistics, natural selection are helpless to account for such designed terror and heartbreak, such an awful symbolic perversion of the innocent being of the world. Frost's details are so diabolically good that it seems criminal to leave some unremarked; but notice how *dimpled*, *fat*, and *white* (all but one; all but one) come from our regular description of any baby; notice how the *heal-all*, because of its name, is the one flower in all the world picked to be the altar for this Devil's Mass; notice how *holding up* the moth brings something ritual and hieratic, a ghostly, ghastly formality, to this priest and its sacrificial victim; notice how terrible to the fingers, how full of the stilling rigor of death, that *white piece of rigid satin cloth* is. And *assorted characters of death and blight* is, like so many things in this poem, sharply ambiguous: *a mixed bunch of actors* or *diverse representative signs*. The tone of the phrase *assorted characters of death and blight* is beautifully developed in the ironic Breakfast-Club-calisthenics, Radio-Kitchen heartiness of *mixed ready to begin the morning right* (which assures us, so unreassuringly, that this isn't any sort of Strindberg *Spook Sonata*, but hard fact), and concludes in the *ingredients* of the witches' broth, giving the soup a sort of cuddly shimmer that the cauldron in *Macbeth* never had; the *broth*, even, is brought to life—we realize that witches' broth *is* broth, to be supped with a long spoon. For sweet-sour, smiling awfulness *snow-drop spider* looks unsurpassable, until we come to the almost obscenely horrible (even the mouth-gestures are utilized) *a flower like froth;* this always used to seem to me the case of the absolutely inescapable effect, until a student of mine said that you could tell how beautiful the flower was because the poet compared it to froth; when I said to her, "But—but—but what does froth *remind* you of?" looking desperately into her blue eyes, she replied: "Fudge. It reminds me of making fudge."

And then, in the victim's own little line, how contradictory and awful everything is: *dead wings carried like a paper kite!* The *dead* and the *wings* work back and forth on each other heartbreakingly, and the contradictory pathos of the *carried* wings is exceeded by that of the matter-of-fact conversion into what has never lived, into a shouldered toy, of the ended life. *What had that flower to do with being white, / The wayside blue and innocent heal-all?* expresses as well as anything ever has the arbitrariness of our guilt, the fact that Original Sin is only Original Accident, so far as the creatures of this world are concerned. And *the wayside blue and innocent heal-all* is, down to the least sound, the last helpless, yearning, trailing-away sigh of too-precarious innocence, of a potentiality cancelled out almost before it began to exist. The *wayside* makes it universal, commonplace, and somehow dearer to us; the *blue* brings in all the associations of the normal negated color (the poem is likely to remind the reader of Melville's chapter on the Whiteness of the Whale, just as Frost may have been reminded); and the *innocent* is given a peculiar force and life by this context, just as the name *heal-all* here comes to sad, ironic, literal life: it healed all, itself it could not heal. The *kindred* is very moving in its half-forgiving ambiguity; and the Biblical *thither in the night* and the conclusive *steered* (with its careful echoes of "To a Water-Fowl" and a thousand sermons) are very moving and very serious in their condemnation, their awful mystery. The partly ambiguous, summing-up *What but design of darkness to appall* comes as something taken for granted, a relief almost, in its mere statement and generalization, after the almost unbearable actuality and particularity of what has come before. And then this whole appalling categorical machinery of reasoning-out, of conviction, of condemnation—it reminds one of the machine in *The Penal Colony*—is suddenly made merely hypothetical, a possible contradicted shadow, by one offhand last-minute qualification: one that dismisses it, but that dismisses it only for a possibility still more terrifying, a whole new random, statistical, astronomical abyss underlying the diabolical machinery of the poem. "In large things, macroscopic phenomena of some real importance," the poem says, "the classical mechanics of design probably *does* operate—though in reverse, so far as the old Argument from Design is concerned; but these little things, things of no real importance, microscopic phenomena like a flower or moth or man or planet or solar system [we have so indissolubly identified ourselves with the moth and flower and spider that we cannot treat our own nature and importance, which theirs symbolize, as fundamentally different from theirs], are governed by the purely statistical laws of quantum mechanics, of random distribution, are they not?" I have given this statement of "what the poem says"—it says much more—an exaggeratedly physical, scientific form because both a metaphorically and literally astronomical view of things is so common, and so unremarked-on, in Frost. This poem, I think most people will admit, makes Pascal's "eternal silence of those infinite spaces" seem the hush between the movements of a cantata. . . .

But one of the strangest and most characteristic, most dismaying and most gratifying, poems any poet has ever written is a poem called "Directive." It shows the coalescence of three of Frost's obsessive themes, those of insolation, of extinction, and of the final limitations of man—is Frost's last word about all three:

> Back out of all this now too much for us,
> Back in a time made simple by the loss
> Of detail, burned, dissolved, and broken off
> Like graveyard marble sculpture in the weather,
> There is a house that is no more a house
> Upon a farm that is no more a farm
> And in a town that is no more a town.
> The road there, if you'll let a guide direct you
> Who only has at heart your getting lost,
> May seem as if it should have been a quarry—
> Great monolithic knees the former town
> Long since gave up pretence of keeping covered.
> And there's a story in a book about it:
> Besides the wear of iron wagon wheels
> The ledges show lines ruled southeast northwest,
> The chisel work of an enormous Glacier
> That braced his feet against the Arctic Pole.
> You must not mind a certain coolness from him
> Still said to haunt this side of Panther Mountain.
> Nor need you mind the serial ordeal
> Of being watched from forty cellar holes
> As if by eye pairs out of forty firkins.
> As for the wood's excitement over you
> That sends light rustle rushes to their leaves,
> Charge that to upstart inexperience.
> Where were they all not twenty years ago?
> They think too much of having shaded out
> A few old pecker-fretted apple trees.
> Make yourself up a cheering song of how
> Someone's road home from work this once was,
> Who may be just ahead on foot
> Or creaking with a buggy load of grain.
> The height of the adventure is the height
> Of country where two village cultures faded
> Into each other. Both of them are lost.
> And if you're lost enough to find yourself
> By now, pull in your ladder road behind you
> And put a sign up CLOSED to all but me.
> Then make yourself at home. The only field
> Now left's no bigger than a harness gall.
> First there's the children's house of make believe,
> Some shattered dishes underneath a pine,
> The playthings in the playhouse of the children.
> Weep for what little things could make them glad.
> Then for the house that is no more a house,
> But only a belilaced cellar hole,
> Now slowly closing like a dent in dough.
> This was no playhouse but a house in earnest.
> Your destination and your destiny's
> A brook that was the water of the house,
> Cold as a spring as yet so near its source,
> Too lofty and original to rage.
> (We know the valley streams that when aroused
> Will leave their tatters hung on barb and thorn.)
> I have kept hidden in the instep arch
> Of an old cedar at the waterside
> A broken drinking goblet like the Grail
> Under a spell so the wrong ones can't find it,
> So can't get saved, as Saint Mark says they mustn't.
> (I stole the goblet from the children's playhouse.)
> Here are your waters and your watering place.
> Drink and be whole again beyond confusion.

There are weak places in the poem, but these are nothing beside so much longing, tenderness, and passive sadness, Frost's understanding that each life is pathetic because it wears away into the death that it at last half-welcomes—that even its salvation, far back at the cold root of things, is make-believe, drunk from a child's broken and stolen goblet, a plaything hidden among the ruins of the lost cultures. Here the waters of Lethe are the waters of childhood, and in their depths, with ambiguous grace, man's end is joined to his beginning. Is the poem consoling or heart-breaking? Very much of both; and its humor and acceptance and humanity, its familiarity and elevation, give it a composed matter-of-fact magnificence. Much of the strangeness of the poem is far under the surface, or else so much on the surface, in the subtlest of details (how many readers will connect the *serial ordeal* of the eye-pairs with the poem's Grail-parody?), that one slides under it unnoticing. But the first wonderful sentence; the six lines about the wood's excitement; the knowledge that produces the sentence beginning *make yourself up a cheering song;* the *both of them are lost;* incidental graces like the *eye-pairs out of forty firkins,* the *harness gall,* the *belilaced cellar-hole* closing *like a dent in dough,* the plays on the word *lost;* the whole description of the children's playhouse, with the mocking (at whom does it mock?) and beautiful *weep for what little things could make them glad;* the grave, terrible *this was no playhouse but a house in earnest;* the four wonderful conclusive sentences—these, and the whole magical and helpless mastery of the poem, are things that many readers have noticed and will notice: the poem is hard to understand, but easy to love. . . .

Frost calls one poem "The Old Barn at the Bottom of the Fogs," and starts out:

> Where's this barn's house? It never had a house,
> Or joined with sheds in ring-around a dooryard.
> The hunter scuffling leaves goes by at dusk,
> The gun reversed that he went out with shouldered.
> The harvest moon and then the hunter's moon.
> Well, the moon after that came one at last
> To close this outpost barn and close the season.
> The fur-thing, muff-thing, rocking in and out
> Across the threshold in the twilight fled him

How can you resist a poet who can begin a poem like this—even if the poem later comes to nothing at all? Nor is it any easier to resist the man who says "To a Moth Seen in Winter," "with false hope seeking the love of kind," "making a labor of flight for one so airy":

> Nor will you find love either nor love you.
> And what I pity in you is something human,
> The old incurable untimeliness,
> Only begetter of all ills that are

What an already-prepared-for, already-familiar-seeming ring the lines have, the ring of that underlying style that great poets so often have in common beneath their own styles! I think that Dante would have read with nothing but admiration for its calm universal precision the wonderful "Acquainted with the Night," a poem in Dante's own form and with some of Dante's own qualities:

I have been one acquainted with the night.
I have walked out in rain—and back in rain.
I have outwalked the furthest city light.

I have looked down the saddest city lane.
I have passed by the watchman on his beat
And dropped my eyes, unwilling to explain.

I have stood still and stopped the sound of feet
When far away an interrupted cry
Came over houses from another street,

But not to call me back or say goodbye;
And further still at an unearthly height,
One luminary clock against the sky

Proclaimed the time was neither wrong nor right.
I have been one acquainted with the night.

Is this a "classical" poem? If *it* isn't, what is? Yet doesn't the poem itself make the question seem ignominious, a question with a fatal lack of magnanimity, of true comprehension and concern? The things in themselves, the poem itself, abide neither our questions nor our categories; they are free. And our own freedom—the freedom to look and not to disregard, the freedom to side against oneself—is treated with delicate and tender imaginativeness in "Time Out":

It took that pause to make him realize
The mountain he was climbing had the slant
As of a book held up before his eyes
(And was a text albeit done in plant).
Dwarf-cornel, gold-thread, and maianthemum,
He followingly fingered as he read,
The flowers fading on the seed to come;
But the thing was the slope it gave his head:
The same for reading as it was for thought,
So different from the hard and level stare
Of enemies defied and battles fought.
It was the obstinately gentle air
That may be clamored at by cause and sect
But it will have its moment to reflect.

. . . I don't want to finish without saying how much *use* Frost's poems are to one, almost in the way that Hardy's are, when one has read them for many years—without saying how little they seem performances, no matter how brilliant or magical, how little things made primarily of words (or of ink and paper, either), and how much things made out of lives and the world that the lives inhabit. For how much this poetry *is* like the world, "the world wherein we find our happiness or not at all," "the world which was ere I was born, the world which lasts when I am dead," the world with its animals and plants and, most of all, its people: people working, thinking about things, falling in love, taking naps; in these poems men are not only the glory and jest and riddle of the world, but also the habit of the world, its strange ordinariness, its ordinary strangeness, and they too trudge down the ruts along which the planets move in their courses. Frost is that rare thing, a complete or representative poet, and not one of the brilliant partial poets who do justice, far more than justice, to a portion of reality, and leave the rest of things forlorn. When you know Frost's poems you know surprisingly well how the world seemed to one man, and what it was to seem that way: the great *Gestalt* that each of us makes from himself and all that isn't himself is very clear, very complicated, very contradictory in the poetry. The grimness and awfulness and untouchable sadness of things, both in the world and in the self, have justice done to them in the poems, but no more justice than is done to the tenderness and love and delight; and everything in between is represented somewhere too, some things willingly and often and other things only as much—in Marianne Moore's delicate phrase—"as one's natural reticence will allow." If some of the poems come out of a cynical commonsense that is only wisdom's backward shadow, others come out of wisdom itself—for it is, still, just possible for that most old-fashioned of old-fashioned things, wisdom, to maintain a marginal existence in our world. If we compare this wisdom with, say, that of the last of the Old Ones, Goethe, we are saddened and frightened at how much the poet's scope has narrowed, at how difficult and partial and idiosyncratic the application of his intelligence has become, at what terrible sacrifices he has had to make in order to avoid making others still more terrible. Yet how many poems, how many more lines, are immediately and supplely responsive with the unseparated unspecialized intelligence that is by now almost as natural to man—that being men have so laboriously created—as dreams and hunger and desire. To have the distance from the most awful and most nearly unbearable parts of the poems, to the most tender, subtle, and loving parts, a distance so great; to have this whole range of being treated with so much humor and sadness and composure, with such plain truth; to see that a man can still include, connect, and make humanly understandable or humanly ununderstandable so *much*—this is one of the freshest and oldest of joys, a joy strong enough to make us forget the limitations and excesses and baseness that these days seem unforgettable, a joy strong enough to make us say, with the Greek poet, that many things in this world are wonderful, but of all these the most wonderful is man.

LIONEL TRILLING
"A Speech on Robert Frost: A Cultural Episode"

Partisan Review, Summer 1959, pp. 445–52

On March 26th (1959) Henry Holt and Company, the publishers of Robert Frost, gave Mr. Frost a dinner at the Waldorf-Astoria in celebration of his eighty-fifth birthday. I was the speaker at the dinner. I am publishing what I said about Mr. Frost not because I think it to be especially interesting in itself but because it made the occasion for a disturbance of some magnitude and I should like to answer the question that has often been put to me: What did I say that could so nearly have approached a scandal?

Some of the substance of my speech was made public by J. Donald Adams in his column in *The New York Times Book Review* of April 12th. Mr. Adams wrote from a copy of my manuscript which, with my permission, had been made available to him by Henry Holt and Company, and he reported with sufficient accuracy those parts of the speech to which he took exception. It should be said of Mr. Adams's reply to me that it took exception only to the critical judgment I had expressed. Mr. Adams did not question my taste or tact except in one small and perhaps facetious instance—he thought it "unfortunate . . . in view of Frost's shock of white hair," that I should have "identified the poet with the Bald Eagle." (But every American worthy of the name knows that the Bald Eagle is not bald at all and that in maturity it is distinguished by its shock of white hair.) Nevertheless the reply of Mr. Adams created the impression with some people that, so far from my having paid tribute to a venerable man at a celebration of his life and achievement, I had actually offered him an affront. I gather that the chief cause of the presumed offense was my having spoken of Mr. Frost as "a terrifying poet."

Certainly what I had said as reported by Mr. Adams

offered an affront to some part of American opinion. It was a very deep affront if I can judge by the letters, published in the *Book Review* of April 26th, which applauded Mr. Adams for his reply to me. There were nine such letters and all of them sounded a note of bitterness, or of personal grievance, or of triumph over my having been so thoroughly taken down by Mr. Adams. I must confess to being surprised by the low personal and intellectual tone of these letters. My estimate of the present state of American culture had not prepared me for it. "Trilling doesn't have the good sense to know when he is out of his field or his depth or whatever it is." "Frost might have had the Nobel Prize if so many New York critics hadn't gone whoring after European gods." "This Trilling fella had it coming to him for some time." "I hope Robert Frost was having a nice plate of buckwheat cakes and Vermont maple syrup as he read Mr. Adams's remarks. He couldn't have done better unless he had taken the so-called professor out to the woodshed." "I am a Freudian psychoanalyst, but I couldn't agree with Mr. Adams more. Imagine calling Frost a 'terrifying poet.' Professor Trilling never got lost in the Freudian wood. He is just enmeshed in a Trilling world." (In his column Mr. Adams had urged me "to come out of the Freudian wood . . . and face the facts of life." It will be seen that I make no mention of Freud in my speech, but I do speak of D. H. Lawrence, and Mr. Adams said that Lawrence was a genius but hadn't understood "the American experience" because, like me, he was "lost in the Freudian wood." Lawrence, of course, hated Freud and took every occasion to denounce him.)

The personal and intellectual quality of the letters is especially interesting because of the professions of the people who wrote them: in addition to the "Freudian psychoanalyst," the writers included the editor of *The Atlantic Monthly*, the publisher of *The Saturday Review*, two fairly well-known poets, a member of the Federal Trade Commission, a well-known and quite literate writer of fiction and biography, a very distinguished literary scholar. Only one of the writers, Mr. Weeks of *The Atlantic Monthly*, knew at first hand, what I had said, having been present at the dinner. He expressed himself as finding my remarks "ill-judged and condescending for an occasion which was intended to be appreciative," and went on to say that "it would have been more appropriate had the introduction been entrusted to W. H. Auden, particularly in view of England's early acceptance of Frost's work, in which case we should have been spared the long Freudian self-analysis which few could have come to hear." All the other writers knew what I had said only from Mr. Adams's reply to it. That the literary scholar was among their number made a circumstance to which I couldn't fail to respond with some unhappiness, for I had first been Professor Emery Neff's student when I was an undergraduate at Columbia College and I had worked in his field and under his direction as a graduate student; I have always thought of Mr. Neff as the teacher from whom I had learned the methods and attitudes of the scholar; that he should so far have abrogated the rule and spirit of scholarship as to write in support of Mr. Adams's rebuke (as he chose to call it) without having seen the text of what I had said disturbed me deeply in a way I shall not now attempt to describe.

I have no doubt that the episode will yield cultural conclusions to whoever wants to draw them.

Because I am publishing the speech as a document, I give it exactly as I spoke it, not even mitigating the donnish humor of the opening paragraphs.

Mr. Rigg, Ladies and Gentlemen
(and I shall address Mr. Frost presently):

I am sure that anyone standing in my place tonight, charged with the happy office of greeting Mr. Frost on his birthday, on his massive, his Sophoclean birthday, would be bound to feel, as I do indeed feel, a considerable measure of diffidence.

For our occasion, although it isn't solemn, is surely momentous. We all of us know that we celebrate something that lies beyond even Mr. Frost's achievement as a poet. No person here tonight, no matter how high his regard for Mr. Frost as a poet may be, is under any illusion that Mr. Frost, at this point in his career, exists in the consciousness of Americans as only a poet. Just what he does exist as may perhaps be best understood by the archaeologists of a few millenniums hence. They will observe, those ardent students of our culture, how, at the time of the vernal equinox, feasts were held to celebrate the birth of this personage, and how, at a later time in the spring, at that ceremony which the ancient North Americans, with their infallible instinct for beauty, called by the lovely name of *Commencement*, it was customary to do him honor by a rite in which it was pretended that he was a scholar, a man of immense learning—a doctor—and no American university was thought to be worthy of the name until it had duly performed this rite, which was quaintly called *conferring a degree*. The time of year at which these ritual observances took place makes it plain to the archaeologists that they are almost certainly not dealing with an historical individual but rather with a solar myth, a fertility figure. They go on to expound the subtle process of myth which is to be observed in the fact that this vernal spirit was called *Frost*, a name which seems to contradict his nature and function. In their effort to explain this anomaly, they take note of evidence which suggests that the early North Americans believed that there were once two brothers, Robert Frost and Jack Frost, of whom one, Jack, remained unregenerate and hostile to mankind, while the other brother became its friend. But of course the archaeologists understand that this is a mere folk-explanation which explains nothing. They say, cogently enough, that mythical figures often embody contradictory principles, that just as Apollo was both destroyer and preserver, so Robert Frost was at one and the same time both ice and sun, and they point to a dark saying attributed to him: "Like a piece of ice on a hot stove, the poem must ride on its own melting."

Thus the ultimate myth. It tells us much about the nature of Robert Frost and I am glad to be able to communicate it to you.

But there is also the myth that is nearer at hand. We do not need to wait upon the archaeologists of the future to understand that Robert Frost exists not only in a human way but also in a mythical way. We know him, and have known him so for many years, as nothing less than a national fact. We have come to think of him as virtually a symbol of America, as something not unlike an articulate, an actually poetic, Bald Eagle. When we undertake to honor him, we do indeed honor him as a poet, but also as a tutelary genius of the nation and as a justification of our national soul.

This mythical existence of Robert Frost determines the nature of our occasion and makes it momentous. It substantiates my statement that anyone who speaks publicly about Mr. Frost tonight must do so under the constraints of an extreme diffidence.

Yet I must be more weighed down by diffidence than many others who might speak here. I must also entertain a doubt of the appropriateness of my speaking here at all. For I cannot help knowing that the manifest America of Robert Frost's poems is not the America that has its place in my own mind. The manifest America of Mr. Frost's poems is rural, and, if I may say so, it is rural in a highly moralized way, in an aggressively moralized way. It thus represents an ideal that is common to many Americans, perhaps especially the Americans of the literary kind, who thus express their distaste for the life of the city and for all that the city implies of excessive complexity, of uncertainty, of anxiety, and of the demand that is made upon intellect to deal with whatever are the causes of complexity, uncertainty, anxiety.

I do not share this ideal. It is true that the image of the old America has a great power over me—that old America with which the America of Mr. Frost's poems seems to be continuous. And I think I know from experience—there are few Americans who do not—how intense can be the pleasure in the hills and the snow, in the meadows and woods and swamps that make the landscape of Mr. Frost's manifest America; and know, too, how great a part this pleasure can play in a man's moral being. But these natural things that give me pleasure constitute my notion of the earthly paradise, they are not the ruling elements of my imagination of actual life. Those elements are urban—I speak here tonight incongruously as a man of the city. I teach in an urban university. The magazine I most enjoy writing for is *Partisan Review*, to which, as I know, there is often imputed an excess of city intellectuality, even to the point of its being thought scarcely American at all.

Of course I have imagination enough to hate the city. And of course I have sensibility enough to be bored and exasperated by the intellectual life that is peculiar to the city, not only as that is lived by others but by myself. But to the essential work that is done by the critical intellect (I use the term in its widest sense), that work which, wherever it is carried on, must sooner or later relate itself to the metropolis or must seek, wherever it is carried on, to create around itself the intensity and variety that traditionally characterize the intellectual life of the metropolis—to that work I give a partisan devotion. I know all that can be charged against the restless, combative, abstract urban intellect: I know perhaps more than is known by its avowed antagonists. I also know that when it flags, something goes out of the nation's spirit, and that if it were to cease, the state of the nation would be much the worse.

It is a fact which I had best confess as simply as possible that for a long time I was alienated from Mr. Frost's great canon of work by what I saw in it, that either itself seemed to denigrate the work of the critical intellect or that gave to its admirers the ground for making the denigration. It was but recently that my resistance, at the behest of better understanding, yielded to admiration—it is probable that there is no one here tonight who has not admired Mr. Frost's poetry for a longer time than I have.

This will begin to explain why I am so especially diffident standing in this place. I have yet more to confess. I have to say that my Frost—*my Frost:* what airs we give ourselves when once we believe that we have come into possession of a poet!—I have to say that my Frost is not the Frost I seem to perceive existing in the minds of so many of his admirers. He is not the Frost who confounds the characteristically modern practice of poetry by his notable democratic simplicity of utterance: on the contrary. He is not the Frost who controverts the bitter modern astonishment at the nature of human life: the opposite is so. He is not the Frost who reassures us by his affirmation of old virtues, simplicities, pieties, and ways of feeling: anything but. I will not go so far as to say that my Frost is not essentially an American poet at all: I believe that he is quite as American as everyone thinks he is, but not in the way that everyone thinks he is.

In the matter of the Americanism of American literature one of my chief guides is that very remarkable critic, D. H. Lawrence. Here are the opening sentences of Lawrence's great outrageous book about classic American literature. "We like to think of the old fashioned American classics as children's books. Just childishness on our part. The old American art speech contains an alien quality which belongs to the American continent and to nowhere else." And this unique alien quality, Lawrence goes on to say, the world has missed. "It is hard to hear a new voice," he says, "as hard as to listen to an unknown language. . . . Why? Out of fear. The world fears a new experience more than it fears anything. It can pigeonhole any idea. But it can't pigeonhole a real new experience. It can only dodge. The world is a great dodger, and the Americans the greatest. Because they dodge their own very selves." I should like to pick up a few more of Lawrence's sentences, feeling the freer to do so because they have an affinity to Mr. Frost's prose manner and substance: "An artist is usually a damned liar, but his art, if it be art, will tell you the truth of his day. And that is all that matters. Away with eternal truth. Truth lives from day to day. . . . The old American artists were hopeless liars. . . . Never trust the artist. Trust the tale. The proper function of the critic is to save the tale from the artist who created it. . . . Now listen to me, don't listen to him. He'll tell you the lie you expect, which is partly your fault for expecting it."

Now in point of fact Robert Frost is *not* a liar. I would not hesitate to say that he was if I thought he was. But no, he is not. In certain of his poems—I shall mention one or two in a moment—he makes it perfectly plain what he is doing; and if we are not aware of what he is doing in other of his poems, where he is not quite so plain, that is not his fault but our own. It is not from him that the tale needs to be saved.

I conceive that Robert Frost is doing in his poems what Lawrence says the great writers of the classic American tradition did. That enterprise of theirs was of an ultimate radicalism. It consisted, Lawrence says, of two things: a disintegration and sloughing off of the old consciousness, by which Lawrence means the old European consciousness, and the forming of a new consciousness underneath.

So radical a work, I need scarcely say, is not carried out by reassurance, nor by the affirmation of old virtues and pieties. It is carried out by the representation of the terrible actualities of life in a new way. I think of Robert Frost as a terrifying poet. Call him, if it makes things any easier, a tragic poet, but it might be useful every now and then to come out from under the shelter of that literary word. The universe that he conceives is a terrifying universe. Read the poem called "Design" and see if you sleep the better for it. Read "Neither Out Far Nor In Deep," which often seems to me the most perfect poem of our time, and see if you are warmed by anything in it except the energy with which emptiness is perceived.

But the *people*, it will be objected, the *people* who inhabit this possibly terrifying universe! About them there is nothing that can terrify; surely the people in Mr. Frost's poems can only reassure us by their integrity and solidity. Perhaps so. But I cannot make the disjunction. It may well be that ultimately they reassure us in some sense, but first they terrify us, or should. We must not be misled about them by the curious tenderness with which they are represented, a tenderness which extends to a recognition of the tenderness which they themselves can often give. But when ever have people been so isolated, so lightning-blasted, so tried down and calcined by life, so reduced, each in his own way, to some last irreducible core of being. Talk of the disintegration and sloughing off of the old consciousness! The people of Robert Frost's poems have done that with a vengeance. Lawrence says that what the Americans refused to accept was "the post-Renaissance humanism of Europe," "the old European spontaneity," "the flowing easy humor of Europe" and that seems to me a good way to describe the people who inhabit Robert Frost's America. In the interests of what great other thing these people have made this rejection we cannot know for certain. But we can guess that it was in the interest of truth, of some truth of the self. This is what they all affirm by their humor (which is so *not* "the easy flowing humor of Europe"), by their irony, by their separateness and isolateness. They affirm *this* of themselves: that they are what they are, that this is their truth, and that if the truth be bare, as truth often is, it is far better than a lie. For me the process by which they arrive at that truth is always terrifying. The manifest America of Mr. Frost's poems may be pastoral; the actual America is tragic.

And what new consciousness is forming underneath? That I do not know, possibly because I have not been long enough habituated to the voice that makes the relatively new experience I am having. I am still preoccupied with the terrifying process of the disintegration and sloughing off of the old consciousness.

Mr. Frost:

I hope that you will not think it graceless of me that on your birthday I have undertaken to say that a great many of your admirers have not understood clearly what you have been doing in your life in poetry. I know that you will not say which of us is in the right of the matter. You will behave like the Secret whose conduct you have described:

> We dance around in a ring and suppose.
> But the Secret sits in the middle and knows.

And I hope that you will not think it graceless of me that on your birthday I have made you out to be a poet who terrifies. When I began to speak I called your birthday Sophoclean and that word has, I think, controlled everything I have said about you. Like you, Sophocles lived to a great age, writing well; and like you, Sophocles was the poet his people loved most. Surely they loved him in some part because he praised their common country. But I think that they loved him chiefly because he made plain to them the terrible things of human life: they felt, perhaps, that only a poet who could make plain the terrible things could possibly give them comfort.

W. H. AUDEN
"Robert Frost"
The Dyer's Hand
1962, pp. 337–53

If asked who said *Beauty is Truth, Truth Beauty!*, a great many readers would answer "Keats." But Keats said nothing of the sort. It is what he said the Grecian Urn said, his description and criticism of a certain kind of work of art, the kind from which the evils and problems of this life, the "heart high sorrowful and cloyed," are deliberately excluded. The Urn, for example, depicts, among other beautiful sights, the citadel of a hill town; it does not depict warfare, the evil which makes the citadel necessary.

Art arises out of our desire for both beauty and truth and our knowledge that they are not identical. One might say that every poem shows some sign of a rivalry between Ariel and Prospero; in every good poem their relation is more or less happy, but it is never without its tensions. The Grecian Urn states Ariel's position; Prospero's has been equally succinctly stated by Dr. Johnson: *The only end of writing is to enable the readers better to enjoy life or better to endure it.*

We want a poem to be beautiful, that is to say, a verbal earthly paradise, a timeless world of pure play, which gives us delight precisely because of its contrast to our historical existence with all its insoluble problems and inescapable suffering; at the same time we want a poem to be true, that is to say, to provide us with some kind of revelation about our life which will show us what life is really like and free us from self-enchantment and deception, and a poet cannot bring us any truth without introducing into his poetry the problematic, the painful, the disorderly, the ugly. Though every poem involves *some* degree of collaboration between Ariel and Prospero, the role of each varies in importance from one poem to another: it is usually possible to say of a poem and, sometimes, of the whole output of a poet, that it is Ariel-dominated or Prospero-dominated.

> Hot sun, cool fire, tempered with sweet air,
> Black shade, fair nurse, shadow my white hair:
> Shine, sun; burn, fire; breathe, air, and ease me;
> Black shade, fair nurse, shroud me and please me:
> Shadow, my sweet nurse, keep me from burning,
> Make not my glad cause, cause for mourning,
> Let not my beauty's fire
> Inflame unstaid desire,
> Nor pierce any bright eye
> That wandereth lightly.
> (George Peele, "Bathsabe's Song.")

> The road at the top of the rise
> Seems to come to an end
> And takes off into the skies.
> So at a distant bend
>
> It seems to go into a wood,
> The place of standing still
> As long as the trees have stood.
> But say what Fancy will,
>
> The mineral drops that explode
> To drive my ton of car
> Are limited to the road.
> They deal with the near and far,
>
> And have almost nothing to do
> With the absolute flight and rest
> The universal blue
> And local green suggest.
> (Robert Frost, "The Middleness of the Road.")

Both poems are written in the first person singular, but the Peele-Bathsabe *I* is very different from the Frost *I*. The first seems anonymous, hardly more than a grammatical form; one cannot imagine meeting Bathsabe at a dinner party. The second *I* names a historical individual in a specific situation—he is driving an automobile in a certain kind of landscape.

Take away what Bathsabe says and she vanishes, for what she says does not seem to be a response to any situation or event. If one asks what her song is about, one cannot give a specific answer, only a vague one:—a beautiful young girl, any beautiful girl, on any sunny morning, half-awake and half-asleep, is reflecting on her beauty with a mixture of self-admiration and pleasing fear, pleasing because she is unaware of any real danger; a girl who was really afraid of a Peeping Tom would sing very differently. If one tries to explain why one likes the song, or any poem of this kind, one finds oneself talking about language, the handling of the rhythm, the pattern of vowels and consonants, the placing of caesuras, epanorthosis, etc.

Frost's poem, on the other hand, is clearly a response to an experience which preceded any words and without which the poem could not have come into being, for the purpose of the poem is to define that experience and draw wisdom from it. Though the beautiful verbal element is not absent—it is a poem, not a passage of informative prose—this is subordinate in importance to the truth of what it says.

If someone suddenly asks me to give him an example of good poetry, it is probably a poem of the Peele sort which will immediately come to my mind: but if I am in a state of emotional excitement, be it joy or grief, and try to think of a poem which is relevant and illuminating to my condition, it is a poem of the Frost sort which I shall be most likely to recall.

Ariel, as Shakespeare has told us, has no passions. That is his glory and his limitation. The earthly paradise is a beautiful place but nothing of serious importance can occur in it.

An anthology selected by Ariel, including only poems like the *Eclogues* of Vergil, *Las Soledades* of Góngora and poets like Campion, Herrick, Mallarmé, would, in the long run, repel us by its narrowness and monotony of feeling: for Ariel's other name is Narcissus.

It can happen that a poem which, when written, was Prospero-dominated, becomes an Ariel poem for later generations. The nursery rhyme *I will sing you One O* may very well originally have been a mnemonic rhyme for teaching sacred lore of the highest importance. The sign that, for us, it has become an Ariel poem is that we have no curiosity about the various persons it refers to: it is as anthropologists not as readers of poetry that we ask who the lily-white boys really were. On the other hand, anything we can learn about the persons whom Dante introduces into *The Divine Comedy*, contributes to our appreciation of his poem.

It is also possible for a poet himself to be mistaken as to the kind of poem he is writing. For example, at first reading, *Lycidas* seems to be by Prospero, for it purports to deal with the most serious matters possible—death, grief, sin, resurrection. But I believe this to be an illusion. On closer inspection, it seems to me that only the robes are Prospero's and that Ariel has dressed up in them for fun, so that it is as irrelevant to ask, "Who is the Pilot of the Galilean Lake?" as it is to ask, "Who is the Pobble who has no toes?" and He who walks the waves is merely an Arcadian shepherd whose name happens to be Christ. If *Lycidas* is read in this way, as if it were a poem by Edward Lear, then it seems to me one of the most beautiful poems in the English language: if, however, it is read as the Prospero poem it apparently claims to be, then it must be condemned, as Dr. Johnson condemned it, for being unfeeling and frivolous, since one expects wisdom and revelation and it provides neither.

The Ariel-dominated poet has one great advantage; he can only fail in one way—his poem may be trivial. The worst one can say of one of his poems is that it needn't have been written. But the Prospero-dominated poet can fail in a number of different ways. Of all English poets, Wordsworth is perhaps the one with the least element of Ariel that is compatible with being a poet at all, and so provides the best examples of what happens when Prospero tries to write entirely by himself.

> The Bird and Cage they both were his:
> 'Twas my Son's bird: and neat and trim
> He kept it; many voyages
> This singing bird has gone with him:
> When last he sailed he left the bird behind;
> As it might be, perhaps from bodings in his mind.

Reading such a passage, one exclaims, "The man can't write," which is something that can never be said about Ariel; when Ariel can't write, he doesn't. But Prospero is capable of graver errors than just being ridiculous; since he is trying to say something which is true, if he fails, the result can be worse than trivial. It can be false, compelling the reader to say, not "This poem need not have been written," but "This poem should not have been written."

Both in theory and practice Frost is a Prospero-dominated poet. In the preface to his *Collected Poems*, he writes:

> The sound is the gold in the ore. Then we will have the sound out alone and dispense with the inessential. We do till we make the discovery that the object in writing poetry is to make all poems sound as different as possible from each other, and the resources for that of vowels, consonants, punctuation, syntax, words, sentences, meter are not enough. We need the help of context—meaning—subject matter. . . . And we are back in poetry as merely one more art of having something to say, sound or unsound. Probably better if sound, because deeper and from wider experience. [A poem] begins in delight and ends in wisdom . . . a clarification of life—not necessarily a great clarification such as sects and cults are founded on, but in a momentary stay against confusion.

His poetic style is what I think Professor C. S. Lewis would call Good Drab. The music is always that of the speaking voice, quiet and sensible, and I cannot think of any other modern poet, except Cavafy, who uses language more simply. He rarely employs metaphors, and there is not a word, not a historical or literary reference in the whole of his work which would be strange to an unbookish boy of fifteen. Yet he manages to make this simple kind of speech express a wide variety of emotion and experience.

> Be that as may be, she was in their song.
> Moreover her voice upon their voices crossed
> Had now persisted in the woods so long
> That probably it would never be lost.
> Never again would bird's song be the same.
> And to do that to birds was why she came.
>
> . . .
>
> I hope if he is where he sees me now
> He's so far off he can't see what I've come to.
> You *can* come down from everything to nothing.
> All is, if I'd a-known when I was young
> And full of it, that this would be the end,
> It doesn't seem as if I'd had the courage
> To make so free and kick up folk's faces.
> I might have, but it doesn't seem as if.

The emotions in the first passage are tender, happy, and its reflections of a kind which could only be made by an educated man. The emotions in the second are violent and tragic, and the speaker a woman with no schooling. Yet the diction in both is equally simple. There are a few words the man uses which the woman would not use herself, but none she could not understand; her syntax is a little cruder than his, but only a little. Yet their two voices sound as distinct as they sound authentic.

Frost's poetic speech is the speech of a mature mind, fully awake and in control of itself; it is not the speech of dream or of uncontrollable passion. Except in reported speech, interjections, imperatives, and rhetorical interrogatives are rare. This does not mean, of course, that his poems are lacking in feeling; again and again, one is aware of strong, even violent, emotion behind what is actually said, but the saying is reticent, the poetry has, as it were, an auditory chastity. It would be impossible for Frost, even if he wished, to produce an unabashed roar of despair, as Shakespeare's tragic heroes so often can, but the man who wrote the following lines has certainly been acquainted with despair.

I have stood still and stopped the sound of feet
When far away an interrupted cry
Came over houses from another street,
But not to call me back or say good-bye.
And further still at an unearthly height
One luminary clock against the sky
Proclaimed the time was neither wrong nor right.
I have been one acquainted with the night.

Every style has its limitations. It would be as impossible to write "Ebauche d'un serpent" in the style of Frost as it would be to write "The Death of the Hired Man" in the style of Valéry. A style, like Frost's which approximates to ordinary speech is necessarily contemporary, the style of a man living in the first half of the twentieth century; it is not well suited, therefore, to subjects from the distant past, in which the difference between then and today is significant, or to mythical subjects which are timeless.

Neither Frost's version of the Job story in A *Masque of Reason* nor his version of the Jonah story in A *Masque of Mercy* seems to me quite to come off; both are a little self-consciously in modern dress.

Nor is such a style well-suited to official public occasions when a poet must speak about and on behalf of the *Civitas Terrena*. Frost's tone of voice, even in his dramatic pieces, is that of a man talking to himself, thinking aloud and hardly aware of an audience. This manner is, of course, like all manners, calculated, and more sophisticated than most. The calculation is sound when the poems are concerned with personal emotions, but when the subject is one of public affairs or ideas of general interest, it may be a miscalculation. "Build Soil, a Political Pastoral," which Frost composed for the National Party Convention at Columbia University in 1932, was much criticized at the time by the Liberal-Left for being reactionary. Reading it today, one wonders what all their fuss was about, but the fireside-chat I'm-a-plain-fellow manner is still irritating. One finds oneself wishing that Columbia had invited Yeats instead; he might have said the most outrageous things, but he would have put on a good act, and that is what we want from a poet when he speaks to us of what concerns us, not as private persons but as citizens. Perhaps Frost himself felt uneasy, for the last two lines of the poem, and the best, run thus:

We're too unseparate. And going home
From company means coming to our senses.

Any poetry which aims at being a clarification of life must be concerned with two questions about which all men, whether they read poetry or not, seek clarification.

1) *Who am I?* What is the difference between man and all other creatures? What relations are possible between them? What is man's status in the universe? What are the conditions of his existence which he must accept as his fate which no wishing can alter?

2) *Whom ought I to become?* What are the characteristics of the hero, the authentic man whom everybody should admire and try to become? Vice versa, what are the characteristics of the churl, the unauthentic man whom everybody should try to avoid becoming?

We all seek answers to these questions which shall be universally valid under all circumstances, but the experience to which we put them are always local both in time and place. What any poet has to say about man's status in nature, for example, depends in part upon the landscape and climate he happens to live in and in part upon the reactions to it of his personal temperament. A poet brought up in the tropics cannot have the same vision as a poet brought up in Hertfordshire and, if they inhabit the same landscape, the chirpy social endomorph will give a different picture of it from that of the melancholic withdrawn ectomorph.

The nature in Frost's poetry is the nature of New England. New England is made of granite, is mountainous, densely wooded, and its soil is poor. It has a long severe winter, a summer that is milder and more pleasant than in most parts of the States, a short and sudden Spring, a slow and theatrically beautiful fall. Since it adjoins the eastern seaboard, it was one of the first areas to be settled but, as soon as the more fertile lands to the West were opened up, it began to lose population. Tourists and city dwellers who can afford a summer home may arrive for the summer, but much land which was once cultivated has gone back to the wild.

One of Frost's favorite images is the image of the abandoned house. In Britain or Europe, a ruin recalls either historical change, political acts like war or enclosure, or, in the case of abandoned mine buildings, a successful past which came to an end, not because nature was too strong, but because she had been robbed of everything she possessed. A ruin in Europe, therefore, tends to arouse reflections about human injustice and greed and the nemesis that overtakes human pride. But in Frost's poetry, a ruin is an image of human heroism, of a defense in the narrow pass against hopeless odds.

I came an errand one cloud-blowing morning
To a slab-built, black-paper-covered house
Of one room and one window and one door,
The only dwelling in a waste cut over
A hundred square miles round it in the mountains:
And that not dwelt in now by men or women.
(It never had been dwelt in, though, by women.)
. . .
Here further up the mountain slope
Than there was ever any hope,
My father built, enclosed a spring,
Strung chains of wall round everything,
Subdued the growth to earth of grass,
And brought our various lives to pass.
A dozen girls and boys we were.
The mountain seemed to like the stir
And made of us a little while—
With always something in her smile.
To-day she wouldn't know our name.
(No girl's of course has stayed the same.)
The mountain pushed us off her knees.
And now her lap is full of trees.

Thumbing through Frost's *Collected Poems,* I find twenty-one in which the season is winter as compared with five in which it is spring, and in two of these there is still snow on the ground; I find twenty-seven in which the time is night and seventeen in which the weather is stormy.

The commonest human situation in his poetry is of one man, or a man and wife, alone in a small isolated house in a snowbound forest after dark.

Where I could think of no thoroughfare,
Away on the mountain up far too high,
A blinding headlight shifted glare
And began to bounce down a granite stair
Like a star fresh-fallen out of the sky,
And I away in my opposite wood
Am touched by that unintimate light
And made feel less alone than I rightly should,
For traveler there could do me no good
Were I in trouble with night tonight.
. . .
We looked and looked, but after all where are we?
Do we know any better where we are,
And how it stands between the night tonight

And a man with a smokey lantern chimney,
How different from the way it ever stood?

In "Two Look at Two," nature, as represented by a buck stag and a doe, responds in sympathy to man, as represented by a boy and girl, but the point of the poem is that this sympathetic response is a miraculous exception. The normal response is that described in "The Most of It."

Some morning from the boulder-broken beach
He would cry out on life that what it wants
Is not its own love back in copy speech,
But counter-love, original response.
And nothing ever came of what he cried
Unless it was the embodiment that crashed
In the cliff's talus on the other side,
And then in the far distant water splashed,
But after a time allowed for it to swim,
Instead of proving human when it neared
And some one else additional to him,
As a great buck it powerfully appeared

Nature, however, is not to Frost, as she was to Melville, malignant.

It must be a little more in favor of man,
Say a fraction of one per cent at least,
Or our number living wouldn't be steadily more.

She is, rather, the Dura Virum Nutrix who, by her apparent indifference and hostility, even, calls forth all man's powers and courage and makes a real man of him.

Courage is not to be confused with romantic daring. It includes caution and cunning,

All we who prefer to live
Have a little whistle we give,
And flash at the least alarm
We dive down under the farm

and even financial prudence,

Better to go down dignified
With boughten friendship at your side
Than none at all. Provide, provide!

There have been Euopean poets who have come to similar conclusions about the isolation of the human condition, and nature's indifference to human values, but, compared with an American, they are at a disadvantage in expressing them. Living as they do in a well, even overpopulated, countryside where, thanks to centuries of cultivation, Mother Earth has acquired human features, they are forced to make abstract philosophical statements or use uncommon atypical images, so that what they say seems to be imposed upon them by theory and temperament rather than by facts. An American poet like Frost, on the other hand, can appeal to facts for which any theory must account and which any temperament must admit.

The Frostian man is isolated not only in space but also in time. In Frost's poems the nostalgic note is seldom, if ever, struck. When he writes a poem about childhood like "Wild Grapes," childhood is not seen as a magical Eden which will all too soon, alas, be lost, but as a school in which the first lessons of adult life are learned. The setting of one of his best long poems, "The Generations of Man," is the ancestral home of the Stark family in the town of Bow, New Hampshire. Bow is a rock-strewn township where farming has fallen off and sproutlands flourish since the axe has gone. The Stark family mansion is by now reduced to an old cellar-hole at the side of a by-road. The occasion described in the poem is a gathering together from all over of the Stark descendants, an advertising stunt thought up by the governor of the state. The characters are a boy Stark and a girl Stark, distant cousins, who meet at the cellar-hole and are immediately attracted to each other. Their conversation turns, naturally, to their common ancestors, but, in fact, they know nothing about them. The boy starts inventing stories and doing imaginary imitations of their voices as a way of courtship, making their ancestors hint at marriage and suggest building a new summer home on the site of the old house. The real past, that is to say, is unknown and unreal to them; its role in the poem is to provide a lucky chance for the living to meet.

Like Gray, Frost has written a poem on a deserted graveyard. Gray is concerned with the possible lives of the unknown dead; the past is more imaginatively exciting to him than the present. But Frost does not try to remember anything; what moves him is that death, which is always a present terror, is no longer present here, having moved on like a pioneer.

It would be easy to be clever
And tell the stones; men hate to die
And have stopped dying now for ever.
I think they would believe the lie.

What he finds valuable in man's temporal existence is the ever-recurrent opportunity of the present moment to make a discovery or a new start.

One of the lies would make it out that nothing
Ever presents itself before us twice.
Where would we be at last if that were so?
Our very life depends on everything's
Recurring till we answer from within.
The thousandth time may prove the charm.

Frost has written a number of pastoral eclogues and, no doubt, has taken a sophisticated pleasure in using what is, by tradition, the most aristocratic and idyllic of all literary forms to depict democratic realities. If the landscape of New England is unarcadian, so is its social life; the leisured class with nothing to do but cultivate its sensibility which the European pastoral presupposes, is simply not there. Of course, as in all societies, social distinctions exist. In New England, Protestants of Anglo-Scotch stock consider themselves a cut above Roman Catholics and those of a Latin race, and the most respectable Protestant denominations are the Congregationalists and the Unitarians. Thus, in "The Axe-Helve," the Yankee farmer is aware of his social condescension in entering the house of his French-Canadian neighbor, Baptiste.

I shouldn't mind his being overjoyed
(If overjoyed he was) at having got me
Where I must judge if what he knew about an axe
That not everybody else knew was to count
For nothing in the measure of a neighbor.
Hard if, though cast away for life with Yankees,
A Frenchman couldn't get his human rating!

And in "Snow," Mrs. Cole passes judgment upon the Evangelical preacher, Meserve.

I detest the thought of him
With his ten children under ten years old.
I hate his wretched little Racker Sect,
All's ever I heard of it, which isn't much.

Yet in both poems the neighbor triumphs over the snob. The Yankee acknowledges Baptiste's superior skill, and the Coles stay up all night in concern until they hear that Meserve has reached home safely through the storm.

In the Frost pastoral, the place of the traditional worldly-wise, world-weary courtier is taken by the literary city dweller, often a college student who has taken a job for the summer on a farm; the rustics he encounters are neither comic bumpkins nor noble savages.

In "A Hundred Collars," a refined shy college professor meets in a small town hotel bedroom a fat whisky-drinking vulgarian who canvasses the farms around on behalf of a local newspaper. If, in the end, the reader's sympathies go to the vulgarian, the vulgarian is not made aesthetically appealing nor the professor unpleasant. The professor means well—he is a democrat, if not at heart, in principle—but he is the victim of a way of life which has narrowed his human sympathies and interests. The vulgarian is redeemed by his uninhibited friendliness which is perfectly genuine, not a professional salesman's manner. Though vulgar, he is not a go-getter.

> 'One would suppose they might not be as glad
> to see you as you are to see them.'
> 'Oh,
> Because I want their dollar? I don't want
> Anything they've got. I never dun.
> I'm there, and they can pay me if they like.
> I go nowhere on purpose: I happen by.'

In "The Code," a town-bred farmer unwittingly offends one of his hired hands.

> 'What is there wrong?'
> 'Something you just now said.'
> 'What did I say?'
> 'About our taking pains.'
> 'To cock the hay—because it's going to shower?
> I said that more than half an hour ago.
> I said it to myself as much as you.'
> 'You didn't know. But James is one big fool.
> He thought you meant to find fault with his work,
> That's what the average farmer would have
> meant.' . . .
> 'He's a fool if that's the way he takes me.'
> 'Don't let it bother you. You've found out something.
> The hand that knows his business won't be told
> To do work better or faster—those two things. . . .'

The ignorance of the town-bred farmer is made use of, not to blame him, but to praise the quality which, after courage, Frost ranks as the highest of the virtues, the self-respect which comes from taking a pride in something. It may be a pride in one's own skill, the pride of the axe-maker Baptiste, the pride of the Hired Man who dies from a broken heart since old age has taken from him the one accomplishment, building a load of hay, which had hitherto prevented him from feeling utterly worthless, or it may be a pride which, from a worldly point of view, is a folly, the pride of the man who has failed as a farmer, burned his house down for the insurance money, bought a telescope with the proceeds and taken a lowly job as a ticket agent on the railroad. The telescope is not a good one, the man is poor, but he is proud of his telescope and happy.

Every poet is at once a representative of his culture and its critic. Frost has never written satires, but it is not hard to guess what, as an American, he approves and disapproves of in his own countrymen. The average American is a stoic and, contrary to what others are apt to conclude from his free-and-easy friendly manner, reticent, far more reticent than the average Englishman about showing his feelings. He believes in independence because he has to; life is too mobile and circumstances change too fast for him to be supported by any fixed frame of family or social relations. In a crisis he will help his neighbor, whoever he may be, but he will regard someone who is always coming for help as a bad neighbor, and he disapproves of all self-pity and nostalgic regret. All these qualities find their expression in Frost's poetry, but there are other American characteristics which are not to be found there, the absence of which implies disapproval; the belief, for instance, that it should be possible, once the right gimmick has been found, to build the New Jerusalem on earth in half an hour. One might describe Frost as a Tory, provided that one remembers that all American political parties are Whigs.

Hardy, Yeats and Frost have all written epitaphs for themselves.

HARDY

> I never cared for life, life cared for me.
> And hence I owe it some fidelity. . . .

YEATS

> Cast a cold eye
> On life and death.
> Horseman, pass by.

FROST

> I would have written of me on my stone
> I had a lover's quarrel with the world.

Of the three, Frost, surely, comes off best. Hardy seems to be stating the Pessimist's Case rather than his real feelings. I never cared . . . *Never?* Now, Mr. Hardy, really! Yeats' horseman is a stage prop; the passer-by is much more likely to be a motorist. But Frost convinces me that he is telling neither more nor less than the truth about himself. And, when it comes to wisdom, is not having a lover's quarrel with life more worthy of Prospero than not caring or looking coldly?

RADCLIFFE SQUIRES
"Weather: Inner and Outer"
The Major Themes of Robert Frost
1963, pp. 21–35

I

One finds it easy to suppose that Robert Frost has always been able to make the kind of poem for which he has been readily admired: the horse, the snow, the dark woods—all in a clear congruency, yet squeezed like clay until allegories of grief and joy spread from between the fingers. To do this is to contain and transform the environment, to make a permanent predicate of what merely happens. It is, ultimately, to conquer nature in the formalities of a drama where man faces some manner of temptation: he is tempted to disappear in the dark woods; he is tempted to climb to heaven. In effect, the temptation is only mildly perverse, mildly self-destructive. The resistance to the temptation is, however, of some intensity, and the triumph lies in refusing to give up any degree of being human in order to become more natural. There is something odd in the triumph, for the conqueror and the conquered, man and nature, are assumed to be conspirators. They have an agreement. They mirror each other.

If the triumph is sly, the desire for the triumph, for the conspiracy, the arrangement, is not. Man has more often than not desired this conspiracy between himself and his outer world. The desire links the metaphysical poet of the seventeenth century with the romantic rhapsodist. Donne's twin compasses and Shelley's Mont Blanc derive from a similar urgency to find in the external nature which defines, contrasts, and opposes a liaison which co-ordinates and affirms. Admirable. Still one must observe that though most of Frost's readers feel that this is the formula which Frost over and over again exploits in his poems, in all reality and in spite of his instinctive desire he contrives this easy unity of man and nature in only a handful of poems, and these poems are not quite his best. The desire may be imperious, but his ability to look upon nature as a friendly mirror is limited to those poems where he is content to do little other than represent nature, to see it intimately, often tenderly, but not to attempt to understand, only to record. This is not to say that Frost does ill to write such a poem. "Blue-Butterfly Day," for example, strikes me as a neglected little masterpiece, as minor and brilliant as Dürer's pieces of sod. The reader must utterly accept the blue butterflies which we are told are:

> flowers that fly and all but sing:
> And now from having ridden out desire
> They lie closed over in the wind and cling
> Where wheels have freshly sliced the April mire.

We are not likely to get a better poetry of observation. It is consummate because of Frost's ability to create, when he will, from experience, which, while depending on the senses, cannot be described as sensuous. There is no impression of the egotistical observer's being important, so that such a poem as "Blue-Butterfly Day" asserts the illusion of being less an observation than a thing in the world, a self. No doubt this great strength in Frost's poetry derives in part from his instinctive insistence on narrowing his poems of observation to one kind of sensation at a time. If he is concerned with the sound of the scythe he largely emphasizes the experience of the ear. If he is concerned with color, then sound and touch are diminished. We neither expect nor find a synesthetic confusion of sensations.

Not all his simple poems are poems of observation, and these require a different narrowing. In "Going for Water," a young couple whose well has gone dry must seek a brook in the woods at night:

> We ran as if to meet the moon
> That slowly dawned behind the trees,
> The barren boughs without the leaves,
> Without the birds, without the breeze.
>
> But once within the wood, we paused
> Like gnomes that hid us from the moon,
> Ready to run to hiding new
> With laughter when she found us soon.
>
> Each laid on other a staying hand
> To listen ere we dared to look,
> And in the hush we joined to make
> We heard, we knew we heard the brook.
>
> A note as from a single place,
> A slender tinkling fall that made
> New drops that floated on the pool
> Like pearls, and now a silver blade.

This poem is of a different order from "Blue-Butterfly Day." The viewpoint is complicated by being dual; the poem is not primarily one of sight or sound. Yet it is a very consciously limited poem. For the environment is severed from any suggestion of a surrounding world. Or say, this poem assumes that the observable world consists of three objects: a dry well, a moonlit woods and a brook, nothing else. The oversimplification gets to heaven through the exportable veracity of the final quatrain. This brook is a small, lonely god, awaiting with grave dignity our witness. No mere concentration, no mere intensification, this apotheosis subdues all other elements. It is a method of limiting.

A similar deification of an object powers the lathe in "The Runaway." Human sympathy, pity, humor, and pride interweave. And yet . . . and yet the world is but a little world, and the focus of attention shapes a divinity:

> A little Morgan had one forefoot on the wall,
> The other curled at his breast. He dipped his head
> And snorted at us. And then he had to bolt.
> We heard the miniature thunder where he fled,
> And we saw him, or thought we saw him, dim and grey,
> Like a shadow against the curtain of falling flakes.
> 'I think the little fellow's afraid of the snow.
> He isn't winter-broken. It isn't play
> With the little fellow at all. He's running away.
> I doubt if even his mother could tell him, "Sakes,
> It's only weather." He'd think she didn't know!
> Where is his mother? He can't be out alone.'
> And now he comes again with clatter of stone,
> And mounts the wall again with whited eyes
> And all his tail that isn't hair up straight.
> He shudders his coat as if to throw off flies.
> 'Whoever it is that leaves him out so late,
> When other creatures have gone to stall and bin,
> Ought to be told to come and take him in.'

Make no mistake. This kind of poetry has a spirit as primitive as magic. No matter what the human observer says, no matter how much the words seem like local color, one only takes the words as an attempt to contain a god. At the same time the wildness of the god, his miniature thunder, escape containment, and in a sudden bouleversement the god seems the cryptic observer rather than the observed. We speak then both truly and sarcastically when we say that the poem is perfectly self-contained. We speak best when we note that the poem presents inarguable authority, the authority which comes from having been there and seen and—even more important—from having been seen. Indeed, this complex authority is at the heart of Frost's seemingly simple powers of observation.

Even so, this very authority makes for Frost an exquisite discontent. The truth is that Frost has not been quite satisfied with what the eye can see when focused briefly, determinedly, within very small purlieus . . . and no questions asked. He has found in the long run that he cannot keep from looking farther than the immediate object and that when he does so, the environment opens upon a bewilderment of landscapes with questions rising like mist. And he has had to parley with these questions, which can be answered not by repeating what he has seen in nature within a limited frame of perception, but only by drifting out among the mists and guessing the way. He sees complexity, inhuman mysteries in nature, and still he desires to find himself the microcosmos of nature. To so see and to so desire has forced Frost to lengthen his poetry, to stretch it from the arresting simplicity of "Blue-Butterfly Day" or the arrested simplicity of "The Runaway" to more intricate conceivings—and what is much more grave to discover in himself and in man generally a complexity to match that of nature. This stretching, which can be described as a growth, is not, however, exactly chronological. That is to say, the early poems are not simple and the later ones complex. Rather, his thought moves back and forth continuously. His poems stop the pendulum at certain arbitrary points. But since the movement itself is perennial, perpetual, he has found it expedient to divide nature into three sorts—the intimate nature of "Blue-Butterfly Day," the outer nature of the lengthened landscape which finally includes intangible galaxies, and, finally, the continuously elongated, searching nature of man, reaching toward both the near and the far nature outside himself. In the division the questions involving relationships between them all arise. And it is to these questions that the most important poems pay attention. Yet the questions, and hence the important poems, are rooted in Frost's apprehension of a discrepancy between an inner or intimate nature and an outer or remote nature.

II

Who would quarrel with the statement that Robert Frost appears to be at his happiest and most comfortable when he turns to direct, spontaneous observation of relatively natural things in an environment which seems writ large? After all, he has proclaimed himself an "environmentalist." One thinks of the domestic temperature of "The Pasture," the stunning simplicity of the little calf so young it totters when its mother licks it. "The Pasture," of course, and other relatively affirmative poems belong to that very work which has brought to Frost a general popularity. A popularity both with women's clubs and school boys—the one not too easy to come by, the other almost impossible. There is no harm in general popularity, nor do I see any reason for attempting to rescue Frost from ladies and school boys. I intend no treachery to him or them in suggesting that these poems are misrepresentative in that they deliberately stop short of the problems which underlie Frost's whole poetic life. They belong, to be sure, in the body of Frost's poetry and as representatives of his intimacy with nature they are valuable, but one's assessment needs to be tempered by a contrast with his two other kinds of nature poetry—first, the kind of poem where to the degree that it tends to desert direct observation it tends to recreate nature. And, secondly, the kind where Frost beholds not genial amity but grim goddesses in the temple of nature.

"The Demiurge's Laugh" is a good place to begin such a contrast. It is a rewarding poem and particularly noteworthy since it is among his early poems. It begins with the characteristic scenic-experiential assuredness which marks much of Frost's poetry. He is "far in the sameness of the wood." (Could anyone but Frost extract so much from the word "sameness"?) But the poem swiftly substitutes for the ordinary character of woods an entirely extraordinary one. Chasing an answer to an unexpressed question (though the reader assumes that the question involves "the riddle of nature"), the poet discovers that he has been pursuing a false god and indeed that he has even passed beyond the object of his search—Demiurge (the Platonic complex of a heartless creator and destroyer), for the god rises "from his wallow" and laughs a laugh which shows that he "utterly couldn't care." At this point Frost abandons his search. The poem has several interesting momentums, but I wish only to emphasize that here when Frost grants himself a freedom from recording naturalistic detail, he creates a supernatural scene where the obscure mechanics of the universe are presented as inharmonious with man's ordinary hopes. On this ground the god is false, yet somehow not less "real," not less powerful.

Frost surprises us by taking the same step even when he does not construct a supernatural occasion. In "Design," he sees (and I have no doubt that this poem reproduces actual experiences or at least combines several) a white spider holding a dead, white moth on an albino form of a normally blue flower. Not the gluttonous spider nor the pitiful moth, but the perversity of the flower's being white perfects the mood of metaphysical disgust in the poem. Nor does it seem to me that Frost stacks the deck. Rather, because the poem strains our credulity it forces us, perhaps paradoxically, to believe in the reality of the poem—the accident of so much whiteness could not, we feel, have been made up; it would have to have happened. And when Frost, like his reader, is caught in the paradox of believing when the circumstances are not entirely believable, the conclusion falls like a white doom:

> What had that flower to do with being white,
> The wayside blue and innocent heal-all?
> What brought the kindred spider to that height,
> Then steered the white moth thither in the night?
> What but design of darkness to appall?—
> If design govern in a thing so small.

In short, even Frost's nearest nature, even the intimate nature of "The Pasture," is able at any moment to furnish examples of an alien interference. And when Frost turns away from tangibles in Vermont, when he gazes at the far edges of the universe, he often replays the theme of the uncaring Demiurge. In "Stars" he may momentarily feel that the constellations have some kinship with man, but shortly their impersonality reveals itself:

> Those stars like some snow-white
> Minerva's snow-white marble eyes
> Without the gift of sight.

Perhaps because he has felt such a separation between himself and the outer cosmos, Frost has tended to give up the hunt when he hears the Demiurge's laugh. No harm in that, but there is something very like harm in his tendency to veer toward an anti-intellectualism when confronted by the uncaring false god who, he fears, may after all be a true god. In that wry poem "The Star-Splitter" Brad McLaughlin burns his house down for the insurance money with which to buy a telescope. The reaction of the poet-narrator is one of amused tolerance toward such dishonesty, and though it is confessed that he and Bradford "said some of the best things we ever said" while they play with the telescope, the final question in the poem is "What good is a telescope?"

> We've looked and looked, but after all where are we?

This disappointing shrug, this pragmatic reluctance, repeated in such poems as "On Looking Up by Chance at the Constellations" and varied in "The Bear," is, however, not the ultimate position. It is a step toward a final consideration; it is a moment, very possibly, of fatigue where he pauses and then steps on. In "Desert Places," for example, there remains some practical scoffing in "They cannot scare me with their empty spaces / Between stars," yet Frost makes a declarative parallel between himself and the vacant stare of space. "I have it in me so much nearer home / To scare myself with my own desert places."

But before he can go on a humble attitude must prevail, humbler than that ironic, insular practicality that smiles at Bradford McLaughlin. He must yield to the mood of separation between himself and star. It is as if he must acknowledge that sudden breaking which is a form of death. He must allow himself the bitter luxury of such a degrading acceptance of distance, separateness in the uncaring universe that his imagination, in order to survive at all, rises to a higher level. It must hold all this negation and purify it. And how very well "An Old Man's Winter Night" holds and purifies! The poem is remarkably better than "The Star-Splitter" because it is committed to the assertion of a self-limiting mood without distraction or facile didacticism. And it has remarkable interest. It begins by observing a separateness between man and a greater, outer nature:

> All out-of-doors looked darkly in at him
> Through the thin frost, almost in separate stars,
> That gathers on the pane in empty rooms.

One tarries to approve the competent observation of the frost-stars. And one may well feel that a spiritual ice is crystallizing with the frost. More importantly, however, the poem proceeds in imbue the old man with a bleakness as devastating as that found in the universe:

> What kept his eyes from giving back the gaze
> Was the lamp tilted near them in his hand.

Age, confusion, emptiness intensify in the poem until they balance the outer night. Indeed, in a poetic shift, the outer night becomes terrified of the old man. Just as impersonal nature becomes the animate observer of man, the old man becomes the impersonal—perhaps depersonified—observer of nature—his vacant peering becomes more eerily inhuman than that of the stars. In equating man's inner terror with that of the whole world the poem nods in the direction of "Desert Places," but beyond it, too, to the perception of an austere unity among all things, to the comity between man and star as in "Lost in Heaven," where the experience of heavenly disorientation becomes exultation. Even so, the goal of Frost's poetry is more than exultation. It is exaltation. There are a few steps more.

III

One perceives elements of strain and efforts at an accommodation of the outer nature from time to time. Frost would come to terms. In "A Star in a Stone-Boat" he smilingly tells of a fallen meteorite carried from where it fell to be used:

> for building stone, and I, as though
> Commanded in a dream, forever go
> To right the wrong that this should have been so.
>
> Yet ask where else it could have gone as well,
> I do not know—I cannot stop to tell:
> He might have left it lying where it fell.
>
> From following walls I never lift my eye
> Except at night to places in the sky
> Where showers of charted meteors let fly.
>
> Some may know what they seek in school and
> church,
> And why they seek it there; for what I search
> I must go measuring stone walls, perch on perch;
>
> Sure that though not a star of death and birth,
> So not to be compared, perhaps, in worth
> To such resorts of life as Mars and Earth,
>
> Though not, I say, a star of death and sin
> It yet has poles, and only needs a spin
> To show its worldly nature and begin
>
> To chafe and shuffle in my calloused palm
> And run off in strange tangents with my arm
> As fish do with the line in first alarm.
>
> Such as it is, it promises the prize
> Of the one world complete in any size
> That I am like to compass, fool or wise.

One savors the self-deprecation at the end, a self-deprecation akin to the anti-intellectuality in "The Star-Splitter," but one also savors the ambiguity with which the poem regards the star. If the poem wonders whether or not it is right to use the fallen star in building a wall, it also wonders whether or not a star may be adopted into the family. It is, after all, a star that can be held in the hand. There is less ambiguity in the little poem "The Freedom of the Moon":

> I put it shining anywhere I please.
> By walking slowly on some evening later,
> I've pulled it from a crate of crooked trees,
> And brought it over glossy water, greater,
> And dropped it in, and seen the image wallow,
> The color run, all sorts of wonder follow.

Less ambiguity and greater presumption. One feels the presumption become sentimentality, as indeed, in an inverted way, the humility borders on sentimentality in "Canis Major":

> The great Overdog.
> That heavenly beast
> With a star in one eye,
> Gives a leap in the east.
>
> . . .
>
> I'm a poor underdog,
> But tonight I will bark
> With the great Overdog
> That romps through the dark.

One does not judge these poems harshly unless he harshly judges Frost's passionate wish to bring men and the farthest reaches of nature together. In the last analysis Frost himself is the victim when the old man and the stars frighten each other with the emotionless incommunication of their gaze. Let them come together! So his poem mutters in its undercurrents. And if Frost cannot quite manage a convergence of the twain, he can discover a moon (which is never so remote to farmer and astronomer alike as stars) in an attitude of love, an attitude suspiciously human. In "Moon Compasses":

> And a masked moon had spread down compass rays
> To a cone mountain in the midnight haze,
> As if the final estimate were hers,
> And as it measured in her calipers,
> The mountain stood exalted in its place.
> So love will take between the hands a face.

So perhaps after all the moon can be adopted into the human family. Yet Frost hardly offers any image which brings the stars into intimate range. Even when ("Fireflies in the Garden") fireflies "emulate" the stars and "Achieve at times a very star-like start," they still cannot "sustain the part." Yet we might remember the mountain that stands "exalted in its place," and we might ask what is involved in the exaltation.

The answer may be too simple, though the effort for Frost of reaching the answer is almost too difficult. Frost tries by pulling down the heavens to elevate man. Too easy, you will say. But, of course. Yet mark how hard it has been for Frost to bring himself to do it. I have already listed some less than satisfying examples. There are others. In the first of these examples, "An Unstamped Letter in Our Rural Mail Box," the narrator is a "tramp astrologer" who sees:

> The largest firedrop ever formed
> From two stars' having coalesced
> Went streaking molten down the west.

And then this highly improbable astronomical accident is paralleled by an inner experience:

> Inside the brain
> Two memories . . . quivered toward each other,
> lipped
> Together, and together slipped;
> And for a moment all was plain
> That men have thought about in vain.

The purpose behind the parallel is clearly that of gathering together the most unique and intimate of experiences with the most unique and remote—in order to transform thought and matter into meta-equivalents. The difficulty with the poem is that it goes on too long beyond its climax and is willfully thrown away in some stringy, overly colloquial lines. It is finally lost altogether in a poor comic rhyme at the end. My second example suffers from similar inadequacies, but they come to us in a different order. "Skeptic" begins in a comic-metaphysical vein:

> Far star that tickles for me my sensitive plate
> And fries a couple of ebon atoms white.

(I have known some who were so misled by the jocularity of this opening that they failed to see how the image drawn from photography merges with an ocular image and deliriously imagined that Frost is speaking of the difficulties of wearing dentures.) The middle section of the poem, after the misplaced cleverness of the opening, asserts in a breathy, naïve voice that Frost does not believe that this nova is the last star nor even that it is "after explosion going away so fast." So far the reader is apt to squirm, but in the last section a startling transfusion—an osmosis—between stars and the human sensibility takes place:

> The universe may or may not be very immense.
> As a matter of fact there are times when I am apt
> To feel it close in tight against my sense
> Like a caul in which I was born and still am wrapped.

The last two lines are among Frost's finest and ought not to have been wasted in an organically impossible and freakish poem. Yet, taking the lines by themselves, they quite majestically and honestly draw together the intimate nature of self and the separate nature of the universe. They achieve this collusion without the mutual terror of old man and cosmos in "An Old Man's Winter Night." And in these lines we glimpse a finished gesture where faith, brought to bay, extends the human mind and heart to the margins of a disappearing God. Heart and mind remain as human as Job.

In effect, then, the desire (and the power) to assemble inner and outer nature in a given poem is essentially Frost's desire to discover balance, or, failing discovery, to *achieve* it. Even in the cozy, nearby landscape of farm and woods, Frost pushes in one direction, one extreme, then backtracks and moves in another direction. He may feel an entire identification or communion in "Hyla Brook," but in another poem, such as "Range-Finding," he may stand aside distressed and removed, refusing yet contemplating the rather Melvillean vision of the grinding necessities of instinct in nature. Because he brings the naturalist's loyalty to truth to his observation of nature he cannot ignore the blunt facts. However, he can bring nature's instinctual, trancelike sprawl ultimately into line with man's conscious idealism, as he does in "Two Look at Two." Here a man and woman see a doe and a buck and are in turn inspected by them. The animals remain animals, the human beings remain human. The two discrete worlds nevertheless momentarily fuse, or at least the wall between them becomes transparent:

> Two had seen two, whichever side you spoke from.
> 'This *must* be all.' It was all. Still they stood,
> A great wave from it going over them,
> As if the earth in one unlooked-for favor
> Had made them certain earth returned their love.

In Frost's poems, then, a pattern emerges. At the level of intimate nature, Frost perceives the heart-warming yet too facile relationships between himself and the superficial aspects of nature. Or, he perceives a frightening severance between himself and the colossal drift of nature. Ultimately, some poems emerge (such as "Two Look at Two") in which he brings the extreme views into equilibrium. At the level of outer nature, he feels inevitable the separation between man and the circling stars. Yet he can, though the effort is exhausting, bring these two worlds together. And in both cases love or faith seems to be the catalyst which while not entering into the combination nevertheless brings it about. Such poems either belong with or preordain Frost's masterpieces. All else is experiment, a walking back and forth on the earth. But a necessary experiment, a necessary perambulation.

FRANK LENTRICCHIA

"Robert Frost and Modern Literary Theory"

Frost Centennial Essays

1973, pp. 315–32

I offer this essay as a theoretical prologue to the study of Robert Frost's poetry and poetics. My key figures and terms are familiar to students of post-Kantian literary theory, but their presence in a study of Frost is likely to appear odd to the many who, with J. Hillis Miller, tend to think that Robert Frost, wherever else he may be located, must most definitely be excluded from the company of the great modern poets. The single most damaging and question-begging critical opinion about Frost today has not been rigorously formulated; it is simply a widespread and casual assumption among the cognoscenti of literary theory that Frost cannot bear sustained theoretical contemplation. I am urging, on the contrary, that the difficulty in Frost's poetics is not absence of depth and modernist sophistication, but too much subtlety. Thus far (and surely to his credit) he has successfully eluded the easy generalizations of the schools.

I find that the most striking feature of Frost's thought is that it unifies what at the surface appear to be mutually exclusive dimensions of the modern literary mind. At the center of Frost's theory is the idea we find in Kant and the Romantics that our mental acts constitute the world of our experience. This notion of mind leads, of course, to the Romantic insistence that the poet's imagination is creative, that poems do not imitate a fully structured, antecedent reality, but rather inform chaos with structure and meaning. Yet, right alongside the Romanticism in Frost stands, paradoxically, the philosophy of common sense realism which posits a real world "out there," independent of our acts of perception. What I take to be the unifying principle in Frost's thinking has its basis in the pragmatism of William James. It is peculiarly the strength of James, that great philosophical mediator, to recognize a difficult real world which plays some determinative role in our lives, while also allowing for the possibility of the active consciousness to carve out, to a certain extent, the world of its desire.

Throughout the essay, I use "landscape" because I believe the concept holds together the divergent philosophical directions in Frost's poetics. The following passage from J. H. Van Den Berg, *The Phenomenological Approach to Psychiatry*, elucidates the definition of both "phenomenology" and "landscape": "The relationship of man and world is so profound, that it is an error to separate them. If we do, then man ceases to be man and the world to be the world. The world is no conglomeration of mere objects to be described in the language of physical science. The world is our home, our habitat, the materialization of our subjectivity. Who wants to become acquainted with man, should listen to the language spoken by the things in his existence. Who wants to describe man should make an analysis of the 'landscape' within which he demonstrates, explains and reveals himself."[1] "Landscape" suggests both a configuration of objects really there in nature and the phenomenological notion that any particular landscape is coherent because the mind of the artist makes it so. And, finally, I shall argue that the special qualities of coherence and the peculiar dominance of this or that object in the landscape are reflections of the artist's subjectivity, his deepest inclinations as a person. "Landscapes" are clues to the essential expression of the poet.

I

As my point of departure I choose Frost's strange and surprising poem "All Revelation":

> A head thrusts in as for the view,
> But where it is it thrusts in from
> Or what it is it thrusts into
> By that Cyb'laean avenue,
> And what can of its coming come,
>
> And whither it will be withdrawn,
> And what take hence or leave behind,
> These things the mind has pondered on
> A moment and still asking gone.
> Strange apparition of the mind!
>
> But the impervious geode
> Was entered, and its inner crust
> Of crystals with a ray cathode
> At every point and facet glowed
> In answer to the mental thrust.

Eyes seeking the response of eyes
Bring out the stars, bring out the flowers,
Thus concentrating earth and skies
So none need be afraid of size.
All revelation has been ours.

Frost's subject in "All Revelation" is a common poetic and philosophical subject after Kant and the Romantics; it is strange and surprising only within the context of most traditional critical thought about Robert Frost. His subject is the act of the mind, the dynamic thrust of consciousness which he evokes in his metaphor of the cathode ray. Because the glowing effect inside the dark cavity of the geode originates from the action of the cathode ray itself, our vision of the geode's interior is inescapably mediated by our very instrument of scientific cognition. Frost shrewdly manages, however, with the first four words of the poem ("A head thrusts in") to suggest that the action of the cathode ray is figurative of human perception in general. In the third stanza the cathode ray emerges as a metaphor for the tendency of human consciousness to be excursive, to reach out, grasp, and shape its world. Frost's metaphoric expansion of the cathode ray is paralleled by his metaphoric expansion of the geode itself. Initially only a "stone nodule," the dictionary signification, Frost makes it mean by the end of the poem something like "our world," "external reality in general." Reuben Brower points out how precise Frost's metaphor is: "geode," in its etymological derivation, means "earth-like"; and this meaning is solidly re-inforced in the phrase "Cyb'laean avenue" (from Cybele, goddess of earth).[2]

One way of reading "All Revelation," then, is to see it as a poet's confronting of the leading idea of post-Kantian epistemology: that the mind is in some part constructive of the world. But there are other, complicating philosophical features in the poem which, once perceived, make a simple Kantian reading impossible to sustain. In the first stanza, for example, a number of questions are bracketed that many traditional philosophers make the central concern of their quests. For Frost, though, the question of the origins of mind ("Where it is it thrusts in from"); the question of the nature of the objective world considered as a thing in itself ("what it is it thrusts into"); and the question of the final and enduring value of the constitutive acts of the mind ("what can of its coming come")—all of these are questions that can be answered only provisionally, if at all. The suggestion is fairly strong, in fact, that when such questions are taken to the metaphysical level they have little pragmatic value for Frost: "These things the mind has pondered on/A moment and still asking gone."

The third and fourth stanzas of the poem particularize a rich philosophical paradox which is crucial to Frost's poems and poetics. By affirming contrary philosophical propositions—by insisting, on the one hand, that consciousness insinuates itself into the world, in part constituting that world (the geode *was* entered, the crystals do "answer" to the "mental thrust"); and by insisting as well (with realists) that the object is out there, independent of the mind (the geode is "impervious," to use Frost's word, and resists flagrant transformation)—Frost asks us to accept a position logically impure and ambiguous, but, for a poet, a position more exciting than what we usually find in either Kantian idealism or common sense realism. When in the last stanza Frost does question the value of this peculiar meeting of mind and object (this "strange apparition"), his answer is pragmatic. Stars and flowers, earth and skies, are there: but consciousness shapes its environment in order to concentrate "the immensities" ("So none need be afraid of size"), make them manageable for the self and thereby supply a psychic need to feel in our confrontations with nature that we are not hopelessly lost and adrift in a world that engulfs and drowns us. The constructive acts of consciousness make the world answer, as Nietzsche reminds us in his extension of Kant, to the desires of our emotional nature; and, specifically, in this poem, to the desire for human continuity and mutuality—"Eyes seeking the response of eyes"—within an inhuman environment.

"All revelation has been ours," reads the last line. It is we who reveal the world—as we desire to see it revealed—and by so doing we reveal the revealing self, we reveal ourselves. It is a characteristic of Frost's poetic stance that he is generally able to maintain the perilous balance which he achieves in "All Revelation," where he can somehow move in and out of the constituting mind. From the "inside" he achieves the kind of vision of a "better nature" demanded by his psychic needs—a vision which I would locate within his "redemptive" act of consciousness. From the "outside" he achieves an ironic self-consciousness which tells him that constitutive visions of a better nature are "apparitions" in the sense of "illusions." The act of ironic consciousness enables Frost to maintain his double vision, his skepticism, and his common sense which let nature be, as it is, and which are, as it turns out, often as psychically healthgiving as his more romantic acts of redemption.

II

On the American intellectual scene at the turn of the century there were basically three philosophical alternatives open to the young Robert Frost: the way of naturalism, which denied creativity and autonomy to human consciousness; the way of Josiah Royce's idealism which guaranteed creative freedom but only within the context of metaphysics that a young, emerging modern mind could not accept; or the via media of William James' pragmatism, which saved the autonomy of consciousness without asking, at the same time, for an acceptance of something like the early Emerson's view of nature and self. Those "redemptive" and "ironic" thrusts of consciousness embedded in "All Revelation," and repeatedly revealed in Frost's poems and urged by his poetics, are illuminatively reflected in the philosophy and psychology of James, who provided Frost with the chief intellectual adventure of his brief Harvard experience at the end of the 1890's.

What was probably basic to the appeal of James for Frost, and for a number of minds that came to maturity at the turn of our century, was that naturalistic toughness which kept James from floating out of time in search for resolutions to human dilemmas. Yet for all his storied hostility toward his Harvard colleague Josiah Royce and toward various idealistic positions, James showed faith—usually associated with a post-Kantian view of mind—in the creative potential of human consciousness which would establish the priority of the human act even in time. James' concept of the freedom of the human act of mind liberates the self from the subjection to the shaping dictates of material reality that seemed demanded by later nineteenth-century naturalism. Joseph Blau has put it this way: James "was a man whose training in the hard-headedness of science never completely subdued his soft-hearted belief that men are not merely automata, strictly determined in a mechanical world, but are, at least to some degree, the makers and shapers of their world."[3] I would characterize the principle of James' philosophical mediation between the tough-mindedness of naturalism and the tender-mindedness of Royce's idealism as "aesthetic": a term by which I mean to suggest that he predicates a freely creative activity of mind. It is doubtful that James' frequent recourse to metaphors which characterize the molding power of consciousness as an artistic process could have failed to catch the eye of the young Robert Frost, then in his formative poetic years.

We might imagine that James' pragmatist reconciliation of scientific naturalism and Royce's idealism saved for Frost the truths of two distinct but not utterly incompatible philosophical traditions. From Royce's Kantian tradition James could accept the proposition that mind actively participates in the constitution of the world of fact without also accepting Royce's idealistic theory of timeless mental categories, or his theory of the Absolute, or his theory that evil is a privation, or his notion that the eternal and temporal orders are continuous. In James' philosophical modernism such issues were dead. And certainly they were dead for Frost. From those of tough-minded persuasion, James could accept the skeptical and common sense view of the world of objects as indeed "out there," as hard, dense, and often dangerous. It is a fundamental postulate of his discussion of the "stream of consciousness" that the objects of consciousness belong to a shareable and independent order.[4] Putting together the Kantian and realist views James could posit an objective world that is yet always caressed and bathed in human consciousness, receiving its final touches from the excursive tendency of consciousness to reach out beyond itself and by so doing insinuate its needs and shapes into the given world.

Though the full philosophical context of his existential phenomenology seems not relevant to Frost's poems, Jean Paul Sartre, who admired James deeply, eloquently articulated a perception of a peculiar duality within human experience which points us to the very center of Frost's poems and James' pragmatism.

> Each of our perceptions is accompanied by the consciousness that human reality is a "revealer," that is, it is through human reality that "there is" being, or, to put it differently, that man is the means by which things are manifested. It is our presence in the world which multiplies relations. It is we who set up a relationship between this tree and that bit of sky. Thanks to us, that star which has been dead for millennia, that quarter moon, and that dark river are disclosed in the unity of a landscape. . . . With each of our acts, the world reveals to us a new face. But, if we know that we are directors of being, we also know that we are not its producers. If we turn away from this landscape, it will sink back; there is no one mad enough to think that it is going to be annihilated. It is we who shall be annihilated, and the earth will remain in its lethargy until another consciousness comes along to awaken it. Thus, to our inner certainty of being "revealers" is added that of being inessential in relation to the thing revealed.[5]

The epistemological emphasis in James which places a premium on the power of human subjectivity to "reveal" and "build out" the world of experience was consistently articulated in his various books. In the first volume of the *Principles of Psychology* (1890) he put it this way: "Out of what is in itself an indistinguishable, swarming *continuum*, devoid of distinction or emphasis, our senses make for us, by attending to this notion and ignoring that, a world full of contrasts, of sharp accents, of abrupt changes, of picturesque light and shade."[6] In another attempt to explain the nature of our perception of the world he said: "if we pass to its aesthetic department, our law is still more obvious. . . . The mind, in short, works on the data it receives very much as a sculptor works on his block of stone."[7] Still, even as he puts forth a view clearly post-Kantian in its suggestion of a creative function for consciousness, James, in his proto-existentialism, refused to accept Kant's importation into the act of knowledge of intersubjective categories of consciousness because he believed that prereflective consciousness was not transpersonal but irreducibly private and that its various constructions of the world flowed from a contingent subjectivity, the interests of an embodied self evolving through time and pressured by place. James separated himself from neo-Kantianism once and for all when he refused to take the notion of the constitutive power of consciousness to what he called the solipsistic conclusion of Kant and the neo-Kantians. Standing now with the tough-minded, he wrote that, for Kant, "Reality becomes a mere empty locus, or unknowable, the so-called Noumenon, the manifold of phenomenon is in the mind. We, on the contrary, put the Multiplicity with the Reality outside. . . ."[8] Without slighting the creative self, James affirms an insight of philosophical realism which the mainstream of post-Kantian idealism cannot affirm: that the pluralistic richness and particularity of the world stands recalcitrantly there, independent of mind, coercing our attention. The basic Kantian insight that man brings meaning into the world in a creative act has been transferred from a static idealistic setting—the eternal geometry of consciousness—to an existential one: the empirical self in a real world.

James envisions the drama of consciousness beginning when mind is confronted by a world which in its destructive unintelligibility seems to call out for a creative intelligence: "the visible surfaces of heaven and earth refuse to be brought by us into any intelligible unity at all. Every phenomenon that we would praise there exists cheek by jowl with some contrary phenomenon. . . ." Such a vision of the face of reality is "poisonous," James concluded—ultimately fatal to psychological serenity—and therefore intolerable. The preservation of our "mental sanity"[9] is directly dependent upon the mind's power to transform its environment, to create for itself something not already there, to take that romantic leap beyond the function that traditional empiricism normally assigned to it. In short, the creative act of the mind in James' philosophy defines the self as the redeemer of brute fact and chaos into human value, pattern, and significance.

III

The crucial metaphor for the creative act of mind in James, that of the process of the sculptor,[10] is strikingly reflected in passages in Frost's letters: "My object is true form—is and always will be. . . . I fight to be allowed to sit cross-legged on the old flint pile and flake a lump into an artifact." Or, more explicitly still: "I thank the Lord for crudity which is rawness, which is raw material. . . . A real artist delights in roughness for what he can do to it. He's the brute who can knock the corners off the marble block. . . ."[11]

Sometimes this sculpting act of consciousness becomes literary in character as it avails itself to the poet's technique. Given our modern fascination for the amalgamatory, ordering powers of metaphor we cannot help recalling Johnson on Cowley, Coleridge on imagination, Eliot on Marvell, and on to the dearest concerns of New Critics and neo–New Critics, when we meet with this in James: "Purely objective truth, truth in whose establishment the function of giving human satisfaction in marrying previous parts of experience with newer parts played no role whatsoever, is nowhere to be found. . . . 'to be true' *means* only to perform this marriage-function."[12]

When James spoke of the "marriage-function" of consciousness he implicitly analogized the creative act of the mind to the dynamic, integrative process of metaphoric activity. For Frost, the metaphoric act of the mind, one of his favorite philosophical themes,[13] is basically a shaping and order-making process. "The only materialist," as he put it, "is the man who gets lost in his material without a gathering metaphor to throw it into shape and order. He is the lost soul." Metaphoric activity is indigenous, Frost frequently suggested, not only to poetic thinking but to all thinking: "Poetry is simply made of metaphor. So also is philosophy—and science, too, for that matter. . . ." One of his more extensive remarks on metaphor occurs in a letter to Louis Untermeyer:

> . . . isn't it a poetical strangeness that while the world was going full blast on the Darwinian metaphors of evolution, survival values and the Devil take the hindmost, a polemical Jew in exile was working up the metaphor of the state's being like a family to displace them from mind and give us a new figure to live by. Marx had the strength not to be overawed by the metaphor in vogue. Life is like battle. But so is it also like shelter. . . . We are all toadies to the fashionable metaphor of the hour. Great is he who imposes the metaphor. . . . There are no logical steps from one to the other. There is no logical connection.[14]

The metaphoric integrations of great thinkers become (for ordinary men) the structures—the "world hypotheses," as Stephen Pepper put it—which condition and frame our understanding of the world of experience. The integrations of metaphor have immediate consequences for our lives. Though it is widely assumed that he evaded the pressures of modern philosophical thought, Frost's epistemological stand on metaphor is precisely parallel to the positions taken by Nietzsche and Hans Vaihinger, two philosophers whose thought is central to the history of modernism.

In a suggestive passage from *Pragmatism* James evokes his sense of human experience as "intolerably confused and gothic," "multitudinous beyond imagination, tangled, muddy, painful and perplexed."[15] The proper response to such a situation, his epistemological principles seem to suggest, is a creative act. In what is probably his fullest single statement on the nature and value of creative activity, the "Letter to *The Amherst Student*," Frost evokes a sense of reality close to what James had evoked in the passage just quoted. Reality in Frost is often projected in psychological language as a place of "excruciations," of "hugeness and confusion," of "black and utter chaos." And the proper response to it is the "figure of order," the "little form which I assert upon it." The order created by any act of consciousness for James and the order created by a specifically artistic act of consciousness for Frost yield similarly therapeutic values. James calls it an inner "ease, peace," and "rest," while Frost sees the process of aesthetic composition as "composing to the spirit," as a release from excruciations.[16] It is ultimately, however, a quality of Frost's tough-mindedness—he places the chaos and the confusion outside the mind, as James had in his criticism of Kant—which underscores the existential urgency of composition, the need for the form-making power of artistic consciousness to come into play.

IV

In the limited post-Kantianism of James and Frost ("limited" because injected with a powerful dose of common sense) consciousness confronts objects which sit out there in a shareable public world. Those objects are not created by the poet's imagination or by the mind of any other human being. We would not be surprised to find in the poems of a man who, say, spent most of his formative and mature years in the countryside of New Hampshire and Vermont, as did Robert Frost, and who shared Frost's literary and philosophical predilections, a recognizably common landscape. The consciousness of our hypothetical poet could have focused, presumably, upon a similar set of objects; his poetic landscape, therefore, would be marked by similar fixed features. So far the tenets of literary realism supply all of the critical procedures that we need. But if we assume that each consciousness is at some level utterly distinct and private—and that is a chief point of the psychology of James and of common sense—then we must assume, as well, that the objects of the perceived world will radiate a different, a special subjective presence, will cohere in ways contingent upon the particular consciousness which has apprehended those objects, and, in apprehending them, enveloped them with the interiority of the perceiving self. The act of perception which represents the landscape is affectively suffused. James supplies a good example for this point. The phenomenon of the "eternal recurrence of the common order," he says, "which so fills a Whitman with mystic satisfaction, is to a Schopenhauer . . . the feeling of an 'awful inner emptiness' from out of which he views it all."[17]

If the world's furniture is partially shaped and revealed by consciousness, then we can expect to find in the world evoked by a particular writer's oeuvre that the furniture—or phenomena—of his imagined world will reveal, or radiate, his revealing consciousness, to extend the theoretical implications of the last line of "All Revelation." And now we have taken a considerable step beyond literary realism because we need a method which can help us grasp the intersection of literature's objective (or mimetic) dimension with its radically subjective (or expressive) one. Georges Poulet has summarized this matter quite clearly:

> Every thought, to be sure, is a thought *of* something. It is turned invincibly towards the somewhere else, toward the outside. Issuing from itself, it appears to leap over a void, meet certain obstacles, explore certain surfaces, and envelop or invade certain objects. It describes and recounts to itself all these objects, and these accounts or these descriptions constitute the inexhaustible objective aspect of literature. But every thought is also simply a thought. It is that which exists in itself, isolatedly, mentally. Whatever its objects may be, thought can never place them, think them, except in the interior of itself.[18]

The following passage from James on the privacy of personal consciousness reveals that the leap from Frost to Poulet is really no leap at all:

> Each of these minds keeps its own thoughts to itself. There is no giving or bartering between them. No thought even comes into direct *sight* of a thought in another personal consciousness than its own. Absolute insulation, irreducible pluralism, is the law. It seems as if the elementary psychic fact were not *thought* or *this thought* or *that thought*, but *my thought*, every thought being *owned*. Neither contemporaneity, nor proximity in space, nor similarity of quality and content are able to fuse thoughts together which are sundered by this barrier of belonging to different personal minds. The breaches between such thoughts are the most absolute breaches in nature.[19]

V

The literary critic may cull from William James some three suggestions to help him close the chasm between the poetry and self of Robert Frost. First, the objects of the perceiver's world are marked by the privacy of his apprehending consciousness; as Van Den Berg puts it, the world is the "materialization of our subjectivity." Secondly, the various objects marked by consciousness are also ordered or arranged by consciousness, and those very arrangements or "landscapes" will be revelations of the poet's needs, his way of looking at things, his personal identity; the constituted landscapes of consciousness thus become keys to interior landscapes, the unique psychological structures of Frost's experience. Thirdly, because consciousness is continuous, the self maintains its identity through time, thereby insuring that the individual poems in the Frost canon, though spread out through the poet's private and public history, are enveloped by a guiding presence which guarantees the wholeness of the poetic corpus.

Studying Robert Frost's interior self as pure interiority is impossible. But we have his poems, and, within them, we have the dominant, fixed objects in his poetic landscape: the things in the real world which he then transferred to and transformed in the poetic medium where they become, inevitably, objects in a poetic landscape. Whether the object is mediated by the consciousness of the lyric "I," or whether the object is mediated by Frost's more fully dramatized selves—the personae of his longer dialogues and monologues—the psychic life of Robert Frost himself is what is ultimately evoked by those fixed objects in his poetic landscape. Philosophically suggested in America by William James, this neo-Romantic expressive poetic that I am urging for Frost is elaborately detailed in the European phenomenological tradition and by several recent American critics. Its basic assumption is that the unique subjectivity *behind* the poem invades the poem itself despite the conventionalizing social and aesthetic forces, the various determinations of his culture at work to dissolve the poet's individual identity as a person. As a critical concept "landscape" becomes synonymous with the poem itself and means always this double thing: not a simple configuration of objects, "out there" in inhuman otherness, but a configuration of objects thoroughly intermeshed with the poet's self. For "poem" read: a linguistic preservation of that landscape-caressing act of consciousness.

"Tree at My Window" is Frost's self-conscious treatment of landscapes, interior and exterior:

> Tree at my window, window tree,
> My sash is lowered when night comes on;
> But let there never be curtain drawn
> Between you and me.
>
> Vague dream-head lifted out of the ground,
> And thing next most diffuse to cloud,
> Not all your light tongues talking aloud
> Could be profound.
>
> But, tree, I have seen you taken and tossed,
> And if you have seen me when I slept,
> You have seen me when I was taken and swept
> And all but lost.
>
> That day she put our heads together,
> Fate had her imagination about her,
> Your head so much concerned with outer,
> Mine with inner, weather.

Something in Frost wants to distinguish landscapes, to mark off "inner" from "outer," subject from object, human from nonhuman; perhaps it is because Frost feels so strongly that the outer landscape is not congenial to the self: the sash, at night, must be lowered, we must stay enclosed for our own good. All of which is to say that this poem, like so many poems by Frost, is grounded in a tough realist's view of things. Yet Frost gives us no unnavigable gulf between subject and object. The sash must be lowered, of course, but the curtain must never be drawn across the window. Thus, between self and not-self Frost places a transparency which allows for an interaction of sorts, as enclosed self and weathered tree take creative looks at one another. The tree, self-like, dreams and speaks; the self, tree-like, is swept and tossed. The intentional, other-directed subjectivity of the poet marks the exterior landscape by naming it "window tree" and "dream-head;" in so naming it he reveals not a deeper "something" interfused with the landscape and with the self, as Wordsworth believed, but only the character of his excursive subjectivity, a subjectivity constituted in the very interaction, the naturalizing of "inner" and the humanizing of "outer."

Frost's subjectivity is in an important (though not metaphysical) sense, romantic; it expresses itself dominantly as a dream-energy which wants to transform (by entering) the landscape it encounters. It tends to be redemptive, though it may be counterredemptive; it desires that all objects become subjects, but only to a point. For the essential Frost is also comic and ironic, and he will allow redemption to go only so far. The "dream-head" is, after all, "vague," the "light tongues" speak meaninglessly because they "utter" nonhuman sound. The poet of ironic consciousness will insist, in a direct thrust at his own redemptive self and at the noumenal confidence of the early Romantics, on the pure object-hood of nature, and in so insisting preserve the integrity of the single, simple subject against the big world beyond self. And that, too, in Frost's poetry, is a lesson derived from the interaction of subjectivity with its environment. The flowing of subject into object is presented by Frost modestly and cautiously—i.e., humorously—as a datum of consciousness (this is the way it feels sometimes) and not as evidence for a metaphysical monism (this is the way it really is with the universe). So, objects will remain objects, even when they are enclosed in subjectivity; subjects will remain subjects, even when they are weathered.

Frost's complex sense of the interrelations and distinctions of interior and exterior landscapes in "Tree at My Window" urges us to modify the Cartesianism that we find in the statements of Poulet and James on the nature of a personal consciousness. If James, anticipating Poulet, appears to refer to Descartes' meditations for the sense of personal consciousness as pure, fully constituted spiritual substance, utterly self-contained and forever inaccessible to the outside and all spatio-temporal definition, then we must correct James with James. For it is one of James' first principles of psychology that consciousness is an outgoing, pragmatic energy that acts upon its environment, and defines itself by its acts. Attempting to mediate extremes, to formulate a position between the Cartesian sense of a subjectivity which is never related, or relatable to an outer environment, and the naturalistic sense of a subjectivity which is nothing but a derivative form of the objective environment, James suggests that the inner citadel of selfhood, the unique subjective character of a personal consciousness, has a real status, but that it can be grasped and known only as it expresses itself, as it is impelled outward to interaction with objective conditions by the pragmatic energy at the very core of consciousness. John Dewey, an admirer of James, would come to say that selfhood is a mere potentiality until it is "both formed and brought to consciousness through interaction with an environment."[20]

In a full-length study I would explore the aesthetic and philosophical dimensions of Frost's poems within the more inclusive context of post-Kantian literary theory in order to define the modern intellectual environment of those poems. In recent organicist theories, the stress is heavily on the shaping force of the poetic medium, on the idea that the discourse of poetry is a special mode of language which reveals a unique world. Extending the range of organicist aesthetic theory with the insights of the phenomenological tradition, the poem becomes a preservation—i.e., a "preserve"—which sustains for our contemplative pleasure the distinctive world—the very life—of the poet's consciousness. If, as James would insist, ordinary consciousness, or mere perception, shapes out the self's world, then for Frost, who is decidedly organicist in his bias, the shaping instrument is decisively language itself. Language, the poem itself, discloses the "inner weather" of Frost's subjective universe in the intersection of self and landscape.

Frost's Jamesian view of self and his organicist tendency in poetics pose a difficult and fascinating question. The question is this: what is the nature and value of that self-sufficient poetic world, which is shaped in language by a constitutive act of his consciousness, vis-à-vis the real world which James and Frost accept as stubbornly there, independent of consciousness? Guided by Frost's Jamesian sympathies and by the several theoretical problems implicitly posed by the poems, I would isolate his response to this key question of modern aesthetics while placing him against the background of some typical modernist answers. At every important theoretical juncture, the significant measurement of Frost's participation in and dissent from major modern theories of imagination is his Jamesian commitment to the powers and limits of human consciousness to recreate its world in accordance with the needs and desires of self. Frost's poetics, his conceptual landscape, as it were, is congruent with the patterns of experience, the interior landscape that I find revealed in his poems; and that very congruency seems to me to be convincing evidence that, the important negative criticism of Yvor Winters and George Nitchie to the contrary, Frost's sensibility is profoundly unified.[21]

Though Frost read William James, and through James came into contact with a number of the salient themes of modernist philosophy and aesthetics, I do not suggest that Frost was "influenced" in the sense that historicists used to say that imaginative writers were "shaped" by the "intellectual backgrounds of the times." Modernism becomes the historical ambience of Frost's work only in the sense that it is what one comes to conceptually if one moves outward from Frost's poems in an attempt to define the ideational milieu of the kinds of consciousness and experience found in Frost.

So Frost is not modernist because he holds self-consciously to certain ideas which we identify with this or that modern philosopher. There are few ideas as such in Frost. Properly speaking, Frost's poems do not "belong" to the intellectual environment we call the "modern mind" because the "modern mind" does not have independent, Platonic existence. It is a thing that his poems have helped to create. The perspectives of modern philosophy and aesthetics are conceptual abstractions from that dense, preideational, primary data of human experience which Frost renders from the inside, as lived.

More than most modern poets Frost needs to have some sort of historical context deliberately constructed for him. (The poems need nothing. It is we, as historical creatures, seeking historical understanding, who need to construct such contexts.) Unlike Stevens, Frost only rarely deals directly with the issues of post-Kantian epistemology; unlike Crane, Williams, and Auden, he only rarely situates us in the modern urban environment; unlike Pound and Eliot, he does not measure in any richly allusive way the modern moment against tradition and the past. And, from the point of view of language and metrical experiment, Frost seems very traditional indeed. In two of the best books about him, he is presented as inhabiting a sort of timeless world. John Lynen sees Frost in the venerable tradition of pastoralism. Reuben Brower, drawing his comparisons from the range of world literature, relates him to the tradition of tough-minded, unflinching writers who see things as they are and do not hesitate to tell the score. Lynen and Brower are both persuasive. Frost inhabits a timeless world as do all poets of high quality. Yet Frost did not exist in a vacuum, and his poems do not present an ahistorical consciousness. What I would call his "implicit poetics" is one way of entering history, of locating the poet in time; "implicit poetics" is a regulative principle which does not help much in explicating the poems, but which does help us to "generalize" the experiential patterns of those poems, and hence to extend the significance of the poems for our times.

Notes

1. J. H. Van Den Berg, *The Phenomenological Approach to Psychiatry* (Springfield: Charles C. Thomas, 1955), 32.
2. Reuben Brower, *The Poetry of Robert Frost* (New York: Oxford University Press, 1963), 140.
3. Joseph Blau, in introduction to *Pragmatism and Other Essays* (New York: Washington Square Press, 1963), xv. The historical relations of Frost and James are traced by Lawrance Thompson in *Robert Frost: The Early Years, 1874–1915* (New York: Holt, Rinehart and Winston, 1966).
4. William James, *Psychology* (New York: Fawcett Publications, 1963), Chap. XI.
5. Jean Paul Sartre, *What Is Literature?*, trans. Bernard Frechtman (New York: Harper & Row, 1965), 32–33.
6. William James, *The Principles of Psychology* (New York: Dover Publications, 1950), I, 284.
7. Ibid., 287, 288.
8. Ibid., 363.
9. William James, *The Will to Believe and Other Essays in Popular Philosophy* (New York: Dover Publications, 1956), 41, 42, 118.
10. For further examples of James' recourse to aesthetic metaphor see: *Pragmatism: A New Way For Some Old Ways of Thinking* (New York: Longmans, Green, & Co., 1907), 61, 64, 65, 256–57, 258; cited below as *Pragmatism*; *A Pluralistic Universe* (New York: Longmans, Green, & Co., 1942), 9–10. For further examples see *The Meaning of Truth: A Sequel to* Pragmatism (New York: Longmans, Green, & Co., 1909), 58, 80.
11. *Selected Letters of Robert Frost*, ed. Lawrance Thompson (New York: Holt, Rinehart and Winston, 1964), 381, 465.
12. James, *Pragmatism*, 64.
13. See: *Selected Letters*, 215; *The Letters of Robert Frost to Louis Untermeyer*, ed. Louis Untermeyer (New York: Holt, Rinehart and Winston, 1963), 189; *Selected Prose of Robert Frost*, ed. Hyde Cox and Edward Connery Lathem (New York: Holt, Rinehart and Winston, 1966), 24, 35, 37–38, 39, 40–41, 49–50; Sidney Cox, *A Swinger of Birches: A Portrait of Robert Frost* (New York: Collier Books, 1957), 18–19, 44, 46, 76.
14. For the quotations in order, see *Selected Prose*, 41; Lawrance Thompson, *Robert Frost: The Years of Triumph, 1915–1938* (New York: Holt, Rinehart and Winston, 1970), 401; *Selected Prose*, 24; Untermeyer, 285.
15. James, *Pragmatism*, 21, 22.
16. For the quotations in order, see *Selected Prose*, 106, 107; quoted in *A Swinger of Birches*, 121.
17. James, *Pragmatism and Other Essays*, 263.
18. Georges Poulet, *The Interior Distance*, trans. Elliot Coleman (Ann Arbor: University of Michigan, 1964), vii.
19. James, *Psychology*, 148.
20. John Dewey, *Art as Experience* (New York: Capricorn Books, 1958), 282.
21. This is the central complaint of George Nitchie, *Human Values in the Poetry of Robert Frost* (Durham: Duke University, 1960).

RICHARD POIRIER
From "A Preview"
Robert Frost
1977, pp. 1–27

Robert Frost's eighty-fifth birthday party in 1959 has since been designated "a cultural episode." It brought into focus certain literary antagonisms having to do with the nature of modernism and it demonstrated the difficulty of placing Frost's achievement within the literature of this century. As the principle speaker that evening, Professor Lionel Trilling of Columbia University chose to call Frost "a terrifying poet." Those who felt they somehow already owned the poet were not grateful for what seemed a compliment. To them it was very late in coming and it suggested, when it did come, not any embarrassment that Trilling and his modernist associates had been tardy in recognizing Frost but rather that most of Frost's supporters had failed, for all their attentiveness, to read their poet the way he ought to be read. There are good reasons for disagreeing with Trilling's characterization of Frost, but no need for the hysterical possessiveness that marked the response to his speech. There was a nagging suspicion that he was simply trying to appropriate Frost to New York. New York meant modernism, construed as a cult in whose eyes the constituents of social and historical reality in America were malignant about half of the time. In fact, that is not what Trilling was doing; much of his work is opposed to this modernist view of reality. It was absurd to suppose that he could be using it as a standard to measure the greatness of anyone.

He was not praising Frost for an ideological stance, unless the attribution of Sophoclean centrality can be called ideological. What he admired in Frost had less to do with the kind of "terrifying" reality created by poems like "Design," "A Servant to Servants," "'Out, Out—,'" "Acquainted with the Night," "The Most of It" than with the literary evidences that Frost had made us *aware* of that reality in a new way. He claimed for Frost a particular kind of literary daring, and though, given the history of American culture, such daring necessarily carries ideological implications, these were not what he principally talked about. Trilling's estimate at the eighty-fifth birthday is worth bringing up now that the hundredth has passed, quite aside from whether it is right or wrong—these are not the only criteria for determining the value of a literary judgment. Rather, he offers a kind of large and crucial argument which calls upon you to decide just how important a poet Frost can be for you. What dimensions can he give your life, what shape can he help you give the time of your life, different as it is from his time? You have, more generally, to decide if Frost belongs in the company with twentieth-century writers of the greatest literary and historical magnitude, and, if he does not, whether this magnitude is not perhaps a form of historical pretension, even historical pretentiousness. Because what Trilling was trying to do was claim that Frost had continued a noble and heroic line of dissent. The line was located in American literature by D. H. Lawrence and, all national differences allowed, enriched by him. Trilling was proposing that Frost was radical in a classic American tradition. That is, Frost was trying to slough off an old inherited European consciousness in order that a new consciousness could come to life from underneath. And this kind of radical enterprise, Trilling added, "is not carried out by reassurance, nor by the affirmation of old verities and pieties. It is carried out by the representation of the terrible actualities of life in a new way."

It is obvious that some of these actualities are present in Frost's poetry; it can be shown that he often represented them in a new way. Granting all that, it still cannot be said, I think, that the consequent experience offered by his work is to any importantly consistent degree the Laurentian experience Trilling claims to find there. Quite the reverse. It is as if the technical genius of Frost, along with an extraordinary originality of mind and force of personality, was meant not to challenge "old verities and pieties" but rather to reinstate them. The whole almost alarmingly intense commitment of psychic and sexual energies to poetic performance turns out in Frost's case to be an effort precisely at the "reassurance" of us and of himself.

If this is true, what can we learn from the fact that in the first quarter of the century Frost was considered—and I think still ought to be—an exponent of the new? We can learn an important cultural lesson, if we do not know it already—that nothing pleases people more than the evidence that, however new the style, however unconventional the sounds, they can carry you nonetheless to conventional meanings. Newness in the arts, when it is popularly acclaimed, almost always confirms the old verities. This was one secret of Frost's success, just as it was a secret, too, of the immense popularity in the 1960's of the Beatles or of Bob Dylan. Their musical and lyrical styles were new to us and were taken by some as evidence also of the emergence of a "new consciousness." After a time, however, it was possible to recognize how conventional, how even learned and affectionately appropriated some of their musical and verbal phrasing really was.

Frost's popularity tells some essential critical and human truth about him. There is no point trying to explain the popularity away, as if it were a misconception prompted by a pose. There is a Frost who has been missed, almost lost, because of the lack of intensity and expectation brought to his poetry by those who know him best. In writing this book I found myself sometimes straining against the familiar in order to reach him where he most intensely lives in his writing. And yet the Frost I got to know was always somehow restoring himself to the lineaments of a massively settled official portrait. What then is "new" about his writing and what is in need of being said about it? Engaging yourself critically with Frost is like taking a trip with an old neighborhood friend and discovering under the stress of travel that he can on occasion be altogether more mysterious than you'd bargained for; he can be more exalted and exalting, yet show all the while flashes of a pettiness you had managed before to overlook; he can be full of wonderful excesses of imagination and generosities of spirit and yet more satisfied, it seems, by his self-control; a man ennobling in his centralities of feeling, which he will nonetheless betray by sudden reversions to formula and platitude. After the trip, you go home again among old friends. And there he sits, the same man to all appearances, whom the others know as well as you do. The difference is that now the persona has itself become, for you, an achievement altogether more powerful, impressive, and interesting in what it includes, the tensions it resolves, the passions it shapes. The others who have never known him to be any different are not so much wrong about him as simply not right enough. They have not, as it were, made the journey out and back, and such a journey is perhaps the central figure for Frost's own poetic enterprise of voice and vision—off into the sublime, back to the domesticated.

So that while the estimate of the so-called general public is necessarily partial and unsatisfactory, it nonetheless represents a kind of truth which criticism cannot afford to ignore. As in the reading of Wordsworth, it is time for criticism to find some way of showing that the surfaces are as important as the depths. The Frost of the best-loved poems is also the Frost who is simultaneously meditating, in a manner often unavailable to the casual reader, on the nature of poetry itself. "Stopping by Woods on a Snowy Evening" is about a central human experience—the enchantments that invite us to surrender ourselves to oblivion; "Mending Wall" is about the opposite impulse, which is to fence yourself in, to form relationships that are really exclusions. But at the same time and in the same terms both poems propose that these human dilemmas are also poetic ones, in the one case the possibly destructive solicitations of the sublime and in the other the claustrophobias of mechanical forms. The poems are about the will to live asserting itself against invitations either to surrender or to constraint, and these, it is intimated, issue as much from the conventions of poetry as from conventions of feeling. The poetry is always showing its alertness not only to the dangers it confronts but also to those it creates.

Frost's poetry can therefore be said to include terror without being itself terrified; it is for the most part reassuring in that it leaves us feeling more rather than less confident about our capacities. His is unlike the poetry of most of his contemporaries, except Lawrence and Stevens, because while you may make your life more complicated by reading it, you do not make your life more unmanageable. You are not led to believe that life is unintelligible or that your capacity to make sense of it merely proves your triviality. Indeed, in his prose, Frost is anxious to suggest that the ordinary sense-making processes are very much like poetic ones, that the making of sense in ordinary activities in analogous, as an art, to the writing of a poem. In "The Constant Symbol," originally used as the preface to the 1946 Modern Library edition of his poems, he remarks that

> Every single poem written regular is a symbol small or great of the way the will has to pitch into commitments deeper and deeper to a rounded conclusion and then be judged for whether any original intention it had has been strongly spent or weakly lost; be it in art, politics, school, church, business, love, or marriage—in a piece of work or in a career. Strongly spent is synonymous with kept.

In this little passage there is much of the essential Frost. Along with a number of clues to his popular appeal, there is a nice sample of why he promises to be more radical than he turns out to be. There is first of all an initial reassurance, that no matter how imposing the title under which he is writing—"The Constant Symbol"—he is still pretty much our friendly neighbor: "every poem written regular." This country language is then followed by a firm, resolute, but still unpretentious rhetorical mounting: "every single poem written regular is a symbol small or great of the way the will has to pitch into commitments." Note, for the unpretentiousness, that the symbol may be "small" as well as "great" and that the thrust toward expansiveness is cheerfully restrained by figures of speech that suggest we are listening to a quite ordinary man. Because if the commitment proposed is a large, rather operatic one ("the will to a rounded conclusion"), the phrase "to pitch into commitments" suggests something not remote from the simple farmyard willingness to "pitch in." Thus the near-grandiloquence of the subsequent "strongly spent or weakly lost" is braced within the realm of anyone's possible daily experience. And lest we miss the point it is made emphatic by the enumeration of those ways outside poetry in which any one of us can be employed. It is all brought to a close, as are many of Frost's poems, by an epigram, something we can take away with us: "Strongly spent is synonymous with kept."

This is an attractive, and above all an adroit performance, a fair enough example of Frost as a writer of prose. Its own "original intent" is to make us assent to a notion which we might ordinarily find presumptuous, namely that poetry is an heroic enterprise and that a poem is made equivalent to a number of activities which belong, as it were, to that real world—of politics, of business—which usually acknowledges poetry, if at all, by condescension. And yet somehow the passage is not a defense of poesy, as if it needed one. It is rather a bit of flattery bestowed by a man of action in poetry on other men of action who, in their own occupations—in which he, of course, also participates—conduct themselves much the way he does. Poetry is not life, but the perfomance in the writing of it can be an image of the proper conduct of life. The exercise of the will *in* poetry, the *writing* of a poem, is analogous to any attempted exercise of will in whatever else one tries to do. This position is not asserted, since the whole point, after all, is that nothing can be carried merely by assertion. One can only "pitch" in "deeper and deeper," and in this passage itself there is a demonstration rather than simply a claim of the validity of what is being said. The validation is implicit in his inclusive suppleness of voice. As in similar moments in Thoreau, the voice here manages to show its facility in the tones and nuances—like the submerged metaphors of sex and love-making, of farming and business—that belong to the tongues, the argots of occupations outside poetry. Frost's intention is not "weakly lost" because it is expended in careful checks and balances of voice by which the reader is convinced that this poet is in all likelihood more articulate in our business than we could hope to be in his.

Frost's critical prose, in lectures or letters, has none of the pretentious deferences by which Eliot communicates his pontifical responsibilities. Rather it seems to gather assurances about poetry by the emotive and injunctive power latent in a vocabulary that is primarily concerned with life: "every . . . poem written regular is a symbol . . . of the way the will," etc. Proposing himself as a master of common as much as of poetic tongues, he would democratize all of these within the equilibriums of a poem or a sentence. He would do this convinced that the authority finally achieved by form in life or in art will be greater than is the authority of any or all of the tongues more randomly combined. This helps explain, I think, why critics have had such a difficult time finding large thematic or philosophical reasons, the reasons of general education and of the humanities, for calling him a great poet. His poems really do not reward explication in the way the poems of Eliot and Yeats do. Criticism works best on him when it gets close, and stays close, when it tries to monitor what is going on in the dialectical play of sounds and metaphors. The poem manages to keep nearly everything to itself—or within the accumulated funds it shares with other poems—and is most alive and fresh in the way sounds and images spend themselves with and on one another.

That is why the poem is itself what he calls "a constant symbol." An especially charming example is "Hyla Brook," which is very much about the proposition that "strongly spent is synonymous with kept." The poem is never penurious or restrictive in the expenditure of any sound or voice within it, either poetic tongues or those of country folk, and it is equally speculative about its metaphors, whether they suggest mystery, as in the proposal that when we are looking for a brook it can be "found groping underground," or whether they offer some mixture of the poetic and familiar, as when the brook is casually compared to poetry within the easy vernacular of the first line.

> By June our brook's run out of song and speed.
> Sought for much after that, it will be found
> Either to have gone groping underground
> (And taken with it all the Hyla breed
> That shouted in the mist a month ago,
> Like ghost of sleigh bells in a ghost of snow)—
> Or flourished and come up in jewelweed,
> Weak foliage that is blown upon and bent,
> Even against the way its waters went.
> Its bed is left a faded paper sheet
> Of dead leaves stuck together by the heat—
> A brook to none but who remembers long.
> This as it will be seen is other far
> Than with brooks taken otherwise in song.
> We love the things we love for what they are.

Another take-away ending, too, it seems, though only those not educated by the poem would want to take it away. Still, the line does mean just what it can simply be supposed to mean. If we love at all truly then probably we do "love the things . . . for what they are." Of course the poem, as a whole development, imposes a weight on the familiar idioms of that line, especially on the word "things" and on the word "what." Very like Thoreau again, in the way common idioms are transformed by a context which nonetheless supports the sounds of those idioms. New England speech is not elevated by this process into poetry; it is shown to *be* poetry as Emerson said it could be. By the end, the brook is many different "things" according to the season. It is even compared to a "faded paper sheet," like something you might write a poem on. This is not a merely fanciful reading, since one of the things the brook is also compared to, twice over, is "song." The brook is many different "things," and to love it therefore for "what" it is, is to love it for being a kind of conundrum.

But we lose the poem, and it is lost to us, if we look beyond the obvious rather than through it. The poem in its sound makes us assent to the likelihood that what we shall have to say about it will belong to the obvious. Much of it, after all, luxuriates in ordinary speech, a near banality of sentiment; the last line could find a place, and probably has, on a sampler. And yet the poem is powerful enough to absorb into itself the sounds of other, more elevated stylistic conventions derived from a kind of poetry Frost knew would be recognizably poetical. Thus, line 5, "Like the ghost of sleigh bells in a ghost of snow"—Reuben Brower, once an Amherst colleague of Frost's and one of his best critics, says that this is "the most exquisite line in the poem." It might well be, if we were encouraged by syntax to read Frost by the line. But we are asked to read him at the very least by the sentence. For Frost, the sentence is the basic unit of voice in a poem. Half or all of some of the shorter poems are made up of a single sentence, "The Silken Tent" being perhaps the best example. When we listen to what Frost calls "the sentence sound," we hear many tongues, including Wordsworthian and Tennysonian poetic tongues, and that truly "exquisite" poetic line is made to accommodate itself to the ordinary vernacular sound of the sentence in which it appears. By the same token, the ordinary vernacular is in turn required to make room for the conventionally poetic.

The wit by which the brook is said to "flourish" by coming up in so frail and common a plant as "jewelweed" should make us wary of trying to isolate any of the items in this *curriculum vitae* of a brook. We cannot separate any detail from the sound of a man talking to other men and woman who are like himself. He is a man who, when he uses a traditional figure (by which if still water or lakes stand for mind, running water stands for eloquence or song), does so in the locution of the neighborhood: "By June our brook's run out of song and speed."

The sound of this poem and the filtering through it of metaphor demonstrate what it means to be "at home in the metaphor," how to make conventionally poetic metaphors and sounds almost casually a part of the ordinary movements of nature and of human speech, how, at last, to tame the extravagant potentialities inherent in any metaphor. It was in this sense that Frost was considered a new poet in 1918, and why he remains still a new, a fresh experience of poetry. He was and is a new poet not, however, because he can be said, in Lawrence's terms, to help us slough off a European consciousness in order to allow the growth of a new one. No such radical consequence can be felt from reading him. Rather, what he does is set about affectionately to make old elements of consciousness—here out of Tennyson and Wordsworth—congenial with the likes of Thoreau, and he then makes all of these live within a humanly simple vernacular which had not, before Frost, been able as easily to accommodate any of them. . . . Here there is a distinctly American egalitarian impulse, along with a regularity in the writing, a commitment to form, which seems to have behind it only the most practical impulses. English poetry is let into the vernacular not to save New Hampshire but rather to save poetry from itself. This is principally why he is a New English rather than a merely English writer.

I used the phrase "at home in the metaphor." It is Frost's, from the most important of his critical talks, "Education by Poetry," and he issues a warning along with it:

> Unless you are at home in the metaphor, unless you've had your proper poetical education in the metaphor, you are not safe anywhere. Because you are not at ease with figurative values: you don't know the metaphor in its strength and weakness. You don't know how far you can expect to ride it and when it may break down with you. You are not safe in science; you are not safe in history.

To "know the metaphor in its strength and weakness"—obviously we are being asked to know more than the mere graphic design of a figure of speech. But we have to begin, as in a poem called "Spring Pools," by knowing at least that much. The poem introduces us to the pools which are then compared to something that has the power to "reflect." Initially, all this seems to imply is that nature "reflects" on itself, that it delights in correspondences and likenesses. But soon thereafter it is borne in on us that this metaphor can be pushed further to quite another meaning of "reflect," as in "Let them think twice." The natural elements are treated as if self-conscious, as if they ought to be narcissistically desirous of freezing or chilling their own "reflected" beauty; as if they should want a moment of delicate balance wholly freed from the further exigencies of time.

> These pools that, though in forests, still reflect
> The total sky almost without defect,
> And like the flowers beside them, chill and shiver,
> Will like the flowers beside them soon be gone.
> And yet not out by any brook or river,
> But up by roots to bring dark foliage on.
>
> The trees that have it in their pent-up buds
> To darken nature and be summer woods—
> Let them think twice before they use their powers
> To blot up and drink up and sweep away
> These flowery waters and these watery flowers
> From snow that melted only yesterday.

This is a rather hazardous poem and raises in an acute way a central and evaded problem about how properly to read Frost. Quite simply, there is a question here, and to some degree in all his work, of his willingness *not* to be ironic, his willingness not to slough off responsibility by ascribing his own confusions of feeling to a "speaker" other than himself or to merely some aspect of himself that has been entrapped, as it were, in a ludicrous situation. The ludicrousness, in turn, is ignored by critics who habitually talk about "situations" as if they were all "dramatic." "Dramatic situation" and "speaker" are terms which I shall have to use now and then, but never, I hope, in order to exempt Frost from the perplexities, absurdities, and contradictions that belong to some of his poems. His greatness depends, I think, in large part on his actually seeking out opportunities for being in untenable positions. In poem after poem he defies the nature of things, lets his metaphors take him too far, and all the while appeals to a kind of decorum by which his excess becomes admirably an evidence of his dependence upon us to go along with him. It is wholly proper that the little poem standing at the head of his collected poems is "The Pasture," with its invitation that we join him on his sorties into the field where he will "rake the leaves away" and see "the little calf / That's standing by the mother." It could be an excursion into poetry, Greek and Latin, and he promises always to return home with us in a line, repeated twice, which is probably, as Lowell Edmunds suggested to me, an imitation of the Greek and Latin metrical phenomenon called bucolic diaresis: "I shan't be gone long.—You come too." Unless we are willing to join his extravagances we have to read a poem like "Spring Pools" as smugly as he, in such a case, would have to perform in it. The poem would thereby become for us an "education by poetry" but of an unappealingly pre-meditated kind. We would have been invited merely to watch someone expose himself to an absurdity because of what was initially a commendable human desire. But the poem is not like that. It is instead an exercise of Frostean "will," pitching in against all logic. William James would have understood the poem in this light.

The speaker—really the mind of the poet going through a representative consultation with itself—realizes that he is to be deprived of his platonic, or, more exactly, eleatic vision of unagitated fusion and oneness, a vision beautifully expressed in Emerson's "Xenophanes." His initial vision, in the first four lines, is of a moment when everything seems in a related state of balance and stillness; he admits to the precariousness of the scene only in the casual euphemism that it will "soon be gone." But then, with the last line before the break in the poem, he acknowledges, in the phrase "up by the roots," a countervailing, brutal reality in the nature of things. It is then that he proposes, in tones at once angry and petulant, a vision of apocalyptic obliteration; he seems innocent of the fact that the things he would preserve do not themselves suffer from a consciousness either of their own uniqueness or of any dangers to it. As the next to last line beautifully suggests in its "reflected" phrasing, the pools and the trees are happily part of one another; they *are* what is happening to them. However, their delicate transitoriness is no more or less engaging than is the voice of the man raised in protest against it. In this on-going process in nature, human nature is a kind of noble impertinence by virtue of its very wrong-headedness. A difference between Frost and Wordsworth should be apparent in the way Frost chooses to characterize the seeming irrelevance here of human consciousness—the poem is feisty rather than brooding; a speaker can hardly be called alienated who is also as blusteringly involved as this one.

Of the many Frostean characteristics illustrated by this poem none is so important as the way the voice can be said to be victimized by its own energies. It is betrayed by grammer as much as by the logical implications of the metaphors on which it insists. Thus, both pools and flowers are said to "chill and shiver." This yoking of a transitive and a normally intransitive verb is a grammatical indication of the forced effort to make things identical when they are only to some extent similar. "Flowers" may "shiver" and so may "pools," but only the latter have the power to "chill." Similarly, nature in the form of "pools" may indeed "reflect"—in more ways than one, it would seem. Frost knew his Milton and how in his poetry (as John Hollander brilliantly illustrates in *Vision and Resonance)* a verb at the end of a line will often create a near enjambment, so that for a moment we cannot be sure whether it is transitive or intransitive. In the hesitation, just before turning into line 2, we can allow for the possibility that the "pools" "reflect" in the sense that they "think"; but once we make the turn, the verb grasps its object, and "reflect" means only "mirror." "Pools" cannot "reflect" the way the speaker can: they cannot remember the past in the present or meditate upon a destructiveness which is in any event a part of the spontaneous creative movement in which they participate. His imperative to the trees, "Let them think twice," following on a dash which suggests some shock of recognition on his part, is simply to cry if not in the dark then in woods that will get dark no matter what he says in admonishment.

In offering an "education by metaphor" the poem does not test out a figure of speech in any dispassionate way or probe the inconsistencies to which it ultimately brings us. We are made to care as much or more for a highly personalized human voice responding to a specific situation, the kind of voice mostly missing from Stevens. It refuses to accommodate itself to the evident breakdown of the metaphor of "reflection." Like other such voiced presences in Frost's poetry, it will submit to nothing, even its own inventions, without sounding off. When Frost says that we must "know the metaphor in its strength and weakness," if we are to be "safe in history," he means that we must test the metaphor, contend with the logic and the limits of it, not just "use" it. And this can be done by the "voice" which made up the metaphor to begin with: "These pools that, though in forests, still reflect / The total sky . . ." Why the plural "forests" and why "total sky"? He is speaking not of some pools in particular, but of pools in his mind, pools of such unusual visionary sharpness as to be immediately present to him, "*these* pools."

The voice, then, is not of a man standing in a wood looking at pools. We have here a fine instance, it seems to me, that the most misleading advice Frost ever gave for the reading of his or of most lyric poetry is that "Everything written is as good as it is dramatic. It need not declare itself in form, but it is drama or nothing . . . spoken by a person in a scene—in character, in a setting. By whom, where and when is the question." In 1929, when this was written as part of his preface to his play, *A Way Out*, Frost was, as ever, anxious to insist upon the speaking voice in his poems, on what for fifteen years he had been propagating as "the sound of sense . . . sentence sounds." Probably the easiest way to get people to look for these elements was with such pointers as "whom, where and when." But the questions "where" and "when" are often useless and sophomoric if applied to poems in which we are asked to imagine a grown man talking in the woods about pools, or trying, on another occasion, to convince us that an oven bird "is a bird everyone has heard."

Voice in Frost is itself a metaphor as it is not, say, in

Auden ("All I have is a voice / To undo the folded lie"). Different on different occasions, voice is a metaphor of a self, of a mind or temperament that engages those other metaphors it creates out of its need to account for whatever is *not* the self. It responds to these—as if they were reality. Like many of Frost's poems, "Spring Pools" is about a man who discovers that even his metaphors about reality, much less any other "truer" forms of it, will not conform to his desires, will not confirm his visions, and not the least because metaphors are as much inherited as are the forests and pools. He is wedded to his metaphors as he might be wedded to a woman who, while a "reflection," is nonetheless, in the words of "The Most of It," "someone else additional to him." He stays with the metaphor, argues with it, for it, against it; he is "in" it to the very end.

Interactions between "voice" and other forms of metaphor, metaphors of otherness, occur everywhere in Frost; they constitute the very substance of his work. Among the forms of interaction can be a tension, noticed in "Hyla Brook," between "voice" which is vernacular, something presumably "taken fresh from talk," and "voice" which is poetic, taken from the poetry of the past, Emerson or Wordsworth, Keats or Tennyson or Shelley. In "All Revelation," for example, Frost shows his capacity for a Yeatsian accent, almost as if he wants to show how masterfully he can resist it, just as at the beginnings of his career in London—at thirty-nine and forty—he chose, after two visits, to avoid the "Monday nights" where Yeats sometimes took the privilege of tinkering with the lines of visiting poets. "All Revelation" is a poem about efforts to penetrate the stuff of life—to discover life through the pleasure of the genitalia, or by the probings of science, or by the faculties of vision—and at the end there is a mounting toward a released largeness of voice not ordinarily heard in Frost:

> A head thrusts in as for the view,
> But where it is it thrusts in from
> Or what it is it thrusts into
> By that Cyb'laean avenue,
> And what can of its coming come,
>
> And whither it will be withdrawn,
> And what take hence or leave behind,
> These things the mind has pondered on
> A moment and still asking gone.
> Strange apparition of the mind!
>
> But the impervious geode
> Was entered, and its inner crust
> Of crystals with a ray cathode
> At every point and facet glowed
> In answer to the mental thrust.
>
> Eyes seeking the response of eyes
> Bring out the stars, bring out the flowers,
> Thus concentrating earth and skies
> So none need be afraid of size.
> All revelation has been ours.

What is especially impressive here is that a demonstrated grandiloquence is made syntactically inseparable from an audacious refusal finally to exercise it, to sound like a Big Poet. The resistance can be felt in the next to the last line: "So none need be afraid of size." That has the characteristic signature of Frost without which the whole passage might be called Yeatsian. Though officially regular iambic the line is largely spondaic. It is far more compacted than any of the others; its tight monosyllabic economies force the voice from the prophetic into a slightly mocking accent, an accent congenial to the meaning of the line, with its suggestion that vision ought to concentrate rather than magnify our experience, ought to make it manageable rather than magnificent. So much so that retrospectively we are forced to concede that the "eyes seeking the response of eyes" may be not the eyes of romantic lovers searching for one another but rather eyes in their primitive state, eyes just beginning to discover their utility, seeking, as do the hands of a baby, for an ordained function in the continual exploration of the world.

The human limits proposed in poetry of this kind are clearly not to be confused with poetic limitations. The poetry discovers its own restraints through successive violations of them, so that the achievement in this instance seems to be snatched from the jaws, the voiced cadence, of visionary rhetoric even while leaving that rhetoric its own glory. In Frost the vernacular almost invariably modifies or includes any more ambitious venture of voice. It is an Emersonian effort to hold the miraculous within the embrace of the quotidian. The sexual play in the poem is indicative of this. Sexuality is simply "there," as it is in so much of Frost's writing—the specific sexual act of "putting in the seed"—but it is syntactically and in every other way made continuous with the general human thrust toward penetration and creativity. Thus, "what can of its comings come" is kept from being quite as specific as it might sound by the initial uncertainty about whether in the first stanza a phallus is exploring a vagina or a child's head is emerging to look into the world.

"Voice" in conflict with metaphor or with other voices—the measure of this requires extreme delicacy because it is a conflict inextricable from love. The voice, when it gets anxious about the metaphor it is using, is, again, involved with what it has helped create or evoke, with versions of reality or of poetry or of the "other" in which the self has chosen to find a "reflection." The abrasions can involve the terrible knowingness of love or of what once was love. Perhaps inevitably, Frost is a great poet of marriage, maybe the greatest since Milton, and of the sexuality that goes with it. This is signally true of the dramatic narratives and less directly of all his poetry. His feelings are saturated with what Wordsworth, in his "Preface to the *Lyrical Ballads*" (1800), calls the perception of "similitude in dissimilitude, and dissimilitude in similitude" upon which depends "our taste and our moral feelings." Poems like "Home Burial" or "The Death of the Hired Man" or "A Servant to Servants" or "West-Running Brook" dramatize marital differences, of taste and feeling (merely teasing differences in "West-Running Brook"), expressed as alleged incapacities of one or another of the partners to speak with adequate sensitivity or in a voice supposedly proper to a situation. Marital voices can become fixed and entrapped within domestic forms, and imaginative freedom, especially for the wives, finds expression in lying or madness, witchery or suicide.

Frost's criticism, in talks and letters, is almost wholly given either to metaphor or to sound, the speaking voice. The first, in its emphasis on the marriage of one thing to another, implies some necessary limit for anything or anyone; the other, the humanly characterized voice, suggests, to the contrary, that the individual voice can have a shaping force, that it can express the will to exceed the limits imposed by "otherness." His poetry is a perpetual debate between, on the one side, the inherent necessity for form in language and in nature, which requires a dialogue of accommodation, and, on the other, the equally inherent human need for excursion beyond form, or (to note how often in Frost the human actions are equivalent to poetic practice) for taking a walk beyond the confines of home.

Form, be it of a poem we read or a home where we live, is, for Frost, all in the making. If it promises security it is only of so relative a kind as to reveal the insecurities around it, insecurities which cannot be made less real by legislation either of government or church. It can be said that for Frost the only possible New Deal occurred in the readjustments immediately after the Fall. We experience the pleasures and reassurances of form in the act of having to create it. "All 'homes" are in finite experience," said William James *(Pragmatism)*, a writer whose works are a treasury of images of which Frost freely availed himself. But James goes on to observe that "finite experiences as such are homeless. Nothing outside the flux secures the issue of it." Form is a gratifying act of will and also a protective one in a universe where we are otherwise freely exposed to chaos, and it can come into existence as a result of the most ordinary human enterprise, the labor of hands as well as of mind. Performances in poetry and performances in an orchard or a field elicit from Frost, as we have seen, the same rhetoric, and part of his great popularity derived, most likely, from his Emersonian capacity to make people feel that in writing a poem he was being *more* like them rather than less. If he was heroic, then so were they in whatever they did to give form to their lives—making a garden, writing a letter, what have you.

Modernism and liberalism, Eliot and Roosevelt, tended, as he saw them, to weaken the human capacity to shape life by proposing the negligible power of individual enterprise. They posited, in their different ways, a situation in which, in the face of overwhelming deteriorations, individual acts of form were made to seem trivial, where people were therefore encouraged to let the form of their lives depend on the provisions of government—"Provide, Provide"—or even on the formal ending of an Upanishad. Frost's feeling about poetry, the making of form, and the—to him—objectionable movements of contemporary thinking all came together in 1935, appropriately a flourishing time for Eliot and for Roosevelt, when Frost wrote a remarkably eloquent letter in reply to a message of congratulation on his sixty-first birthday from *The Amherst Student:*

> Fortunately we don't need to know how bad the age is. There is something we can always be doing without reference to how good or how bad the age is. There is at least so much good in the world that it admits of form and the making of form. And not only admits of it, but calls for it. We people are thrust forward out of the suggestions of form in the rolling clouds of nature. In us nature reaches its height of form and through us exceeds itself. When in doubt there is always form for us to go on with. Anyone who has achieved the least form to be sure of it, is lost to the larger excruciations. I think it must stroke faith in the right way. The artist[,] the poet[,] might be expected to be the most aware of such assurance. But it is really everybody's sanity to feel it and live by it. Fortunately, too, no forms are more engrossing[,] gratifying, comforting, staying than those lesser ones we throw off, like vortex rings of smoke, all our individual enterprise and needing nobody's co-operation: a basket, a letter, a garden, a room, an idea, a picture, a poem. For these we haven't to get a team together before we can play.
>
> The background in hugeness and confusion shading away from where we stand in black and utter chaos; and against the background any small man-made figure of order and concentration. What pleasanter than that this should be so? Unless we are novelists or economists we don't worry about this confusion; we look out on [it] with an instrument or tackle it to reduce it. It is partly because we are afraid it might prove too much for us and our blend of democratic-republican-socialist-communist-anarchist party. But it is more because we like it, we were born to it, born used to it and have practical reasons for wanting it there. To me any little form I assert upon it is velvet, as the saying is, and to be considered for how much more it is than nothing. If I were a Platonist I should have to consider it, I suppose, for how much less it is than everything.

William James would recognize this as the prose of what he called "tough-mindedness." Frost casts his lot with "the truth that," according to James, "grows up inside of all finite experiences." These experiences "lean on each other, but the whole of them, if whole there be, leans on nothing" *(Pragmatism)*. For Frost, there is a disinclination to "lean" on anyone else even for "co-operation." As he would have it, form is very much a lonely enterprise of unremarkable or even invisible industry. And it is perhaps no more lasting than "vortex rings of smoke"—even blowing *these* can apparently count for something. There is no yearning in his work for ultimates, none of the desire to "tighten this loose universe" which James (in a passage that points toward Frost's poem "Design") ascribed to the "tender minded." What they want, said James, with persuasive dismissiveness, is

> Something to support the finite many, to tie it to, to unify and anchor it. Something *un*exposed to accident, something eternal and unalterable. The mutable in experience must be founded on immutability. Behind our *de facto* world, our world in act, there must be a *de jure* duplicate fixed and previous, with all that can happen here already there *in posse*, every drop of blood, every smallest item, appointed and provided, stamped and branded, without chance of variation. The negatives that haunt our ideals here below must themselves be negated in the absolutely Real. This alone makes the universe solid. This is the resting deep. We live upon the stormy surface; but with this our anchor holds, for it grapples rocky bottom. This is Wordsworth's "eternal peace abiding at the heart of endless agitation." This is Vivekananda's mystic One of which I read to you. This is Reality, with the big R, reality that makes the timeless claim, reality to which defeat can't happen *(Pragmatism)*.

We come closest to the spirit of Frost's work whenever as readers we get into the action, the performance of the poem, joining him especially in those movements by which he keeps a poem from "tightening up." There are disclaimers embedded in assertions ("For once, then, something"); conciliating understatements that call for correction ("And to do that to birds was why she came," he says of Eve in "Never Again Would Birds' Song Be the Same"); evasive tactics in the use of words like "almost" and "somehow," of "unless" and especially "as if" ("As if the earth in one unlooked-for favor / Had made them certain earth returned their love," in "Two Look at Two"); predilections for negatives which evoke the reality being denied ("Not bluebells gracing a tunnel mouth— / Not lupine living on sand and drouth" in "A Passing Glimpse"); ascriptions of perception or capacity where none exist ("The aim was song—the wind could see" in "The Aim Was Song"); open-ended endings ("If design govern in a thing so small," "Design"). He is wonderfully exciting in the daring with which he chooses to show that a poem is "less than everything" because, given the nature of things and language, it is difficult enough to be "more than nothing." Frost's is a profound, philosophical use of language, an ultimately austere one which nonetheless provides for its own opportunities of excess. He succeeds in being closer to certain aspects of twentieth-century philosophy—he would have appreciated such a title as Stanley Cavell's *Must We Mean What We Say*—than to the literary modernism of Eliot and Yeats.

HERBERT MARKS

"The Counter-Intelligence of Robert Frost"

Yale Review, Summer 1982, pp. 554–78

I. Why the Stars Twinkle

When Robert Frost presents himself to the reader in the late poem "Directive" as one "who only has at heart your getting lost," or has the Keeper in *A Masque of Mercy* declare to his fugitive alter ego, "Some people want you not to understand them, / But I want you to understand me wrong," he is playing on the interaction of revelation and concealment—a theological commonplace, consecrated for English literature in Touchstone's demonstration that "the truest poetry is the most faining. . . ." The problem of feigning figures prominently in all Frost's work, as a stylistic tendency toward the gnomic, but also as a theme. Consider a less obvious clue, the preface he wrote in 1924 to the little-known *Memoirs of the Notorious Stephen Burroughs*, in which he praises the Massachusetts impostor for his "sophisticated wickedness, the kind that knows its grounds and can twinkle." Burroughs had a flair for irony, and Frost, musing toward the end of the essay on his conversion to Catholicism, appears to have recognized their shared affinities:

> I should like to have heard his reasons for winding up in the Catholic Church. I can conceive of their being honest. Probably he was tired of his uncharted freedom out of jail and wanted to be moral and a Puritan again as when a child, but this time under a cover where he couldn't be made fun of by the intellectuals. The course might commend itself to the modern Puritan (what there is left of the modern Puritan).

Though couched humorously, two serious notions are here advanced in defense of Burrough's "hypocrisy." One is the necessity of concealment, the other is the flaccidity of unconstrained freedom, and, taken together, they are among the central articles of Frost's own personal and poetic creed.

The canny style of engagement is characteristic of Frost, who like Bel's favorite poet in *A Masque of Mercy* seems to have espoused a "doctrine of the Seven Poses." "We like to talk in parables and in hints and in indirections," he explained to an audience at Amherst College, "whether from diffidence or some other instinct." Perhaps the instinct is self-preservation, or, less starkly, the desire to rival God, whose glory it is to conceal things, according to the biblical proverb. Its counterpart, in any case, is the instinct to seek things out, called by the same proverb the glory of kings; and it is disheartening to observe that in our less regal moods we tend to relegate each other's evasions to the realm of confessional hide-and-seek—as when Lawrance Thompson, in his introduction to Frost's letters, presumes to excuse the poet's "masks" by reminding us of his "excruciating sensitivities." Three critical dicta are accordingly in order: that masking is not necessarily a personal symptom; that poetry can exist only as veiled or elusive meaning—Frost has called it metaphor; and that these two precepts imply one another. Admittedly, Frost often provokes some reductive psychologizing even as he reprehends it: one thinks of his admonition to Sidney Cox, "I have written to keep the over curious out of the secret places of my mind." But the invitation, "You come too," at the front of the collected poems is of another, more generous order, and we misprize it badly if we suppose that poetic masks are something behind which it is our privilege or duty to peer. As Frost pointedly remarked in a letter to Thompson, "The right virtue of a natural reader is the nice ability to tell always when a poem is being figurative. . . . A little of the low-down on motivation goes a long way."

This is not to deny that personal anxieties, including a fear of exposure, contributed to the shaping of Frost's personae. Yet his reasons for resisting biographical criticism go beyond the desire for privacy, and informers whetted by such seemingly transparent poses as the folksy philosopher or the good grey poet would do well to pause before exposing themselves. For Frost, any effort to go behind the masks is finally not only slavish but futile; for the "true person" is an endlessly receding ideal valuable as a stimulus or cure, but proof against definition., A similar premise underlies Frost's resolve to "spoil" his correspondence with Cox "by throwing us into confusion the way God threw the speech of the builders of the tower of Babel into confusion." What sounds like arrogant mystagogy is at bottom a shrewd reminder that the confusion of tongues and the fall of the tower were manifestations of an already extant condition: that given the state of Noah's descendants, our projects for arriving anywhere directly must collapse of their own accord. The cadres at Babel failed to reach heaven by reason of the same law that preserves or isolates the author from his readers, or the friend from his familiar; and these varied restrictions are finally inseparable. When Frost's Jonah confesses, "I think I may have got God wrong entirely," the Keeper only echoes in reply, "All of us get each other pretty wrong."

If the face-to-face vision of God and the poet relieved of his personae are interchangeable fictions, it is their mythical complement, the naked or public muse, who flits through "Paul's Wife," a poem that explores the necessity of concealment from multiple vantage points. Frost's strategy in the poem is clever. His yarning narrator, after posing the problem of Paul's refusal to be questioned about his rumored marriage, first relates a series of anonymous explanations, for the most part based on the self-defeating view that Paul really has no wife, or that "the obscurity's a fraud to cover nothing," to quote Job's words from *A Masque of Reason*. Ideally, such reductiveness should serve as a warning, but the more generous observations of the backwoods magister Murphy elicit a second variety of interpretive shortcuts, this time from the reader.

The story he tells is that Paul took a log the mill had rejected, carved out the pith and carried it to the pond, where it dissolved and reemerged a girl. Recognition followed, and the couple set off for a niche in the mountains, pursued at a distance by Murphy and his gang of spying loggers. There the new bride shone like a star, till shouts of tribute and a flying bottle broke the charm, and the girl vanished. As usual with Frost, the apparently simple report abounds with symbols and mythical echoes. The contrasts between the mill and the jackknife, the empty bottle and the transfiguring pond, trade on familiar Frostian emblems; while the generation of Paul's native Anadyomene from the pithy log corresponds nicely to the birth of Venus in Hesiod. But the serious difficulty, and with it the real interest of the poem, only begins with the conclusion, in which Murphy finally offers his own interpretation of Paul's evasiveness:

> Paul put on all those airs
> About his wife to keep her to himself.
> Paul was what's called a terrible possessor.
> Owning a wife with him meant owning her.
> She wasn't anybody else's business,
> Either to praise her, or so much as name her,
> And he'd thank people not to think of her.
> Murphy's idea was that a man like Paul
> Wouldn't be spoken to about a wife
> In any way the world knew how to speak.

At first, these lines seem to echo the arguments from self-preservation and delicacy of feeling suggested by Thompson. Accordingly, they compel two trains of thought: one psychological, about the makeup of the "man like Paul" so leery of intrusion; the second political, about the makeup of the world to which his elusiveness is the fit response. Such readings, like the arguments they would have Murphy echoing, are not so much invalid as incomplete. They allow us to suppose that, given a tougher hide, or a world somehow smarter or better mannered, Paul would have been glad to haul his wife back to camp and, like Len the husband in "A Servant to Servants," compel her to cook for the boys. They neglect, in other words, that necessary correspondence between masking and metaphor—the idea that since language is by nature metaphorical, it must inevitably conceal or misrepresent whatever it tries to convey. Ultimately, for Frost, "*any* way the world knew how to speak" to Paul about his wife must have sounded like slander.

I have been suggesting that a basic theme of Frost's work is the paradoxical alliance of truth and concealment. Another, as I shall try to show, speaks to the mutual dependence of freedom and restraint. In a sense, these two antitheses really express a single paradox, the first in epistemological, the second in physical (or ethical) terms. But I prefer to acknowledge the difference between them, and so the power necessary to yoke them together; for it is precisely here, in the fact that Frost's vision spanned both poles embracing the physical and the mental and making them cohere, that his accomplishment is most impressive.

Perhaps the finest product of this coherence is "The Silken Tent," a poem that conveys both the interdependence of freedom and restraint and, when read allusively, the higher economics of feigning:

> She is as in a field a silken tent
> At midday when a sunny summer breeze
> Has dried the dew and all its ropes relent,
> So that in guys it gently sways at ease,
> And its supporting central cedar pole,
> That is its pinnacle to heavenward
> And signifies the sureness of the soul,
> Seems to owe naught to any single cord,
> But strictly held by none, is loosely bound
> By countless silken ties of love and thought
> To everything on earth the compass round,
> And only by one's going slightly taut
> In the capriciousness of summer air
> Is of the slightest bondage made aware.

The tent is a figure for poetic incarnation, and the fourteen lines of the poem, which uses the restrictions and compartmentalizations of the Shakespearean sonnet to achieve its single sentence, seem themselves a formal embodiment of the meaning they convey. This correspondence of form to content is reflected in the smallest details: the description of the central pole, for example, which is placed in the central quatrain; or the final couplet, which illustrates its own slight "bondage" to formal restraints by "going taut" as preannounced. On a larger scale, the whole sonnet unfolds within the bounds set by the initial simile, in illustration of the inevitable impingement, restrictive yet sustaining, of metaphor on direct expression. As the momentum of the sentence develops, we are tempted to forget such a flexible parenthesis, just as we tend for the most part to ignore the frames within which our thoughts and feelings run their course. Twice therefore Frost brings us back to the ground of reality by calling attention to the metaphorical relation with deliberate gestures which are themselves "silken ties." In line 7, the central pole is surprised at its work of fictional identification and exposed for what it really is, an index that "signifies." The second time, in line 10, the relation no longer needs to be enforced: So close is the control that it is allowed to dissolve—the fusion the poem sets out to interdict taking place, by leave, at the very moment its ban resounds most clearly. It is a wonderful moment, the love and thought which are the soul's rarest ornaments merging with the ties that keep the tent erect in a necessarily contingent freedom. The balanced tensions, appropriately, are both erotic and metaphysical. The gracefulness enveloping the figure binds with its earthward pull the virile thrust toward the sublime, so that the complete structure remains at once open toward, yet apt to withstand, the animating breeze as it presides over the conclusion.

Not the least of Frost's triumphs here is his transvaluation of "the earthly tent," a prominent image in ascetic literature used by Paul in his Second Letter to the Corinthians to figure the temporary abode of the soul. For Paul, the tent suggests the eventuality of being "swallowed up" into a "heavenly dwelling"; in the sonnet, all hint of the provisional is banished. To be sure, Frost preserves the Pauline delight in paradox, but he fosters it for its own sake, unabashedly, rather than in the name of what transcends or resolves it. Where one senses cautious denigration behind Paul's testimony that "we have this treasure in earthen vessels," in Frost's revision, physical embodiment becomes an occasion for pure celebration: not the "earthly" but the "silken" tent.

Especially in Frost's earlier work, the power of such biblical echoes comes from their compression—the layers of connotation through which they are forced to pass. Symbolic locus of the illimitable shekinah in the Pentateuch, figure in John for the indwelling of the Logos, associated with poetic incarnation in *Paradise Regained* and Emerson's "Terminus," the tent is a potentially cumbersome legacy which Frost, by his very reticence, manages to appropriate. In the late poem "Kitty Hawk," by contrast, the economic parallel between poetics and Christology comes to the surface in lines that stand as a sort of creedal summary, a type of the poet's conviction, expressed in "A Constant Symbol," that "the very words of the dictionary are a restriction to make the best of or stay out of and be silent." Frost's claim that "God's own descent / Into flesh" was intended to show the virtue of spending strongly presumes on the strength of sixty years' work, and as often in his last poems, the irony of the reduction borders on persiflage. The ostensibly Platonic description of the soul's birth in "The Trial by Existence" is likewise indebted to the Christic paradox, but less openly and hence to greater effect:

> And from a cliff-top is proclaimed
> The gathering of the souls for birth,
> The trial by existence named,
> The obscuration upon earth.

Here, the limitation or misrepresentation Frost considered an essential feature of language is identified by means of a syntactic ambiguity with the act or process of becoming at all. The dodge centers appropriately on the rime-word "named," which may be read either as a predicate of "trial," or, by a Latinate inversion, as qualifying "existence"—the submission to language thus constituting the trial. Emerson too, in Frost's favorite poem "Uriel," likened the career of poetic speech to "the procession of the soul in matter," but Frost, at least in this early piece, makes more of its restrictive or concealing effects—of an "obscuration" derived via tradition from the spending of the preexistent Word.

Perhaps the counterpart to these passages is the vision of Far-away Meadow at the end of "The Last Mowing"—to me, the most poignant lines Frost ever wrote—in which all sense of trial is momentarily laid aside, and a wistful consummation is realized in the obviation of language:

> The place for the moment is ours
> For you, oh tumultuous flowers,
> To go to waste and go wild in,
> All shapes and colors of flowers,
> I needn't call you by name.

The last two lines are an unusual instance of what Richard Poirier has called "negative designation"; of the way Frost's "visionary impulse . . . gets affirmed by an act of denial." For the most part, Frost would have agreed with Stevens, "All sorts of flowers. That's the sentimentalist," and it is rare to see him treating his longing—"this limitless trait in the hearts of men"—without irony. Or rather, since even here the poet's imagined moment of intimacy is ironically predicated on hearsay, it is rare to feel that despite all odds it is the longing that has triumphed.

More typical is the parodistic treatment one finds in "An Empty Threat," a deflation of the sublime in the mode of Keats's "A Song about Myself," and Thoreau's "The Old Marlborough Road." Keats, we remember, took "A Book / Full of vowels / And a shirt / With some towels . . . / And follow'd his nose to the North"—only to find the ground there as hard as in England. Thoreau, more cautious, recognized before he set out that roving was a spiritual appetite best indulged at home, that one "can get enough gravel / On the Old Marlborough Road"—though the announcement, characteristically, was only to be posted along the Road itself. Like them, Frost knows that the desire to go beyond home, to dispense with the bounds of place or the particular, is apt to confound itself unless tethered to reality. Freedom, communion, transfiguration, the lures that impel the mythical journey, are for him only vapid delusions until embodied in specific forms. His venture north to the realm of "snow and mist / That doesn't exist" in search of a fabulous father figure is thus, as his title tells us, "an empty threat" from the start:

> I stay;
> But it isn't as if . . .

The ensuing description of Hudson's Bay, despite the indicative mode, is idle fantasy, though one senses that in the canvas of Frost's oeuvre such fantasy works as a vanishing point, imposing its perspective on everything before it.

Like the brilliance of Far-away Meadow, or the mystic's cloud of unknowing to which it bears a humorous resemblance, the imagined vastness of Hudson's Bay is unobstructed by language. As a result, thought founders, and instinctual calls take the place of articulate sound. At times however, our ears play tricks on us—"The seal yelp / On an ice cake. / It's not men by some mistake?"—and we fancy ourselves perhaps in the vicinity of an Over-Soul, or on the ridge of the Alps, our rational, disjunctive light of sense usurped by the power of Imagination. To be sure, there is always a companion presence, but even he is an incarnate ambiguity:

> His name's Joe,
> Alias John,
> And between what he doesn't know
> And won't tell
> About where Henry Hudson's gone,
> I can't say he's much help;
> But we get on.

Like the *absconditus* Henry Hudson, whose secret he may or may not share, this "French Indian Esquimau" with the double identity is a familiar, though sadly diminished, figure. As a final comment on the pretensions of unific intuition, Frost has cast him as a trapper, not of souls, but of furs—"off setting traps," which, true to tradition, he baits with his own person—"In one himself perhaps."

In sum, Hudson's Bay is a vacuous happy hunting ground, and Frost is suspicious of its infinite spaces. "Supreme merit," as he tells us in "Kitty Hawk," lies "in risking spirit / In substantiation," in sacrificing possibility for the sake of attainment. Despite the opaqueness of the medium, his ideals must be embodied and his intuitions expressed; and he leaves it to those he later labels "monists" to "end up in the universal Whole / As unoriginal as any rabbit." For the staunch individualist, absorption in this trackless au delà would constitute a defeat, a surrender to that dream of "easy gold" which he had already rejected in his early masterpiece "Mowing." There, "Anything more than the truth would have seemed too weak / To the earnest love that laid the swale in rows"—where swale is a trope for meaning, and rows for the formal constraints of language essential to its cultivation.

Nevertheless, Frost is far from impervious to the temptation he derides; for, as Poirier notes, he is at once morally committed to the necessities of form and "congenitally impatient with form and with limits." Thus, the scrupulous reservation in the last lines of "An Empty Threat" only intensifies the impression of sincere regret:

> Better defeat almost,
> If seen clear,
> Than life's victories of doubt
> That need endless talk talk
> To make them out.

It is the dilemma of a professed "anti-Platonist," vacillating between admiration for our daedal embodiments—for the assertion of form upon chaos—and malaise at their speciousness:

> At one extreme agreeing with one Greek
> At the other agreeing with another Greek. . . .
> A baggy figure, equally pathetic
> When sedentary and when peripatetic.
> ("The Bear")

II. *The Serpent's Tale*

This deep ambivalence toward the status of the Ideal appears most tellingly in Frost's poems about women, many of whom seem to transcend their situations even as they succumb to them. I think it was Williams who once said that he never passed a homely woman without thinking of Helen of Troy. In Frost's case, the fata morgana was Eve. One suspects that at the deepest level he had identified with Milton's Adam and considered himself somehow to blame for her plight. But his fixation has a literary etiology as well; for he found in the myth of the fall the necessary premise and justification for his thoughts on concealment. Once more, one might cite the theologians, who likewise needed a fall from paradise to sustain a doctrine of incarnation.

Fallen man resigns himself with reluctance to the necessity of concealment. Like the lion's carcase, our stubborn refusal to accept dissimilation breeds its swarm of regrets and desires, nourishing the poetic urge to create a language pure enough to present ourselves intact. This urge the myth explains as our residual awareness of an unfallen state. But Frost is no Gnostic, and his work is no post-lapsarian lament for lost perfection. He is willing to embrace his predicament, to entertain with earlier Stoics a notion of design. He even takes pleasure in the opportunity for self-exertion this predicament provides—a frankly pagan attitude which goes against his own Wordsworthian ideas on how poems are conceived, *sola gratia* so to speak, merrily sinning against the systematic logic of the *felix culpa*. But consistency was never Frost's hobgoblin. "You know how I am about chapter and verse," he wrote in a late letter to Victor Reichert, "somewhat irresponsible some would say. I went wielding the phrase *culpa felix* to my own purposes for a long time before I pinned myself down to what it may originally have meant in Church history."

As I have been suggesting, Frost's purposes were metaphysical as well as dramatic, and this equivocacy is reflected in his responses and allusions to the story of Eve—in its Miltonic no less than its biblical form. Since the extraterrestrial was no longer available, however, Frost was forced to localize the cosmic drama within the human part of the story. This he did by adopting the more readily camouflaged topos of the eternal feminine, or consort as muse. His heroines, like Joyce's women, remain unfallen; or rather, like Joyce's women, they remain elusive—now ideal, now vilified.

The clearest expression of this double configuration is to be found in the three "garden of Eden" poems from the section of *A Witness Tree* suggestively entitled "One or Two." The first, "The Most of It," reads like a meditation on Adam's life before Eve's creation. Everything within call is too exactly itself. There is the self, and there is the buck, the utterly other; but there is no mediating term, nothing to initiate the work of analogy and, therewith, the possibility of creative response. "Never Again Would Birds' Song Be the Same," the central leaf of the triptych, testifies to the difference made by Eve's arrival. Here the garden setting is more explicit, though Eve herself, like the ideal she represents, remains a phantasm, visible only through the eyes of the poem's grammatical subject, who is, like the poet or reader of poetry, a descendant of fallen Adam:

> He would declare and could himself believe
> That the birds there in all the garden round
> From having heard the daylong voice of Eve
> Had added to their own an oversound,
> Her tone of meaning but without the words.

In a sense, Frost's Eve is the positive counterpart of the empty threat of Hudson's Bay. As "inarticulate" as Williams's "Beautiful Thing" shimmering through the common fabric of *Paterson*, she moves in a world indifferent to names, made resonant, as the world in "The Most of It" was not, by her ineffable but musical presence. With her transforming power, she resembles too the transcendent creative principle solicited by Milton in his invocation to Urania, "The meaning, not the name, I call," a phrase echoed clearly in the fifth line of the poem. It seems to join there with the more diffused melody of Virgil's first eclogue ("Formosam resonare doces Amaryllida silvas") to mythologize the pathetic fallacy—or perhaps to mock Dr. Johnson's English translation ("And the wood rings with Amarillis' name"), for it is precisely because it is not denominative, not limed in an onomastic net, that Eve's "tone of meaning" is so all-pervasive.

Analogies to this familiar antithesis of pure and embodied meaning from the realm of poetic practice are suggested by Frost's essay, "The Figure a Poem Makes." Though the figuration is different, the alignment of the terms with revelation and concealment, or freedom and restraint, remains the same. To begin with, Frost likens the "sound" of a poem to "the gold in the ore," separable in theory though not in fact from the allegedly "inessential" contextual or verbal meaning. He then splits each of his terms in two and demonstrates the same interdependence between the halves—the conjunction of melody and meter (which recalls Milton's wedding of Voice and Verse in "At a Solemn Musick") standing to the ordering of sounds as the conjunction of "wildness" and "theme" stands to the ordering of ideas: "Just as the first mystery was how a poem could have a tune in such a straightness as meter, so the second mystery is how a poem can have wildness and at the same time a subject that shall be fulfilled." In each case, Frost conceives of the second term as imposing some limitation on the first, and the figures are all potentially metonymic for the relation of meaning and words.

In Frost's version, the fall of Eve, dramatized in the final poem of the group, will thus be represented as a fall into words. Such a development is anticipated at the end of "Never Again," where we see Eve bound for the first time by the notion of design—impressed, as it were, into the service of poetry: "And to do that to birds was why she came." The functional purpose imposed on her is less onerous perhaps than those borne by her literary sisters, but we feel it to be an outrage nonetheless. That Frost himself saw it this way is made clear by the placement of "The Subverted Flower," with its account of an actual, though abortive, impressment. I say placement, because we know from Thompson that the first draft of the poem was composed in Derry, more than thirty years before its inclusion in *A Witness Tree*. However, not only its position in the published sequence, but the parallels within the poem itself to the temptation scenes from Book Nine of *Paradise Lost* invite us to read it as a complement to the idealized vision of Eve presented in the sonnet.

Toward the end of "Never again," the venue shifts quietly from the garden to the woods—a topographical change that subtly shadows the succession of generations and, by implication, the definitive change of aeons. At the beginning of "The Subverted Flower," Eve has already wandered outside the "garden wall" into the fallen world. The characteristic response of that world is an act of shameful self-exposure—illustrative, as I hope will be clear by now, of that purer enthusiasm, which, whether it neglect the demands of decorum or the astringencies of metaphor, inevitably ends in confusion. As usual, the analogy between sexual and poetic fruition (or frustration) looms closest, and one can trace a probable connection between Frost's attitude toward the exhibitionist in the poem and the suggestion he makes in "The Constant Symbol" that poetry "be judged for whether any original intention it had has been strongly spent or weakly lost. . . . Strongly spent," he concludes, "is synonymous with kept"—and to keep is to keep concealed.

It is not his will but the progressive overtness of his behavior that finally costs Eve's assailant his human dignity. As initially presented with his command of the past subjunctive, he is not only forceful but controlled, and the courtly trope that signals his desire could as well be his contrivance as the poet's:

> She drew back; he was calm:
> 'It is this that had the power.'
> And he lashed his open palm
> With the tender-headed flower.

Only when he relinquishes these powers of speech and indirection does the impression of crudeness take over. The flower's seed is openly spilt before the girl—and by now the trope is clearly the poet's—till we are left with the naked thing, unaccommodated man at large:

> She looked and saw the worst.
> And the dog or what it was,
> Obeying bestial laws,
> A coward save at night,
> Turned from the place and ran.
> She heard him stumble first
> And use his hands in flight.
> She heard him bark outright.

This sudden revulsion, which expresses itself as flight to cover, is, Frost would suggest, no more than the rigor of natural law against whatever ignores its preservative order—a rigor akin to that which made Milton's Adam, on waking from his first debauch to apprehend his nakedness, and in it the reality of his transgression, cry: "Cover me ye pines / Ye cedars, with innumerable boughs / Hide me. . . ."

In Paradise the admission was consequential; in twentieth-century New England it is simply another instance of a well-established pattern. The question of the girl's role in the episode that brings about this backlash is accordingly the more interesting of the poem's two foci. At the end, of course, the man's degeneracy will redound upon her as well; yet for all the foam on her chin, she remains technically inviolate, like the Anadyomene in "Paul's Wife." In fact, the darkest implications of the poem only become apparent when we recognize that it is precisely her inviolability that brings the episode to its wretched consummation. There is nothing necessarily vicious about the man's original appeal. Rather, like the ambiguous central trope itself, it may be a prelude to fruitfulness. The degradation is gradual; and a closer look suggests that each step is precipitated by her failure to respond:

He smiled for her to smile,
But she was either blind
Or willfully unkind . . .
She was standing to the waist
In goldenrod and brake,
Her shining hair displaced.
He stretched her either arm
As if she made it ache
To clasp her—not to harm;
As if he could not spare
To touch her neck and hair.
'If this has come to us
And not to me alone—'
So she thought she heard him say;
Though with every word he spoke
His lips were sucked and blown
And the effort made him choke
Like a tiger at a bone.
She had to lean away.

Her uncertainty about his speech is particularly significant, as it seems to mirror Eve's initial wonder, when flattered by the Serpent in *Paradise Lost*, at hearing "language of Man pronounc't / By Tongue of Brute." Indeed, the word "brute" occurs four lines later in Frost; but the image here is inverted, for it is actually the girl's reception of the broken words that puts their status as language in question. Likewise, the demeaning description of his manner of speaking, which we tend to read as her impression, anticipates, rather than reflects, his dehumanization. Her "shining hair" is sufficient to suggest a mythical or ideal beauty, which to the man who fails to appreciate its inaccessibility is potentially pernicious. It is a cold allure, and, though embodied conventionally in an image of woman, strangely akin in its fatality to that foreignness that Stevens figured more portentously in his northern lights. It too can be seen as the serpent's nest, the poetic equivalent of evil's source, "responsible" for educing what Emerson has called the "tragedy of incapacity." Thus, the ominous opening words of the poem, "She drew back," reverberate, once the catastrophe is sure, in indictment of the girl:

A girl could only see
That a flower had marred a man,
But what she could not see
Was that the flower might be
Other than base and fetid:
That the flower had done but part,
And what the flower began
Her own too meager heart
Had terribly completed.

Of course, the very venture beyond the garden wall into the wild field of flowers was already an invitation to trouble. In Milton's poem, Adam reproaches Eve with "that strange / Desire of wand'ring," and throughout Frost's work the same figure is used to signify that "extra-vagant" longing for perfect freedom which if not restrained brings inevitable calamity. In first-person poems like "Into My Own," "The Sound of Trees," "An Empty Threat," "Stopping by Woods," "Come In," and many more, the poet himself wisely resists this longing—either by subordinating it as contrary to fact or relegating it to an indefinite future—but the women in the narratives are often less circumspect. The foreboding that one feels for the wife at the door in "Home Burial" or for the wife in "A Servant to Servants," who could "Drop everything and live out on the ground," is justified by the effect of the fugitive daughter's extravagance in "The Housekeeper," and more terribly by the fate of the woman in "The Hill Wife," who on a sudden "impulse" wanders from the loneliness of a barren marriage to a solitude beyond bound or bourn:

She rested on a log and tossed
  The fresh chips,
With a song only to herself
  On her lips.

And once she went to break a bough
  Of black alder.
She strayed so far she scarcely heard
  When he called her—

And didn't answer—didn't speak—
  Or return.

The emphasis on reticence here is typical; for it is their reluctance to compromise themselves with words that gives to so many of Frost's heroines the air of innocence or of nobility incommensurate with the meanness of their lives. By the same token, so long as she keeps silent, the girl in "The Subverted Flower" manages, despite the poet's indictment, to preserve a virginal purity. Unlike the woman in "The Hill Wife," however, she is alert to the call from home—to the repercussions of her absence if not of her presence—and so, in the end, as her passage from pregnant silence to sterile and profane speech makes manifest, her purity perishes while she survives. This passage is carefully anticipated by an awakening of her other senses, corresponding to the simultaneous decline in the man's speech and sight (note that at the end he stumbles and has to "use his hands in flight"). Thus, whereas she begins as if "blind" and with uncertain hearing ("she thought she heard him say"), in the second half of the poem she actively "looks," "sees," or "hears" in five successive sentences before—with Eve, her eyes how opened, and her mind how darkened—she finally accedes to her own voice:

And oh, for one so young
The bitter words she spit
Like some tenacious bit
That will not leave the tongue.
She plucked her lips for it,
And still the horror clung.
Her mother wiped the foam
From her chin, picked up her comb
And drew her backward home.

The irony is that this accession is itself a decline. Language here is compared to a "bit"—a restraint unknown to the "tiger at a bone," but alien too to Eve in Paradise. Just as the man's flight and submersion in animality were fit retribution for his presumptive self-exposure, so this figurative curb requites the young Eve for her provocative will to wander. Again, one is reminded of Milton's lines: "restraint she will not brook, / And left to herself, if evil thence ensue, / She first his weak indulgence will accuse." To complete the parallel only two things need be added: that her outburst merits pity as well as reproof, and that the responsibility for the evil wrought is mutual.

In *Paradise Lost*, where the ultimate responsibility for evil—for the struggle between passion and reason (or freedom and restraint)—lies outside the human sphere altogether, this second point is less salient. Given the reality of the angelic order, Milton was able to construct a noncommutative chain of influence with Eve, both tempted and tempting, in the center, and the Serpent and Adam at either end (though the fact that Adam initiates their dalliance after the fall doubtless anticipates a new reciprocity). For Frost, however, responsibility is confined to the human sphere, and temptation is thus viciously reciprocal from the start. If Adam is tempted, Eve must be the temptress, *and* vice versa. Although narrative devices and interpolated comments challenging the more obvious reading of the incident both tend to exonerate the man, his culpability is reestablished at a deeper level by the structural parallels between his progress and that of Milton's Tempter: for example, that both prosper through ambiguity until their intentions are realized, or that both then abandon human speech and withdraw. There is Miltonic precedent too for the way Frost aligns perception with speech and uses them to create the chiastic pattern in which the tempter's powers wane as the tempted's revive.

In the end, both masculine and feminine narrative lines circle back on themselves and interlock, until there is no way of telling whether the "subverted flower" of the title is the girl or the man, or simply the prospect of coalescence represented by the nameless flowers of Far-away Meadow. In place of that prospect, we are given a cage of moral ambiguities, reminiscent of the mirrored boxes of Hawthorne or Henry James, whose paradise-lost view of reality Frost shares, as he shares their fascination with emblems and their insistence on craftsmanship. He shares too their respectful impatience with Emerson, of whom he once wrote in criticism that "he could see the 'good of evil born' but he couldn't bring himself to say the evil of good born." If we accept the inaccessible girl with the shining hair as another embodiment of the beautiful thing, then the tale of degradation Frost here tells so powerfully brings that criticism to life.

Admittedly, this sequence of poems shows Frost at his most dialectical. For the most part, the women in the narrative poems have long since been requited for their kinship with Eve, and rather than obscure them further, Frost prefers to let them shine as they can. Despite their subject or "fallen" state—generally suggested by the bond of marriage or economic dependence—their speech and vision tend to remain chaste. At its extreme, this chastity threatens to become a cutting-off of all relation, as when the wife in "Home Burial," convinced of her husband's inner blindness, rejects his attempts at rapprochement and, in a line that recalls the conclusion of "Paul's Wife," forbids him to even mention their buried child:

> [He:] 'A man can't speak of his own child that's dead.'
> [She:] 'You can't because you don't know how to speak.'

But usually it is more benevolent; the granddaughter in "The Generations of Men" simply "using her eyes" to read the true profile of the stranger beside her, or the wife in "West-Running Brook" responding with a name to the gay wave in the stream on which her husband discourses. It is as though the poisoned fruit which destroyed their hopes had left their desires still pure, so that they themselves might become a source of nourishment. To be sure, the "sound of meaning" is now all but inaudible. As the wife "with a houseful of hungry men to feed" admits in "A Servant to Servants":

> There's nothing but a voice-like left inside
> That seems to tell me how I ought to feel,
> And would feel if I wasn't all gone wrong

—for she is as tightly confined by life's contingencies as her mad uncle was by his hickory cage. Yet for all their obscurity, they are never devious or indirect, but remain—if only by their passive endurance—priestesses of the ideal. One might call them hobbled transcendentalists, or remembering their potential balefulness, follow Frost's wrier lead and dub them witches, who though perched between two worlds—as the Pauper Witch of Grafton between her battling towns—must in the end, along with Eve, "come down from everything to nothing."

III. The Longest Way Round

The fall from Eden, like the fall of the tower of Babel, was a fall into confusion. The late poem "Directive," which ends with an invitation to "Drink and be whole again beyond confusion," has usually been read as Frost's program for a poetic sacrament that would carry us beyond our fallen state. However, the text bristles with warnings that should caution us against accepting its apparent assertions too quickly. Of these, the most striking is the allusion to St. Mark which immediately precedes the conclusion. The symbolic itinerary has been completed, and the poet has brought us to his rustic equivalent of the eternal source or waters of life:

> I have kept hidden in the instep arch
> Of an old cedar at the waterside
> A broken drinking goblet like the Grail
> Under a spell so the wrong ones can't find it,
> So can't get saved, as Saint Mark says they mustn't.

The patent reference is to the lines following the parable of the sower, in which Jesus is represented as expounding the necessity of concealment: "And he said unto them, Unto you it is given to know the mystery of the kingdom of God: but unto them that are without, all these things are done in parables: That seeing they may see, and not perceive; and hearing they may hear, and not understand. . . ." An allusion to the same passage in the roughly contemporaneous essay "A Romantic Chasm" makes it clear that for Frost the outsiders or "wrong ones" are those who lack the patience or dexterity to follow that constant "word-shift by metaphor" which keeps the language of poetry from ever meaning simply what it says.

Elitist postures can be exasperating, and it may be argued that "Directive," like the other blank-verse narratives in which the "I" dissociates itself didactically from the reader ("New Hampshire," "The White-Tailed Hornet,"), ends up imposing its purpose rather than "discovering" it the way Frost says a good poem should. Nevertheless, the prerogatives Frost is claiming here are not his own but, as in the tower of Babel letter where he identifies himself with God, those which the mystery of poetry enjoins on its initiates. Moreover, the very flagrance of his posing is our clue that it hides an underlying motive. As should be clear by now, Frost's allusions are far subtler than those flaunted vermiculations to which the "more difficult" modernists have accustomed us. In the case of "Directive," I believe the poetic target is Wordsworth's *Excur-*

sion, and the scriptural stalking-horse is intended simultaneously to publish and to disguise its presence.

This double function begins with the mention of the Grail; for Frost's "broken goblet" is meant to redeem the "useless fragment of a wooden bowl, / Green with the moss of years," which the Wanderer finds by the hidden spring in Book One of Wordsworth's poem. Wordsworth's fragment is "useless" in that the Wanderer will not drink from it. Instead it becomes the focus of the elegiac impulse that dominates this part of the work: a figure, more tentative than the Boy of Winander whom it anticipates, for the poetic self in the obligatory act of dying vicariously in order to be reborn. Echoes of the Wordsworthian dialectic are clearest in the opening lines of Frost's poem, where explicitly elegiac gestures—unless read tongue-in-cheek as the subsequent lapse in diction invites—prepare us for an excursion along the *via negativa*:

Back out of all this now too much for us,
Back in a time made simple by the loss
Of detail, burned, dissolved, and broken off
Like graveyard marble sculpture in the weather,
There is a house that is no more a house
Upon a farm that is no more a farm
And in a town that is no more a town.

From *Lycidas* to Stevens's dirge for the tropical planter in *Notes toward a Supreme Fiction*, such secularized paradox is at the heart of the sublime tradition in English and American poetry. Frost, however, is a poet of "counter-love," for whom the supreme fiction has not to be imagined but discovered—and not in ostentatious isolation, but working "whether together or apart" in inevitable league with others. He thus revises the Wordsworthian itinerary by putting the fragment to use. To speak in parables, the bowl outside Wordsworth's ruined cottage resembles the corn of wheat that must die in order to bear; the broken goblet in Frost, like the faithful servant's talent, is a counter for pragmatic exchange.

Like the Gospel parables themselves, "Directive" can be read in two ways. It can be interpreted point for point (allegorically); or it can be construed in its entirety as illustrating a single conviction (the way form criticism insists Jesus' parables were originally meant to be taken). The latter approach suggests an alternative to the sacramental reading of the poem; for search as we may, the only integrating conviction—the only common term between Frost's poem and experience—is the certainty of fragmentation. That is, read as parable, the poem invites us to achieve the only wholeness possible by becoming reconciled to the imperfect. It offers us a road—later called a ladder—that "may seem as if it should have been a quarry," glacial etchings in the rock, cellar holes, a field eroded to the size of a harness gall, and, in its midst, a "children's house of make believe," with some "shattered dishes" and the broken goblet used to draw the water. These analects become more meaningful when read with an eye to their individual histories—especially in Frost's own poems. Thus, if we move to an "allegorical" reading, the "ladder road" recalls the two-pointed ladder of metaphor that points toward heaven in "After Apple Picking"; the glacier "that braced his feet against the Arctic Pole" is a manifestation or emissary of the same elusive unnameable that haunts the polar mind in "An Empty Threat"; and the traces it leaves on the ledges run "southeast northwest" by reason of the same imaginative westering that makes all "zest / To materialize / By on-penetration" run in the same direction in "Kitty Hawk."

This fragmentary style of reference seems especially fitting in a poem that would vindicate process. As Frost writes in "The Prerequisites," "A poem is best read in the light of all the other poems ever written. We read A the better to read B. . . . Progress is not the aim, but circulation." Moreover, his determination in "The Lesson for Today," to "take [his] incompleteness with the rest," shows that he recognized the limitations of the approach. And yet a close explicator could still argue that the aim of "Directive" is to transcend and so perfect its fragments: that the counterplot I have been tracing is only its *praeparatio evangelica*. The final question is thus whether "the road there," so similar to the dialectical path of the quest romance, leads to some determinate source, or whether our gift at journey's end is just the preacher's vexing wisdom. Does one really come back to the original word or only to another departure?

The answer hinges on our reading of the final phrase, "beyond confusion." The word "confusion" occurs frequently in Frost's work, where it usually connotes disorder and defeat. The reference to the confusion of Babel in Frost's letter to Cox, for example, and the description of "the background in hugeness and confusion shading away from where we stand into black and utter chaos" in his letter to *The Amherst Student* both depend on this usage. If this is the only sense intended in "Directive," then the final line exceeds without question Frost's own definition of a poem's end as "a momentary stay against confusion." The invitation to "drink and be whole again" would be a call to unmediated vision—a call to ascend from Babel not by the two-pointed ladder of metaphor, but directly. But "confusion" may have another meaning, as exemplified in the final line of Frost's early poem "Rose Pogonias:"

We raised a simple prayer
  Before we left the spot,
That in the general mowing
  That place might be forgot;
Or if not all so favored,
  Obtain such grace of hours,
That none should mow the grass there
  While so confused with flowers.

Here Frost, the student of Latin poetry, is punning on the etymologically prior sense of blending or fusing together in the manner of Milton, for whom the original sense of a Latinate word often points back toward an unfallen world ("with mazy error," "sapient fruit"). Allowing that the same etymological play is active in the final line of "Directive," Frost's invitation to wholeness is qualified by an antithetical intimation that the only wholeness or health we can know is to be free from the illusory ideal of perfection—to accept, with full knowledge of its inadequacy, the wisdom of concealment and restraint.

A similar ambiguity is active in Job's lines from *A Masque of Reason*, written about the same time:

Yet I suppose what seems to us confusion
Is not confusion, but the form of forms,
The serpent's tail stuck down the serpent's throat,
Which is the symbol of eternity.

One thinks in reading them of Coleridge's remarks to Joseph Cottle (7 March 1815) that "the common end of all *narrative*, nay, of *all* Poems, is to convert a series into a *Whole*: to make those events, which in real or imagined History move on a strait Line, assume to our Understandings a *circular* motion—the snake with its Tail in its Mouth." Yet presumably there is an undercurrent in Frost's version that links it to the unconverted and unconverting circles of Emerson's "Uriel," the "greatest Western [i.e., American] poem yet," as Job goes on immediately to say. My own conclusion is that within the contest of Frost's poem Job is a weak reader whose word must be completed by that of his wife. (Thyatira, after the New Testament city famed for its witches), who knows the world as the "hard place" where man "can try himself / And find out whether he is any good." For Frost, the "tail stuck down the serpent's throat" is the tale Eve swallowed in the garden, the false promise of a prematurely perfected vision. In eternity, perhaps, Uriel's cry will be heard, the series will be converted, and the circle will focus to a single point. In the meantime, that symbol remains a figure; for the fruit that brought the dualities of good and evil to Eve and her descendants also brought duplicity—the coats of skins—and metaphor to bind them together.

"There is throughout nature," wrote Emerson, "something mocking, something that leads us on and on. . . . We live in a system of approximations. Every end is prospective of some other end." "Directive" is a parable of hermeneutic circulation. True, the search for understanding must begin with our initial faith that some sense is there to be discovered: that *la dive bouteille* when pieced together will not be found empty. But what if we find it half-empty? And if so, should we call it half-empty or half-full? That, to recall a teacher's words, was the oven bird's dilemma—the "diminished thing" and what to make of it. The traditional reading of "Directive" approaches it from the half-full side, as a parable of sufficiency, an affirmation of the power of poetry to embody real meanings in which the properly initiated may happily come to share. It makes the hermeneutical circle a sacramental *temenos*, a magic precinct where source and terminus coalesce. But it misses the critical ambiguity. A reading that achieves its source can only be an icon or an artifact. Frost's sovereign principle of metaphor is, on the contrary, a machine for displacement, and every attained meaning must redeem a correspondent loss.

Late in his career, Frost recounted the history of his own life-long engagement to this hard truth in a narrative poem, "The Discovery of the Madeiras," and placed it at the end of "One or Two." For all its apparent urbanity, the story of the fugitive lovers has the terrible rigor of a sphinx's riddle; for the interpolated tale of the slave couple sacrificed on the high seas is really a parable of the lovers' own fate. Their responses to the oracle differ, however: she withdraws from its harshness, and, constant to some incommunicable ideal, dies "of thought" on a nameless island; he, more bold, dares to conceive it, and so sails on, having buried her there and written, as marriage lines, an epitaph. In the end, his gesture is naturally misread; the island is named for him, not for her. But that, as Frost tells us is "neither here nor there"; for history too is a choice of figments.

LAURENCE PERRINE

"Robert Frost's 'The Hill Wife': Evidence, Inference, and Speculation in the Interpretation of Fiction"

College Literature, Winter 1983, pp. 1–15

> "The art of reading poetry is the art of taking hints when hints are hinted and not taking them when they aren't hinted." (Robert Frost in a reading at Berkeley, California, 1965)

In this paper I have two goals: one specific, and one general. Specifically, I wish to dispute a widespread, and I believe incorrect, reading of Robert Frost's poem "The Hill Wife." More generally, I wish to explore the boundaries between the legitimate and the illegitimate in the interpretation of fiction: or, more precisely, to distinguish between what can be known, what can be inferred, what represents idle speculation, and what must be rejected as misinterpretation. Admittedly the boundaries between these four areas are not hard and fast. They are not like political boundaries dividing state from state on a map, but like those indeterminate divisions on a spectrum or rainbow, in which the areas being divided flow into each other. The areas are nevertheless definable. What can be known rests upon incontrovertible evidence; legitimate inference rests upon sufficient evidence to outweigh contrary suggestion; speculation rests upon no evidence at all; misinterpretation is contrary to evidence. There may be disagreements, of course, about what constitutes evidence. "The Hill Wife" provides a good subject for demonstration, first because, though it is relatively short, its structural division into five separated sections poses special problems. Many interpretive questions have to do with what goes on outside the "frame" of a story; and this one has five frames.

Let me begin by noting two differences between literature and life.

(1) People in life are real. They are tied to past and present by an infinite number of historical and social relationships. What is presently unknown about them can often be discovered by investigation. Their ancestors can be traced by genealogical investigation, their credit standings by institutional investigation, the state of their internal organs by medical examination. People in fiction, on the other hand, exist only on paper. What can be known about them is only what can be known or inferred from the author's words set down on paper. Their ties to past and present are finite and limited. If a work of fiction says nothing about a character's ancestors, that character in a sense has no ancestors.

That last statement, however, represents an extremist position. A more moderate, more supportable position, is only that we can know nothing about his ancestors. Let me draw an analogy from art. A painting is surrounded by a frame. The function of the frame is to separate its subject from all those infinite relationships that it would have in real life—to announce, as it were, that this *is* a work of art, not a segment of reality. Leonardo da Vinci's *Mona Lisa* pictures the face, neck, bust, arms and hands of a woman. She wears a dress of brown material. Her hair is parted in the middle and falls over her shoulders on either side of her face. We are not shown her legs or her back. The observer assumes, however, that she *has* legs and a back. He assumes also that her dress covers her backside as well as her front and that she is not bald on the back of her head. These are warrantable inferences to be drawn from the painting. On the other hand, such questions as, Does she have a mole on her left shoulder blade? and What color are her shoes? are meaningless. Any assumption we make about what is *not* in the painting must be the natural continuation of something that *is* in the painting.

Of course certain kinds of art do *attempt* to create an illusion of reality. In a motion picture the buildings along the village street may actually be photographs of pasteboard fronts, but we are meant to regard them as solid buildings, and an interpretation which declared that the bank robber went with drawn revolver through a pasteboard front and emerged at the rear of the MGM lot would be a distortion of the "reality" created by the movie. If we turn the painting of Mona Lisa around, we find only boards and blank canvas, no dress, no shoulder blades, and certainly no mole. Art, literature, and film, in short, create fictional worlds. These worlds in some respects may simulate the real world, but they differ from the real world in being limited, finite, self-contained. Any inferences drawn about those fictional worlds must be extensions of evidence actually depicted in them. Their only "reality" is that which they themselves create.

(2) A second distinction between literature and life is that anything found in the work of literature—if it is an achieved

work—has been put there by the writer's design. We should assume that it is there for a purpose, not by accident, that it has some relation to the rest of the fictional world. Sometimes, especially in great work, it may have more relevance than the writer consciously realized; but, even in minor work, it is not there for no reason at all. The same is not true of any detail from a segment cut off from the continuum that constitutes real life. If in real life, a smashed flower pot is found in the potting-shed of the house in which a man has been murdered in his bed, there is probably no relation between the two events. In a murder mystery, however, if a smashed flower pot is mentioned as having been found in the potting-shed, we can assume that it has some connection with the murder. It is a clue, even if only a false clue to cast suspicion on the wrong person. It is there for a purpose.

"The Hill Wife"[1] is the story of the progressive mental break-down of a young wife living with her young farmer husband in an isolated hill district. The story is told in five sections, each with its own title. In two of the sections the speaker is the wife herself; in the other three it is the poet acting as omniscient narrator. The five sections are spaced in time, each presenting a small episode or sample of the wife's life and behavior. It is as if a move director had shot a continuous film of the woman's life and then had severely edited it, cutting out all but five brief portions, which he then pieced together to represent the whole.

In section I, the wife comments to her husband on their loneliness. In the absence of people they have turned to birds for companionship, and feel sadder than they ought to when the birds depart on their southern migration in autumn, and gladder than they ought to when the birds return in spring. The wife knows that this is no real companionship, and no adequate substitute for human friendship, for the birds care nothing about them. The birds do not really fly round the house to "say good-by" before leaving, and when they return their concern is only with their own lives—mating and nesting and finding food—they do not reciprocate the feelings of the wife and her husband.

In section II the poet, or narrator, tells us of a habit the young couple have formed when they return late at night to their lonely house after a journey begun earlier in the day. First they rattle the key in the lock so as to give any intruder—human, animal, or bird—warning and a chance to get away before they enter. They then leave the front door wide open and light the lamp inside before closing the door.

The "house fear" exhibited in this section represents a movement toward irrational behavior. Fear of the dark is common among children, but these two are adults. If the door is locked when they arrive home, it is unlikely that anything would be inside large enough to be dangerous. A thief would have looted the house by daylight and not lurked in the dark. A bird or small animal down the chimney would present no real danger. The precautions they take are probably not unique among people living in isolated districts, but they hardly represent the norm.

In section III the wife is again the speaker, and her reactions this time are paranoid. A tramp has been to the house and asked for food. The wife is speaking to her husband after the tramp's departure. She is worried by the smile that appeared on the tramp's face when they gave him bread. At least she interpreted it as a smile, though her asking her husband for confirmation and her exclamation "I was sure!" really indicate uncertainty. Still, the title of the section (supplied by the poet) is "The Smile," and it would be natural for the tramp to smile out of gratitude for receiving the bread. Significantly, this rational explanation is almost the only she doesn't give. Instead, she interprets the smile as one of mockery, and advances wildly improbable reasons why the tramp might have mocked them: because they are poor (the tramp is poor), because he might have seized the bread instead of allowing them to give it to him, because they are married, or because they are very young—and he has a vision of them old and dead. The last two lines reveal how disproportionate her fears have grown. What conceivable reasons could the tramp have for watching them from the woods down the road? They have nothing that he could want, and, if they did (by her own reasoning), he might just have seized it and walked off with it.

Section IV reveals that the irrational fears manifested in sections II and III are rooted deep in her psyche. They find expressions in an obsessive dream—a dream expressing fear not of the wildly improbable but of the impossible. Finding no words adequate to express her terror of the dark pine tree outside their bedroom, which, when the wind blows, brushes against the window as if trying to undo the latch and get in, she has a recurrent nightmare in which she imagines it succeeding.

What does she dream it will do when it enters? We are not told. We know only that it is something dreadful and presumably requires the use of "hands"—her or the poet's metaphor for the needle-clusters that brush across the glass. Kidnap her perhaps? Rape her? Strangle her? Any of these, or any two, or all three possibly—but here we are in the realm of speculation, for the poem provides no evidence. We do not even know, indeed, whether the horrible deed is done to *her only* or to *them*. The argument for the former is external: nightmare fears are most often personal; the argument for the latter is internal: her fears in section III, like her anxieties in section I, concern the two of them, not herself alone.

In the final section, the hill wife, having little to occupy her in the house, follows her husband for company at his work. Idly she sits on a log and tosses wood chips, or goes to the trees to break off a bough of black alder. Absent-spiritedly she strays almost beyond the sound of his voice, and then, when he calls, instead of answering, she suddenly runs and hides in the thick fern growths. The husband searches everywhere, but never finds her, dead or alive. "Sudden and swift and light" the ties of love and marriage give away, and the husband learns of "finalities" other than death—the finalities of an ended relationship.

In my discussion so far, except for speculation about the content of the hill wife's recurrent dream, I have stuck to what can be known about the poem or what can be almost certainly inferred. I now wish to illustrate further the processes of knowing, inferring, and speculating by addressing specific questions to the poem.

1. *What is the geographical locale of the poem?* The setting is hill country, sparsely populated, its scattered farms too far apart to allow for easy neighborly visits between households. It is "wild" country. Such farms as exist are small and difficult to cultivate, and what level patches there are must be cleared and kept clear of trees. Indeed, this is marginal farm land. The wife and her husband are poor, as she reveals in section III; and the husband does all the farm work himself—he has no hired help. Though there is a road past the farm, few travel it, and even fewer stop—the tramp's doing so in section III is an exception that makes a notable impact on the hill wife. All of this may be known or legitimately inferred from the internal evidence of the poem.

If we examine the poem in its context in Frost's work, we can be even more specific. It appeared in his third book, *Mountain Interval*. The immediately preceding book had been entitled *North of Boston*. The ensuing book would be *New Hampshire*, whose title poem is an encomium to that state, by a poet "At present . . . living in Vermont." The poems in *North of Boston* and *Mountain Interval* all belong, or could easily belong, to rural New England. Where place names are mentioned, they almost invariably are in New Hampshire or Vermont.[2] From this evidence, which exists outside the poem, we can infer with some assurance that the setting is northern New England, probably Vermont or New Hampshire.

2. *What is the poem's setting in time?* Since the poem is neither futuristic nor "historical" in genre, it can with almost complete assurance be located within the confines of Frost's own New England experience preceding its composition. In a copy of *Mountain Interval*, in the Library of Congress, Frost has indicated the actual year of composition for each of the five sections of the poem: 1905, 1906, 1913, 1916, 1913.[3] Since the first section introduces the theme of loneliness central to the poem, and since Frost first moved from urban Massachusetts to a farm in New Hamsphire in 1900, it seems reasonable to perceive the poem as set roughly between the years 1900–1905, though an earlier date is possible.

What was the state of technological culture in 1905? Automobiles had entered American life but were rarely seen in the isolated hill regions of Vermont and New Hamsphire, if for no other reason than lack of good roads and service stations.[4] Telephones were in general use in populated areas but were only beginning to become available in rural areas.[5] Electric lighting was common in cities but almost unknown in rural areas.[6] In short, technological history suggests that we are dealing with an essentially pre-automobile, pre-telephone, and pre-electric-light culture.

The poem supports these assumptions. If automobiles had been available, visits from kinsfolk and friends might have been common: the farm would have been less "lonely." The wife does not alleviate this loneliness by making telephone calls to friends, and, when she disappears at the end of the poem, the husband does not place calls to neighbors, kinsfolk, or police; instead he "looked everywhere" and he "asked her mother's house / Was she there." When the couple returns to their dark house in section II they do not flip a switch or "turn on" a light, they *light* the lamp, probably an oil–kerosene lamp.

3. *How old are the hill wife and her husband and how long have they been married?* In the middle section of the poem, the wife imagines that the tramp may have mocked at them "for being wed,/Or being very young." The two ideas, by their juxtaposition, seem associated in her mind. In the first section they were married and even younger. The first section occurs in the fall, for the wife's words are occasioned by the departure of the birds on their southern migration. But she mentions also the previous spring, when the birds had returned from the South, and she seems to speak of the sadness and gladness felt by herself and her husband over these goings and comings, at least the goings, as emotions they have experienced more than once. A legitimate inference is that they have been married, at the beginning of the poem, for at least half a year, more probably for a whole year, and possibly longer. According to Census Bureau estimates, the median age of females at their first marriage in rural areas of New England in 1910 was 21.9.[7] Since the wife refers to herself and her husband in section III as being "very" young, it is a legitimate inference that theirs was a teen-age marriage. A further inference is that neither of the two has had much education. The wife has apparently no intellectual or craft-hobby interests to keep her in the house when her work is done. It is unlikely that their house has many books.

4. *How much time does the action of the poem cover?* Time references in the poem are vague. In no section of the poem is there any reference to snow. In section I, however, it is fall, for the birds are migrating. In section II the weather has turned cold, for husband and wife return to a house with the "fire gone gray." When they left it, it was cold enough to justify leaving a warm fire burning in the grate, which has subsequently gone out. Neither section III nor section IV contains any indication of time of year except the negative one that in III the road is passable, not mired in mud nor drifted deep in snow. Section V is set in the spring, for the husband is plowing, the weather is mild enough for the wife to stroll after him and sit on a log without discomfort, and the fern is thick enough to hide in. On grounds of aesthetic symmetry, a reader tends to assume that the five sections of the poem are more or less equally spaced in time, though no internal evidence proves this, and sections II and IV refer to habitual or recurrent events rather than particular ones. What are we left with then? With a certainty that the poem begins in the fall and ends in the spring; with knowledge that section III, in which the wife describes her husband and herself as "very" young, cannot be too far removed in time for section I; and with an aesthetic probability that section III occurs approximately midway between sections I and V. On this evidence the time elaspsed between section I and section V is not less than half a year and probably not more than a year and a half. Of these alternatives the latter is more likely, for it would put the tramp's visit in summer rather than in winter, would allow more time for key-rattling rituals after distant trips (which cannot have been frequent) to become habitual, and would make more plausible the psychic distance traveled by the wife between her relative sanity in section I and her mental breakdown in section V. Though these are fragile inferences, they are more than mere speculation.

5. *What happened to the hill wife?* This is the first question asked by most readers after first reading the poem. "Did she go crazy?" "Did she commit suicide?" Well, yes, she went "crazy" in a sense—but the connotations of the word, suggesting raving lunacy, leave me acutely uncomfortable. "Insane," "psychotic," "mad"—somehow all the accepted terms, though preferable to "crazy," leave me dissatisfied. But certainly her disappearance represents the completion of the hill wife's mental breakdown. On sudden impulse, without plan or forethought, without suitcase, change of clothing, food, or money, she flees from her lonely life on the farm. Did she commit suicide? We cannot know. She may as easily have plunged into the forest, tripped over a root, and drowned in a pool. She may have died from hunger or exposure. She may have been picked up by a stranger and carried off. But all this is mere speculation, for no evidence in the poem allows even an inference: the wife's story ends with her disappearance. A fictional rather than a real person, she literally has no existence beyond her disappearance. Even here, however, though all speculation is critically meaningless, some speculations are less justifiable than others, for they are not only without evidence, they defy evidence. The wife's progress during the poem has been steadily downward. By every aesthetic and logical consideration, any extrapolation of her progress beyond the frame of the poem should continue downward. It would be misinterpretation to suppose that she found her way to some strange village, got a job there, and gradually made a healthy adjustment to a new reality. Her fear of strangers, her mental derangement, and above all, the design of the poem all testify against any such conclusion. But in any case, it is impossible to extrapolate accurately from the evidence.

6. *To what extent does the husband share his wife's loneliness and fears?* In section 1 the wife assumes that her

husband fully shares her feelings about the birds. It is unlikely that a wife so sensitive to her own feelings could be completely mistaken about her husband's, and indeed there is no reason to believe that he is not also saddened by the departure of the birds in the fall and gladdened by their return in the spring. She would not make such an assumption unless he had expressed such feelings, at least to the extent of concurring in hers. But, since she is the one who brings up the subject of their over-concern, it is probable that his loneliness is less intense than hers. With all the farm work to do, he has less time to brood on their solitude. Time does not lie heavy on his hands.

Section II, since it is spoken by the poet as omniscient narrator, does not present the problem of gauging the speaker's understanding, but it does present the problem of gauging his meaning. "Always," he tells us, "this they learned. . . ." The adverb "Always" begins both the first and second lines, and the phrase "they learned" is used three times in this section, once at the end of a line, twice at the beginnings of lines. These emphatic repetitions give the short lyric an almost obsessive quality. "They learned to rattle the lock and key . . . They learned to leave the house door wide / Until they had lit the lamp inside." The author tells us emphatically that "They" learned, but he does not tell us how they learned, and, in fact, when we examine the lines again, we must notice something unusual about the pronoun "They." Surely, the author does not mean us to believe that unlocking the front door was a collaborative enterprise or that it took two of them to light the lamp? Is it not more likely that *he* learned "to rattle the lock and key" and to leave the door open and light the lamp while *she* waited outside until it was lit? What *they* learned was that this procedure was the most effective way to minimize *her* fears. Whether he to any degree shared these fears may be a matter of speculation, but we find it hard to believe that he shared *her* fear in section III that the tramp may be watching from the woods, and we know that he does not share her fear in section IV that the pine tree will get inside the house. In short, the *fears* expressed in the poem are primarily if not entirely hers.

7. *What causes the hill wife's breakdown?* The poem is quite explicit about the immediate cause. Her breakdown is the effect of loneliness acting upon a sensitive nature. The first section, entitled "Loneliness," expresses the wife's concern that she and her husband rely too much on birds for companionship. And even the birds disappear in the winter. In section II the couple return to "the lonely house" from a distant errand or visit. In section V the poet plainly states: "It was too lonely for her there, / And too wild." Loneliness is the chief cause. Loneliness alone, however, does not produce such swift dramatic changes in stable natures. The husband is as alone as she, but he does not go mad. There are contributing causes. The wife has too little to occupy her hands and her mind. There is little work to do about the house. There is no child to care for. The wife is young, uneducated, and without intellectual or creative interests. When her domestic chores are finished, she has nothing to do. Yet even these additional circumstances are insufficient explanation. Frost's main concern in the poem is in tracing the effects of a "wild" and "lonely" environment on a sensitive and unstable personality, not in probing the deep causes of that instability. But he does provide one additional clue. After the wife's disappearance the husband searches "everywhere" and asks "at her mother's house / Was she there." The poet, without a change in meter, could as easily have had him ask "at her parents' house" or "at her father's house." His choice of "mother's house" implies that the wife has been brought up in a one-parent household. How long the father has been absent, and whether he died, divorced, or simply "went off," can be matter only for speculation; there is nothing in the poem to *prove* that he has not departed recently, perhaps even *after* his daughter's marriage. But here we apply the principle that nothing appears in an achieved work of art except by the author's design. If the poet chose the word *mother's* instead of *parents'*, he did so for a reason, and the only reason that suggests itself is to provide some explanation for the wife's instability. The inference is therefore warranted that the father has been missing for some time. Mental instability usually has its roots in childhood.

We now come to the question where I wish to dispute the majority opinion.

8. *Is the husband significantly to blame for his wife's breakdown?* If this question is raised during a group discussion, the answer is almost invariably a chorus of "Yesses." And almost invariably that modern cliché is dragged in about "a breakdown in communication." "He does not communicate with her." "She cannot tell him about her recurrent nightmare." A bevy of published critics swell the chorus. "The psychological analysis . . . hinges on the growing failure of the man to sympathize with the woman's accumulated psychosis" (Lawrance Thompson).[8] The husband's "neglect must take a share of the blame for her collapse" (Elaine Barry).[9] "Because it was her husband who brought her there, leaves her all day, and fails to understand and alleviate the terror of her life, he becomes one of the forces, perhaps the chief one, which locks her inside herself" (Linda Ray Pratt).[10] "The hill wife spoke her delicate irrational feminine thoughts to a man who was dumb to her need of his insight" (Elizabeth Shepley Sergeant).[11] The poem is "a miniscule novel or drama, psychologically controlled, portraying the dissatisfactions and tensions of a love affair" (F. X. Shea, S. J.).[12]

Lack of communication, failure of sympathy. But where in the poem are these failures indicated? If the husband does not speak to his wife's fears, it is because he is never given a chance. Sections I and III, both of which show the wife communicating freely to her husband, are both written according to the dramatic monologue convention in which the reader hears the words of only one speaker in a dialogue. It is called a "dramatic" monologue precisely because two speakers are involved. It is called a "monologue" because only one of them is heard. Yet section I of Frost's poem clearly implies previous conversation on the subject of birds. And if the husband does not respond to his wife, in this section or in section III, it is because the poem ends before he has a chance to. In section IV we are *not* told that the wife could not or did not tell her husband about her dream, we are told only that she could not find adequate words (a saying "dark enough") to describe the depth of her terror, and we are "told" (here the implication is strong enough for certainty)[13] that he was not afraid of the tree, either sleeping or waking. We can neither know nor infer whether or not she told him about her dream or what comfort he offered or did not offer if she did. I return to my analogy between the structure of this poem and that of a movie made by editing out all but five brief portions from a continuous film of the hill wife's life. Those parts of that film which reveal what the husband may or may not have said all lie on the cutting room floor. For the movie-goer, they do not exist. They are not part of the presented fictional world.[14]

But not only is the lack-of-communication, lack-of-concern theory unbased on evidence, it goes against evidence. That evidence exists, first and foremost, in how the wife speaks to her husband in sections I and III. In both she speaks openly and freely, without fear that her remarks will be scorned, scoffed at, or received in silence. There is no slightest hint in her tone of resentment, blame or alienation. On the contrary she includes him in a harmonious community of two, indicated by her use of the plural pronoun. In section I it is "we" who are too glad for the birds' return and too sad at their departure. In section III it is "we" who gave the tramp bread, and "us" whom the tramp "mocked" for being "poor" or "being wed" or "being very young." Nothing she says suggests any division between them.

Nor do their actions imply any division between them. Section I implies that the husband at least incurred and probably shared in her sorrow and joy over the departures and returns of the birds. Section II shows that he does what he can to mitigate her "house fear" when they return home after dark. Section III suggests that they were at one in answering the tramp's request by offering bread. In section IV, though he sleeps soundly while she has nightmares, they lie side by side on the same bed,[15] and her dream-fears may as plausibly concern what the pine might do to *them* as to *her* alone. In section V, because she is lonely in the house by herself, she follows her husband around at his work, simply to be in his company. In this section, also, the husband is given his one chance in the poem to say something, and he does. When she strays beyond his sight, he calls to her. When she does not answer, he goes to look for her. What more can one ask? An unconcerned husband would shrug his shoulders and say to himself, "Oh, she'll be back"—and go on working.

The most elaborate analysis of this poem in terms unfavorable to the husband is made by Frank Lentricchia in his recent book, *Robert Frost: Modern Poetics and the Landscape of Self.*[16] Lentricchia begins sensibly enough by observing that the poem's fragments "hint at complex troubles too deeply buried in the psyche to be examined." But then, ignoring his own *caveat*, he proceeds to examine them. "A latent paranoia, aggravated and exposed perhaps by the sexual shock of marriage, shows itself in the hill wife's dreams." He is surely right about the latent paranoia, but its aggravation by "the sexual shock of marriage" is sheer speculation, as Lentricchia betrays in his qualifying "perhaps." "In Part I," he goes on to say, "the wife remarks on the cleavage of the human world from the natural world. Then, with the natural world as a reflector of what ought to be, she suggests implicitly another, more disturbing cleavage within her relationship with her husband." In Part I the wife certainly remarks that the birds are preoccupied with their own affairs and unconcerned with the human world, but any indication that she takes the natural world "as a reflector of what ought to be" or that "she suggests implicitly another, more disturbing cleavage within her relationship with her husband" comes out of Lentricchia's own mind rather than out of the poem. Lentricchia then surmises, "It is more likely the absence of deep, empathetic perception from her husband's end of the relationship, rather than alienation from nature, that is at the root of her trouble." A number of things may be said about this statement: first, her complaint about nature, if she has one, is not that she is alienated from it (she is glad when the birds are around) but that it is alienated from her (a fancy way for saying that birds are unconcerned with human lives and therefore can't substitute for people); second, "the root of her trouble," as Lentricchia has himself already confessed in his statement about "latent paranoia," predates her marriage and lies probably somewhere in her childhood; third, though Lentricchia adroitly protects himself with that indeterminate adjective "deep," the "absence of . . . empathetic perception from her husband's end of the relationship" has no evidential basis in the poem.

The centerpiece for Lentricchia's reading is the dream in section IV, which he gives a Freudian interpretation. "The 'dark pine' is decidedly phallic and the house is a representation of the female genitals, suggesting what in particular about marriage troubles this young woman." If one is sympathetic with Freudian analysis, this interpretation may sound quite plausible, but only because Lentricchia has prepared us for it with his proposal of "sexual shock" at marriage, which we have seen to be sheer speculation, and with his suggestion that the "root" of her trouble is her husband's lack of empathetic perception, which is contrary to evidence. Lentricchia had introduced both notions with qualifiers like "perhaps" and "more likely," but now he takes them as givens and connects them into a pattern which sounds plausible because it *is* a pattern. A major objection, in addition to the absence of evidential support, is that Frost himself was not sympathetic with Freudian analysis. In "New Hampshire" he reports with comic scorn his conversation "with a New York alec / About the new school of the pseudo-phallic."[17] If one insists on interpreting the dream symbolically, one should do so in terms of the poem itself rather than in terms of unsupported hypotheses and an external speculative system which the poet himself despised. The pine tree may be taken to represent the natural wildness of the place—that wildness which the hill wife so fears in section II and which the poet names in section V. The house represents the human and domestic. In her dream the hill wife expresses her dread that this lonely wilderness may destroy her human identity and her domestic establishment.

But, declares Elaine Barry, the husband "is insensitive . . . to his wife's incipient breakdown."[18] Says Sidney Cox, "The husband might have had more feelers out."[19] It cannot be denied that the husband is taken by surprise:

> Sudden and swift and light as that
>   The ties gave,
> And he learned of finalities
>   Besides the grave.

No doubt a more perceptive husband might have foreseen his wife's breakdown, but even if he had, what could have been done . . . ? Could he take her to a psychiatrist? There were no psychiatrists then in Vermont and New Hampshire, and, if there had been, the husband could not have afforded them. Could he sell the farm and set up shop in the village? Easily said but not easily done by, say, a 20-year-old with less than a high school education who had probably known no occupation but farming in his life. But even as we pass this minimal judgment on the husband, let us examine once more the final section. It is related by the poet as omniscient narrator. He not only tells us what happens in it but generalizes about causes: "It was too lonely for her there, / And too wild." He titles the section "The Impulse," indicating that the wife's final action was indeed a spur-of-the-moment, unpremeditated move. In the last two lines of the section, he moves, for the first time in the poem, into the husband's mind and tells us what the husband learned. But what about the penultimate two lines, the lines that tell us the ties gave "Sudden and swift and light as that"? They occur as the poet is moving *into* the husband's mind but before he is demonstrably *in* it. They thus occupy an ambiguous position and seem to describe the final event from both the husband's *and* the poet's point of view. For *both* it was "sudden and swift and light as that." But how can this be? Has not the poet throughout the poem been showing us the *gradual* breakdown of the wife? Indeed he has. Does he not contradict himself, then, to call it "sudden"? Indeed he does. But it is a meaningful paradox and illuminates human nature. It reminds me, for instance, of how many mornings I can tie my shoes with a frayed shoestring and yet be startled when it breaks. In other words, the husband's failure to foresee the wife's insanity in her irrational fears and her loneliness is a typically human failure. We may justifiably fault him for that failure, but we should not too complacently assume that we, in his place, should of course have done better. Frost's poem is not about an oversensitive wife mismatched with an insensitive husband. It is about the effects of solitude and wilderness on a young wife already physically frail. More broadly, it is about the sadness of things. It does not ask us to point a finger of blame.

Notes

1. *The Poetry of Robert Frost*, ed. Edward Connery Lathem (New York: Holt, 1969), pp. 126–129. All references are to this edition. ("The Hill Wife," as mentioned in the text of the article, was first published in Frost's third book, *Mountain Interval*. It is also included in *The Norton Anthology of Poetry*—the shorter edition as well as the larger—eds. Allison, Barrows, Blake, et al.; and in *The Norton Anthology of Modern Poetry*, eds. Ellmann and O'Clair; and in *The Harper Anthology of Poetry*, ed. John F. Nims.)
2. In *North of Boston* "The Mountain," "A Hundred Collars," "A Servant to Servants," "The Code," and "The Generations of Men" all contain place-names relating them to Vermont or New Hampshire. In *Mountain Interval* "Hyla Brook" and "'Out, Out—'" likewise do. "The Vanishing Red" is placed in Acton, Massachusetts, northwest of Boston and about fifteen miles from the New Hampshire boundary. "Bond and Free" has no geographical locale. "Range-Finding," said by Frost to have been written circa 1902 "in time of profound peace" (*Selected Letters of Robert Frost*, ed. Lawrance Thompson [New York: Holt, 1964], p. 220) is unplaced in time and could be as easily imagined as having happened, say, in Huddleton or Bennington, Vermont, during the American Revolution, as anywhere else.
3. Lawrance Thompson, *Robert Frost: The Years of Triumph* (New York: Holt, 1970), p. 541.
4. Vermont began requiring registration of motor vehicles in 1904, New Hampshire in 1905. In 1905 there were 78,000 motor vehicles registered in the entire United States (James J. Flink, *America Adopts the Automobile, 1895–1910* [Cambridge, Mass.: MIT Press, 1970], pp. 167, 58). In 1904, of two million miles of American roads, only 141 miles were paved (Merrill Denison, *The Power to Go* [Garden City, N.Y.: Doubleday, 1956], p. 15).
5. "The telephone gradually began to make its way over the hills in increasing numbers about 1910. For the housewife it meant social emancipation. No one in the most remote back road could be lonesome with sixteen neighbors on the line." The New England Telephone and Telegraph in two-page advertisements in 1910 said, in part: "Perhaps the farmer himself does not realize the loneliness of a woman on an isolated farm remote from neighbors and friends. Without a telephone she talks with them only occasionally. With a telephone in the house conversation is possible at any time" (W. Storrs Lee, *The Green Mountains of Vermont* [New York, Holt, 1955], p. 114).
6. "As late as 1935, when Franklin D. Roosevelt began the Rural Electrification Administration, only one farm in every ten in the United States had commercial electric service" (*World Book Encyclopedia* [Chicago, 1960], XV, 483).
7. Telephone conversation, August, 1979.
8. *Fire and Ice* (New York: Holt, 1942), p. 118.
9. *Robert Frost* (New York: Frederick Ungar, 1973), p. 37.
10. "Prosody as Meaning in Frost's 'The Hill Wife,'" in *Gone Into If Not Explained*, ed. Greg Kuzma (Crete, Nebraska: Best Cellar Press, 1976), p. 108. One should notice the number of speculations on which this judgment is based. The husband is to be blamed because "he brought her there." This is to assume that the wife was ignorant of her husband's prospects when they got married, that she went with him against her will, and that she had already shown symptoms indicating that it was a bad place to take her. The assertion that he "leaves her all day" is a further speculation, and a weak one. On a farm as small as theirs, it is improbable that the husband would not return for lunch; he is there when the tramp stops, whenever that is; and he takes his wife with him when he goes to town (section II). But even to the extent that the assertion may be true, it brands a virtue as a vice. The husband is held guilty for toiling long hours to feed, clothe, and shelter the two of them.
11. *Robert Frost: The Trial by Existence* (New York: Holt, 1960), p. 238.
12. "'The Hill Wife': A Romance," *The English Record*, 16 (Feb. 1966), 36.
13. The lines "only one of the two / Was afraid in an oft-repeated dream / Of what the tree might do" clearly require the reader to draw an inference. But there is no doubt about the inference to be drawn. That it is the wife who has the "oft-repeated dream" is supported by three indisputable facts: (a) The poem, as indicated by its title, is primarily about the wife; (b) This section follows three sections devoted to the wife's increasingly distressful anxieties or fears; (c) The section begins with the statement that "She" had "no saying dark enough" for the pine outside their window. It is interesting and instructive that we can be more certain about the exact meaning of these lines than we can of the apparently straightforward statements: "*They* learned to rattle the lock and key" and "*They* learned to leave the house door wide" (italics mine).
14. F. X. Shea, previously cited as having expanded the subject of Frost's poem into "a miniscule novel or drama . . . portraying the dissatisfactions and tensions of a love affair," expands his thesis by declaring, "'Her word' . . . is always a sensitive one. He, being unheard, may be presumed to be lumpish, work-ridden, obtuse." Here is a critic who not only knows that Mona Lisa has a mole on her left shoulder-blade but can tell you its exact location, size, and color. For him the whole poem adds up to "the familiar conflict, the quicksilver feminine against the incurious, self-centered, masculine temperament." In his effort to reduce the poem to "the familiar"—a kind of rural replication of Ibsen's *Doll's House*—Shea minimizes the effect of natural environment.
15. We are *told* only that they share the same bedroom. My inference that they share the same is based on my historical sense that twin beds for married couples had not yet come into fashion, especially in rural New England. The 1897 Sears Roebuck mail-order catalogue (reprinted by Chelsea House, New York, 1968), under bed room suits, iron beds, and wood beds, shows only double beds except for expressly-labled folding cots and child's beds (pp. 654–656, 659–660).
16. Durham, N.C.: Duke Univ. Press, 1975, pp. 69–72.
17. *The Poetry of Robert Frost*, p. 170. According to Daniel Smythe, in *Robert Frost Speaks Out* (New York: Twayne, 1964), p. 53, Frost once told a lady that "A Brook in the City" was "his one and only Freudian poem." In it he had mentioned "a repressed creek." Reginald L. Cook, in *Robert Frost: A Living Voice* (Amherst: Univ. of Massachusetts Press, 1974), p. 201, and Lawrance Thompson, in *Robert Frost: The Years of Triumph* (New York: Holt, 1970), p. 651, comment on Frost's lack of sympathy for Freud's psychological theories. Frost clearly thought them reductive of human nature, introducing the "downward comparisons" that he criticized in "The White-Tailed Hornet." Thompson quotes a college reporter's account of a Frost talk on "Metaphors": "Freud's metaphor is that life is nothing but appetite, alimentary or sexual" (p. 624). Cook transcribes a tape recording of a Frost talk at Bread Loaf. After a reference to "Freudian ideas," Frost says: "Look, I've written a whole book without the word *sex* in it. Just think of that. [Applause] And that doesn't mean I've left everything out. [Laughter]" (p. 140).
18. *Robert Frost*, p. 65.
19. *A Swinger of Birches* (New York: New York Univ. Press, 1957), p. 152.

AP/WIDE WORLD PHOTOS

WILLIAM GADDIS

AP/WIDE WORLD PHOTOS

ROBERT FROST

AP/WIDE WORLD PHOTOS

BRUCE JAY FRIEDMAN

ALICE DUNN/AP/WIDE WORLD PHOTOS

GEORGE GARRETT

APWIDE WORLD PHOTOS

JOHN GARDNER

UPI/BETTMANN NEWSPHOTOS

JEAN GARRIGUE

UPI/BETTMANN NEWSPHOTOS

HAMLIN GARLAND

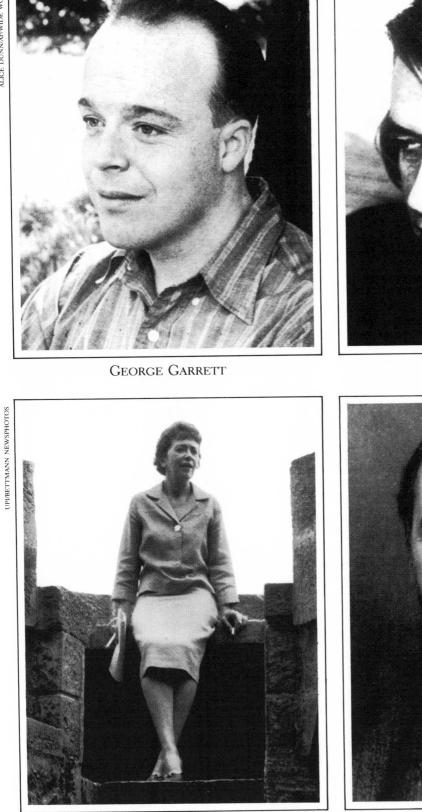

HENRY BLAKE FULLER

1857–1929

Henry Blake Fuller was a native Chicagoan. He was born on January 9, 1857, the son of George Wood Fuller, a banker, and Josephine Sanford Fuller; his family was related to the famous Transcendentalist intellectual Margaret Fuller. Henry Blake Fuller attended the Chicago High School. He worked for a time at banking, then set out for Europe to study music and architecture. A less than outstanding student, he nevertheless developed a profound admiration for European culture, to which most of his writing pays homage. His first novel, *The Chevalier of Pensieri-Vani* (1890), was a great success, but the subsequent *Châtelaine of La Trinité* (1891) was less well received. Fuller also wrote two Chicago-based novels, one of which, *The Cliff-Dwellers* (1893), was widely acclaimed for its depiction of the city. He returned to his home town in 1896 to assume his father's former position in banking, and although he remained in the Midwest almost constantly until his death, he maintained an Old World attitude toward America. In 1899 he privately published satiric verses aimed at President McKinley (*The New Flag*).

Fuller performed reviewing and editorial services for the Chicago *Evening Post* book review section, the *Record-Herald*, and the famous *Poetry: A Magazine of Verse*. Shortly before his death on July 28, 1929, he published a philosophical travelogue called *Gardens of This World* (1929).

It seems to me that every intelligent reader of Mr. Henry B. Fuller's ⟨*The Cliff-Dwellers*⟩ must feel that it is a work of very great power, however he feels about it otherwise. He may like it or dislike it very much, and he may or may not approve of its method, but he cannot deny that its art has reproduced with unerring distinctness the life it has dealt with. I myself like the book extremely, and I feel it a sort of privilege, which I am afraid would take the uncomfortable shape of a neglected duty if foregone, to testify of my pleasure in it, my admiration of it. . . .

Of course it is a study of Chicago from one point of view only, and no one but the groundlings who exult and the groundlings who repine will accuse Chicago of being altogether the Chicago of the Cliff Dwellers. But it is not the least of the miracles which that mighty population has wrought that it has, in the short sixty years of its existence, produced an artist who can portray its ugliness with such masterly skill, with such masterly conscience. As yet, no New-Yorker has begun to do as much for New York, no Bostonian for Boston. Chicago may feel no thrill of vanity in Mr. Fuller's work, but I can fancy her quite large-minded enough to feel a glow of pride in it.

If we would match him in his grasp of local conditions, ideals, characters, we must not stop short of Paris, where Zola has not dealt more epically with the facts of life about him. Mr. Fuller, who has kept scrupulously to the Anglo-Saxon decencies, has not himself stopped short of Paris in adopting Zola's methods with Zola's principles of art. His passage from the nebulous romanticism of *The Chevalier of Pensieri-Vani*, to the intense electric glare of the realism in *The Cliff-Dwellers*, might have almost an effect of violence, if the transit had been accomplished with less artistic success, less æsthetic completeness. As it is, his former triumph, pretty and pleasing as it was, is relegated to complete oblivion in the reader's consciousness, which is filled to the utmost with a sense of this. In reading it you cannot imagine the writer to have ever thought otherwise than realistically, or to have wrought in lines less bold and definite than these. The lines have not only boldness and definition, but they have a largeness, a grand and primitive simplicity, which I have hinted in the notion of something epic in the performance. As the Trojan War transacts the *Iliad*, as the Franco-Prussian war transacts the *Débâcle*, the vast twenty-storied edifice which houses them transacts the story of *The Cliff-Dwellers*. Whether Mr. Fuller went to Homer or went to Zola for his open secret, or whether, as is much more likely, he imagined this kind of motive for himself, there is no doubt but he is like them both in it, and is of the eldest and best tradition of fiction with them.—WILLIAM DEAN HOWELLS, *HB*, Oct. 28, 1893, p. 883

The peculiar strength and the peculiar weakness of Henry B. Fuller lie in his faithful habit of being a dilettante. A generation ago, when the æsthetic poets and critics were in bloom, Mr. Fuller in *The Chevalier of Pensieri-Vani* and *The Châtelaine of La Trinité* played with sentimental pilgrimages in Italy or the Alps, packing his narratives with the most affectionate kind of archæology and yet forever scrutinizing them with a Yankee smile. A little later, when Howells's followers had become more numerous, Mr. Fuller joined them with minute, accurate, amused representations of Chicago in *The Cliff-Dwellers* and *With the Procession*. Then, as if bored with longer flights, he settled himself to writing sharp-eyed stories concerning the life of art as conducted in Chicago—*Under the Skylights*—and of Americans traveling in Europe—*From the Other side, Waldo Trench and Others*. After *Spoon River Anthology* Mr. Fuller took such hints from its method as he needed in the pungent dramatic sketches of *Lines Long and Short*. One of these sketches, called "Postponement," has autobiography, it may be guessed, in its ironic, wistful record of a Midwestern American who all his life longed and planned to live in Europe but who found himself ready to gratify his desire only in the dread summer of 1914, when peace departed from the earth to stay away, he saw, at least as long as he could hope to live. There is the note of intimate experience, if not of autobiography, in these lucid words spoken about the hero of *On the Stairs*: "he wanted to be an artist and give himself out; he wanted to be a gentleman and hold himself in. An entangling, ruinous paradox."

Fate, if not fatalism, has kept Mr. Fuller, this dreamer about old lands, always resident in the noisiest city of the newest land and always less, it seems, than thoroughly expressive. Had there been more passion in his constitution he might, perhaps, have either detached himself from Chicago altogether or submerged himself in it to a point of reconciliation. But passion is precisely what Mr. Fuller seems to lack or to be chary of. He dwells above the furies. As one consequence his books, interesting as every one of them is, suffer from the absence of emphasis. His utterance comes in the tone of an intelligent drawl. Spiritually in exile, he lives somewhat unconcerned with the drama of existence surrounding him, as if his gaze were farther off. Yet though deficiency in passion has made Mr. Fuller an amateur, it has allowed him the longest tether in the exercise of a free, penetrating intelligence. He is not lightly jostled out of his equilibrium by petty irritations or swept off his feet by those torrents of ready emotion which sweep through popular fiction by their own momentum. Whenever, in *A Daughter of the Middle Border*, Hamlin Garland brings Mr. Fuller into his story, there is communicated the sense of a vivid intellect somehow keeping its counsel and yet throwing off rays of suggestion and illumination.

Without much question it is by his critical faculties that Mr. Fuller excels. He has the poetic energy to construct, but less frequently to create. Such endowments invite him to the composition of memoirs. He has, indeed, in *On the Stairs*, produced the memoirs, in the form of a novel, of a Chicagoan who could never adapt himself to his native habitat and who gradually sees the control of life slipping out of his hands to those of other, more potent, more decisive, less divided men. But suppose Mr. Fuller were to surrender the ironic veil of fiction behind which he has preferred to hide his own spiritual adventures! Suppose he were avowedly to write the history of the arts and letters in Chicago! Suppose he were, rather more confidingly, to trace the career of an actual, attentive dilettante in his thunderous town!—CARL VAN DOREN, "New Style," *Contemporary American Novelists 1900–1920*, 1922, pp. 138–40

Henry Fuller . . . refused to be labeled or to walk in his own footsteps. Catalogued as a romanticist by his first two books—a delicately satirical romanticist if you will—he set out, in his next two, to prove himself a modern realist of as stern a mood as Norris or Dreiser could be capable of; and his satirical weapon, a sheathed rapier in *Pensieri-Vani*, became a bludgeon in *The Cliff-Dwellers*. Mr. Robert Morss Lovett, in the *New Republic*, thinks that Fuller was not instinctively a satirist, but that the Spanish War and its Philippine consequences embittered him and dried up his creative energy. But I feel that the satiric quality of his humor was evident from the first, long before the Spanish war, and that political events had a merely superficial effect on his serenity. The truth lay nearer home, in that love and hatred of his native city which was a fundamental motive in a life singularly aloof from passionate experience. His youth had been starved and beaten to the earth by Chicago's preoccupation with "business"; he had escaped to Italy in the flesh for brief travels, and his imagination, taking refuge in "that lovely land" after his return, had consoled itself by writing a masterpiece to celebrate its beauty. Now he turned another facet of his mind upon the city which had tried to make a commercial slave of him, and proceeded to punish its materialistic ideals.

. . . Henry Fuller never quite took the plunge into life. For him human passion was impossible as a personal experience—he stood outside its arena, looking on at its frantic action with an amused and indulgent—indeed a somewhat wistful—tolerance. The wisdom of a keen observer combined with an ever-present sense of humor to make him instinctively a satirist, a satirist not bitter but sympathetic and benign. Such portrait sketches as those of Chicagoans in *Under the Skylights*, and of travelling Americans in *From the Other Side* and *Waldo Trench and Others*, were slight and unpretentious indulgences of this mood—very true and trenchant outlines of familiar types, with just a touch of caricature. And his later brief novels—*On the Stairs* and *Bertram Cope's Year*—were little more. . . .

During ⟨the⟩ progress of a friendship both personal and professional I discovered gradually the unselfish sweetness of a spirit that could not, however endowed with a gift for beautiful utterance, reveal its true quality to the world. There was in its deepest recesses an unconquerable reticence—Henry Fuller found it impossible to tell his whole story. He could not give himself away, and therefore it may be that the greatest book of which his genius was capable was never written, the book which would have brought the world to his feet in complete accord.—HARRIET MONROE, "Henry B. Fuller," *Poetry*, Oct. 1929, pp. 36–41

The finest of all the Chicago writers of ⟨the 1890s⟩ was Henry B. Fuller, who had won high praise with two books of European travel, *The Chevalier of Pensieri-Vani* and *The Châtelaine de La Trinité*, romances as far from Eugene Field's column and George Ade's stories in slang as any works by an American author could possibly be. In him the mid-West owned a stylist of continental rank and quality, but few knew it. I didn't know it—then. Deep in a fight for "Veritism" I had little patience with Fuller's leisurely romances of Europe, and hence, during my first year in Chicago, he and I walked our separate ways, "He havin' his opinion of me and me havin' my opinion of him." To him I was a rude anarch of the prairie, preaching a subversive social and literary creed, whereas he, to my thinking, was a literary trifler who despised his native town and wasted valuable time dreaming of French château and Italian castles.

As a recent adoptive citizen of Chicago, I resented this hypercritical attitude of a native son. Without the sense to perceive that Fuller's fine art was precisely what the city most needed as a counterpoise to its tasteless journalism, I went about saying that an aspiring use of local color was of more value than a derivative romance no matter how exquisite.

"We must have fiction as new in design as our skyscrapers," I repeated, and then quite unexpectedly Fuller took me at my word and published a novel which had the definition of a steel tower wherein all of the characters were connected in one way or another with the newest of our architectural monstrosities. He called his novel *The Cliff-Dwellers*, and I, recognizing that he had beaten the realists at their own game, at once wrote to him acknowledging the art as well as the truth of the book, a letter which drew from him a reply so characteristic and so intellectually arrogant, that it should be read at this point.

"My dear sir" (he began with cool aloofness), "I have to thank you for yours of the 17th in regard to *The Cliff-Dwellers*. The book is to be taken really as a sort of wrist exercise" (observe the implication of this) "preparatory, perhaps, to something better in the future. At the same time, I have no fixed literary creed; on the other hand I experience now and then a disposition not to use the same model too many times running. I am equally indebted to Mr. Howells and Mr. Boyeson, as well as yourself, for a generous welcome." (Here he felt that he had gone too far in compliance and checked himself, adding a contemptuous qualification) "There are a good many ways to skin a cat, and the realistic way, I dare say, is as good a way as any.

"I shall take pleasure in meeting you here next month. Yours very truly, H. B. FULLER."

In this fashion we began an acquaintance which was to ripen into friendship. He wore at this time a full brown beard and carried himself with fastidious grace, a small, alert gentleman who resented the mental and physical bad smells and the raucous noises of his native town. He studied me at our first meeting with bright eyes aslant as if only half liking my appearance, whilst I felt in him something puzzling and remote. He was reported to be more European than mid-Western, a man of independent means who had traveled widely in Italy and France. That he was the best informed man of all my acquaintances in Chicago was evident, although he made no direct display of his acquirements. He said little and his sentences were short, precisely controlled, and pertinent. He had little patience with fuzzy pretentiousness. Intellectually arrogant but never bitter, he worked away on the book to which he had alluded and when it came out a year later I found in it a mellower quality than I had hitherto perceived in him.

Masterly in the precision of its phrase, its characterizations, and its humor, *With the Procession*, in my judgment, ranks with Howells's *A Modern Instance* and *Silas Lapham*. Cosmopolitan in its technique, it made all other stories of Chicago seem raw and crude.

Here was a novelist after my own rules! Choosing a local subject, he brought to bear upon it a literary technique which could be matched only by the best French or English masters.—HAMLIN GARLAND, "Henry B. Fuller," *Roadside Meetings*, 1930, pp. 265–68

. . . ⟨T⟩he realistic procession moves on to 1895, when Chicago presented Henry B. Fuller and his *With the Procession*, quite as sound a piece of realism as that or any other decade has produced. In fact, Fuller appears to have introduced for the first time the purely American realistic novel. In it he pictures the era following the Civil War and, through the labors and psychology of his characters and the post–Civil War commercial and social atmospheres, we are permitted to glimpse the true Chicago American scope of the day. In fact, in that book much more than in the hundreds of lesser and negligible commentaries that have succeeded it, we are already in touch with the beginnings of Big Business and its attendant social milieu. If there is such a thing as the father of American realism, Henry B. Fuller is that man. . . .

It was Henry B. Fuller himself who, in 1913, explained to me why he had not gone on with his work. The reason was, as he then stated it, that he was most vociferously and outrageously assailed by a puritan or romantic and mentally undernourished band of critics, who had proceeded to shout that his contributions were not only libels on life but worthless as reading matter. In his own Chicago world and circle of friends he had been met with not only personal disapproval but contumely. Sensitive to, as well as fond of, the society of which he was a part, as he explained to me, and finding himself facing social as well as literary ostracism, he desisted.—THEODORE DREISER, "The Great American Novel," *ASp*, Dec. 1932, p. 1

For Fuller the city, not Nature, gives the senses infinite room.

His transvaluation of the agrarian myth, with its concomitant image of the city's suffocating bounds, projects a discovery of the city's machine-made beauty. Fuller's Chicago novels, *The Cliff-Dwellers* (1893) and *With The Procession* (1895), celebrate an industrialized city, the mechanized antitype of America's mythical garden. Like his contemporary, the Chicago architect Louis Sullivan, he shapes his spatial aesthetics out of the technological conditions of his time. Chicago's modern architecture, especially the towering skyscrapers built in the 1890s, created a new sense of urban space: urban vistas now pierced and fragmented nature, obliterating the land that in terms of America's pastoral myth was boundless. By abandoning and subverting that myth, Fuller perceived that the city's infinite vistas evoked a pleasing terror—a modern, technological sublime.

Functionalist assumptions inform Fuller's reading of Chicago's architecture and the urban landscape. Fully conscious that Chicago, "of all the very large cities in the world, is the only one that has been built together under completely modern conditions," he nevertheless urged architects and city-planners to stamp Chicago with the impress of machine-made "new materials." His weekly newspaper columns in the Chicago *Evening Post* bristled with attacks on architecture that "reeks with far-fetched picturesqueness and foolish illogical effectism" or that "revels in the falsification of construction and material." The modern city, his rejection of the picturesque suggests, could not be made over in the image of a garden or contained by time-worn architectural forms. In this embrace of modernism, he anticipates Hart Crane's contentious demand that literature "absorb the machine" and "surrender . . . temporarily, to the sensations of urban life."

This is not to say Fuller willingly surrendered his sensibilities to every assault his city might mount. What he pleaded for and worked at in his fiction was the assimilation of the modern city into art. His novels, even today, teach the reader how to see the city's beauty and spatial form. To be sure, he had his doubts about using the city of Chicago as a literary subject: "Who wants to read about this repellent town?" he once asked William Dean Howells. No modern writer—one now assumes—asks himself, as Fuller certainly did, whether an urban landscape seemingly void of meaning and beauty is worthy of fictional treatment, whether its denatured surface might compose an aesthetically significant pattern. Fuller's vision of the city's chaos, unlike that of contemporary novelists such as Saul Bellow or Thomas Pynchon, springs from a consciousness of genteel aesthetics: that is, the belief that art should present a vision of *ideal* beauty and harmony. . . .

By covertly comparing the city's skyscrapers and mechanized landscapes to phantom pastoral gardens and picture book Gothic, Fuller ⟨in *With the Procession*⟩ comes close to seeing the city as a place of wondrous possibility, a modern and man-made Arcadia. His parodic strategy counters, overwhelms, and finally demolishes the genteel platitudes he places in Truesdale's mouth. The cult of ideality with the pastoral ideal falls before his satire. The novelty of his urban aesthetics stands in bold outline when it is remembered that not until 1908 did the Ash Can school of painters first begin to give visual form to the American city. Fuller does not precisely anticipate their imagery, though he, like John Sloan and George Bellows (who in 1913 titled a painting "Cliff Dwellers"), sees the city as possessing a peculiar beauty heretofore ignored or derided. He, thus, annexes and assimilates into the realm of the aesthetic the vast reality of the modern city, impressing its form with his own vision.

What Fuller saw in Chicago fit few of the established literary forms, yet he did not turn away or betray his impressions. Waking from the dream that America was a pastoral garden, the late nineteenth century found that their world was really a mechanized and industrialized city. The city landscape that emerges in Fuller's novels, nevertheless, reflects what few American writers of the nineteenth century had grasped or made vivid.—GUY SZUBERLA, "Making the Sublime Mechanical: Henry Blake Fuller's Chicago," *AmSt*, Spring 1973, pp. 83–92

JOHN FARRAR
"The Literary Spotlight, XXVII: Henry Blake Fuller"

Bookman (New York), February 1924, pp. 645–49

In a brilliant sentence wherein he gives us the character and temperament of the hero of his *Chevalier of Pensieri-Vani* Henry Blake Fuller also thus partly describes himself: "He was sufficient unto himself, exempt from the burdens of wealth, the chafings of domestic relations, the chains of affairs, the martyrdom of great ambition and the dwarfing provincialism that comes from a settled home."

So sufficient is he unto himself that it is only with the greatest difficulty that one can unearth anything about him. Those who have known him for a great number of years as intimately as Mr. Fuller can be known, can tell you very little except that he is a charming gentleman. He is exempt from the burdens of wealth, though he has an income from some property in Chicago which suffices amply for his needs. Far from being chafed by domestic relations, he hasn't even a permanent residence. His address is set down in *Who's Who* simply as "Chicago". He is constantly changing his lodgings, whose location he keeps not only from acquaintances he would avoid but from his closest associates. He receives his mail ordinarily at the office of *Poetry: A Magazine of Verse*. That he does not suffer the martyrdom of great ambition is evidenced by the dilettante character of his whole career. He spent a great part of his youth abroad and seems rather to have yearned wistfully for Italy all his life. That he is utterly lacking in the provincialism that comes from a settled home is perhaps one reason why his excellent novels shoot over the hearts and heads of the public: he is in life but not of it, and that aloofness of the author which gives so great an air or artistic detachment to his work is, in the last analysis, the elusiveness of personality in a man whose zest is very tepid.

It is all very well to declaim bitterly against the general reader's neglect of an artist, but it is an eminently sensible procedure now and then to take pains to discover to what extent the artist himself is responsible for this neglect. Mr. Fuller's first great literary master, Stendhal, is hard put to it even at this late day to muster that handful of appreciative readers who, he said, would not only understand his work but would cherish it as being unique. Irony and satire, especially if they are refined over subtly, have never a general appeal; and the irony and satire of Mr. Fuller's novels are not ensanguined by any passion whatever. Stendhal, literary caviar as he is, had animated and driving emotions: he worshiped Napoleon, and his Julien Sorel is the first great avatar of the Nietzschean superman. Mr. Fuller has, apparently, not even any inclinations, to say nothing of worship, concerning any person or thing. There is no palpable idea in his work; there is only a pervading and gentlemanly diffidence. And diffidence is the last thing in the world to excite the general reader. What it all comes down to, I am afraid, is that Mr. Fuller is deficient in vitality, that vitality which makes pages glow with human warmth and animates the reader with sympathy or distaste. Critics will never quarrel over Mr. Fuller's merits; they will either acknowledge them without passion or remain indifferent to them. And the public, I suspect, will continue to exist in happy ignorance of the dozen books with which he has honored American literature.

Within the last year I have observed a phenomenon which gives credence to my impression that Mr. Fuller's shyness and self isolation is that of a disappointed man. He has begun of a sudden to appear as a prolific reviewer; his analyses and estimates of books appear simultaneously in a half dozen publications; at sixty four years of age he seems to have decided belatedly to impress his name, if only by repetition, upon the minds of American readers. Throughout his career as a writer he has been an occasional contributor of reviews and papers to the literary magazines; but these appearances were so few and far between that the cumulative effect was never great enough to keep an audience aware of his existence. Every once in a while he would be referred to by some critic as the "late H. B. Fuller": and his achievements were somehow thought of as belonging to the last century, even though his last novel, *Bertram Cope's Year,* was published as late as 1919.

I believe that if Mr. Fuller had had his present urge to be useful in the literary scene when he was a younger man he would not only have been much better known as a writer but would have endowed his novels with just that animation which they lack. He had no need ever to struggle for a living; he prepared himself for a profession only in a dilettante way by studying music and architecture and wrote his first novel without any bread and butter urgency. He has never held any job except that as an honorary advisory editor of *Poetry: A Magazine of Verse*. In this capacity, Harriet Monroe tells me, he is faithful, punctual, and efficient: he is at his desk several mornings out of a week, reading poetry in manuscript, dictating letters of rejection, discussing with the other editors the verse which is to be used in the forthcoming issue of the magazine. But this again is a sort of make believe employment; there is no suggestion of professionalism in his editing, his journalism, his criticism, or, indeed, in his fiction making. He has had, in fine, no real work to do in his life. Possessed, like his Chevalier, of a temperament opposed to all restrictions upon his freedom, scouting the obligations imposed by great ambition, domestic life, augmented wealth, and a permanent home, he practically cut himself free from life altogether. He has not even had his Chevalier's flair for adventurous activity. His career in the flesh no less than in fiction seems to be characterized entirely by an austerely passionless curiosity.

In person Mr. Fuller is a furtive little fellow with a neatly trimmed white beard and white hair; his skin is smooth and white; his voice is soft and hesitant; his eyes gleam with amused inquisitiveness; and he is always perfectly shod and tailored. He is neat, gracious, charming, excessively quiet. At any gathering, at tea or dinner, he never takes part in general discussion; at best, if he says anything, it is to one or two people whom he has withdrawn or who have withdrawn him into a corner. He chuckles, rather one suspects, from nervousness and shyness than from actual mirth; he chuckles a great deal when there is nothing particularly to chuckle about. In any discussion he is much more concerned with drawing out the other fellow than with expressing any opinion himself. When he does express an opinion orally he circumscribes it with reservations and puts it forth, as it were, tentatively, as though ready to withdraw it on second thought.

He is deeply interested in young people, and for a bachelor and recluse he has an extraordinary habit of keeping in touch with the children and grandchildren of his friends. If there is a boy or girl in the family of his circle of acquaintances who is being graduated at high school or college, Mr. Fuller somehow learns of it and, on graduation night, is always to be found in the first row, beaming in a sort of proprietary or parental pride. He follows the activities of the literary youngsters with a sympathy and understanding which is unusual among men past middle age. He has, so far as I know, never uttered a deprecatory, admonitory, or shocked word against the younger generation. So alive is he to what is being done by the younger men that not long ago he wrote a highly appreciative article pointing out the peculiar merits of a dozen or so of the most eccentric and revolutionary of the young modern poets.

II

Mr. Fuller's first novel, *The Chevalier of Pensieri-Vani*, was written as long ago as 1886. It did not find a publisher until 1890, when it came out anonymously. When the second edition of the book was issued he attached his name to it. A year later appeared his *Châtelaine of La Trinité*, which, like the first novel, was a romantic comedy, with a touch of the gentlest raillery, the scene laid in Italy. In his next two novels, *The Cliff-Dwellers* (1893) and *With the Procession* (1895), he took up the realistic manner and applied it to stories of contemporary life in Chicago. In these books no less than in his earlier ones, however, a tincture of Stendhalian irony, heightened perhaps by Mr. Fuller's instinctive repugnance for the crudeness and garishness of the Chicago of those days, gave his books, if not a bite, at least a nip. In the books he published between 1895 and the advent of the world war—*From the Other Side, The Last Refuge, Under the Skylights*, and *Waldo Trench and Others*—there is the same exquisite design, the same polished style, the same quiet humor and delicate irony which distinguish all his work, and the same absence of any glow that would give his work force and character. Then there was a period of nine years when nothing, except a few articles here and there, appeared under his name. In 1917 he brought out a book of humorous and experimental verse, parodies and adaptations of the manner of the free verse writers. The book, many items of which had already appeared in Bert Leston Taylor's "Line-o-Type" column in the Chicago *Tribune*, was called *Lines Long and Short*. Then in 1918 he wrote a novel in strict conformity to his theory that no novel should exceed 60,000 words in length, wherein he developed two contrasting figures of equal importance to his story, one of them the vital and successful, though crude, man of action and the other an artist in temperament, unassertive, withdrawn from life. In this novel there seems to have dawned upon him the first realization of what I believe to be the failure of his own career—the failure to make a choice between two roads. If he was to stay in Chicago and use the fiction material at hand in such a way as to give it great significance and meaning, it would have been necessary for him to accept Chicago with fewer regrets that it was not Florence or Milan. If he was to expatriate himself it would have been necessary to do it as thoroughly as did Henry James. In *On the Stairs* he showed for the first time his understanding that vitalilty and driving purpose, however crude, is naturally more admirable than ineffectiveness, however cultured and beautifully mannered.

It may be said that *Bertram Cope's Year*, in so far as it was read and understood at all, shocked Mr. Fuller's friends so painfully that they silenced it into limbo. It is a story, delicately done with the most exquisite taste, of a sublimated irregular affection. It received scant and unintelligent notice from the reviewers and, though it was filled with dynamite scrupulously packed, it fell as harmless as a dud, only to be whispered about here and there by grave people who wondered why Mr. Fuller should choose such a theme. Since then he has written no novels or, if he has written some, he has not published them. Diffidence again and disappointment have conspired to keep his name only a name in our contemporary literature. He has the sensibility and intelligence, the subtlety and delicacy, to produce artistic masterpieces but he lacks temper and gusto—vitality. This is all the more lamentable in that we have in our American literature an abundance of vitality, but not enough of the qualities which Mr. Fuller possesses in a high degree.

William Gaddis

1922–

William Thomas Gaddis was born in Manhattan on December 29, 1922, and attended schools in Connecticut and on Long Island. As a student at Harvard he contributed a wide range of writings to the *Lampoon*, which he edited in 1944, earning himself a reputation as a humorist. After leaving college in 1945 without a degree, he worked for two years for the *New Yorker* before setting off on a series of travels in Central America and Europe. He lived for two years in Spain and for a year in Paris, where he wrote radio programs for UNESCO.

Returning to New York in 1951, Gaddis worked as a freelance writer while developing and revising his first novel, *The Recognitions*, which appeared in 1955. While this work failed to gain him a wide audience or much critical acclaim, it did secure him a grant from the National Institute of Arts and Letters in 1963. In the 1960s he continued freelance writing for a pharmaceutical firm and for magazines, while working on material for his second novel, *JR*, which won him the National Book Award for the best novel of 1975. In 1977 Gaddis was Distinguished Visiting Professor at Bard College, and he has also taught at summer writing workshops. He received a Guggenheim Fellowship in 1981 and a MacArthur Prize in 1982.

A reclusive man who lets little of his private life be known, Gaddis, who has two grown children from a previous marriage, lives in a village north of New York City.

Q: There seems to be a noticeable undercurrent of autobiography in your fiction. Both Willie in *The Recognitions* and especially Thomas Eigen in *JR* bear more than a passing resemblance to their author. Yet you are also one of the most reticent of writers, avoiding publicity of any kind. What are your views on the place of autobiography in artistic creation and to what extent is Thomas Eigen a portrait of the artist?

A: The question of autobiographical sources in fiction

has always seemed to me one of the more tiresome going, usually what simply amounts to gossip and about as reliable, not that we don't all relish gossip. But it can be as inviting a trap for the bounty hunters as tracing down literary sources. A lot of it seems to spring from this urge to scrimp and ice the creative act, the creative personality, you get the extremes in nonsensically detailed questionnaires that show up in the mail, what is your favourite colour? on which side of the paper do you write? Because finally the work itself is going to stand or fall uniquely on its own. Does knowing Dreiser's intimate biographical details make his writing any the less clumsy? or knowing Butler's finally have much to do with an appreciation of *The Way of All Flesh?* And how do you search out the 'portrait of the artist' in a really great novel, is it Dmitri rather than Ivan? or Alyosha? even Smerdyakov? No, characters all draw on some contradictory level of their author's life, as sure as Basil Seal lurked close as thieves under all that houndstooth suiting near to Tony Last.

Q: You have said that you enjoy writing, but you have never discussed your writing habits. Do you keep a journal or notebooks? Do you have preferences as to when and where you work, etc.?

A: Have I said I enjoy writing? Some high moment and I probably did, but it's nearer what Pascal, was it he? as I have it at second hand, said about no man differing more from another than he does from himself at another time. That incidentally may better explain a phenomenon like *The Brothers Karamazov*. It certainly helps to explain my distaste for interviews, though this one may serve to set the record straight on a few points.

Q: It's been said *The Recognitions* was edited down to its present size from a much longer manuscript. Is it true that you fundamentally agreed with the cuts suggested by your editors at Harcourt, Brace & World? How did the abandoned material differ from that in the final version? Have you come to regret any of the deletions? Did *JR* go through a similar process of editing? What part do revisions play in your compositional method?

A: The story that *The Recognitions* was edited down to its present size from a much longer manuscript must have gained currency from a hasty review of my papers by someone who came across fragments there that I'd rejected myself. In a work of that length and time in the writing some of it was rewritten repeatedly, some scarcely at all, some cut, tossed out, recovered and placed elsewhere, some later inserted, some sequences worried at and tossed out entire. I suppose someday someone will really sit down and go through the whole heap of notes, queries, revisions, rewrites, corrected galleys, it's nothing I've an appetite for. At any rate, to my best recollection once the finished manuscript was turned in to the publisher (which was, incidentally, Harcourt, Brace & Co., not Harcourt, Brace & World), editorial attentions to it had very little to do with its published length which may, in fact, with some of my last minute inserts have come out even longer. The only cutting suggestion I remember acceding to involved one long party too many, so I worked it into another long party which I'm sure was an improvement. In the case of *JR* there was no editorial tampering at all.

Q: The pervasive and distinctive authorial voice of *The Recognitions* gives way in *JR* to a self-effacing voice that seems to serve only functional purposes. Also in *JR* there is an increased dependence on dialogue. For verisimilitude in *Lolita*, Nabokov "travelled in school buses to listen to the talk of schoolgirls." Did you take any special measures to hear and note the speech patterns of any of the wide variety of people who speak in *JR?*

A: Style and content must match, must be complementary, accounting in part for a difference between the two books, though the lack of a conventional narrative style had already jarred a good many readers of *The Recognitions* when it appeared, as its hapless reviews show. *JR* was started as a story which quickly proved unsatisfactory, inspired—here's the legitimate gossip—by the postwar desecration of the Long Island village of Massapequa where my family had had property since around 1910, take a look at it now and you'll see all the book's worst hopes realized. In approaching *JR* as a novel, I was at pains to remove the author's presence from the start as must be obvious. This was partly by way of what I mentioned earlier, obliging the thing to stand on its own, take its own chances. But it was also by way of setting up a problem, a risk, in order to sustain my own interest, especially since the largely uninterrupted dialogue raised the further risk of presenting a convincing sense of real time without the conventional chapter breaks, white spaces, such narrative intrusions as A week later . . . How some of the writers I come across get through their books without dying of boredom is beyond me. As for what you call speech patterns, one is always listening and has got an ear or hasn't, and without one, unless perhaps in dealing with an unfamiliar language and culture, no amount of your special measures like riding around on school buses will get you out of the swamp. Stanley Elkin for instance has an ear; C. P. Snow hadn't. You see what I mean.

Q: At the time *JR* was published, it was reported that you had just finished a Western screenplay—a genre that seems to be worlds apart from your novels. What led you to write the screenplay? Was it ever filmed? Apart from the two novels, are there other pieces that you've written but have not published?

A: That screenplay was an exercise and although the idea still intrigues me a good deal it's on the shelf. So is what started as a Civil War novel and became a long cumbersome play called *Once at Antietam*, which I put a year or two into at some point when I'd laid *JR* aside unfinished. And so is a long project that may never see more of the light than its opening pages in *JR* under the guise of Gibbs' *Agapé Agape*, if anyone bothers to stitch them together. I'd like to think of it all, what's eventually completed and what isn't, in terms of Samuel Butler's books 'coming to him wanting to be written.' It was also said of him that he wrote in order to have something to read in his old age and I've always rather liked that too.

Q: Your novels abound with literary allusions, and many who seem to be your favorite authors are mentioned or quoted. What authors do you read and admire that would not be obvious from your novels? Which writers, in or out of the American tradition, do you feel a kinship with?

A: I imagine that some day I'll sit down to try to sort out the writers whose work I've liked, or like, and why, and may have influenced mine, but right now it's a distraction that serves no purpose of mine however much it might yours though I even wonder about that. So for all the queries about literary allusions, artistic creation, writing habits and the rest of it, I'd just leave you with Keats' lines: "It is true that in the height of enthusiasm I have been cheated into some fine passages; but that is not the thing."—WILLIAM GADDIS, Interview by John Kuehl, Steven Moore, *RCF*, Summer 1982, pp. 4–6

BERNARD BENSTOCK

From "On William Gaddis: In Recognition of James Joyce"

Wisconsin Studies in Contemporary Literature
Summer 1965, pp. 177–89

The role of the critic rarely included prophecy, but more often analysis of that which already existed before him, and it is to his credit that he has resigned himself with equanimity to that function, pointing with pride to Aristotle, the greatest of those noted for locking the barn door after the event. Unable to perform the rare service of a John the Baptist, the critic aspires at least to be Johnny-come-lately, depending upon the appearance of some vital piece of evidence to suddenly mark a boundary, so that like Yeats's golden bird he may sing "of what is past, or passing, or to come." The 1955 publication of William Gaddis's *The Recognitions* found the critic of any such aspirations looking the other way, and it is only belated recognition of *The Recognitions* that may now indicate some definite guidelines to the course open to the contemporary novel. And for those who consider the achievements of James Joyce in perfecting many vital aspects of the modern novel—only to bemoan the absence of any major successors to Joyce—a closer examination of Gaddis's first and only novel to date should do much to emphasize the pervasiveness of the Joycean influence and perhaps indicate tendencies of what is to come.

What Joyce has accomplished in prose fiction is now history. First, a volume of short stories, each of which depends solely for its effect on the accuracy of the interrelationship of the individual character and his particular environment, and each of which avoids the storyteller's pitfalls of accident, coincidence, false connectives, supernatural suggestions, single-dimensional conflicts, artificial climaxes, and unnatural resolutions which have marked the limited art form in lesser hands. These fourteen stories are in turn capped by an exercise in the novella rarely duplicated since, a novella which logically extends the boundaries of the short story to duplicate the scope of the novel. The entire set of these, the volume called *Dubliners*, moreover, forms a logical sequence to present a totality of sociological examination of Joyce's worlds—local, international, universal. Thereafter, the novel, *A Portrait of the Artist as a Young Man*, presents a definitive amalgam of the novel of a young man's experience while growing up, the development of the artist in contemporary society, a criticism of the social malaise of the times, a work simultaneously psychological and sociological, investigating social, private, political, religious and artistic roots, again accomplishing a totality greater than the sum total of its parts. Beyond this Joyce went on to perfect the complete modern novel, satisfying all of Northrop Frye's "four types of fiction"[1] simultaneously—romance, novel, confession, catalogue—and blending the naturalistic with the psychological, the conscious stream of thought with the unconscious whirlpool, while still thoroughly developing the pattern of surface events. Thus, with the publication in 1922 of *Ulysses*, all previous tendencies in the development of the novel since Fielding were successfully amalgamated into a single, unified work, an inimitable book which was nonetheless imitated, becoming the single most important influence in the European and American novel for several decades. And finally, with *Finnegans Wake* Joyce left even his most devoted imitators behind, having ventured into a realm of such personal synthesis of techniques that none could successfully follow.

When imitation becomes impossible, it usually follows that a reaction develops instead, but in the case of James Joyce such a reaction could hardly be fruitful: against which Joyce is one to react? the naturalistic Joyce? the symbolistic Joyce? the Joyce of "scrupulous meanness" or the Joyce of "mandarin"[2] involutions? the poet? the storyteller? the chronicler? the moral amoralist or the immoral moralist? With James Joyce, I am suggesting, the twentieth century has produced its most consummate literary artist, and it is to William Gaddis's credit that he has sought and found in Joyce both a direction toward the future and a definite delineation of what has been accomplished, so that *The Recognitions* at once acknowledges its debt and proclaims its individuality. Gaddis is able to do this because the basic element of his work is the delicate balance between originality and imitation, and the book itself as such is able to *be* a living example of what it *means*. The Stephen Dedalus who goes "to encounter for the millionth time the reality of experience and to forge in the smithy of my soul the uncreated conscience of my race" (P 53)[3] is the William Gaddis who goes forth in *The Recognitions* for the million-and-first-time; the Penman Shem who "scrabbled and scratched and scriobbled and skrevened nameless shamelessness about everybody ever he met" (FW 182) and who "did but study with stolen fruit how cutely to copy all their various styles of signature so as one day to utter an epical forged cheque on the public for his own private profit" (FW 181) is the Wyatt Gwyon of *The Recognitions* whose originality as an artist depends upon the faithfulness with which he copies the great Flemish Old Masters, duplicating with a fanaticism beyond the capacity of the non-epical forger the state of mind, soul, and social conditions which determined their work. In order to create his own work of art, Gaddis found it first necessary to exorcise the spectre of James Joyce hovering over the contemporary novel, and like his protagonist Wyatt, Gaddis knew that he could not free himself of the infernal spirit until he first sold himself without qualifications to that demon. *The Recognitions* is one of the most singularly original novels of recent years, and it manages to become just that only when Gaddis pays his full debt to James Joyce.

What immediately impresses the reader of *The Recognitions* is the integrity of its author (a factor which the benighted daily reviewers took to be audacity and treated as such): the book is close to a thousand pages long—rather extravagant for a first novel; few if any concessions are made to the lazy reader, the digest reader, or the literal reader. No flattering photograph of the author graces the dust jacket, and as Gaddis comments within the book about a novel being discussed by his characters: "For some crotchety reason there was no picture of the author looking pensive sucking a pipe, sans gêne with a cigarette, sang-froid with no necktie, plastered across the back" (R 936). Obviously the book in question is Gaddis's own, and the pattern of the novel containing the character who is the author creating the novel in question is a familiar one to us, from Gide's *Counterfeiters* where Edouard is writing *The Counterfeiters* to Joyce's *Finnegans Wake* where Shem is composing a "most moraculous jeere-myhead sindbook for all the peoples" (FW 229), tentatively titled a "warping process" (FW 497).

It is essentially the basic theme of "the counterfeit" in contemporary life which most impresses us in Gaddis's debt to both Gide's book and the Joyce canon, particularly *Finnegans Wake*. The renowned forger of the nineteenth century, known as Jim the Penman, reforged by Sir Charles Young in his play of that name, and adopted again by Joyce as a prototype for his Shem, reappears in *The Recognitions* as a venerated hero of

Gaddis's counterfeiter, Mr. Sinisterra, who includes him in his pantheon of great forgers, but with no more awareness of the "real" name of the "penman" than can be found in the *Wake.* It is the fictional character, the facsimile, that Gaddis uses, but not without acknowledging that it is to Joyce that the real allusion refers: "I miss him when a great artist dies like that," says Mr. Sinisterra. "He was no bum. It's no place for bums to get into, but they're ruining it every day. There hardly is a single old master left, a real craftsman, like Johnny, or Jim the Penman. And me. I haven't had a notice in the *Detector* in fourteen years" (R 519). That "real craftsman" bears a strong echo of *il miglior fabbro.*

In relating the story of the development of the artist in an alien society, Gaddis returns to a pattern basically familiar to us: like Stephen Dedalus, Wyatt Gwyon is a sensitive child, whose childhood is highlighted by an important illness and by the conflict between his father and his Aunt May (a successor to the Dante Riordan of A *Portrait*), the "aunt" representing narrow-minded, parochial religiosity; like Stephen he is considered for the priesthood (in this case the ministry), but severs his religious umbilical cord to become the artist, the forger. (Significantly enough, Protestant Wyatt moves mysteriously toward Catholicism, confusing the word "priesthood" for "ministry," whereas Stephen the lapsed Catholic is mistaken for a Protestant minister in *Ulysses* because of his Latin Quarter hat.) And like Stephen, Wyatt's name is Stephen; that was the name his parents had chosen for him before he was born, but it was forgotten when Aunt May suggested the name of Wyatt. The quest in *The Recognitions* can be seen in terms of Wyatt's search for his Stephen-self: as he moves away from his inherited and conditioned identity he loses his name entirely; at the Christmas tree bonfire the policeman democratically addresses him as "Jack," and then "Father," as Wyatt is mistakenly identified as a priest (like Stephen he dresses in black). Thereafter his wife and others call him "you" and refer to him only in the third person pronoun, so that after page 118 he is never called Wyatt again. Returning home for the last time, he facetiously introduces himself as the Reverend Gilbert Sullivan to the church ladies, and later in Spain contemptuously gives the legendary name of Sam Hall to Mr. Sinisterra. But Sinisterra has a false Swiss passport with the name Stephan Asche, and repeatedly uses that for him (it should be remembered that on the night of the bonfire a Spanish waiter named Esteban considered him "*muy flamenco*"—an appropriate designation for the dedicated forger of Flemish painters). Wyatt in Spain is then Stephan-Estaban-Stephen, the last becoming the name Gaddis goes on to use for him, returning him full circle to the Stephen he should have been.

But most important, like Stephen Dedalus, Gaddis's protagonist is St. Stephen, the first Christian martyr. As a child Wyatt accidentally kills a wren with a well-aimed stone; he buries the bird and succeeds in forgetting the incident, until he accidentally exhumes it during his early adolescence. During his mysterious fever, he confesses the stoning to his father, who informs him: "why, a wren, you know, the missionaries themselves, the early Christian missionaries used to have it hunted down, hunted down and killed, they . . . the wren was looked on as a king, and that . . . they couldn't have that" (R 47). When Wyatt returns home for the last time he repeats the story back again to his father: "I'll go out like the early Christian missionaries did at Christmas, to hunt down the wren and kill him, yes, when the wren was king" (R 430). When we last see Wyatt, at the monastery in Spain about to embark again as a wanderer, he catches a bird in his hand and almost strangles it before he allows it to fly free: this symbol obviously does double service as a dove and as a wren in Gaddis's blend of Christian symbolism. The wren motif is of course well-known to the reader of *Finnegans Wake*, where the chant of "The wren, the wren, the king of all birds, St. Stephen's Day was caught in the furze" is disguised in such incarnations as: "the rann, the rann, the king of all ranns" (FW 44), "a rum a rum, the ram of all harns" (FW 256) and "the bear, the boer, the king of all boors, sir Humphrey his knave we met on the moors!" (FW 430) Both Stephens then are recognizable as the wren, the scapegoat, the sacrificial lamb, the uncrowned king, the creative *Demiurgos* that rivals the God of the Creation, the first martyr of the true religion and the surviving martyr of the true art and the false art which both Joyce and Gaddis offer in lieu of religion.

Wyatt's wanderings, gropings and demon-driven fantasies relate essentially to the all-important search for the transubstantial father which underlies *Ulysses.* His mother's death weighs heavily upon him and her spectre visits him at home; while he goes abroad to search for it at her Spanish burial place, he associates it with the wren he killed and buried, and it is certainly her emanation that flies into his hand at the monastery. He suspects himself somehow guilty of her death apparently, as does Stephen Dedalus of his mother's death, having refused her wish that he pray at her deathbed (except that Wyatt was only four when his mother died, Stephen twenty-one). But it is primarily the search for the father that preoccupies them both, although in both cases their consubstantial fathers are alive. Both deny their own fathers, Wyatt stealing and selling his father's Bosch tabletop to finance his escape from divinity school and expedition to Munich to study painting, Stephen escaping to Paris, and when returned home by his mother's illness, moving to the Martello tower after her death. Somewhat against his wishes Stephen is claimed by Leopold Bloom, as is Wyatt by Mr. Sinisterra, but Gaddis's approach here is more parody than parallel, since the sinister Sinisterra (an ardent Catholic incidentally) attempts to rescue Wyatt (to keep him away from excessive drinking, loose women, careless spending and general dissipation) in order that he might be useful in perpetrating the final great forgery of the old man's career. The same Sinisterra had previously been mistakenly claimed as father by Otto, who serves in *The Recognitions* as a watered-down imitation of Wyatt: Otto had expected to meet his real father, Mr. Pivner, for the first time in his life, but encounters Sinisterra instead, who mistakes him for the appointed "pusher" of his counterfeit money. By book's end, however, Otto is ensnared by the evil Dr. Fell, much in the same way that Tony Last is trapped by the Dickens enthusiast in *A Handful of Dust*, while Pivner, in jail for counterfeiting, receives filial letters from his office boy, Eddie Zefnic. The parallels with *Ulysses* are apparent; the parody is broad. Wyatt and Otto wander like "Japhet in search of a father" (U 16), Mulligan's phrase for Stephen, and as Stephen traverses the Dublin terrain, Wyatt describes himself in Spain: "In this country, without ever leaving Spain, a whole Odyssey within its boundaries, a whole Odyssey without Ulysses" (R 816). He too envisions a "Penelope spinning a web somewhere, and tearing it out at night, and waiting" (R 898), and his attitude toward rivals and usurpers parallels Bloom's: "not slaying the suitors, no never, but to supersede where they failed, lie down where they left" (R 898). . . .

Like Joyce, Gaddis has adopted for his use a type of vast comic novel, balancing the serious introspection of Wyatt with an assortment of comic figures (American cousins surely of

"Pisser" Burke, "Nosey" Flynn, the Citizen, and Cashel Boyle O'Connor Fitzmaurice Tisdall Farrell) who constantly act out a parody of Wyatt's involvement. *The Recognitions*, in effect, is divided into three fairly distinct voices: Wyatt's situation, especially when he confronts his father and the later father-figure Basil Valentine, is essentially the serious novel which underlies all other parts of the book, with his involvements with Esther and Esme as minor modulations of this voice. But when he is confronted by less heroic people (Recktall Brown and Sinisterra, and finally Ludy), what exists is a gentle parody when it is Otto who shoulders the burden of the sensitive young writer in contact with Esther, Esme and Brown. Finally, there is the vast human sub-comedy which provides the surfaces of *The Recognitions*, the huge array of human frauds, plagiarists, forgers, counterfeiters, counterfeits, homosexuals, religious fanatics, philistines, tourists—the corrupt and the corrupters in their interchangeable Malebolgean environments. When Bloom measures the distances between himself and the esthete on one side and the philistine on the other ("Those literary etherial people they are all. Dreamy, cloudy, symbolistic. Esthetes they are. I wouldn't be surprised if it was that kind of food you see produces the like waves of the brain the poetical. For example one of those policemen sweating Irish stew into their shirts; you couldn't squeeze a line of poetry out of him. Don't know what poetry is even. Must be in a certain mood."—U 154), he is unconsciously setting up the basic tensions of *Ulysses*, the distance between himself and Stephen on one hand and between himself and the vast cast of cloddish characters arranged for comic contrast on the other, a pattern paralleled by Gaddis in *The Recognitions*. If any attempts have been made in the twentieth century to fulfill Fielding's requirements for a prose comic epic, Joyce and Gaddis have made the most obvious contributions.

At various instances in *Ulysses* and in the *Wake* Joyce indulges himself in thinking aloud about his craft, offering plan and perspective to his reader, and commenting on his technique while exercising it. Such indulgences are encountered at only a handful of places in Gaddis's book, but they are equally significant. In the Spanish restaurant Wyatt complains to Esther about the limitations in most contemporary fiction and his own theory of the novel (R 113–114):

> . . . all of a sudden bang! something breaks. Then you have to stop and put the pieces together again. But you never can put them back together quite the same way. You stop when you can and expose things, and leave them within reach, and others come on by themselves, and they break, and even then you may put the pieces aside just out of reach until you can bring them back and show them, put together slightly different, maybe a little more enduring, until you've broken it and picked up the pieces enough times, and you have the whole thing in all its dimensions. But the discipline, the detail, it's just . . . sometimes the accumulation is too much to bear.

Later in the book Wyatt and Valentine combine their ideas to form a pattern of the type of novel that *The Recognitions* turns out to be, in which the contrast of major and minor voices sets the perspective of the Joycean non-hero in full dimensions with his environment (R 263):

> —Like . . . as though I were reading a novel, yes. And then, reading it, but the hero fails to appear, fails to be working out some plan of comedy or, disaster? All the materials are there, yes. The sounds, the images, telephones and telephone numbers? The ships and subways, the . . . the . . .
>
> —The half-known people, Valentine, interrupted easily, —who miss the subways and lose each other's telephone numbers? Cavorting about dressed in the absurd costumes of the author's chaotic imagination, talking about each other . . .
>
> —Yes, while I wait. I wait. Where is he? Listen, he's there all the time. None of them moves, but it reflects him, none of them . . . reacts, but to react with him, none of them hates but to hate with him, to hate him, and loving . . . none of them loves, but, loving . . .

If *The Recognitions* as a work of literary art points in any direction it seems to point toward the many-faceted novel which pits its protagonist, a cerebral, visceral, and introspective center, against a vast backdrop which reflects him, parodies him, and complements him, especially if that complement is comic and ironic. But even if it does not indicate any new direction, *The Recognitions* nonetheless leaves William Gaddis in the position of having created a rare and unusual book which in its imitation of the master achieves a unique originality for its creator, and in exploring a new terrain still pays respectful homage to James Joyce.

Notes

1. Northrop Frye, *Anatomy of Criticism* (Princeton, N. J., 1957), p. 314.
2. The term is Cyril Connolly's.
3. Parenthetical designations are for the pages in the following primary sources: P = *A Portrait of the Artist as a Young Man* (New York, 1956); R = *The Recognitions* (Cleveland, 1962); D = *Dubliners* (New York, 1958); U = *Ulysses* (London, 1958); FW = *Finnegans Wake* (New York, 1947).

PETER WILLIAM KOENIG

"Recognizing Gaddis' *Recognitions*"

Contemporary Literature, Winter 1975, pp. 61–72

Tony Tanner recently concluded his critical survey of American fiction between 1950 and 1970 by claiming that William Gaddis' *The Recognitions* (1955) inaugurated an entire period of American fiction.[1] Tanner's conclusion culminates a long, largely underground history for Gaddis' gigantic novel about forgers and counterfeiters, phony art, onanistic sex, and the false rhetoric of all kinds of religions. Still, few outside of a coterie of devoted followers have read or even heard of *The Recognitions*. Although it surfaced briefly at various times during the last twenty odd years, making its way onto an occasional college reading list, relatively little has been written about the perplexing novel since the initial, antagonistic reviews.[2] A satire so fastidious in its condemnation of the entire modern world—a deliberate counterfeit which itself borrows at random from hundreds of sources and satirizes such living persons as then Senator Richard Nixon[3]—of necessity had to provoke exasperated responses. Because reviewers attacked the novel as being too long, complicated, and nihilistic, the public at large ignored it. We have now had, however, access to some of Gaddis' manuscripts, which may help *The Recognitions* find its rightful above-ground reputation.

The manuscripts reveal Gaddis' intent to satirize the book reviewing world of the 1950s for preferring the kind of work being done by Hemingway and other popular writers of the time. Thus he made no attempt to accommodate reviewers or readers and went so far as to predict they would not read his 956-page long, involuted, fragmented, self-consciously demanding novel: "—You reading that? both asked at once, withdrawing in surprise.—No. I'm just reviewing it."[4] Gaddis deliberately increased the reader's difficulties at every turn, compounding the injury by discussing the fate of artists "caught in the toils of unsympathetic critics" (p.5). His self-fulfilled prophecy was confirmed by reviewers and public, and his fate lamented the year after by John Aldridge, who claimed there should have been a Malcolm Cowley to do for Gaddis what that prophetic critic did for the young Faulkner. Aldridge wrote: "*The Recognitions* received indifferent to stupid notice in the leading New York literary supplements, and . . . [was] allowed to pass from publication into oblivion with nothing in between to arrest [its] passage."[5]

A Greenwich Village journalist, writing under the pseudonym of "Jack Green," devoted several issues of his hand-printed *newspaper*[6] to excoriating the original reviewers and defending *The Recognitions* as a great novel. However, even after Bernard Benstock published the first critical article, entitled, "On William Gaddis: In Recognition of James Joyce," in 1965, the novel remained largely unknown and unavailable.[7] In 1968, Karl Shapiro planned to devote an issue of *Prairie Schooner* to it, in which "[w]riters, critics, and scholars from all over the world were going to contribute to the resurrection of this gigantic, all but unknown American masterpiece of a novel,"[8] but Shapiro became embroiled in a censorship dispute and forfeited editorship before the tribute materialized. In 1971, the novelist and critic David Madden edited a book entitled *Rediscoveries* to which he contributed a final essay, "On *The Recognitions*," declaring it "a perfect prototype of the neglected novel."[9] Tony Tanner, in the same year, concluded *City of Words* by stating that "*The Recognitions* remains very underrated," remarking in a footnote, "The critical neglect of this book is really extraordinary. . . . But the book is immensely rich and funny and it certainly deserves much more attention."[10]

As Tanner correctly indicates, Gaddis intended *The Recognitions* to be funny as well as serious, but the reviewers seemed so irritated by his technique and intimidated by his erudition that they could not distinguish Gaddis' philosophical pessimism from his dark humor. The comic-grotesque plot begins with a woman named Camilla getting acute appendicitis on board a ship bound for Spain from Boston in the early 1900s. Frank Sinisterra, a second-rate counterfeiter of twenty-dollar bills, must perform the surgery, because he has masqueraded as the ship's doctor to escape counterfeiting charges in the United States. Camilla naturally perishes, leaving her husband, the Protestant Reverend Gwyon, alone in Spain when the ship lands, to seek solace in Spain's Catholic monasteries. It also leaves her son, Wyatt Gwyon (then three), to be raised by his puritanical Aunt May, who makes him feel so guilty about his tremendous talent for drawing that she renders him incapable of everything except copying.

The rest of the novel takes place in the early 1940s. Wyatt's path is crossed by scores of characters who are all themselves conscious or unconscious forgers, including the Devil himself in the comic person of Recktall Brown,[11] who operates a forgery ring in New York with the homosexual art critic, Basil Valentine. Wyatt creates the art forgeries, Brown plants them in old houses, then buys them at auctions, and Valentine attacks the discoveries as frauds, then publicly retracts and pretends to be persuaded of their authenticity. Finally the public, who Brown claims wants to be duped, buys the forgeries for vast amounts of money, believing that they have acquired something genuine and meaningful from the past. Wyatt ultimately renounces this attempt on his part to patch up the past, and although he continues to search for redemption, he never explicitly finds it. This brought from some reviewers the intitial charge of nihilism.

To understand Gaddis' relationship to his characters, and thus his philosophical motive in writing the novel, we are helped by knowing how Gaddis conceived of it originally. *The Recognitions* began as a much smaller and less complicated work, passing through a major evolutionary stage during the seven years Gaddis spent writing it. Gaddis says in his notes: "When I started this thing . . . it was to be a good deal shorter, and quite explicitly a parody on the FAUST story, except the artist taking the place of the learned doctor."[12] Gaddis later explained that Wyatt was to have all talent as Faust had all knowledge, yet not be able to find what was worth doing.[13] This plight—of limitless talent, limited by the age in which it lives—was experienced by an actual painter of the late 1940s, Hans Van Meegeren, on whom Gaddis may have modeled Wyatt.[14] The authorities threw Van Meegeren into jail for forging Dutch Renaissance masterpieces, but like Wyatt, his forgeries seemed so inspired and "authentic" that when he confessed, he was not believed, and had to prove that he had painted them. Like Faust and Wyatt, Van Meegeren seemed to be a man of immense talent, but no genius for finding his own salvation.

The Faust parody remained uppermost in Gaddis' mind as he traveled from New York to Mexico, Panama and through Central America in 1947, until roughly the time he reached Spain in 1948.[15] Here Gaddis read James Frazer's *The Golden Bough*, and the novel entered its second major stage. Frazer's pioneering anthropological work demonstrates how religions spring from earlier myths, fitting perfectly with Gaddis' idea of the modern world as a counterfeit—or possibly inspiring it. In any case, Frazer led Gaddis to discover that Goethe's *Faust* originally derived from the Clementine *Recognitions*, a rambling third-century theological tract of unknown authorship, dealing with Clement's life and search for salvation. Gaddis adapted the title, broadening the conception of his novel to the story of a wandering, at times misguided hero, whose search for salvation would record the multifarious borrowings and counterfeits of modern culture. Gaddis notes, "I think this book will have to be on voyaging, all the myth & metaphor of that in modern times" (*Notes*). Thus from a limited Faust parody, his novel expanded into an epical, theoretically limitless pilgrimage of recognitions parodying the immense *Recognitions of Clement*.

Basil Valentine provides the key for Gaddis' parody of the Clementine *Recognitions* in the following phone conversation:

> Yes. The What? *The Recognitions?* No, its Clement of *Rome*. Mostly talk, talk, talk. The young man's deepest concern is for the immortality of his soul, he goes to Egypt to find the magicians and learn their secrets. It's been referred to as the first Christian novel. What? Yes, its really the beginning of the whole Faust legend. But one can hardly . . . eh? My, your friend is writing for a rather small audience, isn't he? (p. 373)

The parallels between Clement's *Recognitions* and Gaddis' parody are reasonably well summarized by Valentine. Wyatt's "deepest concern is for the immortality of his soul," and he goes to Egypt (Paris, New York, Germany, Spain, Africa) "to find the magicians and learn their secrets." The parody deviates from the original in that "Egypt" is *everywhere* in the modern world, false magicians abound, and recognition comes only ambiguously or not at all. No Saint Peter exists, as in the original *Recognitions*, to defend spiritual authenticity from the doubting Devil, Simon Magus (Recktall Brown). *The Recognitions* examines the complex problem of salvation, a problem which Gaddis sees as stemming from the "Modernism heresy" (p. 178), the rationalist interpretation of history, which does not allow for meaningful suffering or redemption. Science, according to Gaddis, works against recognition of the need for suffering, as does its therapeutic extension, psychoanalysis. Religion tries to work toward salvation but fails, because like science, it is only a counterfeit of an earlier impulse and ability to wonder and believe. Modern art too, with its worship on the one hand of the past, and on the other of unbridled originality, has forgotten its earlier, painstaking function of recording genuine wonder and dread. Thus all of our modern occupations, institutions, and amusements seem in Gaddis' parody to be the counterfeit secrets of a pagan Egypt, where mere magic replaces true mystery and renders belief impossible.

The Recognitions probes the question of personal salvation of the modern world with the scholastic thoroughness of Clement's theological tract. Wyatt represents what Gaddis defines in his notes as "the self who could do more," a concept derived from a verse by Michelangelo, which he has one of his characters attempt to translate:

O God, O God, O God,
Who has taken me from myself
from me myself
Who was closest (closer) to me
And could do more than I
most about me
What can I do?
(p. 322)

Wyatt, whose wife, Esther, constantly reminds him, "You could do more," suggests the self-who-could-do-more to all the other characters, and they in turn represent missing parts of him. Gaddis calls Wyatt "he" during most of the novel to emphasize this composite role. Wyatt says he lives in a novel where the hero never appears (a novel like *The Recognitions*), yet none of the other characters moves "but it reflects him" (p. 263). They all think about Wyatt, and, "costumed in the regalia of their weary imaginations, he appeared and vanished in a series of images which, compacted, might have formed a remarkable fellow indeed" (p. 85).

Far more suggestive and full of potential, but deluded and a counterfeiter like the rest, Wyatt thinks of himself as an alchemist, recognizing that alchemy "wasn't just making gold" (p. 129), but was originally the search for the redemption of matter. For Wyatt it represents a spiritual quest such as medieval alchemists made when they saw "in gold the image of the sun, spun in the earth by its countless revolutions, then, when the sun might yet be taken for the image of God" (pp. 131–2). Gaddis writes in his notes: "First there is the ideal. Then the crash of reality; and chaos and death. Then resurrection, in which the two, working together, achieve redemption. *Wyatt then is the alchemist; there's no nearer parallel*" (*Notes*, my italics). Gaddis' search for the ideal goes back to what he calls in his notes "those perfect forms of neo-platonism," and in *The Recognitions* "a time before death entered the world, before accident, before magic, and before magic despaired, to become religion" (pp. 11–12). Wyatt chooses the alchemist—part magician, part priest, part scientist—to reunite all these fragmented modern approaches and go back as far as possible to original truth.

Although the attempt to escape from counterfeiting truth is doomed from the beginning, failing to attempt it leaves reality unredeemed, and this unredeemed state is represented by Recktall Brown: "Brown is reality. Brown is matter; and all concerning him, matter that, as forgery or falsification of the ideal, is to be redeemed" (*Notes*). Wyatt, as alchemist, comes closest of all the characters to redeeming reality. Next closest may be his father, whom Gaddis describes as "the religionist-magician": "Reverend Gwyon's importance is again the oldest problem of a man set to preach what no longer satisfies, bent finally to attempt to effect a change which will give significance, all this in the religious sphere" (*Notes*). Valentine, on the other end of the religious spectrum, is described by Gaddis as "the Gnostic magician," the rational skeptic who refuses "to grant the worth of matter, that is, of other people" (*Notes*). Wyatt's selfish wife parallels Valentine "as sleep does waking" (*Notes*). She is "destined to contain redemption (but not be it)" (*Notes*), doomed to sleep with many men but love none, just as Valentine dies an insomniac, reason doomed to itself.

Some of the characters, such as Wyatt's model, Esme, and the simple Catholic believer, Stanley, come closer to the ideal, because the grand illusions of Materialism (Brown), Art (Wyatt), Religion (Gwyon), and so on do not beset them. The simple ideal which they possess is the ability to love, and although Esme is addicted to heroin and Stanley caught up by Catholicism, they still do care unselfishly about other people, not joining in what Gaddis calls the "ritual denial of the ripe knowledge that we are drawing away from one another, that we share only one thing, share the fear of belonging to another, or to others, or to God" (p. 103). Stanley and Esme fall in love briefly (Wyatt spurns her love), but Esme dies from kissing the diseased foot of Saint Peter's statue, and Stanley is buried in the collapsing Italian church where he had come to dedicate his organ mass for his dead mother. Clearly, the world around them is not conducive to the survival of any ideal, it is so full of unhealthy and dangerously impermanent counterfeits, of unordered spiritual, sexual, and creative impulses.

Through this unhealthy, uncertain world, Wyatt attempts to journey from the counterfeit to the genuine, from sin to redemption, chaos to design. The structure of Gaddis' novel symbolizes voyage and return, dislocation and reestablishment, lost recognitions and found. Gaddis felt that "It should be 'apparently' broken up, because that is the nature of the problem it attempts to investigate, that is, the separating of things today without love" (*Notes*). To make the novel "'apparently' broken up," Gaddis employs montage or broken narrative, skipping from place to place without connections, consciously imitating a film.[16] But the fragmentary scenes return at strategic points in the novel, producing surprises by recurrence, and an overall sense of completeness.

Gaddis' symbolic use of structure in fragmenting and then reuniting his fictional world is best exemplified by his treatment of the martyr-saint theme, the most important one in the novel. The major authentic martyr-saint is Wyatt, the main subplot the making of a counterfeit saint out of a dead Spanish girl. Whereas the original *Recognitions* of Clement describes the making of a true saint out of Clement, Gaddis shows the preposterous difficulties involved in Wyatt's becoming a saint through martyrdom in the twentieth century. He does this by creating a structural model of modern, secular chaos.

Gaddis begins with a small detail, a photograph on the Spanish grave next to Camilla's, of "a little cross-eyed girl in long white stockings" (p. 7). He explains that she was "brutally assaulted on her way home from her first communion" by a man "infected with a disease which he believed such intercourse with a virgin would cure" (p. 16). The local pharmacist tells Reverend Gwyon after Camilla's funeral that the little town needs a patron saint, and "our Little Girl" could be made into one were it not for the enormous expense of canonization. Reverend Gwyon does not take the hint, however, and the subject seems closed, until twenty years and hundreds of pages later, Mr. Pivner—the father of one of Wyatt's friends—is engaging in his perennial reading of the evening newspaper. He glances at "a feature story (*exclusive*) on the imminent canonization of a Spanish child, a feature not because the little girl was soon to be a saint, but because she had been raped and murdered" (p. 291). The article has taken up the story from forty years ago, complete with pictures of the little girl and the murderer, under the pretext of reporting the upcoming canonization.

Once again the Little Girl disappears from sight until, some 500 pages later, the advertising executive "Ellery"—one of Esther's lovers who replaced Wyatt when he left her—discovers that he is being sued by the man pictured in the article as the murderer. It seems that the newspaper printed the photograph of a "respectable business man and professor" (p. 740) by mistake. Finally, when fleeing from Brown's counterfeit ring at the end of the novel, Wyatt visits his mother's unmarked grave in Spain. He is told about the exhumation of the Little Girl buried next to Camilla, and the peculiar fact that when they "took her out of the graveyard here to put her somewhere else when she was beatified they thought she look[ed] kind of big for an eleven-year-old girl" (p. 791). Only when we realize Camilla has been mistakenly exhumed and canonized instead of the Little Girl, do the apparently random trivial details take on meaning, revealing that "the little girl in white stockings" is really one of the unifying images of the novel. The reader learns this through a structural sense of details recognized as strategic, spatial intervals.[17]

At the same time he is building up to the sham canonization, Gaddis drops hints that Wyatt might, in another age, have been a genuine martyr-saint. He mentions in the first chapter that Wyatt was to be named "Stephen" "for the name's sake of the first Christian martyr" (p. 27), but Aunt May unrecognizingly changed it to "Wyatt." Aunt May, whose only contact with saints has been through her Calvinist upbringing, lectures Wyatt threateningly about their lives, forcing him to feel too unworthy for any hope of emulating them. Wyatt's father offers him a far more suggestive model of sainthood in the person of the martyred Saint Clement, who died by drowning with an anchor tied to his neck.[18] Years later Valentine cynically predicts Wyatt will be drowned (p. 262), as he is—by his guilt, and by the chaotic world in which he lives.

Wyatt symbolically acts out his martyrdom, dreaming his hair has caught fire and repeatedly cutting himself shaving. Esther, who does not understand the "precision of suffering" (p. 112), suggests Wyatt get an electric shaver. Despite hints of possible martyrdom, the reader doubts Wyatt will ever achieve his destiny. However, isolated details come together surprisingly in the final pages, when Gaddis begins calling Wyatt "Stephen," his original martyr-name. In the monastery where his father stayed grieving Camilla's loss, Wyatt undertakes his final work—the restoration of a painting of Saint Dominic. When we last glimpse Stephen, on a Spanish hillside, he catches a bird in his hand, saying, "I could tell you about Saint Dominic plucking alive the sparrow that interrupted his preaching" (p. 898). Seemingly, a wren Wyatt actually killed as a child—a part of his horrible "guilt," which he buried along with his drawings in the yard—has only "interrupted his preaching." He accepts guilt as something that must be "lived through," and embraces the idea of loving a child, who is "not love but borne out of love" (p. 897–98). Wyatt reveals a pair of earrings, presumably his mother's, which he wishes to give to someone, possibly to a daughter by the prostitute Pastora, whom he met in Spain. Gaddis originally planned to make this ending explicit, as his notes indicate:

> I say I don't want the end to seem trite, an easy way out; because I don't want it to sound as though Wyatt has finally found his place in company with a simple stupid and comparatively unattractive woman who loves him. . . . I simply want the intimation that, in starting a drawing of his daughter, Wyatt, seeing her in her trust and faith (love), is *beginning*. He may not yet understand, but the least we can do is start him, after all this, on the right way, where the things that mattered, not simply no longer matter, but no longer exist. (*Notes*)

Gaddis finally decided, however, that even this ending would be facile and left only hints of it in the final version. He chose instead to emphasize Wyatt's drowning, Clement-like martyrdom, alluding to it in Wyatt's recognition: "I've been a voyage starting at the bottom of the sea" (p. 895). Thus in the final pages, all the suggestions of Wyatt's martyrdom and possible salvation coalesce, briefly and fragmentedly, as Wyatt believed from the first that recognitions occur. To quote David Madden on Gaddis' structural technique: "The achievement of the orchestration of Gaddis' technical devices is the creation, for the most attentive reader, of a sense of simultaneity, cohering not, as for most works of art, in a compressed, poetic image, but in a mental, and perhaps spiritual, state of recognition."[19]

About the time Gaddis completed *The Recognitions* in 1949, he wrote a revealing provisional prefatory note in which he asked:

> Then, what is sacrilege? If it is nothing more than a rebellion against dogma, it is eventually as meaningless as the dogma it defies. . . . Only a religious person can perpetrate sacrilege: and if its blasphemy reaches the heart of the question; if it investigates deeply enough to unfold, not the pattern, but the materials of the pattern, and the necessity of a pattern; if it questions so deeply that the doubt it arouses is frightening and cannot be dismissed; then it has done its true sacrilegious work, in the service of its adversary: the only service that nihilism can ever perform. (*Notes*, edited for spelling)

As this statement reveals, Gaddis considers himself "a religious person" on one hand, and a blasphemous nihilist on the other. Like his hero Wyatt, he is an artist of religious concerns in a nonreligious age. This explains what is most puzzling about *The Recognitions*—why Gaddis opens his novel with an epigraph about nothing being vain or without significance as concerns God, and then attacks every form of religion and faith. He believes that all their myths fail to give meaning to modern life and that he must hasten the collapse, lay bare the emptiness, "to betray the lack of pattern and still its final, if seemingly fortuitous persistence." He uses *Recognitions of Clement* to symbolize a lost spiritual integrity, a personal search for redemption. *The Recognitions* itself is a search for redemption, in which Gaddis seeks to avoid his characters' "hazardous assurance" (p. 55), and to "unfold, not the pattern, but the materials of a pattern, and the necessity of a pattern." The novel offers no final answers to the questions it raises, but its questions do penetrate "so deeply that the doubt it arouses is frightening and cannot be dismissed." The very suggestiveness and structure of his questioning constitutes a partial answer.

Like Alexander Solzhenitsyn in *The First Circle*, Gaddis seeks to produce a consciousness of Heaven through a massive recognition of Dantesque Hell. He chose the yew tree growing outside Reverend Gwyon's study to symbolize suffering opening hopefully onto truth, and he writes of a collapsing church, symbol of a collapsing faith, at the end of the novel: "Everything moved, and even falling, soared in atonement."[20] In his remarkable final lines, Gaddis signed a most unusual and appropriate farewell to his own work. He knew the thanks he would receive for reviving a fragmented, splintered image of the dark-leafed yew tree from which the Cross was cut: "He was the only person caught in the collapse, and afterward, most of his work was recovered too, and it is still spoken of . . . with high regard, though seldom played" (p. 956). If Gaddis was "caught in the collapse," then perhaps we can say that at this point his work has at least begun to be recovered.

Professor Tanner summarizes the importance of *The Recognitions* by stating that "the problems Gaddis raises and the themes he explores seem . . . to be at the heart of American Literature, and in looking back to Hawthorne while it looks ahead to Pynchon, his novel reminds us of the continuities which we might otherwise, perhaps, overlook."[21] Gaddis deals with Hawthorne's problems, permanently rooted in the American consciousness, of too much guilt and not enough morality. In showing how intertwined are the confidence men and the innocents in American life, Gaddis also places himself directly in the tradition of Melville.[22] On the other hand, Tanner asserts that *The Recognitions* inaugurates a new period of American fiction, "in which the theme of fictions/recognitions has come to occupy the forefront of the American writer's consciousness."[23] Certainly *The Recognitions* is among the first, along with the novels of Nabokov, Nin, and Hawkes, to deal in an original way with the post-war world. It is one of the first "cold war novels," in which the hero never appears or the battle never takes place, and yet one feels that great tensions are abroad and enormous consequences at stake. In this it foreshadows the novels of Pynchon, as well as many others, a masterfully crafted prototype of contemporary American fiction as well as a satirically prophetic picture of American life.

Notes

1. Tony Tanner, *City of Words: American Fiction, 1950–1970* (London: Cape, 1971).
2. Leslie Fiedler, when asked why he did not include Gaddis' novel in his *Love and Death in the American Novel*, replied: "The reason I did not write about *Recognitions* in my study of the American novel is that I did not have a firm opinion about it, and I still do not" (Letter, July 21, 1970).
3. Richard Nixon is "Dick," a glib and bungling young minister in *The Recognitions*.
4. William Gaddis, *The Recognitions* (New York: Harcourt, Brace, 1955), p. 936. All further references to *The Recognitions* will be to this edition, indicated in the text in parentheses.
5. John W. Aldridge, *In Search of Heresy* (New York: McGraw-Hill, 1956), p. 201.
6. Jack Green, *newspaper*, New York, 1960–62.
7. Bernard Benstock, "On William Gaddis: In *Recognition* of James Joyce," *Wisconsin Studies in Contemporary Literature*, 6 (Summer 1965), pp. 177–89. American paperback editions followed the hardcover first edition at these intervals: 1962, Meridian; 1970, Harvest; 1974, Avon.
8. Karl Shapiro, *To Abolish Children and Other Essays* (Chicago: Quadrangle Books, 1968), p. 231.
9. David Madden, "On William Gaddis' *The Recognitions*," *Rediscoveries*, ed. David Madden (New York: Crown Publishers, 1971). p. 304.
10. Tanner, p. 393.
11. An obvious pun, referring to Brown's gross, anal-retentive collector's personality. Valentine, whose name plays with his sexual predilection, is named after a heretic who denied Christ (as he does Wyatt). "Gwyon" comes from a word in Robert Graves's *The White Goddess* which means *leader*. Sinisterra is sinister, and is succeeded by his son Chaby (shabby). Aunt May is a wintry old spinster, and so on. Gaddis deliberately gives Wyatt a name which suggests nothing in particular.
12. William Gaddis, notes for *The Recognitions*, 1945–51, used here with permission from the author. Gaddis has in his possession a multiplicity of notes, largely unpaginated, undated, and arranged in no systematized fashion. References will be indicated as *Notes* in the text.
13. Interview, March 23, 1970.
14. Gaddis credits Gilbert Highet with this analysis of Van Meegeren. Gilbert Highet, "Artistic Forgeries II," transcribed radio broadcast WQXR, 1959.
15. The travels of Gaddis' characters, from Harvard to New York, Central America, Spain, Paris, Germany and Africa, are autobiographically based.
16. Gaddis at one time made films for the army.
17. For a discussion of literary spatialism which includes reference to *The Recognitions*, see Sharon Spencer's *Space, Time and Structure in the Modern Novel* (New York: New York Univ. Press, 1971).
18. This Saint Clement is different from the alleged author of the Clementine *Recognitions*. Gaddis delights in "counterfeiting" names, and encouraging the reader to initially confuse them.
19. Madden, p. 304.
20. A parody of the last lines of Rilke's *Duino Elegies*.
21. Tanner, p. 400.
22. R. W. B. Lewis mentions *The Recognitions* in his Afterword to the Signet Classic edition of *The Confidence Man*, 1964.
23. Tanner, p. 393.

STEVEN WEISENBERGER

From "Contra Naturam?: Usury in William Gaddis's *JR*"
Money Talks: Language and Lucre in American Fiction
ed. Roy Male
1981, pp. 93–109

William Gaddis is the author of two Big Books. By this designation I mean that *The Recognitions* (1955) and *JR* (1975) stand in a brotherly relation to *Moby-Dick*, *Ulysses*, *The Sot-Weed Factor*, and *Gravity's Rainbow*. They tend to put us off by their sheer bulk, five hundred pages long at least, like tirelessly constructed monuments to knowledge and wit. We finish reading one and echo Samuel Johnson on *Paradise Lost*: "None ever wished it any longer than it is." Yet the Big Book is demonstrably the most important (and ironic) kind being written in America, and Gaddis's two are masterful examples of the form. Strange to say, then, that with the exception of a National Book Award for his second novel, Gaddis's writing receives little recognition and scarcely any critical discussion. Five years after its publication, *JR*, a brilliantly funny and accessible book, stands unnoticed.[1]

This is not the place for a full-length consideration of Big Books, needful as that is, but a few remarks on the form will help preface my discussion of *JR*.[2] First, Big Books concern themselves with Man's attempted mastery of Nature, but the frame for Man's struggle is Commerce: whaling, travelling salesmanship, colonizing Maryland, building rockets. This is particularly so in American varieties of the form, whose authors are still laying siege against our old Whiggish optimism about making and marketing commodities. Like Melville, they start to exclaim "Ah Bartleby! Ah humanity!", then they set to work on a book Big enough to properly do it.

Narrative tension in a Big Book arises when the claims of imaginative freedom, usually in the person of an artist, are made to correlate with natural necessity, that is, Commerce as the need of people to be useful by turning Nature's riches into gain. Yet the needs of Commerce and those of Art never square with each other, and so the artist discovers his eternally painful relationship with Nature—not in mastery but in estrangement. He may even display his estrangement like a badge, as in *Humboldt's Gift*, where Citrine's hammered-in Mercedes-Benz becomes just such a figure. And at the end, the revelation of the artist's struggle does make identities clear: *this* is the right use of imagination, we say at the conclusion; or, this is the true artist and here the test of genuine art. Thus, as *Gravity's Rainbow* concludes Pynchon is affirming the imaginative spark—compassion—that links characters together and lifts them above the traps of technology and into "systems of caring." And in *The Octopus*, Norris adopts the long view on Preston's failed battle against the railroaders: "Falseness dies," he writes in the last paragraph. Commerce, as a degenerative system of exchange, always takes this kind of moral drubbing at the end of the Big Book. In the final scenes of Robert Coover's *The Public Burning* it resembles nothing less than a sideshow metastasized into banal, murderous demagoguery. And I think that, despite all the talk about where to "place" it, *The Executioner's Song* precisely fits this description. In Norman Mailer's hands Gary Gilmore becomes a type of the artist (he was a painter) who cannot fit, shoplifts for the heck of it, commits senseless murder, but still *articulates* his own death. That is why Mailer has to include his Afterword; he has to indicate that his book, unlike what all the other hacks might have done with a congeries of tapes and letters, is the true artistic rendering of Gilmore's story.

This is the mode Gaddis works in, and I suspect we have only begun to appreciate its value. I intend chiefly to open several lines of approach to a fine novel that we have neglected, yet I also hope the following discussion will suggest lines of inquiry into Big Books as a genre. The questions after all are fascinating: What are the structural resources of storytelling in a Post-industrial leviathan such as America? Where *do* artists fit in, if anywhere? In what ways do we confuse Art and Money?

Depreciation is the principal topic of Gaddis's *JR*. In this novel the desire for commercial and transcendental wealth—for money and artworks—brings into play two related difficulties: the apparent similarity (even identity) of money and language, and the degeneration of monetary and artistic wealth inside a system based on principles of usury. To Gaddis, when money talks, things fall apart. Using money depreciates real wealth and using language depreciates meaning, thus nullifying Art. Edward Bast, the artist-figure in *JR*, finds himself struggling to be free of the institutional usury that wastes his creative vitality, but his crucial discovery is that usury itself is the state of Nature. Usury is not *contra naturam*, as we may have thought from reading *The Merchant of Venice* or Ezra Pound's *Cantos*. No, it partakes of nature's vast commerce, for even molecules exchange particles and yield up energy (interest) during the transaction. Pound's condemnations in Canto 45 ("with usura the line grows thick"; it is "CONTRA NATURAM") reveal a limitation to Bast because he sees it is everything outside Art, everything in usurious Nature, that is inexorably diminishing in worth.

More accurately, not Bast but the structural patterning of *JR* as a Big Book makes these discoveries for us. At first glance this seems absurd, for the writing in *JR* is utterly seamless, without any familiar narrative divisions. Spatio-temporal transitions occur without warning, often in the midst of sentences. That is, when characters speak sentences. Owing to the flux of events they rarely surpass the phrase level of utterance, and Gaddis segues one voice into another with no identifying marks, so that *JR* reads like an extended transcription of tape-recorded noise. One character repeats a bit of financial jargon, "accelerated depreciation," that aptly describes the state of language in this novel, where everyone seems hell-bent on voicing cliché, tautology, cant, obscenity, nonsense.

Yet standing against this chaos of narration are remarkable intricacies of reference and structure. I want to trace three fields of reference basic to *JR*, these being Wagner's *Ring*, Empedocles's cosmology, and entropy theory. Taken together they represent synecdochically the branches of human knowledge—in art, philosophy, and natural philosophy—that Gaddis relates to his central theme of depreciation or usury. These references mediate our reading of the structural oppositions on which the novel depends. They indicate (on the one hand) a commercial Nature run amok with greed, strife and chaos, and (on the other) the struggles of the artist to create inherently useless and self-sufficient works. As I have indicated, this is the crucial test of a Big Book, and Gaddis shapes the triumph of his protagonist, Edward Bast, into the touchstone with which we may tell the truth of human motives and the genuineness of Art.

What Homer's *Odyssey* is to Joyce's *Ulysses*, Richard Wagner's *Der Ring des Nibelungen* is to *JR*. The *Ring* cycle serves as mythic sub-text to the fictional plot, and Gaddis introduces the parallels between them early in the book. The opening scene involving Bast's great aunts abruptly shifts to a Brooklyn school where we meet the main characters.[3] These include Jack Gibbs, seen lecturing on information theory and the Second Law of Thermodynamics to eighth-grade students who can't even spell the word "e-n-t-r-o-p-y," as well as Edward Bast, working as a composer-in-residence at the school, seen attempting to direct a class of sixth graders in "The Rhinegold." One of Bast's pupils is J. R. Vansant, who first appears in a glass phone booth, "motionless but for fragmenting finger and opposable thumb opening, closing, the worn snap of an old change purse" (p. 31). He is a runny-nosed, disheveled kid obsessed with the hollow promises of mail-order fortunes, a boy whom the kindly describe as someone hungering and desolate for success and the cynical as someone "about as touching as a bull shark" (p. 246). In the school's presentation of "The Rhinegold," and in the novel, JR plays Alberich, the grotesque, gnomish creature who renounces love for the power to enslave men by possessing the Nibelung Ring. As in the operas, Gaddis holds up love as the source of all beneficent creativity, and when JR shouts his lines in rehearsal—"Hark floods! Love I renounce forever!" (p. 36)—Gaddis signals the genesis of what will become, in the phenomenally short span of just three months, the "JR Family of Companies," an international consortium of cut-throat business interests capable of disrupting the life of every character in the novel. Read as a fable of business, *JR* (like the *Ring*) represents the origins of American commerce as a little monster, Primal Greed, living inside all of us.

References to Wagner are scattered throughout the first scenes of *JR*, but they all center on the depletion of love as a twilight age in Nature. Shortly after his renunciation of love, JR attends Mrs. Joubert's field trip to the Wall Street skyscraper Valhalla where a confrontation with the gods of finance ensues. In Crawley, a stock-broker who hunts wild pigs "with lances" (p. 88), he meets one of Wotan's spearmen. But it is at best a faltering Valhalla: a stockholder's suit is pending against the Diamond Cable branch of the business, which the class buys a share of; and "Monty" Moncrief (they all have redundant names, like "Dave" Davidoff) rushes about battling corporate "brush fires." The *Götterdammerung* cannot be far off. Amy Joubert, the daughter of Governor Cates (Wotan in this Valhalla), seems to sense an impending collapse. As

Brunnhilde, she represents the gods' estrangement from their own better selves, for she is loving, dignified, aloof and sensitive, but the Valhallans mock her for all that and press her into business deals designed to salvage the family wealth.

JR moves through this faltering Valhalla and sees it as a fabulous game, as though Gaddis meant for us to take Wagner literally when he wrote of the Rhinegold that it is "worthless, except when you play."[4] Moncrief explains to him the crass objectives to this financial game—"I'd just say boys and girls, as long as you're in the game you may as well play to win" (p. 107)—which gives JR the idea that anything goes so long as you can bend a rule to cover yourself. He will be repeating Moncrief's dictum until the novel's end. He also learns a pair of simple rules from Amy's father: "buy for credit sell for cash," Cates tells him in the executive toilet; the second rule is, the "money is credit" that makes more gain possible (pp. 108–09). It is a vicious, usurious circle, and yet precisely that set of rules confers on JR a Ring-like power over mankind. His empire begins from ads in mail-order catalogues. Clipping coupons and operating from the school phone booth, he works a deal to buy four and a half million surplus picnic forks from the United States Air Force, on credit, and sell them to the Army at a wild profit. Business booms. JR acquires bankrupt companies, empty mining claims, an entire New England mill town full of pensioned-off employees, quantities of pork bellies, flawed Chinese sweaters, plastic flowers, an unfinished ship hull as a tax write off, a chain of nursing homes that feed business to another chain of funeral parlors, the Bast family company that makes piano rolls, and a subsidiary of it that manufactures sheep-gut condoms. The JR Corp. is built up from the incomplete, the obsolete, the fruitless, the dead.

The risible part of it is that JR succeeds because he mimics the gods of Commerce so well, following the clichéd laws of their game to the letter. The irony is, like Alberich, he becomes a joke in Valhalla. Looking over a class picture taken when Mrs. Joubert's class visited Diamond Cable, Davidoff points to JR and laughs: "look at this one, down in front here holding up the stock certificate," he says, "ever see so much greed confined in one small face?" (p. 461). What they don't know, by the mid-point in the story, is that they are now on the job for JR, who whips them to work across the invisible distances of telephone connections, like Alberich flogging his Nibelungs to work in the mines. They simply know him as "The Boss," and grant that "he does the grunting and we do the work" (p. 526). By the end, JR has almost brought down Valhalla itself, a fact that he takes delight in when they begin to make the *Wall Street Journal*: "JR Corp. appears threatened by a credit squeeze whose dramatic repercussions could be felt throughout the corporate world" (pp. 649–50). Thus, the fearful thing is that the monster in JR is capable of witlessly bringing down the world.

Against all his artistic principles, Bast allows JR to blandish him until there is no choice but to serve the company that can't even spell his name properly (it comes out "Edwerd" on Bast's business cards). The business grows on Bast like a cancer. He begins to sound more and more like JR when he talks, and throughout Bast's frenzied work JR keeps assuring him that it is all designed to give him money so he will have freedom to do his artwork. Bast finally rejects their corporate success in a climactic scene when, his voice nearly gone from pneumonia, he manages to scream at JR: "you ruin everything you touch . . . why not smash everything? . . . the JR Family of Companies bringing America its full share of holy shit! . . . you can't get up to their level so you drag them down to yours" (pp. 658–59). In the end, the JR Corporation symbolizes everything wasteful and excremental transformed through Commerce into a mockery of the sacred. And while Bast eventually frees himself to go his own artistic way there is the troubling fact that JR, stripped of his empire by the I.R.S. and the S.E.C., will doubtless rise again like Hagen the son of Alberich. When last we hear him on the telephone, JR excitedly spells out his plans for a lecture tour of college campuses. Thus we finish *JR* with a sense of foreboding. This Alberich, whom Wagner decribed as a "darksome foe of love," only needs maturity to bring on the final *Götterdammerung*.

The technique of Gaddis's allusions to Alberich can be formulated in this way: he begins with a constituting scene, the school children's rehearsal of "The Rhinegold," then follows with less explicit references that nevertheless map the overall *Ring* myth onto JR's progress. This means that J. R. Vansant, like Alberich, will disappear from the action for lengthy periods when our attention shifts to Gaddis's mock-hero, Bast.

And if JR represents a composite of Wagner's Alberich/ Hagen characters, then Bast embodies both the Siegmund and Siegfried characters from the *Ring*. Once more Gaddis introduces these parallels with a constituting scene, which occurs when Bast and his step-sister, Stella Angel, attempt intercourse in the upstairs room of a tower behind the Bast home. We have thus moved further into the *Ring* cycle, for countless details link Bast and Stella to Siegmund and Sieglinda in Act One of "The Valkyrie": claps of thunder overhead as they fall onto the bed, flashes of lightening when Bast enters her, the high tower recalling Hunding's mountaintop retreat, and Bast carrying for years in his memory the image of Stella swimming naked, like Siegmund, who claims that Sieglinda is the "picture long hid in my heart."[5] These details all stem from Wagner, but Gaddis includes a crucial departure from the opera. Bast's spur-of-the-moment tryst with Stella ends in *coitus interruptus* when her dim-witted husband, Norman, stumbles into the tower. ("Sorry, it's a hell of a way to meet you," he says on page 140, ignorant of what's been going on upstairs.) There is a deeper irony, too, in the fact that while Bast's passions are serendipitous and purely romantic, Stella has engineered the seduction to obtain certain legal papers from her half-brother. Nevertheless, Bast thinks he has discovered in their stormy tryst a recognition of the *Ring* myth. He sits down at his piano and begins pounding out "the Ring motif" and singing Sieglinda's lines from the libretto (p. 142). Stella ought to get the gist of Bast's wild behavior because she has been reading a book called *Wagner: Man and Artist*, yet she is blinded from this artistic connection by her greed. And Bast is simply too naive at this point in the novel to question Stella's cold-hearted motives. Still, while Bast may not be a stencil of Siegmund here, the offspring of their frustrated coupling will be a new Bast who makes his way into the greedy world, literally parentless (as we will see), like Siegfried.

After this scene, the allusions to the operas become more generalized, as Bast drifts into the maelstrom of the JR Corporation, becomes its chief agent, even scores a fortune for JR while his musical compositions lie uncompleted. Gaddis suggests that Bast's sojourn inside the monolith of Commerce parallels Siegfried's battle with Fafner, from whom he may win the power of the Rhinegold. Bast also defeats a dragon, insofar as he pulls off a series of coups for JR, and like his Wagnerian counterpart the victory sets his blood aflame. Siegfried's amazed cry—"Rushing flows my feverish blood!"—becomes in Bast a literal fever brought on by exhaustion and pneumonia. The ills of capitalism injure him just as they finally stab Siegfried in the back.

Sick with pneumonia, Bast burns with a fever like

Siegfried's corpse flaming on its funeral pyre in "The Twilight of the Gods." This, coupled with the increasing frequency of Jack Gibbs God-damning everything in the last sections of the novel, seems to anticipate a *Götterdammerung* very close indeed to Wagner's tragic ending. Moreover, Governor Cates (Wotan) has also been brought low by the press of business. As the novel closes he is admitted into the same hospital room Bast is preparing to leave for repair work on his artificial heart. (Surely there is a metaphor in that.) But here occurs another important departure from the *Ring* myth, for Gaddis's Siegfried does not die. When Bast recovers he redeems not only his health but his Art, a triumph Gaddis figures in Bast's retrieving the musical scores he had tossed in a trash can out of despair. In this moment, Gaddis affirms the power of Art to stand alone, even to atone for a world gasping from JR's "holy shit."

The aptness of Gaddis's taking on the *Ring* myth reveals itself in other ways, too. Wagner was exiled from Germany during the 1850's for his socialist activities, and this opposition to the ills of capitalism, which first took shape in a pamphlet attacking the corruption of Art by monetary values (*Art and Revolution*, written in 1849), soon took dramatic form in the *Ring* cycle. His librettos center on renunciations of love, both fraternal and romantic, in the presence of greed, and this becomes Gaddis's main theme in *JR*, where love is all just money and calculated talk. We see it in numerous adult characters such as Amy Joubert, Jack Gibbs and Tom Eigen, all of whom haggle over their divorce settlements. Usury also subverts the children's love. When Marion Eigen asks her son David, "Do you love me?" he replies that he does, yet the child acts bewildered when she asks further, "How much?": "Some money . . . ?", he wonders (p. 267). Gaddis is careful, like Wagner, to put the blame for this depreciation on the parents. Bast, for example, inherits the struggle in his artistic soul from his father and grandfather, and from a division in his entire family between beauty and business, just as Siegfried inherited his struggle and loss from Siegmund and Wotan.

Yet Gaddis needs to take another step. Perhaps because there is no symbol within *Der Ring des Nibelungen* for the triumph of Art over Money, Gaddis steps outside Wagner's myth to consider the composer himself. Like Wagner, Bast becomes a true artist because he translates the experience of monetary corruption first into a kind of exile, when he refuses to speak with any of the people around his hospital bed, and the next into works of Art. Bast's finished compositions symbolize the power of Art to transform waste and strife into harmony. They are loving acts.

But there exists a blacker dilemma. *JR* argues that usury and strife are conditions of Nature, even language, which threatens to leave Art very little indeed. In this debate Jack Gibbs plays interlocutor, a role so large and overwhelmingly cynical in the novel that he almost dominates the book, like Satan in *Paradise Lost*. As the disintegrating moral center in this book, Jack's mind, like his coat pockets that bulge from a salmagundi of random notesheets, bursts with disparate knowledge only Gaddis can form into art. Jack's frenzied expostulations on Empedocles and entropy deepen our sense of Wagner's twilight age and argue that the cosmos as a whole is running down from sheer use.

Empedocles first enters *JR* by way of a bogus Greek inscription over the school entrance way—"ΕΒΦΜ ΣΑΟΗ ΑθθΦΒΡ"(p. 20)—which is not only meaningless, it is also unpronounceable. Jack supplied it to the blockheads running the school. They don't know what it might be, yet they admire the grandeur of the Greek letters anyway and one even proposes to use it as the epigraph of his "psychometric" volume on learning, if he can only find out what it means. So where does it come from? Jack throws out a red herring: "You might try Empedocles . . . I think it's a fragment from the second generation of his cosmology, maybe even the first . . . when limbs and parts of bodies were wandering around everywhere separately heads without necks, arms without shoulders, unattached eyes looking for foreheads" (p. 45; my ellipses).[6] This bait does come from Empedocles, and while Jack's paraphrase is right enough he is intentionally off-track on several counts. The letters mean nothing; Empedocles does shed an interesting light on the world of *JR*, but Jack doubtless has in mind the "third generation" of the cosmology when things are coming apart at the seams, not the first or second generation. Of course the simple point in his joke is that language has disintegrated at the joints, but there is more behind it.

In the first place, Jack probably intends that pied inscription to serve as a curse on the school. In his beautiful study of Greek religions, *Persephone*, Gunther Zuntz describes the Hellenic practice of burying the dead with metal lamellae carrying inscriptions. The so-called Orphic Gold Leaves bore poetic lines while leaden pieces, known as the *defixonum tabellae*, bore inscriptions corrupted beyond sense, like Jack's letters. Zuntz speculates that these were popular charms, "articles of mass consumption; objects of beadle's trade like the pictures of the Madonna and of Saints sold at Roman Catholic churches. This fact . . . implies that they came to be appreciated as material objects rather than as carriers of any words engraved on them."[7] He theorizes that the curses were associated with the myth of Kore's descent into Dis, and that they were doubtless directed against certain of the deceased's survivors above-ground. This supernatural power of the lead lamellae would explain why Jack always thinks of his Greek letters and Empedocles when he rides the subway: "looks like the God damn dawn of the world in here necks without heads, arms seeking shoulders, only God damned person lived here's Empedocles" (p. 406). These moments always occur after Jack has left the school, and they suggest that he means to execrate the school administrators' obsession with money (gold). In fact, during one of these underground journeys Jack makes the connection between Empedocles, the subway and his bogus inscription, then notices a vending machine that flattens pennies into lucky charms bearing The Lord's Prayer. The machine has "OUT OF ORDER scrawled across it" (p. 161). At moments like this, signification in *JR* seems to spread wall-to-wall.

In the second place, Jack's references to Empedocles dovetail neatly with the "Twilight of the Gods" motif from Wagner and, as we will see, with Jack's ideas on entropy. In Empedocles's cyclical cosmology the world-process is governed by opposing forces of Love (Amity), and Hatred (Strife). The process begins, and ends, in a condition he terms the "Sphairos," or sphere, an apex of creation where no elemental distinctions exist, no differentiations of beings, no becoming or decaying. It represents a starting point in the cosmic cycle, because the workings of Strife in the first generation begin to differentiate reality until, in the second, Amity brings balance and harmony, eliminating monsters that grew when disparate limbs attached themselves to the wrong bodies. Thirdly, Strife reasserts its power and once again the cosmos enters a disintegrating, twilight age before, at the last, being again expresses itself as a Sphairos. Now Jack suggests to the dunces running the school that they should try Empedocles's "second generation . . . maybe even the first," but there are some interesting distinctions arising here. With one hand Jack is surely playing to their eternal optimism about education (a business) and how it brings order and harmony to the mind, while with the other hand he is surely pointing to the third generation, of Strife, which Empedocles describes as a "joyless place" where "works without result run away like water," a place of wrath, greed, envy and sickness. It is a place where Ugliness has defeated Beauty, Talk has drowned out Silence, and Greed has killed Love. Empedocles calls these adverse qualities "Banes," and nothing could more accurately describe the grim conditions at the school JR attends. . . .

"Money . . . ? in a voice that rustled": with this first phrase in *JR*, Gaddis indicates that he means to question our assumptions about money and language. And with JR's repeated needling of Bast—"I just thought maybe we could use each other you know?"—the context of that original query widens until it includes all of Art in its relations to Commerce. One answer we can now consider is that the two are virtually equivalent, that money as a semiological system compares with the semiological systems of writing, painting, music, even for that matter the physiochemical system underpinning all Nature. Faced with that realization, the artist becomes an anachronism if he does not acknowledge the universality of usury in all he knows and makes. His precious romanticist notions about how "All art depends upon exquisite and delicate sensibility and such constant turmoil must ultimately be destructive" (p. 289); his desire to be original, as the Romantics understood that term; and lastly his expectation that in Nature he shall learn harmony: all of that melts away. The dilemma remaining is a quintessentially Postmodern formulation. For here is a novel in which people are feverishly imploring each other, over a ceaseless din, to "Listen!", and yet their only recourse *appears* to be, as George Steiner has observed in another connection, a profound silence.

Gaddis's answer is that one should slam neither one's door nor one's mouth. While Bast lies sick in his hospital bed, he listens speechlessly to a fellow patient with the wonderful name of Isidore Duncan, a man whose career—and Bast knows it—was demolished by the JR Family of Companies. Duncan reviles the world for the full range of sins we have witnessed in the novel, and he does so in the most coherent, uninterrupted discourse of the book. His theme, like Gibbs's, is the utter depreciation of value. Bast listens to these tirades with one ear and with the other attends to the music in his mind, a kind of split he has been well conditioned to, and the result is a sheaf of musical compositions that Duncan appreciates and encourages. Bast doesn't speak for some time, and then it is to agree with Duncan that nothing may be worth undertaking because the world only uses things up anyway. It takes several paragraphs of this before Bast realizes that Duncan has died in the night and he has been speaking to a corpse. Bast tosses his musical scores away, then feels a change of heart. I think what happens at this moment is that something Gibbs once told him has finally taken hold. Months previous, Gibbs had advised Bast that "the better among us bear each other in mind" (p. 290). And it rings true. For all his cynicism and fruitless effort, the one redeeming quality in Jack Gibbs is his compassion. For compassion is the imaginative exchange Usury cannot touch, and no doubt that is what Duncan had in mind when he advised Bast that "if you want to make a million you don't have to understand money, what you have to understand is people's fears about money" (p. 683). What people fear is the renunciation of love symbolized in the gnomish creature of J. R. Vansant.

At the last, Edward Bast's compositions can stand on their own for the delightfully human reason that a ruined manufacturer from a place called Zanesville liked the idea of his making them. The artist need not put his work in bondage to any interest beyond that, or to any interest beyond the work's recognition of its own design. Such recognitions, as Gaddis made abundantly clear in his first novel, come from the artist's assimilation of the past, even, one must say, his use of it, and it is only in this sense that the artist breaches Oscar Wilde's dictum: "All art is quite useless."

Gaddis's work is faithful to these precepts in every detail. *JR* is long, and it is difficult as Big Books tend to be. It tries our patience with every turn and transition. Yet if we can appreciate the art of Wagner's *Der Ring des Nibelungen* I believe we may come to appreciate *JR* in a similar spirit. *JR* is an astonishing book, and given the attention equal to the patient decades over which it was composed, this novel yields.

Notes

1. The published criticism on Gaddis: Joseph S. Salemi, "To Soar in Atonement: Art as Expiation in Gaddis's *The Recognitions*," *Novel*, 10 (1977), 127–36; John Stark, "William Gaddis: Just Recognition," *The Hollins Critic*, 14 (1977), 1–12; Charles Leslie Banning, "William Gaddis's *JR*: The Organization of Chaos and the Chaos of Organization," *Paunch*, 42/43 (1975), 153–65—the only essay, and a very early one indeed, to discuss *JR* at any length.
2. For example, it would be interesting to distinguish the Big Book from what may well be a sub-species—the encyclopedic narrative. Working from Mikhail Bakhtin's seminal study, *Rabelais and His World* (Cambridge, Mass.: M.I.T., 1975), Edward Mendelson begins to define that form during his essay on Pynchon, "Gravity's Encyclopedia," in George Levine and David Leverenz's *Mindful Pleasures: Essays on Thomas Pynchon* (Boston: Little Brown, 1976), pp. 161–95.
3. The transition occurs on p. 18. All references to *JR* are from the edition published by Knopf (New York: 1975) and will be cited parenthetically in the essay.
4. I have used Stewart Robb's translation of *The Ring of the Nibelung* (New York: Dutton, 1960). This line occurs in "The Rhinegold," Scene One, p. 13.
5. Ibid., p. 92. Bast's recollection of Stella swimming also recalls Sieglinda's statement in Act One of "The Valkyrie": "A brook I looked in / gave back my face— / and now again I behold it; / what once the pool did reveal / now is reflected by you."
6. See *Die Fragmente der Vorsokratiker*, ed. and tr. H. Diels, rev. by Walther Kranz (Dublin/Zurich: Wiedemann, 1952). Jack gives a fair rendering of fragments 57 and 60 of MS 31B.
7. See Gunther Zuntz, *Persephone: Three Essays on Religion and Thought in Magna Graecia* (Oxford: Clarendon, 1971), p. 351. My thanks to Guy Davenport for calling my attention to the Orphic leaves.

THOMAS LeCLAIR

From "William Gaddis, *JR*, and the Art of Excess"

Modern Fiction Studies, Winter 1981–82, pp. 587–98

The 772 small-print pages of Barth's *LETTERS* raise once more at decade's end a question often asked of American fiction in the 1970s: how much is too much? The question has been put to Pynchon's *Gravity's Rainbow*, Heller's *Something Happened*, McElroy's *Lookout Cartridge*, DeLillo's *Ratner's Star*, and Coover's *The Public Burning*, among others, and it is a question that has particularly affected the reputation, as well as the writing, of William Gaddis, whose 726-page *JR* was published in 1975. One answer is offered by a minor character in *JR*: the recording of "longer works of fiction now dismissed as classics and remaining largely unread due to the effort involved in reading and turning any more than two hundred pages."[1] Reviewers with two-week deadlines naturally prefer the short masterpiece, the new *Gatsby*, but quarterly-thinking critics have also complained that these novels are overly long, self-indulgent, excessive. Writing about *JR*, George Steiner grumbled that the avant-garde American novel "has become elephantine in dimension."[2] Whereas dinosaurs might well be avoided, elephants—and whales—seem to be fine mammalian models for fiction with important purposes. What critics of these novels consider excess is, I think, what places them in the first rank of fiction in the '70s. *JR* is my case in point. . . .

Of the novels I've named, Gaddis' *JR* takes the most chances with its excess. Gaddis' vision of America is of a land of excess, of quantitative values and uncontrolled bigness, a place where time, people, and language are atomized. Whereas Pynchon, Coover, and others share aspects of this vision, *JR*, more than any of their books, imitates what it hates, relentlessly insists that the reader occupy in fiction what he inhabits in America. The excess of *JR* is its consistency: about the proliferating opportunities for the waste of American energies, the novel is itself prodigal and is composed almost entirely in the language of waste, the gibbering jargons and double-talk in which America does its business. We have our bricoleurs of waste: Barthelme has been compared to Wallace Stevens' Man on the Dump, and Vonnegut in *Breakfast of Champions* drawns an anus through which we are to imagine his book moving. But *JR* is an audacious act of imaginative totalism, a book that exceeds the limits of conventional satire to create a "runaway system," a new and instructive set of fictional relations.[3]

Other novelists I've mentioned have published either popular or conventionally scaled works, safety platforms for their experiments with excess. With Gaddis, the excess of *JR* is partially a response to the reception given the excess of his only other book, *The Recognitions*, published in 1955, Deep in *JR*, Gaddis has a Public Relations man read titles and reviewers' blurbs from an invented publisher's trade list. The seven titles are anagrams of *The Recognitions*, and the comments are from its reviews. Qualities for which *The Recognitions* was criticized in the quoted reviews—too long, too imposing, too negative, too talky—Gaddis makes central in the composition of *JR*. Attacked by Maxwell Geismer ("M Axswill Gummer" reviewing "O! Chittering Ones") in the *Saturday Review* for ignorance of life—"the outside world of American life is described so imperfectly and so superficially as to make us feel that the novelist himself has never known it" (p. 515)—Gaddis documents in *JR* has comprehensive knowledge of the "outside world" of education and commerce, the environment incapable of nourishing *The Recognitions* and the environment in which Gaddis worked while writing *JR*. Milton Rugoff ("Milton R. Goth" in the *New York Herald Tribune Book Review*) thought *The Recognitions*, despite its profound and multiple basis for indicting falsity, was "a projection of private discontent" (p. 515). In *JR* Gaddis directly expresses his personal discontent by using his unrecognized novel as an example of cultural wastefulness. The writer Thomas Eigen has a name (*eigen* is German for characteristic, self), a past (a long and long-neglected novel), and a job writing speeches for executives that suggest he is a version of the author of *The Recognitions*. Although Eigen receives no support for his achievement, Gaddis does not indulge himself in the portrait. Like the other artists in *JR*—and in *The Recognitions*—Eigen is treated harshly. His complaints about his "shoot the pianist" culture are often rationalizations for his own self-absorption and lack of a artistic commitment. Outrage does energize *JR*, and some of it is personal but not, as John Gardner accused in his review of the book, private and uncontrolled.[4] What Gaddis suggests of his past is measured and representative of the larger cultural issues he pursues. . . .

The art of excess works by contraction and expansion: reduction of the possibilities for stylistic, formal, or thematic variety, then a proliferation of materials within the chosen constraints. The exhaustive development of certain words or concepts exemplifies this process. *LETTERS* is about letters in all their manifestations—alphabet, history, literature. In *Something Happened*, Heller repeats and transforms his title phrase to create a refrain for failed causal investigation. "Recognition" is given extended permutation in *The Recognitions*. The privileged word and concept of *JR* is waste. Very early in the novel Gaddis has a character summarize the subject: "what America's all about, waste disposal and all"[5] (p. 27). A few pages later, the range of Gaddis' interest in waste—from art to business to individuals—is economically and wittily presented by quickly cutting across three channels of televised lessons on silk worms, industry, and the human body:

> "—beautiful colors, but the smell of this waste silk fermenting is so offensive that . . ."
> "—improving production knowhow and eliminating waste is the cause of human better . . ."
> "—elimination of waste and is fitted with a muscular mechanism, or sphincter . . ."(p. 51)

The Random House unabridged dictionary lists five primary meanings of *waste* as a transitive verb:

1. To consume, spend, or employ uselessly or without adequate return;
2. To fail or neglect to use;
3. To destroy or consume gradually;
4. To wear down or reduce in bodily substance, health, or strength;
5. To devastate or ruin.

As a noun, *waste* also means barren tract, garbage, and excrement; as adjective, superfluous and excessive. A wastrel is not only a wasteful person, but is also a waif, an abandoned child. Every one of these meanings is dramatized in *JR*, including the last, which describes the title character J. R. Vansant, an eleven-year-old poor and abandoned boy who creates his business empire out of the leftover materials and rubbish of the conglomerate with which he ends up competing. His empire and the American enterprise it imitates have as their consequences the other meanings of *waste:* things and people are uselessly consumed; talents are neglected; the land is laid waste. Garbage and excrement are major motifs. And that last meaning of *waste*—excessive—is everywhere in evidence.

To accommodate and to reinforce all of the meanings of *waste*, Gaddis constructs *JR* as a set of nestling analogues in which a large master system is replicated by smaller systems within it. This is a method, composition by analogue and recursion, that gives *JR* and other works of excess, most notably *Ratner's Star*, *Lookout Cartridge*, and *LETTERS*, a vertical development that complements the linear movement of plot. The master system of *JR* is a "runaway system," a term coined by Gregory Bateson in *Steps to an Ecology of Mind* and developed by Anthony Wilden in *System and Structure:*

> The present relationship of the industrial system and those who control it (state or private capitalism) to the biosocial environment (to me, to you, to nature, to its "resources") is known as a positive feedback or runaway relationship: the more you have, the more you get. Unlike the primary control system of nature, negative feedback, which seeks out deviation and neutralizes or transforms it, positive feedback increases the deviations. . . . In the short run, this is

> fine for those who invest their money at compound interest or who draw their profits from underdeveloped countries, but in nature, all runaway systems (such as a forest fire or a supernova) are inexorably controlled, in the long run, by negative feedback at a second level.[6]

This eventual negative feedback, Wilden goes on to say, brings elaboration of a new ecological system of extinction. In mechanical or social systems that imitate the negative feedback of natural ecology, a governor is built in to trip off destructive runaway processes. In *JR*, the industrial conglomerate that reaches into every area of the world and the book is headed by Governor John "Black Jack" Cates, whose name is appropriate in several ways. *Cates* is an archaic word meaning buy or seize; *Governor* suggests the interlocking of business and politics as well as the control on any system of growth. Choosing to develop in some detail J. R.'s empire, Gaddis can only suggest through Cates's hyperactivity and his blizzards of orders to underlings the enormous extent of his influence. What is clear, though, from these indirect means is that Cates is an ironic "governor," for his obsessional drive for expanded production, organization, and control increases positive feedback—"the more you have, the more you get"—in the economic system. Temporary setbacks, changes, and threats occur, but they do not interrupt the growth of Cates's conglomerate or the increase in deviations between rich and poor, developed and undeveloped countries, the powerful few and the powerless many. One of Cates's motives is the reduction of waste, which, he says, "shows an undisciplined strain of mind" (p. 110). Considering competition wasteful, Cates uses any means he can to diminish variety and enlarge the power of his conglomerate toward monopoly. In attempting to rid his system of waste, he reduces the chances for a natural homeostatic balancing of economic processes and accelerates toward an ultimate waste the runaway system he is supposed to be "governing."

The JR Corporation is both a small analogue of Cates's operations and a prophetic example of the eventual fate of the runaway. Runaway systems produce on a graph what are called "J-curves," steeply accelerating lines of ascent to which Gaddis may be alluding in J. R.'s rapid rise. J. R.'s last name, Vansant, also fits the role Gaddis has him play: Vansant suggests vanguard, the new "saint" of American life. Begun with the waste materials of Cates's conglomerate and helped by the mistakes of Cates's over-extended employees, J. R.'s corporation, with its chain of unhealthy products, old-age homes, drug companies, funeral homes, and cemeteries, is a primer version of the consumer necropolis that Cates constructs. The rules are credit, investment, unrestrained growth, rapid turnover, and exploitation of resources, consumers, employees, and the institutions of government. As J. R.'s holdings increase and his influence proliferates, his attitudes toward expansion and control come to resemble Cates's. "You can't just play to play," says J. R., "because the rules are only for if you're playing to win which that's the only rules there are" (p. 301). Even when J. R.'s three-month empire begins to weaken, because it too naively and rapidly imitates the runaway process of the larger economic system, he cannot bear to cut back growth. He keeps accumulating companies, products, and employees. Finally he blames himself for not thinking in larger terms; his lament comments on the system, its rule and result, he wishes he had more ambitiously imitated: "how did I know the more you can spend the more you get, I mean I should have only went after all this here cost-plus stuff right at the start! Like I mean these here little booklets they never tell you how you get to take this percent of the more you can *waste* . . ." (p. 663; my emphasis). When J. R. loses his holdings near the novel's end, they are subsumed into Cates's conglomerate, thus contributing further to runaway bigness. That the JR Corporation, headed by an eleven-year-old and represented by a musician, could exist as long as it does and grow as fast as it does implies that the processes in which it takes part are indeed "runaway," out of human control. In fact, both J. R. and Cates are insubstantial figures: J. R. a phantom voice on the phone, Cates a collection of V-like spare parts. They are the Horatio Alger story at its two extremes: ragged youth and old age, and the book moves to this rhythm. *JR* begins in the school, where J. R. is trained to profit, moves to the adult corporate world, and concludes in a hospital where the aged and the prematurely wasted have their end. Set against this natural cycle, however, are the economic processes which continue on, despite changes in people, toward an explosion rather than a rounding off. Gaddis' cutting back and forth among a large number of characters, almost all of whom have as their motives catching up with or staying ahead of the economy, further reduces the importance of individuals and emphasizes the processes at their expense.

The consequences of the runaway in *JR*—and in America—are summarized by Anthony Wilden: "Through unlimited imposition of order and organization, it (industrial capitalism) drives the biosphere and sociosphere to disorder and disorganization. Capital thus becomes equivalent to rigidity, to bound energy, to waste."[7] Entropy is Gaddis' term for these results. An instructional film reminds Jack Gibbs's students and readers that "Energy may be changed but not destroyed" (p. 20). In the runaway system, the free energies of individuals are used by—bound to—large, powerful governmental and commercial institutions such as Cates's, thus increasing their complexity and organization, qualities that are negentropic. The effect is entropy in individual lives: energy is unavailable to do private work; families and individuals break down, degenerate, waste away. As private lives in *JR* tend toward a probable state of fragmentation, the runaway system, ironically, moves toward a unity or sameness that also is finally entropic. By swallowing up education and art, and by imposing its quantitative values on sources of other values, business destroys activities that are needed for negative feedback and its own preservation. Cates and J. R. at first tolerate education and art, as though they were a form of useful, harmless competition, but by the end of the novel both tycoons have lost their patience and have contributed to the further degeneration of teachers and artists. Cates's books are full of advertisements; J. R.'s radio station displaces serious music because it does not pay. Characters who owned independent businesses, worked for the schools, supported themselves, or drifted in a hand-to-mouth existence, even the nonexistent Grynzspan, end up working for J. R. or Cates. Size and organization create a consistency—an absence of flexibility and variety—that ultimately leads to the waste Wilden notes. . . .

Most of the characters are oblivious to the runaway system they live within, but even the character who most fully recognizes the causes and effects of the runaway—Jack Gibbs—cannot resist it. As the major character, the voice with the most complete history and authority, Gibbs replicates many of the themes I've discussed. Given his reference to Norbert Wiener (p. 402), his name recalls Josiah Gibbs, the nineteenth-century scientist who, according to Wiener, introduced probability and contingency into physics: "In Gibbs' universe," says Wiener, "order is least probable, chaos most probable."[8] Jack Gibbs's life also tends toward disorder. Like he is abandoned as a child. He begins working for a small family business representative. Attempting to stay financially even, Gibbs cheats and gambles; he neglects his child and his book. His clothes and speech are equally tattered. Acute critic of waste, Gibbs personifies it.

"*Endropy*," as one of Gibbs's students spells *entropy*, suggests the destruction, deterioration, sickness, and end products that characterize the numerous motifs Gaddis uses to underline the results of the runaway system.[9] As Cates, J. R., and their employees manipulate people, property, and paper into new organizations, Gaddis laces the novel with combinations of waste. The land is being stripped and paved, mined out and filled up with pollution. Long Island is a "leaching field" (p. 673). Gibbs says he used to know every line of *The Waste Land*; now he lives in it. Throughout *JR*, objects are breaking or falling apart; musical instruments, cars, furniture, buildings, toys, and plumbing get demolished. Papers, coins, pages—any kind of material that needs to be sorted—are spilled or shuffled into random piles. Mail is shredded. Shoes are mismatched; clothes are torn or soiled: suits ripped, pants vomited on or urinated on. The apartment where Bast, Gibbs, and Eigen try to work is a rubbish heap of unused and unusable products. Garbage and excrement mark urban and suburban settings. Scenes take place in toilets; shit is found in Bast's piano, in J. R.'s speech ("holy shit"), and secretly spelled in a JR Corporation logo. Most of the major characters are ill during the few months of the novel's present. Bast ends in a hospital, along with Cates, Angel, and a minor character named Duncan; Eigen is sick; Schramm kills himself; Hyde and others are injured in the many accidents that occur. Gibbs summarizes the physical world of *JR* with an allusion to Empedocles: "only audience sit through it's Empedocles, shambling creatures with countless hands eyes wandering around looking for a God damned forehead parts joining up all wrong" (p. 407). Even love scenes are described with this same fragmentation of body parts: no person seems whole or fully purposeful. These motifs occur most frequently in Gaddis' occasional transitional passages, such as the following:

> Bast halted there on the far platform hit before and behind like an invalid in a hotel fire, looking, one way, the other, finally dropping his shoulders and his eyes to dead rivulets leading toward stairs, up them catching breath at the top against uneaten frankfurters turning with venemous patience on a counter grill, more stairs and the street, where the sole of his shoe took up its flapping cadence windblown past ranked garbage cans capped at merry angles down the hill to a doorway lighted, like the rest, by a bulb so dim he cast no shadow as he entered, pursuing a broken refrain up the stairs and down linoleum worn through by fatigue, pausing to move mail with his foot before fitting the long iron key and lifting the door on the sound of running water. (p. 362)

Here the details of waste pile atop each other, rapidly accumulating as Gaddis' long sentence pushes through its participial clauses. The character Bast is diminished as an agent: he is like an invalid, weak before large forces, passive to unpleasant sensations. The physical world has a mocking, malignant presence. The passage thus represents in miniature the cumulative mass in *JR* and the effects it has on character and reader.

For Gaddis composing and for the critic judging the success of *JR*, the critical questions were and are: how to present disorder and waste without contributing to them? How to make the reader apprehend anew the familiar materials of contemporary commerce? The solution—and the achievement of *JR*—is to have the test imitate in its form and style the runaway system it is about. This ambition for full correspondence between technique and material is shared by other artists of excess. Concerned with the meaning of opposites, DeLillo breaks *Ratner's Star* into two halves, makes it a binary book. Coover's *The Public Burning* is a series of circus acts because he saw the Rosenberg case as a circus of hysteria. John Gardner has articulated the traditionalist complaint against some of these novels of excess—that they self-indulgently eschew communication—but I believe that the motive for excess in *JR* and the others is a radically felt need to communicate new, large, even planetary and possibly saving visions of contemporary existence.[10] *Gravity's Rainbow, LETTERS, Ratner's Star, Lookout Cartridge, JR*, and, less obviously, *Something Happened* and *The Public Burning* have been significantly influenced by contemporary science, especially cybernetics and systems theory. Perhaps more than any other generation of American novelists, these writers understand the importance of form and medium in communication. Attempting to reconstruct basic categories of intellectual experience, they deform old modes and create new models to make the reader *formally* aware of and participate in processes that underlie or surround the personal relations traditional fiction takes as its subject. There is urgency in the excess, a sense that codes of representation and metonymy have failed, that radical new communication is necessary for survival, not just the survival of the novel as a form but the survival of the author and audience. This urgency and Gaddis' outrage are why *JR* is not just about a runaway system but *is* a runaway, a system of fiction characterized by growth through positive feedback, mass, fragmentation at local, personal levels, order at high and abstract levels of organization, and a lack of flexibility and variety. Sentence to sentence, page to page, the surfaces of *JR* are fragmented, atomized by interruption, confusion, and rapid cutting. These surfaces seem to be ruled by positive feedback: the more we have, the more we get of the same kind of language. Gaddis absents himself from the text, giving the illusion that it is ungoverned, rapidly creating itself out of itself. Materials accumulate to massiveness, but without any qualitative change in the surface. One of the epigraphs Gibbs collects—"life is all middle" (p. 486)—is appropriate for *JR*; although the novel follows the rise and fall of J. R.'s empire, it is only a small part of the middle of the larger processes Gaddis continually makes us aware of. Large conceptual orders—the organization of analogue and motif I've discussed—do simultaneously come into existence, but, as in the runaway system, these orders are principles by which the book grows rather than static patterns to which the materials conform. Order seems the preparation for or condition of more disorder. The reader cannot integrate all the book's details; he can only understand the process that generates them. What is diminished in the text, as in the world it is about, is the human scale. Significant action and continuity are disrupted by fragmentation and subsumed in the larger systems Gaddis constructs. Early in the novel, a suburb is described as a place where "things came scaled down to wieldy size" (p. 17); but *JR* is about the city and the multi-national corporation where mass and multiplicity have changed the scale of experience. Minute trivialization and enormous power, consistent in their waste, are the proportions of the runaway and of *JR*.

Notes

1. William Gaddis, *JR* (New York: Knopf, 1975), p. 527; subsequent references are in parentheses in the text.
2. George Steiner, review of *JR*, *The New Yorker*, 26 January 1976, p. 109.

3. A "runaway system" is defined below and in Anthony Wilden, *System and Structure* (London: Tavistock, 1972).
4. John Gardner, review of *JR*, *The New York Review of Books*, 10 June 1976, pp. 35–40.
5. William Gaddis, *The Recognitions* (New York: Avon, 1974).
6. Wilden, pp. 208–209.
7. Wilden, p. 394.
8. Norbert Wiener, *The Human Use of Human Beings* (New York: Avon, 1967), p. 20.
9. Susan Strehle Klemtner, "'For a Very Small Audience': The Fiction of William Gaddis," *Critique*, 19 (1978), pp. 61–73, discusses some of the motifs in greater detail.
10. John Gardner, *On Moral Fiction* (New York: Basic Books, 1978).

MAVIS GALLANT

1922–

Mavis Gallant, whose father was English and whose mother was of mixed German-Rumanian-Breton background, was born in Montreal, Canada, on August 11, 1922. After the early death of her father, she had an unsettled childhood, attending a large number of different schools and growing up bilingual in English and French. She wrote poems from childhood, and from the age of nineteen produced stories, plays, and novels, at first without attempting to publish. After working as a reporter for the Montreal *Standard* from 1944 to 1950, she began publishing stories in the *New Yorker* in 1951.

Gallant's first collection of stories, *The Other Paris*, appeared in 1956, and five further volumes have followed, including *The Pegnitz Junction* (1973) and *From the Fifteenth District* (1979). She has also published the novels *Green Water, Green Sky* (1959) and *A Fairly Good Time* (1970), and her play *What Is to Be Done?* was produced in 1982.

In recent years Gallant, who lives in Paris, has achieved increasing recognition. She has been decorated with the Order of Canada, and in 1982 received the Governor-General's Award for literature. She was writer-in-residence at the University of Toronto in 1983–84, and in 1984 was awarded an honorary doctorate by the University of St. Anne, Nova Scotia.

It is hard to tell the novella from the eight short stories in this new and excellent collection of Mavis Gallant's fiction *From the Fifteenth District*. Four out of the eight short stories are about as long as the novella, and all of the pieces here (which originally appeared in *The New Yorker*) show a novelist's imagination at work, spanning a large public world and penetrating many private ones. Gallant ranges over the European scene since the mid-1930s, but never strays far from World War II. That war haunts almost every story; it is an approaching conflict, an upheaval which has just ended, leaving the world in disarray, or a distant but persistent memory which still undermines the postwar era of peace.

Most of the characters who inhabit this unsettled international world are exiles from their homelands, not by force or by design, but by virtue merely of circumstances, dire and not so dire. Gallant traces their personal histories in stories that proceed at an unhurried pace, accruing details and nuances about pasts, places, relationships, and inner lives. The most telling details are those that reveal what her characters selectively remember or forget about their pasts.

What Carmela, the young Italian protagonist of the novella, "The Four Seasons," remembered "for the present, was one smile, one gesture, one man's calm blessing." But rather than being the legacy of composure it seems, the calm blessing is a more disturbing sign. It is the parting gesture of a foreign Jewish doctor being deported as Mussolini clamps down and the war spreads—a war which bewildered Carmela during the year she spent as nanny to an expatriot English family. In Gallant's web of contrasting perceptions and political tensions, the doctor's gesture resists simple reading. For the doctor, it is perhaps a mature acknowledgement of powers beyond his control and understanding; for the bystander Carmela, Gallant suggests, it is a youthful, too easy recollection that threatens to absolve her of an effort to understand—that year, that war or that man.

The usually unheroic drama between personal and public histories which takes place in many of the stories is played out most clearly in one of the longer stories, "Remission." Englishman Alec Webb, once a prisoner of war and now unsuited to life in the fast-paced crowded postwar world, retreats to the Riviera to die a very slow death. While he declines, his wife, uprooted there with their family, instinctively and none too nobly finds a "foothold in the nineteen-fifties." Gallant starkly contrasts these two characters accommodations to the passage of time. In other stories, her characters variously adapt to and resist their circumstances—the vicissitudes of the hotel business in southern France during the war, a return from a prisoner-of-war camp, a son's emigration. Gallant's characters lose and find one another as they cross and recross national borders, live through wars—travels and trouble usually beyond the scope of short fiction.—A. H., *NR*, Aug. 25, 1979, p. 39

In *Home Truths* most of Mrs. Gallant's Canadians are either bound by convention or wasted by efforts to transcend a culture they perceive as imitative, provincial and second-rate. The struggle to wrench a personal identity out of a skewed national identity can lead her to create grotesques and buffoons: matrons, Red Queens, who wear pearl earrings like the Duchess of Kent's. ("Brooches pinned to their cashmere cardigans carried some daft message about the Empire.") Bertie Knox, clerk and mimic, can do any Canadian accent, but during World War II he keeps a photograph of himself over his desk "in full kilt, Highland Light Infantry, 1917: he had gone 'home,' to a completely unknown Old Country, and joined up there." And the worldly Dr. Chauchard, upper-bourgeois French, whose "sitting-room-converted-to-waiting-room had on display landmarks of Paris, identified in two languages:

Le Petit Palais—The Petit Palais
Place Vendôme—Place Vendôme
Rue de la Paix—Rue de la Paix

as if the engraver had known they would find their way to a wall in Montreal." Hilarious, but it is more than touchingly ironic nonsense, given the passions that later brought about a significant separatist movement in Canada.

With few exceptions, these stories are set in the late 1930's and 40's. Mrs. Gallant has a sharp sense of history. Incidents are carefully dated—Prohibition, Depression, treaties, the entrance of Canada into "Hitler's war." She writes of a Canada that was and makes good use of her Red Queens and clownish clerks to set up cultural pretensions and longings. She's funny and perceptive on houses, on dress—the customs of a country in which you could almost never be right.

Quick as she is with telling details—flat nasal accents, ugly reddish-brown streets—Mrs. Gallant never patronizes her country. There is no complicit wink at the reader, no easy put-down—the mere reference to shopping mall, beer brand, K-Mart, the smart visual that asks for the conditioned response in too many American stories of recent years. Her Canadians are as particular and complex as Eudora Welty's Moodys and MacLains. When she uses types—the cold godmother, the remittance man—it is to redefine an attitude, correct a memory. The godmother, who disowns the grown child, is boozy, chill. Caught up in her war work, she is amusing, crisp about her aging Yorkshire terrier:

"'I would like it if Minnie could hang on until the end of the war,' Georgie said. 'I'm sure she'd like the victory parades and the bands. But she's thirteen, so I don't know.'

"That was the way she and my parents and their friends had talked to each other. The duller, the more earnest, the more literal generation I stood for seemed to crowd the worn white room, and to darken it further."

Here the built-in answer to the past once again requires that you say what you are.

In "Varieties of Exile," the disreputable or younger son sent out from England—the remittance man—is played off against the real refugees who flood into Montreal. These "Belgians, French, Catholic German, Socialist German, Jewish German, Czech" come to Linnet Muir, she admits, "straight out of the twilit Socialist-literary landscape of my reading and my desires." The story is about Linnet's willful idea that people must behave according to the script in her head. The refugees are romantic. The remittance man she meets on a commuter train is not. Looking back, she can date her discovery that life does not adhere to literary models, nor can she peg people, get them all down. The refugees are busily assimilating, even taking out Canadian passports. The remittance man—vaguely intellectual, a woolly socialist—she has written off. But he appears heroically in casualty lists as "Maj. Francis Cairns, dead of wounds in Italy."

The stiff set of mind placed like a template on life is seen again in "Virus X," a wandering story in which a smug young woman, Lottie Benz, comes to Paris with the conclusion to her thesis drawn before she does the research. Confronted with Vera, a young Ukrainian woman from home who has had an illegitimate baby and is now knocking around Europe, Lottie's scholarship crumbles. She never gets to the libraries where she intends to prove that minority groups can be integrated "without a loss of ethnic characteristics." Like the Poles in Canada, with their Easter eggs. . . .

"You crazy or something?" Vera asks. It is a fairly comic piece that could turn predictable—Vera, freewheeling and triumphant; Lottie, unstable, giddy with her props gone—but Mrs. Gallant resists any route that might echo a thesis, "trying to stick people in it" (Vera's words). It is characteristic of the best stories in *Home Truths* that there is always another rule to be broken, another limit to be crossed. Lottie does not write a word of her inane study, but she composes, in her head, open, insightful letters, never to be mailed to her dull fiancé. She is not courageous—she will return to Canada and marry this man she does not care for. Like the flu that has disoriented her, Europe is over, and her honest, imaginative words will never be said.

Mrs. Gallant has a remarkable sense of place. Her snowy streets and stark row houses are as carefully drawn as Elizabeth Bowen's English cities in wartime. Her men and women do not live their exacting stories in a void. Where you are is as important as what you are. It's more than atmosphere—whether you find Paris, Geneva, the south of France liberating, therefore possible, or whether you live thinly in those cities as an outsider, but know that going home will never do. She is as sure of her Montreal as Joyce was of his Dublin—that it is the place from which the stories flow.—MAUREEN HOWARD, "When the Identity Is the Crisis," *NYTBR*, May 5, 1985, p. 26

GEORGE WOODCOCK

From "Memory, Imagination, Artifice: The Late Short Fictions of Mavis Gallant"
The World of Canadian Writing
1980, pp. 93–114

je suis seul, isolé, expatrié au milieu de ma famille et dans ma patrie! (Blaise Cendrars)

Absolute plausibility, though not mimesis as such, I take to be one of the principal goals of fiction. The vision, no matter how fantastic, must convince the reader through its self-consistency. And absolute plausibility demands absolute artifice, not faith to actuality, which is why Flaubert outshines Zola and Chekhov outlives Guy de Maupassant. It is also why Mavis Gallant, though little recognized in Canada, outwrites most other Canadians. If I had to define her short fictions—novellas and short stories—setting aside obvious matters of theme and narrative construction, I would—and shall—talk about the impeccable verbal texture and the marvellous painterly surface of the scene imagined through the translucent veil of words, the kind of surface that derives from a close and highly visual sense of the interrelationship of sharply observed detail.

It would need a whole volume for the kind of study that might examine and relate the autonomous worlds of all Mavis Gallant's short fictions, of which there must be about a hundred, by no means all of them collected into volumes. In this essay I have decided to restrict myself to sixteen stories, which fall into three rather clearly defined groups in terms of terrain and theme. They are all fairly late stories, the first of them dating from the early 1960s and most from the 1970s, at least in terms of publication. Given Mavis Gallant's inclination to work intermittently on stories over long periods, the date of publication is not an entirely reliable clue to the time when writing first began, though it usually is an indication of the completion point of the work which emerges out of the long process of reordering and reduction to which every story by Gallant is subjected almost as if it were sculpture.

These sixteen stories all concern people who in some way or another are alone, isolated, expatriated, even when they remain within their families or return to their fatherlands. One of the most significant features of Mavis Gallant's fiction is that, while she has never restricted herself to writing about Canada or about Canadians, and has written more than most creators of fiction on people of other cultures whose inner lives she could enter only imaginatively, she has never, during her period as a mature writer, written from immediate observation of people living in her here-and-now. Distance in time and place seem always necessary.

Almost all the stories I shall be discussing have been written in Paris, where Gallant has lived most of the time since she left Canada in 1950. By now she has so lived herself into the Gallic environment that most of her friends speak French, and the depth of her involvement in French affairs was shown very clearly in "The Events in May: A Paris Notebook" (*The New Yorker,* 14 September, 21 September 1968), which recounted her adventures and observations during the abortive revolutionary situation of 1968 in France.

The "Notebook" dealt almost exclusively with French people and their reactions to events around them, and it showed the same sharp observation of action, speech and setting that one finds in Gallant's stories. There were parts, one felt, that only needed to be taken out of the linear diary form and reshaped by the helical patterning of memory for them to become the nuclei of excellent stories. Perhaps one day they will, but up to now Mavis Gallant has rarely written in fiction about these Parisians among whom she lives. What happens when she infrequently does so is shown in "The Cost of Living," where the two young French bohemians of the story (only one of them a Parisian) are less important than the two Australian sisters whom they exploit and whose education in "the cost of living"—to be interpreted emotionally as well as financially—provides the theme as well as the title of the story.

Similarly, though Mavis Gallant has written on occasion about Canadians in Europe, who usually find it hard to accept the lifestyles they encounter (or avoid encountering), it took her twenty years after her departure from Montreal to turn to the imaginative reconstruction of the vanished city of her childhood and youth, in the five interlinked Linnet Muir stories which have appeared in *The New Yorker* but are as yet uncollected. These examples of memory transmuted, which in intention at least bring Mavis Gallant very close to the Proust she has admired so greatly, form one group among the stories I shall be discussing.

It is virtually impossible to escape memory as a potent factor in Mavis Gallant's stories, and the next group of fictions, while they do not draw on the memory of personal experience, are imaginative constructions in which remembered observations and remembered history play a great part. They concern the Germans (a people Mavis Gallant does not know from experience as well as she knows the Canadians or the French or even the English), and specifically the post-Nazi Germans. One novella and six stories are here involved. The novella and five of the stories comprise the volume entitled *The Pegnitz Junction;* one other German story, "The Latehomecomer," appeared in *The New Yorker* (8 July 1974), but so far it has not been collected.

. . . "An Unmarried Man's Summer" is the tale of Walter Henderson, a harmless homosexual living on the Riviera with his Italian valet Angelo, a repellent youth whom Walter rescued from slum life when he was still a graceful boy. Walter has not always been what we see him in the present of the story, when he is living in the villa called Les Anémones (where only irises grow), pursuing an empty routine "where nothing could be more upsetting than a punctured tire or more thrilling than a sunny day." The story coils from past into present and back to past again, telling us through flash after flash of memory about Walter's past, about the wartime heroism he has chosen to forget, about the childhood which in the summer of the story comes galloping back when his beloved sister and her born-to-failure Anglo-Irish husband, on their way home from an effort at farming in South Africa, plant themselves on him with their two undisciplined children.

There is a sharp ironic tone to "An Unmarried Man's Summer," in which Gallant is pursuing one of her favourite aims, to reveal the inconsistency between expectations—particularly romantic expectations—and reality. Summers are the dullest times in Walter's years, when his phone never rings because the rich ladies on whom he dances attendance have gone away to avoid the hordes of summer vacationers, whom he escapes by hiding in his villa with Angelo and his old cat, William of Orange. Theoretically, the arrival of his sister, to whom he was once deeply attached, should relieve the seasonal tedium. In fact, it merely disrupts Walter's routine of life-avoidance and tangles the web of illusion in which he prefers to remain suspended.

Walter's brother-in-law is coarse and boring. His sister perpetually criticizes him, trying to show up the emptiness of his parasitic existence. And parents and children alike spoil Angelo, who turns under their influence into a sulky lout far different from the appealing boy Walter had thought he would always remain; they even try to entice him away to work on the farm they propose to start in England. When they go, leaving behind them a discontented and intolerable Angelo, the summer is ended, the rich ladies come back, and Walter remakes the invasion into a series of amusing stories as he returns to the empty relationships that make his life.

> He tells his stories in peaceful dining rooms, to a circle of loving, attentive faces. He is surrounded by the faces of women. Their eyes are fixed on him dotingly, but in homage to another man: a young lover killed in the 1914 war; an adored but faithless son.

People in Mavis Gallant's stories tend to live vicariously and on a surface whose perturbations show their inner storms; tend to reveal pathos rather than tragedy. What she writes is a kind of comedy of manners, dry as Austen, sharp as Peacock. Her characters have tragic flaws enough, but catastrophe always looms, either in past or future, and rarely materializes in the present of the stories. People are not seen to die, though deaths may be remembered or foreseen or happen in the distance. And, as in Greek tragedy, a great power is often built up by the mere sense of violence offstage or of doom impending but delayed.

A good example of this aspect of Mavis Gallant's work is "The Four Seasons," a story about expatriates on the Italian Riviera, seen through the eyes of Carmela, an Italian village girl who becomes a maid to the Unwins, a feckless English couple living rather meagrely by providing a variety of services—a real estate bureau, hand printing, etc.—for the local foreign community. The story is bounded by Carmela's arrival one Easter and her departure a year afterwards, and the stages of her experience are marked by sections corresponding to the four seasons of the title—spring, summer, autumn, winter, with a final section devoted to the spring of her departure when Italy enters World War II and the English leave.

On one level it is the story of Carmela's education through her encounter with these always incomprehensible foreigners. On the other it is a picture of expatriate society seen through Carmela's eyes; the distancing her view provides enables us to watch from the outside, as we would in a theatre, the behavior of these people who reveal themselves by what they say and do, not by what they think. In this sense the story is very dramatic, its key scenes being passages of dialogue that take place mostly in rooms and in which some people who deeply influence the action are spoken of but never appear. The use of Carmela as an observer enables us to gain a close knowledge of expatriate behavior without too many scenes in which characters are directly involved. To give one example, a great deal is made by English ladies of the rash pulpit remarks of the new young clergyman in view of the difficult political situation in this year of European war, but we are never taken to church and we encounter the priest only twice, once in Mrs. Unwin's house and once in a café. Yet by the reactions of the expatriates we are able to understand not only their prejudices but also the fears they hardly dare express.

For behind all that goes on overtly, behind the chitchat in villas and the compulsive cheeseparing manoeuvres of the Unwins (who live with vague scandals in their background), stands the reality of war. Nobody is killed, and when Italy finally enters the conflict it looks as though the English colony will all escape, even if they are beggared in the process. Only the Jews are arrested, yet even their fates are in suspension, threatened but not consummated. Near the Franco-Italian border Carmela sees the wise and amiable Dr. Chaffee being led under armed guard.

> As though he had seen on her face an expression he wanted, he halted, smiled, shook his head. He was saying "No" to something. Terrified, she peeked again, and this time he lifted his hand, palm outward, in a curious greeting that was not a salute. He was pushed on. She never saw him again.

In the end it is not the Unwins who have exploited her that Carmela most vividly remembers, but this encounter whose tragic intimations she appears to sense: "What she retained, for the present, was one smile, one gesture, one man's calm blessing."

"Irina" takes us out of the moribund society of English expatriates on the Riviera to the between-world of Switzerland that is the frontier of the Germany of *The Pegnitz Junction*. Irina's own origins are not Germanic but Russian-Swiss, and there is a clue to them in the fact that two months before the story appeared in *The New Yorker* Mavis Gallant published in the *New York Times Book Review* (6 October 1974) an extensive review of *Daughter of a Revolutionary*, whose central figure is Natalie Herzen: after associating with those formidable revolutionaries, Michael Bakunin and Sergei Nechaev, Natalie lived out her long life as a Swiss lady of Russian birth and independent means. Irina's antecedents are deliberately left rather vague, to show how far, until widowed, she fell in the shadow of her husband, Richard Notte, one of those dynamically boring European literary men, rather like Romain Rolland, who were on the right side in every good cause, writing, speaking, signing manifestos, and behaving with profligate generosity to everyone but their own families, who were expected to exist in self-sacrificing austerity.

> He could on occasion enjoy wine and praise and restaurants and good-looking women, but these festive outbreaks were on the rim of his real life, as remote from his children—as strange and distorted to them—as some other country's colonial wars.

The early part of "Irina" is seen through the eyes of a third person narrator; it is a look at the literary life, and significantly it is an outside look. Gallant, as she remarked to Geoffrey Hancock in an interview published in the *Canadian Fiction Magazine* (No. 28, 1978), found after she had written the story that she identified not with her fellow writer, the formidable Notte, but with Irina, his patient wife. And this implicit rejection of the great man of letters prompts one to remark, in parenthesis, how little of the conventionally literary there is in Gallant's attitude or even her work. She avoids literary circles and has no theories about writing; she does not compose self-consciously in advance, but, as she reveals in the interview I have already mentioned, writes it all down in a compulsive rush and then reduces and polishes; it is then that her power of artifice comes into play and the composition that emerges is likely to be spatial like a painting rather than linear like conventional fiction, and the visual appeal to the mind's eye is as important in it as the verbal appeal to the mind's ear. There is perhaps a vestige of Gallant's past of left-wing enthusiasms in Notte, but that past she has abandoned completely, and this may be why she attaches it to a male writer made safely dead by the time the story begins. Her mature work is in no way male and ideological; it is feminine and intuitive, and the rightness of detail and surface which are so striking come not from intellectual deliberation but from a sense of rightness as irrational but as true as absolute pitch.

"In loving and unloving families alike," the narrator remarks, "the same problem arises after a death. What to do about the widow?" Irina in fact arranges matters quietly but very much to her own satisfaction, so that it is she whom we find in control of the posthumous fate of Notte's papers, and displaying a caustic and independent good sense in assessing their importance. Yet her children still feel obliged to carry out a kind of King-Lear-in-miniature act by entertaining her by turns at Christmas. Finally the Christmas comes when every son and daughter is abroad or engaged or in trouble, and there is nowhere for Irina to go. The solution is to send Riri, her grandson, to spend the season with her, and the boy sets off with great self-sufficiency, arriving to find that his grandmother already has a visitor, an old Englishman named Mr. Aiken. The rest of the story is seen a little through Irina's eyes, but mainly through Riri's, and what the child's eye reveals is the liberation which can come with someone else's death, for Irina now follows a vague and comfortable life that is very much her own, indulging without needing them, her children's anxieties about her, thinking a little of the great Notte—her recollections of whom bore Riri—but finding in her renewed friendship with Aiken the sweet pleasure of looking down a path her life might have taken but did not. Hers is the marvellous self-sufficiency which realizes that "anything can be settled for a few days a time, but not for longer."

In the four stories I have been discussing, memory is important both as method and content, and the past, whose relationship to the present may seem as much spatial as chronological, is vitally there in our awareness. To an even greater extent this is true of the Linnet Muir stories, which are nothing less than deep immersions in memory, divings into a sunken world. A condition in which memory takes one constantly between past and present seems to Gallant a normal state of mind. And that gives a special significance to the group of stories about Germany, mostly included in *The Pegnitz Junction*, which are quite different from anything else she has written.

They are about people whose memories have become atrophied; about people who have drawn blinds over the past.

In writing such anti-Proustian stories Mavis Gallant was deliberately abandoning the very approach through reminiscence, with all its possibilities of suggestive indirection, which she had used so successfully in her earlier stories. She was entering into situations where the present had to be observed and recorded directly and starkly since memory had become so shrivelled and distorted that only what was before one's eye could give a clue to the past. Memory can play a part only in the limited sense of the author's remembered observations. Such a rigorous departure from an accustomed manner is a test, and Mavis Gallant passed it well; her German stories are some of her most impressive, and I think she is right when she says to Geoffrey Hancock that the novella "The Pegnitz Junction" is "the best thing I've ever written."

In the same interview, Gallant traces these stories to her interest in "the war and Fascism" and sees their origin in a set of photographs of concentration camp victims which she was given to write a newspaper story about before she left Montreal. Once she had got over the immediate horror, the deeper questions began occurring to her. "What we absolutely had to find out was what has happened in a civilized country, why the barriers of culture, of religion, hadn't held, what had broken down and why." The questions remained with her and she went to Germany "like a spy" to find out for herself. "*The Pegnitz Junction*," she says, "is not a book about Fascism, but it's certainly a book about where it came from."

In the last paragraph I have repeated what Mavis Gallant says elsewhere because she presents in her stories something different from what I have seen through my own experience of marrying into a German family and of having gone to the country to live at fairly close quarters with Germans at least every other year since 1950. In my view, what Mavis Gallant really discovered, and what she presents in these stories, is not where "Fascism" (I would prefer the exacter word *Nazism*) came from, since that world of Nazi origins hardly exists in the memories of Germans who are not historians, but rather the emerging world of modern Germany which the Nazi age like a black curtain has cut off from the traditional past, so that only men in their eighties talk of "the good old Kaiserzeit" and nobody talks of the Weimar age.

I shall deal especially with "The Pegnitz Junction" itself, since this novella has a unique interest on a number of levels, but first I would say that what strikes me most about the other German stories is that they are almost all about people whose pasts have been mentally and even physically obliterated: people in other words who are exiled in the most dreaded way of all, by being banished from themselves. As the narrator says in "An Alien Flower," when she talks about her daughter born since the war: "I saw then that Roma's myths might include misery and sadness, but my myths were bombed, vanished and whatever remained had to be cleaned and polished and kept bright."

The central character of "An Alien Flower" is a girl named Bibi, doomed to the suicide that eventually overtakes her, who comes to western Germany out of Silesia by way of refugee camps, having lost a past she may have forgotten deliberately, or involuntarily—we are never sure which.

> She never mentioned her family or said how they had died. I could only guess that they must have vanished in the normal way of a recent period—killed at the front, or lost without trace in the east, or burned alive in air raids. Who were the Brünings? Was she ashamed of them? Were they Socialists, radicals, troublemakers, black-marketeers, prostitutes, wife-beaters, informers, Witnesses of Jehovah? . . . Whoever the Brünings were, Bibi was their survivor, and she was as pure as the rest of us in the sense that she was alone, swept clean of friends and childhood myths and of childhood itself. But someone, at some time, must have existed and must have called her Bibi. A diminutive is not a thing you invent for yourself.

The use of the word "pure" in this context is significant, since it expresses the desire to see suffering as expiation, but it has a certain grim irony when one associates it with the narrator's remark that: "Anyone who had ever known me or loved me had been killed in one period of seven weeks." The idea of purification and the idea of forgetting or losing the past are closely linked in these stories. In "The Old Friends," a police commissioner has a sentimental attachment to an actress, Helena, cherished in West Germany as a token Jewess, one who as a child inexplicably survived the death camps. "Her true dream is of purification, of the river never profaned, from which she wakes astonished—for the real error was not that she was sent away but that she is here, in a garden, alive." As for the commissioner, knowing "like any policeman . . . one meaning for every word," he cannot deny the horror of the experiences forced on his friend as a child, but he seeks desperately in his mind for a reason to think it all a mistake, something for which a single erring bureaucrat could be punished, rather than something for which his people as a whole might bear some responsibility.

> He would like it to have been, somehow, not German. When she says that she was moved through transit camps on the edge of the old Germany, then he can say, 'So, most of it was on foreign soil!' He wants to hear how hated the guards were when they were Slovak, or Ukrainian. The vast complex of camps in Silesia is on land that has become Polish now, so it is as if those camps had never been German at all. Each time she says a foreign place-name he is forgiven, absolved. What does it matter to her? Reality was confounded long ago.

Then there is Ernst, the demobilized Foreign Legionary in "Ernst in Civilian Clothes," whom we encounter in the Paris flat of his friend Willi; Ernst is about to return to the Germany he left as a teenage prisoner many years before. Ernst, we are told,

> knows more than Willi because he has been a soldier all his life. He knows there are no limits to folly and pain, except fatigue and the failing of imagination. He has always known more than Willi, but he can be of no help to him, because of his own life-saving powers of forgetfulness.

When Thomas Bestermann, in "The Latehomecomer," returns from France, where he has stayed too long because the records of his past (and hence his official identity) were lost, he meets a man named Willy Wehler who with a certain peasant cunning ("All Willy had to do was sniff the air") has managed to slip through the Nazi age without becoming as scarred as most survivors.

> He pushed back his chair (in later years he would be able to push a table away with his stomach) and got to his feet. He had to tip his head to look up into my eyes. He said he wanted to give me advice that would be useful to me as a latehomecomer. His advice was to forget. "Forget everything," he said. "Forget, forget, forget. That was what I said to my good neighbour Herr Silber when I bought his wife's topaz brooch and earrings before he emigrated to Palestine. I said, 'Dear Herr Silber, look forward, never back, and forget, forget, forget.'"

In "An Autobiography" the narrator, a schoolmistress in Switzerland whose German professor father was shot by Russians in Hungary, had met in her poor refugee days a boy named Peter who as a child—like Helena in "The Old Friends"—miraculously escaped death by being arbitrarily taken out of one of the contingents of Jews headed for the gas chambers. Now when she is firmly settled in the womb-like refuge of Switzerland, she encounters Peter once again and realizes that he has become a mythomane, constantly changing his past to suit the company, but for that reason uneasy with someone who knew him in his actual past.

> But I had travelled nearly as much as Peter, and over some of the same frontiers. He could not impress me. . . . He knew it was no good talking about the past, because we were certain to remember it differently. He daren't be nostalgic about anything, because of his inventions. He would never be certain if the memory he was feeling tender about was true.

And even during that German past which everyone in Mavis Gallant's stories wants to avoid or to remember as it never was, those fared best who had the power of shedding their earlier pasts and hence their identities. An example is Uncle Theo, an amiable Schweikish nobody in the Bavarian story, "O Lasting Peace." Uncle Theo avoided involvement in the war almost literally by losing himself. When he went for his medical examination he found that all the physical defects he could rake up were insufficient to get him rejected.

> He put on his clothes, still arguing, and was told to take a file with his name on it to a room upstairs. It was on his way up that he had his revelation. Everything concerning his person was in that file. If the file disappeared, then Uncle Theo did, too. He turned and walked straight out of the front door. He did not destroy the file, in case they should come round asking; he intended to say he had not understood the instructions. No one came, and soon after this his workroom was bombed and the file became ashes. When Uncle Theo was arrested it was for quite another reason, having to do with black-market connections. He went first to prison, then, when the jail was bombed, to a camp. Here he wore on his striped jacket the black sleeve patch that meant "anti-social." It is generally thought that he wore the red patch, meaning "political." As things are now, it gives him status.

And so Uncle Theo lives on, a survivor by evasion who enjoys the repute and pension of a hero in a Germany that does not want to remember too precisely.

A striking feature of Gallant's German stories is the importance of childhood. There are those whose lives are shaped by ruined childhoods—Bibi and Helena, Thomas the latehomecomer who was bearing arms in his teens, and Ernst who was incorporated as a boy in the Werewolves. But children also seem to offer promise of a future in which there will be a memory of a real past, and it is significant that both the character Michael in "An Alien Flower" and Thomas in "The Latehomecomer" will marry girls who are mere children in the present of the stories. This is the generation that will again be able to think of "misery and sadness."

In "The Pegnitz Junction" we are on the verge of this world where renewal may be thought of. One of the important characters is the little boy Bert, four years old. And the central figure is Christine, eighteen years old and so too young to have any personal memory of the Nazi past. She comes indeed from a place where the re-creation of an older past has made it unnecessary to remember what went on more recently: "a small bombed baroque German city, where all that was worthwhile keeping had been rebuilt and which now looked as pink and golden as a pretty child and as new as morning." Yet she does not need to ignore the real past because she does not know much about it; she carries with her a volume of the writings of Dietrich Boenhoffer, one of the anti-Nazi martyrs.

It is through Christine that "The Pegnitz Junction" assumes its special quality. It is the most experimental of Gallant's works, in which she makes no attempt at that special Gallant realism where the web of memory provides the mental links that make for plausibility. Here she is trying to create, in a structure as much dramatic as fictional, a kind of psychic membrane in which recollection is replaced by telepathy.

Christine, it is obvious from the description which opens the story, is the kind of person who becomes a psychic medium or around whom poltergeist phenomena are likely to happen.

> She had a striking density of expression in photographs, though she seemed unchanging and passive in life, and had caught sight of her own face looking totally empty-minded when, in fact, her thoughts and feelings were pushing her in some wild direction. She had heard a man say of her that you could leave her in a cafe for two hours and come back to find she was still smoking the same cigarette.

Although Christine is engaged to a theological student, she is erotically involved with Herbert, and with him and his son, Little Bert, she makes a trip to Paris. The main part of the novella is devoted to a frustrating journey home which takes them to the Pegnitz Junction. There is an airport strike at Orly, so they return by train. When they change at the German border they find that railway movements have been diverted because of heath fires, and instead of going straight home they must travel in a great arc, changing at a station close up to the barbed wire and watchtowers of East Germany, and finally reaching Pegnitz Junction, where the train to Berlin should be awaiting them. It is not, and when the novella ends they are still at Pegnitz, waiting.

"The Pegnitz Junction" is a work of much complexity, and deserves an essay of its own. I will be content to dwell on three aspects that mark its distinctiveness among Mavis Gallant's stories. The first is the intrusion of what appears to be a much stronger element of intentional symbolism than one finds elsewhere in Mavis Gallant's writings. One cannot avoid seeing the train journey as an elaborate figure, representing the wanderings, without an as yet assured destination, of a Germany which has not recovered a sense of its role in history and, indeed, fears what that role might be if it were discovered.

Then there is the peculiar relationship between Christine and the other passengers. With Herbert it is mostly a simple matter of conversation and her inner thoughts about their relationship, and with Little Bert it is a question of exchanging fantasies. But with the other people encountered on the journey Christine falls into a state of psychic openness, so that messages are exchanged, and their flows of thought emerge to mulitply the range of viewpoints.

Their immediate fellow passengers are a Norwegian professional singer with a mania for yogic breathing and an old woman who is constantly munching food from the large bags she has brought with her. The Norwegian, occupied with singing and breathing, has merely a few comments to offer, but from the mind of the old woman there emerges an extraordinary unspoken monologue. Surprisingly—in the context of these stories—it is a reminiscent one that reconstructs a past elsewhere; she lived through the dark years in America and came back to Germany to bury her husband and water his grave after the war ended. But there are remoter messages which trip the levers of Christine's telepathic sense. When the train stops at a level crossing, she suddenly enters the minds of the people waiting, and at the station on the East German border she catches a refugee's memories of the girl in his lost village. Then, at Pegnitz Junction, there is the pregnant country girl who pretends to be an American army wife, from whom Christine receives the strangest message of all: the contents of a letter about racketeering in PX stores from one GI to another that she is carrying in her bag. Not only does this technique give a dramatic quality to the novella, since it becomes so largely a pattern of voices heard in the mind's ear, but there is a cinematic element in the way the outer, visible and audible world cuts away from the inner world and back again; one is reminded of Mavis Gallant's days in a NFB cutting room.

Finally, there is the centrality of the child, Little Bert, who is present and intervening throughout the novella, occasionally making an Emperor's-clothes remark of penetrating aptness, but most of the time involved in his fantasy of the life of the sponge he calls Bruno, which he shares with Christine, but over which he seeks to maintain control, so that he rejects versions of Bruno's adventures that go beyond his ideas of plausibility. For Bruno after all—as Bert makes clear on occasion—is merely a sponge to which he has given a life. History—the irradiation of actuality by imagination—seems to be stirring in this infant mind.

The final group of stories I am discussing is the Linnet Muir cycle, set in Montreal between the 1920s and the 1940s. Mavis Gallant had already used Montreal as a setting in her novella of the 1950s, "Its Image in a Mirror" (included in *My Heart Is Broken*) and in stories like "Bernadette," written at the same period. But the Linnet Muir stories, which have not all been published and will presumably form a volume on their own, are so closely interlinked that one sees them as the chronologically discontinuous chapters in a major novel avowedly devoted to *la recherche du temps perdu*.

I use the Proustian phrase deliberately, since Mavis Gallant's own account of the origin of the stories in the Hancock interview leaves little doubt that an impulse of involuntary memory set them moving and that in general they represent a release of the imagination into memory and the past, after the self-disciplines of writing about the world of *The Pegnitz Junction* where times seems irretrievably lost.

The Linnet Muir stories are no more autobiographical than Proust's great fictional quest, and no less so. Linnet Muir is about as near to Mavis Gallant as the linnet (a modest English songbird) is to the mavis, which is the Scottish name for the magnificent European song thrush. There are things in common between writer and character, and just as many dissimilarities. Gallant, like Linnet, spent her childhood in Montreal where she was born. Her father died when she was young, and at the age of eighteen one of the first things she did on returning to Montreal—this was 1940—was to try and find out how he died. A few people and a few incidents thus stepped from real life into the stories. But everything has been reshaped and transmuted in the imagination so that what emerges is a work of fiction on several levels. It is a portrait of Linnet Muir as a child isolated in her family, and later as a young woman between eighteen and twenty isolated in her fatherland. But it is even more, as Gallant herself has insisted, a reconstruction of a city and a way of life which have now been irrevocably engulfed in time past but which, as Gallant has said, were "unique in North America, if not the world" because the two Montreals, the French and the Anglo-Scottish, were so completely shut off from each other. And, since in this way these stories form a fiction about a collectivity rather than about individuals, one of their striking features is that the narrator, through whose consciousness everything is seen and who is the one continuing character, does not stand out more vividly in our minds than most of the other characters; all of them, down to the slightest, are portrayed with an almost pre-Raphaelite sharpness of vision.

I am not sure how many of the stories in the sequence are yet to be published; certainly we have not had the "very, very long story . . . about the war" which Mavis Gallant talks of and which is intended to terminate the series. But what we do have is already an extraordinary addition to that peculiarly Canadian type of fiction concerned with the changing relationships of cultural groups.

In order of appearance in *The New Yorker*, which I assume is roughly the order of completion, the first story, "In Youth Is Pleasure," sets the theme by showing Linnet in search of the lost world of her childhood. A girl of eighteen, having suffered the contemptuous ignorance of Americans about the country above their borders, she returns to Montreal with a few dollars and immense self-confidence. Almost without thought, she seeks out the French-Canadian nurse of her childhood, and is given unquestioning hospitality. But when she moves into the other Montreal, that of her own people, and tries to find out about her father, she encounters reserve, distrust, even fear. The search for her father is significant in view of Gallant's own theory that perhaps the one distinctive Canadian theme is to be found in the role of the father, who in our literature seems always more important than the mother. Linnet remembers her mother in somewhat derogatory terms as a person who "smiled, talked, charmed anyone she didn't happen to be related to, swam in scandal like a partisan among the people." But the search for the father is, in a very real sense, the beginning of Linnet's search for truth. She never really does find out how he died; all she can assemble is a cluster of conflicting rumours and theories, so that she is never sure whether he actually died of the tuberculosis of the spine that attacked him in his early thirties or shot himself with a revolver she remembered seeing in a drawer in her childhood. In the end she shapes the past in her own mind: "I thought he had died of homesickness; sickness for England was the consumption, the gun, the everything." She realizes all at once that this is not her past. "I had looked into a drawer that did not belong to me." But what she finds in the process is that the world which saw him die with such indifference was a narrow provincial world where wealth and influence were the only virtues, the world of the Montreal tycoons.

"Between Zero and One" and "Varieties of Exile" are further stories about Linnet's experiences when she returns to Montreal, and they are dedicated to obsolescent kinds of people. In the first story Linnet works in a Montreal draughtsman's office (as Jean Price does in "Its Image in the Mirror") and all the people around her, until a woman bitter from a failed marriage joins the staff, are either men too old to fight in World War II but full of recollections of an earlier conflict, or unfit men. It is an entirely English world—an office that does not contain a single francophone, a collection of men with the prejudices of their time who neither know nor wish to know the other nation that shares Quebec with them. Canada, for them, is English; its loyalties are imperial. And they have accepted limitations for themselves as well as for their world. It is a world to which Linnet does not belong, any more than does Frank Cairns, the remittance man in "Varieties of Exile," with whom she strikes up the precarious relationship of two people out of their place and world when she encounters him on the train going from her summer lodgings into Montreal. Frank and his kind, the castoff young men of English families, were the nearest thing in Canada to the superfluous men of Russian literature, and as a species they vanished when World War II dried up the flow of cash from home and most of them went back to fight for a country that had thrown them out. Strangely enough, if the men in the office taught Linnet how narrow life can be made, Frank Cairns, who seems happy only when he is going home, helps to open her mind with his own restless questing, and when she hears of his death she is happy that "he would never need to return to the commuting train and the loneliness and be forced to relive his own past."

All these three stories display memory doubly at work. Linnet the narrator is looking back thirty years to another Linnet exploring a lost Montreal whose doom was sealed by the social changes World War II began in Canada. But the Linnet of thirty years ago in turn is remembering, seeing her own childhood again as she experiences aspects of the city of which she was unaware when she lived protected in the family which is the subject of the two stories that follow and that up to the present complete the published cycle: "Voices Lost in the Snow" and "The Doctor." They are stories of a family of the age between the wars: father and mother still young, but already separated by work ("I do not know where my father spent his working life; just elsewhere") and by relationships, for in "Voices Lost in the Snow" the father, who is already dying though nobody knows it, takes the child to see a woman, an estranged friend of her mother, with whom he still maintains contact.

In these stories, once again, we have the sharp visuality of Gallant's earlier work, and the gripping evocations of a Montreal that has long vanished beneath the blows of the wrecker's ball.

> The reddish brown of the stone houses, the curve and slope of the streets, the constantly changing sky were satisfactory in a way that I now realize must have been aesthetically comfortable. This is what I saw when I read 'city' in a book; I had no means of knowing that 'city' one day would also mean drab, filthy, flat, or that city blocks could turn into dull squares without mystery.

As "The Doctor" shows, Linnet's family inhabits a shifting frontier territory where the two cultures of Montreal meet, as they rarely do elsewhere.

> This overlapping in one room of French and English, of Catholic and Protestant—my parents' way of being, and so to me life itself—was as unlikely, as unnatural to the Montreal climate as a school of tropical fish. Only later would I discover that most other people simply floated in mossy little ponds labelled "French and Catholic" or "English and Protestant," never wondering what it might be like to step ashore, or wondering, perhaps, but weighing up the danger. To be out of a pond is to be in unmapped territory.

A frequent guest to her parents' house is Dr. Chauchard, who in another role is the pediatrician attending Linnet at the age of eight. The bicultural salons are dominated by a flamboyant Mrs. Erskine, who has been the wife of two unsuccessful diplomats and moves in Montreal society escorted by Chauchard (now transformed into genial Uncle Raoul) and various attendant young Québecois intellectuals. But even such encounters take place in a no-man's-land so insecure that the common language is always English, and Linnet does not know, until Dr. Chauchard dies, that he had another life in which he was a notable Québec poet, as she discovers on seeing his obituaries, one for the pious member of his family, one for the doctor, one for the writer.

> That third notice was an earthquake, the collapse of the cities we build over the past to cover seams and cracks we cannot account for. He must have been writing when my parents knew him. Why they neglected to speak of it is something too shameful to dwell on; he probably never mentioned it, knowing they would believe it impossible. French books were from France; English books from England or the United States. It would not have entered their minds that the languages they heard spoken around them could be written, too.

Vignettes of a dead time; of a lost world; of a vanished city. Yet it is easy to lay too much stress on the social-historical nature of the Linnet Muir stories. (Though Gallant herself gives some support to such emphasis when she talks of the "political" nature of her stories.) They are so successful as records of an age because they are inhabited by people so carefully drawn and individually realized that the past comes alive, in its superbly evoked setting, as experience even more than as history. And that is the true rediscovery of time.

JOHN GARDNER

1933–1982

John Champlin Gardner, Jr., was born on a farm in Batavia, New York, on July 21, 1933. After graduating with a B.A. from Washington University, St. Louis, in 1955, he went on to receive a Ph.D. from the State University of Iowa in 1958. His subsequent teaching career in medieval literature and creative writing took him to colleges and universities throughout the country, his last position being at the State University of New York at Binghamton.

Gardner wrote fiction for fifteen years before succeeding in publishing his first novel, *The Resurrection*, in 1966, but the years that followed saw a prolific output of fiction. His third novel, *Grendel*, appeared in 1971, and *October Light* (1976) won him the National Book Critics Circle Award for fiction. His final novel, *Mickelsson's Ghosts*, was published in 1982. As well as novels, he also produced short stories, collected in *The King's Indian* (1974) and *The Art of Living* (1981). An epic poem, *Jason and Medeia*, appeared in 1973, and a radio play, *The Temptation Game*, in 1980. Gardner wrote several books for children and three opera libretti, and his *Poems* were published in 1978.

Although best-known for his creative writing, Gardner was also a respected scholar, writing several works on medieval literature and publishing a modern English version of *The Complete Works of the Gawain-Poet* in 1965. A polemical theoretical book, *On Moral Fiction* (1978), made him a controversial spokesman for the moral responsibility of literature. He was also the founder and editor of the magazine *MSS.*

Gardner was married twice and had two children from his first marriage. Four days before a planned third marriage he died in a motorcycle accident on September 14, 1982, near his home in Susquehanna, Pennsylvania.

General

The best key, although a reductive one, to John Gardner's fiction is the narrator's question in *Jason and Medeia:* "Is nothing serious?" In his fiction Gardner engages us in a search for the answer to this question, a search to determine if life is nothing more than a series of comical, meaningless exercises. A representative of order and one of disorder, an adherent to forms and a believer in magical chaos, conduct the quest through a series of bizarre confrontations. The encounters occur in two types of setting; mythic or everyday American. Three of his novels, *The Wreckage of Agathon* (1970), *Grendel* (1971), and *Jason and Medeia* (1973), are set in the mythic past; another three, *The Resurrection* (1966), *The Sunlight Dialogues* (1972), and *Nickel Mountain* (1973), take place in Batavia, New York, or its middle-American analogue. *The King's Indian* (1974) is a curious mixture of the two. Mythic and quotidian realities inevitably merge in Gardner's work. The answer to his question lies in the merging of contradictions: "the true measure of human adaptability is man's power to find, despite overwhelming arguments, something in himself to love." Man is ridiculous, his actions are absurd; but such perception and his ability to love regardless grant man his seriousness.

Gardner is, of course, telling us nothing new. He recreates new forms and revitalizes old ones for a new perception of the often-conducted search for meaning. His astoundingly visual prose, his reworking of myths, and his resurrection of old forms (pastoral novel, epic poem) shock us out of our complacency about the nearly exhausted question and its equally repetitive answer. His use of magic and deformity, of the mythic and the common, and his insistence on the positive power of love transport a tired search into an active playground. We swing with him on the merry-go-round, laughing at our childish maneuvers. Gardner lets us laugh precisely because we are laughable, and only in our ability to laugh can we approach our seriousness. The ridiculous and the serious are inseparable in his fiction; operating simultaneously with and against each other, they bring us into Gardner's funhouse and out into his gravity.

The ridiculous is emphasized by a special kind of deformity, based on the ludicrous. Grendel, the horrible, hairy monster, symbol of deformed humanity, yells "Mama" when in trouble; the Sunlight Man, disfigured by facial scars, smells and has a bag full of magical tricks. In *Grendel*, the monster, speaking the language of humans, faces the mythic hero, Beowulf, and in *The Sunlight Dialogues*, the Sunlight Man, madman and magician, confronts the town's representative of law and order, Police Chief Clumly. Agathon, in *The Wreckage of Agathon*, defines the ensuing struggle between order and disorder as one between himself and his jailer: "My very existence, for him, is criticism. My paunch condemns his asceticism; my timid, wholly irrelevant grins deny the iron-chained order of his soul." Antagonistic non-order and protagonistic order repeatedly merge in Gardner's fiction; the deformity of the one merges with and defines the conformity of the other. He brings them together and concerns himself with articulating the result of the confrontation:

> A black tree with a double trunk—two trees
> Grown into one—throws up its blurred branches.
> The two trunks in their infinitesimal dance of growth
> Have turned completely about one another, their
> join
> A slowly twisted scar.

Disparate at first, the deformed anarchists and the conformed heroes of law and order are inextricably joined, not without pain and not without healing. For, after all, in *The Resurrection* Gardner has quoted Stevens' "Connoisseur of Chaos":

> A. A violent order is disorder; and
> B. A great disorder is an order. These
> Two things are one.

Try as we might to order life by formula, it contains its inscrutabilities. What matters in these meetings is not who wins but what fusion can occur. Both sides are right and wrong; order is as ridiculous as non-order. In their fusion, in the interstices between contradictions, lies the meaning.

Accident necessarily plays a large part in Gardner's fiction; fusion depends on accident as much as anything else, but it is not negative; it rings with the positive value of chaos. Gardner sets us straight as Chandler, in *The Resurrection*, sets himself straight. Having searched for the order of beauty, he realizes "It was not the beauty of the world one must affirm but *the world*, the buzzing blooming confusion itself. He had slipped from celebrating what was to the celebration of empty celebration." Gardner is going to celebrate the onion smell of Agathon, the magical insanity of the Sunlight Man, the givers of law and order, and the cacophony of a deaf piano teacher: life in all its shoddiness and wonderful absurdity.—JUDY SMITH MURR, "John Gardner's Order and Disorder," *Crt*, Vol. 18, No. 2 (1976), pp. 97–99

At the time of its writing, Gardner was reasonably satisfied with the quality of "The Old Men," but the twenty intervening years dimmed, in his eyes, the book's value. He has described it as "a bad book . . . full of flaws and weak writing." In many ways this is true. It is an ambitious book, perhaps over-populated and sprawling, barely structured, with many of its resolutions unearned. The writing is at times naïve, embarrassingly overcomplex and overplayed, and shamefully melodramatic. Still it is an important work in that it reveals the shapes of things to come. It is, certainly, "early Gardner," the product of a twenty-five-year-old writer, but it is buttressed by nearly ten years of fiction apprenticeship, of story-writing and story-telling.

Part of the importance of "The Old Men" lies in its relation to the remainder of the Gardner canon. It is the touchstone for comparison, for from it can be traced certain patterns of development, various growths and recessions. It is an obvious source for subject and idea in the later works; places, names, and themes spring up in more recent novels and stories that first appeared in this dissertation-novel. Gardner, quite early on, seemed to know where he wished to go in his fiction, and "The Old Men" serves as a literary roadsign, pointing out thematic direction to his works to come.

Most apparent is the mere geography: the Catskill Mountains. "The Old Men" is part, one might say, of a Catskill pair whose other half is the novel *Nickel Mountain*. The Mohawk Valley of New York provides the setting for both novels, and in both books we find looming over the characters the forested humps of Crow and Nickel Mountain. The names are invented, but the awesome physicality of the mountains is authentic. For Gardner, as for Cooper, the Catskills and their environs offer a proving ground for the testing of men and women and their ideas.

Among these ideas is the inevitability of old age and death, of mortality. Beneath the near agelessness of the hills, all too age-conscious humanity struggles to outwit (or outwait) the finality of dying. It is a theme later dealt with in *The Resurrection*, *Grendel*, *Nickel Mountain*, and *October Light*, and is perhaps Gardner's prime philosophic concern.

Also present is the notion of ghosts and visions, of dreams and nightmares. The human imagination is a creative force and is shaped, so Gardner maintains, by personal belief and development. The ability to envision the immaterial and the questionable is important for Gardner. His visionaries are special and peculiar people, ones marked for private but important destinies. We see this idea played upon again in *The Resurrection*, *Nickel Mountain*, *The King's Indian*, *October Light*, *The Art of Living*, and *Mickelsson's Ghosts*, wherein certain characters possess certain imaginative qualities that are explored and annotated.

There also are characters in almost every Gardner fiction, and beginning in "The Old Men," who are forced to confront the shocks of accident and grief. The universe is causal, but surprising; events are related to one another in causal sequence, but that sequence does not always reveal itself to human rationality or knowledge. The seer is the rare talent who can reach back far enough into history, unravel the connections, and make predictions and pronouncements upon the future. Most of us, however, are caught unawares by the mishaps of the cosmos and so often assume unnecessary responsibility for actions that hold no relation to us. In "The Old Men," as well as in *The Resurrection*, *The Wreckage of Agathon*, *Grendel*, *Nickel Mountain*, and *October Light*, people know logical and illogical suffering, the kinds of pain that come in a volatile world.

To combat this felt anguish, Gardner offers love—an old solution, but not, in Gardner's case, a sentimental one. Wounds are salved by strength of community, constancy of faith, temperance of ideals. Love and hate spring from the same source, and are often the weird progeny of each other. Such love-hate relationships are at work in "The Old Men," where they generate much of the book's physical and psychological action; and they reappear in every one of Gardner's later works of adult fiction.

Finally, there are other, lesser ideas that randomly turn up in Gardner's fiction and that first appear in "The Old Men." There is the notion of youthful perversity and iniquity (*The Resurrection*, *Nickel Mountain*, *October Light*); the sterility of institutionalized religion (*Nickel Mountain*, *The King's Indian*, *Freddy's Book*) and the revitalizing force of art, particularly music (*The Resurrection*, *Grendel*, *The King's Indian*, *October Light*, *The Art of Living*); and the idea of "modeling," or character formation based on role models (*The Resurrection*, *October Light*). In short, there is an impressive quantity of technical and intellectual substance that has made its way from "The Old Men," in whatever recarved form, into Gardner's later writings. "The Old Men" is a marred work, but hardly one to be benignly swept off into a corner, mused at as a curious but ultimately jejune piece of craft.—GREGORY L. MORRIS, " 'The Old Men,' " *A World of Order and Light: The Fiction of John Gardner*, 1984, 6–8

Works

NOVELS AND SHORT STORIES

The Sunlight Dialogues and *The Wreckage of Agathon* share a similar theme, in which the metaphysical focus of the earlier novels is replaced by a social focus. Both novels are about the inadequacy of law and the need for justice, the narrowness of codified rules and the need for a broader human understanding. In *The Sunlight Dialogues*, the police chief of Batavia, Fred Clumly, arrests a strangely burned man who calls himself the Sunlight Man. We learn that he is Taggert Hodge, a member of a prominent Batavia family. After Hodge escapes from jail, Clumly meets with him four times for the dialogues. He is equally mystified by the man's adept magic tricks and by his condemnation of the injustice of the legal system that Clumly has unquestioningly served. The Sunlight Man says,

> Your laws are irrelevant, stupid, inhuman. I mean you support civilization by a kind of averaging. . . . There is good and evil in the world, but they have nothing to do with your courts. . . . I care about *every single case*. You care about nothing but the *average*. I love justice, you love law.

After the last dialogue, Clumly chooses to let the Sunlight Man escape, validating the principle of understanding beyond law that Hodge has advocated. When Hodge returns to the police station to surrender, he is shot dead by a young officer.

Like *The Sunlight Dialogues*, *The Wreckage of Agathon* begins with an arrest. Agathon, the Seer of Sparta, is jailed with his disciple, whom he calls Peeker, because he has opposed the rigid laws of Lykourgos. The narrative consists of the writings of Agathon and Peeker while they are in prison; Agathon reminisces about the two women in his life—his wife Tuka, his lover Iona—and the two lawgivers he has watched—Solon of Athens, Lykourgos of Sparta. Solon, the humanist, repeals Draco's severe laws which punished small crimes with death; Lykourgos believes, in contrast, that even loitering should be punished by death because "It purifies the blood. . . . That's the beginning and end of Law and Order." Agathon rejects Lykourgos's version of legality in favor of the same kind of justice the Sunlight Man advocates. He argues that Lykourgos's laws express only the qualities of their maker and "force all men into the nature of the lawgiver, each man sadly abnegating his real nature, that being outlawed." Agathon's protest, like the Sunlight Man's, is answered by imprisonment and ends in pointless death. He catches the plague from rats in his jail cell and dies soon after a futile rescue.

The Sunlight Man and Agathon question the laws from a stance of alienation. Agathon is literally an alien, because he is an Athenian sent by Solon to Sparta, where he remains to hound Lykourgos. The Sunlight Man has, through a series of personal tragedies, become alienated from his own culture: "the world you support is foul," he tells Clumly, "and, personally, I opt out." Both figures act out their alienation with a series of clowning gestures; they mock society half in an earnest attempt to improve it, half in despair. Agathon speaks of a "rage so black and indifferent to life that my natural cowardice left me," which leads him to mock the Spartans: "The clowning despair would rush over me, the total indifference to anything but the monstrous foolishness of human beings, and in a flash—or a giggle—I was at them." Similarly, the Sunlight Man mocks Clumly, the representative of "the coldly reasonable unreason of officialdom," with his magic tricks and wit: "With a part of his mind he was resolved to go straight to the heart of the matter when he met with Clumly. Another part insisted upon preparation for jokes, the laughter of despair." Both figures, then, joke in the black humor mood of rage, indifference, and despair.

Though both novels suggest the kind of affirmative vision that remains constant through Gardner's career, its locus is changed from the protagonists' celebration of life to the legacy of understanding they leave for others. Unlike Chandler and Soames, the Sunlight Man and Agathon do not affirm "the buzzing blooming confusion" or the "holiness of things." Rather, they rage against the inadequacy of systems, they mock the self-righteous complacency of people who believe they know the truth, and they despair of their own inability to create anything better. The Sunlight Man ends the last dialogue with a vision of apocalypse, in which life is destroyed rather than affirmed: "The age that is coming will be the last age of man, the destruction of everything. . . . Hell's jaws will yawn and the cities will sink, and there will be not a trace." Agathon dies with a hopeless inability to find the consoling forgiveness of Chandler's "No harm"; instead, his last words suggest a vision of absurdity. "Whoo*ee* am I scared! I must think of some last, solemn, sententious word. Cocklebur. Ox."

The alienated mockery of each figure has created a mature, complex understanding in other characters, and such legacy provides the source of affirmation. *The Sunlight Dialogues* traces the growth of Chief Clumly, under Hodge's tutelage, from self-righteousness to compassion. Clumly has earned a reputation for inflexibility: "'A man of principle,' people said, which was to say as inflexible as a chunk of steel, with a heart so cold that if you touched it you'd stick as your fingers stick to iron at twenty below zero." By the end of the novel, however, Clumly has seen the inadequacy of his own principles and the need for flexibility and forgiveness:

> "We may be dead wrong about the whole kaboodle," he said wearily. . . . "We have to stay awake, as best we can, and be ready to obey the laws as best as we're able to see them. That's it. That's the whole thing. . . . Blessed are the meek, by which I mean all of us, including the Sunlight Man."

Clumly has learned what the Sunlight Man taught, that justice is obscure and that compassion is the only adequate response to the gloomy confusion of human motives. Clumly's growth localizes and justifies the tentative affirmation, the hope for blessing, that the novel offers with its ending.

Like Clumly, Agathon's disciple Peeker inherits wisdom and understanding from his mentor. Early in the novel, he is often frustrated and impatient with Agathon: "He was a fool, and I was ashamed of him. He was a troublemaker"; later he prays, "Dear gods, please in the next life make Agathon a cow." Peeker's judgments are usually faulty. Though clearly he and Agathon are political prisoners who will not be freed, Peeker naively believes an appeal has been filed and is shocked to learn he was wrong: "It reeled me. I thought it had been going on for weeks." Gradually, however, Peeker grows toward a more complex understanding of Agathon and a more mature vision of the world: "I understand him better and better"; and near the end he wonders: "How many years have I lived in this one deadly summer? I feel older than Akhilles's ghost, and more filled with sorrow, despair." Finally, he takes the manuscript to Agathon's wife, Tuka, in Athens and demonstrates both understanding and forgiveness. Out of his increased maturity emerges the fully earned affirmation at the end of the novel, as Tuka turns to him with the final judgment, "You do me good!" The novel affirms Peeker's legacy from Agathon of a kind of wisdom earned through alienation and clowning despair.

These two novels from the second phase of Gardner's career share more than the thematic link of their concern with law and order. Both revolve around a jail setting; *The Sunlight Dialogues* preserves the contemporary New York locale of the first two novels, while *The Wreckage of Agathon* moves back about 2,500 years to Sparta. Yet the prison cells of both novels are fundamentally alike in spite of the differences of time and space, and the cell works as a controlling metaphor of human experience in both novels. In form, each of the novels replaces the realistic conventions of the earlier works with more experimental techniques. Both play with contrasting narrative perspectives; *The Wreckage of Agathon* contrasts the first-person accounts of mentor and disciple, and *The Sunlight Dialogues* shifts among the consciousnesses of several major and minor characters in the third person. Both works are dialogues of a sort between opposed perspectives on the same events: the Sunlight Man's dialogues with Clumly are echoed in Agathon's dialogues with Peeker.

Finally, both works are self-conscious about their status as fiction. In *The Sunlight Dialogues*, Millie Hodge reminds us of her existence as a character: "She realized, briefly, that she was merely a character in an endless, meaningless novel"; and the Sunlight Man defines the future as the next page of that novel: "There's always the future, p. 656." The novel concludes with the suggestion, common in contemporary fiction, of the truth of its own artifice: "All this, though some may consider it strange, mere fiction, is the truth." *The Wreckage of Agathon* concludes, after the Seer's death, with the judgments of Iona and Tuka on his writings—the characters, then, are judging the novel in which they appear. Iona says to Peeker, "Have you any idea . . . how much of this is pure fiction? . . . No matter, don't think about it. One could do worse than become a caricature in a senseless, complicated lie." The reminder of his fictionality leaves Peeker seeing his own consciousness in multiple layers: "After I'd lain down I began to cry, purposely and crossly, conscious of my consciousness of crying." Tuka also judges the manuscript a fictional lie, saying that Agathon has left out the version of himself she knew. These admissions of the fictionality of Agathon's self-portrait serve as self-conscious reminders of the novels's status as artifice. In these two novels, artificially constructed truths survive and, indeed, benefit from the authorial admission of the lie.—SUSAN STREHLE, "John Gardner's Novels: Affirmation and the Alien," *Crt*, Vol. 18, No. 2 (1976), pp. 88–92

John Gardner is a genuinely eclectic novelist whose books consistently display an impressive range despite their determined articulation of a repeated constitutive theme. It is disclosed variously by several of his protagonists:

A drunken seer staggers blithely to his death, crushed by a zealot's city-state, "filled . . . with an overwhelming sense of the boundless stupidity of things" (*The Wreckage of Agathon*).

A devastated idealist mocks the hollowness of Golden Rules: "Don't hope, don't love: don't expect and don't give"—and the innocent who debates his fatalism can only temporize, thus: "We may be wrong about the whole thing. . . . We have to stay awake, as best we can, and be ready to obey the laws as best as we're able to see them. That's it. That's the whole thing" (*The Sunlight Dialogues*).

The monster who engages the hero Beowulf amuses himself with arbitrary slaughter, having determined that "the world was nothing: a mechanical chaos of brute enmity on which we stupidly impose our hopes and fears" (*Grendel*).

An epic adventurer perceives menacing patterns in experience and finds himself "caught in irrelevant forms," victimized by "dark gods,/conflicting absolutes, timeless and co-existent, who battle /like atoms seething in a cauldron, each against all, to assert /their raucous finales" (*Jason and Medeia*).

The contestants in a geriatric half-comic war of opposed principles concur, separately, in their impatience with hoary idealistic panaceas—"All life . . . is a brief and hopeless struggle against the pull of the earth"—and the dreamy blandishments of culture—"It was covering, all covering, mere bright paint over rotting barn walls" (*October Light*).

One may say the message is existential. The voyage traveled by Gardner's heroes and villains constitutes man's search for meaning and permanence in a universe which asserts their irrelevance and ignores him. Successive books examine the idea of ultimate absurdity from the viewpoints of wildly differing individual seekers; their creator appears to be examining the consequences, in a variety of social and historical contexts, of the lessons they learn. Some of Gardner's people (and nonhumans as well) are destroyed by what they come to know; others persevere in spite of it. Their author's own opinion must be inferred. My guess is that he is obsessively interested in the tension between social order and individual freedom, that he has decided that civil utopias are unmanageable, and that he therefore poses for his readers situations which ask them whether the alternative of isolated personal freedom may be substituted for these as a desirable goal. . . .

His most recent books reveal Gardner's virtues and defects in unruly profusion and in almost equal measure. *The King's Indian* (1974) includes most of his short stories. They are artful redevelopments of themes and situations borrowed from Poe, Browning, Kafka, Melville, and other writers. Even allusions to Lewis Carroll appear in the three "Tales of Queen Louisa," rambunctious Graustarkian romances which liken the "accidents" of status and rule to the kind of unexplainable sorcery that can make a rosebush bloom in winter or transform a monarch into a toad (and back again).

Several stories ("The Temptation of St. Ivo," "Pastoral Care," "The Warden") mislead their protagonists into anticipating that their traumas will conclude in some kind of sensible comprehension—then reduce them to dejected frustration when meaninglessness asserts itself. A more pleasing course is steered by the hero of "John Napper Sailing through the Universe": a real person, the illustrator of *The Sunlight Dialogues*, Gardner notes approvingly that his friend is a burly visionary who's able to reject the logical consequences of his perception of things: "At the edge of self-destruction, John Napper had . . . jumped back. He would make up the world from scratch. Let there be light, a splendid garden. He would fabricate treasure maps. And he'd come to believe it. . . . It was majestic! Also nonsense."

The protagonist of "The King's Indian" has "learned early in life that any man not firmly committed to a single point of view is as apt a philosopher as anybody else." This modest wisdom allows survival (if nothing more) to Jonathan Upchurch, a vigorous adventurer shanghaied, out of New Bedford, onto a ghostly whaler which appears to be the exact double of a ship that sank many years before. Of course the *Jerusalem* may be the "dead ship" herself; its crew may be ghosts wandering through a chaotic otherworld which has false sides, ready-made, to overturn in the face of all presumptions of rational answers to men's questions. The entire story could even be a joke played on its hearer by the narrator, Upchurch (A phlegmatic angel hovers nearby, eavesdropping; we needn't expect untainted verisimilitude). The tale is an exuberant nineteenth-century romance drenched in existentialism. Its prophets and profiteers cannot reap benefits from their own stratagems. No man can harness the mysteries thrashing about in the seas. It teases us with the information that the "King's Indian" is a classic chess move—but also lets that title phrase imply an ideal composite, mingling orderly intelligence with unlettered instinct: the double strength derived from the matched excellences of master and servant. The man who surfaces above these confusions and lives to tell us of them has done so because he accepts knowing there are no paradises, earthly or celestial; that, in spite of such knowledge, "a wise man settles for, say, Ithaca."

Such wisdom comes slowly to the protagonists of Gardner's latest novel, *October Light* (1976). They are elderly James Page and his sister Sally, both widowed, living together (and also apart) in a Vermont farmhouse. Sally is a "liberal," disgusted by her brother's "patriotic" rejection of the modern world. When James shoots her television set, their skirmishes of temperament burgeon into pitched battle: Sally rejects opportunities to leave the bedroom where she is imprisoned ("no use making peace with tyranny"). Relatives and neighbors can effect no compromise; the "war" escalates—even though James falls asleep on the toilet, and Sally occupies herself in skimming a "trashy best-seller."

This "interior" novel (whose plot alternates with the main one) is a flippant antiromance about a drug-smuggling ship, the *Indomitable*, and its pursuing antagonist—and "double"—the *Militant* (whose crew are blacks and foreigners). It contains a farrago of allegorized "messages": a social/racial confrontation (owing a bit to Melville's *Benito Cereno*); a tale of rampant capitalism (individual liberty) hamstrung by liberal attitudinizing; ironic proof that charitable impulses wreak havoc, when they aim to do good; examples of how things change when directionless malcontents assume responsibility. Sally had been drawn to the book for its breezy jeremiads against conventional morality. But it fizzles to a futilitarian nonconclusion (besides, pages are missing: this may be less than the whole story); she concedes it makes no more sense (and no less) than her brother's stuffy manifestoes.

The climax of repentant reconciliations is simply unbelievable. And despite some pointed internal references (to 1975 or later) the novel reads like a close cousin to *The Resurrection* and *Nickel Mountain*—which it resembles in its use of a rural setting, broadly drawn characters who embody symbolic oppositions, and dreadfully clumsy ironies (a theological discussion carried on over the interruptions of people passing by to use the bathroom; an argument on race relations shouted through a locked door). I think this is a rewritten version of a novel which has been around Gardner's workroom for several years. And I'm not sure that it is inappropriate to suggest that its unacknowledged literary models are *Silas Marner* and *A Christmas Carol*.

October Light is ambitious and reasonably sprightly but fails to satisfy the expectations it raises. The epigraphs are reverberant quotations from Founding Fathers; the novel's melodramatic outcome teaches James Page and his sister to surrender their flinty prejudices, admit how their stubbornness has insulated them from reality, and concede that right and wrong are more complicated than they have opined. Thus this bicentennial salute implies that America's battle for independence was not rewarded by any dramatic increase of vision. Gardner's personified forces perceive things in "October light"—a phenomenon native to New England late in the year: a sharp autumnal clarity which arranges hitherto blurred objects in unambiguous focus. The point is that it arrives late in the year; that the clarity (if it be such) is relative in the eye of the beholder.

A few summary remarks. When John Gardner uses his characters as mouthpieces, his readers must feel like sinners who encounter at the gateway to Hell a three-headed dog who doesn't guard against intruders but instead tugs them headlong into the place. The impulse behind his early novels was preferable: to show uncertain protagonists swept up in life's confusion and struggle, surviving their ordeals with an understanding that experience is a mystery not to be too easily understood. Therefore I hope that the unevenness of his recent work reflects an ongoing process of choosing how best to dramatize his characters' assumption of ironic pessimism. It is difficult to believe in the reality of characters who are seemingly born knowing that whatever happens to them will end up being of no consequence. We care more for the ones who live life and learn from it.

There is a real (and I think disturbing) mystery about Gardner's fiction. Are the stories which show his people growing into knowledge newly published work in an early mode that he unwisely has now abandoned? Or is he relaxing his thematic hold on characters, permitting them to be persons as well as ideas and symbols? I choose the latter alternative and will await further stories (like *The Sunlight Dialogues*, *Grendel*, "The King's Indian") told, or retold, for the purpose of reminding us that we have no choice but to accept our burden of incompleteness and study the outrageous ambitiousness of stubborn humans through the imperfect human medium: "not the sunlight, but the sunlight entrapped in the cloud"—October light.—BRUCE ALLEN, "Settling for Ithaca," *SwR*, Summer 1977, pp. 520–31

> And if the Babe is born a Boy
> He's given to a Woman Old,
> Who nails him down upon a rock,
> Catches his shrieks in cups of gold.

Prefatory quotations often provide useful clues to influences and sources, yet, in the case of John Gardner's *Grendel* (1971), critics have been slow to explore the possibilities raised by this epigraph from Blake. While a number of discussions devoted to Gardner's adaptation of *Beowulf* was to be expected, no detailed examination of his debt to Blake has appeared, despite the presence in his novel of scarcely veiled allusions to such well-known works as "The Mental Traveller," *The Marriage of Heaven and Hell*, and *Visions of the Daughters of Albion*. Instead, recent commentary on sources and analogues has linked the book with *Beowulf*, Baudelaire, Existentialism, and Chaucer, without mention of Blake. On closer examination, however, Blake proves a subsidiary though vital source of literary inspiration to Gardner, for Blakean motifs play a significant part in strengthening the novel's pessimistic vision.

The epigraph from "The Mental Traveller" at once acknowledges Gardner's general debt to Blake and alludes to a work presenting a related vision. No other poem of Blake's is as despairingly pessimistic in its portrayal of man's corporeal existence. Caught in the endless vegetative cycle, mankind is presented as rapacious, selfish, and cruel: characteristics dominant also in *Grendel*. From the cradle through old age, Blake's Male and Female are locked into a living hell of reciprocal exploitation, so that even the "positive" achievements in the cycle are based on sexual repression and emotional cannibalism. Similarly in *Grendel*, the heroism and idealism celebrated in the Shaper's alluring songs cloak brutal deeds which issue in the incessant despoliation of nature and mankind. Furthermore, Gardner recaptures the inescapable cyclic movement of "The Mental Traveller" in his precise, twelve-chapter progress through the signs of the Zodiac, beginning with Aries. Here, as elsewhere, not only the action of the ram is determined, but the narrative rhythm and, by implication, existence itself. Hence we hear of the encounter with the bull in Chapter Two under the sign of Taurus, of the treacherous nephew Hrothulf in Scorpio-Chapter Nine, and of the Geats arriving by sea in Aquarius-Chapter Eleven, so that by the end of the narrative, the reader shares the deterministic insight that marked Grendel's opening reference to life as being "Locked in the deadly progression of moon and stars."

The Blake quotation should, ideally, alert the reader to major preoccupations which the works have in common. A reader familiar with "The Mental Traveller" may perhaps more quickly grasp the primary means and specific aims of the novelist's satiric strategy, because both works offer a radical critique of mankind through personae who depart from and yet share basic human characteristics. Blake's speaker sees man in the species, and his vision is presented by semi-human, semi-ideational figures: "I traveled thro' a Land of Men/A Land of Men & Women too/And heard & saw such dreadful things/As cold Earth wanderers never knew." Their designations as Male and Female, together with the vitality of their actions, compel us to associate them with human interaction, while their deeds sufficiently contravene the limits of human existence to suggest a symbolic dimension. Again in *Grendel* the main persona is at once dissimilar (a monster) and similar, in that he shares emotions, thoughts, and language with the recognizably human characters. The dragon summarizes the relationship in words applicable to the personae of Blake's poem:

> You are, so to speak, the brute existent by which they learn to define themselves. The exile, captivity, death they shrink from—the blunt facts of their mortality, their abandonment—that's what you make them recognize, embrace! You *are* mankind, or man's condition.

Both works thus challenge the reader to recognize himself in their brutal portraits; and the Blakean epigraph arguably underscores this satiric aspect of *Grendel*, while it clearly prepares the reader for the novel's overwhelmingly deterministic vision.

Apart from inviting such comparisons which highlight *Grendel's* central themes, the epigraph also implicitly directs attention to a crucial alteration in narrative persective between Gardner's novel and his Blakean source. Critics agree that the speaker in "The Mental Traveller" is one of Blake's "Immortals," who from his vantage point in eternity dilates on the woes of fallen existence. Hence, he can perceive those states which immutably constitute man's corporeal lot, or what is constant in the midst of flux. As Blake explains in *A Vision of the Last Judgment*:

> These States Exist now Man Passes on but States remain for Ever he passes thro them like a traveller who may as well suppose that the places he has passed thro exist no more as a Man may suppose that the States he has passed thro Exist no more Every Thing is Eternal.

But *Grendel* systematically denies all hope of eternity and divinity. Consequently, the narrator, although more prescient than ordinary mortals, is equally entrapped in the vegetative flux. Even the all-powerful dragon is denied the boon of immutability and is comparable with Blake's bard in *Songs of*

Experience, who "Present, Past & Future sees," but does not enjoy the creative visionary capacity ascribed to the bard in *Jerusalem*, who is actively engaged in redeeming man from the deadly corporeal cycles. This limiting of perspective is, of course, dictated by the novel's nihilistic thrust, and we shall witness it in all Gardner's reshaping of Blakean material.

The effect of annulling Blake's eternal perspective is best demonstrated by Gardner's adaptation of a key scene from *The Marriage of Heaven and Hell*. On Plates Seventeen and Eighteen, Blake's narrator recounts how "an Angel came . . . to shew me my eternal lot." Then follows a descent long and arduous, "till a void boundless as a nether sky appeard beneath us. & we held by the roots of trees and hung over this immensity." "Sitting in the twisted roots of an oak," he is vouchsafed an image of hellish torment:

> . . . beneath us at an immense distance was the sun, black but shining; round it were fiery tracks on which revolv'd vast spiders, crawling after their prey; . . . I now asked my companion which was my eternal lot? he said, between the black & white spiders.

In *Grendel*, the details of this scene are gradually introduced in one of the book's most important sequences, beginning with Grendel's confrontation with the dragon, where he succumbs to a premonitory death-swoon:

> His eye burst open like a hole, to hush me. I closed my mouth. The eye was terrible, lowering toward me. I felt as if I were tumbling down into it—dropping endlessly down through a soundless void. He let me fall, down and down toward a black sun and spiders, though he knew I was beginning to die.

The narrator has already undergone a similar descent, associated with mental darkness—"I made my mind a blank"—and with a fall "through earth and sea," to reach this place of fear, which suitably generates the cryptic vision of his final end. But the reader must wait another fifty pages before the initial association of death with a plunge towards a black sun and spiders is amplified. Here Grendel, wishing to fall to the dragon in another metaphoric quest for knowledge that resides beyond the grave, is granted instead only a vague intimation which, however, recalls image by image Blake's work:

> I recall something. A void boundless as a nether sky. I hang by the twisted roots of an oak, looking down into immensity. Vastly far away I see the sun, black but shining, and slowly revolving around it there are spiders. I pause in my tracks, puzzled—though not stirred—by what I see. . . . It is just some dream. I move on, uneasy; waiting.

A reader, unaware of Gardner's direct debt to Blake for this scene, would see it simply as an augury of impending annihilation, to which the doomed Grendel is necessarily blind. But the deterministic suggestions, both here and in the vision's subsequent appearances, are greatly reinforced by recognizing the changes Gardner has made in his source. In *The Marriage of Heaven and Hell* the scene is part of a carefully controlled dialectical structure, which effects a radical reassessment of religious and moral norms. Energy, desire, contraries, and the devil are here positive factors, and the traditional vision of damnation is dismissed as an "angelic" imposition. Upon the Angel's departure, the speaker finds himself "sitting on a pleasant bank beside a river by moon light hearing a harper who sung to the harp, & his theme was, The man who never alters his opinion is like standing water, & breeds reptiles of the mind." *Grendel*, however, has no redeeming vision. Instead, the nightmare images of oak roots and the bottomless void, heralding Grendel's imminent death, reappear with increasing frequency in his encounters with Beowulf. Moreover, when an alternative vision of nature is offered to his own, its vernal and regenerative images are belied both by their speaker and by their murderous purpose. Beowulf is presented as being strangely mechanical, even mad, and he whispers his vision to Grendel to destroy and not to save him:

> It's coming, my brother. Believe it or not. Though you murder the world, turn plains to stone, transmogrify life into I and it, strong searching roots will crack your cave and rain will cleanse it: The world will burn green, sperm build again. My promise. Time is the mind, . . . By that I kill you.

Here, as in *The Marriage of Heaven and Hell*, the antagonists quite literally "impose on one another" their personal visions, although in *Grendel* opposition is no longer an indication of true friendship, and even conventional images of regeneration assume a death-dealing function in keeping with the work's nihilistic vision. . . .

Gardner . . . no more slavishly follows his Blakean sources than he does the Anglo-Saxon original. In his hands, both become ingredients in a new fiction that seeks to express an essentially contemporary sensibility. In place of the noble heroes of *Beowulf* and their fierce loyalty to the ring-giver, we see a society divided, suspicious, bloody, and self-tormenting. Instead of Blake's overriding vision of regeneration and eternity, we find ourselves pitifully locked into mindless, corporeal existence, where "It is the business of rams to be rams and goats to be goats, the business of shapers to sing and of kings to rule." While *Beowulf* provides Gardner with the basic outline and characters of his story, Blake's highly pictorial imagination affords a wealth of related images, conveying the quintessence of fallen existence or what he termed man's eternal sleep. In Gardner's novel, however, the final awakening brings extinction, not redemption, and confirms that narrator's worst forebodings. The opening epigraph from "The Mental Traveller," therefore, acknowledges a crucial debt to Blake and even underscores its precise nature. *Grendel* offers no minute particle opening into infinity, no heaven in a wildflower. Rather, it is a closely textured artifact whose apparent expansion or unfolding leads us full circle, thereby challenging the reader to relate his personal vision to Grendel's and to learn—lest again "all be done" as the narrator has told.—MICHAEL ACKLAND, "Blakean Sources in John Gardner's *Grendel*," *Crt*, Vol. 23, No. 1 (1981), pp. 57–65

In ⟨*The Resurrection* and *Grendel*⟩ and other early works, Gardner gives his readers a considerable advantage over luckless Grendel and his like. He peoples (or monsters) his tales with narrators and characters who demonstrate and often explain for us the limited point of view of his protagonists. James Chandler may begin as a stereotype of the philosophy professor, but his wife, family, friends, and enemies enlarge and complicate his point of view, keeping us always aware of its limitations. Though Grendel's primordial ideas often fail him, they are taken over, developed, and judged by that didactic dragon with fire in his eyes and Nietzsche in his heart.

Even in *October Light* (1976), the most complex and fully realized of Gardner's earlier novels, the reader has access to information from which each of the two central characters is excluded. Here again, Gardner uses several points of view to consider the effect on human lives of certain perceptual categories, ontic commitments, and conventional epistemologies. These focus his characters' experience and help them to make it intelligible, but they also limit both experience and intelligibility. In this novel Gardner sets forth a literary correlative for this multiplicity and interaction of points of view: he uses several literary genres juxtaposed in various ways to free his central characters from the parochial illusion that one point of view or epistemology is natural and valid, all others mistaken or perverse. He does not free them from all convention and genre; such total freedom would render the world incomprehensible and the character silent. The many genres—realistic novel, trash novel, fable, popular history, songs and poems of country reciters, sermon, legend, ghost story, and parable—emancipate the character from reliance on any single one and widen his or her point of view. It is an emancipation from genre achieved through a multiplicity of genres. But the reader is freed long before the character and has access to points of view other and better than that of the central characters.

In *Mickelsson's Ghosts*, however, Gardner demands more of his readers than he ever has before and significantly extends his technique of juxtaposing genres in order to free his central character from complete dependence upon a single epistemology. The danger of this technique, of course, is that the work will become an anthology rather than a novel, and several perceptive reviewers, most of whom had admired Gardner's earlier work, have raised the question of whether this novel is finally incoherent: a campus novel, gothic novel, historical novel, pastoral, detective thriller, love story, ghost story, journey into the occult, and novel of modern *angst*—all not quite rolled into one. They rightly note the many genres and themes and the confusion of the central character. The question is whether Mickelsson's confusions are shared by Gardner or whether they are part of a larger unity.

Gardner's earlier works afford us a useful context for this question. The unity of these works has always been less thematic than epistemological. And the multiplicity of points of view, epistemologies, and genres has served to liberate his central characters from exclusive dependence upon any single one. In conversation, Gardner described *Mickelsson's Ghosts* as a philosophical novel, very much in the tradition of Melville. A glance at *Moby-Dick*, for example, reveals that Melville also mixed genres (etymology, extracts, cetology, drama, and multiple soliloquies) to free Ishmael from his personal and epistemological isolation. Playing with genres in novels that are themselves about modes of interpretation is a dangerous game, and one might argue that doing so was one of the causes of Melville's contemporary failure—a failure Gardner seems to have reenacted, judging from the current reception of *Mickelsson's Ghosts*. If we attempt to impose on this large novel the rigid prescriptions of *On Moral Fiction*, they will, of course, not accommodate it, and the novel will seem immense and incoherent. But if we reflect that Gardner's previous novels centered not on the inculcation of morality but on the liberation of point of view, then we can begin to understand the coherence of his career, the point of his last long novel, and the depth of his conviction that—as he wrote in a letter to his son—"all tragedy is a limited point of view."

In *Mickelsson's Ghosts*, Peter Mickelsson is the only center of consciousness. As Robert Towers notes in his review, "the reader is immersed in the personality of this increasingly desperate man for nearly six hundred pages; no direct access is allowed to the awareness or perspective of any other character." Though Towers considers this focus yet another flaw in the novel, it is I think an appropriate, though daring, extension of Gardner's earlier work. He has put his readers into the predicament in which we ordinarily find his characters, but this time with a dominant point of view. If we are to recognize the limitations of this point of view, we must do so from evidence implicit in the narrative action of the novel itself, never made explicit by other characters, seasonal reference points, traditions, or a synecdochic novel-within-the-novel, in which the structure of the larger work will be made easier to recognize. Here we are stuck with Mickelsson, and he is in a bad way. . . .

Unlike ⟨the Garrets⟩, Mickelsson is beginning to be freed from isolation and cliché by ⟨the novel's⟩ bizarre events, which challenge his narrow epistemology, and by his interactions with larger communities, interactions brought on by his "quest decision" to buy the house. He is no longer confined to the conventions of the campus novel—one of which is, of course, centered on the gossamer fragility of the professor's mind and its gradual breakdown. As he confronts the harsh realities of life, he learns that, yes, there are indeed more things in heaven and earth than are dreamt of in his philosophy—simple rationalism alternating with reductions of Nietzsche—a philosophy quite likely to impair even a good mind. In this phase, Mickelsson makes the old mistake of attempting to posit the isolated self as a ground for perception and discourse. When he finds, predictably enough, that he cannot base his interpretations and values in his own reason, he despairs. This destructive cliché applies to Mickelsson only before he buys the house, however; once he is in the house, he enters larger communities that contain many conventions but transcend any single one. So Tim Booker, who sells him the house, is a real-estate agent, male nurse, and self-proclaimed good witch, who in his healing combines witchly lore with rather more familiar arts learned as a medic in Vietnam. From these disparate bits and pieces of familiar conventions, he assembles a rich yet coherent life, a work of originality. And John Pearson, the neighbor who first tells Mickelsson that the house is haunted, is a hunter, farmer, reader, and dowser, who helps him to look for water on his property.

Gardner has written to his son that he considers the novelist a dowser, using means he cannot quite understand to find something that is really there: "Dowsing makes sense only in the sense that one can see that it works and, having seen that, can make up nonsensical theories as to why." Gardner assumes that the dowsing devices "allow the total mind, with its inherent psychic capacities, to know," but he spends less time on this assumption than on the analog to fiction, arguing that no novelist, whatever his theory of form, "can doubt that there is a form waiting for his work to find it, a necessary arrangement and affirmation." In this novel, however, Pearson's dowsing does not work—even though the water is really there, waiting in a spring under the house itself and found eventually through the familiar devices of memory and reason. The implication, then, is not that clairvoyance, witchcraft, and dowsing are more useful than observation and reason but rather that in Mickelsson's world no single epistemology or point of view or genre is adequate to the complexity of his experience. If he is to continue on what Gardner has called his "quest," he must become capable of seeing through more than one window on the world, more than one point of view.

The central story is how Mickelsson progresses on the quest itself, a quest that combines all the genres mentioned earlier into a coherent and compendious whole as the novel builds to its ending at Jessica's party. Jessica Stark is herself a combination of genres. She carries the name of Shylock's daughter, who ran off to marry a Christian, and the name of one of the most famous and colorful families in New England. Both Jewish mother and Yankee pragmatist, she gives Mickelsson some money, helps him answer his mail, loves him, and puts him back in touch with several communities. They make love at her party while, outside the door of their room, friends converse and, outside the house, the larger world joins spirit and matter, mundane and bizarre, in a shower of small miracles.

There is no suggestion that Mickelsson's quest is over or that he and Jessica will live happily ever after. But he has moved from a life of sterility and despair to one of variety and action. One indication of the distance he has come is his final encounter with Edmund Lawler, a colleague to whom he was similar at the beginning of the book. Both were solitary professors who lived only for learning. Lawler, who remained alone, turns up at Mickelsson's house, pulls a gun, and forces him to dismantle the house he had just reconstructed. Lawler announces that he is a Mormon, a member of the elite Tribe of Dan, and that he has come to cover up any evidence there may be of some dark scandal involving Joseph Smith. They do not find anything, but Lawler is undeterred. He shoots Mickelsson's cat and is prepared to kill not only Mickelsson but an adult and child who come knocking at the door.

Like the philosophical isolato he is, Lawler comes up with a justification. Mormonism is a good thing because it allows people certitude and community; the height of Mormonism is the Tribe of Dan, the hit squad to which he belongs; of course, for reasons of security each member of the Tribe must remain completely alone, cut off not only from the Gentiles but also from all other Mormons. This sort of reasoning gives philosophy a bad name and is reminiscent of the undergraduate joke about the International Order of Solipsists, which of course never meets because none of its members believes in the existence of the others. Mickelsson, whose powers of recognition have improved over the course of the book, sensibly inquires how Lawler can know that he is not simply deluded. Lawler dismisses the question, but we need not. Lawler's epistemology renders his identity uncheckable and keeps him utterly alone, able only to wax nostalgic about such great historical murders as the massacre at Mountain Meadows (which may or may not have been committed by the Tribe of Dan, which may or may not exist) and to shoot passing strangers for the greater glory of a private and curious God.

Whatever the precise ontological status of Mickelsson's ghosts, they have saved him from that, and he can go against Lawler with a cunning that combines the football player, clairvoyant, and philosopher. The many genres have freed him from the one. Even his philosophy has improved. In sum, then, Mickelsson's thoughts, throughout most of the novel, are indeed incoherent, but Gardner's novel about a lost philosopher needing to ground his thought in an interpretive community that will free him from his tragically limited point of view is quite coherent and will stand among his major fictions.

. . . From the start ⟨Gardner⟩ used genres to free his main characters from the confines of genre, to lead the individual character to participation in and understanding of larger segments of the human community. In his books he insisted on including illustrations, poems, songs, photographs, and he worried over choices of typeface and composition in the attempt to build these many components into a harmonious whole. He evinced the same complexity in his own career: writing novels, short stories, plays, poems, opera libretti, scholarship, criticism, theory, translations, and children's books. In his fictions he created individual characters in masterfully realistic settings, then attempted to join that individuality to larger communities and to combine that realistic core with myth, fable, and legend. Often he succeeded, and his best works—among them *Grendel*, *October Light*, and *Mickelsson's Ghosts*—will endure in the canon of American literature.—ROBERT DALY, "John Gardner and the Emancipation of Genres," *GR*, Summer 1983, pp. 421–28

CHILDREN'S LITERATURE

As John Gardner himself remarked recently in an interview, the critical response to his children's books has generally been respectful but unenthusiastic. As a prolific scholar, critic and novelist, he stirs some awe in reviewers, but no one seems to believe that his children's stories will appeal deeply to children. The children's literature journals have been fairly appreciative; periodicals with a broader focus are a little impatient. For example, in *The Sewanee Review*, Bruce Allen writes: "Fanciful and clever as they are, the [fairy] tales remain ironic jokes which assert a breezy relativism. . . . My own children think the story ["The Shape-Shifters of Shorm"] makes no sense whatsoever. John Gardner might approve."

Given his intrepidity as a writer and his concern with the loss of morality in art, it is not surprising that Gardner would try at some point to reach young readers. Moreover, with his interest in the medieval literary tradition and its moral, ironic, and leisurely modes of story telling, the fairy tale and the "collection" of stories would naturally appeal to him. And in fact all five children's works follow the tradition: three are fairy tale collections, one is a book of nonsense verse entitled *A Child's Bestiary* and the last, *In the Suicide Mountains*, is a full-length work in the fairy tale mode. All are marked by Gardner's obvious talent and inventiveness, but all are partial failures.

The "Preface" to *A Child's Bestiary* explains:

A *Bestiary*, or Book of Beasts,
Is a thing full of high morality.
In the Middle Ages, such books were the rage.
If you can't find the moral, turn the page.

Following as well in the more modern tradition of Hillaire Belloc's *The Bad Child's Book of Beasts* (1896), Ogden Nash, and other modern nonsense writers for children, Gardner's book is comic, often satirical, and even occasionally "of high morality."

The House Mouse lives upon crackers and cheese;
The Church Mouse lives on *Ecclesiastes*.
The House Mouse's life is all song and laughter;
The Church Mouse will gather his crackers hereafter.

He includes the conventional be-kind-to-animals joke—"For animals have feelings too,/And furthermore, they bite" ("Introduction")—and has a few modern words to say about the smug hunter who thinks he's smarter than the musk ox but who, unlike the musk ox, will end up in a rest home. Though the poems are entertaining, they don't scan well, and in a collection of nonsense verse, where the wit is generated largely by the contrast between the absurdity of the content and the precision and elegance of the lines, this is a serious flaw. The idiosyncratic shifts in mood and meter might appeal to adults, but children, who read this kind of poem as much for the rhythm as for the words, might find them confusing.

Gardner's three small volumes of fairy tales, *Dragon, Dragon and Other Tales* (1975), *Gudgekin the Thistle Girl and Other Tales* (1976) and *The King of the Hummingbirds and Other Tales* (1977), are more substantial and reflect his interest in the form. Fairy tales clearly delineate what is good and what is evil, and Gardner is interested in the moral side of stories. He claims that literature should give us hope and models of how to act and think, that fantasy, in particular, provides sunlight, where so much modern realistic fiction for children is bleak and gloomy. He likes the simplicity of fairy tales and their focus on what is timeless and true. What he objects to is what he considers the oversimplified classist assumptions of traditional fairy tales, that there are good people and bad people, and that the good ones embody the virtues espoused by the aristocracy. He claims that "solutions in my stories do not come about because of the wonderful power of the true-born aristocrat." In his tales good characters can and often do perform evil deeds to survive; and cunning and necessity, which Gardner considers middle-class virtues, are highly valued.

It is not surprising, then, to find him applying modern novelistic techniques to the traditional fairy tale. The novel, having evolved as a middle-class form, serves Gardner in challenging traditional assumptions about heroism. His characters are not merely good or bad; they are depressed, bored, self-denying. As a novelist, he is interested in what inspires heroic impulses, what motivates destructive behavior. The result is a fusion of realism and fantasy. Gardner explores the extraordinariness of the ordinary the way Hans Christian Andersen did in his fairy tales, though Gardner rarely achieves the kind of emotional intensity or sympathy inspired by Andersen's stories or the power of Andersen's bite. Gardner's satirical touch is light; his tales are comic. Their peculiar blend of psychologizing and philosophizing with the plentiful details which specify and individualize characters and incidents creates much of their wit and humor. Gardner's Cinderella, Gudgekin the thistle girl, for example, needs to undergo a kind of psychotherapy with her fairy godmother before she achieves the right state of mind to accept her prince. In "The Shape-Shifters of Shorm," a tale about protean-like characters, the hero requests as his reward a "round-trip ticket to Brussels," and in the end, "changed his name to Zobrowski and dropped out of sight." Gardner's particular mixture of the archetypal and the mundane reflects his personal vision of life: that the world often appears chaotic, that we don't really know what is going on, and therefore, that any action we decide upon may appear absurd and undermine a sense of meaning and order in the world. Like many contemporary writers, then, his sense of heroism is relative and reflects an essential uncertainty about ethics and codes of behavior. . . .

At the center of Gardner's reflections on the nature of goodness and evil ⟨in *In the Suicide Mountains*⟩ is his conviction that it is love which can save us. The cure for the despair of all the characters in the story is the discovery of the love and sense of responsibility for someone else that can hold forth the promise of fulfillment and shift one's attention from oneself to another. It offers an end to the self-absorption and rage we have come to call narcissism. It is only this which allows one to transcend the anxiety of living with uncertainty, with the unfathomable depths of illusion and unknowable causes. It is love which helps one transcend the rational—all the reasons, for example, that one can list for committing suicide. He offers love to his readers in the face of good that is always tainted with evil, of wisdom that comes from the most suspect source, of babies who carry with them the heritage of sin, the mark of the misfit, who have as much potential for despair and evil as for achievement and goodness.

That the book encompasses all this is certainly to its credit. But it is in many ways a trying work. Interspersed throughout the story are four tales which Gardner adapted from a Russian folktale collection and from Grimm. Presumably included to let art reveal truths about life, they are all told by the abbot—the fourth, with its miraculous happy ending, in his fresh, new condition as baby—and they encompass a wide range of human relationships. But as they are not directly related to the larger story, they feel intrusive. When Christopher asks the abbot why he tells them, the abbot replies—coyly, since this is a book full of didacticism, of morals and ever more subtle morals—"'As the world rolls on, I grow less and less interested in the moral.'" But then he goes on to explain anyway. The inclusion of these tales seems an indulgence on Gardner's part. The work, particularly considering its intended audience, demands boundaries, and Gardner ignores them in his continuing efforts to present life's complexities. Even the fertility of his language eventually works against him, so that at a certain point each fresh metaphor or tender observation seems a little less interesting than the one before it. And though romances are often characterized by subtle examinations of character, there is nonetheless a clash between the story's medieval form and setting and Gardner's self-consciously upbeat and somewhat precious sensibility.

Certainly we would like our children to read and enjoy a book with such substance. But they probably won't sit still for it. It is truly neither a children's book nor one for adults. Adults will clearly read it at one remove, watching Gardner the teacher explain the half-obvious, and children may get lost. Finally, and this is true of the other books as well, the work feels contrived. Though Gardner's vision is full and complex, and though the book is unusual, it and the other volumes read like what they probably are: Gardner's experiments in one more area of literature.—Geraldine DeLuca, Roni Nator, "Modern Moralities for Children," *John Gardner*, eds. Robert A. Morace, Kathryn VanSpanckeren, 1982, pp. 89–96

⟨*In the Suicide Mountains*⟩ is particularly useful for understanding Gardner and his differences from the post-moderns. Even though in it Gardner puts to particular use techniques of self-consciousness and metafiction, he also uses conventions of the traditional fairy tale, and fairy tales use plots primarily to point out a moral. Gardner uses the Russian fairy tales to this end, and he uses his own plot similarly to fulfill his commitment to moral literature. Story telling in this book, as in other novels by John Gardner, has several specific functions. First, it demonstrates that language, the language of books or television, can and does communicate about essential matters of existence. Second, Gardner uses story telling to illustrate points he believes to be true about moral fiction. Third, the fable provides Gardner with the opportunity to observe that the possibilities of literature to deal with both universal human experience and present human concerns are limitless. His selection of different story-telling devices in his various novels exemplifies this further: the frame convention in *October Light*, the memoirs of *The Wreckage of Agathon*, the fictive characters in *Grendel*, and the Russian fairy tales in *In the Suicide Mountains*, to name a few. Gardner's characters tell stories for the same reason he does, to illustrate a point believed by the author to be meaningful to humanity and moral in both its intent and concepts.

Story telling is a central activity in the works of the post-moderns also; however, its function in writers such as Nabokov, Borges, Pinter, and Barth differs from its function in the novels of John Gardner. In the short stories and novels by these post-moderns, one function of story telling is to demonstrate that language refers to the mind of the user, and only problematically to the world. "Lost in the Funhouse" clearly shows Barth's belief that writing fiction is problematic not only because the old forms do not suit modern experience, but also because fictions reflect more about the process of creating fictions than they do about the world. Whereas in the fiction of John Gardner, the language is intended to refer to the world, in the fiction of many post-moderns, the language is intended to refer to the story it creates and the process by which it creates itself.

For John Gardner, it is not the purpose of art to point out that we are living a fiction, an idea which Gardner says leads to despair and hopelessness, nor is it the purpose of art simply to entertain. Rather, the purpose of art is to inspire people to live with greater joy, to love with greater depth, and to fulfill their talents however unique they may be. The story of *In the Suicide Mountains* demonstrates this.—ANGELA A. RAPKIN, "John Gardner's Novels," *John Gardner*, ed. Beatrice Mendez-Egle, 1983, pp. 8–9

LIBRETTI

Our working relationship (between the composer and Gardner) was . . . established from the beginning. Here was John's attitude toward music's role in opera in black and white. Let the libretto lead with an initial metaphor and a skeleton, then retreat and observe how the composer moves into them, ready all the while to bolster, patch, delete, add, all in response to the needs of the music and without deviating from the philosophical purpose, except where the music sheds new light on it. In this way, two can work in much the way that one artist alone must, allowing the work the freedom to discover itself in progress. Too much from the librettist, and the composer's discoveries cannot enter into the finished work. John, from the beginning, displayed a deference to the music and the vision of the composer that was somewhat miraculous. "Like two lobes of the same brain," is his description of our method.

He told me later that even the idea of *Frankenstein* came about as a result of elements which he heard in my music. I have since seen how different are the librettos done by him for other composers, each aimed at the particular strengths of the composer for whom it is intended. I would have had great difficulty, for example, writing the music for *William Wilson*, where John's libretto for this aria-centered opera was in part shaped by the style of its composer, Louis Calabro. By the time we came to *Rumpelstiltskin*, his instincts concerning my traits had become so developed that almost nothing needed to be revised, and it was completed in about the amount of time it took to copy it out.

Nothing so easy happened with *Frankenstein* during the eight or nine years it took to complete. It required long intervals given over not only to devising a workable method for collaboration but also to expanding our capacities for so great a subject. The later *Rumpelstiltskin* deals with fumbling goodness emerging from human fallibility and with the celebration of the kind of boasting fifth-graders do. But *Frankenstein* concerns nothing less than the dilemma of life and art, and with painful difficulty I had to rise to John's scale. Once the first draft was in hand, there began an endless series of confrontations, almost over every line. We acted out scenes and defended our positions, he holding out for philosophic unity and I for dramatic situations, visual configurations, or musical opportunities.

I don't know if literature is more flexible than music, as John maintains, or if he simply had a better technique than I had. I do think that some of the opera's weaknesses are probably due to my insistence on certain points—for example, that singers need enough to sing to justify their presence. And I know that he almost always compromised in my favor, though not always in the way I had expected. Whenever sacrifice was necessary, it was the libretto that suffered it and not the music. Mostly, however, as will be apparent in the examples that follow, John's supple talent was able to adjust to my demands while at the same time to improve what he already had written. . . .

Our understanding of each other's work patterns has lead to much easier collaboration since *Frankenstein*. We can now work over long distances and come together only as the completion date nears, if necessary. *Rumpelstiltskin* was conceived together in concept, but I did not see John again until the month of the first performance. When I read the libretto, I heard music instantly, so naturally did it lend itself to my musical style. Telephone calls were all that were necessary for the small adjustments. We are now working on a one-act comedy with a small cast and I have the text of a large opera based on the Pied Piper awaiting the right moment. In both of these I still feel the freedom to let the music go where it must, confident that John can make good on whatever "dire bastardy" I perform. It occurs to me to wonder if other composers have enjoyed such a luxury.—JOSEPH BABER, "John Gardner, Librettist," *John Gardner*, eds. Robert A. Morace, Kathryn VanSpanckeren, 1982, pp. 99–105

CRITICAL THEORY

It is not surprising . . . to find Gardner publishing *On Moral Fiction*, a theoretical/critical book which will probably be quoted as widely as Gass's *Fiction and the Figures of Life* was a few years ago, not because Gardner's formulations of the new fictional conservatism are particularly brilliant but because he articulates feelings and tastes many disgruntled readers share. Gass's essays had an elegant uselessness; Gardner's appeal is plain talk and righteousness. I have heard "Kill the Aestheticians" murmured in my university library. Gardner responds to this kind of frustration with academic jargon by using words, such as Beauty, Truth, and Goodness, that most critics walked away from years ago. These abstractions come to have a sludge-like quality, Gardner's distinctions often lack precision (a favorite pejorative is "creepy"), and his readings of recent fiction are sometimes militantly unimaginative. But *On Moral Fiction* is still a necessary book because its earnest force requires even the reader who resists it page by page to examine his assumptions about fiction and because no other writer—Tom Wolfe in *The Painted Word* excepted—has reminded us recently that art is by and for human beings. . . .

I think Gardner's assessment of the current literary scene is substantially accurate if our contemporaries are measured against classic or even classic modern writers. His judgments would also be true of the fiction written in the 1870s. Still, we do need to recognize that very few of our writers have the heart or ambition to be a Melville or a Pynchon. Even Gardner's prescriptions could be persuasive had he not vitiated the basic force of his argument with an inconsistent definition of moral fiction, with narrow assumptions, inflated claims, and limited sympathies. Gardner defines moral fiction both by the exploratory, mimetic process of its composition and by the healthy effects it has without fully considering that a "moral" process can and sometimes does produce a negative, even a nihilistic work. His assumptions—that ordinary language is adequate for interesting fiction, that art communicates very much like other discourses, that the reader should fall into fiction as into a dream—are insistently naive, but even more difficult to accept is Gardner's pride. He proclaims that art and criticism are the only ordering agencies left in our culture, that "true" art—and not just the best art—is necessarily moral, and that the artist is the only true critic. As a reader of his fellow novelists, Gardner is sometimes pettish (his comments on Bellow and Updike), occasionally sloppy, and at least once flatly wrong—when he mistakes what happened in Heller's *Something Happened*. There is little sympathy for satirists, creators of indirect affirmations, and makers of imaginative ornaments. In a world where everything and everyone is used, ordered for a purpose,

Gardner would make fiction one more operation, the most efficient persuasion. He forgets fun.

On Moral Fiction does not collapse through its many weaknesses because, ultimately, Gardner sides with great art, an ambitious humane art that displays the writer's love for his craft, his world, and his readers. However, when some of Gardner's notions about character and communication become the premises of an academic criticism . . . the result is disastrous for the novel: art becomes therapy, fiction equals sociology, and the novel dies for sure.—THOMAS LECLAIR, "Moral Criticism," *CoL*, Autumn 1979, pp. 509–11

Gardner's method of proceeding ⟨in *On Moral Fiction*⟩ is simply rhetorical, proscriptive, and viscerally personal, laying down rules and cautels: Others "may be brilliant artists, with positions exactly as absolute as, say, mine. But they are wrong." Authors who write to suit Gardner create "true art"; those who do not, compose "false art," "bad art," something akin to "heresy"; they are "trivial and false"; they produce the "mediocre"—"commercial slickness, misplaced cleverness, posturing, wild floundering—dullness." Their work "lacks conviction"; they demonstrate a "lack of concern" (for whatever). But most of all, such work distressingly displays "errors," is devised by "nihilists, cynics, and merdistes." It "supports death and slavery." The art that Gardner mislikes, Gardner tells us in his flume, "must be driven out." For such evil authors are "usurpers of space that belongs to the sons of God."

Gardner in his screaming and dreaming commences to sound Manichaean; and he himself appears as Melchior, the Magi prince of light, who will sort the good and the evil out for us. (Elsewhere he mentions, in passing, that he himself and "the people I knew—my parents and friends—were as high-minded and decent as any poet." All to the good for his little parochial group. For standards of excellence he hath not far to seek.) In any event, his rather generalized, pious, and myopic categories of goodness allow him to condemn most of the major figures of contemporary literature: Lawrence, Hemingway, Durrell, Nabokov, Porter, Mailer, Beckett, Bellow, Pynchon, Gass, Albee, Vonnegut, Barth, Barthelme, Heller, Gaddis, Updike, Roth, and Coover. To some degree, on the other hand, Gardner approves of "perhaps" Malamud, "conceivably" portions of Cheever, a modicum of Welty, John Fowles, Italo Calvino, Larry Woiwode, Mark Halpern, Grace Paley, Guy Davenport, and Samuel Hazo.

Naturally enough, Gardner aspires to be U. S. Marshall in this territory, and to make the world safe for True Fictioneers. "The only available rules," by his curious method of criticism, "are those of the gunfighter." He shoots first, and asks questions later (if at all). Nor can we nicely examine into his criteria. For, "unfortunately, one can expect no precision . . . in these matters, since the man who really knows cannot prove he knows." He can only do a lot of fancy gunslinging and perform shoot-'em'-up, ego-tripping pyrotechnics, aspiring as he does to make gunfighting "a little more orderly, a little more deadly."

Needless to say, all of this parlous stridency and handing-down of Tablets is arrant nonsense—and embarrassing nonsense, at that. Serious art need *not* present the ideal or the real (Gardner confusedly has it doing both at the same time); it is enough if it intensely scrutinizes human states of aspiration, states of being, states of mind. Nor should the fictioneer merely paint the roseate and the unsubstantial. As Hugo Rahner, S.J., recently argued, in favoring the tempering of seriousness with humor and laughter, we have been "thrust" into the midst of this evil (and yet so lovely) world, into this noisy, merry (because mostly so mortally sad) world." Serious fiction, like the serious life, must come to terms with every aspect of that reality—its pleasure *and* its pain, its beauty *and* its ugliness.

It is unfortunate that a promising writer of fiction himself (author of the ambitious *Grendel* and *October Light*) here descends so fully into hasty, slovenly prose and careless, ridiculous propositions. With an anticlimax, Gardner pronounces against his opponents that "Honest feeling has been replaced by needless screaming, pompous foolishness, self-centered repetitiousness, misuse of the vocabulary." What could better express the situation of Gardner himself? "What has gone wrong?" Gardner elsewhere queries. "Why is it that even those of our writers who insist that they care about argument are for the most part incapable of constructing an argument that will hold?" It may be so of others, but, alas, it is a question poignantly applicable to Mr. Gardner's own *On Moral Fiction*. What has gone wrong indeed?—JOHN R. CLARK, ANNA LYDIA MOTTO, *Thought*, June 1980, p. 243

Gardner maintains that his basic message ⟨in *On Moral Fiction*⟩ is "as old as the hills," but he is correct only to a point. His view of literature, for example, echoes (without the Calvinist perspective on human goodness) Sidney's evaluation of poetry, whose "final end is to lead and draw us to as high a perfection as our degenerate souls, made worse by their clay lodgings, can be capable of." Sidney, however, assumes that the poet teaches deliberately, that the message made sweet by his verse has been consciously chosen. Gardner will have none of this. Because he lives in an age when literature has been more often thought about expressively than affectively, Gardner apparently is inclined to see the morality of fiction as the result of a process rather than of an intention to enlighten, persuade, or move. In fact, he sees such intention as an impediment to imaginative creation. "Art," he proclaims, "is as original and important as it is precisely because it does not start out with clear knowledge of what it means to say." What fiction "says" then must emerge from the act of saying itself: "moral fiction communicates meaning discovered by the process of fiction's creation."

Gardner, to be sure, is somewhat unclear on this point. He does grant that "some good and 'serious' fiction is merely first-class propaganda—fiction in which the writer knows before he starts what it is that he means to say." This concession, which is made apropos of medieval writers like Chaucer, is imprecise. How are we to reconcile the notions of "propaganda" (can this be art at all according to Gardner's definition?) and "good fiction"? One might also wonder how writers such as Chaucer can in any sense be considered propagandists, since their beliefs and ideas were nearly universally shared by their audiences. This fuzzy thinking points to a larger problem with *On Moral Fiction*.

And that is that Gardner never details what is defective about literature with a consciously-contrived moral message. His comment that "didacticism inevitably simplifies morality and thus misses it" seems to point the way toward an answer, but this argument is never further explained or provided with examples. Since Gardner, moreover, holds up the *Divine Comedy* as an example of what he means by "moral fiction," surely he needs either to re-define didacticism in some way to exclude Dante or to provide evidence that the letter to Can Grande is a forgery. But not only is Gardner vague about didacticism; he is vague also about the process of unconscious moral writing (whatever that might be, since I believe we are not to include the influence of the Holy Ghost). How does not thinking about what he wants to say help the writer produce a morally more complex (and hence more satisfactory) result? We are never told. And certainly this is a difficult position to defend, assuming with Gardner that the end of fiction is the communication of the proper ideas and values to the reader. Such a view makes the human brain a perverse organ and language a strange instrument, for it maintains that we speak better without knowing what we are saying and think better if we, in a sense, avoid thinking. Of course, this way of looking at language and its role within the creative process would suit well the aestheticist position, with its intentional and affective fallacies. But Gardner does not maintain that fiction should be and not mean. He agrees essentially with theorists such as E. D. Hirsch, Jr., that a literary work, like other speech acts, embodies a discoverable intention or message. He simply asserts that such a message, if it is to be truly moral, must be revealed to the writer by what he writes.

Although Gardner makes exceptions for writers from earlier periods, acknowledging that didactic intent and artistic success are not always incompatible, he makes none, as far as I can tell, for more modern authors. In fact, he never discusses how a book such as Steinbeck's *Grapes of Wrath*, generally acknowledged as an important and successful work of fiction despite its obvious moralizing intentions, fails to communicate a truly moral message. The only "failure" of this kind addressed specifically is Saul Bellow's. Bellow, we are told, violates the canons of moral fiction by having his characters occasionally serve as the mouthpieces for opinions that have nothing to do "with the progress of the action or the values under test." But what Gardner objects to here is surely a lack of artistry not related directly to the didactic impulse, for we are led to think that Bellow would be a better writer if the opinions he made his characters mouth were dramatically appropriate. Although Bellow is thus accused more of a failure of technique than of a faulty intention, Gardner does end by calling his novels "sprawling works of advice, not art," a judgment that smacks more of art for art's sake than literature as guiding lamp. In any case, Gardner never illustrates how didacticism simplifies and thus misses true morality.

And perhaps this is so for a very obvious reason. That didacticism serves poorly the needs of moral vision is a position which, if one considers the full range of Western literature, is difficult to establish. Because he bases his discussion of moral fiction on writers like Dante and Tolstoy and finds it necessary to exclude Chaucer and other medieval artists from the general pronouncement against deliberate moralizing, Gardner must surely sense this himself. A more reasonable formulation might suggest that instruction and art are not necessarily opposed aims, but may be and frequently are reconciled by writers with deeply moral consciences and truly imaginative gifts. The question is more one of technique and proper balance (as the Bellow example seems to indicate) than one of general principles. The fact is that Gardner, like many writers today, is antipathetic to didactic intent. This antipathy is itself traditional and can be traced at least as far as the aesthetic movement in the late nineteenth century. The irony is that it is this antipathy which has, in large measure, produced the *crise morale* in fiction-making against which Gardner himself so eloquently fulminates.

I do not deny that moral fiction can be produced unconsciously, by the working of the imagination alone. Such seems the case in writers like Graham Greene, in whose writing the force of imagining itself wrenches idiosyncrasy and experience into a pattern that can enlighten and move. But the imagination (and here the vast bulk of literature Gardner cites is substantial proof), if unaided by a conscious intent to produce "valid models for imitation," can just as likely, perhaps even more likely, produce escapist fiction and works that cynically attack traditional values, the kinds of works that Gardner scorns. As he himself suggests, there is nothing in the process of creation itself to insure the appropriate impact of the finished work on the reader; failure seems more likely than success since Gardner can suggest no one more recent than Tolstoy as a writer of moral fiction. The fault which an intentionally didactic writer such as Bellow may commit is to fall, at times, into the role of essayist-lecturer. Gardner is, of course, perceptive about this, though it leaves one mystified about his enthusiasm for Tolstoy, whose fiction is full of essays and lectures. But such a flaw seems a small price to pay for fiction that otherwise fulfills the functions Gardner outlines for it. Bellow's work, he admits, is "boldly opposed to those trashy popular philosophies we so often encounter in other writers' work."

On Moral Fiction, finally, attempts to preserve and reconcile two different ways of looking at literature. On the one hand, Gardner wishes to safeguard the autonomy of imaginative creation, its freedom from any intention to communicate overtly or be controlled by such an intention. This is the freedom demanded by the aestheticists. Thus for Gardner the opposite of art is propaganda, with its prescribed contest. He views, for example, the essay and novel as opposed forms, though the history of the novel suggests a certain affinity between them. On the other hand, he deplores contemporary works which do not serve the moral function of sustaining life by providing a "benevolent vision of the possible." Art, and particularly fiction, is for him a weapon to be used in the struggle against disorder and chaos. *On Moral Fiction*, however, is a strange call to arms. For the book says to the writers it addresses: "Write moral fiction since we need it. But, for God's sake, don't think about morality when you're writing."

Though essentially a *cri de coeur* with only a very loose kind of argument, *On Moral Fiction* deserves the attention it has received from the academic and artistic communities because its message is well worth listening to at a time when the basic assumptions of our literary tradition—and moral enlightenment is perhaps the most important of these—are being discarded on every side. But Gardner's rejection of didacticism certainly will not facilitate a return to the tradition he thinks we have wrongly abandoned. And we can best see why this is true if we examine some of Gardner's own fiction.

. . . Gardner provides no device ⟨in *Grendel*⟩, in the way of character or action, to evaluate the protagonist's faults or to point the way toward a remedy for them. And it can certainly be maintained, as I have tried to do here, that the novel systematically attacks the one means of escape from the human dilemma that the poem holds out: literature. *On Moral Fiction* tells us that art is a weapon against the trolls of disorder; in *Grendel* the troll protagonist reduces moral fiction to self-aggrandizing delusion. I think it can be said that the problem with *Grendel*, speaking morally, is that it was written with no clear intention other than an imaginative one: to approach the *Beowulf* legend with the modern novelists's viewpoint. But imaginative intentions do not always produce moral fiction.

If we are to return to a tradition of moral fiction, we must put aside the aestheticist bias against didacticism. For didacticism need not be the enemy of art; it simply means the desire, from high-minded motive, to uphold the good and persuade others of the right. Such an intention, our literary tradition suggests, is not contrary to artistic value. If fiction is to be a true mirror for us, it must also be a lamp and forthrightly light up the darkness, and not be content with the hope that the imagination of its own accord can save us from ourselves. —R. BARTON PALMER, "The Problem with Gardner's *On Moral Fiction*," *Ren*, Spring 1982, pp. 161–72

SAMUEL COALE
"'Into the Farther Darkness':
The Manichaean Pastoralism of John Gardner"
John Gardner, eds. Robert A. Morace and Kathryn VanSpanckeren
1982, pp. 15–27

> Sometimes when he was not in a mood to read he would stand at the window and watch the snow. On windy nights the snow hurtled down through the mountain's darkness and into the blue-white glow of the diner and the pink glitter of the neon sign and away again into the farther darkness and the woods on the other side of the highway. . . . At last, he would sink down on the bed and would lie there solid as a mountain, moving only his nose and lips a little, troubled by dreams.[1]

This second paragraph from John Gardner's 1973 novel, *Nickel Mountain*, conjures up the psychic landscape of his fiction. Man and nature seem to encounter one another, quietly, almost in a state of trance but never fully overwhelming each other, as if Robert Frost had walked into a darker wood and stood to listen and watch. Here Henry Soames is described as "solid as a mountain," but that's the closest identity Gardner seeks between man and nature in this dark and remote moment. The diner seems an outpost in a great wood, a clean, well-lighted place inside some great mystery whose presence can only be suggested by the presence of the great mountain and the falling snow. Gardner subtitled *Nickel Mountain* "A Pastoral Novel." The book, begun when he was an undergraduate as a kind of tribute to his father and the "apple-knockers" of New York State,[2] where he grew up, clearly reveals that pastoral quality and shape, those forms and traditions within which he viewed his own work.

The term *pastoral* has been bandied about so much, like so many critical rubrics, that it has often lost its usefulness and seems permanently elusive. There remain distinct attributes, however, which we can identify and discuss. Leo Marx and Richard Chase, among others, have discovered the patterns of pastoralism in the best of American literature, which, when seen in relation to Gardner's work, clearly place him in that ongoing and "mainline" tradition. A close look at some of Gardner's novels will reveal how much a part of this tradition his fiction is.

As far back as Theocritus and Vergil, the pastoral as an art form has usually included the recognizable pastoral landscape: a cool garden, suggesting repose, tranquility, the cool shade of self-sufficiency and calm. Man slipping into the garden seeks the restoration of some former, better self. Yet a basic ambivalence remains. That pastoral shade remains an illusion, a conjured-up place that lures us only because we know it cannot last; our conjuring it only makes it clear that such a place, if ever there was one, has already disappeared and vanished. To surrender too completely to its call would be to sacrifice our own fragile egos to that natural cool shade and to lose our own identities in a place where silent nature rules and we do not. As Eleanor Leach suggests, "this failure to satisfy the same longings that give it birth is, in fact, the major source of complexity in pastoral."[3]

Pastoral themes or "impulses" also require a pastoral form. Theocritus and Vergil employed singing contests and soliloquies about love, failed or otherwise. These confrontations between two characters, these laments and praises about the fickleness of Eros, provide the drama of their pastorals. We will see below how Gardner has also employed this basic pattern of confrontation.

Rosenmeyer believes that there is "a unique pastoral mood," which he goes on to define as "detachment," that manner of writing which relies on "showing rather than telling."[4] Such a mood does not suggest great romantic moments of transcendental union and interpenetration of man and universe but rather a quieter confrontation in which both man and nature stand off from one another and "observe" each other. The rhythm of that second paragraph from *Nickel Mountain*—the soothing repetition of the "ands" in the second sentence, which suggest an almost romantic all-inclusiveness of the snow (despite the fact that it "hurtled" down)—may soften the mood, but the mood of Henry Soames remains detached, almost impersonal. His reading suggests involvement; when unwilling or unable to read, he turns to look at nature. While some semblance of relief and beauty is suggested, nevertheless Soames retires with his own separate troubled dreams. Nature here, unlike its role in most romantic poetry, has not soothed and comforted at all.

Leach has suggested that the disruption of pastoral tranquility "is the ultimate justification of its existence."[5] Leo Marx, in his discussion of the American pattern of pastoralism, views this disruption not so much as an outside force shattering the pastoral shade, thereby destroying it, but as "a habit of defining reality as a *contradiction* between radically opposed forces."[6] This habit he sees as the essence of the greatest of American literature. "The trope of the interrupted idyll" permeates American literature, as the aggressively masculine machine becomes "a sudden, shocking intruder" upon a "tender, feminine, and submissive" garden.[7]

Richard Chase, in an illuminating comment on Hofstadter's "folklore of Populism," clearly defines the "radical disunities" in American culture in terms which, for the sake of our argument, bring together both the pastoral impulse—restoration, escape, regeneration—and the pastoral form—Theocritus's dialogues, Vergil's confrontations, the encounter with nature. The pastoral impulse can be seen in "what Mr. Hofstadter calls the 'agrarian myth' that ever since the time of Jefferson has haunted the mind . . . of reformers and intellectuals."[8]

> This "myth" involves the idea of a pastoral golden age—a time of plain living, independence, self-sufficiency and closeness to the soil—an idea which has been celebrated in various ways by innumerable American writers. Second, there is the mythology of Calvinism which . . . has always infused Protestantism, even the non-Calvinist sects, with its particular kind of Manichaean demonology.[9]

The pastoral golden-age myth has provided American literature, according to Chase, with its surfeit of nostalgic idyll, however elusive, lost, and momentary that idyll might be: "It is restorative . . . it may even bring a moral regeneration. But the pastoral experience is rather an escape from society and the complexities of one's own being" and tends to call up certain elegiac feelings.[10] The Calvinist myth provides American literature with its melodramatic confrontations, reflecting the Manichaean dualisms between light and darkness, order and chaos. Both idyll and melodrama create a literature more heavily romantic than novelistic in its fictional narratives. And finally many American writers "seem content to oppose the disorder and rawness of their culture with a scrupulous art-consciousness, with aesthetic forms—which do, of course, often broaden out into moral significance."[11]

The best of most American literature has always attempted

to reconcile the pastoral impulse with the Manichaean confrontation, or at least to present the two in a kind of unreconciled head-on encounter, capable at best of achieving some wary kind of equilibrium and at worst resulting in complete alienation and disorder.

Perhaps Leo Marx summed it up best: "Our writers, instead of being concerned with social verisimilitude, with manners and customs, have fashioned their own kind of melodramatic, Manichaean, all-questioning fable, romance, or idyll, in which they carry us, in a bold leap, beyond everyday social experience into an abstract realm of morality and metaphysics,"[12] John Gardner's fiction belongs squarely in this tradition of the American fable, that tradition which Faulkner best described when he referred to the subject of his fiction as the human heart in conflict with itself.

In its narrative form, the nineteenth-century American Romance relied heavily on allegory to frame its tale. It exposed the driven individual, the self-willed man, as if foreshadowing the industrial future at that time. The basic morality was clear: the ungodly, godlike man or woman was a threat to all humanity and to the ideas of Christian brotherhood and love that ideally sustained it. "Villains" included Ahab, the Puritan community, Westervelt, Judge Pynchon, Chillingworth, and in a later, more complicated guise, Thomas Sutpen. Against these, Hawthorne envisioned a human brotherhood linked by sin and oftentimes the conventional pieties of his day; Melville strove for some Keatsian "negative capability," in which inconsistencies and contraries could somehow acquire a human equilibrium; and Faulkner seemed to have hope in endurance and survival as a major step toward man's prevailing.

In the twentieth century—fragmented by Freud and literary modernism—chaos and anarchy, not order, seem to be the twin threats to man's existence. Contemporary writers like Gardner seem to favor some semblance of order as opposed to some kind of emotional anarchy; Clumly the cop, however changed and alerted, survives the assaults of Taggert Hodge in *The Sunlight Dialogues*. Contemporary writers also rely more upon an ambiguous and often blurred symbolism, as opposed to allegory, to reveal their often uncertain views about the man of will and control. Here the morality itself is far more uncertain, if not downright reversed from traditional norms. One only has to compare Gardner's ambiguous attitudes toward Taggert Hodge the magician, the fabricator of artifices and delights, with Hawthorne's attitude toward the mesmerist Westervelt.

Gardner's basic morality and narrative structures, however "invaded" by modern techniques—the novel within the novel, the self-conscious posturing of the author, the outward display of artifice—seem to parallel Hawthorne's, Melville's, and Faulkner's: he tends to "side" with love and communion, however fleeting these may be, in conflict with the self-controlled will, or at least he describes the ongoing dialectical struggle between them, the very "crisis-pattern" of the nineteenth-century Romance.

In his quixotic but often penetrating diatribe, *On Moral Fiction*, Gardner proclaims that in fiction "the interaction of characters is everything."[13] The American Romance has always contained characters larger than life, invested in many instances with a single absorbing interest, often bordering on certain symbolic types, such as the evil temptress and the evil father figure. Characters should not be mere "stick figures . . . where plot is kept minimal and controlled by message" (p. 60), for "literature tells archetypal stories in an attempt to understand once more their truth—translate their wisdom for another generation" (p. 66), and the artist is expected to penetrate "what is common in human experience throughout time" (p. 125). Art becomes a process, an evolution of angles of vision on time-honored human conflicts, a repository of "eternal verities" (p. 19), and the Romantic poet or artist therefore "imitated in finite art the divine created act" (p. 37). This morality of fiction results in a traditional narrative form, which reveals the ongoing conflict between two forms of behavior: "The Ishmael-Ahab conflict continues, however modified, in the confrontations between Clumly and Hodge in *The Sunlight Dialogues*, James and Sally Page in *October Light*, James Chandler and John Horne in *The Resurrection*, Henry Soames and George Loomis in *Nickel Mountain*, and Jonathan Upchurch and Dr. Luther Flint in "The King's Indian." These confrontations take place in the pastoral landscapes of upstate New York, Vermont, Nickel Mountain and, although not at all wholly pastoral, the sea.

The garden and the machine confront each other anew in Gardner's fiction. The voice of the garden, linked to the pastoral impulse with its love of nature and poetic longings, confronts the voice of the machine, linked to the darker Manichaean belief that the world is mere accident, brute force controls all history, and only outright manipulation will keep things running. The basic pattern of dialogue between the classical/medieval hope for regeneration and redemption, linked to light and often magic, and the modern nihilistic certainty of gloom and despair, linked to darkness and often black magic, informs the basic narrative structure of Gardner's fiction. These voices set off against one another—the human heart in conflict with itself—set up a counterpoint in his fiction, which slowly works itself out in the process of the confrontation itself. Fiction becomes a "dream unfolding in the mind,"[14] a spell cast by both opposing camps, defining each other by the pattern of dialogue and conflict between them. As Will Hodge suggests, "whether the crimes of cops or of robbers: it was necessary, merely, that order prevail for those who were left, when the deadly process had run itself down; necessary to rebuild."[15]

Gardner's classic confrontation can be seen in *Grendel*. Grendel represents the voice of brute force, "a mechanical chaos of casual, brute enmity" and rage, doomed to the unrelenting "cold mechanics of stars," against which all else must be defined.[16] The Shaper, the poet with his harp inventing tales of Gods and men and heroic deeds, represents communion and celebration, however much his words often seem to Grendel mere webs and masks averting the cold reality of existence. Grendel, seduced by harp strings, dies at the hand of the hero, who proclaims, *"The world will burn green, sperm build again. My promise . . . by that I kill you"* (p. 170). The poet's role may be similar to the magician's, mixing both mechanical devices and authentic vision, both artifice and heroic ideal: he alone may be capable of healing the split between the garden and the machine, of welding a sturdy reconciliation between Manichaean opposites, of making, as the old priest Ork suggests, "the solemnity and grandeur of the universe rise through the slow process of unification in which the diversities of existence are utilized, and nothing, *nothing* is lost" (p. 133).

In Gardner's fiction that "slow process of unification" is most likely to occur in a traditional, pastoral setting. In *Nickel Mountain* the landscape fulfills those traditional pastoral attributes. Man is freer in the country than in the city: "It was different in the country, where a man's life or a family's past was not so quickly swallowed up, where the ordinariness of thinking creatures was obvious only when you thought a minute, not an inescapable conclusion that crushed the soul the way pavement shattered men's arches" (p. 179). He is closely involved with birth, death, weddings, those ceremonial rituals that come and go with the seasons. Country rules remain basic, "the rules that a child should have a father, that a wife should have a husband, and that a man trying to kill himself should be stopped" (p. 213). Each chapter begins with a particular season, and the rhythms of the earth never change: " 'Progress, they say. But th' earth don't know about progress' " (p. 242). The world is re-created in its basic and natural simplicity:

> It was as if one had slipped back into the comfortable world pictured in old engravings. . . . The world would seem small and close when dark came, too—sounds would seem to come from close at hand and the mountains ten miles away seemed almost on top of you . . . the trees and hills were like something alive, not threatening, exactly, because Henry had known them all his life, but not friendly, either: hostile, but not in any hurry, conscious that time was on their side. . . . (pp. 152–53)

"Some change, subtle and terrible" (p. 218) and an aura of doom stalk this "burned-over district" of upstate New York—complete with Simon Bale's devil-obsessed religious fundamentalism (matching the stark hostility-friendliness of external nature)—but Nickel Mountain—"That was where the real hills were, and the river, cool, deep with echoes of spring water dripping into it and sliding from its banks!" (p. 59)—suggests a particular vantage point wherein the Manichaean confrontation is reconciled. George Loomis, inveterate collector, emotional and physical cripple, harps on " 'the whole secret of human progress, pure meanness' " (p. 148), but Henry Soames, who drives up the mountain often, believes in communion, marries the pregnant Callie, and discovers that "his vision [was] not something apart from the world but the world itself transmuted" (p. 301). If Loomis derides a world of sheer accident, Soames comes to believe in and experience "the holiness of things (his father's phrase), the idea of magical change" rooted firmly in the landscape around him (p. 302). Garden and machine are reconciled from this pastoral vantage point:

> This side of the trees there were flat acres of winter wheat and peas and hay and stretches of new-plowed ground. It was like a garden, in the gold light of late afternoon; it was exactly what Paradise ought to be like: a tractor humming along far below him, small, on the seat a boy with a wide straw hat: to the right of the tractor, red and white cows moving slowly down the lane to a big gray barn with clean white trim. With a little imagination a man could put angels in the sky . . . it would be as if he were discovering the place for the first time: a natural garden that had been the same for a thousand thousand years. (pp. 169–70)

In *Nickel Mountain* on board a train we catch a glimpse "of a bearded, scarred face" on his way to Batavia (p. 268). Taggert Hodge may be on his way toward his confrontation with Fred Clumly in *The Sunlight Dialogues*, Gardner's most complete and thorough re-creation of the Manichaean duplicity of all things, as suggested by the character of the petty thief Benson/Boyle: "The opposition came suddenly clear to him—the violent, lawless bearded man, the violent policeman. It was, he saw with unspeakable clarity, a picture of his life" (p. 549). The landscape proclaims both doom and pastoral reconciliation in an uneasy alliance with one another:

> Something about the land, or the York State land as it used to be—the near horizons lifting up their high-angled screens between folded valleys, the days full of clouds forever drifting, ominous and beckoning, sliding past green-gray summits and throwing their strange shapes over the tilted fields, sunny elms inexorably darkened by the march of shadow from the straight-edged slopes. "Stand up and seize," the land said; "or rise and prophesy, cock your ears to the invisible." At the edge of the dark woodlots facing on swamps where no mortal trespasser could ever be expected, there were signs KEEP OUT: THIS MEANS YOU. (p. 370)

Natural scenes shimmer with an inherent grace. Arthur Hodge, Sr., describes *"twenty-four geese/en route from swamp to swamp, encountering a dome/at twilight, passing and touching an unseen mark"* and suggests to Taggert that they represent *"the pure idea of holiness"* (p. 240). And David, Ben Hodge's hired boy, playing on milkcan covers fills "the mindless, sullen air" with "wings" (p. 413). Truth becomes that carefully detailed, pastoral scene, as experienced by Millie Hodge:

> She knew well enough, on days like this, where the truth lay. It was the physical pattern in the carpet, where the blue-black lines intersected the brown and where figures of roses showed their threads; in the broken putty on the windowpanes, in the angular shadows inside the glass of a doorknob, in the infinite complexity of lines in the bark of trees, in the dust in the sunbeams: substance calling beyond itself to substance. (p. 430)

In *The Sunlight Dialogues* Gardner achieves that equilibrium between "radical disunities," that fully wrought balance between the pastoral idyll and Calvinist/Manichaean melodrama, which lies at the heart of the greatest of American literature. Here Clumly, the benevolent watchdog, and Taggert Hodge, the Babylonian anarchist, confront one another in a series of dialogues representing the contradictory impulses of western and, in particular, American culture. The dialogue, in fact, becomes Gardner's basic narrative structure, his basic aesthetic form, in the book. The Babylonian holiness of matter confronts the Judeo-Christian holiness of spirit. The Babylonian love of substance opposes the Judeo-Christian "idle speculation" about abstract relationships between soul and flesh (p. 413). An impersonal universe confronts that "grand American responsibility" for right and wrong (p. 323). Clumly finally realizes that " 'we must all be vigilant against growing indifferent to people less fortunate. . . . We have to stay awake, as best we can, and be ready to obey the laws as best as we're able to see them. That's it. That's the whole thing' " (pp. 670, 672). No winners or losers but a constant juggling of contraries, a balance of irreconcilable positions, a continued vigilance in the unrelenting encounter between the "radical disunities" of American culture. The Manichaean interpenetration of each becomes the only certainty, although the pastoral vantage point points the way toward armed reconciliation.

The "radical disunities" of *The Sunlight Dialogues* can be clearly seen in the family tree of Gardner's Faulknerian Hodge clan. The Hon. Arthur Hodge, Sr., the Congressman, is the patriarch, a Renaissance man of both visionary capabilities and practical "know-how"; "if he was an idealist, bookish, he knew trades, too; knew the talk of farmers at the feedmill"; he enjoyed the "invariable good luck in the conspiracy of outer events" (pp. 134–35). But in his four sons there had occurred "a kind of power failure" (p. 576). Will, Sr., is a Batavian attorney, a patcher, a mender; Art, Jr., is an electrician with Niagara Electric, "a good man, gentle, not a mystical bone in his great square body" (p. 174). Son Taggert, the Sunlight Man, is of course the complete crazed visionary, "beaten by the conspiracy of events" (p. 136), and brother Ben "was a dreamer, a poet, an occasional visiting preacher at country churches from here to good news where. He was blind to the accelerating demolition all around him" (p. 143). Will, Sr.'s, two sons, Will, Jr., and Luke, complete the fragmentation and decline of the Hodge family, for Will, Jr., is a Buffalo attorney, a chaser after debtors, "the Congressman through the looking-glass, then, turned inside out, gone dark," (p. 344), and Luke is an ineffectual, romantic visionary, suspended between his brother Will and his cousin Ben, "knowing they were both right but mutually exclusive, as antithetical as the black trees hanging motionless over the motionless water and under the dead, luminescent sky" (p. 636).

The balanced vision between idealism and circumstance, poetic and practical truth, of Stony Hill Farm, has broken down. Pastoral reconciliation has collapsed, leaving poetic insight and practical knowledge as separate, decayed fragments of a once-functioning whole. As the Reverend Willby laments, "our civilization is built on work, and to do well in it we must repress our desire to loll about . . . our puritan ethic in one form or another, is at the heart of the American *problem*" (p. 269). And as Will, Jr., realizes, faith is "an outreaching of the mind beyond what it immediately possesses. Self-transcendence. But the reach did not imply the existence of the thing reached for. One knew it even as one reached" (p. 348). Inside the stone walls of Stony Hill Farm, that pastoral keep, "self-contained and self-perpetuating, even as serene—or so it had seemed to Will Jr's childish eyes—as Heaven itself," lay "a garden for idealism" (p. 338). Outside those walls lies a Manichaean world "gone dark" (p. 344).

The pattern exists as well in Gardner's more recent novel, *October Light* (1976), in which James and Sally Page launch their battle for personal supremacy. The "radical disunities" continue to collide. The English teacher, Estelle Parks, recalls Wordsworth's "Tintern Abbey," his subdued yet powerful celebration of "*A presence that disturbs . . . a sense sublime/ Of something far more deeply interfused . . . A motion and a spirit, that impels/All thinking things, all objects of all thought.*"[17] Ruth Thomas contemplates more modern dilemmas when suddenly she recites Arnold's famous lines: "*And we are here as on a darkling plain/Swept with confused alarms of struggle and flight,/Where ignorant armies clash by night*" (p. 235). Arnold's dark vision clashes with Wordsworth's "light of setting suns . . . and the living air." Later on Ruth recites the poem, "The Opossum," which celebrates the crafty designs survivors are heir to. When exhorted by His Son to destroy the opossum, because he is a killer, a weary and crafty God replies, "'*Peace and Justice are right' . . . And whispered to the 'Possum, 'Lie down. Play dead'*" (p. 261). Between polar opposites, strategic retreat may be the only apparent salvation in a chaotic world.

In the novel Gardner contrasts the point of view of existence found in the main narrative of *October Light* with that found in *The Smugglers of Lost Soul's Rock*: "'There are only two kinds of books in the world. . . . There are books that desperately struggle to prove there's some holy, miraculous meaning to it all and desperately deny that everything in the world's mere belts and gears . . . and there are books that say the opposite'" (p. 273). *October Light*, with its pastoral setting, opts for the former of these two books. Locking time, "obscurely magical, a sign of elves working" (p. 122), suggests the same kind of pastoral landscape as in Frost's "Mending Wall." The Vermont village reminds James Page of one of Grandma Moses's paintings, and Norman Rockwell's determination to paint "this safe, sunlit village in Vermont where they were still in the nineteenth century" rests solely on the pastoral impulse to escape the complex illnesses of the modern world "as if his pictures might check the decay" (p. 424). And yet despite this sentimentalized pastoralism, reconciliation with the landscape and truth still seems the firm reply to the nihilistic, existentialist maneuverings of the creatures on Lost Souls' Rock. In "Ed's Song" the recurring and eternal pattern of the seasons are recounted like the most hopeful and holy of rituals, and good poems are as exactly true as a good window-sash or a horse. In the novel Page is upbraided because of "his excessive Yankee pride in workmanship, his greed, his refusal to stop and simply look, the way Ed Thomas had looked" (p. 432). To "simply look" could be the advice of the dedicated pastoralist. Although Page can't explain why he doesn't shoot the bear he confronts at the end of the novel, the reason is clear to the reader. Page's heart, like the season that surrounds him, is unlocking slowly.

In *The Resurrection* James Chandler, the dying associate professor of philosophy, experiences a kind of pastoral revelation. He senses "the manyness of things grown familiar and therefore one. . . . He felt such inexpressible joy: He felt intensely what later he would learn words to explain, the interpenetration of the universe and himself. For if he was distinct from all he saw, he was also the sum of it."[18] And in "The King's Indian," Jonathan Upchurch—loving not the "flat and mathematical" landscape of northern Illinois but the beauty, "dark with timber and bluffs and the slide of big rivers," of southern Illinois—triumphs over Luther Flint's maniacal, mechanical maneuverings.[19] Here Gardner presents the image of the King's Indian, which suggests both a move in chess and a state of visionary awareness, of pastoral revelation: "Human consciousness, in the ordinary case, is the artificial wall we build of perceptions and *con*ceptions, a hull of words and accepted opinions that keeps out the vast, consuming sea. . . . A mushroom or one raw emotion (such as love) can blast that wall to smithereens. . . . I become, that instant, the King's Indian: Nothing is waste, nothing unfecund" (p. 242). In much the same way does Gardner describe his book as both "a celebration of all literature and life" and "a funeral crypt" (p. 316).

Gardner wishes to side with John Napper, in the short story, "John Napper Sailing Through the Universe," who declares, "Let there be light, a splendid garden" (p. 133). Gardner's pastoral ideals and re-creations of the landscapes of upstate New York and Vermont clearly indicate that urge for restoration and reconciliation in the human spirit. At the same time he shares the modern view that "there is no purity or innocence in theaters, or in forests, or in oceans— and no wickedness, either. Only survival, only cunning and secrecy" (pp. 318–21). His attempt to strike a balance between the opposing poles of innocence and wickedness, or better yet to reconcile these two opposite points of view within some pastoral landscape, however circumscribed and momentary, places him firmly within the mainstream of American literature.

What Henry James referred to as American literature's "rich passion for extremes" can be found in Gardner's fiction. Gardner's hope for human communion and love, however fragmentary and diminished, remains undaunted. He is clearly reworking the American fable for our own troubled contemporary times and not merely delighting in structuralist and "post-modernist" techniques for their own artificer's delight. Like Hawthorne, Melville, and Faulkner before him, he seems intent on dispelling anew the notion of a special American innocence, yet at the same time recognizing the pull and enchantment of the pastoral impulses implicit in that American myth. He's aware of the precariousness in that farther darkness and uses his pastoralism as a vantage point from which to observe and re-create the American heart's unrelenting conflict with itself.

Notes

1. *Nickel Mountain* (New York: Knopf, 1973), p. 3. All page references are to this edition.
2. Conversation with John Gardner, 31 March 1979; cited below as conversation.
3. Eleanor Winsor Leach, *Vergil's Eclogues; Landscapes of Experience* (Ithaca: Cornell Univ. Press, 1974), p. 32.
4. Thomas G. Rosenmeyer, *The Green Cabinet: Theocritus and the European Pastoral Lyric* (Berkeley: Univ. of California Press), p. 15.
5. Leach, p. 36.
6. Leo Marx, *The Machine in the Garden* (New York: Oxford Univ. Press, 1964), pp. 344–45.
7. Marx, pp. 27, 29.
8. Richard Chase, *The American Novel and Its Tradition* (Garden City: Doubleday, 1957), p. 201.
9. Chase, pp. 201–2.
10. Chase, p. 184.
11. Chase, p. 5.
12. Marx, p. 343.
13. *On Moral Fiction* (New York: Basic Books, 1978), p. 92. All page references are to this edition.
14. Conversation.
15. *The Sunlight Dialogues* (New York: Knopf, 1972), p. 644. All page references are to this edition.
16. *Grendel* (New York: Knopf, 1971), pp. 21–22, 9. All page references are to this edition.
17. *October Light* (New York: Knopf, 1976), pp. 201–2. All page references are to this edition.
18. *The Resurrection*, 2nd ed. (New York: Ballantine, 1974), p. 133.
19. *The King's Indian: Stories and Tales* (New York: Knopf, 1974), p. 202. All page references are to this edition.

LEONARD BUTTS

From "The Process of 'Moral Fiction': Protagonist as Artist in John Gardner's Novels"
John Gardner, ed. Beatrice Mendez-Egle
1983, pp. 13–24

In a recent anthology of commentaries, reviews, and short stories collected by Joe David Bellamy under the title *Moral Fiction*, writers and critics were asked to respond to John Gardner's *On Moral Fiction*. Nearly all of the respondents, including such notables as John Updike, Joyce Carol Oates, and John Barth, offered not, as Bellamy suggested, reactions to Gardner's theory, but their own individual definitions of "moral fiction." In fact, most of Bellamy's respondents confessed they had not even read Gardner's book.[1] In this light it is difficult to assess the validity of what Bellamy hoped would be informed and intelligent responses to *On Moral Fiction*, yet Bellamy's collection does serve to point out how often critics and writers are reacting to the phrase "moral fiction" rather than to John Gardner's use of the term as it applies to literature. It is also apparent that use of the word "moral" sends many who have read Gardner's book into wild, emotional condemnations or praises, but often for the wrong reasons. As with other well-worn terms—romanticism, classicism, realism—pejorative applications of the word "moral" have supplanted artistic, critical, and philosophical usage to such an extent that the word is crippled when pressed into a literary context. Despite the glee or grumbling of those who see Gardner's book as propaganda for fundamentalist religious beliefs or conservative political or literary stances, Gardner's theory of moral fiction has little to do with God or country or didactic fiction. Those who condemn or praise *On Moral Fiction* for these reasons have not understood Gardner's methods or purpose as a critic and a novelist.

Nevertheless, John Gardner's use of the word "moral" to define fiction containing some essence of universal truth can be gotten at through a statement that appears more than once in *On Moral Fiction*. "Art discovers by its *process* what it means to say."[2] If we keep in mind that the discovery of truth, assuming it exists, is reached in the *process* of creating, then much of the criticism leveled at Gardner for supposedly imposing an artificial order upon works of fiction can be eliminated. To suggest that a novel must have a "happy ending" or "present a moral" to be a work of "moral fiction" is to misinterpret completely Gardner's use of the phrase. In the same sense, to imply that because in one of Gardner's works the protagonist dies, in another is murdered, and in still another kills and eats a dog Gardner's fiction violates his own "moral principles" is also a misreading. Morality or truth, Gardner maintains, is not discovered in a novel's final lines, nor is it revealed entirely in any one character's actions. Morality or truth is discovered in the *process* of creating and in the *process* of reading a piece of fiction. It is the sum of a novel's or story's effect, what Aristotle calls its "exegesis,' that determines its moral qualities.

As an artist, a creator, Gardner uses his imagination to test values, to get at the truth. Art works, he argues, through an evolutionary process which ends in intense ordering. In this analogy, the imagination acts as a form of natural selection through which all experience is filtered and ordered. It is with the imagination that values are tested and truth, inherent morality, discovered. Only those valued strong enough to withstand this testing survive and are passed on to the reader. If this process is "true," the art created from it will "naturally" instruct, raise human consciousness, and offer a sense of wholeness or unity. Gardner's theory of fiction, then, is based on the Romantic belief that the poet's imagination allows contact with "something far more deeply interfused," that within oneself exists an intuitive or implied mode for individual and social action. When the power of an artist's imagination is misdirected outward or fails all together, if an artist is no longer able to look within himself and rediscover Dante's "liberating feeling" or Faulkner's "eternal verities," if he is no longer able to distinguish between intellectual game playing and truth, then as an artist of lasting stature he will not survive even though his immediate influence on an audience and on other artists may be very great.[3]

Hemingway says begin with one true sentence and the rest will follow. Gardner reiterates this idea in discussing the process of fiction writing. This process, of course, is never seen directly in the work of fiction, although it may be discovered to some extent in the study of manuscripts and revisions of a work. What Gardner attempts in his own fiction is to allow us to see that every individual is, in a sense, an artist, that each person contains a kernel of truth which can be tapped through use of his or her imagination. In each of Gardner's novels we discover a protagonist in the midst of a physical and or spiritual crisis, like Dante facing the dark wood. In attempting to wrest himself from such a situation, the individual asks himself do solutions exist, if so what are they, and will they work. He also often encounters impasses or is misdirected by flaws in his own character or personality. But eventually, since, as Gardner importantly points out, art is *not* merely a mirror held up to reality, the protagonist discovers some meaning, some order, some truth in his life. By "quietly looking and listening," as Gardner phrases it, the protagonist realizes through contact with the world and by deep introspection certain values which eventually allow him to move toward a higher level of perception, an aesthetic wholeness that is itself morality or truth.

This search and discovery, it seems to me, parallels the process Gardner believes an artist undergoes in creating a work of art. The purpose of Gardner's own "moral fiction" then is to discover what meaning life holds for us all, and not, as those who accuse him of writing didactically believe, to impose an external scheme of behavior upon everyone. In putting commonly held beliefs and values to the test, Gardner's fiction reveals amid crisis, chaos, and death not a simple rosy panacea of optimistic outcome, but a process or method whereby those truths worth holding onto and passing on to future generations may be discovered. If then we view each of Gardner's protagonists as an artist and his life as a work of art, we can more clearly understand what Gardner intends in his use of the phrase "moral fiction."

Four of Gardner's novels, *The Resurrection*, *Nickel Mountain*, *October Light*, *and Mickelsson's Ghosts*, serve to illustrate his methods. Each of the novels' main characters can be viewed as an artist in search of some order to stand in opposition to chaos, to hold off "for a little while," as Gardner says, "the twilight of the gods and us" (MF, 3). In working toward an aesthetic wholeness of vision, Gardner's characters, in the way artists create works of lasting value, make life art.

In *The Resurrection*, Gardner makes fine distinctions between intellectual idealism and imaginative insight, revealing how the former, didactic in its aim, can mislead even the most well-intentioned artist. The novel's protagonist James Chandler is, as Gardner reveals, an idealist. Living in San Francisco, surrounded by the fellowship of his family, friends, and work, in a serene state of disassociation from the harsher conditions of urban poverty and injustice, Chandler is sequestered within an "ivory tower" of his own design, even to the extent that he views himself as a kind of modern day hero. "His concern with metaphysics in an age of analysis made him a man born too late for his time, a harmless lunatic all of whose energy and skill went into a heroic battling, by the laws of an intricate and obsolete code, against whatever he could contrive in the way of dragons."[4] When Chandler is confronted not with an abstract conceptualization of death but with the absolute inevitability of his own death from leukemia, his philosophical dragons are reduced to a very real foe he cannot defeat, and the fortress of life he has created crumbles.

When the satisfaction of his California lifestyle evaporates with the news that he has an incurable disease, Chandler, with his wife and three daughters, retreats across country to his childhood home of Batavia, New York, where his mother still lives, hoping he might discover some of the stability and security associated with his youth. "Something must be certain," he thinks aloud as he wanders through his hometown, already sensing the fact that this search for material representations of the stability of his childhood is futile. As with philosophical systems, Chandler discovers, an individual's past, as well as the historical past, is merely an artificially imposed order which crumbles with the passage of time. Ironically, his philosophy, the new book he is rushing to complete, is an attempt to reinhabit the "uninhabited castles" of order imposed upon life by all philosophers. What Chandler finds in his own life, and death, is that no one rigid philosophical system can survive because the metaphysic and social ethic is continually changing. Any "system" is self-defeating because it ignores the process of a changing reality to which "ideas" never entirely correspond. Intellectually, Chandler believes it is good that time erases differences, yet he no longer finds such a belief "a sufficiently comforting vision" when he is faced with his own death. "It was good," he says of his idealism, his belief in progress, "but it was not all right" (R, 36).

Although Chandler cannot rationally, or consciously, come to terms with the change about to disrupt his life, his dreams suggest there is a path of understanding. His dreams become "an imaginative work of selection and arrangement." When he awakes, he dismisses the feeling of unity derived from them, "but . . . something came to him, or rather hovered in the periphery of his inner vision, so to speak, an idea he could not quite catch hold of, but one that was right—that much he could feel—some insight that might be, at least for him, revolutionary" (R, 123). Chandler's blindness is caused by his philosophical training, his attempts to rationally order and explain even the workings of his own imagination. When he has a purely intuitive moment, an epiphany, in which he experiences "a sudden release, an unexpected joy" "the soul's sublime acceptance of lawless, proliferating substance, things and their motions" (R, 229), he tries to conceptualize it, to force it somehow into the logical construct of his new book.

In his rush to grasp some meaning in his life, and made ever weaker by disease and the drugs which slow but cannot cure it, Chandler further isolates himself from the love of family and concern of friends, values he overlooks because of their purely emotional nature. Not until he coldly rejects the love offered by Viola, a strange, young woman who is the caretaker of his mother's elderly neighbors, does he realize his failure. Only when Chandler's intellectual guard is lowered by the effects of disease upon his rational faculties and by Viola's confession of love does his life rise to an intense and certain unity with all things. "All this time it had been right there in front of him and he'd missed it. It was not the beauty of the world one must affirm but *the world*, the buzzing blooming confusion itself. He had slipped from celebrating what was to the celebration of empty celebration . . . *One must make life art*" (R, 229). With this knowledge, James Chandler moves off to die at the feet of a strange, young girl who loves him rather than among his immediate family. He accepts himself and the world in "all of its lawless proliferation and decay," and achieves, if only momentarily, the aesthetic wholeness for which he has been searching.

Chandler as artist-philosopher dedicates his life to pure aestheticism, art for art's sake, an ideal in a society ruled by analysis and utilitarian values. His cause is noble, yet he slips out of touch with what it is to be human. He becomes, in Gardner's terms, one of those artists who is content to experiment with style or form to the exclusion of universal truths. The price he pays is isolation from humanity and difficulty in dealing with the truth when it is presented in human terms—love and death. James Chandler learns that "the highest state a man can achieve is one of aesthetic wholeness, for the end of aesthetic evolution, wholeness, is analogous to the end of religious evolution, saintliness, that state in which one is capable of embracing all experience as holy and some experience as more holy" (R, 202). All of Gardner's protagonists journey toward this state of wholeness in which they are able to affirm not just individual conceptions of what one thinks life *means*, but all of what life is, in William

James's phrase, "the world, the buzzing blooming confusion itself" (R, 202). . . .

Although a great deal of attention has been drawn to Gardner's work because of his use of the word "moral" in discussing literature of lasting value, a reader must look beyond the emotional crossfire of critics and reviewers to the underlying theory of art developed in *On Moral Fiction*, a theory based on the tradition of content as the focus of fiction. Gardner's book, it seems to me, could have as easily been titled "On Truthful Fiction," for it asks is there a morality or truth suitable as an ideal which writers should aspire to communicate in creating works of art or is there no universal morality or truth except an individual's objective existential conclusions about life? Gardner's answer supports the writer's responsibility to his own artistic aims but not without an acknowledgment of his readers' and society's needs. Thus art of "moral" stature might be said to have certain limitations. Gardner, however, does not mean a writer should not challenge his audience or explore new ideas or experiment with style or popularize to communicate, for his own fiction attempts all of these things.

By his use of the word "moral" to define those values inherent in a work of art that allow it to remain flexible enough to survive the changing nature of reality, John Gardner emphasizes the process of creating a lasting work of art. That art orders reality, even for the purest aesthete, is difficult to deny. All artists, through their imaginations, order the world into moments of intensity during which people and their values are tested. If the artist creates without testing, then the outcome is predetermined and the result is susceptible to crumbling beneath the pressure of a constantly changing world. If the artist becomes more interested in structure or form than in ideas and values, then the result may be a work whose only worth is in its vastly complex superstructure. Art, as ethician David Maguire says in *The Moral Choice*, "is not just a work of uninvolved intellectuality but is rather immersed by its nature in feeling, in a sense of fittingness, of contrast, and even in a sense of the macabre. It invokes an intuitive sense of correspondence that can be cultivated only in lived experience. At times it will body forth apparitions which have been stirring inarticulately in group consciousness. At times it will resonate from the uniqueness of a heroic soul. Always art will involve us at many levels of our psyche and in ways that are only partially chartable."[5]

Maguire's conception of art is reiterated in *On Moral Fiction* when Gardner says, "the artist who begins with a doctrine to promulgate, instead of a rabble of ideas and emotions, is beaten before he starts" (MF, 14). It also seems to me that the artist who ends his work as a rabble of ideas and emotions is just as much a failure. "True art," Gardner would say, is not exactly a mirror of reality, nor is it merely a dabbling in ideas or language. "True art," "moral fiction," "clarifies life, establishes models of human action, casts nets toward the future, carefully judges right and wrong directions, celebrates and mourns" (MF, 100).

Notes

1. Joe David Bellamy, ed., *Moral Fiction: An Anthology* (Canton, N.Y.: St. Lawrence Univ. Press, 1980). Bellamy's collection is, on the whole disappointing for those interested in evaluations of *On Moral Fiction* as a serious theory of art.
2. John Gardner, *On Moral Fiction* (New York: Basic Books, 1977), p. 14.
3. *On Moral Fiction*. This summary is essentially the thesis of the opening chapters. All further references will be made in the text, MF.
4. John Gardner, *The Resurrection* (New York: Ballantine Books, 1966), p. 11. All further references will be made in the text, R.
5. David Maguire, *The Moral Choice* (Garden City, N.Y.: Doubleday, 1978), p. 110.

Hamlin Garland

1860–1940

Born near West Salem, Wisconsin, on September 14, 1860, Hannibal Hamlin Garland grew up in the rural Midwest, and had to divide his time between the pursuit of education and work on his father's farm. In 1884 he moved to Boston in search of a better life, and supported himself by teaching while studying literature, economics, and social science.

After publishing stories in the *Arena*, Garland issued his first collection, *Main-Travelled Roads*, in 1891. His early fiction reveals deep sympathy for the hardships of the farmers in the West, and he engaged actively in the reform movement, campaigning for the People's Party in Iowa in 1892 and lecturing about farmers' grievances in other parts of the country. His novels in these years exposed political corruption, or, as in *Rose of Dutcher's Coolly* (1895), described the spoliation of the country, but after propounding realism in art and democratic literature in *Crumbling Idols* (1894), he distanced himself from controversy and politics.

Visiting England in 1899, Garland met many leading authors, and on his return home increasingly sought social and literary respectability. Travels in the Rocky Mountains made him an authority on the American Indian, and enabled him to write *The Captain of the Gray-Horse Troop* (1902). A further area of interest was psychic phenomena, reflected in a number of novels, including *The Shadow World* (1908). A relatively unproductive period was broken by the appearance in 1917 of the autobiographical work *A Son of the Middle Border*, which secured him election to the American Academy of Arts and Letters. A second volume of autobiography, *A Daughter of the Middle Border* (1921), won him a Pulitzer Prize, and Garland remained within this genre for the remainder of his life.

After writing nearly fifty books in his long career, Garland died on March 4, 1940, at his home in Los Angeles, California.

General

Fiction as yet in the United States strikes me . . . as most curious when most confined and most local; this is so much the case that when it is even abjectly passive to surrounding conditions I find it capable of yielding an interest that almost makes me dread undue enlargement. There are moments when we are tempted to say that there is nothing like saturation—to pronounce it a safer thing than talent. I find myself rejoicing, for example, in Mr. Hamlin Garland, a case of saturation so precious as to have almost the value of genius. There are moods in which we seem to see that the painter, of whatever sort, is most for us when he is most, so to speak, the soaked sponge of his air and time; and of Mr. Hamlin Garland—as to whom I hasten to parenthesize that there are many other things to remember, things for which I almost impatiently await the first occasion—I express his price, to my own taste, with all honour if I call him the soaked sponge of Wisconsin.—HENRY JAMES, "American Letter," *Lit*, April 9, 1898, p. 422

The case of Hamlin Garland belongs to pathos in the grand manner, as you will discover on reading his autobiography, *A Son of the Middle Border.* What ails him is a vision of beauty, a seductive strain of bawdy music over the hills. He is a sort of mail Mary MacLane, but without either Mary's capacity for picturesque blasphemy or her skill at plain English. The vision, in his youth, tore him from his prairie plow and set him to clawing the anthills at the foot of Parnassus. He became an elocutionist—what, in modern times, would be called a chautauquan. He aspired to write for the *Atlantic Monthly.* He fell under the spell of the Boston *aluminados* of 1885, which is as if one were to take fire from a June-bug. Finally, after embracing the Single Tax, he achieved a couple of depressing story-books, earnest, honest and full of indignation.

American criticism, which always mistakes a poignant document for æsthetic form and organization, greeted these moral volumes as works of art, and so Garland found himself an accepted artist and has made shift to be an artist ever since. No more grotesque miscasting of a diligent and worthy man is recorded in profane history. He has no more feeling for the intrinsic dignity of beauty, no more comprehension of it as a thing in itself, than a policeman. He is, and always has been, a moralist endeavoring ineptly to translate his messianic passion into æsthetic terms and always failing. *A Son of the Middle Border,* undoubtedly the best of all his books, projects his failure brilliantly. It is, in substance, a document of considerable value—a naïve and often highly illuminating contribution to the history of the American peasantry. It is, in form, a thoroughly third-rate piece of writing—amateurish, flat, banal, repellent. Garland gets facts into it; he gets the relentless sincerity of the rustic Puritan; he gets a sort of evangelical passion. But he doesn't get any charm. He doesn't get any beauty.

In such a career, as in such a book, there is something profoundly pathetic. One follows the progress of the man with a constant sense that he is steering by faulty compasses, that fate is leading him into paths too steep and rocky—nay, too dark and lovely—for him. An awareness of beauty is there, and a wistful desire to embrace it, but the confident gusto of the artist is always lacking. What one encounters in its place is the enthusiasm of the pedagogue, the desire to yank the world up to the soaring Methodist level, the hot yearning to displace old ideas, for example, the Single Tax and spook-chasing. The natural goal of the man was the evangelical stump. He was led astray when those Boston Brahmins of the last generation, enchanted by his sophomoric platitudes about Shakespeare, set him up as a critic of the arts, and then as an imaginative artist. He should have gone back to the saleratus belt, taken to the chautauquas, preached his foreordained perunas, got himself into Congress, and so helped to save the republic from the demons that beset it. What a gladiator he would have made against the Plunderbund, the White Slave Traffic, the Rum Demon, the Kaiser! What a rival to the Hon. Claude Kitchin, the Rev. Dr. Newell Dwight Hillis!

His worst work, I daresay, is in some of his fiction—for example, in *The Forester's Daughter.* But my own favorite among his books is *The Shadow World,* a record of his communings with the gaseous precipitates of the departed. He takes great pains at the start to assure us that he is a man of alert intelligence and without prejudices or superstitions. He has no patience, it appears, with those idiots who swallow the buffooneries of spiritualist mediums too greedily. For him the scientific method—the method which examines all evidence cynically and keeps on doubting until the accumulated proof, piled mountain-high, sweeps down in an overwhelming avalanche. . . . Thus he proceeds to the haunted chamber and begins his dalliance with the banshees. They touch him with clammy, spectral hands; they wring music for him out of locked pianos; they throw heavy tables about the room; they give him messages from the golden shore and make him the butt of their coarse, transcendental humor. Through it all he sits tightly and solemnly, his mind open and his verdict up his sleeve. He is belligerently agnostic, and calls attention to it proudly. . . . Then, in the end, he gives himself away. One of his fellow "scientists," more frankly credulous, expresses the belief that real scientists will soon prove the existence of spooks. "I hope they will," says the agnostic Mr. Garland. . . .

Well, let us not laugh. The believing mind is a curious thing. It must absorb its endless rations of balderdash, or perish. . . . *A Son of the Middle Border* is less amusing, but a good deal more respectable. It is an honest book. There is some bragging in it, of course, but not too much. It tells an interesting story. It radiates hard effort and earnest purpose. . . . But what a devastating exposure of a member of the American Academy of Arts and Letters!—H. L. MENCKEN, "Six Members of the Institute," *Prejudices: First Series,* 1919, pp. 134–38

To a later generation that never knew the pioneer hardships of the Middle border, Hamlin Garland seems strangely remote and old-fashioned; yet his intellectual antecedents are both ancient and honorable. At bottom he is an idealist of the old Jeffersonian breed, an earnest soul devoid of humor, who loves beauty and is mightily concerned about justice in the world where fate first set him, turned rebel and threw in his lot with the poor and the exploited. As a young man, consumed with a desire to speak for his people, he espoused a somber realism, for only by and through the truth could he hope to dislodge from men's minds the misconceptions that stood in the way of justice. The Middle Border had no spokesman at the court of letters and if he could gain a hearing there he must not betray his father's household by glossing ungainly reality; he must depict the life of the western farmer as it was lived under the summer sun and the winter cold, what harvests were brought to crib and what sort of wealth was finally gathered.

And yet in the light of his total work one hesitates to call Garland a realist. Perhaps more justly he might be called a thwarted romantic, and his early rebellious realism be traced to its source in a passionate refusal to be denied the beauty that should be a portion of any rational way of living; for when later he found himself in a land of nobler horizons, unsoiled as yet by crude frontier exploitation, when he looked out upon vast mountain ranges and felt the warm sun on the gray plains, he discovered there the romance of his dreams and fell to describing the strange splendors with the gusto of a naïve romantic. *Main-Travelled Roads* and *Prairie Folks* are the protest of one oppressed with the meanness of a world that takes such heavy toll of human happiness; *Her Mountain Lover* is the expression of a frank romantic who glories in the nobility of nature's noblemen; and *The Captain of the Gray-Horse Troop* is a tale in which romance is justified by ethics and the hero discovers in the protection of a weaker race the deepest satisfactions of life. Beauty is excellent, but beauty should walk hand in hand with service—not art for art's sake, but art subdued to the higher good of humanity.

Between these extremes of a stark realism and an ethical romanticism, stand two books, separated by many years and great changes, that embody in more finished form the theme which after all was the master passion of Garland's life—the Middle Border and the rebellions it bred. *Rose of Dutcher's Coolly* is a full-length portrait of an idealist in revolt against the narrowness of farm life, and *A Son of the Middle Border* is an idyll of the past, autobiography done in mellower years when the passions of youth have been subdued to less exigent demands. These books, together with the sketches of *Main-Travelled Roads* and the militant critical theory of *Crumbling Idols*, contain pretty much the whole of Hamlin Garland that after years have cared to remember—the saga of the Middle Border in the days of its great rebellion when the earlier hopes of boundless prosperity were turning to ashes in the mouth.

The striking originality of Garland's work, that sets it apart from other studies of the local-color school, sprang from the sincerity of his reaction to environment. His intellectual development followed the needs of his ardent, inquisitive nature. After quitting the little Academy at Osage, Iowa, he went forth in quest of an education that should explain to him the meaning of life as he had known it. In this search he was singularly fortunate. He was his own mentor and he took what he needed. Boston had long been the Mecca of his dreams and when he found himself there—having made a pious pilgrimage as Howells had done a generation earlier—he threw himself upon his studies with ascetic zeal. Fortunately he enrolled in the Boston Public Library instead of at Harvard, and his formless radicalisms there found food in plenty. Though he lived in Boston some ten years and made friends, he never penetrated the inner literary sanctuary. A somewhat forlorn outsider, unknown and unvouched for, he found no welcome as Howells and Twain had found, and he never entered the pleasant circles where Holmes and Lowell and Fields and Norton and Aldrich and Howells held sway.

Perhaps that fact unconsciously determined his scornful rejection of the Boston genteel in literature; at any rate his denial of the sovereignty of the New England literary rulers left him free to follow other masters who seemed to him more significant. In his bleak little room his ear had caught the greater voices then sounding in Europe and America. His masters were men of intellectual horizons unbounded by Beacon Street and Harvard Square: Taine and Ibsen and Björnson, Turgenev and Tolstoi, Zola and Millet, Darwin and Spencer and Fiske, Walt Whitman and Henry George, and the later Howells with his deeper sociological concern and graver realism. His three great masters came finally to be Whitman, Spencer and Henry George. To these greater names should be added that of Edward Eggleston, who had been his boyhood idol, and that of Joseph Kirkland, who did much to stimulate and guite his earliest sketches. He did not absorb all these men had to give. He could not stretch his provincial mind suddenly to compass the intellectual realm of his masters. But something he got and that something, woven into the fabric of his thinking, was to make him free. It was the best school of the times, and from his studies Hamlin Garland emerged an uncompromising radical, one of a group of eager young men who gathered about B. O. Flower, and in the sympathetic pages of the *Arena* published their divers radicalisms to a hostile world. He was ready to proclaim new social and literary creeds, ready to go forth to do battle for democratic justice and a democratic art.—VERNON LOUIS PARRINGTON, "Hamlin Garland and the Middle Border," *Main Currents of American Thought*, Vol. 3, 1930, pp. 291–93

That Garland, when he came to Boston, was already inclined to a natural rather than a supernatural view of life, is indicated by his previous interest in Ingersoll and Taine. Now, in Boston, it was to the nineteenth-century scientists and their interpreters that he naturally turned—to Fiske, to Darwin, and, most of all, to Herbert Spencer. From these masters, however, Garland did not derive, for himself, a scientific method of thought. Instead, he accepted, almost without question, the main conclusions of Spencer. He came to look upon Spencer as the greatest living thinker, and he accepted the authority of the Synthetic Philosophy as that of a new and more plausible Bible which, to him, endued the universe with a rationally acceptable harmony and order.

Under such influences, the remnants of Garland's belief in Christian theology, including his belief in an after-life, sloughed quietly away; but the loss of the elder faith brought to him no such suffering as it had brought, say, to Carlyle. For within Spencer's Synthetic Philosophy had lingered much of the optimism of the Enlightenment, and in the thought of Garland, as in that of other Spencerians, the idea of the evolving of all things from the simple to the complex was fused with an assumption of indefinite progress. The belief that the evolutionary process extends to human society gave sanction to Garland's radicalism and instructed him to welcome reform. The belief that the evolutionary process extends also to the arts—he once planned to write literary histories of the evolution of English and American ideals—gave sanction to his bold disregard of many established classics and to his attempt to strike out a literary way of his own—Veritism. The loss of any faith in a future life only called for a more vigorous attempt to make the present life tolerable; the individualism of Spencer, which might have stood in the way of Garland's interest in any socialistic program of economic reform, only confirmed him in his discipleship to Henry George; and, in short, the Synthetic Philosophy furnished, with Garland, a most favorable nourishment for the growth of literary and economic radicalism.

In the forming of his scheme of aesthetics, Garland drew upon sources more complex and varied than those which had contributed to his general philosophy. Of the European critics and artists, Taine attracted him by his naturalistic interpretation of literary history, Eugene Véron by his opposition to the French Academy, and Max Nordau by his savage treatment of the "Conventional Lies" of our civilization. Garland admired, too, the great dramatists and novelists of Norway and Russia, whom he regarded as being "almost at the very summit" of modern authorship. Of the American authors, Whitman, whose *Leaves of Grass* he read in 1883, "changed the world" for him, taught him the "mystery of the near at hand," and let loose upon him "the spiritual significance of America." Besides the poetry of Whitman, Garland read also the *Specimen Days* and especially the vigorous *Democratic Vistas*, with its caustic romantic critique of the commercialism of the Gilded Age. Whitman himself he visited in Camden, approaching the elder poet with the respect due to "one of the very greatest literary personalities of the century." Of other American authors, it was chiefly Howells who taught him to look upon fiction as a fine art. Above all, however, he studied the works of the local colorists—Eggleston, Kirkland, in fact, almost every significant author of American regional fiction; and it is from this literary type that his own earliest work most immediately derives.

No less curiously instructive than these influences which Garland accepted are those which he rejected; for, if there were certain masters whom he admired, there were others against whom he was more or less consciously in revolt. The New England school he reffered to as "eminent but bookish"; men like Bulwer, Scott, and Hugo he disliked because of their "aristocracy." Many of the classics of the past, he felt, had by the inescapable processes of social evolution lost their validity for the present: "Shakespeare, Wordsworth, Dante, Milton, are fading away into mere names—books we should read but seldom do." In this complex of rejection and assimilation, it is difficult, of course, to find any very systematic set of principles; but of one main drift we may be reasonably sure: Garland accepted and assimilated chiefly those influences he thought pertinent to the shaping of a literature which should deal powerfully, truthfully, and, if possible, beautifully, with the secular life of his contemporary America; and those influences which he felt inimical to a realistic literary treatment of our democracy, he rejected.

From such materials, and from their interaction with his own personality, Garland developed his own, individual scheme of aesthetics—a fusion of insurgency, realism, and ethical earnestness. As an insurgent—that is, as a rebellious individualist—he holds first of all that the true artist must be a creator, not an imitator. Excessive bookishness hinders rather than helps the artist. He may be warped or destroyed by libraries; he is made by vital contact with life. In the task of creation, he must free himself from the dominance of literary centers; he must thrust aside all models, even living writers, and "consciously stand alone" before life and before nature. Rebellion is therefore prerequisite to creation; "the iconoclast is a necessity."

Moreover, only by such independence of mind can an author arrive at that entire truthfulness for which Garland preferred a stronger name than realism—Veritism. The essence of Veritism is complete sincerity in the treatment of such phases of contemporary life as are known to the author. To the apprentice writer, Garland's counsel is,

> Write of the things of which you know most, and for which you care most. By so doing you will be true to yourself, true to your locality, and true to your time.

By this basic principle of truthfulness, Garland's emphasis on the value of local color in literature is, to his own mind at least, justified. The presence of local color in a work of fiction means that the writer "spontaneously reflects the life that goes on around him"; it gives a novel "such quality of texture and background that it could not have been written in any other place or by anyone else than a native." Because of the organic union of truthfulness and local color, the latter is "demonstrably the life of fiction," and is a factor in the greatness of many of the classics both of modern and of ancient times.
—WALTER FULLER TAYLOR, "Hamlin Garland," *The Economic Novel in America*, 1942, pp. 151–54

Works

. . . ⟨W⟩e must not be impatient of any writer who continues a short-story writer when he might freely become a novelist. Now that a writer can profitably do so, he may prefer to grow his fiction on the dwarf stock. He may plausibly contend that this was the original stock, and that the *novella* was a short story many ages before its name was appropriated by the standard variety, the duodecimo American, or the three-volume English; that Boccaccio was a world-wide celebrity five centuries before George Eliot was known to be a woman. To be sure, we might come back at him with the Greek romancers; we might ask him what he had to say to the interminable tales of Heliodorus and Longus, and the rest, and then not let him say.

But no such controversy is necessary to the enjoyment of the half dozen volumes of short stories at hand, and we gladly postpone it till we have nothing to talk about. At present we have only too much to talk about in a book so robust and terribly serious as Mr. Hamlin Garland's volume called *Main-Travelled Roads*. That is what they call the highways in the part of the West that Mr. Garland comes from and writes about; and these stories are full of the bitter and burning dust, the foul and trampled slush, of the common avenues of life, the life of the men who hopelessly and cheerlessly make the wealth that enriches the alien and the idler, and impoverishes the producer.

If any one is still at a loss to account for that uprising of the farmers in the West which is the translation of the Peasants' War into modern and republican terms, let him read *Main-Travelled Roads*, and he will begin to understand, unless, indeed, Mr. Garland is painting the exceptional rather than the average. The stories are full of those gaunt, grim, sordid, pathetic, ferocious figures, whom our satirists find so easy to caricature as Hayseeds, and whose blind groping for fairer conditions is so grotesque to the newspapers and so menacing to the politicians. They feel that something is wrong, and they know that the wrong is not theirs. The type caught in Mr. Garland's book is not pretty; it is ugly and often ridiculous; but it is heart-breaking in its rude despair.

The story of a farm mortgage, as it is told in the powerful sketch "Under the Lion's Paw," is a lesson in political economy, as well as a tragedy of the darkest cast. "The Return of the Private" is a satire of the keenest edge, as well as a tender and mournful idyl of the unknown soldier who comes back after the war with no blare of welcoming trumpets or flash of streaming flags, but foot-sore, heart-sore, with no stake in the country he has helped to make safe and rich but the poor man's chance to snatch an uncertain subsistence from the furrows he left for the battle-field.

"Up the Coolly," however, is the story which most pitilessly of all accuses our vaunted conditions, wherein every man has the chance to rise above his brother and make himself richer than his fellows. It shows us once for all what the risen man may be, and portrays in his good-natured selfishness and indifference that favorite ideal of our system. The successful brother comes back to the old farmstead, prosperous, handsome, well-dressed, and full of patronizing sentiment for his boyhood days there, and he cannot understand why his brother, whom hard work and corroding mortgages have eaten all the joy out of, gives him a grudging and surly welcome. It is a tremendous situation, and it is the allegory of the whole world's civilization: the upper dog and the under dog are everywhere, and the under dog nowhere likes it.

But the allegorical effects are not the primary intent of Mr.

Garland's work: it is a work of art, first of all, and we think of fine art; though the material will strike many gentilities as coarse and common. In one of the stories, "Among the Corn-Rows," there is a good deal of burly, broad-shouldered humor of a fresh and native kind; in "Mr. Ripley's Trip" is a delicate touch, like that of Miss Wilkins; but Mr. Garland's touches are his own, here and elsewhere. He has a certain harshness and bluntness, an indifference to the more delicate charms of style, and he has still to learn that though the thistle is full of an unrecognized poetry, the rose has a poetry, too, that even over-praise cannot spoil. But he has a fine courage to leave a fact with the reader, ungarnished and unvarnished, which is almost the rarest trait in an Anglo-Saxon writer, so infantile and feeble is the custom of our art; and this attains tragical sublimity in the opening sketch, "A Branch Road," where the lover who has quarrelled with his betrothed comes back to find her mismated and miserable, such a farm wife as Mr. Garland has alone dared to draw, and tempts the broken-hearted drudge away from her loveless home. It is all morally wrong, but the author leaves you to say that yourself. He knows that his business was with those two people, their passions and their probabilities. —W. D. HOWELLS, "Introduction" (1891) to *Main-Travelled Roads*, 1899, pp. 3–6

Garland came closer to portraying the spirit of the frontier in his autobiographical works . . . than in his fiction. Beginning with his *A Son of the Middle Border*, which appeared in 1917, and continuing in *A Daughter of the Middle Border*, *Trail-Makers of the Middle Border*, and *Back Trailers*, he told the story of the Garland family from the time of their emigration West toward the middle of the last century to their return East in the twentieth century. While Garland's autobiographical writing like his fiction is without æsthetic distinction, it is so rich in intimate detail and historical insight that it is very likely that the picture which it has provided of the frontier background will endure. Telling us as he did in *Roadside Meetings*, that "Horace Greeley's *Go West, Young Man, Go West*, had been the marching orders under which the Garlands and McClintocks and all their neighbors had been moving for forty years," he has related in his various autobiographical narratives the experiences of that family and the fate of his soul. Above all, his work has been consistently realistic—that is at least within the province of what he has considered realism. The frontier he described was not the frontier of romance, but the frontier of defeat. As in his stories in *Main-Travelled Roads*, the hardness of the farmer's life in the West, the oppression of the land laws, the vicious successes of the speculators, stand out in his autobiographical works and give them their realistic—or veritistic—challenge. In his description of Richard, in *Trail-Makers of the Middle Border*, Garland has caught successfully the petty bourgeois psychology of the young frontiersman:

> Like the youth in the city who from his garret hears the roar of vast enterprises and imaginatively shares them, so this young Yankee, working for wages on a raft, imagined himself a part of the upbuilding of a great state, and was happy in the belief. In all this he was typical of his generation.

But that psychology did not survive. The idealism of that generation turned into the disillusionment of the next. The father who had started out full of hope and heroism found himself desolate of spirit and a few decades later. Land taxes weighed down upon him and made his life into a constant struggle to meet them. The old pioneer days when he had been "so patriotic, so confident, so sanguine of the country's future" had passed. In their stead had come the days of despair and defeat. "He had come a long way from the buoyant faith of '66," Garland wrote in description of his father's later years, "and the change in him was typical of the change in the West in America."—V. F. CALVERTON, "The Frontier Force," *The Liberation of American Literature*, 1932, pp. 345–46

Jason Edwards: An Average Man is a caricature of orthodox dualism locked in mortal combat with the forces of scientific materialism. It is a novel of protest against the crushing forces of economic determinism as they operate in Boston industry and in western prairie farming. In Boston, Jason is squeezed to the edge of starvation between rising rents and falling wages. He and those like him are doomed to horrible squalor and misery. Conditions are described in passages of surprising power:

> . . . as Edwards looked in at the foundry door on his way back, about five o'clock, men were "pouring." It was a grew-some sight. With grimy, sooty shirts, open at the throat, in a temperature of deadly heat, they toiled like demons. There was little humanity in their faces, as the dazzling metal threw a dull-red glow on them.
>
> Here and there, with warning shouts, they ran, bent like gnomes, with pots of shining, flame-colored liquid lighting their grimy faces. Here toiled two stalwart fellows, with a huge pot between them; with hoarse shouts they drew up beside a huge "flask" or moulding-box. The skimmer pushed away the slag, the radiant metal leaped out and down into the sand, sending spurts of yellow-blue flame out of a half-hundred crevices . . . Jason Edwards remained a long time looking at this scene. Its terror came in upon him as never before. That men should toil like that for ten dollars per week . . . was horrible.

So Jason takes his family west—to fall into the clutches of heartless capitalists who control all the land near the railroad and hold mortgages on seventy per cent of the farms, farms which, drought-cursed and sun-baked, fail to support the poor souls who toil upon them. Here, after intolerable privations, Edwards's daughter pleads with the mortgage holder:

> "Then take the land!" cried Alice, despairingly, "Don't delude us with the idea of ownership where we're only tenants."
>
> "But we don't want the land," explained the judge. "All we want is the interest. We've got more land than we know what to do with."
>
> He had made it too plain. The girl's face lifted, lit by a bitter indignant smile—
>
> "I see! It's cheaper to let us think we own the land than it is to pay us wages. You're right—your system is perfect—and heartless. It means death to us all and all like us!" she said, as the whole truth came upon her.

Such lines show the mixture of moral indignation and economic determinism so characteristic of Garland's early work.

These passages suggest a novel in the Zola tradition, with the bitter consequences inevitably following. But this matter of mortgages and foreclosures is not the plot of *Jason Edwards*. The plot is concerned with the activities of Jason's daughter, Alice, who is confronted by various difficult choices between love and duty. In Boston, where she has trained her voice and her manners so well that she has risen quite above her economic class, she inspires the love of a rising Bostonian who offers her culture and security if she will stay behind and marry him instead of going west with the family. Duty wins, but the undaunted hero follows Alice and proposes again. His arrival at the town nearest Edwards's farm is the occasion for a chapter or two of expository dialogue from which the reader again learns how bad are conditions and how cruel the men who prey upon their fellows. But the deterministic forces are not shown in operation—they are merely discussed—and they have only the most rudimentary relation to the plot. The action continues to turn upon questions of love against duty. When the hero proposes a second time, duty again triumphs in Alice's refusal. But as the hero is driving away, nature saves the day with a hailstorm and cloudburst which destroy the wheat and prostrate the old man with a stroke. These catastrophes satisfy the frontiersman's sense of honor and make it reputable for Jason to abandon the unequal struggle and return to the green East to live with his daughter and son-in-law.

Genteel elegance and romantic compromise prevent Garland from carrying the grim expectations of his situation through to their tragic consequences. It would be attractive to explain this structural collapse by invoking the eager spirit of American democracy—to say that the West was bold and confident and that the writer was carried along by this spirit to renounce the "pessimistic determinism" of European naturalism. But this patriotic explanation will not do. Returning to the comfortable East to live with genteel culture is not a victory for the pioneer spirit but an abandonment of it. A happy ending of this sort does not express frontier optimism. Paradoxically, a grimly tragic "naturalistic" ending would have revealed the author's belief in the ultimate triumph of democracy over natural and institutional obstacles. It would have demonstrated his eagerness to present the hard facts in all their hardness, so that democracy would know exactly what had to be done. Such a pessimistic conclusion would have been an affirmation because it was intellectually bold and consistent. The happy ending of *Jason Edwards* shows that Garland was already yearning to abandon the hard life of a radical for the comfortable prestige of literary circles. His failure to manage the implications of determinism, in his plots, must not, therefore, be laid merely to the fact that he was not a master of naturalistic techniques or not entirely sure of the philosophy. The same uncertainties appear in criticism of the American novel of 1920 to 1940. Those who wrote most honestly, most courageously, and most notably in the tradition of American idealism were accused of pessimism and of undermining America's faith in her destiny. The accusation was genteel.
—CHARLES CHILD WALCUTT, "Adumbrations: Harold Frederic and Hamlin Garland," *American Literary Naturalism, a Divided Stream*, 1956, pp. 57–60

JAMES K. FOLSOM
From "The Vanishing American"
The American Western Novel
1966, pp. 149–55

In many ways Hamlin Garland's Indian studies are a transition between traditional and modern literary treatments of the Indian. Both "The Silent Eaters"—a fictionalized biography of Sitting Bull—and the short stories which together make up *The Book of the American Indian* (1923) are written out of a feeling of indignation over unjust treatment of the Indian; and both as well have a very definite social reference which, in the weakest of the stories, deteriorates into a thinly disguised program of social action. Yet this program is significantly different from earlier fictional discussions of the Indian problem; for, as Garland sees, the problem itself has changed. No longer is it conceived in terms of how best to defeat the Indians; rather it has become the question of how best to rehabilitate a defeated enemy. "The Silent Eaters" and the stories *The Book of the American Indian* are rather specifically concerned with providing answers to this problem and the method of explication Garland uses is closely related to the idea of Indian conversion mentioned previously. Garland, however, sees that the question of whether the old ways are "good" or "bad" must be approached differently in order for it to have any relevance to the actual world. As a result, the standard plot of escape fiction, the story of the reactionary old chief who is replaced by the modern progressive young Indian is put in a different perspective. Where the escapist plot concerns itself primarily with the events leading to the subjugation of the Indian, after which he is converted, Garland focuses primarily upon the Indian's condition after his subjugation, and hence emphasizes the absolute necessity for his conversion; and where the escapist plot concerns itself primarily with the description of unmotivated event, Garland's primary concern is with the nature of the process of conversion.

This is most clearly seen in "The Silent Eaters," which in format most closely resembles the escapist plot. In this biographical account of the Sioux chief Sitting Bull, Garland presents an expanded metaphor for the decline of the Sioux nation, from its early proud self-sufficiency to its final utter dependence upon the whites. Garland tells his story with considerable skill, especially when he succeeds in generalizing the character of Sitting Bull from that of a conventional "bad" Indian into a sympathetic type of the Sioux nation in general. And just here is the focus of Garland's story; for "The Silent Eaters" universalizes the particular figure of Sitting Bull into a general statement of the nature of that historic process which has inevitably ended with the triumph of the whites and the subjugation of the Indians.

Such a focus enables Garland to establish a double point of view toward his material. While he can admire Sitting Bull's courage, resourcefulness, and so on, at the same time he may consistently condemn these qualities as out of place in the white world inevitably to come. Hence Sitting Bull can be personally admired, but at the same time the position for which he stands need not be affirmed. Garland establishes this double viewpoint by means of his narrator, a young Sioux Indian named Iapi. When Sitting Bull finally surrenders, Iapi is befriended by a Lieutenant Davies of the U. S. Army, who gives him the opportunity for education in the white man's ways, even sending him East to study. Lieutenant Davies has a great respect both for the Indians as a race and for education as a means to ameliorate their unhappy reservation conditions. "The plains Indian was a perfect adaptation of organism to environment," he once tells Iapi, who also tells us that "he looked upon each people as the product of its conditions." The moral is not far to seek, nor does it escape Iapi. Now that the environment is changed, the organism must change with it, and Iapi's role must be that of the educator of his people.

The creation of the character of Iapi is Garland's only major fictional tampering with the historic facts of the life of Sitting Bull. Such a character as Iapi, however, is admirably suited for telling Sitting Bull's story. He is first of all an Indian, and his white ways are only superimposed upon the virtues of what Lieutenant Davies calls "a wonderful race." Hence he can be sympathetic to Indian ways without appearing condescending, and at the same time need not pretend to be anything other than outraged over the excesses and outrages which various whites perpetrate upon his people. His white schooling, on the other hand, has given him another perspective on Indian history which enables him to interpret Sitting Bull not in a personal light but in an historic one. From this historic perspective Sitting Bull, however admirably he may appear as a character, is nevertheless the voice of the past. "He epitomized the epic, tragic story of my kind," Iapi sums up. "His life spanned the gulf between the days of our freedom and the death of every custom native to us. He saw the invader come and he watched the buffalo disappear. Within the half century of his conscious life he witnessed greater changes and comprehended more of my tribe's tragic history than any other red man." But this elegy for Sitting Bull and the heroic past is alloyed with optimism; for the future belongs to Iapi.

The present pessimism and future optimism which Garland notes as the process of Indian history in "The Silent Eaters" are by no means confined to this least fictional of his treatments of the Indian. The historic process of evolution described specifically (and by Lieutenant Davies, at least, in pseudo-scientific Social Darwinian terms) here is also clearly illustrated by the various stories in *The Book of the American Indian*.

The general philosophical burden of these various tales is that, like it or not, the Indian must change. This is emphasized by a recurrent image which is made explicit in a number of the stories, that the Indian's trial has ended, and that the white man's road is the only one left for the Indians to follow. Even when not explicit, this image is always close to the surface. For instance, "Wahiah—A Spartan Mother" tells of the necessity for Indian children to adopt the white man's ways. In this story Wahiah realizes that she must send her son Atokan to the Indian school, no matter how much the reactionary Indians may disapprove of it. When Atokan refuses to go, the schoolteacher gives him a whipping, and Wahiah, in a clearly symbolic gesture, breaks the boy's bow and arrows, his "symbols of freedom," and after saying only "Obey" leaves Atokan at the school.

The theme is most clearly stated in one of the best stories in the book, "Rising Wolf—Ghost Dancer." Rising Wolf, who tells the story of his life himself, recounts how as a young brave he had become a medicine man. He had an honorable position in the tribe before the white men came and, Garland makes clear, he was no cynical prestidigitator but one who sincerely believed in the value of his medicine. After the Indian defeat, Rising Wolf and the rest of his tribe had been sent to a reservation where all had heard of the Ghost Dance. To a medicine man and hence presumably something of an authority on the subject, the idea of the Ghost Dance seemed to make some sense, and he became a convert. The Ghost Dance, Rising Wolf and the other Indians believed, was to operate by magic. The Indians were to dance for four days, and on the fourth day the white men would disappear and the buffalo return, and all Indians, alive or dead, would be reunited on the rejuvenated earth.

The ending of the story describes, in a very sensitively handled tragicomic manner, the Dance itself. The whites, fearing that the gathering dancers represent a threat to civil order, send soldiers to watch lest the dance prove hostile in intent. Of course the Indians, confident of their "medicine," are peaceable in the extreme. For four days they dance, and when they have finished Rising Wolf retires to rest satisfied with a job well done and sure that when he wakes the following morning the whites will have vanished and the buffalo returned.

When he awakes the millennium has unaccountably been delayed; the whites are still there. Convinced by the visible proof that the Ghost Dance in particular and Indian medicine in general have both been in error, he renounces them and resolves to take up white ways. The conclusion of the story is worth examination in detail.

> "When I rose, it was morning. I flung off my blanket, and looked down on the valley where the tepees of the white soldiers stood. I heard their drums and their music. I had made up my mind. The white man's trail was wide and dusty by reason of many feet passing thereon, but it was long. The trail of my people was ended.
>
> I said, "I will follow the white man's trail. I will make him my friend, but I will not bend my neck to his burdens. I will be cunning as the coyote. I will ask him to help me to understand his ways, and then I will prepare the way for my children. Maybe they will outrun the white man in his own shoes. Anyhow, there are but two ways. One leads to hunger and death, the other leads where the poor white man lives. Beyond is the happy hunting ground, where the white man cannot go."

The general similarity between the conclusion of "Rising Wolf" and the more detailed interpretation of history in "The Silent Eaters" is obvious. What is perhaps not so obvious are the implications inherent in Garland's choice of Rising Wolf for his hero. In the character of Rising Wolf, Garland has combined the two points of view represented in "The Silent Eaters" by Sitting Bull and Iapi. By making Rising Wolf first a medicine man and then a believer in the Ghost Dance, Garland has made him symbolically stand for the most reactionary and unprogressive elements in the old order; his conversion to white ways, however anthropologically dubious and psychologically untenable it may seem, represents Garland's deeply held belief that the Indian can be made to accept these ways. Even the most reactionary Indian, when once he understands the hard facts of history, can adjust to the new life forced on him by its inevitable processes.

Garland's insistence upon the inevitability of change relieves him from the fictional necessity to choose sides and accept either white or red ways without qualification; he need not categorically defend or excuse either whites or Indians. Hence villains as well as heroes can be either white or red, and in fact there are many white villians in *The Book of the American Indian*. As a general rule, these white villians are missionaries, for whom Garland had little respect. The general tone of *The Book of the American Indian* is, if not exactly anti-religious, certainly anti-clerical and anti-missionary. One of the most poignant stories, "The Iron Kiva," clearly shows Garland's typical attitude; it tells of two Indian children who kill themselves rather than let the white missionary take them away to school in the East. Significantly, the children like the idea of the white man's school, but distrust and fear the missionaries.

Garland's white heroes are usually Indian agents and schoolteachers, whose tolerance and kindliness stand in none too subtle contrast to missionary bigotry. The agents and schoolteachers are sympathetic to those Indian ways which are not immediately harmful and do not stand in the way of the Indians' education. They view the process of education as basically one of training the Indians in the use of unfamiliar skills which he will need to survive in the white man's world. The missionaries, in contrast, view the educational process as one of total ruthless eradication of Indian customs. Without sympathy for or understanding of the Indians, the missionaries are helpless either to convert them or to ameliorate their lot. Th rehabilitate the Indian, Garland says, it is not necessary to turn him into a white man; Indian customs need not be entirely blotted out, as the missionaries would have it. The Indian desperately needs training in the general skills of civilized life, for in order to survive he must become literate and learn how to use the white man's agricultural tools. But further than this, education should not go; it is possible to assent to the truth of mathematics without swearing undying allegiance to the Apostles' Creed.

Ultimately Garland's point is that the Indian can and should be allowed to have the best of both white and red worlds. Like Iapi and Rising Wolf, the modern Indian can keep the cultural traditions of his fathers and combine them successfully with the demands of life in a world dominated by white values. Perhaps, as Rising Wolf suggests, if he is cunning enough he can outstrip the white man on his own grounds.

This is true of all the stories in *The Book of the American Indian* with the exception of the best one, "The Story of Howling Wolf." In this somber tale the often complacent "long view" of history which justifies particular present hardship is subjected to serious qualification. When the story opens Howling Wolf hates white men because his brother had been killed for sport by cowboys seven years before. He has never forgiven the white and has taken a vow to kill the men responsible for his brother's death, but the Indian agent manages to talk him out of his lust for vengeance. Howling Wolf is strongly influenced by the example of the Indian agent, with whom he makes friends, and, renouncing his savage ways, determines to turn himself into the kind of Indian white men will respect. He even gets the agent to write him a paper which, he ingenuously thinks, "will tell [all men] that my heart is made good." This paper, which he carries with him as a sort of passport, says "I am Howling Wolf. Long I hated the white man. Now my heart is good and I want to make friends with all the white man. These are my words. [Signed] Howling Wolf."

Armed with his passport, Howling Wolf does what a sober, industrious Indian should and gets a job hauling hides. But when he transports a wagonload of hides to town the whites laugh at him and spurn his offers of friendship. A cowboy picks a fight with him and fires a wild shot which hits another white man in the knee. The outraged citizenry assume that Howling Wolf has fired the shot, and are all for lynching him until he gives them the paper which, when they read it, cools their anger, and they compromise their earlier position by throwing Howling Wolf into jail on more or less general principles. The agent's efforts to have Howling Wolf released are futile. One day Howling Wolf, who has borne up patiently throughout the whole affair, is taken from jail by the sheriff, who wants to attend a baseball game and is afraid to leave the Indian unattended. Howling Wolf thinks he is being taken to his execution, so he tries to escape; but he is apprehended by a group of cowboys who lasso him and drag him behind their horses for amusement. A Catholic priest manages to make the cowboys stop, albeit only after Howling Wolf has apparently been dragged to death. Though he finally recovers, he is "so battered, so misshapen that his own wife did not know him." Howling Wolf's attempt to civilize himself has ended disastrously; he will speak only to the priest and the agent, and when he dies no white man knows where his grave is hidden.

In any ways "The Story of Howling Wolf" is an exact inversion of the other stories in *The Book of the American Indian*. Howling Wolf's story, like Iapi's and Rising Wolf's, is a description of education; but what he learns stands in direct opposition to the lesson the other progressive Indians have been taught. Howling Wolf's education is much like Sitting Bull's; that the whites are cruel, selfish, and not to be trusted.

The most sobering aspect of "The Story of Howling Wolf" and what sets it apart from the other stories is Garland's conception of the limited possibilities for goodness in the nature of man. In the brutal and savaged "civilized" world to which Howling Wolf is introduced, there is little room for the optimism which Garland elsewhere shows. Evil in this story is not a product of the conflict between different social values, a conflict which, the other stories lead us to believe, can be smoothed away when one set of social values disappears; rather evil is understood as an expression of the bestiality in man, and social values are not its causes but the ways in which it is made manifest in the world. To such a view history cannot possibly appear optimistic; for all hopes of meliorating human life depend upon the assumption that man's character can be changed for the better. In "The Story of Howling Wolf" such is simply not the case. The parable of history in this story resembles that in the Leatherstocking Tales. Change is certain, but it does not represent progress; history records the frustration of hope.

STANLEY R. HARRISON

"Hamlin Garland and the Double Vision of Naturalism"

Studies in Short Fiction, Fall 1969, pp. 548–56

It is strange that the compelling fascination of literary naturalism resides in its somber tone and its non-exit circumstance when, in fact, it is excitation of hope and the potential for escape that create the naturalistic vibration.[1] Naturalism, whether of the hard or soft, pessimistic or optimistic variety, is a mature fiction of counterpoint that derives its vitality from contrast and its ironic poignancy from the futile struggle to achieve or maintain an enclosed area of freedom. The forces of civilization that pursue a Huck and a Jim, for example, are ominous in themselves, but they are dramatically so when set over against the exhilarating sense of freedom enjoyed by the two wanderers. The vibrations in the novel are set in motion as the tranquility of the river intensifies the madness of the shore and as the violent sounds of land punctuate the pristine stillness of the waters. Similarly, the romantic sense of freedom inspired by the awesomeness of the San Joaquin Valley is as much the essence of Norris's naturalistic impulse in *The Octopus* as is the invincible and destructive force of the railroad itself. The city lights in *Sister Carrie* also set up a dilation, for they hold out the promise of escape from the dreariness of poverty, and yet they occasion nothing more than the frustration of desire and the perversion of value. Even Crane's *Maggie*, a deliberate charting of despair, frustration, and futility, emits its own strange polar vibrations as Maggie is led down the primrose path to her inevitable end. In a world of disorderliness and physical infirmity, brutality and evil, death is her only possible release; her only solace is in the serenity of the black void where illusions of hope do not penetrate and where life ceases in the pathetic dignity of anonymity. Blackness conveys the despair of existence, but, paradoxically, it also offers the hope of extinction, and Maggie, given but one opportunity to determine her own destiny, seeks this salvation and traces her descent into darkness. Death, then, hardly the antithesis of desire, is desire itself; it is the center of freedom to Maggie, as the river is to Huck, the city to Carrie, and the San Joaquin Valley to Presley.

Hamlin Garland presents the vibrations of hope and despair, naturalism's double vision of life and death, in possibly the most complex fashion of all. In the midst of the destructive economic and natural forces that swirl through his short stories, he provides, not one, but three havens of liberation for his prairie folk and main-travelled roaders: they find respite and transcendent wonder in the physical beauty indigenous to the landscape, spiritual satisfaction in their tragic anger and in their own humanity, and hope in the possibility of eventual escape. These well-defined areas of freedom, though elusive, invest his stories with vital dramatic contrast and poignant want; they provide the necessary naturalistic counterpart to total despair and abject surrender.

The life aspects of Garland's shorter works finds an outlet in the release of affections quickened by the sweet freshness, the airy lightness, and the calm enchantment of an untainted natural scene.[2] To travel his road, his "panorama of delight," is to remain motionless, "to lean back in a reclining-chair and whirl away in a breezy July day, past lakes, groves of oak, past fields of barley being reaped, past hay-fields, where the heavy grass is toppling before the swift sickle." It is "a road full of delicious surprises, where down a sudden vista lakes open, or a distant wooded hill looms darkly blue, or swift streams, foaming deep down the solid rock, send whiffs of cool breezes in at the window. It has majesty, breadth. The farming has nothing apparently petty about it. All seems vigorous, youthful, and prosperous." Seldom is this sylvan scene without the vibrancy or serenity of either man or nature. There are windless September dawns greeted by the ringing and clear voices of young, jubilant, happy lovers. There are June days in which no trees waver, no grass rustles, and there is scarcely a sound of human life; but there is the faint and melancholy movement of the wind in the short grass coupled with the wild sounds of prairie voices. Larks, gophers, falling plovers, swift winged prairie-pigeons, lonely ducks, and jays dissonantly yoke their infrequent whistles, fluttering cries, rapid whirs, mournful quacks, and noisy screams into a major theme supported by a choral murmur of ground birds, snipes, and insects; on such days, the air literally pulsates with sounds of life.

Garland complements the vibrations of sound with a canvas of startling color. Purple, orange, and a yellow-green are the prevailing tones of his backdrop, but there is not a flush, no matter how striking in appearance, that is not represented. Red lilies dramatically star the grass with their hues of fire; the sun sets upon the rich brown of wooded areas; shadows of a few scattered clouds slide down upon green and purpled slopes; dazzling sunlight flames along velvety grass, settles upon distant purple peaks, and streams across the blue mist in shoots of gold and crimson. The colors are in flux and their patterns kaleidoscopically change with a shift to a different perspective, a different season, a different time of day. In the autumn, the roads are a smooth gray-white; at dawn, the sun's light effects fleeting banners of rose and pale green through the fallen leaves; and shortly before midday in July colors lose their lustre as they resolve into the dullness of black shadow upon brown earth.

Nature, in its magnificence of color and sound, is to Garland what the Mississipi River was to Twain—a testament to life—and Garland utilizes it, as did Twain, to celebrate its wonder and to provide contrast for the infirmities that mar its beauty. His vision alternates between the splendors of the colorfully vibrant scene and the dingy quality, the drab appearance of the humans who people the setting. In only an instant, he submerges the beautiful and peaceful valley from view: "In the midst of oceans of land, floods of sunshine and gulfs of verdure, the farmer lives in two or three small rooms. Poverty's eternal cordon is ever round the poor."

"The goodness and glory of God was in the very air, the bitterness and oppression of man in every line of her face," writes Garland; and nowhere is his basic theme, that of the oppression of the individual in the midst of the richness of Western life, more tersely expressed, more dramatically stated. One senses the pathos and dullness reflected by the sordid and squalid structures that house the people. A prodigal son returns to the farm after an absence of years and observes that it is "humble enough—a small white story-and-a-half structure, with a wing set in the midst of a few locust trees; a small drab-colored barn with a sagging ridge-pole; a barnyard full of mud, in which a few cows were standing, fighting the flies and waiting to be milked. An old man was pumping water at the well; the pigs were squealing from a pen near by; a child was crying. Instantly the beautiful, peaceful valley was forgotten. A sickening chill struck . . . the soul." Within the houses, the mawkish furnishings convey an air of despondency. There are plaster walls of gold, cheap washstands and three-piece wash sets encircled with blue bands, rectangular windows and vulgar green shades, warped tables, and calico-covered furniture. There are no books in the musty little rooms, only an occasional newspaper, and perhaps the paper on the walls in floral patterns of strange and gaudy color is the most saddening aspect of all, for it is the one concession to gayety and luxuriousness in the blank, bare sheds that provide a functional shelter from the rain, but convey none of the warmth of a home. The only audible sounds within are the rhythmical hissing of the occasional raindrop spattering upon the hot stove and the hum of the swarming flies driven inside to seek the warmth of a dreary kitchen.

Such is the dismal character of the shelters that not even the cool, natural breezes can penetrate and afford a temporary relief. There is a sense of stifling and suffocation; there is nothing other than the still and sultry air that induces a tired feeling, but not one conducive to restful sleep. The very pathos of human misery, of good men suffering in the midst of plenty, produces a moment of despair that prevents the intake of breath as surely as does the frightfully close air, and Garland's characters know of this sensation: "Howard went slowly around the corner of the house, past a vilely smelling rain-barrel, toward the west. A gray-haired woman was sitting in a rocking-chair on the porch, her hands in her lap, her eyes fixed on the faintly yellow sky, against which the hills stood, dim purple silhouettes, and on which the locust trees were etched as fine as lace. There was sorrow, resignation, and a sort of dumb despair in her attitude. Howard stood, his throat swelling till it seemed as if he would suffocate."

As striking as the contrast is between the liveliness of nature and the oppressiveness of the atmosphere, between the majesty of nature and the crude hovels of nature's caretakers, Garland's portraits of physical debility in the presence of nature's vigorous force create an even more discordant uneasiness and contribute an even more frightening quality of emotional experience to his landscape. The severity of the farmhands' labors and the meagerness of their compensation combined with an attitude of resignation, an intuition of hopelessness, and an understanding that change and flexibility have no application to their lives effects a premature deadening of the soul and depletion of the body and creates a race of catatonic embodiments. Henry Adams observed that woman, as a force, was unknown in America, that an American Venus would never dare exist. Possibly she would have endeavored if she had only possessed the energy or if her life force had not been previously drained by the agony of labor and the callousness of rejection. Garland's women are thin and weary and bent; their wrists are red, their necks sinewy, their hands gaunt and knotted, worn and discolored; a skeletal appearance further distinguishes them as does the droop of their lips and the glaze of their eyes. Not atypical is Lucretia Burns:

> . . . she was middle-aged, distorted with work and child-bearing, and looked faded and worn as one of

> the boulders that lay beside the pasture fence near where she sat milking a large white cow.
>
> She had no shawl or hat and no shoes, for it was still muddy in the little yard, where the cattle stood patiently fighting the flies and mosquitoes swarming into their skins, already wet with blood. The evening was oppressive with its heat, and a ring of just-seen thunder-heads gave premonitions of an approaching storm.
>
> She rose from the cow's side at last, and, taking her pails of foaming milk, staggered toward the gate. The two pails hung from her lean arms, her bare feet slipped on the filthy ground, her greasy and faded calico dress showed her tired, swollen ankles, and the mosquitoes swarmed mercilessly on her neck and bedded themselves in her colorless hair.
>
> The children were quarreling at the well, and the sound of blows could be heard. Calves were querulously calling for their milk, and little turkeys, lost in a tangle of grass, were piping plaintively.
>
> The sun just setting struck through a long, low rift like a boy peeping beneath the eaves of a huge roof. It's light brought out Lucretia's face as she leaned her sallow forehead on the top bar of the gate and looked toward the west.
>
> It was a pitifully worn, almost tragic face—long, thin, sallow, hollow-eyed. The mouth had long since lost the power to shape itself into a kiss, and had a droop at the corners which seemed to announce a breaking-down at any moment into a despairing wail. The collarless neck and sharp shoulders showed painfully.

Possibly more distressing than the femininity and sex that are denied the woman is the youth that is denied the young. This is no longer the nostalgic world of Tom Sawyer, wherein the adolescence of youth parallels the immaturity of the nation, and the child is encouraged in his indulgences because early maturing and assumption of responsibility have not yet become necessary to servival. The Civil War has intervened, some fifty years have passed, industrialization has become a fact, mobility and flexibility have undergone stabilization, opportunities have diminished, landlordism has introduced the severities of tenant farming, fertile tracts have long since been laid claim to, wealth has become consolidated, and the adventure of settling the land has given way to the drudgery of cultivating it; progress has introduced hardship and inequity.

The almost premature growth thrust upon the nation and the consequent confusion visited upon the individual make participation in toil by all who are able a requisite for family survival. No longer permitted the pleasures of idle fancy and the opportunities for leisurely adventure, youth has to serve rather than be served, and their energies of dissipation are converted into labors of responsibility. A nightmare of resignation and horror replaces a childish dream of conquest. Garland writes with feeling of this "pathetic but common figure—this boy on the American farm, where there is no law against child labor. To see him in his coarse clothing, his huge boots, and his ragged cap, as he staggered with a pail of water from the well, or trudged in the cold and cheerless dawn out into the frosty field behind his team, gave the city-bred visitor a sharp pang of sympathetic pain. Yet Haskins loved his boy, and would have saved him from this if he could, but he could not." The bent and weighted shoulders of these children are the inherited results of a brutal and fruitless labor.

Garland's characters find themselves in a pitiful and frustrating situation, for nature's paradise is constantly within their sight; yet they are powerless to reach it from their side of the East Gate. Only those who remain ignorant of their expulsion and oblivious to the closed nature of their universe—and there are some, though few indeed—preserve their hope and find in the act of defiance an outlet for emotional expression. Though no qualitative change is in the offing, the rebellion, short lived and transitory as it is, provides it own purpose and meaning. The reflections of the emaciated and sick army private's wife as she stares at their ill-kept, encumbered farm erupt into thoughts of violence and rebellion: "While the millionaire sent his money to England for safe-keeping, this man, with his girl-wife and three babies, left them on a mortgaged farm, and went away to fight for an idea. It was foolish, but it was sublime for all that. That was three years before, and the young wife, sitting on the well-curb on this bright Sabbath harvest morning, was righteously rebellious." Lucretia, the wife of Sim Burns, overburdened by weariness and withered from lack of affection, challenges her husband with intense anger. "She was ripe for an explosion like this," Garland quietly comments. "She seized upon it with eagerness." There are others, also. Grand McClane speakes in a "gruff tone, full of rebellion," and Haskins, denied the rewards of his labor by Butler, the successful landlord, strikes back with the violence of rational hatred: "'I think you're a thief and a liar!' shouted Haskins, leaping up. 'A black-hearted houn'!' Butler's smile maddened him; with a sudden leap he caught a fork in his hands, and whirled it in the air. 'You'll never rob another man, damn ye!' he grated through his teeth, a look of pitiless ferocity in his accusing eyes. Butler shrank and quivered, expecting the blow; stood, held hypnotized by the eyes of the man he had a moment before despised—a man transformed into an avenging demon."

The moment of challenge, a tragic conflict, is a human triumph, but it is only a moment; it expends itself and the discontent resolves into an eternity of despair. There is no reaffirmation, only resignation and futility made more pathetic for the awareness of a moment's triumph. Private Smith's wife shapes her rebellious thoughts as she waits "on the edge of despair"; Lucretia Burns makes her peace, for there is no alternative, "'no hope of anything better'"; Grant McClane's flame subsides with the awareness that life provides no escapes: "'I've come to the conclusion that life's a failure for ninety-nine percent of us. You can't help me now. It's too late.'" And Haskins, refusing to descend the chain of being, surrenders to his own humanity: "But in the deadly hush between the lift of the weapon and its fall there came a gush of faint, childish laughter and then across the range of his vision, far away and dim, he saw the sun-bright head of his baby girl, as, with the pretty, tottering run of a two-year-old, she moved across the grass of the dooryard. His hands relaxed: the fork fell to the ground; his head lowered."

Rebellion and hope are illusory, nature merely taunts, and only one exit remains, but that escape lies outside the pale of Garland's Middle Border. Severance from the society itself is the coveted result of this strange alternative, and an inversion of morality is the frightening means to its attainment. After a seven-year absence, and still obsessed by the lovely image of Agnes, the girl he left behind, Will Hannan returns to the land of his youth. Evidence of decay and disillusion offends his sensibilities, but none more so than the sight of Agnes, now a woman of many years and negligible charm. "She was worn and wasted incredibly. The blue of her eyes seemed dimmed and faded by weeping, and the old-time scarlet of her lips had been washed away. The sinews of her neck showed painfully when she turned her head, and her trembling hands were worn, discolored, and lumpy at the joints. . . . Once or twice Agnes smiled, with just a little flash of the old-time sunny temper. But there was no dimple in the cheek now, and the smile had more suggestion of an invalid—or even a skeleton." Motivated by a curious response of guilt, emotional responsibility, and affection for the past image, Will persuades Agnes to desert her husband, home, and bondage, and travel to Europe with him, and the sanction of God is given the act of immorality: "'We can make this experience count for us yet. But we mustn't let a mistake ruin us—it should teach us. What right has any one to keep you in a hole? God don't expect a toad to stay in a stump and starve if it can get out. He don't ask the snakes to suffer as you do.'"

Theirs is an act of cowardice and a violation of the marriage rite, but it is not cowardice to forsake that place where hope no longer exists, and it is not immoral to preserve life and build anew. In the face of the perversion of life itself, values can hardly be maintained as absolute. Old truths must be sacrificed to new Christians, who understand that the cowardly act is the courageous one, the immoral act the moral one, for it carries with it the hope of a new life, a new resurrection:

> He flung the door wide open. "See the sunlight out there shining on that field of wheat? That's where I'll take you—out into the sunshine. You shall see it shining on the Bay of Naples. Come, get on your hat; don't take anything more'n you actually need. Leave the past behind you . . ."
>
> "That closes the door on your sufferings," he said, smiling down at her. "Good-by to it all."
>
> The baby laughed and stretched out its hands toward the light.
>
> "Boo, boo!" he cried.
>
> "What's he talking about?"
>
> She smiled in perfect trust and fearlessness, seeing her child's face beside his own. "He says it's beautiful."
>
> "Oh, he does! I can't follow his French accent."
>
> She smiled again, in spite of herself. Will shuddered with a thrill of fear, she was so weak and worn. But the sun shone on the dazzling, rustling wheat, the fathomless sky, blue as a sea, bent above them—and the world lay before them.

Consistently enough with this reversal of moral current, and but one-hundred years after the fact of freedom, the New World surrenders its tired, its worn, its tempest tossed to the haven of a hopefully less brutal Old World. But for those who are aware of the barriers, for whom there is a knowledge or an intuition of a closed existence and an entrapment, there can be no escape; there can be neither purpose nor passion, as this is the way the world will end. Resignation is their only strength; pathos, their only commitment: "'These people live lives but little higher than their cattle—are forced to live so. Their hopes and aspirations are crushed out, their souls are twisted and deformed just as toil twists and deforms their bodies.'" And this waste is all the more pathetic and poignant, for life incongruously ebbs not far removed from nature's pulsations. In his prose of contrast, Garland writes:

> The sky was magically beautiful over all this squalor and toil and bitterness, from five till seven—a moving hour. Again the falling sun streamed in broad banners across the valleys; again the blue mist lay far down the Coolly over the river; the cattle called from the hills in the moistening sonorous air; the bells came in a pleasant tangle of sound; the air pulsed with the deepening chorus of katydids and other nocturnal singers.
>
> Sweet and deep as the very springs of his life was all this to the soul of the elder brother; but in the midst of it, the younger man, in ill-smelling clothes and great boots that chafed his feet, went out to milk the cows,—on whose legs the flies and mosquitoes swarmed, bloated with blood,—to sit by the hot side of a cow and be lashed with her tail as she tried frantically to keep the savage insects from eating her raw.

Despair is the property of naturalism and death is its end, but the celebration of life is its counterpoint; and Garland held to this double vision of man's existence throughout his Middle Border years.

Notes

1. The first sentence of Rod Horton and Herbert Edwards' chapter on "Literary Naturalism" in *Backgrounds of American Literary Thought* (New York, 1952), conveys the idea of their entire discussion: "Naturalism in literature is the product of despair" (p. 246). Vernon Parrington, in *Main Currents of American Thought* (New York, 1946), III, 323 ff., catalogues the criteria of the naturalistic novel and also stresses its philosophical determinism and pessimistic attitude; Lars Ahnebrink does the same in his *The Beginnings of Naturalism in American Fiction* (Cambridge, Mass., 1950). Henry Steele Commager chooses the same emphasis of despair when he insists that "It was because the air of the nineties and of the new century was already heavy with pessimism that artists found it so easy to take refuge in scientific doctrines which seemed to provide some ultimate justification for that pessimism" *The American Mind* (New Haven, 1950), pp. 108–109. Even Donald Pizer, who takes issue with the simplistic view—naturalism equals despair—has little to contribute to a complex view other than the obvious remainder that the naturalist also discovers in this world of desperation "those qualities of man usually associated with the heroic or adventurous, such as acts of violence and passion, involving sexual adventure or bodily strength" "Nineteenth-Century American Naturalism: An Essay in Definition," *Bucknell Review*, XIII (1965), 2.
2. Since my purpose is not to present an analysis of Garland's individual works, but to create a montage of his naturalistic world, I have dispensed with the footnoting of direct quotations and have paraphrased many passages with the intention always in mind to remain faithful to the tone, feeling, and thought of the original. The impression that follows is gathered from the stories Garland wrote *circa* 1890 and collected in *Main-Travelled Roads* (New York, 1891) and *Prairie Folks* (Chicago, 1895).

George Garrett

1929–

George Palmer Garrett, Jr., was born in Orlando, Florida, on June 11, 1929, and was educated at Sewanee Military Academy and Hill School before entering Princeton University in 1947. After graduating in 1952, he saw military service in Europe, returning to Princeton to take an M.A. in 1956. He has taught at many institutions, including the University of Virginia, Columbia University, and the University of Michigan.

Garrett's first publication, *The Reverend Ghost: Poems* (1957), won him the *Sewanee Review* fellowship in poetry and the Prix de Rome of the American Academy of Arts and Letters. *King of the Mountain*, a collection of stories, appeared in 1958, and his first novel, *The Finished Man*, one year later. A Ford Foundation grant in drama enabled him to work on *Garden Spot, U.S.A.*, produced in Houston in 1962, but since then, apart from screenplays, he has concentrated on poetry and fiction.

Garrett's biggest success to date, the historical novel *Death of the Fox*, was published in 1971, and his latest novel, *The Succession: A Novel of Elizabeth and James*, in 1983. Notable among his collections of short stories is *Cold Ground Was My Bed Last Night* (1964). *The Collected Poems of George Garrett* appeared in 1984.

Garrett has also edited poetry and fiction by new authors, and was poetry editor of the *Transatlantic Review* from 1958 to 1971. An Episcopalian, he is married with three children.

Works

SHORT STORIES

This first book by George Garrett ⟨*King of the Mountain*⟩ begins in innocence, with a boy's whimper, and ends in evil, with a bang. Long before the bang comes you will know that the author is out of the top of the literary drawer.

Mr. Garrett is aware, as was the young Hemingway, of the attraction of the first person singular and the second plural ("Ask me why I pick that time and I'll tell you"), of the sense of immediacy and intimacy the confidential technique can produce, of the power it has, like the sudden use of Christian names, to engage your full attention. But Mr. Garrett is no mere charmer. In some, twenty stories he says more, and more forcefully, than is commonly said in as many full-length novels. Every page of *King of the Mountain* rings true, and the author has some profound and terrible tales to tell.

The subjects of the stories can be roughly divided between father-son relationships and war, or rather the effects of war upon its survivors. Some stories are likely to make the middle-aged feel old. "Our generation," says the narrator of "The Seacoast of Bohemia," which is Greenwich Village, "had come to life after the war." For Mr. Garrett, who comes from Florida, there have been two wars: the American Civil War and Hitler's war. For those to whom memories of the Kaiser's war are still very much alive, it may come as something of a shock to learn that Garrett himself is an Occupation veteran who will be 30 next year.

His is the generation that was conceived in the Depression, "that anxious time" when, in the center of Florida, the scene of the title-story, a child learned the meaning of bitterness by having to watch as a mob beat his father into a cripple for publicly criticizing the Ku Klux Klan. This story has something of the chilling violence, the authority and the power of the work of Robert Penn Warren and James Baldwin. That no Negro figures prominently in its pages, that no one is likely to guess the awful irony of its denouement, only enhances the story's stature as a work of art.

Blurb writers are unpredictable people. Here only the first three stories are mentioned by name: the two very brief ones, about women, are perhaps the least memorable in the volume, while the third, a tale of courage and cowardice involving a boy and his father, is described as having "apparent in every word . . . the surge of adolescence within the boy." Readers allergic to surges should turn a deaf ear.

For most people, I think, it's the bang with which this book ends that will remain longest in the memory. These are Occupation stories appearing collectively under the title: "What's the Purpose of the Bayonet?" "The Art of Courtly Love" is about a D.P., a German refugee war-widow in Austria whom the American narrator is determined to seduce. Which he does. Only to discover that the woman has an Austrian lover. How the American then behaves makes reading only a few degrees less appalling than the behavior of Americans to Americans and Austrians to Austrians in the seven blood-and-terror pages that follow.

As indictments of war, of the military system, these three short tales talk very loud. Courage of a high order, moreover, was required to write them, for if you write in the first person, and as truly as Mr. Garrett, you are likely to be associated with your "I." But this author is out to fool no one. As the American lover says: "You can fool yourself quicker in a dozen ways than it takes to tell about it." And he knows that what he has said is a cliché.—JAMES STERN, "With a Whimper and a Bang," *NYTBR*, March 2, 1958, p. 4

Mr. Garrett's stories ⟨in *King of the Mountain*⟩ are derived from boyhood, under-graduate days, and service in the U.S. Army of Occupation in Austria. His experiences come to rest in a quiet academic life haunted by memories of Europe's defeated and the manners of conquerors. The book is marked by a unity of theme and comment, and has a distinction of finish and style. It is important as one of the few serious literary efforts arising from the "occupation-generation". While the question of the individual versus the fixed system does not interest the author, he is sensitive to human relations and the effect on personality and behaviour of the military or professorial career. He does not share the melodramatic despair which has characterized so many American novels about U.S. army life after the last war.

. . . His stories are neat and calculated, embodying all

the principles of short story construction taught in creative writing courses. They are so neat that their point is often sacrificed, as in the final anecdote, for example, entitled "Torment". The sudden climax of this story (and of the entire book) is a visually described scene which should be a synthesis of horror, a picture worthy of Dante's inferno: to the strain of military band music Austrian police beat a group of prostitutes bloody because "There is no severe penalty for prostitution. They try to scare them." This image is meant to illustrate the degree to which men's souls can be warped by continual exposure to casual cruelty, the sadistic hangover of modern war. But the objective brevity of style makes the incident read like a shocked undergraduate's account of an orgy at a fraternity dance.

Mr. Garrett has given great care to choosing words and polishing sentences, which unfortunately leads to flatness rather than a sharp pithiness of impact. Many descriptions fall within the "pale bulging muscles" and "broad powerful body" type of thing: Too often the "right" word is the ordinary word.

Least successful is the group of stories about American girls entitled "Four Women." They never come into focus and the symbolism on which they lean seems forced. For instance, a girl pregnant while unhappily married watches a carnival strong man break out of chains, then rejoins her faithless husband. The failure of these stories lies in the author's lack of understanding; he has created types, not characters with dimension. Mr. Garrett is more convincing when he portrays the victimized women of occupied Europe. Compassion does help a writer.—JOAN FOX, *CF*, Aug. 1958, p. 119

NOVELS

George Garrett's *The Finished Man* is about the imperfect world of politics, that border land between high aspiration and low cunning. The fastidious shrink from its compromises, its calculation, its histrionic self-exploitation; others enjoy the tactical surrender of principle, the illusionist's sense of risk and power, the frankness of open ambition. Judge Royle is a man who has come up from poverty, fought his way into political office, and married well. He is a man of just and violent feeling, directness and courage; he has been disenchanted in the way his wife has been sold to him by a distinguished but selfish family, but he has sacrificed his wife and children to his own drive. Jojo, his elder son, has drifted away into a nocturnal voice on a disk-jockey program, as jealously free of commitment as his father has been dedicated to it. The Royles cannot accept the cost of politics: Mrs. Royle and her daughter at the close are leaving for Europe and the comforts of a gracious past.

Mike Royle attaches himself to Senator Parker in a fight for reelection. Parker has created an image of himself which he has come to believe. As success begins to slip away he is ready to adopt any device for holding it. He introduces Vivian Blanch as a campaign adviser; she is an unhappy woman, incapable of simplicity or love, who has made herself a kind of priestess of the unreal. The novel is concerned with Parker's campaign, which opens with a shrewd double-crossing of his opponent and is met with similar maneuvers, the worst of which involves the sacrifice of Judge Royle's life in a futile diversionary candidacy.

The dominant note of the book is its insistence upon a double view of man; he is, in Frost's words, a "diminished thing," and what to make of him is Mike Royle's problem. "This isn't an age for heroes," Jojo says. "Whenever we get a hero, he's a caricature." Or there is Mike's view of the defeated Senator: "This isn't how a tragedy ends up—King Lear dead drunk, dreaming that he's a cave man." (The Senator's cuff links have comic and tragic masks upon them.) There is the wryness of Atkins, the reporter ("the most beautiful thing in the world is a stack of clean laundry") who is perpetually affronted by finding "a virtue is just a vice in disguise." Or the "deep hurt" of Judge Royle "gored on the horns of appearance and reality," raising pigs in his retirement ("The stink of a man—once you get your nose trained to detect it—is the foulest thing in creation"). The possibility of truth keeps getting lost in the absurd gesture or theatrical rhetoric: "No matter how naked or honest you got, you still felt dressed up like the emperor in the fairy tale."

Garrett might have done better to dramatize these perceptions rather than give them so many voices. The action is complex and lively; but it always wants to be discussed, like a drama school play, after the performance. Mike Royle's coming to awareness is not, after all, very interesting in itself, if only because he seems to exist for the sake of the observations he can make. To have built those observations into the pattern of action and image would have made for a far more stylized book but one with stronger coherence and perhaps subtler characterization. For in this version the characters tend to take positions, and they soon flatten into spokesmen or rather obvious symbols. Mike Royle, like many counterparts in recent novels, is so enmeshed in the action as to discern its import only slowly and painfully; yet he is sufficiently detached to expatiate in terms of high generality, laced with vivid colloquialism. since he has neither a strongly defined personality (such as Bellow and Nabokov have lately presented) nor a subtle and original mind (such as C. P. Snow can suggest), he becomes a latter-day Man of Sensibility. And when he strikes a somewhat febrile and ironic note, he does not count the words. But Mike Royle is scarcely the worst of his kind, and the book has much in it to demand strong praise. There are several fine dramatic scenes, a few memorable characters, and altogether a richness of conception that can afford to be wasteful. There have been better first novels, but this is the kind that promises an interesting, and perhaps important, career.—MARTIN PRICE, "Six Recent Novels," *YR*, Sept. 1959, pp. 126–27

The "Fox" of George Garrett's splendid new novel ⟨*Death of the Fox*⟩ is Sir Walter Ralegh, that colorful and elusive figure—soldier, seafarer, historian, poet, courtier—whose life seems "a figment of the renaissance-imagination" and whose death marked the end of England's most glorious age. *Death of the Fox* is no ordinary work of historical fiction, no sword-and-buckler romance after the manner of Shellabarger and Costain. The creation of a gifted lyric poet, it is not a novel in any conventional sense at all, but rather a moving elegy to a vanished ideal of grace and heroism, and more essentially a lyric celebration of the transforming, revivifying powers of the imagination, through which the past may be made to live again and to nourish the present moment. Which is not to say that the book is without characters and a story. From the pages of *Death of the Fox* Ralegh emerges vivid and multifarious, seen, like Elizabeth in her secret chamber of mirrors, reflected both in the fluid stream of his own imagined consciousness and in the thoughts of those whose lives he touched in various ways: Henry Yelverton, James the King, Sir Lewis Stukely, Bacon, the mariners he sailed with and the headsman who killed him. Garrett has made Ralegh believable as a man—brave yet crafty, beset by fears yet playful and affectionate—but it is equally clear that, as he came to haunt the corners of Garrett's imagination during the twenty years in which the book was being conceived and finally written, Ralegh was more an idea than an individual. He became for Garrett a means of defining the nobility of the human spirit and the powers of the human imagination. For the true subject of *Death of the Fox* is the meaning of Time, flowing like the Thames from the heart of England past Windsor and Hampton and the Tower to the sea, ever changing yet ever the same, connecting past and present, disappearing into eternity; and the meaning of Poetry, like Adam's dream, to which Keats compared the poetic imagination, endowing the shadowy forms of history with palpable life. In our own unrelievedly prosaic and inconoclastic times, when noise is music and to burn a flag a poetic act, Garrett's book is a refreshing anomaly. The virtues it prizes are those only Faulkner in our century could manage to evoke convincingly—those "ancient and immitigable truths of the heart": courage and honor, piety and love, wit and eloquence and, rarest of all, wisdom. It is the *idea* of Ralegh that matters here, for the man himself, steady and fine and eloquent in affliction, is ultimately admirable for what he implies about the possibility of dignity and grace in a fallen world. He is real enough, as I have said—no fugitive from a latter-day *Faerie Queene*—but he is also a kind of metaphor, flesh and blood enacting the dream that gave them life.

"Dream" suggests the quality and tone of *Death of the Fox*, and it is the word Garrett himself has chosen to hint at the meaning of the book, whose subject, finally, is the relationship between fact and fiction, history and the imagination. In an essay on the evolution of his novel which he contributed to *New Literary History* in the spring of 1970—an essay entitled, "Dreaming with Adam: Notes on Imaginary History"—Garrett saw his problem in writing the book as one of approaching "the renaissance-imagination," of which Ralegh in a sense was the creation, through a commitment of his own imagination: "The proper theme of the work, then, is the human imagination, the possibility, limits and variety of imaginative experience . . . the possibility of imagining lives and spirits of other human beings, living or dead, without assaulting their essential and, anyway, ineffable mystery, to dream again in recapitulation the dream of Adam. . . ." The haunting, fluent lyricism of Garrett's prose—a narrative voice reminiscent of Faulkner's incantatory evocations of past time, yet simpler in its rhythms and more vividly poetic—is well suited to this purpose. The book has the quality of revery, of the flow and movement of the mind insulated from the disturbing pressures of actuality and musing upon bright, pure shapes of its own creation; it is not by chance, surely, that the opening chapters present Yelverton, James, and Ralegh in their beds, caught between waking and sleeping, in those moments when time past takes possession of the mind to become part of the present. This is not a narrative of action but of thought. The one *act* of the book occurs on the final page: the sudden blow of the axe that ended Ralegh's life and, fittingly, ends as well the poet's dream of that life.

There is action and life aplenty in *Death of the Fox*, but it is not of the swashbuckling variety. This is a work of art, capacious, profound, exquisite. Garrett imaginatively summons up an age that has had an irresistible allure for lovers of history and literature; the research required to make this astonishing bit if conjuring credible would have cooled the ardor of the most zealous professional scholar. Not only the events of Ralegh's life and times, but the descriptions of costumes and furniture, buildings and sailing ships are accurately detailed. But the facts are there primarily to engage the fancy, through which alone the characters of fiction, or the figures of history, may live and move and have their being. One is *there*, sensibly, with James at Burghley's estate in Hertfordshire, or with Bacon at York House in the Strand, or with Ralegh at Winchester or in the Tower. It is the kind of translation from abstraction to sensuous reality that one hopes for in reading fiction, and that one so rarely finds—a translation effected, like history itself, through the play of the imagination. Like Ralegh, Garrett is both historian and poet. But because he is a poet primarily, *Death of the Fox* will do for the reader what John Stow's *Survey* did for the imprisoned Ralegh, through the imagination liberating him from the tyranny of the present moment to move through a terrain forever closed to him in actuality, substantiating, as Garrett has Ralegh express it, "the dark dream of a world." This is one of the most beautiful and moving novels I have read in a long while.—MARTIN C. BATTESTIN, *GR*, Winter 1971, pp. 511–13

F. H. GRIFFIN TAYLOR

From "A Point in Time, a Place in Space"

Sewanee Review, Spring 1969, pp. 308–12

George Garrett would seem to share with Juvenal an appreciation of the virtues of the backwater, an admiration for simple loyalties, and a propensity for what Winston Churchill called the harsh laugh of the soldier. In the note with which he prefaces ⟨*For a Bitter Season*⟩, he says: "I resist a desire to leap upon the circus bandwagon, the float of one 'school' or another. For the aim of these is to make the poet, whether as prophet or charmer, into a respected or respectable citizen. At the moment of Truth the Priests and Pharisees, like the King and the Procurator and even the dancing Princess, are conspicuously absent. Under the circumstances it seems better to kneel in the shadow with the rest of the common soldiers and shoot craps, better in fact to crap out and lose all when the prize is beyond price."

Mr. Garrett's allusion to the soldiers' game of chance is not accidental. Elsewhere he has said that "the only certainty is perpetual uncertainty: knowledge that the only thing unchanging is change itself." In stating what some scientist have propounded for a generation or so, Mr. Garrett is deliberately accepting a notion that belongs to his own present. It is a notion Robbe-Grillet has popularized; and Flaubert made it a central theme of *L'Éducation sentimentale*. But where Flaubert (like to a certain extent, perhaps, Mr. Lowell) detested the men and women he saw around him, Mr. Garrett has observed that "there is no text that says that God cannot look with love upon the stupid, the cruel, the vulgar, the hypocritical and the guilty." Mr. Garrett is a Southerner who, after having lived in other places and countries, has decided to live in the South, and has committed himself to his native region in fact as well as in name. In this he follows the example of, among others, William Faulkner and Flannery O'Connor. He does not, as perhaps he should not, attempt to explicate the principles on which he takes his stand, but he is very clear as to what he does not accept. He especially rejects "the grand hypocritical spirit which erupted in New England"—though presumably he does not deny the love of God to those who fostered it. Of his fiction, Professor William Robinson has written (in *Red Clay Reader*) that it "speaks for a hard-nosed moral realism which . . . achieves its happiness as art by exposing and accepting 'a less exalted view of man' ". As a poet Mr. Garrett is committed not to ideas nor abstract concepts, but to a place and its people.

Mr. Garrett has chosen to stand on familiar ground. He is not unconscious of his task to give shape to and if necessary to defend the views of his region as he sees it in the present. Acceptance of the present seems to be central to his position. He does not dwell on the past at all. At the same time he also exemplifies that *prise de conscience* of men of letters signalized by Baudelaire's proclamation of "*ma blessure*", since which the locus of the struggle has been at least partly in the artist himself. Thus a recurrent theme in these poems is the need to recognize one's own imperfection, one's own disfigurement. The "wounded man" in the poem of that name wishes to hide until his scars are healed.

> Oh, I will be back again, bright-eyed,
> singing a terrible new song.

But this will not work. He must confront "his pain's true name" and live with it. Learning to accept disfigurement, shame, obesity, the frailities of advancing age—these are the constantly recurring themes of these poems. The poet also accepts the occasional ignominy and the contumely not infrequently the lot of the artist in our time, not infrequently, he suggests, deserved. Yet Mr. Garrett is not cut off from others; he is not lonely nor isolated, as Mr. Lowell is, for as a Southerner he is always aware of the society of which he is a part. He perceives the social fabric and his place in it with a sense that never sleeps. Thus, for instance, a favorite subject with him is Susanna and the elders; but it is the elders who especially fascinate him. So too in "Ventriloquist's Dummy":

> Let me tell you a thing or two.
> But first you must learn to bear
> with stiff ways and a splintery tongue.

Images of man as wooden crowd the poems. Mr. Garrett is especially fond of Daphne, patron goddess of all wooden soldiers. The poet too is wooden, but

> Believe me, I'd rather talk
> in my own voice even though it is most like
> the creak and groan of trees in the wind,
> no more and no less.

He calls his book *For a Bitter Season*, and with justice. It is singular for its compassion and affection for others. His laughter is sometimes wry, and sometimes reminiscent of François Villon, especially in "Romantic" and "Some Women". Man is flawed by his vanity, his inconsistency, his blindness in love, his folly, his death. The poet accepts these things and accepts the place in which he finds himself and has chosen to be, but without abandoning hope—"we have lived too long with fear"—for out of these things and this place grow his poems, his children, and all the things he loves. The place he lives in may sometimes most resemble a compost heap, but he loves it for what grows in it.

> And we are fountains of foolish tears
> to flood and green the world again.

Mr. Garrett's interest in all that goes on around him is mirrored in the variety of his poems. He does not disdain the trivial. On the contrary, he seems to have a special affection for, and shows much of his humor and gaiety, in the poems he has deliberately made to be throwaways. They are not properly in the category of light verse, because in them one senses that the poet's intention is to say, "Let's not be so solemn, let's not write every line as though it were imperishable when we know very well that much of our verse, all of it perhaps, will, like ourselves, perish very soon." They serve to remind us that any poet's best efforts owe much to the countless other poems that have been written by him and discarded along the way; owe much to the poems that have been written by others, too.

> And if we're going to tell the truth,
> we'd better gut the pocketbooks
> of all the poets who tried and failed.
> As we pass by their honored biers,
> we'll pick the pennies from their eyes.

> This is, however, merely petty theft
> in an age when thievery
> is so refined it calls itself
> Success.

He neither advocates nor condemns this practice. He simply recognizes it in "Egyptian Gold". In this poem about the pickpockets of Rome, and in "Crows at Paestum", Mr. Garrett's gifts show to their best advantage. Both poems move effortlessly from the simple (often for Mr. Garrett at least faintly ridiculous) to the sublime. In both, on the deserted hillside overlooking Paestum and in the crowded Roman piazza, the poet sees himself as part of the teeming present and the speaking past. He yearns for no more perfect state of affairs. He eyes the present with all its imperfections and leaves the reader in no doubt about what he approves and what he does not. It is plain that he has known the loneliness and estrangement men experience in a mechanized society. Knowing the metropolis and its undeniable importance for the artist, he has elected to live in and write out of his own country where men are loved or hated as men and not as fleeting abstractions.

Having chosen his ground, then what? This is a time when the poet's station has been usurped by the synthetic voice, anonymous, superficial, corporate, and irresponsible, of the weekly newsmagazine; yet also a time when poets are scribbling more furiously and knowledgeably than ever. Mr. Garrett is tempted by the desire

> not to add another voice
> to the damned cacophony
> cacophony of the damned
> makers of verses,

and he does not exempt himself from being one of them. It is good to learn in "Manifesto" that he has, if not overcome, at least decided to profit by the temptation. In wealthy countries poets proliferate. According to James Russell Lowell, in his essay on Lessing, there were said to be eight hundred authors living and writing in Zürich in 1760. Not all at any time have had the resolution, the generosity of spirit, and the gaiety displayed in this volume by Mr. Garrett.

JOSEPH W. TURNER

From "History and Imagination in George Garrett's *Death of the Fox*"

Critique, Volume 22, Number 2 (1980), pp. 37–46

To get Ralegh right, as Garrett sees it, entails preserving the mysteries and contradictions of his character. No single narrative perspective nor uncontested theory will suffice. Rather, *Death of the Fox* piles interpretation upon interpretation, capturing multiple responses to the man with constant shifts in point of view. Though the focus is on Ralegh's progress to the scaffold, the novel follows all of the characters, great and small, whose fortunes intersect at this moment and whose attitudes toward the Fox—both in the present and in former times—color their perceptions and determine their actions.

To Yelverton, the King's cautious Attorney General who will conduct the hearing, Ralegh is one of those great men, "first to catch the eye" because they "rise above their peers like the tallest tree of the forest" but also, and for the same reason, first "to be cut down."[1] Imprisoned in the Tower with his fate already determined, the Fox can do him no harm, Yelverton believes, since the once mighty courtier has squandered his position and power on vain hopes. The King, by contrast, still hates and fears Ralegh, even now that the Fox is old and seemingly at the King's mercy. Terrified of treason and assassinations, having known more than his share of both, James views his prisoner first as a fearless and, therefore, a dangerous man. Between these two extremes, the reflections of other characters cast Ralegh in other lights: that of the hardened soldier and crafty courtier, known to Apsley, Lord Lieutenant of the Tower, who "kept Ralegh more as guest than prisoner" (137); or that of the "poor fellow whom Fortune has ill used," seen by Peter Rush, Yelverton's servant, before he sees the sadly altered Ralegh approaching Westminister (226).

More than simply conveying the diversity of attitudes toward the man, however, these shifting perspectives dramatize the difficulty of ever getting Ralegh right. If to know the Fox is the ambition the novel sets for itself, it is also the riddle each character must solve to attain his own goal. From top to bottom, the characters' success in Ralegh's execution depends on foreseeing the consequences of their actions. Yelverton, who has served the King faithfully, for instance, has every reason to expect continued good fortune, provided he can conduct the sentencing of Ralegh without any embarrassment to James. To prepare for the role, he has studied the mistakes of the King's former attorney, Edward Coke, at Ralegh's first trial in 1603. Having read and re-read the records, much like a careful historian, Yelverton is ready for the Ralegh who had pleaded his case like a lawyer, daring to attack the learned Coke on his own grounds. He understands how Coke had lost control, allowing the Fox to put the King and the Law on trial. If his research has prepared him to foil the Ralegh of old, Yelverton is still no match for the Fox. Expecting a dazzling display of wit and finery, like that in the first trial, he is caught unawares when the hearing turns out to be "brief beyond anticipation." Ralegh appears dressed in old and ill-fitting clothes, looking to all the world like a broken man or poor comedian, and he submits himself to the Court's judgment and the King's mercy, pleading not with words "so much as with his life, his body and soul" (236).

Despite all his research, Yelverton fails to understand the man. All he can see—and this only belatedly—is the similarity amid differences: "Both times Ralegh astonished his antagonists" (235). Had he been more perceptive, he at least could have anticipated his surprise; far better men than Yelverton, after all, had been outfoxed before: "If Coke could not have foreseen how the trial would change beyond strategy and expectation," he observes while reviewing the records, "then no man could" (18). Yelverton, however, does not apply the lesson to himself, believing that his cautious style and worldly wisdom will serve him well. Though these defenses hold to a point, he fails to escape the confrontation with Ralegh unscathed. In his opening remarks, the Attorney General allows himself one flight of fancy—the simile of the falling star, intended at once to exonerate the King and to honor Ralegh: "He has been a star at which all the world has gazed. But stars may fall. . . . Nay, they *must* fall when they trouble the sphere wherein they abide!" (232). Ever the ironic poet, Ralegh seizes the opening; thanking the attorney for the "nice figure of speech," he elaborates the comparison: "A star in the firmament, however bright it may be, is but one of many. We look and behold it in its proper place, and that is sufficient. But mark this: whenever a star falls, it burns so bright it dazzles the eyes of the world" (239–40). Ralegh's gloss of the simile could not have been more prophetic, and if Yelverton's unwilling contribution to his adversary's defense has any irony, it extends with even greater force to James, who was far more perceptive than the cautious lawyer and yet unable or unwilling to fathom the consequences of the execution, even after the Fox had drawn them out for him.

One of the many instances in the novel of the failure to set the imagination free, the scene demonstrates how foolish, if not dangerous, one can be to assume with Yelverton that he has finally "found the keys to the man" (236). The lesson that many of Ralegh's contemporaries learned at their own expense is one that Garrett builds into the structure as well as the action of *Death of the Fox*. Having set out to re-create the last days of Ralegh's life, he intentionally disrupts the narrative to construct a detailed historical framework for his novel. In Part Three, as the soldier, sailor, and courtier converse directly with the reader about Ralegh's life and the reigns of Elizabeth and James, the novelist provides the necessary documented evidence to bring into focus, if not into question, his own interpretation of Ralegh's character. . . .

Instead of solving the riddle of the Fox, Part Three thus compounds our sense of it. Each interpretation takes us closer to the truth and further in the conviction that Ralegh is too imposing a figure, too contradictory and complex, for anyone to see him all at once. Only a composite picture will do, and that imperfectly. Like those who knew Elizabeth but fail to "give true testimony" about the former queen, then, Garrett's many voices in *Death of the Fox* are "all false witnesses." Each is incapable of the whole truth, though the "sum" of their "witnessing may be true" (529). As much as the novel is dedicated to that possibility, however, it preserves in Part Three a sense of its ultimate failure, a testimony to the truth of its subject and its truthfulness to that subject.

Instead of universalizing the particular, then, Garrett reverses the conventional method, moving from the common ground of Ralegh's humanity to the uniqueness of his personality. Were this its only contemporary application, the novel would still be quite an accomplishment—proof that knowledge of the past can enhance the life of the present without weakening or distorting the differences between the two. Yet Garrett pursues the question one step further. Since the goal is to recover the Fox in his individuality, the relevance of the novel comes to be found in the effort to see the world through the eyes of another man in another time. Given that we are moderns, what can we gain in making Ralegh our contemporary? Fashioning him in our own image would be the easiest of tasks, hardly worth doing, since those who remain "clothed in the garments" of their "own concerns" are both imprisoned and impoverished by the refusal to set the imagination free. The proper function of the historical novel, then, becomes the extension of the reader's sensibilities, its relevance residing as much in the act of imaginative sympathy as in the insights it produces: "To live well in the present demands as much imagination as can be mustered," and though "one may choose to deny that one's present world is in any part fictitious," the past "is chiefly fiction and must be imagined before it can exist."[2] . . .

What is remarkable about *Death of the Fox*, then, is not the problems that Garrett had to wrestle with in writing the novel. Any historical novelist faces just as many, if not the same, rhetorical choices. His achievement, rather, lies in the recognition that the difficulties inherent in the genre can be turned to the novelist's advantage, not by overriding them with unchecked claims to imaginative freedom but by incorporating them within the very texture and structure of the novel. Only with such generic self-consciousness can the historical novelist devise an appropriate form for the interplay of history and imagination—no less the essence of his subject than the source of his difficulties.

Notes

1. George Garrett, *Death of the Fox* (Garden City: Doubleday, 1971), p. 16. Subsequent references are to this edition. (Throughout the essay I have followed Garrett's spelling of "Ralegh," if only for consistency.)
2. George Garrett, "Dreaming with Adam: Notes on Imaginary History," *New Literary History*, 1 (1970), 421.

JEAN GARRIGUE

1914–1972

Jean Garrigue was born on December 8, 1914, in Evansville, Indiana; her family name was Garrigus, but she later restored the original French spelling. After graduating with a B.A. from the University of Chicago in 1937, she edited a weekly newspaper before taking an M.A. at the University of Iowa in 1943.

Garrigue's first publication, "Thirty-six Poems and a Few Songs," appeared in *Five Young Poets of 1944*. Following the collection *The Monument Rose* (1953), she won a Rockefeller grant in creative writing in 1954 and other awards, including a Guggenheim Fellowship in 1960. She lived and traveled in Europe for several short periods in the 1950s and 1960s, and was a lecturer and poet-in-residence at a variety of colleges and institutions, including the New School for Social Research in New York, the University of Connecticut, and Smith College. Her poems *Country without Maps* (1964) won her the Emily Clark Balch first prize in 1966.

Apart from poetry, Garrigue also contributed short stories to *Cross-Sections* (1947) and to *New World Writing* (1954). Other volumes of poems include *A Water Walk by Villa d'Este* (1959), *New and Selected Poems* (1967), and *Studies for an Actress* (1973), which appeared after her death of Hodgkins disease on December 27, 1972.

Jean Garrigue's *The Ego and the Centaur* gathers up poems that have been widely published in literary quarterlies. Miss Garrigue writes with disarming smoothness and ease, but is skilled at the unexpected and short-circuiting phrase—the phrase that suddenly plunges the poem into obscurity. She is good at detail, but the reader is constantly being thwarted by her labored nouns, verbs, and adjectives, her thumping resolutions, and her lack of transition. She is evidently a pupil of Wallace Stevens, but her emotional key is fixed at a medium position, and she states emotion rather than projects it. —LOUISE BOGAN, *NY*, Sept. 13, 1947, pp. 118–19

As when in the wheelhouse of the Onawa one elects the north west passage to great San Juan Island, heading through discreet passages to Friday Harbor, and consults the chart with intent to leave a Red Light on our left and turns on automatic compass as one makes headway, and trusting to slither through Deception Pass, feeling the roil of waters on the flanks, the dangerous turbulence, forgetting for the time the trials of navigators from Vancouver's time, happy to have the tide as aid from stern, so one looks to the chart of female poets of this century, not forgetting historical markers of previous days, and, as one steers the long cruise through beautiful islands of the mind, putting over a boat perchance in a blue bay to scout out a land of humming-birds; so one studies the marked headlands of creative effort, and chooses a course where it is deep.

Deeps to the eye are not deeps to the chart, for, as the eye divines a blue-green vastness of fair water ahead and, if sense were trusted, would turn the ship straight across a broad bent, nevertheless intelligence directs the eye to the knowledge of the chart-maker, accepting to turn from false fathoms which would wreck him were his eyes trusted, to the usable deeps, as known, in this vast expanse of water surrounding the beautiful sky-buoyed North West Islands.

Thus one approaches female poets, as a voyage of wondrous potentiality, for as they are fair, so they are a voyage in blue depth with green islands of resinous cedar and scent of the myrtle. So they are perilous if erroneously approached; so do they yield riches to the senses of the true mariner, if their secrets are observed and respected so that they may be fully savored.

There is a restraint on the sea, a withholding of total expense of being, lest the latent power of the waters extend one in emergency. We stand ready, but do not wish reproof. We ride upon the sea of poetry in the same way, in a system of tensions, able to be free, as on a voyage of delicate and strong enchantment among enticing prospects, soul-satisfying progressions, a charged complexity of enjoyment.

The new poetry of Jean Garrigue ⟨in *The Monument Rose*⟩ is such a sea and such an enchantment, a voyage of hers in perfections and balances of self-saying, in waters clean and lithe that give us vigorous joy to ride their new-found, fresh-seen metaphors, and feel that honest dance of mind and heart of hers, in its cool, free play, and deep sincerity.

"Dialogue á Quatre" is of such elegance and such perfection that it sits upon the page as if it might be three hundred years old or more, out of Spenser maybe, something timeless. "Song for a Marriage" and "Address to the Migrations" are Garrigue-true too. Other poems have statements somewhat in the manner of her anthologized pieces. Her overtones are of Hopkins and Thomas. The last line of "Song for a Marriage," "That strike of the moon's white side down Babylon," brings Crane to life again. And if on our voyage of her fine individuality and wit-inducement our eyes are struck by virid, embased, enshaped, swound, aestival, orgulous, Florilegium, Arcana coelestia, it is the sun-diamond glitter on the sea.—RICHARD EBERHART, "In the Blue Depth," *NR*, Nov. 2, 1953, p. 29

It takes but a few lines of Jean Garrigue's second volume ⟨*The Monument Rose*⟩ to hear a really significant voice sing out with deep internal drama and verbal excitement. Her book opens on an intense level, for her poetry is as immediately vibrant in structure and language as it is solid in its emotional intention. There is variety, and an air for the tomorrow of a book in the color and sensuality of her mood-driven interplays of meaning.

There is a continuity here that remains, startling you with its variations and heady nuances. And if Jean Garrigue bears any resemblance to Dylan Thomas and Rimbaud, it is a resemblance that all good poets have when the language they use serves to unite them despite their own differences and distinctions.

Unfortunately, so much has been taken out of the entertainment values of poetry by the interjection of all spurious intellect or an oblique front for servicing all the winds of politics, that poetry has often become a homeless bastard. It has either been in hock to a blueprint and a social program, or it has been a literary pilgrim waiting at some theological pawnshop. Necessarily this review rests on a contrast of intentions. Seen from this point of view, juxtaposed to Rosten's work, Garrigue's poetry is a distinct joy before it is everything else in the human catalogue and the literary program. It is poetry first, exciting, intoxicating, and even entertaining, if I may be allowed that happy thought.

Her line, long and fluent, falls cleanly and clearly in its Elizabethan yet modern control. Too well aware of the need for vision, Garrigue says, with elegiac soberness—

> Winds blow up, bear down, the gulfs are torn
> We ride the nether music of the fall.
> In instance is the vision: words, be blood
> Or we are murmurs to the gravestone knell.
> Ghosts of our gods, ancestral fall!
> She holds my earth there in her arms this while
> Where slips the old moon from the new moon's shell.
> Blow night to me and let come this hour
> That strike of the moon's white side down Babylon.

Nature, like love, is the universal catch-all. But when Garrigue writes on either theme she employs her vast sensorium and obtains some beautiful relationships.

> That blue, that dark, dark, green-dark blue
> By this mid-sunlight pierced whose shafts and rifts
> From delicate armories thinned do bend
> Across the dredged green crest.

In the same poem, later, she says:

> That is dark-blue, that is dark-green blue,
> Flesh of timber wrung through
> As lilac enflasked in its smoky color
> Gives up on the white alphabet of the river—

And about love, this:

> What's love that's always strong?
> Beasts from the Antipodes spring down!
> And hoydens leap like lions over beaches!
> Love is the friend whose faithfulness is wit,
> Is best your mimic when you tongue-tied vow,
> Aloof when you win and surly when you stammer,
> Cries I do not understand you, and
> Corrects your right answer.
>
> Indulges with contempt your sweet tooth at the fair,
> Gives you fearful rides on the roller coaster,
> Greets you like a sovereign when you've come
> An hour, but puts the green toad in your bed
> Just as soon thereafter.
> Your sober love turns tomcat in the bar.

Being inventive, sensual, and lyrical—word-inventive—her language is often just as startling as her imagery and her original phrasing, the essential elements if poetry is to remain alive and not become just a sentimental sewer. Even originality is not enough if it is merely sensational or extravagant; but when originality is allied to a critical intelligence and is imbedded in the systematic values of poetry, then poetry renews itself and the reader, adding another page to literature's uncertain history. Jean Garrigue has done that, if modestly, with a dignified attitude and an exciting air.—HARRY ROSKOLENKO, "The Shadow Is Not the Rose," *Poetry*, Dec. 1953, pp. 177–79

Once ⟨Jean Garrigue⟩ . . . has established her ornate, periodic style, she maintains it with remarkable skill and grace ⟨in *A Water Walk by Villa d'Este*⟩. Here is the beginning of "Primer of an Italian Journey," a sort of variation upon "L'Allegro":

> And here is sorrow, pleasure's son,
> Come on soon and once again.
> What did I do to beget him?
> Greenness grows; on hills with towers
> Fields are patched in royal squares
> Of the reddest flower known.
> And in those wide-spaced groves
> Vines strung taut between the trees
> Make such hazards down the rows
> A tennis-courting bird might play
> At flying gauntlets every way
> While vines strung up and down the boughs
> Turn simple tree forks into lyres.

That is lovely; one could open the book to almost any page and set one's finger upon just such a passage.

And that is one of the troubles: so much elegance, so much eloquence, so much polish. Soon the lines stop making sense; one is carried away much as he might be with Poe. Or perhaps one needs to be carried farther. At any rate, I have a sense of being between stools.

Miss Garrigue appears to have learned from Milton much of how to sustain a long sentence, spun out and strung to dry over the line endings until it envelops whole paragraphs. At times she even seems ready to challenge him in the non-stop sentence derby. And it is true that Milton's mature language has qualities of elegance often unrelated to the qualities of the thing he is talking about. But that is because, as he tells us, he cannot fully describe that greater Reality which is his full subject. After making every attempt to describe it philosophically, he must go on (through the music of his verse) to suggest that the real meaning is something beyond anything he can ever *say*.

Miss Garrigue's language, similarly, directs us from the thing talked about. Yet she makes no more extended attempt to define a greater Reality than what we find in "The Rose Tree":

> There was an instant when delight
> Lived for the pure rose tree
> Then all became as one
> With the rose tree in the sun
> Time, and you were overcome
> By such transparency.
> Time, and let me dream
> This instant may come again.

At the same time, her language is not so magical, so completely dislocated an incantation, that we forget the denotation of the words to be swept up into celebration—as we might be in some of the poems of Dylan Thomas (another of her influences) or of Hart Crane. To say the same thing another way, the eloquence of Milton and Thomas distracts us from the thing being said only to redirect us toward the true object and meaning (the Reality of God or the reality of our own exultation). Miss Garrigue's eloquence seems an end in itself. There is a danger that all objects and meanings may evaporate; there is a triple danger that in this absence the subject will come to be the virtuoso performance of the poet herself. This would be exactly the wrong sort of distraction.

But this sounds unkinder than what I mean. These are good poems and show Miss Garrigue as a very large talent. She herself suggests that she is aware of the problem; one section of the book contains simpler, somewhat Frost-derivative poems which try to break away from the rolling, easy cadences of the rest of the book. I don't think this solves the problem, but I think that we have every reason to expect some remarkable poems to come out of her struggles with it.—W. D. SNODGRASS, *HdR*, Spring 1960, pp. 128–29

Jean Garrigue . . . throws herself somewhat too willingly on the mercy of the court ⟨in *A Water Walk by Villa d'Este*⟩. Single lines, sudden perfect phrasings, real poetic breath—should one not be content with this? In the abstract there is more in Miss Garrigue than in many contemporary poets, yet it remains abstract and fragmentary, a playing of scales rather than a virtuoso incantation:

> Your name wearing water in cloud and flame
> The world bearing flowers out of your name
> Or in the dim sleep nothing borne
> But the sound of waters racing your blood:
> And the running of waters and the dim
> Bemused confession of waters fortelling your
> coming.

She takes too much after her paradigm of water; one is never sure of the vessel, the total form of the poem. Yet the gathering up of the last verse's movement through the interposition of a second adjective ("Bemused"), and the syncopation of waters (6th and 7th syllables) with waters (7th and 8th syllables) shows her ability to make us forget meaning in favor of movement, though this may create meanings of its own:

> Bells and their tongues wait
> Birds in the Bell of the bush their small songs halt.

The birds are suddenly seen as the *tongues* of the bush. A whole poem may be spun out of her sense for movement—"Night talk" is the cadenza of an exceptionally airy imagination, which trusts itself to the air as her poem on the fountains of the Villa d'Este to water. Her finest effects come while forging a rhythm which slows time, which goes against nature's will for change present even on the calmest day:

> These days, so calm and perfect, haunt my blood,
> Palms surging, fine blades in the wind,
> Palms surging, fountains blowing, hurt my blood
> By worn stone seats, by grassy obelisk,
> Or by those walls where stand anonymous gods,
> Broken of hand or of the living parts

But she cannot sustain the moment, and does not have Keats' mythology to explore its dialectic.

Two poems, in fact, the "Discourse from Firenze" and "Soliloquy in the Cemetery of Père Lachaise," deplore the loss of the ancient gods and the freedom of the Renaissance or Keatsian artist who took from the heaven of man's imagination whatever he wanted, Christian or Pagan or mingled forms. She calls on the cemetery ornaments of Père Lachaise to come alive, not for the sake of the buried but for the sake of poetry. Yet she knows (although she does not always accept her own conclusion) that the modern poet must walk naked. "The passion is to keep the ignorance up," she remarks in her most finished poem ("The land we did not know"). Reduced to the moments and figures of her own mind, she runs the same dangers as Denise Levertov. Her psychological songs (e.g. "I sought from love") are not succesful in replacing the Allegory of Love with modern and subtler dramatizations. When she does not frankly strow "The flower of the moment upon the river/Our only libation," she skirts the mock classical, as in "A garland of trumpets." But the latter is saved by its meditative rhythm, the slow-motion effects most organic in her:

> Held, beheld all in a dream,
> The fishermen dark as the sea,
> Foam-dappled, wading the shallows
> Clear to transparency,
> Lightly driving their boats out to sea.

The rhythm is more evocative than the words, and Miss Garrigue shows she is familiar with Wallace Stevens' "necessary angel," whose sight gives the earth a second birth in sight. I suppose my disappointments in her volume are the obverse of a real promise, her being so close and yet still so far from "the idea of the real/That more real than the real gave the real its power." ("A discourse from Firenze.")—GEOFFREY HARTMAN, "Les Belles Dames sans Merci," *KR*, Autumn 1960, pp. 694–96

I have never in my life used the word "poetess," which strikes me as a diminishing term, calculated to introduce a superfluous sexual qualification. Neither do I like to talk about "women poets," as though they constituted a separate species. However, I am compelled by the exigencies of space to make use of whatever groupings seem economical enough to justify their artificiality. Jean Garrigue's third book, *A Water Walk by Villa d'Este*, confirms my impression that here is a wildly gifted poet, the most baroque and (in the best sense) outlandish of spirits, who demonstrates to a T Blake's disturbing dictum, "The road of excess leads to the palace of wisdom." She is our one lyric poet who makes ecstasy her home. Her world of angels, demons, ghosts, moon and roses, fabulous beasts and birds, fireworks and fountains would seem extravagant and false if a real anguish, countered by the most sumptuous of joys, did not hold them together.—STANLEY KUNITZ, *Harper's*, Sept. 1960, p. 101

Jean Garrigue's ways can be, to get the carping over with first, very irritating indeed; the following passage, beginning of "The Opera of the Heart: Overture," has successfully resisted my ardent pursuit of sense, especially as to the references of "this," "your," and "you" and the reason why it is all posed as a question:

> Music at this, for whom the kings throw dice
> Or favor your wild beauty by that sky
> They know the gods appareled white with stars
> Who stung and pale, indifferent as those maps you
> rule,
> Are then appointed by our passioned wills, know
> you?

But this doesn't happen often, so I'd take it that I've simply missed something, which is not unheard of, and go on.

The world of *The Monument Rose* is romantic in its richness and strangeness and curious elaboration of detail—"Flesh of timber wrung through / As lilac enflasked in its smoky color / Gives up on the white alphabet of the river"—but to speak of Keats in this connection would be to neglect the energetic wit that checks this tendency to linger, and keeps it under pressure sometimes suggestive of Pope, as in this about Valentine's Day: "For this is heart's ease day, when dear-my-loves / Blood-bright or velvet-sewn, adorn the door / Or smash their pretty triumphs on the floor." Most of all, though, and for all the elegance in particular words, the character of this poetry is just where it belongs, in the play between rhythm and syntax, the wave-motion, so to say, which makes the identity of passage after passage and makes all one and most fine. This thing, the weaving and stitching, is the most neglected part of poetry at present, but attention to it is a mark of mastery, and the gift for it, the melodiousness which is, as Coleridge claimed, the final and distinguishing sign of a poet, is something Miss Garrigue wonderfully has:

> If you should wander by the ports and parks
> Where goes my mistress, say for me
> When greet the flowers her sumptuous head more
> sumptuously
> Than clouds bringing their rain by distant steppes
> To the green turfs of seiges dust has wrought
> Or by the fountains where the light has spent
> Its elements by archways lavishly—

Here, as elsewhere, with a certain consciousness and deliberate slight mockery, the verse refers to the madrigalists, and to the tradition out of Italy; in general her idea of meter goes back to a time when the English line was a lighter and slighter thing than the dramatists made it, with more hesitations, charming uncertainties of stress, the time of Wyatt, and in Miss Garrigue's hand is capable of fine surprises and syncopations:

> Love is the friend whose faithfulness is wit,
> Is best your mimic when you tongue-tied vow,
> Aloof when you win and surly when you stammer,
> Cries I do not understand you, and
> Corrects your right answer.

—HOWARD NEMEROV, *Poetry and Fiction*, 1963, pp. 212–13

Jean Garrigue is endowed with a metaphysical temper of mind. Her characteristic fragility is a super-sensitiveness to physical experience of the world. In many of her early poems, the obsessive need of her spirit to keep the upper hand over sensory experience defeats her ear and her eye, while the vigorous sensuosity of her language at its best is dispersed in trance, giving way to the language and dreamy essences. But her later development, from book to book, indicates a steady and valiant strengthening of those elements in her art which can secure a foothold, a vital anchorage, in the world of living forms.

"A Dream," an ambitious new poem ⟨from *New and Selected Poems*⟩, journeys into an ultra-real awakeness *within* the dream: a deepening trance in which fantasy is slowly divested of its dim outlines, and all that is vague and abstract in our mutual dream-life is pared and peeled away, layer by layer, like so many skins. Suddenly, we are inside the "tent of cloud or snow / Not unlike a sailing silk", inside the body of the dream looking out, flowing, unable to pinpoint the exact moment when the delicate osmosis of entry drew us irresistibly into the circulatory life of the poem's deep vessels. Whatever seemed blurred, out of focus, in the vision—at the poem's outset—has grown, through a chain of subtle transformations, to be supernaturally clear, luminous, at the finish.

A brash new underground personality emerges in several of Miss Garrigue's new poems: the cat-like grovelling saboteur of "Police of the Dead Day" ("Ignorant of all but my skin, I may be skinned— / And it is possible for the sake of the pelt, alive—"); the homeless and despoiled mongrel of "Proem" ("I turn / And cur-like snarl at what I'd once cherished"); and the owlish solitary of "Nth Invitation." In these poems, there is a hoarse rasping defiance, with no loss of Garrigue's accustomed feminine grace, that results in a toughening of voice. The most impressive incarnation of her new identity is the guerrilla infighter of a number of successful political poems, most notably "Written in London after a Protest Parade."

Miss Garrigue is perhaps more skilled than any other poet writing today with the power to dramatize emotional thresholds between jeopardy and renewal. She has a genius for returning to life's viable starting points following defeats, disappointments, hovering over the twin craters of frustrated love and failed art, owning up to the bleakest shortcomings in the self. In poem after poem, her subject is the failure of events in daily life ever to measure up to her spirit's esthetic craving for perfectability. In "The Flux of Autumn," the poem that ends the book, her art is conceived as a religion which takes the fierce impact of natural beauty on the senses as a first step in the strenuous discipline of achieving her sensibility. The process involves a series of selective denials of the heart's pleasure, yielding to the higher demands of the dream: "The shadow of a bird has crossed my heart / That we are these, these living things, enough!" She relentlessly subjects her keenest life-experiences to the refining "restless eye" of her dream-life. It is because she is able to enjoy all living beauties so much, strictly for themselves, that one is assured of the tragic heroism of her deprivations, of the demands her theology imposes on her responsive being. Her triumph is one of restraint, a succession of inured resistances to all pleasures easy of access, delaying and forestalling her natural gift for spiritual uplift until she has reached the supreme moment in which we are able to "think all things are full of gods". She will settle for nothing short of that arrival, and if she has had to sacrifice the more fashionable virtues of poetry in our time—expressiveness and immediacy—to evolve a middle range, a plateau, of vision (halfway between the language of feelings particularized and the language of elusive dream-states), we can only be as grateful for the qualities her art withholds as for those it affords, for there are rewards to be secured in reading her best poems of a kind that can be found in no other body of work.
—LAWRENCE LIEBERMAN, "The Body of the Dream," *Poetry*, May 1968, pp. 121–23

ROSEMARY TONKS
"Cutting the Marble"

New York Review of Books, October 4, 1973, pp. 8–10

This ⟨*Studies for an Actress*⟩ is ⟨Jean Garrigue's⟩ last book of poems; she died in December, 1972. We follow her into romantic territory, but we have misgivings when we observe that she has grasped the nettle in an overtly poetic manner which has been fatal to so many other good poets before her.

Romantics (and not only romantics) tend to be lazy about first principles. By a continuous process of effort on many levels, a poem is shaken free from all that is not the poem. This is the first step, done is possible well away from a sheet of paper. It is *the* work, brutal, classical precision work to isolate, develop, and organize. Everything important is decided there and then, in order to get a poem out alive from the rapid, egocentric thought-flow of the normal mind. It's especially hard on lyric-romantic writers who have already swallowed the world and all its poets entire. Every burr sticks to their verses.

It emerges gradually that Miss Garrigue has taken up her rich, mannered style with her eyes open. There are prose stanzas in this book in which that style is dropped, and they are good. But they do not contain those lines of poetry which appear in her other verse. Her style, then, is the only way in which she can realize her potential for certain thoughts; thoughts which cannot form in the mind unless the emotional conditions are propitious to them and the clock is turned back. They cannot form in this mind and be recognized as poetry unless they resemble what has already been poetry. For she has no vision of a lyric poetry which is new in kind.

Having made these reservations, we must try to look at her work on its own terms, and there will be rewards which will make the effort worth while. With regard to other voices in her poetry, this is a good moment to remind ourselves of the continuous tradition of licensed romantic borrowing throughout history; without it, our best poets would be out of court straight away. We learn to think and feel for ourselves only by first thinking the thoughts of others, and feeling what they felt. By these means, we learn what it is to do these things.

There are some bunglers, of course. Keats, young, ill, and in a hurry, lifted words and mood from the first four lines of one of the Epodes of Horace in order to get off the ground with "Ode to a Nightingale" (Epode no. XIV, in Dr. John Marshall's translation: "Why 'tis that languorous sloth can thus so strongly bind / My inmost heart and mind, / As though some Lethé draught, I down parched throat had cast"). Rimbaud's "Le Bateau ivre" began in stanza thirteen of "La Bouteille à la mer" by Alfred de Vigny. Dylan Thomas took over Edith Sitwell's territory and vocabulary. And so on. But each of these poets managed to pull a whole poem out of the pie which we recognize to be *sui generis*.

One essential aspect of Miss Garrigue's work is the presence in it of unseen forces, in the Yeatsian sense. The flowing of a mysterious charged current, especially near water or in lonely places. She is content to record it as part of her experience, interprets it pantheistically, and regards herself as part of its experience in turn. From her text it is doubtful whether she had any deeper or more exact knowledge, and she abandons mysticism the moment it no longer serves her literary purpose.

In her case this was certainly the right decision. The subject carries for most people dangerously airy-fairy overtones. Although paradoxically they also believe that this is what poetry is really about. Perhaps they dimly comprehend that human development is morally related to other worlds, other dimensions, which they only sense. We can only measure the importance of these strange influences by noting what happens when we are cut off from them; shut away in cities, locked into our own thoughts, which harden like concrete, we become angry and ill. Whatever the case may be, they assisted Miss Garrigue to write a fine poem, "There is a Dark River," from an early book *The Monument Rose*. Between what is actually seen, and what is only felt, she is able to intimate an other-worldly aliveness collected under dark trees.

> There is a dark river flows under a bridge
> Making an elbowed turn where the swallows skim
> Indescribably dark in rain,

sets the scene, and although Yeats's influence is soaked into her lines here:

> Those oblivion-haunted ones who wrote
> Memorable words on the window pane,
> What but the diamond's firmness gives them name?
> And yet because they did it
> The field is thick with spirit.

due to the beauty of the expression, the poem manages to assert itself, and in the end holds its own.

In her last book she has made an effort to bring both sensibility and manner up to date; possibly she had at last woken up to the fact that her traditional poetic abilities were strangling her. The mixture is of old and new. But she begins to know herself well enough to hear her own voice. Here it is in this good opening of "The Grand Canyon":

> Where is the restaurant car?
> I am lonely under the fluorescent light
> as a cook waddles in her smoky region visible through
>   an open arch
> and someone is pounding, pounding
> whatever it is that is being pounded

The poem goes on to describe the canyon throughout nine extremely long stanzas. Nevertheless, there is in general a much greater variety of line treatment, much firmer ground in the way of angular, dense description. She has been forced by the subject, a wholly American subject, to write a non-European poem. There is no precedent for gathering up the whole by intuition. The material defies it in any case. Thus she is thrown back on herself and writes an original poem. As a consequence, there is only one appearance of Yeats, a mere not, a long-legged insect (never, even for Yeats, a successful image) worked into a context entirely foreign to it in the last stanza when invention was beginning to flag. The poem softens shortly afterward and closes on a conceit; and although this is welded on to the new-look verses so that the join can hardly be seen, it has in fact nothing to do with the poem's primary conception and logic. In a natural desire to finish off by transcending gross matter, she loosens her grip and the old habits of mind reassert themselves:

> under those clouds that like water lilies
> enclose within them this silence received
> that they graze upon and are gone.

Miss Garrigue's line always sees further possibilities in itself, and the irrelevancies it produces, which are then carefully embedded in the poems, are usually the best part. In which case they *are* the poem, and the poem is the irrelevance. Here is one of her striking images: "the wind walked on the roof like a boy"—not factually accurate, but carrying an original concept of a wind (with more of Jean Giono than Dylan Thomas to it) to which we can assent. At the end of the same poem ("After Reading *The Country of the Pointed Fire*"), we get "As the wind threw itself about in the bushes and shouted / And another day fresh as a cedar started." This is aesthetically satisfying. The wind, which has been personalized, now has a life of its own. The characteristics, borrowed from a boy, are amplified and add a dimension which is valid, and the poem is refreshed and lifted out of the commonplace by them.

Still, it is unwise to base a whole method of composition on a talent for phrase-making—that is a stock-in-trade merely. Now this poet has written a number of ballads and songs, and the form of these, for the above reason, is not on her side. It rejects utterly verbal fantastification and imprecise meaning. The surface of a ballad must be as tight as a drum; it is virtually plotless, the plot is one emotion. Burns goes in deeply with "My love is like a red red rose," and continues to refine the same emotion to the core, so that what began by touching us on a physical level ends by moving us spiritually. He makes the work easy; but it's a matter of temperament to be able to do so.

Two points should especially be mentioned with regard to Miss Garrigue's last work. In taking her step forward the poet has uncovered a gift for quick portraits:

> That man going around the corner, his pants blown
>   out by the wind,
> That pottering, grey-faced bakery dog,

(which comes from "Free-Floating Report"), and for genuine insight. Although she had this in early days, it was often so badly placed that it might as well not have been there at all. The use of certain words, which inexorably draw after them other words of the same sort, obliterated it. Even now she does her best to destroy it by insipid diction, which is not the equal of the content in the following lines (from "For Jenny and Roger"):

> Nor is their thought known to them
> Till the other gives the truth away,
> They are hidden from their thought
> Till the other finds it out.

These are worth all the struggles with an overweight baggage of derivative elegies, nocturnes, laments, soliloquies, dialogues, notes, and incantations.

WILLIAM H. GASS

1924–

William Howard Gass was born in Fargo, North Dakota, on July 30, 1924, and grew up in Warren, Ohio. Determined from an early age to be a writer, he majored in philosophy at Kenyon College, graduating in 1947 after serving with the U.S. Navy in the Pacific from 1943 to 1946. As a graduate student at Cornell, he trained as a philosopher of language, writing his Ph.D. dissertation on metaphor. He taught at Purdue University from 1955 to 1969, since when he has been at Washington University in St. Louis.

Gass's first stories were published in *Accent*, and "The Triumph of Israbestis Tott" brought him the Longview Foundation award in fiction in 1959. After receiving a Rockefeller Foundation grant in fiction in 1965, he published his first novel, *Omensetter's Luck*, in 1966. *In the Heart of the Heart of the Country*, a volume of short stories, followed in 1968, and *Willie Masters' Lonesome Wife* in 1971. Gass has also published essays on aesthetics, in *Fiction and the Figures of Life* (1970), and philosophical works, notably *On Being Blue* (1976). His most recent book is *The Habitations of the Word* (1984).

Gass has traveled abroad, visiting England in 1966 and Portugal in 1970. He has been married twice and has five children. Other honors he has won include a Guggenheim Fellowship in 1969, and the National Institute of Arts and Letters prize for literature in 1975.

WILLIAM H. GASS
Interview by Carole Spearin McCauley
Falcon, Winter 1972, pp. 35–45

Most philosophers don't write fiction. Or (if you're a cynic), fictions are all they write.

William Gass is and does both—a philosopher who writes fiction, a writer whose aims and work have been deeply influenced by his philosophical training. His imaginative and experimental use of language and narrative technique in a variety of books has earned him both acclaim and dismissal during the years since parts of his first novel, *Omensetter's Luck*, appeared in *Accent Magazine*. Susan Sontag: "William Gass has written an extraordinary, stunning, beautiful book. I admire him and it very much."

Richard Gilman: "William Gass is not a comfortable writer. He's not immediately available. His work yields up new truths of our experience instead of repeating words of the past."

Born in North Dakota in 1924, Mr. Gass was educated at Kenyon College and Cornell University (Ph.D.). He is currently professor of philosophy at Washington University, St. Louis. His published works are *Omensetter's Luck, In the Heart of the Heart of the Country, Fiction and the Figures of Life*, and *Willie Masters' Lonesome Wife (Triquarterly*, 1968, and Knopf, 1971). His literary criticism appears frequently in *New American Review* and *New York Review of Books*.

A long excerpt from *The Tunnel*, his work in progress, appeared in *Triquarterly* (No. 20, Winter, 1971).

Some quotations from *Fiction and the Figures of Life:*

". . . how absurd these views are which think of fiction as a mirror or a window onto life—as actually creative of living creatures. . . ."

". . . there are no events but words in fiction."

"The advantage the creator of fiction has over the moral philosopher is that the writer is concerned with the exhibition of objects, thoughts, feelings, and actions where they are free from the puzzling disorders of the real and the need to come to conclusions about them."

Interviewer: From your literary criticism (including the above) it seems the philosopher side of you mistrusts the fiction-writing side because the fiction process involves the deliberate telling of lies, the setting forth of actions and people that never happened. How do you reckon with this dilemma?

Gass: I don't distrust the artist as artist at all. I distrust people, including artists, who make pretentious claims for literature as a source of knowledge.

This was the half of Plato's complaint against the poets which I accept. I see no reason to regard literature as a superior source of truth, or even as a reliable source of truth at all. Going to it is dangerous precisely because it provides a sense of verification (a feeling) without the fact of verification (the validating process). Plato was simply too exclusive about his values. He took knowledge to be the supreme good. Consequently he had to banish the poets (for the most part). The appeal to literature as a source of truth is pernicious. Truth suffers, but more than that, literature suffers. It is taken to be an undiscipled and sophistic sociology, psychology, metaphysics, ethics, etc., etc.

When I speak of telling lies, I speak ironically.

Interviewer: It seems as if you desire your fictional characters to exist as pure essences, as ideas that the reader can apply to his own life, provided he doesn't assume they really exist beyond the page. *Fiction and the Figures of Life*: "Though the handbooks try to tell us how to create characters, they carefully never tell us we are making images, illusions, imitations. Gatsby is not an imitation, for there is nothing he imitates."

How did you arrive at this position, which puts you squarely against what most writers desire—and against all that advice to young writers to create "real characters in real situations"?

Gass: Most writers? Most writers of what sort? There is some truth to this, but it is also partly a myth about writers spread by critics and other advertisers who know nothing about the art of writing. "The only reality is the translation of one's ideas into rhythm and beautiful movements." Colette is a writer many would expect to be on an opposite side, but she isn't at all, and this is really true for most serious artists.

That advice to young writers—who is giving it? Teachers in writing workshops, journalists, editors, hacks. As a student of philosophy I've put in a great deal of time on the nature of language and belong, rather vaguely, to a school of linguistic philosophy which is extremely skeptical about the nature of language itself.

Interviewer: In *Fiction and the Figures of Life* you find a "fear of feeling" in the work of some writers in our current literary pantheon such as Hawkes, Barthelme, Coover, Barth, Nabokov, Borges. That they "neglect the full responsive reach of their readers." So if you don't want the reader to "care" in the old sense of where-Hamlet-is-when-he's-not-onpage-or-onstage, then what is it exactly you want the reader to feel?

Gass: I want him to feel the way he feels when he listens to music—when he listens properly, that is. My complaint about Barth, Borges, and Beckett is simply that occasionally their fictions, conceived as establishing a metaphorical relationship between the reader and the world they are creating, leave the reader too passive. But such words are misleading. I have little patience with the "creative reader."

I mean this: some metaphors work in one direction—the predicate upon the subject. When I say that her skin was like silk, I am using the concept silk to interpenetrate and organize the idea of skin. Some metaphors, however, interact—both terms are resonant. If Hardy writes, "She tamed the wildest flowers," then not only has "she" become an animal trainer, the flowers have become animals. Nor has "taming" been left untouched, for such taming is now seen in terms of gardening. Now if fictions are metaphors or models, then perhaps they should occasionally "fictionalize" the reader.

Interviewer: In the words of Kohler, *The Tunnel's* narrator: "My subject's far too serious for scholarship, for history, and I must find another form before I let what's captive in me out. Imagine: history not serious enough, causality too comical, chronology insufficiently precise."

Does fiction writing interest you as the alternative? Like philosophy and Aristotle's "poetry," it can strive after the universal rather than the particular.

Gass: This is Kohler's problem, not mine. History, as I see it, can strive for the universal. My objection to it is simply that it rarely, reasonably, does. Many of my attitudes toward history are expressed by Lévi-Strauss. For me fiction isn't an alternative to anything, however, and it doesn't strive for universals. It merely makes particular things out of universals.

History, philosophy, fiction, like mathematics or physics, are for me all equally important, all difficult to do, rarely well done, each requiring its own disciplines, techniques, skills, and very different in aim. When Kohler says his subject is too serious for scholarship, etc., he means it is too personal, that the modes he mentions won't satisfy him. It reflects *his* mood.

Interviewer: Wittgenstein defines philosophy as "a battle against the bewitchment of our intelligence by means of language." Does this relate to your own concerns in fiction or philosophy?

Gass: I think philosophy is more than this, but it certainly should be this. It has often been busy bewitching. Philosophy ought to spend more time than it has showing how little we need it—it and other foolish sets of opinions. I believe much of what has passed for philosophy, theology, etc., in the past is nonsense. Sometimes beautiful nonsense, if you enjoy myths of the mind as I enjoy them. Beliefs are a luxury and most of them are wicked gibberish.

Philosophical ideas can, however, provide the writer with complex centers of meaning, rich bases to work from. But you must *play* with them primarily because of the danger that what you're saying might be so. Constructing fictions as if the philosophy they're based on *were* so usually leads to falseness.

Interviewer: How or where did you get the material for the characters and Ohio setting of *Omensetter's Luck?* For example, was Omensetter or Jethro Furber or the father in "The Pedersen Kid" modelled on someone you knew (who actually existed)?

Gass: I made it up. I know nothing whatever of Ohio river towns and care less. The only time I ever used a "model" in writing was when, as a formal device, and to amuse myself, I chose to get the facts about "B" in "In the Heart of the Heart of the Country" exactly right. Models interfere with the imagination. Which is better—to play train with a square wooden block, or a scale model? If you have a model, whether a person or a scene, even an idea, you tend to find yourself bent by that model when the work you are doing at any time should be obedient only to itself. Of course writers get ideas from models all the time and, occasionally, so do I, but they have to be able to leave the given behind. I generally take no chances and work "in the dark"—model-less.

Omensetter isn't really set in Ohio; that is the point.

Interviewer: In your essay in *Afterwords: Novelists on Their Novels* you wrote, ". . . the illusion might wrap itself like a sheet around its occupant, so that Omensetter might become a ghost even to himself." Did you intend Omensetter to remain the mystery that many people find him—because we never get inside him directly?

Despite Omensetter's "luck," does his baby die?

Gass: Omensetter is a reflector. People use him the way they use their gods or other public figures—like ink blots—and upon them they project their hopes and fears. Who cared to know Omensetter? And when their hopes were dashed, they blamed the image in the mirror. So of course Omensetter is a mystery and he had to be left, in a sense, blank. Readers are now doing to him exactly what the characters in the book did.

No. His baby doesn't die. Omensetter is a lucky man.

Interviewer: I notice a total difference in tone from something like passionate optimism (people's lives and deaths matter, America matters) in *Omensetter's Luck*, compared to the narrator's disenchantment in *The Tunnel*. How do you explain this?

Gass: The tonal difference is due to the differences in the books. The narrator in *The Tunnel* is disenchanted, but, again, that's his problem. I have always been disenchanted, although I am probably less bitter about things now than I was when I wrote *Omensetter's Luck*. I'm personally happier. But *The Tunnel* will be a very bitter book. I thought *Omensetter's Luck* pretty bitter, too. Also you've only seen fragments from *The Tunnel*. If you saw more of it, your feeling about the tone might change.

Interviewer: Do you feel America has lost its Omensetters, the people who know how to live naturally, unintellectually? Why or why not?

Gass: America never had its Omensetters. There aren't any such human felines. Such creatures are a part of the American myth. What we are losing is our belief in such things. Beliefs lost are minds cleaned. I applaud the development.

Interviewer: You seem to have the kind of mind that brews fiction from massive amounts of stream of consciousness (Jethro Furber, Israbetis Tott). Do you have a method for keeping up the white heat, the Molly Bloom effect?

Gass: No method for "white heat." Whenever I find myself working at white heat, I stop until I cool off. I write very slowly, laboriously, without exhilaration, without pleasure, though with a great deal of tension and exasperation. I fuss over little bits, scarcely ever see beyond my nose, and consequently bump it constantly.

Interviewer: Do you do much "research" to complete

your fiction, make it real by revisiting "the scene of the crime," hunting out people who resemble your characters, etc.?

Gass: No research. I collect words. Twelve different names for "whore" among the Romans. Thirty-five names for cloths and silk stuffs. Etc. Sometimes I even use what I've collected. Or an old book will suggest something. But there are no "scenes" to revisit, except for "B"; and I wouldn't think of doing that while writing; because, as I said, my choice of factuality in that case was purely formal. I collected real names for clubs, for example, and amused myself by arranging them. Part of the game was not to invent any. It would have been like cheating at solitaire.

Interviewer: Do you intend, as part of the fun, that the "Masters" in *Willie Masters' Lonesome Wife* could refer to William Masters of the St. Louis sex research? Or that "Kohler" in *The Tunnel* means "miner" in German?

Gass: I began *Willie* and wrote most of it in 1966, before I'd ever heard of Masters and Johnson. Scarcely before I'd ever heard of St. Louis. The jokes are there—in Goethe, in Shakespeare, etc.

The choice of "Kohler," however, was deliberate. Miner in the tunnel . . . yes.

Interviewer: Do you have a writing schedule? Are you able to write every day? Do you do any sort of warmup exercises? What do you do if you get blocked?

Gass: I have a schedule for writing whenever I have enough free time that having such a schedule seems realistic—when I'm off because of a grant or during the summer. I used to be able to write nearly every day, but that has become impossible. I don't do warmup exercises, but I do try to stop only when I've left some fingers pointing to the future—some lines I can begin my next day's work by starting with. If I have to start cold, with entirely new material (new sentences, I mean), then I have trouble.

I don't really get blocked. That is: I don't find that I sit and stare at the page and nothing comes. Not for long. But I have blocks in the sense that I allow things to distract me so that for a long time I won't work. It is the same as a block, though perhaps not so immediately distressing.

Interviewer: Did you have to write for many years before you succeeded in being published?

Gass: I began writing seriously (I always wanted to write, planned on it, etc.) in 1951. I wrote "The Pedersen Kid" and the opening parts of *Omensetter* in '51–52. I didn't get published until *Accent* devoted an issue to my work in 1958. *Omensetter* didn't get written for a long time, but it wasn't published until 1966. "The Pedersen Kid" (finished in '51) had to wait until 1961. Even *Willie* waited from 1966 to '68. "In the Heart" waited. They all wait. So that it is generally true that most of my stuff is old when it appears—old to me, that is.

Interviewer: What do you like to read? Are there any authors you've learned something from?

Gass: I am an omnivorous reader. My library is that of a dedicated dilettante. I might, on any given day, be reading a book about bees, or about epistemology, or about the brain, or about the theory of signs, or about odd native tribes, or odd psychological states, or sexual positions, or who knows—travel, geography, biography . . . I like letters, diaries, journals, gossip, and therefore history. I read less and less poetry, though I get to Rilke almost every day. I rarely read fiction and generally don't enjoy it. I usually read it because I have to. Lately, most of my reading has been of that sort. I read X because I have to shoot off my mouth about it—teaching, reviewing—and I'm sick of it.

I've learned from so many I couldn't even begin to list the essential. As far as my own writing goes, from poets mostly, from philosophers, of course, because they supply me with material, and from stylists in general, whether Sir Thomas Browne, Hobbes, Stein, Joyce, James, Ford, or Colette.

Interviewer: Do you enjoy any of the other arts?

Gass: I enjoy all of them, especially perhaps ballet (when pure and not mucked up) and architecture. I was an opera nut when young. That's tailed off. I haunt museums when I can. In one sense, painting has influenced my theory of art more than almost anything, music my practice of it.

Interviewer: Do you write poetry or plays?

Gass: I wrote terrible poetry in my youth. I write doggerel now. I am a rotten poet and have absolutely no talent for it.

I haven't the dramatic imagination at all. Even my characters tend to turn away from one another and talk to the void. This, along with my inability to narrate, is my most serious defect (I think) as a writer and incidentally as a person. I am (though I wasn't especially raised as one) a Protestant, wholly inner-directed, and concerned only too exclusively with *my* salvation, *my* relation to the beautiful, *my* state of mind, body, soul . . . The interactions which interest me tend to be interactions between parts of my own being. One could, I suppose, try to get a little drama out of that. Besides the drama is a mug's game. Actors are enemies. The theater is cheap, divided in its source of control. It would drive me crazy.

Interviewer: Do political issues on campus or among students interest you for their fictional possibilities? That is, there's terrible pressure on fiction to "be relevant" today, to deal with "today's real issues" instead of rural people or private consciousness. So we have Norman Mailer making his career as a sort of hippy-fascist weathercock telling us how tomorrow's winds will blow in America. How do you deal with this pressure to "be relevant"?

Gass: Art is never concerned with such things. Relevance is meaningless to it. A work of art is made to last as a valuable being in the world. As such it may develop, over time, useful relations to the world; but just as human beings ultimately must find their values in themselves, so works of art must *be relevant by being*. There have always been Mailers because culture requires its human talismans. These procedures and activities are as different from art as weeds from differential equations. I feel no pressure to be relevant.

I am, of course, as a person, interested in these public matters, and I am frequently taken from my work to engage in them. They are, indeed, often far more important than myself and my private playthings. Dante was "relevant" but fortunately he triumphed over it.

Interviewer: Is teaching a stimulus to your writing—or something that just takes time from it? I know that you received the Hovde Prize for excellence in teaching in 1967.

Gass: It used to be. I think I fed on the students. They have been an enormous help to me in every way, but my interest in teaching grows less—I think mainly because my toleration of the monkey business which attends it grows less. Now I often feel that it just takes time. But I really enjoy lecturing (not teaching); I never really enjoyed teaching. I enjoy talking to the material. And if I'm not doing that aloud, I'm doing it silently. It's nice to get paid for it.

Interviewer: Someone from the Midwest (even New Jersey!) can feel discriminated against by the New York literary establishment, perhaps criticized for being provincial, unsophisticated, whatever. Has this kind of treatment ever afflicted you?

Gass: When I go to New York City, I feel I'm going to the provinces. What is sophisticated about literary New York? How much of importance goes on there? It is filled with commercial hacks and their pimps. There are, of course, many cultivated people—people who have their values straight, who know even more about Valéry and Peguy, say, than about Mailer or Updike—but most of them mistake the literary froth for the body of the beer.

Literature doesn't take place in New York. It takes place in writers' heads and on their pages all over the world. From the literary point of view, New Yorkers live in the servants' quarters. No, I haven't been afflicted. Literature is where the Faulkners are. No Faulkner is in New York and if he were, he wouldn't be known. I snub them.

Interviewer: Did you have to submit *Omensetter's Luck* to many publishers before it was noticed by New American Library and other people in New York?

Gass: I think *Omensetter's Luck* went to twelve publishers (so much for New York sophistication). New American Library didn't notice it. It takes no notice of books. David Segal saw the book early on. Tried to get it published at McGraw Hill, finally succeeded at NAL. If it hadn't been for my agent, Lynn Nesbit, and for David, it probably would still be unpublished, and so would all the rest of my stuff.

Interviewer: Did they suggest or require many revisions?

Gass: David suggested a few revisions—nothing major—most wise suggestions from him. I do my own work and do not permit other people to interfere with it. Editors occasionally ask for cuts, and sometimes I submit to them (for magazine publication). Anyone who requires revisions has simply rejected the manuscript as far as I'm concerned. Some (a few) wanted to do that with *Omensetter's Luck.*

Interviewer: How do you generally revise your work? Just two drafts or many more?

Gass: I work not by writing but by rewriting. Each sentence has many drafts. Eventually there is a paragraph. This gets many drafts. Eventually there is a page. This gets many drafts. And so on. I have about 300 pages of *The Tunnel.* But in a few days I start over redrafting them—from the beginning.

Writing isn't easy for me. That's why I have to answer your questions in pidgin, for if I began to worry about what I was saying and the way I was saying it—well, I'd never answer your questions. I would never emerge from # 1. So I'm a poor correspondent. I deliberately butcher matters. Write wretchedly. Turn no phrases. Speak telegraphese.

Interviewer: How do you feel about *The Tunnel* compared with *Omensetter's Luck?* Progression or enlargement?

Gass: The Tunnel is a crucial work for me. All my work up to it I have privately thought of as exercises and preparations. This was a dodge, of course, but it did work. How can you fail when you are simply practicing, learning, experimenting? I can't hide behind that dodge anymore. Further, in this business it is no honor to finish second. Now I shall find out whether I am any good.

Certainly I hope that *The Tunnel* will be better than *OL*. *OL* made compromises. I trust that *The Tunnel* will not. I hope that it will be really original in form and in effect, although mere originality is not what I'm after.

OL made compromises because it still sometimes treated fiction as if it were an imitation of some factual form. *OL* made only sporadic steps at establishing its own form.

Fiction has traditionally and characteristically borrowed its forms from letters, journals, diaries, autobiographies, histories, travelogues, news stories, backyard gossip, etc. It has simply *pretended* to be one or other of them. The history of fiction is in part a record of the efforts of its authors to create for fiction its own forms. Poetry has its own. It didn't borrow the ode from somebody. Now the novel is imagined news, imagined psychological or sociological case studies, imagined history . . . feigned, I should say, not imagined. As Rilke shattered the journal form with *Malte*, and Joyce created his own for *Ulysses* and *Finnegan*, I should like to create mine.

Interviewer: Do you have any advice for beginning writers? Do you recommend fiction writing classes? Would you ever teach creative writing? If so, what would be your approach?

Gass: My advice for beginning writers is first to recognize that writers differ a great deal in their own natures and in the nature of their talent and that little advice which is general can be of much value. Learn not to take advice. Look to yourself. Make yourself worthy of trust.

No art can be taught, though some techniques sometimes can. Writing classes help some, don't others. It depends, again, on the kind of person you are. Do whatever works. It wouldn't have worked for me and I am personally suspicious of them. I've taught creative writing (a little) but I would never make a habit of it. All that attention wasted on poor work? Better to speak of the good things and learn from that. So my approach would be flight.

Interviewer: Can you estimate when your book *The Tunnel* will be finished or published?

Gass: I began *The Tunnel* in 1966. I imagine it is several years away yet. Who knows, perhaps it will be such a good book no one will want to publish it. I live on that hope.

WILLIAM H. GASS

"Groping for Trouts"

The World within the Word

1976, pp. 262–65

> Yonder man is carried to prison.
> Well; what has he done?
> A woman.
> But what's his offense?
> Groping for trouts in a peculiar river.

I want to begin with a problem that's also a bit of history. It may at first appear as far from my topic—art and order—as the Andes are from their valleys, or as such remote and glacial mountain slopes must seem to some swimmer whose nose is full of salt. The problem concerns the measurement of nature, and I don't in the least mind saying that on any number of counts it's like groping for trouts in a peculiar river.

We have each seen the motion in bodies. We ourselves live. The newsboy delivers the daily paper. The dime which has slipped from our fist runs into a tightening spiral till, like a bug, we flat it with out foot. Spirits rise, rumors travel, hopes fade. The flesh crawls, felts and satins roughen, and when we lick our ice cream we can even taste the melt. Yes, Heraclitus calls the tune, and like the sound of an accordion is the noisy meeting and passing of trains.

The movements everywhere around us—in us—seem, well . . . too numerous, too vague, too fragile and transitory to number, and that's terribly unsettling, for we always feel threatened when confronted with something we can't count. Why should we be surprised, then, to find out that creating and defending a connection between what William James called the buzzing, blooming confusion of normal consciousness—of daily life with its unstimulating bumps, its teaseless, enervating grinds—and the clear and orderly silences of mathematics, a connection which will give us meaning, security, and management, in one lump sum, is what our science—is what our art, law, love, and magic—is principally about?

That newspaper—we might mistake it for the white wings of a passing pigeon. Do we see the line it draws? Think how Galileo would have rendered it. He'd notice neither newspaper nor pigeon. He discovered that the distance which the paper might be tossed could be expressed—how wonderful his image—as the area of a rectangle. The match-up was astonishing: Velocity could be laid out on one side, time on another, and since he knew so much more about rectangles than he did about motion, his little Euclidean model (for that's what he'd managed), to the degree it held firm, would immediately make a science of physical movement possible . . . in terms of dots and dashes, points and paths . . . and he went on to describe all evenly accelerating motion in the cool and classic language of the triangle. Had Dante been more daring? I think not.

Now imagine that Alice (the girl conceived by Carroll—minister, poet, and logician), having eaten what she's been told to and drunk according to instructions, is swelling as she tiptoes through the tunnel, and imagine in addition that there is a light like those which warn low planes of towers, chimneys, or intrusive steeples, attached to the top of her head. Can't we see her as an elongating wand whose end is then a point upon a curve? A most monstrous metaphor, yet inspired. Any curve, Descartes decided, could be considered to enclose a set of lines whose ends like trimmed logs lay against it. Only moments later, so it seemed, so swift is thought translated into history, Descartes had devised a language to describe these points and lines, these curved and squares, in numbers. Every place upon a line had its address, and with that went directions: you went along Rue X a while, and then up Y till you were there. As simple as children, but all quite absurd, for motion only alters the overlaps of colors—we know that; there is nothing rectangular about passage; and surely squares and curves are never numbers—abstract, inert, and purely relational; they stretch their legs like cats. Yet in a generation (we speak now like the critics), Galileo, Fermat, and Descartes had first created, then speeded up, mechanics. Beyond the Pythagoreans' wildest dreams, motion had become number.

Again: how was it managed? The paperboy's paper is dispensed with. It becomes a point; its flight, a line. That curve itself is seen to be a row of dots, or so we might conceive a string of pearls if we were mathematically inclined. Next, each dot is said to represent the top of a slat, a vertical fixed like a post in the plane of the paperboy's feet. A picket fence, in short, has unfolded from his throw. If you prefer: it's a Venetian blind on its side, on edge. But no, the tip of each post is the elbow of an angle, the corner of that old friend, area, again, and thus this simple little daily act is actually, in our new poetry and picture book, exactly like a perfect fan of cards. Plato's intuition has been confirmed: the world we know and swim in is everywhere it flows a qualitative expression of serene, unchanging quantitative laws. The ambiguity of "point" makes many of these verses possible. Who knows? it may be the peak of a witch's cap, the climax of the geometer's cone. *Point*: it is truly a word to wonder at, this minute mark like a prick, this place in space less large than a hair's end or the sound of a silent clock, this piercing part and particular of discourse, this dimensionless speck which has been spelled, alone in English, sixteen different ways already—should we not salute it?

So yonder man is carried to prison. Shakespeare measures matter in quite another way. This sort of sexuality is seen as poaching . . . poaching in a peculiar river. The term is technical, and requires that we feel for the fish with our hands beneath an overhanging bank. "Fish must be grop't for, and be tickled too," Bunyan writes. When Hamlet tells Horatio how

> Up from my cabin,
> My sea-gown scarf'd about me, in the dark
> Groped I to find them

he is using "groped" less precisely, more generally, than in this passage from *Measure for Measure*. Tickling is apparently essential to it, for Maria awaits Malvolio, whom she plans to dupe, with the words: ". . . here comes the trout that must be caught with tickling." And what was thought as *peculiar* then was, in particular, private property.

For instance.

We hate to think that through much of our life we window-shop and rarely purchase. Therefore, I suppose, it does dismay us to discover that of all the time we spend on sex—in thought, dreams, deed, in word, desire, or feeling—there is so little spending done to show for it that nothing's bought. Yet I notice how predictably I've put it. I should be ashamed. First I spoke of spending time, and when I spoke of sperm—our sacred future—in the same way. Well, time is money, don't we say? and maybe our seeds are simply many pennies. Both, at least, are quantities—methods of accounting, blueprints, masterplots—and perhaps Protagoras really meant to tell us that man is the measurer of all things, not merely the measure, for I honestly believe it is his principal concern.

LARRY McCAFFERY
From "The Art of Metafiction: *Willie Masters' Lonesome Wife*"

Critique, Volume 18, Number 2 (1976), pp. 24–34

Gass's basic intention in *Willie Masters'* is to build a work which will literally embody an idea he has elsewhere stated:

> It seems a country-headed thing to say: that literature is language, that stories and the places and the people in them are merely made of words as chairs are made of smoothed sticks and sometimes of cloth or metal tubes. . . . That novels should be made of words, and merely words, is shocking really. It's as though you had discovered that your wife were made of rubber: the bliss of all those years, the fears . . . from sponge.[1]

Gass never allows the reader to forget that literature is made of words and nothing else; here the words themselves are constantly called to our attention, their sensuous qualities emphasized in nearly every imaginable fashion. Indeed, the narrator of the work—the "Lonesome Wife" of the title—is that lady language herself. Although the narrative has no real plot, the "events" occur while Babs makes love to a particularly unresponsive lover named Gelvin—suggesting the central metaphor of the whole work: that a parallel exists—or should exist—between a woman and her lover, between the work of art and the artist, and between a book and its reader. The unifying metaphor is evident even before we open the book: on the front cover is a frontal photograph of a naked woman; on the back cover is a corresponding photograph of the back-side of the same woman. Gass, thus, invites one to enter his work of art—a woman made of words and paper—with the same sort of excitement, participation, and creative energy as one would enter a woman's body in sexual intercourse. The poet-narrator of Gass's short story, "In the Heart of the Heart of the Country," explains why the metaphor is appropriate when he says "Poetry, like love, is—in and out—a physical caress."[2]

Babs puts it more bluntly: "How close in the end is a cunt to a concept; we enter both with joy" (White Section, 4). Unfortunately, as we discover from Babs, all too frequently those who enter her do so without enthusiasm, often seemingly unaware that she is there at all.

As an appropriate extension of the metaphor, the central orderings of the work are very loosely the stages of sexual intercourse. In order to embody these parallels more closely, Gass uses the color and texture of the page to indicate subtle alterations in Babs' mind rather than relying on traditional chapter divisions and pagination. Even the page itself is not ordered in the usual linear fashion; instead, typographical variations establish a different visual order for each individual page. The first eight pages, for example, are printed on blue, thin paper with very little texture; these pages suggest the rather slow beginning of intercourse and Babs' playful, low-intensity thoughts and remembrances. The next twelve pages are thicker, more fully textured, and olive in color; this section, which is also the most varied in typography and graphics, corresponds to the rising stages of Babs' sexual excitement and her wildly divergent thoughts. Next follows eight red pages, with paper of the same texture as the first section, suggesting the climax of intercourse and the direct, intensely intellectual climax of Babs' thoughts about language. Finally, the fourth section uses a thick, high-gloss white paper like that of expensive magazines; these pages parallel Babs' empty, lonely feelings after intercourse when she realizes how inadequate the experience has been.

Reinforcing the feelings produced by color and texture are the photographs of Babs' nude body throughout the book. The first section opens with a picture of her upper torso and face, with her mouth eagerly awaiting the printer's phallic S-block. As the book continues, her face becomes less prominent and her body itself is emphasized. The photo at the beginning of the White Section (4) shows Babs curled up in fetal position, with her head resting upon her knees in a position indicating her sad, lonely feeling of resignation.

By far the most intricately developed device used by Babs to call attention to her slighted charms is the wide variety of type styles and other graphic devices with which she constructs herself.[3] One of the functions of the typographic changes—at least in the Blue and Red Sections (1 and 3)—is to indicate different levels of consciousness in Babs' mind. The opening Blue Section, for instance, is divided into three monologues printed mainly in separate, standard typefaces: roman, italic, and boldface. With these typographic aids, we can separate the strands of Babs' thoughts roughly as follows: the roman sections deal with her memories about the past and her concern with words; the italic sections indicate her memories of her first sexual encounter; and the boldface sections present her views about the nature of fundamental body processes and their relation to her aspirations for "saintly love." The Blue Section (1) can be read largely as an ordinary narrative, from top to bottom, left to right; the different typefaces, however, enable us to read each level of Babs' thought as a whole (by reading all the italics as a unit, then reading the boldface sections together). In the Olive and Red Sections (2 and 3), however, the graphics and typography destroy any linear response; Gass's aim in using such techniques is to achieve, like Joyce in *Ulysses*, a freedom from many of the language's traditionally imposed rules of syntax, diction, and punctuation. To help emphasize the incredible versatility of human consciousness, Joyce relied (most notably in the "Cyclops" and the "Oxen of the Sun" episodes) on linguistic parody of earlier styles. Like his fellow Irishman, Laurence Sterne, Joyce was quite willing to use unusual typographic devices to help present his parodies. The devices—Sterne's blank and marbled pages, Joyce's headlines, question-and-answer format, the typographic formality of the "Circe" episode—are foreign to the "pure" storyteller but are available to a writer by the nature of books and print alone. Hugh Kenner has persuasively argued that Joyce hoped to liberate the narration of *Ulysses* from the typographical conventions of ordinary narratives and notes that the linear, one-dimensional method of presenting most books simply could not do justice to Joyce's expansive view of language: "There is something mechanical, Joyce never lets us forget, about all reductions of speech to arrangement of 26 letters. We see him playing in every possible way with the spatial organization of printed marks."[4] Kenner's remarks are perceptive, although he overstates his point when he says that Joyce experimented with printed marks "in every possible way." Gass's work, written fifty years later (in the Age of McLuhan—himself a Joyce scholar), carries the methods of typographic freedom to a much fuller development.

Gass's intentions in *Willie Masters'* can be compared to Joyce's in other ways. Like Joyce's presentation of a parodic history of English styles in the "Oxen of the Sun" section, Gass's work is practically a history of typography. One of Gass's original intentions for *Willie Masters'* was to reproduce the first-edition typeface of any lines quoted from other works; this proved impractical, but type styles are found from nearly every period since Gutenberg, ranging from pre-printing-press calligraphy to old German gothic, Victorian typeface, and modern advertising boldface.

In addition to mimicking typefaces, Gass presents many other typographic conventions, often with parodic intent. One amusing example is found in the Olive Section (2) in which a one-act play is presented with all the rigid typographic formality usually found in a written transcription of a play. Babs provides asterisked comments and explanations about stage directions, costumes, and props. These remarks begin in very small type, but as the play progress the typeface becomes larger and bolder. Gradually the number of asterisks before each aside becomes impossible to keep up with, and the comments themselves become so large that the text of the play is crowded off the page—to make room for a page containing only large, star-shaped asterisks. Gass thus pokes fun at a typographic convention in much the same way as John Barth did (with quotation marks) in "The Menelaid." Gass also uses the asterisks for reasons we do not usually expect—for their *visual appeal*. As Babs notes, "these asterisks are the prettiest things in print" (Olive Section, 2). Throughout the Olive and Red Sections (2 and 3) are examples of many other typographic variations: concrete poems, quoted dialogue inscribed in comic-book style, pages which resemble eye-charts, a Burroughs' newspaper "cut-up," and even the representations of coffee-stains.

In addition to drawing attention to how words look, Babs makes us examine the way we read words. In particular, she reminds us that the Western conventions of reading—left-to-right, top-to-bottom, from first page to last—are all merely conventions. Indeed, as Michael Butor has pointed out, even in Western cultures we are probably more familiar with books which do not rely on linear development (like dictionaries, manuals, or encyclopedias) than we realize: "It is a misconception for us to think that the only kind of book are those which transcribe a discourse running from start to finish, a narrative or essay, in which it is natural to read by starting on the first page in order to finish on the last."[5] In *Willie Masters'*, especially in the Olive and Red Section (2 and 3), Gass typographically makes ordinary reading impossible. In the Red Section (3), for example, Babs begins four or five narratives on a single page. In order to follow these largely unrelated narratives, each presented in a different typeface, we cannot begin at the top of the page and read down; instead, we are forced to follow one section from page to page and then go back to the beginning for the second narrative. Like Joyce who forces us to page backwards and forwards to check and cross-check references, Gass is taking advantage of what Kenner has termed "the book as book"[6]; the book's advantage lies in the fact that we can go backwards and forwards rather than being forced to move ever forward—as we are with a movie or a spoken narrative. The use of asterisks and marginal glosses indicates Gass's willingness to take advantage of the expressive possibilities of Babs' form as words on a printed page; he uses a typographical method to deflect the eye from its usual horizontal/vertical network. Kenner has defined the effect in discussing the use of footnotes:

> The man who composes a footnote, and sends it to the printer along with his text, has discovered among the devices of printed language something analogous to counterpoint: a way of speaking in two voices at once, or of ballasting or modifying or even bombarding with exceptions his own discourse without interrupting it. It is a step in the direction of discontinuity; of organizing blocks of discourse simultaneously in space rather than consecutively in time.[7]

Especially in the Red Section (3) of *Willie Masters'*, our eye is never allowed to move easily on the page from left-to-right and top-to-bottom; instead we turn from page to page, backwards and forwards, moving our eye up and down in response to footnotes or asterisks, from left to right to check marginal glosses, and occasionally "standing back" to observe the organization of the page as a whole (as when we note that one is shaped like a Christmas tree, another like an eye-chart). The effect achieved here is remarkably close to Kenner's description of "blocks of discourse" organized "simultaneously in space rather than consecutively in time."

The last—and most significant—method used by Babs to call attention to herself is also probably the least radical of her strategies. It is produced by the sensual, highly poetic quality of the language which she uses to create herself. This non-typographic method of focusing our attention on the words before us is often used by poets. In ordinary discourse and in the language of realistically motivated fiction, words do not usually call attention to themselves. The reason, as Valery has explained, is that calling attention to words *as words* defeats the utility-function of ordinary language:

> Current, level language, the language that is used for a purpose, flies to its purpose, flies to its meaning, to its purely mental translation, and is lost in it. . . . Its form, its auditive aspect, is only a stage that the mind runs past without stopping. If pitch, if rhythm are present, they are there for the sake of sense, they occur only for the moment . . . for meaning is its final aim.[8]

In ordinary discourse and in most fiction, words are used mainly as vehicles to refer us to a world (real or imaginary), and the words themselves remain invisible: as Babs says, "The usual view is that you see through me, through what I am really—significant sound" (Red Section, 3). Babs, however, resembles the stereotyped woman in being vain about her physical qualities and resentful when she is used but not noticed. Babs shares with Valéry (to whom Gass seems to owe much of his esthetics) the view that when words are placed in an esthetic context (as in a poem) their utility is sacrificed in favor of a unity of sound and sense:

> Again there is in every act of imagination a disdain of utility, and a glorious, free show of human strength; for the man of imagination dares to make things for no better reason than they please him—because he *lives*. And everywhere, again, he seeks out unity: in the word he unifies both sound and sense; . . .between words and things he further makes a bond so that symbols seem to contain their objects. (Red Section, 3)

Like Barthelme's Snow White, who wishes "there were some words in the world that were not the words I always hear,"[9] Babs is bored with her own existence as she usually finds it: "Why aren't there any decent words?" she exclaims at one point in the Blue Section (1); and in a footnote to the play in the Olive Section (2), she compares the "dreary words" of ordinary prose to ordinary action, which often loses all subtlety and beauty as it strains to make itself understood to an audience "all of whom are in the second balcony." Too often, claims Babs, writers—and readers—seem unaware that words make up the body of all literature. At one point she comments on the necessity of the writer accepting the medium in which he works. The passage is typical of the lyrical, highly "poetic" language favored by Babs throughout her monologue:

> You are your body—you do not choose the feet you walk in—and the poet is his language. He sees the world, and words form in his eyes just like the streams and trees there. He feels everything verbally. Objects, passions, actions—I myself believe that the true kiss comprises a secret exchange of words, for the mouth was made by God to give form and sound to syllables; permit us to make, as our souls move, the magic music of names, for to say Cecilia, even in secret, is to make love. (Olive Section, 2)

These remarks not only direct our attention to the nature of the words on the page but also reinforce the sexual parallels that have been suggested. Even as we read these words, we have "in secret" been making love—and hopefully our response has been better than Gelvin's.

If poetry is the language which Babs is trying to realize herself in, she admits that she rarely finds lovers appreciative enough to create her properly. When Gelvin leaves, she says: "he did not, in his address, at any time, construct me. He made nothing, I swear. Empty I began, and empty I remained" (White Section, 4). Indeed, she even observes some inadequacies in our own response when she asks: "Is that any way to make love to a lady, a lonely one at that, used formerly to having put the choicest portions of her privates flowered out in pots and vases" (Red Secton, 3). The main problem, as Babs observes, is simply that we have forgotten how to make love appreciatively:

> You can't make love like that anymore—make love or manuscript. Yet I have put my hand upon this body, here as no man ever has, and I have even felt my pencil stir, grow great with blood. But never has it swollen up in love. It moves in anger, always, against its paper. (Red Section, 3)

Today readers and writers alike approach lady language in the wrong spirit. The pencil, the writer's phallic instrument of creation, grows great nowadays only with blood, never with love. After intercourse, Babs is left alone; she sits and ponders her fate: "They've done, the holy office over, and they turn their back on me, I'm what they left, their turds in the toilet. Anyway, I mustn't wonder why they don't return. Maybe I should put a turnstile in" (Red Section, 3).

Lonely and often ignored, Babs spends a good deal of time considering her own nature. Like many twentieth-century philosophers, she is very interested in the relationship between words and the world. In the Olive Section (2) she quotes (or quasi-quotes) John Locke's discussion of the way in which language develops from sense to impression to perception to concept. Locke shows the way our understanding sorts out our perceptions, and then concludes that we give proper names to things "being such as men have an occasion to mark particularly."[10] Babs has obviously taken Locke to heart, for she is constantly musing over the appropriateness of names in just this fashion. She wonders, for instance, why men do not assign proper names to various parts of their anatomy:

> They ought to name their noses like they named their pricks. Why not their ears too?—they frequently stick out. This is my morose Slave nose, Czar Nicholas. And these twins in my mirror, Rueben and Antony, they have large soft lobes. . . . If you had nice pleasant names for yourself all over, you might feel more at home, more among friends. (Blue Section, 1)

The passage shows that Babs confers upon language the same magical potency which Stephen Dedalus gave it in *A Portrait of the Artist as a Young Man*: she exalts the habit of verbal association into a principle for the arrangement of experience. Of course, she is right—words help arrange our experience and often exhibit the power to make us "feel more at home, more among friends." Naming something gives us a sort of power over it, just as we become the master of a situation by putting it into words. On the other hand, Babs confronts "the terror of terminology" (Blue Section, 1) when she considers specific occasions when words fail to suggest what they are supposed to. As might be expected, Babs' example of an inappropriate word is drawn from a sexual context: "Screw—they say *screw*—what an idea! did any of them ever? It's the lady who wooves and woggles. Nail—bang—sure—*nail* is nearer theirs" (Blue Section, 1).

Because of her envy of poetic language, Babs is especially interested in circumstances—as with the language of Shakespeare or any great poet—where words become something more than simply Lockean devices for calling to mind concepts. Babs thinks a good deal about the "poetic ideal": the word which lies midway between the "words of nature" (which constitute reality) and the words of ordinary language (which are nothing in themselves but arbitrary symbols which direct our minds elsewhere). Babs explains her view of what qualities ordinary words have:

> What's in a name but letters, eh? and everyone owns *them*. . . . the sound SUN or the figures S, U, N, are purely arbitrary modes of recalling their objects, and they have the further advantage of being nothing *per se*, for while the sun, itself, is large and orange and boiling, the sight and the sound, SUN, is but a hiss drawn up through the nose. (Olive Section, 2)

At times Babs tries to exploit the sound of words at the expense of their sense (or referential quality) in a way which may remind us of the symbolist poets. For example, she takes one of her favorite words ("catafalque") and repeats it for several lines; she follows up by creating a lovely-sounding but totally nonsensical poem: "catafalque catafalque neighborly mew/ Ozenfant Valery leonine nu" (Olive Section, 2). What Babs is obviously looking for, especially in creating herself, is the kind of fusion of sound and sense found in the best poets. She says admiringly of Shakespeare at one point that "Now the language of Shakespeare . . . not merely recalls the cold notion of the thing, it expresses and becomes a part of its reality, so that the sight and sound, SUN, in Shakespeare is warm and orange and greater than the page it lies on" (Olive Section, 2). Nearly all the strategies of *Willie Masters'* are closely related to the idea that in literature words should not merely point somewhere else but should be admired for themselves.

Willie Masters', then, is a remarkably pure example of metafiction. As we watch "imagination imagining itself imagine" (Blue Section, 1), we are witnessing a work self-consciously create itself out of the materials at hand—words. After Babs has endured still another unsatisfactory encounter (with Gelvin—but possibly with us as well), she sums up some of the problems she faces by quoting Dryden:

> The rest I have forgot; for cares and time
> Change all things, and untune my soul to rhyme.
> I could have once sung down a summer's sun;
> But now the chime of poetry is done;
> My voice grows hoarse; I feel the notes decay,
> As if the wolves had seen me first today
> (White Section, 4)

Babs finishes the poem by adding a final, optimistic line of her own—she will "make a start against the darkness anyway." In the concluding pages Babs makes an eloquent plea for a new kind of language capable of provoking the kind of loving response she so desires. Her plea concludes her narrative and provides a brilliant example of the sort of language she is calling for:

> Then let us have a language worthy of our world, a democratic style where rich and well-born nouns can roister with some sluttish verb yet find themselves content and uncomplained of. We want a diction which contains the quaint, the rare, the technical, the obsolete, the old, the lent, the nonce, the local slang of the street, in neighborly confinement. Our tone should suit our time: uncommon quiet dashed with common thunder. It should be as young and quick and sweet and dangerous as we are. Experimental and expansive . . . it will give new glasses to new eyes, and put those plots and patterns down we find our modern lot in. Metaphor must be its god now gods are metaphors. . . . It's not the languid pissing prose we got, we need; but poetry, the human muse, full up, erect and on the charge, impetuous and hot and loud and wild like Messalina going to the stews, or those damn rockets streaming headstrong into stars. (White Section, 4)

As the best metafiction does, *Willie Masters' Lonesome Wife* forces us to examine the nature of fiction-making from new perspectives. If Babs (and Gass) have succeeded, our attention has been focused on the act of reading words in a way we probably have not experienced before. The steady concern with the *stuff* of fiction, words, makes Gass's work unique among metafictions which have appeared thus far. At the end of the book, we encounter a reminder from Gass stamped onto the page: "YOU HAVE FALLEN INTO ART—RETURN TO LIFE." When we do return to life, we have, hopefully, a new appreciation—perhaps even love—of that lonesome lady in Gass's title.

Notes

1. William Gass, "The Medium of Fiction," *Fiction and the Figures of Life* (New York: Random House, 1972), p. 27.
2. William Gass, "In the Heart of the Heart of the Country," *In the Heart of the Heart of the Country and Other Stories* (New York: Harper and Row, 1968), p. 202.
3. Among contemporary works of fiction which have used typographic experimentation, the most interesting are Michael Butor's

Mobile (1963), Steve Katz's *The Exaggerations of Peter Prince* (1968), Raymond Federman's *Double or Nothing* (1971), and Kobo Abe's *The Box Man* (1974).
4. Hugh Kenner, *Flaubert, Joyce, and Beckett: The Stoic Comedians* (London: W. H. Allen, 1964), p. 47.
5. Michael Butor, "The Book as Object," *Inventory* (New York: Simon and Schuster, 1968), p. 44.
6. Kenner, p. 47; Butor refers to basically the same thing with his term "the book as object."
7. Kenner, p. 40.
8. Paul Valéry, "Discourse on the Declamation of Verse," *Selected Writings* (New York: New Directions, 1964), p. 157.
9. Donald Barthelme, *Snow White* (New York: Atheneum, 1967), p. 6.
10. John Locke, *An Essay concerning Human Understanding* (Book II, Chapter XI, Section 9), *Selections* (Chicago: Univ. of Chicago Press, 1956), p. 144.

NED FRENCH
"Against the Grain: Theory and Practice in the Work of William H. Gass"
Iowa Review, Winter 1976, pp. 86–106

The times are full of contradictions. People *feel* happy and tell you as much, but they are not. Classes are at war, and so are friends and lovers. Families and workplaces are at odds with each other—and with us. Such contradictions, which slip in among the products of our work, have become the subject and the fact of our best fiction—making it complicated, ambivalent, and too often inaccessible. Some of this fiction is written by William H. Gass.

Of course, ever since the novel came to birth amid the contradictions of a rising capitalism, it has been what Lukács, Auerbach, and Goldmann have aptly called the "problematic" genre. It has always contained tensions between realism and romance, mimesis and illusion, type and individual, description and prescription, content and form. But today the situation is intensifying: the novelist is both more cut off from society and more involved in its contradictions. We shouldn't be surprised, therefore, to find in Gass's work a major discrepancy between the theory of his essays and the practice of his fiction—a discrepancy that also makes for difficulty, disturbance, and beauty within the fiction itself. Richard Gilman detected this problem when he wrote that *Omensetter's Luck* was caught between "ambitions and recalcitrances," "discovery and nostalgia."[1] And Gass himself has warned us that he is "one whose views seem stretched like a wet string between passion and detachment, refusal and commitment, tradition and departure."[2] I want here to examine some implications of that self-conscious tension as it informs what I take to be the work of a major writer.

Anyone familiar with Gass's essays will have been struck by certain of their shining and upsetting sentences:

> There are no descriptions in fiction, there are only constructions, and the principles which govern these constructions are persistently philosophical.[3]
>
> It seems a country-headed thing to say: that literature is language, that stories and the places and people in them are merely made of words as chairs are made of smoothed sticks and sometimes of cloth or metal tubes.[4]
>
> In our hearts we know what actually surrounds the statue. The same surrounds every other work of art: empty space and silence.[5]
>
> Hamlet is a mouth, a vocabulary.[6]

I confess that these sentences are taken out of context and that the contexts "constructed" by Gass sometimes compel us to agree with him. Nevertheless, we squirm more often than we put a check in the margin. Such sentences seem to assume the victory for New Criticism. People with whom we do not agree would applaud them. We blink and look again, but the sentences do not go away. So, for comfort, we turn to the fiction—*Omensetter*, the stories, the fragments from *The Tunnel*. John Gardner's common sense seems to support us in this. Of the opinions in Gass's essays, he writes: "They give the reader things to think about while reading Gass's fiction. To think about for half a sentence, before he [or she] gets swept away."[7]

One explanation of this incongruity in Gass is that maintaining such a theory is a corrective for certain tendencies in his own habits of composition—tendencies toward overwriting or turgidity. To say this sounds as if we are psychologizing (as Gass says we psychologize about Hamlet), but nevertheless, I think we can proceed, remembering that such activities do have their place. Gardner allows that if the "front" of Gass's mind is preoccupied with these formalist theories, the "back" of it "keeps pumping in emotion" when he sits down to his fiction. Gardner definitely accounts for something here, but he also makes it sound as if Gass's writing is automatic, which it most assuredly is not. This confusion is really not Gardner's: his letter is a concise reply to an extended polemic by Gass. Much of the problem results from the easy reduction we make of the standard Freudian terms. The interplay between the conscious and unconscious factors of creation is often tactfully and euphemistically placed under a single heading such as "taste" or "talent." Gass himself does this.

> Neither keeping the unities nor dissolving them is of any use, nor is loyalty to symmetry, harmony, balance, or coherence. A consistent image can be dull, and an inconsistent one both noble and exciting. You have to taste to tell.[8]

In one conversation, he is even more candid.

> One of the things that you really have to do when you are waiting is forget all the crap you've been talking about in theory, because what is important is the work and not your bloody theory. The theory is a protective device. . . . Although you may be interested in talking about work and developing some kind of theory, that is a separate interest, and a very suspicious one. As soon as you get caught up and start writing to a program, you have got to constantly sort of feel the work and experience the taste at the same time. You worry whether you are coming or going.[9]

But this second statement is also hyperbole. Gass's theory is more than "crap" or a mere "protective device." It is an integral part of his world view and his creative process. There is a sense in which his theory is his conscience, if not his consciousness. Useful, appropriate and necessary in certain ways, it is not however sufficient. Exactly because it is insufficient Gass must resort to the elusive idea of "taste." Similarly, New Criticism teaches us how to read, but not how to criticize or live. Of Gass's theory (that nothing exists except what's on the page, and, thus, that a character is only words or noises, a vocabulary), Gardner admits that it contains some truth "or Gass wouldn't have said it." But, Gardner continues, fiction is more than its theory and more than its words, for fortunately we fill in with details, employing "*empathy*, a philosophically mysterious process." Consciousness focuses, but the whole world (a material totality) continues to exist and though we focus on the part, we are aware of the whole. Or, in reference to fiction, the sum of the metaphors is more than their total. Gardner emphasizes the element of synecdoche which is ever-present in the process of language. Gass, whose Ph.D. thesis was entitled "A Philosophical Investigation of Metaphor," does not overlook this element. Elsewhere, we find him sounding quite a lot like Gardner:

> But metaphor is more than a process of inference; it is also a form of presentation or display.[10]
>
> A metaphorical system can itself be interpreted metaphorically, and that one again in terms of another, and another, on and on until positive wonders have been constructed. A simple scene, a sudden flash, can be used metaphorically, to represent a whole—and there are simply a million possibilities.[11]

What Gass does not acknowledge is that this chain reaction set off by the "sudden flash" does not slow down for language and its meanings. Psychologically, the process is called symbolization. Gass denies that there are any images when he reads, claiming that it's "just words."[12] Elsewhere, however, in his laudatory review of William Thompson's study of the role of imagination in the Easter Rebellion, he agrees with this epigram on epistemology by Thompson: "The consequences of an event take place in the mind, and the mind holds on best to images."[13] Reading also is an event. There is a conflict here between Gass's usual emphasis on words and meanings, and the layman's terms for symbolization, this rendering of a "simple scene" with its "million possibilities." Such terms refer often to image-making—the "theater of the mind" or the "mind's eye."

"Represent a whole"—strange talk from one whose theory is ostensibly *not* representational or mimetic. What Gass reminds himself about here (and what Gardner is reminding Gass about) is that truth resides in both camps, or rather, in the interaction between them. Philosophically (and we must remember that Gass is a philosopher), this interaction has led to the amalgam of abstract, speculative idealism and vulgar, deterministic materialism that Marx developed into dialectical materialism. Aesthetically, most of this interaction has yet to be systematized, but it has led to Brecht's practical discovery that illusion is needed in order to truly and critically represent. In criticism, it may have led to Lucien Goldmann's combination of formalism and socio-historical analysis. The contradictions of our society to which I alluded at the outset are not unconnected to the split between the theory and practice of so much fiction.

> Writers are seldom recognized as empiricists, idealists, skeptics, or stoics, though they ought—I mean, now, in terms of the principles of their constructions, for Sartre is everywhere recognized as an existentialist leaning left, but few have noticed that the construction of his novels is utterly bourgeois.[14]

Gass is everywhere recognized as a theoretician leaning toward formalism, but the construction of his novels is realist.

I bring this up in this way because the play between Gass's theory and his fiction has its social aspect. As Robert Kiley expresses it, "Mr. Gass is not a fastidious esthete or a doctrinal fanatic. He is a moderate man—an artist—pressed to extremes by circumstances."[15] But what are the circumstances? They involve the competition which the novel faces from television, movies, cassettes, and other media, and the consequent degradation of people and their culture which this seems to signal. For Gass, the threat lies also in a certain kind of novel—those books which "trade in slogan and clichés, fads and whims, the slippery and easy, the smart and the latest."[16] The circumstances have called forth best-selling novels on murder in Kansas, anthrosophy, life in the suburbs, "the negro question, the drug question, the jewish question, the catholic question."[17] Gass's particularly acerbic reviews of Updike and Roth show where he stands on fashion, "relevance" and popularity. He is driven to the position of equating realism with journalism and pornography. His avoidance of the topical leads him to deny subject matter and content almost completely, dismissing them as "just a way of organizing."[18]

On the New York literary market, he is equally trenchant: "When I go to New York City, I feel I'm going to the provinces. What is sophisticated about literary New York? How much of importance goes on there? It is filled with commercial hacks and their pimps."[19] Presented with these circumstances, Gass constructs his elaborate *defense of poesy*. His defense, however, is ultimately of the people for whom the work of art can be an aid—society, reader, artist.

> The aim of the artist ought to be to bring into the world objects which do not already exist there, and objects which are especially worthy of love. . . . *he* [or *she*, i.e., the artist] is valuable to society if what he produces is valuable to it.[20]

Confusion arises because value is so hard to measure. The measures of the market (popularity, relevance, marketability) infect even the "purest" art. Thus, in trying to create a worthy addition to reality, Gass counters with the stringent criteria of his formalist theory. Sounding like an aesthete, his position is, however, not one of retreat. He is polemical, awesomely devoted and very hard working.[21] We have seen the situation before. Ernst Fischer has described the progressive element in this kind of contradictory stance.

> *L'art pour l'art*—the attitude adopted by that great and fundamentally realistic poet, Baudelaire—is also a protest against the vulgar utilitarianism, the dreary business preoccupations of the bourgeoisie. It arose from the artist's determination not to produce commodities in a world where everything becomes a saleable commodity.[22]

Socially, the first consequence of such a position is the ambivalent relationship one then has with one's readers. Where are they to be found when you don't want them to buy the book, when you don't want the book to be popular and therefore consumed? The object may be worthy of love, but love itself is difficult—"love (someone save the word, I am unable)."[23] Thus, we find Gass at one point asking fictional theory to take up the question of "the recreative power of the skillful reader"[24] and at another admitting that he has "little patience with the 'creative reader.'"[25] The difference between these two kinds of readers (and the kinds of writers that appeal to them) is a fine one, and one that both writer and reader must constantly struggle to distinguish. "Often these things are matters of a little more or a little less."[26] To look at it another way, the distinction has to do with whether the "books act on us" and make us "too much a passive term" (as Gass suggests is sometimes the case with the work of Beckett, Borges and Barth[27], or whether, in the phrase by Arnold Bennett that Gass is so fond of quoting, the books "test us." The classic, the book that tests us, first of all gives us an "invitation." Then, with its figurative system, it "achieves . . . the reader's ardent whole participation" in both art and life. It neither toys with us nor asks us to toy with it, but rather calls for rethinking and real changes. The difference is between being challenged and being ordered. It is at this point that Gass quotes Rilke's famous line on the conclusion of such an ardent, artistic process: "You must change your life."[28] We might supplement this only with a quote from Mary Wollstonecraft: "Labor to reform thyself to reform the World."[29]

In searching for the way in which the novel might make a difference, Gass comes to the conclusion that the writing and reading of novels should be like teaching (or testing) and like loving. The writer's relationship to the reader then, if it is good, is full and reciprocal, proceeding dialectically, illuminating both the subject and the participants. Such a process can only be long and difficult, full of scrutiny, commitment and caring. This is a Romantic and romantic notion.

> Listen, Furber said, when I was a little boy and learning letters—A . . . B . . . C . . . , love was never taught to me, I couldn't spell it, the O was always missing, or the V, so I wrote love like live, or lure, or late, or law, or liar.[30]

Much study and hard work are needed to avoid the games and lies that prohibit real learning and loving. "We live, most of us, amidst lies, deceits, and confusions. A work of art may not utter the truth, but it must be honest."[31] It is little wonder then that it was so long before *Omensetter's Luck* was ventured forth as an invitation, metaphorical system and test. We always doubt that we are worthy of love or able to teach. Trust comes hard. "Unfortunately this book was not written to have readers. It was written to *not* have readers, while still deserving them."[32]

This problem of audience is, as I mentioned, a social problem. Yet, as Kohler discovers in *The Tunnel*, the personal life is also social and a part of history. To be denied an audience when one is deserving is a problem to which we correctly grant a certain magnitude, but just as excruciating is the fact that the same set of contradictions alienates each of us from our self. Thus, in "The Artist and Society," we find this schizophrenic slip: "Naturally the artist is an enemy of the state. . . . As a man he may long for action; he may feel injustice like a burn; and certainly he may speak out."[33] Riddle, possible story for Borges: when is a writer not a person? Possible answers: when the writer is writing, acting or speaking out. But elsewhere, in reference to Valéry and Wittgenstein, Gass presents philosophy and poetry as activities "where every word allowed to remain in a line represented a series of acts of the poet, or proposals and withdrawals which, in agony, at last, issued in this one, and how no one word was final, how the work was never over, never done, but only, in grief, abandoned as it sometimes had to be . . ."[34] Because the situation is not static and no one solution will hold, the emphasis, over time, is less on the individual answer than on the continual struggle to answer. Again, Gass tries to move beyond the topical to the truly lasting and exemplary work. Unity, stamina and courage are sought beyond mere impressions and effects. This is true for both life and art. With Coleridge, Gass can settle for nothing less than "what we—what each of us—should somehow be: a complete particular man [or woman]." This must be the concern because "nonpersons unperson persons. They kill. For them no one is human."[35]

The stakes, we can see, are high. When writing is an activity and a *raison d'etre*, ethics and aesthetics merge. When the ethical and political concern is this strong, everything, or almost everything, hinges on every word. To be exemplary is to write exemplary fictions.[36] Gass quotes Karl Kraus to make this point: "I cannot get myself to accept that a whole sentence can ever come from half a man [or woman]."[37] The implications of such a statement can be paralyzing. Agraphia becomes a real hazard. Certain names group themselves around Gass, and we can only worry. Coleridge is often characterized as having possessed the largest unfulfilled potential in English literature. Wittgenstein and Valéry both experienced long silences. With Lowry, some similarities become especially haunting.[38] Both the *Volcano* and the *Omensetter* were ten years in the making. Lowry's manuscript was burned, Gass's stolen. One can be pitted against one's self, so that nothing gets written, let alone published. "Writing. Not writing. Twin terrors."[39] Thus, it is reassuring to welcome each new essay or piece of *The Tunnel*. A healthy difference between Gass and these others starts to become clear as we watch him observing Valéry, for after devoting a score of his life only to precise, formalistic and quasi-mathematical theories of aesthetics, Valéry could finally return to poetry,

> working—in the phrase of Huysmans, one novelist he allowed himself to admire—always *au rebours* against the grain, and correcting in himself a severe and weakening lean in the direction of the mystical and romantic.[40]

Then, in conversation, almost as if it is his secret, the key to his ability to produce, Gass admits, "I'm basically a romantic. I'm a romantic writer and a formalist in theory. So, working against the grain all the time in this way, I try to get something that will stand straight up."[41] Romantic (realist?) and formalist—this also is a relationship which is full and reciprocal, and proceeding dialectically.

That Gass's work is proceeding is what is so encouraging. With the realization that it is on-going we can return to the fiction, ready to start through it again and have the next set of a "million possibilities" flash up before us. Going back, for instance, to the opening of the fabulous section on graffiti in "The Clairvoyant" (1964), we see that even then, Gass was working against the grain:

> I am an inveterate pencil carver and I consequently understand the qualities of wood. I know how, for instance, the grain will cause the most determined line to quake and wiggle. My first attempt to engrave the letter *c* in the Covenant plank left a very bent and shaken *l*, though you would never guess it now, the original is so overlaid with flourishes. The secret is to proceed by a series of gentle scratches, repeated often; never an impatient deep gouge which the wood will surely put a crick in, but always the patiently light scratch.[42]

For Gass, so deeply concerned with writing as a form and as a figure of life, it now seems inevitable that he would have taken on the immense metafictional project of which "The Clairvoyant" and *Willie Masters'* were to have been parts.[43]

The Pedersen Kid was conceived under the influence of Gertrude Stein as an exercise in small units, "patiently light scratches." It is more than a formal exercise, however, for in Gass, content and form are always one and the same, as Wittgenstein said ethics and aesthetics are. Or, to phrase it in a more Coleridgean way, form and content must be fused in imagination. Thus, on the level of theme or content, *The Pedersen Kid* is about Jorge's battle to stay in touch with himself and to love others. Wrapped in the blizzard and separated from his family by distrust, Jorge is driven in on himself until the very end when, finally, after a series of catastrophes, he is "warm inside and out, burning up inside and out, with joy."[44] His joy, however, is ironically and dramatically undermined by the story's violence. Jorge's final encompassing of the "inside and out" (that previously disorienting fluctuation between solipsism and selflessness) is in some ways analogous to the final position of the writer who after a series of acts, proposals and withdrawals, finally, in joy and grief, abandons himself to one statement. The gentle, repetitious prose of *The Pedersen Kid* exemplifies such a series of acts.

Gass did not rest, of course, with the small units of *The Pedersen Kid*. Since that story's simple understated sentences, he has turned increasingly to rhetoric. The change has been so thorough at times one might even say the "original is overlaid with flourishes," or as Mary Ellmann has put it, there is in Gass's work a "contrary allegiance to extravagance . . . a deliberate rhetorical swinging-out beyond previous bounds."[45] There are dangerous tendencies toward histrionics in such projects, but in spite of the risks, Gass has extended and accelerated his use of figurative language in order to range more easily through moods, voices, and dramatic situations. While Gass's metaphors alternate beautifully between the sensuous and the witty, Jethro Furber, his fictional embodiment of rhetoric,[46] struggles with isolation, desire, power and jealousy on his way to his confrontation with Omensetter. Within the story, Furber experiences the dangers of rhetoric. Once, he had felt that "yes, words were superior; they maintained a superior control; they touched without your touching; they were at once the bait, the hook, the line, the pole, and the water in between."[47] Then, the rhetoric sours into lies and "all his speeches" become "beautiful barriers of words."[48] He cracks up.

Furber's experience demonstrates to us the problems inherent in rhetorical language. Linguistically, figurative language is a language of relationships, correspondences and levels of meaning. Psychologically, as in Furber's case, it is a language of highs and lows, the epiphanies in the garden with Pike's stone as well as the final confused fall. Throughout Gass's work the reasons for the rhetoric have had first of all to do with the levels of meaning it allows to operate simultaneously. The French structuralist Gérard Gennette has described this phenomenon quite succinctly.

> Every figure is translatable, and carries its translations, visible in its transparence, like a watermark or palimpsest, under its apparent text. Rhetoric is tied to this duplicity of language.[49]

Duplicity—doubleness, something more than simply one, or deceit.

In *The Tunnel*, multiplicity is the key, as Kohler's rhetoric moves beyond Furber's. In such a book, the themes will have to be more varied and dense in order to handle the rhetoric (or vice versa). In *The Tunnel*, we also know that these themes will be more explicitly historical and political than they have been before in Gass's work. Politics are apparent in the earlier pieces. The relationship between Henry and Omensetter was one of the lyrical worshipper confronting and being possessed by the myth of grace, but it was also a landlord-tenant relationship. "Icicles" deals with property relationships.[50] "In the Heart" occasionally tends toward a kind of pastoral anarchism. Tott raised the questions of the historical convincingly enough that Roger Shattuck has claimed[51] the "moral" of *Omensetter* is this thought of Tott's:

> Imagine growing up in a world where only generals and geniuses, empires and companies, had histories, not your own town or grandfather, house or Samantha—none of the things you'd loved.[52]

In *The Tunnel*, the other histories will be told, at least figuratively. The fantastic inventories of things and names, the typographical experiments, the flip-flopping puns, the ellipses, the alliteration, the iambic rhythms, the sight rhymes, the dirty limericks and the ironic jumps of Gass's prose will this time be moving Professor Kohler's rhetorical consciousness through a history of "Fascism in all those little places."[53] The pieces we have seen so far have shown Kohler dealing with the politics of bedrooms, marriages, families, classrooms, academic departments, publishing, childhood, hometowns, and the self.

> My customary tone is scholarly. I always move with care. And I've been praised for weight, the substance of my thought. But it's not the way I feel I want to speak now, and I realize (I've come to it as I write) that my subject's far too serious for scholarship, for history, and I must find another form before I let what's captive in me out.[54]

The form is all new for Kohler perhaps, but for Gass it is part of a progression. Form and content—one and the same, and still the same: writing against one's self so as to write well and writing out of one's self toward another.

Notes

1. *The Confusion of Realms* (New York: Random House, 1969), p. 70.
2. *Fiction and the Figures of Life* (New York: Alfred A. Knopf, 1970), p. xii.
3. William H. Gass, "A Letter to the Editor," in Thomas McKormack, ed., *Afterwords: Novelists on Their Novels* (New York: Harper and Row Publishers, 1969), pp. 88–105.
4. *Fiction and the Figures of Life*, p. 27.
5. Ibid., p. 49.
6. *Afterwords*, p. 92.
7. "Correspondence," *New American Review*, 9 (April, 1970), p. 235.
8. *Fiction and the Figures of Life*, p. 241.
9. "Against the Grain: A Conversation with William H. Gass," conducted by Ned French and David Keyser, *Harvard Advocate*, CVI, 4 (Winter, 1973), pp. 8–16.
10. *Fiction and the Figures of Life*, p. 63.
11. *Afterwords*, p. 94.
12. "Against the Grain: A Conversation with William H. Gass," p. 10.
13. *Fiction and the Figures of Life*, p. 267.
14. Ibid., pp. 25–26.
15. Review of *Fiction and the Figures of Life*, *The New York Times Book Review*, February 21, 1971, p. 26.
16. *Afterwords*, pp. 90–91.
17. Ibid., p. 91.
18. "Against the Grain: A Conversation with William H. Gass," p. 16.
19. "Fiction Needn't Say Things—It Should *Make* Them out of Words: An Interview with William H. Gass," conducted by Carole Spearin McCauley, *The Falcon*, 5 (Winter, 1972), pp. 34–35.
20. *Fiction and the Figures of Life*, pp. 284–285.
21. See Stanley Elkin's comments on his good friend's work habits and the exercises he performs in practicing sentences in Scott Sanders, "An Interview with Stanley Elkin," *Contemporary Literature*, XVI, 2 (Spring, 1975), p. 135.
22. *The Necessity of Art: A Marxist Approach* (Baltimore: Penguin Books, 1964), p. 68.
23. William H. Gass, "We Have Not Lived the Right Life," *New American Review*, 5 (April, 1969), pp. 30.
24. *Fiction and the Figures of Life*, p. 25.
25. "Fiction Needn't Say Things— It Should *Make* Them out of Words: An Interview with William H. Gass," p. 37.
26. *Fiction and the Figures of Life*, p. 75.
27. Ibid., pp. 73–74.
28. Ibid., p. 76.
29. *A Vindication of the Rights of Woman* (New York: W. W. Norton and Co., 1967).
30. William H. Gass, *Omensetter's Luck* (New York: New American Library, 1966), p. 298.
31. *Fiction and the Figures of Life*, p. 282.
32. *Afterwords*, p. 105.
33. *Fiction and the Figures of Life*, p. 287.
34. Ibid., p. 249.
35. Ibid., p. 283.
36. Gass is not alone here, even among contemporary writers. See Robert Coover's preface to his "Seven Exemplary Fictions" in *Pricksongs & Descants: Fictions* (New York: E. P. Dutton, 1969), pp. 76–79.

37. *Fiction and the Figures of Life*, p. 252.
38. Frederick Busch has examined some of the thematic similarities between *Under the Volcano* and "In the Heart of the Heart of the Country" in one of the best articles on Gass's work—"But This Is What It Is Like to Live in Hell: William H. Gass's 'In the Heart of the Heart of the Country,'" *Modern Fiction Studies*, XIX, 1 (Spring, 1973), pp. 97–108.
39. William H. Gass, "The Doomed in Their Sinking," *New York Review of Books*, XVII 9 (May 18, 1972), pp. 3–4.
40. William H. Gass, "Paul Valéry: Crisis and Resolution," *New York Times Book Review*, August 20, 1972, p. 16.
41. "Against the Grain: A Conversation with William H. Gass," p. 16.
42. William H. Gass, "The Clairvoyant," *Location*, I, 2 (Summer, 1964), pp. 64–66.
43. For a beautifully compact article on Gass as one of four writers of metafiction, see Robert Scholes, "Metafiction," The *Iowa Review*, I, 4 (Fall, 1970) pp. 100–115.
44. William H. Gass, *In the Heart of the Heart of the Country* (New York: Harper and Row, 1968), p. 79.
45. *Thinking About Women* (New York: Harcourt Brace Jovanovich, 1968), p. 173.
46. *Afterwords*, p. 96.
47. *Omensetter's Luck*, p. 138.
48. Ibid., p. 231.
49. *Figures* (Paris: Seuil, 1966), p. 211, as trans. and quoted by Robert Scholes, *Structuralism in Literature: An Introduction* (New Haven: Yale, 1974), p. 161.
50. See Patricia Kane, "A Point of Law in William Gass's 'Icicles,'" *Notes on Contemporary Literature*, I, 2 (March, 1971), pp. 7–8.
51. "Fiction à la Mode," *New York Review of Books*, VI, 11 (June 23, 1966), p. 25.
52. *Omensetter's Luck*, p. 27.
53. "Against the Grain: A Conversation with William Gass," p. 16.
54. "We Have Not Lived the Right Life," p. 24.

ALLEN GINSBERG

1926–

Allen Ginsberg was born in Newark, New Jersey, on June 3, 1926. His childhood was marked by the poverty of the Depression and by the decline into insanity of his mother, who died in a mental hospital in 1958. As a student at Columbia University, he was involved in the beginnings of the Beat movement, associating with William Burroughs and Jack Kerouac. After graduating with a B.A. in 1948, he worked on and off as a market research consultant in New York and, from 1954, in San Francisco. There he met Lawrence Ferlinghetti, who brought out Ginsberg's *Howl and Other Poems* in the City Lights Pocket Poets Series in 1956. The resulting obscenity trial, in which the judge ruled in favor of the publisher, brought Ginsberg immense publicity.

In 1957 Ginsberg traveled in Europe, and in 1960 in South America. In these years he experimented with marijuana and hallucinogenic drugs such as LSD, which he defended as an aid to poetic creation and consciousness expansion; parts of *Kaddish and Other Poems, 1958–1960* were written under the influence of drugs.

Travels from 1961 to 1963 took Ginsberg through Europe and Israel to India, where he studied Hindu thought and meditational practices with Indian holy men. In 1965 he visited Eastern Europe, and was crowned King of the May in Prague before being expelled by the Czechoslovakian authorities. Back in America, he promoted "flower power", spoke against war on college campuses, and was a leading figure at literary happenings. In the 1970s he remained active in political protests, such as anti-nuclear demonstrations, and in poetic events, often working with music. He toured with Bob Dylan in 1975, and later performed with the New Wave group, The Clash, and has recorded his own blues music and lyrics.

In spite of the diversity of his other activities, to which may be added occasional film appearances, Ginsberg has produced a large amount of poetry. *Planet News, 1961–1967*, appeared in 1968, and *The Fall of America: Poems of These States, 1965–1971*, in 1972, winning him a National Book Award in 1974. *Mind Breaths: Poems, 1972–1977*, and *Plutonian Odes, 1977–1980*, were followed by *Collected Poems, 1947–80* in 1984.

Ginsberg's long-enduring relationship with Peter Orlovsky finds expression in *Straight Heart's Delight* (1980). A practicing Buddhist since the early 1970s, he teaches meditation and poetry in the summers at the Naropa Institute in Boulder, Colorado.

The most remarkable poem of the young group ⟨of San Francisco poets⟩, written during the past year, is *Howl*, by Allen Ginsberg, a 29-year-old poet who is the son of Louis Ginsberg, a poet known to newspaper readers in the East. Ginsberg comes from Brooklyn; he studied at Columbia; after years of apprenticeship to usual forms, he developed his brave new medium. This poem has created a furor of praise or abuse whenever read or heard. It is a powerful work, cutting through to dynamic meaning. Ginsberg thinks he is going forward by going back to the methods of Whitman.

My first reaction was that it is based on destructive violence. It is profoundly Jewish in temper. It is Biblical in its repetitive grammatical build-up. It is a howl against everything in our mechanistic civilization which kills the spirit, assuming that the louder you shout the more likely you are to be heard. It lays bare the nerves of suffering and spiritual struggle. Its positive force and energy come from a redemptive quality of love, although it destructively catalogues evils of our time from physical deprivation to madness.—RICHARD EBERHART, "West Coast Rhythms," *NYTBR*, Sept. 2, 1956, p. 18

It is only fair to Allen Ginsberg . . . to remark on the utter lack of decorum of any kind in his dreadful little volume. I believe that the title of his long poem, "Howl," is meant to be a noun, but I can't help taking it as an imperative. The poem itself is a confession of the poet's faith, done into some 112 paragraph-like lines, in the ravings of a lunatic friend (to whom it is dedicated), and in the irregularities in the lives of those of his friends who populate his rather disturbed pantheon. . . . A kind of climax was reached for me, in a long section of screams about "Moloch!", at a rare point of self-referential lucidity: "Dreams! adorations! illuminations! religions! the whole boatload of sensitive bullshit!" *Howl* seems to have emerged under the influence of a kind of literary *Festspiel* held at frequent intervals on the West Coast, in the course of which various poets, "with radiant cool eyes," undoubtedly, read their works before audiences of writhing and adoring youths. "Howl" and the other longer poems in this book, including "America," "Sunflower Sutra," "In the Baggage Room at Greyhound" and some dismal pastiches of William Carlos Williams (who wrote a brief reminiscence of the poet to introduce this volume), all proclaim, in a hopped-up and improvised tone, that nothing seems to be worth saying save in a hopped-up and improvised tone. There are also avowed post-Poundian pacts with Walt Whitman and Apollinaire, and perhaps an unacknowledged one with Lautréamont. I don't know; Mr. Ginsberg prefaces *Howl* with a long dedication to some of his fellow-writers that reads just like his poems ("To . . . William Seward Burroughs, author of *Naked Lunch*, an endless novel which will drive everybody mad"), and in the book he alludes to a "spontaneous bop prosody." Perhaps this is as good a characterization of his work as any.

I have spent this much time on a very short and very tiresome book for two reasons. The first of these is involved with the fact that Mr. Ginsberg and his circle are being given a certain amount of touting by those who disapprove of what Horace Gregory, writing in these pages last fall, christened "The Poetry of Suburbia." If it turns out to be to anybody's profit, I shouldn't be a bit surprised if *Howl* and its eventual progeny were accorded some milder version of the celebration Colin Wilson has received in England. This may not be a real danger, however. If it suddenly appeared that there were no possible worlds between suburbia and subterranea, I expect most of us would go underground. But this is not quite yet the case, and the publicity seems regrettable, in view of the fact (my second reason for dealing with him here) that Allen Ginsberg has a real talent and a marvelous ear. It shows up in some of the funniest and most grotesque lines of "Howl," and even without knowing his profound and carefully organized earlier writing (unpublished in book form), one might suspect a good poet lurking behind the modish façade of a frantic and *talentlos* avant-garde.

The same might be said of all the poems in *Howl* as was remarked in a recent film, upon a doting eulogy of a heel by one of his toadies: "Phony, but sincere."—JOHN HOLLANDER, "Poetry Chronicle," *PR*, Winter 1957, pp. 296–98

Allen Ginsberg speaks of himself as having turned aside "to follow my Romantic inspiration—Hebraic-Melvillian bardic breath." That he is a very literary poet is the most obvious of his qualities. He cites Blake and Shelley, Whitman and Hart Crane, as well as Pound and W. C. Williams, those more baleful influences on recent verse fashion. In his best poems, "America" in the *Howl* pamphlet, and "Death to Van Gogh's Ear!" in this volume ⟨*Kaddish*⟩, he does establish himself as a legitimate though querulous follower of the main Romantic tradition in poetry, the line that in English runs from Blake and Wordsworth to "The Broken Tower" of Crane. But his major efforts, *Howl* and *Kaddish*, are certainly failures, and *Kaddish* a pathetic one.

Ginsberg's genuine poetic flaws are not in structure or in the control of rhetoric. Granted his tradition, he has a surer grasp of the shape of his poem and a firmer diction than almost all of his academic contemporaries, so many of whom have condemned him as formless. A little sympathetic study will establish that most of his larger poems move with inevitable continuity, finding their unity by repetitive techniques akin to those of Christopher Smart's *Jubilate Agno*. Smart's model was ultimately the King James Bible, which is the dominant influence on the technique of Blake and perhaps of Whitman. Ginsberg is hardly a biblical poet, but clearly he is trying to write a kind of religious poetry, and just as clearly he has read the displaced religious poetry of romanticism with some technical profit.

The sadness is that his content, and not his form, is largely and increasingly out of control. His dominant notion as to form derives from Blake's "Exuberance is Beauty," the belief that the energy embodied in poetry finds only its outward boundary in reason and order, and can make that boundary where it will, at the limit of the poet's informing desire. But Blake's exuberance is the result of powerful imaginative control over the content of his own experience and visualization. Ginsberg is ruined poetically by his wilful addiction to a voluntaristic chaos, by a childish social dialectic as pernicious as any he seeks to escape. The ruin is very evident in *Kaddish*, a poem that is a prayer for the death anniversary of Ginsberg's mother, and also (as the title implies) an attempt at a sanctification of the name of God.

The poem opens, movingly, with the son and poet walking the streets of the city, remembering the death of his mother three years before. It passes, through sustained and harrowing memories of childhood and youth, to an agonized summary of the helplessness of love confronted by the separating power of mental disease. Having faced these horrors, the poet seeks some consolation, some radiance that can impinge upon the mystery of mortality. Ginsberg's epigraph is from *Adonais*, and he arouses in the reader some expectation that all this pathos and sorrow have been evoked toward some imaginative end. But this is what he gives us as a climax to his poem:

> Lord Lord great Eye that stares on all and moves in a
>   black cloud
> caw caw strange cry of Beings flung up into sky over
>   the waving trees
> Lord Lord O Grinder of giant Beyonds my voice in a
>   boundless field in Sheol

All that is human about these lines is in the circumstances of their incoherence. Their single grace is in the irony, however unintended, of their self-reference. We have suffered an experience akin to but not our own, only to discover that its subject has nothing to say. Why then has he written his poem? Ginsberg's voice, which seemed to have possibilities of relevance, will at this rate soon enough constitute a boundless field of Sheol.—HAROLD BLOOM, "On Ginsberg's *Kaddish*" (1961), *The Ringers in the Tower*, 1971, pp. 213–15

It is a little misleading, I think, to speak of Ginsberg in terms of a movement, and to attempt to define his achievement in light of what he and the other "beats" have thought or said they stood for. He stands alone, or almost alone, surely, in his preference for the long, swinging line that breaks the verse pattern expected by the eye; and his thick columns of prose-verse surmounted by single-word titles like "Howl" make quite the opposite design on the page from the tau cross shape of the poems we have already seen (such as the one by Creeley, for instance) whose diet-slim bodies are sometimes surmounted by titles longer than their lines (say, "All That Is Lovely in Men"). Besides, in terms of merit, he stands out above those who cluster about him and with whom he is sometimes driven to identify himself out of personal loyalty or programmatic solidarity: a closing of ranks against the "squares."

Finally, it is he alone who has single-handedly, in less than a decade, moved to the center of the national scene, capturing the newest anthologies and pre-empting the imaginations of the young; so that at a moment when his own talent already seems (quickly, quickly) to be flickering out, a resistance to his influence is beginning among even younger poets, annoyed at how difficult it has become to be printed in certain little magazines without accepting his poetic credo, or at least affecting his style. Some older critics, on the other hand, have never accepted him at all, quoting against him his own worst efforts, which are very bad indeed; and yet no one, entrenched critic or competitive new poet, can deny that since the appearance of *Howl* it has been made clear at least that Walt Whitman is *not* dead, the Whitmanian tradition not exhausted. The question once smugly closed by Blackmur, Tate, and company has been reopened and placed high on the poetic agenda of the moment. Perhaps this, after all, is the cause of the often irrational rejection of Ginsberg by those who would find it easy enough to accept a young poet, but cannot abide honoring in him the influence of an old one they had long since written off.

Everything about Ginsberg is, however, blatantly Whitmanian: his meter resolutely anti-iambic, his line-groupings stubbornly anti-stanzaic, his diction aggressively colloquial and American, his voice public. The title of his first book was, we remember, *Howl;* and though the Whitmanian roar has become in him a little shrill and tearful, it is no less obnoxiously loud. Yet he is a follower of Whitman along utterly unforeseen lines, owing no debt to such professional Westerners as Sandburg or Masters, much less to the Popular Front or liberal-Philistine bards, who long claimed exclusively to represent the Master. The Whitman he emulates is the "dirty beast" out of the East who once shocked even Emerson; and he manages to be dirtier and more bestial, a deliberately shocking, bourgeois-baiting celebrator of a kind of sexuality which the most enlightened post-Freudian man-of-the-world finds it difficult to condone.

. . . ⟨I⟩t must be confessed that though there is no joy in Ginsberg, there is a good deal of humor; for he never quite forgets how funny it is to be a Jewish, homosexual Walt Whitman, a parody of a white Indian, the bearded secular saint, into which Whitman's first followers had transformed him. It is not in the egregious self-pity and uncertain tone of the title poem of *Howl* that one finds the authentic Ginsberg, the Whitman no one had expected; but in "America," his *Leaves of Grass* one hundred years later, a poem comic enough to be appropriate to our time:

> America I used to be a communist when I was a kid
> I'm not sorry.
> I smoke marijuana every chance I get.
> I sit in my house for days on end and stare at the roses
> in the closet.
> When I go to Chinatown I get drunk and never get
> laid.
> My mind is made up there's going to be trouble.
> You should have seen me reading Marx.
> My psychoanalyst thinks I'm perfectly right.
> I won't say the Lord's Prayer.
> I have mystical visions and cosmic vibrations.
> America I still haven't told you what you did to
> Uncle Max after he came over from Russia.
> America is this correct?
> I'd better get right down to the job.
> It's true I don't want to join the Army or turn lathes
> in precision parts factories, I'm nearsighted and
> psychopathic anyway.
> America I'm putting my queer shoulder to the wheel.

There are jokes on Ginsberg, however, as well as in him; and the greatest of all, of course, is his success. Who could not have foreseen the pictures in *Life*, the fellowships to Chile or the Peloponnesus or whatever, the journey to Israel (with required verses on Martin Buber and Gershom Scholem), the pilgrimage to the banks of the Ganges (reported fully in *Esquire*). Nobody is to blame, nobody has betrayed anybody, it is simply the way it goes in America. "America," says Ginsberg, "I still haven't told you what you did to Uncle Max after he came over from Russia." Nor what it did to Uncle Max's nephew after he returned east from San Francisco—not yet, not quite, not ever. So far, Ginsberg has resisted a regular teaching job, but not the occasional lectures at New York's City College and Columbia, not the appearances at writers' conferences, nor the speeches at benefits for sympathetic little magazines.—LESLIE A. FIEDLER, "Into the Cafes: A Kind of Solution," *Waiting for the End*, 1964, pp. 241–45

His original intention as a poet was to achieve an emotional breakthrough of individual, subjective feeling and values as a way of overcoming the Kafkian intimidation of the fifties. Relying on natural speech and spontaneous transcriptions, Ginsberg sought a nonliterary poetry based on the facts of daily existence. Jazz, abstract painting, Zen and haiku, writers like William Carlos Williams and Kerouac, Apollinaire and Artaud, Lorca and Neruda, were to influence his development of a new measure that corresponded more closely to the body's breath than to the artifice of iambics. The result for Ginsberg, as it had been for Gertrude Stein earlier in the century, was composition as creation, that is, the act of writing itself leading to a pursuit of the unknown rather than to a recovery of the already revealed. As with Burroughs and Kerouac, form would not be predetermined, but would follow the sequence of perception in the course of the writing, even if the route became as irrational, intuitive, and discontinuous as the shape of the mind itself. Syntax, therefore, would not accord with the imposed logic of grammar, but would correspond to the essentially nonsequential flow of the mind. As the mind does not perceive in the orderly arrangement of expository prose, it becomes almost a pretentious fiction to write a poem or a story as if it did. . . .

The reviews of *Howl* document Ginsberg's position in American letters through the sixties. John Hollander, poet and professor, writing in a spirit of evident distrust for what he felt was a modish façade of avant-garde posturing, deplored in *Partisan Review* the "utter lack of decorum of any kind in his dreadful little volume." James Dickey, in *Sewanee Review*, established Ginsberg as the very citadel of modern Babel, and found the poem full of meaningless utterances. Dickey, at least, had the grace to allow that Ginsberg was capable of "a confused but believable passion for values." Even Michael Rumaker, reviewing *Howl* for the *Black Mountain Review*, certainly a friendly organ, had few words of praise. Rumaker perversely read Ginsberg according to the expectations of New Criticism (exactly what Ginsberg was reacting against!) and found only imprecision everywhere. For Rumaker, the title poem especially was corrupted by "sentimentality, bathos,

Buddha and hollow talk of eternity." The poem was uncontained, its language cumbersome and hysterical, but its most unforgivable quality was that it tried to use art to induce spiritual values.—JOHN TYTELL, "Allen Ginsberg and the Messianic Tradition," *Naked Angels*, 1976, pp. 214–20

Allen Ginsberg's poems of the 1970's are a marvel, his new book, *Mind Breaths*, presenting a half dozen poems, probably more, that are first-rate Ginsberg. The fact that they are as good as anything he has ever written delights me (and I hope, many others), because I feel that his poems of the 1960's in *The Fall of America* were generally not so good, too full of random, unassimilated political rage; neither were his experiments with consciously composed blues a few years ago, as I remarked at the time.

You know how Ginsberg writes. Long circular movements, syntax irregular and interfused, catalogues of parallel thoughts and images extending sometimes for pages: chants, oracles, body-rhythms. Hopeless to try quoting them in a review. To excerpt a few lines would serve no purpose, and it would be a positive disservice to the poem.

But let me describe one poem from the new book, called "Ego Confession." A wonderful poem; I've read it five times. It is a mockery throughout: a mockery first of the convention of confessional poetry in recent decades, and then a mockery of the poet himself; it lays bare all his fantastic desires, to be the great poet, the great saint, to stop war, to eradicate viciousness, to gather in from the universal spirit that singing tenderness that will unite us all, etc., etc.; and it is, finally, a mockery of us, the readers and bystanders, silly, fantasizing, unavoidably messianic creatures that we are.

Yet the mockery transcends itself, not at the end of the poem, but all the way through, each statement moving in a process of self-transcension toward the higher compassionate understanding that makes our silliness sane, our pathos holy, our "ego confessions" authentic significations of human spiritual desire. The poem is infused with passionate tenderness. . . .

Ginsberg is no simple poet, though some people would like him to be—in fact, the technical means by which he achieves his effects are difficult, even obscure. Consider structure. Categorically speaking, there are three kinds in poetry: first, conventional structure imposed from without; second, archetypal structure risen from within; and third, random structure derived, again, from without. In reality these categories are far from explicit, and they shift and meld together; yet I do believe that all great poems, no matter how rigid or free in their styles and appearances, fall within the second category, and this includes the best of Ginsberg's earliest work (though whether or not those poems are truly "great" is something we won't know in our lifetimes).

In his poems of the 1960's Ginsberg strayed into the third category. Structure was derived from random external events, newspaper stories or things seen from the window of an airplane. The result too often was declaration, not poetry. The structure, if it was structure at all, was disintegrative, literally incoherent.

But now he has returned to poems of the imagination, poems arising from within, complexes of feeling that come to consciousness with their own structure already in them. This doesn't mean that they are of necessity profoundly mythological, in the Jungian sense. No, the political feeling of the 60's—and of the present—can be as much a part of these inherent complexes as anything else. But the structures are integrated, assimilated; they are products of Ginsberg's unified, multiplex personality. As a result, he can now utter explicit political curses against the whole nark segment of modern life in such a way that they not only become genuine political statements but also function esthetically and commensurately as elements of his entire poetic vision. They are part of the prophesying. And this has been at least one of the chief poetic objectives through all ages, from Homer and Isaiah down to our own time. —HAYDEN CARRUTH, "Chants, Oracles, Body-Rhythms," *NYTBR*, March 19, 1978, pp. 15, 39

PAUL PORTUGÉS

From "The Heightened Awareness of a Prophet"
The Visionary Poetics of Allen Ginsberg

1978, pp. 78–83

His interest in breath and natural breathing units . . . began early. However, it was not fully realized until he had written the "Moloch" section of "Howl," which was composed under the influence of peyote during his exploration of extraordinary states of consciousness:

> I had an apt. on Nob Hill, got high on Peyote, & saw an image of the robot skullface of Moloch in the upper stories of a big hotel glaring into my window . . . I wandered down Powell Street muttering, "Moloch, Moloch" all night & wrote *Howl* II nearly intact in cafeteria at foot of Drake Hotel, deep in the hellish vale.[1]

The "hellish vale" is a combination of peyote and the meditative practice of focusing attention to induce the prophetic illuminative seizure. After writing the "Moloch" section, Ginsberg realized the rhythmic units were based on his breathing (aligned with thought units); he believed that anyone reading Part II (i.e., the "Moloch" section) properly, would have to *breathe* exactly the way he was breathing while in the heightened state of awareness, the "hellish vale." He had unconsciously transcribed his prophetic vision into rhythmic units that corresponded to his "breathing physiological spasm."[2] The amazing thing about this theory-practice is that it actually works. When the reader says the units aloud, in an excited mood, making sure he breathes with each rhythmic break, the experience can actually approach Ginsberg's original breath-mind-feeling patterns. Therefore, by going through the same breathing "spasm" the reader "would presumably catalyze in himself the same *affects* or emotions."[3]

> Moloch the incomprehensible prison! Moloch the crossbone soulless jailhouse and Congress of sorrows! Moloch whose buildings are judgement! Moloch the vast stone of war! Moloch the stunned governments![4]

Ginsberg believes that his visionary episodes in Harlem were partly a result of his unconscious syncopation with Blake's breath units while he was reading "The Little Girl Lost," et al., that eventful night:

> So you find in Blake or any good poetry a series of vowels which if you pronounce them in proper sequence *with the breathing* indicated by the punctuation, as in . . . "Howl," the Moloch section . . . you find a yogic breathing. Yogic's a bad word 'cause it's un-American—you find a "phys.-ed" breathing that, *if reproduced by the reader*, following the poet's commas and exclamation points and following long long long breaths, will get you high physiologically . . . will actually deliver a buzz like grass, or higher. And so I think that's what happened to me in a way with Blake.[5]

By following the rhythmic units, as indicated by punctuation (as Ginsberg did in 1948 while reading Blake), the reader can actually experience the "prophetic illuminative seizure" that Ginsberg underwent on peyote and transferred into the "Moloch" section of "Howl." The underlying assumption of this theory is that breath is ultimately the "director" of an individual's emotional pattern, that in pronouncing the words and repeating the breathing patterns the reader will experience the emotion the poet is trying to convey. Putting it in a simple formula, it would be something like this: Ginsberg's rhythmic units are dictated by his breathing patterns; the breathing patterns in turn are controlled by the particular emotion he is experiencing; thus, the emotions give rise to the breath which is notated by rhythmic units separated by punctuation and articulated in words. Language, in this schema, the language of poetry, becomes an extension of the physiology of the body. As Ginsberg puts it:

> Mainly from this point of view: that the words we pronounce do connect finally to our body, connect to our breathing, particularly, and breathing connects to feeling, feeling articulated in language. Poetry is a rhythmic vocal articulation of feeling and the content of poetry is feeling as well as whatever else you would call it if it were removed from feeling—I suppose conditioned reflex language chain associations.[6]

So he realized, after writing the "Moloch" section, that it was possible for him to give forth prophetic rhapsodies and change consciousness by carefully inducing in his reader the same breathing units he was experiencing during his meditative illuminative writing periods—"you can teach breathing . . . inspiration being a matter of breath."[7]

Ginsberg's first great experiment in *consciously* writing inspired poetry, which notates breathing patterns, is to be found in Part II of "Kaddish." Here Ginsberg uses the dash as indication of his breath units, trying to coordinate breath with thought (words) in order accurately to express the illuminative state of mind he was experiencing in the painful recall of his life with his mother Naomi. Once again, to ensure heightened consciousness, Ginsberg used drugs to stimulate his awareness and help him achieve, not only "all day long attention," but on this occasion, almost two days of intense meditative concentration. (He used injections of amphetamine to keep him going, "plus a little bit of morphine, plus some dexedrine later, because it was all in one long sitting."[8]) The use of amphetamines helped him attain the "peculiar metaphysical tinge" he was after in recording his prophecy of death and doom—using, as he had so often, the method of minute particulars to capture the essence of Naomi's life and death:

> . . . the language intuitively chosen as in trance & dream, the rhythms rising thru breath from belly to breast, the hymn completed in tears, the movement of the physical poetry demanding and receiving decades of life while chanting Kaddish the names of Death in many mind-worlds the self seeing the Key to life found at last in our own self.[9]

"Kaddish" is a "physical poetry" with "the rhythms rising thru breath" becoming feelings, i.e., from the body ("belly") to the "breast" (emotions). As in the "Moloch" section of "Howl," the notation is made to correspond to the emotions by a careful use of punctuation to indicate breathing units:

> Your last night in the darkness of the Bronx—I phone-called—thru hospital to secret police.
>
> That came, when you and I were alone, shrieking at Elanor in my ear—who breathed hard in her own bed, got thin—
>
> Now will forget, the doorknock, at your fright of spies,—Law advancing, on my honor—Eternity entering the room—you running to the bathroom undressed, hiding in protest from the last heroic fate—
>
> staring at my eyes, betrayed—the final cops of madness rescuing me—from your foot against the broken heart of Elanor[10]

The dashes indicate Ginsberg's breath while he was composing. If the reader reads the poem with this in mind, the theory is that he will experience the same, or similar, "metaphysical tinge" that Ginsberg underwent while writing about and remembering his mother. The *Word*, language, actually becomes a spiritual alchemy, where the reader is catalyzed, by the manipulation of breathing units in the poem, to experience "the same *affects* or emotions."[11]

Ginsberg would experiment with this method of writing throughout the sixties, refining the accuracy of notation with the use of an Uher tape recorder (which was given to him by Bob Dylan). He realized that he could be true to his breath and thought by dictating the poem and transcribing it later, carefully indicating (by punctuation or line arrangement) the breath and thought units as they were accurately recorded on tape. He could tell where the thought and breath broke because the Uher made a clicking sound every time he turned it off, which meant he had completed one thought-breath and was beginning another. So, his dedication to his theory during these experiments with the tape recorder resulted in an absolute accuracy, to the point of being able to record the mind in its natural rate of flow (impossible if he were writing in longhand, or using a typewriter, because both methods would impose their own rhythms, due to the time factor, or—in the case of the typewriter—the rhythms of the machine would impinge on the rhythms of natural thought and breath[12]). An example of his use of coordinating rhythmic units with the aid of the Uher recorder is the poem "Wichita Vortex Sutra" (1966), which was written in a series of very long meditative sittings while he was traveling through Kansas—dictating his poem as he went:

That the rest of earth is unseen,
                                        an outer universe invisible,
        Unknown except thru
                                        language
                                                airprint
                                                        magic images
or prophecy of the secret
                heart the same
                in Waterville as Saigon one human form[13]

Listening to the actual recording, it became clear that Ginsberg, instead of using dashes as he did in "Kaddish," notated breath and thought breaks by line arrangement. In other words, when the line breaks, the actual breath and thought breaks. After each break there was a click on the tape, indicting end of thought-breath. The poem actually *sounded* like this:

That the rest of earth is unseen (Click!)
                                        an outer universe invisible (Click!)
        Unknown (Click!) except thru
                                (Click!) language
                                        (Click!) airprint
                                                (Click!) magic images
or prophecy of the secret (Click!)
                heart the same (Click!)
                in Waterville as Saigon one human form (Click!)

Ginsberg has described the method of transcription he used in this poem as follows:

> So when transcribing, I pay attention to the clicking on and off of the machine, which is . . . the

> equivalent of how they arrive in the mind and how they're vocalized on the tape recorder.[14]

He finally arrived at a method of composition that didn't interfere with his attempts accurately to "pronounce aloud the thoughts that are going through the head."[15] With the tape recorder, he managed to unite thought and breath in a vivid, accurate transcription of the mind and the emotions that, when read as notated, would cause a parallel thought-emotion-breath in the reader. This was an ideal way for him to communicate his prophetic consciousness, achieved by long sessions of meditation and years devoted to consciousness exploration. He had learned a method of catalyzing emotions in his readers that might achieve for them the catalyzed visionary state that Blake had induced in him. After twenty years, an important technical experiment had yielded a method of writing in a deep, illuminative seizure, with minimal interference, from the time of thought-breath-feeling to actual transcription. The use of his Uher tape recorder allowed him to pursue "the sacred art of writing"[16] as a meditation exercise which would "bring on a recall of detailed consciousness that is an approximation of high consciousness. High epiphanous mind."[17] The actual method of transcription facilitated the goal of getting "deeper and deeper into your own central consciousness"[18] and achieving the transmission of a prophetic consciousness. This is a method of composition where "writing is a yoga that invokes Lord mind."[19]

Notes

1. Allen Ginsberg, "Notes on Finally Recording 'Howl,'" *A Casebook on the Beat*, ed. Thomas Parkinson (New York: Thomas Y. Crowell Company, 1961), p. 29.
2. Allen Ginsberg, *Improvised Poetics*, ed. Mark Robison (San Francisco: Anonymous Press, 1961), p. 22.
3. Allen Ginsberg, "A Talk with Allen Ginsberg," ed. Alison Colbert, *Partisan Review* XXXVI, No. 3 (1971), p. 297.
4. Allen Ginsberg, *Howl and Other Poems* (San Francisco: City Lights Books, 1956), p. 17.
5. Allen Ginsberg, *Allen Verbatim: Lectures on Poetry, Politics, Consciousness*, ed. Gordon Ball (New York: McGraw-Hill, 1974), p. 23.
6. Ibid., p. 28.
7. Ibid., p. 109.
8. Ibid., p. 47.
9. Allen Ginsberg, "How *Kaddish* Happened," in *The Poetics of the New American Poetry*, ed. Donald Allen and Warren Tallman (New York: Grove Press, Inc., 1973), p. 347.
10. Allen Ginsberg, *Kaddish and Other Poems: 1958–1960* (San Francisco: City Lights Books, 1961), p. 27.
11. Allen Ginsberg, unpublished interview, July 1976.
12. This use of breath and its parallel to thought was something Olson demanded in his essay "Projective Verse."
13. Allen Ginsberg, *Planet News* (San Francisco: City Lights Books, 1968), pp. 123–24.
14. Allen Ginsberg, *Improvised Poetics*, p. 14.
15. Ibid., p. 4.
16. Allen Ginsberg, "Craft Interview with Allen Ginsberg," *The Craft of Poetry*, ed. William Packard (New York: Doubleday, 1974), p. 73.
17. Ibid., p. 73.
18. Ibid., p. 73.
19. Ibid., p. 73.

MARK SHECHNER
"The Survival of Allen Ginsberg"

Partisan Review, January 1979, pp. 105–12

We have three new books from Allen Ginsberg: a selection of recent poems, a second transcription of entries from his vast store of journals, and an exchange of letters with Neal Cassady, who was once the elusive object of his tumultuous affections. But there is nothing especially new here; two of the books are retrospective forays over known territory. For years Ginsberg has been the most accessible of our writers, and has conducted his affairs very much in the open, if remarkably beyond the reach of talk shows, bookchat, and general literary blather. Nor do the poems break any new ground, imaginatively or technically. They put forth the standard brew of homosexuality, metaphysics, pacifism, political outrage, muddled prophecy, and homemade Buddhism that is as familiar now as the morning coffee, and about as alarming.

Ginsberg has long since graduated from being a subterranean and "know-nothing Bohemian" to being everyone's favorite prophet. He is our anarchist-in-residence, queer and avuncular, whose tirades against imperial warfare, official repression, and hard dope, and open passion for nubile young boys are disarmed and domesticated by his irony. Even Diana Trilling, who is ever on the alert for bad influences on the young, has preferred to remember him, in *We Must March My Darlings*, as a warm and comforting presence in the sixties. As an added ingratiating feature, Ginsberg is that rarest of figures among American poets, a survivor, working vigorously into his fifties, despite the script he was handed early in life which called for a spectacular crack-up or a slow descent into alcohol or madness in the grand American tradition. He was cut out to be a *poète maudit:* a Poe, a John Berryman, a Delmore Schwartz, a Sylvia Plath, a Jack Kerouac or Norman Mailer (whose chief claim to attention these days is the novel he *can't* write), and much of his initial impact in the fifties came from the impression, which he cultivated, that he had privileged insight into the tragic fate of the imagination in America: "I saw the best minds of my generation destroyed by madness." But, unlike Kerouac, he eventually recoiled from the allure of self-destruction, and saved us, in the bargain, from another tiresome lesson in how America treats her poets, and yet another spellbinding case-history in poetry as a by-product of terminal euphoria. He was finally too ironic and willful for martyrdom, and, despite his rages against America and her wars, too enamored of the *idea* of America (which has been bound up for him with the idea of Walt Whitman) to renege on his initial promise: "America I'm putting my queer shoulder to the wheel."

Special credit for Ginsberg's survival must go to his Buddhism, which has taught him how to marshall and conserve his energies, and has given him the emotional ballast to stand up against crushing psychic pressures. The air of wise passiveness that attends his public appearances these days is a deliberate calm, a steady vigilance over his own seething emotions, which he has learned to hold in check and sublimate into a sonorous and agitated delivery. In a recent poem on the subject of being mugged in his own neighborhood ("Mugging," in *Mind Breaths*) Ginsberg tells of surrendering to a troop of young thugs while frantically intoning a mantra to keep his own terror and rage under control: "I went down shouting Om Ah Hūm to gangs of lovers on the stoop watching." But whatever such a containment of rage has contributed to his durability and his public figure—that is, the instructional example—it has brought little to the poetry save a treasury of liquid phrases to be sprinkled over a poem like spices over stew, for piquancy. They scan wonderfully, while lending an air of mystical illumination. Thus a few poems in *Mind Breaths* are graced with such sweet cadences as "Bom Bom! Shivaye! Ram Nam Satyahey! Om Ganipatti, Om Saraswati Hrih Sowha!" which, for most of us, might just as well be "Polly wolly doodle all the day." Yet, despite suggestions of Tagore or Lao-Tze that hang like smog over his poetry, Ginsberg has kept faith with his original mentors—Williams, Whitman, and Blake—and nothing he has done since the poems in *Kaddish* (1961) shows any advance in vision or skill.

In *Mind Breaths*, except for a strange bit of romantic allegory, "Contest of Bards," which Ginsberg himself has hailed as a visitation from the muse, but whose studied Blakeisms ("Icy intellect fir'y beauty wreck") sound false to an ear trained on his more colloquial, American line, most of the poems seem like refrains from prior books, and at lower levels of inspiration at that. This is Ginsberg's coolest book; its moments of agitation, at any rate, are not up to what we remember. The spontaneous composition that was a boon to earlier poetry, summoning up the rhythmic power of the long, bardic line in "Howl," "Kaddish," and "Wichita Vortex Sutra," looks more and more like a recipe for surefire inspiration: a shortcut to the poetic high. But the paraphernalia of inspiration that works so well for Ginsberg in performance—what with the harmonium and the receptivity of audiences just dying for enchantment—are no guarantee of poetry that is effective in print, especially now that Ginsberg devotes so much of his attention to pure voice and pure breath. Only his old sexual frankness still comes alive, and that because of the aggressive punch of the sexual image, rather than from any freshness of insight or depth of meaning. "Under the world there's a lot / of ass, a lot of cunt / a lot of mouths and cocks, / under the world there's a lot of come, and a lot of saliva dripping into brooks" makes its point with the same aggressiveness that Ginsberg could always summon up when in a lousy mood, even if the final result here isn't very interesting.

At this stage of the game, at fifty-two, rather than try to push ahead poetically, Ginsberg has taken to doubling back upon himself, and the journals, correspondence, memoirs, and *obiter dicta* (see Gordon Ball's *Allen Verbatim*) that now crowd the market suggest that what we can look forward to at this point are neither new breakthroughs in poetry nor further refinements, but Ginsberg's efforts to clarify his image and reaffirm his claim upon a place in American cultural history. I suspect that Ginsberg understands these days that he matters less as a poet than as a figure, an exemplary life. Certainly he has become influential without being consistently great, or even consistently engaging as a writer, and most of us can count on one hand the poems that survive rereading, let alone study. As an exemplary figure, though, Ginsberg is something else again, and it is to the clarification of the example that the journals and letters are dedicated.

But in what sense is such a life admirable? Surely not in its conspicuous alienation nor the rootlessness that has made of Ginsberg a wandering Jew (or Buddhist-Jew) by default, and certainly not in the homosexuality as such, even though as a campaigner for sexual pluralism Ginsberg has been instrumental in creating the current social climate in which coming out is considered a positive personal gesture. What surely is exemplary on Ginsberg's part is the risk he has taken in placing his own sexual nature out in the open: proclaiming it, writing about it, worrying over it, and insisting on its right to gratification, thus keeping himself clear of the enervating compromises of closet homosexuality. Ginsberg's acceptance of his own constitution as the very condition of his life and his poetry is certainly one of the sources of his strength and durability. Blakean that he is, he has not let himself be undermined by his own repressed desires.

But Ginsberg's long involvement with mind-altering drugs is more problematic. His exalted testimonials on behalf of his pharmacological experiments gave sanction, not only to the indiscriminate use of drugs in the sixties, but to their glorification as the elixir of cosmic consciousness. Though Ginsberg has campaigned against heroin, and now writes, "Nobody saves America by sniffing cocaine," his basic line on dope, as on everything nelse, has been the libertarian one: *laissez faire*, and let every man find out for himself. But hallucinogenic drugs once meant more to him than just another degree of human freedom; they conveniently suited his romance with madness, which, as Kerouac shrewdly saw, served his need to justify his mother. Though he eventually outgrew his illusions about redemptive insanity and took up spiritual self-discipline after the Indian trip in 1962–63, he had already contributed enormously and disastrously to the myth of the madman as antinomian saint "who drove crosscountry seventytwo hours to find out if I had a vision or you had a vision or he had a vision to find out eternity." Some of those visions, we now know, were the mental image of neurons boiling away in the skull. The dope revolution blew minds as the price of expanding consciousness, and whether the benefits were worth the costs, which are still being toted up in mental hospitals across the country, is largely a question of how one came through the experience.

Yet all this in Ginsberg: the aggressive homosexuality, the rootlessness, the anarchism, the celebrated expeditions in search of a better hallucinogen, cannot be seen apart from what is exemplary in him, for they are, however ambiguous, his efforts at salvation. They are what he had to attain and then had to get beyond. The accumulating documentation of his life is slowly amounting to the authentication of a saint's life, a history of beatitude whose theme, like that of all saints' lives, is crisis, conversion, and trial. The famous Blake vision, of which we have a half dozen accounts, is like Paul's vision on the road to Damascus or Martin Luther's fit in the choir, a token of election, and the torments that follow are steps in the realization of the mission. The mother's madness had to be suffered and purged; the humiliating love for Neal Cassady had to be indulged and worked through; imprisonment and institutionalization had to be endured and made use of; shame and guilt had to be embraced and transcended. Such experience was an apprenticeship in failure, and in light of the dismal lessons with which he was imbued, Ginsberg's heroism lies not in his oversold resistance to political power or social convention but in his refusal of the original emotional ground rules of his life. He altered the deadly prognosis: by way of Blake and Buddhism he became that mythic American, the self-made man, an anarchist Horatio Alger. More bookish, more assiduously literary than the other Beats, he rescued himself through his reading. Little wonder that he is honored these days in the academy, to whose basic values he is seemingly so anathema, for he is a living defense of the literary life, a man who was saved by books.

These journals and letters, by and large, have little to teach about Ginsberg's survival, but much to show us about his early desperation. The *Journals* cover two periods, 1952 to 1956, and 1959 to February 1962, the eve of Ginsberg's departure for India. The *Indian Journals*, which were the first to be published (1970), take up where these leave off. The correspondence with Neal Cassady extends farther back, to 1947 and the dark years at Columbia, and plots the vicissitudes of that difficult relationship into 1963. The Ginsberg who emerges from these pages is the lost and driven young poet seeking resolution of his conflicts through determined reading, mysticism, and the pursuit of sexual experience.

The letters to Neal, especially the very earliest ones, are the most moving and readable of these documents. Ginsberg's mysticism would later throw a haze of metaphysics over the emotions, and parts of the journals make for very tough going. But the letters are direct and ardent, if confused, full of passionate declarations of emotional dependency and pleas for punishment and love. Writing in 1947, a year after they had first met in New York, Ginsberg declared, "I am lonely, Neal, alone, and always I am frightened. I need someone to love me and kiss me & sleep with me; I am only a child and have the mind of a child. I have been miserable without you because I had depended on you to take care of me for love of me, and now that you have altogether rejected me, what can I do, what can I do?" I scarcely know of more abject appeals for love anywhere in literature or published correspondence. Yet even at his most desolate, Ginsberg would turn his sexual dependency into intellectual advantage, urging Neal, in a postscript to one letter, to read *Nightwood*, *Wings of the Dove*, and *The Idiot*. Cassady, who had been educated on Denver's skid row, where he earned an advanced degree in brutality and deprivation, was vulnerable to learning, and Ginsberg knew how to gain leverage over him with demonstrations of Columbia erudition. The letters reveal the emotional quid pro quo of homosexuality, the give and take of power that became for Ginsberg the very principle of psychic accounting, by which his paranoia and sense of persecution could give way to prophetic exaltation. His later messianism came out of his early masochism, his transcendence out of his lessons in abasement. But in their relationship Ginsberg was always the pursuer and Cassady the pursued. Cassady was, after all, married during most of this period, three times, in fact, and always seemed to have a woman in tow.

It is easy to understand the appeal of Cassady for someone like Ginsberg, though Cassady's magic does not come through in the letters. He was not an intellectual or even a reader; he tried to write and, for the most part, failed, and even his letters are garbled. "I hate words," he confessed to Ginsberg. "They are too much." Even then, some of the autobiographical fragments collected in his sole book, *The First Third*, are fascinating for the life they describe. What captivated Ginsberg and Kerouac was the rough and ready masculinity, the pose of complete male competence. They were Reichians, and he was their man of raw libido, at ease with his sexual urges, undisturbed by homosexuality though a success with women, and untempted by the appeals of comfort and responsibility. Also, he was almost a dead ringer for Kerouac, which surely played into the latter's exalted conception of him. Kerouac turned him into a myth through the superhuman figures of Dean Moriarty and Cody Pomeray; Gary Snyder saw him as the last cowboy, a Jedediah Smith entrapped by the encircling modern world; Ginsberg just loved him. He was their link to frontier manhood, their own hotrod buckaroo, though they understood too that his skid row disorientation was an alienation not unlike their own. He was born to lose. After his marriage to his second wife, Carolyn, in 1949, he wrote to Ginsberg, "From what I can understand of them your doldrums are fine. All I can see is the long, continuous doldrum I'm in." By means of fast cars, fast living, and women, he was always in flight from the doldrums, and, thanks to Kerouac, his frenetic journeying became his contribution to literature. He introduced Kerouac to an authentic American high, the high of the open road, the ecstatic illusion of omnipotence one gets during an all-night drive across the endless plains, with the radio tuned in to half the country. The rolling cadenzas of *On the Road* owe everything to Cassady and his cars, as do the rhythm and flow of Ginsberg's highway poems, which are among his best: "The Green Automobile" (*Reality Sandwiches*), which is a poem about Cassady, "Wichita Vortex Sutra" (*Planet News*), and the cross-country "vortex" poems in *The Fall of America*.

But the open road is only a high between starting point and destination, and in fleeing from oneself one never gets more than a few miles ahead. Cassady's urgent activity was only to buy time away from his confusion and congenital bad luck. Indeed, while Burroughs and Lucien Carr could get away with, literally, murder, Cassady would eventually get caught for possession and sale of marijuana, and wind up doing two years at San Quentin, from 1958 to 1960. After his release he was reduced to doing his routine in caricature, driving the bus for Ken Kesey and his Merry Pranksters, hitting the road as a comic imitation of himself. In 1967 he drifted down to Mexico, where he died, in February 1968, apparently from a fatal mixture of alcohol and barbiturates.

But Ginsberg and Cassady had already begun to drift apart after their reunion in 1954. Ginsberg met Peter Orlovsky, while Cassady tried to attend to his family and his job as a railroad brakeman for the Southern Pacific. In the mid-fifties, Ginsberg was also discovering his own strength and direction, consigning his torments to his poetry and spiritualizing his emotions. The movement of the journals is away from the lucid, personal, and tormented style of the early letters toward an elliptical and mystagogic style that is difficult to penetrate. Relationships fade and are replaced by casual impressions and dreams; almost half the contents of these journals are Ginsberg's transcriptions of his own dreams, though without the associations that might make them available to the average reader. Indeed, there is a refractory quality to these journals, and the *Indian Journals* are the most resistant of them all. Despite their assiduous documentation of the inner life, they obscure personal qualities in a blizzard of fragmentary notations. The disturbing aspect of these journals is the absence of any familiar ground of "sensibility" or sustained thought between pure notation and pure desire, unless the metaphysics, which is applied with such assurance, qualifies as thought. Ginsberg's imagination shuttles back and forth between observation and longing, while social relations and social thinking are consigned to the background. Consider, for example, how important Peter Orlovsky has been in Ginsberg's life and yet how strangely little we learn about him in any of these journals. But then the journals have little to say about anyone with whom Ginsberg has been deeply involved. The metaphysical crowds out the social and eventually even the personal, just as dream transcription supercedes conversation. The journals document the victory of the religious imagination over the social.

The appeal of Ginsberg in the sixties lay in the appearance he gave of seeing through or around or beyond the veils and corruptions of ordinary social thought. It was not then evident, as it now is, that such transcendence was in fact a falling short of social reality, and that what seemed in the poetry a deeper penetration into the mysteries of being was really a narrowing of emotional range and a painful shyness about people. We expect poetry that is sufficiently inspired to leap from one plane of meaning to another, to zoom upward from sensory data to the higher realms, but what seems like thrilling prophecy when spoken in Biblical accents does not satisfy in the form of a journal entry. Which is another way of saying that the journals and most of the letters to Neal are intrinsically uninteresting except for the light they shed on other things that may matter to us: Ginsberg's poetry, or American social history in the postwar decades.

So, I must cast my praise of these books in somewhat negative terms. There is no reason for Ginsberg not to have published such journals and letters, nor to withhold the additional materials which will soon be forthcoming. Public self-examination of this sort is a rare and valuable gesture, even when, as in this case, the social value of the gesture far exceeds the intellectual impact of what is actually disclosed. Understandably, a confession, even to oneself, is a bargain struck with the superego to permit some more difficult and compromising knowledge to be withheld, though it is odd to find such a case in which primal fears and sexual anxieties are laid bare and social relations suppressed. But that reversal is part of the antinomian meaning of Ginsberg's life. He has always done things differently than the rest of us.

MARJORIE PERLOFF

"A Lion in Our Living Room"

American Poetry Review, March–April 1985, pp. 35–46

> I saw the best minds of my generation destroyed by
> madness, starving hysterical naked,
> dragging themselves through the negro streets at
> dawn looking for an angry fix.

In the New York of the late fifties, Frank O'Hara, hearing Allen Ginsberg declaim the now classic opening of "Howl," turned, so the story goes, to his neighbor and whispered, "I wonder who Allen has in mind?"

The question is not mere camp. What O'Hara meant, no doubt, is that, despite the unversalizing gesture, the roll call of "best minds . . . destroyed by madness," the real hero of "Howl," the "angelheaded hipster"

> who poverty and tatters and hollow-eyed and high sat
> up smoking in the supernatural darkness of cold-
> water flats floating across the tops of cities contem-
> plating jazz

was a single lonely and bookish young man named Allen Ginsberg, writing, like the Francois Villon of "The Testament," in the thirtieth year of his life, when he felt himself to be beyond shame. "Howl," that is to say, is less Ginsberg's "Ode to the Confederate Dead" or his elegy for Carl Solomon (institutionalized, like Ginsberg's own mother Naomi, in a mental hospital), than it is the most harrowing as well as the funniest of autobiographies.

To put it more accurately: "Howl" is one link in the larger autobiographical chain which constitutes Allen Ginsberg's poetry. In the "Author's Preface, Reader's Manual" that opens his canonical eight-hundred-page *Collected Poems* (an elegant edition by Harper and Row, whose back cover bears the photograph of a charmingly rabbinical Allen Ginsberg, holding a packet of the seven small black-and-white City Lights volumes in which the bulk of his poetry has appeared from 1956 to the present), Ginsberg announces, "Herein author has assembled all his poetry books published to date rearranged in straight chronological order to compose an autobiography." Indeed, the *Collected Poems* has an index of proper names so that the reader can trace the evolving relationship of Ginsberg and, say, Neal Cassady or can look up what the poet said about his grandmother, Rebecca Ginsberg (four references).

The "straight chronological" arrangement gives a startling new shape to a life we have so far perceived only in bits and pieces. Thus the "youthful poetries" (1945–1952) originally published in *The Gates of Wrath* (1972) and *Empty Mirror* (1961) are now combined, the "imperfect literary rhymes" of the former interspersed with the "raw-sketch practice poems" of the latter so that "Disparate simultaneous early styles juxtaposed [will] aid recognition of a grounded mode of writing encouraged by Dr. Williams, 'No ideas but in things.'" Again, Ginsberg has arranged the volume so that the "Travel poems Calcutta-Saigon-Angkor-Wat-Japan, 1963, mixed through three separate books, now cohere in sequence," and he takes pains to alert us to the continuity of the "Cross-country Auto Poesy chronicle [that] starts 1965 at Northwest border." The ten sections of the book, we are told, "roughly indicat[e] time, geography, and motif or 'season' of experience"; the book, as a whole, is meant to portray "poetic energy as cyclic, the continuum a panorama of valleys and plateaus with peaks of inspiration every few years."

These brief hints are not just rationalizations, designed to "make it cohere." To read Ginsberg's *Collected Poems* in 1985 is something of a shock—a *frisson* of pure pleasure. Was our poetry really this energetic, this powerful and immediate just a few short decades ago? Did the poet really dream of a "Green Automobile," in which he could take his lover "riding/over the Rockies . . . riding/all night long until dawn"? At a time when so much of our poetry wears white gloves, when the main precept often seems to be "Proceed with caution!", Ginsberg's poetic trajectory is a marvel to behold. Vortex, as Ginsberg's mentor Ezra Pound put it, is ENERGY!

This energy has not always been appreciated. The more theoretical studies of modern and postmodern poetry and poetics—Hillis Miller's *Poets of Reality*, Charles Altieri's *Enlarging the Temple*, Hugh Kenner's *The Pound Era* and *A Homemade World*, and, for that matter, my own *Poetics of Indeterminacy*—have tended to ignore Ginsberg's achievement, perhaps in reaction to the journalistic overkill devoted to the Beat Generation. "In 'A Supermarket in California'," says Denis Donoghue, "Ginsberg had done everything that is required of a poet except the one essential thing—to write his poem."[1] And in an essay called "The Sorrows of American-Jewish Poetry," Harold Bloom declares:

> The chanter of *Howl*, *Kaddish*, and many lesser litanies is as much beyond the reach of criticism as Norman Mailer; both have been raised to that bad eminence where every fresh failure is certain of acclaim as an event, something that has happened and so is news, like floods, fires, and other stimulating disasters. The genuine painfulness of reading through *Kaddish* is not an *imaginative* suffering for the reader, but is precisely akin to the agony we sustain when we are compelled to watch the hysteria of strangers.[2]

The charge of formlessness, of poetry as mere rant will no doubt continue to haunt Ginsberg, but the publication of his *Collected Poems* should do much to dispel it. Indeed, to read one's way through the "valleys and plateaus" of these eight-hundred pages is to be reminded how fatuous are the legends that have grown up around Allen Ginsberg, legends for which the poet's own *ex-cathedra* pronouncements have been at least partially responsible.

The first such myth is that Ginsberg's poetry is a straight transcription of visionary speech. As he himself insists in the Preface, "'First thought, best thought.' Spontaneous insight—the sequence of thought-forms passing naturally through ordinary mind—was always motif and method of these compositions." Ginsberg has been making this claim for years: in the *Paris Review* interview with Tom Clark (1965), he explains:

> We all talk among ourselves and we have common understandings, and we say anything we want to say. . . . So then—what happens if you make a distinction between what you tell your friends and what you tell your Muse? The problem is to break down that distinction: when you approach the Muse to talk as frankly as you would talk with yourself or with your friends. . . . That meant . . . a complete revision of what literature was supposed to be. . . . It's the ability to commit to writing, to *write*, the same way that you are![3]

Such comments have often been taken at face value. In a study of the Beats called *Naked Angels* (1976), John Tytell commends Ginsberg's *Paris Review* commentary for its "great clarity" and remarks:

> Prematurely conscious of the potentials for lying on a national scale, the Beats raised the standard of honesty no matter what the artistic consequences. . . . [They] passionately embraced the extreme of uncontained release and denounced superimposed and confining forms. . . . The desire to remove the literary superego was a sign of how the Beats would struggle with the conditioning influences of language; in many ways it represented a fulfillment of the romantic credo as formulated in the preface to the *Lyrical Ballads* in which Coleridge and Wordsworth promised to use the language of ordinary men.[4]

"Uncontained release"? The removal of "the literary superego"? Here is a little diary-poem of 1955 called "A Strange New Cottage in Berkeley," originally designed as a prelude to the famous "A Supermarket in California" and now restored to its proper place:

> All afternoon cutting bramble blackberries off a tottering brown fence under a low branch with its rotten old apricots miscellaneous under the leaves,
> fixing the drip in the intricate gut machinery of a new toilet;
> found a good coffeepot in the vines by the porch, rolled a big tire out of the scarlet bushes, hid my marijuana;
> wet the flowers, playing the sunlit water each to each, returning for godly extra drops for the stringbeans and daisies;
> three times walked round the grass and sighed absently;
> my reward, when the garden fed me its plums from the form of a small tree in the corner.,
> an angel thoughtful of my stomach, and my dry and lovelorn tongue.

Perhaps the first thing to notice here is that "the sequence of thought-forms passing naturally through ordinary mind" would not include the title, "A Strange New Cottage in Berkeley," a title that serves as the focal point for the catalogue that follows. For it is, of course, the poet who is "strange" and "new" to his surroundings and hence lonely in his solitude, even as he senses himself to be on the brink of something "new" that he longs for. Ginsberg in conversation with Burroughs or Kerouac or Corso might talk about the same activities—cutting brambles from the fence, fixing the toilet, watering the flowers—but hardly in the sequence found in the poem, a sequence that moves carefully from the ordinary to the strange and that culminates in the high style of "an angel thoughtful of my stomach, and my dry and lovelorn tongue."

The sequence of images moves from without to within, from the bramble blackberries on the fence to the "dry and lovelorn tongue" that craves the fruit of the garden. The first three lines present images that seem to be in accord with the great American work ethic, the natural desire to "fix up the place," to create order. But Ginsberg as boy scout imperceptibly gives way to Ginsberg the resourceful tramp, finding "a good coffeepot in the vines by the porch, roll[ing] a big tire out of the scarlet bushes," and then Ginsberg, the bad Beat boy, hiding his marijuana in anticipation of the times to come. The pragmatic and the visionary here go hand in hand: to "wet the flowers, playing the sunlit water each to each," becomes a rite of initiation, a rite confirmed in the line "three times walked round the garden and sighed absently."

This self-portrayal makes us smile. The poet as lord of the manor surveying his domain is, of course, a scared young man, "absently" dreaming of lost and future love. But "absence" also paves the way for the influx of spirit, for the vision of the plum tree in the corner of the garden as "an angel thoughtful of my stomach, and my dry and lovelorn tongue."

Such wry conjuctions of the ordinary and the "strange," of grubby fact and vision, are typical of Ginsberg. There is a touch of the Jewish clown in the make-up of this poet-prophet. In the Appendix to the *Collected Poems*, we find a photograph of Naomi, Allen, and Louis Ginsberg taken at the New York World's Fair on June 15, 1940. The bespectacled adolescent looks like nothing so much as a nice Jewish boy on an outing with his respectable parents, although even here Naomi's expression beneath her rakish black hat is decidedly odd, and Louis, holding a neat umbrella, has the smile of the insecure. The homely urban kid with glasses is, in any case, still very much a part of the bardic young poet who arrives in Berkeley looking for freedom and love. The ethos of rehabilitating the "good coffeepot" found in the vines and the automobile tire beneath the burning bush is still the ethos of the Paterson, New Jersey, streets, indeed, of the Lower East Side where Louis and Naomi grew up. The poet's angel, it would seem, is ready to be "thoughtful of [his] stomach," because he has not wasted his material substance. Waste not, as it were, want not.

"Waste not, want not" is, for that matter, the adage that comes to mind as one reads Ginsberg's early poems and journals. A second common Ginsberg myth dispelled by a reading of the *Collected Poems* is that the conventional verse forms of the poet's youth were, at best, a false start, a kind of straitjacket he had to shed in order to find his "real self" in the long, loose sweeping line of "Howl"—a line purportedly derived from Blake, Whitman, and the Bible. In his famous letter of 1949 to his mentor, William Carlos Williams (the letter reproduced by Williams in *Paterson IV*), Ginsberg writes: "I do not know if you will like my poetry or not—that is how far your own inventive persistence excludes less independent or youthful attempts to perfect, renew, transfigure, and make contemporarily real an old style of lyric machinery, which I use to record the struggle with imagination of the clouds."[5] Williams, who had little tolerance for fixed verse forms, replied with the terse comment, "In this mode perfection is basic." Ginsberg took the hint: the poems of *Empty Mirror* (1952) abandon verse forms completely; the new line is created by breaking the prose of his journals into lines of verse.[6] This time Williams responded enthusiastically. In his Introduction to *Empty Mirror*, he writes:

> The lines are superbly all alike. Most people, most critics would call them prose—they have an infinite variety, perfectly regular; they are all alike and yet

none is like the other. It is like the monotony of our
lives that is made up of the front pages of newspapers
and the first (aging) 3 lines of the *Inferno*.

And from here, so the story usually goes, it was just a short step to the "breath unit" of "Howl," the long jazz-inspired line first heard in Ginsberg's reading at the Six Gallery in San Francisco in 1956, a line the poet himself has described as moving according to "natural inspiration of the moment . . . disparate thinks put down together, shorthand notations of visual imagery, juxtapositions of hydrogen juke-box. . . . Mind is shapely, Art is shapely."[7]

Hip as this sounds, the fact is that Ginsberg has always been the most careful of prosodists[8] and that the metrical forms of *The Gates of Wrath* have never been entirely abandoned. Indeed, by the late seventies, Ginsberg was once again writing ballad quatrains like the following:

LACK LOVE

Love wears down to bare truth
My heart hurt me much in youth
Now I hear my real heart beat
Strong and hollow thump of meat

I felt my heart wrong as an ache
Sore in dreams and raw awake
I'd kiss each new love on the chest
Trembling hug him breast to breast

Kiss his belly, kiss his eye
Kiss his ruddy boyish thigh
Kiss his feet kiss his pink cheek
Kiss behind him naked meek.

This harks back thirty years to such poems as "A Western Ballad":

When I died, love, when I died
my heart was broken in your care;
I never suffered love so fair
as now I suffer and abide
when I died, love, when I died.

Or to the even earlier "An Eastern Ballad," dated 1945–49:

I speak of love that comes to mind:
The moon is faithful, although blind;
She moves in thought she cannot speak.
Perfect care has made her bleak.

It could (and has) been argued that Ginsberg's recent return to the "simple" ballad form of his repressed youth marks a loss of poetic power, a retreat into the pleasant and easy. But since the circular arrangement of the *Collected Poems* is Ginsberg's own, we can take it to signify that, for this poet, as for Pound before him, "poetry withers and 'dries out' when it leaves music . . . too far behind it."[9] Consider lines 3–4 of "An Eastern Ballad," one of the first poems Ginsberg wrote and preserved:

She móves in thóught‖she cánnot spéak.
Pérfect cáre has máde hêr bléak.

The twenty-year-old poet who placed the caesura in the third line and who foreshortened the fourth, beginning, in Blakean fashion, with a trochee, was already a very accomplished poet. The consonance of "Per"/"care"/"her," the alliteration of "has"/"her," the assonance of *e*'s and *a*'s—all culminating in the rhyme "speak"/"bleak"—this is a poetic debut that bears watching, no matter how hackneyed the image of the blind moon and the theme of lost love. Side by side with such songs, we find "prosaic" poems like "Paterson" (1949), which begins:

What do I want in these rooms papered with visions
of money?
How much can I make by cutting my hair? If I put
new heels on my shoes,
bathe my body reeking of masturbation and sweat,
layer upon layer of excrement.

This jaunty self-mocking opening immediately brings to mind Frank O'Hara, who was still an undergraduate at Harvard and quite unknown to Ginsberg in 1949. After listing all the Establishment institutions to be rejected ("employment bureaus," "statistical cubicles," "cloakrooms of the smiling gods of psychiatry," and so on), Ginsberg launches into a long catalogue of what he would rather be doing:

rather jar my body down the road, crying by a diner
in the Western sun;
rather crawl on my naked belly over the tincans of
Cincinnati;
rather drag a rotten railroad tie to a Golgotha in the
Rockies;
rather, crowned with thorns in Galveston, nailed
hand and foot in Los Angeles, raised up to die in
Denver,
pierced in the side in Chicago, perished and tombed
in New Orleans and resurrected in 1958 somewhere on Garret Mountain,
come down roaring in a blaze of hot cars and
garbage,
streetcorner Evangel in front of City Hall, surrounded by statues of agonized lions,
with a mouthful of shit, and the hair rising on my
scalp,
screaming and dancing in praise of Eternity annihilating the sidewalk, annihilating reality,
screaming and dancing against the orchestra in the
destructible ballroom of the world,
blood streaming from my belly and shoulders
flooding the city with its hideous ecstasy, rolling over
the pavements and highways
by the bayoux and forests and derricks leaving my
flesh and my bones hanging on the trees.

Here, seven years before the performance of "Howl" in San Francisco, is the Ginsberg mode in embryo; the long anapestic line built on the anaphora of "rather" (as the "Howl" line builds on the anaphora of "who"), the cataloguing of American place names, the reference to ugly reality ("the tincans of Cincinnati," "a rotten railroad tie," "hot cars and garbage"), the conjunction of the physical ("mouthful of shit") and the spiritual ("hair rising on my scalp,/screaming and dancing in praise of Eternity"). Indeed, some of the phrasing of "Paterson" (e.g., "to die in Denver") reappears almost verbatim in "Howl."

But toward the close, "Paterson" goes sosmewhat limp. Such phrases as "the destructible ballroom of the world" and "hideous ecstasy" are hackneyed, and the Whitmanian conclusion, "by the bayoux and forests and derricks leaving my flesh and my bones hanging on the trees," has not quite been earned by the preceding catalogue: the speaker is too angry at the world to become a seer, too preoccupied with himself to enter the life of the bayoux and forests and derricks.

Indeed, the feat of "Howl" is that it pays homage to Whitman and Williams even as it transforms their characteristic rhythms and images. Consider the following sequence:

who júmped ôff the Bróoklyn Brídge‖thîs áctually
háppened‖and wálked awáy ûnknówn and for-
gótten into the ghóstly dáze of Chínatôwn sóup
álleywâys & fíretrûcks,‖not êven óne frêe béer,
who sáng oût of their wíndows in despáir,‖féll oût of
the súbway wíndow,‖júmped in the fílthy Pas-
sáic,‖leáped on négroes,‖críed âll óver the
stréet,‖dánced on bróken wineglâsses báref̆ôot
smáshed phónogrâph récords of nostálgic Éuro-

> péan 1́930́s Gérman jázz‖fínished the whískey and
> thréw ûp gróaning into the blóody tóilet,‖móans
> in their éars and the blást of colóssal stéam
> whîstles,
> who bárreled dówn the híghways of the pást jóurney-
> ing to eâch óther's hótrôd-Gólgôtha‖jáil-sólitude
> wátch‖or Bírmingham jázz incarnátion.

Compare this to Whitman's "Song of Myself":

> Wálking the páth wórn in the gráss and béat through
> the léaves of the brúsh,
> Where the quáil is whístling betwíxt the wóods and
> the whéat-lôt,
> Where the bát flíes in the Séventh-mônth éve,
> ‖where the gréat góldbûg dróps through the
> dárk,
> Where the bróok puts oút of the róots of the ôld trée
> and flóws to the méadow. . . .

Whitman's rhythm is characterized by its flow, its forward thrust. Phrase succeeds parallel phrase with only the slightest of pauses between them, and the predominant anapests and amphibrachs are linked by alliteration and assonance. In contrast, Ginsberg's line moves forward only to go into reverse. His mode is a curious amalgam of graphic realistic reference and surrealist image, a mix, so to speak, of Williams ("No ideas but in things," as Ginsberg repeatedly tells us) and the high style of the Great (English) Tradition, learned from Mark Van Doren and other professors at Columbia and filtered through Hart Crane. "The ghostly daze of Chinatown," "the highways of the past," "moans in their ears"—such phrases could and did appear in *The Gates of Wrath*, as could such poetic diction as "unknown and forgotten," "in despair," "journeying," and "solitude." But in "Howl," this elegant language quickly modulates into parenthetical statements like "this actually happened" or "not even one free beer." Here is the speech base we hear so much about, but notice that Ginsberg's clotted catalogues—"Chinatown soup alleyways & firetrucks" or "each other's hotrod-Golgotha jail-solitude watch"—are closer to the proto-Dada style of Apollinaire and Cendrars than to Whitman. The rhythmic contour of such phrases is one of intentional clash:

> êach óther's hótrôd-Gólgôtha jáil-sólitude wátch

where the opposition of voiced and voiceless stop *(d + g)* or liquid and spirant *(l + s)* forces the reader to pause and draw breath.

Throughout "Howl," we hear this oppositional rhythm, a bumping and grinding that vocalizes the poet's feverish intensity. But in the "Footnote to Howl," written some time after the completion of the poem, the clash of energies gives way to something much more predictable:

> Holy the solitudes of skyscrapers and pavements!
> Holy the cafeterias filled with the millions! Holy
> the mysterious rivers of tears under the streets!

Evidently Ginsberg added the "Footnote" to counter the criticism (made, among others, by his father) that the poem propounded no positive values.[10] But the "Holy! Holy! Holy!" conclusion (set over against the "Moloch" litany of the preceding section) has an air of willed assertion: everything is too easily and too inexplicably "holy" and beautiful. The long lines now consist of no more than a series of neatly parallel phrases ("Holy New York Holy San Francisco Holy Peoria"), phrases that have none of the bite of such earlier sequences as "Peyote solidities of halls, backyard green tree cemetery dawns, wine drunkenness over the rooftops, storefront boroughs of teahead joyride neon blinking traffic light, sun and moon and tree vibrations"). I mention this because poems like the "Footnote to Howl" have been imitated by countless Ginsberg disciples, whereas the linear structure of "Howl" itself is all but inimitable in its density.

The question of density brings me to a third myth, which has to do with the interpretation of the poet's voice. Simply put, this is the myth that, from "Howl" onward, Ginsberg writes a poetry of vatic inspiration coupled with a searing denunciation of modern Capitalist society as the embodiment of the spiritual death brought on by a culture bent on "visions of money." Only the transformation of consciousness, whether induced by drugs or poetry or Buddhist meditation, can bring the poet to a cosmic vision of the essence of things. Ginsberg, according to this myth, is a poet-prophet in the tradition of Plotinus, Blake, and Mahayana Tibetan Buddhism. The negative side of this myth (and we hear this often too) is that Ginsberg's claim to vision is dubious, that his drug-induced poems or Buddhist mantras make pretentious claims for what is in fact no more than free association, and that his political ideology is at best naive and at worst merely foolish, as when he exclaims: "Birdbrain runs the World/Birdbrain is the ultimate product of Capitalism/Birdbrain chief bureaucrat of Russia, yawning" ("Plutonian Ode").

Interestingly, the controversy over the value of Ginsberg's prophetic mode tends to bypass the role of the comic, the absurd in his poetry. What the *Collected Poems* shows us is that Ginsberg is, finally, a very *funny* poet. To read "Howl" as a serious indictment of American culture, a culture that denies the possibility of spirtual illumination, is to ignore the poet's self-deprecatory humor, his ability to laugh at himself and at his friends. When, in a 1976 reading of the poem at the Naropa Institute in Boulder, Colorado, Ginsberg came to the line:

> who reappeared on the West Coast investigating the
> FBI in beards and shorts with his pacifist eyes
> sexy in their dark skin passing out incom-
> prehensible leaflets

the audience laughed delightedly, no doubt at the non-sequitur of referring to "the big pacifist eyes" as "sexy," as well as to the open question of what those "incomprehensible leaflets" did, in fact, contain.[11] Or again, the line, "who cut their wrists three times successively unsuccessfully, gave up and were forced to open antique stores where they thought they were growing old and cried," is playful in its insinuation that the youthful slitting of the wrists was all bravado, a Chaplinesque gesture designed to protect the "best minds of my generation" from the middle-class boredom that turned out to be precisely their fate.

"Howl" is replete with images of young men who thought "the cosmos instinctively vibrated at their feet in Kansas," who were dragged off roofs "waving genitals and manuscripts," who furnished their rooms with "orange crates of theology," who jumped off Brooklyn Bridge only to walk away "unknown and forgotten" and be rewarded with "not even one free beer," who made "harlequin speech[es] of suicide, demanding instantaneous lobotomy," and "who were given instead the concrete void of insulin Metrazol electricity hydrotherapy psychotherapy occupational therapy pingpong & amnesia." It is in many ways an elegy for the poet's youth, for the time when opposition was all, when taking risks was daily fun, designed to *épater* one's parents and teachers. Part I of "Howl" presents Ginsberg in the role of urban Jewish Huck Finn, the street-wise kid who refuses to obey those boring, hypocritical grown-ups. The same voice speaks to us in "A Supermarket in California," where we find "Aisles full of husbands! Wives in the avocados, babies in the tomatoes!" Or again, in "America," where the poet exclaims, "America after all it is you and I who are perfect not the next world," but then admits that, "There must be some other way to settle this argument."

The other side of such clowning is, as in a Chaplin film, a terrible sadness, the emptiness of having no one for whom to perform. Consider the opening of "Transcription of Organ Music," written in Berkeley in 1955:

> The flower in the glass peanut bottle formerly in the
> kitchen crooked to take a place in the light,
> the closet door open because I used it before, it
> kindly stayed open waiting for me, its owner.
> I began to feel my misery in pallet on floor, listening
> to music, my misery, that's why I want to sing.
> The room closed down on me, I expected the
> presence of the Creator, I saw my gray painted
> walls and ceiling, they contained my room, they
> contained me
> as the sky contained my garden,
> I opened my door
> The rambler vine climbed up the cottage post,
> the leaves in the night still where the day had placed
> them, the animal heads of the flowers where they
> had arisen
> to think at the sun

Here the poet is himself the "flower in the glass peanut bottle" straining crookedly "to take a place in the light." Nothing happens. Like the young men of "Howl" who "cowered in unshaven rooms in underwear," the "I" finds himself in a room that "closed down on me," and opening the door leads to no influx of spirit. Everything remains exactly as it was: rambler vine, leaves, flowers, and, inside the house, "My books . . . waiting in space where I placed them . . . my words piled up, my texts, my manuscripts, my loves."

In the lines that follow, the lonely poet attempts to cheer himself up by contemplating, "the red blossoms in the night light" of a bush "peering in the window." In a moment of Laurentian communion he tries to assume the position of the leaves "upturned top float to the sky to receive." But Ginsberg's is a sensibility that communes with people, not with flowers, (unless, of course, a Jack Kerouac is sitting close by, as in "Sunflower Sutra"), and so nothing changes. "The light socket is crudely attached to the ceiling, after the house was built, to receive a plug which sticks in it all right, and serves my phonograph now." Indeed, "There are unused electricity plugs all over my house if I ever need them." And worst, for a poet who needs friends and lovers, "The telephone—sad to relate—sits on the floor—I haven't the money to get it connected."

In *The Visionary Poetics of Allen Ginsberg*, Paul Portugés argues that "Transcription of Organ Music" records a "transcendental, prophetic experience," that the poet "masterfully uses his physical surroundings to force himself into a visionary state."[12] True, the poem ends with the lines:

> I want people to bow as they see me and say he
> is gifted with poetry, he has seen the presence of the
> Creator.
> And the Creator gave me a shot of his presence
> to gratify my wish, so as not to cheat me of my
> yearning for him.

But in the context of the unused electric plugs, unconnected telephone, and the masturbatory fantasy about the kitchen door as "hole [that] will admit me," the telling thing is that the poet wants "people to bow as they see me," he wants *others* to *know* that "he is gifted with poetry," that "he has seen the presence of the Creator." Like the Lawrence of *Birds, Beasts and Flowers*, Ginsberg has a strong sense of theater. Even at his most introspective, he does not forget to play to the stands.

The Chaplinesque mode with its rapid shifts from sadness to laughter and back again is brought to perfection in such poems of the late fifties as "In the Baggage Room at Greyhound," which culminates in the lines:

> A swarm of baggage sitting by the counter as the
> transcontinental bus pulls in.
> The clock registering 12:15 A.M., May 9, 1956, the
> second hand moving forward, red.
> Getting ready to load my last bus—Farewell, Walnut
> Creek Richmond Vallejo Portland Pacific High-
> way
> Fleet-footed Quicksilver, god of transience.
> One last package sits lone at midnight sticking up out
> of the Coast rack high as the dusty fluorescent
> light.
> The wage they pay is too low to live on. Tragedy
> reduced to numbers
> This for the poor shepherds. I am a communist.
> Farewell ye Greyhound where I suffered so much,
> hurt my knee and scraped my hand and built my
> pectoral muscles big as vagina.

Here is the Ginsberg signature: the careful location of the self in place and time, the rollcall of place names as if the very naming process could conjure up godhead, the sudden political gesture ("The wage they pay is too low to live on. . . . I am a communist")—all finally giving way to the burlesque of the tough-guy boast about "pectoral muscles big as vagina."

II

Ginsberg's autobiography takes him from these exquisite anatomies of loneliness to the more public (and sometimes strident) pronouncements of *Planet News* (1968) and *The Fall of America* (1973). Between these two modes there is "Kaddish" (1961), at once Ginsberg's most highly praised and his least typical poem. So close is the poet of "Kaddish" to the story he tells about his mother Naomi's mental breakdowns and remissions, her "mad" episodes, her relationship with her weak husband and her adolescent son, that we respond to his terrible disclosures with a certain astonished embarrassment, embarrassment that any man would be willing to describe his own mother as follows:

> One night, sudden attack—her noise in the
> bathroom—like croaking up her soul—con-
> vulsions and red vomit coming out of her
> mouth—diarrhea water exploding from her be-
> hind—on all fours in front of the toilet—urine
> running between her legs—left retching on the
> tile floor smeared with her black feces—
> unfainted—
> At forty, varicosed, nude, fat, doomed, hiding
> outside the apartment door near the elevator
> calling Police, yelling for her girlfriend Rose to
> help. . . .

How the twelve-year-old Allen Ginsberg coped with this situation, how years later, Naomi no longer recognized him when he visited her on the mental ward, and how, "2 days after her death," he found a letter from her saying: "The key is in the window, the key is in the sunlight at the window—I have the key—Get married Allen don't take drugs—the key is in the bars, in the sunlight in the window"—these tales are moving, even harrowing, but no one would wish this portion of Ginsberg's autobiography any longer. On the contrary, it seems that the Ginsberg of "Kaddish" is writing somewhat against the grain. He had, no doubt, to get the Freudian drama off his chest, but in his best and most characteristic poems, the "family" is that of male comrades, the band of brothers whose lives intersect with his. With the exception of Naomi and Aunt

Rose, women play no role in Ginsberg's poetry. Indeed, Woman is the absence that haunts the poet's worst moments. In "This Form of Life Need Sex" (1961), we read:

I will have to accept women
if I want to continue the race,
kiss breasts, accept
strange hairy lips behind
buttocks,
Look in questioning womanly eyes
answer soft cheeks.

And because he cannot in fact accept women in any sense:

Between me and oblivion an unknown
woman stands;
Not the Muse but living meat-phantom,
a mystery scary as my fanged god.

This is Ginsberg at his least attractive: his equation of Woman and Death, his references to "the one hole that repelled me 1937 on," call into question, it seems to me, his protest poems about the oppressive "Fathers in office in these industries" ("War Profit Litany"), his references to the "Corporate voices [that] jabber on electric networks building/body-pain, chemical ataxia, physical slavery" ("Pentagon Exorcism"). For Ginsberg does not reject the patriarchal world; he merely wants to replace one set of fathers with a more congenial one, for example the "peasant manhoods [of Vietnam, who] burn in black & white forest" on the TV screen. One of the low points in the volume is a poem of 1970 called "Ecologue," which begins:

In a thousand years, if there's History
America'll be remembered as a nasty little Country
full of Pricks, thorny hothouse rose
Cultivated by the Yellow Gardeners.
"Chairman Mao" for all his politics, head of a
Billion
folk, important old & huge
Nixon a dude, specialized on his industrial
Island, a clean paranoiac Mechanic.

Our "nasty little Country" is metaphorized as the female rose; it is the rose that is, in an all too obvious pun, "full of Pricks." In this context, the homage to Chairman Mao as "head of a Billion/folk, important old & huge," has a "macho" ring: it brings to mind Ezra Pound's adulation of "old Muss" (Mussolini). Today, in the reign of Mao's enemy, Comrade Deng, Ginsberg's simple-minded opposition of the good Mao to the bad Nixon is hardly compelling.

What is compelling in the later (and, on the whole, lesser) poems is Ginsberg's extraordinary sense of the moment, of being, so to speak, at the center of the vortex. Read as an autobiography, the *Collected Poems* is a kind of ironic Horatio Alger story. The hero of this narrative learns how to take every liability of his childhood and turn it into an asset. The homely little kid with glasses becomes a bearded, exotically attractive guru-figure, and then, just when everyone expects him to appear in Indian dress and beads, he dons suit and tie, cuts his hair, and looks, for all the world, like everyone's cuddly Jewish uncle. The dreary lower-middle class setting of Paterson, New Jersey, gives way to the cross-country and cross-continent journeys that take the poet to Big Sur and Benares, to Calcutta and Katmandu. Yet these travels have never produced, as they have for so many writers and artists, a scorn for one's native place. Ginsberg is just as celebratory of Wichita, Kansas, as of Macchu Picchu, just as attentive to the sights and sounds on the New York subway as on the Patna-Benares express. Again, his homosexuality, surely a source of guilt and shame for a Jewish boy growing up in America in the forties, becomes, by the time of *Howl* and *Planet News*, the source of a new-found strength: it allows Ginsberg to play a double role. On the one hand, his sexual otherness calls into question the complacent "masculinity" of the straight men who are in power. On the other, it is a source of vulnerability, bringing the "famous poet" down to the reader's level. For, despite all his celebrity, here is a man whose lovers continue to leave him, who can never get enough sex, who, in his mid-fifties, can still complain:

Rarer and rarer
Boys give me favor
Older and older
Love grows bolder

Or:

It's not the most romantic
dream to be so frantic
for young men's bodies,
a fine sugar daddy
blest respected known
but left to bed alone.

If love is often a failure, there is consolation in friendship. Like the Yeats of "The Municipal Gallery Revisited," Ginsberg might well declare, "Say that the glory was I had such friends." The poor and lonely Columbia undergraduate, masturbating in his Harlem room, grows up to count among his friends Jack Kerouac and William Burroughs, Gary Snyder and Robert Creeley, Frank O'Hara and John Ashbery. Having made a convert of Williams at the outset of his career, twenty years later Ginsberg takes on Pound. Calling on the Great Poet in Venice at a time when Pound no longer speaks, Ginsberg cajoles the old man into commenting on the *Cantos* ("It's all tags and patches") and introduces his attentive listener to songs by Dylan and the Beatles.

A great deal of fuss has been made about the role of drugs in Ginsberg's work: he himself has conscientiously noted which poem was written on which drug—Part II of "Howl" on peyote, "Kaddish" on methedrine, "Wales Visitation" on LSD, and so on. But here again, Ginsberg's history, as presented in the *Collected Poems*, is a kind of Fortunate Fall. As a child, we learn in "Kaddish," his response to the food prepared by his mother was one of disgust:

Serving me meanwhile, a plate of cold fish—chopped raw cabbage dript with tapwater—smelly tomatoes—week-old health food—grated beets & carrots with leaky juice, warm—more and more disconsolate food—I can't eat it for nausea sometimes—the Charity of her hands stinking with Manhattan, madness, desire to please me, cold undercooked fish—pale red near the bones. Her smells—and often naked in the room, so that I stare ahead, or turn a book ignoring her.

To escape from this world is, at first, to go West, to the "Supermarket in California" with its "peaches and . . . penumbras," its avocados and giant melons, so unlike the "grated beets & carrots with leaky juice" of his childhood. In poems like "Sunflower Sutra" and "Sather Gate Illumination," the poet's new "mad locomotive riverbank sunset Frisco hilly tincan evening sitdown vision" is, at least in part, induced by the ingestion of exotic food and drugs. "Float[ing] on the sweetened scene of trees & humans" at Berkeley, he exclaims:

My stomach is light, I relax, new sentences spring forth out of the scene to describe spontaneous forms of Time—trees, sleeping dogs, airplanes wandering thru the air, negroes with the lunch books of anxiety, apples and sandwiches, lunchtime, icecream, Timeless—

Apples, sandwiches, ice cream under the trees—it is a far cry from the "cold undercooked fish" his mother fed him. "Kaddish" is followed, not coincidentally, I think, by the three drug poems, "Mescaline," "Lysergic Acid," and "I Beg You Come Back & Be Cheerful," as if to say that, with the death of his mother, he is now free to do as he pleases.

But not quite. Unlike Kerouac or Neil Cassady, unlike the countless Beat poets who OD'd or drank themselves to death, Ginsberg emerges in the *Collected Poems* as the ultimate survivor. There is something of the professor (and also of the once good boy who ate his chicken soup) in his disciplined experimentation with drugs, the careful accounts made in his journals of his precise physical reactions. By the early seventies, the fascination with drugs had largely given way to the absorption in the discipline of Buddhist meditation.

And here again, Ginsberg has responded to the challenge with a certain pragmatism. If Buddhism has been useful to him, he has not exactly retired to a monastery. In conversation with Paul Portugés, he is candid about his inability to fully follow the Tibetan doctrine of nonattachment to the ego. As he puts it, "[Buddhist practice] is just a question of learning a sharper, more experienced way of recognizing and appreciating what's already in your head. It doesn't require a big breakthrough or anything like that."[13]

So, in the seventies, we find the poet returning more frequently to the scene of the crime, to the old neighborhood on New York's Lower East Side where Naomi once walked. In a charming poem called "Mugging" (1974), which begins:

> Tonight I walked out of my red apartment door on
> East tenth street's dusk—

we see Ginsberg strolling down his familiar street, calmly observing the local sights and sounds, when something happens:

> Walked past a taxicab controlling the bottle strewn curb—
> past young fellows with their umbrella handles & canes leaning against a ravaged Buick
> —and as I looked at the crowd of kids on the stoop—a boy stepped up, put his arm around my neck—
> tenderly I thought for a moment, squeezed harder, his umbrella handle against my skull,
> and his friends took my arm, a young brown companion tripped his foot 'gainst my ankle—
> as I went down shouting Om Ah Hūm to gangs of lovers on the stoop watching slowly appreciating, why this is a raid, these strangers mean strange business with what—my pockets, bald head, broken-healed-bone leg, my softshoes, my heart—
> Have they knives? Om Ah Hūm—Have they sharp metal wood to shove in eye ear ass? Om Ah Hūm. . . .

The spectacle of Ginsberg, once himself the hoodlum suspended from Columbia for writing "Butler has no balls" on his dorm window, now middle-aged and bald, wearing "a neat orlon shirt" and carrying a "woolen bag of poetry address calendar & Leary-lawyer notes," the spectacle of this man suddenly being knocked down by a gang of slum kids and trying to calm himself by chanting a mantra, is both funny and touching. For the irony is that the once wild poet has become a member of the Establishment and he knows it. His "snakeskin wallet" ("actually plastic," he explains apologetically) contains "70 dollars" as well as "dreary plastic contents—Amex card & Manf. Hanover Trust Credit too—business card from Mr. Spears British Home Minister Drug Squad—my draft card—membership ACLU & Naropa Institute Instructor's identification."

The metamorphosis the poet has undergone is rather like the metamorphosis of the little black-and-white City Lights pocket books into the big fat *Collected Poems* selling for $27.50. But so good-humored is Ginsberg about his new role as "sixty-year-old smiling public man," that we can only smile too. As he rises from "the cardboard mattress" where the boys have thrown him, having carried off his wallet and Seiko Hong Kong wrist watch, he remarks ruefully: "Om Ah Hūm didn't stop em enough,/the tone of voice too loud." And there is the further irony that they took his "valuables," but "my shoulder bag with 10,000 dollars full of poetry left on the broken floor."

So much for being a poet. He gets up, picks up his glasses from the step where he had the good sense to deposit them even as he was dragged into the store, and surveys the now wholly defamiliarized scene:

> Whole street a bombed-out face, building rows' eyes & teeth missing
> burned apartments half the long block, gutted cellars, hallways' charred beams. . . .

The chanting of "Om Ah Hūm" now gives way to a more Western Jeremiad: "Oh hopeless city of idiots empty eyed staring afraid." In the poet's imagination, the "honking neighborhood" is transformed into a surreal and frozen landscape: the poem's final image is of an "old lady with frayed paper bags/sitting in the tin-boarded doorframe of a dead house."

"Mugging" may be read as an elegy for the lost New York of the fifties, a New York in which people still spoke to their neighbors and chatted on their tenement steps. But it avoids sentimentality by turning the poet's situation into comedy. The image of Ginsberg, down on the ground and deprived of his glasses, trying to chant Buddhist mantras so as to pacify his teen-age assailants, carries on the tradition of "Howl."

III

In recent years, as I have noted earlier, Ginsberg has returned to the short ballad stanzas of his yough. Having written so expansively for decades, he now shows a penchant for the minimal, as in a poem called "For Creeley's Ear," which begins with the stanza:

> The whole
> weight of
> everything
> too much

Such minimal lyrics may be profitably read against a new text by John Cage, called "Writing through Howl for A.G. on his Sixtieth Birthday." Commissioned for a birthday festschrift that will appear in 1986,[14] "Writing through Howl," which is dated, Ginsberg style, "through Asia and home to New York, January-April 1984," functions as a fascinating commentary on its parent text, even as it creates a new poetic construct of a very different sort.

"Writing through Howl" is what Cage calls a *mesostic*, which is to say that the acrostic "ALLEN GINSBERG" runs down the middle of the page rather than at the left margin. "Howl" is subjected to I Ching chance operations and the mesostic follows the rule that "A *given letter capitalized does not occur between it and the preceding capitalized letter.*"[15] Thus the word "saw" ("I saw") gives us the first letter of "Allen," and the second letter, *l*, is taken from "themselves," the "l" of "hysterical" not counting because the word also contains an *a*. When the "writing through" is completed, the process begins again, this time using what Cage calls the "rubble," that is, the words that were not used the first time around. So the first word that contains an "a" is "madness," and the first "l" that qualifies comes in "cold-water flats." By the ninth and last time of "writing through," we have the tiny mesostic "Allen"—

Angry
soLidities
battaL ion
thE
aNd

which nicely characterizes Ginsberg's stance: the "Lion" ready to spring from the larger "battaLion," and "thE end" that becomes, for Ginsberg, "the aNd," in keeping with his faith in the rhetoric of accumulation. But—and here is where Cage is so interesting—Ginsberg himself would never use such a phrase any more than he would use so abstract a designation as "Angry soLidities." "Starry dynamo," "unshaven rooms," "incomparable blind streets"—with Ginsberg, we still know where we are.

"Writing for the first time through Howl" begins like this:

sAw
themseLves
Looking for
hipstErs
starry dyNamo
hiGh sat
theIr
heaveN
Saw
puBlishing
odEs on
Rooms
listeninGto the terror
beArds returning through
Laredo
beLt
for nEw york
iN
druGs
wIth
alcohol aNd
ballS
Bind
in thEmind
towaRd
illuminatinG
dAwns
bLinking
Light
thE
wiNter
liGht
endless rIde

Here Ginsberg's dense, clotted, overwrought line gives way to stark reduction, a reduction that leaves a great deal to the reader's imagination. We don't know, for example, who it is that is "Looking for hipstErs," for we are given only flashes of a starry dyNamo," of a Miltonic " hiGh sat/theIr/heaveN," of "beArds returning through/Laredo." Ginsberg's snowballing and sonorous chant here becomes the trill of "Blind/in thE mind/towaRd/illuminatinG/dAwns/bLinking/Light," a trill followed by the echo "thE/wiNter/liGht," and then a kind of breath pause and the addition, "endless rIde."

Further on, we get such stanzas as

visionAry
onLY
supernaturaL
Ecstasy
iN
streetliGht

Or:

Gaunt
waI tresses
loNely petticoat
eSpecially
Blood
on thEsnowbank docks
foR
floodliGht

By the time we get to the third writing through, we get little fragments like:

stArving
fLoating
contempLating jazz

or:

theIr
bloNde
loSt
loveBoys
thE
thRee

Cage's stanzas leave a good deal open (e.g., who are "the three"?) but they are by no means to be taken as non-sensical. When, for example, the "lonely petticoat" of the "Gaunt/ waItresses" is metonymically related to "Blood/on thE snowbank docks," a new narrative possibility is suggested. Think of the promising plots that might contain these elements! Or again, when we read "incomprehensibLe/capitaLism/ distributEd/iN/deliGht," we are struck by the realization that the stanza provides an ironic commentary on Ginsberg's own wholesale diatribes against the System.

Emblematically, "Howl" and "Writing through Howl" provide us with two interesting poetic alternatives. Ginsberg's is a mode of continuity: however surrealist, jarring, hilarious, horrendous his conjunction of images may be, he regards the poem as a living *whole* with, somewhat surprisingly, a beginning, middle, and end. "Howl" moves from the "I saw . . ." sequence to the diatribe against Moloch (II) to the resolution of "Carl Solomon! I'm with you in Rockland" (III), with the Footnote "Holy! Holy! Holy!" as an even more elaborate (and, I think, unnecessary) coda. Similarly, "Sunflower Sutra" moves from the despair of "I walked" to the final "evening sitdown vision," and "America" ends on the triumphant assertion, "America, I'm putting my queer shoulder to the wheel."

Ginsberg, we may conclude, is never the poet of collage, of fragment, of layering and splicing. As such, his poetry now looks, for all its references to "cock" and "balls," reassuringly traditional. This may well be what Cage is implying in his gently ironic mesostics, featuring, as they do, the primacy of the word over its referent. But Cage's poetic text is also an act of homage, in that it isolates key words and phrases like "in the goldhorn shadow" so as to make us more aware of their peculiar density. "Writing through Howl" is thus a fitting tribute to the author of the *Collected Poems*, which is itself a great memorial to the middle of our century.

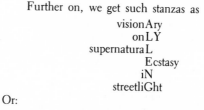

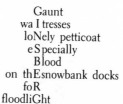

Notes

1. *Connoisseurs of Chaos: Ideas of Order in Modern American Poetry* (New York: Macmillan, 1965), p. 49.
2. *Figures of Capable Imagination* (New York: Seabury Press, 1976), p. 260.
3. *Writers at Work: The* Paris Review *Interviews, Third Series*, ed. George Plimpton (New York: Viking Press, 1968), pp. 287–88.
4. See John Tytell, "The Broken Circuit," in Jack Kerouac, *On the Road: Text and Criticism*, ed. Scott Donaldson (New York: Viking Penguin, 1979), pp. 327–328.
5. See Williams, *Paterson* (New York: New Directions, 1963), p. 174. The letter is reprinted as the Preface to *The Gates of Wrath: Rhymed Poems 1948–1951* (Bolinas: Grey Fox Press, 1972).
6. On this point, see James E. B. Breslin, *From Modern to Contemporary: American Poetry, 1945–65* (Chicago: University of Chicago Press, 1984), pp. 88–92.
7. "Notes for *Howl and Other Poems*," in *The Poetics of the New American Poetry*, ed. Donald M. Allen and Warren Tallman (New York: Grove Press, 1973), p. 319.
8. For a discussion of the function of stress, syllable count, breath units, and stanza forms, both in his own poetry and in that of poets ranging from Campion and Milton to Williams, Moore, and Creeley, see "Improvised Poetics" (1971) and "An Exposition of William Carlos Williams' Poetic Practice" (1976), both in *Composed on the Tongue*, ed. Donald Allen (Bolinas: Grey Fox Press, 1980), pp. 18–62, 118–153.
9. "Vers Libre and Arnold Dolmetsch" (1918), in *Literary Essays of Ezra Pound*, ed. T.S. Eliot (London: Faber and Faber, 1954), p. 437. Ginsberg quotes this passage in "Improvised Poetics," p. 59.
10. In a 1956 letter cited by James Breslin *(From Modern to Contemporary*, pp. 104–105), Louis Ginsberg wrote his son: "['Howl'] has violence; it has life, it has *vitality*. In my opinion, it is a one-sided neurotic view of life; it has not enough glad, Whitmanian affirmations."
11. See Allen Ginsberg and Anne Waldman, *Beauty and the Beast, Naropa Institute Recordings* (Boulder, Colorado, 1976).
12. (Santa Barbara: Ross-Ericson, 1978), p. 76.
13. *The Visionary Poetics of Allen Ginsberg*, p. 162.
14. I have a copy of the manuscript from which John Cage has kindly permitted me to quote. The editor of the forthcoming festschrift is Bill Morgan.
15. See Cage, "Foreword," M, *Writings '67–72* (Middletown, Conn.: 1973). The particular rules and terminology (e.g. "rubble") used here were discussed with Mr. Cage on 21 January 1985.

Ellen Glasgow

1874–1945

Ellen Anderson Gholson Glasgow was born in Richmond, Virginia, on April 22, 1874 (according to some sources, 1873). Because of ill health in childhood, she was educated privately, and began writing at age seven. When she was sixteen her hearing began to fade, a weakness about which she was sensitive all her life. In 1896 she made the first of many trips to Europe, visiting England, Scotland, and France.

Glasgow's first novel, *The Descendant*, which appeared anonymously in 1897, was set in New York, but starting with *The Voice of the People* (1900) she drew mainly on her intimate knowledge of Virginian society. In the early twentieth century she participated in the women's suffrage movement, but she was never a thorough-going feminist. A lifelong resident of Richmond, she was active in humane social campaigns and was President of the Richmond SPCA from 1924 to 1945. Though she never married, she was engaged twice, in 1907 and in 1917.

Glasgow enjoyed both popular and critical acclaim in the course of a long and productive writing career. Among her many novels are *Virginia* (1913), *Barren Ground* (1925), *They Stooped to Folly* (1929), *The Sheltered Life* (1932), and *Vein of Iron* (1935). The 1930s brought her declining health but many honors, including honorary doctorates, and election to the National Institute of Arts and Letters in 1932 and the American Academy of Arts and letters in 1938. *In This Our Life* (1941) won her the Pulitzer Prize. A book on the nature and writing of fiction, *A Certain Measure*, was published in 1943, and her autobiography, *The Woman Within*, appeared posthumously in 1954.

Ellen Glasgow died in Richmond on November 21, 1945.

Personal

Miss Glasgow's home is at No. 1 West Main Street, Richmond, a tall, square, gray-walled mansion in a most incongruous setting. The house is old and spacious and is situated on a plot of ground shaded by magnolias and enlivened in the summertime with a profusion of flowers. There is a high wall in the rear and an iron fence encloses the yard on the side and front. But this charming old residence is surrounded by garages, chain stores, lunchrooms, bakeries, laundries, fruit stores, and small shops. For "commercial progress" has overtaken the old residential section of Richmond, and the house at No. 1 West Main Street is one of the few ancient houses of the section that have not been demolished.

Miss Ellen Glasgow was born in this house. All of her novels, with the exception of *Life and Gabriella*, were written in a room on thde second floor which is set aside as her workroom. The sides of this room are occupied by bookcases, except for a niche in which fits a cabinet of glass and mahogany, where she keeps her collection of porcelain dogs. There is a fireplace, a Hepplewhite couch, a straight chair before which sits a small table, on which stands a typewriter directly under a shaded light supported by a wrought-iron standing lamp.

In one corner, where the sunlight falls through two windows, is Miss Glasgow's work desk, a heavy, beautiful piece of old colonial design. On this desk there is a china vase containing a great number of cork-bodied pens with stub points. Over the mantelpiece there is a Botticelli print and about the room there are many paintings and pictures of dogs. Miss Glasgow loves dogs, and, besides her collection of china dogs, paintings, bronze medallions, and photographs of dogs, she has two large and fluffy and very animated Sealyhams.

The walls of the hallway and living rooms are ivory and gray and the furnishings of Sheraton and Hepplewhite, with Chinese hangings and oriental rugs adding touches of color.

Miss Glasgow uses a typewriter and usually makes her first draft by typing it out herself. This draft she submits to a thorough revision with her stub pen and gives the result to Miss Bennett, her secretary, to retype. She invariably attends to her correspondence in longhand, writing large, full-bodied letters, slanting slightly to the right.

She as a person is witty and charming, with an unquenchable spirit of gay irony. Her eyes twinkle with an amused vivacity, and her conversation is studded with general and specific ideas expressed with subtlety and verbal resourcefulness. One of the subjects about which she grows grave and indignant is that of Prohibition. She told me that it embittered her to hear old Virginia gentlemen who once prided themselves on their knowledge of the various grades of bourbon talking about their new shipments of "corn," their palates ruined, their urbanity coarsened, and their mint juleps a vile parody of the mint julep of former times. And over the murders committed by Federal Prohibition enforcement officers she flames with the anger of outraged justice. A most gracious and hospitable hostess who entertains her guests in the grand manner of old Southern traditions, she took precaution to stock a fine collection of wines and spirits before the Eighteenth Amendment went into effect, and it is a source of anxiety to her that this cellar is steadily diminishing with no hope of its being replenished with anything like its quality.

The authoress in unorthodox in her opinions and as free from sentimentality as was Jane Austen. She made her somewhat sensational debut as a novelist at eighteen, when she published *The Descendant*, a novel in which she broke away from the sentimental tradition in American fiction. She has lived through the final stages of Victorian hypocrisy and has seen the expansion of the privileges and rights of women; and she has seen the South emerge from its old lethargy and take part in the brisk go-getterism of the North. And she has reservations about both eras. She finds many of the professed ideals of the Victorian age preposterous; but Fundamentalism, Prohibition, and real-estate subdivisions she finds have destroyed one of the old rules of life in the South, which was to live and let live.

Miss Glasgow has dedicated her most recent novel, *They Stooped to Folly*, to James Branch Cabel. Mr. Cabell had dedicated *Something about Eve* to her. They are old friends, and the Cabells are often guests at Miss Glasgow's home and Miss Glasgow is often a guest at the Cabell home in Monument Avenue.

She tells me that every time she publishes a novel, some of her readers in Richmond accuse her of having used real persons in her book; but all the events she has ever recorded in fiction have been imaginary and although, like other novelists, she draws upon the character of this actual person and that one for traits, none of her characters has existed as a whole except in her imagination.

They Stooped to Folly Miss Glasgow describes as a comedy of morals. It is more than that. It is the lively history of three generations in the South from the days when, as she says: "Being ruined was not a biological fact but a state of mind," to the present, when the whole is a personal affair, one's own business. *They Stooped to Folly* is being sponsored by the Literary Guild for August. It is characteristic of Ellen Glasgow that she sympathizes not with Poor Aunt Agatha who stooped to folly in an earnest age, nor Amy Dalrymple, mid-Victorian flirt, but with Milly Burden, a young stenographer, who sinned as if it were her own private affair; and that she blames Southern men for the "harlot or Madonna" concept that has brought tragedy to so many Southern women.

Miss Glasgow is plump and bronze-haired; she has brown eyes and a short but ample nose, slightly retroussé. Her lips are neither thick nor thin, although they appear thin when stretched into her frequent and engaging smile. She likes to dress in lively colors and to carry of an evening a large purple fan of ostrich feathers and to wear brightly colored shoes.

Her favorite poet is Alice Meynell and her favorite novelists are Tolstoi, Dostoevski, and Jane Austen, all of whom have influenced her work. She is generous and benevolent, intensely feminine, and endowed with that complete ignorance of money matters, which, somehow, miraculously enables her to get the fattest sort of contracts and the most desirable terms from editors and publishers. She is ruled over by a kindly despot, her secretary, Miss Bennett, who sometimes seems to regard her as an improvident child.

One night when Mr. Cabell and I were admiring Miss Glasgow's collection of porcelain dogs, Miss Glasgow, in a burst of generosity, offered Mr. Cabell one of the dogs he expressly admired. Mr. Cabell collects representations of all sorts of creatures: cows, lions, horses, dogs, elephants, rhinoceroses, cats, lizards, in glass, amber, bronze, porcelain, terra cotta, and plaster of paris. When he got downstairs with the treasure Miss Glasgow had given him, he took care not to let the porcelain dog out of his hands for more than a few seconds and not to let Miss Bennett have it at all, for he rightly feared that Miss Bennett would at once restore it to its former owner and tell him that he could not have it. For Miss Bennett upbraided Miss Glasgow for giving it to him.—BURTON RASCOE, "Ellen Glasgow at Home" (1928), *We Were Interrupted*, 1947, pp. 303–6

General

Here was a little girl of an almost morbidly sensitive and imaginative sort, set down in a Virginia that had been reduced by the fortunes of war to a kind of aching chaos, socially, politically and economically, and was trying desperately to fashion a new social order out of the black stumps and smouldering brands of the old. The easy way, obviously, was to seize upon a few simple principles, a set of bold and easy patterns, and give them, by a sort of acclamation, the authority of Sinai. But many of them, alas, would not work, and not a few of them were plainly false, so what issued out of the struggle was no more than a mass of gaudy artificialities, comforting to the simple but immensely unpleasant to the intelligent. Among the intelligent was the little Glasgow girl, a decorous pigtail down her back. She revolted against the blather, but had no philosophy to meet it. "I excelled only in imaginary adventures. . . . I saw painful sights. . . . The tragedy of life and the pathos which is worse than tragedy worked their way into my nerves."

Escape came at the hands of a teacher encountered in Richmond—a sort of miraculous accident. He recalls forcibly the bearded youth who, at the same time, was arousing and inflaming young Frank Harris in faraway Kansas. Dead at twenty-six, he yet managed in his short years to cover a vast area of reading, and, what is more important, a vast area of genuine thinking, centering on what was then called political economy, but running up hill and down dale in all directions. Miss Glasgow herself was but sixteen when she encountered this extraordinary pedagogue, but she was ripe for him, and whan he presently passed out of her life and his own he left her with something closely resembling a philosophy. It is with her yet, and every one of her long series of books is informed by it. It is a kind of skepticism that is pungent without being harsh; at least two-thirds of it is simple tolerance. "I believe that the quality of belief is more important than the quantity, that the world could do very well with fewer and better beliefs, and that a reasonable doubt is the safety-valve of civilization."

One may applaud this platform without forgetting how seditious it must have seemed in the Virginia of thirty years ago. But Miss Glasgow, having once mounted it, did not budge an inch. Some day the history of her novels in her home-town must be written. They began as scandals of high voltage, and it was years before Richmond was ready to admit that there was anything in them save a violent enmity to the true, the good and the beautiful. As the news gradually oozed over the Potomac that they were regarded with high politeness in the North there was some reconsideration of this position, but it was not actually abandoned until comparatively recent years. To this day, indeed, Virginia is a bit uneasy about its most distinguished living daughter, and even her appearance in all the solemn panoply of Collected Works will probably leave her something of a suspicious character. For skepticism, save in a few walled towns, of which Richmond is surely not one, is still a kind of wickedness in the South. The thing most esteemed down there, whether by the hidalgos who weep for the lost Golden Age or by the peasants who sweat and pant for the New Jerusalem, is the will to believe.

Frankly, I do not blame the Virginians for stopping cautiously short of taking Miss Glasgow to their arms, and covering her with proud kisses. For the plain fact is that the whole canon of her works is little more or less than a magnificent *reductio ad absurdum* of their traditional metaphysic. Thrown among them, and essentially of them despite her struggle against the bond, she has had at them at close range, and only too many of her shots have hit them in almost pathologically tender places. In her gallery all of the salient figures of the Virginia zoölogy stalk about under glaring lights, and when she has done with them there is little left to know about them—and not too much that is made known is reassuring. She has, in brief, set herself the task of depicting a civilization in its last gasps, and though her people have their share of universality they are still intrinsically Virginians, and hardly imaginable outside their spooky rose-gardens and musty parlors. They remain so even when the spirit of progress seizes them, and they try to take on the ways and habits of mind of the outside world. Surely the polyandrous Edmonia Bredalbane, in *The Romantic Comedians*, seems, at first glance, to be anything but provincial. But that is only at first glance. Soon it appears that she is Virginian in every corpuscle, despite all her far rides on her witch's broomstick. One parts from her quite sure that this witch, precisely, could not have happened anywhere else on earth.

Miss Glasgow's Richmond colleague, Mr. Cabell, has gone in, at intervals, for the same pitiless illumination of the local scene. There are, indeed, obvious resemblances between *The Rivet in Grandfather's Neck* and the Glasgow novels, though there are also important differences. But Cabell has thus come to close quarters with his fellow Democrats only at longish intervals; for the most part he has contented himself with doing them, as it were, at second hand, in the form of mural figures in a gaseous Virginia of his own imagining. This transformation has improved their looks and augmented their store of ideas, but it has left a good many of them disquietingly unVirginian, or, at all events, Virginian only to specialists in the species. I daresay that Miss Glasgow herself reads the Cabell books with a kind of understanding denied to the rest of us. If so, she gets double value for her money, and both times it is high value. As for herself, she avoids the hazes of allegory. Her portraits may not be exactly photographs, but certainly there is a blistering realism in them, and as she herself hints in some of her prefaces . . . they were made, in many cases, from models who once actually breathed the Virginia air.
—H. L. MENCKEN, "A Southern Skeptic," *AM*, Aug. 1933, pp. 504–5

The advantages that she brought to her task and ambition were indeed considerable. Out of her wide reading she selected the mightiest and probably the best models to guide her in her recreation of the Virginia scene. She used Hardy as her master in rustic atmosphere, George Eliot as her guide in morality, Maupassant for plot, and Tolstoi for everything. She had the richest source material that any author could wish, consisting simply of a whole state and its whole history, a state, too, that occupies the center of our eastern geography and of our history and that not coincidentally has produced more Presidents than any other. And the social range among Miss Glasgow's characters is far greater than that of most twentieth-century novelists, suggesting that of such Victorians as Trollope, Dickens, Elizabeth Gaskell, and, again, George Eliot.

She not only considered every social group, but she covered wide varieties within each. In the top ranks of the old hierarchy she showed aristocrats in their glory, such as Major Lightfoot, and aristocrats in their decay, such as Beverly Brooke (in *The Ancient Law*). She showed them turning to the new world of business and dominating it, such as General Bolingbroke, and turning to the same world to be dominated and ultimately vulgarized by it, such as William Fitzroy. She showed aristocrats surviving into our own time, such as Judge Honeywell and Virginius Littlepage, having made the necessary adjustments and compromises, respectable, prosperous, but curiously unsatisfied, and she showed aristocrats like Asa Timberlake, who have been beaten into mediocrity and have failed in life without even the consolation and romance of a picturesque decay. Among the women of this world she created such magnificent anachronisms as Mrs. Blake, such noble, docile, and submissive wives as Virginia Pendleton, such apparently submissive but actually dominating mothers as Mrs. Gay, and such a reconstructed success in the North as Gabriella Carr.

In the middle ranks we find the rising businessman, Ben Starr, the risen politician, Gideon Vetch, the corrupt overseer, Bill Fletcher, the poor philosopher, John Fincastle, the "yeoman" farmers, Dorinda Oakley and Nathan Pedlar, the thriving miller, Abel Revercomb, and, among the lower orders, the "poor white" Burr family, the Starrs from whose midst Ben rises, the victims of the Richmond slums whom Stephen Culpeper is made to visit, the village prostitute and her idiot son in *Vein of Iron*, and, of course, all the Negro servants. Despite what has already been said about the limitations of Miss Glasgow's characterization of Negroes, the servants in her novels are absolutely alive and convincing. In at least one instance, that of the maid and companion to Dorinda in *Barren Ground*, the characterization is as successful as of any of the author's other women.

Miss Glasgow had the same range in scenery that she had in human beings, and she could make the transfer without difficulty from the grim mountains and valleys of *Vein of Iron* to the interminable fields of broomsedge in *Barren Ground* and thence to the comfortable mansions of Richmond and to the smaller gentility of Petersburg and Williamsburg. Highly individual in American letters is her ability to pass with equal authority from country to city, from rusticity to sophistication, from the tobacco field to the drawing room, from irony to tragedy.

Yet for all her gifts and advantages she does not stand in the very first rank of American novelists. She was unable sufficiently to pull the tapestry of fiction over her personal grievances and approbations. The latter are always peeping out at the oddest times and in the oddest places. It is strange that a novelist of such cultivation and such fecundity and one who was also such a student of her craft should not have seen her own glaring faults. How is it possible that the woman who could imagine the brilliant repartee of Edmonia Bredalbane, which annihilates every vestige of pretentiousness in Queenborough, should not have torn up the dreary sermon that is called *The Builders?* How could the author of prose which conveys all the beauty and mystery of the desolate countryside in *Barren Ground* have written the tired purple passages in earlier novels which describe the animal charm of handsome men and women in terms that might have been lifted from the very women's magazines that she so violently despised? How, moreover, could she have failed to see that her own bitterness on the subject of men was reflected in her heroines to the point of warping the whole picture of their lives? The mystery of Ellen Glasgow is not so much how she could be so good a writer as how she could on occasion be so bad a one.—LOUIS AUCHINCLOSS, *Ellen Glasgow,* 1964, pp. 40–43

FREDERICK P. W. McDOWELL
"Conclusion"
Ellen Glasgow and the Ironic Art of Fiction
1960, pp. 229–34

"In seeking and in finding there is not ever an end, nor is there an end in seeking and in not finding." These words of Asa Timberlake in *In This Our Life* might have been Ellen Glasgow's own comment upon her intellectual life and her career as writer. Her capacity for spiritual enlargement and growth allowed her to do some of her best work in her fifties. In her sixties, creative force and flexibility of mind diminished with *Vein of Iron* and *In This Our Life;* but these books, along with *A Certain Measure,* do reveal that her ever-dissatisfied spirit was still searching for the truth and an adequate form for conveying it. Undoubtedly this same truth-seeking impulse, eager to achieve viable outward expression, led to the writing of *The Woman Within* during these years.

Something of a Jamesian concentration of purpose—or of a Dreiserian persistence—effectively stayed with Miss Glasgow and allowed her to renew herself and do excellent work even after, at various times during her career, she had written one or more relatively inferior novels. Like that of James, her good work is spread over an extended period; and within their somewhat constricted limits, her books reveal a greater range of interest—from the vivaciously witty to the profoundly serious—than do those of most of her contemporaries. Nor did her creative force in fiction spend itself so rapidly as in the case of Sinclair Lewis and Sherwood Anderson. In her combination of irony with the tragic sense, of analytic perceptiveness with emotional depth, of detached satiric intelligence with pervasive human sympathy, she looks back to Henry James and forward to Southern writers as various as Caroline Gordon, Katherine Anne Porter, Eudora Welty, William Faulkner, and Robert Penn Warren. Like practically all these writers whom she foreshadows, Ellen Glasgow was chiefly interested in depicting with candor and sympathy "the dignity of greatness and the pitiable corruption of human nature."[1]

In her early revolt against the sentimental tendency of the South to obscure the social actuality and to avoid the moral implications of such evasion, she analyzed with honesty the inadequacies of Virginia life in the present and the immediate past. Unlike her more genteel predecessors in Southern letters, she saw that, as a writer with genuine artistic aspirations, she could not compromise with present truth in the interest of preserving romantic nostalgia. Still her emancipation from deep feeling with somewhat sentimental overtones was never complete—perhaps fortunately so, if we remember the emotional richness as well as the realistic force of her best novels.

Like most of the realists who immediately preceded her or who were prominent during her early career, she felt that an honest confronting of the facts did not invalidate the reality of the spirit. A modernist and a relativist toward the specific moral issue, she was haunted, too, by the absolutes of the Christian tradition whose relevance she in part rejected: "a few sublime virtues or, more accurately perhaps, a few ideas of sublime virtues . . . called truth, justice, courage, loyalty, compassion."[2] Although she was responsive as a realist to the flux of experience, she found that the pragmatic was by itself insufficient without a philosophy to govern it. The self-within-the-self which resisted change was replete for Ellen Glasgow with a supernal reality outside time, a reality which might impart some deeper meaning to her confrontations with actuality in time. As a result of the fervor with which Miss Glasgow led the detached solitary life of the spirit, she was often able to illuminate profoundly both what she had imagined and what had, in point of fact, happened to her. Like Henry James, she thought that fact as such and its imaginative representation in art were distinct, if related entities.

The spirit in its austere confines could often assign the actual to its most meaningful place in the larger patterns of experience; at other times such dispassionate intelligence might cause a distortion of the actual by failing to apprehend it fully or by applying an inappropriate standard to it. When, therefore, the brooding mind failed to converge precisely upon an empirically defined reality or when a dogmatic version of this reality was insisted upon, sentimentality occurred in Miss Glasgow's fiction. Both kinds of sentimentality are prominent in her last two novels and in the least successful of the early ones, and sometimes they even mar her best work. In *The Ancient Law* Daniel Ordway luxuriates in an ideal world of the suffering spirit, with the result that his struggles are too disembodied to be real. On the other hand, Miss Glasgow's positive view on how things ought to be ordered in actual life resulted in the priggish heroine of *Life and Gabriella,* who determines too expeditiously the exact course of her career. If dispassionate intensity of vision gave rise to the splendid rhythms of the opening chapters of *Barren Ground* and to its intermittent epic grandeur, this same intensity, fastened upon Dorinda Oakley's aspiring spirit, made her too radically competent in achieving her success, too reliably gallant after the advent of adversity, and too complacently certain of her own values.

Another result of Ellen Glasgow's excessive preoccupation with the self within was a recoil from disturbing circumstances without. At times, then, she became defeatist in her own attitude when the actual fell short of ideal expectation and when irony offered an inadequate refuge for her sensitive spirit.

As a result, an intermittent exasperation with her aristocratic characters sometimes breaks through the generally maintained objective delineation of their lives, even in such excellent novels as *The Deliverance* or *The Sheltered Life*; and the tableaus from modern life in her last two novels are distorted through jaundiced regret at life's failure to square with her own predilections. An obsessive concern with the personal life within, similar to her own, also marks her self-conscious characters—as various as Christopher Blake, Dorinda Oakley, General Archbald, and Asa Timberlake—who, in their articulate alienation, are tied too closely at some points to Miss Glasgow herself. Some of these figures find reality too much for them as did Miss Glasgow upon occasion. Yet she never gave in to circumstance and admitted defeat when external pressures seemed gratuitously hostile to her. She is at once sympathetic toward, and critical of, such men in her fiction as Oliver Treadwell in *Virginia*, Ralph McBride in *Vein of Iron*, and Craig Fleming in *In This Our Life*, all of whom find that they are unable to order their lives harmoniously and are inclined to drift morally.

Upon occasion, this retreat from actuality in Miss Glasgow or in her central characters led to a false estimate of things as they are. For this reason, Miss Glasgow's struggling central characters often succeed because they ought to, not because they convincingly master circumstances; her somewhat ascetic moral idealism caused her either to dwell excessively upon the beauties of renouncing the love that exists or to be scornful of its deficiencies; and her high valuation of social concord led her to overemphasize the views of her elder spokesmen such as Tucker Corbin, General Archbald, and John Fincastle.

If Miss Glasgow's fiction is at times subservient to the facts or at others nebulously connected with them, it is sometimes pallid in being abstractly intellectual. Too much explicit satire and irony are present in novels like *The Romantic Comedians* and *They Stooped to Folly* for there to be much blood in them. Most of her central characters are interested in ideas, but frequently at an elementary level, the level of sententious moralizing or of the platitude. Such individuals, while they perhaps inadequately record Miss Glasgow's own intellectuality, nevertheless demonstrate that her mind is derivative and eclectic rather than profoundly original. Their lucubrations clog the weaker novels like *The Wheel of Life* and *The Builders*, impair the effectiveness of a potentially fine work like *Vein of Iron*, or detract from the full force of strong novels like *The Deliverance* and *Barren Ground*. In Miss Glasgow's fiction, philosophical speculation is often only tenuously related to the psyche of a created character, with the result that the character's ideas are too easily separable from the depths of his being. Some of the emotions expressed in her work, especially those deriving from worldly success, from sexual experience, from inner aspiration or personal fulfillment, and from her own philosophical idealism, also lose vitality through being too directly intellectualized. This is true even of General Archbald's deeply felt musings over his existence, which are forceful so long as they deal with incidents in his past rather than with his "philosophy of life." Miss Glasgow's best insights were intuitive and imaginative rather than intellectual; and she was at her best, therefore, when realistically and cynically she analyzed characters and social relationships, not ideas. The quality so characteristic of Miss Glasgow herself, the "austerity [which] prolongs the vision of delight,"[3] becomes, in fact, the enemy of delight, and comports more suitably with the rendition of emotions associated with disenchantment, neurotic indisposition, psychological antagonism, self-seeking, inner martyrdom, and spiritual unfulfillment. This austerity was also translated into her high valuation, too abstractly stated in the fiction, of fortitude. In fact, characters like Abel Revercomb, Gabriella Carr, and Ada Fincastle feel the need of enduring deprivation more compulsively than their individual situations warrant.

Inflexible prejudice or overemphatic abstraction might at times prevent Miss Glasgow from perceiving exactly the tangible and intangible realities; nevertheless, Miss Glasgow's grasp of fact at other times was strongly pragmatic. This practical sense helped engender her gospel of fortitude which is, in essence, a provisional philosophy imposed by the moral obligation to exist without a more dynamic faith and to endure the worst. Miss Glasgow's novels were written partly out of the Anglo-Saxon ethical tradition with its emphasis upon the active powers in man's moral nature. As a result, most of her characters reveal an inability to resign themselves passively to fate, and are driven therefore by an urgent need to impress their own individualities upon hostile circumstances. Like Thomas Hardy's, Miss Glasgow's central, spiritually perceptive characters strive to maintain a sense of equanimity, even though their personal universe may crumble. Despite a failure at times to see some facts clearly, Miss Glasgow possessed a critical acuity sufficiently strong to distinguish illusion from reality. She possessed, moreover, a well-developed sense of humor which was awake both to the perversities apt to govern the individual's existence and to the absurdities present even in a cosmos governed by natural laws. These two intellectual attributes in Miss Glasgow induced in her a conviction that an absolute pessimism was too pretentious to provide a balanced interpretation of experience. Again, considerations, largely pragmatic, may have determined initially the quality and intensity of her youthful revolt, since she declared that it was easier for the intellectual in the South to break with tradition than to endure it. The only practical alternative to coming to terms with her family was to rebel from it.

When her inner spirit inexorably informed external reality, Miss Glasgow achieved the full perfection of *Virginia* and *The Sheltered Life*, the delicacy and ironic strength of *They Stooped to Folly* and *The Romantic Comedians*, and the bitter intensity and serene detachment of the best parts of *The Deliverance*, *Barren Ground*, *In This Our Life*, and *The Miller of Old Church*. In these novels Miss Glasgow was at least partly successful in fusing her artist's fastidious vision with appropriate outer concretions, in reconciling, to the greatest extent possible, the "truth of fiction" and the "truth of life."

An ironic detachment from experience, in conjunction with an idealistic commitment to a flexible but strongly apprehended spiritual principle operating within and outside the self, helped give her books their authentic quality. At the same time, sentimental lapses were also encouraged by this same idealism, and a lack of felt reality by this same detachment. She is at her best when, in *The Deliverance*, *Virginia*, *They Stooped to Folly*, and *The Sheltered Life*, the conditions which surround the characters merge with them in their development until inner and outer realities virtually become one and reach full fruition in this interplay. When such full identification of scene with agent is not achieved, a separation occurs between style and subject, with the result that her novels then are either overwritten or wrongly felt. Miss Glasgow's accomplishments and limitations as a writer are best suggested in her own judgment of another Southern writer, Edgar Allan Poe, whose elusive merits she contrasts with his inadequacies:

> Poe is, to a large extent, a distillation of the Southern. The formalism of his tone, the classical

element in his poetry and in many of his stories, the drift toward rhetoric, the aloof and elusive intensity,—all these qualities are Southern. And in his more serious faults of overwriting, sentimental exaggeration, and lapses, now and then, into a pompous or florid style, he belongs to his epoch and even more to his South.[4]

Miss Glasgow is a transitional figure in the development of our literature, standing as she does between the romanticism of the local color writers and the genteel realism of Howells or Mary Wilkins Freeman on the one hand, and the revolutionary naturalism of Theodore Dreiser and the psychological immediacy of Faulkner on the other hand. Lacking the full vigor of Dreiser and Lewis, the crisp intellectuality of Mrs. Wharton, and the poetic intensity, at their best, of Sherwood Anderson and Willa Cather, she is, in her finest work, distinguished for her mordant sense of social reality and for the precision of her ironic intelligence. Of her nineteen novels, a half dozen are truly distinguished, both for their incidental insights into human nature and for their comprehensive interpretation of human life. The exactness of perception in Henry James at his best was denied to Miss Glasgow, for she never achieved James's command of the self, and consequently of medium; but at her best she explored as deeply as he the subtle relationships existing between personality and environment. The six or seven novels which represent Miss Glasgow at her best are substantial in a way that the achievement of her more erratic contemporaries is not. When all qualifications have been made, Ellen Glasgow emerges as a complex and impressive writer; and one can agree with N. Elizabeth Monroe and Maxwell Geismar that she has been underestimated.[5]

Her talents as a craftsman of fiction are manifold: an ability to envision living characters, a sharp sense of the psychological impact of various individualities upon each other, a skill at fusing her characters with scene, a starkness and concentration of energy in her climactic episodes, an animistic sensitivity toward nature, a gift of witty and exact phrasing and of economy of characterization, and a feeling for structure and narrative pace in the novel. More important still, the creation of a believable universe from out the Virginia past in her best novels, their undeniable insight into the human heart and their pervasive spiritual light and grace, give them a permanent place in our literature. In these novels, one must acknowledge that Ellen Glasgow manifested with ironic lucidity the qualities which she most sought to express as a writer: "Humanity and distinction, reality and art."[6]

Notes

1. Letter to Van Wyck Brooks, Sept. 7, 1944, *Letters of Ellen Glasgow*, ed. Blair H. Rouse (New York: Harcourt, Brace & Co., 1958), p. 353. In a recent stimulating essay, C. Hugh Holman indicates those qualities in Ellen Glasgow's mind and art which are in their essence Southern and which anticipated the work of major present-day Southern writers: "a sense of evil, a pessimism about man's potential, a tragic sense of life, a deep-rooted sense of the interplay of past and present, a peculiar sensitivity to time as a complex element in narrative art, a sense of place as a dramatic dimension, and a thorough-going belief in the intrinsic value of art as an end in itself, with an attendant Aristotelian concern with forms and techniques" ("Ellen Glasgow and the Southern Literary Tradition," *Virginia in History and Tradition*, ed. R. C. Simonini, Jr. [Farmville, Virginia: Publications of Longwood College, 1958], p. 102).
2. "What I Believe," *Nation*, CXXXVI (Apr. 12, 1933), p. 406.
3. "Mr. Cabell as a Moralist," *New York Herald Tribune Books*, I (Nov. 2, 1924), p. 2.
4. *A Certain Measure: An Interpretation of Prose Fiction* (New York: Harcourt, Brace & Co., 1943), p. 132.
5. "Ellen Glasgow: Ironist of Manners," *Fifty Years of the American Novel*, ed. Harold C. Gardiner, S.J. (1951); "Ellen Glasgow's Private History," *Nation*, CLXXIX (Nov. 13, 1954), 425.
6. Letter to Bessie Z. Jones, May 9, 1938, *Letters*, p. 240.

MONIQUE PARENT FRAZEE

From "Ellen Glasgow as Feminist"
Ellen Glasgow: Centennial Essays
ed. M. Thomas Inge
1976, pp. 180–87

Miss Glasgow's consciousness of being a person entitled to her own way of thinking began early, with her double rebellion . . . against father and religion. Her first open act of emancipation was her refusal to accompany him to church one Sunday. The next step was an effort to decide on her own culture. At this point, "I read what Father . . . feared and hated rather than what I, myself, enjoyed. Right or wrong, I could not be moved. . . . Over and over I repeated my variation of the modern creed: not 'my life is my own!' as youth cries today, but 'my mind is my own!' "[1] The absence of school training encouraged her drift from conformity. Her native curiosity assisted her in mastering the most arduous material, philosophy, economy, literature. Other Southern women had written books: sweet novels for young ladies, or history books to the glory of the Confederacy. She completed her intellectual liberation by writing exactly what she wanted to write, without sparing her people, her times, the South, or the opinions of gentility. *The Descendant*, the most daring of all her novels in this respect—situations, characters, happenings—marked her declaration of independence. Intentions are clear: the newspaper edited by the rebellious hero is called the *Iconoclast*. The hero himself is a social outcast, a "bastard" whose birth forces him to leave his community, and he ends up in jail for murder. The heroine is an artist, sure enough; no "nice girl" could accept concubinage with the hero and retain the reader's sympathy. In this unconventional couple, the woman is by far the stronger; however, she becomes for a while a victim of the male, since their cohabitation causes her talent to wither temporarily. Separation restores her to herself: woman triumphs if she is left alone. The tract is complete; it will not be presented again in this simplistic form.

The fundamental claim, however, blatant in this first novel, will reappear throughout the works to come: woman's desire to be herself, to exploit her potentialities, to lead her own life. If she is more often than not frustrated in this goal, it is because society offers more examples of women impeded by men's wills than the contrary. We have seen Virginia sinking under traditional sex roles, unmarried girls smothered by spinsterhood, widows dependent on the older generation for survival, abandoned women crushed by mundane disapproval. Children throw rocks at Ada, unmarried and pregnant; Dorinda runs away when she discovers her predicament. Yet both will rise up, fight, and win the battle against male domination. The weapon is courage, drawing on the old sources of Southern fortitude. But, in terms of feminism, there is a huge difference between the two heroines.

Dorinda is the archetype of the liberated woman. The daughter of an improvident farmer (the father here is the image of irresponsibility, poor, ignorant, incompetent, stubborn, totally unimaginative, his mind closed to progress), the innocent girl is seduced by her fiancé (the lover is weak, unsettled, alcoholic, cowardly, easily persuaded to marry another girl when threatened by the latter's brothers). After a welcome miscarriage and two years' absence from home (today she would have had an abortion), Dorinda returns to her barren land, makes it productive, achieves economic independence and financial prosperity. The male, rejected and unnecessary, is seen in a totally negative light. Dorinda could be any woman today, successful in any career. Her contempt for men never relents. She ends up contriving the ultimate humiliation of her seducer. In the guise of charity, she rescues his degenerate body from the poorhouse and buys his land, a superfluous addition to her own. Eventually, for economic convenience, she has married a kind, insipid eunuch with a ludicrous face; his death leaves her untouched. Dorinda, once the victim, has become the victor; but her triumph is only complete through her negation of man.

"Dorinda was free to grow, to change, to work out her own destiny," says the author.[2] So far, the feminist theory is satisfied. But then the story moves toward a dubious demonstration. Were Dorinda happy, all would be well; but she is not. To achieve success, she had to learn "to live without joy . . . to live gallantly, without delight."[3] In other words, she had to steel herself against the fundamental urges of woman toward happiness. Like Dreiser's Sister Carrie, who, at the zenith of her career, success, and economic independence, sighs over some wistful sense of loss, Dorinda, mature and rich, confesses that "success, achievement, victory over fate, all these things were nothing beside that imperishable illusion. Love was the only thing that made life desirable, and love was irrevocably lost to her."[4] A passing weakness or a revelation of the truth? She checks herself and concludes: "Though in a measure destiny had defeated her, for it had given her none of the gifts she had asked of it, still her failure was one of those defeats . . . which are victories."[5] Defeat—failure—victory—all one, what a confused philosophy is this? "None of the gifts she had asked": what were those mysterious gifts? Ada in *Vein of Iron* gives us a clue.

Ada's story begins in the same way. She is pregnant and abandoned by her fiancé. However, she keeps her baby, raises him through shame and love, and later marries her seducer. They remain poor—his nervous instability and the Depression assure that. Sickness and poverty are ever present; yet her fortitude endures, and her final cry of feminine triumph is "O Ralph, we have been happy together." "Yes," he answers reluctantly, because it has been all her doing, not his, "we've had a poor life . . . but we've been happy together."[6] Ada has had "the gifts of life" which Dorinda denied herself. She has retained her femininity by keeping her heart alive, at whatever cost. Stronger than her partner, she props his softness with her energy, tempers his bitterness with her affection; she is his moral support, and finds joy in this feminine role. Here is the catch, the vicious circle of destiny. Love being the only thing that makes life worthwhile to a woman, and man the only partner to give and receive love, whenever man is found wanting, woman is doomed to unhappiness. But is happiness a right? Virginia thought so, "unquestionably,"[7] feeling, with Milly Burden, Jenny Blair, Roy, Stanley, and others, that "craving for happiness" deep in their nature. But in *They Stooped to Folly*, it is an old man who replies with restrictive pessimism: "Remember, my child, that happiness is not a right but a blessing."[8]

Let us recapitulate the fate of woman in the hands of Ellen Glasgow. Virginia cherished her role of slave and perished in despair. Gabriella rebelled and flourished, but ultimately slipped back into matrimony. Dorinda fought and conquered, but in the process killed her heart and all chance of happiness. More flexible, Ada submitted to her emotional demands and ultimately found happiness. Which of these four women reflects most the feministic spirit of the author?

Raised like Virginia and faithful to that line of conduct, free, independent, and prosperous like Dorinda, Ellen Glasgow appears as an intellectual counterpart of the latter. Proud and tortured, "the woman within" retraces the same emotional struggle; she seems to have paid the same price in her desperate search for serenity. Perhaps she found peace—happiness never. But in the light of recent progress in Women's Lib, we may venture this suggestion: today, Ellen Glasgow would *not* publish *The Woman Within*. She would not flaunt her victimization. She would not assume the part of melodramatic endurance. She probably would turn to more sensible and positive means of psychological liberation. Times have changed; new solutions, new outlets have opened that were taboo then. Divorce was still considered a catastrophe for women. We have mentioned lesbianism before: let us hasten to say that, in all of Ellen Glasgow's writings, there is not the slightest indication, even remotely subconscious, in situations, characters, imagery, commentary, or terminology, that a republic of women would be a desirable thing. There is not one of her heroines (practically all victims of men) who did not obscurely wish that males be greater so as to be more adequate mates. Contempt for men never bars women from wanting them. Then why aren't they greatest? Why are they all so uniformly mediocre, second-rate, if not scoundrels?

In that pale gallery of unimpressive men, very few are masculine enough to be rich and influential—and those who are, are tough, scornful, cruel, insensitive, like Cyrus Treadwell; most are economic failures; the lovers are weak, selfish, spineless, alcoholic. Shall we speak of a prejudice, a bias against manhood? Let us open the very first novel, *The Descendant*; the first men to appear who, we shall learn later, have good hearts and common sense, are thus depicted: a minister of the church is "small" (no comment), "ill-omened" (without any subsequent evidence of this), "chinless" (a sign of degeneracy), "ignorant" (Michael, the pig boy, will soon outwit his master's theology). The farmer who employs Michael is "a negative character" (although good and virtuous), "since to be wicked necessitates action."[9] We may ponder on this qualifier, persistent throughout the novels as applied to men: *negative*.

Negative, the oncoming farmers of the same breed such as Burr and Oakley; the rare intellectuals, such as Michael Akershem, Anthony Algarcife, Ralph McBride, who cannot control their intelligence and impulses; negative, the nice young gentlemen, such as Dudley Webb, Roger Adams, Arthur Peyton, David Blackburn, John Benham, Craig Fleming; even more so, the weaklings lost in alcohol and vice, Will Fletcher, Arnold Kemper, Jonathan Gay, Oliver Treadwell, Jason Greylock, Martin Welding, George Birdsong. The few men of character, their foils, Nick Burr, Ben Starr, Abel Revercomb, Gideon Vetch, and the reformed ones, Dan Montjoy, Daniel Ordway, Christopher Blake, fail to come out for want of proper characterization.

Such is not the case, however, for a handful of older men who (with the brilliant exception of Gamaliel Honeywell, the sexagenarian "romantic comedian") escape the damning, as if age alone would confer on men dignity and psychological depth. Shall we ask Miss Glasgow whether this is due to wisdom acquired by experience or to the decline of virility? Take for example John Fincastle, the gentle philosopher, and Asa Timberlake, two of her finest male characterizations. Both suffer and endure, but fail to achieve the stature of minor episodic characters who die a heroic death. John Fincastle writes books of subversive philosophy that will never be published, keeps his family in poverty, gives them the example of passive fortitude in the face of adversity, and finally starves to death. He does not fight; he can never confront his human responsibilities. Lost in his dreams, he elicits pity, not admiration. Asa Timberlake, unredeemed by any intellectual achievement, is even more a failure. Unable as he is to satisfy his wife, to raise and support his daughters morally, he represents a male version of the exploited woman, of the hopeless wife, enduring the odds of life and finding relief only in his final flight from home. Few books are as devoid of happiness as *In This Our Life*. Strange to say, Asa was Miss Glasgow's favorite hero, her epitome of manhood. Isn't it significant? She tried to persuade us that his endurance had secured him moral victory: "That Asa should be regarded as my idea of failure by so many . . . readers [including me] proves . . . that we are in danger of forgetting that character is an end in itself."[10] Poignantly illustrated in Faulkner's *Wild Palms*, the demonstration here is pale and unconvincing. There is a creative way of enduring, an ultimate victory in suffering accepted *for* a purpose; but Asa does not know for what, or what else he could do. Unlike Prometheus or Sisyphus, he buys no future of liberty for anybody, and his final freedom is acquired at the price of desertion, not redemption. So in the end these two also remain insignificant and negative. They are the typical production of female creativity, revealing an innate difficulty in achieving greatness in male characterization. Here we face a bias common to most women novelists, even more flagrant with feminists, this more or less conscious determination to belittle man in order to magnify woman. This is all the more regrettable as the purpose defeats itself and the demonstration comes to nought. The more mediocre the male partners, the less convincing becomes the superiority of women to dominate or defeat them.

We may wonder how these superwomen (Dorinda for example) would react to true men. But, like the radical feminists, Miss Glasgow tends to deny the existence of the species and views the superior man as a figment of female imagination and credulity. We shall not open the debate at this stage, but we may ask: what do women gain in conquering such poor terrain? We may tentatively conclude that hers is a shortcoming in creative art more than a flaw in feminism. Probably Ellen Glasgow thought obscurely with Anaïs Nin that, notwithstanding the defective quality of men, perhaps because of it, women should take the responsibility for their lives, and, by doing so, would "feel less helpless than when we put the blame on society or man. . . . To take destiny into our own hands is more inspiring than expecting others to direct our destiny for us."[11] Her indictment of men's passivity is meant to stimulate women's as well:

> This passivity can be converted to creative will. . . . To become man, or like man, is no solution. There is far too much imitation of man in the Women's Movement. That is merely a displacement of power. . . . The women who truly identify with their oppressor, as the cliché goes, are the women who are acting like men, masculinizing themselves, not those who seek to convert or transform man. There is no liberation of one group at the expense of another. Liberation can only come totally and in unison.[12]

This statement, made in 1972 by an older woman of letters, pictures much of what Miss Glasgow's feminism was and might be today. Yes to the emancipation of woman's intelligence, spirit, self-accomplishment, self-responsibility. No to her masculinization, no to the cancellation of her femininity. Woman's liberation should not be won at the expense of her past privileges or personal values. It is safe to believe that Miss Glasgow would forgo none of the Southern traditional manners: courtesy, chivalry, social graces, "a yellow rose on the breakfast tray," the right of women to be beautiful and attractive. Even if beauty comes second to character, all her favorite heroines have interesting features, "a beauty less of flesh than of spirit."[13] Moral beauty, artistic beauty, demands self-discipline and taste. "The whole truth must embrace the interior world as well as external appearances."[14] She would no doubt reject the "external appearances" of many women liberators today: the cult of homeliness, the coarse loud voices, the angry tones, the unwashed bodies, the ugly clothes, the masculine gait, the unisex haircut, slovenliness, promiscuity, aggressive separateness. These things she would deplore as ungainly masks to deeper truths, with the risk of doing disservice to the cause of true feminism. Radicalism stands at the opposite of measure and good taste. Radicalism has to work for immediate efficiency, with hits and blows and violence in order to burst open recalcitrant doors. Ellen Glasgow hated violence; she chose more subdued means of action: moderate, disciplined, gentle; yet, under her velvet glove, one feels the iron hand of conviction, the cutting edge of her wit and satire. These were not the least of her weapons, particularly in dethroning the male idol in a man-made world, from the *Iconoclast* of her youthful years to "the romantic comedians" of her sunset laughter. This major aspect of her talent was left deliberately untouched in the present paper, because revolutionists cannot afford humor; comedy is an insult to the seriousness of their purpose. But Miss Glasgow would sacrifice to no restrictive militantism. Strong, with unfathomable mental reserves of "blood and irony,"[15] she was able to plead aptly for the cause of feminism and lose nothing of her femininity. In the final analysis, in behavior as in writing, Ellen Glasgow stood for aesthetics and placed her loyalty first and last in literature as "experience illuminated . . . an interpretation of life."[16]

Notes

1. *The Woman Within* (New York: Harcourt, Brace, 1954), pp. 92–93.
2. *A Certain Measure* (New York: Harcourt, Brace, 1943), p. 155.
3. Ibid., pp. 154–55.
4. *Barren Ground* (Garden City, N.Y.: Grosset & Dunlap, 1925), p. 446.
5. Ibid., p. 447.
6. *Vein of Iron* (New York: Harcourt, Brace, 1935), p. 462.
7. *Virginia* (New York: Doubleday, Page, 1913), p. 33.
8. (Garden City, N.Y.: Doubleday, Doran, 1929), p. 114.
9. *The Descendant* (New York: Harper & Bros., 1897), pp. 4, 20, 11.
10. *A Certain Measure*, p. 253.
11. L. R. Edwards, M. Heath, and L. Baskin, eds., *Woman: An Issue* (Boston: Little, Brown & Co., 1972), p. 25.
12. Ibid., p. 28.
13. "The Difference," in *The Shadowy Third* (Garden City, N.Y.: Doubleday, Page, 1923), p. 227. Also, *The Builders* (Garden City, N.Y.: Doubleday, Page, 1919), p. 115, and Betty Ambler *(The Battle-Ground)*, Gabriella *(Life and Gabriella)*, Caroline Meade *(The Builders)*, Laura Wilde *(The Wheel of Life)*, Milly *(The Ancient Law)*, Ada *(Vein of Iron)*.
14. *A Certain Measure*, p. 28.
15. Ibid., p. 28.
16. Ibid., pp. 14–15.

RICHARD GRAY

From "The Social and Historical Context"
The Literature of Memory
1977, pp. 28–34

Glasgow's convictions underwent several changes during the course of her life, and they were always qualified by her commitment as a writer to the presentation of diverse human forms, but her initial stance at least, the point from which all explorations started, was a simple one and understandable. It was to accept, quite happily, the premise that the old feudal order was in the last stages of decay, as a fact and an idea, and that the "plain man" of the land was "building the structure . . . of the future" that would replace it. That done, Glasgow then went on to develop two fictional strategies which she hoped would enable her to investigate the implications of her premise, and dramatize them. One strategy invited comedy, a satirical inventory of the weaknesses of the "aristocratical" person—the aim being, in effect, to show how "stationary and antiquated"[1] he was, and how imperative it was to replace him. The other, by contrast, was more in the heroic line. It required the writer to concentrate her attention on the poorer white and the qualities, latent in his character, that appeared to guarantee his eventual success—and this as a prelude to the presentation of his actual success story. Necessarily, the result of using two such different strategies was to create two different types of novel; Glasgow herself liked to refer to them as "novels of history" or "of the town" on the one hand, and "novels of the country" on the other. But despite all their differences, the same optimism usually managed to shine through them both and betray their common authorship; satire and heroic tale were equally shaped by the conviction that the small farm was about to secure the state.

Just what that meant as far as the state was concerned was something Glasgow implied in her portrait of the farmer characters, all of whom tended to be variations on certain themes. They belonged, so the author argued, to a tradition going back to the colonial years, which had given them stern lessons in self-reliance and the capacity to endure. The life of the husbandman was defined by its rigor, and this had bred a common resilience in all men of his type; a "vein of iron" running so deep that his "secret self" "could not yield, could not bend, could not be broken,"[2] even under enormous pressure. He would stand fast in a decaying environment, and perhaps use it to his advantage. In some ways, of course, this was no more than a rehearsal of conventional notions about the resilience of country folk—as faded as the pastoral dream, if rather different in its assumptions. But in the best of her heroic novels, Glasgow managed to go beyond the accepted and encompass an almost mystical belief in the efficacy of direct contact with the earth. The religious motive and the utilitarian were then combined in such a way as to strengthen them both. Here is an example of what I mean from one of her best novels, *Barren Ground*. It bears comparison with the more uninhibited moments in Jefferson's *Notes on Virginia*.

> The storm and the hag-ridden dreams of the night were over, and the land which had forgotten was waiting to take her back to its heart. Endurance. Fortitude. The spirit of the land was flowing into her, and her own spirit, strengthened and refreshed, was flowing out again toward life. This was the permanent self, she knew. This was what remained to her after the years had taken their bloom.[3]

The point about this passage, I think, is that Dorinda Oakley, the heroine of the novel and the person who achieves the particular recognition described here, is not simply any woman experiencing a moment of transcendent contact with nature, but a farmer's daughter rediscovering her proper vocation. Her perception is of the good life as a special mode of behavior, with its own blessings and sanctions attached to it, and it is upon this that her resurrection of the spirit depends.

This association of a program for political and social action with what can only be described as the vision of a new moral order received its complement in Glasgow's comedies of manners. And here, too, the success of the enterprise depended on her ability to personalize the action; in other words, to make the specific movement of the narrative—in this case the charting of a decline rather than a resurrection—seem dramatically inevitable and individually relevant rather than the result of some preconceived design. *The Romantic Comedians* was perhaps the best of her novels describing the collapse of the old patriarchal order. In it the fate of the central character, Judge Gamaliel Bland of Richmond, Virginia, emerged as the only possible one if the demands of dramatic justice were to be met. The novel unfolded the Judge's unfortunate marriage to a woman half his age, whom, in accordance with the dictates of the chivalric code, he had idealized completely and quite inaccurately into a creature of fragile innocence. Cuckolded, and then abandoned, his rewards were those of the innocent hypocrite; and for both the innocence and the hypocrisy Ellen Glasgow blamed the society that had fostered him. The social point was more or less explicit in the Judge's subsequent meditations on his wife's infidelity.

> If only women had been satisfied to remain protected! . . . If only they had been satisfied to wait in patience, not to seek after happiness! For it seemed to him . . . that there could be nothing nobler than the beauty of long waiting and wifely tolerance . . . surely it was not too much to insist that the true feminine character had never flowered more perfectly than in the sheltered garden of Southern tradition.[4]

There is a nice balance in this passage between personal misunderstanding and the social mechanisms that have created it, a balance characteristic of its author at her best. And through it all shines the perception that the ironic conflicts contained in an attitude like the Judge's were as responsible for the collapse of an entire class as were the more obvious factors of invasion and economic ruin.

That does not mean to say Glasgow was not interested in such factors; of course she was. She had to be, actually, because of her belief that the personal and social dramas of the South were inseparable. The private face was related to the public place in nearly all of her fiction; and this required her to devote at least some attention to the activities of the meeting house and marketplace. A few of her books even went beyond this, openly concerning themselves with political themes, and in such cases the larger implications of Glasgow's message were stated with a clarity and insistence that approached the polemical. Her story, *The Voice of the People*, for instance, read (as its title suggests) like a program for action. Its hero, Nicholas Burr, was a "po' white" of uncertain origins whom Glasgow described rising to the position of state governor, thanks to sheer effort and the vigor of his character. One reason offered for the ease with which he attained this eminence was the dormancy and apathy of the ruling class, so hypnotized by its "dream of the past," apparently, as to be unaware of the changes taking place around it. But even if it had been aware of them, the author argued, the consequences would have been the same, the "mental thinness, emotional dryness," and "intrinsic weakness" of the "old feudal order" being such that it could offer little more than a token opposition in any circumstances.[5] To call this situation one of conflict would be to overdramatize it. Like a morality play, *The Voice of the People* presented a battle, between a gallery of fools and a protagonist graced with all the advantages of a culture hero, which was over before it had begun. The reader hardly had to read to the end to know that the triumph of the plain man would be complete.

The triumph was a peculiar one, however, because it was fictional in the most limited and limiting sense possible—a product of wish fulfillment rather than engagement with historical fact. That was why Glasgow's contemporaries only had to look around them to discover forces calculated to deny her dream, and make prophecies like those in *The Voice of the People* seem ridiculous. The New South, as we have seen, was to be nothing like the society Ellen Glasgow anticipated. It was not, as it turned out, a place populated by happy farmers, but another witness to the industrial age, with a financial and technological structure to rival any of its neighbors'. The very fact that the industrialized North had defeated the rural South in the Civil War had tended to ensure this, and yet Glasgow would not acknowledge it. Seeing something of what was happening around her, she nevertheless failed to see the whole; and occasionally she seemed quite willful in her refusal to do so. Certainly, her blindness in this connection should not be exaggerated. Even in her earlier novels she betrayed some awareness of the possibility that things might not develop as she had expected. It was implicit, among other things, in her portraits of the businessmen occupying the periphery in some of the novels: a certain Cyrus Treadwell, for instance, one of the minor figures in *Virginia*, who was said to be so controlled by the "shibboleth" of success as to "resemble a machine" deprived even of the "ordinary animal capacity for pleasure."[6] But, unnerving as the thoughts aroused by such characters might be, they scarcely affected the prophetic core of the narrative. For anything more than a few symptoms of apprehension, the isolated warning flag, the reader had to wait for Ellen Glasgow's last book, *In This Our Life*, which was published several years after the others.

The event was worth waiting for, since what the novel represented was a complete volte-face—a reversal of all the predictions Glasgow had previously made. The reasons for this change were obvious enough, perhaps: by the time that Glasgow came to write *In This Our Life* the New South, and the recognition of its character contained in the literature of the "renaissance," were both established facts. The course of a new society had been charted and could no longer be ignored. But that did not make the change any the less surprising, in some of its ramifications at least, or any the less significant either. The book was a testimony to hope betrayed, and its personal basis was only nominally concealed by the use of a male surrogate for the author, called Asa Timberlake. Asa, a gentleman of the old school, was not so much a protagonist as a central consciousness, observing and commenting on the activities of the characters placed around him. And most of his comments were reserved for the members of his own family—the younger members, that is, through whom Glasgow projected her vision of contemporary life. Needless to say, they were nearly all in the negative. His children and grandchildren, as Asa saw it, were eccentrics, deviations from the traditional norms who demonstrated by their deviation the "general breaking-up in the pattern of life" to which they belonged. They had lost touch with the controls normally placed on human behavior, with inherited codes and systems of belief; and they had nothing with which to fill in the gap that was left except their own random impulses. "Responsibility and integrity" had disappeared, as facts and standards of judgment, and all that remained to distinguish one man from another was "the superiority . . . a very wide margin of vested interests . . . [could] confer"—in other words, the cash nexus. An interesting corollary of this situation, according to Glasgow, was that in a way Asa's young relatives had ceased to exist at all. Lacking any code other than the fiscal, they lacked whole and functioning personalities; and lacking this, they lacked reality. Like the "unreal, unsubstantial"[7] houses in which they lived, they offered nothing more than a series of appearances, empty gestures, and meaningless façades.

The verdict was a damning one, a diatribe without qualification, and what made it all the more so was the standpoint from which it was delivered. Asa, like his creator, was an old person living in a strange new world, which he hardly understood and certainly did not like. It was natural, then, that he should turn to his memories for relief—and as a means of confirming the deficiencies of his contemporaries. This was the basic strategy of the book—to judge times present in terms of a comparison with times gone by, and so use the heroic impulse as a means of satire. The past was mythologized rather than the future, and then accepted as a yardstick, something to which existing circumstances could be compared and found wanting. There could be no doubt about this, that Asa and Ellen Glasgow were criticizing the New South with reference to the Old. Nor could there be much doubt that the particular form the Old South assumed in the novel tended to identify it with the aristocratic idea. It was, to use some of the words favored by Asa, a society characterized by its "elegance, grace, dignity and beauty,"[8] a perfect feudal type. Asa's own father was taken as its paradigm, a man as accomplished as Kennedy's Frank Meriwether and as gracious as Wirt's portrait of Richard Henry Lee. This passage, describing his relationship with his employees, will serve to illustrate.

> In the old days his father had known the name and face of every man he employed. One and all, he and his men belonged to a single social unit, which . . . was held together by some vital bond of human relation. . . . There had been injustice . . . but one had dealt with flesh and blood, not with a list of printed names.[9]

The contrast proposed here is between a social structure that supposedly expresses the personal values of "family feeling" and romantic love, and one that reduces all motives to the economic—the "human" and "vital" on one hand, and on the other the mechanical. Perhaps that sounds familiar. It should, since it represents an only slightly modified version of the conflict described in the work of John Taylor of Caroline; and that in itself may suggest how Glasgow had altered in her attitude toward the "old feudal order."

The situation was steeped in irony, like something from one of her own comic novels. Ellen Glasgow, the self-appointed advocate of the plain man, had ended her creative life with a novel that celebrated the virtues of the old patriarchy. Turning her back on her own arguments, she had endorsed the cultural myth from which she had once revolted and the tradition she had dismissed as anachronistic. It was a strange course, but in its very strangeness something of a representative one as well. For, after all, weren't her own alterations paralleled throughout the entire South? And didn't the change in her opinions repeat the drastic transformations of attitude that followed the Revolution? Just after the Civil War, and as we have seen just after the Revolution too, there was a feeling in the region that the plain farmer was about to seize the day. The feeling was not universal, to be sure, but it was very widespread; and it was encouraged in both periods by the recognition that certain sections of the plantation community, if not all of it, had fallen into serious difficulties. The old order seemed to be changing, making way for the new, and this necessarily stimulated the growth of utopian visions. Things did not work out as expected, however, either in John Taylor's time or Ellen Glasgow's. Hopes for the future were disappointed, as far, at least, as they involved the resurrection of subsistence farming, and it was only natural for some people to seek relief from their disappointment in a comforting dream of the past. The dominant tendency, it seemed, was toward a different kind of progressivism from the one anticipated, in which progress was identified with industrialization; and in this situation the agrarian might well feel justified in becoming a reactionary. Certainly, Ellen Glasgow felt justified. Moving across from one side of the regional tradition to the other she declared, "I was a radical when everyone else . . . was conservative, and now I am a conservative when other people appear to be radical."[10] The remark located the change that had taken place in her thinking accurately enough, but it did so with a touch of bravado that tended to distort other things. For whatever Glasgow might have liked to think, she was no more of a special case in her old age than she had been in her youth. *In This Our Life*, as we have seen, was a book written at the crossroads, a witness to the sense of disorientation suffered by its author. As such it belonged to the New South, the age of paradox and upheaval, in exactly the same way that a book like *The Voice of the People* had belonged to the optimism of an earlier period. Perhaps it would be simplistic to assume a straight equation between Ellen Glasgow in her last years and the writers, a generation younger than her, who participated in the Southern "renaissance." Quite apart from anything else, they were in closer touch with the problems of the new society than she could ever be. Still, it remains true that the dilemma with which she was eventually confronted compared with their dilemma; and that her interest in the resources of her past, or the uses of nostalgia, offered only a slightly less sophisticated version of their own.

Notes

1. *The Builders* (London, 1919), p. 112.
2. *Barren Ground* (London, 1925), p. 509; *Vein of Iron* (London, 1936), p. 126.
3. *Barren Ground*, p. 509. Cf. *The Deliverance* (New York, 1904), p. 125.
4. *The Romantic Comedians* (London, 1926), p. 319. Cf. *The Ancient Law* (London, 1908) pp. 95–103.
5. *The Voice of the People* (New York, 1900), p. 13. Cf. *The Miller of the Old Church* (London, 1911), p. 16; *One Man in His Time* (London, 1922), pp. 22, 92.
6. *Virginia* (London, 1913), p. 122.
7. *In This Our Life* (London, 1941), pp. 31, 32, 55, 122, 148, 218.
8. Ibid., p. 111.
9. Ibid., p. 13.
10. *The Woman Within* (London, 1955), p. 42. Ellen Glasgow had never explicitly denied the existence of the "cavalier" planter in ante-bellum times (indeed, in *The Battle-Ground* [London, 1902] she had gone far toward accepting it); only his relevance to post-bellum society.

Gail Godwin

1937–

Gail Kathleen Godwin was born on June 18, 1937, in Birmingham, Alabama, and was raised by her divorced mother and widowed grandmother near Asheville, North Carolina. After graduating with a B.A. from the University of North Carolina, she joined the staff of the Miami *Herald* for one year. From 1962 to 1965 she worked with the U.S. Travel Service at the American Embassy in London, returning to America to study at the University of Iowa. Since graduating with a Ph.D. in 1971, she has taught at writers workshops and at Vassar College and Columbia University.

Godwin's first novel, *The Perfectionists*, was published in 1970, followed by *Glass People* in 1972 and *The Odd Woman* in 1974. In 1974 she received a grant from the National Endowment for the Arts, and in 1975 a Guggenheim Fellowship. *Dream Children*, a collection of stories, appeared in 1976, and *Violet Clay* in 1978. More recent work includes the novels *A Mother and Two Daughters* (1982) and *The Finishing School* (1984), and the stories *Mr Bedford and the Muses* (1983). Godwin has also written three libretti, with music by Robert Starer.

Godwin has been married twice, and has spent time in Spain and Denmark as well as England. She currently lives in Woodstock, New York.

Works

THE PERFECTIONISTS

Truly unconventional writing has nothing to do with hallucinatory prose adventures, or tricks of style, or self-conscious appearances by the writer in his own work; it is only a matter of discovery or rediscovery, a revelation of surprising and therefore "unconventional" emotions within a framework that may appear absolutely ordinary. What point is there to "experimental" writing when it reveals to us familiar ideas, familiar faces? Much of what passes today for experimental writing is simply derivative, taken over from Sartre, Ionesco, Beckett and others; it is certainly not "experimental" in the sense in which it tries out new visions of the world.

The Perfectionists, an engrossing and mysterious first novel, is a perfectly structured story, with chapters that follow one another logically, characters that are recognizably human and with whom we can "identify"; the narrative movement that contains the several meager—but awful—events of the novel's two weeks is conventional, traditional, even classic. A reader knows where he is going with these people—or thinks he knows—and so, when the novel comes to an abrupt end, when the final vision is set before him, the sense of mystery he comes away with is all the more haunting because there does not seem anything hidden, anything that might explain the several doomed "perfectionists."

Along with being nicely readable in form and style, *The Perfectionists* is also something of a suspense story. Its main characters are locked in a bizarre triangle: a young wife, her husband and his illegitimate child, a little boy named Robin. The wife, Dane, is newly married and unsure of her husband, herself, the meaning of marriage, the meaning of life—she questions everything, constantly, an unhappy woman whose intelligence vies with her dark, inert, pessimistic vision of life, at such variance with the dynamic role her husband expects her to play in their "perfect" marriage. She is very human, this miserable young wife, and even when she is less than admirable—leafing through her husband's notes, searching a friend's bureau drawers—she engages our sympathy. Like one of those restless, nervous, unappeasable women in the fiction of Doris Lessing, Dane is heroic in her very misery. "Oh God, I don't want to be ordinary," she cries, though she is sinking into intellectual and spiritual inertia, approaching total deterioration.

In a superficially experimental novel, the experience of deterioration would be thrust out at us in fragments; but in *The Perfectionists* it is offered to us with a deceptive calm, as we might endure it ourselves, as days blend into days, constituting a "marriage," a "relationship," a "friendship," or the frustrating "motherhood" Dane must attempt. Her husband's child is demonic. He will not speak to her; he hardly acknowledges her existence. Her already difficult marriage—to this self-styled psychotherapist who is perhaps a genius, perhaps a fool—is subjected to a terrific strain by the boy. . . .

The subject of *The Perfectionists* is the paranoid tragedy of our contemporary worship of self-consciousness, of constant analysis. It is a most intelligent and engrossing novel, and introduces a young writer of exciting talent.—JOYCE CAROL OATES, *NYTBR*, June 7, 1970, pp. 5, 51

THE ODD WOMAN

At the time of Gail Godwin's first novel she amused people by saying, "I think everyone should have more apocalypses in their daily lives." That novel, *The Perfectionists*, and her next, *Glass People*, were short, evocative entertainments with sophisticated techniques. Like Godwin's statement, they suggested a breathless schoolgirl's approach to life and literature. She loaded them with symbols, but the books were too well constructed to be top-heavy. The "apocalypses" were sexual: beloved sex objects were angels in human form; the emotional pain lumped onto sex was sacred. By the end of *Glass People*, when the heroine was dressed by her husband as a Byzantine madonna and he knelt to worship at her feet, the divinity of sex was made explicit.

Godwin is now trying to rid her work of divinity fetishes. The title character of *The Odd Woman* is perfectly capable of thinking that everyone needs more daily apocalypses. . . .

Like several recent novels, *The Odd Woman* owes much of its dialectic structure to Doris Lessing's *Children of Violence* pentalogy, in which Martha Quest explores herself and the world around her over many years and two continents. Martha was often as exasperating a character as Jane, but we stayed with the slow parts of her story because Lessing's emotional and intellectual sweep invited confidence. The confidence was justified by the imaginative completion of *The Four-Gated City*. Godwin merely confirms our fears that Jane's tentativeness won't lead to a confrontation with anything outside itself. *The Odd Woman*'s schematic organization is unpleasantly rigid, and Godwin has little to say.

Jane responds to students too frequently with a quote that doesn't answer anything, and she evades her own basic questions by thinking of characters with whom she wants to identify. *The Odd Woman* is full of literary allusions that backfire. When Jane compares herself to Isabel Archer or Gwendolen Harleth, we see the foolishness of the comparison; and we may wish that we were back reading *The Portrait of a Lady* or *Daniel Deronda*.

Dwelling on literature as a way of stalemating one's self is a potentially interesting subject for a novel, but I was never convinced that Godwin was aware of the problem. Jane approaches life as though it were a doctoral thesis that could be completed with mental note cards, and Godwin presents all of Jane's literary references so solemnly that the novel is footnoted like a thesis. The title is a footnote: Gissing's *The Odd Women*, which Jane is preparing to teach, is evoked so frequently that it becomes Godwin's novel-within-a-novel. Jane, trying to work out her life, makes a chart of Gissing's characters and the solutions they found. Gissing's 19th-century feminists and unhappy spinsters have problems that offer Jane no help with hers; but before Jane reaches that conclusion, Godwin has spent an inordinate number of words on a novel that is like her own only in the use of "odd" to mean "unmarried."

The flaws of *The Odd Woman* are crippling, but I may have made the book seem less promising than it is. One is always aware of Godwin's struggle with the demands she had made on herself, and there are places where her novelist's intelligence breaks through Jane's meetings with Gabriel and their bedroom clashes are shaped by a good, tense interplay. Her attempt to find a dress in Saks is harrowingly real. In the successful scenes Godwin is turning to the tone of her earlier work and I'm not suggesting that she should simply go back to what she is good at. She was right to know that she couldn't grow as a writer by continuing with those little fables about sexual apocalypses and exquisite neuroses. But now she has to find a subject.—JOHN ALFRED AVANT, *NR*, Jan. 25, 1975, pp. 26–27

The "new" woman's novel provides some of the best fiction available today. Major novels have always achieved lasting importance because they deal with questions immediately concerning their readers, with characters who are fully realized human beings struggling with problems which have no easy answers. In recent years women novelists, in a tradition reaching from Rebecca West through Doris Lessing to the militantly feminist books of Marge Piercy and Erica Jong, have attempted to describe heroines who have achieved a hard-won selfhood in a male-oriented world. This is certainly a subject of prime importance today, but most recent novels have failed to reach true excellence because of an underlying stridency, an understandable desire to incite rather than to entertain.

Gail Godwin, a young and enormously talented writer, has now succeeded in writing a "woman's novel" of universal interest. . . .

⟨*The Odd Woman*⟩ is funny and true. Godwin's narrative gifts enable us to accompany Jane on her attempt to make herself more chic by buying some clothes at Saks. All women have had Jane's experience shopping: a large and intimidating store, masses of clothing, a dressing room mirror which reveals degrading bulges, and dowdiness—who *are* those other women, who know exactly what they want?

Later, Jane's erotic fantasies in bed with Gabriel are so unself-conscious and entertaining that we rejoice. The whole idea of a woman's emotional response to lovemaking has been so little talked about until recently that it is a surprise to see it described so naturally.

Almost all of the women Jane knows are intelligent and aggressive. Her mother, Kitty, supported the family when Jane was a child by teaching and writing true confession stories. Her heroines had to be chaste nurse-secretary types, and Godwin's satirical discussion of the genre is incisive. The new generation, however, recognizes no limits. Jane's colleague, Sonia Marks, is an eminent scholar, and Gerda is the Compleat Feminist (her household is a much more believable collective than the one in Marge Piercy's *Small Changes*).

But if the women are strong, so too are the men, in their own ways. Despite the cliché that authors never describe both sexes with equal skill, Godwin does manage to create both men and women with believable individual characteristics. Ray, Jane's stepfather, the archetypical self-made man, is a possessive parent but a comforting husband. Hugo Von Vorst, an aged actor famous in Clifford family legend as the road company villain who stole Great Aunt Cleva and then abandoned her, turns out to be a vain but entertaining man surviving with her cat Ethel in a vandalized apartment house. Gabriel seems an almost dreamlike character: Jane half-believes she has created him out of her own fantasies or needs.

Even Gabriel's specialty, the pre-Raphaelite Brotherhood, has its dreamlike qualities. Godwin knows the Nineteenth Century specialty of her two major characters, and the authenticity of her background adds to our enjoyment. Indeed, the texture of university life, with its term papers, student conferences, and academic gossip makes this one of the finest novels of Academia—much better, because fresher and less bitter, than Mary McCarthy's *Groves of Academe*. Jane's attempts to cope with her students—the hippie, the combined physics major who writes papers she finds profound but cannot quite understand, the black Portia, who deserves an F but is the first of her family to get to college—will be familiar to every teacher.

But most important is Jane. Introspective, highly articulate, loving, perceptive, she fights through the complex relationships of family, friends, and lover, to find and strengthen herself. Her refusal to become dependent on anyone is a courageous assertion of the value of individual growth. Gail Godwin has given us a heroine to admire fully, in a rich novel that is a joy to read.—ELSA PENDLETON, "Struggle for Self," *Prog*, Feb. 1975, pp. 57–58

Gail Godwin has received lots of praise from lots of names for her first two novels, but the latest one ⟨*The Odd Woman*⟩ (and how fast they come!) is a solemn 400-page bore, for all its occasional attempts at self-irony. It's hard to care much about Jane Clifford, Eng lit prof who fifteen years ago would have been turning out articles on Spenser or Milton for *PMLA* and is today respectably "into" George Eliot and George Gissing, while having a less-than-torrid affair with a married prof who is into Ruskin. As the title suggests, the Gissing-gimmick is worked all too steadily through the book, since our heroine tends to carry around the master's novel wherever she goes, which gets her into conversations like this with her brilliant friend Sonia ("Chilled white wine would be lovely . . . Only, I have to save some of my wits for later, because I want to grade all my papers tonight") who riffles through *The Odd Women*:

> "Any good? You're using it for the spring course, aren't you."
>
> "It's a tough little book. Inelegant, maybe, but I like it.
> It will work well in the course. What I like about Gissing is that he lets his characters think. They come to horrible ends, most of them, but they keep track of themselves so beautifully along the way. And he writes women well. He doesn't keep the sexual-ironic distance of many male writers when writing about female characters."
>
> "Or female writers writing about male characters," added Sonia.
>
> "We must be fair, mustn't we?" Ellen Glasgow makes her men seem such fools. Now there's a challenge. *Barren Ground*. . . . It's the book which tests the mettle of the sincerest militant.

No doubt, but if there are people who talk like this in life they should avoid getting themselves into novels. Committed to writing women well, Gail Godwin could use lots more sexual-ironic distance in testing the mettle of her sincerest heroine. —WILLIAM H. PRITCHARD, "Novel Sex and Violence," *HdR*, Spring 1975, p. 151

DREAM CHILDREN

To find one of Gail Godwin's stories in an anthology or magazine is a pleasure, and equally a challenge. She possesses an enormous command of technique, together with a much rarer command of appropriateness: like Donald Barthelme, Gail Godwin will use any means necessary for her purpose. Also like Barthelme, she demonstrates that the methods of 'experimental' fiction are out of the breadboard stage and available for normal use.

Why is it, then, that reading straight through *Dream Children* is noticeably enervating? Qualities emerge that were not visible in individual stories: to begin with, a cloying, insistent rhythm of incantation, a lilting prolixity used to bridge tricky caesuras of plot and feeling. This is the clue to a deeper evasiveness which, once suspected, is confirmed. The 'modern' techniques of summary ('Notes for a Story'), present tense, montage, numbered paragraphs, are opportunities not only to realise an idea, but also to avoid working it through. In 'The Legacy of the Motes,' a young academic is blocked in his research into metaphysical conceits by 'muscae volitantes,' spots before the eyes in the shape of wings. Ten years later he realises their meaning; their implications 'began opening up to him like flowers, one by one; there seemed to be no end to them, their paradoxes, their analogies . . .' And this is all we get. Surely the author should either put up or shut up.

Having stated these ambiguities, I can see a partial resolution. The recurring theme of *Dream Children* is the aperçu that collapses in upon itself if one tries to make it do everyday work: as with the Sussex vicar in 'An Intermediate Stop' who turns his epiphanic vision into a book, then into a lecture tour—and finally stares uncomprehendingly at meaningless lecture notes. Gail Godwin is a mystic, with a mystic's cunning in pointing at the inexpressible. *Dream Children* should be read one or two stories at a time to avoid the jadedness from too many words about silence.—NICK TOTTON, "Camouflage," *Spec*, Jan. 15, 1977, p. 21

Dream Children, Gail Godwin's first collection of stories, may disappoint or even dismay readers who admired *The Odd Woman*. My own admiration for that novel was a little uneasy; though Godwin can be eloquent and witty, her effects depend mainly on amassing incidents and thoughts, and her work can be ponderous and sentimental. In *The Odd Woman* the accumulation adds up, finally, even though it is not a continuously active or engaging book.

The stories, I'm afraid, expose further deficiencies that aren't evident in the longer and denser novel. A number of them seem exercises in fantasy-making which ought not to be memorialized in hard covers—a rather coy rehearsing of Swift's relations with Vanessa, Varina, and Stella ("Why Does a Great Man Love?"), a mawkish account of a woman's gradual withdrawal from her affectionate husband and son, whom she rewards with a magnificent outburst of cooking, laundry, and "creative writing" before death claims her ("A Sorrowful Woman"). Godwin writes semi-surreal tales of women leaving home to observe their own life from an apartment across the street ("Nobody's Home"), being abandoned temporarily or permanently by their lovers ("Death in Puerto Vallarta," "My Lover, His Summer Vacation"), becoming a more than willing object of gang-rape in an airport VIP lounge ("Layover"). Some themes recur in these stories—dead children and lost lovers, female gigantism, sexual attraction to and damage from older men, writers constructing fictions or dreams—but Godwin's use of the short story form doesn't succeed in giving them clear meaning.

Godwin can be very good—and sometimes very funny—when she attaches her characters' feelings to the conditions of their culture:

> "I have to stop by the damn supermarket," Gretchen's mother said, "and you know, no matter what I fix he won't be satisfied." Her mother's library books were digging into Gretchen's rear so she restacked them, examining the titles: SF Nebula awards, a novel called *Other Orbits* with a dust jacket from one of Hieronymus Bosch's more gruesome panels, and a book on the medieval mind. . . . She began to read. "You're going to ruin your eyes," her grandmother said through the rear-view mirror. Gretchen thought of Borges and Joyce and Homer and Milton and wished she could fall in love with a really good man. ("Some Side Effects of Time Travel")

When she confines herself to relatively conventional modes, where inner feeling and outer circumstance each have their rights preserved, she does quite well, as in "False Lights," a brief exchange of letters between a writer's first and second wives, with very different ideas about what they do or don't have in common. In "An Intermediate Stop," a young British clergyman, author of a bestseller about his own mystical experience of God, finds a richer kind of beatitude while lecturing at a small women's college in the American South.

The first and last stories in the book show rather neatly the limitations of this writer. Both concern apparently secure women living in the country north of New York City, one with a TV-producer husband, and the other with a playwright lover; but from these similar cases very different stories emerge. . . .

"Dream Children" is better than summary makes it sound, but it remains a little too close in tone and intensity to the emotional conventions of a familiar kind of commercial women's fiction to earn its professions of seriousness. I much prefer "Notes for a Story," which, though done mostly in outline, mixes emotional intensity with intelligent ironic control. . . . The ending is inconclusive but credibly mixes remorse with an exhilarating acceptance of the hostility both women have concealed for so long. This incident, in effect the climax of a longer story which hasn't fully been written and suggesting a novel's greater amplitude, reminds us that Gail Godwin is a very considerable writer indeed.—THOMAS R. EDWARDS, "The Short View," *NYRB*, April 1, 1976, pp. 34–35

VIOLET CLAY

What ⟨is wrong in the current vogue for fiction about getting back to nature⟩ finds poignant expression in Gail Godwin's newest novel, *Violet Clay*, a terrifying example of sentimentality in the disguise of contemporary sensibility. Violet, whose name embodies the antithesis between a shrinking and an earthy persona, is an uncanny cross between Melanie Wilkes and Little Audrey. An orphan, she has been raised in a Charleston mansion by her grandmother, who has lost her fortune and taken to drink. Violet is a painter; having failed to crash the New York art scene, she makes a life of equivocation, and paints book jackets for lurid romances, sometimes using herself as a model. She swigs vodka, engages in disengagement with various men, and admires her Uncle Ambrose, who has written one good novel during the war and malingered ever since. Clearly the Gothic fiction, with which she is working and which she transmutes in fantasy into the travesty of her own life, is the past which she has to transcend. And clearly Uncle Ambrose is the symbol of all its most attractive and pernicious aspects, its dependent gentility, its dilettantism, its exploitation of women, its exploitation by women, its reliance on war and excitement for meaning, and, above all, to state the obvious, its maleness.

And there lies trouble; for Uncle Ambrose is as poor a spokesman for the male as Violet is for the female, neither of them having quite made it to flesh and blood. Pursued by none of the furies which in fact wreck the lives and work of artists, subject to none of the banal irritations of real life, they are no more than cardboard placards on which to write unconvincing messages. None of the novel's characters has been translated by Godwin's imagination into credibility. They speak to each other in prolix and tendentious conversations, so unedited by personality that they are droll; especially those between Violet and Milo, a neuter personage of such excruciating unreality that he makes one long for a Milton Berle female impersonation, just to get one's bearings back. When Uncle Ambrose commits suicide, Violet takes over his cabin in the Adirondacks, and makes the leap back to nature *de rigueur* for ladies of the late 1970s attempting to establish independent careers. In the woods, for reasons never made clear, she finds meaning and inspiration in the example of the sinewy young woman next door, whom I suspect, though I hope I am wrong, of standing for the Woman of the Future. This person's name is, of course, Sam, and she has, of course, survived triumphantly a history of rape and incest intended to jar, as it does, against the heroine's own self-indulgent progress, as patrician frivolity meets *lumpen*-squalor.

Well, to be fair, a lot of this is the fault of bad writing, an inability to describe exactly or to transcribe the sound of different voices into anything resembling living language. "I know this is not the evening for looking on the bright side of things," says poor Milo, "what with this tragic news you've just learned, but as far as your leaving Harrow House is concerned, I think it might turn out to be a blessing in disguise. For so long you've wanted to paint your own things." And Violet conforts herself, "humorously" yet, with this stunning sentence: "Well at least . . . I'm not in the middle of South Dakota with nothing but the clothes on my back and a trio of rapists' seeds batting it out for ascendancy in my womb.'" I weep for the pen of a cartoonist, or the pencil of an editor.

But there is worse than this, the basis from which the flabby language, the insubstantial characters, the odd lapses of taste seem to spring; the novel is simply half-baked, half-created, and so far from inevitable that one reads it constantly reminding oneself that it could easily have been avoided. Violet Clay's struggle to become an artist has nothing to do with such pompous motivations as vision or sensitivity or the compulsion to express deep and paradoxical passions. Heavens no! It is the result of a moderate facility and the immoderate impatience of Eve to take a bite of the Big Apple. If the book carries any conviction with it, it is that Violet's esthetic is pretty much molded by her author's, a schoolgirl sensibility in search of vocation. Gail Godwin has been regarded highly as a novelist for some time, certainly since *The Odd Woman* was published in 1974, and I wonder unhappily how much of that regard is due to the fashionable nature of her themes, which can create, without feeling for character, language, ambience, or moral significance, a job lot of current concerns that passes as "Women's Fiction."—EDITH MILTON, *NR*, July 8, 1978, pp. 40–41

There is nothing of the extreme or simple-minded about Gail Godwin, and one would expect from the author of *The Odd Woman* careful and leisurely portraiture, balanced attitudes towards the sexes and experience generally, as well as much sincerity and an absence of humor. The new novel ⟨Violet Clay⟩ seems to me to have something seriously wrong with it, not so much for what it includes as for what it lacks. What's askew in its tone may be gathered from the concluding sentences, informing us that "Meanwhile that limitless radiance which eludes us all spins on, taking our day with it, teasing and turning us for a time in its vibrant dimensions, continuing to spread its blind effulgence when we have gone." I realize that a Fitzgerald or a Faulkner manage not to sink under such diction, but Gail Godwin's quite straightforward manner of telling Violet Clay's story (a flashback here, another one there, now back to the present again), plus the rather claustrophobic nature of her "I" narrative, introduces an embarrassing lyricism that you wish somebody, if not the author, could be critical and ironic about: "The color of Ivor's body was a surprise too; it was a warm russet color, like a winter apple. I had expected it to be white and withdrawn, like his face. And my dream had been prescient: he was warm. He was magnanimously warm, and as firm and as sure of my response as if he'd been my appointed fate." Somehow I felt as if I were watching a sadly romantic, "serious" TV or movie bit. And though *Violet Clay* introduces many characters, moves the heroine around here and there, I couldn't see what interesting purposes were being served other than getting a novel written. Page by page it simply was not entertaining.—WILLIAM H. PRITCHARD, "Telling Stories," *HdR*, Autumn 1978, p. 521

A number of novels spawned by the women's movement have focused on growth out of oppressive or inadequate relationships; instead, Gail Godwin has chosen for her subject the options on the far side of such political and sexual emancipations. In *The Odd Woman* (her last novel), she examined with intelligence and wit the question of how an attractive, single, professional woman achieves a sense of purpose and integrity in a life style that is not altogether willed. *Violet Clay* extends those themes adroitly, as Godwin poses the relationship between independence and talent. . . .

What makes Violet's own progress so absorbing is that the novel opens into an inner detective story: what led to Ambrose's disillusionment and ultimate defeat? Violet pieces together the circumstances of his life, slowly determining the lesson in it for herself as she confronts her own inner demons and illusions—her fears of failure and of total dedication to uncertain artistic potentialities. . . .

In examining the deeper anxieties accompanying the pursuit of any true vocation, Godwin gives an artful if occasionally cerebral portrait of the difficult route toward autonomy. The story of Violet's growth as a painter resonates for any person concerned with the balances between security and risk, between the limits and the inspiration of one's deepest dreams; between settling for too little and demanding too much of oneself. As Violet faces her inner resources in the reflected image of her uncle's puzzling life, she refers to the "shape-shifting" creations or discoveries of any life, those crucial transformations of personality that not only express the essential self but that, by translating potentialities into actual expression, propel one toward deeper actualization.—ROBERTA RUBENSTEIN, "Adventures in Self-Discovery," *Prog*, Oct. 1978, p. 56

Godwin has a knack for certain kinds of observation. She sees the ways in which women subvert and smother their own ambitions. And she knows all the contemporary (and ignoble) manifestations of boredom, envy, social intimidation, loneliness, and procrastination—the last of which dominates her heroine's life.

A novel about procrastination, about a woman with inflated ideas about herself who at the same time doesn't take herself seriously enough, about a woman who is starting late, who gives herself an ultimatum and rises from her lethargy, who becomes wise about her demons ("little creatures like the ones in Bosch . . . those are somebody else's demons. They've already been given a shape. . . . Whereas, it is the nature of personal demons to be the last thing you imagine."), who gets her perspective and sense of proportion from relationships which are not romantic—is a novel worth having, and Godwin is canny enough to have chosen to write it.

Yet her management of these timely subjects is often clumsy enough to make us wince. Her plot creaks with the weight of her intentions, her transitions are awkward, and her characters, strained through the grid of her plan for them, are painfully thin. Violet's first person narrative—chatty, ironic, self-denigrating—is so wry that it nearly makes us indifferent to what happens, and we are grateful for the liberation from inertia that occurs at the end of the book, not so much because it provides an upbeat ending, but because it brings to a halt the grinding ironic tone of voice in which the book is written. It is only at the end, too, that Violet becomes believable as an artist. Until then her identity as a painter seems merely researched, and her career as an illustrator doesn't merit her anguish or our interest. In the last pages, however, as she lives out her ultimatum, taking the time and space to paint, Violet speaks about the painting process in a way that is plausible and attentive, giving herself instructions that Godwin herself might heed as a writer:

> She appears to be crafted out of the light, so continuously and harmoniously do the parts of her body mesh with its contours. And yet I need her outline too. Otherwise it will be just blobs of light. . . . (Yet) the main thing is to get the model sketched in and then, quickly, over the pencil outline, try to capture those fugitive contours of light. Yes, leave out the book. That's too particular.
>
> —LYNN LURIA-SUKENICK, "Four Novels," *PR*, 1980, pp. 291–92

A MOTHER AND TWO DAUGHTERS

. . . *A Mother and Two Daughters* demonstrates, once again, Gail Godwin's uncommon generosity as a storyteller. She is openhanded—she's positively spendthrift—with her tales. The most insignificant character travels on a stream of absorbing histories, past love affairs, coincidences, recurring themes. Just look at the story of Nell's semi-seduction before her marriage;

or of how old Uncle Osmond lost his nose in World War I; or of Lydia's cold-blooded pursuit of her husband-to-be. Any one of these plots could possibly have been a novel on its own, or at least a short story, but Gail Godwin doesn't measure things out so penuriously. When you read one of her novels, you have a feeling of abundance.

Is *A Mother and Two Daughters* as good as *The Odd Woman?*

Is that even a fair question to ask?

The Odd Woman remains one of my all-time favorites, perhaps partly because of the element of surprise—I read it before I knew how much one could expect of Gail Godwin. *A Mother and Two Daughters* lacks that element, of course, and it suffers too from what seems to me an unnecessary summary epilogue—an epilogue that leaps too far ahead, ties things up too suddenly, and takes place, moreover, in 1984 (I don't want to sound pessimistic, but how is she so sure there's going to *be* a 1984?).

There is one improvement, though. In *A Mother and Two Daughters*, the male characters have real depth and texture. Dear Leonard Strickland and Cate's redneck millionaire suitor, and Lydia's sweetly stuffy husband and her earnest lover—all are solidly believable. For the first time, Gail Godwin's men are equal to her women. And that's saying something.—ANNE TYLER, "All in the Family," *NR*, Feb. 17, 1982, p. 40

Gail Godwin's latest (and longest) novel ⟨*A Mother and Two Daughters*⟩ has its flaws, as annoying as they are unnecessary, but the complex pattern it weaves, the subtle analyses of motive and memory it sustains and the rich evocation of place and time it provides should render readers benevolent toward its stylistic lapses. Indeed, the book's strengths and weaknesses are bound together as inextricably as the lives of the title characters; and the title itself, provocative in its banality, promises neither more nor less than what the author delivers: a detailed portrayal of the interlocked crises that alternately unite and divide the lives of three contemporary women.

The novel begins and ends with a party. But where the first commemorates an old order dying and concludes with a fatal accident, the latter celebrates a wedding and a new order being born. It is a measure of Gail Godwin's skill as a novelist that these disparate notes harmonize rather than clash; the story is a comedy in the classic sense, moving from dispersion to reunion and, indeed, the final gathering on the lawn with minstrels playing could as easily be set in Illyria or the Forest of Arden as in rural North Carolina. But the specific questions under discussion and the circumstances of the women's lives are unmistakably late 20th-century American: mid-life identity crises, academic vagabondage, interracial permutations. Nell Strickland and her two daughters, Cate and Lydia, perform their family dance of estrangement and reconciliation to the music of a society so rapidly in transition that even massive physical landmarks have simply disappeared, like the hill in the middle of Mountain City, or been transformed beyond recognition, like the orchard of Nell's private school now part of a shopping mall. Fragile human constructs like marriage or civility or contractual obligations fare less well still. Left a widow early in the novel, Nell struggles both to remember and to go on living for her own sake and that of her daughters whose lives show the scars of the wider conflict. Cate, the elder, is going on 40 and has already put several teaching positions and two husbands behind her. Independence is her passion. Lydia, younger and more conservative, has only recently broken the ordered progress of her life, walking out on a successful and devoted husband to test her own powers. The tension between the two sisters, never dormant for very long, grows more acute as Lydia's fortunes wax and Cate's wane, sexually as well as professionally; the result is, literally and figuratively, a conflagration whose scorch marks never fully heal.

Stated as boldly as that, the triangular structure of the novel could seem trite and contrived, especially when Lydia's two boys are presented as chiastic replicas of their mother and aunt. But that would be to see the skeleton and miss the body. Gail Godwin has fleshed out her story with a remarkable collection of secondary characters (mid-America's plenty) and a lavish display of sensuous and psychological detail. If every sentence does not certify its own inevitability, as even the phrases do, for example, in Shirley Hazzard's *The Transit of Venus*, still the sheer accumulation of incident and description, of psychological perception and social comment gives the novel a density that pulls the reader into this particular story while, at the same time, expanding awareness of cognate mysteries in his or her own life.

On one page, for instance, we follow Nell's progress from comforting thoughts of detachment ("being nobody"), through imagined homily to her daughters and swift rejection of such advice as ill-timed, to a final, ruefully ironic realization: "Here am I, plotting how I can resume the running of their lives—as if they weren't old enough to do it for themselves. Some 'nobody' I am!" And all this while Nell navigates, in fact and memory, the shopping mall that sits atop the cherished crabapple orchard of her youth.

This kind of compression redeems the novel's tendency toward sprawl where dialogue grows, topsy-like, into set speeches, and information, once conveyed, is repeated as if the reader were *expected* to be nodding. In fact, such is the force of Godwin's narrative and descriptive instincts that even the excess baggage is willingly borne in our desire to finish the journey with Nell, Cate and Lydia. On the way, as in John Updike's most recent novel, we meet more than enough recognizable (and usable) parts of our recent past to make it all, detours included, well worth the price of the trip.—JOHN B. BRESLIN, *Am*, April 17, 1982, p. 305

SUSAN E. LORSCH

From "Gail Godwin's *The Odd Woman:* Literature and the Retreat from Life"

Critique, Volume 20, Number 2 (1978), pp. 21–32

Gail Godwin's *The Odd Woman* (1974) does not at first glance seem to be in the currently popular mode of self-conscious fiction—and perhaps for this reason has not attracted the critical attention it deserves. Neither a work as involuted as one by Borges nor a *Künstlerroman*, *The Odd Woman* centers on the relation between literature and life, especially on the effect that literature—and the lies it often tells—has on those who believe it. Of special interest is the novel's focus on fiction's traditional portrayal of women and its effect on women's relations with and reactions to men.

For Jane Clifford, the protagonist of *The Odd Woman*, words possess an almost magical quality. The novel opens with Jane lying in bed trying to overcome her usual insomnia by pondering the written records of sleeplessness left by other insomniacs. To Jane, words seem imbued with the power to heal, the power to influence life:

> she believed in them deeply. The articulation, interpretation, appreciation, and preservation of good words. She believed in their power. If you truly named something, you had that degree of control over it. . . . The right word or the wrong word could change a person's life, the course of the world.[1]

As Jane admits to herself, "everything for her is measured in words" (211).

To Jane, a professor of English, literature serves as far more than simply vocation or avocation. It is not just an object of perception but conditions her very mode of seeing. She views her own life through the refracting filter of literature. Jane's mother, Kitty, oversimplifies matters when she accuses Jane of looking up her life in books (137), but Jane interweaves her life with books; she experiences her life through literature, through the books she has so entirely assimilated. A teacher of Romantic and Victorian literature, Jane has lived since graduate school "more in the nineteenth century than in her own" (27). For Jane the worlds of fiction and the "real" world are one: she admits to a student that, gazing at the moon, she might perhaps perceive it through Coleridge's poetry (13). Climbing off this student's motorcycle, she "made a point of thanking him with the formality of a Jane Austen heroine climbing decorously from a carriage" (11).

Jane not only experiences literary worlds as real, she treats the actual world as if it were an aesthetic creation. The anecdotes of her family history become the formative stories of Jane's present as well as her past, serving as simply so much more fiction for her to analyze and interpret. Jane dwells, for example, on "Kitty's train story" (26), Edith's fainting story, and Cleva's escape story. Her astute friend Gerda, criticizing Jane's conception of her family history, asserts that Jane transforms her relatives into symbols and their stories into myths (29). Jane creates her own personal yet widely allusive fictions. . . .

In addition to the story of Edith fainting away at the feet of her husband-to-be, Hans, with the words "life is a disease," and the story of Kitty's decision finally to rid herself of all that loose change, the story of Cleva's elopement and subsequent death influences Jane tremendously. In 1905 Cleva ran off with an actor in a melodrama passing through town, had an illegitimate child, and

> returned ten months later, in a coffin. Her death remained a mystery. Hans had gone to New York on the night train and returned with the coffin and the infant girl, after Edith had received a note from Cleva, scrawled in pencil on the back of a torn theatre program: "*Sister I am in grave trouble please can somebody come the villain has left me*," and an address. (17).

The force of the story for Jane issues in part from the fact that she has a tangible written relic of the episode over which she can and does ruminate at length: the note from Cleva to Edith. In support of Jane's belief that life and art are indeed continuous, the melodrama in which Cleva's "villain" acted is aptly *The Fatal Wedding*. Taking off from the title and comparing Cleva's story to Edith's life, Jane agrees with Edith in concluding that "You had your choice: a disastrous ending with a Villain; a satisfactory ending with a Good Man. The message was simple" (17). Jane believes that, like art, the actual world is composed of heroes and villains, and she casts her life accordingly. Ray Sparks acts the part of a villain (67) along with two of Jane's elementary school teachers (110). At a Modern Language Association seminar, Gabriel and Zimmer play hero and villain respectively (175).

At the end of *The Odd Woman* Jane tracks down and visits Von Vorst, the villain of *The Fatal Wedding* and the man with whom, she has supposed all her life, Cleva ran off. Contrary to all Jane's expectations and the scenario she had prepared herself for, Von Vorst does not act the part of the villain. When Jane returns home, the truth of the encounter hits her in a shocking revelation: the villain in life, the man who carried Cleva off, may not have been the villain of the play in which he acted: Cleva's lover may not have been Von Vorst: "Did 'villain' in 1906 simply mean the person you hated because he had hurt you—as 'son of a bitch,' 'prick,' 'bastard' meant today—regardless of what mild creature played Villain or Man About Town on the stage?" (337). The man with whom Cleva ran off may well have been Edwin Merchant, who played the part of the hero and "happy husband" in the melodrama.

Finally, the full insight that the literary world has no necessary correlation with the actual world bursts on Jane. Villains in art need not be villains in life. Moreover, her insight confirms the truth of Jane's early wondering whether or not the concept of the self is itself a myth—"Characters were not so wholly good or bad, heroes or villains, anymore" (15), whether or not the very notion of personality—the staple of fiction—is itself false. As the concepts of personality of heroes and villains die, so does "all the stuff of novels" (223) on which Jane depends to give meaning to her life.

Unfortunately, *The Odd Woman* does not end on an optimistic note of lessons learned. Jane will try to incorporate Edwin Merchant as villain into a new mythology rather than give up the belief, so central to her, that art accurately reflects and comments on life (338). The revelation comes too late for thirty-two-year-old Jane Clifford. Even though she has—however half-heartedly—managed to break off her unhealthy relationship with Gabriel, she remains an "odd woman" still. The novel closes with the snow falling, reminding us of Jane's retreat when writing her dissertation, and pointing to another such frozen retreat from the actual world (345).

Godwin seems to offer a forceful indictment of literature and the harmful effects it can have on its readers. Jane can never be happy except, perhaps, in the safe world of the imagination, the only world which can begin to fulfill the expectations literature has fostered in her. We must go on to ask how Godwin can escape her own indictment of literature, whether her message does not undermine the very novel in which it is embodied. Gissing's novel first gives voice to the charge against fiction and the lies it tells to women, and he would probably defend his own novel against the charge by asserting that it counteracts those lies, offering women bleak truth instead. As Jane notes, Gissing's novel displays his "unrelenting pessimism. It was one of the few nineteenth-century novels she could think of in which every main female character who was allowed to live through the last page had to do so alone. The book's ending depressed her utterly" (21). Godwin might find her defense against the charge she, too, levels against literature in pointing to the pessimistic ending of Jane's story as an example of the truth-telling that we must require from contemporary fiction. Godwin, however, has some of the Jane Clifford in her, and her novel still embodies some of the old attractive lies.

In Sonia Marks we have a fairy-tale figure, the woman who represents something special to Jane, who is a "winner" (36). Not only the mistress of an attractive and interesting man (unlike Ray Sparks) who manages to become his wife and a mother, Sonia proves a popular and spell-binding professor of literature who never had to sell out like Kitty and write *Love Short Stories* or give up her dreams. According to Jane, Sonia has it all. Here we have the woman in "real" life who fulfills all the promises fiction offers, and Godwin does not undercut or deny Jane's vision of Sonia. Perhaps, she admits, we *can* have it all; Godwin yearns to believe the conventional fictions that tell us that men and women do fall in love and live happily ever after. Gerda's pragmatic economic point of view may be right, but we still join Godwin in favoring Jane, the "heroine" of *The*

Odd Woman and the focus of our sympathies, who has not given up love like Gerda (326).

Finally, Godwin proves unwilling to choose the outer life over the life of the imagination in a decision that her novel—Sonia Marks notwithstanding—argues will prove necessary. Like Jane, Godwin's narrator prefers "building your own interior castle" (7) to living in the actual world. Godwin's novel closes not with Jane Clifford, a hopeless, albeit sympathetic case, but with her neighbor, a man (interestingly) who, more than anyone else in the novel, represents the escape from life and the immersion in art and the world of the imagination:

> He kept bird-feeders. A modern-day hermit if there ever was one, he worked in the library's Special Collections and kept to himself. [Jane] had watched him often from her window, frail, nervously alert, refilling those feeders. At night, after the rest of the street was long asleep, she heard him playing Mozart. (32)

Despite her convincing quarrel with the literary imagination, Godwin ends *The Odd Woman* with the beautiful and simple image of Jane lying in bed listening to this man take elements of the actual world and transform them into something far more precious—art:

> All was silent, safe and still. [Jane's] heartbeat slowed from melodramatic terror to its usual insomniac tick. From the little concrete house behind came the barely audible tinkle of a soul at the piano, trying to organize the loneliness and the weather and the long night into something of abiding shape and beauty. (345)

Notes

1. Gail Godwin, *The Odd Woman* (1974; rpt. New York: Berkley, 1976), p. 1. Subsequent references are to this edition.

HERBERT GOLD

1924–

Herbert Gold was born on March 9, 1924, in Cleveland, Ohio, as the son of a Jewish Russian immigrant who had become a successful businessman. After serving in U.S. Army Intelligence in World War II, he graduated with a B.A. from Columbia University, and went on to receive an M.A. in 1948. A Fulbright Fellowship enabled him to study philosophy at the Sorbonne from 1949 to 1951, before taking up a position at Western Reserve University.

Gold's first novel, *Birth of a Hero*, appeared in 1951, and his third, *The Man Who Was Not With It*, later re-issued in paperback as *The Wild Life*, in 1956. In the years that followed he received a number of awards, including a Guggenheim Fellowship in 1957, a grant from the National Institute of Arts and Letters in 1958, and a Ford Theatre Fellowship in 1960. In the 1950s and 1960s he held teaching positions at colleges and universities including Cornell, Berkeley, Harvard and Stanford. A volume of short stories, *Love and Like*, was published in 1960, and a second, *The Magic Will*, in 1971. He has written two collections of essays, *The Age of Happy Problems* (1962) and *A Walk on the West Side: California on the Brink* (1981), which reflects on the state where he has lived since 1963.

The bulk of Gold's output has been long fiction, and his later novels include *Fathers: A Novel in the Form of a Memoir* (1967), *Swiftie the Magician* (1974), *He/She* (1980), *Family: A Novel in the Form of a Memoir* (1981), *True Love* (1982), which won him the Commonwealth Club Award, and *Mister White Eyes* (1984). An autobiography, *My Last Two Thousand Years*, appeared in 1972, and much of his fiction draws on his experiences of childhood in Cleveland, life on the West Coast, and the break-ups of his two marriages, in 1956 and 1975.

In his critical writings Herbert Gold has referred to fiction as the exploration of human possibility, and his novels and short stories demonstrate what he means. In particular he has been concerned with the effect of love on personality. His first three novels, though in other ways they are strikingly different, have a common theme: in each a man learns to love and at the same time comes to terms with himself. It is hard to tell which comes first, love or self-discovery. Indeed, Gold seems to be saying that each is the prerequisite of the other: only the person who is capable of love can accept himself, and, conversely, only the person with self-knowledge and self-respect is capable of a fruitful relationship with others. Somehow a miracle has to happen, and in *Birth of a Hero*, *The Prospect before Us*, and *The Man Who Was Not With It*, Gold has examined some of the ways in which the transformation takes place. In his fourth novel, *The Optimist*, on the other hand, he has shown us a man who learns neither lesson, a man who remains alienated both from himself and from others.

Therefore Be Bold continues the study of love, and this time Gold is scrutinizing the love of adolescents. It is a theme that often has been treated humorously though sometimes with morbid seriousness. Gold is serious enough but a long way from being morbid. There are comic episodes in the book, and the narrator, who is looking back over twenty years, knows as well as anyone that he and his boyhood friends were making fools of themselves in a variety of ways. But at the same time he feels both tenderness and respect, and he has a sense that anything is possible for these boys and girls.

. . . Gold has fashioned for this book an original style, and the style is responsible for much of its power. He has always had a good ear, and some of the talk—conversations of Dan's parents, for instance, or the adolescents' talk at the party—is wonderful. But it is in descriptive and reflective passages that his style is most distinctive. He employs many devices, including Joycean puns and bits of verse, but what he chiefly relies on is imagery of startling boldness. Here, for example, is Chuck Hastings at the party: "In some respects he resembled a mummy—the shriveled yellow skin, the hand and head too large for a wasted body, the bottomless eye sockets of thought beyond the Nile. But his agile Adam's apple and point-making finger made him less the Styx-swimmer dog-paddling toward Coptic limbos than a high school intellectual intimidating the navel-eyed little girl." This is high-pitched, to be sure, but the point is that Gold keeps it up and keeps it up. He has been working steadily towards greater freedom and freshness in the use of words, not for the sake of shocking the reader but in order to rouse him out of lethargy, in order to compel him to see more clearly and feel more strongly. One may feel that he is not always successful and yet respond sharply to the total effect. The book vibrates with energy. It is full of the hopefulness and courage of the young, full of belief in love, full of the sense of human possibility.—GRANVILLE HICKS, "Literary Horizons: Amour, Amour, Amour," *SR*, Oct. 1, 1960, p. 15

. . . ⟨An⟩ uneasy, ironic qualification may be sensed in the style of ⟨*The Optimist* (1959)⟩. Gold's style tends to possess verve, color, pace. It has its mannerisms too: a facile, aphoristic turn of expression, an elliptic trick of striking off-key rhythms, a touch of false glamor, even where genuine sentiment is called for. But these are quirks of sensibility. The real difficulty is more subtle. It is that the style tries to give hope and humor to dramatic material weighed down by genuine desperation. The bounce of words cannot conceal a fairly bleak spectacle of loneliness and frustration. Hence the glibness of Burr's affirmative editorials on life. His rapt comment on Frank, the sergeant who sells obscene pictures and traffics in the black markets of Paris, is one of numerous examples. (The comment reminds us of the more convincing statement of Bellow's Augie March on laughing Jacqueline, the Norman maid.) Frank may have "a paltry and unprotected heart," as Burr thinks, but the wonder or gaiety of life cannot be caught and dismissed in an elegant phrase. What joy the events and actions of the novel lack, the style seeks to create unaided. *The Optimist* remains, in this sense, a self-created metaphor of hope, and an ironic act of dissection. A severely diminished man, the hero still wants more of everything. Metaphor and action, we see, suffer from the disunity of the age; nor can illusion and reality be entertained in a common perspective. Irony, which endeavors to reconcile opposites, also assumes that things, at bottom, are irreconcilable. But perhaps this is the way things really are. —IHAB HASSAN, "Encounter with Possibility," *Radical Innocence*, 1961, p. 187

The attempt to poeticize the wandering naturalistic American Joe and give him moralistic resolution takes other forms. In the quite over-written but best novel of Herbert Gold, *The Man Who Was Not With It*, Bud Williams, a young carnival barker and part-orphan, gains his education into moral identity on the road and in the loving elaborated underside of life. The wandering, father-defying, drug addiction, sexual voyeurism, crime and varied gross experiences elucidate such aphorisms as "You drink from the cup of wisdom? I fell into it." Hitch-hiking, the carnival-world's parody of the business society, and a prolonged nightmarish drive in a jalopy with a demonic father-figure in the back seat, fill the cup. The wisdom, however, is that the ordinary American Joe learns the hard way back to being the urban worker and family man that he originally rebelled against being. Degradation and the road, not convention and culture, provide the truest way to adaption and acceptance. "Down is the long way up." Slanged-over Heraclitean wisdom summarizes the traditional violations and final affirmations of monogamy, loyalty, honesty, filial acceptance, forgiveness and going back home again. The road through extremity provides the leap of faith into ordinary moral life by which the con-man can, once again, become an authentic "mark." "There's a good and with it way to be not with it, too"—which means that you can be a rebel without being rebellious. Acceptance of present day American life seems, in a good many clever writers, to require some such fideistic paradoxes to reconcile the rebelliously intelligent and sensitive to the ostensible social order. The maturity which such rebels reach for eschews the carnival morality of the fast-buck and the con-man's hard-sell to empty success. They also learn to despise the pretty but compulsive and willfully ambitious—and therefore sexually counterfeit—middle-class girl. However, in giving up their larcenous artistry and longing flights they tend to identify their own contradictions with those of the society, achieving an urbane disenchantment that allows them to be neither vicious nor defiant.—KINGSLEY WIDMER, "Contemporary American Outcasts," *The Literary Rebel*, 1965, pp. 126–27

Herbert Gold's open feeling and generous sympathy in *Fathers* are initially appealing . . . and I admired the self-criticism apparent in Mr. Gold's new quieter style: the strenuous lyricism, the boastful emotionality of the earlier work have been subdued. But to my taste they have not been transmuted into the genuinely imaginative love and insight that *Fathers* needs. I wish I could feel more enthusiastic about a novel so humane in intention and so courageously direct in its approach to large simple feelings. But sympathy and piety can be willful too; quiet acceptance can be only an assertion, though it may be the right assertion. Mr. Gold wants to honor his father in honest terms, to bridge by faith the "abyss" of incommunicability between paternal and filial love, to express filial love by imagining what can never be experienced—the sufficiency of paternal love. And he fashions a highly attractive image of his father's energy and freedom, above all of his father's charm. But in so doing he makes himself too small—or so it seems to me, and Mr. Gold's frank autobiographical novel seems to ask for a similarly frank response from his reader. The father is a man of fact and commercial action, of will and property, the son's values are opposed, and this opposition is meant to be important. But Mr. Gold underplays his own values to protect his father. This seems to me false piety to begin with, and it badly upsets the balance of the book: it makes the son's imagination of his father's virtues too fluent. There is far too much charm and far too little boredom, annoyance, pain, anger or shame, and therefore what we actually see of the father's nature and his relationship with the son doesn't begin to justify large language about the abyss of incommunicability. Nor do I feel much pressure behind that language in itself:

> My father did better than to lecture me in general. He took charge at a moment when I needed him to take charge. He did not understand power or love, but they were his familiars. Lacking the language for them, he dwelled in these commodities as if they were houses. Cut off from his own family at age thirteen, he lived in the world of do and make. How could he talk to sons? Nothing to say but: "Go out. I give you the stars." And of course no words even for that. "I give you the sky, the earth, the stars, and your freedom. It's all out there." No words.
>
> And how to show that he was generous? With money and energy. He swam in the motel pool with my daughters on his back. He seemed like one of

> those ageless Galápagos tortoises, living rocks which burgeon out of the sea, encrusted with the centuries, stubbornly enduring and waddling about their beachy turf.

This is a late moment in the novel, when the father is trying to save his son's marriage, and what the writer has in mind, obviously enough, is a statement of achieved recognition and clear declaration, a lyrical directness of insight. But shouldn't the language seem to have cost him more, and to make a more exact sense? The word "familiars" sounds more meaningful than it is, and I have trouble connecting its meaning with the sentence that follows. But the more important question is about the painful element in the father's behavior that the passage claims to have understood and accepted. What is that element, what needed such imaginative understanding as to justify this *vox humana* tone when understanding has been achieved? It cannot surely have been just the father's lack of sophisticated self-awareness about love or the language of love; it must, just as surely, have been that the father's behavior diminished the son, denied him dignity as a person and a man? Why isn't this mentioned? The second sentence protests too much and too easily; the lyrical amplification of the father's unspoken generosity is decisively sentimental; the grandiloquent metaphor of the Galápagos tortoise is self-conscious fine writing. I think Mr. Gold has sold himself short, and the sad thing is that he has also encouraged our disbelief in the father he hoped to honor.—ROBERT GARVIS, "Varieties of the Will," *HdR*, Summer 1967, pp. 329–30

. . . It would be nice to report that in *Swiftie the Magician* Herbert Gold has somehow redeemed a career that hasn't seemed to get anywhere for quite a few years and books. It turns out, however, that after he finished writing about his father and his boyhood in Cleveland, Gold never really had materials for a novel, and *Swiftie* is notable mostly as an honorable holding action, a serious attempt to do the work he still can do. It is self-consciously about the sixties, Camelot in New York, flower children in California, everyone splitting at the end. It was not a good decade to be With It unless one was very young, and Gold's hero suffers because he has only ambition and slick talent to keep him going, and this isn't enough to keep him from doing what everyone else does. Gold himself suffers because he wants to use the hero to see and comment on the scene while at the same time indicating that this vision is limited, and he just isn't interested enough in his not interesting hero to work out his relation to hero and scene carefully. Which leaves him with his commentary, some of which I found rather good, much better than that in Gold's *Age of Happy Problems*, though as the following will show, the good commentary tends to lapse rather too often into easy satire:

> In London Karen would have been distinctly another class—the pretty shopgirl who becomes a model. But this was the time of Swinging London everyplace, when nobody comes first, nobody comes from anyplace but Liverpool. . . . The childhood sound of leaves on windows was, for Karen, the sound of tires spitting gravel as the short-order motel visitors pulled up to pay their three-hour rental to her father. The trailers stayed longer, the Shevies and Pontiacs were brief about it. When she saw tumbleweed on television, the old west, cowboys, Indians, lawmen, she never guessed it was the same tumbleweed which slipped across the freeway to float in the swimming pool. It was Karen who stood there with a scoop, cursing her teenie curses at age thirteen (fuckit, fuckit, fuckit) and cleaning the Polyduramite-Spartan-Aqualon pool.

Commentary that knows neither fictional surroundings nor the integrity of a vision almost always is going to have troubles with tone and sustenance, but Gold tries hard here to keep it all going, and he knows enough now to see that *Swiftie* must be a short book; no mammoth Helleresque insistences for him. So even as it disappoints, it does not depress.—ROGER SALE, "Fooling Around, and Serious Business," *HdR*, Winter 1974–75, pp. 628–29

Waiting for Cordelia is soggy with stale crumbs from the bottom of the Great American Crackerbarrel—'perfection means you are what you are'—and the earth-mother heroine is too sweet'n'sad to be true. When she is not big-heartedly giving her clients 'specials' at a cut price, Cordelia is 'squeezing away at the fret in her heart'. Al is a sad sack, too. He wants 'to link my stiff wet lonely soul with the welcoming wet soul of someone'. There is altogether too much 'wet soul' in this ramblingly episodic book. Gold is at his best when he abandons his folksy philosophising and just tells funny stories. Have you heard the one about the girl who sent her widowed mother, as a birthday present, a catalogue for 'Adult Eros Industries' featuring such sex-aids as 'finger extensions for sanitary sensuality'?—JOHN MELLORS, "Roman Road," *LT*, Sept. 7, 1978, p. 319

HARRY T. MOORE
"The Fiction of Herbert Gold"
Contemporary American Novelists, ed. Harry T. Moore
1964, pp. 170–81

A television producer once said to Herbert Gold, "I don't think you understand what we want. We want happy stories about happy people with happy problems." Gold in his fiction often displays a fine sense of comedy, but his characters don't have happy problems. Even at his poorest—and there are times when his people and situations don't rise above the commonplace—Herbert Gold never serves up the fake hopes and wistful outcomes of the popular-entertainment serial. If he calls one of his novels *The Optimist*, his intent is ironical.

And if he plays rather freely with irony, he can also be nostalgic, as in *Therefore Be Bold* and in such short stories as "The Heart of the Artichoke." But he lacks sentimentalism, that condition whose bedazzled victim simply expects too much of life. Gold's latest novel is called *Salt:* beyond certain symbolic and leitmotiv uses of the title-word in that particular book, the idea it suggests covers a good part of his writing, which is so often strong-tasting and somewhat acrid.

Another feature of his work which is always noticeable is his use of language. Herbert Gold is a neat stylist, sometimes too neat. He can upon occasion master words, use them to bring out exactly what he needs to say about people and incidents; but he often slips too easily into rhetoric. He has a sensitivity for the nuances of speech and can frequently catch the precise accent, rhythm, and tone of dialogue and dialect. But here too he can slip, simply by making the characters themselves speak a little too brightly, as for example in *Salt*. On the other hand, in *The Man Who Was Not With It*, Gold's use of carnival idiom is exactly in key. He shows its tricks of insincerity, an important part of the story, but also displays its force in expressing the deepest feelings of the people who speak it.

In a specific consideration of Gold's fiction, perhaps the best place to begin is with the collection of short stories he brought out in 1960, after he had published four novels. This collection, *Love and Like*, is in one sense a summary of Gold's career, even extending beyond that volume and into his fifth and sixth novels. Fortunately it contains much of Herbert Gold at his best, and can therefore indicate why he is worth talking about here. Similarly, his book of essays, *The Age of Happy Problems* (1962), helps toward a fuller understanding of Gold's fiction.

The gem among the *Love and Like* stories is "The Heart of the Artichoke," of which Gold has written that it "was personally crucial because it gave me a sense that I was now my own man. I had written other stories and a first novel, *Birth of a Hero*, but with this story I felt that I had discovered myself as a writer in some conclusive way." He has also said of this product of 1951, "by writing it I learned to be a writer. I had a sense of mastering my experience. Not just examining, not just using, but *riding* my world, with full sense of my faculties in the open air . . . After writing a heavily influenced, heavily constructed first novel—to prove I could learn from others—I was ready to throw a rock at the Henry James hive, a rock even at the great juicy Dostoyevsky swarm, and secrete my own gathered sweets into my own homemade jug."

The story, tender without being sentimental, is the first-person narrative of Daniel Berman, a Jewish grocer's son in Cleveland. It concerns his conflicts with his parents and his pubescent fixation upon a girl he meets at school. The blonde little Pattie Donahue has "aquarium eyes, profoundly green, profoundly empty, and a mouth like a two-cent Bull's Eye candy, and pale transparent fingers busy as fins"—which anticipates the imagery and symbolism taken from marine life in some of the later work. In the "Artichoke" story these devices are at least right for the ruefully humorous evocation of the ecstasies and miseries of a twelve-year-old boy's vision of an unattainable girl. Daniel Berman knows he is "no Culver Academy athlete calling for Pattie Donahue in his uniform at Christmastime"—Daniel, who has to work in his father's store, is what Pattie, not with contempt but with realism, calls a grocery boy. Daniel at the end of the story engages his father in a physical struggle whose meaning he realizes only with the passing of the years, when he writes the experience down.

Daniel Berman and his strikingly portrayed family appear in other stories in *Love and Like*, one of them ("Aristotle and the Hired Thugs") a brisk tale of the father's adventures in bargaining with truck farmers in the Cleveland marketplace during the depression. But most of the stories, including the one that gives the book its title, are about a young man who in the accumulation of experience becomes almost mythically representative. He is the lower-bourgeois intellectual of the junior-executive, assistant-professor generation, and maybe he is, under different names, various phases of Daniel Berman grown up.

In the *Love and Like* stories, under those different names but carrying a single temperament, he has wife troubles, visits France or Haiti on grants, tangles with his girl students, and wistfully thinks of the child or children taken from him by divorce. He earnestly confronts a gallery of richly assorted characters, including several versions of the embittered wife, a retired French colonel of fascist persuasion, an attractive but treacherous Finnish girl of the hipster faith, a pathetic husband of the "other woman," and some robust Haitians. They and others help to make these stories in their totality a crowded and lively chronicle of a young American's wide range of experience.

Here and there a failure appears, such as "Susannah at the Beach." With echoes of the Apocrypha, this allegory of innocence tells of a girl who accidentally rips her bathing suit open while diving and then, after jeers from a coarse lakeside beach crowd, swims out toward the horizon and probable suicide, for which her motivation is as flimsy as her easily shredded beachwear. Gold also includes a story about a messiah, one Jim Curtis (note the initials), who at thirty-three enters upon his ministry. Although more imaginatively credible than the "Susannah" episode, this story again indicates that the heavily symbolic and the transcendental have their dangers for such writers as Herbert Gold, who work most effectively in the tangible but, when they try to soar, all too often get caught in skytraps.

But in the stories about little Daniel Berman and the various young men whom I have designated as representative, Gold avoids both the mood sketch and the tricky ending. He shows that he can dramatically develop his people and project his scene in a narrative which, although complete in its limited space, often suggests the massiveness of a novel. Gold has noted that there is a difference between short stories (really just "a peek") and novels, which have a larger mission ("to explore possibility"). Yet the stories, in accumulation—except for the two I have called failures—have somewhat the effect of a novel and its "possibility." This is one of the main reasons why *Love and Like* is more than just another collection of stories and may be used to help give perspective to Herbert Gold's entire career so far.

The same year as his "Artichoke" story, 1951, he brought out his first novel, *Birth of a Hero*, a quite different kind of work, the book he referred to as being somewhat derivative and deliberately formal. This is one of his rare fictional efforts in which stylistic effects are muted. Reuben Flair, a middle-aged lawyer, has never realized his potential; when a good-looking neighbor, Lydia Fortiner, who passes for a widow, states that Flair is really a hero, Mrs. Flair says, "He's my husband. Why should he be a hero?" Flair has a love affair with Lydia, in itself unheroic, though it is the first time he has really been in love. There is a comic complication when Lydia's brother, Larry, turns up and camps on the Flairs. A mockery of the heroic, he fascinates them, in their different ways, with his rapid-fire and sometimes shocking anecdotes of his life as a drifter. But the situation can't last, for Larry finally reveals that he is really Lydia's husband. But he can't go on, either, and takes poison. The Flairs resume their marriage, with Reuben apparently becoming a better husband and father, heroic in rather unheroic and everyday activities. As a first novel, it is unusually mature. Reread today, it seems less exciting than when it first came out, and seemed so "promising." Nevertheless, the reader can still admire the author's grasp of character and at times his inventiveness. Ultimately, however, the story is an exploration of the commonplace which doesn't quite transfigure the commonplace.

The next book, *The Prospect Before Us* (1954), is considerably flashier. And it is in many ways a good story; not the traditional let-down of a young man's second novel. Once again avoiding autobiographical elements such as those which predominate in the short stories, Gold deals with a type of man quite different from a young writer just turning thirty. This is an immigrant hotel owner in Cleveland's honky-tonk district. He is fairly successful until confronted with a problem when the "Association" that is fighting racial discrimination moves an attractive Negro girl into the hotel of which Harry Bowers is so proud. The guests make threats and then begin to move out; Harry Bowers stands firm against them and the rival association of businessmen which threatens him. Even the official representatives of the community, the police, mistreat him. The girl, Claire Farren, is isolated from her own people as she lives on in the almost-deserted hotel. Harry too is cut off, and he is drawn erotically to Claire.

But what of the hotel, which has become a liability? Harry's rootless and disaffected roomclerk, Jake, insinuates to him that the building could be burned down for its insurance. Harry slowly yields to this idea and involves his weak brother in the plot. On the night of the fire, Harry mistakenly believes that Claire is in the building, and when he rushes in to rescue her he goes to his villain's and hero's death. This is melodrama rather than anything that might be said to resemble the tragic, and it is a resolving of the story which, along with the often-too-rhetorical language of the style, reduces the value of the book. For there is much in it that is expertly done, particularly the technical details of hotel operation; the author has made himself thoroughly familiar with the milieu and its properties.

Yet there is always that intrusive rhetoric: "The eyes of Jake roamed the dogdays morning sky with a conman's monkeyshine tricks of gaze, doomed to flesh but yearning away from it, asking faith and please-believe-me." In another passage of description and motive, the author writes of Jake: "He giggled and teased, and wiggle-waggled his chin and his Bailey Brothers pants behind, and pleaded across the counter to Harry: Hurry up and love me quick, somebody." Of course much of this may be excused as the work of a young writer groping toward expressional skill.

The most striking episode in the novel doesn't take place at Harry's Green Glade Hotel, but rather in Nancy's notch house, which is the opposite of Harry Bowers' place, even to the point of its being in the good part of the city rather than in the skid-row section. At Nancy's, sexual acts are performed before a small group of spectators. One girl who is watching runs out to vomit. Harry Bowers, who doesn't vomit and stays to watch, sees a mingling of black and white (Negro man, white girl) that underscores his relation with Claire. And the very name of the proprietor, Nancy, suggests another parallel: the implicit homosexuality of Jake and the unconscious homosexuality of Harry's brother, Morris. Indeed, the book is excellently plotted, marred somewhat by the ending (Jake dies in the fire also) and considerably by its extravagant idiom, of which examples have been given.

Gold's next novel, *The Man Who Was Not With It*, came out in 1956 and, because I consider it his best, will save discussion of it for later, meanwhile dealing with *The Optimist*, *Therefore Be Bold*, and *Salt*. Burr Fuller, the center of attention in *The Optimist* (1959), is one of today's schizoid Americans who at mid-life find themselves split between an urge to make slow but steady progress and a compulsion to keep speeding frantically ahead. This kind of American futility has so often been presented that it can now be taken as a basis for serious literature only when the treatment of it sounds new depths. *The Optimist* doesn't do that; it is mostly a skillful reflection of surfaces.

The first part of the story is by far the more successful in its treatment of even such overworked themes as campus life and the second world war. The University of Michigan phase of Burr's youthful experience has some sardonic bits of anthropological value: fraternity life and campus eroticism. In describing Burr's army years, Gold's gift of realistic observation is given full play. In his use of dialogue here he shows that he has an eager and expert ear for regional varieties of speech, and among his characters in that first part of the book he includes some out-of-the-way personalities of the kind that appeared so zestfully in his first three novels.

After the war, there is a ten-year hiatus in the story, 1946–56, and from this point on the narrative never quite picks up again as it takes Burr through the later stages of an unhappy marriage. He is a successful lawyer in Detroit who decides to run for Congress; outwardly he seems to be a man of principle but inwardly he is tricky. His former campus sweetheart, now his wife and the mother of his two children, is hungry for barbiturates and the psychoanalyst's couch. Burr in the sweep of his political campaign takes on an attractive young mistress, and the complications which result make the evasive optimist aware of the jagged division in his nature. But this last part of the book, with its suburban agonizings and all too sketchily presented picture of politics, fails to fulfill the promise of the first part. These later sections fail to bring to the hackneyed themes the freshness they need.

Little can be said about Gold's next novel, *Therefore Be Bold* (1960), except that it is charming. It is also unambitious and indeed hardly seems to be a novel at all, but rather a memoir of what it was like to be adolescent in Cleveland in the 1930s. Daniel Berman reappears, along with some of his friends, including the attractive Pattie Donahue, with her fin-like hands; Pattie plays a very small part here, and a brief epilogue reveals that she later became a social worker. Most of the book is a joyous, youthful romp; Dan Berman is interested in the verse-writing Eva Masters, who has an antisemitic father. In portraying her family, Herbert Gold once again draws upon the marine imagery through which he often sees people: "The Masters home was a house of crabs. They obscurely swarmed; they moved sideways over each other, claws everywhere." But Dan evades their claws, and he isn't taken by the finny hands of Pattie Donahue, but rather by the harpist's fingers of Lucille Lake, whom he will ultimately marry. This book, which took its author more than ten years to write its less than two hundred and fifty pages, is an attempt to see life through the hot-eyed innocence of youth. The vision may not be deep, but the picture of adolescent, depression-era morals is vital and attractive.

Salt (1963) is highly ambitious and, except for a surprisingly strong conclusion, seems to me somewhat of a failure, at least in not realizing all the ambitions it implicitly announces. It is the story of two men and a woman. Peter Hatten, a young Wall Street broker, plays girls as he plays the market, and in order to keep in shape practices juggling, a tricky pastime. The other leading male character is Peter's friend, Daniel Shaper, who appeared in the story "Love and Like" as the young man with a broken marriage who had gone to revisit his native Cleveland and exercise his right to see his children occasionally. He might well be Daniel Berman grown up and living in New York, working for a successful semi-intellectual magazine. The girl in *Salt* is Barbara Jones, up from the South. Peter has known her first and becomes weary of her; Dan becomes serious about her. Peter can't go on telling her he loves her—even the most strenuous juggling is easier—but Dan is essentially a family man, despite the unfortunate experience of his first marriage.

Salt is, among other things, an attempt at a full picture of New York life, or rather of the part of it where young Wall Streeters and Madison Avenuers play. Some of the characters are makers of pornographic films, but they are only comic background figures whose activities are a symbolic commentary on Peter's Casanova-like adventures. For Peter's love life is extensive and is devoutly described—Herbert Gold is the sharpest girl-watcher among American novelists. Peter knows a varied gallery of girls, and as Mr. Gold graphically shows him putting them through their paces, the book becomes among other things a Baedeker of the sex lives of young Americans living in Manhattan. Peter can't help going back to Barbara once, even after she has seriously become Dan's girl; so Dan beats up the juggler-athlete in a ferocious sidewalk fight. After this display, he has an even harder fight to win back Barbara, who has returned to her home in Virginia. "Peter's smart," she tells Dan, "he believes love is impossible. He tried his best to teach us. He did his best to convince us." But Dan, who believes in love, breaks through the barriers Barbara has put up. He offers marriage, but not in New York. Dan, whose thoughts and phrasing sometimes come from the Bible, tells Barbara she is the salt of the earth. This is in contrast to one of Peter's fantasies about himself in which the salt of the sea is his element and he is a quick fish swimming above "the monumental excrescences of tiny shellfish"; and in another of his fantasies he thinks of a continuous poker game, which he knows is crooked—and yet "he felt himself yearning to swim in it." Barbara and Dan are of a different substance and outlook; it is only after Dan's proposal that she tells him she is expecting his child.

The ending, as I noted before, has strength, with Dan accepting Barbara's lapse—she doesn't want to be "forgiven," so he merely "accepts." Unfortunately, however, the author, in attempting to show the falsity of New York existence, is too often too slick. The people he introduces are mostly fringe types of journalism, television, and show business, and far too epigrammatically clever. Some of their behavior reflects the results of the author's shrewd observation, but their speech is always sprinkled with verbal gold dust; the people talk like characters put forth by Scott Fitzgerald before he matured. That this level of New York social existence is glittering and brittle, the reader would hardly dispute, but the total effect of its representation here is one of a high artificiality, in which the dialogue makes the purposeful artificiality of the characters into something not always believable. That is, if one may use the expression, they are often just too artificially artificial. In these passages the author is of course trying for satire, and while he occasionally succeeds—once again, through the actions rather than the speech of his people—the satire is not sharply enough fanged to bite very deep.

Salt nevertheless shows Herbert Gold as still a writer of more than promise. Not long after completing it, he went to Haiti, the setting of some of his short stories, to work on what will apparently be a different kind of novel. He is still ambitiously trying. And while we wait for this further work, we have *The Man Who Was Not With It* as evidence of what Gold can accomplish when he brings together his varied gifts—observation, comedy, and ear for dialogue. And the moral implications usually found in Gold's fiction are all emphatically present in this book.

The novel tells the story of Bud Williams' two sojourns with a smalltime carnival, and of his return home between the two. Motherless, he had run away from the father he didn't like, but even in the life of the "Wide World and Tuscaloosa Too Shows" he hadn't found security and had become a dope addict. Then, forceful interference by the carnie's barker, Grack (Gracchus), cures him. Bud goes back home to Pittsburgh and an unsuccessful visit with his father; then heads south to pick up the show again. Relationships change; the small daughter of Pauline, the fortune teller, has budded: "She was a female already, and I knew I had been away for many months. She turned red at the sight of me. At last someone meant welcome home." Grack, the substitute father, is no longer there; Bud marries Joy Deland, Pauline's daughter, in one of the carnival tents, with a small-town Southern minister presiding. That night, Bud finds a thief trying to open the carnival owner's safe and says, "Hello, Grack. Did you know I got married tonight?" Bud and Joy drive north for their honeymoon, aiming for Niagara Falls and the border of Canada, the native country of "Frenchie" Grack, who goes with them from motel to motel. Joy is pregnant. A stop in Cleveland includes a visit to Nancy's notch house, which Gold had written about earlier in *The Prospect before Us*. Calamities abound: Joy loses her child, and Bud loses his desperate fight to cure Grack of the drug addiction into which he has sunk; he fights to help him, in the phrasing of this milieu, kick the habit. Grack winds up in the arms of the police, and Bud and Joy settle in Pittsburgh, friends now of Bud's father, and have a son, whom Bud's father wants brought up "to be with it." But even for people who have, in carnie lingo, become squares, this isn't easy.

The Man Who Was Not With It—in the few years of its paperback existence rather wildly called *The Wild Life*—is a book to which synopsis can't do justice. It can merely indicate some of the main trends of the story. Herbert Gold has marvelously captured carnival life, with its lures for markers and its fights with rubes, all the excitement and tinsel and struggle. Grack is the most successful of the author's vitalistic characters, and to hear him giving his pitch on the midway, with his "lookee" and his "hee hee hee" and "ho ho ho," is to be in the gusty atmosphere of the fairgrounds. In having Bud tell the story in carnie slang, Gold makes full use of his own ability to handle colorful idiom. It crackles. But the language isn't flashed just for its own sake; it is organic. Through it, the author is able to present nuances of character and investigate the depths of his particular kind of people in a way which would have been less intimate with straight language. Herbert Gold's tendency toward the bizarre in style exactly matches the subject matter in this book.

Let me say once again that the whole novel needs to be read for its story to be appreciated. And it is a good story, one of a redemption or partial redemption, and of a failing attempt at redemption. To use this last word is to oversimplify, something which Herbert Gold avoids doing in this story. But the word is a kind of semaphore to indicate partially what happens in the novel. And such matters, involving important changes in character, are never simple, as Bud carefully suggests at the end of the book. Commenting on his father's wish to have his grandson brought up "to be with it," Bud concludes: "Joy and I had other ideas. We will not—and cannot—pull our son out of the way of our own hard times. They go on. There's a good and with it way to be not with it, too."

A number of good novels came out of America in the 1950s. *The Man Who Was Not With It* ranks among the best of them. It is reassuring to know that Herbert Gold, who is in his early forties, is still trying, despite some recent rather harsh, or at least unappreciative, criticisms of his work. He has the potential. And he has not succumbed to the temptation that besets so many of our authors: to write about happy problems.

AP/WIDE WORLD PHOTOS

HERBERT GOLD

AP/WIDE WORLD PHOTOS

ELLEN GLASGOW

UPI/BETTMANN NEWSPHOTOS

ALLEN GINSBERG

AP/WIDE WORLD PHOTOS

GAIL GODWIN

JOHN GRUEN/AP/WIDE WORLD PHOTOS

HORACE GREGORY

AP/WIDE WORLD PHOTOS

ZANE GREY

AP/WIDE WORLD PHOTOS

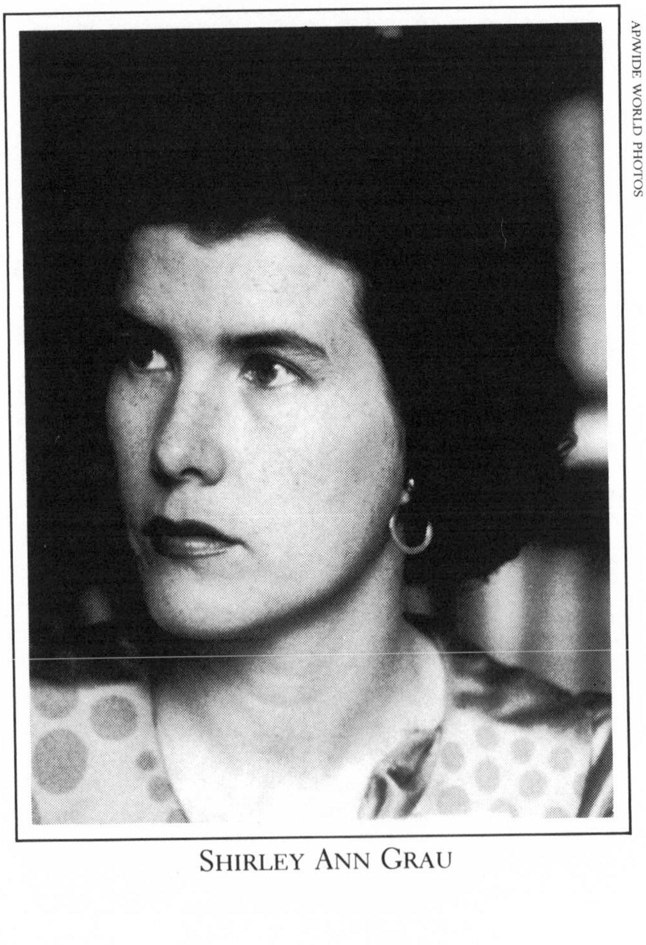

SHIRLEY ANN GRAU

Paul Goodman

1911–1972

Paul Goodman was born in New York City on September 9, 1911. His father, a failing businessman, abandoned the family before his birth, and he was raised mainly by his older sister. After an outstanding high school career, he majored in philosophy at the City College of New York, graduating in 1931. He later studied literature and philosophy at the University of Chicago from 1936 to 1940, completing his doctorate in 1954.

Determined from an early age to be a writer, Goodman was irregularly employed in the 1930s and 1940s while working on poetry, fiction, and other projects. Having received a fellowship from the American Council of Learned Societies in 1940, he published a volume of poems, *Stoplight*, in 1941, his first novel, *The Grand Piano*, in 1942, and a collection of stories, *The Facts of Life*, in 1945. His developing anarchist views are expressed in the essays *Art and Social Nature* (1946), and the following year a book on urban planning, *Communitas*, written with his brother Percival, was published. Goodman taught intermittently, but ran into trouble on account of his overt homosexuality. From 1946 he received psychoanalytic therapy, and from 1950 to 1960 practiced as a therapist himself. His book *Gestalt Therapy*, written with F. S. Perls and R. Hefferline, appeared in 1951.

It was as a social critic that Goodman achieved prominence in the 1960s. *Growing Up Absurd: Problems of Youth in the Organized System* (1960) made him famous, and further works attacking social and educational institutions followed, such as *Compulsory Mis-Education* (1964). He became active in protest movements, speaking out against nationalism, war, and state interference in individual sex life.

In addition to his writings on education, politics, moral philosophy, religion, and psychology, Goodman continued to produce poetry, fiction, and drama. *The Empire City*, a multiple novel, appeared in 1959, the memoir-novel *Making Do* in 1963, and the stories *Adam and His Works* in 1968. *Three Plays* (1965) comprises *The Young Disciple*, produced in 1955, *Faustina*, produced in 1952, and *Jonah*, produced in 1966. *The Lordly Hudson: Collected Poems* was published in 1962, and a final *Collected Poems* posthumously in 1974.

Goodman, who lived for the most part in New York City and at his farm near North Stratford, New Hampshire, began a common-law marriage with Sally Duchsten in 1945. The couple had one son, who died in 1967, and they were still together at the time of Goodman's death of a heart attack at his home in New Hampshire on August 2, 1972.

Goodman's poetry, as one might expect from his career as a critic of American mores and institutions, is filled with forthright political statement, following the model of Wordsworth and Shelley in such matters. His 'April 1962' begins:

> My countrymen have now become too base,
> I give them up. I cannot speak with men
> not my equals.

This is Goodman at his bluntest. One sees a subtler, though equally heartfelt, expression of his views in 'The Lordly Hudson,' title poem of his 1962 collected volume. For many years he has advanced a half-mystical conception of the relation between our civilization and its neglect of the resources that should be made available to the citizenry. The passionate outcry of this poem is an indirect protest but at the same time a spontaneous outburst of love for the river—patriotic love, in fact—and pain at its neglect:

> Be still, heart! no one needs your passionate
> suffrage to select this glory,
> this is our lordly Hudson hardly flowing
> under the green-grown cliffs.

One might view Goodman's work as in some degree a throwback to the romantic and polemical style of the best popular poets of the last century. To some extent his refusal to internalize the ills of the age as thoroughly as many other modern poets do, obliterating their character as social issues and offering up their own psyches as more interesting symbolic substitutes, points toward such a throwback. But there is a thoroughly contemporary side to his poetic style and thought as well. It is seen in the lighthearted sequence 'Poems of My Lambretta,' which has to do with the poet and his motorbike. The doughty, slangy tone Goodman employs is not merely for the sake of humor and immediacy. He is, rather, presenting himself as a chivalric figure, vulnerable and dauntless despite his weaknesses and despite the demeaning world he inhabits—a New York Don Quixote, in short. The bike has a pennant, sewn for him by his lady; he prays to Castor and Pollux ('from cops preserve me') and rides out for adventure. His pride is provincial but noble:

> I never had to jam the brakes
> for I am a New Yorker bred,
> the light is green all my road.

A more introspectively moving note is introduced in the third poem of the sequence, which begins confessionally and ends in exaltation; the speaker here is at once Paul Goodman and the poet of this age, swiftly carried through the débris of the modern with his head stll full of the past:

> Dirty and faded
>   is the banner of my bike
> and tattered in the winds
>   of journey like
> my self-esteem my soiled
>   repute my faded hope.

But at the end:

on glad our windy way
  nowhere, going forty!
Flapping is my flag,
  faded torn and dirty,
and on the buddy-seat
  there rides Catullus dead
and speaks to me in gusts of shouts,
  I dare not turn my head.

Finally, Goodman has written still more inward poems that bring his work into rapport with the confessional tendency of the age—particularly his poems about love, both homosexual and normal, and poems like 'Long Lines' that recall the sonnets of Wordsworth (or the tone of his and Coleridge's odes) but are thoroughly modern in their dislocations of syntax and of the hexameter pattern, their shifts of focus, their specific diction, and, most important, their essential attitude:

The heavy glacier and the terrifying Alps
that simply I cannot, nor do I know the pass,
block me from Italy. As winter closes in,
just to survive I hole up in this hovel
with food that has no taste, no one to make love to
but fantasies and masturbating, sometimes sobbing
South! South! where white the torrent splashes down
past Lugano.

—M. L. ROSENTHAL, "Epilogue: American Continuities and Crosscurrents," *The New Poets*, 1967, pp. 313–16

He had been a hero of mine for so long that I was not in the least surprised when he became famous, and always a little surprised that people seemed to take him for granted. The first book of his I ever read—I was sixteen—was a collection of stories called *The Break-up of Our Camp*, published by New Directions. Within a year I had read everything he'd written, and from then on started keeping up. There is no living American writer for whom I have felt the same simple curiosity to read as quickly as possible *anything* he wrote, on any subject. That I mostly agreed with what he thought was not the main reason; there are other writers I agree with to whom I am not so loyal. It was that voice of his that seduced me—that direct, cranky, egotistical, generous American voice.

Many writers in English insist on saturating their writing with an idiosyncratic voice. If Norman Mailer is the most brilliant writer of his generation, it is surely by reason of the authority and eccentricity of his voice; and yet I for one have always found that voice too baroque, somehow fabricated. I admire Mailer as a writer, but I don't really believe in his voice. Paul Goodman's voice is the real thing. There has not been such a convincing, genuine, singular voice in our language since D. H. Lawrence. Paul Goodman's voice touched everything he wrote about with intensity, interest, and his own terribly appealing sureness and awkwardness. What he wrote was a nervy mixture of syntactical stiffness and verbal felicity; he was capable of writing sentences of a wonderful purity of style and vivacity of language, and also capable of writing so sloppily and clumsily that one imagined he must be doing it on purpose. But it never mattered. It was his voice, that is to say, his intelligence and the poetry of his intelligence incarnated, which kept me a loyal and passionate addict. Though he was not often graceful as a writer, his writing and his mind were touched with grace.

There is a terrible, mean American resentment toward someone who tries to do a lot of things. The fact that Paul Goodman wrote poetry and plays and novels as well as social criticism, that he wrote books on intellectual specialties guarded by academic and professional dragons, such as city planning, education, literary criticism, psychiatry, was held against him. His being an academic freeloader and an outlaw psychiatrist, while also being so smart about universities and human nature, outraged many people. That ingratitude is and always was astonishing to me.

. . . It has never been clear to most people, I think, what an extraordinary figure he was. He could do almost anything, and tried to do almost everything a writer can do. Though his fiction became increasingly didactic and unpoetic, he continued to grow as a poet of considerable and entirely unfashionable sensibility; one day people will discover what good poetry he wrote. Most of what he said in his essays about people, cities, and the feel of life is true. His so-called amateurism is identical with his genius: that amateurism enabled him to bring to the questions of schooling, psychiatry, and citizenship an extraordinary, curmudgeonly accuracy of insight and freedom to envisage practical change.—SUSAN SONTAG, "On Paul Goodman," *NYRB*, Sept. 21, 1972, p. 10

According to George Dennison, there is to be found in all of Goodman's work the same insistent theme, "the search for harmony of the life made by man and the life not made but given." In his essays he could exhort or propose (one of his books consists of letters written to various newspapers and journals), and thus participate in what was "made by man"; for poetry he reserved the "given," the world in what often seemed to him its intransigence and even cruelty. Poem after poem laments the irrational society fashioned by Adam (his antonomasia for man), the tedious errors of history:

What is it with this race that does not learn?
I am weary for meaning and they tire
my soul with great deeds. Yet I cannot turn
my eyes from the stupid story in despair:
since I have undertaken to be born,
Adam, Adam is my one desire.

His anger against those responsible for Vietnam is no less constant; everywhere he sees "the vast wreck of common sense and justice," and is torn between patriotism and intense resentment. The world of his concerns, humane and cultured, was violated so consistently that there were times when he could only complain, and bitterly. . . .

In *Speaking and Language*, subtitled (echoing Sidney and Shelley) "Defence of Poetry," Goodman emphasized the importance of colloquial speech in his writing. He was a master of idiom, a brilliant stylist who knew how to turn language into a subtle instrument responsive to what he saw. One of his most original poems, "Epode. The New Bus Terminal," celebrates in ironic high style the completion of the Port Authority, alternating between the grandiose ("this new / this marvel where the buses overhead / roar to the provinces") and the demotic ("so I came inside / out of the lousy season"). In this he was like Delmore Schwartz, whose comic, exaggerated poetry took advantage of the tradition in order to satirize or elevate his subject.

More than Schwartz, though, I would say that Goodman's poems resemble Berryman's late religious phase. Less metered, less intense than Berryman's "Address to the Lord," much of Goodman's poetry is in the form of prayer, the wish to speak directly with God. His theology was uncomplicated, wanting only explanations about why things were as they were, and was expressed, like all his poetry, in the most economical speech possible. Toward the end of his life, he seems to have become resigned to a condition he was powerless to alter:

Despairing to be happy any more,
on the other hand I am not much in pain,
I can work, and sometimes from my pen
such lovely sentences of English pour
as I am proud of for their casual grandeur
nor will, when I am dead, they be forgotten;
I look about and I am as most men as happy.
Yet my spirit is still sore
with disappointment of the paradise
lost that I could not enter; a hard question
haunts me. "Is life worth it as it is?"

Because he wrote so copiously, these poems vacillate between Utopian hope and a sort of Nietzschean stubbornness; one can learn from them nearly all the details of Goodman's own life, the trials encountered, the successes and loss.

I don't mean to make too large a claim for these poems. They depend on what he called elsewhere "the glorification of simple overt acts," and often require patience to read through simply because their intentions are so limited. Goodman wrote poetry with a deliberate awkwardness. Perhaps he thought it would be more democratic to practice a style so plain and rude. His own estimate of his work was rather high; but he was surely accurate in this lines:

I have among the Americans
the gift of honest speech
that says how a thing is
—if I do not, who will do it?

—JAMES ATLAS, "First Person," *NR*, March 2, 1974, p. 31

As a writer, Goodman was a naturalist who analyzed human behavior and thought, often using his own as a model on which to center investigation. He was a Gestaltist, and his insistence was to see an object in its field, particularly where field and object touch. He became widely known in 1960 for *Growing Up Absurd*, an analysis of youth gangs, junior executives and Beats, written at the time *Life* magazine was running inspirational pieces on "Our National Purpose," and the nations were fighting the cold war. In this book Goodman argued that people had hardly any world to live in, even less to devote themselves to except, perhaps, the little life in the stances their egos had managed to eke out for them.

He, too, had etched, as a poet and writer, a self from the blocks of his intelligence and passion:

Fatherless I was, nobody offered
me to the muses. I imposed on them.

And done it in a world that he felt hindered not only his but most people's fundamental needs. He did not take seriously such a notion as a nation's providing a purpose. Psychologist and anarchist, Goodman knew that the realities of nations take one too far from actual experience and satisfaction (or disappointment) and, therefore, become dangerous. His poetry often records an encounter, in himself, where words and experience become each other, where experience is named into being and the boundaries of the self are discovered.—NEIL HEIMS, "Who Sang the Lordly Hudson," *Nation*, June 29, 1974, pp. 824–25

KINGSLEY WIDMER
From "Several American Perplexes"
The Literary Rebel
1965, pp. 188–92

The alienation from most literary merit as well as incisive human context marks most of the poetry collected in *The Lordly Hudson*. From the title on, the scenes and forms are quaintly synthetic and this Goodman cannot, in contrast to some of his contemporaries, wittily play with because he lacks "natural" talent: a dead ear ("poetical" often), lack of sensory responses, taste for the flat generality, earnest sentimentality, and no redeeming concreteness. Only a few idiosyncrasies manage to find their own shape: the middle-aged bitterness around a sentimental image ("Birthday Cake"), the gross and therefore sometimes effective flatness about self-importance (several of the "Sentences for Mathew Ready"), and the reversal of poetic pretension in an apostrophe to his penis ("Dishonored Sex").[1] The love poems, the narratives of things never seen, and the prayers to something or other may have some private therapeutic significance. The fantastic self-conceit—the major subject of his verse—makes Goodman deserve the insult he unironically asks for: finally my country-men/ will make of me a statue in the park."[2] Often as a writer (as well as for this characteristically garbled syntax) he deserves to be stuck alive into a concrete pedestal.

Yet his very weirdness makes Goodman a suggestive voice, despite the absurd literary pretensions. As he rightly notes of himself, his "words and behavior [sometimes have] a random freedom that unsettles people" in a provocative way.[3] Social "edification" (his word) from the fanciful perspective of a dissociated utopian roughjack of letters can be, like a drunk giving a demonstration of first-aid, both unintentionally comic and didactically salutary. In endless angry moral ruminations, from the anarchist theorizing in rather academic terms of *Art and Social Nature*[4] through the cranky-perceptive letters to editors and officials collected in *The Society I Live in Is Mine*[5] (with righteous footnotes added), Goodman hectors all ways of the villainous "Organized System." In the main, the monster is damned for being too unimaginatively organized and too much of a system, i.e., not a confrontable and responsive human entity.

For an example of Dr. Goodman's quaint mixture of almost pedantic radical earnestness and of angrily whimsical eccentricity, we might note several of the motifs of *The Community of Scholars*. This academic critique charges after the "phony" ideology and bureaucratization of American higher education, and effectively cuts down a good many academic spokesmen. In an earlier (and excellent) piece on the modern academic man and his "freedom," Goodman held to view the university schizophrenia which so often submerges the rebellious intellectual in the organizational bureaucrat.[6] In his longer study, he elaborates the theme in a programmatic assault on the replacement of intellectual communion, especially of students and teachers, by "a community of administrators and scholars with administrative mentalities, company men and time-servers."[7] Outside the usual institutional loyalties and ambitions, he can be devastatingly apt on the pseudo-democracy of higher education with its administered concensus and ideologies which encourage mediocre teaching and intellectual vapidity. He raises the obvious, but usually ignored, drastic criticisms of officials, hierarchies, grades, credits, academic gamesmanship, and other authoritarian formalizations, which tend to devalue content, skill and responsiveness.[8] Conclusion: do away with them: no more ornate programs, ranks, big buildings, staffs, credits, grades, administrators and psuedo-intellectuals. An admirable extremity!

But Goodman is opposed to destructive criticism; as he announces elsewhere, "negative criticism insults and disheartens."[9] So he offers a "constructive" program—"secession." The pacifistic academic civil war can be waged by dedicated teachers and their protégés going away from the organized schools (but staying close enough to use the libraries) to form new, unadministered, "communities of scholars." Rebellious in its extreme refusal but oddly archaic in actual form, Goodman's proposal up-dates romantic notions of the Medieval university. Such a movement might have a refreshing openness to it, and could serve as an impetus to several small liberal arts colleges, though of course it would make only the most peripheral marks on the vast technician factories, research ranches, bureaucratic apprenticeship programs, cultural rest homes, genteel spectacles, class institutes—and occasional teaching and thought—which comprise the higher learning in America.

For those who would with equal earnestness reply to this unwitty Veblen that "No doubt much of this should be changed, but that really means a social revolution," his probable answer would be, "Of course. Let's get communally started." A utopian revolutionary demand thus gets lightly disguised as a practical pedagogical proposal. Such is Goodman's strategy. Actually, a report on a real educational situation might be rather more to the point, and have less over-insistent mannerisms of practicality in his mish-mash presentation, but Goodman aims at less revolutionary practice and utopian thought than rebellious irritant in the thickly hypocritical rhetoric of current higher education.

Another deceptively simple rebel motif appears in *The Community of Scholars*. Goodman really seeks to bring into community the alienated intellectuals, and rightly polemicizes against the organizers and imitations who are much the cause of the alienation. His major twist to his arguments on almost everything—and he argues about almost everything—is an individualistic anti-individualism. Ideas of community, whether about poetry or about stores, provide his persistent answer—partly a reaction against his own fractured consciousness, partly the Jewish sense of the community as the deepest entity, partly the legacy of the radical social ideologies' attacks on atomization by industrialist-capitalist-modernist forces. His educational example comes in arguing that "veteran" masters of professions should be teachers of communities of followers. (He must strangely pretend that philosophical, artistic and religious passions constitute recognizable professions in our society.) And he adds: "it is importantly because they are not on the faculty that artists and writers are so individualistic and fragmented as to be almost treasonable in co-operation with *l'infame*."[10] For the moment, he has amusingly forgotten that academic faculties belong to the infamous Organized System. (A present plethora of writer-artist academics also does not substantiate his point.) And then that curious equation of the "individualistic" and "treasonable."

To counter the Organized System, Goodman demands his smaller organized systems, euphemistically known as communities, run by egotistical master "professionals" instead of bland administrators. Rather than debate which system, in practice, would be nastier to individual freedom—one could sometimes prefer the large, educationally irrelevant, and bumbling educationists since their confusions, willy-nilly, allow some pedagogical and personal freedom—we should grant that Goodman yearns for something else. Once again, a literary rebel dreams of a religious caste of dedicated ones with independent identity and communal place and power. The historical-minded sceptic will note that Goodman never explores the tragic qualities of social change—not only the often disproportionate human price, but the transformation of utopias into anti-utopias. Even the large and shifty Organized System allows certain freedoms almost never permitted in small, and probably inherently self-tightening, communities. His anti-individualistic and anti-rebellious side comes out, for just one example, when Goodman talks about actual rather than ideal academies. He recommends "taking stupid rules whence they come, refraining anger." More specifically, he urges biting on a pipe to keep quiet. His natural obstreperousness, however, also leads him to admitting that this is "craven advice," and "spirit-breaking and probably even unhealthy."[11] Ruins a lot of pipes, too.

Notes

1. Paul Goodman, *The Lordly Hudson* (New York, 1962), p. 132; Parts 46 and 51 of "Mathew Ready"; and p. 158.
2. Ibid., p. 223; see, also, pp. 30, 43, 45, 56, 57, 77, 91, 157, 163, etc.
3. Paul Goodman, *Drawing the Line* (New York, 1962), p. 87. The best essay in this collection is the critique of liberal professors and similar people failing to act, "The Ineffectuality of Some Intelligent People," pp. 97 ff.
4. Paul Goodman (New York, 1946). The social essays are reprinted in *Drawing the Line.*
5. Paul Goodman (New York, 1963).
6. Paul Goodman, "The Freedom to Be Academic," *Growing Up Absurd* (New York, 1962), pp. 256 ff.
7. Paul Goodman, *The Community of Scholars* (New York, 1962), p. 74.
8. But Goodman is sometimes more earnest than serious, and does not probe the issues. He fails to note, for a representative example, that grading systems partly impersonalize—and free the intransigent from—the vicious "laying on of hands" traditions of academic recommendations and sycophancy. Similarly, much of the "value" of administrative neutralization of values is in allowing contradictory values, and people, to exist, which would not happen (especially to the best and rebellious) if a likely pedagogical ideology were in control. The freest places are rarely the small and committed institutions—and this probably applies broad scale through out social organizations.
9. *Drawing the Line*, p. 41—one of his hedges on drawing the line.
10. *The Community of Scholars*, p. 139. I discuss Goodman's academic piece at such length less from personal bias than because it expresses some of the basic concern of the rebellious intellectual with his own place in society, and has some paradigmatic value for all social organizations. I am not denying his basic point that much of our educational system and style is an outrageously hypocritical fraud carrying us toward "1984."
11. Ibid., p. 162.

EMILE CAPOUYE
"The Poet as Prophet"

Parnassus: Poetry in Review, Fall-Winter 1974, pp. 23–30

While he lived, Paul Goodman had little reputation as a poet, just as he had little reputation as a political thinker in the generally accepted sense of the term. There was misunderstanding in both cases. His well known activity as a social critic, dealing with moral, psychological, and cultural issues, tended to obscure his public character as artist, though he had written verse, short stories, plays, and the long novel, *The Empire City*. Indeed, he was known only to a small circle before the publication of *Growing Up Absurd*, the book that made him justly famous because it pointed out that the ideal of a vocation was no longer available to young Americans. He was right in saying so, and persuasive about what he took to be the consequences of that state of affairs. Even those readers to whom the discipline of a vocation was not an attractive ideal—and there must have been many such, for when the good is not to be had it is self-preservation not to hanker for it—could recognize Goodman's description of the psychological deformations and the social problems that were features of their own experience, even if they were not prepared to attribute those troubles to the absence of a directing passion. Accordingly, *Growing Up Absurd* put its seal upon Goodman's life thereafter. Much of his poetry, his plays, and his short fiction was issued in book form for the first time because of the success of that essay in sociology, and the novel, *Making Do*, might never have been conceived—let alone published—if the author had not come to be regarded by commercial publishers as a commercial property. But his more strictly literary works were naturally looked upon as mere by-blows of his talent, which had been classified once and for all as a talent for a particular kind of social analysis.

Goodman himself contributed to the general impression that his social insight had no political dimensions, and no political consequences. First, he made frequent and explicit denials of interest or competence in politics. In that connection, the anarchist tradition with which he identified himself had been accustomed to denounce politics as an activity—meaning the system of ideological pressure, regimentation, demagoguery, and parliamentary play-acting which was and is the dominant politics of the West. Goodman departed from his natural Aristotelian bent on this point out of a similarly short-sighted assumption that the politics he saw around him necessarily exhausted the practical and theoretical possibilities for the conduct of our public business. I recall Goodman's saying, in addressing a public gathering during the 1960's, that the white students who traveled to the South to take part in the integration movement then underway were mistakenly engaging in politics, in an activity that was not authentic because not personal to them. He added that instead of minding other people's business, they ought to deal with the problems they found on their own campuses, and agitate for the abolition of parietal rules and the legalization of marijuana. On that occasion, at any rate, Goodman felt that the issue of public decency posed by the status, in law and custom, of black Americans, could not be a genuine concern of whites—so narrowly did he define politics. Nevertheless, it is hardly conceivable that if he had been pressed on this general question, he would not have agreed with the Greek definition that makes man a political animal rather than a featherless biped—a creature, that is, who fashions organized societies at least partly by design, and whose accomplishments in those undertakings can be usefully criticized as better or worse.

Further, Goodman was eager to be loved and praised, perhaps more than most, because he had never said goodbye to his own feelings, and for that reason he felt his long eclipse to be a kind of painful exile. His special ambition was to be of use, and the pain of living for so long with that ideal unrealized may have made him diffident about those powers of his that were not blindingly obvious, at least to him. In talking about politics, which he persistently called by other names, diffidence sometimes made him sound arch, as if by way of apology. Or it allowed him to advance proposals that he called practical, without paying a decent attention to the revolution in our practice that would be a necessary precondition for instituting any of these. His political insight was profound. So much is clear from his shrewd diagnosis of our social troubles. But his political will was enfeebled, for he was a man of his time and experienced the discouragements that we all labor under.

And finally, another powerful reason why Goodman's talents in political speculation and poetry, too, have not been generally admitted is inherent in the nature of those talents as he expressed them. His powers, his very originality, had a homegrown, provincial cast, a Thoreauvian streak of cussedness that, as occasion offered, showed him foolish or sublime. He was very much taken with his own discoveries, which is one sign of genius, and prone to think them universally applicable—which can be another. At the same time he often chose to publish them in terms cranky enough to defeat their possible usefulness to his fellows. He wrote a book on the theory of literary criticism that drew its main categories from the work of Richard McKeon, and from that dark-lantern of a philosopher Goodman borrowed beams that he transmuted into something "not light but rather darkness visible," casting a glow of corposants and swamp-fire on familiar texts. The wonder is that shapes define themselves somehow in the murk, and persist when the book is closed and daylight returns: the work is as suggestive as it is unintelligible.

As a practical critic, however, Goodman was often first-rate. An example that shows him at the height of his powers is the essay on Hemingway's style that appeared some two years ago in the *New York Review of Books*. In it he analyzes the way in which Hemingway puts the words together, and like a good Aristotelian he describes the purpose that imposes the form: the effect upon the reader, and the moral and psychological satisfactions that, consciously or unconsciously, his author is pursuing. Characteristically, Goodman starts with what is near at hand, the choice of words and the shape of the sentences, remarks in passing that the Bible is the immediate source of Hemingway's method—an observation that in other hands could flower into a doctoral thesis—and directs our attention to what these literary questions have to do with the shape of our lives. The limpidity of the writing may disguise, for readers who have not considered these matters before, the depth and penetration of the essay. The even-tempered tone suggests that these are things that everyone knows, and indeed when Goodman has finished, his readers know them.

For provincial singularity of mind he was not unlike McKeon—or for that matter B. F. Skinner—save that his public discourse betrays a sense of humor, and that he was apt to chuck a notion into the discussion because it had occurred to him, departing in that way from the crookshank consistency of the one man and the monomaniac reasonableness of the other. But something of their perverse confidence in the luminous character of their private mysteries afflicts Paul Goodman's poetry, as it does often his political expedients, and his insistence that they are in fact expedient, and his denial that they are in any way political. But again, assurance is the first virtue of the poet or the lawgiver. In any case, his poems and his social designs, of extraordinary interest in themselves, are of a piece. Their congruent powers and limitations stand forth clearly when the two bodies of work are held in contemplation together. Considering one, we find hints of the best use to make of the other. And since the author of both is mostly disprized as a poet, or sayer of true things, and as a political thinker, or sayer of true things, it would be worthwhile to discuss those two functions of the man. But that is not the purpose of this essay.

To turn to the poetry, then, it is on the whole understandable that in any discussion of poets and "the state of poetry," Paul Goodman's name is not likely to be mentioned. He was in one respect remarkably unliterary, for he was always out of fashion; it is no small part of the literary gift to be interested in saying what an audience, any audience, is ready to hear. Goodman's contemporaries were not his audience—he was too simple, too impersonal, too patriotic for their taste. Mostly he addressed himself to a synod of the dead, or at least the unregenerate. For modern as he was in his appetite for "problems" and "solutions," he was archaic in his sense of what poetry is. The work itself is marked by his conception of it. He understood it as prophecy, which does not deal in problems or solutions, nor in those problems cut to the poor man's purse which inform the greater part of contemporary verse—the moods of the poet, his velleities of feeling, the monumentalization of the sentient ego—all things sanctified by the psychoanalytic religion. (I speak here of Goodman's best work. Like any other good poet, he wrote hundreds of honest trifles, some rubbish, and a scant handful of verses that showed him to be a master.) Prophecy, on the contrary, deals with the common life and fate. It is addressed to the common aspiration, and is intrinsically public. That is true of Paul Goodman's poems. Even though he writes in an age when the altars are abandoned, there is no received form of worship, and he must sometimes invent rites and mysteries that inevitably give a gnomic air to his utterance.

If he declared himself no politician, he certainly never denied his conviction of poetic election. His daemon addressed him as "most excellent poet," and he was frank to tell us so. He said it often in verse, referring with suitable modesty to "excellent sentences I make, better than any other man's"—and here it is clear that he meant not verses merely, but *sententiae*, opinions wrought with art and application, shibboleths for the host and sayings for the faithful. Apparently, too, he confessed his gift in casual conversation with the appropriate strangers. I met him at a gathering some thirteen years ago, and on his learning that I worked for a publisher who had undertaken to issue a good number of books of verse, he told me that I ought to interest myself in his work, for he wrote the best sonnets since Wordsworth. I thought him mad. But it turned out that he was acute about his own work. At least it appears to me that he wrote the best "Wordsworthian" sonnets since, say, Matthew Arnold. He is clumsy like Wordsworth, and sometimes as touchingly splendid.

What are the signs of his election? To start with the obvious, he has an instinct for rhetoric. He most often begins a sonnet by blurting out the most important thing he has to say. He is in good company. Shakespeare: Not marble nor the monuments of kings. . . . Milton: Avenge, O Lord, thy slaughtered saints! Goodman: My countrymen have now become too base. I give them up. What soldiers understand as the advantage of surprise, what musicians call in martial phrase "the attack," is one of Goodman's gifts. He does his hemming and hawing offstage. The poem is the occasion for vatic utterance, and he emerges like the Pythian priestess from the cave, wreathed in smoke and crying out what the god has given her to say. Then, too, his rhetoric turns without strain to a kind of homely grandeur, most Wordsworth-like. Even in a jocular sonnet, the sestet runs to a bardic strain.

> Dan, who adorns richly like duchesses
> ladies with sleek furs in our northern snows
> —the sea-lion that lay blotted on the flows,
> the mink that darted in the leafless trees:
> yet are not strong and heavy coats like these
> fitter for males, that have been the clothes
> of shepherds and woodmen and made grandiose
> the stature of kings during solemnities?
> Then as I see on our not vivid street
> spare men among the falling flakes flit by,
> I think, let Dan resume to glorify
> our knights with furs and make my city proud
> like seaports whither came the Hansa fleet,
> Hamburg, Luebeck, and Nijni-Novgorod.
> ("For Dan, the Furrier")

And the sestets especially of the first two of the group called "Four Sonnets":

> But *this* face of pain
> is mine, which I and all my family have;
> my mother wears it in her southern grave,
> my sister grown old woman has it, and
> my brother building buildings rich and grand.

And,

> Oh, when He bound my arms behind my back
> and threw me in the sea, I heard Him call
> "Swim! swim!" and so I have swum to this hour
> hopeless in cold water rough and black
> where many have already drowned and all
> *shall* drown in the swells that sink and tower.

In these times, an inversion like those post-positive adjectives in the last line of the first of these sestets is a form of audacity on the part of an educated man. Goodman does not come to it out of a penury of rhymes. He knows the device is ancient, but because it is good, clear English, he knows it will serve again. In the last line of the second sestet, the rhyme may well have led him to make the discovery, but he knows how not to reject the surprising order of the concluding verbs. The view from land is of surges that tower and sink. Goodman's view is that of the man in the sea's maw. The strength of the line confirms his saying that his history has been that struggle; the poem is no longer a poet's metaphor.

The power of Goodman's rhetoric comes from its directness. We are surprised to find anyone so direct. Has not language been given to us so that we may dissemble? Goodman's assumption is that the poet is not distinguished by imagination but by his sense of fact. He does not put on airs, and especially not airs of sophistication. He tells us what the fact is. Sometimes, when the poet is Goodman, he tells us prosily, and sometimes with an unbecoming air of reproof—"Telling the Americans how it is." One is tempted to answer, "We'll have a medal struck in the morning." But however self-gratulatory Goodman may be about his practice, telling us how it is with us is indeed his practice—poetry is prophecy.

Direct and hopelessly unsophisticated, Goodman's rhetoric draws upon powerful emotions like patriotism, which is no longer in repute with us but is a form of self-respect for all that. How many since the time of Whitman have written a decent poem about New York? Goodman has written a great one: "The Lordly Hudson."

> "Driver, what stream is it?" I asked, well knowing
> it was our lordly Hudson hardly flowing,
> "It is our lordly Hudson hardly flowing,"
> he said, "under the green-grown cliffs."
>
> Be still, heart! no one needs your passionate
> suffrage to select this glory,
> this is our lordly Hudson hardly flowing
> under the green-grown cliffs.
>
> "Driver! has this a peer in Europe or the East?"
> "No, no!" he said. Home! home!
> be quiet, heart! this is our lordly Hudson
> and has no peer in Europe or the East,
>
> this is our lordly Hudson hardly flowing
> under the green-grown cliffs
> and has no peer in Europe or the East.
> Be quiet, heart! home! home!

CAROLINE GORDON

1895–1981

Caroline Gordon was born on a tobacco farm in Todd County, Kentucky, on October 6, 1895. Her early education at a boys' school run by her father led to a lifelong interest in classical literature. After taking a B.A. at Bethany College, West Virginia, in 1916, she taught at a high school and in 1920 became a journalist. In 1924 she met the poet Allen Tate, whom she married later that year. After moving to New York City she became secretary to Ford Madox Ford, who encouraged and criticized her writing. In 1928 Tate won a Guggenheim Fellowship, and the couple traveled to Paris, where they met Gertrude Stein, the Fitzgeralds, and Ernest Hemingway. Returning to America in 1930, the Tates settled on Benfolly Farm in Tennessee, where Gordon completed her first novel, *Penhally*, in 1931.

Having won a Guggenheim Fellowship in 1932, Gordon returned to France with her husband and worked on a second novel, *Aleck Maury, Sportsman*, which appeared in 1934. By this time the Tates were back at Benfolly and active in the Agrarian movement. Two further novels date from this period, *None Shall Look Back* and *The Garden of Adonis*, both published in 1937. In 1938 Gordon was writer-in-residence at Greensboro College in North Carolina, and then moved on to Princeton when her husband took up a teaching position there. Gordon and Tate were divorced in 1959.

Gordon converted to Roman Catholicism in 1947, and her religion was an important influence on her subsequent work, including *The Strange Children* (1951) and *The Malefactors* (1956), which draw on her experiences in Paris. Her non-fiction includes *How to Read a Novel* (1957) and *A Good Soldier: A Key to the Novels of Ford Madox Ford* (1963). Her final novel, *The Glory of Hera*, was published in 1972, and *The Collected Stories of Caroline Gordon* appeared posthumously in 1981. Gordon gave generous and untiring help to younger writers later in her career. She died on April 11, 1981, in San Cristóbal de las Casas, Chiapas, Mexico.

General

The five novels which culminate in *Green Centuries* have much in common. With the exception of *Aleck Maury, Sportsman*, they exhibit a consistent movement towards tragedy, although only *None Shall Look Back* fulfills the movement. And the novels are conceived in a kind of grand design against the enveloping action of history. With these five books behind her, Miss Gordon had the choice of "filling out" her subject, perhaps using some of the characters she had already invented, or else of extending it by moving to another post of observation. Her second group of novels—*The Women on the Porch* (1944), *The Strange Children* (1951), and *The Malefactors* (1956)—does both. These books are set against the history of the South, like their predecessors, but only indirectly. And their mode is finally Christian comedy. About the time that she published *The Women on the Porch* Miss Gordon was beginning to doubt whether a "regional" literature in the South would continue much longer; it was her opinion that the renaissance in letters was coming to its end. Probably with some such feeling about her subject she has steadily widened its reference. Two of the stories of this period, for example, are set in Europe and North Africa. And the last three novels, beginning with *The Women on the Porch*, are written out of a knowledge of Europe as well as the United States.

With the complexity of subject has come a new boldness of technique. These novels are more Jamesian than the earlier ones—the point of view is more strictly controlled—but they also draw extensively on the resources of poetry, such as *The Waste Land*, which lies back of *The Women on the Porch*, and Dante's *Purgatorio*, which informs *The Malefactors* to some extent. Miss Gordon was converted to the Roman Catholic Church even before she wrote *The Strange Children*, and that fact has its obvious repercussions in her latest novels. *The Malefactors*, especially, makes the highest demands on her talent, because here she tries to dramatize the actual experience of a religious conversion in her poet-hero, Tom Claiborne.

Having remarked the technical range of Miss Gordon's novels, we should not assume that she has been the virtuoso. On the contrary, her stylistic shifts are an index to the scale of her work. Her eight novels and her stories and even her critical essays compose a genuine *oeuvre*. Using the materials accessible to her (her own life, the history of her family, the history of her region), she has built up an impressive image of Western man and the crisis which his restlessness has created. We can see one instance of this restlessness in Rion Outlaw and his dream of infinite space. But there are scarcely any institutional forms to restrain him. Chapman, the sophisticated historian in *The Women on the Porch*, is the latest version of Rion Outlaw, and *his* dream of infinite space is a nightmare. Nearly all of Miss Gordon's heroes are aware of the general plight, but Chapman and Stephen Lewis and Tom Claiborne are intensely conscious of a failing in their lives, and their meditations take the form of an interior drama.

Most of Miss Gordon's heroes (and many of her heroines) are fleeing from some kind of historical ruin—the exceptions are old Nicholas Llewellyn and Fontaine Allard and even Mister Ben Allard in *The Garden of Adonis*, but even these patriarchs cannot check the force of disruption very long. Miss Gordon seems to be saying that it was a mistake to make such an absolute commitment to the order of history. Aleck Maury perhaps understands this failure, and as classicist and sportsman he can still act the Aeneas who will never found another Troy. But even the sportsman's instinct for ritual as a barrier against the ruins of time cannot be counted on, and Jim Carter, a flawed sportsman-hero in *The Garden of Adonis*, hardly even makes the attempt. In *The Strange Children* we see the futility (or at least the irony) of the effort to perpetuate a history already ruined. Here and even more in *The Malefactors* Miss Gordon is saying that redemption must lie in another order of existence, and of course she finally makes no secret of her Christian emphasis. But the ruin is easier to dramatize than the act of redemption.

If the imagery of flight permeates her books, what is the counter-image, the emblem of stasis, even of fulfillment? That is a natural image which most frequently takes the form of a tree. (Like Yeats she seems to arrive at this image very easily.) Perhaps the most "typical" moments in Miss Gordon's fiction occur when her heroes step out of time, as it were, and contemplate the forest. There is the moment when young John Llewellyn, shot from his horse at Shiloh, watches a young maple leaf floating through the center of the destruction. Or there is Mister Ben Allard sitting under his favorite sugar tree and dreaming of his dead sweetheart. In *The Malefactors* the symbol of the natural order becomes more than that: Claiborne "stared at the copper beech tree as if he could find the answer there," and "he had felt that those dusky boughs harbored Presences." No other American writer has so patiently described the surfaces of trees, even the striations of leaves, or made so much of them. The tree as an image of "wholeness" yields a meaning to him who contemplates it lovingly, Miss Gordon seems to say, and the moment of stasis can perhaps be an intimation of something divine. The tragedy of historical ruin could be redeemed—so the movement from *Penhally* to *The Malefactors* suggests. . . .

Meanwhile Miss Gordon and several of her contemporaries carry on the tradition of the Impressionist masters, which still assumes that a public reality is accessible to a private vision. No one can say what this tradition will finally come to represent, but for the moment one can applaud Miss Gordon for her devotion to her chosen mission; her place in the line of succession should be secure, and one says this knowing that her career is not finished. Her desire for excellence has been an admirable thing—ASHLEY BROWN, "The Achievement of Caroline Gordon," *SHR*, Summer 1968, pp. 287–89

Gordon's early work, beginning with "Summer Dust" (1929) up through her fifth novel, *Green Centuries* (1941), depicts heroic characters struggling to assert order and meaning in a shadowed world. At the heart of these heroes' solitary stands against death and disintegration lie a stoic acceptance of man's depravity and a desire to forge a code of courageous dignity. As heroic and noble as these characters are, the dark forces of life inevitably destroy them and—we understand now—their fragile edifices of order. Gordon's strong bond of sympathy with her heroes (derived primarily from her extensive early education in the classics), allowed her to maintain a healthy tension between her dark vision of existence and her need to assert some vestige of meaning amidst life's pain; this tension helped prevent her works from becoming merely shrill cries against the world's unfairness.

Sometime in the early 1940s Gordon's thought and art began to shift. With *The Women on the Porch* (1944) and several stories which followed until her conversion to Roman Catholicism in 1947, she began searching for a larger system of order which would transcend personal heroics. Where these works, like her earlier fiction, center on the difficult quests for order in a threatening world, now disorder is finally brought into check; emerging from crises of despair, Gordon's heroes arrive at the understanding that an overarching tradition exists, rooted in eternity, which can bring them the unifying order they seek. Gordon at this point seemed to be unsure of the nature of this tradition, at times suggesting it rested with Christianity (*The Women on the Porch*), at others with classicism ("The Olive Garden," reprinted, fortunately, for the first time in *The Collected Stories*). Probably because she was herself wavering between accepting one of these two traditions, she was able to keep her fiction free from easy reconciliations and heavy-handed dogma—elements which flawed Gordon's fiction during the next few years.

In 1947 Gordon joined the Roman Catholic Church, a step which gave her a tradition and authority by which to structure her life and art. With her newly embraced faith, Gordon believed, her art took on a greater depth and profundity, since it now took on what Flannery O'Connor called "the added dimension"—that is, the Church's vision of world and eternity. Whether or not Gordon's artistic vision deepened is an arguable point, but clearly her work from this period—notably her two novels *The Strange Children* (1951) and *The Malefactors* (1956) and her long story "Emmanuele! Emmanuele!" (1954)—took a new shape. While these works are more openly concerned with the transcendent, they lack the deeply felt love for heroic struggle which gave her earlier work such strength. Rather than celebrating man's valiant efforts to achieve private dignity, the post-conversion works show such struggles as rooted in vanity and destructive pride. Only by abandoning these personal struggles and by giving oneself to the Church, these works suggest, can a person achieve fulfillment and unity.

To communicate her religious vision to an audience she saw as secular and unsympathetic, Gordon adopted strategies of shock and distortion; these she hoped would compel her readers to abandon literal interpretation and look beyond to the religious message embodied in the work. Unfortunately Gordon's strategy, usually centering on a dramatic and unprepared for conversion experience near the end of the work, often appears forced and unconvincing, the result of her didacticism rather than her fidelity to human experience. The reader feels cheated rather than enlightened.

After *The Malefactors* (1956) and up until her death in 1981, Gordon struck out with her fiction in a new radical direction: she tried to merge her Christian and classical visions. Following the lead of Jacques Maritain, she developed a definition of Christian art based on archetypal patterns rather than on literal subject matter. Great literature, she now believed, "comes into being when one of those timeless patterns reveals itself in time and conflict in which human beings are involved"; and true artists are those who intuit these archetypal patterns and structure their work by them on some deep level. Works so constructed, Gordon said, were ultimately Christian because since archetypes embody the full range of human endeavor, they finally lead to the Christian mysteries. With her new theory of fiction came a renewed interest in heroes, whom she now likened to the ancient battlers; from wrestling with evil, Gordon's heroes gained knowledge which could lead them to the discovery of God. Perhaps because she was trying to accomplish too much, most of the work from this period ("One Against Thebes" is an exception), is sketchy and uneven, written as if from a tentative hand. *The Glory of Hera* (1972), her only novel from this period, suffers from these faults. . . .

With *Aleck Maury, Sportsman*, Gordon follows the exploits of a Southern sportsman—Maury is based on her father—who rejects the modern world and seeks order and meaning through the ritual of the hunt. In one sense the novel is a paean—a song of celebration to a grand old man, his love for the hunt, his zest for life. It is a statement of Gordon's love for her father and her recognition of the beauty of his life. But at the same time, working against this glorification of Maury, is a critical recognition, rooted in a modern perspective, of the ultimate futility and irrelevance of Maury's life. From this point of view, the novel becomes a statement of Gordon's rejection of her father. Together these two viewpoints working against each other give the novel searching depth and tremendous feeling.

. . . In the joyous last scene of the novel, Maury, now a hobbling old man, is lighting out once more for the river. Like his forebear Huck Finn, Maury makes good his escape from the snares of civilization, here his daughter and son-in-law (figures clearly based on Gordon and Allen Tate), who want him to move in with them. Though Maury knows that death will finally catch up with him, he is happy to be on the run, to fish as many streams and rivers as possible before his time is up.

What a fine ending to this great novel! With it Gordon affirms her respect and admiration for her father's life, while at the same time realizing its shortcomings and knowing full well that this is not the life for her. Her deep feelings are underscored by the contrast between the passionate Maury and the rather stiff and pedantic versions of herself and Tate, Sally Maury and her husband. His life is better than mine, Gordon seems to say in this novel. This knowledge of her father's full life and her efforts to resolve her own attitudes towards that life are central to *Aleck Maury, Sportsman*, and indeed much of Caroline Gordon's work. Always the seeker, Gordon in a large sense emulated her father, not by taking to the woods, but by sitting at the writer's table, where like him she sought to establish with her art an essentially private order or unity of existence. Her vision of her father's courage and knowledge amidst the chaos of modern society is, I believe, one of the driving forces behind her writing. I don't think it was merely a coincidence when later in life, after Gordon became a Roman Catholic—a move embodying her desire for a larger system of order—one of the first stories she wrote, "The Presence," shows Aleck Maury too discovering the Church. She wanted him along for her journey—ROBERT H. BRINKMEYER, JR., "New Caroline Gordon Books," *SLJ*, Spring 1982, pp. 63–68

Among those who have influenced Caroline Gordon's thought and work, Dante, Carl Jung, James Joyce, and T. S. Eliot all hold that the phenomenal world reveals subjective truths—a notion related to Gordon and Tate's concepts of fiction. Their endorsement of symbolic naturalism is based on the philosophical tenet that one does not understand reality by merely projecting one's feelings and ideas onto the natural world; rather, one perceives that a higher order, which is "supernatural" in the broadest sense, interpenetrates the physical. In other words, the individual sees *through* nature and society to larger patterns; and this complex reality, which subsumes the physical and the psychic worlds, is timeless, though—for human minds—inextricable from immediate, concrete experience. Here, Gordon's affinity with Jung is evident. Commenting on the archetypal nature of an incident in her short story "The Captive," she has deemed Jung "much more interesting than Freud because . . . he believes that the archetype is operating right now." By her own admission, Jungian archetypes also help to form the pattern in *The Glory of Hera*.

Through her preoccupation with vision in the later novels, Caroline Gordon investigates these archetypal structures and shows how inextricably linked are subjective and objective experience. Because perception is not merely eyesight but a larger awareness of the physical world, compounded by intuitions of an eternal order governing both nature and human society, in *The Women on the Porch*, *The Strange Children*, and *The Malefactors* Gordon often relies on exaggerated and distorted perception to suggest the importance of these intuited realities: flashbacks are sometimes hallucinatory; dreams are treated as facts, given much the same stature that Jung would bestow on them; and the imaginations of the protagonists often grant them fanciful or grotesque, but nonetheless true, images of reality. While the distortion of time and the symbolic content of these subjective experiences at first suggest dissociation, even mental collapse or immaturity, they indicate finally an enduring and universal reality that the subconscious can discover.

Frequently, the protagonists who see this complex reality are artistic, in keeping with Jung's observation that the poet "knows that a purposiveness out-reaching human ends is the life-giving secret for man; he has a presentiment of incomprehensible happenings in the pleroma. In short, he sees something of that psychic world that strikes terror into the savage and the barbarian." There is nothing reductive in Jung's choice of words: "the savage" and "the barbarian" are examples of original or primal man—one who is not protected by "the shield of science and the armour of reason" and consequently is closer to subjective truths. Similarly, Gordon stresses the universality of experience between more "primitive" peoples and moderns, even implying in *Green Centuries*, for example, that there is more beauty and directness in the rituals and faith of the Indians than in those of the pioneers.

Analyzing the grotesque, William Van O'Connor has described this "American genre" as "seeking, seemingly in perverse ways, the sublime." Although his list of American writers manifesting this concern does not include Caroline Gordon, her preoccupation with the visionary affiliates her with other contemporary southern writers who employ the grotesque to correct the prevailing dissociation of feeling and thought. Gordon's characters may not be actual freaks as are, say, Cousin Lymon in *The Ballad of the Sad Café*, Hazel Motes in *Wise Blood*, or Popeye in *Sanctuary*. Yet she does share with these writers what William Van O'Connor defines as a belief "that man carries in his unconscious mind not merely wilfulness or the need to indulge himself, but a deep bestiality and dark irrationality."

Jim Chapman's anger and jealousy turn him into a kind of monster in *The Women on the Porch*, so that he nearly strangles his wife. But the grotesque quality in Caroline Gordon's fiction is less often expressed in such outwardly violent behavior. More frequently there is a violence of revelation—a psychic explosion as an old way of seeing the world is destroyed and a more comprehensive meaning is perceived. As in Eudora Welty's fiction, for example, where subjective and objective worlds seem to collide whenever a character tries to control reality, to limit it by reason or by rationalizing the inexplicable away (*e.g.*, "The Green Curtain," "A Memory")—dreams, memories, and intuitions in Gordon's novels attest to a psychic reality that cannot be permanently repressed without irreparably damaging the individual.

The strength with which the repressed subconscious erupts not only indicates how much violence the individual has done to his psyche in damming up such powerful forces but also serves as a measure of the true awfulness and awesomeness of those forces. Carl Jung describes the terrible encounters that the visionary work of art seeks to record: "The primordial experiences rend from top to bottom the curtain upon which is painted the picture of an ordered world, and allow a glimpse into the unfathomed abyss of what has not yet become." A confrontation with and an appreciation of mystery is the final result. Paradoxically, that recognition of human limitation is also the realization of human possibility—"the life-giving secret for man."

A novelist who strives to convey this "presentiment of

incomprehensible happenings in the pleroma"—moreover, a Christian novelist whose faith urges the individual to recognize human limitations and accept a greater ineffable order—has the difficult task of revealing in everyday life a transcendent reality. In attempting to share revelation, the novelist's aims are akin to those of the prophet. So, Flannery O'Connor defines "the prophetic vision" of the novelist as "a matter of seeing near things with their extensions of meaning and thus of seeing far things close up. The prophet is a realist of distances, and it is this kind of realism that you find in the best modern instances of the grotesque."

Since the novelist perceives a reality that others do not acknowledge, her efforts to portray that vision often necessitate shocking the reader—through exposure to the freakish, the violent, the crazy, the terrible. Flannery O'Connor thus justifies her use of the grotesque: "The novelist with Christian concerns will find in modern life distortions which are repugnant to him, and his problem will be to make these appear as distortions to an audience which is used to seeing them as natural; and he may well be forced to take ever more violent means to get his vision across to this hostile audience. . . . Then you have to make your vision apparent by shock—to the hard of hearing you shout, and for the almost-blind you draw large and startling figures." In a letter to Flannery O'Connor, written in November, 1951, Caroline Gordon remarks similarly on the younger novelist's freakish characters: "But homosexuality, childishness, freakishness—in the end, I think it comes to *fatherlessness*—is rampant in the world today. And you are giving us a terrifying picture of the modern world, so your book is full of freaks."

There is an important distinction in Gordon's thinking between a keen-sighted writer like O'Connor who exposes the freakishness in the world and a freakish writer who projects his distorted vision as the true picture of reality. For example, Gordon insists that homosexuality be depicted as an aberration and cites Proust as an author who does just that. In other words, the novelist is responsible for portraying a moral universe and for revealing as abnormalities what she regards as moral and spiritual failures. *The Strange Children* as well as *The Women on the Porch* and *The Malefactors* fulfill these aims by labeling "homosexuality," "childishness," and "freakishness" as misguided, compensatory behavior for fatherlessness; and for Gordon, whether this fatherlessness means, on the literal level, the want of a rational and just human father or the want of an internalized faculty to direct the individual, it is ultimately the absence of divine guidance and spiritual purpose. While Flannery O'Connor's characters and plots may appear more grotesque than do Caroline Gordon's, both novelists strive to show moral "distortions which are repugnant" and to write the "kind of fiction [that] will always be pushing its own limits outward toward the limits of mystery." In *The Women on the Porch*, that mystery must be perceived by both husband and wife before they can be reunited with a fuller understanding of the significance of their marriage.—ROSE ANN C. FRAISTAT, "The Later Novels," *Caroline Gordon as Novelist and Women of Letters*, 1984, pp. 98–102

Works

NOVELS

. . . ⟨W⟩hen I say that *Penhally* is the best American novel that I know I need not be taken as appraising. I must not be taken as saying that *Penhally* is a better novel than *The Spoils of Poynton*, or a better piece of work than *The Red Badge of Courage* or even than *The House of the Seven Gables*. It curiously unites attributes of all those works.

. . . As befits the work of a woman who has served a long apprenticeship to her art *Penhally*, though dealing with the tragedy of a race and the disappearance of a deeply in-bitten civilization, is a work of great composure and tranquility. Great art is never harrowing; its emotions are large in outline, overwhelming, gradual. It is these qualities in Mrs. Tate's work that makes me reserve for her book the epithet "novel". The novel is a thing of form and of gradual but inevitable growth into that form. It is in short a classical phenomenon, a piece of slow moulding, like the Winged Victory.

Penhally is the triumphant tragedy of a house and the vindication of a mode of life. It is an achievement at once of erudition and of sombre and smouldering passion. It is distinguished by the afterglow of the Greek-Roman-Anglo-Saxon classicism that marked the old South off from all other lands.

> He suddenly saw his father, a tall, stooped man in a suit of gray homespun, standing book in hand under the poplar tree. . . . "*Nunc te, Bacche, canam*," he said, smiling, and bending took the glass from the boy's hand.

There is the epitome of all the civilization of the old South in those four lines on the fourth page of Mrs. Tate's book. And we may find there the reason why, until right up to the present generation, the South has hardly produced any works of art . . . and why its most prominent writers of the imagination are women. The classics have this deterrent effect on their postulants: their perfectionism, when partaken of in an atmosphere of material suavity, makes all further intellectual effort seem not only useless but contemptible. So you had the Oxford don of the English eighteenth century, with his port, his shining naperies, his silver candlesticks by whose light he read Tully, Flaccus and the *Persephone Rapta*. So you had Nicholas Llewellyn's father who in the first years of the nineteenth century emigrated from overcrowded Virginia to a then new South, in that wilderness built Penhally, and there, after that effort, sat under his poplar tree, read Virgil, drank juleps that were brought to him at intervals by a little Negro, and put upon his estate the entail that was eventually to bring Penhally to humiliation. For, in the end it became a Northern millionaires' country club.

Penhally is thus the epic of a house and its fugitive generations of inhabitants. It is an epic, not what it is fashionable to call a saga, since the doom is pronounced in the first few words. It is a novel, not a book of fiction nor a piece of "literature of escape", because it is so constructed that every word of it leads on to the appointed end. Its themes are woven and interwoven, the story progresses forward in action and back in memory so that the sort of shimmer that attaches to life attaches also to the life of the book. Just as you may be a little vague as to the men and women who attended on your youth so you may be a little vague about the innumerable names of Llewellyns of Penhally, of Rosemead or of Virginia. But the figures themselves are alive, passionate, sombre, intolerant, foolish or weak.

. . . *Penhally* differs from other historical works which are written from the outside and are at best *tours de force*—more or less cold re-constitutions. It unites itself to the living school of autobiographic writers in that it is a piece of autobiography. Mrs. Tate has from her earliest days so lived herself into the past of her race and region that her whole being is compact of the passions, the follies, the exaggerations, the classicisms, the excesses, the gallantries and the leadings of forlorn hopes that brought the Old South to its end. She does not have to document herself in order to evoke Morgan's cavalry raids or conditions of life amongst the slaves in the be-hollyhocked Quarters. She has so lived in the past that it is from her own experience that she distils these things.

So *Penhally* is a chronicle of reality. It is as real as Mr. Davis's projection of Chicago, Mr. Wescott's of Wisconsin or Miss Roberts's of the migratory South of today. Her characters have none of the historic over-emphasis that distinguishes the usual romance of escape. Her Southern girls are not over-dimitied, her gallants not over-spurred, her great proprietors not over-lavish. They are in short everyday people—but people of an everyday that is not today. That is a great literary achievement—and a great service to the republic the chief of whose needs is to know how life is constituted.

I do not have to trust myself to write about Mrs. Tate's writing—which profoundly moves me. The first paragraph of her book will prove everything that I could say:

> The shadows that laced the gravelled walk shifted and flowed away between his boot soles like water. He plunged through them as a horse plunges through a shallow stream. Passing the big sugar tree he tapped it smartly with his cane. It must be rotten at the heart by this time though it did not sound hollow. It has been an old tree when little Sister Georgina—dead twenty years ago in August 1807—no. 1808—made her doll's playhouse between its roots out of broken china and the white pebbles that lay at the bottom of the spring. The trees grew too close here. Any wind storm might send them crashing down on the roof. Mister Piper would not come for love or money in August, when people were having their cisterns cleaned. The big sugar tree would have to go, and the big poplar, and the young oak. There would be a vista then, from the dining-room windows of the house clean through to the big road. He turned to look over the lawn—a woman was crying.

I do not think that one need ask for better writing—and I do not know of many first paragraphs of novels that more skilfully get in an atmosphere. It could hardly be bettered —Ford Madox Ford, "A Stage in American Literature," *Bkm*, Dec. 1931, pp. 374–76

Caroline Gordon's talent is what may be termed *intensive* rather than *extensive*. The talent of a writer like Sinclair Lewis or Evelyn Scott, for instance, is of the extensive order: it works by accumulating illustration, and it primarily depends for its success on the degree of structural sense the writer possesses and the degree to which the writer is committed to a single vigorous leading conception by which situations can be defined. . . .

Caroline Gordon's first novel, *Penhally*, shows, like ⟨Evelyn Scott's⟩ *The Wave*, a kind of discrepancy between the intention and the method of execution: it, apparently, was conceived along lines of the extensive and executed along lines of the intensive treatment. Whatever dissatisfaction, despite the brilliance of sections, may be felt with the novel as a whole possibly derives from this situation. (Or perhaps the author labored under a more mechanical difficulty, the difficulty of discovering a technique for compressing the enormous amount of material at hand into a book of ordinary scale.). . . The *extensive* treatment triumphs in its logic, its exposition; the *intensive*, as in the case of Caroline Gordon's story "Old Red," triumphs in its poetry, that is, in its sudden and illuminating perception, which can re-order a body of experience. The special power of Caroline Gordon's new novel, *Aleck Maury, Sportsman*, inheres in the development of this treatment. . . .

The book is a simple chronicle, with no plot in the ordinary meaning of the term. But even for a reader who is no sportsman the author has managed to convey an almost unflagging excitement and a sense of participation in that delight by which Aleck Maury lives. It is difficult to account for the success of the book on this score; it can only be remarked that the author is capable of presenting a natural and social background without effort or over-emphasis, of ordering a narrative with extraordinary skill, and of maintaining suspense concerning an apparently trivial subject. The focus is rarely wrong, and the action slackens only once, in the section dealing with the Ozarks. But the real force of the novel derives from something other than the overt objective: there is the sense of a full and intense emotional life, which is never insisted upon, rarely stated, but implied, somehow, on almost every page. The birth of the first child, the drowning of the son, and the death of the wife are scenes unsurpassed in contemporary fiction for discipline of execution or fullness of effect. . . .

The story . . . is in the form of an autobiography. It is one measure of Caroline Gordon's success that her dramatic sense is able to sustain a long first-person narrative for such different characters as the pioneer woman in "The Captive," the sportsman in *Aleck Maury*, or the 'I' of "Tom Rivers." In each of these instances the style is different and appropriate, descending to the conventional only once, in "Tom Rivers," and then but momentarily. In each case the author has set herself a precise stylistic problem based on a conception of character. She has not attempted to develop a trademark or a manner; her writing is peculiarly selfless, and therein lies its cunning and its distinction. The 'I' in much work by Hemingway is always essentially the same person, whether he is writing about the war in Italy, drinking in Paris, or bull-fighting in Spain; that is, he always assigns himself the same post of observation. That post of observation is selected with a high sense of strategy, and I do not mean to underrate Hemingway's very considerable literary gifts. But the style, on occasion, can become personal in a bad sense, that is, mannered and trademarked: it is the trademark only, a sort of self-parody, that he has been selling to the magazine *Esquire* and that appears in the weaker pieces of *Winner Take Nothing*. The principle by which Caroline Gordon has composed her fiction seems, theoretically at least, to be sounder, for it should define the problem of the discipline of composition on a more objective basis, a basis that should provide in future productions a great variety of effect. But for the present it can be said that the problem has been satisfactorily solved for *Aleck Maury*: the success of the book is that it is not Caroline Gordon's novel, but, after all, the autobiography of Aleck Maury—Robert Penn Warren, "The Fiction of Caroline Gordon, *SWR*, Winter 1935, pp. 5–10

⟨One⟩ form of opportunism is sometimes at present called "interpreting history correctly"—that is, having the foresight to get on the bandwagon and make the most of the parade. With such shabbiness Miss Gordon has nothing to do. Her ⟨*None Shall Look Back*⟩ is a legend in praise of heroes, of those who fought well and lost their battle, and their lives. . . .

Miss Gordon's heart is fixed on the memory of those men who died in a single, superbly fought lost cause, in nothing diminished for being lost, and this devotion has focused her feelings and imagination to a point of fire. She states clearly in every line of her story her mystical faith that what a man lives by, he must if the time comes, die for; to live beyond or to acknowledge defeat is to die twice, and shamefully. The motive of this faith is the pride of Lucifer and Miss Gordon makes no pretense, either for herself or for her characters, to the maudlin virtue of humility in questions of principle.

All-seeing as an ancient chronicler, she has created a panorama of a society engaged in battle for its life. The author moves about, a disembodied spectator timing her presence expertly, over her familiar territory, Kentucky, Georgia, Tennessee, Mississippi. Time, 1860 to 1864, dates which are, after 1776, the most portentous in the history of this country. Having chosen to observe from all points of view, rather than to stand on a knoll above the battle and watch a set procession of events through a field glass, she makes her scenes move rapidly from Federal lines to Confederate, from hospitals to prisons, to the plantations; the effect could easily have become diffuse without firm handling, and the central inalterable sympathies of the chronicler herself. She might have done the neat conventional thing, and told her story through the adventures of her unlucky young pair of lovers, Lucy Churchill and her cousin, Rives Allard. But they take their proper places in the midst of a tragedy of which their own tragedy is only a part. . . .

The Allard family is a center, or rather, a point of departure and return; in the beginning they are clearly seen, alive, each one a human being with his individual destiny, which gradually is merged with the destiny of his time and place. Their ends are symbolically exact: the old man lapses into the escape of imbecility, the old mother into perpetual blind grief, Rives into death in battle, Jim into moral dry rot, Lucy into numbness. . . .

This seems to me in a great many ways a better book than *Penhally* or *Aleck Maury, Sportsman*, Miss Gordon's other two novels. The good firm style, at once homely, rhythmical and distinguished, is in all three of them, but at its best, so far, in *None Shall Look Back*. It is true I know her story by heart, but I have never heard it told better. The effect is of brilliant, instant life; there is a clear daylight over a landscape I need not close my eyes to see, peopled with figures I know well. I have always known the end, as I know the end of so many tales of love, and heroism, and death. In this retelling, it all happened only yesterday. Those men on the field are not buried yet, those women have just put on their mourning.—KATHERINE ANNE PORTER, "Dulce et Decorum Est," *NR*, March 31, 1937, pp. 244–45

Miss Gordon's most recent novel *The Malefactors* (1956), though unquestionably a brilliant novel, does not seem to me to succeed. Not because it repeats earlier situations and not because the symbolism is excessive, though both assertions are true. It does not succeed for the reason that it is too logical. It took the only direction which seemed open for her fiction to take: Miss Gordon tried to combine her feeling for the concrete, earthy life with her feeling for the underground stream of salvation. It comes out as a kind of impossible Fundamentalist-Catholicism. What is too logical in art is too impossible. But I hasten to add that I am glad Miss Gordon wrote *The Malefactors*. It is exactly the kind of work a serious writer often has to create before he can rise above his previous attainment. It takes courage to write such a book. But once it is done, the self, having paid its dues to the mind, may return to the uncertainties, the mysteries that John Keats properly recommended, and find again the metaphoric schemata by which to investigate once again all of the intricacies that Henry James was willing to call simply "life." We know from a sample in this present issue of *The Southern Review* and from a sample last year in The *Sewanee Review* that Miss Gordon has written new work, two new works, in fact. We have every reason to look forward to them with excitement and faith.—RADCLIFFE SQUIRES, "The Underground Stream: A Note on Caroline Gordon's Fiction," *SoR*, April 1971, p. 478

Ashley Brown has already made a convincing case for seeing *The Malefactors* as a Christian comedy by paralleling the novel's action to that in Dante's *Purgatorio*. The novel is, indeed, a story of conversion, not only for the protagonist, Tom Claiborne, but also for most of the major characters in the book. Yet while a reading of *The Malefactors* in terms of a general comic movement toward conversion structured along Dantean lines is indeed illuminating, it does not say all about the specific configuration of image, consciousness, and action that constitutes its dramatic life. For conversion is both the theme of *The Malefactors* and its governing principle of dramatic composition. And the brilliantly seamless quality of Miss Gordon's art in this novel derives from her power to enact in the process of creation that very conversion which is its subject. Such a power of vision, I hope to show, has as its source a belief in the Christian Incarnation and Redemption. The *process* of redemption directs not only the general thematic movement of the novel, but also the process of composition itself, so that *The Malefactors* is no less than a dramatic rendition of the Christiaan vision of history.

This vision of history is rendered through the configuration of image, consciousness, and action in the novel, but the configuration operates within a general design comprising three orders, or levels, of reality—natural, classical, and Christian. . . . ⟨I⟩t will be helpful to recall their general lineaments. By "natural order" I mean, of course, that conception of reality which sees existence, including man in his fallen condition, as totally governed by the laws of nature—birth, fruition, death. The limitations of such a conception are obvious. The "classical order" envisions a higher world of human activity modeled on the heroic pattern and evoked through legend and memory. But even here the vision of history and the human situation, though exalted, is nevertheless circumscribed within the natural order. For as Romano Guardini has stated, "Classical man knew nothing of a being existing beyond the world: as a result he was neither able to view or shape his world from a vantage point which transcended it."

The Christian conception of history and the human situation, in sharp contrast with the natural and classical views, posits a new and higher kind of knowledge—divine revelation—which makes possible man's participation in supernatural mystery, and enables him to conceptualize his experience from a standpoint outside his world. History is revealed as having a definite beginning emanating from a personal act of God (the Creation), a factual point of transforming apotheosis (Christ's Incarnation, Death, and Resurrection), and a fixed end (the Final Judgment). With the Incarnation, human history becomes the history of Christ's penetration and transformation of the natural world, in a process of redemption moved forward by man's willing participation in it. At the core of this process is the new freedom and grace created by the Redemption, which nurtures the divine life in man. It is this vision which serves as the absolute model for both the theme *and* the artistic practice of conversion in *The Malefactors*.

Looking at the novel in terms of its general, comic movement, one can easily see how it is structured in terms of these three orders, or visions, of reality. In the course of the narrative the major characters move in and through the natural order, with its classical trappings, to a confrontation with the supernatural embodied in the Christian vision; or to state the matter differently, the world of nature in the novel is finally circumscribed and defined by the Christian perspective. One can readily see this by noting the progress of Tom Claiborne and his wife Vera from their life at Blenker's Brook early in the novel to their final anticipated reunion at Mary Farm, the land consecrated to Christian service. Their life at Blenker's Brook is a pagan and decadent submission to the natural order, a sterile round in which Vera, aided by Max Shull, indulges in an idolatrous preoccupation with nature—her prize bull, Bud—while Tom, a lapsed poet and critic, sinks into drunkenness and despair. Claiborne despises their life at Blenker's Brook, and rightly so, for he sees it accurately as a degradation of the human spirit and a travesty of the heroic ideal envisioned in classical myth. Images of a better past—both personal and mythical—constantly haunt his memory, but memory as an ordering instrument within consciousness is not enough to save him. Claiborne lacks grace; the efforts of his human will alone are useless, and his impotence as a poet is intrinsically related to his spiritual impotence as a man. Without grace, he cannot rise above the natural level of existence, whose logical end, as he well knows, is death. It is toward the reception of divine grace that Claiborne is "converted" in his return to Mary Farm at the end of the novel.

Although the general movement of *The Malefactors* is from the natural/classical to the Christian perspective, the three orders or ways of perceiving human experience are not to be seen, of course, as rigidly exclusive of one another or, from a temporal standpoint, as consecutive. To say simply that Miss Gordon evokes the natural, classical, and Christian orders as a means of defining the action of the novel does not sufficiently explain *how* these three orders, or levels, exist in dynamic relationship with each other in the work. The point, for her art—which is indistinguishable from her vision—is crucial. Merely to say that Miss Gordon uses the three orders to heighten the significance of the narrative is a crude caricature of her art. Rather, the three orders are visions of reality which exist *simultaneously* in the human consciousness as possibilities to be enacted through knowledge and choice, a situation which will be clear, I think, in my discussion of the focal point of the novel, Tom Claiborne's interior development.

What makes possible from an artistic standpoint the *dynamic* relationship between the three visions of reality is not, however, merely the concentration of point of view in a central intelligence, important as that is. The dynamic is realized because Miss Gordon's dramatic sense is analogical and Christological. Her imagination contains the same quality which Biblical exegetes practice in their four-fold reading of the Scriptures, the same quality Dante described in his famous letter to Can Grande de la Scala: an analogical vision of reality which enables a single image or action to "contain" at one and the same time multiple levels of meaning. This is the metaphysical basis of her dramatic technique, a technique in exact correspondence with the vision informing the work. —JOHN F. DESMOND, "*The Malefactors*: Caroline Gordon's Redemptive Vision," *Ren*, Autumn 1982, pp. 17–19

SHORT STORIES

The structure of the novel is large enough to accommodate almost any genuine talent, however undisciplined; and though the greatest novelists are skillful and learned as well as gifted, even a figure like Theodore Dreiser, whose works are sprawling and primitive like massive pueblos, has earned a permanent place in the history of American literature. But the short story demands a special piety, a studied devotion to the intricate technique of fiction; and consequently only the finest craftsmen can successfully practice this special art. For within its narrow confines one cannot play loose and free with point of view or bury a bad sentence; a writer may make up his own rules but he must follow them to the letter or incur the scorn of the perceptive reader. For this reason, no more than a handful of modern writers have produced short stories which are both technically sound and rich in fictional values.

Such a writer is Caroline Gordon, whose artistic discipline has always been adequate to control the wide range of vision she brings to her fiction. Indeed she tends to crowd into her stories more than their formal limitations would seem to permit: the total experience of a region's history, the hero's archetypal struggle, the complexity of modern aesthetics. In every instance, however, she succeeds in bringing the broad scope of her narrative into focus and in creating the ideal fictional moment, when form and subject are at war and the outcome hangs forever in the balance.

Yet there is a classic simplicity in most of her short stories, an unusual economy of incident and detail which decorously masks their essential thematic complexity. Even the prose is, for the most part, spare in its diction and syntax, particularly in the first-person narratives, dominated by a tone that is quiet and conversational, the intimate language of the piazza on a warm summer evening.

And it is in this quality that one finds a clue to the origins of Miss Gordon's narrative virtue. For she is still in touch with the oral tradition which in her formative years was a vital element of family life. Like William Faulkner and Katherine Anne Porter, with whom she has much in common, her experience of the nature of being begins in the family, with its concrete relationships, its sense of wholeness, its collective memory. In fact, many of her stories are the artistic rendition of incidents involving her father, her brother, and more distant connections, events which formed a significant part of her earliest and most important understanding of the world. For Southern writers of her generation, the family was a natural symbol of the order of existence, the basic analogue for everything of importance; and therefore it provided a key to the meaning of community, history, politics, morality, the transcendent and timeless.

Thus to render the family was to come to terms with all of these larger considerations simultaneously and to do so as concretely and as unselfconsciously as possible in the post-Cartesian world, which is, after all, the world of fiction. For if anything survived of an earlier and more coherent order, it survived in a rural agrarian society which still held fast to some concept, however dimmed, of *pietas*, the tripartite virtue which informed western civilization until the late renaissance and undergirded the works of Homer, Virgil, Dante, and Shakespeare.

It was no problem, then, for Miss Gordon and her Southern contemporaries to move, say, from family history to regional history; for they were, after all, one and the same thing, the latter almost perfectly preserved in the former. And so the reader finds her first volume of stories *The Forest of the South* (1945) not only the Aleck Maury stories, based on the life of Miss Gordon's father, but also tales of the Civil War and Reconstruction, which undoubtedly originated in anecdotes that came to her by way of family reminiscences.

Indeed, every narrative in *The Forest of the South* and in *Old Red and Other Stories* (1963) has the unmistakable ingredients of life itself, those sharp and singular details which one immediately recognizes as containing truths beyond the province of the mere "angelic imagination." Thus Miss Gordon's fiction moves *toward* abstraction rather than proceeds from it, and is always symbolic rather than purely literal or purely allegorical. For this reason she never falsifies the world as, for example, Shirley Jackson does in order to serve the tyranny of intellect. Heart and head in Miss Gordon's work never come to blows; and neither betrays the steady, uncompromising senses, which are the primary means of fictional understanding. In other words, her artistic vision is whole and inviolable, which can be said of few modern writers.—THOMAS H. LANDESS, "Introduction" to *The Short Fiction of Caroline Gordon*, 1972, pp. 1–2

Henry James once said that, in writing about fiction, "one speaks best from one's own taste, and I may therefore venture to say that the air of reality (solidity of specification) seems to me the supreme virtue of a novel—the merit on which its other merits helplessly and submissively depend." Though James here refers to the novel, what he says would inevitably apply to the short story and may serve as our golden text in an introduction to the short stories of Caroline Gordon. Her stories show to a superlative degree "solidity of specification," even if the land she knows so well lies thousands of miles and hundreds of years from the great country houses, shaven lawns, family-portrait galleries, and Sèvres which so enchanted James. . . .

The stories in ⟨*The Collected Stories of Caroline Gordon*⟩ may be divided into the central and peripheral. The peripheral are relatively few, with two long examples, "The Captive" (the story of a white woman captured by Indians) and "Emmanuele! Emmanuele!" (laid in North Africa and France), and some several short pieces involving the Civil War. The central stories, more numerous, refer to ⟨Southeast Kentucky⟩, and in these the enclosing sense of the land combines with the enclosing sense of family and kin. It is true that, at all levels of society in the South, the sense of kinship, of the clan, of the family, hung on long after it died elsewhere, and hung on with so strong a sense of obligation that to the outsider it seems—or not too long ago seemed—nonsense or mystique. Caroline Gordon's stories are set just before the breakdown of the sense of family. "Still," she writes in "Tom Rivers," "in a large family connection such as ours every member, no matter how remotely related or how unimportant, had his place and a sort of record in memory. . . . We sit here under the trees all afternoon and talk about people we used to know: Cousin Owen, who walked from house to house, carrying his teeth in a basket . . . Cousin Henry Hord, who was deafened by cannonading in the Civil War and lost all his property by ill-advised investments and had to live with any of the kin who would put up with him." And then there is the last great family reunion, of five hundred members from all over the country, including one who had made it rich and provided all the whiskey—this scene narrated by a little girl, who hears her father, Professor Maury (who had only "married into" the family), remark: "All these mediocre people, getting together to congratulate themselves on their mediocrity!"

But beside the absurd or pretentious side of this world flowers story after story that is humorous (directly so as in "The Petrified Woman"), touching, or shocking. The artist here, sometimes by assuming the child's vision, shows the complexity of life. Few stories can match "The Enemies" or "The Long Day" for shock, or for a more subtle kind of shock, scarcely less powerful on reflection, at the end of "The Burning Eyes," in which a child goes on his first possum hunt. Or the muted conclusion of "One More Time," with its tangle of emotion at the end, especially for Professor Maury. He is old and slow now, his whole life now given to fishing and the study of expertise of fellow sportsmen, and at a fishing resort he meets a man whose strength is failing. The story ends with the body of the frail fellow sportsman at the bottom of the Blue Pool, with dumbbells in his pockets. This, of course, is a companion piece to "The Last Day in the Field" (which we may take to be that of Professor Maury, who, feeling his age, gives up the field entirely for the stream). It is his narrative: ". . . I shot too quick. It swerved over the thicket and I let go with the second barrel. It staggered, then zoomed up. Up, up, up, over the rim of the hill and above the tallest hickories. I saw it there for a second, its wings black against the gold light, before, wings still spread, it came whirling down, like an autumn leaf, like the leaves that were everywhere about us, all over the ground." (How subtle the touch of the word *us* here! The implied identification of the dying bird rising against the gold light, and the old man in his last act of a sport he lived for.) Subtlety of effect, poetic subtlety somehow entwined with a lucent prose, is one of the qualities of this writer. And sometimes it requires more than a second casual look. . . .

The stories gathered in *The Collected Stories of Caroline Gordon* are more than admirable examples of the "solidity of specification." They are dramatic examples of man in contact with man, and man in contact with nature; of living sympathy; of a disciplined style as unpretentious and clear as running water, but shot through with glints of wit, humor, pity, and poetry. Caroline Gordon belongs in that group of Southern women who have been enriching our literature uniquely in this century—all so different in spirit, attitude, and method, but all with the rare gift of the teller of the tale.—ROBERT PENN WARREN, "Introduction" to *The Collected Stories of Caroline Gordon*, 1981, pp. ix–xiii

JAMES I. ROCKS

"The Mind and Art of Caroline Gordon"

Mississippi Quarterly, Winter 1967, pp. 2–15

It is now a well-established fact that Miss Gordon worked in the literary tradition of Gustave Flaubert and Henry James. Any estimate of her work must indicate how she appropriated that tradition, what she then did with it in writing her own fiction, and to what degree it might have helped or hindered her own creative expression. Like many of the writers of the emerging Southern Renaissance, Miss Gordon took seriously the problems of fictional form. And like them she sought for a myth to replace the ethic of a defeated ante-bellum South. Order and authority are, indeed, the props of her mind and art.

. . . When Miss Gordon chose the men of the Flaubertian tradition as her literary mentors, she believed that their methodology offered the soundest principles for a craft of fiction. Well read in and rather glib about these writers, she set out to pattern her fiction on their practice, with an eye on Aristotelian terminology, and later, after her conversion to Catholicism, on the idea of a Christian art as discussed in the writings of the Catholic philosopher Jacques Maritain.[1] And when she wrote about her tradition, she tended to codify the ideas of Flaubert, James, Ford, and Conrad, setting down elaborate charts and tables, definitions and descriptions whereby the novice, whether he be student or amateur writer, might learn those techniques which come closest to guaranteeing artistic success.

. . . In her own fiction the Jamesian central intelligence is the principal informative technique. Occasionally, as in the Aleck Maury stories, she utilizes the first person. Aleck himself is like the country humorist who relies conspicuously on the oral mode of communication, relating his experiences to a silent if at times amusedly disdainful audience; yet he betrays a reticence that is not typical of those humorists. Her first-person narrators, such as the young man in "Her Quaint Honour," are variations of Aleck; diction and metaphor are always appropriate to their agrarian view of life.

Only rarely, however, does Miss Gordon employ the technique of the concealed narrator.[2] This subtle but complicated method reaches perfection in stories—which she values highly—by men in the Flaubertian literary tradition: "Un Coeur simple," "The Open Boat," "The Dead," and "The Beast in the Jungle." Her own "To Thy Chamber Window, Sweet" (1934), for example, ranks with these stories; not only is the story a skillful exercise in this technique—proof, therefore, that she can handle the method of the concealed narrator exceptionally well—but, furthermore, the story pictures Aleck Maury from a different and revealing angle, thus enhancing the reader's understanding of this intriguing man. Finally, Miss Gordon utilizes one central intelligence, as in *The Malefactors*, or more than a half dozen, as in *The Women on the Porch* (1944). In her criticism she states, as did James, that adherence to one, perhaps several, posts of observation is requisite for longer fiction, but in her own works, however, she frequently uses more intelligences than James used in his later fiction.

Occasionally she shifts the point of view from the established center of vision for one sentence or for a rather lengthy section; such changes usually enhance meaning by divulging the narrator's lack of self-knowledge. Often she uses several different posts of observation in order to present various philosophical positions, for she, like Ford, who said that the novelist must be judicious by presenting opposing ideas,[3] desires her novel to be a dialectic. These instances of narrative shift add variety to her best fiction and are usually completely justifiable. Only in rare instances, as in the conclusion to *The Strange Children*, does an alteration break the tone; uniformity of tone is necessary in fiction, according to Miss Gordon, and is effected, as she would argue, through consistency in narrative point of view. The intrusion of an obviously omniscient narrator, in her opinion a device to be avoided, comes occasionally in panoramas where time needs to be foreshortened. *None Shall Look Back* has passages of marked unevenness in the "Long View," particularly in the battle scenes, which lack the dramatic focus of similar scenes in *The Red Badge of Courage*. Crane's novel, having purportedly been influenced by *La Chartreuse de Parme*, shows, in Miss Gordon's opinion, an important advance over Stendhal in the dramatic handling of battle scenes.[4] Her own war novel fails, however, in the very scenic qualities that she considers so effective in Crane's work.

A reading of Miss Gordon's fiction must take into account the masterful way in which she utilizes centers of vision, particularly in works like "To Thy Chamber Window, Sweet" and *The Strange Children*. Her manipulation is as conscious and meaningful as in James's best work, from which she obviously learned much, and offers excellent examples for students of the novel who want to examine the practical illustration of a working esthetic. In Miss Gordon's fiction itself there is little development to be noted in the method of handling narrative point of view. Her first story, "Summer Dust" (1929), and her first novel, *Penhally* (1931), are evidence that she mastered the technique well before marketing her fiction. The products of an apprenticeship have never appeared (if there are any). Her fiction shows that she learned her methods before beginning to publish, rather than seeking modes in the course of her writing career.

In matters of style a development, particularly in the novels, can be indicated. Style is, of course, an adjunct to point of view, because the choice of narrator determines the quality of the narration, a fact of which Miss Gordon has been completely aware, since she is careful to distinguish between levels of diction befitting the social backgrounds of her reflector characters. If a character speaks idiomatically or ungrammatically, as in "The Captive," the narration retains these qualities. Unlike her mentor James she chooses intelligences from different classes of society, choices which would reflect her opinion that the subtlety of an observer does not depend upon his belonging to the Brahmin or moneyed class, as it often does in the case of James.

The balance and cadence of Miss Gordon's style, with its emphasis on the right word and the active detail, are more reminiscent of, say, Willa Cather[5] (not to mention Southern female writers like Katherine Anne Porter or Eudora Welty) than of Faulkner or Wolfe. Some of Miss Gordon's characters fall into the oral tradition of anecdote tellers, but they are not orators, and even those ante-bellum gentlemen in her fiction who might be politically inclined tone down their speeches—at least as Miss Gordon styles them. More than the convolutions and ambiguities of James, Ford, or even Conrad, the concrete exactitude of Flaubert influenced Miss Gordon, as did the rigorous classicism of Latin and Greek authors in whom she read extensively.[6]

Although Miss Gordon's usual style is one of clarity and precision, utilizing a simple vocabulary and short sentences, in divulging the deep recesses of her characters' minds, she occasionally writes with a style that is more fluid, rich, and varied. *The Women on the Porch* is a distinguished example of her more complex style, which is noticeable in the last three novels. In the short stories written from the mid-'forties on there is diversity, likewise, although it is rather difficult to point to any particular story which marks the beginning of a new technique or style. "Old Red," for example, which appeared quite early in her career, is as mature in form and style as anything she wrote later. The majority of her stories were written from 1929 to 1945, when the collection *The Forest of the South* was published, bringing together most of those early stories. Some of the relatively few new stories written after 1945, including "The Petrified Woman" (1947), "The Presence" (1948), "Emmanuele! Emmanuele!" (1954), and "One against Thebes" (1961), were added to numerous notable early ones for the latest collection, *Old Red and Other Stories* (1963).

In matters of style, one must look, then, at the novels (and at the stories published from her novel in progress) to find any apparent development. Miss Gordon's fiction does take on a new dimension in the mid-'thirties with *The Garden of Adonis* (1937) and "The Brilliant Leaves." Thereafter the novels are built on some mythic superstructure derived from the classics, folklore, or religion. Symbolism and archetypal patterns, the use of which she considers essential if a work of art is to endure, occur more frequently; in a story like "The Brilliant Leaves" symbolic naturalism provides a key to meaning.

Despite the mythic character of her later work she certainly does not write in the vein of Wolfe, Faulkner, or William Styron, all of whose fiction draws attention to itself through its style. Miss Gordon criticizes Faulkner for succumbing to his own rhetoric.[7] But the same can be said of her, for her carefully wrought style is as manneristic in its own way as is Faulkner's. If we know the actual world through style, as Allen Tate says in "The Hovering Fly,"[8] if materials are defined by form, then it can be said that Miss Gordon's careful structure and style illustrate not simply her regard for precision, clarity, and order but also her fundamental view—a view appropriated in large part from Jacques Maritain—that the artist must recognize some coherent pattern out of the shifting planes of a seemingly disjointed reality.

If Miss Gordon's fiction does not illustrate a search for new narrative techniques with which to inform her materials, it does present a quest for meaning and value. She wrote her early novels and stories in order to dramatize—indirectly, to advance—the agrarian worldview, which was at that very moment receiving a certain notoriety through the social criticism of Tate and others. Her fiction was to some degree a defense of traditions on the wane, with the aim of "educating" her audience—as Ford would have the author do[9]—to understand a culture which existed, for non-Southerners at least, only as an exotic world of fantasy. She recreated moments in history, like the Civil War, which figures directly or indirectly as the crisis in all of her fiction, and devised characters, like the Allard family—all of which would serve as components in her dramatized dialogue on the Southern ethic. But as her career progressed Miss Gordon became uneasy in her myth of conservative agrarianism and began to question it openly in later novels, such as *The Garden of Adonis* and *The Women on the Porch*, in an effort to find a more permanent, absolute system of truth. This quest—if not the idea itself or quest—is the larger theme of her fiction.

Miss Gordon has remarked meaningfully: "My stories, I think, are all one story. . . . Like most fiction writers, I seem to spend my life contemplating the same set of events."[10] Her novels and stories do form a larger narrative, of which each unit is either one telling of the same story or an enlargement upon the basic theme, which is, as Miss Gordon herself has explained, the scheme of Redemption or the interworkings of natural and supernatural grace.[11] More specifically her plot is the dramatization of a culture in transition and the search for values to replace those destroyed in a particular moment of crisis.

In *Green Centuries* she depicts one aspect of the settlement of the South, in both *The Garden of Adonis* and *The Women on the Porch*, the twentieth-century deterioration of the South, using the same families throughout to indicate a continuation of the Southern tradition in its various phases. Men like the Llewellyns, the Allards, and Aleck Maury are heroes, in her opinion, because they struggled to defend and perpetuate a way of life. The women, who are their guides, spur them on to achievement but exact an allegiance, a reciprocated love that cannot stand the test of political disunity, chaos, and loss—the agents of moral breakdown in many of her male characters. In the central subject of the man-woman relationship carnal love often replaces spiritual love because of rootlessness or escape from one's rightful world. Her men are in quest of values in the alien world about them but will find permanence, instead, in a higher religious myth through the ministrations of women, as *The Malefactors* shows. Since man cannot, finally, redeem himself in the natural world, as the Aleck Maury stories imply, he must find salvation through the myth of religion and thus prepare himself for the supernatural gift of grace as a recipient both charitable and humble.

Robert Heilman says that Miss Gordon's stories "expand into the myth of a recurrent character,"[12] one who, it should be added, is in continual search for meaning and understanding in his milieu. It is in the family circle, she contends, that the fiction writer will find the subjects for the conflicts in his fiction,[13] and, indeed, all of her characters operate within the family unit. Her own family often served as the inspiration for these characters,[14] a fact particularly evident in the novel and stories centering around Aleck Maury. Elsewhere in her fiction, as in "Summer Dust," "The Petrified Woman," and *The Strange Children*, Miss Gordon speaks through the mask of the character Sarah. Because of her use of this persona, Miss Gordon's fiction exemplifies the unalterable truth about literature and its creator: an artist's life informs his product, which can itself be a source for the deeper understanding of the writer.

Miss Gordon's own figure in the carpet, that is, her recurrent themes and methods, reveals an obsession with the same fundamental story. Her fiction dramatizes the myth of the South, as Cooper's does that of Western migration, James's of Old and New World culture, Proust's of French social change at the end of the nineteenth century. Beginning, in thematic order, with *Green Centuries* and ending with *The Malefactors*, Miss Gordon's fiction shows the movement from loss to acquisition, from rootlesness to stability, from chaos to order, from matter to spirit. In *Green Centuries* the antagonistic natural world drives the exile to certain destruction as he escapes his past (finally, himself) in the pursuit of the unknown. This theme of the natural world as opponent reappears later in *The Garden of Adonis* and particularly in *The Women on the Porch*, as does the central concept of the failure of love between man and woman, in part the result of destroyed cultures or man's warped view of new and different economic systems.

The Southern ethic provides a stable code, according to Miss Gordon, but in *None Shall Look Back* the Civil War forces the postbellum Southerner in two directions: either to cling to the tatters of the agrarian culture of the Old South but still readapt to new realities, or to reconstruct the New South along commercial lines. The conflict between these ethics, as they form the crux of *None Shall Look Back* and *Penhally*, provides a central dialectic in Miss Gordon's fiction. She admits with difficulty that the New South will ultimately be taken over by the commercialists—but not without a struggle, like agrarian Chance Llewellyn's symbolic murder of his materialistic brother in *Penhally*. Chance is an agrarian hero of the New South, as General Nathan Bedford Forrest was of the Old South—men for whom Miss Gordon has infinite respect because they confront the enemy and will fight to the death, even as they are aware that their chance for victory is slim.[15]

The agrarian world, however, can stultify and warp its inhabitants. Salvation in that world, even as an escape from the oppressive, self-pitying past, can be only tentative for a man like Aleck Maury, who—along with Tom Claiborne in *The Malefactors* and Lucy in *The Strange Children*, among others—finds few if any values from the dead past, which seems to smother his every attempt to enjoy the experiences of the moment. Claiborne's malaise is of a special kind, however, for he has nothing at all to which he can turn; a victim in a world dissociated, he—like most of Miss Gordon's men—becomes estranged from the woman who might well be able to focus his vision on the one and true reality. By a series of trials and errors Claiborne reaches the goal of his quest—the knight after the fair lady, who in this case turns out to be the Beatrice-like Vera or, finally, the Virgin Mary. Love brings forth and, in turn, depends on the state of grace, the capacity for charity, sympathy, and understanding; without these qualities no man can find sustenance in any reality.

Miss Gordon's men are beset by such insurmountable problems that they are often made to appear weak and ineffectual, when in fact they are meant, in her opinion, to represent heroic endeavor. Except for General Forrest, Aleck Maury, Kevin Reardon in *The Strange Children*, and several of the Allards and the Llewellyns, it is the women characters who generally tend to exhibit a more indomitable will and greater endurance in the face of some disaster. Miss Gordon exhibits a surer hand with women characters, and in her fiction they appear more complete and plausible psychologically. On the other hand, the men, those who founder and fall, ultimately look to a woman as an agent of moral regeneration. The men—particularly the intellectuals, who lack any passionate involvement—suffer a kind of emasculation, so that as a group in Miss Gordon's fiction they appear in a very bad light indeed. The reader becomes impatient with many of her male characters because she tends to upset the conventional pattern of man-woman relationships—man as dominant principle, woman in a subservient role. Her views of woman as moral guardian and the embodiment of truth and of man as pursuer and defender are not conducive to easy acceptance, either for the male reader who sees himself as the dominant individual or for the female reader who rather likes her man to assume that role. The reader becomes incredulous when the men in her fiction are forever bewitched by their women. Miss Gordon herself reacts in like manner towards the similar female temptation of men in Ford's fiction.[16] And such an attitude of disbelief is inevitable in the reader of her own work.

Despite the essentially optimistic cast of Miss Gordon's fiction (the themes of quest, heroism, salvation) there is a constant note of impending disaster, loss, death, or alienation present in all of her novels and stories. Because of the nature of the man-woman relationship, she usually portrays vicious love, not virtuous love, as James said George Sand did.[17] Like James in his handling of evil, Miss Gordon suggests the hatred, bitterness, and cruelty of the estranged married couples. There is, in fact, more illicit sex in her fiction than there is chastity, which—even in the novels about the Old South—is considered with tacit indifference, as if it were an outdated moral idea. Adultery predominates in her fiction as a kind of license that grows out of an estrangement in the once virtuous love of man and wife. Premarital sex and adulterous affairs are usually expressions of what the participants think is genuine love, but even when they do serve to reveal the true nature and meaning of human relationships, more often than not some misfortune results from these acts. Miss Gordon's moral vision is not unlike George Eliot's in that she shows how spiritual love can deteriorate into vicious and petty acts of spite.

Miss Gordon's characters do ultimately learn, if not always enact, the conditions and attributes of virtuous love. The reunion between man and woman, argues in the last two novels, is more easily effected under the moral influence of the Christian way of life. The testing of love, often caused by a cultural crisis, is but one example of the manifestations of alienation present in her fiction. Estrangement within the family, of one man from his culture, or between ethics creates a conflict that can be remedied only through the submission of one antagonist. This capitulation ends, at times, with death or, more frequently, with the even greater pain of emotional annihilation, the death-in-life state. And for this reason there is, as Heilman has noted, an "insistent awareness of death" in Miss Gordon's work, thus explaining the elegiac tone that Eisinger senses therein.[18] Miss Gordon's fiction consistently shows that the quest for a new reality, myth, or authority exacts some loss on the part of the seeker. This pattern of experience is, however, a source of knowledge for her characters—and, as she ultimately hopes, for her readers.

. . . Miss Gordon's technique so rigidly informs her materials that much of the vitality is robbed from the emotions. Usually she treats a scene of dramatic significance in an indirect, suggestive, elliptical manner, often effectively controlling the emotions in that scene. Instead of containing the intensity, and thus heightening it, the technique, however, often merely smothers it. These climaxes, toward which the action of the plot is always skillfully directed, are often disappointing because they are understated; as big scenes they need scope and power, not a feeling of anticlimax. Such crucial scenes lack the drama that she often insists upon in her own critical statement. For example, Miss Gordon maintains that in the confrontation between Becky, Rawdon, and Lord Steyne in *Vanity Fair* Thackeray deliberately avoids the possibility of an exciting clash.[19] As he purportedly lost his nerve at this point, so does Miss Gordon at many moments of intense emotion. Because of this failure to effect the full range of possible feeling, it would seem that her limitations as an artist rest primarily with an inability to abandon herself during these scenes. At any rate, her genius does not carry her through the climaxes.[20]

Those scenes which fall off are always competent, if not often effective, yet her stylization tends to check the emotions to such an extent that the reader feels robbed of the response he was expecting; the letdown may simply be disappointing. Such a novel as *None Shall Look Back*, for example, although technically her poorest work, is perhaps her most sincere effort, because the struggle to define her Southern ethic at its crisis of the Civil War is revealed in the somewhat faltering method. One other fault of Miss Gordon as an artist may also result from emphasis on technique, or conversely may explain the reason why she has adhered so closely to fictional methods. Despite a variety of individualized characters, whose lives are chronicled in the Fordian manner of weaving fact and revelation throughout the course of the narrative, these characters, particularly the men, never come fully alive. Except for Aleck Maury, most of them seem to be vehicles of Miss Gordon's thought, always carefully characterized yet somehow dominated by technique. Even when a character is a central intelligence, the method whereby his complete personality might be revealed, he is controlled by method instead of determining it himself. Miss Gordon simply does not have the power to put vitality, expansiveness, and intensity into her characters, even into her agrarian heroes and heroines, who leave with the reader the final impression of potentiality unrevealed.

Like Katherine Anne Porter or Eudora Welty, Miss Gordon works best with the small unit, the short story; individual chapters in the novels, like the meetinghouse scene in *The Garden of Adonis*, are excellent, but when it comes to the complete work, the totality is less than the sum of its parts. This weakness is related, to be sure, to her inability to enliven her characters or to sustain the climactic scenes. In discussing the faults of the amateur writer Miss Gordon comments: "The structure of his narrative collapses for lack of proper proportion in its parts, however 'good' each part may be in isolation."[22] This failing is noticeable in her longer fiction, which, it soon becomes evident to the reader, reveals a conscious attempt at over-all unity and cohesion. She is successful to a large degree because where instinctive ability ends, hard work takes over. Her fiction is the product of painfully careful craftsmanship, particularly in those areas where artistic genius can usually command the materials.

Miss Gordon is certainly an author of second rank in the flourishing Southern Renaissance. But had she written nothing else, novels like *Penhally*, *Green Centuries*, *The Women on the Porch*, and *The Strange Children*, or stories like "Old Red," "The Brilliant Leaves," and "The Presence" would suffice to place her in a high position among her distinguished confreres. As an interpretation of the Southern way of life her total work stands comparison with even as penetrating a voice as Faulkner, whom she continually praises with justifiable pride, not only as a touchstone of Southern fiction but as a master within the mainstream of modern literature. Like Faulkner, Miss Gordon is a descendant of the great realistic school, whose members, so she would argue, have made fiction a genre to rival poetry and drama, which itself, as she states in her criticism, provided innumerable criteria for fiction.

As an expounder of the human condition in general she has recreated a particular world or social milieu which envelops the universal action of mankind. Through the technique of symbolic naturalism she has dramatized the meanings of existence as they are revealed in the conduct of life. Especially in matters of narrative technique, which is, finally, both the achievement and the shortcoming of her complete work, Miss Gordon reveals the primacy of conscious craftsmanship, the need for the artist to concern himself with the "how" and the "why" as well as the "what" of fiction. For the materials of her fiction she drew from a rich cultural tradition, for the techniques from a—perhaps the—foremost literary tradition.

Notes

1. For her appropriation of Aristotle, see the appendices to the 1950 and 1960 editions of the anthology, *The House of Fiction*, and *How to Read a Novel* (New York, 1957), Chapter 3. For the influence of Maritain, particularly his *Art et scolastique*, see *How to Read a Novel*, "Some Readings and Misreadings, *Sewanee Review*, LXI (Summer 1953), 384–407; "Mr. Verver, Our National Hero," *Sewanee Review*, LXIII (Winter 1955), 29–47; "Flannery O'Connor's *Wise Blood*," *Critique*, II, no. 3 (1958), 3–10; and "Letters to a Monk," *Ramparts*, III (December 1964), 4–10.
2. For a discussion of this particular narrative point of view, see *The House of Fiction* (1960), pp. 442–443.
3. *Joseph Conrad: A Personal Remembrance* (Boston, 1924), pp. 223–224.
4. "Stephen Crane," *Accent*, IX (Spring 1949), 153–157; for additional comment on panorama and scene, see *How to Read a Novel*, Chapter 5; and the appendices to *The House of Fiction* anthologies.
5. Miss Gordon says that Willa Cather excels in recreating common speech, an attribute of Miss Cather's style that Miss Gordon possesses as well, if not to an even more proficient degree ("A Virginian in Prairie Country," *New York Times Book Review*, March 8, 1958, p. 1).
6. For the influence of Flaubert, see *How to Read a Novel* and "Notes on Faulkner and Flaubert," *Hudson Review*, I (Summer 1948), 222–231; for that of the classics, see "How I Learned to Write Novels," *Books on Trial*, XV (November 1956), 111–112, 160–163.
7. "Mr. Faulkner's Southern Saga," *New York Times Book Review*, May 5, 1946, p. 45.
8. *Collected Essays* (Denver, 1959), p. 156; one of Tate's few essays on fiction, "The Post of Observation in Fiction," *Maryland Quarterly*, I. no. 2 (1944), 61–64, is an imaginative statement of Miss Gordon's critical position as enunciated in a dozen or so of her more verbose and at times simplistic critical articles and books.
9. *Portraits from Life* (Boston, 1937), pp. 219–220, and *The Critical Attitude* (London, 1911), Chapter 2.
10. Harry R. Warfel, *American Novelists of Today* (New York, 1951), p. 178. Miss Gordon says that Ford also told the same story over each time he wrote. His novels, she argues, deal with the attraction between the sexes, the men usually bewitched by women who are the belles-dames-sans-merci type ("The Story of Ford Madox Ford," *New York Times Book Review*, September 17, 1950, pp. 1, 22, and *A Good Soldier: A Key to the Novels of Ford Madox-Ford* [Davis, Calif., 1963], pp. 2–4). This is the nature of the man-woman conflict in Miss Gordon's own works, which must, therefore, have been thematically inspired in part by Ford's novels.
11. "Letters to a Monk," p. 10. This is the theme of all literature, she says, from the Greek tragedians on down.
12. "The Southern Temper," in *Southern Renascence: The Literature of the Modern South*, ed. Louis D. Rubin, Jr., and Robert D. Jacobs (Baltimore, 1953), p. 11.
13. *How to Read a Novel*, p. 207.
14. An experience of her younger brother provided the material for "Her Quaint Honour," so she recounts in the recent essay "Cock-Crow," a chapter from an autobiographical novel in progress to be entitled *A Narrow Heart: The Portrait of a Woman (Southern Review*, I, n.s. [Summer 1965], 556). This work will undoubtedly provide a significant insight into her mind and art.
15. Miss Gordon's hero-worship—not to mention a resurgence of chauvinism, a reaffirmation of agrarianism, and a nostalgia for the lost glories of the ante-bellum South—is particularly apparent in "Cock-Crow."
16. *A Good Soldier: A Key to the Novels of Ford Madox Ford*, p. 4.
17. *French Poets and Novelists* (London, 1904), p. 171.
18. "The Southern Temper," p. 7, and *Fiction of the Forties* (Chicago, 1963), p. 186.
19. *The House of Fiction* (1950), p. 623.
20. See Eisinger, p. 193, to this effect. José Ortega y Gasset, in *The Dehumanization of Art* (Garden City, N. Y., 1956), argues that contemporary art is more interested in esthetics and style and shuns the lived realities, thus causing the masses to turn away from literature: ". . . to stylize means to deform reality, to derealize; style involves dehumanization" (p. 23). Although Ortega argues that excessive stylization robs a work of its power to recreate life, he does subscribe, in *Notes on the Novel*, to the impressionistic doctrine of authorial impersonality in the sense that the novelist should present the facts about his character so that the reader can discover and define him for himself.
21. This part appeared earlier as "A Morning's Favor," *Southern Review*, I (Fall 1935), 271–280.
22. *The House of Fiction* (1950), p. 635.

Mary Gordon

1949–

Mary Catherine Gordon was born on Long Island on December 8, 1949, and grew up in Queens, New York. Her mother was a New York Catholic of Irish descent, and her father, who died when she was eight, was a Jew from Ohio who had converted to Catholicism. After attending the Holy Name of Mary School in Valley Stream, New York, and the Mary Louis Academy, Gordon enrolled at Barnard College, graduating with a B.A. in 1971. She wrote poetry from an early age, but turned to prose while in the writing program at Syracuse University, where she took an M.A. in 1973 and met and married her first husband.

Gordon began her first novel, *Final Payments*, while teaching composition at Dutchess Community College in Poughkeepsie, New York. After several rejections and considerable revision, the novel achieved critical and popular success when published in 1978, selling more than a million copies in paperback by the end of 1979 and winning her the Kafka Prize in 1980. A second novel, *The Company of Women*, appeared in 1981, and *Men and Angels* in 1985. Gordon has also published short stories in magazines and continues to write poetry. She has one child from her second marriage, to Arthur Cash, a professor of English.

Works

FINAL PAYMENTS

Mary Gordon's much-praised *Final Payments* may be the best American feminist novel yet, though its thematic emphases are skillfully concealed beneath its wry surface picturing of an Irish Catholic girl who "gives up her life" for her invalid father, nervously edges back into reality after his death, then chooses renunciation again (for "having put myself at the center of the universe")—in a drastic penitential act that is simply unbelievable in pure narrative terms (though it does deftly dramatize women's reluctance to claim all they're entitled to).

The overall shape of Gordon's story is itself an eloquent comment on the nature of woman's fate. The simple declarative style, with its emotion-charged repetitions, generates great intensity. And, not least of all, Gordon's spectacular verbal skill allows her heroine to express complex emotional and intellectual attitudes with great precision. *Final Payments* is, owing to the tactical error I have mentioned, not all it might have been—but is quite good enough to demonstrate that Mary Gordon is one of the most gifted writers of her generation.—BRUCE ALLEN, "First Novels," *SwR*, Fall 1978, p. 616

Final Payments is a well-made, realistic novel of refined sensibility and moral scruple, informed by the values of orthodox Christianity—qualities one does not expect from the debut of a young American writer these days. It was in fact very well received in the United States, but the publishers cannily solicited a pre-publication endorsement from Margaret Drabble rather than from one of the fashionable American women writers. Anything more different from the school of Jong could hardly be imagined; but there is a perceptible affinity between *Final Payments* and, say, *The Needle's Eye*. In both writers the primary source of interest and concern is the effort of an ironic and fastidious female sensibility to be good. . . .

At this point ⟨when Isabel is seduced⟩ the novel, so firmly and freshly written at the outset, threatens to turn soft at the core, like a sleepy pear. The main trouble is the character of Hugh, and it may be some measure of the author's inability to make anything of him that the heroine is peculiarly attracted by his back, so that he spends much of the novel with his face inscrutably averted from us.

Ms Gordon tries hard to compensate for this thinness of characterization by passages of discreetly erotic lyricism and anguished introspection by the heroine which only push the novel dangerously in the direction of superior women's magazine fiction. But it recovers its poise and power splendidly in the last eighty pages. Hugh's wife, urged on by the jealous John, attacks Isabel in the most public way, and Isabel, so accustomed to having the reputation of a "good woman", is unable to tolerate the role of seductress and homebreaker. She renounces her lover and runs off to another town to care for the charmless, spiteful Margaret, her father's former housekeeper. Masochistically she sinks back into the mean, ugly, repressive Catholic subculture of her youth. That this is a neurotic, rather than a spiritual development, is clearly signalled by her obsessive eating and drinking. It says much for the power of Ms Gordon's writing that the reader feels a genuine sense of dismay at the spectacle of the heroine's physical and mental decline, and a genuine sense of relief when she finally allows herself to be rescued from it.

In one sense *Final Payments* is a study in the power of traditional Catholicism over those who were indoctrinated in it at an impressionable age. The heroine's utter subservience to her father is obviously a microcosm of the power structure of the authoritarian, paternalistic pre-Conciliar Church; and her renunciation of her lover a desperate attempt to recover the assurance of personal salvation that she enjoyed as a result of her self-mortifying service. In the end the heroine breaks the suffocating grip of the Catholic ghetto, and opts for a more open and humanistic ethic. Yet the novel is steeped in nostalgia for, as well as nausea at that kind of Catholicism, and the undoubted distinction of its writing owes much to the high-cultural equivalent of the Catholic ghetto—the "Catholic Novel" of Greene, Mauriac, Bernanos, Bloy, with its characteristic fondness for aphorisms that are subversive of liberal, materialistic assumptions. "I was angry at myself," says the heroine at one point, "for making the equation, my father's equation, the Church's equation, between suffering and value", but the equation seems stronger than her anger and ultimately impervious to it. The heroine feels obliged to ransom herself, in the end, by giving all her money to Margaret, and it is by no means clear whether the author means us to see this as an authentic or a neurotic gesture.

I have emphasized the Catholic theme because it interests me particularly, but *Final Payments* is a rich, thoughtful, stylishly-written novel that should have a more than parochial appeal. The progress of its author will be worth watching. —DAVID LODGE, "The Arms of the Church," *TLS*, Sept. 1, 1978, p. 965

⟨Mary Gordon's⟩ presence as a novelist is hard to resist, and . . . it appeals to quite different sorts of readers. I say this on the basis of having spoken to some of those readers, of different sex, age and convictions, all of whom liked the book. Unlike the case with respect to, say, Doris Lessing, Mary McCarthy, or even Margaret Drabble, no one seems to be put off or offended or bored by Mary Gordon.

. . . ⟨The plot of *Final Payments*⟩ is described by the first-person narrator, and I remember that the author has been quoted as saying that Elizabeth Hardwick, with whom she studied writing at Barnard, had advised her that first, rather than third person was the right form for *Final Payments*. True enough; a central reason for the novel's charm and a measure of its limits.

Hear this speaker on the novel's first page, describing the priests who attended her father's funeral:

> They prided themselves on being out of the ordinary. . . . One of their jokes was that non-Catholics thought that they argued about how many angels could dance on the head of a pin, not knowing that this was a ridiculous question: angels were pure spirits; they did not dance. No, it was the important questions that absorbed them. They argued about baptism of desire, knocking dishes of pickles onto the carpet in their ardor. They determined the precise

> nature of the Transubstantiation, fumbling for my name as I freshened their drinks.

Beyond the precision of syntax and the strongly-felt rhythmic pace, the passage lives in its juxtaposing, without raising an eyebrow, the baptism of desire with pickles on a carpet, or the dead, middle-class word "freshened" with argument about Transubstantiation. The narrator is very secure here, has ordered her past experience into revealing comic and ironic formulations; and the novel is strong, dignified and funny too, when it is thus reflective.

When by contrast Isabel is living in the present, and turns her mind to people and subjects other than her father, priests, life in the old Queens apartment, Mary Gordon sometimes has a problem. She's fine when dealing with the old people on welfare whom Isabel goes around to interview; they can be presented as grotesquely or humorously or sadly affecting, can be characterized with the sharpness of one-dimensional life—as Jane Austen and Dickens were good at doing. But with her two girl-friends (and I use the word deliberately, since there is a lovely spirit of high school-best pals affection that hangs over them) and with Bad John (the man who, in an admired line, handles her breast "as if he had been making a meatball"—there is a lot about breasts in this novel) or Good Hugh of the "beautiful, classical back," she sometimes seems to be flailing the narrative along:

> I called Liz. Why had we stayed away from one another? When we lived a hundred miles apart we were closer; we had had telephone calls that were like works of art, full of color and definite line. They had helped me. I wanted to tell Liz now, more than she could possibly know. I had been trying to remember what my life had been like, how I had got through it. Hugh had been helping me; it was terribly important, he said, that I remember.

Nothing wrong with this, but maybe not quite enough right with it; compared to the prose standards she sets elsewhere these sentences are not fully enough written, the characters not quite there.

But the novel is strong at its end, as Mary Gordon manages to prevent this Jane Eyre from going out into the world and reducing it to the dimensions of her own mind. Again, humor is terribly important in keeping things sane, as on the last page when Isabel, returned from her term of penance at the abominable Catholic, Margaret Casey's, confronts her friends who have come to take her away from it all and presumably back to life. While staying at Margaret's, the heroine has gotten fat, sloppy, and had her hair done into a Bubble Cut, most chastening of former styles and beyond almost anyone's nostalgia:

> Liz looked at me, her eyes flicking up and down in quick judgment.
>
> "Who did your hair? Annette Funicello?"
>
> The three of us laughed. It was a miracle to me, the solidity of that joke. Even the cutting edge of it was a miracle.

The cutting edge of this novel is similarly solid, and like all really solid things—like laughter—miraculous. There will be more, and more difficult books, to come from Mary Gordon, for which and for whom we should be pleased.—William Pritchard, "Telling Stories," *HdR*, Autumn 1978, pp. 525–27

'I thought how easy it would be to kill a woman like that. You could lure her with coffee and doughnuts and then poison her or bash her skull in. To watch her die would be perfectly enjoyable.'

This disturbing reflection by the heroine and narrator of Mary Gordon's much-praised first novel ⟨*Final Payments*⟩ occurs to her while she is on her way to dedicate her life to caring for the person she likes least in the world. The offence of the unknown woman at the bus station is that 'she caught my eye and laughed like an animal', presumably a hyena since such behaviour is zoologically uncommon. In any case—a point we will return to—the simile is gratuitously imprecise. The murderous impulse is significant since *Final Payments* is a work of casuistry concerned to examine the conflicting demands of morality, especially Catholic morality. Isabel Moore, the heroine, blunders about, discharging ruin and agonizing about whether she is behaving well. It would be reassuring to feel that Mary Gordon knew she had created a Pharisaic monster and would dissociate herself from sympathy with Isabel's lethal spiritual struggles. This is not made clear and I was left with the feeling that perhaps Isabel was intended by her creator to represent Heroic Virtue or something of the kind.

. . . The characters in this book are static, in the sense that at the core of their being lies not a psychology but a morality. They are almost 'humours'. Thus, although they interact they cannot change or evolve. Liz, the hard-bitten, but soft-hearted, girl-friend will grunt wise-cracks to the end of time. Judgement day will discover Margaret still reeking sourly and muttering envious complaint masked as devout solicitude. Isabel herself is essentially the idea of moral dilemma who will bounce indefinitely from socket to socket of the Catholic pinball machine with her shiny steel surface unscarred by earthly experience. The fundamental impulse behind *Final Payments*, adequately implied by the title, is eschatalogical rather than fictional.

This is matched by a curious feature of the writing: the image without real content. The offending lady at the bus terminal who 'laughed like an animal' is credited with patches in her hair 'the colour of egg yolks', 'eyes . . . the colour of a chemical', 'a face the colour of egg whites' and so on. Ignoring the obsessive egg comparisons, which might well haunt a childless woman, these similes seem to express a refusal to collaborate with mere matter and, although certain excellent passages reveal Mary Gordon's talent for description, generally speaking the novel is set in a kind of featureless limbo.

Readers will rightly suspect by now that I didn't much enjoy this book. It seemed to me to be theology posing as fiction, a hybrid form which compounds the tedium of the former with the imprecision of the latter to the advantage of neither. Nevertheless, a case, and even a strong one, can be made for the defence. Mary Gordon is a natural writer who has enough authority over language, imaginative strength and eye for character to furnish a splendid novel. The vignettes in which Isabel explores a variety of bewildered old folk lodged with sometimes negligent, sometimes caring hosts, struck me as excellent. There is no doubt that *Final Payments* is an auspicious debut for a woman of twenty-eight and little doubt that its author will speak to us again. My own hope is that next time her voice will be less that of the casuist than of the novelist.—Paul Ableman, "Last Things," *Spec*, Jan. 13, 1979, pp. 23–24

The idea which informs ⟨*Final Payments*⟩ is neither unfamiliar nor bad. Everyone has sooner or later to assume responsibility for himself, and in our society this is as likely as not to mean a break with the past. The generation gap and the turn away from formal religion are themes frequently exploited in twentieth-century fiction. One difficulty Gordon encounters in handling her material is a failure to achieve any degree of objectivity: the old father, the priests who surround him, the Catholic community, the church itself are delineated with unrelieved scorn. Can the church really have such a devastating effect on all who are touched by it as Gordon's book seems to imply? Are all Catholics, from the politicians in Boston to the brahmins in New Orleans to the grape pickers in California, living twisted thwarted lives which can be redeemed only by a break with the old superstitions? It seems doubtful that such should be the case, and I think one of the first lessons any writer has to learn is to treat his antagonist with respect. The best literature encompasses our common humanity.

A trouble in *Final Payments* is that no one's humanity is more than minimally achieved. Isabel is a particularly bloodless and, for me, unattractive main character. I realize that her lack of motivation, her coldness, her apparent inability to know or to manage herself are offered as evidence of the state in which her father and the church have left her. Her vapid unprepossessing presence is in itself the conflict of the action. Her promise at the end to be a new human being, a nice girl, but one who has been freed from the old debilitating loyalties, is the resolution. She moves from sexual independence, which she cannot endure, to a return to a parodic kind of piety, to, in the last few pages of the book, the second phase of freedom which I have mentioned above. Whether or not this sort of spiritual and psychological progress would lead Isabel to the happiness she desires remains a question because she, along with all the other characters, is poorly drawn, and because the novel is poorly written in all its dimensions. I have mentioned the poverty of characterization, which can scarcely be exaggerated. The sentences in *Final Payments* are undistinguished and devoid of energy. The passion we are told about is never matched by either the thoughts and perceptions of the people or the thrust of the language. In some cases, as in that of Margaret, who kept house for and wanted to marry Professor Moore, serious efforts at character portrayal evolve into unintentional farce. A truism of literary theory is that bad conception leads to bad technique: so it is in *Final Payments*.—WALTER SULLIVAN, "Model Citizens and Marginal Cases: Heroes of the Day," *SwR*, Spring 1979, pp. 339–40

THE COMPANY OF WOMEN

Keen, enthusiastic, self-centered, condescending to her elders (her mother's friends and the priest ceaselessly cosset her), Felicitas Taylor ⟨in *The Company of Women*⟩ has to be brought down, and at length she is. A not entirely believable, self-hating professor of Marx cynically deflowers her, and Felicitas finds herself pregnant.

It's the kind of experience that often leads one's "own adult person" to say an everlasting Nay, but, happily, matters come out differently in *The Company of Women*. At the moment of narrative crisis, when Felicitas returns home with the bad news of her pregnancy and her gullibility, she instantly receives from her elders the gift of loving pardon. We don't watch the onset of a seed time of embitterment; neither do we watch Felicitas trading off sophisticated skepticism or comprehension of dominance as the price of being loved and pitied in her misfortune. We see, instead, that in welcoming her home with whole heart, Felicitas's guardians have not observed strict logic. (Strict logic dictates that when those condescended to as inferior see a chance to humiliate their oppressors, they do so unhesitatingly.) And the balance of the narrative proves, as it carries closer to the present the story of the heroine's relationships with other men and women, that Felicitas has learned an enriching lesson her elders' swift generosity is meant to teach: forbearance is among the world's great things.

No single character in *The Company of Women* seems to me as energetically drawn as the half-dozen major parties in *Final Payments*. (The four adult women are nearly interchangeable: each time the narration turned to one of them, I found myself obliged to leaf backward to check her identity.) And the atmosphere lacks tautness and edge. But there's a sweet and old-fashioned tolerance at the book's core that's highly likable. Miss Gordon chooses for her epigraph Auden's beautiful poem "The Common Life," the tricky closing lines of which claim:

> though truth and love
> can never really differ, when they seem to,
> the subaltern should be truth.

The charm of *The Company of Women* lies in the warmth of its acceptance of the simple dailiness of forgiveness, and in the directness of its reminder—we can't have too many such reminders, it seems—that, even now, truth and logic luckily often don't compel.—BENJAMIN DEMOTT, "Women without Men," *At*, March 1981, pp. 89–90

Since the rise and predominance of the art novel, the documentary aspect of fiction—regarded in the nineteenth century as a major strength of the genre—has figured little in critical discourse except among Marxists. Yet, stubbornly, the appeal of the documentary persists—and not only among unsophisticated readers. It is an impurity that cannot be strained out by the most finely textured filter of linguistically based criticism. Just as readers were once eager to be told *what it is like* to live in a coal mining town or to work in a grog shop in a Paris slum or to make one's way up as a businessman in Boston, so we still yearn for the revelation of modes of existence that are relatively unfamiliar, even when they involve large numbers of people living in our midst.

Too often, of course, the fiction that in these days gratifies that yearning has no literary pretensions whatsoever. What is it like to have grown up in an Irish-Catholic neighborhood in Queens, in a house that "had always been full of priests"? An exotic way of life? Hardly—except perhaps to the excessively secularized purveyors and consumers of "serious" literary culture. Yet I suspect that the careful, indeed loving, documentation of the mores of this world, arousing as it does the staring curiosity of the outsider and the pained or delighted recognition of the insider, had a good deal to do with the popular success of Mary Gordon's first novel, *Final Payments*.

Fortunately for her reputation, there was much more to the novel than that. Though imperfectly resolved, *Final Payments* is clearly the work of a gifted novelist, a writer whose stylistic attainments are on a level with her intelligence and insight. The story of the venturing into life of a "good Catholic girl" of thirty, who had devoted the previous eleven years to the unremitting care of her once formidable, then invalided, father, was in itself moving, and the moral perplexities she faced were handled with subtlety, humor, and compassion until the plot took a melodramatic turn that damaged the credibility of the last third of the book. Her new novel, *The Company of Women*, is likewise a fascinating document, likewise a work at once excellent and flawed. Though it is to some degree a reworking of the themes of the earlier novel, *The Company of Women* is, in its structure and scope, a very different sort of book. . . .

The theme of reconciliation—of the need for charity toward oneself as well as toward others—is merely one of the many themes explored in *The Company of Women*. The role of women in relation to male authority and to the Church, the rhythms of submission and rebellion, the perception of human love as a form of entrapment, the conflicting needs for shelter and escape—such are some of the preoccupations of this most *thoughtful* of recent novels. This thematic abundance is more successfully realized in short episodes and ruminations than dramatized in the compelling sweep of a major action. Mary Gordon is a reflective, even meditative novelist, and the effective sustaining of a plot is not among her strengths, either here or in *Final Payments*. There were times when I felt that the themes had escaped the narrative frame designed to contain them and scattered in several directions at once.

The Company of Women, with its extraordinary marshalling of forces in the opening section, promises more than it is ever able to deliver. Yet there is so much in this novel to admire and enjoy, to make the reading of it memorable. I will conclude with one striking example of Mary Gordon's artistry: her remarkable tact in handling the psychological alignments of the novel without so much as a Freudian nudge in the reader's ribs. She feels no compulsion to comment on or to underscore in any way what can be seen as Felicitas's quest for a father-surrogate or the veiled eroticism in the relationship between Father Cyprian and his flock. The veiling is thick indeed. Father Cyprian examines his spiritual state with great scrupulosity and precision and with never a consciously sexual thought; even his covert misogyny and his longing for an impassioned male friendship (such as he once enjoyed with Charlotte's long-dead husband) are given an entirely religious coloration. His tools are those of Catholic introspection, tools handed down from one priestly generation to the next. And not one of the older women voices the slightest concern or regret over the absence of sexual contact in their lives; better off without it, they would say. It is left for us to meditate, if we choose, upon the odd twists and turnings of sublimation. —ROBERT TOWERS, "Reconciliations," *NYRB*, March 19, 1981, pp. 7–8

Most books are so boring that I raise my glass to anyone who can write a novel which it is impossible to put down. Mary Gordon has done so. Only sleep and hunger interrupted my reading of *The Company of Women*. It was completely gripping from beginning to end.

But books which you cannot put down do not necessarily give you any pleasure. When clever novelists hold your attention they, and not you, are in control. It might be like transportation to Heaven. Or, as in the case of *The Company of Women*, it might be like being stuck in a lift with a crowd of people that you loathe.

I deeply loathed all the people in this book. I hated the heroine, who is a vain, selfish girl called Felicitas with a big bottom and a grudge against her pious Catholic upbringing. I hated the conceited slob of a college professor who initiates her into the sordid habits of promiscuous sex. I hated the way they all spoke, with 'shit' and 'fuck' so prodigally and unnecessarily used as punctuation. But more than the slob's world, I hated the world Felicitas tried to escape from: an oppressively Catholic world in which she is taught to feel guilty for preferring Protestant writers like Jane Austen to Thomas Merton or *The Sacred Heart Messenger*. Yet, however ghastly they all were, I read on; and the reason was that they were all evoked with such wit and narrative *panache*.

Actually, the book starts out with all the promise of a novel by Barbara Pym, if you can imagine Miss Pym's genius being translated into an American Roman Catholic setting. . . .

What will happen? Will Father Cyprian fall in love with Felicitas, or she with him? Are we to be treated to a sort of Papist *Lolita* or a spiritual re-run of *Heidi?* Both interesting possibilities.

Having dangled them under our noses, it has to be said that Mary Gordon does not really give us our money's worth. We turn a page and find we have jumped six years to 1969. That subtle novel—the relationship between Felicitas and Cyprian—was actually a bit beyond Mary Gordon's range. Little Felicitas is now a college kid, and the rest of the story is a very predictable and slushy business. She falls in love with one of the college lecturers. She loses her virginity. She moves into a sort of commune where there are hippies who take drugs, and dogs called Ho, Che and Jesus. She sleeps around, rather aimlessly, she finds herself to be pregnant (off-stage America invades Cambodia); she cannot face the abortion clinic and goes home to her mother.

It is all perfectly competently done: you keep turning the pages. But, really it was rather a let-down, after the subtle and interesting opening section to be palmed off with the dull old questions of female orgasm and abortion and all the other stuff of which Fiction is made. After that, you only need a cliché ending, which Mary Gordon neatly provides. Felicitas as a young mother herself, has repeated for her daughter the overpowering relationship she had with her mother. And the child, Linda, has begun to dote on the dying Father Cyprian.—A. N. WILSON, "Overfrocked Priest," *Spec*, July 4, 1981, pp. 23–24

MEN AND ANGELS

The title and the second epigraph of Mary Gordon's third novel, *Men and Angels*, are taken, characteristically, from the Bible, from the familiar passage in I Corinthians: "Though I speak with the tongues of men and of angels, and have not charity, I am become as sounding brass, or a tinkling cymbal." And in this novel Miss Gordon returns once more to a problem that dominated much of *Final Payments*, the problem of loving the unlovely. . . .

In *Men and Angels* a similar relationship of symbiotic dependence ⟨to that in *Final Payments*⟩ is portrayed again between the attractive and the unattractive, the powerful and the powerless, the loved and the unloved; the nature and limits of human love are explored, as before, against a background that contains at least the possibility of the limitless love of God. Isabel, leaving her lover, argues "If we can love the people we think are most unlovable, if we can get out of this ring of accident, of attraction, then it's a pure act, love; then we mean something, we stand for something." The protagonist of *Men and Angels*, Anne Foster, a mother and an art historian, is less ambitious spiritually, yet she too is deeply perplexed by the knowledge that although she is generally considered a "good" person, she cannot bring herself to love her mother's helper, Laura Post. She can treat her well, she can be fair to her, she can make her a birthday cake and buy her boots, but she cannot love her. . . .

This is a deliberately domestic, at times claustrophobic novel, with the rewiring of the house by an attractive electrician and a school Christmas dance recital presented as major events. The daily social life, the network of neighbors, the small-town flirtations and adulteries, the gossip and jealousies are sketched in so suggestively that the reader at times shares Anne's impatience with the confines of her world. Anne's escape is in her work: through the career of Caroline Watson she enters a bolder, brighter landscape of the imagination, a country of freedom—for Caroline was not only an important artist, she was also (although primarily a painter of the domestic life) a Bad Mother.

Suburban Anne is of course a Good Mother, who puts her children first most of the time and is preoccupied with keeping them safe. She loves them with a tellingly evoked physical passion, she returns with pleasure from reading Caroline's letters to "that other life, beautiful and heavy-scented as a dark fruit that grew up in shadow, the life of the family," and she worries constantly about the justice and wisdom of her own behavior toward them. Miss Gordon's rich, informal, imagery-packed prose beautifully reveals the poetry of domesticity, and her language dramatizes the small inner movements of the maternal heart. . . .

It is not clear whether Miss Gordon convicts Anne of spiritual hubris in her efforts to placate Laura and her own conscience, and thus blames her for precipitating the tragedy. Had she recognized the limitations of human love, maybe she would not have driven Laura over the edge. Unlike Miss Gordon's two earlier heroines, Isabel and Felicitas (in *The Company of Women)*, Anne is not religious. She is a representative, 20th-century woman, "rational, responsible for herself, for her own acts and her own marriage," unable to appeal to higher authority or to shelter behind sanctions. She is embarrassed by and does not understand people who claim to have "a religious life" and is puzzled when Caroline Watson's intelligent, sophisticated, mature daughter-in-law, whom she much admires, reveals herself as a churchgoer. Anne's husband (a shadowy and largely absent figure) regards a religious disposition as an odd human trait "quite randomly bestowed, like buckteeth or perfect pitch," whereas Anne regards it as "something powerful and incomprehensible" that made people "monsters of persecution, angels of self-sacrifice."

Anne herself is neither monster nor angel, although she is given to fantasizing about the extent of sacrifice she would embrace on her children's behalf. Her ruling passion, as she herself says, is maternity, and her creator provides in the novel several examples of the ill that falls to children whose mothers lack this passion. Yet behind the portrayal of Anne's maternal feeling lurks the sense that such devotion could be dangerous, could even, perhaps, be wrong: that it excludes other lives with other imperatives. It is possible that Anne's feeling for her children is as fanatical, as perverse, as Laura's for God. Laura, on the first page of the novel, is dwelling on a text from Isaiah: "Can a woman forget her sucking child, that she should have no compassion on the child of her womb? Even these may forget, yet I will not forget you." Even these forget, as Laura's mother had forgotten, as Caroline Watson forgot. Anne Foster judges Caroline Watson harshly for this, but the violence of her own preoccupation with her children nevertheless disturbs her: it is not wholly innocent, although it is natural. Moreover, it constrains and limits her. It interferes with her working life, it prevents her from making courageous decisions, it diminishes as well as enlarges her. . . .

A moral life, a religious life, an artistic life, a family life. Miss Gordon contrasts these at times mutually exclusive ways of being and of seeing with subtlety and feeling. She is reaching for a sense of wholeness, for the possibility of inclusion rather than exclusion, for a way of connecting the different passages of existence, and her book asks questions rather than provides answers. It disturbs, rather than reassures, for it demonstrates that family life itself, that safest, most traditional, most approved of female choices, is not a sanctuary: it is, perpetually, a dangerous place.—MARGARET DRABBLE, "The Limits of Mother Love," *NYTBR*, March 31, 1985, pp. 1, 30–31

WILFRID SHEED
From "The Defector's Secrets"

New York Review of Books, June 1, 1978, pp. 14–15

Mary Gordon's *Final Payments* is much more than the latest thing in Catholic novels . . . but it does show brilliantly the effects of the new dispensation on American Catholic fiction. It gives a picture of certain Catholic lives (its aim is convent-school modest) more ambiguous than anything either a loyalist or a heretic would have had a mind to produce a few years ago. In the European manner, the Church is seen not as a good place or a bad place, with batteries of the best lawyers to prove both at once, but as a multilayered poem or vision which dominates your life equally whether you believe it or not: which doesn't even seem to need your belief once it has made its point. Santayana once called himself "a Catholic atheist," as if there were a rubric even for that, if all else fails.

Gordon's heroine, Isabel Moore, is an ex-Catholic who still carries the vision on her person like radiation. She has sacrificed her life from nineteen to thirty to a fanatical right-wing father, nursing him through strokes and dotage, like a nun presiding over the last days of the pre-Vatican Church. But, like such a nun, she doesn't regret a minute of it. By secular consensus, the old man sounds as murderous as Jaweh (God is not a liberal): a McCarthyite reactionary, who accepts his own and other people's sufferings with inhuman serenity—placed next to the City of God, they are less than nothing. And unblinkingly, he has broken his own daughter's life, driving away her first boyfriend with Jove-like curses, and accepting her sacrifice as if he were God himself. The worst of him is that, senile or not, he knows exactly what he is doing.

Yet astonishingly he emerges as the most impressive and attractive character in the book—especially astonishing since he is never on stage but has to dominate from the clouds, and from memory. Gordon has conveyed his mere emanations, his perfectionism, his intelligence, his sheer size of spirit so well that the reader too half-sees that after him the outside world would seem trashy and pointless. The religious vocation has been made incarnate.

Which means that Isabel cannot begin to explain it to her friends. Her father the Church dies at last, and she finds them waiting for an explanation. Where has she been all these years? A father fixation? Female masochism? She finds the questions themselves trashy, and unanswerable. Her answer must be acted out. The novel is an exploration of whether the years with God were wasted.

The nun-parallel needn't be pushed too far. But it pushes very well, even on a prosy level. For instance, after her father's death, Isabel becomes dazzled by the clothes women are wearing, as if she had been literally locked in with the old man. Although she had been seeing a worldly friend all that time, they had apparently never once talked fashion. Likewise, she is suddenly perplexed by the minutiae of housekeeping, although she has been doing it herself for eleven years, albeit sloppily. If all this does not make her a nun-in-disguise, it might as well. If Gordon's point is that *all* Catholic girls are nuns in disguise she certainly goes to extremes to prove it.

More seriously, if we take the nun away and make Isabel's father too much less than God, we land at the level of her friends' questions, and find ourselves reading yet another book about female masochism. The surrender of the soul to God knows no sex, but looking after a cranky old man usually does. And this is decisively not a book about that. Or not *just* a book about that.

The author's problem here is to get the book out of the heroine's head, where everything works perfectly, and into situations where her actual existence can be verified. Since Isabel is telling the story herself, her outside self has to be deduced from the looks on her friends' faces, and their stabbing conversation, which is perhaps the hardest task in fiction.

For this reason, many first-person narrators never develop an outside at all. Isabel develops plenty, almost as if Gordon has started from the outside and worked her way in. Isabel comes across as an overgrown schoolgirl, in equal parts snippy and ardent. Her friends find her vaguely "strong," masochism or not, and wise in an unfocused sort of way. She seems extravagantly both to need help and to overflow with it. The question, as with the wisdom of LSD or opium, is whether the experience of a religious love can be applied to anything else, or must constantly return to itself. "My father is dead," she repeats grimly to herself. She *cannot* return to that. Her love, fastidiously fashioned for one purpose, one sacrament, is at large now, ravening for an object. And so the book begins.

The world of sex fails predictably—but rather more, owing to an author's lapse, than it has to. Gordon's own master is Jane Austen, and she shares some of Austen's difficulties at depicting young men. Most writers can at least render you a passable cad, but Gordon (put this down to her art perhaps) seems edifyingly never to have met one. Her villain is too awful to be true, although he is some sort of social work administrator, and a good one, he hasn't a decent bone in his body. When in a fit of muddled ardor she allows him to seduce her, he responds with all the grace of a tire salesman: "You were really dying for it, weren't you. . . . I was afraid I was going to have to pop your cherry," etc. And later when she decides that it is high time to repel his brutish advances, he goes off vowing vengeance like Dick Dastard in "Tied to the Railroad Track: a drama." There is no need for this even in plot terms; he could have had his vengeance without ever calling it that.

Her Mr. Right fails more by omission. Outside of a "classic back" and a walk that demands nothing (I had trouble picturing this), he is hard to get a handle on. His fits of petulance are less masterful than they are presumably intended to be, and indeed verge uncomfortably toward the cad's childishness. The only explanation, outside of late-blooming sex, for the man's fitful hold on Isabel is that he reminds her of her father—but this is a tactic of despair. *Someone* had better remind her of her father around here, or she'll boil over and fling herself into his grave.

Fortunately the men take up very little space, and are perhaps about what you'd expect on the first day out of the convent when everybody you meet seems a little more significant than they ever will again. In fact, Gordon seems less sure with her own generation in general. Isabel's two women friends, though adequate, are respectively too pale like her hero and too narrowly drawn like her villain. But she makes up for this triumphantly with the people Isabel really would know well: old people, who replicate her father, in that they're dying and helpless, and teeming with strategy.

She takes a job with the swinish social worker, which entails visiting these people and checking on their nursing care. Now at last she can use her eleven years of wisdom. The Christian proposition is that you must love the unlovable, or it doesn't count. Anyone can love the lovable, it is like sending money to the rich; but Christ has located himself like a Hans Andersen prince in the sick, the poor, and the ugly, the people who actually need it, and who have a million ways of warding it off.

Mary Gordon's gallery of addled old people is funny, exact, various: her intense, humorous prose, which gets her over some thin ice with the other characters, here finds its subject, and seems magically to become more mature and sure of itself as if the author became older around old people. Having sacrificed her youth once, Isabel seems anxious to get on with her own old age, and her concept of sacrifice oddly includes getting fat, slatternly, and helpless. Yet for all her introspection, she sees this as duty, not as a contagious disease like leprosy.

That senility is catching might be called an accidental theme, strong but not quite the point. Nor is the book precisely about Isabel's scruples, encyclopedic though these be. It is more about such matters as the *arrogance* of loving the unlovable, and the resourcefulness of the latter in breaking their saviors: hence the hard-faced nurse and the wily invalid, the survivors of the nursing home wars; hence their victims.

Worse yet, Isabel discovers that loving the unlovable is largely a charade one plays for one's own benefit: because for all her quivering sensibility she doesn't seem to be helping them in the least. The happy ones would be happy anywhere, she decides, while the mean ones would still be trapped in their meanness. "People were happy, people were unhappy, for reasons no one could see, no one could do much about." And what one could do was so random and intellectually unplannable. She shows an old man her breasts on request, and bureaucratically facilitates the death of an old woman—not the things she was raised to do, but the things that need doing. Charity is small and tactical and has nothing whatever to do with any conceivable government program she is supposed to be working on. It is, as she always thought, one person sacrificing everything to give just a tiny bit to another, with the only reward being the cold comfort of being thought "good."

With her father's cranky absolutism (he is a jealous god), she finally rejects even this reward as a stain on Charity and moves in with an old woman who hates her and who gobbles love without tasting it like a tapeworm, the *reductio ad absurdum* of her father. Margaret Casey used in fact to be her father's housekeeper, and had wanted in a dim, crafty way to marry the old man, and Isabel had gotten her fired years ago. So our heroine can be punished for this now too. Miss Casey even does Isabel the kindness of bad-mouthing her so that nobody can see her by-now spotfree sacrifice. Her humiliation is as thorough as anything in *The Story of O.*

Yet sacrifice for its own sake is idolatry, and she cannot enjoy even that, like a good pagan, for long. Her father, her justification, is dead: she cannot see his face any more. Which means that this is not religious abnegation and transcendence, but vulgar masochism, something the old man would have despised. A nun without a God is a fool. Isabel comes to see this by way of an interior monologue—and as anyone knows who has tried it, it is terribly difficult to show a convincing change of heart in this form. In Gordon's case, it might be a little more convincing with a little less talk. Because the novel has been so sturdily set up that it doesn't need captions, Isabel's doddering pastor, Father Mulcahy, indicates that such super-Christianity is wrong, and a boozy shake of the head from him is quite enough.

In the end, Isabel seems to accept the regular world of loving the lovables, who will certainly give her as much chance to sacrifice and suffer as all the old people put together. But she still carries her strange, pseudo-nun's equipment with her. For instance, she cannot understand property, or why people should be collectors; she has no patience with nature, a quirk common to those who have once seen nature as a mere shadow of God. Even with her girlfriends, she is happiest talking of schooldays when they were all Catholics together. When that narcotic is used up, she will be as hard on them as she is on herself, a pain and comfort like religion itself. In any plausible sequel one pictures her at permanently perplexed odds with the secular world, still going about her father's business.

It is entirely appropriate that *Final Payments* should be written in a comic mode. "She was performing her Catholic high school girl trick of comedy instead of intimacy," Isabel says of a friend. And this is the convention Isabel herself must work with, where danger is marked by jokes, and it is no accident that her model is Austen, the patron writer of the cloistered. The Austen method which seems so cool is not that far removed from eighteenth-century bullying; it will sacrifice anyone for a laugh. And the convent and the Catholic family need laughs too. Thus, if Isabel's ultra-monster, Margaret Casey, seems a bit too horrible, too infallibly horrible, to swallow, it is partly because of Isabel's burning attention and need for a joke.

The heroine's chaste bitchiness adds a little something to each miserable character until we have a comedy: as Austen made comedy of the puddingy gentry of western England. And when the characters flag, Gordon takes over herself, like Austen; and *makes* them funny. "Never once in those years did I wake up of my own accord. It was Margaret, always, knocking on my door like some rodent trapped behind a wall." "Father Mulcahy was clean as a piglet bathed in milk. His black hat was brushed as smooth as the skin of a fruit; his white hair, so thin that the hard, pink skull showed beneath it like a flagstone floor, looked as though the color had been taken out of it purposefully through a series of washings." The cadences are grave, unfacetious: a tragedy could be written in such prose. It is as if the jokes are being paid for even as they're being made. Even at her most carefree when she has one of her old ladies cheerily piping, "blow it out your ass," Gordon's effect is reverberantly sad.

These are the conditions Mary Gordon has set herself—that the story must be sad, the telling funny—and they appear quite inevitable. This was the style of the sardonic priest and the wry nun of the period, the ones who hid their feelings because they were so tumultuous. If God really has died as a presence to many Christians in this century, even as a grouchy demanding presence, this still seems like the best way to talk about it.

William Goyen

1915–1983

Charles William Goyen was born on April 24, 1915, in Trinity, Texas, and grew up from the age of seven in Houston. He received a B.A. in 1937 and an M.A. in Comparative Literature in 1939 from Rice University (then called Rice Institute), and taught for one year at the University of Houston before joining the U.S. Navy in 1940. Determined after the war to be a writer, he settled briefly in Taos, New Mexico, where he met Frieda Lawrence and other members of the D. H. Lawrence commune, and worked on short stories and his first novel. His story "A Parable of Perez" appeared in the *New Directions* annual in 1947, and in 1949 he published his first book, a translation of Albert Cossery's *Les Fainéants* (The Lazy Ones).

In 1949 Goyen visited England on the invitation of Stephen Spender, returning to live in Manhattan the next year, when his novel *The House of Breath* was published. He won Guggenheim Fellowships in 1951 and 1952, and worked on a volume of short stories, *Ghost and Flesh* (1952), and on a stage version of his novel, which was produced off-Broadway in 1954. After a year in Rome he taught at the New School for Social Research in New York from 1955 until 1960. His second novel, *In a Farther Country*, appeared in 1955, and his play *The Diamond Rattler* was produced in Boston in 1960. More stories were published the same year, in *The Faces of Blood Kindred*, and the comic novel *The Fair Sister* followed in 1963. Goyen was playwright-in-residence at the Lincoln Center Repertory Company in 1963–64, and his play *Christy* was produced in New York in 1964. He won ASCAP Awards for musical compositions in 1965, 1966, and 1968, but from 1966 to 1971, while a senior editor at McGraw-Hill, experienced a less productive period.

In the 1970s Goyen taught intermittently at Brown University, and was also writer-in-residence at Princeton. A non-fictional work, *A Book of Jesus*, was published in 1973, and a further novel, *Come, The Restorer* in 1974. *Collected Stories* appeared in 1975, the short novel *Wonderful Plant* in 1980, and the novel *Arcadio* posthumously in 1983.

Goyen married the actress Doris Roberts in 1963. He died of leukemia on August 29, 1983, in Los Angeles, where he had lived since 1975.

Personal

Interviewer: In the Introduction to your *Selected Writings*, you stated that you began writing at the age of sixteen, at a time when you were also interested in composing and dancing and other art forms. Why writing as a career rather than one of the other arts?

Goyen: My foremost ambition, as a very young person, was to be a composer, but my father was strongly opposed to my studying music—that was for girls. He was from a sawmill family who made strict a division between a male's work and a female's. (The result was quite a confusion of sex-roles in later life: incapable men and over-sexed women among his own brothers and sisters.) He was so violently against my studying music that he would not allow me even to play the piano in our house. Only my sister was allowed to put a finger to the keyboard . . . the piano had been bought for her. My sister quickly tired of her instrument, and when my father was away from the house, I merrily played away, improving upon my sister's Etudes—which I had learned by ear—and indulging in grand Mozartian fantasies. In the novel *The House of Breath*, Boy Ganchion secretly plays a "cardboard piano," a paper keyboard pasted on a piece of cardboard in a hidden corner. I actually did this as a boy. My mother secretly cut it out of the local newspaper and sent off a coupon for beginners' music lessons. I straightaway devised Liszt-like concerti and romantic overtures. And so silent arts were mine: I began writing. No one could hear that, or know that I was doing it, even as with the cardboard piano.

Interviewer: You weren't having to write under the covers with a flashlight, were you?

Goyen: You know, I *was* playing my music under the quilt at night, quite literally. I had a little record player and I played what music I could under the quilt and later wrote that way. So I did write under the sheets.

Interviewer: What was your father's reaction to writing?

Goyen: Something of the same. He discovered it some years later, when I was an undergraduate at Rice University in Houston. He found me writing plays, and to him the theatre, like the piano, was an engine of corruption which bred effeminate men (God knows he was generally right, I came to see), sexual libertines (right again!), and a band of gypsies flaunting their shadowed eyes and tinselled tights at reality. When my first novel was published, my father's fears and accusations were justified—despite the success of the book—and he was outraged to the point of not speaking to me for nearly a year.

This could, of course, have been because the book was mostly about his own family—the sawmill family I spoke of earlier. My father, his brothers, his father, everybody else were lumber people, around mills . . . and forests. I went around the sawmills with him, you see, and saw all that. He loved trees so! My God, he would . . . he'd just *touch* trees . . . they were human beings. He would smell wood and trees. He just loved them. He knew wood. He was really meant for that.

Poor beloved man, though, he later came around to my side and became the scourge of local bookstores, making weekly rounds to check the stock of my book. He must have bought a hundred copies for his lumbermen friends. God knows what *they* thought of it. Before he died he had become my ardent admirer, and my *Selected Writings* is dedicated to him.

Interviewer: Do you agree with the theory that an unhappy childhood is essential to the formation of exceptional gifts? Were you genuinely unhappy?

Goyen: How could it have been any other way? My own nature was one that would have made it that way. It was a melancholy childhood. It was a childhood that was searching for—or that *needed*—every kind of compensation it could get. I think that's what makes an artist. So that I looked for compensation to fulfill what was not there. . .

Interviewer: Do you think of the novel as a lot of short stories, or as one big story? Or does it depend upon the novel?

Goyen: It might. But it seems to me that the unified novel, the organic entity that we call a novel, is a series of parts. How could it not be? I generally make the parts the way you make those individual medallions that go into quilts. All separate and as perfect as I can make them, but knowing that my quilt becomes a whole when I have finished the parts. It is the *design* that's the hardest. Sometimes it takes me a long time to see, or discover, what the parts are to form or make.

Interviewer: Does the completion of one "medallion" lead to another?

Goyen: No, the completion of one medallion does not usually lead to another. They seem to generate, or materialize, out of themselves and are self-sufficient, not coupled to, or, often, even related to, any other piece. That seems to be what my writing job is: to discover this relationship of parts. Madness, of course, comes from not being able to discover any connection, any relationship at all! And the most disastrous thing that can happen is to *make up*, to *fake*, connections. In a beautiful quilt it looks like the medallions really grow out of one another, organic, the way petals and leaves grow. The problem, then, is to graft the living pieces to one another so that they finally become a living whole. That is the way I've had to work, whatever it means.

Interviewer: Have you made medallions that did not fit into a final quilt?

Goyen: There's rarely been anything left over, that is, medallions that didn't fit into the final quilt. If the pieces didn't all come together, the whole failed. It's really as though all the pieces were around, hidden, waiting to be discovered, and there were just enough for the design on hand. If, in rare cases, something was left over, one tried to use it as some sort of preamble or "postlude"—that sort of fussy thing. It never worked, even when one felt it was such "fine" writing that it should be kept in. It's this kind of exhibitionism of bad taste that's harmed some good work by good writers.

Interviewer: So you started writing under a quilt and you came out producing quilts.

Goyen: Producing them is right.

Interviewer: How else would you describe your own writing, or your style?

Goyen: As a kind of singing. I don't say this because others have said it. But we've spoken of my work as song, earlier, the musicality of my writing and its form. It's impossible for me not to write that way. I write in cadence—that could be very bad. Just as in the theatre, when an actor in rehearsal discovers that lines in a speech rhyme, he or the director is horrified. Someone in the back of the theatre will scream out, "Couplet! Couplet!", meaning, "It rhymes! It rhymes!"

Now, when I speak of writing in cadence, I obviously don't mean "Couplet! Couplet!" Nor am I concerned with alliteration or any kind of fancy language. But I am concerned with the *flow* of language (the influence of Proust). I think of my writing as having to do with singing people: people singing of their lives, generally, arias. The song is the human experience that attracts me and moves me to write.

Interviewer: Are you concentrating now on short stories or novels?

Goyen: I have less an urge to write the short story, and more of a concern with writing The Book. It has nothing to do with anything but my own lack of need for the very short form and a deep love for the book itself, for a longer piece of writing.

Interviewer: Some may say you achieved both in *Ghost and Flesh*—a book of short stories which, on rereading, seems a total book rather than a collection of pieces. Was it conceived as a book, or was it a true gathering?

Goyen: No, it was conceived as a book, it truly was. A sort of song cycle, really, that made up a single, unified work, a thematic unity like Schubert's *Die Winterreise* (which influenced *The House of Breath*—an early Marian Anderson recording. Frieda Lawrence first made it known to me, that is, the poem on which the songs were based).

Ghost and Flesh . . . you can see in those stories . . . wow . . . quite surreal and I loved those, and when that was finished and published, I kind of went off the beam. I think the book made me quite mad; writing it, the obsession of that book; but, on the other hand, *The House of Breath* did not. And that's an obsessed book, you see. It's hard to say these things but something always pulled me through. Of course my critics might say, he *should* have gone mad.—WILLIAM GOYEN, Interview by Robert Phillips, *PRev*, Winter 1976, pp. 60–62, 92–95

Works

NOVELS

William Goyen's *The House of Breath*, a first novel, begins with a rather dismaying rush of words and some self-conscious mannerisms, notably a kind of nudging parenthesis, but it soon settles down and becomes a style of some power as well as readability. The title refers to a house in an East Texas village, the past life of which is evoked, partly through a narrator who spent his boyhood there, and partly through the reflective monologues of the people who have lived in it. The pervading tone of the book is thus one of nostalgic reminiscence. This would normally be discouraging, because the emotional urgency of nostalgia is so often mistaken for inspiration, and yet it is one of the hardest moods to communicate. But here is one author who has boldly faced material that dozens of writers have failed with and made something of it. There is some fine and sensitive description of the woods and the river and the farm animals and the changing seasons, and an intricate but clearly developed pattern of themes and symbols is built up somewhat after the manner of Virginia Woolf. The house is thought of as haunted by its memories, and the monologues are extracted from it as though Yeats were right, and it was possible to sink into an *anima mundi* where one could tune in on a psychic ether of memory and points of brooding return. It sounds ectoplasmic, but it has been skillfully done, and when we finish this remarkable book we have a panorama of a dozen interconnected and brilliantly summarized lives.

The author has an acute ear for the slurred elisions, agglutinative syntax and somnolent rhythms of vernacular speech, and he is particularly successful with females and the female mood of querulous patience. He has also discovered that when East Texas lifts up its voice in complaint the result is very suggestive of a banshee wail, which adds point to his scheme. He appears to be a little afraid that his characters will not get enough sympathy from the reader unless he insists on their claims to it. At any rate his genuine humor seems a bit furtive and some of his symbolism is over-italicized—the village the house is in is called Charity, for instance, which evidently means something, and there are other traces of portentousness. But these are trifles in a book that gets an extraordinary amount said in its hundred and eighty pages, a book which, if it remains something of a stunt, is an outstandingly clever and successful one.—NORTHROP FRYE, "Notes on Several Occasions," *HdR*, Winter 1951, pp. 614–15

In his novel *House of Breath*, William Goyen writes: "That people could come into the world in a place they could not at first even name and had never known before; and that out of a nameless and unknown place they could grow and move around in it until its name they knew and called with love, and call it HOME, and put roots there and love others there; so that whenever they left this place they would sing homesick songs about it and write poems of yearning for it, like a lover; . . ." The soil in which chance had sown the human plant was of no importance. And against this background of nothingness human values grow! Inversely, if beyond memories, we pursue our dreams to their very end, in this pre-memory it is as though nothingness caressed and penetrated being, as though it gently unbound the ties of being. We ask ourselves if what has been, was. Have facts really the *value* that memory gives them? Distant memory only recalls them by giving them a value, a halo, of happiness. But let this value be effaced, and the facts cease to exist. Did they ever exist? Something unreal seeps into the reality of the recollections that are on the borderline between our own personal history and an indefinite pre-history, in the exact place where, after us, the childhood home comes to life in us. For before us—Goyen makes us understand this—it was quite anonymous. It was a place that was lost in the world. Thus, on the threshold of our space, before the era of our own time, we hover between awareness of being and loss of being. And the entire reality of memory becomes spectral.

But it would seem that this element of unreality in the dreams of memory affects the dreamer when he is faced with the most concrete things, as with the stone house to which he returns at night, his thoughts on mundane things. William Goyen understands this unreality of reality: "So this is why when often as you came home to it, down the road in a mist of rain, it seemed as if the house were founded on the most fragile web of breath and you had blown it. Then you thought it might not exist at all as built by carpenter's hands, nor had ever; and that it was only an idea of breath breathed out by you who, with that same breath that had blown it, could blow it all away." In a passage like this, imagination, memory and perception exchange functions. The image is created through co-operation between real and unreal, with the help of the functions of the real and the unreal. To use the implements of dialectical logic for studying, not this alternative, but this fusion, of opposites, would be quite useless, for they would produce the anatomy of a living thing. But if a house is a living value, it must integrate an element of unreality. All values must remain vulnerable, and those that do not are dead.—GASTON BACHELARD, "House and Universe," *The Poetics of Space*, tr. Maria Jolas, 1964, pp. 58–59

SHORT STORIES

Above the Mason-Dixon line, hardly a ghost to speak of turns up in contemporary American writing. But below that line, ghosts swarm in a thousand forms: the ghostly father of Thomas Wolfe, the ghostly Confederacy of William Faulkner, the ghostly lover of Elizabeth Hardwicke, the ghostly cafés and army posts of Carson McCullers. In his second book, a collection of eight short stories ⟨*Ghost and Flesh*⟩, William Goyen demonstrates that this ghostly Southern literary tradition extends as far west as Texas, where he grew up. His ghosts are lost figures and faces out of his childhood.

Goyen's method, in all but three of these stories, is to chase his phantoms through a lush word-thicket reminiscent of the prose rhapsodies of Thomas Wolfe, calling on them to reveal themselves, occasionally flushing some of the freshest images in post-war fiction, but seldom catching more than a fleeting glimpse of the shadowy figures he is after.

Among the three stories in which Goyen allows his characters to act out their lives without the misting intrusion of a narrator's comment, "The White Rooster," a shrewd, cruel tale of murder, is the best. In it an irritable housewife named Marcy Samuels finds her life burdened with a snooping invalid father-in-law in her house and an impudent stray white rooster outside in her pansy bed. Marcy sees the poaching rooster as her poaching father-in-law's surrogate and sets out to kill him.

Grandpa Samuels, sensing his involvement, sets out to prevent this. Goyen's fresh-faced colloquial style runs like a riotous red ribbon of humor through a dark design woven around a housewife's murder by an old man who believes that old roosters never die.

"What there is to tell about," writes Goyen in one of the long monologues that serves as the remaining five stories, "is *what was not seen.*" He follows this dictum out the window and into an airy prose filled with cloudy shapes and crossed with bright flights of poetry. At one point he is a daring young man on a flying trapeze lying awake in a San Francisco hotel room, kneading his past for meaning. At another he lets a grieving widow tell the story of why her dead husband "comes ridin' onto the sleepinporch every night regular as clockwork." At still another he finds overwhelming significance in a slight childhood incident involving a kite. More ghost than flesh, most of Goyen's people drift undramatized through a smog of loneliness—bodiless voices speaking of murder, madness and emasculation.—Robert Lowry, "A Smog of Loneliness," *NYTBR*, Feb. 10, 1952, p. 5

ERNST ROBERT CURTIUS

"William Goyen" (1952)

Essays on European Literature, tr. M. Koval

1973, pp. 456–64

Here ⟨*The House of Breath*⟩ is the fledgling work of a young American. I have rendered it into German because spiritual currents flow through it that I should like to transmit.

A house in the remote southwest of the United States, a long-decayed house with its family relations and its fortunes, is erected here by the power of the spirit. Breath is respiration, breath is the breath of life, breath is the creative spirit moving upon the waters; it carries the word, it spans the abysses of human solitude, it builds palaces, cathedrals, worlds of ideas. Franz Werfel has expressed it in hymnic tones:

> Lausche Du, horche Du, höre!
> In der Nacht ist der Einklang des Atems los,
> Der Atem, die Eintracht des Busens ist gross.
> Atem schwebt
> Über Feindschaft finsterer Chöre.
> Atem ist Wesen vom höchsten Hauch.
> Nicht der Wind, der sich taucht
> In Weid, Wald und Strauch,
> Nicht das Wehn, vor dem die Blätter sich drehn . . .
> Gottes Hauch wird im Atem der Menschen geboren.
>
> [Listen, hearken, hear! In the night the harmony of the breath is free, breath, the concord of the bosom, is vast. Breath floats above the hostility of tenebrous choirs. Breath is the essence of the highest inspiration. Not the wind that plunges into meadow, wood, and hedge, not the blast before which the leaves dance . . . God's breath is born in the breath of men.]

The truth expressed in these ten lines we shall encounter once more in Goyen's book, and it evidently means so much to him that he refers the readers to it in his title and harps on it again and again through the leitmotif technique of the work. The breath with which he builds the house of his childhood belongs to the region outlined by Werfel's stanza.

The house of which Goyen tells is located in the small town of Charity, Texas. Perhaps this place will one day be recorded on those maps of the soul in which Proust's Combray as well as Joyce's Dublin are inscribed. The house faces a meadow (soon oil rigs will root it up). Herds graze there (before they must make way for the oil wells), giving the children of the house that intimacy with animal nature which has been associated with the human realm since the Garden of Eden, and which responds to the natural in man. The pasture is sown in bitterweed; and it is as if bitterness had become a part of the milk on which the children were raised. But sometimes its effect is like that of the enchanted grass of which Glaucus, the Fisherman, partook (Ovid tells his story): all of a sudden his heart was shaken and he was seized by an irresistible longing for a different element. He said farewell to the earth, on which he would never again set foot, plunged into the waters, and was transformed. So the adolescent Folner is transformed when the circus spreads its tent on the meadow, with its tinsel display of wild and colorful life, which Folner will follow into tawdriness, corruption, and death. This magic also seduces Christy, carried out to sea or into the deep woods. Also Sue Emma; also Berryben; also the small boy who is the narrator of these destinies. All the children break with house and home and custom; only the old remain to wait and watch. They are the prisoners of the house, aging and decaying and rotting with it, until it becomes food for the elements and for the hordes of uncannily quiet, greedy insects.

The bitterweed meadow slopes down to the bottomlands of the river. The river plays a generative and destructive role in the lives of the people of Charity. It is older than man and animals; it is the God of buried cycles of time; it is the elemental power that demands its prey and casts its spell. Immersion in it brings thrills of bliss (Novalis could speak of the "supernal bliss of all that flows" and of the "outpourings of the primal waters within us") but it also brings death. The river is one of the central characters in the book. Another is the wood on the other side of the river, or rather the woods, those endless regions of wild forest in which Christy goes bird-hunting; where death lurks and blood flows; where, if anywhere, the heart could disclose its secret—if it could find the language or the ear to listen. The wild wood of Charity conceals enigmas like the wood of Arthurian legend.

The elements of nature not only constitute the background of this book, they are also demonic participants in the action. The element of water is in it as river and sea; the element of earth as meadow and wood. Associated with them is the air as breath; as the amphibious element which belongs to both spirit and nature. Alive in William Goyen is a primal affinity with the first things of creation ("O I am leaf and I am wind and I am light"). He has the keen senses of the woodsman, whom no creak or rustle can elude. He registers the sensual qualities of natural things, and it is as though he himself had experienced, from within, the cycle of germination, budding, flowering, and withering of all created matter. We seem to be hearing the voice of an aboriginal America that is being constantly pushed back by industrial civilization and forced to languish in its big cities.

To plunge into the river and into the wilderness of the woods; to escape from the house and its ties of guilt and suffering, of bodily decay and dullness; from the spiritual corruption of the old but also from the self-destruction of the young through vice, revolt, aberration: this is the thorny path of the boy whose story is related in this book. But he struggles through, and roses will bloom for him, because he has had courage.

Courage: this means to obey the lesson of life. In order to do so we must first take life's measure completely: must reach its heights by flying like the bird; must penetrate its depths like the fish (this book cannot be understood if its animal symbolism is overlooked). We must be able to change elements like that legendary fisherman who became a sea-god. Alternation between air, earth, water: alternation between sinking and rising again: the fabric of the book is shot through with the drama of man and the elements. Otey's intact maidenhood is swallowed up by water; but her last breath sprays the body of her beloved as with a shower of diamonds. To plunge into the deadly deep; but also to bring up its treasure, shelter it and help it toward the light—this is what we recognize as the demands of life but also as the mission of art. From all the world's darkness, from all its regions of misery, the spirit rises again like the pearl diver, laden with responsibility toward its own vision of the depths. Only it must first dress its finds and shape them. What it brings to light is raw material: an amalgam of sense and soul. This booty from the deep must be fused and annealed. Art is alchemy; a higher stage of chemistry. It carries on and sublimates the process of life, which is itself a "great mysterious chemistry." Human beings react upon each other like acids, salts, and sulphur; everything acts upon everything else; in this process the stuff of human life is transformed and enhanced. It is refined in pain, in wisdom, and in love.

But first its hardness must be broken. Life, experience, guilt break the human being. Youth means the destruction of the magic of childhood; that is why it is the bitterest time of life. A broken world has been given to us to live in. That is how it presents itself to the artist, that is how he suffers it. He sifts these fragments and splinters; he sifts them, saving the most precious. These he polishes and fits together with long patience. Out of these bits of mosaic he pieces together his picture. So on his part he restores the unity and wholeness of the world.

A fledgling work—but a mature one. We are accustomed to a first novel being an eruption in which ore, slag, and ashes are whirled up together; or a so-called confession; or the reaction to the shock of growing pains on the nerves. Goyen's art is of a different sort. He has pledged himself to silence and waiting: to wait until he should find the word, "strong, small, but hard as a stone," which would utter his loneliness to the world; to wait until the breath which the house breathed in him should become speech; till this breath should take form and become matter pliant and capable of being transformed into an image. The genesis of a work of art is a two-sided process. It is the response to an inner impulse that makes itself felt as suffering and as a goad to the spirit; at the same time it responds to a demand that the unspoken existence of things makes upon the artist. "Lost time" wants to be recovered, the decayed house wants to be rebuilt. For these things the artist must find the word, the word that is both a touching and a naming. The title, *House of Breath*, comprises this polarity. The breath of lived life has merged with the breath of the artist. William Goyen had the power to attend this moment. He was able to wait because this breath was energy, an energy that wanted to be caught and directed so as to become the driving force of a power station. This energy had to be harnessed by a generator and converted into communication: communication through discourse, not through outcry or puling. Communication is something else and something more than mere "expression," which today is often considered an adequate validation of the artist. Communication means demonstration and construction of a spiritual content. The goal to which it aspires is "a full clear statement, a singing, a round, strong, clear song of total meaning, a language within language, responding each to each forever in the memory of each man."

For the artist everything depends on whether this conversion into spirit and language is successful. It is for this that he struggles and experiments, for this that he suffers and chooses the way of greatest resistance. For this he sacrifices the easy solutions and mechanical aids. This is the ordeal by which he is tested, and, if he stands the test, he wins the highest prize: he becomes real and substantial. He is redeemed from his solitude, connected with the world and the flow of its energies. And his work is the bridge to other men. He has vaulted the stream and stands now on the farther shore.

The artist must assume this burden of sorrow in an obtuse world, under a leaden sky. Not many choose this path. But those who do have the vocation.

Like all modern art Goyen's book is the testimony and result of a sincerity that refuses to draw the line at cruelty. Bodies and souls are displayed with their wounds, their scars, their disintegrating tissue, their shames. In some artists such unmasking is cynical or bitter. In some it purports to be the ultimate truth about life, art being the only exception: an art which sees its nobility in hardness of form and of heart. Flaubert, Valery, Joyce are the saints of this kind of art. Goyen too lays bare the cancer of the flesh and of the soul; he too proclaims the passion of man. But with him suffering and torment include compassion. The tragic agony is carried through to the catharsis. The harmony with the elemental power of earth operates in this book as a stream that washes away all stains, that purifies and heals. Folner has died of the bitterweed of the Charity meadow. But he will be healed beyond death on a meadow bright with clarity. What does the river tell us once we have learned to understand its language? "Everything flows into everything and carries with it and within it all lives of its life and others' life and all is a murmuring and whispering of things changing into each other, breeding and searching and reaching and withdrawing and dying. Whatever crossing is made each over other, by boat or bridge or swimming, is to another side; and whatever drowning is dying and sinking back into a womb, and what salvation or rescue of the perishing in waters or wickedness, dead or alive, is a union of silence or rejoicing; and to drop down into any of us, into depths (in river or self or well or cellar) is to lower into truth and sorrow. But we are purged, to plunge beneath a flood is to lose all guilty stains and to rise is to be purified. And we are to keep turning the wheels we turn, we are wind we are water we are yearning; we are to keep rising and falling, hovering at our own marks, then falling, then rising." The children in this book have grown up in the ecstatic piety and otherworldly hope of the Methodist Church. Stanzas of hymns, full of nostalgia for the golden city of heaven, reverberate within them. All this turns to dust along with the dream images of childhood. But a longing for redemption, a trust remains, even if its form has been completely changed. It has been transmuted into the blowing of the breath that restores wholeness:

> Gottes Hauch wird im Atem der Menschen geboren.
>
> [God's breath is born in the breath of men.]

If I have set Goyen's novel beside Werfel's lines (which Goyen has undoubtedly never read) or beside the sibylline words of Novalis, it was in order to point out a spiritual law. There are emotional realities that can only be discovered through the poets (this is perhaps the essential function of poetry). And one of the functions of criticism might be to register such discoveries; to draw the lines connecting explorers widely separated in space, time, and culture, who knew nothing of one another and yet shaped their course for the same islands and were guided on their voyage by the same stars. Such a view of literature might, within its modest limits (yet also guided by a clear sense of responsibility), assist in the great task appointed to mankind since the Tower of Babel: the restoration of unity. Separation, division, fragmentation are evil and lead to death. Connection, completion, conjunction restore the fullness of life; they lead to goodness and love. They are two opposing principles, as separation and conjunction are two complementary operations of alchemy. The law of separation and reunion also prevails throughout Goyen's book.

It is no accident that this book recalls poetry. The element of poetry entirely pervades Goyen's novel. It is not as if it had isolated "lyrical passages." No, it's very substance is poetic in nature. Everything that the author experiences presents itself to him in the aggregate state of poetry; a primary poetry in which the epic and the lyric have not yet been sundered. The mode of discourse is not descriptive but imaginative. This is already shown by the title. Mingling with the human voices is the voice of the river, the voice of the fountain, the voice of the wind. Goyen's mode of lyrical epic is related to myth and legend. The muse of the book is the blind girl sitting on a blue, rolling, cosmic sphere, bent over her lyre, and reciting her memories in a lyric lament (Greek myth makes the Muses the daughters of memory). She is a cosmogonic muse. She knows all the legends of genesis and all history. She could speak of heroic expeditions and of the founding of cities; of errant voyages and of the quest for salvation. *The House of Breath* tells us of Charity and East Texas; when it ranges farther, it only crosses the border of the neighboring state of Louisiana. And yet this book is something other than a local novel. What we are given here is not regionalism. The language and the landscape of East Texas are only the ground here of a fabric in which living and neighboring people talk and move. In the kitchen of the house at Charity hangs a map of the world. To the boy whose story is related to us the outlines of the countries and continents seemed like the organs of a human body. The articulation and conformation of the earth has impressed itself with the utmost vividness upon his child's consciousness. In the sleepy town of Charity he has had an intuitive apprehension of the wide world and known that he himself was part of it. That is why this novel of a childhood has become a book containing a universal experience.

Since 1920 the American novel has been discovered in Europe, and that is good. But since 1945 it has become the fashion, with the result that the reading public has formed a conventional idea of this branch of world literature that it now wishes to have confirmed. This notion is confused and naïve—like most of the ideas that Europeans have about America (and Americans about Europe). From the American novel we expect brutality and cynicism; intellectual over-refinement; but also primeval eruptions; morbidity and neurosis. In William Goyen's book we shall find very different elements of substantive poetry (as I have already said); harmony with the deepest simplicities of existence; reunion of sexuality with love; but also an artistic discipline that is more reminiscent of Flaubert, Proust, Joyce than of Melville, Wolfe, Faulkner.

It seemed more important to me to bring out some of the personal characteristics of William Goyen than to investigate his place in American literature of the 1950s (which will be done by others). Moreover, I believe that we form an erroneous conception of American literary sociology when we apply European conditions to the enormous transatlantic community. The loneliness of the young American who indentures his life to literature, let alone to poetry, is absolutely distinct from that of his European colleague, and infinitely more cruel. To endure it requires heroism. That is why it pleases me all the more that William Goyen's first book has been favorably received in America and England, and that it can now be submitted to German readers. For as André Gide said of Charles-Louis Philippe: "Cette fois, c'est un vrai."

SHIRLEY ANN GRAU

1929–

Shirley Ann Grau was born on July 8, 1929, in New Orleans. After attending Booth Academy in Montgomery, Alabama, and the Ursuline Academy in New Orleans, she studied at Sophie Newcomb College, Tulane University's college for women, graduating with a B.A. in 1950. She stayed on at Tulane as a graduate student for one year, but then devoted herself full-time to writing. Having sold a few short stories to magazines in 1953, she considered moving to New York but remained in New Orleans, and in 1955 married James Kern Feibleman, professor of philosophy at Tulane University.

Grau's first book, *The Black Prince and Other Stories*, was sold out within two weeks of its first printing in 1954, and was a success with the critics as well. Further stories and essays appeared in periodicals in the following years, before her first novel, *The Hard Blue Sky*, was published in 1958. *The House on Coliseum Street* followed in 1961, and Grau's third novel, *Keepers of the House* (1964), won her the Pulitzer Prize. She taught creative writing at the University of New Orleans in 1969–70, but for the most part has remained absorbed by writing and family life. Later works include the novels *The Condor Passes* (1971) and *Evidence of Love* (1977), and a second collection of stories, *The Wind Shifting West* (1973).

Grau and Feibleman have four children. They live in Metarie, New Orleans, and spend their summers at Martha's Vineyard.

A well-made novel is a matter of form, of design—and very difficult design and form at that. It is not accident that the folk of *Hard Blue Sky*, for instance, are island folk, framed by the sea and the low sky, their lives touched accidentally and sparingly by people not of the island. It is an isolation that provides focus and adds to depth perception; we can see better what is held for us in its own special frame. It is art, too, that the storm that gathers itself as these pages turn is not given to us at the end; it is the tension and fire of the internal storm-stresses against this impending background that are important, not the background itself. These tensions the author is perceptive enough not to drown out with the dramatic over-sweep of the literal storm. So too with the interlacing of lives. Here accident and art must seem to concur, if there is to be design, as in Annie's gravitation to the outsider, Inky, rather than to the island boy Perique and his sullen dedication. These relationships are intimate, personal, yes, but they take on substance too in proportion as they become more than that, as they move out from what they have been toward what they may become. By this relating of inner world to outer world, and of that outer to a further, as in Annie's final leaving of the island, the structure of the book extends itself into structures of meaning.

Form, design, is perhaps not the essence of art, but art without form is nothing, is merely protean. Indeed, it is unimaginable. In view of this, again, the indifference of publishers and reviewers alike to the primary constituents of art is a grave threat to the future of the novel.

The fine awareness of the interplay among characters all of whom in a good novel must be inter-relating figures seen each in full dimension—this seems more and more a recessive gene in the publisher's consciousness, seems less and less a matter of interest to the jaded reviewers. Indeed, I wonder lately how many reviewers have much notion of what a novel *is*, or is for.

Hard Blue Sky is conscious of its legitimacy as a novel in the same way that Elizabeth Bowen's *Death of the Heart*, or to leap-frog titles, Carson McCullers' magnificent *The Heart Is a Lonely Hunter*, is conscious of its legitimacy in the field. It embodies and makes use of the large fund of technical resources and awareness of form that are aspects of all fine art at its highest reaches. This is, of course, a learned and recognized thing—not the sweepings of inspiration or the loose outpour of "a talent." It represents a longer coming-to, a larger and much more sustained effort toward the deliberate, planned mastery of a craft than most who "want to write" are willing ever even to attempt. The unfolding of Annie and of Annie's world, and the simultaneous making-known to the reader the lives and worlds of the figures among whom Annie grows and moves—Julius, and Adele and Claudie; Annie's father, and of course Inky—how can we know except by mastery of a complex craft where and how to place the bits of this mosaic so the light will fall just right, so the whole will come to life through the intricate relating of all its parts to each other?—so that event and person will fall together with just the right, chiming note? It is this sort of thing that measures quality in a novel. And it is this sort of thing that we have grown indifferent to, in reading and in reviewing.

Both the best and the worst of *Hard Blue Sky* come from Miss Grau's own achieved awareness, not from any overlay of training or any of the "influences" that are the thin gruel of many professional critics. The best, I think, is the quality of her awareness. It has to do, a lot of it, with her recognition as writer that these figures in this landscape in these attitudes add up to something, become a total meaning that is pertinent to lives all unlike these. Annie, edging her way in the nightwind along the perilous convent roof ledge, figures with superb poetic artistry the recognition of what happens to all of us who go out past our depth; like Annie; like Henry. Sometimes, like Annie, we make it out and back. Other times the going is like Henry's going. It is so slightly done, so deftly and unpretentiously written in, that assay of Annie's, we might not notice the configuration of the night journey. But it is here, and it is this kind of fine management that is the most promising aspect of Miss Grau's art of the novel. This awareness, this management, wind on through the tenuousness of these lives; the flexible durability of Julius, the perishable quality both of Inky and of the slim white yacht that is what there is of home for Inky; the tenacious reach for life, and the meanings given life by its insecurity—these too are parts of that admirable complexity of awareness that Miss Grau has brought to her book.—JOHN DILLON HUSBAND, *NMQ*, Spring 1958, pp. 62–65

Joan ⟨in *The House on Coliseum Street*⟩ exists in a relativistic world where genuine feelings must be replaced by social and self deceptions. The act of destroying the career of the man she loves is without emotional engagement, and as a result her intellectual reflections are marked by hesitant non-introspection. Her principal tone is detachment, but Joan struggles vaguely toward integration by identifying herself with the tiny floating seaweed that was her child, and by symbolically admitting a need for wholeness in her desperate desire for another child. But she cannot reach conscious self-knowledge because she finds herself in a morally irresponsible world.

Formal education has failed, except symbolically. The instructor offers marriage merely to protect his job. Another phase of her scrambled liberal education, he is exciting, compelling, empty. Like her intellectual initiation, her psychological one (love) is only ritual—changing classes or "making love"—because the larger implications of her actions are not apprehended. The school's dean fulfills part of her need for self-identification while becoming the agency which protects her from it. When he contributes a patriarchal moral view, he makes actual her idealization of her lost father.

But Miss Grau's subject—a sterile society's self-conviction that evil can be negated by not acknowledging it—cannot be treated in sixty thousand words dealing primarily with a non-introspective protagonist confronted with clichés that substitute for real people—from the bitchy sister to the Victorian dean. This suggests that the world of Miss Grau is too pat, too unrealized, and we wonder if this is not purposeful, a way to insure her conclusions. Though she writes with almost Hemingwayesque scenic skill, the author has formed her characters to conform to a generalization about life, rather than letting the density and ambiguity of human experience make its own comment through artistic rendering.—JACK DEBELLIS, "Two Southern Novels and a Diversion," *SwR*, Oct.–Dec. 1962, p. 692

In Shirley Ann Grau's *The House on Coliseum Street*, a girl named Joan moves through life in a trance which partially excludes me. My senses are dulled—not because Miss Grau doesn't recognize the power of the physical world, but because most of her observations do not make it vivid; consciously, it seems to me, she chooses those which do not. How to make real a character such as Joan (a truly dull girl), and still be faithful to Joan's dullness? I respect the limitations Miss Grau has imposed upon herself as a novelist, but Joan's temperament does not meet mine anywhere. I understand her, she is recognizable, and what is there is honest, but instead of seeing the world through Joan's eyes in such a way that Joan herself might be real to me, I see her only as a pitiable girl whose sensual perceptions are mainly compulsive. Her sense of smell, for instance, is phenomenally accurate, yet the author is willing to stop as soon as the object is identified. We get the name of the perfume, the fact of the hidden cigar butt, the fact of the rats in the walls, and that's about all; what this finally does to me is not to prove Joan's world to my nose but to convince me that Joan is a good smeller—much the way statistics prove to me that Mickey Mantle is a good batter—and once again I'm outside of Joan, observing her, not her world, through my eyes (nose).

Another indication that Miss Grau has consciously handicapped herself is her use of sentence fragments. She uses these stylistic devices so often that I began, against my will, to count them. Again she is being scrupulously faithful to her heroine's limitations, and I respect her for it at the same time that I am uncomfortably aware of style.

The book is serious and, as well as it can within the limits Miss Grau has imposed upon herself, reveals certain truths about certain women. At one point Joan says of her ex-lover, "Anyhow, he ought to be nibbled to death by ducks." Read man for the food here, and Miss Grau supplies a house full of horribly fluttery, hungry little beaks.—THOMAS WILLIAMS, "Ducks, Ships, Custard, and a King," *KR*, Winter 1962, pp. 184–85

Plot aside, ⟨*The Keepers of the House*⟩ is a Southern novel all right, and one often beautifully written: the flowers and trees in all their semi-tropical variety and abundance; the kin that connect and connect until you think everyone is related to everyone else; the swamps and rivers and bayous—much of the region is graced with water enough to make its rich and black or copper-red land seem fresher than the rest of American soil; the birds, grateful in their wide assortments for the temperate climate—herons rising out of a bleak patch of wet, wild grassland and ranging near moss dripping oaks are an unforgettable sight; the special food and the names for the food; and everywhere the special relationship, grounded in history, buttressed by customs, insisted upon by laws, of Negroes and whites, so close to one another, so dependent upon one another, so mutually frightened. . . .

Shirley Ann Grau has been demonstrating her gifts as a sensitive observer of human development and growth for some time now. With a few words she can establish a mood, mixing man's emotions with appropriate reflections of them in landscape. She knows her heavy, low Southern moon, her Southern turtles and snakes and herb gardens. She knows the old houses with their long windows and the nodding breezes which come upon thankful, clammy skin. She knows the people, knows the ambiguities of race relations, the devices, pretenses, ironies, absurdities, and incredible frustrations, all of them constant reminders of the mind's capacity for illusion, rationalization and even delusion under an irrational but powerfully coercive social and economic system. She knows the Negro as an emotional alternative for the white man's personal loneliness or isolation. She knows the white man as an awesome, enviable attraction for many Negroes. She knows how a Negro mistress must silently and discreetly grieve at her white man's death; and she knows the rising warmth and fear which struggle in a white man when he begins to respect a Negro rather than use one.

Most significantly, she writes at a time when she can know some answers, too. For this is a novel which in its own sudden and firm way has a statement to make. Robert is, after all, the composite Northerner, the outsider, black and white, and the South has its reasons to fear and hate him. The author does not shirk the complicated nature of the problem. Her segregationist is no demon, but any region's ambitious, aggressive politician. He can be tender with Negroes, affectionate with his family, can even disbelieve his own racist talk. How many Americans can really get very smug with him or about his adjustment to his society? And who can deny his wife her anger at what this "outside agitator" has done? . . .

Still, the author does not back and fill between a story crying out for change in the ways Negroes and whites get along with one another and justifiable criticism of those whose efforts at change merely lead to worsened strife in the future. She gathers herself together and ends her story by insisting that deceptions exposed are ultimately if painfully better than compromises and falsehoods endured. Robert may have been gratuitous and ignorant in his intervention but his action reveals to the white community and to the wife of its segregationist politician the reality they have so long dodged. The town learns that economic ruin follows violence. A wife learns what she had really sensed all along, her husband's faulty, compromised nature.

It is said that people are tired of the South and the Southern novel. Yet, I wonder where else in this country past history and present social conflict conspire to bring forth so much of the evil in people, so much of the dignity possible in people, so much of the "pity and terror" in the human condition. Looking at people living elsewhere, in bureaucratized passivity and efficiency, in faceless bustle, in cliché-riddled "progressive" comfort or sophisticated but paralysed bewilderment, we can turn to the South in horror and fascination, and on those counts alone, in some hope. —ROBERT COLES, "Mood and Revelation in the South," *NR*, April 18, 1964, pp. 17–19

Shirley Ann Grau has kept herself as far out of ⟨*The Condor Passes*⟩ as is consistent with writing it. Feeling and interpretation are just as lively in her as in Mr. ⟨Robert Penn⟩ Warren or any other good writer, but she holds them in abeyance, their time will come but not yet. Each incident is given with as much fullness as its participants deserve, but it is surrounded by silence; either it justifies itself or it does not. If the acts and events are not as opulent as they would be in Utopia, so much the worse, they must do the best they can, the novelist is not going to pretend that they are more than they are.

The theme is given in the title. "What's a condor?" someone asks, and the Old Man answers, "A big bird . . . a black bird. They used to fill the feathers with gold after he was dead." I can't see that the symbol does anything for the book, and Miss Grau comes back to it at the end for no good reason. The novel already has nearly as much as it needs, for theme: money and a family to spend it. If *The Condor Passes* is more variously interesting than, say, ⟨Warren's⟩ *Meet Me in the Green Glen*, one reason is that Miss Grau's narrative voice keeps its mouth shut until it has something true and relevant to say. Another is that the pertinent feelings and interpretations come from the several characters, individually, or they do not come at all. Each character is given his day in court, beginning with Stanley, forty-four, the useful Negro in Gulf Springs, Mississippi. But Stanley is small stuff, the big man is Thomas Henry Oliver, without him there would be no story. Thereafter the saga includes his wife Stephanie, his girl Helen Ware, his children Anna and Margaret, his servant Robert Caillet, Robert's marriage, sundry affairs, and a boy Anthony who drowns himself.

One of the chief graces of the book is the imaginative

control with which Miss Grau moves the story from Stanley to the Old Man to Robert to Anna to Margaret to Anthony and back at last to Robert and Stanley. Each viewpoint is held with just enough emphasis to define it, there is no impression of force or excess. Perhaps Margaret gets more space than she is worth, but generally Miss Grau is judicious in these allowances. She is fair even to characters who have done little to deserve justice, but she does not lick their boots. Anna, for instance: a character of force, much of it deadly, devoted to the art of possession. I recall with special pleasure a scene, the day before Anna's wedding, when she wanders through the house that she means to buy. "This is me," she reflects, "I make things belong to me."

Miss Grau's policy is clear. She is determined to give her characters free range, subject only to the limitations implicit in the nature of things. As for their own natures, they are welcome to do what they like with what they own. So the novel hovers upon questions of property, possession, rights, duties, needs, license. Miss Grau attends to her art with a corresponding sense of law and limitation. She does whatever she can manage with characters, she invents new characters when she feels in need of them. If there is something that her characters cannot reasonably see or feel, her novel must do without it; that she, the novelist, can see or feel it is not enough reason for including it. In short, whatever cannot be achieved by attending to a large family of characters had better be left alone.

Miss Grau works by concentrating on one thing, one character, at a time, and her art is exhilarating in its precision. But she is not exceptionally good when it is a question of latitude. *The Condor Passes* is a family saga, and much of it takes place in New Orleans, but it is hard to feel that New Orleans makes any difference or that the saga would have been another thing if it had happened in Detroit. Again the years are marked, there are references to Robert away in England, fighting his war, but it might as well be another war and another country for all the difference it makes. The book has very little feeling for the millions of lives that it does not describe. Every episode is vividly illuminated, but there is very little sense of a world and a time between the lights. The public world does not press upon Miss Grau's private people, and we could be forgiven for thinking that it has gone away. The characters have lively relations to one another, and equally lively relations to themselves, but they do not bump against strangers, they are rarely aware of a world going about its alien business, indifferent to the Olivers.

Miss Grau tells us, in each case, what she thinks we ought to know, and nothing more. Her tact is blessed. But she virtually conceals from us, while the novel lasts, the fact that other forms of reality are present, even if we do not see them. She nearly prevents us from knowing those forms of reality which James called "the things we cannot possibly *not* know, sooner or later, in one way or another." In a richer novel we would hear noises which we would not interpret, except in the ordinary way as the buzz of things. *The Condor Passes* is all foreground, very little background, everything is presented in the same degree of lucidity, that is, a high degree. But after a while the lucidity begins to oppress, and I think we would believe more if we were shown less, or if a little public confusion were to assert itself against the private gleam. —Denis Donoghue, "Life Sentence," *NYRB*, Dec. 2, 1971, pp. 28–29

Evidence of Love, Shirley Ann Grau's fifth novel, is told through the viewpoint of three characters. Words spoken by Edward Milton Henley begin and end the novel. The middle sections are spoken by Henley's son, Stephen, and by Stephen's wife, Lucy. Grau uses a similar point of view in the Pulitzer Prize–winning *The Hard Blue Sky* (1964) and in *The Condor Passes* (1971). But whereas the earlier novels are tied to place and time, *Evidence of Love* operates like much contemporary fiction on a plane where space and time are intrareferential, turning back on themselves. In addition, though we hear voices and through them a story is told, the meaning of the novel derives not so much from the voices or the story but rather from the silences between the voices and from the gaps in the story. It is in these silences and these gaps that various shadows reside as they are projected from and reflected in recurrent motifs that cluster in montage patterns providing the novel with its underlying structure.

Grau uses a quotation from Wallace Stevens' "Le Monocle de Mon Oncle" to suggest the course the novel will take;

I pursued,
And still pursue, the origin and course
Of love, but until now I never knew
That fluttering things have so distinct a shade.

At surface the novel is an embodiment of the various characters' search for love. Edward Milton Henley buys lover after lover, provides gifts for his son and finally independence for his son's widow. Stephen, depleted early in his life of sexual desire, pursues Lucy, also depleted, and their marriage becomes for Stephen a "visceral sympathy of acquired identity." Lucy marries Harold Evans (her first husband) for love, but instead of union comes isolation, and instead of completion and its concomitant freedom comes a dependence which she abhors. Love, finally, is seen as misconception, and evidence of love illusory. Lucy comes to understanding: "There is no one I care about, no one I need worry about." For the first time in her life she is content.

The search for love turns out to be a quest for order and understanding that can only come through an apprehension of shadows, which in this novel are presented as reflected and reflecting images. The theme is caught early in the novel. . . .

The novel ends with a cogent restatement of theme where Grau repeats the montage patterns. Plunged back into Henley's voice and consciousness, the reader finds time and space convoluted, life and death merged. "'Things,' Henley says, 'become one and the same.'" He thinks of himself as curling like a leaf "as it disappears into dust." But the natural cycle is not enough. He seeks the transcendent. Once, when he was younger, he had a drug-induced vision of heaven, where he "danced with the gods" and was "perfect, complete. Like a circle." It is this heaven that he sought and continues to seek in death. While Henley dies, Lucy sits reading *House and Garden*. The old man moves in and out of consciousness: "I am I suppose, flickering like a lightbulb." As Henley dies, a greenish light in thickening glow sags down from the ceiling like a mosquito net.

Evidence of Love is a finely crafted, tightly woven, and powerful novel by a major American author whose works deserve far better treatment than they have received in myriad reviews. Shirley Ann Grau won't be confined, and as *Evidence of Love* indicates, her novels are the better for it.—Mary Rohrberger, "'So Distinct a Shade': Shirley Ann Grau's *Evidence of Love*," *SoR*, Winter 1978, pp. 195–98

ALWYN BERLAND

From "The Fiction of Shirley Ann Grau"

Critique, Volume 6, Number 1 (1963), pp. 78–84

Shirley Ann Grau has published three books: a collection of short stories, *The Black Prince*, 1955, and two novels: *The Hard Blue Sky*, 1958, and *The House on Coliseum Street*, 1961. They are all of them perceptive works, well-written, precocious, versatile in range, and—all three—less achieved than promising. *The Black Prince* impressed many people, including apparently its publisher (Knopf), since only three of the nine stories had appeared in magazines; we have all heard often enough to accept as inevitable truth the dogma that book publishers are properly wary of short story collections, especially those of unknown writers. The publisher was right to publish, of course, and a number of critics were quick to support that decision, though sometimes in rather strange terms. For instance, Carl Van Vechten wrote (I quote from that most suspicious of sources, the back cover of the paperback edition): "A most remarkable book, in the best tradition of Chekhov and Katherine Mansfield." I should amend this, I think, to read: "A most interesting book, curiously unlike the tradition of Chekhov and Katherine Mansfield except insofar as all three write short stories, and all three eschew one traditional, and rigid, conception of *plot*." If less satisfactory for paperback purposes than the other, I think it a fairly accurate description of all three of Miss Grau's books.

Miss Grau was born in New Orleans which, together with its surrounding rural areas and nearby fishing islands, is the setting for all of her work. Of the nine stories in *The Black Prince*, five are about Negroes, four about middle-class and more or less urban whites. The stories about Negroes have a certain convincing solidity of detail, by which I mean that they reveal a sharp eye, and ear, for convincing gesture and idiom, for the characteristics of a different mode of experience. Their limitation is that they *remain* different, seen as by a perceptive outsider, a (gifted) fictional anthropologist who is sensitive to the nuances of behavior in his hosts, but who never is able to forget in his own nervous system that he is a guest. The story which seems to me the best of this group, and of the volume, is the title story, a fantasy, circumspectly realistic in execution, about one Stanley Albert Thompson, the prince-of-darkness-as-handsome-"buck," who courts successfully a rather diffident Negro girl whose name is Alberta (significant?). His qualities are mainly the extremes of all the virtues admired by the characters in this story, and in all the others: chest expansion, readiness of cash, talent with the razor and in bed. The story is sustained by a kind of folkloristic tone, and humor, lacking in the other stories, as well as by the texture of the writing, which is everywhere Miss Grau's strongest appeal. Although less arch than many other excursions into low life, as for instance Steinbeck's *Tortilla Flat*, the effect is much the same: a visit to a small planet.

. . . ⟨"White Girl, Fine Girl"⟩ is told with skill (although perhaps the treatment of the brother is too rhetorical near the end), and while reading one is convinced. But the story ends—and this is a problem so general in Miss Grau's work that I will return to this point later—with a kind of meaningless inconsequence: the sum of the parts *should* have been more substantial than the whole.

These stories, and the others about Negroes, share an interesting common note: their characters are almost totally indifferent to each other, except sexually. No other relationship—and I exclude that of physical violence—takes on any real dimension or resonance. This consistent brutality of relationship coupled with the fineness of execution in the stories gives them the effect of photographic reductions: everything is clear, precise, accurate in its isolated details, and smaller than life.

The stories about whites are somewhat more various, although they are all "initiation" stories. In all but one of them, children bump against, rather than encounter, the portals of adult damnation. In the one exception, "The Bright Day," a newly married woman instead of a child is the victim. The feel of the story is not much different except that she is, more than are the children, herself an active agent in the loss of innocence.

The Hard Blue Sky is more ambitious and more satisfactory. Its setting is a Gulf Island near the mouth of the Mississippi, which Miss Grau has peopled with a large number of fishermen and their wives and children. The islanders are loosely Cajun in tradition, though now mixed French, Spanish, Indian and Negro. Like most strongly marked and isolated people, they are largely interbred, "nearly all related, one way or the other." Their ethos stems not from the American Puritan past, but from the Mediterranean. They move in what is less a novel than a series of inter-related short stories or sketches. These deal, sometimes brilliantly, with the representative life of the island: the loss of a teenager, Henry Livaudais, in the unexplored marshes; an older widowed fisherman, Al Landry, who returns with a new wife from the outside; his daughter Annie's groping into her first adolescent relationships to the world and to sex. . . .

The novel's weakness is in a sense anticipated by the short story collection. There is so much more building up than there is *dénouement*, so much more preparation than the event itself ever supports. The metaphors of architecture are always dangerous when applied to literature, but it is an architectural defect which Miss Grau's talent suffers from. The good Chekhov story represents a marriage of atmosphere, incident, tone and effect, in which as in all inspired marriages no one member dominates another. The harmony of parts, in themselves often rather frail, makes a substantial whole. In Miss Grau's work, too often the effect is as of a construction done in beautifully polished stone, that just escapes emotional or intellectual shape because the artist withdraws before the keystone is added. Curiously enough, Miss Grau leaves the impression that she knows what she is doing. The absence of keystone, whether unifying symbol, or theme, or resolving incident, seems not accidental but deliberate. She builds *toward* these, and then stops. No one (and I am being disingenuous) wants to erect a rigid aesthetic and then condemn an author for not living up to it. I am not interested in an *a priori* scheme that might justify (or not justify) Miss Grau's strategy, but in the rather grubbily pragmatic fact that the strategy just doesn't work.

For all that, there are fine moments in *The Hard Blue Sky*; moments that, for all their arbitrariness in relation to the whole, take on the dimension of solidly realized fiction. Annie Landry, sent by her perplexed father to a New Orleans convent, rooms with an exotic South American girl who has (apparently nightly) amatory adventures after dark. Annie, yearning for if not experience at least the knowledge of experience, stalks the lover across the ledges of the convent in a scene which, in summary, sounds like *The Hunchback of Notre Dame*, gargoyles and all, but which in the novel is very freshly and convincingly realized. Also, there is a good semi-comic episode involving the islanders' maneuvres to get the mainland priest to minister against his will to their superstitions about the teenager lost in the marshes; and balancing that, a beautiful and tender account of his family's reactions to their loss.

In many ways, the least satisfactory character in *The Hard Blue Sky* is the adolescent Annie Landry, who suffers, it seems to me, too much the sullenness and meanness and passivity of the teenager fumbling into her world, and too little the poetry. Her initiations into sex—like those of Miss Grau's other characters—are seen as dull necessity or joyless compulsion. In this, as indeed in a number of other ways, Annie Landry prepares us for the central character of Miss Grau's latest novel, *The House on Coliseum Street.*

Here we are in New Orleans itself, in an old house once wealthy and still prosperous, dominated by Aurelie, Joan Mitchell's mother, who has five daughters, one commemorating each of her successive alliances. Her second daughter, Joan Mitchell, is the wealthiest of the group; her father has left an iron-clad will which gives her an advantage resented by the others, especially by Doris, the oldest. Joan Mitchell shares with the less fortunate and less educated Annie Landry many of the same qualities: an intermittent disposition to sever connections with immediate reality in favor of hallucination or "trance"; a rather dumb passivity; an apparent tendency to "stalk" lovers at night; a strong desire for sex which, when it comes, seems rather flat and dull: there is a good deal of smoothing of hairs with automatic hands. Both girls, finally, come to us as *given;* they act credibly enough, on the whole, but the reportage is so external that one never feels the necessity for their actions; they might just as well play at arbitrary *x* as at arbitrary *z.* A certain dull opacity of character seems to spill over into their characterizations, which ought to be another matter.

. . . Miss Grau's gifts of observation are very good; her technical skills (at least in the textural sense) are first-rate. She knows her characters behavioristically, and sometimes from areas within. But so far, at least, her vision is essentially a mimetic one; she has a sense of how the world goes, and she manipulates her characters to move that way. What is missing is the firm center, the center of a vision, and hence the conviction of why her characters behave as they do. Inevitably, then, she moves *for* them, and they behave as they do because, finally, she tells them to. What she tells them constitutes certainly some of the better fiction of her uncommitted generation. This gives us all the more reason for hoping that one day she will move to the center, where we cannot tell the dancer from the dance.

ANN PEARSON

"Shirley Ann Grau: Nature Is the Vision"

Critique, Volume 17, Number 2 (1975), pp. 47–58

To one whose interest was piqued by scattered passages in *The Keepers of the House*, the more recent publication of Shirley Ann Grau's *The Condor Passes* and *The Wind Shifting West* has turned curiosity into absolute puzzlement. What, if any, overall purpose does this talented writer have in her fiction? Her fine eye for natural detail and ability to understand a variety of characters are so appealing that she stands far above the usual story teller. Yet even the dedicated reader caught in her spell must finally wonder, after the book is closed and the mind takes over from the disengaged imagination, what her world is about. Is she really, as one critic suggested as long ago as 1965, "largely without a dominant theme or an explicit philosophical view"?[1]

In particular, two questions haunt anyone who reads Grau's stories or novels: what is the function of natural setting in her work, and how does it contribute to any thematic purpose in her fiction? The first question is less elusive than the latter since nature frequently permeates her novels and stories and becomes a force that forever surrounds the lives of her characters. The other question, however, is a puzzling one that seems to elude the reader every time it seems just within his grasp. A close examination of her work seems to yield only one plausible suggestion: she is portraying a world dominated by the seasons that only obliquely has meaning. Her only definable vision of the world lies in her perception of the ever present closeness of nature, that "hard blue sky" which rules the lives of her characters. Thus, nature is her vision, the focal point of her best fiction.

The dominance of natural setting is certainly not uncommon among Southern writers, but unlike Glasgow and O'Connor, who romanticize and personify nature to suit their purpose, Grau's treatment of natural surroundings has a chilly impersonality—in spite of the steamy earth that is her region, the bayous of Louisiana and the Gulf Coast of Alabama. Her innumerable swamps, marshes, and forests are described objectively, never filtered through an imagination given to moonlight and magnolia.

The problematic result of her impartiality is that nature becomes meaningless, and, in turn, so does much of her fiction. The natural world regulates the lives of her characters, but its very rhythm has in and of itself no meaning that molds her work into a meaningful whole. As a critic noted several years ago, "This persistent strain of the magnitude and power of natural forces in Miss Grau's work achieves an almost naturalistic reduction of the status of man to a biological cipher insignificant among other forms of life."[2] Perhaps she is, then, the most pessimistic southern contemporary, for her characters move, love, and die amid bright foliage, immense wealth, or grinding poverty, yet they rarely perceive a transcendent joy that reconciles them with the natural order.

The function of nature in Grau's work has developed in the course of her career. Her fine eye for setting is evident in her first work, the collection of stories entitled *The Black Prince* (1955). Nearly every story begins with the scene of the action carefully described, but rarely are the characters related to their surroundings. As in so much of her fiction, "There is so much more building up than there is *dénouement*, so much more preparation than the event itself ever supports."[3] However, her fine grasp of poignant daily brushes with the natural world are obvious in such stories as "Miss Yellow Eyes," in which the young Negro girl who is the narrator describes the cold: "There was a heavy frost like mold on the riverside slant of the levee. I stopped and pulled a clover and touched it to my lips and felt the sting of ice."[4] In "The Girl with the Flaxen Hair" a recurrent phrase used to describe the mythically dashing grandfather of the young girl relates the fictional courage of the man to the larger glory of nature: the Senator's boots were always "shiny as water in the sun" (144). In spite of such inspired touches, the natural descriptions rarely prove to be more than a nice stroke on a flat canvas. One brief exception occurs, however, in "Fever Flower," a telling study of a beautiful, egotistical woman whose perception of life is limited to order and worldly goods. She is too self-centered to be pitied; the pathos lies in the effect she will have on her small daughter, Maureen. One brief description late in the story when Hugh, the father, takes Maureen to a tropical garden has more than passing significance: "And then the orchids, a whole wall of them with their great spreading petals reaching into the heat. 'See,' Hugh told Maureen. 'Pretty. Just the color of your dress.' The blooms were forced to grow to gigantic size in half the time; they were beautiful and exotic and they didn't last" (176).

The orchids apparently hint at the destiny of Maureen, who, though beautiful, grows up to lead the empty life of her mother.

These early astute, though erratic, glimpses of nature against which her characters play out their meager destinies are more fully embroidered in Grau's first novel, *The Hard Blue Sky* (1958), whose title indicates the dominance of the elements over the lives of the poor fishermen of the Isle aux Chiens. In this rather aimless novel about the daily lives of common people Grau seems less concerned about what her characters do than the background against which they do it. As in many of her stories, the opening pages of the novel are devoted to a thorough description of the setting that yet shows no signs of having been filtered through an ordering imagination. The characters' closeness to their environment is especially made evident in the youthful awareness of the grocer, Julius Arcenaux, who told his mother: "I hear the sun come up in the morning; and I hear the leaves come out the stalk; and I hear the worms crawling in the ground. And when I sit and watch a moonflower open, I can hear that, me."[5] His awareness has no larger significance to him even as a youth, for the moonflower only "creaks, like" (59), and to the middle-aged grocer of the novel, "That had been such a long time ago" (59). Still, unconsciously, he sees all the events of his life in terms of the seasons: he met his wife in the winter when "The ball of the chinaberry trees were yellow and falling" (62).

The natural setting is ever present to other characters in the novel, though often nature, because it is not imaginatively ordered by the author, seems more like the cardboard backdrop for a school play than a living phantasmagoria. In one vivid scene Annie Landry's early curiosity about sex is highlighted by natural objects when, at the convent school in New Orleans, she secretly follows her roommate, Beatriz, to a rendezvous: "It was a bright night, with an almost full moon. There was just a sliver gone. The trees, which came up to the level of the second story, were still and silver-colored" (130). At the end of the novel when she leaves the island to marry Inky D'Alfonso, her surroundings have never brought meaning to her life; they are a *donnée* without significance: "Things happened, she thought, and you did whatever it was you had to do to meet them. And they went on past you. . . . She was waiting, waiting for things to happen to her. Things that could be handled and changed" (427). But in Grau's world things are neither handled nor changed; they are seasonal and without human significance.

Grau comes closest to a direct statement of her belief in an indifferent universe in several passages involving Cecile, the attractive daughter of Julius Arcenaux. In a reflective mood, Cecile takes her baby to the north edge of the island and sits looking at the sky: a "hard blue sky, whitened a little by the sun. She stared at it, thinking how hard and solid it looked like a blue cup put over the ground" (285). Finally, thinking of young Henry Livaudais' senseless death in the marshes, she says out loud to the emptiness: "It don't even matter that we been alive" (286). Leaving, she throws a brick at the sky and turns toward home, "not waiting to see it fall" (287). In *The Hard Blue Sky* the characters are caught in the blue cup of the sky that imposes a natural order on their lives, but the order fails to give their lives any intrinsic meaning. Consequently, the novel itself lacks a coherence that can justify the lengthy recitation of social and natural detail.

Nature, however indifferent, is not so dominant in her next novel, *The House on Coliseum Street* (1961). Set in New Orleans and centered around Joan Mitchell, a wealthy girl hopelessly floundering for some form or meaning to her life, the novel is a sharp departure from the predominantly backwater setting of her earlier work. True to her earlier form, Grau opens the novel with a natural description, a summer thunderstorm on the Gulf. It seems, momentarily, to bring a surge of excitement to Joan, who watches its approach from her aunt's gazebo: "She could see the rain, a grey haze like smoke, at Dolphin Island, some five miles offshore. She could smell it now too, the wonderful exciting smell of coming rain. The quiver in the air grew stronger."[6] The rain's promise of excitement, however, is never fulfilled: "In ten minutes the first drops came, big tadpole-shaped drops that plopped and exploded with sharp, distinct sounds. And then the rain itself—windless sheets, straight down, luminous grey, fish-colored. The roof began to leak" (4). After it passes it leaves only the same indifferent landscape: "The squall passed over slowly. On the other side the sun was bright and hard and the sky was brilliant cloudless blue" (5). Joan is left again with her guilt over her recent abortion.

The longest passage in the novel devoted to the natural landscape describes the grounds of the college in New Orleans where Joan attends summer school. She is shocked by the aggressiveness of the summer foliage that seems to defy human control: "Under the fierce June sun and the heavy rains, the staff of gardeners made no headway. . . . She studied the cut blades and fancied that she could see them begin to grow again, leaping up from under the path of the mower" (62). Like Julius Arcenaux she "could feel it growing . . . even under the pavement" (62). Nature seems grotesquely out of control, reflecting Joan's emotional disarray: "The bed of zinnias had gone wild, too. They grew at right angles to the ground, like mad children crawling along on hands and knees" (62).

Such personification is rare, and nature is not consistently linked with Joan either literally or imaginatively. Only once does it seem to presage events (and thus mesh with human affairs). When she meets Michael Kern, a young instructor, one day on the campus and he asks her out, their surroundings hint at the beginning of a satisfactory relation: "A large redbird was building an out-of-season nest in the sprawling gnarled crape myrtle. The tree itself was just coming into bloom. The fat green buds were beginning to burst open into ruffled white flowers" (101). Again, as in the opening scene, nature's promises are not fulfilled for Joan, and her short affair with Kern ends with the abortion that only intensifies her confusion. Setting is less intrusive in *The House on Coliseum Street* than in *The Hard Blue Sky*, but it is occasionally coupled with the emotional life of the protagonist. Still, it does not add sufficient depth to a character who is, unfortunately, drowning in emotional shallows.

In Grau's most recent two novels, *The Keepers of the House* (1964) and *The Condor Passes* (1971), a more artistic use of setting is directly related to the inner workings of her characters. *The Keepers of the House*, her best novel to date and winner of the Pulitzer Prize, is set in a small town in Alabama, and it resembles *The Hard Blue Sky* in its rural setting and the omnipresence of nature. It rises above the aimlessness of the earlier novel in that, in the best tradition of Southern fiction, the ambiance of the land is incorporated with the burden of the past which Abigail Mason Tolliver must cope with in the present. The novel opens with a fine description of a bleak Southern November evening that reflects the despair of Abigail, who, deserted by her husband, must defend alone the Howland family acres that have been disgraced by her grandfather's miscegenation: "November evenings are quiet and still and dry. The frost-stripped trees and the bleached grasses glisten and shine in the small light. In the winter-emptied fields granite outcroppings gleam white and stark. The bones of the earth, old people call them."[7] Even in her despair she finds a sense of permanence in the landscape: "I have the illusion that I am sitting here, dead. That I am like the granite outcroppings, the bones of the earth, fleshless and eternal" (4). She also feels a continuity with the generations before her who owned the land: "They sat on this porch and looked out across the fields, resting from the heat of the day, letting their eyes run over the soft turns of the land until they reached the dark woods" (5).

A human significance is suggested in the response to the land, but it is never fully allowed. In the words of the Negro woman whom Howland secretly marries: "Things came in a certain form and that was all there was to it" (103). *The Keepers of the House* is also Grau's most successful novel in artistically employing natural detail.

In *The Condor Passes*, Grau appears to be attempting to do more with natural setting than she has in her earlier works. With the imagistic use of birds and tropical flowers, she makes an effort to unite a work that, unfortunately, was too broadly conceived. The central theme of the corruptive power of money on a variety of individuals is never quite brought under control. The chief image of the book lies, of course, in the condor, a bird believed by the Indians to carry messages to the other world. It is also associated with money, for as Thomas Henry Oliver, the patriarch of the novel, recounts shortly before his death, "They'd fill the quills with gold dust and bury them with the dead; that way the spirit would always have money."[8] Both the "Old Man," as Oliver is called, and his black servant, Stanley, are compared to birds, particularly the condor; they are the only two characters to withstand the corrupting influence of the Old Man's money. Their likeness to birds seems to link them to a natural force that enables them to prevail.

Stanley is described imagistically as a blackbird. In terms of the legend he is a messenger in whose hands the Old Man leaves gold. He seems to be the force of the Old Man who will survive after his death—the continuation of his vitality and integrated spirit. The vitality of the condor is also expressed in several descriptions of the Old Man, who is the condor of the title. His eyes were bright, "hooded like a bird's—quick as a bird's too, flashing open to catch you watching" (13).

Besides the Old Man's identity with the condor, he is also closely associated with the greenhouse and its huge bird cage that his daughter, Margaret, builds for him in his home. The Old Man is first introduced in the greenhouse in the second chapter of the novel, and he dies in it at the end. The humid greenhouse with its birds and exotic flowers seems to be the force of nature that feeds and drives the Old Man. Every morning with strict regularity Stanley must purge the bird cage of sick birds. To Stanley "Everything in the house had a fixed and ordered pattern. Unchangeable" (11); it seems somehow a simulacrum of the regularity of nature that the Old Man's wealth is able to imitate in the humid greenhouse. Only Stanley remotely perceives the Old Man's symbiosis with the greenhouse: "Maybe, when the Old Man sits in his greenhouse and looks at the shiny leaves hanging in the thick wet air, maybe he really can see something that makes one place mean more to him than another. I don't know" (384). At the end of the novel, when the Old Man dies in the greenhouse, he is linked with nature. Stanley waits for his death: "Total black surrounded them, sightless and close with the feel of wet leaves and wet ground, its only sound the steady rattle of rain on the glass roof" (418).

On the other hand, Robert Caillet, a Cajun the Old Man had raised from poverty and married to his daughter, is corrupted by the Old Man's money, and his degeneration is partially revealed in his rejection of nature. On a trip west with the Old Man and his family shortly before he marries Anna, he finds himself loving the flowers, but his new response to nature appalls him: "I am going queer, he told himself, when flowers begin to mean something to me" (154). His early temerity increases until he is an alcoholic womanizer spoiled by the Old Man's wealth. His ultimate disintegration is suggested at the close of the novel when he retreats to the greenhouse to sleep off a hangover. Later, when Stanley finds him there urinating on one of the expensive plants, he says: "That's what I think of the whole thing, Stanley, . . . Look at that funny fiddle-leaf tree, and that one over there—it's got red veins running under the leaves. I've been sitting in the chair looking at it; damnedest thing. I never noticed it before. Take a leak, that's about what they're worth" (395).

The Condor Passes is an ambitious work in its use of bird and nature imagery and in its scope. It also reveals Grau's perception of nature as a vitalizing force as opposed to the indifference of the hard blue sky. In spite of the strengths of the novel, one is still left without a meaningful whole, chiefly because her imagery is not extended to include other major characters whose lives run down an assortment of blind alleys.

Unfortunately, Grau has sidestepped her earlier promise again in the collection of short stories, *The Wind Shifting West* (1973). In a selection of sixteen pieces that range in subject from an aging wife's first infidelity in the title story to a teenager's first acquaintance with death, she reveals that her powers of description are still intact; but with only a few exceptions, the well-described scene is not integrated with the action.

Her descriptions of nature reflect ideas established in the earlier works, though not in any particular pattern. In "Homecoming" the presence of nature implies life and vitality, while the absence of it suggests death. The west porch of the old house where the action takes place is covered with flowers, but the south porch is "bare and clear, no vines, no planting."[9] It is a "porch for old people" (42). The description, however, has little relation to the story, which involves a young girl's response to the death of a boy in Vietnam. An old woman is described, like the Old Man in *The Condor Passes*, as birdlike, "eyes hooded like a bird's, fingers like birds' claws" (47), but this description, too, is incidental to the story.

Nature invigorates the story "Three," about another young girl who cannot accept the death of her husband in Vietnam. She associates the happiness of their first meetings with long walks, and to dispel her depression on a beautiful day, she retraces their steps: "At once she began to feel better; she lengthened her stride, the air swirling around her" (87). Nature also soothes as implied in the haunting "The Last Gas Station" in which the narrator says of the place where his family used to live in happier times, "there were tall trees, real tall trees where you could lie on your back and watch the sun spin in the leaves" (126); where he lives now has only scrub, a setting in which the family gradually disintegrates.

Animal imagery is also used on one occasion in "Sea Change" to describe a character's state of mind. In despair after seeing her husband off for his third tour of duty in Vietnam, the central character goes to bed with a pilot who befriends her at the airport. Afterwards, "her mind stole out, prowling like a cat in the shadows, searching. And it found that there was nothing on any side of her, that she hung like a point, like a star in the empty sky" (180). The cat image further develops her despair: "And the cat that wore her mind found a dried empty shrimp shell mixed in the seawrack on a beach somewhere, empty beach, wet and cold, and began to play with it, to slap it back and forth with its paw. The shell rattled like a dry gourd" (180). The animal here is used to express emptiness instead of vitality as with the birds in *The Condor Passes*.

The eternal seasonal changes that order the lives of common people are again, as in *The Hard Blue Sky*, skillfully detailed in "The Man Outside." The lives of the numerous children and their mother are lived in strict accordance with the seasons of the year that are unquestioningly accepted. As in the earlier novel, the detail has no final significance. Other stories, such as "The Wind Shifting West," "The Long Afternoon," and "Pillow of Stone" all offer developed natural descriptions that never tie the stories together.

Of the sixteen stories, only four make any attempt to integrate setting with theme, and only two of these are really successful. In "The Beach Party" a teenaged girl learns to accept the brutality of life in the course of an evening on the beach. She encounters the presence of death for the first time when a young diver drowns, and she sees him brought up on the sand. At the beginning of the story she is "afraid of the ocean. It had something to do with the dark color, with the sound and the motion of the surf" (71). By the end of the story she still fears the ocean, but she accepts it as a natural part of life which she perceives as both cruel and desirable: "She saw the dark mark on the sand where the diver had lain. She wondered why that did not bother her more, but it seemed no more horrible than everything else. . . . Than the sharp smell of a man's sweat, or the angular pressure of another body" (81).

A young girl's first exposure to death is also the theme of "The Land and the Water." When three neighborhood children are lost in a fog in a small boat and drown, the girl is touched for the first time by the terror of death. She goes down to the water alone before dawn on the day after the bodies are found: "It [the water] looked heavy and oily and impenetrable. I tried to imagine what would be under it. . . . There would be horseshoe crabs and hermit crabs . . . and the eels. I kept telling myself that that was all" (124). But the tragedy has changed her view of the ocean: "I couldn't seem to keep my thoughts straight. I kept wondering what it must be like to be dead and cold and down in the sand" (124). Even back in the security of the house, she has the feeling of being touched by death, "Something that was wet, that had come from the water, something that had splashed me as it went past" (125).

These two stories are successful to a large degree because the descriptions serve throughout to implement the theme. The last two stories in the collection, however, are not so successful, though descriptions of natural objects are used thematically. "The Way Back" treats the end of a brief affair: in the last pages of this very short story, the woman, while driving home after the affair is over, looks at an acorn she has picked up and reflects that "Life is the same in me as in anything else. Trees come out of acorns, no matter how unlikely that seems" (224). The affair, however, has produced nothing, "The tree was still in the acorn, and love hadn't grown either" (224). The analogy, injected in the last half of the story, is too stilted to carry off the situation, itself too vaguely drawn to be convincing. The final story, "Stanley," has obvious relations to *The Condor Passes*. Here the Old Man is again carefully described sitting in the greenhouse that Stanley must purge of dead birds with a terrible regularity. The moist greenhouse is repellent and seems to be suffocating the decaying old man, apparently devoid of any spiritual energy. He is only aroused momentarily from his senile lethargy by the flight overhead of a red tail hawk that he mistakes for a condor. The condor conjures up for him memories of his youth in South America but has no deeper implication. Consequently, the portrayal of the Old Man in the story is only a pale reflection of the interesting characterization in the novel.

The Wind Shifting West shows no slackening of Grau's skill as an artist. Certainly, considering the effective portraying of different types of characters and viewpoints, it is a virtuoso performance. Nevertheless, her flaws persist, for in only two stories does she merge setting with action to create an artistic whole. Again, she is content to tot up the trivia of daily existence that, in the end, adds up to very little.

From the examination of nature in her work as a whole one can see that Grau has a fairly explicit philosophical view. The indifference of nature is her vision, and its impartial description contributes to a generalized theme in her work of its unalterable presence. However, her vision is blurred primarily by her undeveloped use of setting. In most of her work, except for parts of her last two novels and occasional stories, the profusion of landscape is misleading. What one critic said about *The Hard Blue Sky* applies to most of her fiction: "What is missing is the firm center, the center of a vision, and hence the conviction of why her characters behave as they do."[10] The chief problem with Shirley Ann Grau's work, then, is that it is concerned primarily with story. She herself has said that she has "no cause and no message."[11] If it is true, she has sold herself short, for she suggests a potential for much more. Her consistent failure to order her plots and settings artistically cheats her audience by giving it an uneven experience. Hailed justifiably in 1955 as one of the most promising of Southern writers, mentioned in 1963 as still showing the potential genius of O'Connor, Capote, and Styron,[12] she is shortchanging herself far more than her readers by delaying the fulfillment of that promise.

Notes

1. Louise Y. Gossett, *Violence in Recent Southern Fiction* (Durham: Duke Univ. Press, 1965), p. 193.
2. Gossett, p. 182.
3. Alwyn Berland, "The Fiction of Shirley Ann Grau," *Critique*, 6, i (1963), 81.
4. Shirley Ann Grau, *The Black Prince* (New York: Knopf, 1955), p. 106.
5. Shirley Ann Grau, *The Hard Blue Sky* (New York: Knopf, 1958), p. 58.
6. Shirley Ann Grau, *The House on Coliseum Street* (New York: Knopf, 1961), p. 3.
7. Shirley Ann Grau, *The Keepers of the House* (New York: Knopf, 1964), p. 3.
8. Shirley Ann Grau, *The Condor Passes* (New York: Knopf, 1971), pp. 397–8.
9. Shirley Ann Grau, *The Wind Shifting West* (New York: Knopf, 1973), p. 42.
10. Berland, p. 84.
11. Earle F. Walbridge, "Shirley Ann Grau," *Wilson Library Bulletin*, 34 (1959), 250.
12. John M. Bradbury, *Renaissance in the South* (Chapel Hill: Univ. of North Carolina Press, 1963), p. 197.

MARY ROHRBERGER

From "Shirley Ann Grau and the Short Story"

Southern Quarterly, Summer 1983, pp. 83–101

The problem with Shirley Ann Grau is that she has consistently refused to stand still and conform to the stereotypes critics and reviewers have created for her. The problem of course, is not hers but ours, for we have consistently failed to understand the complexity of her statements and the excellence of her forms. Rather than try here to treat the corpus of her fiction, I have decided to examine the short stories, starting with the earliest and coming to ones she is currently working on for collection in a new anthology. My hope is to demonstrate not only her extraordinary skill in the short story genre, but also the development of that skill, and by so doing to stimulate a continuation of the recent flurry of scholarly activity devoted to examination of her work.

Had critics and reviewers been familiar with Grau's first published stories, their initial judgments concerning her proper métier might have been different, for the stories published during her college years exhibit a range more in line with catholic than regionalist tendencies. . . .

The Black Prince, published by Knopf in 1955, contains nine stories, three of which were published earlier: "Joshua" in *The New Yorker;* "White Girl, Fine Girl," in *New World Writing* and "The Black Prince," in *The New Mexico Quarterly.* Several differences are apparent among the stories published in *Carnival* and the stories published in *The Black Prince:* the later stories are considerably longer; more fully developed plots follow either the traditional or the epiphanic line; more characters are involved and they are developed in more complex ways. Despite the additional complexities made possible by the additional length, however, basic devices remain the same. The writing style remains poetic and evocative; images still cluster into patterns, subsurfaces function in analogical modes.

In the move to longer stories, Grau's effort was toward a more careful and precise rendering of the experiential, while at the same time holding to that rich suggestiveness made possible by symbolic structures. The distinction to be made is not exactly between the romantic and the realistic or the intuitive and the empirical. That would be too easy. Rather, it is more between the direct and the subtle. What Grau was aiming for was a realistic rendering of a total experience, but only if "total experience" is taken to mean a meshing of the affective and the cognitive. Grau makes the point herself in her comment on "The Black Prince" prepared for an anthology of literature:

> Fiction, as I see it, is basically and always realistic. What else can it be? I know nothing beyond my experience and the experiences of people like me. If my expression becomes too personal, my symbols too intimate, my readers no longer understand. The demands of communication force me—partially at least—into the common mold of thought. I find myself dancing around the edges of meaning, trying to cut off a bit of the truth here, a bit there, trying to express, to shake the limitations of experience, above all to communicate my vision of the world. And, like most writers, I sometimes lose patience and abandon the reasonable realistic paths for the simple direct truths of myth-making.[1]

In this comment made thirteen years after the publication of *The Black Prince*, Grau was not suggesting that "The Black Prince" is easier to understand than stories which do not partake of the quality of legend. She uses both the words "direct" and "oblique" to describe her method and she is talking about means of communicating.

I should like to extend her points by suggesting that the "college" stories in their brevity and concentration on essence, are marked by a common analogical mode. Indeed, most of the stories in *The Black Prince* collection are closer to the dream mode than to the realistic. Five of the stories portray black characters in situations common to folk ballads. The other pieces of the collection, with the exception of "Fever Flower," are initiation stories, told in the first person by a white adolescent (two female and one male). But even these in one way or another partake of the stuff of legend. There is a pattern whereby Grau moves increasingly toward the more realistic, but we need to remember that the stories in *The Black Prince* are also early stories. And though movement can be seen away from the college stories, similarities persist. . . .

At its publication *The Black Prince* received rave reviews from all of the right critics and places. But though the critics wrote in superlatives, the superlatives were based in initial impressions, and no one went further in an effort to analyze the stories to see just where their merits lay. Indeed, the major impression that the critics seem to have taken away with them was that the stories were written by a young Southern woman and that she would carry on the tradition of Southern writers, especially women, and take her place among other Southern regionalist writers of the time. Novels followed the publication of *The Black Prince*, all published by Knopf: *The Hard Blue Sky* (1958), *The House on Coliseum Street* (1961), the Pulitzer Prize winning *The Keepers of the House* (1964), *The Condor Passes* (1971)—each succeeding one better than the last, though it was becoming more and more difficult for reviewers to make their assumptions about Grau's work jibe with the work she was producing. And all the while she continued to write short stories, publishing them regularly both in the popular magazines and in the literary journals. A number of these were collected in the volume, *The Wind Shifting West* (1973).

Stories in *The Wind Shifting West* demonstrate many of Grau's mature interests, as well as her continuing and remarkable narrative skill in the genre of the short story and her ability to handle forms and points of view extraordinary in their range and gradation. A fiction that can loosely be classified as a "ghost story" ("Three") or one in the "science fiction" mode ("The Last Gas Station") take their place in the same collection with pieces of topical interest ("The Other Way," "Eight O'Clock One Morning"), with stories that circle back to Grau's earlier interests typified in *The Black Prince* ("Pillow of Stone"), to those that adumbrate novels to come ("The Patriarch," anticipating *Evidence of Love*, 1977, and "Stanley," *The Condor Passes)*, and with stories, including several of the above, that demonstrate a continuing effort to hide the technical and formal underpinnings in a dazzling and seemingly effortless surface display. The volume also exhibits virtuosity in perspectives employed. Whereas point of view in *The Black Prince* was basically limited to children or primitives, viewpoint in *The Wind Shifting West* extends to include people of all ages, both sexes, and different social classes in a variety of settings. . . .

As a short story writer, Grau's talent is immense though not revealed by a simple surface reading, for what is beneath the surfaces and interacting with them is what is characteristic of the short story genre, and Grau has mastered the genre.

Southern female writer she is, by accident of birth and genes. Southern regionalist writer, she is not. Nor are her skills confined to revealing and commenting on "the genuinely native particulars of a scene" in time, as Frederick J. Hoffman would have it.[2] Rather, like that of other important writers, her work transcends particulars, excellent as she is at rendering them.

Notes

1. See Mary Rohrberger, Samuel H. Woods, Jr., and Bernard F. Dukore, *An Introduction to Literature* (New York: Random House, 1968), 320–21.
2. See *The Art of Southern Fiction* (Carbondale: Southern Illinois Univ. Press, 1967), 28.

Horace Gregory

1898–1982

Horace Gregory was born in Milwaukee, Wisconsin, on April 10, 1898. He was of a mixed German and Anglican stock. Gregory's paternal relations were mainly academics and scholars, and they helped to establish Milwaukee's intellectual circle. Gregory studied at the German-English Academy, the Milwaukee School of Fine Arts, and the University of Wisconsin, where he received his degree in 1923. He was an ardent student of classical literature. In college he began writing poetry, influenced by his readings in Pope and Landor. After graduating he went to New York and published some strict formal verses in magazines.

But Gregory became gradually disillusioned with mere formal grace and intelligence. In 1930 he published *Chelsea Rooming House*, a collection of poems which attempted to reconcile his classical influences with contemporary speech and the modern experience. A translation of Catullus followed, another effort to contemporize and revitalize classicism. Other volumes of poetry included *No Retreat* (1933), *Poems: 1930–1940* (1941), and *Collected Poems* (1964—Bollingen Prize, 1965).

In 1925 Gregory married the poet Marya Zaturenska, who later received a Pulitzer Prize for her collection of verses, *Cold Morning Sky*. The couple had one son and one daughter. Gregory taught at Sarah Lawrence College from 1934 until his retirement in 1960. He died on March 11, 1982.

Horace Gregory's *Poems: 1930–1940* is a selection from three previous books, to which new poems have been added. Gregory is of the post-Eliot school which tends to see man moving rudderless, like a ghost, or man building himself into a rather theatrical myth, lost in the labyrinth of the modern world. Gregory's tone is always completely literary, and his effects are based on contrasting this tone with the modern (chiefly urban) scene. Similar effects Rilke and Eliot learned from Baudelaire. The two things which such effects demand, in order really to come off, are a weight of terrible emotion behind them and the gifts of a true lyric poet. Gregory writes well, and his chosen manner improves as he goes along, but his poetry has a definite Graeco-Roman air about it, the air of a tendency pushed to its limits, of writing-in-the-manner-of-writing. No roughness of subject can help this manner. Nothing can break through it. It is lifeless, it is "literature." Poetry must stay outside the museum, no matter how "modern" that museum may be. It must sound, as someone has said, as though at one time in its existence it had flowed from the end of a human arm.—Louise Bogan, NY, April 12, 1941, p. 85

New York was Gregory's waste land: more particularly, the neighborhood of Chelsea, he writes in the prefatory note to his *Collected Poems*, "bounded by the West River docks and a stretch of 'Hell's Kitchen'; on the east by Fifth Avenue; on the south by Greenwich Village; on the north by the garment industries and trade." Drawing upon the drifters, the dreamers, the down-and-outers, the would-be suicides, the sad and despairing who walked the streets of the city, upon those frozen between its "metallic sky and brilliant iron lake," and those entrapped in a limbo of concrete and steel, he set out not to symbolize but to show through symbols the actuality of civilized man's spiritual and physical poverty, his emotional and physical crippling.

In inveighing against these, at the same time empathizing with them, Gregory came closer to the primitive idealism of D. H. Lawrence (about whom he wrote a book in 1933) than to the metaphysics of Eliot, the city-poet. Eliot saw the essential tragedy of our age in its dissociation from traditional, cultural values and sought regeneration through the old myths supplied by history and religion; Lawrence (ever the iconoclast both of culture and eschatology) sought to free man from the prison of his own intellect and the pressures of industrial, urban society through the self-renewing myth of the individual and the new myth of the unconscious. In the truest sense, both glimpsed the apocalypse, but refused to allow man to be swept over the abyss without at least dragging with him the chains of salvation.

Gregory was to develop throughout the thirties (in *Chelsea Rooming House*, and in the two succeeding volumes, *No Retreat* [1933] and *Chorus for Survival* [1935]) his own corollary to such ideas; and before the decade was out, was to arrive, through the successive stations of his pilgrimage, at his own mythic vision. Rejecting Eliot's dogmatism, doubts, ambiguities, and eventual refuge in the church, he was to gradually assimilate Eliot's central poetic technique, discovering some partial hope for civilization in the "eruption of timeless myths into modern life"; rejecting Lawrence's messianic fervor, he was to recast belief in the "selfless, stoic, enduring man" whom Lawrence (in his *Studies in Classic*

American Literature) found to be the quintessential product of the American mythopoeic genius.—Robert K. Moriss, "The Resurrected Vision: Horace Gregory's Thirties Poems," *MPS*, Spring 1973, pp. 75–76

M. L. ROSENTHAL

From "The 'Pure' Poetry of Horace Gregory"

Modern Poetry Studies, Spring 1973, pp. 44–55

The best poetry of Horace Gregory is neither sensational nor experimental nor chic. It is elegantly right in its simplicity of method and "pure" in its freedom from tendentiousness. Gregory's translations of Catullus and Ovid are from this standpoint his most impressive work. They surpass all other modern English verse-translations of these Latin poets. In their phrasing and formal effects they are true to their originals, while at the same time they are colloquially natural; in short, they are classical in the most accurate sense. Gregory learned from Pound how to repossess a poem in a foreign tongue and make it one's own, a modern poem recalling the tone and style and rhythmic basis of the original without becoming stilted and dull and idiomatically impossible in the process.

That truthfulness to his material and to its inner formal demands marks the most memorable original work by Gregory. While his work does not always succeed, his effort is toward a difficult end—to find both a pitch of speech and a lyrical *song* quality appropriate to the dramatic situation of the poem. One has a sense of enormous energies being refined and directed toward the simple yet elusive aim of "getting at" something that remains hidden after all. Such an effort cannot always be controlled or sustained, but when it does find its own proper direction we get something shimmering and incomparable—not "great" but quite beautifully of its own kind.

Of the poems that achieve this success, or very nearly do so, I would select seven especially for comment: in *Chelsea Rooming House* (1930), "Longface Mahoney Discusses Heaven" and "Interior: The Suburbs"; in *Chorus for Survival* (1935), poem "Five" ("Under the stone I saw them flow"); in *Fortune for Mirabel* (1941), "Four Monologues from *The Passion of M'Phail*"; in *The Door in the Desert* (1951), "Elizabeth at the Piano" and "Opera, Opera!"; and in *Medusa in Gramercy Park* (1961), "Flight to the Hebrides." All these poems share a certain despair and sense of failure, either at loss through the passing of time or at the plain feeling of failure on the speaker's part. They are nostalgic, elegiac, and wittily rueful not merely at the loss of life's great possibilities but at the loss (or unattainability) of its more ordinary desires and expectations. One can see easily enough the social criticism and humane compassion in most of these poems; less easily perhaps, the half-identification of the poet with most of his protagonists in a transposition of personal motifs that blocks off his giving us anything like "confessional" poetry. A lifelong struggle with illness is like a lifelong acknowledgement of other kinds of disadvantage. The reason, the meaning, lies hidden from purposeful intelligence. In Gregory's quietly heroic life a powerful psyche has made triumphs for him that less endowed men could never realize; the co-presence of suffering and passionate, sensitive will is projected onto speakers like the pathetic dreamer Longface Mahoney, the inspired loser M'Phail, and the hunted criminal in "Flight to the Hebrides." But Gregory's purity as an artist is of the sort that makes him shun the self-portrait. The closest he comes is in the poem "Interior: The Suburbs," in *Chelsea Rooming House*.

And that is not so very close. The word "I" does not enter this poem; instead, "the mind" is the protagonist. It is the mind for which "there is no rest . . . in a small house." It is the mind that "moves, looking for God" in all the impossibly petty resources of the suburban house: fixing its eye "on the bed," then focusing on "a cracked egg at breakfast," on an arm chair, and on "a fly asleep upon the ceiling." It is the mind that cannot conquer except through complete rejection of life as it is ordered and through the dubious release of death:

> There is no victory in the mind
> but desperate valor
> shattering the four walls,
> disintegrating human love
> until the iron-lidded mysterious eye
> (lowered carefully with the frail body
> under churchyard gardens)
> stares upward, luminous, inevitable,
> piercing solar magnitudes
> on a fine morning.

What strikes me about the dominant emotion of this poem is its violent frustration, as if it were a poem of "survival" of the post-concentration-camp era. The violent frustration finds no release in the form, as it would in some of Sylvia Plath's or Allen Ginsberg's poems. It is a quality of the mind's situation, while the free-verse stanzas hold the potential disorder under control through their precision of figurative language and of diction generally and their somewhat distantly observing speaker. The *words* for the feeling are present—"desperate," "shattering," "disintegrating"—but the overall form and the tone contain and repress it. If one asks for *whom* "there is no rest for the mind in a small house" (*any* small house? under *any* human circumstances?), the answer would have to be: "For a quite special kind of person." And if one asks what the "desperate valor" is that is the only possible kind of victory, it seems to be the result of devotion to an impersonal aim ("disintegrating human love") that will transform the devotee into a universal or cosmic principal himself. Pressing very hard here, in a slightly unmannerly fashion, we should have to insist that the poem refers to the poet's own highly unique circumstances—either that, or the dramatic circumstances are not a sufficient explanation of the extreme state of feeling expressed. But the poem does not set out to bring us to this personal clarification, and that is why, despite its brilliant effects in the closing stanza, which I have quoted, one still feels there is something left unaccounted for, an affect without basis, a modulation toward the sentimental such as one finds in many of the other early poems.

"Longface Mahoney Discusses Heaven," which opens the first book, is quite another matter. This is a monologue in which the protagonist, a down-and-outer possibly in jail, dreams of what it would be really to escape to a state of heavenly transport. At first he thinks of the Alpine and South Sea visions of travel posters, but then he pictures a truer "heaven":

> set up in the air, safe, a room in a hotel.
> A brass bed, military hairbrushes,
> a couple of coats, trousers, maybe a dress
> on a chair or draped on the floor.

This, of course, is a sort of minimum subsistence heaven: a room to stay in, neat clothes to wear, a woman to love. If the poem ended here, it would be not sentimental but true to the Bowery fantasies of a Longface Mahoney. But Longface dreams of more. It will be a place "where marriage nights are kept," and where the "neat girl" with him will like him for himself. His language changes into that of a romantic lover—

> Maybe this isn't heaven but near
> to something like it,

more like love coming up in elevators
and nothing to think about except, O God,
you love her now and it makes no difference
if it isn't spring. All seasons are warm
in the warm air
and the brass bed is always there.

From these imagined heights, finally, we are brought down to the world of the speaker's daily fears in which the dream has no place—

If you've done something
and the cops get you afterwards, you
can't remember the place again,
away from cops and streets—
it's all unreal—
the warm air, a dream
that couldn't save you now.
No one would care
to hear about it

The originality of this poem lies in its lyrical improvisations on the materials of a dramatic monologue. Consistency of character is not the issue here as it would be in a Browning monologue. The key lies in the use of the imagined speaker and circumstance as a central point of reference while the dynamics of the poem move us from the music of stock daydreams in a world of deprived men to that of imagined romantic ecstasy transcending the literal and the realistic in a way that Longface Mahoney himself would not be likely to grasp and then finally to the music of loss and despair with which the poem ends. In an earlier discussion of Gregory, I used the term "lyrical monologue" for his characteristic form. Gregory's "self-expression" or "confessional" aspect reveals itself more in the song-quality of his poems than in their explicit subject-matter and personae. It is the melody of entrapment by existence, of soaring dreams, and then of a plunge into depressive vision—an emotional orchestration caught at the expense, as it were, of his supposed speaking character.

I have selected poem "Five" for special comment in the twelve-part sequence *Chorus for Survival*, published in mid-Depression. A study of the whole sequence would have to concern itself with Gregory's attempt, in it, to fuse a large number of disparate motifs and points of poetic reference. Among these is a familiar desire on the part of the literary Left in the Thirties to link Marxian and revolutionary perspectives with native American ones (Emerson, Whitman) and, in turn, with the sense of the deepest European religious and literary traditions as living presences in the sense advanced by Pound and Eliot. Poem "One" reflects Gregory's studies in Latin verse, especially Catullus, at the University of Wisconsin, and there are many echoes of Hart Crane and some of Yeats. Not a single one of the twelve poems lacks beautiful lines or passages, though all but "Five" (and possibly "Eleven," though it, too, is weakened by a few derivative notes) are marred by obvious notes from other poets or self-conscious rhetoric. Poem "Five" itself makes use of the Poundian and *Waste Land* image of the crowds returning home, in New York City, after work as a vision of terror, darkness, and loss. But it is not the mere employment of a motif already used by other poets—in this instance not only the two older contemporaries but behind them Wordsworth and, still further back, Dante and Homer—that makes work derivative; it is domination by another poet's idiom, possession by his very tone of insistence. In "Five" Gregory's own music makes a clear place for itself, not strikingly original but pure in the way it picks up a tradition and creates its own variation:

Under the stone I saw them flow,
express Times Square at five o'clock,
eyes set in darkness, trampling down
all under, limbs and bodies driven
in crowds, crowds over crowds, the street
exit in starlight and dark air
to empty rooms, to empty arms,
wallpaper gardens flowering there,
error and loss upon the walls.

The contemporary American moment, the New York City rush-hour crowds, the assimilation into the lyric form of flat colloquial phrasing ("express Times Square," "exit," "wallpaper") that projects a big-city world of mobs in motion and the desolation of the literal—all are present and active in these syntactically breathless lines. And again, the elusively personal note comes through. Does everyone in the crowds arrive home "to empty rooms, to empty arms"? Of course not, but the speaker has projected his own desolation and isolation onto the scene, as I suppose Eliot did in "Preludes," because the scene is not simply realistic but is a passionately realized, fairly complex image whose symbolism has more to do with a private psychological state than with objective and empirical knowledge. Who knows what the real meaning of one's dismay at the sight of a scene such as is described at the beginning of "Five" may be? In the opening stanza of "Five" that I have quoted, the poem begins a visionary descent into deeper and deeper states of anomie and self-obliteration. In the course of the two succeeding stanzas, clarity and focus are deliberately lost and a state of confused and disturbed nightmare-awareness is induced. The idea of underground travel by "express" train becomes a motif whose elements are speed and disjointed, compulsive repetition without control. The poem's ending will illustrate the way the original formulation, which began dissolving very early on, disintegrates into effects of paradox and bleakness reflecting a lost self far more than a universal human condition:

Riderless home, shoulder to head,
feet on concrete and steel to ride
Times Square at morning and repeat
tomorrow's five o'clock in crowds
(red light and green for speed) descend,
break entrance home to love or hate
(I read the answer to the door)
the destination marked "Return,
no stop till here; this is the end."

If one compares Gregory's style here with, say, George Barker's, one can see that even when he experiments with an atmosphere of dislocation and derangement he does sustain *formal* clarity. The impact of a succession of lines with neither caesura nor end-stop, together with the parenthetical self-interruptions and the shifts of syntax without transition, is of the state of awareness I have described. The specific images are those natural to the given original scene of the vision, though they no longer form an ordered and intact whole. It is interesting that poem "Four" begins with the striking lines:

Ask no return for love that's given
embracing mistress, wife or friend.

"Four" fades quickly away into sentimentally nostalgic complaint and finally into facile affirmation, but "Five" in its bitter disorder, its emphasis on loss ("empty rooms" and "empty arms"), and its play on the word "return" handles the same conception of unrewarded life as that in "Four" with far more concentrated if delphic intensity.

Implicit in "Five" are the themes most richly developed by the more mature Gregory in "Four Monologues from *The*

Passion of M'Phail." These are the waste of the speaker's own genius or life-energy, the comparably unrealized lives he sees in the world about him, the persistence of belief in possibility that the psyche reveals ("waiting for hope (like love) here for an hour / invisible, then gone"), and the mysterious relation of that persistence to our sense of time. "The passion of M'Phail" is a punning phrase. Gregory gives his speakers Irish names that reflect his own family background; and the "failure" implied in the pun is of a piece with the failures to accept, to adjust, to feel at home in the world, presented in his poems generally. The thought of Gregory himself is unavoidable, if one has met him, when one reads these monologues. Not that M'Phail is in any direct sense an embodiment of the poet, but it is hard not to think of Gregory's physical presence—frail, shaking, blazing with a fierce yet impersonal excitement, fixing his audience with fiery, haunted eyes and uttering his thoughts in a boyishly sepulchral voice, at once mid-Western and Yeatsian—when one reads the beginning of M'Phail's first speech:

> Do I have to prove that I can sell anything?
> You can see it in my eyes, the way I brush my hair,
> even when I need a drink and can't stop talking.

This brilliant opening "Monologue" is probably the most successful projection of the daydreams of failure in our poetry. The failure consists, not in a weakness of personality but in the conception of the self as something that has to be "sold" for life to mean anything. M'Phail presents himself as the artist *par excellence* of such salesmanship:

> I can sell the power in my eyes that makes life grow
> where not even one blade of grass has grown before

and:

> I can sell snowbright
> dead women gleaming through shop windows,
> or diamond horseshoe naked dancing girls

and:

> I almost love the way I sell
> my lips, my blood, my heart: and leave them there,
> and no one else can sell such pity and such glory,
> such light, such hope
> even down to the last magnificent,
> half-forgotten love affair.

The parallel that is being drawn, between the demonically dedicated salesman and the artist, is unmistakable though not directly stated. The implicit criticism of a social assumption that one must always be "selling" oneself as if personality and spirit were market commodities, and of a ruthless social process that does indeed make commodities of us all, involves the artist quite as much as the salesman. It is presented with beautiful and powerful irony, becoming by the end of the poem a plaint for all the rich and varied tones of life that are not allowed to come into experience for their own sakes. The speaker's exaltation is a transport of irony, superbly elegiac. The two middle "Monologues" sustain the mood at a lower pitch. M'Phail becomes obsessed with the idea of ordinary people who bear accidental resemblances to the famous—"the lunch-room bus boy who looked like Orson Welles," for instance—and with the "sweepstake invisible but real" that cheats them and the rest of us of life's common rewards. Then in the fourth "Monologue," the exaltation of defeat goes beyond irony into the piercing reconciliation of the sensitive and imaginative ultimate speaker, M'Phail's creator, that enables him to say:

> I am not the same as other men;
> I must live to wake beyond the fears of hope
> into an hour that does not quite arrive

That side of the "Four Monologues" that is a sardonic yet compassionate treatment of the American success-dream, and at the same time a lament for the brevity and elusiveness of all mankind's bright joys and dreams, has many antecedents and parallels: moments in Whitman and even in Dickinson, the dominant notes in Robinson and Masters, the harsh and humorous poignancy of Kenneth Fearing. None of these matched Gregory in this matter of catching the essential music of one modern condition of awareness. Gregory has well understood our state of so valuing private personality that our selfbetrayal in a culture of "selling" can lead to tragic joy of a Yeatsian kind. In fact, there are interesting resemblances between Yeats's play *The King's Threshold* and the M'Phail sequence. The claims made in the play for the poets as creators of the very sense of value, and the triumphant acceptance there of the defeat of Seanchan, the master poet, bear a certain resemblance to the succession of attitudes in the "Monologues." Gregory's phrasing also at times resembles Yeats's as may be seen in the passage I have quoted. There may well be a remote or indirect influence here, or the sources may lie elsewhere. My point has less to do with influence than with Gregory's having reached a certain pitch of musicality and of tone that makes his achievement in this poem comparable with that of Yeats. . . .

All these poems cope imaginatively and spiritedly with the vision of a death-driven world. All "disprove" the value of illusion yet cherish it. The absolute darkness of the human condition is at times equated with the inevitability of death, as in "Flight to the Hebrides," an abrasively quick-moving short story in verse not altogether unlike Hemingway's "The Killers." One has the sense of the determined displacement, by the poet, of an original personal confrontation of death in it, and the substitution of a poetic narrative about a fugitive from justice or at least from an overweening feeling of guilt. Holding terror at bay, while finding room for buoyancy of thought and for the transcending of his death-absorption, has been Gregory's main poetic enterprise. He has never deceived himself in the face of the pressure of this enterprise or of life, and he has handled the theme of mortality with candor and dauntlessness.

ZANE GREY

1875–1939

Pearl Zane Gray was born on January 31, 1875, in Zanesville, Ohio, a city named in honor of a maternal ancestor who had distinguished himself in the Revolutionary War. After the family moved to Columbus, Ohio, in 1890, Gray worked as an itinerant tooth-puller before entering the dental school of the University of Pennsylvania on a baseball scholarship. Graduating in 1896, he practiced dentistry in New York City until his marriage to Lina Roth in 1905 enabled him to move to Lackawaxen, Pennsylvania, and write full-time under the name of Zane Grey.

Though he sold a few articles on fishing and baseball, his fiction was at first consistently rejected, and he considered returning to dentistry until he made a trip to the Arizona ranch of J. C. "Buffalo" Jones in 1907. This journey instilled in him a deep fascination with the West, and provided the basis of his novel *The Last of the Plainsmen* (1908) and of future works. *Riders of the Purple Sage* (1912) established Grey as a best-selling author, and was followed by a string of successes including *The Light of Western Stars* (1914), *The Lone Star Ranger* (1915), *The Border Legion* (1916), *The U. P. Trail* (1918), and *Man of the Forest* (1920). Three of his novels were filmed in 1918, and Grey moved to California to be near the movie business and good fishing grounds, settling in Altadena in 1920.

Always a keen angler, Grey purchased his own boat in 1924, and made trips to fishing grounds in the Pacific and later to New Zealand and Australia. At one time he held several world records, notably for marlin, tuna, and swordfish; among his books on fishing are *An American Angler in Australia* (1937) and *Adventures in Fishing* (1952). He also traveled extensively in the American West, gaining first-hand knowledge of the country and conditions of life for use in his books.

Grey's vast output of prose includes fifty-six novels of the West, which have been immensely popular in America and Europe, and have been the basis for more than 100 films. His later novels include *Call of the Canyon* (1924), *The Thundering Herd* (1925), *Code of the West* (1935), and *West of the Pecos* (1937). He was also the author of baseball stories and books on hunting. He died of a heart attack on October 23, 1939, in Altadena, California.

ZANE GREY
From "What the Desert Means to Me"

American Magazine, November 1924, pp. 5–7

Places inspire me in some sense as they did Stevenson. I love wild canyons—dry, fragrant, stone-walled, with their green-choked niches and gold-tipped ramparts. I love to get high on a promontory and gaze for hours out over a vast desert reach, lonely and grand, with its far-flung distances and its colors.

I love the great pine and the spruce forests, with their spicy tang and dreamy peace, their murmuring streams and wild creatures.

The Grand Canyon appalled and depressed, yet exalted me. Never yet have I attempted to write of it as I hope to.

The lonely, white, winding shore line of Long Key, a coral islet in Florida, always inspired me to write. I have wandered there many profitable hours.

Clemente Island in the Pacific calls and calls me to come again to its bleak black bluffs, its tawny wild-oats slopes, its bare desert heights, its white-wreathed rocks and crawling curves of surf; its haunting sound of the restless and eternal sea; its lofty crags where the eagles nest, and its almost inaccessible ledges where wild goats sleep; its canyons of silence and loneliness.

Death Valley is a place to face one's soul—aloof, terrible, desolate, the naked iron-riven earth showing its travail. The sage slopes of the Painted Desert is the place for the purple that is the most beautiful of colors. Among features of nature I love color best.

All of which is to say that my romances are simply the expression of my feeling for places.

The desert, of course, has been most compelling and most illuminating to me. The lure of the silent waste places of the earth, how inexplicable and tremendous! Why do men sacrifice love, home, civilization for the solitude of the lonely land? How infinite the fascination of death and decay and desolation—the secret of the desert!

It took me many years of experience and meditation to make sure that I was not laboring under imagination or delusion. But I was not obsessed by a feeling for some unknown thing, for the desert is a reality. It casts an actual spell.

Nothing in civilized life can cast the spell of enchantment, can grip men's souls and terrify women's hearts like the desert.

It has to do, then, with the dominating power of wild, lonely, desolate places.

Study of myself, in relation to the wilderness, disclosed many strange facts that took years to understand. I preferred to ride, walk, hunt, alone, when that was possible. The lonely places seemed to be mine, and I was jealous of them. Always I was watching and listening. All my life I have done this; but it was never significant until I became a writer and began to peer into my heart.

On trips to the desert, of which I have had many, there was always an hour or a moment of every day or evening when I went alone to some ridge or hill, or into the cedars or the sage, there to listen and to watch. This seemed to me to be a communion with the strange affinity of the desert.

I had contracted a habit which I followed without thinking. But when I actually did think of it the interpretation held aloof. Why did a vague happiness attend me in the solitudes?

It became an imperative thing for me to find out what took place in my mind during these idle, dreaming hours. The mystery augmented with the discovery that at such moments and hours I did nothing—nothing but gaze over the desolate desert, over the beautiful purple-sage uplands, listening to the wind in the cedars, the rustling sand along the rock, the scream of an eagle or cry of a lonely bird. I hardly knew I was there.

This peculiar state at last became known to me, and I grew to have a strange and fleeting power to exercise it voluntarily. Practice made it possible for me to make this a thinking act, to capture it as in a flash of lightning.

At Catalina Island for several years during May and June I used to climb the mountain trail that overlooks the Pacific, and here a thousand times I shut my eyes and gave myself over to sensorial perceptions. When I grasped the thing, always I felt it followed by a swift, vague joy.

Then I knew I had found the secret of the idle hours.

Profound thought reduced this state to a mere listening, watching, feeling, smelling of the open. It assumed staggering proportions, for I began to feel that I had got on the track of the desert influence.

During these lonely hours I was mostly a civilized man, but the fleeting trances belonged to the savage past. I was a savage. I could bring back for a brief instant the sensitory state of the progenitors of the human race.

Thus I seemed to be able to revert to the animal. But in reality it was not that, rather the intense waiting, watchful perception of the animal.

Nature developed man according to the biological facts of evolution. Therefore all the instincts of the ages have been his heritage. When I had a gun in my hands and was hunting meat to eat, why was the chase so thrilling, exciting, driving the hot blood in gusts over my body?

I recalled my boyhood days, when, like all boys, I killed for the sake of killing, until conscience intervened. Is not conscience the difference between savage and the civilized man—the greatest factor in human progress?

In every man and woman there survives the red blood of our ancestors, the primitive instincts. In these hides the secret of the eloquent and tremendous influence of the desert. The wide, open spaces, the lonely hills, the desolate, rocky wastes, the shifting sands and painted steppes, the stark-naked canyons—all these places of the desert with their loneliness and silence and solitude awake the instincts of the primitive age of man.

I realized that men toiled over the desert, some on transient journeys which were unforgettable, and others who wandered all their lives there, never for a moment understanding the fleeting trance-like transformation back to the savage.

Men take to the desert permanently: prospectors for gold, wanderers because of crime or ruined lives, seekers for the unattainable, thinking these were the things that chained them to their martyrdom. But the truth lay vastly deeper, deep as the instinct of the savage. Men love the forbidding and desolate desert because of the ineradicable and unconscious wildness of savage nature in them.

No visitors to the desert can escape this influence, though but few ever will realize the meaning of the thrill of joy that returns in memory of the desert, and the vague regret. I have met women who lived along the edge of the barren lands, hating the desolate, glaring, lonely void, yet conscious of a nameless charm.

Men once lived in trees. They descended to the ground to walk upright. They took to caves, and then spread over the face of the earth. Nature is the mother of every man.

Harness the cave-man—yes! as Doctor Fosdick so eloquently preaches; but do not kill him. Something of the wild and primitive should forever remain instinctive in the human race. All the joy of the senses lives in this law. The sweetness of the childhood of the race comes back in this thoughtless watching and listening. Perhaps the spirit of this marvelous nature is in reality God.

T. K. WHIPPLE

"American Sagas" (1925)

Study Out the Land

1943, pp. 19–29

As everyone knows, the latest fad of the intelligentsia is discovering the United States. This is the cult of which Mr. Gilbert Seldes is high priest. He and his acolytes wax analytic and aesthetic over Charlie Chaplin, Fanny Brice, Krazy Kat, Ring Lardner, and "How Come You Do Me Like You Do Do Do." And, indeed, why not? The rest of us may be amused at the delighted surprise with which recent graduates of Harvard "discover" what everyone else has been familiar with since earliest childhood—but the fact remains that Mr. Seldes has secured for our popular arts a recognition that they never had before. Already jazz has invaded Carnegie Hall, and before long everyone may be attending recitals not of Lithuanian, Swedish, and Bantu folk songs only, but of American as well. The Negro spirituals have arrived; why not the ballads of cowboys, lumberjacks, and Kentucky mountaineers?

While the boom is on, I wish to put in a word for the tales of the American folk. In Paris, according to hearsay, one of the more recent literary finds is James Oliver Curwood, whose art is discussed at length in periodicals and reviews. My own nominee, however, for the position of American *tusitala* is not Mr. Curwood, but Zane Grey. Mr. Grey has received justice only from his millions of devoted readers—and some of them, I fear, have been shamefaced in their enthusiasm. The critics and reviewers have been persistently upstage in their treatment of Mr. Grey; they have lectured him for lacking qualities which there was no reason for him to possess, and have ignored most of the qualities in which he is conspicuous. The Boston *Transcript* complains that "he does not ask his readers to think for themselves"; Mr. Burton Rascoe asks sorrowfully: "Do Mr. Grey's readers believe in the existence of such people as Mr. Grey depicts; do they accept the code of conduct implicit in Mr. Grey's novels?"

One thing at least is clear: Mr. Grey himself emphatically believes in the truthfulness of his record. Above all else he prides himself upon his accuracy as a historian. In the foreword to *To the Last Man* he says: "My long labors have been devoted to making stories resemble the times they depict. I have loved the West for its vastness, its contrast, its beauty and color and life, for its wildness and violence, and for the fact that I have seen how it developed great men and women who died unknown and unsung." And he asks: "How can the truth be told about the pioneering of the West if the struggle, the fight, the blood be left out? How can a novel be stirring and thrilling, as were those times, unless it be full of sensation?" One must admire and be thankful for Mr. Grey's faith in his own veracity; but to share it is impossible. Zane Grey should never be considered as a realist. To Mr. Rascoe's questions, I can answer for only one reader, but I should say that I no more believe in the existence of such people as Mr. Grey's than I believe in the existence of the shepherds of Theocritus; I no more accept the code of conduct implicit in Mr. Grey's novels than I do the code of conduct implicit in Congreve's comedies. At the very start I grant that Mr. Grey does not portray the world as I know it, that he is not an expert psychologist, that his is no refined art in the subtle use of words—that in competition with Henry James, Jane Austen, George Eliot, and Laurence Sterne he is nowhere.

But what of it? There is no reason for comparing him with anyone, unless perhaps with competitors in his own genre. If he must be classified, however, let it be with the authors of *Beowulf* and of the Icelandic sagas. Mr. Grey's work is a primitive epic, and has the characteristics of other primitive epics. His art is archaic, with the traits of all archaic art. His style, for example, has the stiffness which comes from an imperfect mastery of the medium. It lacks fluency and facility; behind it always we feel a pressure toward expression, a striving for a freer and easier utterance. Herein lies much of the charm of all early art—in that the technique lags somewhat behind the impulse. On the whole, it is preferable to the later condition, when the technique is matured and the impulse meager. Mr. Grey's style has also the stiffness of traditional and conventional forms; his writing is encrusted with set phrases which may be called epic formulae, or, if you insist, clichés. These familiar locutions he uses as if they were new, to him at least—as if they were happy discoveries of his own. So behind all his impeded utterance there makes itself felt an effort toward truth of expression—truth, that is, to his own vision, for we must never ask of him truth to the actual world as we know it.

That Zane Grey has narrative power no one has denied, but not everyone is pleased with his type of story. To a reader whose taste has been formed on Howells and Bennett, Mr. Grey's tales seem somewhat strong. They are, of course, sensational melodrama, as "improbable" as plays by Elizabethan dramatists. They roar along over the mightiest stage that the author has been able to contrive for them. They tell of battle and bloodshed, of desperate pursuits and hair-breadth escapes, of mortal feuds and murder and sudden death, of adventures in which life is constantly the stake. These stories move on the grand scale; they are lavish in primitive, epic events. Mr. Grey does not dodge big scenes and crises, in which plot and passion come to a head; he has a distinct liking for intense situations, and he has the power which Stevenson so admired of projecting these high moments in memorable pictures. In *Riders of the Purple Sage*, when Lassiter throws his guns on the Mormon band and saves the Gentile youth, when Venters from his hiding place in the mysterious canyon watches the robbers ride through the waterfall, when at last Lassiter rolls the stone which crushes his pursuers and forever shuts the outlet from Surprise Valley—these are scenes which linger in the mind. Very different, obviously, is this art from Mrs. Wharton's when she condenses the tragedy of three lives into the breaking of a pickle dish, and from Sinclair Lewis' as he takes Babbitt through a typical day at the office. But what of that? Though melodrama is not in style at the moment, the human taste for tremendous happenings is not likely to die for some centuries yet. Mr. Grey has the courage of his innocence in tackling difficulties which cautious realists know enough to avoid.

And no more than in his stories does he dodge the heroic in his characters. His people are all larger than life size. They may be called cowpunchers, prospectors, ranchers, rangers, rustlers, highwaymen, but they are akin to Sigurd, Beowulf, and Robin Hood. Just at present, heroism, of all literary motifs, happens to be the most unfashionable, and disillusionment is all the cry. But it is tenable surely that the heroic is not incompatible with literary merit, and perhaps even that a naïve belief in human greatness is a positive asset to literature. Certainly of the writings in the past which humanity has singled out for special favor most have this element, notoriously strong in all early literature.

Of these heroic figures Mr. Grey's portrayal is crude and roughhewn. Their speech is often far from the talk of actual men and women; we are as much—and as little—conscious of the writer's working in a literary convention as when we read a play in blank verse. His characterization has no subtlety or finesse; but, like his style, it is true—again, of course, I mean true to the author's own conception. That conception of human nature is a simple one; he sees it as a battle of passions with one another and with the will, a struggle of love and hate, of remorse and revenge, of blood lust, honor, friendship, anger, grief—all on a grand scale and all incalculable and mysterious. The people themselves are amazed and incredulous at what they find in their own souls. A good illustration of Mr. Grey's psychological analysis is the following from *The Lone Star Ranger:*

> Then came realization. . . . He was the gunman, the gun-thrower, the gun-fighter, passionate and terrible. His father's blood, that dark and fierce strain, his mother's spirit, that strong and unquenchable spirit of the surviving pioneer—these had been in him; and the killings, one after another, the wild and haunted years, had made him, absolutely in spite of his will, the gunman. He realized it now, bitterly, hopelessly. The thing he had intelligence enough to hate he had become. At last he shuddered under the driving, ruthless, inhuman blood-lust of the gunman.

In Zane Grey's conception of human nature nothing is more curious than his view of sex. In *Riders of the Purple Sage* a young man and a girl live alone together for weeks in a secret canyon; in *The Lone Star Ranger* the hero rescues an innocent girl from a gang of bandits and roams about Texas with her for a long time—and all as harmlessly as in *The Faerie Queene* Una and the Red Cross Knight go traveling together. Nothing shows more clearly how far away Mr. Grey's world is from actuality; his Texas is not in the Union, but in fairyland. His heroes, to be sure, have occasional fierce struggles with their "baser natures"—a difficulty, by the way, from which his heroines are exempt. Not all his women, however, are altogether pure; from time to time a seductress crosses the path of the hero, who usually regards her with indifference. These women, incidentally, are often among the best-drawn of Mr. Grey's characters. In his treatment of sex as in other respects Mr. Grey is simple and naïve; his conventions are as remote as those of the medieval Courts of Love, and must be taken for granted along with the other assumptions of his imaginary world.

Mr. Grey's heroic ideal looks a little strange in the twentieth century. It is; it belongs more naturally to the sixth century; it is the brutal ideal of the barbarian, of the Anglo-Saxons before they left their continental homes. Like them, Mr. Grey cares above all things for physical strength, for prowess in battle and expertness with weapons, for courage and fortitude and strength of will, for ability to control oneself and others. Where the Anglo-Saxon emphasized loyalty in thegn and generosity in earl, Mr. Grey more democratically insists on loyalty and generosity between friends, and on independence and self-reliance. And to this code he adds an element which is no doubt a kind of residuum from Christianity: he likes to see hatred and desire for vengeance supplanted by forgiveness and love. The process of purification or redemption is a favorite theme of his; sometimes it is brought about by the influence of a noble and unselfish man or by the love of a pure and innocent girl, but more often by the cleansing effect of nature in the rough. If one is to take Mr. Grey's ethics at all seriously, one must of course find fault with them; although such morals are better, no doubt, than those inculcated by Benjamin Franklin or Mr. Ben Hecht, still one would no more care to have one's sons adopt Mr. Grey's *beau idéal* than one would care to have one's sons adopt, say, the *Saga of Burnt Njal* as a program of life. Without wishing, however, to return to the human ideals of the Bronze Age, we may insist that a storyteller's merit is not dependent on the validity of the lessons which he teaches. There is something of the savage in most of us, so that we can respond imaginatively to Mr. Grey without our all rushing off to the wilds to be made men of.

Not that Mr. Grey regards nature as always a beneficent force. Rather, he portrays it as an acid test of those elemental traits of character which he admires. It kills off the weaklings, and among the strong it makes the bad worse and the good better. Nature to him is somewhat as God is to a Calvinist—ruthlessly favoring the elect and damning the damned. Mr. Grey sees in nature the great primal force which molds human lives. Not even Thomas Hardy lays more stress on the effect of natural environment. The stories themselves are subsidiary to the background: "My inspiration to write," says Mr. Grey, "has always come from nature. Character and action are subordinate to setting." This setting of desert, forest, mountain, and canyon, great cliffs and endless plains, has been made familiar to us all by the movies if not by travel; but as seen through Mr. Grey's marveling and enhancing eyes it all takes on a fresh and unreal greatness and wonder. For his descriptive power is as generally recognized as his narrative skill; indeed, it would be hard for anyone so overflowing with zest and with almost religious adoration to fail in description. Mr. Grey's faculty of wonder, his sense of mystery, is strong; it shows itself in his feeling for the strangeness of human personality and also more outwardly in the air of strangeness with which he invests his lonely wanderers or outlaws who from time to time appear out of the unknown—but most of all it shows itself in his feeling for the marvelous in nature. So far as he indicates a religion, it is a form of nature worship; when he is face to face with the more grandiose aspects of the earth's surface, he feels himself in the presence of God.

Mr. Grey differs from many nature lovers, that is to say, in that his fervor is altogether genuine. His enthusiasm is not assumed because it is the proper thing; on the contrary, he feels much more than he can manage to express. And here, I think, we come to the secret of his superiority to most of his contemporaries and competitors: he is sincere and thoroughly in earnest. He really cares, he gets excited about what he is writing. His books have not the look of hackwork. It is true that they are uneven, that he has not been immune to the influences of his own popularity and of the movies, that he must often have worked hastily and carelessly—but he has never written falsely. He is genuine and true to himself, an artist after his fashion. Furthermore, he possesses a powerful imagination, of the mythmaking type which glorifies and enlarges all that it touches, and in his best work, such as *Riders of the Purple Sage*, he uses his imagination to the utmost. The whole story, the situations and people and settings, are fully living in his mind, and he gets them into words as best he can. Of course he has an amazing, an incredible simplicity and unsophistication of mind, a childlike naïveté—but that is what makes him what he is, a fashioner of heroic myths. At the present moment, when the primitive is all the vogue in the arts, and Viennese and Parisian sculptors are doing their best to be archaic, in Zane Grey we have a real, not a would-be, primitive miraculously dropped among us; yet we accord him no recognition at all—except an astounding popularity.

If, that is, his popularity is astounding—if it is not, rather, what should be expected. Most Americans seem to have a strongly ingrained hankering for the primitive and a good deal of the childlike quality of mind, possibly as an inheritance from our three centuries of pioneering. Whenever a holiday comes along, we reproduce primitive conditions and play at pioneering as much as possible. The age of the pioneers, especially in the West, is taking on more and more the air of a heroic and mythic period. The glorification of the redblooded he-man, the pioneer ideal, is a national trait, and even those who have learned better cannot rid themselves of a sneaking respect for the brute in their hearts. If you doubt the simplicity and innocence of Americans, watch their reactions to Michael Arlen and Jean Cocteau and their forlorn efforts to imitate Ronald Firbank and to understand and admire *Ulysses*. They are like stray Vandals wandering bewildered through the streets of Byzantium. Only the pure in heart could be so impressed by decay and corruption, just as only a man from an Iowa village could have written *The Blind Bow-Boy*. No, the American forte is not sophisticated disillusion—it is much more likely to be something on the order of Zane Grey's work. Of course everyone is at liberty not to like such literature, which belongs by right to the infancy of the race, and to disagree with Mr. Grey's view of the world. Indeed, if one asks of books a valid criticism of life as we experience it, Mr. Grey has little to offer. But let us look at him for what he is, rather than what he is not. Then, whether or not we happen to care for his work, I think we must grant him a certain merit in his own way. We turn to him not for insight into human nature and human problems nor for refinements of art, but simply for crude epic stories, as we might to an old Norse skald, maker of the sagas of the folk.

GARY TOPPING

From "Zane Grey's West"

The Popular Western

eds. Richard W. Etulain and Michael T. Marsden

1974, pp. 42–45

Perhaps Grey's most original contribution to the view of the West found in his novels was his Darwinism. Other Western novelists could wax eloquent over the nobility of the mountain man and cowboy, but Grey attempted to explain in detail just how it was that the Western environment operated to create such people.

Although Grey later claimed to have "devoured" the works of Darwin as a youth, they do not seem to have induced the kind of mystical conversion in him as they did in other young men of his time. Rather, they seem to have offered simply a convenient rationale for the Western phenomena he observed, a rationale that could be expressed in the common intellectual currency of the time.[1] Moreover, Grey's Darwinism owed more to Darwin himself than to Spencer and the other Social Darwinists, in spite of the fact that Grey also used Darwinism as a basis for social theory. Contact with raw nature was the vital factor in Grey's West, not the strife of man versus man emphasized by the Spencerians. The following passage, in which Grey describes the relationship of man to nature, makes this clear:

> Men once lived in trees. They descended to the ground to walk upright. They took to caves, and then spread over the face of the earth. Nature is the mother of every man. If the primitive were eliminated from man there would be no more progress. Harness the cave-man, yes . . . but do not kill

> him. Something of the wild and primitive should remain instinctive in the human race. All the joy of the senses lives in this law.[2]

Further, at the risk of digressing too far, one can see the extent to which nature was, to Grey, not only the philosophical explanation for his Western characters but also a great cause, by simply quoting an example of the way in which he wrote about nature. Nature in his novels is the one great fact of Western life that cannot be ignored or cheated. The following passage occurs in describing an Eastern girl's wagon ride in the pre-dawn desert:

> A puff of cold wind struck [Madeline's] face and she shivered. Florence noticed her and pulled up the second robe and tucked it closely round her up to her chin.
>
> "If we have a little wind you'll sure feel it," said the Western girl.
>
> Madeline replied that she already felt it. The wind appeared to penetrate the robes. It was cold, pure, nipping. It was so thin she had to breathe as fast as if she were under ordinary exertion. It hurt her nose and made her lungs ache.[3]

A standard Zane Grey plot for expounding his Darwinian West is the story of an Easterner who comes to live in the West and is gradually educated to Western ways. Comparing the two ways of life, the Easterner realizes the essential artificiality of his former life and is converted to the primal wholesomeness of Western life. Grey's 1920 novel *The Man of the Forest* represents one of his most ambitious and successful assaults upon that theme and will serve here as an example.

The story hinges on the sheep versus cattle conflict. Al Auchincloss, a lone cattle rancher in sheep country, is about to die and his former partner, the unscrupulous sheep rancher Beasley, plots to take over the ranch. His strategy is to have Auchincloss's niece, Helen Rayner, kidnapped on her way west to prepare for succeeding her uncle. He is frustrated in his plan since Milt Dale, a lone hunter, accidentally overheard Beasley discussing the plot with the outlaw gang he has hired to do the work. Dale is temporarily out of favor with Auchincloss, so he acts alone, abducting Helen and her sister before the outlaws can get to them. He holds them in his isolated mountain valley until it is safe to deliver them to their uncle. Inevitably, Dale falls in love with Helen and gives up his lonely life to marry her and to help dispose of Beasley.

Helen's initiation into Western life occurs during her stay in Dale's hideout. She marvels at Dale's courage and manly abilities in dealing with the outlaws and wild animals in the forest. Dale is willing to explain to her the reasons why life alone in the forest has created such a magnificent specimen of manhood as himself. "Strife," he explains, is

> the meanin' of all creation, an' the salvation. If you're quick to see, you'll learn that the nature here in the wilds is the same as that of men—only men are no longer cannibals. Trees fight to live—birds fight—animals fight—men fight. They all live off one another. An' it's this fightin' that brings them all closer an' closer to bein' perfect. But nothin' will ever be perfect.

When Helen protests in terms of the morality and values of her Eastern education, Dale rebukes her harshly. "I must live and fulfill my mission," she objects, "my work in the civilized world." "A woman's mission," Dale counters, "is to have children. The female of any species has only one mission—to reproduce its kind. An' Nature has only one mission—toward greater strength, virility, efficiency—absolute perfection, which is unattainable." When she asks, "What of the mental and spiritual development of man and woman," Dale replies brutally, "Both are direct obstacles to the design of Nature."[4]

Eventually Auchincloss shows up and escorts the girls to his ranch. Left alone that winter, Dale becomes the victim of some of Helen's rebuttals and even of his own Darwinism. First, he acknowledges that he cannot account for such things as pain and suffering. Also, he cannot account for the seeming meaninglessness of a cosmos that has no end but the perpetuation and perfection of itself. These two problems can only be solved by religion or some other philosophy, as Helen had pointed out to him.

Ironically, however, Dale comes to realize that he has not even lived according to his own Darwinist ideas. The highest glory of the natural order, he realizes, is manifested in the group, not the individual. A lone wolf is of no use, but a wolf pack can reproduce, seek food together and provide defense and other mutual assistance that benefits the race. Thus, he reasons, society is to man what the ecosystem is to nature. This social imperative is the basic progressive force in Grey's novels. Even his semi-outlaw gunmen are heroes only because they can justify their violent acts in the name of social improvement.[5]

Conversely, Grey's villains violate their social responsibility, which puts them out of harmony with nature and makes their destruction inevitable. Beasley is a good example. One of Dale's cowboy friends explains to Helen that "it's the nature of happenin's that Beasley passes away before his prime. Them of his breed don't live old in the West." In another novel, the hero observes the cowardice and immorality of one of the villains and wonders how "a man of his mind [had] ever lived so long and gone so far among the exacting conditions of the Southwest."[6]

Without really approving of them, Grey does seem at times to allow his villains a certain perverse grandeur and to dispose of them under dramatic and glorious circumstances. In *Riders of the Purple Sage*, for example, the outlaw Oldring perishes under the superior speed and accuracy of Bern Venters' guns. Likewise, the band of cruel Mormons who kidnap little Fay Larkin die in an orgy of glorious vengeance wreaked by Lassiter's pistols and the huge avalanche he creates by pushing over the Balancing Rock.[7]

But Grey showed little sympathy of any kind for the dudes in his novels. Boyd Harvey, a dude in *The Light of Western Stars*, is a good example. He avoids all strenuous activity, rides whenever he can to avoid walking, and has a pale complexion that even the Western sun cannot darken. Grey condemns him in classic Darwinian terms: "If he ever had any sons they would be like him, only a generation more toward the inevitable extinction of his race." Gene Stewart, the hero, is a manly cowboy who thrills the heroine by quite opposite qualities, such as "his potential *[sic]* youth and promise of things to be, red-blooded deeds, both of flesh and spirit. In him she saw the strength of his forefathers unimpaired." Above all, Grey hated the flappers of the 1920s as an example of everything artificial and phony in Eastern life. In *The Call of the Canyon*, the heroine is a converted flapper who delivers a long tirade against her former way of life:

> I positively hate that phrase "modern feminine unrest!" It smacks of ultra—ultra—Oh! I don't know what . . . this unrest means speed-mad, excitement-mad, fad-mad, dress-mad, or I should say *un*dress-mad, culture-mad, and Heaven knows what else. The women of our set are idle, luxurious, selfish, pleasure-craving, lazy, useless, work-and-children shirking, absolutely no good.[8]

There is one final aspect of Grey's West in which his

Darwinism proved effective. Social convention since the time of Cooper had prevented Western literary heroes, no matter how noble, from marrying genteel heroines. Nature's nobleman was simply not noble enough to be linked with an Eastern aristocrat.[9] Thanks partly to a great deal of social leveling since Cooper's day, Grey had a much easier time reconciling nature's nobility with society's genteel, but the problem still existed. Owen Wister had shown that a solution was possible in *The Virginian*, but the effects of Western environment were still not enough in that novel to render the hero acceptable without assistance from other factors.[10]

Often Grey could simply ignore the problem, since literary convention no longer demanded a truly genteel heroine. When he chose to face the issue directly, however, as in *The Light of Western Stars*, he resorted to his Darwinism for the solution. Madeline Hammond, the heroine, is truly aristocratic and protests strongly, early in the novel, when she learns that her brother is engaged to marry a common Western girl. When she falls in love with the cowboy Gene Stewart, she realizes that his success in the process of natural selection is sufficient to compensate for his humble ancestry. "All her Eastern lovers," she recalls, "who had the graces that made them her equals in the sight of the world were without the only great essential [natural nobility] that a lonely hard life had given Stewart. Nature here struck a just balance."[11]

How then can we characterize in general terms Zane Grey's West? First, it is a romanticized creation directly in line with the mythical tradition dating back to the eighteenth century. Although to say, with Whipple, that Grey's Texas is in fairyland rather than the Union is a bit extreme, it is true that Grey never really appreciated the West on its own terms. He saw the West the way he did, one might say, because he saw the East the way he did.

Secondly, however, Grey has never received due credit for the comparatively high degree of realism in his books. His cowboys, for example, actually raise cattle, get tired, dirty and drunk, and curse, albeit mildly, when angry.

Finally, Grey was philosophically a child of his times. In an age that extolled moral incorruptibility, the manly virtues and "the strenuous life," Grey's novels revealed a world in which those values reigned supreme.

Notes

1. Zane Grey, "Breaking Through: The Story of My Life," *The American Magazine*, July, 1924, p. 78. Richard Hofstadter's *Social Darwinism in American Thought* (Philadelphia: University of Pennsylvania Press, 1944) discusses the wide acceptance and applications of Darwinist social theory in America during Grey's youth and early writing career.
2. Zane Grey, "What the Desert Means to Me," *The American Magazine*, November, 1924, p. 7.
3. Zane Grey, *The Light of Western Stars* (New York: Grosset & Dunlap, 1914), pp. 46–47.
4. Zane Grey, *The Man of the Forest* (New York: Grosset & Dunlap, 1920), pp. 126, 132–33.
5. Ibid., p. 202. See *Riders of the Purple Sage* (New York: Grosset & Dunlap, 1912), p. 326, and *Lone Star Ranger* (New York: Grosset & Dunlap, 1915), pp. 137–42 (for examples of the social conscience of Grey's gunman-heroes).
6. Grey, *The Man of the Forest*, p. 234; *Lone Star Ranger*, p. 289.
7. *Riders of the Purple Sage*, pp. 259–60, 326–35.
8. Grey, *The Light of Western Stars*, p. 256; *The Call of the Canyon* (New York: Grosset & Dunlap, 1921), p. 229.
9. On this problem in Cooper's novels, see Henry Nash Smith, *Virgin Land: The American West as Symbol and Myth* (New York: Alfred A. Knopf, 1950), pp. 64–76, and his introduction to Cooper's *The Prairie* (New York: Holt, Rinehart & Winston, 1950), pp. v–xx.
10. The Virginian's pursuit of Molly Wood's hand is facilitated by his Southern background and a considerable Westernization on her part.
11. Grey, *The Light of Western Stars*, p. 161.

A. B. Guthrie, Jr.

1901–

Albert Bertram Guthrie, Jr., was born on January 13, 1901, in Bedford, Indiana. Six months later his family moved to Choteau, Montana, where Guthrie's father was a high school principal. In 1919 Guthrie began his studies at the University of Washington in Seattle, but transferred after one year to the University of Montana at Missoula, where he completed a degree in Journalism in 1923. After graduating he traveled to Mexico and worked in the rice harvest, then found temporary employment in California before returning to Montana in 1924 as a census-taker for the U.S. Forestry Service. In 1926 he joined the staff of the *Lexington Leader* in Kentucky, remaining with the newspaper until 1947.

Guthrie began work on his first novel, *Murders at Moon Dance*, in 1936. After its publication in 1943 he applied successfully for a Nieman Fellowship to Harvard, where he studied in 1944–45 and worked on *The Big Sky*, published in 1947. His third novel, *The Way West* (1949), won him the Pulitzer Prize.

In the 1950s Guthrie worked in Hollywood, writing the screenplays for *Shane* and *The Kentuckian*. Having moved back to Montana in 1953, he completed a fourth novel, *These Thousand Hills*, in 1956. A volume of short stories, *The Big It*, appeared in 1960, and his autobiography, *The Blue Hen's Chick*, in 1965. *Arfive* (1970) continued his series of Western novels and won him the Western Heritage Wrangler Award. Further novels include *The Last Valley* (1975) and *Fair Land, Fair Land* (1982). Guthrie won the Golden Saddleman Award of the Western Writers of America in 1978, and the Montana Governor's Award for Distinguished Achievement in the Arts in 1982.

His first marriage having ended in divorce in 1962, Guthrie remarried in 1969, and his second wife illustrated his short stories for children, *Once Upon a Pond* (1973).

In *The Big Sky* Mr. Guthrie gave shape to a tale heavy with important but little-related incident, by sticking so closely to Boone Caudill as to secure nearly the selective continuity of the first-person view. In *The Way West* his structural problem is just the contrary one of maintaining life in a narrow line which is necessarily narrow and dangerously protracted, and it must be solved by the reverse and much more difficult means of the multiple viewpoint. Mr. Guthrie succeeds in this complicated task with an apparent simplicity which is proof enough of his mastery. He avoids the threat of separation inherent in the multiple approach, by gradually focussing the viewpoint, even as the wagon train itself is gradually, by experience along the 2,000-mile route, drawn together from its beginnings as a loose collection of heterogeneous and sometimes even hostile units, the solvent and the penniless, farmers and merchants, Southerners and New Englanders, politicians and loners, loud-mouths and close-mouths, Catholics, Protestants, free-thinkers, into a single, efficient, and purposeful entity, pioneers only, and able tools of the leader's will. . . .

This superior achievement in structure is complemented, to my mind, by an equal improvement in the writing. In *The Big Sky*, Mr. Guthrie sometimes came near, in his major scenes, to degenerating into free verse, and then, in order to maintain his tone, was forced to hurry and inflate traditional passages until the reader was rushed past understanding, and even, at times, to the point where the language parted with the realities behind it. In *The Way West*, on the contrary, he has made use of an even, well-paced prose, perfectly suited to the movement of the train, and never once, that I can remember, detached from the experience it presents. Some readers will miss the magnificent but often nearly isolated canvases of *The Big Sky*, both scenic and dramatic, but I promise that if they will bear with the first difference, they will find the slow, bit-by-bit accumulation of *The Way West* even more effective before they are done with it, and more memorable afterwards. It is a medium in keeping with the structure, and both are admirably suited to the patient, increasingly stirring ascent toward the Divide of the miniature America that is Mr. Guthrie's wagon train on what has now become Mr. Guthrie's Oregon Trail.—WALTER VAN TILBURG CLARK, "Emigrants on the Oregon Trail," *SR*, Oct. 8, 1949, pp. 21–22

On one level *The Big Sky* is entertaining melodrama, the Old West of hunting and trapping, Indian fighting, violence and sudden death. On another it is a novel of atmosphere, its pages lovely and luminous with the sense of great spaces and empty skies conveyed in images of sunset-flushed peaks, stormy winter nights, green river valleys, autumn moons; a land where "one day and another it was pretty much the same, and it was all good." But the true meaning of Guthrie's novel comes through, not in action or landscape painting, but in an unexposed pattern of ideas and images bringing the whole into proper focus.

We can make no greater demand upon the art of the novelist than this: Granted the imaginative reality of his story, he must convey upon the level of significant meaning some truth about human conduct and its consequences. Because Guthrie tries to answer this demand, his novel has moral value beyond mere entertainment. His sense of form allows no surprises of technique, and his style is at times uncertain, but no one could doubt the seriousness of his purpose. He writes about the frontier, a subject and an experience which concerns us all, though we may be separated from it by generations. The physical frontier has reached its dead end, but its emotional and moral forces are still unspent. We take certain habits of our minds and nerves from the frontier experience; it gave us as well our tormenting restlessness, our social and racial tensions, and the sense of loneliness which Europeans have often noted, a feeling of isolation and lostness that Willa Cather lightly touched upon but which runs like a despairing refrain through the novels of Thomas Wolfe.

The story of westward expansion is the fundamental American experience. It gives life and drama to our history and confirms our unity and progress as a nation. But we have grown used to seeing the frontier only in its broad and generous outlines, as De Tocqueville viewed it and Walt Whitman hymned it, the dramatic spectacle of pathfinders marching toward the Pacific, and civilization following in their footsteps. The frontier was a historical reality, but it was also myth, a summons to adventure, the promise of a better life, the second chance. If myth was to sustain the illusion of a fat present and a heroic past, it had to leave out whatever fails to flatter national self-esteem. What was missing from the noble view of the pioneer was the sense of human values, the appalling waste of the human spirit and effort, and the emotional erosion which frontier life imposed. The realistic writer must always restore the cost of hardship and the casual cruelty of things to the story of the frontier.

Guthrie is a realist. Boone Caudill was a mountain man. That is the whole point of his social and aesthetic significance, for the mountain man was the "white Injun," the product of his environment. He brought the skills of woodcraft to the point of highest development on this continent. In a region where his life often depended on his ability to interpret instantly and unerringly the slightest sound or motion, he outwitted the Indian on his home ground. Instinct became his compass and barometer. To supply furs for traders who exploited him, he covered every mountain, river, and valley in a territory spanning a third of a continent. Breaking trails where the settler would soon follow, he reduced the perspectives of history from centuries to decades. His equipment was meager—a horse, a few traps, a gun, powder, lead, salt. On occasion he survived for months with nothing but a knife. He had no use for the money his furs brought him, and he wasted his catch on liquor, cards, squaws. He added a new symbol of loneliness—the mountains—to the American experience. Their silence and emptiness ate into him, and in his tensed spirit he reverted to savagery. Having invented the phrase that the only good Indian is a dead one, he killed and scalped to justify his belief. Dehumanized, ferocious, he took his pleasures at the yearly rendezvous and then fled back to his mountains. Thoreau wrote, "Eastward I go only by force; but westward I go free." The mountain man lived this text in ways undreamed of by Concord's naturalist-sage. There was always the road back, but few ever took it for long; the mountain man expected to go on until he lost his hair in some sudden ambush or until the streams were trapped out and the settlers moved in. And in the end he despoiled the land which made him a free man.

The mountain man was the master of his environment but not of himself. Like Boone Caudill, he was unable to endure human relationships and social institutions. In him we see American individualism in its most extreme and elemental form trying to get away, to break all ties with the past. His struggle became psychic, because his need to conquer the wilderness turned into a wish to destroy. The ravages of the machine age did no more than complete the processes he began. Since the frontier is the deeply possessed national experience within the common consciousness, we owe to him in part the restlessness, the flaring violence, the communal shame and guilt, the inner fears, and secret loneliness which agitate our society today.

Guthrie has been fortunate in that the stories he has to tell lend themselves to the use of historical images, the kind of symbolic figure for which other writers capable of more subtle and aesthetic effects often search in vain. In *The Big Sky* his image is the mountain man, solitary, morose, fiercely independent, given to wild humors and murderous rages. All the lesser symbols of the novel—the frontier court which aroused Boone Caudill's resentment of law and order, the beaver which looked at him with quick, frightened eyes in the moment of dying, Boone's quest for Teal Eye, the blind child, the spoiled paradise—tend toward a fuller understanding of the trapper's place in the landscape and history of the West.—DAYTON KOHLER, "A. B. Guthrie, Jr., and the West," *CE*, Feb. 1951, pp. 252–53

The Big Sky is a long, easy-gaited, smooth-running novel which seems unimpressive enough at first, which builds its effects slowly, fitting its separate ideas and episodes together as snugly as the porcupine quills on a buckskin shirt. As one follows Mr. Guthrie's stirring story deeper and deeper into the wilderness, one realizes with increasing certainty that this is not just another combination of research and adventure, that here is a magical re-creation of a lost world and a rare capacity to convey its essential quality. If that sadly overworked word, epic, had not been so debased by indiscriminate misuse, *The Big Sky* could be called an epic of the Mountain Men. Tarnation! Let's just call it an epic, anyway. How is a word going to get back its proper dignity if we are afraid to use it at all?—ORVILLE PRESCOTT, "The Art of Historical Fiction: Richter, Guthrie," *In My Opinion*, 1952, pp. 141–42

There are ways in which ⟨*These Thousand Hills*⟩ is not so strong a book as either of its predecessors, and only too often the task of sustaining a long, planned series, especially within the arbitrary frame of history, can weary an author into dead writing and formula plotting. But, if there are signs of less successful work in *These Thousand Hills*, it is also, in itself and in what it makes clearer about *The Big Sky* and *The Way West*, the sufficient proof that they have not resulted from any cheapening of intention or weakening of will. . . .

The Big Sky tells the story of the mountain men. True, but more to the point, it does so by means of a profound re-creation of the life, internal and external, from its rebellious beginnings to its shadowy passing, of one highly credible, complete mountain man, Boone Caudill. And this concern for the individual, even though he may be at the same time a representative of his kind, creates a strong, unbroken narrative movement, though it presents an aimless wandering, almost unconscious life, for which the simple fact of being is almost enough. And, of equal importance, presents it as dominated by that splendid, vast and impersonal wilderness which creates it and which makes simple being enough. . . .

It would appear . . . that Mr. Guthrie has sought to embody the spirit of each era of his series in the kind of man created by that era and most important to it. It would also appear that he has sought to give the very form of each book a reinforcing likeness to that spirit—for *The Big Sky*, a world vast, loose and scenic; for *The Way West*, a world narrow and moving, and for *These Thousand Hills* a world tight, various, uncertain and contentious. And if *These Thousand Hills* does not move with quite the certainty and power of its predecessors, it seems likely that the difference results, not from any faltering on Mr. Guthrie's part, but from the nature of his materials. It may be that it is not possible to render the complexities of an era of increasing density, involvement and moral debate with the same unity or within the same scope that will serve the wanderings of a lone or the progress of a single, obsessive passion, and that Mr. Guthrie will be forced, as his chronicle continues, to move a little more slowly, to deal, book by book, with phases, not epochs, with men representative of phases, not of an age entire.

It is to be hoped that the chronicle will continue. What emerges above all from a consideration of *These Thousand Hills* and a glance back at *The Big Sky* and *The Way West* is the fact that Mr. Guthrie is moved by a fictional purpose as high and valid as his historical purpose is big, and that the two are soundly related, that he is writing, out of the real events of a real world, something like a spiritual epic of the Northwest. —WALTER VAN TILBURG CLARK, "When Settlers Begin to Take Over," *NYTBR*, Nov. 18, 1956, pp. 1, 54

The Big Sky does not merely celebrate the paradisiacal quality of the mountain man's life: like other Edens, this one becomes a paradise lost. Deliberately setting his novel at the moment when beaver were vanishing and settlers were starting over South Pass, Guthrie skillfully chooses his events and characters to give sharp impact to the ponderous historical process by which the mountain man's frontier gave way to the settler's frontier. Dick Summers' nostalgia, expressed in eloquent passages of internal monologue while Dick rides out of the mountains for the last time, is one method Guthrie uses to underscore the tragic loss of the wilderness paradise. More important is the private tragedy which Boone brings upon himself by giving in, Othello-like, to his suspicions, killing his comrade and repudiating his Indian wife. Shocked and numb, Boone returns temporarily to the East, only to discover that although he has ruined his wilderness home, he cannot tolerate taking another home in civilization. Rough, inexpressive, unresigned, able to grieve only through increased violence, Boone leaves our vision, "weaving big and dark into the darkness." We know from Dick Summers' last words that Boone's private tragedy is the tragedy of the mountain man generally. And there is nothing to prevent any American, especially if he is a Westerner, from associating the destruction of this particular frontier at this particular moment with the vanishing of all frontiers and with the destruction of the continental wilderness.

The Big Sky is a celebration of the tragic loss of the freedom, violence, and natural religion that the Romantic era associated with the frontier. This novel has, I believe, a claim to greatness. It is, first of all, technically accomplished. Its strong authenticity, its realism, and its effective devices for giving sharp point to a gradual historical process produce a tragic effect that is both cathartic and exaltive. . . . *The Big Sky* calls us not only to purge our grief for what is lost but to experience in new intensity what the lost value has meant to us. . . .

Some may reject *The Big Sky* for its tragic celebration of values considered sentimental and soft-minded. But until the West and America at large purge themselves definitively of their Romantic feelings, the appeal of *The Big Sky* will remain strong. There is some evidence that they will not purge themselves. . . . The saga of the vanished frontier is the cloth in which the West drapes its existential grief. If a brooding sense of absolute guilt is the regional grief of New England, if nationhood lost in civil war is the regional grief of the South, then as surely the loss of the frontier is the regional grief of the West. Because it expresses this grief so admirably, I believe *The Big Sky* will endure.—LEVI S. PETERSON, "Tragedy and Western American Literature," *WAL*, Winter 1972, pp. 247–49

RICHARD ASTRO
"*The Big Sky* and the Limits of Wilderness Fiction"

Western American Literature, Summer 1974, pp. 105–14

A decade ago, John Milton, Editor of the *South Dakota Review*, conducted a symposium on the Western novel in which he asked such accomplished Western writers as Frank Waters, Frederick Manfred, Walter Van Tilburg Clark and Vardis Fisher whether the subject matter and/or regional setting of Western fiction poses any special problems for the Western novelist. Some of the answers Milton received were to be expected: that Eastern and urban critics cannot understand Western and non-urban fiction and so treat it lightly or ignore it altogether, and that the formula Western has undermined serious Western writing and has made it a little suspect with sophisticated readers and critics. But the most important response to the question from these writers was that in those historical novels which record the great conflicts between civilization and wilderness, between primitivism and progress, there is simply no room for the kind of thorough-going exploration of the inward aspects of human personality through which complete characterizations are generally achieved. As novelist Michael Straight has observed about the characters in his own writing, "I could not spend much of my time hidden under their beds."[1]

Frederick Manfred has pointed to the importance of setting in Western fiction by insisting that "it's place that writes your books."[2] And Manfred is, of course, correct to a point. But even a cursory glance at the classics of British and American fiction reminds one that great novels are not written about places, but about people; that as Frank Waters so succinctly notes, "characterization is the test of all novels wherever their settings are laid. Great literature does not rely upon action, the intricacies of plot structure, the manipulations of events. It depends upon the unfoldment of character."[3] And, Waters laments, "few Western novels meet the test."

> It has been far easier to depend upon the built-in drama of Indian depredations, cattle and sheep wars, battles over water rights and mining claims, of pushing through railroads, and damming wild rivers. Stock characters easily manipulated are sufficient: the Trapper, Trader, and Mountain Man, the Settler, the dashing Dragoon, the renegade Mormon, the Cattle King, the Prospector, the Outlaw, and above all, the savage Redskin.[4]

There are, of course, characters in Western novels who do "meet the test." There is, for example, Waters' own Martiniano in *The Man Who Killed the Deer* or Kesey's Hank Stamper in *Sometimes a Great Notion*. But these are contemporary "Westerners," by definition protected from the kind of stock characterizations which constitute the formula Western. But even in the best Western wilderness novels, there are effectively drawn characters who escape the stereotypes. And it is here that we must turn to A. B. Guthrie's Boone Caudill in *The Big Sky* who, far from being an "epic knight in buckskin,"[5] is a real-life figure whose behavior as a mountain man fully reflects Guthrie's knowledge of and adherence to the facts of frontier history. And yet, while a genuine character who is neither sentimentalized nor unrealistically intellectualized, Caudill is deprived in a way which is peculiar to the Western wilderness novel; his shortcomings as a man explain the inherent limitations of this kind of fiction.

Put broadly, the American West is space, and Boone Caudill is an Adam who lives in the Edenic expanse of total possibility which is space and which is somehow outside of that more complex area of existence we call time. Caudill becomes a victim of his landscape; the isolated man in a neutral and indifferent universe. He is driven from his Eden by his own ferocity and thrust into the world of time which he can neither understand nor control.

There has been a persistent tendency to read *The Big Sky* as Western tragedy, as Guthrie's lament over the loss of freedom along a closing frontier. Set in that epic moment when tens of thousands of emigrants were flooding across the Great Plains in search of a better life in Oregon's lush Columbia River valleys, the book has been interpreted as a depiction of the mountain man's life as paradise and as a record of the transformation of the wilderness into a paradise lost.[6] But this approach assumes *a priori* that for Guthrie wilderness is indeed paradise, and that Boone Caudill, the archetypal man of the wilds, is totally fulfilled in nature. A more careful reading of *The Big Sky* clearly disproves this view. It explains precisely why the book is not a nostalgic look back at a lost past, but a hard-headed study of human behavior in which Guthrie concludes that man alone cannot achieve the conditions of life necessary for total happiness. Instead, and here is the crux of Guthrie's thesis in the novel, Emerson's "plain old Adam," that "simple genuine self against the whole world" is restricted by a defect in knowledge to a life of pre-or semi-consciousness. Consequently, he is prohibited from growing to the kind of mature consciousness which characterizes the most memorable figures in American fiction.

From the beginning of the novel when Boone flees his home in Kentucky, he dreams of a life lived entirely in the open, a "free and easy" existence, "with time all a man's own and none to say no to him."[7] The story sweeps up the Missouri, through Ree and Sioux country and into the lands of the Blackfeet, and Boone stands alone on the brown earth beneath the Big Sky, "with a free, wild feeling in his chest, as if they were the ceiling and floor of a home that was all his own." (123) With only Jim Deakins and Dick Summers as companions, Boone finds that the solitary life suits him well—"this life along the streams and in the hills." (170) And whereas Jim longs to "put out for St. Louis or Taos or anywhere that people were," (170–171) Boone shuns the more settled areas along the frontier where he feels "strange and uneasy and caged in." (171) Indeed, Boone is transformed into a new-world Adam, a man reborn in utter innocence in a land which resembles "the beginning of the world . . . high and lonesome and far off from men's doings." (223)

But Boone is an odd and a sullen Adam. And the land of the Big Sky, far from ennobling him, makes his "mind small" and his "heart tight." It is true, of course, that even as a boy in Kentucky he was strange and quiet. But his years as a mountain man make him even more morose, so that "there wasn't much fun in Boone. He was a sober man, and tight-mouthed, without any give in him. . . ." (217) Jim Deakins, who never really seemed cut out to be a mountain man, is a thinker, a man who, when it came to an idea, would tip it over "to see what was underneath." (124) But Boone practices the precept that the key to a mountain man's survival depends upon his always being ready to act without thinking. Boone "figured it was better to take what came and not trouble the mind with questions there was no answer to." (124)

Gradually, Boone becomes a man who is "like an animal, like a young bull that traveled alone, satisfied just by earth and water and trees and the sky over him. It was as if he talked to the country for company, and the country talked to him, and as if that was enough." (185) Guthrie's point, though, is that it is not enough.

For one thing, the years during which Guthrie sets the latter part of his novel recall that era when two ways of life came into serious and unavoidable conflict. The early 1840's marked what has become known as the "take-off" and the subsequent incursion of history (and time) into the frontier. In 1843, John Gilpin carried his doctrine of the "untransacted destiny" to Oregon with Fremont. And in that same year, Guthrie's Elisha Peabody (a name that to Boone "tasted strange on the tongue and sounded strange in the ear" [273]) makes a similar journey, intent upon "being realized, long hence" in Oregon's Willamette Valley. Shunning the mountain man's interest in beaver, Peabody is the prophet of material progress, the harbinger of civilization. "'It's development I'm interested in, future development,'" (277) he tells the mountain men. And when Boone and Jim point out that the land of the Big Sky belongs to the Indians who "live off it, and enjoy themselves and all," Peabody points to their failure to "civilize" the West as "'justification for invasion, peaceful if possible, forcible if necessary, by people who can and will capitalize on opportunity.'" (278)

> "Nothing shall stop us. British? Spanish? Mexicans? None of them. By every reasonable standard the land is ours—by geography, contiguity, natural expansion. Why, it's destiny, that's what it is—inevitable destiny." (279)

Indeed, Peabody looks to the future and sees "carts and four-wheeled wagons piled with settler's goods, bound for the fertile valleys of the Columbia." (287) And some day, he reflects, "'maybe in our own time, the steam railway will be heard clanking over this pass, carrying passengers three hundred miles in twenty-four hours.'" (289)

To Boone and to Jim, such prophecies mean nothing. "'It's ag'in nature,'" Deakins reflects. And Boone insists that Peabody's head has "'room for the damndest notions.'" (289) The fact is, of course, that Boone (and to a lesser extent Jim) are blind to the historical process which defines the world of time. For Boone, "time didn't flow at all, but just stood still while a body moved around in it." (28) When, as early as 1837, a fellow hunter named Russell suggests that a wave of settlers will eventually cover the Northwest territories and destroy the lifestyles of its current inhabitants, Boone replies with incredible naivete, "'what ud settlers do out here?'" (200) And when the settlers envisioned by Russell begin to come, Boone incredulously aids in the destruction of his own way of life by serving as a scout for the merchants of progress. Unable to understand or cope with the fact of a closing frontier, Boone goes empty and numb. He had been "'in the hills so long he's growed dumb like one and his tongue no good but to lick with.'" (345)

To make matters worse, Boone's animal-like suspicion of people leads him to kill his best friend Deakins and repudiate his Eve-like Indian wife, Teal Eye. And in the end he becomes a sad man who looks without seeing and who lets his mind go without thinking. The Oregon wagon trains roll over Boone's paradise, and Boone, for whom all feeling has died, leaves his Eden and walks back aimlessly into his Kentucky past.

Of course, Boone must experience what all weary travelers have learned: that you can't go home again, particularly when home is a house which must smother a man who "had got the smell and look and feeling of the mountains in him." (367) And so Boone wanders off again, stopping briefly at the home of Dick Summers (who years earlier left the Big Sky to marry and settle down to a life of farming) where he finds no solace for his sense of dislocation. He ends up a lumpish man for whom all of life ("'the whole caboodle,'" as he tells Summers) has been utterly spoiled and irretrievably lost.

Boone Caudill is a victim of his own Adamic innocence. Cast out of Eden into a world he neither loves nor understands, he is unable to cope with the fact of change. As the world weary Dick Summers tells him, "'Everything we done it looks like we done against ourselves.'" And so, in the larger view, *The Big Sky* is really Guthrie's testament to the bankruptcy of primitivism. Guthrie's Adam is not one of Whitman's children who is divine "inside and out and I make Holy whatever I touch." Instead, Boone is an innocent in need of experience, but prohibited from that experience by the life-style he has chosen. He is flat, colorless and undramatic, evidence of the fact that primal purity is cheerless.

In his significant study of the American Adam, R. W. B. Lewis suggests that one of the most important problems of American life which is given expression in our literature concerns the fate of the American innocent in the new-world garden.[8] And Lewis points out that our most mature writers have portrayed man's journey from innocence to mature consciousness occurring as the result of some sort of engagement with evil. Lewis discusses the works of Hawthorne and Melville and indicates that for them, as for many writers, the complex world of time serves as a metaphor for the experience of evil. In his analysis of Melville's *Billy Budd*, for example, Lewis suggests that Melville celebrates the fall of Adam (Billy) on the *H.M.S. Indomitable* and indicates how, through the fall, Billy is transfigured into a new Adam (Christ) whose death redeems the world.

Similarly, in his discussion of Hawthorne's *The Marble Faun*, Lewis notes that for Hawthorne maturity results through a kind of conscious recognition which restores the self to its right relation with the world. Hawthorne's Donatello is a simpleton in Arcadia. Though he resides in Rome, he speaks with a "rusticity of accent, and an unshaped sort of utterance,"[9] and in demeanor and disposition resembles the famous Faun of Praxiteles. He lives "in the merriment of woods and streams; living as our four-footed kindred do—as mankind did in its innocent childhood, before sin, sorrow, or mortality itself had ever been thought of." (18) Indeed, Donatello, much like Boone, is a man "who had nothing to do with time." (19)

But also like Boone, he commits a crime of passion—murdering a specter of a man who haunts his beloved Miriam. And he too finds that his crime destroys his happiness. Initially, Donatello flees Rome to a rural retreat, but the burden of his guilt drives him back. And in Rome, where there are sermons even in the streets of the city, he makes an adjustment to time which offers a control for life. In short, Hawthorne's sylvan faun grows up in sadness but in truth, and he becomes a man of feeling and intelligence. Facing the certainty of arrest, conviction and a long prison sentence, Donatello commits himself to the "delicate moral atmosphere" of Rome and, with help from dedicated and intellectually sophisticated friends who care deeply about him, he develops a growing "intellectual power and moral sense." A soul is "breathed into him," and he moves beyond the tower of tragedy "toward a state of higher development." And here, says Hawthorne, is the riddle of humanity: that the soul's growth must take its first impulse amid remorse and pain. If the rest of mankind were in accordance with the genial nature of the primitive, the world might be a paradise to genial natures like Donatello. But, the novelist laments,

> It seems the moral of his story that human beings of Donatello's character, compounded especially for happiness, have no longer any business on earth, or elsewhere. Life has grown so sadly serious, that such

> men must change their nature, or else perish, like the antediluvian creatures, that required, as the condition of their existence, a more summer-like atmosphere than ours. (328–329)

For Donatello, in Rome amid friends who understand and care, change and growth are possible. Consequently, Hawthorne's story is one of the fortunate fall as his Adam attains a "higher, brighter, and profounder happiness than our lost birthright gave. . . ." (311) But for Boone Caudill, an adjustment to time is not possible. Guthrie's "arcadian simpleton" has no Rome nor any far-visioned friends. Cut off from society, largely through his own choosing, he cannot undergo Donatello's tragic rise.

Francis Parkman once noted that the history of America is the history of loss in a world where the possibility of tragedy is central.[10] But this tragedy has purpose only if the meaning of the loss is understood and if from it there come successive stages of personal growth. Hence, there is no tragedy in *The Big Sky* because after Boone kills Deakins and deserts Teal Eye, he leaves his garden and enters a personal wasteland. He becomes one of those characters T. S. Eliot depicts walking in circles—seeing nothing, knowing nothing. His violent dream of primitive freedom comes to an abrupt end because he reaches the extremity of his conquests and is unable to "give, control and sympathize." Like Robert Montgomery Bird's Nathan Slaughter in *Nick of the Woods,* another innocent who suffers a collision with evil, he is alienated from the world of open possibility. And like Slaughter and unlike Donatello, he is a victim of the wilderness, for the condition which rendered him solitary has prohibited his growth to manhood. There are no virtues forced upon Boone because of his impudent crimes. Incapable of meaningful social contact, his hollow ship collides and sinks on the island of his aloneness. He is one of Hawthorne's "antediluvian creatures" who must eventually perish.

It might be argued that although Guthrie uses Boone to criticize one mountain man's inflexibility, his unwillingness to change, he does present in Dick Summers (an "easy man, without the dark streak of violence that ran so often in mountain men" [116]), the seasoned and articulate mountain man who first leads Boone into Blackfoot country, a man who understands and can cope with the facts of history. It is true, of course, that Summers does "live in his head a good part of the time." (185) He understands the inevitable incursion of time on the frontier and the fact that "beaver was poor doings now, and rendezvous was pinching out, and there was talk about farms over on the Columbia." (15) And he acknowledges that because they belonged to another time, perhaps the "mountain man best close out too." (195)

Summers leaves the mountains in favor of a life of farming, a sort of "middle state" where he might live out his years in peace and contentment. And yet, while he sees the past receding before him, drawing off "farther and farther, like a point on a fair shore," Summers' attempts at personal salvation, though less violent, are not much more successful than are those of Boone. For Summers had lost "the happy feeling, the strong doing, the fresh taste for things. . . ." (12) He "walked stooped, dragging his feet a little," (377) and "he was old and changed." (378) And for all the comforts of home and family, he is a beaten and lonesome man who belonged to another time and who sees "everything behind him and nothing ahead." His insight is wistful, not tragic, and he is no more successful than is Boone in adjusting to the fact of change or to the onslaught of history.

American literature at its best has been a dialectic in which our writers have defined the American experience as a series of conflicts and contradictions between contrasting ways of life. And perhaps the drive toward abstraction in the best works of a Hawthorne, a Melville, a James and a Twain is attributable to the fact that the central conflicts throughout the history of American civilization—between innocence and experience, between primitivism and progress—can be resolved only in oblique, morally equivocal ways. With respect to the belief that personal well being is synonymous with a free, uninhibited life away from the complexities of "civilized" society, a Hawthorne, a Melville, and a Twain can understand and portray the infantile and anarchic primitivism of a Donatello, a Redburn, or a young Huck Finn. But they similarly show through a series of tensions in their works how this simple primitivism gives way to a growth in character that clarifies and enriches experience. And Huck Finn on and near the Mississippi, Ishmael on the *Pequod*, and Hester Prynne in Salem grow to a consciousness *in society* as the conflicts and contradictions are resolved, however indefinite those resolutions must be. They become fully-developed, multi-dimensional characters who share the complicated needs, the acute problems of us all, and who make the adjustments and adaptations necessary for a full and meaningful life.

But in Western wilderness novels, particularly in those set in the times just before the closing of the frontier, a final resolution of the conflict is impossible, because the physical conditions necessary for that resolution do not exist. The best wilderness novelists—A. B. Guthrie, Vardis Fisher and Frederick Manfred—can create exciting plots which are true to history, and interesting, one-dimensional characters who live in unbounded space. And by so doing, they present a valuable record of what once was. But because their characters are cut-off and alone, by choice deprived of the kind of meaningful social contact which leads one from innocence to experience, they are limited by their medium. In short, the wilderness novel simply cannot transcend its occasion. If we read the best of them as period pieces about what Guthrie calls "the engaging, rude, admirable, odious, thoughtless, resourceful, loyal, sinful, smart, stupid, courageous character that he [the mountain man] was and had to be,"[11] we are on safe ground. To ask more from Guthrie or from any wilderness novelist is to demand more than they can legitimately provide.

Notes

1. Michael Straight in an interview with John Milton, reprinted from the Autumn, 1964, issue of the *South Dakota Review* in Taylor's *The Literature of the American West*, p. 28.
2. Frederick Manfred in conversation with Richard Astro, October 13, 1973.
3. Frank Waters in an interview with John Milton, reprinted from the Autumn, 1964, issue of the *South Dakota Review* in Taylor's *The Literature of the American West*, p. 28.
4. Ibid., pp. 28–29.
5. Don D. Walker, "The Mountain Man as Literary Hero," *Western American Literature*, I (Spring, 1966), pp. 15–25.
6. Levi S. Peterson, "Tragedy and Western American Literature," *Western American Literature*, VI (Winter, 1972), p. 247.
7. A. B. Guthrie, Jr., *The Big Sky*, Sentry Books edition (Boston: Houghton Mifflin, 1947), p. 201. All further citations from *The Big Sky* refer to this edition and are identified by page number in the text.
8. R. W. B. Lewis, *The American Adam* (Chicago: University of Chicago Press, 1955).
9. Nathaniel Hawthorne, *The Marble Faun* (New York: New American Library, 1961), p. 17. All further citations from *The Marble Faun* refer to this edition and are identified by page number in the text.
10. See Lewis, *The American Adam*, pp. 168–173.
11. A. B. Guthrie, Jr. "Why Write about the West?" *Western American Literature*, VII (Fall, 1972), p. 164.

Marilyn Hacker

1942–

Marilyn Hacker was born in New York City on November 27, 1942. After attending the Bronx High School of Science, she studied at the Washington Square College of New York University, graduating with a B.A. in 1964. She has worked as a teacher and a book editor, and was editor of *City* from 1967 to 1970 and co-editor of the SF anthology series *Quark* in 1970–71. From 1971 to 1976 she was an antiquarian bookseller in London.

Hacker's first published poetry was privately printed in the late 1960s; one such volume, *Highway Sandwiches* (1970), was written with Thomas M. Disch and Charles Platt. Her first commercially published collection, *Presentation Piece* (1974), was the Lamont Poetry Selection of the Academy of American Poets, and won her the National Book Award for Poetry in 1975. *Separations* followed in 1976, *Taking Notice* in 1980, and *Assumptions* in 1985. In 1976–77 she held the Jenny McKeen Moore fellowship for writers at George Washington University; she has also received a Creative Artists Public Service Grant, and in 1980 a Guggenheim Fellowship.

Hacker has lived in San Francisco and Mexico City, as well as New York and London. From 1961 to 1974 she was married to SF author Samuel R. Delany; they have one daughter.

Personal

1.

I believe
in Higher Gossip; shifting states of soul
revealed in nervous tics, beer and bon mots:
what do you think he thinks, I want to know.
(Separations)

Marilyn invites biography, almost inveigles it. Her poems are full of hints and indiscretions, of first names and mysterious initials. They abound in snapshots of exotic cities, honkytonks, and pleasant post-Impressionist interiors verdant with houseplants, all of them quietly waiting the captioner's hand: "Here is Marilyn with X," "Marilyn drinking at the Ys's party," "Marilyn in Arizona with C and T," "Marilyn's apartment on Natoma Street."

Not that she is a tease. Though she offers more (and more interesting) particulars than the last (Lowell-time) generation of poets who sang the song of themselves, she proffers only what the poems autonomously demand for, as they say, their own full being. Why these excuses, anyhow? Writers wouldn't write if they didn't want to be, somehow or other, objects of curiosity.

2.

Not having gone the academic route, Marilyn's milieu has been whatever she could manage, which meant, for a long time, the bohemias first of New York, where she grew up and went to NYU, and later, electively, of San Francisco. Not an uncommon fate, and not necessarily a bad one, representing, as it does, one of the few forms of freedom available to those of us who lack an independent income. It does seem odd, in more jaundiced moments, to hear Marilyn celebrating Clancy's Bar or the Old Reliable in such heroic, highly decorated terms, as if we'd all just stepped out of a Mucha poster and were on our way to the Guermantes for dinner.

To be fair, she has her jaundiced moments too, when she can be quite withering concerning the size of her friends' incomes and appetites. Witness this reminiscence of two "drunk poets" in San Francisco:

One nurses the
brandy while his boy
friend does cartwheels. They
want to be taken to dinner. We
can't afford it. They
try being ebullient. We
really can't afford it.
(Aquatic Park, 1967)

3.

Radical honesty, the present touchstone for poetic content, is a ticklish business. Too much reticence and it is as if the poet were cheating at cards; too little and the audience flees the theater of such cruelties. Marilyn's mix of high soliloquy and small beer, of arched brow and archetype, is just right, the maximum distance a spark can be made to leap. Again and again, the eye is dazzled by the brilliance.

4.

. . . Chip ⟨Delany⟩ and Marilyn went to high school together, were married remarkably young and stayed married for better and for worse, for richer, for poorer, in sickness and in health, together and apart till this very day. The marriage was also, in a real sense, a business partnership, for they went through the years of apprenticeship and journeyman work, each of them under the other's daily scrutiny, like Jesuits in their novitiate; an exacting regimen but, by the evidence, an effective one. . . .

8.

A friend who knows them both quite well was sure that the first fourteen (italic) lines of "Prism and Lens" were by Chip. My own sense of it is that the couplets have the unmistakable stamp of Marilyn, but I see what he means. The allegorical/erotic stances of the figures in these lines, together with their Botticelli-by-way-of-Beardsley style of ornament is very much like Chip in his more baroque moments: "the pale autumnal queen" and "their laurel arms" are turns of phrase that would be at home in *Dhalgren*, as well as all the physiological grue—the scabs, the reopened wounds, the salt rubbed into them.

9.

For both of them, though in differing degrees and for different reasons, this mannered style and raunchy content constituted a risk and a defiance. Consider the modes of poetry that were Editor's Choices in the late '50's and early '60's, when Marilyn began to write. There was the Black Mountain school of crisp, gnomic solemnity that blurred, northwestwards, into the prairie-wide affirmations of the Black Sparrow Press. There was also, loosely allied with these, the demotic surrealism of the New York School, just then burgeoning into its second generation. Besides these "open" styles indigenous to bohemia there was the closed (as in door, or corporation) style of the Academy and the *New Yorker*. Even here it was a rule that one's fancy clothes should be cut on very modest lines. Satin, feathers, and all such *fin-de-siècle* fineries were to be avoided, because (it was held) that was how poetry had gone wrong.

Eventually, as we know, Marilyn had her way, fineries and all. *Presentation Piece* was accepted in the spirit in which it was offered. The Academy opened its doors. It was the Lamont Poetry Selection for 1973. The dustjacket has a long encomium by Richard Howard. Reviewers dithered. Finally, an N.B.A.

On the way to her apotheosis, though, there were some rough passages and the occasional Slough of Despond. Her collected rejections would doubtless embarrass many a proud editor. (I can lay claim myself to having turned down "The Osiris Complex," on the grounds that I didn't understand it.) It *is* painful to witness nincompoops like X, Y and Z covered with laurels and Guggenheims, while one's own deathless mss. become dog-eared or vanish into the littlest of little magazines. No younger poets can entirely escape the dark thoughts that such unhappy comparisons give rise to. Paranoia is an occupational disease.

What was denied Marilyn was not simply recognition of the merits of her poetry, but specifically recognition that she was, verily, a child prodigy. "Chanson de l'enfant prodigue," written when she was fifteen, came out in *Poetry* when she was thirty.

Chip, meanwhile, was being celebrated by a chorus of critical voices as the best sf writer of the age, the boy wonder in whose books were united all that was viable from the past and all that was valid in the experimental vagaries of the present.

Not that Marilyn wouldn't have celebrated him in just the same terms. But still. When you're hungry it's hard to watch people eating.—THOMAS M. DISCH, "A la recherche de Marilyn Hacker," *LitM*, Summer 1975, pp. 5–9

Works

PRESENTATION PIECE

. . . Marilyn Hacker can, and frequently does, compose sonnets, villanelles, and sestinas with proficiency and with great versatility. As is always the case with such a poet, her unconstrained free forms are superior. The blurb (on *Presentation Piece*), by Richard Howard, therefore more than a blurb, describes her as having "intensity of craftsmanship" (yes!), also as being "witty, desperate." Witty, for sure. Desperate? So too Bloom described Hollander as giving us "a style fit for our despair." Despair is desperately fashionable (that should be a warning) and I suppose we all do have our private despairs, but must we keep checking them to make sure they are desperate enough? I suspect Marilyn Hacker of sometimes playing up to this theme with her recurrent nightmare of a third presence, generally or mostly male, who keeps pushing her or somebody out of some lover's bed: as in "Alba: September"

> and woke because your lover, holding you
> diagonally on the bed, was shoving me
> between the mattress and the wall, determinedly
> asleep. Clever Jean-Paul imagined hell
> unloving threesies in a cheap hotel.
> No room in that bed.

And the theme haunts a long sequence called "The Navigators." But there is another mood, as in "The Art of the Novel" . . . "I always /gossip in poems, mostly about myself".

. . . A rather long poem dedicated to Janis Joplin is the most moving piece in the book, but there are many admirable poems. We hear, for instance, the cool burnished phrases of Nimue propositioning Merlin within the frame of a sestina. This is an impressive new talent.—RICHMOND LATTIMORE, "Poetry Chronicle," *HdR*, Autumn 1974, pp. 467–68

. . . Marilyn Hacker stands squarely, and very elegantly, in the indirect T. S. Eliot line. She is sharp-eyed and -edged, cool, very acute about sophistication and its falsities, and very witty. Her wit is at its best when it is at one with her humor and her good humor. *Presentation Piece* shows a great many skills, and doesn't just show them off. At times, it does wax philosophical about what poetry deeply is—but then elsewhere it furnishes the best sort of self-criticism; poems which are likewise about poetry but are rich with comedy and insinuation. The exquisitely sinister sestina, "Untoward Occurrence at Embassy Poetry Reading," for instance, which pays back its tacit debt to W. H. Auden tenfold; or the sardonic sonnet "Apologia pro opere suo," which begins:

> It appears that almost all the poets who slighted
> the theme of Unrequited Love to say
> how more of the land than That Boy or That Lady
> lay
> were poets whom somebody had, in fact, requited.

She is a most deft rhymestress—the feminine form of "rhymester," which Marilyn Hacker may dislike (when she lists her interests and causes, she juxtaposes houseplants and radical feminism), compresses rhythm and prosody ("stress") with rhyme. There is a weird amplitude of spirit in her steely erotic poetry, as in the cheerful city grubbiness of "Elektra on Third Avenue"; or the mock-prim suggestive silence (total, just where you least expect it) of "Pornographic Poem"; or the laconic crackle of "Imaginary Translation II"; or the seductive accents of "Nimue to Merlin"; or (best of all) the rhythmic disintegration into a hurrying longing, which gives itself away, of "She Bitches About Boys":

> To live on charm, one must be courteous.
> To live on others' love, one must be lovable.
> Some get away with murder being beautiful.
> Girls love a sick child or a healthy animal.
> A man who's both itches them like an incubus,
> but I, for one, have had a bellyful
> of giving reassurances and obvious
> advice with scrambled eggs and cereal;
> then bad debts, broken dates and lecherous
> onanistic dreams of estival
> nights when some high-strung, well-hung penurious
> boy, not knowing what he'd get, could be more
> generous.

Estival: it is a cool word for those summer nights, but the air of these poems is generous.—CHRISTOPHER RICKS, *NYTBR*, Jan. 12, 1975, p. 2

Marilyn Hacker's work is much closer to modernism than Rosalie Colie's, and yet among the most impressive things in *Presentation Piece* are the seven sestinas she has managed to place among the prodigious pages of this remarkable first book—seven delightful, dexterous, almost off-handed renderings of the toughest form the English poets brought home in their saddlebags from the south of France—the kind of poem worth trying at least once, and if you are a poet of special invention, why not try it seven times? Along with the sestinas are several sonnets, including a "crown" of sonnets—all in a contemporary voice, however strictly patterned—a couple of villanelles, numerous pieces in other forms, and a good many in the most supple free-verse. From the sound of it this may seem a collection of school-figures, and Ms. Hacker, indeed, has made a stunning first impression; but it seems to me a healthy sign that a younger poet should have expended what must have been an enormous inventive energy in order to make just a first impression of this magnitude. It reveals both intelligence and respect for intelligence—both her own and her reader's. I myself am tired of the talky, sloppy, thrown-together plainsongs we are given by nine-tenths of the poets who constitute the various "scenes" of contemporary poetry. Reading Marilyn Hacker's book makes me realize, as if for the first time, that so much of the stuff so many of the others give us is dull and painful and downright hurtful to the spirit, because it derides the spirit in the most unedifying way, and then insults my intelligence by presuming I will call it poetry. Poetry is an art and the art comes by intelligence: Marilyn Hacker knows that, and as a result—sestinas aside—she gives us poems that are flawless acts of speech as well as works of art in the strongest possible sense: she is at work in these poems and what she is working is the art—working it, putting it to the test, but not working it over. I hope some others of her generation may observe how much her work has strengthened the art they say they practice. A little work wouldn't kill them either. —MICHAEL HEFFERNAN, *Com*, Aug. 15, 1975, p. 347

SEPARATIONS

. . . I think all readers who aren't categorically opposed to traditional forms will find most of ⟨*Separations*⟩ a real pleasure. Hacker writes in free forms sometimes, but she especially likes sonnets, she writes a lot of them, tough sonnets, humorous or half-humorous, with very skillful interweaving of true rhymes, off-rhymes, and no rhymes, and she likes sestinas too, and villanelles, and even canzones, the hardest of all foreign forms. I don't see how anyone who knows versification can help but admire and relish her abilities. Notice, for instance, how remarkably well she disguises the padding needed in any rhymed poem to make the lines come out right. With great syntactical diversity and with an immense vocabulary from which to choose her padded words, she makes the unnecessary seem not only necessary but natural, which is half the art of the poetic artificer.

Add to this her thematic adultness and intelligence, her compelling poems of lust, anger and grief, her sense of experience truly lived, and you have a formidable poet to contend with. *Separations* is the work of a woman whose body and mind are functioning at high intensity, perfectly coordinated. You can't draw the line between sensation and idea—a rare achievement.—HAYDEN CARRUTH, *NYTBR*, Aug. 8, 1976, p. 13

⟨*Separations*⟩ has five sections. It does not seem accidental that, with the exception of one part of the fourth section, "Prism and Lens," all the solid poems are in the third part, and that the third part is basically centered around Miss Hacker's personal life, directly and immediately. Let no one take that for a comment about the proper subject matter for poetry: there is no such thing. Nor should it be taken as in any sense a comment about the kind of poetry which women either can or should write. It is simply a descriptive fact. When Miss Hacker tackles themes of a more cosmic order, as in "After the Revolution," visual acuity and metaphorical clarity give way to clotted straining: "thick sap oozes amber marbled cream." In "Birmingham" we are told of a "a doped rag / cloying his blind runnelled face / after the black melting from there to here, / purple moss over the glistening / surface of a foreign afternoon." . . .

But I think there is even more to the problem. Different times have different modal, and even modish, conceptions of what the Poet must be like. Almost two centuries ago William Wordsworth wrote, with piercing accuracy, that the truly fine poet must create the taste by which he is appreciated; his analysis makes it plain that the truly fine poet must therefore wait for recognition—not because he sets out to be more modish than the rest, but on the contrary because he follows no mode except his own, because he creates out of what he is. Miss Hacker's generation has necessarily created a different mode of poet-ness; a good deal of her difficulty in this book, I suspect, is that she is excessively influenced by that mode, trying far too hard and far too earnestly to fit into it. "I've put my child to bed. I cannot eat. / This death is on my hands. This meat dead meat." The tone, even the rhythms are what might be called the Universal (or New York) Sixties/Seventies Mode. But what underlies this passage? Simply enough, the notion that her grief for her brother's death is so great that the meat she has cooked for supper becomes inedible to her, reminding her gruesomely of the dead meat of her brother's body. I do not see how anyone can find this notion credible. And if the notion is *in*credible, then the poetry is unreal. And if the poetry is unreal, what on earth good is it? "The delicate purgation of a tongue / turned back over purgation: paradox / within a more intriguing paradox / of involuted mouth." I'm not nearly so sure, here, what the notion is. What I do see clearly, however, is that Miss Hacker is playing with fashionable tools, as indeed she does frequently. Poetry is playing, certainly, but with *some* reality, some warm-blooded connection, underlying the game. I can't find anything of the sort, here. And when Miss Hacker writes "The moon is always fading / above them. Stars in intaglio / imprint a pattern on their upturned brows. / Loosely, their fingers latch. The star-seared mark / glows bloody effulgence in the dark"—well, I neither believe her nor care. It's all contrived thunder and lightning, mechanical, cold, essentially meaningless and deeply un-felt.

Neither full diagnosis nor the prescription of a cure is the place, nor is it within the competence, of a brief review. I should like it to be plain that my complaints are based primarily on Miss Hacker's abilities, not on her failures. That is, when I find a poet who can write the kind of opening strophe I shall quote in a moment, and then I find that this same poet more often than not does not write with the control, the clarity, and the full-blooded heat of this same passage, but writes instead in a make-believe style of make-believe feelings and make-believe ideas, using mostly modish language—then I am concerned for the poet and for poetry, and I am obliged to protest. Here, finally, is the opening strophe of "Alba: March," and if Miss Hacker wrote anywhere near this well most or even much of the time, this would have been a celebratory rather than a largely condemnatory review: "Coming home to the white / morning light in my studio. Ten o'clock; / down the block construction workers stop / for coffee, beer, a drop of booze. It's cold; / they trample frozen mud. White / sunlight quivers in my head, / slivers in puddles breaking last night's freeze. / I finger keys in my wooly pocket, holding / a grocery bag striped golden with light."—JOYCE BELLAMY, *DQ*, Autumn 1976, pp. 154–56

Although there are still a few poems which betray her apprenticeship, sounding like exercises or baring influences, Hacker extends her technical mastery and increases her self-confidence measurably in *Separations*. Spinning out sonnets, sestinas, villanelles, canzones, couplets, fixed and free forms, lyrics and narratives in generous portions, she displays an impressive virtuosity and vitality of language.

All of this technical skill is in the service of a dark, somewhat sordid urban vision which is sometimes lightened, but more often further darkened, by love. Raking her forms across the separations of death, distance, and unreturned love, Hacker attempts, as she says, to "maul the pain / to shape":

> Hating words, I fumble words
> into a bridge, a path, a wall.

The book is pervaded by a sense of disappointed aubade, a wakening to a cold and grimy morning after a night of love remembered more for its pain than for its comfort:

> Satisfied lovers eat big breakfasts. I
> want black coffee and a cigarette
> to dull this cottonmouth. Nine-ten. The wet-
> faced construction workers hunkered by
> the Pioneer Grill grin as I walk past.
> You tried to be sleeping when I left
> your room. The sweaty blanket hugged the cleft
> between your buttocks. Now a crowd of fast
> clouds scutters across the cautious sky
> above the Fillmore West. We didn't make
> it this time. Maybe it will take
> another year. If you still want to try.
> We try, and fail again, and try, and fail.
> I'll be back home an hour before the mail.

Hacker can strike other notes as well, as in "Imaginary Translation," "After Catullus," the marvelous sestina "La vie de chateau," or as here in "Occasional Verses":

> "Your breasts are like melons, your mouth like dark plums,"
> said Petrarch. Said Laura, "Why can't we be chums?"
>
> "You move like a Phoenix on fire," said John.
> "I'm off dancing," said Fanny. "You *do* carry on."
>
> "Your glance is a torrent and I die of thirst,"
> said William. Said Maud, "Revolution comes first."

But despite these other tones and voices, the great preponderance of poems are somber and preoccupied with loss, most of them winding their way around eventually to the same conclusion—"Predictably, it's cold." And it is in this preoccupation and narrowness of vision that my troubles with this poetry lie; for while I admire the sureness of technique, I keep asking myself why it must be all that damp and dreary, unrelieved by any of the ordinary compensations of life. These poems have, as Richard Howard has said of another poet's work, "the conviction of sordor without the conviction of grandeur", and so, exhausted by all the mauling and fumbling, dirtied by stained sheets and grimy streets, I come away from the book feeling as if I should take a bath. Hacker, in short, takes her losses too seriously, nursing her grievances and dwelling on them with the single-mindedness of a Malvolio, and Olivia's advice would seem to apply to her as well: "To be generous, guiltless, and of free disposition, is to take those things for birdbolts which you deem cannon bullets." The power of language that Hacker possesses deserves a more balanced vision.—ROBERT HOLLAND, "Six or Seven Fools," *Poetry*, Feb. 1977, pp. 292–93

Because of its title, one might expect ⟨*Separations*⟩ to be concerned with getting rid of the past. "What a trash to annihilate each decade," Sylvia Plath wrote. But the poems in this volume, rather than radical departures, are really imaginative reclaimings of poetic territory once owned by the formalists. Word got around that the structures in this area were haunted, disreputable, and even Sylvia Plath gets a hard look once in a while for her early villanelles and sonnets. It is a shock, therefore, to read Hacker and find her courageously entering the realm protected by the Covering Cherub, choosing old forms—often in meter and rhyme—to make her wit work. Few have been willing to do this recently, and one remembers only too well Kenneth Rexroth's statement that to write a sonnet in these times is a Fascist act.

Nevertheless, last year's National Book Award winner clearly has some support for her kind of undertaking. Perhaps we are now ready to consider seriously what J. V. Cunningham once wrote: "We have written to vary or violate the old line, for regularity we feel is meaningless and irregularity meaningful. But a generation of poets, acting on the principles and practice of significant variation, have at last nothing to vary from. The last variation is regularity."

I must admit that I am grateful to see a woman up to these old tricks. There are certainly a number of good books of young women's poems which are not dominated by meter and rhyme. I think of Margaret Atwood, of Miriam Levine's *To Know We Are Living*, and especially Eloise Klein Healy's *Building Some Changes*, which deserves wider circulation than Peace Press in Los Angeles can probably give it. However, Hacker's is the most unusual of these books, because she has taken the past seriously in a way none of the others have. In the imaginary city so many of her poems inhabit, the lovers (past and present possibly) meet again. Although they may "clink / snifters, wax quotable near 'Time,' then go / home their discrete and solitary ways," the rendezvous itself demands our attention. What one is separating from (the past) is as important as the terms of the separation. There is always the refusal but again the temptation to take the past too seriously.

Hacker herself has a wonderful poem about her own relation to formal techniques which are usually thought of now as belonging to the past:

> I still balk at my preference for rhyme which hounds
> me like an inarticulate and homely lover whom
> I wish would wait
> outside; no, he can meet my friends this time,
> screw vanity, I love him, he's my own obsession.
> Angular
> child, I have to tell them who you are,
> and love you so much they will envy us
> and want you so much they will want you too.

Obviously if she is going to introduce us to this anonymous angular child, she sees herself as refashioning these metrical structures in a way which will allow us to meet them without a sense of familiarity. She will do this not so small thing in her own way, to rephrase Adrienne Rich. She will be her own woman, she tells us.

Writing like a woman these days has often, though not always, meant treating male-female relations with anger or irony. And Marilyn Hacker sometimes does this, as in the ironic ending of "Two Farewells":

> "Try to turn
> boys into men," Circe said,
> "and they behave like pigs."

But Hacker's work is fundamentally female in the sense that it is part of a tradition of American women poets. Her poetry carries the burden of the past with it in a different way from that of any of the other contemporary women poets I know of. Reading the opening stanzas of "The Terrible Children," the echoes of Louise Bogan are inescapable:

> You, who never tasted the fruit,
> who woke wide and immobile in blue fire
> now, stretched to silence on the singing wire,
> fall through limed fissures, naked, rigid, mute,
> while summer children underneath the tree
> gather the thick-dropped apples where they lie.

"The Song of Liadan" with its image cluster of silver, crystal, and gauntlets, lies in a direct line with Elinor Wylie's poetry. Who, knowing Wylie's work, could read

And I am silver
and barren.
Brocade. Our hands clasped in a truce of gauntlets
a silence above song

without thinking of Wylie's "Gauntlet" poems and the line: "And I am barren in a barren land" from "Sequence." "A silence above song" could easily have been written by either Wylie or Teasdale. Brocade? Is it Dickinson or Amy Lowell? In fact the whole theme of incomplete renunciation and the nun figure Liadan who embodies it here, takes us back to the work of Dickinson, Teasdale, Wylie and Bogan.

There is much to praise in this book. I especially like "Geographer" and parts of "Prism and Lens" but the poetic misprision, to use Bloom's term, which is Hacker's need to misuse the past in the interests of her own present, does not always work successfully for her. A woman poet who chooses to reify the past tradition of female formalists stands in an uneasy position given the shift of our poetic diction toward the conversational and colloquial. Thus we get lines which are too literary: "Precocious cold sullies our gelid sheets." In other poems, such as "Birmingham," an overly refined insight like:

The vision of his change: a doped rag
cloying his blind runnelled face
after the black melting from there to here,

gives way to a harsher tone. The combination of the two is disorienting, as though we were hearing a single voice speaking from two different directions at once.

I found it very useful to have the Caedmon record of Hacker reading as a supplement to the book. Most of the recorded poems are from *Presentation Piece*, her first book, but one hears on the record the voice which sometimes falters in the poems on the page: original, insistent, witty, it is a pitiless voice, a voice which would not give way to pressures from either the Right or the Left—a good voice, I think, for a poet.

There is some talk that, since Marilyn Hacker has now returned from living in England, she will begin to loosen up a little. I hope not. It is certainly true that sometimes one feels that the poems are stretched as taut as a high wire between the colloquial and the purely literary. Any false step means disaster, and every poet makes a false step once in a while. But it is much easier to keep one's balance writing discursively with that ironic deadpan so common to young women poets these days. Their books are much more solid in their footing than hers, less risky. Hers make us gasp and sometimes groan. But one is moved by her statement that she should own up to her inarticulate and homely lover. It has the ring of authenticity in it: "Love drives its rackety blue caravan / right to the edge." —CHERYL WALKER, "Choosing Old Forms," *Nation*, Sept. 18, 1976, pp. 250–52

TAKING NOTICE

Thematically, the poems in *Taking Notice*, by Marilyn Hacker, betray their imprisonment in the material present. Although there is much talk about the merging of affectionate bodies and the approach to others as objects of adoration and desire, the poems do not imitate the transport to which they frequently refer. Neither are they meditations at one remove from the experience; the mood of the volume is one of manic vigilance before the monotony of the present. The most characteristic rhetorical device is the catalogue of highly textured, usually exotic things, arranged in a kind of glossy ad for poetic "taste":

Two blue glasses of neat
whiskey, epoxy-mended Japanese
ashtray accruing Marlboro and Gauloise
butts, umber and Prussian blue ceramic cups
of Zabar's French Roast, cooling. You acquired
a paunch; I am almost skinny
as I'd like to be. You are probably
right, leaving. We've been here
thousands of miles away, hundreds of times before.

There is here no beauty that makes the heart yearn, no broad consciousness guiding the verses, and no spiritual truth. There are only things. . . .

In another respect, the prosodic, these poems are ill-written. Marilyn Hacker is trying to use stringent rhyming forms like heroic and tetrameter couplets, canzoni, sonnets, and quatrains; but she has thrown off the fetters of the accentual-syllabic line, counting sometimes stress and sometimes syllables, and sometimes counting both ways in the same poem. Lacking any consistent attitude toward the line, her rhymes become abstract exercises, since the line has not been poised to register and savor them. I quote from the sestet of a sonnet:

We came for the day
on a hot bus from Avignon. A Swedish child hurls a chalk boulder; a tall girl,
his sister, twelve, tanned, crouches to finger shell-
whorls bedded in rock-moss. We find our way
here where we can; we take away what we need.

The chopped-off line breaks are committed with arrogance, not wit. In an accentual-syllabic poem, it is not enough to "count out": the line must also loosely embrace the rhythm it asserts, by maintaining its own unity. Although there is an end-line pause after "a tall girl" in the stanza above, it is a nominal pause inasmuch as the phrase has further—and equivalent—qualifiers, "a tall girl, his sister, twelve, tanned, crouches. . . ." These frequent phrase-bracketings work against any priority of line break over comma. The other line breaks in the stanza are yet more abstract, creating the typographical image of a poetic stanza, but no lines of poetry. The obsession with details (the hot bus, Avignon, the chalk boulder, the aspect of the two children, the "shell-whorls bedded in rock-moss") is peculiarly inward; the flat stage props repel the reader's attention; and the outrageously contrived rhymes (like Swed-/need) sound both amateurish and dispirited.—MARY KINZIE, "A Generation of Silver," *APR*, July–Aug. 1981, p. 13

Marilyn Hacker's conception of language has shifted from a position close to Louise Glück's to a position that justifies Isabella Gardner's assumptions more convincingly than Gardner has been able to do. In Hacker's first two volumes, words are felt to create distance from the world of the body, as they do for Glück, but unlike Glück, Hacker passionately wishes to be in touch with the body. Fortunately, she is also in love with words, so that in *Taking Notice* her project becomes not the peeling away of words that she occasionally threatens in her early work, but rather the creation of

words as physical
as waking with hungry skin, an extravagant
shudder to touch, like a branchy plant
palming the window with bright leaves.
("Sequence")

To achieve this unity of word and thing, Hacker must overcome the sense of exile that interferes with Isabella Gardner's attempts to use language in a similar way. For

Hacker, return from exile involves her acceptance of herself as a woman and of the primacy of her love for a woman, conditions which Louise Glück explicitly struggles against.

Since sexual orientation has in so many ways become a political issue, it seems necessary to recall that we are dealing with poetry, which may at some levels be inseparable from politics, but which arises in emotional realities which preclude both politics and aesthetics because they preclude choice. It would be as wrong to claim that, either for the sake of poetry or politics, Glück *should* choose to be a lesbian, as it would be to claim that Hacker *has* chosen so. Hacker humorously points out the absurdity of such a position through the remark of a friend:

> if you could take a *pill*
> to be a Lesbian, you'd
> walk on down the street and home
> in on Ms. Wrong before you got to the post office!
> ("Little Green-Eyed Suite")

Taking Notice is the record not of a decision but of a private experience that is transformed into a public experience through Hacker's use of language. In my view that transformation, which is all that a critic can judge, not only preserves the life of the experience but gives life to language in some startling ways.

There is much craftsmanship to admire here, as there is in Glück, but the chief strength of Hacker's volume lies in its cumulative effect. Numerous individual poems fail to come off. Unlike Glück and Gardner, Hacker does not handle personae well, so that what would feel like the strangeness of truth in Hacker's own voice sounds like mere contrivance in "The Hang-Glider's Daughter." An air of contrivance also arises occasionally when Hacker's verbal facility degenerates into slickness, as it seems to do for instance in "Sonnet" or "Burnham Beeches." On the whole her poems benefit from their ability to absorb the details of daily life, but arrested absorption appears as conspicuous consumption. Gauloises packs are prominently discarded, and a Volvo is parked in the first line of one poem about as unobtrusively as my neighbor's Rolls is left out in the driveway. . . .

The traditional and the new are not antithetical for Hacker. The culminating discovery of the "Taking Notice" sequence is the possibility that "persistent love demands change," in contrast to the conventional notion of fidelity which seeks a love that is permanent rather than "persistent." One reason for making the sequence mark off the course of a year, through changing seasons, is that Hacker wants to enter time. Unlike Louise Glück, she wants her language to do so as well, which Hacker accomplishes by building cumulative effects, by tying verse to occasions, and, most important, by balancing the suppleness of natural speech, words as they are spoken in time, against the rigidity of fixed forms like the sonnet. Hacker owes a debt to Adrienne Rich for the conception that "the moment of change is the only poem," but many poets will owe a debt to Hacker for her demonstration that fulfillment of that conception does not entail rejection of a "male" poetic tradition, though it does require rejection of the view that the tradition is solely male. As Hacker writes in "Introductory Lines":

> We always crafted language just as they did.
> We have the use, and we reclaim the credit.

In this regard, too, Marilyn Hacker has returned from exile.
—TERENCE DIGGORY, "Three Women Exiles," *Salm*, Fall 1981, pp. 151–54

DONALD HALL

1928–

Donald Hall was born on September 20, 1928, in Hamden, Connecticut, where his family operated a dairy business. His childhood was divided between his home in Hamden and his mother's family's farm in New Hampshire. That early exposure to New England farm life left a deep impression on Hall, who later recorded his New Hampshire reminiscences in the prose work *String Too Short to Be Saved*. But Hall is primarily a poet. He began writing seriously, he says, at twelve, and published his first verses at sixteen in small magazines. He spent two years at Phillips Exeter, and entered Harvard at nineteen. There he worked on the *Advocate* with the poet Robert Bly and studied theoretical prosody. He took a one-year fellowship at Christ Church, Oxford, and received his B.Litt. in 1953. On his return from Oxford, Hall married Kirby Thompson, a Radcliffe contemporary. The couple had two children, and were subsequently divorced.

Hall's early career was spent largely on writing fellowships, first at Stanford, then Harvard. He later joined the faculty of the University of Michigan, but focused more on writing than on academics. His early poetry was formal and detached, but he has progressed steadily toward a looser and more expressive form. In recent years Hall has given up teaching to return to the New Hampshire farmlands with his wife, the poet Jane Kenyon. He is a freelance writer.

Hall's collections of verse include *Exiles and Marriages* (1955, Academy of American Poets' Lamont Poetry Selection), *A Roof of Tiger Lilies* (1964), *A Blue Wing: Selected Poems 1964–1974* (1975), and *Kicking the Leaves* (1978).

Donald Hall's first book *Exiles and Marriages* reveals his early achievement of an attractive fluency of poetic statement. His sixty-one poems range widely in subject and tone, indicating skilled technique and dedication to his craft. What unity this book displays comes from the concern, constant in the best poems, to define the mind that made them. Mr. Hall's poetry, unlike much recent verse, is frankly personal. He traces the record of his own growing, gives grave and affectionate tribute to ancestors and places that have shaped his life, and writes unabashedly of his love and marriage. As the book ends, the poet, watching his infant son, thinks again of his own childhood and its comforting or frightening illusions, to which he knows he can never return. This is the "exile" indicated in the title of his book and of his Newdigate Prize poem; it is the theme he most consistently writes well of, there and in "A Child's Garden," "The Sleeping Giant," and "A Relic of the Sea."

Elsewhere, however, the diversity of his offerings exacts a price. Much of the light verse seems the arpeggios, not the cadenzi, of a young virtuoso: satire may not be the metier of this predominantly lyrical talent. What gives the best of Mr. Hall's poems their special charm is their poise and easy grace, yet these virtues are sometimes jeopardized by a stance too relaxed and a diction not consistently his own. "The beasts are real whose shapes I walk among," he writes, but the beasts are few, and those are asserted, not evoked. "Lycanthropy Revisited" is a witty exception.

In "Apology" Hall looks ahead: "There is a virtue which I must achieve . . . A singleness, whose excellence must leave / This personal mountain for a greater range." Whatever singleness Mr. Hall achieves, the considerable skills evident in this engaging book are an assurance that he will come to his "greater range" well prepared. With singleness may come more concentration and intensity. Such a poem as "Passage to Worship" may be indicative of what Mr. Hall will turn to:

> Those several times she cleaved my dark,
> Silver and homeless, I from sleep
> Rose up, and tried to touch or mark
> That storied personage with deep
> Unmotivated love. My days were full,
> My halting days were full of rage,
> Resisting in my heart the pull
> Toward reverence or pilgrimage.
> But now this blinding sheeted bird
> Or goddess stood at my bed's head,
> Demanding worship, and no word
> But honoring the steadfast dead.

—D. G. Hoffman, *SR*, Feb. 18, 1956, p. 39

In the Guggenheim exhibition now at the Tate Gallery there is a picture by René Magritte which is good in a way that I find puzzling. It is a large canvas, and shows a housefront at night, lit by a single street-lamp whose light hardly reaches to the eaves. Above the roof, tree-tops are silhouetted black and lacy against the sky of a sunny spring day, filled with small, soft, very white clouds, and utterly unnocturnal. It is odd how much at home that sky seems with the night scene beneath, as though the artificial, paradoxical, conjunction of opposites which is the basis of the picture had been softened somehow into naturalism. It works brilliantly as a metaphor, bringing together feelings common to its two elements, whose real diversity is emphasised, however, by the use of different styles for house and sky. Unity of ideas counts for more than diversity of style. It is just here, though, that the puzzle arises: if the force of the picture lies in its idea, in what could be understood of it even before it was painted, then it is difficult to see what is contributed by *these* particular brush-strokes, by *this* suggestion of light, to the general theme. Style is so far overshadowed by initial conception that the traditional terms of criticism, which lay importance on the unique nature of the work of art and on individual interpretation, seem not to be quite applicable.

Similar kinds of puzzle arise in these three recent books of verse (*A Roof of Tiger Lilies*, by Donald Hall; *Poems Ancient and Modern*, by Peter Porter; *Selected Poems*, by Anne Sexton)—not that their authors want very much to be puzzling, but that their poems happen to be mysterious in the way their subject-matter shapes its form. This kind of mysteriousness has become not uncommon recently; the traditional formal patterns of verse favoured ten years ago have now been abandoned largely by younger poets in preference for free and syllabic forms so self-effacing that their expressive function is in doubt. Donald Hall is a poet who succeeds where many have failed, and *A Roof of Tiger Lilies* is an excellent book, but from the point of view of form and rhythm it remains mystifying. He writes with an eloquent simplicity that puts questions of metric firmly to one side; to praise him for his style would be like congratulating Pascal on his: not wrong, but largely irrelevant to the matters in hand. He does not decorate his poems; they speak for themselves with a kind of Puritan gravity and intentness, which surely owes something to their author's New Hampshire childhood.

They return again and again to the subject of death:

> Like an old man,
> whatever I touch I turn
> to the story of death.

Death is ambiguously symbolised by snow, which "must / come down, even if it struggles / to stay in the air with the strength / of the wind." It is cold, gradual and has an absolute purity in its whiteness; it preludes the birth of the year as surely as it delays it. It gathers slowly and cannot be prevented:

> the snow keeps falling
> and something will always be falling.

In another poem we are told of the poet's father that "his early death grew inside him / like snow piling on the grass." Mr. Hall's best poems all have this note of unforced sadness.

The short lines which I have quoted suggest that though he uses great simplicity of technique it is far from unsophisticated. Death *grows* as snow *piles*; the two verbs don't really match up, and so deftly hint at the uneasiness with which death's place in the economy of life is viewed. By placing together *I touch* and *I turn* Mr. Hall suggests what was at once the gift and curse of Midas; by ending two successive lines emphatically with *falling*, he demonstrates how that word's very sound and meaning refuse to accept stress. His style is full of felicities; the likeness to Magritte lies in one's not seeing how the felicities are rooted in this way of saying things only. Each poem is a sequence of more or less simple statements which fall together—like snow—and hint at the contours of feeling beneath. One is at once satisfied and baffled by the bareness of his poems.

The shorter ones are, on the whole, noticeably less good, perhaps because they are not able to use repetition and contrast with such unostentatious cunning. They have to be more explicit, and their simplicity seems more artificial. Even the longer pieces become at times sentimental, as though Mr. Hall's tight-lipped curb on obvious feelings were too difficult to maintain. "The Old Pilot's Death," for example, is fanciful and evasive:

> In the distance, circling
> in a beam of late sun like birds migrating,
> there are thin wings of a thousand biplanes.
> He banks and flies to join them.

This does not represent the general level of achievement; the best poems are continuously, yet mutely, surprising but right—these lines from "New Hampshire" may give an idea:

> Fat honey bees
> meander among raspberries where a quarrel
> of vines crawls into the spilled body of a plane.

The mind enters a series of shocks in reading this simple, descriptive sentence. First it is lulled by the *meandering* of the bees and then jolted awake by the *quarrel*. But the quarrel turns out to be only metaphorical—only *vines*. The vines, however, *crawl* like insects dabbling in something *spilled* (raspberry jam, perhaps; the innocence of the bees seems to be invoked here). The fact that it is a *body* that has been spilled changes one's reaction yet again; only the body of a *plane*, of course, but the human disaster, already suggested by the quarrel, effectively darkens the natural scene. These successive shocks are held in check by the syllabic line, whose irregular stresses are deployed to soften the blows as they come. Both *vines* and *crawls* are stressed yet juxtaposed—"a quarrel of *vines crawls*"—and this modifies the force with which their meaning strikes us. Mr. Hall is astonishingly good at this sort of thing; he uses syllabic verse with such skill that one neglects to ask why he chose it in the first place. But if you ask the question, it is mystifying; the poems exist suspended in mid-air, with no general context of feeling or norm of rhythm to which to refer.—Martin Dodsworth, "Puzzlers," *Enc*, March 1965, pp. 83–86

Although Donald Hall's new book ⟨*The Alligator Bride*⟩ offers work both recent and early (the latter somewhat revised) and although it clearly shows his poetic manner shifting to accommodate, or at least to accompany, the changing styles of 20 years, certain features are consistent from beginning to end; consistent and curiously old-fashioned. We are reminded of the period when Hall began to write, the late forties and early fifties.

The past, Hall says, is better than the present. Grandfathers are superior to fathers, middle-aged lovers make better love than young lovers. The values of early generations of New Hampshire farmers were more humane and reasonable than the values of their descendants. In his own life the poet's progress toward middle age, or even old age, brings him nearer to freedom, discovery, and a wise appreciation of pleasure.

Yet because this progress ends in death, and because past values are irretrievably past, Hall's attitude is touched with inevitable irony. His celebration of pleasure is imbued with a sense of loss. He is, in short, hung up on the conventional dilemma of metaphysical poets, which he meets by conventional means: his poems are elegiac in tone, and civil, subdued and orderly in manner. The alternative, he would say, is insanity.

There is obvious truth in this, and obvious importance too. We are reminded, almost with shock, of the time not long ago when men in their forties were still called young and our heroes were mostly older than that by far. But this is not the truth that most Americans want to hear today. Nor is Hall's poetic decorum, with its roots in literary tradition, what attracts their notice. His recent work, for instance, has been more successful in England than in the United States and has been broadcast on the B.B.C.

A second point concerns Hall's attitude toward natural objects. For him they are things to be manipulated in the poet's favor, "objective correlatives." A stone, tree, bird or animal is significant only as it transmits meanings from outside itself, meanings which are verbally imposed. This is the attitude of Yeats, Eliot, and many great poets of 40 years ago. Call it Neo-Symbolism or Post-Symbolism if you will; it is still Symbolism, and its roots are deep in the Transcendental past.

To the great majority of American poets today, however, working under the influence of Pound, Williams, Zukofsky and the Black Mountain school, this view is not only wrong but evil. The objects of our world have their own meanings, natural meanings, which poets have no right to manipulate. Instead the poet's work is to represent the objects in their pristine self-hood, not as symbols of his feeling but as counterparts, or simple presences.

The philosophical differences between these views are too important to be condensed in a book review, though obviously they are related to the larger questions of man's place in the universe and our deepening ecological crisis. The point here is that, next to the clear-cut poems of the objectivists, Hall's symbolic poems, even his leanest and sharpest, are likely to seem murky and portentous by comparison.

Yet sometimes it is easier to judge a poet who is out of fashion than one who is in. If a poem projects through its facade of quaintness, so to speak, and genuinely touches us, then probably it is a success. How great a success doesn't matter; we call it, loosely but reasonably, a good poem. Hall's most famous poem, his early "Elegy for Wesley Wells," in which the poet grieves for the death of a New Hampshire farmer and the values he represents, is not a good poem. We can no longer accept such overstuffed, factitious lines as:

> His dogs will whimper through the webby barn
> Where spiders close his tools in a pale gauze.

Some of us never accepted them. But a few of Hall's poems from the middle and later parts of his book do break through: "The Snow," "The Stump," "The Long River," "Swan," perhaps three or four others. These, more cleanly written and less derivative than the early poems, have attracted strong advocates and many readers, and doubtless have earned a place, in the New England tradition.

Finally the reviewer must apologize for writing about Donald Hall as if he were finished. He is still in his early forties, a young man by his own standards. But the fault is partly his, for giving us his *Poems New and Selected* with such an air of finality.—Hayden Carruth, *NYTBR*, Sept. 13, 1970, p. 38

The Man in the Dead Machine

High on a slope in New Guinea
the Grumman Hellcat
lodges among bright vines
as thick as arms. In 1942,
the clenched hand of a pilot
glided it here
where no one has ever been.

In the cockpit the helmeted
skeleton sits
upright, held
by dry sinews at neck
and shoulder, and webbing
that straps the pelvic cross
to the cracked
leather of the seat, and the breastbone
to the canvas cover
of the parachute.

Or say that the shrapnel
missed him, he flew
back to the carrier, and every
morning takes his chair, his pale
hands on the black arms, and sits
upright, held
by the firm webbing.

Interviewer: "The Man in the Dead Machine" has a speculative cast to it, almost a fantasy quality. Tell us what made you choose such a subject for your poem.

Donald Hall: The subject matter chooses *you*, really. I can tell you how it began. I was driving along the New York Thruway, alone. Suddenly I had an intense visual image. Most of my poems begin with language, with words, rhythm. But this one began with a really strong vision. I had the vision of a crashed airplane; well, not really *crashed*, landed pretty intact, in a jungle, with vines growing all around it and a skeleton upright in the cockpit. I pulled over to the side of the road, illegally (unless a poem is an emergency, which for a poet it is). I pulled over and wrote down a prose paragraph describing what I'd just seen. I recognized that it was an image of how I felt in my life, then. It wasn't a good patch. I didn't do much about the image for many months. Perhaps a year afterward I began to work on it. I began with the introduction and then the description of the skeleton, which was the strongest thing. Then I wanted to bring him back into the contemporary world, to say that it made no matter whether he was dead or alive. I had all sorts of terrible ideas, like calling it his identical twin, who was wandering around in New York City. I couldn't get it right. Until finally, I saw again what you can do in poetry: use the possibility of fantasy, of dreams. Or say, "Suppose I was lying?" Why not say that? It makes no difference.

I had other problems in writing it. For instance, when it first came out in a magazine, it didn't read "his pale/hands on the black arms," it read "every/morning takes the train, his pale/hands on the black case." I like the assonance there, with "case," and "train," and "pale." I like the sound of it. But it came to me that it looked like another poet attacking the businessmen, another poet attacking the commuters. Well, I can do that if I want to, but that's not what I wanted to do, this time, at all. I wanted to implicate *everybody:* me, you, *everybody*, in this sense of being "the man in the dead machine." I didn't want to limit it to a social class.

I.: That suggests that "The Man in the Dead Machine" is apolitical. But what do you think about poets who write so much on political subjects, let's say about the Indo-China War?

D.H.: I don't have any general feeling. I think some of Robert Bly's work, which includes the Vietnam war, is fantastically good—"The Teeth Mother Naked at Last," the long poem, is terrific, and so are some of the shorter ones. But poems are never *about* anything. I mean, what's "The Man in the Dead Machine" about? Is it about the middle-aged man, the Second World War? I don't know what it's about except that it embodies a feeling. It's pretty much a single feeling, but not entirely. The spider web is never mentioned in that poem, but the skeleton is like a fly in a web, a spider's web; webbing is mentioned, but not a spider's web, and then there are those vines like arms: I think of the mother embrace—that embrace is death also. The mother spider.

In order to write with the Vietnam war as part of your subject, or as an ostensible subject, or a beginning to it, the event has to touch something in your own life, your inner life, very strongly. For instance, when someone asked him, "Are you a pacifist?" Sigmund Freud answered, "No, I'm not aggressive enough." Now in order to write out of the misery and horror of the Vietnam war, you have to have a lot of murder in you. If you want to write out of indignation, go write an editorial, go run a political campaign—that's great—but indignation is not going to make poetry. Poetry has to come out of something in you, part of which was there even when you were two or three years old.

I.: Does that explain Bly's "Small Boned Bodies"?

D.H.: Yes. That's a poem of intense fantasy, the fantasy of making things tinier or larger, like Alice in Wonderland. It's one of the characteristics of the infantile mind, the ability to change the size of things. It comes about probably because the baby is so aware of disparities: his own smallness against the hugeness of the giants that hover over him.

I.: Does that suggest that poets have child-like minds?

D.H.: Poets are people who have to be in touch with that part of themselves. There's power in that kind of thinking—the prerational thinking, as opposed to the kind of thinking that begins about ten, eleven, and twelve. Prerational thinking has power for transformation, for understanding; it has the power of dream. There's an incredible source of energy of dream thinking. That's not actually to *be* a child. It is, from time to time, to think like one, to let your mind perform like a child's. Still it's to be a man, a more complete man.

I.: You're talking about an aesthetic for modern poetry, as distinct from earlier poetries. Words that describe the impact of the modern poem like "epiphany" or "transport" or "gut feeling," are taking the place of words like "theme" or "idea." Do you agree?

D.H.: Yes, but I'm not sure it's a difference in poets; it may be a difference in the critics.

I.: That opens up a whole new bag of beans, doesn't it?

D.H.: It's a difference in the way we talk *about* poetry, more than it's a difference in the way we write it. I think there's a fantastic continuity in lyric poetry, from the early Greeks to the present. Remember that poem by Robert Graves, "To Juan at the Winter Solstice"? It begins, "There is one story and one story only." Sometimes I think that all poetry is one story. And that story is: transform yourself, release yourself from the control of civilization. That's why Plato had to kick it out of the *Republic*. Plato was absolutely reasonable to do so. . . .
—DONALD HALL, Interview by Gregory Fitz Gerald, Rodney Parshall, *Goatfoot, Milktongue, Twinbird*, 1978, pp. 76–80

1. Some Premises

First, in connection with oppositions:

1. Any quality of poetry can be used for a number of purposes, including opposed purposes. Thus, concentration on technique has often been used to trivialize content, by poets afraid of what they will learn about themselves. But concentration on technique can absorb the attention while unacknowledged material enters the language; so technique can facilitate inspiration.

On the other hand, a poet can subscribe to an anti-technical doctrine of inspiration in a way that simply substitutes one technique for another. Surrealism can become as formulaic as a pastoral elegy.

2. When a poet says he is doing *north*, look and see if he is not actually doing *south*. Chances are that his bent is so entirely *south* that he must swear total allegiance to *north* in order to include the globe.

3. Energy arises from conflict. Without conflict, no energy. Yin and yang. Dark and light. Pleasure and pain. No synthesis without thesis and antithesis. Conflict of course need not be binary but may include a number of terms.

4. Every present event that moves us deeply connects in our psyches with something (or things) in the past. The analogy is the two pieces of carbon that make an arc light. When they come close enough, the spark leaps across. The one mourning is all mourning; "After the first death, there is no other." This generalization applies to the composition of poems (writing), and to the recomposition of poems (reading).

5. The way out is the same as the way in. To investigate

the process of making a poem is not merely an exercise in curiosity or gossip, but an attempt to understand the nature of literature. In the act of reading, the reader undergoes a process—largely without awareness, as the author was largely without intention—which resembles, like a slightly fainter copy of the original, the process of discovery or recovery that the poet went through in his madness or inspiration.

And then, more general:

6. A poem is one man's inside talking to another man's inside. It may *also* be reasonable man talking to reasonable man, but if it is not inside talking to inside, it is not a poem. This inside speaks through the second language of poetry, the unintended language. Sometimes, as in surrealism, the second language is the only language. It is the ancient prong of carbon in the arc light. We all share more when we are five years old than when we are twenty-five; more at five minutes than at five years. The second language allows poetry to be universal.

7. *Lyric poetry, typically, has one goal and one message, which is to urge the condition of inwardness, the "inside" from which its own structure derives.*—DONALD HALL, "Goatfoot, Milktongue, Twinbird: The Psychic Origins of Poetic Form," *Goatfoot, Milktongue, Twinbird*, 1978, pp. 117–19

. . . Donald Hall's ⟨*Remembering Poets: Reminiscences and Opinions*⟩ is mainly a gathering of well-told anecdotes about the author's relations with Frost, Pound, Eliot, and Dylan Thomas. Hall deserves praise for the care he has taken to verify his information, to be accurate, to complete stories of which he knew only a part at first hand. The care is visible everywhere but most attractively in the author's frankness about himself. The refusal to cover up his blunders deepens the appeal and the humor of the narrative. His good nature and appreciativeness give it coherence. Readers in general, and young readers in particular, who hesitate to dip into poetry of any sort will find themselves reaching for the works of Hall's subjects as they yield to the charm of his voice.

That they will discover much about the poetry itself is less certain. Hall is aware of the limitations of his approach, and insists that one must not confuse the personality of a genius with his work. Yet for all his experience as a poet, Hall rarely shows much penetration or independent judgment when he acts as a critic. Biography is an efficient method of getting into the meaning and shape of works of art so long as the biographer is obsessed with the creative imagination of his subject.

Naturally, the characters of his four poets fascinate Hall and infuse drama into his accounts of them. We hear Dylan Thomas talk about Yeats; we observe the competitiveness of Frost; we see Eliot reluctantly shaking hands with Oscar Williams; and we learn about the obstacles Hall met when he tried to get lecture engagements for Pound in America. Some of the anecdotes move one deeply, like the report of Thomas planning to give up poetry for prose because he could make more money from prose. One also learns much from Hall about the career of a poet in our time—the mechanical, financial, and emotional problems of winning the attention of deafened ears.

But the paragraphs of comment on individual poems, of judgments about the *oeuvre* of a poet, or of generalization about the art of poetry are not incisive enough. The psychological and moral observations are more often honest than profound. Hall's notions about the relation of culture to society seldom enlighten one—for example, his speculation that if Thomas had lived in a society which "valued life over death," he might not have drunk himself into disaster.

For readers concerned with poetry itself, the most absorbing parts of the book will be the interviews with Eliot and Pound, which have been published before. But scrupulous as they are, these in turn remain less than they might appear to be. They bring us (as the whole book does) the speech of men at the end of their careers. Even the sympathy and intelligence of Mr. Hall cannot transform them into the young, creative innovators whom we yearn to know.

Besides, these men had already put their self-portraits on public display, and consciously or not were preserving them while answering Hall's questions (as he perfectly realized). Finally, they had fallible memories. Eliot told Hall that he had sold the manuscripts of *The Waste Land* to John Quinn. In fact, we know from the correspondence published by Valerie Eliot in her edition that Eliot refused to sell those manuscripts to his benefactor and insisted on making him a present of them. It was other manuscripts that Quinn succeeded in buying from Eliot.—IRVING EHRENPREIS, *NYRB*, Dec. 7, 1978, pp. 16–19

By definition, the literary memoir presupposes an intimate connection between a writer's life and his work: a look, a gesture, a particular conversation, an observed eccentricity, a remembered incident—all these provide potential insights into the work itself. It is all the more curious that Donald Hall, who modestly refers to his memoirs of Dylan Thomas, Robert Frost, T.S. Eliot, and Ezra Pound as "literary gossip," repeatedly denies that such a connection exists and urges us to "split poem from poet." "If a poet is great," he argues, "the poem is the poet at his or her greatest, and the man or woman in person will never equal the poem created. . . . Great poets may tell lies all day and all night. . . . Conversely, I have known a hundred poets who were decent and apparently honest people in daily life . . . who . . . stole the voices of dead poets and the ideas of live friends." Or again, "The poet in his own skin will never equal the poems."

But why then write literary gossip? What good does it do us to know that Pound didn't know his way around Rome or that Thomas bullied his wife or that Frost worried about what suit to wear to a reading? Hall's "gossip" is, moreover, fairly thin because, unlike such literary memorialists as Ford Madox Ford writing on the young D.H. Lawrence, or Bertrand Russell commenting on the deadlock between Eliot and his wife, or A. Alvarez recalling the last dark days of Sylvia Plath, Donald Hall, by his own admission, barely knew the four poets who are his subject. His role was, from the beginning, that of middleman: it was Hall who arranged the poetry readings, who brought the car around, who made introductions, who interviewed Eliot and Pound for the *Paris Review*. Frost and Eliot expressed a polite if rather perfunctory interest in Hall's own poems; Thomas and Pound had never read them.

If Hall's book is short on anecdote, it is long on general reflections as to the "meaning" of poets' lives; not for nothing is his book subtitled *Reminiscences and Opinions*. His central thesis is that "The poet who survives is the poet to celebrate." "In our culture," he notes, "an artist's self-destructiveness is counted admirable, praiseworthy, a guarantee of sincerity. There seems to be an assumption . . . that it is natural to want to destroy yourself; that health is bourgeois or conventional." Hall deplores this cult of the suicidal artist. "Thomas," he declares, "was a minor poet, rather than a major one, because he was a drunk," whereas Eliot, Pound, and Frost survived heroically and therefore became great poets.

Hall is quite right, I think, to debunk the myth of art as self-destruction, a myth propagated by such studies as A. Alvarez's *The Savage God* (1972) and reinforced by the actual suicides of Sylvia Plath, Anne Sexton, and John Berryman. But I am not sure that Hall's own view of poetic "survival" is any more satisfactory than the one he opposes. . . . If Hall's theorizing repeatedly flounders, as I think it does, it is perhaps because his set of memoirs is only ostensibly about Thomas, Frost, Eliot, and Pound. Hall's real subject is himself, as his conclusion "Gladness and Madness" reveals. "Artists of vast ambition seldom die happy," Hall announced, leaving us to wonder who it is that does die happy. "Most people," he continues, "avoid [the poet's] despair at the end of life by following simple maxims: don't be ambitious; take it easy; be a *good* father, mother, citizen. . . ." But the poet can't take this way out. "You will never be any good as a poet unless you arrange your life and your values in the hope of writing great poems—always knowing . . . that you may well have 'messed up your life' for nothing."

Here Hall gives himself away. Throughout the book, he has been assuming, rather naively, that poets "arrange their lives and values in the hope of writing great poems," evidently because this is what he himself did. An extraordinarily precocious boy, Hall "decided to become a poet" at 14. By the time he was 16, he had already published poems in Little Magazines; later he was an editor of the Harvard *Advocate* and won an important fellowship to Oxford. He became a well-known anthologist, editor, interviewer, and critic—a genuine man of letters. But I think it is not unfair to say that, despite all his "arranging," Hall has not lived up to his early poetic promise.

Perhaps this doesn't matter. Hall himself insists: "This book records a portion of my education. Whether my own poems look worthy in retrospect is irrelevant: I grew up as a poet, for better or worse, among other poets." But Hall's evaluations of his poetic fathers suggest that the status of his own poems is not, after all, irrelevant. He longs to convince us that the aspiring poet cannot help but "mess up a part of his own life or the lives of others"—"for the selfish sake" of his art. He believes, in short, that the aspiration toward greatness—his own aspiration—is in itself admirable; the sufferings it may cause others or himself are justified so long as he endures, survives, dares to continue.

Such Romantic glorification of the poet's enterprise (as distinct from the production of good poems) is perhaps just as misguided as the cult of self-destruction. *Remembering Poets* is an oddly dispiriting book for it demonstrates, quite unwittingly, that becoming a poet is one thing, and wanting and *planning* to become one, quite another. As for "literary gossip," one wishes that Donald Hall had chosen to give us some juicy tales about the poets of his own time and place. "John Ashberry, Kenneth Koch, and Frank O'Hara at the Harvard *Advocate*"—there is a literary memoir I should like to read.—MARJORIE PERLOFF, *NR*, May 6, 1978, pp. 30–32

DASHIELL HAMMETT

1894–1961

Samuel Dashiell Hammett was born on May 27, 1894, in St. Mary's County, Maryland, and grew up in Baltimore, where his family moved in 1901. Leaving school in 1908, he drifted from job to job before becoming an operative for Pinkerton's Detective Agency in 1915. His career was interrupted by service with the U.S. Army Ambulance Corps in 1918–19 and by illness; although highly rated by Pinkerton's, he resigned his position in 1922. By this time he had moved to San Francisco and married, and in the following years barely supported himself and his family by writing short stories, book reviews, and advertising copy.

From 1923 Hammett's stories, drawing on his experiences as a detective, appeared in the popular magazine *Black Mask*, and it was here that his first three full-length novels, *Red Harvest*, *The Dain Curse* (both 1929), and *The Maltese Falcon* (1930), first appeared, in serial form. With his national reputation firmly established, he gave up magazine work and in 1930 accepted an offer to write movie stories. The Hollywood social scene accentuated his already marked habits of heavy drinking, gambling, and womanizing, which a lifelong liaison with Lillian Hellman, whose playwriting career he decisively encouraged, did little to diminish. His fourth novel, *The Glass Key*, was published in 1931, and *The Thin Man* in 1934, after which, despite many plans, he was unable to complete another novel.

From 1937 Hammett was increasingly involved in various left-wing causes. In 1940 he was named chairman of the Communist-affiliated Committee on Election Rights; after serving in the Aleutians in World War II, he became President of the Civil Rights Congress in 1946 and began an association with the Jefferson School of Social Science in New York which lasted until 1955. In 1951 he served a six-month jail sentence for refusing to testify about the Civil Rights Congress bail fund, and in 1953 he was interrogated by the McCarthy Committee. His last years were made still more difficult by financial troubles and declining health; he suffered a heart attack in 1955, and died of lung cancer on January 10, 1961.

Personal

I said to Hammett there is something that is puzzling. In the nineteenth century the men when they were writing did invent all kinds and a great number of men. The women on the other hand never could invent women they always made the women be themselves seen splendidly or sadly or heroically or beautifully or despairingly or gently, and they never could make any other kind of woman. From Charlotte Brontë to George Eliot and many years later this was true. Now in the twentieth century it is the men who do it. The men all write about themselves, they are always themselves as strong or weak or mysterious or passionate or drunk or controlled but always themselves as the women used to do in the nineteenth century. Now you yourself always do it now why is it. He said it's simple. In the nineteenth century men were confident, the women were not but in the twentieth century the men have no confidence and so they have to make themselves as you say more beautiful more intriguing more everything and they cannot make any other man because they have to hold on to themselves not having any confidence. Now I he went on have even thought of doing a father and a son to see if in that way I could make another one. That's interesting I said.—GERTRUDE STEIN, *Everybody's Autobiography*, 1937, p. 5

He had made up honor early in his life and stuck with his rules, fierce in the protection of them. In 1951 he went to jail because he and two other trustees of the bail bond fund of the Civil Rights Congress refused to reveal the names of the contributors to the fund. The truth was that Hammett had never been in the office of the Committee and did not know the name of a single contributor. The night before he was to appear in court, I said, "Why don't you say that you don't know the names?" "No," he said, "I can't say that." "Why?" "I don't know why." After we had a nervous silence, he said, "I guess it has something to do with keeping my word, but I don't want to talk about that. Nothing much will happen, although I think we'll go to jail for a while, but you're not to worry because—" and then suddenly I couldn't understand him because the voice had dropped and the words were coming in a most untypical nervous rush. I said I couldn't hear him, and he raised his voice and dropped his head. "I hate this damn kind of talk, but maybe I better tell you that if it were more than jail, if it were my life, I would give it for what I think democracy is and I don't let cops or judges tell me what I think democracy is." Then he went home to bed, and the next day he went to jail. —LILLIAN HELLMAN, "Introduction" to *The Big Knockover* by Dashiell Hammett, 1966, pp. x–xi

General

The ascendancy of the job in the lives of Americans—just this is the chief concern of Dashiell Hammett's art. When tuberculosis forced him to return to writing, it was his job experience that he drew upon; and his knowledge of the life of detectives could fit easily into a literary form that had at least as much in common with a production plan as with art. As soon as he got a "better" job, he stopped writing. And, as we shall see, the Job determines the behavior of his fictional characters just as much as it has set the course of his own life. . . .

There is an obvious coincidence between the beginning of Hammett's sojourn in Hollywood and the *de facto* end of his literary effort. Moreover, his job in the West Coast magic factories (at a reported fifteen hundred dollars a week) is not strictly a writing one; he is employed as a trouble-shooter, patching up scripts and expediting stories, often when the film is already before the cameras. Until 1938 Hammett seems to have been exclusively occupied with his joy-ride on the Hollywood gravytrain, but in that year—it was the height of the Popular Front period—he was seized by "political consciousness." Already forty-four, he had spent six of his best years in Hollywood instead of writing his play, and thus was more or less ready for religion.

Unlike many victims of the Popular Front, Hammett went on following the Communists—up hill and down dale: Popular Front—No Front—Second Front. We can only assume that his need is great. During the war he was president of the League of American Writers and as such occupied himself lining up talent behind war activities in general and the Second Front in particular. He also joined the army. At present he serves as head of the New York branch of the Civil Rights Congress, a Stalinist "front" organization; most recently his name turned up as a sponsor of the Cultural and Scientific Conference for World Peace, held in New York in March. . . .

The Op is primarily a job-holder: all the stories in which he appears begin with an assignment and end when he has completed it. To an extent, *competence* replaces moral stature as the criterion of an individual's worth. The only persons who gain any respect from the Op are those who behave competently—and all such, criminal or otherwise, are accorded some respect. This attitude is applied to women as well as men. In *The Dain Curse*, the Op is attracted deeply only to the woman who has capacity and realism—and he fears her for the same reason. So Woman enters the Hammett picture as desirable not merely for her beauty, but also for her ability to live independently, capably—unmarried, in other words.

But the moral question is not disposed of so easily. Hammett's masculine figures are continually running up against a certain basic situation in which their relation to evil must be defined. In *Red Harvest*, for instance, the detective doing his job is confronted with a condition of evil much bigger than himself. He cannot ignore it since his job is to deal with it. On the other hand, he cannot act morally in any full sense because his particular relation, as a paid agent, to crime and its attendant evils gives him no logical justification for overstepping the bounds of his "job." Through some clever prompting by the Continental Op, the gangsters—whose rule is the evil in *Red Harvest*—destroy each other in their own ways. But it becomes a very bloody business, as the title suggests. And the Op's lost alternative, of perhaps having resolved the situation—and performed his job with less bloodshed, grows in poignancy. He begins to doubt his own motivation: perhaps the means by which a job is done matter as much as the actual accomplishment of the job.

One of the most suggestive aspects of this situation is that the Op's client hinders rather than aids him in resolving the evil. For the client is the capitalist who opened the city to the gangsters in the first place to break a strike. (This ambiguous relation to the client is characteristic in that it further isolates the detectives; suspicion is imbedded like a muscle in Hammett's characters, and lying is the primary form of communication between them. In two of the novels, the murderer is an old friend of the detective.) If the Op were not simply *employed*—that is, if he were really concerned with combating evil—he would have to fight against his client directly, to get at the evil's source. As it is, he confines his attention to his "job," which he carries out with an almost bloodthirsty determination that proceeds from an unwillingness to go beyond it. This relation to the job is perhaps typically American.

What is wrong with the character of the Op—this

American—is that he almost never wrestles with personal motives of his own. The private eye has no private life. He simply wants to do his job well. One might think he was in it for the money—but his salary is never made known, is apparently not large, and he isn't even *tempted* to steal. Each story contains at least one fabulously beautiful woman—but the Op goes marching on. If he is a philosopher of some peculiarly American *acte gratuit*, a connoisseur of crime and violence, we never know it, since we are never permitted to know his thoughts. So, while this character often holds a strong primitive fascination because he represents an attempt at a realistic image of a human being who succeeds (survives not too painfully) in an environment of modern anxiety, he is, ultimately, too disinterested—too little involved—to be real.

It is interesting, in view of the importance of job-doing to the detective, to remark the reasons for this lack of personal motivation. What the Op has as a substitute for motives is a more or less total projection of himself into the violent environment of crime and death. And by "projection" I mean that he surrenders his emotions to the world outside while dissociating them from his own purposeful, responsible self; he becomes a kind of sensation-seeker. So, despite all the *Sturm und Drang* of his life, it remains an essentially vicarious one, because the *moral* problem—the matter of individual responsibility or decision-making in a situation where society has defaulted morally—is never even faced, much less resolved. The question of doing or not doing a job competently seems to have replaced the whole larger question of good and evil. The Op catches criminals because it is his job to do so, not because they are criminals. At the same time, it is still important that his job is to catch criminals; just any job will not do: the Op has the same relation to the experience of his job, its violence and excitement, the catharsis it affords, as has the ordinary consumer of mass culture to the detective stories and movies he bolts down with such regularity and in such abundance. His satisfactions require a rejection of moral responsibility—but this in itself requires that he be involved in a situation charged with moral significance—which exists for him solely that it may be rejected.

. . . Hammett, in *The Glass Key*, got only as far as the experience of the vital need of knowing (beyond the horizon of the job). He then collapsed—quite completely. Instead of following his literary problem where it was leading him, he preferred to follow his new-found Hollywoodism down whatever paths of pleasure *it* might take him. He postponed the attempt to resolve those problems with which life had presented him. But it was, it could be, only a postponement, and after a few years he came upon Stalinism—that fake consciousness, fake resolution, perfect apposite of Hollywoodism—and crossed the t's of his lost art.—DAVID T. BAZELON, "Dashiell Hammett's 'Private Eye,'" *Cmty*, May 1949, pp. 467–72

Ideology is, by contrast, an *escape* from personal responsibility. Someone like Whittaker Chambers wanted to be told what to do, wanted to be History's slave. Ideologues want to be certified by others as respectable—if not by the Committee or the Party, then by the ADA. They want their hates to be dictated by the national program. The radical thinks of virtuous people, while the ideologue thinks of orthodoxy. The radical hates vicious and harmful people, while the ideologue hates heretical ideas, no matter how "nice" the possessors of those ideas may be. The radical tries to uphold a private kind of honor in a rotten world—like Hammett's "private eyes," serving society without respecting it, seeing men and not just abstract Crime in the victims of their hunt. Hammett wielded that most self-wounding of human instruments, irony; and ironists make terrible crusaders. The worst thing one could have wished on the mousy world of Communist ideologues in America was a dozen more Hammetts.—GARRY WILLS, "Introduction" to *Scoundrel Time* by Lillian Hellman, 1976, pp. 31–32

Hammett wrote at first (and almost to the end) for people with a sharp, aggressive attitude to life. They were not afraid of the seamy side of things; they lived there. Violence did not dismay them; it was right down their street. Hammett gave murder back to the kind of people that commit it for reasons, not just to provide a corpse; and with the means at hand, not hand-wrought dueling pistols, curare, and tropical fish. He put these people down on paper as they were, and he made them talk and think in the language they customarily used for these purposes.

He had a literary style, but his audience didn't know it, because it was in a language not supposed to be capable of such refinements. They thought they were getting a good meaty melodrama written in the kind of lingo they imagined they spoke themselves. It was, in a sense, but it was much more. All language begins with speech, and the speech of common men at that, but when it develops to the point of becoming a literary medium it only looks like speech. Hammett's style at its worst was as formalized as a page of *Marius the Epicurean;* at its best it could say almost anything. I believe this style, which does not belong to Hammett or to anybody, but is the American language (and not even exclusively that any more), can say things he did not know how to say, or feel the need of saying. In his hands it had no overtones, left no echo, evoked no image beyond a distant hill.

Hammett is said to have lacked heart; yet the story he himself thought the most of is the record of a man's devotion to a friend. He was spare, frugal, hard-boiled, but he did over and over again what only the best writers can ever do at all. He wrote scenes that seemed never to have been written before. —RAYMOND CHANDLER, "The Simple Art of Murder," *At*, December 1944, p. 58

Fitzgerald said he was haunted by the conviction that Ring Lardner "got less percentage of himself on paper than any other American author of the first flight." Hammett got even less on paper, so much less that his rank is uncertain. His use of language is, certainly, "first flight." He did for American slang—the argots of hobos, cowboys, seamen, boxers, longshoremen, miners, Wobblies, and, of course, cops and robbers—what Mark Twain had previously done for the American vernacular: used it on the level of art. Hammett never merely played lexicographer to the underworld. He selected the witty, colorful elements of the jargon and used them naturally, knowledgeably, without dazzling or digressing for the sake of innovation but always to advance his story. In "Fly Paper," for example, as the Op tries to figure out where a criminal has fled, he reasons:

> The big man was a yegg. San Francisco was on fire for him. The yegg instinct would be to use a rattler to get away from trouble. The freight yards were in this end of town. Maybe he would be shifty enough to lie low instead of trying to powder. In that case, he probably hadn't crossed Market Street at all. If he stuck, there would still be a chance of picking him up tomorrow. If he was hightailing, it was catch him now or not at all.

As for commonplace profanities, Hammett would skirt them with a graceful précis such as "He called her four unlovely names, the mildest of which was, 'a dumb twist.'" Occasionally he would slip in a newly coined obscenity to test his editor's conversance with the everchanging language. One editor failed to blue-pencil the word "gunsel." He took it to mean a gunman's young assistant; it actually meant a homosexual hanger-on. Other writers of detective stories, emulators of Hammett, repeated the editor's mistake and began using "gunsel" in the inaccurate sense. Their errors stuck and the word, when it is used nowadays, is usually used incorrectly.

The imitators proliferated and Hammett soon became typecast as "the founder of the hard-boiled school of detective fiction." It might be useful to consider his work in terms of what had come before. Twain had made the literary break with Europe, but those in the first flush of freedom always look back to make sure the bonds are really broken, and that's what Twain did in *The Innocents Abroad*. Hammett was second-generation free of the genteel tradition; to him "abroad" meant across the Pacific, not the Atlantic. . . .

Understatement, coolness if you will, enables Hammett to keep some distance from his characters, He needs the distance because, shades of Twain, he is torn between fondness for human beings and disgust over their depravity. Hammett's Op is frequently turning in women whom he would not turn down, Sam Spade does so in *The Maltese Falcon*. The Op, in "Blood Money," shoots a young colleague whom he particularly likes when the colleague turns to crime (because *he* cannot resist a girl). In *The Dain Curse*, a man whom the Op was once "chummy with" turns out to be the villain. Thus the style based on understatement lends itself to an understatement of theme, freeing Hammett from the sentimentality and good-against-evil framework of the traditional mystery. To the Op each case is just a job, not a moral crusade.—FREDERICK H. GARDNER, "Return of the Continental Op," *Nation*, Oct. 31, 1966, p. 455

⟨H⟩is best novels, *Red Harvest* and *The Glass Key*, are not really detective stories at all. They are political; they are about what happens and how it feels when the gangsters take over. *Red Harvest*, for example, is set in an ugly Western mining town which is virtually owned by one man:

> For forty years old Elihu Willson . . . had owned Personville, heart, soul, skin and guts. He was president and majority stockholder of the Personville Mining Corporation, ditto of the First National Bank, owner of the *Morning Herald* and *Evening Herald*, the city's only newspapers, and at least part owner of nearly every other enterprise of any importance. Along with these pieces of property he owned a United States senator, a couple of representatives, the governor, the mayor, and most of the state legislature. Elihu Willson was Personville, and he was almost the whole state.

That ironic acceptance of how things are dictates Hammett's tone and pervades the whole story, however savage it becomes. Willson has had trouble from the Wobblies; to break their strikes he has imported gunmen. But the hoods have found the pickings too good to leave, and gradually they have slid out of his control. So Willson reluctantly allows a private eye in on the act. He, the narrator, is forty, overweight, thick with booze, and more or less without principles.

With a kind of blank cunning, like a good poker-player, he sets the gangs against each other. There are twenty murders before the place is finally tidied up. Only one is a normal 'mystery', and that is cleared up early. The real interest is in the effect of all this carnage on the narrator:

> 'This damned burg's getting me. If I don't get away soon I'll be going blood-simple like the natives. . . . I've arranged a killing or two in my time, when they were necessary. But this is the first time I ever got the fever. . . . Look. I sat at Willson's table tonight and played them like you'd play trout, and got just as much fun out of it. I looked at Noonan and knew he hadn't a chance in a thousand of living another day because of what I had done to him, and I laughed, and felt warm and happy inside. That's not me. . . . After twenty years of messing around with crime I can look at any sort of murder without seeing anything in it but my bread and butter, the day's work. But this getting a rear out of planning deaths is not natural to me.'

This has less in common with Agatha Christie than with *The Revenger's Tragedy*. The killings are not a game or a puzzle or a joke. Instead, they are at one with the obsessional, illicit drinking, the drug-taking, the police beatings-up—all casual symptoms of prevailing corruption.

You have only to compare this with factual histories of prohibition and its legacy (see *Murder, Inc.*, 1951, by Burton B. Turkus, Assistant D.A. of New York) to see that Hammett exaggerated nothing: indeed, he may even have toned down the realities. Yet his massacres are intriguing neither as social history nor because they cater so nicely to our sadistic fantasies—as do his imitators, in descending order from Raymond Chandler to Mickey Spillane. The fascination of Hammett's writing is that it makes the killing somehow different, accepted, habitual, part, as he says, of 'the day's work'. It has the ordinariness of real nihilism. And this makes him seem peculiarly close to us, though we now accept violence on a grander scale and expect our politicians not to be owned by gangsters but themselves to behave like gangsters.

God forbid I should foist any large moral significance on thrillers dealing mostly with American small-town politics. But Hammett has a genius, and part of it lies in his ability to make corruption seem normal without ever quite endorsing it. His heroes have all undergone that brutalizing which Lawrence called 'the breaking of the heart'; and obscurely they know it. Hence the conventional barriers are down between the goodies and baddies. Those laconic, wise-cracking investigators may see all, know all, and handle themselves with startling confidence, but they are essentially no better, no worse, than the crooks they outwit. The narrator in *Red Harvest* becomes 'blood-simple'; Ned Beaumont, in *The Glass Key*, is an underworld figure, henchman of a political boss; Sam Spade in *The Maltese Falcon* and Nick Charles in *The Thin Man*, in their controlled, cynical, alcoholic ways, both qualify as psychopaths. All are liars when it suits them, all are indifferent to murder, all are marginally corrupt. They win out only because they are more able, more canny and, above all, more thorough-going with their contempt. Such toughness makes them seem impregnable, but it is also a burden. At moments, fatigue and distaste for themselves comes over them like a sickness. It is as though, the habitual violence pulled them psychically apart and they then had to reassemble themselves through booze and cunning and patience. You can sense Hammett's own illness through all that hard-boiled glitter.

It is his steady refusal to expect anything beyond the immediate, and usually rather nasty, situation, or to presume on any values anywhere, that makes for the curious distinction of his style: the wit, the flair for essential details, the suppressed, pared-down, indifferent clarity. His achievement is to have evolved a prose in which the most grotesque or shocking details are handled as though they were matters of routine, part of the job. Granted, Hemingway's simplicity was devoted to much the same end and was capable of far greater subtleties; but it was also a deeply literary device, almost dandified at times, something he had learned the hard way from Gertrude Stein. Hammett, too, was a writer of considerable deliberation and skill, but he made his taut style, like his ear for gangsterese, sound as though it were something he had come by in the grind of being a Pinkerton's agent. He seems less to have evolved his style than to have earned it.

Maybe this is what makes him so sympathetic. At the moment, the serious arts are faced with gloomy choices: either they are tense with despair at the confusion of all the values on which they were traditionally based, or they are anxiously—and suicidally—scrambling aboard the pop wagon. Dashiell Hammett, who had no cultural pretensions at all, provides a hard-minded alternative: his books have artistic concentrations without literariness, they achieve their purity from their absence of values. They are meticulous, witty, authentic and utterly nihilistic. It may not be high art, but it is a relief. —A. ALVAREZ, "Dashiell Hammett" (1966), *Beyond All This Fiddle*, 1968, 210–12

Hammett's style was, almost from the beginning, original: bone-dry, drained of colour, lacking delicacy but full of power, a perfect style for describing violent action without moral comment. It is true that at the beginning this was pretty well all he could do. As Richard Layman perceptively says, the "hard-boiled" fiction in *Black Mask* sprang from the naturalistic writing of Dreiser and Frank Norris, but "departed from naturalism in its lack of sympathy for people in the miserable, pitiful, and horrible circumstances it described". There is not much sympathy anywhere in Hammett, and most of the early stories are distinctive only in the style that he came to dislike near the end of his life. They are as stylistically original as the early Hemingway stories which they precede, but are bare, intricate bones of plot, lacking the flesh of human feeling. From *Red Harvest* onwards this is no longer true. All of the novels, even the inferior *The Dain Curse*, have their distinctive felicities, but most unusual are the sexual attractiveness of Dinah Brand in *Red Harvest*, conveyed through her big bloodshot blue eyes, uneven lipstick, coarseness and untidiness, and the emotional relationship between Ned Beaumont and Paul Madvig in *The Glass Key*, given in terms of what remains unsaid between them. Hammett's treatment of sex was also remarkably frank for the time. The most marked example of this is the question Nora asks Nick when he has tangled with Mimi Jorgensen: "When you were wrestling with Mimi, didn't you have an erection?" The question, and his answer, "Oh, a little", were omitted from the English edition. . . .

One returns to the puzzle of Hammett's reasons for giving up writing. Nunnally Johnson, who is mentioned in the biography as a drinking companion, but was apparently not consulted by Mr. Layman, is in no doubt about the answer:

> Hammett told me that he stopped writing because he saw no more reason to write when he not only had all the money he needed but was assured of all that he would ever need for the remainder of his life. This turned out to be a mistake, but it was a sound enough belief at the time. . . .
>
> Apparently there was nothing in writing that interested him but the money. . . . He had no impulse to tell any more stories, no ambition to accomplish more as a writer, no interest in keeping his name alive, or any other vanity about himself or his work. . . . If there is a precedent for a decision like this in a writer I have never heard of it . . . I can't tell you how awed I was and always have been by such astonishing resolution.

Well, it's an explanation, and one that echoes a remark made by a character in a Hammett screenplay: "I'm in the game for money. Sure, I'm always on the make." It is, however, contradicted by much that Hammett himself said and did. He wrote to Blanche Knopf when she accepted *Red Harvest* that he hoped to be the first person to make "literature" out of the detective story, and the revisions he made between magazine and book publications show how seriously he took what he was doing. In one of his few public critical pronouncements he praised the virtues of directness and literal accuracy: "The contemporary novelist's job is to take pieces of life and arrange them on paper", and the less ornament they contained the better. There are several indications that he had a bitter knowledge of his failing talent, like the speech he wrote for a play of Hellman's, where a retired General speaks of the turning point, the moment when you can "do the work you've never done, think the way you'd never thought, have what you've never had", and says that you either train for that moment or fritter yourself away. "I've frittered myself away." He let his publishers announce new books, books which would not be crime stories, but so far as is known never got beyond providing titles for them. There is a first draft of *The Thin Man*, the sixty-odd pages of which suggest a more interesting, less flippant book than the one Hammett wrote. His last attempt at fiction, "Tulip", is a fragment of 12,500 words, abandoned in 1952 or 1953, and he must have recognized that it was a piece of sub-Hemingway writing. The last words are neatly symbolic: "If you are tired you ought to rest, I think, and not try to fool yourself and your customers with colored bubbles."

Hammett was a man who never fooled himself, although he sometimes kidded other people. Probably it would be true to say that he gave up writing partly because he felt his talent had gone, partly because he had a strong impulse towards self-destruction, partly because for a long time he didn't need the money. But while he was writing he recognized, like Chandler and Macdonald, that if you want the crime story to be taken seriously, you must yourself be serious about what you are doing. Given an original talent plus that essential seriousness, you can afford a reasonable ration of guns and gangsters, obscure motives and bloody murders, and still produce something that can stake a claim to be called art.—JULIAN SYMONS, "The Tough Guy at the Typewriter," *TLS*, June 5, 1981, pp. 619–20

Works

Red Harvest takes us to America . . . and to an almost inconceivable world. The English novelist who wants to write a story of peril and adventure has to go some distance from ordinary life. The municipal troubles of a small town would be of no service to him. The American novelist is luckier, for he can take the train from New York or Chicago and, if Mr. Hammett is to be believed, find mediæval violence and uncertainty co-existent with a good tram service. . . . ⟨T⟩he mere fact that an author of obvious intelligence can write such a tale and persuade an American publisher to print it throws a valuable light on American conditions. If there is anywhere on the American continent remotely like Personville, then it is a sociological phenomenon which we must take into our reckoning, and I cannot believe that Mr. Hammett has made up Personville purely out of his desire to have a background for sensational happenings.—UNSIGNED, "New Novels," *NS*, July 27, 1929, p. 500

Until the coming of Mr. Dashiell Hammett in *Red Harvest*, and now in *The Maltese Falcon*, the memorable detectives were gentlemen. The ever-delightful M. Lecoq and his copy, Mr. Sherlock Holmes, are fair gods against the gnomes. Their only worthy successor, Father Brown, is a priest. Scratch every other detective and you'll find a M. Lecoq. Now comes Mr.

Hammett's tough guy in *Red Harvest* and his Sam Spade in *The Maltese Falcon*, and you find the Pinkerton operative as a scoundrel without pity or remorse, taking his whiffs of drink and his casual amours between catching crooks, treating the police with a cynical contempt, always getting his crook by foul and fearless means, above the law like a satyr—and Mr. Hammett describing his deeds in a glistening and fascinating prose as "American" as Lardner's, and every bit as original in musical rhythm and bawdy humor.

There is nothing like these books in the whole range of detective fiction. The plots don't matter so much. The art does; and there is an absolute distinction of real art. It is (in its small way) like Wagner writing about the gnomes in *Rheingold*. The gnomes have an eloquence of speech and a fascinating mystery of disclosure. Don't get me wrong, bo. It's not the tawdry gum-shoeing of the ten-cent magazine. It is the genuine presence of the myth. The *events* of *The Maltese Falcon* may have happened that way in "real" life. No one save Mr. Hammett could have woven them to such a silver-steely mesh.—DONALD DOUGLAS, "Not One Hoot for the Law," *NR*, April 9, 1930, p. 226

It is true that Mr. Hammett displays that touch of rare genius in his selection of undistinguished titles for his mystery stories—*The Maltese Falcon* and *The Glass Key*, his new one, sound like something by Carolyn Wells. It is true that had the literary lads got past those names and cracked the pages, they would have found the plots to be so many nuisances; confusing to madness, as in *Red Harvest*; fanciful to nausea, as in *The Maltese Falcon*; or, as in the case of the newly-published *The Glass Key*, so tired that even this reviewer, who in infancy was let drop by a nurse with the result that she has ever since been mystified by amateur coin-tricks, was able to guess the identity of the murderer from the middle of the book. It is true that he has all the mannerisms of Hemingway, with no inch of Hemingway's scope nor flicker of Hemingway's beauty. It is true that when he seeks to set down a swift, assured, well-bred young woman, he devises speeches for her such as are only equalled by the talk Mr. Theodore Dreiser compiled for his society flapper in *An American Tragedy*. It is true that he is so hard-boiled you could roll him on the White House lawn. And it is also true that he is a good, hell-bent, cold-hearted writer, with a clear eye for the ways of hard women and a fine ear for the words of hard men, and his books are exciting and powerful and—if I may filch the word from the booksy ones—pulsing. It is difficult to conclude an outburst like this. All I can say is that anybody who doesn't read him misses much of modern America. And hot that sounds!

Dashiell Hammett is as American as a sawed-off shotgun. He is as immediate as a special extra. Brutal he is, but his brutality, for what he must write, is clean and necessary, and there is in his work none of the smirking and swaggering savageries of a Hecht or a Bodenheim. He does his readers the infinite courtesy of allowing them to supply descriptions and analyses for themselves. He sets down only what his characters say, and what they do. It is not, I suppose, any too safe a recipe for those who cannot create characters; but Dashiell Hammett can and does and has and, I hope, will. On gentle ladies he is, in a word, rotten; but maybe sometime he will do a novel without a mystery plot, and so no doggy girls need come into it. But it is denied us who read to have everything, and it is little enough to let him have his ladies and his mysteries, if he will give us such characters as Sam Spade, in *The Maltese Falcon*, and such scenes as the beating-up of Ned Beaumont in *The Glass Key*.—DOROTHY PARKER (as "Constant Reader"), "Oh, Look—Two Good Books!," *NY*, April 25, 1931, p. 91

STEVEN MARCUS
From "Introduction"
The Continental Op by Dashiell Hammett
1974, pp. xv–xxix

I was first introduced to Dashiell Hammett by Humphrey Bogart. I was twelve years old at the time, and mention the occasion because I take it to be exemplary, that I share this experience with countless others. (Earlier than this, at the very dawn of consciousness, I can recall William Powell and Myrna Loy and a small dog on a leash and an audience full of adults laughing; but that had nothing to do with Hammett or anything else as far as I was concerned.) What was striking about the event was that it was one of the first encounters I can consciously recall with the experience of moral ambiguity. Here was this detective you were supposed to like—and did like—behaving and speaking in peculiar and unexpected ways. He acted up to the cops, partly for real, partly as a ruse. He connived with crooks, for his own ends and perhaps even for some of theirs. He slept with his partner's wife, fell in love with a lady crook, and then refused to save her from the police, even though he could have. Which side was he on? Was he on any side apart from his own? And which or what side was that? The experience was not only morally ambiguous; it was morally complex and enigmatic as well. The impression it made was a lasting one.

Years later, after having read *The Maltese Falcon* and seen the movie again and then reread the novel, I could begin to understand why the impact of the film had been so memorable, much more so than that of most other movies. The director, John Huston, had had the wit to recognize the power, sharpness, integrity, and bite of Hammett's prose—particularly the dialogue—and the film script consists almost entirely of speech taken directly and without modification from the written novel. Moreover, this unusual situation is complicated still further. In selecting with notable intelligence the relevant scenes and passages from the novel, Huston had to make certain omissions. Paradoxically, however, one of the things that he chose to omit was the most important or central moment in the entire novel. It is also one of the central moments in all of Hammett's writing. I think we can make use of this oddly "lost" passage as a means of entry into Hammett's vision or imagination of the world.

It occurs as Spade is becoming involved with Brigid O'Shaughnessy in her struggle with the other thieves, and it is his way of communicating to her his sense of how the world and life go. His way is to tell her a story from his own experience. The form this story takes is that of a parable. It is a parable about a man named Flitcraft. Flitcraft was a successful, happily married, stable, and utterly respectable real-estate dealer in Tacoma. One day he went out to lunch and never returned. No reason could be found for his disappearance, and no account of it could be made. "'He went like that,' Spade said, 'like a fist when you open your hand.'"

Five years later Mrs. Flitcraft came to the agency at which Spade was working and told them that "'she had seen a man in Spokane who looked a lot like her husband.'" Spade went off to investigate and found that it was indeed Flitcraft. He had been living in Spokane for a couple of years under the name of Charles Pierce. He had a successful automobile business, a wife, a baby son, a suburban home, and usually played golf after four in the afternoon, just as he had in Tacoma. Spade and he sat down to talk the matter over. Flitcraft, Spade recounts, "had no feeling of guilt. He had left his family well provided for, and what he had done seemed to him perfectly reasonable. The only thing that bothered him was a doubt that he could make that reasonableness clear" to his interlocutor. When Flitcraft went out to lunch that day five years before in Tacoma, "'he passed an office-building that was being put up. . . . A beam or something fell eight or ten stories down and smacked the sidewalk alongside him.'" A chip of smashed sidewalk flew up and took a piece of skin off his cheek. He was otherwise unharmed. He stood there "'scared stiff,'" he told Spade, "'but he was more shocked than really frightened. He felt like somebody had taken the lid off life and let him look at the works.'"

Until that very moment Flitcraft had been "'a good citizen and a good husband and father, not by any outer compulsion, but simply because he was a man who was most comfortable in step with his surroundings. . . . The life he knew was a clean orderly sane responsible affair. Now a falling beam had shown him that life was fundamentally none of these things. . . . What disturbed him was the discovery that in sensibly ordering his affairs he had got out of step, and not into step, with life.'" By the time he had finished lunch, he had reached the decision "'that he would change his life at random by simply going away.'" He went off that afternoon, wandered around for a couple of years, then drifted back to the Northwest, "'settled in Spokane and got married. His second wife didn't look like the first, but they were more alike than they were different.'" And the same held true of his second life. Spade then moves on to his conclusion: "'He wasn't sorry for what he had done. It seemed reasonable enough to him. I don't think he even knew he had settled back into the same groove that he had jumped out of in Tacoma. But that's the part of it I always liked. He adjusted himself to beams falling, and then no more of them fell, and he adjusted himself to their not falling.'" End of parable. Brigid of course understands nothing of this, as Spade doubtless knew beforehand. Yet what he has been telling her has to do with the forces and beliefs and contingencies that guide his conduct and supply a structure to his apparently enigmatic behavior.

To begin with, we may note that such a sustained passage is not the kind of thing we ordinarily expect in a detective story or novel about crime. That it is there, and that comparable passages occur in all of Hammett's best work, clearly suggests the kind of transformation that Hammett was performing on this popular genre of writing. The transformation was in the direction of literature. And what the passage in question is about among other things is the ethical irrationality of existence, the ethical unintelligibility of the world. For Flitcraft the falling beam "had taken the lid off life and let him look at the works." The works are that life is inscrutable, opaque, irresponsible, and arbitrary—that human existence does not correspond in its actuality to the way we live it. For most of us live as if existence itself were ordered, ethical, and rational. As a direct result of his realization in experience that it is not, Flitcraft leaves his wife and children and goes off. He acts irrationally and at random, in accordance with the nature of existence. When after a couple of years of wandering aimlessly about he decides to establish a new life, he simply reproduces the old one he had supposedly repudiated and abandoned; that is to say, he behaves again as if life were orderly, meaningful, and rational, and "adjusts" to it. And this, with fine irony, is the part of it, Spade says, that he "'always liked,'" which means the part that he liked best. For here we come upon the unfathomable and most mysteriously irrational part of it all—how despite everything we have learned and everything we know, men will persist in behaving and trying to behave sanely, rationally, sensibly, and responsibly. And we will continue to persist even when we know that there is no logical or metaphysical, no discoverable or demonstrable reason for doing so.[1] It is this sense of sustained contradiction that is close to the center—or to one of the centers—of Hammett's work. The contradiction is not ethical alone; it is metaphysical as well. And it is not merely sustained; it is sustained with pleasure. For Hammett and Spade and the Op, the sustainment in consciousness of such contradictions is an indispensable part of their existence and of their pleasure in that existence.

That this pleasure is itself complex, ambiguous, and problematic becomes apparent as one simply describes the conditions under which it exists. And the complexity, ambiguity, and sense of the problematical are not confined to such moments of "revelation"—or set pieces—as the parable of Flitcraft. They permeate Hammett's work and act as formative elements in its structure, including its deep structure. Hammett's work went through considerable and interesting development in the course of his career for twelve years as a writer. He also wrote in a considerable variety of forms and worked out a variety of narrative devices and strategies. At the same time, his work considered as a whole reveals a remarkable kind of coherence. In order to further the understanding of that coherence, we can propose for the purposes of the present analysis to construct a kind of "ideal type" of a Hammett or Op story. Which is not to say or to imply in the least that he wrote according to a formula, but that an authentic imaginative vision lay beneath and informed the structure of his work.

Such an ideal-typical description runs as follows. The Op is called in or sent out on a case. Something has been stolen, someone is missing, some dire circumstance is impending, someone has been murdered—it doesn't matter. The Op interviews the person or persons most immediately accessible. They may be innocent or guilty—it doesn't matter; it is an indifferent circumstance. Guilty or innocent, they provide the Op with an account of what they know, of what they assert really happened. The Op begins to investigate; he compares these accounts with others that he gathers; he snoops about; he does research; he shadows people, arranges confrontations between those who want to avoid one another, and so on. What he soon discovers is that the "reality" that anyone involved will swear to is in fact itself a construction, a fabrication, a fiction, a faked and alternate reality—and that it has been gotten together before he ever arrived on the scene. And the Op's work therefore is to deconstruct, decompose, deplot and defictionalize that "reality" and to construct or reconstruct out of it a true fiction, i.e., an account of what "really" happened.

It should be quite evident that there is a reflexive and coordinate relation between the activities of the Op and the activities of Hammett, the writer. Yet the depth and problematic character of this self-reflexive process begin to be revealed when we observe that the reconstruction or true fiction created and arrived at by the Op at the end of the story is no more plausible—nor is it meant to be—than the stories that have been told to him by all parties, guilty or innocent, in the course of his work. The Op may catch the real thief or collar the actual crook—that is not entirely to the point. What is to the point is that the story, account, or chain of events that the Op winds up with as "reality" is no more plausible and no less ambiguous than the stories that he meets with at the outset and later. What Hammett has done—unlike most writers of detective or crime stories before him or since—is to include as part of the contingent and dramatic consciousness of his narrative the circumstance that the work of the detective is itself a fiction-making activity, a discovery or creation by fabrication of something new in the world, or hidden, latent, potential, or as yet undeveloped within it. The typical "classical" detective story—unlike Hammett's—can be described as a formal game with certain specified rules of transformation. What ordinarily happens is that the detective is faced with a situation of inadequate, false, misleading, and ambiguous information. And the story as a whole is an exercise in disambiguation—with the final scenes being a ratiocinative demonstration that the butler did it (or not); these scenes achieve a conclusive, reassuring clarity of explanation, wherein everything is set straight, and the game we have been party to is brought to its appropriate end. But this, as we have already seen, is not what ordinarily happens in Hammett or with the Op.

What happens is that the Op almost invariably walks into a situation that has already been elaborately fabricated or framed. And his characteristic response to his sense that he is dealing with a series of deceptions or fictions is—to use the words that he uses himself repeatedly—"to stir things up." This corresponds integrally, both as metaphor and in logical structure, to what happened in the parable of Flitcraft. When the falling beam just misses Flitcraft, "he felt like somebody had taken the lid off life." The Op lives with the uninterrupted awareness that for him the lid has been taken off life. When the lid has been lifted, the logical thing to do is to "stir things up"—which is what he does.[2] He actively undertakes to deconstruct, decompose, and thus demystify the fictional—and therefore false—reality created by the characters, crooks or not, with whom he is involved. More often than not he tries to substitute his own fictional-hypothetical representation for theirs—and this representation may also be "true" or mistaken, or both at once. In any event, his major effort is to make the fictions of others visible as fictions, inventions, concealments, falsehoods, and mystifications. When a fiction becomes visible as such, it begins to dissolve and disappear, and presumably should reveal behind it the "real" reality that was there all the time and that it was masking. Yet what happens in Hammett is that what is revealed as "reality" is a still further fiction-masking activity—in the first place the Op's, and behind that yet another, the consciousness present in many of the Op stories and all the novels that Dashiell Hammett, the writer, is continually doing the same thing as the Op and all the other characters in the fiction he is creating. That is to say, he is making a fiction (in writing) in the real world; and this fiction, like the real world itself, is coherent but not necessarily rational. What one both begins and ends with, then, is a story, a narrative, a coherent yet questionable account of the world. This problematic penetrates to the bottom of Hammett's narrative imagination and shapes a number of its deeper processes—in *The Dain Curse*, for example, it is the chief topic of explicit debate that runs throughout the entire novel.

Yet Hammett's writing is still more complex and integral than this. For the unresolvable paradoxes and dilemmas that we have just been describing in terms of narrative structure and consciousness are reproduced once again in Hammett's vision and representation of society, of the social world in which the Op lives. At this point we must recall that Hammett is a writer of the 1920's and that this was the era of Prohibition. American society had in effect committed itself to a vast collective fiction. Even more, this fiction was false not merely in the sense that it was made up or did not in fact correspond to reality; it was false in the sense that it was corrupt and corrupting as well. During this period every time an American took a drink he was helping to undermine the law, and American society had covertly committed itself to what was in practice collaborative illegality.[3] There is a kind of epiphany of these circumstances in "The Golden Horseshoe." The Op is on a case that takes him to Tijuana. In a bar there, he reads a sign:

ONLY GENUINE PRE-WAR AMERICAN AND
BRITISH WHISKEYS SERVED HERE

He responds by remarking that "I was trying to count how many lies could be found in those nine words, and had reached four, with promise of more," when he is interrupted by some call to action. That sign and the Op's response to it describe part of the existential character of the social world represented by Hammett.

Another part of that representation is expressed in another kind of story or idea that Hammett returned to repeatedly. The twenties were also the great period of organized crime and organized criminal gangs in America, and one of Hammett's obsessive imaginations was the notion of organized crime or gangs taking over an entire society and running it as if it were an ordinary society doing business as usual. In other words, society itself would become a fiction, concealing and belying the actuality of what was controlling it and perverting it from within. One can thus make out quite early in this native American writer a proto-Marxist critical representation of how a certain kind of society works. Actually, the point of view is pre- rather than proto-Marxist, and the social world as it is dramatized in many of these stories is Hobbesian rather than Marxist.[4] It is a world of universal warfare, the war of each against all, and of all against all. The only thing that prevents the criminal ascendancy from turning into permanent tyranny is that the crooks who take over society cannot cooperate with one another, repeatedly fall out with each other, and return to the Hobbesian anarchy out of which they have momentarily arisen. The social world as imagined by Hammett runs on a principle that is the direct opposite of that postulated by Erik Erikson as the fundamental and enabling condition for human existence. In Hammett, society and social relations are dominated by the principle of basic mistrust. As one of his detectives remarks, speaking for himself and for virtually every other character in Hammett's writing, "I trust no one."

When Hammett turns to the respectable world, the world of respectable society, of affluence and influence, of open personal and political power, he finds only more of the same. The respectability of respectable American society is as much a fiction and a fraud as the phony respectable society fabricated by the criminals. Indeed, he unwaveringly represents the world of crime as a reproduction in both structure and detail of the modern capitalist society that it depends on, preys off, and is part of. But Hammett does something even more radical than this. He not only continually juxtaposes and connects the ambiguously fictional worlds of art and of writing with the fraudulently fictional worlds of society; he connects them, juxtaposes them, and sees them in dizzying and baffling interaction. He does this in many ways and on many occasions. One of them, for example, is the Maltese Falcon itself, which turns out to be and contains within itself the history of capitalism. It is originally a piece of plunder, part of what Marx called the "primitive accumulation"; when its gold encrusted with gems is painted over, it becomes a mystified object, a commodity itself; it is a piece of property that belongs to no one—whoever possesses it does not really own it. At the same time it is another fiction, a representation or work of art—which turns out itself to be a fake, since it is made of lead. It is a *rara avis* indeed. As is the fiction in which it is created and contained, the novel by Hammett.

It is into this bottomlessly equivocal, endlessly fraudulent, and brutally acquisitive world that Hammett precipitates the Op. There is nothing glamorous about him. Short, thick-set, balding, between thirty-five and forty, he has no name, no home, no personal existence apart from his work. He is, and he regards himself as, "the hired man" of official and respectable society, who is paid so much per day to clean it up and rescue it from the crooks and thieves who are perpetually threatening to take it over. Yet what he—and the reader—just as perpetually learn is that the respectable society that employs him is itself inveterately vicious, deceitful, culpable, crooked, and degraded. How then is the Op to be preserved, to preserve itself, from being contaminated by both the world he works against and the world he is hired to work for?

To begin with, the Op lives by a code. This code consists in the first instance of the rules laid down by the Continental Agency, and they are "rather strict." The most important of them by far is that no operative in the employ of the Agency is ever allowed to take or collect part of a reward that may be attached to the solution of a case. Since he cannot directly enrich himself through his professional skills, he is saved from at least the characteristic corruption of modern society—the corruption that is connected with its fundamental acquisitive structure. At the same time, the Op is a special case of the Protestant ethic, for his entire existence is bound up in and expressed by his work, his vocation. He likes his work, and it is honest work, done as much for enjoyment and the exercise of his skills and abilities as it is for personal gain and self-sustainment. The work is something of an end in itself, and this circumstance also serves to protect him, as does his deliberate refusal to use high-class and fancy moral language about anything. The work is an end in itself and is therefore something more than work alone. As Spade says, in a passage that is the culmination of many such passages in Hammett:

> "I'm a detective and expecting me to run criminals down and then let them go free is like asking a dog to catch a rabbit and let it go. It can be done, all right, and sometimes it is done, but it's not the natural thing."

Being a detective, then, entails more than fulfilling a social function or performing a social role. Being a detective is the realization of an identity, for there are components in it which are beyond or beneath society—and cannot be touched by it—and beyond and beneath reason. There is something "natural" about it. Yet if we recall that the nature thus being expressed is that of a man-hunter, and Hammett's apt metaphor compels us to do so, and that the state of society as it is represented in Hammett's writing reminds us of the state of nature in Hobbes, we see that even here Hammett does not release his sense of the complex and the contradictory, and is making no simple-minded appeal to some benign idea of the "natural."

And indeed the Op is not finally or fully protected by his work, his job, his vocation. (We have all had to relearn with bitterness what multitudes of wickedness "doing one's job" can cover). Max Weber has memorably remarked that "the decisive means for politics is violence." In Hammett's depiction of modern American society, violence is the decisive means indeed, along with fraud, deceit, treachery, betrayal, and general, endemic unscrupulousness. Such means are in no sense alien to Hammett's detective. As the Op says, "'detecting is a hard business, and you use whatever tools come to hand.'" In other words, there is a paradoxical tension and unceasing interplay in Hammett's stories between means and ends; relations between the two are never secure or stable. And as Max Weber further remarked, in his great essay "Politics as a Vocation": "the world is governed by demons, and he who lets himself in for . . . power and force as means, contracts with diabolic powers, and for his action it is *not* true that good can follow only from good and evil only from evil, but that often the opposite is true. Anyone who fails to see this is, indeed, a political infant." Neither Hammett nor the Op is an infant; yet no one can be so grown up and inured to experience that he can escape the consequences that attach to the deliberate use of violent and dubious means.

These consequences are of various orders. "Good" ends themselves can be transformed and perverted by the use of vicious or indiscriminate means (I am leaving to one side those even more perplexing instances in Hammett in which the ends pursued by the Op correspond with ends desired by a corrupted yet respectable official society.) The consequences are also visible inwardly, on the inner being of the agent of such means, the Op himself. The violence begins to get to him:

> I began to throw my right fist into him.
> I liked that. His belly was flabby, and it got softer every time I hit it. I hit it often.

Another side of this set of irresolvable moral predicaments is revealed when we see that the Op's toughness is not merely a carapace within which feelings of tenderness and humanity can be nourished and preserved. The toughness is toughness through and through, and as the Op continues his career, and continues to live by the means he does, he tends to become more callous and less and less able to feel. At the very end, awaiting him, he knows, is the prospect of becoming like his boss, the head of the Agency, the Old Man, "with his gentle eyes behind gold spectacles and his mild smile, hiding the fact that fifty years of sleuthing had left him without any feelings at all on any subject." This is the price exacted by the use of such means in such a world; these are the consequences of living fully in a society moved by the principle of basic mistrust. "Whoever fights monsters," writes Nietzsche, "should see to it that in the process he does not become a monster. And when you look long into an abyss, the abyss also looks into you." The abyss looks into Hammett, the Old Man, and the Op.

It is through such complex devices as I have merely sketched here that Hammett was able to raise the crime story into literature. He did it over a period of ten years. Yet the strain was finally too much to bear—that shifting, entangled, and equilibrated state of contradictions out of which his creativity arose and which it expressed could no longer be sustained. His creative career ends when he is no longer able to handle the literary, social, and moral opacities, instabilities, and contradictions that characterize all his best work. His life then splits apart and goes in the two opposite directions that were implicit in his earlier, creative phase, but that the creativity held suspended and in poised yet fluid tension. His politics go in one direction; the way he made his living went in another—he became a hack writer, and then finally no writer at all. That is another story. Yet for ten years he was able to do what almost no other writer in this genre has ever done so well—he was able to really write, to construct a vision of a world in words, to know that the writing was about the real world and referred to it and was part of it; and at the same time he was able to be self-consciously aware that the whole thing was problematical and about itself and "only" writing as well. For ten years, in other words, he was a true creator of fiction.

Notes

1. It can hardly be an accident that the new name that Hammett gives to Flitcraft is that of an American philosopher—with two vowels reversed—who was deeply involved in just such speculations.
2. These homely metaphors go deep into Hammett's life. One of the few things that he could recall from his childhood past was his

mother's repeated advice that a woman who wasn't good in the kitchen wasn't likely to be much good in any other room in the house.

3. Matters were even murkier than this. The Eighteenth Amendment to the Constitution was in effect from January 1920 to December 1933, nearly fourteen years. During this period Americans were forbidden under penalty of law to manufacture, sell, or transport any intoxicating liquor. At the same time no one was forbidden to buy or drink such liquor. In other words, Americans were virtually being solicited by their own laws to support an illegal trade in liquor, even while Congress was passing the Volstead Act, which was intended to prevent such a trade.
4. Again it can hardly be regarded as an accident that the name Hammett gives to the town taken over by the criminals in *Red Harvest* is "Personville"—pronounced "Poisonville." And what else is Personville except Leviathan, the "artificial man" represented by Hobbes as the image of society itself.

JOHN G. CAWELTI

From "Hammett, Chandler, and Spillane"
Adventure, Mystery, and Romance
1976, pp. 163–66

Chandler's insistence that Hammett is primarily a "realist in murder" must be seen in its context as a defense of the hard-boiled story against the classical genre of complex puzzles and clues. The main ground of Chandler's defense is that the classical story lost contact with reality in its development of intriguing and mystifying puzzles solved by a gentlemanly amateur detective whom, as Chandler puts it, "the English police seem to endure . . . with their customary stoicism; but I shudder to think of what the boys down at the Homicide Bureau in my city would do to him."[1] But is it really the case that a Hammett novel like *The Maltese Falcon*, which revolves around a mysterious age-old treasure, eccentric villains, and complex webs of intrigue, is more "realistic" than the detective novels of Dorothy Sayers with their ordinary settings, their relatively plausible motivations, and their rich texture of manners and local color? Such an assertion surely exemplifies that American literary tendency to identify the "real" with the violent, the sordid, and the brutal aspects of life. As Lionel Trilling points out in his analysis of this tendency in Theodore Dreiser and Vernon Parrington, such an identification can be just as arbitrary and limited a view of "reality" as the more philosophical or genteel perspectives it set out to attack.[2] If one approaches the Hammett canon without accepting the premise that toughness and violence are supremely real, the fantastic nature of most of his stories becomes clear. The Continental Op creates and controls a revolution in a mysterious Balkan country in a story tougher in style but no more plausible in incident than the popular Graustarkian romances of the early twentieth century. A criminal genius named Pappadoupolous (but clearly a Hammett version of Doyle's Professor Moriarty) brings an army of gangsters to San Francisco, pulls off a bank robbery that involves a pitched battle with the entire city police force, and then succeeds in killing off the great majority of his henchmen before he is finally brought to bay by the Op. The Op becomes involved in the tangled affairs of the Leggett family, which are so bizarre that they even involve a family curse. In one of the climactic moments of this story the Op confronts a maddened prophet who is about to sacrifice the heroine on the altar of his temple, a setting as gothic as anything out of *The Mysteries of Udolpho*. To say that such characters, actions, and settings are more realistic than the advertising agencies, country villages, or university quadrangles of Dorothy Sayers cannot withstand serious scrutiny.

Far from being a straightforward realist who rescued the detective story from sterile littérateurs and gave it back to the actual world, Hammett was an extremely literary writer. His work shows both an awareness of earlier literary models and a continual interest in such literary effects as irony and paradox. One of his earliest published works, "Memoirs of a Private Detective," though based on Hammett's own experiences as a Pinkerton operative, implies a perspective shaped as much by the elegant, fin-de-siècle cynicism of writers like Ambrose Bierce as by the direct perception of life. Though Hammett probably had more practical experiences as a detective than any other writer of mystery novels, his presentation of his own career takes the form of brief, delicately turned paradoxes that have a flavor something between *The Devil's Dictionary* and an O. Henry story.

> Wishing to get some information from members of the W.C.T.U. in an Oregon city, I introduced myself as the secretary of the Butte City Purity League. One of them read me a long discourse on the erotic effects of cigarettes upon young girls. Subsequent experiments proved this trip worthless.[3]

As he developed as a writer, Hammett lost some of the aroma of the *décadence*, not so much because his attention focused more directly on life, but because his literary models changed. Hammett's early stories grew directly out of the pulp tradition and many of them, like *Red Harvest*, resemble westerns as much as they do detective stories. Even at this time Hammett occasionally experimented with the transformation of other traditional literary types into his own hard-boiled mode. This became a standard practice in his later novels. Thus, *The Dain Curse* makes use of a wide variety of gothic traditions—the family curse, the mysterious temple with its secret passages and ghosts, religious maniacs, the tragedy on the beetling cliffs—while *The Maltese Falcon* reflects the great tradition of stories of hidden treasure like "The Gold-Bug" and *Treasure Island* with Cairo and Gutman playing the role of Long John Silver. *The Thin Man* embodies a more contemporaneous literary tradition, the novel of high society and urban sophistication. The quality of its dialogue, setting, and general tone of breezy hauteur suggests that it was at least partly modeled on the novels and stories of F. Scott Fitzgerald.

In part Hammett may have felt that his employment of the hard-boiled detective in stories that owed so much to established literary traditions added respectability and dignity to the saga of the tough-guy hero in such a way as to make his adventures more acceptable to a cultivated, middle-class reading public. It would not be the first time that a pulp writer had tried to add tone to his creations by wrapping them in a literary toga. Hammett's contemporary Max Brand (Frederick Faust) even went so far as to construct an entire western called *Hired Guns* using the plot and characters of the *Iliad* in cowboy costumes (a ten-year range war between two families that started in an argument over a young lady named Ellen). But this is only part of the story. Hammett's use of these traditional literary materials is more often ironic than straightforward, satirical rather than serious. Hammett continually builds up conventional literary moods and then punctures them with the flat, rasping cynicism of the private eye who has seen it all before and knows it is phony. In the famous climax of *The Maltese Falcon*, Sam Spade unmasks Brigid O'Shaughnessy as the killer, accusing her of having used him to save her neck. Brigid, however, still hopes to capitalize on the romance that has grown up between the two:

> "Yes, but—oh, sweetheart!—it wasn't only that. I would have come back to you sooner or later. From the first instant I saw you I knew—"

> Spade said tenderly: "You angel! Well, if you get a good break you'll be out of San Quentin in twenty years and you can come back to me then." She took her cheek away from his, drawing her head far back to stare up without comprehension at him. He was pale. He said tenderly: "I hope to God they don't hang you, precious, by that sweet neck." He slid his hands up to caress her throat.[4]

Sam's flat refusal—"I won't play the sap for you"—shatters the world of romantic illusion that Brigid has woven about the attraction between herself and Sam and dissipates the haze of dashing adventure with which she has cloaked the sordid reality of her pursuit of the falcon. This sort of ironic contrast between romantic fantasies and real violence and ugliness permeates *The Maltese Falcon* as it does much of Hammett's work. We see it in the way Cairo and Gutman's exotic elegance has an underside of petty and sordid ruthlessness, or in the way Spade refuses to accept any of the noble motives that various characters seek to ascribe to him; for example, though Sam insists on tracking down the killer of his partner, Miles Archer, he makes it clear that he does so not out of affection or loyalty, but as a matter of good business: "When one of your organization gets killed it's bad business to let the killer get away with it. It's bad all around—bad for that one organization, bad for every detective everywhere." Perhaps, most powerfully of all, Hammett's pervasively flat, hard-edged, and laconic vernacular style with its denial of the lyrical effects cultivated by vernacular stylists like Hemingway or, in a different way, by Hammett's fellow hard-boiled writer Raymond Chandler, runs against the breathless excitement of his stories. Even the most fantastic episodes retain the solid, cold, slightly tired tone in which Hammett's detectives narrate their adventures. Everything is calmly weighed and measured:

> It was a diamond all right, shining in the grass half a dozen feet from the blue brick walk. It was small, not more than a quarter of a carat in weight, and unmounted. I put it in my pocket and began searching the lawn as closely as I could without going at it on all fours.[5]
>
> He came in, looking and acting as if I were St. Peter letting him into Heaven. I closed the door and led him through the lobby, down the main corridor. So far as we could see we had the joint to ourselves. And then we didn't. Gabrielle Leggett came around a corner just ahead of us. She was barefooted. Her only clothing was a yellow silk nightgown that was splashed with dark stains. In both hands, held out in front of her as she walked, she carried a large dagger, almost a sword. It was red and wet. Her hands and bare arms were red and wet. There was a dab of blood on one of her cheeks. Her eyes were clear, bright, and calm. Her small forehead was smooth, her mouth and chin firmly set. She walked up to me, her untroubled gaze holding my probably troubled one, and said evenly, just as if she had expected to find me there, had come there to find me: "Take it. It is evidence. I killed him."
>
> I said: "Huh?"[6]

The stylistic combination that these passages exemplify—utterly fantastic incidents described in nearly emotionless, lucidly descriptive vernacular prose—has a surrealistic flavor, like those paintings by Dali where flaming giraffes and melting watches are rendered with the most carefully drawn "realistic" detail. This interweaving of flat realism and wild fantasy seems to grow out of Hammett's basic sense of life: the vision of an irrational cosmos, in which all the rules, all the seeming solidity of matter, routine, and custom can be overturned in a moment, pervades his work from beginning to end.

Notes

1. Raymond Chandler, "The Simple Art of Murder," in Haycraft, ed., *The Art of the Mystery Story* (New York: Simon & Schuster, 1946), p. 234.
2. Lionel Trilling, "Reality in America," in *The Liberal Imagination* (Garden City, N.Y.: Doubleday Anchor Books, 1953).
3. Quoted in Haycraft, p. 417.
4. Dashiell Hammett, *The Maltese Falcon* (New York: Perma Books, 1957), p. 173.
5. Dashiell Hammett, *The Dain Curse* (New York: Perma Books, 1961), p. 3.
6. Ibid., p. 72.

DIANE JOHNSON

From *Dashiell Hammett: A Life*

1983, pp. xviii–xx, 37–38

Introduction

The question of paternity is central to Hammett's work. This theme, or issue, involves the conflict between generations, identity, the handing down of skill and wisdom, the usurpation of authority, the transfer of power. In some of his early stories, set in the tuberculosis hospital where Hammett was sent after his military service, a young, powerless soldier ("I" or "Slim") joins others in defying or combating figures of authority—doctors or orderlies—and in situations where they cannot win they drift off like yearlings from a herd. Hammett's first detective, the Op, is as plump and nameless as a newborn; he exists only in relation to a powerful father, the Old Man of the Continental Agency, whose rules are "rather strict" and who, like an implacable god, has "no feelings at all on any subject." And like the Old Man, other fathers in Hammett's early work prevail over sons; it may be the father who is sexually involved with a young woman, like Leopold Gantvoort in "The Tenth Claw"; or a father who is a sexual rival of his son. Most strangely—for it is a theme unusual in literature—the central crime in two of his novels, *The Glass Key* and *Red Harvest*, is the murder of a son by his father.

This vision of authority as evil and menacing also forms the basis of Hammett's politics and may even provide a clue to why he stopped writing—as an unconscious means of defying the fatherly editors who so enthusiastically fostered and championed him. His stories are dramatizations of conflict with authority born of the discovery that authority is flawed. Fathers are not gods; they kill; the law is corrupt; and the rich and powerful are the worst people.

Hammett was a Marxist, and this fact has encouraged various critics to identify his and other hard-boiled detective stories with Marxism (and sometimes fascism). It is true that *Red Harvest* can be seen as an indictment of capitalist society, but it presents no socialist program and no real idea of social change. The point is to describe the corruption and observe the protagonist in his attempt to make little temporary corrections for the sake of the endeavor, without much hope that they will endure, and to do this by the rules he makes up, which are not the rules of society.

Tough-guy politics might better be described as disillusioned populism. The methods adopted by the Op and others continue to appeal to us because they begin from a widespread perception of society and authority: "Available though it is to the appeal of patriotism during times of national crisis, much of the political sentiment of Americans remains crystallized in the image of little people, lost now without a party or a program. . . . The neopopulists' politics is that of frustration and a desire to set things right, at least temporarily, by any means, the simpler the better."[1] And so the Op retains his charm today. The more complex mutations of Hammett's hero into Spade, Ned Beaumont and Nick Charles arise from Hammett's personal history and dramatize his attitude to authority.

During his life, Dashiell Hammett was a popular figure, often identified with his creations. He was like the hero of a book—tall, handsome, talented and flamboyant, a former private eye turned writer and playboy. Eventually he was to be regarded as a political villain dedicated to the overthrow of the government, and he would finally lead the life of a forgotten and penniless recluse. During all these phases he was the same person, always his own man. But he was also the embodiment of certain contradictions and tensions typical of his generation and nationality, an individual, yet curiously typical too. His fascination for so many is perhaps like that of Humphrey Bogart, especially the Bogart as Spade, world-weary and unsurprised, a survivor.[2]

Like other men born in the nineteenth century within the traditions of the Catholic Church, Southern manhood and American patriotism, Hammett was heir to beliefs and values that, though they did not seem appropriate to the world he found, he believed in and could not abandon. To make sense of a contradictory world, he embodied the contradictions in his own life; his behavior was both virtuous and libertine. He was to be rich and poor; unfaithful while faithful; a patriotic Communist, an ascetic hedonist. All of these contradictions gave his life a certain fascination, and, even more, a certain familiarity. There was something peculiarly American about it that can be better presented perhaps than summarized. At each decade of his life he did the American thing—went West before World War I when young men went West, joined the army, went West again to San Francisco during the twenties and the heyday of gangsters and prohibition, went to Hollywood in the glamorous thirties, when Hollywood was at its peak, to war again in the forties, and in the fifties, during the witch-hunts, to jail. He presented himself gamely to history and bore its depredations cheerfully, for he had a strange and sweet nature and knew what the Continental Op knew when he woke up beside the dead body of Dinah Brand with an ice pick in his hand: no one is to be trusted, least of all yourself. . . .

1921–1923 Starting Out in San Francisco

In February 1922 he entered Munson's Business College, a secretarial school, to learn newspaper reporting. His tuition and a small stipend were paid by the Vocational Rehabilitation Bureau. He also managed to get a small sum for Jose and the baby. His negotiations with the Veterans Bureau became, as well as a necessity, an obsession.

At his sickest, in the hospital in Tacoma, Hammett had received $80 a month, which was reduced to $40 a month when he went to the convalescent hospital in San Diego. When he left the hospital, probably in May of 1921, he was given $20 a month, as though he were better; but "Maximum improvement achieved" wasn't the same as better—in fact, it implied he would never be better. Later the rehabilitation people had told him that though he was accepted in Vocational School, he wasn't well enough for Vocational School. The illogic, the indifference of this, infuriated him. Sitting in a lonely room in Seattle,[3] he wrote the Veterans Bureau, and he continued to do so after he and Jose had moved to Eddy Street. But he could not make the government see the unfairness that he saw: that he was now a sick person, likely to die, who had had wonderful plans and aims. The boy who took to the road at fourteen, veteran of stakeouts and mining camps and wide-open towns, must now lead the quiet and semi-invalid life of a secretarial student, would-be writer and advertising man—all pursuits that kept him indoors at his typewriter. Here he was, in a tiny, dingy apartment over bootleggers, with a new baby, a trustful little nurse wife, and no money. He was twenty-eight and would soon be thirty. He had the artist's indignation at the world's indifference, its inability to distinguish him from the other rowdy soldiers, the other little boys at the blacking factory. He, this precious I, this distinct, perceptive being. Like Dickens' complaints, years after he had worked in the blacking factory, Hammett's injured tone creeps into his letters to indifferent bureaucrats, and sounds in his stories: "Paul left the post-office carrying his monthly compensation check, in its unmistakable narrow manila envelope with the mocking bold-faced instructions to postmasters should the addressee have died meanwhile."[4]

Loyal service got you nothing, not from the government, not from Pinkerton's. He would always hate the government, and people in authority. If you were faithful to the job you said you'd do for them, it was only because you had pride in your word and your work. This was the way he himself behaved, expecting nothing, and the way his fictional heroes would behave. They would expect nothing, would not be surprised at the indifference of the higher-ups to the private soldier, the miner, the member of the guild, the operative on his cold watch. And yet these lonely servants took pride in their lot to serve if the higher-ups were on the side of higher good. Hammett was in every sense an enlisted man. He knew better than to ask for anything in return. Yet if driven by need he would sometimes ask, and it was his fate that he would always be denied.

Notes

1. John M. Reilly, "The Politics of Tough Guy Mysteries," *University of Dayton Review*, vol. 10, 1973.
2. André Bazin, "Mort d'Humphrey Bogart," *Cahiers du Cinéma*, Février 1957, p. 81: *"quand il entre dans le film c'est déjà l'aube blême du lendemain, dérisoirement victorieux du macabre combat avec l'ange, le visage marqué par ce qu'il a vu et la démarche lourde de tout ce qu'il sait. Ayant dix fois triomphé de sa mort, il survivra bien sans doute pour nous une fois de plus."*
3. Hammett was presumably there for Pinkerton; he stayed at 1117 Third Avenue.
4. "Holiday," in *Woman in the Dark*. First published in *The New Pearsons*, July 1923, pp. 30–32.

AP/WIDE WORLD PHOTOS

Dashiell Hammett

AP/WIDE WORLD PHOTOS

A. B. Guthrie, Jr.

AP/WIDE WORLD PHOTOS

Marilyn Hacker

AP/WIDE WORLD PHOTOS

LORRAINE HANSBERRY

AP/WIDE WORLD PHOTOS

JOHN HAWKES

AP/WIDE WORLD PHOTOS

MARK HARRIS

Lorraine Hansberry

1930–1965

Born in Chicago, Illinois, on May 19, 1930, Lorraine Vivian Hansberry came from a well-to-do black family. Her father bought a house in a white neighborhood in 1938, and in spite of hostility fought his case all the way to the Supreme Court for the right to live there. Even after his death in 1946, prominent black artists and politicians were frequent guests. Hansberry studied art, English, and stage design at the University of Wisconsin, but left without a degree in 1950. Moving to New York later that year, she began to write full time for *Freedom* magazine in 1951. Her articles on Africa and on civil rights issues affecting blacks, women, and the poor, and her speeches to civil rights and other groups, made her a prominent young spokeswoman for progressive causes. After marrying Robert Nemiroff in 1953 she continued to contribute articles to *Freedom*, and taught at the Jefferson School of Social Science.

Hansberry's first play, *A Raisin in the Sun*, begun in 1956 and completed in 1958, received tryouts in New Haven, Philadelphia, and Chicago before opening on Broadway in March 1959. The play won the New York Drama Critics Circle Award that year, and received 530 performances in a nineteen-month run. Hansberry's screenplay for the film version won a Cannes Film Festival award in 1961. Her second play, *The Sign in Sidney Brustein's Window*, opened in October 1964, and in spite of difficulties was kept running by friends and admirers until the playwright's death of cancer on January 12, 1965.

In spite of their divorce in 1964, Hansberry named Nemiroff her literary executor. His program of excerpts from her plays, journals, speeches, and letters, *To Be Young, Gifted and Black: Lorraine Hansberry in Her Own Words*, was presented off-Broadway in 1969, and his edition of *Les Blancs: The Collected Last Plays of Lorraine Hansberry*, which includes *The Drinking Gourd* and *What Use Are Flowers?* as well as the title play, was published in 1972.

Personal

Good evening. I am very pleased to have been invited to be a part of this program, and—

(Smiling)

—and I hope it isn't premature. That is, this *is* a Writers' Conference, a Negro Writers Conference to be exact; I am, clearly, a Negro—but I'm not sure yet how much of a writer I am. I suppose I have been invited because my first play will be opening soon (that is, *if* they give us a theater). I think I like it, but I've no idea what the public will think of it. Still, for the moment, let's presume I am a writer.

(Now she refers to the typed speech she has been carrying)

I must share with you a part of a conversation I had with a young New York intellectual a year ago in my living room in Greenwich Village. He was a young man I had known, not well but for a number of years, who was, by way of description, an ex-Communist, a scholar and a serious student of philosophy and literature, and whom I consider to possess quite a fine and exceptionally alert mind. In any case, he and I had wandered conversationally into the realm of discussion which haunts the days of humankind everywhere: the destruction or survival of the human race.

"Why," he said to me, "are you so sure the human race *should* go on? You do not believe in a prior arrangement of life on this planet. You know perfectly well that the *reason* for survival does not exist in nature!"

I was somewhat taken aback by the severity that this kind of feeling has apparently reached among a generation that presumably should be lying on its back in the spring woods somewhere, contemplating lyrics of love and daring and the wonder of wild lilies.

I answered him the only way I could: that man is unique in the universe, the only creature who has in fact the power to transform the universe. Therefore, it did not seem unthinkable to me that man might just do what the apes never will—*impose* the reason for life on life. That is what I said to my friend. I wish to live because life has within it that which is good, that which is beautiful, and that which is love. Therefore, since I have known all of these things, I have found them to be reason enough and—I wish to live. Moreover, because this is so, I wish others to live for generations and generations and generations and generations.

I was born on the Southside of Chicago. I was born black and a female. I was born in a depression after one world war, and came into my adolescence during another. While I was still in my teens the first atom bombs were dropped on human beings at Nagasaki and Hiroshima, and by the time I was twenty-three years old my government and that of the Soviet Union had entered actively into the worst conflict of nerves in human history—the Cold War.

I have lost friends and relatives through cancer, lynching and war. I have been personally the victim of physical attack which was the offspring of racial and political hysteria. I have worked with the handicapped and seen the ravages of congenital diseases that we have not yet conquered because we spend our time and ingenuity in far less purposeful wars. I see daily on the streets of New York, street gangs and prostitutes and beggars; I know people afflicted with drug addiction and alcoholism and mental illness; I have, like all of you, on a thousand occasions seen indescribable displays of man's very real inhumanity to man; and I have come to maturity, as we all must, knowing that greed and malice, indifference to human misery and, perhaps above all else, ignorance—the prime ancient and persistent enemy of man—abound in this world.

I say all of this to say that one cannot live with sighted eyes and feeling heart and not know and react to the miseries which afflict this world.

I have given you this account so that you know that what I write is not based on the assumption of idyllic possibilities or innocent assessments of the true nature of life—but, rather, my own personal view that, posing one against the other, I think that the human race does command its own destiny and that that destiny can eventually embrace the stars.—LORRAINE HANSBERRY, *To Be Young, Gifted, and Black*, 1969, pp. 10–11

We had a talk recently with Lorraine Hansberry, the twenty-eight-year-old author of the hit play *A Raisin in the Sun*. Miss Hansberry is a relaxed, soft-voiced young lady with an intelligent and pretty face, a particularly vertical hairdo, and large brown eyes, so dark and so deep that you get lost in them. At her request, we met her in a midtown restaurant, so that she could get away from her telephone. "The telephone has become a little strange thing with a life of its own," she told us, calmly enough. "It's just incredible! I had the number changed, and gave it to, roughly, twelve people. Then I get a call from a stranger saying, 'This is So-and-So, of the B.B.C.'! It's the flush of success. Thomas Wolfe wrote a detailed description of it in *You Can't Go Home Again*. I must say he told the truth. I enjoy it, actually, so much. I'm thrilled, and all of us associated with the play are thrilled. Meanwhile, it does keep you awfully *busy*. What sort of happens is you just hear from *everybody!*" . . .

Miss Hansberry told us that she had written her play between her twenty-sixth and twenty-seventh birthdays, and it had taken her three months. "I'd been writing an awful lot of plays—about three, I guess—and this happened to be one of them," she told us. "We all know now that people like the play, including the critics. Most of what was written about the play was reasonable and fine, but I don't agree that this play, as some people have assumed, has turned out the way it has because just about everybody associated with it was a Negro. I'm pleased to say that we went to great pains to get the best director and the best actors for this particular play. And I like to think I wrote the play out of a specific intellectual point of view. I'm aware of the existence of Anouilh, Beckett, Durrenmatt, and Brecht, but I believe, with O'Casey, that a real drama has to do with audience involvement and achieving the emotional transformation of people on the stage. I believe that ideas *can* be transmitted emotionally." . . .

"I mostly went to Jim Crow schools, on the Southside of Chicago, which meant half-day schools, and to this day I can't count. My parents were some peculiar kind of democrats. They could afford to send us to private schools, but they didn't believe in it. I went to three grade schools—Felsenthal, Betsy Ross, and A. O. Sexton, the last of them in a white neighborhood, where Daddy bought a house when I was eight. My mother is a remarkable woman, with great courage. She sat in that house for eight months with us—while Daddy spent most of his time in Washington fighting his case—in what was, to put it mildly, a very hostile neighborhood. I was on the porch one day with my sister, swinging my legs, when a mob gathered. We went inside, and while we were in our living room, a brick came crashing through the window with such force it embedded itself in the opposite wall. I was the one the brick almost hit. I went to Englewood High School and then to the University of Wisconsin for two years. Then I just got tired of going to school and quit and came to New York, in the summer of 1950. The theatre came into my life like *k-pow!*" Miss Hansberry knocked a fist into the palm of her other hand. "In Chicago, on my early dates, I was taken to see shows like *The Tempest*, *Othello*, and *Dark of the Moon*, which absolutely flipped me, with all that witch-doctor stuff, which I still adore. In college, I saw plays by Strindberg and Ibsen for the first time, and they were important to me. I was intrigued by the theatre. Mine was the same old story—sort of hanging around little acting groups, and developing the feeling that the theatre embraces everything I like all at one time. I've always assumed I had something to tell people. Now I think of myself as a playwright."—UNSIGNED, "Playwright," *NY*, May 9, 1959, pp. 33–35

⟨Sweet Lorraine:⟩ That's the way I always felt about her, and so I won't apologize for calling her that now. *She* understood it: in that far too brief a time when we walked and talked and laughed and drank together, sometimes in the streets and bars and restaurants of the Village, sometimes at her house, sometimes at my house, sometimes gracelessly fleeing the houses of others; and sometimes seeming, for anyone who didn't know us, to be having a knockdown, drag-out battle. We spent a lot of time arguing about history and tremendously related subjects in her Bleecker Street and, later, Waverly Place flat. And often, just when I was certain that she was about to throw me out, as being altogether too rowdy a type, she would stand up, her hands on her hips (for these down-home sessions she always wore slacks) and pick up my empty glass as though she intended to throw it at me. Then she would walk into the kitchen, saying, with a haughty toss of her head, "Really, Jimmy. You ain't *right*, child!" With which stern put-down, she would hand me another drink and launch into a brilliant analysis of just why I wasn't "right." I would often stagger down her stairs as the sun came up, usually in the middle of a paragraph and always in the middle of a laugh. That marvelous laugh. That marvelous face. I loved her, she was my sister and my comrade. Her going did not so much make me lonely as make me realize how lonely we were. We had that respect for each other which perhaps is only felt by people on the same side of the barricades, listening to the accumulating thunder of the hooves of horses and the treads of tanks.

The first time I ever saw Lorraine was at the Actors' Studio, in the winter of '57–58. She was there as an observer of the Workshop Production of *Giovanni's Room*. She sat way up in the bleachers, taking on some of the biggest names in the American theater because she had liked the play and they, in the main, hadn't. I was enormously grateful to her, she seemed to speak for me; and afterwards she talked to me with a gentleness and generosity never to be forgotten. A small, shy, determined person, with that strength dictated by absolutely impersonal ambition: she was not trying to "make it"—she was trying to keep the faith.

We really met, however, in Philadelphia, in 1959, when *A Raisin in the Sun* was at the beginning of its amazing career. Much has been written about this play; I personally feel that it will demand a far less guilty and constricted people than the present-day Americans to be able to assess it at all; as an historical achievement, anyway, no one can gainsay its importance. What is relevant here is that I had never in my life seen so many black people in the theater. And the reason was that never before, in the entire history of the American theater, had so much of the truth of black people's lives been seen on the stage. Black people ignored the theater because the theater had always ignored them.

But, in *Raisin*, black people recognized that house and all the people in it—the mother, the son, the daughter and the daughter-in-law, and supplied the play with an interpretative element which could not be present in the minds of white people: a kind of claustrophobic terror, created not only by their knowledge of the house but by their knowledge of the streets. And when the curtain came down, Lorraine and I found ourselves in the backstage alley, where she was immediately mobbed. I produced a pen and Lorraine handed me her handbag and began signing autographs. "It only happens once," she said. I stood there and watched. I watched the people, who loved Lorraine for what she had brought to them;

and watched Lorraine, who loved the people for what they brought to *her.* It was not, for her, a matter of being admired. She was being corroborated and confirmed. She was wise enough and honest enough to recognize that black American artists are a very special case. One is not merely an artist and one is not judged merely as an artist: the black people crowding around Lorraine, whether or not they considered her an artist, assuredly considered her a witness. This country's concept of art and artists has the effect, scarcely worth mentioning by now, of isolating the artist from the people. One can see the effect of this in the irrelevance of so much of the work produced by celebrated white artists; but the effect of this isolation on a black artist is absolutely fatal. He *is,* already, as a black American citizen, isolated from most of his white countrymen. At the crucial hour, he can hardly look to his artistic peers for help, for they do not know enough about him to be able to correct him. To continue to grow, to remain in touch with himself, he needs the support of that community from which, however, all of the pressures of American life incessantly conspire to remove him. And when he is effectively removed, he falls silent—and the people have lost another hope.—JAMES BALDWIN, "Sweet Lorraine," *To Be Young, Gifted, and Black,* 1969, pp. ix–xii

Works

In literature as in life, no doubt, dominant traits may be expected to reappear in alternate generations. Just as children may favor their grandparents more than their parents, in ways at least, young writers sometimes seem to reach back past their immediate predecessors for examples and blood ties with earlier kin.

Thus the newest crop of Negro writers in the United States show more traits in common with the writers of the Harlem Renaissance than the famous WPA group who were their literary parents, so to speak.

Despite the ringing success of Richard Wright, Frank Yerby, and Willard Motley, bellwethers of the little flock nourished by WPA writer's projects, and such gifted colleagues of theirs as Roi Ottley, Margaret Walker and Gwendolyn Brooks, one searches in vain among the newest Negro writers today for any who could qualify as their artistic progeny, or even as their disciples. Well, almost in vain. Lorraine Hansberry, the exciting author of *Raisin in the Sun,* is in some very fundamental literary ways related to the sturdy author of *Native Son, Black Boy* and *Uncle Tom's Children.*

Even the Hansberry-Wright link, however, which is by no means limited to the way in which they have drawn upon their common Chicago background for subject matter, is marked by notable differences. Miss Hansberry's star came up unheralded. Nothing from her typewriter had been published or produced prior to *Raisin in the Sun.* The critical and popular approval which followed this event made her famous, and the rejoicing this occasioned can only be compared to the kudos which followed Richard Wright's sunburst a little more than a decade earlier. But her recognition was based on a play. *Native Son* was a novel, *Black Boy* an autobiography, *Uncle Tom's Children* a collection of stories. And the two authors, though they had both spent crucial years of their lives in the Chicago jungle, if that's the word for the South Side of those days, were separated by more than just a span of time in their development.

Richard Wright's young manhood in Chicago was poverty ridden. Lorraine Hansberry's family was well-to-do by South Side standards. Her father was in the real estate business. He could, in a manner of speaking, have owned or managed the rental property in which Bigger Thomas killed the rat with the frying pan. How his perceptive daughter came to see the human turmoil in those sub-standard quarters through eyes of sympathy and deep understanding has not been told. Miss Hansberry's subsequent writing has consisted mainly of articles in periodicals. It has not tended toward autobiography.

A lesser writer, one imagines, particularly a lesser Negro writer in the United States, might have been in a hurry, given her talents and background, to give the world a picture of debutants' balls, and gracious living to compensate for the ugliness Richard Wright had forced before the eyes of millions of readers, to the embarrassment of our favored few. She also avoided the equally unwise assumption that more of the same material that Wright had presented would prove to be equally arresting when presented by her, equally instructive. But it doesn't work that way without the addition of new elements, and the new Hansberry ingredient was *technique.*

In the theatre, a medium that demands a maximum of know-how, usually attained only after long and painful apprenticeship, years of heartbreaking trial and error, she showed up at first bow with complete control of her tools and her craft. This was little short of startling. Self-educated Richard Wright had been a toiling, sometimes almost awkward manipulator of the devices of composition. He had won over this disadvantage by sheer power. In Lorraine Hansberry's case this particular shoe seemed to be on the other foot.—ARNA BONTEMPS, "The New Black Renaissance," *ND,* Nov. 1961, pp. 53–54

I commend *Les Blancs* to your immediate attention, not so much as a great piece of theater (which it may or may not be) but, more significantly, as an incredibly moving experience. Or, perhaps, as an extended moment in one's life not easily forgotten or regularly discovered in a commercial theater that takes such pains to protect us from knowing who and what and where we are in 20th-century America.

I use the phrase "moving experience" to convey something other than a conventional, perhaps comforting and sentimental sense of beauty or warmth. *Les Blancs* offers few if any of these things. Rather, I wish to suggest a response to the playwright's awareness and exploration of a more contemporaneous reality: ugliness recognized, filth and perversity definitively perceived, in that social order most people will recognize under its formal title—Western Civilization.

I was deeply affected by Lorraine Hansberry's design for the direction this play was intended to take: an examination of urgent forces existing in close proximity to one another, of a flesh and blood encounter between those who have and those who cannot have, of revelations that are no longer avoidable, and of dangers never again to be ignored or casually regarded.

"Moving" in *that* fashion. In such a way as to polarize an opening night audience into separate camps, not so much camps of color, of Black and White, although that, too, was part of it. The play divides people into sectors inhabited on the one hand by those who recognize clearly that a struggle exists in the world today that is about the liberation of oppressed peoples, a struggle to be supported at all costs. In the other camp live those who still accept as real the soothing mythology that oppression can be dealt with reasonably—particularly by Black people—if Blacks will just bear in mind the value of polite, calm and continuing use of the democratic process.

A Black man, Tshembe Matoseh, returns to his home in an unnamed African country. He is a day too late for the funeral of his father, a tribal chieftain. Tshembe has been to Europe and America, acquiring that bizarre form of obedience training that imperialists stubbornly insist on referring to as education. His country is in turmoil. Blacks are demanding independence, freedom from the colonial yoke. Quickly, Tshembe becomes the classic man-in-the-middle, torn between an allegiance to Black liberation and loyalty to those who taught him all too well to accept himself as an enlightened if not noble savage.

Tshembe has left his wife, a European, in London with their child, and he longs to return to them. However, the Black freedom-fighters view his homecoming as the answer to a void in their leadership. An American journalist arrives, intending to write of the difficulties that attend the emergence of independence-minded Black Africa. Charlie Morris is both a writer and a white liberal (if that designation still has validity) whose effort to establish friendship and a meaningful dialogue with Tshembe forms the core of the play. Their lengthy, probing conversations are responsible for the structuring of those mutually exclusive philosophical command posts that offer havens for the haves and have-nots.

Morris wants Tshembe to get off his back with all his hints of white guilt and responsibility. It is Morris's contention that he cannot shoulder the sins of his fathers. "I've got my own sins to deal with." In the mind of Charlie Morris (and how many others?) enough conversation and enough Scotch whisky *can* obliterate a history he has never really examined—the history that Tshembe has lived. For the Black man, Western society's talking goes on while *his* life is bartered, violated or destroyed.

The relationship between Tshembe and Charlie Morris is doomed to failure as long as white men are still at work lacerating the hills of any Black homeland in search of new mines, new gold or diamonds. While Charlie offers, benevolently, to pay for the drinks. . . .

The play is flawed—what play not completed by its original author would not be? Yet, beyond the imperfection of its ragged perimeters, or its frequently awkward transitional sections and fitfully episodic construction, there is a persistent glow, an illumination. Somewhere, past performance, staging and written speech, resides that brilliant, anguished consciousness of Lorraine Hansberry, at work in the long nights of troubled times, struggling to make sense out of an insane situation, aware—way ahead of the rest of us—that there is no compromise with evil, there is only the fight for decency. If even Uncle Sam must die toward that end, *Les Blancs* implies, then send *him* to the wall.—CLAYTON RILEY, "An Incredibly Moving Experience," *NYT*, Nov. 29, 1970, Sec. 2, p. 3

C. W. E. BIGSBY

From "Lorraine Hansberry"

Confrontation and Commitment: A Study of Contemporary American Drama 1959–1966

1967, pp. 156–65

Lorraine Hansberry's first play, *A Raisin in the Sun*, was awarded the New York Drama Critics' Prize for 1959–60. For all its sympathy, humour and humanity, however, it remains disappointing—the more so when compared with the achievement of her second play, *The Sign in Sidney Brustein's Window*. Yet it passes considerably beyond the trivial music-hall dramas of Langston Hughes and does something to capture the sad dilemma of Negro and white alike without lapsing into the bitter hatred of Richard Wright or the psychodrama of O'Neill's *All God's Chillun Got Wings*. Its weakness is essentially that of much of Broadway naturalism. It is an unhappy crossbreed of social protest and re-assuring resolution. Trying to escape the bitterness of Wright, Hansberry betrays herself into radical simplification and ill-defined affirmation. Like Saul Bellow she senses the validity of affirmation before she can justify it as a logical implication of her play's action.

A Raisin in the Sun is set in Chicago's Southside 'sometime between World War II and the present'. The Younger family live in a roach-infested building so overcrowded that they have to share the bathroom with another family while Travis the only son of Walter and Ruth Younger, has to sleep on a sofa in the living room. Yet the central factor of the play is not poverty but indignity and self-hatred. The survival of the family is dependent on their ability to accomodate themselves to the white world. Walter works as a chauffeur while his wife works as a maid. To both of them accommodation to the point of servility is required for the very right to work. James Baldwin has indicated the cost to the individual of accepting one's life on another's terms, 'one of the prices an American Negro pays—or can pay—for what is called his "acceptance" is a profound, almost ineradicable self hatred.'[1] *A Raisin in the Sun* is primarily a study of such self-hatred, emphasised here, as Baldwin saw it emphasised in an article called 'Alas, Poor Richard', by a confrontation between the enervated American Negro and the dignified self-confidence of the African.

There is a story by Richard Wright called 'Man of All Work' in which a Negro man dresses up as a woman in order to get work as a cook. His action emphasises what Baldwin has called 'the demoralisation of the Negro male'[2] when his position as breadwinner is necessarily usurped by the woman. It is this agony with which Walter Younger lives. He has been desexualised and his dignity has been crushed. It is this knowledge which underlies his bitter disgust and self-contempt. 'I'm thirty-five years old; I been married eleven years and I got a boy who sleeps in the living room—and all I got to give him is stories about how rich white people live'.[3] When a ten thousand dollar insurance matures on his father's death he has to watch the money pass into his mother's hands—a final blow to both his dreams and his manhood. '*You* the head of this family. You run our lives like you want to.' (R.S. p. 165.)

Richard Wright, sensing the emasculation of the Negro trapped in the physical ghetto of Chicago and the cage of self-contempt alike, had seen in violence both the Negro's attempt to re-assert himself and an expression of white oppression. Bigger Thomas, who kills, decapitates and incinerates a white woman thereby achieves a measure of self-awareness which had previously escaped him. Hansberry's play is set in the same locale. Its sense of desperation is the same. Walter Younger's emasculation is pushed to the point at which he condones his wife's attempt to secure an abortion. Yet where Wright created in Bigger Thomas a hardening of the stereotype, which was in effect a spring-board for an exegesis of communist doctrine, Hansberry, writing some twenty years later, is concerned with demonstrating human resilience. The gulf between the two writers is in part that dictated by the changing social position of the American Negro but more fundamentally it is indicative of Lorraine Hansberry's belief in the pointlessness of despair and hatred. Indeed Hansberry's play is essentially an attempt to turn Wright's novel on its head. Where he had examined the potential for violence, Hansberry sees this as a potential which once realised can only lead to stasis. Both works start with an alarm-clock ringing in the stifling atmosphere of Chicago's coloured ghetto. Yet whereas Bigger Thomas wakes up to the inexorability of his fate, Walter becomes conscious of the existence of other levels than the purely material. The sense of urgency presaged by the initial alarm is as much the key-note of Hansberry's play as it is of Wright's novel yet while the alarm functions as a threat in the latter it functions as a promise in the former.

The play's title is taken from a poem by Langston Hughes—a poem which expresses the sense of kinetic energy and tension which underlies the frustrations of the American Negro, an energy which can be turned into violence, self-destruction, despair or genuine realisation:

What happens to a dream deferred?
Does it dry up
Like a raisin in the sun?
Or fester like a sore—
And then run?
Does it stink like rotten meat?
Or crust and sugar over—
Like a syrupy sweet?

Maybe it just sags
Like a heavy load.

Or does it explode?

(R.S. p. 101.)

The dreams of the Youngers are sharpened and pointed by the indignity and self-hatred which is their racial inheritance. Walter dreams of owning a store and thus becoming independent of the system of which he is the victim, while his sister-in-law, impressed by the need for compassion, wants to become a doctor. Lena Younger, Walter's mother, however, is concerned only with the disintegration of the family. When the money arrives she places a deposit on a new house. The decision drives Walter into a despairing disaffiliation.

Walter Younger's sullen cynicism, which, like Willy Loman's confused mind, grants value only to wealth and power, is balanced by his sister-in-law's passionate belief in the feasibility of change and the need for compassion. Beneatha has a strong sense of racial pride compounded with humanistic commitment. Intensely aware of her racial origins she associates with Asagai, an African student, and steeps herself in the culture of her forbears. When Asagai gives her the nickname Alaiyo, 'one who needs more than bread', it is both an ironical comment on her intensity and an indication that Hansberry's concern is less with the poverty of the Youngers than with the need for spiritual replenishment which can only come with a return of dignity. Yet when Walter squanders the money which was to have paid for her medical training Beneatha lapses into despair and the compassion which she had shown evaporates as had Ruth's hope and Walter's ambitions. Like Sidney Brustein in Hansberry's second play, forced to confront present reality, she slips into the cant of nihilism. She projects her personal disappointments onto a universal scale and Asagai identifies the questions which obsess her. 'What good is struggle; what good is anything? Where are we all going? And why are we bothering?' (R.S. p. 191.)

The personal and familial crises are finally resolved by the open challenge offered by the white world. Karl Lindner, whose name suggests non-American origins, is the representative of the white community into which the family had planned to move. He offers to buy the house from them at a profit. The insult is delivered with courtesy but it stings Walter into a response which simultaneously gives him back his dignity and commits him to an involvement which he had sought to escape. Thus in a sense this is a fulfilment of Asagai's prophesy. In speaking of his own political future in Africa he had said, 'They who might kill me even . . . actually replenish me!' (R.S. p. 192.)

Yet while leaving the Youngers committed to 'new levels of struggle'[4] Miss Hansberry brings about this partial resolution through something of a specious *deus ex machina*. Although she is as antipathetic towards a life printed on dollar bills as Odets had been, it is clear that the spiritual regeneration of the Younger family is ultimately contingent on a ten thousand dollar check, for it is only the money which makes it possible for them to challenge the system under which they have suffered. In making it the necessary prerequisite for their return to dignity and pride Hansberry would seem to demean the faith in human potential which she is ostensibly endorsing. Walter, again like Willy Loman, far from rejecting the system which is oppressing him wholeheartedly embraces it. He rejects the cause of social commitment and compassion and places his faith in the power of money. It is the unintentional irony of this play however that he proves to be right, 'You all want everybody to carry a flag and a spear and sing some marching songs, huh? You wanna spend your life looking into things and trying to find the right and the wrong part . . . There ain't no causes—there ain't nothing but taking in this world, and he who takes most is smartest—and it don't make a damn bit of difference how.' (R.S. p. 198.) Without the insurance check not only would the dreams have been left to shrivel like raisins in the sun but so would Beneatha's compassion and Walter's courage. Indeed Walter's final conversion, or, as Hansberry would put it, the eventual realisation of his potential, is itself as unconvincing as Biff's similar conversion in *Death of a Salesman*. Her true declaration of faith is, however, embodied in the person of Asagai, the least convincing of the play's characters. This African revolutionary is used by Lorraine Hansberry as a point of reference—as the realisation of the dignity and commitment which exists in Walter only as potential. When Walter, returning home drunk, had leapt onto a table and shouted out the words of a defiant nationalism he had been establishing a contact with the African which served at the same time as a source of contrast and promise. Yet Asagai's self-assurance remains untested. His confident assertion of progress and redemption remains unreal precisely because we do not see him, as we do the Youngers, brought face to face with frustration.

The relationship between the American Negro and the African remains, as Baldwin had in part anticipated it would, a complex arrangement of subtle misunderstandings. Particularly in the nineteen-twenties' 'Negro Renaissance' Africa was seen as a pagan but innocent land. . . .

While this romantic view of Africa repelled both the Christian and the communist whose approach to that continent was coloured by their own ideology, it was a view which seems to have seized the imagination of many writers. . . . If Hansberry mocks the naïveté with which Beneatha tries to adopt African modes of dress and general culture she leaves unchallenged the assumption that those values stem from a purer source. Yet Asagai's vitality and enthusiasm spring from his own dreams which differ in kind from Walter's only in magnitude and in the fact that they are never put to the test. We see Walter balance his manhood against a dream of success but Asagai remains nothing but an oracle whose declarations make sense only to those who are faithful to the stereotype African of Bennett and Cuney, rich in wisdom and standing, like the noble savage, as a reminder of primal innocence. Asagai's declaration of the inevitability of change built on courage and compassion, a declaration which clearly represents Lorraine Hansberry's own faith, remains as unconvincing as do the circumstances of Walter's change of heart, 'things will happen, slowly and swiftly. At times it will seem that nothing changes at all . . . and then again . . . the sudden dramatic events which make history leap into the future. And then quiet again . . . And I even will have moments when I wonder if the quiet was not better than all that death and hatred. But . . . I will not wonder long.' (R.S. pp. 191–2.)'

Lorraine Hansberry dedicates her second and last play, *The Sign in Sidney Brustein's Window*, to 'the committed everywhere' and in doing so expresses not only her own personal philosophy but also her conception of the purpose of art. From her play, however, it becomes apparent that commitment does not mean for her exactly what it had for Brecht or even Rice and Odets, neither does it mean that intransigent alignment with sectional interests which undermines the drama of LeRoi Jones. The commitment of which she speaks is one to life rather than death, hope rather than despair and to human potential rather than human failure. Her enemy is thus neither the rich industrialist nor the racial bigot but rather the indifferent and the self-deceived. In terms of art her enemy is Camus and the theatre of the absurd so that *The Sign in Sidney Brustein's Window* is as much a statement of artistic responsibilities as of social inadequacies. Indeed in many ways it is a dramatic equivalent of Tynan's assault on Ionesco for while he was working, like Brecht, from a Marxist premise, Hansberry's rejection of the absurd is based on a similar desire (already noted in the drama of confrontation of which this play is essentially a part) to re-constitute the humanist heresy of belief in man.

The Sidney Brustein of the title is a liberal who fluctuates between the two poles of liberalism; Thoreauesque dissociation and enthusiastic political involvement. The play effectively spells out the inadequacies and ultimately the futility of both these extremes. In essence Sidney Brustein is but another of the American heroes in search of primal innocence waging a holy war and deeply wounding those around him. . . . Baldwin has said that, 'People who shut their eyes to reality simply invite their own destruction, and anyone who insists on remaining in a state of innocence long after that innocence is dead turns himself into a monster.'[5] In effect this is a savagely accurate picture of Sidney Brustein, as indeed it is of Miller's Quentin. For Sidney, in clutching naïvely at what he imagines to be innocence becomes insensitive, blind alike to the crumbling of his marriage and the halting despair of his sister-in-law. His relationship with his wife, Iris, is strained because he refuses to recognise the reality of the world but chooses rather to remould it, and her, to suit his own personal vision. On the one hand he tends to lapse into a romantic dream of man as innocent and free spirit suitably removed from the conventional corruption of the city. In this mood he takes Huck Finn as an archetype of noble dissociation and sees Iris as a mountain nymph. On the other hand he throws himself with naïve faith into political activism. There is a bitter desperation in Iris's demand to know which role she should play—Margaret Mead or Barbara Allen—for her life is lived as a counterpart to her husband's and his sudden and impractical enthusiasms throw an increasing strain on their relationship. The crisis between Sidney and his wife is ultimately a crisis of Sidney's liberalism. For Iris rebels against the sterility of a life which gravitates around idealistic dreams and facile crusades—a life of philosophical speculation and meaningless activity entirely lacking in a commitment which means anything more than an irresponsible game and which achieves nothing more than the exchange of one corruption for another.

At the beginning of the play Sidney, who has just admitted to the failure of one of his impractical schemes, is prevailed upon to use a newspaper which he has bought to support a reform candidate in a local election. He accepts the campaign as a further diversion and the sign which he puts in his window (a sign pledging support for the reform candidate) is less evidence of his faith in the possibility of change than of a self-justifying sense of the righteousness of protest. He tells Mavis, his sister-in-law, that to change one politician for another 'is to participate in some expression of the people's about the way things are'.[6] The act of protest is sufficient and when his candidate is elected he is genuinely amazed for, Hansberry suggests, Sidney's liberalism is the exercise of conscience without attendant responsibility. Indeed he remains blithely unaware, until informed by his wife, that he has secured the election of a candidate who has sold out to the machine, for his vision of the world is still founded on the absolutes of former decades. It takes the professional cynicism of a playwright friend to point out that '"the good guys" and "the bad guys" went out with World War Two'. (S.B. p. 59.)

Lorraine Hansberry's portrait of bewildered liberalism, however, far from constituting an attack on liberals, as Richard Gilman suggests in his review of the play, lies at the very centre of a drama which is essentially concerned with the plight of the individual in a society in which commitment is considered passé. In an article in *The New York Sunday Times* she describes her sense of this dilemma and sees it as the crux of her play:

> Few things are more natural than that the tortures of the *engagé* should attract me thematically. Being 34 years old at this writing means that I am of the generation which grew up in the swirl and dash of the Sartre-Camus debate of the post-war years. The silhouette of the Western intellectual poised in hesitation before the flames of involvement was an accurate symbolism of some of my closest friends, some of whom crossed each other leaping in and out, for instance, of the Communist Party. Others searched, as agonizingly, for the ultimate justification of their lives in the abstractions flowing out of London and Paris. Still others were contorted into seeking a meaningful repudiation of *all* justifications of anything and had, accordingly, turned to Zen, action painting or even just Jack Kerouac . . . It is the climate and mood of such intellectuals . . . which constitute the core of a play called *The Sign in Sidney Brustein's Window.*[7]

Lorraine Hansberry is acutely aware of the temper of the decade in which she is writing. In the 1930's theatres had been created for a popular and vital social drama in which there had been no apparent conflict between the demands of drama and those of the practical idealist. The theatre of the fifties, however, was dominated by the absurd to which social concern was at best irrelevent and at worst a symptom of man's self-destructive optimism. When Sidney rages, in the second act, against a world in which anger and passion have been transmuted into neurosis and anaesthetised unconcern he is voicing equally the bewilderment of his age: 'Yes, by all means hand me the chloroform of my passions; the sweetening of my conscience; the balm of my glands. Oh blessed age! That has provided that I need never live again in the full temper of my rage . . . Wrath has become a poisoned gastric juice in the intestine. One does not *smite* evil any more: one holds one's gut, thus—and takes a pill.' (S.B. p. 96.)

If Hansberry is critical of liberalism which is nothing more than naïve self-expression she is equally critical of disinterest which masquerades under the guise of liberal tolerance. Iris epitomises this attitude which constitutes the other side of the liberal coin. It takes Mavis to point out the implications of this moral disengagement. When Iris takes as her maxim, 'Live and let live, that's all,' Mavis retorts, 'That's just a shoddy little way of trying to avoid responsibility in the world.' (S.B. p. 57.) This desire for non-involvement is further emphasised, rather too pointedly, by Iris's surname, Parodus, an implication which

Mavis again underlines. Parodus, as she points out, is the Greek word for chorus, '. . . the chorus is always there, commenting . . . watching and being.' (S.B. p. 103.) Iris's form of moral dissociation makes no distinctions between Sidney's naïve absolutism and a commitment which is more fundamental. When Alton, a Negro friend of theirs, is offended by what he takes to be prejudice on their part Iris attacks him, assuming that his commitment is of the same nature as Sidney's. 'You and the causes all the time. It's phoney as hell! . . . The country is full of people who dropped it when they could'. (S.B. pp. 40–1.) Hansberry's laconic stage direction appended to this speech identifies the author's attitude. She describes the substance of the speech as 'Pragmatic bohemia'. (S.B. p. 41.)

Lorraine Hansberry's involvement with the plight of the Negro is subsumed here in a more general concern. The human failure which is evidenced in the hardening of prejudice in racial matters becomes for her indicative of a more fundamental failure which underlies alike the capricious enthusiasm of Sidney Brustein and the disaffiliation of Iris. The commitment which she urges, and in which all the play's characters fail, is a devotion to humanity which goes beyond a desire for political and moral freedoms.

Notes

1. *Nobody Knows My Name* (New York, 1961), p. 175.
2. Ibid., p. 153.
3. Lorraine Hansberry, *A Raisin in the Sun*, *Four Contemporary American Plays*, ed. Bennet Cerf (New York, 1961), p. 115. All future references to this play will be abbreviated to 'R.S.' and incorporated into the text.
4. Robert Nemerov, 'Introduction,' *The Sign in Sidney Brustein's Window* (New York, 1965,) p. xxi.
5. *Notes of a Native Son* (New York, 1955), p. 165.
6. Lorraine Hansberry, *The Sign in Sidney Brustein's Window* (New York, 1965), p. 60. All future references to this play will be abbreviated to 'S.B.' and incorporated into the text.
7. 'Introduction', *The Sign in Sidney Brustein's Window*, pp. xv–xvi.

MARK HARRIS

1922–

The son of American-born Jews, Mark Harris Finkelstein was born in Mount Vernon, New York, on November 19, 1922. Because discrimination made it difficult to gain employment, he dropped his final name in 1940, and found work as a journalist. His experiences in the U.S. Army, in which he served reluctantly in 1943–44, made him a determined pacifist and campaigner for civil rights. While in the army he started work on his first novel, *Trumpet to the World*, which was published in 1946. After the war Harris married and went to study at the University of Denver, receiving his B.A. in 1950, and at the University of Minnesota, where he gained his Ph.D. in 1956. He taught English at San Francisco State College from 1954 to 1968, and since then has served on the faculty of a number of universities, including Purdue University, the University of Pittsburgh, and Arizona State University. In 1957–58 he was a Fulbright professor at the University of Hiroshima, and in 1964 attended the Dartmouth Conference in Kurashiki, Japan, as a U.S. delegate.

Harris is best known for his novels about baseball player Henry Wiggen, beginning with *The Southpaw* (1953), followed by *Bang the Drum Slowly* (1956), *A Ticket for a Seamstitch* (1957), and most recently *It Looked Like for Ever* (1979). Other works include the novels *Something about a Soldier* (1957), *The Goy* (1970), and *Killing Everybody* (1973), and the play *Friedman and Son*, written while on a Ford Foundation grant in 1961. He has also written volumes of autobiography, notably *Twentyone Twice* (1966), which records his experiences on a Peace Corps assignment in 1965, and *Best Father Ever Invented* (1976). His most recent novel, *Lying in Bed* (1984), is a sequel to *Wake Up, Stupid* (1959).

Showing a deplorable lack of consideration for reviewers, Mark Harris refuses to be classified. Three of his books—*The Southpaw, Bang the Drum Slowly,* and *A Ticket for a Seamstitch*—have established him pretty clearly as the foremost contemporary writer of novels about baseball. A tidy pigeon-hole, but Mr. Harris has shown little inclination to stay quietly in it. Like his master, Ring Lardner, in his baseball books he has usually managed to convey the impression that the unpretentiousness of his subject-matter is no measure of the scope of his literary intentions. Nor has it always been the measure of his achievements; the national pastime has served him as a diamond-shaped window on a larger world.

In *Something about a Soldier* Mr. Harris is off the reservation. It is a World War II novel, and an odd and unusual one. It is the sort of second World War novel that we have seen very seldom up to now, and may see more often from now on—a sort in which the writer has little interest in recording the raw shock of experience, aiming rather at imposing form on material that, through a period of years, he has been turning over and over in his mind.

Mr. Harris' hero is Jacob Epp, the 17-year-old ex-star of the Perkinsville (N. Y.) High School debating team. Jacob's Army career begins with an incoherent argument with a fellow-draftee in a train, in the course of which one of the lenses of his spectacles is broken. At the camp in Georgia that turns out to be the train's destination, a PX counter girl offers him a piece of flashlight glass to replace the lens. He is delighted with this gift, and the two strike up a friendship on the strength of it. He tries to get the authorities to change his name to Epstein, which it was before he changed it to get a job a few months earlier. It is in this endeavor, frustrated by bureaucracy, that Jacob begins to find out something about the Army, and something about himself.

The rest is an amiable nightmare in which some magic always prevents the worst from happening. Brimming with naive idealism, Jacob unexpectedly finds himself a courier for what seems to be the Communist party. (He successfully breaks this tie by saying to a fellow comrade, "My enthusiasm is waning.") He becomes engaged in a competition—or as nearly a competition as is possible, considering how different their intentions are—with his battery captain for the love of the PX girl (who loves them both). He goes on maneuvers, goes A.W.O.L., and is captured and put in solitary, where he tries to starve himself to death. Eventually, Jacob's battery goes overseas and is annihilated: he, meanwhile, has been separated from the Army—not noticeably kicking and screaming—via the psychiatric ward. His ailment is not insanity but innocence.

Jacob is not the good soldier Schweik; his resistance to authority is not so much passive as inadvertent. We cannot admire him or even feel very sorry for him, and some may itch to beat some sense into him; but we can certainly laugh at him. Mr. Harris' short novel falls short of complete effectiveness; its style is sometimes arch, its point of view sentimental. Its redeeming features are its deftly drawn characters and its passages of wild humor.

A.W.O.L. from baseball, Mark Harris is as exasperating as, and a good deal more promising than, Private Epp-Epstein.—JOHN BROOKS, "A Ward Case of Innocence," *NYTBR*, Oct. 27, 1957, pp. 5, 42

We have not had a novel from Mark Harris since he published *Wake Up, Stupid* in 1959. That was his sixth novel, following the youthful *Trumpet to the World*, the three baseball novels (*The Southpaw, Bang the Drum Slowly,* and *A Ticket for a Seamstitch*), and *Something about a Soldier*, which is my favorite. There were no books for four years, and then came a play, *Friedman and Son*, with a long and revealing autobiographical preface. Next came a piece of journalism with a good deal of autobiography in it, *Mark the Glove Boy*, an account of Harris's experiences while covering Richard Nixon's campaign for Governor of California. Now we have *Twentyone Twice*, which describes the author's adventures as a special investigator for the Peace Corps. From this, incidentally, it appears that what Harris has chiefly been working on during this period is an autobiography.

Twentyone Twice is in the form of a journal, and the entries were supposedly—and, for all I know, actually—written day by day from November 8, 1964, to February 2, 1965. Harris, it appears, had kept a journal sporadically for a long time, circulating copies of it among several friends, according to an elaborate formula described here in detail. This is the first paragraph of the first entry: "Sunday, November 8. Today, on the fourth anniversary of the election of John F. Kennedy as President of the United States, I resume my Journal, it having lain idle since August 10, 1963. The event the present Phase is designed to cover is my journey somewhere in the world for the Peace Corps, an arm of our government, an instrument of what Kennedy called 'national purpose.'"

The opening entry is necessarily a summary of what happened to Harris while the journal lay idle. He tells about his literary activities, his trip to Japan, and the beginnings of his Peace Corps mission. On July 28, 1964, he had a telephone call from Sargent Shriver, who said that he had liked *Mark the Glove Boy* and felt that Harris was "the kind of person who could examine the work of the Peace Corps and say useful things about it," strictly for "internal" circulation. (I understand that many such investigations are carried out in the course of any year.) Harris having expressed interest, the bureaucratic machine began slowly to roll.

The book is divided into two parts, the first and longer being called "United States Phase." For five months Harris was kept dangling while he was being investigated by the FBI and by a psychiatrist and while the Peace Corps administration decided what, if anything, it wanted to do with him. Finally, on January 8, he set forth for an African country he calls Kongohno. Although it had been expected that he would spend at least five weeks in Africa, he was there less than half that time. When he got home, he decided to submit his journal in lieu of the expected report.

Harris suggests that the Peace Corps administrators were not exactly delighted with his efforts as an investigator, and I see no reason why they should have been. I don't suppose that there are more than fifty pages in the book based on actual observation of the Peace Corps workers and their labors in Kongohno, and these are not particularly revealing. One point Harris did make. In Washington he was told about certain workers who were classified as "Risks" and asked to talk with them. He met them, and he liked them, and he was convinced that most of them were doing a good job. Moreover, he saw and said that the Peace Corps, by its nature, was bound to attract the kind of young people who are likely to be regarded as "Risks" by the FBI, and that it could not fulfill its purposes without them.

In general, however, we learn more about Mark Harris than we do about the Peace Corps, and he is more interesting on the first topic than on the second. He does not present himself in a heroic role; on the contrary, he is as much the butt of his own humor as any of the characters in his novels. We see him as cantankerous, crotchety, whimsical, self-pitying, quick to take umbrage, and in many ways a bad boy. If he made only a superficial investigation of the Peace Corps, he studied himself with care and candor.

In explaining why he was a problem for the FBI, Harris writes: "I want to observe that the politics and the mental state are related, that I was disgusted in the army by the contradictions between proclamations of democracy on the one hand, and the treatment of Negroes on the other. This was in the South. I couldn't ride with this contradiction emotionally, and the emotions turned to politics, so that for several years thereafter I flirted with the Communists."

Trumpet to the World was his only specifically political novel, but the theme that was to occupy him for years was dissent. His second book, a biography of Vachel Lindsay, *City of Discontent*, presents an idealistic poet who will not compromise. Henry Wiggen, hero of the baseball novels, is not only a first-rate pitcher and an excellent wisecracker; he is a rebel, and he learns compassion. *Something about a Soldier*, which must be largely autobiographical, tells what happens to an idealistic boy in the army. The hero of *Wake Up, Stupid* is in rebellion against both the academic and the literary establishments.

In the preface to *Friedman and Son* Harris wrote: "That summer, 1959 . . . my emptiness had begun to worry me. I was composed and mellow, and the living was easy. All that had been on my mind I had discharged in a novel, *Wake Up, Stupid*, published in July, and so successful in its way that it was soon to carry me beyond accustomed comforts. All my useful grievances were submerged beneath this new experience, transforming my petulance to amiability."

What the Peace Corps experience did was to convince Harris that he really hadn't gone soft and conservative. Even while he was being investigated by the FBI, he cautiously supported the demonstrating students in Berkeley. The fact that the FBI men seemed to look on him as a dangerous radical boosted his self-esteem. Best of all, the young people in the

Peace Corps, the ones classified as "Risks," accepted him as one of themselves. The journal, he says, shows "how my youthful instincts remain with me though I am twice my age:" I hope he feels better from here on.

The book also shows that there is a lot of idealism left in the work, whatever cynics say. The idealists, as Harris makes clear, are often hard to get along with, and their motives must always be scrutinized, by themselves and by others; but it would be an even lousier world without them.—GRANVILLE HICKS, "Eye on the Peace Corps," *SR*, Oct. 8, 1966, pp. 95–96

The trouble with Mark Harris is that he can't shake Mark Harris. In other guises, notably the three splendid 1950's Henry Wiggen baseball novels (of which *Bang the Drum Slowly* is the best known), he is a funny, perceptive, moving writer. But when an autobiographical or self-analytical impulse strikes him, he descends into a curious blend of whining self-flagellation and intellectual chest-thumping. He has been that way for a decade, especially in a ghastly stab at personal journalism, *Mark the Glove Boy*, and in the long introduction to his autobiographical play, *Friedman & Son*. *The Goy* suggests that the cloud of self-indulgence is beginning to lift, but it still hovers.

One would almost think that Harris and John Updike had been passing secret messages in the night. In *Bech*, Updike, quintessential goy, celebrates the "Jewishness" he feels lurking within himself. In *The Goy*, Harris, né Finkelstein, explores goyism from the opposite end. Both say the same thing: in these unpleasant times, there is much to be said, morally and ethically, for being a Jew.

The Goy is Dr. Westrum, first name not supplied (though occasionally nicknamed "Wes," which might surprise a certain erstwhile Mets manager). He is, at 50, a celebrated scholar, author of the blockbuster *A History of the Past World*, laboring now on *A History of the Present World*, a breath-by-breath journal of his daily life intended to prove his conviction that history is "accessible only by a study of persons, of individual men and women consumed by private goals and passions, seeking glory in their own time by the humiliation of particular enemies, not by a study of reigning theories of existence but by the study of lovers and mistresses, wives and fathers and children."

Now lion-in-residence at what one takes to be Columbia, Westrum was born in the heart of high-corn America. Coming to Manhattan as a young man he soon "fell among Jews, he rejoiced, he admired them to extravagance, he envied them their talk, their frankness, their uncensored passion, the unfenced limits of their debate, partaking without repaying in kind, sitting silent and seeming cold, not because he chose that way but because he was incapable of passion. And he married into them as soon as he could."

For the archetypically uptight Gentile Westrum (and the point is not without its truth, *viz.*, Updike), there is a hope of release in immersing himself in Jews: Beatrice, his wife; Tikvah, his gentle brother-in-law; his unnamed mistress, all the rest. Himself "alien, Gentile, smelling of horses and guns and the Jewish-hating Ku Klux Klan," Westrum turns to Jewishness for warmth and humanity. Yet his Gentile reserve keeps his yearnings and compassions from escaping; instead, he cynically uses the open-hearted acceptance he meets among Jews as lever for fabricating a lie, passing himself off "as the man of labor, sobriety, industry, control, and rugged quietude"—or, Wasp incarnate.

Driven into "imagined exile" by his inability to express affection to Tikvah, he packs up Beatrice and their son Terence (Harris uses personal and place names ironically, usually heavy-handedly) and heads for the Middle America of his birth, where he hopes to obtain a seat at a splendidly antiseptic think tank. The journey back into the heart of the heart of the country brings him into confrontation with his goyish heritage of bigotry and violence. Moving uneasily between the Jews of the think tank and the Middle American birthplace he has fled ("'Oh, it's a nice little fascist town,' said Westrum . . . , 'White Protestant, no Jews, Catholics, Negroes, poor, liquor, speeding, smoke, dirt, unions, third parties . . ."), he is forced to acknowledge, and attempt to exorcise, hatred and violence within himself. In so doing he comes to understand the true meaning of a pacifism he has articulated but never adequately felt; and thus in the end the novel achieves an unexpectedly emphatic, rather impressive, antiwar expression.

Harris takes Westrum on his journey with some skill. His secondary characters are fine (in particular the secretary Miss Sanantone, the think-tank staffers Benstock and Weinberg, the boy Terence) and the measured pace at which they become fully revealed is enticing. Harris's sense of humor is still functioning (though a bit out of shape), but his prose is inconsistent, ranging from the stilted ("At Brest lived Westrum's mother and father. There Westrum was born") to the improbably Faulkneresque (". . . in a voice as low as his father's, speaking of that moment now for the first time, which he had never spoken of before but carried in his heart only, nor forgotten it, nor buried it; but saved it and preserved it to present to his father at such a moment as this, a threat of foreclosure, a debt undeniable"). The prose in its thickness is like the novels it is too intense, too much jammed into too little, not enough breathing-room for the reader.

The Goy is, obviously, heavily political, a repudiation of Mr. Agnew's America. Its admiration for the special moral and human qualities of Jewishness is, I think, well-founded; yet its portrait of goyism is painted with too sweeping a brush, oversimplified and even gratuitously venomous. It is my suspicion, unkind though it may seem (it is not so intended), that the ethnic agonizing of *The Goy* is part and parcel with the ethnic identity struggle Mark Harris has been putting on public display these many years. He is a better novelist as Henry Wiggen, though where that leaves the identity struggle, I do not know.—JONATHAN YARDLEY, "Dr. Westrum's Search for Identity," *NYTBR*, Oct. 18, 1970, pp. 50–51

WILLIAM J. SCHAFER

From "Mark Harris: Versions of (American) Pastoral"

Critique, Volume 19, Number 1 (1977), pp. 28–48

Mark Harris, over the past thirty years, has produced a large group of fine novels, too many to survey easily in one essay.[1] His work has garnered good reviews and some general reputation; he is known as an exceptional essayist and journalist, and he has taught creative writing for years in San Francisco and in the Midwest. Yet his work is rarely discussed in surveys of "new" fiction or promising writers; he is rarely grouped with the Jewish writers of the 1950's renaissance[2] and has seemed to work in isolation from a critical audience. He might be passed over as a quirky offshoot of vernacular Americana, down the road that Mark Twain and Ring Lardner took, but all through the 1950's and '60's Mark Harris worked his own individual territory, explored the intricate maze in the heart of America, and wrote some of the finest comic fiction of those decades.

Some persistent themes run through Harris's novels from

his first, *Trumpet to the World* (1946), to his most recent, *Killing Everybody* (1973). Among the basic concerns of his fiction are: the variety and multiplicity of American life, and its corollary demands for tolerance and understanding; the collision of young innocence with the world of hard experience; the uniqueness of the individual and the completeness of imaginative experience. All the novels deal directly or indirectly with tensions between pluralist and conformist patterns in American life and with the response of the individual to demands of his culture. The early novels take the familiar shape of the *Bildungsroman*—the baseball trilogy *(The Southpaw, Bang the Drum Slowly,* and *A Ticket for a Seamstitch), Trumpet to the World,* and *Something about a Soldier* are all variants on the education-of-a-youth theme, drawing on Harris's own autobiography for central motives. In a direct sense all of Harris's writings have sprung from autobiography, although only *Mark the Glove Boy* and *Twentyone Twice* take conventional autobiographical forms.

From the beginning of his career as a novelist, when he wrote *Trumpet to the World* (1946), a shaky but energetic story of a black man in the South discovering his identity and mission in life, Harris has worked with scenes and situations he knew firsthand. He has described his apprenticeship as a novelist very clearly, noting the inception of *Trumpet to the World* in his own Army experiences during World War II.[3] The novel strikes a keynote of radical political consciousness coupled with an intense awareness of American themes and ideas, a strong emotional focus on problems of the underdog in a WASP society. Ten years later, Harris circled back to this basic story in *Something about a Soldier* (1957), using a viewpoint much closer to his own private experience but working with the same milieu and concerns. In the intervening decade, Harris's style and craftsmanship matured markedly, and *Something about a Soldier* emerges as a small classic of pacifism and the continual dialectic of innocence and experience in American life. The training ground for Harris had been primarily his three Henry Wiggen baseball novels, providing him a pattern of interests and problems in the novel form. The baseball novels forced Harris to concentrate on the shape and demands of first-person, vernacular narratives, on modes of folk-thought and -speech, and on methods for imagining his own personal experience in the ritualistic, conservative world of bigtime baseball. When he finished the baseball stories, Harris knew expertly how to become another character and still incorporate his own experiences and viewpoint into the novel framework. He learned to mold a highly characteristic prose style into various informal but flexible "unliterary" shapes, as Mark Twain learned through jackleg journalism, frontier tall tales, and *Huckleberry Finn* the infinite variety of American story-telling dialects.

Harris also seemed to move from the overtly propagandistic demands of *Trumpet to the World,* with its lengthy discussion of racism, military brutality, war and pacifism, and other socio-political themes, to a world apolitical and becoming anachronistic—the great American national pastime, baseball, already by the 1950's being shoved into the wax museum of American history. However, instead of abandoning his early themes, Harris was discovering ways to reuse, refine, and extend them. By choosing such a hierarchic and traditional American interest as baseball, long the most decorous and genteel WASP sport, Harris developed a microcosm inside which he could portray the subsurface tensions and divergences in our national life. Using big-league baseball as "the moral equivalent of war," as a mural-sized cartoon and metaphor for American life, he was freed to construct a serio-comic commentary on the national character revealed on the playing fields of mid-America.

In *The Southpaw* (1953) Harris created his new world—the New York Mammoths and their roster of heroes, along with Henry W. Wiggen, the central consciousness who is the mock-writer of the vernacular tales. The stories ring with echoes of Lardner's *You Know Me, Al,* but the novels range more widely than Lardner's experiments with the loopy surrealism of semi-literate sports figures and are less exercises in modernized frontier-humor styles. Beyond Wiggen's struggles with the American language and his earnest recording of the hard facts of his first year's work in the big leagues, a significant theme is of self-discovery and developing consciousness. Wiggen is the classic country bumpkin of folklore, coming from Harris's own upstate New York region into the intensely competitive and frantic world of professional athletics, comprehending his own mind and heart in the process. Wiggen learns he has the physical gifts to win, but he must grow mentally and spiritually in his year's seasoning with the Mammoths to comprehend other dimensions of the game—and of his life. Baseball is an imaginative catalyst that delivers the man encased in Henry Wiggen's boyhood.

Henry, an archetypal American boy, has been raised on the child's-eye view of baseball as an Olympic context of giant heroic figures. In his season with the Mammoths he perceives the players as the worried, neurotic, aging men they are, and his ideals are deflated, one by one. The game, on a sandlot, is an idyl of vigorous freedom; on the professional turf it is a struggle for income, for survival, in raw Hobbesian terms. His skills are no longer esthetic gestures but marketable commodities, his talent no longer an individualistic activity but part of a highly structured corporate enterprise. Henry, as a left-handed pitcher in a right-handed world, has become the drive-train in a delicate and expensive machine, and new responsibilities descend on him. Most important are challenges to his mind and beliefs: he finds his heroes, Sad Sam Yale and Ugly Jones, to be cantankerous, egotistical relics, utterly unlike the idealized "biographies" palmed off on boys. He finds the management to be sharks, capitalists who exploit the players for every raw nickel of profit. He finds fans and sports reporters to be brutal, parasitical, and ultimately boring. The juice of heroism runs out of the game as the season becomes a grueling pennant race. The team members are rubbed raw under pressure, and the ugliness of group life surfaces in all its manifestations of hatred, tension, and stupidity. Yet *The Southpaw* is not simply a debunking of one episode in the American dream, for Wiggen finds positive values in the game and the players, examples of grace under pressure important to his maturation.

The game of baseball, as Harris develops it through Wiggen's mind, is a version of pastoral—a microcosmic, slightly simplified version of society stylized and shaped into a formal mold. The swains here are the players, each of whom has a viewpoint, an individual attitude toward life, to contribute to the dialogue. The artificial stresses and crises of the game, laid out in its neatly hieratic pattern of innings and outs, runs and hits, and errors, strikes, and balls, give Harris a framework for a dramatic tale and a metaphor or central image refracting American values which most interest him. The comic motion of Harris's fiction revolves around games, gamesmanship, strategies for winning and losing, for living. The central figure of *Wake Up, Stupid* (1959), Lee Youngdahl, ex-boxer turned English professor, meditates on American literature and finds this formula:

> What is it that thrusts Mark Twain and Sherwood Anderson into one stream, and Henry James into another? . . . It has so much to do with a man's early relationship to the society of boys and games—

> that miniature of our larger society of men and business, with its codes and rules, its provision for imagination within those rules, with winning, losing, timing, bluffing, feinting, jockeying, with directness of aim and speech and with coming back off the floor again. (179)

Harris flows with the stream of Twain and Anderson—and Lardner, Hemingway, and all other American literary sportsmen.

Yet Henry Wiggen finds himself in a world much harsher than his idealized vision of sport: the pastoral myth does not correspond to the realities of daily life, and the heroes of boyhood seen close-up are shrunken, vulnerable men much like himself. Further, the game itself is not the clean, simple pattern of Henry's mind. Competition and cooperation collide fiercely in professional athletics, and Henry learns rapidly that he is part of a large system, an impersonal organization, not a band of happy warriors staving off time and death. When he first visits the Mammoths' front office in *The Southpaw*, an anonymous clerk puts him firmly in his place:

> "The reason I am laughing," said the man, "is this," and he went over to the wall where there was three green cabinets, and he begun to slide some drawers out as far as they would go, and he run his hand up and down the papers in the drawer. "Records," he said. "Every one of these papers is a record on some kid that thinks he is another Joe DiMaggio or another Honus Wagner. They are just names. Your name is somewhere amongst them. How do we know who you are except just a name? You are but another name." (77)

The pattern of rejection and demythicizing continues when Henry confronts his teammates. He realizes that to keep the myth alive for himself he can depend only on his own strength and talents. The tension between real and ideal versions of experience pushes Henry toward self-discovery.

In the second novel of the baseball trilogy, *Bang the Drum Slowly* (1956), Henry Wiggen is no longer the upstart acolyte but a veteran. He is thus able to turn outside himself and his own experience to view a teammate, Bruce Pearson, the subject of the story. Pearson is an awkward, dull-witted catcher, naturally gifted but unable to bring his abilities into focus: "He was not interested in going any place in baseball, then and maybe never, playing only for the kicks and what little cash was in it" (27). Pearson learns he is dying of Hodgkin's disease, and he tells Wiggen, the only Mammoth who can tolerate his rural stolidity. The burden of Pearson's secret and Henry's responsibility to the man are the basis for the story, which shows us Henry slowly instilling a sense of identity and worth in Pearson, teaching him to become a dedicated baseball player in the face of imminent, inevitable death. We already know from *The Southpaw* that Wiggen is a conscious pacifist, a man who believes in justice and social equality. In this novel, we see that his compassion extends further, into empathy for a man written off as a hopeless case in all senses.

Bang the Drum Slowly turns, like Housman's "To An Athlete Dying Young," around the pity and mystery of the unconscious young struck down untimely. Pearson is one of the faceless, semi-anonymous rankers of baseball, no star, no personality, an average plugging ballplayer, but Wiggen pays attention to him, to his story. Persistently, Wiggen demands respect for Pearson from his teammates, and he finally is forced to reveal Bruce's secret to them, one by one. Predictably, their attitudes of contempt or indifference change when they realize Bruce is dying, yet their change is not simply an illustration of the flags of hypocrisy unfurled in the face of mortality. The *fact* of death is brought home to the players, and Pearson's predicament galvanizes the floundering team and inspires them to win the pennant race. Pearson becomes a symbol for them, and they rally as if to show him that superhuman efforts can vanquish even death. Pearson, however, dies alone and friendless after the season, cast off like the superannuated players who fret about their meager savings and blank futures. The baseball machine, the reality behind the pastoral dream, has ground up another individual. Wiggen reflects bitterly on the loneliness in death in the last paragraphs of the novel:

> In my Arcturus Calendar for October 7 it says, "De Soto visited Georgia, 1540." This hands me a laugh. Bruce Pearson also visited Georgia. I was his pallbear, me and two fellows from the crate and box plant and some town boys, and that was all. There were flowers from the club, but no *person* from the club. They could of sent somebody.
>
> He was not a bad fellow, no worse than most and probably better than some, and not a bad ballplayer neither when they give him a chance, when they laid off him long enough. From here on in I rag nobody. (243)

Henry has learned how the team's petty hazing and bickering cut into personality, how rivalries, grudges, and small hatreds of the hermetic life erode the common will of the players. He may be the only man on the Mammoths to understand, through his intense personal concern for Bruce Pearson and the life-and-death involvement he has had with the dying catcher.

Pushing Wiggen's enlightenment further is the last brief book in the trilogy. *A Ticket for a Seamstitch* (1957), which again shows Wiggen in close interaction with another figure, Pearson's replacement, Piney Woods. Woods is a polar opposite, temperamentally, from Pearson, a carefree extrovert who rides a motorcycle, plays a guitar, and dresses up in a gaudy cowboy suit. Where *Bang the Drum Slowly* introduced the fact of death into the pastoral landscape *(Et in Arcadia ego)*, *A Ticket for a Seamstitch* deals with romantic love, the traditional pastoral topic, and, specifically, with idealized love, Piney Woods' fantasy romance with a woman fan who vows to spend her life's savings to travel across the U.S. to see her hero (Wiggen) play. Woods conceives a passion for the correspondent and urges her on her cross-country odyssey. When she appears, she is (of course) the archetypal blind date, the big letdown from Woods' juvenile fantasy:

> She has nice skin [Wiggen narrates]. You might as well say that for her, and decent hair and eyes and nose, average, nothing below average and nothing too much above, just exactly the average kind of girl you bump into everywhere you turn, waitresses and photo retouchers and switchboard girls, girls on trains and girls on planes, girls in depots and restaurants and nightclubs, girls in banks and insurance offices and tax offices, girls in the newspaper business and girls in the book business, girls selling tickets to the movies and girls tearing them in half at the door, girls in Queen City and all the towns of the Four-State Mountain League, and girls in New York and Chicago, girls, girls, girls, everywhere I go. (104)

Wiggen sees the seamstitch clearly as someone from the big world outside baseball, the nonmythic, nonheroic world of average women working at menial jobs to finance a little vicarious romance. The seamstitch arrives in time for the top-of-the-season Fourth of July game, which ends in bathos, like "Casey at the Bat," with Piney Woods blasting a mighty ball right into a fielder's glove to lose the game and break Wiggen's winning streak. Everything has gone wrong with the heroic vision, which has become translated into mock-heroic; Orlando is no longer the virginal shining knight but the silly lovestruck oaf running naked thorugh the woods, gabbling.

A Ticket for a Seamstitch explicitly describes illusion and disillusionment, the chasm between appearance and reality in the baseball world. It develops two parallel stories of unreasonable expectations—the seamstitch's illusions about the heroism and chivalry of the players, and Piney Woods' naive, teenage views of women and love. The fair maiden turns out to be the average young woman, and she discovers that her idols are insensitive, hardworking professionals, not demigods. After the loss of the Fourth of July game, Wiggen meditates on appearance and reality, on the disparity between the player's view and the fan's view:

> They were fairly quiet—the fans I mean—1,000's and 1,000's of clucks, out the exits, out across the field, stopping by home plate and sizing up the fences like they do, and stopping by the hill and looking down towards home. And the fences look far, while home plate looks close from the hill. They think the pitcher got the best of things. Maybe so. But the fences are closer than they look, and the spaces behind you are wide, and the batter got wood in his hand, and maybe you are strong, for you got to be strong to pitch, but the batter is also strong, and the ball is lively, and you got a brain, yes, but the batter also got a brain, and you guess him, and he guesses you, and one of you got to lose the decision on every guess. If the both of you are lucky you guess right enough times, and you keep your job, which is what it also is, your job I mean, your rent and your baby-food. (137–8)

The comparison of visions makes Harris's last baseball novel a more overt comment on the discrepancies in the American dream than the earlier novel.

Harris's development of the three baseball stories gave him a strong grasp on a vernacular novel form refined very carefully through the persona of Henry Wiggen. Wiggen is an alert, skeptical, but basically moral intelligence afloat in a maelstrom of powerful psychological and physical conflicts. His observations and protracted analyses of his teammates run through his narratives about the summer seasons to form a sensitive picture of American mores and folkways in the middle of the Cold War. Wiggen is the "ideal simple man" of pastoral needed to give us a lucid insight into a complex society. He is at once a very average individual (like his own summary of the seamstitch) and an eccentric individualist willing to hold and defend unpopular positions and to champion outcasts like Bruce Pearson or the lonely seamstitch. His running arguments with himself are on "situational ethics," like Huck Finn's soliloquies on the raft. Wiggen arrives at his beliefs through constant skeptical testing, but he stands by them regardless of pressure. He defends his pacifism intelligently, opposes the racism of teammates, maintains a stoutly realistic view of his capabilities. But he is still in love with the game, with his boyhood's innocent vision of life, and the double vision keeps him alive and healthy. He does not lapse into the mindless apathy or cynicism of some players. He is a balanced man, competent and insightful but subject to the pressures and agonies of his peers. Like the pastoral swain, he is *in* the environment and *above* it at once, dealing with hard reality and with the mental landscape of ideals simultaneously. The creation of Wiggen and the baseball stories helped Harris grow as a novelist, for he used the techniques of the stories more subtly and indirectly in his later fiction.

After the baseball novels, Harris turned to more versions of his own story, two of his finest comic inventions: *Something about a Soldier* (1957) and *Wake Up, Stupid* (1959). The novels are complementary, like opposed mirrors or bookends framing a shelfload of ideas. Versions of war and peace from the still center of the Eisenhower era, they develop Harris's meditations on his own experience and its relation to the American soul. *Something about a Soldier* reworks Harris's own World War II adventures, but it is also a skilfully developed *bildungsroman* about maturation and a young man's emerging recognition of Freud's two great psychic poles, love and death. It chronicles the brief Army career of Jacob Epp (Epstein), who moves in a matter of a few months in 1943 from being an unshaped high-school debater and near-genius with no experience of life to a fully formed man aware of his mortality, the possibility of genuine love, and the discreteness of his own mind and conscience in a complex social order. He has collided with the rigid conservatism of the Army, found a father-figure in a sympathetic commanding officer, fallen in love with a local girl, confronted social injustice in the racist attitudes around a Southern Army post, run away from the Army, been committed for medical observation, and finally achieved insight into himself while on hunger strike in the Army prison.

Jacob Epstein collides with troublesome inequities as soon as he enters the Army. He struggles to adjust to the broad spectrum of human types around him, to follow Army discipline (earning the honorary title of "Chickenshit" from his peers), to understand the complex world he has been hurled into. His system overloads, and he breaks down when he perceives discrepancies in his life: the government for which he yearns to become a perfect fighting machine allows discrimination against Negroes to go unchecked around the Army base; his superiors wish him not to be an intelligent and creative individual but to be a quiet and untroubling presence (a "good soldier" in the stoic sense), not to buck the system; his peers have no clear idea why they will fight and die but meander toward their common fate without ideology, without faith or comfort. Jacob is tangled in paradox, knowing the Army is necessary to stamp out Hitler's mad rampage through Europe and his killing of the Jews, yet loathing the Army for its blind authoritarian inhumanity, its insensitivity to him and to all weak and oppressed, the young men in his company doomed to die for reasons beyond their comprehension. In his agony of rationalizing, Jacob slips beyond the bounds of his young experience.

> As the days passed, he began to see that his act was futile, and he knew that to persist in futility was a mark of madness. Yet he persisted, and he understood now the fearful meaning of the phrase *to lose one's mind*, to have it go off by a power divorced from reason, to have it float away and be lost, like a balloon, or to roll away and be lost, like a ball. His mind was floating and rolling and becoming lost, or so he thought, in those days. (59)

The childish imagery marks the turning of Jacob's life, as he moves from childhood into a kind of madness which becomes wisdom.

The force which redeems Jacob is also irrational—love. He is loved by Joleen Davis, a local girl, and by Captain Dodd, his commanding officer. Each sees Jacob's basic innocence and goodness, and each tries to show him he is not destined to be a soldier. He is too blind to himself to understand what they tell him about life and love. He is champion of abstract causes, thinks out rational problems, is *correct* in all things. Everyone tells him that he will die in Europe, that soldiers are made to die—not to be heroes, not to enforce justice. Jacob dreams on, reading, thinking, becoming a communist messenger without ever understanding communism or what he is doing. He pastes stickers crying for social justice over the town and the base. Jacob is too timid to love Joleen, even though she obviously wants him to take her. He refuses to understand that Captain Dodd has seduced her; he hears and sees selectively, idealizing the war, himself, Joleen, the Captain.

Slowly, Jacob realizes the imminence of his own death and the futility of his participation in war. He realizes the cosmic injustice of his position: "as he would be neither oppressed nor oppressor, so now his heart renounced killing equally with dying. But this he could not express" (62). Jacob's games are in his mind: chess, puzzles, debating, and argumentation. But they are games nonetheless, on the same order as Henry Wiggen's athleticism. War, however, is not a game nor a neat ritualized pattern governed by rules and decorum. It is—as Tolstoy has assured us—a succession of chaotic blunders, accidents big and small, over which no single man has dominion, to which reason, rules, and methods of play do not apply. Jacob's rigid, orderly mind begins to admit this principle. He begins to understand that love and hate are beyond reason's sway, that war represents the supreme irrationality. All that is demanded is his life, the one possession he is not prepared to relinquish without struggle. Galvanized by the news of his best friend's death in the Air Force, by his struggle with his conscience, by his inability to love Joleen in fact as well as in fancy, Jacob runs from the Army to think. In his flight begins his enlightenment. He flees to catch up with himself and becomes a figure like Job's messenger escaping the holocaust.

Epstein is pitted against his immediate superior, Sergeant Toat, a kind of mirror-image alter-ego, all the things Jacob is not—coarse, dull, committed to the Army and the war, seemingly on the side of death. Yet Toat feels a bemused sorrow over Jacob's plight, and when he is sent to escort Jacob back to the base after his flight, Toat becomes drunk, maudlin, and violent by turns, realizing that Jacob will live and he will die. Even before Jacob's decision to abandon the Army, Toat tries to describe Jacob's dilemma to him:

> Look at me. Bring your mind in focus. For your own good I'm telling you, I'm describing, I'm saying it's a long war ahead and I see you and it is night and you are laying in the distance with the air full of lead. They're coming over the hills at you, and under the trees, and you wish you knew a way to protect, but you do not know, and you will say Jesus God how I wish I knew a way to protect because now my days are done and life is gone, no more eating no more drinking no more screwing all the pretty girls no more reading out of books or movie shows. Jesus God you will say, how I wish I knew what my Sergeant taught me, you'll say, I am about to die when instead of dying I should of listened to what they taught me down there, and you'll die, Epp, and it's nothing to me. Think of yourself dead. Think! (60)

Jacob, like his namesake, must wrestle with his angel alone, however, and Toat's vivid plea is only realized later when Jacob can meditate deeply on war and death and love and the self.

Something about a Soldier describes the awakening of a young mind and conscience to the facts of life and death, to the possibilities of experience. Jacob grows from a brilliant boy skilled in the abstractions of logic and forensics into a man confronting the narrow facts of his own existence. His mind pushes away the meaning of death when the data of the war begin to impinge on him:

> He was startled to think of his own death. Death was not a thing that happened to him but to aged and useless people like his Grandma Epstein and to wicked people in electric chairs and to foolish people carelessly crossing streets, or in wartime in round and nameless numbers, so many and so many at Waterloo and Bull Run, always in round numbers in textbooks, but never to himself whose death was unbelievable. (17)

As in *The Red Badge of Courage*, the naive young soldier is brought to look upon the face of war—in Harris's novel not through the direct experience of battle but through the experience of others, the love and concern of Epstein's fellows. Unlike Crane's boy giving a classic account of the battle of Chancellorsville, Jacob never sees the monster in full view, but he learns from its effects all around him. Only after the war does he find out his battery was wiped out, all dead. His strategic retreat from the jaws of death was not an illusion, a failure, but the course of truth. Yet the experience itself was its own vindication, as it transformed Jacob from aimless boy into thoughtful man. From destruction Jacob seized life and love.

Notes

1. Subsequent references to Mark Harris's books are to the following editions: *Trumpet to the World* (New York: Reynal and Hitchcock, 1946), *The Southpaw* (Indianapolis: Bobbs-Merrill, 1953). *Bang the Drum Slowly* (New York: Knopf, 1956), *A Ticket for a Seamstitch* (New York: Knopf, 1957), *Wake Up, Stupid* (New York: Knopf, 1959), *Mark the Glove Boy* (New York: Macmillan, 1964), *Twentyone Twice* (Boston: Little, Brown, 1966), *The Goy* (New York: Dial Press, 1970), *Killing Everybody* (New York: Dial Press, 1973).
2. In an analysis of the current literary situation, Richard Kostelanetz, *The End of Intelligent Writing* (New York: Sheed and Ward, 1974), pp. 33–34, makes a point of citing Mark Harris as a prime case of neglect.
3. Mark Harris, "How to Write," in Thomas McCormack, ed., *Afterwords* (New York: Harper & Row, 1969), pp. 65–79.

JOHN HAWKES

1925–

John Clendennin Burne Hawkes, Jr., was born on August 17, 1925, in Stamford, and grew up in Connecticut and Alaska. He entered Harvard University in 1943, and had a volume of poems, *Fiasco Hall*, published privately the same year. After service as an ambulance driver in Italy and Germany in 1944–45, he returned to Harvard, completing his B.A. in 1949. Until 1955 he worked for Harvard University Press, and then taught at the university for three years. Since 1958 he has been a professor of English at Brown University.

Hawkes's first long fiction, *Charivari*, appeared in *New Directions 11* in 1949; a surrealistic examination of a modern marriage, it remained unreprinted until 1969. His first novel in book form, *The Cannibal* (1949), is set in Germany, his second, *The Beetle Leg* (1951), in a fictionalized American west, and the two short novels, *The Goose on the Grave* and *The Owl* (1954), in Italy. These early works secured him an underground reputation as an avant-garde writer, but it was *The Lime Twig* (1961) which brought him a wider audience. A Guggenheim Fellowship and a grant from the National Institute of Arts and Letters, both in 1962, enabled him to spend ten months in the West Indies, where he worked on *Second Skin* (1964), which was runner-up for a National Book Award. He spent 1964–65 in San Francisco on a Ford Foundation Fellowship, writing short plays published in *The Innocent Party* (1966). A Rockefeller Foundation Fellowship financed extended trips to Greece and France in 1968. A collection of shorter fictions, *Lunar Landscapes*, appeared in 1969. *The Blood Oranges* (1971) won him the Paris Prix du Meilleur Livre Étranger. *Death, Sleep and the Traveller* was published in 1974, followed by *Travesty* (1976), *The Passion Artist* (1979), and *Virginie: Her Two Lives* (1982). *Humors of Blood and Skin*, a reader with selections by the author from his novels, short stories, and work-in-progress, appeared in 1984.

John Hawkes married in 1947, and has four children.

General

Hawkes' "experimentalism" is . . . his own rather than that of yesterday's avant-garde rehashed; he is no more an echoer of other men's revolts than he is a subscriber to the recent drift toward neo-middlebrow sentimentality. He is a lonely eccentric, a genuine unique—a not uncommon American case, or at least one that used to be not uncommon; though now, I fear, loneliness has become as difficult to maintain among us as failure. Yet John Hawkes has managed both, is perhaps (after the publication of three books and on the verge of that of the fourth) the least read novelist of substantial merit in the United States.

. . . Hawkes may be an unpopular writer, but he is not an esoteric one; for the places he defines are the places in which we all live between sleeping and waking, and the pleasures he affords are the pleasures of returning to those places between waking and sleeping.

He is, in short, a Gothic novelist; but this means one who makes terror rather than love the center of his work, knowing all the while, of course, that there can be no terror without the hope for love and love's defeat. In *The Cannibal*, *The Beetle Leg*, and *The Goose on the Grave* he has pursued through certain lunar landscapes (called variously Germany or the American West or Italy) his vision of horror and baffled passion; nor has his failure to reach a wide audience shaken his faith in his themes.

. . . ⟨T⟩he final achievement of Hawkes' art ⟨is⟩ his detachment from that long literary tradition which assumes that consciousness is continuous, that experience reaches us in a series of framed and unified scenes, and that—in life as well as books—we are aware simultaneously of details and the context in which we confront them.

Such a set of assumptions seems scarcely tenable in a post-Freudian, post-Einsteinian world; and we cling to it more, perhaps, out of piety toward the literature of the past than out of respect for life in the present. In the world of Hawkes' fiction, however, we are forced to abandon such traditional presumptions and the security we find in hanging on to them. His characters move not from scene to scene but in and out of focus; for they float in a space whose essence is indistinctness, endure in a time which refuses either to begin or end. To be sure, certain details are rendered with a more than normal, an almost painful clarity (quite suddenly a white horse dangles in mid-air before us, vividly defined, or we are gazing close up, at a pair of speckled buttocks), but the contexts which give them meaning and location are blurred by fog or alcohol, by darkness or weariness or the failure of attention. It is all, in short, quite like the consciousness we live by but do not record in books—untidy, half-focused, disarrayed.

The order which retrospectively we *impose* on our awareness of events (by an effort of the will and imagination so unflagging that we are no more conscious of it than of our breathing) Hawkes decomposes. For the sake of art and the truth, he dissolves the rational universe which we are driven, for the sake of sanity and peace, to manufacture out of the chaos of memory, impression, reflex and fantasy that threatens eternally to engulf us. Yet he does not abandon all form in his quest for the illusion of formlessness; in the random conjunction of reason and madness, blur and focus, he finds occasions for wit and grace. Counterfeits of insanity (automatic writing, the scrawls of the drunk and doped) are finally boring; while the compositions of the actually insane are in the end merely documents, terrible and depressing. Hawkes gives us neither of these surrenders to unreason but rather reason's last desperate attempt to know what unreason is; and in such knowledge there are possibilities not only for poetry and power but for pleasure as well.—LESLIE A. FIEDLER, "The Pleasures of John Hawkes," Introduction to *The Lime Twig*, 1961, pp. viii–xiv

His style of describing a scene and telling a story is adapted to his world of decay and deteriorated values. Hawkes tells his stories in fragments of memory, past and present flowing through each other in images, in recalled episodes. Even in those stories in which he provides a narrator, like *The Cannibal* and *The Owl*, the narrative is discontinuous, the sensory details apparently disconnected on any but an emotional, dream-like level. His descriptive technique is something like that of the movies; by focusing sharply on small details and sustaining the apparently trivial close-up in more words than the reader would expect, he is able to haunt an entire scene. For example, more than mere desolation affects the reader from the following image, in a passage from *The Cannibal* describing the streets of Spitzen-on-the-Dien, a defeated German town in 1945: "Bookstores and chemists' shops were smashed and pages from open books beat back and forth in the wind, while from split sides of decorated paper boxes a soft cheap powder was blown along the streets like fine snow. Papier mâché candies were trampled underfoot." Also, the recurrence of images (snow and dogs are two examples from *The Cannibal*) gives the sense of dream, of a psychic order, imposed upon and accenting the physical and moral disorder of the world.—ALAN TRACHTENBERG, "Barth and Hawkes: Two Fabulists," *Crt*, Fall 1963, p. 5

Hawkes' novels are full of unexplained events, untold histories that leave you with questions that cannot be answered. There is no pretense to that verisimilitude which gives you a rounded, completed world; on the contrary, his are angular, elliptical, incomplete worlds which have to leave you unsatisfied if you expect answers to all questions, but which do satisfy you once you realize that there are no answers. Not that there's any coy holding back on Hawkes' part: he could not possibly explain the ritual in the cemetery or that of the iguana on Catalina Kate's back in *Second Skin;* or the sinister priest's ritual at the end of *The Goose on the Grave*; or those of Il Gufo in *The Owl*. Most important of all, he cannot give you the motivations, the psychology of any of his characters. Like ⟨Nathanael⟩ West, and perhaps he gets it from West, Hawkes rejects psychological analysis willfully. To turn to his latest book, *Second Skin*, for a moment, consider Skipper and his father; Skipper and his mother; Skipper and his wife; Skipper and his daughter; Skipper and his son-in-law; Skipper and Tremlow; Skipper and Sonny; Skipper and Pixie; Skipper and Kate: explain love. Skipper and his wife, his daughter, Tremlow, Miranda, Captain Red, Jomo: explain hate, or, better still, despair. And certainly the same kinds of permutation and combination hold in *The Lime Twig*. "Freud is your Bulfinch; you cannot learn from him," Nathanael West once wrote. That is, the Greeks had no need for a textbook explicating their mythology; we have no need for one of psycho-sexual behavior. Hawkes can present his comic, violent rituals and the Freudian myths that give rise to them: he cannot explain them, except as Freud would, and that's not the novelist's job, or the critic's. Finally, every one of Hawkes' characters, and every one of those incredibly imagined incidents in all his books stands like a crux in a medieval manuscript: explain as you like, the crux stands, open to innumerable other possibilities, substantial as only a word on paper can be.—ROBERT I. EDENBAUM, "John Hawkes: *The Lime Twig* and Other Tenuous Horrors," *MR*, Summer 1966, pp. 471–72

The integrity of John Hawkes's voice and painful grace of his conceits are standards by which most recent American fiction is revealed to be not serious. Yet as about some powerful dreams and extraordinary waking experiences, one is likely to find oneself with little to *say* about Hawkes's works, for all the strength of one's response to them, beyond such banalities—but heartfelt!—as:

They're quite original. To mention Céline, Faulkner, Nathanael West, Djuna Barnes, Henry James, or the Symbolists, any of whom may come to mind as one reads *The Lime Twig, The Goose on the Grave*, and the rest, is to see how little after all one can lay hold of in the way of antecedents to Hawkes's voice and vision. He reminds one of no one, really; in the landscape of our fiction he stands improbably as Gibraltar: unaccountable, astonishing, formidable, sui generis and self-sufficient, at once familiar and exotic, flowers in its cracks and monkeys on its back.

They're quite different. They burden the spirit, weigh hard on the sensibility. Characteristically dark, they are in places downright opaque. Even *Second Skin*—the most luminous and, for Hawkes, even joyous of the novels—is no larky read; of *The Owl*, my favorite, I can absorb no more than seven pages at a time, so spirit-spending is the intensity of the prose. But if this difficulty is some barrier to explication—I wouldn't care to *teach* Hawkes's fiction, or attempt a critical essay—it is none to admiration. I'll understand *Ada* better when Alfred Appel annotates her; Stuart Gilbert's key to *Finnegans Wake* really does unlock some doors—but I love Nabokov's girl before I understand her, and roamed amazed in Joyce's corridors while still keyless. When the literary ornithologists write a Field Guide to Hawkes I'll read it gratefully, but as one already rapt in his flights, to learn not how to love them but to know how perhaps to account for their hold.

They're quite beautiful, as not all important writing is. And though his dramaturgic and choreographic imagination is extraordinary, the beauty is principally in Hawkes's language: in the diction, the cadences, the obscure meticulous passion of his narrative voice. Events the most outrageous are refracted through a dense and beautiful rhetoric which distances, dignifies, and fixes them—and makes them altogether plausible even as it heightens their comedy or terror. His telling voice is the singularity and chief richness of this great contemporary American writer who lives modestly among us. There's not one I more admire.—JOHN BARTH, "A Tribute to John Hawkes," *HA*, Oct. 1970, p. 11.

Works

If I skim over John Hawkes' *The Lime Twig*, it is in despair at my inability to convey its imaginative brilliance, its appreciation of the possibilities that lurk somewhere outside Eliot House. If you have ever read *Brighton Rock* while in a peyote trance, you may have some notion—I don't know—of what *The Lime Twig* is like. It is peopled by characters who come to live out their own nightmares. . . .

As in a dream, gratuitous horror mounts upon gratuitous horror; every scene unfolds like those nightmares in which, as one tries to cope with the rattlesnakes underfoot, a faceless body hurtles down an air-shaft somewhere in the distance. But the power of *The Lime Twig* is that the action takes place exactly on the *brink* of nightmare: it is not quite hallucination, and therefore nothing from which you can wake up; it is every waking wish carried to its logical extreme, and what Dora and Larry and Hencher and Michael and Margaret are screaming is simply *mon semblable, mon frére*. In brief, *The Lime Twig* made me more than happy, for the first time in some time, to set aside the *Hollywood Reporter*.—JOAN DIDION, "Notes from a Helpless Reader," *NaR*, July 15, 1961, p. 22

Like Hawkes's other novels, *Second Skin* is a relatively short book, with extreme compactness. But where his previous books have stressed horror, *Second Skin* is ebullient and joyous; it is, in short, about horror surmounted by lushness and love. The past is the locale of horror; there Skipper belonged to a family with an incredible talent for death; there took place the suicides of Skipper's father, his wife and his daughter, Cassandra, and the murder of his son-in-law, Fernandez.

The present is the scene of Dionysian mellowness; now, as Skipper reminisces about his past, he is ensconced on an unnamed tropical island in a large, new informal family with an equally extreme talent for life, whose principal members are the pregnant Catalina Kate and Sonny, his former mess boy, who is now his best friend and possibly (if Skipper is not), the father of Catalina Kate's baby. *Second Skin* is thus about two things simultaneously—a second life, and a first life seen through the perspective of the second. The book ends after the birth of Catalina Kate's baby amid beautiful harmonies of flesh and friendship.

Hawkes manages to talk about all this horror and joy without being either abstract or poetic (in the sense in which this is a vice for the novelist). *Second Skin* is full of the most exact observation, of beautifully realized though not chronologically ordered 'scenes.' . . .

Hawkes is an exact, wonderfully visual writer. Yet, precisely, he does not rely on his story to be self-evident. One has only to compare his treatment, in *Second Skin*, of the theme of a man shedding an old life for a more joyous and sensuous one with Bernard Malamud's recent *A New Life* to see the difference. Malamud's novel is shallow because it contains no point of view larger or more interesting than the very ordinary hero's very ordinary personal psychology. Hawkes's novel is compelling because Skipper is not so much an ordinary man (a realistic character in a realistic novel) as a palpable vessel of viscera and juices, his life not so much a story as a frieze of fleshy details. Hawkes does not just report the facts of vigor and renewal; his style enacts them.

For it is always, in a Hawkes novel, the style. He is the master of an immensely artful, corrugated surface of language—a looped, virile, restless style that really *is* the story. One usually speaks of an author's style, of course. But it's not enough to praise or disparage style; one must note the role of style in a given work. In some writers—say, Dostoyevsky or Dreiser—style is fairly unimportant; to say, therefore, that Dostoyevsky or Dreiser were sloppy or indifferent stylists is to say little against their work, which proposes quite different merits. But in a writer like Hawkes (like two other, very different, very good American writers, Djuna Barnes and Edward Dahlberg) style is—virtually—all. In *Second Skin*, style is the living incarnated form of the author's intelligence; everything is poured into it. Therefore, to say Hawkes's style is beautiful is scarcely to speak of something accessory. It is to speak of the life and intention of his books.

What makes Hawkes's books, however fine, still small scale, less than great? For me, these novels, with their intricate and allusively narrated plots, somehow fail wholly to connect with their major themes. The plot—vis-à-vis the theme—seems overgrown; as exotic details proliferate, the effects tend to cancel each other out. Then there is that persistent trait of understating the emotion of a violent scene, and Hawkes's habit of dramatizing the periphery rather than the center of an event. Sometimes I long to see some plain masonry behind the creeping vines and tendrils. But these are reservations which it is no doubt ungrateful to raise at this moment. The important thing to say now is that Hawkes is an extraordinary and admirable writer, and that in *Second Skin* he has written a beautiful book which is a worthy successor to his previous work.—SUSAN SONTAG, "A New Life for an Old One," *NYTBR*, April 5, 1964, p. 5

The story ⟨*Second Skin*⟩, "like to a murdering-piece in many places gives me superfluous death." The suicides and murder carry no demonic strain, no Faulknerian doom; there could be more or less or, conceivably, none. Skipper could have had other "casualties" against which to pose his present life. The structure seems akin to that of a 19th Century opera libretto, without architectural imperative, easily alterable, condensable, expansible, primarily a provider of occasions for arias, ensemble pieces, ballet.

The arias and so on that Hawkes supplies are not "big" in terms of sweep and surge. The mutiny, for example, seems to be taking place underwater in slow motion. To Hawkes the novel is a machine for turning experience into images, and he uses his dramatic moments as bases for constructs of supple, gorgeous prose. There is little sense of fate in Skipper's unhappy life; we feel instead that Hawkes simply wanted to write a series of highly subjective scenes about a man experiencing various deaths and remembering them in various contexts.

His reliance on his prose as such is certainly not misplaced. His figuration, selectivity, his ear and eye are extraordinarily fine and untiring. But one flaw in his method is that it spreads. He seemingly forgets when he is not in a "scene," and he gives almost everything the same rich treatment. Virtually every millimeter of the book's fabric goes under the microscope of his intensified vision. For instance, when Skipper and his daughter are traveling on a bus at night, she hands him a sandwich:

> She moved—my daughter, my museum piece—and hoisted the sack onto her lap and opened it, the brown paper stained with the mysterious dark oil stains of mayonnaise and tearing, disintegrating beneath her tiny white efficient fingers. Brisk fingers, mushy brown paper sack, food for the journey. She unwrapped a sandwich, for a moment posed with it—delicate woman, ghostly morsel of white bread and meat—then put it into my free hand which was outstretched and waiting. The bread was cold, moist, crushed thin with the imprint of dear Sonny's palm; the lettuce was a wrinkled leaf of soft green skin, the bits of pimiento were little gouts of jellied blood, the chicken was smooth, white, curved to the missing bone. I tasted it, sandwich smeared with moonlight, nibbled one wet edge—sweet art of the mess boy—then shoved the whole thing into my dry and smiling mouth and lay there chewing up Sonny's lifetime, swallowing, licking my fingers.

It is remarkable imagistic writing. It can be analyzed in terms of its internal rhythms, the intricacy of the recurrent and varied figures in that small space, the sense of wholeness of each phrase, each sentence, the cumulation of the whole passage. It might almost stand, typographically rearranged, as a poem. But in a novel, still enslaved as we no doubt are by conditioning of the past, we recognize the beauties at the same time that another lobe is thinking: "For God's sake, it's only a sandwich. Eat it, and let's move on." Thus this method tends to flatten the topography of the book. For all Hawkes' care to include peaks of climax, the long prairie of sandwiches, etc., is bathed in the same golden light as the peaks.

Another peril in his method is indicated by V. S. Pritchett's recent brisk comment on William Golding's new novel:

> The inside view inflates the novelist at the expense of his people. And seen from the inside as "thinkers" and so on, novelists are bores. The more distinguished the more boring. Novelists are not entitled to these personal gratifications. I do not believe that theories of "contemporary alienation", the "human

> crisis", or "our loneliness", etc., justify him in disposing of character. It is, at any rate, nine-tenths of our destiny.

The parallels between Golding and Hawkes are inexact but existent. For "thinkers," read "feelers," for "human crisis," read "crisis in the novel." Hawkes is not, like the Englishman, a dramatist of philosophical views, but his work is equally internal, equally far (in Irving Howe's phrase) from "the reality of *other minds*, minds quite unlike his own." The boredom—exquisite boredom, perhaps, in this case—of the solipsist scrutinizing his nerve-ends is inevitable.

The novel resolves to a solo virtuoso performance with props of people and incidents. Thus Hawkes disappoints in some measure even the reader seasoned by the "new" novel, perhaps because this author's sensibilities raise expectations of insight, of emotional effect, instead of well-articulated autism. I dare not aspire to Pritchett's note of pronunciamento, but perhaps I may suggest that Hawkes' definition of the novel is ineluctably and stringently circumscribed. Whatever his subject matter in this book, Hawkes seems primarily concentrated on its rendering, rather than its realization in us. The medium becomes to a considerable degree the object. Thus, although *Second Skin* certainly has other aims, it *seems* to exist for the sake of its admittedly exceptional prose.—STANLEY KAUFFMANN, "Further Adventures of the Novel," *NR*, June 6, 1964, pp. 20–22

Charivari, Hawkes's first fiction, found the voice for all the rest. It is a caprice about a 40-year-old bridegroom's flight from family and marriage into hallucination. And it boils with rhetoric. The ideas—about vacant sex, caste and incomprehensible human motivation—seem to evaporate into language. Hawkes began *Charivari* on a working vacation in Montana while soaking his feet, afflicted by cowboy boots, in chemicals. The experience turned earnest, and the physical discomfort and Montana dryness seem to have been abstracted into the novella. A work that gives pain, it shows Hawkes's first sighting of himself and his world of cracked mirrors.

In *The Cannibal* Hawkes found theme and story to convey a wider terror. Completed, as was *Charivari*, in Albert Guérard's class at Harvard, it prophesies a neo-Gothic Germany rising out of the ashes of two world wars. A single American G.I. on a motorcycle, Leevey, rules a third of the burnt-out Third Reich. At a point in this panorama of the dislocated and pathological, Leevey is murdered by Zizendorf, a Nazi who lives in a boarding house in tiny Spitzen-on-the-Dein. The house, its occupants, their behavior suggest an epidemic of horrors attacking Europe. The town is "as shriveled in structure and as decomposed as an ox tongue black with ants." A monkey screams, "Dark is life, dark, dark is death." The local undertaker runs out of embalming fluid for the stacked corpses. One character desperately plays the tuba all night long.

Out of this surrealist dream of evil articulated in cascades of images—more murder, desiccated eroticism, insane delusions, preparation for a feast on a boy's body—Zizendorf emerges as Germany's new Führer. Hawkes wrote the novel after reading an account of German cannibalism in *Time* magazine. "I thought I was telling a perfectly straight story," he later said. "I wasn't really concerned at all with what kind of fiction I was writing. I was just trying to write." The shock of war revisited Hawkes in memory and detonated an explosion of imagination and recalled destruction. The apocalyptic revelation of *The Cannibal* is unique in American fiction that came out of that war.

Hawkes's works immediately after *The Cannibal* are symbols and situations, literary memoranda on the world as a moral death factory. *The Beetle Leg* ⟨1951⟩ came, like *Charivari*, from Hawkes's summer in Montana, where he worked on the construction of the Fort Peck irrigation dam. A laborer accidentally buried in the dam's mountain of dirt was never found. "I got to thinking of him as swimming around in that sea of mud," Hawkes says. In the novel Hawkes places this death at the center of a trance-like demonology and draws his monsters into vague association with the landslide. *The Beetle Leg* parodies the exhausted Western—dumb Indians, bad doctors, and Red Devil motorcyclists for savages. Mythically it reproduces purgatory: damned souls, wasteland, no exit. —WEBSTER SCHOTT, "John Hawkes, American Original," *NYTBR*, May 29, 1966, p. 4

Mr. Hawkes's book ⟨*The Lime Twig*⟩ transposes the sounds of excitement into the key of terror. He writes not to make us see but to make us fear. Indeed, a churlish reader who insisted upon a story would be well advised to go back to *Brighton Rock*. If you were to read Mr. Hawkes for the story, as Johnson said of Richardson, your impatience would be so much fretted that you would hang yourself. Johnson then advised Boswell to read Richardson for the sentiment, but this procedure in reading Mr. Hawkes's book will go unrewarded.

"You suffer *The Lime Twig* like a dream", Flannery O'Connor once wrote, a Gothic writer responding to one of her fellowship. In this tale, events have the kind of weight they would acquire in a nightmare. If there is a logic of metaphor, there is a logic of image. Mr. Hawkes is given to these forms of logic. So in *The Lime Twig*, as in Mr. Hawkes's *The Cannibal*, the plot is allowed to submit its proposals only when every consideration of image and metaphor has been fulfilled. Thick beats Margaret with a truncheon, Banks is trampled to death by the horses, Cowles's throat is cut; but these episodes may be understood not as events but as images. The image does not refer to anything in particular but to everything in general which shares the nature of the image. The procedure is Symbolist, as comparison with the procedures of T. S. Eliot's early poems would show. What apears as empirical detail is empirical only in appearance. . . . After a while, the effects begin to sound predictable:

> For now he was drunk, drunk into a stupor of civility and strength, that state of brutal calm, and only a little trickle of sweat behind the ear betrayed his drunkenness.

The rhetoric is high for its occasion, as if Mr. Hawkes could not run the risk of letting it speak for itself. Generally in *The Lime Twig* the chosen ground of rhetoric is very high: the result is that when rhetorical control falters, the sentences are propelled only by their own insistence. There are some magnificent passages in the book, but the work as a whole is uneven. Mr. Hawkes is an experimental writer, full of daring and high flight, but *The Lime Twig* is often self-indulgent in the exercise of its rhetoric. To say that among contemporary works of fiction it is unusually impressive is to say the obvious.—UNSIGNED, "Into the Atmosphere," *TLS*, Aug. 29, 1968, p. 929

John Hawkes's *The Blood Oranges* fails because it is the work of a contemptible imagination. Hawkes has always seemed to me more an unadmitted voyeur of horror than its calm delineator, but in this new novel the pretense that what is being described is horrifying is dropped, and we have only the nightmare of a narrator unable to see how awful he is. . . .

Hawkes has many admirers, which means some will note that I have completely missed the fact that it is all a put-on;

some others will suspect I am guilty of all those sins that Hawkes's narrator so cleverly exposes in your ordinary man. So be. But when horror becomes a pastime it should announce itself or at least know itself; when reticence and shyness become the great human vices, then their opposites should be clearly and ably defended; when the man who does not want his wife sleeping around makes her wear a rusty and viciously designed chastity belt, then narrator and author should not imagine it is chastity's fault; when life is insistently joyless it should not be called good, or even particularly tolerable; when people stop mattering to a novelist, the writing will suffer and the writer should stop.—ROGER SALE, "What Went Wrong?," *NYRB*, Oct. 21, 1971, p. 3

IRVING MALIN
From "Self-Love"
New American Gothic
1962, pp. 38–44

Unlike the other writers already discussed, John Hawkes has not received recognition for his Gothic talent. Perhaps he is less popular because his fiction appears completely out-of-focus. He prefers to present characters who "float in a space where essence is indistinctness, endure in a time which refuses either to begin or end."[1] What is at the center of his "conjunction of reason and madness, blur and focus"?[2] One of the chief concerns of Hawkes is narcissism. In *The Cannibal* he presents an overwhelming study of Germany in 1914 and 1945. Like Mrs. McCullers and Miss O'Connor he shows us that the community is often a monstrous reflection of individual lovers. The narrator is Zizendorf. Zizendorf resembles the others who have neglected everything except one abstraction: he must kill the American soldier who guards his sector. His mission, he proclaims, is based on love of the fatherland: "The rise of the German people and their reconstruction is no longer questionable—the land, the Teutonic land, gives birth to the strongest of races, the Teutonic race." But Hawkes shows us that underneath Zizendorf's will to power is great anxiety. The German asserts leadership because he needs adulation and respect which will enhance his self-love. He plays a role; the other weaklings around him believe in the grotesque illusion: they become loyal followers. "Success is almost ours." Ironically enough, Zizendorf's victim, Leevey, is also self-centered. He likes being "overseer for a sector of land that was one-third of the nation," although he "frowns with the responsibility." The American reflects his German counterpart in neglecting common humanity. He simply regards Germans as instruments to be manipulated—like the slut he uses.

The title of the novel refers, then, to the narcissistic cannibalism that eats the community. Hawkes, however, introduces an actual cannibal who, like Enoch Emory, exaggerates the already grotesque situation. The Duke pursues a boy, slashes him, and takes the fragments to his house for dinner. His inhumanity is pictured in the following way: "The very fact that it was not a deer or a possum made the thing hard to skin . . . ; its infernal humanness carried over even in death and made the carcass just as difficult as the human being had itself been. Every time a bone broke his prize became mangled, every piece that was lost in the mud made the whole thing defective, more imperfect in death." The Duke believes in ordered perfection. By seeking this perfection (which is never achieved) he loses his humanity: *he* becomes "mangled" and "defective."

I have suggested that a recurrent image in new American Gothic is the "mechanical." Hawkes suggests the horror of Germany by using almost obsessively such imagery. We have seen the methodical cannibalism of the Duke. Akin to it is the insistence on the institution. In the very first sentence we see "its delicate and isolated buildings trembling over the gravel and cinder floor of the valley." The institution opens at the end of the novel when "public spirit" revives it. The insane asylum—like the rigid army camp of Mrs. McCullers (in "The Displaced Person")—is a proper setting for narcissistic compulsion. The entire landscape of *The Cannibal* is cluttered with metallic, nonhuman elements: hatchets, motorcycles, and steel canes.

Animals emerge to engulf humanity. We read: "The town . . . was as shriveled in structure and as decomposed as an oxen's tongue black with ants." Food is unappetizing: "sleek" sausages "bulged like pig's hind legs." Dogs pursue the train: "these dogs ran with the train, nipped at the tie rods, snapped at the lantern from the caboose, and carrying on conversation with the running wheels, begged to be let into the common parlor." The Merchant's corpse is pictured: "in his open mouth there rested a large cocoon, vividly protruding and white, which moved sometimes as if it were alive." The emphasis on the animalistic and the mechanical influences our attitude toward the characters. Hawkes presents an inhuman world in which people are trapped; they cannot rise above what Albert J. Guérard calls "impotent mechanical ruttings."[3] They are Bosch-like creatures.

Hawkes also uses animalistic imagery in *The Owl*. Here the hangman of a strangely medieval town is viewed as the owl. History has decreed that his escutcheon bear the bird: "with wisdom, horns, and field rodent half-destroyed, hardly visible under the talons." He falls in love with the dynastic role, and he always acts like a cruel bird. He preys on the weak community under his mountain-top castle. A Zizendorf, he drowns in his reflection as he "assumed rule to the archaic slow drumming of the nocturnal thick wings . . . bearing instantaneously the pain of authority."

As in *The Cannibal* stone and metal replace the human element. Thus we are given a lengthy description of the castle which images the "iron-edged view of the world" possessed by its master. Even the ritual hanging emphasizes "chains" and "bolts" for the victim. (Actually there are two victims: the hangman and the hanged.) The vital sun is "urged down the spires of the scaffold." The landscape is dominated by the "power of blackness." The hangman's black hood symbolizes his refusal to see humanity clearly; he prefers to recognize weakness, sin, guilt. But the people who live under his rule are attracted to the hood—"all their thoughts and feelings, the very grayness of hair, vanished when the hangman put on his black cape." The hangman watches the "coming of dark from the high tower."

In this inhuman, suffocating, iron world Hawkes introduces Antonia. Because the hangman delights in attacking the "normal," the living, he loves the girl. He refuses to allow her to marry the prisoner. He uses her as does Leevey the slut to consolidate his power. Antonia, attracted and repelled like all of the citizens, succumbs to him and consequently loses her chance for marriage and health. At the end of the novelette, we see Antonia with "altered" complexion: "the rest of her days would be spent with the manual for the virgins not yet released to marriage."

The Owl stresses the "covenant" between hangman and hanged, lover and loved, in a metaphoric way. It could have been a much greater work if Hawkes had made us understand why the narcissistic urge erupts. As do Capote and Mrs.

McCullers he presents a stylized closed circle or—to use his words—a "demon's iron halo." But why do some love their halo? And how did they get it?

The Lime Twig, Hawkes' latest novel, presents the same theme: the inhuman reflection of narcissism. Leslie Fiedler has defined it as "the fact that love breeding terror is itself the final terror."[4] The first lover we meet is Hencher. A weak son who lives with his mother, he can never grow up. He likes the security she offers him (even when he is middle-aged). Never able to separate himself from her while she is alive, he must continue to live with her after death. He returns to the old rooming house; he eats the same food. He falls in love with "past glory" but it is evident that he really loves his sick, effeminate nature. It is all he has. Hencher lives a circular, compulsive life. He circles back to the rooming house where he lived with his mother. He "prowls" through the apartment: "I found her [Margaret's] small tube of cosmetic for the lips and, in the lavatory, drew a red circle with it round each of my eyes." Earlier he enters an airplane which has crashed and settles the pilot's "helmet securely on his own smooth head." He returns always to the womb.

His circular life drowns Mr. and Mrs. Banks. Because of his own dream-like state, Banks submits to Hencher's crazy plea to steal a horse. By doing so, he can become his unreal, glamorized reflection—that of sportsman and lover. Banks flees from "suffocating" marriage to the race track—another violent circle. Mrs. Banks also lives in a fragmented world. She cannot live without her husband. The love is too unnatural to remain intact. Margaret is a child: the only way she can exist is by becoming her husband (as Hencher becomes his mother). She waits patiently for him to return; she becomes "dead to the world."

Responsible for the tragedies—Hencher is kicked to death by the horse; Margaret is beaten by one thief; Michael falls onto the track before the field of horses—are thieves. Hawkes shows us that they are narcissists who will themselves to power. Larry is in charge. He cares only about himself, using weaklings to help him assert power. (As in *The Owl* and *The Cannibal* slave and master are two sides of the same coin.) In spite of overwhelming pride, Larry is as compulsive and dream-like as Hencher and Michael Banks. He must have Little Dora and the others idolize him: "Larry turned slowly round so they could see, and there was the gun's blue butt, the dazzling links of steel, the hairless and swarthy torso."

Again Hawkes uses the mechanical to reinforce the inhuman compulsion of narcissists. Note the "dazzling links of steel" mentioned above. The entire existence of Larry is dominated by steel or stone. When we first see him, he is described as "heavy as a horse cart of stone." Later we see his "vest of linked steel, shiny, weighing about five pounds." There is repeated emphasis on material (as in *The Cannibal*). Margaret becomes a "white sheet"; Hencher wears elastic sleeves on his thighs; the thieves cut the "stuffing in bulky sawdust layers away from the frame of the furniture." In this nonliving world action is either violent or automatic (often both): in the steam room we see "only a lower world of turning and crawling and drowning men." Michael Banks "pumps the hand" of Syb, his dancing partner. Thick's arm "quivers" as he pounds Margaret with the "truncheon." The "riders coming knee to knee with tangle of sticks and the noise" kill Banks. Leslie Fiedler is surely correct when he states that Hawkes gives us the "consciousness we live by but do not record in books—untidy, half-focused, disarrayed."[5] At the center of this consciousness lies the pool of Narcissus.

Notes

1. Leslie Fiedler, "The Pleasures of John Hawkes," intro. to *The Lime Twig* (New York: New Directions, 1961), p. ix.
2. Ibid., p. xiv.
3. Albert J. Guérard, "Introduction," *The Cannibal* (New York: New Directions, 1949), p. xiv.
4. Leslie Fiedler, p. xi.
5. Ibid., p. xiv.

JOHN HAWKES

From an interview by John J. Enck

Wisconsin Studies in Contemporary Literature
Summer 1965, pp. 142–55

Enck: As you know, the "avant-garde" was a rather popular concept about twenty years ago, but seems to be less so now. Do you have any views on the writer as experimenter?

Hawkes: Of course I think of myself as an experimental writer. But it's unfortunate that the term "experimental" has been used so often by reviewers as a pejorative label intended to dismiss as eccentric or private or excessively difficult the work in question. My own fiction is not merely eccentric or private and is not nearly so difficult as it's been made out to be. I should think that every writer, no matter what kind of fiction writer he may be or may aspire to be, writes in order to create the future. Every fiction of any value has about it something new. At any rate, the function of the true innovator or specifically experimental writer is to keep prose alive and constantly to test in the sharpest way possible the range of our human sympathies and constantly to destroy mere surface morality. What else were we trying to get at?

Enck: The concept of the avante-garde.

Hawkes: America has never had what we think of as the avant-garde. Gertrude Stein, Djuna Barnes, whose novel *Nightwood* I admire enormously, Henry Miller—no doubt these are experimental writers. But I don't think we've ever had in this country anything like the literary community of the French Surrealists or the present day French anti-novelists. And I'm not sure such a community would be desirable. On the other hand, in the past few years we've probably heard more than ever before about an existing avant-garde in America—we've witnessed the initial community of Beat writers, we're witnessing now what we might call the secondary community of Beat writers, recently many of us have defended *The Tropic of Cancer*. But I confess I find no danger, no true sense of threat, no possibility of sharp artistic upheaval in this essentially topical and jargonistic rebellion. Henry Miller's view of experience is better than most, Edward Dahlberg is a remarkably gifted writer who has still not received full recognition, I for one appreciate Norman Mailer's pugilistic stance. But none of this has much to do with the novel, and so far Beat activity in general seems to me to have resulted in sentimentality or dead language. My own concept of "avant-garde" has to do with something constant which we find running through prose fiction from Quevedo, the Spanish picaresque writer, and Thomas Nashe at the beginnings of the English novel, down through Lautréamont, Céline, Nathanael West, Flannery O'Connor, James Purdy, Joseph Heller, myself. This constant is a quality of coldness, detachment, ruthless determination to face up to the enormities of ugliness and potential failure within ourselves and in the world around us, and to bring to this exposure a savage or saving comic spirit and the saving beauties of language. The need is to maintain the truth of the fractured picture; to expose, ridicule, attack, but always to create and to throw into new light our potential for violence and absurdity as well as for graceful action. I don't like soft, loose prose or fiction which tries to cope too directly with life itself or is based indulgently on personal experience. On the other hand, we ought to respect resistance to commonplace authority wherever we find it, and this attitude at least is evident in the Beat world. But I suppose I regret so much attention being spent on the essentially flatulent products of a popular cult. A writer who truly and greatly sustains us is Nabokov. . . .

Enck: An aspect of your work that I have always appreciated, which I think many other critics have not, is the comic element. You have referred several times to comic writing—would you like to say something more about what you regard as the importance of comedy in your work?

Hawkes: I'm grateful to you for viewing my fiction as comic. Men like Guérard have written about the wit and black humor in my novels, but I think you're right that reviewers in general have concentrated on the grotesque and nightmarish qualities of my work, have made me out to be a somber writer dealing only with pain, perversion, and despair. Comedy puts all this into a very different perspective, I think. Of course I don't mean to apologize for the disturbing nature of my fiction by calling it comic, and certainly don't mean to minimize the terror with which this writing confronts the reader—my aim has always been the opposite, never to let the reader (or myself) off the hook, so to speak, never to let him think that the picture is any less black than it is or that there is any easy way out of the nightmare of human existence. But though I'd be the first to admit to sadistic impulses in the creative process, I must say that my writing is not mere indulgence in violence or derangement, is hardly intended simply to shock. As I say, comedy, which is often closely related to poetic uses of language, is what makes the difference for me. I think that the comic method functions in several ways: on the one hand it serves to create sympathy, compassion, and on the other it's a means for judging human failings as severely as possible; it's a way of exposing evil (one of the pure words I mean to preserve) and of persuading the reader that even he may not be exempt from evil; and of course comic distortion tells us that anything is possible and hence expands the limits of our imaginations. Comic vision always suggests futurity, I think, always suggests a certain hope in the limitless energies of life itself. In *Second Skin* I tried consciously to write a novel that couldn't be mistaken for anything but a comic novel. I wanted to expose clearly what I thought was central to my fictional efforts but had been generally overlooked in *The Cannibal, The Lime Twig, The Beetle Leg*. Obviously Faulkner was one of the greatest of all comic writers—Nabokov is a living example of comic genius. . . .

Enck: To what degree are you worried about structure in your novels? Do you generally think of your novels in terms of a formal structure of the narrator, or do you discover structure as you write?

Hawkes: My novels are not highly plotted, but certainly they're elaborately structured. I began to write fiction on the assumption that the true enemies of the novel were plot, character, setting, and theme, and having once abandoned these familiar ways of thinking about fiction, totality of vision or structure was really all that remained. And structure—verbal and psychological coherence—is still my largest concern as a writer. Related or corresponding event, recurring image and recurring action, these constitute the essential substance or meaningful density of my writing. However, as I suggested before, this kind of structure can't be planned in advance but can only be discovered in the writing process itself. The success of the effort depends on the degree and quality of consciousness that can be brought to bear on fully liberated materials of the unconscious. I'm trying to hold in balance poetic and novelistic methods in order to make the novel a more valid and pleasurable experience. Of course it's obvious that from *The Cannibal* to *Second Skin* I've moved from nearly pure vision to a kind of work that appears to resemble much more closely the conventional novel. In a sense there was no other direction to take, but in part this shift came about, I think, from an increasing need to parody the conventional novel. As far as the first-person narrator goes, I've worked my way slowly toward that method by a series of semi-conscious impulses and sheer accidents. *The Cannibal* was written in the third person, but in revision I found myself (perversely or not) wishing to project myself into the fiction and to become identified with its most criminal and, in a conventional sense, least sympathetic spokesman, the neo-Nazi leader of the hallucinated uprising. I simply went through the manuscript and changed the pronouns from third to first person, so that the neo-Nazi Zizendorf became the teller of those absurd and violent events. The result was interesting, I think, not because *The Cannibal* became a genuine example of first-person fiction, but because its "narrator" naturally possessed an unusual omniscience, while the authorial consciousness was given specific definition, definition in terms of humor and "black" intelligence. When I finished *The Beetle Leg* (a third-person novel), I added a prologue spoken in the first person by a rather foolish and sadistic sheriff, and this was my first effort to render an actual human voice. Similarly, Hencher's first-person prologue in *The Lime Twig* (also a third-person novel) was an afterthought, but his was a fully created voice that dramatized a character conceived in a certain depth. This prologue led me directly to *Second Skin* which, as you know, is narrated throughout in the first person by Skipper who, as I say, had his basis in Hencher. . . .

Enck: We can have a last question. In *The Lime Twig* you killed off Michael Banks and Margaret, the gang survive, at the end the detectives do not accomplish much. Despite what you've said about comedy, this novel doesn't appear to be very hopeful. Would you care to comment on this problem?

Hawkes: For me the blackest fictions liberate the truest novelistic sympathy. When Michael is killed the whole world collapses with him, and comically—that is, the race track is littered with the bodies of the fallen jockeys and horses. And at the moment of Margaret's death, Larry, the head of the gang, is speaking comically about his hopes of journeying to a new world full of lime trees. (It's a journey which he won't be able to take of course, since his gigantic plan has failed.) But at any rate Michael has destroyed the "golden bowl" of earthly pleasure and destructive dream and has atoned for his betrayal of Margaret. This ending along with the novel's general pairing off of sensual and destructive experiences to me suggests a kind of hope. The fictional rhythm itself is in a way hopeful. But I admit I'm reluctant to argue too strongly for the necessity of hope.

Enck: What about the detectives? Are they anything more than comic?

Hawkes: The detectives represent law and order, or the baffled and banal mind at large. Specifically, and along with Sidney Slyter, they may be seen as images of the absurd and lonely author himself. Even the author is not exempt from judgment in my fiction. But at least the detectives, in trying to learn what the reader has presumably learned already (and it's clear, I think, that these obtuse men from Scotland Yard will never solve the "crime"), are attempting to complete the cycle of mysterious experience. At least they, like ourselves, will go on hunting for clues.

CHRISTOPHER RICKS
"Chamber of Horrors"

New Statesman, March 11, 1966, pp. 339–40

'A waxen tableau, no doubt the product of a slight and romantic fancy.' When John Hawkes put those words into the mouth of Skipper, the narrator of his new novel, it must have been with some sense that *Second Skin* would probably be similarly patronised, with the reviewers admiring an indisputable skill (waxen tableaux are hard to create) and yet puzzling at a romantic pointlessness. Not that the visionary memory which elicits from Skipper this flash of self-revulsion is in fact merely slight and romantic—it catches with a comic lyricism the child's memory (fantasy?) of his mother being driven away in a primitive car, the car 'severe and tangled like a complicated golden insect', the mother 'raising a soft white arm as if to wave'. There is an idyllic frailty about this moment, which follows hard on the black absurdity of his father's shooting himself in the lavatory, and is immediately followed by an anecdote which takes up 'waxen tableau' with a vengeance:

> My mother, unable to bear the sound of the death-dealing shot—it must have lodged in her head like a shadow of the bullet that entered my father's—deafened herself one muggy night, desperately, painfully, by filling both lovely ears with the melted wax from one of our dining-room candles.

Yet when we think of all the horrors that are perpetrated in Mr Hawkes's novels, as in all those modern 'Gothic' novels which Leslie Fiedler so admires, we may be inclined to take that waxen tableau in a harsher sense. It was Shaw, contemptuous of all the *grand guignol* which he saw in Jacobean tragedy, who fixed John Webster as a 'Tussaud Laureate'. Do the murders, suicides, mutilations, perversions, in *Second Skin* add up to more than a Chamber of Horrors? What is in question is not Mr Hawkes's talent or imagination—he can write with a precise intensity on a range of subjects and emotions. The account in *Second Skin* of what it feels like to be tattooed, the pages which describe the difficulty of removing an iguana that has clamped itself to someone's back—these evocations are certainly not less than *tours de force*. But as with the violent happenings of *The Duchess of Malfi*, we find it necessary to ask what saves such writing from mere sensationalism.

Part of the answer would be the sense of humour. Humour is no guarantee of moral *bona fides*, but it does change *Second Skin* into something very different from Jacobean tragedy. To laugh at Webster is to annihilate him (as amateur theatricals are always demonstrating), whereas the poised ostentation of Mr Hawkes's style both invites and then freezes our laughter. It is the same with the purple patches: they know they are purple, and they choose—not succumb to—the cadences of blank verse. The decadent romanticism is not self-indulgent but is *about* self-indulgence:

> I heard the firmness of the dreaming voice,
> The breath control of the determined heart,
> The whisper dying out for emphasis,
> Hoping to keep her feathery voice alive.
> The darkest hour at the end of the night watch,
> When sleep is only a bright immensity.
> 'But wasn't Cassandra still my teenage bomb?
> And wasn't this precisely what I loved?'

That, and much more, you can assemble from less than two pages of prose. The rhythms are luxuriantly enervated, but they are not inadvertent—Mr Hawkes's subject here is the romantic, intense, but preposterous and precarious love between father and grown-up daughter, a relationship which is tinged with incest but perhaps not more so than is commonplace.

Is it an accident that the father-daughter relationship should be a recurring obsession of Dickens, and that it should be Dickens whose prose most notoriously falls into blank verse? Gabriel Pearson has a fine analysis of this phenomenon in *The Old Curiosity Shop* (a novel in which sentimentality, humour, romance, deformity and terror create a world not unlike Mr Hawkes's), and he shows that the blank verse is sometimes altogether apt: 'The primitive quality of the feeling is breathtaking: yet there is a corresponding mythic strength which is appropriately rendered in metre.'

Mythic, yes. And it was surely the main gap in Leslie Fiedler's brilliant study of *Love and Death in the American Novel* that he seemed concerned with only one sense of the word 'mythic'. He says practically nothing about classical mythology and its relevance to these Gothic horrors. Mr Fiedler sometimes writes as if the American imagination had created its terror from nothing but its Gothic predecessors and its own guilt. 'The importance in our literature of brother-sister incest and necrophilia,' the 'obsession with death, incest and homosexuality'—these are true things to remark, but what needs also to be remarked is the similarity of such Gothicism to the doings of classical mythology. A father behaves so cruelly that the mother gives her son a knife with which the father is castrated as he is about to make love to the mother. A man finds that he has been made to eat his own son, runs away in terror, and later rapes his own daughter. A man who loses a competition is flayed alive. A treacherous servant is forced to cut off his own flesh, cook it, and eat it. The violence and perversion of such classical stories provide an analogue for the American Gothic. The myths of Greece and Rome, too, can share in Mr Fiedler's observation that 'the great works of American fiction are notoriously at home in the children's section of the library.'

It is precisely the child's trustingness—dreadfully, fatally, persisting even in the adult—which creates the hideous terror of Mr Hawkes's earlier novel, *The Lime Twig*, a story of racehorses and gangsters which suffers from the inevitable comparison with *Brighton Rock* but which has at times a remarkable force. The woman strapped to the bed and tortured by a sadist cannot believe that this can happen to her. Surely being innocent must save you—but it doesn't, because there is no cosmic headmaster. If there were, he might resemble Saturn. It is the same with Mr Hawkes's first novel, *The Cannibal*, a distorted picture of Germany after the war, an eerie landscape of real and unreal cruelties. 'Throughout these winters Madame Snow could not believe that the worst would come.' But sometimes the worst will come, and not to believe so is one of the marks of weakness and of woe. At intervals throughout *The Cannibal* we catch glimpses of the Duke stalking a boy. We expect rape, but we meet cannibalism.

Too much need not be made of the fact that the desperate daughter in *Second Skin* is named Cassandra. On his first page Mr Hawkes offers us not only classical allusions but also one of those strange fantasies of sex-change which figure so prominently in the myths.

> Had I been born my mother's daughter instead of son—and the thought is not so improbable, after all, and causes me neither pain, fear nor embarrassment when I give it my casual and interested contempla-

> tion—I would not have matured into a muscular and self-willed Clytemnestra but rather into a large and innocent Iphigenia betrayed on the beach. A large and slow-eyed and smiling Iphigenia, to be sure, even more full to the knife than that real girl struck down once on the actual shore. Yet I am convincined that in my case I should have been spared. All but sacrificed I should have lived, somehow, in my hapless way; to bleed but not to bleed to death would have been my fate, forgiving them all while attempting to wipe the smoking knife on the bottom of my thick yellow skirt.

A father, a daughter and a wife all of whom commit suicide, and a son-in-law cruelly murdered—the tale is told through dimly-lit flashbacks, and it is true that Skipper was in a way right to be 'convinced that in my case I should have been spared.' He is not one of nature's murderees, and yet Mr Hawkes never allows us to forget that the conviction that in our case we shall somehow be spared is one of our most foolish assurances.

But the mock-heroic in the style is comic, even if not only so, and it shows that the mythical nature of the horror is related to the other attributes which save *Second Skin* from sensationalism: its humour and its fully-conscious poeticising. If we want a parallel from the past, it will not be Jacobean tragedy but the Elizabethan minor epic, where Ovid's tales of violence and perversion, the 'heady riots, incests, rapes' of Marlowe, were made into something new, something that did not deny the cruelty but was determined to find a cool way of reducing cruelty's power to drive us mad. The ambition of Mr Hawkes's writing is not the impure one of making us tolerate violence, but that of helping us to find violence endurable.

The counterpart in classical mythology is also relevant to one of the first and most acute analyses of American Gothic fiction, an essay which still has not received recognition as a critical classic. Writing in the *Edinburgh Review* in 1829, William Hazlitt used the Gothic novels of Charles Brockden Brown in order to point the contrast with English fiction. The superstitions of England both authenticated and mitigated the violence of her fiction, as Hazlitt pointed out half-mockingly: 'Not a castle without the stain of blood upon its floor or winding steps: not a glen without its ambush or its feat of arms: not a lake without its Lady!' But the Gothic terrors of Charles Brockden Brown were exaggerated just because they were created from scratch:

> They are full (to disease) of imagination—but it is forced, violent, and shocking. This is to be expected, we apprehend, in attempts of this kind in a country like America, where there is, generally speaking, no *natural imagination*. The mind must be excited by overstraining, by pulleys and levers.

And because of the lack of a potent superstition in America, 'the writer is obliged to make up by incessant rodomontade, and face-making.'

Certainly the modern Gothic novelists have too often gone in for rodomontade and face-making. The success of so much of Mr Hawkes's writing—the feeling that he is a caricaturist rather than a parodist—has to do with his ability to make classical mythology take the place of that shared superstition which Hazlitt rightly saw as responsible for the hectic rhetoric of terror. But the peace to which Skipper finally comes, after the brutalities of a naval mutiny and of a suicide in the motel, is that which goes with his work artificially-inseminating cows, and *Second Skin* also succeeds because of its ability to impart warmth and esteem to such work. It has its failures, most obviously a dissipating fragmentariness which prevents the whole novel from ever becoming more than the sum of its best parts. But the neglect of Hawkes in this country makes it more important to remark the successes of this fastidious and frightening novelist.

ROBERT SCHOLES

"John Hawkes as Novelist: The Example of the Owl"

Hollins Critic, June 1977, pp. 1–10

For over twenty-five years John Hawkes has been a unique voice in American letters. Belonging to no school, following no fashion, he has paid the price exacted of such loners by the literary establishment. He has been reviewed capriciously, embarrassed by unconsidered praise and attacked with ill-tempered venom. His admirers have been mostly his fellow writers, some English teachers, and their students. Recently he has been more honored abroad than at home. For better or worse, he has been taken up by the French, who can see in his writing connections to the surrealists, to Faulkner, and to their own *nouveau roman*. Perhaps they will teach us to appreciate him, as they taught us to appreciate jazz music, Edgar Poe, William Faulkner, and the American films of the studio era.

Meanwhile we must do the best we can to understand him ourselves, which involves measuring his strengths and weaknesses as a writer, and sorting out his best work from his less successful efforts. This discussion is intended as a part of that sorting out. *The Owl* originally appeared in 1954, in a double volume with another short novel, also set in Italy, called *The Goose on the Grave*. That these two works are of unequal quality has become increasingly apparent over the years. *The Goose on the Grave* suffers from a murky atmosphere, a lack of focus and coherence, as if indeed it were written by someone who felt (as Hawkes has claimed to feel) that plot, character, setting, and theme are the worst enemies of the novel. *The Owl* is altogether different. It is tightly organized. It is strong precisely in plot, character, setting, and theme. Which suggests that with Hawkes, as with many other writers, we will do well to take D. H. Lawrence's advice and not trust the teller but the tale. After its first publication, *The Owl* was reprinted in *Lunar Landscapes*, a collection of short novels and stories of which it is fair to say that *The Owl* is its only entirely successful work.

The Owl is one of the very best of Hawkes' fictions, and probably the best introduction to his work. His method has always been to work with strong images that can be developed into scenes of nightmarish power and vividness, and then to seek some means of connecting these scenes in a coherent and developmental way. Because he starts with images rather than with a story, his work *is* different from conventionally plotted fiction, though this is not the same thing as being without plot altogether. Over the years, as his work has developed, he has turned more and more to the unifying voice of a single narrator as a way of giving coherence to the events of his narrative. At the same time, his fiction, which began with an emphasis on terror, violence, and death, has moved from those horrors toward a lush eroticism, initiated in the closing section of *Second Skin* and continued in *The Blood Oranges* and *Death, Sleep and the Traveller*. Even *Travesty*, which moves toward death, draws most of its strength from its slightly over-ripe eroticism—what the French, in speaking of the decadence that brings the grapes of Sauternes to their highest pitch of sweetness, call *la pourriture noble*.

The Owl is about rottenness, also, but there is no suggestion in it of what Walter Pater liked to call "a sweet and comely decadence." Only the narrator of the book finds anything sweet and comely in his world, and he is clearly a monster. He is, in fact, the epitome of fascism, at once hangman and dictator, ruling over a decaying little world with absolute and terrible authority. *The Owl* is an imaginative probe into the heart of Italian fascism, with its deep roots in Imperial Rome and the Roman Catholic church. The novel is localized and historicized, as is much of Hawkes's best work, especially his early novels. The England of *The Lime Twig* (1961), the American West of *The Beetle Leg* (1951), the Germany of *The Cannibal* (1949), and the Italy of *The Owl* (1954) are imaginative settings, to be sure, rather than documentaries of social realities. But they are attempts to reach a kind of depth, a kind of truth about human experience, which is based on historical and cultural processes. The narrator of *The Owl* is as much connected to a particular heritage as the speaker of Browning's "My Last Duchess" though he is not so precisely located in time and space. It is relevant to think of Browning here, for Hawkes has come to specialize in the extended dramatic monologue. Like Browning, he is drawn to the strange and the perverse, and he delights in immersing his readers in the voice and vision of a character whose consciousness is disturbing to "normal" sensibilities. The point of this immersion in the abhorrent is to force readers to acknowledge a kind of complicity, to admit that something in us resonates to all sorts of monstrous measures, even as we recognize and condemn the evil consciousness for what it is. As a literary strategy this requires great delicacy and control. Both the horrible complicity and the shudder of condemnation must be actively aroused by the text and maintained in a precarious balance. In *The Owl* Hawkes manages this feat as well as anywhere in his work.

The narrator, whose voice is our guide to Sasso Fetore (Tomb Stench), is calm, orotund, and self-righteous. Il Gufo (The Owl) has the title of Hangman but is also *de facto* ruler of his village kingdom. Laws were made in the past and they are not to be broken or revised. They mainly take the form of "interdicts, cried or posted, 'Blaspheme no more. Il Gufo.'" In the extremity and consistency of his ruthless complacency, Il Gufo approaches the condition of ridiculousness. He threatens to become a comic figure more than once in the course of his narrative. We read his words with a repressed giggle, a blend of abhorrence and amusement, tempered with fear. This creature is a construct, obviously, a talking fiction—grotesque, macabre, absurd. But such fabrications have stalked our real world all too frequently. Here—in fiction—it is tolerable, but it masks a reality all too like its own false face. And there is a power and an attraction in this evil. The marriageable women in the village are drawn to Il Gufo and their fathers eye him with hope. But he already has his "tall lady," the gallows, and he is forever true to her. As an unknown voice tells one of these fathers in the opening lines of the book,

> *"Him?"*
> *Think not of him for your daughter Signore, nor for her sister either. There will be none for him. Not him. He has taken his gallows, the noose and knot, to marry."*

The story of *The Owl* is simple and fierce. The town of Sasso Fetore has lost its young men—apparently in a war. As the fathers are reduced to thinking of the Hangman himself as the only candidate for their daughters' hands and dowries, a captured soldier is brought to the town and imprisoned in the Hangman's fortress. The prisoner, who is foreign and never speaks, becomes an object of hope for these fathers and their daughters. But the Hangman has other plans for him. Sasso Fetore is an infertile wasteland; Il Gufo is its king:

> Without mass violence, Sasso Fetore was still unmerciful. It was visible in the moonlight, purposeful as an avalanche of rock and snow. Here in the cellars and under roofs as far as the boundary, the old men slept in their stockings and the others, confident wives, warmed wedding bands in their armpits. Politically, historically, Sasso Fetore was an eternal Sabbath.

This lunar landscape reveals a town so gripped by law and order that it is almost dead: "As a prosecuted law with the ashes of suffering and memory carried off on the wind, Sasso Fetore was a judgment passed upon the lava, long out of date, was the more intolerant and severe." Even the "cloud formations over Sasso Fetore were consistent of color, large and geometric, the clear head of a Roman heaven." The Hangman rules here by law:

> to the hangman went the souls of death's peasants, to him were bonded the lineage of a few artisans and not least the clarity of such a high place, a long firm line of rule. If there was decay, it was only in the walls falling away from proclamations hundreds of years old, still readable, still clear and binding.

Though the walls may crumble, the proclamations survive and hold the living in their iron grip. The geometry of the sky, the clarity of the view, and the persistence of law shape the village and bind it to the hangman's will. Its history began with "a primitive monastic order whose members worked in strict obedience and were the first inhabitants of the province." As the hangman says, "The immense King's evil of history lay over the territory." He breathes this atmosphere and it refreshes him. He keeps a pet owl of his own, and when it attacks a young woman who had dared disturb its privacy, implanting its claws in her scalp, "circumsizing the brain," the hangman takes it to his arm and comforts it, sending the girl home without a thought for her:

> But I wet and smoothed the feathers under the triangle of his beak with my tongue and he regained himself, once more folded into his nocturnal shape, and only the eyes did not relent. I gave him a large rat and slept near him the night.

When the Hangman dreams, he sees his country as a tiny green mountain under three white flags:

> The country was no larger than the flags and as perfect. The road was a bright red line winding to the three precipices and the capital of rigid existence. And the flags were moving, fluttering, the motion of life anchored safely to one place.

This orderly vision of a country no larger than its flags, of life anchored safely, turns into a nightmare. The flags disintegrate into shreds and the hunchbacked village fisherman's voice comes out of the sky, concealed in the rays of the sun. He says, "'The fish are running well, Master,' with mockery in his voice." Fertility is the enemy of law and order. The fasces, ancient Roman symbol of justice borne by the Hangman's ward Pucento, symbolizes the power of the law, which is the power of punishment. When the Prisoner arrives, awakening hopes of fertility and fecundation in the hearts of the village's young women and their fathers, the Hangman meets this threat to the eternal Sabbath with the full power of the law and all his authority. He turns the prisoner over to the tender mercies of the prefect, with his live coals and his four hooks of punishment, but he does not concern himself with these "temporary arrangements." He thinks of something more permanent—his gallows:

> The tall lady stood below in the court almost as if she were taking the sun. Now she had no rope. Her place had been appointed by men who with trepidation paced off the earth and tested it upon their knees under her shadow, a shadow taken to earth and remaining there. The scaffold itself, shaped like a tool of castigation, was constructed to support the dead weight of an ox if we came to hang oxen. She was of wood and black as a black ark, calm by nature, conceived by old men with beards and velvet caps, simple and geometric as frescoes of the creation of the world.

The village possesses another landmark, a statue of "the Donna," a different sort of lady, who represents the softer side of the old religion—mercy as opposed to justice. Says the Hangman, "Surely the Donna made the scaffold majestic." The Donna suits the "soft flesh" of the peasants, but the law gives "bony strength to the lover of Donna and legend":

> the character and the code, right upon right, crashed into the pale heart when the culprit hanged, her prayers for him so soft as hardly to be heard. She saved none—salvation not being to the purpose. . . .

The statue of the Donna is not given a prominent place in the village. It stands before a cave in the burned forest—"an idol whose nights were spent with a few small deer and speechless animals," says the Hangman. When someone reddens the statue's cheeks with blood, the Hangman is offended and simply rides past on his donkey and kicks her off her pedestal. After this, the scaffold is the only "lady" in Sasso Fetore.

If the softness of the Donna disturbs the Hangman, the unruly nature of sexuality is even more abhorrent to him. Indeed, when the cheeks of the Donna are reddened, he treats the statue like a painted whore rather than a vandalized icon. Later, one of the most deeply and distressingly imagined scenes in all Hawkes's fiction is based upon the tension between the bodily vigor of sex and the mental power of law. In this scene the villagers hold a pathetic remnant of a fair below the Hangman's ramparts: "The fair was pitched directly below the fortress, in good view, and for the benefit of the prisoner up there." The Hangman doesn't like fairs. As he puts it,

> History had forbade the fair, a guise for flirting and the dissatisfaction of a sex—the fair invoked only when the measures of the fathers failed. I listened to the festival, the ribaldry of the viol da gamba, the concert of bushes. How could it be anything but an ill omen, the distraction and the gaiety of woman preceded the fall of man.

The Hangman detests women, seeing in them, as Judeo-Christian tradition has taught him to see it, the source of all human evil, which stems from Eve's breaking of the first law. He watches them coming to the fair:

> They stumbled, the swaying shanks of hair, the flaming red scarves binding torso or hips and the cantilevering, the maneuvering of the skirts. Newly shod and gowned, the purple and green of earth and sky became warm in their presence; all that was female, unnatural in congregation, came into the open air walking as geese who know the penalty awaiting the thief who catches them.

This hatred of the feminine, and of the sexuality associated with it, is not a mere aberration of the Hangman's mind. Hawkes is not presenting to us an individual case study in this portrait but the deep mentality of an entire culture. The primitive monastic order that founded the community is the source of this hatred of the female and of the flesh itself. And it is the monks who initiated the grotesque ritual which dominates the fair:

> On their leaning instruments the musicians played the seldom heard 'March of the White Dog.' This whole breed had once been deprived and whipped, tied ascetically by the lay brothers on the slopes. The bitches were destroyed. And the rest, heavy of organ and never altered with the knife, day after day were beaten during the brothers' prayers, commanded to be pure unmercifully. The dogs tasted of blood given in mean measure but were not permitted the lather, the howl, the reckless male-letting of their species. Beaten across the quarters, they were taught by the monks the blind, perfectly executed gavotte.

At the fair, the "sole remaining dog" is led in this "devilish dog's fandango" by Pucento, the Hangman's ward and lictor, bearer of the fasces itself. Boy and dog complete geometric figures, "a square and then a circle," all the while "straining to duplicate the measure, the ruthless footstep of the past."

In this scene, which mingles elements of the grotesque and macabre so powerfully, we find that perverse preoccupation with sexuality which characterizes all puritanisms. From the monkish thwarters of canine sexuality to the Hangman himself is only a step. In bending the poor beasts' motions to the mathematical rhythms of the gavotte and the abstract figures of square and circle the monks impose law upon nature—a law which defines itself as the opposite of nature, which becomes "law" by virtue of perverting nature. What the Hangman never tells us, of course, but what comes through his every gesture and word, is the immense and perverse pleasure this fascist takes in the stifling of what is natural and pleasurable in others. And the Hangman's ultimate pleasure is in his ultimate power. The taking of life is his consummation. The gallows is indeed his "lady."

The scene at the fair is followed by the attempt of Antonina, the most eligible young woman in the village, to win the Hangman himself as her husband. He climbs the hill of the fortress with her and she offers herself to him: "Honorable Hangman. Carino. Il Gufo. It is you I love." And this is perhaps the most terrifying thing of all: that the woman should be drawn to that very power, attracted by that very hatred of all things lawless, feminine, and natural, to offer herself to this macabre creature. What happens is grotesque, turning intensity to comedy:

> Antonina rolled stiff on the brown hilltop and the skirts loosened, lifted by the wind. She pushed her fingers into the bent grass and dragged her hair on the silt and stones. Her slender belly thrashed like all cloistered civilization among weed, root, in the wild of the crow's nest. I reached into the sheltered thighs touching this bone and that and felt for what all women carried. High and close to her person, secreted, I found Antonina's purse which she had hid there longer than seven years, that which they fastened to the girls when young. What was there more?

The language reeks of sexuality here, but the deed performed is only a financial transaction or an act of theft. He takes her purse but leaves her person, touches her bones but ignores her flesh. Antonina's father tries to regard this as an act of betrothal. Il Gufo gives him no more satisfaction than he gave the daughter.

It is not my purpose here to examine the entire novel or even to offer a coherent interpretation of it. That is better left to the individual reader in any case, who will find much of interest in scenes involving or concerning the prisoner, such as the extraordinary "judgment supper" in which is enacted the corruption of Christianity, as if its founder had not been a victim but the executioner himself. The Prisoner in this novel comes as a potential redeemer, one who might restore fertility to this tomblike and infertile world. But this salvation is not acceptable. The Hangman is in love with death, which constitutes for him the most perfect order of all. He is not a venal sadist. It is the Prefect who plies his hooks and fingers his truncheon. The Hangman is beyond this. He serves the Law and follows the book from which a "hangman knew the terms and directions, the means and methods to destroy a man." He loves not pain but destruction itself. The execution of the prisoner, when it comes, is preceded by a lavish feast, altogether different from the simple meal of fish at the judgment supper—a feast so rare and stimulating that it brings back "the effulgent memory of execution, step by step, dismal, endless, powerful as a beam that transcends our indulgence on the earth, in Sasso Fetore."

To the Hangman, the world itself, the whole earth is Sasso Fetore, a stinking tomb. Behind his hatred of life, of the unruly, the sexual, the natural, is a terrible fastidiousness. Execution cleanses the earth, purifies it. As he rides through his world, or contemplates it from what he calls "the absolute clarity of my vantage above," he sees the men as so many "Garibaldis burning in a cold and wintry piazza"; he sees the hunchback's daughter as "a girl who should have been burned in Sasso Fetore." For whatever appears to threaten order, whether the libertarian politics of a Garibaldi or the apparent sexuality of a girl, Il Gufo has one response: purification by fire. For others, the scaffold will do. But *all* are guilty, *all* must be punished, as they were even "in the time when there were men to hang and those to spare, with clemency for neither." What the Hangman hates is life itself.

This portrayal of repressive fascism is, as I have tried to suggest, at once terrible and comic, bizarre in its extremity but profoundly accurate in probing the philosophical and emotional roots of this mentality as embodied in the Hangman. It is of course an imaginative construct rather than a case study, an emblem rather than a portrait. In saying that plot, character, setting, and theme were the enemies of the novel, Hawkes was hyperbolically and provocatively protesting against certain traditional ways of approaching the construction of fiction. But the only true justification for surrealism in art is that it destroys certain surface plausibilities in order to liberate realities that are habitually concealed by habits of vision attuned only to the surface itself. And this is precisely what Hawkes accomplishes in *The Owl*. It is time to recognize that achievement.

Robert Hayden

1913–1980

Born Asa Bundy Sheffey on August 4, 1913, in Detroit, Michigan, Robert Earl Hayden received his name from the foster parents who reared him from infancy. After graduating from high school, he was variously employed before entering Detroit City College (now Wayne State University) on a scholarship in 1932. From 1936 to 1940 he worked as a writer and researcher of black history and folklore on the WPA Federal Writers' Project in Detroit, and studied part-time at the University of Michigan. In 1938 he won the university's Hopwood Award for poetry, and after publishing a book of poems, *Heart-Shape in the Dust*, in 1940, he moved to Ann Arbor in 1941 to complete his education. After gaining his B.A. in 1942 and his M.A. in 1944, he stayed on to teach for two years before joining the faculty of Fisk University in Nashville, Tennessee, in 1946.

In 1948 Hayden established the Counterpoise Press at Fisk to encourage creative writing, particularly by black Americans. Although he wrote *The Lion and the Archer* in collaboration with Myron O'Higgins in 1948 and published a brief collection of poems, *Figure of Time*, in 1955, his heavy teaching load limited his production, and he found little recognition in America. However, his poems were translated widely, and his growing reputation abroad led to the publication in London of his second major book, *A Ballad of Remembrance* (1962), which won him the Grand Prize for Poetry at the First World Festival of Negro Arts in Dakar, Senegal, in 1966. The same year his *Selected Poems* were issued in New York, followed in 1970 by *Words in the Mourning Time*, and in 1972 by *The Night-Blooming Cereus*. Hayden returned to the University of Michigan as professor of English in 1969, and for the rest of his life was much in demand as a visiting lecturer and poet. *Angle of Ascent: New and Selected Poems* appeared in 1975, the year in which he was elected a Fellow of the Academy of American Poets. From 1976 to 1978 he was poetry consultant to the Library of Congress, and in his last years he received several honorary doctorates.

A practising Baha'i since 1942, Hayden was poetry editor of the Baha'i quarterly journal *World Order* from 1967 until his death on February 25, 1980. A collection of his last poems, *American Journal*, was published in 1982.

⟨Writing about being an American Negro⟩ . . . presents a growing problem for poetry. The subject matter is inescapable—and if one is a Negro, he will not wish to escape it. The subject matter is explosive and elemental; hard stuff for poets, it provides a discouraging paradox: the more you face it, the more you are driven to one of two extremes—sentimentality or hyper-erudition. Hughes or McKay would illustrate the former; Tolson, the latter. Hayden is saddled with both. ⟨In *Selected Poems*⟩ he oscillates from semi-dialect blues and corrupted ballads to Poundian notation; predictably, he resorts to the former for portraits of his childhood, family, and friends, and to the latter for "historical evidence" poems describing the white man's burden. Predictably, too, with a subject so fearfully basic and seemingly insoluble, Hayden is capable of high eclecticism when dealing with salvation (on the theological plane); witness his poems concerned with the Baha'i faith, a prominent nineteenth-century Persian sect whose leader was martyred. Might not the example of Jesus have sufficed? For the white man, probably.

Hayden is as gifted a poet as most we have; his problem is not one of talent but frame of reference. It is fascinating, moving, and finally devastating that the finest verse in his book is spoken by a Spanish sailor, a witness of the *Amistad* mutiny, who describes the slaughter of their captors by "murderous Africans". This speech the sailor delivers to American officials, saying at one point:

> We find it paradoxical indeed
> that you whose wealth, whose tree of liberty
> are rooted in the labor of your slaves
> should suffer the august John Quincy Adams
> to speak with so much passion of the right
> of chattel slaves to kill their lawful masters

Hayden is a superb ironist in this passage. The crime of it is he has not chosen his forte; it has chosen him.—DAVID GALLER, *Poetry*, July 1967, pp. 268–69

The recent publication of Robert Hayden's new book of poems, *Words in the Mourning Time*, once again brings us the work of one of the most underrated and unrecognized poets in America. Until the publication of *Selected Poems* in 1966, Hayden was unrepresented by a book of his own poems, except for two small, privately printed books and a volume published in England. Now 57 years old, he has had to wait too long for the recognition that his work has merited for 20 years. But that is primarily because he is black.

If there was scarcely a market for black writers before the sixties, black poets must have been regarded as something odd indeed, particularly a poet who refused to be pressed into anyone's preconceived mold of what a black poet should be. Yet, Hayden persevered—teaching, writing, publishing where he could and giving occasional readings.

When I entered Fisk University in the fall of 1956, he had already been there 10 years in that miasma of black bourgeois gentility. On the campus, he was regarded as just another instructor in the English department, teaching 15 hours of classes a week, from two sections of freshman English to American literature to creative writing. No one at Fisk had the vaguest notion of what a poet's function was, not that they gave it any thought. Yet, somehow, Hayden continued to believe—in himself and poetry—though no one except his wife and a few students and friends in New York ever cared.

Within these circumstances, being a poet could bring him no joy. Despite his pain and loneliness, he always made it clear to those of us who were foolish enough to think that we wanted to write that perhaps our experiences would be different. In creative writing classes, he tried to teach us that words were our principal tool and no matter how important we considered our "message" to be, it was the words that expressed it. Assuming that we had something to say, the importance of saying it as well as our ability allowed us could never be underestimated.

When I read his poetry I know that I am in the presence of a man who honors language. His images give the reader a new experience of the world. In his *Selected Poems* are found such lines as: "Graveblack vultures encircle afternoon"; "palm-leaf knives of sunlight"; "autumn hills /in blazonry of farewell scarlet." And in *Words in the Mourning Time* these lines appear: "His injured childhood bullied him"; "Good brooms had swept /the mist away." He chooses words with the care of a sculptor chipping into marble and, in his poem "El-Hajj Malik El-Shabazz," from "Words in the Mourning Time," a vivid historical portrait of Malcolm X is presented in six short lines:

> He X'd his name, became his people's anger,
> exhorted them to vengeance for their past;
> rebuked, admonished them,
> their scourger, who
> would shame them, drive them from
> the lush ice gardens of their servitude.

Such a simple phrase—"He X'd his name"—but it sets up reverberations that extend back to August of 1619.

I left Nashville in 1961, and though I saw Mr. Hayden a few times afterwards, our relationship slowly diminished. I, his "son," had to find my own way, and he found new "sons" in succeeding classes. The last time I saw him was in May, 1966. I was working for the Student Non-Violent Coordinating Committee and had just come from the meeting in which Stokely Carmichael had been elected chairman. Black power was just a few weeks away, but Mr. Hayden had already felt the heat of its approaching flames. At a writers' conference held at Fisk a few weeks before, he had been severely attacked as an "Uncle Tom" by the students and other writers. When I walked into his house, his first words to me were a tirade against "the nationalists."

He had also just been awarded the Grand Prize for Poetry at the First World Festival of Negro Arts at Dakar, Senegal. That honor was not enough, however, to offset being rejected and attacked by black students and black writers. He had always insisted on being known as a poet, not a black poet, and he could be belligerent about it. I listened to him again as he angrily maintained that there was "no such thing as black literature. There's good literature and there's bad. And that's all!" I couldn't wholly agree then (and I'm still not sure), nor could I understand why he was so vociferous in denying that he was a black poet. After all, he was the man who had written "Middle Passage," "Frederick Douglass" and "Runagate Runagate," three of the finest poems about the black experience in the English language. Why couldn't he admit that he was a black poet?

To be a black artist has always been difficult. The mere fact that he is black means that he is associated with a "cause." It is his birthright, whether he wants it to be or not. Yet, while no one expects Philip Roth, for example, to be a spokesman for Jews, it is the black writer's fate to have his work judged more on the basis of racial content than artistic merit. This is because whites only grant the right of individuality to whites. A black is not an individual; he is the representative of a "cause." Unfortunately, black concur in this evaluation. They see each other as "causes" and have little, if any, use for a black writer who does not concern himself with "the cause." Both races think the black writer is a priest, offering absolution to whites or leading blacks to the holy wars.

The prevailing black esthetic was summarized succinctly by Ron Karenga when he said, "All art must reflect and support the Black Revolution and any art that does not discuss and contribute to the revolution is invalid. Black art must expose the enemy, praise the people and support the revolution." In other words, art should be the voice of political ideology and the black artist must comply or find himself with an indifferent white audience and no black one.

To a black artist, like Mr. Hayden, who was not conceived or reborn in the womb of black power, such thinking is not only repugnant, it is a direct assault upon art itself. By its very nature, art is revolutionary, because it seeks to change the consciousness, perceptions and very beings of those who open themselves to it. Its revolutionary nature, however, can only be mortally wounded if it must meet political prescriptions. That, however, is now being demanded of the black artist.

Robert Hayden refuses to be defined by anything other than the demands of his craft. He does not want to be restricted solely to the black experience or have his work judged on the basis of its relevance to the black political struggle. First and foremost, he is not a pawn in some kind of neo-medieval morality play. His task is, in his words, merely that which has always been the poet's task: "to reflect and illuminate the truth of human experience."

Now, I know that his desire to be regarded as nothing more or less than a poet was not a denial of his blackness, but the only way he knew of saying that blackness was not big enough to contain him. He wanted to live in the universe. In the ninth part of the title poem of *Words in the Mourning Time*, he writes:

> We must not be frightened nor cajoled
> into accepting evil as deliverance from evil.
> We must go on struggling to be human,
> though monsters of abstractions
> police and threaten us.
>
> Reclaim now, now renew the vision of
> a human world where godliness
> is possible and man
> is neither gook nigger honkey wop nor kike
> but man
> permitted to be man.

If we ever reach that time when man is permitted to be man, one of the reasons will be men and women like this poet, Robert Hayden, who, when pressed into the most terrifying corners of loneliness, refused to capitulate to those, who in the screaming agony of their own pain and loneliness, could do nothing but return evil for evil.—JULIUS LESTER, *NYTBR*, Jan. 24, 1971, pp. 5, 22

This ⟨*Angle of Ascent*⟩ is Robert Hayden's sixth book of poems, its appearance auspiciously occurring almost simultaneously with his election as the 1975 Fellow of the Academy of American Poets for "distinguished poetic achievement"; an award that has been a long time in coming. Hayden was born and raised in Detroit and grew up as one who feared "those who feared the riot-squad of statistics." A Spanish major in college, he studied with Auden at the University of Michigan, where Hayden has taught since 1969. There he won the Hopwood prize for a sequence of poems tentatively entitled, "The Black Spear." In those poems are the seeds of his bicentennial classic, "Middle Passage," and other highlights like the rhythmically accented sonnet that ends *Angle of Ascent*, "Frederick Douglass":

> Oh, not with statues' rhetoric,
> not with legends and poems and wreaths of bronze
> alone,
> but with the lives grown out of his life, the lives
> fleshing his dream of the beautiful, needful thing.

Hayden has always been a symbolist poet struggling with historical fact, his rigorous portraits of people and places providing the synaptic leap into the interior landscape of the soul, where prayer for illumination and perfection are focused on the oneness of mankind. Having committed himself to the improvement of language, he has sometimes been falsely accused of timidity of commitment to the black struggle because of his refusal to "politicize" his work for expedient and transient goals. But it is Hayden's poetry that best captures the Afro-American tradition of the black hero, from the slave narratives and testimonials of Douglass, Harriet Tubman, Sojourner Truth, to musicians and jazz singers such as Bessie Smith, Billie Holiday, Miles Davis. Hayden is the master conversationalist and handler of idiom; his perfect pitch is always pointed toward heroic action and his central images are almost always an embracing of kin. He has never abandoned his people. One might find them on St. Antoine Street, where Hayden lived as a boy with his foster parents, making visits to local stores, seeing synagogues become black churches ("But the synagogue became/New Calvary"), or just catching glimpses:

> then Elk parades and big splendiforous
> Jack Johnson in his diamond limousine
> set the ghetto burgeoning
> with fantasies
> of Ethiopia spreading her gorgeous wings.

Though Hayden has not written about his mother directly, it is her voice that informs his love of detail and spice; he alludes to her passing in "Approximations" ("In dead of winter /wept beside your open grave./Falling snow."), an approximate haiku fused with his own experience. He has been critical of his own slow pace in turning out poems, of what he has summarized as "slim offerings over four decades." But his own assessments should include the *teachableness* of this volume to an increasing public audience. From Detroit's Paradise Valley—

> The sporting people
> along St. Antoine—
> that scufflers'
> paradise of ironies—bet salty money
> on his righteous hook and jap

—to the composite persona parceled from asides he got from his mother—

> A shotgun on his shoulder
> his woman big with child and
> shrieking curses after him,
>
> Joe Finn came down from
> Allegheny wilderness
> to join Abe Lincoln's men.
>
> Goddamning it survives the
> slaughter at the Crater.
> Disappears in to his name

—Hayden is the poet of perfect pitch.

His living in the South for 22 years while at Fisk University accounts in part for his small output:

> Here symbol houses
> where the brutal dream lives out its lengthy
> dying. Here the past, adored and unforgiven. Here
> the past—
> soulscape, Old Testament battleground
> of warring shades whose weapons kill.

Hayden could not accommodate or adjust himself to the "Locus" of segregation, the nightmare landscape everpresent in our history.

His experiments with the ballad form have produced singular achievements—*ballads in spirit* in the language, with dramatic tension and economy that adapt to his personal view of history:

> And purified, I rose and prayed and returned after a
> time
> to the blazing fields, to the humbleness.
> And bided my time.

Hayden's "The Ballad of Nat Turner," written before the Turner controversy of the late sixties, demonstrates how he does this, dwelling on the high points of the mysterious and archaic roots of black folk rhythms.

His search for kinfolk is the permanent condition of his poetry and his personality:

> And when he gets to where the voices were—
> Don't cry, his dollbaby wife implores;
> I know where they are, don't cry.
> We'll go and find them, we'll go
> and ask them for your name again.
> —("'Mystery Boy' Looks for Kin in Nashville")

Or in "Belsen, Day of Liberation":

> Her parents and her dolls destroyed, Her childhood foreclosed,
> she watched the foreign soldiers from the sunlit windows whose black bars
> Were crooked crosses inked upon her pallid face.
> "Liebchen, Liebchen, you should be in bed."
> —But she felt ill no longer.

Hayden memorializes the experiences of Rosey Poole, who at Fisk told a black convocation how people in concentration camps wanted to pray but could not agree on what prayers; "they sang Negro spirituals and poems by Negro Poets," she told them.

Angle of Ascent is a book that is told. The title comes from the poem "For a Young Artist," which grew out of a conversation with a young musician set upon "astral projection," the attempt to live and create on the highest spiritual plane. Hayden's answer is to find transcendence *living among the living*. In "Stars" Sojourner Truth "Comes walking barefoot / out of slavery / ancestress / childless mother/ following the stars / her mind a star," giving testimony to Hayden's living "angle of ascent / achieved."—MICHAEL S. HARPER, "A Symbolist Poet Struggling with Historical Fact," *NYTBR*, Feb. 22, 1976, pp. 34–35

Offered the chance that all selections offer, to expunge, silently, the errors and excesses of early work, Robert Hayden has retained all but two of the poems which formed his 1966 *Selected Poems*. This is a poet secure about the past, and the past work. That work, continued here by eight new poems and the bulk of two interim volumes, has shifted its emphasis, gradually, from narrative to symbolism. The earlier poems, heavily dependent on story, have broken down now entirely into words, some of rich personal association: "Plowdens, Finns, / Shefeys, Haydens, / Westerfields. / / Pennsylvania gothic, / Kentucky homespun, / Virginia baroque." The new poems have a spareness that resists first reading, but which eventually rewards with the radiance of hard-earned, hard-edged memory. Of a night-blooming cereus:

> Lunar presence,
> foredoomed, already dying,
> it charged the room
> with plangency
> older than human
> cries, ancient as prayers
> invoking Osiris, Krishna,
> Tezcátlipóca.

Hayden exploits the classics and the contemporary, historical anecdote and personal encounter, to demonstrate that what grants history poignancy—that it cannot be altered—also gives pathos to the personal. His explorations of Black history appear in choice of subject matter and a slight widening of technique to include occasional swatches of song and dialect, rather than as impenetrable anger or voguish posture. He produces homages to both Mark Van Doren and Malcolm X; his poems conjure up a variety of lives caught in the desperation of poverty, or that of decadence. His most extreme emotions, and successes, reserved for the era that began with the arrival of slaves in America and ended with the Civil War and Reconstruction, produce a number of serious, haunted poems, including "The Dream," "The Ballad of Sue Ellen Westerfield," and the stunning "Middle Passage."

"Middle Passage" is a deceptive piece, a perfectly modulated pastiche of voices contained in diary, deposition, and reminiscence, that has for its subject the slave trade between Africa and America. The poem exhibits a toughness of language and a variety of method, including prose, parody, and prayer, that create effects of horror and anger in service of a passage through history, the "voyage through death / to life upon these shores."

> Sails flashing to the winds like weapons,
> sharks following the moans the fever and the dying;
> horror the corposant and compass rose.
> *Deep in the festering hold thy father lies,*
> *of his bones New England pews are made,*
> *those are altar lights that were his eyes.*
> ". . . A plague among
> our blacks—Ophthalmia: blindness—& we
> have jettisoned the blind to no avail.
> It spreads, the terrifying sickness spreads.
> Its claws have scratched sight from the Capt.'s eyes
> & there is blindness in the fo'c'sle . . ."

As "Shuttles in the rocking loom of history, / the dark ships move, the dark ships move"; woven from the mingling of many tales, many terrors, is a display of the moral blindness at slavery's heart, of self-interest that destroys the self and breaks men like twigs. "Middle Passage" is the best contemporary poem I have read on slavery. It is a singular performance, one which Hayden's later poems have not matched, in part because it is a poem whose special construction does not invite imitation.

Hayden has not discovered other methods rich enough to encompass public or private history so well. The defects which mar his poetry include compositional tics (repetition, for example: "the name he never can he never can repeat") and, especially in the newer poems, occasional opaqueness. Some recent poems are contrived from feelings so momentary that only a fleeting satisfaction is achieved. At worst, in the new work the phrases break up, the words fly apart, and the associative structure holds no meaning. The poems may shatter into component images, individually attractive but fragmentary. There are few first-rate metaphors; the poems that remain in the mind persuade by narrative, not image. As one moves through the book, it is disconcerting to find the older poems last. Such an ordering places the newer poems, whose methods are smaller, and which should be seen as the product of development, at a disadvantage; as the older poems drape themselves in description and narration, the newer work seems insubstantial.—WILLIAM LOGAN, "Language against Fear," *Poetry*, July 1977, pp. 226–28

WILBURN WILLIAMS, JR.
"Covenant of Timelessness and Time"
Chant of Saints
eds. Michael S. Harper and Robert B. Stepto
1979, pp. 66–84

I

The appearance of Robert Hayden's *Angle of Ascent* is something of a problematic event for students of the Afro-American tradition in poetry, for while it gives us occasion to review and pay homage to the best work of one of our finest poets, it insistently calls to mind the appalling tardiness of our recognition of his achievement. A meticulous craftsman whose exacting standards severely limit the amount of his published verse, Robert Hayden has steadily accumulated over the course of three decades a body of poetry so distinctive in character and harmonious in development that its very existence seems more fated than willed, the organic issue of a natural principle rather than the deliberate artifice of a human imagination.[1] But in spite of official honors—Hayden is now the poetry consultant at the Library of Congress and a Fellow of the Academy of American Poets—and a formidable reputation among critics, Hayden has received surprisingly little notice in print. Unless we suffer another of those sad fits of inattention that have so far limited Hayden's readership, *Angle of Ascent* should win for him the regard he has long deserved. With the exception of *Heart-Shape in the Dust*, the apprenticeship collection of 1940, poetry from every previous work of Hayden's is represented here, and we can see clearly the remarkable fertility of the symbolist's union with the historian, the bipolar extremes of Hayden's singular poetic genius.

Robert Hayden is a poet whose symbolistic imagination is intent on divining the shape of a transcendent order of spirit and grace that might redeem a world bent on its own destruction. His memory, assailed by the discontinuities created by its own fallibility, is equally determined to catch and preserve every shadow and echo of the actual human experience in which our terribleness stands revealed. In poem after poem Hayden deftly balances the conflicting claims of the ideal and the actual. Spiritual enlightenment in his poetry is never the reward of evasion of material fact. The realities of imagination and the actualities of history are bound together in an alliance that makes neither thinkable without the other. Robert Hayden's poetry proposes that if it is in the higher order of spirit that the gross actualities of life find their true meaning, it is also true that that transcendent realm is meaningful to man only as it is visibly incarnate on the plane of his experience.

Viewed as a theory of poetics, Hayden's characteristic method of composition will hardly strike anyone as unique. His preoccupation with the relationship between natural and spiritual facts puts him squarely in the American tradition emanating from Emerson; we are not at all amazed, therefore, when we find correspondences between his work and that of figures like Dickinson and Melville. The brief lyric "Snow," for instance (all page references in this essay are to *Angle of Ascent*, New York, 1975):

> Smooths and burdens,
> endangers, hardens.
>
> Erases, revises.
> Extemporizes
>
> Vistas of lunar solitude.
> Builds, embellishes a mood.
>
> (p. 84)

recalls the Dickinson of "It sifts from Leaden Sieves—."[2] But the brooding presence of death lurking behind the brave outward show of a playful wit that is common in Dickinson is uncharacteristic of Hayden, and a comparison with Melville casts more light on his habitual concerns. In "El-Hajj Malik El-Shabazz" Malcolm X is likened to Ahab—"Rejecting Ahab, he was of Ahab's tribe. / 'Strike through the mask!'" (p. 57)—and "The Diver" (pp. 75–76) closely parallels Chapter 92 of Melville's *White-Jacket*. To be sure, Hayden's speaker and Melville's narrator are impelled by distinctly different motives. The former's descent is a conscious act, a matter of deliberate choice, whereas White-Jacket's one-hundred-foot fall into a nighttime sea cannot be ascribed to his sensible will, however strong his subconscious longing for death might be. Yet the underlying pattern of each man's ordeal is the same. The approach to death is paradoxically felt as a profound intensification of life. Death takes, or at least seems to promise to take, both men to the very core of life. Thus White-Jacket in his precipitous drop "toward the infallible center of the terraqueous globe" finds all he has seen, read, heard, thought, and felt seemingly "intensified in one fixed idea in [his] soul." Yielding to the soft embrace of the sea, he is shocked into revulsion of death almost purely by chance—"of a sudden some fashionless form" brushes his side, tingling his nerves with the thrill of being alive.[3] In like manner, Hayden's diver's longing to be united with "those hidden ones" in a kind of well-being that lies so deep as to be beyond the reach of articulate speech, his passion to "have / done with self and / every dinning / vain complexity," can be satisfied only if he tears away the mask that sustains his life. The intricate contrapuntal development of the poem brings an overwhelming extremity of feeling to the critical moment that finds the diver poised between life and death. His going down is both easeful and swift, a plunge into water and a flight through air. The flower creatures of the deep flash and shimmer yet are at the same time mere "lost images / fadingly remembered." The dead ship, a lifeless hulk deceptively encrusted with the animate "moss of bryozoans," swarms with forms of life that are themselves voracious instruments of death. And what liberates the diver from this labyrinthine and potentially annihilating swirl of contradictory instincts and perceptions is never clear. As is the case with White-Jacket, he "somehow" begins the "measured rise," no nearer to winning the object of his quest but presumably possessed of a deeper, more disciplined capacity for experience. ("Measured" is decidedly meant to make us think of the poet's subordination to the rules of his craft.)

The most fruitful area of comparison between Hayden and Melville is to be found in their tellingly different attitudes toward the symbolistic enterprise itself. Committed to reconciling within the ambiguous flux of poetic language the warring oppositions created by the divisiveness of discursive logic, the symbolist finds himself necessarily presupposing the very terms of order—subject and object, mind and matter, spirit and nature—his method seeks to erase.[4] Because the symbolist's stance is such a difficult posture to keep, the idea of the artist as acrobat and the conception of his craft as a dance of language are conventional figures in modern literature and criticism. In Hayden, however, the drama of the symbolist's tightrope walk is objectified infrequently. The sumbolist's striving for balance is not seen in what Hayden's speakers do but is heard in how they talk: tone assumes the burden that topic might bear. Hayden's characteristically soft-spoken and fluid voice derives much of its power from the evident contrast between the maelstrom of anguish out of which it originates and the quiet reflecting pool of talk into which it is inevitably channeled.

Interestingly enough, when Hayden does write poetry in which the action is clearly analogous to the symbolist's task of wizarding a track through a jungle of contraries, the prevailing tone is not his customary seriousness. In "The Performers," the modesty of two high-rise window cleaners subtly mocks the speaker's misuse of their daring as a pretext for a kind of absurd metaphysical strutting that his own desk-bound timidity will not allow (p. 27). In "The Lions" an animal trainer whose mentality is a peculiar blend of Schopenhauerian wilfulness and transcendentalist vision breaks out into an ebullient speech that is at once divinely rapturous and somehow wildly funny:

> And in the kingdom-cage
> as I make my lions leap,
> through nimbus-fire leap,
> oh, as I see them leap—
> unsparing beauty that
> creates and serves my will,
> the savage real that clues
> my vision of the real—
> my soul exults and Holy cries
> and Holy Holy cries, he said.
> (p. 64)

Yet whenever Robert Hayden loses his artistic balance, his fall is not likely to be in Melville's direction. The enormous gulf between the unified paradise of the symbolistic imagination and the outright hellishness of a world rife with division, the gulf which drew Ahab and Pierre to their deaths and drowned Melville the writer in silence, poses no threat to Hayden. Hayden's peril comes from a different quarter, and it comes disguised as his salvation. It is precisely Hayden's faith in the ultimate redemptiveness of the universal and timeless order of spirit that threatens to kill the life of his art. Insofar as his poetry is concerned, Hayden's God and Devil are one. The blinding light of faith can shrivel up the sensuous specificity of poetry just as surely as it can enkindle the life of the world of inert fact. Hayden's divergence from Melville here is nowhere more apparent than in "Theme and Variation." Readers of Hayden will recognize the voice of the Heraclitus-like stranger who delivers the poem's wisdom as the poet's own:

> I sense, he said, the lurking rush, the sly
> transcience flickering at the edge of things.
> I've spied from the corner of my eye
> upon the striptease of reality.
>
> There is, there is, he said, an imminence
> that turns to curiosa all I know;
> that changes light to rainbow darkness
> wherein God waylays and empowers.
> (P. 115)

Set the above lines against this sentence from the famous last paragraph of "The Whiteness of the Whale" in *Moby-Dick:*

> And when we consider that other theory of the natural philosophers, that all other earthly hues—every stately or lovely emblazoning—the sweet tinges of sunset skies and woods; yea, and the gilded velvets of butterflies, and the butterfly cheeks of young girls; all these are but subtle deceits, not actually inherent in substances, but only laid on from without; so that all deified Nature absolutely paints like the harlot, whose allurements cover nothing but the charnel-house within; and when we proceed further, and consider that the mystical cosmetic which produces every one of her hues, the great principle of light, forever remains white or colourless in itself, and if operating without medium upon matter, would touch all objects, evaj tulips and roses, with its own blank tinge—pondering all this, the palsied universe lies before us a leper; and like wilful travellers in Lapland, who refuse to wear coloured and colouring glasses upon their eyes, so the wretched infidel gazes himself blind at the monumental white shroud that wraps all the prospect around him.

Hayden's stranger reverses Ishmael on every point. His perceptions nourish belief; Ishmael's skepticism and doubt. He is pious and Ishmael is blasphemous. Melville's Nature dresses while Hayden's disrobes. The former's adornment is emblematic of a diabolical deceitfulness; the latter's nudity points to a sanctuary of grace. Where Melville's eye strips away delusory hues to gaze in horror upon the "blank tinge" of a "palsied" and leprous universe, Hayden's eye spies out an indwelling spirit that transforms an undifferentiated light into a sacredly tinged darkness wherein man discovers his hope and his blessing. But here Hayden can no more be accused of a naive optimism than Melville can be charged with blind cynicism. The ironic intimation of violent assault reverberating in "waylays" checks the stranger's rush into the plenitude of divine imminence, maintaining the poem's complexity and integrity.

Nevertheless, the point remains that the beneficent banditry of Hayden's divinity has far more in common with the onslaughts of Donne's Three-Personed God than with anything ever done by the maddeningly elusive Jehovah of Melville. Hayden's supreme highwayman is more apt to strip the poet of his facts than to rob him of his faith, which might be heaven for religion but certainly hell for poetry. As much is evident in the increasingly sparing detail and more cryptic utterance that marks the poet's recent work. At his best Hayden composes poetry that is paradoxically both rich in statement and ascetic in temperament. In "Stars" and the Akhenaten section of "Two Egyptian Portrait Masks," however, an abstract and unconvincing expression of acute religious belief shows only a marginal relation to the concrete particularities of human experience. The latter verse segment plainly suffers in contrast to the paean to Nefert-iti that precedes it. Meditating on the carving of a woman

> whose burntout
> loveliness alive in stone
> is like the fire of precious stones
>
> dynastic
> death (gold mask and vulture wings)
> charmed her with so she would never die
> (p. 16)

the poet tersely harmonizes a succession of discordant sensations. But in the Akhenaten companion piece, the poet's contemplativeness has no equivalent object on which it can focus—admittedly, it would take an extraordinary imagination to bridge the gap between the majesty of Akenaten's dream of human oneness and the fat hips and bloated abdomens of the Pharaoh's Karnak colossi—and consequently the poetry lacks force:

> Aten
> multi-single like the sun
> reflecting Him by Him
>
> reflected.
> Anubis howled. The royal prophet reeled
> under the dazzling weight
>
> of vision,
> exalted—maddened?—the spirit moving
> in his heart: Aten Jahveh Allah God.
> (p. 17)

Certainly there is nothing in this like the faultless description of death as "dynastic," a brilliant conceit whereby Hayden associates the idea of the unbroken hereditary transfer of power from generation to generation with the eternal dominion of death, thus finding death's very indomitability dependent upon the principle of generation, or life. What Emerson, the one indispensable figure in any discussion of American symbolism, once said about the poet's duty is patently applicable to Robert Hayden, and it can serve both as an accurate representation of what Hayden does in his best work and as a necessary corrective to the etherealizing proclivities of Hayden's symbolist genius:

> The poet, like the electric rod, must reach from a point nearer the sky than all surrounding objects, down to the earth, and into the dark wet soil, or neither is of use. The poet must not only converse with pure thought, but he must demonstrate it almost to the senses. His words must be pictures, his verses must be spheres and cubes, to be seen and smelled and handled.[5]

II

However much we might like to dwell on the manifold possibilities of Hayden's symbolism, particularly in relation to the practices of Yeats and Eliot (to whom he sometimes alludes) and to Auden (whom he has said was a key factor in his growth as a poet[6]), no discussion of his poetry can avoid the question of the place a sense of history occupies in his work. Every reader is quick to detect a pervasive sense of the past and a powerful elegiac strain in his work. In the most thorough examination of Hayden's poetry we have, Charles T. Davis has recounted the crucial contribution of Hayden's extensive research in the slave trade to "Middle Passage," and he has called attention to the importance of Hayden's grasp of the Afro-American folk tradition to "O Daedalus, Fly Away Home," "The Ballad of Nat Turner," and "Runagate Runagate."[7] Aware of the paradox, Hayden has referred to himself as a "romantic realist," a symbolist compelled to be realistic, and Michael Harper has called him a "symbolist poet struggling with the facts of history."[8] Now, nothing is perhaps more tempting or more mistaken than to infer from all this that the historian in Hayden is at odds with the symbolist. A close reading of the poetry will not support such a conclusion. Because of the popularity of "Middle Passage" and "Runagate Runagate"—poems unmistakably black in subject matter and sometimes identifiably black in use of language—the historical impulse in Hayden is understandably allied in the minds of many readers with the poet's pride in his own blackness. Since Hayden's recognition of his blackness is widely (and, we think, most aberrantly) perceived as a grudging one, the symbolist in Hayden is often viewed as the enemy of his essentially historical, and black, muse. If that Bob Hayden only knew better, the argument (it is hardly reasoning) goes, he would leave that symbolism stuff alone (the poetry of *The Night-Blooming Cereus*, for example) and get back to his roots. Certainly Hayden's insistence that he be judged as a poet and not as a Negro poet only exacerbates this misapprehension, and no appeal to the extensive exploitation of symbolism in the spirituals and the blues is likely to quiet the suspicion that Hayden's symbolist clings parasitically to the creativity of his black historian.[9]

But while it is easy to see that the symbolistic method is operative in poems as disparate as "Middle Passage" and "The Night-Blooming Cereus," it is not so evident that Hayden's historical sensibility is also at work in poems that have no obvious connection with historical incidents. To apprehend the unity of Hayden's entire body of work, it is necessary to understand that his fascination with history is but one part of a more comprehensive entrancement in the mystery of time. Robert Hayden is clearly more intrigued by the process of change, the paradoxes of permanence and evanescence, than the particular substances that undergo change. Here we are interested in the psychological and artistic implications of his dramatic re-creations of historical events, and not just in the nature of the events themselves. Throughout the poetry of Hayden we encounter a memory and an imagination pitted against the losses time's passage inevitably entails. We meet a consciousness struggling to retain the finest nuances of its own experience and seeking to enter into the experience of others from whom it is alienated by time and space. The fundamental source of Hayden's productivity, the wellspring of his poetic activity, lies in the ability of the human memory to negotiate the distance between time past and time present and the capacity of a profoundly sympathetic imagination to transcend the space between self and other. The complex interactions generated by the life of memory and imagination define the basic unity of Hayden's work.

But while we think that Hayden's obsession with time is, in a sense, larger than his deep involvement in the Afro-American past, it would be foolish to deny the special place black American history occupies in his development as a poet. The 1940s, the years in which Hayden patiently studied the annals of his black past, are also the years in which he matured as artist.[10] To simply live in a culture with a sense of the past as notoriously shallow as this one's is burden enough. A black like Hayden, the fierceness of whose need to know his history is matched only by the ponderousness of the mass of distortion and fabrication under which his past lies buried, finds that even the truthful accounts of the black American experience, which cannot really take him farther back than the eighteenth century anyway, give him the composite picture of a collectivity, rather than detailed portraits of individuals. It can hardly seem an accident to him that historians have until recently slighted the value of the slave narratives, documents that shake him with a revelation more awesome than any truth contained in the most complete compilation of data seen even in the wildest dreams of the maddest cliometrician. When he looks at his mental picture of Representative Afro-American Man, he sees that it is a mosaic formed of bits of the lives of many men, and there are moments when he wonders whether the portrait typifies the truth of art or the deceit of artifice. The face is formed of fragments themselves faceless; the sacred text of his people's experience an accretion of footnotes culled from the profane texts of another's. His past is pregnant with a significance that it is incapable of giving birth to. It is a speechless past peopled with renowned personalities who are ironically impersonal:

> Name in a footnote. Faceless name.
> Moot hero shrouded in Betsy Ross
> and Garvey flags—propped up
> by bayonets, forever falling.
> ("Crispus Attucks," p. 20)

Viewed in this somber light, the primary significance of Hayden's famous poems of Cinquez, Turner, Tubman, and Douglass resides in the poet's imaginative attempt to reforge his present's broken links with the past. The past, Hayden says, need not be past at all. His speakers confront their history as active participants in its making, and not as distant onlookers bemoaning their isolation; the past is carried into the present. Although the poet's mind ventures backward in time, the poems themselves invariably close with a statement or action that points forward to the reader's present. The progress of "Middle Passage" is through death "to life upon these shores," and the reader leaves the poem with his attention riveted to *this* life on *these* shores just as much as it is fixed on the historical reality of the slave trade. The man we leave at the conclusion of "The Ballad of Nat Turner" has his revolution still before him. "Runagate Runagate" ends with an invitation, "Come ride-a my train," whose rhythm subtly anticipates the action to be undertaken, and the powerful assertion of yet another intention to act—"Mean mean mean to be free" (p. 130). The accentual sonnet to Frederick Douglass is poetry that moves like the beating of a living heart. The poet emphasizes that the dead hero is still a vital force. The first long periodic sentence seems to resist coming to an end. The poem celebrates not a man who has been, but a man still coming into being. Although commemorative in nature, it does not so much elegize a past as prophesy a future. Frederick Douglass, the poet, and all enslaved humanity are united in one generative process:

> When it is finally ours, this freedom, this liberty, this
> beautiful
> and terrible thing, needful to man as air,
> usable as earth; when it belongs at last to all,
> when it is truly instinct, brain matter, diastole,
> systole,
> reflex action; when it is finally won; when it is more
> than the gaudy mumbo jumbo of politicians:
> this man, this Douglass, this former slave, this Negro
> beaten to his knees, exiled, visioning a world
> where none is lonely, none hunted, alien,
> this man, superb in love and logic, this man
> shall be remembered. Oh, not with statues' rhetoric,
> not with legends and poems and wreaths of bronze
> alone,
> but with the lives grown out of his life, the lives
> fleshing his dream of the beautiful, needful thing.
> (p. 131)

A great deal of Hayden's success in undoing the dislocations of time and space can be attributed to his poet-speakers' uncanny ability to give themselves over to the actuality they contemplate. They become what they behold; known object and knowing subject unite. Like psychic mediums, his speakers obliterate distinctions between self and other; the dead and distant take possession of their voices. Take for example these lines from "The Dream (1863)":

> That evening Sinda thought she heard the drums
> and hobbled from her cabin to the yard.
> The quarters now were lonely-still in willow dusk
> after the morning's ragged jubilo,
> when laughing crying singing the folks went off
> with Marse Lincum's soldier boys.
> But Sinda hiding would not follow them: those
> Buckras with their ornery
> funning, cussed commands, oh they were not
> were not
> the hosts the dream had promised her.
> (p. 36)

The poem is obviously a third-person narrative, but the space separating narrator and actor is frequently violated. The speaker's voice modulates effortlessly into the cadences of the slaves. "Marse Lincum," "Buckra," and "ornery" are words heard in the accents of the slaves. The pathos of the cry "oh they were not were not" is so extraordinary because, syntax notwithstanding, it is Sinda's own voice we hear, and not the poet's. In six lines in "The Rabbi" Hayden gives a virtuoso demonstration of the resources of his voice:

> And I learned schwartze too
> And schnapps, which schwartzes bought
> on credit from "Jew Baby."
> Tippling ironists laughed and said
> he'd soon be rich as Rothschild
> From their swinish Saturdays.
> (p. 81)

In the first two lines the poet's retrospective view of the blacks of his youth is clearly refracted through the cultural lens of the Jews he knew. By the end of the third line, however, his perspective has shifted, and it is now the Jews who are being looked upon from a black point of view. "Credit" is the pivotal term in this transition, for it not only allows the speaker to describe objectively the economic relationship of black to Jew but also lets him draw on the powerful connotations this word has in the Afro-American speech community. The last three lines of indirect quotation, framed by two jocularly incongruous phrases that are clearly of the poet's own making, indicate that the speaker finally assumes an amused posture independent of the viewpoint of either black or Jew, but remarkably sensitive to both. And there is a social morality implicit in this display of Hayden's multivocal talents. What might at first seem to be merely a technical device has enormous ethical implications. When the poet says in the last stanza,

> But the synagogue became
> New Calvary.
> The rabbi bore my friends off
> in his prayer shawl
> (p. 81)

he means for us to see that the loss of his childhood friends Hirschel and Molly is part of a wholesale separation of black and Jew, a separation that will brook no opposition from considerations as flimsy as one human being's love for another. "New Calvary," tellingly isolated in a single line, is not only the name of the black church that succeeds the synagogue. It represents too a place and an action. It is the hill where Christianity and Jewry part ways, the site where Hayden's ideal of human oneness is sacrificed, a modern reenactment of that old attempt at redemption that ironically, bitterly, only sped man in his fall out of unity into division.

But there is a sinister dimension to this intercourse between self and other, present and past. Robert Hayden knows, and this is a sign of his strength, that openness is also vulnerability, that the past in which one finds possibilities of inspiration and renewal can exert a malignant influence on the present. In "A Ballad of Remembrance" the poet is besieged by specters pressing upon him the value of their individual adaptations to American racism. The Zulu King urges accommodation, the gunmetal priestess preaches hate, and a motley contingent of saints, angels, and mermaids, blind to the realities of evil, chime out a song of naive love. These competing voices drive the poet to the brink of madness. In "Tour 5" an autumn ride into the country becomes a frightening excursion into a surreal world alive with ancient conflicts between black, white, and red men. In "Locus" the Southland lies wasted under the blight of its own history. The present abdicates to the superior force of the past. The redbuds are "like momentary trees / of an illusionist"; there is a "violent metamorphosis, / with every blossom turning / deadly and memorial soldiers." Life here is stunted, reality the bondsman of a dream of disaster. The past forecloses its mortgage on the future:

> Here spareness, rankness, harsh
> brilliances; beauty of what's hardbitten,
> knotted, stinted, flourishing
> in despite, on thorny meagerness
> thriving, twisting into grace.

Here symbol houses
where the brutal dream lives out its lengthy
dying. Here the past, adored and
—unforgiven. Here the past—
soulscape, Old Testament battleground
of warring shades whose weapons kill.

(p. 45)

Closely related to Hayden's interest in the cunning ironies of history is his anxiety for the fate of myth and religion in the modern world. This concern provides the motivation of some of his best poetry. Take "Full Moon," for example, which we quote in full:

No longer throne of a goddess to whom we pray,
no longer the bubble house of childhood's
tumbling Mother Goose man,

The emphatic moon ascends—
the brilliant challenger of rocket experts,
the white hope of communications men.

Some I love who are dead
were watchers of the moon and knew its lore;
planted seeds, trimmed their hair,

Pierced their ears for gold hoop earrings
as it waxed or waned.
It shines tonight upon their graves.

And burned in the garden of Gethsemane,
its light made holy by the dazzling tears
with which it mingled.

And spread its radiance on the exile's path
of Him who was the Glorious One,
its light made holy by His holiness.

Already a mooted goal and tomorrow perhaps
an arms base, a livid sector,
the full moon dominates the dark.

(p. 79)

The world we encounter here is radically impoverished. The slow process by which the rise of positivistic science has emptied Nature of all religious significance is recapitulated in the fall of childhood's illusions before the advance of adult skepticism. For contemporary man, the moon exists only as a means of flaunting the triumphs of his technological vanity. But the poet sees in this diminished moon an analogue to the deprivations death has exacted from him, and with this crucial recognition of a mutuality of fates begins the movement toward recovery. Like the breathtaking expansion of meaning we witness in Eliot's "Sweeney among the Nightingales" when we leap from the nightingales "singing near / The Convent of the Sacred Heart" to those that "sang within the bloody wood / When Agamemnon cried aloud,"[11] there is a startling intensification of feeling in the transition from a light that "shines tonight upon their graves" to the light that "burned in the garden of Gethsemane." But Hayden knows that this age looks upon Jesus Christ and the prophet Baha'u'llah (The Glorious One of the penultimate stanza and the founder of Hayden's Baha'i faith) with a cynical regard, and that any appeal to them to restore the significance of a degraded Nature would sound highly artificial and entirely unconvincing. Like Flannery O'Connor, who frequently discerns in overt denials of faith ironic avowals of the existence of God, Hayden subverts the materialism of technology to make a claim for the reality of spirit. The moon that is now meaningless will once again become all-meaningful, he says, not as the throne of a benign deity or as an object of harmless childish fancies, but as an arms base that can end all life. The meaning that has been lost to the achievement of science reasserts itself with a vengeance by means of that very same achievement. This ironic turn of events is itself fully in keeping with the traditional view of the moon as the symbol of eternal recurrence. The full weight of this paradox is felt in the critical word "livid," on which a whole world of ambiguities turns. As meaning ashen or pallid, livid is both a forthright description of a full moon and suggestive of the moon's fearful retreat before the press of technology. As meaning black and blue, livid, in conjunction with the reference to the moon as "the white hope of communications men," suggests a moon bruised and discolored by the assaults of the Jack Johnsons of science. As a synonym for enraged or angry, livid further elaborates upon the implied meanings of this prize-fighting metaphor, and, by connecting it to the ominous possibilities of the moon's use as an arms base, subtly transforms the earlier reference to the moon as victim into an image of the moon as aggressor. And when we finally consider livid as meaning red, that satellite's consequence as an object of martial reverence is fully revealed, for the red moon is the moon foreseen by John of Patmos, and its appearance announces the coming of God in His wrath, the destruction of nations and the end of time.

III

When we review the entire course of Hayden's development, the importance of the poet as historian seems to lessen drastically over time. In his last two volumes of verse, only "Beginnings" immediately strikes us as aspiring to the largeness of historical vision of a "Full Moon" or the early explorations of the Afro-American past for which Hayden is chiefly known. What we feel is responsible for this change is not something so simple as the symbolist's displacement of the historian, but a growing preoccupation in the historian with ever smaller units of time. Having exhausted his examination of the problematic interactions of present and past, Hayden's historian is free to chronicle the mystery of change itself. Instead of feeling obliged to overcome the effects of change, he is more and more fascinated by single moments of metamorphosis. This is clearly the case in the poetry of *The Night-Blooming Cereus*. Standing before the "Arachne" of the black sculptor Richard Hunt, the poet is transfixed by the impenetrable mystery of the total change of essence he witnesses. At the same time his language manages to evoke Arachne's terror, it confesses, by the violent juxtaposition of concepts of motion and stasis, the human and the animal, birth and death, the singular incapacity of rational terms to represent adequately such an event:

In goggling terror fleeing powerless to flee
  Arachne not yet arachnid and no longer woman
    in the moment's centrifuge of dying
      becoming

(p. 23)

The capacity of short-lived and seemingly trivial events to manifest truths of exceptional import is shown in "The Night-Blooming Cereus." The speaker initially anticipates the blooming of that flower with a casual disregard for the miracle it will actually be. He and his companion are, in effect, two decadent intellectuals whose interest in the "primitive" is really just a shallow trafficking in the exotic. For them the blossoming sanctions hedonistic indulgence: they will paint themselves and "dance / in honor of archaic mysteries." Yet so much more than they can possibly imagine depends on the appearance of that blossom. When the bud unfolds, the phenomenon of its transformation enlarges into the enigma of eternal recurrence, the riddle of the cyclical alternation of life and death. And the blasphemous are reduced to near speechlessness:

Lunar presence
foredoomed, already dying,
it charged the room
  with plangency

older than human
cries, ancient as prayers
invoking Osiris, Krishna,
Tezcátlipóca.
We spoke
in whispers when
we spoke
at all

(p. 26)

Just as Hayden's historian's engrossment with the epochal modulates into an absorption with the momentary, there is a parallel shift of his focus away from the history of a people to the biographies of individuals, away from the public figures of the past to persons who are the poet's contemporaries. The boxer Tiger Flowers and the artist Betsy Graves Reyneau take the place of Nat Turner and Harriet Tubman. If the personages that engage him impress us as having little relation to the main currents of our history, they clearly arouse anxieties in him that nothing less than a total reconsideration of the nature of history itself can assuage. Just as Hayden's early historian is compelled to personalize the past he confronts, his later one is compelled to objectivize his own subjectivity. His private anguish never locks him into the sterile dead-end of solipsism; it impels him outward into the world. "The Peacock Room," Hayden tells us, grew out of an intense emotional experience. A visit to that room designed by Whistler excited painful recollections of his dead friend Betsy Graves Reyneau, who had been given a party in the same room on her twelfth birthday.[12] Contemplating the rival claims of art and life,

Ars Longa Which is crueller
Vita Brevis life or art?

the poet seeks shelter in Whistler's "lyric space," as he once did in the glow "of the lamp shaped like a rose" his "mother would light / . . . some nights to keep / Raw-Head-And-Bloody-Bones away." But he knows that the dreadful facts of the nightmare that is our history—"Hiroshima Watts My Lai"—scorn "the vision chambered in gold." The very title of the poem, however, has already hinted that his meditations will not issue into a simplistic espousal of art's advantages over life. The peacock is an ambiguous figure. The legendary incorruptibility of the bird's flesh has led to its adoption as a type of immortality and an image of the Resurrected Christ; but as the emblem of Pride, the root of all evil, the bird has always had ominous connotations in Christian culture. These intimations of evil remind the poet of the artist driven mad by Whistler's triumph, and the Peacock Room is transformed in his mind from sanctuary to chamber of horrors. The echoes of Stevens's "Domination of Black" and Poe's "Raven" heighten the poet's fears:

With shadow cries
the peacocks flutter down,
their spread tails concealing her,
then folding, drooping to reveal
her eyeless, old—Med School
cadaver, flesh-object
pickled in formaldehyde,
who was artist, compassionate,
clear-eyed. Who was belovéd friend.
No more. No more.

The paradox of a lasting art that mocks man's fragility at the same time that it realizes his dream of immortality is resolved in the beatific, enigmatic smile of the Bodhisattva ("one whose being—sattva—is enlightenment—bodhi"):

What is art?
What is life?
What the Peacock Room?
Rose-leaves and ashes drift
its portals, gently spinning toward
a bronze Bodhisattva's ancient smile.

(pp. 28–29)

In a remarkable way, "Beginning," the first poem of *Angle of Ascent*, re-enacts the course of the fruitful collaboration of Hayden's historian and symbolist. The historian summons up the essential facts of the poet's ancestry, and the symbolist imediately translates them into the terms of art:

Plowdens, Finns,
Sheffeys, Haydens,
Westerfields.

Pennsylvania gothic,
Kentucky homespun,
Virginia baroque.

As the poem moves forward in time, the ancestors are particularized. Joe Finn appears "to join Abe Lincoln's men" and "disappears into his name." Greatgrandma Easter lingers longer before the poet's gaze, and she is remembered not for the role she took in an historic conflict, but for her individual qualities: "She was more than six feet tall. At ninety could / still chop and tote firewood." The progression toward individuation that accompanies the poem's movement to the present—the sharpness of focus of the portrait of an ancestor is a direct function of that ancestor's nearness to the poet's own present—is paralleled by a growth in the poet's awareness of the figurative possibilities of language. As the historian's field of view contracts, the symbolist's artfulness becomes increasingly apparent. As we move from summaries of the entire lives of Joe Finn and Greatgrandma Easter to select moments in the lives of the poet's aunts, the symbolist's reveling in words for the beauty of their sound and rhythm becomes more evident:

Melissabelle and Sarah Jane
oh they took all the prizes one Hallowe'en.
And we'll let the calico curtain fall
on Pocahontas and the Corncob Queen
dancing the figures the callers call—
Sashay, ladies, promenade, all.

But when the poet himself finally appears, a curious—but, for Robert Hayden, characteristic—change occurs. The historian reasserts his centrality (the concluding piece is called "The Crystal Cave Elegy"), and the poem's steady flow toward life and the present is momentarily reversed in commemoration of the death of the miner Floyd Collins. The symbolist's increasing involvement in the resources of his art does not end in an autistic preoccupation with the poet's inner life but finally turns outward in prayer for the liberation of Collins. The timeless paradise of the imagination is invoked to release humanity from the limitations of time:

Poor game loner
trapped in the rock
of Crystal Cave, as
once in Kentucky coal-
mine dark (I taste the
darkness yet)
my greenhorn dream of
life. Alive down there
in his grave. Open
for him, blue door.

(p. 5)

The province of the poet is neither the realist's moonscape of inert matter nor the romantic's starfire of pure spirit, but the middle kingdom of actual earth that unites the two. Robert Hayden's symbolist and historian long ago joined hands to seize this fertile territory as their own. Together they have kept it up very well.

Notes

1. This meticulousness poses problems for the critic. Robert Hayden frequently revises his work, and a poem in one collection can appear in considerably altered form in a later collection. In general, Hayden's revisions involve deletions; he characteristically seeks greater economy of expression. His revisions could form the topic of a separate essay. To avoid confusion among variants, all our references are to poems as they appear in *Angle of Ascent* (New York, 1975). Page numbers after quotations pertain to this volume.
2. Thomas H. Johnson, ed., *Final Harvest: Emily Dickinson's Poems* (Boston, 1962), p. 59. The Dickinson influence here might not be direct. It is quite possible, given the extraordinary likeness Hayden's "Witch Doctor" bears to Gwendolyn Brooks's well-known "The Sundays of Satin-Legs Smith," that the Dickinson influence is filtered through Brooks, particularly the Brooks of *Annie Allen* where one finds poems ("A light and diplomatic bird," for example) that are virtually indistinguishable from the work of Dickinson's own hand.
3. Herman Melville, *White-Jacket: The World in a Man-of-War* (New York, 1952), p. 370.
4. Charles Feidelson, Jr., *Symbolism and American Literature* (Chicago, 1953), p. 71.
5. Quoted in F. O. Matthiessen, *American Renaissance* (New York, 1941), p. 54.
6. John O'Brien, ed., *Interviews with Black Writers* (New York, 1973), p. 114.
7. Charles T. Davis, "Robert Hayden's Use of History," in Donald Gibson, ed., *Modern Black Poets* (Englewood Cliffs, N.J., 1973), pp. 96–111.
8. *New York Times Book Review*, February 22, 1976, p. 34.
9. Hayden's insistence that he is a poet who happens to be Negro, made most dramatically at the Fisk University Centennial Writers' Conference in 1966, inevitably calls to mind the stance taken by Countee Cullen in the Foreword to *Caroling Dusk* (New York, 1927). Hayden was enamored of Cullen as an undergraduate, and the careful reader can detect significant correspondences between "The Ballad of Nat Turner" and "The Shroud of Color." Yet when Cullen rejected the idea of a black poetry in favor of a poetry written by blacks, his equation of a black movement in poetry with disease clearly indicated how much he underestimated the possibilities for poetry in black American culture and how much he was intimidated by the richness of the Anglo-American poetic tradition: "to say that the pulse beat of their [i.e., the blacks'] verse shows generally such a fever, or the symptoms of such an ague, will prove on closer examination merely the moment's exaggeration of a physician anxious to establish a new literary ailment." Hayden throughout his career has prized his independence, but he has never hesitated to exploit the possibilities for poetry in Afro-American culture. At any rate, Melvin B. Tolson, the magnificent and neglected black poet who rose in opposition to Hayden at Fisk to say that blackness is prior to poetry, has himself been accused of denying his own blackness. No issue in Afro-American letters has to date generated more heat or less light than the question of what "black poet" means.
10. For the assertion that Hayden was especially concerned with Afro-American history during the 1940s, we refer the reader to Davis, "Hayden's Use of History," p. 97. Proof that Hayden reached his maturity during these years is to be found in the difference between the stiff poetry of *Heart-Shape in the Dust* and the elastic verse of *The Lion and the Archer* (New York, 1948).
11. T. S. Eliot, *The Waste Land and Other Poems* (1922; rpt. New York: 1962), p. 26.
12. O'Brien, *Interviews*, pp. 120–22.

ANTHONY HECHT

1923–

Anthony Evan Hecht was born in New York City on January 16, 1923. After graduating with a B.A. from Bard College in 1944, he served with the U.S. Army in Europe and Japan, returning to America to teach for a year at Kenyon College before gaining an M.A. from Columbia University in 1950. In 1951 he held the Prix de Rome Fellowship, and translated poems by Rilke which were set by Lukas Foss as the cantata *A Parable of Death*. He has also translated poems by Baudelaire and Apollinaire.

Hecht's first collection of poems, *A Summoning of Stones*, was published in 1954, and the same year he won a Guggenheim Fellowship, with a second in 1959. He held teaching positions at a number of colleges before settling at the University of Rochester in 1967 as professor of poetry and rhetoric. His second major publication, *The Hard Hours* (1967), won him both the Russell Loines Award and the Pulitzer Prize for Poetry in 1968. In 1971 he was a Fulbright professor in Brazil, and he was visiting professor at Harvard in 1973 and at Yale in 1977. *Millions of Strange Shadows* appeared in 1977, and *The Venetian Vespers* in 1979. From 1982 to 1984 Hecht was poetry consultant to the Library of Congress, and in 1983 he was made a trustee of the American Academy in Rome. His other publications include a translation of *Seven against Thebes* by Aeschylus (1973) and *A Love for Four Voices: Homage to Franz Josef Haydn* (1983).

Hecht, who has been married twice and has three children, lives in Rochester, New York.

Personal

I once served on a rather distinguished literary jury that had the noble task of disposing of large sums of money as literary awards in all fields—fiction, non-fiction and poetry. It was our general procedure to begin with an enormous list of candidates submitted by knowledgable persons, to which the jury was entitled to add any names it cared to, and then by surgical elimination to work down to final choices. One day, as we were paring away, somebody noticed that there were very few fiction writers left, while there was a very considerable number of poets still unscratched. Admitting that this presented problems, I nevertheless declared myself pleased by the thought that there were so many very good and deserving poets now writing. One of the other jurers, a well-known writer of fiction and criticism, observed with absolutely citric mordancy, "Perhaps that's because poetry is so much easier to write than fiction."

There followed a pronounced silence, not thoughtful but embarrassed. But there has been time since to be thoughtful, and what is saddening is that my fellow juror was right. While novelists must labor under the compulsion to *invent*, to create fictional personages, put them in provocative situations, contrive actions and reactions and eventualities, poets have more and more retreated into undisguised narcissism and documentary literalness until, as things now go, a poet may be congratulated for being truthful, candid or confessional, but he is rarely told that he is, nor is he expected to be, imaginative or inventive. Imagination these days seems to belong entirely to the realm of prose.

The general tendency to self-absorption began around the same time that poets started going mad, and for some of the same reasons. It was itself an index of professional unpleasantness. With what must seem deliberate petulance, poets were saying, in effect: If no one else will pay attention to me, I will focus entirely upon myself, upon my sensitive reactions to inoffensive, non-human things, and to hell with everyone else. This can easily lead to oddness. And while the modern reader may think it odd that John Donne should have posed for his funeral monument wearing his shroud, it is far more sane and humble than some of the nutty behavior or boring introspection now offered as both *Dichtung* and *Wahrheit*.

Their tiny and loyal readership aside, if poets provoke any interest whatever on the part of the general public, that interest is not in poetry *per se* but in the poets' lives, which are widely held, on the basis of considerable evidence, to be highly peculiar and unsavory. Aware of this prying and voyeuristic curiosity, T. S. Eliot and W. H. Auden expressly forbade biographies to be written of them, and so stipulated in their wills. Auden often declared that he did not want more attention paid to the idiosyncrasies of his life than to the poems in which he hoped to redeem himself from his faults. Both poets, as things turned out, were unable to have their wills respected. Insinuating memoirs and recollections were published, and in Auden's case a detailed and responsible biography was brought out by Humphrey Carpenter. All this would have greatly pained not only the dead poets but the New Critics of some years ago, who kept telling us that the lives of the poets were of no concern to us and irrelevant to their poems. That pious notion, too, has been moderated or altogether abandoned by such critics as David Kalstone, William Pritchard and Lawrence Lipking.

But, if the fashions of criticism change, the status of the poet in society remains precisely as obscure as when Randall Jarrell raised his eloquent cry in the essay "The Obscurity of the Poet": The rewards are small, the neglect or indifference enormous. So how and why did I get into this racket?

Hard to say. Quite early in my life I learned a song, taught to me, I must suppose, by someone with a bad cold, because for years I thought the words went:

My body lies over the ocean,
My body lies over the sea,
My body lies over the ocean,
O bring back my body to me.

Being a thoughtful child, I brooded upon this, like darkness upon the face of the deep. It bespoke a remarkable spiritual condition, possibly a ghoulish one. What was my body doing out there, anyway? Was it getting wet? And where was *I* in the meantime? These questions absorbed me at an age when I was supposed to be getting down some elementary facts about American history. I had a vision of my body in mid-Atlantic, hanging unsupported just about three feet above the whitecaps, looking as if you could pass steel hoops along it from end to end by way of demonstrating that there were no wires or hidden brackets. It was very cold, and getting dark.

But, though all the germs of a mystic experience were present, they did not consolidate into any interest in poetry, or anything else, for that matter. I was conspicuous for mediocrity throughout my school years—so conspicuous that my worried parents sent me off for two days of aptitude tests at the Pratt Institute. I was curious about the results myself, and by no means confident, so I kept prodding my parents who, as it turned out, were trying to keep from me the bleakness of the findings. But at last they had no recourse except to let me know that Pratt had said decisively that I had no aptitudes whatever. And this only confirmed a fairly uniform opinion of teachers and family with which I was painfully obliged to agree.

So I may have been more astonished than anyone else when I fell in love with poetry in my freshman year at college. And, though I had never attempted anything but doggerel verse of the very lowest order, I told my parents that I intended to become a poet. Had I said that I'd settled upon a career of burglary, they might have been pained but would at least have credited me with a cool, prudential instinct for survival. As it was, they were genuinely alarmed; and sought help. When I next visited home, there were guests at dinner, my parents' only "literary" friends, Ted and Helen Geisel. Ted is the celebrated cartoonist known as Dr. Seuss. Given his calling, I suspected nothing, and the dinner conversation was diverting and innocent enough. But, when we rose from the table, Ted led me into the living room, his hand gentle upon my shoulder, and asked, "Well now, what is it you want to do with you life?" Instantly I was alerted to the likelihood of parental intrigue.

I suppose I could have answered that the question came a trifle prematurely to a boy of 17, but I was a guileless young fellow, and, besides, my curiosity was aroused. So I confessed candidly that I wanted to become a poet. Ted replied, "That's fine. I think that's wonderful. And I have some advice I'd like to give you. I think the very first thing you should do is read the life of Joseph Pulitzer." This was not what I had expected. I thanked Ted for his advice and found occasion to withdraw. I could not immediately see the relevance of the life of a newspaper publisher to a career in poetry; but it was my shrewd guess that, given my parents' undisguised anxiety, there must have been something in that biography that would be gravely discouraging. So I resolved quite firmly never to read it, and I never have. This policy seems to have served me well, and I commend it unreservedly to all young poets.—ANTHONY HECHT, "Masters of Unpleasantness," *NYTBR*, Feb. 7, 1982, pp. 3, 25

Works

A *Summoning of Stones* is Mr. Hecht's first volume of poetry. It shows him to be a poet of great charm, possibly even too great charm, for when these poems fall below Mr. Hecht's highest standard, as of course they occasionally do, it is always because his witty fancy gets out of control. This may be partly the fault of the period style, of which Mr. Hecht has a remarkable mastery.

We have, after all, been living for nearly half a century in an almost continuous poetic revolution, a preservation of the dialect of the tribe by drastic surgery. During the last decade or so, this revolution seems to have been slowing down; as it does, poets become more interested in mastering the established style and using it than in making an entirely new style for themselves. In poets like Mr. Hecht and, say, Richard Wilbur, the period style seems to be emerging pretty clearly. It is an eclectic style, a composite of means developed by various earlier 20th Century poets; you can hear the echoes, as you hear Yeats in Mr. Hecht's

> So that pale mistress or high-busted bawd
> Could smile and spit into the eye of death,

and Stevens in

> Deep in the phosphorous waters of the bay,
> Or in the wind, or pointing cedar tree,
> Or its own ramified complexity,

and Crane in

> as the gulls hover
> Winged with their life, above the harbor wall,
> Tracing inflected silence.

Such a style offers the poet a great range of resources for "extending his remarks"; indeed, its mastery almost forces such an extension on him, whether his subject calls for it or not, just as Milton's style forced grandeur on him even when the occasion—no fear lest dinner cool—hardly required it. This is the danger of our period style. But it is a fine style when the occasion is right and the poet's remarks are good enough and sufficiently controlled.

It is sometimes said that, thanks to the established style of the period, no Elizabethan could write a bad lyric. This is very far from true, as any reader of Tottel's *Miscellany* knows. And it is not the estblished style which makes Mr. Hecht's poems interesting; it only determines their kind. Mr. Hecht makes them good. The distinction is clear in "La Condition Botanique." This is a poem "about" botanical gardens; it belongs to what is by now almost a conventional kind, a poem in which, while apparently making meticulous and even scientifically accurate observations about the obvious subject, the poet gradually builds up a system of assertions about life as a whole. Auden provides all sorts of examples of the kind:

> O season of repetition and return . . .
> How lucid the image in your shining well
> Of a limpid day, how eloquent your streams
> Of lives without language, the cell maneuvres and the molecular bustle.

"La Condition Botanique" begins:

> Romans, rheumatic, gouty, came
> To bathe in Ischian springs where water steamed,
> Puffed and enlarged their bold imperial thoughts.

It goes on to instance other peoples who love the luxury of steam baths and, in the third stanza, finally makes its transition to botanical gardens by remarking that, for all their refinement, these people have known

> Nothing of the more delicate sweat
> Of plants, breathing their scented oxygen upon
> Brooklyn's botanical gardens, roofed with glass and run
> So to the pleasures of each leafy pet,
> Manured, addressed in Latin, so
> To its thermostatic happiness—
> Spreading its green innocence to the ground
> Where pipes, like Satan masquerading as the snake,
> Coil and uncoil their frightful liquid length, and make
> Gurglings of love mixed with a rumbling sound
> Of sharp intestinal distress—
> So to its pleasure, as I said,
> That. . . .

How complicated and yet how clear and controlled the structure of this sentence is: "The Romans and the rest knew nothing of the sweat of plants, plants which breath on the greenhouses, which are run so to the pleasures of the plants, so to their happiness—which spreads to the ground where pipes do this and that—so to the pleasures of the plants that . . ." The clause which follows upon "that" runs to eighteen more lines of equally complicated and equally controlled sentence structure. This syntactical virtuosity is what the period style provides for the poet if he can learn it. Its use is to provide the maximum syntactical opportunity for what is the main interest of this kind of poem, the only apparently incidental detail. The poet has to be able to make such detail good enough or the poem becomes a monumental bore. Mr. Hecht is able to; in spite of the apparent randomness of his observations, they all fall together finally. Satan remains below; the flowers thrive "as in the lot first given to Man, / Sans interruption,"

> And we, like disinherited heirs,
> Old Adam, can inspect the void estate
> At visiting hours: the unconditional garden spot,
> The effortless innocence preserved, for God knows what,
> And think as we depart by the toll gate:
> No one has lived here these five thousand years.

Mr. Hecht likes to apply this style to such subjects as botanical gardens, and he has poems on "The Gardens of the Villa d'Este," on "A Roman Holiday," and on the Frick Museum. He also likes abstract elements like Air or Water. But he knows too how to make this style work for "A Discourse Concerning Temptation" or pain, for narrative, like the one of Samuel Sewall's wooing, for a soldier's soliloquy ("Christmas Is Coming") or an elegy for dead companions ("Drinking Song"). He has considerable range, but he is committed to the established style, of which he might have said what he actually says of something slightly different:

> This was not lavish if you bear in mind
> That dynasties of fishes, swimming before mankind,
> Felt in the pressure of their element
> What Leonardo charted in a brook:
> How nature first declared for the baroque
> In her design of water currents.

—ARTHUR MIZENER, *KR*, Summer 1954, pp. 479–81

Anthony Hecht's new volume, *The Hard Hours*, is . . . , in effect, selected poems: a third of the poems are reprinted from Hecht's first volume, *A Summoning of Stones* (1954), and another third have already appeared in two or three standard anthologies. This latter fact is a tribute to Hecht's craftsmanship: his poems are anthologized before there are enough of them to fill a single volume.

In any case, this volume represents Hecht's career from its beginning (the earliest copyright in 1948) and allows us to see the basic argument that underlies most of his poetry: facing the biological conditions of decay and destructiveness and the historical facts of mass savagery, man tries to construct "rites and ceremonies" by which to know his condition, combat his weakness and despair, and achieve civility. Hecht's favorite images for man's biological condition come from the insect world, an insidious and yet microscopically elaborate world in which man sees his own reflection. In "Alceste in the Wilderness", for example, he imagines Molière's misanthrope escaping to the jungle and finding there a microcosm of the hypocritical world he has fled:

> Before the bees have diagrammed their comb
> Within the skill, before summer has cracked

The back of Daphnis, naked, polychrome,
Versailles shall see the tempered exile home,
Peruked and stately for the final act.

The analogous image from history is the slaughter of the innocents. In " 'It Out-Herod's Herod. Pray You, Avoid It' ", a father, seeing himself reflected in his children's eyes as a television hero-protector, muses:

Yet by quite other laws
My children make their case;
Half God, half Santa Claus,
But with my voice and face,

A hero comes to save
The poorman, beggarman, thief,
And make the world behave
And put an end to grief.

And that their sleep be sound
I say this childermas
Who could not, at one time,
Have saved them from the gas.

The horror of historical chance is all the more concentrated for the nonchalance with which it is mentioned; and the "childermas", even if ultimately insufficient, is quietly noble.

Hecht is a highly accomplished formalist, but form is not an ultimate value. "Nothing," he says in "Three Prompters from the Wings," "is purely itself / But is linked with its antidote/In cold self-mockery—/A fact with which only those / Born with a Comic sense/Can learn to content themselves." This describes the broadest use of form in Hecht's poems: it holds together, in harsh comic fusion, the self-mocking opposites; it rarely resolves them. Often the tension issues from a comic inappropriateness of rhetoric, as in the description, in "A Vow", of a miscarriage ("In the third month, a sudden flow of blood./The mirth of tabrets ceaseth, and the joy/Also of the harp"), or as in the liturgy, in "Pig", to the swine into whom a thousand demons were driven ("O Swine that takest away our sins/That takest away").

Whatever the tactic—and his approaches are many—the strategy is basically the same: Hecht works against the grain, but so smoothly that we almost fail to notice. He gives us valved emotion; rather than direct expression of feeling, he presents, in magnificent variety of forms, the artifices we construct in the face of our historical and biological condition. Thus we get both formal brilliance and intense, often bitter, irony—and, more difficult to trace, a humane and kindly sympathy for man, inadequate as he struggles against destruction.—RICHARD A. JOHNSON, *SwR*, Autumn 1968, pp. 684–85

In its clear-eyed mercy toward human weakness, Anthony Hecht's poetry goes from strength to strength. *The Venetian Vespers* is at once an intense corroboration and an ample extension of his subtle, supple talents. Nothing humane is alien to him.

The poems' self-respect is at one with their unenvious respect for other poets, so that there is nothing intrinsically startling (except the new delight) about some of the shapes they take: the two vivid versions from the Russian poet Joseph Brodsky, or the two from Horace—the blithe ingratiations of "Application for a Grant" and the sardonic warning of "An Old Malediction," in which Horace's Pyrrha is seen in all her marine predatoriness as piranha. Then there is a handful—but how warm and capable of earnest grasping is this living hand—of short poems that are fostered alike by beauty and fear. But it is the four long poems that confirm Hecht as a poet of the widest apprehensions and comprehensions, and this without the gigantism that so haunts American poetic ambition.

"The Grapes" tells of a moment of hallucinatory clarity when a chambermaid contemplates the light on the grapes within a bowl, and suddenly and unarguably knows the desolation of her life: "There was nothing left for me now, nothing but years." "The Deodand" brings into appalling but justified juxtaposition Renoir's painting "Parisians Dressed in Algerian Costume" and a brutal incident of the Algerian war. "The Short End" calls up the frigid vacancy and torrid death of a woman ensconced in drinking and pillow-collecting, "trying to figure what went wrong." And "The Venetian Vespers" is a 30-page monologue in which an American expatriate—morbid, musing, witty, doomed—expatiates upon the various legacies which buoy him up and which lay him low: his uncle's money, "some genetic swamp," the father never known.

Succinct and poignant, and with a steely unsentimentality despite its width of concern for all concerned, the title poem constitutes the quintessence of an entire novel. The plot—an unforgivable yet hideously natural family betrayal—is direct, and yet it is released, with touching reluctance, only indirectly and piecemeal. "The Venetian Vespers" ends, after legitimately availing itself of *The Merchant of Venice*, of T. S. Eliot's lurid Venice in "Burbank with a Baedeker: Bleistein with a Cigar" and of *Death in Venice*, with the undying worm of self-disgust. Yet it does not disgust us, this moribundity in Venice. Gazing on the great clouds,

I look and look,
As though I could be saved simply by looking—
I, who have never earned my way, who am
No better than a viral parasite,
Or the lees of the Venetian underworld,
Foolish and muddled in my later years,
Who was never even at one time a wise child.

Hecht has genius in his command of rhythms, above all, where an imagined self-command falters and yet does not break.

One would need his powers of economy to get far enough in praise. There is much to be said about the illuminations that he gets from light in all its diversity; this book is, among much else, an anthology of light, from the author of that harrowing and enduring poem " 'More Light! More Light!' " (in *The Hard Hours*). His effects of light need their contexts, but one important thing about them is that light is seldom transparent for Hecht. There is a strong affiliation between this sense of light—not only as the medium of all attention but as itself an object of conscious attention—and Hecht's new relation to his own medium.

He began, 25 years ago, as the welder and wielder of a highly self-conscious language, able to take on Wallace Stevens ("Le Monocle de Mon Oncle") at his own game: "Le Masseur de Ma Soeur." Then, at the time of his Pulitzer Prize for *The Hard Hours* (1967), he gained the praise of Ted Hughes: "This most fastidious and elegant of poets shed every artifice and began to write with absolute raw simplicity and directness." Hecht's latest work, though, returns to a language that is not directly transparent (and that repeatedly speaks explicitly of brilliance, polish and scintillation) but that draws attention to itself. Verbalism and mannerism, tensed against much else, are now more deeply available themselves for exploration as well as for exploring with. This is the opposite of a fiasco.

Ho fatto un fiasco, which is to say,
I've made a sort of bottle of my life,
A frangible and a transparent failure.

Such poetry is transparently a success, but it is not (because "frangible" does attend to itself as a word) a success of transparency, You are conscious of the glass, and Hecht's art is to show that this may show you things which you'd otherwise not have seen.

A note on the notes appended to this volume: they are strange. They tell you that when the poem quotes Byron, Byron is being quoted. But they do not let on, for instance, to what is behind these lines:

O that the soul should tie its shoes, the mind
Should wash its hands in a sink, that a small grain
Of immortality should fit itself
With dentures.

Walter Bagehot: "The soul ties its shoes: the mind washes its hands in a basin. All is incongruous." But there is an essential congruity between allusion as itself a form of inheritance and the dark inheritance that flickers throughout this splendid poem of light and dark.—CHRISTOPHER RICKS, "Poets Who Have Learned Their Trade," *NYTBR*, Dec. 1, 1979, pp. 1, 44–45

There are only a half-dozen poets writing today with the technical prowess, moral intelligence, and exuberant gravity of Dr. Johnson's masters. Anthony Hecht is one of them. Much of his new book ⟨*The Venetian Vespers*⟩ started elsewhere, and he has made his own—a brace of caustic imitations of Horace, one of Ronsard, and two padded but affecting translations from the Russian of Joseph Brodsky. There are ten original poems as well, four of some length. The shorter poems show off Hecht's celebrated ability to move through a network of images and abstract ideas—whether exotic or familiar—by means of nimbly rhymed, occasionally very intricate stanzas, each an added shade of feeling or feat of association. But longer poems have always elicited—in these new instances, in a cultivated but pulsing blank verse—his most intriguing and commanding work. The four in this book all, in one way or another, conform to a model established earlier by Hecht, from "A Hill" in *The Hard Hours* (1967) to "Apprehensions" in *Millions of Strange Shadows* (1977). Each turns on an unexpected but sad or even grotesque epiphany, some dark transformation scene during which is revealed the world's horror or the speaker's dread. In "The Grapes," for instance, a no longer young chambermaid in a two-star French resort hotel, leafing through an old glossy magazine and daydreaming about a bellboy who has taken no notice of her, suddenly sees her future in a crystal bowl of grapes: "And I seemed to know/In my blood the meaning of sidereal time/And know my little life had crested./ There was nothing left for me now, nothing but years." Nothing but tears, she might have said, since time has stopped for her, fixed in memories of old images. That is the case, too, with the forlorn protagonist of "The Short End," an overweight, alcoholic, empty-headed housewife who wears double knits and sits alone in a conversation pit. The harshness of Hecht's Swiftian satire nearly overwhelms the care and concern of his character study. So too, when the impact of his poems depends on raw sensationalism, on sheer pity and terror—as "The Deodand" does—then I find them less sympathetic and illuminating than merely lacerating.

"The Short End," though, also reminds one of Hecht's capacity for the irrational or demonic as both subject and effect—a capacity usually unacknowledged by his critics, who prefer to praise (or not) his polish and equanimity. After several disconcerting episodes, the poem rises to an eerie, gripping hallucination. The reader is left unnerved, without knowing quite how or why. Just the reverse is true of the long (809 lines) title poem, also episodic but built to a resonant, plangent finale. The speaker is a retired American failure, living out his days in Venice ("The world's most louche and artificial city") and indulging a series of voluntary memories—the deaths of his parents, of a fellow soldier—that keep returning him to the "wilderness/Natural but alien and unpitying" that is his personal history. Set against that are the city's own past history and present blandishments. Like many other Hecht poems, this is a poem about survival, the unwitting, even unwanted survival of those spots of time that constitute the self. It is also a poem—more keen and magnanimous than any Hecht has written before—about salvation and paradise, the lost paradise that Proust says is the only true one. Like Proust, Hecht—or rather, his speaker of whom we grow so fond—searches for it in art itself, in the dome of St. Mark's or the furnaces of Murano. And finds it finally in himself, in the primary artistic act of attention—as when he contemplates the clouds out his window:

Great stadiums, grandstands and amphitheaters,
The tufted, opulent litters of the gods
They seem; or laundered bunting, well-dressed wigs,
Harvests of milk-white, Chinese peonies
That visibly rebuke our stinginess.
For all their ghostly presences, they take on
A colorful nobility at evening.
Off to the east the sky begins to turn
Lilac so pale it seems a mood of gray,
Gradually, like the death of virtuous men.
Streaks of electrum richly underline
The slow, flat-bottomed hulls, those floated lobes
Between which quills and spokes of light fan out
Into carnelian reds and nectarines,
Nearing a citron brilliance at the center,
The searing furnace of the glory hole
That fires and fuses clouds of muscatel
With pencilings of gold. I look and look,
As though I could be saved simply by looking.

The description having saved the moment, it saves—or so we deem it should—the man. And to have drawn us into that redeeming enterprise, as Hecht has so intimately, is only permitted the finest artist.—J. D. MCCLATCHY, "Summaries and Evidence," *PR*, 1980, pp. 643–44

Anthony Hecht chose as his early mentors T. S. Eliot in spirit and W. H. Auden in technique. Many another poet of the generation of the 1950's abandoned a formal style in mid-career to embrace an ostensibly more radical poetic; Hecht has never wavered. He has, if anything, rather narrowed than expanded and varied the range of themes and emotions in his work; and as his career progresses, much that appeared freely chosen in his early poems comes increasingly to seem the product of an ever more constricting necessity.

Hecht's poetic burden is a deep-seated ambivalence toward sexuality, usually expressed in poems that violently alternate or uneasily hover between attraction to and repulsion from the sexual world. Poem after poem takes the form of a long, overrich description abruptly juxtaposed to some threatening or repulsive matter. Hecht means to seduce the reader into complicity with the poem's imagined lusts, the better to shock him by the grotesque reversal at its close. Hecht frequently conceals the sexual nature of that theme by a kind of reverse synecdoche in which he represents sexuality by the more general emblem of natural beauty; in such poems the closing peripety usually invokes a memory of some horror of public and political dimensions:

As in a water-surface I behold
    The first, soft, peach decree
Of light, its pale, inaudible commands.
I stand beneath a pine-tree in the cold,
Just before dawn, somewhere in Germany,
A cold, wet Garand rifle in my hands.

Alongside those ambivalent meditations Hecht has written, throughout his career, a certain kind of "vision" poem. "A

Hill," from his first book, *A Summoning of Stones*, and "The Grapes," from *The Venetian Vespers*, though separated by twenty-five years, nevertheless come to the same resolution—a moment of heightened consciousness that, instead of irradiating and renewing the world, reveals its barrenness and poverty:

> And I seemed to know
> In my blood the meaning of sidereal time
> And know my little life had somehow crested.
> There was nothing for me now, nothing but years.

What indicates the years that divide those poems is not a difference in imaginative strategy but a difference in tone. The earlier poem hesitates at the edges of its vision with something of the shock of real discovery; the later seems resigned to its moment of reduction long before that anticlimax is reached.

"The Venetian Vespers," title poem and centerpiece of this volume, recalls the high modernist mode both in its organization, a dramatic monologue grouping discrete passages around a thematic center, and in the situation of its speaker, a cultured but world-weary man whose energy and will have failed. This lengthy "Gerontion" comprehensively renders the quality of self-loathing and pained consciousness it sets out to portray, but is perhaps not so successful in convincing us of the value of that undertaking. Dwelling at such lengths on neurotic states is not without its dangers, and it may be questioned whether this dissection of the "gross, intestinal wormings of the brain" is wholly consistent with good imaginative hygiene.

Hecht is almost unique among his contemporaries in having an alive, and alert, sense of sin. Hecht finds Eros and Thanatos inextricably mingled, and both irredeemably corrupted by their belonging to the natural world. Hecht's anti-naturalism resembles that of T. S. Eliot, a fear of the harrowing experience of the realm of flesh. Whether any poet who persists in that theme must inevitably become merely compulsive may be questioned. Hecht has persisted in it, at the cost of growing progressively darker, less balanced. It may seem strange to assert that so formal—and technically accomplished—a poet has failed to digest completely his poetic material. Yet throughout his career Hecht's individual obsessions have pressed harder on his poems, ultimately, than the needs of the poetic imagination he certainly possesses. Despite all of Hecht's verbal sense and facility, it is not without a certain relief that we turn from this world where every pleasure can be bought only with an excess of pain, where resignation is the only authentic stance.—VERNON SHETLEY, "Take But Degree Away," *Poetry*, Feb. 1981, pp. 297–98

ASHLEY BROWN
"The Poetry of Anthony Hecht"

Ploughshares, Volume 4, Number 3 (1978), pp. 9–25

THE NIGHTINGALE

> What is it to be free? The unconfined
> Lose purpose, strength, and at the last, the mind.
> (Anthony Hecht: a couplet to accompany Aesop)

The American poets who were born up and down the 1920s have come into their full powers and fame well before now, though the contours of some careers have emerged rather slowly. Most of them were presented in Richard Howard's brilliant commentaries in *Alone with America* almost ten years ago. Mr. Howard didn't mean to write literary history, and indeed he avoided the issue and perhaps emphasized his forty-one subjects' aloneness by arranging them in alphabetical order. But there is something to be said for a sense of period; in recollection one thinks of the common urgencies and possibilities in the literary scene of a generation ago: the enveloping action, as it were, that the craft of poetry would make actual. As a contemporary, born in the same year as Anthony Hecht, Louis Simpson, Denise Levertov, Daniel Hoffman, and James Dickey (not a bad year), I can hardly pretend to be disinterested about poets whose work I have watched for three decades.

In the late 1940s those I read most immediately were Hecht, James Merrill, and Edgar Bowers, the latter in my opinion the most neglected member of his generation—neglected, that is, by almost everybody outside the circle created by Yvor Winters, his teacher and champion. They came together in one number of *The Hudson Review* in 1949, I remember. They were precocious in their different ways. They had been in the Army during the War and had much to write about amidst the ruins of Europe, but I think that only Mr. Bowers had got hold of his subject at that time. His special focus of experience comes out in the conclusion of "The Stoic," which is addressed to a German friend:

> You must, with so much known, have been afraid
> And chosen such a mind of constant will,
> Which, though all time corrode with constant hurt,
> Remains, until it occupies no space,
> That which it is; and passionless, inert,
> Becomes at last no meaning and no place.

Earlier in the same poem he evokes

> Eternal Venice sinking by degrees
> Into the very water that she lights;
> Reflected in canals, the lucid dome
> Of Marie dell' Salute at your feet,
> Her triple spires disfigured by the foam.

Venice, after the War, became a kind of *mise en scéne* for various states of mind (Mr. Bowers returns to it in the second of his beautiful "Italian Guide-Book" poems), just as it was the place for important premieres and exhibitions. But who could have foreseen then that Mr. Merrill, with his dazzling verbal gift, would eventually perfect the comedy of manners in our generation and bring us, in the climactic sections of *The Book of Ephraim*, the grandeurs and trivia of Venice as we know it? Or that Mr. Hecht would write "The Venetian Vespers," a great meditation on the tragic displacements of our century?

I have tended to put Mr. Hecht somewhere between Mr. Bowers and Mr. Merrill all these years, just as a way of defining his special poetic qualities. He partakes of the moral penetration of the one and the wit of the other, to my way of thinking. But this is too easily said, just as these qualities are too easily named, and Anthony Hecht was his own man from the beginning. He is a New Yorker, born the day before St. Anthony's Day in January, and he took his degrees at Bard College and Columbia. After Bard he went to the War in Europe and Japan as an infantry rifleman for three years—an experience that has deeply affected his poetry. Then he turned to John Crowe Ransom at Kenyon College, like several others of his generation, and his first poems that I read came out in *The Kenyon Review* for Spring 1947, where he was Tony Hecht. These early pieces have not been reprinted, but they are entirely competent and Mr. Hecht should certainly put them in a future edition of his Collected Poems. They are called "Once Removed" and "To a Soldier Killed in Germany." Looking back at them from the vantage point of the later Hecht, one is inclined to say that they are very direct treatments of their subjects—quite understandably the work of a twenty-three-year-old recently under fire. The second poem begins with characteristic strength of feeling keyed up by a formal stanza:

> On a small town, twitching with life and death,
> The sun pours his consuming acid down

On broken monuments, the shattered fist
Of Hitler's figure, stoney carrion kissed
By the devouring light, and near this town
They stitched your lips and cut away your breath.

A recurring image in the poems, early and late, is "stone" or some variant of it: nature inert and shattered: ". . . this broken landscape tied by the wind together." In retrospect this seems to point toward Mr. Hecht's first book, *A Summoning of Stones* (1954), which takes its title from a phrase by Santayana implying that the poet's duty is ". . . to call the stones themselves to their ideal places, and enchant the very substance and skeleton of the world." (Mr. Hecht uses it as his epigraph.) Someone studying the poems might explore the imagery at length and observe its permutations, but just the titles of the three collections suggest a kind of progression: *A Summoning of Stones, The Hard Hours*, and *Millions of Strange Shadows*.

By Autumn of 1947 Mr. Hecht was Anthony in *The Kenyon Review*, and he had moved on to the University of Iowa, another literary mecca of the period. I suppose it was his Kenyon year that left traces of Ransom in a few of the early poems and perhaps gentled them. "A Valentine," for instance:

Surely the frost will gain
Upon its essence, and execute
Its little bravery of cardinal red.

Or "Songs for the Air":

We may consider every cloud a lake
Transmogrified, its character unselfed

Few would dare to use "transmogrified" after Ransom's "Janet Waking," though I think Mr. Hecht gets away with it. These are only momentary details of style, however, an episode. Like Robert Lowell before him, he was affected more decisively by another Fugitive, Allen Tate. He never sounds like Tate nor assumes the high oratorical mode that is part of the southerner's inheritance. One might place his "Samuel Sewall" beside Tate's "Mr. Pope" to see the difference. What I have in mind is a certain "cut" in the poetic line:

Now take him, Virgin Muse, up the deeper stream:
As a lost bee returning to the hive,
Cell after honeyed cell of sounding dream—
Swimmer of noonday, lean for the perfect dive
To the dead Mother's face, whose subtile down
You had not seen take amber light alive.

These are the final tercets of Tate's "The Maimed Man," which opened *The Partisan Review* for May-June 1952, at a time when Mr. Hecht was perfecting his style. One line—"Swimmer of noonday, lean for the perfect dive"—represents the kind of poetry, taut and rhythmically alert, that he was already approaching. There is a further consideration here. In his prose tribute to Allen Tate (*The Sewanee Review*, Autumn, 1959), Mr. Hecht says that what he finally realized from his teacher (which Mr. Tate was for a time) was ". . . the way a poem's total design is modulated and given its energy, not by local ingredients tastefully combined, but by the richness, toughness and density of some sustaining vision of life . . ." And this, I think, describes the way in which we should finally approach Mr. Hecht.

In 1952 there were other presences on the scene, notably Stevens and Auden. Stevens' rhetoric is occasionally overpowering for young poets, or it used to be. Mr. Hecht seems to have been playful about this older contemporary, who is often treated rather solemnly in the Age of Bloom; so I judge from the first group of poems in *A Summoning of Stones*. In "La Condition Botanique" he speaks of

hopeful dreams,
Peach-colored, practical, to decorate the bones, with
schemes
Of life insurance, Ice-Cream-After-Death

Then "Divisions upon a Ground," which is a parody of "Le Monocle de Mon Oncle," was reprinted in *The Hard Hours* as "Le Masseur de Ma Soeur." "The Place of Pain in the Universe," an amusing meditation in a dentist's office, surely refers to the first section of *Esthetique du Mal*, where Stevens has his hero brooding at Naples in the shadow of Vesuvius:

He tried to remember the phrases: pain
Audible at noon, pain torturing itself,
Pain killing pain on the very point of pain.

As for Auden, one might say that the big set-pieces of *A Summoning of Stones*, "La Condition Botanique" and "The Gardens of the Villa d'Este," could not have existed as they do without the example of Auden's virtuosity from *The Sea and the Mirror* onward. Although the interest in elaborate, even "baroque" poetry during the 1950s was entirely characteristic of the period (James Merrill was an outstanding practitioner even then), Mr. Hecht had been reading Auden since 1937 at the age of fourteen and presumably was ahead of everyone else. But he never succumbed to the Auden manner of speech, which of course has always existed on several levels. It was a matter of formal perfection, the pleasure in the finished poem. (Mr. Hecht's interesting remarks on Auden can be found in *The Hudson Review* for Spring 1968.)

"The Gardens of the Villa d'Este" is a Fifties poem in another obvious way. Around 1950, a Holy Year, the American literati moved over the Alps to Italy, which quickly became the great good place that France had been for the Twenties. (Mr. Hecht was awarded a writing fellowship at the American Academy in Rome in 1951.) Poems about baroque fountains and gardens began to turn up in the literary quarterlies quite regularly. Mr. Hecht's garden is anything but *nature morte*; its delightful eroticism is immediately announced and carried through seventeen intricate stanzas. This is a serious poem, too, and toward the end of the movement slows down; the poet reflects:

For thus it was designed:
Controlled disorder at the heart
Of everything, the paradox, the old
Oxymoronic itch to set the formal strictures
Within a natural context, where the tension lectures
Us on our mortal state, and by controlled
Disorder, labors to keep art
From being too refined.

It is tempting to pursue the wit of this stanza in several directions, and no doubt some readers have taken it as a *jeu d'esprit* of the New Criticism (Brook's paradox, Tate's tension, Warren's pure and impure poetry, etc.) long before now. But the stanza should direct our attention to Marvell's Garden (the important literary reference), hence back to Eden itself. Richard Howard says that all the poems in *A Summoning of Stones* ". . . are illuminated by a primal vision which asserts, beyond growth as beyond decay, beyond accident as beyond purpose, that there is a significant ordering in experience, fall from it as we must . . ." and this theme would naturally find its fulfillment in "The Gardens of the Villa d'Este." An analogous way of approaching the poem is by way of the water that pours over the stone and gushes from the fountains: "Clear liquid arcs of benefice and aid." This composes a counter-image to the "broken monuments" and "stoney carrion" of the earliest poems. I don't agree with some readers of *A Summoning of Stones* (for instance the late Louise Bogan in *The New*

Yorker) who saw the Italian poems, especially the "Villa d'Este," as simply a celebration of elegance, however exuberant. The "controlled disorder" is really one phase of a larger and quite important subject, as Mr. Howard says.

In *A Summoning of Stones* and again in *The Hard Hours* (1967), Mr. Hecht places the "Villa d'Este" soon after "Christmas is Coming," a remarkable poem on several counts. It is one of the few things that he wrote in blank verse in those days (like Yeats and Tate he usually required rhymed stanzas), but certain words like *cold* and *pain* are carefully deployed half a dozen times in a poem of forty-nine lines, and the effect is almost formal. This procedure is continued by the old verse that is inserted and then repeated in fragments:

Christmas is coming. The goose is getting fat.
Please put a penny in the Old Man's hat.

The strange landscape of the poem isn't identified; it could be the setting for the Battle of the Bulge, where so many of one's contemporaries were frostbitten in December, 1944:

Where is the pain? The sense is frozen up,
And fingers cannot recognize the grass,
Cannot distinguish their own character,
Being blind with cold, being stiffened by the cold;
Must find out thistles to remember pain.
Keep to the frozen ground or else be killed.
Yet crawling one encounters in the dark
The frosty carcasses of birds, their feet
And wings all glazed. And still we crawl to learn
Where pain was lost, how to recover pain.
Reach for the brambles, crawl to them and reach,
Clutching for thorns, search carefully to feel
The point of thorns, life's crown, *the Old Man's hat.*

This almost refers back to "The Place of Pain in the Universe," with its echo of *Esthetique du Mal*, and it could be considered a "tragic" version of the same theme. By this time Mr. Hecht had begun to present his subject through a kind of indirection: the old verse, a plea for charity out of the more genial world of Dickens, say, cuts across the eerie landscape to maximum effect. And the serious wit of these last lines introduces a religious perspective that is new in his poetry and that certainly anticipates a great deal.

Leaving aside a number of fine individual achievements in *A Summoning of Stones*, "La Condition Botanique" for one and "Alceste in the Wilderness" for another, I turn to *The Hard Hours*. The title suggests a crisis or at any rate a holding action in the poet's private life, but the general subject is much larger than that, and eventually personal and public destinies merge. The setting is usually urban now: Manhattan with its casual violence and its high bourgeois culture on which the civilized mind can still draw: Central Park and the Frick Collection:

Daily the prowling sunlight whets its knife
Along the sidewalk. We almost never meet.
In the Rembrandt dark he lifts his amber life.
My bar is somewhat further down the street.

The big set-piece of the volume is "Rites and Ceremonies." Here the poet reaches beyond his own circumstances and the public atrocities of our time towards the "richness, toughness and density of some sustaining vision of life" that he mentions in his tribute to Allen Tate. The range of his subject is large—say the whole sweep of western history. It is sometimes very unpleasant, and at one point he remarks: "The contemplation of horror is not edifying, / Neither does it strengthen the soul." He has permitted himself a new rhythmic and stanzaic freedom that carries him through ten pages, and the intensity of feeling often pushes against the restraints of the stanzas, as in the long passage on Buchenwald. But it is a "controlled disorder" at every stage. The third section, which begins with the caustic lines I have already quoted, is entitled "The Dream." After a preliminary passage, which touches on the martydoms of three saints, we move to the Corso in Rome and the homesick poet du Bellay at Carnival time; now we settle into a sequence of five-line stanzas that concludes:

Du Bellay, poet, take no thought of them;
And yet they too are exiles, and have said
Through many generations, long since dead,
"*If I forget thee, O Jerusalem, . . .*"
Still, others have been scourged and buffeted
And worse. Think rather, if you must,
Of Piranesian, elegiac woes,
Rome's grand declensions, that all-but-speaking dust.
Or think of the young gallants and their lust.
Or wait for the next heat, the buffaloes.

Du Bellay, the homesick spectator, is I suppose a surrogate for Mr. Hecht at this point, and in fact Mr. Hecht has already allowed him to speak in the marvelous version of "Heureux qui, comme Ulysse, a fait un bon voyage . . ." that he has placed just before "Rites and Ceremonies."

This is the most ambitious poem in *The Hard Hours*, its center, and perhaps some tentative statement of Mr. Hecht's theme is in order at this point. By far the best review of the book that I recall was Carol Johnson's in *Art International* (Lugano, 1968). Miss Johnson said that ". . . if it has seemed nearly impossible for Americans to attain to tragedy without self-pitying stridence or comedy without vulgarity, we now have Mr. Hecht's poem to allay that pessimistic expectation and remind us in what proximity wit and tragedy reside—providing civilization survives them." It is "the tragic vision," then, a term we are apt to be uncomfortable with, that we have to take into account here. Many of the poems in this collection have public subjects; I suspect the ones that have had the most impact are "Behold the Lilies of the Field," which is placed near the beginning, and "More Light! More Light!" which comes near the end. They remind us that human viciousness has been a recurring feature of history. (Occasionally, in reading Mr. Hecht, I have thought of D.W. Griffith's panoramic movie *Intolerance.)* In the first case the appalling execution of the Roman Emperor Valerian (253–260 A.D.) erupts into a session on the modern psychiatrist's couch, and the patient identifies himself with this ancient humiliation. The public subject, that is, becomes the physical image of a private malaise. In "More Light!" the poet juxtaposes the execution of a religious martyr in 16th Century England ("Permitted at least his pitiful dignity") and a peculiarly brutal incident at Buchenwald. He has insisted on confronting these horrors, but in the second stance with a sardonic wit that governs, as Carol Johnson says, the tragedy. "More Light! more light!": these were Goethe's last words, and light figures prominently throughout the poem.

But it would be mistaken to restrict Mr. Hecht to a bleak view of experience. The tragic vision itself, or rather the romantic melancholy which it could lead to, is beautifully parodied in "The Dover Bitch: A Criticism of Life." Although Mr. Hecht has the utmost respect for Arnold (I believe that when he reads to audiences he always takes up "Dover Beach" before his own poem), he seems to suggest that melancholy is a passive state of mind that could be otherwise dealt with by the modern intelligence. One might suppose that his main reference for the tragic vision would be *King Lear*, the play which has had a special fascination for the post-war world, but it seems to be the *Oedipus at Kolonos*, the great classic of reconciliation, which he is translating as a work-in-progress. His version of the chorus in praise of Kolonos has already appeared in *Millions of Strange Shadows*, and I quote the final stanzas, which I think bear out Richard Howard's thesis that in Anthony Hecht's poetry ". . . there is a significant ordering in experience, fall from it as we must . . ."

O Lord Poseidon, you have doubly blessed us
with healing skills, on these roads first bestowing
the bit that gentles horses, the controlling curb and
the bridle,
and the carved, feathering oar that skims and dances
like the white nymphs of water, conferring mastery
of ocean roads, among the spume and wind-blown
prancing of stallions.

An intensely personal poem, "The Vow," which stands just before du Bellay's "Heureux qui, comme Ulysse . . ." makes a connection with the *Oedipus at Kolonos* in another way. The subject is a dead unborn child. The poem is so carefully built up in forty lines that partial quotation would do it violence; I must refer the reader to *The Hard Hours*. About fifteen years ago Mr. Hecht picked this as his favorite for *Poet's Choice*, an anthology edited by Paul Engle and Joseph Langland. In the course of a short commentary he mentions a poem on the same subject in Lowell's first book, *Land of Unlikeness*. This would be "The Boston Nativity," a harshly satirical piece from Lowell's early Catholic period. Mr. Hecht's poem owes nothing to Lowell except, as he explains, the courage of the "difficult" subject. Where Lowell tends to contract his poem through his abrasive tone, Mr. Hecht expands backward, as it were, through the Judaic-Greek traditions, and the unborn child speaks with an "aged, bitter, Sophoclean wisdom." I quote a passage from Robert Fitzgerald's translation of the *Oedipus* to make the connection: a kind of background for Mr. Hecht's poem:

Not to be born beats all philosophy.
The second best is to have seen the light
And then to go back quickly whence we came.
The feathery follies of his youth once over,
What trouble is beyond the range of man?
What heavy burden will he not endure?

In "Three Prompters from the Wings," a triptych in which Atropos, Clotho, and Lachesis take us through the stages of Oedipus' career (they represent the future, the present, and the past), Clotho submits the "tragic vision" to this comment:

Nothing is purely itself
But is linked with its antidote
In cold self-mockery—
A fact with which only those
Born with a Cosmic sense
Can learn to content themselves.
While heroes die to maintain
Some part of existence clean
And incontaminate.

Here Mr. Hecht approaches the later Yeats, as much in his assertive trimeters as in anything else. (Yeats of course also did a version of the *Oedipus at Kolonos* that is connected with *his* sense of the tragic.) Mr. Hecht's wit isn't always sardonic by any means. In the last lines of "The Vow," addressed to the unborn child, he remarks, audaciously yet tenderly:

If that ghost was a girl's, I swear to it:
Your mother shall be far more blessed than you.
And if a boy's, I swear: The flames are lit
That shall refine us: they shall not destroy
A living hair.
Your younger brothers shall confirm in joy
This that I swear.

The poet's first two sons are named Jason and Adam, and in fact they have already appeared in a pair of charming poems where they re-enact their mythical roles in random childish gestures. But the childhood world merges, through the television set, with the fearful possibilities of the public world, and at the end of the last poem in *The Hard Hours* ("It Out-Herods Herod. Pray You, Avoid It") the father offers this curt prayer:

And that their sleep be sound
I say this childermas
Who could not, at one time,
Have saved them from the gas.

The last decade has been a glorious period of creativity for Mr. Hecht. A bit to one side of his poems, but closely related to them in ways that I have already suggested, is the translation of *Seven against Thebes* that he did in collaboration with Helen Bacon (Oxford University Press, 1973). The translation with its introduction is clearly an important event in classical studies; that is, it makes accessible a dramatic masterpiece which hasn't been treated as handsomely as Aeschylus' other works. As poetry, the Hecht-Bacon version is superb: see, for instance, the long choral passage in trimeters (lines 927-1109) with its pentameter interlude. I now think that Mr. Hecht, after Yeats, is the master of the trimeter line in English poetry.

The translation was undertaken at the American Academy in Rome, and modern unclassical Rome is the setting for "The Cost," the first poem in *Millions of Strange Shadows:*

Instinct with joy, a young Italian banks
Smoothly around the base
Of Trajan's column, feeling between his flanks
That cool, efficient beast,
His Vespa, at one with him in a centaur's race,
Fresh, from a Lapith feast,
And his Lapith girl behind him. Both of them lean
With easy nonchalance
Over samphire-tufted cliffs which, though unseen,
Are known, as the body knows
New risks and tilts, terrors and loves and wants,
Deeply inside its clothes.

Although the barbarians are everywhere now, the poet seems to have relaxed his severity, and indeed there is a kind of joy in physicality that runs through many of the poems in this collection: "Somebody's Life" and "Swan Dive" for instance. But youthful instinct could be "the secret gaudery of self-love," and in "The Feast of Stephen" physicality becomes sinister: Saul watches as the young thugs move in on the first Christian martyr:

And in between their sleek, converging bodies,
Brilliantly oiled and burnished by the sun,
He catches a brief glimpse of bloodied hair
And hears an unintelligible prayer.

Youth and age figure prominently in these poems, and it is part of Mr. Hecht's great talent to be able to move with ease among accumulated memories. He does this as though he were riffling through a heap of photographs, deciding what to discard, what to preserve, and actual photographs are the focal points of several poems. In "Dichtung und Wahrheit" he takes up the subject with a certain hesitation:

The Discus Thrower's marble heave,
Captured in mid-career,
That polished poise, that Parian arm
Sleeved only in the air,
Vesalian musculature, white
As the mid-winter moon—
This, and the clumsy snapshot of
An infantry platoon,

Those grubby and indifferent men,
Lounging in bivouac,
Their rifles aimless in their laps,
Stop history in its tracks.

This poem is on a "high" subject: the "sacred discipline" that might "give breath back to the past." In "Exile," dedicated to the Russian poet Joseph Brodsky in America, his Egypt, the local scene is brought to the exile's attention thus:

Look, though, at the blank, expressionless faces
Here is this photograph by Walker Evans.
These are the faces that everywhere surround you;
They have all the emptiness of gravel pits.

But this harsh first impression is gentled, and then one realizes that it would be the poet's privilege, in this instance, to give breath back to the *present:*

This is Egypt, Joseph, the old school of the soul.
You will recognize the rank smell of a stable
And the soft patience in a donkey's eyes,
Telling you you are welcome and at home.

"A Birthday Poem," one of Anthony Hecht's finest achievements, is in a sense about the act of perception itself. It is late June, and he peers through the "golden dazzle" at a swarm of midges, his mind open to possibilities. Perspective, the great invention (or was it discovery?) of the Renaissance, sets off ranges of space, as in a Crucifixion scene by Mantegna. The midges give way to the "blurred, unfathomed background tint" in a Holbein group portrait (a more secular age now). Then space shifts into time through "the gears of tense," and the poet comes to rest with a photograph of his wife as a child:

You are four years old here in this photograph.
You are turned out in style,
In a pair of bright red sneakers, a birthday gift.
You are looking down at them with a smile
Of pride and admiration, half
Wonder and half joy, at the right and the left.
The picture is black and white, mere light and shade.
Even the sneakers' red
Has washed away in acids. A voice is spent,
Echoing down the ages in my head:
What is your substance, whereof are you made,
That millions of strange shadows on you tend?

And the poet allows Shakespeare (Sonnet 53) to speak for him, as he has previously brought du Bellay and the others into the conversation, as it were. It is a moment of supreme poetic tact.

The longest poems in the new volume, "Green: An Epistle," and "Apprehensions," have already been much admired. "Apprehensions" especially seems to mark the direction that Mr. Hecht's poetry is taking: the long blank-verse monologue that admits a surprising amount of personal history. The passage about the childhood experience on Lexington Avenue in "Apprehensions" bears out the idea of a "primal vision" or what Auden (who is actually quoted) calls "The Vision of Dame Kind." It is beautifully sustained, a poem in itself, but Mr. Hecht has put it in a dramatic context that makes it so much more than a moment remembered. It is true, as Richard Howard remarks (in *Poetry*, November 1977), that prose is "no longer rejected" in these recent poems, but I think that the poet's impulse to write lyric is as strong as ever. These are the final stanzas of "The Lull," the last poem of all:

The seamed, impastoed bark,
The cool, imperial certainty of stone,
Antique leaf-lace, all these are bathed in a dark
Mushroom and mineral odor of their own,
Their inwardness made clear and sure
As voice and fingerprint and signature.
The rain, of course, will come
With grandstand flourishes and hullabaloo,
The silvered street, flashbulb and kettledrum,
To douse and rouse the citizens, to strew
Its rhinestones randomly, piecemeal.
But for the moment the whole world is real.

This lovely coda, a moment of repose before another onslaught of experience, makes the case for formal poetry as much as anything being written today. Its author has in many ways carried forward and modified a kind of tradition that I associate mainly with Tate and Auden, the leading members of the second generation of modernists (if we have Stevens, Pound, and Eliot in the first generation). He has dealt with the terrible divisiveness of the age with an extraordinary honesty and grace—what Auden called for in "The Shield of Achilles." My sense of the current scene is that his kind of poetry will matter a great deal from now on, after a period of rather shameless opportunism, and what is so reassuring is that he is writing better than ever.

ROGER GARFITT

"Contrary Attractions"

Times Literary Supplement, May 30, 1980, p. 623

Narrative has always been the conscience of Anthony Hecht's poetry. He is an instinctive decorator, a court jeweller among wordsmiths, who from time to time submits himself to a bare narration. Bare, because the facts are beyond the aid of artifice. They are narratives of atrocity, the flaying alive of the Emperor Valerian, the stoning of Stephen, or, most particularly, the persecution of the Jews throughout hisory, culminating in the concentration camps. It is as if the power of invention, the skill and the delight in artifice, is a gift that could be used in any way at all; whereas narrative is a vocation, a moral imperative, that determines how the gift is to be used.

One can see the process clearly at work in "The Odds", a poem from his previous collection *Millions of Strange Shadows* (1977). The poem opens with three stanzas in evocation of a snowfall, stanzas full of an affectionate invention. Appearances seem poised for celebration. But the fourth and fifth stanzas introduce a different order of vision, a moral vision that sees the snowfall as

A sort of stagy show
Put on by a spoiled, eccentric millionaire.
Lacking the craft and choice that go
With weighed precision, meditated care,
Into a work of art, these are the spent,
Loose, aimless squander fogs of the discontent.
Like the blind, headlong cells,
Crowding towards dreams of life, only to die
In dark fallopian canals,
Or that wild strew of bodies at My Lai.
Thick drifts, huddled embankments at our door
Pile up in this eleventh year of war.

The poem seems to have taken a radically different direction, in answer to Hecht's political conscience, and to his abiding sense of the extravagance and waste of the life process. Only then, startlingly, in the face of all "the odds" that have deliberately been stacked against it, the poem *does* turn towards celebration, and towards a much more profound celebration than we had anticipated:

Yet to these April snows,
This rashness, those incalculable odds,
The costly and cold-blooded shows
Of blind perversity or spend-thrift gods
My son is born, and in his mother's eyes
Turns the whole war and winter into lies.

Further difficulties are invoked in the penultimate stanza, but the poem drives through to a concluding image that combines its first innocence with its final knowledge, an image of

those crystal balls
With Christmas storms of manageable size,
A chalk precipitate that shawls
Antlers and roof and gifts beyond surmise,
A tiny settlement among those powers
That shape our world, but that are never ours.

Conscience implies deliberation, and there surely is an element of deliberation here, a determination to confront all the kinds of evidence available to the poet. But there is also temperament, the involuntary attraction of the sensibility towards a particular atmosphere or quality, that in Hecht is often a quality of light. In the opening poem of *The Hard Hours* (1967), Hecht describes the vision of "A Hill" that suddenly broke into his consciousness. One minute he was

with some friends
Picking my way through a warm sunlit piazza
In the early morning. A clear fretwork of shadows
From huge umbrellas littered the pavement and made
A sort of lucent shallows in which was moored
A small navy of carts. Books, coins, old maps,
Cheap landscapes and ugly religious prints
Were all on sale. The colours and noise
Like the flying hands were gestures of exultation,
So that even the bargaining
Rose to the ear like a voluble godliness.

The next minute, Hecht goes on to say,

pushcarts and people dissolved
And even the great Farnese Palace itself
Was gone, for all its marble; in its place
Was a hill, mole-colored and bare.

It seems to me that the contrast there is very akin to the contrast between artifice and narrative in Hecht. On the one hand there is the attraction towards the "gestures of exultation", the "voluble godliness", that whole shimmer of surfaces that Hecht catches so beautifully in much of his work. On the other hand there is the haunting by "the plain bitterness of what I had seen", as by that hill, "mole-colored and bare."

What is impressive is the thoroughness with which Hecht has explored that ambivalence and sought to harness the opposing attractions within a poetry that can contain them both. Even that hill's bare light is in itself ambiguous. In *Millions of Strange Shadows* it is twice celebrated, in "After the Rain" as "a Spartan fairness . . . A light so pure and just", and in "The Lull" as "Some shadowless, unfocussed light/In which all things come into their own right". Whereas in "Auspices" in the new collection it belongs more straightforwardly to "the wilds/Of loneliness, huge, vacant, sour and plain" where "The fearfullest desolations of the soul/Image themselves as local and abiding". "Auspices" is perhaps a little too straightforward: in the two earlier poems there is a wresting of meaning from that bare light, an arguing against the grain, that seems to produce a more subtle verse movement.

Hecht is at his best in exploring the contrariness of the soul's attractions. The best of his short poems, "The Odds" or "A Birthday Poem", have always been able to set delight against foreboding, celebration against self-knowledge: but in his previous collections that contrariness has as often been evident in the interplay between different kinds of poem. In the interplay, for instance, between "The Origin of Centaurs" in *The Hard Hours* and "Goliardic Song" in *Millions of Strange Shadows*. Above all, in the interplay between invention and narrative, between poems of an intricate surface, like the play of light on water, and bare documentary poems, the facts of history as a submerged reef. The major departure of *The Venetian Vespers* is the use of narrative fiction—fiction rather than fact—in an attempt to explore the full range of contraries within a single extended poem.

There are three narrative fictions, "The Grapes", "The Short End", and the title poem, all three centred around oppositions of light and colour that are also oppositions of mood and experience. Of these it is the title poem that is the most ambitious and the most problematic.

The first two sections of "The Venetian Vespers" are beautifully written. The subtlety of construction, around images of bubbles in water, bubbles in Venetian glass, could make a study in itself. In the stream of consciousness of a man in his declining years, "an expatriate American,/Living off an annuity", we quickly recognize the characteristic landscape of Hechtian desolation—but delineated with a quite conclusive eloquence, as if images that have obsessed him all his life are now receiving their definitive statement:

And over all
The dust of oblivion finer than milled flour
Where chips of brick, clinkers and old iron
Burn in their slow, invisible decay.
Or else it is late afternoon in autumn,
The sunlight rusting on the western fronts
Of a long row of Victorian brick houses,
Untenanted, presumably condemned
Their brownstone grapes and their grand entablatures,
Their straining caryatid muscle-men
Rendered at once ridiculous and sad
By the black scars of zigzag fire escapes
That double themselves in isometric shadows.
And all their vacancy is given voice
By the endless flapping of one window-shade.

The other side of Hecht's talent, his ability to present "the soul being drenched in fine particulars", is represented in Sections III and IV by superlative descriptions of the interior of St Mark's and of a thunderstorm in the piazza outside. But the brilliance of those particulars is rapidly undercut: clearly the hill is winning against the piazza, and one is not allowed to escape for long "into the refuge of the present tense".

The narrator's past, the reef in his consciousness, emerges in Section V—at which point the narrative reverts to a plainness reminiscent of Hecht's documentary style. But this is fiction, and the very plainness of the narration seems to highlight the limitations of the plot, which is an awkward contrivance, at once extraordinary and not entirely removed from bathos. But there is a weakness of construction here in any case, a weakness that raises a general question about the possibilities of narrative fiction in contemporary poetry.

The opening sections of "The Venetian Vespers" are so rich in image and intimation that one reads them as one would read any poem, as if they belonged to us all, as if they were part of the general history of human sensibility. Their value is the degree to which they seem to illuminate our own experience, the extent to which they are universal. Once that universality is confined, and related to one particular life history, let alone so singular a life history, we begin to lose interest. In the case of "The Venetian Vespers" this effect is compounded by the diminution of linguistic interest as the poem proceeds. The later sections are meant to explain and illumine the earlier sections: but in poetry explanation and illumination tend to be in inverse ratio. "The Venetian Vespers" is so constructed that it offers the reader a progressively diminishing return.

The other two narrative fictions do not pose this problem, because they do not venture beyond the play of consciousness, which is our common ground. There is a useful comparison here with David Harsent's long poem "Dreams of the Dead" (the title poem of his collection of that name), which is successful precisely because it exploits the dream motif, where there is no distinction between image and event. I am really suggesting that there is something in the expectation we bring to poetry nowadays that resists the fictive element—except at the level of folk tale or myth, at the level of the archetype.

"The Venetian Vespers" is seriously flawed, but it is by no means a negligible work. Even the plot has a kind of Hardy-an pessimism, the sense of a fault so deep that it is cellular, in the very nature of the life process. This is a theme that Hecht first explored in "Green: An Epistle", and which he recapitulates briefly in Section III of "The Venetian Vespers". He touches on it again memorably in "A Cast of Light", a poem set at a Father's Day picnic during which he notices "A maple bough of web-foot, golden greens./Found by an angled shaft/Of late sunlight" where mosses

in all innocence pursue their cottage
Industry of photosynthesis.
Yet only for twenty minutes or so today,
On a summer afternoon,
Does the splendid lancet reach to them, or sink
To these dim bottoms, making its chancy way,
As through the barrier reef of some lagoon
In sea-green darkness, by a wavering chink,
Down, neatly probing like an accurate paw
Or a notched and beveled key,
Through the huge cave-roof of giant oak and pine.
And the heart goes numb in a tide of fear and awe
For those we cherish, their hopes, their frailty,
Their shadowy fate's unfathomable design.

There is something akin to Hardy, too, in Hecht's use of neutralities of light, interludes of dusk or predawn, atmospheres of mist or snow, when appearances become permeable, open to the imagination's hauntings. In Hecht such moments form those intersections of artifice and conscience where his finest work is done. In *The Venetian Vespers*, "Still Life" and "Persistences" are poems of that kind and quality.

I would not want to end without drawing attention to "The Deodand", a fictive extension of documentary that seems to open up new possibilities in this area, and to Anthony Hecht's versions of two poems by Joseph Brodsky, which friends who read Russian tell me are among the very few translations in English to convey something of the music of the original.

Ben Hecht

1894–1964

The son of Russian immigrants, Ben Hecht was born in New York City on February 28, 1894. After attending high school in Wisconsin, he became a journalist with the *Chicago Journal*, moving to the *Chicago Daily News* in 1914. In 1918 he went to Berlin as his newspaper's correspondent, sending back imaginative and sparkling reports. Back in America, he became a prominent figure in the Chicago "literary renaissance," notably through his novel *Erik Dorn* (1921). More popular works followed—including *Fantazius Mallare* (1922), for which he was fined for obscenity, and the detective novel *The Florentine Dagger* (1923)—as well as the more serious *Humpty Dumpty* (1924). He drew on his experience as a journalist to write short stories included in the volumes *1001 Afternoons in Chicago* (1922) and *Tales of Chicago Streets* (1924).

In 1924 Hecht moved to New York to concentrate on writing for the stage in collaboration with other authors. His best-known play, *The Front Page*, written with Charles MacArthur, was produced in New York in 1928. From 1930 he was one of Hollywood's most successful and highly paid screenwriters. He won Academy Awards for *Underworld* (1927) and *The Scoundrel* (1935), and in his career worked on more than sixty film scripts. He continued to write fiction, though *A Jew in Love* (1931), which earned him the reputation of a Jewish anti-Semite, was his last serious novel.

In his later years, Hecht turned increasingly to non-fiction. *A Flag Is Born*, advocating a free Palestinian state, was published in 1946. His autobiography, *A Child of the Century* (1954), was followed by a biography of MacArthur, *Charlie* (1957). Hecht's last two works were volumes of correspondence and reminiscences, *Gaily, Gaily* (1963) and *Letters from Bohemia* (1964). He died in New York City on April 18, 1964.

Personal

Keith Preston and I had wandered rather aimlessly to Ben's room in an ancient building that ran back to the days of the great fire. A strange, Dickensian sort of pile, like those that appear in the funereal prints of the sixties and seventies, a place in which the appearance of Abraham Lincoln and Stephen Douglas even to-day would not seem out of harmony. Quaint, old-fashioned mahogany elevator cages, still propelled by a tug at a cable; a great wide court roofed over with a skylight and surrounded by heavy mahogany balustrades. Offices that permit a glimpse of old, high-backed secretaries with pigeon holes stuffed with musty, yellowing papers; of men, bearded and unkempt, bent over wide blue blotters frayed and covered with inkstains. Insurance; real estate; steamship agencies; the law. Two doors at the right—the second door is his—through the first one discerns a tailor in shirt sleeves industriously applying a steam press to pantaloons. His workshop—a strange anachronism. Across the street the false Corinthian pillars of a modern city hall, and just beyond that the thousand glowing candles of an office building encased in terra cotta. But here, within his walls, great hangings of green burlap depending from the ceiling, and soft mats of thick, green wool just underfoot, and deep enveloping chairs and soft lights and hours for idling. And Ben Hecht, sunk down within the generous arms of a deep leather chair, saying in a melodious monotone: "I've got something to read to you boys. My first act. Yes, I'm doing another play for Leo. We stayed up until daybreak to try it out, and here it is. Quattrocento this time. Florence, Venice, Rome, Milan; swords, loves, swashbuckling, romance. Leo likes that sort. Gives him a chance to make love gracefully and swashbuckle all over the place."

And then he reads. A play on the life of Benvenuto Cellini, as revealed by himself in his incomparable memoirs. A swashbuckler with a soul. A mountebank with a heart. An acrobat with love and laughter and hope and tears. And an artist. Thus Ben Hecht has captured him and portrayed him. He reads on, and we listen.

And how he reads! You are attracted by his fecundity, his versatility, his humanness, his shifting aims. You wonder, as you listen: What next? Where? And how? Already at thirty he is the most talked about, the most praised, the most reviled of the Chicago group. Already at thirty he defies analysis. Stay away from him and you will judge him harshly. Come close to him and his gentleness, his knowledge of human motives and acts, his kindliness, robs you of an objective judgment. His acerbic criticism, on paper, stings; spoken, it amuses. To-day, condemned by some, vilified by others, praised by those who know him best, he stands as a strangely aloof, irreconcilable figure in American writing, an example of the new, uncompromising spirit born with Dreiser, of the new unassimilated spirit that has bade defiance to the New England tradition within the last twenty years. And yet he is one of us, born on our soil, nurtured in our middle west, educated in our public schools; the product of living in a crowded, rude, tempestuous city, a representative of the shifting, restless, uncatalogued writers of the new age.—HARRY HANSEN, "Ben Hecht, Pagliacci of the Fire Escape," *Midwest Portraits*, 1923, pp. 307–9

General

Ben Hecht lends himself easily to identification. His idiosyncrasies as an individual are well known. His gift of words convinces one that he, like O. Henry, also considered Webster's *Unabridged Dictionary* as the most useful of all books. His pranks are supposed to have inspired the Spewacks in their delineation of the dramatists in *Boy Meets Girl*. He has long been known as an incessant, fascinating, cynical, and iconoclastic conversationalist.

It is not surprising that the heroes of *Erik Dorn* and of *To Quito and Back* are both writers, that they both exude epigrams as easily as the average person exudes banalities, that they are both restless, both escaping from unwanted wives, both incapable of making firm decisions, both capable of attracting the opposite sex, and both extremely unhappy. Why does Hecht seem so preoccupied with epigrammatic speech, with the minutiae of sex, with escaping from one's first wife, with indecision? These elements are not confirmed to the first and last work. In *Gargoyles* (1922) the sensuality of the hero George Basine is given an almost case-history presentation. In *A Jew in Love* (1931) the sexual equipment, experience and conquests of the Jewish publisher, Jo Boshere, are catalogued with a verisimilitude more frequently found in the numbered cases of Krafft-Ebing.

Sixteen years, however, of world changes have made a difference. Erik Dorn lived through the German revolution and the founding of the Bavarian Soviet Republic, but returned to America unmoved by the impact of the social upheavals in Europe. Alexander Sterns of *To Quito and Back* dies fighting in the cause of social revolution. Hecht and his hero have realized that in the world of today one cannot stand by calmly without taking sides. Although Sterns says "We're always on the right side in discussions but never on any side of the barricades," he finally stops talking and fights for his ideals.

In the evolution of Hecht's heroes, one perceives the evolution of Ben Hecht. His first novel, and his short stories written at the beginning of his career, reveal a talent astoundingly rich in language, unrestrained as to artistic form, emotional, attuned to the miseries of the world and intensely subjective. Thus one finds in his early collections of short stories, *Tales of Chicago Streets* (1924) and *Broken Necks* (1924), narratives that abound in treatments of the sordidness, the material and spiritual decay of the poverty-stricken areas of Chicago. We note also the strivings for a meaning in life, for some philosophy of existence which will make life significant and hence endurable. The story "Life," for example, deals with Moisse the dramatist's musings on the emptiness of life. —JOSEPH MERSAND, "Ben Hecht," *Traditions in American Literature*, 1939, pp. 114–16

Hecht's iconoclasm about and his contempt for ideas does not mean that he is devoid of them. He isn't. But generally his ideas are banal. They repeat what he has said in the yesterday of his own youth. His autobiography ⟨*A Child of the Century*⟩ is a concoction, an improvised literary cocktail. Everything in life is an occasion for Hecht to sound off, and he fills too many pages with the wind of his prejudices. He tells us what he thinks of ideas and philosophy, of life, love, literature, politics, politicians, Democracy, Communism, Germans and Germany, the Cold War, Jews, Palestine, Zionism, Irgon (the Hebrew Terrorist movement which fought for a Palestinian State), Hollywood, marriages, mistresses, wives, seductions, Chicago, New York, and sundry other matters. All of this could be more interesting if Ben Hecht had more interesting opinions and ideas. But he doesn't and the steam of his phrases, the arrogance of his judgments, and the staleness of many of his prejudices do him a disservice. For Ben Hecht is a gifted writer though he hurts his work because of his easy iconoclasm, his ready-to-wear, medium-priced cynicism, and his deficiency in a clearer sense of values. . . .

1001 Afternoons in Chicago helped me to become more aware of, let us say, the poetry of the street. Its high-voltage figures of speech attracted me. Frequently, the young and aspiring writer sees the use of figures of speech, the coining of phrases, as the sign of literary talent. I did. Ben Hecht could make phrases. Harry Hansen, in *Midwest Portraits*, characterized him as a Pagliacci of the fire escapes. *1001 Afternoons in Chicago* consists of sketches. They are short and Hecht's talents were fresh; he had an exuberance and flair. His novels *Erik Dorn* and *Humpty Dumpty* were frustrating. They exuded a sense of the present, of life going on immediately in one's own time, and there was some excitement in this. (What little sense of books and culture I had had come to me, almost as though by osmosis, from the dead Victorian past.) There was a frankness about sex but the cynicism, the iconoclasm, the verbal posturings, the lack of empathy frustrated me. A newspaper man can look at people and happenings; he can cast a cold and jaundiced eye at politicians; he can watch hangings;

he can dig into tales of rape and murder; and he can do a good piece of reporting without having to identify deeply with the people who are subjects of his stories. A fair number of journalists tend to develop what sometimes seems to be an occupational trait—they tend to regard what happens as though it occurred so that they could do a story. The world is a show made for them. Hecht often gives the impression that this is an integral feature of the way he looks at life. Journalism is an honorable and socially useful profession. I do not intend to denegate it. But what I have observed might help explain why it is often so difficult for journalists to write novels. This may be the case in Hecht's novels. *Count Bruga* was an exception but it is a special kind of book. The chief protagonist is a poet who acts and talks much like a once well-known Chicago poet. The character is bizarre and Hecht has a lively and enthusiastic feeling for the bizarre.

Behind the frustration I found in Hecht's early novels, there was not only a limited power to identify; there was too little sympathy. Sympathy is usually significant because it is the means of making human emotions important. I discovered Sherwood Anderson and Theodore Dreiser after Hecht. In them, I found not cleverness or a keenness for a grotesque surface of life or an iconoclasm that helped me feel a false sense of superiority to others; but rather, in them, I encountered a seriousness of feeling about human emotions, human tragedies, about the struggle, often so blundering, which we all make to live out our life span. There are some writers who can produce out of negative emotions, who can arouse and move us. Céline, in *Journey to the End of Night* and *Death on the Installment Plan*, is one. But Céline hates and hates deeply. His hatred, in fact, is so intense that it carries its own antidote. As we read, we can purge ourselves of hatred. Ben Hecht doesn't hate; he flings out phrases of contempt. He laughs. He falls into quick scorn; is facilely negative. He is something of a Chicago Hupmann without any real cultivation or depth of feeling. . . .

One man he deeply admired was H. L. Mencken. He shares many of Mencken's attitudes. While having the energy, there is none of the Mencken gusto in Hecht's assaults on booberty. Also, unlike Mencken, Hecht gives no evidence of having read as much as Mencken. Thus, Mencken's views are grounded on a more serious foundation than Hecht's.

Seen now and in the past, Ben Hecht appears a man of talent, of easy prejudices, and without values. Unlike in the twenties, he cannot today stimulate youth. He has seen and reported the grotesque and sordid but it now appears on his pages as something too familiar.

He writes: "Except for my relation to God, I have not changed in forty years. I have not become different as an adult."

It seems a shame that a man of talent who has had the opportunities in life that Ben Hecht has had would be pleased to keep sitting on what he styles as his "Pedestal of Sameness."

This comes as a strange boast from a man who defends—even rants against—the destruction of individuality in our country. Iconoclasm can be as conventional as conventionality. And this child of the century appears to be a conventional iconoclast. The "half-alive ones," the mob, the people drowned by the "tidal wave of education"—they have not changed. But here is one of the not-half-alive, here is one of the alive ones; and he does not give us a great outpouring of his aliveness.

Talent could be better used.—JAMES T. FARRELL, "The Mind of Ben Hecht" (1955), *Literary Essays: 1954–1974*, ed. Jack Alan Robbins, 1976, pp. 70–76

One can't help speaking of Mr. Hecht as a "case," if only because that is how he presents himself. He is one of those writers who step between the printed page and the reader, exploiting their own personalities, coaxing us to be interested in this or that because of our undoubted interest in *them*. The advent of television has put this kind of writer in a stronger position—as a "personality," that is; as an artist, I am not sure that it has not weakened him still further.

With those three sentences I leave the public Mr. Hecht; and I feel justified in doing so, because as a literary critic I am concerned with the private Mr. Hecht, the one who communicates with me in the quietness of my armchair. The exploitation of the personality is still there, but it recedes into the perspective of a literary device. If a man writing a story decides to bring himself in as a character, there is no reason why he shouldn't. If he puts a certain amount of energy into implying that he, the story-teller, is a man of the world, moves in circles unknown to his desk-bound brethren, gets around and meets people generally, that is simply one more ingredient in the flavoring of the story.

Mr. Hecht generally manages to give his stories a top-dressing of this kind, and usually it doesn't come amiss, especially when he is in his O. Henry vein, writing about the teeming and shifting world of Manhattan. O. Henry is the basis here, with flecks of Hemingway in the constant reminders that the writer is a man of action and no mere word-merchant. But neither of these two influences goes at all deep. Mr. Hecht's heart is elsewhere. His eyes, for all their shrewd Manhattan glitter, are in reality fixed far away, on a vision he had once and has never ceased to stare after.

In a word, Mr. Hecht is a romantic. Not just any kind of romantic, but a Wildean romantic, a man of the nineties. If, instead of being a mid-twentieth century New Yorker, he had been a *fin de siècle* Londoner, he would have been faithfully present, week in and week out, at the Cheshire Cheese. His figure would have been a familiar one in the bars of Fleet Street, where he would have made an attentive listener to the monologues in Lionel Johnson. Possibly Mr. Hecht's would be the hands that raised Johnson's lifeless body after his last fatal fall from a stool in one of these same bars. He would have known Yeats, Beardsley, and Richard Le Gallienne.

That is Mr. Hecht's misfortune. Owing to an unaccountable kink in the time-corridor, he slipped sixty-five years and landed on the wrong side of the Atlantic into the bargain. As a man of the nineties, he has never been very comfortable in the surroundings that Fate wrongly issued him with. For all his talk of prize-fighters and night-clubs, for all his Runyonesque familiarity with the sidewalks of little old N.Y., his heart is back there with the aesthetes carrying lilies down the Strand and the *poètes maudits* dying young for the sake of an adjective. . . .

Like his fellow aesthetes, Mr. Hecht is a good deal preoccupied with "the artist" as a human type. To the nineties it seemed that the artist was the only survivor from the wreck of their century: the decay of religious belief, and a growing sense of the futility of well-meaning social engineering, left the artist as the one significant figure but also doomed him to discontent. As Yeats asked,

> What portion in the world can the artist have
> That has awakened from the common dream,
> But dissipation and despair?

During the last fifty years, this idea has come in for a good deal of stringent criticism. Both in the occasional masterpieces like *Tonio Kröger* and in the broad day-to-day stream of literature and criticism, the notion of the absinthe-drinking *poète maudit* has been not so much attacked as quietly superseded. Mr. Hecht, however, still holds to it loyally. . . .

The trouble, in short, with this disengaged, "aesthetic" attitude is simply that it is not sufficiently interesting. There are too many important areas of human experience which it does not touch upon. It was justifiable for Wilde to say, coolly, that "all art is completely useless," because he came at the tail-end of a long period during which art had been insistently urged, by every kind of public spokesman, to be instructive and profitable in the crudest way. Nevertheless, as we well know, art is *not* "useless." Only Mr. Hecht's dream-people, they of the brittle epigrams and the eternally tired souls, think it is, and both art and life have a way of revenging themselves on such people. —JOHN WAIN, "Ben Hecht" (1959), *The Critic as Artist*, ed. Gilbert A. Harrison, 1972, pp. 343–48

Works

In *Fantazius Mallare* and *The Kingdom of Evil*, Mr. Hecht paints the logical conclusion of tendencies which he has remorselessly observed in his own mind; he projects upon the screen of his imagination his own type of mind swollen to gigantic proportions by the disease incipient in it; he paints the elephantiasis of evil. Beneath the grandiose phrases and images of an occasionally impressive symbolism, one can trace readily enough the excitable, imaginative journalist, in whom excessive journalism and undigested modern literature have produced an atrophy of the normal emotional faculties, aspiring toward a super-humanity through the repudiation of all normal human sentiments and the untrammeled expansion of curiosity and libidinous desire. Mr. Hecht himself appears to have little sense of the necessity of the laws and conventions which more or less govern human society. The ordinary mortal, tolerably comfortable, moderately law-abiding, appears to his inflamed imagination, haunted by Crucifixion imagery, as a pitiable, contemptible, horribly agonizing wretch, self-nailed on a cross and writhing under a self-imposed crown of thorns. Fantazius Mallare, by selling his soul to the devil, and entering the kingdom of evil, aspires to become a free spirit; and in theory should transcend human limitations and enjoy a godlike expansion of experience. But Mr. Hecht is, I believe, an honest explorer and reporter of this realm of consciousness. As a matter of fact, his Fantazius attains no godlike experience. He attains no freedom. He becomes the beaten and bleeding slave of an amorphous demoniacal deity, which he recognizes as the horrible enlargement of his own lusts. He has left man in his "maggotism," to find the superman only a magnified maggot.—STUART SHERMAN, "Ben Hecht and the Superman," *Critical Woodcuts*, 1926, pp. 69–70

Among the men writing for the American theatre, Mr. Ben Hecht is one of the most sharply ironical and bitingly honest. As in Mr. Kaufman's case, it also comes as a surprise, therefore, to find his name combined with that of a gentleman named Fowler on the exhibit called *The Great Magoo*. That is, it comes as a surprise unless one recalls that Mr. Hecht has lately been in literary contact with Hollywood and unless one recalls, further, that the newspapers not so long ago noted that he had been commissioned to do a scenario suitable to the talents of Mr. James Cagney. That *The Great Magoo*, accordingly, was written less for the stage than for the subsequent screen is more or less apparent.

The play, as shown on the stage, is exactly the soufflé of smut and sentimentality that is so close to the movie impresarios' hearts. It combines, in alternating doses, assaults upon the humor of such persons as are wont to go into paroxysms of ribald laughter at the public mention of a water-closet and upon the somewhat tenderer sensibilities of such—they are usually one and the same—as experience an inner fluttering at the spectacle of a baffled and noble love at length coming into its own. At bottom, the theme is one which, if he encountered it in anyone else's play, would cause Hecht to let out a yell of derision that would blast all the stone quarries in his native Nyack, to wit, the theme of the harlot redeemed by Pure Love. Laying hold of the ancient claptrap—and with what seems to be a straight face, as the writing of the sentimental passages is the best in the play—Hecht and his partner have sought to conceal their boyish shame by obstreperously embellishing its outer fringe with words, phrases and bits of business that would drive Lady Chatterley's lover right into the arms of Jane Austen. This embellishment has an air of unmistakable insincerity and dishonesty. It suggests the loud self-incriminations as to his own canine genealogy on the part of a man who has hit his thumb with a hammer. It has all the ring of the monosyllabic snort of an abashed little boy who has been surprised by his comrades in the act of kissing the school-teacher. It is, in short, jingo. Well, not all of it, for there is one scene into which it fits properly and honestly—a scene wherein the miscellaneously constituted young wife of a champion flag-pole-sitter entertains, with some difficulty, a midnight caller while her husband spies upon her bedchamber from his somewhat distant perch with a pair of powerful binoculars. This is good low comedy and the manner of its expression is legitimate. But the rest is merely college-boy washroom stuff.

And what is more, it is sadly out-dated. Listening to the Hecht-Fowler lower vocabulary takes one back to the theatre of a half dozen years or more ago, when a multitude of young men, bursting with gleeful shouts the restraining chains of the earlier stage, let go nightly with such a torrent of deity-damning, mother-derogating, sex-celebrating *mots* that, when eleven o'clock came around, the auditor didn't know whether to reach under the chair for his hat or under the bar for the bar-towel. The drama has changed a lot since then. And the Messrs. Hecht and Fowler, though they may not realize it, today look dramatically very much like sailors with their hands on their hips.—GEORGE JEAN NATHAN, "Several Writers for the Theatre," *Passing Judgments*, 1935, pp. 161–63

Erik Dorn is a man who seems, to himself, to be a perfect translation of his country and his day: one who has lived since boyhood in a changeless vacuum waiting for something to happen, a contact to overtake him or reality to seize him. But nothing has hapened at all.

"What the hell am I talking about?" he finally asks himself at thirty: "I'm like men will all be years later, when their emotions are finally absorbed by the ingenious surfaces they've surrounded themselves with, and life lies forever buried behind the inventions of engineers, scientists, and businessmen. This business of being empty is all there is to life."

Could it be that somebody is kidding us? Could it be that Dorn's changeless vacuum is only a hideout from the winds of passion? Could it be that his claim to emptiness is a boasting made of fear?

What did Dorn fear? It was not fear or dread.

". . . the elastic distortion of crowds winding and unwinding under the tumult of windows gave him the feeling of a geometrical emptiness. . . . No drawn picture stirred him to the extent that did the tapestry of a city street. No music aroused the elation in him that did the curious beat upon his eyes of window rows, of vari-shaped building walls whose oblongs and squares translated themselves in his thought into a species of unmelodious but perfect sound. . . ." Dorn had achieved almost complete indifference to literature and especially toward painting.

"'Nothing' was a word his thought tripped on. He was used to mumbling it to himself as he walked alone in the streets. And at his desk it often came to him and repeated itself . . . his thought murmured 'nothing, nothing,' and a sadness drew itself into his heart."

Yet excepting Charles Louis-Philippe, in *Bubu de Montparnasse*, no other writer of modern times has caught the beat of a great city with such simplicity:

"In the evening when women stand washing dishes in the kitchens of the city, men light their tobacco and open newspapers. Later, the women gather up the crumpled sheets and read. . . . Tick, say the words and tock say the juries. Tick-tock, the cell door and the scaffold drop. Streets and windows, paintings of the Virgin Mary, beds of the fifty-cent prostitutes, cannon at Verdun and police whistles on crossings; the Pope in Rome, the President in Washington, the man hunting the alleys for a handout, the langorous women breeding in ornamental beds—all say a tick-tock."

As in no other American novel is the relationship between the book's hero and the novelist revealed so lucidly.

For as Erik Dorn had once held an appreciation of all things in life and art "which filled him with the emotion of symmetry" and had seen streets and crowds "pleasantly blurred and in motion," yet now saw all things as "an arrested cinematograph; grotesquely detailed and with the meaning of motion out of it," so everyone who has witnessed those scenarios revealing life as an arrested film, under Hecht's name, may perceive the relationship readily. *Erik Dorn* is a demonstration of this relationship.

For no American yet has written a novel this good yet this bad. This is the one work of serious literature we have that by the same token stands as a literary hoax. *Erik Dorn* is so true that nobody but his creator could have made him so spurious. No other writer has written a novel anything like it—and yet it resembles many novels. . . .

"What is literature?" Jean-Paul Sartre once inquired.

One might reply—"*Erik Dorn.*"

And if someone then asked—"What is *not* literature?" the answer might also be—"*Erik Dorn.*"

For the value that is derived from the novel today is not within the novel itself, but from the curiously prophetic shadow that a book, written half a century ago, now casts across our own strange times.—NELSON ALGREN, "*Erik Dorn:* A Thousand and One Afternoons in Nada," *Erik Dorn*, 1963, pp. viii–xvii

---

DOUG FETHERLING

From "1001 Afternoons in Hollywood"

The Five Lives of Ben Hecht

1977, pp. 94–99

Hecht faced many problems as a movie writer. The most important, aside from the one of literary morale, was that writing for the movies forced him to be a writer of parts rather than a whole. That fact overshadowed even a sorrier one—that he was forced into writing many things in which he had no particular interest and for which he had no special skill. Hollywood work tended to dilute his various selves—the Bohemian and the Sophisticate, for example—and to show them one at a time rather than in force, all together.

The effect was destructive except when it involved him with directors who complemented him and he them. These were generally either action directors, who appealed to Hecht's Chicago cynicism and toughness, or European ones, who were more sardonic than cynical and used the side of him that was the Sophisticate. The most imporant director of the first kind was certainly Howard Hawks.

Hawks was an intelligent tough guy who liked to play up that part of his intelligence that was rugged and practical. He was a pragmatist. His direction reached its height as a mirror of his own ideas—for instance, in the way he used Humphrey Bogart in *To Have and Have Not* or *The Big Sleep:* as a thoroughly professional fellow who gets a difficult job done without ostentation, who thinks he knows something about women, especially when they are independent types like himself but with the violence taken away, and who enjoys above all the companionship of fellow pros, whatever their sex. That crossing of sexual lines, often ignored by critics, is interesting if one considers that it was Hawks' idea to use a female Hildy Johnson in *His Girl Friday*.

Such an outlook on professionalism and comradeship was a small part of Hecht, but the greater part of his affinity with Hawks. Another bond between them, and one loosely related to the first, was that both men dreaded nothing so much as the prospect of being labelled tame and middle class. They fought against that fate (Hawks rather more blindly than Hecht) by associating themselves in life and in their work with loners, outcasts, outlaws and all manner of anti-authoritarian figures. These similar attitudes, combined with the fact that both were at the height of their Hollywood success, made their working together somehow natural. When such a collaboration came about in 1931, a year in which Hollywood produced fifty-one gangster features, it was only logical that their first project should be a film on the Chicago crime wars.

The picture was *Scarface*, which the Hays office would force them to subtitle "Shame of a Nation" and otherwise lace with phony moralistic canards. The film was produced by Howard Hughes, whom Hawks would work for again in 1943 on the famous Jane Russell sex-western *The Outlaw*, for which Hecht would co-author the script without credit. At the time of *Scarface*, Hughes was merely a multimillionaire, not the supposed billionaire he became later. Fearing Hughes might go bankrupt at any moment, Hecht demanded payment of one thousand dollars each writing day, in cash. In that way, he stood to lose only a day's work if Hughes should suddenly go belly up.

Hughes had purchased the rights to *Scarface*, a rather incredible novel by the young pulp writer, Armitage Trail. In the end only the title of the book was retained. Hecht's script was an original in more than even the usual sense. Although he was writing of Chicago again, he was now writing, in the light of *Public Enemy* and *Little Caesar*, of a criminal lifestyle that had run rampant after his departure.

Both Hecht and Hawks have said that the film was an attempt to superimpose the story of Al Capone on the story of the Borgias. While the film has as much of the Borgian incest element as they could slip past the censors, it is clearly more relevant to contemporary news than to Renaissance Europe. It is the story of the ruthless rise of Tony Camonte (Paul Muni) to the top of the gangster heap and of his ultimate capture and death. Although Capone's biography had little to do with the story, the title of the film and Muni's facial scars left no doubt in the audience's minds of the intent.

The scars were in the shape of xs. Part of the renown of the film is the way Hecht and Hawks made the x a running symbol, just as newspaper photographs of the day used the device to denote the spot where bodies lay. The opening credits roll over an x. A fallen gangster flays his arms in an x. There are many more instances. Perhaps the most famous occurs in the scene in which a gangster is gunned down in a bowling alley. The ball, which he has let loose of just as the bullets strike him, leaves two pins standing for a moment. But then they totter and finally collapse, in the shape of an x.

Scarface would have an effect on actual gangsters much as *The Front Page* had on newspapermen. Four years after the film was released, gangsters in Chicago, inspired by *Scarface*, gunned down a rival in a bowling alley. The victim was Machine Gun Jack McGurn (another Italian with an Irish *nom de guerre*) who had engineered the St. Valentine's Day Massacre in 1929, an event caricatured in Hecht's script.

Just as the stage production of *The Front Page* had done, *Scarface* established the careers of many persons involved in it, for better or for worse. Its success prompted Muni to forsake the theatre for films, most notably for a long series of biographical pictures. George Raft, who played Muni's bodyguard and was seen tossing a coin in the air repeatedly, went on to make a long list of gangster films. His coin-tossing became a favourite bit of business for impressionists and, ultimately, a sad bit of self-parody for the actor himself. Hawks would grow professionally over the decades to become the great American action director, with his tough western, detective and war films. Hecht, for his part, would strive for a happy compromise with Hollywood by working with people who could best realize on film the Chicago anti-hero side of his personality.

The action directors were by nature adventurers, either physically or vicariously. For example, Raoul Walsh (with whom Hecht never worked, it seems) had been a seaman and a cowboy before going to work for Griffith, who sent him to film the Mexican Revolution. Others, such as John Ford, Henry Hathaway and William Wellman, possessed much the same free spirit and anti-middle class attitudes. With each of them, however, the stance took a different form. Thus Hecht's writing for each also took a different form and resulted in a different kind of script.

Ford, for instance, was the most serious of the lot. Like the others he had a remarkably pronounced sense of history. He would harken back to a time of what he imagined were clear-cut moral codes and clear distinctions between good and evil. He put that concept into play by sometimes representing history as Nature and pitting against it the ruggedest type of individual. Hecht wrote only one film for him, the John Hall–Dorothy Lamour vehicle, *The Hurricane*, in which exactly this idea is played out against a South Seas background.

For Hathaway, who was a sort of a lesser, more muddled Hawks, Hecht wrote four diverse films. They illustrate Hathaway's scattergun work and Hecht's failure with such a director to produce anything more than a good script well-filmed, rather than a collaboration between writer and director. The films were *China Girl* (1942), a farfetched World War Two adventure; *Kiss of Death* (1947), a gangster film resting on the power of the script and perhaps the last first-rate piece of film writing Hecht did; *Legend of the Lost* (1957), another adventure, set in North Africa and likewise more interesting for the Hecht touches; and *Circus World* (1964), the last Hecht film released before his death and interesting hardly at all.

On most of these films Hecht was left pretty much alone. That is, he was left to write, at best, merely a good script in the abstract, without the magic which might otherwise have resulted between the script and the camera. Such a situation, however, allows one to trace the evolution of certain recurring elements in Hecht's screenwriting and his writing generally. *Kiss of Death*, for example, is, like *Underworld*, a film about a thief masquerading as a more glamourous kind of criminal. This time the masquerade is Hecht's doing, not the director's. The thief, Victor Mature, is apprehended as the logical result of the storyline, not as a concession to the censors. Once captured, he squeals on his colleagues. There is no romanticizing of his virtues or failings as there had been in *Underworld* and to a lesser extent in *Scarface*. The essential integrity of the story differs from Hecht's *Underworld* story (as distinct from Robert Lee's finished script) by being the work of a much more mature writer.

Legend of the Lost is another example of a change in Hecht as he grew older. The Hechtian man of such works from the 1920s as *1001 Afternoons in Chicago*, *Broken Necks* and *Erik Dorn* was bitter about his own failure to find a place in a stupid world. Now the same character has grown older and more tolerant of himself and others. He is also perhaps (as in *To Quito and Back* from the late 1930s) somewhat more desperate. In *Legend of the Lost*, he is, in the unlikely person of John Wayne, a tired soldier of fortune in Timbuctoo hired by Sophia Loren to help find a hidden treasure. Eventually they stumble upon the deserted Holy City of Opher, once a Roman outpost, and in a typically Hechtian piece of irony, discover the jewels while digging for water needed to remain alive.

The Wayne character is a man who knows human nature and doesn't like it. He remains largely silent whereas once he would have been noisy and iconoclastic. Loren, however, thinks he is a bit of a rogue, and tells him, "Every place you go is a barroom." Actually he is no rogue at all but spiritually a newspaperman. He is an older, wearier version of the nameless diarist of *1001 Afternoons in Chicago*, who in this film has substituted his reporter's fedora for the garb of a tough but half-hearted fortune-seeker.

This multifarious character at first appears to be one of Hecht's cinematic inventions. Actually, he is a much older Hecht stock figure brought to Hollywood from his own books and his own life and disguised a bit along the way. The same is true of that character's kindred spirit, the screen newspaperman who is really a younger Hecht recycled again and again, generally for comic effect. He turns up as a reporter in the person of Fredric March in Wellman's *Nothing Sacred* and as a former reporter turned press agent (Roscoe Karns) in Hawks' version of *Twentieth Century*. He is also the bumbling but cuddly foreign correspondent (Stuart Irwin) in Hecht's Oscar-winning script for *Viva Villa!*, with Wallace Beery in the title role.

Many former newspapermen who became screenwriters used that character, of course. The creature was generally shown as a wisecracking nuisance who never took off his hat. (Frank McHugh of the Warner stable must have played the part dozens of times.) Including the character was a way of adding to the mayhem of 1930s comedies. It owes most of its existence to the originals of *The Front Page*, for this Hecht-Hollywood "invention" was actually born in Hecht's pre-Hollywood days.

The fact that Hawks would direct three comedies propelled by such characters—*Twentieth Century*, *His Girl Friday*, and, to a lesser extent, *Viva Villa!*—is a good indication of why the Hecht-Hawks collaboration was the most successful writer-director match either of them ever knew. Hawks taught Hecht a great deal about how to put both power and subtlety into films, knowledge Hecht employed when he became a director himself. Hecht in turn encouraged Hawks to develop the quality most notably absent in the films he made with other people: a sense of humour. Coming from Hecht it was a backhanded, epigrammatic and rapid-fire sense of humour, but it added a great deal to their relationship. It nearly succeeded for a time in making Hawks a more European, less American director. It almost made him a Sophisticate: almost but not quite.

ROBERT A. HEINLEIN

1907–

Robert Anson Heinlein was born on July 7, 1907, in Butler, Missouri, and spent his childhood in Kansas City. In 1929 he graduated from the United States Naval Academy, and from then until 1934 served as an officer on several ships including the aircraft carrier U.S.S. *Lexington*. In 1934 ill health forced his retirement from the Navy. For the next five years he sold real estate, involved himself in politics and silver-mining speculation, and studied physics at U.C.L.A.; in 1939 he wrote and sold his first story, "Life-Line," to John W. Campbell for *Astounding*.

Over the next three years Heinlein, with Campbell's guidance and support, moved from complete obscurity to a position of unrivaled dominance in SF, producing in that time four novels plus so many short stories that several were published pseudonymously in order to avoid having more than one story under Heinlein's own name appear in any single magazine issue. All this fiction from Heinlein's first period, as well as most of his later work, has been reprinted in book form; much of it forms the nucleus to his "Future History" sequence, collected in the 1966 omnibus volume *The Past through Tomorrow*. Other work in these years ranged from SF-adventure potboilers such as *Sixth Column* (1941) to sophisticated fantasies ("They," 1941; "The Devil Makes the Law," 1942). The core of Heinlein's SF, however, was and has remained matter-of-fact, provocative "hard SF" like *Beyond This Horizon* (1942).

In 1942 Heinlein left writing to work as a civilian engineer for the Navy in Philadelphia. In 1947 he returned to SF, publishing a string of short stories in the *Saturday Evening Post* in addition to more novels and short works in the SF magazines. Throughout the 1950s he also wrote several SF novels for teenagers; later re-issued without the juvenile-market packaging, some of them (notably *The Star Beast*, 1954, *Time for the Stars*, 1956, and *Citizen of the Galaxy*, 1957) have retained the interest of critics and adult readers as well. In 1956 he published one of his best-regarded novels, *Double Star*.

In 1959 Heinlein's career took a new direction with the explicitly militaristic *Starship Troopers*. This was followed in 1961 by the campus bestseller *Stranger in a Strange Land*. Heinlein's subsequent work, while reaching a much larger audience than most SF, has been marked by greater and greater emphasis on complex political and religious polemics. Further novels include *Glory Road* (1963), *Farnham's Freehold* (1964), *The Moon Is a Harsh Mistress* (1966) and *I Will Fear No Evil* (1970). In 1973 Heinlein capped his long-neglected "Future History" series with *Time Enough for Love*, the "memoirs" of Lazarus Long, protagonist of *Methuselah's Children* (1941). Following an extended illness, in 1980 he published *The Number of the Beast—*, a complex science-fantasy involving many characters from his own and other writers' previous works. Since then he has published two relatively conventional SF novels, *Friday* (1982) and *Job: A Comedy of Justice* (1984).

Heinlein has also published several collections of short fiction, notably *The Green Hills of Earth* (1951), *6 × H* (1959; also published as *The Unpleasant Profession of Jonathan Hoag*), and *Expanded Universe* (1980). This last also features a number of short essays presenting Heinlein's views on writing and politics throughout various stages of his career.

Robert A. Heinlein has been Guest of Honor at three World SF Conventions, in 1941, 1961, and 1976. He has won SF's prestigious Hugo award four times. He lives in Santa Cruz, California, with his wife Virginia, to whom he has been married since 1948.

Personal

The audience that gathered in the Kaufmann Auditorium was predominantly college age, long-haired, and bluejeaned, and it had obviously come not to disagree but to worship. Some of them had been reading Heinlein since they were ten years old. But if his more recent novels had led them to expect an elderly mirror image of themselves—a gray-bearded guru in love beads—they soon realized their mistake. Heinlein, who lives in northern California, arrived onstage in a black tuxedo and fancy dress shirt. The sparse hair around his ears was clipped short, and he was sporting a neat, pencil-thin black mustache in the style of the early Ronald Colman. Standing behind the lectern, he looked exactly like what he is: a retired naval officer with a background in engineering. And instead of talking about the provocative ideas in his recent books he chose to talk about the five rules of successful writing he had learned back in the old days when he almost single-handedly filled issue after issue of pulp magazines like *Astounding Science Fiction*. The five rules, he said, are: "You must write, you must finish what you write, you must place it on the market, you must not rewrite it (unless an editor guarantees to buy the rewrite), and you must leave it on the market until it sells." By following these rules, Heinlein has produced thirty-eight books, which, in all their trade editions, fill a bookcase in his house four feet wide and eleven feet high. Heinlein said that his working habits were quite simple. He writes fourteen hours a day, seven days a week, until a book is finished. He also keeps a log of his working time; the shortest time he ever spent on a trade book was thirteen days, the longest time was a hundred and eight days. Dialogue is no problem. "Once I hear the voice of my characters, I just take down what they're saying," he explained.

In the question period after his talk, several people in the audience tried to get him to discuss his own fiction. Someone asked him why in the nineteen-sixties he had suddenly started writing so freely about sex, and he said, "Because there was no market for sex in science fiction before then." When someone asked him what the most important influence on his career had been, he replied, without hesitation, "Money!" And when someone asked him whether he wrote with a specific "ideal reader" in mind, he said, "A writer is like a beggar with a bowl. No one *has* to read fiction. A man can always spend his spare cash on beer. The reader I have in mind is someone who bought my book instead of a six-pack of beer. My purpose is to be entertaining enough to get him to do it again."

The audience did not seem at all alienated by Heinlein's Portrait of the Writer as a Grub Street Hack. When he was done, a large crowd gathered around him, waving copies of his books to be autographed. For nearly an hour, Heinlein graciously obliged all comers. Watching the scene, we were reminded of a classic theme of science fiction—the "first contact" between Earthmen and another race of intelligent beings somewhere in interstellar space. The other beings may look like giant spiders or blobs of mucus, but it turns out that they think we look pretty funny, too.—UNSIGNED, "The Talk of the Town," NY, July 1, 1974, p. 18

At this moment Bob Tucker came by to tell us to keep our speeches short because Ghod was due to appear unexpectedly at exactly 9:45: in fact we needn't even go up to the dais. While Ethel and I were discussing the implications of these three statements Hamling got involved in conversation with his neighbours across the table. . . . When our turn came we decided to go up to the dais so that at least we wouldn't be invisible as well as inaudible. Having arrived at the microphone I made to feel in my pocket for my notes and pulled out a couple of pieces of lettuce I had taken off my plate for the purpose. But this little throwaway gag was half hidden by the high lectern and noticed by only one fan with good eyesight and an even better memory, who giggled perceptively. However the rest of my bit went over quite well, so that I began to think I might get the hang of this speechmaking business if I didn't hate it so much. Then I waited while Madeleine ⟨Willis⟩ said her few but sincere words of thanks and escorted her back to our table. There we relaxed, ready now to enjoy the best of the banquet, the Sturgeon.

We did, though I thought the business with his wife's book a little chi-chi, and its spontaneity suspect. But it was a remarkable performance, not only in content but in structure. Being of a cynical turn of mind as far as speechmaking ⟨professional SF writers⟩ are concerned, I had conjectured that the imminent Ghod would be Heinlein, and listened attentively from this point of view as the thread of ⟨Theodore⟩ Sturgeon's discourse unrolled. Sure enough, at exactly 9:45 he reached the exact point at which Heinlein's name should occur. It did, and I looked expectantly at the door. But nothing happened. Sturgeon carried on without the slightest hesitation, and half an hour later had again reached a point where Heinlein's name naturally arose. Now to write a good speech is not difficult for a man who can write like Sturgeon. To be able to deliver it so well is an added gift that seems almost unfair. But to be able to take a speech apart in mid-air and reassemble it, and to do it so well that people afterwards who don't even know he did it praise the speech for its structure, is quite awe-inspiring.

Heinlein's entrance was certainly dramatic, but I thought his white dinner suit almost too theatrical for a man who had travelled vast distances at breakneck speed to arrive unexpectedly in the nick of time. However, fortunately for my peace of mind Steve Schultheis, who is an authority on all sartorial matters, explained everything to me later in Santa Barbara. It is of course perfectly true that, as every good little neofan believes, Heinlein struggles each year through sleet, hail, rain, snow and mud in his exquisite evening dress, climbing mountains, fording rivers, scrambling over fences, trudging through fields, hacking his way through undergrowth and fighting his way along alleys, in his desperate efforts to get to the ⟨World Science Fiction⟩ Convention on time. And it cannot be denied that in the course of these heroic journeys even a man like Heinlein must occasionally be in danger of getting a speck of dust on his clothing. But what I had not realised is that he is not alone. He is closely followed, Steve revealed, every step of the way by a devoted retainer who used to be a batman on Heinlein's aircraft carrier and thus acquired the ability of intercepting every speck of dirt before it reaches his master's person. He ceases from his dedicated task only at the very door of the Convention Hall, where he waits humbly clutching the well-worn little long leather Hugobag.

These appearances of Heinlein are becoming one of the most charming traditions of fandom. They remind me of a series of faan-fiction stories I once started based on the theory that conventions are becoming more and more stylised, and will eventually develop into something like carnival or circus, or the British Christmas Pantomime. The Heinlein Manifestation would make a fine conclusion to any such performance. The distribution to the audience of favors and of gaily coloured but inedible food symbols would be the prelude to a series of ritual incantations before a number of silver spaceship-shaped objects, which would culminate in a blinding flash and the miraculous apparition of The Heinlein in a technicolor tuxedo. After the Bob-Up, as they call it backstage where they operate the trapdoor, there would be a knockabout comedy turn involving other traditional characters like The Doctor and The Surgeon and The Tucker and The Clerk and The Farmer, and then The Heinlein would wrest one or more of the silver objects from them and disappear with demoniacal laughter in another flash and puff of smoke. The children will love it, and indeed The Heinlein does re-appear for them in a number of smaller tents simultaneously, like Santa Claus in department stores, where he gives autographs to those who bring serial wrappers.

Next morning over noon coffee I mentioned to Sid Coleman that I'd heard Heinlein was up already receiving visitors again. "He isn't up already," said Sid, "he hasn't been to bed already." We contemplated for a moment in silence the thought of Heinlein after that long journey sitting up all night talking to fans, and still at it. "You know," said Sid, "it's possible that one of the most admirable things about Heinlein is his insincerity." He went on to point out that for years Heinlein had had, literally and metaphorically, no time for fans; and that we had never been informed as to what brought about his sudden conversion. A nasty cynical person might speculate it was because he had suddenly realised that the acclaim of fandom might be of some practical advantage to him. But, Sid pointed out, if this cultivation of fans was coldly deliberate, how much should we respect him for his strength of will, and how much more for the perfection with which he does it?

After this conversation with Sid I decided to go up and judge for myself. I hadn't meant to, because I needed all the time I had and more to see the people I had really come to meet; and I had nothing worth saying to Heinlein that wouldn't involve us in a long argument. But watching him, and then talking to him, I found it was impossible either to dislike the man or fail to admire him. I couldn't detect any phoniness in his friendliness. Even if it did originate in an act of policy, I think he is still a man we can like as well as admire. A great man will first try to change his environment, but if this is impossible he will adapt himself to it. It is possible that Heinlein, having made up his mind to get on with fans, set himself to see what there was in us to like, and succeeded. —WALTER A. WILLIS, "Chicago Chicago," *Hyphen*, Sept. 1963, pp. 17–20

General

Robert A. Heinlein has that attribute which the mathematician Hermann Weyl calls "the inexhaustibility of real things": whatever you say about him, I find, turns out to be only partly true. If you point to his innate conservatism, as evidenced in the old-time finance of "The Man Who Sold the Moon" ⟨1950⟩, you may feel smug for as much as a minute, until you remember the rampantly radical monetary system of *Beyond This Horizon*. . . .

With due caution, then, let me say that in art, at least, Heinlein seems to be as conservative as they come. He believes in a plain tale well told. Although he fancies his own Yukon-style verses, or used to, he has no patience with poetry-in-a-garret. The people he writes about are healthy, uninhibited and positive, a totally different breed from the neurasthenic heroes of many of his colleagues. In a field whose most brilliant and well-established writers seem to flip sooner or later, Heinlein is preeminently sane.—DAMON KNIGHT, "One Sane Man: Robert A. Heinlein" (1960), *In Search of Wonder*, 1967, p. 76

What is most interesting for my purposes about all ⟨of Heinlein's⟩ recent novels . . . is that in them the editorializing has become blatant (sometimes, as in *Farnham's Freehold*, to the near-extinction of the story), so that it is no longer necessary to apply any sort of detective work to the problem of what Heinlein thinks; he tells you, and at length. In particular, the political conservatism of Dan Davis and his twins has intensified into a reactionary radicalism indistinguishable, except for the intelligence with which it is defended, from the positions of the John Birch Society and the Minutemen. In short, it is no longer possible to pretend that Dan Davis' attitudes are those of a *persona* adopted solely for literary purposes.

Heinlein is already unique in science-fiction history in many important respects, and his political development further sets him off from his fellow practitioners. From H. G. Wells on, the main current of social thought in science fiction has been liberal, even, despite some preoccupation with the Superman, egalitarian—so thoroughly that, as Kingsley Amis complains, many of the liberal assumptions have gone underground and become clichés, to the frequent impediment of both logic and imagination. Thus even Heinlein's worst recent novels (especially *Farnham's Freehold*) exert a shock effect all out of proportion to the dwindling amount of craftsmanship that has gone into them.

It seems unlikely, however, that this aspect of Heinlein's *curriculum vitae* will have anything like the influence upon his peers that his previous innovations did. "The gulf between us," as a Heinlein superman remarks, "is narrow but it is deep." —JAMES BLISH (as "William Atheling, Jr."), "Afterword (1967)" to "First Person Singular: Heinlein, Son of Heinlein" (1957), *More Issues at Hand*, 1970, pp. 57–58

Critics have noticed Heinlein's *laissez faire* "philosophy," passing it off as primitive. What they have not noticed, however, is that this philosophy is rooted in much deeper soil, in patterns that are both cultural and mythical. The advent of religion in ⟨*Stranger in a Strange Land*⟩ and the other later novels is no accident, nor is the harshly Calvinistic nature of this creed. Calvinistic figurations are present in Heinlein's earliest stories—they run throughout his work in one form or another. These variations, however, are important: there are three discernable phases. The first, essentially but not exclusively that of the early stories and novellas, could be called the Puritan phase—Heinlein's emphasis in these stories is on worldly hierarchies of the elect. At the point, in the juvenile novels, where predestination and conventional heroic patterns meet, we have a second, more "democratic" phase: the rule of the visionary company gives way momentarily to the possibility of Everyman as hero. The third phase, that of *Stranger* and its kindred novels, is more purely Calvinist. The mechanisms of election are reaffirmed; but, as with the Everyman hero, the group also pales before the all-absorbing problem of superman before grace.

The organization of the various secret societies in early Heinlein stories reminds one of the Puritan Church of our founding fathers. Within these groups, emphasis is always placed on covenantal relationships. Strangely, none of them is the least bit anarchistic—one might expect it of rugged individualists. On the contrary, members are ever careful to establish, and observe to the letter, all kinds of binding sacraments. The ending of "Gulf" ⟨1949⟩ in fact, shows hero and heroine completing their "mission impossible" with a marriage ceremony. They say their vows (a third listener acts as "witness") as doom rushes upon them. What matter if death do them part at once—a memorial marker is erected on the spot to preserve their union. The pragmatic shaping power of the forms has become the important thing, far more than any mystical core they once may have had.

In Heinlein's latest novels, however, such groups wane beside the rising star of one supreme existence, and we find something comparable to Calvinist "supernatural grace." Election, as in Michael Smith's sudden conversion, overleaps regular channels, elides everything into one epiphanic moment. This contrasts with the early stories, where, if election takes place, it is analagous to what was once called "common grace," the form most amenable to the worldly Puritans because it sanctioned their theocratic order. Its path was visible both in the ritual and social structures of their group—it was God's will incarnate. Indeed, Heinlein's characters in these stories do little more than act out such concrete designs of providence. The thrust of election is both worldly and functional; its result is a firm and efficient social hierarchy.

The roots of Heinlein's basic pattern go deep into the American past. They can be found at that point where the social forces of the Puritan Church and the new mercantile elite of the Enlightenment cross and blend, where church member and property owner meet. Indeed, behind the seemingly "democratic" facade of "inner light" grace stands the Puritan theocracy, interpreting their own worldly success as a sign of election. In the same way, behind the Enlightened doctrine of "liberty and justice for all" lies the basic inequality of entrepreneurial society; add this to the sanction of Puritan doctrine, and it becomes incontestable; add a "Darwinian" sanction, and it becomes hereditary as well. Heinlein holds up the same masks of freedom and individual liberty. And yet he despises the incompetent and weak, the democratic processes that enfranchise what he calls "homo sap."

In taking up the juvenile adventure, Heinlein must adopt quite a contrary pattern. However unlikely the channel, through it he taps a tradition that, if not egalitarian, is eminently humanistic. Heroic action at least implies that man makes his way in the world through moral qualities that many humans (not just the happy few) recognize and to some extent possess. The novels in which Heinlein develops this pattern are full of a strange tension. Can the individual help shape his destiny through willed action? Or are deeds futile in a fallen world? Is not election rather irrational and unearnable, a gift beyond all sense of personal merit? Born of this tension, perhaps, is the new emphasis, in Heinlein's novels of the 1960s and 1970s on the ambiguities of election. Out of it rises the new Heinlein hero: supreme man alone before his hidden god.—GEORGE EDGAR SLUSSER, *The Classic Years of Robert A. Heinlein*, 1977, pp. 7–8

If we look at ⟨*Time Enough for Love*'s⟩ mythic structure, deeper even than Freudian-therapeutic readings of the oedipal material, there are forces operating that unify the book despite disharmonies in value systems and even artistic flaws and ideological irritations. First of all, Lazarus is an epic hero, even if he lacks the tragic grandeur and high style of the classical models. He leads his people to salvation (first the flight of the Howards; then the diaspora, which he and Libby made possible; then the colonizations of Secundus and Tertius), he fights monsters, displays extraordinary courage and self-sacrifice, and generally serves as a model of wisdom, love, and bravery for his culture. It can even be argued that the automatic and often cloying reverence he receives from all "good" characters (a feature much objected to by reviewers) is a symbol of Lazarus' status as a demigod-hero. Next, Lazarus is Everyman as well—a role not necessarily in conflict with his job as hero—in his struggle with fundamental questions of value and meaning and his failure to gain control over the conflicting parts of systems that solve pieces of the puzzle. In his many lives he follows all possible paths (see *Time Enough for Love*, "Variations on a Theme III," for a list with comments of some of his careers), gathering much information about How but little about Why. Last, and most powerful, is the shape of the novel itself. The content motif of return is also an important structural feature, and even without a Freudian analysis, it is plain that Lazarus' healing is tied up with reliving his past and finally traveling into it bodily to confront his childhood and Maureen. To say that Lazarus wants to die because he is tired of life—that he is bored—is to say that he has been wounded by the experience of being, by the fact of existence. After being teased and nursed back to life, his death at the end of "Coda" should be tragic, or at least ironic—the completion of a process that his family of healers could only interrupt, not deny altogether. But Lazarus does not die; he is resurrected after experiencing a vision of ambiguous import; and Tamara (confused with Maureen in Lazarus' mind and symbolically identified with her in the novel) tells him what we all know of all heroes, mortal or not: "'You cannot die'" (*Time Enough for Love*, "Coda IV").

So Lazarus is reborn. The pattern is complete, the circle of life to death to new life is closed, and Lazarus has truly returned. In the face of this mythic pattern, the tensions between the philosophical systems are unimportant—it is the fact of the recurrence of life, of the reality of the process, whatever its Why, that provides the power for this book. Even if there are no answers, the search is satisfying; even if in the static plenum of Andy Libby's mathematical universe there is no causality, the man-monkey keeps asking How and even Why.

This is not to say that there is no leaning toward one side or the other. Despite the failure of the novel to supply a systematic, consistent philosophy on the rational level, I am left with the conviction that all the explanations of species survival as the universal morality are meaningless without the immediate experience that life itself—survival—is worthwhile in its own terms; that is, I believe that *emotionally* the book resolves in favor of the aesthetic way. Whatever the validity of the Gray Voice vision, there is an interesting reference in the Voice's advice to Lazarus to start the game over again—"'You cannot exhaust her infinite variety'" ("Coda II"). Ignoring for the moment who or what else "she" might be in a solipsist metaphysic, she is symbolically Cleopatra, as unmistakable a representative of the erotically and *intrinsically* desirable as we could want, a sign that time exists for love and not the other way around.—RUSSELL LETSON, "The Returns of Lazarus Long," *Robert A. Heinlein*, eds. Joseph D. Olander, Martin Harry Greenberg, 1978, pp. 220–21

Heinlein, in the ultimate analysis, doesn't sound ⟨in *Expanded Universe*⟩ like the savage militarist who so worries certain fans. His defence of *Sixth Column/The Day After Tomorrow* (the one where a few red-blooded American boys equipped with magic technology zap a vast occupation force of slant-eyed tyrants) as a potboiler written under the yoke of ⟨John W. Campbell⟩ is fair enough. His defence of *Starship Troopers*' peculiar franchise system (only veterans vote) involves an explanation that "veteran" merely means a retired civil servant . . . ho hum. He comes down strongly *against* conscription, volunteer armies having *esprit de corps* and thus being better. The Heinlein that finally emerges is not too far removed from the bold pioneer, the unquenchable "free man" he so admires, who is unafraid to speak his mind, who vows never to "leave my quarters without being properly armed" (introduction), and is supremely competent in all the minutiae of survival. Since such a person does not exactly find the fullest scope for expression of his talents in today's America, it follows that Heinlein should have a soft spot for para-military organizations which still value the pioneering arts—I refer, of course, to the Boy Scouts. Looking closer still, is one wrong to imagine a certain gloating in so very many pieces wherein Heinlein sees the ruin of civilization-as-we-know-it—sees his favourite Survival Types coming into their own at last and muscling their dauntless way through the wilderness?

Now, it seems that Heinlein identifies with America itself as a Survival Type—as a pioneer nation scratching out its liberty in hostile surroundings (i.e. the rest of us). Once he saw America as a global policeman—"Solution Unsatisfactory", again—and, now that ideal seems impossible, the country is visualized as a Free Man in the wilderness of wild communists, socialists, OPEC profiteers and so on. Perhaps it's just as well that America does not heed his sermons and—bar a few little CIA activities—is content to sit there "fat, dumb and happy". An America animated anew by the pioneering spirit would fit about as well in this crowded world as a revived and pioneering Britain, or Rome.

Expanded Universe, then, is less for the sf reader than the Heinlein student. Its author once reshaped the world of pulp sf with the greatest of ease; but, as shown in "The Happy Days Ahead", the instant pulp solution looks less convincing in the real world. Now, trying to alter this real world by preaching sterner virtues to a decadent America, Heinlein cuts a less impressive figure . . . never quite a bore, but perilously close to being a crank.—DAVE LANGFORD, *Fndtn*, Oct. 1981, pp. 110–11

Heinlein's influence on modern science fiction is so pervasive that modern critics attempting to wrestle with that influence find themselves dealing with an object rather like a sky or an ocean. In many respects Heinlein's limits are the horizons of science fiction. The bulk of his most influential work was done largely before any academic scholarship in the field got its methodological legs fully under itself in the '60s. And that bulk *is* large. To come to terms with Heinlein one must be prepared to examine deeply over 20 of his more than 40 published volumes; nor does this mean slighting any of the rest. Basically, however, what he has provided science fiction with is a countless number of rhetorical figures for dramatizing the range of SF concerns. These are the rhetorical turns that still provide most SF readers with the particular thrill that is science fiction's special pleasure: a fact about a character (her race; his gender; whether or not someone happens to be wearing clothes) that current society considers of defining import is placed at such a point in the narrative that it not only surprises the reader, but also demonstrates how unimportant such concerns have become to this particular future world; a historical reference is casually dropped that lets the reader know that some present historical trend has completely reversed; another reference, made by a character, suddenly reveals that the future world has completely misinterpreted or forgotten some historical fact that is a commonplace of our world, and the fallibility of "history" is pointed out. These are Heinlein's.

. . . ⟨W⟩hat distresses one about the Heinlein argument in general, when it is presented in narrative form, is that it so frequently takes the form of a gentlemanly assertion: "Just suppose the situation around X (war, race, what-have-you) were P, Q, and R; now under those conditions, wouldn't behavior Y be logical and justified?"—where behavior Y just *happens* to be an extreme version of the most conservative, if not fascistic, program. Our argument is never with the truth value of Heinlein's syllogism: Yes, *if* P, Q, and R were the case, then behavior Y *would* be pragmatically justifiable. Our argument is rather with the premises: Since P, Q, and R are *not* the situation of the present world, why continually pick fictional situations, bolstered by science-fictional distortions, to justify behavior that is patently *in*appropriate for the real world? And Heinlein's unerring ability to see precisely how the real world would have to be changed to make such conservative behavior appropriate begins to suggest that his repeated use of science fiction to this end represents what existentialist critics used to call "bad faith." One assumes Heinlein's answer to this argument is simply that the science-fiction parts of the distortion, at any rate, *are* possible in the future, if not probable; we must be prepared.

Well, Marx's favorite novelist was Balzac—an avowed Royalist. And Heinlein is one of mine. A basic tenet of Heinlein's philosophy has been quoted by Damon Knight in his fine introduction to the "Future History" stories ("Future History" is Campbell's term, not Heinlein's) *The Past through Tomorrow*; this is a good place to set it out because it contours a good deal of the quibbling one is likely to get into over Heinlein's "politics":

> When any government, or any church for that matter, undertakes to say to its subjects, "This you may not read, this you must not see, this you are forbidden to know," the end result is tyranny and oppression, no matter how holy the motives. Mighty little force is needed to control a man whose mind has been hoodwinked; contrariwise, no amount of force can control a free man, a man whose mind is free. No, not the rack, nor fission bombs, not anything—you can't conquer a free man; the most you can do is kill him.

Heinlein and I might well quibble over what constitutes "hoodwinking," or what one's social responsibility to the "hoodwinked" is; still, if you put Heinlein's statement up and asked me to sign, I would. Clearly, then, there is an agreement—a tribute to the man who, as much as any writer while I was growing up, taught me to argue with the accepted version.

. . . My own feeling . . . is that to encounter Heinlein significantly, one must be prepared to take on the seven novels running from *Double Star* (1956) through *The Moon Is a Harsh Mistress* (1966), as well as all the shorter works contained in *The Past through Tomorrow* (copyright 1966; it contains stories and novels written between 1939 and 1962). Only then will we have a proper acquaintance with the writerly concerns and patterns that will allow us to appreciate fully what is deeply serious in the dozen "juvenile" novels, what is profoundly inventive in some of his more ephemeral earlier works, or what is patently authentic in the more recent didactic ones. This seems to me the only way to cut up the sky (or the ocean) Heinlein's work makes over (or around) the whole of contemporary science fiction.—SAMUEL R. DELANY, "Heinlein," *Starboard Wine*, 1984, pp. 38–44

BRIAN W. ALDISS
From "After the Impossible Happened"
Billion Year Spree: The True History of Science Fiction
1973, pp. 269–74

Heinlein's transition from magazine writer to novelist is dramatic. His great and rare virtue is that he has never been content to repeat a winner or rely on a formula; and this, as we know from our study of Edgar Rice Burroughs, is a way of defying popularity. Nevertheless, wide popularity has been his.

He is very much a pulp writer made good, sometimes with his strong power drives half-rationalised into a right-wing political philosophy, as in *Starship Troopers* (1959), a sentimental view of what it is like to train and fight as an infantryman in a future war. Anyone who has trained and fought in a past war will recognise the way Heinlein prettifies his picture. But realism is not Heinlein's vein, although he has an adroit way of dropping in a telling detail when needed, sometimes giving the illusion of realism. This technique is notably effective in his boys' novels, such as *Starman Jones* (1953), where close analysis of character and motive is not demanded.

For my taste, Heinlein's most enjoyable novel is *Double Star*, which first ran as a serial in *Astounding* in 1956. *Double Star* is a hymn to behaviourism. For once Heinlein begins with a "little" man, almost a Wellsian Cockney, a pathetic failed actor, Lawrence Smith, who liked to style himself Lorenzo the Great.

Because of his chance resemblance to Bonforte, one of the leading politicians of the solar system, Lorenzo is forced to impersonate the politician and take on his powers, until he eventually becomes the man himself, clad in his personality and office. People in other Heinlein novels often have to fit into unaccustomed roles, become revolutionaries, become space troopers, wear slugs on their backs, or—like Smith in *I Will Fear No Evil*—live in a woman's body.

Heinlein's grasp of politics has always been remarkably frail, and the political issues concerning liberty which lie close to the heart of *Double Star* are absurdly falsified by the coarsely impractical methods the politicians employ. Thus, Lorenzo is shanghaied into playing his role, while Bonforte is kidnapped by the opposing party, the Humanists. This Chicago gangsterism is rendered the more silly because an effort is made to model political procedures on British parliamentary method: Bonforte is a Right Honourable, and "leader of the loyal opposition."[1]

Despite this monstrous drawback, *Double Star* survives somehow because at its centre is the process whereby Lorenzo becomes Bonforte, and Heinlein handles this with a clarity he is rarely able to sustain in his other adult novels. The scene on Mars where Lorenzo as Bonforte goes to be adopted into a Martian Nest (rare honour for Earthmen) is effective. There are parallels between this novel and Hope's *Prisoner of Zenda*.

In a juvenile novel, *Red Planet* (1949), Heinlein presents another effective picture of Mars. Heinlein is obscurely moved by Mars. As a thinker, he is primitive; perhaps this is the source of his appeal. The critic Panshin says that "Heinlein's idea of liberty is wolfish and thoroughgoing."[2] Although it is true that several of his novels are about revolution and wars, this does not make of Heinlein a Zapata. The dark and blood-red planet shines only in the complex universe of his own mind; his ideas of liberty boil down to what a man can grasp for himself.

More nonsense has been written about Heinlein than about any other sf writer. He is not a particularly good storyteller, his characters are often indistinguishable, his style is banal, and to compare him with Kipling is absurd. A better comparison is with Nevil Shute, who also loved machines and added mysticism to his formulae; but Shute is more readable.

Shute, however, is not as interesting as a character. The interest in Heinlein's writing lies in the complexity of Heinlein's character as revealed through the long autobiography of his novels. He is a particular case of that magic-inducing not-growing-up which marks so many sf writers.

And this is best exemplified in his best novel, *Stranger in a Strange Land* (1961). Though it is a faulty book, Heinlein's energy and audacity are turned to full volume. It also is an ambitious book and that, too, one respects.

Mars hangs just below the horizon again.

The central figure of *Stranger in a Strange Land* is Valentine Michael Smith, twenty-five years old and a distant relation of Tarzan; he was born on Mars and brought up by Martians. Back on Earth, his strange Martian ways threaten political stability. He is even better equipped than Tarzan, materially and mentally—materially because oddities of his birth have left him heir to several considerable fortunes and have possibly made him owner of Mars as well; mentally, because he has picked up all sorts of psi powers, learnt from his Martian parents.

Although the novel is by no means "a searing indictment of Western Civilization," as the blurb on one edition would have it, it does pitch in heartily against many of our idiocies, just as the early Tarzan books did.

But the odd attraction of *Stranger* is that it mixes the Burroughs tradition with the Peacock–Aldous Huxley tradition. It is full of discussions of religion and morals and free love. For Smith comes under the protection of Jubal Harshaw, a rich old eccentric know-all, who holds forth about everything under the Sun. He is a distant and tiresome relation of Propter in *After Many a Summer* (and is later to spawn the even more distant and tiresome Chad Mulligan in *Stand on Zanzibar*).

Smith's ideas of sharing come from his Martian Nest, which sounds much like the Martian Nest in *Double Star*.

All the characters talk a great deal, their verbosity only exceeded by the characters in *I Will Fear No Evil*. Here's a sample, where Jubal and Ben discuss Smith's rejection of conventional moral codes, and Jubal calls Smith a "poor boy."

> "Jubal, he is *not* a boy, he's a man."
>
> "Is he a 'man'? This poor ersatz Martian is saying that sex is a way to be happy. Sex *should* be a means of happiness. Ben, the worst thing about sex is that we use it to hurt each other. It ought *never* to hurt; it should bring happiness, or at least, pleasure.
>
> "The code says, 'Thou shalt not covet thy neighbor's wife.' The result? Reluctant chastity, adultery, jealousy, bitterness, blows and sometimes murder, broken homes and twisted children—and furtive little passes degrading to woman and man. Is this Commandment ever obeyed? If a man swore on his own Bible that he refrained from coveting his neighbor's wife *because* the code forbade it, I would suspect either self-deception or subnormal sexuality. Any male virile enough to sire a child has coveted many women, whether he acts or not.
>
> "Now comes Mike and says: 'There is no need to covet my wife . . . *love* her! There's no limit to her love, we have everything to gain—and nothing to lose but fear and guilt and hatred and jealousy.' The proposition is incredible. So far as I recall only pre-civilization Eskimos were this naive—and they were so isolated that they were almost 'Men from Mars' themselves. But we gave them our 'virtues' and now they have chastity and adultery just like the rest of us. Ben, what did they gain?"
>
> "I wouldn't care to be an Eskimo."
>
> "Nor I. Spoiled fish makes me bilious."
>
> "I had in mind soap and water. I guess I'm effete." (Chapter 33)

Smith also has a number of psi powers at his command, from the ability to slow his heartbeats, to psychokinesis, to making objects vanish—and those objects include clothes, guns, and human beings.[3] He is also represented as being of high intellect *and* is a great success with the girls. In fact, as James Blish knowingly puts it, Smith "can work every major miracle, and most of the minor ones, which are currently orthodox in Campbellian science fiction."[4]

So Smith is ideally equipped by his author to found a new religion—and he does. After "discorporating" quite a few troublesome people, Smith allows himself to be killed by the mob, and discorporates on to the astral level himself.[5]

Stranger in a Strange Land has an odd fascination, despite its faults; it reminds one of Huxley's *Island* in its attempt to offer a schema for better living, but one imagines that Huxley would have been horrified by its barely concealed power fantasy. One might go even further than Blish (who was writing at time of publication) and say that *Stranger* in fact represents the apotheosis of Campbellian science fiction, and so of the long pulp tradition.

Stranger has a strange case history. When first published, it did not sell very well, although, within the sf field, it collected a Hugo. It slowly got up a head of steam and became one of the campus best sellers, along with *Lord of the Flies* and *Lord of the Rings*, spreading then to Underground success.

⟨Alexei⟩ Panshin, writing possibly in 1965, has a startlingly prophetic thing to say. Speaking of the fact that the religious premises of Heinlein's novel are untrue, and superpowers do not exist, he adds, ". . . without these anyone who attempts to practise the book's religion (which includes mass sex relations) is headed for trouble. In other words, the religion has no point for anybody."[6]

The sixties, so good for so many people in the West, began with the success of *Lolita* and the trial of *Lady Chatterley* and ended with the trial of the hippie murderer Charles Manson, whose family messily took care of Sharon Tate and other victims, and whose career magnificently encapsulates all the slummier manifestations of the decade. Manson's grotesque "religion" was compounded of many straws drifting in the atmosphere, among them Bible texts and Beatles music and drugs. He also picked up some Scientology from a defrocked renegade from that movement—and we recall with pride that Scientology, too, was the brain child of an sf writer, L. Ron

Hubbard, alias René LaFayette. *And*, in the words of Manson's biographer,

> . . . another book that helped provide a theoretical basis for Manson's family was *Stranger in a Strange Land* by Robert Heinlein. . . . Initially, Manson borrowed a lot of terminology and ideas from this book—not, hopefully, including the ritual cannibalism described therein. Manson, however, was to identify with the hero of the book, one Valentine Michael Smith [Manson's first follower's child was named Valentine Michael Manson]—a person who, in the course of building a religious movement, took to killing or "discorporating" his enemies. . . . To this day Manson's followers hold water-sharing ceremonies.[7]

Of course, only a moralist would be silly enough to imagine, during the Vietnam War, that the Sharon Tate murders and all the rest of Manson's odious mumbo-jumbo might be any sort of logical end result of the well-established and respectable pulp tradition of the all-powerful male, so largely epitomised in Campbell's swaggering intergalactic heroes.

Before leaving Heinlein, one more thing remains to be said. Old-time fans still think of him as a hardware specialist. In fact, he moved over very early to writing a different kind of sf, and one, I believe, much more in tune with the sixties and seventies—a variant which we may call Life-Style Sf[8]; that is to say, a fiction which places the emphasis on experimental modes of living more in accord with, or forced on us by, pressures of modern living.

Notes

1. Despite which, one critic claims this novel is "not melodramatic, but sure and real." The remark occurs in Chap. 3 of Alexei Panshin's *Heinlein in Dimension: A Critical Analysis*, Chicago, 1968. This is a long, honourable, and painstaking study of Heinlein's work, recommended simply as a popular guide. But Panshin has no grasp of critical method, or of what makes literature. His own prose style is blind to grace and meaning; "By 2075 one assumes that everybody will talk enough differently from the present to need translation into our terms."
2. Panshin, op. cit., Chap. 7.
3. A lively discussion of the wish-fulfilment aspects of the novel is contained in Dr. Robert Plank's article, "Omnipotent Cannibals: Thoughts on Reading Robert Heinlein's *Stranger in a Strange Land*," *Riverside Quarterly*, Vol. 5, No. 1 ⟨1971⟩.
4. James Blish, "Cathedrals in Space," in *The Issue at Hand* ⟨(1964)⟩.
5. It is interesting to compare Heinlein's novel, written before the hippie thing, with my own *Barefoot in the Head* (1969). In the latter, the entire culture is freaked out after the Acid Head War, and the central character, Charteris, is elevated to the role of Messiah. But such power as he has comes from abnegation and, when he finds himself on the brink of believing in his ability to work miracles, he deliberately throws away the Christ role.
6. Panshin, op. cit., Chap. 4, portions of which appeared in *Riverside Quarterly* in 1965. Which demonstrates that Panshin has some of the qualities needed to criticise sf, *pace* Note 1!
7. From Chap. 1, Sec. 1 of Ed Sanders' *The Family: The Story of Charles Manson's Dune Buggy Attack Battalion*, New York, 1971. Manson was also turned on by Dr. Eric Berne's *Transactional Analysis* and the Beatles' totally innocuous "I Wanna Hold Your Hand."
8. As far as I know, this coinage is first used in my Afterword, "A Day in the Life-Style of . . ." in *Best SF: 1971*, edited by Harry Harrison and Brian Aldiss, where it is applied to such novels as Luke Rhinehart's *The Dice Man*.

GEORGE EDGAR SLUSSER

From *Robert A. Heinlein: Stranger in His Own Land*

1976, pp. 48–62

The Deification of Lazarus Long

Time Enough for Love (1973) is an immense novel built around one man, Lazarus Long, Senior of the Howard Families. In his many 'lives' and incarnations, Lazarus is the hero of this vast *roman-a-tiroirs*. *Time* returns to the world of Heinlein's earliest fiction. *Methuselah's Children* ⟨rev. ed., 1958⟩, to which this book is nominally the sequel, lies at the center of a cycle of stories intended to depict the 'Future History' of human civilization. Heinlein reorganized this Balzacian epic in his recent collection, *The Past through Tomorrow* (1966), which includes the famous chart of names, places, and events prominent in his imaginary scheme. *Time Enough* is presented as the capstone of this Future History. Not surprisingly, many characters from earlier works make new (if brief) appearances here. Johann Smith's brain transplant is even mentioned in passing, although *I Will Fear* is not formally part of this saga. Apparently Heinlein would tell us that all his novels are 'history' in this same sense. Indeed, each of his stories can, if necessary, be classified according to the names and dates on the master chart. Obviously, Heinlein intends Lazarus, whose existence spans the entire period, to be both center and circumference of this mighty fictional structure.

Like *Stranger*, Heinlein's latest novel makes extensive use of forms and devices borrowed from the didactic fiction of the eighteenth century. Again, the exemplary thrust is elided. The novel is fashioned of diaries, inserted documents, sayings, and aphorisms; there are even footnotes, and an 'editor' who supposedly has rearranged all the miscellaneous materials into unified form. Each of the tales is intended to illustrate some aspect of Long's exemplary life. There is, however, only a semblance of progression. The novel does not narrate his becoming so much as celebrate his being. Overriding these linear expectations is a 'musical' structure which is openly circular. Chapter headings announce "Variations on a Theme," or "Counterpoint." The final story of Lazarus' return to the Earth of his past is titled "Da Capo." This novel, Heinlein is telling us, has fugal form. In essence, there will be different temporal and spatial arrangements of a single basic theme—diversity in unity. In terms of progression, the work inscribes a circle: in the end, we return to the beginning. All possibility of heroic action is gone forever. Even the polar dynamic has given way to open exaltation of the singular. There is one hero, one theme, and one world—and all these are one: Lazarus Long. It is a novel of solipsism.

At first glance, Heinlein may seem to be redecorating old material with a profusion of structural novelties. Not only is *Time Enough* well crafted, but its ambitions are vast and well-executed. Heinlein would do nothing less than merge the two axes of his fictional universe. Lazarus's life covers the whole range of his adventure tales, and absorbs them all. In the vertical sense, he subsumes all other exemplary figures in Heinlein. *Time*, in fact, is intended to be a truly philosophical novel. As far as the destiny of mankind is concerned, it begins not *in medias res*, but at the end. An ancient Lazarus ponders Hamlet's dilemma: to be or not to be. This old man has not only done everything there is to do, but through his 'family,' he has brought civilization to a state where even the 'evil' of death is no more. But if death was a quandary for Smith, the possibility of endless life is one for Lazarus. The hero of *Methuselah's Children* struggled to survive, and the challenge gave value to his life. Now, however, with nothing left to accomplish, no adventures to be had, Lazarus wonders (and all mankind with him) what he has to live for. He faces a new, and more insidious enemy—boredom.

Stranger elides the tragic possibilities of death. If it occurs at all, it becomes, in the larger perspective of human destiny, merely another step on the way, not a harrowing finality. *Time Enough* begins beyond death. Man's science has now defeated Johann Smith's enemy. The human race, in fact, has entered a utopian phase. Along with death, it seems, man has done away with the need for God: the idea of immortality in Heaven has simply become irrelevant. Michael Smith's gospel was: "Thou art God"; Lazarus, however, now discovers the danger in being a god. To replace destiny is to become static; on the contrary, man thrives only in a dynamic situation. The old hero of *Methuselah's Children*, who rejected paradise in favor of struggle and the unknown, is still alive in this new world at the end of time.

All decisions have apparently been made: man has reached a state of rest. Evolution has abolished the heroic world, and, it seems, has broken the Calvinistic hegemony as well. Not only has man conquered death, but he himself forsees and arranges all 'surprises' now. Lazarus's actions will prove, however, that man has not reached his destiny. Heinlein's latest novel does not suspend the Calvinistic pattern, but reaffirms it. In this static world, Lazarus has apparently found the one choice that remains: to die. But his situation is falsely existential. As it turns out, he does not choose, but is 'tricked' into continuing his existence. And this is a most fortunate occurrence, for Lazarus's ensuing experiments, his search for a *raison d'être*, lead the intrepid voyager to new, unheard-of discoveries. If man's possibilities again prove unlimited, it is clear that this man of action also does not guide, but is being guided. Science may aid Lazarus in his new search. Yet without this initial 'grace,' man's efforts will invariably flounder. The proof lies in the book's initial situation: man masters the physical universe, only to find himself faced with even graver problems—matters (in Lazarus's words) of a 'spiritual' nature. Once more, the course of this novel is governed by 'serendipity.' Heinlein may want us to exclaim: "a mighty maze, but not without a plan!" Lazarus's journey back from utopia, if anything, reverses these terms. Even more than for Johann Smith, the plan leads Heinlein's hero into a nightmarish maze. Long's quest to relieve spiritual anxieties only takes him deeper and deeper into the prison of matter; in his search to expand man's horizons, he loses himself in the labyrinth of his own personality.

Time Enough for Love advances on two parallel levels: the past world of Lazarus's adventures, and the present one of metaphysical boredom. In the latter, Heinlein describes a "sensually polymorphous" culture in which Lazarus is a "living fossil." The exotic and erotic world of Ishtar and Galahad (the 'bed-names' of two of his descendants) is static. Age is now mainly a cosmetic problem. In direct contradiction to Michael Smith's philosophy, gender is now considered unimportant in sexual relationships: indeed, Ishtar is surprised (pleasantly) when her partner for "seven hours of ecstasy" turns out to be male. Reproduction is under perfect genetic control, and has become an 'art.' The sex change of *I Will Fear* is mentioned in passing as something utterly barbaric. Such matters are now routinely accomplished through cloning. Genetic engineering will allow Long to make his first experiments in life beyond death.

Paradoxically, however, the direction Lazarus takes is not (as we might expect) expansive, but contractive. The title of the novel presents two terms: time and love. Its grammatical logic relates them not in linear but in polar fashion: they are rhythmically dependent on each other. Lazarus has all the time he wants. We would hope to see a new center, love, expanding to fill this periphery of time, thus giving value and meaning to what otherwise is a material void. Just the opposite happens, however. As the novel progresses, Lazarus gradually draws the external world completely into himself. If this is love, it is solely of self. In turn, expansion from this center seeks to people time and space with more images of the self. As ancestor of the Howard Families, Lazarus is the seed from which this world has sprung. In the various action tales, we watch him as, step by step, he shapes it throughout history. Now he would give it a soul, a basic rhythm at its heart. What we have, instead, is Narcissus and his mirror.

Long's taste for life is restored at first by the possibility of rectifying certain errors of time. Men can be rejuvenated indefinitely, but no one can completely turn back the clock. Lazarus is offered a way to fill in an important gap. Through cloning, he can now have the sisters he never had. The twins that result are, paradoxically, both sister and daughter. The cloned cells are implanted in host mothers, Ishtar and Hamadryad, both of whom are Long's mistresses. Johann Smith, through luck, became a woman, and thus was able to bear his own child. Long does not need to do this. These children have no biological contact with women at all: the role of mother has been subverted to that of carrier. And yet these outward forms are scrupulously maintained. Love-making here is divorced from conception, and even becomes a travesty of it. These children are genetically identical with the hero; they *are* Lazarus. Nevertheless, he goes through all the forms of being father to himself. In a sense, he must, for the biological processes demand that this prolongation of self be carried and raised as a daughter. Within the recurring rhythms of life, the same individual reproduces himself endlessly.

Because everyone is related to Lazarus in some way or other, incest is a constant danger in his world. Or perhaps, in the manner of Heinlein's fortunate paradoxes, it is a blessing. Heinlein cultivates these paradoxes on both levels of narration. In one of the inserted tales, Lazarus tells of the "twins who weren't." These creatures are 'diploid complements,' products of genetic manipulation. Long rescues them from a circus freak show, and takes them into space. Again, we have a Heinlein novel in miniature. Following this active beginning, we bog down in technicalities. These healthy adolescents are ignorant of the 'facts of life,' and all in love with each other. Many pages are devoted to Lazarus's proving that these 'facts' are wrong: they can indeed marry and have offspring. In fact, he shows (with interminable statistics) that Joe is really the *best* possible mate for his sister. Wonders never cease. Even more astonishing is Lazarus's parallel love-making with his own sister-daughters. This time it is his turn to be convinced by irrefutable logic: "We are artifical constructs, and the *soi-disant* 'incest' mores of another time and utterly different circumstances don't apply to us . . . that's just an excuse to avoid something you don't want to do. Coupling with us might be masturbation, but it can't be incest, because we aren't your sisters. We aren't even your kin in any normal sense; we're you. Every gene of us comes from you." Here is an odd variation on the Pygmalion myth—the ideal woman turns out to be another form of the creator himself—and a strangely solipsistic mode of masturbation. The inspiration only appears to be another; it is really the self.

In the *da capo* episodes, Heinlein explores the ultimate form of incest—love of mother. Long journeys back in time to the place of his origin. As a mature man (he has undergone rejuvenation), he faces himself as a small boy, and sees his mother as a possible lover. Another ersatz family is formed—an ideal that can never be, but is miraculously realized in the flesh. Son and father stare at each other as mirror images. The time shift has, simultaneously, created this pair of doubles, and also the conditions which will break them apart. In their ensuing rivalry for the mother's affections, the two men fight over the source of their own life. In this scene, Heinlein perfects the art of titillation. Will Lazarus seduce his mother and conceive himself? This cannot be—Lazarus is already born, and the mother is pregnant with another: here is double protection against contamination from the future. In spite of this, however, the drama of seduction is elaborately acted out. The mother falls in love, and would have Lazarus at exactly the same spot, and in the same clothes and position that she had used that wild night years before when she had conceived him. This re-enactment, happily, is thwarted *in extremis* by none other than Lazarus himself—the little pest has sneaked a ride in his mother's car. Is Heinlein parodying his own doctrine of predestination here? We seem to be closing the circle, but at the last minute, good luck twists things, and we have a spiral. Here, as in all the other episodes, incest only appears to stifle—in stranger and stranger ways, the dynamic of the universe still carries things forward. The ultimate Heinleinian paradox is this: man can lose himself in contemplation of his own image, and yet be part of a vital ongoing dynamic.

The drama in these scenes is contrived. The reader is titillated by the possibility of disaster, only to be pulled back in time. The inserted tales are of the same sort. Here, however, it is Long himself who plays destiny. The stories both illustrate his talents for manipulation, and give him the opportunity to voice his wisdom. In the diploid twins episode, for example, Llita is made pregnant by her brother, and Lazarus deploys a fantastic array of intellectual fireworks to resolve this seemingly impossible situation. In fact, the only intrigue we have in this scene is his logical advance: step by step, we breathlessly await the result. The crisis over, another immediately arises: now the twin's own children have grown up, and want to marry each other, just like Mom and Dad. Once again Lazarus comes to the rescue. He gives a lesson: "Starting cold on the complexities of genetics with persons who don't even know elementary biology is like trying to explain multidimensional matrix algebra to someone who has to take his shoes off to count above ten." The specialist is needed to resolve situations only the specialist can dream of. Lazarus, of course, manages; the youngsters pair off, in genetically acceptable fashion.

More than ever, Heinlein seems to take a prurient delight in all these proceedings. He appears to savor the scientific lectures on the facts of life (why else dwell ad nauseam on such banalities?). Through the eyes of Lazarus, he looks tenderly on as sexual matches are made between diverse adolescents in the name of technology or family integrity. And there are always ready-made families on hand to work with. For example, the problem of incipient incest arises a second time, mirror fashion, in the pioneering episode with Lazarus and his 'ephemeral' beloved Dora. The family is isolated, and the sexual awakening of the adolescents poses a danger to the group. Needless to say, Long steps in with diversionary games (idle hands are the devil's play), until real help arrives in the form of another big family. Then the matchmaking begins in earnest.

Time Enough for Love is more than a sequel to *Methuselah's Children*; it reaches across the span of Heinlein's career to answer questions left unanswered in this earlier novel. In *Methuselah*, the Howard Families flee Earth to escape persecution: their longevity makes them the object of envy among more ephemeral mankind. They land on the Elysian world of the Little People. Eldorado, however, is not for man; the Family begins to stagnate there for lack of challenge and adversity. Lazarus rallies those settlers whose wills have not been permanently crippled, and takes them back to Earth. Once again, relativity and luck save the day. When these voyagers get home, they find that Earth scientists (inspired by the colonists' example) have discovered a means of extending life. Ironically, this new development creates a situation much like that on the Elysian planet: longevity brings widespread conservatism and fear of change. These, along with overpopulation, mark the decline of Earth's civilization. There is no promised land, apparently, for this new Moses and his chosen people: Lazarus must again head for the stars.

In *Time Enough*, the Elysian world of the earlier book has become universal. Ironically, it is man's very strivings and refusals that have ultimately brought him to this impasse once again. This time, however, the circle seems air-tight. Action and adventure are things of history and memory. Lazarus's one pleasure lies in recollecting his past. In his story of the trek over Hopeless Pass, he dwells lovingly on the long list of articles (now all obsolete) he needed for survival. His latest homestead on 'Boondock' has been designed to resemble a Pompeiian villa, complete with elaborate Roman baths. The past has now become merely a lifeless decoration, an artifice at the service of ever more sophisticated eroticism. What does a man like Lazarus have to live for in such a world?

In *Methuselah's Children*, Mary Sperling, faced with a similar dilemma, defected to the Little People. Lazarus now recalls the incident with horror: rejuvenation was not unlimited at that time, and Mary had succumbed to the onslaughts of old age. Her attraction to the Little People was understandable. In their way, they had conquered death; the individual was absorbed into a collective consciousness that transcended the limits of any one body. Any such dissolution of self in the totality of man is anathema to Lazarus. His view (strongly tainted by the Calvinist doctrine of election) is radically different: not only is the individual spirit inviolate, but so is the body itself. Indeed, the spirit is not the issue here. Mary keeps her spiritual integrity; Lazarus can still talk to a 'Mary Sperling,' and receive an answer. The odious thing is that she must share her body with every other mind; the shell has become no more than a walking zombie.

Lazarus's actions in *Time Enough for Love* constitute a protracted answer to Mary's actions. She had chosen out of fear, and had thrown away her very self. Lazarus claims to act out of 'love,' and apotheosizes the self, expanding it to embrace and absorb that collective periphery Mary and the Little People had occupied. Lazarus becomes the world, quite literally. With each new act of love, he subdues a more recalcitrant pocket of resistance, reduces another duality to that unity which is himself. His multitudinous incarnations throughout history, and his prolific family life, make him the fountainhead of mankind. Now he lives to tighten the bonds between himself and his offspring even more. These bonds are always physical: bodies cloned from his are rejoined to it through fornication. The impossible barriers of time and space are neatly elided as Lazarus carries on his affair with his mother. Michael Smith made great promises for copulation. Now, in the person of Lazarus Long, it becomes the act through which space and time are physically conquered. Mary Sperling's denial of self was hardly altruistic. Lazarus's love requires no giving at all, except to self.

Heinlein has much to say about love in this book. One statement made by Maureen comes to the heart of the matter:

"She liked herself . . . and liking yourself was the necessary first step toward loving other people." In reality, it is the all-consuming step. Lazarus's constant concern for his myriad families, his patriarchal complex, his fascination with mirror twins and doubles, his obsession with incest—all are manifestations of an all-devouring solipsism. All the women Lazarus loves are either created or recreated in an image he alone provides. The most interesting example is that of Minerva, the computer-become-woman. As Long tells the computer the story of his love for Dora Brandon, an 'ephemeral,' Minerva falls in love with him. The computer can have such human yearnings (we are told) because man has made it in his own image—the machine becomes but another face in this gallery of fictional mirrors. The only thing denied it is Eros. To feel lust, the machine must become flesh and blood. Minerva chooses this option, and abandons a timeless world for one which, in comparison, is quite ephemeral. Thus, in a reverse sense, she takes the same step Dora did when she married Lazarus centuries earlier: eternity and transcience are drawn to the center point which is Lazarus Long. The ties between Minerva and Dora run deeper still. In the course of a chance conversation, the computer asks Lazarus to describe what he would like 'her' to look like if 'she' should become a woman. The portrait he gives is that of Dora. When Minerva finally steps forth in human form, his description has been brought to life: Dora is reborn in Minerva's most unusual 'flesh.' And when these two make love, time and space are literally abolished. It is more than serendipity. In becoming 'Dora,' the machine has conformed absolutely to the wishes of Lazarus. In a sense, then, 'she' too becomes but another projection of Long's ever-present self.

Heinlein carries this theme to even greater heights. The most recalcitrant antitheses are abolished. With his cloned sisters, the lover can play both roles at once: "If we love you—and we do—and if you love us—and you do, some, in your own chinchy and cautious fashion—it's Narcissus loving himself. But this time, if you could only see it, that Narcissist love could be consummated." Lazarus's adventures with his mother destroy further barriers in time as well as space. In coupling with her, he joins himself to the very same life force which originally produced him. Heinlein stops short of having Lazarus actually father himself: the first cause must remain both inviolate and mysterious, an inimitable act of grace. But, by linking with the same force that bore him, he physically encompasses everything in between. In his greatest understatement, he says: "I'm a solipsist at heart." The full significance of this confession is revealed on the last page of the book. Lazarus seems to have met his end at last on this battlefield of the past. But the time paradox is, of course, on his side: he cannot be here when he belongs there. We learn, however, that there is another reason for his indestructibility: he belongs everywhere. He awakens to the sound of a 'Gray Voice': "You are you, playing chess with yourself, and again you have checkmated yourself."

Lazarus's initial question, "Why should man live?" is answered with a tautology: "living is." All of history, drawn to this point which is Lazarus Long, becomes one huge *carpe diem*: "Life is too long when one is not enjoying now. You recall when I was not and wished to terminate it. Your skill—and trickery, my darling—changed that and again I savor now. But perhaps I never told you that I approached even my first rejuvenation with misgiving, afraid that it would make my body young without making my spirit young again—and don't bother to tell me that 'spirit' is a null-word; I know that it is undefinable . . . but it means something to me." In spite of this declaration of faith, 'spirit' remains a 'null-word' here. Lazarus's universe consists of a first cause—that moment of grace out of which the chosen company of Howard's evolve—and an ongoing, seemingly open-ended dynamic. The only soul in this machine (we are told) is human intelligence itself, and it is shaped in the processes of natural selection, led onward by recurring strokes of good fortune. These have, by now, come to be as predictable and mechnical as Heinlein's 'evolution' itself. We expect Lazarus to be 'tricked'; we expect paradox to save the day. The world of *Time Enough* is one of endless matter, of quantity and extension. Long's spirit is not elevated, it is rejuvenated. Love does not transcend this world; on the contrary, it becomes the means of reducing all things to one point. Basically, this novel offers the same message as *Stranger*: "thou art god." When he hears the 'Gray Voice,' Lazarus thinks for a moment that it might be God; he asks to see its face, and is told: "Try a mirror." But if there is no God; there is no 'other' here either—only an all-loving Lazarus staring at himself. The only double the hero has, apparently, is the author looking back at him. Lazarus's Missouri childhood has obvious autobiographical overtones. The deification of Lazarus Long must be, without a doubt, Heinlein's consummate solipsism.

There remains, nevertheless, a 'Gray Voice,' and it is more than Lazarus simply talking to himself. Brooding over the destiny of the hero is the familiar Calvinist theology. It informs the mystery that surrounds Lazarus's origins. He was born a normal man, in a world where scientific breeding and rejuvenation techniques did not exist. Why then has he lived so long? His life is a puzzle that even the most advanced genetics of the future cannot answer. The only solution to this enigma is grace: at this arbitrary point in time and space, some power enters the biological processes of nature, and the Howard Families are born. If there is a plan, its contours lie beyond human logic and reason.

But if Lazarus is the first cause, what is the final cause, the end of this destiny? For Long, the end is death; and he, unlike Johann Smith ⟨in *I Will Fear No Evil*⟩, appears ready to meet it. However, the structural rhythms of *Time Enough* tell us quite the opposite. Lazarus assures us that he fears no evil; the entire novel is shaped around rejection of the valley of shadow. Ironically, horror of the unknown has led Heinlein to create an even more terrifying eternity this side of the tomb. The 'Gray Voice' may tell Lazarus: "There is no time, there is no space. What was, is, and ever will be." Actually, there is nothing but time and space in his universe: Lazarus lives on to twist and turn forever in these infernal circles and spirals. The hero's name is itself most significant: intended, perhaps, as ironic defiance. The name in Hebrew means 'God has helped,' and Lazarus has indeed proved that he alone is God. The name merely marks off the appalling limits of Long's universe. *I Will Fear No Evil* was a novel about raising the dead. Science may have advanced far beyond Dr. Frankenstein, but the results of Smith's experiment remain the same—he is still a monster. The Biblical Lazarus comes back to life in the flesh; the miracle of restoration is meant to prefigure the far greater one of resurrection of the spirit. Heinlein's 'Voice,' in proclaiming to his Lazarus, "You cannot die," dooms him at the same time to remain forever, on Earth or in the stars, a walking corpse.

Heinlein's latest novel leaves no doubt as to the frightful extent of his materialism. His anxiety is not (to use Baudelaire's expression) that man may never get free of this world of things and numbers; rather, that he might escape too soon, meeting in death a maker whose chosen being he may not be at all. In avoiding the chance of some unknown Hell, Heinlein's hero plunges into a Dantesque nightmare of his own making. Long before him, another man of science, Blaise Pascal, saw the danger in this position: "Physcial science will not console me for the ignorance of morality in the time of affliction." Lazarus faces problems of a 'moral' order: man's position in the universe and his inadequacies. But this brave hero is at heart a moral coward. If Lazarus quests, it is not for spiritual finality, but for material exotica: he becomes a connoisseur of more and more involuted excuses not to die. Johann Smith's 'affliction' was physical; Lazarus's claims to be metaphysical. And yet the answers that come back to console him are invariably materialistic: more stars, more time, more love that is merely onanistic sex. But can an inexhaustible string of planets console even one man's anxiety? It was Emerson who saw that travelling solves nothing: man carries his problems with him wherever he goes. Ironically, as Lazarus expands, his human limitations only expand with him.

Once again, there is a surface and an undercurrent. On the face of things, Heinlein extols Lazarus's glorious destiny, preaching serendipity and the fortunate paradox. This time, however, the facade cannot conceal the much grimmer Calvinist patterns at work. In spite of the surface optimism, Lazarus's fate is a clear sign. In seeking to pre-empt destiny, the human intellect only falls further, dividing things even more. This hero reduces divisions only by isolating himself; in his ultimate solipsism, Lazarus comes to occupy the position of Lucifer himself. Heinlein clearly did not intend this to be. In a sense, though the author himself has undergone an analagous fall. *Time Enough* is a novel about an old hero, written by an old man. In it we witness the dissolution of the materialist creed before the onslaught of age and death. The only response to mortality has become a more and more frenized cleaving to the body. This may throw new light on Heinlein lurking behind the endless sermons on freedom, there seems to be a fear that his heroes are really slaves; and behind the obsession with election, a fear that they are really damned. Heinlein is and always has been beset by Calvinist trepidations. This latest novel only reveals to what degrees the prophet of optimism and self-reliance has been, all along, a stranger in his own land.

Afterword

Robert Heinlein may write more novels. However, it is safe to assume that, whatever their form, they will be little different in purpose and design from *Time Enough for Love*. All the earlier modes and forms are summed up in its dense texture; they, along with Heinlein's hero, have grown irrevocably old. Taking this work as capstone, his vast production may be studied and assessed as a whole. In discussing Heinlein's achievement, Scholes and Rabkin, in their recent study *Science Fiction: History, Science, Vision*, put the emphasis elsewhere than on literary excellence: "Students of American culture and values will do well to consider [Heinlein], for his contradictions and confusions are very much our own—as is his energy and the optimism that lies below his 'neo-pessimistic' facade." I have tried to examine Heinlein in this perspective. In light of the persistent Romantic and Calvinist undercurrents in his work, however, this description must be qualified. If there is optimism, it is for the elect only; for the common mass of men, there was never any hope, biologically or spiritually. And even for the chosen few, there is, in his latest novels, an increasing fear of death and an unwillingness to expose this unique individuality to what may lie beyond. The dynamic existence they substitute is merely an empty whirl of molecules. What characterizes a work like *Time Enough* (and all Heinlein novels to one degree or another) is a 'neo-optimism.' Beneath the facade of energy and purpose—which Heinlein must touch up more and more with fabulous feats of science and fantastic paradoxes—lies a realm of soulless perpetual motion. Heinlein's true land is materialist America. Out of its hopes and fears, he has fashioned, perhaps without knowing it, a new circle in hell.

H. BRUCE FRANKLIN

From "New Frontiers: 1947–59"

Robert A. Heinlein: America as Science Fiction

1980, pp. 120–24

"All You Zombies—" is Heinlein's most ingenious short story, and, I think, his finest. It is also his last to date, except for three pieces scattered between 1962 and 1973. A fitting climax to Heinlein's mastery of the short-story genre, "All You Zombies—" recapitulates and integrates many of his most significant themes and leaves us with a brilliant vision into the tangled contradictions at the heart of his achievement.

Like "By His Bootstraps" (1941) and *The Door into Summer* (1957), the story weaves an intricate web of time travel in which the narrator meets himself going and coming. In his avatar as narrator and governing consciousness, he is a colonel on a recruiting mission, sent from the headquarters of the Temporal Bureau in 1993 on an involuted series of time-travel hops back into a past that can be saved only by active manipulation of crucial events by Bureau "operatives" and "agents."

In a New York City bar named "Pop's Place" back (or forward, since the story was published in 1959) in 1970, he ensnares "the Unmarried Mother," a twenty-five-year-old man who makes a living by writing short stories for confession magazines. The Unmarried Mother had begun her present life as a one-month-old baby girl in an orphanage in 1945, been seduced in 1963, and given birth to a baby girl in 1964. This had ruined her prospective career in the Women's Emergency National Corps, Hospitality & Entertainment Section (W.E.N.C.H.E.S.), the forerunners of the Women's Hospitality Order Refortifying & Encouraging Spacemen of 1973, for the cesarian operation necessary to deliver the baby had revealed a complete set of male organs, leading the doctors to change her into a man. Our narrator takes the Unmarried Mother back to 1963, where that confession writer turns out to be the man who had seduced his former self and fathered her baby girl. While these two are making love, the narrator leaps forward in 1964 to kidnap the baby and backward into 1945 to plant her on the steps of the orphanage where she is to grow up to be Jane, the Unmarried Mother. He returns to 1963 on the night of the seduction to pick up the young short-story writer, whom he has recruited as a future temporal agent: " 'That's all, son,' I announced quietly. 'I'm going to pick you up.' " The young man is badly shaken by all his new knowledge about himself, and the narrator reveals why: " 'It's a shock to have it proved to you that you can't resist seducing yourself.' "

The narrator, of course, turns out to be the final avatar of baby Jane, the Unmarried Mother, and the sneaky seducer. Thus "he" is daughter and mother, son and father. By seducing himself, he manages to have sex as a male with himself as his own mother and also as his own daughter, and as a female with himself as his own son and also his own father. This fantasy is almost as far as narcissism can go.

It is also almost as far as the bourgeois cult of the lone, self-created individual can go. The narrator is the ultimate self-made man, the logical end point of the epoch based on the belief that "*I* think, therefore, *I* am." At the end of the story, the narrator, going to his lonely bed in the year 1992, muses on the ring he wears—"The Worm Ouroboros . . . the World Snake that eats its own tail, forever without end," an emblem of his own cosmic loneliness in a solipsistic void:

> The Snake That Eats Its Own Tail, Forever and Ever . . . I *know* where *I* came from—but *where did all you zombies come from?*
>
> I felt a headache coming on, but a headache powder is one thing I do not take. I did once—and you all went away.
>
> So I crawled into bed and whistled out the light.
>
> *You* aren't there at all. There isn't anybody but me—Jane—here alone in the dark.
>
> I miss you dreadfully!

On one level, the narrator is deprived of the love of other human beings within the fictive universe of the story. Self-created, loving only other forms of himself, he loathes the very products of his own labors. On another level, the products of his own labors are indeed fictions, because the narrator is in more than one sense an author, and the "*you*" he can see only as "zombies" are we, the readers. Is it an idle coincidence that the young man he retrieves from the past is a hack short-story writer selling his works "at four cents a word," a rate Heinlein had earned as a young man? "'Business is okay,'" he says, "'I write 'em, they print 'em, I eat.'" The narrator toys with his knowledge of the Unmarried Mother's stories written from "the woman's angle." Is this a little inside joke about Heinlein's short stories narrated by a teenaged girl and published in magazines for girls? When the Unmarried Mother defiantly states what he does for a living he puts it in these terms: "'I write confession stories.'" And consciously or not, the characters created by a fiction maker are all embodiments of the author.

This particular writer has been forced, because of a physiological problem, to give up a future career in the service. But then his future self offers him the opportunity of a lifetime, in many senses. He can give up his hack-writing career and join the most important service of all time, the Temporal Bureau, whose job is nothing less than saving the world—over and over again.

Here we must begin to recognize some deep similarities and differences between *Starship Troopers* and "All You Zombies—." Just as the novel glorifies militarism, the short story exposes its hollow core. Just as the novel revels in death and destruction, the short story seeks to evade and escape the horrors of war and the history that Heinlein perceives in the future.

When the narrator reports in, with his new recruit in tow, to "the duty sergeant" in the "Sub Rockies Base" of 1985, he indicates that they too may be interchangeable: "he did what I said—thinking, no doubt, that the next time we met he might be the colonel and I the sergeant." The sergeant assures the Unmarried Mother that he will enjoy his career in the service: "'Look at me—born in 1917—still around, still young, still enjoying life.'" Nineteen seventeen, of course, is the year the United States entered World War I. The next date in the story is September 20, 1945, the day the colonel places Jane, then a month-old baby, on the steps of the orphanage. This is the month after the surrender of Japan ends World War II. World War III *would* have taken place in 1963 (four years after the publication of the story), the year in which the colonel arranges the seduction of Jane by the Unmarried Mother, except for the self-sacrificing service of our lone hero:

> It's rough, but somebody must do it and it's very hard to recruit anyone in the later years, since the Mistake of 1972. Can you think of a better source than to pick people all fouled up where they are and give them well-paid, interesting (even though dangerous) work in a necessary cause? Everybody knows now why the Fizzle War of 1963 fizzled. The bomb with New York's number on it didn't go off, a hundred other things didn't go as planned—all arranged by the likes of me.

Without the ceaseless work of the operatives of the Temporal Bureau, history would develop as it appears to Heinlein to be developing. Thus the Mistake of 1972 apparently leads to "a nasty period . . . 1974 with its strict rationing and forced labor" (like the world of "zombie recruiters" projected in the future of *The Door into Summer*).

Instead of the "freedom" of voluntary self-sacrifice and cooperation presented by *Starship Troopers*, "All You Zombies—" presents a deterministic maze that leads nowhere but to a series of holes in a dike constructed to hold back the flood of history. Instead of the intense passion that binds the Troopers of the Mobile Infantry to each other, to their mission, and to their glorious history and future, "All You Zombies—" offers us the loveless solipsism of the ultimate narcissist, the self-created individual spinning out webs of fiction in which he wanders alone, not even believing in the existence of his audience.

JOSEPH HELLER

1923–

Joseph Heller grew up in Coney Island. He was born in Brooklyn on May 1, 1923, and stayed there until the Second World War, when he served as a bomber for the U.S. Army Air Force in Corsica. He left the service a lieutenant and enrolled in New York University. Heller received his B.A. in 1948, and his M.A. from Columbia the following year. He was awarded a Fulbright Fellowship at Oxford from 1949 to 1950. He began writing stories as an undergraduate, and some of these were published in *Esquire* and *The Atlantic*. He taught English composition for two years at Pennsylvania State University, then returned to New York as an advertising copywriter. In 1955 he published the first chapter of a novel in *New World Writing;* that chapter appeared under the title "Catch-18." It was republished in 1961 as the opening of Heller's most famous work, the novel

Catch-22. *Catch-22*, which grimly satirized Heller's war experiences, provoked such controversy that his subsequent writings have all been overshadowed by it. But his anti–Viet Nam experimental drama, *We Bombed in New Haven*, demonstrated Heller's versatility. He went on to publish two more novels in a cynical vein, attacking corporate bureaucracy and the American political scene: *Something Happened* (1966) and *Good as Gold* (1979).

Heller has written and collaborated on a number of screenplays for film and television.

Catch-22 has much passion, comic and fervent, but it gasps for want of craft and sensibility. A portrait gallery, a collection of anecdotes, some of them wonderful, a parade of scenes, some of them finely assembled, a series of descriptions, yes, but the book is no novel. One can say that it is much too long, because its material—the cavortings and miseries of an American bomber squadron stationed in late World War II Italy—is repetitive and monotonous. Or one can say that it is too short because none of its many interesting characters and actions is given enough play to become a controlling interest. Its author, Joseph Heller, is like a brilliant painter who decides to throw all the ideas in his sketchbooks onto one canvas, relying on their charm and shock to compensate for the lack of design. —RICHARD G. STERN, "Bombers Away," *NYTBR*, Oct. 22, 1961, p. 5.

Now beyond a doubt, of all the books discussed here, the one which most cheats evaluation is Joseph Heller's *Catch-22*. It was the book which took me longest to finish, and I almost gave it up. Yet I think that a year from now I may remember it more vividly than *The Thin Red Line*. Because it is an original. There's no book like it anyone has read. Yet it's maddening. It reminds one of a Jackson Pollock painting eight feet high, twenty feet long. Like yard goods, one could cut it anywhere. One could take out a hundred pages anywhere from the middle of *Catch-22*, and not even the author could be certain they were gone. Yet the length and similarity of one page to another gives a curious meat-and-potatoes to the madness; building upon itself the book becomes substantial until the last fifty pages grow suddenly and surprisingly powerful, only to be marred by an ending over the last five pages which is hysterical, sentimental and wall-eyed for Hollywood.

This is the skin of the reaction. If I were a major critic, it would be a virtuoso performance to write a definitive piece on *Catch-22*. It would take ten thousand words or more. Because Heller is carrying his reader on a more consistent voyage through Hell than any American writer before him (except Burroughs who has already made the trip and now sells choice seats in the auditorium), and so the analysis of Joseph H.'s Hell would require a discussion of other varieties of inferno and whether they do more than this author's tour.

Catch-22 is a nightmare about an American bomber squadron on a made-up island off Italy. Its hero is a bombardier named Yossarian who has flown fifty missions and wants out. On this premise is tattooed the events of the novel, fifty characters, two thousand frustrations (an average of four or five to the page), and one simple motif: more frustration. Yossarian's colonel wants to impress his general and so raises the number of missions to fifty-five. When the pilots have fifty-four, the figure is lifted to sixty. They are going for eighty by the time the book has been done. On the way every character goes through a routine *on every page* which is as formal as a little peasant figure in a folk dance. Back in school, we had a joke we used to repeat. It went:

"Whom are you talking about?"
"Herbert Hoover."
"Never heard of him."
"Never heard of whom?"
"Herbert Hoover."
"Who's he?"
"He's the man you mentioned."
"Never heard of Herbert Hoover."

So it went. So goes *Catch-22*. It's the rock and roll of novels. One finds its ancestor in Basic Training. We were ordered to have clean sheets for Saturday inspection. But one week we were given no clean sheets from the Post laundry so we slept on our mattress covers, which got dirty. After inspection, the platoon was restricted to quarters. "You didn't have clean sheets," our sergeant said.

"How could we have clean sheets if the clean sheets didn't come?"

"How do I know?" said the sergeant. "The regulations say you gotta have clean sheets."

"But we can't have clean sheets if there are no clean sheets."

"That," said the sergeant, "is tough shit."

Which is what *Catch-22* should have been called. The Army is a village of colliding bureaucracies whose colliding orders cook up impossibilities. Heller takes this one good joke and exploits it into two thousand variations of the same good joke, but in the act he somehow creates a rational vision of the modern world. Yet the crisis of reason is that it can no longer comprehend the modern world. Heller demonstrates that a rational man devoted to reason must arrive at the conclusion that either the world is mad and he is the only sane man in it, or (and this is the weakness of *Catch-22*—it never explores this possibility) the sane man is not really sane because his rational propositions are without existential reason.

On page 178, there is a discussion about God.

> ". . . how much reverence can you have for a Supreme Being who finds it necessary to include such phenomena as phlegm and tooth decay in His divine system of creation. . . . Why in the world did He ever create pain?"
>
> "Pain?" Lieutenant Scheisskopf's wife pounced upon the word victoriously. "Pain is a useful symptom. Pain is a warning to us of bodily dangers."
>
> . . . "Why couldn't he have used a doorbell instead to notify us, or one of His celestial choirs?"

Right there is planted the farthest advance of the flag of reason in his cosmology. Heller does not look for any answer, but there is an answer which might go that God gave us pain for the same reason the discovery of tranquilizers was undertaken by the Devil: if we have an immortal soul some of us come close to it only through pain. A season of sickness can be preferable to a flight from disease, for it discourages the onrush of a death which begins in the center of oneself.

Give talent its due. *Catch-22* is the debut of a writer with merry gifts. Heller may yet become Gogol. But what makes one hesitate to call his first novel great or even major is that he has only grasped the inferior aspect of Hell. What is most unendurable is not the military world of total frustration so much as the midnight frustration of the half world, Baldwin's other country, where a man may have time to hear his soul, and time to go deaf, even be forced to contemplate himself as he becomes deadened before his death. (Much as Hemingway may have been.) That is when one becomes aware of the anguish, the existential *angst*, which wars enable one to forget. It is that other death—without war—where one dies by a failure of nerve, which opens the bloodiest vents of Hell. And that is a novel none of us has yet come back alive to write. —NORMAN MAILER, "Part Two: Lions," *Cannibals and Christians*, 1966, pp. 117–19

The essence of such novels as Joseph Heller's *Catch-22* and Kurt Vonnegut's *Slaughterhouse-Five, or The Children's Crusade* is that though both are ostensibly about the 1941–1945 war, in which both writers served, they are really about The Next War, and thus about a war which will be without limits and without meaning, a war that will end only when no one is alive to fight it. The theme of *Catch-22* in particular is the total craziness of war, the craziness of all those who submit to it, and the struggle to survive by the one man, Yossarian, who knows the difference between his sanity and the insanity of the system. But how can one construct fictional meaning, narrative progression, out of a system in which virtually everyone but the hero assents to madness, willingly falls into the role of the madman-who-pretends-to-be-sane? The answer is that *Catch-22* is about the hypothesis of a totally rejectable world, a difficult subject, perhaps impossible so long as the "world" is undifferentiated, confused with man's angry heart itself—but expressive of the political uselessness many Americans have felt about themselves since World War II. So Heller, who combines the virtuousness of a total pacifist with the mocking pseudo-rationality of traditional Jewish humor, has to fetch up one sight gag after another. "The dead man in Yossarian's tent was simply not easy to live with." "General Dreedle was incensed by General Peckem's recent directive requiring all tents in the Mediterranean theater of operations to be pitched along parallel lines with entrances facing back proudly toward the Washington monument." The book moves by Yossarian's asking sensible, human, logical questions about war to which the answers are madly inconsequent. Heller himself is the straight man on this lunatic stage, Yossarian the one human being in this farcically antihuman setup. The jokes are variations on the classic Yiddish story of the totally innocent recruit who pokes his head over the trench, discovers that everyone is firing away, and cries out in wonder—"One can get killed here!"

Yet the impressive emotion in *Catch-22* is not "black humor," the "totally absurd," those current articles of liberal politics, but horror. Whenever the book veers back to its primal scene, a bombardier's evisceration in a plane being smashed by flak, a scene given us directly and piteously, we recognize what makes *Catch-22* disturbing. The gags are a strained effort to articulate the imminence of *anyone's* death now by violence, and it is just this that makes it impossible to "describe war" in traditional literary ways. Despite the running gags, the telltale quality of *Catch-22* is that it doesn't move, it can't. The buried-alive feeling of being caught in a plane under attack, of seeing one's partner eviscerated, produces the total impotence of being unable to move, to escape. And this horror-cold immobililty is reproduced not in the static, self-conscious distortion of the gags but in the violence of the straight, "serious" passages:

> The forward bombardier would have liked to be a ball turret gunner. That was where he wanted to be if he had to be there at all, instead of hung out there in front like some goddamned cantilevered goldfish bowl while the goddam foul black tiers of flak were bursting and booming and billowing all around and above and below him in a climbing, cracking, staggered, banging, phantasmagorical, cosmological wickedness that jarred and tossed and shivered, clattered and pierced, and threatened to annihilate them all in one splinter of a second in one vast flash of fire.

The urgent emotion in Heller's book is thus every individual's sense today of being directly in the line of fire, of being trapped, of war not as an affair of groups in which *we* may escape, but as my and your nemesis. The psychology in *Catch-22* is that of a man being led to execution, of a gallows humor in which the rope around one's neck feels all too real (and is plainly stamped General Issue). This sense of oneself not as a soldier in a large protective group but as an isolated wretch doomed to die *unaccountably* is more and more a feature of literature about World War II.—ALFRED KAZIN, "The Decline of War," *Bright Book of Life*, 1973, pp. 84–87

If *Something Happened* turns out to be of slight interest in itself, it is of wider interest in demonstrating that fiction written under the assumptions of the post-Modernist sensibility cannot sustain itself over the length of a large novel. A Donald Barthelme can float a story or sketch under these same assumptions for eight or ten pages on sheer brilliance. But at greater length, things tend to flatten out—the literature of exhaustion itself in the end proves exhausting to read. In Joseph Heller's case there is an irony here that an ironist such as himself might perhaps appreciate. Thirteen years in transit, when the milk train of his second novel finally arrived at its destination the cargo had gone sour.—JOSEPH EPSTEIN, "Joseph Heller's Milk Train: Nothing More to Express," *WPBW*, Oct. 6, 1974, pp. 1–2

Joseph Heller's long-awaited second novel, *Something Happened*, was the best book I read this year. Not because it's perfect ("A novel is a prose narrative of some length that has something wrong with it" in Randall Jarrell's handy definition) but because it interested and bothered me most; it sticks in my mind and won't be settled. The craven Bob Slocum, circling and recircling the question of what went wrong with his life, is a comical and disturbing success. "I wish," he says, "I knew what to wish." I sometimes wished I were elsewhere—rereading *Catch-22* for instance—but this is a prodigious book.—WALTER CLEMONS, "The Best of '74," *Nwk*, Dec. 30, 1974, p. 63

Catch-22 is probably the finest novel published since World War II. *Catch-22* is the great representative document of our era, linking high and low culture, with its extraordinary double-helix form, its all-American G.I.-comedy characters, its echoes of Twain, Faulkner, Hemingway, Miller and Celine. Its only rival is Pynchon's gargantuan *Gravity's Rainbow*—much larger, more learned and intelligent, but top-heavy, and a colder, deadly work of art. (I should add that if *Catch-22* recalls Dickens in its comic fertility and complex form, then Heller's second novel, *Something Happened*, seems an impressive if tortuous attempt to rewrite Henry James—to provide a counterpart to *The Portrait of a Lady*, to chart the postwar civilian hell of narcissism.)—RICHARD LOCKE, "What I Like," *NYTBR*, May 15, 1977, p. 37

Though sometimes seen as a movement towards non-referentiality, the experimental drive of the Sixties and Seventies was indeed much concerned with responding to modern history. It has been haunted everywhere by the image of disabling war, and the note of absurdism and black humour has been crucial throughout. Thus a founding text for the Sixties was Joseph Heller's *Catch-22*, about a group of flyers in a corrupt and benighted Italy carrying out an unremitting series of wartime missions to no apparent intent. Heller's nihilist-absurdist mode was hardly new to American fiction; related images of grotesque absurdity go back to Melville (especially his *The Confidence Man*), Mark Twain, Nathanael West. But the absurdism of *Catch-22* comes from a modern senselessness and is a direct reaction to contemporary history and institutions; the 'catch-22' of the title derives from the U.S. Air Force's view that, to get out of combat duty, you must be certified insane, but, since anyone who wants to avoid combat duty must be sane, it is impossible to get out of combat duty. It is an image of the way man is bound to the system as machine; similar absurd formulae provide the book's structure and become its prime source of black humour. If such bondage is absurd, the only response can be wry anarchy, a perception that there are no just causes, only our corrupt technological system operating unideologically against an enemy system. Enemies are death-bringing forces which are either evaded or not; death is pervasive and purpose absent; the army is staffed by freaks programmed to perform senseless acts; technology, system, and death, rather than culture, morals, values, or significant politics, surround men in this world; 'There are now fifty or sixty countries fighting in this war. Surely so many countries can't *all* be worth dying for,' the book observes. The alternative to the system becomes personal survival, since 'The spirit gone, man is garbage', and all intelligence goes into the skills of evasion—a principle exemplified by the book's hero, Captain Yossarian.

Catch-22 is, like many of the new American novels, a book of systematic denaturing, by society, capitalism, the war organization, disfiguration, de-identification, dehumanization, and death, as well as by the text itself. Comedy creates both the denaturing—the system of paper laws which insists that record is prior to fact, unreality precedes reality, the human being is a function of his role and may suffer every possible humiliation and manipulation—and its alternative, the sense of the absurd which constitutes revolt. Heller's book turns on a comic proliferation of absurd characters: Milo Minderbender, the classic entrepreneur and confidence man; Major Major, who runs his office by only seeing people in it when he is out, and who earns promotion to Major Major Major; Lieutenant Scheisskopf, whose aim is to produce the perfect military parade, and who does it through attaching technological devices to the men; ex-Pfc Wintergreen, the mail clerk, who is actually running the war. In this world of dehumanization and death, insanity is contagious, and madness both a system and a means of recuperation. There is a pervasive sense of pain and tragedy: Yossarian, inspecting his experiences in the dark ruined city of Rome, finds the Eternal City eternal only in its continuous and chaotic suffering; here too the rule of catch-22 prevails, for God has created a lousy world filled with unnecessary suffering. So survival requires an equal power of absurdity, a manipulation of language. Yossarian decides to live forever or die in the attempt; people are, he believes, trying to murder him, which he can prove because 'strangers he didn't know shot at him with cannons every time he flew into the air to drop bombs on them'. A paranoid with reasons, he finally pursues the possibilities of survival through desertion; but to the end escape remains an elusive and absurd possibility.—MALCOLM BRADBURY, "Postmoderns and Others," *The Modern American Novel*, 1983, pp. 164–66

A good title isn't exactly a seal of approval, but a bad one will seriously detract from a novel's aura. Interestingly, a 'brilliant' title, like *Hangover Square* or *The Ballad of the Sad Café*, is almost a guarantor of very minor work. It appears that the classic titles give substance to an idea that, when it comes, seems to have been there all along: *Pride and Prejudice*, *Hard Times*, *A Portrait of the Artist as a Young Man*, *Lolita*. To risk a Hollywood intonation, Joseph Heller's titles vary in quality, and in some sense gauge the quality of the books they give a name to.

The catchy and catching *Catch-22* put its finger on a central modern absurdity, and the catchphrase passed straight into the language. Even more weighty and haunting, in my view, is *Something Happened*, a novel whose refrain is one of unlocatable loss ('something did happen to me somewhere that robbed me of confidence and courage'), a novel where nothing happens until the end, the fateful accident presaged by a random cry in the street: 'Something happened!' With *Good as Gold* the Heller stamp starts to smudge: Bruce Gold is the cheerfully venal hero, and all novels that pun on a character's name tend to seem, well, a bit Sharpe-ish, like *Blott on the Landscape*. It has to be said, too, that *God Knows* sounds particularly flat and perfunctory; it sounds like a God-awful movie starring some grinning octogenarian. Perhaps *God's Wounds* might have been better (for the novel is dark); and no doubt the obvious contender, *The Book of David*, was disqualified by E. L. Doctorow's *The Book of Daniel*.

At first, *God Knows* feels like God's gift to readers. All novelists in every book are looking for a voice—the right voice in the right place at the right time—and Heller, at first, seems to have found the perfect, the consummate medium. Here he gives us the deathbed memoir of King David ('I've got the best story in the Bible. Where's the competition?'), filtered without apology or embarrassment through the modern, urban, decadent and paranoid consciousness of Joseph Heller. While the comic possibilities are infinite, they are not the only possibilities on view, Heller being a comic writer whose chief interest is pain. David, at 70, fading, receding, seems the true instrument for Heller's brand of envenomed elegy. 'The older I get, the less interest I take in my children and, for that matter, in everyone and everything else.' Or, in a more familiar cadence: 'I get up with the fucking cricket.'

With a justified smirk Heller furtively maps out his fictional island. And what riches are there, what streams and melons and ores! David agrees that it was odd of God to choose the Jews—but why didn't He *give* them anything? He gave them bread without scarcity

> and that's all that He gave us, along with a complicated set of restrictive dietary laws that have not made life easier. To the *goyim* He gives bacon, sweet pork, juicy sirloin, and rare prime ribs of beef. To us He gives a pastrami. . . . Some Promised Land. The honey was there, but the milk we brought in with our goats. To people in California, God gives a magnificent coastline, a movie industry, and Beverly Hills. To us He gives sand. To Cannes He gives a plush film festival. We get the PLO.

Each joke is earned, prepared for and exquisitely timed. When the prose rolls along in its high old style, we brace ourselves for the deflations. Here is the effect, in miniature: 'And the anger of Moses was kindled and he demanded of the Lord: "God damn it, where am I supposed to get the flesh to feed them?"' The interfolding of the ancestral voice with the voice of blasphemous modernity provides the main technical business of the novel. And, for a while, Heller has it pat.

The favourite targets are lined up against the wall: sex, cruelty, Jewishness, and universal injustice (for which God is a handy embodiment). 'Like cunnilingus, tending sheep is dark and lonely work; but someone has to do it'—where the first two elements are ordinary enough, and the third is pure genius. 'Are you crazy?' David asks his new mistress Abishag. 'I'm a married man! I don't want Michal, Abigail, Ahinoam, Maccah, Haggith, Abital, or Eglah to find out about us.' David's trials are universal: 'Evil would rise up against me in my own house. So what? This was an eventuality taken for granted by every Jewish parent.' But he is also a man of his times: 'When my lovely daughter Tamar was raped by her half brother Amon, I was upset, naturally. Mainly, though, I was annoyed.' After all, as he points out later, 'She's only a girl.' I was one happy reviewer until page 70 or so (a fifth of the way through), at which point the novel curls up and dies.

Something happened. God knows what. Initially one assumes that the joke has simply run its course, and that the novel is maintained only by the inertia of its ambition. But in fact the joke, the premise, is boundlessly strong: it is the ambition that fails and retracts. Significantly, the two thematic counterweights to the main action—God and the present day—fade without trace into the vast and sandy background. 'God and I had a pretty good relationship,' muses David, 'until he killed the kid.' And indeed God was a lively presence, a nasty piece of work ('the Lord, of course, is not a shepherd, not mine or anyone else's'), a divine underwriter of the nihilism we first glimpsed in *Catch-22*. To the question 'Why me?' He jovially answers, 'Why not?' As David says, 'Go figure Him out.' David never does. Between him and his maker there is only silence, which is poignant, and Biblical; but it doesn't fill the pages.

What does fill the pages? Writing that transcends mere repetition and aspires to outright tautology. Here's an accelerated foretaste: 'lugubrious dirge,' 'pensive reverie,' 'vacillating perplexity,' 'seditious uprising,' 'domineering viragoes,' 'henpecking shrews,' 'sullen grievance and simmering fury,' 'gloating taunts and malignant insults,' 'loathed me incessantly with an animosity that was unappeasable,' 'tantrums of petulance and tempestuous discharges of irrational antipathies.' The units of spluttering cliché sometimes achieve paragraph-status. They get bigger and bigger, and, alas, say less and less.

No reader should be asked to witness an author's private grapplings with his Thesaurus. Comic effervescence having been stilled, Heller is left alone with his material—i.e., oft-told yarns from the holy book of a bronze-age nomadic tribe. He churns on through the chaff long after the inspiration has been ground to dust. The *donnée* of *God Knows* must have seemed as lithe and deft as the young David with his sling; the finished book looks more like 'the big bastard' Goliath, brawny, apoplectic, and easily toppled.

The unedifying truth is that Joseph Heller, like all the best athletes, needs a manager, a coach. It is common knowledge that he had one (his editor at Knopf) until part-way through *Good as Gold*, when Heller switched houses. The unforgiving genius still flares, and the book is worth the price of admission for the first few pages alone. In at least two senses, though, Heller's novels simply refuse to get better.—MARTIN AMIS, "Book of David," *Obs*, Nov. 18, 1984, p. 29

ROBERT BRUSTEIN

"The Logic of Survival in a Lunatic World"

New Republic, November 13, 1961, pp. 11–13

> The man who declares that survival at all costs is the end of existence is morally dead, because he's prepared to sacrifice all other values which give life its meaning.
>
> (Sidney Hook)
>
> ". . . It's better to die on one's feet than live on one's knees," Nately retorted with triumphant and lofty conviction. "I guess you've heard that saying before."
>
> "Yes, I certainly have," mused the treacherous old man, smiling again. "But I'm afraid you have it backward. It is better to *live* on one's feet than die on one's knees. *That* is the way the saying goes."
>
> *(Catch-22)*

Like all superlative works of comedy—and I am ready to argue that this is one of the most bitterly funny works in the language—*Catch-22* is based on an unconventional but utterly convincing internal logic. In the very opening pages, when we come upon a number of Air Force officers malingering in a hospital—one censoring all the modifiers out of enlisted men's letters and signing the censor's name "Washington Irving," another pursuing tedious conversations with boring Texans in order to increase his life span by making time pass slowly, still another storing horse chestnuts in his cheeks to give himself a look of innocence—it seems obvious that an inordinate number of Joseph Heller's characters are, by all conventional standards, mad. It is a triumph of Mr. Heller's skill that he is so quickly able to persuade us 1) that the most lunatic are the most logical, and 2) that it is our conventional standards which lack any logical consistency. The sanest looney of them all is the apparently harebrained central character, an American bombardier of Syrian extraction named Captain John Yossarian, who is based on a mythical Italian island (Pianosa) during World War II. For while many of his fellow officers seem indifferent to their own survival, and most of his superior officers are overtly hostile to his, Yossarian is animated solely by a desperate determination to stay alive:

> It was a vile and muddy war, and Yossarian could have lived without it—lived forever, perhaps. Only a fraction of his countrymen would give up their lives to win it, and it was not his ambition to be among them. . . . That men would die was a matter of necessity; *which* men would die, though, was a matter of circumstance, and Yossarian was willing to be the victim of anything but circumstance.

The single narrative thread in this crazy patchwork of anecdotes, episodes, and character portraits traces Yossarian's herculean efforts—through caution, cowardice, defiance, subterfuge, strategem, and subversion, through feigning illness, goofing off, and poisoning the company's food with laundry soap—to avoid being victimized by circumstance, a force represented in the book as Catch-22. For Catch-22 is the unwritten loophole in every written law which empowers the authorities to revoke your rights whenever it suits their cruel whims; it is, in short, the principle of absolute evil in a malevolent, mechanical, and incompetent world. Because of Catch-22, justice is mocked, the innocent are victimized, and Yossarian's squadron is forced to fly more than double the number of missions prescribed by Air Force code. Dogged by Catch-22, Yossarian becomes the anguished witness to the ghoulish slaughter of his crew members and the destruction of all his closest friends, until finally his fear of death becomes so intense that he refuses to wear a uniform, after his own has been besplattered with the guts of his dying gunner, and receives a medal standing naked in formation. From this point on, Yossarian's logic becomes so pure that everyone thinks him mad, for it is the logic of sheer survival, dedicated to keeping him alive in a world noisily clamoring for his annihilation.

According to this logic, Yossarian is surrounded on all sides by hostile forces: his enemies are distinguished less by their nationality than by their ability to get him killed. Thus, Yossarian feels a blind, electric rage against the Germans whenever they hurl flak at his easily penetrated plane; but he feels an equally profound hatred for those of his own countrymen who exercise an arbitrary power over his life and well-being. Heller's huge cast of characters, therefore, is dominated by a large number of comic malignities, *genus Americanum*, drawn with a grotesqueness so audacious that they somehow transcend caricature entirely and become vividly authentic. These include Colonel Cathcart, Yossarian's commanding officer, whose consuming ambition to get his picture in the *Saturday Evening Post* motivates him to volunteer his command for every dangerous command, and to initiate prayers during briefing sessions ("I don't want any of this Kingdom of God or Valley of Death stuff. That's all too negative. . . . Couldn't we pray for a tighter bomb pattern?"), an idea he abandons only when he learns enlisted men pray to the same God; General Peckem, head of Special Services, whose strategic objective is to replace General Dreedle, the wing commander, capturing every bomber group in the US Air Force ("If dropping bombs on the enemy isn't a special service, I wonder what in the world is"); Captain Black, the squadron intelligence officer, who inaugurates the Glorious Loyalty Oath Crusade in order to discomfort a rival, forcing all officers (except the rival, who is thereupon declared a Communist) to sign a new oath whenever they get their flak suits, their pay checks, or their haircuts; Lieutenant Scheisskopf, paragon of the parade ground, whose admiration for efficient formations makes him scheme to screw nickel-alloy swivels into every cadet's back for perfect ninety degree turns; and cadres of sadistic officers, club-happy MPs, and muddleheaded agents of the CID, two of whom, popping in and out of rooms like farcical private eyes, look for Washington Irving throughout the action, finally pinning the rap on the innocent chaplain.

These are Yossarian's antagonists, all of them reduced to a single exaggerated humor, and all identified by their totally mechanical attitude towards human life. Heller has a profound hatred for this kind of military mind, further anatomized in a wacky scene before the Action Board which displays his (and their) animosity in a manner both hilarious and scarifying. But Heller, at war with much larger forces than the army, has provided his book with much wider implications than a war novel. For the author (apparently sharing the Italian belief that vengeance is a dish which tastes best cold) has been nourishing his grudges for so long that they have expanded to include the post-war American world. Through the agency of grotesque comedy, Heller has found a way to confront the humbug, hypocrisy, cruelty, and sheer stupidity of our mass society—qualities which have made the few other American who care almost speechless with baffled rage—and through some miracle of prestidigitation, Pianosa has become a satirical microcosm for many of the macrocosmic idiocies of our time. Thus, the author flourishes his Juvenalian scourge at government-subsidized agriculture (and farmers, one of whom "spent every penny he didn't earn on new land to increase the amount of alfalfa he did not grow"); at the exploitation of American Indians, evicted from their oil-rich land; at smug psychiatrists; at bureaucrats and patriots; at acquisitive war widows; at high-spirited American boys; and especially, and most vindictively, at war profiteers.

This last satirical flourish, aimed at the whole mystique of corporation capitalism, is embodied in the fantastic adventures of Milo Minderbinder, the company mess officer, and a paradigm of good natured Jonsonian cupidity. Anxious to put the war on a businesslike basis, Milo has formed a syndicate designed to corner the world market on all available foodstuffs, which he then sells to army messhalls at huge profits. Heady with success (his deals have made him Mayor of every town in Sicily, Vice-Shah of Oran, Caliph of Baghdad, Imam of Damascus, and the Sheik of Araby), Milo soon expands his activities, forming a private army which he hires out to the highest bidder. The climax of Milo's career comes when he fulfills a contract with the Germans to bomb and strafe his own outfit, directing his planes from the Pianosa control tower and justifying the action with the stirring war cry: "What's good for the syndicate is good for the country." Milo has almost succeeded in his ambition to pre-empt the field of war for private enterprise when he makes a fatal mistake: he has cornered the entire Egyptian cotton market and is unable to unload it anywhere. Having failed to pass it off to his own messhall in the form of chocolate-covered cotton, Milo is finally persuaded by Yossarian to bribe the American government to take it off his hands: "If you run into trouble, just tell everybody that the security of the country requires a strong domestic Egyptian cotton speculating industry." The Minderbinder sections—in showing the basic incompatibility of idealism and economics by satirizing the patriotic cant which usually accompanies American greed—illustrate the procedure of the entire book: the ruthless ridicule of hypocrisy through a technique of farce-fantasy, beneath which the demon of satire lurks, prodding fat behinds with a red-hot pitchfork.

It should be abundantly clear, then, that *Catch-22*, despite some of the most outrageous sequences since *A Night at the Opera*, is an intensely serious work. Heller has certain technical similarities to the Marx Brothers, Max Schulman, Kingsley Amis, Al Capp, and S. J. Perelman, but his mordant intelligence, closer to that of Nathanael West, penetrates the surface of the merely funny to expose a world of ruthless self-advancement, gruesome cruelty, and flagrant disregard for human life—a world, in short, very much like our own as seen through a magnifying glass, distorted for more perfect accuracy. Considering his indifference to surface reality, it is absurd to judge Heller by standards of psychological realism (or, for that matter, by conventional artistic standards at all, since his book is as formless as any picaresque epic). He is concerned entirely with that thin boundary of the surreal, the borderline between hilarity and horror, which, much like the apparent formlessness of the unconscious, has its own special integrity and coherence. Thus, Heller will never use comedy for its own sake; each joke has a wider significance in the intricate pattern, so that laughter becomes a prologue for some grotesque revelation. This gives the reader an effect of surrealistic dislocation, intensified by a wierd, rather flat, impersonal style full of complicated reversals, swift transitions, abrupt shifts in chronological time, and manipulated identities (*e.g.* if a private named Major Major Major is promoted to Major by a faulty IBM machine, or if a malingerer, sitting out a doomed mission, is declared dead through a bureaucratic error, then this remains their permanent fate), as if all mankind was determined by a mad and merciless mechanism.

Thus, Heller often manages to heighten the macabre obscenity of total war much more effectively through its gruesome comic aspects than if he had written realistic descriptions. And thus, the most delicate pressure is enough to send us over the line from farce into phantasmagoria. In the climactic chapter, in fact, the book leaves comedy altogether and becomes an eerie nightmare of terror. Here, Yossarian, walking through the streets of Rome as though through an Inferno, observes soldiers molesting drunken women, fathers beating ragged children, policemen clubbing innocent bystanders until the whole world seems swallowed up in the maw of evil:

> The night was filled with horrors, and he thought he knew how Christ must have felt as he walked through the world, like a psychiatrist through a ward of nuts, like a victim through a prison of thieves. . . . Mobs . . . mobs of policemen. . . . Mobs with clubs were in control everywhere.

Here, as the book leaves the war behind, it is finally apparent that Heller's comedy is his artistic response to his vision of transcendent evil, as if the escape route of laughter were the only recourse from a malignant world.

It is this world, which cannot be divided into boundaries or ideologies, that Yossarian has determined to resist. And so when his fear and disgust have reached the breaking point, he simply refuses to fly another mission. Asked by a superior what would happen if everybody felt the same way, Yossarian exercises his definitive logic, and answers, "Then I'd be a damned fool to feel any other way." Having concluded a separate peace, Yossarian maintains it in the face of derision, ostracism, psychological pressure, and the threat of court martial. When he is finally permitted to go home if he will only agree to a shabby deal white-washing Colonel Cathcart, however, he finds himself impaled on two impossible alternatives. But his unique logic, helped along by the precedent of an even more logical friend, makes him conclude that desertion is the better part of valor; and so (after an inspirational sequence which is the weakest thing in the book) he takes off for neutral Sweden—the only place left in the world, outside of England, where "mobs with clubs" are not in control.

Yossarian's expedient is not very flattering to our national ideals, being defeatist, selfish, cowardly, and unheroic. On the other hand, it is one of those sublime expressions of anarchic individualism without which all national ideals are pretty hollow anyway. Since the mass State, whether totalitarian or democratic, has grown increasingly hostile to Falstaffian irresponsibility, Yossarian's anti-heroism is, in fact, a kind of inverted heroism which we would do well to ponder. For, contrary to the armchair pronouncements of patriotic ideologues, Yossarian's obsessive concern for survival makes him not only *not* morally dead, but one of the most morally vibrant figures in recent literature—and a giant of the will beside those weary, wise and wistful prodigals in contemporary novels who always accommodate sadly to American life. I believe that Jospeh Heller is one of the most extraordinary talents now among us. He has Mailer's combustible radicalism without his passion for violence and self-glorification; he has Bellow's gusto with his compulsion to affirm the unaffirmable; and he has Salinger's wit without his coquettish self-consciousness. Finding his absolutes in the freedom to *be*, in a world dominated by cruelty, carnage, inhumanity, and a rage to destroy itself, Heller has come upon a new morality based on an old ideal, the morality of refusal. Perhaps—now that Catch-22 has found its most deadly nuclear form—we have reached the point where even the logic of survival is unworkable. But at least we can still contemplate the influence of its liberating honesty on a free, rebellious spirit in this explosive, bitter, subversive, brilliant book.

KURT VONNEGUT, JR.
"Joseph Heller's Extraordinary Novel about an Ordinary Man"

New York Times Book Review, October 6, 1974, pp. 1–3

The company that made a movie out of Joseph Heller's first novel, *Catch-22*, had to assemble what became the 11th or 12th largest bomber force on the planet at the time. If somebody wants to make a movie out of his second novel, *Something Happened*, he can get most of his props at Bloomingdale's—a few beds, a few desks, some tables and chairs.

Life is a whole lot smaller and cheaper in this second book. It has shrunk to the size of a grave, almost.

Mark Twain is said to have felt that his existence was all pretty much downhill from his adventures as a Mississippi riverboat pilot. Mr. Heller's two novels, when considered in sequence, might be taken as a similar statement about an entire white, middle-class generation of American males, my generation, Mr. Heller's generation, Herman Wouk's generation, Norman Mailer's generation, Irwin Shaw's generation, Vance Bourjaily's generation, James Jones's generation, and on and on—that for them everything has been downhill since World War II, as absurd and bloody as it often was.

Both books are full of excellent jokes, but neither one is funny. Taken together, they tell a tale of pain and disappointments experienced by mediocre men of good will.

Mr. Heller is a first-rate humorist who cripples his own jokes intentionally—with the unhappiness of the characters who perceive them. He also insists on dealing with only the most hackneyed themes. After a thousand World War II airplane novels had been published and pulped, he gave us yet another one, which was gradually acknowledged as a sanely crazy masterpiece.

Now he offers us the thousand-and-first version of *The Hucksters* or *The Man in the Gray Flannel Suit.*

There is a nattily-dressed, sourly witty middle-management executive named Robert Slocum, he tells us, who lives in a nice house in Connecticut with a wife, a daughter and two sons. Slocum works in Manhattan in the communications racket. He is restless. He mourns the missed opportunities of his youth. He is itchy for raises and promotions, even though he despises his company and the jobs he does. He commits unsatisfying adulteries now and then at sales conferences in resort areas, during long lunch hours, or while pretending to work late at the office.

He is exhausted.

He dreads old age.

Mr. Heller's rewriting of this written-to-death situation took him 12 years. It comes out as a monologue by Slocum. Nobody else gets to talk, except as reported by Slocum. And Slocum's sentences are so alike in shape and texture, from the beginning to the end of the book, that I imagined a man who was making an enormous statue out of sheet metal. He was shaping it with millions of identical taps from a ball-peen hammer.

Each dent was a fact, a depressingly ordinary fact.

"My wife is a good person, really, or used to be," says Slocum near the beginning, "and sometimes I'm sorry for her. She drinks during the day and flirts, or tries to, at parties we go to in the evening, although she doesn't know how."

"I have given my daughter a car of her own," he says near the end. "Her spirits seem to be picking up."

Slocum does his deadly best to persuade us, with his tap-tap-tapping of facts, that he is compelled to be as unhappy as he is, not because of enemies or flaws in his own character, but because of the facts.

What have these tedious facts done to him? They have required that he respond to them, since he is a man of good will. And responding and responding and responding to them has left him petrified with boredom and drained of any capacity for joyfulness, now that he is deep into middle age.

Only one fact among the millions is clearly horrible. Only

one distinguishes Slocum's bad luck from that of his neighbors. His youngest child is an incurable imbecile.

Slocum is heartless about the child. "I no longer think of Derek as one of my children," he says. "Or even as mine. I try not to think of him at all. This is becoming easier, even at home when he is nearby with the rest of us, making noise with some red cradle toy or making unintelligible sounds as he endeavors to speak. By now, I don't even know his name. The children don't care for him, either."

Mr. Heller might have here, or at least somewhere in his book, used conventional, Chekhovian techniques for making us love a sometimes wicked man. He might have said that Slocum was drunk or tired after a bad day at the office when he spoke so heartlessly or that he whispered his heartlessness only to himself or to a stranger he would never see again. But Slocum is invariably sober and deliberate during his monologue, does not seem to give a damn who hears what he says. Judging from his selection of unromantic episodes and attitudes, it is his wish that we dislike him.

And we gratify that wish.

Is this book any good? Yes. It is splendidly put together and hypnotic to read. it is as clear and hard-edged as a cut diamond. Mr. Heller's concentration and patience are so evident on every page that one can only say that *Something Happened* is at all points precisely what he hoped it would be.

The book may be marketed under false pretenses, which is all right with me. I have already seen (British) sales-promotion materials which suggest that we have been ravenous for a new Heller book because we want to laugh some more. This is as good a way as any to get people to read one of the unhappiest books ever written.

Something Happened is so astonishingly pessimistic, in fact, that it can be called a daring experiment. Depictions of utter hopelessness in literature have been acceptable up to now only in small doses, in short-story form, as in Franz Kafka's "The Metamorphosis," Shirley Jackson's "The Lottery," or John D. MacDonald's "The Hangover," to name a treasured few. As far as I know, though, Joseph Heller is the first major American writer to deal with unrelieved misery at novel length. Even more rashly, he leaves his major character, Slocum, essentially unchanged at the end.

A middle-aged woman who had just finished *Something Happened* in galleys said to me the other day that she thought it was a reply to all the recent books by women about the unrewardingness of housewives' lives. And Slocum does seem to argue that he is entitled to at least as much unhappiness as any woman he knows. His wife, after all, has to adapt to only one sort of hell, the domestic torture chamber in Connecticut, in which he, too, must writhe at night and on weekends, when he isn't committing adultery. But he must also go regularly to his office, where pain is inflicted on all the nerve centers which were neglected by the tormentors at home.

(The place where Slocum works, incidentally, is unnamed, and its products and services are undescribed. But I had a friend of a friend of an acquaintance ask Mr. Heller if he minded naming Slocum's employers. Mr. Heller replied with all possible speed and openness, "Time, Incorporated." So we have a small scoop.)

Just as Mr. Heller is uninterested in tying a tin can to anything as localized as a company with a familiar name, so is he far above the complaining contests going on between men and women these days. He began this book way back in 1962, and there have been countless gut-ripping news items and confrontations since then. But Heller's man Slocum is deaf and blind to them. He receives signals from only three sources: his office, his memory and home.

And, on the basis of these signals alone, he is able to say, apparently in all seriousness: "The world just doesn't work. It's an idea whose time is gone."

This is black humor indeed—with the humor removed.

Robert Slocum was in the Air Force in Italy during World War II, by the way. He was especially happy there while demonstrating his unflagging virility to prostitutes. So it was also with John Yossarian, the hero of *Catch-22*, whose present whereabouts are unknown.

There will be a molasses-like cautiousness about accepting this book as an important one. It took more than a year for *Catch-22* to gather a band of enthusiasts. I myself was cautious about that book. I am cautious again.

The uneasiness which many people will feel about liking *Something Happened* has roots which are deep. It is no casual thing to swallow a book by Joseph Heller, for he is, whether he intends to be or not, a maker of myths. (One way to do this, surely, is to be the final and most brilliant teller of an oft-told tale.) *Catch-22* is now the dominant myth about Americans in the war against fascism. *Something Happened*, if swallowed, could become the dominant myth about the middle-class veterans who came home from that war to become heads of nuclear families. The proposed myth has it that those families were pathetically vulnerable and suffocating. It says that the heads of them commonly took jobs which were vaguely dishonorable or at least stultifying, in order to make as much money as they could for their little families, and they used that money in futile attempts to buy safety and happiness. The proposed myth says that they lost their dignity and their will to live in the process.

It says they are hideously tired now.

To accept a new myth about ourselves is to simplify our memories—and to place our stamp of approval on what might become an epitaph for our era in the shorthand of history. This, in my opinion, is why critics often condemn our most significant books and poems and plays when they first appear, while praising feebler creations. The birth of a new myth fills them with primitive dread, for myths are so effective.

Well—I have now suppressed my own dread. I have thought dispassionately about *Something Happened*, and I am now content to have it shown to future generations as a spooky sort of summary of what my generation of nebulously clever white people experienced, and what we, within the cage of those experiences, then did with our lives.

And I am counting on a backlash. I expect younger readers to love Robert Slocum—on the grounds that he couldn't possibly be as morally repellent and socially useless as he claims to be.

People a lot younger than I am may even be able to laugh at Slocum in an affectionate way, something I am unable to do. They may even see comedy in his tragic and foolish belief that he is totally responsible for the happiness or unhappiness of the members of his tiny family.

They may even see some nobility in him, as an old soldier who has been brought to emotional ruin at last by the aging process and civilian life.

As for myself: I can't crack a smile when he says, ostensibly about the positions in which he sleeps, "I have exchanged the position of the fetus for the position of the corpse." And I am so anxious for Slocum to say something good about life that I read hope into lines meant to be supremely ironical, such as when he says this: "I know at last what I want to be when I grow up. When I grow up I want to be a little boy."

What is perhaps Slocum's most memorable speech mourns not his own generation but the one after his, in the person of his sullen, teen-age daughter. "There was a cheerful baby girl in a high chair in my house once," he says, "who ate and drank with a hearty appetite and laughed a lot with spontaneous zest: she isn't here now; and there is no trace of her anywhere."

We keep reading this overly long book, even though there is no rise and fall in passion and language, because it is structured as a suspense novel. The puzzle which seduces us is this one: Which of several possible tragedies will result from so much unhappiness? The author picks a good one.

I say that this is the most memorable, and therefore the most permanent variation on a familiar theme, in that it says baldly what the other variations only implied, what the other variations tried with desperate sentimentality not to imply: That many lives, judged by the standards of the people who live them, are simply not worth living.

JOSEPH HELLER

"Martin Amis in Conversation with Joseph Heller"

New Review, November 1975, pp. 55–59

Amis: Currently you're averaging one book every decade or so. It's easy to get an image of you hanging about the place polishing three lines a day, like Virgil. And yet your prose, for all its deliberateness, doesn't sniff of the lamp. How do you write? Are you just slow, or do you get clogged?

Heller: Well, one of the problems is that I think—and write—pretty much like I talk: slow and not very coherent. I don't have an instinctive command of a literary language, I don't think with a literary language. What I have to do is use my natural form of writing—which is as conversational as writing a letter to a friend or talking to him on the telephone—and then go back and liven it up some, make it more polished and considered. Then I have to go back *again* to check that it's still spontaneous and conversational. I write maybe thirty lines a day. I have a two-hour work-stand which I can sometimes stretch to two-and-a-half if I'm in the middle of a dialogue and know how it's going to come out. But if I worked any longer than that the prose would lose what polish it has and become sloppy, imprecise and diffuse. So it's 10 to 12 in the morning, except in the final stages, when some of the tension and insecurity lifts and you can complete the last third or quarter much more rapidly. At the moment I'm working pretty briskly on a third novel, and I think I'm going to like it. I'm in the habit. I started writing it ten months ago and I have 50 typewritten pages, which is three chapters, and a handwritten version of the fourth. When I get back, in about two weeks, I will read through what I have and I think I will like it enough to go ahead with it. It will be a short book, a funny book, more in keeping with the lighter novels of Evelyn Waugh and Kingsley Amis than with the gloom and anxiety of *Something Happened*—much closer to the comedy of *Catch-22*, but without that book's pessimism and 'philosophical' underpinning. A departure.

Amis: A departure from what, exactly? In what senses, if any, are *Catch-22* and *Something Happened* the products of the same preoccupations? On the face of it, of course, they are radically dissimilar books. One is about war; it is lurching and surrealistic, full of heightened characterisation and grotesque incident. The other is about peace; it is intimate, glazed, monotone—you might even say that the point of *Something Happened* is that nothing ever happens in it. Do you think it possible to argue, though, that both novels are largely about the same thing—in short, going crazy? Yossarian, the exploited and flak-shocked hero of *Catch-22*, virtually has madness thrust upon him, whereas Bob Slocum, the shabby, furtive, lugubrious ad-exec hero of *Something Happened*, has to cope only with the more self-willed horrors of peace, and seems therefore to be creating and generating madness from within. Does this make any sense to you as a link between the books?

Heller: I would say that madness is certainly a component of both books, but it is not what they are 'about'. And, again, they look at madness quite differently—one in a stylised, literary way, the other with total realism. I think madness is present only thematically or symbolically in *Catch-22*. With the exception of Dunbar, who has after all taken a bad knock on the head, I can't recall there being anybody too close to what might be called a state of psychosis or breakdown. Yossarian, yes, on those occasions when he suffers some kind of shock and goes into hospital in a state of what I call hysterical anxiety. But he soon recovers and then comes out and does go back to combat.

Amis: I assume you're being paradoxical? Or do you say this in order to anticipate, and so pre-empt, a literal-minded reading of the book? By almost anybody's standards, everyone in *Catch-22*—*except* Yossarian—is irretrievably insane. But no doubt you'd reply that they are merely mild eccentrics reacting sanely to the insanity of war.

Heller: Yes and no. I do regard them as eccentrics, and very heightened eccentrics, but they're in that novel to achieve a less literal (and more literary) effect than that of mass-hysteria. I wanted to recruit a cast of eccentrics or 'types' who would have virtually no precursors in the tradition of realistic fiction. They would be the caricatures produced by war: Hungry Joe would be one type, and Dobbs would be another, and Orr would be another, and the Colonels would be others. Their various mental conditions were just part of realising an idea rather than producing a commentary on deracination. I regarded them as cartoon eccentrics, not real people intended to represent mental aberration and collapse. You'd have to be suffering from a compassion problem to use up much time feeling sorry for them.

Amis: In *Something Happened*, on the other hand, psychological accuracy (and particularity) is of basic structural importance—it is used to shape and present the whole argument of the book. Bob Slocum's knowing but guileless narration, with its flashbacks, blocks, traumata and repressions, is surely meant to be as revelatory of perverse and wayward mental states as the therapy sessions of Alex Portnoy. Or would you say that Slocum's neuroses are the appropriate responses to the anxieties of peace?

Heller: Bob Slocum is certainly very close to madness, and madness is a very real thing in *Something Happened*. It is written from the point of view of someone so close to madness that he no longer has the ability to control what to think about. There are passages in the book where I strongly indicate that Bob himself no longer appreciates the distinction between what is and what isn't; as narrator, Bob transcribes his own auditory hallucinations, so that parts of the dialogue are in fact imagined conversations. No, the threat of madness is vividly real for Bob, which makes the world of *Something Happened* entirely different from that of *Catch-22*. *Something Happened* is about the processes of Bob Slocum's mind, underlaid, from my point of view, by what knowledge I do have of psychology, psychiatry and psychotherapy.

Amis: Doesn't it make *you* at all nervous to subject a novel to a psychiatric schema? Psychological accuracy is after all not the same thing as literary shape. Don't you think that by your fidelity to Bob's thought processes, which are necessarily often ponderous, hectoring, irrelevant, obsessive and repetitive, you might be in danger of making the book those things too? For instance, it made the book longer than it perhaps needed to be. A lot of reviewers over here complained about the length, suggested convenient cuts, and so on. Does this bother you?

Heller: People say it's a long book. That's an accurate statement. The book is long. The same criticism was made of *Catch-22* when it came out, by the way. The initial reviews of *Catch-22* in the States were mostly very unfavourable—people said that it wasn't a novel, that it shouldn't have been published, that it was too long. Too long for some and not long enough for others. It is a long novel. As for *Something Happened*, I can justify its length the same way I can justify the whole book—by the psychological nature of Bob Slocum. Slocum is a person whose memory is fixed obsessively on three or four stages of his life; in his thoughts he keeps returning to those moments, and also longs to recapture the happier periods in between that he can't recall any more. That's not unusual in the workings of human minds—we remember our humiliations and feelings of unhappiness for a lifetime, I think.

But to answer your previous question, I wouldn't go so far as to say that I followed a psychological structure. That's not how books get written. Psychological accuracy is what you end up with if you're fortunate, not what you set out to achieve. In fact, many of the nuances of Bob's thought and speech habits, which I put in just because I thought they'd be effective, were later pointed out to me by psychologists and linguists as being of psychological significance. For instance, the only member of Slocum's family who is given a name in the book (the rest are 'my boy', 'my girl', 'my wife') is the brain-damaged younger son, who is given the rather stark name of 'Derek'. I'm told that people in Bob's state will habitually name things which they want to dissociate themselves from, and not name things which they love and want to protect. Similarly, Bob's use of infantilisms—phrases like 'I get the willies', and his habit of putting 'ha, ha' in parentheses after every one of his despairing jokes—was also later pointed out to me as being typical of Bob's condition. Satisfying though all this may be, however, I think it's hardly more than a lucky accident so far as I'm concerned. Probably I don't write novels the way other people do. I get an idea, and the only thing that attracts me about that idea is that I think it would make a good novel. The subject-matter itself doesn't attract me, though in the absence of that subject-matter I wouldn't proceed. I didn't choose war as the subject of *Catch-22* and I didn't choose whatever is the subject of *Something Happened*. I just feel very lucky to get an idea for a novel that I think I can write.

Amis: Regardless, then, of extra-literary considerations? Again several reviewers over here found themselves gratuitously disgusted by Bob's brutal and sickly ways—or ways of thought. Why write 570 pages about a monster? seemed to be a fairly well-represented view. Caroline Blackwood in the *TLS*, I remember, as well as calling the hero 'Bob' throughout her review, also called him mean, sick, chauvinistic, etc. Perhaps they felt that you identified with Bob, endorsed him as a character.

Heller: Well, readers were more sympathetic to Bob than the reviewers were—or even than I was—and this shores up my feeling that the author's conception of what he is doing is no more accurate than the reader's. Or even less so: I would believe in the collective impression of an audience being a more accurate description of a book than any critique. As it happens, I myself thought of Bob as an incredibly contemptible person for whom I had no conscious sympathy whatever when I was writing about him. I mean, the way I have him behave is *awful*. So I was surprised when handing in the early sections to my agent and my editor and a few other people, to have them react instantaneously with phrases like "poor Slocum', 'poor Bob', and to be so thoroughly moved by the unhappiness he was experiencing. That took me by surprise at first, but by now I feel sorry for him myself too. I have a better understanding of Bob now than I had when I was writing about him. He's not evil or corrupt, after all; he tries like hell to get on with his family, and his behaviour at his work is close to irreproachable. When he behaves badly he feels bad. And anyway it's not what he does so much as what he says and thinks: that's what causes the problems.

Amis: You could, mind you, extend Bob's roll-call of sins to include the most heinous of all: murder. As well as all the venial stuff—the sneaky office politics. Bob's extreme callousness about the 'idiot' Derek, his routine nights of lies and booze and sex—there comes a point in the final pages of the novel where you make it very tempting to infer that Bob has taken the life of his elder son, the member of his family he loves most, as an act of *vengeance*. Bob's boy has been run over; Bob rushes up to him in the street and sees his son's face and body covered in holes with blood pouring out of them: through some desperate protective instinct Bob picks him up and hugs him violently in his arms—and we later learn that the boy died from asphyxiation, and not from his superficial injuries. Fair enough. But by this stage you've made it clear that Bob's boy has begun to move away from Bob and that Bob bitterly resents it. Immediately before the accident you have Slocum say:

> I want my little boy back too.
> I don't want to lose him.
> I do.
> 'Something happened!'

Something has happened at last, as Bob is summoned to the scene of the accident. The incident could hardly be more cruelly ironic: but don't you think that this would have to weigh with a strictly moral reading of Bob and your attitude towards him?

Heller: It is part of it, and to be candid with you it is a part that I was not aware of consciously when I wrote it. I suppose it got in on the level of psychological understanding rather than deliberate intention. Again, it took somebody else to point it out to me. I got a letter from Bruno Bettelheim, in which he explained that Bob is about to lose the main love relationship in his life, and that the incident described in the book would be credible psychologically as Bob's wild attempt to *preserve* that relationship. I was surprised, too, to see that I had prepared for such an interpretation in the text immediately before the incident. When Bob mislays his boy on the beach he says, 'I could have killed him', and by this stage the sheer suspense of Bob's anxieties is getting too much for him to bear: 'I wish whatever's going to happen would happen already,' he keeps thinking. Yes, it's part of it.

Amis: So far as I know none of the British critics noticed the implication, though it would certainly have fuelled those of them who feared for Bob's—and your own—spiritual hygiene. However, I'd take it that you would dismiss moral objections to the book as essentially extra-literary objections.

Heller: Well, I'd be very upset if I were accused of writing an immoral book. There is a high moral content in *Catch-22* and I think an extremely high moral content in *Something Happened*. It's quite specific in *Catch-22*—I made it easy to tell the good guys from the bad guys. At the end of the book, with the war almost won, Yossarian finds that the moral of the life of action is to desert from it, and with my sanction. You might disagree with me, in that we can argue, but there is morality involved and I know what I'm doing. It's my idea of conscience and it coincides with Bob's idea of it in *Something Happened*, in which an extremely exacting, at times peremptory, conscience is at work throughout. When Slocum does something wrong he feels guilty about it. In fact, he feels guilty without knowing what he's done wrong, and feels guilty sometimes even when he's done right. I think that Bob's own retributive thought processes, as established in the body of the book, supply all the moral the book needs.

Amis: Yes—and how can you punish a reprehensible character anyway? You can either have him tritely punished or improbably converted, and who is going to believe that any more? What you do need to do, though, and I think you do this very clearly in *Something Happened*, is to establish your detachment, or disinterestedness, with regard to your narrator. But with general readers as much as critics the narratorial 'I' has a habit of becoming *you*. Like Bob, you worked for several years in an advertising agency; and, like him, you have a boy, a girl, and a long marriage. I know you started to write about Bob with feelings of contempt for him, but it's certainly possible to write a novel out of a nugget of self-contempt. Did people assume that there was a good deal of self-revelation in *Something Happened*? Is there any?

Heller: People certainly thought there was. When I handed the early sections of the novel in to my editor at Knopf he would say things like, 'Joe, this is so fucking convincing, but I *know* you don't feel this way.' That kind of reaction was so common that when a magazine wanted to take an excerpt I wouldn't let them have it; it was the chapter about Bob's wife and, read in isolation, I thought it might cause considerable embarrassment to *my* wife. In fact, the book is written in the *manner* of self-revelation: everything in it is meant to be self-revelatory, but it's not me who's being revealed. I used plenty of my own experience in it, but the mind the book is about is not my mind. And maybe I succeeded here to an extent that goes beyond the point of what might be called commercial caution, because everybody made it pretty clear what a harrowing experience it was to read the book.

Amis: Some final questions. I spoke earlier of 'the horrors of peace' in *Something Happened* being equivalent to the horrors of war in *Catch-22*. At one point Slocum says, unnervingly: 'It was after the war, I think, that the struggle really began.' How widespread is the malaise of inertia and anxiety in present-day America? At another point Slocum says, 'I've got the decline of American civilisation . . . to carry around on these poor shoulders of mine.' Is Bob bluffing? How much have he and America got in common?

Heller: In many ways they're very much alike, Bob and America. I did not intend Bob to be symbolic of, or representative of, the upper echelons of American life, though not in any obvious or over-rationalised sense. Things are simplified by war, at least they were by World War Two. It was easy for every American to know what to think and what to do after Pearl Harbour. You knew who the bad guys were and who the good guys were and you had some idea of the dangers involved. If Slocum had been in Yossarian's war, it would have been morally and emotionally very simple for him. You're either afraid or not, or only a bit afraid, or so afraid that you can't go into combat. But the struggle of what to do with yourself after the war is more complicated for somebody like Slocum—or even for somebody like Kurt Vonnegut, who reviewed the book sympathetically in the *Sunday Times*. It's the end of what other people have called the American Dream, the wastelands that await the person who succeeds. Affluence combined with leisure does seem to produce clinical neurosis in a great many Americans. I grew up in what was called the Depression mentality. College had a different function than it has for the people going there now. The idea was to go to work as quickly as you could, advance as quickly as you could, get into the professional classes and win salary raises and rapid promotions. By doing this you would be handsome and sane, your wife would be beautiful, your children would be healthy and happy. Having achieved what we were told to strive for, we find that we're middle-aged and unstable, our marriages are likely to be unsatisfactory, and our children are miserable. And then there's nowhere else to turn. Remember when Slocum says, 'I wish I knew what to wish'? That's the problem for people who have a choice of things, but no longer know what things they want to wish for.

LEONARD MICHAELS

"Bruce Gold's American Experience"

New York Times Book Review, March 11, 1979, pp. 1, 24–25

In his diary Kafka asks, "What have I in common with Jews?" Immediately he answers, "I have hardly anything in common with myself and should stand very quietly in a corner, content that I can breathe." Thus, failure to identify with his people inspires a joke about failure to identify with himself. The same failure, and the same joke extremely elaborated, describes much of Joseph Heller's third novel, *Good as Gold*.

As the title boasts, *Good as Gold* is a dazzling commodity. It is in fact another big book about Jews—literally about a Jewish professor, Bruce Gold, who has an idea for a book about the Jewish experience in America. He sells the idea to friends of his in publishing, two sleazy, conniving opportunists. One is Lieberman: a "fat, round, vulgar face" with "tiny eyes." He edits a small intellectual magazine. The other is Pomoroy, a grimly serious, intelligent editor at a "faintly disreputable" publishing house. Both see the Jewish book as potentially lucrative, but while Lieberman wants it to be sensational, containing such things as what it feels like for a Jewish man to have sexual intercourse with "gentile girls," Pomoroy wants Gold to write a book "useful to colleges and libraries." In any case, Gold's idea for the Jewish book, which occupies him through the first chapter, is never realized because he does too many other things.

He goes to family dinners and parties, he jogs, he visits his doctor, he has love affairs, he converses with friends, he travels between Washington and New York, he teaches a class at his college, he eats frequently and thinks much about food, his life, marriage, careers of famous men in government, and the novel climaxes in a nightmarish flurry of adulterous activity. Though Gold never writes his book, we finally have the book he lives, *Good as Gold*. It is indeed about Jews and a lot more, and it satisfies the requests of vulgar Lieberman and grimly serious Pomoroy, for it is both high and low in comic spirit. It contains much truth as well as gross, slapstick lunacy.

While the title speaks ironically about Bruce Gold's intention to make money on the Jewish experience, it also mocks him with paradox, suggesting in his very name problems of identity and value. How good is Gold? Is Gold good? (As for Bruce, a Gaelic name, what is a Jew doing with it?) Beyond all this doubleness, the novel has a double plot that reflects its deepest subject, alienation—being what you are not, feeling what you don't feel, thinking what you don't think, living a life that is not yours. Essentially, then, *Good as Gold* is about some American Jews, their bastardized existence, their sense of congenital inauthenticity. Kafka's agonies of personal identity are brought up to date by Heller and remade American—bold and commercial.

Virtually everything about his hero is ambivalent or inconsistent. Gold is a middle-aged Jew, bored by his professorial duties, who yearns for a glamorous job in Washington among politicians he finds contemptible. Though he is the author of books, essays, stories, poems and reviews, he knows that none of them is distinguished by moral character, personal depth, brains or talent; and, for this reason, he can be said to consider himself contemptible. Despite his deficiencies—or, as Heller suggests, because of them—he wins invitations to speak before groups of university students and businessmen. Gold is married to a decent, dumpy, obedient, all-enduring Jewish woman named Belle, who "would never fight or say anything wrong at home or do anything wrong outside," and was always "kind and practical and so good to the children and family." Of course, Gold is continually adulterous and he wants to marry a tall Gentile blonde whose character is defined by robotlike promiscuity, fast cars and horses.

Most important to the description of Gold is his oppressive family. Much of the time in the novel is spent with them, mainly at the dinner table in scenes that are delightfully theatrical and funny; they probably could be staged with little change. The family characters tend to be hilariously obnoxious, especially Gold's father—a narcissistic tyrannical fool—and Gold's older brother, a goodhearted ignoramus who infuriates Gold with displays of smug, idiotic erudition. For example:

> "It's really one of the great miracles of nature, isn't it? The way vultures, or gizzards, as they sometimes are called—"
>
> "Buzzards," growled Gold, without looking up.
>
> "What'd I say?"
>
> "Gizzards."
>
> "How strange," said Sid. "I meant buzzards, of course—how vultures are able to locate dying animals from five or ten miles away—even though all of them, from the moment they're born, are always totally blind."

There are also several doting sisters; one beloved debauched younger sister; three enervating children; and an insane stepmother who may live forever as a possession of the English language. Here Gold meets her for the first time:

> "And what," he said in his most courtly manner, "Would you like us to call you?"
>
> "I would like you treat me as my own children do," Gussie Gold replied with graciousness equal to his own. "I would like to think of you all as my very own children. Please call me Mother."
>
> "Very well, Mother," Gold agreed. "Welcome to the family."
>
> "I'm not your mother," she snapped.

Along with Lieberman, Pomoroy and other amusing, revolting Jewish friends from his youth in Coney Island, the family determines one plot of the novel that is exquisitely realistic—that is, grotesque, witty, lugubriously banal. Its Jewish characters are comically limited, but they suffer, they have pasts, they have interior lives, and they constitute the roots, trunk and branches of Gold's inescapable, basic identity. He wants, nevertheless, to escape it. Given his family and friends, it is hard to blame him for this, but only death can make it possible. At the end of the novel, when someone close to him dies, he sinks into a sort of ambiguous reconciliation with himself.

The Protestant characters in the novel, in contrast to the Jews, are essentially unproblematic and mechanical. They determine most of the other plot, which is mainly fantastic but includes an astounding vision of our leaders in Washington. Astounding because, while fantastic, it doesn't seem incorrect. Among these characters is Ralph Newsome, who went to college with Gold and now works for the President. He is the purest, least problematic Protestant in the novel. Here he tempts Gold toward Washington, the stronghold of American venality and blond power:

> "All of us want you working with us as soon as possible after the people above us decide whether they want you working here at all."
>
> "As what?" said Gold, who already knew the answer was ardently yes.
>
> "Oh, I don't know," said Ralph. "We probably could start you right in as a spokesman."
>
> "A spokesman?" Gold was abruptly doubtful. It sounded like something athletic. "What's a spokesman?"
>
> "Oh, Bruce, you must know. That's what I've been when I haven't been doing something else. A government spokesman, an unnamed source. . . . In a month or two, we can move you up."
>
> "To what?"
>
> "Well, if nothing else, to a senior official."

These temptations are offered several times, always with greater intensity, and eventually Newsome sees no reason Bruce Gold can't be Secretary of State or head of NATO. Given Heller's picture of Washington—full of lazy, unprincipled, prurient careerists—there is no reason Gold couldn't be Secretary of State. Indeed, it is one of Heller's triumphs in the novel that he makes this observation convincing and perhaps more valuable to our understanding of our Government than a library of Presidential papers. In this respect, *Good as Gold* is certainly "useful to colleges and libraries."

In contrast to Gold's ambivalent character, there is at least one figure in the novel who is absolutely who he is, a man of ultimate authenticity: Hugh Biddle Conover, an old dying Protestant of infinite wealth, father of the woman Gold wants to marry. Father and daughter, Gold imagines, can be instrumental in getting him a job in Washington, in the President's inner circle. The realistic-Jewish-plot and the fantastic-Protestant-plot, as separate from each other as Gold is from himself, come together with concentrated ferocity when Gold visits Conover's immense estate (seven acres under the roof of one house) to ask for the hand of his immensely tall, blonde daughter. Conover refers to gold with various Jewish names. He doesn't discriminate, you might say, regarding Jews:

> "How does it feel, Dr. Gold, to know you've already failed your children and probably your grandchildren as well—to realize you've already deprived these innocent descendants of yours of the chance to enter good society?"
>
> Gold echoed him with disdain. "Good society?"
>
> "Yes, Shapiro, you know what I mean. I'm in it and you're not. My family is and yours isn't. You have aspirations and regrets and feelings of inferiority and I don't. What are you doing in here with me?"

Here and elsewhere, Conover's speeches are too flatly punishing to be terribly funny. Long, detailed, precise, full of venomous hatred, they are not only impossible in reality, but the hatred seems finally to exceed the comic situation. This happens again in an extended comment Gold makes on the career of Henry Kissinger. In both cases the satirical animus is focused on loathsome qualities of Jews, but the book is essentially about Jews, especially those like Gold, who wants to escape his identity while exploiting it, particularly by making a lot of money on a big book about Jews. Heller himself is implicated, but only insofar as *Good as Gold* is about such books and the people who write them. He exploits the exploiters. He has his cake and eats it, too. Indeed, the novel self-consciously comments on itself in the title and in other places, and thus seems literally to feed on itself.

Conover's denunciation of Gold is echoed by many other people: Gold's stepmother says he has a "screw loose"; his father introduces him as "the brother of my son Sid"; his daughter tortures him in small mean ways; his doctor teases him sadistically about his decreptitude; his lover says he has middle-aged attitudes toward sex; the narrator describes him as a scheming mediocrity, a disillusioned, deeply compromised, mealy-mouthed fraud; and Gold thinks less of himself than anyone else does. He is perhaps the most exposed, humiliated hero of our day.

What distinguishes Conover from Gold's other detractors is that his comments are based on the contrast between Gold and himself, but we understand that he is finally only a noise named Conover, the product of Gold's fears and self-hate. The same is more or less true of other Protestants in the novel, including Conover's daughter, whose immense height, beauty, blondeness and blithely brainless promiscuity are so exaggerated as to guarantee her unreality and allow the treatment she receives. For example, during the visit to Conover's estate, she pleads with Gold not to use her sexually, thus suggesting what he wants—revenge against her father and sexual-social violation. The point is that, just as Conover's racism comes from the mind of Gold, so does the pleading of his daughter specify Gold's own desire to ravish and soil. Later, she tells him he can tie her up and do whatever he likes to her, as if she fancies herself the creature of his masturbatory Jewish imagination. The narrator describes Gold, in relation to her, as "rapacious and calculating," but he seems also sadistic, impotent and slimy.

Father and daughter, comic Protestants of Gold's imagination, play the same role Jews once played in the Protestant imagination. The reversal is much apparent in contemporary movies and novels, but Jewish artists can be trusted to balance attacks on Protestants with lots of anti-Semitism. For these satirists the truth of our American life lies between ugly and funny. In Lenny Bruce, Woody Allen and others, a powerful satirical convention has been established, and it is just what Heller says, ironically: good as gold. His novel comments on itself constantly, and the merciless denunciation of his scapegoat hero is the price Heller pays for his artistic conscience.

It's a little embarrassing to confess that I was not tough enough to laugh always at such vile objects as Conover, his daughter, Gold's friends and others who represent us to ourselves in a morally degenerate society. "Look too long into the abyss," says Nietzsche, "and the abyss will look into you." Anyhow, the self-conscious complexities of the novel make it inconsistently funny and sometimes tiresome.

However Protestants are conceived and treated, it is one of the themes of *Good as Gold* that Jews violate themselves in their relations with such unreal creatures of their own minds, especially when Jews yearn for tall blondes and jobs in Washington, where successful Jews are "slaves." The chief example, for Gold, is Kissinger, about whom Gold plans to write a book called *The Little Prussian*. He is so obsessed with Kissinger that, among the great variety of scenes, we find a long, detailed account of Kissinger's career, written by Gold. It is full of Yiddish name-calling and so rich in moral revulsion as to seem like a voodoo incantation intended to make the real man sicken and die. Kissinger is described by Gold, with evidence taken from newspapers, as self-demeaning, sycophantic, sanctimonious, incompetent, self-seeking, power-crazy, murderous and like a Nazi. According to Gold's father, it is possible Kissinger isn't a Jew. This is relevant to the novel's paradoxical, ironical character, because it gives the final twist to the relations between Bruce Gold, an imaginary hero, and the real living Kissinger, a non-Jewish Jew married in fact to a tall blonde. In brief: Bruce Gold yearns to escape what he is so that he can become what he isn't, which is precisely what he hates. He nearly succeeds, nearly becomes a Washington non-Jewish Jew, a rich, powerful slave with a tall blonde wife.

The way Heller plays with this psycho-physical transmogrification of his hero is remarkably impressive, and I suspect that Bruce Gold is a uniquely original hero. Has there ever been one who is the self-despising alter ego of a world-famous person? A hero who exists, in his very essence, relatively? At the core of its satirical vision, *Good as Gold* seems to have combined Einstein's theory of relativity with Kafka's agonies.

Lillian Hellman

1905–1984

Lillian Hellman was born in New Orleans on June 20, 1905. Her parents, Max and Julia Newhouse Hellman, were native Southerners. The family moved to New York City when Hellman was still a child, but she returned frequently to New Orleans and received some schooling there. She attended New York University for three years but did not graduate. Later she studied briefly at Columbia, but did not receive a degree there, either. From 1924 to 1925 she read manuscripts for the publishing house of Horace Liveright, and mixed in literary circles.

In 1925 she married the playwright Arthur Kober. Hellman had been writing fiction since her youth; in her twenties she began publishing stories, articles, and reviews. Hellman and Kober were divorced in 1932. That same year she began to study writing with the mystery writer Dashiell

Hammett. Hellman and Hammett became lovers, a relationship which continued until Hammett's death. It was he who first encouraged Hellman to write what would become her first major literary achievement, the play *The Children's Hour,* produced in 1934. *The Little Foxes* followed in 1939, continuing Hellman's theme of societal hypocrisy and corruption. She was politically left-wing, and visited the Soviet Union as an honored guest in 1945. Seven years later she was called to testify before the House Un-American Activities Committee. She denied being a Communist but refused to say if she had ever been a member of the Communist Party. She also refused to testify about the political activities of her friends. Her dealings with HUAC, described in her 1976 memoir *Scoundrel Time,* were widely applauded for their integrity.

Hellman stopped writing plays in the early 1960s, but in her last years she wrote three volumes of widely acclaimed memoirs: *An Unfinished Woman* (1969), *Pentimento* (1974), and *Scoundrel Time* (1976). She died on June 30, 1984, of a heart attack.

Personal

Lillian Hellman has long been known as a moral force, almost an institution of conscience for the rest of us—but my view is that her influence, and her help to us, derive rather from something larger: the picture she gives of a *life* force.

It is the complexity of this organism that stuns and quickens us. Energy, gifts put to work, anger, wit, potent sexuality, wild generosity, a laugh that can split your eardrums, fire in every action, drama in every anecdote, a ferocious sense of justice, personal loyalty raised to the power of passion, fantastic legs and easily turned ankles, smart clothes, a strong stomach, an affinity with the mothering sea, vanity but scorn of all conceit, love of money and gladness in parting with it, a hidden religious streak but an open hatred of piety, a yearning for compliments but a loathing for flattery, fine cookery, a smashing style in speech and manners, unflagging curiosity, fully liberated female aggressiveness when it is needed yet a whiff, now and then, of old-fashioned feminine masochism, fear however of nothing but being afraid, prankishness, flirtatious eyes, a libertine spirit, Puritanism, rebelliousness.

Rebelliousness above all. Rebelliousness is an essence of her vitality—that creative sort of dissatisfaction which shouts out, "Life ought to be better than this!" Every great artist is a rebel. The maker's search for new forms—for ways of testing the givens—is in her a fierce rebellion against what has been accepted and acclaimed and taken for granted. And a deep, deep rebellious anger against the great cheat of human existence, which is death, feeds her love of life and gives bite to her enjoyment of every minute of it. This rebelliousness, this anger, Lillian Hellman has in unusually great measure, and they are at the heart of the complex vibrancy we feel in her.

But all the attributes I have listed are only the beginnings of her variousness. She has experienced so much! She has had an abortion. She has been analyzed. She has been, and still is, an ambulatory chimney. She drinks her whiskey neat. She has been married and divorced. She has picked up vast amounts of higgledy-piggledy learning, such as how to decapitate a snapping turtle, and I understand that as soon as she completes her dissertation, said to be startlingly rich in research, she will have earned the degree of Doctor of Carnal Knowledge. This is in spite of the fact that during a long black period of American history she imposed celibacy on herself. She will admit, if pressed, that she was the sweetest-smelling baby in New Orleans. As a child she knew gangsters and whores. She has been a liberated woman ever since she played hookey from grade school and perched with her fantasies in the hidden fig tree in the yard of her aunts' boarding house. She is so liberated that she is not at all afraid of the kitchen. She can pluck and cook a goose and her spaghetti with clam sauce begs belief. She can use an embroidery hoop. She knows how to use a gun. She cares with a passion whether bedsheets are clean. She grows the most amazing roses which are widely thought to be homosexual. She speaks very loud to foreigners, believing the language barrier can be pierced with decibels. She scarfs her food with splendid animal relish, and I can tell you that she has not vomited since May 23, 1952. She must have caught several thousand fish by now, yet she still squeals like a child when she boats a strong blue. I know no living human being whom so many people consider to be their one best friend. . . .

We must come back around the circle now to the rebelliousness, the life-force anger, with which Miss Hellman does live, still growing every day. There was a year of sharp turn toward rebelliousness in her, when she was 13 or 14. By the late 1930s or early '40s, she had realized that no political party would be able to contain this quality of hers. Yet the pepper in her psyche—her touchiness, her hatred of being physically pushed even by accident, her out-of-control anger whenever she feels she has been dealt with unjustly—all have contributed in the end to her being radically political while essentially remaining outside formal politics. Radically, I mean, in the sense of "at the root." She cuts through all ideologies to their taproot: to the decency their adherents universally profess, but almost never deliver. "Since when," she has written, "do you have to agree with people to defend them from injustice?" Her response to McCarthyism was not ideological, it was, "I will not do this indecent thing. Go jump in the lake." Richard Nixon has testified under oath that her Committee for Public Justice frightened J. Edgar Hoover into discontinuing illegal wiretaps. How? By shaming.

Lillian Hellman is popular now, and needed now, because her stern code touches the national nerve at just the right moment—after Nixonism . . . before what?

Important as this is, our need for her, as I suggested at the outset, is far larger than that. In her plays, in her writings, out of memory, above all in her juicy, resonant, headlong, passionate self, she gives us glimpses of *all* the possibilities of life on this mixed-up earth. In return we can only thank her, honor her, and try to live as wholeheartedly as she does.—John Hersey, "Lillian Hellman," *NR*, Sept. 18, 1976, pp. 25–27

General

It was with *Days to Come*, or perhaps it was with *The Little Foxes*—this forgetting has its cheery side—that I began to examine the two descriptions that some critics have found so handy for me: the plays are too well-made, the plays are melodramas. By the well-made play, I think is meant the play whose effects are contrived, whose threads are knit tighter than the threads in life and so do not convince.

Obviously, I can have no argument with those whom my plays do not convince. Something does not convince you. Very well, and that is all. But if they convince you, or partly convince you, then the dislike of their being well-made makes little sense. The theatre has limitations: it is a tight, unbending, unfluid, meager form in which to write. And for these reasons, compared to the novel, it is a second-rate form. (I speak of the form, not the content.) Let us admit that. Having admitted it—a step forward, since most of us are anxious to claim the medium by which we earn a living is a fine and fancy thing—we can stop the pretentious lie that the stage is unhampered. What the author has to say is unhampered: his means of saying it are not. He may do without scenery, he may use actors not as people but as animals or clouds, and he still must *pretend* the empty stage is a garden or an arena, and he still must *pretend* that living people are animals. He has three walls of a theatre and he has begun his pretense with the always rather comic notion that the audience is the fourth wall. He must pretend and he must represent. And if there is something vaguely awry, for me, about the pretense of representation—since by the nature of the stage it can never be done away with—it is not that I wish to deny to other writers their variations of the form, but that, for me, the realistic form has interested me most.

Within this form there must be tricks—the theatre is a trick—and they are, I think, only bad when they are used trickily and stop you short. But if they are there, simple, and come to hand, they are justified. In the last act of *Watch on the Rhine*, Kurt Müller is about to leave. He wants to say good-bye to his children who are upstairs. He asks his wife to bring them down. Now it is most probable that in real life a man would go upstairs, find the children in their room, say good-bye there. But it semed to me, when this problem came up, that kind of un-well-madeness was not worth the candle. It seemed messy to ring in another set, to bring down the curtain, to interfere with a mood and a temper. The playwright, unlike the novelist, must—and here is where I think the charge of well-madeness should be made—trick up the scene. This is how he has to work. It is too bad, but it is not his fault. If he is good, and drives ahead, it will not matter much. If he is not good, the situation will worry him, and he will begin to pretend it doesn't exist and, by so pretending, fret and lengthen it.

I think the word melodrama, in our time, has come to be used in an almost illiterate manner. By definition it is a violent dramatic piece, with a happy ending. But I think we can add that it uses its violence for no purpose, to point no moral, to say nothing, in say-nothing's worse sense. (This, of course, does not mean, even by inference, that violence plus the *desire* to say something will raise the level of the work. A great many bad writers want to say something: their intention may make them fine men, but it does not make them fine writers. Winning the girl, getting the job, vanquishing the slight foe, are not enough.) But when violence is actually the needed stuff of the work and comes toward a large enough end, it has been and always will be in the good writer's field. George Moore said there was so much in *War and Peace* that Tolstoi must surely have awakened in the night frightened that he had left out a yacht race or a High Mass. There is a needed return to the correct use of the word melodrama. It is only then the critic will be able to find out whether a writer justifies his use of violence, and to scale him against those who have used it.

I do not want to talk here of *Watch on the Rhine*. Only eleven months have gone by since it was finished, and that is not time enough for me to see it clearly. Even now, of course, I know many ideas should have come clearer, many speeches cleaner, many things should have been said with more depth and understanding. I have not wanted to write here any final word on the plays. Some day, perhaps. Some day when I have greater faith that I will be the writer I now, on January 14, 1942, want to be. In any case, while there is much in all the plays that is wrong—and it did not hurt me to see it last night, as it once would have hurt me to half-see it—this much has been right: I tried. I did the best I could do at the time each play was written. Within the limitations of my own mind and nature, my own understanding, my own knowledge, it was the best I could do with what I had. If I did not hope to grow, I would not hope to live.—LILLIAN HELLMAN, "Introduction" to *Four Plays*, 1942, pp. x–xii

Lillian Hellman wrote eight original plays, four adaptations of plays or stories by others, and wrote or collaborated on more than seven screenplays. The original plays fall into two principal groups, based on Hellman's view of human action and motivation—a highly moral view, interpreting both action and the failure to act in terms of good and evil.

The first two plays became signposts, marking the directions to be taken by the later plays. *The Children's Hour* concerned active evil—here the ruin of two women by the spreading of a malicious lie. The drama pointed the way toward the three plays whose chief characters are despoilers—those who exploit or destroy others for their own purposes. Hellman's second play, *Days to Come*, was not so much about the despoilers—the evildoers themselves—as about those characters who, well-meaning or not, stand by and allow the despoilers to accomplish their destructive aims. Often these bystanders may be the victims of their own naiveté or lack of self-knowledge.

The despoiler plays are *The Little Foxes*, *Another Part of the Forest*, and *Watch on the Rhine*. Each is a tightly constructed drama, leading to a violent climax that is the result of evildoing. Most of the characters are clearly defined as evil or good, harmful or harmless. But the so-called bystander plays—*The Searching Wind*, *The Autumn Garden*, and *Toys in the Attic*—are as different from the despoilers in structure as they are in theme. The action is slower, the plot more discursive and low-keyed, moving more within the characters and the events that befall them, than through their actions. For most of these people are unable to act positively or with conviction. They let things happen and they become the passive victims of the despoilers and themselves. Despoilers and bystanders appear in some form in all the plays, but Hellman clearly differentiates between evil as a positive, rapacious force in the first group, and evil as the negative failure of good in the second. . . .

Hellman declared for realism at the beginning of her career, and left it only in a couple of adaptations, late in that career. In the introduction to her first published collection (*Four Plays*, 1942) she stated her position. Her argument in that essay is directed at the criticism that she writes "well-made plays"—plays depending upon the careful structuring of events to create suspense, or as she defines it: "the play whose effects are contrived, whose threads are knit tighter than the threads in life and so do not convince." This charge was leveled at much of her work, and her answer was always to the effect that drama as a form demands contrivance, and what does it matter if the play is contrived, as long as it *is* convincing? For the stage, says Hellman, is a

> tight, unbending, unfluid, meager form in which to write. . . . [The author] has three walls of a theatre and he has begun his pretense with the always rather comic notion that the audience is the fourth wall. He must pretend and he must represent. And if there is something vaguely awry, for me, about the pretense of representation . . . it is not that I wish to deny to other writers their variations of the form, but that, for me, the realistic form has interested me most.

As to "well-madeness," the theater itself is a trick, according to Hellman, and demands that the playwright "trick up the scene."

This statement, written in 1942, remains definitive. It was not until many years later in the memoirs, and occasionally in interviews, that Hellman spoke again about her playwriting, and about the two men who helped launch her career. Herman Shumlin, for whom she had once read scripts, became the producer of her first five plays. Dashiell Hammett taught her the need for discipline, objectivity, and constant rewriting. This was always to be hard work for Hellman, but she felt that she had an instinct for theater: that the "second-rate form" came naturally to her, while the novel form did not. The memoirs were to be her novel, but they, too, sometimes took the form of plays or screenplays—instinctively theatrical, instinctively well-made.—DORIS V. FALK, "Hellman's Dramatic Mode—'The Theater Is a Trick,'" *Lillian Hellman*, 1978, pp. 29–34

A generation of theater-goers and theater students have been conditioned to associate the name Hellman with the terms "well-made play," "melodrama," "social protest." If this cultural reflex persists, then Hellman's metaphor of fashion in the theater will continue to describe her critical reputation.

An unnecessary stumbling block to a fresh perception of Hellman is the "political" label. Although, as Jacob Adler comments, "to one assessing her as an artist, politics—particularly her political problems in the Fifties—seems almost entirely beside the point," political partisanship is not likely to subside in the foreseeable future.

The Hellman vision is nonetheless moral, not political. Robert Corrigan and John Gassner arrived independently at the same judgment: Gassner said, "Miss Hellman concerns herself generally with damnation as a state of the soul, and a case might be made out for saying that her real theme, whether she knew it or not, is 'original sin' in a modern context, which brings her closer to such contemporary Catholic writers as Mauriac than to Bernard Shaw or Karl Marx." Corrigan concluded that "she cannot be considered, as she so often is, a social writer; rather, she is interested in showing damnation as a state of the soul, a condition that cannot be reformed out of existence or dissolved by sentimentality or easy optimism."

Murray Kempton said that Hellman's behavior before the House committee was partly determined by her sense of how things would look in due course. For "in due course" substitute the "days to come" of the Old Testament, days determined by human actions today. Engagement, commitment, self-knowledge, and self-acknowledgment of responsibility are the virtues Hellman urges on her audiences and readers. If the memoirs had never been written, the moral vision is clear in play after play.

As critics of the memoirs have pointed out, Hellman's moral vision is inseparable from the ironic vision and voice. Though obviously more overt in the memoirs, the voice is there in the plays. And, "[a]s soon as an ironic voice has been used to any extent in any work of any kind," says Wayne Booth, "readers inevitably begin to take interest and pleasure in that voice—in the tasks it assigns and the qualities it provides; it thus becomes part of whatever is seen as the controlling context."

In *The Context and Craft of Drama*, James Rosenberg raises a pertinent question: "why must generic classification necessarily degenerate into a game of hierarchies? Is it not enough to perceive that there are various modes of perception . . . ?" What we should recognize is "a way of seeing, not a trick of writing."

Any final judgment must include a perception of Hellman as ironist, with a way of seeing, and seeing again. This is not to say that such an awareness will necessarily cause a reader to prefer Hellman to other major American playwrights. But it should prevent one's judging her by inapplicable criteria. To "rank" Hellman in a Williams-Miller-Odets-whoever list is, as she might put it, "a losing game." In the modern American theater Lillian Hellman is *sui generis*, and a careful reading of her plays reveals that those generally considered her best (*The Little Foxes, The Autumn Garden, Toys in the Attic*—to which list might be added *Watch on the Rhine* and *Another Part of the Forest*) are the most fully ironic (and novelistic). By the same criteria, *Pentimento*, in which Hellman most completely employs fictional techniques and a controlling ironic voice, is the superior memoir.

D. C. Muecke has described irony as "intellectual rather than musical, nearer to the mind than to the senses, reflective and self-conscious rather than lyrical and self-absorbed," having the qualities of "fine prose rather than . . . lyric poetry." Readers and audiences with no predilection for irony will perhaps prefer Arthur Miller's pathos of the common man, or perhaps Tennessee Williams' poetry of the sensitive, bruised soul. There will always be those, however, who will turn to Lillian Hellman for a view of life trenchantly expressed, often moving, frequently funny, uncomfortably accurate in its ironic vision of the fools met in the forest—and the fools *those* fools meet. In judging Lillian Hellman's work, critics might abandon the automatic genre labeling and examine her way of seeing and her appraisal of things seen, remembering that there is more than one valid way of looking at a blackbird. And a writer.—KATHERINE LEDERER, "An Ironic Vision," *Lillian Hellman*, 1979, pp. 137–39

Works

It is my belief that Lillian Hellman's *The Autumn Garden* is the most deftly constructed, the most maturely thought, the most scrupulously written play produced here in a long time; I do not think that, because I directed it, I should refrain from saying this. Moreover, since Miss Hellman is one of the most important American playwrights, I feel that criticism of her latest play should attempt to confront it on the high level of its ambition.

The Autumn Garden has the density of a big novel. If this is a fault, to complain about it is like complaining, as a folk saying puts it, that the bride is too beautiful. The play is dense because Miss Hellman has tried to construct it not along the usual lines of a cumulatively progressive single story, but as a compact tissue of life unraveled with the apparent casualness of ordinary behavior. Ten people's lives are disclosed, and what holds their interlocking stories together is the author's theme and point of view.

To make a formula of it, what Miss Hellman is saying in *The Autumn Garden* is that each of our lives constitutes a decisive act, and that when the chain of these acts reaches a certain point—around the middle years—no sudden movement of our will is likely to alter the shape and meaning of what we have made. To hope, as most of us do, that though we dream one thing and do another, it will come out all right in the end, come out satisfactorily according to some abstract conception we have fuzzily projected in our imagination, is to indulge in a lie that will finally rob us of pleasure, dignity and substance.

A play's ideology is not precisely the same thing as its content. What is significant in *The Autumn Garden* is not so much its thematic emphasis as Miss Hellman's approach, her feeling about most of us of the educated near-upper class. We are earnest, we yearn, but we are not serious, we have no clear purpose. We have no binding commitments to ourselves or to others; we are attached to nothing. We allow ourselves to be deviated because we do not know exactly where we want to go.

This is not, as Miss Hellman suggests her thought in terms of her characters, simply a matter of high moral aims. The dilettante painter of her play, an intellectual lightweight and universal flirt, is actually less damaged than the intelligent Crossman whose words are always sounder than those of the others. The painter wants little more than what he does, while Crossman satisfies himself with "understanding" everything except that he is wasting his life and that his "honesty" has no object except to hide his own futility from himself.

The people of *The Autumn Garden* are ordinary, nice people, average to their class—but in this sense they are representative of far more of us than we care to believe. Miss Hellman finds none of them bad, but in the light of their own sweet earnestness, rather silly. They are unwittingly self-condemned, even before they are socially condemned, because they are not intelligent in relation to any total human objective. They are idealists whose ideals are conventions and chimeras rather than goals. They will wither and disappear in a mist of empty sighs.

Against these people, Miss Hellman pits the half-European Sophie, a normal girl who wants only to do an honest job back in the grim environment of her native land, where things are not pretty or "good," but concrete, unromanticized, real. Miss Hellman does not make a heroine of this girl; in fact she makes her rather sharp, shrewd, decently matter-of-fact and not above taking advantage—with a certain humor and pride that some might mistake for cynicism—of the folly of the sentimentalists around her.

The Autumn Garden is lucid, witty, incisive, dramatic, unquestionably the subtlest and most probing of Miss Hellman's plays. If it has a limitation, it is a philosophic or spiritual limitation which is part of her objectivity. The author is just with her characters; she sees them with a certain smiling asperity, an astringent, almost cruel, clarity. But she is unable to reveal in their weakness that which still makes them part of what is blessed and great in life. The blunderers in Chekhov are brothers in our nobility even as in our abjectness. The characters in *The Autumn Garden* are our equals only in what we do not respect about ourselves. Miss Hellman refuses to be "metaphysical," poetic or soft. She will not embrace her people; she does not believe they deserve her (or our) love. Love is present only through the ache of its absence. Miss Hellman is a fine artist; she will be a finer one when she melts.—Harold Clurman, "Lillian Hellman's Garden," *NR*, March 26, 1951, pp. 21–22

Miss Hellman's most recent play, *The Autumn Garden* (1951), is at the same time her most ineffectual, her most baffling and her most psychoanalytic. Although Freudian interpretation can help to explain it, it cannot give the play the dynamic plot development which it lacks. *The Autumn Garden* is a muted, obscure play with the characters moving through decadence, sterility and emptiness as in Chekhov's world, but without the Russian's warmth and affection for his characters. A more appropriate comparison is perhaps with Schnitzler's autumnal play of approaching death, *The Lonely Way*.

The scene is an aristocratic Southern summer boarding house, but without any local color of the South. The assembled characters have little dynamic connection with each other, except that each is in search of some kind of meaning for his empty life: General Griggs, a retired officer, is married to a scatterbrained and flirtatious wife whom he wants to divorce; Edward Crossman, who had loved Constance but never married her, is now a cynical book publisher who remarks that, "Medical statistics show that sixty-one percent of those who improve have bought our book on Dianetics and smoke Iglewitz cigarettes." Constance brings her niece, Sophie, over from Germany and tries to get her married to Frederick Ellis, a passive-dependent youth with a dominant mother. Frederick develops an attachment instead for a Mr. Payson, and wants his mother to pay for Mr. Payson's passage to Europe with them. His homosexuality is on the unconscious level, however, and he is deeply hurt to learn Mr. Payson's true motives. Frederick's grandmother is a perceptive old lady who knows that her daughter ". . . will never want him to marry. And she will never know it."

Constance's former lover, Nick, returns to her life with his wife, Nina, and Constance would resume her love for him. But he proceeds to get sardonically drunk and tries to seduce Sophie. He passes out mumbling his love to a Julie who must have figured somewhere in his past. The next morning Nina and Nick quarrel and almost split up over his behavior; but they are tied together with unconscious bonds which will reconcile them.

The relationship of Nick and Nina is astutely depicted as that of a weak, passive-dependent man, destined always to be unfaithful and to return repentant to his wife, whose unconscious masochism requires just such a man-child. As Fred's old grandmother observes to Nick, shaking his hand off her shoulder, "You're a toucher. You constantly touch people or lean on them. Little moments of sensuality. One should have sensuality whole or not at all. Don't you find pecking at it ungratifying? There are many of you: the touchers and the leaners. All since the depression, is my theory." The grandmother's theory of the leaner or toucher suggests the psychiatric concepts of Harry Stack Sullivan.

The most sympathetic character up until now has been Sophie; but even she is doomed to betray a sour side of her nature. She would use Nick's attempted seduction as an excuse to blackmail him for $5000 with which to return to Germany. Miss Hellman seemed determined to remind us that the human personality is composed of sadistic and aggressive as well as tender and generous impulses in a subtle balance. With her back to the wall in a hostile, foreign land, Sophie uses her wits to advantage, a familiar trademark of Hellman's characters.

The resolution is as inconclusive as these lives have been. Nick and Nina are reunited and will pay Sophie her blackmail money. Griggs cannot leave his wife when she announces that she has a serious heart condition; he isn't even sure that he doesn't welcome the doctor's verdict, as it helps rationalize his own ambivalence and indecision. Disturbed as he faces the end of his unfulfilled life, he finds himself wishing to see his sister again—a regression to Oedipal infantile emotions:

> *Griggs:* I really want to see her because she looks like my mother. The last six months I've thought a lot about my mother. If I could just go back to her for a day. Crazy at my age . . .
>
> *Crossman:* I know. We all do at times. Age has nothing to do with it. It's when we're in trouble.

Constance is left alone as all of her guests go their ways in a scene of disintegration reminiscent of the end of *The Cherry Orchard*. All the moments of crisis and decision have been missed. Even Crossman, whose unfulfilled love for Constance has warped his life, does not want to marry her now; he apologizes:

> *Crossman:* Sorry I fooled you and sorry I fooled myself. And I've never liked liars—least of all those who lie to themselves.
>
> *Constance:* Never mind. Most of us lie to ourselves, darling, most of us.

The Autumn Garden is a poignantly sad play of the discovery of the lies or rationalizations by which a group of people have lived—only to learn in the autumn of life that their ego-defenses were only excuses for not doing what they could not or would not will. With profound psychoanalytic perception, Miss Hellman has laid bare the dependency of humans upon each other and upon various rationalizations. If the material somehow eludes Miss Hellman's customarily tight dramaturgy, and if she gives us no single character with whom we can fully empathize, nevertheless *The Autumn Garden* is a masterful attempt to look deep into tragic, empty lives which lacked only self-awareness.

The Autumn Garden marks a step forward in psychology for Lillian Hellman, enlarging her grasp of unconscious motivation beyond the sado-masochism which permeated the Hubbard plays. The theme of latent inversion, too, is suggested in a number of her plays. The task of bringing together in one play the complex and deeply perceived motives of *The Autumn Garden* and the superbly structured theatrical tension of *The Little Foxes* remains the task which Miss Hellman's talents give promise of fulfilling.—W. DAVID SIEVERS, "Freudian Fraternity of the Thirties," *Freud on Broadway*, 1955, pp. 287–89

The rancorous structure of interpersonal relationships in *The Children's Hour* is patterned after the structure of human association in the Venice of Shakespeare's *Merchant*. This can best be described as a victim-victimizer syndrome, the most concrete representation of which is the relationship between Antonio and Shylock. Antonio is convinced that his harsh treatment of Shylock is "just," because the Jew's interest rates are harsh. As victim, Shylock suffers from spiritual agony, feelings of persecution, and desires revenge. If he is able to consummate his wish, Shylock will become the victimizer of the man who originally victimized him. That the victim-victimizer syndrome is finally self-destructive is seen in the courtroom scene, when each victimizer in turn is reduced to the position of victim. Shylock's demand for Antonio's life is turned against him when Portia reminds the court that an alien Jew must suffer the death penalty if he plots against the life of a Venetian citizen. The Duke and Antonio destroy the vicious circle by showing mercy to Shylock.

In the first two acts of her play, Hellman develops three relationships which are characterized by the circular form and destructive content of the victim-victimizer syndrome; these pairs are; Karen Wright—Mary Tilford, Martha Dobie—Lily Mortar, and Amelia Tilford—Wright/Dobie. In *The Merchant*, a Jew who is socially inferior to a Christian is mistreated by the Christian and attempts to use the Duke—the land's highest authority—as a vehicle for his revenge. In *The Children's Hour*, an adolescent pupil who is socially inferior to an adult teacher is mistreated by the teacher and proceeds to use Lancet's most influential citizen—the powerful matron Amelia Tilford—as a vehicle for her revenge. Finally, in the much criticized third act, Hellman, like Shakespeare, posits mercy as the only solution to the moral dilemma which is created when we deal justly with each other. . . .

The two traditional criticisms of *The Children's Hour*'s last act are that Mary Tilford is the central interest of the play and so should not be missing at its conclusion; and that the final "summing up" (Hellman's words) is tedious. However, Mary Tilford is not the central interest of the play; a certain perverse structure of human relationships is. Moreover, if critics paid more attention to what Hellman is "summing up," they would find that the conclusion of the play is a structurally necessary resolution, not a tedious reiteration of previous materials. Jacob H. Adler has noted that *The Children's Hour*, like *The Wild Duck*, "ends not with . . . [a] suicide but with a brief discussion pinning down the issues as a result of the suicide."

Works as diverse as Aeschylus' *Oresteia*, Shakespeare's *Measure for Measure*, and Melville's *Billy Budd* have dealt with the dichotomy between primitive justice and mercy. Although *The Children's Hour* is certainly a less monumental work of art than any of these, it is within its limits a wholly successful moral play. Hellman suggests that adults are too often "children." While infantile revenge is matter of course in men's dealings with each other, Hellman shows a last-act discovery—Karen Wright's discovery of a more mature concept of compassion.—PHILIP M. ARMATO, "Good and Evil in Lillian Hellman's *The Children's Hour*," *ETJ*, Dec. 1973, pp. 444–47

As melodrama, *The Little Foxes* teeters between the slick and the substantial. By the slick I mean a skill in theatrical manipulations which make our responses too easy; Miss Hellman puts together a smooth succession of clichés and gimmicks to which we are vulnerable if we let slip that vigilance which is the price of freedom in the theater. By the substantial I mean a sense of reality which has some continuing power to gain assent. The slick predominates. Of the dramatic versions of "The love of money is the root of all evil" *The Little Foxes* has the most clear-cut division between bad guys (the brothers Ben and Oscar Hubbard, their sister Regina Giddens, and Oscar's son Leo) and good guys (Oscar's wife Birdie, Regina's husband Horace and her daughter Alexandra, and their black servants Addie and Cal). The Hubbards have got rich in business, and they have no scruples about getting richer; they scorn their less money-minded spouses. Their plots and counterplots, including robbing Horace and outsmarting each other, move ahead briskly, the over-all expectedness combined with entertaining unexpectedness of detail. (Surprise: Horace plans, by writing a new will, to turn their robbery of him into a punishment of his wife. Surprise: he dies (with help) before the will is written. Surprise: Regina uses her knowledge of the robbery to make her brothers toe the financial mark and cut her in for more profits than they intended. Surprise: Alexandra revolts against Regina, and brother Ben hints that he may still get the upper hand of Regina by learning a little more about Horace's death.) There are no surprises of character in the calculating Hubbards or in the nicer people, who are sensitive, musical, socially conscious, not very happy, and rather the worse for wear because of the Hubbards. There is pathos: Birdie drinks alone; Horace is at death's door because of a bad heart; Alexandra is pushed around by her scheming mother. Obviously we can do nothing but side with decent underdog Davids against tough-skinned Goliaths. Characters get new light on what others are up to, but none on themselves. Instead of the drama of divided personality we have the theater of duplicity in action; the clever deployment of single-track personalities invites numerous alternating responses rather than complex ones. The execution is strictly monopathic.

What is substantial is Miss Hellman's sense of the intensity of monetary self-seeking, of love of power, of how it works and what it leads to. She tries for the general validity that lies beyond stereotypes. Ben tells Regina that "the world is open . . . for people like you and me. . . . There are hundreds of Hubbards sitting in rooms like this throughout the country" (III). Insofar as this applies to the twentieth century or to the "new South," the realm is that of social documentation. A truth more general than historical appears in a common element in *The Little Foxes* and Jonson's *The Fox*: in both there is the foxiness of the acquisitive operating against each other—the persuasive irony of dishonor among thieves. This complexity crops up effectively in the final situation: as the Hubbards look ahead to a fatter world, they also face each other, and that means no final peace or certainty about advantages gained. This is a touch of the black comedy that we saw in Becque. But the dividedness of appeal achieved by Becque is not produced by the final confrontation of the Hubbards; they simply make us wonder which of them will be cleverer in the next round.

Death appears, almost inevitably. In *Everyman*, death was an opportunity for spiritual reassessment, and in *The Vultures*, for the predators to move in on the vulnerable; in *The Little Foxes*, death is a made opportunity: Regina assists an ailing husband out of a troubled life. The action stays on the melodramatic level: Regina is untroubled by restraining imperatives. —ROBERT BECHTOLD HEILMAN, "Dramas of Money," *The Iceman, the Arsonist and the Troubled Agent*, 1973, pp. 301–2

Lillian Hellman's *Scoundrel Time* has been more than a big seller: it has convinced the generation that has grown up since the Fifties that the author was virtually alone in refusing to name past or present Communist party members to the House Un-American Activities Committee, that the only issue in 1952 was whether you were personally a baddie instead of a hero like her great love Dashiell Hammett. Hammett went to jail for refusing to name the donors of a fund set up to support Communists, the Civil Rights Congress.

It was not only the young who adored *Scoundrel Time*: it was that great body of liberal Americans who are either inattentive to historical facts or have never known them. Studs Terkel said of Hellman, "Let it be recorded that she is merely great." The many adoring reviews of *Scoundrel Time*—most of them quoting Hellman's remark "I cannot and will not cut my conscience to fit this year's fashions"—were ignorant and simpleminded; Hellman's celebration of herself and Hammett was accepted uncritically. The book was sentimental and evasive in its portrait of Hammett. It was totally in error in stating that the documents in Whittaker Chambers' famous pumpkin that nailed Alger Hiss were of no significance. (The pumpkin contained microfilms—two of them reproductions of State Department memoranda to which Hiss had access—plus copies of cables initialed by Hiss.) Hellman obfuscated the fact that H.U.A.C. dismissed her after a little more than an hour because she took the Fifth Amendment when there was no need to: she steadfastly denied ever having been a Communist party member, so there would have been no legal force to her naming anybody. And the book featured a historical introduction by Garry Wills, formerly an extreme rightist and a proponent of war against the Communist forces of evil, who now acclaimed Hellman as the greatest woman dramatist in all American history and, with the same discrimination, proceeded to blame the cold war and McCarthyism entirely on Truman. . . .

The success of *Scoundrel Time* is due in part to Hellman's long-standing grievance against government in America. This cannot but please a generation sickened by Vietnam, Watergate, governmental snooping, taxation on every civic level. The young, unlike old leftists and ex-leftists now in their seventies, have no interest in Russia but are understandably suspicious of their own government, so overgrown, unwieldy, secretive, demanding, hideously costly. . . . Lillian Hellman has been dramatizing herself ever since she stopped writing plays. She can dramatize anything about herself and she has done herself, Dashiell Hammett, her old retainers, the many people she hates, with a Broadway skill that is a mixture of social snottiness and glib liberalism. A large audience—if it includes many people who disagree with her if they ever think about it—finds her so-called memoirs irresistible.

If you wonder how a nonfiction book can have so much dialogue and why there should be so many baddies in her innocent life, the answer is that Broadway will rewrite anything. . . .

Hellman is easy on herself and Hammett, exquisitely nasty to those with whom she disagrees. Henry Wallace didn't seem to know that Communists were running his 1948 campaign until she told him. What she does then is mark him down for being dumb; pushes him down even more for being a stingy rube in restaurants; scorns his wife for serving a ridiculous supper of one egg on shredded wheat. She then caps the performance by explaining to Wallace that the Communists running him "'don't . . . mean any harm; they're stubborn men.' 'I see,' he said, and that was that." But it isn't. *Scoundrel Time* is historically a fraud, artistically a put-up job and emotionally packed with meanness. Oh, these ancient positions and position takers! These glib morality plays about goodies and baddies in a world where millions have died, will go on dying, for not taking the correct "line"!

It cannot be said of Lillian Hellman, as was said of Henry James, that she has a mind so fine that "no idea can violate it." She is full of ideas. So, in another bad time, her book has pleased all those who think that Stalin lived in the time of Ivan the Terrible and that her taking the Fifth Amendment in 1952 gives political sanction and importance in the 1970's to her self-approval and her every dogged resentment.—ALFRED KAZIN, "The Legend of Lillian Hellman," *Esquire*, Aug. 1977, pp. 28–34

BARRETT H. CLARK
From "Lillian Hellman"

College English, December 1944, pp. 127–33

To understand one important aspect of the work of Lillian Hellman, it should be pointed out that, while she was never associated with any theater group that discussed, wrote, or produced radical propaganda plays, all but one of her works belong in the camp of the earnest thinkers—the propagandists. To say this without qualification, however, is to miss the point. Though she never wrote a play merely to entertain an audience, to win fame, or to make money, she never wrote a line without trying to say something that would help man to escape or offset the effects of ignorance and wrong thinking. In a word, she is an idealist, and a philosopher. But, if that were all, she would hardly be worth talking about: she is also an artist, a playwright whose "message" is invariably, though not always skilfully, integrated into works which hold us by those qualities of truth without which all the good ideas in the mind of man are of no avail.

The first of her plays to be seen in the theater was *The Children's Hour.* Produced and directed by Herman Shumlin (she never had any other producer or director) in November, 1934, this somber drama had a long and successful run. The theme, as the author tells us, is "good and evil." Rather, I believe, evil alone. The evil here, as in the character of Iago, is a kind of unattached and almost meaningless power. It is like a phenomenon of nature, which cannot be eradicated, hardly perhaps even dealt with. It differs from all the other evils Miss Hellman has so skilfully and meaningfully set forth in her later plays. For instance, in *The Little Foxes* and *Watch on the Rhine*, the forces set in opposition, the good against the evil, are pretty evenly matched, since in each case the evil is shown not only to be rooted in what is understood but to be something about which it is humanly possible to take a definite stand. The child Mary in *The Children's Hour* precipitates a tragedy out of her own malice, yet she is scarcely responsible; she is almost a monster, and, as such, the drama that follows is in a way accidental. True, a part of the responsibility lies with Mrs. Tilford, the child's grandmother, but her responsibility is only indirect and, to that extent, attenuated and weak.

A study in evil, yes, and an amazingly tense and artfully constructed drama, yet weakened because the emotions it precipitates remain partly sterile. . . .

It is a little puzzling that *The Children's Hour*, so effective as pure drama, but so remotely concerned with any issue likely to appeal to anyone so deeply concerned with man and his destiny, should have preceded the other four plays, every one of which is inescapably "moral" in all its implications. Miss Hellman says that she is "a moral writer, often too moral a writer." Which is another way of saying that she writes her plays in order to demonstrate what is wrong with life and how a better way of life may be found and won. . . .

There are traces in *Days to Come*, especially in the last act, of the mood that was to sound the note in the entire action of *The Little Foxes*. It is an easy progression into the first act of the latter play, which came to the stage in 1939 and enjoyed a long run. In most respects *The Little Foxes* is the most mature and satisfactory of its author's five plays. Here the artist is nearly always in command of the moralist, or shall we say that the moral backbone of the play is completely fused with the skeleton of the plot. The playwright has, as Henry James phrased it, buried her tools after making good use of them. Details of planting and preparation seem more casual, the direction of the plot is never too obvious, and the dialogue is exactly right. It possesses a rhythmical quality which is never intrusive and a surface realistic quality that makes us forget it is the work of a conscious and determined and scrupulous writer. . . .

Watch on the Rhine, first produced in 1941, was probably even more popular than *The Little Foxes*. It is by all odds the most human of all the Hellman plays, the warmest and in some ways the most understanding. For one thing it has a full-length hero, again a man who "works for other men." He is articulate in a wholly winning manner, and he goes out of his way to stress his unimportance; besides, the enemy is not capitalism, or the privileged members of society, but fascism at its melodramatic worst. Kurt, the little German who gives up his work, his wife and children, and is ready to give up his life in order to crush what threatens all we believe in, could scarcely have been anything but sympathetic.

And again I call attention to the "villain" Teck, the Romanian aristocrat who blackmails his hosts into buying him off when he discovers who Kurt is and what he is trying to do. Teck is no lay figure; he does not even represent fascism: he is no more than a pitiful little rat, himself a victim. But the author wastes no hatred upon him; she even goes out of her way to make him understandable, and she likewise endows him with some remnants of human decency. In a word, she has learned that to symbolize a situation it is not necessary to assume the manner or dramatize the gestures of contempt. The fact speaks for itself when the fact is wholly and understandably embodied in speech and action.

Certain critics have accused the author of this play and of *The Little Foxes* of being melodramatic. It is true that in both plays there are scenes which, if stripped of their significance, would indeed be pure melodrama. Take the scene in which Kurt kills Teck or, in the earlier play, that in which Regina allows her husband to die while she stands watching him. Pure melodrama, both scenes, in the hands of a writer who conceived them in vacuo, for their own sakes alone; but melodrama is melodramatic not because it is violent or striking but because it uses violence for violence' sake. Miss Hellman seems a little reluctant to use violence as she has consistently done, even apologetic, as though she were saying, "You see what happens in such situations? I didn't invent them; that's what I see." Kurt's words after he strangles Teck reflect, I feel, the playwright's own attitude.

Perhaps, I am not sure, Miss Hellman may have pondered the charge of melodrama when she came to shape the ideas and develop the characters of her latest play, *The Searching Wind*. Here, too, is violence, but a kind of violence only vaguely felt; not a necessary ingredient of that part of her story that was to be told on the stage. Among the elements that go to round out the background are some that we recognize from earlier plays, persons like Moses Taney, the wise old man who closely parallels the deceased but immanent figure of Joshua Farrelly in *Watch on the Rhine*; and Sam, the young generation who speaks for the author as Julie did in *Days to Come*, and the youngsters in *Watch on the Rhine*. The theme in *The Searching Wind* is neither so obvious nor so clearly stated as it was in *Watch on the Rhine*, because by its very nature it is hardly susceptible of perfect definition. When Moses finds himself in the midst of the *fait accompli* of Mussolini's capture of Rome, he says: "I knew most of this years ago. But I should have known before that, and I did. But I didn't know I did. All night long I've been trying to find out when I should have known." There is the heart of the problem Miss Hellman has sought to elucidate, if not to solve. Why have the men of good will and courage and intelligence allowed the destroyers of freedom and the dignity of man to get the upper hand, and how has it come about that little or nothing was attempted besides appeasement? How many of us knew what was happening, and what prevented our killing the evil before it took root and spread? An episodic play of the ordinary kind could do little but remind us of twenty years' newspaper headlines, and an episodic scene would have had to be added to point the moral. So the ever seeking playwright, not content with spinning a little fable and tacking an appendix onto it, conceived a dramatic structure which should combine a personal knot of conflicting wills with a roughly parallel knot showing how a world-wide situation was only an amplified personal drama on a large scale. Cassie, Emily, and Alex, all seeking to understand their relationships one to the other, are in the same sort of dilemma that the world faced twenty years ago and about which the enemies of fascism were unable to do anything effective until a world war resulted.

In order to resolve the personal problem, or rather to merge it into the world problem, the author has faced, and partly solved, technical difficulties far greater than she had ever before tried to handle. It would not do to stress the parallel too strongly, because, after all, the story is told in terms of surface realism, and anything like a *raisonneur* added to the story would destroy the needed illusion. We therefore watch her stalking her prey—her theme—precisely as certain minor characters, like the Negro servant and the French butler, seem to be looking for something they do not themselves understand. The underlying idea is so simple that Miss Hellman approaches it with some hesitancy, and, except for the one passage quoted, she does not return to it directly until the very end of the play. True, Emily is throughout striving to learn how Cassie feels and in what way Cassie's affair with her (Emily's) husband affects all three participants in the situation, and at one point stresses the need for getting things straight, but all she says is: "We've started it; let's finish it. . . . It's time to find out." But the author, having established on a solid dramatic basis the *personal* drama—a drama in itself complete—resists the temptation to point out that what was wrong with individuals is precisely what is wrong with nations.

When the play is nearly ended, we are in the presence of a situation not unlike those in the concluding scenes of *Days to Come* and *The Little Foxes*. Here Sam, a little like Julie and a little like Alexandra, Sam the young soldier who is heir to the mistakes of his predecessors, cries out upon his parents and grandparents, that is, upon his elders who have caused him to fight in another war and to lose a leg in the process: "I don't want any more of my father's mistakes. . . . I am ashamed of you both, and that's the truth. I don't want to be ashamed that way again. I don't like losing my leg. . . . I'm scared—but everybody's welcome to it as long as it means a little something and helps to bring us out someplace."

That *The Searching Wind* is neither so appealing nor so wholly satisfactory as *The Little Foxes* or *Watch on the Rhine*, that its means of achieving revelation are somewhat awkward, and that its implications are not entirely convincing—this is not very important: the play relies to a remarkable extent on the characterization and not on the story, on the dialogue and not on the plot; it needs no violence other than the violence precipitated by the impact of person on person, idea upon idea. Most notable, however, is the author's own attitude toward the problem she wants to set forth. She is no longer the special pleader for this or that type of reform, and she is evidently not ridden by the notion that all you have to do to win the Good Life is to eradicate the evil men and substitute the good. "I love this place," says Sam, and Sam speaks for the author, "and I don't want any more fancy fooling around with it." This place is, of course, our country, or perhaps all those countries in which our way of life is held to be the best.

Lillian Hellman has been writing plays for only a little over a decade; she has pretty well mastered the tools that every dramatist must use in order to gain the attention of the public; she is conscious of the limitations of the drama medium, and she has found out at moments how to make the best of them. She is still unwilling to use her talent except directly in the service of humanity. It is possible, I am convinced, for her to speak just as eloquently on behalf of the oppressed and the blind if she is willing to forget the immediate good to be won by this reform or that and to concentrate on the far more difficult and rewarding task of illuminating the world she knows *as she sees it*, through the power of her imagination, without insisting too much on guiding and instructing it. It is questionable whether the preacher ever did anything as effectively as the poet.

MARVIN FELHEIM

"*The Autumn Garden*: Mechanics and Dialects"

Modern Drama, September 1960, pp. 191–95

I

Probably no play of the American theater (and I am including that feeble adaptation *The Wisteria Trees*) is more completely Chekhovian than Lillian Hellman's recent and most charming original drama, *The Autumn Garden*. Although the piece was only mildly successful when presented during the 1950–1951 season on Broadway, to the discerning (and here I quote Alan Downer) it is "Miss Hellman's most original play."

The Autumn Garden is remarkable for its skill. Miss Hellman herself (in her Introduction to *Four Plays*) lists the two faults most enumerated by her critics: that her plays are "too well-made" and that they are "melodramas." These two limitations are strikingly absent from *The Autumn Garden*. As a matter of fact, the play successfully contradicts Miss Hellman's own statements about the nature of drama. In her Introduction, she states: "The theatre has limitations: it is a tight, unbending, unfluid, meager form in which to write." But *The Autumn Garden* is just the opposite kind of drama; it is loose in structure, bends easily but without break, is fluid and, far from being meager, overflows with characters and situations; indeed, so diffuse is the play that a first reading presents the same difficulties as does *The Cherry Orchard*: one must keep a finger poised to search out identities in the cast of characters.

In all of Miss Hellman's first six plays, the initial situation is presented in terms of some kind of problem, and in three of these pieces (*Days to Come*, *The Little Foxes* and *Watch on the Rhine*) the first actors the audience sees and hears are servants behaving in the traditional opening scene fashion. The Negro servants, Addie and Cal, who are on stage in the first scene of *The Little Foxes*, are there to give us a feeling of elegance and richness and a sense of power, all of which help establish the character of Regina Giddens before her delayed entrance allows her really to dominate the stage. In *The Autumn Garden*, the opening is quite different. "On stage at rise of curtain" are six of the main persons of the play. They do not direct their conversation or their actions toward any one situation, but indeed are behaving in a manner which we have come to call Chekhovian. Each is concerned with himself, his own problems. We, the audience, seem to have interrupted a series of activities which have been going on for some time: the marital problems of Rose and Benjamin Griggs; the complex emotional and financial relationships between old Mrs. Ellis, her daughter-in-law and her grandson; the grandson's involvements with a novelist friend and with his fiancée, the refugee, Sophie Tuckerman; Edward Crossman's peculiar and lonely position. Finally, there is the setting itself, "the Tuckerman house in a summer resort on the Gulf of Mexico, about one hundred miles from New Orleans." The house serves a symbolic function, just as do the houses of Madame Ranevsky in *The Cherry Orchard*, of Sorin in *The Seagull* and of the Prosorovs in *The Three Sisters*. It is the old home to which cling many memories but which has grown somewhat shabby with the passage of time; it is the autumn garden where flashes of brightness only emphasize the proximity of wintery sterility.

In both *The Children's Hour* and *The Little Foxes*, widely regarded as Miss Hellman's best plays, once the initial situation has been established, the whole movement of the plays is direct and without embellishment toward the climax. Both are "well-made" plays in the narrow sense that in neither are there any characters or any actions which to do not contribute directly to the unfolding of the central incident. Here we might consult Miss Hellman's definition; "by the well-made play," she writes, "I think is meant the play whose effects are contrived, whose threads are knit tighter than the threads in life and so do not convince." But all art is contrived and better organized than life. The trouble in *The Children's Hour* and *The Little Foxes* is that the contrivances are too obvious; they are *theatrically* convincing, but they do not have the high artistry which makes them consistent with themselves, true not to life but to dramatic art; the contrivances in these pieces render them merely realistic, good enough for exciting (even meaningful) theater, but not great art. Again, Miss Hellman's words suffice. The dramatist, she asserts, "must represent." These plays do, merely.

The Autumn Garden does all this and more. Without seeming to, in this play Miss Hellman organizes her materials in terms of artistic principles, dramatic principles (what Coleridge called "organic" principles). The realism is to the essence of human existence, not to the representation of life. There are many threads of action and of thought playing through *The Autumn Garden*. By the end of Act One, we have established the moral and artistic principle upon which the play is based: people must do the best they can; to do less is immoral. And Miss Hellman, as she hastens to admit, is "a moral writer." But the difference in *The Autumn Garden* is that the moral is within the situation and within the characters, not superimposed upon them by a skillful playwright. (This is the kind of thing David Magarshack refers to in his exciting study, *Chekhov the Dramatist*. Pointing out that "the chorus element" is "an indispensable feature of the play of indirect-action," he maintains that it is the characters themselves who perform the choral function, of moral judgment on the action. "Characters," he asserts, "assume the mantle of the chorus whenever their inner life bursts through the outer shell of their everyday appearance and overflows into a torrent of words." And when this occurs, the characters move from the world of realism into the world of art. For they are then not merely human beings but become also human symbols.) Nick Denery and Rose Griggs are both immoral and selfish people, but their immorality is a matter of degree inasmuch as all of the characters are to some extent tainted (or human). Perhaps one could say it in this way: in this play, Lillian Hellman lets her characters alone to act out their destinies, regarding them only with love and understanding; in her earlier play, she took sides; one can list the characters she admires and those whose behavior and beliefs she dislikes; in *Days to Come*, for example, she admits she even tried to balance characteristics: good against bad, well against sick, complex against simple. In *The Autumn Garden*, she does not make this kind of breakdown. The result is true complexity, both in dialectics and mechanics.

II

Mechanically, *The Autumn Garden* has Chekhovian grace. The characters all belong on the set: each has a legitimate reason for being at the Tuckerman house at this particular moment in history; each is searching for the meaning of life, and for love. Some are weak, some a little stronger, but one cannot make lists or easy judgments; this, in other words, is not melodrama; these are people, not puppets. In Act One, Rose and Benjamin Griggs, a retired general, are involved in analyzing their marriage; they have never understood one another, nor do they now; they are doomed perennials. Mrs. Ellis is an aged matriarch using her money for her own selfish pleasures and her tongue to criticize; her dependent daughter-in-law and her grandson are unhappily caught in their emotional mother-son relationship; the grandson is further involved with an unsuccessful (and evidently homosexual) novelist and finally with his fiancée, the refugee Sophie, half European and wise beyond her years; in both relationships young Frederick Ellis is an innocent; he is a good example of the consequences of "momism." Then there is Constance Tuckerman, who runs this genteel boarding house; she is a sentimentalist, living on dreams and good works, understanding neither. Into this charged atmosphere, where indeed the blooms are withering on the vines, come the Denerys, Nick and Nina, cosmopolites and sophisticates, up to their old tricks; they live on her money but they amuse each other by their little cruelties at the expense of other people. Finally, there is Ned Crossman, observer of life, lonely and drunken.

These people arrive and depart constantly. The superficial stage action consists of noise and bustle; the director is provided with inexhaustible opportunities for stage effects of the most varied sort. This movement supplies the external tension, a tension partly produced by confusion and stir, but a tension which accurately mirrors the inner states of mind and emotions of the characters.

This is a Chekhovian cast, appropriately set in the American South; they are upper middle-class people, with their roots in money and traditions, but caught in the essential tragedy, the tragedy of life. This is not Shakespearean; it is Chekhovian. It is social drama, not classical tragedy. As such, it has two necessary dialectical principles. First of all, as Miss Hellman reminds us, it is "sharp comedy. . . . The world these people [she is discussing *The Cherry Orchard*] made for themselves would have to end in a whimper." But, and here is the second significant point, even though the dramatist does foresee the end of this world, he has what Miss Hellman calls "the artist-scientist hope" for a better one. The pity and terror are present, but they are not for the single, noble (however representative) individual, the Hamlet or the Lear; the pity and the terror are spread out, they are for all. Pity and terror have been democratized and made the proper subject for prose.

The Autumn Garden is written in prose. By the very nature of the medium, the tragic intensity and, to a lesser degree, the tragic nobility of the characters and their situations are rendered less magnificent than if the play were phrased in poetry. In one sense, this is a purely mechanical problem. But prose can take on certain of the qualities of poetry, or, I should say, certain poetic devices are available to the prose writer, particularly to the dramatist. Perhaps the most significant of these is symbolism. In *Days to Come* (a play whose shortcomings Miss Hellman admits, but, as she says, "with all that is wrong, all the confusion, the jumble, the attempt to do too much, I stand on the side of *Days to Come*"), one of the characters says: "I don't like autumn anymore. The river is full of leaves and it was too cold to walk very far." This speech, as any clever sophomore could tell us, has symbolic overtones. In *The Autumn Garden*, aside from a few incidental references to roots and trees, there is no mention of a garden, but the title adds a necessary symbolic note to the whole play. Miss Hellman has used a number of such titles, particularly those which emphasize the organic, natural aspects of human existence: in both *The Searching Wind* and *Another Part of the Forest*, she has used the significant relationship between man and nature to extend the meaning of her dramas. So in *The Autumn Garden*, the symbolism inherent in the title adds a poetic dimension to the scope of the play.

In fact, this is my central point: that the kind of drama we have in *The Autumn Garden* is the only kind which makes for modern tragedy. It is not merely psychological (as in Tennessee Williams) nor sociological (as in Arthur Miller) but it is artistic (poetic) and moral—and all in the Chekhovian sense. And so Miss Hellman's movement in this direction is a movement toward seriousness. As one New York critic ironically put it, Miss Hellman is "our most promising playwright."

That Miss Hellman should have moved from the "well-made" play in the direction of Chekhov is not surprising; for a sensitive individual, this was a logical development. Further, it was natural in light of the life-long study which Miss Hellman has made of Chekhov, a devotion which culminated in her edition of *The Selected Letters of Chekhov*, published in 1955. In her various editorial notes, Miss Hellman pays tribute to Chekhov's "common sense," to his workmanship, and to his "deep social ideals"; of all his plays she thinks *The Three Sisters* is the greatest. These opinions throw some light on *The Autumn Garden*, for they support our idea of its careful design and, in particular, they give a point of reference. For the central themes of the two plays are similar: nostalgia for a no-longer existent past and the individual's frustrating search for love and the meaning of life. The central "message" of both *The Autumn Garden* and *The Three Sisters* is also the same: the inevitability of disaster in the kind of world presented. Miss Hellman has quoted this pertinent remark from one of the letters: "A reasoned life without a definite outlook is not a life, but a burden and a horror."

ALLAN LEWIS
From "The Survivors of the Depression"
American Plays and Playwrights
1965, pp. 106–9

The problem of good and evil is basic to all of Hellman's work, but in her own plays the well-intentioned are destroyed by "the little foxes," who are always around to "eat the earth." The evidence of a satiric touch, so rare in contemporary theatre, was reinforced by her dramatization later of *My Mother, My Father, and Me.* Her adaptation of Emmanuel Robles' *Montserrat* (1949) and Jean Anouilh's *The Lark* led to the charge that her talent was exhausted and she had been reduced to rewriting the works of others. *Toys in the Attic* (1960) put such fears to rest.

In *The Children's Hour* and *The Little Foxes* the forces of evil are clearly marked. Mary Tilford, the malicious brat, destroys good people in a world where evil is too prone to be accepted In Regina, all human values have been destroyed by the lust for power and money. Mary confesses, but the harm has already been done. Regina triumphs, and her only defeat is her rejection by her daughter. In *Toys in the Attic,* Cyrus Warkins, the millionaire, is the one consciously malicious character, and he never appears. People who are outwardly good, who presumably sacrifice their lives for others, are now the instruments of human suffering. Misplaced or possessive love can destroy. Julian is beat up physically and his pride broken through the actions of a spinster sister who secretly prefers to keep him close to her, and by a silly, sex-hungry wife who mistakenly fears Julian will leave her. Both loves are selfish and devastating. The innocent are the tragic victims—Karen and Horace and Anna.

Hellman's dark world of those who triumph through a calculated disregard of moral values is as grim and full of pain as in the most extreme theatre of the absurd. Her dramas differ in that they are portraits of people and not of abstract symbols. Events are causative, and the individual the product of his environment. Her one effort to dramatize immediate social forces resulted in her weakest play, *Days to Come,* an obeisance to the times, in which workers and capitalists line up in opposing ranks.

In her best plays, the cycle of New Orleans family dramas, specific historic events are left in the background, implying the conditions of modern civilization which alter human motives, and the major interest is focused on richly developed, multi-faceted characters involved with forces they dimly understand. Rarely are these protagonists heroic. Kurt in *Watch on the Rhine* is an exception. In the fervent years, his heroism stirred a willing audience. Today he is far too noble to be convincing. His cause is just, but his absolute certainty of righteousness removes him from tragic stature. Regina, her most memorable creation, is a savage, determined woman. Carrie, of *Toys in the Attic,* is quietly obsessive. Julian is a well-intentioned, none too capable young man who finds an easy way to get rich and runs foul of a husband's jealousy and his own wife's innocence. Good characters are more difficult to portray dramatically. Albertine, the wealthy southern aristocrat, and Henry, her Negro consort, are admirable in their philosophic calm and mature understanding, but are nebulous figures.

Lillian Hellman's strength lies in the dramatic power she can extract from the realistic form. *The Little Foxes,* like *Ghosts,* is almost flawless in economy and structure, realization of character, and pertinence of dialogue. Characters generate events and in turn are influenced by them. *Toys in the Attic* has a weak first act with too much preparation for what follows, but its final resolution is explosive. Hellman's mastery of technique has led to the accusation that her plays are too contrived, too adroitly arranged by the author. Such charges are valid, but it is a pleasure to watch the work of a skilled craftsman. All writers rearrange life and impose their own will on the chaos of reality. The test in the realistic theatre is whether the characters appear to be self-propelled, as they do in *The Little Foxes,* a masterpiece of the Ibsen-influenced theatre. *Toys in the Attic* shows bits of the machinery, perhaps because family plays of psychological insight have become too familiar, but is so artfully contrived that it becomes compelling drama. Hellman does not use her skill to exhibit technical prowess, but to expose the extent to which greed and avarice have corrupted the human soul. She strives for a Chekhovian complex of frustrated and unhappy people, but her use of violence and sexuality brings her closer to Tennessee Williams. At the end of the second act, Anna, the older sister, tells Carrie that her need for Julian is incestuous. Carrie has asked for the truth, which is what she least wants to hear: "When you love, truly love, you take your chances on being hated by speaking out the truth." Anna replies, "All right. I'll take my chance and tell you that you want to sleep with him and always have."

Hellman's bitter complaint is that greed and avarice have eroded love, and that the cause is a social system in which human relations are a product for sale. She is a moralist, and her major weakness, by her own confession, is the obvious addition of the moral, either by an all too obvious explanatory speech or through an arranged resolution that borders on the melodramatic. *The Children's Hour* could have ended with Martha's suicide. The visit of the grandmother, which follows, and the hammering away by Karen that she has come to relieve her conscience are superfluous and aesthetically disturbing. Kurt's final speech in *Watch on the Rhine* about the need to kill if necessary, to destroy Hitlerism, has already been implicitly stated in what went before. *Toys in the Attic* avoids this weakness, and as Julian moans that he "will have to start all over again," we know that he will forever be cared for by his sisters.

Most writers who master the well-made play can ill afford to experiment in other directions. Failure on Broadway is too catastrophic. Odets never varied. Hellman took a chance in *My Mother, My Father, and Me,* and though the piece was not a financial success, it indicated a surprising gift for humor. The play is a travesty of American middle-class life, with abundant laughter, absurd situations, and high comedy, and is expressionist in form. It was probably poorly received because of its failure to concentrate on a few targets, for it lashes out bitterly on all fronts, bordering at times on the petulant and vindictive without reason. Hellman deserted her psychological introspection to concentrate on comic-strip stereotypes in a wild extravaganza of the Jewish family plagued by wealth and removed from dedication to any vital issue. The dominant mother, the complaining and submissive father, the crazy grandmother who is more sane than the rest, the bohemian son, are all here. The scenes shift from the family home to an old folks' asylum, to an Indian reservation to which the young Berney escapes to find American roots. He will spend the rest of his life making silver bracelets and selling blankets to middle-class tourists. He informs the audience that his father

> is back in the shoe business, and seems to be doing
> all right with what he calls an 'Honor' shoe, a shoe to
> be buried in, a shoe in honor of the dead

and that his mother was wild when he left and sent him a postcard saying:

> The eye that mocks the father and does not obey the mother, the ravens shall pick it out, and the young eagles shall eat it.

He giggles and adds, "There are plenty of eagles and ravens here, but nothing's happened." "Nothing's happened" distinguishes the comfortable sixties from the Depression era. Most writers of the thirties had something to say, but didn't say it too well. Most writers of today have little to say and say it extremely well.

Hellman's alert sensitivity is able to find varying means to express her major theme. Her problem is her loss of certainty. Her attacks have become negative and as impotent as Rona in *My Mother, My Father, and Me*. When she was stimulated by the social upheaval of the thirties she wrote a powerful drama in human terms, *The Little Foxes*, in which an entire society in decay is revealed. It ranks with Gorky's *Yegor Bulitchev* and Henry Becque's *Les Corbeaux*.

JAMES EATMAN

From "The Image of American Destiny: *The Little Foxes*"

Players Magazine, December–January 1973, pp. 71–73

The Little Foxes is strikingly related to traditional accounts of the history of the period: its central action is a microcosmic version of a society in transition from agrarianism to industrialization. . . .

Since the process of establishing a cotton mill is a mainspring for the plot of *The Little Foxes*, the play treats a socioeconomic strategy critical to the times. The milieu of the play becomes especially convincing through Hellman's depiction of a broad range of social impulses accompanying the early industrialization of the South.[1] Regina represents the aspiration of upward social mobility, in planning to establish herself in wealthy Chicago society. Ben and Oscar represent the entrepreneurs who could pursue their private business interests in the name of Southern economic growth. Mr. Marshall typifies the Northern capitalists who, by 1900, were increasingly attracted to investment in burgeoning Southern industry. Birdie represents the disintegration of the old aristocracy, in having naively lost to the Hubbards her family's plantation, Lionnet. Addie symbolizes the social status of the black population, for whom "freedom," in the postbellum South, often meant only the choice of servitude as an alternative to starvation and vagrancy. And finally, Horace and Alexandra represent the beginning of social reform. Horace dies trying to stop the Hubbards from what he calls "pounding the bones"[2] of their town to make dividends while Alexandra plans to continue her father's cause.

The play offers possibilities for a psychological interpretation of the Hubbards in terms of the predatory instinct. But the focus of the dramatic argument is the *effect* of their predacity on others in their immediate circle and in their community. Near the end of the play, the context of the Hubbard story is broadened to include American society in general, as Ben predicts that the ever flourishing Hubbard-types will eventually own the country. Thus, *The Little Foxes* exemplifies the dramaturgy of social realism—an examination of representative human response to a social environment. In this instance, the social environment is dominated by economic reorganization, and the responses range from predacity to passivity to antipredacity. Each of these attitudes has strong moral implications. While Hellman's historiography provides the factual material of the play, the dramatic action is based on the development and conflict of moral values.

To assess *The Little Foxes* as merely a compelling struggle between the forces of good and evil is to underestimate the ambiguity of the moral positions implied by the play. The victims of the Hubbard machinations—represented by Birdie, Addie, Horace, and Alexandra—are appealingly sympathetic, but they are deficient as moral agents. Birdie quietly evades her painful environment by drinking and covert protest against the Hubbards. But at least she is willing to acknowledge her moral weakness in an attempt to spare her young niece Alexandra of a similar plight. In Birdie's last scene in the play, she confesses to Alexandra that she has been drinking privately for a long time. When Alexandra says she will still always love her, Birdie retorts:

> Well, don't. Don't love me. Because in twenty years you'll just be like me. They'll do all the same things to you. [. . .] You know what? In twenty-two years I haven't had a whole day of happiness.[3]

Addie, also, does no more than quietly complain about the Hubbards. She says:

> Yeah, they got mighty well-off cheating niggers. Well, there are people who eat the earth and eat all the people on it like in the Bible with the locusts. And other people who stand around and watch them eat it. *(Softly)* Sometimes I think it ain't right to stand and watch them do it.[4]

Edifying as this sentiment may be, Addie herself violates it, in a sense, by remaining a "loyal" servant to the Hubbards. She too "stands around and watches" while they despoil. Even though her chances for self-maintenance outside the Hubbard circle are probably limited, Addie has more freedom in choosing her circumstances than she had before the Emancipation Proclamation (1862). As for Horace, his decision to stand up against the Hubbards may be admirable, but it has taken him some twenty years to reach that decision. Moreover, his attempt to thwart Regina's financial hopes by using the Hubbard-like tactics of secrecy and evasion does not enhance his moral position. Alexandra experiences a moral awakening, but it would be premature to assume that she will carry out her stated intentions. Summarily, the morality that can be extrapolated from the actions of these four characters is humane but largely ineffectual.

As for the morality of the Hubbards themselves, special pleading cannot substantially justify their exploitation, which culminates in the death of Horace. Yet for all their excesses they are by no means anomalous to their moment in history. In a sense, their actions manifest the ethics of progress—namely, that traditional morality must be modified or set aside to accommodate the momentum of much needed economic progress. W. J. Cash and other historians have viewed the application of the ethics of progress as apparently necessary to the growth of Southern industry in this period.[5] Thus, the Hubbards, whatever their methods or goals, were potentially contributors to the recovery of Southern economy by their promise of a cotton mill.

All the major characters of *The Little Foxes*, then, may be interpreted as morally ambiguous in varying degrees. But the play remains essentially a judicial instrument. And the case against the Hubbards is virtually complete, since Miss Hellman does little to acknowledge the potential beneficence of the ethics of progress.[6] The play implies that the four sympathetic characters have moral strengths and weaknesses, but the Hubbards are pictured primarily in terms of the injustices they cause. The resultant condemnatory tone, which is the moral dominant of the play, is plausible within the dramatic framework, but not particularly characteristic of the historical period. From the 1880's onward, the recovery of Southern morale was predicated on an upswing in the economy. Since the cotton mills had great financial promise, their organizers were hailed as the salvation of society, and public enthusiasm for economic expansion continued to prevail through the beginning of the twentieth century[7]—the temporal setting of Hellman's play. But the Hubbards (even if they had *not* been partly responsible for Horace's death) emerge as a menace to society. Why does a play so meticulously accurate in historical detail evade the spirit of the age by exposing the underside of the cotton mill interest?

Miss Hellman, in choosing excessively predatory Hubbards as protagonists, posts a moral perspective that can most adequately be traced to sources outside the period of the play. One of those sources is the tradition of social realism in the drama. In both form and content, *The Little Foxes* strongly resembles two of Henrik Ibsen's plays, which are considered definitive examples of social realism. In *The Pillars of Society* (1877) and *An Enemy of the People* (1882), Ibsen, like Miss Hellman, is far more concerned with the moral crises fostered by rapid industrialization than with the benefits of economic progress.

A second and perhaps more direct explanation of the moral perspective of *The Little Foxes* is the political climate of the period when the play was written, the 1930's. The free enterprise system, a cornerstone of the American experiment, was viewed with increasing skepticism by many American intellectuals of this period.[8] Charles A. Beard and other historians argue that economic collapse and mass unemployment, both of which the decade inherited from the Panic of 1929, were partly attributable to the abuse of free enterprise by private interests. Increased governmental control was often proposed as a solution to the problem.[9] Freely interpreted according to the politico-economic critique of these writers, the Hubbards' exploitation might be seen as a "harmful side-effect" of laissez-faire economics, and the moral perspective of the play thus reflects the skepticism of the 1930's. However, if the Hubbards represent dark excesses made possible by laissez-faire, the corrective explicitly offered by the play is not more government control (nor an alternate political system), but the firm assertion of personal integrity by those exploited. The play emphasizes that the Hubbards have thrived not only because they are industrious, but also because their opponents have been listless.

If *The Little Foxes* tests a historical era with a moral perspective rooted outside the era, then the play gains in its value as social history, in one important sense. Moral perspectives are, after all, as much a part of social history as economic pursuits. By examining an age of progess according to views from an age of skepticism, Miss Hellman reconstructs a crucial dilemma for American liberal democracy then and now: how to uphold both private freedom and public concern when the two are at odds.

A recurring manifestation of this dilemma—privately-based economic expansion which encroaches on the public interest—is the sociopolitical substance of the play. Specifically, the play expresses the dilemma in terms of a moral tension between a form of materialism (represented by Regina and her brothers) and a form of humanitarianism (represented by Alexandra and the other Hubbard-dissenters). The confrontation between Regina and Alexandra at the end of the play epitomizes the moral tension of the whole. By this time, Alexandra has been motivated toward humanitarianism and the critical scrutiny of human motives by the troubled acquiescence of Addie, the impassioned warning of Birdie, and the fatal defiance of Horace. Responding to the dictate of her newly-found critical spirit, Alexandra declares that she will leave her mother, but the real challenge that she sets for herself is not merely to escape the Hubbards but to fight against the methods and consequences of their predatory materialism. Despite Alexandra's defection, Regina reaffirms the goal she has pursued throughout the play. She has finally arranged to get the money necessary for her to join the beau monde of Chicago.

Thus, the plot of *The Little Foxes* is structured by the development of a humanitarian ethic in tandem with the operation of a materialistic ethic. Because the two ethical patterns are presented in different stages of maturation and application, the conflict between them is unequal and, as it turns out, unresolved. By the time Alexandra has acquired the strength and insight necessary for confrontation, the cotton mill project and all it has come to symbolize seems assured of success. But the temporal present at the conclusion of the play is heavily charged with a sense of the future. At the threshold of adulthood, Alexandra is poised for a struggle, in spite of events in the play which might easily have discouraged her. As for Regina's future, she expects to transcend her background—particularly the conflicts she has endured—by joining a different society. But Regina's "victory" is hardly conclusive. Although it is established that the family will control the business, Ben insinuates that he intends to vie with her for a larger share of the eventual proceeds. Also, Regina's morale is weakened, at least temporarily, by Alexandra's rejection of her. Thus, in the final scene the moral conflict is expressed at a higher valence, rather than resolved.

Ultimately *The Little Foxes* may be interpreted as a rational assessment of the historical forces it dramatizes. Given its dramatic premises, the play stringently adheres to causality and probability and thus reflects the spirit of objectivity which Emile Zola considered imperative to dramatic realism. The final scene prominently manifests this rational process by offering no facile resolution of the complex moral conflict which structures the play or of the democratic dilemma which that conflict represents. Hellman's rational process serves to strengthen the validity of the play's moral stance (i.e., the preoccupation with detrimental effects of economic expansion). By a synthesis of rational formulation and moral commitment, *The Little Foxes* gains particular authority in casting an image of American destiny—the continuing dialectic of the privileges versus the responsibilities of liberal democracy.

Notes

1. For an analysis of the impact of industrialization on democratic societies, see Reinhold Niebuhr and Paul E. Sigmund, *The Dramatic Experience: Past and Prospects* (New York: Praeger, 1969), pp. 26–49.
2. Lillian Hellman, *The Collected Plays* (Boston: Little, Brown, 1972), p. 176.
3. Ibid., p. 183.
4. Ibid., p. 182.
5. See W. J. Cash, *The Mind of the South* (New York: Knopf, 1941), pp. 191–93; Broadus Mitchell and George Sinclair Mitchell, *The Industrial Revolution in the South* (Baltimore: Johns Hopkins Press, 1930), pp. 238 and 247–48.
6. For example, the poor whites, who were expected to be among the principal beneficiaries of economic progress (Mitchell and Mitchell, pp. 245–48), are the only large class of Southerners not represented in the persons of the play.
7. Cash, pp. 193 and 215.
8. See Gerald Rabkin, *Drama and Commitment: Politics in the American Theatre of the Thirties* (Bloomington: Indiana Univ. Press, 1964), pp. 18–41.
9. See Charles A. Beard, "The Myth of Rugged American Individualism," *Harper's Magazine*, 164 (Dec. 1931), pp. 13–22.

Ernest Hemingway

1899–1961

Ernest Miller Hemingway was born on July 21, 1899, at Oak Park, near Chicago. At high school he distinguished himself only in English and sport, and after graduation went into journalism. Because of defective vision he was unable to join the armed forces in World War I, but went to Italy as an ambulance driver with the Red Cross. On his return to America he joined the staff of the *Toronto Star*, and in 1920 went to Paris as European correspondent. There he soon began to make a name for himself among the expatriate community, enjoying the friendship of Ezra Pound and Gertrude Stein, among others.

The year 1923 saw the publication of Hemingway's first book, *Three Stories and Ten Poems*, and his first visit to Spain, the origin of a life-long fascination with bullfighting. In the following years he established his reputation with the critics and the general public with *In Our Time* (1925), *The Sun Also Rises* (known in Britain as *Fiesta*) (1926), and *Men without Women* (1927). Having moved back to America briefly, to Key West, Florida, Hemingway discovered a passion for big-game fishing, enhancing his already tough personal image. In 1929, after his return to Paris, *A Farewell to Arms* was published to rave reviews; this was the first of his books to be filmed, in 1932.

With his literary standing undisputed, Hemingway adopted an increasingly domineering attitude towards critics and colleagues. His tough image was further nurtured by a well-earned reputation for hard drinking and by an African safari in 1932. In 1937 he went back to Spain as a journalist, and was celebrated as an ally by the Loyalists in their fight against Franco. In 1940 the literary fruits of this experience appeared in *For Whom the Bell Tolls*, which achieved a great commercial success. In 1941 he visited China to cover the Sino-Japanese War, and in 1944 was in England to report on the war in Europe. After the Allied invasion of France, he was soon involved more actively than his brief career as a war correspondent allowed; although reprimanded for his active participation, he is reported to have shown considerable bravery.

After the war Hemingway lived mainly in Cuba. The publication of *The Old Man and the Sea* in 1952 rescued his waning reputation and won him the Pulitzer Prize, followed in 1954 by the Nobel Prize. A second safari, in 1954, was marred by two plane crashes, and Hemingway returned to Cuba in ill health. Following the revolution in 1959 he moved to Ketchum, Idaho, where, after signs of mental disorder and in poor physical health, he shot himself on July 2, 1961.

Ernest Hemingway was married four times, and had three sons. Among his other works are: *Death in the Afternoon* (1932); *Green Hills of Africa* (1935); *To Have and Have Not* (1937); *The Fifth Column* (1938); *Across the River and into the Trees* (1950); and *A Moveable Feast* (1965), a posthumous volume of reminiscences about his years in Paris in the 1920s.

Personal

Dear Sherwood:

You sound like a man well beloved of Jesus. Lots of things happen here. Gertrude Stein and me are just like brothers and we see a lot of her. Read the preface you wrote for her new book and like it very much. It made a big hit with Gertrude. Hash says to tell you, quotes, that things have come to a pretty pass between her and Lewy-close quotes. My operatives keep a pretty close eye on the pair of them.

Joyce has a most god-damn wonderful book ⟨*Ulysses*⟩. It'll probably reach you in time. Meantime the report is that he and all his family are starving but you can find the whole celtic crew of them every night in Michaud's where Binney [Hadley] and I can only afford to go about once a week.

Gertrude Stein says Joyce reminds her of an old woman out in San Francisco. The woman's son struck it rich as hell in the Klondyke and the old woman went around wringing her hands and saying, "Oh my poor Joey! My poor Joey! He's got so much money!" The damned Irish, they have to moan about something or other, but you never heard of an Irishman starving.

Pound took six of my poems and sent them wit a letter to Thayer, Scofield, that is, you've heard of him maybe. Pound thinks I'm a swell poet. He also took a story for the *Little Review*.

I've been teaching Pound to box wit little success. He habitually leads wit his chin and has the general grace of the crayfish or crawfish. He's willing but short winded. Going over there this afternoon for another session but there aint much job in it as I have to shadow box between rounds to get up a sweat. Pound sweats well, though, I'll say that for him. Besides it's pretty sporting of him to risk his dignity and his critical reputation at something that he don't know nothing about. He's really a good guy, Pound, wit a fine bitter tongue onto him. He's written a good review of *Ulysses* for April *Dial*.
—Ernest Hemingway, Letter to Sherwood Anderson (March 9, 1922), *Ernest Hemingway: Selected Letters 1917–1961*, ed. Carlos Baker, 1981, p. 62

Those were the brave times in Paris when William Bird and I, and I daresay Hemingway too believed, I don't know why, that salvation could be found in leaving out capitals. We printed and published in a domed wine-vault, exceedingly old and cramped, on the Ile St. Louis with a grey view on the Seine below the Quais. It must have been salvation we aspired to for thoughts of fortune seldom came near us and Fortune herself, never. Publisher Bird printed his books beautifully at a great old seventeenth-century press and we all took hands at pulling its immense levers about. I "edited" in a gallery like a bird-cage at the top of the vault. It was so low that I could never stand up. Ezra also "edited" somewhere, I daresay, in the rue Notre

JAY KAY KLEIN

ROBERT A. HEINLEIN

AP/WIDE WORLD PHOTOS

ANTHONY HECHT

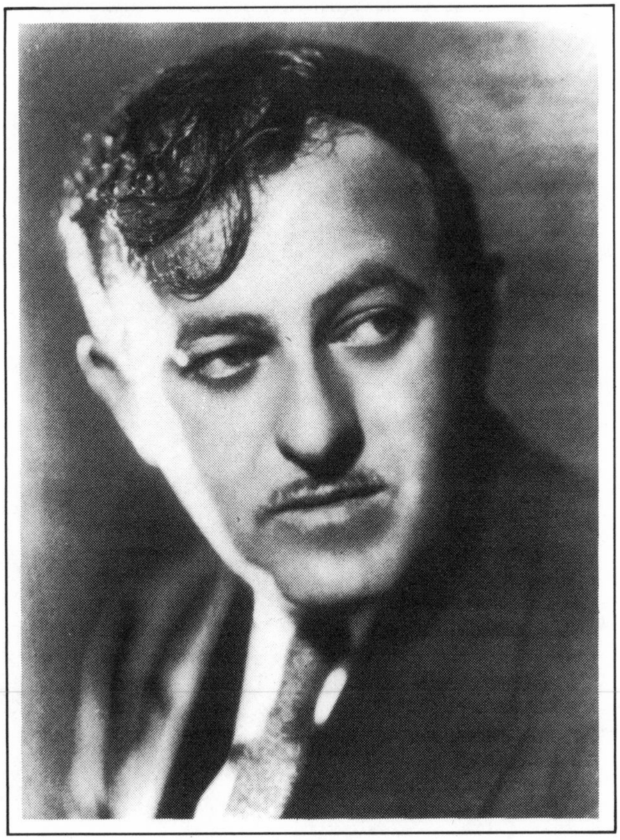

UPI/BETTMANN NEWSPHOTOS

BEN HECHT

APWIDE WORLD PHOTOS

LILLIAN HELLMAN

APWIDE WORLD PHOTOS

ERNEST HEMINGWAY

APWIDE WORLD PHOTOS

JOSEPH HELLER

Dame des Champs. At any rate the last page but one of *In Our Time*—or perhaps it is the *feuille de garde*, carries the announcement:

Here ends *The Inquest* into the state of
contemporary English prose, as
edited by EZRA POUND and printed at
the THREE MOUNTAINS PRESS. The six
works constituting the series are:
Indiscretions *of* Ezra Pound
Women and Men *by* Ford Madox Ford
Elimus *by* B. C. Windeler
with Designs *by* D. Shakespear
The Great American Novel
by William Carlos Williams
England *by* B. M. G. Adams
In Our Time *by* Ernest Hemingway
with portrait *by* Henry Strater.

Mr. Pound, you perceive did believe in CAPITALS and so obviously did one half of Hemingway for his other book of the same date—a blue-grey pamphlet—announces itself all in capitals of great baldness. (They are I believe of the style called *sans-sérif*):

THREE STORIES
& TEN POEMS
ERNEST HEMINGWAY

it calls itself without even a *'by'* in italics. There is no date or publisher's or distributor's name or address on the title page but the back of the half-title bears the small notices

Copyright 1923 by the author
Published by
Contact Publishing Co.

and the last page but one has the announcement

PRINTED AT DIJON
BY
MAURICE DARANTIERE
M. CX. XXIII

This copy bears an inscription in the handwriting of Mr. Hemingway to the effect that it was given to me in Paris by himself in 924. That seems almost an exaggeration in antedating.

Anyhow, I read first IN OUR TIME and then MY OLD MAN in TEN STORIES both in 1923. . . .

Those were exciting times in Paris. The Young-American literature that today forms the most important phase of the literary world anywhere was getting itself born there. And those were birth-throes!

Young America from the limitless prairies leapt, released, on Paris. They stampeded with the madness of colts when you let down the slip-rails between dried pasture and green. The noise of their advancing drowned all sounds. Their innumerable forms hid the very trees on the boulevards. Their perpetual motion made you dizzy. The falling plane-leaves that are the distinguishing mark of grey, quiet Paris, were crushed under foot and vanished like flakes of snow in tormented seas.

I might have been described as—by comparison—a nice, quiet gentleman for an elderly tea-party. And there I was between, as it were, the too quiet æstheticisms of William Bird, publisher supported by Ezra Pound, poet-editor, and, at the other extreme, Robert McAlmon damn-your-damn-highbrow-eyes author-publisher, backed by a whole Horde of Montparnasse from anywhere between North Dakota and Missouri. . . . You should have seen those Thursday tea-parties at the uncapitalled *transatlantic review* offices! The French speak of "la semaine à deux jeudis" . . . the week with two Thursdays in it. Mine seemed to contain sixty, judging by the noise, lung-power, crashing in, and denunciation. They sat on forms—school benches—cramped round Bird's great hand press. On the top of it was an iron eagle. A seventeenth-century eagle!

Where exactly between William Bird, hand-printer and publisher and Robert McAlmon, nine-hundred horse power linotype-publisher Hemingway came in I never quite found out. He was presented to me by Ezra and Bill Bird and had rather the aspect of an Eton-Oxford, husky-ish young captain of a midland regiment of His Britannic Majesty. In that capacity he entered the phalanxes of the *transatlantic review.* I forget what his official title was. He was perhaps joint-editor—or an advisory or consulting or vetoing editor. Of those there was a considerable company. I, I have omitted to say, was supposed to be Editor in Chief. They all shouted at me: I did not know how to write, or knew too much to be able to write, or did not know how to edit, or keep accounts, or sing *'Franky & Johnny,'* or order a dinner. The ceiling was vaulted, the plane-leaves drifted down on the quays outside; the grey Seine flowed softly.

Into the animated din would drift Hemingway, balancing on the point of his toes, feinting at my head with hands as large as hams and relating sinister stories of Paris landlords. He told them with singularly choice words in a slow voice. He still struck me as disciplined. Even captains of his majesty's fifth fusiliers are sometimes amateur pugilists and now and then dance on their toe-points in private. I noticed less however of Eton and Oxford. He seemed more a creature of wild adventures amongst steers in infinitudes.—FORD MADOX FORD, "Introduction" to *A Farewell to Arms*, 1929, pp. x–xiv

The first thing that happened when we were back in Paris was Hemingway with a letter of introduction from Sherwood Anderson.

I remember very well the impression I had of Hemingway that first afternoon. He was an extraordinarily good-looking young man, twenty-three years old. It was not long after that that everybody was twenty-six. It became the period of being twenty-six. During the next two or three years all the young men were twenty-six years old. It was the right age apparently for that time and place. There were one or two under twenty, for example George Lynes but they did not count as Gertrude Stein carefully explained to them. If they were young men they were twenty-six. Later on, much later on they were twenty-one and twenty-two.

So Hemingway was twenty-three, rather foreign looking, with passionately interested, rather than interesting eyes. He sat in front of Gertrude Stein and listened and looked.

They talked then, and more and more, a great deal together. He asked her to come and spend an evening in their apartment and look at his work. Hemingway had then and has always a very good instinct for finding apartments in strange but pleasing localities and good femmes de ménage and good food. This his first apartment was just off the place du Tertre. We spent the evening there and he and Gertrude Stein went over all the writing he had done up to that time. He had begun the novel that it was inevitable he would begin and there were the little poems afterwards printed by McAlmon in the Contract Edition. Gertrude Stein rather liked the poems, they were direct, Kiplingesque, but the novel she found wanting. There is a great deal of description in this, she said, and not particularly good description. Begin over again and concentrate, she said.

Hemingway was at this time Paris correspondent for a canadian newspaper. He was obliged there to express what he called the canadian viewpoint.

He and Gertrude Stein used to walk together and talk

together a great deal. One day she said to him, look here, you say you and your wife have a little money between you. Is it enough to live on if you live quietly. Yes, he said. Well, she said, then do it. If you keep on doing newspaper work you will never see things, you will only see words and that will not do, that is of course if you intend to be a writer. Hemingway said he undoubtedly intended to be a writer. He and his wife went away on a trip and shortly after Hemingway turned up alone. He came to the house about ten o'clock in the morning and he stayed, he stayed for lunch, he stayed all afternoon, he stayed for dinner and he stayed until about ten o'clock at night and then all of a sudden he announced that his wife was enceinte and then with great bitterness, and I, I am too young to be a father. We consoled him as best we could and sent him on his way.

When they came back Hemingway said that he had made up his mind. They would go back to America and he would work hard for a year and with what he would earn and what they had they would settle down and he would give up newspaper work and make himself a writer. They went away and well within the prescribed year they came back with a new born baby. Newspaper work was over. . . .

We had heard that Ford was in Paris, but we had not happened to meet. Gertrude Stein had however seen copies of the Transatlantic and found it interesting but had thought nothing further about it.

Hemingway came in then very excited and said that Ford wanted something of Gertrude Stein's for the next number and he, Hemingway, wanted The Making of Americans to be run in it as a serial and he had to have the first fifty pages at once. Gertrude Stein was of course quite overcome with her excitement at this idea, but there was no copy of the manuscript except the one that we had had bound. That makes no difference, said Hemingway, I will copy it. And he and I between us did copy it and it was printed in the next number of the Transatlantic. So for the first time a piece of the monumental work which was the beginning, really the beginning of modern writing, was printed, and we were very happy. Later on when things were difficult between Gertrude Stein and Hemingway, she always remembered with gratitude that after all it was Hemingway who first caused to be printed a piece of The Making of Americans. She always says, yes sure I have a weakness for Hemingway. After all he was the first of the young men to knock at my door and he did make Ford print the first piece of The Making of Americans.

I myself have not so much confidence that Hemingway did do this. I have never known what the story is but I have always been certain that there was some other story behind it all. That is the way I feel about it.

Gertrude Stein and Sherwood Anderson are very funny on the subject of Hemingway. The last time that Sherwood was in Paris they often talked about him. Hemingway had been formed by the two of them and they were both a little proud and a little ashamed of the work of their minds. Hemingway had at one moment, when he had repudiated Sherwood Anderson and all his works, written him a letter in the name of american literature which he, Hemingway, in company with his contemporaries was about to save, telling Sherwood just what he, Hemingway thought about Sherwood's work, and, that thinking, was in no sense complimentary. When Sherwood came to Paris Hemingway naturally was afraid. Sherwood as naturally was not.—GERTRUDE STEIN, *The Autobiography of Alice B. Toklas*, 1933, pp. 212–16

One of the writers to arrive at the Press office was Ernest Hemingway, a black-haired, bushy-mustached, hairy-handed giant, who did not belie the impression one might have of his appearance from his novels. In his behavior he seemed at first to be acting the part of a Hemingway hero.

I wondered how this man, whose art concealed under its apparent huskiness a deliberation and delicacy like Turgenev, could show so little of his inner sensibility in his outward behavior. But one afternoon, when he and I were walking through the streets of Valencia, I caught a glimpse of the esthetic Hemingway, whose presence I suspected. I had happened to mention that I had no books in Valencia and that the bookshops were empty of all but Spanish and a little French literature. In one bookshop, I went on, I had seen a novel which I had never read, Stendhal's *La Chartreuse de Parme*, and I did not know whether to buy it. Hemingway said that he thought the account at the beginning of the hero, Fabrice, wandering lost in the middle of the Battle of Waterloo, with which *La Chartreuse* opens is perhaps the best, though the most apparently casual, description of war in literature. For war is often really like that, a boy lost in the middle of an action, not knowing which side will win, hardly knowing that a battle is going on. He warmed to the theme of Stendhal, and soon I realized that he had that kind of literary sensibility which the professional critic, or the don, nearly always lacks. He saw literature not just as "good writing," but as the unceasing interrelationship of the words on the page with the life within and beyond them—the battle, the landscape or the love affair. For him, writing was a kind of wrestling of the writer armed with a pen, as a huntsman with his spear, with his living material. I mentioned the battle scenes in Shakespeare. "Why do you talk to me about Shakespeare?" he asked with annoyance. "Don't you realize I don't read books?" and he changed the conversation to—was it boxing? Shortly after this he was saying that his chief purpose in coming to Spain was to discover whether he had lost his nerve under conditions of warfare which had developed since Caporetto. By now we had reached a *taverna* on the shore. We went in and found some gypsy players. Hemingway seized a guitar and started singing Spanish songs. He had become the Hemingway character again.

He told me often that I was "too squeamish," by which, I suppose, he meant "yeller." Yet on one occasion he came down heavily on my side. K——, on sick leave from the Brigade, used to hobble around the cafés where the journalists met, leaning on a stick. Whenever there were arguments about Communism this man attacked me viciously, and most people knew that his motive was to draw attention to the fact that my name was linked with that of Jimmy. As K—— was believed by all the journalists to be a hero, these attacks were humiliating. After a particularly acrimonious discussion, Hemingway took me aside and said: "Stephen, don't you worry about K——. I know his type. He's just a malingerer. He's yeller." He then gave me an outline of K——'s story, which became, in the telling, such excellent Hemingway that I begged him to write it. He said: "I give the idea to you. Why don't you write it?" And from that we went on to make a compact that we would both write the same story. Of course, neither of us did so, and now I forget what it was. All I remember is the curious fact of receiving Hemingway's support in a situation where I should never have expected it. For I had to accept the humiliation of knowing that I was not on the side of the heroes. This was a difficult attitude to maintain, because as my experience of Spain deepened I found myself more and more appreciative of the difficulties of the people . . . who were strong, even whilst I wrote often in defense of the weak.—STEPHEN SPENDER, *World within World*, 1948, pp. 208–10

A customer we liked, one who gave us no trouble, was that young man you saw almost every morning over there in a corner at Shakespeare and Company, reading the magazines or Captain Marryat or some other book. This was Ernest Hemingway, who turned up in Paris, as I remember, late in 1921. My "best customer," he called himself, a title that no one disputed with him. Great was our esteem for a customer who was not only a regular visitor, but spent money on books, a trait very pleasing to the proprietor of a small book business.

However, he would have endeared himself to me just as much if he hadn't spent a penny in my establishment. I felt the warmest friendship for Ernest Hemingway from the day we met.

Sherwood Anderson, in Chicago, had given his "young friends Mr. and Mrs. Ernest Hemingway" a letter of introduction to me. I have it still, and it reads as follows:

> I am writing this note to make you acquainted with my friend Ernest Hemingway, who with Mrs. Hemingway is going to Paris to live, and will ask him to drop it in the mails when he arrives there.
>
> Mr. Hemingway is an American writer instinctively in touch with everything worth while going on here and I know you will find both Mr. and Mrs. Hemingway delightful people to know.

But the Hemingways and I had known each other for some time before they remembered to produce Anderson's letter. Hemingway just walked in one day.

I looked up and saw a tall, dark young fellow with a small mustache, and heard him say, in a deep, deep voice, that he was Ernest Hemingway. I invited him to sit down, and, drawing him out, I learned that he was from Chicago originally. I also learned that he had spent two years in a military hospital, getting back the use of his leg. What had happened to his leg? Well, he told me apologetically, like a boy confessing he had been in a scrap, he had got wounded in the knee, fighting in Italy. Would I care to see it? Of course I would. So business at Shakespeare and Company was suspended while he removed his shoe and sock, and showed me the dreadful scars covering his leg and foot. The knee was the worst hurt, but the foot seemed to have been badly injured, too, from a burst of shrapnel, he said. In the hospital, they had thought he was done for; there was even some question of administering the last sacraments. But this was changed, with his feeble consent, to baptism—"just in case they were right."

So Hemingway was baptized. Baptized or not—and I am going to say this whether Hemingway shoots me or not—I have always felt that he was a deeply religious man. Hemingway was a great pal of Joyce's, and Joyce remarked to me one day that he thought it was a mistake, Hemingway's thinking himself such a tough fellow and ⟨Robert⟩ McAlmon trying to pass himself off as the sensitive type. It was the other way round, he thought. So Joyce found you out, Hemingway!

Hemingway confided to me that before he was out of high school, when he was still "a boy in short pants," his father had died suddenly and in tragic circumstances, leaving him a gun as a sole legacy. He found himself the head of a family, his mother and brothers and sister dependent on him. He had to leave school and begin making a living. He earned his first money in a boxing match, but, from what I gathered, didn't linger in this career. He spoke rather bitterly of his boyhood.

He didn't tell me much about his life after he left school. He earned his living at various jobs, including newspaper work, I believe, then went over to Canada and enlisted in the armed forces. He was so young he had to fake his age to be accepted.

Hemingway was a widely educated young man, who knew many countries and several languages; and he had learned it all at first hand, not in universities. He seemed to me to have gone a great deal farther and faster than any of the young writers I knew. In spite of a certain boyishness, he was exceptionally wise and self-reliant. In Paris, Hemingway had a job as sports correspondent for the Toronto *Star.* No doubt he was already trying his hand at writing fiction. . . .

Hemingway's readers were usually won over by a first contact. I remember Jonathan Cape's enthusiasm over his first Hemingway. Mr. Cape, Colonel Lawrence's and Joyce's publisher in England, asked me, on one of his visits to Paris, what American he should publish. "Here, read Hemingway!" I said—and that is how Mr. Cape became Hemingway's English publisher.

Hemingway was serious and competent in whatever he did, even when he went in for the care of an infant. After a brief visit to Canada, Hadley and Hemingway came back bringing another "best customer," John Hadley Hemingway. Dropping in one morning and seeing him giving the baby his bath, I was amazed at his deft handling of Bumby. Hemingway *père* was justly proud, and asked me if I didn't think he had a future as a nursemaid.

Bumby was frequenting Shakespeare and Company before he could walk. Holding his son carefully, though sometimes upside down, Hemingway went on reading the latest periodicals, which required some technique, I must say. As for Bumby, anything was all right as long as he was with his adored Papa. His first steps were to what he called "Sylver Beach's." I can see them, father and son, coming along hand in hand up the street. Bumby, hoisted on a high stool, observed his old man gravely, never showing any impatience, waiting to be lifted from his high perch at last; it must have seemed a long wait sometimes. Then I would watch the two of them as they set off, not for home, since they had to keep out of Hadley's way till the housekeeping was done, but to the bistrot around the corner; there, seated at a table, their drinks before them—Bumby's was a grenadine—they went over all the questions of the day.

Everybody at that time had been in Spain, and varied were the impressions. Gertrude Stein and Alice B. Toklas had found it very amusing. Others had gone to a bullfight, been shocked, and come away before the end. The bullfight had been written up from the moral and the sexual point of view, and as a bright-colored sport, picturesque and all that. The Spanish themselves usually found anything foreigners said about *los toros* bewildering and, besides, technically unsound.

Hemingway, unlike the others, set out to learn and to write about the bulls in his usual serious, competent manner. So we have, in *Death in the Afternoon*, a complete treatise on bullfighting, one that my Spanish friends, the most difficult to please, have acknowledged as excellent.. And some of Hemingway's finest writing is in this book.

Good writers are so rare that if I were a critic, I would only try to point out what I think makes them reliable and enjoyable. For how can anyone explain the mystery of creation?

Hemingway can take any amount of criticism—from himself; he is his own severest critic, but, like all his fellow-writers, he is hypersensitive to the criticism of others. It's true that some critics are terribly expert in sticking the sharp penpoint into the victim and are delighted when he squirms. Wyndham Lewis succeeded in making Joyce squirm. And his article on Hemingway entitled "The Dumb Ox," which the subject of it picked up in my bookshop, I regret to say, roused him to such anger that he punched the heads off three dozen tulips, a birthday gift. As a result, the vase upset its contents over the books, after which Hemingway sat down at my desk and wrote a check payable to Sylvia Beach for a sum that covered the damage twice over.

As a bookseller and librarian, I paid more attention to titles perhaps than others who simply rush past the threshold of a book without ringing the bell. I think Hemingway's titles should be awarded first prize in any contest. Each of them is a poem, and their mysterious power over readers contributes to Hemingway's success. His titles have a life of their own, and they have enriched the American vocabulary.—SLYVIA BEACH, "My Best Customer," *Shakespeare and Company*, 1956, pp. 77–83

After my parents were divorced, and my father remarried, he moved to Cuba. Marty found them a wonderful old house about nine miles outside of Havana. It was situated on twenty acres of some of the loveliest land I've seen. Mango trees lined the driveway leading up to the house, and tall royal palms grew beside the path leading down to the swimming pool in back. Flowers and bougainvillea vines bloomed all over. Hummingbirds made their tiny neat square nests in the tropical foliage, and I could watch for hours a mother sitting on her eggs, one of the most regally beautiful sights I've ever seen. The rambling, one-story Spanish colonial house was perched on the highest point of land in the area, and had a wonderful view of the lights of Havana. It was called Finca Vigía, or Lookout Farm, though we simply called it the Finca.

It was hard to believe that anyone could produce in such a place, and for many of the years that I visited Havana, I never thought of my father as a working writer. I knew that he had written books in the past, because he was Hemingway the Writer; but I never saw him at work, and I had doubts mixed with hero worship. Although I suppressed them as much as possible, they kept popping to the surface. Was he a phony? He was always talking about his work but when did he do it?

I'd get up around eight-thirty during those summer vacations, have a leisurely breakfast, and then a swim. By the time I made it up to the big house around ten, there was papa, a Scotch and soda in his hand, bidding me a cheerful good morning.

"What do you want to do today, Gig? I haven't planned anything definite yet. Maybe we could have lunch at the Floridita, and then shoot a few practice pigeons in the afternoon. Gregorio called to say it's too rough for fishing. When he cancels this early it means the winds already are at gale force and the sea will be rough all day. Think about it, and then we'll make definite plans.

"Maybe we should just take it easy today," he would say, looking closer at me with concern. "You don't look so good. Are you coming down with something, old pal?"

"I feel like I'm coming up with something, papa. It almost feels like I'm seasick."

"I'll fix you a bloody mary. You've just got a hangover." He would sound relieved. From the time I was ten or eleven, he let me drink as much as I wanted, having confidence that I would set my own limits.

"Maybe you should cut down on the drinking? If you don't—" his voice rose in mock seriousness—"discipline must be enforced. We can't send you back to Mother at the end of the summer with the D.T.'s."

We'd usually have been up fairly late drinking the night before and I would think I'd done pretty well to be awake by eight-thirty. My head may have been buzzing, but I was still up. My father would always look great, as if he'd slept a baby's sleep in a soundproof room with his eyes covered by black patches. Somemtimes I could explain it to myself satisfactorily, remembering how he'd fallen asleep with the Scotch in his hand going down slowly to rest on the arm of the chair. But more often there just wasn't any explanation, except, as I learned, his remarkable metabolism. I was certain he hadn't gotten up before me. But he had.

It was his habit, my older brothers later told me, to get up every morning of his adult life around five-thirty or six, when the first light woke him. He'd work for four or five hours. If, after a couple of hours, he saw that his writing wasn't going well he'd knock off the serious stuff and answer letters. He loved writing letters, because they gave him a chance to relax from "the awful responsibility of writing," or, as he sometimes called it, "the responsibility of awful writing." In his letters he didn't have to worry about how a passage sounded or was constructed, and he could joke and gossip and give well-intended (and usually solicited) advice.—GREGORY HEMINGWAY, "Havana," *Papa: A Personal Memoir*, 1976, pp. 47–52

In marked contrast to his sixtieth, Ernest's sixty-first birthday came and went like a shadow. He seldom left the apartment, and set up a card table in a corner of the living room to serve as an office. Charles Scribner conferred with him there. Among his few visits outside were a trip to an eye doctor and a lunch at Toots Shor's with Lenny Lyons, Jimmy Cannon, and ⟨A. E.⟩ Hotchner. Hotchner had been negotiating with Twentieth Century Fox for a film play, *The World of Nick Adams*, based on his television adaptations of some of the stories, strung together in a pseudo-biographical sequence. Ernest was dissatisfied with the preliminary offer of $100,000 and insisted that Hotchner hold out for $900,000. If this figure suggested delusions of grandeur, the depressive phase was very close. On July 31st he wrote his son Bumby that he was not in good shape and that his eyes were bothering him badly. He added that he wished he did not have to go to Spain at all.

He did not need to go and he should not have gone. But he kept insisting that Antonio needed him. After several postponements, he got aboard the overnight TWA jet for Lisbon and Madrid. His seat companion was a Chicago attorney named Luis Kutner, with whom he had once corresponded about the release of Ezra Pound. Like ⟨Andrew⟩ Turnbull in October, Kutner was astonished to discover that this unsure and quiet man was not the "robust, virile, aggressive" hero of popular legend. When the plane reached Madrid, Ernest was fatigued and upset by the sudden change in time zones. He conferred briefly with Bill Lang, the Paris representative of *Life* magazine, and then drove off with Bill Davis for two days' rest at La Consula.

The Davises had seen him in most of his moods, but none like this. He showed the symptoms of extreme nervous depression: fear, loneliness, ennui, suspicion of the motives of others, insomnia, guilt, remorse, and failure of memory. He had been in Spain only ten days when his letters to his wife complained of cramps and nightmares. At the end of the two weeks he said flatly that he feared a "complete physical and nervous crack up from deadly overwork." It had been his lifelong habit to awaken cheerfully. Now each day seemed like a nightmare seventy-two hours long. "Woke bad today," he said on the 19th. Although he spoke of being lonely, new faces made him nervous. The whole bullfight business seemed "corrupt" and "unimportant." Everybody in it was "as egotistical as Sinsky ⟨Juan Sinsky Dunabeita⟩ at his worst." He even suspected that ⟨Luis Miguel⟩ Dominguín was secretly conspiring against Antonio ⟨Ordóñez⟩. Yet he was much worried that his *Life* article had been unfair to Dominguín. When the first installment of "The Dangerous Summer" reached him by airmail early in September, he recoiled in anguish at the grinning cover portrait, calling it a "horrible face." He felt "ashamed and sick" to have done such a job, and was full of remorse at having made "such a mess." He wrote Mary repeatedly, calling her "poor blessed kitten," and saying that he now realized why she had hated Spain so much in the summer of 1959. He wished that she were with him now to keep him from "cracking up."

At his urgent request and at the invitation of Annie Davis, Mary sent Valerie over to help him with his mail. She arrived calm and cheerful to find him at the opposite extreme. Antonio had sustained a concussion when a bull dumped him at Bilbao, and Carmen ⟨Ordóñez⟩ had had a miscarriage. Ernest said that he was sick of it all to the marrow of his bones: the only reason he stuck it out was that every time he had been this bad before he had managed to rise out of it into a "belle époque" of writing. He was still hoping to repeat the process, and could not bring himself to face the fact that never before in his life had he been half so "bad" as he was now. . . .

Mary had been advised to stay at home in Ketchum. She had locked all the guns in the storage room in the basement, but the two threats of suicide made her more doubtful than ever that Ernest was receiving proper treatment in Rochester. In mid-May she told Betty and Otto Bruce that she was so exhausted with worry that she would like to spend a month in cold storage. But real rest was out of the question. Late in May she went to New York to consult with the eminent psychiatrist who had arranged for Ernest's first admission to Mayo Clinic. She had been there less than a week when she was called to Rochester at Ernest's request. He had been complaining that he had no girl at the hospital. But the visit was not a success. She had made a list of questions to ask Dr. Rome. His answers did not satisfy her. Ernest presented one front to the doctors and quite another to her. She was dismayed to learn that Dr. Rome thought him ready to be discharged. Back in New York, she tried to arrange his transfer to a psychiatric institute in Hartford, Connecticut. The Mayo Clinic advised against the move. Ernest's old paper, *The Kansas City Star,* reported on May 31st that his condition was improving. Mary knew otherwise but was powerless to act. The impasse dragged on into the month of June.

There were still ways of getting to him. A man named Herbert Wellington had written a fisherman's guide to the waters of the Yellowstone. Charlie Scribner sent Ernest a copy. He read it avidly and asked Scribner to send another copy to Bumby in San Francisco. It set him dreaming of the old days at the Nordquist ranch beside the Clark's Fork of the Yellowstone. Scribner also reported that all of Ernest's books were selling very well. This, said Ernest, made him "feel very good." Work was his life. He was hoping soon to return to Ketchum and start to work again.

Dr. Saviers's nine-year-old son Fritz was hospitalized in Denver. He was suffering from nonspecific myocarditis and the prognosis was poor. George ⟨Saviers⟩ said that a note from Ernest might help to cheer him up. "Dear Fritz," wrote Ernest, "I was terribly sorry to hear this morning in a note from your father that you were laid up in Denver for a few days more and speed off this note to tell you how much I hope you'll be feeling better. It has been very hot and muggy here in Rochester but the last two days it has turned cool and lovely with the nights wonderful for sleeping. The country is beautiful around here and I've had a chance to see some wonderful country along the Mississippi where they used to drive the logs in the old lumbering days and the trails where the pioneers came north. Saw some good bass jump in the river. I never knew anything about the upper Mississippi before and it is really a very beautiful country and there are plenty of pheasants and ducks in the fall. But not as many as in Idaho and I hope we'll both be back there shortly and can joke about our hospital experiences together. Best always to you, old timer, from your good friend who misses you very much./Mister Papa./"

The talk of returning to Idaho was not a dream. Ernest had convinced his doctors that he was fit to be discharged. When Mary reached Rochester, she knew that an enormous mistake was being made. But Ernest was eager to be off and she felt that she must comply. She telephoned George Brown in New York. He flew to Rochester to drive them home to Ketchum. Mary rented a Buick from Hertz and they set off on the morning of June 26th. Ernest sat beside George in the front seat, watching the road. The first day all went well. They covered 300 miles and spent the night at a motel in Mitchell, South Dakota. On the 27th, however, Ernest's delusions returned. Mary had bought some wine so that they could have a picnic lunch along the way. He kept worrying that state troopers would arrest them for carrying alcoholic beverages. By noon he began to talk of where they would spend the night. Such problems had never bothered him before. Mary must call ahead to make a reservation. Each day thereafter he was so insistent that once or twice she dropped coins into telephones to simulate calls she never made. They often stopped for the day at two or three in the afternoon. It took them five days to cover 1700 miles.

They reached Ketchum on Friday, June 30th. Mary slept in the front bedroom and Ernest in the back. George Brown stayed in the cinder-block guesthouse beside the parking area outside the kitchen door. Next morning Ernest and George drove out to the hospital to see George Saviers. George said that Fritz had been pleased with Ernest's letter. The child had been spending a few days at home but that night George would have to take him back to Denver on the train. Ernest walked over to see Don Anderson at his Sun Valley office. Don was not there and they drove home. In the afternoon, Chuck Atkinson came over to see Ernest, and they talked for an hour, standing out on the front porch. Clara Spiegel wanted them to come to dinner. Ernest refused. He invited Clara for Sunday dinner instead. Ernest and Mary took George Brown to the Christiania Restaurant beside Chuck Atkinson's motel. Ernest sat in a corner facing the room. He said little but did not seem morose. The restaurant filled with Saturday-night diners. They left early and returned to the house. Almost at once Ernest began to prepare for bed. He was brushing his teeth in the bathroom adjoining his bedroom when Mary suddenly remembered a gay Italian song: *"Tutti mi chiamano bionda"*—"They all call me blond." She sang it to Ernest and he joined her in the closing line. He put on his blue pajamas and snapped on the reading light beside his bed. Mary went to sleep in the big front room.

Sunday morning dawned bright and cloudless. Ernest awoke early as always. He put on the red "Emperor's robe" and padded softly down the carpeted stairway. The early sunlight lay in pools on the living-room floor. He had noticed that the guns were locked up in the basement. But the keys, as he well knew, were on the window ledge above the kitchen sink. He tiptoed down the basement stairs and unlocked the storage room. It smelled as dank as a grave. He chose a double-barreled Boss shotgun with a tight choke. He had used it for years of pigeon shooting. He took some shells from one of the boxes in the storage room, closed and locked the door, and climbed the basement stairs. If he saw the bright day outside, it did not deter him. He crossed the living room to the front foyer, a shrinelike entryway five feet by seven, with oak-paneled walls and a floor of linoleum tile. He had held for years to his maxim: *"il faut (d'abord) durer."* Now it had been succeeded by another: *"il faut (après tout) mourir."* The idea, if not the phrase, filled all his mind. He slipped in two shells, lowered the gun butt carefully to the floor, leaned forward, pressed the twin barrels against his forehead just above the eyebrows, and tripped both triggers.—CARLOS BAKER, "Journey Down," *Ernest Hemingway: A Life Story*, 1969, pp. 553–62

General

Vague rumours attach themselves to people's names. Of Mr. Hemingway, we know that he is an American living in France, an 'advanced' writer, we suspect, connected with what is called a movement, though which of the many we own that we do not know. It will be well to make a little more certain of these matters by reading first Mr. Hemingway's earlier book, *The Sun Also Rises*, and it soon becomes clear from this that, if Mr. Hemingway is 'advanced', it is not in the way that is to us most interesting. A prejudice of which the reader would do well to take account is here exposed; the critic is a modernist. Yes, the excuse would be because the moderns make us aware of what we feel subconsciously; they are truer to our own experience; they even anticipate it, and this gives us a particular excitement. But nothing new is revealed about any of the characters in *The Sun Also Rises*. They come before us shaped, proportioned, weighed, exactly as the characters of Maupassant are shaped and proportioned. They are seen from the old angle; the old reticences, the old relations between author and character are observed.

But the critic has the grace to reflect that this demand for new aspects and new perspectives may well be overdone. It may become whimsical. It may become foolish. For why should not art be traditional as well as original? Are we not attaching too much importance to an excitement which, though agreeable, may not be valuable in itself, so that we are led to make the fatal mistake of overriding the writer's gift?

At any rate, Mr. Hemingway is not modern in the sense given; and it would appear from his first novel that this rumour of modernity must have sprung from his subject matter and from his treatment of it rather than from any fundamental novelty in his conception of the art of fiction. It is a bare, abrupt, outspoken book. Life as people live it in Paris in 1927 or even in 1928 is described as we of this age do describe life (it is here that we steal a march upon the Victorians) openly, frankly, without prudery, but also without surprise. The immoralities and moralities of Paris are described as we are apt to hear them spoken of in private life. Such candour is modern and it is admirable. Then, for qualities grow together in art as in life, we find attached to this admirable frankness an equal bareness of style. Nobody speaks for more than a line or two. Half a line is mostly sufficient. If a hill or a town is described (and there is always some reason for its description) there it is, exactly and literally built up of little facts, literal enough, but chosen, as the final sharpness of the outline proves, with the utmost care. Therefore, a few words like these: 'The grain was just beginning to ripen and the fields were full of poppies. The pasture land was green and there were fine trees, and sometimes big rivers and chateaux off in the trees'—which have a curious force. Each word pulls its weight in the sentence. And the prevailing atmosphere is fine and sharp, like that of winter days when the boughs are bare against the sky. (But if we had to choose one sentence with which to describe what Mr. Hemingway attempts and sometimes achieves, we should quote a passage from a description of a bullfight: 'Romero never made any contortions, always it was straight and pure and natural in line. The others twisted themselves like corkscrews, their elbows raised and leaned against the flanks of the bull after his horns had passed, to give a faked look of danger. Afterwards, all that was faked turned bad and gave an unpleasant feeling. Romero's bullfighting gave real emotion, because he kept the absolute purity of line in his movements and always quietly and calmly let the horns pass him close each time.') Mr. Hemingway's writing, one might paraphrase, gives us now and then a real emotion, because he keeps absolute purity of line in his movements and lets the horns (which are truth, fact, reality) pass him close each time. But there is something faked, too, which turns bad and gives an unpleasant feeling—that also we must face in course of time. . . .

There are in *Men without Women* many stories which, if life were longer, one would wish to read again. Most of them indeed are so competent, so efficient, and so bare of superfluity that one wonders why they do not make a deeper dent in the mind than they do. Take the pathetic story of the Major whose wife died—'In Another Country'; or the sardonic story of a conversation in a railway carriage—'A Canary for One'; or stories like 'The Undefeated' and 'Fifty Grand' which are full of the sordidness and heroism of bull-fighting and boxing—all of these are good trenchant stories, quick, terse, and strong. If one had not summoned the ghosts of Tchekov, Mérimée, and Maupassant, no doubt one would be enthusiastic. As it is, one looks about for something, fails to find something, and so is brought again to the old familiar business of ringing impressions on the counter, and asking what is wrong?

For some reason the book of short stories does not seem to us to go as deep or to promise as much as the novel. Perhaps it is the excessive use of dialogue, for Mr. Hemingway's use of it is surely excessive. A writer will always be chary of dialogue because dialogue puts the most violent pressure upon the reader's attention. He has to hear, to see, to supply the right tone, and to fill in the background from what the characters say without any help from the author. Therefore, when fictitious people are allowed to speak it must be because they have something so important to say that it stimulates the reader to do rather more than his share of the work of creation. But, although Mr. Hemingway keeps us under the fire of dialogue constantly, his people, half the time, are saying what the author could say much more economically for them. At last we are inclined to cry out with the little girl in 'Hills Like White Elephants': 'Would you please please please please please please stop talking?'

And probably it is this superfluity of dialogue which leads to that other fault which is always lying in wait for the writer of short stories: the lack of proportion. A paragraph in excess will make these little craft lopsided and will bring about that blurred effect which, when one is out for clarity and point, so baffles the reader. And both these faults, the tendency to flood the page with unnecessary dialogue and the lack of sharp, unmistakable points by which we can take hold of the story, come from the more fundamental fact that, though Mr. Hemingway is brilliantly and enormously skilful, he lets his dexterity, like the bullfighter's cloak, get between him and the fact. For in truth story-writing has much in common with bullfighting. One may twist one's self like a corkscrew and go through every sort of contortion so that the public thinks one is running every risk and displaying superb gallantry. But the true writer stands close up to the bull and lets the horns—call them life, truth, reality, whatever you like—pass him close each time.

Mr. Hemingway, then, is courageous; he is candid; he is

highly skilled; he plants words precisely where he wishes; he has moments of bare and nervous beauty; he is modern in manner but not in vision; he is self-consciously virile; his talent has contracted rather than expanded; compared with his novel his stories are a little dry and sterile. So we sum him up. So we reveal some of the prejudices, the instincts and the fallacies out of which what it pleases us to call criticism is made.—VIRGINIA WOOLF, "An Essay in Criticism," *NYHT*, Oct. 9, 1927, pp. 1, 3

Dear Mr. Perkins:

Thanks for your letter and the clipping. I'm very worried about ⟨F. Scott Fitzgerald⟩ and wish I were over there and could try and get him in some sort of shape. But I won't mention your having written.

About serialization—let's not think about it until the 1st draft is done. Thanks just the same.

The Virginia Woolf review ⟨*New York Herald Tribune Books*, Oct. 9, 1927⟩ was damned irritating—She belongs to a group of Bloomsbury people who are all over 40 and have taken on themselves the burden of being modern and all very promising and saviours of letters. When they are all busy at it they dislike what they consider the intrusion of anybody much under 40 into the business, though God knows one doesn't wish to intrude. They live for their Literary Reputations and believe the best way to keep them is to try and slur off or impute [impugn] the honesty of anyone coming up.

Of course where they are right is that literary reputations in ones life time are plants that can be nurtured—and blighted and they do their best to nurture theirs and their friends and throw off on the others. Well God be with them though I would have enjoyed taking the clothes off Virginia Woolf this noon and permitting her to walk down the Avenue de l'Opéra letting every one, truth, reality, whatever she liked—pass her close each time.

The deliberate twisting of the blurb was what angered me—that and the imputation that I faked and cheated etc. I was glad I did not get it when I was having one of those hellish depressions when you feel you can never write again.—ERNEST HEMINGWAY, Letter to Maxwell Perkins (Nov. 1, 1927), *Ernest Hemingway: Selected Letters 1917–1961*, ed. Carlos Baker, 1981, pp. 264–65

What about the Old Lady? She's gone. We threw her out of the book, finally. A little late you say. Yes, perhaps a little late. What about the horses? They are what people always like to talk about in regard to the bullfight. Has there been enough about the horses? Plenty about the horses, you say. They like it all but the poor horses. Should we try to raise the general tone? What about higher things?

Mr. Aldous Huxley writing in an essay entitled "Foreheads Villainous Low" commences: "In [naming a book by this writer] Mr. H. ventures, once, to name an Old Master. There is a phrase, quite admirably expressive [here Mr. Huxley inserts a compliment], a single phrase, no more, about 'the bitter nail-holes' of Mantegna's Christs; then quickly, quickly, appalled by his own temerity, the author passes on (as Mrs. Gaskell might hastily have passed on, if she had somehow been betrayed into mentioning a water-closet), passes on, shamefacedly, to speak once more of Lower Things.

"There was a time, not so long ago, when the stupid and uneducated aspired to be thought intelligent and cultured. The current of aspiration has changed its direction. It is not at all uncommon now to find intelligent and cultured people doing their best to feign stupidity and to conceal the fact that they have received an education"—and more; more in Mr. Huxley's best educated vein which is a highly educated vein indeed.

What about that, you say? Mr. Huxley scores there, all right, all right. What have you to say to that? Let me answer truly. On reading that in Mr. Huxley's book I obtained a copy of the volume he refers to and looked through it and could not find the quotation he mentions. It may be there, but I did not have the patience nor the interest to find it, since the book was finished and nothing to be done. It sounds very much like the sort of thing one tries to remove in going over the manuscript. I believe it is more than a question of the simulation or avoidance of the appearance of culture. When writing a novel a writer should create living people; people not characters. A *character* is a caricature. If a writer can make people live there may be no great characters in his book, but it is possible that his book will remain as a whole; as an entity; as a novel. If the people the writer is making talk of old masters; of music; of modern painting; of letters; or of science then they should talk of those subjects in the novel. If they do not talk of those subjects and the writer makes them talk of them he is a faker, and if he talks about them himself to show how much he knows then he is showing off. No matter how good a phrase or a simile he may have if he puts it in where it is not absolutely necessary and irreplaceable he is spoiling his work for egotism. Prose is architecture, not interior decoration, and the Baroque is over. For a writer to put his own intellectual musings, which he might sell for a low price as essays, into the mouths of artificially constructed characters which are more remunerative when issued as people in a novel is good economics, perhaps, but does not make literature. People in a novel, not skillfully constructed *characters*, must be projected from the writer's assimilated experience, from his knowledge, from his head, from his heart and from all there is of him. If he ever has luck as well as seriousness and gets them out entire they will have more than one dimension and they will last a long time. A good writer should know as near everything as possible. Naturally he will not. A great enough writer seems to be born with knowledge. But he really is not; he has only been born with the ability to learn in a quicker ratio to the passage of time than other men and without conscious application, and with an intelligence to accept or reject what is already presented as knowledge. There are some things which cannot be learned quickly and time, which is all we have, must be paid heavily for their acquiring. They are the very simplest things and because it takes a man's life to know them the little new that each man gets from life is very costly and the only heritage he has to leave. Every novel which is truly written contributes to the total of knowledge which is there at the disposal of the next writer who comes, but the next writer must pay, always, a certain nominal percentage in experience to be able to understand and assimilate what is available as his birthright and what he must, in turn, take his departure from. If a writer of prose knows enough about what he is writing about he may omit things that he knows and the reader, if the writer is writing truly enough, will have a feeling of those things as strongly as though the writer had stated them. The dignity of movement of an ice-berg is due to only one-eighth of it being above water. A writer who omits things because he does not know them only makes hollow places in his writing. A writer who appreciates the seriousness of writing so little that he is anxious to make people see he is formally educated, cultured or well-bred is merely a popinjay. And this too remember; a serious writer is not to be confounded with a solemn writer. A serious writer may be a hawk or a buzzard or even a popinjay, but a solemn writer is always a bloody owl.—ERNEST HEMINGWAY, *Death in the Afternoon*, 1932, pp. 190–92

Then ahead we saw a big fire and as we came up and passed, I made out a truck beside the road. I told Kamau to stop and go back and as we backed into the firelight there was a short, bandy-legged man with a Tyroler hat, leather shorts, and an open shirt standing before an un-hooded engine in a crowd of natives.

"Can we help?" I asked him.

"No," he said. "Unless you are a mechanic. It has taken a dislike to me. All engines dislike me."

"Do you think it could be the timer? It sounded as though it might be a timing knock when you went past us."

"I think it is much worse than that. It sounds to be something very bad."

"If you can get to our camp we have a mechanic."

"How far is it?"

"About twenty miles."

"In the morning I will try it. Now I am afraid to make it go farther with that noise of death inside. It is trying to die because it dislikes me. Well, I dislike it too. But if I die it would not annoy it."

"Will you have a drink?" I held out the flask. "Hemingway is my name."

"Kandisky," he said and bowed. "Hemingway is a name I have heard. Where? Where have I heard it? Oh, yes. The *dichter.* You know Hemingway the poet?"

"Where did you read him?"

"In the *Querschnitt.*"

"That is me," I said, very pleased. The *Querschnitt* was a German magazine I had written some rather obscene poems for, and published a long story in, years before I could sell anything in America.

"This is very strange," the man in the Tyroler hat said. "Tell me, what do you think of ⟨Joachim⟩ Ringelnatz?"

"He is splendid."

"So. You like Ringelnatz. Good. What do you think of Heinrich Mann?"

"He is no good."

"You believe it?"

"All I know is that I cannot read him."

"He is no good at all. I see we have things in common. What are you doing here?"

"Shooting."

"Not ivory, I hope."

"No. For kudu."

"Why should any man shoot a kudu? You, an intelligent man, a poet, to shoot kudu."

"I haven't shot any yet," I said. "But we've been hunting them hard now for ten days. We would have got one tonight if it hadn't been for your lorry."

"That poor lorry. But you should hunt for a year. At the end of that time you have shot everything and you are sorry for it. To hunt for one special animal is nonsense. Why do you do it?"

"I like to do it."

"Of course, if you *like* to do it. Tell me, what do you really think of Rilke?"

"I have read only the one thing."

"Which?"

"The Cornet."

"You liked it?"

"Yes."

"I have no patience with it. It is snobbery. Valery, yes. I see the point of Valery; although there is much snobbery too. Well at least you do not kill elephants."

"I'd kill a big enough one."

"How big?"

"A seventy pounder. Maybe smaller."

"I see there are things we do not agree on. But it is a pleasure to meet one of the great old *Querschnitt* group. Tell me what is Joyce like? I have not the money to buy it. Sinclair Lewis is nothing. I bought it. No. No. Tell me tomorrow. You do not mind if I am camped near? You are with friends? You have a white hunter?"

"With my wife. We would be delighted. Yes, a white hunter."

"Why is he not out with you?"

"He believes you should hunt kudu alone."

"It is better not to hunt them at all. What is he? English?"

"Yes."

"Bloody English?"

"No. Very nice. You will like him."

"You must go. I must not keep you. Perhaps I will see you tomorrow. It was very strange that we should meet."

"Yes," I said. "Have them look at the truck tomorrow. Anything we can do."

"Good night," he said. "Good trip."

"Good night," I said. We started off and I saw him walking toward the fire waving an arm at the natives. I had not asked him why he had twenty up-country natives with him, nor where he was going. Looking back, I had asked him nothing. I do not like to ask questions, and where I was brought up it was not polite. But here, we had not seen a white man for two weeks, not since we had left Babati to go south, and then to run into one on this road where you met only an occasional Indian trader and the steady migration of the natives out of the famine country, to have him look like a caricature of Benchley in Tyrolean costume, to have him know your name, to call you a poet, to have read the *Querschnitt*, to be an admirer of Joachim Ringelnatz and to want to talk about Rilke, was too fantastic to deal with. So, just then, to crown this fantasy, the lights of the car showed three tall, conical, mounds of something smoking in the road ahead. I motioned to Kamau to stop, and putting on the brakes we skidded just short of them. They were from two to three feet high and when I touched one it was quite warm.

"*Tembo,*" M'Cola said.

It was dung from elephants that had just crossed the road, and in the cold of the evening you could see it steaming. In a little while we were in camp. . . .

I was thinking how real that Russia of the time of our Civil War was, as real as any other place, as Michigan, or the prairie north of town and the woods around Evans's game farm, of how, through Turgenieff, I knew that I had lived there, as I had been in the family Buddenbrooks, and had climbed in and out of her window in *Le Rouge et le noir,* or the morning we had come in the gates of Paris and seen Salcède torn apart by the horses at the Place de Grèves. I saw all that. And it was me they did not break on the rack that time because I had been polite to the executioner the time they killed Coconas and me, and I remember the Eve of St. Bartholomew's and how we hunted Huguenots that night, and when they trapped me at her house that time, and no feeling more true than finding the gate of the Louvre being closed, nor of looking down at his body in the water where he fell from the mast, and always, Italy, better than any book, lying in the chestnut woods, and in the fall mist behind the Duomo going across the town to the Ospedale Maggiore, the nails in my boots on the cobbles, and in the Spring sudden showers in the mountains and the smell of the regiment like a copper coin in your mouth. So in the heat the train stopped at Dezenzano and there was Lago de Garda and those troops are the Czech Legion, and the next time it was raining, and the next time it was in the dark, and the next time you passed it riding in a truck, and the next time you were coming from somewhere else, and the next time you walked to it in the dark from Sermione. For we have been there in the books and out of the books—and where we go, if we are any good, there you can go as we have been. A country, finally, erodes and the dust blows away, the people all die and none of them were of any importance permanently, except those who practised the arts, and these now wish to cease their work because it is too lonely, too hard to do, and is not fashionable. A thousand years makes economics silly and a work of art endures forever, but it is very difficult to do and now it is not fashionable. People do not want to do it any more because they will be out of fashion and the lice who crawl on literature will not praise them. Also it is very hard to do. So what? So I would go on reading about the river that the Tartars came across when raiding, and the drunken old hunter and the girl and how it was then in the different seasons.—ERNEST HEMINGWAY, *The Green Hills of Africa*, 1935, pp. 6–10, 108–9

His brilliant and seductive novels are a deliberate simplification of the complex cross-currents of his environment, and as such represent most attractive avenues of escape for irresponsible people. His characters are men and women at the end of their tether, the leisure class of a disintegrating world who have ceased to believe in anything and are shown to us as pursuing violent physical pleasure as an end in itself. They move as in a dream, drugged by a mysticism of pure action, the mindless somnambulists of a vaguely voluptuous 'blood-consciousness'. Their attitude to things is a studied indifference, a kind of 'aprés moi la déluge'. Eat, drink, make love, horse-race, bull-fight, catch trout—anything rather than think. This is why Hemingway, who writes with a freshness and vitality unknown to the English novel, is at first so exhilarating, till one begins to realize that all this violent activity, pursued as an end in itself, is quite meaningless, a kind of life that can only have one conclusion: 'Well, boy, I guess I'll beat it. It isn't fun any more. Everything's gone to hell inside me.' Such is the inevitable conclusion of the whole array of these charming, brilliant and empty novels and stories, *A Farewell to Arms*, *The Sun Also Rises*, *Death in the Afternoon*, *Men without Women*. It isn't fun any more! Everything's gone to hell inside me. The emptiness of this leisure class life finds even more cynical, hardboiled expression in Hemingway's follower O'Hara, with his *Appointment in Samara* and *Butterfield 8*.—PHILIP HENDERSON, "The Romantic Novel: America," *The Novel Today: Studies in Contemporary Attitudes*, 1936, pp. 136–37

Hemingway's difficulties as a writer arise from the limitations of realism. His style, derived from Huck Finn, Stein, Anderson with perhaps a dash of Firbank, is the antithesis of fine writing. It is a style in which the body talks rather than the mind, one admirable for rendering emotions; love, fear, joy of battle, despair, sexual appetite, but impoverished for intellectual purposes. Hemingway is fortunate in possessing a physique which is at home in the world of boxing, bull-fighting and big game shooting, fields closed to most writers and especially to Mandarins; he is supreme in the domain of violence and his opportunity will be to write the great book (and there have been no signs of one so far), about the Spanish war. Hemingway's tragedy as an artist is that he has not had the versatility to run away fast enough from his imitators. The talkies that facilitated his success brought on a flood of talkie-novels, the trick of being tough, the knack of writing entirely in dialogue interrupted only by a few sentimental landscapes caught on and with each bad copy the prestige of the original was affected. A Picasso would have done something different; Hemingway could only indulge in invective against his critics—and do it again. His colleagues in American realism, Dos Passos, O'Hara, Caldwell, have found the same difficulties and the Hemingway style is now confined to sporting journalists on the daily papers, advertising men with literary ambitions, cinema critics and the writers of thrillers. The first you-man sentence of the *Portrait of the Artist*, "when you wet the bed first it is warm, then it gets cold", a sentence intended to represent the simple body-conscious needs of early childhood, after dominating fiction for years, would seem to have had its day.

Lewis has attacked Hemingway for being a "dumb ox", for choosing stupid inarticulate heroes who are the passive victims of circumstance rather than active and intelligent masters of their fate. Yet at the period at which Hemingway wrote his best books it was necessary to be a dumb ox. It was the only way to escape from Chelsea's Apes of God and from Bloomsbury's Sacred Geese.—CYRIL CONNOLLY, "The New Vernacular," *Enemies of Promise*, 1938, pp. 63–66

The parallels which exist between Hemingway and ⟨Stephen⟩ Crane as human beings are so numerous and exact that they will go a long way toward explaining why the two men so resemble each other as prose stylists, and even on occasion as poets. Both Hemingway and Crane began very young their careers as reporters, and quickly became foreign correspondents. They traveled widely, and to the same places: Key West, the American West and Cuba; Europe, a Greco-Turkish War, and so on. Mainly they journeyed to wars, when they were able. Both had very religious mothers, neither ever quite got over the death of his father, and both rebelled in various ways against their families. Each childhood was marred by the painful experience of violence; and it was eventually in warfare, sought out and embraced, that each man found a fascinating formalization of violence, and his essential metaphor for life. Both made an art of their preoccupations, and sought above all things the varied meanings of war. Chiefly they were compelled to learn what it had to teach them about themselves, and to test themselves against it, to make of danger a kind of mystic ceremony, or rite, or crucible. The results were identical. Each man found violence, pitted himself against it in terror, sought courage for its own sake, and was cited for its uneasy attainment. They worried at great length the problems of the relation of fear to bravery, and in the end they acted with a similarity that is startling. The pictures of Hemingway's behavior under fire in the Second World War are identical with those of Crane in Cuba, where the earlier reporter took suicidal risks in what appear to be truly desperate attempts to get hit.

Often dedicated in their attitudes and their work to the annihilation of romantic idealisms and lies, both men seem themselves romantic individualists. Both stubbornly self-reliant, they disdained those who would not strike out for themselves, and as a result both held unpopular attitudes toward people who condoned or awaited a social reliance. Both opposed and insulted respectability, violated in dress, language, frankness and behavior the genteel traditions of their periods, and developed defiant affections for people in disrepute. Partly as a result, both men became the victims of gossip and found their characters the subjects of hot debate. They livened our literary scene with their color, and—lonely, handsome to women, and a bit heroic—watched legends grow from their personalities and adventures. Crane had no devotion to bullfighting, but he was an amateur athlete of note; he also loved to shoot and was good at it. He ended his career in the midst of friends, fame, wealth, partial expatriation and small animals at Brede Place—the perfect precedent for Finca Vigía. Crane's whole dark view of existence, of man damaged and alone in a hostile, violent world, of life as one long war which we seek out and challenge in fear and controlled panic—it is all an amazing forecast of Hemingway.

The work which Stephen Crane tore out of his sickness was rescued from the obscurity into which it had fallen after his death in 1900 at a moment which could not have been more perfectly timed for Hemingway than it was. Damaged himself, and in every imaginable way prepared to find in Crane what would have most meaning for him, Hemingway was in 1921 learning how to write the things Crane had written. This was the year in which Vincent Starrett selected among Crane's nearly forgotten stories and brought out a volume called *Men, Women and Boats*. A friend of Hemingway's, Ford Madox Ford, called these the "best short stories in English," and the young writer could not possibly have missed them.

At any rate it does not look as though he missed them. In Crane he could find his own strict sense of personal integrity and honesty, exercised in a rigorous effort to look for himself directly and immediately at things, so that he might see them as if they had not been seen before. Here was a writer who must have worked on the theory that a complete honesty of vision would mean a new originality, so false are our clichés and our commonplace attitudes, and the notion was validated by the results on paper. Here, as he would hope for himself, the effort had resulted in a concentrated, exclusive and brilliant prose style, simple, bare and tense. Here were vivid, clear impressions and perceptions, fresh pictures of the sensuous surface of life, and a precision and originality in language. Here too a sense of tight design, a startling immediacy in description and even (in *The Red Badge of Courage*) a fascinated, glaring picture of a battlefield corpse, compulsive and intense. In Crane he could see also an attempt to make dialogue a true imitation of colloquial American speech (though it often failed) and could always feel sharply the country in the background—"the places and how the weather was." Here there were even the laconic, understated endings to stories that people complained were "pointless."

In the *Green Hills* Hemingway chose two stories for special praise—"The Open Boat" and "The Blue Hotel." The first of these is often called Crane's masterpiece; at times it sounds enough like Hemingway to have been written by him. There are several such places, but take one in which Crane's ear did not fail him:

> . . . the cook and the correspondent argued as to the difference between a life-saving station and a house of refuge. The cook had said: "There's a house of refuge just north of the Mosquito Inlet Light, and as soon as they see us they'll come off in their boat and pick us up."
>
> "As soon as who sees us?" said the correspondent.
>
> "The crew," said the cook.
>
> "Houses of refuge don't have crews," said the correspondent. "As I understand them, they are only places where clothes and grub are stored for the benefit of shipwrecked people. They don't carry crews."
>
> "Oh, yes, they do," said the cook.
>
> "No, they don't," said the correspondent.
>
> "Well, we're not there yet, anyhow," said the oiler, in the stern.
>
> "Well," said the cook, "perhaps it's not a house of refuge that I'm thinking of as being near Mosquito Inlet Light; perhaps it's a life-saving station."
>
> "We're not there yet," said the oiler in the stern.

Here is all the flatness, and yet all the cadence, too, of Hemingway's famous conversation. Here is the realistic yet mannered effect, the same terse and unliterary tone, the same repetitions of words, phrases and statements, and the same muted tension.

"The Blue Hotel" has as many resemblances, particularly to "The Killers," and has in addition a dead Swede propped up in front of a cash register—a device Hemingway used in "An Alpine Idyll" and reused in *The Fifth Column*. But it is a story that Hemingway failed to mention which most clearly establishes his great debt to Crane. This is "An Episode of War," and it is enlightening to compare it with a story of Hemingway's like "A Clean Well-Lighted Place," which has all the "monotony," the regularly rising and falling cadence, the depressed tone and the razor-edged impressions and perceptions for which Hemingway is famous.

"A Clean Well-Lighted Place" is a fairly "typical" Hemingway story. An old man has tried to commit suicide, and has failed even in this. He sits alone in a café until late at night an unsympathetic waiter sends him along, and closes the place. Another waiter is the central figure in the story, and he feels quite differently from his colleague about those who need a clean, well-lighted café to sit up late in. There is little else in life to help support it. "Hail nothing full of nothing, nothing is with thee," he thinks, echoing Mr. Frazer as he heads homeward in the realization that there is nothing else he can do but go to his room and to bed. The story ends with a characteristic understatement.

> Now, without thinking further, he would go home to his room. He would lie in the bed and finally, with daylight, he would go to sleep. After all, he said to himself, it is probably only insomnia. Many must have it.

Crane's story is of a lieutenant who, while distributing a ration of coffee, is suddenly shot in the arm. The wound is not serious, but in the confusion of battle it is not properly cared for, and the arm is amputated. With the same flat, reserved, depressed understatement and absolute lack of comment for which Hemingway is well known, Crane ends "An Episode of War":

> And this is the story of how the lieutenant lost his arm. When he reached home, his sisters, his mother, his wife, sobbed for a long time at the sight of the flat sleeve. "Oh, well," he said, standing shamefaced amid these tears, "I don't suppose it matters so much as all that."

"After all, he said to himself, it is probably only insomnia. Many must have it."

Hemingway "had no basic relation to any prewar culture," wrote Alfred Kazin in his *On Native Grounds*. But Hemingway himself knows better than this, and with the praise he bestowed in the *Green Hills* he has acknowledged his relations. If we will read this praise as an admission of indebtedness, and read his attacks of other writers who are supposed to have influenced him as a refusal to admit anything, then a kind of sense can be made of this process of casting off immediate and familiar forebears, while taking on older ones. This is by no means to say that Hemingway learned nothing from his friends in Paris. It is to say instead that whatever he may have been taught there was an extension of what he could have learned at home. The route which goes from Twain to Crane and Hemingway has no uncharted areas which needed to be negotiated by a transatlantic crossing.
—PHILIP YOUNG, "The Origin and Meaning of a Style," *Ernest Hemingway*, 1952, pp. 162–67

Hemingway is a limited writer. But he has knocked his way among the immortals by his tight, poignant style, giving the young twentieth century a voice and a manner. He is a journalist transforming the report into art. He is a boy eternally trying to prove himself a man. He is modern man, driven by a warring world to survive in himself. He is the existential battler, the knight in the turtle-necked sweater, who has discovered the ultimate romance in fighting hopeless odds among the ashes of our temples.

And because we all respond to the romantic dream of embattled self, which is at the center of Hemingway's best work, Hemingway will continue to be read and will continue, in his way, to be great. He has found, in himself, our own soft romantic center, our sweet dream of despair, and toughened it into bravery. He has caught man's essential nagging belief—aggravated by a nihilistic, skeptical, and uncertain period—that we do not get all we deserve, that we are made for something better than brutality and death, that our virtues ought to be rewarded by some supreme and deathless love and by some grandeur that neither the rubble of two wars nor the glitter of the suburbs can supply.

Hemingway is the apostle of the faith that is lost, the faith that had already begun to erode by the middle of the nineteenth century. He is the American expression of the British Henley who wrote:

> Out of the night that covers me,
> Black as the Pit from pole to pole,
> I thank whatever gods may be
> For my unconquerable soul.

Like Henley, the Hemingway hero tends to be covered by night; he, too, neither winces nor cries aloud. But only late in his career does Hemingway's hero acquire anything like an unconquerable soul, as the unbowed head is bloodied. The soul of his early hero is conquered indeed, and he moves as if stunned.

Early and late, Hemingway's God is only a forlorn possibility. The sea of Christian faith had drained away over the edges of the modern world, as Matthew Arnold had perceived in "Dover Beach" a half-century earlier (Philip Young also sees Arnold's pertinence), leaving neither joy, nor love, nor light, nor certitude, nor peace, nor help for pain—leaving nothing but a cry for constancy between a man and a woman standing on a darkening plain

> Swept with confused alarms of struggle and flight,
> Where ignorant armies clash by night.

Hemingway has toughened up all this to our taste. And he will continue to speak for the lost pitiful soul in all of us, as we cry out against a world that occasionally seems incapable of giving us what we so deeply and selfishly want—an attitude disguised in a brave way, in a far land, so that we can have our romance without noticing it and can believe that we are being real and tough.

Self-pity remains at the Hemingway core, but the surface is progressively covered over by a rind of courage. A tougher hero begins to predominate. Hemingway's early hero, to simplify, personifies self-pity; his later one personifies courage. The early one is beaten and passive; the later one stays unbeaten because active. The early one is young; the later one is (at least as youth would see him) old. Philip Young has taken the first hero as the only one, has seen the second only, as a subsidiary figure, a "code hero," and has seen Hemingway's growth in the true hero's ability to learn the code. And certainly Mr. Young has been illuminating. I have indeed despaired of acknowledging his work—and that of Carlos Baker and Charles Fenton—in any just detail. Nevertheless, I prefer to see in Hemingway two different modes, the soft and the hard, the inner and the outer, and to see two distinct heroes—the early, beaten one, and the emerging unbeaten one, the man who is, in Hemingway's own term, "undefeated" in spite of loss.

Hemingway's early hero, Nick Adams and his successors, is a young man blown out of society and belief by shellfire in the First World War. The world now seems cruel, whimsical, senseless, with no meaning nor plan. However bleak, the energy and truth in these early stories comes from the state of mind of the young hero. We can accept the hero's attitude of defeat, his sad, drifting despair—because he is young. These stories of the defeated hero tell in extreme form the sadness and disillusion that any young person knows at some time or another, in some way or another, as he wakes up into life. The First World War simply put this disillusion on Hemingway and his generation in a sudden and shocking way. And Hemingway's fictive transposition is memorable and probably enduring. This is Hemingway's first mode. The tune is soft, sad, and sweet.

But Hemingway's second mode is different. The irony has a braver twang. Although "The Undefeated" appears early (summer, 1925)—indeed even several months before Nick Adams and *In Our Time* reached print—the undefeated mode develops slowly, not predominating until *To Have and Have Not* (1935). But thereafter the undefeated loser is Hemingway's hero, though rendered imperfect by streaks of the old defeat, until his triumph in *The Old Man and the Sea*. The undefeated loser represents an existential step up from the depths, or forward from the wall. If man seems to be beaten by a world without meaning, at least he has his courage, at least he can act. As John Killinger has recently shown in *Hemingway and the Dead Gods*, Hemingway has a great deal of the existentialist in him. Hemingway's existentialistic affirmation, however, is late, and it is further qualified by the fact that his undefeated losers, at their strongest, are all men of the lower classes, men of limited understanding, unable to see the world widely enough, it seems, to despair of hopeless situations. When Hemingway tries to move his undefeated man up the scale of intelligence, he loses him in the old Hemingway; we hear the old inner murmur of self-pity.

To see Hemingway as a writer of two opposing modes, never happily reconciled, may prove helpful. In fact, this duality of modes matches exactly the slightly schizophrenic personality apparent in Hemingway from the first, as Robert McAlmon's remembrance of the young Hemingway in Paris suggests:

> Hemingway was a type not easy to size up. At times he was deliberately hard-boiled and case-hardened; again he appeared deliberately innocent, sentimental, the hurt, soft, but fairly sensitive boy trying to conceal hurt, wanting to be brave, not bitter or cynical but being somewhat of both, and somehow on the defensive, suspicions lurking in his peering analytic glances at a person with whom he was talking. He approached a café with a small-boy, tough-guy swagger, and before strangers of whom he was doubtful a potential snarl of scorn played on his large-lipped, rather loose mouth.

The very tension in Hemingway's prose expresses his struggle to keep himself together, to integrate the soft and the hard, to heal the abysmal uncertainty. And so the undefeated loser emerges in Hemingway's works as a sign of confidence and maturity, never wholly won. The undefeated loser may serve as an index for some of Hemingway's failures and may help to distinguish some of his triumphs, played on one string or the other.
—SHERIDAN BAKER, "Introduction" to *Ernest Hemingway: An Introduction and Interpretation*, 1967, 1–3

. . . Hemingway explained the process of getting it down by chronicling his work habits and routines. There was for him a kind of inductive magic in the way he went about writing. Part of the vision and feeling of how to render it came from the way it was approached. Rule one was to work alone. Both seeing and writing were for individuals, not schools or organizations. Incidental reasons for such work were that others distracted the writer from the concentration needed for making his truth and, as he noted while condemning the pseudo-artists of Montmartre and Montparnasse, one had to be careful not to betray himself into substituting public talk and public display for actual writing. And in groups one lost his certainty of how he felt; he was likely to accept the group's feeling for his own. Particularly was this true if the group had its own favorite theories. Watching Reginald Rowe puzzle alone over his paintings in Cuba, Hemingway noted that "as long as an artist is puzzled he has a chance." For a writer with a tragic sense, working alone was the most efficient way to combat the passage of time; time was always short for the artist and the wasting of it became more and more the unforgivable sin. Indeed, the writer, he said in his Nobel Prize speech, had to "face eternity, or the lack of it, each day."

His second rule was to avoid talking about his work while he was doing it. Indeed, he told Harvey Breit, he disliked talking about completed work because such talk destroyed his pleasure in having done it, and requests to explain it made him feel he had not succeeded in conveying the experience. But to talk about work in progress was to endanger the work. One could talk away his vision, lose the excitement and the mystery of creating before the creation was fully realized, and dissipate the inner tensions that helped get the created experience into writing. The problem was not wholly internal, though. In his writing as in his feeling and thought, Hemingway recognized the power of mysterious external forces on him. That he was superstitious about such powers was evident in remarks like that in *A Moveable Feast*: " 'We're always lucky,' I said [to Hadley] and like a fool I did not knock on wood. There was wood everywhere in that apartment to knock on too." He carried horse chestnuts and rabbit feet for luck and knocked on wood whenever he made proud statements that might offend lurking forces. About his work and his life he practiced a kind of language magic that might be explained away by psychoanalysts but was more than figuratively real to him. Language could either make things real or keep them from being real. Circumstance apparently determined the way the magic worked. In one of his articles on Louis Quintanilla and in another on Gulf fishing he illustrated how talk induced reality. Quintanilla, he said, lost the product of his life's work in painting when his studio was destroyed by bombs in Madrid and found the loss too overwhelming to talk about. Hemingway's coxswain and assistant on the fishing boat *Pilar*, he noted, had an animistic belief about certain hooks, lures, and lines they used, cursed and abused them like sensate beings when they failed, and practiced a kind of incantatory magic on the lines when a large fish was hooked: "Oh, God the bread of my children!" he would chant. "Joseph and Mary look at the bread of my children jump! There it goes the bread of my children! He'll never stop the bread the bread of my children!" That Hemingway thought language could make feeling unreal was evident when he noted in the preface to *The Great Crusade* that he could not write about Hans, commander of the Eleventh Brigade: "We have too much together for me ever to risk losing any of it by trying to write about it." But the important thing was for the writer not to be "spooked," he said, by talking too much and too unwisely.

Rule three was to wake early, work while his mind was fresh and he could concentrate, to work hard while he worked, then stop. The idea was, he said, to stop when he knew what would come next and not exhaust his imagination. He had exhausted himself while writing his first novel in six weeks and had had to spend extra months rewriting it. Later he found that his imagination functioned like a well, which is "where your 'juice' is. Nobody knows what it is made of, least of all yourself. What you know is if you have it or you have to wait for it to come back." To avoid dry periods he learned "never to empty the well of my writing, but always to stop when there was still something in the deep part of the well, and let it refill at night from the springs that fed it." Another part of the rule was to avoid conscious thinking or worrying about the writing until his next session at the writing board. His mind might, perhaps should, continue to work unconsciously, but he read, fished, and continued observing other things to keep his mind off the next day's writing. That way, he said, all his energy went into the writing.

Rule four was that if one did not worry his work as a dog does a bone, he went fresh to the making of it each day and the coherence of the invention depended on sustaining freshness of insight rather than a thought-out plan. He reread each morning what he had written the day before, sometimes read the entire work up to that point if it was not too long, and began again creating within the illusion offered by the work. But, as he said and wrote on several occasions, he seldom knew what was going to happen when he began to write: "I start to make it up and have happen what would have to happen as it goes along." This was as true for novels as for stories. While writing *A Farewell To Arms* and *For Whom the Bell Tolls*, he knew in a very general way what the logic of the story was but "didn't know what was going to happen for sure. . . . I as inventing." He demonstrated the influence of daily experience on day-to-day creation of his fiction when he incorporated family experience in the narrative progress of *A Farewell to Arms*. His wife gave birth to their son by Caesarean section while he was working through the first draft of that novel, and he saw the terrors of a Caesarean birth for Frederic and Catherine's child as imaginatively logical for the novel and made that part of the inventing. In writing *The Old Man and the Sea*, he said, he began knowing "two or three things about the situation, but I didn't know the story. . . . I didn't even know if that big fish was going to bite for the old man when it started smelling around the bait. I had to write on inventing out of knowledge."

Rule five was even more practical. In essence, it was to work slowly. For Hemingway, it was necessary to live the experience as he created and wrote it, and sometimes, as he remembered in *A Moveable Feast*, he wrote only a paragraph in a morning's work. The thing to do was to avoid being facile. He found it useful to write in pencil except for occasional passages of dialogue which he did on the typewriter. Such slow work, he said, gave him more chances to make sure that all the sensations and emotions became available to the reader. Typing up the scenes later gave him another opportunity to revise for vividness, and he did not mind revising for effect even at the proofreading stage. The trick was to keep the writing fluid as long as possible. . . .

He learned, Hemingway said, not only from great writers. The great painters were his teachers too; they taught how to see and how to pattern one's vision. In actual numbers of expressions of debt and influence, Hemingway had more to say about painters than writers. "I learn as much from painters about how to write as from writers," he told ⟨George⟩ Plimpton. He went to the Luxembourg Museum on foodless lunch hours to study the paintings, particularly those of Cézanne, and found that hunger sharpened his perceptions of the way artists worked. Besides, he had no money for food and the free museum was a powerful teacher for a struggling young man who had stopped his formal education after high school. But an even more fundamental reason for his learning from paintings, he noted on several occasions, was that he wished almost as much to be a painter as a writer. "If I could be something else, I'd like to be a painter," he told Robert Manning on a misty, painter's afternoon. Some emotional states he thought could better be conveyed in paint than in prose. To sense how a picador felt after seeing large bulls in the corrals before a *corrida*, he wrote in *Death in the Afternoon*, one had to see a picture: "If I could draw I would make a picture of a table at the café during a feria with the banderilleros sitting before lunch reading the papers, a boot-black at work, a waiter hurrying somewhere and two returning picadors, one a big brown-faced, dark-browed man usually very cheerful and a great joker, the other a gray-haired, neat, hawk-nosed, trim-waisted little man, both of them looking the absolute embodiment of gloom and depression." The wish was indicative of a key characteristic of Hemingway's invention. He thought and worked in terms of scenes, though they had more movement and fluidity than most painters could suggest. . . .

Still another indication of the way he learned from paintings could be seen in his frequent allusion to paintings as a way of evoking scene-consciousness in his writing, both fictional and nonfictional. In his descriptive accounts, for example, he saw the view from the restaurant and river at Bas Meudon near Paris as a scene from Sisley, and again at the Aranjuez restaurant during his travels on the Ordóñez-Dominguín circuit he saw a view of the Tajo River as though Sisley had painted it. In the kudu country of Africa, he noted in 1935, there were parks that looked as though they came out of André Masson's pictures. In Aranjuez at fiesta time the colorful townspeople made the city "Velázquez to the edge and then straight Goya to the bull ring." In Paris the saffron-hued tank wagons working on the Rue Cardinal Lemoine "looked like Braque paintings." And to tell in shorthand what one of his chauffeurs was like in Madrid during the siege, he noted that Tomás looked like a "particularly unattractive, very mature dwarf out of Velázquez, put into a suit of blue dungarees." For scenes of violence he almost always turned to Goya. The broken-legged horses and mules left to drown at Smyrna during the Greco-Turkish war, he noted, called for a Goya to depict them. In his fiction, to cite only a few instances, he used painting and art allusions to evoke scenes and moods. Pablo's proud horse, Robert Jordan notes, "looked as though he had come out of a painting by Velázquez"; and at Velázquez 63, Madrid headquarters of the idealistic International Brigade, Robert Jordan remembers having the religious feeling he knew when looking at Chartres Cathedral windows or seeing paintings by Mantegna, El Greco, and Breughel in the Prado. In *Across the River and into the Trees* Richard Cantwell thinks of death as having a face only Hieronymous Bosch could paint, sees the Venetian market place as if it had been done by Dutch genre painters, and in his elegiac mood sees the Grand Canal "as grey as though Degas had painted it on one of his greyest days." Painting allusions also lent themselves to ironical statement in fiction. The idealistic young Hungarian in "The Revolutionist" carries with him reproductions of saintly paintings by Giotto, Masaccio, and Piero della Francesca but cannot like the bitter Mantegnas, favorites of his Italian mentor, who has become disillusioned about prospects for revolution in Italy. In *A Farewell to Arms*, when Frederic Henry and Catherine Barkley flee to Switzerland while posing as architecture and art students, they cynically review their clichés on artists in case they are questioned: "Rubens. . . . Large and fat. . . . Titian. . . . Titian-haired. . . . Mantegna. . . . Very bitter . . . lots of nail holes." And with their alibi still in mind after interrogation by the Swiss police, Frederic looks at his raw hands and comments cynically that at least there is no hole in his side.

Hemingway's further insight into the relationship between fiction and painting could be seen in his comments on having his own work illustrated. Charles Scribner, he wrote in the introduction for the 1948 edition of *A Farewell to Arms*, had asked him how he felt about such a prospect. Hemingway's answer indicated his recognition that the two arts met on the level of invention, not observation. Unless the illustrator had a better sense of invention than the writer had, the result would be to limit the imaginative overtones of the novel. What he preferred was to have pictures with their own centers of meaning and let the book and pictures complement each other. "If I could write a book that took place in the Bahamas, I would like it to be illustrated by Winslow Homer, provided he did no illustrating but simply painted the Bahamas and what he saw there. If I were Guy de Maupassant, a good job to have dead or alive, I would like my work to be illustrated by the drawings and paintings of Toulouse-Lautrec, some outdoor scenes of the middle time of Renoir and have them leave my Norman landscapes alone because no painter ever did them better."

If his most instructive analogies for writing came from painting, Hemingway found it useful to think in terms of other arts as well. His family background in music and his own intensive training in music while a boy provided other insights which he later acknowledged. He told George Plimpton that writers should learn what they could from composers on the use of harmony and counterpoint. He provided an example in his interview with Lillian Ross: "In the first paragraph of 'Farewell,' I used the word 'and' consciously over and over the way Mr. Johann Sebastian Bach used a note in music when he was emitting counterpoint. I can almost write like Mr. Johann sometimes—or, anyway, so he would like it." His counter-pointing of two narative lines in the last third of *For Whom the Bell Tolls*—the partisans' last preparations for the attack on the bridge and Andrés' attempt to ascend the chain of command to reach General Golz—was another instance of his using such strategies from music.

What he learned from the art of bullfighting was both technical and theoretical. His preference for the simple, unadorned line of action with all its meaning implicit, not pointed out either by gesture or by verbalization, was of course a value he shared with the best matadors and *aficionados*, whether or not he learned it at the bull ring. But the fundamental insight behind such a preference was one he could see dramatized at the bull ring and could carry over into his seeing and creating. It was, ironically enough, the decadence of bullfighting rather than its flowering that afforded the insight. The decadent style in bullfighting came with the emphasis on capework rather than on killing the bull. As the popular matadors put on more and more florid shows with their capes, using the butterfly pass and all the other passes with names ending in *illa* and *ina*, they left the true meaning of capework to be carried out by the picadors and banderilleros; that is, to prepare the bull for killing. And with such decadent styles the matadors finally made killing the bull a virtual anticlimax. They emphasized the manner of execution instead of the end result; they ignored the effect of the *suertes* on the bull. To Hemingway it was too often that way with writing also.

Style in writing, as he noted more than once, was keyed to efficiency, to attaining the end result of effect on the reader, of giving him the sense of reality that both the good writer and the good bullfighter could provide. But style for itself was meretricious and narcissistic.—ROBERT O. STEPHENS, "Hemingway's Aesthetic Thought: The Art of Seeing," *Hemingway's Nonfiction: The Public Voice*, 1968, pp. 219–27

Works

Of all the work by the young men who have sprung up since 1920 one book survives—*The Enormous Room* by E. E. Cummings. It is scarcely a novel; it doesn't deal with the American scene; it was swamped in the mediocre downpour, isolated—forgotten. But it lives on, because those few who cause books to live have not been able to endure the thought of its mortality. Two other books, both about the war, complete the possible salvage from the work of the younger generation—*Through the Wheat* and *Three Soldiers*, but the former despite its fine last chapters doesn't stand up as well as *Les Croix de bois* and *The Red Badge of Courage*, while the latter is marred by its pervasive flavor of contemporary indignation. But as an augury that someone has profited by this dismal record of high hope and stale failure comes the first work of Ernest Hemingway.

In Our Time consists of fourteen stories, short and long, with fifteen vivid miniatures interpolated between them. When I try to think of any contemporary American short stories as good as "Big Two-Hearted River," the last one in the book, only Gertrude Stein's "Melanctha," Anderson's "The Egg," and Lardner's "Golden Honeymoon" come to mind. It is the account of a boy on a fishing trip—he hikes, pitches his tent, cooks dinner, sleeps, and next morning casts for trout. Nothing more—but I read it with the most breathless unwilling interest I have experienced since Conrad first bent my reluctant eyes upon the sea.

The hero, Nick, runs through nearly all the stories, until the book takes on almost an autobiographical tint—in fact "My Old Man," one of the two in which this element seems entirely absent, is the least successful of all. Some of the stories show influences but they are invariably absorbed and transmuted, while in "My Old Man" there is an echo of Anderson's way of thinking in those sentimental "horse stories," which inaugurated his respectability and also his decline four years ago.

But with "The Doctor and the Doctor's Wife," "The End of Something," "The Three Day Blow," "Mr. and Mrs. Elliot," and "Soldier's Home" you are immediately aware of something temperamentally new. In the first of these a man is backed down by a half breed Indian after committing himself to a fight. The quality of humiliation in the story is so intense that it immediately calls up every such incident in the reader's past. Without the aid of a comment or a pointing finger one knows exactly the sharp emotion of young Nick who watches the scene.

The next two stories describe an experience at the last edge of adolescence. You are constantly aware of the continual snapping of ties that is going on around Nick. In the half stewed, immature conversation before the fire you watch the awakening of that vast unrest that descends upon the emotional type at about eighteen. Again there is not a single recourse to exposition. As in "Big Two-Hearted River," a picture—sharp, nostalgic, tense—develops before your eyes. When the picture is complete a light seems to snap out, the story is over. There is no tail, no sudden change of pace at the end to throw into relief what has gone before.

Nick leaves home penniless; you have a glimpse of him lying wounded in the street of a battered Italian town, and later of a love affair with a nurse on a hospital roof in Milan. Then in one of the best of the stories he is home again. The last glimpse of him is when his mother asks him, with all the bitter world in his heart, to kneel down beside her in the dining room in Puritan prayer.

Anyone who first looks through the short interpolated sketches will hardly fail to read the stories themselves. "The Garden at Mons" and "The Barricade" are profound essays upon the English officer, written on a postage stamp. "The King of Greece's Tea Party," "The Shooting of the Cabinet Ministers," and "The Cigar-Store Robbery" particularly fascinated me, as they did when Edmund Wilson first showed them to me in an earlier pamphlet, over two years ago.

Disregard the rather ill considered blurbs upon the cover. It is sufficient that here is no raw food served up by the railroad restaurants of California and Wisconsin. In the best of these dishes there is not a bit to spare. And many of us who have grown weary of admonitions to "watch this man or that" have felt a sort of renewal of excitement at these stories wherein Ernest Hemingway turns a corner into the street.—F. SCOTT FITZGERALD, "How to Waste Material: A Note on My Generation," *Afternoon of an Author*, 1920, pp. 120–22

Last June, when *The Torrents of Spring* was published, it was my pleasure to confess that the author, Ernest Hemingway, had enabled me to distinguish him from the surrounding Americans in Paris who contribute to esoteric Franco-American magazines, and now and then publish a volume in France which would not pass the vigilant scrutiny of American or English printers. The fact that one very great book, to wit, James Joyce's *Ulysses*, was published in that manner had never converted me to the notion that any book printed in English in France must necessarily be the masterpiece of an expatriate and misunderstood genius. When Mr. Hemingway brought out his first volume of short stories, *In Our Time*, I felt that anything he had to say might well be said over the imprint of an American publisher, and that he ought on no account to become the victim of that spurious fame attaching to books published in France and barred from this country.

With remarkable foresight Mr. Hemingway made the supreme sacrifice for an American of his generation; he left Paris for a few weeks and rested his feet upon the barren soil of his native land. He rested them long enough to interest one of the oldest and most dignified publishing houses in America in two manuscripts, of which the second, *The Sun Also Rises*, has just appeared in direct and apostolic succession to *The Torrents of Spring*. The latter, I may say, was regarded coldly by those who take their Sherwood Anderson straight, and it was even said that the author was that creature who is sharper than a serpent's tooth, namely, a thankless child. Mr. Hemingway, it seems, was an admirer, nay, a disciple, of Mr. Anderson, and in parodying him, he was biting the literary hand that had been outstretched to feed him at the outset of a great career. It was my impartial opinion that this base ingratitude was a hopeful sign of conversion.

The Sun Also Rises is a first offering from the convert, for which I return thanks unto the gods who thus touch the hearts of wayward men. The aura of æstheticism no longer lingers about Mr. Hemingway. Innocent of his past, one would never guess that he once toyed with synthetic heresies and bowed down to æsthetic idols of wood and stone. What one felt as a potential quality of certain stories in *In Our Time* is here realized with masterly cunning. It all looks so simple! He hasn't even a story to tell. There are no witty and no purple patches. Yet, when the book is finished, the reader has heard a story, his mind has been titillated by something which must obviously have been the author's sense of humor, and flashes of scenes remain in the memory despite his refusal to do more than hint at what he sees.

In the first place, Ernest Hemingway writes dialogue so effectively that he has merely to allow one to hear the sound of a character's voice in order to plant him vividly before the reader. Those familiar with the particular world of Paris which is the axis of the narrative will further note with amusement how Mr. Hemingway has managed to introduce several easily identified people, of minor importance intrinsically, but of deep importance as typical phenomena. Robert Cohn, who learned boxing "painfully and thoroughly to counteract the feeling of inferiority and shyness he had felt on being treated as a Jew at Princeton," is something more than an impression of a certain American editor in exile. His portrait becomes at Mr. Hemingway's hands an amazing character study.

Another figure who lives intensely in these pages, although her activities consist mainly of having drinks, lovers, and passionate moments of sincerity with the author's *alter ego*, is Lady Ashley, a perfect product of that postwar world of which Mr. Hemingway is the brilliant chronicler. After all that we have suffered from novelists intent on describing hard-boiled flappers, Ernest Hemingway comes along with his modern version of *la femme de trente ans*, and we know more about the eternal feminine, model 1926, than ever before. If there are people who wonder why six cocktails grow where one grew before, this book will tell them. The consumption of liquor to the square inch in *The Sun Also Rises* reaches maximum pressure, and just as these characters would not exist without their frequent and generous libations, so, I think, Mr. Hemingway's story could not be told within the limits of what is so preposterously known in this country as "Law Enforcement"—meaning usually the illegal imposition of one measure.

Mr. Hemingway is not merely a student of expatriate alcoholism, he is a bullfighting connoisseur, and when his group of tragic comedians arrive in Pamplona for the *fiesta*, he dwells with an expert's affection upon every aspect of the affair without once giving the impression that he is determined to show how much he knows. He enters into the technicalities and leaves the picturesque to emerge as best it can, and it does emerge more truly and impressively than from any bravura passage. The reason being that the technical details of a bullfight are no more and no less to the author than the details of the innumerable drinks and dishes consumed in the course of that hectic week. All these matters are equal in the sight of Mr. Hemingway, and with the utmost gravity, certain in managing his effects, he carefully records exactly what each person drinks or does.

The technique of this book is fascinating. When one is not swept along by astonishing dialogue, subtle, obvious, profound, and commonplace,—but always alive,—one is listening to careful enumeration of little facts whose cumulative effect is to give them the importance of remarkable incidents. The description of Pamplona during the festival week is reporting of the most laconic type. We are told what preparations are made, we see the bulls being unloaded from the train, the peasants swarming in from the countryside, and we are plunged into tavern brawls and carouses. At no time does the author attempt to "write up" his scenes, but in the end one has the feeling of having spent the week there.

In the midst of all this Mr. Hemingway never loses sight of his psychological *déracinés*, who so strongly merge their highly complicated modern selves in the stream of elementary consciousness. Remote as they seem from the setting, they are a part of it. Fishing in Spain or drinking at Zelli's, these American men express themselves, the curious syncopated rhythm of their lives, just as Frances, the American girl, endures in a nagging scene outside a café, and Brett, the Englishwoman, bares her soul in fierce moments of tortured feeling. Ernest Hemingway has so completely realized his types and mastered his medium that he triumphantly adds a new chapter to the story which Scott Fitzgerald began in *This Side of Paradise*.—ERNEST BOYD, "Readers and Writers," *Ind*, Nov. 20, 1926, p. 594

The present novel ⟨*The Sun Also Rises*⟩ by the author of *In Our Time* supports the recent prophecy that he will be the "big man in American letters." At the time the prophecy was delivered it was meaningless because it was equivocal. Many of the possible interpretations now being eliminated, we fear it has turned out to mean something which we shall all regret. Mr. Hemingway has written a book that will be talked about, praised, perhaps imitated; it has already been received in something of that cautiously critical spirit which the followers of Henry James so notoriously maintain toward the master. Mr. Hemingway has produced a successful novel, but not without returning some violence upon the integrity achieved in his first book. He decided for reasons of his own to write a popular novel, or he wrote the only novel which he could write.

To choose the latter conjecture is to clear his intentions, obviously at the cost of impugning his art. One infers moreover that although sentimentality appears explicitly for the first time in his prose, it must have always been there. Its history can be constructed. The method used in *In Our Time* was *pointilliste*, and the sentimentality was submerged. With great skill he reversed the usual and most general formula of prose fiction: instead of selecting the details of physical background and of human behavior for the intensification of a dramatic situation, he employed the minimum of drama for the greatest possible intensification of the observed object. The reference of emphasis for the observed object was therefore not the action; rather, the reference of the action was the object, and the action could be impure or incomplete without risk of detection. It could be mixed and incoherent; it could be brought in when it was advantageous to observation, or left out. The exception, important as such, in Mr. Hemingway's work is the story "Mr. and Mrs. Elliot." Here the definite dramatic conflict inherent in a sexual relation emerged as fantasy, and significantly; presumably he could not handle it otherwise without giving himself away.

In *The Sun Also Rises*, a full-length novel, Mr. Hemingway could not escape such leading situations, and he had besides to approach them with a kind of seriousness. He fails. It is not that Mr. Hemingway is, in the term which he uses in fine contempt for the big word, hard-boiled; it is that he is not hard-boiled enough, in the artistic sense. No one can dispute with a writer the significance he derives from his subject-matter; one can only point out that the significance is mixed or incomplete. Brett is a nymphomaniac; Robert Cohn, a most offensive cad; both are puppets. For the emphasis is false; Hemingway doesn't fill out his characters and let them stand for themselves; he isolates one or two chief traits which reduce them to caricature. His perception of the physical object is direct and accurate; his vision of character, singularly oblique. And he actually betrays the interior machinery of his hard-boiled attitude: "It is awfully easy to be hard-boiled about everything in the daytime, but at night it is another thing," says Jake, the sexually impotent, musing on the futile accessibility of Brett. The history of his sentimentality is thus complete.

There are certain devices exploited in the book which do

not improve it; they extend its appeal. Robert Cohn is not only a bounder, he is a Jewish bounder. The other bounders, like Mike, Mr. Hemingway for some reason spares. He also spares Brett—another device—for while her pleasant folly need not be flogged, it equally need not be condoned; she becomes the attractive wayward lady of Sir Arthur Pinero and Michael Arlen. Petronius's Circe, the archetype of all the Bretts, was neither appealing nor deformed.

Mr. Hemingway has for some time been in the habit of throwing pebbles at the great—which recalls Mr. Pope's couplet about his contemporary Mr. Dennis. The habit was formed in *The Torrents of Spring*, where it was amusing. It is disconcerting in the present novel; it strains the context; and one suspects that Mr. Hemingway protests too much. The point he seems to be making is that he is morally superior, for instance, to Mr. Mencken, but it is not yet clear just why. —ALLEN TATE, "Hard-Boiled," *Nation*, Dec. 15, 1926, pp. 642–44

In Our Time is the last of the four American books, and Mr. Hemingway has accepted the goal. He keeps on making flights, but he has no illusion about landing anywhere. He knows it will be nowhere every time.

In Our Time calls itself a book of stories, but it isn't that. It is a series of successive sketches from a man's life, and makes a fragmentary novel. The first scenes, by one of the big lakes in America—probably Superior—are the best; when Nick is a boy. Then come fragments of war—on the Italian front. Then a soldier back home, very late, in the little town way west in Oklahoma. Then a young American and wife in post-war Europe; a long sketch about an American jockey in Milan and Paris; then Nick is back again in the Lake Superior region, getting off the train at a burnt-out town, and tramping across the empty country to camp by a trout-stream. Trout is the one passion life has left him—and this won't last long.

It is a short book: and it does not pretend to be about one man. But it is. It is as much as we need know of the man's life. The sketches are short, sharp, vivid, and most of them excellent. (The "mottoes" in front seem a little affected.) And these few sketches are enough to create the man and all his history: we need know no more.

Nick is a type one meets in the more wild and woolly regions of the United States. He is the remains of the lone trapper and cowboy. Nowadays he is educated, and through with everything. It is a state of *conscious*, accepted indifference to everything except freedom from work and the moment's interest. Mr. Hemingway does it extremely well. Nothing matters. Everything happens. One wants to keep oneself loose. Avoid one thing only: getting connected up. Don't get connected up. If you get held by anything, break it. Don't be held. Break it, and get away. Don't get away with the idea of getting somewhere else. Just get away, for the sake of getting away. Beat it! "Well, boy, I guess I'll beat it." Ah, the pleasure in saying that!

Mr. Hemingway's sketches, for this reason, are excellent: so short, like striking a match, lighting a brief sensational cigarette, and it's over. His young love-affair ends as one throws a cigarette-end away. "It isn't fun any more."—"Everything's gone to hell inside me."

It is really honest. And it explains a great deal of sentimentality. When a thing has gone to hell inside you, your sentimentalism tries to pretend it hasn't. But Mr. Hemingway is through with the sentimentalism. "It isn't fun any more. I guess I'll beat it."

And he beats it, to somewhere else. In the end he'll be a sort of tramp, endlessly moving on for the sake of moving away from where he is. This is a negative goal, and Mr. Hemingway is really good, because he's perfectly straight about it. He is like Krebs, in that devastating Oklahoma sketch: he doesn't love anybody, and it nauseates him to have to pretend he does. He doesn't even *want* to love anybody; he doesn't want to go anywhere, he doesn't want to do anything. He wants just to lounge around and maintain a healthy state of nothingness inside himself, and an attitude of negation to everything outside himself. And why shouldn't he, since that is exactly and sincerely what he feels? If he really *doesn't* care, then why should he care? Anyhow, he doesn't.—D. H. LAWRENCE, "*In Our Time*" (1927), *Selected Literary Criticism*, 1932, pp. 427–28

There are gorgeous pages in Ernest Hemingway's book about bullfights ⟨*Death in the Afternoon*⟩—big humor and reckless straight talk of what things are, genuinely heavy ferocity against prattle of what they are not. Hemingway is a full-sized man hewing his way with flying strokes of the poet's broad axe which I greatly admire. Nevertheless, there is an unconscionable quantity of bull—to put it as decorously as possible—poured and plastered all over what he writes about bullfights. By bull I mean juvenile romantic gushing and sentimentalizing of simple facts.

For example, it is well known and fairly obvious that bulls do not run and gallop about the pasture; they stand solid "dominating the landscape with their confidence" as Hemingway brilliantly says. Therefore when they have dashed about the ring some minutes, tossed a few horses, repeatedly charged and attempted to gore a man and thrown their heads off because he turned out to be a rag, they soon get winded and their tongues hang out and they pant. Certain bulls, however, for reasons more or less accidental, go through the ordeal in a small area without much running and therefore get tired in the muscles before they get winded. These bulls do not hang their tongues out and pant. This plain fact, which would be obvious to anybody without smoke in his eyes, is romanticized by Hemingway to mean that some bulls are so "brave" that they will never let their tongues out, but hold their mouths "tight shut to keep the blood in" even after they are stabbed to death and until they drop. This is not juvenile romanticism, it is child's fairy-story writing. And yet Hemingway asks us to believe that what drew him to bullfights was the desire to put down "what really happened in action; what the actual things were which produced the emotion that you experienced."

In pursuit of this rigorous aim he informs us that bullfights are "so well ordered and so strongly disciplined by ritual that a person feeling the whole tragedy cannot separate the minor comic-tragedy of the horse so as to feel it emotionally." And he generalizes: "The *aficionado*, or lover of the bullfight, may be said, broadly, then, to be one who has this sense of the tragedy and ritual of the fight so that the minor aspects are not important except as they relate to the whole." Which is just the kind of sentimental poppycock most regularly dished out by those Art nannies and pale-eyed professors of poetry whom Hemingway above all men despises. Hemingway himself makes plain through his book that the performance itself is not an artistic tragedy as often as one time out of a hundred. When it is, there is about one man out of a thousand in the grandstand who would know what you were talking about if you started in on "the whole tragedy" as opposed to the "minor comic-tragedy of the horse." The *aficionado*, or bullfight fan, is the Spanish equivalent of the American baseball fan. He reacts the same way to the same kind of things. If you could get the authorization to put on a bullfight in the Yankee Stadium, you would see approximately the same crowd there that you do now, and they would behave, after a little instruction from our star reporters and radio announcers, just about the way the Spanish crowd behaves. And there would not be—"broadly"—the kind of people, if there are such people, who can see an infuriated bull charge across a bull ring, ram his horns into the private end of a horse's belly and rip him clear up to the ribs, lifting and tossing his rider boldly in the air and over against the fence with the same motion, and keep their attention so occupied with the "whole tragedy" that they cannot "separate" this enough to "feel it emotionally." Bullfights are not wholly bad, but sentimentalizing over them in the name of art-form and ritual is.

Whatever art may be, a bullfight is not art in exactly that particular which exempts art from those rules of decent conduct which make life possible and civilization a hope—namely, that its representations are not real. A bullfight—foolishly so called by the English for it does not except for a moment resemble a fight—is real life. It is men tormenting and killing a bull; it is a bull being tormented and killed.

And if it is not "art" in a sense to justify Hemingway's undiscriminating recourse to this term, still less is it "tragedy" in a sense to sustain the elevated emotions which he hopes to pump over it with this portentous term.—MAX EASTMAN, "Bull in the Afternoon," *NR*, June 7, 1933, pp. 94–95

"The writer has attempted to write an absolutely true book to see whether the shape of a country and the pattern of a month's action can, if truly presented, compete with a work of the imagination." So Mr. Hemingway describes his intention ⟨in *The Green Hills of Africa*⟩, in a preface that is shorter than the average sentence that follows it. Later, in one of the "bloody literary discussions," he praises prose that is "without tricks and without cheating"—a phrase which sums up an ambition that has been constant in all his work. Then he records his satisfaction "when you write well and truly of something and know impersonally you have written in that way and those who are paid to read it and report on it do not like the subject so they say it is all a fake." In another passage, "the lice who crawl on literature will not praise" a work of art. Either the reviewers have been getting under his skin or he is uneasy about this book.

Mr. Hemingway should have his answer: *Green Hills of Africa* cannot compete with his works of the imagination. It is not exactly a poor book, but it is certainly far from a good one. The trouble is that it has few fine and no extraordinary passages, and long parts of it are dull. And being bored by Ernest Hemingway is a new experience for readers and reviewers alike. The queer thing is that this novelty springs from the same intense literary self-consciousness that has been a large part of the effectiveness of his books up to now. He kills this one by being too assiduously an experimental artist in prose, out to register sensation and find the right words for the countryside and activity and emotion, and, by way of the bush and the campfires and the rhinoceros dung, carry his prose to the "fourth and fifth dimension that can be gotten." He has reverted to his café-table-talk days, he is being arty, and Africa isn't a good place for it.

Only about forty percent of the book is devoted to the shape of the country and the pattern of action. That part isn't too good. He is magnificent when he is rendering the emotions of the hunt and the kill, but those passages are less frequent than long, confusing, over-written descriptions, and these are lush and very tiresome. Besides, there are a lot of tricks and some cheating. Mr. Hemingway plunges into the rhetoric he has monotonously denounced, and he overlays a good many bits of plain brush-work with very eloquent and highly literary researches into past time.

The rest of it runs about twenty percent literary discussion, twenty percent exhibitionism, and twenty percent straight fiction technique gratefully brought into this unimaginative effort. The literary discussion, though it contains some precious plums, is mostly bad; the exhibitionism is unfailingly good. Mr. Hemingway is not qualified for analytical thought. His flat judgments and especially his papal rules and by-laws are superficial when they aren't plain cockeyed. He has written about writing, probably, more than any other writer of his time: he is much better at writing and we should all be richer if he would stick to it. But he is a first-rate humorist, and the clowning is excellent. When he gives us Hemingway in the sulks, Hemingway with the braggies, Hemingway amused or angered by the gun-bearers, Hemingway getting tight, Hemingway at the latrine, Hemingway being hard-boiled, or brutal, or swaggering, or ruthless, Hemingway kidding someone or getting sore at someone—the book comes to life. It comes to life, in fact, whenever he forgets about the shape of the country and the pattern of action, and brings some people on the stage. . . .

The big news for literature, however, is that, stylistically, there is a new period of Hemingway. He seems to be fighting a one-man revolution to carry prose back to *The Anatomy of Melancholy* or beyond. There have been omens of it before now, of course, and Mr. Hemingway, in his café-table days, pondered Gertrude Stein to his own gain. The repetitious Stein of *Tender Buttons* doesn't show up here, but the Stein who is out to get four or five dimensions into prose is pretty obvious. But he also appears to have been reading a prose translation of the *Odyssey* too closely, and something that sounds like a German translation of Hemingway. With the result that whereas the typical Hemingway sentence used to run three to a line it now runs three to a page. And whereas he used to simplify vocabulary in order to be wholly clear, he now simplifies grammar till the result looks like a marriage between an e. e. cummings simultaneity and one of those ground-mists of Sherwood Anderson's that Mr. Hemingway was burlesquing ten years ago.

The prize sentence in the book runs forty-six lines, the one I should like to quote as typical ("Now, heavy socks . . ." p. 95), though less than half that long is still too long, and a comparatively straightforward one must serve. "Going downhill steeply made these Spanish shooting boots short in the toe and there was an old argument, about this length of boot and whether the bootmaker, whose part I had taken, unwittingly, first, only as interpreter, and finally embraced his theory patriotically as a whole and, I believed, by logic, had overcome it by adding onto the heel."

This is simpler than most, but it shows the new phase. Usually the material is not so factual as this and we are supposed to get, besides the sense, some muscular effort or some effect of color or movement that is latent in pace and rhythm rather than in words. But, however earnest the intention, the result is a kind of etymological gas that is just bad writing. The five-word sentences of *The Sun Also Rises* were better. You know where you stood with them, and what Mr. Hemingway was saying. He ought to leave the fourth dimension to Ouspensky and give us prose.

An unimportant book. A pretty small book for a big man to write. One hopes that this is just a valley and that something the size of *Death in the Afternoon* is on the other side. —BERNARD DE VOTO, "Hemingway in the Valley," *SRL*, Oct. 26, 1935, p. 5

What was for long the sign of Ernest Hemingway's work—the curious tension between subject matter and style, between the themes of violence and the perfectly controlled prose—has gone. Hemingway was extraordinary among modern prose writers for exactly this reason, that he pressed his style into the service of his subject matter in a rather special way: the style was the immediate representation of the moral attitude of the author toward his material, it objectified the author's values and thus in itself was comment in writing otherwise unhampered by comment. When, however, the subject matter began to change—from violent experience itself to the expressed evaluation of violence—the manner began to change. The separation seems to take place in the story, "The Snows of Kilimanjaro," but it is in the novel *To Have and Have Not*, that the fumbling transition is clearest. The first third of this book is superb narrative in the old manner; but as Hemingway lets himself into the theme proper thereafter, the book begins to break down, and the end is a debacle, the noisy collapse of a style and technique simply unable to support their matter. Before, the style in itself was moral comment; with a change in moral attitude, that style was necessarily disrupted. In *For Whom the Bell Tolls* we may witness a new style, less brilliant but more flexible, as it integrates itself. That is a very exciting literary spectacle.

The Sun Also Rises was a representation of the life that Hemingway lived and enjoyed and out of which his values came. The characters in this novel—without belief, without relation to a cultural or national past, without ideological relation to the future—submerge themselves in extravagant sensation and view life as a losing game, a sport like bullfighting which, while it is more nearly tragedy than sport because death is inevitable, is interesting only if it observes strict rules. Hemingway epitomized this not very difficult matter when, in an author's note in *Scribner's Magazine*, he once said, "I've known some very wonderful people who even though they were going directly to the grave . . . managed to put up a very fine performance enroute." This "fine performance" is the sporting attitude, and it is dramatized in the gesture of Lady Ashley when she gives up her lover: "You know I feel rather damned good, Jake . . . it makes one feel rather good deciding not to be a bitch. . . . It's sort of what we have instead of God." Jake has himself observed that morality is what makes you feel good afterwards. Brett feels "rather damned good" because she has behaved according to the tenets of that negative morality, that emphasis on the "performance en route," the *manner* of living, which the group has substituted for belief.

The preoccupation with bullfighting is not accidental; bullfighting is at once the most violent and the most stylized of sports. Its entire excitement depends on the degree to which the matador exposes himself to death *within the rules*. It disregards consequences, regards performance. Both are important. Courage, or unconcern for disaster, is a moral virtue: the best bullfighter works closest to the horns; the best man disregards present and impending catastrophe. Syphilis, the occupational disease of bullfighters, "of all people who lead lives in which a disregard of consequences dominate," is nearly commended. A blundering display of courage, however, is absurd: the matador should "increase the amount of the danger of death"

> *within the rules provided for his protection*. . . . it is to his credit if he does something that he knows how to do in a highly dangerous but still geometrically possible manner. It is to his discredit if he runs danger through ignorance, through disregard of the fundamental rules.

Courage stylized, *style*, then, matters finally, and the experienced spectator looks for this; "what they seek is honesty and true, not tricked, emotion and always classicism and the purity of execution of all the suertes, and . . . they want no sweetening." Since the performance is a matter of the fighter's honor, bullfighting is a *moral* art, and style a *moral* matter.

> So far, about morals, [writes Hemingway] I know only that what is moral is what you feel good after and what is immoral is what you feel bad after and judged by these moral standards . . . the bullfight is very moral to me.

In *The Sun Also Rises*, Romero, who "fakes" nothing in the fight, who has "the old thing, the holding of his purity of line through the maximum of exposure," is the one character who makes the others feel fine: he is the representation of artistic, hence of moral excellence.

All this carried directly over into Hemingway's concept of prose and into his own prose. The definition of morality and Brett's dramatization of it; the important counterpoint between danger and performance; the concept of art as moral insofar as its style is "honest" or "true" or "pure"—this complex is translated as follows:

> It is much more difficult than poetry. . . . It can be written, *without tricks* and *without cheating. With nothing that will go bad afterwards*. . . . First, there must be talent. . . . Then there must be discipline. . . . Then there must be . . . an *absolute conscience* as unchanging as the standard meter in Paris, to prevent *faking*.

The style which made Hemingway famous—with its ascetic suppression of ornament and figure, its insistence on the objective and the unreflective (for good fighters do not talk), its habit of understatement (or sportsmen boast), the directness and the brevity of its syntactical constructions, its muscularity, the sharpness of its staccato and repetitive effects, "the purity of its line under the maximum of exposure," that is, its continued poise under the weight of event or feeling—this style is an exact transfiguration of Hemingway's moral attitude toward a peculiarly violent and chaotic experience. His style, in effect, is what he had instead of God.

Until God came.

Now that the evidence is in, the position taken by Edmund Wilson some time ago in *The Atlantic Monthly* is indefensible. Mr. Wilson argued that Hemingway's political persuasion was no persuasion at all, but a simple transfer from object to object of the desire to kill: kudu to fascist. No one would seriously contend, I think, that the very motive of *For Whom The Bell Tolls* is not a tremendous sense of man's dignity and worth, an urgent awareness of the necessity of man's freedom, a nearly poetic realization of man's *collective* virtues. Indeed, the individual vanishes in the political whole, but vanishes precisely to defend his dignity, his freedom, his virtue. In spite of the ominous premium which the title seems to place on individuality, the real theme of this book is the relative unimportance of individuality and the superb importance of the political whole. (For fascists are men, too, and even when the bell tolls for them, it tolls for me, I believe; but the fascists in this book have scarcely any meaning as personalities, merely represent The Enemy.) Hemingway's title portends nothing more than that which we have all known: that the doom of Republican Spain was our doom. This novel is no *War and Peace*, no *Dynasts;* it is realistic, political, and deeply partisan. The defects of characterization are the conventional defects of partisan novels, in which personalities always threaten to vanish in abstractions, as, half the time, the woman Pilar becomes a Spanish Gaea, Robert Jordan any vaguely attractive

American, and Maria that perfect sexual creature of the private Hemingway mythology. As in so many partisan novels it is the minor characters, who bear no burden but their own, who are excellent: Sordo, the good old man Anselmo, the insane Marty, the politically exhausted Pablo, this last a magnificent portrait, and a dozen more. About their cause, which is his, Hemingway writes with a zealot's passion. And the old mould is as useless to him—as meaningless—as the old insistence on the individual's isolation, on the private pursuit of his pleasures, and on the exercise of his wholly private virtues. If the early books pled for sporting conduct on violent occasions, this book pleads the moral necessity of political violence. A different thing; indeed, a different writer.

Here is none of the grace of *The Sun Also Rises*, none of the precise perfection of stories such as "A Clean, Well-Lighted Place." This is by no means a perfect technical performance. The severe compression of the old work gives way to nearly complete relaxation. The first effect of this relaxation is evident in the pace of the narrative itself, which is leisurely. The second effect is in the fulness of detail, which Hemingway's sentences can suddenly accommodate. And the third effect is in the sentences themselves, which employ a wide variety of cadences, almost entirely new, and which are short and long, truncated and sinuous, bare or copious as they are needed. To my taste, this syntactical loosening up is almost excessive, for it quickly ramifies in many directions. Understatement is gone and overstatement too often replaces it; we are reminded of Hemingway's own remark that "the dignity of movement of an iceberg is due to only one-eighth of it being above water." The older objectivity of style held the narrative in check in a way that this narrative is not held in check; and to this fact we may attribute many long passages of reflection not particularly well-written and not particularly necessary to the story, long reveries with which the older Hemingway would have had nothing to do. This easy method of exposition is a technical device which the older style made a luxury; here it is everywhere, and largely wasted.

Thus we gain and we lose. Because it is another story, this story could not have been told at all in the older style, and so, in the future, the flexibility of this new style, with its broader subject matter, gives us a bigger writer. How much do we care if, in relaxing, this style also sprawls sometimes, sometimes even snores a little in the sun? It is possible that moral greatness and the best manners are incompatible.—MARK SCHORER, "The Background of a Style," *KR*, Winter 1941, pp. 101–9

Mr. Ernest Hemingway's long-expected novel (*Across the River and into the Trees*) has been out for some weeks, and has already been conspicuously reviewed by all the leading critics. It is now impossible to approach it without some prejudice either against the book itself or against its critics, for in England their disapproval has been unanimous. They have been smug, condescending, derisive, some with unconcealed glee, some with an affectation of pity; all are agreed that there is a great failure to celebrate. It is the culmination of a whispering campaign of some years' duration, that "Hemingway is finished."

I read the reviews before I read the book, and I was in the mood to make the best of it. Mr. Hemingway is one of the most original and powerful of living writers. Even if he had written a completely fatuous book, this was not the way to treat it. What, in fact, he has done is to write a story entirely characteristic of himself, not his best book, perhaps his worst, but still something very much better than most of the work to which the same critics give their tepid applause.

It is the story of the death of an old soldier. He knows he is mortally ill, and he chooses to spend his last days in and near Venice, shooting and making love. The book is largely a monologue. The veteran ruminates bitterly over old battles. He exults in his young mistress. And all is written in that pungent vernacular which Mr. Hemingway should have patented.

It may be conceded at once that the hero is not an attractive character. He is a boor and a bore, jocular, humorless, self-centered, arrogant; he rose to command a brigade, but he is consumed by the under-dog's resentment of his superiors both in the army and elsewhere; the last man, in fact, to choose as one's companion in Venice. But these reviewers have been telling us for years that we must not judge novels by the amiability of their characters, any more than we must judge pictures by the beauty of their subjects. Mr. Hemingway makes a full, strong portrait of his obnoxious hero.

The heroine, a very young Venetian, is strangely unchaperoned. If social conventions have indeed relaxed so much since I was last in that city, this young lady's behavior provides ample evidence that the traditional, rigid code was highly desirable. But are our reviewers the right people to complain of her goings-on? I think it is the troubador in Mr. Hemingway which impels him to ennoble his heroines. He did the same thing in his first, startlingly brilliant *Fiesta*. There is a strong affinity between that book and this. How it delighted and impressed us a quarter of a century ago! How flatly we accept the same gifts today!

Of course, between then and now there have been the shoals of imitators. It was so easy. You have to be an accomplished writer to imitate Henry James. Any journalist can produce a not quite passible imitation of Mr. Hemingway. But it was not only the inventions in technique that impressed us in *Fiesta*. It was the mood. English literature is peculiarly rich in first-class Philistine novelists—Surtees and Mr. P. G. Wodehouse, for example. But their characters were always happy. Mr. Hemingway has melancholy, a sense of doom. His men and women are as sad as those huge, soulless apes that huddle in their cages at the zoo. And that mood is still with us.

Across the River and into the Trees is the nemesis of the philistine. The hero is fifty-one years of age, when the civilized man is just beginning the most fruitful period of his life. But the philistine is done for, a "beat-up old bastard," as he expresses it. He has lived for sport and drink and love-making and professional success, and now there is nothing left for him. He has to be decorated with a physical, mortal illness as with a medal. In accentuation of the pathos of his position, he regards himself as rather cultured and sophisticated. He has been places. He is one with that baffled, bibulous crew of *Fiesta* who thought they were plunging deep into the heart of Europe by getting on friendly terms with barmen; who thought their café pick-ups the flower of decadent European aristocracy. He believes he is the sort of guy for whom the Old Masters painted, and to hell with the art experts.

All of the faults of this latest book were abundantly present in the first; and most of the merits of the first are here again. Why has there been this concerted attack on Mr. Hemingway?

It began a few months ago with a softening-up blitz in the *New Yorker*. That widely-read paper attached a female reporter to Mr. Hemingway to study him while he was on a holiday in New York. She ate and drank, went shopping and visited art galleries with him, and took careful note of every silly or vulgar thing he said or did during his spree. One might suppose that only a megalomaniac or a simpleton would expose himself to such an ordeal. She made a complete ass of him, of course; not altogether a lovable ass, either. I have never met Mr. Hemingway, but I think it probable that his own boisterous manners have contributed to his present unpopularity.

He has really done almost everything to render himself a "beat-up old bastard." His reputation was unassailable in 1936. Then with much trumpeting, he went to Madrid and Barcelona. Here was something greater than bull-fights and *bistros.* The greatest modern writer was devoting his art to the greatest modern theme. Picasso had painted Guernica; Messrs. Auden and Spender had written something or other; now the great warrior-artist of the New World was going to write the Modern Epic. But it did not turn out like that. *For Whom the Bell Tolls* was not at all what the Socialists wanted. They had been busy denying atrocities; Mr. Hemingway described them in detail with relish. They had denied the presence of Russians; Mr. Hemingway led us straight into the front-door of the Gaylord Hotel. He made Marty and la Passionaria as comic as any *New Yorker* correspondent could have done. From then on he was on the wrong side of the barricades for the Socialists, while his pounding revolutionary heart still drove him from civilization.

His sense of superiority to Americans combined with his sense of inferiority to Europeans to give him the sort of patriotism which pleased no one. He could not abide the urban commercial development of his own country; he supposed, rather rightly, that the English were snooty about him, and the French wanted only his dollars. He had a Kiplingesque delight in the technicalities of every trade but his own. He remained, of course, an admirable technician, but, while he could talk for nights to fishermen about their tackle, he was nauseated by the jargon of other writers. Indeed, in this book he uses an American novelist as the typic contrast to his hero; a seedy, industrious fellow in the same hotel, sober, with no young mistress and no scars of battle, and no rollicking jokes with the servants.

When the second war came Mr. Hemingway could not be a soldier, and he despised war-correspondents; he became a war-correspondent. There is plenty to account for the bitterness and frustration of his present work. But our critics thrive on bitterness and frustration. They have forgotten that they once raised clenched fists to the red flag in Barcelona. Not more than a handful have been physically assaulted by the man. Why do they all hate him so?

I believe the truth is that they have detected in him something they find quite unforgivable—Decent Feeling. Behind all the bluster and cursing and fisticuffs he has an elementary sense of chivalry—respect for women, pity for the weak, love of honor—which keeps breaking in. There is a form of high, supercilious caddishness which is all the rage nowadays in literary circles. That is what the critics seek in vain in this book, and that is why their complaints are so loud and confident.—EVELYN WAUGH, "The Case of Mr. Hemingway," *Com,* Nov. 3, 1950, pp. 97–98

The only guts that are mentioned in this story ⟨*The Old Man and the Sea*⟩ are the veritable entrails of fish, but we are nevertheless reminded on every page that Hemingway once defined this favorite word, in its metaphorical use, as "grace under pressure." Grace, in the fullest sense, is the possession of this old man, just as grace was precisely what Colonel Cantwell, in *Across the River and into the Trees,* was totally without. But here it is, complete and absolute, the very breath of this old man, so thoroughly his in his essence as in his *ambiente,* that it can only be there under pressure as at all other times, and indeed, even under the greatest pressure, he hardly alters. Grace, by which one means now not the old stiff upper lip (this old man's upper lip is not so very stiff) which came to some of the older heroes a little easily sometimes, a quality more nearly a manner of speaking than of being; not that now, but benignity, nothing less, and beautifully, masterfully presented, so that the satisfaction one has in this creation is plain happiness, and then, I suppose, gratitude.

The old man has a Franciscan quality that so pervades his habit of thought as to support and give the body of dramatic plausibility, even inevitability to the suggestion of Christian martyrdom which comes at the end. Early in the story, when the old man is being helped by the boy, he thanks him for the food he gives him. "He was too simple to wonder when he had attained humility. But he knew he had attained it and he knew it was not disgraceful and it carried no loss of true pride." Humility—the assumption, without self-consciousness and therefore without sentimentality—is the old man's strength.

> He was very fond of flying fish as they were his principal friends on the ocean. He was sorry for the birds, especially the small delicate dark terns that were always flying and looking and almost never finding, and he thought, "The birds have a harder life than we do except for the robber birds and the heavy strong ones. Why did they make birds so delicate and fine as those sea swallows when the ocean can be so cruel? She is kind and very beautiful. But she can be so cruel and it comes so suddenly and such birds that fly, dipping and hunting, with their small sad voices are made too delicately for the sea."

And again, now of porpoises, and then of the marlin itself:

> "They are good," he said. "They play and make jokes and love one another. They are our brothers like the flying fish."
>
> Then he began to pity the great fish that he had hooked. He is wonderful and strange and who knows how old he is, he thought. Never have I had such a strong fish nor one who acted so strangely. Perhaps he is too wise to jump. He could ruin me by jumping or by a wild rush. But perhaps he has been hooked many times before and he knows that this is how he should make his fight. He cannot know that it is only one man against him, nor that it is an old man. But what a great fish he is. . . . I wonder if he has any plans or if he is just as desperate as I am?

And thus, with a kind of Biblical abstraction that always assumes the independence of all things in their own character from his character, which is likewise independent and separate (in this recognition lie the true sources of brotherhood as of pity), he speaks to a bird, to his fish, and to the parts of his own body, his hands and his head. With a few wavering exceptions, Hemingway sustains the perilous poise of all this with great beauty over pits of possible bathos.

Everywhere the book is being called a classic. In at least one sense, the word cannot be applied, for here and there, where the writing wavers, its pure lucidity is muddied by all that hulking personality which, at his worst, Hemingway has made all too familiar. I do not have in mind the talk about baseball, which has bothered at least one reviewer. "The basball" is a near obsession with most Caribbean natives but we do not have to know this to accept the old man's interest as his own rather than as Hemingway's. (After all, DiMaggio's father *was* a fisherman, as the old man tells us, and the sword of the marlin is "as long as a baseball bat.") But a murky paragraph that has to do with "mysticism about turtles" is a case in point. Or a sentence such as this: "He did not truly feel good because the pain from the cord across his back had almost passed pain and gone into a dullness that he mistrusted"—is it a quibble to suggest that the word "truly" and its location spoil this sentence, jar us out of the mind of the old man whom we are coming to know into the reflection that we've read Hemingway before? Or a brief passage such as this:

> After he judged that his right hand had been in the water long enough he took it out and looked at it.
>
> "It is not bad," he said. "And pain does not matter to a man. . . .
>
> "You did not do so badly for something worthless," he said to his left hand. "But there was a moment when I could not find you."
>
> Why was I not born with two good hands? he thought. Perhaps it was my fault in not training that one properly. But God knows he has had enough chances to learn. He did not do so badly in the night, though, and he has only cramped once. If he cramps again let the line cut him off.

The last sentence tells us with dramatic concreteness what the generalization, "pain does not matter to a man," which is really Hemingway's, does not tell us at all. It should not have been written, precisely because what *is* written must make *us* speak that conclusion, it should be our generalization from his evidence.

But the old man seldom lapses into dramatic falseness. In his age, alone at sea, he has taken to speaking aloud, and instead of dialogue between characters by which most fiction moves, this story moves by little dialogues in the old man himself, the exchange of what is spoken and what is not spoken. This is almost a running drama between that which is only possible and that which is real:

> "Fish," he said, "I love you and respect you very much. But I will kill you dead before this day ends."
>
> Let us hope so, he thought.

The threat of over-generalization is almost always in the spoken words, which, then, are immediately rooted in actuality by the reservations of the unspoken. And of course, Hemingway's incredible gift for writing of the natural life serves the same function. Whether he is describing plankton, jelly fish, the sucking fish that swim in the shadow of the marlin, the gutting of a dolphin that contains two flying fish, or turtles, they are all always there before us, actualities, and the old man is an actuality among them.

The novel is nearly a fable. The best fiction, at its heart, always is, of course, but with his particular diction and syntax, Hemingway's stories approach fable more directly than most, and never so directly as here. It is the quality of his fiction at its very best, the marvelous simplicity of line. ("'Be calm and strong, old man', he said.") There has been another strain in his fiction, to be sure—his personal ambition to become a character in a tall tale, folklore as opposed to fable. That is the weaker man pushing aside the great novelist. The strain glimmers once in this story, when we are told of the old man's feat of strength in his youth: "They had gone one day and one night with their elbows on a chalk line on the table and their forearms straight up and their hands gripped tight." Take it away.

The true quality of fable is first of all in the style, in the degree of abstraction, which is not only in some ways Biblical but is always tending toward the proverbial rhythm. ("The setting of the sun is a difficult time for fish.") Next, it is in the simplicity of the narrative, and in the beautiful proportion (about three-fourths to one-fourth) of its rise and fall. Finally, of course, it is in the moral significance of the narrative, this fine story of an ancient who goes too far out, "beyond the boundaries of permitted aspiration," as Conrad put it ("You violated your luck when you went too far outside," the old man thinks), and encounters his destiny:

> His choice had been to stay in the deep dark water far out beyond all snares and traps and treacheries. My choice was to go there to find him beyond all people. Beyond all people in the world. Now we are joined together and have been since noon. And no one to help either one of us.

In this isolation, he wins a Conradian victory, which means destruction and triumph. We permit his martyrdom because he has earned it. His sigh is "just a noise such as a man might make, involuntarily, feeling the nail go through his hands and into the wood." He stumbles under the weight of his mast when he carries it across his shoulder, up a hill. He sleeps, finally, "with his arms out straight and the palms of his hands up." There is more than this, and for those who, like this reviewer, believe that Hemingway's art, when it is art, is absolutely incomparable, and that he is unquestionably the greatest craftsman in the American novel in this century, something that is perhaps even more interesting. For this appears to be not only a moral fable, but a parable, and all the controlled passion in the story, all the taut excitement in the prose come, I believe, from the parable. It is an old man catching a fish, yes, but it is also a great artist in the act of mastering his subject, and, more than that, of actually writing about that struggle. Nothing is more important than his craft, and it is beloved; but because it must be struggled with and mastered, it is also a foe, enemy to all self-indulgence, to all looseness of feeling, all laxness of style, all soft pomposities.

> "I am a strange old man."
>
> "But are you strong enough now for a truly big fish?"
>
> "I think so. And there are many tricks."

Hemingway, who has always known the tricks, is strong enough now to have mastered his greatest subject. "I could not fail myself and die on a fish like this," the old man reflects. They win together, the great character, the big writer.—MARK SCHORER, "With Grace under Pressure," *NR*, Oct. 6, 1952, pp. 19–20

Here ⟨in *The Dangerous Summer*⟩ we have a great writer who set out to write an epilogue that turned into a book-length manuscript that died of unwieldiness but was years later edited to its literary essence and became a book, truly, and is here with us now, and is good.

The epilogue was conceived by Ernest Hemingway in 1959 to conclude a new edition of his 1932 treatise on bullfighting as life and art, *Death in the Afternoon*. Life magazine editors heard of his plan and asked him to expand the piece into an article of a few thousand words, which they hoped to publish as successfully as they had published his novella, *The Old Man and the Sea*.

Hemingway's subject for the epilogue was the *mano a mano* (or hand-to-hand, a duel) between Spain's two leading matadors, Luis Miguel Dominguín and his brother-in-law, Antonio Ordóñez. Hemingway wrote to his close friend A. E. Hotchner: "It looked like one or the other of the men might be killed and Life wanted coverage of it. Instead, it turned out to be the gradual destruction of one person by another with all the things that led up to it and made it. I had to establish the personality and the art and the basic differences between the two great artists and then show what happened, and you can't do that in 4,000 words."

This was Hemingway's way of apologizing for having extended the epilogue to 688 typed pages covered with 108,746 words. What had happened was that he turned both the *mano a mano* and the epilogue into a quest for, and a statement about, his own youth, his own heroism, his own art, his own immortality; for he was dying, psychically and artistically, and he seems to have intuited that.

Hemingway had begun his writing career in journalism and though he denigrated it in later life ("Journalism, after a point has been reached, can be a daily self-destruction for a serious creative writer"), he never really left it. The last two books on which he worked so diligently before his death in 1961 were this one and his superb nonfiction sketches of Paris in the 1920's, *A Moveable Feast*.

He lived all his life with his own *mano a mano* between nonfiction and fiction, primarily believing that fiction was supreme. He told George Plimpton that "you make something through your invention that is not a representation but a whole new thing truer than anything true and alive, and you make it alive, and if you make it well enough, you give it immortality."

In an author's note to his 1935 book on big-game hunting, *The Green Hills of Africa*, he also wrote this: "The writer has attempted to write an absolutely true book to see whether the shape of a country and the pattern of a month's action can, if truly presented, compete with a work of the imagination."

His use of the novelist's tools—dialogue, scene construction, interior monologues—in *The Green Hills* was the style that such New Journalists as Gay Talese and Tom Wolfe would popularize so abundantly well in the 1960's. Hemingway's Ego Journalism, wherein the writer's point of view is more important to the reader than the subject matter, would be carried to splendid new heights in a later generation by writers like Hunter Thompson and Norman Mailer.

The Green Hills of Hemingway, however, was only a valiant failure. The book perished in the bush from overkill: too much hunting detail, too much bang-bang banality, insufficient story. By contrast, his two fictional stories of Africa, "The Snows of Kilimanjaro" and "The Short Happy Life of Francis Macomber," were both masterworks.

By 1959, when Hemingway was 60 years old, his plan to write the bullfight epilogue trapped him anew in journalism, and he went to Spain. He followed the *corridas* (afternoons of bullfighting) in which Dominguín and Ordóñez fought the bulls. He worked manically at recording the small and large details of it all, wrote voluminously for five months and in September 1960 published three articles in Life.

I remember the articles. I looked forward to them but could not read them. I don't think I finished even one of the three. The great Hemingway had resuscitated all the boredom I'd felt in reading *The Green Hills*. This was also the response of Life's other readers. The articles were a disaster. Nevertheless, plans continued at Hemingway's publishing house, Charles Scribner's Sons, to publish a book from the material. For many reasons, chief among them Hemingway's suicide in 1961, the book remained a manuscript with elephantiasis until now, 26 years after the writing. . . . Mr. Michener had access to the entire original manuscript and says it is so excessively detailed that most readers would not finish it. Hemingway knew it was far too long. Mr. Hotchner went to see him in Havana and reported that Hemingway, not trusting Life's editors to cut his work, had labored for 21 full days by himself and cut only 278 words.

Hemingway plaintively asked for Mr. Hotchner's help in the cutting but then strangely rejected all suggested cuts with explanations in writing to Mr. Hotchner, who was in the same room with him. Hemingway's mind was out of control and would get progressively worse. His vaunted ability to leave out what was irrelevant, his great talent for synthesis, were malfunctioning. Mr. Hotchner pressed on, but Hemingway continued to resist. "What I've written is Proustian in its cumulative effect, and if we eliminate detail we destroy that effect," he told Mr. Hotchner.

On the fourth day of talk Hemingway yielded, the cutting began, and 54,916 words were excised. These are Mr. Hotchner's figures, and they differ somewhat from Mr. Michener's; but then Mr. Hotchner did the cutting. The residual manuscript went to Life and formed the basis for the three articles. Charles A. Scribner Jr. said earlier this year that he tried to cut the script to publishable size in later years, eventually giving it to a Scribners editor named Michael Pietsch, who reduced it to its present size, "a wonderful job" by Mr. Scribner's lights.

And so here is Hemingway—who derided F. Scott Fitzgerald's "gigantic, preposterous" outline for *The Last Tycoon* and wrote that Fitzgerald would never have finished the book—unable to finish his own run-away journalism. Here is Hemingway—calling Thomas Wolfe the "over-bloated Lil Abner of literature" and saying that if Wolfe's editor (and his own), Maxwell Perkins of Scribners, "had not cut one-half million words out of Mr. Wolfe everybody would know how he was"—psychopathically viewing his own rampant verbosity as sacrosanct.—WILLIAM KENNEDY, "The Last Olé," *NYTBR*, June 9, 1985, pp. 1, 32

EDMUND WILSON
"The Sportsman's Tragedy" (1927)
The Shores of Light
1952, pp. 339–44

The reputation of Ernest Hemingway has, in a very short time, assumed such proportions that it has already become fashionable to disparage him. Yet it seems to me that he has received in America very little intelligent criticism. One finds Mr. Lee Wilson Dodd, for example, in the *Saturday Review of Literature*, with his usual gentle trepidation in the presence of contemporary vitality, deciding with a sigh of relief that, after all, Mr. Hemingway (a young man who has published only three books) is not really Tolstoy or Shakespeare, and describing his subjects as follows: "The people he observes with fascinated fixation and then makes live before us are . . . all very much alike: bull-fighters, bruisers, touts, gunmen, professional soldiers, prostitutes, hard drinkers, dope-fiends. . . . For what they may or may not be intellectually, aesthetically, or morally worth, he makes his facts ours." In the *Nation*, Mr. Joseph Wood Krutch, whose review is more sympathetic than Mr. Dodd's, describes Mr. Hemingway as follows: "Spiritually the distinguishing mark of Mr. Hemingway's work is a weariness too great to be aware of anything but sensations. . . . Mr. Hemingway tells us, both by his choice of subject and by the method which he employs, that life is an affair of mean tragedies. . . . In his hands the subject-matter of literature becomes sordid little catastrophes in the lives of very vulgar people." I do not know whether these critics of *Men without Women* have never read Mr. Hemingway's other two books or whether they have simply forgotten them. Do the stories in *In Our Time* and *The Sun Also Rises* actually answer to these descriptions? Does *Men without Women* answer to them? The hero of *In Our Time*, who appears once or twice in this new volume of stories, and the hero of *The Sun Also Rises* are both highly civilized persons of rather complex temperament and extreme sensibility. In what way can they be said to be "very vulgar people"? And can the adventures of even the old bull-fighter in such a piece as "The Undefeated" correctly be called a "sordid little catastrophe"?

One of the stories in *Men without Women* also appeared in the *American Caravan*, and was thus twice exposed to the reviewers; yet in all the reviews I have read I cannot remember one which seemed to me to give an accurate account of it. "An Alpine Idyl" has usually been mentioned as a simple tale of horror or a tale of brutality, or something of the sort. Let us examine this story a moment. Two young men have been skiing in the Alps. It is spring and the sun is terrifically strong; but in the shade, the sweat freezes in their underclothes. They have begun to find this oppressive and are glad to get down to an inn. On their way, they have passed a funeral, and at the inn they hear the story behind it. The woman who is dead was a peasant's wife who had died during the winter, but the house had been snowbound, and the husband had not been able to bring her out till spring. The man had put the body in the woodshed, laying it on a pile of logs; but when he had had to use the wood, he had stood the corpse up in a corner, and had later got into the habit of hanging the lantern in its mouth. Why, we ask ourselves now for a moment, have we been told about the skiing expedition? Then, immediately, we realize that Hemingway, with his masterly relevance in indirection, has, by telling us of the tourists' oppression, supplied us with the explanation of the brutalization of the peasant. But it is not the mere fact of this brutalization that makes the point of the story. We do not see the point till the end. The peasant comes on to the inn, but he refuses to drink with them there and goes on to another inn. " 'He didn't want to drink with me,' said the sexton. 'He didn't want to drink with me, after he knew about his wife,' said the innkeeper." In a similar way, it is true that "A Pursuit Race" is, as Mr. Dodd would say, a story about a dope-fiend; but what is much more important, it is also a story of a man who has just lost a desperate moral struggle. It is given its point by the final paragraph, in which the manager of the burlesque show, understanding that the struggle has been lost and pitying his recreant advance man, goes away without waking him up. So, in "A Simple Inquiry"—a glimpse of one aspect of army life: that strange demoralization that may bring with it a kind of stoicism—the significance of the incident lies in the fact that the major refrains from dismissing the boy who has just refused his advances.

It would appear, then, that Hemingway's world is not quite so rudimentary as Mr. Krutch or Mr. Dodd represents it. Even when he is dealing with primitive types—as he by no means always is—his drama almost always turns on some principle of courage, of pity, of honor— in short, of sportsmanship, in its largest human sense—which he is able to bring to light in them. I do not say that the world that Mr. Hemingway depicts is not, on the whole, a bad world; it *is* a bad world, and a world where much is suffered. Mr. Hemingway's feelings about this world, his criticism of what goes on in it, are, for all his misleadingly simple and matter-of-fact style, rather subtle and complicated; but he has, it seems to me, made it plain enough what sort of ideas and emotions he is trying to communicate. His first book was called *In Our Time*, and it was a sequence of short stories about a sensitive and healthy boy in the American Northwest. We were, I take it, to contrast these two series. When Mr. Hemingway gave them this title, he meant to tell us that life was barbarous even in the twentieth century; and that the man who sees the cabinet ministers shot and who finds himself potting the Germans from behind the "absolutely topping" barricade has had to come a long way from the boy who, with the fresh responses of youth, so much enjoyed the three days' fishing trip at Big Two-Hearted River. Yet *has* he really come so far? Is not the principle of life itself essentially ruthless and cruel? What is the difference between the gusto of the soldier shooting down his fellow humans and the gusto of the young fisherman hooking grasshoppers to catch trout? Ernest Hemingway is primarily preoccupied with these problems of natural cruelty and its inevitable obverse of suffering.

The barbarity of the world since the war is also the theme of his next book, *The Sun Also Rises*. By his title and by the quotations which he prefixes to this novel, he makes it plain what moral judgment we are to pass on the events he describes: "You are all a lost generation." What gives the book its profound unity and its disquieting effectiveness is the intimate relation established between the Spanish fiesta, with its revelry, its bull-fighting and its processions, and the atrocious behavior of the group of holiday-making British and Americans who have come down from Paris to enjoy it. In the heartlessness of these people, in their treatment of one another, do we not find the same principle at work as in the pagan orgy of the festival? Is not the brutal persecution of the Jew as much a natural casualty as the fate of the man who is gored by the bull on his way to visit the bull-ring? The whole interest of *The Sun Also Rises* lies in the attempts of the hero and the heroine to disengage themselves from this world, or rather to arrive at some method of living in it in such a way as to satisfy some code of their own. The real story is that of their attempts to do this—attempts by which, in such a world, they are always bound to lose out in everything except honor. I do not agree, as has sometimes been said, that the behavior of the people in *The Sun Also Rises* is typical of only a small special class of American and British expatriates. I believe that it is more or less typical of certain phases of the whole western world today; and the title *In Our Time* could have been applied to it with as much appropriateness as it was to its predecessor.

Ernest Hemingway's attitude, however, toward the cruelties and treacheries he describes is quite different from anything else that one remembers in a similar connection. He has nothing of the liberating impulse involved in the romantic's indignation:[1] he does not, like Byron, identifying himself with the Prisoner of Chillon, bid the stones of any earthly cell "appeal from tyranny to God"; nor, like Shelley, invite the winds to "wail for the world's wrong." Nor has he even that grim and repressed, but still generous, still passionate feeling which we find in the pessimist-realists—in Thomas Hardy's Tess, in Maupassant's "Boule de suif," even in those infrequent scenes of Flaubert by which one's resentment is kindled at the spectacle of an old farm servant or of a young working-class girl at the mercy of the bourgeoisie. In his treatment of the war, for example, Mr. Hemingway is as far as possible from John Dos Passos or Henri Barbusse. His point of view, his state of mind, is a curious one, and one typical, I think, of "our time"; he seems so broken in to the human agonies, and, though even against his will, so impassively, so hopelessly, resigned to them, that the only protest of which he is capable is, as it were, the grin and the curse of the sportsman who loses the game. Nor are we always quite sure on which side Mr. Hemingway is betting. We do sometimes feel a suspicion that the conflict we are witnessing is a set-up, with the manager backing the barbarian. Yet to speak in these terms of Mr. Hemingway is really to misrepresent him. He is not, of course, a moralist staging a melodrama, but an artist exhibiting situations the values of which are not simple. Mr. Hemingway enjoys bull-fighting, as he enjoys skiing, racing and prize-fights; and he is unremittingly conscious of the fact that, from the point of view of life as a sport, all that seems most painful in it is somehow very closely bound up with what he finds to be most enjoyable. The peculiar conflicts of feeling which arise in a temperament of this kind are the subject of Mr. Hemingway's fiction. The most remarkable effects of this fiction, effects unlike those of anyone else, are those, as in the fishing-trip in *The Sun Also Rises*, by which we are made to feel, behind the appetite for the physical world, the tragedy or the falsity of a moral relation. The inescapable consciousness of this does not arouse Hemingway to passionate violence; but it poisons him and makes him sick, and thus invests with a sinister quality—a quality perhaps new in fiction—the sunlight and the green summer landscapes of *The Sun Also Rises*. Thus, if Hemingway is oppressive, as Mr. Dodd complains, it is because he himself is oppressed. And we may find in him—in the clairvoyant's crystal of a polished incomparable art—the image of the common oppression.

Notes

1. This liberating impulse, however, was later to be brought out in Hemingway by the Spanish Civil War.

ROBERT PENN WARREN
From "Ernest Hemingway" (1944–47)
Selected Essays
1958, pp. 80–118

In May, 1929, in *Scribner's Magazine*, the first installment of *A Farewell to Arms* appeared. The novel was completed in the issue of October, and was published in book form the same year. Ernest Hemingway was already regarded, by a limited literary public, as a writer of extraordinary freshness and power, as one of the makers, indeed, of a new American fiction. *A Farewell to Arms* more than justified the early enthusiasm of the connoisseurs for Hemingway, and extended his reputation from them to the public at large. Its great importance was at once acknowledged, and its reputation has survived through the changing fashions and interests of many years.

What was the immediate cause of its appeal?—It told a truth about the first world war, and a truth about the generation who had fought it and whose lives, because of the war, had been wrenched from the expected pattern and the old values. Other writers had told or were to tell similar truths about this war. John Dos Passos in *Three Soldiers*, E. E. Cummings in *The Enormous Room*, William Faulkner in *Soldier's Pay*, Maxwell Anderson and Laurence Stallings in *What Price Glory?* All these writers had presented the pathos and endurance and gallantry of the individual caught and mangled in the great anonymous mechanism of a modern war fought for reasons that the individual could not understand, found insufficient to justify the event, or believed to be no reasons at all. And *A Farewell to Arms* was not the first book to record the plight of the men and women who, because of the war, had been unable to come to terms with life in the old way. Hemingway himself in *The Sun Also Rises*, 1926, had given the picture of the dislocated life of young English and American expatriates in the bars of Paris, the "lost generation," as Gertrude Stein defined them. But before that, F. Scott Fitzgerald, who had been no nearer to the war than an officers' training camp, had written of the lost generation. For the young people about whom Fitzgerald wrote, even when they were not veterans and even when their love stories were enacted in parked cars, fraternity houses, and country clubs and not in the cafés and hotels of Paris, were like Hemingway's expatriates under the shadow of the war and were groping to find some satisfaction in a world from which the old values had been withdrawn. Hemingway's expatriates had turned their backs on the glitter of the Great Boom of the 1920's, and Fitzgerald's young men were usually drawn to the romance of wealth and indulgence, but this difference is superficial. If Hemingway's young men begin by repudiating the Great Boom, Fitzgerald's young men end with disappointment in what even success has to offer. "All the sad young men" of Fitzgerald—to take the title of one of his collections of stories—and the "lost generation" of Hemingway are seekers for landmarks and bearings in a terrain for which the maps have been mislaid.

A Farewell to Arms, which appeared ten years after the first world war and on the eve of the collapse of the Great Boom, seemed to sum up and bring to focus an inner meaning of the decade being finished. It worked thus, not because it disclosed the end results that the life of the decade was producing—the discontents and disasters that were beginning to be noticed even by unreflective people—but because it cut back to the beginning of the process, to the moment that had held within itself the explanation of the subsequent process.

Those who had grown up in the war, or in its shadow could look back nostalgically, as it were, to the lost moment of innocence of motive and purity of emotion. If those things had been tarnished or manhandled by the later business of living, they had, at least, existed, and on a grand scale. If they had been tarnished or manhandled, it was not through the fault of the individual who looked back to see the image of the old simple and heroic self in Frederick or Catherine, but through the impersonal grindings of the great machine of the universe. *A Farewell to Arms* served, in a way, as the great romantic alibi for a generation, and for those who aped and emulated that generation. It showed how cynicism or disillusionment, failure of spirit or the worship of material success, debauchery or despair, might have been grounded in heroism, simplicity, and fidelity that had met unmerited defeat. The early tragedy could cast a kind of flattering and extenuating afterglow over what had come later. The battlefields of *A Farewell to Arms* explained the bars of *The Sun Also Rises*—and explained the young Krebs, of the story "Soldier's Home," who came back home to a Middle-Western town to accept his own slow disintegration.

This is not said in disparagement of *A Farewell to Arms*. It is, after all, a compliment to the hypnotic force of the book. For the hypnotic force of the book was felt from the first, and it is not unusual for such a book to be relished by its first readers for superficial reasons and not for the essential virtues that may engage those who come to it later. . . .

In the years after the war Hemingway set about learning, quite consciously and with rigorous self-discipline, the craft and art of writing. During most of his apprenticeship he lived in Paris, one of the great number of expatriates who were drawn to the artistic capital of the world to learn to be writers, painters, sculptors, or dancers, or simply to enjoy on a low monetary exchange the freedom of life away from American or British conventions. "Young America," writes Ford Madox Ford, "from the limitless prairies leapt, released, on Paris. They stampeded with the madness of colts when you let down the slip-rails between dried pasture and green. The noise of their advancing drowned all sounds. Their innumerable forms hid the very trees on the boulevards. Their perpetual motion made you dizzy." And of Hemingway himself: "He was presented to me by Ezra [Pound] and Bill Bird and had rather the aspect of an Eton-Oxford, huskyish young captain of a midland regiment of His Britannic Majesty. . . . Into that animated din would drift Hemingway, balancing on the point of his toes, feinting at my head with hands as large as hams and relating sinister stories of Paris landlords. He told them with singularly choice words in a slow voice."[1]

The originality and force of Hemingway's early stories, published in little magazines and in limited editions in France, were recognized from the first by many who made their acquaintance. The seeds of his later work were in those stories of *In Our Time*, concerned chiefly with scenes of inland American life and a boy's growing awareness of that life in contrast to vivid flashes of the disorder and brutality of the war years and the immediate post-war years in Europe. There are both contrast and continuity between the two elements of *In Our Time*. There is the contrast between the lyric rendering of one aspect of the boyhood world and the realistic rendering of the world of war, but there is also a continuity, because in the boyhood world there are recurring intimations of the blackness into which experience can lead even in the peaceful setting of Michigan.

With the publication of *The Sun Also Rises*, in 1926, Hemingway's work reached a wider audience, and at the same time defined more clearly the line his genius was to follow and his role as one of the spokesmen for a generation. But *A Farewell to Arms* gave him his first substantial popular success and established his reputation. It was a brilliant and compelling novel; it provided the great alibi; it crowned the success story of the American boy from the Middle West, who had hunted and fished, played football in high school, been a newspaper reporter, gone to war and been wounded and decorated, wandered exotic lands as a foreign correspondent, lived the free life of the Latin Quarter of Paris, and, at the age of thirty, written a best seller—athlete, sportsman, correspondent, soldier, adventurer, and author.

It would be possible and even profitable to discuss *A Farewell to Arms* in isolation from Hemingway's other work. But Hemingway is a peculiarly personal writer, and for all the apparent objectivity and self-suppression in his method as a writer, his work, to an uncommon degree, forms a continuous whole. One part explains and interprets another part. It is true that there have been changes between early and late work, that there has been an increasing self-consciousness, that attitudes and methods that in the beginning were instinctive and simple have become calculated and elaborated. But the best way to understand one of his books is, nevertheless, to compare it with both earlier and later pieces and seek to discern motives and methods that underlie all of his work.

Perhaps the simplest way into the whole question is to consider what kind of world Hemingway writes about. A writer may write about his special world merely because he happens to know that world, but he may also write about that special world because it best dramatizes for him the issues and questions that are his fundamental concerns—because, in other words, that special world has a kind of symbolic significance for him. There is often—if we discount mere literary fashion and imitation—an inner and necessary reason for the writer's choice of his characters and situations. What situations and characters does Hemingway write about?

They are usually violent. There is the hard-drinking and sexually promiscuous world of *The Sun Also Rises*; the chaotic and brutal world of war, as in *A Farewell to Arms*, *For Whom the Bell Tolls*, many of the inserted sketches of *In Our Time*, the play *The Fifth Column*, and some of the stories; the world of sport, as in "Fifty Grand," "My Old Man," "The Undefeated," "The Snows of Kilimanjaro"; the world of crime, as in "The Killers," "The Gambler, the Nun, and the Radio," and *To Have and Have Not*. Even when the situation of a story does not fall into one of these categories, it usually involves a desperate risk, and behind it is the shadow of ruin, physical or spiritual. As for the typical characters, they are usually tough men, experienced in the hard worlds they inhabit, and not obviously given to emotional display or sensitive shrinking—men like Rinaldi or Frederick Henry of *A Farewell to Arms*, Robert Jordan of *For Whom the Bell Tolls*, Harry Morgan of *To Have and Have Not*, the big-game hunter of "The Snows of Kilimanjaro," the old bullfighter of "The Undefeated," or the pugilist of "Fifty Grand." Or if the typical character is not of this seasoned order, he is a very young man, or boy, first entering the violent world and learning his first adjustment to it.

We have said that the shadow of ruin is behind the typical Hemingway situation. The typical character faces defeat or death. But out of defeat or death the character usually manages to salvage something. And here we discover Hemingway's special interest in such situations and characters. His heroes are not squealers, welchers, compromisers, or cowards, and when they confront defeat they realize that the stance they take, the stoic endurance, the stiff upper lip mean a kind of victory. If they are to be defeated they are defeated upon their own terms; some of them have even courted their defeat; and certainly they have maintained, even in the practical defeat, an ideal of themselves—some definition of how a man should behave, formulated or unformulated—by which they have lived. They represent some notion of a code, some notion of honor, that makes a man a man, and that distinguishes him from people who merely follow their random impulses and who are, by consequence, "messy."

In case after case, we can illustrate this "principle of sportsmanship," as Edmund Wilson has called it, at the center of a story or novel. Robert Jordan, in *For Whom the Bell Tolls*, is somehow happy as he lies, wounded, behind the machine gun that is to cover the escape of his friends and his sweetheart from Franco's Fascists. The old bullfighter, in "The Undefeated," continues his incompetent fight even under the jeers and hoots of the crowd, until the bull is dead and he himself is mortally hurt. Francis Macomber, the rich young sportsman who goes lion-hunting in "The Short, Happy Life of Francis Macomber," and who has funked it and bolted before a wounded lion, at last learns the lesson that the code of the hunter demands that he go into the bush after an animal he has wounded. Brett, the heroine of *The Sun Also Rises*, gives up Romero, the young bullfighter with whom she is in love, because she knows she will ruin him, and her tight-lipped remark to Jake, the newspaper man who is the narrator of the novel, might almost serve as the motto of Hemingway's work: "You know it makes one feel rather good deciding not to be a bitch."

It is the discipline of the code that makes man human, a sense of style or good form. This applies not only in isolated, dramatic cases such as those listed above, but is a more pervasive thing that can give meaning, partially at least, to the confusions of living. The discipline of the soldier, the form of the athlete, the gameness of the sportsman, the technique of an artist can give some sense of the human order, and can achieve a moral significance. And here we see how Hemingway's concern with war and sport crosses his concern with literary style. If a writer can get the kind of style at which Hemingway, in *Green Hills of Africa*, professes to aim, then "nothing else matters. It is more important than anything else he can do." It is more important because, ultimately, it is a moral achievement. And no doubt for this reason, as well as for the reason of Henry James's concern with cruxes of a moral code, he is, as he says in *Green Hills of Africa,* an admirer of the work of Henry James, the devoted stylist.

But to return to the subject of Hemingway's world: the code and the discipline are important because they can give meaning to life that otherwise seems to have no meaning or justification. In other words, in a world without supernatural sanctions, in the God-abandoned world of modernity, man can realize an ideal meaning only in so far as he can define and maintain the code. The effort to do so, however limited and imperfect it may be, is the characteristically human effort and provides the tragic or pitiful human story. Hemingway's attitude on this point is much like that of Robert Louis Stevenson in "Pulvis et Umbra":

> Poor soul, here for so little, cast among so many hardships, filled with desires so incommensurate and so inconsistent, savagely surrounded, savagely descended, irremediably condemned to prey upon his fellow lives: who should have blamed him had he been of a piece with his destiny and a being merely barbarous? And we look and behold him instead, filled with imperfect virtues . . . an ideal of decency, to which he would rise if it were possible; a limit of shame, below which, if it be possible, he will not stoop. . . . Man is indeed marked for failure in his effort to do right. But where the best consistently miscarry how tenfold more remarkable that all should continue to strive; and surely we should find it both touching and inspiriting, that in a field from which success is banished, our race should not cease to labor. . . . It matters not where we look, under what climate we observe him, in what stage of society, in what depth of ignorance, burthened with what erroneous morality; by campfires in Assiniboia, the snow powdering his shoulders, the wind plucking his blanket, as he sits, passing the ceremonial calumet and uttering his grave opinions like a Roman senator; on ships at sea, a man inured to hardship and vile pleasures, his brightest hope a fiddle in a tavern and a bedizened trull who sells herself to rob him, and he for all that, simple, innocent, cheerful, kindly like a child, constant to toil, brave to drown, for others; . . . in the brothel, the discard of society, living mainly on strong drink, fed with affronts, a fool, a thief, the comrade of thieves, and even here keeping the point of honor and the touch of pity, often repaying the world's scorn with service, often standing firm upon a scruple, and at a certain cost, rejecting riches:—everywhere some virtue cherished or affected, everywhere some decency of thought or carriage, everywhere the ensign of man's ineffectual goodness! . . . under every circumstance of failure, without hope, without help, without thanks, still obscurely fighting the lost fight of virtue, still clinging, in the brothel or on the scaffold, to some rag of honor, the poor jewel of their souls! They may seek to escape, and yet they cannot; it is not alone their privilege and glory, but their doom; they are condemned to some nobility.

Hemingway's code is more rigorous than Stevenson's and perhaps he finds fewer devoted to it, but, like Stevenson, he can find his characteristic hero and characteristic story among the discards of society, and, like Stevenson, is aware of the touching irony of that fact. But for the moment the important thing in the parallel is that, for Stevenson, the world in which this drama of pitiful aspiration and stoic endurance is played out, is apparently a violent and meaningless world—"our rotary island loaded with predatory life and more drenched with blood . . . than ever mutinied ship, scuds through space."

Neither Hemingway nor Stevenson invented this world. It had already appeared in literature before their time, and that is a way of saying that this cheerless vision had already begun to trouble men. It is the world we find pictured (and denied) in Tennyson's "In Memoriam"—the world in which human conduct is a product of "dying Nature's earth and lime." It is the world pictured (and not denied) in Hardy and Housman, a world that seems to be presided over by blind Doomsters (if by anybody), as Hardy put it in his poem "Hap," or made by some brute and blackguard (if by anybody), as Housman put it in his poem "The Chestnut Casts Its Flambeaux." It is the world of Zola or Dreiser or Conrad or Faulkner. It is the world of, to use Bertrand Russell's phrase, "secular hurryings through space." It is the God-abandoned world, the world of Nature-as-all. We know where the literary men got this picture. They got it from the scientists of the nineteenth century. This is Hemingway's world, too, the world with nothing at center.

Over against this particular version of the naturalistic view of the world, there was, of course, an argument for Divine Intelligence and a Divine purpose, an argument that based itself on the beautiful system of nature, on natural law. The closely knit order of the natural world, so the argument ran, implies a Divine Intelligence. But if one calls Hemingway's attention to the fact that the natural world is a world of order, his reply is on record in a story called "A Natural History of the Dead." There he quotes from the traveler Mungo Park, who, naked and starving in an African desert, observed a beautiful little moss-flower and meditated thus:

> Can the Being who planted, watered, and brought to perfection, in this obscure part of the world, a thing which appears of so small importance, look with unconcern upon the situation and suffering of creatures formed after his own image? Surely not. Reflections like these would not allow me to despair: I started up and, disregarding both hunger and fatigue, travelled forward, assured that relief was at hand; and I was not disappointed.

And Hemingway continues:

> With a disposition to wonder and adore in like manner, as Bishop Stanley says [the author of *A Familiar History of Birds*], can any branch of Natural History be studied without increasing that faith, love and hope which we also, everyone of us, need in our journey through the wilderness of life? Let us therefore see what inspiration we may derive from the dead.

Then Hemingway presents the picture of a modern battlefield, where the bloated and decaying bodies give a perfect example of the natural order of chemistry—but scarcely an argument for faith, hope, and love. That picture is his answer to the argument that the order of nature implies meaning in the world.

In one of the stories, "A Clean, Well-Lighted Place," we find the best description of what underlies Hemingway's world of violent action. In the early stages of the story we see an old man sitting late in a Spanish café. Two waiters are speaking of him.

> "Last week he tried to commit suicide," one waiter said.
>
> "Why?"
>
> "He was in despair."
>
> "What about?"
>
> "Nothing."

"How do you know it was nothing?"

"He has plenty of money."

The despair beyond plenty of money—or beyond all the other gifts of the world: its nature becomes a little clearer at the end of the story when the older of the two waiters is left alone, reluctant too to leave the clean, well-lighted place:

> Turning off the electric light he continued the conversation with himself. It is the light of course but it is necessary that the place be clean and pleasant. You do not want music. Certainly you do not want music. Nor can you stand before a bar with dignity although that is all that is provided for these hours. What did he fear? It was not fear or dread. It was a nothing that he knew too well. It was all a nothing and a man was nothing too. It was only that and light was all it needed and a certain cleanness and order. Some lived in it and never felt it but he knew it all was nada y pues nada y nada y pues nada. Our nada who art in nada, nada be thy name thy kingdom nada thy will be nada in nada as it is in nada. Give us this nada our daily nada and nada us our nada as we nada our nadas and nada us not into nada but deliver us from nada; pues nada. Hail nothing full of nothing, nothing is with thee. He smiled and stood before a bar with a shining steam pressure coffee machine.
>
> "What's yours?" asked the barman.
>
> "Nada."

At the end the old waiter is ready to go home:

> Now, without thinking further, he would go home to his room. He would lie in bed and finally, with daylight, he would go to sleep. After all, he said to himself, it is probably only insomnia. Many must have it.

And the sleepless man—the man obsessed by death, by the meaninglessness of the world, by nothingness, by nada—is one of the recurring symbols in the work of Hemingway. In this phase Hemingway is a religious writer. The despair beyond plenty of money, the despair that makes a sleeplessness beyond insomnia, is the despair felt by a man who hungers for the sense of order and assurance that men seem to find in religious faith, but who cannot find grounds for his faith.

Another recurring symbol is the violent man. But the sleepless man and the violent man are not contradictory; they are complementary symbols. They represent phases of the same question, the same hungering for meaning in the world. The sleepless man is the man brooding upon nada, upon chaos, upon Nature-as-all. (For Nature-as-all equals moral chaos; even its bulls and lions and kudu are not admired by Hemingway as creatures of conscious self-discipline; their courage has a meaning only in so far as it symbolizes human courage.) The violent man is the man taking an action appropriate to the realization of the fact of nada. He is, in other words, engaged in the effort to discover human values in a naturalistic world.

Before we proceed with this line of discussion, it might be asked, "Why does Hemingway feel that the quest necessarily involves violence?" Now, at one level, the answer to this question would involve the whole matter of the bias toward violence in modern literature. But let us take it in its more immediate reference. The typical Hemingway hero is the man aware, or in the process of becoming aware, of nada. Death is the great nada. Therefore whatever code or creed the hero gets must, to be good, stick even in the face of death. It has to be good in the bull ring or on the battlefield and not merely in the study or lecture room. In fact, Hemingway is anti-intellectual, and has a great contempt for any type of solution arrived at without the testings of immediate experience.

So aside from the question of a dramatic sense that would favor violence, and aside from the mere matter of personal temperament (for Hemingway describes himself on more than one occasion as obsessed by death), the presentation of violence is appropriate in his work because death is the great nada. In taking violent risks man confronts in dramatic terms the issue of nada that is implicit in all of Hemingway's world.

But to return to our general line of discussion. There are two aspects to this violence that is involved in the quest of the Hemingway hero, two aspects that seem to represent an ambivalent attitude toward nature.

First, there is the conscious sinking into nature, as we may call it. On this line of reasoning we would find something like this: if there is at center only nada, then the only sure compensation in life, the only reality, is gratification of appetite, the relish of sensation.

Continually in the stories and novels one finds such sentences as this from *Green Hills of Africa*: ". . . drinking this, the first one of the day, the finest one there is, and looking at the thick bush we passed in the dark, feeling the cool wind of the night and smelling the good smell of Africa, I was altogether happy." What is constantly interesting in such sentences is the fact that happiness, a notion that we traditionally connect with a complicated state of being, with notions of virtue, of achievement, etc., is here equated with a set of merely agreeable sensations. For instance, in "Cross-Country Snow," one of the boys, George, says to the other, Nick, who in story after story is a sort of shadow of Hemingway himself, "Maybe we'll never go skiing again, Nick." And Nick replies, "We've got to. It isn't worth while if you can't." The sensations of skiing are the end of life. Or in another story, "Big Two-Hearted River: Part II," a story that is full of the sensation-as-happiness theme, we find this remark about Nick, who has been wading in a trout stream: "Nick climbed out onto the meadow and stood, water running down his trousers and out of his shoes, his shoes squelchy. He went over and sat on the logs. He did not want to rush his sensations any." The careful relish of sensation—that is what counts, always.

This intense awareness of the world of the senses is, of course, one of the things that made the early work of Hemingway seem, upon its first impact, so fresh and pure. Physical nature is nowhere rendered with greater vividness than in his work, and probably his only competitors in this department of literature are William Faulkner, among the modern, and Henry David Thoreau, among the older American writers. The meadows, forests, lakes, and trout streams of America, and the arid, sculpturesque mountains of Spain, appear with astonishing immediacy, an immediacy not dependent upon descriptive flourishes. But not only the appearance of landscape is important; a great deal of the freshness comes from the discrimination of sensation, the coldness of water in the "squelchy" shoes after wading, the tangy smell of dry sagebrush, the "cleanly" smell of grease and oil on a field piece.[2] Hemingway's appreciation of the aesthetic qualities of the physical world is important, but a peculiar poignancy is implicit in the rendering of those qualities; the beauty of the physical world is a background for the human predicament, and the very relishing of the beauty is merely a kind of desperate and momentary compensation possible in the midst of the predicament.

This careful relishing of the world of the senses comes to a climax in drinking and sex. Drink is the "giant-killer," the weapon against man's thought of nada. And so is sex, for that matter, though when sexual attraction achieves the status of love, the process is one that attempts to achieve a meaning rather than to forget meaninglessness in the world. In terms of drinking and sex, the typical Hemingway hero is a man of monel-metal stomach and Homeric prowess in the arts of love. And the typical situation is love, with some drinking, against the background of nada—of civilization gone to pot, of war, or of death—as we get it in all of the novels in one form or another, and in many of the stories.

It is important to remember, however, that the sinking into nature, even at the level of drinking and mere sexuality, is a self-conscious act. It is not the random gratification of appetite. We see this quite clearly in *The Sun Also Rises* in the contrast between Cohn, who is merely a random dabbler in the world of sensation, who is merely trying to amuse himself, and the initiates like Jake and Brett, who are aware of the nada at the center of things and whose dissipations, therefore, have a philosophical significance. The initiate in Hemingway's world raises the gratification of appetite to the level of a cult and a discipline.

The cult of sensation, as we have already indicated, passes over very readily into the cult of true love, for the typical love story is presented primarily in terms of the cult of sensation. (*A Farewell to Arms*, as we shall see when we come to a detailed study of that novel, is closely concerned with this transition.) Even in the cult of true love it is the moment that counts, and the individual. There is never any past or future to the love stories, and the lovers are always isolated, not moving within the framework of obligations of an ordinary human society. The notion of the cult—a secret cult composed of those who have been initiated into the secret of nada—is constantly played up.

In *A Farewell to Arms*, for instance, Catherine and Frederick are two against the world, a world that is, literally as well as figuratively, an alien world. The peculiar relationship between Frederick and the priest takes on a new significance if viewed in terms of the secret cult. We shall come to this topic later, but for the moment we can say that the priest is a priest of Divine Love, the subject about which he and Frederick converse in the hospital, and that Frederick himself is a kind of priest, one of the initiate in the end, of the cult of profane love. This same pattern of two against the world with an understanding confidant or interpreter, reappears in *For Whom the Bell Tolls*—with Pilar, the gipsy woman who understands "love," substituting for the priest of *A Farewell to Arms*.

The initiates of the cult of love are those who are aware of nada, but their effort, as members of the cult, is to find a meaning to put in place of the nada. That is, there is an attempt to make the relationship of love take on a religious significance in so far as it can give meaning to life. This general topic is not new with the work of Hemingway. It is one of the literary themes of the nineteenth century—and has, as a matter of fact, a longer history than that.

If the cult of love arises from and states itself in the language of the cult of sensation, it is an extension of the sinking-into-nature aspect of the typical Hemingway violence; but in so far as it involves a discipline and a search for a "faith," it leads us to the second aspect of the typical violence.

The violence, although in its first aspect it represents a sinking into nature, at the same time, in its second aspect, represents a conquest of nature, and of nada in man. It represents such a conquest, not because of the fact of violence, but because the violence appears in terms of a discipline, a style, and a code. It is, as we have already seen, in terms of a self-imposed discipline that the heroes make one gallant, though limited, effort to redeem the incoherence of the world: they attempt to impose some form upon the disorder of their lives, the technique of the bullfighter or sportsman, the discipline of the soldier, the fidelity of the lover, or even the code of the gangster, which, though brutal and apparently dehumanizing, has its own ethic. (Ole Anderson, in "The Killers," is willing to take his medicine without whining, and even recognizes some necessity and justice in his plight. Or the dying Mexican, in "The Gambler, the Nun, and the Radio," refuses to squeal despite the detective's argument: "One can, with honor, denounce one's assailant.")

If it is said that Frederick in *A Farewell to Arms* does not, when he deserts, exhibit the discipline of the soldier, the answer is simple: his obligation has been constantly presented as an obligation to the men in his immediate command, and he and the men in his command have never recognized an obligation to the total war—they recognize no meaning in the war and are bound together only by a squad sense and by their immediate respect for each other; when Frederick is separated from his men his obligation is gone. His true obligation then becomes the fidelity of Catherine.

The discipline, the form, is never quite capable of subduing the world, but fidelity to it is part of the gallantry of defeat. By fidelity to it the hero manages to keep one small place "clean" and "well-lighted," and manages to retain, or achieve for one last moment, his dignity. There should be, as the old Spanish waiter reflects, a "clean, well-lighted place" where one could keep one's dignity at the late hour.

We have said earlier that the typical Hemingway character is tough and, apparently, insensitive. But only apparently, for the fidelity to a code, to the discipline, may be the index to a sensitivity that allows the characters to see, at moments, their true plight. At times, and usually at times of stress, it is the tough man in the Hemingway world, the disciplined man, who is actually aware of pathos or tragedy. The individual toughness (which may be taken to be the private discipline demanded by the world) may find itself in conflict with the natural human reactions; but the Hemingway hero, though he may be aware of the claims of the natural reaction, the spontaneous human emotion, cannot surrender to it because he knows that the only way to hold on to the definition of himself, to "honor" or "dignity," is to maintain the discipline, the code. For example, when pity appears in the Hemingway world—as in "The Pursuit Race"—it does not appear in its maximum but in its minimum manifestation.

What this means in terms of style and method is the use of understatement. This understatement, stemming from the contrast between the sensitivity and the superimposed discipline, is a constant aspect of the work, an aspect that was caught in a cartoon in the *New Yorker*. The cartoon showed a brawny, muscle-knotted forearm and a hairy hand that clutched a rose. It was entitled "The Soul of Ernest Hemingway." Just as there is a margin of victory in the defeat of the Hemingway characters, so there is a little margin of sensitivity in their brutal and apparently insensitive world. Hence we have the ironical circumstance—a central circumstance in creating the pervasive irony of Hemingway's work—that the revelation of the values characteristic of his work arises from the most unpromising people and the most unpromising situations—the little streak of poetry or pathos in "The Pursuit Race," "The Killers," "My Old Man," "A Clean, Well-Lighted Place," or "The Undefeated." We have a perfect example of it in the last-named story. After the defeat of the old bullfighter, who is lying wounded on an operating table, Zurito, the picador, is about to cut off the old fellow's pigtail, the mark of his profession. But when the wounded man starts up, despite his pain, and says, "You couldn't do a thing like that," Zurito says, "I was joking." Zurito becomes aware that, after all, the old bullfighter is, in a way, undefeated, and deserves to die with his coleta on.

This locating of the poetic, the pathetic, or the tragic in the unpromising person or situation is not unique with Hemingway. It is something with which we are acquainted in a great deal of our literature since the Romantic Movement. In such literature, the sensibility is played down, and an anti-romantic surface sheathes the work; the point is in the contrast. The impulse that led Hemingway to the simple character is akin to the one that drew Wordsworth to the same choice. Wordsworth felt that his unsophisticated peasants were more honest in their responses than the cultivated man, and were therefore more poetic. Instead of Wordsworth's peasant we have in Hemingway's work the bullfighter, the soldier, the revolutionist, the sportsman, and the gangster; instead of Wordsworth's children we have the young men like Nick, the person just on the verge of being initiated into the world. There are, of course, differences between the approach of Wordsworth and that of Hemingway, but there is little difference on the point of marginal sensibility. In one sense, both are anti-intellectual, and in such poems as "Resolution and Independence" or "Michael" one finds even closer ties.

I have just indicated a similarity between Wordsworth and Hemingway on the grounds of a romantic anti-intellectualism. But with Hemingway it is far more profound and radical than with Wordsworth. All we have to do to see the difference is to put Wordsworth's Preface to the *Lyrical Ballads* over against any number of passages from Hemingway. The intellectualism of the eighteenth century had merely put a veil of stereotyped language over the world and a veil of snobbism over a large area of human experience. That is Wordsworth's indictment. But Hemingway's indictment of the intellectualism of the past is that it wound up in the mire and blood of 1914 to 1918; that it was a pack of lies leading to death. We can put over against the Preface of Wordsworth, a passage from *A Farewell to Arms:*

> I was always embarrassed by the words sacred, glorious, and sacrifice and the expression in vain. We had heard them, sometimes standing in the rain almost out of earshot, so that only the shouted words came through, and had read them, on proclamations that were slapped up by billposters over other proclamations, now for a long time, and I had seen nothing sacred, and the things that were glorious had no glory and the sacrifices were like the stockyards at Chicago if nothing was done with the meat except to bury it. There were many words that you could not stand to hear and finally only the names of places had dignity. . . . Abstract words such as glory, honor, courage, or hallow were obscene beside the concrete names of villages, the numbers of roads, the names of rivers, the numbers of regiments and the dates.

I do not mean to say that the general revolution in style, and the revolt against the particular intellectualism of the nineteenth century, was a result of the first world war. As a matter of fact, that revolt was going on long before the war, but for Hemingway, and for many others, the war gave the situation a peculiar depth and urgency.

Perhaps we might scale the matter thus: Wordsworth was a revolutionist—he truly had a new view of the world—but his revolutionary view left great tracts of the world untouched; the Church of England, for instance. Arnold and Tennyson, a generation or so later, though not revolutionists themselves, are much more profoundly stirred by the revolutionary situation than ever Wordsworth was; that is, the area of the world involved in the debate was for them greater. Institutions are called into question in a more fundamental way. But they managed to hang on to their English God and their English institutions. With Hardy, the area of disturbance has grown greater, and what can be salvaged is much less. He, like the earlier Victorians, had a strong sense of community to sustain him in the face of the universe that was for him, as not finally for Arnold and Tennyson, unfriendly, or at least neutral and Godless. But his was a secret community, different from that of social institutions. It was a human communion that, as a matter of fact, was constantly being violated by institutions. Their violation of it is, in fact, a constant source of subject matter and a constant spring of irony. Nevertheless, Hardy could refer to himself as a meliorist. He could not keep company with Wordsworth or Tennyson or Arnold; and when Hardy, having been elected an Honorary Fellow of Magdalene College, Cambridge, was to be formally admitted, the Master, Doctor Donaldson (as we know from A. C. Benson's *Diary)* was much afraid that Hardy might dislike the religious service. The occasion, however, went off very well, even though Hardy, after impressing the Master with his knowledge of ecclesiastical music, did remark, "Of course it's only a sentiment to me now." Hardy listened to a sermon by the Archdeacon of Zanzibar, who declared that God was "a God of *desire*—who both hated and loved—not a mild or impersonal force." But even though Hardy could not accept the God of the Bishop of Zanzibar, he still had faith in the constructive power of the secret community.

Now, in Hemingway we see something very like Hardy's secret community, but one much smaller, one whose definition has become much more specialized. Its members are those who know the code. They recognize each other, they know the password and the secret grip, but they are few in number, and each is set off against the world like a wounded lion ringed round by waiting hyenas (*Green Hills of Africa* gives us the hyena symbol—the animal whose death is comic because it is all hideously "appetite": wounded, it eats its own intestines). Furthermore, this secret community is not constructive; Hemingway is no meliorist. In fact, there are hints that somewhere in the back of his mind, and in behind his work, there is a kind of Spenglerian view of history: our civilization is running down. We get this most explicitly in *Green Hills of Africa:*

> A continent ages quickly once we come. The natives live in harmony with it. But the foreigner destroys, cuts down the trees, drains the water, so that the water supply is altered and in a short time the soil, once the sod is turned under, is cropped out and, next, it starts to blow away as it has blown away in every old country and as I had seen it start to blow in Canada. The earth gets tired of being exploited. A country wears out quickly unless man puts back in it all his residue and that of all his beasts. When he quits using beasts and uses machines, the earth defeats him quickly. The machine can't reproduce, nor does it fertilize the soil, and it eats what he cannot raise. A country was made to be as we found it. We are the intruders and after we are dead we may have ruined it but it will still be there and we don't know what the next changes are. I suppose they all end up like Mongolia.
>
> I would come back to Africa but not to make a living from it. . . . But I would come back to where it pleased me to live; to really live. Not just let my life pass. Our people went to America because that was the place for them to go then. It had been a

> good country and we had made a bloody mess of it and I would go, now, somewhere else as we had always had the right to go somewhere else and as we had always gone. You could always come back. Let the others come to America who did not know that they had come too late. Our people had seen it at its best and fought for it when it was well worth fighting for. Now I would go somewhere else.

This is the most explicit statement, but the view is implicit in case after case. The general human community, the general human project, has gone to pot. There is only the little secret community of, paradoxically enough, individualists who have resigned from the general community, and who are strong enough to live without any of the illusions, lies, and big words of the herd. At least, this is the case up to the novel *To Have and Have Not*, which appeared in 1937. In that novel and in *For Whom the Bell Tolls*, Hemingway attempts to bring his individualistic hero back to society, to give him a common stake with the fate of other men.

But to return to the matter of Wordsworth and Hemingway. What in Wordsworth is merely simple or innocent is in Hemingway violent: the gangster or bullfighter replaces the leech-gatherer or the child. Hemingway's world is a more disordered world, and the sensibility of his characters is more ironically in contrast with their world. The most immediate consideration here is the playing down of the sensibility as such, the sheathing of it in the code of toughness. Gertrude Stein's tribute is here relevant: "Hemingway is the shyest and proudest and sweetest-smelling storyteller of my reading." But this shyness manifests itself in the irony. In this, of course, Hemingway's irony corresponds to the Byronic irony. But the relation to Byron is even more fundamental. The pity is valid only when it is wrung from the man who has been seasoned by experience. Therefore a premium is placed on the fact of violent experience. The "dumb ox" character, commented on by Wyndham Lewis, represents the Wordsworthian peasant; the character with the code of the tough guy, the initiate, the man cultivating honor, gallantry, and recklessness, represents the Byronic aristocrat.

The failures of Hemingway, like his successes, are rooted in this situation. The successes occur in those instances where Hemingway accepts the essential limitations of his premises—that is, when there is an equilibrium between the dramatization and the characteristic Hemingway "point," when the system of ironies and understatements is coherent. On the other hand, the failures occur when we feel that Hemingway has not respected the limitations of his premises—that is, when the dramatization seems to be "rigged" and the violence, therefore, merely theatrical. The characteristic irony, or understatement, in such cases, seems to be too self-conscious. For example, let us glance at Hemingway's most spectacular failure, *To Have and Have Not*. The point of the novel is based on the contrast between the smuggler and the rich owners of the yachts along the quay. But the irony is essentially an irony without any center of reference. It is superficial, for, as Philip Rahv indicates, the only difference between the smuggler and the rich is that the rich were successful in their buccaneering. The revelation that comes to the smuggler dying in his launch—"a man alone ain't got no . . . chance"—is a meaningless revelation, for it has no reference to the actual dramatization. It is, finally, a failure in intellectual analysis of the situation.

There is, I believe, a good chance that *For Whom the Bell Tolls* will not turn out to be Hemingway's best novel (an honor I should reserve for *A Farewell to Arms*) primarily because in this most ambitious of the novels Hemingway does not accept the limitations of his premises. I do not mean to imply that it is on a level with *To Have and Have Not*. There is a subtler irony in the later novel. I have pointed out that the irony in *To Have and Have Not* is that of the contrast between the smuggler and the rich in the yachts along the pier; that is, it is a simple irony, in direct line with the ostensible surface direction of the story. But the irony in *For Whom the Bell Tolls* runs counter to the ostensible surface direction of the story. As surface, we have a conflict between the forces of light and the forces of darkness, freedom versus fascism, etc. Hero and heroine are clearly and completely and romantically aligned on the side of light. We are prepared to see the Fascist atrocities and the general human kindness of the Loyalists. It happens to work out the other way. The scene of horror is the massacre by the Loyalists, not by the Fascists. Again, in the attack on El Sordo's hill by the Fascists, we are introduced to a young Fascist lieutenant, whose bosom friend is killed in the attack. We are suddenly given this little human glimpse—against the grain of the surface. But this incident, we discover later, is preparation for the very end of the novel. We leave the hero lying wounded, preparing to cover the retreat of his friends. The man who is over the sights of the machine gun as the book ends is the Fascist lieutenant, whom we have been made to know as a man, not as a monster. This general ironical conditioning of the overt story line is reflected also in the attitude of Anselmo, who kills but cannot believe in killing. In other words, the irony here is much more functional, and more complicated, than that of *To Have and Have Not;* the irony affirms that the human values may transcend the party lines.

Much has been said to the effect that *To Have and Have Not* and *For Whom the Bell Tolls* represent a basic change of point of view, an enlargement of what I have called the secret community. Now no doubt that is the intention behind both books, but the temper of both books, the good one and the bad one, is the old temper, the cast of characters is the old cast, and the assumptions lying far below the explicit intention are the old assumptions.

The monotony and self-imitation, into which Hemingway's work sometimes falls, are again an effect of a failure in dramatization. Hemingway, apparently, can dramatize his "point" in only one basic situation and with only one set of characters. He has, as we have seen, only two key characters, with certain variations from them by way of contrast or counterpoint. His best women characters, by the way, are those who most nearly approximate the men; that is, they embody the masculine virtues and point of view characteristic of Hemingway's work.

But the monotony is not merely a monotony deriving from the characters as types; it derives, rather, from the limitations of the author's sensibility, which seems to come alive in only one issue. A more flexible sensibility, one capable of making nicer discriminations, might discover great variety in such key characters and situations. But Hemingway's successes are due, in part at least, to the close co-ordination that he sometimes achieves between the character and the situation, and the sensibility as it reflects itself in the style.

The style characteristically is simple, even to the point of monotony. The characteristic sentence is simple, or compound; and if compound, there is no implied subtlety in the co-ordination of the clauses. The paragraph structure is, characteristically, based on simple sequence. There is an obvious relation between this style and the characters and situations with which the author is concerned—a relation of dramatic decorum. (There are, on the other hand, examples, especially in the novels, of other, more fluent, lyrical effects, but even here this fluency is founded on the conjunction *and;* it is a rhythmical and not a logical fluency. And the lyrical quality is simply a manifestation of that marginal sensibility, as can be demonstrated by an analysis of the occasions on which it appears.)

But there is a more fundamental aspect of the question, an aspect that involves not the sensibility of the characters but the sensibility of the author. The short, simple rhythms, the succession of co-ordinate clauses, the general lack of subordination—all suggest a dislocated and ununified world. The figures who live in this world live a sort of hand-to-mouth existence perceptually, and conceptually they hardly live at all. Subordination implies some exercise of discrimination—the sifting of reality through the intellect. But in Hemingway we see a romantic anti-intellectualism.

In Wordsworth, too, we see this strain of anti-intellectualism. He, too, wishes to clear away the distorting sophistications of the intellect, and to keep his eyes on the object. The formulations of the intellect create the "veil of familiarity" that he would clear away. His mode, too, was to take unpromising material and reveal in it the lyric potentiality. He, too, was interested in the margin of sensibility. He, too, wished to respect the facts, and could have understood Hemingway's rejection of the big abstract words in favor of "the concrete names of villages, the numbers of roads, the names of rivers, the numbers of regiments and the dates."

The passage from *A Farewell to Arms* from which the above quotation comes is, of course, the passage most commonly used to explain the attitude behind Hemingway's style. But we can put with it other passages of a similar import, and best of all a sentence from the story "Soldier's Home." Krebs, the boy who has been through the war and who comes back home to find himself cut off from life, had "acquired the nausea in regard to experience that is the result of untruth or exaggeration." He is a casualty, not of bullet or bayonet, but of the big, abstract words. Hemingway's style is, in a way, an attempt to provide an antidote for that "nausea."

A Farewell to Arms is a love story. It is a compelling story at the merely personal level, but it is much more compelling and significant when we see the figures of the lovers silhouetted against the flame-streaked blackness of war, of a collapsing world, of nada. For there is a story behind the love story. That story is the quest for meaning and certitude in a world that seems to offer nothing of the sort. It is, in a sense, a religious book; if it does not offer a religious solution it is nevertheless conditioned by the religious problem.

The very first scene of the book, though seemingly casual, is important if we are to understand the deeper motivations of the story. It is the scene at the officers' mess where the captain baits the priest. "Priest every night five against one," the captain explains to Frederick. But Frederick, we see in this and later scenes, takes no part in the baiting. There is a bond between him and the priest, a bond that they both recognize. This becomes clear when, after the officers have advised Frederick where he should go on his leave to find the best girls, the priest turns to him and says that he would like to have him to go to Abruzzi, his own province:

> "There is good hunting. You would like the people and though it is cold it is clear and dry. You could stay with my family. My father is a famous hunter."
>
> "Come on," said the captain. "We go whorehouse before it shuts."
>
> "Goodnight," I said to the priest.
>
> "Goodnight," he said.

In this preliminary contrast between the officers, who invite the hero to go the brothel, and the priest, who invites him to go to the cold, clear, dry country, we have in its simplest form the issue of the novel.

Frederick does go with the officers that night, and on his leave he does go to the cities, "to the smoke of cafés and nights when the room whirled and you needed to look at the wall to make it stop, nights in bed, drunk, when you knew that that was all there was, and the strange excitement of waking and not knowing who it was with you, and the world all unreal in the dark and so exciting that you must resume again unknowing and not caring in the night, sure that this was all and all and all and not caring." Frederick, at the opening of the novel, lives in the world of random and meaningless appetite, knowing that it is all and all and all, or thinking that he knows that. But behind that there is a dissatisfaction and disgust. Upon his return from his leave, sitting in the officers' mess, he tries to tell the priest how he is sorry that he had not gone to the clear, cold, dry country—the priest's home, which takes on the shadowy symbolic significance of another kind of life, another view of the world. The priest had always known that other country.

> He had always known what I did not know and what, when I learned it, I was always able to forget. But I did not know that then, although I learned it later.

What Frederick learns later is the story behind the love story of the book.

But this theme is not merely stated at the opening of the novel and then absorbed into the action. It appears later, at crucial points, to define the line of meaning in the action. When, for example, Frederick is wounded, the priest visits him in the hospital. Their conversation makes even plainer the religious background of the novel. The priest has said that he would like to go back after the war to the Abruzzi. He continues:

> "It does not matter. But there in my country it is understood that a man may love God. It is not a dirty joke."
>
> "I understand."
>
> He looked at me and smiled.
>
> "You understand but you do not love God."
>
> "No."
>
> "You do not love Him at all?" he asked.
>
> "I am afraid of him in the night sometimes."
>
> "You should love Him."
>
> "I don't love much."
>
> "Yes," he said. "You do. What you tell me about in the nights. That is not love. That is only passion and lust. When you love you wish to do things for. You wish to sacrifice for. You wish to serve."
>
> "I don't love."
>
> "You will. I know you will. Then you will be happy."

We have here two important items. First, there is the definition of Frederick as the sleepless man, the man haunted by nada. Second, at this stage in the novel, the end of Book I, the true meaning of the love story with Catherine has not yet been defined. It is still at the level of appetite. The priest's role is to indicate the next stage of the story, the discovery of the true nature of love, the "wish to do things for." And he accomplishes this by indicating a parallel between secular love and Divine Love, a parallel which implies Frederick's quest for meaning and certitude. And to emphasize further this idea, Frederick, after the priest leaves, muses on the high, clean country of the Abruzzi, the priest's home that has already been endowed with the symbolic significance of the religious view of the world.

In the middle of Book II (chapter xviii), in which the love story begins to take on the significance that the priest had predicted, the point is indicated by a bit of dialogue between the lovers.

> "Couldn't we be married privately some way? Then if anything happened to me or if you had a child."
>
> "There's no way to be married except by church or state. We are married privately. You see, darling, it would mean everything to me if I had any religion. But I haven't any religion."
>
> "You gave me the Saint Anthony."
>
> "That was for luck. Some one gave it to me."
>
> "Then nothing worries you?"
>
> "Only being sent away from you. You're my religion. You're all I've got."

Again, toward the end of Book IV (chapter xxxv), just before Frederick and Catherine make their escape into Switzerland, Frederick is talking with a friend, the old Count Greffi, who has just said that he thought H. G. Wells's novel *Mr. Britling Sees It Through* a very good study of the English middle-class soul. But Frederick twists the word *soul* into another meaning.

> "I don't know about the soul."
>
> "Poor boy. We none of us know about the soul. Are you *Croyant?*"
>
> "At night."

Later in the same conversation the Count returns to the topic:

> "And if you ever become devout pray for me if I am dead. I am asking several of my friends to do that. I had expected to become devout myself but it has not come." I thought he smiled sadly but I could not tell. He was so old and his face was very wrinkled, so that a smile used so many lines that all gradations were lost.
>
> "I might become very devout," I said. "Anyway, I will pray for you."
>
> "I had always expected to become devout. All my family died very devout. But somehow it does not come."
>
> "It's too early."
>
> "Maybe it is too late. Perhaps I have outlived my religious feeling."
>
> "My own comes only at night."
>
> "Then too you are in love. Do not forget that is a religious feeling."

So here we find, again, Frederick defined as the sleepless man, and the relation established between secular love and Divine Love.

In the end, with the death of Catherine, Frederick discovers that the attempt to find a substitute for universal meaning in the limited meaning of the personal relationship is doomed to failure. It is doomed because it is liable to all the accidents of a world in which human beings are like the ants running back and forth on a log burning in a campfire and in which death is, as Catherine says just before her own death, "just a dirty trick." But this is not to deny the value of the effort, or to deny the value of the discipline, the code, the stoic endurance, the things that make it true—or half true—that "nothing ever happens to the brave."

This question of the characteristic discipline takes us back to the beginning of the book, and to the context from which Frederick's effort arises. We have already mentioned the contrast between the officers of the mess and the priest. It is a contrast between the man who is aware of the issue of meaning in life and those who are unaware of it, who give themselves over to the mere flow of accident, the contrast between the disciplined and the undisciplined. But the contrast is not merely between the priest and the officers. Frederick's friend, the surgeon Rinaldi, is another who is on the same "side" of the contrast as the priest. He may go to the brothel with his brother officers, he may even bait the priest a little, but his personal relationship with Frederick indicates his affiliations; he is one of the initiate. Furthermore, he has the dsicipline of his profession, and, as we have seen, in the Hemingway world, the discipline that seems to be merely technical, the style of the artist or the form of the athlete or bullfighter, may be an index to a moral value. "Already," Rinaldi says, "I am only happy when I am working." (Already the seeking of pleasure in sensation is inadequate for Rinaldi.) This point appears more sharply in the remarks about the doctor who first attends to Frederick's wounded leg. He is incompetent and does not wish to take the responsibility for a decision.

> Before he came back three doctors came into the room. I have noticed that doctors who fail in the practice of medicine have a tendency to seek one another's company and aid in consultation. A doctor who cannot take out your appendix properly will recommend to you a doctor who will be unable to remove your tonsils with success. These were three such doctors.

In contrast with them there is Doctor Valentini, who is competent, who is willing to take responsibility, and who, as a kind of mark of his role, speaks the same lingo, with the same bantering, ironical tone, as Rinaldi—the tone that is the mark of the initiate.

So we have the world of the novel divided into two groups, the initiate and the uninitiate, the aware and the unaware, the disciplined and the undisciplined. In the first group are Frederick, Catherine, Rinaldi, Valentini, Count Greffi, the old man who cut the paper silhouettes "for pleasure," and Passini, Manera, and the other ambulance men in Frederick's command. In the second group are the officers of the mess, the incompetent doctors, the "legitimate hero" Ettore, and the "patriots"—all the people who do not know what is really at stake, who are deluded by the big words, who do not have the discipline. They are the messy people, the people who surrender to the flow and illusion of things. It is this second group who provide the context of the novel, and more especially the context from which Frederick moves toward his final complete awareness.

The final awareness means, as we have said, that the individual is thrown back upon his private discipline and his private capacity to endure. The hero cuts himself off from the herd, the confused world, which symbolically appears as the routed army at Caporetto. And, as Malcolm Cowley has pointed out,[3] the plunge into the flooded Tagliamento, when Frederick escapes from the battle police, has the significance of a rite. By this "baptism" Frederick is reborn into another world; he comes out into the world of the man alone, no longer supported by and involved in society.

> Anger was washed away in the river along with my obligation. Although that ceased when the carabiniere put his hands on my collar. I would like to have had the uniform off although I did not care much about the outward forms. I had taken off the stars, but that was for convenience. It was no point of honor. I was not against them. I was through. I wished them all the luck. There were the good ones, and the brave ones, and the calm ones and the sensible ones, and they deserved it. But it was not my

> show any more and I wished this bloody train would get to Maestre and I would eat and stop thinking.

So Frederick, by a decision, does what the boy[4] Nick does as the result of the accident of a wound. He makes a "separate peace." And from the waters of the flooded Tagliamento arises the Hemingway hero in his purest form, with human history and obligation washed away, ready to enact the last phase of his appropriate drama, and learn from his inevitable defeat the lesson of lonely fortitude.

This is not the time to attempt to give a final appraisal of Hemingway's work as a whole or even of this particular novel—if there is ever a time for a "final" appraisal. But we may touch on some of the objections which have been brought against his work.

First, there is the objection that his work is immoral or dirty or disgusting. This objection appeared in various quarters against *A Farewell to Arms* at the time of its first publication. For instance, Robert Herrick wrote that if suppression were to be justified at all it would be justified in this case. He said that the book had no significance, was merely a "lustful indulgence," and smelled of the "boudoir," and summarized his view by calling it "garbage."[5] That objection has, for the most part, died out, but its echoes can still be occasionally heard, and now and then at rare intervals some bigot or high-minded but uninstructed moralist will object to the inclusion of *A Farewell to Arms* in a college course.

The answer to this moralistic objection is fundamentally an answer to the charge that the book has no meaning. The answer would seek to establish the fact that the book does deal seriously with a moral and philosophical issue, which, for better or worse, does exist in the modern world in substantially the terms presented by Hemingway. This means that the book, even if it does not end with a solution that is generally acceptable, still embodies a moral effort and is another document of the human effort to achieve ideal values. As for the bad effect it may have on some readers, the best answer is perhaps to be found in a quotation from Thomas Hardy, who is now sanctified but whose most famous novels, *Tess of the D'Urbervilles* and *Jude the Obscure*, once suffered the attacks of the dogmatic moralists, and one of whose books was burned by a bishop:

> Of the effects of such sincere presentation on weak minds, when the courses of the characters are not exemplary and the rewards and punishments ill adjusted to deserts, it is not our duty to consider too closely. A novel which does moral injury to a dozen imbeciles, and has bracing results upon intellects of normal vigor, can justify its existence; and probably a novel was never written by the purest-minded author for which there could not be found some moral invalid or other whom it was capable of harming.[6]

Second, there is the objection that Hemingway's work, especially of the period before *To Have and Have Not*, has no social relevance, that it is off the main stream of modern life, and that it has no concern with the economic structure of society. Critics who hold this general view regard Hemingway, like Joseph Conrad and perhaps like Henry James, as an exotic. There are several possible lines of retort to this objection. One line is well stated in the following passage by David Daiches if we substitute the name of Hemingway for Conrad:

> Thus it is no reproach to Conrad that he does not concern himself at all with the economic and social background underlying human relationships in modern civilization, for he never sets out to study those relationships. The Marxists cannot accuse him of cowardice or falsification, because in this case the charge is not relevant [though it might be relevant to *To Have and Have Not* or to *For Whom the Bell Tolls*]. That, from the point of view of the man with a theory, there are accidents in history, no one can deny. And if a writer chooses to discuss those accidents rather than the events which follow the main stream of historical causation, the economic, or other, determinist can only shrug his shoulder and maintain that these events are less instructive to the students than are the major events which he chooses to study; but he cannot accuse the writer of falsehood or distortion.[7]

That much is granted by one of the ablest critics of the group who would find Hemingway an exotic. But a second line of retort would fix on the word *instructive* in the foregoing passage, and would ask what kind of instruction, if any, is to be expected of fiction, as fiction. Is the kind of instruction expected of fiction in direct competition, at the same level, with the kind of instruction offered in Political Science I or Economics II? If that is the case, then out with Shakespeare and Keats and in with Upton Sinclair.

Perhaps *instruction* is not a relevant word, after all, for this case. This is a very thorny and debatable question, but it can be ventured that what good fiction gives us is the stimulation of a powerful image of human nature trying to fulfill itself, and not instruction in an abstract sense. The economic man and political man are important aspects of human nature and may well constitute part of the *materials* of fiction. Neither the economic nor the political man is the complete man; other concerns may still be important enough to engage the attention of a writer—such concerns as love, death, courage, the point of honor, and the moral scruple. A man has to live with other men in terms not only of economic and political arrangements but also of moral arrangements; and he has to live with himself, he has to define himself. It can truly be said that these concerns are all interrelated in fact, but it might be dangerously dogmatic to insist that a writer should not bring one aspect into sharp, dramatic focus.

And it might be dangerously dogmatic to insist that Hemingway's ideas are not relevant to modern life. The mere fact that they exist and have stirred a great many people is a testimony to their relevance. Or to introduce a variation on that theme, it might be dogmatic to object to his work on the ground that he has few basic ideas. The history of literature seems to show that good artists may have very few *basic* ideas. They may have many ideas, but the ideas do not lead a life of democratic give-and-take, of genial camaraderie. No, there are usually one or two basic, obsessive ones. Like Savonarola, the artist may well say: "*Le mie cose erano poche e grandi.*" And the ideas of the artist are grand simply because they are intensely felt, intensely realized—not because they are, by objective standards, by public, statistical standards, "important." No, that kind of public, statistical importance may be a condition of their being grand but is not of the special essence of their grandeur. (Perhaps not even the condition—perhaps the grandeur inheres in the fact that the artistic work shows us a parable of meaning—how idea is felt and how passion becomes idea through order.)

An artist may need few basic ideas, but in assessing his work we must introduce another criterion in addition to that of intensity. We must introduce the criterion of area. An artist's basic ideas do not operate in splendid isolation; to a greater or lesser degree, they prove themselves by their conquest of other ideas. Or again differently, the focus is a focus of experience, and the area of experience involved gives us another criterion of condition, the criterion of area. Perhaps an example would be helpful here. We have said that Hemingway is concerned with the scruple of honor, that this is a basic idea in his work. But we find that he applies this idea to a relatively small area of experience. In fact, we never see a story in which the issue involves the problem of definition of the scruple, nor do we ever see a story in which honor calls for a slow, grinding, day-to-day conquest of nagging difficulties. In other words, the idea is submitted to the test of a relatively small area of experience, to experience of a hand-picked sort, and to characters of a limited range.

But within that range, within the area in which he finds congenial material and in which competing ideas do not intrude themselves too strongly, Hemingway's expressive capacity is very powerful and the degree of intensity is very great. He is concerned not to report variety of human nature or human situation, or to analyze the forces operating in society, but to communicate a certain feeling about, a certain attitude toward, a special issue. That is, he is essentially a lyric rather than a dramatic writer, and for the lyric writer virtue depends upon the intensity with which the personal vision is rendered rather than upon the creation of a variety of characters whose visions are in conflict among themselves. And though Hemingway has not given—and never intended to give—a documented diagnosis of our age, he has given us one of the most compelling symbols of a personal response to our age.

Notes

1. Introduction to the Modern Library edition of *A Farewell to Arms* (New York, 1932).
2. Commented on by Ford Madox Ford in his introduction to the Modern Library edition of *A Farewell to Arms*.
3. Introduction to the *Portable Hemingway*, The Viking Press, 1944. In this general connection one may consider the strategic advantage that Hemingway has in that it is the Italian army from which his hero deserts. If his hero had, for instance, deserted from the American army, the American reader's resistance to accepting the act would have been much greater—the reader's own immediate loyalties, etc., would have been betrayed by Frederick's act. And by the same token the resistance to the symbolic meaning of the act—the resigning from society—would have been much greater. The reader is led to accept the act because the desertion is from a "foreign" army. The point is indicated in a passage of dialogue between Frederick and Catherine. Frederick complains that he doesn't want them to have to live in secret and on the run like criminals.

   "I feel like a criminal. I've deserted from the army."
   "Darling, *please* be sensible. It's not deserting from the army. It's only the Italian army."

   It may be objected that since Hemingway himself saw service on the Italian front it is only natural that his story should be laid there and that by consequence the fact has no symbolic significance and no significance as fictional strategy. But the fact that circumstances of personal history dictated the setting of the story does not prevent the author from seizing on and using the advantages inherent in the situation.
4. *In Our Time*, chapter vi.
5. "What Is Dirt?," *Bookman*, November, 1929.
6. "The Profitable Reading of Fiction," in *Life and Art, Essays, Notes and Letters* (New York, 1925).
7. For a contrary view of the work of Conrad, see my *Selected Essays*, p. 31.

CARLOS BAKER

From "The Mountain and the Plain"

Ernest Hemingway: The Writer as Artist

1952, pp. 94–116

"Learn about the human heart and the human mind in war from this book."
(Hemingway, in another connection.[1])

I. Landscape in Gorizia

The opening chapter of Hemingway's second novel, *A Farewell to Arms*, is a generically rendered landscape with thousands of moving figures. It does much more than start the book. It helps to establish the dominant mood (which is one of doom), plants a series of important images for future symbolic cultivation, and subtly compels the reader into the position of detached observer.

"In the late summer of that year we lived in a house in a village that looked across the river and the plain to the mountains. In the bed of the river there were pebbles and boulders, dry and white in the sun, and the water was clear and swiftly moving and blue in the channels. Troops went by the house and down the road and the dust they raised powdered the leaves of the trees. The trunks of the trees too were dusty and the leaves fell early that year and we saw the troops marching along the road and the dust rising and leaves, stirred by the breeze, falling and the soldiers marching and afterward the road bare and white, except for the leaves."

The first sentence here fixes the reader in a house in the village where he can take a long view across the river and the plain to the distant mountains. Although he does not realize it yet, the plain and the mountains (not to mention the river and the trees, the dust and the leaves) have a fundamental value as symbols. The autumnal tone of the language is important in establishing the autumnal mood of the chapter. The landscape itself has the further importance of serving as a general setting for the whole first part of the novel. Under these values, and of basic structural importance, are the elemental images which compose this remarkable introductory chapter.

The second sentence, which draws attention from the mountainous background to the bed of the river in the middle distance, produces a sense of clearness, dryness, whiteness, and sunniness which is to grow very subtly under the artist's hands until it merges with one of the novel's two dominant symbols, the mountain-image. The other major symbol is the plain. Throughout the sub-structure of the book it is opposed to the mountain-image. Down this plain the river flows. Across it, on the dusty road among the trees, pass the men-at-war, faceless and voiceless and unidentified against the background of the spreading plain.

In the third and fourth sentences of this beautifully managed paragraph the march-past of troops and vehicles begins. From the reader's elevated vantage-point, looking down on the plain, the river, and the road, the continuously parading men are reduced in size and scale—made to seem smaller, more pitiful, more pathetic, more like wraiths blown down the wind, than would be true if the reader were brought close enough to overhear their conversation or see them as individualized personalities.

Between the first and fourth sentences, moreover, Hemingway accomplishes the transition from late summer to autumn—an inexorability of seasonal change which prepares the way for the study in doom on which he is embarked. Here again the natural elements take on a symbolic function. In the late summer we have the dust; in the early autumn the dust and the leaves falling; and through them both the marching troops impersonally seen. The reminder, through the dust, of the words of the funeral service in the prayer-book is fortified by the second natural symbol, the falling leaves. They dry out, fall, decay, and become part of the dust. Into the dust is where the troops are going—some of them soon, all of them eventually.

The short first chapter closes with winter, and the establishment of rain as a symbol of disaster. "At the start of the winter came the permanent rain and with the rain came the cholera. But it was checked and in the end only seven thousand died of it in the army." Already, now in the winter, seven thousand of the wraiths have vanished underground. The permanent rain lays the dust and rots the leaves as if they had never existed. There is no excellent beauty, even in the country around Gorizia, that has not some sadness to it. And there is hardly a natural beauty in the whole first chapter of *A Farewell to Arms* which has not some symbolic function in Hemingway's first study in doom.

II. Not in Our Stars

To call *A Farewell to Arms* a "first" study in doom might seem unfair to *The Sun Also Rises*. But the total effect of the first novel, whatever its author's intention, is closer to that of tragicomedy than of tragedy. The tragic sense of life exists in the undertones of *The Sun Also Rises*. Its surface tone is, however, somewhere within the broad range of the comic. Reading it, one is oftener reminded of the tragi-comic irony of a work like Chaucer's *Troilus and Criseyde* than, say, the tragic irony of the Greeks and the Elizabethans. The operation of pity—again as in Chaucer—is carefully equivocal, somehow in itself a phase of irony, and under a restraint so nearly complete that it can scarcely move. Possibly because of the nature of the material, possibly because of the cultivated habit of understatement, one does not find in *The Sun Also Rises* the degree of emotional commitment which becomes visible in *A Farewell to Arms*. . . .

In the midst of life, runs the Book of Common Prayer, we are in death. "During the time I was writing the first draft," said Hemingway in 1948, "my second son Patrick was delivered in Kansas City by Caesarean section, and while I was rewriting my father killed himself in Oak Park, Illinois. . . . I remember all these things happening and all the places we lived in and the fine times and the bad times we had in that year. But much more vividly I remember living in the book and making up what happened in it every day. Making the country and the people and the things that happened I was happier than I had ever been. Each day I read the book through from the beginning to the point where I went on writing and each day I stopped when I was still going good and when I knew what would happen next. The fact that the book was a tragic one did not make me unhappy since I believed that life was a tragedy and knew it could only have one end. But finding you were able to make something up; to create truly enough so that it made you happy to read it; and to do this every day you worked was something that gave a greater pleasure than any I had ever known. Beside it nothing else mattered."[2]

The appearance of *A Farewell to Arms* in book form on September 27, 1929, marked the inception of Hemingway's still lengthening career as one of the very few great tragic writers in twentieth-century fiction. His next book, *Death in the Afternoon*, furthered his exploration into the esthetics of tragedy. Through the 1930's he continued at intervals to wrestle with the problem. *To Have and Have Not* (though with limited success) examined the tragic implications of social and political decay. *For Whom the Bell Tolls* attacked a similar problem on an epic and international scale. Ten years after that, at the age of fifty, Hemingway rounded out a full twenty years of work in tragedy with his character-study of Colonel Richard Cantwell.

The position occupied by *A Farewell to Arms* among Hemingway's tragic writings may be suggested by the fact that he once referred to the story of Lieutenant Frederick Henry and Catherine Barkley as his *Romeo and Juliet*.[3] The most obvious parallel is that Henry and Catherine, like their Elizabethan prototypes, might be seen as star-crossed lovers. Hemingway might also have been thinking of how rapidly Romeo and Juliet, whose affair has begun as a mere flirtation, pass over into the status of relatively mature lovers. In the third place, he may have meant to imply that his own lovers, caught in the tragic pattern of the war on the Austrian-Italian front, are not far different from the young victims of the Montague-Capulet family feud.

Neither in *Romeo and Juliet* nor in *A Farewell to Arms* is the catastrophe a direct and logical result of the immoral social situation. Catherine's bodily structure, which precludes a normal delivery for her baby, is an unfortunate biological accident. The death of Shakespeare's lovers is also precipitated by an accident—the detention of the message-bearing friar. The student of esthetics, recognizing another kind of logic in art than that of mathematical cause-and-effect, may however conclude that Catherine's death, like that of Juliet, shows a kind of artistic inevitability. Except by a large indirection, the war does not kill Catherine any more than the Veronese feud kills Juliet. But in the emotional experience of the novel, Catherine's dying is directly associated and interwoven with the whole tragic pattern of fatigue and suffering, loneliness, defeat and doom, of which the war is itself the broad social manifestation. And one might make a similar argument about *Romeo and Juliet*.

In application to Frederick and Catherine, the phrase "star-crossed lovers" needs some qualification. It does not mean that they are the victims of an actual malevolent metaphysical power. All their crises are caused by forces which human beings have set in motion. During Frederick's understandably bitter ruminations while Catherine lies dying in the Lausanne hospital, fatalistic thoughts do, quite naturally, cross his mind. But he does not, in the end, blame anything called "Fate" for Catherine's death. The pain of her labor reminds him that her pregnancy has been comfortable and apparently normal; the present biological struggle is perhaps a way of evening things up. "So now they got her in the end. You never got away with anything." But he immediately rejects his own inference: that is, that her sufferings in labor are a punishment for sinful pleasures. Scientifically considered, the child is simply a by-product of good nights in Milan—and there is never a pretence that they were not good. The parents do not happen to be formally married; still, the pain of the child-bearing would have been just as it is even if they had been married fifty times. In short, the pain is natural, inevitable, and without either moral or metaphysical significance. The anonymous "they" is nothing but a name for the way things are.

A little later Frederick Henry bitterly compares the human predicament first to a game and then to a swarm of ants on a log in a campfire. Both are homely and unbookish metaphors such as would naturally occur to any young American male at a comparable time. Living now seems to be a war-like game, played "for keeps," where to be tagged out is to die. Here again, there is a moral implication in the idea of being caught off base—trying to steal third, say, when the infield situation and the number of outs make it wiser to stay on second. "They threw you in and told you the rules and the first time they caught you off base they killed you." One trouble, of course, is that the player rarely has time enough to learn by long experience; his fatal error may come in the second half of the first inning, which is about as far as Catherine seems likely to go. Even those who survive long enough to learn the rules may be killed through the operation of chance or the accidents of the game. Death may, in short, come "gratuitously" without the slightest reference to "the rules."

It is plainly a gratuitous death which comes to the ants on the burning log in Frederick's remembered campfire. Some immediately die in flame, as Catherine is now dying. Others, like Lieutenant Henry, who has survived a trench-mortar explosion, will manage to get away, their bodies permanently scarred, their future course uncertain—except that they will die in the end. Still others, unharmed, will swarm on the still cool end of the log until the fire at last reaches them. If a Hardyan President of the Immortals takes any notice of them, He does little enough for their relief. He is like Frederick Henry pouring water on the burning campfire log—not to save the ants but only to empty a cup.

Catherine's suffering and death prove nothing except that she should not have become pregnant. But she had to become pregnant in order to find out that becoming pregnant was unwise. Death is a penalty for ignorance of "the rules": it is also a fact which has nothing to do with rule or reason. Death is the fire which, in conclusion, burns us all, and it may singe us along the way. Frederick Henry's ruminations simply go to show that if he and Catherine seem star-crossed, it is only because Catherine is biologically double-crossed, Europe is war-crossed, and life is death-crossed.[4]

III. Home and Not-Home

As its first chapter suggests, the natural-mythological structure which informs *A Farewell to Arms* is in some ways comparable to the Burguete-Montparnasse, Catholic-Pagan, and Romero-Cohn contrasts of *The Sun Also Rises*. One has the impression, however, of greater assurance, subtlety, and complexity in the second novel, as if the writing of the first had strengthened and consolidated Hemingway's powers and given him new insights into this method for controlling materials from below.

Despite the insistent, denotative matter-of-factness at the surface of the presentation, the subsurface activity of *A Farewell to Arms* is organized connotatively around two poles. By a process of accrual and coagulation, the images tend to build round the opposed concepts of Home and Not-Home. Neither, of course, is truly conceptualistic; each is a kind of poetic intuition, charged with emotional values and woven, like a cable, of many strands. The Home-concept, for example, is associated with the mountains; with dry-cold weather; with peace and quiet; with love, dignity, health, happiness, and the good life; and with worship or at least the consciousness of God. The Not-Home concept is associated with low-lying plains; with rain and fog; with obscenity, indignity, disease, suffering, nervousness, war and death; and with irreligion.

The motto of William Bird's Three Mountains Press in Paris, which printed Hemingway's *in our time*, was "Levavi oculos meos in montes." The line might also have served as an epigraph for *A Farewell to Arms*. Merely introduced in the first sentence of the first chapter, the mountain-image begins to develop important associations as early as Chapter Two. Learning that Frederick Henry is to go on leave, the young priest urges him to visit Capracotta in the Abruzzi. "There," he says, "is good hunting. You would like the people and though it is cold, it is clear and dry. You could stay with my family. My father is a famous hunter." But the lowlander infantry captain interrupts: "Come on," he says in pidgin Italian to Frederick Henry. "We go whorehouse before it shuts."[5]

After Henry's return from the leave, during which he has been almost everywhere else on the Italian peninsula *except* Abruzzi, the mountain-image gets further backing from another low-land contrast. "I had wanted," says he, "to go to Abruzzi. I had gone to no place where the roads were frozen and hard as iron, where it was clear cold and dry and the snow was dry and powdery and haretracks in the snow and the peasants took off their hats and called you Lord and there was good hunting. I had gone to no such place but to the smoke of cafés and nights when the room whirled and you needed to look at the wall to make it stop, nights in bed, drunk, when you knew that that was all there was."

Throughout Book I, Hemingway quietly consolidates the mountain-image. On the way up towards the Isonzo from Gorizia, Frederick looks across the river and the plain to the Julian and Carnic Alps. "I looked to the north at the two ranges of mountains, green and dark to the snow-line and then white and lovely in the sun. Then, as the road mounted along the ridge, I saw a third range of mountains, higher snow mountains, that looked chalky white and furrowed, with strange planes, and then there were mountains far beyond all these that you could hardly tell if you really saw."[6] Like Pope in the celebrated "Alps on Alps arise" passage, Hemingway is using the mountains symbolically. Years later, in "The Snows of Kilimanjaro," he would use the mighty peak of East Africa as a natural image of immortality, just as in *The Green Hills of Africa* he would build his narrative in part upon a contrast between the hill-country and the Serengetti Plain. When Frederick Henry lowers his eyes from the far-off ranges, he sees the plain and the river, the war-making equipment, and "the broken houses of the little town" which is to be occupied, if anything is left of it to occupy, during the coming attack. Already now, a few dozen pages into the book, the mountain-image has developed associations; with the man of God and his homeland, with clear dry cold and snow, with polite and kindly people, with hospitality, and with natural beauty. Already it has its oppositions: the lowland obscenities of the priest-baiting captain, cheap cafés, one-night prostitutes, drunkenness, destruction, and the war.

When the trench-mortar explosion nearly kills Henry, the priest comes to visit him in the field-hospital, and the Abruzzi homeland acquires a religious association. "There in my country," says the priest, "it is understood that a man may love God. It is not a dirty joke." Repeating, for emphasis, the effect of the priest's first account of the highland country, Hemingway allows Frederick to develop in his mind's eye an idyllic picture of the priest's home-ground.

"At Capracotta, he had told me, there were trout in the stream below the town. It was forbidden to play the flute at night . . . because it was bad for the girls to hear. . . . Aquila was a fine town. It was cool in the summer at night and the spring in Abruzzi was the most beautiful in Italy. But what was lovely was the fall to go hunting through the chestnut woods. The birds were all good because they fed on grapes, and you never took a lunch because the peasants were always honored if you would eat with them in their houses. . . ."[7]

By the close of Book I, largely through the agency of the priest, a complex connection has come clear between the idea of Home and the combination of high ground, cold weather, love, and the love of God. Throughout, Hemingway has worked solely by suggestion, implication, and quiet repetition, putting the reader into potential awareness, readying him for what is to come.

The next step is to bring Catherine Barkley by degrees into the center of the image. Her love affair with Henry begins as a "rotten game" of war-time seduction. Still emotionally unstable and at loose nervous ends from her fiancé's death, Catherine is a comparatively easy conquest. But in the American hospital at Milan, following Henry's ordeal by fire at the front not far from the Isonzo, the casual affair becomes an honorable though unpriested marriage. Because she can make a "home" of any room she occupies—and Henry several times alludes to this power of hers—Catherine naturally moves into association with ideas of home, love, and happiness. She does not really reach the center of the mountain-image until, on the heels of Frederick's harrowing low-land experiences during the retreat from Caporetto, the lovers move to Switzerland. Catherine is the first to go, and Henry follows her there as if she were the genius of the mountains, beckoning him on. Soon they are settled into a supremely happy life in the winterland on the mountainside above Montreux. Catherine's death occurs at Lausanne, after the March rains and the approaching need for a good lying-in hospital have driven the young couple down from their magic mountain—the closest approximation to the priest's fair homeland in the Abruzzi that they are ever to know.

The total structure of the novel is developed, in fact, around the series of contrasting situations already outlined. To Gorizia, the Not-Home of war, succeeds the Home which Catherine and Frederick make together in the Milan Hospital. The Not-Home of the grim retreat from the Isonzo is followed by the quiet and happy retreat which the lovers share above Montreux. Home ends for Frederick Henry when he leaves Catherine dead in the Lausanne Hospital.

Developed for an esthetic purpose, Hemingway's contrasting images have also a moral value. Although he has nothing to say about the images themselves, Mr. Ludwig Lewisohn is undoubtedly correct in saying that *A Farewell to Arms* "proves once again the ultimate identity of the moral and the esthetic." In this critic's view, Hemingway "transcended the moral nihilism of the school he had himself helped to form" by the very intensity of his feelings for the contrast of love and war. "The simply wrought fable," Lewisohn continues, ignoring all the symbolic complexities yet still making a just appraisal, "has two culminations—the laconic and terrible one in which the activity of the battle police brings to an end the epically delineated retreat of the Italian army with its classically curbed rage and pity . . . and that other and final culmination in Switzerland with its blending in so simple and moving a fashion of the eternal notes of love and death." The operation of the underlying imagery, once its purposes are understood, doubly underscores Mr. Lewisohn's point that there is no moral nihilism in the central story of *A Farewell to Arms.*[8]

The use of rain as a kind of symbolic obligato in the novel has been widely and properly admired. Less apparent to the cursory reader is the way in which the whole idea of climate is related to the natural-mythological structure. (Hemingway's clusters of associated images produce emotional "climates" also, but they are better experienced than reduced by critical descriptions.) The rains begin in Italy during October, just before Henry's return to Gorizia after his recovery from his wounds. The rains continue, at first steadily, then intermittently, throughout the disastrous retreat, Henry's flight to Stresa, and the time of his reunion with Catherine. When they awaken the morning after their reunion night, the rain has stopped, light floods the window, and Henry, looking out in the fresh early morning, can see Lake Maggiore in the sun "with the mountains beyond." Towards these mountains the lovers now depart.

Not until they are settled in idyllic hibernation in their rented chalet above Montreux are they really out of the rain. As if to emphasize by climatic accompaniment their "confused alarums of struggle and flight," the rain has swept over them during their escape up the lake in an open boat. Once in the mountains, however, they are out of the lowlands, out of danger, out of the huge, tired debacle of the war. Above Montreux, as in the priest's homeland of Abruzzi, the ridges are "iron-hard with the frost." The deep snow isolates them, and gives them a feeling of domestic safety, tranquillity, and invulnerability.

For several months the rainless idyll continues. "We lived through the months of January and February and the winter was very fine and we were very happy. There had been short thaws when the wind blew warm and the snow softened and the air felt like spring, but always the clear, hard cold had come again and the winter had returned. In March came the first break in the winter. In the night it started raining."

The reader has been prepared to recognize some kind of disaster-symbol in the return of the rains. Much as in *Romeo and Juliet*, several earlier premonitions of doom have been inserted at intervals. "I'm afraid of the rain," says Catherine in the Milan Hospital one summer night, "because sometimes I see me dead in it." In the fall, just before Henry returns to the front, they are in a Milan hotel. During a break in the conversation the sound of falling rain comes in. A motor car klaxons, and Henry quotes Marvell: "At my back I always hear Time's wingèd chariot hurrying near." He must soon take a cab to catch the train that will project him, though he does not know it yet, into the disaster of the great retreat. Months later, in Lausanne, the Marvell lines echo hollowly: "We knew the baby was very close now and it gave us both a feeling *as though something were hurrying us and we could not lose any time together.*" (Italics added.) The sound of the rain continues like an undersong until, with Catherine dead in the hospital room (not unlike that other happy one where their child was conceived), Henry walks back to the hotel in the rain.[9]

One further reinforcement of the central symbolic structure is provided by the contrast between the priest and the doctor, the man of God and the man without God. In line with the reminiscence of *Romeo and Juliet*, it may not be fantastic to see them respectively as the Friar Lawrence and the Mercutio of Hemingway's novel. The marked contrast between the two men becomes especially apparent when Henry returns to the Gorizia area following his discharge from the hospital.

The return to Gorizia is a sharp come-down. After the "home-feeling" of the hospital and the hotel in Milan, the old army post seems less like home than ever. The tenor of life there has noticeably changed. A kind of damp-rot afflicts morale. The major, bringing Henry up to date on the state of affairs, plays dismally on the word *bad*. It has been a "bad summer." It was "very bad" on the Bainsizza plateau: "We lost three cars. . . . You wouldn't believe how bad it's been. . . . You were lucky to be hit when you were. . . . Next year will be worse. . . ." As if he were not fully convinced by the Major's despair, Henry picks up the word: "Is it so bad?" The answer is yes. "It is so bad and worse. Go get cleaned up and find your friend Rinaldi."

With Rinaldi the doctor, things also are bad, a fact which has been borne in upon the major so strongly that he thinks of Rinaldi when he mentions the word *bad*. Things are not bad for Rinaldi from a professional point of view, for he has operated on so many casualties that he has become "a lovely surgeon." Still, he is not the old Mercutio-like and mercurial Rinaldi. If mercury enters into his picture at all it is because he has syphilis, or thinks he has. He is treating himself for it and is beginning to entertain certain delusions of persecution. Except for his work, and the temporary opiates of drink and prostitutes, both of which interfere with his work, Rinaldi, the man of the plain, the man without God, is a man without resources.

With the priest, the man from the Abruzzi highlands, tacitly reintroduced as a contrast for Rinaldi, things are not so bad. "He was the same as ever," says Henry at their meeting, "small and brown and compact-looking." He is much more sure of himself than formerly, though in a modest way. When Rinaldi, in the absence of the foul-mouthed captain, takes up the former indoor game of priest-baiting, the priest is not perturbed. "I could see," says Henry, "that the baiting did not touch him now."

Out of the evils of the past summer the priest has even contrived to gather a nascent hope. Officers and men, he thinks, are gentling down because they "realize the war" as never before. When this happens, the fighting cannot continue for very much longer. Henry, playing half-heartedly the *advocatus diaboli*, argues that what the priest calls "gentling down" is really nothing but the feeling of defeat: "It is in defeat that we become Christian . . . like Our Lord." Henry is maintaining that after the fearless courage of His ministry, Our Lord's gentleness and His refusal to fight against the full brunt of the experience on Calvary became the ideal of Christian meekness. If Peter had rescued Christ Jesus from the Garden, suggests Henry, Christian ethics might be something different. But the priest, who is as compact as he looks, knows otherwise. Our Lord would not have changed in any way. From that knowledge and belief comes the priest's own strength. He has resources which Dr. Rinaldi, the man without God, does not possess.[10]

The priest-doctor contrast is carried out in the sacred-versus-profane-love antithesis which is quietly emphasized in the novel. Through the agency of Rinaldi the love affair begins at a fairly low level. The doctor introduces Frederick to Catherine, and takes a jocularly profane view of the early infatuation, seeming to doubt that it can ever be anything but an unvarnished war-time seduction. On the other hand, the background symbols of home and true love and high ground suggest that the lovers' idyllic life in Switzerland is carried on under the spiritual aegis of the priest. Neither Rinaldi nor the priest appears in the latter part of the book. But when, having been driven to the lowlands by the rains of spring, Catherine enters the hospital, it is naturally enough a doctor who takes over. And though this doctor does all he can to save her life, Catherine dies.

Projected in actualistic terms and a matter-of-fact tone, telling the truth about the effects of war in human life, *A Farewell to Arms* is entirely and even exclusively acceptable as a naturalistic narrative of what happened. To read it only as such, however, is to miss the controlling symbolism: the deep central antithesis between the image of life and home (the mountain) and the image of war and death (the plain).

IV. The Female of the Species

Coleridge once made the questionable remark that in Shakespeare "it is the perfection of woman to be characterless. Every one wishes a Desdemona or Ophelia for a wife—creatures who, though they may not always understand you, do always feel [for] you and feel with you."[11] To make so inordinate a generalization, Coleridge was obliged to ignore the better than half of Shakespeare's "perfect" women who are anything but characterless.

The modern reader, brought up on similar generalizations about the heroines of Hemingway, may wish to reconsider the problem. The most frequent adverse comment on Hemingway's fictional heroines is that they tend to embody two extremes, ignoring the middle ground. This fact is taken to be a kind of sin of omission, the belief being that most of their real-life sisters congregate and operate precisely in the area which Hemingway chooses not to invade at all.

The strictures of Mr. Edmund Wilson may be taken as typical of a recurrent critical position. He puts the argument in terms of a still-to-be-written chapter on the resemblances between Hemingway and Kipling. The two writers seem to him to share in "certain assumptions about society" with particular reference to the position of women. Kipling and Hemingway show, says Mr. Wilson, "much the same split attitude toward women. Kipling anticipates Hemingway in his beliefs that 'he travels fastest who travels alone' and that 'the female of the species is more deadly than the male'; and Hemingway seems to reflect Kipling in the submissive infra-Anglo-Saxon women that make his heroes such perfect mistresses. The most striking example of this is the amoeba-like little Spanish girl, Maria, in *For Whom the Bell Tolls*. Like the docile native 'wives' of English officials in the early stories of Kipling, she lives only to serve her lord and to merge her identity with his; and this love affair with a woman in a sleeping-bag, lacking completely the kind of give and take that goes on between real men and women, has the all-too-perfect felicity of a youthful erotic dream."[12]

The relevance of this commentary is that it underscores the idea of the two extremes in Hemingway's fictional treatment of women. In one group are the "deadly" females. Their best-realized (because most sympathetically presented and most roundly characterized) representative is Brett Ashley. The horrible example would presumably be someone like Margot Macomber, who is really and literally deadly. In varying degrees—and the fact that it is a matter of degree ought to be noticed—these women are selfish, corrupt, and predatory. They are "bad" for the men with whom they are involved. At the other extreme would stand the allegedly docile and submissive mistress-types, of whom Catherine Barkley and Maria are the conspicuous examples. These, for Mr. Wilson, are incredible wish-projections, youthfully erotic dream-girls, or impossibly romantic ideals of wife-hood. They bear, it seems, little resemblance to the women with whom one is acquainted. Where now, Mr. Wilson seems to be asking, are the day-by-day vagaries, the captious bickerings, the charming or enraging anfractuosities which combine to produce the "normal" or "real" married state? The greater number of the female kind obviously occupy some realm intermediate between the Becky Sharps and the Amelia Sedleys, between the pole of Goneril and Regan and the pole of Ophelia and Desdemona. By his failure, or his tacit refusal, to depict realistically the occupants of this realm and to use them as the heroines of his fiction, Hemingway has somehow failed in his obligation to present things as they are.

This point of view naturally affects Mr. Wilson's judgment of *A Farewell to Arms*. On the whole he finds the novel to be "a less serious affair" than Hemingway's previous work. Catherine Barkley and Frederick Henry, at least during the period of their Swiss idyll, strike him as "not in themselves convincing as human personalities." For him their relationship is merely an idealization, "the abstraction of a lyric emotion."[13] Mr. Cowley evidently shares this view. "To me," writes Mr. Cowley, "[Catherine] is only a woman at the beginning of the book, in her near madness"—as if, perhaps, some degree of emotional instability were a criterion of credibility in the portrait of a fictional heroine.[14]

For those who find it hard to accept Mr. Wilson's view of

Catherine as an abstraction and of Maria as an amoeba, four practical points might well be made. The first has to do with the relation of Brett Ashley and Catherine Barkley to what Mr. Wilson might call the Great Infra-Anglo-Saxon tradition of fictional heroines. It is of some interest to observe that Mr. Wilson's strictures on the heroines of Hemingway could be applied with equal justice, not only to the heroines of Kipling but also to a considerable number of other heroines throughout the history of English and American fiction. Hemingway shares with many predecessors an outlook indubitably masculine, a certain chivalric attitude not without ironic overtones, and a disinclination to interest himself in what may be called the prosaisms of the female world.

The second point is that through a method of comparative portraiture, Hemingway carefully establishes a moral norm of womanly behavior. Then, whether by ethical intent or by temperamental attitude, he uses the established norm as a means of computing various degrees of departure from it. Depending on their own views in this area, readers may find Hemingway's "norm-women" less interesting and less credible than their "abnormal" cousins. For the inveterate reader of fiction and narrative poetry it is perhaps a psychological truism that the *femme fatale*, the general type of the temptress, seems more "interesting" than the stable heroine.

In the early work of Hemingway the point is well illustrated by the contrast between Brett and Catherine. There are, to begin with, certain resemblances. Like Brett, Catherine is an Englishwoman; like Brett, she is beautiful, tall, and blonde. She talks as Brett does, stressing certain words which in print are italicized. Like Brett, she has lost her own true love early in the war, and her emotions, like her way of life, have become confused as a result of the bereavement. But here the resemblances stop.

Brett's neurosis drives her from bar to bar, from man to man, and from city to city. None of it is any good: her polygamy, with or without benefit of justices of the peace, leads only to more of the same, as one drink leads to another in the endless round. Brett is not "good" for the men she knows. Romero wants her to let her hair grow out, to become more feminine, to marry and live with him. The basic abnormality at work in Brett opposes such feminization. She is the short-haired companion of men, wearing a man's felt hat, calling herself a "chap." She does not really like other women, and neither has nor wishes to have any real friends among them. She is never happier than in the Pamplona wineshop, the center of raucous masculine singing, as if she were a half-woman half in love with damnation.

Catherine Barkley, on the other hand, is all woman. At once dependent and independent, she half-mothers, half-mistresses Frederick Henry. She wants no other life than with him, no other man than he. She drinks little and displays none of Brett's geographical restlessness. She is temperamentally monogamous. Where she is, home is. Even the red-plush hotel room in Milan (which for several minutes makes her feel like a whore) is changed by her presence until she herself can feel at home in it. "In a little while," says her lover, "the room felt like our own home. My room at the hospital had been our own home and this room was our home too in the same way." Trying at first to help her out of the harlot-feeling, Henry kisses her and assures her, "You're my good girl." "I'm certainly yours," says Catherine, wryly. But she is also, and preeminently, a "good girl"—even more so, for example, than Hardy's Tess, who was so designated on the title page.[15] As if Hemingway were looking back for contrast to the Circean figure of his first novel, Rinaldi refers to Catherine as "your lovely cool . . . English goddess." But she is a woman, not a goddess. She rescues, pities, comforts, companions, and sustains, just as she in turn is rescued from the "craziness" induced by her lover's death when she has finally involved herself sufficiently in Henry's growing love. Her hair is long; she dresses like a woman and gets on well with other women like her friend Ferguson. Yet she is evidently happiest alone with her husband. She would be unhappy and possibly frightened on the wine-cask in Pamplona. She is at ease in Milan in the midst of a war because she is a young woman in the midst of love. Like Maria, she is a completing agent for the hero, and is in turn completed by her association with him. But Brett, on the other hand, is an agent of depletion, as she herself realizes, and as her unselfish renunciation of Romero is presumably meant to show.[16]

The third point to be made about Hemingway's heroines is that they are, on the whole, an aspect of the poetry of things. It is perhaps a sign of an attitude innately chivalric that they are never written off, as sometimes happened in Kipling, as mere bundles of rags, bones, and hanks of hair. Even Margot Macomber, in the bottomless slough of her bitch-hood, is seen to be "damned beautiful." The treatment of Catherine, like that of Brett, shows in Hemingway a fundamental indisposition to render his heroines "reductively." And if one argues that he nowhere seems to commit himself to the emancipation of women, or to become in the usual sense of the term an ardent feminist, the answer would be, perhaps, that his women are truly emancipated only through an idea or ideal of service. His heroines, to make the statement exactly, are meant to show a symbolic or ritualistic function in the service of the artist and the service of man.

The final point grows naturally out of the preceding ones. It is, in brief, that all of Hemingway's heroines, like all of his heroes, are placed in a special kind of accelerated world. We do not see them puttering in their kitchens, but only dreaming of that as a desirable possibility. They are never presented as harassed mothers; their entire orientation tends to be, in this connection, premarital. Wars and revolutions, the inevitable enemies of peace and domesticity, set them adrift or destroy their lives. Yet they contrive to embody the image of home, the idea if not the actuality of the married state, and where they are, whatever the outward threats, home is.

Mr. Wilson's feeling that Catherine is not convincing as a human personality, his belief that her love affair with Frederick Henry is an "abstraction of lyric emotion," may be partly explained by the fact that a majority of the characters in the first two novels are oddly rootless. With a few notable exceptions like Robert Cohn, Brett Ashley, or the priest from Abruzzi, they seem on the whole to possess no genealogies or previous biographies. We know nothing about Henry's background, and next to nothing about Catherine Barkley's. Like Jake Barnes, Bill Gorton, and Dr. Rinaldi, they seem to come from nowhere, move into the now and here, and depart again for nowhere after the elapsed time of the novels. They have substance and cast shadows, but they lack the full perspective and chiaroscuro that one finds among most of the people in *For Whom the Bell Tolls*. We are seldom permitted to know them in depth. The inclination is to accept them for what they do more than for what they are. They are the men and women of action, the meaning of whose lives must be sought in the kind of actions in which they are involved, very much, again, as in *Romeo and Juliet*.

This feeling about the characters can be accounted for in two different ways. One has to do with Hemingway's esthetic assumptions as of 1928–1929; the other is a natural consequence of the kind of stories he chose to tell. His working assumption that character is revealed through action will, if rigorously adhered to, produce the kind of fiction in which characterization-in-depth is in a measure sacrificed to the exigencies of narrative movement. Even there, however, it is advisable to notice that a close reading of any of the early books reveals far more in the way of nuances of light and shade, or in subtle shifts of motivation, than one at first imagined was there. This half-concealed power is easily explained by what is now acknowledged in all quarters: Hemingway's carefully controlled habit of understatement. As for the second explanation, it might be pointed out that nearly all the important characters in the first two novels are "displaced persons"—either men fighting a war far from their former home-environments, or aliens in foreign lands whose ties with nearly everything they have known before are now severed—for better or for worse, but severed.

These two explanations, the esthetic and the "geographical," may throw some further light into the reasons behind Mr. Wilson's strictures. If Hemingway had not yet met head-on the problem of characterization-in-depth, perhaps it was unfair to ask a writer who had done so much so brilliantly that he should do so much more. He had developed a memorably individualized style—whittled it, as MacLeish said, from the hard wood of a walnut stick. He showed an unerring ability to keep his narratives in motion. Finally, he had achieved mastery of that special combination of naturalistic and symbolic truth-telling which was the despair of those who could (and so frequently did) imitate his style and his narrative manner.

In the absence of other evidence, it is probably wisest to assume that Hemingway knew what he was doing. That he could draw a character fully, roundedly, and quickly is proved by a dozen minor portraits in the first two books—Cohn's acidulous mistress, for example, or Brett's friend Mippipopoulos, or the wonderful old Count Greffi, with whom Henry plays at billiards and philosophy in the hotel at Stresa, or the Milanese surgeon who does the operation on Henry's leg after the affair of the trench mortar, a surgeon who seems, and is, four times as good as the three old-maiden doctors who have wisely wagged their heads an hour before and advised Henry to wait six months for the operation. These are only four examples, but they are enough to show that the ability to draw character was by no means lacking in the Hemingway of 1929. If he went no deeper into the backgrounds of his displaced persons, he went as deeply as he needed to do for the purposes of his narrative. And the paring-out of the superfluous had always been one of his special addictions.

There is, finally, a *tendenz* in *A Farewell to Arms* which helps to account for the opinion that Hemingway has somehow failed in his attempt to present Catherine as a credible characterization. In a large and general way, the whole movement of the novel is from concretion towards abstraction. This became apparent in our consideration of the wonderfully complex opening chapter, and the importance of the observation is enhanced by what happens in the closing chapters of the book. The fact that the whole story is projected in actualistic terms ought not finally to obscure the symbolic mythos on which it is built and from which a great part of its emotional power derives. Catherine may be taken as an English girl who has a Juliet-like liaison with a young American officer. Similarly, one may read the novel as a naturalistic narrative of what happened to a small group of people on the Italian front during the years 1917–1918.

In the central antithesis between the image of life, love, and home (the mountain), and the image of war and death (the plain), Catherine however has a symbolic part to play. It is indeed required of her that she should become, as the novel moves on towards its dénouement, more of an abstraction of love than a down-to-earth portrait of an actual woman in love and in pain. The truly sympathetic reader may feel that she is a woman, too. But if she does move in the direction of abstraction, one might argue that the *tendenz* of the novel is in this respect symbolically and emotionally justified. For when Frederick Henry has closed the door of the hospital room in order to be alone with his dead wife Catherine, he learns at once, as if by that act, the finality and totality of his loss. It is the loss of a life, of a love, of a home. Saying good bye is "like saying good bye to a statue." The loved woman has become in death an abstract unvital image of her living self, a marble memorial to all that has gone without hope of recovery. Her death exactly completes the symbolic structure, the edifice of tragedy so carefully erected. This structure is essentially poetic in conception and execution. It is achieved without obvious insistence or belaboring of the point, but it is indubitably achieved for any reader who has found his way into the true heart of the book. And it is this achievement which enables Hemingway's first study in doom to succeed as something far more than an exercise in romantic naturalism. Next to *For Whom the Bell Tolls*, it is his best novel.

Notes

1. Hemingway, *Men at War*, introd., p. xx.
2. See Hemingway's introduction, dated June 30, 1948, to the illustrated edition of *FTA*, New York, Scribner's, 1948, pp. vii–viii. Hemingway seems to be in error when he gives the impression that the original publication date was "the day the stock market crashed"—that is, October 30, 1929. The book had been published September 27th. For an excellent review of *FTA* following publication, see Malcolm Cowley, *New York Herald Tribune Books*, October 6, 1929, pp. 1 and 6.
3. The *Romeo and Juliet* comment is quoted by Edmund Wilson in "Ernest Hemingway: Bourdon Gauge of Morale," which first appeared in the *Atlantic Monthly* 164 (July 1939), pp. 36–46. The essay was collected in *The Wound and the Bow*, New York, 1941, and reprinted by J. K. M. McCaffery, ed., *Ernest Hemingway: The Man and His Work*, New York, 1950, pp. 236–257. Further page-references to this essay will be to the McCaffery reprint only.

   In *A Farewell to Arms* Hemingway was dealing imaginatively but also retrospectively with his own first adult love affair, which had taken place in Milan at the base hospital during his recuperation there in the late summer and autumn of 1918. Harold Loeb alludes to it in *The Way It Was*, New York, 1959, pp. 219–220, stating erroneously that the girl was English. She was in fact Agnes von Kurowsky, an American of Polish ancestry working as a Red Cross nurse. It was she who voluntarily ended the association by letter after Hemingway's return to the United States early in 1919. I am indebted for materials documenting this episode to Mr. J. C. Buck. The portrait of Catherine Barkley appears to have been influenced by Hemingway's recollections of his first wife, Hadley Richardson. His second wife, Pauline Pfeiffer, was delivered of a son by Caesarean section in Kansas City in 1928 while Hemingway was at work on the novel. See his introduction to the illustrated edition of *FTA* (New York, Scribner's, 1948), p. vii. The manner of Catherine's death was perhaps suggested to Hemingway by this experience. But the portrait of Catherine seems to have been founded chiefly on his remembrance of the Red Cross nurse in Milan. Ten years later, when he was readying *The Fifth Column and the First Forty-Nine Stories* for publication, Hemingway directed Maxwell Perkins to change the name of the nurse in "A Very Short Story" from Ag (for Agnes) to Luz—on the grounds that the name Ag was libellous. EH to ⟨Maxwell Perkins⟩, 7/12/38. Perkins complied. It is therefore quite clear, as many have surmised, that the central episode of "A Very Short Story" is connected with the love affair in *A Farewell to Arms*.
4. On Catherine's bad luck, see *FTA*, pp. 342, 350.
5. *FTA*, pp. 9, 13.

6. *FTA*, p. 48.
7. *FTA*, p. 78.
8. *Expression in America*, New York, 1932, p. 519.
9. *FTA*, pp. 135, 165, 267, 326, and 332 show, in order, the various premonitions and the obligato use of rain. Malcolm Cowley was one of the first of Hemingway's critics to point to his symbolic use of weather. See *The Portable Hemingway*, New York, 1944, introd., p. xvi.
10. On the low morale among the Italian troops, see *FTA*, pp. 174–175. On Rinaldi's affliction, see p. 181. On the priest's firmness, see pp. 183–184.
11. Coleridge, *Table Talk*, in *Works*, ed. Shedd, vol. 6, p. 349.
12. McCaffery, op.cit., p. 254, note.
13. Ibid., p. 242.
14. Malcolm Cowley to Carlos Baker, 10/20/51.
15. On Catherine's connection with the "home-feeling," see *FTA*, p. 163. Rinaldi's remark on her goddess-like qualities is on p. 71.
16. Mr. Theodore Bardacke has an interesting essay on "Hemingway's Women" in McCaffery, op.cit., pp. 340–351. Among its contributions is a discussion of Hemingway's "symbolic" use of long and short hair as a mark of femininity or the relative lack of it. The point is of special interest in connection with Maria, who has been raped and shorn by the fascists. The growing-out of her hair is a reminder of her gradual return to mental and physical health under the double tutelage of Pilar and Roberto.

ROGER ASSELINEAU

From "Hemingway, or 'Sartor Resartus' Once More"
The Transcendentalist Constant in American Literature
1980, pp. 137–52

Though history never quite repeats itself, the same causes to a large extent produce the same effects and thus, other things being equal, the Napoleonic wars and the so-called Great War both resulted in the same general collapse of political, moral, religious, and aesthetic structures, brought about the same crash of commonly accepted values, and created the same spiritual vacuum. Carlyle and Bernanos, Francis Scott Fitzgerald and Musset, Byron and Hemingway were all equally "enfants du siècle," "children of the century." They all suffered from the same "mal du siècle." "Tout était vide,"[1] "everything was empty," Musset complained, and, a hundred years later, Scott Fitzgerald's "sad young men" echoed his complaint and similarly lamented because they found "all Gods dead, all wars fought, all faiths in man shaken."[2] They were, as he also said, "cynical rather than revolutionary, tired of great causes."[3] Some of them were so tired and sick to nausea that they committed suicide. Harry Crosby in particular, who had come to Europe believing that "God [had] ordained this war . . . and when it's over the world will be a finer, cleaner, and squarer place."[4] He served as an ambulance driver like E. E. Cummings, John Dos Passos, and Hemingway, but on the French, not on "the picturesque front,"[5] and he never succeeded in forgetting the horrors he had seen. He felt so miserable in the Waste Land of the postwar world that, though immensely rich and in principle happily married, he committed suicide in 1929.

It was indeed a "lost generation" in more senses than one. Yet, Hemingway among others survived the Great War for over forty years and, after appearing as the cynical and disillusioned Byron of the twentieth century, ultimately turned into a new "teacher of athletes" and a "professeur d'énergie" à la Barrès. A rather surprising change and a very spectacular recovery, which we can follow step by step in his works, since his novels make up an interminable *Bildungsroman* whose hero is always himself. In his early short stories he offers us a portrait of the artist as a boy and a young man, perhaps symbolically called Nick Adams, a combination of Nick, the Devil, and Adam or prelapsarian innocence in the Garden of Eden. Frederick Henry, Jake Barnes, Harry Morgan, Robert Jordan, Colonel Cantwell, Santiago, the Old Man, and Thomas Hudson, the painter, are all avatars of himself. They grow old with him—whereas the heroines, on the contrary, remain eternally young. His protagonists were projections of himself as he would have liked to be—and to some extent really was, at least potentially. Their adventures, which he partly lived and partly "invented truly," to borrow his own phrase, constitute, as it were, *The Education of Nick Adams*, a fascinating record of his experiences, a lifelong *Erlebnis*, rather than a piece of intellectual history like *The Education of Henry Adams*. His fiction, in other words, provides us with a graph of his evolution from innocence to experience through despair and cynicism, and the hard-won equilibrium of his middle years up to the apparent serenity of his old age. His life and his works were carried away by a dialectical movement which, to some extent, parallels the movement of *Sartor Resartus*, although less dramatically and with a less resounding "everlasting yea." After the "idyllic" passage of youth, we get under way and witness the "sorrows" of Frederick, visit the "Centre of Indifference," and eventually reach (or hear) the "everlasting no." It is indispensable to distinguish these various stages for the sake of logic and clarity, though, of course they sometimes overlap chronologically.

"Happy season of childhood!" exclaims Teufelsdröckh.[6] It is hard to say whether Hemingway's childhood was happy, but it certainly was a period of enforced innocence. He was born at Oak Park in the suburbs of Chicago, but there was then almost a difference in kind between the two places. Chicago was Hell and Oak Park a modern—and improved—version of the Garden of Eden, for, as the saying was, it was the place where the saloons stopped and the churches began. Both of Hemingway's parents were ardently religious, and one of his paternal uncles was a missionary in China. His mother was a devout Episcopalian and his father a stern Congregationalist and a strict disciplinarian. For him, right was right and wrong was wrong. There were no half measures. When young Ernest used coarse language, he was sent upstairs to wash his mouth with toilet soap. Hemingway senior believed that dancing, card playing, and gambling were wrong, and he absolutely disapproved of smoking and drinking alcoholic beverages. Young Ernest thus spent an artificially sheltered childhood in a vice-proof, teetotaling community where virtue and high moral ideals were compulsory. The only times when he had a chance to live a more natural and less restrained life were during the summer holidays, when he could fish and shoot and swim like a young savage "up in Michigan." In Oak Park, he had no choice but to be a "clean young American," a God-fearing young man, completely cut off from reality, pent-up in the closest approximation to the American dream that could then be found in the United States.

This phase of idyllic innocence could not last forever. It ended rather abruptly when, after serving a six months' apprenticeship as a cub reporter on the staff of the Kansas City *Star*, Hemingway suddenly found himself right in the middle of World War I on the Italian front, a new innocent abroad whose untried idealism was unexpectedly confronted with the sordid reality of war. "I was an awful dope when I went to the last war," he was to say later on, "I can remember just thinking that we were the home team and the Austrians were the visiting team."[7] He had enlisted as a volunteer ambulance driver, because he wanted to watch the game. And at first he was delighted. He arrived in Paris just as the city was being bombarded by Big Bertha and, as soon as a shell blew up, he took a taxi and rushed to the scene to contemplate the damage.

In Milan, he was equally lucky. A big munitions-factory exploded when he got there and he had to help pick up the dead—mostly women—and gather shapeless human fragments from trees and barbed wire fences. This baptism of war, for all his bravado, gave him a considerable shock. He got over it at the time, but soon made other disconcerting discoveries—notably that women are not necessarily angels and soldiers generally are no choirboys. There were houses of ill repute behind the front to bolster up the morale of the troops. Far from being outlawed, they were quasi-official institutions: some were intended for officers and others for enlisted men. Frederick Henry occasionally visited them, but, when he came back, Rinaldi taunted him: "I know you are the fine good Anglo-Saxon boy, I know. You are the remorse boy, I know. I will wait till I see the Anglo-Saxon brushing away harlotry with a toothbrush."[8] But Anglo-Saxon hygiene was powerless to obliterate Latin—or human—corruption. All the illusions of the young midwestern innocent were destroyed in quick succession. Hemingway presently found out that modern armies were not made up of heroes, but of unwilling civilians caught in the cogs of a ruthless machine and compelled to go to the front lines whether they liked it or not. If they resisted, they were shot by the military police. The only way out was a self-inflicted wound, and many tried it with various degrees of ingenuity and success. Gallantry did not exist. The bravest troops, the Alpini, the Bersaglieri, had been known to run away. "There is nothing worse than war," Passini concludes in *A Farewell to Arms.*[9] Far from ennobling, it debases everything it touches.

This direct experience of the evils of war à la Goya was soon completed by a personal encounter with death. In July 1918, at Fossalta di Piave, while engaged in the rather unheroic occupation of eating a piece of cheese, Hemingway was very severely wounded by an Austrian shell and machine-gun fire, and nearly killed. He has recounted it in *A Farewell to Arms:* ". . . there was a flash, as a blast-furnace door is swung open, and a roar that started white and went red and on and on in a rushing wind. I tried to breathe but my breath would not come and I felt myself rush bodily out of myself and out and out and all the time bodily in the wind. I went out swiftly, all of myself and I knew I was dead and that it had all been a mistake to think you just died. Then I floated, and instead of going on I felt myself slide back. I breathed and I was back."[10]

This was an ambiguous experience. On the one hand, Hemingway very proudly found out that he could "take it" as well as anyone else: he had been initiated and—without any irony—had received "the red badge of courage." But, on the other hand, he had also made the startling discovery that he was mortal. "When you go to war as a boy," he wrote in 1942, "you have a great illusion of immortality. Other people can get killed, not you. It can happen to other people; but not to you. Then when you are badly wounded the first time you lose that illusion and you know it can happen to you. After being severely wounded two weeks before my nineteenth birthday I had a bad time. . . ."[11] Until then death had been an abstraction to him, now it was a reality, and a frightening and horrible reality at that, which gave him nightmares and insomnia to such an extent that for weeks and even months afterward he could not go to sleep without a light in his room.

When he returned to the United States in 1919, he was a much sobered and very disillusioned young man. Though feted at first as a war hero by his home town, he did not feel at home at all. He was unable to adjust himself to a society whose principles he now regarded as a mere sham. His parents took it for granted that after a brief respite he could carry on as if nothing had happened. But he could not bring himself to do it. Like Krebs, the hero of "Soldier's Home," he felt "angry," "sick and vaguely nauseated," and his parents reacted very much like those of Krebs. "Unless you, my son Ernest, come to yourself; cease your lazy loafing and pleasure-seeking . . . and neglecting your duties to God, and your Savior, Jesus Christ . . . there is nothing for you but bankruptcy—you have overdrawn,"[12] his mother wrote to him. So, like Krebs, he decided to run away. At the earliest opportunity, he turned his back on puritan America, prohibition, moral purity, the myth of success, and all the rest of it, and left for Paris.

There, although outwardly happy and hard at work, he went through his "centre of indifference," his nihilistic period. Every day was not a moveable feast. More than once, in the solitude of his "mansarde" (garret) on rue du Cardinal Lemoine, he must have been licking his psychic wounds far from the crowd of his noisy and unthinking fellow expatriates. The war which he had just gone through and which still lingered in the Balkans and Turkey had debased all the things he believed in. As he wrote in *A Farewell to Arms:* "I was always embarrassed by the words sacred, glorious and sacrifice and the expression in vain. We had heard them, sometimes standing in the rain almost out of earshot, so that only the shouted words came through, and had read them on proclamations that were slapped up by bill posters over other proclamations . . . and I had seen nothing sacred, and the things that were glorious had no glory and the sacrifices were like the stockyards at Chicago if nothing was done with the meat except to bury it . . . finally only the names of places had dignity. . . . Abstract words such as glory, courage, or hallow were obscene beside the concrete names of villages, the numbers of roads, the names of rivers."[13] All the traditional values had thus become devalued and were just as worthless as German currency. As John Peale Bishop, one of Hemingway's exact contemporaries and the prototype of Tom d'Invilliers in *This Side of Paradise,* noted: "The most tragic thing about the war was not that it made so many dead men, but that it destroyed the tragedy of death. Not only did the young suffer in the war, but every abstraction that would have sustained and given dignity to their suffering. The war made the traditional morality unacceptable . . . so that at its end, the survivors were left to face, as they could, a world without values."[14]

This kind of disillusionment was general. In France a slightly older veteran, Georges Bernanos, reached much the same conclusion: ". . . we were so sick of phoney blah, of Right and Justice and Morale, that we didn't know any more how to speak to kids; we didn't dare any more; it seemed to us we were reciting by heart articles from the Military Gazette, passed by the censor. My foot!"[15]

The bottom seemed to have dropped out of everything. The world was empty, life absurd and meaningless, since the war had reduced men to the condition of passive, expendable things herded en masse into the vast slaughterhouses of the western world. The individual felt like Frederick Henry, "lonely and empty,"[16] alienated from the society into which he happened to be born, a stranger, in short. Even the word "soul" had lost its meaning and sounded obscene and dirty.[17] "I do not know about the soul," says Frederick Henry. "We none of us knows," answers his interlocutor, Count Greffi, and this was nearly the only occasion when Hemingway ever used the word "soul" in his fiction.[18] His characters are men and women without souls. They are more ashamed of their souls than of their bodies. He wrote almost as if the word had become completely obsolete.

And no wonder, since the lost generation practically lived in a godless world—very much like the one which Carlyle described in *Sartor Resartus*: "*Aus der Ewigkeit, zu der Ewigkeit hin*: from Eternity, onwards to Eternity! These are Apparitions: what else? Are they not souls rendered visible: in Bodies, that took shape and will lose it, melting into air?"[19] In the same way, Hemingway's characters are only very provisionally staying in "a clean, well-lighted place," but they will sooner or later be engulfed forever in nothingness. As the Spanish waiter philosophizes in "A Clean, Well-Lighted Place": "What did he fear? . . . It was a nothing that he knew too well. It was all a nothing and a man was nothing too. It was only that and light was all it needed and a certain closeness and order. Some lived in it and never felt it but he knew it all was nada y pues nada y pues nada." He goes on parodying the Lord's Prayer: "Our nada who art in nada, nada be thy name, thy Kingdom nada, thy will be nada in nada as it is in nada. Give us this nada our daily nada and nada us our nada as we nada our nadas and nada us not into nada but deliver us from nada y pues nada."[20] It is quite likely that Hemingway was here playing on the words nada and dada, and wanted to suggest by this almost nonsensical use of the Spanish word for "nothing" that his own brand of nihilism was just as desolate and despairing as that of Tristan Tzara and all the other dadaists.

At this point Hemingway's position is fundamentally identical with that of the Ecclesiast: "All is vanity. . . . One generation passeth away, and another generation cometh, but the earth abideth for ever. The sun also ariseth. . . ."[21] *The Sun Also Rises* and Jake Barnes and Lady Brett Ashley and the others strut and fret their hour upon the stage and then are heard no more, to take up the words that Macbeth used when he realized his delusion. The situation of man in the Waste Land of the postwar world was desperate too. If you did not share the faith of the priest from the Abruzzi, the only sensible thing to do was to destroy yourself like Rinaldi by drinking too much and / or making love indiscriminately and catching syphilis—"self-destruction day by day,"[22] Rinaldi called it.

Hemingway, however, found another way out, since he survived the Great War until 1961. Like Dr. Teufelsdröckh, he could probably have said: "From Suicide a certain after shine (*Nachschein*) of Christianity withheld me."[23] After touching the bottom, he gave a kick and rose to the surface again. He could not live interminably in a spiritual vacuum. Absolute nihilism is an untenable position. In a way, as Edgar Johnson has pointed out, his scepticism of the immediate postwar years, other things being equal, corresponds to Descartes's provisional doubt, which he used as "a stage preparatory to a new departure,"[24] as a *tabula rasa* on which to build a truer and more harmonious conception of life.

The first remedies which Hemingway applied to his trauma were mere anaesthetics. All abstractions being debased, Thought with a capital *T* having led to disaster,[25] only concrete things, only the physical world mattered. "I lay down on the bed and tried to stop from thinking,[26] said Frederick Henry, and he added: "I was not made to think. I was made to eat. My God, yes. Eat and drink and sleep with Catherine."[27] In other words, if you wanted to save yourself, there was only one thing for you to do: you must become wholly engrossed in concrete, material activities. Hemingway has explained this strategy in particular in "Big Two-Hearted River." In doing so, he was quite literally following the advice of the Ecclesiast: "There is nothing better for a man than that he should eat and drink, and that he should make his soul enjoy good in his labour."[28] This is why he became a connoisseur of food and wines and alcoholic drinks of all kinds. In fact, his characters enjoy drinking so much and so convincingly that it is impossible to read his books without feeling thirsty. And they drink so often and at such regular intervals that it gives the reader a sense of duration. Alcohol in Hemingway's novels serves the same purpose as a clepsydra or water clock. It reminds us of the flight of time. The drinks taken by the characters are a kind of temporal punctuation, whereas hunting and fishing become the supreme diversion, especially in *Green Hills of Africa*, which culminates in a sort of quest for the unicorn in the form of a perfect kudu.

Thus Hemingway's instinctive, visceral reaction after his European ordeal was to cling to life, to imbibe it greedily through all his senses. Life is indeed better than nothing in his eyes. However disappointing, tragic, and unsatisfactory the form of existence to which we are condemned here below may be, it is infinitely better than the terrible nothingness in which we are doomed sooner or later to be engulfed. "Do you value life?" asks Count Greffi. "Yes," answers Frederick. "So do I," says Count Greffi, "because it is all I have."[29]

But Hemingway and his heroes soon realized that this desperate hedonism, this deliberate epicureanism did not suffice. The pleasures of the flesh or the satisfaction you derive from a well-done job can only be palliatives or sedatives, pastimes in the Pascalian sense of the word, drugs, "opiums of the people," to use Karl Marx's phrase. This is the discovery which Frazer, the writer in "The Gambler, the Nun and the Radio," is supposed to make while staying in the hospital: "Yes, and music is the opium of the people. Old Mount-to-the-head [i.e., Karl Marx] had not thought of that. . . . But drink was a sovereign opium of the people, oh, an excellent opium. Although some people prefer the radio, another opium of the people, a cheap one he had just been using. . . ."

But no one can live on *panem et circenses* alone. As the Ecclesiast had already found out: "To every thing there is a season, and a time to every purpose under the heaven. A time to kill and a time to heal; a time to break down and a time to build up."[30] Remembering his wartime emotions in tranquillity, Hemingway discovered that war, in fact, does not destroy everything. Like an acid it corrodes and removes all that is soft and unprotected and thus gives a stronger relief to what remains. It etches, as it were, the men who survive its contact. It is a touchstone and a test. It tries your mettle. It gives you a chance to find out whether you can look death in the face or not. It teaches you how to control fear—all fear being in the last analysis the fear of death. Courage, then, ceases to be an abstract word. It becomes a reality, one of the few realities that count—which you can learn only through experience. So those who have gone through the ordeal of war, even if they have been scorched and partly broken, are almost different in kind from their fellow men. They are even stronger in the places where they were originally broken. They have been initiated into the quasi-secret society of those who know what life really means and is. They belong to "El Ordine Militar, Nobile y Esperituoso de los Caballeros de Brusadelli," founded by Colonel Cantwell. They are natural aristocrats regardless of their social origins. The Gran Maestro is the headwaiter of the Gritti Hotel in Venice and he is the Italian counterpart, one World War later, of the manager of the Hotel Montoya in Pamplona in *The Sun Also Rises*. Of course Jake Barnes belongs to it and so do Pilar, that pillar of strength, Count Mippipopoulos, Kandisky, the Austrian hunter in *Green Hills of Africa*, and Santiago, the old man of the sea. On the contrary, Robert Cohn, for all his phsyical bravery and skill at boxing, will forever remain an outsider, "indignus entrare in nostro docto corpore," because he has never been to war,[31] just as Sherwood Anderson and Gertrude Stein were for the same reason forever disqualified from treating certain essential subjects in Hemingway's opinion.[32]

All the veterans of foreign wars who appear in Hemingway's fiction are united by a common belief in an unwritten code. They are morally and physically very tough. They can take it. They keep a stiff upper lip. They grin and bear it. They refuse to discuss their own emotions and despise loquacious swaggerers like Robert Cohn. They hate gushing. They believe in self-control and self-imposed discipline. They have reached true wisdom in the etymological meaning of the word "wisdom." They are those who know—who know that they are mortal and that sooner or later life ends in death. They know that man—whatever he does—will sooner or later be crushed by the hostile forces which surround him and is bound to be defeated—defeated, but not vanquished, for, like Pascal, they believe in the dignity of man, "a mere reed, and the weakest that can be found on earth, but even when the universe crushes him, man is still nobler than what kills him, for he knows that he is dying, while the advantage that the universe has over him, the universe is unaware of it."[33]

Most of the values extolled by Hemingway are British sportsmen's values (he always admired the British in this respect), but they are combined with that Spanish sense of death which he has exalted in *Death in the Afternoon*. He regarded bullfighting as a ritual, a *memento mori* implicitly understood by all *aficionados*, and he contrasted the American dream of life as a perpetual pursuit of happiness and an endless flight from death, and the thought of death with the Spanish conception of life as the austere contemplation of mortality. This is a constant contrast in his fiction. It sets Harry Morgan, the heroic smuggler, against Richard Gordon, the soft intellectual, the "hollow man."

Living in conformity with this code, playing the game is a purely gratuitous activity. No reward is promised and no material gain is procured. "Winner take nothing." But the heroes feel a deep and intense satisfaction when they have behaved as they think they should have. For Hemingway this new form of stoicism is its own reward. As he hated preaching and despised didacticism, he always refused to define a new set of values explicitly or to use "big words" in his turn. But he affirmed again and again that what is moral is "what you feel good after," as even Lady Brett Ashley ultimately finds out.[34] For Jake Barnes, immorality is "things that made you disgusted afterwards,"[35] and, in *Death in the Afternoon*, we are told again that "so far, about morals, I know only that what is moral is what you feel good after and what is immoral is what you feel bad after."[36]

Hemingway thus replaced the traditional abstract principles of morality by a set of subjective values passionately believed in by his heroes. These values, however were not actually new; they were often nothing but some of the old values stripped of "bunk," "debunked," as the phrase was. (It appeared during the interwar years, which was a rather significant symptom.) His moral was morals without any moralizing, in other words, a return to fundamental moral values without sententiousness or righteousness: "I hated anyone who was righteous at all, or who had ever been righteous. I hated all righteous bastards," Hemingway declared in *Green Hills of Africa*.[37] War, that manmade machine for crushing hundreds of thousands and millions of men, had taught him modesty and humility. It had taught him, among other things, that man is a puny, short-lived creature, whereas "the earth abideth for ever." The business of living is too difficult. No one can set himself up as a teacher or preacher. Everyone must work out his own salvation by himself. "Let those who want to save the world, if they can see it clear, do it," he concluded in *Death in the Afternoon*.[38]

Yet, though he had signed "a separate peace" with mankind at the end of World War I, he gradually rediscovered the meaning and value of human solidarity, that sense of human solidarity which Frederick Henry felt so instinctively that, though very seriously wounded himself, he carried one of his comrades-in-arms on his back to the nearest dressing station through the bombardment. During the depression years, distressed by the helplessness and sufferings of the veterans who were reduced to living on public charity in camps in Florida, he reached the same conclusion as Harry Morgan, the hero of *To Have and Have Not*: "No matter how, a man alone ain't got no bloody chance."[39] This tolled the knell of his rebellious individualism. The rise of fascism and nazism, the progress of a more and more dictatorial form of communism made it impossible for a man of good will—and will—to remain indifferent. So Robert Jordan, instead of denouncing "holy abstractions," like his predecessors decided to join the "crusade" against political oppression:

> That was the only word for it although it was a word that had been so worn and abused that it no longer gave its true meaning. You felt, in spite of all bureaucracy and inefficiency and party strife something that was like the feeling you expected to have and did not have after your first communion. It was a feeling of consecration to a duty toward all the oppressed of the world which would be difficult and embarrassing to talk about as a religious experience, and yet it was as authentic as when you heard Bach, or stood in Chartres Cathedral [Nick Adams here follows in Henry Adams's footsteps] or the cathedral at León and saw the lights coming through the great windows, or when you saw Mantegna, Greco, Brueghel in the Prado. It gave you a part of something you could believe in wholly, and in which you felt an absolute brotherhood.[40]

Over the centuries Hemingway then joined hands with a Christian preacher named John Donne who had proclaimed from his pulpit in St. Paul's cathedral: "No man is an Iland, intire of itself, every man is a peece of the Continent, a part of the maine . . . therefore never send to know for whom the bell tolls; It tolls for thee. . . ."

Actually, even at the height of his rebellion, Hemingway had never quite believed that man is an island entire of itself, for he never doubted Love or called it in question. He never ceased to capitalize it—mentally at least. In the middle of universal chaos it always remained intact, a permanent and indestructible value. Love is an oasis in his heroes' lives, where they can rest and forget the nada which surrounds them by transcending the limitations of time and escaping into eternity, for lust is on the level of the body, but love belongs to the realm of the spirit, as Frederick Henry finds out by passing from the one to the other. (Malraux declared that *A Farewell to Arms* was the most beautiful love story that had appeared since *The Charterhouse of Parma*.) Jake Barnes, for his part, dreams of love. Harry Morgan experiences it without expressing it. Robert Jordan both experiences and expresses it: "When I am with Maria I love her so that I feel, literally, as though I would die and I never believed in that nor thought that it could happen."[41] "What you have with Maria," he soliloquizes, "whether it lasts just through today and a part of to-morrow, or whether it lasts for a long life is the most important thing that can happen to a human being. There will always be people who say it does not exist because they cannot have it. But I tell you it is true and that you have it and that you are lucky even if you die to-morrow."[42] "I suppose it is possible to live as full a life in seventy hours as in seventy years. . . . So that if your life trades its seventy years for seventy hours I have that *value* now and I am lucky enough to know it."[43]

In Hemingway's universe, Love is thus an ideal and almost mythical value. He was in love with love and dreamed of it, but he may very well never have encountered it himself—except perhaps once with his first wife.[44] Anyway, it is worth noting that all his wives were American, whereas the women his heroes fall in love with are always submissive, absolutely passive European women. For his part, he could love them only from a distance. They were idols he worshipped without ever daring to touch them, perhaps for fear they might vanish away. Curiously enough, Marlene Dietrich was one of his lifelong idols, and, after World War II, he found another in the person of a Venetian girl called Adriana Ivancich, who served as a model for Renata, but he was less fortunate than Colonel Cantwell; his relationship with her remained purely platonic. Love as he conceived it belonged to the realm of essences, but did not exist on the level of mere existence.

He went still further, for *The Old Man and the Sea* describes an apotheosis of Love. Love ceases to be addressed to Woman only. It becomes the love of all animate and inanimate things which the old man feels for the little bird which rests for a few minutes on his boat and the big fish, his victim, and the young lions which he sees in his dreams innocently gamboling on African beaches as in the days of the Garden of Eden.

Notes

1. *La Confession d'un enfant du siècle* (Paris: G. Charpentier, 1856), Part I, chap. 2.
2. Quoted by Alfred Kazin, *On Native Grounds* (New York: Harcourt, Brace, 1942), p. 324.
3. *This Side of Paradise.*
4. Quoted by Frederick J. Hoffman, *The Twenties* (New York: Collier Books, 1962), p. 75.
5. I.e., the Italian front. Hemingway used the phrase in *A Farewell to Arms.*
6. Thomas Carlyle, *Sartor Resartus,* 1836, Book II, chapter 2.
7. Carlos Baker, *Ernest Hemingway—A Life Story* (New York: Scribner, 1969), p. 38.
8. *A Farewell to Arms,* chap. 25.
9. Ibid., chap. 8.
10. Ibid., chap. 9.
11. Introduction to *Men at War* (London: Fontana Books, 1966), p. 7.
12. Quoted by Carlos Baker, op. cit., p. 72.
13. *A Farewell to Arms,* chap. 27.
14. "The Missing All," quoted by John K. M. McCaffery, ed., *E. Hemingway: The Man and His Work* (Cleveland: World, 1950), p. 304. This essay originally appeared in the *Virginia Quarterly,* vol. XIII, no. 1 (Winter 1937).
15. ". . . Nous en avions tellement plein le dos des bobards à la mie de pain, et du Droit et de la Justice, et du Moral, que nous ne savions plus parler aux gosses, nous n'osions plus, nous nous faisions l'effet de réciter par coeur un article du Bulletin des Armées, visé par la censure—des clous!" *Nouvelles Littéraires,* vol. XLVII, no. 2176 (June 5, 1969), p. 11A.
16. *A Farewell to Arms,* end of chap. 7.
17. This disaffection to the word "soul" was quite widespread among young writers after World War I. Aldous Huxley expressed a similar repugnance in a conversation with Professor Louis Cazamian.
18. He used the word again, however, in his very last novel, *Islands in the Stream* (New York: Scribner, 1970), p. 100 and especially p. 191: "What he needs is to work well to save his soul. I don't know anything about souls. But he misplaced his the first time he went out to the Coast." He did not know what a soul was, but he did know that it could be saved or lost.
19. *Sartor Resartus,* Book I, chap. 3.
20. "A Clean, Well-Lighted Place."
21. Ecclesiastes I: 2, 4–5. Thomas Wolfe, though belonging to a slightly younger generation, at times shared Hemingway's fundamental pessimism: "In everlasting terms—those of eternity—you and the Preacher may be right: for there is no greater wisdom than the wisdom of the *Ecclesiastes,* no acceptance finally so true as the acceptance of the rock. Man was born to live, to suffer, and to die, and what befalls him is a tragic lot. There is no denying this in the final end. But we must, dear Fox, deny it all along the way." Quoted by Maxwell Geismar in his introduction to the *Portable Thomas Wolfe* (New York: Viking, 1946), p. 25
22. *A Farewell to Arms,* chap. 25.
23. *Sartor Resartus,* Book I, chap. 7.
24. "Farewell the Separate Peace," in John K. M. McCaffery, op cit., p. 137.
25. Introduction to *Men at War,* p. 12.
26. *A Farewell to Arms,* chap. 35.
27. Ibid., chap. 32.
28. Ecclesiastes II:24.
29. *A Farewell to Arms,* chap. 35.
30. Ecclesiastes III: 1, 3.
31. Robert Cohn is in a way a prefiguration of some of Saul Bellow's and Malamud's heroes. No wonder Bellow has in his turn rejected Hemingway and his code of WASP values.
32. Cf. this passage in *The Green Hills of Africa* (chap. 4), in which Hemingway discusses Tolstoy's early novel, *Sevastopol:* "It was a very young book and had one fine description in it, when the French take the redoubt and I thought about Tolstoy and what a great advantage an experience of war was to a writer. It was one of the major subjects and certainly one of the hardest to write truly of and those writers who had not seen it were always very jealous and tried to make it seem unimportant, or abnormal, or a disease as a subject, while, really, it was just something quite irreplaceable that they had missed."
33. Pascal, *Pensées* (Léon Brunschvicg, ed., no. 347): "L'homme n'est qu'un roseau pensant, le plus faible de la nature . . . mais quand l'univers l'écraserait, l'homme serait encore plus noble que ce qui le tue, parce qu'il sait qu'il meurt et l'avantage que l'univers a sur lui, l'univers n'en sait rien."
34. Last page but one of *The Sun Also Rises.*
35. Ibid., chap. 14.
36. *Death in the Afternoon.*
37. *Green Hills of Africa,* chap. 5.
38. *Death in the Afternoon,* last page.
39. *To Have and Have Not,* chap. 15.
40. *For Whom the Bell Tolls,* chap. 18.
41. Ibid., chap. 13.
42. Ibid., chap. 36.
43. Ibid., chap. 13. The italics are mine.
44. Cf. *Islands in the Stream:* ". . . he was still in love with the first woman he had been in love with" (p. 8).
45. *Sartor Resartus,* Book II, chap. IX.
46. Ibid.
47. *Green Hills of Africa,* Part I, chap. 1.
48. Pascal, though a good Christian, feared nada as much as Hemingway and confessed that "le silence éternel des espaces infinis" (the eternal silence of infinite space) inspired him with awe. (*Pensées,* Léon Brunschvicg, ed., thoughts no. 205, 206).
49. The theme of universal love is taken up again in *Islands in the Stream,* when David, Thomas Hudson's youngest son, like Santiago, catches a big fish and fights with him just as epically. Hemingway makes him say afterward: "In the worst parts, when I was the tiredest I couldn't tell which was him and which was me. . . . Then I began to love him more than anything on earth. . . . I loved him so much when I saw him coming up that I couldn't stand it" (pp. 142–43).

O. Henry
William Sydney Porter

1862–1910

O. Henry was born William Sydney Porter in Greensboro, North Carolina, on September 11, 1862. His father, Algernon Sydney Porter, practiced medicine; his mother, Mary Virginia Swaim Porter, wrote poems. She died of tuberculosis when O. Henry was three years old. He was brought up by a maiden aunt, and went to work in his uncle's drugstore at the age of fifteen. In 1882 poor health sent him to Texas, where he stayed on the ranch of some family friends. For the next two years he studied bronco-busting and foreign languages. O. Henry then moved to Austin, where he was a pharmacist, a clerk, a draftsman, and finally a banker. He became popular for his storytelling, singing, and cartooning. In July 1887 he eloped with Athol Estes, with whom he had one daughter, Margaret. His writing career began when he bought out a small paper for $250 and renamed it *The Rolling Stone;* although the paper was not a success, he continued to write and publish, producing freelance articles and short stories to supplement his income.

In 1892 scandal struck the First National Bank of Austin where O. Henry was working. The bank was notoriously mismanaged and, very probably through no fault of his own, O. Henry was indicted for embezzling funds. He went to Houston to await his trial, and took a position as a reporter. When his summons finally came in 1896 O. Henry set off for Austin, but inexplicably changed course midway and hopped on a train to New Orleans. He traveled with some outlaws through Central and South America, but returned to be with his gravely ill wife in 1897. Athol Porter died after a few months, and O. Henry was convicted and sent to the Ohio Penitentiary at Columbus. He spent three and a half years in prison, where he led a relatively unrestricted life as a pharmacist and prolific story writer. It was here that he adopted the pen name whose origin has caused much speculation, retaining it after his release. He spent his later years in Pittsburgh and New York, drinking a great deal of whiskey and producing a great deal of prose. His collections of fiction include *Cabbages and Kings* (1904), *The Four Million* (1906), and *Strictly Business* (1910).

In 1907 he married Sara Lindsay Coleman, a childhood friend. The couple returned to North Carolina on account of O. Henry's failing health. On a visit to New York in 1910 O. Henry collapsed and was hospitalized. He died of tuberculosis on June 5 of that year.

Personal

I should like to explore the possibility that "O. Henry" is actually an unsuspected trick name based on a clever pun. O. Henry's penchant for puns, word coinage, and surprise endings are all familiar to his readers, but his special interest in onomastics, particularly trick names, merits closer attention. The utilization of such names as Alfred E. Ricks, seller of phoney stocks, under the name A. L. Fredericks in "The Man Higher Up," and Michob Ader revealed to be Mike O'Bader in "The Door of Unrest" are examples of static anagrams. Elsewhere names which involve phonetic and orthographic manipulation include, among others: S. Q. Lapius (Esculapius); Homer K. M. (Omar Kayyam); Lee Andrews, swimmer of Hell's Point (Leander-Hellespont); the genie Roc-Ef-El-Er; the Caliph Kar-Neg-Ghe, and Shamrock Jolnes etc.

O. Henry executes a clever onomastic pun in "The Rose of Dixie" as he plays on the word "rose" and the name T. Roosevelt, i.e., THE [odore] ROOS[evelt]. Current-Garcia remarks that just before his death from cirrhosis, O. Henry displayed sharp wit upon being rushed to Polytechnic Hospital. When an attendant asked for his name, O. Henry purportedly replied: "Call me Dennis. My name will be Dennis in the morning." Although the statement is unexplained, one may surmise that O. Henry was playing on the name Dennis—Gr. *Dionys-os,* "god of wine." But if DENNIS is viewed as a retrograde anagram and MORNING taken as a homophonic pun, another reading would be: "Call me Dennis. My name will be SINNED [against] in the MOURNING."

What pun may William S. Porter have had in mind when he created his pseudonym in the Ohio Penitentiary? Given the circumstances, did the humorist indulge in a private joke by taking his *pen name* from the name of the *pen*[itentiary] where he was serving his time? A simple zigzagging of the letters into a symmetrical pattern produces:

OH EN EN RY
IOP IT TIA

The letters of the top row, with synthesis of the "EN" components, yield the renowned pseudonym as a static anagram: OH EN EN RY > OH EN RY > O. HENRY. Is this new perspective the key to the genesis of William S. Porter's pseudonym?—Fred Abrams, "The Pseudonym 'O. Henry': A New Perspective," *SSF,* Summer 1978, p. 329

General

The elements of his art were not many. One notes first of all that his stories are generally trivial as stories—mere anecdotes. Any one of his *World* pieces may be reduced to the compass of a commercial traveler's "good one." And not even this figment of plot is the vital thing about the story: it is the style of the telling—O. Henry stands first of all for manner, and the chief ingredient of this manner is humor. He should be rated first of all as a humorist, as much so as even Artemus Ward or Mark Twain. . . .

The second element of his art came from his journalistic sense. He knew the public for which he was writing—Mr. Everybody—and catered to his whims. To his boon companion, Al Jennings, train robber and yeggman with literary aspirations, he wrote in 1902 this advice: "We have got to respect the conventions and delusions of the public to a certain extent. . . . In order to please John Wanamaker, we will have to assume a virtue that we do not possess. Comment on the moral side of the proposition as little as possible. Do not claim that holding up trains is the only business a gentleman would engage in, and, on the contrary, do not depreciate a profession that is really only financiering with spurs on." He knew precisely how much of the sugar of sentimentality the great average reading public must have, and how much of the pepper of sensation, and the salt of facts, and the salad dressing of romance. He had, moreover, the newspaper man's horror of heaviness, of surplusage, of the commonplace. The story must have "snap," "go," up-to-dateness to the moment; a "punch" in every sentence.

The third conspicuous element in his art is closely allied to the second—form, technique. He studied Maupassant, but Maupassant in turn might have added a certain glow to the cold finish of his own tales, could he have studied O. Henry. The American certainly was the more original of the two. Not enough has been made of the ingrained Americanism of the man. No one, not even Mark Twain, was more a product of our own soil. He was a finished oral story-teller of the Western hotel-foyer type before he had ever written a word of fiction. In every company "mixed" and "unmixed," there are stories, anecdotes *apropos*, Abraham-Lincolnlike modern instances cleverly told—it is a peculiar evolution of our Western civilization. A "good one" is followed by "another one" and still another and better one, and the soul of them all is humor, and the technique is the technique of the short story. The "nub" of the narrative is held to the last moment and then greeted with a roar of laughter. The embroidery of the tale, the skill in concealing the final crux, and the color and the momentum of it all depend upon the narrator. O. Henry is the crowned chief of the ancient American order of *That Reminds Me of Another*. To read him is at times almost to feel his physical presence. He slaps you on the shoulder, asks your advice on points of grammar and the wording of quotations, and you can almost hear his laugh when he springs his final ending. His art is the art of Poe: he has no thought beyond the immediate effect of his tale upon his reader. Poe often left his audience quivering with horror; O. Henry leaves them chuckling with laughter.

The last distinctive element in his art is the strangest of all the strange paradoxes connected with O. Henry. In this unschooled druggist, this cowboy and Main Street clerk, this Texas funny man, one would hardly expect to find verbal precision and wide range of vocabulary. Modern slang he used with outrageous abandon, but everywhere amid the slang are felicities of expression and strange verbal flavors that amaze one. Not even Henry James could choose words more fastidiously or use them more accurately. And yet should one attempt to illustrate this quality of his style one could find only sentences or at most paragraphs. Not one of his stories as a whole can be singled out for its distinction of phrase and its uniformity of beautiful style. The Momus that ruled his pen suffered few serious interludes. One can never trust him. A paragraph of beauty ends in a caper; one reads a whole page at the height of Emerson, only to find its author grinning through a horse collar at the end; one may discover what seems at last a completely serious story of real life—yet beware! Until its closing sentence "The Guardian of the Accolade" is a beautiful tale of the Old South, but the last sentence turns the whole of it into vaudeville—a whole story written beautifully with no other intent than deliberate preparation for a single vulgar moment of suprise. What he might have done had he dropped his harlequin pen and done serious work at the height of his powers we may not say. We know, however, that he had, whenever he deigned to use it with seriousness, a vocabulary like a backwoodsman's rifle: every word striking the red with a precision that gives to the reader a continual thrill.

But brilliant as were the possibility of his powers, and distinctive as was his technique, his final place can never be high even among the writers of short stories. He did not take literature seriously: he was a victim of Momus and the swift ephemeral press. His undoubted powers were completely debauched by it. He became exclusively an entertainer, with no thought but of the moment, and no art save that which brought instant effect upon his reader. To accomplish that he would sacrifice everything, even the truth. One never reads his tales for their material—incident for its own sake—as one does Jack London's or Kipling's; nor do we read them because of the characters as one does Mary E. Wilkins's or Alice Brown's; nor for seeing life exactly as life is as one reads Garland or Norris: one reads them for the narcotic effects they produce. These tales of South America, of picaresque adventurers and New York shop girls—two hundred and forty-five of them in all—are not necessarily the truth: they are *opera bouffe*. His gentle grafters may have been suggested by actual men he had met in the Ohio prison, but they are not alive: they never could have been alive . . . .

He worked without truth, without moral consciousness, and without a philosophy of life. He created no characters: he worked with puppets, lay figures without souls—we see them moving before us, but we know them not at all; they are *x*, *y*, and *z* in his rambles in absurdity. He was a harlequin Poe with modern laughter in place of gloom: much that we have charged up against him we have also charged up against the creator of "The Gold-Bug" and "The Black Cat," but he was utterly without Poe's reverence for the literature of power, he was without his simplicity, without his universality, without his ability to stand with the great serious literary creators of the world.—FRED LEWIS PATTEE, "O. Henry and the Handbooks," *The Development of the American Short Story*, 1923, pp. 360–64

Want, and the fever of the huge American city, drove him, whipped him on. He wrote too much—some years as many as fifty or sixty stories. This is why his work is uneven. True, even among his weakest lines there will be an occasional glint of true O. Henry gold. But then, the same carbon produces both coal and graphite and diamonds. At any rate, O. Henry has produced diamonds, and this brings him into the vicinity of such masters of the short story as Chekhov and Maupassant. And it must be said that O. Henry's technique—at least in his best works—is sharper, bolder, and more modern than that of many short-story writers who have already assumed their place as classics.

A pungent language, glittering with an eccentric and unexpected symbolism, is the first thing that captures the attention of O. Henry's reader. And this is not the dead, mechanical eccentricity found in the symbols of the Imagists. In O. Henry the image is always *internally* linked to the basic tonality of his character, incident, or entire story. This is why all his epithets or images, even when seemingly incongruous or far-fetched, are convincing and hypnotic. The housekeeper of a rooming house (in the story "The Furnished Room") has a "throat lined with fur." At first the image is difficult to assimilate; but as the story proceeds, it is varied, becoming sharpened with each variation. Now it is simply a "furry throat," or "she said in her furriest tones"—and the cloying figure of the housekeeper, never described in detail as it would have been by the old narrative method, is etched in the imagination of the reader.

O. Henry achieves especially striking effects by employing the device which can most accurately be described as that of the *integrating image* (in analyzing literary prose we are compelled to create our terminology afresh). Thus, in the story "The Defeat of the City," Miss Alicia Van Der Pool is "cool, white and inaccessible as the Matterhorn." The Matterhorn—the basic image—is developed as the story goes on; it becomes ramified and embraces almost the entire story broadly and integrally: "The social Alps that ranged about her . . . reached only to her knees." And Robert Walmsley attains this Matterhorn. But, even if he has found that the traveler who reaches the mountaintop finds the highest peaks swathed in a thick veil of cloud and snow, he manages to conceal his chills. "Robert Walmsley was proud of his wife; although while one of his hands shook his guests' the other held tightly to his alpenstock and thermometer."

Similarly, the story "Squaring the Circle" is permeated with the integrating image: nature is a circle, the city a square. In "A Comedy in Rubber," the image is of the rubbernecks as a special tribe, and so on.

O. Henry's kind of story approaches most closely the *skaz* form (to this day, one of the favorite forms in the Russian short story): the free, spontaneous language of speech, digressions, purely American coinages of the street variety, which cannot be found in any dictionary. His, however, is not that ultimate, complete *skaz* form from which the author is absent, in which the author is but another character, and even the author's comments are given in a language close to that of the milieu depicted.

But all these are the static aspects of a work of art. The urban reader, who grew up in the mad whirl of the modern city, cannot be satisfied with only the static elements; he demands the dynamics of plot. Hence all that yellow sea of criminal and detective literature, usually crude and unartistic verbally. In O. Henry, brilliant language is usually combined with dynamic plot. His favorite compositional device is the surprise ending. Sometimes the effect of surprise is achieved by the author with the aid of what may be called the *false denouement:* in the plot syllogism, the reader is deliberately led to the wrong conclusion, and then, somewhere at the end, there is a sudden sharp turn, and an altogether different denouement reveals itself (in the stories, "The Rathskeller and the Rose," "Squaring the Circle," "The Hiding of Black Bill"). Very complex and subtle compositional methods may be found in O. Henry's novel, *Cabbages and Kings*.

Unfortunately, the composition of O. Henry's stories, especially in the endings, suffers from sameness. The chronic surprise loses its point; the surprise is expected, and the exception becomes the rule. The reader has much the same feeling as he experiences under Wilde's shower of paradoxes: in the end he sees that each paradox is but a truism turned inside out.—Yevgeny Zamyatin, "O. Henry" (1923), *A Soviet Heretic*, ed. and tr. Mirra Ginsburg, 1970, pp. 293–95

O. Henry belongs to the scintillating pleiad of American authors who came to the fore at the turn of the century. Their works give powerful and expressive reflection to the turbulent, dynamic epoch when the United States became—as O. Henry derisively dubbed her—the greatest hard-currency and gold-reserve power in the world.

After a difficult, deprived youth and after being thrown into jail on an unproved charge of embezzling funds (his literary career practically began in prison), O. Henry knew all too well what lay behind the sumptuously advertised showcase of American democracy. In "New Baghdad," as he was wont to call New York, if you wanted to save your skin, you had to beware of the fellow on the neighboring bench or behind the counter, in the next room or in the house across the street, on the nearest corner or in a passing cab. In short, you had to be on guard against anybody sitting, drinking, sleeping, walking or riding next to you.

It would seem that O. Henry, past master of the humorous short story, could hardly describe anything so ruthlessly. If we are to believe his other stories, in that mad monotonous struggle for existence waged in the "New Baghdad" of his day there could also be spots of good luck. But O. Henry mocked at them. Even when giving his short stories a happy ending, he derided the American philistine who demanded that he concede that much to him. . . .

The Big City in his panorama stands aggressively in the fore. He once remarked that he had written of the things the giant city had whispered, trumpeted and shouted to him. In his short stories you can hear that music: the blatant voices of hired newspaper writers and advertising agencies that shape the minds of the philistines, the bawling of hard-boiled politicians and demagogues, the whispers and complaints of those who have been dumped to the bottom of society or are docilely dragging out a drab existence in the hope of somehow making ends meet. O. Henry's stories often mention those vain naive hopes, the dreams that never come true. Even if they do, the very incredibility of the fact only confirms the illusory quality of the dreams. . . .

In depicting the Big City in all its frightening grandeur and cynicism, O. Henry did not yield to the demands of the rapacious laws of the society of his time. He made the reader see the cruel senselessness, inhumaneness and abnormality of the life his heroes led. He gave a general idea of the absurdity of the system under which dire poverty was the source of the amassing of fantastic wealth, and under which the rich became slaves of their millions and lost all human semblance. For O. Henry they were leaches who sucked their capital out of the poor, to whom they paid a pittance so that they might keep body and soul together and help the rich make their millions. . . .

On the other hand, he had many warm words for those who stood behind the counters of other people's shops and slaved at other people's factories.—Roman Samarin, "O. Henry—'A Really Remarkable Writer,'" *SvR*, Dec. 1962, pp. 55–57

Henry James can reveal both the surface and the depth of natural events, but his page-long discussions and explanations of his characters all work against the short-story form. Later, Edith Wharton produced some talented versions of condensed Henry James. O. Henry comes as the complete antidote to over-refined discussion: extremely American, the very epitome of the fast talker, fizzing with entertaining phrases, challenging the reader to a game of guessing the twist ending. Here is one example of O. Henry getting a story under way with his bright-as-a-button style, and very talkative, very personal patter. This is the opening of 'The Trimmed Lamp'.

> Of course there are two sides to the question. Let us look at the other. We often hear 'shop girls' spoken of. No such persons exist. There are girls who work in shops. They make their living that way. But why turn their occupation into an adjective? Let us be fair. We do not refer to the girls who live on Fifth Avenue as 'marriage girls'.
>
> Lou and Nancy were chums. They came to the big city to find work because there was not enough to

eat at their homes to go around. Nancy was nineteen, Lou was twenty. . . . I would beg you to step forward and be introduced to them. Meddlesome reader: My lady friends Miss Nancy and Miss Lou.

O. Henry's stories contain some very real people saying some very real and amusing things. For all his surface humanity, however, he is apt to deal in ready-packaged notions, and ironies that are 'cute' rather than profound. He is an entertainer, with flashes of profundity, and he puts the stamp on the slick professional magazine story, which American writers themselves have often attacked in the last two generations, not only for being shallow but for tempting good writers away from their better selves, to play tricks at which they become all too competent.—T. O. BEACHCROFT, "The American Point of View," *The Modest Art: A Survey of the Short Story in English*, 1968, pp. 239–40

In the early years of this century the short story in America seemed to be in danger of disappearing altogether or, rather, into the swamps of daily journalism and magazine fiction. The great name was that of O. Henry, who had an enormous and mainly bad influence for many years on writers on both sides of the Atlantic. In his own country he was a kind of popular poet of New York City, which he celebrated as the modern Babylon. He wrote more than six hundred stories, and although this may remind us of Chekhov's beginning, he never graduated beyond Chekhov's early stage. A typical story is 'While the Auto Waits', the action of which takes place in a quiet, small park in New York City. . . .

The story is an example of formula-writing. O. Henry was the master of what has been called the trick-ending. He was not its inventor but he taught thousands of magazine writers in the United States and Britain for a generation or more how to do it. He reduced the short story precisely to a trick, his reward being the naive reader's gasp of surprise at the end.—WALTER ALLEN, *The Short Story in English*, 1981, pp. 59–60

CESARE PAVESE

"O. Henry; or, The Literary Trick" (1932)
American Literature: Essays and Opinions
tr. Edwin Fussell
1970, pp. 79–90

The excellent selection and translation that Giacomo Prampolini has recently made of O. Henry once more puts before us one of the most perplexing personalities in American civilization. Until now this capricious storyteller has been a little too much maltreated by us in illustrated magazines and the like, which every so often for want of news had recourse to his Thousand and One Nights. From there, translating by ear, cutting and reinforcing, they continued to dig out disconcerting and almost anonymous pages that for good or ill imported a little animation into the midst of the tired lucubrations of our storytellers. But this vulgarization of O. Henry has served a little too much to disseminate among us what in America, where at least they read O. Henry in whole volumes, is by now a widespread inclination: the suspicion that not all that dazzle of inexhaustible invention is of good quality, that O. Henry wrote too many brilliant stories. And at the twenty-first you shout "Stop!"

Still, who hasn't shouted "Stop!" at some point with any short-story writer? These things are like the collections, which were once the fashion, of epigrams and sonnets: they have to be read in small doses, on the installment plan. Except that on these terms O. Henry would be tiresome, not insofar as he was a short-story writer but insofar as he was a writer. His tales, we are now sure, end with a bang because they are *empty*, because in them puns and paradoxes are the trumpery of a barren inner life.

Let it lie—for the time being—the "inner life": I can personally declare that to read O. Henry is almost always entertaining and that you always have before you a most sympathetic kind of man who, as full of brio as one of his many heroes is full of whiskey, continues to recount little anecdotes and witticisms and adventures with a cordiality and a spirit quite exceptional. So that those who deplore the fact that O. Henry has created nothing, no *character*, are at least this one time wrong: a character there is, alive and speaking—even too much so—who at every moment has something of his own to say and (outrageously!) almost always says it well: O. Henry or, to his friends, William S. Porter. A writer even needs to be a little listened to, and if anyone had said to O. Henry's face that he wanted more aching humanity, or whatever, O. Henry surely would have told him to take it easier, because to insist on certain fixed ideas is to risk losing what little there is and to vex the soul over what little there is not.

For O. Henry is honest. He doesn't try to bluff, as so many of his most attractive characters do, but from the early pages of his best book there is revealed the trick, if trick it is and not rather the unconstraint of every artist worthy of the name:

> 'Tis contrary to art and philosophy to give you the information. . . . The art of narrative consists in concealing from your audience everything it wants to know until after you expose your favorite opinions on topics foreign to the subject. A good story is like a bitter pill with the sugar coating inside of it. I will begin, if you please, with a horoscope. *(Cabbages and Kings)*

Now such a confession, made where it is made, can clarify O. Henry's intentions and techniques. In the first place, he does not come from a cultivated society like that of a Maupassant or a Flaubert, and therefore he never dreamed of longing for an impersonal, realistic, or primitivistic literature. Not that one recipe is preferable to another, what is important is to say something with whatever recipe one uses; but it is useful in the present instance clearly to distinguish O. Henry from those others, because too many readers, not finding him another Maupassant, have rejected him. O. Henry clearly tells you that he conceives the short story as an oblique discourse, as a series of verbal and structural tricks that seem and are not, as a continuous comment and byplay of the narrator to the actions of his characters: so much so that, as I have already noticed, the character who leaps most conspicuously to the eye in his pages is the speaker himself.

Now this fact has deeper and more complicated roots than may appear. And if the reader of O. Henry's stories would think again about the cultural atmosphere from which these stories are drawn, many things might seem to him obvious that presently annoy him, since the singular nature of the writer was entirely conditioned by the intellectual moment into which he was born. He who thinks back to the only period of American letters at all well known in Europe, the period—naturally—of Poe and Emerson (1830–1850), will seem to find himself in absolutely another continent than the one of which O. Henry gives us an idea in his writings (1900–1910). The earlier writers had made a center of New England, nourishing themselves on European culture, while vitally transforming it, and ignoring all the great territory and the future variety of races in the nation. Then the polished speech of the best seventeenth-century English traditions prevailed, together with the writer shut in a tower to ruminate the almost invariably occult sciences, in short, the Puritan province of anti-Puritan rebels, aristocratic and isolated.

Consider instead the age of O. Henry. Roosevelt's administration has yielded its fruits: America is henceforth a single nation from the Atlantic to the Pacific, no more Puritan than necessary, with the business of the chosen people to excuse its conquests and its new riches, and it is so sure of itself, so much a "melting pot," that it dares to receive, in order to naturalize them, even the Armenians, the Negroes, and the Chinese. The cultural centers are henceforth spread through the whole huge country, with the consequence of a slight diffusion of forces, although a youthful simplicity—and not a poverty—of spirits just then sings its most frenetic hymns to the élan vital (Jack London). There no longer exists an Athens of the United States, New England. The new centers are as numerous as the free play of races, released from every traditional barrier, knows how to produce: California, with Norris and London; the Center (Chicago), with Sinclair and young Dreiser; New York, finally, with the first movies and O. Henry. One thing of immense significance and importance is the transfer of the movie studios from New York to California that occurs just at the end of this period, around 1912. The whole American territory is henceforward in this way crisscrossed by intellectual currents. Before, up to 1850, America was divided into two worlds: the New England which thought and wrote, and the West, broadly understood, from the Alleghenies to Wyoming and Texas, which conquered and broke ground. The former, slightly skeptical literary aristocrats, the latter, rough illiterate Puritans who chewed tobacco and fought with their fists.

This is not the place to tell the whole story. Suffice it to say that from Poe you get to O. Henry through a half century of revolutions: trappers, miners, new cities, new states, the War of Secession, contingents of Germans, Swedes, Italians, territorial conquests, industrialism, oil and coal, corn, the unrestrained love of life as life, no longer as mere thought or the printed page. The earlier New England dies because the English public forgets how to read, it no longer knows English well, much less the polished English of Boston or of Richmond, or it no longer has time to waste getting to the bottom of philosophies. The powerful body of the U.S.A. begins to look about restlessly, to search for writers who speak of its own life, who will tell it something more than the gambling parlor, or the racecourse, or the fever of work. But clearly: something more, not something different. The new short stories that triumph in all the American newspapers from 1870 to 1910 are essentially humorous or anyhow full of action and "suspense." It has been rightly said that the America of this period seeks in its short stories a duplicate of the emotions of Luna Park: distorting mirrors, chutes, thrills, clowns, sleight of hand, laughs, and noise. Elsewhere, mainly in the states of the Center (Illinois, Indiana, Wisconsin), there will be coming into vogue gloomy novels of which the whole interest consists in the attempt to give a grayly faithful reproduction of reality: from this vogue Dreiser will issue. Immediately after, from 1900 on, there enters the picture the tastes for the social question, these too more life than literature: the rally, the strike, the organization, the revolution *(The Iron Heel, Metropolis)*—tastes that persisted into the renaissance of 1912, which will be essentially a deepening of the new cultural centers on the basis of more vital problems. But this is another subject altogether.

Finally, this literature that culminates in the "prince" O. Henry has a new charactersitic: it is a dialect literature. It is a curious kind of dialect, because we Italians imagine dialects to be local and we would have looked for a dialect literature rather from New England. But in America dialect is the colloquial speech spoken by everybody in contrast to the cultivated and upper-class English taught in the schools. Localisms (as they say over there) hardly exist in their language. Reasons: the youth of this language and the intricacy of communications which from one day to the next causes the New Yorker to live in California or the Great Laker in Florida. The dialect quality of the short stories from Mark Twain to O. Henry comes from the need to speak to a rather democratic public (miners, sometimes), and in any case always to speak to a bourgeoisie which tends toward solidity and wants to understand and to recognize itself in its newspapers. Because of course from Mark Twain to O. Henry all the literature that lives is journalistic.

It would certainly be sufficient, then, if it happened in poetry as in the cultivation of fruit, to define the O. Henry story as the final literary manifestation of that period which begins with the crude pages of anonymous miners where witticisms in dialect serve to cheer up a people rather trivial and rather tired of existence. But, I repeat, poetry is not a cultivation of fruit, and it has not yet been proved that a fine example of it arises from long seasons of selection and grafting; and so it happens that, having explained everything, it is just as well to begin again at the beginning and to ask yourself once more: Has O. Henry really "created something"? Or is he not rather the "light," "skin-deep," "fantastic" writer, and in the worst sense of these words?

Let us return to those previously mentioned *Cabbages and Kings*. This is a sequence of stories collected in a novel. The setting of the novel is already a proof of the new American cosmopolitanism and imperialism. A tiny Central American republic, Anchuria, easily turned upside down by factions, governed by Spanish types full of high-sounding words and essentially understood in terms of their own "price." O. Henry's hand begins to reveal itself in the way this material is treated: the events are seen from Coralio, a small town of many huts and a few residences on the shores of the Spanish Main, where American consuls and traders in bananas, rubber, and shoes assist the various local revolutions, helping them along, and attributing to them so much importance as is permitted a discreet citizen of the United States who doesn't too much believe in the politics even of his own country. The atmosphere of the tale is above all the blessed indolence of that sky and sea, where everything can happen and nothing does, or at least it leaves no trace and, as a president falls or a Christian dies, a hundred thousand of them could fall and die and the novel would always be the same. Therefore, its nature is excellent, clearly revealed in episodes, in varied stories.

O. Henry's notorious "insufficiencies," then, the mechanical quality of the action, the cerebral trickiness in the presentation of the adventures, must surely be quite plainly exemplified in this free and easy plot. Thus, for example, the fact that the two characters (President Miraflores and the actress Isabel, who have run off with government funds) imminent in and dominating the whole book, are not at all who they are thought to be, and that they have succeeded in escaping, and that their place is taken by two Americans, a father and daughter who have run off from their country with money from an insurance company, this fact appears to be only an oddity, a contrivance of the storyteller's, the final unexpected happening desired by the slightly gross and childish taste of the public. But after it has been said that the book is entirely constructed like the ordinary card castle, what has been revealed about O. Henry except what he himself has already too hastily confessed? The lecture can be repeated for each of the chapter-stories which comprise the book and for every other story that

O. Henry ever wrote. We always find in him, in the structure of the action, these overturnings of values, these paradoxes, these bluffs.

And it is at this point that the critical labor ought to begin. What else should we expect from O. Henry but mechanical actions? And this (you observe) would be a defect as fatal as the other defect of even the most highly esteemed writers, in whom are found only fragments of observations, of "material," and the plot, the construction, is either nonexistent or virtually nonexistent. But reread, with that kind of goodwill indispensable to any enjoyment, the whole book of which I speak—for the moment the hundreds of other short stories aren't important—reflect upon it a bit, keeping in mind the historical bases that have been alluded to, and I am convinced that in the end you will begin to have doubts about the theory of the trick. Have we not before us instead a bizarre and delightful kind of writer who sees the entire universe as a bewildering stylization and who, far from inventing paradoxical adventures because he doesn't know what to say, feels these paradoxes as the very substance of life?

In sum, specific historical conditions suggested to O. Henry a certain taste, a certain manner; they imposed upon him, in short, certain themes. And why can't O. Henry have made of these themes poetry, a genuine creation, that is to say, a genuine *form* of a lively sensibility, of what can seem to be but is only at the beginning a trick (the aforementioned substitution of characters in *Cabbages and Kings*), which makes an expression or a myth of the oddity and relativity and fundamental illogic of life?

The conclusion of the adventure of Miraflores and Isabel is characteristic; saved by a misunderstanding, they are constrained by it to live far away a fictitious and almost unbearable life. To conclude the various strands of the narrative, O. Henry has imagined a little cinematographic scene.

> THE WRITING ON THE SANDS
>
> SCENE—*The Beach at Nice*. A woman, beautiful, still young, exquisitely clothed, complacent, poised, reclines near the water, idly scrawling letters in the sand with the staff of her silken parasol. The beauty of her face is audacious; her languid pose is one that you feel to be impermanent—you wait, expectant, for her to spring or glide or crawl, like a panther that has unaccountably become stock-still. She idly scrawls in the sand; and the word that she always writes is "Isabel." A man sits a few yards away. You can see that they are companions, even if no longer comrades. His face is dark and smooth, and almost inscrutable—but not quite. The two speak little together. The man also scratches on the sand with his cane. And the word that he writes is "Anchuria." And then he looks out where the Mediterranean and the sky intermingle, with death in his gaze.

This would not seem to be cerebral. The account of the tricks in the action has naturally been exaggerated. Many times the O. Henry story presents only a humorous stylization of persons or events, or it is odd only in the way that a scene is perceived, an opinion expressed, or the "philosophy" of an event treated.

So we enter the real heart of the question about the "inner life" of O. Henry, a question that seems to me potentially answered already by the reply to the charges of trickery in the action—except that many people still, especially in America, boldly distinguish action from characters, characters from style, style from content. Returning therefore to the point of departure, imagine O. Henry as the American night owl who has lived by his wits in all the states of the Union and beyond, carefully saving up that little store of riches which enables him to rattle off stories in an unsophisticated manner, with his legs under the table, all his impressions of existence condensed in jokes, in demonstrations of good-humored paradoxes, and sometimes moved by a friendship, by a sorrow, by a distant sacrifice; only thus shall we have before us his "inner life."

All O. Henry's heroes, we notice, are from New York, or are provincials like himself who have made their apprenticeship through the whole nation and now end, experienced and tolerant, taking shelter in old Manhattan. These persons are naturally not monuments of psycholology or pyres of passion: the language that describes them, the tone of the narrative, the good-natured intimacy of the recollection, everything conspires to reduce their proportions, everything casts over O. Henry's events a faint shade of jest and of "philosophy"—which permits no creative luxury, in the usual sense of the term. In the act of conversing, O. Henry describes his types; he gives a brush stroke and then he stops—looks at the listener—makes an observation on some related memory, winks with his eyes, gestures with his hands, changes the position of his cigar, gives another brush stroke. For it is not O. Henry's intention to describe such or such another character in the name of humanity; he tends simply to represent in the most direct and least pedantic way possible a memory of something incredible, curious, paradoxical. The principle that comprehends and unifies all his narrative art is just this, the knowing exposition of something intellectually unusual, bizarre, "queer."

In his characters no other law of unity can be found. There are vagabonds in his stories, genial burglars, melancholy gentlemen, drunks, naive young girls, déclassé nobles, politicians, prostitutes of strict morals, young wives desperate out of spite, assassins: all the scum and the flower of the American melting pot. But not even the appeal of the beatitude of liquor and indolence, the most common appeal in O. Henry's world, is sufficient to pull together all these characters. Their real affinity consists only in their strangeness, in the oddity of their cases, sometimes sad, almost always cheerful, more or less resigned. Here is an example. A decayed gentleman, reduced to sleeping on park benches and living by his wits, feels winter coming on in New York. What to do? Get himself arrested; three months on Staten Island; security and repose. How to get himself arrested? He tries to eat in a hotel, without money: they don't denounce him, they beat him. He tries to smash the window of a store, and accuses himself: they don't believe him. He tries to molest a lady: it's all right with her! Evening comes; the "never-wuzzer" walks desperately through the streets. He stops before a church. He hears an organ. Gentle thoughts begin to stir in his head, childhood, illusions, the abject present. He has made a decision: tomorrow he will go to work and reform his life. At that moment, a policeman, finding him without identification papers, arrests him. Three months of "repose" on Staten Island. A thousand such tales could be recounted. No need to be afraid of declaring that O. Henry exists precisely and only in the ironic and slightly saddened sense of these paradoxical contrasts.

Granted this conception of the short story—conversation at a bar about some chance happening—it follows that often it will be worth less as a unified story than in certain of its details: a mocking image, an exclamation, a scene. This, if anything, is somewhat the defect of O. Henry, not that other one of the "superficial action." You could make a whole list of expressions, of descriptive mannerisms, of crackling, well-turned, and quite fantastic epithets: their only defect is that they can be so easily detached and collected. But for every one of these slightly external expressions, how many there are of the utmost felicity! This can be verified on simply opening the book, and I don't at the moment want to go big-game hunting after flies. O. Henry's is a real "dialect" humor; no manufactured language would sustain so volcanic and continuous a shower of phrases and words. In this respect, O. Henry is truly the Rabelais of the United States. And also in the taste, half erudite and half popular, for letting things go, for living happily—la Devinière, the liquor store—the two resemble each other.

As Rabelais seems to be, more than an initiator, the necessary crown of a gauloise tradition that was essentially expressed in the fabliaux, so O. Henry concludes the carefree youth of the American novella or "short story." This genre (let us for once speak of genre), born with those early humorists of the miners' newspapers, carried to its first triumphs by punsters and dialect writers as notable as Artemus Ward, had already excelled in the hands of Mark Twain and Bret Harte, the self-conscious pioneers of the new literature no longer New England but national. At the time of O. Henry, everyone was writing short stories. The genre had enriched itself; no longer were there only stories half-humorous and half-sentimental, but Ambrose Bierce, for instance, was imitating, rather badly, in fact, Poe, and Jack London—everybody knows what Jack London was doing.

O. Henry found his tone with a rare security and timeliness. Of all the writers of his age, it was he who was also best suited to speak in a newspaper to the *whole* nation. The veins of the bizarre and of the cosmopolitan which he opened up were, even in their precise delimitations, the most comprehensive epitome of every short fictional effort up to then achieved in the new nation. And if although, like Rabelais, he concludes a period in such a manner that no one had to stop there any longer and other tendencies were developed, still, the language, the expressive American spirit, by him exemplified and justified in a thousand ways, could easily survive him. And indeed the generation that follows O. Henry—Dreiser, Lindsay, Lee Masters, Sandburg, Lewis, Anderson—doesn't forget the lesson, and in its work of interpretation and re-creation of the U.S.A. will carry to its termination the great linguistic revolution, and this will definitively become in new hands the conscious instrument for an exploration entirely intellectual.

WALTER EVANS

"'A Municipal Report': O. Henry and Postmodernism"

Tennessee Studies in Literature, 1981, pp. 101–16

What can be said for O. Henry? In the face of modern critics' alternate heated denunciation and glacial indifference to his work can a contemporary construct any reasonable case for O. Henry's significance in the Postmodern era? The case now extant certainly does more harm than good; a few critics have rather fruitlessly explored most conventional avenues of literary appreciation seeking to praise O. Henry in the ways they praise other writers.[1] But since, on the whole, his work won't really support much informed praise of characterization, setting, theme, influence—or even trick endings—modern criticism has wasted very little approval on O. Henry.

Yet, surprisingly enough, a remarkably strong case for O. Henry's significance exists if one cares to make it. As a first step one need do little more than call to mind many of America's most imaginative and talented contemporary writers: Nabokov, Barth, Barthelme, Coover, Gass, and the many other Postmoderns artistically heir to such innovators as Laurence Sterne and James Joyce. The characteristics by which such writers identify themselves, the patterns according to which they construct their works, and the standards by which they prefer to be judged could not more harmoniously blend with the O. Henry canon.

How are we to understand the term Postmodern? I employ it here as the least restrictive and dogmatic of several terms commonly applied to contemporary American avant-garde fiction. While Postmodern[2] seems to me the most widely accepted term, some critics speak of "metafiction" and "fabulation;"[3] "parafiction"[4] has appeared, as have "Super-Fiction"[5] and "surfiction"[6] and "anti-novel/anti-story"[7] and "irrealism"[8] and "anti-realism"[9] and the not yet popular "bossa-nova"[10]—among others. I cannot stop to anatomize the anatomizers; footnotes can guide any readers curious and intrepid enough to dare exploring innovative fiction's taxonomic heart of darkness.[11]

I don't wish to be misunderstood as implying that Postmodernist writers restrict themselves to some dogmatic party line, but prominent among the tendencies[12] which do seem to characterize many of their fictions are:

—a pervasive and intense self consciousness;[13]
—a fondness for significant allusions, often copious or extended, to art/literature which exist in the "real" world;[14]
—innovative structural patterns irrelevant to "plot" in the traditional sense;[15]
—deliberate use of stereotypes, particularly of character;[16]
—style marked by evident artificiality and verbal play ("linguistic foregrounding");[17]
—metafictional references to storytelling;[18]
—toyings with "reality" as in the imposture motif, determinism, coincidence;[19]
—and parody.[20]

Enough, for now, about Postmodernism. What about O. Henry? Critics like to praise originality as long as the work in question is not too original. It would appear that, as far as his current reputation is concerned, O. Henry made the mistake of writing too innovatively half a century too soon. We may condemn him on traditional grounds, but must—or so it seems to me—praise him on Postmodernist grounds. Perhaps the best test case for O. Henry's significance in Postmodern terms can be made on the basis of "A Municipal Report,"[21] a story frequently reprinted even today, and in 1914 chosen in a *New York Times* poll as the best American short story ever written. I don't personally endorse the poll's results, but certainly few more innovative, more technically fascinating short stories have ever been written.

In O. Henry's first, most immediate, and most modest challenge to tradition, "A Municipal Report" commences with two epigraphs. Some earlier writers favored similar beginnings. Poe, for instance, was fond of prepping his reader with brief quotations from other writers—fond enough to fabricate them (as in "Ligeia") when he couldn't locate precisely the phrase he desired. But O. Henry prefaced "A Municipal Report" quite uniquely, so far as I know, in a couple of respects. For one thing, he employed two epigraphs rather than one:

> The cities are full of pride,
> Challenging each to each—
> This from her mountainside,
> That from her burthened beach.
> (R. Kipling)

> Fancy a novel about Chicago or Buffalo, let us say, or Nashville, Tennessee! There are just three big cities in the United States that are "story cities"—New York, of course, New Orleans, and, best of the lot, San Francisco. (Frank Norris)

The first of the epigraphs, Kipling's, functions rather as one might expect—as a thematic prologue. But the second, by

Norris,[22] operates like none other I can recall in a short story—quite literally as a "challenge" to be accepted. The implied conflict between Kipling and Norris, O. Henry proceeds to elaborate in his first two paragraphs, declaring: "it is a bold and rash deed to challenge in one sentence history, romance, and Rand and McNally."

Does all this really matter?

It seems to me absolutely fundamental—for at one sweep he immediately indicates that the narrative to follow functions as a kind of demonstration rather than as a purer fiction, rather than as an essentially mimetic fiction, rather than primarily as a rendering of human experience. O. Henry immediately follows his acknowledgment of Norris's challenge to a Nashville setting with the word: "Nashville." O. Henry thus unambiguously prepares us to identify the story's stimulus as rhetorical.

The story's rhetorical focus (more what one expects of an essay than of a short story), indicated with these contradictory epigraphs, O. Henry then underlines in the first couple of pages with references to a wide variety of writers and literary works. Kipling he quotes somewhat incorrectly: "East is east and west is San Francisco." *The Arabian Nights* (by all accounts O. Henry's favorite book, as it seems to be John Barth's[23]) he alludes to in describing San Francisco as "the Bagdad of the New World." The Old Testament provides a reference to Adam and Eve; Shakespeare supplies "'tis enough—'twill serve" (from Mercutio's death speech in *Romeo and Juliet)*; a reference to Sidney Carton calls up Dickens's own tale of two cities, neither of them on Norris's list—nor do Norris's cities figure prominently in the Bible, *The Arabian Nights*, works of Kipling, Shakespeare, or any of the other writers the story mentions with almost Nabokovian enthusiasm: Irving, Tennyson, Lamb, Chaucer, Hazlitt, Marcus Aurelius, Montaigne, and Hood. Thus, with his copious literary references and allusions, throughout "A Municipal Report," O. Henry constantly foregrounds the rhetorical dimension of the fiction he's creating before our very eyes.

So much, for now, for the epigraphs and allusions. Much more impressive, daring, and original is a pattern not of allusion but of quotation which he employs to rhetorically structure the piece, or at least one dimension of the piece. In fact, O. Henry creates in "A Municipal Report" a unique contrapuntal pattern of coordinated structures: one a tale of selfless devotion, pitiful pride, and justifiable homicide; the other O. Henry's self-conscious reaction to Norris's challenge. The latter dimension, that dominating the story's title, O. Henry repeatedly reintroduces to the reader's mind by a series of quotations, presumably from some Rand McNally guide to American cities:

> Nashville—A city, port of delivery, and the capital of the State of Tennessee, is on the Cumberland River and on the N. C. & St. L. and the L. & N. railroads. This city is regarded as the most important educational centre in the South.

Throughout the first two-thirds of his story O. Henry scatters five similar quotations. This first, referring to the river, the railroads, and education, O. Henry immediately exploits by discussing the area's moisture, his arrival by train, and the commencement of his education regarding the city itself. The second quotation, describing Nashville's "undulating grounds" and streets and lights, O. Henry counterpoints by describing a nighttime cab ride through the hilly streets, meanwhile mentioning many of the area's lights. The next quotation, referring to a local Civil War battle, prefaces a paragraph of military metaphors (involving "marksmanship" and "battle" and "enemy" etc.), introducing the hotel cuspidors and the associated character who later turns out to be the villain, a vainglorious professional Southerner, Major Wentworth Caswell. After suffering interminable delay at the bar because of Caswell's disquisitions on the Civil War and on genealogy, the narrator escapes to his lonely room where, as he removes a shoe and drops it on the floor, he determines that Nashville must be a colorless city, "Just a good, ordinary, hum-drum, business town."

The next guidebook quotation identifies Nashville as a manufacturing and business center—specifically mentioning shoes and boots, thus keying the transition. The general topic of the quotation—business—appears in the next paragraph when the narrator identifies his "own business," arranging for a Miss Azalea Adair to write regularly for a Northern literary magazine. A Negro cabman dressed in tatters drives the narrator the mile and a half over "uneven brick paving" to his "business" destination, Miss Adair's home.

The subsequent quotation appropriately describes Nashville's linear dimensions, miles of streets, paved and unpaved, and waterworks. Arriving at their destination the cabman charges two dollars rather than the fifty cents he deserves: "I *has* to have two dollars to-night and business is mighty po'" (p. 1213). The narrator identifies himself (to cabman and reader) as a Southerner who feels compelled to pay because of "inheritance." Inside, he meets Miss Azalea Adair, fifty years old, impoverished, "a descendant of the cavaliers." She charms him too much for talk of business and he makes an appointment to see her again the next afternoon, incidentally remarking (again O. Henry prods Norris, though so far the latter seems to have been correct) that in her hometown "few things out of the ordinary ever happen" (p. 1213).

The last quotation describes Nashville's extensive trade in shoes, hollow ware, and flour. Moments later Miss Adair rings for an unshod Negro girl and, handing her one of the very torn dollar bills the narrator only minutes before gave the cabman, orders the girl "to Mr. Baker's store on the corner" to buy tea and sugar cakes.

Interpolating in every few pages of narrative such radically alien material as these quotations strikes me as absolutely unique in two respects: the quotations' mere presence and their function. Many other stories contain interpolated tales of Fieldingesque comments by a narrator. In "Benito Cereno," the closest (though distant) antecedent example I can recall of a similar technique, Melville appends "extracts" translated from the official Spanish documents which his narrator identifies as designed to "shed light on the preceding narrative" and clear up certain details. Scholars have written reams of contradictory opinions on these "extracts" and their function, but it seems reasonable to conclude that finally they shed more darkness than light and—though illuminating specific details—underline the complexity of reality. In any event, Melville's body of appended materials (1) is immediately and directly relevant to the story, and (2) appears in a single body at the end.

In contrast, O. Henry's interpolated material (1) appears to have only the most marginal relevance, and (2) appears not in a body but scattered throughout the story.

So much for their presence: I know of no short story writer before O. Henry who has done anything like it. Barthelme comes later.

Now, how do these interpolations function? In at least three crucial ways. First, rhetorically the quotations guard in the reader's consciousness Norris's city challenge which O. Henry accepts so enthusiastically in producing "A Municipal Report." The quotations remind us again and again that we are experiencing a rhetorical construct; they repeatedly puncture the pure narrative dream, the mimetic illusion, the willing suspension of disbelief so much more important to every earlier American short story I can recall.

Second, the interpolations function as a structuring device, introducing the motifs of imagery and the details of setting and physical action which undergird the first two-thirds of the story.[24] O. Henry cleverly and imaginatively matches our progress through the story to our progress through the quotations: (1) railroads, water, and education; (2) hills and streetlights; (3) Civil War battle experiences; (4) business; (5) extent of the city and its streets; (6) the trade in shoes, hollow ware, and flour. Significantly, when the "plot" really begins to develop in the last third of the story the quotations disappear and the structuring principle reverts to a traditional tactic, casual action.

Third, and not at all obvious, is the possibility that O. Henry means to imply (tweaking Norris's nose, as it were) that O. Henry himself, as writer, has been no closer to Nashville than an almanac or encyclopedia or city guide could take him.[25] Absolutely nothing in the story seems in the least specific to Nashville. The streets, hotel, hills, run-down mansion could exist with perfectly equal credibility in dozens of American cities—only the drizzle he describes so vigorously lends the fictional city anything approaching unique personality—and his emphatic hyperbole finally achieves a level of abstraction on which the drizzle could represent that of almost any Southern (only because of the honeysuckle) city: "Take of London fog 30 parts; malaria 10 parts; gas leaks 20 parts; dewdrops gathered in a brick yard at sunrise, 25 parts; odor of honeysuckle 15 parts. Mix" (p. 1209). The quotations function as do no other elements of the story: to endorse the title, "A Municipal Report," and make the story seem uniquely Nashvillian. Yet a close reader can hardly avoid two conclusions: (1) almanac quotations from a regionful of cities could have set the scene with equal effect. (2) O. Henry not only realizes the fact, but rubs in it both Norris's nose and the reader's.

The setting of "A Municipal Report" leads to another interesting aspect of O. Henry's work: the intense avoidance of realism. In his case the opposite of realism is not dreamlike imagination or fantasy but pure artifice, though some might prefer the term artificiality. It may be that O. Henry's writing skills were too limited for him ever to rise above stereotypes of setting, character, and dialogue. On the other hand, few marks of a writer's skill matter more than his ability to disguise or triumph over his inevitable limitations. In describing the characters of "A Municipal Report," as in many of his other stories, O. Henry didn't merely employ stereotypes; he insisted on explicitly pointing out to the reader that the stereotypes are stereotypes, the cliches cliches. The narrator says of Major Caswell, for example, "I knew him for a type the moment my eyes suffered from the sight of him" (p. 1210). O. Henry more subtly—but hardly less pointedly—indicates cliche elements of Miss Azalea Adair's personality by describing her "reception room": "Yes, there was a picture on the wall, a colored crayon drawing of a cluster of pansies. I looked around for the portrait of Andrew Jackson and the pine-cone hanging basket but they were not there" (p. 1213).

O. Henry deserves no credit for relying on types, but he reveals creditable ingenuity in admitting their existence to the reader; he both solicits and merits the respect we pay to the successful puppeteer or muppeteer or magician or "illusionist." O. Henry doesn't really ask us to suspend our disbelief (as we never believe that doves turn to silk scarves) so much as to appreciate the skill and artifice of the acknowledged illusion. As with "The Gift of the Magi," we are charmed not because we believe, but because the artifice could not be more perfectly, more delightfully artificial.

His self-conscious narrative style convinces as little as his self-conscious characters, but shares the same energetic, almost narcissistic striving for effect that pleases so much when it succeeds.

> On an extemporized couch of empty boxes and chairs was stretched the mortal corporeality of Major Wentworth Caswell. A doctor was testing him for the mortal ingredient. His decision was that it was conspicuous by its absence.
>
> The erstwhile Major had been found dead on a dark street and brought by curious and ennuied citizens to the drug store. The late human being had been engaged in terrific battle—. . . . (p. 1217)

If O. Henry's style seems awkward, if he seems less committed to imaginatively using language than he is to misusing it, perhaps he shares more with Donald Barthelme than we suspect. Discussing his own story "Paraguay," Barthelme said he particularly likes its "misuse of language": "Every writer in the country can write a beautiful sentence, or a hundred. What I am interested in is the ugly sentence that is also somehow beautiful."[26]

The following sentence is not a mistake. In "A Municipal Report" as in many of his best stories, O. Henry's style achieves the same emphatic lack of naturalism, of realism, of credibility as his characters and his plots. O. Henry's charm, more than that, O. Henry's best claim to genius, lies in his self-conscious artificiality. From the first page to the last of "A Municipal Report" he charms the reader (one who reads him without prejudice) with rhetorical games ("East is east and west is San Francisco"), often not dissimilar to those of such writers as Sterne and Joyce, games in America wrongly traced back no earlier than Nabokov and the Postmoderns.

Inspired verbal play O. Henry demonstrated from his earliest fictions. Humor in his early *Rolling Stone* pieces, the humor magazine he edited in Austin, often involved fractured quotes, malaprops, spoonerisms, outrageous puns, and imaginative respellings. The style owes more to regional humorists like Charles Farrar Browne (of Artemus Ward), David Locke (of Petroleum V. Nasby), and Henry Shaw (of Josh Billings) than to the genius of Joyce (who after all came after O. Henry, not the other way around). But no American prose writer—certainly no previous short story writer—devoted more energy to verbal play, or derived more success from it. As brief examples (from various stories), consider a few of his delightfully warped Latin phrases: a railroad station uproar continues "Ad noisyam;" when rubes gather, Broadway becomes the "Yappian Way." Caesar's famous opening lines O. Henry translates himself: "Omnis Gallia in tres partes divisa est: we will need all of our gall in devising means to tree them parties." He does much more with Shakespeare.[27]

We've investigated several aspects of formal innovation in "A Municipal Report," among them: (1) a heavy, almost Nabokovian, reliance on literary allusions; (2) a Barthian structural pattern devoted more to an encyclopedic profile of a city (at least for the first two-thirds) than to a mimetic treatment of human experience; (3) a Barthelmesque preponderance of stereotypes so self-consciously underlined as to draw exaggerated attention to their function as stereotypes; (4) a focus as insistent as William Gass's (though, of course, their premises differ radically) on language as artificial construct of self-sufficient significance. Let us consider a fifth.

These self-conscious, rather Barthian or Borgesian references to storytelling in "The Gift of the Magi" and elsewhere in his canon abound in "A Municipal Report" as well, but here their context more than ever emphasizes their "deconstructive" function of playfully calling into question the basic concepts of traditional fiction. In the space of three paragraphs, for instance, O. Henry plays a variety of Borgesian epistemological games in asides to the reader.

"I must tell you how I came to be in Nashville, and I assure you the digression brings as much tedium to me as it does to you" (p. 1211). In the first place, direct addresses to the reader in the second person seem far less common in short stories than in long. More interesting, however, is the reference to a "digression," for in fact—in traditional short story terms—"A Municipal Report" so far consists of nothing *but* digressions. The narrator here promises exposition which a reader hungering for traditional fiction (assuming such a reader is still reading) must regard at this point as an unexpected treasure trove. On one level O. Henry is simply teasing. On another, however, the comments *are* digressions, for O. Henry and the sympathetic reader are most concerned with his jazzlike improvisations and experiments with traditional formal expectations. The exposition here introduced *is* a digression in that in a sense it is merely a sop to convention, essentially distinct from the story's technically innovative heart and soul.

In a second example of his epistemological play, the narrator tells us one morning he breakfasted on "chicken livers *en brochette* (try them if you can find that hotel)" (p. 1211). In narrative fiction such asides commonly call upon the "Dear Reader's" personal experiences or knowledge, asking him or her to draw on these for help in understanding the fiction at hand. Much rarer, some asides will imply that the reader's experiences and those of the fictional characters exist in the same level of reality (an implication the reader may have noticed a character in a railway station or at some soiree, for example). Rarer still in long fiction but especially rare in stories are references which boldly underline the unreality of a fiction—Thackeray's famous description of his *Vanity Fair* characters as puppets, for example. O. Henry seems even more innovative in bridging the last two possibilities. The story opened in answer to Norris's rhetorical challenge about the impossibility of a Nashville story. O. Henry here issues his own oblique challenge to the reader, a challenge which straddles the question of how real the hotel actually is.

A third comment mentions "the story that is so long in coming, because you can hardly expect anything to happen in Nashville" (p. 1211). Here, as at numerous points in "A Municipal Report," O. Henry refers to his story as a "story" and recalls the Norris challenge. The excitement O. Henry cultivates, the suspense for which he intrigues, the interest and anticipation he creates focus not on any of the characters or their situations so much as they focus on O. Henry's ability (so far in serious doubt for a traditional reader) to tell a story, to vanquish Norris. The few critics who have written on the story[28] seem not quite to understand what O. Henry was about, but they intuitively show more respect for the challenge and response than for the characters—as did O. Henry himself in a precis describing the story for an editor before he wrote it: "The whole scheme is to show that an absolutely prosaic and conventional town (such as Nashville) can equal San Francisco, Bagdad or Paris when it comes to a human story" (Langford, p. 225).

We have already covered several areas that demonstrate O. Henry's close artistic links to the Postmodernists; others to be mentioned only briefly include the theme of illusion or imposture, determinism, coincidence, and parody.

Long ago "appearance versus reality" sank to a critical bromide on a level with Christ figures; even accepting the concept's critical vulgarization, certainly the theme of illusion, a toying with reality, functions much more significantly in the work of such Postmodernists as Nabokov and Borges than in that of most earlier twentieth-century American writers. No question intrigued O. Henry more, in Gerald Langford's terms, than "the situation of the imposter or wearer of a disguise" (p. 94). Eugene Current-Garcia endorses the theme's significance: "without doubt the theme of pretense—the desire to pose for what one is not, if only for a few moments and regardless of the price exacted—is the most persistent one in O. Henry's writing; for it crops up again and again in nearly all his stories from the earliest to the last few he left unfinished at his death" (p. 124). Most of *The Gentle Grafter* stories involve con men; many other stories involve impoverished scions masquerading as wealthy aristocrats ("The Renaissance at Charleroi"), ordinary Americans as sophisticates ("A Cosmopolite in a Cafe"), rivals in love as trusted confidants ("The Love-Philtre of Ikey Schoenstein"), cowards as desperadoes ("The Passing of Black Eagle"), criminals as solid citizens ("A Retrieved Reformation"). The list of impostures he develops extends almost endlessly.

In "A Municipal Report" the imposture motif involves Miss Azalea Adair's valiant, heartrending, and childishly futile pretense of maintaining the elite standard of living she'd formerly been accustomed to. Caswell also pretends he's well-to-do and living on an "inheritance." A more significant imposture involves Old Caesar's unsuccessful attempts to pass himself off as a selfish uninvolved cabdriver rather than a selflessly loyal retainer, and his more successful attempt (only the narrator and the reader find him out) to conceal his final identity as murderer. Significantly, the narrator guards Old Caesar's secret guilt as zealously as O. Henry's friends guarded his own background of embezzlement, conviction, and imprisonment.[29]

Only one theme rivals imposture in O. Henry's work: "the idea of fate as the one unavoidable reality of life" (Langford, p. 94), the idea "that destiny or fate imposes inescapable roles on the individual" (Current-Garcia, p. 75). One can easily link the notions of fate and the paradoxical fitness of O. Henry's routine trick endings. I find equally interesting, however, O. Henry's emphatically pronounced fondness for a rather ordinary story, "Roads of Destiny," which consists of one beginning and three alternate endings: in each the poet David Mignot dies shot by the pistol of the Marquis de Beaupertuys. Gerald Langford's biography cogently develops the theme of fatalism through O. Henry's life (for instance, pp. 94, 232, 247), certainly after the prison term, but most impressively before. Nabokov, of course, repeatedly plays with the concept, in "Signs and Symbols," for example; and in stories like "The Garden of Forking Paths," Borges invokes fate and determinism with a profound artistry. O. Henry undeniably equals them in sincerity and commitment to the premise.

Coincidence, often outrageous coincidence, functions significantly in the great majority of O. Henry's stories, much as in the stories of many contemporary avante-garde writers. It may sound strange to relate coincidence and fate, but Nabokov, Borges, and other Postmodernists constantly juxtapose the two (as in the stories mentioned above). The word "juxtapose" may betray deeper links, however, for in O. Henry as in the Postmodernists and others, coincidence normally functions as an agent of fate. What other agent but fated coincidence selected Old Caesar as the narrator's cabman? What other agent determined that the hotel boor, the narrator's first Nashville acquaintance, would be the villainous husband of the woman he sought? What other agent chose such a fortuitous moment for rigor mortis to allow Caswell's dead hand to release the button torn from Caesar's coat, a moment when the narrator—the only man who would immediately recognize it, understand its significance, and desire to protect its owner—could conceal it from prying eyes?

Parody also distinguishes the Postmodernists, and few writers have parodied others—or themselves—more enthusiastically and repeatedly than O. Henry. Among his earliest ventures were the burlesques and satires of his *Rolling Stone*. Later and more successfully, he parodied popular romantic fiction in "Best-Seller," crime stories in "Tommy's Burglar," his own work in "A Dinner at———" which he subtitled, "The Adventures of an Author with His Own Hero," anticipating Pirandello *(Six Characters in Search of an Author)*. He wrote many other parodies, and the mass of his stories contain at least moments of self-mockery. In "The Gift of the Magi," for example, Della receives twenty dollars for her hair: "Oh, and the next two hours tripped by on rosy wings. Forget the hashed metaphor."

We have identified in O. Henry's work a great variety of the characteristics identified with Postmodernism: a pervasive self-consciousness, fondness for allusions, innovative structural pattern, deliberate use of stereotypes, style marked by evident artificiality and verbal play ("linguistic foregrounding"), metafictional references to storytelling, toyings with "reality" as in the imposture motif, determinism, coincidence, and finally parody. But apart from the criteria of Postmodernism as evidenced in "A Municipal Report," do grounds for honest praise of O. Henry exist? I think so—in two very important areas.

For one thing, the works of O. Henry have entered the American imagination on the most fundamental level. He generated material which has since become almost folklore. Like a great many other Americans, long before I'd ever read any of his stories I'd absorbed by osmosis story patterns he created: the tramp who vainly seeks imprisonment so he can spend a comfortable winter, then decides to reform at the very moment he's arrested for loitering ("The Cop and the Anthem"); the kidnapped child so wild his abductors have to pay the father to take him back ("The Ransom of Red Chief"); the reformed safecracker who exposes himself to imprisonment by cracking a safe which traps a child ("A Retrieved Reformation"); the husband who sells his prized watch to buy his wife some expensive combs, while she has cut and sold her hair to buy him a watch fob—the story of "The Gift of the Magi," like so many of his others, is more familiar to Americans and holds more genuine mythic value than almost any forgotten tales of Greeks or Romans or Norsemen.

Undeniably, O. Henry has become a permanent part of the American imagination, one good reason to value him. Another is his originality. No one reading an O. Henry story could reasonably mistake it for a story by any other writer. Poe's definitive essay on the tale (in his 1842 review of *Twice-Told Tales)* proclaims "invention, creation, imagination, originality" to be a single trait, a "trait which, in the literature of fiction, is positively worth all the rest." From the beginnings through Barthelme, America has never produced a more unique fiction writer than O. Henry.

O. Henry published "A Municipal Report" six months before his death at the age of 47. In those last few months of his life he often spoke of great work he intended to do, work which would tower over anything he had yet produced. I doubt now, as I have always doubted, that O. Henry could produce anything we could value by the conventional standards which critics like Brooks and Warren have taught us to honor. The standards by which Nabokov and Barth and Gass and Coover and Barthelme are honored differ radically from Brooks and Warren's, however, and by these O. Henry had it in him, I think, to produce work of genius.

"A Municipal Report" seems to me close to such work, but even if it falls short, it is a fascinating and incredibly innovative short story. O. Henry himself once seemed to me a formerly overrated and now justly forgotten hack. On a closer look he seems a neglected, prescient, premodern master of Postmodern fiction.

Notes

1. Eugene Current-Garcia, for example, in *O. Henry (William Sydney Porter)* (New York: Twayne, 1965), bravely praises the realism of O. Henry's Western and New York settings (p. 98; pp. 77ff), but few of the examples Current-Garcia quotes range far from stereotype. Van Wyck Brooks in *The Confident Years* (New York: Dutton, 1952) also praises O. Henry's treatment of New York (pp. 276ff), but even his biographer Gerald Langford in *Alias O. Henry* (New York: Macmillan, 1957) describes O. Henry's interest in New York as superficial (pp. 218–19). How superficial? O. Henry produced the New York setting as authentically in "No Story" as in any of his stories, well before he had even seen the city (Langford, p. 150). In *Understanding Fiction* (2nd ed., New York: Appleton-Century-Crofts, 1943, 1959; pp. 95–98), Cleanth Brooks and Robert Penn Warren's absolutely relentless attack on O. Henry generally and on setting in "The Furnished Room" specifically seems finally more acute, if almost frightening in its studious mercilessness, than either Current-Garcia's or Van Wyck Brooks' analysis. As for characterization, Stephen Leacock in "The Amazing Genius of O. Henry" (reprinted in *The Complete Works of O. Henry* [New York: Doubleday, Page, 1927], pp. 1339–48) rather idiosyncratically perceives "a depth of understanding of the human heart as only genius can make manifest" (p. 1342). But H.L. Mencken much more accurately observes that in "the whole canon of O. Henry's work you will not find a single recognizable human character; his people are unanimously marionettes" (quoted in Langford, p. xiv). Indeed, few credit him with producing more than vibrant types. A.H. Quinn in *American Fiction* (New York: Appleton-Century-Crofts, 1936) praises O. Henry's themes, but in the very act of praising he unintentionally condemns them by underlining the stories' unrelieved sentimentality. Quinn lauds, for example, "his deep sympathy for the underdog, for youth striving for a taste of joy before the humdrum of existence settles down, for the loyalty of true love, illumined by sacrifice" (p. 547). In their introduction to *The Best Short Stories of O. Henry* (New York: Modern Library, 1945), Bennet Cerf and Van Cartmell take the most common route of praising O. Henry for having "introduced to the public a relatively new device—the surprise or 'twist' ending" (p. ix). But Current-Garcia admits O. Henry added nothing significant to the technique, which "entered the short story with the emergence of the form itself and was developed at the hands of many writers from Washington Irving on" (p. 138; see Graves Glenwood Clark's unpublished Master's thesis for Columbia University, 1930: "The Development of the Surprise Ending in the American Short Story from Washington Irving through O. Henry").

In the absence of praiseworthy elements in a writer's work, some indefatigable critics must inevitably take the predictable tack of praising him for his influence. Unfortunately for O. Henry, however, even in Current-Garcia's evaluation his "contribution to a developing form of literary art" is "dated" (p. 5). On the other hand, what influence O. Henry had seems to have been essentially perverse. Frederick Lewis Pattee in *The Development of the American Short Story* (New York: Harper and Brothers, 1923) damns O. Henry for destroying the short story's spirit, for making it "mechanistic"; in his words: "the novice was inspired to codify his laws and imitate his devices" (p. 368). So, any influence O. Henry may have had was bad, but fortunately temporary. Ironically, the impulse O. Henry gave to a primary focus on structure, technique, workmanship, helped prepare the ground for the New Critics' emphasis on a similar perspective as the most legitimate and most important for literary criticism. Of course, from this perspective Brooks and Warren and other New Critics have vigorously damned him.

Only one man seems to have discovered a legitimate critical perspective from which we may honestly praise O. Henry. Over half a century ago, in 1925, the Russian Formalist Boris Eichenbaum (or Ejxenbaum or Eikenbaum) wrote an indispensable article, "O. Henry and the Theory of the Short Story," which has only recently been translated into English by I.R. Titunik (Michigan Slavic Contributions; Ann Arbor: Department of Slavic Languages and Literatures, University of Michigan, 1968). Eichenbaum's focus on O. Henry's predilection for metafictional parody has deeply influenced my own essay. The Russians' immense enthusiasm for O. Henry in the 1920's and implications of the Formalists' critical theories (Titunik observes that Eichenbaum is well-known in Slavic circles and his "work is a perennial source of interest and stimulation for all Slavists everywhere"; p. 31) can hardly have escaped a young exile studying Russian literature at Cambridge University during these years—Vladimir Nabokov.

2. I shall attempt to keep footnotes to a minimum (despite appearances to the contrary) by citing only one example to support each statement about Postmodernism in the text. See Gerald Graff, "Babbit at the Abyss: The Social Context of Postmodern American Fiction," *Tri-Quarterly*, 33 (1975), 307–37.
3. See Robert Scholes, "Metafiction," *Iowa Review*, I (1970), 100–115; and *The Fabulators* (New York: Oxford, 1967) or *Fabulation and Metafiction* (Urbana: Univ. of Illinois Press, 1979).
4. James Rother, "Parafiction: The Adjacent Universe of Barth, Barthelme, Pynchon, and Nabokov," *Boundary* 2, V (1976), 21–43.
5. Jerome Klinkowitz, *The Life of Fiction* (Urbana: Univ. of Illinois Press, 1977); Klinkowitz clarifies the term by asserting that it's like "what twelve ounces of Miller beer does when it chases your shot of brandy, while the jukebox belts out Eric Clapton and the parking lot fills up with Formula Firebirds and turbo-charged Camaros" (p. 3).
6. *Surfiction: Fiction Now . . . and Tomorrow*, ed. by Raymond Federman (Chicago: Swallow, 1975).
7. Philip Stevick, *Anti-Story* (New York: Free Press, 1971); his introduction lists some of the phenomena this new fiction is anti: mimesis, "reality," event, subject, the middle range of experience, analysis, meaning, scale.
8. John Barth borrows the term from Jorge Luis Borges; see, for instance, Joe David Bellamy, *SuperFiction* (New York: Vintage, 1975), p. 5.
9. Albert J. Guerard, "Notes on the Rhetoric of Anti-Realist Fiction," *Tri-Quarterly*, 30 (1974); Guerard emphasizes contemporary writers' discontent with old-fashioned notions regarding "reality," and "the inherited novel form, and of the very act of fictionizing" (p. 14), and notes certain anti-realist impulses and rhetorical aims: "Self-consciousness and anxiety over the fiction-making process, and over the relation of fiction to reality; Nabokovian involution" (p. 21); "Formal discontinuity: the impulse to fragment form, consciousness" (p. 23); "Absurd reasoning. Eruption of the absurd amid the banal, or vice versa" (p. 24); "Phenomenological fiction: notation, meditation, monologue" (p. 24); "verve, *vis comica*, a sense of play" (p. 27).
10. Ronald Suckenick in *Surfiction*: "Needless to say the Bossa Nova has no plot, no story, no character, no chronological sequence, no verisimilitude, no imitation, no allegory, no symbolism, no subject matter, no 'meaning.' It resists interpretation. . . . The Bossa Nova is non-representational—it represents itself. . . . we should direct our attention to the surface of a work, and such techniques as graphic and typographical variations, in calling the reader's attention to the technological reality of the book, are useful in keeping his mind on that surface instead of undermining it with profundities" (pp. 43–45).
11. Guerard, Stevick, and Scholes seem to me the best of the guides mentioned above; and, of course, Tony Tanner in *City of Words* (New York: Harper, 1971).
12. One trait which seems to characterize many of these fictions but not the work of O. Henry is a pervasive social and cultural pessimism, an overwhelming sense of entropy, what Malcolm Bradbury calls "a sense of absolute historical apocalypse" (in *Possibilities: Essays on the State of the Novel* [London: Oxford Univ. Press, 1973], p. 26). In my opinion O. Henry was on the one hand too egocentric to seriously question the state of contemporary culture, on the other too committed (though there are some exceptions in his work) to shoring up his marketability by endorsing conventional optimistic pieties.
13. See Robert Alter, "The Self-Conscious Moment: Reflections on the Aftermath of Modernism," *Tri-Quarterly*, 33 (1975), 209–30.
14. A tendency familiar to readers of Nabokov and Borges, the godfathers of Postmodernism, as well as to readers of their heirs.
15. John Barth observes that his "Perseid," like some of his other work, "is based upon a rather complicated structure which is almost, but not quite, completely arbitrary. . . . the Fibonnaci series of numbers as it manifests itself in the logarithmic spiral" (see James McKenzie, ed., "Pole-Vaulting in Top Hats: A Public Conversation with John Barth, William Gass, and Ishmael Reed," *Modern Fiction Studies*, 22 [1976], 131–51; p. 137). Similarly, William Gass has pointed out that structurally his "In the Heart of the Heart of the Country" imitates Yeats' "Sailing to Byzantium"; "That's a little kind of imposed formality that I did to help shape the work" ("Pole-Vaulting," p. 147).
16. See Morris Dickstein, "Fiction Hot and Cool: Dilemmas of the Experimental Writer," *Tri-Quarterly*, 33 (1975), 257–72. See also Guerard.
17. See the introduction to Tanner's *City of Words*.
18. See Scholes on metafiction.
19. See Guerard; imposture and/or fluctuating personality is a favorite theme of Postmodernists, beginning with Nabokov and Borges and reaching a kind of high point in Thomas Pynchon's *V*.
20. Postmodernists are fond even of self-parody; see, for instance, Richard Poirier, "The Politics of Self-Parody," *Partisan Review*, 35 (1968), 339–53.
21. Originally published December 1909 in *Hampton's Magazine*; reprinted in *The Complete Works of O. Henry* (New York: Doubleday, Page, 1927), pp. 1208–17.
22. O. Henry probably came across the Norris quotation in the August 1909 *Putnam's Magazine*. The issue carried a photograph portrait of O. Henry on p. 632 and on 633 a reference to Norris's stories about San Francisco and his remark that fewer good ones seem to have been written about New York, though "Mr. Janvier and O. Henry have written some delightful ones" (p. 633). The obverse of the O. Henry portrait (p. 631) contains the quotation from Norris which serves as the second epigraph to "A Municipal Report." O. Henry has subtracted a comma after Chicago, however, and boosted Norris's period after Tennessee to an exclamation point. In fact, pp. 629–33 of *Putnam's* ramble on about Norris in general and specifically a collection of Norris's stories, *The Third Circle*, which the columnist ("The Lounger") has just received. The Norris quotation which O. Henry seems to have borrowed from *Putnam's*, the *Putnam's* columnist has taken from the first paragraph of Norris's story, "The House with the Blinds" (see Frank Norris, *The Third Circle* [and] *A Deal in Wheat* [Port Washington, N.Y.: Kennikat Press, 1909, 1928], Vol. IV of *The Complete Works of Frank Norris*), p. 11.
23. See, for example, Current-Garcia, pp. 74, 146; and Langford pp. 78, 80, 169, 173, 199. Barth often refers to the book, as in his frequently reprinted, "The Literature of Exhaustion," and in "Pole-Vaulting," p. 137.
24. See the remarks on Gass and Barth in n. 15.
25. In fact, O. Henry had been in Nashville. I quote from a letter from Allison Ensor: "In the fall of 1904, O. Henry visited Nashville, staying at the Maxwell House Hotel and seeing his daughter Margaret, then a student at what became Belmont College and living with the Boyers family at 1403 Division Street. The whole matter of the O. Henry visit is discussed in H.B. Teeter, 'Stranger in the Town,' *Nashville Tennessean Magazine*, Dec. 9, 1951, pp. 6–7, and Dec. 16, 1951, pp. 5, 28. 'A Municipal Report' was first published in *Hampton's Magazine*, with illustrations which show a clearer knowledge of Nashville than any demonstrated in the story."
26. In Rust Hills, ed., *Writer's Choice* (New York: David McKay, 1974), pp. 25–26.

27. Current-Garcia documents a great range of O. Henry's verbal play, pp. 141–49; see also Edward C. Echols, "O. Henry's 'Shaker of Attic Salt,'" *Classical Journal*, 43(1948), 488–89; and "O. Henry and the Classics—II," *Classical Journal*, 44(1948–49), 209–10; see also, William B. Gates, "O. Henry and Shakespeare," *Shakespeare Association Bulletin*, 19(1944), 20–25.
28. For instance, Kenneth Kempton, *The Short Story* (Cambridge, Mass.: Harvard Univ. Press, 1947), pp. 94–98, who feels O. Henry might more wisely have thrown away his beginning; see also Current-Garcia, pp. 59–60.
29. Langford repeatedly makes the point in his biography; for typical examples see the essays by Page and Leacock in *The Complete Works*.

JOSEPHINE HERBST

1892–1969

Josephine Frey Herbst was born on March 5, 1892, in Sioux City, Iowa. The daughter of an unsuccessful small-town businessman, she held a variety of jobs while attending four different colleges, eventually receiving her degree in 1918 from the University of California at Berkeley. After working in New York as an editorial reader for H. L. Mencken's *The Smart Set*, she lived for two years among the urban poor in Berlin, writing short stories and an unpublished novel. While in Paris she met John Herrmann, also a writer, whom she later married; they returned to New York together in 1924. Her first novel, *Nothing Is Sacred* (1928), received considerable attention; it was followed in 1929 by *Money for Love*.

During the Great Depression of the 1930s, Herbst and her husband were increasingly active in radical political circles. As a journalist she covered a farm strike in Iowa and an auto workers' strike in Michigan, interviewed Cuban revolutionaries in the hills above Havana, and reported on the Nazi consolidation of power from Germany in 1935 and on the Spanish Civil War from Madrid and Barcelona in 1937. During this same period she wrote the three interconnected novels of the "Trexler trilogy": *Pity Is Not Enough* (1933), *The Executioner Waits* (1934), and *Rope of Gold* (1939). Heavily autobiographical like most of her fiction, the narrative interweaves events in the lives of Herbst and her family with stories of earlier generations of Herbsts and Freys, simultaneously relating her characters' struggles to larger political and economic issues and historical developments in the United States; the period covered ranges from just after the Civil War up through the mid-1930s.

In 1941, while working for the federal Office of the Coordinator of Information (the Donovan Committee), Herbst was abruptly fired as a result of an FBI investigation of her political connections. The investigation continued for some years. John Herrmann had joined the Communist Party in the '30s, and was an associate of Whittaker Chambers and possibly Alger Hiss as well; though Herbst and her husband had by then been separated for some years, she was nevertheless "graylisted" and went into semi-retirement. She continued writing, and received a Rockefeller Foundation grant in 1965 and an award from the National Institute of Arts and Letters in 1966, but her literary reputation lapsed into complete obscurity. Only recently has her work again received attention.

Her last project, her extensive memoirs, was unfinished at the time of her death. She died on January 25, 1969, in New York City.

Josephine Herbst's novel, *Nothing Is Sacred*, which will be issued in September by Coward, McCann, took command of my intelligence with its first sentence when I read it in manuscript and it continued to exercise its singular quality of impressive interest until now it has found its publisher and I have read it right through again in proofs. That is due not to the interest of the subject but to the sheer skill of its narrator. There is no reason—no reason in the world—why I, hardened European as I am—should be interested in and should be kept reading far into the night twice running by the affairs of a quite undistinguished family in a quite indistinguishable American small town—but that is what has happened to me.

You see if a book begins: "'Can I talk to you a minute!' said Harry Norland to his mother-in-law. He stood in the kitchen doorway with his hat on", you are given at once a sense of interest as strong as you receive at the opening of a good detective story and the person who so begins a book will have the sense to carry it on at the same pitch of interest. There is no reason why the story of a small-town family should not be as interesting as any detective-romance—the trouble usually is that the narrators of such tales begin with the thesis that the life described has by them been found uninteresting and that they must therefore make an uninteresting story out of it. But the actual livers of such lives seldom find them uninteresting *per se*—or it might be truer to say that the dwellers in small towns seldom find small-town life as such other than thrilling with its struggles for precedence, local renown, prosperity and the rest. They may of course have intervals of dullness—but who has not? But the fact that they continue to live in small towns and that small towns continue to exist is the proof that their inhabitants find there an interest in life that is not apparent to the outsider.

That really is the problem that is before the modern novelist. If the novel in the future as in the past can only exist with the unusual, the hero, the type, or the demi-god for its sole pabulum it must in a more and more standardizing world end by losing all contact with life—and by dying as a form of art. And that is the problem that Mrs. Herbst has attacked and triumphantly overthrown. For me at least she has done this, and I do not believe that as reader I differ much from the ordinary reader of light fiction: I mean that when I do surrender to reading a book I surrender just as fully as any child reading Hans Andersen or any commuter reading "Sherlock Holmes".

I have been, twice, just as thrilled to know whether Harry Norland made good the club-money that he had embezzled as to know who committed any murder anywhere—just as thrilled, twice, to know how his mother-in-law was going, once again, to get the resulting mortgage off her house; and I have twice been left speculating as to how Mr. Winter, after his wife's death, liked living by turns with his daughters and their families, and saying to myself: "Perhaps he will—because in the end they are very decent, dutiful girls—or perhaps he won't because he is an old man of strong character and they are all rather nervous people . . ." The problems of these quite commonplace people become, in short, one's own problems during the reading of the book, and one leaves them with a pang of regret—for the destroyed contents of the ragbags of a lifetime in the attic, and of regret as if one were moving into another town and leaving people whom on the whole one liked and respected. In short this is the sort of novel that I want to see make its mark—for the sake of the art of the novel, which is an art I love. I hope it may *faire école*, find thousands of readers, and earn for its writer glory enough to make her continue to go on doing this. And I don't know that, if I wanted to impress a foreign audience with what the native American really is—a normal, honest, wrong-headed, rightly-inspired, undulled—above all undulled!—American that I really like, I don't know that it isn't *Nothing Is Sacred* that I would give to those Dagos. For there stands out in this book a quality of family solidarity, of family dutifulness and above all of family consideration between sensitive individuals such as rarely swims to the surface in the more tumultuously manifest features of life here. I know, I mean, that it exists and is touching and beautiful, but I don't know where—if it isn't in *Nothing is Sacred*—I should put my finger on the expression of it.—FORD MADOX FORD, "A Distinguished First Novel," *B&B*, Sept. 1928, pp. 87–88

The Executioner Waits is a solidly constructed novel-machine. Each part functions for the whole, each character is fitted into the total effect, there is hardly a paragraph that exists for its own sake. A great number of characters are set before the reader, their lives are recounted in such a way as to fit them into the economic history of the times. No character can escape Miss Herbst's purpose or get her to relax her remorseless science. The result is a book that is difficult to read and that, after it has been read, it is impossible not to admire for its clarity and organization.

The problem Miss Herbst has undertaken is to describe the effect of the economic class antagonisms of the contemporary world on the lives of a middle-class family. The Trexler family is made up of limbs that are economically sound, of some that are economically frail, but all of them are emotionally rotten. It branches out with sons, daughters, sons-in-law, daughters-in-law across the America of our time. It speaks the American language. (Miss Herbst has a superb ear for the way Americans actually talk and a style that is able to convey it.) But the Trexler family and practically everyone else in *The Executioner Waits* are as inhuman as the parts of a machine. They have hardly any emotions that are not mechanically caused by economic problems or social conventions; they have no fancies, humors, caprices; they are dead and gestureless; except that practical problems attack them, they would not stir.

. . . Miss Herbst has overplayed her propagandist's hand. A people such as she describes is not worth saving. Moreover, one feels that Miss Herbst *requires* her characters to be dull-witted, feelingless, and dead. For she describes them only in terms of their habits. As a great word has it, we are only heroes momentarily. Moments of wonder and doubt even the most automatic of us must experience at some time or other. Not so Miss Herbst's characters. The social purport of *The Executioner Waits*—analysis of the economic pressure on the American middle classes—requires of course a disclosure of what is habitual in the middle-class reaction to economic stress. But one can describe any class in terms of its automatisms. True enough, Miss Herbst manages to pump a little enthusiasm and life into those of her characters who find themselves on the side of the workers. But it is not easy for her to handle a living and inventive organism.

. . . The fact that Miss Herbst writes without warmth or scorn, that she does not even have any hatred for her characters, proves, it seems to me, that there is a subtle affinity between her talents as a writer and their lack of talent as human beings. To put it frankly, it occurs to me that Miss Herbst's writing equipment necessitates a talentless humanity such as she describes.

But once we suspect that Miss Herbst has something to gain as a writer by the defects of the people she writes about, it becomes difficult to have faith in her vision. The question arises: In a society of supermen and superwomen would not Miss Herbst find novel-writing too adventuresome an art? In, let us say, a classless society in which men and women are free and creative, in which the élan of their lives would correspond only to a rhapsodic, laughter-loving style in art, would not Miss Herbst find reality not dull enough for her talents? A harsh judgment.—LIONEL ABEL, "A Technician of Mediocrity," *Nation*, Oct. 31, 1934, pp. 514–16

The proletarian novel is a novel written under the influence of dialectic materialism from the point of view of the class-conscious proletariat.

The bourgeois novel is either (1) a novel of escape written under the influence of idealistic philosophy or (2) a novel of despondency written under the influence of pragmatism or (3) a novel combining elements of both. . . . These three types exist in time: *i.e.* the first tends to be supplemented by the second, and the third reflects the rise of fascism: *i.e.*, in the third type certain aspects of contemporary society are recognized with disgust and then distorted by the optimism of an idealistic (Nietzschean) interpretation.

Insofar as the bourgeois novel is concerned with the proletariat, it is pessimistic; insofar as the proletarian novel is concerned with the bourgeoisie, it is pessimistic; but though the bourgeois novel may be pessimistic about the bourgeoisie, the proletarian novel is never pessimistic about the class-conscious proletariat. This is by reason of the fact that both by observation of American life and by Marxist theory the proletariat is defined as class-conscious when it acts in the belief that only its conscious cooperation is necessary to promote the immediate direction of history towards the dictatorship of the proletariat. Therefore at the present moment in American history the proletarian is synonymous with the revolutionary novel: *i.e.*, the revolutionary novel is the proletarian novel considered from its political rather than its social or its æsthetic aspect. . . .

At present, the proletarian novel at its best represents that region of American life where the skilled worker merges with the petty bourgeoisie: *i.e.*, where the worker has once had a bourgeois education and a bourgeois point of view and where the petty bourgeois is coming to discard his bourgeois education and point of view. The line of distinction, therefore, is delicate between two such masterly novels as Cantwell's *Land of Plenty* (in which the skilled worker is becoming conscious of his power) and Herbst's *The Executioner Waits*, in which the petty bourgeois is becoming conscious of his belonging with the proletariat.

At the present moment, therefore, the proletarian novels that have received the most praise are novels "from the point of view" of the class-conscious proletariat, but are actually written by and for the petty bourgeoisie who have achieved or are achieving this point of view under the pressure of events.

But this definition of the proletarian novel purports to be dialectic in part since it represents a direction rather than sets up a norm. As events change we may expect a change in emphasis: *i.e.*, a continued shift of focal interest more and more upon the proletariat itself. MacLeish's *Panic* could not have been written five years ago and we may predict that nothing like it can possibly appear two years hence. We may predict also that Miss Herbst will in future novels shift her focus from the middle bourgeois members of the family she is treating towards the problems and interests of its simon pure proletarians.

With this change in emphasis will come changes in the technique of writing either (1) away from the great bourgeois styles, such as the stream of consciousness or (2) towards a new utilization of them which will make them under the new emphasis the more communicative and the more self-consistent or (3) (as I think the more probable) first in the first direction and later in the second.

. . . ⟨T⟩he whole novel is only an episode in a conflict to be continued in time, but a conflict to be continued definitely in a certain direction, to a certain outcome, to the establishment of the dictatorship of the proletariat. This "open" form, however, is not "open" in the romantic sense since the direction is established, and is not into a world of absolute ideas but rather into a new stage in the materialistic development of history. This fact determines the note of belief and optimism which must define the conclusion of the proletarian novel.

Therefore, every proletarian novel craves its sequel. Every proletarian novel is an historical novel, but one which recognizes that we can know only the history of our own times and never with sufficient intimacy for the purpose of fiction either the distant past or the distant future. It represents the span of experience of its author and of his age seen thru the philosophy of dialectic materialism at a peculiar moment in the progress of history.—EDWIN BERRY BURGUM, "Discussion," from "What Is a Proletarian Novel?," *Partisan Review*, July–Aug. 1935, pp. 8–11

Of the many things that distinguish the "Trexler trilogy" from comparable trilogies of the Depression era such as James Farrell's *Studs Lonigan* or John Dos Passos' *USA*, perhaps the most important is the centrality of women. From the grandmother of the first volume, to the mother of the second, to the daughters of the second and third, it is the female line whose experience provides the link between the generations. In addition to the portraits of the nineteenth-century women, "Mem" and Anne, the portraits of Victoria and Rosamond are among the earliest representations of modern women in American fiction. The modernity of Victoria and Rosamond consists, above all, in their desire for independence. "Don't be stupid and shut your eyes and imagine that the only things in life worth while come from men and what people call romance," cautions Anne in one of the foreshadowing interchapters of the first volume, and the girls do not. They seek not only love, but work. In passages which clearly capture a frustration not unknown today, they see all their efforts to get an education end only in business school and the chance to "sit solemnly at some business man's feet while he cleared his throat and began "Yours of the 19th received and contents noted." Nor do they find love any easier. Rosamond, though she is married, dies as a result of an accidental, unaffordable pregnancy—something that actually happened to the youngest, favorite sister of Josephine Herbst—and Victoria's bohemian affair with Jonathan Chance is very uncertain. The women are bold, but they are vulnerable. The protections of their mother's era are gone. This is not the image of the 1920s as it has come down to us in works largely written by men: it is women from their own point of view, in which one of the implications of freedom is the possibility of ending up alone.

But *The Executioner Waits* is not only a novel of women. Like *Pity Is Not Enough* it is also an historical novel: specifically a novel of the early twentieth-century radical movement. In the sense that *Pity is Not Enough* is "about" capitalism, *The Executioner Waits* is "about" the rise of opposition to capitalism during the 1920s. . . .

The chief incarnation of capitalism in *The Executioner Waits* is the successful but selfish banker David Trexler, who has so much but gives so little to his family. The youngest brother of "Poor" (but generous) Joe, and poor (but generous) Anne, he is very much their moral opposite. His self-satisfied but self-deluded character is perhaps best captured in the scene in which he imagines his neighbors remarking to one another on his all-too-modest good works: "There goes Mr. Trexler, the philanthropist, he does so many nice things, and all so quietly." Another representative of capitalism is the philistine father of Jonathan Chance who would rather write his son moralistic, self-serving letters than trouble to understand him. ("It was . . . a horrible example of the way people were warped all out of shape to find out that a father could have it in his power to help his son and not help him," thinks Victoria, to which "People get different when they begin to get money. You were lucky to have parents who didn't have much," is Jonathan's response.) What is interesting about these portraits, as in so much of the writing of Josephine Herbst, is how close to the real-life originals they came. Relatives of Herbst's uncle Daniel Fry found her representation of the Oregon banker perfectly apt. The letter denouncing Jonathan Chance's life of "vice and vagabondism" and stopping a check previously proffered to help buy a house is a letter the real father of Herbst's real husband John Herrmann actually wrote. . . . So harsh they may at times read like stereotypes, Herbst's capitalists were nonetheless not invented. She was interested in the relationships between money and social control both in and out of the family and she found plenty of evidence for her perceptions. If the portraits seem exaggerated, remember: it was not a very subtle era.—ELINOR LANGER, "Introduction" to *The Executioner Waits*, 1985, pp. vii–ix

EDWIN BERRY BURGUM
"A Significant Revolutionary Novel"
Partisan Review, January-February 1935, pp. 82–83

The title of Miss Herbst's latest novel ⟨*The Executioner Waits*⟩ means, I take it, that the executioner waits for the great middle class. So many Americans belong to this class by descent and by income that the implications of this book make it one of the most absorbing novels of the season. It is a more faithful reproduction of our actual experiences during the years of depression than Sinclair Lewis was for the years of prosperity, since it is free from the distortion both of satire and of conscious propaganda. It pictures the progress of impoverishment in the way in which it is coming to most of us, so gradually that we are loath to admit it. Our incomes are periodically reduced. The rents from our little properties are so uncertain as to leave scant profit after increasing taxes are paid. We find it harder to get new jobs at the same time that we contribute to the support of a larger number of relatives, most of whom are neither aged nor infirm. The adage to be thrifty, to labor incessantly and thus guarantee the reward of a tranquil old age; the old adages no longer work. At this point we visit our really prosperous relatives, only to find them repeating the advice and keeping their incomes to themselves. We become conscious that class distinctions are gradually and with a cruelty that is often unrecognized supplanting the ties of blood once believed so sacred and now generally functioning in proportion to mutual poverty. *The Executioner Waits* is the most damaging criticism yet published in the form of fiction of the theory of capitalistic individualism as applied to the petty bourgeoisie.

But the value of the book is not simply that these sociological reflections are embedded in it. It is rather that they are embedded in it after the manner appropriate to fiction as an esthetic medium. Nowhere, to my recollection, are these statements actually made in the book, but they lie behind the action of the novel and give form to its accumulation. Miss Herbst is writing of the family of Anne Wendel and of those of her brothers and sisters, her brothers-in-law and sisters-in-law, and her cousins and her aunts. It would be impossible for her within the limits of a single volume to philosophize successfully about the activities of so many people. Where philosophy intrudes, it is in the conversation of her characters. For she knows better than most novelists that people do "talk philosophy," and better than most propagandists that when they do, it is normally a generalization of their own experiences with the aid of whatever formal philosophy in the air at the moment seems to explain them. She has doubtless been led to this insight by another shrewd observation from life: that persons without the leisure of the wealthy actually do find other matters vital besides sex and recreation and culture. Mr. Galsworthy rarely brought business into his *Forsythe Saga*, and Henry James thought it positively beneath the attention of the novelist. When novelists of the middle class have done so, it has been usually, as in Balzac, Dickens, and Lewis, in the spirit of satire, which is of course the spirit in which the aristocratic view-point would regard it once it decided to regard it at all. Miss Herbst, on the contrary, weaves it into her book precisely as it is woven into the family life of our petty bourgeoisie, where it is as real and necessary an interest as finding a mate, and tremendously more real and necessary than gossiping about the neighbors or discussing the latest women's club lecture. And yet no two of her families have quite the same problems or quite the same outlook upon them. It is true that a direct dialectic opposition becomes apparent to the reader through the natural grouping of these families according to generation. But it is not a simple dichotomy. The older group holds to the theory of capitalistic individualism. And those of the older generation who have not followed it are the least prosperous and respected. But, on the other hand, those of the younger generation who command our respect are those who are conscious of the present inadequacy of the system, out of whose own problem of survival is arising a social attitude and explanation. Whereas the younger characters who still adhere to the theory of the older are no more successful, no more happy, and much more shrivelled and crabbed in personality than their contemporaries who do not. But here again the contrast is an inference of the reader since Miss Herbst leaves us amid the rich plenty of incident and individual characterization.

In previous novels, Miss Herbst has had the same interest in practical life and has employed the same technique. But she has never before displayed them so adequately; for she has not, let us say, in *Pity Is Not Enough*, applied them to a material with which she has been sufficiently acquainted. *Pity Is Not Enough* deals with the youth of Anne Wendel and especially with the career of her brother who became involved in Reconstruction politics in the South. Since she does not, in fact, cannot know, intimately the particular circumstances of life at this now remote period, and sees the personalities of the era only through the eyes of history and family legend, because of the very nature of her method, this earlier novel failed to become realized. In place of detail in human personality, she gave, as Dreiser did in *An American Tragedy*, detail observed from the newspapers or other documents. But with her economy in the use of detail, as far as any individual character out of the many on her canvas is concerned, her objective method, when applied to history, became a failure. If it is to her credit as an artist that she has nevertheless insisted upon the method natural to her talent, it is to the credit of her insight that in this later novel she has brought to it the contemporary material in which alone it can properly function. The artifice and superficiality which, despite her intention, are present in *Pity Is Not Enough* have now given way, and in *The Executioner Waits*, Miss Herbst has developed into one of our most significant novelists.

WALTER B. RIDEOUT
From "Forgotten Images of the Thirties: Josephine Herbst"
Literary Review, Fall 1983, pp. 30–36

In his book *Man against Myth*, published thirty-odd years ago, the philosopher Barrows Dunham compressed a summary of the American Depression decade into a single striking sentence which I would give much to have written myself: "The Nineteen-Thirties began in hunger and ended in blood." That is a melodramatic sentence, granted, but in its raw, hurtful concision it cuts directly to two great negative essentials of that decade. . . .

Still, . . . there were at least two great positive essentials about the nineteen thirties which that superb sentence of Dunham's had to omit or lose its sharp historical insight and its impact as language. These essentials were the deep, widespread sympathy for others suffering the same disasters, and the hope for a better society.

Nowhere in the literature written in that decade is this double sense of the times, the negative and the positive, better given, it seems to me, than by the now largely forgotten

Josephine Herbst in her now largely forgotten trilogy of novels about the Trexler family published individually as *Pity Is Not Enough* (1933), *The Executioner Waits* (1934), and *Rope of Gold* (1939). One reason why these linked novels are now so little known may be that they were never brought together in a single massive volume like Dos Passos's *U.S.A.*, which Herbst's trilogy superficially resembles, and a reason why Herbst herself is now so little known is certainly that in the thirties she became and, until her death in 1969, remained a political radical. . . .

Because she is so little known, it is essential first to place Herbst the human being in relation to her time and to the subject matter of her trilogy. Born in Sioux City, Iowa, in 1892, she was of that extraordinary generation which came of age in the 1910s and made American literature come of age in the 1920s.[1] Her father was an unsuccessful small business man, and the family—she was the third of four daughters—was poor. The most significant influence on her as person and author, especially of the trilogy, was her mother, a natural storyteller whose tales were often about her own people, the Freys, and—I am quoting Herbst—about "their rovings. All of her family of her own generation had spread thru the country, penetrating the South, West and Far West."[2]

> I was brought up on my mother's nostalgia for the East; and her admiration for those members of her family who had ventured, often to their downfall, dramatized for me my entire conception of American life. . . . The family for generations had kept diaries and letters, and the first inkling I had of the complexity and significance of people in relation to each other and the world came from these documents. Living seemed constantly fertilized and damned by the tragic burden one generation passed to the next.[3]

The Freys were to become, sometimes literally, the Trexlers of the trilogy, and the stories of their wanderings were to provide that sense which the trilogy so strongly communicates of how intermeshed are the destinies of individual, family, social class, and nation.[4]

. . . Herbst began to receive critical attention with her first two novels, *Nothing Is Sacred* (1928) and *Money for Love* (1929), two "Twentyish" attacks on the bankruptcy of American middle-class ideals based, as she saw them, on a pervasive greed for material success. Herrmann's failure to develop his writing career as productively would be one of the reasons for the couple's painful separation in 1935.

Along with certain other literary rebels of the twenties they were politically radicalized early in the Depression, Herrmann joining the Communist Party, Herbst becoming a fellow-traveler though retaining her characteristic independence of mind. Already in 1928 they had bought a farmhouse in Erwinna, Bucks County, Pennsylvania; and throughout the thirties Herbst used this home as a base from which to travel around the United States and abroad in order to observe and report for various magazines, often *The New Masses*, on what was happening among the dispossessed and angry—among the miners of Bloody Harlan County, Kentucky, in 1931; among farmers in the Midwest Dustbowl; among the Cuban peasants defending their plots of mountain land against Batista and the sugar companies during the general strike of 1935; among the anti-Nazi Underground fighters in Germany; among the Michigan automobile workers in their CIO-led sitdown strikes of 1937; among the Loyalist soldiers of the Spanish Republic resisting the Fascist armies under Franco. (In her independent, skeptical radical way she agreed more with Dos Passos than with Hemingway as to what the Communists were up to in Spain.)

In between her travels and her journalism, which became sources for many of the events in *Rope of Gold*, she worked on her Trexler trilogy, finding in the combination of past and ongoing present the best way to use her extensive and complex material. Going back into family record and legend, coming up to personal experience contemporary with her writing about it, she made the individual and family microcosm both reflect and illuminate the social and national macrocosm over some three-quarters of a century of American history, from just after the Civil War to just before, as we now know, the outbreak in Europe of the Second World War. . . .

Scornful as any 1920s satirist of the American middle-class, Mencken's "booboisie," with its hollow values and aspirations, she tempered that scorn with compassion and understanding for her mainly middle-class characters, whose lives she knew vividly from her mother's endless stories about them. Though she fictionalized them, these were members over the generations of her own family, most of them persons driven by internal desires and external forces they were not equipped to comprehend. Pity for them was not enough, but she sympathized with them while simultaneously showing them as they were and, frequently, condemning them. As with members of her own close-knit family, there were a few she intensely disliked, but most of them she could fiercely love as well as fiercely scold. Through this double feeling about her family, real and fictional, she would be able, as author writing about them in the 1930s, to combine an unblinking recognition of violence and failure with a profound human sympathy and a hope for a better world for people to live in.

As the personal and historical events of the developing trilogy came nearer to the time when she was writing of them—and for the last volume even largely occurred after the time when she had written the first volume—her design and double feeling persisted, reinforced both by her radical experience and her radical reading.

. . . For all the real influence of Marxism in her thought, her radicalism was and remained very much a homegrown, grassroots, feisty Midwestern rebelliousness; and it was, to the great benefit of her fiction, usually undogmatic and always grounded in human feeling despite the clarity and firmness of her intellectual convictions. To give the most significant of many examples: Victoria Wendel and Jonathan Chance are drawn together in volume two of the trilogy partly because of their common rebellion against things as they are, just as Josephine Herbst and John Herrmann were in actual life, and their marriage ends in volume three with as much emotional devastation for both as did Josephine and John's in 1935, the year after volume two was published.

Herbst was a ruthlessly honest person in her life; and in her fiction the devotion of two individuals to working for a better society does not, as in some false, doctrinally schematic novels, prevent their passionate love from turning into a shattering psycho-sexual conflict. Individuals are as they complicatedly are, Herbst implies, and even the coming of a classless society will not automatically guarantee universal harmony, even between lovers.

Taken as a whole, the Trexler trilogy achieves many of its meanings through its successive depiction of the lives of two major characters, members of the family who never meet since the older, Joseph Trexler, dies in 1896, the year that his niece, Victoria Wendel, is born; but a closer examination of *Pity Is Not Enough* will serve to indicate something of Herbst's ideological design and, as well, the inventiveness of her technique. This first volume, which covers the period from 1868 to 1896, actually begins with a four-page section subtitled "Oxtail 1905"—Oxtail being the fictitious name for Sioux City, Iowa, and 1905 being, though we do not learn this until later, the year in which Victoria Wendel is nine years old. Anne Wendel, mother of four girls, comforts her young daughters, as they all take refuge in a cellar once during the cyclone season, with stories of "the dead and gone Trexlers and Joe, the most generous brother, poor Joe."[5] The unnamed narrator of this section, who refers to the four sisters as "we" and who, it will later be understood, is Victoria Wendel, tells how all four girls continue to be fascinated by the stories about this generous uncle and puzzled as to why their mother always refers to him fondly and sadly as "poor Joe," who as some kind of fugitive took the alias of Victor Dorne. (Victoria, it will become clear, was named after Joe's assumed name because of his deathbed wish, thus establishing a connection that Herbst will develop by occasional reference to it for the rest of the trilogy.)

After this out-of-chronology introduction, *Pity Is Not Enough* is primarily concerned with the life story of Joe Trexler and its impact on the rest of the Trexler family, in which his sister Anne, who will later marry Amos Wendel and bear four girl children, is herself growing up from childhood. In 1868, Joe, aged nineteen, leaves Philadelphia for the South, where, as Herbst puts it, "Northern armies still had the whip hand, Northern politicians were running states to please their pocketbooks" (p. 5). Settling in Atlanta, Joe becomes involved in the politics and graft of a railroad line, having decided in his naive self-confidence that "fortunes were like continents in Columbus's day, just waiting to be discovered" (p. 72). Briefly he profits from the corrupt operations of the railroad and generously—hence "generous Joe"—sends money and expensive gifts home to his loyal family; but the corrupt operations are exposed, the higher-ups in the fraud make him the fall guy, and Joe returns North a fugitive from justice. He goes first to Canada, then to Colorado under the assumed name of Victor Dorne, and finally to the Black Hills during the gold rush of the mid-70s, where he eventually goes insane as the result of frustration over lost opportunities to make a fortune, the physical hardships of mining, and an ill-considered marriage. In sum, "poor Joe."

But Joe, we begin to perceive as Herbst unobtrusively nudges us toward an understanding of the meaning of his life, is more than the beloved, unfortunate brother of Anne Trexler Wendel; to be abstract about it, as Herbst in her fiction definitely is not, he is to be read as symbolic both of the pervasive corruption of the capitalist system and of the decline of old-fashioned American individualism in the second half of the 19th Century. The alias of "Victor" is obviously an unintended irony on his part; his niece Victoria must grow up in a twentieth-century America that he, and the many others he represents, helped to create.

Interspersed with the events of Joe's life are sequences about the lives of other Trexlers, which extend Herbst's analysis of national history via family history during this period. One series of sequences shows Anne Trexler growing up, marrying Amos Wendel, moving to Iowa with him, starting a family, seeing her husband fail in a small business, faithfully and lovingly enduring with him a life at the poverty line. In counterpoint to this story of American middle-class failure is the American success story of the youngest of Anne's brothers, the self-centered and greedy David Trexler, born in 1859, the year, one recalls, of Darwin's *Origin of Species*. His exploitative rise to upper-middle-class wealth, David reassures himself, exemplifies the survival of the fittest.

A third series of sequences is contained in the five more interpolated chapters subtitled "Oxtail" and a final one subtitled "Seattle 1918." These give more details of Amos and Anne Wendel's life and that of the four Wendel girls as they grow up. The last leaps ahead, beyond the 1905 of the introductory chapter, to the final year of World War I and the year following when the two youngest Wendel daughters, Rosamond and Victoria, now in their early twenties, are working in Seattle and, unlike the other people at their boarding house, are sympathetic with the unions when they go out in the city's general strike of 1919. Victoria's career as rebel and then radical has begun.

Herbst's technique of interpolating these chapters is further developed in *The Executioner Waits* and *Rope of Gold*, and the device provides throughout the trilogy an unusual and unusually powerful effect. The main narrative, or narratives, of the trilogy reaches back in family and American history to 1868—indeed in a few instances deals with Trexler ancestors who flourished before the Civil War—and comes up to 1937. The interpolated chapters in each volume, on the other hand, describe events, some fictional, some actual, which are consistently ahead chronologically in relation to the narrative. The result is to give the reader a richly complex sense of time. . . .

In *The Executioner Waits* and *Rope of Gold*, furthermore, the interpolated chapters do not deal with the Wendels, not even, except indirectly, with the highly autobiographical figure of Victoria. Instead they are vignettes describing events drawn from the Depression decade itself, instances of the angry dispossessed in various parts of the United States, of Cuba, of Spain rebelling against oppression, events such as Herbst herself had witnessed but which she does not specify herself (nor Victoria) as observing. Since the time between the events of the narrative and the events of the interpolated chapters becomes progressively shorter and shorter throughout the two later volumes, Herbst conveys an extraordinary sense, not only of how the fates of individuals and of nation are intricately linked, but also of the speed and intensity with which the narrative present rushes climactically toward a future which was actually within a contemporary reader's own immediate experience or awareness—and which a reader now readily recovers through a knowledge of history and with the added perspective of one who knows how the 1930s did in fact end.

Since *Pity Is Not Enough* had established the ideological direction and the fictional technique of the trilogy, Herbst's task in *The Executioner Waits* and *Rope of Gold* was to bring the Trexler and American pasts ever closer toward convergence in the novelist's and her country's present, a convergence which would dramatize her passionate hope throughout the thirties that the disintegration of her own middle-class family might be related dialectically to working-class integration and that the classless society would become an historical reality. Post-thirties history, as we of course now know, has not worked out that way in the United States; but Herbst would not be the first or only writer (or historian or philosopher or political thinker) to misread the direction of social processes. The point, however, is that her depiction of these processes is vivid with concrete circumstance and is imaginatively powerful. . . .

Josephine Herbst knew because she had seen it that the thirties began in hunger, and she foresaw that they might end in blood; but quite as certainly she understood that the past of an individual, a family, a nation lays living as well as dead hands on the present, shaping it toward a future in which oppression is resisted but in which there is also compassion for others. Here are the images of the thirties that are too often forgotten, and should not be forgotten. Herbst's most lasting achievement is to recall them to us.

Notes

1. Elinor Langer has established Herbst's year of birth as 1892, not the often cited 1897. See her entry on Herbst in Barbara Sicherman and Carol Hurd Green, eds., *Notable American Women: The Modern Period: A Biographical Dictionary* (Cambridge, Mass.: Belknap Press of Harvard University Press, 1980), p. 335.
2. Stanley J. Kunitz, ed., *Authors Today and Yesterday* (N.Y.: H.W. Wilson, 1933), p. 308.
3. Stanley J. Kunitz and Howard Haycraft, eds., *Twentieth Century Authors: A Biographical Dictionary of Modern Literature* (N.Y.: H.W. Wilson, 1942), p. 641.
4. For this formulation of intermeshed destinies and for the observation on the function of time in the trilogy I am indebted to Dion Kempthorne, whose excellent doctoral dissertation on Herbst's writing I had the pleasure of directing in the early 1970s.
5. *Pity Is Not Enough* (N.Y.: Harcourt, Brace, 1933), p. 1. Subsequent page references are given in parentheses after the quotation.

JOSEPH HERGESHEIMER

1880–1954

Joseph Hergesheimer was born in Pennsylvania on February 15, 1880. His parents, Joseph and Helen MacKellan Hergesheimer, were Philadelphia Protestants of German and Scots descent. Hergesheimer's early education was parochial and sheltered: he attended a small orthodox Quaker school until he was sixteen. Hergesheimer went on to study for a time at the Pennsylvania Academy of Fine Arts, without receiving much encouragement. In 1907 he married Dorothy Hemphill. They never had any children. Hergesheimer wrote steadily, professionally, from 1914 until his sixtieth year. He lived a simple, austere life in an old stone house in Pennsylvania, writing his volumes of novels, history, biography, stories, and criticism. He achieved his greatest success with his elevated historical and romance novels, such as *The Lay Anthony* (1914), *The Three Black Pennys* (1917), *Cytherea* (1922), and *Swords and Roses* (1929).

In 1940 Hergesheimer abruptly retired as a novelist, announcing his own satisfaction with his accomplishment. He spent his last years with his wife at a house in Stone Harbor, New Jersey. He died on April 25, 1954, of complications from diabetes and arteriosclerosis. He was buried in West Chester, Pennsylvania.

Personal

To the author of *Linda Condon* life has become in all its hours a refinement of sensuous experiences. Food is only incidentally sustenance. The clothes that supply warmth and protection should be pleasant to see and touch. And a house is less than nothing if it is conceived of only as a shelter. It is an expression of the complete man, the resort in which his soul expands, an asylum of the spirit. For this American, used to the amplitudes and the amenities from childhood, a house must be incarnate age and rock-bound stability. In the perpetuation of the past it must give grounds for criticism of the present. It must be so stable that it receives only on sufferance the resident of the moment. And it must be exacting in its demands on him, reaching out through him and securing from their hiding places in the past the chairs and tables and chests and rugs and pewter and glass that inevitably belong to it. It must be the work of art that life itself should be, surrounded by turf and tree and plant and shrub that perennially renew the past and beautify the passing moment. It must form the motivation for the literary art of the writer in it, so that he writes to support it, gathers data in its interest, brings his rewards to its hearthstone as to an exacting mistress, and finds that for his own reward he has "a house to live in that upholds him with an inviolable whispered calm."

The calm that comes to him is born of the fact that the house prolongs the quiet of an early Quaker pastoral in the midst of a tumultuous present, and that it promotes the spirit of the patriot, as that spirit roots itself in the love of the land and the fireside, depresses him with a sense of the social disintegration now in process, and reawakens in him the faith of the federalist, who is nearest to the traditions that prevailed when the house was builded, and who is most skeptical about the democratic experiment that would in time substitute bungalows and flats for homesteads that stand foursquare against the winds of innovation.

So he installs himself in such a homestead (and he tells all about it in the pages entitled *From an Old House*—though oddly enough they were not written from it but from a rented room in the town), and once installed here, he weighs past and present in the balance. He is a Presbyterian child of a rich, aristocratic past, the kind of past to which Linda Condon, born of the Lowries, returned when she became Linda Hallet. What he cherishes from this past is not the religious belief but the capacity for enjoyment, and an admiration for the independence of mind and action that belongs to the well-intrenched aristocrat. He misses just these traits in the present. He knows very well that his father and grandfather would look askance at his writings. His grandfather would detest *Cytherea*, regard *Linda* as a mad performance, and pass *The Lay Anthony* without a word. He would approve the backgrounds of *The Three Black Pennys*, *Java Head*, and *Balisand*; but *Mountain Blood* he would fully understand because it is so completely Presbyterian. . . .

In a passage of self-analysis Mr. Hergesheimer makes himself imperatively quotable on the subject of his characters: "I didn't particularly, the truth was, admire my own character; I should not—except for the ability of work—have chosen it. I liked calmness and I wasn't calm; I liked fidelity, and except to

O. HENRY (WILLIAM SYDNEY PORTER)

JOSEPH HERGESHEIMER

JOSEPHINE HERBST

AP/WIDE WORLD PHOTOS

PATRICIA HIGHSMITH

AP/WIDE WORLD PHOTOS

JOHN HERSEY

AP/WIDE WORLD PHOTOS

DUBOSE HEYWARD

my writing, I wasn't conspicuous for it; I liked hardness of body, a condition I hadn't the perseverance to keep; I liked, for myself, in vain, a distinguished resolution in bearing and mind." So, lacking these characteristics himself, he says, they seemed uncommonly desirable to him, and he made them live on paper. But he omits from this passage another trait which does belong to himself—a highly developed formality coupled with an inherent independence of mind and conduct. It is the heritage of the non-conformist aristocrat. It belongs to all the black Pennys, but no less to Isabel Penny who is the product of supercultivation yet resiliently strong as a Damascus blade. It belongs to Linda Hallet, who, like Isabel, could with unraised pulse defy her husband in behalf of palpitant youth. It is a part of Richard Bale, who on the morning of a duel to the death can tell his wife only by indirection of his sentiment, too deep for words, which possesses him for his home and his homestead. It is a part, and the larger part, of Tao Yuen, who comes from a civilization measured by millenniums and whose implicit but unmistakable vitality is never betrayed into outward expression. These characters are all the natural creations of an author who could say for himself, "A complete formality, it seemed to me, provided a mask behind which the individual could rest, retire, unwearied by the endless fatigue of personal contacts."

He surrounded himself with complete formality in architecture and furniture, and dominated by that portion of himself which is his home, he resolved after early wanderings of the imagination never again in his writing to depart from the traditions of America, to stray from the mood of Dower House. It is a mood not dissimilar to that of *The House of the Seven Gables*, a mood which can be re-created from the past of all the seaboard towns from Salem to New Orleans. Yet he did not do this with the resolution of the historical novelist. He had rather chosen—or acknowledged—the idiom in which he must write, and was concerned with the facts only as they were expressive of the mood. Fancy could create a background which never was on land or sea, like the exotic backgrounds of Poe, but imagination can act as Hawthorne's did, and connect "a bygone time with the very present that is flitting away from us," prolonging a legend, to continue with Hawthorne's words, "from an epoch now gray in the distance, down into our own broad sunlight, and bringing along with it some of its legendary mist." As the mood is timeless and as the idiom is only that of thought and action, Mr. Hergesheimer, like Hawthorne, speaks in the language of his own day, in the perennial idiom of good English, abjuring the archaisms of the past. And the perennial idioms of life are expressed, partly in fine capacities to enjoy the best of life's sights and sounds, and partly in finer capacities for strength and constancy and courage.

Like Hawthorne again, he seldom forgets that "the very present is flitting away from us." It is an inevitable feeling for characters whose eyes are focused on the past. There is a minor key prevailing through his pages, the key sounded on the entrance of Jasper Penny, "conscious of the invidious beginning weariness of accumulating years," and on the entrance of Richard Bale, just past thirty but weary of the strife of years, aware that life has but the frail duration of a flower, and that the finest quality of a flower is its fragrance. To Jasper and Richard a renewal of youth is offered and mockingly withheld. The hand of the past is on them both as the present slips away.—PERCY H. BOYNTON, "Joseph Hergesheimer," *More Contemporary Americans*, 1927, pp. 139–44

Joe, when he cares to, talks as well as he writes, with a quite spontaneous choice of words sufficiently accurate to be taken by a stenographer as they are spoken by him. He employs the vernacular as frequently as anyone else, but in serious conversation or letter-writing he is as impatient as Elinor Wylie with vulgar or misapplied phraseology. Once, in reference to a friend of ours, he wrote: "A letter came . . . this morning, containing, among other things, the word comfy," and I could see through the written lines Joe's black countenance. No one that I know smiles quite so radiantly or looks so completely cross. He has a pure passion for words, their beauty, their ugliness, and their fitness. "Please keep every lovely [flower] name you think of for me," he once wrote me when I was in the country in Virginia. He cannot endure what he calls solemn conversation. "Solemn," by the way, is the word wherewith he utterly damns a person. He prefers frank frivolity to solemnity, but his ideal person is, in his own words, by turns "lightly serious or seriously light." "There are two courses of conduct superior to all others," he once wrote me: "to be profoundly serious with charm, or to be as charming as a fresh muslin gown very profoundly." He loves every smooth, gleaming surface of life and joyously adopts each new form which luxury can assume. Mencken, whose habits are of the simplest, is constantly diverted by this trait of Joe's, and once wrote me when his friend was travelling gaily and expensively through the Far West: "I gather that Hergesheimer is touring the country clubs, exhibiting his solid gold dress coat, and shooting dice to pay his expenses." Again he said, when Joe's purely perfect American house was mentioned: "Hergy belongs in a Chinese cosy corner, draped in scarlet." The Dower House, his home in West Chester, is a complete disclosure of Joe's double soul. In him, again as in Elinor Wylie, run two parallel strains. An almost Oriental passion for colour, for softness, for the feel of fabrics, for every fine scent, exquisite taste, and elaborate form, resulting in books like *San Cristóbal de la Habana* and *The Bright Shawl;* and an even more dominating passion for the clean austerity of an earlier America, for a Greek clarity of outline, for a beauty not to be physically grasped, resulting in books like *Linda Condon* and *Quiet Cities.* Early America is Joe's land of refuge, his Utopia, as Poictesme is Mr. Cabell's. "That which was lovely and is lost" is the sum of his desires. Existent, attainable loveliness leaves him disappointed and slightly annoyed. He goes with the zest of a child to parties, in the spirit that the Germans have best described as "immer kindlich," hoping perpetually to find something really magical, something æsthetically satisfying; but he says, in exasperation: "I never do. It's never there." He returns always to his close green gardens, his quiet white walls, his old stone house, filled with calmly flawless eighteenth-century form in all its furnishings. And there he finds again a temporary contentment in another addition to his long list of beautiful books. Books not exactly romantic, not exactly realistic, not exactly ironic, not in the least philosophic; books which beautifully and perfectly present the lovely surfaces, the decorative and rather heartless persons who most engage him; persons who move in an ordered, ornamental land, not exactly early America, not exactly modern America, actually, as W. L. George once said, "Hergesheimer Land."—EMILY CLARK, "Joseph Hergesheimer," *Innocence Abroad*, 1931, pp. 104–6

General

Unlike Mrs. Wharton he had a rather austere childhood, and this bred in him, not loyalty to an aristocratic ideal, but an ambition for beauty and luxury. At first his longing for beauty partly redeemed his work, despite the turgidity of his style. In *The Lay Anthony* he succeeded in suggesting the irrational but by no means unappealing idealism of a young boy, just as a little later in *Linda Condon* he gave some substance to his vision of the desirable but unattainable woman. This work was romantic, but frankly and freshly and not unpleasantly so. But even such mild magic could not keep long its potency. Hergesheimer's love of luxury overcame his love of beauty, and his aspirations reduced themselves to a formula. In *The Three Black Pennys* and *Java Head* he had projected his romantic visions into the past, and in portions of these novels, as in some of his short stories, he suggested a kind of life in which beauty played a conspicuous part. But even here he frequently yielded to the temptation to find his beauty in mere ornamentation, in the houses, the furnishings, the clothes. This zeal for decoration dominated *The Bright Shawl* and *Balisand* and had become an obsession by the time he wrote *Quiet Cities*. In the novels of contemporary life, such as *Cytherea* and *The Party Dress*, his passion for physical luxury nakedly revealed itself as simply the vulgar longing of the idle rich for conspicuous waste. His stories, many of which were printed in *The Saturday Evening Post*, might almost have appeared as part and parcel of the magazine's advertising. To this, then, his romantic dreams reduced themselves—to a gross satisfaction in expensive dresses, rare wines, and ornate furniture. His pessimism, which at first remotely recalled the dignity of Conrad's philosophy, became an obvious pose, an attempt to mask his porky complacence.—GRANVILLE HICKS, "Two Roads," *The Great Tradition*, 1933, pp. 219–20

Hergesheimer is one of the most difficult of our novelists to evaluate fairly. It would be absurd to say that he cannot create character, yet there are scenes in even his best novels in which the people seem altogether unreal. Perhaps the fundamental difficulty is that individual character does not seem very important to him; he "didn't much believe in the triumph or importance of the individual"; even the Pennys were to him like the notes in a piece of music, and valued individually in quite that way. He even persuaded himself that not to be interested in the individual was somehow "classical." Hergesheimer admitted frankly that he made his characters up to embody the qualities he admired but failed to find in himself—calmness, fidelity, hardness of body, "a distinguished resolution in body and mind," and, in the case of women, "a warm rich vitality of being." The women especially were created for his "personal reassurance and pleasure." But "the business of being a woman is universal and not individual." Lee Randon does not even remember Savina as an individual, once she has served his need—and destroyed him.

Hergesheimer's admirers insist that he is, above all things, the novelist of spiritual integrity, and there are books, like *Java Head*, of which this is certainly true. The influence of Conrad seems to have been important at this point. Others find themselves so stifled and smothered in fabrics, so worn out with physical sensation that values disappear altogether. Many years ago, Fanny Butcher spoke of his "five-sensitive writing."

Some of this carries over from Hergesheimer's experience as a painter. He has "used words precisely in the way I had used colors, striving for the same effects." But this is not all. And the $500,000 that *The Saturday Evening Post* paid him for his stories seems to have made it easier for him to become seduced by the luxury which intellectually he can only despise.

Hergesheimer does not like the age in which his lot has been cast; he may record its infidelities but he does not approve of them; he cannot rid himself of the notion that values were lost somehow with a simpler, less sophisticated America. Yet, in a sense, his love for this older America is a sentimental love, for he has no real anchors in the past. He clings tenaciously, as he himself has observed, only to its more superficial aspects: its faith is gone, but he remembers "the hour of its supper" and "its amazing breakfasts." Unfortunately a man cannot fend off a welter of materialism with even the finest and rarest antiques; neither is Duncan Phyfe one of the names given among men whereby we must be saved.

There is a deep division here in Hergesheimer himself. He disliked the "literary pathology" and the "arrogant materialism" of his time, but he did not like the things the libertarians were attacking much better; his antipuritanism, his negative reaction to his narrow religious upbringing delivered him over to the very forces that were destroying the things he loved. As time went on, he felt himself out of harmony with his contemporaries; he was even shocked by them, despite his "not inconsiderable experience." He did not wish to reform them, but he accepted himself as having dated, and he wanted to rest.

Art itself began to retreat from him; indeed, he was getting "damned sick" of art. He had never been able to read many of the English novelists, but in *The Lay Anthony* he had gone out of his way to call "Heart of Darkness" the most beautiful story of our time. In later years he lost the ability to read Conrad; he seems to have lost the ability to read all novelists except his friend and admirer Cabell. He had tried to cling to values in fiction even after they had grown dim in life. When he wrote *The Three Black Pennys*, he still saw that, in a satisfying work of art at least, consequences must follow Howat's adultery; he could not have been sure of that at a later date. *Linda Condon* seems to be a study in spiritual experience; actually it means only that, through Pleydon's adoration, Linda has somehow had her beauty perpetuated—surely not a very worthy goal to which to dedicate one's life! By 1931 Hergesheimer saw the novel itself as "dying." Three years later, at fifty-four, he published his last book.—EDWARD WAGENKNECHT, "In the Second Decade," *Cavalcade of the American Novel*, 1952, pp. 309–11

H. L. MENCKEN

From "Four Makers of Tales"

Prejudices: Fifth Series

1926, pp. 42–49

This gentleman, like Conrad, has been slated very waspishly because his English is sometimes in contempt of Lindley Murray. Once, a few years back, a grammarian writing in the *New Republic* formally excommunicated him for it. A number of his offending locutions were cited, all of them, it must be admitted, instantly recognizable as pathological and against God by any suburban schoolma'm. *Soit!* The plain truth is that Hergesheimer, when it comes to the ultimate delicacies of English grammar, is an ignoramus, as he is when it comes to the niceties of Swedenborgian theology. I doubt that he could tell a noun in the nominative case from a noun in the objective. But neither could any other man who writes as well as he does. Such esoteric knowledge is the exclusive possession of grammarians, whose pride in it runs in direct ratio its inaccuracy, unimportance and imbecility. English grammar as a science thus takes its place with phrenology and the New Thought: the more a grammarian knows of it, the less he is worth listening to. Mastering such blowsy nonsense is one thing, and writing sound English is quite another thing, and the two achievements seem to be impossible to the same man. As Anatole France once remarked, nearly all first-rate writers write "bad French"—or "bad English." Joseph Conrad did. France himself did. Dreiser does. Henry James did. Dickens did. Shakespeare did. Thus Hergesheimer need not repine. He is sinful, but in good company. He writes English that is "bad," but also English that is curiously musical, fluent, chromatic, various and caressing. There is in even the worst of his *Saturday Evening Post* novelettes for Main Street a fine feeling for the inner savor of words—a keen ear for their subtler and more fragile harmonies. In *Cytherea*, which I like beyond all his works—even beyond *The Three Black Pennys* and *Java Head*—they are handled in so adept and ingenious a way, with so much delicacy and originality, that it is no wonder they offer an intolerable affront to pedagogues.

This novel, as I say, seems to me to be the best that Hergesheimer has yet done. His best writing is in it, and his best observation. What interests him fundamentally is the conflict between the natural impulses of men and women and the conventions of the society that they are parts of. The struggles he depicts are not between heroes and villains, dukes and peasants, patriots and spies, but between the desire to be happy and the desire to be respected. It is, perhaps, a tribute to the sly humor of God that whichever way the battle goes, the result is bound to be disastrous to the man himself. If, seeking happiness in a world that is jealous of it and so frowns upon it, he sacrifices the good will of his fellow men, he always finds in the end that happiness is not happiness at all without it. And if, grabbing the other horn of the dilemma, he sacrifices the free play of his instincts to the respect of those fellow men, he finds that he has also sacrificed his respect for himself. Hergesheimer is no seer. He does not presume to solve the problem; he merely states it with agreeable variations and in the light of a compassionate irony. In *Cytherea* it takes the ancient form of the sexual triangle—old material, but here treated, despite the underlying skepticism, with a new illumination. What we are asked to observe is a marriage in which all the customary causes follow instead of precede their customary effects. To the eye of the world, and even, perhaps, to the eye of the secondary figures in it, the Randon-Grove affair is no more than a standard-model adultery, orthodox in its origin and in its course. Lee Randon, with an amiable and faithful wife, Fanny, at home in Eastlake, Pa., in the County-Club Belt, with two charming children at her knee, goes to the hell-hole known as New York, falls in love with the sinister Mrs. Savina Grove, and forthwith bolts with her to Cuba, there to encounter a just retribution in the form of her grotesque death. But that is precisely what does *not* happen—that is, interiorly. Savina actually has little more to do with the flight of Randon than the Pullman Company which hauls him southward. It is already inevitable when he leaves Eastlake for New York, almost unaware of her existence. Its springs are to be sought in the very normalcy that it so profoundly outrages. He is the victim, like Fanny, his wife, of a marriage that has turned upon and devoured itself.

Hergesheimer was never more convincing than in his anatomizing of this *débâcle*. He is too impatient, and perhaps too fine an artist, to do it in the conventional realistic manner of piling up small detail. Instead he launches into it with a bold sagittal section, and at once the play of forces becomes comprehensible. What ails Randon, in brief, is that he has a wife who is a shade too good. Beautiful, dutiful, amiable, virtuous, yes. But not provocative enough—not sufficiently the lady of scarlet in the chemise of snowy white. Worse, a touch of stupid blindness is in her: she can see the honest business man, but she can't see the romantic lurking within him. When Randon, at a country-club dance, sits out a hoe-down with some flashy houri on the stairs, all that Fanny can see in it is a vulgar matter, like kissing a chambermaid behind the door. Even when Randon brings home the doll, Cytherea, and gives it a place of honor in their house, and begins mooning over it strangely, she is unable to account for the business in any terms save those of transient silliness. The truth is that Cytherea is to Randon what La Belle Ettarre is to Cabell's Felix Kennaston—his alter-flame in a dun world, his visualization of the unattainable, his symbol of what might have been. In her presence he communes secretly with the outlaw hidden beneath the chairman of executive committees, the gypsy concealed in the sound Americano. One day, bent upon God's work (specifically, upon breaking up a nefarious affair between a neighboring Rotarian and a moving-picture lady), he encounters the aforesaid Savina Grove, accidentally brushes her patella with his own, get an incandescent glare in return, discovers to his horror that she is the living image of Cytherea—and ten days later is aboard the Key West Express with her, bound for San Cristóbal de la Habana, and the fires eternal.

A matter, fundamentally, of coincidence. Savina, too, has her Cytherea, though not projected into a doll. She too has toiled up the long slope of a flabby marriage, and come at last to the high crags where the air is thin, and a sudden giddiness may be looked for. To call the thing a love affair, in the ordinary sense, is rather fantastic; its very endearments are forced and mawkish. What Randon wants is not more love, but an escape from the bonds and penalties of love—a leap into pure adventure. And what Savina wants, as she very frankly confesses, is the same thing. If a concrete lover must go with it, then that lover must be everything that the decorous William Loyd Grove is not—violent, exigent, savage, inordinate, even a bit gross. I doubt that Savina gets her wish any more than Randon gets his. Good business men make but indifferent Grand Turks, even when they are in revolt: it is the tragedy of Western civilization. And there is no deliverance from the bonds of habit and appearance, even with a mistress. Ten days after he reaches Havana, Randon is almost as securely married as he was at Eastlake. Worse, Eastlake itself reaches out its long arm and begins to punish him, and Savina with him. The conventions of Christendom, alas, are not to be spat upon. Far back in the Cuban hinterland, in a squalid little sugar town, it is a photograph of Fanny that gives a final touch of gruesomeness to the drama of Randon and Savina. There, overtaken in her sin by that banal likeness of the enemy she has never seen, she dies her preposterous death. An ending profoundly ironical. A curtain that gives a final touch of macabre humor to a tale that, from first to last, is full of the spirit of high comedy. Hergesheimer never devised one more sardonically amusing, and he never told one with greater skill.

The reviewers, contemplating it, were shocked by his hedonism in trivialities—his unctuous manner of recording the flavor of a drink, the sheen of a fabric, the set of a skirt, the furnishings of a room. In all that, I suppose, they saw something Babylonish, and against the Constitution. But this hedonism is really as essential a part of Hergesheimer as moral purpose is part of a Puritan. He looks upon the world, not as a trial of virtue, but as a beautiful experience—in part, indeed, as a downright voluptuous experience. If it is elevating to the soul to observe the fine colors of a sunset, then why is it not quite as elevating to observe the fine colors of a woman's hair, the silk of her frock, a piece of old mahogany, a Jack Rose cocktail? Here it is not actually Hergesheimer's delight in beauty that gives offense, but his inability to differentiate between the beauty that is also the good and the true, and the beauty that is simply beauty. As for me, I incline to go with him in his heresy. It constitutes a valuable antidote to the moral obsession which still hangs over American letters, despite the collapse of the Puritan *Kultur*. It still seems a bit foreign and bizarre, but that is because we have yet to achieve a complete emancipation from the International Sunday-school Lessons. In *Cytherea*, as in *Java Head*, it gives a warm and exotic glow to the narrative. That narrative is always recounted, not by a moralist, but by an artist. He knows how to give an episode color and reality by the artful use of words and the images that they bring up—how to manage the tempo, the play of light, the surrounding harmonies. This investiture is always as much a part of his story as his tale itself. So is his English style, so abhorrent to grammarians. When he writes a sentence that is a bit artificial and complex, it is because he is describing something that is itself a bit artificial and complex. When he varies his rhythms suddenly and sharply, it is not because he is unable to write in the monotonous sing-song of a rhetoric professor, but because he doesn't want to write that way. Whatever such a man writes is *ipso facto* good English. It is not for pedagogues to criticise it, but to try to comprehend it and teach it. The delusion to the contrary is the cause of much folly.

J. B. PRIESTLEY

From "Joseph Hergesheimer"

London Mercury, May 1926, pp. 63–70

II

He began as a painter and still brings to literature a painter's eye, delighted with colours and shapes and textures, the more luxurious the better. At times he can be positively cloying, burying his people under a heap of bright stuffs and dazzling bric-à-brac. Opening his *Linda Condon* at random, we are asked to remark, in two pages, "morocco beauty-cases and powder-boxes," "slipper and garter buckles extravagant in exquisite metals and workings," "limousines with dove-coloured upholstery and crystal vases of maidenhair fern and moss-roses," "black chocolates from painted boxes ruffled in rose silk," "a restaurant of Circassian walnut and velvet carpets," "eggs elaborate with truffles and French pastry." We begin to feel slightly dizzy and sick. But in such passages the still-life painter and the lover of mere luxury and magnificence join hands, with a somewhat unfortunate result. For the most part, however, the painter in him only directs his attention to the play of light and shadow, the shape and colour, bidding him see how a "twilight like blue dust sifted into the shallow fold of the thickly wooded hills," how "the Spanish oaks were hung with patches of wine red, the sumach was brilliant in the darkening undergrowth," how "a pattern of wild geese, flying low and unconcerned above the hills, wavered against the serene, ashen evening." But his passion for these things, though born with the painter, is really a literary one, like that of the earlier Keats. This delight of the eye is an essential part of the world he creates, and the beautiful things in it are not merely so much captivating form and colour but so many centres round which there thickly cluster all manner of associations, sentiments, memories, and are too, if you will, symbols, exquisitely embodying an idea.

It is easy to see why he is in danger of being dismissed as "decorative." This appeal to the eye, this richly brocaded texture in his presentation, seems to exist independently of the story, the drama, that is being unfolded. Thus, no matter how great the crisis in his narrative, the murmurous flow of his descriptive prose goes on, poured out like thick cream; the reader is asked to notice this patch of colour, that exquisite shape; and there is no attempt, or little attempt, to present the scene as it filters through the agonised minds of the actors in it. The longest story of the three in *Gold and Iron* begins with a description of a young lawyer sitting in his office. He has arrived at a crisis, for he has suddenly realised that so far he has been a failure, and that he has no alternative but to begin his life all over again. There he sits in despair:

> He was staring sombrely, with an immobile, thin, dark countenance, at the white plaster wall before him. Close by his right shoulder a window opened on a tranquil street, where the vermilion maple buds were splitting; and beyond the window a door was ajar on a plank sidewalk. Some shelves held crumbling yellow calf-bound volumes, a few new, with glazed black labels; at the back was a small cannon stove, with an elbow of pipe let into the plaster; a large steel engraving of Chief Justice Marshall hung on the wall; and in a farther corner a careless pile of paper, folded in dockets or tied with casual string, was collecting a grey film of neglect. A small banjo clock, with a brass-railed pediment, and an elongated picture in colour of the Exchange at Manchester, traced the regular, monotonous passage of minutes into hours.

There is certainly no trace of subjective treatment here. Faced with this cool determined picture-making on the part of the narrator, we find it difficult to realise that the man there is in a mood of utter despair. What are vermilion maple buds and the rest to him? Make us realise his state of mind, we demand, before worrying us with yellow calf-bound volumes and small banjo clocks and other things in which there is no trace of human misery.

Yet though this practice of heavily brocading his narrative with description runs through all his work, we are not left with any sense of failure in their drama. There is something false in the opening of that story mentioned above, and there we do feel that description and drama are at war with one another, but that is because the story is not typical of its author. We feel that it has not been primarily conceived as a "setting" as most of the others have. There was not present in the initial conception that crinoline-candelabra-bright shawl element, the brilliant intriguing surface, the visual feast, we noticed in connection with the Cuban romance and discovered to be an essential part of the world he creates. With him there is no "story" first and then "setting" afterwards. The two arrive together, and this richness of texture in the narrative is as much a part of it as the drama, and indeed perhaps more. He has told us that "houses and night and hills were often more vivid to me than the people in or out of them," and he might have added furniture and clothes and curtains and jewelled ornaments, whatever lovingly caught his eye and made him dream, to the list of things more vivid. When we find him, in his solitary travel book, wandering through the streets of Havana that he pictures so artfully, brooding over the bright images before him, beginning to dream, we are at least half-way towards his fiction. One step further and the dream is dramatised, around some central mood of the dreamer, himself turned into its chief personage (though still remaining the painter of the scene), a few other figures added, and the story is before us.

He has not only travelled in space for his settings but also in time, in particular to the eighteenth century and the middle of the nineteenth. From all these voyages he has returned rich in spoil, and there has been something like genius in his choice of places and periods; the Massachusetts coast during its great sailing days or rather (and better) at the end of those days, in *Java Head*; the three glimpses, one eighteenth-century, one mid-nineteenth, and one present-day, of the Pennsylvanian iron fields, in *The Three Black Pennys*; the Havana of the 'Eighties, in *The Bright Shawl*; the late eighteenth-century Virginia, in *Balisand*. Thus he has succeeded—and it is no small part of his accomplishment, though he does not appear to have been given much credit for it—in exploiting the picturesque possibilities of America, dowering the past life of his own and neighbouring states with a romantic charm and a glamour excelling those of his fellow authors who still laboured at romances of medieval Florence or Pompadour's France. America has had, of course, an historical-romantic past for her novelists for some time, but now, thanks to Hergesheimer, she has achieved an æsthetic-romantic past in fiction, a notable step forward for her and one that will probably have very important consequences in her literature. There are two motives for ever in operation behind the writing of fiction: one is the desire to escape from the life about one, the other is the desire to criticise that life. In some novelists, the desire to escape is easily the predominant motive; in others criticism takes precedence; and in a few there is something like a balance. This æsthetic-romantic past obviously provides the American novelist with an excellent new method of escape, for which purpose Hergesheimer has made use of it. But it also, indirectly and more subtly, provides him with a method, an oblique but effective method, of criticism, for which purpose again Hergesheimer has made use of it.

IV

. . . He is one of those writers (and perhaps Thackeray is the best example of them) who are able, without any apparent effort, to present growth and decay, the ebb and flow of time, itself a dimension, as it were, of the narrative; who do not, as so many lesser writers do, present a static scene and then when they wish to show the changes of time jerk the whole thing forward in a most irritating and unconvincing fashion. Hardly anywhere in modern fiction will you find the ebbing out of time, the slow changes and fading of life, so cunningly suggested as they are in *The Three Black Pennys*, *Linda Condon*, and *Balisand*. It would be interesting too, to return to the two motives of escape and criticism (or revolt) and to see how Hergesheimer, apparently all intent upon the first, has also provided the second with an outlet, so that while he might appear to be one of the few detached artists among a horde of shouting rebels, actually his own little revolt, indirect, oblique, though it may be, is one of the most effective. There is as much damaging criticism of the "hundred per cent American" tradition implied in these highly coloured romances as there is in any of the so-called novels of revolt. Nor would it be difficult to show that deliberate reaction against that tradition is responsible for much of the weakness of Hergesheimer's attitude, its narrowness and deliberate over-emphasis of certain aspects of life. But with the adequacy and value of the romantic-æsthetic philosophy of life we are fortunately not concerned here, though we are at liberty to point out that there are signs that Hergesheimer, whose *Balisand* is only less successful than one or two of the earlier novels because it tries to do much more, is now broadening the basis of that philosophy. This means that in the future he is less likely to be in danger, always the danger of humourless æsthetes, of periodical collapse, of suddenly appearing to us not as a conscientious and very considerable literary artist but as a fatuous little man solemnly fussing about gilt clocks and shimmering underclothes. And even so far he has the satisfaction of knowing that he is one of the handful of modern novelists who have widened the scope of the art of fiction, for while he has given his narratives a purely objective, solidly rounded appearance, leaving them as vivid in the memory as a real experience, he has also made his fiction as subjective in essence as a lyric. He has been equally successful with both the brocade and the dream, leaving the one shining in our hands while the other goes filtering through our minds, our imagination being thus doubly captured for a while by his vision of life.

JOHN HERSEY

1914–

John Richard Hersey spent most of his childhood in China. He was born in Tientsin on June 17, 1914. His father, Roscoe Monroe Hersey, was a Y.M.C.A. secretary in China. His mother, Grace Baird Hersey, was a missionary. Hersey spoke Chinese, and traveled around the world with his mother. At the age of ten he came to the United States, where he attended Hotchkiss School, then Yale. He took his B.A. in 1936 and studied for a year at Clare College, Cambridge. On returning to America Hersey served for one year as personal secretary to Sinclair Lewis. In 1940 he married Frances Ann Cannon, with whom he later had four children.

During World War II Hersey worked as a war correspondent for *Time* and *Life* magazines. The material for his journalism also served as the basis for his novels. His first book, *Men on Bataan*, was published in 1942. Two more war novels appeared in the next two years, and A *Bell for Adano* (1944) received the Pulitzer prize in 1945. The highly acclaimed *Hiroshima* was published by the *New Yorker* in 1946, and then in book form. Later works include *The Wall* (1950), *The Marmot Drive* (1953), *The War Lover* (1959), *The Child Buyer* (1960), and *The Writer's Craft* (1974).

In the fifties Hersey renewed his association with Yale University—this time as a fellow—and continued his prolific output of journalistic novels and essays. His first marriage ended in 1958. A short time later Hersey married Barbara Day Addams Kaufman. They have one child.

A Bell for Adano, by John Hersey, makes very good reading in its capable and wholly unpretentious fashion. It is the story of Major Victor Joppolo, an American of Italian descent who, for a few weeks last summer, was the senior civil-affairs officer and acting mayor of a Sicilian town. He was a good man and he did his best for the people of Adano, feeding them, teaching them democracy and even finding a new bell for their city hall; but he came into conflict with an essentially Prussian major-general, bearing some faint resemblance to Old Blood and Guts. The result was that Joppolo was ordered back to Algiers and probably lost his commission. Except for a wistful little love affair, that is the whole framework of the novel; it is filled out with the incidents of daily life in a town occupied by American forces. Some of these are extremely moving. It would be hard to forget Father Pensovecchio's first sermon to his congregation after the town was taken, and still harder to forget the Italian prisoners of war returning to their homes:

> They did not break into a run. Their happiness was terrifying; they walked slowly toward their women. . . . The women ran toward the men. There was equal happiness on both sides, it just happened that most of the men knew their women would be there, whereas some of the women were not sure that their men would be there. That was the difference.

Often you wonder how it is that Hersey knows his Sicilians so well, considering that he was born in China and has done most of his reporting in the Far East (he is the author of *Men on Bataan* and *Into the Valley*). He came to Sicily with the invading army and stayed there hardly longer than Major Joppolo. On the other hand, he is a good observer, and you suspect him of filling in the gaps with his literary memories. His Sicilians sometimes act like John Steinbeck's *paisanos,* so that you aren't quite sure whether you are in Adano or Tortilla Flat. His style also has overtones of Steinbeck—not to mention Hemingway, as in the passage quoted above—but he is saved by being a competent craftsman in his own right. Notwithstanding its self-imposed limitations of time and knowledge, *A Bell for Adano* is an entertaining story, a candid report from behind the lines and an effective tract. To demand that it be a soundly constructed novel as well would be asking too much.—MALCOLM COWLEY, "Novels after the War," *NR,* Feb. 14, 1944, p. 216

By now, you have doubtless heard that last week's *New Yorker* devoted its entire space to one subject for the first time in the history of that periodical. The subject is the atomic bombing of Hiroshima; the author is John Hersey; and we understand the magazine sold out on most newsstands within a few hours of its appearance. If so, the public showed discernment. Hersey's piece is certainly one of the great classics of the war; if it is eligible for a Pulitzer Prize and doesn't get it, the judges should go and take a Rorschach.

Everyone has read the statistics on what happened at Hiroshima (statistics which Hersey says gravely underestimated the actual damage). But figures have no grappling hooks with which to take hold of dim human imagination. With the simplicity of genius, this author had the idea of doing what many other journalists should have thought of long ago: he has reduced the story of the bombing to its effect on the lives of six people in Hiroshima, and their relatives and friends: Miss Toshiko Sasaki, a clerk in the East Asia Tin Works; Dr. Masakazu Fujii, a physician; Mrs. Hatsuyo Nakamura, impoverished widow of a tailor killed in battle; Father Wilhelm Kleinsorge, a German missionary priest; Dr. Terufumi Sasaki; and the Reverend Mr. Kiyoshi Tanimoto, pastor of a Japanese Methodist Church.

Hersey, with indefatigable research, and the great abilities demonstrated in his earlier war books, *Into the Valley* and *A Bell for Adano,* has sorted out the personal experiences of each of these people and of those with whom they were in close contact during and after the bombing. In a series of vignettes, he tells where each was at 15 minutes past 8 A.M. on August 6, 1945, when the bomb went off, and what happened to them during the minutes, hours, days and weeks thereafter. He moves from one personal narrative to another so that the time sequence of all six stories is carried forward simultaneously. The general effect is a little like that of Thornton Wilder's *The Bridge of San Luis Rey;* except that Hersey's story is true and indescribably tragic, not only for Hiroshima but for the world which must live henceforth under the shadow of the threat of more bombings of the same character, though far more serious since, as he reports, the Hiroshima bomb was a little one, of uranium, and today we can make bigger, plutonium ones. . . .

Hersey does no editorializing, passes no judgments; he does not try to say whether the atomic bombing of Japan was justified, or to compare its results with, for instance, the sack of Nanking. He just tells the story. If we could be sure the Hiroshima and Nagasaki atomic bombs were the last ever to fall on an inhabited place, we could read it as we read of the eruptions of Krakatoa and Mt. Pelee. It is the grim conviction so many of us feel that what happened in Japan may be a foretaste of what is in store for many others, including ourselves, that gives Hersey's words their terrible import. —BRUCE BLIVEN, *NR,* Sept. 9, 1946, pp. 300–301

Since it will leave newspaper reviewers in a state of superior bewilderment, this novel is likely to be tagged a parable; I think it more accurate to call it a catastrophe. About the best that can be said for *The Marmot Drive* is that Mr. Hersey has made an intense effort to shake off those journalistic mannerisms which marred his previous novels. But he has replaced them with a large repertoire of literary mannerisms, of the sort one finds in novels about crises in the suburbs. The two most dangerous temptations for ambitious novelists today are Rich Prose and Symbolism, and Mr. Hersey is in a fair way to having succumbed to both.

Simply as writing *The Marmot Drive* is remarkable. Mr. Hersey's poetic style: a young man laughs "like a concupiscent rooster who feels his loins stir as the earth rolls to morning." Mr. Hersey's clever style: "Eben's mother . . . a woman with a face that seemed to be compounded of skim milk and strained virtue." Mr. Hersey's caustic style: his heroine, flirting with the wrong man, tries "with quick dry talk to make a eunuch of [him]." Mr. Hersey's contemplative style: "There was a mole on the side of his chin, a small black badge as impossible to hide or forget as grief." Mr. Hersey's philosophical style: "The houses were gathered together in townhood, but they seemed to insist upon their separateness, their privacy. . . ."

The central figure of the novel is Hester, a New York girl, bright, lively, restless. One summer weekend she visits the Connecticut town of Tunxis, where the family of her boy friend, Eben, is to look her over. Thus far the relationship between Hester and Eben has been, to her sense of things, alarmingly chaste, and she reaches Tunxis in a condition of aggressive uneasiness. Then begins her trial, the exposure of a fundamentally innocent mind to those local hatreds and passions which go so deep into the past of the town that a stranger caught among them can only suffer in silence.

For some years Tunxis has been pestered by invasions of marmots, and now Matthew Avered, Eben's father and the

Town Selectman, proposes a drive to destroy the animals. When the ceremony-chase is over, few marmots have been found, which suggests that the threat may have been imaginary, but meanwhile the more destructive impulses of the hunters have been released. The elder Avered has come dangerously close to making a pass at Hester—his restraint disappoints her; and at the end, when the townsmen propose to give him "a light public whippin'" as scourge for his private misdemeanor, he meekly accepts it in the mistaken belief that he is being punished for his public failure. Appalled, Hester flees, overcome by a sense of failure.

Mr. Hersey apparently had some symbolic scheme in mind when he wrote this story. At first I thought it might be a political symbolism: the marmots suddenly become aggressively imperialist, one Tunxis citizen suggests that "the trouble had begun . . . during the last century, when the railroad had been put in" and adds that "they calculate Tunxis is on the wane . . . they're movin' in on us." But the not very arresting possibility that Mr. Hersey intends a comment on the times soon loses its force; and when we are told that Aunty Dorcas, a spry thing of ninety-one, has killed a hawk with her own hands (or does she just imagine she has?) we know we are on the familiar, slippery symbolic ground of private impulse, dominating will and—who would dare doubt it?—Good and Evil.

But it hardly matters what the symbolic scheme of the book is, whether an oblique topical reference or a reworking of a Greek myth or anything else. For what is the point of investigating a novel's symbolic dimension or possible moral significance when on the plane of represented life, its play of action and character, it is entirely flimsy and boring? The major characters dissolve into a stream of anxieties and musings, the minor ones are ferociously eccentric; and neither matter.—IRVING HOWE, "Symbolic Suburbia," *NR*, Nov. 16, 1953, p. 17

Mr. Hersey's bland parable of a Yankee engineer's odyssey up the Yangtze ⟨*A Single Pebble*⟩ is, in intent, a simple symbolic tragedy of crossed perspectives, East *vs.* West, both taken at the level of the typical if not the stereotype, both meant to be illuminated when the typical reaches out for the heroic. And why not? If the perspectives are crossed with passion, if the heroism compels assent, if the characters can be themselves beyond the symbolic burdens they happen to carry, common ground—the tragic sense of life firm below the topsoil of culture—is there for the claiming. And this is what Mr. Hersey's action tries to claim, "the sense of elation at the moment of despair," when the dying hero, a dead loss to himself, becomes a great light to others. This is hard, tragic ground, hard to get to, hard to hold, but known unmistakably by its hardness too—the firm action, the bedrock certainty of significant conduct, the sure purchase on passion going *somewhere* yet not quite *anyhow*. Were Mr. Hersey's attempts more modest, his bland and pleasant narrative might do, but it is tragedy that is missing here, the story foundering on a blandness so pervasive—in the characters, in the limpness of perception and the leached ideas, in the stricken fuzziness of his tragic sense and the flatfooted march of his prose—that little more than a husk of tragedy survives. If, at first, we respond, it is to the intimation of the tragic, the feel of a generous and large intent; but in the end, if it is tragedy and not dying falls we require, *A Single Pebble* must seem a disappointing book.

Yet the plot is well-conceived; there is competence in the construction, and the prose, especially in descriptive passages, is capable of power. The story itself is a simple one, narrated by a callow and naïve American engineer whose easy optimism and vague and generous bigotry—he sounds like a mind molded entirely from *Life* editorials—it is the purpose of the action to instruct and mellow. Sent to the Yangtze to look for dam-sites, he goes upstream by junk, and in the course of his trip is brought into close contact with the Chinese who work the river. Slowly he begins to understand the alien river-culture, its tragic waste of human life and effort and the necessary fatalism of the trackers; and this understanding in turn enlarges as the engineer begins to see in the life of the chief tracker, Old Pebble, the possibility of heroism, a life lived with courage in the teeth of a necessity that makes fatalists of ordinary men. Stimulated by his conviction of sympathy, he excitedly unfolds to Old Pebble his vision of a dam; and Old Pebble, recognizing the threat to the way of life of the river and thereby the threat to the honor he has so precariously asserted, destroys himself, falls or slips out of life at the peak of his greatness. His death is, depending upon how you read it, an act of self-sacrifice to the river before the staggering, blasphemous rightness of the engineer's vision, or an act of final heroic self-assertion, beyond the comprehension of men of meaner motives. The engineer, understanding at last the sacrificial intent of Old Pebble's act, turns in his report, only to be branded as impractical by his firm.

The crucial difficulty here is not so much with the moral underpinnings of the tragedy, but in the absence of particularity, the failure of the tragedy to declare itself in particular lives, lives with precise motives and purposes, coming via passion on bigger purposes up to the point of heroism. Particularity here is swamped in symbolism, and the symbolic apparatus is particularly murky in the case of Old Pebble and his death. Pebble's halo is the heroic; he is clearly marked off—in size, generosity, courage and passion—from the fatalistic trackers. Yet the central act of the book—his death—is dark, indeed, inexplicable as sacrifice really, for it is hard to see any earthly good to this sacrifice; and if he stumbles merely, why, this is worse. Heroes die for hopes, or reasons, or because they must; Old Pebble *might* die to save his honor, but his honor suffers no immediate threat; and he *might* die to convert the engineer, to demonstrate by the careless grandeur of his gesture by both his insignificance and his value.

But he appears to die because Mr. Hersey's novel requires a death, some gesture that will mellow with *lacrimae rerum* the Luce-mind of this engineer. And Old Pebble must get bad marks for his knowledge of men, if he hopes that this dark way of dying will register rightly on the engineer's dullheadedness. Which is to say that Mr. Hersey's novel works backward, not forward; works from a notion of tragedy as the piety that goes with a lump in the throat and builds toward it, syllogistically, rather than following significant passion to its unknown terminus. And similarly with Old Pebble's death; for Mr. Hersey seems to me to have confused the meaning of heroism with the hero's motives: the resonance of heroic death *is* big, meaningful but also a mystery, but God help the would-be hero whose motives are a mystery. Because Old Pebble dies for no good reason, it is hard to know the meaning of his death or to accept the significance Mr. Hersey wants us to place upon it. The consequences upon the engineer, of course, supply the answer, but we recognize a put-up job: underneath the sluggish perceptions of this slowpoke engineer beats the heart of an amateur Buddhist.

If the tragedy is *a priori* and limp, the ideas on which the novel rests are essentially pieties, made amiable by apparent candor and humility, but limp and without relevance to the action. Thus the progress of the engineer's conversion is contrived more by passive observation than by action, its stages marked by symbolic gestures which evade, without reinforcing, the novelist's work. The most crippling pieties, however, are those which derive from public life—the journalistic drive in Mr. Hersey which allows his novel to slide constantly away from public life without ever becoming political either, but a kind of UNESCO miracle-play inculcating tolerance.

The characters get short shrift. Thus the engineer never achieves anything resembling a personality: identity has been usurped by Mr. Hersey's need for a public American of the generous, open-minded, forward-looking, and now tragedy-requiring stereotype. If Old Pebble alone survives as a character, I suspect it is because Mr. Hersey's mystique of heroism saves him from being cut from the public cloth. In compensation for so much publicity, Mr. Hersey introduces a little love, but love is as limp as the language of the novel, without power to affect the tragedy and designed to sustain the illusion that these characters are capable of private emotions too.

In short, a bland book, generous in intent, but everywhere crippled by a debased notion of the tragic and human passion, committed to a sense of dignity it refuses to explore except by mystique. As performance, it belongs to that growing genre of *le roman complaisant*, everyone's Eskimo-wife of a novel trotted out to please all comers and fit all tastes with a tidy pretense of passion. Those who dislike involvement will like it.—WILLIAM ARROWSMITH, "More Bland Than Mellow," *NR*, Aug. 13, 1956, pp. 19–20

As a matter of fact, ⟨Nelson Algren's⟩ *A Walk on the Wild Side* and ⟨Hersey's⟩ *A Single Pebble*, beneath certain striking superficial differences, define a common literary tradition—an important one in America. In both, the role of the imagination has been yielded up on the one hand to documentation and on the other, to sentimentality; in both, the purpose of the novel has been converted from revelation to liberal uplift; in both, the cliché of the common man is celebrated once more, the nobility of the lost memorialized; in both, that is to say, the writer on the make, the man aiming at success, blubbers ceremonially over the virtues of failure.

Hersey's brief fable of an American engineer's trip up the Yangtze in the 1920s and of his learning to respect the wisdom of the illiterate and the heroism of the brutal poor—takes up once more the new revised version of the White Man's Burden: his need to demean himself in order to atone for his former conviction of superiority. I must confess in all frankness that I find Hersey's sentiments so piously unexceptionable as to be intolerable. There is something maddening to ordinary sinners in being told so mildly and firmly that we must be humble, that we must close the gap, that we must bring to the Orient not merely techniques but understanding, and not merely cold understanding but the comprehension which includes a lump in the throat. "Elations with despair," Hersey calls the sentimental indulgence he takes for wisdom, "a palpable ache that somehow gave me comfort." The mild-mannered masochisms behind his high-minded façade, like the more strident sadism behind Algren's politics, ends by making me queasy; though, indeed, I am never sure who should be despised, Hersey for being so pious or me for being appalled by that piety.

I am sure, at any rate, that he is not a novelist; that he writes fiction (or pretends to) only as a strategy for getting his point of view before more people. There is in him no poetry or invention, only the patient, slick exposition of facts, plus the desire to stay on the side of the angels of the latest headline—Warsaw Jews or Japanese peasants or Chinese boatmen. But the writer, as Kierkegaard somewhere pointed out, casts out devils only by the aid of the devil. For reporting of a superior order, however, for restrained but effective descriptions of the wild Yangtze gorges, for little observations on the Chinese character (on a popularizing level) the present small book has a certain value. And yet one surely has the right to feel offended at being told once more that the Chinese find offensive our habit of blowing our noses into little rags that we put into our pockets. This is the standard example one gives to a twelve-year-old in a first "adult" discussion on cultural differences and prejudice. If one does not object to being lectured at like an intelligent adolescent, and finds quite inoffensive the journalist's pretense to be writing a novel (by sketching a love affair in lightly against the moralizing and the scenery) there is no reason why he should not enjoy Hersey's book. . . .

Hersey . . . is stylistically well-behaved, almost impeccable. He sports not a back-alley but a Brooks Brothers prose: the modest well-made style of the man who does not want to call undue attention to himself but feels obliged to live up to a certain aesthetic class standard: "I spent a year preparing myself for the trip. I applied myself to learn Mandarin Chinese and got a fair fluency in it. I read all I could find on the Yangtze; I learned of its mad rise and fall. . . ." These are the sentences of one secure enough to know that even if he begins each monotonous period with a subject, everyone will know he does it because he *wants* to, because he would consider it vulgar to avoid such simplicity. I am, however, helplessly reminded of the Latin satirist's tag: "Desiring to appear simple, he succeeds."—LESLIE FIEDLER, "The Novel in The Post-Political World," *PR*, Summer 1956, pp. 360–63

John Hersey's new novel, *The War Lover*, a Book-of-the-Month Club selection, is, to all intents and purposes, a conventional story that tells of five months in the lives of a Flying Fortress crew stationed in England in 1943. But one soon discovers that the story is only a detailed disguise for a solemn, passionate sermon against war. Moreover, it is the sort of sermon one can hear any Sunday in a thousand up-to-date churches, for, in addition to intoning the standard virtues, it is heavily powdered with Freud. The protagonists in the sermon are Buzz Marrow, the pilot of the plane, and his best friend and co-pilot, Charles Boman. Marrow at first is seen as the invincible warrior. A big, meaty man, he is a superb and fearless flier, a heroic lover, and a swaggering extrovert. Boman is small, quiet, thoughtful, and mouselike. But Marrow, it turns out, is riddled with worms. A coward since childhood, he has coated himself with bluster and seeming virility, which in the end fall away, revealing a maniac who, we were told, would kill death itself were he able. As Marrow shrinks, Boman swells into a cool, honorable, and courageous man who knows that in killing others he is also killing himself. Fortunately, Mr. Hersey pauses here and there to catch his breath. During these respites, we learn what every inch of a B-17 was like (Mr. Hersey shares Hemingway's ability to make the smallest nut and bolt a dramatic event), how it was operated, what marvels the sky affords at twenty thousand feet, what the terrors of air warfare are. Although Mr. Hersey's sermon becomes a bellow toward the end of the book, the novelist in him suddenly gains the upper hand and there is a long description of the plane—crippled and faltering, with one man dead and another missing—coming home from a mission deep in Germany that is, in all its essentials, a remarkably sustained piece of writing. Indeed, it comes very close to persuading one that the book is what its author intended it to be—the war novel to top all war novels.—WHITNEY BALLIETT, *NY*, Dec. 19, 1959, p. 140

Taken as a work of the imagination, as giving any kind of illusion of life or reality, *The Child Buyer* is sheer nightmare. The characters are talkative grotesques, air-filled monsters, bobbing and swaying like balloons in the Macy parade on a windy Thanksgiving. There are no stable objects for the mind to hold to, except when the characters are talking about the natural sciences. The people—or non-people—are consistent only in their general smart-aleckness and in their total collapse into venality at the end of the book. In this respect Hersey's novel is like Friedrich Dürrenmatt's play *The Visit*.

The visitor in this instance is the resourceful agent of a great corporation who arrives in a typical American town to buy a ten-year-old genius named Barry Rudd. The agent, just to make things picturesque, turns up in old-fashioned plus-fours and riding a tiny collapsible motorcycle. In a detective story all the principal characters except the detective have to be unpleasant at the beginning, displaying enough resentment or greed so that any one of them may be supposed capable of the crime. *The Child Buyer* moves in the opposite direction. During much of the action—or talk, rather—some characters, mostly women, appear to be working in the interests of good, humanity, non-conformism, free intelligence. But then at the end, everyone sells out to the agent, this after learning that the corporation will destroy the bright boy as a human being by the most repulsive methods straight out of Huxley's *Brave New World*.

The educators who sound sensible and the educators who talk ridiculous jargon succumb alike in the most unfeeling way. We don't know where we are, or what psychological and social forces can be used to achieve what Hersey wants. These are supposed to be typical parents, teachers, school administrators, PTA officials, all as pictured on Norman Rockwell covers. Certainly we thought that we could count on Dr. Gozar, a woman of boundless energy, apparently utterly devoted to Barry and creativity and the experimental sciences. But she collapses, too. Only Barry Rudd and his tough friend Charles Perkonian retain some dignity. They are an erudite Tom Sawyer and a hipster-tongued Huckleberry Finn alone against the whole world of their elders.

To refer to names this way is to suggest that there are living characters in the novel. But they are all turned into grotesques by the slick, glib, machine-turned talk, varying and interchangeable from character to character. The novel purports to be the bare record of hearings before a state senatorial investigating committee. The author pretends not to describe or narrate, but only to report what was said. The speakers are permitted a few speech eccentricities, corresponding to the agent's plus-fours and collapsible motor cycle. But then—except for Charles Perkonian and an imbecile Senator, who don't know from nuttin'—they launch into long, complex sentences, full of colorful description that is pure Hersey. As a faithful reader of transcripts of Congressional hearings, I have never observed any such oral flights. Dr. Gozar tells the Senators or "a weasel gliding along, like the slippery hope in a thief's heart, beside a stone wall near a hen coop: the gaping mouths of baby robins, uptilted triangles, in a nest in dangerous springtime." Barry gives us two pages on the way trees look in October—"the incredible orange glow of hard maples—like the inside of a Halloween pumpkin when the candle's lit." The committee counsel feels impelled to describe the hotel desk with "its long slab of black-veined soapstone supported on interlacing aluminum M's." There is much fun with polysyllablic humor, with Barry's scientific terms and the jargon of the educationalists. Some of the facts of science which are introduced are very interesting, for instance the sex habits of the stickleback fish.

Seen beyond the torrents of talk, the action of the novel is all on the Tom Sawyer level. Dr. Gozar releases a stink bomb at a PTA meeting; the Child Buyer urges high school kids to throw slops at the Rudd house and break windows; as part of a plot worked out with Charles Perkonian, Barry plays doctor with a little girl in the school principal's storeroom. Of the social and political forces in America we learn as little as we do in *Advise and Consent*, a novel which *The Child Buyer* in many ways resembles.

Of the "ideas" in *The Child Buyer* it is not my place here to speak. But if it is a question of an imaginative encounter with unreal beings living in various kinds of rapport with the real world of nature, then I must say that I feel more at home with Tolkien's hobbits or Bronte's Heathcliffe and Katherine, than I do with my fellow Americans as Mr. Hersey conceives them.—ROBERT GORLAM DAVIS, "An Arrangement in Black and White," *NR*, Oct. 10, 1960, p. 24

Is John Hersey a novelist or a journalist? The question, first asked a quarter of a century ago with the appearance of *Men on Bataan*, has been again raised with each of his succeeding books. Later ones—*The Child Buyer, The Lotus Eater*, for example—have strengthened the impression that his books are a kind of dramatized reporting. *Under the Eye of the Storm* should win over all remaining doubting Thomases.

For here there is not one shred of plot—none of the strong story line that made, say, A *Bell for Adano or The War Lover* wonderfully entertaining reading. Nor are there any true-to-life (or even true-about-life) characters like the heroic Major Joppolo. Indeed, Hersey has brought types rather than flesh-and-blood characters into this book.

Chief among these is Tom Medlar, a medical doctor who "regarded himself as a humanist, a vitalist; he believed in an inner flame, a secret life, intuition, love, whispers in the night, and crushing fallibility." Opposite Tom is Flicker Hamden, self-styled genius of the computer, who "characterized anything Medlar said as 'rickety, antiquated Bergsonian idiocy' and extolled electrical intellectuality and wanted every mortal to be plugged in to a vast cybernetic system of data-sifting, problem-solving, and decision-making."

Then there are the wives: Audrey Medlar and Dottie Hamden—but they are of only passing interest. They serve as foils, for Tom especially, whose inability to understand either of these uncomplicated women reinforces our picture of him as a man hopelessly out of touch with life—and lacking the intellect to realize it.

These four are gathered aboard Tom's ancient yawl *Harmony* for what is hoped to be a leisurely cruise of Block Island Sound. But a hurricane (which had been predicted would pass out to sea far to the south) suddenly strikes. The leisurely cruise then becomes a kind of voyage of discovery as this latter-day Thoreau and this modern man of science try desperately to work together to save *Harmony* and her crew.

By now, of course, symbol hunters will be gleefully off and running. There are just too many obvious signs to slip by unnoticed. One thinks immediately of Melville's notion that a ship is a microcosm of the world; of the great storm that suggests the conflict between Tom and Flicker; of the connotations of the name *Harmony;* and so on.

In the hands of a writer less skillful than Hersey, such clichés would spell complete disaster. But he is, of course, a pro, and his sure, spare style, his characteristic restraint, his probing journalist's eye almost surmount these difficulties. His description of the storm is especially impressive. One can almost feel the pull of the wind, the wrench of the boat as she is flung about the sea. But this is not enough: *Under the Eye of the Storm* is not supposed to be a meteorological study, but an introspective look at people under stress. And once Hersey's relentless and minute probing of Tom (and Flick) is done, we still know they are cardboard figures, hardly worth the effort. —JOHN WARNER, "Novelist or Journalist?," *Harper's*, May 1967, p. 116

So urgently significant is this book ⟨*The Algiers Motel Incident*⟩, say both the hard and paperback publishers, that finished copies were ready less than six weeks after submission of the completed manuscript. And the author is so transmuted by his evangelical role that for the first time he is putting himself—I, John Hersey—into his journalism: ". . . this account is too urgent, too complex, too dangerous to too many people to be told in a way that might leave doubts strewn along its path; I cannot afford, this time, the luxury of invisibility." He could, presumably, at Hiroshima.

The present account is of an incident that took place at the Algiers Motel on the third night of the Detroit riots in the summer of 1967. Responding to a telephone report of sniping, Detroit police officers, state troopers, National Guardsmen and a Negro private guard invaded the motel and for an hour questioned ten black men and two white girls, none of whom were armed. When the interrogators left, three young men—Carl Cooper, Auburey Pollard, and Fred Temple—had been shot to death. The rest, including the two girls, had been gleefully, severely beaten. As Hersey demonstrates, there had in fact been no sniping in the area and the three black men were executed "for being thought to be pimps, for being considered punks, for making out with white girls . . . for being, all and all, black young men and part of the black rage of the time."

To prove this, Hersey involved himself in months of research, and his book shifts swiftly, though not always clearly, between interviews, extracts from court records, and his own reportage. Despite the occasional confusions in chronology, Hersey's analysis leaves no doubt as to the innocence of the victims (they weren't even pimps) although we are still not sure exactly which cop executed which black. But tying up the case neatly is not the point. Hersey sees in this episode "all the mythic themes of racial strife in the United States: the arm of the law taking the law into its own hands; interracial sex; the subtle poison of racist thinking by 'decent' men who deny that they are racists; the societal limbo into which so many young black men have been driven ever since slavery in our country; ambiguous justice in the courts. . . ."

But we already know this. Certainly blacks know it, as by now do most whites. Ah, but whites do not *experience* justice by color, and it is Hersey's innocent conviction that by writing in lacerating detail about this prototypical act of savagery on our colonials, he may help bring change. The remedy for unequal justice "is in the minds of men . . . I do believe that every scrap of understanding, every door-crack glimmer of illumination, every thread that may lead not just to survival of the races but to health—all should be shared as soon as possible. There is so much to be done in so little time . . . I bid you to read on . . . and see whether you are not pretty well purged of pity and terror as you follow this tale of humble citizens to its unresolved ending."

I pretty well felt pity and some vicarious terror and much rage as I read on, but I feel the same emotions reading the daily papers. For this kind of journalism to do more than conjugate the obvious requires a writer who both puts himself into his journalism and is also complex enough (Norman Mailer, for example) to dig so deeply into his subjects and into his own ambiguities as to return sufficiently altered by the experience to reflect in himself "the mythic themes of racial strife in the United States." Hersey does neither. From his time in Detroit, he claims that he "learned all sorts of new things, both about reality and about myself." But there is hardly anything of Hersey in this book. He remains essentially the faceless, careful, selective observer of *Hiroshima* (the difference then was that those facts were terrifyingly new). As for the "reality" outside himself, surely Hersey knew before Detroit that some cops are racists and killers besides. Surely he knew the courts are quicksand for the black poor, especially in a time of riot.

Hersey's interviews with the families and friends of the executed young men faithfully reflect their anger and pain and do tell us something of "the societal limbo" in which many black young men live; but this is only competent journalism with none of "the shock of revelation" the publishers proclaim. The fierce complaints about the police, the courts, the schools are all commonplace now—even on prime-time television. But there are also interviews with the three policemen most directly involved, and those sections promise fresher information because cops are seldom asked who they are. These, however, are flat monologues—shards of autobiography; accounts of police practices; a sense of bewildered injury that they, guardians of the law, have suddenly become vulnerable to the law. The most committed cop of the three is the most corrupted by the symbiotic relationship between his own instincts and those of the pimps and whores who had become his particular specialty in line of duty. But him too we know only superficially.

The alleged transmogrification of these "ordinary" policemen (and they are indeed the banality of evil) into sadistic killers that night at the Algiers Motel is not explored by Hersey beyond the cool extracts from his conversations with them. He tells us they turned into werewolves, but not in any way that can make us get inside their heads and skins. *He* cannot get inside, and that is why this book is only efficient, surface journalism. Hersey has written many novels, but there is no sign here of the authentic novelist's compulsive leaps of imagination; his relentless (however compassionate) curiosity; his capacity to understand, for instance, how a white cop can be devoted to his family and also be able deliberately, perhaps ecstatically, to shoot off the genitals of the executed black men.

There is a mythic quality to the incident at the Algiers Motel, as there is to incidents endemic to ghetto life every day. But to make that mythic quality part of the white experience of this country is probably beyond the power of any writer now. Some whites can come part of the way toward feeling as they think blacks do, but not very far. And to the extent that they have been moved in this direction by books, it has been by Ralph Ellison, the early James Baldwin, Malcolm X, and Eldridge Cleaver. The diligent reporting of John Hersey is only reporting, and myths are apprehended in quite another way—those who bear, interpret and eventually destroy them are at least as large as life as they make myth palpable. Ordinary journalism by barely visible reporters reduces life to incident. And that is what Hersey has done. After all the pages of *The Algiers Motel Incident*, we know only a little more specifically what the Kerner Report has already told us generally. We have names to attach to victims and executioners, but they will be forgotten, as those of "humble citizens" in incidents reported in newspapers are forgotten.—NAT HENTOFF, "Waking Up the White Folks Again," *NR*, July 20, 1968, pp. 36–39

John Hersey's *A Bell for Adano* (1944) is a competently concocted confection about an Italian-American school drop-out from a tough New York neighborhood who emerges as a kind of modern saint when he is put in charge of the military government of a small Italian town. His personality is adequately suggested by this description:

> Major Joppolo's desire for popularity in Adano stuck out all over him. It was not just that he wanted to do a good job, and felt that popularity was one sign that he had. It was not much tied up with wanting the Americans to be well received, though he did want that. It was mainly that he himself wanted to be liked.

His technique for winning friends and influencing people is illustrated by his treatment of some roughneck soldiers who have destroyed some art treasures in a private home, "The Major said: 'I'm going to make this your punishment: to have this man's unhappiness on your conscience, and from now on to keep his house as clean as if everything in it belongs to your own mother.'"

Hersey, who was later to achieve his greatest renown for his report on the first atomic bombing, *Hiroshima* (first printed in its entirety as the sole contents of one issue of the *New Yorker)*, is another able reporter. His account of the operation of the black market, for example, provides valuable information about "what it was like," but when he tries to create characters, this novel—like his subsequent ones—degenerates into timely soap opera. Hersey never tells us, for example, how Joppolo—in view of his background—develops his remarkable tact and insight; Hersey just thinks it would be nice if such a man existed, so he invents him. The novel is useful today only as pathetic evidence of what war-time Americans—uncomfortable in their role of world conquerors—could be prevailed upon to accept as serious literature. . . .

The difference between a Hersey and a Michener is that the Hersey is incurably deluded that his fables are FRAUGHT WITH SIGNIFICANCE—he is the descendant of the revivalist preacher seeking through print a larger congregation; Michener does not take himself that seriously. He may garnish his tale with a banal little moral about the way of the wicked world, but his real relish is in the telling. He cannot conceive a grand design; rather he specializes in details. . . .

Michener's popularity is, however, well deserved. The regrettable thing about American writing today is that there are few men around with his talents as a raconteur and too many around waiting like Hersey to pound a moral into our heads. If Michener's diverting works are recognized for what they are, they might be used to lure back to reading some of the people scared off by the pomposities of the Herseys.—WARREN FRENCH, "Fiction: A Handful of Survivors," *The Forties: Fiction, Poetry, Drama*, ed. Warren French, 1969, pp. 15–17

The murderous glare of the American Hiroshima Bomb, the single most destructive moment of that part of the twentieth century Eurasian barbarism quaintly labeled World War II, casts a peculiar light on some literary as well as moral faiths. Surveying the writings linked to the atomic bomb must impress us with how dimly literature reflects and comprehends the actual. Even the obvious symbol of the mushroom-cloud rising above a hundred thousand dead humans (and another hundred thousand dying and crippled)—rather a better sign of the end than anything in *Revelation*—carries but small affective power. At best, the art of the word can only provide a paltry, and probably falsified, reality.

Many of the inadequacies of our forms of imagination apply, of course, to the related experiences. How memoralize, extend into moral dialects, or in any way humanly realize the fate of the millions of Jews (and the forgotten Gypsies) murdered in the Nazi "Final Solution"? And the similar millions of the Stalinist Russian slave-labor exterminations? How, indeed, comprehend any major fact of the continuous sanctioned violence of our century and its victims, of which the killed and wounded (a hundred million?) indicate only a part of the man-made suffering. Nor do the integral and pervasive political terror, social exploitation, technological dehumanization and moral viciousness find appropriate expression. When our actualities provide the standards, the study of our culture must mostly note inadequacy and mendacity.

One way to reduce the vast horror to recognizable scale takes the form of the documentary-novel. This fusion of journalism and fictional art now provides the stock genre for exceptional events—invasion, the fall of a city, technological exploits, rural murder, and other man-made catastrophes. Refusing the individual integration of the personal "memoir" or the responsible factual organization of the public "history," the documentary-novel uses fiction's devices of vivid description, curious anecdote, character sketch, imagined dialogue and stylized narrative. Yet it claims literal truth. Most of these documentary-novels come out too patently artful, not least in their indebtedness to the cinema for multiple and cross-cut narration and visual heightening. Perhaps more damaging, the view of character tends to the reductive; persons appear as random and representative topical figures, diverse only within a normative evaluation of the event and almost never as commanding and exceptional individuals. People serve as manipulatable material for an author whose superior editorial stance, professionally masqueraded as disinterested sympathy, inherently implies contempt. The economy and polish and consistency of the documentary-novel (in contrast to true documents) indicates a drastic editing down, and out, of much of human response.

Given the scale of the events and the refusal of individual focus, the fictional verisimilitude (right down to brand names and a nearly surreal over-exactness on odd details) must falsify the reality. The author's pose of merely recording and reporting allows him to obscure personal evaluation, attenuate intellectual reflection, abstain from moral argument and abnegate poetic meditation. Such decorous and unthoughtful fictionalized reportage illustrates not only the limitations of commercial authorship but of the popular audiences and our standard exploitative publication which combines over-indulgence with undernourishment. The documentary-novel is itself a technological exploit; it expertly and vividly "communicates" but at the price of a considerable reduction in human response and relevance.

Such is John Hersey's *Hiroshima*. In its dozens of editions and millions of copies, this montage of half a dozen recitals of victim-survivors seems to have been crucial, even to many Japanese, in setting the attitude—most essentially the lack of adequate attitude—to the American atomic bombing of Hiroshima and Nagasaki. *Hiroshima* is, of course, competently written, blandly sympathetic, reasonably vivid and weirdly understated and depersonalized in its synthetically interwoven narratives and pathetic anecdotes of destruction and shock. Artful detail substitutes for moral intelligence. The unreflective and finally rather decorous treatment, part of which may be blamed on the parochial sophistication of the *New Yorker* audience for whom it was written (and perhaps on the editing of Harold Ross and William Shawn), manages to suggest some of the commonplaces of horror but loses fuller individual response as well as any larger issue.

Many lesser technicians than Hersey have done documentary narratives of and around the Bomb. And still continue to, two decades later. Some are rather quirky, as with Robert Trumbull's imitation, *Nine Who Survived Hiroshima and Nagasaki*. The assumption of this montage of narratives and rather thin reflections is that if surviving one atomic bombing is something special, then surviving two is profundity. But the most profound response reported there may be that of the one double survivor who was too "bitter" to provide human interest data.

The related atomic events (building the Bomb, testing the Bomb, poisoning Japanese fishermen, rebuilding Hiroshima, etc.) appear in similar narrative reportage (by Daniel Lang, Ralph Lapp, Lansing Lamont, and others). Even some poets fell back on heightening documentation. For example, Thomas Merton's *Original Child Bomb*, "Points for Meditation to Be Scratched on the Walls of a Cave," simply and awkwardly takes forty-one paragraphs of commonplace facts about the bombing as constituting a poetic indictment. Is the horror and guilt so great that no thought and imagination can be made relevant? While a factual narrative can be valuable when based in an individual sensibility and commitment (thus Lester Atwell's *Private* provides some of the more insightful literature about American army experience in Europe in World War II), psuedo-objectivity ends quite inadequate.

Literature, we sometimes forget because of our "positivistic" bias, cannot achieve awareness by merely describing. The documentary fictions, for all their exactingly dramatized reportage, must miss many of the crucial experiences. In the *naif* accounts of survivors (for example, those presented by Takashi Nagai, *We of Nagasaki*) appears an insistent theme little found in the documentary novels or hardly any of the American discussions: "survival guilt." As we also find in the European "death camp" literature, this guilt remains pervasive and scarring. The fear and shock and brutalization in the bombing made kindly people walk away from the thirsty screams of their friends, mothers abandon their children, sensitive men ignore the women they loved. This permanently crippling revelation about one's self and about others separates the remembering *hibak'sha* from those who did not undergo the experience. One knows, then, that man is not a worthy creature. No mere detailing and dramatization will explore this guilty knowledge, this bitter human dimension basic to so much of our warfare.—KINGSLEY WIDMER, "American Apocalypse: Notes on the Bomb and the Failure of Imagination," *The Forties: Fiction, Poetry, Drama*, ed. Warren French, 1969 pp. 141–44

There is scarcely a moment these days when such authors of the Sentimental Liberal Protest Novel as Irwin Shaw, John Hersey, Budd Schulberg, and James Michener are not fighting for slots on the list of best sellers; since in our time left-of-center politics has become, by virtue of converting all its political content to sentiment, the reigning belief of the educated middle classes. In our genteel age, the class struggle has been translated from a confrontation of workers and bosses on the barricades to a contest between certain invisible or remote exploiters and all the rest of us—a contest in which more tears are shed than blood. The writer dedicated to portraying that struggle is no longer the man in the work shirt rolled to the elbow and open at the neck, but the man ashamed of his gray flannel suit—the searcher out and defender of Victims. For the image of man which possesses the genteel conscience is the image of the Victim: the snubbed Jew, the oppressed Negro, the starving Chinese, the atom-scarred Japanese, the betrayed Hungarian, the misunderstood paraplegic. For each Victim there is an appropriate book, a last indignity: *Gentlemen's Agreement*, *The Wall*, *The Bridge at Andau*, *The Last Pebble*, *One Hour*. Even the War Novel is recast in the prevailing form, captured, like *The Young Lions*, for piety, protest, and self-pity. In the end, we are left with the sense that wars are fought and armies organized (in representative platoons, with all minorities duly represented) so that the persecuted Jew or tormented Italian can shame his fellows by proving his unforeseen valor in the end.

Having only a single theme, of a rather simple-minded sort, the Sentimental Protestors are driven to eke it out, to conceal its stereotypical bareness with up-to-date details and topical references. Their eyes are constantly on the headlines; and before the ink is dry, Michener and Hersey are already embarked for the scene of the latest indignity—or at least racing for their typewriters! It is a somewhat comic contest, with the whole reading world breathlessly waiting to discover who will get Little Rock first, who the Puerto Ricans. But what is the ersatz morality which sustains the protest fictionists, from Hersey-Shaw to Jones-Algren, from the soft-sell defenders of the dark-skinned people to the tough apologists for maximum security prisoners and minor hoods? It is the theory that the "Little Man" must be defended against the great and powerful, merely because he is little and "wants only to be left alone." Little! Surely no more degrading label has ever been invented for the exploited, none which has so combined pathos and condescension: the little Jew, the little shopkeeper, the little mixed-up kid, the bewildered little pusher of dope, the little pimp trying to establish himself against the competition of the big operators. . . . Against so abject a surrender to sentiment, one wants to cry out in the terrible words of the Old Testament, "Thou shalt not honor the poor man in his cause." But who could be heard over the voices of those storming their book counters for copies of *Exodus* and *Hawaii?* —LESLIE FIEDLER, "No! In Thunder," *The Novel: Modern Essays in Criticism*, ed. Robert Murray Davis, 1969, pp. 317–19

When John Hersey's account of six survivors of Hiroshima appeared in the Aug. 31, 1946, issue of *The New Yorker* it caused a sensation. For the first time the entire editorial space was devoted to a single article. The magazine was overwhelmed by requests for reprints. Albert Einstein asked for 1,000 copies. Newspapers throughout the country clamored for the rights, which were granted provided all profits went to the Red Cross. The book, a few months later, was acclaimed as a modern classic. (It has recently been reprinted in paperback by Bantam Books.) The Book-of-the-Month Club sent out free copies to hundreds of thousands of its subscribers.

All this acclaim appeared when most Americans regarded the Japanese as brutes, brainwashed by their leaders who were as evil as the Nazis. We had treated our own Japanese-Americans as enemy aliens, applauding President Franklin Roosevelt for incarcerating them in "relocation camps." Liberals, progressives and Communists joined in praise of this action. The American Civil Liberties Union supported the imprisonment and the Supreme Court upheld its legality.

Spurred by propaganda, almost all of us were swept up in the passions of war and fear of the Yellow Peril; and so there were few protests when Gen. Curtis LeMay began scattering firebombs on the tinderbox buildings of Japan. In one night an estimated 120,000 men, women and children were incinerated in Tokyo. Time described the fire-bombings as "a dream come true," which proved that "properly kindled, Japanese cities will burn like autumn leaves." The fire-bombings continued, wiping out city after city and consigning to terrible death more hundreds of thousands of civilians. And then on Aug. 6, 1945, the first atom bomb was dropped on Hiroshima. Seconds later some 100,000 human beings were dead and an equal number were dying of burns, injuries and a new terrifying disease—radiation poisoning.

There was jubilation throughout the Western world. We

were all convinced that "the Japs" deserved what they got because of the sneak attack on Pearl Harbor and such atrocities as the Bataan Death March of American prisoners of war in the Philippines. With the surrender of Japan nine days after the first bomb fell, we lost our fear of the Japanese. Now the task was to rehabilitate the Japanese in our own image and punish their leaders. We promptly executed Lt. Gen. Masaharu Homma, who conquered the Philippines, and Gen. Tomoyuki Yamashita, the last commander of the Philippines, and launched the War Crimes Trial in Tokyo to deal with Gen. Hideki Tojo, the Japanese Premier, and other leading criminals. It was against this background that John Hersey's *Hiroshima* appeared. Riveted by the ghastly details, those of us who had hated the Japanese for almost five years finally realized that Mr. Hersey's six protagonists were fellow human beings.

The years have not dimmed the luster or import of what Mr. Hersey wrote 40 years ago.—JOHN TOLAND, "Beyond the Brink of Destruction," *NYTBR*, Aug. 7, 1985, pp. 3, 24

ELIZABETH JANEWAY

From "The High Price of Good Intentions"

Christian Science Monitor, February 4, 1965, p. 11

When is it morally right to lie? The question is prompted by the flood of recent novels which center on the Negro question (race question if you'd rather) or in some way make use of it. Almost all of them have fallen away from the first duty of literature, which is the discovery and exposition of the truth about a human situation; and to fall away from the search for truth, for any reason whatsoever, is to fall into falsity. Almost all these books have chosen to expound a thesis, to make a point by shock, to underline (and overvalue) events, to awaken consciences. This being their first aim, the authors almost inevitably choose the telling and terrifying anecdote instead of the revealing one.

Almost all have been written by convinced and angry men with high and closed minds (except, of course, the ones that have been written simply to cash in on the excitement). Certainly there are a few totally honest books in the genre, written by men who are not trying to preach or to persuade but to understand—there come to mind Ralph Ellison's *Invisible Man*, Peter Peibleman's *A Place without Shadows*, William Styron's *Lie Down in Darkness*. This doesn't exhaust the list, but it isn't a long one. It seems to me that its scantiness is a considerable disservice both to literature and to the difficult task of working our way toward a solution of the race (or Negro) problem.

John Hersey's new novel, *White Lotus*, and *Many Thousands Gone* by Ronald L. Fair, which is described as "An American Fable," are both books of enormously good intentions. Neither is a novel, as Fair acknowledges, and as Hersey certainly does not claim: the jacket of *White Lotus* speaks of it as "a parable" and "a human document." It is unfair, then, to judge them by the strict standards of fiction and to complain naively (as some reviewers have done) that Hersey's characters are unconvincing or not fully realized. Hersey and Fair have deliberately chosen to deal in parable and fable (personally, I feel that this is a huge and crippling mistake, but they have a right to act on their decisions) and so they are committed to dealing in types rather than rounded individuals.

The question, then, comes down to this: are the types they have chosen (of characters and of situations) the most meaningful, the closest to the center of the problem, the ones that grip the facts best and weave them together most tightly, most pointedly, and without distorting them: If so, the parable will work. It will bypass the fictional method, in which meaning is never told directly but communicated by action, and will strike home to the moral center of the human mind and spirit, as Bunyan and Swift do. But if not. . . .

I am very much afraid that in the case of both these books the weight comes down, in the end, on the negative side. Fair, a Negro, is arguing that the Negro problem had best be settled by Negroes alone, and through violence (retaliatory violence, of course). This is an understandable position. But it is the premise with which this book begins, and not its conclusion. Fair has it in his mind from the beginning, and this inhibits him from developing it, and thus leading his readers to a fervent or a reluctant acceptance of it. . . .

Hersey is a cooler hand and a better writer. As I say, I regret his decision to turn his back on fiction, because when he uses fictional methods fully (he uses them in part here) he knows what he is doing and produces powerful books; he is not just "a magnificent journalist," as his old employer, *Time*, alleges. And there is no denying that *White Lotus* incorporates a considerable act of creation.

Hersey has imagined a race of White Americans enslaved by conquesting Chinese. Some time in the 18th or 19th century, America slipped sideways out of history and into barbarism, after losing a war to a triumphant Chinese power. Slave raiders bring coffles of captive whites to the West Coast, where they are crammed into slaveships and ferried across the Pacific to be sold to the citizens of the Celestial Empire as house servants and field hands.

Hersey then telescopes history (and history, after all, sometimes telescopes itself, as in 19th-century Japan and 20th-century Russia). He records the backwash of a Civil War, Emancipation, villeinage, the beginnings of industrialization, a peasant revolt (unfulfilled), a proletarian revolt (aborted), and the growth and early successes of peaceful resistance, which appeals to the half-forgotten Buddhist ethics of the Chinese much as Martin Luther King appeals to the half-forgotten Christian ethics of our era.

Hersey's thesis half coincides with, half contradicts Fair's. He too asserts that an enslaved people must win their freedom themselves. (History and I are not so sure; we believe that economic change and political accident get into it.) Hersey's Chinese Abolitionists, however, are crazy fanatics, more interested in saving their own souls than in liberating the whites (read Negroes); and his modern Chinese (read white) liberals are hangers-on, resented and distrusted.

Hersey differs from Fair in arguing for the use of peaceful, not violent methods. I can imagine some cynical Negroes declaring that this is because he is white and (further) that this again is the reason why his book is a choice of the Book-of-the-Month Club. Granted that no one, not even the judges of the Book-of-the-Month Club, can fully analyze their own motives. I doubt that Hersey's plea for nonviolence is related to the color of his skin. Rather, he believes in it for the reasons that Tolstoy, Gandhi, Toynbee and King do—that it works (or so they think) and violence doesn't. Basically, this is the Christian position too when the Christian position contemplates action in today's world.

The trouble with Hersey's book is that he, like Fair, is writing from a predetermined belief. He is not searching for truth, but expounding it. And though the background of this long story is fascinating, drawn from meticulous research and Hersey's own boyhood memories of China, his characters again are not merely types. In fact, the central one, White Lotus, is hardly there at all. She is simply the person to whom things happen. They are interesting things, but for them to happen fully, they need a human response and it isn't forthcoming. White Lotus is rather like the Gallup Poll rolled up into one person and reacting in a median way, or a walking Nielsen rating, and she deadens the book and vulgarizes it in a way, which is certainly the last thing that Hersey intends. If he had allowed her a little of his own sensitivity, a touch of character, it wouldn't have happened.

Then what is to be done by a writer with a concern for the times, who wants (as they used to say) to engage himself? Is parable useless now? Didn't Camus, for one, bring it off? Camus, however, was dealing not with the changing events of an external situation but with the permanent confrontation of man and life. And there are those, like Simone de Beauvoir, who dispute his success. In any case, parable is an intensely difficult genre to use, for all that it looks so deceptively simple. Much more than in fiction, where the test of plausibility continually controls the writer's intentions, parable adapts to misuse, to well-intentioned wandering from the truth, to oversimplification, to wish fulfillment.

So I am afraid that my own answer to the question with which I began this review is that it is never—in literature—morally right to lie, and always incapacitating. Truth is not easily come by, particularly in a situation so charged with emotion as that we face today. But there is no substitute for it. I would go further. Hersey and Fair have both moved outside of "mere" literature and are suggesting remedies for an historical situation that calls for political action. To act on the basis of misinformation, personal emotions (including guilt), and sociological myth is to invite error. Once upon a time we were promised that if we knew the truth, the truth would make us free. At any rate, nothing else will.

DuBose Heyward

1885–1940

Although he was a direct descendant of Judge Thomas Heyward, a signer of the Declaration of Independence, DuBose Heyward began life in dire circumstances. He was born August 31, 1885. His father, Edwin W. Heyward, died two years after Heyward's birth. His mother, Jane DuBose Heyward, sent the boy to work selling papers at the age of nine. Heyward quit school at fourteen, worked as a clerk, and contracted polio which left him paralyzed from his eighteenth to his twenty-first year. On recovering, he worked as a cotton checker and then as an insurance salesman, but the work strained his delicate health. He began writing stories in 1917, and found a patron, John Bennett, the following year. In 1921 Heyward began visiting McDowell Writers' Colony in New Hampshire, where he met the aspiring playwright Dorothy Kuhns. They married the following year.

Heyward had continued selling insurance, and writing poems in his spare time. His new wife encouraged him to abandon all other work and to go to the mountains to complete his first novel. The result was *Porgy*, Heyward's most famous work. *Porgy* enjoyed enormous success, first as a novel and later as an adaptation for the stage and an opera by George Gershwin *(Porgy and Bess)*. Heyward wrote several works of fiction and drama, usually focusing on the Gullah black population of South Carolina. These include *Mamba's Daughters* (1929), *The Half Pint Flask* (1929), and *Peter Ashley* (1932).

Heyward was often mistakenly identified as a black author, and is still regarded as a major figure in the Harlem Renaissance. He and his wife had one daughter, and settled in South Carolina. Heyward suffered a fatal heart attack near his summer home in Tryon, North Carolina, on June 16, 1940.

DONALD DAVIDSON
"An Author Divided against Himself" (1929)
The Spyglass: Views and Reviews, 1924–1930
ed. John Tyree Fain
1963, pp. 29–34

DuBose Heyward has enjoyed a considerable popularity in the last few years, and has been looked on as a leader among the new writers who have brought the South forward in literary matters. That the popularity is well deserved, I think no one can deny. But Mr. Heyward's third novel, *Mamba's Daughters*, shows him to be wavering between the demands of his own artistic integrity and the demands made by outside influences, including no doubt the public, the metropolitan critics, and the publishers—all three as likely to operate for ill as for good.

The memorable *Porgy* was first of all a good story. Perhaps it did not rise to great heights, but in an even, mellow tone it unfolded the drama of an obscure and pathetic life, strong in the primitive values for which our jaded civilization is now greedy. It was faithful to the Negro character it depicted, as Thomas Nelson Page and others were faithful in the old days. Yet it has a novelty of attitude. The Negro was allowed to stand forth as a human being in his own right, with the white world not merely put in the background but shoved completely out of view. The slight tone of indulgence that Southern writers have used toward the Negro was almost entirely absent, though it was replaced by a somewhat elusive tone partaking of the peculiar modern sentimentalism affected nowadays. Furthermore, *Porgy* dealt with the Gullah Negro, a regional type belonging to the Carolina coast and not widely known. It was published at a time when it got the full advantage of New York's sudden fancy for Negro art of all sorts, and indeed for everything pertaining to Negro life.

The second novel, *Angel*, toyed with Fundamentalist themes against the social background of the North Carolina mountains. It did not go well, for it was somehow artificial. It had little conviction of purpose. It was not a very good story. But public interest in Mr. Heyward's work continued, for the play, *Porgy*, made from the novel by Mr. Heyward and his wife Dorothy, entered on a very successful run in New York and proved in many ways to be even more interesting and satisfactory, from the artistic standpoint, than the novel. There is also Mr. Heyward's poetry to be considered. His *Skylines and Horizons* and *Carolina Chansons* stand at the beginning of the poetry revival in the South. His work as leader and organizer of the Poetry Society of South Carolina was notable in many ways. Since he has now apparently gone over entirely from poetry to fiction, I do not need to prolong critical comment, except to observe that his poetry, like his fiction, is regional. It exploits the Negro, the mountaineer, the picturesque ways of Charleston. It reflects fine feelings and good taste and has a gentle lyrical charm. But it never shows great strength or originality.

Considering Mr. Heyward, then, as a regionalist, we are obliged to ask some primary questions. If we observe the works of Hardy or of the European novelists of the soil, or, in this country, of Elizabeth Madox Roberts and Julia Peterkin—all, in my opinion, true regionalists—we see at once that they write of their chosen section as if no other region existed. They bring to their interpretation of a locale no extraneous attitudes, being quite unconcerned about special "problems" and contemporary manias. They have no particular philosophy devised for an occasion merely and applicable only to mountaineers, cowboys or English milkmaids. But these special types are accepted as human beings, costume and place being pervasive but incidental; and whatever philosophy is applied is a philosophy of humanity in the large. Singularly enough, these writers get their universality by narrowing their gaze to the extremely particular.

Without wishing to put myself in too authoritative an attitude, I am nevertheless forced to believe that Mr. Heyward does not resemble the writers I have mentioned. As a regionalist, he does not possess their traits. And *Mamba's Daughters* is example enough.

If I did not know Mr. Heyward is the author, I could easily have imagined the book to have been written by some fly-by-night millionaire novelist from the Riviera or Gopher Prairie, who put his yacht into Charleston harbor for the winter season and picked up enough local color to fill out his contract for a fifteenth best-selling novel. Not that DuBose Heyward does not know his Charleston! Not that he does not depict it accurately and with enough humor to make us like him and it, even in spite of his faults! But the voice and tone are not the voice and tone of DuBose Heyward. They are of New York. They echo its fashionable platitudes about the Negro and to some extent play up to its curiosity about Charleston. The book, in brief, though seeming to be an "inside" interpretation, is without the passionate absorption in the subject that we must demand of a regional novelist. It is written as if to order.

As such, it is a rather astonishing mixture of things. First of all, there is the story of Mamba, the old crone from the vulgar Negro set who attaches herself to the patrician Wentworths and makes herself an indispensable retainer by shrewd ways that Negroes have. She is a real creation, as well conceived as Porgy, or better. What Mamba does is by way of sacrificial labor for her daughter, Hagar, a giant incoherent child of earth, and more especially for her granddaughter, Lissa. The story of Hagar and Mamba alone would have been enough to make a fine book, and I feel that Mr. Heyward has erred greatly in not sticking to their simple tale.

But there is also the mixture. We are shown the pathetic secrets of the proud-but-poor Wentworths, and in much too obvious contrast to them the tawdrier secrets of a family of wealthy social climbers from the North. The mother of this latter family attempts in vain to break into the exclusive St. Cecilia circle. Victory is attained only when the father, a coolly efficient businessman, maneuvers a business deal to the advantage of the Charleston men, and through them wins the coveted entry. The son of the Wentworths succumbs to the charm of a Northern girl, whose love brings him to his real self—and he vanishes weakly, rather vaguely, into the mists of New York. The unholy system by which workers in the phosphate mines are kept under the company's thumb is revealed; in this there is a little more than a hint of doctrinaire attitudes, and though the whole episode involving Hagar, young Wentworth, and others, has its dramatic and lively parts, it is rather detached from the main story. Then there is the story of Lissa, Mamba's talented granddaughter. She works her way into Negro aristocracy in Charleston and finally flees to New York after Hagar's sacrificial death and there her golden soprano charms exclusive circles and plays a distinguished part in making a new art. This last strand of narrative, especially inorganic, is an unexplainably pat echo of the Harlem school of rhapsody and propaganda, very surprising in Mr. Heyward.

The general treatment, too, smacks of conceptions extra-Charlestonian rather than indigenous. On one side is white Charleston, consciously patrician, idealized against the background of its romantic past, but a little infertile and chilly, yielding gradually before the onset of a commercial, hustling world. On the other side are the Negroes—full of primitive strength and zest, superstitious but humorous and wise, somewhat abused yet on the whole pampered and indulged by the white folks, curiously faithful to the "quality" white folks and to Negro codes at the same time. In this contrast, as in occasional touches on social conditions, Mr. Heyward ceases to be a local colorist and leans in the direction of sociology.

Reluctantly, one comes to the conclusion that in *Mamba's Daughters*, despite many excellent strokes of character and incident, Mr. Heyward has faltered uncertainly. He is divided against himself, and it is still impossible to say what he is going to make of himself. But in justice to him—and he is a writer for whom one would cheerfully make every possible excuse—it is well to remember that *Mamba's Daughters* was first published serially. In the serialization, a stretching and filling out process may have occurred to the great disadvantage of the book and the disappointment of those who wish Mr. Heyward well.

ANTHONY HARRIGAN

From "DuBose Heyward: Memorialist and Realist"

Georgia Review, Fall 1951, pp. 336–44

I

DuBose Heyward's finest and most significant works of fiction are *Porgy* and *Mamba's Daughters*. These novels are a memorial to the Gullah Negro of the Carolina Low-Country. The memorial is constituted of affection and understanding—affection in token of the Negro's faithfulness and understanding of his struggle. Since the First World War many thousands of Negros have left the old Rich Coast and gone to live in Harlem and the Negro quarters of the large Northern cities. The new Negro cannot understand the tragic connection between his ancestors and the Low-Country planter class. Nevertheless, *Porgy* and *Mamba's Daughters* are a testament to this lost relationship. Sterling A. Brown, the Negro social historian, has termed this relationship: "a mystical cult of mutual affection."

The relationships between people separated by race is the central issue of these novels and constitutes a major theme of Southern writing. At a time when the stability of the relationships between whites and blacks is decreasing, the question of relationships must be considered anew—the breakdown of the old social order and the consequent dislocation of the ruling and servant classes. Heyward's attitude towards the Negro and this changing relationship is the attitude typical of his class. In an essay, "The Negro in the Low-Country," he wrote eloquently of the Negro in his part of the South:

> . . . we [in America] have forgotten that there can be such a thing as pride of caste among the lowly, that there could exist in a man who had been born a servant and expected to die a servant a self-respect equally as great, and as jealously guarded as that enjoyed by the master, and yet, paradoxically, this very cleavage between the ruling and the servant classes in the South which has imposed an obligation to respect the dignity of each other has constituted the bond which has held the two classes together in affection and mutual understanding through the vicissitudes of two and a half centuries.

Heyward did not find the Negro better or worse than the whites, merely different. But he was keenly alive to the differences between the races. Delving into the inmost qualities of the black race, he showed the deepest insight and grasped the essence of the black man's soul.

> . . . we must remember that the Negro probably to a greater extent than any other living race is possessed of a genius for forming happy human relationships, for inspiring affection, for instinctively divining the mood of the one with whom he comes in contact, and of accommodating his own mood to that of the other.

It is important to bear in mind, however, that Heyward was primarily concerned with the Negro of his own day—not with the Negro of ante-bellum times. And he was profoundly mindful of the fact that the Negro of his own lifetime was groping towards a strange new destiny in America. His awareness of the latter is most evident in *Mamba's Daughters*. He puts the following words into Mamba's mouth when the old Negro woman asks Mrs. Wentworth for a letter stating that she was an old family servant of the Wentworths: "Tain't fuh me, Miss. Ah kin tek care ob Mamba. But time is changin'. Nigger gots tuh git diff'ent kind ob sense now tuh git long."

Later in the novel when Hagar decides to kill herself and is speaking to the crowd in the company store at the phosphate works, Heyward has Hagar say,

> "Time comin' when nigger goin' worry jes like white folks, an' den Gawd show 'em what to do when he trouble get too deep fur he to walk t'rough."

Yet in *Mamba's Daughters* the *age of anxiety* has touched but the upper levels of Charleston's Negro world. Of the great mass of the blacks, Heyward wrote:

> The corrosion of hidden sin did not mark the faces, for the consciences that might have been sitting in judgement had not yet been scourged into consciousness.

It is perfectly clear that despite his sympathy for the struggle the Negro was making to improve himself, Heyward had deep misgivings as to the future that awaited the race. He was too keen an observer of contemporary life and too acutely aware of the pitiful inadequacy of it in comparison with the old mode of life in the American republic to hold any foolish notions of automatic progress and human betterment through so oversimple a device as a change in social institutions and class structure. Nevertheless, he realized that the Low-Country Negro, the Negro in *Porgy* and *Mamba's Daughters*, was heeding the call of an illusory new modern world. He understood that certain types of change could not be resisted and that the black race was certain to be absorbed into the cruel and destructive way of life prevailing in so many portions of the country.

> We watch him [the Negro] with his family, his unquestioning belief in a personal God, his spontaneous abandonment to emotion, his faith in his simple destiny. And seeing these things, out of our own fuller and sadder knowledge, we wonder whether he will be happier when the last of the bonds are severed and finally and triumphantly he has conformed to the stereotyped pattern of American success.

However, DuBose Heyward was not exclusively concerned with the relationships between the races. He was also greatly interested in the relationship of the artist to his society and the standard of literary taste. In an essay entitled "The New Note in Southern Literature" which he prepared prior to publication of the first of his novels he gave a forthright exposition of his ideas:

> In spite of its lynchings, its paternity of the Klan, its evolution trials, and its legislatures that naively exclude chewing tobacco from taxation, the south is artistically, probably the most civilized section of America; and for the reason that it has a large, if reticent aristocracy which possesses a congenial feeling for beauty and a tolerant attitude towards the artist.

. . . The truly fine works of fiction written by modern Southern writers have all been tragic and based upon the lives of passionate characters. Inasmuch as the civilization of the Southern states has not required endless action in life, it is understandable that endless motivation has not been required in its literature. Because there is a fixed code between the races and within each racial group, character interpretation does not have to be carried to the lengths to which it is carried in Northern fiction. *Porgy* is an excellent example of the tragic novel with a passionate character as a central figure.

Porgy is the story of a crippled beggar who lives in the ruined grandeur which is Catfish Row in the old city of Charleston. He drives his goat-cart through the streets every day, returning at night with the money he has collected. Heyward wrote of Porgy and Porgy's era in which "the profession was one with a tradition." As he explained in the opening pages of the book:

> A man begged, presumably, because he was hungry, much as a man of more energetic temperament became a stevedore from the same cause. His plea for help produced the simple reactions of a generous impulse, a movement of the hand, and a gift of a coin, instead of the elaborate and terrifying processes of organized philanthropy. His antecedents and his mental age were his own affair, and, in the majority of cases, he was as happily oblivious of one as he was of the other.

One night there is a crap game and Crown, a giant Negro stevedore, kills another Negro. Crown flees the city. Heyward gives a superb description of the dead man's room with the corpse laid out in the center and the women singing dirges until neighbors place sufficient money in a saucer to insure the murdered man a decent burial. There is a great sweeping scene which reveals the Negro's primitive passion and which comes to a fabulous end with the mourners in the dingy room bursting forth in the jubilant spiritual "Oh, I gots a little brudder in de new grabe-yard what outshine de sun." Sympathetically and compassionately Heyward describes the funeral cortege with its "odd fusion of comedy and tragedy so inextricably a part of Negro life in its deepest moments." The funeral comes to an end and the crowd dashes madly from the burial ground inasmuch as there is a superstition that "De las' man in de grabe yahd goin' tuh be de nex' one tuh git buried." The story then proceeds to the incarceration of an old Negro man by the name of Peter and the confiscation of his few belongings by the dishonest merchants. Heyward's description of this constitutes one of the rare bitter moments in the novel: a moment in which he strikes at the middle class white man's injustice in his dealings with the Negro. Heyward says of the man who takes away old Peter's wagon that he exhibited "a contract, dated three years previous, by which Peter was to pay two dollars a week for an indefinite period, on an exorbitant purchase price. Failure to pay any installment would cause the property to revert to the seller. It all looked thoroughly legal." Heyward cites the irony of the situation which is that one of the few belongings left by the swindling merchants is a chromo of The Great Emanicipator.

Later in the summer of the same year, Bess, who is Crown's woman, comes to live with Porgy in Catfish Row. After she has been living with Porgy a while, there takes place "the grand parade and picnic of the Sons and Daughters of Repent Ye Saith the Lord" and the trip aboard a stern-wheel excursion boat to Kiawah Island, which is south of Charleston. His comment on the parade is excellent:

> Out of its fetters of civilization this people has risen suddenly, amazingly. Exotic as the Congo, and still able to abandon themselves utterly to the wild joy of fantastic play, they had taken the reticent, old Anglo-Saxon town and stamped their mood swiftly and indelibly into its heart. Then they passed, leaving behind them a wistful envy among those who watched them go—those whom the ages had rendered old and wise.

Bess encounters Crown on Kiawah and makes plans to join him after the cotton crop is sent to the city. This action is followed by the magnificent hurricane scene—the most superb piece of writing in all of Heyward's fiction. The end follows soon after with the killing of Crown by Porgy and the loss of Bess when she is taken aboard a river boat by some Negro boatmen. And in this manner the story comes to an end.

Porgy is the story of a Negro's inner life, the years of complete peace and eventually the moments of passion and extreme violence. *Porgy* is, after a fashion, the story of all the black men of the South. One cannot escape its symbolism and the fact that the central characters embody so many of the expectations and disappointments of the race.

Many years before Heyward published any fiction he wrote for the *Reviewer* an article which may be properly considered in relation to *Porgy:*

> . . . Are they an aeon behind, or an aeon ahead of us? Who knows? But one thing is certain: the reformer will have them in the fullness of time. They will surely be cleaned, married, conventionalized. They will be taken from the fields, and given to machines, their instinctive feeling for the way that leads to happiness, saved as it is from selfishness, by humour and genuine kindness of heart, will be supplanted by a stifling moral straitjacket. They will languish, but they will submit, because they will be trained into a habit of thought that makes blind submission a virtue. . . . And my stevedore, there out of the window, I look at him again. I cannot see him a joke. Most certainly I cannot contort him into a menace, I can only be profoundly sorry for him, for there he sits in the sunshine unconsciously awaiting his supreme tragedy. He is about to be saved.

II

Sixteen years ago Gerald W. Johnson wrote: "The case of DuBose Heyward is peculiarly interesting because his work, like that of R. L. Stevenson, represents a triumph of acute observation." It is true that *Mamba's Daughters* is not the typical regional novel. Heyward carefully observes the present. His theme embraces more than the elements of *loss:* destructive family conflicts, the forced sale of an ancestral property, the breakdown of tradition. *Mamba's Daughters* is not a sorrowful tale about the old ruling class which is so often pictured as devoid of will power and courage with which to meet the problems of a new era. Fundamentally, it is a story of development and change on the part of both the black and white races.

This novel is exceedingly complex in comparison with *Porgy.* It covers a period of twenty-odd years, and the action sheds light on several utterly different worlds: everything from aristocratic white Charleston to wealthy Harlem circles. The reader has revealed to him the respective modes of living of the old Charleston families, the Negroes of the servant class, the Northern, newly rich, educated Negroes of the post First World War era, the white "crackers," and the workers in the phosphate mining camps. The bare outline of the story is built around the figure of Mamba, a sly, indomitable old Negro woman who insinuates herself into a poor but exceedingly proud Charleston family. Her purpose is to develop the habits and contacts necessary to obtain a job with a wealthy social-climbing Northern family. This job would enable her to educate Lissa, her granddaughter, who is the child of Hagar, a simple-minded giantess. Mamba's intriguing and Hagar's labour in the phosphate diggings make possible Lissa's education and training as a singer. The novel is also the story of St. Julien de C. Wentworth, only son in the poor but aristocratic family with which Mamba allies herself. Saint has a decided inclination towards the arts. His family depends upon him, however, and he has to find employment in the phosphate mining camp. Lissa's family sacrifices everything in order that she may attain a place in the world. In the case of the Wentworths, it is the young man who has to make the sacrifice. Saint assumes the family's financial obligations. Lissa eventually is an artistic success in New York and attains stardom in a Negro opera. The price of Lissa's success is, however, the suicide of Hagar and the confession of a murder the giant Negro woman did not commit. Her purpose in this was to prevent Lissa becoming involved in a situation which might be disastrous to her career. Saint's difficulties are removed with the event of a happy marriage.

The characters of Mamba and Hagar are the dual source of the novel's power. Mamba's shrewdness and Hagar's strength bring about their victory as regards Lissa. This victory is achieved in a world that is compounded of poverty, drunkenness, poor-white scoundrels, villainous Negros, and callous policemen. These two elemental beings strive together to bring into being an utterly new creature.

In discussing Heyward's presentation of the Negro world,

one must stress his realization of the existence of the educated Negro in the South. He wrote in *Mamba's Daughters*:

> In the old city that was so strong in its class consciousness among the white it was singular that there was so little realization of the fact, that, across the colour line, there existed much the same state of affairs. . . . Far above, in the life of the aristocracy, the new freedom was beginning to be manifest, smashing conventional usage; talking its Freud and Jung—rearranging moral standards, and explaining lapses in its pat psychological jargon. But in the Monday Night Music Club ladies were ladies, those who were pale enough blushed, a leg was still a limb—and a gentleman asked permission to smoke cigarettes.

Heyward was perfectly well aware of the fact that these Negroes were pioneers of a definite sort, fashioning standards for their less educated brethren and learning new behavior.

He described the Negro with realism. But he did not write with equal realism of the white race and the class to which he belonged. One receives the impression when reading his novels that he felt no limitations in his portrait of the black race. But his analysis of Charlestonians is deficient in the critical spirit. It is as if he were speaking to his first cousin about the manners of his second cousin. The writing is too restrained and protective. Stringfellow Barr writes that "Aristocracy exists only where there is faith in the worthwhileness of some intangible values." Perhaps these intangible values were too vivid in his thoughts when he sat down to describe his own kind of human being. One is led to think of Heyward's description of the character of Saint:

> But the past had reached dead hands after him, guiding him imperceptibly this way and that. Forces that had driven forward in grooves for generations had pulled against his amorphous longings, his only half-realized dreams—had held him true to form and tradition.

There is part of the answer to the question of the imperfectness of his characterization of Charlestonians of his class. Too many of the unpleasant facts are omitted. With that in mind, Gerald W. Johnson wrote of him:

"He can evoke Paradise, but he cannot, or will not, raise Hell; and that is both his strength and his weakness." But, nevertheless, his characterization of the Negro is superb.

Other Southern writers have dealt more completely with the aristocratic Southern white. But Heyward was at once the most eloquent memorialist of the older type Negro and the most compassionate observer of the new.

WILLIAM H. SLAVICK

From "The Vision and the Achievement"

DuBose Heyward

1981, pp. 165–68

Heyward's role in the Southern Renascence is a minor but special one. Ellen Glasgow argued that the South's greatest needs were "blood and irony," the one "because Southern culture had strained too far from its roots in the earth," the other because she thought irony "the safest antidote to sentimental decay."[1] Faulkner's Negroes, yeoman farmers, and tragic vision provided the blood, and Glasgow's ironic vision, as Hugh Holman observes, "lay bare the inner nature of the social order" of the South which was the subject of her novels of manners.[2] A Charlestonian, Heyward could not share the mythical vision of Faulkner's South; he belonged to that city's eighteenth-century conservative tradition to which the Civil War was not the Apocalypse; Charleston, after all, was "the city that care forgot." Heyward could see the evils of crass commercialism and feel some of Mencken's barbs hit home, but he did not, as Allen Tate, see the South as a peculiar battleground of Western values and the modern spirit. He could not distance himself enough from Charleston's decadent aristocracy to offer the ironic criticism of his world that Glasgow could of hers.

The voice frequently heard in *Peter Ashley* suggests that Heyward might have been an ironist. But there is as much sentimentality as irony in Heyward, and he is more often and better defined as a memorialist and as often as a realist.

Like Faulkner, Heyward sees from without and feels from within, but the ambiguous response in Heyward lacks the creative conflict; Heyward's perspective remains more discrete.[3] His feelings have more to do with manners than moral passion.

Heyward's role, then, is transitional, memorializing and criticizing, telling the truth—not all of it but enough to be called courageous for his time. He is less the Glasgow ironist, Faulkner moralist, or Stribling satirist than the mannered Charleston stoic who is largely resigned to the imperfections of the world in his gratitude for its blessings or to the hopelessness of affecting the future—but not quite always resigned. Heyward's special brew was a combination of this inborn aristocratic conservatism; the local colorist's nostalgia for the traditional, particularly the primitive qualities of the Negro; that eighteenth-century southern stoicism that hesitates to judge or strongly criticize; an honest recognition of the practical evils that follow from the doctrine of white supremacy; and a recognition of the change that was upon the region, whether it wanted such change or not, and of the inability of the aristocracy to meet such change effectively. It might be called social realism.

Central in Heyward's contribution to the Southern Renascence is his truth-telling, in the first years after it had become possible to "tell the actual truth about any phase of life in the South." [4] Latter-day readers will find Heyward's truth selective and pallid, and his style and point of view are sometimes a challenge to that truth. But "Gamesters All," *Porgy*, *Angel*, and *Mamba's Daughters* are not lacking in a certain investment of courage. At least enough of Catfish Row, the elemental mountaineers' struggle, and the phosphate mines is there to guess the whole truth. Then, in *Peter Ashley*, he dares tell the less than heroic truth about how some—at least one—of the gallant heroes of the Confederate army came to be there in the first place: against his better judgment. And in *Lost Morning* there is no mistaking the vulgar nouveau-riche decadence that has engulfed whole communities and the frustration of the artist caught in it. Still, by viewing the reality of Negro urban life in *Porgy* largely apart from the moral issues involved in white exploitation and social irresponsibility—and apart from the historical context of black experience, Heyward has his truth . . . without alienating a Southern audience. The same strategy carries over into *Mamba's Daughters* where Saint's class, ineffectual conventional Christianity, and a stoic acceptance of the status quo obscure the burning social questions raised by the difficulties Mamba and her daughters face. It is truth within limits; the reader does not encounter anywhere an adequate image of that oppressive and brutal conformity experienced throughout the South in the early twentieth century. *Brass Ankle* is the nearest approximation.

Yet, Heyward's work reflects the truth of his childhood experience of poverty, of his clerkship in a hardware store, of his waterfront observation, of his summers in the mountains, of the firsthand accounts he heard of what the Sumter prelude was really like, and of the new aristocracy he as surely met in the 1930s as a defeated Felix Hollister met it in Exeter.

Assessment of Heyward's criticism of his world—and appreciation of the origin of that criticism—is assisted by returning to Donald Davidson's question about why Heyward's studies of Negro life are "so palpably tinged with latter-day abolitionism." Davidson's concern was what he saw, in certain southern works, Heyward's included, to be "a dissociation of the artist from his environment, resulting in a literature of mingled protest and escape."[5] Davidson answers his own question about Heyward extremely well: "The Southern tradition in which these writers would share has been discredited and made artistically inaccessible; and the ideas, modes, attitudes that discredited it, largely not southern, have been current and could be used."[6]

And whose ideas discredited it? Ironically, where the Nashville academics could discount H. L. Mencken as a "vulgar rhetorician," DuBose Heyward, as this study has shown, repeatedly adopts a perspective consistent with Mencken's iconoclastic stance and his campaign to "free" the Southern mind.[7] *Angel* is a good example. Heyward sees little of value in the backwoods life of Thunder Cove; in ridiculing Thornley's revival as an emotional orgy, he fails to acknowledge anything genuine in Fundamentalist Protestantism; he scorns the mechanical and uniformly tawdry lives of the mill folk. And, like Mencken, he has nothing to put in place of what he scorns, save the indomitable spirits of Buck and Angel. Again, in *Mamba's Daughters*, Heyward sees the inadequacies of the life Charleston's whites inherit but offers only a healthy mercantile career as an inferior alternative—and escape for blacks. Nor are the religious values of Mamba and Hagar duly credited as motives until the play version. *Peter Ashley* probes the closed Southern mind—sympathetically but without mercy. Southern provincialism in Rivertown has no redeeming features, and in Exeter the modern secular world is fully realized and dominant; Hollister at his best is part of it, too, if hostile to the commercialism. As Davidson observes, Heyward's treatment of the South—The Negro, race relations, Puritanism, or whatever—serves to confirm Mencken's narrow view of the South as reflecting "bigotry, ignorance, hatred, superstition, every sort of blackness" as opposed to "sense."[8] Heyward appears to need Mencken to begin to see meanings in what he so well observes.

Whatever prompts Heyward's insight, when he is finished, the illusion of the white aristocracy's superiority is dispelled. But Heyward also goes beyond Mencken's concerns to recognize certain primitive Negro strengths and qualities, particularly rhythm, community spirit, and a *joie de vivre*, as well as such sad realities of black life as Hagar's pathetic self-hatred and the self-deprecation of Row inhabitants who see themselves as "just niggers." Also, the relentless inroads of modern industrialism and progress are reflected in the changing economics of the aristocracy, the aspirations of the urban Negros, the invasion of the mountains, the incorporation of Rivertown, the modernization of the city ("Chant for an Old Town"), and the bourgeois respectability that rules Exeter. The truth of Heyward's vision is primarily social, for the struggles of his characters are chiefly with society or representatives of it.

Notes

1. A *Certain Measure* (New York: Harcourt, Brace, 1943), p. 28.
2. *Three Modes of Modern Southern Fiction* (Athens: University of Georgia Press, 1966), p. 19.
3. See Frank Durham, "The Southern Literary Tradition: Shadow or Substance," *South Atlantic Quarterly* 67 (Summer 1968): 467.
4. Julia Peterkin, "Southern View-Point," *North American Review* 244 (Winter 1937–38): 392.
5. Donald Davidson, "The Artist as Southerner," *Saturday Review of Literature* 2 (May 15, 1962): 782.
6. "A Mirror for Artists," in Twelve Southerners, *I'll Take My Stand* (1930; rpt. New York: Harper, 1962), pp. 58–59.
7. Davidson, *Southern Writers in the Modern World* (Athens: University of Georgia Press, 1958), p. 30; Fred C. Hobson, *Serpent in Eden: H. L. Mencken and the South* (Chapel Hill: University of North Carolina Press, 1973), pp. 109, 148–52.
8. The characterization of Mencken's view is his, not Davidson's. See "Aftermath," *Baltimore Evening Sun*, September 14, 1925, cited in Hobson, p. 151.

Patricia Highsmith

1921–

Mary Patricia Highsmith was born in Fort Worth, Texas, on January 19, 1921, and grew up in New York. Her parents, who separated before she was born, were both commercial artists, as was her stepfather, whose name she adopted after her mother's remarriage, and she herself engaged in drawing and painting before deciding to devote herself to writing. After receiving a B.A. from Barnard College in 1942, she worked as a freelance writer on comic books while publishing occasional short stories. Her first novel, *Strangers on a Train* (1950), provided the basis for one of Alfred Hitchcock's finest films, and *The Talented Mr. Ripley* (1955) also became a film under the title *Purple Noon*. Ripley is her most enduring character, appearing in four novels, the most recent of which, *The Boy Who Followed Ripley*, was published in 1980.

Highsmith has received more recognition in Europe than in America, and after visits in the 1950s has lived in France and England since 1963. In 1957 she was awarded the Grand Prix de Littérature Policière, and in 1964 the Crime Writers' Silver Dagger. Her fiction, including *The Cry of the Owl* (1962), *Those Who Walk Away* (1967), and *Ripley Under Ground* (1971), deals mainly with the psychology of crime, though in later works, such as *Edith's Diary* (1977), she has extended her range to include other psychological studies. Apart from novels, she has also published collections of short stories, including *The Snail-Watcher and Other Stories* (1970) and *The Black House* (1981), and in 1966 produced the theoretical work *Plotting and Writing Suspense Fiction*.

Patricia Highsmith lives alone and continues to travel widely.

General

Because she writes murder stories Patricia Highsmith is usually reviewed under some such heading as 'Crime Corner' or 'Murder Ration'. It is true that reviewers nearly always place her first in the list, and concede that her books are good novels as well as effective thrillers; but the essential distinction remains unmade. The point is, her writing is quite free from any element of fantasy. The very phrase 'murder story' implies some degree or other of stylisation; there are countless gradations between the cosy vicarage puzzle and the sexy Californian blood-bath, but all are highly formal. Facetious reticence at one extreme, baroque callousness at the other—both are designed to distract attention from the inconvenient reality of murder, which in such books is a pretext rather than a theme. Thus the least trivial of all subjects has become, in popular fiction, synonymous with triviality.

Miss Highsmith writes murder stories which are literally that: stories about murder. They are about what drives people to kill and about what the event of murder is like for the killer and for the people connected with him and his victim. It is rare for death to occur in a Highsmith novel until at least a third of the book is past; often it is reserved for the very end. When it takes place, her readers are made aware not only of the horror, but also of the *embarrassment* following an act of destructive violence; it is as if a person one knows quite well were suddenly killed by somebody else one knows quite well. And although Miss Highsmith makes the most scrupulous psychological preparation for her murders, so that their eruption is never unconvincing, yet the effect on her readers is shocking in the same kind of way as the experience of murder would be in life. For very rarely, in life, can murder be expected: yet it happens.

Guilt is her theme, and she approaches it through two contrasting heroes. These may be simplified as the guilty man who has justified his guilt and the innocent man who feels himself to be guilty. Both appeared in her first and most famous novel, *Strangers on a Train:* the soft, plausible charmer who is really a psychopath and the shy bungler who allows himself to be engulfed in a nightmare from which he is too ineffectual (and perhaps basically unwilling) to extricate himself. Variations on one or other of these mutually attractive figures dominate her later books: *The Blunderer, A Game for the Living* and *The Cry of the Owl* concentrate on the victim of malign events who is hypnotised into immobility by the horror of his situation; while *The Talented Mr Ripley, Deep Water* and *This Sweet Sickness* provide full-length portraits of the well-spoken young man, somehow incomplete and yet not apparently sinister, who slithers into mania and murder. The books in the first group also contain a detective whose behaviour is capricious, irrational yet depressingly dogged; this figure is the more menacing because he is invariably wrong. Miss Highsmith specialises in male characters, but two types of women recur throughout her work: the bitch and the nice girl. The bitch (Melinda in *Deep Water,* Nickie in *The Cry of the Owl)* can be a creature of Strindbergian venom, compensating for some mysterious sexual outrage or disappointment by the total destruction of a man. The nice girl (Marge in *Mr Ripley,* Effie in *This Sweet Sickness,* Jenny in *The Cry of the Owl)* is intense, affectionate, rather arty, and fatally unsuspicious.

There is no doubt that Miss Highsmith's extraordinary gifts are demonstrated most successfully in the novels of the second group, where the psychopath takes precedence over the blunderer: *The Talented Mr Ripley, Deep Water, This Sweet Sickness.* Her unemphatic style makes a highly effective medium for the unsettling view of life which she expresses. As Tom, Vic and David become increasingly absorbed in their obsessions, we gradually share them; the well-meaning, trusting figures who surround them seem to be separated from us by glass; so does the 'ordinary' background which Miss Highsmith can suggest with such economy and atmospheric subtlety. Her moral detachment raises disturbing questions, both about the nature of evil and the point where madness starts. David, in *This Sweet Sickness,* nourishes a hopeless love for Annabelle and will not take no for an answer: when does his attitude cease to be romantic fidelity and become dangerous delusion? At a much earlier point than any of his associates realise. Similarly, Vic in *Deep Water* has been humiliated for so long by Melinda that some violent action on his part might be both morally and socially excusable; but he hesitates before taking it, and when he does it is in a hideous form. It is possible to sympathise with David and Vic and to be frightened by them at the same time. Strangely enough, the one hero who is allowed by Miss Highsmith to escape unpunished (and with whom it is hard for the reader not to feel at least a certain complicity) is the most wicked of all: Tom Ripley, morally a terrifying blank, whose urge to acquire the trappings of another man's personality involves him in two successful murders and a fraud so mad and so intricate that it defies discovery. This thrilling novel sheds more light on 'the problem of identity' than many solemn approaches to a fashionable theme.

In her new novel, *The Cry of the Owl,* she is writing well below top form: but even so, she still maintains an exciting pitch of narrative tension. Here the main Highsmith archetypes are re-arranged in a complex pattern to produce her characteristic atmosphere, which is not so much one of nightmare as of the grey small hours when reality is seen in all its unpalatable clarity. The blunderer is divorced from the bitch, who has decided to ruin him. The nice girl falls obsessively in love with the blunderer, and is herself loved by the psychopath, who joins forces with the bitch in a revenge no less destructive for being insanely irresponsible. The book is a study of things getting out of control. Miss Highsmith's plots are often praised for being ingenious, but they are never tidy; chance, coincidence, silly misunderstandings play their part, as they do in life. She knows that people do not always act in their own best interests, and that their motives are more obscure than psychological novelists often care to admit. Her peculiar brand of horror comes less from the inevitability of disaster, than from the ease with which it might have been avoided. The evil of her agents is answered by the impotence of her patients—this is not the attraction of opposites, but in some subtle way the call of like to like. When they finally clash in climactic catastrophe, the reader's sense of satisfaction may derive from sources as dark as those which motivate Patricia Highsmith's destroyers and their fascinated victims.—FRANCIS WYNDHAM, "Miss Highsmith," *NS,* May 31, 1963, pp. 833–34

The suspense writer can improve his lot and the reputation of the suspense novel by putting into his books the qualities that have always made books good—insight, character, an opening of new horizons for the imagination of the reader. I do not speak, in this paragraph, about mystery books, because they are out of my line, and it is a characteristic of them that the identity of the murderer is withheld, or at any rate his character as murderer is not deeply explored, if at all. If a suspense writer is going to write about murderers and victims, about people in the vortex of this awful whirl of events, he should do more than describe brutality and gore and the gooseflesh in the night. He should throw some light on his characters' minds; he should be interested in justice or the absence of it in the world we live in; he should be interested in the morality, good and bad, that exists today; he should be interested in human cowardice or courage, and not merely as forces to push his plot this way and that. In a word, his people should be real. This seriousness may sound at variance with the element of playing that I mentioned in regard to plot, but it is not, since I am talking of another matter. The spirit of playing is necessary in plotting to permit freedom of the imagination. It is also necessary in inventing characters. But once one *has* the characters in mind, and the plot, the characters should be given most serious consideration, and one should pay attention to what they are doing and why, and if one does not explain it—and it may be artistically bad to explain too much—then a writer should know why his characters behave as they do and should be able to answer this question to himself. It is by this that insight is born, by this that the book acquires value. Insight is not something found in psychology books; it is in every creative person. And—see Dostoyevsky—writers are decades ahead of the textbooks, anyway.

It often happens that a writer has a theme or a pattern in his books, and he should be aware of this, though again not in a hampering way. He should be aware of it so as to exploit it well, and so as not to repeat it without realizing it. Some writers' themes may be a quest for something—a father one never knew, the pot of gold which does not exist at the foot of the rainbow. Others may have a recurrent girl-in-distress motif, which starts them off plotting, and without which they are not exactly comfortable writing. Another is a doomed love or a doomed marriage. Mine is the relationship between two men, usually quite different in make-up, sometimes obviously the good and the evil, sometimes merely ill-matched friends. I might have realized this theme in myself at least by the middle of *Strangers on a Train*, but it was a friend, a newspaperman, who pointed it out to me when I was twenty-six and just beginning *Strangers*, a man who had seen the manuscript of my first effort at twenty-two that I have already mentioned, the book that was never finished. This was about a rich, spoiled boy, and a poor boy who wanted to be a painter. They were fifteen years old in the book. As if that weren't enough, there were two minor characters, a tough, athletic boy who seldom attended school (and then only to shock the school with things like the bloated corpse of a drowned dog he had found on the banks of the East River) and a puny, clever boy who giggled a great deal and adored him and was always in his company. The two-men theme turned up also in *The Blunderer, The Talented Mr. Ripley*, in *A Game for the Living*, and *The Two Faces of January*, and raises its head a little in *The Glass Cell* in the curious comrades-in-social-defiance attitude between Carter and Gawill. So in six books out of ten it has turned up, certainly in my "best" books in public opinion. Natural themes cannot be sought or strained for; they appear. Unless one is in danger of repeating oneself, they should be used to the fullest, because a writer will write better making use of what is, for some strange reason, innate.

For example, the one really dull book I have written was my fifth, *A Game for the Living*, in which the murderer (of the girl found dead in Chapter One) is but dimly introduced early in the story. He is not to be suspected. Another man, whom we know much better, confesses, though his confession is not entirely believed. The real murderer is off-scene mostly, so *A Game for the Living* became a "mystery who-dunnit" in a way—definitely not my forte. I had tried to do something different from what I had been doing, but this caused me to leave out certain elements that are vital for me: surprise, speed of action, the stretching of the reader's credulity, and above all that intimacy with the murderer himself. I am not an inventor of puzzles, nor do I like secrets. The result, after rewriting the book four times in a grueling year of work, was mediocrity. I always say to foreign publishers, and to publishers who contemplate a reprint, "This is my worst book, so please think twice before you buy it." However, I believe that any story can be told properly, using some of the writer's stronger points, but the writer must first be aware of what his stronger points are. I disobeyed my natural laws in this boring book, and it was unforgivable of me.

I have said little about other people's suspense books, mainly because I seldom read them, and so I am unqualified to say that certain suspense books are good, very good, or why. I like best Graham Greene's entertainments, mainly because they are intelligent, and their prose is very skillful. He is also a moralist, even in his entertainments, and I am interested in morality, providing it isn't preached. There is no doubt that a study of the whole field of "the best" in suspense writing, whatever that is, can be of benefit professionally to a suspense writer, but I would just as soon not pursue this study. After all, I do not take myself seriously as a suspense writer as to category, and I am not interested in seeing how another writer handled a difficult theme successfully, because I cannot keep his or her example in my mind when I am faced with my typewriter and my own problem. I read Graham Greene's novels for pleasure, but I do not ever think of imitating him or even of being guided by him—except that I would like to have his talent for *le mot juste*, a gift that can be admired in Flaubert, too. And given this laziness about studying my own field, it is easy to rationalize and excuse it by telling myself I believe I run a danger of copying if I read other people's suspense books. I don't really believe this. There is no enthusiasm in copying, and without enthusiasm, one can't write a decent book.
—PATRICIA HIGHSMITH, "Some Notes on Suspense in General," *Plotting and Writing Suspense Fiction*, 1972, pp. 143–47

For most of her career, reviewers have been urging Patricia Highsmith to have a go at writing a Real Novel. Disheartening advice for her, presumably, since these same reviewers were simultaneously announcing to the world that the books she *had* published possessed gifts and insights well beyond the scope of most Real Novelists. She had, it was repeatedly proclaimed, much narrative power, psychological subtlety, ingenuity of composition, elegance of prose style, understanding of American middle class *mores*, etc. To have that lot credited to your account and still somehow be in the red—well, that's what comes of joining the Crime Writers' Association at an early age. If you've asked people not to take you seriously, they'll jump at the chance.

Unfair, without a doubt. And yet Patricia Highsmith has always to some extent collaborated in her own pigeon-holing; in lots of casual-looking ways she has acceded to the requirements of her genre. Even her most original creations—the Ripley tales, *Deep Water, Strangers on a Train*—have a more than ample supply of stock detective-yarn ingredients, and there has often been an air of market-conscious haste about her treatment of minor characters, brochure-ish foreign settings, coincidences wrenched in order to clear up any loose ends that she can't be bothered properly to follow through, and so on. Many of her novels of the Sixties seemed content to mimic the most striking of the habits or mannerisms that she had mastered in her first half-dozen books; there even seemed to be a weariness in this, a resigned willingness to let mere incident take over, to rest content with plumping out the crime-novel formula with a bit of her by then celebrated understanding of the obsessed psyche.

It was only with the re-emergence of the Ripley character in *Ripley under Ground* that Miss Highsmith seemed to recover the intensity, and the intense curiosity, that had made even the most formula-ridden stretches of her early work so chilling. The Ripley-Greenleaf balance of insufficiencies had been repeated on and off in later novels—Ray Garrett/Edward Coleman in *Those Who Walk Away* and Rydal Keenor/Chester MacFarlane in *The Two Faces of January* are typical instances of the Highsmith pre-occupation with weirdly spellbound male relationships—but it was never given quite the same subtlety and animation. The triumph of Ripley is that his paranoia is supportive; he genuinely believes that there's an injustice in the ordering of things—why, having equipped me with all else in such abundance, does nature withhold the one gift I need to make me absolutely perfect? Not just withhold it, but turn around and hand it out to someone who in every other respect is worthless, barely fit to live? A lot of people feel this way; it's an obsession that lurks somewhere at the heart of even the most forlorn and sluggish grumble. In most, it merely makes for sulks; in Ripley, it produces a series of neat, untroubled homicides.

And this is so often the mode in which Highsmith excels; she persuades us that it really could go either way. 'It' may vary, but the suspense is at some level common to us all, however humdrum, well-ordered or bogged down we pride ourselves on having managed to become. Up to now, Miss Highsmith has chosen to alert us by exhibiting the spirals of frightful and outlandish consequence that it's possible to get caught up in, and—with Ripley—how it's all too easy to be awful. In *Edith's Diary*, the matter is approached from, as it were, the far end of the tunnel. Instead of moving outwards from the banal to the spectacular, we are led deeper and deeper into the heart of the banal, to where the real horror is of what's utterly familiar. Miss Highsmith employs her dead-pan suspense techniques to unfold the day-to-day, year-to-year, minutiae of a life that's almost wholly passive, a life that is defined in nearly every detail by its obligations, its rituals, its chores, its ever-darkening banality.

Edith is a well-off, Left-progressive, middle-middle-class housewife, a busy and capable manager, a loyal wife, and a genial and tolerant mother to her only child. When the book opens, the family is packing to leave for a new house in the country, where Brett's salary will be lower but the air less polluted, where there will be space for the boy to grow up in and opportunity for her and Brett to start their own Left-progressive town newspaper and in their small way maybe do some good. It sounds a reliable recipe for a distinctive type of American good life. Edith writes optimistically about the move in the diary she's been keeping for some years.

It's a fairly typical Highsmith opening, so when the packing is interrupted briefly by the sound of the boy Cliffie tormenting the cat, or when Edith reflects idly on an ugly dream she's had a few nights earlier, we settle down to wait for the menace to start building up. And this is more or less where we stay throughout the book. Things happen: Brett's old uncle is moved into the house and proves demanding and irritating; Cliffie grows more and more sullen and disaffected; Brett falls in love with his secretary and goes off with her; there are deaths in the family and quarrels with neighbours; there are the impinging political upheavals of Vietnam, Watergate, and so on.

Summed up, it's a fairly ordinary sequence of events; and, although the neutral, itemising clarity of Highsmith's prose hints all the time that an eruption is just around the corner, the book's real shock effect is registered precisely through the steady lifelessness of the lives it so inertly charts. Gradually we are made aware that there are two ways of describing Edith's life, and that the second way—the way that sees it as horribly devoured by odious dependents—is the way Edith can't afford to contemplate. Hence her diary, in which she invents a successful career for her son, arranges a satisfactory marriage, two fine children, frequent loving visits to the old homestead. The keeping of the diary and the clinging to the last meticulous, desperate detail of her imprisoning routine is what she hopes will keep her sane; and, of course, if that effort fails, she'll be the last to know. As the pressure intensifies, the most mundane domestic function is made to seem like an icy little melodrama. It's not going to be easy from now on for Miss Highsmith to scare us with mere murder.—LOUIS FINGER, "Mere Murder," *NS*, July 1, 1977, pp. 23–24

Works

Miss Highsmith is a crime novelist whose books one can reread many times. There are very few of whom one can say that. She is a writer who has created a world of her own—a world claustrophobic and irrational which we enter each time with a sense of personal danger, with the head half turned over the shoulder, even with a certain reluctance, for these are cruel pleasures we are going to experience, until somewhere about the third chapter the frontier is closed behind us, we cannot retreat, we are doomed to live till the story's end with another of her long series of wanted men.

It makes the tension worse that we are never sure whether even the worst of them, like the talented Mr. Ripley, won't get away with it or that the relatively innocent won't suffer like the blunderer Walter or the relatively guilty escape altogether like Sydney Bartleby in *The Story-Teller.* This is a world without moral endings. It has nothing in common with the heroic world of her peers, Hammett and Chandler, and her detectives (sometimes monsters of cruelty like the American Lieutenant Corby of *The Blunderer* or dull sympathetic rational characters like the British Inspector Brockway) have nothing in common with the romantic and disillusioned private eyes who will always, we know, triumph finally over evil and see that justice is done, even though they may have to send a mistress to the chair.

Nothing is certain when we have crossed *this* frontier. It is not the world as we once believed we knew it, but it is frighteningly more real to us than the house next door. Actions are sudden and impromptu and the motives sometimes so inexplicable that we simply have to accept them on trust. I believe because it is impossible. Her characters are irrational, and they leap to life in their very lack of reason; suddenly we realise how unbelievably rational most fictional characters are as they lead their lives from A to Z, like commuters always taking the same train. The motives of these are never inexplicable because they are so drearily obvious. The characters are as flat as a mathematical symbol. We accepted them as real once, but when we look back at them from Miss Highsmith's side of the frontier, we realise that our world was not really as rational as all that. Suddenly with a sense of fear we think, "Perhaps I really belong *here*," and going out into the familiar street we pass with a shiver of apprehension the offices of the American Express, the centre, for so many of Miss Highsmith's dubious men, of their rootless European experience, where letters are to be picked up (though the name on the envelope is probably false) and travellers' cheques are to be cashed (with a forged signature).

Miss Highsmith's short stories do not let us down, though we may be able sometimes to brush them off more easily because of their brevity. We haven't lived with them long enough to be totally absorbed. Miss Highsmith is the poet of apprehension rather than fear. Fear after a time, as we all learned in the blitz, is narcotic, it can lull one by fatigue into sleep, but apprehension nags at the nerves gently and inescapably. We have to learn to live with it. Miss Highsmith's finest novel to my mind is *The Tremor of Forgery*, and if I were to be asked what it is about I would reply, "Apprehension."

In her short stories Miss Highsmith has naturally to adopt a different method. She is after the quick kill rather than the slow encirclement of the reader, and how admirably and with what field-craft, she hunts us down. Some of these stories were written twenty years ago before her first novel, *Strangers on a Train*, but we have no sense that she is learning her craft by false starts, by trial and error. "The Heroine," published nearly a quarter of a century ago, is as much a study of apprehension as her last novel. We can feel how dangerous (and irrational) the young nurse is from her first interview. We want to cry to the parents, "Get rid of her before it's too late."

My own favourite in this collection is the story "When the Fleet Was in at Mobile" with the moving horror of its close when all we had foreseen was a simple little case of murder—here is Miss Highsmith at her claustrophobic best. "The Terrapin," a late Highsmith, is a cruel story of childhood which can bear comparison with Saki's masterpiece, "Stredni Vashtar," and for pure physical horror, which is an emotion rarely evoked by Miss Highsmith, "The Snail-Watcher" would be hard to beat. Mr. Knoppert has the same attitude to his snails as Miss Highsmith to human beings. He watches them with the same emotionless curiosity as Miss Highsmith watches the talented Mr. Ripley.

> Mr. Knoppert had wandered into the kitchen one evening for a bite of something before dinner, and had happened to notice that a couple of snails in the china bowl on the drainboard were behaving very oddly. Standing more or less on their tails, they were weaving before each other for all the world like a pair of snakes hypnotised by a flute player. A moment later, their faces came together in a kiss of voluptuous intensity. Mr. Knoppert bent closer and studied them from all angles. Something else was happening: a protuberance like an ear was appearing on the right side of the head of both snails. His instinct told him that he was watching a sexual activity of some sort.

—GRAHAM GREENE, "Introduction" to *The Snail-Watcher and Other Stories*, 1970, pp. xi–xiv

Twelve years back *The Talented Mr Ripley* was made into a very good film *Plein soleil* by René Clement. Now Ripley, the amoral impersonator and something of a spark in his day, is back between covers and the effect is stifling.

This time ⟨in *Ripley under Ground*⟩ he's forced to disguise himself as a great painter Derwatt, who's in fact been dead for years, but who's been posthumously forged by a neurotic admirer called Bernard Tufts. Ripley and a corrupt art gallery have profited from the deception, which is bolstered with the colourful fiction that Derwatt is alive and living in an inaccessible village in Mexico.

This amiable fraud is threatened when an American client of the gallery notices an inconsistency in the work and flies over to England to investigate. To try and satisfy the man it's suddenly necessary to resurrect Derwatt, and Ripley volunteers to leave his comfortable French life (which he established in the previous volume) in order to impersonate the great man. But the American is not deceived by the false Derwatt's assertion that none of his work has been forged, so Ripley is driven to a horrifying murder and to burying the American in the grounds of his beautiful French home.

The story so far is ingenious and convincing, tightly written and superbly sustained as long as it keeps its sense of danger. Particularly good is the way you feel the warmth of wealth's embrace, the physical comfort Ripley lives in, and the instinctive way he reacts to its being threatened. But the narrative is strained to contain diversions about the pressure forging puts on Bernard's personality. After all this forging is he truly himself or another man etc? You can imagine. These always elegant inquiries into the nature of artistic personality are basically dull as hell, and the tension of the story is dissipated when the book becomes fascinated with the minds of Ripley and Tufts; for Tufts's mind is dull and Ripley's mind seems numb, jotting little intellectual queries in its margin, but never really coming to terms with what it's doing.

You realise once this investigation is under way that nothing in the story is going to develop and all you're going to get is permutations. Sure enough, the end is determinedly inconsequential. This ties in regrettably with the way Miss Highsmith has recently been writing, particularly in *The Tremor of Forgery*, which is almost a total anti-thriller: the whole nature of the threat to Ingham the artist is that it is unspecified, vague, half-sensed and unsettling. The strings of the narrative, here as there, cannot be pulled together. They make no patterns. In both cases the demand of the thriller that it keeps a sense of infinite possibility and the inevitability of the psychology seem at odds. The openness of the story and the closedness of the characters jam. The pity is that in avoiding the patness of a lot of thriller narrative, Miss Highsmith puts in its place an intellectual patness—too simply asking familiar questions. And the way nothing ties up seems as studied as the most ridiculously unlikely examples of detective narrative. —DAVID HARE, "David Hare on Crime Fiction," *Spec*, Jan. 30, 1971, p. 161

Taken (which it could but I don't think should be) purely as a novel of suspense, *A Dog's Ransom* is a virtuoso piece. Miss Highsmith is in such command that she can actually do without mystery and still compel you to read urgently on. (The only sleight-of-hand comes from the printers, who, in a small extra-canonical miracle, transform Châteauneuf du Pape into a claret by spelling it Château Neuf.)

The first 45 pages do not disclose the identity of the person who sends Ed and Greta Reynolds anonymous letters, then causes the disappearance of their black poodle Lisa during her evening run in Riverside Park, and finally collects 1,000 dollars of supposed ransom. Even, however, while he goes unlocated, his actions define him as a petty psychopath. It is less a surprise than a completely realised confirmation when the narrative endows his personality with a name and a local, indeed brilliantly narrowed-down, bodily habitation, and goes on to dispose of even the one remaining mystery, the fate of the poodle, through the reflections of the psychopath's unfeeling, non-moral consciousness.

What *A Dog's Ransom* counts on, to carry the reader, is

the soundness of its construction. Before quite renouncing mystery by entering the psychopath's mind, it establishes the strategic centres from which it is going to explore the responses forced from the sane by erratic and lunatic acts of violence. Ed Reynolds is at first unambivalent, concerned simply and reasonably for the safety of his dog. The narrative builds up his plausibility by an engaging circumstantialness about his actions; and by the same token it evokes, without needing to describe, the physical grittiness and social unease of New York: 'He had just come from the office, and as he let the water rinse away the soap, he thought: "I'm washing my hands of the subway and also of that damned letter."'

Ed's quasi-parental responsibility for his dog is reinforced by the fact that, a year before the story opens, his grown-up daughter has died by violence. This looks like an item of merely worldly-wise plotting, a device to hook the sympathy even of readers cold towards dogs. But it turns out to be a structural necessity in the design, carrying the book deeper into its theme and also creating a contrasting link between Ed and the narrative's other chief centre of consciousness, which resides in Patrolman Clarence Duhamell.

Duhamell is a realistically elastic and amorphous personality. He aspires to be good, and has indeed chosen deliberately to be a 'good cop' in the sense of eschewing the corruption practised by his colleagues. Impressed by the patent fact that Ed, in the altruism of his immediate relationships, simply *is* good, Duhamell involves himself in the case of the poodle, to which he is not assigned. He wants to help Ed and, in doing so, to act out his own large but unshaped aspirations towards being a parent and protector of society as a whole. But Duhamell traps himself into making an attack on violence that is itself violent. Ed is riven by moral ambivalence towards the 'help' Duhamell affords him. And Duhamell fails to get away with committing evil for the ironic reason that he is, precisely, not one of the bad cops.

The 'analyses' which often come with miniature music scores ('at bar 97 the second theme returns and is elaborated') may be dogmatic, inflexibly academic and sometimes plain wrong, but they have the virtue of strongly implying to listeners that a symphony or concerto is a design as well as entertainment and/or the self-expression of a soul. It crosses my mind that good novels will not be restored to the respect they deserve, and pretentious ones won't cease to debase the currency, until publishers include a structural analysis in the blurb.

The intellectual effort that goes into (and the intellectual profit that a reader can take from) a novel lies not in the overt statements of the narrative and dialogue but in the power of the thought incarnated in the design. No more than it describes New York does *A Dog's Ransom* make statements about society and violence. Yet it is a profound act of thought on the theme of violence seducing its opponents into violence. Statistics might affirm that the problem is most acute in New York: *A Dog's Ransom* can achieve the *imaginative* rightness of being set there. Sociology and reporting, with their wide scatter, can set out contradictions in moral attitudes: *A Dog's Ransom* performs the indispensable function of fiction by taking the reader deep into the ironies of his own ambivalence.—BRIGID BROPHY, "Poodle," *LT*, May 11, 1972, p. 627

Man is beastly to animal, animal retaliates and destroys man. Sometimes it is an individual animal: an elephant turning on her keeper, a dog on his owner, a camel on his driver; sometimes it is a swarm of smaller animals—hamsters or battery chickens—taking revenge on an individual for man's collective cruelty to nature. Even if the title of this collection of stories (*The Animal-Lover's Book of Beastly Murder*) were not a give-away, the pattern becomes predictable after the second piece. Surprise and suspense, essential in horror fiction, receive fatal injuries from the blunt instrument of repetition.

Describing a story in Patricia Highsmith's previous collection *Eleven*, Graham Greene said that "for pure physical horror, which is an emotion rarely evoked by Miss Highsmith, 'The Snail-Watcher' would be hard to beat". But here, in order to give us our kicks, Miss Highsmith resorts to physical horror in every story but one—"Notes from a Respectable Cockroach", a piece of beetle's eye-view social criticism. Elsewhere even the physical horrors are repetitive: The smaller animals go for the eyes, nose and throat; then, if not disturbed, they clean the flesh off the skeleton. The larger just trample and squash their victims, while medium-sized ones sometimes trip them up, causing them to crack their skulls or drown in a handy bit of water. The most elaborate killing mechanism occurs in "There I Was Stuck with Bugsie" where a dog bites through the tube of an asthma mask belonging to the odious Bugsie, who has inherited him from his beloved but defunct first owner. Even here there is not much surprise, however: the asthma machine has been planted with uncharacteristic clumsiness earlier on in the story.

The Siamese cat operates in Acapulco, the camel in a fictionalized Morocco, the rat in Venice, the ferret in Touraine, the pig in the Lot; all classy locations, but they do not make up for the lack of a proper thrill. There is only one real attempt to establish a social milieu: "Bugsie" is set in the chic New York artistic and theatrical world, but it is observed through the eyes of the dog, whose vision is naturally limited.

With the exception of Harry in "Harry: A Ferret" (by far the most subtle piece) all the single animals are anthropomorphized, and some tell the tale in the first person. But Miss Highsmith has not made up her mind about how sophisticated their intelligence is supposed to be. In "Chorus Girl's Absolutely Final Performance", for instance, the elephant's devoted keeper, Steve, retires and dies. He is replaced by a young brute (same plot as "Bugsie") whom the elephant eventually savages. She has to be killed, and in her last moments she sees Steve in a vision: "I know that I am dying", she says, "because I know that Steve is dead." Too much conceptual thinking, you might say, for a beast who has previously described a space heater as a "box with a cord attached which blew hot air". (By going in for talking animals, Miss Highsmith exposes herself to the threat of cuteness and sentimentality, and it must be admitted that they make a number of kills.)

One of Miss Highsmith's previous books is dedicated to a cat, and in *A Dog's Ransom* the reader has to accept that kidnapping and killing a dog are more or less in the same category of crime as murder. Miss Highsmith is apologetic about this: "a dog, a daughter", muses the bereaved owner, "there should be a difference, yet the feeling was much the same". If the animal story is to be used as a cautionary fable, or as a disguise for social or moral criticism, then it must surely be cool as La Fontaine is cool—or even Hugh Lofting; if it is to be a horror tale, then it had better stick to unemotive creatures like snails, birds, or ferrets; and if it is to carry a load of mysticism like *Moby-Dick*, then the animals must not be chatty. In this book Miss Highsmith's feeling for animals, or the excess of it, has put her off her usual clean and masterly stroke.—GABRIELE ANNAN, "Our Dumb Friends," *TLS*, July 11, 1975, p. 784

ADDITIONAL READING

STANLEY ELKIN

Bargen, Doris G. *The Fiction of Stanley Elkin*. Frankfurt: Lang, 1980.

———. "Stanley Elkin's *The Franchiser.*" *Studies in American Jewish Literature* 2 (1983): 132–43.

Bernt, Phyllis and Joseph Bernt. "Stanley Elkin on Fiction: An Interview." *Prairie Schooner* 5 (1976): 14–25.

Clayton, Jay. "An Interview with Stanley Elkin." *Contemporary Literature* 24, (1983): 1–12.

Ditsky, John. "'Death Grotesque as Life': The Fiction of Stanley Elkin." *Hollins Critic* 19 (June 1982): 1–11.

Duncan, Jeffrey L. "A Conversation with Stanley Elkin and William Gass." *Iowa Review* 7 (1976): 48–77.

Edinger, Harry G. "Bears in Three Contemporary Fictions." *Humanities Association Review* 28 (1977): 141–50.

Edwards, Thomas R. Review of *Searches and Seizures*. *New York Times Book Review*, 21 October 1973, p. 3.

Elkin, Stanley. "Representation and Performance." In *Representation and Performance in Postmodern Fiction*, ed. Maurice Couturier. Montpellier: Delta, 1983.

Guttmann, Allen. "Stanley Elkin's Orphans." *Massachusetts Review* 7 (1966): 597–600.

Hardaway, Francine O. "The Power of the Guest: Stanley Elkin's Fiction." *Rocky Mountain Review of Language and Literature* 32 (1978): 234–45.

Olderman, Raymond M. "The Six Crises of Dick Gibson." *Iowa Review* 7 (1976): 127–40.

RALPH ELLISON

Alter, Robert. "The Apocalyptic Temper." *Commentary* 41 (June 1966): 61–66.

Bone, Robert A. *The Negro Novel in America*. New Haven: Yale University Press, 1958, pp. 196–212.

Boskin, Joseph. "The Life and Death of Sambo." *Journal of Popular Culture* 4 (1971): 647–57.

Clarke, John Henrik. "The Visible Dimension of *Invisible Man*." *Black World* 20 (1970): 27–30.

Furay, Michael. "Negritude—A Romantic Myth." *New Republic*, 2 July 1966, pp. 32–35.

Gross, Theodore L. *The Heroic Ideal in American Literature*. New York: Oxford University Press, 1971, pp. 148–79.

Miller, Stuart. *The Picaresque Novel*. Cleveland: Case Western Reserve University, 1967.

Nower, Joyce. "The Traditions of Negro Literature in the United States." *Negro American Literature Forum* 3 (1969): 5–12.

Sanders, Archie D. "Odysseus in Black." *CLA Journal* 13 (1970): 217–28.

Walker, James. "What Do You Say Now, Ralph Ellison?" *Black Creation* 1 (1970): 16–18.

Weinberg, Helen. *The New Novel in America*. Ithaca, NY: Cornell University Press, 1970, pp. 186–91.

WILLIAM EVERSON

Everson, William, "Foreword" to *The Birth of a Poet*. Santa Barbara: Black Sparrow Press, pp. v–vi.

Gelpi, Albert. "Everson/Antoninus: Contending with the Shadow." In *The Veritable Years* by William Everson. Santa Barbara: Black Sparrow Press, 1978, p. 361.

Haslam, G. Review of *Archetype West*. *Western American Literature* 12 (1977): 161.

Kherdian, David. "Brother Antoninus." In *Six Poets of the San Francisco Renaissance*. Fresno: Giligia Press, 1965, pp. 133–51.

Saroyan, A. Review of *Archetype West*. *Village Voice*, 16 May 1977, p. 73.

JAMES T. FARRELL

Branch, Edgar M. *A Bibliography of James T. Farrell's Writings, 1921–1957*. Philadelphia: University of Pennsylvania Press, 1959.

———. *James T. Farrell*. Minneapolis: University of Minnesota Press, 1963.

Frohock, William H. *The Novel of Violence in America, 1920–1950*. Dallas: Southern Methodist University Press, 1958.

Glicksberg, Charles I. "The Criticism of James T. Farrell." *Southwest Review* 35 (1950): 189–96.

Grattan, C. Hartley. "James T. Farrell: Moralist." *Harper's Magazine* 209 (October 1954): 93–98.

Gregory, Horace. "James T. Farrell: Beyond the Provinces of Art." *New World Writing* 5 (April 1954): 52–65.

Mitchell, Richard. "*Studs Lonigan:* Research in Morality." *Centennial Review* 5 (1962): 202–14.

WILLIAM FAULKNER

Adams, Richard Perrill, *Faulkner: Myth and Motion*. Princeton: Princeton University Press, 1968.

Backman, Melvin. *Faulkner: The Major Years: A Critical Study*. Bloomington: Indiana University Press, 1966.

Blotner, Joseph. *Faulkner: A Biography*. New York: Random House, 1974.

Coughlan, Robert. *The Private World of William Faulkner*. New York: Harper, 1954.

Cullen, John B., and Floyd C. Watkins. *Old Times in the Faulkner Country*. Chapel Hill: University of North Carolina Press, 1961.

Everett, Walter K. *Faulkner's Art and Characters*. Woodbury, NY: Barron's Educational Series, 1969.

Faulkner, John. *My Brother Bill: An Affectionate Reminiscence*. New York: Trident Press, 1963.

Hoffman, Frederick John, ed. *William Faulkner: Three Decades of Criticism*. East Lansing: Michigan State University Press, 1960.

Kerr, Elizabeth M. *Yoknapatawpha: Faulkner's "Little Postage Stamp of Native Soil."* New York: Fordham University Press, 1969.

Malin, Irving. *William Faulkner: An Interpretation*. Stanford: Stanford University Press, 1957.

Meriwether, James B., and Michael Millgate, eds. *Lion in the Garden: Interviews with William Faulkner 1926–1962*. New York: Random House, 1968.

Schmitter, Dean Morgan. *William Faulkner: A Collection of Criticism*. New York: McGraw-Hill, 1973.

Slatoff, Walter Jacob. *Quest for Failure: A Study of William Faulkner*. Ithaca, NY: Cornell University Press, 1960.

Watson, James Gray. *The Snopes Dilemma: Faulkner's Trilogy*. Coral Gables: University of Miami Press, 1970.

EDNA FERBER

Banning, Margaret Culkin. *Saturday Review*, 4 February 1939, p. 5.

Gilbert, Julie Goldsmith. *Ferber: A Biography*. Garden City, NY: Doubleday, 1978.

Van Doren, Dorothy. *Nation*, 23 April 1930, p. 494.

LAWRENCE FERLINGHETTI

Cherkovski, Neeli. *Ferlinghetti: A Biography*. Garden City, NY: Doubleday, 1969.

Kennedy, X. J. Review of *Starting from San Francisco*. *New York Times Book Review*, April 29, 1962, p. 30.

Jouffroy, Alain. "Introduction à la 'Beat Generation.'" *Les Temps Modernes* 20 (1964): 961–99.

Podhoretz, Norman. "The Beat Generation." *Esquire* 50 (1958): 148–50.

Sutton, Walter. *American Free Verse: The Modern Revolution*. New York: New Directions, 1973.

Tucker, Martin. "A Novel from the World of Modern Beatdom." *Commonweal*, 3 February 1961, pp. 488–89.

F. SCOTT FITZGERALD

Bruccoli, Matthew J. *The Composition of* Tender Is the Night: *A Study of the Manuscripts*. Pittsburgh: University of Pittsburgh Press, 1963.

Bryer, Jackson R. *The Critical Reputation of F. Scott Fitzgerald: A Biographical Study*. Hamden, CT: Archon Books, 1967.

Cowley, Malcolm. "Breakdown." *New Republic*, 6 June 1934, pp. 105–6.

Hoffman, Frederick J., ed. The Great Gatsby: *A Study*. New York: Scribner's, 1962.

Lehan, Richard D. *F. Scott Fitzgerald and the Craft of Fiction*. Carbondale: Southern Illinois University Press, 1965.

Miller, James E. *F. Scott Fitzgerald: His Art and His Technique*. New York: New York University Press, 1964.

Mizener, Arthur. *The Far Side of Paradise: A Biography of F. Scott Fitzgerald*. Boston: Houghton Mifflin, 1965.

Turnbull, Andrew. *Scott Fitzgerald*. New York: Scribner's, 1962.

ROBERT FITZGERALD

Bagg, Robert. "Translating the Abyss: On Robert Fitzgerald's *Odyssey*." *Arion* 8 (1969): 51–65.

Brinnin, John Malcolm. *Yale Review* 46 (1957): 455.

Humphries, Rolfe. *New Republic*, 6 March 1944, p. 324.

Vazakis, Byron. "Contemporary Classicist." *Saturday Review*, 13 April 1957, pp. 462–64.

JOHN GOULD FLETCHER

Davidson, Donald. "In Memory of John Gould Fletcher." *Poetry* 77 (1950): 154–61.

Dudley, Dorothy. "Poet as Theorist." *Poetry* 9 (1916): 43–47.

Faulkerson, Baucum. "John Gould Fletcher." *Sewanee Review* 46 (1938): 275–87.

Gregory, Horace. "Hours in a Poet's Life Cycle." *New York Herald Tribune Review of Books*, 29 December 1935, pp. 6–7.

Henderson, Alice Corbin. "Irradiations—Sand and Spray." *Poetry* 7 (1915): 44–47.

Hughes, Glenn. *Imagism and the Imagists: A Study in Modern Poetry*. Stanford: Stanford University Press, 1931.

Jack, Peter Monro. "John Gould Fletcher: The Imagist and the Man." *New Times Book Review*, 5 December 1931, pp. 33–35.

Lowell, Amy. *Tendencies in Modern American Poetry*. New York: Macmillan, 1917.

Monroe, Harriet. "John Gould Fletcher." *Poetry* 27 (1926): 206–10.

Simon, Charlie May. *Johnswood*. New York: E. P. Dutton, 1953.

Yarnell, D. A. "John Gould Fletcher." *University Review* 3 (1936): 110–13.

CAROLYN FORCHÉ

Gray, Paul. *Time*, 15 March 1982, p. 83.

Juhasz, Suzanne. *Library Journal*, 15 April 1976, p. 1023.

Lipari, J. A. *Library Journal*, 1 March 1982, p. 552.

McCann, W. L. *Christian Century*, 27 October 1982, p. 1084.

ROBERT FRANCIS

Beaulieu, Linda H. "Robert Francis on Henry Thoreau." *Thoreau Society Bulletin* 139 (1977): 3–4.

Field, Fall 1981, pp. 1–26. (The first half of this issue is dedicated to the poetry of Robert Francis.)

Francis, Robert. *Pot Shots at Poetry*. Ann Arbor: University of Michigan Press, 1980.

Francis, Robert. "Robert Francis Worksheets." *Malahat Review* 4 (1967): 114–18.

MARY E. WILKINS FREEMAN

Brand, Alice Glarden. "Mary Wilkins Freeman: Misanthropy as Propaganda." *New England Quarterly* 50 (1977): 83–100.

Foster, Edward. *Mary E. Wilkins Freeman*. New York: Hendricks House, 1956.

Hamblen, Abigail Ann. *The New England Art of Mary E. Wilkins Freeman*. Amherst, MA: Green Knight Press, 1966.

Herron, Ima Honaker. *The Small Town in American Literature*. Durham, NC: Duke University Press, 1939.

Quinn, Arthur Hobson. *American Fiction: An Historical and Critical Survey*. New York: D. Appleton-Century, 1936.

Westbrook, Perry D. *Mary Wilkins Freeman*. New York: Twayne, 1967.

BRUCE JAY FRIEDMAN

Chester, Alfred. "Submitting, Not Rising to the Heroic Gesture." *New York Herald Tribune Books*, 23 September 1962, p. 8.

Gilman, Richard. "Who Needs Critics?" *New Republic*, 17 February 1968, pp. 25–26.

Greenfield, Josh. "Bruce Jay Friedman Is Hanging by His Thumbs." *New York Times Magazine*, 14 January 1968, pp. 30–42.

Larner, Jeremy. "Compulsion to Toughness." *Nation*, 1 December 1962, pp. 380–81.

Schultz, Max. *Bruce Jay Friedman*. New York: Twayne, 1974.

ROBERT FROST

Borroff, Marie. *Language and the Poet*. Chicago: University of Chicago Press, 1979.

Brower, Reuben. *The Poetry of Robert Frost*. New York: Oxford University Press, 1963.

Donoghue, Denis. "The Limitations of Robert Frost." *Twentieth Century* 166 (1959): 13–22.

Lowell, Amy. *Tendencies in Modern American Poetry*. New York: Macmillan, 1917.

Munson, Gorham B. *Robert Frost: A Study in Sensibility and Good Sense*. New York: Doran, 1927.

Tharpe, Jack, ed. *Frost Centennial Essays*. Volumes II and III. Jackson: University Press of Mississippi, 1976 and 1978.

Thompson, Lawrance. *Fire and Ice: The Art and Thought of Robert Frost*. New York: Holt, 1942.
Waggoner, Hyatt H. *The Heel of Elohim*. Norman: University of Oklahoma Press, 1950.
Warren, Robert Penn. *Selected Essays*. New York: Random House, 1958.

HENRY BLAKE FULLER

Bowron, Bernard R., Jr. *Henry B. Fuller of Chicago*. Westport, CT: Greenwood Press, 1974.
Lawrence, Elwood P. "Fuller of Chicago: A Study in Frustration." *American Quarterly* 16 (1954): 137–47.
Lovett, Robert Morss. "Fuller of Chicago." *New Republic*, 21 August 1929, pp. 16–18.
Morgan, Anna, ed. *Tributes to Henry B. Fuller from Friends in Whose Minds He Will Live Always*. Chicago: Ralph Fletcher Seymour, 1929.
Silet, Charles L. P. *Henry Blake Fuller and Hamlin Garland: A Reference Guide*. Boston: G. K. Hall, 1977.
Wilson, Edmund. "Henry B. Fuller: The Art of Making It Flat." *New Yorker*, 23 May 1970, pp. 112–39.

WILLIAM GADDIS

Aldridge, John W. *The American Novel and the Way We Live Now*. London: Oxford University Press, 1983, pp. 46–52.
Banning, Charles Leslie. "William Gaddis's *JR*: The Organization of Chaos and the Chaos of Organization." *Paunch* 42/43 (1975): 153–65.
Kuehl, John, and Steven Moore, eds. *In Recognition of William Gaddis*. Syracuse: Syracuse University Press, 1984.
Lathrop, Kathleen L. "Comic-Ironic Parallels in William Gaddis's *The Recognitions*." *Review of Contemporary Fiction* 2 (Summer 1982): 32–40.
Madden, David. "William Gaddis's *The Recognitions*." In *Rediscoveries*, ed. David Madden. New York: Crown, 1971, pp. 291–304.
Moore, Steven. *A Reader's Guide to William Gaddis's* The Recognitions. Lincoln: University of Nebraska Press, 1982.
Stark, John. "William Gaddis: Just Recognition." *Hollins Critic* 14 (April 1977): 1–12.

MAVIS GALLANT

Auchincloss, Eve. *New York Review of Books*, 25 June 1964, p. 14.
Gill, Brendan. "Holding On." *New Yorker*, 19 September 1970, p. 132.
Price, Martin. *Yale Review* 49 (1959): 283.
Theroux, Paul. *New Statesman*, 8 March 1974, p. 334.

JOHN GARDNER

Bellamy, Joe David. *The New Fiction: Interviews with Innovative American Writers*. Urbana: University of Illinois Press, 1974.
Butts, Leonard C. "Locking and Unlocking: Nature as Moral Center in John Gardner's *October Light*." *Critique* 22, No. 3 (1980): 47–60.
DeMott, Benjamin. "A Philosophical Novel of Academe." *New York Times Book Review*, 20 June 1982, pp. 1, 26.
Ellis, Helen B., and Warren U. Ober. "*Grendel* and Blake: The Contraries of Existence." *English Studies in Canada* 3 (1977): 87–102.
Harris, Richard C. "Ecclesiastical Wisdom and *Nickel Mountain*." *Twentieth Century Literature* 26 (1980): 424–31.
Howell, John M. *John Gardner: A Bibliographical Profile*. Carbondale: Southern Illinois University Press, 1980.
Milosh, Joseph. "John Gardner's *Grendel*: Sources and Analogues." *Contemporary Literature* 19 (1978): 48–57.

HAMLIN GARLAND

Bryer, Jackson R.; Harding, Eugene; and Rees, Robert A. *Hamlin Garland and the Critics: An Annotated Bibliography*. Troy, NY: Whitson, 1973.
Duffy, Bernard I. "Hamlin Garland's Decline from Realism." *American Literature* 25 (1953): 69–74.
Gish, Robert. *Hamlin Garland: The Far West*. Boise: Boise State University, 1978.
Holloway, Jean. *Hamlin Garland: A Biography*. Austin: University of Texas Press, 1960.
Keiser, Albert. "Travelling the White Man's Road." In *The Indian in American Literature*. New York: Oxford University Press, 1933, pp. 279–92.
McCullough, Joseph B. *Hamlin Garland*. Boston: Twayne, 1978.
Morgan, H. Wayne. "Hamlin Garland: The Rebel as Escapist." In *American Writers in Rebellion*. New York: Hill & Wang, 1965, pp. 76–103.
Pizer, Donald. *Hamlin Garland's Early Work and Career*. Berkeley: University of California Press, 1960.
Reamer, Owen J. "Garland and the Indians." *New Mexico Quarterly* 34 (1964): 257–80.
Sherman, Caroline B. "The Development of American Rural Fiction." *Agricultural History* 12 (1938): 67–76.
Silet, Charles L. P. *Henry Blake Fuller and Hamlin Garland: A Reference Guide*. Boston: G. K. Hall, 1977.

GEORGE GARRETT

Dickey, William. "Revelations and Homilies." *Poetry* (1961): 127–28.
LeSage, Laurent. "Writers' Games with Dames." *Saturday Review*, 3 September 1966, pp. 36–37.
Lieberman, Laurence. "Poetry Chronicle." *Poetry* 112 (1968): 340.
Maloff, Saul. "Archetype and Enigma." *New York Times Book Review*, 4 September 1966, p. 20.
Moynahan, Julian. Review of *Death of the Fox*. *New York Times Books Review*, 26 September 1971, pp. 52–53.
Silver, Adele Z. Review of *Death of the Fox*. *Saturday Review*, 2 October 1971, p. 48.
Stegner, Wallace. "Stories for Lazy Hours." *Saturday Review*, 14 June 1958, p. 38.

JEAN GARRIGUE

Bock, Frederick. "And a Variable Compass." *Poetry* 106 (1965): 229–31.
Holmes, Theodore. "The Wine-Transfiguring World." *Poetry* 96 (1960): 118–20.

WILLIAM H. GASS

Howard, Richard. "Nothing But the Truth." *New Republic*, 18 May 1968, pp. 27–28.
O'Connell, Shaun. "The Stone and the Sermon." *Nation*, 9 May 1966, p. 563.
Tanner, Tony. *City of Words: American Fiction, 1950–1970*. New York: Harper & Row, 1971, pp. 269–72.

ALLEN GINSBERG

Carroll, Paul. "I Lift My Voice Aloud, / Make Mantra of American Language Now . . . I Here Declare the End of the War!" In *The Poem in Its Skin*. Chicago: Follet, 1968, pp. 80–101.

Henry, William A. III. "In New York: *Howl* Becomes a Hoot." *Time*, 7 December 1981, p. 8.

Hunsberger, Bruce. "Kit Smart's Howl." *Wisconsin Studies in Contemporary Literature* 6 (1965): 34–44.

Hyde, Lewis, ed. *On the Poetry of Allen Ginsberg*. Ann Arbor: University of Michigan Press, 1984.

Kramer, Jane. *Allen Ginsberg in America*. New York: Random House, 1969.

Kraus, Michelle P. *Allen Ginsberg: An Annotated Bibliography, 1969–1977*. Metuchen, NJ: The Scarecrow Press, 1980.

Rosenthal, M. L. "Allen Ginsberg." In *The New Poets*. New York: Oxford University Press, 1967, pp. 89–112.

Williams, William Carlos. "Howl for Carl Solomon." Introduction to *Howl* by Allen Ginsberg. San Francisco: City Lights, 1956, pp. 7–8.

ELLEN GLASGOW

Godbold, E. Stanly, Jr. *Ellen Glasgow and the Woman Within*. Baton Rouge: Louisiana State University Press, 1972.

Jones, Anne Goodwyn. "Ellen Glasgow: The Perfect Mould." In *Tomorrow Is Another Day*. Baton Rouge: Louisiana State University Press, 1981, pp. 225–70.

Kelly, William W. *Ellen Glasgow: A Bibliography*. Charlottesville: Bibliographical Society of Virginia/University Press of Virginia, 1964.

Myer, Elizabeth Gallup. *The Social Situation of Women in the Novels of Ellen Glasgow*. Hicksville, NY: Exposition Press, 1978.

Raper, Julius Rowan. *From the Sunken Garden: The Fiction of Ellen Glasgow, 1916–1945*. Baton Rouge: Louisiana State University Press, 1980.

———. *Without Shelter: The Early Career of Ellen Glasgow*. Baton Rouge: Louisiana State University Press, 1971.

Rouse, Blair. *Ellen Glasgow*. New York: Twayne, 1962.

Santas, Joan Foster. *Ellen Glasgow's American Dream*. Charlottesville: University Press of Virginia, 1965.

Thiebaux, Marcelle. *Ellen Glasgow*. New York: Ungar, 1982.

Wagner, Linda W. *Ellen Glasgow: Beyond Convention*. Austin: University of Texas Press, 1982.

GAIL GODWIN

Gaston, Karen C. "'Beauty and the Beast' in Gail Godwin's *Glass People*." *Critique* 21, No. 3 (1980): 94–110.

Kearns, Kathleen. Review of *Mr. Bedford and the Muses*. *New Republic*, 18 December 1983, pp. 38–39.

Sage, Lorna. "The Villain's Demise." *Times Literary Supplement*, 15 September 1978, p. 1011.

Taliaferro, Frances. "'Dream Daughter' Grown Up." *New York Times*, 27 January 1985, p. 7.

Unsigned. "Headstrong." *Times Literary Supplement*, 23 July 1971, p. 850.

Unsigned. Review of *Glass People*. *New York Times Book Review*, 15 October 1972, pp. 38–39.

HERBERT GOLD

Gold, Herbert. "Postface: An Aftermath about These Stories." In *Love and Like*. New York: Dial Press, 1960, pp. 301–7.

Gordon, David J. "Trust and Treachery." *Yale Review* 57 (1967): 105–7.

Serlen, Ellen. "The American Dream: From F. Scott Fitzgerald to Herbert Gold." *Midamerica* 4 (1977): 122–37.

Solotaroff, Theodore. "Remember Those Tissues They Wrapped the Fruit In . . . ?" In *The Red Hot Vacuum*. New York: Atheneum, 1970, pp. 237–41.

PAUL GOODMAN

Gitlin, Todd. "Paul Goodman, Poet." *Commentary* 59 (March 1975): 24–26.

Rich, Adrienne. "Caryatid: A Column." *American Poetry Review* 2 (January–February 1973): 16–17.

Roszak, Theodore. "Exploring Utopia." In *The Making of a Counter Culture*. Garden City, NY: Doubleday, 1969, pp. 178–204.

Steiner, George. "On Paul Goodman." *Commentary* 36 (August 1963): 158–63.

Widmer, Kingsley. *Paul Goodman*. Boston: Twayne, 1980.

CAROLINE GORDON

Baker, Howard. "The Strategems of Caroline Gordon, or, the Art of the Novel and the Novelty of Myth." *Southern Review* 9 (1973): 523–49.

Cheney, Brainard. "Caroline Gordon's Ontological Quest." *Renascence* 16 (1963): 3–12.

Cowan, Bainard. "The Serpent's Coils: How to Read Caroline Gordon's Later Fiction." *Southern Review* 16 (1980): 281–98.

Critique 1, No. 1 (1956). Special issue on Gordon.

Fletcher, Marie. "The Fate of Women in a Changing South: A Persistent Theme in the Fiction of Caroline Gordon." *Mississippi Quarterly* 21 (1967): 17–28.

Golden, Robert E. and Mary C. Sullivan. *Flannery O'Connor and Caroline Gordon: A Reference Guide*. Boston: G. K. Hall, 1977.

MARY GORDON

Craig, Patricia. "Paperbacks in Brief." *Times Literary Supplement*, 26 November 1985, p. 1318.

May, John R. Review of *Final Payments*. *America*, 11 November 1978, p. 339.

Unsigned. Review of *The Company of Women*. *New York Times Book Review*, 27 December 1981, p. 17.

WILLIAM GOYEN

Barr, Donald. Review of *In a Farther Country*. *New York Times*, 24 July 1955, p. 17.

Breit, Harvey. "A Talk with William Goyen." *New York Times Book Review*, 10 September 1950, p. 12.

Mohrt, Michel. "Preface" to "Le Coq Blanc." *Le Table Ronde* 63 (1953): 53–55.

Pickrel, Paul. Review of *House of Breath*. *Yale Review* 40 (1950): 192.

Porter, Katherine Anne. Review of *House of Breath*. *New York Times*, 20 August 1950, p. 17.

Prescott, Orville. "The Young Decadents." In *In My Opinion*. New York: Bobbs-Merrill, 1950, pp. 110–19.

Stern, Daniel. "On William Goyen's *The House of Breath*." In *Rediscoveries*, ed. David Madden. New York: Crown, 1971, pp. 256–69.

Sühnel, Rudolf. "Die Wiederentdeckung des Wunderbaren: William Goyen zum Gruss anlässlich seines Deutschlandbesuches." *Die Neueren Sprachen* No. 6 (1962): 249–55.

SHIRLEY ANN GRAU

Donogue, H. E. F. "Shirley Ann Grau." *Publishers Weekly*, 3 December 1973, pp. 10–13.

Going, William T. "Alabama Geography in Shirley Ann Grau's *The Keepers of the House.*" *Alabama Review* 20 (1967): 62–68.

Gossett, Louise Y. *Violence in Recent Southern Fiction.* Durham, NC: Duke University Press, 1967.

Hoffman, Frederick J. *The Art of Southern Fiction: A Study of Some Modern Novelists.* Carbondale: Southern Illinois University Press, 1967.

Keith, Don. L. "Shirley Ann Grau: Chasing the Creative Muse through the Land of the Lotus Eaters." *Louisiana Renaissance* 1 (1977): 18–19, 44.

Trachtman, Paul "Rotten Roots." *Progressive* 28 (1964): 41–43.

HORACE GREGORY

Phillips, Robert. "The Quick-Change Artist: Notes on Horace Gregory's Poetic Imagery." *Modern Poetry Studies* 4 (1973): 60–74.

Rosenthal, M. L. "Three Poets in Focus." *New Republic,* 10 December 1951, pp. 28–29.

Wagner, Linda W. "Horace Gregory: Voice in Action." *Modern Poetry Studies* 4 (1974): 13–22.

ZANE GREY

Folsom, James K. *The American Western Novel.* New Haven: College and University Press, 1966.

Gruber, Frank. *Zane Grey: A Biography.* New York: World, 1970.

Jackson, Carlton. *Zane Grey.* New York: Twayne, 1973.

Karr, Jean. *Zane Grey: Man of the West.* New York: Greenberg, 1949.

Le Gallienne, Richard. "Zane Grey." *New York Times Book Review,* 15 February 1920, pp. 94, 97.

Nye, Russel. *The Unembarrassed Muse: The Popular Arts in America.* New York: Dial Press, 1970.

Ronald, Ann. *Zane Grey.* Boise: Boise State University, 1975.

Scott, Kenneth W. *Zane Grey, Born to the West: A Reference Guide.* Boston: G. K. Hall, 1979.

A. B. GUTHRIE, JR.

Coon, Gilbert D. "A. B. Guthrie, Jr.'s Tetralogy: An American Synthesis." *North Dakota Quarterly* 44 (1976): 73–80.

Etulain, Richard W. "A. B. Guthrie: A Bibliography." *Western American Literature* 4 (1969): 133–38.

Ford, Thomas W. *A. B. Guthrie, Jr.* Austin, TX: Steck–Vaughn, 1968.

Guthrie, A. B., Jr. *The Blue Hen's Chick.* New York: McGraw–Hill, 1965.

Stewart, Donald C. "A. B. Guthrie's Vanishing Paradise: An Essay on Historical Fiction." *Journal of the West* 15 (1976): 83–96.

Williams, John. "The 'Western': Definition of the Myth." *Nation,* 18 November 1961, pp. 401–6.

MARILYN HACKER

Brown, Rosellen. "Spellbinders." *Parnassus: Poetry in Review* 6 (1977): 219–23.

Howard, Ben. "Naturalist, Feminist, Professor." *Poetry* 126 (1975): 46–47.

McClatchy, J. D. "Figures in the Landscape." *Poetry* 138 (1981): 231–33.

Molesworth, Charles. "Fondled Memories." *New York Times Book Review,* 12 October 1980, pp. 14, 36–37.

Pritchard, William H. "More Poetry Matters." *Hudson Review* 29 (1976): 453–63.

DONALD HALL

Brownjohn, Alan. Review of *Remembering Poets: Reminiscences and Opinions. Encounter* 53 (August 1979): 45.

Davenport, Guy. *Seeing Shelley Plain. National Review,* 7 July 1978, pp. 844–46.

Rice, H. C. K. Review of *Remembering Poets: Reminiscences and Opinions. New York Times Book Review,* 11 November 1979, p. 51.

DASHIELL HAMMETT

Eames, Hugh. "Sam Spade." In *Sleuths, Inc.* Philadelphia: J. B. Lippincott, 1978, pp. 98–140.

Gores, Joe. *Hammett: A Novel.* New York: Putnam, 1975.

Gregory, Sinda. *Private Investigations: The Novels of Dashiell Hammett.* Carbondale: Southern Illinois University Press, 1985.

Layman, Richard. *Dashiell Hammett: A Descriptive Bibliography.* Pittsburgh: University of Pittsburgh Press, 1979.

Madden, David, ed. *Tough Guy Writers of the Thirties.* Carbondale: Southern Illinois University Press, 1968.

Nolan, William F. *Hammett: A Life at the Edge.* New York: Congdon & Weed, 1983.

Sale, Roger. "Dashiell Hammett." In *On Not Being Good Enough.* New York: Oxford University Press, 1979, pp. 73–80.

Spitzer, E. E. "With Corporal Hammett on Adak." *Nation,* 5 January 1974, pp. 6–9.

Wolfe, Peter. *Beams Falling: The Art of Dashiell Hammett.* Bowling Green, OH: Bowling Green University Popular Press, 1980.

LORRAINE HANSBERRY

Clurman, Harold. Review of *Les Blancs. Nation,* 30 November 1970, pp. 237–47.

Hentoff, Nat. "They Fought—They Fought." *New York Times,* 25 May 1969, sec. 2, pp. 1, 18.

Isaacs, Harold. "Five Writers and Their African Ancestors, Part II." *Phylon* 21 (1960): 317–36.

Kerr, Walter. "Vivid, Stinging, Alive." *New York Times,* 29 November 1970, sec. 2, p. 3.

Walker, Alice. "One Child of One's Own." *Ms.,* August 1979, pp. 47–50, 72–75.

MARK HARRIS

Baker, Carlos. "The Wires Burn and the Mail Flies Hot and Heavy." *New York Times Book Review,* 19 July 1959, pp. 4–5.

Dayle, Robert. "Henry Was a Southpaw." *New York Times Book Review,* 18 March 1956, p. 5.

Hicks, Granville, "Portrait of a Nonconformist." *Saturday Review,* 18 July 1959, p. 13.

Sylvester, Henry. "Touching All Bases." *New York Times Book Review,* 12 April 1953, p. 4.

Walbridge, Earle. "Mark Harris." *Wilson Library Bulletin* 33 (1959): 716.

JOHN HAWKES

Busch, Frederick. *Hawkes: A Guide to His Fictions.* Syracuse, NY: Syracuse University Press, 1973.

Greiner, Donald J. *Comic Terror: The Novels of John Hawkes.* Memphis, TN: Memphis State University Press, 1973.

Guérard, Albert J. "The Prose Style of John Hawkes." *Critique* 6, No. 2 (Fall 1963): 19–29.

Hryciw, Carol. *John Hawkes: An Annotated Bibliography.*

With Four Introductions by John Hawkes. Metuchen, NJ: Scarecrow Press, 1977.
Rovit, Earl. "The Fiction of John Hawkes: An Introductory View." *Modern Fiction Studies* 11 (1964): 150–62.
Scholes, Robert. *Fabulation and Metafiction*. Urbana: University of Illinois Press, 1979.
Warner, John M. "The 'Internalized Quest Romance' in Hawkes' *The Lime Twig*." *Modern Fiction Studies* 19 (1973): 89–95.

ROBERT HAYDEN

Davis, Charles T. "Robert Hayden's Use of History." In *Modern Black Poets*. Englewood Cliffs, NJ: Prentice Hall, 1973, pp. 96–111.
Fetrow, Fred. *Robert Hayden*. Boston: Twayne, 1984.
Harper, Michael S. "Remembering Robert E. Hayden." *Carleton Miscellany* 18 (1980): 231–34.
Turco, Lewis. "*Angle of Ascent*: The Poetry of Robert Hayden." *Michigan Quarterly Review* 16 (1977): 199–219.

ANTHONY HECHT

Bloom, Harold. "The Year's Books Part 1." *New Republic*, 27 November 1977, p. 25.
Gerber, Philip J. "An Interview with Anthony Hecht." *Mediterranean Review* 1 (1979): 3–9.
Oppenheimer, Joel. "Fate of Grace." *Village Voice*, 18 February 1980, pp. 44–45.
Perloff, Marjorie. *Far Point* 2 (1969): 45–51.
Pettingell, Pheobe. "On Poetry: Anthony Hecht's Transmutations." *New Leader*, 17 December 1979, pp. 22–23.

BEN HECHT

Baldwin, C. C. "Ben Hecht." In *The Men Who Make Our Novels*. Rev. ed. New York: Dodd, Mead, 1925, pp. 219–26.
Hecht, Ben. *A Child of the Century*. New York: Simon & Schuster, 1954.
Karsner, David. "Ben Hecht." In *Sixteen Authors to One*. New York: Lewis Copeland, 1928, pp. 235–45.
Martin, Heffrey Brown. *Ben Hecht: Hollywood Screenwriter*. Ann Arbor, MI: UMI Research Press, 1985.
Ravitz, Abe C. "Ballyhoo, Gargoyles, and Firecrackers: Ben Hecht's Aesthetic Calliope." *Journal of Popular Culture* 1 (1967): 37–51.

ROBERT A. HEINLEIN

Christopher, Joe R. "Lazarus, Come Forth from That Tomb!" *Riverside Quarterly* 6 (1975): 190–97.
Christopher, Joe R. "Methuselah, out of Heinlein, by Shaw." *Shaw Review* 16 (1973): 79–88.
Panshin, Alexei. *Heinlein in Dimension*. Chicago: Advent, 1968.
———, and Cory Panshin. "The Death of Science Fiction: A Dream." In *SF in Dimension*. Chicago: Advent, 1980, pp. 318–97.
———. "Reading Heinlein Subjectively." In *SF in Dimension*. Chicago: Advent, 1980, pp. 93–126.
Perkins, James Ashbrook. "MYCROFTXX is Alive and Well: The Ambiguous Ending of *The Moon Is a Harsh Mistress*." *Notes on Contemporary Literature* 5 (1975): 13–15.
Rogers, Ivor A. "Robert Heinlein: Folklorist of Outer Space." In *Robert A. Heinlein*, ed. Joseph D. Olander and Martin Harry Greenberg. New York: Taplinger, 1978, pp. 222–39.
Schuman, Samuel. "Vladimir Nabokov's *Invitation to a Beheading* and Robert Heinlein's 'They.'" *Twentieth Century Literature* 9 (1973): 99–106.
Smith, Philip E., II. "The Evolution of Politics and the Politics of Evolution." In *Robert A. Heinlein*, ed. Joseph D. Olander and Martin Harry Greenberg. New York: Taplinger, 1978, pp. 131–71.
Wolfe, Gary K. "Autoplastic and Alloplastic Adaptations in Science Fiction: 'Waldo' and 'Desertion.'" In *Coordinates: Placing Science Fiction and Fantasy*, ed. George E. Slusser, Eric S. Rabkin, and Robert Scholes. Carbondale: Southern Illinois University Press, 1983, pp. 65–79.

JOSEPH HELLER

Aldridge, John. "Vision of Man Raging in a Vacuum." *Saturday Review*, 19 October 1974, pp. 18–21.
Beatty, Jack. Review of *Good as Gold*. *New Republic*, 10 March 1979, pp. 42–44.
Kennedy, William. "Endlessly Honest Confession." *New Republic*, 19 October 1974, pp. 17–19.
Searles, George. "*Something Happened*: A New Direction for Joseph Heller." *Critique* 18, No. 3 (1977): 74–81.
Wiseltier, Leon. "Schlock of Recognition." *New Republic*, 29 October 1984, pp. 31–33.

LILLIAN HELLMAN

Adler, Jacob H. *Lillian Hellman*. Austin: Steck-Vaughn, 1969.
———. "Miss Hellman's Two Sisters." *Educational Theatre Journal* 15 (1963): 112–17.
Adler, Renata. "The Guest Word." *New York Times Book Review*, 9 July 1972, p. 39.
Broc, Mary Lynn. "Bohemian Bumps into Calvin: The Deception of Passivity in Lillian Hellman's Drama." *Southern Quarterly* 19 (1981): 26–41.
Holmin, Lorena Ross. *The Dramatic Works of Lillian Hellman. Studia Anglistica Upsaliensa* 10 (1973).
Plimpton, George, ed. *Writers at Work: The* Paris Review *Interviews: Third Series*. New York: Viking Press, 1967.
Rubin, Louis, Jr., and Robert D. Jacobs, eds. *South: Modern Literature in Its Cultural Setting*. Garden City, NY: Doubleday, 1961.
Samuels, Charles Thomas. Review of *Collected Plays*. *New York Times Book Review*, 9 July 1972, p. 39.
Underwood, June O. "Experimental Form and Female Archetypes: Lillian Hellman's *Pentimento*." *Publications of the Missouri Philological Association* 5 (1980): 49–53.
Wagner, Linda W. "Lillian Hellman: Autobiography and Truth." *Southern Review* 19 (1983): 275–88.

ERNEST HEMINGWAY

Baker, Carlos. *Hemingway and His Critics: An International Anthology*. New York: Hill & Wang, 1961.
Benson, Jackson S. *Hemingway: The Writer's Art of Self-Defense*. Minneapolis: University of Minnesota Press, 1969.
Bridgman, Richard. *The Colloquial Style in American Literature*. New York: Oxford University Press, 1966, pp. 195–230.
Brooks, Cleanth, and Warren, Robert Penn. "The Killers." In *Understanding Fiction*, New York: Appleton-Crofts, 1959, pp. 303–12.
Callaghan, Morley. *That Summer in Paris: Memories of Tangled Friendships with Hemingway, Fitzgerald, and Some Others*. New York: Coward–McCann, 1963.
Castillo–Puche, J. L. *Hemingway in Spain: A Personal*

Reminiscence of Hemingway's Years in Spain by His Friend. Garden City, NY: Doubleday, 1974.
De Falco, Joseph. *The Hero in Hemingway's Short Stories*. Pittsburgh: University of Pittsburgh Press, 1963.
Donaldson, Scott. *By Force of Will: The Life and Art of Ernest Hemingway*. New York: Viking Press, 1977.
Hoffman, Frederick J. *The Twenties*. New York: Viking Press, 1955.
Hotchner, A. E. *Papa Hemingway: the Ecstasy and the Sorrow*. New York: Morrow, 1983.
Kazin, Alfred. "Hemingway the Painter." *An American Procession*. New York: Knopf, 1984.
Lynn, K. S. "Hemingway's Private War." In *The Air Line to Seattle*. Chicago: University of Chicago Press, 1983.
MacLeish, Archibald. *A Continuing Journey*. Boston: Houghton Mifflin, 1968, pp. 307–12.
McCaffery, John K. M., ed. *Ernest Hemingway: The Man and His Work*. Cleveland: World, 1950.
Ross, Lillian. *Portrait of Ernest Hemingway*. New York: Simon & Schuster, 1961.
Stephens, Robert O., ed. *Ernest Hemingway: The Critical Reception*. New York: Burt Franklin, 1977.

O. HENRY

Beachcroft, T. O. *The Modest Art: A Survey of the Short Story in English*. London: Oxford University Press, 1961.
Current-García, Eugene. *O. Henry*. New York: Twayne, 1965.
Harris, Richard C. *William Sydney Porter (O. Henry): A Reference Guide*. Boston: G. K. Hall, 1980.
Long, E. Hudson. *O. Henry: American Realist*. Austin, TX: Steck-Vaughn, 1970.
Marks, Patricia. "O. Henry and Dickens: Elsie in the Bleak House of Moral Decay." *English Language Notes* 12 (1974): 35–37.
Monteiro, George. "Hemingway, O. Henry, and the Surprise Ending." *Prarie Schooner* 47 (1973): 296–302.
O'Connor, Richard. *O. Henry: The Legendary Life of William Sydney Porter*. Garden City, NY: Doubleday, 1970.
Rea, John A. "The Idea for O. Henry's 'Gift of the Magi.'" *Southern Humanities Review* 7 (1973): 311–14.
Starke, Catherine Juanita. *Black Portraiture in American Fiction: Stock Characters, Archetypes, and Individuals*. New York: Basic Books, 1971.

JOSEPHINE HERBST

Herbst, Josephine. "Counterblast." *Nation*, 11 March 1931, pp. 275–76.
Jones, Howard Mumford. "The Fallacy of 'Advanced' Fiction." *Saturday Review*, 28 February 1948, pp. 15–16, 31–32.
Kazin, Alfred. "Josephine Herbst (1897–1969)." *New York Review of Books*, 27 March 1969, pp. 19–20.
Langer, Elinor. *Josephine Herbst*. New York: Atlantic/Little, Brown, 1984.
Schneider, Isidor. "The Fetish of Simplicity." *Nation*, 18 February 1931, pp. 184–86.

JOSEPH HERGESHEIMER

Baldwin, C. C. "Joseph Hergesheimer." In *The Men Who Make Our Novels*. Rev. ed. New York: Dodd, Mead, 1925, pp. 227–42.
Beach, Joseph Warren. "Incoherence in the Aesthete: Mr. Joseph Hergesheimer." In *The Outlook for American Prose*. Chicago: University of Chicago Press, 1926, pp. 37–41.
Garnett, Edward. "A Note on Two American Novelists." In *Friday Nights*. London: Jonathan Cape, 1922, pp. 335–41.
Hatcher, Harlan. "Facing Two Worlds: Joseph Hergesheimer." In *Creating the Modern American Novel*. New York: Farrar & Rinehart, 1935, pp. 202–10.
Hartwick, Harry. "Costumes by Hergesheimer." In *The Foreground of American Fiction*. New York: American Book Co., 1934, pp. 187–99.
Swire, H. L. R. *A Bibliography of the Works of Joseph Hergesheimer*. Philadelphia: Centaur Book Shop, 1922.

JOHN HERSEY

Aldrich, Nelson. Review of *Too Far to Walk*. *Book Week*, March 13, 1966, p. 5.
Daiches, David. "Record and Testament." *Commentary* 9 (1950): 385–88.
Fadiman, Clifton. Review of *Men on Bataan*. *New Yorker*, 6 June 1942, p. 78.
Hatch, Robert. "The Man Who Attends Catastrophes." *New Republic*, 3 April 1950, p. 18.
Hicks, Granville, "John Hersey's Message." *Saturday Review*, 3 October 1959, p. 59.
Huse, Nancy Lyman. *John Hersey and James Agee: A Reference Guide*. Boston: G. K. Hall, 1978.
Sanders, David. *John Hersey*. New York: Twayne, 1967.
Weeks, Edward. Review of *A Bell for Adano*. *Atlantic* 173 (April 1944): 127.
———. Review of *The Conspiracy*. *Atlantic* 229 (March 1972): 106–7.

DUBOSE HEYWARD

Allen, Hervey. *DuBose Heyward: A Critical and Biographical Sketch*. New York: Doran, 1926.
Clark, Emily. "DuBose Heyward." In *Innocence Abroad*. New York: Knopf, 1931, pp. 235–50.
Durham, Frank. *DuBose Heyward: The Man Who Wrote* Porgy. Columbia: University of South Carolina Press, 1954.
———. "DuBose Heyward's 'Lost' Short Stories." *Studies in Short Fiction* 2 (1965): 157–63.

PATRICIA HIGHSMITH

Callendar, Newgate. "Criminals at Large." *New York Times Book Review*, 3 September 1972, p. 22.
Elliott, Janice. "Black Wonderland." *New Statesman*, 24 January 1969, pp. 124–25.
Fenton, James. "Spoils." *New Statesman*, 10 July 1970, p. 28.
Grumbach, Doris. "Fine Print." *New Republic*, 29 June 1974, p. 33.
Wood, Michael. "A Heavy Legacy." *New York Review of Books*, 15 September 1977, p. 32.

ACKNOWLEDGMENTS

Advent:Publishers. DAMON KNIGHT, "One Sane Man: Robert A. Heinlein," *In Search of Wonder*, copyright © 1967 by Damon Knight. Reprinted by permission of Advent: Publishers, Inc., and Damon Knight.

America. JOHN B. BRESLIN, April 17, 1982, copyright © 1982. JAMES FINN COTTER, July 25, 1981, copyright © 1981, 1982. Reprinted by permission of America Press, Inc.

American Magazine. ZANE GREY, "What the Desert Means to Me," Vol. 98, No. 5 (Nov. 1924), copyright © 1924.

The American Mercury. H. L. MENCKEN, "A Southern Skeptic," Vol. 29, No. 4 (Aug. 1933), copyright © 1933.

The American Poetry Review. MARY KINZIE, "A Generation of Silver," July–Aug. 1981, copyright © 1981. J. D. MCCLATCHY, "Speaking of Hollander," Sept.–Oct. 1982, copyright © 1982. MARJORIE PERLOFF, "A Lion in Our Living Room," March–April 1985, copyright © 1985.

The American Scholar. R. W. B. LEWIS, "Genius and Sheer Fudge," Autumn 1972, copyright © 1972. MARK VAN DOREN, "The Permanence of Robert Frost," Spring 1936, copyright © 1936 by the United Chapters of Phi Beta Kappa. Reprinted by permission of *The American Scholar* and Dorothy Van Doren.

The American Spectator. THEODORE DREISER, "The Great American Novel," Vol. 1, No. 1 (Dec. 1932), copyright © 1932.

American Studies. GUY SZUBERLA, "Making the Sublime Mechanical: Henry Blake Fuller's Chicago," Vol. 14, No. 1 (Spring 1973), copyright © 1973 by Midcontinent American Studies Research Association, The University of Kansas.

Atheneum Publishers, Inc. MARIUS BEWLEY, "Scott Fitzgerald: The Apprentice Fiction," *Masks and Mirrors*, copyright © 1965, 1970 by Marius Bewley.

The Atlantic. CONRAD AIKEN, "William Faulkner: The Novel as Form," Nov. 1939, copyright © 1939 by the Atlantic Monthly Co., Boston. RAYMOND CHANDLER, "The Simple Art of Murder," Dec. 1944, copyright © 1944 by The Atlantic Monthly Co., Boston. STOYAN CHRISTOWE, Oct. 1947, copyright © 1947 by The Atlantic Monthly Co., Boston. BENJAMIN DEMOTT, "Women without Men," March 1981, copyright © 1981. ROBERT FITZGERALD, "The Third Kind of Knowledge," June 1980, copyright © 1980 by The Atlantic Monthly Co., Boston. EDWARD GARNETT, "A New American Poet," Aug. 1915, copyright © 1915 by The Atlantic Monthly Co., Boston.

Beacon Press. GASTON BACHELARD, "House and Universe," *The Poetics of Space*, copyright © 1964. LESLIE A. FIEDLER, "Some Notes on F. Scott Fitzgerald," *An End to Innocence*, copyright © 1955 by Leslie A. Fiedler. Reprinted by permission of Stein & Day Publishers.

The Bobbs-Merrill Co., Inc. ORVILLE PRESCOTT, "The Art of Historical Fiction: Richter, Guthrie," *In My Opinion*, copyright © 1952 by Orville Prescott.

The Bodley Head. J. B. PRIESTLEY, "Introduction" to *The Bodley Head Fitzgerald, Volume 1*, copyright © 1958. Reprinted by permission of The Bodley Head Ltd.

Book Forum. CARL E. SHERMAN, "Man Working," 1977, copyright © 1977.

The Bookman (New York). FREDERIC TABER COOPER, Vol. 33, No. 4, (June 1911), copyright © 1911. JOHN FARRAR, "The Literary Spotlight, XXVII: Henry Blake Fuller," Vol. 58, No. 6 (Feb. 1924), copyright © 1924. FORD MADOX FORD, "A Stage in American Literature," Vol. 74, No. 4 (Dec. 1931), copyright © 1931. JOHN MACY, "The Passing of the Yankee," Vol. 73, No. 6 (Aug. 1931), copyright © 1931.

Books & Bookmen. FORD MADOX FORD, "A Distinguished First Novel," Sept. 1928, copyright © 1928 by Books and Bookmen.

The Borgo Press. GEORGE EDGAR SLUSSER, *The Classic Years of Robert A. Heinlein*, copyright © 1977 by George Edgar Slusser. GEORGE EDGAR SLUSSER, *Robert A. Heinlein: Stranger in His Own Land*, copyright © 1976, 1977 by George Edgar Slusser.

Bowling Green University Popular Press. GARY TOPPING, "Zane Grey's West," *The Popular Western*, eds. Richard W. Etulain and Michael T. Marsden, copyright © 1974 by Bowling Green University Popular Press.

Butler & Tanner Ltd. PHILIP HENDERSON, "Ernest Hemingway," *The Novel Today: Studies in Contemporary Attitudes*, copyright © 1936.

CLA Journal. ARTHUR P. DAVIS, "Langston Hughes: Cool Poet," June 1968, copyright © 1968. JAMES A. EMMANUEL, "The Literary Experiments of Langston Hughes," June 1968, copyright © 1968. BLYDEN JACKSON, "A Word about Simple," June 1968, copyright © 1968.

The Canadian Forum. JOAN FOX, Aug. 1958, copyright © 1958.

Jonathan Cape Ltd. C. DAY LEWIS, "Preface" to *Selected Poems of Robert Frost*, copyright © 1936. EDWIN MUIR, "Preface" to *Selected Poems of Robert Frost*, copyright © 1936.

The Christian Science Monitor. ELIZABETH JANEWAY, "The High Price of Good Intentions," Feb. 4, 1965, copyright © 1965.

College and University Press. JAMES K. FOLSOM, "The Vanishing American," *The American Western Novel*, copyright © 1966 by College and University Press Services, Inc.

College English. BARRETT H. CLARK, "Lillian Hellman," Vol. 6, No. 3 (Dec. 1944), copyright © 1944 by the National Council of Teachers of English. Reprinted by permission of the publisher. DAYTON KOHLER, "A. B. Guthrie, Jr., and the West," Vol. 12, No. 5 (Feb. 1951), copyright © 1951 by the National Council of Teachers of English. Reprinted by permission of the publisher.

College Literature. LAURENCE PERRINE, "Robert Frost's 'The Hill Wife': Evidence, Inference and Speculation in the Interpretation of Fiction," Winter 1983, copyright © 1983.

Columbia University Press. ONWUCHEKWA JEMIE, "Hughes' Black Esthetic," "Conclusion," *Langston Hughes: An Introduction to the Poetry*, copyright © 1973, 1976 by Columbia University Press.

Commentary. ROBERT ALTER, "The Critic as Poet," Sept. 1975, copyright © 1975 by Robert Alter. Reprinted by permission of Robert Alter. DONALD T. BAZELON, "Dashiell Hammett's 'Private Eye,'" May 1949, copyright © 1949 by *Commentary*. Reprinted by permission; all rights reserved. SAUL BELLOW, "Man Underground," June 1952, copyright © 1952. ROBERT PENN WARREN, "The Unity of Experience," May 1965, copyright © 1965 by *Commentary*. Reprinted by permission; all rights reserved.

Commonweal. CLAIRE HAHN, May 9, 1975, copyright © 1975 by *Commonweal*. MICHAEL HEFFERNAN, Aug. 15, 1975, copyright © 1975 by *Commonweal*. EVELYN WAUGH, "The Case of Mr. Hemingway," Nov. 3, 1950, copyright © 1950 by *Commonweal*. LEONARD WOLF, "The Shaded Eye," April 26, 1957, copyright © 1957 by *Commonweal*.

Cornell University Press. WALTER J. SLATOFF, "Conclusions," *Quest for Failure: A Study of William Faulkner*, copyright © 1960 by Cornell University Press.

Cranium Press. SAMUEL CHARTERS, "Brother Antoninus," *Some Poems/Poets*, copyright © 1971.

Critique. MICHAEL ACKLAND, "Blakean Sources in John Gardner's *Grendel*," Vol. 23, No. 1 (1981), copyright © 1981 by James Young. ALWYN BERLAND, "The Fiction of Shirley Ann Grau," Vol. 6, No. 1 (Spring 1963), copyright © 1963 by James Young. ROBERT EDWARD COLBERT, "The American Salesman as Pitchman and Poet in the Fiction of Stanley Elkin," Vol. 21, No. 2 (1979), copyright © 1979 by James Young. SUSAN E. LORSCH, "Gail Godwin's *The Odd Woman:* Literature and the Retreat from Life," Vol. 20, No. 2 (1978), copyright © 1978 by James Young. LARRY MCCAFFERY, "The Art of Metafiction: William Gass' *Willie Masters' Lonesome Wife*," Vol. 19, No. 1 (1976), copyright © 1976 by James Young. LARRY MCCAFFERY, "Stanley Elkin's Recovery of the Ordinary," Vol. 21, No. 2 (1979), copyright © 1979 by James Young. JUDY SMITH MURR, "John Gardner's Order and Disorder: *Grendel* and *The Sunlight Dialogues*," Vol. 18, No. 2 (1976), copyright © 1976 by James Young. ANN PEARSON, "Shirley Ann Grau: Nature Is the Vision," Vol. 17, No. 2 (1975), copyright © 1975 by James Young. WILLIAM SCHAFER, "Mark Harris: Versions of (American) Pastoral," Vol. 19, No. 1 (1977), copyright © 1977 by James Young. SUSAN STREHLE, "John

Gardner's Novels: Affirmation and the Alien," Vol. 18, No. 2 (1976), copyright © 1976 by James Young. ALAN TRACHTENBERG, "Barth and Hawkes: Two Fabulists," Vol. 6, No. 2 (Fall 1963), copyright © 1963 by James Young. JOSEPH W. TURNER, "History and Imagination in George Garrett's Death of the Fox," Vol. 22, No. 2 (1980), copyright © 1980 by James Young.

Crown Publishers, Inc. ALLAN LEWIS, "The Survivors of the Depression," *American Plays and Playwrights*, copyright © 1965 by Allan Lewis.

Denver Quarterly. JOYCE BELLAMY, Vol. 11, No. 3 (Autumn 1976), copyright © 1976 by The University of Denver. Reprinted by permission of *Denver Quarterly*.

The Dial Press. NORMAN MAILER, "Part Two: Lines," *Cannibals and Christians*, copyright © 1966.

Doubleday & Co. BRIAN W. ALDISS, "After the Impossible Happened," *Billion Year Spree: The True History of Science Fiction*, copyright © 1973 by Brian W. Aldiss. GRAHAM GREENE, "Introduction" to *The Snail-Watcher and Other Stories* by Patricia Highsmith, copyright © 1970 by Patricia Highsmith. BURTON RASCOE, "Ellen Glasgow at Home," *We Were Interrupted*, copyright © 1947 by Burton Rascoe.

Dragon Press. SAMUEL R. DELANY, "Heinlein," *Starboard Wine*, copyright © 1984 by Samuel R. Delany. Reprinted by permission of the author and his agents, Henry Morrison, Inc.

E. P. Dutton, Inc. VAN WYCK BROOKS, "Country Pictures," *New England: Indian Summer 1865–1915*, copyright © 1940, 1950 by Van Wyck Brooks, renewed 1968, 1978 by Gladys Brooks.

Educational Theatre Journal. PHILIP M. ARMATO, "Good and Evil in Lillian Hellman's *The Children's Hour*," Vol. 25, No. 4 (Dec. 1973), copyright © 1973.

Encounter. JONATHAN RABAN, "Taking Possession," Feb. 1975, copyright © 1975.

Esquire. F. SCOTT FITZGERALD, "The Crack-Up," Feb. 1936, copyright © 1936. ALFRED KAZIN, "The Legend of Lillian Hellman," Aug. 1977, copyright © 1977.

Everett/Edwards Inc. WARREN FRENCH, "Fiction: A Handful of Survivors," KINGSLEY WIDMER, "American Apocalypse: Notes on the Bomb and the Failure of American Imagination," *The Forties: Fiction, Poetry, Drama*, ed. Warren French, copyright © 1969 by Warren French.

The Falcon. WILLIAM H. GASS, Interview by Carole Spearin McCauley, Winter 1972, copyright © 1972.

Farrar, Straus & Giroux, Inc. ROBERT PENN WARREN, "Introduction" to *The Collected Stories of Caroline Gordon*, copyright © 1981 by Robert Penn Warren. EDMUND WILSON, "F. Scott Fitzgerald," "The Sportsman's Tragedy," *The Shores of Light*, copyright © 1952 by Edmund Wilson.

Field. ROBERT WALLACE, "The Excellence of 'Excellence,'" No. 25 (Fall 1981), copyright © 1981.

Foundation: The Review of Science Fiction. DAVE LANGFORD, No. 23 (Oct. 1981), copyright © 1981 by The Science Fiction Foundation.

The Georgia Review. MARTIN C. BATTESTIN, Winter 1971, copyright © 1971. DAVID BROMWICH, Fall 1975, copyright © 1975. ALFRED CORN, Summer 1977, copyright © 1977. ROBERT DALY, "John Gardner and the Emancipation of Genres," Summer 1983, copyright © 1983. ANTHONY HARRIGAN, "DuBose Heyward: Memorialist and Realist," Fall 1951, copyright © 1951.

G. K. Hall & Co. EDGAR M. BRANCH, "Conclusion," *James T. Farrell*, copyright © 1971 by Twayne Publishers. KATHERINE LEDERER, "An Ironic Vision," *Lillian Hellman*, copyright © 1979 by G. K. Hall & Co. WILLIAM H. SLAVICK, "The Vision and the Achievement," *DuBose Heyward*, copyright © 1981 by G. K. Hall & Co.

Harcourt Brace Jovanovich. SYLVIA BEACH, "My Best Customer," *Shakespeare and Company*, copyright © 1956 by Sylvia Beach. HARRY HANSEN, "Ben Hecht, Pagliacci of the Fire Escape," *Midwest Portraits*, copyright © 1923 by Harcourt, Brace & Co. VERNON LOUIS PARRINGTON, "Hamlin Garland and the Middle Border," *Main Currents of American Thought*, copyright © 1930 by Harcourt, Brace & Co. STEPHEN SPENDER, *World within World*, copyright © 1948, 1949, 1951 by Stephen Spender. VIRGINIA WOOLF, "An Essay in Criticism," *Granite and Rainbow*, copyright © 1958 by Leonard Woolf.

Harper and Row. W. D. HOWELLS, "Introduction," *Main-Travelled Roads* by Hamlin Garland, copyright © 1893, 1899 by Hamlin Garland. FRED LEWIS PATTEE, "O. Henry and the Handbooks," *The Development of the American Short Story*, copyright © 1923 by Harper & Brothers. TONY TANNER, "The Music of Invisibility," *City of Words: American Fiction, 1950–1970*, copyright © 1971 by Tony Tanner.

Harper's. STANLEY KUNITZ, Sept. 1960, copyright © 1960. JOHN WARNER, "Novelist or Journalist?," May 1967, copyright © 1967.

Harper's Bazaar. WILLIAM DEAN HOWELLS, Oct. 28, 1893, copyright © 1893.

The Harvard Advocate. JOHN BARTH, "A Tribute to John Hawkes," Vol. 104, No. 2 (October 1970), copyright © 1970 by *The Harvard Advocate*.

The Harvester Press Ltd. BERNDT OSTENDORF, "Oral Tradition and the Quest for Literacy," *Black Literature in White America*, copyright © 1982.

Hermitage House. W. DAVID SIEVERS, "Freudian Fraternity of the Thirties," *Freud on Broadway: A History of Psychoanalysis and the American Dream*, copyright © 1955 by W. David Sievers.

The Hollins Critic. JOHN ALEXANDER ALLEN, "Another Country: The Poetry of Daniel Hoffman," Vol. 15, No. 4 (October 1978), copyright © 1978. HOWARD NELSON, "Many Unnoticed Notes on Robert Francis's Poetry," Vol. 14, No. 4 (October 1977), copyright © 1977. ROBERT SCHOLES, "John Hawkes as Novelist: The Example of the Owl," Vol. 14, No. 3 (June 1977), copyright © 1977.

Holt, Rinehart & Winston, Inc. SHERIDAN BAKER, "Introduction" to *Ernest Hemingway: An Introduction and Interpretation*, copyright © 1967 by Holt, Rinehart & Winston, Inc. ELAINE BARRY, "Introduction" to *Robert Frost*, copyright © 1973 by Holt, Rinehart & Winston, Inc. REGINALD L. COOK, *The Dimensions of Robert Frost*, copyright © 1958 by Holt, Rinehart & Winston, Inc. ROBERT FROST, JOHN F. KENNEDY, *Selected Letters of Robert Frost*, ed. Lawrance Thompson, copyright © 1960 by Holt, Rinehart & Winston, Inc. ROBERT FROST, "The Figure a Poem Makes," *Selected Poems of Robert Frost*, copyright © 1963 by Holt, Rinehart & Winston, Inc. ROBERT GRAVES, "Introduction" to *Selected Poems of Robert Frost*, copyright © 1963 by Holt, Rinehart & Winston, Inc. LAWRANCE THOMPSON, "Introduction" to *Robert Frost*, copyright © 1970 by Holt, Rinehart & Winston, Inc. MAURICE THOMPSON, Letter to W. H. Ward, March 10, 1894, *Recognition of Robert Frost*, ed. Richard Thornton, copyright © 1937 by Henry Holt & Co. EDWARD WAGENKNECHT, "In the Second Decade," *Cavalcade of the American Novel*, copyright © 1952 by Henry Holt and Co. PHILIP YOUNG, "The Origins and Meaning of a Style," *Ernest Hemingway*, copyright © 1952 by Philip Young.

Houghton Mifflin Co. GREGORY H. HEMINGWAY, "Havana," *Papa: A Personal Memoir*, copyright © 1976 by Gregory H. Hemingway. PAUL ELMER MORE, "Hawthorne: Looking Before and After," *Shelburne Essays: Second Series*, copyright © 1905 by Paul Elmer More.

The Hudson Review. HAYDEN CARRUTH, Vol. 24, No. 2 (Summer 1971), copyright © 1971. JAMES FINN COTTER, "Familiar Poetry," Vol. 32, No. 1 (Spring 1979), copyright © 1979. JAMES FINN COTTER, Vol. 35, No. 3 (Autumn 1982), copyright © 1982. NORTHROP FRYE, Vol. 4, No. 4 (Winter 1951), copyright © 1951. ROBERT GRAVIS, "Varieties of the Will," Vol. 20, No. 2 (Summer 1967), copyright © 1967. RICHMOND LATTIMORE, "Poetry Chronicle," Vol. 27, No. 3 (Autumn 1974), copyright © 1974. WILLIAM H. PRITCHARD, "More Poetry Matters," Vol. 29, No. 3 (Autumn 1976) copyright © 1976. WILLIAM H. PRITCHARD, "Novel Sex and Violence," Vol. 28, No. 1 (Spring 1975), copyright © 1975. WILLIAM H. PRITCHARD, "Poetry Matters," Vol. 26, No. 3 (Autumn 1973), copyright © 1973. WILLIAM H. PRITCHARD, "Telling Stories," Vol. 31, No. 3 (Autumn 1978), copyright © 1978. ROGER SALE, "Fooling Around and Serious Business," Vol. 27, No. 4 (Winter 1974–75), copyright © 1974. W. D. SNODGRASS, Vol. 13, No. 1 (Spring 1960), copyright © 1960. EUDORA WELTY, "In Yoknapatawpha," Vol. 2, No. 4 (Winter 1949), copyright © 1949.

Hyphen. WALTER A. WILLIS, "Chicago Chicago," No. 34 (Sept. 1963), copyright © 1963 by Walter A. Willis.
The Independent. ERNEST BOYD, "Readers and Writers," Nov. 20, 1926, copyright © 1926.
International Magazine Co. EDNA FERBER, "Foreword" to "The Gay Old Dog," *My Story That I Like Best*, ed. Ray Long, copyright © 1925 by International Magazine Co.
The Iowa Review. NED FRENCH, "Against the Grain: Theory and Practice in the Work of William H. Gass," Winter 1976, copyright © 1976.
The Johns Hopkins University Press. RICHARD GRAY, "The Social and Historical Context," *The Literature of Memory*, copyright © 1977 by Richard Gray. DAVID MINTER, "Preface" to *William Faulkner: His Life and Work*, copyright © 1980 by The Johns Hopkins University Press.
Kennikat Press. JAMES T. FARRELL, "F. Scott Fitzgerald and His Romanticism," "The Mind of Ben Hecht," *Literary Essays: 1954–1974*, ed. Jack Alan Robbins, copyright © 1976 by Kennikat Press. VICTOR STRANDBERG, "Between Truth and Fact: Symbols of Identity," *A Faulkner Overview: Six Perspectives*, copyright © 1981 by Kennikat Press.
The Kenyon Review. HAROLD BLOOM, "The White Light of Trope: An Essay on John Hollander's *Spectral Emanations*," Winter 1979, copyright © 1979. LAWRENCE BOWLING, "Faulkner: Technique of *The Sound and the Fury*," Autumn 1948, copyright © 1948. GEOFFREY HARTMAN, "Les Belles Dames Sans Merci," Autumn 1960, copyright © 1960. ARTHUR MIZENER, Summer 1954, copyright © 1954. GEORGE MARION O'DONNELL, "Faulkner's Mythology," Summer 1939, copyright © 1939. PHILIP BLAIR RICE, "Faulkner's Crucifixion," Autumn 1954, copyright © 1954.
Alfred A. Knopf. CONRAD AIKEN, "Possessor and Possessed: John Gould Fletcher," *Secpticisms*, copyright © 1919 by Alfred A. Knopf. EMILY CLARK, "Joseph Hergesheimer," *Innocence Abroad*, copyright © 1931 by Alfred A. Knopf. WILLIAM GASS, "Groping for Tracts," *The World within the Word*, copyright © 1976 by Alfred A. Knopf. HUGH KENNER, "The Promised Land," *A Homemade World: The American Modernist Writers*, copyright © 1975 by Hugh Kenner. ALFRED KAZIN, "Retrospect 1937: The Twenties and the Great American Thing," *An American Procession*, copyright © 1984 by Alfred Kazin. ARTHUR MACHEN, *Hieroglyphics: A Note upon Ecstasy in Literature*, copyright © 1923 by Alfred A. Knopf. H. L. MENCKEN, "Six Members of the Institute," *Prejudices: First Series*, copyright © 1919 by Alfred A. Knopf. H. L. MENCKEN, "Four Makers of Tales," *Prejudices: Fifth Series*, copyright © 1926 by Alfred A. Knopf. GEORGE JEAN NATHAN, "Several Writers for the Theatre," *Passing Judgments*, copyright © 1933, 1934, 1935 by George Jean Nathan.
J. Laughlin. JOHN DOS PASSOS, "A Note on Fitzgerald," EDMUND WILSON, "Dedication," *The Crack-Up* by F. Scott Fitzgerald and others, copyright © 1945 by J. Laughlin.
Lester & Orpen, Ltd. DOUG FETHERLING, "1001 Afternoons in Hollywood," *The Five Lives of Ben Hecht*, copyright © 1977 by Doug Fetherling.
J. B. Lippincott Co. EDWARD MARGOLIES, "History as Blues: Ralph Ellison's *Invisible Man*," "Race and Sex: The Novels of Chester Himes," *Native Sons*, copyright © 1968 by Edward Margolies.
The Listener. BRIGID BROPHY, "Poodle," May 11, 1972, copyright © 1972 by British Broadcasting Corporation. JOHN MELLORS, "Roman Road," Sept. 7, 1978, copyright © 1978 by British Broadcasting Corporation.
Literary Review. WALTER B. RIDEOUT, "Forgotten Images of the Thirties: Josephine Herbst," Vol. 27, No. 1 (Fall 1983), copyright © 1983 by Literary Review.
Literature. HENRY JAMES, "American Letter," April 9, 1898, copyright © 1898.
Little, Brown & Co. ALFRED KAZIN, "The Decline of War," *Bright Book of Life*, copyright © 1971. F. D. REEVE, *Robert Frost in Russia*, copyright © 1963. GARRY WILLS, "Introduction" to *Scoundrel Time* by Lillian Hellman, copyright © 1976 by Garry Wills.
The Little Magazine. THOMAS M. DISCH (as "Tom Disch"), "A la Recherche de Marilyn Hacker," Vol. 9, No. 3 (Summer 1975), copyright © 1975 by *The Little Magazine*.
Liveright Publishing Corporation. JOHN WAIN, "Ben Hecht," *The Critic as Artist*, ed. Gilbert A. Harrison, copyright © 1959 by Harrison-Blaine, Inc., copyright © 1972 by Liveright Publishing Corporation.
London Magazine. LOUIS SIMPSON, "Californian Poets," Feb.-March 1972, copyright © 1972.
London Mercury. J. B. PRIESTLEY, "Joseph Hergesheimer," May 1926, copyright © 1926.
Louisiana State University Press. JOHN WILLIAM CORRINGTON, "Lawrence Ferlinghetti," *Nine Essays in Modern Literature*, ed. Donald E. Stanford, copyright © 1965 by Louisiana State University Press. ROSE ANN C. FRAISTAT, "The Later Novels," *Caroline Gordon as Novelist and Woman of Letters*, copyright © 1984 by Louisiana State University Press.
McGraw-Hill Book Co. JOHN TYTELL, "Allen Ginsberg and the Messianic Tradition," *Naked Angels*, copyright © 1976 by John Tytell.
Macmillan Publishing Co. (New York). CYRIL CONNOLLY, "Predicament," *Enemies of Promise*, copyright © 1938, 1948 by Cyril Connolly. HAMLIN GARLAND, "Henry B. Fuller," *Roadside Meetings*, copyright © 1930 by Hamlin Garland. GRANVILLE HICKS, "Two Roads," *The Great Tradition*, copyright © 1933 by Macmillan Publishing Co. CARL VAN DOREN, "New Style," *Twentieth-Century American Novelists 1900–1920*, copyright © 1922 by Macmillan Publishing Co.
The Massachusetts Review. ROBERT I. EDENBAUM, "John Hawkes: *The Lime Twig* and Other Tenuous Horrors," Vol. 7, No. 3 (Summer 1966), copyright © 1966 by The Massachusetts Review, Inc. JOHN HOLMES, "Constants Carried Forward: Naturalness in Robert Francis' Poems," copyright © 1960 by The Massachusetts Review, Inc.
Mississippi Quarterly. JAMES E. ROCKS, "The Mind and Art of Caroline Gordon," Vol. 21, No. 1 (Winter 1967), copyright © 1967.
Modern Chapbooks. JOSEPH MERSAND, "Ben Hecht," *Traditions in American Literature*, copyright © 1939 by Joseph Mersand.
Modern Drama. MARVIN FELHEIM, "*The Autumn Garden*: Mechanics and Dialectics," Vol. 3, No. 2 (Sept. 1960), copyright © 1960.
Modern Fiction Studies. A. E. DYSON, "*The Great Gatsby*: Thirty-Six Years After," Spring 1961, copyright © 1961. THOMAS LECLAIR, "William Gaddis, *JR*, and the Art of Excess," Winter 1981–82, copyright © 1981.
Modern Language Notes. EDWARD HONIG, "A Conversation with Robert Fitzgerald," No. 91 (1976), copyright © 1976.
Modern Poetry Studies. ROBERT K. MORRIS, "The Resurrected Vision: Horace Gregory's Thirties Poems," Vol. 4, No. 1 (Spring 1973), copyright © 1973. M. L. ROSENTHAL, "The 'Pure' Poetry of Horace Gregory," Vol. 4, No. 1 (Spring 1973), copyright © 1973.
The Nation. LIONEL ABEL, "A Technician of Mediocrity," Oct. 31, 1934, copyright © 1934. NELSON ALGREN, "The Radical Innocent," Sept. 21, 1964, copyright © 1964. FREDERICK H. GARDNER, "Return of the Continental Op," Oct. 31, 1966, copyright © 1966. NEIL HIMES, "Who Sang the Lordly Hudson," June 26, 1974, copyright © 1974. KATHA POLLITT, "Poems and Public Subjects," May 8, 1982, copyright © 1982. ALLEN TATE, "Hard-Boiled," Dec. 15, 1926, copyright © 1926. LIONEL TRILLING, "The McCaslins of Mississippi," May 30, 1942, copyright © 1942. CHERYL WALKER, "Choosing Old Forms," Sept. 18, 1976, copyright © 1976.
National Review. JOAN DIDION, "Notes from a Helpless Reader," July 15, 1961, copyright © 1961. HUGH KENNER, "Mirror of Language," April 25, 1975, copyright © 1975.
Negro Digest. ARNA BONTEMPS, "The New Black Renaissance," Nov. 1961, copyright © 1961.
New Directions Publishing Corp. LESLIE A. FIEDLER, "The Pleasures of John Hawkes," Introduction to *The Lime Twig* by John Hawkes, copyright © 1961 by New Directions, Inc. EZRA POUND, "Robert Frost," *Literary Essays*, copyright © 1918, 1920, 1935 by Ezra Pound. KENNETH REXROTH, "Introduction" to *The Residual Years* by William Everson, copyright © 1948 by New Directions, Inc.
The New England Quarterly. ALLEN GUTTMANN, Vol. 35, No. 1 (March 1962), copyright © 1962.
The New Republic. A. H., Aug. 25, 1979, copyright © 1979. WILLIAM ARROWSMITH, "More Bland Than Mellow," Aug. 13, 1956, copyright © 1956. JAMES ATLAS, "First Person," March 2, 1974,

copyright © 1974. JOHN ALFRED AVANT, Jan. 25, 1975, copyright © 1975. BRUCE BLIVEN, Sept. 9, 1946, copyright © 1946. ROBERT BRUSTEIN, "The Logic of Survival in a Lunatic World," Nov. 13, 1961, copyright © 1961. HAROLD CLURMAN, "Lillian Hellman's Garden," March 26, 1951, copyright © 1951. ROBERT COLES, "Mood and Revelation in the South," April 18, 1964, copyright © 1964. MALCOLM COWLEY, "The Case against Mr. Frost," Sept. 11 and 18, 1944, copyright © 1944. MALCOLM COWLEY, "Go Down to Faulkner's Land," June 29, 1942, copyright © 1942. MALCOLM COWLEY, "Novels after the War," Feb. 14, 1944, copyright © 1944. ROBERT GORHAM DAVIS, "An Arrangement in Black and White," Oct. 10, 1960, copyright © 1960. DONALD DOUGLAS, "Not One Hoot for the Law," April 9, 1930, copyright © 1930. MAX EASTMAN, "Bull in the Afternoon," June 7, 1933, copyright © 1933. RICHARD EBERHART, "In the Blue Depth," Nov. 2, 1953, copyright © 1953. RICHARD GILMAN, "Anatomy of a Hit," Oct. 28, 1967, copyright © 1967. NAT HENTOFF, "Waking Up the White Folks Again," July 20, 1968, copyright © 1968. JOHN HERSEY, "Lillian Hellman," Sept. 18, 1976, copyright © 1976. IRVING HOWE, "Symbolic Suburbia," Nov. 16, 1953, copyright © 1953. JOSEPHINE JACOBSEN, "A Rich Fusion," April 6, 1974, copyright © 1974. STANLEY KAUFFMANN, "Frightened Writer," Oct. 8, 1960, copyright © 1960. STANLEY KAUFFMANN, "Further Adventures of the Novel," June 6, 1964, copyright © 1964. AMY LOWELL, Feb. 20, 1915, copyright © 1915. WILLIAM MCFEE, "Life on the Mississippi—New Style," Sept. 15, 1926, copyright © 1926. T. S. MATTHEWS, "Novels by Weight," March 6, 1935, copyright © 1935. EDITH MILTON, July 8, 1978, copyright © 1978. MARJORIE PERLOFF, May 6, 1978, copyright © 1978. KATHERINE ANNE PORTER, "Dulce et Decorum Est," March 31, 1937, copyright © 1937. ISAAC ROSENFELD, "With Best Intentions," Dec. 31, 1945, copyright © 1945. R. V. A. S., May 12, 1920, copyright © 1920. MARK SCHORER, "With Grace under Pressure," Oct. 6, 1952, copyright © 1952. JAMES THURBER, "Taps at Assembly," Feb. 9, 1942, copyright © 1942. ANNE TYLER, "All in the Family," Feb. 17, 1982, copyright © 1982.

The New Review. MARTIN AMIS, "Interview with Joseph Heller," copyright © 1975.

The New Statesman and Nation. LOUIS FINGER, "Mere Murder," July 1, 1977, copyright © 1977. CHRISTOPHER RICKS, "Chamber of Horrors," March 11, 1966, copyright © 1966. FRANCIS WYNDHAM, "Miss Highsmith," May 31, 1963, copyright © 1963. UNSIGNED, "New Novels," July 27, 1929, copyright © 1929.

New York Review of Books. DENIS DONOGHUE, "Life Sentence," Dec. 2, 1971, copyright © 1971. THOMAS R. EDWARDS, "The Short View," April 1, 1976, copyright © 1976. ROGER SALE, "What Went Wrong," Oct. 21, 1971, copyright © 1971. WILFRED SHEED, "The Defector's Secrets," June 1, 1978, copyright © 1978. SUSAN SONTAG, "On Paul Goodman," Sept. 21, 1972, copyright © 1972. ROSEMARY TONKS, "Cutting the Marble," Oct. 4, 1973, copyright © 1973. ROBERT TOWERS, "Reconciliations," March 19, 1981, copyright © 1981. GORE VIDAL, "F. Scott Fitzgerald's Case," May 1, 1980, copyright © 1980.

The New York Times Co. MAX APPLE, "Having Their Last Good Time," March 24, 1985, copyright © 1985 by The New York Times Co. JAMES BALDWIN, "Sermons and Blues," March 29, 1959, copyright © 1959 by The New York Times Co. JOHN BARKHAM, "Where It's the Biggest and Bestest," Sept. 28, 1952, copyright © 1952 by The New York Times Co. JOSEPH WARREN BEACH, "The Dilemma of a Black Man in a White World," Dec. 2, 1945, copyright © 1945 by The New York Times Co. HAROLD BEAVER, "Snapshots and Artworks," March 18, 1984, copyright © 1984 by The New York Times Co. JOHN BROOKS, "A Ward Case of Innocence," Oct. 27, 1957, copyright © 1957 by The New York Times Co. HAYDEN CARRUTH, "Chants, Oracles, Body-Rhythms," March 19, 1978, copyright © 1978 by The New York Times Co. HAYDEN CARRUTH, Aug. 8, 1976, copyright © 1976 by The New York Times Co. HAYDEN CARRUTH, Sept. 13, 1970, copyright © 1970 by The New York Times Co. WALTER VAN TILLBURG CLARK, "When Settlers Begin to Take Over," Nov. 18, 1956, copyright © 1956 by The New York Times Co. BABETTE DEUTSCH, "Waste Land of Harlem," May 6, 1951, copyright © 1951 by The New York Times Co. MARGARET DRABBLE, "The Limits of Mother Love," March 31, 1985, copyright © 1985 by The New York Times Co. MARTIN DUBERMAN, "Literary Summitry," Jan. 13, 1985, copyright © 1985 by The New York Times Co. RICHARD EBERHART, "West Coast Rhythms," Sept. 2, 1956, copyright © 1956 by The New York Times Co. IRVING EHRENPREIS, Dec. 7, 1978, copyright © 1978 by The New York Times Co. HORACE GREGORY, "A Noble Homer Who Almost Never Was," April 16, 1961, copyright © 1961 by The New York Times Co. MICHAEL S. HARPER, "A Symbolist Poet Struggling with Historical Fact," Feb. 22, 1976, copyright © 1976 by The New York Times Co. ANTHONY HECHT, "Masters of Unpleasantness," Feb. 2, 1982, copyright © 1982 by The New York Times Co. D. G. HOFFMAN, Jan. 10, 1960, copyright © 1960 by The New York Times Co. JOHN HOLLANDER, Feb. 13, 1972, copyright © 1972 by The New York Times Co. MAUREEN HOWARD, "When the Identity Is the Crisis," May 5, 1985, copyright © 1985 by The New York Times Co. JOHN IRVING, "An Exposé of Heaven and Hell," June 10, 1979, copyright © 1979 by The New York Times Co. WILLIAM KENNEDY, "The Last Olé," June 9, 1985, copyright © 1985 by The New York Times Co. LOUIS KRONENBERGER, "*Show Boat* Is High Romance," Aug. 22, 1926, copyright © 1926 by The New York Times Co. JULIUS LESTER, Jan. 24, 1971, copyright © 1971 by The New York Times Co. RICHARD LOCKE, "What I Like," May 15, 1977, copyright © 1977 by The New York Times Co. ROBERT LOWRY, "A Smog of Loneliness," Feb. 10, 1957, copyright © 1957 by The New York Times Co. JAMES MACBRIDE, "Thirty-one by Ferber," Feb. 16, 1947, copyright © 1947 by The New York Times Co. LEONARD MICHAELS, "Bruce Gold's American Experience," March 11, 1979, copyright © 1979 by The New York Times Co. JOYCE CAROL OATES, June 7, 1970, copyright © 1970 by The New York Times Co. JOYCE CAROL OATES, April 4, 1982, copyright © 1982 by The New York Times Co. CHRISTOPHER RICKS, "Poets Who Have Learned Their Trade," Dec. 1, 1979, copyright © 1979 by The New York Times Co. CHRISTOPHER RICKS, Jan. 12, 1975, copyright © 1975 by The New York Times Co. CLAYTON RILEY, "An Incredibly Moving Experience," Nov. 29, 1970, copyright © 1970 by The New York Times Co. WEBSTER SCHOTT, "John Hawkes, American Original," May 29, 1966, copyright © 1966 by The New York Times Co. C. H. SISSON, "Accepting a Heroic Challenge," Oct. 16, 1983, copyright © 1983 by The New York Times Co. SUSAN SONTAG, "A New Life for an Old One," April 5, 1964, copyright © 1964 by The New York Times Co. JAMES STERN, "With a Whimper and a Bang," March 2, 1958, copyright © 1958 by The New York Times Co. RICHARD G. STERN, "Bombers Away," Oct. 22, 1961, copyright © 1961 by The New York Times Co. JOHN TOLAND, "Beyond the Brink of Destruction," Aug. 4, 1985, copyright © 1985 by The New York Times Co. HELEN VENDLER, April 6, 1975, copyright © 1975 by The New York Times Co. KURT VONNEGUT, JR., "Joseph Heller's Extraordinary Novel about an Ordinary Man," Oct. 6, 1974, copyright © 1974 by The New York Times Co. JONATHAN YARDLEY, "Dr. Westrum's Search for Identity," Oct. 18, 1970, copyright © 1970 by The New York Times Co. PAUL ZWEIG, Oct. 17, 1971, copyright © 1971 by The New York Times Co.

New York Tribune. ZELDA SAYRE (FITZGERALD), "Friend Husband's Latest," April 2, 1922, copyright © 1922.

New York University Press. ROGER ASSELINEAU, "Hemingway, or 'Sartor Resartus' Once More," *The Transcendentalist Constant in American Literature*, copyright © 1980 by New York University Press. JONATHAN BAUMBACH, "Nightmare of a Native Son," *The Landscape of Nightmare*, copyright © 1965. WILLIAM MILES, "Isolation in Langston Hughes' *Soul Gone Home*," *Five Black Writers*, copyright © 1970 by New York University Press. ALAN M. WALD, "The Literary Record," *James T. Farrell: The Revolutionary Socialist Years*, copyright © 1978 by New York University Press.

The New Yorker. WHITNEY BALLIETT, Dec. 19, 1959, copyright © 1959. LOUISE BOGAN, April 12, 1941, copyright © 1941. LOUISE BOGAN, Sept. 13, 1947, copyright © 1947. DOROTHY PARKER (as Constant Reader), "Oh, Look—Two Good Books!," April 25, 1931, copyright © 1931. EDMUND WILSON, "William Faulkner's Reply to the Civil Rights Program," Oct, 23, 1948, copyright ©

1948. UNSIGNED, "Playwright," May 9, 1959, copyright © 1959. UNSIGNED, "The Talk of the Town," July 1, 1974, copyright © 1974.

Newsweek. WALTER CLEMONS, "The Best of '74," Dec. 30, 1974, copyright © 1974.

The Observer. MARTIN AMIS, "The Book of David," Nov. 18, 1984, copyright © 1984.

Opportunity. COUNTEE CULLEN, "Poet on Poet," Feb. 1926, copyright © 1926.

Oxford University Press. WALTER ALLEN, *The Short Story in English*, copyright © 1981 by Walter Allen. T. O. BEACHCROFT, "The American Point of View," *The Modest Art: A Survey of the Short Story in English*, copyright © 1963 by Oxford University Press. MALCOLM BRADBURY, "Postmoderns and Others," *The Modern American Novel*, copyright © 1983. H. BRUCE FRANKLIN, "New Frontiers: 1947–59," *Robert A. Heinlein: America as Science Fiction*, copyright © 1980 by Oxford University Press. RICHARD POIRIER, "A Preview," Robert Frost, copyright © 1984. M. L. ROSENTHAL, "Epilogue: American Continuities and Crosscurrents," *The New Poets*, copyright © 1967 by M. L. Rosenthal.

PMLA. ILSE DUSOIR LIND, "The Design and Meaning of *Absalom, Absalom!*," Dec. 1955, copyright © 1955 by the Modern Language Association of America.

Pan American University. LEONARD BUTTS, "The Process of 'Moral Fiction': Protagonist as Artist in John Gardner's Novels," ANGELA A. RAPKIN, "John Gardner's Novels: Post-Modern Structures in the Service of Moral Fiction," *John Gardner: True Art, Moral Art*, ed. Beatrice Mendez-Engle, copyright © 1983 by the School of Humanities, Pan American University.

The Paris Review. RALPH ELLISON, Interview by Alford Chester, Spring 1955, copyright © 1955. WILLIAM GOYEN, "William Goyen: The Art of Fiction LXIII," Winter 1976, copyright © 1976.

Parnassus: Poetry in Review. EMILE CAPONYE, "The Poet as Prophet," Fall–Winter 1974, copyright © 1974 by *Parnassus: Poetry in Review*. JUDITH GLEASON, "The Lesson of Bread," Spring–Summer 1982, copyright © 1982 by *Parnassus: Poetry in Review*.

The Partisan Review. EDWIN BERRY BURGUM, "Discussion" from "What Is a Proletarian Novel," July–August 1935, copyright © 1935. EDWIN BERRY BURGUM, "A Significant Revolutionary Novel," January–February 1935, copyright © 1935. LESLIE FIEDLER, "The Novel in the Post-Political World," Summer 1956, copyright © 1956. ELIZABETH HARDWICK, "Faulkner and the South Today," October 1948, copyright © 1948. JOHN HOLLANDER, "Poetry Chronicle," Winter 1957, copyright © 1957 by *The Partisan Review*. LYNN LURIA-SUKENICK, "Four Novels," 1980, copyright © 1980. J. D. MCCLATCHY, "Summaries and Evidence," 1980, copyright © 1980. MARK SHECHNER, "The Survival of Allen Ginsberg," January 1979, copyright © 1979. LIONEL TRILLING, "A Speech on Robert Frost," Summer 1959, copyright © 1959.

Pennsylvania State University Press. JAMES L. POTTER, *Robert Frost Handbook*, copyright © 1980.

Philosophical Library. JEAN-PAUL SARTRE, "On *The Sound and the Fury*: Time in the Work of William Faulkner," *Literary Essays*, tr. Annette Michelson, copyright © 1957.

Players Magazine. JAMES EATMAN, "The Image of American Destiny: *The Little Foxes*," Vol. 48, No. 2 (Dec.–Jan. 1973), copyright © 1973.

Ploughshares. ASHLEY BROWN, "The Poetry of Anthony Hecht," copyright © 1978.

Poetry. R. P. BLACKMUR, "Versions of Fletcher," March 1936, copyright © 1936. HAYDEN CARRUTH, Nov. 1958, copyright © 1958. TURNER CASSITY, Dec. 1963, copyright © 1963. BABETTE DEUTSCH, "A Lost Address," Sept. 1938, copyright © 1938. AVID GALLER, July 1967, copyright © 1967. ALICE CORBIN HENDERSON, "Two Books by Fletcher," March 1919, copyright © 1919. ROBERT HOLLAND, "Six or Seven Fools," Feb. 1977, copyright © 1977. BEN KIMPEL, "John Gould Fletcher in Retrospect," Aug. 1954, copyright © 1954. LAURENCE LIEBERMAN, "The Body of the Dream," May 1968, copyright © 1968. WILLIAM GOYEN, "Language against Fear," July 1977, copyright © 1977. HARRIET MONROE, "Henry B. Fuller," Oct. 1929, copyright © 1929. SAMUEL FRENCH MORSE, "The Time Made Good," May 1957, copyright © 1957. HARRY ROSKOLENKO, "The Shadow Is Not the Rose," Dec. 1953, copyright © 1953. DONALD SHEEHAN, "Numquam Minus Solus Quam Solus," Jan. 1971, copyright © 1971. VERNON SHETLEY, "Take But Degree Away," Feb. 1981, copyright © 1981.

Prentice-Hall, Inc. JAMES BALDWIN, "Sweet Lorraine," *To Be Young, Gifted and Black*, copyright © 1969 by James Baldwin. LESLIE FIEDLER, "No! In Thunder," *The Novel: Modern Essays in Criticism*, ed. Robert Murray Davis, copyright © 1969 by Prentice-Hall, Inc. LORRAINE HANSBERRY, "Prologue: Measure Him Right, Child," *To Be Young, Gifted and Black*, copyright © 1969 by Robert Nemiroff.

Princeton University Press. CARLOS BAKER, "The Mountain and the Plain," *Ernest Hemingway: The Writer as Artist*, copyright © 1952, 1956, 1963 by Carlos Baker. ERNST ROBERT CURTIUS, "William Goyen," *Essays on European Literature*, copyright © 1973. IHAB HASSAN, "Encounter with Possibility," *Radical Innocence*, copyright © 1961 by Princeton University Press.

The Progressive. ELSA PENDLETON, "Struggle for Self," Vol. 39, No. 2 (Feb. 1975), copyright © 1975. ROBERT RUBENSTEIN, "Adventures in Self-Discovery," Vol. 42, No. 10 (Oct. 1978), copyright © 1979.

Random House, Inc. W. H. AUDEN, "Robert Frost," *The Dyer's Hand*, copyright © 1964. BENNETT CERF, *At Random*, copyright © 1977 by Random House. WILLIAM FAULKNER, Address upon receiving the Noble Prize, *Essays, Speeches and Public Letters*, ed. James B. Merriwether, copyright © 1965 by Random House. WILLIAM FAULKNER, *Selected Letters of William Faulkner*, ed. Joseph Blotner, copyright © 1977 by Joseph Blotner. FORD MADOX FORD, "Introduction" to *A Farewell to Arms*, copyright © 1932 by Modern Library. WILLIAM GOYEN, "Introduction" to *Selected Writings of William Goyen*, copyright © 1974 by William Goyen. LILLIAN HELLMAN, "Introduction" to *The Big Knockover* by Dashiell Hammett, copyright © 1966 by Lillian Hellman. LILLIAN HELLMAN, "Introduction" to *Four Plays*, copyright © 1942 by Modern Library. RANDALL JARRELL, "To the Laodiceans," *Poetry and the Age*, copyright © 1953. DIANE JOHNSON, *Dashiell Hammett: A Life*, copyright © 1983 by Diane Johnson. STEVEN MARCUS, "Introduction" to *The Continental Op* by Dashiell Hammett, copyright © 1974 by Steven Marcus. GERTRUDE STEIN, *The Autobiography of Alice B. Toklas*, copyright © 1933, 1960 by Alice B. Toklas. GERTRUDE STEIN, *Everybody's Autobiography*, copyright © 1937 by Random House. ROBERT PENN WARREN, "Ernest Hemingway," "William Faulkner," *Selected Essays*, copyright © 1941, 1946 by Robert Penn Warren.

Renascence. JOHN F. DESMOND, "*The Malefactors*: Caroline Gordon's Redemptive Vision," Vol. 35, No. 1 (Autumn 1982), copyright © 1982. R. BURTON PALMER, "The Problem with Gardner's *On Moral Fiction*," Vol. 34, No. 3 (Spring 1982), copyright © 1982.

Reporter. GEORGE STEINER, "The Lyre and the Pen," Feb. 16, 1961, copyright © 1961.

Review of Contemporary Fiction. JOHN KUEHLE, STEVEN MORE, "An Interview with William Gaddis," Summer 1982, copyright © 1982.

Reynal & Hitchcock. ALFRED KAZIN, "The Revival of Naturalism," *On Native Grounds*, copyright © 1942 by Alfred Kazin.

Ross-Erikson Publishers. PAUL PORTUGÉS, "The Heightened Awareness of a Prophet," *The Visionary Poetics of Allen Ginsberg*, copyright © 1978 by Paul Portugés.

Rutgers University Press. HOWARD NEMEROV, *Poetry and Fiction*, copyright © 1963 by Rutgers, The State University.

Salmagundi. TERENCE DIGGORY, "Three Women Exiles," No. 54 (Fall 1981), copyright © 1981 by Skidmore College.

Saturday Review. WALTER VAN TILBURG CLARK, "Emigrants on the Oregon Trail," Oct. 8, 1949, copyright © 1949. MARTIN DODSWORTH, "Puzzles," March 1965, copyright © 1965. GRANVILLE HICKS, "Domestic Felicity?," Sept. 24, 1966, copyright © 1966. GRANVILLE HICKS, "Eye on the Peace Corps," Oct. 8, 1966, copyright © 1966. GRANVILLE HICKS, "Literary Horizons: Amour, Amour, Amour," Oct. 1, 1960, copyright © 1960. EDWARD MARGOLIES, "America's Dark Pessimism," March 22, 1969, copyright © 1969. JOSEPH SLATKIN, "Wizards and New-Born Gods," Jan. 7, 1961, copyright © 1961.

Saturday Review (London). BERNARD DE VOTO, "Hemingway in the Valley," Oct. 26, 1935, copyright © 1935.

The Scarecrow Press, Inc. LEE BARTLETT, "God's Crooked Lines: William Everson and C. G. Jung," *William Everson*, copyright © 1983.

Charles Scribner's Sons. CARLOS BAKER, "Journey Down," *Ernest Hemingway: A Life Story*, copyright © 1968 by Carlos Baker, 1969 by Carlos Baker and Mary Hemingway. V. F. CALVERTON, "The Frontier Force," *The Liberation of American Literature*, copyright © 1932 by Charles Scribner's Sons. F. SCOTT FITZGERALD, "How to Waste Material: A Note on My Generation," *Afternoon of an Author*, copyright © 1958 by Charles Scribner's Sons. ERNEST HEMINGWAY, *Death in the Afternoon*, copyright © 1932 by Charles Scribner's Sons. ERNEST HEMINGWAY, *The Green Hills of Africa*, copyright © 1935 by Charles Scribner's Sons. ERNEST HEMINGWAY, *Ernest Hemingway: Selected Letters 1917–1961*, copyright © 1981 by the Ernest Hemingway Foundation, 1981 by Carlos Baker. STUART SHERMAN, "Ben Hecht and the Superman," *Critical Woodcuts*, copyright © 1926 by Charles Scribner's Sons.

The Sewanee Review. BRUCE ALLEN, "First Novels," Vol. 86, No. 4 (Fall 1978), copyright © 1978. BRUCE ALLEN, "Settling for Ithaca," Vol. 85, No. 3 (Summer 1977), copyright © 1977. JACK DE BELLIS, "Two Southern Novels and a Diversion," Vol. 70, No. 4 (Oct.–Dec. 1962), copyright © 1962. R. P. DICKEY, "The New Genteel Tradition in American Poetry," Vol. 82, No. 4 (Fall 1974), copyright © 1974. RICHARD A. JOHNSON, Vol. 76, No. 4 (Autumn 1968), copyright © 1968. WALTER SULLIVAN, "Model Citizens and Marginal Cases: Heroes of the Day," Vol. 87, No. 2 (Spring 1979), copyright © 1979. WALTER SULLIVAN, "The Novel in the Gnostic Twilight," Vol. 78, No. 4 (Oct. 1970), copyright © 1970. F. H. GRIFFIN TAYLOR, "A Point in Time, a Place in Space," Vol. 77, No. 2 (Spring 1969), copyright © 1969. YVOR WINTERS, "Robert Frost: or, the Spiritual Drifter as Poet," Vol. 56, No. 3 (Aug. 1948), copyright © 1948.

The Smart Set. H. L. MENCKEN, August 1920, copyright © 1920.

The South Atlantic Quarterly. CARL BENSON, "Thematic Design in *Light in August*," Oct. 1954, copyright © 1954.

Southern Humanities Review. ASHLEY BROWN, "The Achievement of Caroline Gordon," Vol. 2, No. 3 (Summer 1968), copyright © 1968.

Southern Illinois University Press. JOSEPH BABER, "John Gardner, Librettist: A Composer's Notes," *John Gardner: Critical Perspectives*, eds. Robert A. Morace, Kathryn VanSpanckeren, copyright © 1982 by The Board of Trustees, Southern Illinois University. SAMUEL COALE, "'Into the Farther Darkness': The Manichaean Pastoralism of John Gardner," *John Gardner: Critical Perspectives*, eds. Robert A. Morace, Kathryn VanSpanckeren, copyright © 1982 by The Board of Trustees, Southern Illinois University. GERALDINE DELUCA, RONI NATOR, "Modern Moralities for Children: John Gardner's Children's Books," *John Gardner: Critical Perspectives*, eds. Robert A. Morace, Kathryn VanSpanckeren, copyright © 1982 by The Board of Trustees, Southern Illinois University. IRVING MALIN, "Self-Love," *New American Gothic*, copyright © 1962 by Southern Illinois University Press. HARRY T. MOORE, "The Fiction of Herbert Gold," *Contemporary American Novelists*, ed. Harry T. Moore, copyright © 1964 by Southern Illinois University Press. KINGSLEY WIDMER, "Contemporary American Outcasts," *The Literary Rebel*, copyright © 1965 by Southern Illinois University Press.

Southern Literary Journal. ROBERT H. BRINKMEYER, JR., "New Caroline Gordon Books," Vol. 14, No. 2 (Spring 1982), copyright © 1982.

Southern Quarterly. MARY ROHRBERGER, "Shirley Ann Grau and the Short Story," Vol. 21, No. 4 (Summer 1982), copyright © 1983.

Southern Review. MARY ROHRBERGER, "'So Distinct a Shade': Shirley Ann Grau's *Evidence of Love*," Vol. 14, No. 1 (Winter 1978), copyright © 1978. MAX F. SCHULTZ, "Towards a Definition of Black Humor," Vol. 9, No. 1 (Winter 1973), copyright © 1973. RADCLIFFE SQUIRES, "The Underground Stream: A Note on Caroline Gordon's Fiction," Vol. 7, No. 2 (April 1971), copyright © 1971.

Southwest Review. ROBERT PENN WARREN, "The Fiction of Caroline Gordon," Vol. 20, No. 2 (Winter 1935), copyright © 1935.

Soviet Review. ROMAN SAMARIN, "O. Henry—'A Really Remarkable Writer,'" Vol. 3, No. 12 (Dec. 1962), copyright © 1962.

The Spectator. PAUL ABLEMAN, "Last Things," Jan. 13, 1979, copyright © 1979. DAVID HARE, "David Hare on Crime Fiction," Jan. 30, 1971, copyright © 1971. NICK TOTTER, "Camouflage," Jan. 15, 1977, copyright © 1977. A. N. WILSON, "Overfrocked Priest," July 4, 1981, copyright © 1981.

State University of New York Press. LESLIE FROST, "Introduction," *New Hampshire's Child*, copyright © 1969.

Stein & Day Publishers. LESLIE A. FIEDLER, "Into the Cafes: A Kind of Solution," *Waiting for the End*, copyright © 1964 by Leslie A. Fiedler.

Frederick A. Stokes & Co. MARGARET LAWRENCE, "Go-Getters," *The School of Femininity*, copyright © 1936 by Frederick A. Stokes & Co.

Studies in Black Literature. LLOYD W. BROWN, "The Portrait of the Artist as a Black American in the Poetry of Langston Hughes," Winter 1974, copyright © 1974 by Mary Washington College.

Studies in Short Fiction. FRED ABRAMS, "The Pseudonym 'O. Henry': A New Perspective," Vol. 15, No. 3 (Summer 1978), copyright © 1978. STANLEY R. HARRISON, "Hamlin Garland and the Double Vision of Naturalism," Vol. 6, No. 5 (Fall 1969), copyright © 1969.

Taplinger Publishing Co., Inc. RUSSELL LETSON, "The Return of Lazarus Long," *Robert A. Heinlein*, eds. Joseph D. Olander and Martin Harry Greenberg, copyright © 1978 by Joseph D. Olander and Martin Harry Greenberg.

Tennessee Studies in Literature. WALTER EVANS, "'A Municipal Report': O. Henry and Postmodernism," Vol. 26 (1981), copyright © 1981 by University of Tennessee Press.

Thought. JOHN R. CLARK, ANNA LYDIA MOTTO, June 1980, copyright © 1980 by Fordham University Press.

Times Literary Supplement. GABRIELE ANNAN, "Our Dumb Friends," July 11, 1975, copyright © 1975. ROGER GARFITT, "Contrary Attractions," May 30, 1980, copyright © 1980. DAVID LODGE, "The Arms of the Church," Sept. 1, 1978, copyright © 1978. JULIAN SYMONS, "The Tough Guy at the Typewriter," June 5, 1981, copyright © 1981. UNSIGNED, "Into the Atmosphere," Aug. 29, 1968, copyright © 1968.

Tudor Publishing Co. ALFRED KREYMBORG, "A Free-Verse Revolt," *A History of American Poetry: Our Singing Strength*, copyright © 1934.

Frederick Ungar Publishing Co., Inc. DORIS V. FALK, "Hellman's Dramatic Mode—'The Theater Is a Trick . . . ,'" *Lillian Hellman*, copyright © 1978 by Frederick Ungar Publishing Co.

The University of California Press. CESARE PAVESE, "O. Henry; or, the Literary Trick," *American Literature: Essays and Opinions*, tr. Edwin Fussell, copyright © 1970 by The Regents of the University of California. T. K. WHIPPLE, "American Sagas," *Study Out the Land*, copyright © 1943 by The Regents of the University of California.

The University of Chicago Press. NELSON ALGREN, "*Erik Dorn:* A Thousand and One Afternoons in Nada," *Erik Dorn*, copyright © 1963 by the University of Chicago. HAROLD BLOOM, "On Ginsberg's *Kaddish*," *The Ringers in the Tower*, copyright © 1971 by the University of Chicago. PERCY H. BOYNTON, "Joseph Hergesheimer," *More Contemporary Americans*, copyright © 1927 by the University of Chicago. JOHN G. CAWELTI, "Hammett, Chandler, and Spillane," *Adventure, Mystery, and Romance*, copyright © 1976 by the University of Chicago. YEVGENY ZAMYATIN, "O. Henry," *A Soviet Heretic*, copyright © 1970 by the University of Chicago.

University of Dallas Press. THOMAS H. LANDERS, "Introduction" to *The Short Fiction of Caroline Gordon*, copyright © 1972 by the University of Dallas Press.

University of Georgia Press. GREGORY L. MORRIS, "The Old Men," *A World of Order and Light: The Fiction of John Gardner*, copyright © 1984 by the University of Georgia Press.

University of Illinois Press. WILBURN WILLIAMS, JR., "Covenant of Timelessness and Time," *Chant of Sounds*, eds. Michael S.

Harper and Robert B. Stepto, copyright © 1979 by the University of Illinois Press.

University of Massachusetts Press. ARTHUR F. KINNEY, "Narrative Consciousness," *Faulkner's Narrative Poetics: Style as Vision*, copyright © 1971 by Arthur F. Kinney, copyright © 1978 by the University of Massachusetts Press.

The University of Michigan Press. ROBERT FRANCIS, "Frost as Mugwump," *Pot Shots at Poetry*, copyright © 1980 by the University of Michigan. DONALD HALL, "An Interview with Gregory Fitzgerald and Rodney Parshall," *Goatfoot, Milktongue, Twinbird*, copyright © 1978 by the University of Michigan. LYALL H. POWERS, "The Yoknapatawpha Comedy," *Faulkner's Yoknapatawpha Comedy*, copyright © 1980 by the University of Michigan. RADCLIFFE SQUIRES, "Weather: Inner and Outer," *The Major Themes of Robert Frost*, copyright © 1963 by the University of Michigan.

University of Minnesota Press. LOUIS AUCHINCLOSS, *Ellen Glasgow*, copyright © 1964 by the University of Minnesota. CHARLES CHILD WALCUTT, "Adumbrations: Harold Frederic and Hamlin Garland," *American Literary Naturalism, a Divided Stream*, copyright © 1956 by the University of Minnesota.

University of Missouri Press. C. W. E. BIGSBY, "Lorraine Hansberry," *Confrontation and Commitment: A Study of Contemporary American Drama*, copyright © 1967 by The Curators of the University of Missouri. EDMUND S. DE CHASCA, "Fletcher's Poetry, 1913–1916," *John Gould Fletcher and Imagism*, copyright © 1978 by The Curators of the University of Missouri.

The University of North Carolina Press. ROBERT O. STEPHENS, "Hemingway's Aesthetic Thought: The Art of Seeing," *Hemingway's Non-Fiction: The Public Voice*, copyright © 1968 by The University of North Carolina Press. WALTER FULLER TAYLOR, "Hamlin Garland," *The Economic Novel in America*, copyright © 1942 by The University of North Carolina Press.

University of Oklahoma Press. STANLEY K. COFFMAN, JR., "'Amygism,'" *Imagism: A Chapter for the History of Modern Poetry*, copyright © 1951 by the University of Oklahoma Press. JOSEPH GOLD, "Introduction," *William Faulkner: A Study in Humanism, from Metaphor to Discourse*, copyright © 1966 by the University of Oklahoma Press. STEVEN WEISENBERGER, "Contra Naturam?: Usury in William Gaddis' *JR*," *Money Talks: Language and Lucre in American Fiction*, ed. R. Male, copyright © 1981 by the University of Oklahoma Press.

University of Washington Press. ROBERT BECHTOLD HEILMAN, "Dramas of Money," *The Iceman, the Arsonist, and the Troubled Agent*, copyright © 1973 by the University of Washington Press. GEORGE WOODCOCK, "Memory, Imagination, Artifice: The Late Short Fictions of Mavis Gallant," *The World of Canadian Writing*, copyright © 1970 by the University of Washington Press.

The University of Wisconsin Press. FREDERICK P. W. MCDOWELL, "Conclusion," *Ellen Glasgow and the Ironic Art of Fiction*, copyright © 1960 by the Regents of the University of Wisconsin.

University Press of Mississippi. HUGH KENNER, "Faulkner and the Avant-Garde," *Faulkner, Modernism and Film*, copyright © 1979 by the University Press of Mississippi. FRANK LENTRICCHIA, "Robert Frost and Modern Literary Theory," *Frost Centennial Essays*, copyright © 1973 by the University Press of Mississippi.

University Press of Virginia. MONIQUE PARENT FRAZEE, "Ellen Glasgow as Feminist," *Ellen Glasgow: Centennial Essays*, ed. M. Thomas Inge, copyright © 1976 by the Rector and Visitors of the University of Virginia.

Vanguard Press. JAMES T. FARRELL, "How *Studs Lonigan* Was Written," *The League of Frightened Philistines*, copyright © 1938 by *The Atlantic Monthly*.

Viking Penguin, Inc. A. ALVAREZ, "Dashiell Hammett," *Beyond All This Fiddle*, copyright © 1968 by A. Alvarez. D. H. LAWRENCE, "In Our Time," *Selected Literary Criticism*, copyright © 1923 by Thomas Seltzer, Inc., copyright © 1932, 1936, 1951, 1955 by Frieda Lawrence, copyright © 1964 by Angelo Ravagli and Montague C. Weekly, copyright © 1964 by the Estate of Frieda Lawrence Ravagli. LIONEL TRILLING, "F. Scott Fitzgerald," *The Liberal Imagination*, copyright © 1950.

Warner Books Inc. ELINOR LANGER, "Introduction" to *The Executioner Waits* by Josephine Herbst, copyright © 1985 by Elinor Langer.

Washington Post Book World. JOSEPH EPSTEIN, "Joseph Heller's Milk Train: Nothing More to Express," Oct. 6, 1974, copyright © 1974. RICHARD POIRIER, "Crossing Poetic Boundaries," Dec. 17, 1978, copyright © 1978.

Wayne State University Press. ALFRED KAZIN, "The Stillness of *Light in August*," *Twelve Original Essays on Great American Novels*, ed. Charles Shapiro, copyright © 1958 by Wayne State University Press.

Western American Literature. RICHARD ASTRO, "*The Big Sky* and the Limits of Wilderness Fiction," Vol. 9, No. 2 (Summer 1974), copyright © 1974 by Western Literature Association. LEVI S. PETERSON, "Tragedy and Western American Literature," Vol. 6, No. 4 (Winter 1972), copyright © 1972 by Western Literature Association.

Weybright & Talley. BARBARA CHRISTIAN, "Ralph Ellison: A Critical Study," *Black Expression*, ed. Addison Gayle, Jr., copyright © 1969.

Whitson Publishing Co. GLENN O. CAREY, "Faulkner and His Carpenter's Hammer," *Faulkner: The Unappeased Imagination*, copyright © 1980 by Glenn O. Carey. Reprinted by permission of Glenn O. Carey.

World Publishing Co. ALFRED KAZIN, "An American Confession," *F. Scott Fitzgerald: The Man and His Work*, copyright © 1951 by World Publishing Co.

The Writer. PATRICIA HIGHSMITH, "Some Notes on Suspense in General," *Plotting and Writing Suspense Fiction* (rev. ed.), copyright © 1966, 1972 by Patricia Highsmith.

The Yale Review. LAURENCE LIEBERMAN, Summer 1968, copyright © 1968. J. D. MCCLATCHY, Spring 1975, copyright © 1975. HERBERT MARKS, "The Counter-Intelligence of Robert Frost," Summer 1982, copyright © 1982. MARTIN PRICE, "Six Recent Novels," Sept. 1959, copyright © 1959.

Yale University Press. W. H. AUDEN, "Foreword" to *An Armada of Thirty Whales* by Daniel G. Hoffman, copyright © 1954 by Daniel G. Hoffman. W. H. AUDEN, "Foreword" to *A Crackling of Thorns* by John Hollander, copyright © 1958 by Yale University Press. ROBERT BONE, "The Contemporary Negro Novel," "Harlem Renaissance," *The Negro Novel in America*, copyright © 1958 by Yale University Press. CLEANTH BROOKS, "The Community and the Pariah," *William Faulkner: The Yoknapatawpha County*, copyright © 1963 by Yale University Press. CLEANTH BROOKS, "William Faulkner: Vision of Good and Evil," *The Hidden God*, copyright © 1963 by Yale University Press. STANLEY KUNITZ, "Foreword" to *Gathering the Tribes* by Carolyn Forche, copyright © 1976 by Yale University Press.